The Washington Almanac of International Trade & Business, 1998

Editors:

Gary P. Osifchin
William O. Scouton

© June 1998
Washington, D.C.

Almanac Publishing, Inc.

For additional information, contact:

Almanac Publishing, Inc.
P.O. Box 3785 - Washington, D.C. 20007.
Phone: 202/296-2297; 888/825-6262. Fax: 202/223-3504.
E-mail: Almanac@almanacpublishing.com

Printed in the United States of America by TechniGraphix, Inc..

ISBN 1-886222-10-X $225

Almanac Publishing, Inc.
Publishers: Stuart D. Serkin, Jeffrey B. Trammell
Executive Vice President: Gary P. Osifchin
Composition Editor: Steven M. Osifchin
Cover design by: Carol Nansel, IMTEK

The Washington Almanac of International Trade & Business, 1998

Editors:
Gary P. Osifchin
William O. Scouton

Composition Editor:
Steven M. Osifchin

Assistant Editors:
Todd Keeler
Jennifer Margiotta
Darren Smith

Research and Production Assistants:
Susan Connochie
Donna Voag

Publishers:
Stuart D. Serkin
Jeffrey B. Trammell

OTHER BOOKS AVAILABLE FROM ALMANAC PUBLISHING

THE ALMANAC OF THE EXECUTIVE BRANCH

On the road to becoming the definitive annual reference on the top players and workings of the Federal Executive Branch, *The Almanac of the Executive Branch* is essential for every Washington watcher. It enables the reader to understand the key administration insiders behind the policy decisions. You will learn firsthand the personal stories about the men and women who are in the news every night. This reference profiles over 800 key decision makers providing educational and professional backgrounds, job responsibilities and photographs. It also includes organizational charts and departmental histories for each of the 14 Cabinet level departments.

(Nov., 1997 Paper. ISBN 1-886222-06-1. $149.00)

THE ALMANAC OF THE UNELECTED

The Almanac of the Unelected is a substantial work of reference profiling over 700 key members of the Congressional committee staff including every committee and subcommittee staff director. The Almanac responds to the growing need for information about the personalities and issues behind these staff-people who are increasingly essential to the functioning of today's Congress and its elected officials.

(April, 1998 Hardbound. ISBN 1-886222-11-8. $275.00)

THE NEW MEMBERS OF CONGRESS ALMANAC

Available December 1, 1998, *The New Members of Congress Almanac* gives you the most comprehensive and insightful look at these new players only days after the election. No other publication offers this much information this soon after the election. Read it to find out key information on each new Member on Capitol Hill who will help reshape virtually every aspect of the Congress -- from committee assignments to the election of the Congressional leadership to the legislative agenda. The book contains a full-page narrative on each of the new Senators and Representatives including: photographs, professional backgrounds, education, biographical sketches, election statistics, district information, voter registration statistics, and political analysis.

(December, 1998. Paperback. ISBN 1-886222-14-2. $39.95)

TABLE OF CONTENTS

FOREWORD

Nearly every business transaction is international now. The world is so interconnected that it is difficult to think any longer in exclusively domestic terms. This book covers a wide array of foreign and domestic contacts in Washington, D.C. and around the U.S. who deal with foreign policy and international business.

Despite the focus on trade and business, *The Washington Almanac of International Trade and Business* is designed for everyone who is interested in international issues. It contains information that can be useful to a wide range of interests. A few examples: the international health research efforts of the Health and Human Services Department; the cooperative scientific and engineering research projects undertaken by the National Science Foundation; and the activities of the Environmental Protection Agency to help foreign countries implement their environmental laws.

The first section, "Foreign Diplomatic Corps in the United States," begins with biographical profiles and photos of each foreign ambassador to the U.S. It also contains a list of the chief commercial contacts at each embassy, complete staff listings for each embassy, and a listing of all foreign consulates in the U.S. It then provides a list of world currencies, time zones, and holidays.

The second section, "The U.S. Government: Who Does What?", begins with a section about "General Export Information". It then lists the foreign policy and foreign trade contacts for each Representative and Senator followed by a list of the Congressional Committees that have jurisdiction over trade legislation and foreign policy. Next, this section lists in alphabetical order all the Executive Branch offices with international responsibilities throughout the Executive Office of the President, the Cabinet Departments, and the Independent Agencies. The section provides information about the responsibilities and jurisdiction of each office; the names of officials with international responsibilities with their titles, addresses, telephone and fax numbers; and substantive, in-depth profiles of numerous senior level officials.

The third section, "Other Entities Dealing with International Trade," begins with a segment on the Multilateral Development Banks and on the International Monetary Fund (IMF). The section lists Washington-based international interest groups, research institutions, foreign agents registered under the Foreign Agents Registration Act (FARA), and the foreign press. Also included is a list of World Trade Centers in the U.S., U.S. Chambers of Commerce Abroad, and Foreign Chambers of Commerce in the U.S. It concludes with a listing of state-government agencies that promote international trade as well as lists of other trade related entities throughout the U.S.

Somewhere in this book every user can find an idea, a name, a telephone or fax number that will be useful in conducting research, in doing business, in placing a story in the foreign press, or in representing a client before the U.S. Government.

Gary P. Osifchin
Editor

Willliam O. Scouton
Editor

The Greater Washington Board of Trade

The Greater Washington Board of Trade is proud to sponsor the 1998 edition of **The Washington Almanac of International Trade & Business.** We are glad to have the opportunity to share with you the valuable information it contains on the tremendous international resources in our home town, the Nation's Capital.

The business community of Greater Washington (covering Northern Virginia, Suburban Maryland, and Washington, D.C.) sometimes takes for granted the international resources in our backyard -- the U.S. Congress and Federal Government agencies that make and implement trade policy, as well as foreign embassies, international private and non-governmental organizations, foreign agents, and multilateral financial institutions such as the World Bank and International Monetary Fund.

We in the Greater Washington business community also have a tendency to take for granted that people outside Greater Washington know what we know -- *that Greater Washington IS a major international business center.* For example,

▶ Three state-of-the-art international airports are located in the Greater Washington Region.

▶ Over 700 foreign corporations have headquarters here.

▶ Greater Washington earns at least $17.6 billion a year from international activities.

▶ Every sector of Greater Washington's $58 billion service economy is involved in international business.

The Greater Washington Initiative promotes Greater Washington as a world class business center and site for business location. The Initiative works with the economic development agencies of Washington, D.C., Northern Virginia, and Suburban Maryland to help companies from around the globe identify local:

- Strategic business partners
- Venture capital contacts
- Public and business leaders
- Site tours, and
- Demographic and real estate information.

For more information on these services, please call 800-555-6783.

Greater Washington Board of Trade
The International Business Council

The premier regional chamber of commerce for Washington D.C., Northern Virginia, and Suburban Maryland, The Greater Washington Board of Trade represents over 1,200 of the region's businesses. The Greater Washington Board of Trade's International Business Council consists of both professional firms that serve international clients and international corporations located in the Greater Washington Region. The International Business Council can put you in contact with private firms and corporations that can connect your business or organization to the international resources in the Washington D.C. region or assist you with international trade policy or business concerns.

1129 20th Street NW
Washington, D.C. 20036-3494
202/857-5992   FAX   202/223-2648

E-mail: AdrienneEdisis@bot.org
Url: http://www.bot.org

Contact: Adrienne Edisis
               Director, International Business Council

The real secret to the success of international business in Greater Washington, however, is knowledge. Greater Washington is a bustling gateway for international business because our *highly educated and international workforce has expertise regarding nearly every economic, business, and legal system in the world.*

The Region consistently produces and attracts an intelligent and educated pool of talent from diverse industries and specialties, with a high degree of international awareness. Greater Washington's population includes:

- *the highest percentage of people with at least a college degree*
  and
- *the largest number of graduate degree holders in the United States.*

In the international arena, Greater Washington has *more institutions and knowledgeable individuals who can facilitate contacts with business leaders and potential customers in overseas markets than any other city-region in the United States.* Conversely, overseas firms can find representatives of U.S. industries from all 50 states in Greater Washington – better access to the U.S. economy than in any other city-region in the world.

To reach professional firms in Greater Washington that can connect you to our Region's international resources or assist you with international trade policy or business issues, please contact The Greater Washington Board of Trade at 202-857-5900 or visit our web site at **www.bot.org** .

The Greater Washington Board of Trade has been the premier regional chamber of commerce for Northern Virginia, Suburban Maryland, and Washington, D.C. since 1889.

For further data and information regarding the Greater Washington Region, please see the web site of The Greater Washington Initiative, the marketing arm of The Greater Washington Board of Trade, at **www.greaterwashington.org** .

Map of Region

Geographically, Greater Washington is strategically located at the heart of the Mid-Atlantic region, encompassing the District of Columbia, Northern Virginia, and Suburban Maryland.

Globally, Greater Washington is the center of policy-making and political power—capital of the most powerful nation in the world.

Economically, Greater Washington is one of the most dynamic regional economies in the United States.

- 1st in Median Income
- 1st in Population with College Degree
- 1st in Per Capita Federal Spending
- 1st in Headquarters for Trade and Professional Associations
- 1st in Percent of Workforce in Executive/Professional Occupations
- 1st in Concentration of Scientists and Engineers
- 1st in High Tech Job Growth
- 1st in Labor Force Participation by Women
- 2nd in NETPLEX Companies and Data Communications
- 2nd in Job Growth Rate during the Eighties
- 3rd in Biotechnology Firms

SECTION I

FOREIGN DIPLOMATIC CORPS IN THE UNITED STATES

"Know your market" — the first rule of salesmanship — is particularly important in doing business abroad because of lack of familiarity with the lay of the land, the people, and the culture. "Foreign Diplomatic Corps in the United States," the first section of *The Washington Almanac of International Trade and Business,* is designed to overcome that problem.

The first segment provides biographical profiles and photos of all but a handful of the foreign Ambassadors to the U.S., and lists the staff of each Embassy as provided by the State Department and confirmed with each Embassy.

The second segment lists the key commercial contact at each Embassy in Washington — the person responsible for facilitating commercial contacts with firms or individuals in the foreign country.

The third segment lists foreign consulates in cities throughout the U.S. where company executives can obtain vital information about doing business with a particular country and travelers can learn about conditions within their country of destination.

The fourth segment provides foreign currencies, country holidays and world time zones.

A final segment provided in prior editions but not in this fourth edition, Country Information, featured basic facts about each country: about its geography, its people, its government, its economy, its communications, and its defense forces. This information is compiled by the Central Intelligence Agency (CIA) in *The World Factbook*, published annually. The CIA no longer makes the information available on disk which is how we provided it in the past. It is now available free however in a fully searchable, user-friendly manner on the worldwide web at www.odci.gov/cia/publications/factbook.

INTRODUCTION

An international capital, Washington D.C. is home to 171 foreign missions to the United States. In addition, six countries maintain diplomatic relations with the U.S. through their embassies in other cities. Ranging in size from a relatively small country like Palau to a large one like the United Kingdom, these embassies are the official channels of communication between the U.S. and the countries of the world. Missions to Washington are headed by an Ambassador who presents credentials to the State Department and is received by the President. The Dean of the Diplomatic Corps in Washington is H.R.H. Prince Bandar Bin Sultan of Saudi Arabia who presented his credentials to President Ronald Reagan on the 24th of October, 1983.

The Ambassadors

Included in this section of the book are profiles and photographs of the foreign ambassadors to the United States organized alphabetically by country. In the absence of an ambassador until the appointment of a successor, a chargé d'Affaires typically heads a country's diplomatic mission and is profiled accordingly. Each profile contains important and insightful information about these individuals including detailed personal, educational, professional, and political backgrounds.

Also included for each country is information about the embassy, including the address, phone, fax, E-mail, and web sites when available.

The Embassy Staff

Over 2,500 people staff the embassies and a complete diplomatic staff list along with their spouse's name is also included here. For purposes of clarity, we have capitalized the last name of each ambassador and staff member. An ambassador is addressed as His Excellency or Her Excellency. Staff members should be addressed typically as Mr. or Ms. with their surname unless a military title like Captain or Colonel is shown.

Members of the diplomatic staff are the members of the staff of the mission having diplomatic rank. Changes in staff occur frequently. The status of personnel listed in this section should be verified with the individual Embassy. The names are not in protocol order of preference.

The diplomatic staff at foreign embassies in the U.S. enjoy full immunity under provisions of the Vienna Convention on Diplomatic Relations. Pertinent provisions of the Convention include the following:

Article 29

The person of a diplomatic agent shall be inviolable. He/she shall not be liable to any form of arrest or detention. The receiving State shall treat him/her with due respect and shall take all appropriate steps to prevent any attack on his/her person, freedom, or dignity.

Article 31

A diplomatic agent shall enjoy full immunity from the criminal jurisdiction of the receiving State. He/she shall also enjoy immunity from civil and administrative jurisdiction, except in the case of:

a) a real action relating to private immovable property situated in the territory of the receiving State, unless he/she holds it on behalf of the sending State for the purposes of the mission;

b) an action relating to succession in which the diplomatic agent is involved as executor, administrator, heir or legatee as a private person and not on behalf of the sending State;

c) an action relating to any professional or commercial activity exercised by the diplomatic agent in the receiving State outside of his/her official functions.

A diplomatic agent's family members are entitled to the same immunities unless they are U.S. nationals.

Albania

Embassy of the Republic of Albania
2100 S. Street, NW
Washington DC 20008
Phone: 202/223-4942
Fax: 202/628-7342

Petrit BUSHATI
Ambassador

Date Credentials Presented: 3/16/98

Born: 10//20/50 in Tirana, Albania

Spouse: Mrs. Liljana Bushati

Petri Bushati, Albania's ambassador to the U.S., began his diplomatic career in the 1983 as first secretary in the Albanian embassy in Vienna, Austria, where he was responsible for press and public relations. He was named his country's ambassador to Sweden and the Nordic countries in 1988.

In 1985, he served as alternate representative to the United Nations International Development Organization and other international organizations at the United Nations Center in Vienna. He worked in the department of European affairs in the ministry of foreign affairs in Tirana in 1987.

After his ambassadorial stint, he returned to the ministry of foreign affairs, where he served as director of the department of multilateral cooperation and international organizations. He became head of the section on the United Nations and international organizations in 1992. In 1994, he represented the ministry at the Institute of International Studies.

Between 1995 and 1997, Bushati was associated with the German Association of Technical Cooperation.

After receiving a University degree in history and philology, the ambassador worked in 1971 as a teacher of English and as an interpreter. From 1973 to 1980, he was with the Albanian Telegraphic Agency, first as a translator and journalist, then as chief of the international press board, and finally as head of the foreign news department.

Bushati has varied experience in United Nations/international cooperation activities including the World Conference of TELECOM in Geneva, Switzerland, in 1979-80; as alternate representative at the United Nations General Assembly; and at international conferences in Geneva on the former Yugoslavia.

The ambassador is married and has two children. He speaks English, German, and French.

STAFF:

Mrs. Zhaneta MANSAKU
Second Secretary
Spouse: Mr. Edmond Mansaku

Mr. Mustafa XHEPHA
Second Secretary
Spouse: Mrs. Aida Xhepha

Mr. Artan HASANAJ
Attaché
Spouse: Mrs. Gentiana Hasanaj

Colonel Dhimiter BINAJ
Defense, Military, Naval and Air Attaché
Spouse: Mrs. Anila Binaj

Algeria

Embassy of the Democratic and
    Popular Republic of Algeria
2118 Kalorama Road, NW
Washington DC 20008
Phone: 202/265-2800
Fax: 202/667-2174
Email: algenews@gwuvm.gwu.edu

Ramtane LAMAMRA
Ambassador

Date Credentials Presented: 7/29/96

Born: 6/15/52 in Amizour, Bejaia, Algeria

Spouse: Mrs. Aicha Lamamra

The title of ambassador is nothing new for Ramtane Lamamra, who held the title as Algeria's Permanent Representative to the United Nations in New York, starting in 1993. Between September 1995 to September 1996, he was vice president of the 50th session of the U.N. General Assembly.

In 1992, he was named ambassador to the Republic of Austria and Permanent Representative to the U.N. office at Vienna. Between 1989 and 1991, he was Algeria's ambassador to Ethiopia and Djibouti and Permanent Representative to the Organization of African Unity (OAU) and to the U.N. Economic Commission for Africa.

Lamamra was vice chairman of the OAU Standing Commission on Refugees in Addis Ababa, Ethiopia, from 1989 to 1991 and the

chairman of the first and second sessions of the OAU committee on conferences in Addis Ababa in 1991-92. He also was chairman of the African Group to Vienna-based International Organizations in 1992 and of the Group of "77" Member States of the United Nations for a one-year term in 1994.

A 1976 graduate of the diplomatic section of École Nationale d'Administration in Algiers, Lamamra speaks three languages---Arabic, French, and English. He is married and has one daughter.

STAFF:

Mr. Mohammed Farid DJEBBARI
Minister (Consular and Cultural)
Spouse: Mrs. Yamina Djebbari

Mr. Abdelmoun'am AHRIZ
Counselor (Political, Agriculture,
    Housing & Infrastructure)
Spouse: Mrs. Ahriz

Mr. Ali ALAOUI
Counselor (Political, Trade and Industry)
Spouse: Mrs. Samira Alaoui

Mr. Belaid BENALI
Counselor (Political)
Spouse: Mrs. Benali

Mr. Mahieddine DJEFFAL
Counselor (Political, Energy and Finance)
Spouse: Mrs. Djeffel

Mr. Kamel HADRI
Counselor (Political, Public Relations
    and Communications)
Spouse: Mrs. Zouina Hadri

Mr. Djilai BELBACHIR
Attaché (Administrative)
Spouse: Mrs. Belbachir

Mr. Khaled BELMIHOUB
Attaché
Spouse: Mrs. Nafissa Belmihoub

Mr. Cherif KHALI
Attaché (Administrative and Financial)
Spouse: Mrs. Dalila Hkali

Mr. Mohamed Larbi RAHMANI
Attaché (Financial)
Spouse: Mrs. Rahmani

Colonel Mohamed LOUNES
Defense, Military, Naval and Air Attaché
Spouse: Mrs. Myriem Lounes

Consular Office
2137 Wyoming Ave., NW
Washington DC 20008

Economic and Administrative Office
2135 Wyoming Ave., NW
Washington DC 20008

Military Office
2133 Wyoming Ave., NW
Washington DC 20008

Andorra

Embassy of Andorra
Two United Nations Plaza, 25th Floor
New York NY 10017
Phone: 212/750-8064
Fax: 212/750-6630

Juli MINOVES-TRIQUELL
Ambassador

Date Credentials Presented: 2/6/96

When Andorra started its diplomatic corps in 1993, Juli Minoves-Triquell was the first recruited Andorran diplomat. Since 1993, Minoves-Triquell has negotiated the establishment of diplomatic relations with 20 countries.

He was named counsellor at the Permanent Mission of the Principality of Andorra immediately after the admission of his country to the United Nations. In May 1994, he was promoted to the rank of minister plenipotentiary and deputy permanent representative. He was head of the mission as chargé d'affaires by ministerial decree until he was appointed the first Andorran ambassador extraordinary and plenipotentiary to the United Nations in August, 1995. In early 1996, he was appointed concurrently as ambassador to the U.S. and Canada.

Throughout his career, Minoves-Triquell has represented Andorra at various international conferences. In March, 1995, he was alternate head of delegation at the World Summit on Social Development in Copenhagen, Denmark. In June, 1994, he was chairman of the Western European and Other States Group at the United Nations, and in November of that year he served as vice-president of the United Nations Pledging Conference for the World Food Program. In March and April, 1995, Minoves-Triquell became president of the Vinci Group, a social and economic debating group of western countries at the U.N. As of September ,1996, he will be president of the Western European and Other States Group at the U.N. for the second time, and will serve as vice-president of the General Assembly during its 51st session.

Minoves-Triquell obtained his undergraduate degree in economic and social sciences from Fribourg University in Switzerland, and attended graduate school at Yale University where he earned a master of arts and a master of philosophy in political science. He was admitted to candidacy for a Ph.D. He also holds a diploma from the Conservatory of Music of Barcelona in piano and music.

He has published one novel *Segles de Memòria* (National Award Fiter I Rossell 1988), and a collection of short stories "Les pedres del diable" (Premi Sant Carles Borromeu 1991).

Angola

Embassy of the Republic of Angola
1615 M St., NW - Suite 900
Washington DC 20036
Phone: 202/785-1156
Fax: 202/785-1258
Email: angola@angola.org
Url: http://www.angola.org

Antonio dos Santos FRANCA
Ambassador

Date Credentials Presented: 9/25/95

Spouse: Mrs. Maria Joao Jardim Franca

Antonio dos Santos Franca played a critical role in the long struggle for Angolan independence as well as the successful diplomatic process which led to peace and international recognition. His distinguished military and peacetime service highlights that role. He remains a special adviser to the president of the Republic of Angola.

Franca holds the rank of general of the army of the Angolan Armed Forces. Since 1974, he has been a member of the Central Committee of MPLA (Movement for the Liberation of Angola) and, in 1977, was appointed to the MPLA's Political Bureau.

After participating in the armed struggle for Angolan independence as a column commander, Franca served in a number of key military posts during the transition period following independence. These included chief of the general staff of the Ninth Motorized Brigade, commander of the presidential regiment, vice minister of defense and commander of the Air Force, chief of staff of the Angolan Armed Forces (1982 to 1990), first vice minister of defense and permanent member of the Council of Defense and Security.

Instrumental in the diplomatic peace process, Franca served as chief of the Angolan delegation for Peace in Southeast Asia (the New York accords), chief of the Military Commission of the Delegation of Angola for the Bicesse Accords, head of the Government Delegation on the Joint Political/Military Commission (CCPM) for Compliance with the Bicesse Accords, and as deputy and member of the permanent commission of the Assembly of the People.

A trained agricultural engineer who has studied both in Angola and abroad, Franca has served as secretary of the Central Committee for Agriculture, Herding, and Fishing. He is an avid soccer player, having played as a student and later as a professional with Associacao Academica de Coimbra and Sporting Club de Portugal. He has served as secretary of the Central Committee for Culture and Sports, as president of the National Military Sports Committee, and as president of the General Assembly of the Central Club of the Armed Forces.

STAFF:

Mr. Matias Bertino MATONDO
First Secretary
Spouse: Mrs. Julia Gualdino Matondo

Mr. Antonio RAFAEL
First Secretary

Mr. Joao Sergio ANDRADE SILVA
Second Secretary (Consular)
Spouse: Mrs. Antonia Silvia Silva

Mr. Baptista Alberto COCA
Second Secretary
Spouse: Mrs. Ivetta Sanchez Dominguez

Mr. Camilo Joao MANUEL
Second Secretary

Ms. Joana Mendes FERNANDES
Third Secretary

Mr. Armando FRANCISCO
Attaché (Press)
Spouse: Mrs. Rosa Giron Guillot

Mr. Agostinho A. FERNANDES
Attaché (Commercial)
Spouse: Mrs. Leopoldina M. S. Fernandes

Ms. Isabel Faria PEREIRA
Attaché (Financial)

General Alberto Correia NETO
Military, Naval and Air Attaché
Spouse: Mrs. Neto

Colonel Francisco Miguel ANTONIO
Assistant Defense and Military Attaché
Spouse: Mrs. Margarida Silveiro Antonio

Antigua & Barbuda

Embassy of Antigua and Barbuda
3216 New Mexico Avenue, NW
Washington DC 20016
Phone: 202/362-5122
Fax: 202/362-5225

Lionel Alexander HURST
Ambassador

Date Credentials Presented: 7/29/96

Born: 12/4/50 in St. John's, Antigua

Lionel Alexander Hurst had an earlier tour of duty in Washington, D.C., having served as first secretary of Antigua and Barbuda's embassy in 1985-86. Between 1988 and 1995, he was his country's Permanent Representative to the United Nations in New York. He was vice president of the 44th session of the U.N. General Assembly.

In 1987-88, Hurst was stationed at the consulate of Antigua and Barbuda in Miami, Fla. Before that, he was executive director of Saint John's (Urban) Development Corporation in St. John's, Antigua, in 1986-87. He was director of an Antigua and Barbuda trade mission in Miami in 1986. In 1985, he served briefly as trade and investment promotion officer in Antigua and Barbuda's Ministry of Economic Development.

After receiving his J.D., with a major in international law, from New York Law School in 1984, Hurst served as assistant to the managing attorney in the Wall Street law firm, Hawkins, Delafield & Wood. He received a B.A. from Brooklyn College in political science and international politics in 1980 and a master's degree in business administration from Long Island University in 1981.

He is married and has four children.

STAFF:

Ms. Deborah LOVELL
Minister-Counselor

Ms. Gracelyn G. HENRY
First Secretary and Consul

Ms. Debbie PROSPER
First Secretary
Spouse: Mr. Kodjo Adadevoh

Argentina

Embassy of the Argentine Republic
1600 New Hampshire Avenue, NW
Washington DC 20009
Phone: 202/939-6400
Fax: 202/332-3171
Email: feeEuu@mrecic.gov.ar
Url: http://emb-eeuu.mrecic.gov.ar

Dr. Diego Ramiro GUELAR
Ambassador

Date Credentials Presented: 9/8/97

Born: 2/24/50

Spouse: Mrs. Diana Custodio Guelar

A lawyer and diplomat, Dr. Diego Ramiro Guelar came to Washington, D.C., as Argentina's ambassador in 1997 after serving as his country's ambassador to Brazil in 1996-97. Between 1989 and 1996, he was Argentina's ambassador to the European Union.

Between 1968 and 1971, Guelar co-founded the National Students Union and served as a national delegate of the school of law at the University of Buenos Aires. He was the national leader of the Peronista Youth between 1973 and 1976. During that period, he also was the delegate of the Justicialista party for the province of Buenos Aires. He was engaged in professional activities connected with workers' unions.

Guelar was elected a national deputy for the Justicialista party in 1983. In 1984, he served as vice president of the committee on the budget and finance of the House of Deputies. He was a member of the committees on finance, constitutional affairs, foreign affairs, and impeachment and general legislation. Between 1985 and 1987, he was the secretary general of the Justicialista Deputies Caucus.

Guelar's career in the private sector included: president of the Foundation for the Agreement on Growth, which specialized in economic and constitutional matters; director of editorials of the newspaper, *La Razón*, in Buenos Aires; director of the chair of European studies at the University of Management and Social Sciences in Buenos Aires; professor at the University of Maastricht in the Netherlands; and vice president of the general assembly of the Institute on European-Latin American Relations.

Between 1973 and 1976, Guelar was an associate professor at the school of law and the school of architecture at the University of Buenos Aires. He served in 1971 as a professor of sociology of the law at the school of law.

The ambassador and his wife, Diana Custodio, have three children.

STAFF:

Mr. Santos GONI-MARENCO
Minister (Deputy Chief of Mission)
Spouse: Mrs. Luz Ojea de Goni

Mr. Ruben Eduardo CARO
Minister(Commercial)
Spouse: Mrs. Maria Cecilia de Caro

Mr. Daniel CHUBURU
Minister
Spouse: Mrs. Araceli Mejica de Chuburu

Mr. Felipe FRYDMAN
Minister

Ms. Noemi C.E. LA GRECA
Minister (Financial)

Mr. Adolfo Dante LOSS
Minister (Press)

Mr. Carlos MAGARINOS
Minister (Economic and Trade)
Spouse: Mrs. Maria Jose Santambrogio de Magarinos

Mr. Jose Domingo MOLINA
Minister (Agriculture)
Spouse: Mrs. Mary Alice Troast

Mr. Jorge Alberto OSELLA
Minister
Spouse: Mrs. Graciela Garcia Moris de Osella

Mr. Rodolfo Ernesto BLACHOWICZ
Counselor
Spouse: Mrs. Amalia Blachowicz

Mr. Julio Alberto CIRINO
Counselor
Spouse: Mrs. Maria Cristina Rinaldi de Cirino

Mr. Horacio C. MENDEZ ITURBIDE
Counselor (Cultural)

Mr. Juan M. MINIERI
Counselor
Spouse: Mrs. Mariana De Achaval de Minieri

Mr. Fernando PERALTA RAMOS
Counselor
Spouse: Mrs. Lucila Arancedo

Mr. Diego Javier TETTAMANTI
Counselor
Spouse: Mrs. Mrs. Alejandra Maria Ruiz de Tettamanti

Mr. Carlos E. WEITZ
Counselor (Financial)
Spouse: Mrs. Myriam P. Krapf

Mr. Eduardo ACEVEDO-DIAZ
First Secretary
Spouse: Mrs. Maria Acevedo Diaz Asua

Mr. Luis Pablo Maria BELTRAMINO
First Secretary
Spouse: Mrs. Maria Mercedes Beltramino

Mr. Luis Ariel CASTILLO
First Secretary

Mr. Enrique Ignacio FERRER-VIEYRA
First Secretary
Spouse: Mrs. Monica Ferrer Vieyra

Mr. Roberto Ramon LAFFORGUE
First Secretary
Spouse: Mrs. Andrea Claudia F.
   de Lafforgue

Mrs. Maria Julia RODRIGUEZ DE MAS
First Secretary
Spouse: Mr. Ivan Mas

Ms. Graciela ABREU
Attaché (Administrative)

Mrs. Elsa Catalina BARONE DE LAMELA
Attaché
Spouse: Mr. Manuel Oscar Lamela

Mrs. Mabel Haydee BOITIER
Attaché (Administrative)
Spouse: Mr. Julio Boitier

Mrs. Silvia S. SPAGNOLO
Attaché (Administrative)
Spouse: Mr. Roger Armand Do Rosario

Mrs. Graciela VARELA DE APUD
Attaché (Administrative)
Spouse: Mr. Jose Antonio Apud

Rear Admiral Norberto Ulises PEREIRO
Defense and Naval Attaché
Spouse: Mrs. Adriana Pereiro

Major General Julio Alberto HANG
Military Attaché & Asst. Defense Attaché
Spouse: Mrs. Adriana Dipaolo de Hang

Major General Ricardo Jose CIASCHINI
Air Attaché and Asst. Defense Attaché
Spouse: Mrs. Lydia Raquel Elena
   Ciaschini

Lt. Colonel Alberto Pablo HOLGADO
Asst. Military Attaché
Spouse: Mrs. Monica Elena Schkliar

Captain Eduardo Luis AVILES
Asst. Naval Attaché
Spouse: Mrs. Maria de la Paz Dominguez
   de Aviles

Commander Oscar Osvaldo
   BRANDEBURGO
Asst. Naval Attaché
Spouse: Mrs. Ana Maria Grisoni
   de Brandeburgo

Commander Jorge Daniel MARQUARDT
Asst. Naval Attaché
Spouse: Mrs. Maria Ileana Flamini
   de Marquardt

Colonel Ernesto Jesus CUELLO

Asst. Air Attaché
Spouse: Mrs. Nora Angelica Soto
   de Cuello

Lt. Colonel Eduardo Jose FERNANDEZ
Asst. Air Attaché
Spouse: Mrs. Ana Maria Kramar
   de Fernandez

Colonel Huberto Horacio TULIAN
Asst. Air Attaché
Spouse: Mrs. Silvia Ramona Tulian

Accounting Section
1718 Connecticut Ave., NW
Suite 200
Washington DC 20009
Phone: 202/265-1673

Office of the Air Attaché
2405 I Street, NW
Washington DC 20037
Phone: 202/452-8500

Consular Section
1718 Connecticut Ave., NW
Suite 200
Washington DC 20009
Phone: 202/797-8826

Cultural Section
1718 Connecticut Ave., NW
Suite 200
Washington DC 20009
Phone: 202/785-4313

**Office of the Economic and
   Trade Representative**
1901 L Street, NW
Suite 606
Washington DC 20036
Phone: 202/265-4557

Financial Office
1901 L Street, NW
Suite 606
Washington DC 20036
Phone: 202/466-3021

Office of the Military Attaché
1810 Connecticut Ave., NW
Washington DC 20009
Phone: 202/667-4900

Office of the Naval Attaché
630 Indiana Ave., NW
Washington DC 20004
Phone: 202/626-2100

Armenia

Embassy of the Republic of Armenia
2225 R St., NW
Washington DC 20008
Phone: 202/319-1976
Fax: 202/319-2982
Email: teni@erols.com
Url: http://www.armeniaemb.org

Rouben Robert SHUGARIAN
Ambassador

Date Credentials Presented: 6/11/93

Born: 10/19/62 in Moscow

Spouse: Mrs. Lilit Karapetian

Prior to his appointment as Ambassador in Washington, Rouben Shugarian was spokesman to the President of the Republic of Armenia and, before that, a foreign affairs aide to the President and an advisor to the Standing Committee on Foreign Relations of the Armenian Parliament. During his early career, Shugarian had taken part in his country's struggle for autonomy, serving from 1989 to 1990 as spokesman for the Information Center of the Armenian National Movement.

Shugarian graduated from the Yerevan Institute of Foreign Languages, where he studied English and Russian. He completed post-graduate studies in philosophy and art at Yerevan State University. Shugarian is married and has two sons.

STAFF:

Mr. Tatoul MARKARIAN
Counselor

Ms. Hasmik HARUTYUNIAN
First Secretary (Political)

Ms. Lillit TOUTKHALIAN
First Secretary

Mr. Michael Georgi BAGRATUNI
Second Secretary (Press and Cultural)
Spouse: Mrs. Rouzan Bagratuni

Mr. Armen YEGANIAN
Third Secretary and Consul
Spouse: Mrs. Maria Yeganian

Australia

Embassy of Australia
1601 Massachusetts Avenue, NW
Washington DC 20036
Phone: 202/797-3000
Fax: 202/797-3168
Url: http://www.austemb.org

Andrew Sharp PEACOCK
Ambassador

Date Credentials Presented: 2/11/97

Born: 2/13/39 in Melbourne, Victoria

Andrew Sharp Peacock served in the Australian Federal Parliament from 1966 to 1994, holding a variety of ministerial portfolios. He began his duties as Australia's ambassador to the U.S. in February 1997.

Peacock's association with the Liberal Party and politics began when he joined the Young Liberals at the age of 17. He was president of the Young Liberal Movement in 1962-63; vice president of the Victorian division of the Liberal Party between 1963 and 1965; and president of the Victorian division of the party in 1965-66. From July 1985 to June 1987, he was chairman of the Pacific Democrat Union and from September 1989 to September 1992 he was chairman of the International Democrat Union.

He entered the Federal Parliament in April 1966 when he won a by-election for the Victorian seat of Kooyong and was reelected at each subsequent general election until his resignation in September 1994.

Peacock held the following ministerial portfolios: minister for the army, 1969-72; minister assisting the prime minister, 1969-71; minister assisting the treasurer, 1971-72; minister for external territories, 1972; minister for environment, 1975; minister for foreign affairs, 1975-1980; minister for industrial relations, 1980-81; and minister for industry and commerce, 1982-83.

In opposition, he held these positions: shadow minister for manufacturing industry, 1972-73; shadow minister for foreign affairs and external territories, 1973-75; leader of the opposition, 1983-85; shadow minister for foreign affairs, 1985-87; deputy leader of the opposition and shadow treasurer, 1987-89; leader of the opposition, 1989-90; shadow attorney-general and shadow minister for justice, 1990-92; shadow minister for trade, 1992-93; and shadow minister for foreign affairs, 1993-94.

He was educated at Scotch College and the University of Melbourne, where he graduated with a degree in law. Before entering parliament, he worked as a barrister, solicitor, and company director.

STAFF:

Mr. Paul T. O'SULLIVAN
Minister (Deputy Chief of Mission)
Spouse: Mrs. Merrily E. O'Sullivan

Mr. Kenneth Miles JORDANA
Minister-Counselor (Political)
Spouse: Mrs. Janette Margaret Ryan

Mr. Paul Charles MORRIS
Minister-Counselor (Agr. & Resources)
Spouse: Mrs. Maren Elizabeth Morris

Mr. Nigel RAY
Minister-Counselor (Economic)
Spouse: Mrs. Christine Ray

Mr. James Y. HASLAM
Counselor (Veterinary)
Spouse: Mrs. Maryanne G. Haslam

Ms. Amanda M. BUCKLEY
Counselor (Public Affairs)

Mr. Patrick William CARROLL
Counselor (Defense Policy)
Spouse: Mrs. Jeanette Mary Carroll

Mr. Laurence Gerard DALY
Counselor (Property)

Mr. Malcolm Linley FERGUSON
Counselor (Admin.) & Consul General
Spouse: Mrs. Lunlana Nganthawee

Mr. Athol G. GARDINER
Counselor (Customs)
Spouse: Mrs. Elizabeth A. Gardiner

Mr. Philip John GARTON
Counselor (Economic)
Spouse: Ms. Rachel Mary Trimmer

Mr. Robert GODFREY
Counselor (Nuclear)
Spouse: Mrs. Lucy Godfrey

Dr. Brandon C. HAMMER
Counselor (Political)
Spouse: Mrs. Inge S. Sugani

Mr. William James HENDERSON
Counselor (Communications and Transp.)
Spouse: Mrs. Michal A. Henderson

Mr. Michael Howard IVES
Counselor (Defense Acquisition & Logistics)

Mr. Graeme LADE
Counselor
Spouse: Mrs. Christine L. Lade

Mr. Howard Adrian LAWLER
Counselor
Spouse: Mrs. Deborah Anne Lawler

Mr. Michael Gerard LYNCH
Counselor
Spouse: Ms. Elizabeth Ann McKenna

Dr. Peter J. MILLER
Counselor (Veterinary)

Spouse: Mrs. Denise Patricia Miller

Mr. Timothy James MOY
Counselor (Political)
Spouse: Mrs. Leanne Erica Moy

Mr. Brendan M. PEARSON
Counselor (Commercial)
Spouse: Mrs. Josephine Pearson

Mr. John C. PRICE
Counselor (Trade Commission)
Spouse: Mrs. Teresa Price

Dr. Peter G. TUCKER
Counselor (Industry, Science & Techn.)
Spouse: Mrs. Nicole M. Tucker

Mr. Barry Edward WELSBY
Counselor (Immigration)

Dr. Raymond WOODWARD
Counselor (Defense Science)
Spouse: Mrs. Annette M. Woodward

Mr. Christian David BENNETT
First Secretary

Mr. Michael FORD
First Secretary (Commercial)

Mr. Alick Hugh LONGHURST
First Secretary (Political)

Mr. Alistair Charles MACLEAN
First Secretary (Commercial)
Spouse: Mrs. Jeanette Lucy O'Connor

Mr. Allen TODD
First Secretary (Technical)
Spouse: Mrs. Monica Todd

Ms. Mary T. WOODS
First Secretary (Immigration)
Spouse: Mr. Robert G. Davis

Mr. David A. COX
Second Secretary

Mr. Peter John DAVEY
Second Secretary

Ms. Denise EARNSHAW
Second Secretary (Immigration)

Mr. J. Scott IRONS
Second Secretary
Spouse: Mrs. Georgina Irons

Ms. Denise Margaret MORGAN
Second Secretary (Political)

Mr. Noel SCOBELL
Second Secretary (Police Liaison)
Spouse: Mrs. Tracey Scobell

Mr. John Michael WOODS
Second Secretary
Spouse: Mrs. Debbie Ann Woods

Mr. Mervyn T. JENKINS
Attaché (Defense Liaison)
Spouse: Mrs. Sandra P. Jenkins

Dr. Gregory C. L. SEARLE
Attaché (Defense Scientific)
Spouse: Mrs. Violetta Searle

Mr. Russell WALLS
Attaché (Defense)
Spouse: Mrs. Marlene Walls

Air Vice Marshal Brandon D. O'LOGHLIN
Defense Attaché
Spouse: Mrs. Helen J. O'Loghlin

Brigadier Simon WILLIS
Military Attaché & Asst. Defense Attaché
Spouse: Mrs. Wendy Willis

Commodore Geoffrey Alfred MORTON
Naval Attaché and Asst. Defense Attaché
Spouse: Mrs. Dianne Rosemary Morton

Commander Peter J. LAUNDER
Asst. Defense Attaché
Spouse: Mrs. Wendy M. Launder

Lt. Colonel Alan MCCLELLAND
Asst. Military Attaché
Spouse: Mrs. Susan McClelland

Commodore Glenn David CURRAN
Asst. Naval Attaché
Spouse: Mrs. Anne M. Curran

Wing Commander Paul John MCCANN
Asst. Naval and Air Attaché
Spouse: Mrs. Corrine Anne McCann

Austria

Embassy of Austria
3524 International Court, NW
Washington DC 20008
Phone: 202/895-6700
Fax: 202/895-6750
Url: http://www.austria.org/web/austria

Dr. Helmut TUERK

Ambassador

Date Credentials Presented: 4/14/93

Born: 04/24/41 in Linz, Austria

Spouse: Dr. Monika Tuerk

Most of Dr. Helmut Tuerk's professional career has been spent working on various aspects of international law, including human rights, international (space, sea and air) law, state property, and negotiations.

He has participated in numerous conferences as an Austrian delegate or delegation head. Among these were the 1983 Second World Conference to Combat Racism and Racial Discrimination, the 1983 United Nations Conference on the Succession of States in Respect of State Property, Archives and Debts, the 1976 United Nations Conference on Territorial Asylum, and numerous air and maritime navigation law conferences.

In 1987 and 1989, Tuerk led the Austrian delegation to the United Nations' Human Rights Commission. He was the head of the 1989 Austrian delegation and chair of the 6th Committee of the 44th United Nations General Assembly. From 1982 to 1993, Tuerk was the Austrian federal government agent before the European Commission on Human Rights and the European Court for Human Rights. Since 1986, he has been a member of the Permanent Court of Arbitration at The Hague.

After commencing his career with the Federal Ministry for Foreign Affairs' international law department in 1965, Tuerk served in embassies and consulates in Hong Kong and West Germany.

The U.S. should continue its strong role in Europe, particularly with respect to military security, according to Tuerk, but he thinks economic and cultural considerations should be emphasized too. He has noted that Austria can serve as a "docking place" for new democracies in Central and Eastern Europe and as a U.S. "gateway" to Central and Eastern Europe.

An exchange student in the United States in 1957 and 1958, Tuerk studied law at the University of Vienna from which he received a J.D. and the College of Europe in Bruges, Belgium.

Tuerk and his wife Dr. Monika Tuerk have three children.

STAFF:

Mr. Franz J. KUGLITSCH
Minister (Deputy Chief of Mission)

Mr. Michael SCHMIDT
Counselor
Spouse: Mrs. Claudia Kryza Gersch

Mr. Martin WEISS
Counselor (Political and Congressional)
Spouse: Mrs. Susanne Weiss

Mr. Stefan Franz Josef SCHOLZ
First Secretary (Trade Policy)
Spouse: Mrs. Angelika Scholz

Mr. Peter PRIES
Counselor (Administrative) & Consul Gen.
Spouse: Mrs. Leopoldine Pries

Mr. Christian GRINSCHGL
Attaché (Administrative)

Mr. Martin G. EICHTINGER
Counselor (Press and Information)
Spouse: Mrs. Kathrin Eichtinger

Mr. Ulf PACHER
Counselor (Press)

Mrs. Teresa INDJEIN
Attaché (Cultural)
Spouse: Mr. Alexandre Indjein

Ms. Isabella WOLTE
Attaché (Scientific)

Mr. Helmut WAGNER
Counselor (Commercial)
Spouse: Mrs. Babro Wagner

Brig. General Guntmar HECK
Defense, Military, Naval and Air Attaché
Spouse: Mrs. Ursula Heck

Colonel Werner KUNERTH
Asst. Defense, Military and Air Attaché
Spouse: Mrs. Gertraud Kunerth

Colonel Timmo UNFRIED
Asst. Defense, Military & Air Attaché
Spouse: Mrs. Doris Unfried

Mr. Thomas NAKLADAL
Asst. Attaché (Defense and Admin.)
Spouse: Mrs. Doris Nakladal

Commercial Counselor
1350 Connecticut Ave., NW
Suite 501
Washington DC 20036
Phone: 202/835-8962

Azerbaijan

Embassy of the Republic of Azerbaijan
927 15th Street, NW, Suite 700
Washington DC 20005
Phone: 202/842-0001
Fax: 202/842-0004

Hafiz Mir Jalal Oglu PASHAYEV

Ambassador

Date Credentials Presented: 4/14/93

Born: 5/2/41 in Baku, Azerbaijan

Spouse: Mrs. Rena Pashayeva

Hafiz Pashayev is the first Ambassador of the Republic of Azerbaijan to the United States. He has noted that Azerbaijan became the first nation in the Near and Middle East to establish an independent, democratic government. The Azerbaijan Democratic Republic was in existence from 1918 to 1920, when it was incorporated by force into the Soviet Union.

Azerbaijan is committed once again to establishing a democratic government and a free market economy, according to Pashayev. He has emphasized that Azerbaijan recognizes such international agreements as the United Nations Charter, the United Nations Covenant on Civil and Political Rights, and the CSCE Helsinki Final Accords on human rights.

Upon presenting his credentials as Ambassador to the United States, Pashayev stated, "I can only hope that during my tenure the United States will become one of the most respected influences and powers in the region, as it uses its power to enhance the healing, arbitration, peace and prosperity for all peoples in this entire complex region of the Caucasus."

In 1984, Pashayev was named full professor at the Academy of Science in Azerbaijan. Prior to his appointment as Ambassador to the United States, Pashayev taught physics at Baku State University and served as director of the Metal Physics Laboratory in the Institute of Physics at the Azerbaijan Academy of Sciences in Baku.

Pashayev received a degree in physics from Baku State University in 1963 and Ph.D. in solid state physics from the Institute of Atomic Energy in Moscow in 1971. In 1975-76, he did research at the University of California at Irvine. He is the author of more than 80 scientific articles and books.

Pashayev is married to Rena Pashyeva, a scholar and professor of Arabic literature and history. They have two children.

STAFF:

Mr. Fakhradin Isa KURBANOV
First Secretary and Consul
Spouse: Mrs. Saida Samedova

Mr. Mahir Chingiz Oglu KHALIFA-ZADE
Second Secretary (Political)
Spouse: Mrs. Samira Javer Gizi
  Khalifa-Zade

Mr. Takhir T. TAGI ZADE
Second Secretary

Mr. Araz Fazil ABBASOV
Third Secretary
Spouse: Mrs. Madina Shamil Mamedova

Mr. Anar Namik ABBASOV
Attaché

Ms. Utarida Izzat HUSSEYNOVA
Attaché

Mr. Yusif Orhan VEZIROV
Attaché

Bahamas

Embassy of The Commonwealth of
  The Bahamas
2220 Massachusetts Avenue, NW
Washington DC 20008
Phone: 202/319-2660
Fax: 202/319-2668

Arlington Griffith BUTLER
Ambassador

Date Credentials Presented: 7/29/96

Born: 1/2/38 in Nassau, The Bahamas

Spouse: Lady Sheila Paulette Butler

Sir Arlington Griffith Butler served as the first speaker of the House of Assembly after The Bahamas gained independence in 1973. Sir Arlington had been in line for the speaker's post, having served as chairman of the Progressive Liberal Party (PLP) and having won election to Parliament in April 1968 and again in 1972. In 1977, he left the PLP, offering himself as an independent candidate for Parliament. He ran on the Free National Movement ticket in 1982 and 1987 and won in the 1992 election when the Free National movement won control of the government. He has served as Minister of Public Safety and Immigration, Transport and Minister of Public Works in the Free National Movement government.

During his public career, Sir Arlington has been chairman of the Broadcasting Corporation of The Bahamas, the gaming board, and the hotel licensing authority. He has been a member of the Committee on the Prerogative of Mercy, the 1973 Independence Committee, and vice president of the Commonwealth Speakers Association.

In the sporting arena, Sir Arlington has, since

1972, been president of The Bahamas Olympic Association. In 1994, he was awarded the Olympic Order of the International Olympic Committee.

Sir Arlington has led or been part of numerous Bahamian sporting delegations to games and meetings all over the world. He is a vice president of The Bahamas Amateur Athletic Association and has served as president of The Bahamas American Football Association and the St. Agnes Cricket Club.

Sir Arlington, who attended The Bahamas Teacher's College, took his first teaching assignment at age 19 with a two-year stint at the Deep Creek All-Age School in South Eleuthera. He subsequently served as principal at several schools before he left The Bahamas in 1961 to attend the University of Loughborough in the United Kingdom. He returned to The Bahamas in 1964 and became a master at Government High School, remaining at that post until 1966. He began to study law in the late 1960s and passed The Bahamas bar in 1974.

Sir Arlington and his wife, the former Sheila Smith of West End, Grand Bahama, have four children.

STAFF:

Ms. Sheila G. CAREY
Minister-Counselor
  (Deputy Chief of Mission) & Consul

Ms. Edda D. DUMONT
First Secretary and Consul
Spouse: Mr. Ronald P. Adolph

Ms. Rhoda Mae JACKSON
First Secretary and Consul

Mr. Eugene TORCHON NEWRY
Second Secretary and Vice Consul
Spouse: Mrs. Yvette Pintard Newry

Ms. Monique Denean MAJOR
Attaché

Bahrain

Embassy of the State of Bahrain
3502 International Drive, NW
Washington DC 20008
Phone: 202/342-0741
Fax: 202/362-2192

Dr. Muhammad ABDUL GHAFFAR
Ambassador

Date Credentials Presented: 2/14/94

Born: 1/15/49 in Manama, Bahrain

*Spouse: Mrs. Mariam Mohmood
      Al-Mahmood*

Muhammad Abdul Ghaffar served as Bahrain's permanent representative to the United Nations in New York for three years before taking his post in Washington. He had been a member of the Bahrain delegation to all sessions of the U.N. General Assembly since 1979.

He has served in a number of positions in Bahrain's Ministry of Foreign Affairs, including senior counsellor, senior first secretary of international affairs and international organization, senior first secretary of the economic directorate, and second secretary in Bahrain's Embassy in Amman, Jordan.

Between 1976 and 1993, he was a participant in the Ministerial and Summit Conferences of the Gulf Cooperation Council, the Arab League, and Non-Aligned Movement.

He received a B.A. in political science from Poona University in India in 1974; a certificate in economics and trade promotion from the Arab Institute for Economic and Social Planning in Kuwait and at the German Foundation for International Development in Germany; an M.A. from the New School for Social Research in New York in 1981; and a Ph.D. from State University of New York at Binghamton in 1991.

He and his wife have five children.

STAFF:

Mr. Abdul Hakim Mohamed BUHIJI
First Secretary (Deputy Chief of Mission)
Spouse: Mrs. Amina Othman Alzayani

Mr. Jaber Fahad ALROMAIHI
First Secretary
Spouse: Mrs. Shaikha Ali Alzeabi

Mr. Yusuf JAMEEL
Second Secretary

Mr. Abdulaziz Mohamed ALRAFAEI
Attaché (Cultural)

Spouse: Mrs. Ebtisam Rashed Alallan
Lt. Colonel Khalifa Ali AL-KHALIFA
Defense, Military, Naval and Air Attaché
Spouse: Mrs. Maryam Mubarak Alkhalifa

Bangladesh

Embassy of the People's Republic
   of Bangladesh
2201 Wisconsin Avenue, NW - #300
Washington DC 20007
Phone: 202/342-8372
Fax: 202/333-4971
Email: BanglaEmb@aol.com
Url: http://members.aol.com/banglaemb/
   index.html

K.M. SHEHABUDDIN
Ambassador

Date Credentials Presented: 2/11/97

Born: 1/13/40

Spouse: Mrs. Khaleda Shehabuddin

A career diplomat, K.M. Shehabuddin came to his post as ambassador to the U.S. in November 1996 from Paris, where he served as Bangladesh's ambassador to France for five years. During that time, he also served as ambassador to Spain and as permanent delegate to UNESCO and the World Tourism Organization.

Shehabuddin, whose career began in the Pakistan foreign service in 1966, was the first Bangladesh diplomat to resign from that organization in April 1971 to take part in the Bangladesh Liberation War. As the first head of the Bangladesh Mission in 1971 to New Delhi, he contributed significantly to the liberation of his country.

He was assigned to various posts in the following capitals: New Delhi, first secretary, chargé d'affaires, 1968-72; Paris, first secretary, 1972-75; Beirut, Lebanon, chargé d'affaires, 1975-76; London, deputy high commissioner, 1979-82; Warsaw, minister, chargé d'affaires, 1983-85 and, from 1985 to 1987, as ambassador (concurrently accredited to Hungary); and ambassador to Kuwait (concurrently accredited to Yemen), 1987-91. His term as ambassador to France ran from 1991 until 1996.

In Bangladesh's foreign ministry, Shehabuddin served as director and director-general on several occasions. He also was joint secretary-in-charge (acting secretary-general, Bangladesh) of the relief and rehabilitation division at the ministry of food in 1982-83. He was promoted to the rank of the secretary of the government's A Category Ambassador in November 1993.

During the Iraqi occupation of Kuwait in 1990, Ambassador Shehabuddin maintained close contact with western embassies in Kuwait and kept the Bangladesh Embassy open for 45 days until Sept. 16, 1990, defying the orders of the occupation forces to close the diplomatic mission before Aug. 24. For his defiance, Shehabuddin was prevented from leaving for Bangladesh by another 15 days until Oct. 1, 1990.

The ambassador has traveled widely as a member of Bangladesh delegations to many countries in South and South-East Asia, the Middle East, Europe, and America. He attended United Nations General Assembly sessions several times.

Shehabuddin holds B.A. and M.A. degrees from Dhaka University.

STAFF:

Ms. Nasim FIRDAUS
Counselor (Deputy Chief of Mission)
Spouse: Mr. Muhit Choudhury

Dr. Quazi Mesbahuddin AHMED
Minister (Economic)
Spouse: Mrs. Rehana Ahmed

Mr. Md. Shahjahan MIAN
Minister (Press)
Spouse: Mrs. Hasina Jahan

Mr. A. M. Yakub ALI
Counselor (Head of Chancery)
Spouse: Mrs. Mehera Yakub

Mr. Mizanur RAHMAN
Counselor (Commercial)
Spouse: Mrs. Monwara Begum

Mr. Mushfiq Us SWALEHEEN
Counselor (Economic)
Spouse: Mrs. Nasrin Sultana Swaleheen

Mr. Jahangir HOSSAIN
First Secretary

Brigadier Mohammed Zikir HOSSAIN
Defense, Military, Naval and Attaché
Spouse: Mrs. Nasreen Begum

Lt. Colonel Zahur UL ALAM
Asst. Defense, Military and Air Attaché
Spouse: Mrs. Anju M. Begum

Barbados

Embassy of Barbados
2144 Wyoming Avenue, NW

Washington DC 20008
Phone: 202/939-9200
Fax: 202/332-7467
Email: barbados@oas.org
Url: http://www.barbados.org

Dr. Courtney N.M. BLACKMAN
Ambassador

Date Credentials Presented: 3/20/95

Born: 3/06/33 in Barbados

Spouse: Gloria Nee McKoy

Courtney N.M. Blackman was an international business consultant for the seven years preceding his posting in Washington. Between 1972 and 1987, he was the governor of the Central Bank of Barbados.

As a consultant, Blackman advised, among others, the Center for Monetary Studies of Latin America and the Caribbean; the Central Bank of Oman; the Governments of Zanzibar, Colombia, and Curacao; the Organization of Eastern Caribbean States; and The Ford Foundation.

As governor of the Central Bank, Blackman managed an institution with assets of $250 million and supervised a staff of 200. He was responsible to the Minister of Finance for the formulation and execution of monetary and balance of payments policy and for the supervision of the financial sector. He served as alternate governor of the IMF between 1973-87.

Blackman received a B.A. in modern history, with honors, at University College of the West Indies and a Ph.D. in money and banking from the Graduate School of Business at Columbia University.

STAFF:

Mr. Ricardo Randolph BROWNE
Minister-Counselor

Miss Annalee C. BABB
First Secretary and Consul

Miss Pamela Veronica STROUDE
Second Secretary

Ms. Rose C. GREAVES
Attaché

Ms. Betty Eulene CALLENDER
Attaché and Vice Consul

Miss Myrtle D. BISHOP
Counselor (Commercial)

Lt. Colonel Jeffrey D. BOSTIC
Defense Attaché

Belarus

Embassy of the Republic of Belarus
1619 New Hampshire Avenue, NW
Washington DC 20009
Phone: 202/986-1604
Fax: 202/986-1805
Email: belaremb@pop.erols.com

Valery V. TSEPKALO
Ambassador

Date Credentials Presented: 5/14/97

Born: 1965 in Grodno, Belarus

Spouse: Mrs. Veronika Tsepkalo

Valery V. Tsepkalo became Belarus' ambassador to the U.S. in 1997 after serving for three years as first deputy minister of foreign affairs in Belarus.

In 1994, he served as advisor to the executive secretary of the Commonwealth of Independent States. In 1993-94, he was an advisor on international affairs to the chairman of the Supreme Council of Belarus. Tsepkalo worked at the ministry of foreign affairs of Belarus in 1992-93. Before that, in 1991, he worked at the USSR Embassy in Finland.

Tsepkalo studied at the Belarusian Technological Institute in Minsk from 1982 to 1984, after which he served in the army for two years. Between 1986 and 1991, he studied at the Moscow State Institute of International Relations.

He has written 40 articles on international security, foreign policy, and the world economy and is the author of a number of publications on Russian nationalism. He has

developed scenarios of globalization of ethnic conflicts in Eurasia and has lectured on the problems of geopolitics and modern international relations and on modern neo-conservatism.

Tsepkalo is the author of the book, *By the Road of the Dragon*, published in 1994, on the experience of economic development of the new industrial nations of South-East Asia.

STAFF:

Mr. Yevgeniy G. BOGOMAZOV
Counselor
Spouse: Mrs. Lyudmilla Bogomazova

Mr. Arkady M. CHEREPANSKY
Counselor
Spouse: Mrs. Ivetta V. Cherepanskaya

Mr. Leanid L. SENNIKAU
Counselor
Spouse: Mrs. Tamara V. Sennikava

Mr. Valentin B. RYBAKOV
First Secretary
Spouse: Mrs. Irina Rybakov

Mr. Vladimir M. SERPIKOV
First Secretary
Spouse: Mrs. Tatyana I. Malevskaya

Mr. Dmitriy Victorovich GRISHCHENKO
Third Secretary & Vice Consul
Spouse: Mrs. Yelena A. Grishchenko

Mr. Valery M. TSYNKEVICH
Third Secretary

Belgium

Embassy of Belgium
3330 Garfield Street, NW
Washington DC 20008
Phone: 202/333-6900
Fax: 202/333-3079
Email: usa@belgium-emb.org
Url: http://www.belgium-emb.org/usa

Andre ADAM
Ambassador

Date Credentials Presented: 11/21/94

Born: 9/10/36

Spouse: Mrs. Danielle David

A veteran of the Belgian Foreign Service, Andre Adam held the post of director general for political affairs in the Ministry of Foreign Affairs for three years before coming to Washington. In that capacity, he presided over the European Union Political Committee.

Adam's other diplomatic assignments included two previous Ambassadorships--to Algeria, starting in 1986, and Zaire, starting in 1990. He entered the Foreign Service in 1962, after which he held positions in Havana, Paris, Kinshasa, and London. In 1979, he became "Chef de Cabinet" of Minister of Foreign Affairs Henri Simonet, and then in 1980, head of the Energy Division of the Ministry of Foreign Affairs.

In 1982, he was named Consul General of Belgium in Los Angeles. As Olympic Attaché for Belgium during the 1984 Olympic Games, he created a Californian non-profit organization to raise funds for the Belgian Olympic team.

Adam has written articles about Belgian export penetration and regional economic policy and other articles about international trade. He is a staunch supporter of European unity and has been instrumental in devising procedures for starting the common foreign and security policy of the European Union after the ratification of the Maastricht Treaty in 1993.

He has a degree in political and diplomatic science and a degree in public administration from the University of Brussels. In addition to his native French, Adam speaks English, Dutch, Spanish, and German.

STAFF:

Mr. Johan C. VERBEKE
Minister (Political and Deputy
  Chief of Mission)
Spouse: Mrs. Catherine Dubois

Mr. Raoul DELCORDE
Minister-Counselor (Economic)
Spouse: Mrs. Fatemeh B. Favadi

Mr. Jan ADRIANSENS
Counselor (Agricultural)
Spouse: Mrs. Francine Hindrickx

Mr. Martin HINOUL
Counselor (Technological, Defense
  Research and Engineering)
Spouse: Mrs. Helena Hinoul-Bieseman

Mr. Rudolf HUYGELEN
First Secretary (Political)
Spouse: Mrs. Ellen Petzel

Mr. Willy MERTENS
First Secretary and Consul

Spouse: Mrs. Jenny D'Haeseleer

Mr. Walter STEVENS
First Secretary (Economic)
Spouse: Mrs. Godelieve Janssens

Mr. Dirk VERHEYEN
First Secretary (Trade)
Spouse: Mrs. Sarita Sterckx

Mr. Pierre DE BAUW
Second Secretary
Spouse: Mrs. Anne-Cecile M. Marechal

Mr. Ivo SCHALBROECK
First Secretary (Political)
Spouse: Mrs. Margareta Ral

Mr. Patrick EVERARTS DE VELP
Attaché (Economic and Commercial)
Spouse: Mrs. Francoise Everarts de Velp

Mr. Peter GROGNARD
Attaché (Science)
Spouse: Mrs. Nathalie Duprez

Mr. Bart Jan HENDRICKX
Attaché
Spouse: Mrs. Lutgart M. Severijns

Mr. Pascal HEUS
Attaché (Communications)
Spouse: Mrs. Chantal Vermeire

Mr. Roland PIETERS
Attaché (Communications)
Spouse: Mrs. Hilde Pieters

Mr. Etienne VAN MOL
Attaché
Spouse: Mrs. Irene Van De Voorde

Mr. Freddy VANBAELEN
Attaché (Communications)
Spouse: Mrs. Myriam Vanbaelen

Brig. General Jozef Filip DE HEYN
Defense, Military, Naval, Air and Defense
Cooperation Attaché
Spouse: Mrs. Virginia Laenen

Lt. Col. Raymond Louis PIERLOT
Asst. Defense, Military, Naval, Air &
  Defense Cooperation Attaché
Spouse: Mrs. Micheline Marie Michaux

Belize

Embassy of Belize
2535 Massachusetts Avenue, NW
Washington DC 20008
Phone: 202/332-9636
Fax: 202/332-6888

James S. MURPHY
Ambassador

Date Credentials Presented: 10/9/96

Born: 7/26/52

Spouse: Mrs. Bessie Tam Murphy

James S. Murphy has been Belize's ambassador to the U.S. since 1996, as well as his country's permanent representative to the Organization of American States and high commissioner to Canada.

He came to Washington, D.C., after serving as community relations officer in the ministry of national security in Belmopan in 1995 and 1996. Before that, he was a teacher in the ministry of education, stationed at Belize Continuation School in Belize City.

Between 1990 and 1994, he was president of St. John's College in Belize City and a lecturer in political science at St. John's College Sixth Form. In the previous two years, he was a lecturer in political science and social ethics at St. John's College Sixth Form. Between 1978 and 1981, he was a lecturer in social studies and religious studies at St. John's College High School in Belize City.

Murphy has a professional diploma in administration and supervision from Fordham University in New York City, 1987-88; a master of theology degree from Weston School of Theology in Cambridge, Mass., 1986-87; a master of divinity degree from Weston School of Theology, 1983-86; a master of arts degree in political science from St. Louis University, St. Louis, Mo., 1981-83; and a bachelor of arts degree in philosophy, cum laude, from St. Louis University, 1974-78.

Murphy is a member of Alpha Sigma Nu (National Jesuit Honour Society) and Pi Sigma Alpha (National Political Science Honour Society).

STAFF:

Mr. Claude Bromwell Fitzgeral HAYLOCK
Minister-Counselor (Deputy Chief of
  Mission)
Spouse: Mrs. Sharon Claudette
  Brennen Haylock

Miss Lauren Laverne QUIROS
Attaché and Consul
Spouse: Mr. Milton A. G. Nieto

Benin

Embassy of the Republic of Benin
2737 Cathedral Avenue, NW
Washington DC 20008
Phone: 202/232-6656
Fax: 202/265-1996

Lucien Edgar TONOUKOUIN
Ambassador

Date Credentials Presented: 11/21/94

Spouse: Mrs. Justine Tonoukouin

Lucien Tonoukouin began his diplomatic career in 1972, serving as the president of Benin's Chief of Protocol and adjunct director of financial and administrative affairs at the Ministry of Foreign Affairs.

Tonoukouin has served as first counsel and chargé d'Affaires in Germany (1976-82), with jurisdiction over Austria, Switzerland, Denmark, Norway, and Sweden, and as ambassador to Ghana (1982-90), with accreditation to Togo and Burkina Faso. Since 1990, he has participated in several delegations from Benin at international conferences in Africa, Europe, Asia, and the U.S.

Educated in France, Tonoukouin received a diploma in international and public administration and a law degree. He is married and the father of four.

STAFF:

Mr. Theodore-Honore AHIMAKIN
Minister-Counselor
Spouse: Mrs. Ahimakin

Ms. Haolatou ASSANI PIO
Counselor

Mr. Blaise Yao AKOTCHENOUDE
First Secretary (Financial and Administrative)
Spouse: Mrs. Akotchenoude

Mr. Kouassi GUIDI
First Secretary (Press and Information)
Spouse: Mrs. Guidi

Bolivia

Embassy of the Republic of Bolivia
3014 Massachusetts Avenue, NW
Washington DC 20008
Phone: 202/483-4410
Fax: 202/328-3712
Email: bolembus@erols.com

Marcelo PEREZ MONASTERIOS

Ambassador

Date Credentials Presented: 12/12/97

Born: 9/27/29 in La Paz, Bolivia

Spouse: Mrs. Elba Reyes Trigo de Perez

Marcelo Perez Monasterios brought 47 years of activism in the private sector with him to his post as Bolivia's ambassador to the U.S. He had also served in the public sector as vice minister in Bolivia's ministry of foreign affairs and worship.

Perez was president and general manager of Sociedad Comercial Andina S.A. (SOCOMAN S.A.) and of Companie Importadora Panamericana (CIPAN S.A.) He was promoter, founder, and former president of the Bolivian Stock Market S.A.

He served as an ambassador in a special mission to the V Centennial Commemoration, and is a former director of the Bolivian Olympic Committee. He was president and advisor to the Confederation of the Andean Chambers of Commerce and was designated president for life of the National Association of Representatives, Importers, and Distributors of Pharmaceuticals (ASOFAR)

Perez is an honorary president for life and a permanent director of the Bolivian Chamber of Commerce and was named a permanent member of the board of directors at the Confederation of Private Entrepreneurs of Bolivia.

He was a former president of the following groups: the Athletic Association of La Paz, the Bolivian Federation of Athletism, the Bolivian Tennis Federation, the Bolivian Junior Chamber, and the board of the Bolivia Mining Corporation. He headed the economic commission for the visit of the Pope to Bolivia as the representative of the Confederation of the Private Entrepreneurs of Bolivia.

Perez has a high school diploma from Colegio Jesuita San Calixto in La Paz. He studied economics at Universidad Mayor de San Andres and specialized in marketing and business administration at universities in the U.S., Chile, and Peru. He and his wife have a son, Marcelo, and three daughters, Mariana, Elba, and Veronica.

Perez was presented the Orden el Libertador San Martin by the president of Argentina. He received a medal and recognition from the Interamerican Council on Trade and Production CICYP and a coat of arms from the City of La Paz for special services.

STAFF:

Mr. Gonzalo AVILA PEDUCASSE
Minister-Counselor (Deputy Chief of Mission)
Spouse: Mrs. Marlene Otazo De Avila

Mrs. Maria TAMAYO DE ARNAL
Minister Counselor

Mr. John Paul MARTIN ROJAS
Counselor (Commercial)
Spouse: Ms. Monica Iturralde De Martin

Ms. Sissy TORRICO CALVIMONTES
Counselor

Mr. Marcelo Javier ALFARO
First Secretary (Legal)

Mr. Carlos Javier IBARGUEN
First Secretary (Commercial)

Ms. Beatriz REVOLLO PACHECO
First Secretary (Consular)

Ms. Maria A. TERRAZAS-ONTIVEROS
First Secretary (Consular)

Mrs. Maria Teresa CAMPERO
Second Secretary
Spouse: Ms. Francisco Pineros

Mrs. Matilde C. BUSCH
Attaché

Colonel Edgar Abel PARDO MONTALVO
Attaché
Spouse: Mrs. Betzabe Benita Velasquez De Pardo

Ms. Aida VALDIVIA
Attaché (Administrative)

Colonel Fernando CALDERON
Military Attaché
Spouse: Mrs. Selvy Calderon

Cap. Alberto SHIOSAKY ESCALANTE
Naval Attaché
Spouse: Mrs. Danyck De Shiosaky

Colonel Oscar MARISCAL
Air Attaché
Spouse: Mrs. Ana Guilarte De Mariscal

Captain Sabad LINO
Asst. Military Attaché
Spouse: Mrs. Ximena Lino

Lt. Carlos VALDIVIA
Asst. Military Attaché
Spouse: Mrs. Elizabeth Sandra Flores

Colonel Antonio LUJAN
Assistant Air Attaché

Spouse: Mrs. Consuelo Lujan

Bosnia & Herzegovina

Embassy of the Republic of
Bosnia and Herzegovina
2109 E Street, NW
Washington DC 20037
Phone: 202/337-1500
Fax: 202/337-1502
Email: emofbih@aol.com
Url: http://www.bosnianembassy.com

Sven ALKALAJ

Ambassador

Date Credentials Presented: 6/23/94

Born: 11/11/48 in Sarajevo

Spouse: Mrs. Naila Alkalaj

Sven Alkalaj became the first Ambassador
to the U.S. of the Republic of Bosnia and
Herzegovina after serving for several months
as Chargé d'Affaires, of the newly opened
Embassy of his country in Washington.

Alkalaj's professional business career has
taken him from Europe to the Far East. He
began his career with Petrolinvest, a Bosnian
engineering company for the design and
construction of refineries and petrochemical
and chemical plants. Later, he worked in
the head office of Energoinvest in Sarajevo,
the largest engineering and exporting
company in the former Yugoslavia, which
operated 20 offices worldwide. He was the
regional manager for the firm's Middle East
and Far East regions. He became the
managing director of Energoinvest in its
Bangkok, Thailand, branch office in 1988.

Alkalaj earned a bachelor of science degree
in mechanical engineering from the
University of Sarajevo in 1974. In 1987, he
earned his master's degree from the same
university in international economics. He is
fluent in French and English, is married, and
has one child.

STAFF:

Mr. Malik SKALJIC

Counselor
Spouse: Mrs. Belma Skaljic

Mr. Sead TIKVINA
First Secretary

Ms. Meliha BASIC
Attaché

Colonel Suad CENGIC
Defense, Military, Naval, & Air Attaché
Spouse: Mrs. Dzenita Cengic

Colonel Miroslav NIKOLIC
Asst. Def., Military, Naval, & Air Attaché
Spouse: Mrs. Jadranka Nikolic

Botswana

Embassy of the Republic of Botswana
3400 International Drive, NW, Suite 7M
Washington DC 20008
Phone: 202/244-4990
Fax: 202/244-4164
Email: botwash@compuserve.com

Archibald Mooketsa MOGWE

Ambassador

Date Credentials Presented: 2/6/96

Born: 8/29/21 in Kanye, Botswana

Spouse: Mrs. Serara S. Mogwe

After Botswana became independent,
Archibald Mooketsa Mogwe served as the
country's first secretary for foreign affairs in
1966. In 1967, he was promoted to the office
of permanent secretary to the President,
secretary to the Cabinet, and head of the
Public Service, a position he held until 1974.
From 1974 to 1984, Mogwe was assigned
the portfolio of minister of external affairs.
Then, in 1994, he became minister for
Mineral Resources and Water Affairs.

Diplomacy is not a new field to Mogwe. As
permanent secretary and minister of external
affairs, he travelled widely, attending
conferences, meetings of Frontline Presidents
involved in the struggle for the liberation of
Angola, Mozambique, Namibia, and
Zimbabwe. He played a vital role in the
creation of the Southern Africa Development
Community (S.A.D.C.).

Mogwe received his secondary and university
education in South Africa obtaining a
bachelor of arts degree. He studied educational
administration at the University of Reading,
Berkshire, U.K., and international relations
at a Foreign Service course at Oxford
University in England.

He has three children---a son and two
daughters.

STAFF:

Mr. Mustaq Agmed MOORAD
Counselor
Spouse: Mrs. Denise Moorad

Mr. John Thomas DIPOWE
First Secretary
Spouse: Mrs. Dipowe

Mr. Clifford MARIBE
First Secretary

Mrs. Seore Alice LASARO
Attaché (Administrative)
Spouse: Mr. Lasaro

Mrs. Seodi Yada KHAMA
Attaché (Education)

Mr. Peloeritle Shakie KEBASWELE
Attaché (Commercial)
Spouse: Mrs. Kebaswele

Lt. Colonel Duke MASILO
Defense, Military and Air Attaché
Spouse: Mrs. Lulu Laone Masilo

Brazil

Brazilian Embassy
3006 Massachusetts Avenue, NW
Washington DC 20008
Phone: 202/238-2700
Fax: 202/238-2827
Url: http://www.brasil.emb.nw.dc.us

Paulo-Tarso FLECHA DE LIMA

Ambassador

Date Credentials Presented: 12/8/93

Born: 7/8/33 in Belo Horizone,
Minas Gerais

Spouse: Mrs. Lucia Martins Flecha de Lima

A career foreign service officer and expert in foreign trade relations, Paulo-Tarso Flecha de Lima has had almost four decades of international experience. Immediately prior to his appointment to Washington, he served as Brazil's Ambassador to the Court of St. James.

During his early career, Flecha de Lima served as a member of the staff of President Juscelino Kubitschek and as chief of staff of the government of the State of Guanabara. His first foreign posting was as Secretary at the Brazilian Embassy in Rome during 1961 and 1962. In the following years, he served as secretary and deputy representative to the Latin American Free Trade Association. After that, he headed the Brazil's New York Trade Promotion Sector from 1969 to 1971.

In 1971, Flecha de Lima was appointed head of Brazil's Trade Promotion Department. During his 13-year tenure, he revamped and modernized overseas support for Brazil's trade and investment promotion activities. In 1984, he became under-secretary for economic and commercial affairs, and in the following year, he was named to the highest post in Brazil's diplomatic service, secretary-general of external relations.

Since then, Flecha de Lima has participated in Presidential trips across North America, Europe, Africa, and Asia, and has served as ambassador on a special negotiation mission to the U.S. concerning bilateral investment. He served later as Brazil's special representative for trade negotiations before his move to London as ambassador.

Flecha de Lima holds a law degree from the University of Brazil in Rio de Janeiro. He is married and has five children.

STAFF:

Mr. Antonio Lisboa Mena GONCALVES
Minister-Counselor (Deputy Chief of Mission)
Spouse: Mrs. Elizabeth Goncalves

Ms. Maria Stela FROTA
Minister-Counselor
Spouse: Mr. Antonio Frota

Mr. Regis P. ARSLANIAN
Minister-Counselor
Spouse: Mrs. Maria Beatriz Arslanian

Mr. Luiz A. F. MACHADO
Counselor
Spouse: Mrs. Vania L.L. Machado

Mr. Marcos V. P. GAMA
Counselor
Spouse: Mrs. Claudia Nunes P. Gama

Mr. Luis Henrique S. LOPES
Counselor
Spouse: Mrs. Dora S. Lopes

Mr. Helio Vitor Ramos FILHO
First Secretary

Mr. Nilo BARROSO NETO
First Secretary
Spouse: Mrs. Maria Hollanda Barroso

Mr. Andre A. CORREA DO LAGO
First Secretary (Cultural)
Spouse: Mrs. Beatrice W.C. do Lago

Mr. Carlos De Abreu E SILVA
First Secretary
Spouse: Mrs. Morganan De Abreu Silva

Mr. Francisco Carlos Soares LUZ
First Secretary

Ms. Wanja Campos Da NOBREGA
First Secretary (Consul)
Spouse: Mr. Aldemo Garcia Junior

Mr. Norberto MORETTI
Second Secretary
Spouse: Mrs. Jacqueline Moretti

Mr. Renato Mosca DE SOUZA
Second Secretary
Spouse: Mrs. Luciana Duarte Paiva Arantes

Ms. Ana Paula Simoes SILVA
Second Secretary

Mr. Jose Raphael AZEREDO
Second Secretary
Spouse: Mrs. Vanessa De Andrade Azeredo

Mr. Philip YANG
Second Secretary

Mr. Rodrigo De Azeredo SANTOS
Second Secretary
Spouse: Mrs. Marilia C. A. Santos

Ms. Maria Elisa R. MAIA
Third Secretary

Mr. Aristides Jose de Souza MARTINS
Attaché
Spouse: Mrs. Martins

Mr. Celso Ricardo Hottum MEIRA
Attaché
Spouse: Mrs. Alice Maria R. Meira

Mr. Dival LARA
Attaché
Spouse: Mrs. Angela M. B. Lara

Mrs. Elida De SOUZA MOORE
Attaché & Vice Consul
Spouse: Mr. Kenneth Moore

Ms. Elgeni STRZELESKI
Attaché
Washington DC 20008

Mr. Jose Raul TEIXEIRA
Attaché
Spouse: Mrs. Teixeira

Mrs. Maria Ester G. CARVALHO
Attaché

Spouse: Mr. Ary Mamede Cruzeiro

Ms. Maria Humbertina NOBREGA
Attaché

Mrs. Maria Leonor Ramos BATES
Attaché
Spouse: Mr. Ronald Leland Bates

Mr. Mauricio Souza LEITE
Attaché

Mr. Patricio PORTO FILHO
Attaché

Ms. Sonia Reis DA COSTA
Attaché

Mrs. Telma Leda Monteiro NORBREGA
Attaché
Spouse: Mr. Carlos O. Victorino

Major General Sergio P. M. CORDEIRO
Military Attaché
Spouse: Mrs. Vera Lucia P. M. Cordeiro

Colonel Renato C. LEMOS
Asst. Military Attaché
Spouse: Mrs. Angela Ramos Lemos

Colonel Paulo Kazunori KOMATSU
Asst. Military Attaché
Spouse: Mrs. Maria Pedrosa Komatsu

Rear Admiral Kleber Luciano De ASSIS
Naval Attaché
Spouse: Mrs. Dolores de Assis

Captain Luiz Umberto MENDONCA
Asst. Naval Attaché
Spouse: Mrs. Albertina Maria Mendonca

Captain Paulo Roberto De Oliveira ELIAS
Asst. Naval Attaché
Spouse: Mrs. Nilce Fonseca Elias

Major General Valdir SOUSA
Air Attaché
Spouse: Mrs. Isa K. Y. Sousa

Colonel Emilio F. DRUMMOND
Asst. Air Attaché
Spouse: Mrs. Regina M. Drummond

Colonel Hiromiti YOSHIOKA
Asst. Air Attaché
Spouse: Mrs. Magdalena K. Yoshioka

Brazilian Aeronautical Commission
1701 22nd. St., NW
Washington DC 20008
Phone: 202/483-4031

Brazilian Army Commission
4632 Wisconsin Ave., NW
Washington DC 20016
Phone: 202/244-5010

Brazilian Naval Commission
5130 MacArthur Blvd., NW
Washington DC 20016-3344
Phone: 202/244-3950

Brunei Darussalam

Embassy of the State of Brunei Darussalam
2600 Virginia Avenue, NW, Suite 300
Washington DC 20037
Phone: 202/342-0159
Fax: 202/342-0158
Email: tutong@erols.com

Pengiran Anak Dato PUTEH
Ambassador

Date Credentials Presented: 5/14/97

Born: 1/19/51

Spouse: Mrs. Datin Kamilah Abdullah

Before coming to Washington, D.C., as
Brunei Darussalam's ambassador to the U.S.
in 1997, Pengiran Anak Dato Puteh served
for ten years as permanent secretary of the
ministry of foreign affairs in Brunei
Darussalam. He served briefly as his
country's ambassador to Japan in 1986.

Puteh's first job in the civil service was in
1976 as an administrative officer for the
public service commission. He became a
senior administrative officer in the
diplomatic service department in 1980. From
1984 to 1986, he was director of the
department of protocol and consular affairs
in the ministry of foreign affairs. He held
the post of deputy permanent secretary in the
ministry briefly before being appointed
permanent secretary.

Puteh received a bachelor of science degree
in psychology from London University in the
United Kingdom (UK) in 1976; a certificate
in diplomacy from Oxford University in the
UK in 1983; and an M.A. degree in
international relations from the Fletcher
School of Law & Diplomacy at Tufts
University in the U.S. in 1986.

Puteh is a member of the board of directors
of Sultan Haji Hassanal Bolkiah Foundation.
He was president of the Brunei Squash
Racquet Association between 1984-86; vice
president of the Brunei Amateur Football
Association in 1988-90; and president of the
Brunei Karate Association, 1991-95. His
hobbies are football, badminton, squash, and
golf. He received the Order of Merit from
Egypt in 1984.

The ambassador and his wife have two
children.

STAFF:

Mr. Shofry ABDUL-GHAFOR
First Secretary
Spouse: Mrs. Misnah Daud

Mrs. Hasney MAT YASSIN
Second Secretary
Spouse: Mr. Hussain Osman

Mr. Buyong ARSHAD
Third Secretary

Mr. Haji Morshidi bin HAJI MD. YUSOF
Third Secretary (Administrative/Finance)
Spouse: Mrs. Hajah Timah Haji Baker

Miss Zabaidah DAUD
Attaché

Mr. Hasnan SERUDIN
Attaché (Communications)
Spouse: Mrs. Adinawati Abdullah

Bulgaria

Embassy of the Republic of Bulgaria
1621 22nd Street, NW
Washington DC 20008
Phone: 202/387-7969
Fax: 202/234-7973
Email: Bulgaria@access.digex.net

Dr. Snezhana BOTUSHAROVA
Ambassador

Date Credentials Presented: 07/11/94

Born: 09/20/55 in Sofia, Bulgaria

Spouse: Mr. Arso Stratiev Doytchev

Before her arrival in Washington, Mrs.
Snezhana Botusharova served in the
Bulgarian National Assembly as deputy
chairman from 1991 to 1994. In 1990-91,
she was a member of the Grand National
Assembly and served on its constitutional and
legislative committees.

Botusharova was an associate professor of
constitutional law at Neofit Rilski University
of Blagoevgrad in 1994. Earlier, she had
been an assistant and associate professor of
constitutional law in the Faculty of Law at
Sofia University, a lawyer with the First Sofia
College of Barristers, and a judge on
Probation in the Sofia City Court.

Botusharova was a NATO research fellow in
1990-91 and a Mexican Autonomous
University fellow in 1989.

She graduated from the Sofia English
Language School in 1974 and from the
Faculty of Law at Sofia University in 1978.

In 1983, she became a doctor of law. She
speaks English, Spanish, Russian, and
French, is married, and has one son.

STAFF:

Mr. Gueorgui KOSTIANEV
Counselor and Consul
Spouse: Mrs. Irina Kostianeva

Mr. Panteley Anguelov PENEV
Counselor (Commercial)

Mr. Petio D. PETEV
Counselor (Political)
Spouse: Mrs. Yoana Lubenova Peteva

Mr. Mihail HRISTOV
Third Secretary (Press)

Mr. Ivan TCHOMAKOV
Attaché

Mr. Kalin Iliev TINTCHEV
Attaché (Political)

Captain Lubomir Deltchev SIMOV
Defense, Military, Naval and Air Attaché
Spouse: Mrs. Natalia Marinova Simova

Mr. Petar TCHAPANOV
Attaché (Administrative)
Spouse: Mrs. Tatiana Todorova
    Tchapanova

Mr. Yordan Kirilov STOYTCHIN
Attaché (Administrative)
Spouse: Mrs. Mariana I. Atanassova-
    Stoytchina

Mr. Dimitar VELEV
Attaché (Administrative)

Mr. Rizva Moustafov ALIEV
Attaché (Administrative)

Burkina Faso

Embassy of Burkina Faso
2340 Massachusetts Avenue, NW
Washington DC 20008
Phone: 202/332-5577
Fax: 202/667-1882

Bruno Nongoma ZIDOUEMBA
Ambassador

Date Credentials Presented: 3/16/98

Born: 1949 in Dargo, Province of Namentinga

Spouse: Mrs. Rosine Mariam Zidouemba

Bruno Nongoma Zidouemba, who has been Burkina Faso's ambassador to several countries, assumed the ambassadorial post in Washington, D.C., in November 1997. He is concurrently his country's ambassador to Argentina, Brazil, Mexico, and Chile.

Between 1994 and 1997, he served as secretary general of the ministry of foreign affairs in Ouagadougou. In the previous five-year period, he was based in Rome as Burkina Faso's ambassador to Italy, Greece, Albania, and Yugoslavia. Between 1984 and 1989, he was based in Copenhagen as ambassador to Denmark, Sweden, Norway and Finland.

Zidouemba was first counsel with the permanent mission of Burkina Faso at the United Nations in New York from 1983 to 1986, moving up from the position of second counsel, which he had held for the previous three years. Before that, he was a member of Burkina Faso's delegation to the United Nations Security Council in New York in 1984-85. Between 1976 and 1980, he was chief of the civil aviation service and minister of public works and urban transportation. He was a professor at the National School for Administration and Justice in Ouagadougou in 1978-79.

In 1994, Zidouemba, operating out of Rome, was president of a group of African ambassadors accredited to the Food and Agricultural Organization and the International Fund for Agricultural Development (FIDA). Also in that year, he was president of a committee to support the programs of the United Nations Economic and Social Council (UNESCO). In 1995-96, he served as president of the secretariat and work group for the 19th conference of the heads of state in France and Africa.

Zidouemba received a doctorate in international relations from the Institute of International Relations of Cameroon. He also holds a degree in history and geography and a master's degree in history from the University of Dakar in Senegal. He studied at the Institute of Economic Development, World Bank, in Washington, D.C., in 1981.

Zidouemba is fluent in French, English, and Spanish and has some fluency in Italian. He and his wife have three children.

STAFF:

Mr. Simplice Honore GUIBILA
Counselor
Spouse: Mrs. Marie Florence Guibila
    Quedraogo

Mrs. Awa Ndeye OUEDRAOGO

Counselor (Cultural)
Spouse: His Excellency Gaetan
    Rimwanguiya Ouedraogo

Mr. Souleymanea OUEDRAOGO
Counselor (Economic)

Mr. Boureima OUEDRAOGO
Attaché (Financial)
Spouse: Mrs. Awa Ouedraogo

Mrs. Cecile Pare TOE
Attaché
Spouse: Mr. Norbert Toe

Mrs. Rosine Mariam ZIDOUEMBA
Attaché
Spouse: His Excellency Bruno Zidouemba

Burundi

Embassy of the Republic of Burundi
2233 Wisconsin Avenue, NW, Suite 212
Washington DC 20007
Phone: 202/342-2574
Fax: 202/342-2578

Thomas Ndikumana

Chargé d'Affaires, ad interim
Minister

Date Credentials Presented: 2/9/98

Burundi's ambassadorship to the U.S. was left vacant with the departure of Ambassador Severin Ntahomvukiye in July 1997. At press time, no successor had been named. The embassy did not respond to requests for biographical information on the chargé d'affaires.

Cambodia

Royal Embassy of Cambodia
4500 16th Street, NW
Washington DC 20011
Phone: 202/726-7742
Fax: 202/726-8381
Email: cambodia@embassy.org
Url: http://www.embassy.org/cambodia

Huoth VAR

Ambassador

Date Credentials Presented: 9/15/95

Born: 12/30/36 in Kompong Cham, Cambodia

Spouse: Mrs. Saudy NY

Prior to his current appointment as ambassador to the U.S. which began in May 1995, Ambassador Var served as Minister of Commerce in the Cambodian government from early 1993 to late 1994. He had been economic advisor to the prime minister of Cambodia from 1992 to 1993.

Var 's early career with the Cambodian government began in 1956 as a senior custom manager in the Ministry of Finance. He remained in that position through 1968, when he became director general of direction of dangerous drug control within the prime minister's office. From 1975 to 1991, Var was the director of international air-freight management in Paris.

The ambassador received his Baccalaureate from Phnom Penh high school. He received an M.S. degree in Economies and Commerce. Later, Var earned a Diploma of Custom and Fiscal Management from the Custom and Fiscal Management Institute in Paris, France. He also received a Diploma of Commercial Enterprise Management.

STAFF:

Mr. Kim Heng MEAS
Counselor (Political)
Spouse: Mrs. Meardey Hout

Mr. Samnom MAO CHAN
Counselor (Economic)
Spouse: Mrs. Norn Phneo

Mr. Hak NOU
First Secretary (Consul and Press)

Mr. Kong PRAK
Attaché (Consular Affairs Accounting)

Mr. Syvatha NGUON
Attaché (Protocol)
Spouse: Mrs. Sokmom Lay

Cameroon

Embassy of the Republic of Cameroon
2349 Massachusetts Avenue, NW
Washington DC 20008
Phone: 202/265-8790
Fax: 202/387-3826

Jerome MENDOUGA

Ambassador

Date Credentials Presented: 6/23/94

Born: 8/15/38 in Yaounde, Cameroon

Spouse: Mrs. Louisette M. R. Mendouga

In the four years before he became ambassador to the United States, Jerome Mendouga, a career diplomat, served as his country's ambassador, concurrently, to Zaire, Burundi, and Rwanda. Mendouga is familiar with Washington, D.C., aving begun his professional life here as a young foreign service officer in the early 1960s.

His career has taken him across Africa, Western and Eastern Europe, and North America. He has participated in various international conferences and negotiations.

Following his initial assignment in Washington, Mendouga served as first secretary and acting chief of mission in Cameroon's Embassy in Ottawa, before returning to his country in 1966 to become acting director of the Ministry of External Relation's Technical and Economic Affairs Section. Later, he was named division chief for international organizations, a position he held until the end of the decade.

Mendouga spent most of the next 14 years abroad, serving as an economic counselor in Moscow, Bonn, and Addis-Ababa, and as head of Cameroon's Economic Mission to the E.C. in Brussels. He received his first ambassadorial posting in 1984 - to Senegal.

In the Organization of African Unity (OAU), Mendouga has chaired three key committees: political and information, liberation, and the committee for the redrafting of the OAU Charter.

Mendouga holds a B.A. in international affairs from the George Washington University School of International Service and has received certificates in diplomacy, economics, and economic development from American University and the Johns Hopkins University. He is married and has six children. Soccer is his hobby, and he is the former president of the famous Cameroon Soccer team, Canon Sportif Yaounde.

STAFF:

Mr. Raymond Ebenezer EPOTE

Minister-Counselor
Spouse: Mrs. Arlett Kesseng A. Mbassa

Mr. Andre-Blaise KESSENG A MBASSA
Counselor (Economic)
Spouse: Mrs. A. Kesseng A. Mbassa

Mr. Crecy TAWAH CHE
Counselor

Mr. Vincent MBULLE ETUE
First Secretary
Spouse: Mrs. Nziege Margaret Mbulle

Mrs. Regina A. BOUDJIHO
Second Secretary (Consular and Protocol)

Mr. Zang A. ETORI
Second Secretary (Financial)
Spouse: Mrs. Therese Etori

Mr. Philippe ONDO ONDO
Second Secretary
Spouse: Mrs. Felicite Ondo Andeme Engo

Mr. Dax BATTOKOK BITYEKI
Attaché (Cultural)
Spouse: Mrs. Julienne Battokok Bityeki

Colonel Mathurin MEILLON
Defense, Military, Naval, and Air Attaché
Spouse: Mrs. Meillon

Lt. Commander Emmanuel CHIKANDO
Asst. Defense, Military, Naval and
   Air Attaché
Spouse: Mrs. Emilienne Njiki Chikando

Canada

Embassy of Canada
501 Pennsylvania Avenue, NW
Washington DC 20001
Phone: 202/682-1740
Fax: 202/682-7726
Url: http://www.cdnemb-wshdc.org

Raymond A.J. CHRETIEN
Ambassador

Date Credentials Presented: 2/14/94

Born: 5/20/42 in Shawinigan, Quebec

Spouse: Mrs. Kay Chretien

Having spent his entire career with the Canadian government, Raymond A.J. Chretien is a lawyer by training. Prior to his posting to Washington, he was Canada's ambassador to Belgium. He has now been in civil and diplomatic sevice for more than a quarter century. He is the nephew of Jean Chretien, the current Canadian prime minister.

After being admitted to the Quebec bar, Chretien entered government service in 1966, joining the Legal Affairs Bureau of the Department of External Affairs (now the Department of Foreign Affairs and International Trade). During the subsequent 12 years, Chretien held positions in Ottawa with the Privy Council Office, the Treasury Board and the Canadian International Development Agency. He also served in diplomatic posts in Beirut and Paris and worked with Canada's Permanent Mission to the U.N. in New York. Chretien received his first ambassadorial assignment in 1978, as his country's representative to Zaire.

In 1981, Chretien returned to Canada. Over the next four years, he held several senior positions within the Ministry of External Affairs, including those of policy director for industry, investments and competition, assistant under secretary for manufacturing, technology, and transportation, and inspector general. In 1985, he became Canada's ambassador to Mexico.

Chretien holds a B.A. from the Seminaire de Jollette and an LL.L from Laval University. He is married to Kay Rousseau and has a daughter and a son.

STAFF:

Mr. Douglas Gordon WADDELL
Minister (Economic) (Deputy Chief of
   Mission)
Spouse: Mrs. Constance Anne Waddell

Mr. Paul FRAZER
Minister (Public Affairs)
Spouse: Dr. Tina Alster

Mr. John HIGGINBOTHAM
Minister (Political)
Spouse: Mrs. Michele Higginbotham

Mr. Jon J. ALLEN
Minister-Counselor (Political)
Spouse: Mrs. Clara Hirsch

Mr. Paul FAUTEUX
Minister-Counselor (Congressional/Legal)
Spouse: Mrs. Lise Andree Provost

Mrs. Astrid Yolanda PREGEL
Minister-Counselor (Commercial)
Spouse: Mr. Abdelkrim Oka

Ms. Colleen Catherine SWORDS
Minister-Counselor
Spouse: Mr. Bjorn Gunnar Johannson

Mr. Jean-Pierre Francois GOMBAY

Counselor (Economic)
Spouse: Mrs. Rose Gombay

Mr. James F. GOULD
Counselor

Mr. Stuart HUGHES
Counselor (Political)

Mr. Daniel JEAN
Counselor (Immigration)
Spouse: Mrs. Line Cote

Mr. Jamal A. KHOKHAR
Counselor (Trade Policy)

Mr. Andre R. LAPORTE
Counselor (Administrative) and Consul
Spouse: Mrs. Nancy L. Galloway

Ms. Eleanor LEWICKI
Counselor

Mr. Ronald Austin MACINTOSH
Counselor (Environment and Fisheries)

Mr. David J. MCLELLAN
Counselor (Energy)
Spouse: Mrs. Yoonkyung Sohn

Mrs. Evelyn PUXLEY
Counselor
Spouse: Mr. James Owen Hyatt

Mr. George RIOUX
Counselor
Spouse: Mrs. Sharon Gray

Mr. Robert James RUTHERFORD
Counselor (Commercial)
Spouse: Mrs. Marianne Rutherford

Mr. Joseph W. SCUBY
Counselor
Spouse: Mrs. Louise Scuby

Mr. Brian A. SMITH
Counselor (Financial)
Spouse: Mrs. Sayoko Yamamoto

Dr. Donald Lionel Patrick STRANGE
Counselor (Science and Technology)
Spouse: Mrs. Shirley Lorraine Thomas

Dr. Ronald S. THOMAS
Counselor (Defense, Research & Develop.)
Spouse: Mrs. Shirley Thomas

Mr. Paul James TRUEMAN
Counselor (Immigration)
Spouse: Mrs. Patricia Gail Trueman

Mr. Terry Sidney WOOD
Counselor
Spouse: Mrs. Carol Ann Wood

Ms. Kathryn Anne ALEONG
First Secretary (Commercial)
Spouse: Mr. Donald Robert Mackay

Mrs. Louise BLAIS
First Secretary (Cultural)
Spouse: Mr. Peter Norman Port Falkner

Mr. Robert Graham CAIRNS
First Secretary (Commercial)
Spouse: Mrs. Karen Thorington

Mr. Thomas Gregory CURRY
First Secretary (Administrative) and
Consul
Spouse: Mrs. Frances Lee Curry

Mr. Nicolas DIMIC
First Secretary
Spouse: Mrs. Nicole G. Gesnot Dimic

Mr. William A. HEWETT
First Secretary (Communication,
Agriculture & Fisheries)
Spouse: Mrs. Jennifer L. Hewett

Mr. Marvin D. HILDEBRAND
First Secretary (Agriculture)
Spouse: Mrs. Linda Hildebrand

Mr. Howard Raphael ISAAC
First Secretary
Spouse: Ms. Alzbeta Klein

Mr. Matthew LEVIN
First Secretary
Spouse: Mrs. Rosalba Levin

Mr. Daniel J. MURPHY
First Secretary (Administrative) & Consul
Spouse: Mrs. Bridget Christina Hayes
   Murphy

Mr. Evhen Eugene RIZOK
First Secretary
Spouse: Mrs. Maria Rizok

Mr. Brian Carl RUMIG
First Secretary
Spouse: Mrs. Allison Merrick

Mr. Randall F. WAHAB
First Secretary
Spouse: Mrs. Maret E. Wahab

Mr. Peter G. BATES
Second Secretary
Spouse: Ms. Margaret I. Gibson

Mr. David Matthew EHINGER
Second Secretary

Mrs. Allison Barbara MERRICK
Second Secretary
Spouse: Mr. Brian Carl Rumig

Ms. Allison Janet SAUNDERS
Second Secretary (Commercial)
Spouse: Mr. A. Ross Murray

Mr. Stewart Ross WHEELER
Third Secretary (Congressional and Legal)

Mr. Robert William ALEXANDER
Third Secretary

Mr. Paul Kenneth CHARLTON
Third Secretary

Ms. Kathleen Ann LANNAN
Third Secretary (Commercial)

Ms. Marie Anne STAMP
Third Secretary
Spouse: Mr. Plamen Tomov Tzvetkov

Mr. Kenneth Joseph ALLEN
Attaché (Administrative)
Spouse: Mrs. Donna Mary Allen

Mr. Graham James BELL
Attaché (Telecommunications)
Spouse: Mrs. Joan Elizabeth Bell

Mr. William H. CUMMINGS
Attaché
Spouse: Ms. Margaret F. Cummings

Mr. Reginald Jon EACRETT
Attaché
Spouse: Mrs. Jean Eacrett

Mrs. Barbara Catherine GIBBONS
Attaché
Spouse: Mr. Richard Joseph Gibbons

Mr. Michael Edwin HENWOOD
Attaché (Head of Security)
Spouse: Mrs. Susan Marie Henwood

Captain Christina Lola HUTCHINS
Attaché (Financial)
Spouse: Mr. Gianni Cucinelli

Mr. Denis Bruno LAMADELEINE
Attaché (Personnel)
Spouse: Mrs. Suzanne Carrolle
Lamadeleine

Mr. Michael B. LEMAY
Attaché
Spouse: Mrs. Ivon Lemay

Sergeant John V. MUISE
Attaché
Spouse: Mrs. Sharon Mary Muise

Mr. Vincent MUOLO
Attaché
Spouse: Mrs. Rita Mary Niles

Mr. Terence James NIELD
Attaché
Spouse: Mrs. Donna Mary Edith Nield

Mr. Michael Norman SAUNDERS
Attaché
Spouse: Ms. Josee Charland

Lt. Colonel Omar VAN ROOYEN
Attaché (Administrative)
Spouse: Mrs. Janice Irene Van Rooyen

Mr. Douglas S. WAKEFIELD
Attaché (Defense Research and
Development)
Spouse: Mrs. Susan F. Wakefield

Mr. Arnold F. WEISBROT
Attaché
Spouse: Mrs. Elizabeth Weisbrot

Lt. Alan ANDERSON
Asst. Attaché (Health, Training & Visits)
Spouse: Mrs. Paulette Anderson

Ms. Zoe Anne BELTER
Asst. Attaché

Major Gregory Dennis CLARK
Asst. Attaché (Air Engineering)
Spouse: Mrs. Johanne Dumont

Major William J. FLEMING
Asst. Attaché (Engineering)
Spouse: Mrs. Vivian Fleming

Major Gerald GAUDREU
Asst. Attaché (Training and Doctrine)
Spouse: Mrs. Jacqueline Gaudreau)

Major Gordon GREAVETTE
Asst. Attaché (Administrative)
Spouse: Mrs. Marguerite Greavette

Lt. Cmdr. Karel Albertus HEEMSKERK
Asst. Attaché (Engineering)
Spouse: Mrs. Penny Suzanne Heemskerk

Lt. Cmdr. Gary Raymond MACKNIGHT
Asst. Attaché (Operations)
Spouse: Mrs. Heather Anne MacKnight

Major Kenneth S. O'BRIEN
Asst. Attaché (Air Operations)
Spouse: Mrs. Cheryl A. O'Brien

Major Terrance PACHAL
Asst. Attaché (Communications and
Electronics)
Spouse: Mrs. Lorraine Pachal

Lt. Colonel Francis Carl Glenn SOUTER
Asst. Attaché
Spouse: Mrs. Elena Souter

Dr. Philip R. STAAL
Asst. Attaché (Defense Research and
Development)
Spouse: Mrs. Grace Ballen

Major General Thomas Frank DE FAYE
Defense Attaché
Spouse: Mrs. Barbara De Faye

Colonel J. Douglas BRISCOE
Military Attaché & Asst. Defense Attaché
Spouse: Mrs. Mary K. Briscoe

Captain Richard William BOWERS
Naval Attaché and Asst. Defense Attaché
Spouse: Mrs. Constance Mary Bowers

Colonel Murray John BERTRAM
Air Attaché and Asst. Defense Attaché
Spouse: Mrs. S. Beryl Bertram

Lt. Colonel Robert George SCOTT
Asst. Defense Cooperation Attaché
Spouse: Mrs. Christa Elisabeth Scott

Lt. Colonel Raymond James TAYLOR
Asst. Defense Attaché
Spouse: Mrs. Judith Taylor

Lt. Colonel Alan J. HOWARD
Asst. Military Attaché
Spouse: Mrs. Sydney K. Howard

Commander John Thomas LEGAARDEN
Asst. Naval Attaché
Spouse: Mrs. Wendy Legaarden

Lt. Colonel Stuart A. BAINES
Asst. Air Attaché
Spouse: Mrs. Mavis M. Baines

Cape Verde

Embassy of the Republic of Cape Verde
3415 Massachusetts Avenue, NW
Washington DC 20007
Phone: 202/965-6820
Fax: 202/965-1207
Email: cvefont@sysnet.net
Url: http://www.capeverdeusembassy.org

Manuel DE MATOS
Chargé d'Affaires, ad interim
Minister.

Date Credentials Presented: 9/23/97

Spouse: Mrs. Fernanda Matos

Cape Verde's ambassadorship to the U.S. was left vacant with the departure of Ambassador Corentino Virgillios Santos in September 1997. At press time, no new ambassador had been appointed. The embassy did not respond to requests for biographical information on the chargé d'affaires.

STAFF:

Mr. Alexandre Guilherme VIEIRA FONTES
Attaché (Commercial)
Spouse: Mrs. Jacqueline Rodrigues Fontes

Central African Republic

Embassy of Central African Republic
1618 22nd Street, NW
Washington DC 20008
Phone: 202/483-7800
Fax: 202/332-9893

Henry KOBA
Ambassador

Date Credentials Presented: 11/21/94

*Born: 8/30/36 in Mbaiki,
Central African Republic*

Spouse: Mrs. Juliette Koba

Henry Koba started his career as a journalist, first as a radio journalist for Radio Centrafrique in 1962, and later as thehHead editor of the same station from 1963 to 1965. After taking part in the Triangular Fellowship Program, in which he served as an economic journalist for the regional U.N. offices in Africa Hall, Addis-Adaba, New York, Rome, and Geneva, he was promoted to general director of Radio Centrafrique in 1966.

Koba's career in government began in 1970, when he became Secretary General of Information. In 1977, he entered the field of diplomacy when he was appointed Diplomatic Adviser with rank of minister's privileges to the Imperial Court. In 1978, he was promoted Secretary of State to the Foreign Affairs Ministry of the Central African Government.

He has held several ambassadorial posts, including ambassadorships to Congo from 1980 to 1982 and to Egypt and Sudan concurrently from 1988 to 1992. He acted as adviser to the Ministry of Foreign Affairs from 1982 to 1988.

Koba holds a diploma in journalism from the "Studio Ecole de l'Ocora" in Paris. He has two honorary distinctions: in 1970, he was appointed Chevalier de l'Ordre National Centrafricain, and in 1991, he was appointed Officier de l'Ordre National Centrafricain.

Koba has taken several educational trips to the U.S. during which he was made an Honorary Citizen of Nashville. He is married and has nine children.

STAFF:

Mr. N'dinga GABA
Counselor
Spouse: Mrs. Gaba

Ms. Lucienne PERRIERE
Counselor (Economic)

Chad

Embassy of the Republic of Chad
2002 R Street, NW
Washington DC 20009
Phone: 202/462-4009
Fax: 202/265-1937

Ahmat MAHAMAT-SALEH
Ambassador

Date Credentials Presented: 3/20/95

*Born: 04/15/46 at Oum-Hadjer Batha
in Chad*

Spouse: Mrs. Mariam Mahamat-Saleh

Mahamat Saleh Ahmat has served in several high posts in the Chad Government since 1978, most recently as Minister of Agriculture and Environment in 1993-94. He also served as Minister of Information, Culture, and Tourism in 1991; Minister of Finance, Buildings, and Materials in 1979; and Minister of Economy and Planning in 1978.

He began his government career in the civil service in 1967 as adjunct prefet of Batha.

Between 1982 and 1990, Ahmat was in

political exile in Nigeria, Benin, and France. He is a member of the National Salvation Committee of the Patriotic Salvation Movement (M.P.S.), the political party of Chad's President Idriss Deby.

Ahmat has attended a number of international conferences, including several ministerial meetings of the Inter-State Committee for Struggle Against the Drought. He represented the Head of State at the Heads of State Summit in Praia, Cape Verde, in 1993. As Chad's governor of the International Monetary Fund, he attended the annual meetings of the IMF and the International Bank of Reconstruction and Development in 1978.

Ahmat received diplomas from the National School of Administration and the International Institute of Public Administration in Paris. He is married and has five children.

STAFF:

Mr. Lemaye FAVITSOU-BOULANDI
Counselor
Spouse: Mrs. Askane Boulandi

Mr. Hassan OUSMANE
Attaché

Chile

Embassy of Chile
1732 Massachusetts Avenue, NW
Washington DC 20036
Phone: 202/785-1746
Fax: 202/887-5579
Email: echileus@radix.net

John BIEHL
Ambassador

Date Credentials Presented: 8/11/94

Born: 9/5/39 in Valparaiso, Chile

Spouse: Mrs. Maria Navarrete

Before coming to Washington, John Biehl, political scientist and university professor, served as director of the United Nations regional program for Latin America and the Caribbean that focuses on improving

governments in the post cold-war world. He was a member of the Organization of American States (OAS) mission for the restoration of democracy in Haiti.

Earlier, over a 14-year period, he directed various U.N. Development Program (UNDP) projects in Costa Rica, Honduras, Panama, Mexico, and Chile.

Biehl was the founding director of the Institute of Political Science of the Catholic University of Chile. He also was associate researcher for the Economic Research Corporation for Latin America and Director of the Center for Development Studies in Santiago, Chile.

Biehl is the author of numerous articles and publications in Chilean and international magazines on development, peace, and the strengthening of democracy. He has lectured on similar subjects at universities in Latin America, the U.S., Canada, and several European countries.

He is married and has six children.

STAFF:

Mr. Daniel CARVALLO
Minister Counselor and Deputy Chief of
    Mission

Mr. Jose Gabriel ZEPEDA
Minister-Counselor
Spouse: Mrs. Rina D. Monroy

Mr. Pablo Rodrigo GAETE
Counselor
Spouse: Mrs. Maria Cristina Larrain

Mr. William P. PATRICKSON
Counselor & Consul
Spouse: Mrs. Sofia Isabel Blanco

Mr. Mario C. MATUS
Counselor (Economic)
Spouse: Mrs. Maria A. Sanchez De Matus

Mr. Eduardo Alejandro SANTOS
Counselor (Agricultural)

Lt. Colonel Douglas MARTINEZ
Counselor (Technical Advisor)

Mr. Guillermo J. ANGUITA
First Secretary
Spouse: Mrs. Cecilia M. Rademacher

Mr. Antonio E. PENA
First Secretary
Spouse: Mrs. Maria Begona Bustamante

Mr. Reme Mauricio HURTADO
Second Secretary
Spouse: Mrs. Milagros Nancy Montesinos
    Arce

Mr. Manuel Franciso GORMAZ
Second Secretary
Spouse: Mrs. Maria Angelica Rochette

Mr. Ricardo Gustavo ROJAS
Second Secretary
Spouse: Mrs. B. Sandra Giacobbe

Mr. Bernardo J. DEL PICO
Third Secretary and Consul

Ms. Maria del Carmen DOMINGUEZ
Third Secretary

Mr. Hernan JOFRE
Attaché (Labor)

Ms. Maria Noilia Odette MAGNET
Attaché (Press)

Mrs. Karen HERRERA
Attaché (Cultural)

Mrs. Maria BOLVARAN DE PINCUS
Attaché (Civil)
Spouse: Mr. Pedro E. Pincus

Dr. Jorge LITVAK
Attaché (Scientific)

Rear Ad. Cristian CIFUENTES CABELLO
Naval Attaché
Office of Naval Attaché
1736 Massachusetts Avenue, NW
Washington DC 20036
Phone: 202/466-2500 Fax: 202/223-9733

Brigadier General Alfredo CANALES
Military Attaché
Office of Military Attaché
2174 Wisconsin Avenue, NW
Washington DC 20007
Phone: 202/965-9662 Fax: 202/965-9704

General Hernan GABRIELLI
Air Attaché
Office of Air Attaché
1029 Vermont Avenue, NW, Suite 1100
Washington DC 20005
Phone: 202/872-1334 Fax: 202/872-1361

China

Embassy of the People's Republic of China
2300 Connecticut Avenue, NW
Washington DC 20008
Phone: 202/328-2500
Fax: 202/588-0032
Url: http://www.china-embassy.org

LI Zhaoxing
Ambassador

Date Credentials Presented: 3/16/98

Born: 10/40 in Shandong Province, China

The People's Republic of China appointed Li Zhaoxing as its ambassador to the U.S. in early 1998. He had been his country's vice minister of foreign affairs for the previous three years.

Between 1992 and 1995, Li served as China's permanent representative and ambassador to the United Nations. In 1993, he was a guest professor of Beijing University and Nankai University. He served as assistant minister of foreign affairs between 1990 and 1992.

His other posts included: assistant minister of foreign affairs, 1990-92; deputy director general and director general of the information department of the Chinese ministry of foreign affairs, 1985-1990; first secretary of the Chinese embassy in the Kingdom of Lesotho, 1983-85; staff member and deputy division chief of the information department of the ministry of foreign affairs, 1977-83; staff member and attaché of the Chinese embassy in Kenya, 1970-77; and staff member of the Chinese People's Institute of Foreign Affairs, 1967-70.

Zhaoxing graduated from Beijing University in 1964. He was a postgraduate student at Beijing Institute of Foreign Languages between 1964 and 1967.

The ambassador is married and has one son.

STAFF:

Mr. ZHOU Wenzhong
Minister (Deputy Chief of Mission)
Spouse: Ms. XIE Shu Min

Mr. DONG Buming
Minister (Administrative)

Mr. JIANG Miao Rui
Minister-Counselor

Mr. LI Gang
Minister-Counselor
Spouse: Ms. LIU Min

Mr. LU Shu Min
Minister-Counselor
Spouse: Ms. GAO Shu Qing

Mr. SHI Jian Xin
Minister-Counselor
Spouse: Ms. HAN De Yu

Mr. CUI Luo Sheng
Counselor

Mr. CUI Zhan Qiao
Counselor
Spouse: Ms. ZHAO Shu Ying

Mr. FU Wei Dong
Counselor

Ms. GAO Jian
Counselor

Mr. HUO Ming Wu
Counselor

Ms. LI Shu Fang
Counselor and Consul General
Spouse: Mr. XIE Yin Gong

Mr. LIN Hui Sheng
Counselor

Mr. PENG Zhandong
Counselor and Deputy Consul General
Spouse: Ms. HE Suzhen

Mr. SHEN Long Hai
Counselor
Spouse: Mrs. LI Jing Yu

Mr. WANG Ke Bin
Counselor
Spouse: Ms. DONG Li Sha

Mr. YE Ruan
Counselor
Spouse: Ms. WANG Ruiyun

Mr. YIN Cheng De
Counselor
Spouse: Mrs. WAN Ling Ying

Mr. YU Shu Ning
Counselor
Spouse: Ms. ZHANG Chun Xiang

Mr. YUE Xiao Yong
Counselor
Spouse: Ms. XU Er Wen

Ms. ZHANG Chun Xiang
Counselor
Spouse: Mr. YU Shu Ning

Mr. ZHANG Ke Yuan
Counselor

Mr. CAI Jin Biao
First Secretary
Spouse: Ms. WANG Jian Qun

Mr. CAO Xue Jun
First Secretary
Spouse: Ms. QIN Shao Jie

Mr. CHEN Qi
First Secretary (Cultural)
Spouse: Ms. CUI Yun Shi

Mr. CHENG Hai Bo
First Secretary
Spouse: Ms. YANG Yi Min

Mr. CUI Qing Ping
First Secretary and Consul
Spouse: Ms. LIANG Xiu Ting

Ms. GAO Shu Qing
First Secretary
Spouse: Mr. LU Shu Min

Mr. GONG Nai Xu
First Secretary
Spouse: Ms. LI Qui Shuang

Mr. GUO Shenwu
First Secretary
Spouse: Ms. WANG Yan

Mr. HE Zhigeng
First Secretary
Spouse: Ms. JIA Ning Jiang

Mr. LI Chao Wei
First Secretary

Spouse: Ms. TU Xiao Wei

Mr. LI Jian Ping
First Secretary

Mr. LI Zhi Min
First Secretary

Mr. LIAO Yong He
First Secretary

Mr. LIN Yi Shun
First Secretary
Spouse: Ms. HUANG Yin Hong

Mr. LIU Minggang
First Secretary
Spouse: Ms. WANG Liwen

Mr. LIU Ren
First Secretary
Spouse: Ms. LI Ling Ou

Mr. LIU Zheng Rong
First Secretary
Spouse: Ms. XIONG Yu Tong

Mr. LU Wen Xiang
First Secretary

Ms. LUAN Li Ying
First Secretary
Spouse: Mr. MA Hai Bo

Mr. LUO Zhao Hui
First Secretary
Spouse: Ms. JIANG Yi Li

Mr. MA Hai Bo
First Secretary
Spouse: Ms. LUAN Li Ying

Mr. MA Kang De
First Secretary
Spouse: Ms. WANG Xiu Ju

Mr. QUIN Decun
First Secretary

Mr. SHEN Wei Lian
First Secretary
Spouse: Ms. LUO Gui Zhu

Mr. SHEN Yong Xian
First Secretary and Consul
Spouse: Ms. ZHANG Qui Min

Mr. SHEN Yun
First Secretary
Spouse: Ms. XI Min

Mr. SUN Jian Hua
First Secretary
Spouse: Ms. LIU Rui Qin

Mr. SUN Wen Qi
First Secretary

Mr. WAN Ji Song
First Secretary

Mr. WANG Dajiang
First Secretary

Spouse: Ms. DONG Yannan

Mr. WANG De Fa
First Secretary
Spouse: Ms. GU Yu Hua

Mr. WANG Xin Cai
First Secretary

Mr. WEI Li Qing
First Secretary

Mr. XING Bing Zheng
First Secretary
Spouse: Ms. ZHANG Yu Ying

Ms. XU Er Wen
First Secretary
Spouse: Mr. YUE Xiao Yong

Mr. XU Yong Ji
First Secretary

Mr. YANG Ji Jian
First Secretary

Mr. YANG Xiyu
First Secretary
Spouse: Ms. DU Xiaolan

Mr. YAO Ji Lin
First Secretary

Ms. YU Wei Xiang
First Secretary

Mr. ZHA Wei Ping
First Secretary

Mr. ZHANG Dong Liang
First Secretary

Mr. ZHANG Zhi Qiang
First Secretary
Spouse: Ms. QU Shu Jing

Mr. ZHOU Chang Yi
First Secretary
Spouse: Ms. ZHU Yan Chun

Mr. CAO Jing Hua
Second Secretary

Mr. CAO Yu
Second Secretary

Mr. CHAO Xiao Liang
Second Secretary

Mr. FU Wei Zhong
Second Secretary
Spouse: Ms. SU Li Li

Ms. GU Yu Hua
Second Secretary
Spouse: Mr. WANG De Fa

Mr. GUO Jing
Second Secretary
Spouse: Ms. GE Shu Yun

Ms. HE Chun Su
Second Secretary

Spouse: Mr. ZHU Hong

Mr. HU Ding Jin
Second Secretary
Spouse: Ms. WANG Wei

Mr. HU Yin Quan
Second Secretary
Spouse: Ms. TAN Xiang Rong

Mr. JIANG Wei
Second Secretary
Spouse: Ms. LAI Qiao Ling

Ms. JIANG Yi Li
Second Secretary
Spouse: Mr. LUO Zhao Hui

Mr. LI Hui
Second Secretary
Spouse: Mrs. YANG Yan

Mr. LI Wei Kun
Second Secretary

Ms. LIU Rui Win
Second Secretary
Spouse: Mr. SUN Jian Hua

Mr. LIU Shichang
Second Secretary and Consul
Spouse: Ms. SHI Qiong

Ms. LIU Yi
Second Secretary
Spouse: Mr. ZHAO Ge

Ms. WANG Jian Qun
Second Secretary
Spouse: Mr. CAI Jin Biao

Mr. WU Ke An
Second Secretary
Spouse: Ms. WU Min Su

Mr. XIA Ya Feng
Second Secretary
Spouse: Ms. MA Qian Li

Mr. XIA Yu Ming
Second Secretary

Mr. XU Fu Cai
Second Secretary and Consul
Spouse: Ms. WEI Xiu Feng

Mr. XU Xiao
Second Secretary
Spouse: Mrs. YANG Yue

Mr. YANG Hong Jin
Second Secretary
Spouse: Ms. ZHANG Jie

Mr. YU Xiao Hai
Second Secretary
Spouse: Ms. KANG Shu Lan

Mr. YUAN You Xin
Second Secretary
Spouse: Ms. WANG Huai Ting

Mr. ZHANG Shou Qing

Second Secretary

Ms. ZHAO Shu Ying
Second Secretary
Spouse: Mr. CUI Zhan Qiao

Mr. ZHENG Hu Qiang
Second Secretary and Consul
Spouse: Ms. GUO Rui Hong

Mr. ZHOU Shan Qing
Second Secretary
Spouse: Ms. ZHANG Xiao Hong

Mr. DING Dian Guo
Third Secretary

Mr. DONG Chuan Ji
Third Secretary and Consul
Spouse: Ms. LI Guo Hong

Colonel WANG Ying Jun
Air Attaché

Mr. GUO Xiao Guang
Third Secretary
Spouse: Ms. XIONG Lian

Ms. LUO Gui Zhu
Third Secretary
Spouse: Mr. SHEN Wei Lian

Mr. SUO Xian Liang
Attaché
Spouse: Ms. MENG Jin Yan

Mr. HONG Xiao Dong
Third Secretary

Mr. LI Guang Ming
Third Secretary
Spouse: Ms. LI Zheng

Ms. WANG Xin Lin
Third Secretary

Ms. WU Min Su
Third Secretary and Vice Consul
Spouse: Mr. WU Ke An

Mr. SUN Long Zhi
Attaché

Mr. WANG Qi
Attaché

Mr. WANG Wen Yong
Attaché

Lt. Colonel LIN Hui Sheng
Asst. Attaché
Spouse: Ms. WANG Haoi Jie

Mr. YIN Zhong Liang
Asst. Attaché

Major General GONG Xian Fu
Defense Attaché
Spouse: Ms. HUA Qun Li

Colonel ZHANG Jian Guo
Military Attaché
Spouse: Ms. SHEN Xiao Li

Captain YANG Yi
Naval Attaché
Spouse: Ms. BAI Xiang Yun

Colonel WANG Han Sheng
Asst. Defense Attaché
Spouse: Ms. SHAO Hong Hua

Colonel LING Zhi Yang
Asst. Military Attaché
Spouse: Ms. GAO Xiao Rong

Colonel REN Fu Mao
Asst. Military Attaché

Colonel TANG Bu Sheng
Asst. Military Attaché

Commander TANG Qiang Hua
Asst. Naval Attaché
Spouse: Ms. WU Wei Li

Lt. Colonel ZHANG Qiang
Asst. Air Attaché
Spouse: Ms. WANG Ping

Defense Attaché Office
2139 Wisconsin Avenue, NW
Washington DC 20007
Phone: 202/295-2500 Fax: 202/338-1690

**Economic and Commercial
 Counselors Office**
2133 Wisconsin Avenue, NW
Washington DC 20007
Phone: 202/625-3380 Fax: 202/337-5864

Education Office
2700/12 Porter Street, NW
Washington DC 20008
Phone: 202/885-0731

Colombia

Embassy of Colombia
2118 Leroy Place, NW
Washington DC 20008
Phone: 202/387-8338
Fax: 202/232-8643
Email: webmaster@columbiaemb.org
Url: http://www.columbiaemb.org/

Juan Carlos ESGUERRA
Ambassador

Date Credentials Presented: 2/11/97

Born: 3/13/49 in Bogotá, Colombia

Spouse: Mrs. Julia Miranda

Juan Carlos Esguerra held the post of minister of defense in Bogotá from 1995 to 1997 before his appointment as Colombia's ambassador to the U.S. He is a lawyer, who has been an associate justice in the constitutional court and dean of a law school.

Early in his career, he held government posts, as secretary general in the ministry of communications in 1974-75 and as vice-

minister of communications in 1975-76. He was associate justice of Consejo de Estado in 1987-88, an associate justice in the constitutional court in 1994-95, and a delegate to the National Constitutional Assembly in 1991.

In academia, he was dean of the Javeriana University School of Law from 1992 to 1995. He served on the University's board of directors and was a member of the law school board. As a professor, he specialized in government contracts, administrative procedure, economic constitutional law, and administrative law. He was also engaged in the private practice of law between 1977 and 1995.

Esguerra was a professor of administrative law from 1987 to 1996 at Externado de Colombia University School of Law. He also taught at Colegio Mayor Nuestra Señora del Rosario School of Law and Los Andes University School of Law. At Cornell University, he was a member of the advisory council to the law school between 1992 and 1997 and a member of the University Council from 1986 to 1990.

Esguerra received his Juris Doctor degree, along with the title of specialist in social and economic sciences, from Javeriana University in 1972. He obtained a master of law degree from Cornell University in the U.S. in 1973 and obtained the title of professor of law from Javeriana University in 1991.

Among his publications are "Termination and Liquidation of Administrative Contracts," Los Andes University law publication; and "The Andean Common Market," his thesis for his degree at Cornell.

The ambassador is married. He speaks Spanish, German, and English.

STAFF:

Ms. Ximena TAPIAS
Minister (Deputy Chief of Mission)
Spouse: Mr. Carlos Rodriguez Aguilar

Mr. Felipe PIZUERO
Minister-Counselor
Spouse: Ms. Clara Lucia Uribe

Mrs. Claudia VACA
Minister-Counselor

Mr. Francisco COY
Counselor
Spouse: Mrs. Gloria Marlene Gomez

Mr. Miguel FADUL
Counselor (Commercial)
Spouse: Mrs. Margarita Bonamusa

Mr. Camilo SALAZAR
Counselor
Spouse: Mrs. Martha Bonett

Mr. Fidel CANO

First Secretary
Spouse: Mrs. Carolina Renteria Rodriguez

Mr. Alfonso LIEVANO
Second Secretary
Spouse: Mrs. Isabel Lievano

Ms. Maria Stella FERNANDEZ
Third Secretary

Mr. Francisco Alberto GONZALEZ
Third Secretary
Spouse: Mrs. Ruth Mery Ariza Lemus

Mrs. Ana Maria PUJANA
Third Secretary
Spouse: Mr. Miguel Ceballos

Colonel German Dario MORENO ACERO
Attaché (Police)
Spouse: Mrs. Narcisa De Vargas Espinosa

Ms. Olga P. REYES
Attaché (Commercial)

Colonel Joaquin BUITRAGO
Asst. Attaché
Spouse: Mrs. Marcela Gonzalez

Major Jose Vicente SEGURA ALFONSO
Asst. Attaché (Police)
Spouse: Mrs. Doris Lucia Rodriguez

General Ramon E. NIEBLES
Defense Attaché
Spouse: Mrs. Nohora De Niebles

Colonel Abelardo GOMEZ
Military Attaché
Spouse: Mrs. Marlene Infante

Vice Admiral Hugo SANCHEZ
Naval Attaché
Spouse: Mrs. Emilia Elena Fonnegra

General Hector Hernando GIL
Air Attaché
Spouse: Mrs. Ruth Maria Quinones de Gil

Colonel Ernesto BELTRAN
Asst. Military Attaché
Spouse: Mrs. Gloria De Beltran

Major Nicacio MARTINEZ
Asst. Military Attaché
Spouse: Mrs. Ines Avella

Major Luis Carlos PERDOMO
Asst. Military Attaché
Spouse: Mrs. Marcela Londono

Lt. Colonel Eduardo PINZON
Asst. Military Attaché
Spouse: Mrs. Vivian Teresa De Pinzon

Lt. Commander Jose Alirio CIFUENTES
Asst. Naval Attaché
Spouse: Mrs. Yolanda Roldan

Colonel Victor Rafael PLATA
Asst. Air Attaché
Spouse: Mrs. Martha Sofia Amado
 de Plata

Office of the Commercial Attaché
1701 Pennsylvania Ave., NW, Suite 560
Washington DC 20006
Phone: 202/463-6679

Comoros

Embassy of the Federal and Islamic
    Republic of the Comoros
336 East 45th Street, 2nd Floor
New York NY 10017
Phone: 212/349-2030
Fax: 212/619-5832

Ahmed DJABIR
Ambassador

Date Credentials Presented: 11/12/97

The Comoros embassy did not respond to
requests for biographical information on the
ambassador.

Congo, Democratic Republic of (formerly Zaire)

Embassy of the Democratic Rep. of Congo
1800 New Hampshire Avenue, NW
Washington DC 20009
Phone: 202/234-7690
Fax: 202//237-0748

Tambo a Kabila MUKENDI
Chargé d'Affaires, ad interim
Minister-Counselor

Date Credentials Presented: 6/26/95

Spouse: Mrs. Muadi Mwendakami

Tambo a Kabila Mukendi has headed the
mission of the Democratic Republic of in
Washington, D.C., since the departure of
Ambassador Tatenene Manata in 1995. The
embassy did not respond to requests for
biographical information.

Congo, Republic of

Embassy of the Republic of Congo
4891 Colorado Avenue, NW
Washington DC 20011
Phone: 202/726-5500
Fax: 202/726-1860

Serge MOMBOULI
Chargé d'Affaires, ad interim
Minister-Counselor

Date Credentials Presented: 2/9/98

The Republic of Congo's ambassadorship to

the U.S. was left vacant with the departure
of Ambassador Dieudonne Antoine-Ganga in
November 1997. At press time, no new
ambassador had been named. The embassy
did not respond to requests for biographical
information on the chargé d'affaires.

STAFF:

Mr. Jean Alain BACKOULAS
Counselor (Cultural)

Mr. Daniel MOUELLET
Counselor
Spouse: Mrs. Josiane Solange Kihoulou

Mr. Auguste BIYO
First Secretary (Financial)
Spouse: Mrs. Nathalie Soline Victoire Biyo

Mr. Mbow AMPHAS-MAMPOUA
Second Secretary (Consular)
Spouse: Mrs. Edith Clemence Amphas-
Mampoua

Mr. Andre TENTOKOLO
Second Secretary (Economic/Commercial)
Spouse: Mrs. Valentine Alexandrouna
    Tentokolo

Costa Rica

Embassy of Costa Rica
2114 S Street, NW
Washington DC 20008
Phone: 202/234-2945
Fax: 202/265-4795

Jaime DARENBLUM
Ambassador

Date Credentials Presented: 5/27/98

Due to the recent arrival of the ambassador,
the embassy did not have biographical
information on Ambassador Darenblum
available for release before press date of this
publication.

STAFF:

Mr. Oscar ACUNA
Minister-Counselor (Economic)
Spouse: Mrs. Ana Teresa Dengo
Benavides

Mrs. Martha Virginia DE PEREA
Minister-Counselor (Cultural)
Spouse: Mr. Alfonso Perea

Mr. Carlos SILVA
Minister-Counselor (Commercial)
Spouse: Mrs. Irene Soler

Mrs. Anik ZURCHER
Counselor
Spouse: Mr. David Ochoa

Ms. Yamile SALAS
First Secretary

Mrs. Estrella BARRANTES
Attaché and Vice Consul
Spouse: Mr. Vincent Jerome Ruddy

Côte D'Ivoire

Embassy of the Republic of Cote d'Ivoire
2424 Massachusetts Avenue, NW
Washington DC 20008
Phone: 202/797-0300
Fax: 202/462-9444

Koffi Moise KOUMOUE
Ambassador

Date Credentials Presented: 6/23/94

Spouse: Mrs. Sounougou Comoe Koumoue

In the twenty years preceding his
appointment as Ambassador to the United
States, Koffi Moise Koumoue served in
various university and government positions.
The first half of his early career was spent in
various teaching positions at the National
University of Côte d'Ivoire in Abidjan where
he worked from 1973 to 1986. and within
the tax administration department

Following his university career, Koumoue
held several cabinet level positions in the
government including Minister of Budget
from 1986-89; Minister of Economy and
Finance from 1989-90; and Minister
Delegate at the Presidency in charge of the
presidential election from 1990-91. His first
diplomatic post was as ambassador to Japan
from 1991 to 1994. He was credentialed as
ambassador to the U.S. in June, 1994 and
subsequently to the Commonwealth of the
Bahamas in June, 1995.

Koumoue received a B.A. in law from the
University of Clermont-Ferrand in France
and is a graduate of the Clermont-Ferrand
Advanced School of Taxation. He holds a
master's in public law from the National
University of Côte d'Ivoire in Abidjan and a
Ph.D. in law and public finance from the
Pantheon/Sorbonne in Paris.

Koumoue and his wife, Sounougou C.
Koumoue, have six children. In his spare
time, the ambassador enjoys reading, writing,
jogging, and walking.

STAFF:

Mr. Yalle AGBRE
Commercial Counselor (NY)
Spouse: Mrs. Clemence Agbre

Mr. Kouakou E. DESHBY
Counselor
Spouse: Mrs. Claudine Kouakou

Mr. Adamoh DJELHI YAHOT
Counselor (Economic)
Spouse: Mrs. Marie Claude Djelhi

Mr. Fry KOUADIO
Counselor
Spouse: Mrs. Kosso Nou Ama Cecile
Kouadio Fry

Mr. John William Leon F. MORRISSON
Counselor (Economic)

Mr. Bah Jeannot ZORO BI
Counselor (Economic)

Mr. Severin Mathias AKEO
First Secretary (Consular/Cultural Affairs)

Mr. Charles Daho TCHIMOU
Second Secretary (Protocol)
Spouse: Mrs. Simone Mlingui Tchimou

Mr. Yao Vincent NZI
Attaché (Financial)
Spouse: Mrs. Bassie Virginie Adja Nzi

Colonel Sory DEMBELE
Military, Naval and Air Attaché

Chancery Annex
2412 Massachusetts Avenue, NW
Washington DC 20008

Croatia

Embassy of the Republic of Croatia
2343 Massachusetts Avenue, NW
Washington DC 20008
Phone: 202/588-5899
Fax: 202/588-8937
Email: amboffice@croatia.emb.org
Url: http://www.croatia.emb.org

Dr. Miomir ZUZUL
Ambassador

Date Credentials Presented: 2/6/96

Born: 6/19/55 in Split, Croatia

Spouse: Mrs. Tatjana Zuzul

Although an ambassador of one of the world's newest democracies, Miomir Zuzul has garnered considerable diplomatic experience. Since 1994, he has been the Croatian President's special envoy for negotiations and work with the Contact Group and other representatives of the international community---a position he continues to hold. His responsibilities have taken him to peace negotiations in Vienna, Paris, and Dayton, Ohio. Zuzul remains head of the Committee for Foreign Policy and International Relations of the Presidential Council of the Republic of Croatia.

Before coming to Washington, Zuzul was Croatia's Permanent Representative to the U.N. office in Geneva, Switzerland; national security adviser to the President of Croatia; and deputy minister of foreign affairs.

Before 1992, when he ventured into diplomacy, Zuzul was a volunteer in the Croatian Army. Prior to enlisting in the army, Zuzul had been head of the University of Zagreb's Department of Developmental Psychology. He also served as dean of that University's faculty of philosophy, starting in 1990. He holds a Ph.D. in behavioral and development psychology from the University of Zagreb, as well as a bachelor's degree and a master's degree.

No stranger to the U.S., Zuzul was a visiting professor at the University of Pittsburgh from 1988 to 1990 during which time he also lectured at several other universities in the U.S. and Europe. He is the author of three books and editor of another three. He has also published more than 50 scientific research papers and has given presentations at more than 30 international scientific conferences.

In addition to his native Croatian, Zuzul speaks fluent English, French, and Italian. He is married to the former Tatjana Bradvica, and has four children, Ivana, Tiona, Mihovil, and Andrija.

STAFF:

Mr. Andrija JAKOVCEVIC
Minister (Deputy Chief of Mission)
Spouse: Mrs. Kacusa Jakovcevic

Dr. Jelena GRCIC POLIC
Minister-Counselor
Spouse: Mrs. Boris Polic

Mr. Aleksander HEINA
Counselor (Economic)
Spouse: Mrs. Zvjezdana Heina

Mrs. Mira MARTINEC
Counselor
Spouse: Mr. Miljenko Martinec

Dr. Kresimir PIRSL
Counselor
Spouse: Mrs. Pirsl

Mr. Marijan GUBIC
First Secretary
Spouse: Ms. Suzana Colina

Mr. Tomislav THUR
First Secretary

Mr. Luka ALERIC
Third Secretary

Captain Robert HRANJ
Defense, Military, Naval and Air Attaché
Spouse: Mrs. Mirjana Hranj

Cuba

Cuban Interests Section
2630 16th Street, NW
Washington DC 20009
Phone: 202/797-8518
Fax: 202/797-8521
Email: cubaseccion@igc.apc.org

Fernando REMIREZ DE ESTENOZ
Counselor

Born: 10/9/51

Spouse: Mrs. Patricia Semidey Rodriguez

Diplomatic relations between the U.S. and Cuba have been severed. Cuba's protecting power in the U.S. is Switzerland and Cuba maintains a small staff at the Swiss Embassy in Washington.

Fernando Remirez de Estenoz was appointed head of the Cuban Interests Section in Washington in October 1995. He retains his post of first deputy at the Ministry of Foreign Affairs of Cuba.

A medical doctor by profession, he has had considerable experience in international affairs. He was appointed to the first deputy post in 1993. Between August 1993 and February 1995, he also served as representative of Cuba to the United Nations. He has headed several official delegations to international events and bilateral visits.

He served as first secretary at the Cuban Embassy in Luanda, Angola, and as an official at the International Relations Department of the Central Committee of the Communist Party of Cuba from 1988 to 1993.

He received the degree of doctor of medicine in 1975 and the degree of licenciate in social sciences in 1984.

STAFF:

Mr. Armando L. COLLAZO IGLESIAS
First Secretary
Spouse: Mrs. Doris Wong Sio

Mr. Fernando PEREZ MAZA
First Secretary
Spouse: Mrs. Ana Belkis Cabrera Arregui

Mr. Dagoberto RODRIGUEZ BARRERA
First Secretary
Spouse: Mrs. Marisabel de Miguel

Mr. Felix WILSON HERNANDEZ
First Secretary

Mr. Roberto GARCIA HERNANDEZ
Second Secretary
Spouse: Mrs. Cynthia Ayala Alcorta

Mr. Eugenio MARTINEZ ENRIQUEZ
Third Secretary

Mr. Sergio M. MARTINEZ GONZALEZ
Third Secretary
Spouse: Mrs. Barbara Suarez del
    Villar Farres

Mr. Luis Roberto MOLINA
ABRAHANTES
Third Secretary
Spouse: Mrs. Elsa Camaroti Duarte

Mr. Rajael Eduardo NORIEGA
    FERNANDEZ
Third Secretary
Spouse: Mrs. Amanda Rodriguez Carro

Mrs. Johana TABLADA DE LA TORRE
Third Secretary

Mr. Alain ALVAREZ AGUERO
Attaché

Mr. Alfredo BORDON DIAZ
Attaché
Spouse: Mrs. Georgina Zuaznabar Sterling

Mr. Jose I. NEYRA CABARROCA
Attaché

Mr. Manuel Angel PINEIRO PEREZ
Attaché

Ms. Lilia ULLA GONZALEZ
Attaché

Embassy of Switzerland, Cuban Annex
2639 16th Street, NW
Washington DC 20009
Phone: 202/797-8609

Cyprus

Embassy of the Republic of Cyprus
2211 R Street, NW
Washington DC 20008
Phone: 202/462-5772
Fax: 202/483-6710

Andros A. NICOLAIDES
Ambassador

Date Credentials Presented: 2/11/97

Born: 8/20/38 in Galata, Cyprus

Spouse: Mrs. Ero Macri Nicolaides

Andros A. Nicolaides, the Republic of Cyprus' ambassador to the U.S. since December 1996, is no stranger to this country, having held two earlier diplomatic posts in Washington, D.C. He also received much of his education in the U.S.

Nicolaides serves as Cyprus' non-resident high commissioner to Canada, as well as non-resident high commissioner to The Bahamas, Barbados, Jamaica, and Guyana, and as non-resident ambassador to Brazil. He also serves as permanent observer to the Organization of American States and represents Cyprus at the World Bank, the International Monetary Fund, and the International Civil Aviation Organization.

In 1992, Nicolaides was named Cyprus' ambassador to the Federal Republic of Germany, with concurrent accreditation to Austria (1992-94), Denmark (1972-95), and the Holy See. Between 1987 and 1991, he was ambassador to Italy with concurrent accreditation to Switzerland and Malta. He returned to Cyprus in 1991 and was appointed roving ambassador during which period he also served as acting permanent-secretary and director of policy planning at the ministry of foreign affairs.

Nicolaides' other diplomatic posts included permanent representative to the United Nations office in Geneva and other international organizations in Switzerland (1983-1987); Cyprus' first high commissioner in India (1979-1983); and minister plenipotentiary, and later, deputy chief of mission of the Cyprus embassy in Washington, D.C. (1974-79). He also was stationed in Washington between 1968 and 1973 as counsellor and later chargé d'affaires, a.i., at the Cyprus embassy.

Nicolaides joined the civil service of Cyprus in 1960 as special assistant to the minister of the interior and served four years. He joined the foreign service in 1964. His first post abroad was London, where he served as political and press officer at the Cyprus High Commission between 1966 and 1968. In

1973 and 1974, he was back in Cyprus, serving in the first political department in the ministry of foreign affairs, in charge of Commonwealth affairs, the Council of Europe, and the European Conference on Security and Cooperation.

Nicolaides was educated in Cyprus, England, and the U.S. He studied journalism in England and international relations, economics and political sciences in the U.S. He completed his undergraduate studies at George Washington University and John Hopkins School of Advanced Studies and did postgraduate studies at the University of Maryland, where he earned an M.A. degree in political science and comparative government.

Among honors received by Nicolaides were the Order of Gorka-Dakshin-Balm, First Class, from the King of Nepal; the Highest Order of Honour from the president of the Republic of Austria; the Knight Commander's Cross (badge and star) of the Order of Merit from the president of the Federal Republic of Germany; and the Knight Grand Cross of the Order of St. Gregory the Great (civil division) from Pope John Paul II.

Nicolaides and his wife have a daughter.

STAFF:

Mr. Andrea S. KAKOURIS
Counselor (Deputy Chief of Mission)
Spouse: Mrs. Kareen Farrell Kakouris

Mr. Milton MILTIADOU
Counselor (Press)

Mr. George CHACALLI
First Secretary and Consul

Czech Republic

Embassy of the Czech Republic
3900 Spring of Freedom Street, NW
Washington DC 20008
Phone: 202/274-9100
Fax: 202/966-8540
Email: washington@embassy.mzv.cz
Url: http://www.czech.cz/washington

Alexandr VONDRA
Ambassador

Date Credentials Presented: 5/14/97

Born: 8/17/61 in Prague

Spouse: Mrs. Martina Vondrova

Before taking his post in Washington, D.C., in 1997, Alexandr Vondra served in several government posts. Between 1990 and 1992, he was the foreign policy adviser to President Vaclav Havel.

In the summer of 1992, he was appointed first deputy minister of international affairs of the Czech Republic, and in January 1993, first deputy minister of foreign affairs. In 1996, he became the chief negotiator for the Czech Republic in preparing the Czech-German Declaration.

From the mid-1980s, Vondra participated in the activities of his country's democratic opposition, focusing on editorial work in samizdat and cooperation with opposition groups in Central and Eastern Europe. Between 1985 and 1987, he also worked in the Naprstek Museum of Asian, African, and American Cultures.

After signing Charter 77, a manifesto to Czechoslovakian authorities protesting that human rights were not being protected, Vondra worked first as a boilerman and later as a computer programmer. In 1989, he became a spokesperson for Charter 77. For organizing demonstrations in January 1989 and circulating the petition, "A Few Sentences," he was sentenced to two months in prison. In November 1989, he was a co-founder of the Civil Forum movement.

Vondra is not a member of any political party. He is fluent in English and Russian. He and his wife have three children.

STAFF:

Mr. Antonin HRADILEK
Minister-Counselor (Deputy Chief of Mission)
Spouse: Mrs. Ana Hradilkova

Mr. Martin WEISS
Second Secretary (Press)
Spouse: Mrs. Katerina Weissova

Mr. Michal SEDLACEK
Counselor (Political)

Mr. Miroslav TOMAN
Counselor (Commercial and Economic)
Spouse: Mrs. Katerina Tomanova

Mr. Jan STARY
Counselor (Cultural)

Mr. Marcel SAUER
Public Affairs
Spouse: Mrs. Martina Leierova

Mr. Jan CIZEK
Counselor and Consul
Spouse: Mr. Hana Cizkova

Colonel Jiri GIESL
Attaché (Military)
Spouse: Mrs. Jana Gieslova

Denmark

Royal Danish Embassy
3200 Whitehaven Street, NW
Washington DC 20008-3683
Phone: 202/234-4300
Fax: 202/328-1470
Email: ambadane@erols.com
Url: http://www.denmarkemb.org

K. Erik TYGESEN
Ambassador

Date Credentials Presented: 9/15/95

Born: 10/24/35

Spouse: Mrs. Ulla V. Tygesen

K. Erik Tygesen, who began his service to his government in 1964, came to Washington, D.C., from Germany, where he represented the Kingdom of Denmark for six years as ambassador. He was Denmark's ambassador to Brazil in 1981-82.

Tygesen began his career as secretary in the Danish Ministry of Agriculture in Copenhagen between 1964 and 1967 and then served as secretary of the Ministry of Foreign Affairs between 1967 and 1969. His first foreign assignment was as secretary of the Royal Danish Embassy in Bangkok between 1979 and 1972.

Tygesen's other posts included economic counselor at the Danish Embassy in Bonn between 1974 and 1977; counselor, Permanent Representation of Denmark at the European Community in Brussels in 1977-78; head of division, Ministry of Foreign Affairs, between 1978-81; under secretary for commerce affairs in the Ministry of Foreign Affairs in 1982-83; and state secretary and the minister's deputy for European and Foreign Economic Affairs in the Ministry of Foreign Affairs between 1983 and 1989.

Tygesen was head of delegation to UNCTAD V in Manila in 1979 and was later elected the first president of OECD's high-level North-South group (1979-81). He was

deputy head of delegation to the United Nations' 11th Special Assembly on Economic Affairs in 1980. Between 1983 and 1989, he was a member of the EC Council of Ministers for Foreign Affairs and the Budget Council, and he chaired the Council of Budget Ministers in 1987. He has headed numerous Danish delegations to international negotiations including the Uruguay Round and the Lome negotiations.

Tygesen received an international baccalaureate at the Cathedral School of Ribe and an M.A. in economics at the University of Copenhagen in 1964.

He was married in 1962 to Ulla Tygesen.

STAFF:

Mr. Svend MADSEN
Minister (Political and Deputy Chief of Mission)
Spouse: Mrs. Anette Hoejberg Christensen

Mr. Lars MOLLER
Minister (Economic)
Spouse: Mrs. Kirsten B. Moller

Mrs. Lis M. FREDERIKSEN
Minister-Counselor (Press and Cultural)

Mr. Jorge Mollegaard KRISTENSEN
Minister-Counselor (Agricultural)
Spouse: Mrs. Eva Y. Kristensen

Mr. Lars KJAER
Counselor (Economic)
Spouse: Mrs. Berit H. Kjaer

Mr. Peter MOLLER
Counselor (Labor Relations)
Spouse: Mrs. Eva T. Moller

Mr. Jorn ANDERSEN
First Secretary (Administrative) & Consul
Spouse: Mrs. Britt Andersen

Mr. Jens Otto HORSLUND
First Secretary (Political)
Spouse: Mrs. Githa Birkegaard Horslund

Mr. Jens LUNDAGER
First Secretary (Financial)
Spouse: Mrs. Lene G. Lundager

Mr. Anders AGERSKOV
Second Secretary (Economic)

Mrs. Lone Fruerskov ANDERSEN
Second Secretary (Political)
Spouse: Mr. Peter Kirkegaard

Mrs. Pernille HAUBROE
Attaché (Commercial) and Consul
Spouse: Mr. Niels Wilhelmsen

Mr. John PEDERSEN
Attaché (Research)
Spouse: Mrs. Inger Merete Sarborg

Mr. Patrick SONDERGAARD
Attaché (Agricultural)

Spouse: Mrs. Patricia Sondergaard

Brig. General Lars C. FYNBO
Defense, Military, Naval, and Air Attaché

Lt. Colonel Tom STOLTENBERG
Asst. Defense, Military, Naval, and
    Air Attaché
Spouse: Mrs. Melody Lynn Stoltenberg

Djibouti

Embassy of the Republic of Djibouti
1156 15th Street, NW - Suite 515
Washington DC 20005
Phone: 202/331-0270
Fax: 202/331-0302

Roble OLHAYE
Ambassador

Date Credentials Presented: 3/22/88

Born: 1944 in Djibouti

Spouse: Mrs. Amina Farah Ahmed Olhaye

A finance expert, Roble Olhaye has spent the bulk of his career in commerce and banking, having begun his diplomatic work as honorary consul to Kenya while still in private industry. In addition to his duties as Ambassador to the U.S., he now serves concurrently as non-resident ambassador to Canada and as Djibouti's permanent representative to the U.N. in New York.

Olhaye began his career in Addis-Ababa, Ethiopia, and spent nearly a decade there in various senior positions in the fields of accountancy, auditing, and taxation. From 1973 until 1980, he worked for a U.S. multinational - TAW International Leasing Corp. of New York - in Kenya, eventually rising to the position of financial controller for Africa. In that position, he traveled extensively throughout Africa and made frequent trips to headquarters in New York.

Between 1980 and 1982, Olhaye served as an independent consultant, dealing primarily with developing incentives for investment in Djibouti, procuring foreign aid, and facilitating multinational joint ventures.

During 1980, Olhaye opened Djibouti's first

diplomatic liaison office in Nairobi, Kenya. In 1982, he founded the Bank of Djibouti and the Middle East - a joint venture with the Middle East Bank of Dubai. He remains on the Bank's board. He began full-time government service in 1985. Olhaye established Djibouti's first full-fledged Embassy in Nairobi.

A certified general accountant, Olhaye was a Fellow of the Association of International Accountants in London and is a Member of the British Institute of Management. He speaks English, French, Arabic, Somali, Amharic, and Swahili. He is married to Amina F. Olhaye and has five children.

STAFF:

Mr. Issa Daher BOURALEH
Second Secretary
Spouse: Mrs. Fozia Ahmed Abaneh

Mr. Hassan Mohamed SOUGAL
Attaché (Financial)
Spouse: Mrs. Hasna Hassan Mohamed

Dominica

Emb. of the Commonwealth of Dominica
3216 New Mexico Avenue, NW
Washington DC 20016
Phone: 202/364-6781
Fax: 202/364-6791

Dr. Nicholas J.O. LIVERPOOL
Ambassador

Date Credentials Presented: 2/16/98

Born: 9/9/34 in Dominica, West Indies

Dominica's non-resident ambassador to the U.S., Dr. Nicholas J. O. Liverpool, is an expert in West Indian law who has served as a consultant to many governments and international organizations.

His most recent previous post was as a member of the Organization of American States' administrative tribunal in 1997. He has worked on commissions and boards to revise the laws of Guyana, Saint Christopher and Nevis, Santa Lucia, Grenada, Belize, the Bahamas, Barbados, Antigua and Barbuda, Dominica, and St. Vincent.

His varied career includes a law practice in Dominica; lecturer in the faculty of law at the University of Ghana, West Africa; judge of the high court in Antigua and Montserrat; justice of appeal, Grenada Court of Appeal; director of the Caribbean Law Institute; justice of appeal, Belize Court of Appeal; justice of appeal, Eastern Caribbean Supreme Court; justice of Appeal, Bahamas Court of Appeal; and dean of the faculty of law, UWI, Cave Hill, Barbados. He has been chairman of the income tax appeal board in Barbados and an advisor to the regional constituent assembly of the Windward Islands.

Liverpool has co-authored three books on legal matters and has written monographs on such subjects as "The History and Development of the St. Lucia Civil Code" and "Legal and Sociological Survey of Land Use and Land Tenure in the Less Developed Countries of Caricom."

Liverpool received an LL.B., with honors from Hull University, which he attended between 1957 and 1960. He studied to become a barrister-at-law from 1958 to 1961 from Inner Temple, and he earned a Ph.D. from Sheffield University, which he attended from 1962 to 1965. He was a research fellow at McGill University in Canada between 1967 and 1969.

The ambassador is married and has five children.

Dominican Republic

Embassy of the Dominican Republic
1715 22nd Street, NW
Washington DC 20008
Phone: 202/332-6280
Fax: 202/265-8057
Email: embdomrepusa@msn.com
Url: http://www.domrep.org

Bernardo VEGA
Ambassador

Date Credentials Presented: 2/11/97

Born: 1938 in Santiago, Dominican Rep.

Bernardo Vega, an economist and author of books on economics, archaeology, anthropology, and history, became the Dominican Republic's ambassador to the U.S. in January 1997.

Vega has represented his country at many international conferences on economic subjects including meetings of central banks, as well as conferences under the auspices of the World Bank, the International Monetary Fund, the Inter-American Development Bank, and the Organization of American States.

From 1962-64, Vega worked as an officer at the ministry of finance, the Industrial Development Corporation, Banco Popular

Dominicano and the Central Bank, where he was economic adviser to the governor. He has been a professor of economics at UASD and PUCMM universities, as well as lecturer at the University of Puerto Rico and the University of the West Indies in Trinidad and Tobago. He was a member of the Monetary Board of the Central Bank from 1977 to 1982. He represented his country, as well as other five nations of the continent, as a deputy in the Group of 20 on Reform of the International Monetary System.

From 1982 to 1984, Vega held the position of governor of the Central Bank of the Dominican Republic. From 1978 to 1982, he served as director general of the Museum of the Dominican Man, having written six books in the fields of archaeology and anthropology. In the field of history, he has published 24 books, four of which won him the National History Prize.

Vega studied in Santo Domingo, England (Downside School), and the United States, where he graduated as an economist at the Wharton School of Finance at the University of Pennsylvania. He also is a graduate of the Institute for Latin American Integration (INTAL) of Buenos Aires.

STAFF:

Mr. Angel GARRIDO
Minister
Spouse: Mrs. Marta Garrido

Mr. Roberto DESPRADEL
Minister-Counselor
Spouse: Mrs. Margarita Rosa Dargam
De Despradel

Mrs. Germania GASKILL
First Secretary
Spouse: Mr. Guilford Gaskill

Ms. Eunice LARA
Attaché (Cultural)

Gen. Jose Miguel Angel SOTO JIMENEZ
Defense, Military, Naval, and Air Attaché
Spouse: Mrs. Mercedes Luisa
Thormannnde Soto

Ecuador

Embassy of Ecuador
2535 15th Street, NW
Washington DC 20009
Phone: 202/234-7200
Fax: 202/667-3482
Email: mecuaa@pop.erols.com
Url: http://www.ecuador.org

Alberto F. MASPONS
Ambassador

Date Credentials Presented: 9/8/97

Born: 6/2/44 in Guayaquil, Ecuador

Spouse: Sylvia Burbano Garcia de Maspons

Alberto F. Maspons brought extensive business experience with him to the post of Ecuador's ambassador to the U.S.

He was production manager of Inedeca C.A., a joint venture with Nestle-Ecuador. Among his other business activities were as production and marketing manager with CIA, Intercambio y Credito, a family company involved in the coffee and cocoa export business; as manager of Incacao C.A., a joint venture with W.R. Grace and Co., New York; as board director in El Rosario S.A., engaged in shrimp growing and a processing factory; and as president of the board with Banco Sociedad General.

He was a director in Ecufinsa S.A., initially a joint venture with the Wells Fargo Bank; and president of the board in Tunlo S.A., a fishing and tuna-processing operation.

Maspons served as president of the Chamber of Industry of Guayaquil; as vice president of the National Federal of Chambers of Industry in Ecuador; as vice president of the Civic Committee of Guayaquil; and as a director of the Ecuador Foundation.

He received a bachelor of mechanical engineering degree in 1965 from the University of Notre Dame in Indiana, where he was a member of the Phi Thau Zigma Mechanical Engineering Honor Society.

Maspons and his wife have two sons, Alberto and Jorge, and two daughters, Maria Laura and Sylvia. Alberto, Jorge, and Sylvia are students at Notre Dame University and Maria Laura is studying at the Academia di Arte y Ofici in Florence, Italy.

STAFF:

Mr. Fernando FLORES
Minister (Deputy Chief of Mission)
Spouse: Mrs. Maria Amparo Flores

Dr. Eduardo BRITO
Counselor (Economic and Commercial)
Spouse: Mrs. Ana Brito

Mr. Giovanni O. DARQUEA
Counselor and Consul
Spouse: Mrs. Aglae V. Darzuea

Dr. Arturo CABREERA
Second Secretary

Miss Mireya MUNOZ
Second Secretary

Mr. Diego M. RAMIREZ
Second Secretary
Spouse: Mrs. Monica A. Ortiz Del Salto

Mrs. Pilar V. CORNEJO
Attaché (Civil)
Spouse: Mr. Carlos Cornejo

Mrs. Elsa Maria MARTINEZ

Attaché (Civil)
Spouse: Mr. Gustavo Martinez

Ms. Lucia ZAMBRANO
Attaché (Civil)

Rear Admiral Edgar GUERRA
Defense Attaché
Spouse: Mrs. Maria Elena Bosano

Colonel Marco CEPEDA
Military Attaché
Spouse: Mrs. Lourdes Quezada

Captain Victor H. ROSERO
Naval Attaché
Spouse: Mrs. Giglia G. Rosero

Colonel Jorge CABEZAS
Air Attaché
Spouse: Mrs. Beatriz Cabezas

Colonel Ignacio DIAZ
Asst. Military Attaché
Spouse: Mrs. Alexandra Tandazo

Captain Jorge E. BASSANTE
Asst. Naval Attaché
Spouse: Mrs. Shirley Arizaga Gonzales

Commander Carolos L. ZURITA
Asst. Naval Attaché
Spouse: Mrs. Magaly N. Zurita

Colonel Washington LASCANO
Asst. Air Attaché
Spouse: Mrs. Emma G. Lascano

Egypt

Embassy of the Arab Republic of Egypt
3521 International Court, NW
Washington DC 20008
Phone: 202/895-5400
Fax: 202/244-4319

Ahmed Maher EL SAYED
Ambassador

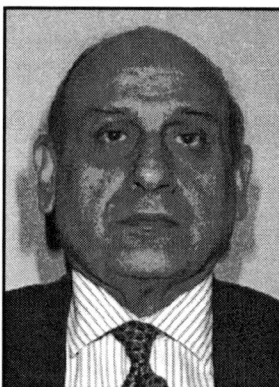

Date Credentials Presented: 9/8/92

Born: 9/14/35

Spouse: Mrs. Maher El Sayed

Having joined the Ministry of Foreign Affairs

in 1957, Ambassador Ahmed El Sayed has spent his entire career in the diplomatic corps.

In his early career, he served in the Egyptian missions to Zurich, Paris, and Kinshasa before becoming an aide to President Sadat's National Security Advisor from 1972 to 1974. After a stint as the minister of the Embassy in Paris and as the chief of Cabinet at the Ministry of Foreign Affairs, El Sayed spent the early 1980s as Egypt's ambassador to Portugal (1980-82) and to Belgium (1982-1984), before returning for senior assignments in the Foreign Ministry. From 1988 to 1992, he was Egyptian ambassador to the Soviet Union and, subsequently, to Russia.

Over the years, the Ambassador has participated in some of Egypt's most crucial foreign dealings, having held Foreign Ministry posts as the director of policy planning and as the director of the legal affairs and international treaties departments. Having participated in the Camp David Peace Negotiation between Egypt and Israel, as well as the negotiations and arbitration over the TABA dispute between Egypt and Israel, El Sayed is no stranger to high-level diplomatic processes.

He holds the following decorations: Pour le Merit, Commander Class, France; Order of the Republic, Second Class, Egypt; Order of Merit, Fourth Class, Egypt; Order of Merit, Third Class, Egypt; and Order of Merit, First Class, Egypt.

The Ambassador speaks fluent English and French and some Russian, in addition to his native Arabic. In 1956, he graduated from Cairo University Faculty of Law. He is married to the former Hoda Agheizi.

STAFF:

Mr. Hamdi S. LOZA
Minister (Deputy of Mission)
Spouse: Mrs. Sherine M. Riad

Mr. Amr Abdel Latif ABOUL ATTA
Counselor

Mr. Hazem A. KHAIRAT
Counselor
Spouse: Mrs. Manal Salaheldin

Mr. Abdel Aziz A. MOUSTAFA
Counselor
Spouse: Mrs. Assad Hanem H. Ahmed

Mr. Ehab M. M. FAWZY
First Secretary
Spouse: Mrs. Eman G. E. Helmy

Mr. Amgad M. ABDEL GHAFFAR
First Secretary
Spouse: Mrs. Laila Ahmed Bahaa Eldin

Ms. Hala A. F. A. EL GHANNAM
First Secretary

Mr. Mahmoud Ahmed Samir SAMY

First Secretary

Mr. Mohamed Taha EL FARNAWANY
Third Secretary
Spouse: Mrs. Yomna Moutafa

Mr. Amr Fathi AL JOWAILY
Third Secretary
Spouse: Mrs. Hanan Mohamed Galal Dowedar

Mr. Karim A. HAGGAG
Third Secretary
Spouse: Mrs. Soha Sayed Abou Zeid Omar

Mr. Walid Mahmoud SHERIF
Attaché

Mr. Mohamed Naguib Z. SHALAN
Attaché (Administrative)
Spouse: Mrs. Rabab F. A. Shalan

Mr. Mohamed A. TOLBA
Attaché (Administrative)

Mr. Magdy A. M. EL SAYED
Attaché (Administrative)
Spouse: Mrs. Amani H. M. Ezzat

Mr. Mahmoud M. M. GAMIL
Attaché (Administrative)
Spouse: Mrs. Azza A. I. Aly

Mr. Osama Zaki HASSAN
Attaché (Administrative)
Spouse: Mrs. Zeinab Aly E. Shibl

Mr. Magdy Abdalla Ibrahim ELSAYED
Attaché (Administrative)
Spouse: Mrs. Hanaa Amin S. Abouel Dahab

Mr. Mohsen A. Z. EL ADAWI
Attaché (Administrative)
Spouse: Mrs. Fatma B. M. El Didi

Mr. Faithi EL BENDARI
Attaché (Administrative)
Spouse: Mrs. Olfat R. Abdelmoneim

Mr. Gaber Sayed MAHMOUD
Attaché (Administrative)

Mr. Said Abdel Sattar Ibrahim MOHAMED
Attaché (Administrative)

Rear Admiral Tarek Ahmed A. A. M. NOOUR
Defense, Military, Naval, and Air Attaché
Spouse: Mrs. Merfat H. G. Azab

Colonel Mohamed Amin F. ISMAIL
Asst. Defense, Military, Naval, and Air Attaché
Spouse: Mrs. Maha Mohamed I. Ali

Lt. Col. Sherif Fouad E. S. M. HEGAZY
Asst. Defense, Military, Naval, and Air Attaché
Spouse: Mrs. Wafaa Ibrahim M. Ibrahim

Major Tarek Hassan EL SEADY

Asst. Attaché (Administrative)
Spouse: Mrs. Mona A. S. Ashor

Major Ahmed Hussein KHIDR
Asst. Attaché (Financial)
Spouse: Mrs. Mona A. Mosbeh

Brigadier General Hazem AWAD
Asst. Attaché (Military Procurement)
Spouse: Mrs. Wafaa M. El Homosany

Colonel Maher Mohamed L. ELSAYED
Asst. Attaché
Spouse: Mrs. Maryam B. A. Mofid

Colonel Essam El Din ABDEL HADY
Asst. Attaché
Spouse: Mrs. Salwa K. Mohamed

Colonel Galal GAAFAR
Asst. Attaché
Spouse: Mrs. Amina S. Abousoud

Lt. Colonel Hesham Farid HOSNY
Asst. Attaché
Spouse: Mrs. Nadia A. Mahmoud

Major Moustafa TAHA
Asst. Attaché
Spouse: Mrs. Omaima E. Shouah

Major Ehab M. HELAL
Asst. Attaché
Spouse: Mrs. Dina A. El Abasery

Major Ahmed Aref ABDEL MOTALEB
Asst. Attaché
Spouse: Mrs. Manal A. Abdel-Moneim

Mr. Alaa Eldin SHALABY
Minister (Economic and Commercial)
Spouse: Mrs. Fekria El Sayed

Mr. Atef HASSAAN
Counselor (Economic and Commercial)
Spouse: Mrs. Amany M. Khalifa

Mr. Said Taha KHALED
First Secretary (Economic & Commercial)
Spouse: Mrs. Hamdiah Elsayed

Mr. Adel ABDEL-SALAM
Second Sec. (Economic & Commercial)
Spouse: Mrs. Sanaa Aly

Mr. Mohamed Abdel Aziz DAWOOD
Second Sec. (Economic & Commercial)

Mr. Abdul Moneim Mohamed AL MASHAT
Counselor (Cultural and Educational)
Spouse: Mrs. Nagwa El Attar

Mrs. Ihsan Abdelsabour WALI
Attaché (Cultural and Educational)
Spouse: Mr. Sayed Ismail M. El Gammal

Mrs. Madeha M. Ghaleb SHOUKRI
Attaché (Administrative)
Spouse: Mr. Ismail M. Ismail

Mrs. Fathia Ahmed SOUDAN
Attaché (Administrative)

Mr. Hassan M. HASSAN
Attaché (Administrative)
Spouse: Mrs. Fatma M. T. Mohamed

Mr. Abdel Aleem EL ABYAD
Minister (Press and Information)
Spouse: Mrs. Akila Saleh

Ms. Basma Hafez MAHMOUD
Attaché (Press and Information)

Mr. Abdel Aziz Mohamed EL KADI
Attaché (Administrative)
Spouse: Mrs. Enayat Abdel Khalik

Mr. Gamal Mahmoud ALI
Attaché (Administrative)
Spouse: Mrs. Hanan Selem

Dr. Samiry I. SULTAN
Counselor (Medical)
Spouse: Mrs. Zeinab Hassan Zekry

Mr. Ahmed Ibrahim KAMAL
Attaché (Administrative)
Spouse: Mrs. Wafaa Rashad

Dr. Mohamed Abbas EL KALLA
Counselor (Agricultural)
Spouse: Mrs. Aida Wafate

Office of Commercial & Economic Affairs
2232 Massachusetts Avenue, NW
Washington DC 20008
Phone: 202/265-9111 Fax: 202/328-4517

Office of Cultural & Educational Affairs
1303 New Hampshire Avenue, NW
Washington DC 20036
Phone: 202/296-3888 Fax: 202/296-3891

Office of the Defense & Military Attaché
2308 Tracy Place, NW
Washington DC 20008
Phone: 202/462-5943 Fax: 202/462-5978

Office of Procurement
5500 16th Street, NW
Washington DC 20011
Phone: 202/726-8006 Fax: 202/829-4909

Office of Press and Information
1666 Connecticut Avenue, NW, 4th Floor
Washington DC 20009
Phone: 202/667-3402 Fax: 202/234-6827

Office of Medical Affairs
3521 International Court, NW
Washington DC 20008
Phone: 202/296-5286 Fax: 202/296-5288

Office of Agricultural Affairs
3521 International Court, NW
Washington DC 20008
Phone: 202/966-2080 Fax: 202/895-5493

El Salvador

Embassy of El Salvador
2308 California Street, NW
Washington DC 20008

Phone: 202/265-9671
Fax: 202/234-3834

René A. LÉON
Ambassador

Date Credentials Presented: 9/8/97

Before taking his post as El Salvador's ambassador to the U.S., Réne A. León served as vice-minister of economy between 1994 and 1997 in San Salvador.

He was responsible for El Salvador's trade policy and international trade negotiations. He represented El Salvador in its first trade policy review session before the World Trade Organization trade policy review body in November 1996. Prior to his appointment as vice-minister of the economy, León served as director of international trade negotiations and economic integration in the ministry of economy.

In the private sector, León was an economic advisor to El Salvador's Chamber of Commerce and Industry and to the National Association of Private Enterprise of El Salvador. He also was a professor of economics at the Universidad Centro-americana José Simeón Cañas (UCA) and advised several private enterprises and international organizations.

The ambassador graduated as an economist from the Universidad Centroamericana José Simeón Cañas (UCA) in San Salvador. As a Fulbright scholar, he then pursued advanced economic studies at the University of Illinois at Urbana-Champaign in Champaign, Ill.

STAFF:

Mrs. Carmen TOBAR
Minister-Counselor (Deputy Chief of Mission)

Ms. Grace M. AWAD
Counselor (Administrative)

Ms. Claudia N. DE BARTOLINI
Counselor (Press and Public Affairs)
Spouse: Mr. Frank Paul Bartolini

Ms. Angela Mathilde DE CRAIK
Counselor

Ms. Johanna HILL
Counselor (Economic Policy)

Second Lt. Zeyda Nissia MARSH
Counselor (Political)

Mr. Werner M. ROMERO
Counselor (Trade and Investment Promo.)

Mr. Walter A. ANAYA E.
First Secretary and Consul General

Mrs. Dora Maria DE AGUILAR
First Secretary
Spouse: Mr. Jose M. Aguilar

Ms. Maria Isabel ROSALES LAGUARDIA
Second Secretary and Vice Consul

Mr. Francisco Javier CALLEJA
Attaché (Commercial)
Spouse: Mrs. Maureen Calleja

Mr. Victor Manuel RODRIGUEZ PREZA
Attaché (Cultural)
Spouse: Mrs. Mercedes Del C. Rodriguez Preza

Ms. Mirian Etelinda VARGAS CASTILLO
Attaché (Cultural)

Colonel Baltazar LOPEZ
Defense, Military, Naval, and Air Attaché
Spouse: Mrs. Susana Lopez

Lt. Colonel Alvaro Antonio PALOMO
Asst. Defense, Military, Naval, and Air Attaché
Spouse: Mrs. Blanca Margarita Palomo

Lt. Colonel Otto Alejandro ROMERO
Asst. Defense, Military, Naval, and Air Attaché
Spouse: Mrs. Ana Consuelo Romero

Office of Consular Affairs
1010 16th St., NW - 3rd Floor
Washington DC 20036
Phone: 202/331-4032

Equatorial Guinea

Embassy of Equatorial Guinea
1511 K Street, NW, Suite 405
Washington DC 20005
Phone: 202/393-0525
Fax: 202/393-0348

Pastor Micha ONDO BILE
Ambassador

Date Credentials Presented: 9/15/95

Born: 12/2/52 in Equatorial Guinea

Spouse: Mrs. Concepcion Angue de Micha Ondo

An engineer by profession, Pastor Micha Ondo Bile worked his way up in the Equatorial Guinean government to the position of secretary-general of the Ministry of Mines and Energy before he was named ambassador to the United States and permanent representative before the United Nations.

In 1977, he received a master of science degree in engineering at the University Institute at the Krivoi-Rog Mines. He is licensed in underground development of natural resources.

Ondo Bile began his career in 1982 as an engineer in the department of mines and hydrocarburetors in Malabo. In 1983, he attended a training course in Washington,

D.C., on continuation, evaluation control, and processing of World Bank projects. He attended a course on "Elastic Petroleum and Natural Gas Reserves" in Peru in 1984 and a course organized under the auspices of the United Nations Development Program in Malabo in 1985. In 1986, he participated in a seminar on negotiation, evaluation, control, and inspection of petroleum contracts in Geneva, Switzerland.

He held the office of director-general of mines and hydrocarburetors from 1984 to 1994 before his promotion to secretary general of the Ministry of Mines and Energy.

Married and the father of six, Ondo Bile speaks Spanish, Russian, French, and English. He is a Knight of the Order of Independence, Second Class, of the Republic of Equatorial Guinea.

STAFF:

Mr. Teodoro BIYOGO NSUE
First Secretary (Deputy Chief of Mission)
Spouse: Mrs. Elena Mensa Abena

Mrs. Mari Cruz EVUNA ANDEME
Attaché (Administrative)

Eritrea

Embassy of the State of Eritrea
1708 New Hampshire Ave., NW
Washington DC 20009
Phone: 202/319-1991
Fax: 202/319-1304
Email: Freweini@embassyeritrea.org

Semere RUSSOM
Ambassador

Date Credentials Presented: 9/8/97

Born: 1943 in Kudoabour, Eritrea

Spouse: Mrs. Alem Abraha Hadgu

Before taking his post as ambassador to the U.S. in July 1997, Semere Russom served in the new nation's ministry of foreign affairs in Asmara as head of the Americas, U.N., and international organizations affairs office.

From 1970 to 1973, Russom was a high school teacher in Asmara after which he was the head of the purchasing department in a private company for three years.

He joined the Eritrean People's Liberation Front (EPLF) in 1975 and held a series of jobs. Between 1978 and 1984, he was head of the EPLF mass administration department for the Sudan region. He was a staff member of EPLF foreign relations in the Sudan between 1985-1989 after which he became assistant head of the research section in the department of security and intelligence of the EPLF. He served as first secretary of the Eritrean Provisional Mission to the Sudan in 1991-92, after which he served in the ministry of foreign affairs when Eritrea became an independent nation in 1993.

Russom has participated in a number of international courses and workshops including a workshop on developments in Germany after unification in Berlin; workshops in the European Union and at NATO headquarters in Belgium; meetings involving several United Nations agencies in Geneva and Switzerland; and seminars on the British Parliament, Foreign Office, the Commonwealth Office, and the British Petroleum Co.

In 1994, Russom went to an international conference on population and development in Cairo. He attended the UN General Assembly and 50th Anniversary of the UN in New York in 1995 and returned the following year for the UN's 51st General Assembly. He has written a dissertation on "Diplomacy in Liberation Movements of the Cold War Era---The Eritrean Experience."

Russom has a B.A. degree from Haile Selassi I University in Addis Ababa, Ethiopia, which he attended from 1965-70. He also studied at Oklahoma State University in 1974 and at Oxford University in Oxford, in a special post-graduate program in diplomatic studies in 1993-94.

STAFF:

Mr. Berhane Asresehei KIDANE
Second Secretary (Administrative)
Spouse: Mrs. Elsa Abraham Haile

Mr. Goitom Sium GHEBREZGHABIHER
Third Secretary (Consular)
Spouse: Mrs. Tblez Abraha Asfaha

Estonia

Embassy of Estonia
2131 Massachusetts Ave., NW
Washington DC 20008
Phone: 202/588-0101
Fax: 202/588-0108
Email: info@estemb.org
Url: http://www.estemb.org

Grigore Kalev STOICESCU
Ambassador

Date Credentials Presented: 5/14/97

Born: 9/2/65 in Constanta, Romania

Spouse: Mrs. Kattri Arge Stoicescu

Grigore-Kalev Stoicescu, a mathematics teacher, prepared himself for serving his country after it became an independent nation in 1991 by attending the Estonian School of Diplomacy, from which he graduated the same year.

He began his diplomatic career in the ministry of foreign affairs in Talinn in the position of first secretary, department of information, where he served in 1991-92. He moved on to become counselor on CSCE Affairs (the CSCE's name has since been changed to the Organization for Security and Cooperation) in the Department of International Organizations in 1992-93.

Stoicescu went to Vienna in 1993 to serve for three years first as counselor and head of mission to the CSCE at Estonia's embassy in Austria and, starting in January 1994, as ambassador to the CSCE. In 1995, he returned to Talinn to take the post of director of the policy planning division of the ministry of foreign affairs.

He taught mathematics at Tartu L Second School in 1989 and later taught mathematics and information science. He received a mathematics degree from Tartu State University in 1990.

Stoicescu, who has no affiliation with a political party, speaks Estonian, Romanian, English, French, Italian, and Russian.

STAFF:

Mr. Lauri LEPIK
First Secretary (Political)

Mr. Mait MARTINSON
First Secretary (Commercial)

Mr. Jaan SALULAID
First Secretary (Economic)
Spouse: Mrs. Maria Claudia Solarte Vasquez

Ethiopia

Embassy of Ethiopia
2134 Kalorama Road, NW
Washington DC 20008
Phone: 202/234-2281
Fax: 202/328-7950
Email: ethiopia@tidalwave.net
Url: http://www.nicom.com/~ethiopia

Berhane GEBRE-CHRISTOS
Ambassador

Date Credentials Presented: 4/2/92

Born: 3/6/53 in Makalle, Ethiopia

Spouse: Mrs. Ketema Redda Gebre-Christos

Berhane Gebre-Christos became the first Ethiopian ambassador to the U.S. since the mid-1970s, following the overthrow of the authoritarian government of Mengistu Haile-Mariam in 1991.

Having joined the Tigray People's Liberation Front (TPLF) in 1976, Gebre-Christos worked in the political department of the organization, before being made the head of its administration and mass movements. He was elected in 1983 to the Front's leadership.

As a member of the TPLF's Foreign Relations Bureau from 1979 to 1991, and as a member of the Foreign Relations Bureau of the Ethiopian Peoples' Revolutionary Democratic Front from 1988 to 1991, Gebre-Christos gained extensive diplomatic experience. In these capacities, he traveled extensively throughout Europe, Asia, Africa, and North America to promote the cause of the Front among government officials, parliaments, international organizations and the public.

After Mengistu Haile-Mariam's overthrow, Gebre-Christos served briefly as the Ethiopian Foreign Ministry's Ambassador at Large.

Gebre-Christos was educated at the Haile Selassie I University and speaks English, Italian, Amharic, and Tigrigna. He is married to Ketema Redda and has three children.

STAFF:

Mr. Fisseha ADUGA
Counselor (Political) and Deputy Chief of Mission
Spouse: Mrs. Desta Mulat

Mr. Tadelle TEFERRA
Counselor (Economic and Financial)
Spouse: Mrs. Messelu Tadesse

Mr. Mohammed Yahya GARAD
Counselor (Trade)
Spouse: Mrs. Nabata Abdullahi Garad

Mr. Ayalew Yimann ERGETE
Counselor
Spouse: Mrs. Semainesh Tesfayohanes

Mr. Ayalew H. MAMO
First Secretary (Political)
Spouse: Mrs. Zewdinesh Kegede

Mr. Gizaw Gebre-Hanna WOLDETSADIK
Second Secretary (Admin. and Financial)
Spouse: Mrs. Almaz Kebede Asfaw

Economic Financial and Trade
1800 K Street, NW, Suite 624
Washington DC 20006
Phone: 202/452-1272 Fax: 202/223-0137

European Union

Delegation of the European Commission
2300 M Street, NW
Washington DC 20037
Phone: 202/862-9500
Fax: 202/429-1766

Hugo PAEMEN
Ambassador

Date Credentials Presented: 2/6/96

Born: 10/28/34 in Erps-Kwerps, Belgium

Spouse: Mrs. Irma Koninckx Paemen

A career diplomat, Hugo Paemen took over the responsibility for the European Commission's Uruguay Round negotiating team in 1987 as deputy director general for external relations and stayed in the post for almost the entire duration of the round.

He served in the Belgian embassies in Geneva, Paris, and Washington, D.C., before

he was appointed chief de cabinet to Viscount Davignon when the latter was appointed vice president of the European Commission in 1978. In 1985, he became the official spokesman of the commission when it was headed by President Jacques Delors.

From 1987 to 1996, Paemen was also a professor at Catholic University of Leuven, where he lectured in European politics. He became a member of the board at the university early in 1996.

Paemen has degrees in philosophy and classics and political and social science. He and his wife, Irma, have six children.

STAFF:

Mr. John B. RICHARDSON
Minister (Deputy Head of Delegation)

Mr. Aslam M. AZIZ
Minister-Counselor (Development)
Spouse: Mrs. Anna Azia

Mr. Lodewijk BRIET
Minister-Counselor (Political)

Mr. Pablo AMOR
Counselor (Science, Techn. and Education)

Mr. Patrice P. LAGET
Counselor (Science, Techn. and Education)

Mr. Bernd LANGEHEINE
Counselor (Trade)

Mr. Reinhard RIEMER
Counselor (Agriculture)

Mr. Werner Kurt SCHULE
Counselor (Economic and Financial)

Mr. Soren Peter SONDERGAARD
Counselor (Press and Public Affairs)
Spouse: Mrs. Sondergaard

Mr. Alessandro FORTINI
First Secretary (Administrative)

Mr. Gerrit DE GRAAF
First Secretary (Trade)

Mr. Anastassios HANIOTIS
First Secretary (Agriculture)

Mr. Anders C. JESSEN
First Secretary (Energy, Environment and Transportation)

Miss Caroline NORMOND
First Secretary (Trade)

Ms. Astrid SCHOMAKER
First Secretary (Trade)

Ms. Mary Catherine BUNYAN
Attaché (Agriculture)

Ms. Marie-Jose J. DE BLOCK
Attaché (Nuclear Supply)

Fiji

Embassy of The Republic of Fiji
2233 Wisconsin Avenue, NW, Suite 240
Washington DC 20007
Phone: 202/337-8320
Fax: 202/337-1996
Email: fijiemb@earthlink.net

Napolioni MASIREWA
Ambassador

Date Credentials Presented: 2/2/97

Born: 6/1/53

Spouse: Mrs. Florence Joanna T. Masirewa

Napolioni Masirewa, the Republic of Fiji's
ambassador to the U.S. since 1997, had
served in the Fijian government as deputy
secretary of home affairs, Fijian affairs and
tourism and as a commissioner of the western
division. He has a B.A. degree in history
and politics from the University of the South
Pacific.

STAFF:

Mr. Emori TUDIA
First Secretary
Spouse: Mrs. Vani Tudia

Ms. Salaseini Lelevawalu VOSAILAGI
Second Secretary

Finland

Embassy of Finland
3301 Massachusetts Avenue, NW
Washington DC 20008
Phone: 202/298-5820
Fax: 202/298-0450
Email: Finland@ix.netcom.com
Url: http://www.finland.org

Jaakko LAAJAVA
Ambassador

Date Credentials Presented: 4/30/96

Born: 6/23/47 in Joensuu, Finland

Spouse: Mrs. Pirjoriitta (Rita) Laajava

Jaakko Laajava came to Washington, D.C.,
from the post of Director General for Political
Affairs for the Ministry of Foreign Affairs
in Helsinki.

He is a career diplomat and has served the
Finnish government since 1971. He started
with the Conference on Security and
Cooperation in Europe (CSCE), also known
as the Helsinki Process. In this context, he
served in Geneva, Belgrade, and Madrid.

In addition to postings at the Finnish
embassies in Yugoslavia, Spain, and Poland,
he has also held senior positions in Helsinki
in arms control, security policy, and
multilateral affairs.

Laajava has attended numerous conference
and negotiations as Finland's delegate. He
has written and taught on matters of foreign
policy and is a graduate of Helsinki
University and the University of Stockholm.
He was also a Harvard Fellow from the
Center for International Affairs between
1985 and 1986.

Laajava is married and has three children
who are university students in Helsinki and
London.

STAFF:

Mr. Teemu TANNER
Minister (Deputy Chief of Mission)
Spouse: Mrs. Kirsimarja Tanner

Ms. Armi HEINONEN
Minister-Counselor (Development Policy)

Mr. Antti TURUNEN
Counselor (Political Affairs)
Spouse: Mrs. Kirsti Turunen

Ms. Kirsti H. KAUPPI
First Secretary (Political Affairs)

Mr. Jyrki IIVONEN
Minister-Counselor (Political-Military)
Spouse: Mrs. Mirja Iivonen

Mr. Jorma KORHONEN
Counselor (Economic)
Spouse: Mrs. Ulla Noroviita-Korhonen

Ms. Leena RITOLA
Second Secretary (Economic)

Mr. Jarmo A. MAKELA
Counselor (Press)
Spouse: Mrs. Kielo Kaarina Karioja
Makela

Ms. Anneli HALONEN
Counselor (Cultural)

Mr. Veikko Juhani KANTOLA
Counselor (Project Promotion)
Spouse: Ms. Birgitta K. Kantola

Mr. Anssi KUJALA
Counselor (Science and Technology)
Spouse: Mrs. Tarja Kujala

Colonel Kari Juhani KOKKONEN
Military Attaché
Spouse: Mrs. Marja-Leena M. Kokkonen

Lt. Commander Markus A. AARNIO
Asst. Military Attaché
Spouse: Mrs. Johanna Koroma

Lt. Colonel Jouni KOSKENMIES
Military Attaché

Ms. Maria SORSA
Second Secretary (Administrative Affairs)

Ms. Anja L. MANN
Attaché (Consular)
Spouse: Mr. Edward Mann

Ms. Sirkka AUVINEN
Events Coordinator

**Office of Defense, Military, Naval and
Air Attaché**
3301 Massachusetts Avenue, NW
Washington DC 20008
Phone: 202/298-5800 Fax: 202/298-6059

F/A-18 Liaison Office
3301 Massachusetts Avenue, NW
Washington DC 20008
Phone: 202/298-5800 Fax: 202/298-6059

Project Promotion Office
3301 Massachusetts Avenue, NW
Washington DC 20008
Phone: 202/298-5877 Fax: 202/298-6041

Technology Center
3301 Massachusetts Avenue, NW
Washington DC 20008
Phone: 202/298-5837 Fax: 202/298-6040

France

Embassy of France
4101 Reservoir Road, NW
Washington DC 20007
Phone: 202/944-6000
Fax: 202/944-6166
Url: http://www.info-france-usa.org

Francois V.
BUJON DE L'ESTANG
Ambassador

Date Credentials Presented: 12/12/95

Born: 1940 in Neuilly sur Seine, France

Spouse: Mrs. Anne M. Bujon de l'Estang

After three years as France's ambassador to Canada, Francois Bujon de l'Estang returned in 1991 to Paris and the private sector.

He served as senior vice president with the Compagnie de Navigation Mixte, a French industrial and financial conglomerate, and Via Banque from November 1991 to October 1992, and simultaneously as chairman and CEO of S.F.I.M., a high-technology electronics and aeronautics company. In 1992, he created FBE International Consultants, a consulting firm specializing in international relations, policy risk analysis, and government counseling.

After graduating from the Institut Politique de Paris and the Ecole Nationale d'Administration, Bujon de l'Estang chose a career with the Ministry of Foreign Affairs, starting in 1966. He was assigned as a special adviser to the president of the republic, Charles de Gaulle. He was deputy to the president's diplomatic adviser and continued to work for General de Gaulle until the latter's resignation in 1969.

He was then posted to the French embassy in the United States where he remained from 1969 to 1973, serving as second and then as first secretary. He moved in 1973 to the French embassy in London where he remained for two years. He returned to Paris, where he was assigned to the Ministry of Industry as adviser on international affairs.

Other government posts held by Bujon de l'Estang include director of international relations for the Atomic Energy Commissariat and chief of staff to Andre Giraud, minister of industry. Between 1986 and 1988, he served as senior adviser to Prime Minister Jacques Chirac for diplomatic affairs, defense, and cooperation.

In the early 1980s, he set up a subsidiary in the United States for the A.F.C. group to develop the production and export of French nuclear material and services. He created Cogema Inc. and set up its offices in Washington, D.C. The firm became one of the main producers of natural uranium in the United States.

A Knight of the Order of the Legion of Honor, Bujon de l'Estang is married to the former Anne de Margerie and is the father of four. In the 1980s, he attended the advanced management program at the Harvard Graduate School of Business Administration.

STAFF:

Mr. Hugues Alban PERNET
Minister (Deputy Chief of Mission)
Spouse: Mrs. Francoise Pernet

Mr. Jean Francois BOITTIN
Minister (Economic and Commercial)

Spouse: Mrs. Sarah Leith Boittin

Mr. Daniel AUDUREAU
Counselor (Paymaster General)
Spouse: Mrs. Michele Audureau

Mr. Jean Michel BOUR
Counselor (Transportation)
Spouse: Mrs. Laurette Bour

Mr. Guy BROISSAND
Counselor
Spouse: Mrs. Pascaline Ginette Broissand

Mr. Pierre BUHLER
Counselor (Cultural)

Mr. Oliver CARON
Counselor
Spouse: Mrs. Marie-Odile Caron

Mr. Noel Jean Pierre CLAUDON
Counselor (Tax)
Spouse: Mrs. Elisabeth G. Claudon

Mr. Alain DE KEGHEL
Counselor and Consul General
Spouse: Mrs. Dominique De Keghel

Mr. Nicolas DE RIVIERE
Counselor
Spouse: Mrs. Meike Bueld

Mr. Roland GALHARAGUE
Counselor

Mr. Pierre GUIGNARD
Counselor (Chief of Staff to Ambassador)
Spouse: Mrs. Maria Carmen Guignard

Mr. Bruno JACTEL
Counselor (Economic and Commercial)
Spouse: Mrs. Ann Jactel

Mr. Jean Pierre LACROIX
Counselor
Spouse: Mrs. Muge Lacroix

Mr. Jean-Francois LACRONIQUE
Counselor (Health)
Spouse: Mrs. Catherine Isabelle LaCronique

Mr. Phillippe LEFORT
Counselor
Spouse: Mrs. Geraldine Lefort

Mr. Daniel LEROY
Counselor (Nuclear and Energy)

Mr. Herve MAGRO
Counselor
Spouse: Mrs. Maria de Fatima Magro

Mr. Bernard MAIZERET
Counselor (Head of Chancery)
Spouse: Mrs. Marie-Jeanne Maizeret

Mr. Hubert MARTIN
Counselor (Labor and Social)
Spouse: Mrs. Dianna Martin

Mr. Jean Marie PAUGAM

Counselor (Commercial)
Spouse: Mrs. Anne Paugam

Mr. Emile PEREZ
Counselor
Spouse: Mrs. Marie Ange Perez

Dr. Serge PLATTARD
Counselor (Scientific and Technology)
Spouse: Mrs. Sylvie Plattard

Mr. Bernard RABATEL
Counselor

Ms. Christine ROBICHON
Counselor

Mr. Bernard ROUX
Counselor (Customs)
Spouse: Mrs. Brigitte Roux

Mr. Bernard VALERO
Counselor (Press and Information)
Spouse: Mrs. Patrizia Sirignano

Mr. Phillippe ARDANAZ
First Secretary
Spouse: Mrs. Isabel Ardanaz

Mr. Jacques CHAMPAGNE DE LABRIOLLE
First Secretary
Spouse: Mrs. Marie Champagne de Labriolle

Mr. Raymond EUGENE
First Secretary
Spouse: Mrs. Arlette Eugene

Miss Marie Pierre GOURVENNEC
First Secretary

Mr. Jean Raphael PEYTREGNET
First Secretary
Spouse: Mrs. Zhun Peytregnet

Ms. Anne Marie ROUX
First Secretary and Consul
Spouse: Mr. Michel Roux

Ms. Emmanuelle BENSIMON
Third Secretary

Mr. Phillippe HUBERT
Third Secretary

Mr. Luc MENARD
Third Secretary
Spouse: Mrs. Isabelle Menard

Mr. Michel PROOST
Third Secretary
Spouse: Mrs. Helene Proost

Mrs. Brigitte ROUX
Third Secretary
Spouse: Mr. Bernard Roux

Mr. Francois BERTIN
Attaché (Scientific and Technology)
Spouse: Mrs. Marie-France Bertin

Mr. Edmond Jean BOULLAY

Attaché (Civil Aviation Safety)
Spouse: Mrs. Jeanne Roberte Boullay

Mrs. Marie-Helene FORGET
Attaché (Legal)
Spouse: Mr. Louis Forget

Mr. Herve JOLY
Attaché (Financial)
Spouse: Mrs. Severine Joly

Mr. Louis LAURENT
Attaché (Space)
Spouse: Mrs. Caroline Laurent

Ms. Regine LOPEZ
Attaché and Vice Consul

Mr. Frederic PARUTA
Attaché (Press)
Spouse: Mrs. Gloria Marina Paruta

Mr. Lazare E. PAUPERT
Attaché (Cultural)
Spouse: Mrs. Anne P. Paupert

Mr. Vito Francis SACCO
Attaché
Spouse: Mrs. Christiane Sacco

Ms. Anne-Marie SEGUIER
Attaché and Vice Consul

Miss Francoise TOURAINE MOULIN
Attaché (Science and Technology)

Mr. Bruno Paul DUPRE
Asst. Attaché (Armament)
Spouse: Mrs. Anne Martine Dupre

Brigadier Gen. Jean Francois LOUVION
Defense Attaché
Spouse: Mrs. Simone Louvion

Captain Robert RANQUET
Defense Cooperation Attaché
Spouse: Mrs. Blandine Ranquet

Colonel Christian VAGANAY
Military Attaché
Spouse: Mrs. Laure Vaganay

Captain Philippe ANGLES
Naval Attaché
Spouse: Mrs. Francoise Angles

Colonel Christian SOULERES
Air Attaché
Spouse: Mrs. Francoise Souleres

Colonel Francois Max COTE
Asst. Defense Cooperation Attaché and
   Asst. Air Attaché
Spouse: Mrs. Veronique Corinne Cote

Captain Frederic Jean JOUREAU
Asst. Defense Cooperation Attaché
Spouse: Mrs. Stephanie Helene Joureau

Major Christophe MARX
Asst. Military Attaché
Spouse: Mrs. Anne Marx

Colonel Dominique ORSINI
Asst. Military Attaché
Spouse: Mrs. Maureen Orsini

Commander Olivier CASENAVE PERE
Asst. Naval Attaché
Spouse: Mrs. Rachel Casenave Pere

Lt. Commander Laurent MOLARD
Asst. Naval Attaché
Spouse: Mrs. Laurence Molard

Gabon

Embassy of the Gabonese Republic
2034 20th Street, NW, Suite 200
Washington DC 20009
Phone: 202/797-1000
Fax: 202/332-0668

Paul BOUNDOUKOU-LATHA
Ambassador

Date Credentials Presented: 9/3/93

Born: 4/23/52 in Mafoungui, Gabon
A career foreign service officer, Paul Boundoukou-Latha rose quickly through the ranks of Gabon's Foreign Affairs Department. Educated in France, the ambassador has worked extensively with European affairs and with international organization issues. Immediately prior to his present appointment, he was Gabon's ambassador to Morocco.

In the Ministry of Foreign Affairs, Boundoukou-Latha held a number of positions, including head of Division for EEC and Western Europe and director for international organizations and multilateral cooperation.

Boundoukou-Latha has expressed the hope that the U.S. can play a key role in helping the developing African nations find solutions for their debt problems and in encouraging Western private sector investment in the Gabonese economy.

He received a master's degree in sociology at the University of Tours in France in 1978. He holds a doctorate in politics and development law from the University of Poitiers in France and an advanced degree

in diplomacy from the Paris School of Law. Among his published works are "Syndication of Immigrant Workers from Black Africa in France," "Contribution to the Study of a Single African Party: the Gabonese Democratic Party," and "International Aid and Development in Gabon," his doctoral dissertation in 1982.

Boundoukou-Latha is the recipient of several state honors: he was named Officier de l'Etoile Equatoriale (Gabon), Officier de l'Ordre National du Merite (France), and Commandeur de l'Ordre d'Ouissam Alaouite (Morocco).

STAFF:

Mrs. Alba BIFFOT
Counselor (Economic)
Spouse: Mr. Tomas Sales

Ms. Marie-Clementine MOUNGALA
Counselor

Mr. Laurent NDONG
Counselor
Spouse: Mrs. Justine Ndong

Mr. Mathurin NGOMONDJAMI
Counselor (Communication)
Spouse: Mrs. Leah Andrea Ermarth

Mr. Fidele Moussavou NGUEMBI
Counselor
Spouse: Mrs. Marie L. Dilindi

Mrs. Aline OBAME
Counselor
Spouse: Mr. J. Christian Obame

Mr. Georges TIGALEKOU
Counselor
Spouse: Mrs. Clotilde Tigalekou

Mrs. Clotilde TIGALEKOU
First Secretary
Spouse: Mr. Georges Tigalekou

Lt. Colonel Anatole AUGOULA
Defense, Military, Navy, and Air Attaché

Gambia

Embassy of The Gambia
1155 15th Street, NW, Suite 1000
Washington DC 20005
Phone: 202/785-1399
Fax: 202/785-1430
Email: gamembdc@gambia.com
Url: http://www.gambia.com

Crispin GREY-JOHNSON
Ambassador

Date Credentials Presented: 9/8/97

Born: 12/7/46

Spouse: Mrs. Sarah Grey-Johnson

Crispin Grey-Johnson worked for 20 years for the United Nations Economic Commission for Africa before assuming his responsibilities as The Gambia's ambassador to the U.S.

Between 1994 and 1996, he served as coordinator for the multidisciplinary regional advisory group in the cabinet office of the executive secretary for the United Nations Economic Commission for Africa in Addis Ababa, Ethiopia. Between 1990 and 1994, he was senior regional advisor in the same office.

Grey-Johnson was an economic affairs officer with the commission between 1981 and 1990. Before that he was an associate economic affairs officer for four years.

Immediately before coming to Washington, D.C., Grey-Johnson was managing director of Galloryaa Farms Ltd. in The Gambia. He started his working career as senior master, head of department, at the Gambia High School in Banjul from 1968-77.

He has published numerous research reports and technical papers on such topics as "Higher Education and the Implementation of the Lagos Plan of Action," "The Employment Crisis in Africa: Issues in Human Resources Development Policy," and "Capacity Building, Strengthening and Retention for Socio-economic Development in Africa: Lessons from Mauritius and Madagascar."

Grey-Johnson holds a B.A. degree in political science and French from McGill University in Canada, 1968; a PGCE in theory and practice of education from Oxford University in England, 1971; and an M.A. degree in human resource development from George Washington University in 1980.

Among fellowships and scholarships received by Grey-Johnson are a U.S. Agency for International Development fellowship in 1980; a UN fellowship for research at the Africa Institute for Economic Development and Planning in Dakar, Senegal, in 1973; an

Overseas Development Agency scholarship from the government of Great Britain, 1970-71; and a Special Commonwealth Africa Aid Programme Scholarship from the Canadian government, 1965-68.

Grey-Johnson is proficient in English and French.

STAFF:

Mr. Malamin K. JUWARA
Minister (Deputy Chief of Mission)
Spouse: Mrs. Fatou Keita

Mrs. Juliana G. BALDEH
First Secretary

Mr. Lamin A. BOJANG
Attaché (Financial)
Spouse: Mrs. Joko Jabang Bojang

Georgia

Embassy of the Republic of Georgia
1511 K Street, NW, Suite 424
Washington DC 20005
Phone: 202/393-5959
Fax: 202/393-6060
Email: 73324.1007@compuserve.com

Dr. Tedo JAPARIDZE
Ambassador

Date Credentials Presented: 1/30/95

Born: 9/18/46 in Tbilisi

Spouse: Mrs. Tamar Japaridze

In addition to being his country's ambassador to the U.S., Tedo Japaridze is also Georgia's mbassador to Canada and Mexico.

Between 1989 and 1992, he served in several positions at Georgia's Ministry of Foreign Affairs, including vice chairman of the Council for UNESCO Affairs; head of the political department; deputy foreign minister; and first deputy foreign minister. Between 1992 and 1994, he served as national security adviser to the Head of State.

Between 1974 and 1989, Japaridze was affiliated with the Institute of USA and Canada at the U.S.S.R. Academy of Sciences

in Moscow.

Japaridze, who completed his studies at Tbilisi State University in 1974, has published in the field of U.S. domestic politics and regional security policy. He speaks English and Russian fluently. He likes sports, particularly basketball, and his hobbies include jazz music and reading history books. He and his wife, Tamar have one son.

STAFF:

Mr. Vassili KATCHARAVA
Minister
Spouse: Mrs. Maia Katcharava

Mr. Roland BERIDZE
Counselor (Consular)
Spouse: Mrs. Inga Paichadze

Mr. Ioseb KHELASHVILI
Counselor
Spouse: Mrs. Tamar Davitashvili

Mr. David SOUMBADZE
Counselor
Spouse: Mrs. Inga Diasamidze

Mr. Gotcha PIPIA
First Secretary
Spouse: Mrs. Maia Khvitia

Mr. Mamouka TSERETELI
First Secretary
Spouse: Mrs. Maia Koupounia

Mr. Mikhail SIAMACHVILI
Second Secretary

Germany

Embassy of the Federal Republic
of Germany
4645 Reservoir Road, NW
Washington DC 20007
Phone: 202/298-4000
Fax: 202/298-4249
Url: http://www.germany-info.org

Juergen CHROBOG
Ambassador

Date Credentials Presented: 4/10/95

Born: 1/28/40 in Hohen-Neuendorf near Berlin

Spouse: Mrs. Magda Gohar Chrobog

Juergen Chrobog came to Washington to be Germany's ambassador to the U.S. from the post of political director of Germany's Federal Foreign Office that he had held for four years.

Between 1984 and 1991, he was spokesman for the Federal Foreign Office, but between 1989 and 1991, he also served as head of the Office of the Foreign Minister. From 1981 to 1983, he was press officer at the Permanent Mission to the European Community in Brussels.

Chrobog entered the Foreign Service in 1972 and served for a year at the Permanent Mission to the United Nations in New York. After that, he went to the Federal Foreign Office in the Office of the Foreign Minister. Between 1977 and 1981, he was deputy chief of mission and economic counselor at the Germany Embassy in Singapore.

Chrobog studied law in Freiburg, Aix-en-Provence and Gottingen, and passed the first state bar examination in 1966. He underwent legal training for the next four years and passed the second state bar exam in 1971, after which he practiced law.

Chrobog is married and has three children.

STAFF:

Mr. Thomas MATUSSEK
Minister (Chief of Mission)
Spouse: Mr. Ursula Maria Matussek

Dr. Harald BRAUN
Minister (Political)

Mr. Volker Hermann SCHLEGEL
Minister (Economic)
Spouse: Mrs. Gabriele Schlegel

Mr. Karl Peter ALBERS
Counselor (Defense Research and
    Engineering Technology)
Spouse: Mrs. Maria Teresa Riera Y
    Bague Albers

Mr. Axel BARRACH
Counselor (Defense Research and
    Engineering Technology)
Spouse: Mrs. Margarete Barrach

Mr. Hans-Georg BERGMANN
Counselor
Spouse: Mrs. Margrit Bergmann

Mr. Joachim BLEICKER
Counselor (Political)

Mr. Manfred Josef Karl BLESS
Counselor
Spouse: Mrs. Martha Kopp Bless

Mr. Dirk BRENGELMANN
Counselor (Political)
Spouse: Mrs. Brigitte Brengelmann

Mr. Gerhard GLOEY
Counselor
Spouse: Mrs. Konstanze Gloey

Mrs. Doris E. GRIMM
Counselor (Finance)
Spouse: Mr. U. Hermann Stiehler

Mr. Johannes Konrad HAINDL
Counselor
Spouse: Mrs. Regina Sophie Haindl

Mr. Benedikt HALLER
Counselor
Spouse: Mrs. Angelika Haller

Mr. Florenz HUNDT
Counselor (Finance)
Spouse: Mrs. Waltraud Hundt

Mrs. Dorothee JANETZKE WENZEL
Counselor
Spouse: Mr. Heinz Dieter Wenzel

Dr. Karin K. KAMMANN KLIPPSTEIN
Counselor
Spouse: Mr. Thomas K. W. Klippstein

Mr. Ullrich KLOECKNER
Counselor (Press)
Spouse: Mrs. Angela Kloeckner

Mr. Detlef LINGEMANN
Counselor
Spouse: Mrs. Ute Lingemann

Dr. Hans-Ulrich SEIDT
Counselor (Cultural)

Mr. Juergen W. MAURER
Counselor
Spouse: Dr. Sabine Vogt

Dr. Karl Heinrich PITZ
Counselor (Labor)

Mr. Heinrich ROSENLEHNER
Counselor
Spouse: Mrs. Ruth Rosenlehner

Mr. Konrad Max SCHARINGER
Counselor (Economic)
Spouse: Mrs. Hildegard Scharinger

Mr. Wolfram Josef SCHOETT
Counselor (Scientific and Technology)
Spouse: Mrs. Barbara Schoett-V. Zwehl

Mr. Claus WUNDERLICH
Counselor
Spouse: Mrs. Christa Wunderlich

Mr. Juergen BORSCH
First Secretary (Political)
Spouse: Mrs. Andrea Borsch

Mr. Guido MELKE
First Secretary (Political)
Spouse: Mrs. Alexandra Melke

Mrs. Heike FULLER
First Secretary
Spouse: Mr. Kurt Fuller

Mr. Karsten D. GEIER
First Secretary (Political)
Spouse: Ms. Tatjana Geier

Mr. Otto GRAF
First Secretary (Scientific and Technology)
Spouse: Mrs. Edlira Graf

Mr. Hubert KNIRSCH
First Secretary
Spouse: Mrs. Eva Maria Knirsch

Mr. Martin KOTTHAUS
First Secretary (Press)

Mr. Ulrich LOCHERER
First Secretary (Administrative)
Spouse: Mrs. Gisela Locherer

Ms. Monika OTTEMEYER
First Secretary (Economic)

Mr. Wolfgang SCHLUMP
First Secretary (Scientific and Technology)

Mr. Ludger A. SIEMES
First Secretary (Political)
Spouse: Mrs. Barbara Siemes

Mr. Thomas TERSTEGEN
First Secretary and Consul General
Spouse: Mrs. Birgit Terstegen

Mr. Hans Leopold VON WINTERFELD
First Secretary (Economic)

Mr. Siegbert Gunther BRUECKNER
Second Secretary
Spouse: Mrs. Monika Brueckner

Mr. Wolfgang EWERT
Second Secretary and Consul
Spouse: Mrs. Mechtild Ewert

Mr. Jens HANEFELD
Second Secretary (Cultural)
Spouse: Mrs. Petra Renate Hanefeld

Mr. Rainer HARMS
Second Secretary
Spouse: Mrs. Anne Claudia Harms

Mr. Reinhold H. NEUKOETTER
Second Secretary
Spouse: Mrs. Annette M. K. Neukoetter

Mr. Karsten RABE
Second Secretary
Spouse: Mrs. Marion Rabe

Mr. Hartwig Gustav ROHRBECK
Second Secretary (Administrative)
Spouse: Mrs. Gudrun Rohrbeck

Mr. Alexander SCHOENFELDER
Second Secretary (Economic)
Spouse: Mrs. Octavia Schoenfelder

Mr. Hans-Juergen WOELK

Second Secretary (Administrative)
Spouse: Mrs. Ilona Woelk

Mr. Gerd Siegfried BUCHSTEINER
Third Secretary (Defense Research & Eng)
Spouse: Mrs. Marlene Buchsteiner

Mrs. Mechtild EWERT
Third Secretary (Press and Information)
Spouse: Mr. Wolfgang Ewert

Mr. Uwe FREUCK
Third Secretary
Spouse: Mrs. Ingrid Freuck

Mr. Erwin GANZER
Third Secretary (Economic)
Spouse: Mrs. Silvia Scharf

Mrs. Petra HANEFELD
Third Secretary (Science and Technology)
Spouse: Mrs. Jens Hanefeld

Mr. Ernst PFEIFLE
Third Secretary

Mr. Peter SCHMAHL
Third Secretary
Spouse: Ms. Brigitte Ruyter Schmahl

Mr. Horst STENDER
Third Secretary (Administrative)
Spouse: Mrs. Bettina Martha Stender

Mr. Anton Manfred WAGNER
Third Secretary (Administrative)
Spouse: Mrs. Hildegard K. M.
    Velling-Wagner

Mr. Bernd WEISER
Third Secretary (Legal and Consular) and
    Vice Consul

Mr. Volker FEY
Attaché
Spouse: Mrs. Petra Fey

Mr. Rainer POSDZIECH
Attaché (Administrative)
Spouse: Mrs. Hildegard Posdziech

Mr. Wolfgang Albert RUENZI
Attaché (Administrative)
Spouse: Mrs. Gabriele Magdalena Ruenzi

Mr. Eduard SCHROEDER
Attaché
Spouse: Mrs. Karin Schroeder

Mr. Helmut ANDERS
Asst. Attaché and Vice Consul
Spouse: Mrs. Linda Anders

Mrs. Gudrun BERGMANN CONSTANTIN
Asst. Attaché (Cultural)
Spouse: Mrs. Roger Constantin

Mr. Klaus BREITGAM
Asst. Attaché

Mr. Juergen BRUEGGEMANN
Asst. Attaché (Defense Research & Eng.)
Spouse: Mrs. Monika Brueggemann

Mr. John HEISE
Asst. Attaché
Spouse: Mrs. Klaudia Heise

Mrs. Theda JERRIHO
Asst. Attaché

Mr. Ingemar JOST
Asst. Attaché
Spouse: Mrs. Ruth Jost

Mr. Hansgeorg KNAUER
Asst. Attaché (Administrative)
Spouse: Mrs. Astrid Knauer

Mr. Detlev KRAUSKOPF
Asst. Attaché
Spouse: Mrs. Helga Krauskopf

Mr. Anton MEINGAST
Asst. Attaché
Spouse: Ms. Hannelore Meingast

Mr. Gerhard Siegfried NOWAK
Asst. Attaché and Vice Consul
Spouse: Mrs. Marie Luise Nowak

Mr. Christoph Guenter RICKSTAT
Asst. Attaché (Administrative)
Spouse: Mrs. Hildegard Rickstat

Mr. Ralf ROSINSKI
Asst. Attaché (Administrative)

Mr. Ingo SALZER
Asst. Attaché (Security)

Mr. Karl Heinz Ernst SCHOBER
Asst. Attaché
Spouse: Mrs. Margaret Anne Schober

Mr. Lothar W. SKUDAYSKI
Asst. Attaché (Finance and Agriculture)
Spouse: Mrs. Brigid Skudayski

Brigadier General Peter N. SCHMITZ
Defense Attaché
Spouse: Mrs. Silvia Schmitz

Colonel Gerhard STELZ
Military Attaché & Asst. Defense Attaché
Spouse: Mrs. Siglinde Stelz

Captain Friedrich JACOBI
Naval Attaché and Asst. Defense Attaché
Spouse: Mrs. Anke Jacobi

Colonel Michael PADBERG
Air Attaché and Asst. Defense Attaché
Spouse: Mrs. Petra Padberg

Major Axel PFAFFENROTH
Asst. Military Attaché
Spouse: Mrs. Karin Pfaffenroth

Commander Gerald Axel MOELLER
Asst. Naval Attaché
Spouse: Mrs. Heidi Moeller

Lt. Colonel Thomas B. HOENIG
Asst. Air Attaché
Spouse: Mrs. Gabriele Hoenig

Ghana

Embassy of Ghana
3512 International Drive, NW
Washington DC 20008
Phone: 202/686-4520
Fax: 202/686-4527
Email: hagan@cais.com
Url: http://www.ghana-embassy.org/

Kobina Arthur KOOMSON
Ambassador

Date Credentials Presented: 11/12/97

Born: 5/20/51 in Elmina, Ghana

Spouse: Mrs. Bertha Helena Koomson

Until his appointment as Ghana's ambassador to the U.S. in November 1997, Koby Arthur Koomson was the president and CEO of Koomson Financial, a tax accounting and management consulting firm in Los Angeles.

He had worked for such Fortune 500 companies as Beatrice Food, Transamerica Insurance and Genstar Corporation as accounting manager and senior cost and financial accountant. He also worked for Groundwater Technologies, Arrowhead Puritas, and Allied Telephone Co. He was a financial and management consultant to many medical and service-oriented businesses.

A native Ghanaian, Koomson was educated at Ghana National College in Cape Coast. He later continued his education at the University of Arkansas in Little Rock, where he graduated with a bachelor's degree in accounting and management.

The ambassador has served on the boards of many non-profit corporations and has a been an activist in the Ghanaian community in the U.S. He served as president of the Ghana Development Fund from 1994 to 1996; and as a minority business opportunity committee member of the Los Angeles mayor's office of economic development in 1996-97. He is vice president of the Ghana Association of Southern California.

Koomson was affiliated with the Los Angeles Chamber of Commerce, the Los Angeles chapter of the American Lung Association, the San Gabriel Pediatrics Inc., the Black Inventions Museum, Rebuild Los Angeles, and the 2nd Annual Black Business Expo, 1990.

Koomson has received awards from the Who's Who Among University Students and Who's Who in the American Business Community. His hobbies are golf, tennis, soccer and listening to classical and African music. He is married with two children.

STAFF:

Mr. Sam AFRIFA KYEI
Minister (Consular)
Spouse: Mrs. Florence Africa Kyei

Mr. Nana EFFAH-APENTENG
Minister-Counselor (Econo. & Political)
Spouse: Mrs. Christina Effah-Apenteng

Mr. Daniel Kwesi Ofori HAGAN
Counselor (Commercial)
Spouse: Mrs. Gloria Hagan

Mr. Kingsley Saka Abdul KARIMU
Counselor (Head of Chancery)
Spouse: Mrs. Kianah Lamisi Karimu

Mr. Emmanuel Kwaku ABU
First Secretary (Administrative)

Ms. Effie BENTSI-ENCHILL
Second Secretary

Mrs. Harriet MENSAH
Attaché (Financial)
Spouse: Mr. James Mensah

Colonel Ebenezer Narteh CATERNOR
Defense, Military, Naval and Air Attaché
Spouse: Mrs. Yaa Amoakoa Caternor

Greece

Embassy of Greece
2221 Massachusetts Avenue, NW
Washington DC 20008
Phone: 202/939-5800
Fax: 202/939-5824

Loucas TSILAS
Ambassador

Date Credentials Presented: 9/3/93

Born: 10/18/39 in Athens, Greece.

Spouse: Mrs. Penelope Kartsonas-Tsilas

Loucas Tsilas' many past diplomatic postings include a period of service in Washington, D.C. from 1975-1979, when he served as counselor at the Greek Embassy.

His other positions included: first secretary in the Greek Embassy in Bucharest; consul of Greece in New Orleans, La.; deputy director of the Department of NATO and European Security Affairs in the Greek Foreign Ministry in Athens; Greek ambassador to South Africa; and director of the Diplomatic Office of the Prime Minister of Greece. He began his career practicing law in Athens between 1963-65.

Tsilas received an M.A. in political science from the State University of Louisiana in New Orleans. He holds degrees in law and economics from the University of Athens. He is the author of several studies, including a major thesis, "System Analysis in International Relations: The Case of the Balkans."

Tsilas served in 1990-1991 as President of the Greek Diplomats' Association. He is fluent in English, French, and Romanian.

Tsilas and his wife have two children.

STAFF:

Mr. Alexios CHRISTOPOULOS
Minister (Deputy Chief of Mission)
Spouse: Mrs. Danae Zachari

Mr. Leonidas ANANIADIS
Minister-Counselor (Commercial & Econo)
Spouse: Mrs. Helma Maria Ananiadis

Mr. Constantin C. CATSAMBIS
Counselor (Political)
Spouse: Mrs. Zoe Catsambis

Mr. Archilles PAPARSENOS
Counselor (Press)
Spouse: Mrs. Anita Paparsenos

Mr. Georgios POUKAMISSAS
Counselor (Political)
Spouse: Mrs. Polyxeni Stathopoulou

Ms. Anna CONSTANTINIDOU
First Secretary

Mr. Theodossis C. DEMETRACOPOULOS
First Secretary (Press)
Spouse: Mrs. Faye Demetracopoulos

Mr. Georgios DIMITRIADIS
First Secretary

Mr. Francois COSTELLENOS
Second Secretary
Spouse: Mrs. Christine Kostellenos

Mr. Panteleimon GASSIOS

Second Secretary (Commercial)
Spouse: Mrs. Maria Tsapepa Gassiou

Mr. Efstathios PAIZIS
Second Secretary and Consul

Mrs. Eudoxia CUTLER
Attaché (Administration)

Mr. Elias D. GALANIS
Attaché (Press)

Mrs. Magdalini KANTARTZI
Attaché (Press)
Spouse: Mr. Nicolaos Kantarzis

Mr. Gerassimos LAZARIS
Attaché (Commercial)
Spouse: Mrs. Georgia Lazari

Mr. Victor PAPADOPOULOS
Attaché (Communications)
Spouse: Mrs. Ourania Papadopoulou

Mrs. Maria PARTSINEVELOU
Attaché (Administrative)
Spouse: Mr. Christos Valakostas

Mr. Evangelos THEOPHILOU
Attaché
Spouse: Mrs. Angelika Theophilou

Mr. Spyrangelos VALLIANATOS
Attaché (Communications)
Spouse: Mrs. Zoe Vallianatos

Brigadier General Georgios SIMOS
Defense Military Attaché
Spouse: Mrs. Maria Simou

Captain Ioannis EGOLFOPOULOS
Naval Attaché
Spouse: Mrs. Maria Roussou

Lt. Colonel Kosmas VOURIS
Air Attaché
Spouse: Mrs. Vassiliki Kokkori

Lt. Colonel Nikolaos TSIROGIANNIS
Asst. Defense and Military Attaché
Spouse: Mrs. Marika Tsirogianni

Commander Andreas TOUSSAS
Asst. Naval Attaché
Spouse: Mrs. Grammatiki Toussa

Lt. Colonel Georgios KOTSILIMBAS
Asst. Air Attaché
Spouse: Mrs. Maria Hatziemmanouil

Office of the Air Attaché
2228 Massachusetts Avenue, NW
Washington DC 20008
Phone: 202/234-0561

Office of the Commercial Counselor
2211 Massachusetts Avenue, NW
Washington DC 20008
Phone: 202/332-2844

Consular Office
2211 Massachusetts Avenue, NW
Washington DC 20008

Phone: 202/232-8222

Office of the Defense & Military Attaché
2228 Massachusetts Avenue, NW
Washington DC 20008
Phone: 202/234-5695

Office of the Economic Counselor
1731 21st Street, NW
Washington DC 20009
Phone: 202/745-7100

Office of the Educational Counselor
1731 21st Street, NW
Washington DC 20009
Phone: 202/332-3196

Office of the Naval Attaché
2228 Massachusetts Avenue, NW
Washington DC 20008
Phone: 202/332-8145

Office of Press and Information
2211 Massachusetts Avenue, NW
Washington DC 20008
Phone: 202/332-2727

Grenada

Embassy of Grenada
1701 New Hampshire Avenue, NW
Washington DC 20009
Phone: 202/265-2561
Fax: 202/265-2468

Denis G. ANTOINE
Ambassador

Date Credentials Presented: 7/29/96

Born: in Grenada

Spouse: Mrs. Marva Antoine

Denis G. Antoine is beginning his second tour of duty in the diplomatic service in Washington, D.C. He served as counsellor, second in command at Grenada's Embassy in Washington from 1986 to 1990.

Antoine began his service to the government of Grenada in the Ministry of Health before migrating to the United States. He studied and worked in this country in the field of education and in management. He has wide experience in education supervision and

human resource development. He served as a program specialist for Consumer and Regulatory Affairs in the District of Columbia government until he returned to the Grenada Embassy in September 1995.

Concerned about a lack of sustained mechanism of engagement with the Caribbean, Antoine has indicated a desire to point Grenada in a direction that will enable the nation to benefit from economic and trade liberalization. He sees the Caribbean as very much a part of the Inter-American System. In light of the fact that the focus on the global agenda minimizes the importance of smaller economies, Antoine believes there must be persistent efforts by the Caribbean to keep smaller economies competitive and secure within the context of a global economy. The impact of globalization must be studied; and multilateral organizations must look at alternative measures of development.

Grenada seeks technical support and cooperation in its effort to achieve sustainable development, according to Antoine, and he sees retention of foreign capital, and human capital as vitally important to building the capacity which would enable a competitive presence.

Antoine received a master's degree in management in 1992 from the National College of Virginia (now NLU). He holds a master's degree in education from the University of District of Columbia.

Antoine and his wife have two children.

STAFF:

Ms. Sibyl ALEXANDER
First Secretary and Consul

Guatemala

Embassy of Guatemala
2220 R Street, NW
Washington DC 20008
Phone: 202/745-4952
Fax: 202/745-1908
Email: Embaguat@sysnet.net

Pedro Miguel LAMPORT
Ambassador

Date Credentials Presented: 4/30/96

Spouse: Mrs. Patricia Lamport

Pedro Miguel Lamport's involvement in Guatemalan political affairs has provided him with first-hand insight into Guatemala's efforts to restore constitutional and democratic government.

Lamport coordinated two key events in his country's restoration of democratic life: the Gran Dialogo Nacional (Grand National Dialogue - the GND) of 1983 and the Instancia Nacional de Consenso (Committee of National Consensus - INC) of 1993. As coordinator and representative of the private sector for the GND, he led the consolidation of the electoral process by establishing the basis for a dialogue involving the labor unions, cooperatives, universities, the entrepreneurial sectors, and the government. During the 1993 institutional crisis, his coordination efforts through the activities of the INC bore fruit as Guatemala soon returned to the constitutional framework.

As the first coordinator of the Special Commission for Peace in 1994-96, Lamport acted as liaison between the private sector and the parties involved in peace process negotiations. He represented the private sector on Guatemala's Monetary Board and led several delegations promoting Central American integration and in negotiating bilateral treaties with Mexico. He has served as vice president of the Guatemalan Social Security Institute.

In the business sector, Lamport has held a variety of positions since 1972. They include president, director, and general manager of several distribution, exporting, insurance, and tourism companies. In 1985, he was elected president of the Guatemalan Chamber of Commerce for a two-year period. Between 1985 and 1987, he presided over CACIF, a private sector coordinating committee for agricultural, commercial, industrial and financial associations.

Lamport has taught finance at the Universidad Francisco Marroquin. He studied economics at Universidad Rafael Landivar and Harvard; international commerce in Antwerp, Belgium; and doctorate-level studies economics at the University of Rochester in New York. He has been a long-time member of the Rotary Club of Guatemala City, having founded the Youth Service organization of the Rotarians in 1967.

STAFF:

Ms. Maria Mercedes ANDRADE
Minister-Counselor

Mr. Arturo R. DUARTE
Minister-Counselor

Mrs. Maria Z. LANDIS
Counselor (Cultural)

Mr. Lionel Valentin MAZA
Counselor

Mr. Alfonso Jose QUINONEZ
Counselor (Legal)

Mrs. Vilma Eugenia AVILA-MEDA
DE GENTRY
First Secretary

Mr. Erwin BENTZEN
First Secretary and Consul
Spouse: Mrs. Rina Hazel Bentzen

Miss Ivonne SANCHEZ
Second Secretary

Ms. Eugenia ALVAREZ
Third Secretary

Ms. Luisa G. CONSTANZA
Third Secretary

Miss Maria Candelaria HERNANDEZ
Third Secretary

Ms. Betty MARROQUIN
Third Secretary

Ms. Maria MAYORA
Third Secretary

Mr. Robert E. ROSENBERG
Attaché (Commercial)

Colonel Cesar A. RUIZ
Defense, Military, Naval and Air Attaché
Spouse: Mrs. Teresa Ruiz

Guinea

Embassy of the Republic of Guinea
2112 Leroy Place, NW
Washington DC 20008
Phone: 202/483-9420
Fax: 202/483-8688

Mohamed Aly THIAM
Ambassador

Date Credentials Presented: 7/29/96

Born: 1/10/51 in Kindia, Guinea

Spouse: Mrs. Irene Marie Hadjimalis

Mohamed Aly Thiam brings with him to
Washington, D.C., ten years of diplomatic
experience. Most recently he was secretary
general in the Ministry of Foreign Affairs in
Guinea; earlier he was director national of
juridical and consular affairs in the ministry.

Thiam represented Guinea in the United
Nations General Assembly between 1987 and
1995. Before the Committee on Human
Rights, he helped prepare a report on the
"Initial Presentation of the Republic of
Guinea on Civil and Political Rights" in
1989. He attended the Worldwide Conference
on Human Rights in Vienna in 1993.

Other international conferences in which he
participated include: the United Nations
Conference on the Refugees and Removed
Populations of Southern Africa in Oslo in
1989; a meeting of the Administrators of the
Ministries of Foreign Affairs in Abidjan in
1993; and a worldwide conference on the
Protection of War Victims in Geneva 1993.

Earlier in his career, Thiam worked in
Guinea's Ministry of Justice. He started as
an assistant judge in the Court of Conakry I
in 1977. Between 1978 and 1980, he was
an examining magistrate in the Court of
Conakry I and was in charge of civil law
courses at the University of Conakry.
Between 1980 and 1984, he was president
of the Regional Court of Siguiri, then served
as Solicitor General at the Supreme Court of
Kankan between 1984 and 1986. In 1986,
he was Judge of Peace in Kissidougou.

Thiam received his baccalaureate degree in
1973 and a diploma for advanced studies
(laws) in 1977. He is married and has seven
children.

STAFF:

Mr. Frederick BANGOURA
Counselor (Economic, Financial and
Consular)
Spouse: Mrs. Cecile Macauley

Mr. Dondo SYLLA
Counselor (Political and Cultural)
Spouse: Mrs. Ramata Kourouma

Ms. Oumou KASSE
Attaché (Administrative)

Lt. Cmdr. Mamadou Alimou DIALLO
Defense, Military, Naval and Air Attaché
Spouse: Mrs. Binta Bokoum Diallo

Guinea-Bissau

Embassy of the Republic of Guinea-Bissau
1511 K Street, NW - Suite 519
Washington DC 20005
Phone: 202/347-3950
Fax: 202/347-3954

Henrique Adrian DA SILVA
Chargé d'Affaires, ad interim

Date Credentials Presented: 5/4/98

Guinea-Bissau's ambassadorship to the U.S.
was left vacant with the departure in May
1998 of Ambassador Rufino Mendes. At
press time, no new ambassador had been
appointed. The embassy did not respond to
requests for biographical information about
the chargé d'affaires.

STAFF:

Mr. Henrique Adriano DA SILVA
Counselor
Spouse: Mrs. Maria Odilia Almeida
Da Silva

Mrs. Ligia Maria C. GARCIA
First Secretary

Mrs. Maria Odilia ALMEIDA DA SILVA
Attaché
Spouse: Mr. Henrique Adriano Da Silva

Guyana

Embassy of Guyana
2490 Tracy Place, NW
Washington DC 20008
Phone: 202/265-6900
Fax: 202/332-1297
Email: guyanaem@erols.com

Dr. Odeen ISHMAEL
Ambassador

Date Credentials Presented: 9/3/93

Born: 1/29/48 in Britannia, Guyana

Spouse: Mrs. Evangeline Ishmael

Since June 1993, Odeen Ishmael has served
both as Guyana's ambassador to the United
States and as ambassador to the Permanent
Representative of Guyana to the Organization
of American States (OAS).

Ishmael previously worked as a teacher in
Guyana. During the 1970s, he served in the
Ministry of Foreign Affairs of Guyana, but
returned to teaching from 1985 to 1993, when
he worked in The Bahamas in secondary and
adult education.

Ishmael has represented Guyana at the

Intercessional Meeting of Caricom Information Ministers in Jamaica in November 1992; the United Nations General Assembly in New York, Oct-Dec. 1993; the Special General Assembly of the OAS in Mexico, February 1994; the 24th Regular Session of the General Assembly of the OAS in Belem, Brazil, June 1994; and the 25th Regular Session of the General Assembly of the OAS in Haiti in June 1995.

At the OAS, he served as chairman of the Permanent Council from Oct. 1 to Dec. 31, 1994. Before that, he had served as vice-chairman of the Permanent Council, and as vice-chairman of the Environmental Committee of the Permanent Council. In 1994, Ishmael served as chairman of the general committee to prepare the OAS draft convention on the situation of persons with disabilities.

In political life, Ishmael served in the Central Committee of the People's Progressive Party (PPP) of Guyana, and in the course of his political work, he participated in international conferences and activities in many different countries. He also assisted in lobbying Guyana's case for electoral reforms in different countries in North and South America, Europe, and the Caribbean. He has written numerous articles on education, Guyanese history, and international political issues which have been published in newspapers and journals in Guyana, the Caribbean, and North America. He has published three books, Problems of the Transition of Education in the Third World, Towards Education Reform in Guyana, and Amerindian Legends of Guyana.

Ishmael holds a B.A., a post-graduate diploma in education, and a Ph.D. in education. He is married and has two children.

STAFF:

Ms. Gillian ROWE
First Secretary

Mrs. Taveta HANIFF
Second Secretary
Spouse: Mr. Mohamed Haniff

Mr. Mohamed ZAMAL
Attaché (Administrative)
Spouse: Mrs. Patricia Bernadette Zamal

Haiti

Embassy of the Republic of Haiti
2311 Massachusetts Avenue, NW
Washington DC 20008
Phone: 202/332-4090
Fax: 202/745-7215
Email: embassy@haiti.org
Url: http://www.haiti.org/embassy/

Louis Harold JOSEPH

Chargé d'Affaires, ad interim

Minister-Counselor

Date Credentials Presented: 12/18/97

Haiti's ambassadorship to the U.S. was left vacant in November 1997 with the departure of Ambassador Jean Casimir. At press time, no new ambassador had been appointed. The embassy did not respond to requests for biographical information on the chargé d'affaires.

STAFF:

Ms. Denise JEAN-LOUIS
Minister-Counselor

Mr. Raymond VALCIN
Minister-Counselor

Mr. Antoine Hanel ELIACIN
Counselor

Mr. Lionel Leonard LAVIOLETTE
Counselor (Cultural and Information)

Mrs. Madeline A. PIERRE DUPITON
Counselor (Economic and Financial)

Ms. Claude AMBROISE
First Secretary

Mrs. Gisele DEPESTRE
First Secretary (Consular)

Mrs. Marie-Claude MALEBRANCHE
First Secretary (Commercial)

Mrs. Raymonde PREVAL BELOT
First Secretary

Holy See

Apostolic Nunciature
3339 Massachusetts Avenue, NW
Washington DC 20008
Phone: 202/333-7121
Fax: 202/337-4036

The Most Reverend Agostino CACCIAVILLAN

Apostolic Pro-Nuncio

Date Credentials Presented: 10/24/90

Born: 8/14/26 near Vicenza, North Italy

Ordained a priest in 1949, Agostino Cacciavillan has served in the diplomatic service of the Holy See for nearly four decades. For three years following his ordination, Cacciavillan served as a parish priest in Bassano del Grappa prior to continuing his studies in Rome.

After joining the diplomatic service of the Holy See in 1959, Cacciavillan spent ten years in the Philippines, Spain and Portugal, before returning to the Vatican Secretariat of State. He served in varying capacities for the next seven years, dealing with personnel matters, the media, and - from 1969 to 1976 - as head of the Documentation and Information Office of the Secretariat of State. From 1976 until his appointment to Washington, Cacciavillan served in the following capacities: Apostolic Pro-Nuncio to Kenya and Apostolic Delegate to the Seychelles (1976-1981); Apostolic Pro-Nuncio to India (1981-1990); the first Apostolic Pro-Nuncio to the Kingdom of Nepal (1985-1990); Apostolic Pro-Nuncio to the United States and Permanent Observer of the Holy See to the OAS (1990).

Cacciavillan holds a master's degree in social sciences from the Pontifical Gregorian University, a doctorate in canon law from the Pontifical Lateran University, and a doctorate in civil law from the University of Rome. He speaks Italian, English, and Spanish.

STAFF:

Monsignor Renato VOLANTE
Counselor

Monsignor Francis Cao MINH-DUNG
Counselor

Monsignor Giorgio LINGUA
First Secretary

Honduras

Embassy of Honduras
3007 Tilden Street, NW
Washington DC 20008
Phone: 202/966-7702
Fax: 202/966-9751

Edgardo DUMAS RODRIGUEZ

Ambassador

Date Credentials Presented: 5/27/98

Due to the recent arrival of the ambassador, the embassy did not have biographical information on the ambassador available for release before press date of this publication.

STAFF:

Mr. Salvador RODEZNO-FUENTES
Minister (Deputy Chief of Mission)
Spouse: Mrs. Elizabeth de Rodezno-Fuentes

Mrs. Margarita DURON DE GALVEZ
Minister-Counselor
Spouse: Mr. Juan Manuel Galvez

Mr. Jose Benjamin ZAPATA
Minister-Counselor (Economic)
Spouse: Mrs. Susan de Zapata

Ms. Norma MEJIA-RODEZNO
Counselor (Political)

Mr. Sergio MONCADA
Counselor (Tourism)

Mr. Felipe S. PAREDES
First Secretary (Consular)
Spouse: Mrs. Alma Paredes

Ms. Yolando MEMBRENO
Third Secretary (Environment)

Mrs. Nilda TORRES
Third Secretary (Commerce)
Spouse: Mrs. Guillermo Torres

Rear Admiral Giordano B. FONTANA
    HEDMAN
Defense, Military, Naval, and Air Attaché

Consular Section
1612 K St., NW, Suite 310
Washington DC 20005
Phone: 202/223-0185 Fax: 202/223-0202

Hungary

Embassy of the Republic of Hungary
3910 Shoemaker Street, NW
Washington DC 20008
Phone: 202/362-6730
Fax: 202/966-8135
Email: huembwas@aol.com
Url: http://www.hungaryemb.org

Dr. Gyorgy BANLAKI
Ambassador

Date Credentials Presented: 11/21/94

Born: 3/21/48 in Budapest, Hungary

Spouse: Mrs. Teresa Banlaki

Dr. Gyorgy Banlaki's diplomatic career, which began in Hungary's Ministry of Foreign Affairs in 1971 at the British Desk, was interrupted in 1990 when he founded the Sawyer Miller Group-Hungary, an American-Hungarian joint venture strategic communications consulting firm.

His last post in the ministry was as consul general in New York, N.Y., between 1986 and 1990. Earlier positions included: assistant attache, London, 1972; secretary of the Hungarian delegation to the International Commission of Control and Supervision, Saigon, 1974; U.S. Desk, later British Desk, 1975-77; press attaché (third secretary, later second secretary), London, 1977-81; and later head of U.S. Desk, 1981-86.

Banlaki is a graduate of Woodrow Wilson High School in Washington, D.C., and he attended his freshman year of college at Howard University in Washington. He received a B.A. from the University of Economics, Budapest, Faculty of International Relations, in 1972 and a doctorate in economics a year later.

He has been married to the former Teresa Konopka since 1971, and they have a daughter, Katalin, who attends American University in Washington, D.C.

STAFF:

Mr. Jozsef TOTH
Counselor (Economic and Trade)
Spouse: Mrs. Maria Toth

Mr. Pal KERTESZ
Counselor (Economic and Trade)
Spouse: Mrs. Ludmilla Kertesz

Mr. Gabor CSABA
Second Secretary (Political Affairs)
Spouse: Mrs. Edit Csaba

Mr. Istvan SZEMENYEI
First Counselor (Science and Technology)
Spouse: Mrs. Gyorgyi Szemenyei

Dr. Jozsef POPP
First Secretary (Agricultural)

Dr. Zoltan BANYASZ
Counselor and Consul
Spouse: Mrs. Marianna Banyasz

Mr. Gyorgy TABORI
First Secretary (Public Affairs)
Spouse: Mrs. Ildiko Taborine

Mr. Gabor SZUCS
Counselor (Law Enforcement)
Spouse: Mrs. Eva Szucs

Mr. Tibor SZILAGYI
Second Secretary (Press and Information)
Spouse: Mrs. Lilli Szilagyi

Mrs. Zsofia TROMBITAS
Second Secretary (Culture and Education)
Spouse: Mrs. Zoltan Tardos

Mr. Viktor SZEDERKENYI
Third Secretary

Spouse: Ms. Adel Keleti

Colonel Tamas TOTH
Defense, Military and Air Attaché
Spouse: Mrs. Veronica Toth

Major Istvan PASZTOR
Asst. Military and Air Attaché
Spouse: Mrs. Melinda Pasztor

Consular Office
3910 Shoemaker Street, NW
Washington DC 20008
Phone: 202/362-6730

Office of the Military and Air Attaché
3910 Shoemaker Street, NW
Washington DC 20008
Phone: 202/362-6730

Commercial Office (Main Office)
2401 Calvert St., NW, Suite 1021
Washington DC 20008
Phone: 202/387-3191 Fax: 202/387-3140

Commercial Office
150 East 58th St., 33rd Floor
New York NY 10021
Phone: 212/752-3060

Iceland

Embassy of Iceland
1156 15th Street, NW, Suite 1200
Washington DC 20005
Phone: 202/265-6653
Fax: 202/265-6656
Email: icemb@udn.sdjr.is
Url: http://www.iceland.org

Jon Baldvin HANNIBALSSON
Ambassador

Date Credentials Presented: 3/16/98

Born: 2/21/39 in Ísafjördur, Iceland

Spouse: Mr. Bryndis Schram Hannibalsson

After serving for seven years as Iceland's minister of foreign affairs and external trade, John Baldvin Hannibalsson was appointed in 1998 as his country's ambassador to the U.S. He is also accredited as ambassador to Canada, Mexico, Argentina, Chile, Venezuela, Uruguay, and Costa Rica.

Hannibalsson was minister of finance between 1987-88 before he became minister of foreign affairs and external trade. He served in Althing, the Icelandic Parliament, from 1982 to 1998 and was the leader of the Social-Democratic Party of Iceland from 1984 to 1996.

Prior to his government service, he was editor-in-chief of Althydubladid, a national daily between 1979 and 1982. He was the rector of Ísafjördur College, which he founded, from 1970 to 1979. From 1964 to 1970, he was a teacher and journalist in

Reykjavik.

Hannibalsson is the editor of books on anthropology and educational policy and the translator of books and articles on economics, history, and international affairs. He has written numerous articles in books, periodicals and newspapers on politics, political biography, economic policy, educational and international issues. Besides his editorship of Althydubladid, he was editor of the Students' Magazine (1960-61), and Free Nation, a political weekly (1964-67). He has been a frequent contributor to radio and television discussion programs.

The ambassador was a member of the European Free Trade Association (EFTA) council of ministers from 1988 to 1995 and was the chair a good part of that time. He was a member of the North Atlantic Council of Ministers, 1988-95; a member of SAMAK, the Coordinating Council of Nordic Social-Democratic Parties and Labour Federations, 1984-96; a member of the Constitutional Reform Council, 1979-84; and a member of the government committee on the transfer of public service institutions to the regions, 1973-75. He was a town-councillor in the Ísafjördur municipality, 1971-78; a member of the government advisory committee preparing for Iceland's membership in EFTA, 1968-70; and chairman of the Radical Students Association, 1960-61.

Hannibalsson received an M.A. degree from Edinburgh University in economics, history, and constitutional law in 1963. He did postgraduate work in labor economics at Stockholm University in 1963-64 and received a diploma in education from the University of Iceland in 1965. He was a Fulbright scholar at Harvard University in 1976-77.

Hannibalsson's wife, Bryndis Schram, is an actress, television producer, and author. They have four children and five grandchildren. Hannibalsson was made an honorary citizen of Vilnius, Lithuania in 1995.

STAFF:

Mr. Sveinn BJORNSSON
Deputy Chief of Mission

Mr. Arnor SIGURJONSSON
Counselor (Defense)

Ms. Sigriour Osk BIRGISDOTTIR
Secretary

Mrs. Sigurbjorg GUOMUNDSDOTTIR
Secretary

Mrs. Guolaug PORLEIFSDOTTIR
Secretary

Mr. Magnus BJARNASON
Commercial Counselor

India

Embassy of India
2107 Massachusetts Avenue, NW
Washington DC 20008
Phone: 202/939-7000
Fax: 202/939-7027

Naresh CHANDRA
Ambassador

Date Credentials Presented: 4/30/96

Naresh Chandra has had a long personal association with the United States. The first of his several visits to this country was in 1963-64. He has been the Indian co-chairman of the U.S.-India Technology Working Group and a member of the Indo-U.S. Economic Sub-Commission, which enabled him to get acquainted with the broad range of Indo-U.S. relations.

In 1992, soon after the economic liberalization program was initiated in India, Chandra led the first official delegation to the U.S. to promote U.S. investments in India. He has attended several important conferences organized subsequently in the U.S. by business development groups.

A career civil servant, Chandra has held a series of important posts. He joined the Indian Administrative Service in May 1956 and served in different capacities, including that of chief secretary in the State of Rajasthan. In between, from May 1981 to May 1984, he was assigned by the Commonwealth Secretariat as adviser on export industrialization and policy, Colombo (Sri Lanka). He was named adviser to the Governor of Jammu and Kashmir in 1986 for eight months.

Between 1987 and 1990, Chandra served in the Federal Indian Government successively as secretary to the Ministries of Water Resources, Defense, and Home (Interior). In December 1990, he became cabinet secretary, the top post in the Indian civil service, from which he retired in July 1992. The next month, he was appointed as senior adviser to the Prime Minister of India. His last assignment was as the governor of the state of Gujarat.

Chandra did post-graduate work in mathematics at Allahabad University and afterwards taught there briefly. He plays golf, bridge, and tennis. He was president of the Delhi Lawn Tennis Association. He is a crossword puzzle enthusiast and has won several international prizes in that arena. He is unmarried.

STAFF:

Mr. Thettalil P. SREENIVASAN
Minister (Deputy Chief of Mission)
Spouse: Mrs. Chandralekha Sreenivasan

Mr. Wajahat HABIBULLAH
Minister (Community Affairs)
Spouse: Mrs. Shahila Habibullah

Mr. Shiv S. MUKHERJEE
Minister (Press, Information and Culture)
Spouse: Mrs. Nalini Mukherjee

Mr. Sudhakar RAO
Minister (Economic)

Mr. Amitava TRIPATHI
Minister
Spouse: Mrs. Suryakakanthi Tripathi

Mrs. Suryakanthi TRIPATHI
Minister (Commerce)
Spouse: Mr. A. Tripathi

Mr. Radha Ranjan DASH
Counselor (Head of Chancery)
Spouse: Mrs. Rita Dash

Mr. Ashok JAIN
Counselor (Science and Technology)
Spouse: Mrs. Sunanda Jain

Ms. Shamma JAIN
Counselor

Mr. Ajit LAL
Counselor (Personnel)
Spouse: Mrs. Rita Lai

Mr. Madhusudan PRASAD
Counselor (Economic)
Spouse: Mrs. Sapna Prasad

Mr. Navdeep S. SURI
Counselor (Political)
Spouse: Mrs. Maninder Suri

Mr. Rayol John AUGUSTUS
First Secretary (Defense Technology)
Spouse: Mrs. Meena Augustus

Mr. Vijayaraghavan RAVINDRAN
First Secretary (Audit)
Spouse: Mrs. Manju Ravindran

Mrs. Reenat SANDHU
First Secretary (Commerce)
Spouse: Mrs. Taranjit Singh Sandhu

Mr. Taranjit Singh SANDHU
First Secretary
Spouse: Mrs. Reenat Sandhu

Mr. Arvind SAXENA
First Secretary (Consular)
Spouse: Mrs. Meera Saxena

Mr. Govind Singh KHAMPA
Second Secretary (Commerce)
Spouse: Mrs. Neema Sangmo

Mr. Hiranand PURKAIT
Second Secretary (Audit)
Spouse: Mrs. Rupa Purkait

Mr. Radha Krishan SHARMA
Second Secretary (Establishment)
Spouse: Mrs. Neelam Sharma

Mr. Kumar V. PRATAP
Third Secretary (Economic)
Spouse: Mrs. Seema Agrawal

Mr. Krishna Chandra BANERJEE
Attaché (Consular)
Spouse: Mrs. Alpana Banerjee

Mr. Jagdish CHAND
Attaché
Spouse: Mrs. Supti Chand

Mr. Subhash CHAND
Attaché
Spouse: Mrs. Raman

Mrs. Manju Bala CHANNAN
Attaché
Spouse: Mr. Yougal Kishore Channan

Mr. Arjun Dev KUKREJA
Attaché (Information)
Spouse: Mrs. Sharda Kukreja

Mr. Lila Dhar PANDEY
Attaché
Spouse: Mrs. Nirmala Pandey

Mr. Surjeet Singh REKHI
Attaché
Spouse: Mrs. Manjit Kaur Rekhi

Mr. Ajay Kumar SHARMA
Attaché (Establishment)
Spouse: Mrs. Sadhana Sharma

Mr. Rakesh Kumar SHARMA
Attaché (Consular)
Spouse: Mrs. Anita Sharma

Mr. Sarb Krishan SHARMA
Attaché (Political)
Spouse: Mrs. Akshma Sharma

Mr. Amar Jit SINGH
Attaché (Administrative)
Spouse: Mrs. Param Jit Kaur

Mr. Gyan SINGH
Attaché
Spouse: Mrs. Rajni Bala

Mr. Jasbir SINGH
Attaché
Spouse: Mrs. Satnam Kaur

Mr. Kuldeep SINGH

Attaché
Spouse: Mrs. Aruna Singh

Mr. Prit Pal SINGH
Attaché
Spouse: Mrs. Gurdeep Kaur

Mr. Virendra SINGH
Attaché (Property and Central Registry)
Spouse: Mrs. Sudesh Singh

Mr. Gyaneshwar SRIVASTAVA
Attaché
Spouse: Mrs. Neeru Srivastava

Mr. Babugey Parayathukattil THOMAS
Attaché
Spouse: Mrs. Bina Thomas

Air Commodore Krishna Bala Krishna
   MENON
Defense and Air Attaché
Spouse: Mrs. Padmini Balakrishna Menon

Brigadier General Arun ROYE
Military Attaché & Asst. Defense Attaché
Spouse: Mrs. Anushiela Roye

Commander Pratap Singh BYCE
Naval Attaché and Asst. Defense Attaché
Spouse: Mrs. Ranjana Byce

Office of Commerce & Supply,
   Passport & Visa Section
2536 Massachusetts Avenue, NW
Washington DC 20008
Phone: 202/939-9806

Indonesia

Embassy of the Republic of Indonesia
2020 Massachusetts Avenue, NW
Washington DC 20036
Phone: 202/775-5200
Fax: 202/775-5365

Dorodjatun KUNTJORO-JAKTI
Ambassador

Dorodjatun Kuntjoro-Jakti is the successor to Ambassador Arifin M. Siregar, who left the post in December 1997. The Indonesian embassy did not respond to requests for biographical information on the new ambassador.

STAFF:

Mr. Judo PRAJITNO
Minister-Counselor (Administrative)
Spouse: Mrs. Mashminatun Judo Prajitno

Mr. Hupudio SUPARDI
Minister-Counselor (Information)
Spouse: Mr. Ni Luh Wayan Aryati Hupudio

Ms. Perwitorini WIJONO
Minister-Counselor (Political)

Mr. Robertus BROTO UTOMO

Counselor (Consul)
Spouse: Mrs. Andrea Bandriyah
   Broto Utomo

Mr. Yani HARYANTO
Counselor (Economic)
Spouse: Mrs. Greta Haryanti Haryanto

Mr. Bintang Parlindungan
   SIMORANGKIR
Counselor (Economic)
Spouse: Mrs. Lelly Darmawarince
   Simorangkir

Mr. Benny BAHANADEWA
First Secretary (Economic)
Spouse: Mrs. Sarwini Bahanadewa

Mr. Bebbo DJAJAKUSUMA
First Secretary (Administrative)
Spouse: Mrs. Nina Kardiana Bebbo
   Djajakusuma

Mr. Akhyar RAIS
First Secretary (Administrative)
Spouse: Mrs. Essy Lusniaty Akhyar

Mr. Mulya WIRANA
First Secretary (Political)

Ms. Nina Saraswati DJAJAPRAWIRA
Third Secretary (Economic)

Mr. Teuku FAIZASYAH
Third Secretary (Economic)
Spouse: Mrs. Andis Erawan

Mr. Aris MUNANDAR
Third Secretary (Political)
Spouse: Mrs. Henny Sulistiawati

Mr. Mohammad Sofwan NAZARUDDIN
Third Secretary

Ms. Siti Sofia SUDARMA
Third Secretary (Consular)

Mr. Herry SUDRADJAT
Third Secretary (Information)
Spouse: Mrs. Ine Wanodyahyu
   Insani Sudrajat

Mr. Priyanto MAWARDI
Attaché (Administrative)
Spouse: Mrs. Indri Lusiana Mawardi

Mr. Yahya Abdul MUHAIMIN
Attaché (Education and Cultural)
Spouse: Mrs. Choifah

Ms. Aleida Margaretha PALENEWEN
Attaché

Mr. Harmen SEMBIRING
Attaché (Commercial)
Spouse: Mrs. Elisabeth Gurusinga

Mr. Patuan Natigor SIAGIAN
Attaché (Agricultural)
Spouse: Mrs. Deanna Simanjuntak Siagian

Mr. Warim SOEDARKO
Attaché (Transp. and Communications)

Spouse: Mrs. Haryati Soedarko

Brigadier General Jat SUDRAJAT
Defense Attaché
Spouse: Mrs. Sally Sudrajat

Colonel I. Gede SARDJANA
Military Attaché
Spouse: Mrs. Atiek Sri Siswathy

Colonel Anthony NOORBANDHY
Naval Attaché
Spouse: Mrs. Hariyantini

Colonel Rodi SUPRASODJO
Air Attaché
Spouse: Mrs. Emmy Setyowati

Iran

Islamic Republic of Iran
2209 Wisconsin Ave., NW
Washington DC 20007
Phone: 202/965-4990
Fax: 202/965-1073

Faramarz FATHNZHAD
Director, Interests Section

Diplomatic relations with Iran have been
severed and Pakistan serves as Iran's
protecting power in the U.S. Mr. Faramarz
Fathnzhad heads the Interests Section of the
Islamic Republic of Iran in Washington.

Iraq

Iraqi Interests Section
1801 P Street, NW
Washington DC 20036
Phone: 202/483-7500
Fax: 202/462-5066

Dr. Khairi O. T. AL ZUBAIDI
Chief of Mission

Spouse: Mrs. Hana I. Rasool

Diplomatic relations with Iraq have been
severed since the Persian Gulf War. Iraq's
protecting power in the U.S. is Algeria. The
chief of mission of the Iraqi Interests Section
is Dr. Khairi Al Zubaidi.

STAFF:

Mr. Fadhel H. HAMED
Third Secretary

Ireland

Embassy of Ireland
2234 Massachusetts Avenue, NW
Washington DC 20008
Phone: 202/462-3939
Fax: 202/232-5993

Sean O'HUIGINN
Ambassador

Date Credentials Presented: 9/8/97

Spouse: Mrs. Bernadette O'Huiginn

"It's a good time to be Irish!" Sean O'Huiginn,
Ireland's ambassador to the U.S., told
Washington International Magazine in March
1998, referring to a renaissance in the arts
in Ireland.

O'Huiginn told the magazine, "There are
many groups in what you might call `civil
society' in Northern Ireland and throughout
the island working very hard at the process
of reconciliation." Noting that the European
Union is devoted to harmonizing processes
throughout Europe, the ambassador said, "In
all areas where that objective succeeds, it
helps, as a byproduct to lessen the differences
between the north and south of Ireland."

In the last ten years, O'Huiginn has been
prominently involved in Anglo-Irish relations,
in particular the conduct of policy relating
to Northern Ireland. From 1987 to 1990, he
led the Irish team of officials assigned to the
Anglo-Irish Secretariat in Belfast (the
primary day-to-day channel of contact
between the two governments of Northern
Ireland).

Between 1991 and 1997, he was head of the
Anglo-Irish Division in Dublin. He was
closely associated with major developments
during the period, including the negotiations
of the Downing Street Declaration (1993),
the Framework Document (1995), the cease
fires called by the Irish Republican Army and
loyalist paramilitaries, and the establishment
of an inclusive talks process open to all the
parties in Northern Ireland.

O'Huiginn joined the Irish foreign service
in 1969. His previous overseas assignments
included Switzerland, New York (consul
general), Saudi Arabia (ambassador) and
Denmark (ambassador).
Since September 1997, he has been Ireland's
ambassador to the U.S. and, on a non-resident
basis, to Mexico, as well.

A native of County Mayo, the ambassador
was educated at St. Jarlath's College in Tuam
in County Galway, University College
Galway, and the University of Bordeaux. He

is married with two children. His wife,
Bernadette, is an accomplished sculptor and
a former television presenter.

STAFF:

Mr. Patrick HENNESSY
Counselor (Political)
Spouse: Mrs. Pauline Hennessy

Mr. Kenneth THOMPSON
Counselor (Economic)

Mr. Adrian O'NEILL
First Secretary (Press)
Spouse: Mrs. Aisling O'Neill

Ms. Catherine M. SLATTERY
First Secretary

Dr. Michael H. MOLONEY
Third Secretary

Ms. Jean MCMANUS
Attaché (Administrative)
Spouse: Mr. Michael O'Halloran

Israel

Embassy of Israel
3514 International Drive, NW
Washington DC 20008
Phone: 202/364-5500
Fax: 202/364-5560
Email: ask@israelemb.org
Url: http://www.israelemb.org/

Lenny BEN-DAVID
Deputy Chief of Mission

Born: in Washington, D.C.

Spouse: Mrs. Rahel Black Ben-David

At press time, Zolman Shoval had been
appointed by Prime Minister Benjamin
Netanyahu as Israel's new ambassador to the
U.S. He was expected to assume his duties
in July or August 1998, according to the
Israeli embassy.

Until that time, Lenny Ben-David heads the
Israeli mission in Washington. Ben-David
assumed his post as Israel's number two
diplomat in Washington, D.C. in August
1997, after being appointed by Prime

Minister Benjamin Netanyahu.

As deputy chief of mission, his duties include relations with the U.S. executive offices of the White House, State Department, and Defense Department as well as the legislative branch. He meets with other diplomatic missions in Washington and maintains ties with the American Jewish community and the media.

Prior to his appointment, Ben-David served as an independent consultant on public and political affairs, advising American and Israel political organizations, charitable and educational organizations, and foreign investors.

Ben-David also held senior posts in the American Israel Public Affairs Committee (AIPAC) for 25 years, in both Washington and Israel. He was hired by AIPAC founder, Si Kenen, and after 10 years of employment in Washington, he opened AIPAC's Israel office in 1982, directing it for almost 15 years. In that capacity, he coordinated the visits of hundreds of members of Congress and political delegations to Israel. In his role as AIPAC's editor of Near East Report, he authored and edited numerous editions of Myths and Facts.

He attended both the Madrid and Cairo peace conferences as an advisor to the conference of presidents. He also traveled extensively in the Middle East and Europe, including visits to Jordan, Qatar, Egypt, and Gaza.

Ben-David is a graduate of Yeshiva University in New York. He received his master's degree in political science from American University in Washington. He also undertook religious studies in Israel and New York.

He and his wife, Rochelle Black, are the parents of six children. Ben-David and two of his sons are medics in the Israeli Defense Force reserves.

STAFF:

Mr. Ohad MARANI
Minister (Economic)
Spouse: Mrs. Rachel Marani

Mr. Itzhak OREN
Minister (Congressional)
Spouse: Mrs. Ruth Oren

Mr. Jeremy NISSIM-ISSACHAROFF
Minister-Counselor
Spouse: Mrs. Kam Nissim-Issacharoff

Mrs. Ceremia PADAN
Minister-Counselor
Spouse: Mr. Uzi Padan

Mr. Jacob SAGIV
Minister-Counselor (Agricultural)
Spouse: Mrs. Tamar Sagiv

Mr. Yoram SHAPIRA

Minister-Counselor (Scientific)
Spouse: Mrs. Ilana Shapira

Mr. Dov SHEFI
Minister-Counselor
Spouse: Mrs. Esther Shefi

Mr. Aharon YAAR
Minister-Counselor
Spouse: Mrs. Devora Yaar

Mr. David AKOV
Counselor (Congressional)
Spouse: Mrs. Tamar Akov

Mr. Uri BIRAN
Counselor
Spouse: Mrs. Neta Biran

Mr. Shlomo COHEN
Counselor
Spouse: Mrs. Yaffa Cohen

Mr. Dror GABAY
Counselor (Administrative) and Consul
Spouse: Mrs. Daphna Murvitz Gabay

Mr. Moshe GILO
Counselor
Spouse: Mrs. Michal Gilo

Mr. Arie REGEV
Counselor
Spouse: Mrs. Celia Regev

Mr. Gadiel BALTIANSKY
First Secretary (Press & Communications)
Spouse: Mrs. Nurit Baltiansky

Mr. Amir SHAY
Second Secretary
Spouse: Mrs. Sigalit Shay

Mr. David SIEGEL
Second Secretary
Spouse: Mrs. Myra Clark Siegel

Mr. Nadav TAMIR
Second Secretary
Spouse: Mrs. Ronit Tamir

Mr. Haim BARZILAY
Attaché
Spouse: Mrs. Hanna Barzilay

Mr. Amir BEN HAIM
Attaché
Spouse: Mrs. Daphna Ben Haim

Mr. Yechezkel LEDER
Attaché (Rep. of Israel National Police)

Mr. Uri PEER
Attaché
Spouse: Mrs. Ruth Peer

Mr. David PIKIELNY
Attaché
Spouse: Mrs. Pnina Rotman Pikielny

Mrs. Sarah RAANAN
Attaché
Spouse: Mr. Gideon Raanan

Mrs. Rachel SHANI
Attaché
Spouse: Mr. Zachi-Zalah Shani

Mr. Nizan TENY
Attaché
Spouse: Mrs. Inbar Teny

Mrs. Yael ZIV
Attaché
Spouse: Mr. Pinhas Zion Ziv

Major General Zeev LIVNE
Defense and Defense Cooperation Attaché
Spouse: Mrs. Amalia Livne

Colonel Yoav HIRSH
Military Attaché
Spouse: Mrs. Vered Hirsh

Captain Yochay BEN YOSEF
Naval Attaché
Spouse: Mrs. Irit Ben Yosef

Brigadier General Avraham BARBER
Air Attaché and Asst. Military Attaché
Spouse: Mrs. Sima Barber

Major Yair BARKAT
Asst. Defense Attaché
Spouse: Mrs. Lior Katz Barkat

Colonel Amikam SHAFRAN
Asst. Defense Cooperation, Military,
  Naval and Air Attaché
Spouse: Mrs. Neta Shafran

Colonel Noam TOREN
Asst. Def. Military, Naval & Air Attaché
Spouse: Mrs. Nurit Toren

Lt. Colonel Lavi Yoav AMIRAM
Asst. Military Air Attaché
Spouse: Mrs. Michal Amiram

Italy

Embassy of Italy
1601 Fuller St., NW
Washington DC 20009
Phone: 202/328-5500
Fax: 202/483-2187
Url: http://www.italyemb.org

Ferdinando SALLEO
Ambassador

Date Credentials Presented: 2/6/96

Born: 1936 in Messina, Sicily

Spouse: Mrs. Anna Maria Salleo

Ferdinando Salleo is the eldest of four in one of Sicily's oldest aristocratic families. His father, Baron Carmelo Salleo, was a landowner and a noted painter.

Salleo joined the Italian foreign service in 1960 and was assigned the political directorate before taking duty at the Italian embassy in Paris in 1963. He returned to Rome and served in the foreign minister's cabinet and at the president's diplomatic office until 1966 when he was posted abroad again to New York as deputy consul general of Italy (1966-69). Between 1969 and 1972, he was assigned to Prague as counsellor at the Italian embassy. His next posting to the U.S. was to the Italian embassy in Washington as counsellor between 1972 and 1974.

He returned to Rome, again to the political directorate of the Foreign Ministry, as head of the NATO department until 1977 when he was assigned as minister to the embassy in Bonn. At the beginning of 1981, he assumed the post of deputy director general of Development Cooperation. Later, he became director general, serving until 1986 when he was appointed Italy's ambassador to the Paris-based Organization for Economic Cooperation and Development.

In 1988, Salleo returned to the Foreign Ministry as director general of economic affairs, and in 1989, he was appointed Italy's ambassador to the Soviet Union. He served in Moscow throughout the events that brought about the disintegration of the USSR. He then became ambassador to Russia and to a number of successor states, serving until 1993. Named director general of political affairs in 1993, he was appointed secretary general of the Foreign Ministry in 1994.

Salleo received a degree in law from the University of Rome in 1959. He was a visiting professor at the University of Florence in political science and economics from 1982 to 1984. He is fluent in Italian, English, French, and German.

Salleo is married to the former Anne Marie Riegler, who was born in Hungary. They have two sons: Carmelo, now with the Italian Central Bank, and Alberto, currently in a post-graduate program at the University California at Berkeley in Materials Science.

Ferdinando and Anne Marie Salleo have a keen interest in the arts and collect drawings and German porcelain.

STAFF:

Mr. Antonio PURI PURINI
Minister (Deputy Chief of Mission)
Spouse: Mrs. Rosanna Puri Purini

Mr. Vittorio TEDESCHI
Minister (Economic)
Spouse: Mrs. Maria Pia Paglino Tedeschi

Mr. Stefano BENAZZO
Counselor
Spouse: Mrs. Daniela Benazzo

Mr. Alessandro DI FRANCO
Counselor (Press and Information)
Spouse: Mrs. Cristina De Franco

Mr. Luca FERRARI
Counselor
Spouse: Mrs. Mariachiara Ferrari

Mr. Filippo FORMICA
Counselor
Spouse: Mrs. Michaela Annemarie
   Werkmeister

Mr. Daniele MANCINI
Counselor
Spouse: Mrs. Anna Rita De Luca Mancini

Mr. Elfsio Luigi MARRAS
Counselor (Economic)
Spouse: Mrs. Sofia Marras

Mr. Stefano STEFANINI
Counselor
Spouse: Mrs. Stephanie E. Stefanini

Mr. Maurizio ZANINI
Counselor (Emigration and Social)
Spouse: Mrs. Patricia Zanini

Mr. Sergio BARBANTI
First Secretary (Press and Information)
Spouse: Mrs. Kathleen Barbanti

Mr. Giuseppe PERRONE
First Secretary

Mr. Mario VATTANI
First Secretary (Economic)

Ms. Maria Rosa CIANNELLA
Second Secretary (Administrative)

Mr. Angelo Alfonso Alberto CICOGNA
Attaché (Financial)
Spouse: Mrs. Giulia Carolina S. Cicogna

Mr. Piero DI PORTO
Attaché (Scientific)
Spouse: Mrs. Anna Maria Di Porto

Dr. Alexander TENENBAUM
Attaché (Scientific)
Spouse: Dr. Sylvia Tenenbaum

Mrs. Maria Livia TOSATO
Attaché (Science)

Brigadier General Giuseppe BERNARDIS
Defense, Air & Defense
   Cooperation Attaché
Spouse: Mrs. Caterina Viol Bernardis

Colonel Fabrizio CASTAGNETTI
Military Attaché
Spouse: Mrs. Teresa Castagnetti

Captain Piero FRANCINI
Naval Attaché

Colonel Ubaldo Giuseppe SERINO
Asst. Defense & Def. Cooperation Attaché
Spouse: Mrs. Antonia Serino

Lt. Colonel Francesco CASTRATARO
Asst. Military Attaché
Spouse: Mrs. Rosa Castrataro

Lt. Colonel Paolo RUGGIERO
Asst. Military Attaché
Spouse: Mrs. Holly Ann Ruggiero

Commander Vincenzo DI LEVA
Asst. Naval Attaché

Lt. Commander Roberto VENTURONI
Asst. Naval Attaché
Spouse: Mrs. Flora Venturoni

Lt. Colonel Giovanni AMMONIACI
Asst. Air Attaché
Spouse: Mrs. Phyllis A. Santleben

Lt. Colonel Roberto FILIPPI
Asst. Air Attaché
Spouse: Mrs. Teresita Pagliani Filippi

Office of the Air Attaché
5301 Wisconsin Ave., NW
Washington DC 20015
Phone: 202/966-3754

Office of the Military Attaché
5301 Wisconsin Ave., NW
Washington DC 20015
Phone: 202/966-4052

Office of the Naval Attaché
5301 Wisconsin Ave., NW
Washington DC 20015
Phone: 202/966-4165

Jamaica

Embassy of Jamaica
1520 New Hampshire Avenue, NW
Washington DC 20036
Phone: 202/452-0660
Fax: 202/452-0081
Email: emjam@sysnet.net

Dr. Richard Leighton BERNAL
Ambassador

Date Credentials Presented: 6/11/91

Born: 11/30/49 in Kingston, Jamaica

Spouse: Mrs. Margaret Ann Reckord Bernal

Economist, banker, university lecturer, and diplomat, Dr. Richard L. Bernal serves not only as Jamaica's ambassador to the United States but as his country's Permanent Representative to the Organization of American States (OAS). Prior to his present assignment, he was chief executive officer of a commercial bank.

Bernal has served the government of Jamaica in various capacities: in the Central Bank, the Planning Institute of Jamaica, and the Ministry of Finance. He has played an important role in the formulation and implementation of policies regarding Jamaica's debt management, structural adjustment, and international trade. Baernal has worked extensively on trade and debt issues of developing countries with an emphasis on Latin America and the Caribbean.

Bernal served as chairman of the OAS's Working Group on the Enterprise for the Americas Initiative. He was Jamaica's representative on the Special Committee of the OAS and the Committee for Hemispheric Financial Issues, and he was chairman of the Working Group on Smaller Economies.

Among the negotiations in which Bernal has been a leading participant on Jamaica's behalf are debt reduction agreements; a Bilateral Framework Agreement between CARICOM and the United States; the U.S./Jamaica Bilateral Investment Treaty; the U.S./Jamaica Intellectual Property Rights Agreement; and loans from multilateral financial institutions (International Monetary Fund, Work Bank, the Inter-American Development Bank) and the U.S. government on program and project funding for Jamaica.

Bernal is the author of numerous policy studies for the government of Jamaica and of papers on economic issues for scholarly publications, including the debt problem, economic adjustment in developing countries, regional integration, U.S./Caribbean relations, foreign policy, and trade policy. He has published more than 70 articles in scholarly journals, books, and monographs. He has also published articles in business and financial periodicals and newspapers, including opinion editorials in The Washington Post, Wall Street Journal, and the Journal of Commerce.

Bernal received a B.S. in economics from the University of the West Indies and a master's degree and a Ph.D., both in economics, from the New School for Social Research in New York.

STAFF:

Mr. Basil K. BRYAN
Minister (Dep. Chief of Mission) & Consul

Spouse: Mrs. Jean Marie Bryan

Mrs. Charlane M. O. MARYNS
Minister (Information) and Consul
Spouse: Mr. Raphael H. M. Maryns

Ms. Pamela Rosemarie COKE
Minister-Counselor and Consul
Spouse: Mr. O'Neil Donovan Hamilton

Mr. Ahan George BROWN
Attaché
Spouse: Mrs. Diane Smith-Brown

Ms. Rolande Simone PRYCE
Attaché (Legal)

Japan

Embassy of Japan
2520 Massachusetts Ave., NW
Washington DC 20008
Phone: 202/238-6700
Fax: 202/328-2187
Url: http://www.embjapan.org

Kunihiko SAITO
Ambassador

Date Credentials Presented: 2/6/96

Born: in 1935 in Toyama, Japan

Spouse: Mrs. Akiko Saito

Kunihiko Saito, who entered the Japanese Ministry of Foreign Affairs (MOFA) in 1958, has held various governmental posts, including an ambassadorship to Iran.

Immediately before coming to Washington, D.C., he served as an adviser to the minister for foreign affairs in 1995. In 1993, he was named vice-minister for foreign affairs. Before that he was deputy minister for foreign affairs. He was assigned as ambassador to Iran in 1989.

Saito's other positions, including the year of his assignment, were as follows: director-general of the Treaties Bureau, Ministry of Foreign Affairs, 1987; deputy director-general of the Treaties Bureau, 1984; director of the Financial Affairs Division, Minister's Secretariat, Ministry of Foreign Affairs, 1982; counselor, Permanent Mission of Japan

to the European Communities, 1978; director of the Treaties Division, Treaties Bureau, Ministry of Foreign Affairs, 1976; director of the Second North America Division, American Affairs Bureau, Ministry of Foreign Affairs, 1973.

Saito, a graduate of the Tokyo University, Faculty of Law, is married and has two sons.

STAFF:

Mr. Hideaki KOBAYASHI
Minister (Deputy Chief of Mission)
Spouse: Mrs. Toshiko Kobayasi

Mr. Ichiro FUJISAKI
Minister (Political)
Spouse: Mrs. Yoriko Fujisaki

Mr. Tadashi IWASHITA
Minister (Financial)
Spouse: Mrs. Naoko Iwashita

Mr. Kazuo KANEKO
Minister

Mr. Seiji KOJIMA
Minister
Spouse: Mrs. Tami Kojima

Mr. Toshinori SHIGEIE
Minister
Spouse: Mrs. Emiko Shigeie

Mr. Toyozo HASHIMOTO
Counselor

Mr. Hidehisa HORINOUCHI
Counselor
Spouse: Mrs. Sabine Horinouchi

Mr. Mitsutaka INAGAKI
Counselor
Spouse: Mrs. Yoshiko Inagaki

Mr. Hajime ITO
Counselor
Spouse: Ms. Miyuki Ito

Mr. Kiyoshi KITA
Counselor

Mr. Takao KURAMOCHI
Counselor
Spouse: Mrs. Yoko Kuramochi

Mr. Junichiro MIYAZAKI
Counselor
Spouse: Mrs. Yoko Miyazaki

Mr. Masao NISHIKAWA
Counselor

Mr. Hiroshi OE
Counselor
Spouse: Mrs. Midori Oe

Mr. Norihiro OKUDA
Counselor (Congress)

Mr. Yoichi OTABE
Counselor

Spouse: Mrs. Kiyoka Otabe

Mr. Relichiro TAKAHASHI
Counselor
Spouse: Mrs. Masako Takahashi

Mr. Yutaka TAKUBO
Counselor (Protocol)
Spouse: Mrs. Sayoko Takubo

Mr. Akihiko TAMURA
Counselor
Spouse: Ms. Yumiko Tamura

Mr. Kaoru YOSHIMURA
Counselor
Spouse: Mrs. Tomoko Yoshimura

Mr. Yoshinori FUJIYAMA
First Secretary
Spouse: Mrs. Mari Fujiyama

Mr. Eiji HABU
First Secretary
Spouse: Ms. Yukiko Habu

Mr. Yuichi HANAWA
First Secretary
Spouse: Mrs. Yoshiko Hanawa

Mr. Hisao INAGAKI
First Secretary
Spouse: Ms. Yuki Inagaki

Mr. Tetsuo KANAI
First Secretary
Spouse: Mrs. Rieko Kanai

Mr. Kenichiro KATAOKA
First Secretary
Spouse: Ms. Keiko Kataoka

Mr. Noriaki KOYAMA
First Secretary
Spouse: Mrs. Kasumi Koyama

Mr. Ichiro MARUYAMA
First Secretary
Spouse: Mrs. Emiko Maruyama

Mr. Kuninori MATSUDA
First Secretary
Spouse: Mrs. Naoko Matsuda

Mr. Noriyuki MATSUKAWA
First Secretary
Spouse: Ms. Mika Matsukawa

Mr. Yukiharu MATSUMOTO
First Secretary and Consul
Spouse: Mrs. Noriko Matsumoto

Mr. Osamu MIZUI
First Secretary
Spouse: Mrs. Yukie Mizui

Ms. Mami MIZUTORI
First Secretary

Mr. Koichi MORITA
First Secretary
Spouse: Mrs. Hatsue Morita

Mr. Kiyofumi MURANO
First Secretary
Spouse: Mrs. Noriko Murano

Mr. Takeo NAKAGAWA
First Secretary
Spouse: Ms. Michiko Nakagawa

Mr. Masahiro OBATA
First Secretary
Spouse: Mrs. Hiroko Obata

Mr. Masahiro OKA
First Secretary (Political)
Spouse: Mrs. Kano Oka

Mr. Seiji OKADA
First Secretary
Spouse: Mrs. Yasuko Okada

Mr. Takeo OKADA
First Secretary
Spouse: Mrs. Fusayo Okada

Mr. Shingo OTA
First Secretary
Spouse: Ms. Hiroko Ota

Mr. Hitoshi OZAWA
First Secretary (Economic)
Spouse: Mrs. Makiko Ozawa

Mr. Junji SHIMADA
First Secretary
Spouse: Ms. Tazuko Sugiyama

Mr. Yukinari SUGIYAMA
First Secretary
Spouse: Ms. Tazuko Sugiyama

Mr. Shinichi TAKASAKI
First Secretary
Spouse: Ms. Mika Takasaki

Mr. Tetsuya TAMAI
First Secretary
Spouse: Ms. Kazuko Tamai

Mr. Masahiro TERAMOTO
First Secretary
Spouse: Mrs. Yumiko Teramoto

Mr. Toshitsugu UESAWA
First Secretary
Spouse: Mrs. Junko Uesawa

Mr. Takeshi YAMAKAWA
First Secretary
Spouse: Ms. Mikine Yamakawa

Mr. Tsuyoshi TAMAMOTO
First Secretary

Mr. Kanji YAMANOUCHI
First Secretary
Spouse: Ms. Yukiko Yamanouchi

Mr. Naomasa YOSHIDA
First Secretary
Spouse: Mrs. Keiko Yoshida

Mr. Mikio HAZUMI
Second Secretary

Spouse: Mrs. Masumi Hazumi

Mr. Shinichi HOSONO
Second Secretary
Spouse: Mrs. Chiaki Hosono

Mr. Toshio KAWAUCHI
Second Secretary

Mr. Koichi MARUYAMA
Second Secretary
Spouse: Mrs. Riko Maruyama

Mr. Motosada MATANO
Second Secretary
Spouse: Ms. Chieko Matano

Mr. Takashi MORIOKA
Second Secretary

Mr. Kaoru NISHIYAMA
Second Secretary
Spouse: Mrs. Tomie Nishiyama

Mrs. Yoshie OTSUKA
Second Secretary
Spouse: Mr. Umio Otsuka

Mr. Takashi SHIMODA
Second Secretary

Mr. Akihiko TAMURA
Second Secretary

Mr. Yuji TERAKADO
Second Secretary
Spouse: Mrs. Hideko Terakado

Mr. Nobuhiko TSUKIYAMA
Second Secretary
Spouse: Mrs. Junko Tsukiyama

Mr. Yasuharu UEDA
Second Secretary (Economic)
Spouse: Mrs. Keiko Ueda

Mr. Koichi YAMASAKI
Second Secretary
Spouse: Ms. Kunie Yamasaki

Mr. Jun EGUCHI
Third Secretary

Ms. Kaori INUI
Third Secretary

Mr. Tomoaki ISHIGAKI
Third Secretary

Mr. Hirotaka MATSUO
Third Secretary

Mr. Daisuke NAMIOKA
Third Secretary
Spouse: Mrs. Ryoko Namioka

Mr. Makoto TAGA
Third Secretary
Spouse: Mrs. Chiaki Taga

Mr. Teruyuki FUNABA
Attaché
Spouse: Mrs. Maki Funaba

Mr. Ken FURUYA
Attaché
Spouse: Mrs. Chie Furuya

Ms. Kiyoko GOTO
Attaché

Ms. Noriko INOUE
Attaché

Mr. Yasushi ISE
Attaché
Spouse: Mrs. Yuri Ise

Mr. Hitoshi KAMIKUBO
Attaché
Spouse: Mrs. Misato Kamikubo

Mr. Yoshihiro KANO
Attaché
Spouse: Ms. Yuki Kano

Mr. Junya KAWAKAMI
Attaché
Spouse: Mrs. Miyuki Kawakami

Mr. Kenichi KINOSHITA
Attaché

Ms. Mayuko KOURA
Attaché

Mr. Koichi MIWA
Attaché
Spouse: Mrs. Hiroe Miwa

Miss Noriko MIYAMOTO
Attaché

Mr. Takashi MURAMATSU
Attaché

Ms. Akiko NODA
Attaché

Mr. Masamichi NOGUCHI
Attaché

Mr. Nobuyuki OGINEZAWA
Attaché

Mr. Akitoshi SAITO
Attaché

Mr. Nobuyuki SHIMAZAKI
Attaché

Mr. Masami SUGAHARA
Attaché

Ms. Midori YAMAMITSU
Attaché
Spouse: Mr. Michael Joseph Otting

Mrs. Yuka YUMOTO
Attaché

Ms. Mayumi ASAKO
Asst. Attaché

Mr. Tamio ITO
Asst. Attaché
Spouse: Mrs. Toshimi Ito

Ms. Michiko MURAKAMI
Asst. Attaché

Mr. Hitoshi OURA
Asst. Attaché

Lt. Colonel Makoto TAKASHIMA
Asst. Air Attaché
Spouse: Mrs. Michiyo Takashima

Lt. Colonel Chiharu NARITA
Asst. Military Attaché
Spouse: Mrs. Masayo Narita

Commander Tetsuo ANDO
Asst. Defense and Naval Attaché
Spouse: Mrs. Hiroko Ando

Colonel Yuji ISHII
Air Attaché
Spouse: Mrs. Tomoko Ishii

Colonel Kazuya HAYASHI
Military Attaché & Assistant
   Defense Attaché
Spouse: Mrs. Mayumi Hayashi

Rear Admiral Fumio OTO
Defense and Naval Attaché
Spouse: Mrs. Michiko Ota

Ms. Eriko YOSHIMURA
Asst. Attaché

Ms. Takako YODA
Asst. Attaché

Ms. Tomoko TONEGAWA
Asst. Attaché

Ms. Chiharu TAKETOMI
Asst. Attaché

Information Center
1155 21st Street, NW
Washington DC 20036
Phone: 202/393-6900

Jordan

Embassy of the Hashemite
   Kingdom of Jordan
3504 International Drive, NW
Washington DC 20008
Phone: 202/966-2664
Fax: 202/966-3110
Url: http://www.jordanembassyus.org/

Dr. Marwan Jamil MUASHER
Ambassador

Date Credentials Presented: 9/8/97

Born: 6/14/56 in Amman, Jordan

Spouse: Mrs. Lynne Muasher

Dr. Marwan Jamil Muasher held a number of posts in Jordan's government before his appointment as his country's ambassador to the U.S. He was minister of information in

1996-97 and ambassador to Israel in 1995-96.

Between 1991 and 1994, Muasher was the spokesman and a member of the Jordanian delegation to the Middle East Peace talks. He was director of the Jordan Information Bureau in Washington, D.C., between 1990 and 1994, and he served as press advisor to the prime minister of Jordan in 1989.

Muasher was a political columnist for the Jordan Times between 1983 and 1990. He was with the ministry of planning for four years, first as head of the computer unit and monitoring unit (1985-87) and later as director of the socio-economic information center, national information system (1987-90). In 1984-85, he was a senior consultant with the Special Systems Company in Amman. He was director of the computer center, Jordan Electric Power Company, in 1984, and assistant research engineer, Research Institute, University of Petroleum and Minerals, in Saudi Arabia in 1983-84.

He attended the American University of Beirut from 1972 to 1975 and holds a B.S. in electrical engineering (1977), an M.S. in computer engineering (1978) and a Ph.D. in computer engineering (1981), all from Purdue University in Indiana.

He and his wife, Lynne, have two children, Omar and Hana.

STAFF:

Mr. Mohamed Ali DAHER NSOUR
Minister (Deputy Chief of Mission)
Spouse: Mrs. Manal S. Shami

His Royal Highness P Talal Bin
   MOHAMMED
Minister
Spouse: Her Royal Highness Princess
   Ghida Talal

Dr. Zaid A. AL SHAMALEH
Counselor (Cultural)
Spouse: Mrs. Rugayya Al Shamaileh

Mr. Elias Samir Gh. MANSOUR
Counselor (Commercial)
Spouse: Mrs. Randa Elias Samir Mansour

Her Royal Highness P Ghida TALAL
Counselor
Spouse: His Royal Highness Prince
   Talal Bin Mohammed

Ms. Rania M. ATALLAH
First Secretary (Press and Info.)

Mr. Ali H. AL AYED
Second Secretary
Spouse: Mrs. Vincenza Al Ayed

Mr. Majed T. H. QATARNEH
Third Secretary
Spouse: Mrs. Tima M. Al Qatarneh

Mr. Ahmad S. AWAD

Attaché (Cultural)

Mr. Saado A. QUAL
Attaché

Brigadier General Hamed S. SARAIREH
Defense, Military, Naval & Air Attaché
Spouse: Mrs. Hamed Saraireh

Lt. Colonel Azzam A. M. EIAD
Asst. Defense, Military, Naval and
   Air Attaché
Spouse: Mrs. Suad Azzam A. M. Ayyat

Captain Maen H. AL LOZI
Asst. Military Attaché
Spouse: Mrs. Shireen Ahmad Hasan
   Nazzal

Information Bureau
2319 Wyoming Avenue, NW
Washington DC 20008
Phone: 202/265-1606 Fax: 202/667-0777

Kazakhstan

Embassy of the Republic of Kazakhstan
3421 Massachusetts Avenue, NW
Washington DC 20008
Phone: 202/333-4504
Fax: 202/333-4509
Email: kazak@intr.net

Bolat K. NURGALIYEV
Ambassador

Date Credentials Presented: 4/30/96

Born: 7/25/51

Spouse: Mrs. Alma Sh. Nurgaliyeva

Before his appointment to Washington, D.C., Bolat K. Nurgaliyev served as deputy foreign minister responsible for the de-nuclearization of Kazakhstan, a top priority of the new independent state's foreign policy in the early years of sovereign decision-making.

Nurgaliyev also held the position of head of the Foreign Ministry's international security and arms control department. He joined the Soviet Ministry of Foreign Affairs in 1980 and occupied different diplomatic posts including the Soviet embassies in Pakistan and India.

Nurgaliyev considers relations between Kazakhstan and the United States to be developing dynamically, based on the Charter of Democratic Partnership of 1994 and the network of 34 specialized agreements covering cooperation in political security, trade, and investment. With such strong legal underpinning, he has stated that the two countries are moving forward in their partnership, considered by the Kazakhstan government as a key element of peace and prosperity in Central Asia.

U.S. involvement in the Kazakhstan market is of crucial importance, according to Nurgaliyev, and he stated there is an attractive business climate for foreign companies in Kazakhstan. He cited the participation of Chevron, Mobil, AT&T, and other prominent U.S. companies in different sectors of the Kazakhstan economy as examples of successful and mutually beneficial projects.

Nurgaliyev is a graduate of the Tselinograd Pedagogical Institute. He speaks fluent English and French. He and his wife, Alma, have two children.

STAFF:

Mr. Kairat K. ABUSSEITOV
Counselor
Spouse: Mrs. Roza Abusseitova

Mrs. Zukhra G. AKISHEVA
First Secretary
Spouse: Mr. Alisher Akishev

Mr. Kanat M. ARENOV
First Secretary
Spouse: Mrs. Rauza Arenova

Mr. Askar S. TAZHIYEV
First Secretary
Spouse: Mrs. Maiya S. Tazhiyeva

Mr. Dostay RAMANKULOV
Second Secretary
Spouse: Mrs. Aliya Ramankulova

Mr. Gabit YERMEKOV
Third Secretary
Spouse: Mrs. Gaukhar Yermekova

Mr. Adel E. ABICHEV
Attaché

Mr. Askar S. BASSIBEKOV
Attaché (Administrative)
Spouse: Mrs. Sariya M. Bassibekova

Mr. Ilyas OMAROV
Attaché

Mr. Bakytzhan ZHOKEBAYEV
Attaché
Spouse: Mrs. Zauresh S. Zhokebayeva

Colonel Yerzhan K. ISSIN
Defense, Military and Air Attaché
Spouse: Mrs. Bulbul B. Issina

Consular Division
3421 Massachusetts Avenue, NW
Washington DC 20007
Phone: 202/333-4507

Kenya

Embassy of the Republic of Kenya
2249 R Street, NW
Washington DC 20008
Phone: 202/387-6101
Fax: 202/462-3829
Email: klqy53a@prodigy.com
Url: http://www.embassyofkenya.com/

Samson K. CHEMAI
Ambassador

Date Credentials Presented: 3/16/98

*Born: 3/6/42 in Nandi District of Rift
   Valley Province*

Spouse: Mrs. Esther Chemai

Kenya's newly appointed ambassador to the U.S., Mexico, and Columbia --- Samson Kipkoech Chemai --- is a technocrat. He came to Washington from Japan, where he was Kenya's ambassador for two years.

After receiving his Cambridge school certificate in 1962 from Kapsabet High School, he joined the then East African Posts and Telecommunications School for a two-year technician's training. Between 1964 and 1967, he attended City and Guilds of London and in 1972 he proceeded to a satellite engineers course in Ahmedabad, India. Upon returning to Kenya, he was appointed a maintenance engineer at the International Maintenance Centre of the then Kenya External Telecommunications (KENEXTEL) after which was promoted to the position of engineer-in-charge.

In 1976, Chemai sat for the professional academic examination offered by the Council of Engineering institutions in the United Kingdom and in 1980 he pursued a further academic course at the U.S. International University from which he obtained a master of science degree in management and organizational development.

He was promoted to the position of deputy

managing director of the Kenya External Telecommunication Company in 1981. The company was merged in 1982 with the Kenya Post and Telecommunications Corporation.

Following the merger, Chemai was appointed head of External (international) Telecommunications Services, a position he held until 1989 when he named head of National (domestic) Telecommunications Services. After organizational restructuring of Kenya Post and Telecommunications in 1990, he was appointed to the newly created post of general manager (corporate planning and engineering) in the corporation.

In 1991, the Central Training School, Mbagathi, was transformed into the Kenya College of Communications Technology vested with autonomous authority to formulate training programs under an independent board of directors. Chemai was appointed the first director and chief executive officer of the new college.

The president of Kenya appointed Chemai managing director and chief executive officer of the Kenya Posts and Telecommunications Corporation in 1993 --- a position he held until his appointment in 1995 as ambassador to Japan.

Chemai recently was awarded the degree of doctor of international relations, honoris causa, by the Newport Asia Pacific University.

STAFF:

Mr. Jacob K. CHUMBA
Counselor (Administrative)
Spouse: Mrs. Salome Jelel Chumba

Mr. Charles M. KANGE
Counselor (Economic)
Spouse: Mrs. Celestine M. Muthui

Mrs. Anne B. NYIKULI
Counselor (Political)
Spouse: Mr. Peter Khamala Nyikuli

Mr. Elmanus A. VODOTI
Counselor (Educational)
Spouse: Mrs. Florence Lodenyi Vodoti

Mr. Joshua Ruto KIPTEPKUT
First Secretary (Education)
Spouse: Mrs. Mary J. Cherop Kiptepkut

Ms. Dorothy Mbulwa MUTUNGA
First Secretary (Immigration)

Mr. Shee Mwasukuti MBWANA
Second Secretary (Administrative)
Spouse: Mrs. Mariamu Ngiza Shee

Mr. John Kilungya MUTIE
Second Secretary (Financial)
Spouse: Mrs. Florence Nduku Kilungya

Mr. Peter Khamala NYIKULI
Attaché (Commercial)
Spouse: Mrs. Ann Belinda Nyikuli

Warrant Officer Geoffrey Ben OTOLO
Attaché (Administrative)
Spouse: Mrs. Beatrice Amondi Otolo

Mr. Enock Alfayo WAMOYO
Attaché (Administrative)
Spouse: Mrs. Jane Nanzala Wamoyo

Colonel Moses C. YATOR
Defense, Military, Naval and Air Attaché
Spouse: Mrs. Alice A. Yator

Korea (Republic of)

Embassy of the Republic of Korea
2450 Massachusetts Avenue, NW
Washington DC 20008
Phone: 202/939-5600
Fax: 202/232-0117
Url: http://korea.emb.washington.dc.us

Hong Koo LEE
Ambassador

Date Credentials Presented: 5/27/98

Born: 5/9/34

Spouse: Mrs. Han-ock Lee

Korea's new ambassador to the U.S., Hong Koo Lee began his career as a political science professor in the U.S. and has held a succession of high political and governmental posts in Korea.

He became a member of the National Assembly and chairman of the New Korea Party (the Grand National Party) in 1996 and was prime minister of Korea in 1994 before which he was deputy prime minister and minister of national unification. In 1991, he was appointed Korea's ambassador to the United Kingdom. He served as a special assistant to the president for political affairs in 1990.

Lee studied at the college of law, Seoul National University, in Seoul in 1953. He graduated from Emory University in Atlanta University in 1959. Then, in 1968, he graduated from Yale University Graduate School in New Haven, Conn., receiving an M.A. and a Ph.D. in political science.

He became an assistant professor of political science at Emory University in 1963. He returned to Korea in 1968 to be a professor in the department of political science at Seoul National University. In 1979, he was named director of the institute of social sciences at that university. He went back to being a professor of political science there in 1980.

Lee was named president of the Korean Association for Communist Studies in 1982. He was a member of the executive committee in the International Political Science Association, beginning in 1985, and, in 1986, was named president of the Korean Political Science Association.

The ambassador is married and has one son and two daughters.

STAFF:

Mr. Chang Ho LEE
Minister (Deputy Chief of Mission)
Spouse: Mrs. Hye Kyung Lee

Mr. Myong Joo CHOE
Minister

Mr. Hyuck CHOI
Minister (Economic)
Spouse: Mrs. Hyae Seung Chung

Mr. Kyu Ho CHOO
Counselor
Spouse: Mrs. Jung Won Choo Song

Mr. Hae Moon CHUNG
Counselor
Spouse: Mrs. Jung Sun Chung

Mr. Soon Young CHUNG
Counselor (Congressional)

Mr. Suk Koo CHUNG
Counselor (Education)
Spouse: Mrs. Soon Ae Chung Myung

Mr. Woon Ki CHUNG
Counselor (Customs)
Spouse: Mrs. Yong An Chung

Mr. Chun Koo HAHN
Counselor (Communications)
Spouse: Mrs. Yung Ock Hahn

Mr. Doug Young JOO
Counselor (Commercial)
Spouse: Mrs. Song Hee Park

Mr. Sung Hwan KIM
Counselor
Spouse: Mrs. Soong Deok Kim

Mr. Sung Yup KIM
Counselor and General Consul
Spouse: Mrs. Ke Soon Kim

Mr. Yoon Hee KIM
Counselor
Spouse: Mrs. Pha Kim

Mr. Young Ho KIM
Counselor (Administrative)
Spouse: Mrs. Min Hee Cho

Mr. In Gyu LEE
Counselor (Legal)
Spouse: Mrs. Min Jeong Lee Kim

Mr. Soo Hyuck LEE
Counselor
Spouse: Mrs. Hye Kyung Lee

Mr. Yum LEE
Counselor
Spouse: Mrs. Ae Yeong Lee

Mr. Yun Joe LEE
Counselor

Spouse: Mrs. Hyun Ok Shin Lee

Mr. You Hyun MOON
Counselor (Scientific)
Spouse: Mrs. Chang Hee Kang

Mr. Kyung Tark PARK
Counselor
Spouse: Mrs. Jae Soon Kang

Mr. Dong Kyu SHIN
Counselor (Financial and Economic)
Spouse: Mrs. Hyun Sook Park

Mr. Onhan SHIN
Counselor (Health and Welfare)
Spouse: Mrs. Myung Hee Shin

Mr. Chan Joon SOHN
Counselor
Spouse: Mrs. Gum Sook Park

Mr. Myung Soo AHN
First Secretary
Spouse: Mrs. Shin Young Ahn

Mr. Jeong Suk CHA
First Secretary
Spouse: Mrs. Su Il Cha Na

Mr. Hyun CHO
First Secretary
Spouse: Mrs. Jeeyoon Cho

Mr. June CHO
First Secretary
Spouse: Mrs. In Sook Cho

Mr. Byung Koo CHOI
First Secretary
Spouse: Mrs. Kyung Soo Kim

Mr. Jang-Hyun CHOI
First Secretary (Maritime)
Spouse: Mrs. Hye-Sook Choi

Mr. Hyun HAN
First Secretary
Spouse: Mrs. Tae Kyung Park

Mr. Man Hee HAN
First Secretary (Construction and
  Transportation)
Spouse: Mrs. Hyun Joo Kim

Mr. Ji In HONG
First Secretary
Spouse: Mrs. Young Mee Hong Kim

Mr. He Beom KIM
First Secretary
Spouse: Mrs. Kim Choi Soo Hyun

Mr. Hong Rak KIM
First Secretary
Spouse: Mrs. Mi Young Kim

Mr. Jae Shin KIM
First Secretary
Spouse: Mrs. Jong Min Kim

Mr. Young Min KIM
First Secretary

Spouse: Mrs. Un Hee Lee

Mr. Hye Min LEE
First Secretary
Spouse: Mrs. Sun Mi Lee

Mr. Hyung Kun LEE
First Secretary
Spouse: Mrs. Yae Bok Lee

Mr. Jae Kap LEE
First Secretary (Labor)
Spouse: Mrs. Seung Jin Lee

Mr. Jeong Gwan LEE
First Secretary
Spouse: Mrs. Jong Ran Lee

Mr. Kyung Woo NAM
First Secretary
Spouse: Mrs. Chung Hee Lim

Mr. Ro Byug PARK
First Secretary
Spouse: Mrs. Seong Rahn Hong

Mr. Sang Hoon PARK
First Secretary and Consul
Spouse: Mrs. Chung Mi Park

Mr. Yoon Hwan SON
First Secretary
Spouse: Mrs. Laan Kyung Kim

Mr. Ha Seong SONG
First Secretary
Spouse: Mrs. Jae Eun Pie

Mr. Chang Seok YANG
First Secretary
Spouse: Mrs. Sook Kyung Lee

Mr. Seung Il CHEONG
Second Secretary
Spouse: Mrs. Yoo Un Cheong Choi

Mr. Byung Hwa CHUNG
Second Secretary
Spouse: Mrs. Jae Kyung Chung

Mr. Byung Wook JO
Second Secretary
Spouse: Mrs. Chi Soo Jo Won

Mr. Gunn KIM
Second Secretary
Spouse: Mrs. Hee Jung Kim

Mr. Myung Yul LEE
Second Secretary and Consul
Spouse: Mrs. Ji Ae Le Bahk

Mr. Seong Hyun MOON
Second Secretary
Spouse: Mrs. Myung Ji Suh

Mr. Ho Ryung O
Second Secretary
Spouse: Mrs. Mi Nam O

Mr. Soon Gu YOON
Second Secretary
Spouse: Mrs. Chan Soon Yoon

Mr. Hyun Ki KIM
Third Secretary
  (Culture and Information)
Spouse: Mrs. Soon Chung Kim

Mr. Joon Chui KIM
Third Secretary

Colonel Jung Soo KIM
Attaché (Defense, Research and
  Development)
Spouse: Mrs. Jung Soon Kim

Mr. Su Han KIM
Attaché
Spouse: Mrs. Jeom Ok Kong

Colonel Dong LEE
Attaché (Logistics)
Spouse: Mrs. Yeon Lee Kim

Brigadier General Seon Kyu KIM
Defense Attaché
Spouse: Mrs. Yeo In Kim

Colonel Jongsoo KIM
Military Attaché
Spouse: Mrs. Hyesoon Kim

Captain Hyung BAI
Naval Attaché
Spouse: Mrs. Man Sook Bai Han

Colonel Hak Soo YOON
Air Attaché
Spouse: Mrs. Hye Kyung Kim

Major Young Moon JUNG
Asst. Defense and Military Attaché
Spouse: Mrs. Ji Yun Rhee

Major Kwang Taek KWON
Asst. Defense and Military Attaché
Spouse: Mrs. Myoung Ae Kwon

Major Sang Bok CHOI
Asst. Naval Attaché
Spouse: Mrs. Ok Ja Choi Park

Major Jin Ho KIM
Asst. Air Attaché
Spouse: Mrs. Hye Kyung Ryu

Chancery Annex
2400 Wilson Boulevard
Arlington VA 22201
Phone: 703/524-9272 Fax: 703/524-9273

Consular Office
2320 Massachusetts Avenue, NW
Washington DC 20008
Phone: 202/939-6497 Fax: 202/342-1597

Education Office
2320 Massachusetts Avenue, NW
Washington DC 20008
Phone: 202/939-5681 Fax: 202/265-2127

Information Office
2370 Massachusetts Avenue, NW
Washington DC 20008
Phone: 202/797-6343 Fax: 202/387-0413

Kuwait

Embassy of the State of Kuwait
2940 Tilden Street, NW
Washington DC 20008
Phone: 202/966-0705
Fax: 202/966-0517

Mohammed Sabah Al-Salim AL-SABAH

Ambassador

Date Credentials Presented: 4/14/93

Born: 10/10/55

Spouse: Mrs. Feryal D. Al-Sabah

An economist by profession, Mohammed Sabah Al-Salim Al-Sabah has taught at Kuwait University since completion of his own education in the U.S. Immediately after completing his doctorate, he was a member of the Harvard University Kuwait Economic Study Team.

Despite his grounding in academia, Al-Sabah has maintained continuous involvement with both government and private consultation, as well as with promoting Kuwaiti relations with the U.S. Since 1987, he has been the chairman of Kuwait's Economic Committee of the Higher Planning Council. In 1988, he became vice chairman of the Kuwait Trading, Contracting, and Investment Company. Following the Iraqi invasion of his country, Al-Sabah was a member of the Higher Consultative Council of the Kuwaiti Government in Exile during 1990 and 1991. The following year, he was a founding member of the Kuwaiti-American Foundation.

Al-Sabah holds a B.A. in economics from Claremont Men's College, and an M.A. and Ph.D. in economics from Harvard University. He speaks English, in addition to his native Arabic. He is married to Feryal D. Al-Sabah and has four children.

STAFF:

Mr. Dhari Ajran Hussain AL AJRAN
Counselor (Deputy Chief of Mission)

Mr. Abdullah AL-BAHER
Counselor (Cultural)

Mr. Adil Hamad AL-AYYAR
Second Secretary (Administrative)

Mr. Raed A. AL-RIFAI
Second Secretary

Mr. Ahmad Salem Ahmad Al-Salem
   AL-WEHAIB
Second Secretary
Spouse: Mrs. Ghadah A.A. Duaij

Mr. Jasem Mohammad ABURAHMAH
Attaché

Spouse: Mrs. Aman Aburahmah

Mr. Mohammad Hassan AL-BADAH
Attaché (Acting Director)
Spouse: Mrs. Nadiah Th.S. Al-Hamlan

Mr. Othman Dawoud AL DAWOUD
Attaché (Political)

Dr. Ahdi Yousef AL GHANIM
Attaché (Health)
Spouse: Mrs. Ibtihaj Abdullah Al Ghanim

Mr. Abdullatif A. AL HENDI
Attaché
Spouse: Mrs. Faizah A. Al Senedy

Dr. Abdulrahman M.M. AL JOUHAR
Attaché (Health)
Spouse: Mrs. Badreyah A. Al Tenaib

Mr. Taraq Eid AL-MEZREM
Attaché (Media)

Mr. Amer A. ALMUTAIRI
Attaché (Diplomatic)
Spouse: Mrs. Nuha Salem Alsudairawi

Mr. Salah Hamdan ALSAIF
Attaché (Press)
Spouse: Mrs. Abeer A.A. Aleisa

Mr. Hamad A.Y.A. AL SHATTI
Attaché
Spouse: Mrs. Ibtesam Kh. E. Al Zenki

Mr. Marzouq Fairouz SAEED
Attaché
Spouse: Mrs. Badreyah Essa

Col. Mohammad Yousef A.Y. ALSOBAIE
Attaché
Spouse: Mrs. Amal A.J.M. Almudhaf

Mr. Abdullah E. HASHEM
Attaché (Cultural)
Spouse: Mrs. Khaulah M. Alasfoor

Cultural Division
3500 International Drive, NW
Washington DC 20008
Phone: 202/364-2100

Health Office
4201 Connecticut Ave., NW, Suite 502
Washington DC 20008
Phone: 202/686-4304

Information Office
2600 Virginia Ave., NW, Suite 404
Washington DC 20037
Phone: 202/338-0211

Liaison Office
3500 International Drive, NW
Washington DC 20008
Phone: 202/364-2200

University Office
3500 International Drive, NW
Washington DC 20008
Phone: 202/363-8055

Kyrgyzstan

Embassy of the Kyrgyz Republic
1732 Wisconsin Avenue, NW
Washington DC 20007
Phone: 202/338-5141
Fax: 202/338-5139
Email: Embassy@kyrgystan.org
Url: http://www.kyrgystan.org

Baktybek ABDRISSAEV

Ambassador

Date Credentials Presented: 2/11/97

Born: 4/17/58

*Spouse: Mrs. Tcholpon Akmatalieva
   AbdrisSaev*

Baktybek Abdrissaev, the Kyrgyz Republic's ambassador to the U.S. since October 1996, is also his country's ambassador to Canada. He is a member of the Kyrgyz Republic's Parliament.

In 1993, Abdrissaev became the head of the international relations department on the president's staff. Earlier, he served as an expert in the department. Kyrgyzstan, whose population is about five million, became an independent country in 1991.

Abdrissaev had been a senior scientific fellow and, before that, a scientific fellow at the Institute of Physics under the Academy of Sciences. In 1987, he was a senior scientific fellow at the Bishkek Polytechnical Institute, where he had completed studies in automatics and telemechanics in 1980 and later pursued post-graduate studies. He has a doctor of sciences degree.

Abdrissaev and his wife, Tcholpon Akmatalieva, have one son, Bectur. The ambassador enjoys classical music and table tennis.

STAFF:

Mr. Erkin MAMKULOV
Counselor
Spouse: Mrs. Aygul Sydykova

Mr. Azamat KERIMBAEV
First Secretary
Spouse: Mrs. Aynura Kerimbaeva

Mr. Oulan DJOUSSOUPOV
Attaché
Spouse: Mrs. Alexandra Kfoussoupova

Consular Section
1511 K Street, NW
Suite 707
Washington DC 20005
Phone: 202/628-0433

Laos

Embassy of the Lao People's
    Democratic Republic
2222 S St., NW
Washington DC 20008
Phone: 202/332-6416
Fax: 202/332-4923
Email: laoemb@erols.com
Url: http://www.laoembassy.com

Khamla SAYACHACK

Chargé d'affaires, ad interim
Counselor

Born: 10/10/50 in Vientiane, Laos

The appointment of a new Lao ambassador
to the U.S. was expected in the summer of
1998 to succeed Hiem Phommachanh, who
had served in the post since 1992. Until that
time the head of mission is Khamla
Sayachack. He came to Washington, D.C.
in May 1997 as counselor, then became
chargé d'affaires in May 1998 upon the
departure of Ambassador Phommachanh.

Before coming to the U.S., Sayachack served
in the ministry of foreign affairs in Vientiane
between 1988 and 1997. Between 1993 and
1997, he was deputy director of the ministry's
consular department. He served as third
secretary to the Lao embassy in Berlin,
Germany, between 1984 and 1987. In 1983-
84, he was stationed at the ministry of foreign
affairs in Vientiane.

Sayacack received a high school diploma in
Vietnam in 1971. Between 1975 and 1981,
he attended the Moscow Institute of
International Relations in Russia, where he
obtained a master of arts degree.

Sayachack is married and has two children.
He speaks Lao, Vietnamese, Russian, and
English.

STAFF:

Mr. Thonglung SAYAVONG
First Secretary (Administrative)
Spouse: Mrs. Khamsinh Sayavong

Mr. Sinchai MANIVANH
Third Secretary (Consular)
Spouse: Mrs. Silivanh Manivanh

Mr. Mai SAYAVONGS
Third Secretary (Economics)
Spouse: Mrs. Soumaly Sayavongs

Mr. Savang VONGSINNASONE
Attaché (Consular)
Spouse: Mrs. Phonthip Vongsinnasone

Mr. Bounty SENVONGSINOUAN
Attaché (Financial)

Latvia

Embassy of Latvia
4325 17th Street, NW
Washington DC 20011
Phone: 202/726-8213
Fax: 202/726-6785
Email: latvia@seas.gwu.edu
Url: http://www.seas.gwu.edu/guest/latvia

Ojars Eriks KALNINS

Ambassador

Date Credentials Presented: 4/14/93

Born: 10/22/49 in Munich, Germany

Spouse: Mrs. Irma Anna Kalnins

An emigrant to the U.S. in 1951 at the age
of two, Ojars E. Kalnins brings to his
ambassadorial position a unique perspective
of the U.S. - as a foreign representative with
an insider's frame of reference and - until
1991, U.S. citizenship.

Immediately prior to his ambassadorial
appointment, he served the Latvian
Government in several capacities: as a
representative for Latvian interests in the
U.S. before the establishment of diplomatic
relations; as a public relations specialist for
the Washington embassy during 1991 to 1992
(during which time relations were re-
established between the U.S. and Latvia);
as minister counselor and deputy chief of
mission of the embassy; and as deputy
permanent representative of the Latvian
Mission to the U.N.

For the five years preceding his work with
the government, Kalnins was intimately
involved with the Latvian community and
with efforts towards Latvian independence.
Serving from 1985 to 1990 as the public
relations director of the American-Latvian
Association, the largest Latvian organization
outside Latvia, he served as a liaison between
the Latvian-American community and the
U.S. Congress and Administration, as well
as with the press and other organizations.
Concurrently, Kalnins served as a consultant
to the World Federation of Free Latvians, as
chairman of the Joint Baltic American
National Committee and, beginning in 1987,
as the American-Latvian Association's

contact with pro-independence leaders and
movements in Latvia. To cement his ties with
Latvia, he renounced his American
citizenship in 1991 after the U.S. recognized
Latvia as an independent nation.

Kalnins met frequently with former
Presidents Bush and Reagan and gave
briefings on Latvia for the State Department,
Congress, the U.S. Information Agency and
for private associations and universities.

A resident of Chicago for most of his life,
Kalnins had been an advertising executive.
Before becoming involved full time with the
promotion of Latvia, he was creative director
for Semel/Kaye and Company.

Kalnins holds a B.A. in philosophy from
Roosevelt University. In addition to his native
Latvian and English, he speaks fluent French.
He has one daughter.

STAFF:

Mr. Einars SEMANIS
Counselor
Spouse: Mrs. Tatyana Semanis

Ms. Agnese LIVENA
Third Secretary (Consular)

Mr. Eldar MAMEDOVS
Second Secretary

Mr. Peteris VINKELIS
Counselor
Spouse: Mrs. Daria Kulagina

Lebanon

Embassy of Lebanon
2560 28th Street, NW
Washington DC 20008
Phone: 202/939-6300
Fax: 202/939-6324
Email: embofleb@aol.com
Url: http://www.embofleb.org

Dr. Mohamad B. Chatah

Ambassador

Date Credentials Presented: 9/8/97

Born: 1951 in Tripoli, Lebanon

Spouse: Mrs. Nadera Mikati Chatah

Before accepting his post as Lebanese ambassador to the U.S. in 1997, Dr. Mohamad B. Chatah was vice governor of the Banque du Liban, a position he had held since his return to Lebanon from the U.S. in early 1993.

A career economist, Chatah was instrumental in setting monetary policy and was involved in the domestic and external financing of the Lebanese government. During his vice governorship of the Banque du Liban, he played an important part in the rebuilding process by chairing a special committee on external debt which included the ministry of finance and the council of development and reconstruction.

The ambassador obtained his B.A. in economics from the American University of Beirut in 1974 and went on to do postgraduate work, which was interrupted at the outset of the Lebanese civil war in 1975. He transferred to the University of Texas at Austin, where he taught and received a Ph.D. in economics in 1983.

Chatah served as a member of the executive board of the International Monetary Fund from 1985 to 1993 where he took part in formulating policies set by the board with regard to lending to member countries, unconditionality, and surveillance, as well as periodic reviews of member countries. He also played a role in the IMF involvement in the global debt crisis during the 1980s.

In his role as advisor to the executive board, Chatah served as a link between IMF management and the Middle East countries including Lebanon.

He was executive director both of the Arab Monetary Fund and the Inter-Arab Trade program from 1994 to 1997.

The ambassador is married to Nadera Mikati and has two children, Ronnie and Omar.

STAFF:

Mr. Victor EL-ZMETER
Counselor (Deputy Chief of Mission)

Mr. Joe RAGGI
First Secretary

Mr. Houssam DIAB
First Secretary and Consul

Lt. Colonel Salim RAAD
Military Attaché

Lesotho

Embassy of the Kingdom of Lesotho
2511 Massachusetts Avenue, NW
Washington DC 20008
Phone: 202/797-5533
Fax: 202/234-6815
Email: lesotho@afrika.com

Eunice M. BULANE
Ambassador

Date Credentials Presented: 1/30/95

Born: 4/22/42

Eunice Malephiri Bulane, an electrical engineer, came to Washington from her position as deputy managing director to the Lesotho Electricity Cooperation (LEC). She began her career with the LEC in 1976 as a power engineer.

Bulane received a technical diploma from the Moscow Power Institute in 1969. From the Bucharest, Rumania, Polytechnic Institute, she earned an M.Sc. degree in electrical engineering in 1976 and a Ph.D. in electro energetic engineering in 1980.

Bulane served as a consultant for the Southern Africa Development Community Rural Electrification Survey, and she has been active in promoting regional power cooperation in the Southern Electric Power Community. Among her publications are "Present Organization of the National Electricity Supply and the Extent of Rural Electrification in Lesotho" and "Hydropower and Solar Energy Technology in Lesotho."

She is affiliated with the Lesotho Association of Engineers and the Lesotho Architects, Engineers and Surveyors Association.

STAFF:

Mr. Ben NTESO
Counselor
Spouse: Mrs. Lebohang Nteso

Miss Itumeleng Gladys RAFUTHO
First Secretary

Mr. Tsepiso Jeffrey MALEFANE
Third Secretary
Ms. Claudia L. MORAKE
Attaché

Liberia

Embassy of the Republic of Liberia
5201 16th Street, NW
Washington DC 20011
Phone: 202/723-0437

Fax: 202/723-0436
Email: Liberia-Embassy@men.com
Url: http://www.liberiaemb.org

Rachel DIGGS
Ambassador

Date Credentials Presented: 5/16/98

Spouse: Dr. Joseph Diggs

Liberia's new ambassador to the U.S., Rachel Diggs, is a graduate of the University of Geneva School of Interpreters who formerly worked on the World Bank staff. She served there for 12 years as a research analyst in the offices of the directors for international relations, strategic planning, and external affairs.

Mrs. Diggs previously served as coordinator to Liberia's minister of finance, Stephen Allen Tolbert, in Liberia, and as a personal assistant in the office of the secretary-general of the United Nations Conference on Trade and Development (UNCTAD) in Geneva, Switzerland.

In 1992, Mrs. Diggs founded a consulting and catering firm based in Reston, Va. She served as the firm's president and CEO until she was named Liberia's ambassador to the U.S.

She is fluent in English, French, and German and has a working knowledge of Italian and Russian.

Mrs. Diggs has been married for 35 years to Dr. Joseph Diggs, a former assistant professor of radiology at Vanderbilt University in Nashville, Tenn., and at George Washington University in Washington, D.C. They have five sons.

STAFF:

Mr. Konah K. BLACKETT
Minister-Counselor

Mr. John S. MORLU
Minister-Counselor (Maritime)
Spouse: Mrs. Arlie Travick-Morlu

Mr. George M. ARKU
Counselor (Maritime)
Spouse: Mrs. Kari H. J. Arku

Mr. Wilfred S. BANACI
Counselor (Educational)
Spouse: Mrs. Alice M. Banaci

Dr. Abdoulaye W. DUKULE
Counselor (Press)
Spouse: Mrs. Enid F. Dukule

Mr. Alexander H.N. WALLACE III
Counselor (Economic & Trade) and Consul

Mr. Abdulah K. DUNBAR
Second Secretary and Vice Consul
Spouse: Mrs. Beatrice Dunbar

Ms. Enid H. SHANNON
First Secretary (Public Affairs)

Mr. Timonty Dweh SIKLO
First Secretary and Consul
Spouse: Mrs. Joyce W. Siklo

Mr. William S. SALLEY
Second Secretary and Vice Consul
Spouse: Mrs. Salley

Ms. Stataria Ethel COOPER
Attaché (Administrative)

Mrs. Ruth Yei KEHLEAY-THOMAS
Attaché
Spouse: Mr. Leon Thomas

Lithuania

Embassy of the Republic of Lithuania
2622 16th Street, NW
Washington DC 20009
Phone: 202/234-5860
Fax: 202/328-0466
Email: admin@1tembassyus.org
Url: http://www.1tembassyus.prg/

Dr. Stasys SAKALAUSKAS
Ambassador

Date Credentials Presented: 11/12/97

Born: 8/19/46 in Kaunas, Lithuania

Spouse: Mrs. Jurate Sakalauskiene

Dr. Stasys Sakalauskas returned in late 1997 to the Lithuanian embassy in Washington, D.C., where he held the post of counselor between 1994 and 1997. Back in Lithuania,

he did a brief stint during 1997 as secretary of the ministry of foreign affairs.

Between 1991 and 1994, Sakalauskas was head of the division of the Americas and desk officer for the American and Asian division of the ministry of foreign affairs. He was an associate professor at Kaunas Technological University between 1984 and 1991 and an assistant at the Kaunas Polytechnic Institute between 1969 and 1984.

Sakalauskas, who has a Ph.D., wrote his thesis in mechanical engineering at North-West Polytechnic Institute in Leningrad, U.S.S.R., in 1982. He received a diploma in mechanical engineering at Kaunas Polytechnic Institute in Lithuania in 1969. He took the diplomats course at Leeds University in the United Kingdom in 1992 and a special course in technical control at Otto von Guericke Technical University in Magdeburg, Germany, in 1987.

The ambassador, who is married and has two sons, speaks English, Russian, Polish, and Lithuanian.

STAFF:

Ms. Dalia GRYBAUSKAITE
Minister

Mr. Darius SEMASKA
Counselor (Political)
Spouse: Mrs. Ausra Semaskiene

Mrs. Ausra SEMASKIENE
Second Secretary (Political)
Spouse: Mr. Darius Semaska

Major Valdemaras SARAPINAS
Defense, Military, Naval and Air Attaché
Spouse: Mrs. Vyte Sarapiniene

Luxembourg

Embassy of Luxembourg
2200 Massachusetts Avenue, NW
Washington DC 20008
Phone: 202/265-4171
Fax: 202/328-8270
Email: ambalux@earthlink.net

Alphonse BERNS
Ambassador

Date Credentials Presented: 11/25/91

Born: 4/9/52

Spouse: Mrs. Christiane Poeker Berns

Having spent his entire career in Luxembourg's diplomatic corps, Alphonse Berns has extensive experience with political and military issues impacting Europe and the U.S.-Europe axis. He began his career at the Ministry of Foreign Affairs in 1977 in the Eastern Europe and CSCE Department and moved on to become deputy permanent

representative for Luxembourg at the Council of Europe in Strasbourg. From 1979 to 1986, he held the same position at his nation's mission to NATO.

In the interval between his years at NATO and his current Washington posting, Berns held senior positions in Luxembourg's Foreign Ministry, from 1986 to 1988 serving as director for Budget, Finance and Administration, and from 1988 to 1991, as director for International Economic Relations and Cooperation. In his present position, Berns is concurrently accredited as ambassador to Canada and to Mexico.

Berns holds a B.A. in international and EEC law from the University of Aix-en-Provence, France, and has pursued post-graduate studies at the European University Center in Nancy, France. He is married to Christiane Poeker and has one son, Thierry, and one daughter, Isabelle.

STAFF:

Mr. Carlo KRIEGER
Minister (Deputy Chief of Mission)
Spouse: Mrs. Nicole Krieger-Loos

Miss Colette KINNEN
Attaché (Administration)

Macedonia

Embassy of the Republic of Macedonia
3050 K Street, NW, Suite 210
Washington DC 20007
Phone: 202/337-3063
Fax: 202/337-3093
Email: rmacedonia@aol.com

Ljubica Z. ACEVSKA
Ambassador

Date Credentials Presented: 2/6/96

*Born: 2/8/57 in Selo Capari,
Republic of Macedonia*

Ljubica Z. Acevska, the first ambassador of Macedonia to the U.S., brings to her position a mix of experience in academia, private enterprise, and politics.

Acevska, who came to the United States in

1966, obtained her bachelor's degree from Ohio State University in international studies in 1980. From 1981 to 1983, she taught classes at the Ohio State Graduate School in international management and introductory East European politics and economics. During this period, she conducted research for the book, The Other Europe, a text that covers the complex history and nationalist issues of Eastern Europe from 1919 to 1945.

Acevska began working with international trading companies in Washington, D.C., in 1983. From 1983 until 1992, she worked in the field of international development and trade as a consultant and managing director.

In January 1992, Acevska, perceiving the need for the Republic of Macedonia to establish diplomatic relations and gain recognition from the U.S., set up an office in Washington, D.C., from which to base contact and communication between the two countries. The same year, she was recognized as the U.S. representative of the Republic of Macedonia.

Since Macedonia was a newly declared independent country, Acevska dedicated herself to promoting economic investment and world recognition for the young republic. From 1992 to 1995, she maintained close contact with the president of Macedonia and the foreign minister. In 1995, she assisted in various negotiations, meetings, and conferences involving the United Nations, the World Bank, the International Monetary Fund, and the Organization for Security and Cooperation in Europe. The culmination of her efforts resulted in the lifting of an economic embargo, mutual recognition between Greece and Macedonia, and the establishment of full diplomatic relations with the U.S.

Acevska continues to promote economic investment and aid for Macedonia. She participates in conferences and round-table discussions; speaks at universities and forums, on radio and television programs; and meets with foreign correspondents. She is a member of the World Affairs Council of Washington, D.C., and the U.S. Business Council for Southeastern Europe, and is a volunteer with various professional and charity organizations.

The ambassador is the recipient of the 1996 alumni medalist award from the Ohio State University Alumni Association for international distinction in service to humanity.

STAFF:

Mr. Oliver KRLIU
First Secretary (Deputy Chief of Mission)
Spouse: Mrs. Sonja Gievaka-Krliu

Mr. Igor POPOV
Second Secretary (Economic and
    Consular Affairs)

Colonel Metodija VANEVSKI
Defense, Army and Air Attaché
Spouse: Mrs. Paraskeva Vanevski

Madagascar

Embassy of the Republic of Madagascar
2374 Massachusetts Avenue, NW
Washington DC 20008
Phone: 202/265-5525
Fax: 202/265-3034
Email: malagasy@embassy.org
Url: http://www.embassy.org/madagascar

Biclair H.G. ANDRIANANTOANDRO
Chargé d'Affaires, ad interim
Counselor

Date Credentials Presented: 3/21/97

Spouse: Mrs. Bakoly Andrianantoandro

Biclair H.G. Andrianantoandro has headed Madagascar's mission to the U.S. since the departure of Ambassador Pierrot Jocelyn Rajaonarivelo in early 1997. The embassy did not respond to requests for biographical information.

STAFF:

Mr. Raymond Alison RASAMOELINA
Counselor
Spouse: Mrs. Lala Marivelo Rasamoelina

Mrs. Bakoly ANDRIANANTOANDRO
Attaché
Spouse: Mr. Biclair Henri
    Andrianantoandro

Mr. Justin MANARINJARA
Attaché (Financial)
Spouse: Mrs. Georgina Manarinjara

Mr. Djazina Henry RAVELOSON
Attaché
Spouse: Mrs. Razafindrasoa Augustine
    Raveloson

Malawi

Embassy of Malawi
2408 Massachusetts Avenue, NW
Washington DC 20008
Phone: 202/797-1007
Fax: 202/265-0976

Willie CHOKANI
Ambassador

Date Credentials Presented: 3/20/95

Born: in Blantyre, Malawi

Spouse: Mrs. Grace Chokani

In Malawi's struggle for freedom and independence from Britain, Willie Chokani was an active participant. He was among the 1,500 Malawians, including Dr. Hastings K. Banda, who were deported by the British to what was then Southern Rhodesia, now Zimbabwe. But on their release, they became the new rulers of their country.

Chokani was a delegate to the Constitutional Conference that ushered in independence of Malawi in 1964. He was an elected Member of Parliament and was appointed Minister of Labor, but he resigned over a disagreement with the style of government of Banda and his policies toward apartheid South Africa and other issues.

Chokani went into self-imposed exile in Zambia, where he was Headmaster of a secondary school in Ndola and later head of Department at the Northern Technical College. With the coming into power of a new and democratically elected government in Malawi to succeed Dr. Banda's regime, Chokani was appointed ambassador to the United States in 1995.

After attending primary and secondary schools in Blantyre, Chokani received his B.A., M.A., and B.Ed degrees at Delhi University. Later, he earned a second M.A. at Leeds University in England.

After university education, Chokani became a teacher and headmaster of a secondary school at his former primary school at Blantyre Mission.

Chokani has been active in Rotary International since 1975. His wife, Grace, is a teacher by profession. He and his wife have three adult children. One is a medical doctor in Malawi; the second, an associate professor in aerospace and mechanical engineering; and the third, a London-trained electronics engineer. The Chokanis have one grandchild.

STAFF:

Mr. Steven G. KAZEMBE
Counselor
Spouse: Mrs. Martha Kazembe

Mr. MacKienzie M. KUMBATIRA
Counselor and Head of Chancery
Spouse: Mrs. Kumbatira

Mr. Renford W. K. GONDWE
First Secretary (Administration)
Spouse: Mrs. Anncy Gondwe

Mrs. Rosta MSAKA
Second Secretary (Administration)

Mrs. Dorothy AMINI
Third Secretary

Malaysia

Embassy of Malaysia
2401 Massachusetts Avenue, NW
Washington DC 20008
Phone: 202/328-2700
Fax: 202/483-7661
Email: embmaldc@erols.com

Dato' Dali Mahmud HASHIM
Ambassador

Date Credentials Presented: 4/30/96

Born: 12/25/40

Spouse: Mrs. Datin Asmara Laini Hashim

A career foreign service officer, Dato' Dali Mahmud Hashim has been a diplomat for more than three decades and has held the rank of ambassador since 1981. Immediately prior to his appointment to Washington, D.C., he served as Malaysia's ambassador to Indonesia.

Dato' Hashim, who joined the diplomatic corps in 1963, served first in the Malaysian Ministry of Foreign Affairs before receiving his first foreign posting to Ottawa, Canada. Over the years, his overseas appointments have included Bonn, Beijing, Tokyo, Bangkok, Pakistan, Moscow, Stockholm, and Brussels.

Dato' Hashim holds a B.A. in economics from the University of Malaya and speaks Malay and English. He is married to Datin Asmara L. Hashim and has two children.

STAFF:

Dr. Fauziah Mohd TAIB
Dep. Chief of Mission, Minister-Counselor

Mr. Mohd. Sidek HASSAN
Minister-Counselor (Economics)
Spouse: Mrs. Wan Noorlina Wan Hussin

Mr. Abd. Hamid OTHMAN
Minister-Counselor
Spouse: Mrs. Wan Meriam Wan Jusoh

Mr. Umardin Hj. Abdul MUTALIB
First Secretary/Head of Chancery
Spouse: Mrs. Faridah Shariff

Mr. Loon Lai CHEONG
Second Secretary
Spouse: Mrs. Cheong Bee Ling

Mr. Mustapha Ong ABDULLAH
Second Secretary (Financial and Admin.)
Spouse: Mrs. Faridah Ong

Mr. Rosli ISMAIL
Third Secretary
Spouse: Mrs. Azlina Abd. Ghani

Mr. Abu Bakar BACHIK
Attaché (Education)
Spouse: Mrs. Hjh. Maimon Abd. Hamid

Mr. Joohari HASHIM
Asst. Attaché (Education)
Spouse: Mrs. Ramlah Musa

Mr. Hamzah BAKAR
Asst. Attaché (Education)
Spouse: Mrs. Naibah Khalid

Mrs. Norani ABDULLAH
Asst. Attaché (Education)
Spouse: Mr. Idrus Paiman

Mr. Noor Shah SAAD
Asst. Attaché (Education)
Spouse: Mrs. Shamsiah Ahmad

Mr. Abdul Ghafar TAIB
Asst. Attaché (Education)
Spouse: Mrs. Rohani Ismail

Mr. Wan Shuaib Wan MOHD.
Asst. Attaché (Education)
Spouse: Mrs. Aishah Omar

Mr. Mohd Yusoff MUSTAPHA
Asst. Attaché (Education)
Spouse: Mrs. Norani Mohd. Yassin

Mr. Yunos Mohd. SALLEH
Asst. Attaché (Education)
Spouse: Mrs. Faridah Yunos

Mr. Mohd. Redzuan HASAN
Accountant
Spouse: Mrs. Ramizan Hj. Yaacob

Ms. Azian AZIZ
Deputy Account Officer

Mr. Ibrahim Abdul RAHMAN

Asst. Account Officer
Spouse: Mrs. Rosnah Usuldin

Mr. Aziz bin SHAFFIE
Principal Development Officer MARA
Spouse: Mrs. Sakinah Mahmood

Mr. Bahaldin Zainal ABIDINE
Development Officer MARA
Spouse: Mrs. Salmah Ajis

Mr. Ramli MUHAMMAD
Development Officer MARA
Spouse: Mrs. Fatimah

Mr. Mohd Fuad Abd. KAHHAR
Asst. Administrative Officer
Spouse: Mrs. Aliah Ngah Tasir

Colonel Chan Sing CHIA
Defense, Military, Naval, and Air Attaché
Spouse: Mrs. Susan Chia

Major Wan Johan Wan HUSSIN
Asst. Defense, Military, Naval, and
  Air Attaché
Spouse: Mrs. Nor Azidah Abd. Malik

Mr. T. THIAGARAJAN
Attaché (Science)
Spouse: Mrs. Pavany Periasamy

Mali

Embassy of the Republic of Mali
2130 R Street, NW
Washington DC 20008
Phone: 202/332-2249
Fax: 202/332-6603
Email: info@mali.emb,nw.dc.us

Cheick Oumar DIARRAH
Ambassador

Date Credentials Presented: 12/12/95

Born: 6/6/54 in Koutiala, Mali

Spouse: Mrs. Fatou Rella Ba Diarrah

Before assuming his post in Washington, D.C., in 1995, Cheick Oumar Diarrah served as an adviser to the prime minister of the Republic of Mali in 1994-95.

Diarrah's other past governmental positions

include: chief of staff of the State Minister in charge of national education, 1992-95; special envoy on mission to the General Delegation of the North of Mali (Leadership in the Transitional Commission on the People's Salvation), 1991-92; and member of the negotiation missions with the Tuareg rebellion, 1991-92.

In 1989-90, Diarrah was a professor at the Center for Adult Training to the Institute of Political Science in Paris. He was an assistant professor at the Department of Law in Brazzaville from 1984 to 1988.

Diarrah has a doctorate in political science from the University of Bordeaux I and a doctorate in African Studies from the same university's Center for Black Africa's Studies. He also has a degree in advanced studies from the Center for Black Africa's Studies and a degree from the Institute of Political Science of Bordeaux.

Diarrah has published: "Toward Mali's Third Republic," 1991; "Mali, Result of a Disastrous Management," 1990; and "The Mali of Modibo Keita," 1986. All were published by Editions L'Harmattan, Paris.

STAFF:

Mr. Claude Sama TOUNKARA
Counselor
Spouse: Mrs. Kadiatoy Tounkara Tounkara

Mr. Mahamane TOURE
Counselor
Spouse: Mrs. Nana Toure

Mr. Mahmane A. MAIGA
Attaché (Financial)
Spouse: Mrs. Mariame Maiga

Malta

Embassy of Malta
2017 Connecticut Avenue, NW
Washington DC 20008
Phone: 202/462-3611
Fax: 202/387-5470
Url: http://www.magnet.mt

Dr. Mark Anthony MICALLEF
Ambassador

Date Credentials Presented: 5/14/97

Born: 1950 in Malta

A connoisseur of art, Dr. Mark Anthony Micallef presented his credentials as Malta's ambassador to the U.S. to President Clinton in May 1997. He also is Malta's ambassador to Canada.

Micallef was the art correspondent of Malta's daily evening newspaper, The Bulletin. His interest in the arts led him to further his studies at Sotheby's in London, where he worked closely with Peter Wilson, chairman

of Sotheby's. Several world record prices were established for works of art procured by him, according to Micallef. His studies in Paris led him to specialize in Russian works of art.

His successful business association with H.R.H. Prince Vittorio Emanuel di Savoia earned him the title, "Cavaliere di San Maurizio e Lazzaro."

Back in Malta, Micallef involved himself in the local art scene, where he remains an active member of Malta's National Heritage Foundation. He has several publications to his name including "Silver and Banqueting in Malta."

Micallef serves on a committee appointed by Malta's ministry of national culture to supervise the restoration in Florence of Caravaggio's "Beheading of St. John the Baptist."

STAFF:

Mr. Alfred A. FARRUGIA
Counselor and Consul General
Spouse: Mrs. Eva Farrugia

Marshall Islands

Embassy of the Republic of the
Marshall Islands
2433 Massachusetts Avenue, NW
Washington DC 20008
Phone: 202/234-5414
Fax: 202/232-3236

Banny DE BRUM
Ambassador

Date Credentials Presented: 4/30/96

Born: 10/13/56 in Majuro, Marshall Islands

Spouse: Mrs. Honor Note

Before his appointment to Washington, D.C., in January 1996, Banny de Brum served for two years as chairman of the Washington Pacific Committee, which consists of representatives from Pacific embassies based in Washington.

In 1992-93, he was chargé d'Affaires to the

Republic of the Marshall Islands Permanent Mission to the United Nations. Before that, he was deputy chief of the Marshall Islands at the embassy in Washington from 1987 to 1995.

Earlier, de Brum worked for the government of the Marshall Islands, first as legislative liaison officer in 1982-83, then as an energy planning officer between 1983 and 1987.

He received a bachelor's degree in sociology at the University of Regis College in Denver, Colo., in 1981. He attended Xavier High School in Truk in the Federated States of Micronesia from 1973 to 1977.

He is married to Honor Note, and they have four children.

Mauritania

Embassy of the Islamic
Republic of Mauritania
2129 Leroy Place, NW
Washington DC 20008
Phone: 202/232-5700
Fax: 202/319-2623
Url: http://www.embassy.org/mauritania

Ahmed Ould SID'AHMED
Ambassador

Date Credentials Presented: 9/8/97

Born: 8/11/49

*Spouse: Mrs. Mone Mint Ahmed Oul
Sid'Ahmed*

Ahmed Ould Sid'Ahmed served as Mauritania's permanent representative and representative to the United Nations in New York for nearly a year before taking his post as his country's ambassador to the U.S. in 1997.

Between 1993 and 1996, he was ambassador to Belgium, the Netherlands, and Luxembourg and representative to the European Union, with residence in Brussels, Belgium. He was ambassador to Senegal, Guinea Bissau, Cape Verde, Guinea, and the Gambia, with residence in Dakar, Senegal, in 1992-93 and ambassador to Egypt, the Sudan, Ethiopia, Somalia, and Djibouti, with residence in Cairo, Egypt, from 1988 to 1990. From 1990 to 1992, he was secretary of state charged with the Mauritania's relations with Tunisia, Algeria, Morocco, and Libya.

Sid'Ahmed began his career as a diplomat in 1973 when he joined Mauritania's ministry of foreign affairs and cooperation. Between 1975 and 1985, he served as second counselor, then first counselor to Mauritania's first mission to the Untied Nations. During this period, he represented his country on the Security Council and the General Assembly; on the United Nations Economic and Social Council; on the World

Food Council; on the Commission of the Rights of Mankind at the United Nations; at the Conference on the Law of the Sea; and at the U.N. Conference on Water in Argentina.

Sid'Ahmed received his primary, secondary, and higher education in Mauritania. He was presented a diploma in 1973 from "l'Ecole Normale Superieure de Nouakchott."

The ambassador is married and has five children. He speaks French, Arabic, and English.

STAFF:

Mr. Abdellahi OULD KEBD
Counselor

Mr. Mohamed M. OULD HAMADI
First Secretary (Financial)
Spouse: Mrs. Mint Hamady Mohamed
    Mahmoud

Mauritius

Embassy of Republic of Mauritius
4301 Connecticut Avenue, NW- Suite 441
Washington DC 20008
Phone: 202/244-1491
Fax: 202/966-0983
Email: mauritius.embassy@MCIONE.com

Chitmansing JESSERAMSING
Ambassador

Date Credentials Presented: 7/29/96

Born: 8/25/33

Spouse: Mrs. Usha Jesseramsing

Chitmansing Jesseramsing returned to Washington, D.C., for the second time as Mauritius' ambassador to the U.S. in June of 1996. He previously served in the post between 1982 and 1993.

Since he left Washington, Jesseramsing was a senior adviser on foreign affairs to Dr. Ramgoolam, a member of parliament who was the leader of the opposition, between September 1994 and December 1995; and subsequently became his senior adviser when he became the Prime Minister of Mauritius

between February and June 1996.

Even before his first ambassadorship to the U.S., Jesseramsing was assigned to Mauritius' embassy in Washington, as minister-counsellor in 1980-81 and as first secretary between 1972 and 1980. Between 1968 and 1972, he was assigned to Mauritius' missions in New York and Washington. He was attached to the prime minister's office in Mauritius in 1967 and 1968. He began his career as an education officer in 1962.

When he was ambassador to the U.S. the first time, Jesseramsing also was accredited to represent his country to Argentina, Brazil, Mexico, Cuba, Canada, Barbados, Jamaica, and Trinidad and Tobago.

Jesseramsing received a B.A., with honors, and an M.A., Delhi University, Delhi, India. He also earned an M.A. from Georgetown University in Washington, D.C. He has certificates in diplomatic studies from Canberra, Australia, and Oxford, England.

He is married and has two children.

STAFF:

Mr. Mahammed Naguib SOOMAUROO
First Secretary
Spouse: Mrs. Firdosse Soomauroo

Mr. Sneddy Neysen UDAIYAN
Second Secretary

Mr. Peter CRAIG
First Secretary (Commercial)
Spouse: Mrs. Amrita Craig

Mr. Rajendrukumar KEJIOU
Attaché (Administrative)

Mexico

Embassy of Mexico
1911 Pennsylvania Avenue, NW
Washington DC 20006
Phone: 202/728-1600
Fax: 202/728-1698

Jesús F. REYES-HEROLES
Ambassador

Date Credentials Presented: 11/12/97

Born: 1952 in Mexico City, Mex.

*Spouse: Mrs. Regina Cardosa de
    Reyes Heroles*

Jesús Reyes-Heroles, Mexico's new ambassador to the U.S., is a prominent businessman and economics professor who has held high political and governmental posts.

He has been president of the board of Petróleos Mexicanos (PEMEX), the Comisión Federal de Electricidad (CFE), and Luz y Fuerza del Centro (LyFC) and has been on the board of directors of a number of other business enterprises. He is a member of the Editorial Council of Comercio Exterior, the foreign trade magazine of Banco Nacional de Comercio Exterior, S.N.C. and of the economic editorial board of Fondo de Cultura Económica.

From 1991 to 1994, he founded and was chairman of the board and CEO of GEA, Grupo de Economistas Asociados, a private consulting firm. In December 1994, he returned to the public sector as president and CEO of Banco Nacional de Obras y Servicios Públicos (BANOBRAS), an infrastructure development bank. In January 1996, he was appointed Mexico's minister of energy.

In 1972, Reyes-Heroles joined the Partido Revolucionario Institucional (PRI). In 1982, he was an advisor to the Institute for Political, Economic and Social Studies of the PRI during the presidential campaign of Miguel de la Madrid. In 1991, he served as a member of the economic affairs commission. In 1994, he was named personal representative of Ernesto Zedillo, presidential candidate of the PRI, at the National Program of Citizens Encounters. That same year he was coordinator of the National Ideology Commission of the PRI, which produced a proposal for the reform of the party.

Reyes-Heroles was an economics professor at the Tecnólogico Autonómo de Mexico (ITAM), the Unversidad Iberoamericana (UIA), and the Matias Romero Institute for Diplomatic Studies. From 1986 to 1991, he was the academic coordinator of the public finance program of the Instituto Nacional de Administración Publica. From 1991 to 1995 he was the academic coordinator of the economics department at UIA. Since 1976, he has contributed position papers and articles to publications, magazines, and newspapers.

In 1975, he worked as a researcher at the economist's office of the president of Banco de México, and in 1980-81, he served as advisor to the deputy director general. In 1982, he was an advisor to the minister of finance. From 1983 to 1988, he held the position of director general for financial planning at the ministry of finance. From 1988 to 1990, he served as chief of staff to the minister of foreign affairs.

Reyes-Heroles holds a bachelor's degree in economics from the Instituto Tecnológico Autonómo de Mexico. His thesis concerning the effect of policy and income redistribution on Mexico's fiscal system won the 1976 Banamex's economics award in the category of research. He pursued law studies at the Universidad Nacional Autonóma de Mexico, but did not apply for the degree. In 1976, he obtained Fulbright and Banco de Mexico scholarships to undertake a doctoral program at the Massachusetts Institute of Technology, where he earned a Ph.D. degree in 1980.

STAFF:

Mr. Francisco DEL RIO LOPEZ
Minister (Deputy Chief of Mission)
Spouse: Mrs. Elena Calero de del Rio

Mr. Mario Gilberto AGUILAR-SANCHEZ
Minister (Environment)

Mr. Jose Luis ALCUDIA GARCIA
Minister (Agricultural and Forestry)

Mr. Salvador CASSIAN SANTOS
Minister (Consular)
Spouse: Mrs. Victoria Eugenia Moran
de Cassian

Mr. Luis Fernando DE LA CALLE PARDO
Minister (Trade)
Spouse: Mrs. Sophie L. Bidalit

Mr. Salvador DE LARA RANGEL
Minister (Economic)
Spouse: Mrs. Ana Maria Gomis-de Lara

Mr. Gustavo GONZALEZ BAEZ
Minister (Attorney General's Office)
Spouse: Mrs. Lourdes Fernandez
de Gonzalez

Mr. Gustavo MOHAR BETANCOURT
Minister (Migration and Border)
Spouse: Mrs. Maria del Carmen
Berreneche Rodriguez

Mr. Francisco J. OLAVARRIA PATINO
Minister

Mr. Alfredo Guillermo PHILLIPS GREENE
Minister (Economic)

Mr. Oscar ROCHA DABROWSKI
Minister (Special Affairs)

Mr. Alvaro RODRIGUEZ TIRADO
Minister (Cultural)
Spouse: Mrs. Maria S. Carreno
de Rodriguez

Mr. Federico SALAS-LOTFE
Minister (Political and Congressional
Relations)

Mr. Jose Antonio ZABALGOITIA TREJO
Minister (Press)
Spouse: Mrs. Lucia Villalobos Barragan

Mrs. Alma America ALFARO-SIERRA
Counselor (Trade)
Spouse: Mr. Jose Luis Tapis Nava

Mrs. Maria E. ESPINOZA LOYA
DE HOUDE
Counselor (Economic)
Spouse: Mr. Michel Houde

Mr. Nestor Eduardo GALVAN ZAMORA
Counselor (Trade)

Ms. Adriana Josefina GOMEZ GOMEZ
Counselor (Press)
Spouse: Mr. Angel Gil Ordonez

Mr. Carlos LARA MEDINILLA
Counselor (Trade)

Mr. Jose Ignacio MADRAZO-BOLIVAR
Counselor (Political and Congressional)
Spouse: Mrs. Margarita de Otaduy
de Madrazo

Mr. Marco Antonio MARTINEZ-MUNOZ
Counselor (Agricultural and Forestry)
Spouse: Mrs. A. Obregon Santacilia
de Martinez

Mr. Miguel MENDEZ BUENOS AIRES
Counselor (Attorney General's Office)
Spouse: Mrs. Elma Alicia Oviedo
Galdaeno

Mr. Carlos MERCADO VILLALOBOS
Counselor
Spouse: Mrs. Patricia C. Zesati Farias

Miss Maria Del Pilar R.
MORALES ARIAS
Counselor (Political and Congressional)

Mr. Rodolfo QUILANTAN ARENAS
Counselor (Legal)
Spouse: Mrs. Patricia Lourdes Tapia
de Quilantan

Mr. Jesus RODRIGUEZ MONTERO
Counselor (Financial)
Spouse: Mrs. Erendira Davalos
de Rodriguez

Mrs. Marcela SERRATO-DE TREVINO
Counselor (Energy)
Spouse: Mr. Jose Trevino-Botti

Mr. Jose Juan TREVINO-BOTTI
Counselor (Trade)
Spouse: Mrs. Marcela Serrato-de Trevino

Mr. Raul URTEAGA TRANI
Counselor (Trade)
Spouse: Mrs. Julia Urteaga

Mr. Raul VALLEJO LARA
Counselor
Spouse: Mrs. Patricia Villafuerte
de Vallejo

Miss Alicia BUENROSTRO MASSIEU
First Secretary

Miss Luz Maria DE LA MORA

First Secretary (Trade)

Mr. Bryan Andrew ELWOOD SALIDO
First Secretary (Trade)

Miss Gabriela M. GERARD RIVERO
First Secretary

Mr. Alejandro MUNOZ LEDO
First Secretary (Financial)

Mr. Ricardo PINEDA ALBARRAN
First Secretary (Migration and Border)
Spouse: Mrs. Silvia Esther Cruz Palma

Mr. Alejandro POZOS-GUERRERO
First Secretary (Trade)
Spouse: Mrs. Araceli Juana Hernandez
Briones

Mr. Arturo CHAVARRIA BALLEZA
Second Secretary (Consular)
Spouse: Mrs. Luz Maria Velasco
de Chavarria

Mr. Rodrigo ENCALADA PEREZ
Second Secretary (Administrative)

Mr. Juan Jose GOMEZ
Second Secretary

Mr. Juan Carlos MENDOZA SANCHEZ
Second Secretary (Office of the Deputy
Chief of Mission)
Spouse: Mrs. Alejandrina Diaz
de Mendoza

Mr. Arturo SARUKHAN-CASAMITJANA
Second Secretary (Political and
Congressional)

Ms. Reyna TORRES MENIVIL
Second Secretary (Political and
Congressional)

Mr. Emilio VARELA HAMUI
Second Secretary (Administrative)
Spouse: Mrs. Perla Crespo de Varela

Mr. Jose Ramon LORENZO
DOMINGUEZ
Third Secretary (Economic)

Mr. Juan Manuel SALDIVAR CANTU
Third Secretary (Cultural)

Ms. Katia Lilia SEGURA CALDERON
Third Secretary (Political and
Congressional)

Ms. Monica Maria A.
VELARDE MENDEZ
Third Secretary (Consular)

Mr. Juan Carlos CARRILLO CABRERA
Attaché (Administrative)
Spouse: Ms. Yolanda Gallegos Rodriguez

Mrs. Lea CORTI
Attaché (Office of the Ambassador)
Spouse: Mr. Jesus Arturo Garcia

Mrs. Martha Graciela DUARTE PINA

Attaché (Office of the Ambassador)

Mrs. Mercedes ESQUIVEL DE ANTUNES
Attaché (Office of the Deputy Chief of
  Mission)
Spouse: Mr. Joao de Deus Barbosa
  Antunes

Mr. Armando FERNANDEZ GALLAGA
Attaché (Agriculture)
Spouse: Mrs. Maria Teresa Gutierrez
  Zamora

Mr. Alberto FONCERRADA BERUMEN
Attaché (Migration and Border)

Miss Liliana GONZALEZ RAMIREZ
Attaché (Press)

Ms. Lourdes VILCHIS PLATAS
Attaché (Consular)

Mr. Jose Martin GARCIA SANJINES
Asst. Attaché (Revenue and Customs)
Spouse: Mrs. Patricia Gomez de Garcia

Mr. Arturo Luis German JESSEL PEREZ
Asst. Attaché (Trade)
Spouse: Mrs. Maria D. Sandoval de Jessel

Mr. Raul Angel SICILIA BARBA
Asst. Attaché (Revenue and Customs)
Spouse: Mrs. Mary Cristi Concha de
  Sicilia

General Eduardo Alejandro MARTINEZ
  ADUNA
Defense, Military, and Air Attaché

Lt. Colonel Raymuto Luis LARIOS SAIZ
Military Attaché
Spouse: Mrs. Guadalupe Gutierrez
  de Larios

Rear Admiral Antonio VAZQUEZ DEL
  MERCADO MUNOZ
Naval Attaché
Spouse: Mrs. Matilde Malpica Valverde

Colonel German NORIEGA MEJIA
Asst. Defense and Air Attaché
Spouse: Mrs. Maria Isabel Velazquez
  de Noriega

Lt. Colonel Juan SAUCEDO ALMAZAN
Asst. Defense Attaché
Spouse: Mrs. Hermelinda Torres
  de Saucedo

Lt. Colonel Lorenzo CANO JIMENEZ
Asst. Military Attaché
Spouse: Mrs. Luisa Fernanda Campillo
  Garcini de Cano

Lt. Colonel Dagoberto ESPINOSA
  RODRIGUEZ
Asst. Military Attaché
Spouse: Mrs. Carmen Elena Fierro
  de Espinosa

Captain Bruno Ismael VARAS REYES
Asst. Naval Attaché
Spouse: Mrs. Matilde Gonzalez de Varas

Agricultural and Forestry Minister
1911 Pennsylvania Avenue, NW
Washington DC 20006
Phone: 202/728-1720 Fax: 202/728-1728

Consular Office
2827 16th Street, NW
Washington DC 20009
Phone: 202/736-1000 Fax: 202/797-8458

Defense, Military and Air Attaché
1911 Pennsylvania Avenue, NW
Washington DC 20006
Phone: 202/728-1740 Fax: 202/728-1741

Financial Counselor
1615 L Street, NW, Suite 310
Washington DC 20005
Phone: 202/338-9010 Fax: 202/338-9244

Naval Attaché
1911 Pennsylvania Avenue, NW
Washington DC 20006
Phone: 202/728-1760 Fax: 202/728-1767

Tourism Minister
1911 Pennsylvania Avenue, NW
Washington DC 20006
Phone: 202/728-1750 Fax: 202/728-1758

Trade Minister
1911 Pennsylvania Avenue, NW
Washington DC 20006
Phone: 202/728-1700 Fax: 202/728-1712

Trade Negotiations
1911 Pennsylvania Avenue, NW
Washington DC 20006
Phone: 202/728-1687 Fax: 202/296-4904

Micronesia

Embassy of the Federated
  States of Micronesia
1725 N Street, NW
Washington DC 20036
Phone: 202/223-4383
Fax: 202/223-4391
Email: fsmamb@aol.com

Jesse Bibiano MAREHALAU
Ambassador

Date Credentials Presented: 2/5/90

Personal: Born 12/25/48

Spouse: Mrs. Martha Lorerang Marehalau

Having begun his career in the Yap state government, within the now Federated States of Micronisia (FSM), Marehalau has since 1980 served the FSM national government as an officer in its foreign service. Prior to that, he had held the positions of assistant fisheries officer and chief of marine resources within the Yap state government.

Since the onset of his foreign service career, Marehalau has served both at home and abroad. Having begun in the Department of External Affairs in Kolonia, Pohnpei, he has since been at varying times the Micronesia's first Permanent Representative to the United Nations, Deputy Representative - and then Representative - of Micronesia to the U.S. and, since 1990, Micronesian Ambassador to the U.S.

As ambassador, Marehalau has worked not only to expand public knowledge of Micronesia and expand support for its continued success as an independent state, but also to aprise U.S. and multilateral institutional investors of opportunities within the Federated States. Along these lines, he has stated that "We are working hard to privatize many areas of our economy and bring a new era of economic well-being and self-sufficiency to our people through increased development of our natural resources. Sustainable development is our principle guiding light."

Marehalau was educated at Chaminade University and the University of Hawaii, both in Honolulu, and at the University of Guam. He speaks Ulithian, Yapese, Trukese and English. He is married and has one son.

STAFF:

Mr. Ringlen P. RINGLEN
Minister (Deputy Chief of Mission)
Spouse: Mrs. Mary Lee Ringlen

Mr. Samson E. PRETRICK
First Secretary (Political and Economic)
Spouse: Mrs. Lavernie L. Pretrick

Moldova

Embassy of the Republic of Moldova
2102 S Street, NW
Washington DC 20008
Phone: 202/667-1130
Fax: 202/667-1204
Email: 103714.2137@CompuServe.com

Nicolae TAU
Ambassador

Date Credentials Presented: 12/09/93

Born: 3/25/48 in Kahul region of Moldova

Spouse: Mrs. Zinaida Tau

Before coming to Washington, Nicolae Tau served as Moldavia's minister of foreign affairs from 1990 to 1993.

Between 1986 and 1990, he was the leader of the Chinisau Communist Party Committee. Before that, he was head of the regional executive authorities, starting in 1978. Between 1970 and 1978, he was engineer, chief engineer, and head of a production association.

Tau studied at the Academy of Social Sciences in Sofia, Bulgaria, between 1981 and 1983 and was awarded a doctor of economics degree. He graduated in 1970 from the State Agrarian University of Moldova in engineering.

Tau is married and has two children. Besides his native Romanian, he speaks English, French, Russian, and Bulgarian.

STAFF:

Mr. Tudor GOIA
Minister-Counselor (Deputy Chief of
    Mission)
Spouse: Mrs. Tamara Goia

Mr. Iurie RENITA
Counselor (Political)
Spouse: Mrs. Lidia Renita

Mr. Andrei BOBOC
First Secretary (Commercial & Economic)
Spouse: Mrs. Marina Boboc

Mr. Andrei POPOV
Second Secretary (Political)
Spouse: Mrs. Natalia Popov

Ms. Svetlana RUSCIUC
Attaché (Chief of Chancery)

Mongolia

Embassy of Mongolia
2833 M Street, NW
Washington DC 20007
Phone: 202/333-7117
Fax: 202/298-9227

Jalbuu CHOINHOR
Ambassador

Date Credentials Presented: 12/12/95

Born: 1/15/44 in Mongolia

Spouse: Mrs. Sanjmyatav Maijargal

For the five years preceding his arrival in Washington, D.C., as ambassador, Jalbuu Choinhor served as Deputy Foreign Minister in Mongolia. He is concurrently Mongolia's non-resident ambassador to Canada.

Choinhor's career with the Mongolian Ministry of Foreign Affairs began in 1970 when he joined the department of international organizations. He stayed in that post for two years, then spent the next three years as part of the Mongolian Permanent Mission to the United Nations office in Geneva. Between 1975 and 1985, he returned to Ulaanbaatar, Mongolia to serve in the ministry's press and information department and the policy planning department. He was director of the Asian Department in the ministry between 1987 and 1990, after which he took the position of deputy minister for foreign affairs.

Choinhor graduated from the Moscow State Institute of International Relations (1970) and holds a Ph.D. in history from the Moscow Diplomatic Academy. In addition to his native Mongolian, Choinhor speaks fluent English and Russian. He and his wife have one daughter, Tserendulam. His hobbies include translation of Shakespeare.

STAFF:

Mr. Khalzkhuu NARANKUU
Counselor (Economic)
Spouse: Mrs. Sukhbaatar Amgalan

Mrs. Ragchaa BAASAN
First Secretary

Mr. Luuzan GENDENBAATAR
Second Secretary
Spouse: Mrs. Darjaa Amgalan

Mr. Jambaljamts OD
Second Secretary
Spouse: Mrs. Surenhuu Munhsuren

Mrs. Bavuusuren BAYASGALAN
Attaché (Trade and Economic)
Spouse: Mr. Nyamjav Batbayer

Colonel Gur RAGCHAA
Defense and Military Attaché
Spouse: Mrs. Dambaravijaa Lhagvasuren

Morocco

Embassy of the Kingdom of Morocco
1601 21st Street, NW
Washington DC 20009
Phone: 202/462-7979
Fax: 202/462-7643
Email: sifamausa@trident.net

Mohamed BENAISSA
Ambassador

Date Credentials Presented: 6/23/93

Born: 1/3/37 in Asilah (Tangiers)

Spouse: Mrs. Laila Hajoui-Benaissa

An expert on world food issues, Mohamed Benaissa has had a long career as a government servant at the national and international levels and as a politician and elected official.

Having begun his career as chargé d'information at Morocco's Permanent Mission to the United Nations in New York, he went on to serve the U.N. itself as an information officer in New York and Addis Ababa. In 1967, he began his association with food concerns, working from 1967 to 1971 as a regional information advisor for the Food and Agriculture Organization (FAO).

Moving on to FAO headquarters in Rome, Benaissa eventually rose to become director of the FAO's information division and in 1975 was named assistant secretary general of the United Nations World Food Conference, which met in both New York and Rome. While continuing his association with food and development issues as an independent consultant, Benaissa entered politics in 1976, when he was elected a councilman of the Asilah City Council. Elected to the Moroccan Parliament the next year, he remained in his seat until 1992, concurrently serving as Mayor of Asilah. From 1985 until his appointment as U.S. ambassador, he was Morocco's Minister of Culture.

In addition to his other responsibilities, Benaissa was chief editor of an Arabic and French daily newspaper. He is the author of "Grains De Peau" (Shoof Publishers, Casablanca, 1974).

Benaissa holds a B.A. in communications from the University of Minnesota. He studied in 1964 at Columbia University as a recipient of a Rockefeller Foundation Fellowship for Communications Research. In addition to his native French and Arabic, he speaks fluent English, Spanish, and Italian. He is married and has five children.

STAFF:

Mr. Mustapha CHERKAOUI
Minister (Deputy Chief of Mission)

Mr. Abdelhamid TOUROUGUI
Counselor
Spouse: Mrs. Khadija Tourougui

Mr. Abdeljebbar AZZAOUI
Counselor

Mr. Thami EL MEZOUARI EL GLAOUI
Counselor (Political)

Mr. Mohamed SALOUI
Counselor
Spouse: Mrs. Kaoutar Saloui

Mr. Rachid Ismaili ALAOUI
First Secretary

Mr. Lahcen BAKHAR
First Secretary

Mr. Tarik EL MESSOUSSI GARTI
First Secretary
Spouse: Mrs. Ihssane Nassereddine

Ms. Amina ELAISSAMI
First Secretary

Mr. Abdelouahed BENMOUNA
Counselor (Paymaster General)
Spouse: Mrs. Rachida Benmouna

Mr. Rahmoune ESSALHI
First Secretary

Ms. Faiza MEHDI
First Secretary

Mr. Noureddine GHIATI
Attaché

General Mohamed EL KOSTALI
Defense, Military, Naval and Air Attaché
Spouse: Mrs. El Kostali

Captain Abdelkader AMAL
Asst. Defense Attaché
Spouse: Mrs. Amal

Press Office
1821 Jefferson Place, NW
Washington DC 20036
Phone: 202/462-7979

Cultural Office
1821 Jefferson Place, NW
Washington DC 20036
Phone: 202/462-7979

Economic Office
1821 Jefferson Place, NW
Washington DC 20036
Phone: 202/462-7979

Consular Office
1821 Jefferson Place, NW
Washington DC 20036
Phone: 202/462-7979

Mozambique

Embassy of the Republic of Mozambique
1990 M Street, NW - Suite 570
Washington DC 20036
Phone: 202/293-7146
Fax: 202/835-0245
Email: embamoc@aol.com

Marcos Geraldo NAMASHULUA
Ambassador

Date Credentials Presented: 7/29/96

Born: 10/15/42 in Mozambique

Spouse: Mrs. Lucia M.P. Namashulua

Marcos Geraldo Namashulua came to Washington, D.C., from Mozambique's Ministry of Foreign Affairs, where he had been director of the division for Asia and Oceania for a year. For the previous 15-year period, he was an officer in the U.N.

Between 1989 and 1991, he was assistant resident representative in the United Nations Development Program, Equatorial Guinea. Then he became a U.N. political affairs officer, first in the division for regional cooperation and self determination between 1991 and 1994 and later in the department of political affairs. He was assigned to the U.N. Secretariat in New York in the division for U.N. Council for Namibia between 1979 and 1989.

Before his U.N. career, Namashulua was in the academic world. He was a lecturer in political science and black studies departments at the University of Massachusetts in 1978-79; an assistant professor in the sociology/political science department at Salem State College in Salem, Mass., in 1977-78; an instructor in African and Afro-American studies at Brandeis University in Waltham, Mass., between 1973 and 1979; and an instructor in the African American studies department at Trenton State University in Trenton, N.J. in 1972-73. He was a foreign languages teacher at Trenton High School in Trenton, N.J. between 1971 and 1973.

After receiving a B.A. in political science from the University of Bridgeport in Bridgeport, Conn., in 1969, Namashulua earned an M.A. in international relations from Fordham University in New York City in 1972. In 1976, he satisfied all requirements toward a Ph.D/ABD in comparative politics at Boston University except for the dissertationon.

Namashulua was president of Uniao Nacional dos Estudantes de Mocambique (UNEMO) in the United States in 1968 and general secretary of the organization between 1972 and 1975. He is a former member of the American Political Science Association, the International Political Science Association, and the African Studies Association.

Namashulua is married and has two children. He is fluent in Portuguese, English, Spanish, Kiswahili, and Makonde and has a working knowledge of French and Latin.

STAFF:

Mrs. Esperanca MACHAVELA
Minister/Counselor
Spouse: Mr. Joaquim Carvelho

Mr. Salvador NAMBURETE
Counselor (Economic)
Spouse: Mrs. Luisa Florencia Namburete

Mr. Salvador ADRIANO
Second Secretary

Mr. Ismael VALIGY
Second Secretary (Consular)

Mrs. Guida ALEGRE
Attaché (Finance)

Myanmar (formerly Burma)

Embassy of the Union of Myanmar
2300 S Street, NW
Washington DC 20008-4089
Phone: 202/332-9044
Fax: 202/332-9046
Url: http://www.myanmar.com

Tin WINN
Ambassador

Date Credentials Presented: 10/9/96

Born: 5/22/42

Spouse: Mrs. Daw Khia Nu

Before coming to Washington as the Union of Myanmar's ambassador, Tin Winn was his country's ambassador to the King of Thailand between 1994 and 1996. The Union of Myanmar formerly was known as Burma.

Winn joined the Army in 1965 and served in various capacities up to the rank of lieutenant colonel. After his retirement from the army, he was appointed ambassador to the Republic of Korea, where he served from 1990 to 1994. Between 1962 and 1965, Winn was a tutor in the department of philosophy at the University of Yangon.

He studied at Yangon University and holds a bachelor of arts degree. He is a registered lawyer. Winn's wife, Daw Khia Nu, is a professor in the department of philosophy at Mawlamyine University. They have one son and two daughters.

The ambassador enjoys reading and golf.

STAFF:

Mr. Thaung TUN
Minister (Deputy Chief of Mission)
Spouse: Mrs. Sanda Lwin

Mr. Khin Maung AYE
Minister-Counselor
Spouse: Mrs. Khin May Oo

Mr. Tha Aung NYUN
First Secretary

Spouse: Mrs. Mar Mar Kyaw

Ms. Hmway Hmway KHYNE
Second Secretary

Mr. Wai LINN
Attaché (Commercial)
Spouse: Mrs. Thein Daw Thein

Mr. Sein NYUNT
Attaché

Ms. Tin Mya WIN
Attaché

Ms. Moe Thu ZAR
Attaché

Colonel Thet WIN
Military, Naval and Air Attaché
Spouse: Mrs. Win Win Yee

Military, Naval, and Air Attaché Office
2300 California Street, NW
Washington DC 20008
Phone: 202/332-1938

Namibia

Embassy of the Republic of Namibia
1605 New Hampshire Avenue, NW
Washington DC 20009
Phone: 202/986-0540
Fax: 202/986-0443
Email: embnamibia@aol.com

Veiccoh K. NGHIWETE
Ambassador

Date Credentials Presented: 10/9/96

Born: 5/28/52

Spouse: Mrs. Julia K. Nghiwete

His country's second ambassador to the U.S. since Namibia gained its independence in 1990, Veiccoh K. Nghiwete is also non-resident high commissioner to Canada. He had participated in the liberation war of Namibia against the apartheid regime of South Africa.

Before and after the independence of his country, he represented Namibia at various regional and international meetings,

seminars, and conferences. He was the high commissioner of his country to the United Kingdom and Northern Ireland from 1991 to mid-1996, serving also as non-resident ambassador to Ireland and Namibia's representative to the Commonwealth secretariat. While stationed in London, he served as a member of the executive committee of the board of directors of the Commonwealth Institute from 1992 to 1995, a member of the board of representatives of the Commonwealth Fund for Technical Cooperation, a board member of the Commonwealth Deaf Society, and as the vice president of the Commonwealth Royal Overseas League from 1991 to 1996.

Nghiwete arrived in Washington, D.C., in 1990 to open an embassy and remained until mid-1991 in the capacity of Namibian chargé d'affaires a.i. Beginning in 1974 he served in various posts for SWAPO (South West African Peoples Organization). From 1988-1990, he was SWAPO's chief representative to the Republic of Zambia and Central Africa. He served as the chief administrative officer for the department of foreign affairs at SWAPO headquarters, based in Luanda, Angola, from 1980 to 1984.

From 1974 to 1980 Nghiwete participated in the liberation war. He was a member of the PLAN (People's Liberation Army of Namibia) military council, and he served as the regional political commissar and the field commander (northern front) in Namibia.

Nghiwete obtained his M.A. degree in economic and diplomatic studies from the University of Keele in the United Kingdom in 1988. He holds a diploma of distinction in computer science from the Hendon Secretarial College (1995); a private pilot certificate from Flight Services at Washington's Dulles Airport (1997); and a post-graduate diploma in economics and international relations from the University of London in 1986. He also holds a high national diploma in public administration and econometrics from South Devon College of Art and Technology, Torquay, UK (1985), and a diploma from Odessa (Ukraine) Military Academy in the former USSR in 1977.

The ambassador is married with five children. His hobbies are soccer, tennis, golf, gardening, and clay pigeon shooting games.

STAFF:

Mr. Usko S. SHIVUTE
Minister-Counselor
Spouse: Mrs. Frieda T. Shivute

Mr. Gerry Wilson MUNYAMA
Counselor (Commercial)
Spouse: Mrs. Selma Namupaafita Munyama

Mr. Immanuel IYAMBO
First Secretary
Spouse: Mrs. Sharon Rudolfine Iyambo

Mrs. N. Elina MATENGU
First Secretary

Mr. Joel EELU
Second Secretary

Ms. Geraldine PETERS
Third Secretary

Nepal

Royal Nepalese Embassy
2131 Leroy Place, NW
Washington DC 20008
Phone: 202/667-4550
Fax: 202/667-5534

Lava Kumar DEVACOTA

Chargé d'Affaires, ad interim

Date Credentials Presented: 9/24/97

Spouse: Mrs. Neeru Devacota

Nepal's ambassadorship to the U.S. was vacated when Ambassador Bhekh Bahadur Thapa left the post in September 1997. A new ambassador was expected to be appointed during the summer of 1998. The embassy did not respond to requests for biographical information on the chargé d'affaires.

STAFF:

Mr. Mukti BHATTA
First Secretary
Spouse: Mrs. Bhatta

Mr. Lekha Nath BHATTARAI
Attaché
Spouse: Mrs. Apsara Bhattarai

Lt. Colonel Pradyumna KATTEL
Military Attaché
Spouse: Mrs. Bana Kattel

Netherlands

Royal Netherlands Embassy
4200 Linnean Avenue, NW
Washington DC 20008
Phone: 202/244-5300
Fax: 202/362-3430
Url: http://www.netherlands_embassy.org

Joris Michael VOS

Ambassador

Date Credentials Presented: 11/12/97

Born: 1940

Spouse: Mrs. Yvonne M. Rydemark Vos

The diplomatic career of Joris Michael Vos, the Netherlands's ambassador to the U.S., has spanned three decades with assignments on four continents. His most recent post was in The Hague as under secretary for political affairs in the ministry of foreign affairs from 1994 until 1996. In the job he chaired the European Union's political committee during the Netherlands presidency of the union in the first half of 1997.

After obtaining a law degree from the University of Utrecht, the Netherlands, Vos began his diplomatic career in 1968 in Prague, Czechoslovakia, where he served for two years as third secretary at the Royal Netherlands embassy. In 1970, he joined the Netherlands embassy in Accra, Ghana, as second secretary. In 1972, he returned to The Hague, and, after an 18-month period at the Middle East desk, he served for four years as the private secretary of the minister of foreign affairs.

In 1977, he was posted to Washington, D.C., as counselor at the Netherlands embassy where he dealt with politico-military affairs. He returned to Europe in 1980 and was stationed for two years as deputy chief of mission at the Netherlands embassy in Belgrade, Yugoslavia. In 1982, he became head of the military cooperation section of the Netherlands ministry of foreign affairs, and later, director of the Atlantic cooperation and security affairs department of the ministry of foreign affairs until 1986. In that year, he was appointed ambassador to Australia, a position he held until 1990 when he became the Netherlands ambassador to the USSR, and from 1991 forward, to the Russian Federation.

The ambassador is married to Yvonne M. Rydemark, who has a degree in history of art from the Courtahuld Institute at London University. They have two children, Sebastian and Annabelle. The ambassador's hobbies are classical music, fine arts, literature, golf, and skiing.

STAFF:

Mr. Robert Jan VAN HOUTUM
Minister (Deputy Chief of Mission)

Mr. Fermin P. CORONEL
Minister (Aruba)
Spouse: Mrs. Marisa Castellano

Mr. Leendert SOLLEVELD
Minister (Economic)

Mr. Herbert Pieter BARNARD
Counselor (Health and Welfare)
Spouse: Mrs. Hermina Cornelia Merkelijn

Ms. Magdalina Anna Jacobs
DE PLANQUE
Counselor (Press and Agriculture)
Spouse: Mr. James C. Humphreys

Mr. Phillip A. DE WAAL
Counselor (Economic)
Spouse: Mrs. Marie Jose de Waal
De Bourayne

Mr. Jan J. GROENEVELD

Counselor (Agriculture)
Spouse: Mrs. Pieternella Maria van
der sar Groeneveld

Mr. Leendert HARTEVELD
Counselor
Spouse: Mrs. Carmen Harteveld Heemels

Mr. Paulus J. M. HOFHUIS
Counselor (Environment)
Spouse: Mrs. Wilhelmina A.P.M. van
den Brekel

Mr. Kees PLANQUE
Counselor (Scientific and Technology)
Spouse: Mrs. Anna Maria Grimbergen

Mr. Antonius M. SCHELLEKENS
Counselor

Mr. Hendrik Jan Jurriaan SCHUWER
Counselor (Political)
Spouse: Mrs. Anna Lena Elisabeth
Boman Schuwer

Mr. Eduard Victor SJERP
Counselor (Transportation)

Mr. Jan Willem A. VAN DEN
WALL BAKE
Counselor (Financial)
Spouse: Mrs. Jasmenka Ilijas

Mr. Rene DE JONG
First Secretary (Administrative)
Spouse: Mrs. Linda de Jong Hottentot

Mr. Jozef L. IJZERMANS
First Secretary (Economic)
Spouse: Mrs. Maria C. T. Derckx

Mrs. Johanna Gerarda Maria RUIGROK
First Secretary (Political)
Spouse: Mr. Everard Peet

Mr. Johan Christiaan VAN DRECHT
First Secretary and Consul
Spouse: Mrs. Kim Hoa van Drecht

Mr. Stefanus VAN WERSCH
First Secretary
Spouse: Mrs. Liliane Ezzat Resk Fawzi

Mr. Lauentius WESTHOFF
First Secretary (Economic)
Spouse: Mrs. Caroline B. F. Havers

Mrs. Maria C. T. DERCKX
Second Secretary (Press and Culture)
Spouse: Mr. Jozef L. Ijzermans

Mr. Abraham GORREE
Second Secretary
Spouse: Mrs. Elisabeth Gorree

Mrs. Johanna SORENSEN
Second Secretary (Political)

Ms. Yvonne RIJNDERS
Attaché and Vice Consul

Mr. Marcus H. SLINGENBERG
Attaché (Agriculture)

Spouse: Mrs. Christiane C.
  Arriens-Slingenberg

Mr. Gerrit VAN DER WEES
Attaché (Science and Technology)
Spouse: Mrs. Mei Chin van der Wees-Chen

Mr. Benedictus EIJBERGEN
Asst. Attaché (Transportation)
Spouse: Mrs. Urmiladebie Garib

Mr. Marinus J. M. GOOS
Asst. Attaché (Def. Cooperation Material)
Spouse: Mrs. Maria J. de Valk Goos

Captain Simon J. BUNT
Defense Cooperation Attaché
Spouse: Mrs. Anne Marie Bunt Schol

Major General Cornelus VAN DEN BURG
Defense & Air Attaché
Spouse: Mrs. Jantje M. van den Burg

Colonel Anthonie Franciscus DE NIJS
Military Attaché & Asst. Defense Attaché
Spouse: Mrs. Maria Hendrika Cornelia
  de Nijs

Captain Wilhelmus Izak WILMS
Naval Attaché and Asst. Defense Attaché
Spouse: Mrs. Pieternella Wilms van Donk

Lt. Colonel Reinhold HARTING
Asst. Military Attaché
Spouse: Mrs. Lauke Maria Schonherr

Commander Freek Sjoerd VLEER
Asst. Naval Attaché
Spouse: Mrs. Jantina Weesing Vleer

Lt. Colonel Johannes SMIT
Asst. Air Attaché
Spouse: Mrs. Gerarda Wendelina Smit Ploeg

New Zealand

Embassy of New Zealand
37 Observatory Circle, NW
Washington DC 20008
Phone: 202/328-4800
Fax: 202/667-5227
Email: nzemb@dc.infi.net
Url: http://www.emb.com/nzemb

L. John WOOD
Ambassador

Date Credentials Presented: 6/23/94

Born: 3/31/44 in Kaikoura, New Zealand

Spouse: Ms. Rosemary Ann Newell

John Wood, who joined his country's Ministry of Foreign Affairs in 1969, served in Washington previously, between 1984-87, as minister, deputy chief of mission. In the interim, between 1987-90, he served as ambassador to Iran with concurrent accreditation to Pakistan and Turkey.

Immediately before coming to Washington, he was deputy secretary for economic and trade relations in the New Zealand Ministry of External Relations and Trade. His other assignments include: director, North Asia Division, Ministry of External Relations and Trade; head, European Division, Ministry of Foreign Affairs; first secretary, later counsellor and consul-general, Bonn, Germany; adviser to the Prime Minister in his Department of International Affairs; and second and later first secretary of the New Zealand Embassy in Tokyo.

Wood earned an M.A. with first class honors from Canterbury University in 1965 and a B.A. with honors from Balliol College (Oxford) in 1968. He is married and has one child.

Wood was scheduled to return to New Zealand in the summer of 1998 when he will be replaced by the former prime minister, J.B. Bolges as ambassador to the U.S.

STAFF:

Mr. George Robert TROUP
Minister (Deputy Chief of Mission)
Spouse: Mrs. Hilary Troup

Mrs. Jan HENDERSON
Counselor (Political)
Spouse: Mr. David Henderson

Dr. Bill JOLLY
Counselor
Spouse: Mrs. Tanya Jolly

Mr. Alwyn Evan MOORES
Counselor (Commercial and Trade
  Commissioner)
Spouse: Mrs. Judith Moores

Mr. Michael GRACE
First Secretary (Admin.) and Consul
Spouse: Mrs. Penelope Anne Grace

Mr. John WILLSON
First Secretary
Spouse: Mrs. Janice Willson

Mr. Philip LEWIN
First Secretary (Trade)
Spouse: Mrs. Carolyn Lewin

Ms. Kirsty GRAHAM
Second Secretary (Political)
Spouse: Mr. Craig Marris

Mr. Tony FAUTUA
Second Secretary (Trade and Economics)
Spouse: Mrs. Ina Fautua

Ms. Emily RICHELTS
Asst. Attaché (Administrative)

Air Commander Maurice MANTTAN
Defense, Naval and Air Attaché
Spouse: Mrs. Lynette Manttan

Lt. Colonel Alan JOHNSTON
Military Attaché & Asst. Defense Attaché
Spouse: Mrs. Julie Johnston

Commander Roger MCDONALD
Asst. Naval Attaché
Spouse: Mrs. Diane McDonald

Wing Commander Terence GREENING
Asst. Air Attaché
Spouse: Mrs. Elizabeth Anne Greening

Nicaragua

Embassy of Nicaragua
1627 New Hampshire Avenue, NW
Washington DC 20009
Phone: 202/939-6570
Fax: 202/939-6542

Francisco Xavier AGUIRRE-SACASA
Ambassador

Date Credentials Presented: 5/14/97

*Spouse: Mrs. Maria de los A.
  Sacasa Aguirre*

Francisco Xavier Aguirre-Sacasa came to his post as Nicaragua's ambassador to the U.S. from the World Bank, which he joined in 1969 under the Young Professionals Program.

Aguirre-Sacasa's most recent position at the World Bank was as director of the operations evaluation department from 1995 to 1997. From 1990 to 1995, he was director of the Central Africa and Indian Ocean department.

His other jobs at the World Bank included: director of external affairs department, 1988-90; senior advisor to the vice president, Latin America, and the Caribbean region, 1987-

88; assistant director for agricultural projects, Latin America and the Caribbean region, 1986-87; chief, trade finance and industry division, Eastern and Southern Africa region, 1983-86; chief, Chile, Ecuador, and Peru division, Latin American and the Caribbean region, 1977-83.

Aguirre-Sacasa received a B.S. in Foreign Service from Georgetown University in Washington, D.C. in 1966 and a J.D. at Harvard University in Cambridge, Mass., in 1969.

He has contributed articles frequently to The Boston Globe, The Christian Science Monitor, The Wall Street Journal, and The Washington Post.

Aguirre-Sacasa has addressed student clubs and graduate seminars at Dartmouth, Georgetown, Harvard, Stanford, Tufts, UCLA, and the University of California at Berkeley. He has spoken to the Royal Tropical Institute in Amsterdam, the Inter-party Group on Development of the British House of Commons, the Pan American Society of Northern California, and the Save the Children Foundation

STAFF:

Mr. Juan M. GARCIA
Minister-Counselor

Mr. Harold RIVAS REYES
Minister-Counselor and Consul General
Spouse: Mrs. Jeanette Rivas

Niger

Embassy of the Republic of Niger
2204 R Street, NW
Washington DC 20008
Phone: 202/483-4224
Fax: 202/483-3169

Joseph DIATTA
Ambassador

Date Credentials Presented: 5/14/97

Born: 5/15/48 in Fadama, Niger

Spouse: Mrs. Haoua Diatta

Joseph Diatta assumed his duties in 1997 as ambassador to the U.S., a post he had held previously between 1982 and 1986. He is also the Republic of Niger's permanent representative to the United Nations.

Diatta, who began his career in Niger's ministry of foreign affairs in 1970, has held a variety of governmental posts. Most recently, he served as special advisor to the president of Niger between 1996 and 1997. He was general secretary, then commissioner ad interim, at the High Commission of the Restoration of Peace between 1994 and 1996. In 1993-94, he served in the cabinet of the ministry.

Diatta's other assignments included: diplomatic advisor of the prime minister; chief executive of the protocol of state for the presidency; and ambassador to the People's Republic of China and non-resident ambassador to Japan, the Democratic Republic of Korea; ambassador to Ethiopia, as well non-resident ambassador to Kenya, Tanzania, Angola, and Mozambique, and permanent representative to the Organization of African Unity (OAU) between 1979 and 1982.

The ambassador has participated in many conferences and international meetings including summits of the Organization of African Union and eleven sessions of the United Nations General Assembly. He has negotiated a number of credit agreements between Niger and the International Development Association.

Diatta was granted the diploma of the International Institute of Public Administration in Paris, diplomatic section, in 1971 and a bachelor of public law degree (equivalent to a master's degree) at the University of Abidjan, Cote d'Ivoire, in 1970.

As a professor at the National Administration College of the Republic of Niger, Diatta taught a course on international organizations. He was a member of the managing board of the Conseil de l'Entente Fund from 1976 to 1978 and a member of the administration council of the multinational company, Air Afrique, from 1976 to 1978.

The ambassador classifies his language skills as "very good" in French, "good" in English, and "average" in Spanish. He is married and has four children.

STAFF:

Mr. Moussa DABAL SOUNA
Counselor

Mr. Boureima KIMSO
Second Secretary (Financial)
Spouse: Mrs. Rabi Kimso

Mr. Aboubacar KABO
Attaché
Spouse: Mrs. Marie Kabo

Lt. Colonel Djibo TAHIROU
Defense Attaché
Spouse: Mrs. Balkissa Tahirou

Nigeria

Embassy of the Federal
   Republic of Nigeria
1333 16th Street, NW
Washington DC 20036
Phone: 202/986-8400
Fax: 202/775-1385

Dr. Alhaji Hassan ADAMU
Ambassador

Date Credentials Presented: 7/29/96

Born: 5/25/40 in Yola, Adamawa State, Nigeria

Spouse: Mrs. Inna Hassan Adamu

Dr. Alhaji Hassan Adamu brings to his post as Nigeria's ambassador to the U.S., a strong business background. Most recently, from 1990, he served as president of the Manufacturers Association of Nigeria (M.A.N.) of which he is a founding member. He was elected first chairman of M.A.N.'s Kano Branch in 1972 and chairman of the North-Eastern Zone in 1985.

Prior to his appointment as ambassador to the U.S., Adamu served on the board of directors of sixteen private companies while holding the chairmanship of eight others. In 1993, he served as Secretary for Power and Steel. His early career began with the Nigerian Ports Authority from 1966-68. He was then with the Northern Nigeria Development Corporation as general manager in Kano in 1971.

In the field of international relations, Adamu has taken part in several presidential delegations during which Nigeria concluded bilateral agreements with The Sudan, France and Germany.

Adamu holds a graduate degree in economics and transport studies as well as a post-graduate degree in transport studies from the University of London. He studied at the General Murtala College, the Yaba College of Technology (Lagos), the Newport College of Technology (South-Wales), and the North Western Polytechnic (University of London). He is the recipient of four honorary doctorate degrees including an LLD from the Clark Atlanta University in Atlanta, Georgia.

He and his wife have fifteen children. He enjoys fishing, reading, riding, and classical music.

STAFF:

Mr. Fungbe Ralf ADERELE
Minister-Counselor
Spouse: Mrs. Modupe O. Aderele

Mr. Adoga ONAH
Minister
Spouse: Mrs. Justina I. Onah

Mr. Ali ABUBAKAR
Counselor
Spouse: Mrs. Mojishola B. Abubakar

Mr. Joseph A. ADEFOLALU
Counselor
Spouse: Mrs. Anire Adefolalu

Mr. Patrick Benson AYENDI
Counselor (Information)
Spouse: Mrs. Afebanye Janet Ayendi

Mr. Aliyu Serki HAMMAN
Counselor
Spouse: Mrs. Aishatu Aliyu

Mr. Halidu Danjuma IBRAHIM
Counselor
Spouse: Mrs. Mariam O. Ibrahim

Mr. Haroum Abubakar IBRAHIM
Counselor
Spouse: Mrs. Fatima Ajus Ibrahim

Mr. Mahdi JIBIR
Counselor
Spouse: Mrs. Safia M. Jibir

Mr. Umar Jika MANA
Counselor
Spouse: Mrs. Mana

Mr. Abubakar ABDULLAHI
Attaché (Information)
Spouse: Mrs. Fatima Abdullahi

Mr. Frank Okonkwor EJEDOGHAOBI
Attaché (Financial)
Spouse: Mrs. Juliana Ejdoghaobi

Chancery Annex
2201 M Street, NW
Washington DC 20037
Phone: 202/822-1500

University Office
2010 Massachusetts Ave., NW
Fourth Floor
Washington DC 20036

Norway

Royal Norwegian Embassy
2720 34th Street, NW
Washington DC 20008-2714
Phone: 202/333-6000
Fax: 202/337-0870

Tom Eric VRAALSEN
Ambassador

Date Credentials Presented: 7/29/96

Born: 1/26/36

Spouse: Mrs. Viebecke Vraalsen

Tom Eric Vraalsen assumed his duties in Washington after a two-year stint as Norway's ambassador to the Court of St. James. He served in 1992 as Assistant Secretary General in the Norwegian Ministry of Foreign Affairs.

Vraalsen, a graduate in business administration, entered the foreign service in 1960. He was assigned as an attaché to the Norwegian Embassy in Beijing in 1962, after which he was named second secretary in his country's embassy in Cairo in 1964.

His other assignments included: executive officer, Ministry of Foreign Affairs, 1967; first secretary, Norwegian Embassy in Beijing, 1969; first secretary, Norwegian Embassy in Manila, 1970; head of division, Ministry of Foreign Affairs, 1971; minister counselor and DCM, Permanent Mission of Norway to the United Nations in New York, 1975; director general (political director), Ministry of Foreign Affairs, 1981; ambassador, Permanent Mission of Norway to the United Nations in New York, 1982.

During a leave of absence from the foreign service, Vraalsen was named Minister of the International Development Cooperation in 1989. Then in 1991, he took the position of director of information for Saga Petroleum.

STAFF:

Mr. Karsten KLEPSVIK
Minister (Deputy Chief of Mission)
Spouse: Mrs. Heidi Klepsvik

Ms. Elisabeth RODERBURG
Minister-Counselor

Mr. Are-Jostein NORHEIM
Minister-Counselor (Political)
Spouse: Mrs. Susana S. Norheim

Mr. Eivind HOMME
Counselor (Press and Cultural)

Mr. Stala RISA
Counselor (Shipping and Civil Aviation)

Spouse: Mrs. Yuen Kwan Risa

Ms. Inga M. W. NYHAMAR
First Secretary (Political)
Spouse: Mr. Tore Nyhamar

Mr. Lars HENIE
Second Secretary (Political)
Spouse: Mrs. Tove Berg

Ms. Berit ENGE
First Secretary (Economic)
Spouse: Mr. Donald Jerome Ridings

Mr. Bjern Brede HANSEN
Second Secretary (Economic)
Spouse: Mrs. Heidi Stien

Ms. Inger RONNING
Second Secretary and Consul

Mr. Odd MOLSTER
Second Secretary (Press and Cultural)
Spouse: Mrs. Eva Marie Loveid
   Roe Molster

Ms. Kristin SKJEFSTAD
Attaché and Vice Consul

Major General Bjorn M. NYGARD
Defense Attaché
Spouse: Mrs. Jorun M. Nygard

Lt. Colonel Stein M. GUNDERSEN
Military, Naval & Asst. Defense Attaché
Spouse: Mrs. Lill Gundersen

Lt. Colonel Kjell A. INGEBRIGTSEN
Defense Cooperation & Air Attaché and
   Asst. Military & Naval Attaché
Spouse: Mrs. Anne-Mari Ingebrigsten

Lt. Cmdr. Christian H. NORDANGER
Asst Military and Naval Attaché
Spouse: Mrs. Kari Beate Nordanger

Captain Rnoaf ENGELIEN
Asst. Defense Cooperation Attaché
Spouse: Mrs. Vibeke Stromme

Mr. Knut RINGSTAD
Counselor (Commercial)
Spouse: Mrs. Marie Ringstad

Mr. Tore LI
Counselor (Science)

Mr. Erling G. RIKHEIM
Counselor (Financial and Economic)
Spouse: Mrs. Anne Kristin Westberg

Ms. Marit ENGEBRETSEN
Counselor (Energy)

Mr. Stein OWE
Counselor (Fisheries)
Spouse: Mrs. Marianne Kjollesdal

Mr. Jan A. OLSEN
Counselor (Political)
Spouse: Mrs. Gro Seglen

Oman

Embassy of the Sultanate of Oman
2535 Belmont Road, NW
Washington DC 20008
Phone: 202/387-1980
Fax: 202/745-4933

Abdulla Mohammed Ageel AL-DHAHAB
Ambassador

Date Credentials Presented: 3/20/95

Born: 1/29/49

Spouse: Mrs. Zakyia Moh'd Amin Abdulla

Abdulla Bin Mohamed Al-Dhahab has had extensive ambassadorial experience, having been, at different times, Oman's ambassador to Sudan, Bahrain, and Great Britain and Northern Ireland, as well as non-resident ambassador to the Republic of Ireland, Zimbabwe, and Zambia. The first of these assignments was in 1978 to Sudan. The last was in 1990 to Great Britain and Northern Ireland.

Al-Dhahab also held various posts in Oman's Ministry of Foreign Affairs, including deputy chief of political affairs, chief of the Asian Department, and chief of the Minister's Department. While resident ambassador to the U.S., he serves concurrently as non-resident ambassador to: Argentina, Brazil, Bolivia, Canada, Chili and Mexico.

Al-Dhahab, who holds a bachelor of law degree, is married and has five children.

STAFF:

Mr. Sayyid Muhammed Harub ABDULLA
First Secretary
Spouse: Mrs. Walliem Al Marjabi

Mr. Badr AL-HINAI
First Secretary
Spouse: Mrs. Shikha Abdulla Zaher
  Al Hinai

Mr. Munther Mahfoodh AL-MANTHERI
First Secretary

Mr. Salim Suhaul Muhad AL-MASHANI
First Secretary
Spouse: Mrs. Noor Ali Mohammed
  A-Mashani

Mr. Khamis AL-SIYABY
Third Secretary (Consular)
Spouse: Mrs. Aziza Al-Seyabi

Mr. Yahya Amur Abdullah AL KIYUMI
Attaché (Cultural)
Spouse: Mrs. Fayiza Abdullah Hamed
  Al Barwani

Mr. Salim AL-MAHROOQY
Attaché (Information)

Spouse: Mrs. Amina Abdullah Al-Hamdan

Colonel Mohammed AL-AJMI
Defense, Military, Naval and Air Attaché

Cultural Office
1717 Massachusetts Ave., NW, Suite 400
Washington DC 20036
Phone: 202/387-2014

Defense Office
1717 Massachusetts Ave., NW, Suite 300
Washington DC 20036
Phone: 202/387-1758

Pakistan

Embassy of Pakistan
2315 Massachusetts Avenue, NW
Washington DC 20008
Phone: 202/939-6200
Fax: 202/387-0484
Email: info@pakistan-embassy.com
Url: http://www.pakistan-embassy.com

Riaz H. KHOKHAR
Ambassador

Date Credentials Presented: 5/14/97

Born: 1942

Spouse: Mrs. Shahnaz Khokhar

Pakistan's ambassador to the U.S., Riaz H. Khokhar, has held a number of posts in his government and abroad since he joined Pakistan's foreign service in 1966.

Before coming to Washington, D.C., in 1997, he had been high commissioner to India for five years. He participated in several rounds of talks at the foreign secretary and defense secretary level between Pakistan and India on Kashmir and Siachen.

From 1989 to 1992, he served as additional secretary (foreign affairs and defense) in the prime minister's secretariat under Prime Ministers Benazir Bhutto, Ghulam Mustafa Jatoi, and Nawaz Sharif. He was Pakistan's ambassador to Bangladesh and Bhutan between 1986 and 1989.

Other positions included: director general (South Asia), ministry of foreign affairs,

Islamabad, and assignments at the Pakistan embassies in New Delhi, India, and in Portugal. In 1976, he traveled extensively with the prime minister on a state visit to China, France, Iran, Turkey, and Saudi Arabia and participated in several international conferences. He also took part in bilateral meetings with the shah of Iran and President Daud of Afghanistan to resolve border problems with Afghanistan.

From 1968 to 1971, Khokhar served as second secretary in Pakistan's embassy in Moscow. From 1971 to 1974, he served in Sweden, Norway, and Denmark. He was assigned to the office of the Prime Minister, Zulfiqar Ali Bhutto from 1974 to 1977.

The ambassador holds a degree of M.A. in international relations. He attended the Civil Service Academy in 1966-67.

STAFF:

Mr. Zamir AKRAM
Minister (Political and Deputy Chief of
  Mission)
Spouse: Mrs. Sadi Akram

Dr. Agha GHAZANFAR
Minister (Economic)

Mr. Faqir Zia MASOOM
Minister-Counselor
Spouse: Mrs. Nameema Zia

Mr. Jalil Abbas JILANI
Counselor (Political)
Spouse: Mrs. Shaista Jilani

Mr. Mohammad Masood KHAN
Counselor (Political)
Spouse: Mrs. Zohra Masood Khan

Mr. Mohammad Zareef KHAN
Counselor
Spouse: Mrs. Aziza Zareef

Mr. Iftikhar HUSAIN
First Secretary (Finance and Accounts)
Spouse: Mrs. Salma Iftikhar

Mr. Abbas KAZMI
First Secretary (Political and Head of
  Chancery)
Spouse: Mrs. Nourin Kazmi

Mr. Muhammad Naeem KHAN
First Secretary
Spouse: Mrs. Anila Naeem Khan

Mr. Javed Jalil KHATTAK
Second Secretary (Political)
Spouse: Mrs. Faiza Khattak

Mr. Syed Abdul RAZZAQ
Third Secretary (Commercial)
Spouse: Mrs. Mussarat Razzaq

Captain Ausaf AHMED
Attaché (Defense Procurement)
Spouse: Mrs. Shamsa Ahmed

Mr. Mohammad AZAM
Attaché (Press)
Spouse: Mrs. Tahina Azam

Colonel Shahid Pervez CHEEMA
Attaché (Defense Procurement)
Spouse: Mrs. Anjum Shahid Cheema

Mr. Mohammad Shafi KHALIQUE
Attaché (Administrative)
Spouse: Mrs. Shahnaz Bibi

Brigadier Syed Muhammad MUJTABA
Defense and Military Attaché
Spouse: Mrs. Azra Mujtaba

Commander Syed ALI
Air Attaché
Spouse: Mrs. Syeda Musaffar

Lt. Colonel Farooq Hameed KHAN
Asst. Military Attaché
Spouse: Mrs. Rubina Farooq

Chancery Annex
2201 R Street, NW
Washington DC 20008
Phone: 202/939-6205

Commercial Office
2201 R Street, NW
Washington DC 20008
Phone: 202/939-6585

Palau

Embassy of the Republic of Palau
1150 18th Street, NW - Suite 750
Washington DC 20036
Phone: 202/452-6814
Fax: 202/452-6281

Hersey KYOTA
Ambassador

Date Credentials Presented: 11/12/97

Spouse: Mrs. Lydia Shmull Kyota

Palau's ambassador to the U.S., Hersey Kyota, came to Washington, D.C., after serving for five years in the Palau National Congress.

As a legislator, he served as chairman of the committee on capital improvements and land

matters and as chairman of the committee on ways and means. He was a member of task forces on a master development plan, on a joint aviation task force, and on a Koror sewer improvement.

Before becoming a legislator himself, Kyota worked as a staff person for the Palau National Congress: as director of the office of the legal counsel for the House of Delegates, 1989-91; as chief clerk of the House of Delegates, 1985-88; and as legal researcher for the House of Delegates, 1981-84.

Between 1992 and 1996, Kyota served on the board of directors in the Association of Pacific Islands Legislature.

Kyota graduated from Palau High School in Koror, Palau, in 1972. He received two degrees from the U.S. International University in San Diego, Calif.: a B.A. degree in social science in 1977 and an M.A. degree in human behavior and leadership in 1979.

The ambassador enjoys fishing, baseball, basketball, reading, and spending quality time with his family.

STAFF:

Mr. David ORRUKEM
First Secretary

Mr. Rhinehart SILAS
Second Secretary

Panama

Embassy of the Republic of Panama
2862 McGill Terrace, NW
Washington DC 20008
Phone: 202/483-1407
Fax: 202/483-8413

Dr. Eloy ALFARO de Alba
Ambassador

Date Credentials Presented: 3/16/98

Spouse: Mrs. Patricia Boyd de Alfaro

Dr. Eloy Alfaro de Alba, a prominent lawyer, served on the legal commission that drafted the enabling law for the Panama Canal

Authority as well as other high-level commissions involving the canal.

He served in 1993 as a member of the legal subcommittee of the Presidential Commission for Canal Affairs, appointed by President Guillermo Endara, which drafted an amendment to the constitution of the Republic of Panama related to the Panama Canal. He was appointed by President Perez Balladares in 1994 to the transition commission for transfer of the Panama Canal and has been a representative of Panama at the consultative committee of the Panama Canal.

Starting in 1994, he was a member of the high-level presidential commission on developing a policy against money laundering. He has been a negotiator for Panama in negotiations to establish a multinational counternarcotics center in Panama. In 1997, he was named to the national foreign relations committee of the ministry of foreign affairs.

A member of the National Bar Association of Panama, Alfaro has been a partner in the law firm, Tapia, Linares & Alfaro. He served as an alternate justice of the Supreme Court of Panama between 1990 and 1997 and was president of the Association of International Lawyers in Panama between 1994 and 1996. He was president of the Banking Law Association of Panama between 1984 and 1986 and was named to the board of directors of the Panamanian Law Institute in 1989.

Alfaro is a former vice president of the Panamanian Committee for Human Rights. He is a member of the board of directors of the Panamanian Institute of Art (Museum of Contemporary Art).

He holds three degrees from Columbia University in New York City: a B.A. degree, 1969; a J.D. from the law school in 1972; and an M.B.A. from the school of business in 1974. He and his wife have three children, Carolina Alfaro Boyd, Eloy Alfaro Boyd, and Federico Alfaro Boyd.

STAFF:

Mr. Fernando ELETA CASANOVAS
Minister-Counselor

Mrs. Maria Isobel ARAMBURU PORRAS
Counselor

Mr. Federico O. BOYD
Counselor (Public Affairs) & Consul Gen.
Spouse: Mrs. Graciela Maria Boyd

Mrs. Raquel ALFARO
Attaché

Mr. Alejandro FERRER
Attaché and Vice Consul
Spouse: Mrs. Iren De Arias

Mrs. Mylene Mayuly MARRONE
Attaché and Vice Consul

Spouse: Mr. Milton Lot Ruiz

Papua New Guinea

Embassy of Papua New Guinea
1615 New Hampshire Avenue, NW
Suite 300
Washington DC 20009
Phone: 202/745-3680
Fax: 202/745-3679

Nagora Y. BOGAN
Ambassador

Date Credentials Presented: 4/30/96

Born: 9/25/56 in Lae, Papua New Guinea

Spouse: Mrs. Nohoranie N. Jimmy-Kepo

Not only does Nagora Bogan represent Papua New Guinea in Washington, D.C., but he also is accredited as the nation's ambassador to Mexico and as high commissioner to Canada.

Bogan took a position in Papua New Guinea's taxation office and gradually worked his way up to chief collector of taxes. Then, in 1992, he was named head of his country's Internal Revenue Commission, which resulted from a merger of the former bureau of the customs and the taxation office.

For three consecutive years, 1988, 1989, and 1990, he was appointed chairman of the government's policy working group on tax and customs. He was also appointed Oceania delegate and committee member of the management committee of the Commonwealth Association of Tax Administration (CATA) at the CATA annual general meeting in Blantyre, Malawi, in 1988 for a three-year term. Later he served as chairman of the CATA management committee. Countries in the Oceania region are Australia, New Zealand, Papua New Guinea, Solomon Islands, Tonga, and Western Samoa.

Bogan received a law degree (LLB) from the University of Papua New Guinea. He went to Sogeri National High School in Port Moresby, after attending primary and high school in Lae.

He is married to Nohoranie Jimmy-Kepo, and they have four children. He is a member of the Lutheran Church.

STAFF:

Mr. Graham MICHAEL
Counselor

Mrs. Barbara AGE
Second Secretary
Spouse: Mr. Frank Tamarua

Miss Helen SANNY
Third Secretary

Paraguay

Embassy of Paraguay
2400 Massachusetts Avenue, NW
Washington DC 20008
Phone: 202/483-6960
Fax: 202/234-4508
Email: embapar@erols.com

Jorge G. PRIETO
Ambassador

Date Credentials Presented: 3/20/95

Born: 11/28/41 in Asuncion, Paraguay

Spouse: Mrs. Dora O. De Prieto

From 1983 until he came to Washington in November 1994, Jorge G. Prieto served as the president of the board of directors for the Electromon Consulting firm, which specializes in energy products, providing potable water, sanitation, industrial infrastructure, and ecology.

Earlier, he was director of administration and finances for the International Consortium of Consultors for the Yacyreta hydroelectric plant. The consortium was led by Harza Engineering Co. of Chicago, Ill. Between 1971 and 1979, he was an engineer for the National Administration for Electricity. In that job, he served as a consultant for the United Nations Program for Development in the UNDP-ANDE project for the reconnaissance of the primary sources for non-conventional energy and industries of high energy consumption--a program sponsored by the U.S. and Canada in 1974.

Prieto also was a professor at the Mechanical Aeronautical School of the Air Force and professor of internal combustion of motors at the Institute of Aeronautical Technology in Brazil. He is a former president of the Paraguayan Center for Engineers and a member of the Paraguayan National Rural Association and the Association of Nerlore Cattle Raising.

He studied aeronautical engineering at Facultad de Ingenieria de la Universidad Nacional de La Plata in Argentina in 1968. He did post-degree studies at the Technological Institute of Aeronautics at ITA in Sao Jose Dos Campos from 1979 to 1971. He also studied hydroelectrical engineering at the Electric Power Development Co. Ltd, in Tokyo, Japan.

Prieto is married and has two children.

STAFF:

Mr. Ricseso CABALLERO
Counselor

Ms. Elianne CIBILS
Counselor

Mr. Enrique INSFERN
First Secretary

Miss Norma CARDOZO
Second Secretary

Mr. Enrique RAMIREZ
Second Secretary

Office of Commercial and Economic Affairs
2400 Massachusetts Avenue, NW
Washington DC 20008
Phone: 202/483-6960

Office of Press and Information Affairs
2400 Massachusetts Avenue, NW
Washington DC 20008
Phone: 202/483-6960

Office of Visa and Consular Affairs
2400 Massachusetts Avenue, NW
Washington DC 20008
Phone: 202/483-6960

Office of the Defense Attaché
2400 Massachusetts Avenue, NW
Washington DC 20008

Peru

Embassy of Peru
1700 Massachusetts Avenue, NW
Washington DC 20036
Phone: 202/833-9860
Fax: 202/659-8124

Ricardo V. LUNA
Ambassador

Date Credentials Presented: 4/14/93

Personal: Born 11/19/40

Spouse: Mrs. Margarita Proano de Luna

A career diplomat, Ricardo V. Luna brings to Washington extensive foreign relations experience at both the bilateral level, having been stationed in North America, Europe, and the Middle East, and at the multilateral level, having served as Peruvian ambassador to the United Nations and as a delegate to the GATT in Geneva.

Luna held various posts in diplomatic missions between 1968-87 in the United Kingdom, Israel, Geneva, Paris, Ecuador, New York, and Washington. In 1984-85, he was Peruvian deputy representative to the U.N. Security Council. He served as under secretary for multilateral affairs at the Foreign Ministry. He was Peruvian National Coordinator of the "Rio Group" and delegate to Rio Group Summits, and was Peruvian ambassador to the United Nations between 1989 and 1992.

Luna sees cooperation from Washington as crucial to Peru's future, because of the U.S.'s "new role of leader of the unipolar system," and because of the example which it sets for future north-south relations.

He received an A.B. in political science from Princeton University in 1962 and a master's degree in international affairs from Columbia University in 1964. He was a fellow (CFIA) at Harvard University, and holds a license from the Peruvian Diplomatic Academy.

Luna and his wife Margarita have a daughter.

STAFF:

Mr. Luis QUESADA
Minister-Counselor (Deputy Chief of
    Mission)

Mrs. Maria Teresa MARINO DE HART
Minister-Counselor (Political & Military)

Mr. Gustavo MEZA CUADRA
Counselor (Economic and Financial)
Spouse: Mrs. Sonia Meza Cuadra

Mr. Francisco J. RIVAROLA
Counselor (Political)
Spouse: Mrs. Maria Elena Rivarola

Ms. Elvira VELASQUEZ
Counselor (Political and Environment)

Mr. Eduardo RIVOLDI
Counselor (Commercial Section and
    Cultural Attaché)
Spouse: Mrs. Carmen Rivoldi

Mr. Augusto ARZUBIAGA
Counselor (Consul)
Spouse: Mrs. Carla Wagner

Mr. Juan DEL CAMPO
First Secretary
Spouse: Mrs. Daniela del Campo

Ms. Cecilia GALARRETA
First Secretary (Political & Congressional
    Liasion)

Mr. Hugo CONTRERAS
Second Secretary (CICAD)

Mr. Alfredo VALENCIA
Minister-Counselor (Economic)
Spouse: Mrs. Julia Valencia

Division General Danfer SUAREZ

Air Attaché

Rear Admiral Carlos Sarmiento DUPUY
Naval Attaché

Division General Santiago Gonzalez
    ORREGO
Military Attaché

Office of the Consul General
1625 Massachusetts Avenue, NW
Washington DC 20036
Phone: 202/462-1084

Office of the Military Attaché
2141 Wisconsin Ave., NW, Suite F
Washington DC 20007
Phone: 202/342-8130

Office of the Naval Attaché
2141 Wisconsin Ave., NW, Suite J
Washington DC 20007
Phone: 202/337-6670

Office of the Air Attaché
2141 Wisconsin Ave., NW, Suite A
Washington DC 20007
Phone: 202/333-1528

Office for Joint Fight Against Drugs
2201 Wisconsin Avenue, NW, Suite 350
Washington DC 20007
Phone: 202/737-5484

Philippines

Embassy of the Philippines
1600 Massachusetts Avenue, NW
Washington DC 20036
Phone: 202/467-9300
Fax: 202/328-7614

Raul Chaves RABE
Ambassador

Date Credentials Presented: 9/3/93

Born: 1/5/40

Spouse: Mrs. Buena Rodriguez Rabe

An attorney by profession, Raul Chaves Rabe began his career in private practice with two firms in the Philippines in the mid-1960s. For the past 25 years, Rabe has served with the Philippines' Department of Foreign

Affairs, both at home and abroad. His career has taken him to Europe, the Middle East, and several times to the U.S.

Joining the foreign service in 1968, Rabe served first in the Office of the United Nations and International Organizations and later with the Consular and Political Office. In 1971, he received his first posting overseas with his country's missions in London and Bucharest.

Rabe returned to Manila in 1979 for two years, working as deputy chief of protocol, before heading abroad again. Between 1981 and 1989, he held positions in Saudi Arabia, Honolulu and Washington, where he ended the decade as deputy chief of mission in the Phillipines' U.S. Embassy. In the years immediately preceding his ambassadorial appointment, Rabe served as director-general for American affairs within the Foreign Department. During 1992, he was his nation's ambassador to Korea.

Rabe holds a B.A. from the University of Santo Tomas in Manila and a bachelor of laws from Ateneo de Manila. He was a Colombo Plan Scholar at the Foreign Service Training Institute in Canberra, Australia, and speaks Filipino, Cebuano, and English. He is married and has a son.

STAFF:

Mr. Antonio I. BASILIO
Minister (Deputy Chief of Mission)
Spouse: Mrs. Agnes P. Basilio

Mrs. Laura Q. DEL ROSARIO
Minister-Counselor
Spouse: Mr. Raul L. Del Rosario

Mr. Tagumpay NANADIEGO
Minister-Counselor (Veterans)
Spouse: Mrs. Adela Veluz Nanadiego

Mrs. Jocelyn BATOON GARCIA
Counselor

Mr. Victor S. GOSIENGFIAO
Counselor (Economic)
Spouse: Mrs. Araceli P. Gosiengfiao

Mr. Eduardo Pablo MAGLAYA
Counselor and Consul General

Mr. Ben Hur C. ONG
Counselor (Administrative) and Consul
Spouse: Mrs. Gloria M. Ong

Mr. Jose Maria EBRO
Second Secretary (Information)

Mr. Leo Moncerate HERRERA-LIM
Second Secretary and Consul
Spouse: Ms. Fidelis C. Gonzales

Mr. Roberto N. AVENTAJADO
Attaché (Political)
Spouse: Mrs. Teresita S. Aventajado

Mr. Samuel BAET

Attaché

Mr. Edgardo CASTRO
Attaché
Spouse: Mrs. Anna Maria C. Castro

Mrs. Maria Hennie X.
  FORNIER-BELONIO
Attaché
Spouse: Mr. Jesus Raul L. Belonio

Mr. Antonio Lucido GARCIA
Attaché (Labor)
Spouse: Mrs. Conchita Garcia

Mr. Manuel G. IMSON
Attaché (Labor)
Spouse: Mrs. Wilhelmina A. Imson

Mr. Victoriano B. LEVISTE
Attaché (Agricultural)
Spouse: Mrs. Leviste

Mr. Jessie Rose D. MABUTAS
Attaché
Spouse: Mr. Marianito Cid Mabutas

Mr. Silverio R. MANGUERRA
Attaché
Spouse: Mrs. Nilda R. Manguerra

Mrs. Malinee G. MARFIL
Attaché

Mr. Plaridel S. ONG
Attaché
Spouse: Mrs. Jean P. Ong

Mr. Roberto A. PALANCA
Attaché
Spouse: Mrs. Anita Abiog-Palanca

Mr. Eduardo Chinsio PARAAN
Attaché
Spouse: Mrs. Maria Antonia Tabunar
  Paraan

Mr. Carlos R. REGALARIO
Attaché
Spouse: Mrs. Eden M. Regalario

Mrs. Amanda SEGOVIA
Attaché
Spouse: Mr. Patricio Segovia

Mrs. Luz B. VALLIDO
Attaché
Spouse: Mr. Roberto P. Vallido

Colonel Danilo Augusto B. FRANCIA
Defense and Naval and Air Attaché
Spouse: Mrs. Arleen Rose A. Francia

Lt. Col. Pedro Cesar C. RAMBOANGA
Military Attaché & Asst. Defense Attaché
Spouse: Mrs. Edita Concipcion A.
  Ramboanga

Office of the Armed Forces Attaché
1600 Massachusetts Avenue, NW
Washington DC 20036
Phone: 202/467-9300

Office of the Commercial Counselor
1600 Massachusetts Avenue, NW
Washington DC 20036
Phone: 202/467-9300

Consular Office
1600 Massachusetts Avenue, NW
Washington DC 20036
Phone: 202/467-9300

Office of the Revenue Attaché
1600 Massachusetts Avenue, NW
Washington DC 20036
Phone: 202/467-9300

Poland

Embassy of the Republic of Poland
2640 16th Street, NW
Washington DC 20009
Phone: 202/234-3800
Fax: 202/328-6271
Email: embpol@dgs.dgsys.com
Url: http://www.polishworld.com/polemb

Jerzy KOZMINSKI
Ambassador

Date Credentials Presented: 6/23/94

Born: 4/20/53

Spouse: Mrs. Irena Kozminska

Before Jerzy Kozminski assumed the post of Poland's ambassador to the U.S., he was first deputy minister at the Polish Ministry of Foreign Affairs, with the rank of Secretary of State.

Since 1989, Kozminski has held other governmental positions. As director general in the Office of the Council of Ministers, he was the closest associate of deputy prime minister and Minister of Finance Leszek Balcerowicz, the author of Poland's radical economic reforms.

In 1991, Kozminski was promoted to the rank of under secretary of state in the prime minister's office, at the same time continuing his work for Deputy Prime Minister Balcerowicz. In the course of 1992 and 1993, while holding the position of under secretary of state, he worked closely with Prime

Minister Hanna Suchocka, organizing and directing the prime minister's special advisory teams for socio-political and economic matters.

An economist by profession, he graduated from the Faculty of Foreign Trade of the Central School of Planning and Statistics (now the Warsaw School of Economics) in Warsaw, and then pursued his academic career there at the Central School's Institute of Foreign Trade Economics.

He became a founding member of the Foundation for Economic Education, established in Warsaw in 1992 with the aim of familiarizing the Polish public and potential entrepreneurs with the functioning of the free market and its institutions.

Kozminski speaks, English, German, and Russian. He is married to Irene Kozminska, who is also an economist, and they have one daughter.

STAFF:

Mr. Andrzej JAROSZYNSKI
Counselor (Deputy Chief of Mission)
Spouse: Mrs. Henryka Dogil-Jaroszynska

Mr. Janusz OMIETANSKI
Counselor
Spouse: Mrs. Joanna Omietanski

Mr. Jakub WOLSKI
Counselor
Spouse: Mrs. Hanna Wolski

Mrs. Alina MAGNUSKA
Counselor (Cultural)

Mr. Andrzej RABCZENKO
Counselor (Science and Technology)
Spouse: Mrs. Zanetta Miluk

Mr. Piotr OGRODZINSKI
Counselor-Minister
Spouse: Mrs. Agata Ogrodzinska

Mr. Artur HARAZ
Second Secretary

Mr. Dariusz WISNIEWSKI
First Secretary
Spouse: Mrs. Ewa Bem Wisniewska

Mr. Krystyna FUSNIK
First Secretary
Spouse: Mr. Adam Fusnik

Mr. Mariusz HANDZLIK
Counselor
Spouse: Mrs. Monika Handzlik

Mr. Michal WYGANOWSKI
First Secretary
Spouse: Mrs. Dorota Wyganowska

Mr. Zbigniew GURZYNSKI
First Secretary
Spouse: Mrs. Irena Gurzynski

Mr. Jaroslaw LASINSKI
First Secretary (Consular)
Spouse: Mrs. Mariola Lasinska

Mr. Jaroslaw KUREK
First Secretary
Spouse: Mrs. Agnieszka
Jerdrzejewska-Kurek

Mr. Mieczyslaw KAMINSKI
Second Secretary
Spouse: Mrs. Malgorzata
Jaglarska-Kaminski

Mr. D. MAJEWSKA
Counselor-Minister
Spouse: Mrs. Monika Majewska

Mr. Ryszard WILCZYNSKI
Counselor (Financial)
Spouse: Mrs. Longawa-Wilczynski

Mr. Andrzej DZIEKONSKI
Attaché (Economic)
Spouse: Mrs. Jolanta Dziekonska

Mr. Andrzej ILCZUK
Attaché (Economic)
Spouse: Mrs. Swietlana Ilczuk

Mrs. Magdalena
BENTKOWSKA-KICZOR
Asst. Attaché (Economic)
Spouse: Mr. Grzegorz Kicor

Mrs. Joanna KRAWCZYK
Asst. Attaché (Financial)

Mr. Andrzej LAGANOWSKI
Counselor (Commercial) (N.Y.)
Spouse: Mrs. Maria
Gadzinowska-Laganowska

Ms. Ewa SALKIEWICZ
First Secretary (Consular)

Colonel Waldemar DZIEGIELEWSKI
Defense, Military, Naval and Air Attaché
Spouse: Mrs. Monika Dziegielewska

Colonel Krzysztof POLKOWSKI
Asst. Defense, Military, Naval and
Air Attaché
Spouse: Mrs. Aleksandra Polkowska

Lt. Colonel Ryszard WOZNIAK
Assistant Military, Naval and Air Attaché
Spouse: Mrs. Grazyna Wozniak

Office of the Economic Counselor
1503 21st St., NW
Washington DC 20036
Phone: 202/467-6690 Fax: 202/833-8343

Office of the Financial Counselor
2640 16th St., NW
Washington DC 20008
Phone: 202/332-8497 Fax: 202/818-9623

Office of the Commercial Counselor
100 Park Ave., 19th Floor
New York NY 10017

Office of the Military Attaché
2224 Wyoming Ave., NW
Washington DC 20008
Phone: 202/232-2303 Fax: 202/483-5785

Office of the Consular Division
2224 Wyoming Ave., NW
Washington DC 20008
Phone: 202/232-4517 Fax: 202/328-2152

Portugal

Embassy of Portugal
2125 Kalorama Road, NW
Washington DC 20008
Phone: 202/328-8610
Fax: 202/462-3726

Fernando ANDRESEN-GUIMARAES
Ambassador

Date Credentials Presented: 5/16/95

Born: 1941 in Lisbon, Portugal

Spouse: Mrs. Graca Andresen-Guimaraes

Fernando Andresen-Guimaraes, who joined the foreign service in 1967, has represented Portugal as ambassador in two other countries: Algeria, from 1988 to 1991; and Iraq from 1986 to 1988.

Between 1992 and 1995, Andresen-Guimaraes was president of the Interministerial Commission on Macau and head of the Portuguese-Chinese Joint Liaison Group. In 1991-92, he was director-general of development aid in the Portuguese Ministry of Foreign Affairs.

Earlier, he was consul-general in Luanda between 1982 and 1986; counsellor, Permanent Mission to the United Nations in New York, between 1978 and 1982; auditor for the NATO Defense College in Rome between 1977-78; first secretary to the Portuguese embassy in London between 1970 and 1973; and secretary of the embassy in Malawi between 1970 and 1973.

Andresen-Guimaraes has a degree in economics from the University of Lisbon. He is married and has two sons.

STAFF:

Mr. Antonio Augusto JORGE MENDES
Minister (Deputy Chief of Mission) &
Permanent Observer to the O.A.S.
Spouse: Mrs. Maria Luis Jorge Mendes

Mr. Rui Alberto M. TERENO
Counselor
Spouse: Mrs. Maria Belchior Tereno

Mr. Jose DUARTE
First Secretary
Spouse: Mrs. Maria Jose Pinto da
Silva Duarte

Mrs. Claudia MOTA PINTO
First Secretary

Mr. Paulo Vizeu PINHEIRO
First Secretary
Spouse: Mrs. Maria Farima P. Vizeu
Pinheiro

Mr. Jose Estevao C. SASPORTES
Counselor (Cultural)

Mr. Carlos Dias SOUTO
Counselor (Industrial and Scientific)
Spouse: Mrs. Brenda Kay Souto

Mr. Diogo Jose VILAS-BOAS
Counselor (Economic)
Spouse: Mrs. Mariana Vilas-Boas

Mrs. Maria Teresa Tarujo de Almeida
GREENWALD
Counselor (Social)
Spouse: Mr. John Greenwald

Mr. Jorge de Fonseca FELNER
DA COSTA
Counselor (Tourism)
Spouse: Mrs. Felner Da Costa

Mr. Antonio CARNEIRO JACINTO
Counselor (Press)

Mrs. Elia Maria de Jesus RODRIGUES
Counselor (Commercial)
Spouse: Mr. Joao Gerardo Mauricio
Wemans

Mrs. Alda Maria Silva FERNANDES
Counselor (Economic)

Mrs. Maria Amelia M.N. HILKER
Attaché and Vice Consul
Spouse: Mr. Hilker

Ms. Ana Maria PIRES MONTEIRO
Attaché (Latin American Affairs)

Mr. Jose Manuel VITAL MORGADO
Attaché (Commercial)
Spouse: Mrs. Vital Morgado

Lt. Colonel Mario De Oliveira CARDOSO
Defense and Military Attaché
Spouse: Mrs. Maria Adelia C. Branco
O. Cardoso

Captain Fernando Vargas MATOS
Naval Attaché
Spouse: Mrs. Merete Regine Werstein
 Vargas de Matos

Lt. Colonel Armando Manuel VIEIRA
Air Attaché
Spouse: Mrs. Maria Irene Vieira

Office of the Naval Attaché
2310 Tracy Place, NW
Washington DC 20008
Phone: 202/234-4483

Office of the Defense and Air Attaché
2310 Tracy Place, NW
Washington DC 20008
Phone: 202/234-5037

Office of the Military Attaché
2310 Tracy Place, NW
Washington DC 20008
Phone: 202/232-7632

Consular Section
2310 Tracy Place, NW
Washington DC 20008
Phone: 202/332-3007

Trade Commission
1900 L St., NW, Suite 401
Washington DC 20006

Qatar

Embassy of the State of Qatar
4200 Wisconsin Ave., NW - Suite 200
Washington DC 20016
Phone: 202/274-1603
Fax: 202/237-0059

Saad Mohammed AL-KOBAISI
Ambassador

Date Credentials Presented: 5/14/97

Born: 1951

*Spouse: Mrs. Huda Abdulla Rashis
 Al-Suwaidi*

The U.S. is the second nation where Saad Mohammed Al-Kobaisi has represented Qatar as ambassador. The first was Turkey from 1992 until 1996.

Al-Kobaisi, who joined Qatar's ministry of foreign affairs in 1980, served as head of his country's delegation to the multilateral committee on arms control and regional security from 1992 until 1997.

His other assignments include: acting director of the political department at the ministry, 1989-90; deputy chief of mission, embassy of Qatar in Tokyo, 1987-89; chargé d'affaires of the embassy of Qatar in Algeria, 1981-84; and member of Qatar's permanent mission to the United Nations in New York, 1981.

From 1975 to 1980, Al-Kobaisi was personal assistant to the chief of police, attaining the rank of major.

The ambassador has two degrees from Central Michigan University: a bachelor's degree in economics, 1975, and an M.A. in political science, 1978.

Al-Kobaisi is married and has two daughters and a son.

STAFF:

Mr. Khalifa Ahmed AL SOWAIDI
Counselor
Spouse: Mrs. Nadia Mohugnod
 Al Ghashish

Mr. Khalid Rashid H. AL-MANSOURI
Second Secretary
Spouse: Mrs. Al-Mansouri

Sheikh Ali Jassim AL THANI
Third Secretary

Mr. Mohammed Saslah AL-MANNAI
Attaché (Cultural)
Spouse: Mrs. Al-Mannai

Mr. Abdulaziz Mohamed Saleh NISHWAR
Attaché (Medical)

Mr. Nasser Ali AS-SAADI
Asst. Attaché (Cultural)
Spouse: Mrs. Fatma Al-Banna

Colonel Hamad Ali Jaber AL MARRI
Defense, Military, Naval and Air Attaché
Spouse: Mrs. Noora A. S. Al Shareef

Office of the Cultural Attaché
4200 Wisconsin Ave., NW, Suite 200
Washington DC 20016

Office of the Medical Attaché
4200 Wisconsin Ave., NW, Suite 200
Washington DC 20016

Romania

Embassy of Romania
1607 23rd Street, NW
Washington DC 20008
Phone: 202/332-4846
Fax: 202/232-4748

Mircea Dan GEOANA
Ambassador

Date Credentials Presented: 2/6/96

Born: 7/14/58 in Bucharest, Romania

Spouse: Mrs. Mihaela Geoana

Before taking his post in Washington, D.C., Mircea Dan Geoana served in the Romanian Ministry of Foreign Affairs as general director for Europe, North America, Asia, the Middle East, Africa, and Latin America. He also was spokesman for the ministry between 1993 and 1996.

Geoana's previous assignments included: counselor to the minister of state, minister of foreign affairs, in 1993; director of the European Affairs Department in the same Ministry and head of the Romanian delegation at the Commission on Security and Cooperation in Europe (CSCE) Committee of Senior officials in 1991; and desk officer at the West European Department in the Ministry of Foreign Affairs, 1990-91.

In 1987-88, he worked for the Department of Foreign Trade at the Ministry of Industry. In 1988-90, as well as between 1983 and 1987, he was an execution and research specialist at the ENERGOMTAJ TRUST in Bucharest.

Geoana attended National College Sfantul Sava in Bucharest. He is a graduate of the Polytechnical Institute of Bucharest, the Law University of Bucharest, and the French Ecole Nationale d'Administration. He was a professor at the National School of Political and Administration Science in Bucharest teaching a European Institutions course and a professor at the Nicolae Titulescu University of Bucharest teaching an international relations course. Geoana received a NATO Research Fellowship on democratic institutions and he is working on a doctorate in world economy at the Bucharest Academy of Economical Sciences.

Geoana is married and has two children and is fluent in English, French, Spanish, and German. His hobbies are literature, music, tennis, and skiing.

STAFF:

Mr. Napoleon POP
Minister-Counselor (DCM)
Spouse: Mrs. Anne Maria

Mr. Adrian CONSTANTINESCU
Minister-Counselor (Economic)
Spouse: Mrs. Ana Constantinescu

Mrs. Iuliana BOGHEZ
Counselor (Consular)

Mrs. Simona Mirela MICULESCU
First Secretary (Press)
Spouse: Mr. Ovid Miculescu

Mr. Constantin MATACHE
First Secretary (Political)
Spouse: Mrs. Raduta Matache

Mr. Cristian MATEI
First Secretary (Cultural)
Spouse: Mrs. Gabriela Matei

Mrs. Raduta MATACHE
Second Secretary (Political)
Spouse: Mr. Constantin Matache

Mr. Alin CRAPATUREANU
Second Secretary (Political)
Spouse: Mrs. Luana Craptureanu

Mr. Cosmin DOBRAN
Second Secretary (Economic)
Spouse: Mrs. Diana Dobran

Ms. Cristina SERBANESCU
Second Secretary (Economic)

Ms. Tatiana MAXIM
Third Secretary (Political)

Mr. Lucian FATU
Second Secretary (Political)
Spouse: Mrs. Luminita Fatu

Mrs. Anca MEDAR
Second Secretary (Economic)
Spouse: Mr. Sergiu Medar

Mr. Gheorghe PREDESCU
Third Secretary (Political)
Spouse: Mrs. Olga Predescu

Mr. Ovidiu GHITA
First Secretary (Political)
Spouse: Mrs. Marilena Ghita

Mr. Victor SERBAN
Attaché (Financial)
Spouse: Mrs. Elisabeta Servan

Lt. Colonel Sergiu Tudor MEDAR
Defense, Military, Naval and Air Attaché
Spouse: Mrs. Medar

Major Petrus BUTU
Asst. Attaché
Spouse: Mrs. Cornelia Butu

Mr. Lupu CORNELIU
Attaché (Financial)
Spouse: Mrs. Marioara Lupu

Office of the Economic Counselor
1607 23rd Street, NW
Washington DC 20008
Phone: 202/232-6593 Fax: 202/332-4858

**Office of the Defense, Military, Navy
and Air Attaché**
1607 23rd Street, NW
Washington DC 20008
Phone: 202/232-6206 Fax: 202/232-4748

Office of Consular Affairs
1607 23rd Street, NW
Washington DC 20008
Phone: 202/332-4846 Fax: 202/332-4848

Russia

Embassy of the Russian Federation
2650 Wisconsin Avenue, NW
Washington DC 20007
Phone: 202/298-5700
Fax: 202/298-5735

Yuli M. VORONTSOV
Ambassador

Date Credentials Presented: 8/11/94

Born: 10/7/29

Spouse: Mrs. Faina A. Vorontsova

Yuli M. Vorontsov served in Washington between 1966 and 1977 as counsellor and later minister-counsellor of the USSR Embassy to the U.S. Since that time, he has been USSR ambassador to India between 1977-83, to France between 1983-86, and to Afghanistan in 1988-89. In addition to his responsibilities in Washington, he now serves as a foreign affairs adviser to President Boris N. Yeltsin and is co-chairman of the Russia-American Bankers Forum.

After joining the diplomatic service in 1952, Vorontsov worked on the staff of the USSR permanent mission to the U.N. Between foreign assignments, he occupied several important posts in the USSR Foreign Ministry. He headed the Soviet delegation to the Belgrade meeting of the Conference on Security and Cooperation in Europe. In 1986, he was appointed first deputy foreign minister of the USSR.

In 1990, Vorontsov was appointed permanent representative of the USSR to the U.N. and representative of the USSR on the Security Council. In December 1991, he became the permanent representative of the Russian Federation to the U.N. and representative of the Russian Federation on the Security Council.

Vorontsov and his wife have one daughter.

STAFF:

Mr. Vladimir I. CHKHIKVISHVILI
Minister-Counselor (Deputy Chief of Mission)

Spouse: Mrs. Olga Viktorvna Chkhikvishvili

Mr. Yuriy V. AKHREMENKO
Minister-Counselor (Trade Representative)
Spouse: Mrs. Nataliya L. Akhremenko

Mr. Nikolay Y. BABICH
Counselor
Spouse: Mrs. Valentina V. Babich

Mr. Vladimir Y. BASHKIROV
Counselor (Political Military)
Spouse: Mrs. Yelena S. Bashkirova

Mr. Valeriy K. BOBUNOV
Counselor (Africa and Administrative)
Spouse: Mrs. Zoia Bobunova

Mr. Sergey Y. CHESTNOY
Counselor (Economic)

Mr. Vladimir Mikhaylovich CHIBIREV
Counselor (Commercial)
Spouse: Mrs. Natalia Chibireva

Mr. Andrey Andreyevich CHUPIN
Counselor
Spouse: Mrs. Natalya Yevgenyevna Chupina

Mr. Aleksandr A. DANILOV
Counselor
Spouse: Mrs. Lyubov A. Danilova

Mr. Aleksandr N. DARCHIYEV
Counselor

Mr. Serguei S. DMITRIYEV
Counselor (Commercial)
Spouse: Mrs. Tatiana A. Dmitrieva

Mr. Vitaliy Nikolayevich DOMORATSKIY
Counselor
Spouse: Mrs. Alla Domoratskaya

Mr. Vladimir G. FOEDORENKO
Counselor (Fisheries)
Spouse: Mrs. Galina Nikolayevna Fedorenko

Mr. Yuriy A. FILATOV
Counselor (Bilateral)
Spouse: Mrs. Galina V. Filatova

Mr. Valentin F. FOMICHEV
Counselor (CIS and Baltics)
Spouse: Mrs. Tayana V. Fomicheva

Mr. Boris Yevgenyevich GOROZHANKIN
Counselor
Spouse: Mrs. Yelena Gorozhankina

Mr. Aleksandr Vitalyevich KHLUNOV
Counselor
Spouse: Mrs. Natalya Aleksandrovna Khlunova

Mr. Aleksandr N. KHUDIN
Counselor
Spouse: Mrs. Lyudmila Y. Khudina

Mr. Mikhail A. KONAROVSKIY

Counselor (Arabian Peninsula, S.W. Asia)
Spouse: Mrs. Inessa A. Konarovskaia

Mr. Nikolai M. KOZLOV
Counselor
Spouse: Mrs. Svetlana N. Kozlova

Mr. Vladimir KUDRYAVTSEV
Counselor

Mr. Grigoriy S. LOGVINOV
Counselor (Asia-Pacific, South Asia)
Spouse: Mrs. Irina N. Logvinova

Mr. Aleksandr V. NOVOSELOV
Counselor (Asst. to the Ambassador)
Spouse: Mrs. Natalia N. Novoselova

Mr. Sergey A. PANCHEKHIN
Counselor
Spouse: Mrs. Nataliya A. Panchekhina

Mr. Vladislav V. POTAPOV
Counselor (Asst. to the Ambassador)
Spouse: Mrs. Marina M. Potapova

Mr. Igor P. RYZHKOV
Counselor (Commercial)
Spouse: Mrs. Irena E. Ryzhkova

Miss Natal'ya P. SEMENIKHINA
Counselor (Public Affairs)

Mr. Vladislav V. SHIMANOVSKIY
Counselor
Spouse: Mrs. Tatyana S. Shimanovskaya

Mr. Mikhail A. SHURGALIN
Counselor (Press and Information)
Spouse: Mrs. Irina Nikolayevna
   Shurgalina

Mr. Petr A. SILANTYEV
Counselor (Information)
Spouse: Mrs. Olga K. Silantyeva

Mr. Pavel P. SOROKIN
Counselor (Agricultural)
Spouse: Mrs. Oksana S. Sorokina

Mr. Aleksandr P. TOLSTOPYATENKO
Counselor and Consul General
Spouse: Mrs. Ylena V. Tolstopyatenko

Mr. Sergey Y. YAKOVLEV
Counselor (Middle East and North Africa)
Spouse: Mrs. Nina V. Yakovleva

Mr. Aleksandr S. YERESKOVSKIY
Counselor (Political-Military)
Spouse: Mrs. Valentina Yereskovskaya

Mr. Anotoliy Ivanovich ZUBEKHIN
Counselor
Spouse: Mrs. Svetlana Nikolayevna
   Zubekhina

Mr. Vladimir Fedorovich ANSIMOV
First Secretary
Spouse: Mrs. Yekaterina G. Ansimova

Mr. Nikolay AVDOSHKIN
First Secretary

Spouse: Mrs. Galina Avdoshkina

Mr. Vladimir BIRYUKOV
First Secretary
Spouse: Mrs. Larisa M. Biryukova

Mr. Artur A. BLINOV
First Secretary
Spouse: Mrs. Yevgeniya A. Blinova

Mr. Aleksandr V. CHUPLYGIN
First Secretary and Consul
Spouse: Mrs. Galina P. Chuplygina

Mr. Aleksey Y. DEDOV
First Secretary
Spouse: Mrs. Larisa A. Dedova

Mr. Vladimir L. FROLOV
First Secretary
Spouse: Mrs. Yelena N. Frolova

Mr. Sergey K. GEYVANDOV
First Secretary
Spouse: Mrs. Irina I. Geyvandova

Mr. Vladimir N. KIRDYANOV
First Secretary
Spouse: Mrs. Galina V. Kirdynova

Mr. Igor N. KUZNETSOV
First Secretary
Spouse: Mrs. Irina Y. Kuznetsova

Mr. Mikhall F. MASLOV
First Secretary
Spouse: Mrs. Viktoriya Y. Maslova

Mr. V. RAZUMOVSKIY
First Secretary
Spouse: Mrs. Olga N. Razumovskaya

Mr. Sergey Y. SACHKO
First Secretary
Spouse: Mrs. Valentina S. Sachko

Mr. Mikhail Y. SHCHENEV
First Secretary
Spouse: Mrs. Nataliya Y. Shcheneva

Mr. Gennadiy I. STEPANOV
First Secretary (Security)
Spouse: Mrs. Vera F. Steponva

Mr. Sergery I. SUKHOV
First Secretary
Spouse: Mrs. Irina Y. Sukova

Mr. Aleksandr M. TRIFONOV
First Secretary
Spouse: Mrs. Lyudmila N. Tifonova

Mr. Aleksandr N. TRUDNENKO
First Secretary
Spouse: Mrs. Olga Leonidovna Trudnenko

Mr. Igor S. VISHNEVETSKIY
First Secretary
Spouse: Mrs. Yekaterina V.
   Vishnevetskaya

Mr. Vladimir I. YERMAKOV
First Secretary

Spouse: Mrs. Olga V. Yermakova

Mr. Sergey V. IVANETS
Second Secretary
Spouse: Mrs. Inna V. Ivanets

Mr. Aleksandr S. IVANOV
Second Secretary (Accounts)
Spouse: Mrs. Tatiana V. Ivanova

Mr. Igor B. IVANOV
Second Secretary
Spouse: Mrs. Tamara V. Ivanova

Mr. Vyacheslav Yuryevich KABANOV
Second Secretary and Consul
Spouse: Mrs. Yelena Alimovna Kabanova

Mr. Igor A. KAZANTSEV
Second Secretary and Consul
Spouse: Mrs. Irina A. Kazantseva

Mr. Yevigeniy V. KHORISHKO
Second Secretary
Spouse: Mrs. Olga V. Khorishko

Mr. Igor Y. KOCHETKOV
Second Secretary
Spouse: Mrs. Anastasiya Vadimovna
   Kochetkova

Mr. Anatoliy Nikolayevich KUTYAVIN
Second Secretary and Consul
Spouse: Mrs. Nataliya Nikolayevna
   Kutyavina

Mr. Anatoliy MIKRYUKOV
Second Secretary
Spouse: Mrs. Irina G. Mikryukova

Mr. Sergey Vladimirovich PETROV
Second Secretary
Spouse: Mrs. Olga A. Petrova

Mr. Peter N. PRIMAK
Second Secretary
Spouse: Mrs. Irina Primak

Mr. Vladimir N. PROKHOROV
Second Secretary

Mr. Aleksander ROMASHKOV
Second Secretary
Spouse: Mrs. Lyudmila V. Romashkova

Mr. Aleksander N. SAMOCHKIN
Second Secretary
Spouse: Mrs. Olga V. Samochkina

Mr. Vadim V. SAVELYEV
Second Secretary and Consul

Mr. Aleksandr I. VARENYA
Second Secretary
Spouse: Mrs. Tatiana G. Varennia

Mr. Dmitriy Y. ASHANIN
Third Secretary
Spouse: Mrs. Tatyana Ashnina

Mr. Yuriy Viktorovich AVERIN
Third Secretary and Vice Consul
Spouse: Mrs. Zinaida Vladimirovna

Averina

Mr. Vladimir Yuryevich BEDRZHITKAYA
Third Secretary
Spouse: Mrs. Galina Pavlovan
    Bedrzhitskaya

Mr. Aleksey Yuryevich CHIBISOV
Third Secretary
Spouse: Mrs. Tatyana Antolyevna
    Chibisova

Mr. Viktor P. DUBENETSKAYA
Third Secretary
Spouse: Mrs. Galina N. Dubenetskaya

Mr. Oleg B. GOGOLEV
Third Secretary
Spouse: Mrs. Yelena G. Gogoleva

Mr. Dmitriy Y. KORYAGIN
Third Secretary
Spouse: Mrs. Elizaveta V. Koryagina

Mr. Vasiliy S. MAKAROV
Third Secretary and Vice Consul
Spouse: Mrs. Nataliya I. Makarova

Mr. Dmitriy P. MIKHEYEV
Third Secretary and Vice Consul
Spouse: Mrs. Viktoriya V. Mikheyeva

Mr. Dmitriy V. NIKOLAYEV
Third Secretary
Spouse: Mrs. Natalia B. Nikolayeva

Mr. Aleksandr S. SHCHEGLOV
Third Secretary
Spouse: Mrs. Valentina V. Shcheglova

Mr. Yuliy Valeryevich SHEVCHENKO
Third Secretary
Spouse: Mrs. Svetlana I. Shevchenko

Mr. Yuliy P. SUBACHEV
Third Secretary
Spouse: Mrs. Yelena G. Subacheva

Mr. Viktor Ivanovich AKIMOV
Attaché
Spouse: Mrs. Raisa Alkesandrovna
    Akimova

Mr. Sergey I. AKSENOV
Attaché
Spouse: Mrs. Nelya A. Aksenova

Mr. Serguei M. ARTAMONOV
Attaché
Spouse: Mrs. Ianina V. Artamonova

Mr. Alexandre N. BARSOUKOV
Attaché
Spouse: Mrs. Valentina I. Baroukova

Mr. Vladimir V. BASIKHIN
Attaché
Spouse: Mrs. Galina I. Basikhina

Ms. Anna P. BOGOMOLOVA
Attaché

Mr. Aleksandr N. BONDAREV

Attaché
Spouse: Mrs. Lyudmila Bondareva

Mr. Yevgeniy Nikolayevich BUBNOV
Attaché
Spouse: Mrs. Irina Petrovna Bubnova

Mr. Aleksandr Ivanovich CHVANOV
Attaché
Spouse: Mrs. Nina Vladimirovna
    Chvanova

Mr. Aleksandr N. DZHORDZHADZE
Attaché

Mr. Mikhail P. KLIMOVSKIY
Attaché
Spouse: Mrs. Svetlana I. Klimovskaya

Mr. Vladimir V. KONONALOV
Attaché
Spouse: Mrs. Olga A. Konovalova

Mr. Aleksandr D. KONSTANTINOV
Attaché
Spouse: Mrs. Lyudmila A. Konstantinov

Mr. Aleksey Vyacheslavovich
    KORZHUYEV
Attaché

Lt. Colonel Sergey V. ZHUKOV
Asst. Air Attaché
Spouse: Mrs. Olga N. Zhukova

Colonel Andrey B. KOLDUNOV
Asst. Air Attaché
Spouse: Mrs. Tatyana Y. Koldunova

Lt. Colonel Nikolay V. BLEDNYKH
Asst. Air Attaché
Spouse: Mrs. Tatyana P. Blednykh

Commander Sergey A. SHERGIN
Asst. Naval Attaché
Spouse: Mrs. Lyudmila I. Shergina

Captain Valeri A. POUSTOVOITOV
Asst. Naval Attaché
Spouse: Mrs. Tatiana N. Pustovoitova

Lt. Commander Pavel A. BELAYAYEV
Asst. Naval Attaché
Spouse: Mrs. Marina N. Belayayeva

Colonel Viktor S. TIMOCHKOV
Asst. Military Attaché
Spouse: Mrs. Olga A. Timochkova

Lt. Colonel Pavel N. SADOVNICHIY
Asst. Military Attaché
Spouse: Mrs. Galina Sadovnichaya

Lt. Colonel Antoliy N. BRUYEV
Asst. Military Attaché
Spouse: Mrs. Irina I. Bruyeva

Major Igor Y. GROSHIKOV
Asst. Defense & Air Attaché
Spouse: Mrs. Tatyana V. Groshikova

Lt. Colonel Aleksandr Valeriyevich
    GRINENKO

Asst. Defense Attaché
Spouse: Mrs. Svetlana Vladimirovna
    Grinenko

Colonel Dmitriy A. BABIYCHUK
Asst. Defense Attaché
Spouse: Mrs. Nina S. Babiychuk

Lt. Colonel Aleksandr A. ANTONOV
Asst. Defense and Military Attaché
Spouse: Mrs. Yelena Y. Antonova

Captain Victor V. ZAIKINE
Naval Attaché
Spouse: Mrs. Tatiana S. Zaikina

Colonel Valeriy V. NYUNIN
Military Attaché
Spouse: Mrs. Natalya T. Nyunina

Mr. Aleksandr Valeryevich ZAYTSEV
Attaché
Spouse: Mrs. Marina Viktorovna Zaytseva

Mr. Viktor A. YAZHLEV
Attaché
Spouse: Mrs. Isabella N. Yazhleva

Mr. Oleg Vitalyevich VINOKUROV
Attaché
Spouse: Mrs. Yuliya S. Vinokurova

Mr. Sergey P. TRUKHIN
Attaché
Spouse: Mrs. Valentina M. Trukhina

Mr. Aleksandr V. TITKIN
Attaché
Spouse: Mrs. Natalya G. Titkina

Mr. Vikto Vladdimirovich STOLYAROV
Attaché
Spouse: Mrs. Alla Dmitriyevna Stolyarova

Mr. Aleksey Leonidovich SOROKIN
Attaché

Mr. Oleg V. SEROV
Attaché
Spouse: Mrs. Darya A. Serova

Mr. Vitaliy A. SEL'DEV
Attaché (Maritime)
Spouse: Mrs. Mariya L. Sel'deva

Mr. Adrey REZNICHENKO
Attaché
Spouse: Mrs. Natalya Y. Reznichenko

Mr. Sergey A. PSHENICHNIY
Attaché
Spouse: Mrs. Viktoriya A. Pshenichnaya

Mr. Aleksandr Vladimirovich OLKHOVOY
Attaché
Spouse: Mrs. Olga Vadimovna Olkhovaya

Mr. Mikhail Y. NEDOSEKIN
Attaché
Spouse: Mrs. Yekaterina A. Nedosekina

Mr. Mikhail V. KUTEPOV
Attaché

Spouse: Mrs. Lyubov M. Kutepova

Mr. Aleksandr A. KOTIKOV
Attaché
Spouse: Mrs. Yelena V. Kotikova

Trade Rep. of the Russian Federation
2001 Connecticut Avenue, NW
Washington DC 20008
Phone: 202/234-8304

Information Office
1706 18th Street, NW
Washington DC 20009
Phone: 202/232-6020

Fisheries Attaché
1609 Decatur Street, NW
Washington DC 20011
Phone: 202/726-3838

Defense, Military, Naval, & Air Attaché
2650 Wisconsin Avenue, NW
Washington DC 20007

Consular Division
1825 Phelps Place, NW
Washington DC 20008
Phone: 202/939-8907

Rwanda

Embassy of the Republic of Rwanda
1714 New Hampshire Avenue, NW
Washington DC 20009
Phone: 202/232-2882
Fax: 202/232-4544

Dr. Theogene RUDASINGWA
Ambassador

Date Credentials Presented: 4/30/96

Born: 2/2/61

Spouse: Mrs. Dorothy Rudasingwa

Along with his ambassadorship, Dr. Theogene Rudasingwa continues to hold the position of secretary-general of the Rwandese Patriotic Army (RPF) to which he was appointed in 1993.

In 1990, Rudasingwa joined the Rwandese Patriotic Army (RPA), the armed wing of the RFP and rose to the rank of major in 1993.

From 1990 to mid-1991, he was an operational doctor in charge of one of the combat units which involved medical and surgical operations for the wounded as well as the general population.

In 1991, he was appointed by the RPF as director of international relations in charge of the Africa region. From 1991 to 1993, he participated in various peace initiatives, including the Arusha negotiations. He also represented the RPF at the Organization of African Unity and the United Nations, and led delegations to the United States and European and African countries to meet, among others, government officials and officers of international organizations.

Rudasingwa grew up and was educated in Uganda. He obtained a degree in medicine and surgery from Makerere University in Kampala, Uganda.

STAFF:

Mr. Joseph W. MUTABOBA
Counselor
Spouse: Mrs. Vicky Mutaboba

Mr. Eugene KAYIHURA
Second Secretary

Saint Kitts & Nevis

Embassy of St. Kitts and Nevis
3216 New Mexico Avenue, NW
Washington DC 20016
Phone: 202/686-2636
Fax: 202/686-5740

Dr. Osbert W. LIBURD
Ambassador

Date Credentials Presented: 5/14/97

Dr. Osbert W. Liburd, Saint Kitts and Nevis' ambassador to the U.S. since 1995, is an expert on agriculture and rural development. He has worked in rural development with small farmers in Africa and the Caribbean and developed appropriate agricultural technologies and techniques for farmers in those regions.

From 1977 to 1982, he was director of agricultural services and rural development for the agricultural missions of the National Council of Churches in New York. From 1982 to 1987, he was the team leader for the Caribbean Agricultural Research and Development Institute. He was a consultant on plant pathology and agronomy from 1983 to 1995.

Liburd earned a B.A. degree in biology, concentrating on zoology, from the College of the Virgin Islands, St. Thomas, the U.S. Virgin Islands, and he received a Ph.D. in plant pathology, concentrating on nematology, from Cornell University in Ithaca, N.Y.

The ambassador enjoys track and field and basketball, tennis, gardening, music, and art. His primary interest is being a national representative of St. Kitts and Nevis.

STAFF:

Mr. A. Kenneth JULES
Minister-Counselor (Deputy Chief of Mission)

Mr. Kutayba Y. ALGHANIM
Minister-Counselor (Economic)

Saint Lucia

Embassy of Saint Lucia
3216 New Mexico Avenue, NW
Washington DC 20016
Phone: 202/364-6792
Fax: 202/364-6723

Sonia Merlyn JOHNNY
Ambassador

Sonia Merlyn Johnny, who served as political and economic attaché in the embassy of Saint Lucia in Washington, D.C., in the 1980s, has returned to the embassy as the country's ambassador to the U.S.

At the embassy between 1984 and 1989, Johnny wrote briefs on U.S.-Latin America political issues and U.S. trade legislation of relevance to Saint Lucia. She also wrote speeches for the ambassador and visiting ministers and lobbied the U.S. Congress on U.S.-Caribbean matters. Before that, Johnny served as chief of the political and economic division of the ministry of foreign affairs in Saint Lucia from 1979 to 1984.

From 1995 until she assumed her responsibilities as ambassador, Johnny was section chief in the tax litigation section of the office of the corporation counsel in Washington, D.C. She also worked in the office of the corporation counsel from 1993 to 1995 in the housing litigation section.

Before that, Johnny was affiliated with two Washington, D.C., law firms---Charles A. Brady & Associates, 1991-93; and Anderson, Kill, Olick & Oshinsky, 1991-92. She also was a law a clerk with two other Washington law firms---Robinson & Geraldo in 1990 and James P. Gittens & Associates in 1989. In 1991, she tutored first-year students at the Georgetown Law Center.

Johnny was an advisor to Saint Lucia's permanent mission to the United Nations in New York in 1981 and served as an alternate representative to the Organization of American States in Washington, D.C., from 1984 to 1989. She is affiliated with the Federal American Inn of Court in Washington, which presents current federal issues before federal judges for critique.

Johnny received a bachelor of arts degree in history and literature with honors from the University of the West Indies in Barbados in 1977 and earned a diploma in international relations from the same college in 1979. She received a master's degree in international public policy from Johns Hopkins School of Advanced Studies in Washington, D.C., in 1987 and a juris doctor from Georgetown University Law Center in Washington in 1991.

STAFF:

Ms. Tahis MEROE
Attaché (Administrative)

Saint Vincent & the Grenadines

Embassy of Saint Vincent and
the Grenadines
3216 New Mexico Avenue, NW
Washington DC 20016
Phone: 202/364-6730
Fax: 202/364-6736

Kingsley Cuthbert Augustine LAYNE
Ambassador

Date Credentials Presented: 2/19/91

Born: 2/7/49 in St. Vincent

Spouse: Mrs. Cornelia M. Layne

As ambassador to the U.S. from the "Gem of the Antilles", Kingsley Layne represents a country whose economy is anchored in agriculture, chiefly banana exports. Although some companies in St. Vincent & the Grenadines are engaged in light manufacturing operations and while tourism is rising in importance, the nation's reliance dominates both internal policy and foreign relations.

Layne has been in almost continuous service directed at improving his country's economic development. In 1989, St. Vincent & the Grenadines had a per capita income of only $1,268.

Layne began his career in 1973 at the Ministry of Trade, Agriculture and Tourism. He moved on in 1975 to become a project manager for the Housing and Land Development Corporation and, in 1977, to the Department of Labor, and from there, to the Registry Department in 1978. His sole venture into the private sector came between 1980 and 1982, when he served as the manager of the St. Vincent Children's Wear Company, after which he was named to the Economic Affairs Secretariat of the Organization of Eastern Caribbean States.

During the five years preceding his Washington assignment, Layne served as permanent secretary of the Ministry of Trade, Industry and Agriculture, as well as with the Ministry of Tourism, Aviation, Culture and Women's Affairs, and the Ministry of Trade and Tourism.

A focus of Layne's work in Washington involves not only the securing of agricultural trade terms favorable to St. Vincent & the Grenadines, but also the promotion of the activities of DEVCO, the Development Corporation established by Parliament in 1970 to encourage investments in St. Vincent & the Grenadines, primarily through the formulation of transnational joint ventures.

Layne holds a B.A. in economics and history from the University of the West Indies.

STAFF:

Ms. Cecily A. NORRIS
Minister-Counselor (Deputy Chief of Mission)

Mr. Frank M. CLARKE
Counselor

Samoa

Embassy of the Independent State of Samoa
820 Second Avenue, Suite 800D
New York NY 10017
Phone: 212/599-6196
Fax: 212/599-0797

Tuiloma Neroni SLADE
Ambassador

Date Credentials Presented: 9/3/93

Born: 4/8/41 in Apia, Western Samoa

Spouse: Mrs. Jeanne Doris Schoenberger Slade

An attorney by training, Tuiloma Neroni Slade has practiced law since 1968 - in private practice and for his country's government and parliament. His career has spanned most of Samoa's history as an independent state since 1962, before which it was a trust territory, administered by New Zealand.

Having begun his career in private law practice in New Zealand, Slade soon returned to his country as legal counsel in the office of the attorney general - a position in which he remained until 1973. At that juncture, he was appointed parliamentary counsel and in 1976, he moved on to become Samoa's attorney general. During the decade prior to his appointment to Washington, Slade was a London resident, serving as deputy director of the legal division of the Commonwealth Secretariat.

Slade studied at Wanganui Technical College in New Zealand, received an LL.B. from Victoria University in Wellington, New Zealand, and speaks English and Samoan. He is married and has a daughter.

STAFF:

Mrs. Andrea Monique
WILLIAMS STEWART
First Secretary
Spouse: Mr. Wilber Sean Apoua Stewart

Saudi Arabia

Embassy of Saudi Arabia
601 New Hampshire Avenue, NW
Washington DC 20037
Phone: 202/342-3800
Fax: 202/944-5983

H.R.H. Prince Bandar Bin Sultan BIN ABDUL AZIZ
Ambassador

Date Credentials Presented: 10/24/83

Born: 3/2/49 at Taif, Saudi Arabia

Spouse: H.R.H. Princess Haifa Bint Faisal

Prince Bandar Bin Sultan Bin Abdul Aziz, who has represented Saudi Arabia in the United States since 1983, is the dean of the diplomatic corps in Washington, D.C. In August 1995, he was promoted to the rank of minister.

Prince Bandar graduated from the British Royal Air Force College at Cranwell, England, in 1968 and was commissioned as a second lieutenant in the Royal Saudi Air Force (RSAF). He received pilot training in the United Kingdom and the United States and has flown numerous fighter aircraft. During his 17-year military career, he attained the rank of lieutenant-colonel, commanded fighter squadrons at three RSAF bases, and undertook management responsibilities in the major RSAF modernization project, Peace Hawk.

In addition, Prince Bandar carried out special assignments in Washington, D.C., during the debates between the U.S. administration and the Congress concerning the sale to Saudi Arabia of F-15s in 1978 and of F-3 AWACS in 1981. In 1982, he was assigned to Washington as the Kingdom's defense attaché.

As special envoy, Prince Bandar negotiated the ceasefire in the Lebanese civil war in 1983. He was the Saudi delegate with the Gulf Cooperation Council observing the 1991 Madrid Peace Talks. In addition, he has been a regular member of the King's delegation to the United Nations General Assembly since 1994.

Prince Bandar completed his post-graduate work in several U.S. professional military schools including staff courses with the Air Command and Staff College at Maxwell Air Force Base in Montgomery, Ala., and with the Industrial College of the Armed Forces at Fort McNair in Washington, D.C. He received his master's degree in international public policy from Johns Hopkins University School of Advanced International Studies in Washington, D.C., in 1980.

Prince Bandar is the son of Prince Sultan Bin Abdul Azia Al-Saud, who held the posts of second deputy premier and minister of defense and aviation. He is married to Princess Haifa Bint Faisal, and they have four sons and four daughters. Prince Bandar has been awarded many medals and decorations, including the Hawk Flying Medal of Aviation, the King Faisal Medal, and the King Abdul Aziz Sash, as well as honors from other nations.

STAFF:

H.R.H. Prince Mohamed Bin Faisal Bin
  Turki AL-SAUD
Minister
Spouse: Mrs. Wafa Fayyad Al-Saud

Mr. Ahmed A. KATTAN
Minister
Spouse: Mrs. Kattan

Mr. Ali M. ALOMARI
Counselor
Spouse: Mrs. Al Daajani

Mr. Zain M.K. AL-ZAHIRY
Counselor
Spouse: Mrs. Murad

Mr. Rihab M. Ibrahim MASSOUD
Counselor

Mr. Mohamad A.M.S. AL-GHAMDI
First Secretary
Spouse: Mrs. Al-Hamdan

Mr. Adel A. AL-JUBEIR
First Secretary

Mr. Majid A. AL DREES
Second Secretary
Spouse: Mrs. Nawal A. Al-Shalhoub

Mr. Abdulaziz A. AL OTHMAN
First Secretary
Spouse: Mrs. Nourah S. Al Helali

Mr. Fouad GASSAS
First Secretary
Spouse: Mrs. Osta

Mr. Khalid J. KATTAN
First Secretary
Spouse: Mrs. Sohair A. Kattan

Mr. Emad A. MADANI
First Secretary
Spouse: Mrs. Madani

Mr. Jamal NASEF
First Secretary
Spouse: Mrs. Al-Muhayawi

Mr. Khaled A. AL FADL
Second Secretary
Spouse: Mrs. Ebstam A. Abdulwahab

Mr. Azzam A. AL-GAIN
Second Secretary
Spouse: Mrs. Basrawi

Mr. Nail Ahmed AL-JUBEIR
Second Secretary

Mr. Abdullah Mohamed AL RASHIDAN
Second Secretary
Spouse: Mrs. Asma A. Al Yaseen

Mr. Saud Homoud AL ZAID
Second Secretary
Spouse: Mrs. Najah Fajad Al-Salloum

Mr. Hamzah Ahmad EDREES
Second Secretary
Spouse: Mrs. Al-Sawi

Mr. Mohammed I. AL ZAMIL
Third Secretary
Spouse: Mrs. Jamilah O. Al Zamil

Mr. Abdulatif Yhia ABDULWAHAB
Attaché (Administrative)
Spouse: Mrs. Gorban

Dr. Saad H. AL ADWANI
Attaché (Administrative)
Spouse: Mrs. Monerah M. Al-Angary

Mr. Bandar Mohammed AL-AIBAN
Attaché
Spouse: Mrs. Al-Jomaih

Dr. Khalik M. AL-AIBAN
Attaché
Spouse: Mrs. Al-Sewilem

Mr. Nassir AL-AJMI
Attaché (Administrative)
Spouse: Mrs. Al Joharah Al-Sudairi

Mr. Abdullah M.N. AL-ATHEL
Attaché (Commercial)
Spouse: Mrs. Feryal Ali Al-Mojhed

Lt. Commander Ateyat Allah AL-BALADI
Attaché (Administrative)
Spouse: Mrs. Latifa M. Al-Baladi

Colonel Sulaiman S. AL-BASSAM
Attaché (Administrative)
Spouse: Mrs. Hend Al-Faris

Mr. Omar A. AL-BASSAM
Attaché (Administrative)
Spouse: Mrs. Al-Bassam

Major Ali S. AL FRAIJI
Attaché (Administrative)
Spouse: Mrs. Soha Saleh A. Al Omair

Dr. Majed H.N. AL-GHESHEYAN
Attaché (Administrative)
Spouse: Mrs. Al-Ghesheyan

Mr. Fahad S. AL-GHOFAILEY
Attaché (Administrative)
Spouse: Mrs. Marian Al-Ashban

Colonel Saleh A. AL-JAWINI
Attaché (Administrative)
Spouse: Mrs. Mariam A. Al-Jawini

Mr. Mohammed A. AL-KOBAILY
Attaché (Administrative)
Spouse: Mrs. Alaf Al-Sorayai

Dr. Fahad Turki AL-MADHY
Attaché (Medical)
Spouse: Mrs. Salwa Al-Khateeb

Captain Nezar M. AL MALEK
Attaché (Administrative)
Spouse: Mrs. Jawaher A. Al Melek

Dr. Mazyed I. AL MAZYED
Attaché (Cultural)
Spouse: Mrs. Wendy M. Al Mazyed

Mr. Mohammed A. A. AL MESFER
Attaché (Administrative)

Mr. Fahad S. AL-MHQANI
Attaché (Administrative)
Spouse: Mrs. Al-Ghazwa E. Al-Otaibi

Mr. Saud Saleh AL-MUHANNA
Attaché
Spouse: Mrs. Amal Mohammed
  Al-Nejaidi

Mr. Salem M. AL MURRI
Attaché

Mr. Saleh A.A. AL-QAHTANI
Attaché
Spouse: Mrs. Khadra H. M. Al Ghamdi

Dr. Nasser I. AL-RASHID
Attaché (Administrative)

Mr. Saleh Abdul-Aziz AL-SAID
Attaché (Administrative)
Spouse: Mrs. Al-Ghadi

His Highness Prince Faisal Bin Turki
   Bin Naser AL SAUD
Attaché

H.R.H. Prince Turki Bin Khalik Bin
   Bin Saad AL-SAUD
Attaché (Administrative)
Spouse: Her Highness Princess Arib
   Bint Fahd Al-Saud

Mr. Talaat AL-SHUBAIKI
Attaché
Spouse: Mrs. Soha Karkadan

Mr. Khaled AL-SOWAILEM
Attaché
Spouse: Mrs. Bushra Al-Khamais

Colonel Abdulrahman I. AL SUWAILEM
Attaché (Administrative)
Spouse: Mrs. Gomasha I. Al-Metawaa

Major Saeed Ali ALGHAMDI
Attaché (Administrative)
Spouse: Mrs. Alghamdi

Lt. Colonel Saud ALOMARI
Attaché (Administrative)
Spouse: Mrs. Joza S.S. Al-Mohamed

Mr. Khalid M.A. ALSAIF
Attaché

Colonel Mohammad ALTHOMALI
Attaché (Administrative)

Brigadier General Abdulaziz Saleh
   M. ASEEL
Attaché (Administrative)
Spouse: Mrs. Thoria Ali Etaiwi

Mr. Mahmoud M. FOSTOUK
Attaché

Major Abdulhafiz A. HORAIB
Attaché (Administrative)
Spouse: Mrs. Fatin M. S. Alhamad

Dr. Abdullah M.Z. KHOUJ
Attaché (Administrative)

Colonel Yahya Ahmed A. MASFUH
Attaché (Administrative)

Mr. Abdullah A. MAWYAH
Attaché (Administrative)
Spouse: Mrs. Hayat Mohammed Rayes

Colonel Saeed Abdulaziz M. MUSHAYT
Attaché (Administrative)
Spouse: Mrs. Mushayt

Mr. Abdulaziz A.M.S. NAZIR
Administrative Attaché (Executive
   Assistant to the Ambassador)

Mr. Saleh Mohammad OBAID
Attaché (Administrative)
Spouse: Mrs. Samiah A. Hamda

Major General Mosleh A. OMAIR
Attaché (Administrative)
Spouse: Mrs. Omair

Mr. Mohammed J. RADWAN
Attaché (Administrative)
Spouse: Mrs. Al-Ayesh

Mr. Hamad H. ALABDALI
Asst. Attaché (Cultural)
Spouse: Mrs. Nadia M. H. Alabdali

Mr. Abdulrahman A. ALHOSAIN
Asst. Attaché (Cultural)
Spouse: Mrs. Alhamdan

Mr. Fahad AL BAWARDY
Asst. Attaché (Cultural)
Spouse: Mrs. Sarah Al Shohaib

Mr. Abdulrahman A. AL-DYEL
Asst. Attaché (Cultural)
Spouse: Mrs. Al-Dyel

Mr. Mohammed Jayez AL ENEZI
Asst. Attaché (Cultural)
Spouse: Mrs. Tahani Al Enezi

Mr. Abdullah J.M. AL-JAMMAZ
Asst. Attaché (Cultural)
Spouse: Mrs. Salwa A. Al-Suwailem

Major Abdulla H. KABLY
Attaché (Administrative)
Spouse: Mrs. Kably

Mr. Mohammed A. AL-KHALAF
Asst. Attaché (Cultural)
Spouse: Mrs. Nora Al-Dawod

Mr. Abdullah Kh. AL-KHODAIR
Asst. Attaché (Administrative)
Spouse: Mrs. Sarah M. Al-Robia

Mr. Abdulrahman AL OMIRAH
Asst. Attaché (Cultural)
Spouse: Mrs. Sarah Alabbas

Mr. Naif AL OTAIBI
Asst. Attaché (Cultural)

Mr. Ahmed A. M. AL RASHEED
Asst. Attaché (Cultural)

Mr. Ahmad Abdullah AL-ASWAD
Asst. Attaché (Cultural)

Mr. Seleh O. AL RAZGAN
Asst. Attaché (Administrative)
Spouse: Mrs. Nora A. M. Alfallaj

Mr. Abdul Muhsin AL SHAIKH
Asst. Attaché (Cultural)

Dr. Feher S. AL-SHARIF
Asst. Attaché (Medical)
Spouse: Mrs. Al-Ghalib

Mr. Muhammed A.S.A. AL TURBAK
Asst. Attaché (Cultural)

Mr. Sameer F. AL-TURKI
Asst. Attaché (Administrative)

Mr. Abdullah I. ALMATROUDI
Asst. Attaché (Cultural)
Spouse: Mrs. Hessah A. Almatroudi

Mr. Neyef A. ALMIZAINY
Asst. Attaché (Administrative)
Spouse: Mrs. Laila Yousef Alewaimer

Mr. Abdulmuhsin F. M. ALSUWAILIM
Asst. Attaché (Cultural)
Spouse: Mrs. Bushra N. Al-Tuwaijri

Mr. Mutasim ASSIDMI
Asst. Attaché (Cultural)
Spouse: Mrs. Abutheyab

Mr. Mohammed FALL
Asst. Attaché

Mr. Mahmoud M. SAAD
Asst. Attaché (Administrative)

Dr. Suliman SINDI
Asst. Attaché (Cultural)
Spouse: Mrs. Faygah Sindi

Mr. Abdul Mannan TURJOMAN
Asst. Attaché (Cultural)

Major General Abdulaziz S.A. AL-SAIF
Defense Attaché
Spouse: Mrs. Haya Dh.H. Al-Hamdan

Colonel Abdullah S. ALHUMAIDAN
Military Attaché
Spouse: Mrs. Al-Eisa

Captain Mogbel Hamad AL-MOGBEL
Naval Attaché
Spouse: Mrs. Al-Hamdan

Lt. Colonel Saleh H.A. AL-ROWAITEE
Air Attaché
Spouse: Mrs. Al-Rowaitee

Captain Abdullah A.I. AL-KHWYTER
Asst. Naval Attaché
Spouse: Mrs. Al-Fraikh

Office of Citizen Services
601 New Hampshire Avenue, NW
Washington DC 20037
Phone: 202/342-7393

Commercial Office
601 New Hampshire Avenue, NW
Washington DC 20037
Phone: 202/337-4088

Information Office
601 New Hampshire Avenue, NW
Washington DC 20037
Phone: 202/342-3800

Saudi Arabian Cultural Mission
601 New Hampshire Avenue, NW
Washington DC 20037
Phone: 202/342-3800

**Office of the Defense & Armed
   Forces Attaché**
1001 30th Street, NW
Washington DC 20007

Phone: 202/857-0122

Senegal

Embassy of the Republic of Senegal
2112 Wyoming Avenue, NW
Washington DC 20008
Phone: 202/234-0540
Fax: 202/332-6315

Mamadou Mansour SECK
Ambassador

Date Credentials Presented: 11/1/93

Born: 7/3/35 in Dakar, Senegal

Mamadou Mansour Seck, a career military officer who holds the rank of lieutenant general, took on his first diplomatic assignment when he became Senegal's ambassador to the U.S.

An officer for more than 30 years, he began his career in 1961 after completing his military education in France. For a decade thereafter, he served as commanding officer of the First Senegalese Air Force, becoming in 1972 the commander of the Air Force.

Seck continued to rise through the ranks of Senegal's military and was named deputy chief of the general staff in 1980, after he was appointed special chief of staff to Senegal's president and chief of staff of the Senegal-Gambia Confederation. Immediately prior to being named ambassador, Seck served as general chief of staff and general Chief of the Confederation.

Mamadou Monsour Seck was educated at St. Cyr Military Academy in France, the Salon Air Force Academy, the French Air War College, and the Institut des Hautes Etudes de la Defense Nationale. In addition to numerous honors bestowed upon him by his own government, Seck has been decorated by France, Gabon, Holland, and Luxembourg.

STAFF:

Mr. Ibrahima SENE
Counselor
Spouse: Mrs. Khadidiatou Samb Sene

Mr. Babacar THIOUNE

Counselor (Education)
Spouse: Mrs. Mame Penda G. Thioune

Mrs. Seynabou Diop FALL
Counsel (Financial)

Mr. Makhtar GUEYE
First Secretary
Spouse: Mrs. Fatou Gueye

Mr. Mamadou Lamine DIOP
First Secretary
Spouse: Mrs. Souadou Drame Diop

Mr. Etienne DIEDHIOU
Attaché

Col. Khaly NIANE
Defense, Military, Naval and Air Attaché

Seychelles

Embassy of the Republic of Seychelles
800 Second Avenue - Suite 4000
New York NY 10017
Phone: 212/972-1785
Fax: 212/972-1786
Email: sycun@undp.org

Claude Sylvestre Anthony MOREL
Ambassador

Date Credentials Presented: 3/16/98

Born: 9/25/56 in Victoria, Mahé, Seychelles

Spouse: Mrs. Margaret Morel

Claude Sylvestre Anthony Morel was promoted in 1998 to the post of ambassador to the U.S. from the position of chargé d'affaires that he had held since 1996. He also represents his country at the United Nations and in Canada.

During 1997, Morel also served as ambassador to the European Communities, Germany, and the Benelux countries, with residence in Brussels, Belgium. Back in Seychelles, he was director general for foreign affairs and international cooperation in the ministry of foreign affairs, planning and environment from 1993 to 1996.

Other assignments include: director general external relations division in the ministry of environment, economic planning and external relations, 1990-93; charge d'affaires, Seychelles Embassy in Paris, 1988-90; director of external relations, department of planning and external relations, 1987-88; chief protocol officer, ministry of planning and external relations, 1983-87; second secretary, ministry of foreign affairs, 1982-83; and assistant international relations officer, ministry of foreign affairs, 1981-82.

Morel has been a member of several Seychelles presidential visits abroad since 1983. He was a member or head of delegation to meetings of the Organization of African Unity, the Commonwealth, La Francophonie, Franco-African Summit, the Non-Aligned Movement, the United Nations General Assembly, and several U.N. specialized agencies.

From 1992 to 1996, he was a board member of the Seychelles Fishing Authority and from 1990 to 1993, a board member of the Seychelles Islands Foundation.

The ambassador attended Seychelles College and Cambridge University between 1964 and 1975. At the University of Lille, France, he received a "Diplôme Supérieur d'Etudes Françaises" and a "Diplôme d'Etudes Universitaires Génerales" in literature and history. He went to the Cairo Institute of Diplomatic Relations in Egypt in 1984 and studied diplomacy at Institut International d'Administration Publique in Paris, the United Nations in Geneva, and the European Commission in Brussels.

He is fluent in English, French, and Creole and enjoys sports, reading, and traveling.

Sierra Leone

Embassy of Sierra Leone
1701 19th Street, NW
Washington DC 20009
Phone: 202/939-9261
Fax: 202/483-1793
Url: http://www.amenhotep4.virtualafrica.
    com/slembassy/

John Ernest LEIGH
Ambassador

Date Credentials Presented: 10/9/96

Spouse: Mrs. Elizabeth Margaret Leigh

John Ernest Leigh, Sierra Leone's ambassador to the U.S. since 1996, actively participated in the democratization process in Sierra Leone which produced the country's first democratically elected government in 30 years in 1996.

Leigh analyzed a proposed Constitution and helped write the Manifesto of the Sierra Leone's Peoples' Party. When the military staged a coup in May 1997 against the new democratic government, Leigh worked to remove the illegal regime and reinstate the elected government---a feat that was accomplished in February 1998.

Leigh has spent much of his life in the U.S. He first came here in 1961 as a student of economics at New York University. He obtained a B.S. degree in economics in 1964; and an M.B.A. in banking and finance in 1966. During his years in New York City, Leigh was active in student affairs, serving as the general-secretary and president of the Sierra Leone Students Union; and secretary-general of the Pan-African Students Union. He also was a member of the New York University chapter of the Congress of Racial Equality and took part in civil rights activities during most of the 1960s.

Following a twelve-month fellowship at the Chase Manhattan Bank in New York, Leigh returned to Freetown, Sierra Leone, in 1967 to work in economic research at the Bank of Sierra Leone. He left when Siaka Stevens was elected president in 1968.

Returning to the United States, Leigh worked for several multinationals based in the New York metropolitan area before accepting a position in Xerox in the Boston, Mass., area. He acquired Xerox's Nigerian publishing subsidiary, African Universities Press, and spent 1975-81 in Nigeria publishing books for schools and colleges in West Africa. In 1981, Leigh again returned to the U.S. and acquired Advertising Corporation of America, which he sold in 1987.

Leigh graduated juris doctor, cum laude, from Suffolk University Law School in Boston and practiced law in Massachusetts and New York.

As an attorney, Leigh devoted a portion of his practice to representing clients pro bono. He successfully represented not only Americans but other nationalities in a variety of areas including criminal law, and immigration law and in civil litigation. His most recent case prior to his appointment as ambassador was the successful prosecution of the New York City Police Department and one of its officers in a civil rights case.

Leigh and his wife have two daughters. He has a son from a previous marriage.

STAFF:

Mr. James George CAULKER
First Secretary (Economic)
Spouse: Mrs. Marian Caulker

Singapore

Embassy of the Republic of Singapore
3501 International Place, NW
Washington DC 20008
Phone: 202/537-3100
Fax: 202/537-0876
Email: singemb@bellatlantic.net

Heng Chee CHAN
Ambassador

Date Credentials Presented: 7/29/96

Prior to her appointment in 1996 as Singapore's ambassador to the U.S., Heng Chee Chan was the Executive Director of the Singapore International Foundation (similar to our Peace Corps) and Director of the Institute of Southeast Asian Studies. From 1989 to 1991 she served as Singapore's Permanent Representative to the United Nations and was concurrently High Commissioner to Canada and Ambassador to Mexico.

Chan has published numerous articles and books on politics in Singapore, on Southeast Asia, and in the area of international security. For her achievements, she has received numerous awards including an Honorary Degree of Doctor of Letters in 1994 from the University of Newcastle, Australia; Singapore's first "Woman of the Year" award in 1991; the National Book Award, non-fiction section in 1986 for A Sensation of Independence: A Political Biography of David Marshall; and the National Book Award, non-fiction section in 1978 for The Dynamics of One Party Dominance: The PAP at the Grassroots.

Chan was a member of The Australian National University/Australian Research Council Joint Review Team of the Institute of Advanced Studies, ANU, Australia in August 1995; an external specialist to review the Center of Asian Studies at The University of Hong Kong in April 1995; and a member of the International Advisory Panel of the East-West Center in Honolulu in August 1993.

She has been a member of the International Advisory Board of the Council on Foreign Relations in New York since 1995 and a council member of the International Institute for Strategic Studies (IISS) in London since July 1993. Chan has also been a committee member of the Singapore National Committee for Security Cooperation in the Asia-Pacific (CSCAP) since August 1993, and a member of the International Council of the Asia Society in New York since 1991.

Chan is on secondment from her post as Professor in the Department of Political Science at the National University in Singapore. She was educated at the University of Singapore and Cornell University in New York.

STAFF:

Mr. Benjamin Jeyaraj WILLIAM
Counselor (Deputy Chief of Mission)

Mr. Leo Ah BANG
Minister-Counselor
Spouse: Mdm Wong Guek Lan

Brigadier General Sin Boon WAH
Defense Attaché
Spouse: Mdm. Maggie Tan

Lt. Colonel John WONG
Counselor (Defense Procurement)
Spouse: Mdm. Ling Chai Joo

Ms. Tan Sui KIM
Counselor

Mr. Ng Teck HEAN
First Secretary
Spouse: Ms. Lynn Mok

Ms. Kathy Sou Tien LAI
Counselor (Economic)
Spouse: Mr. Enrique Castanon

Ms. Hon Myn Serena WONG
First Secretary

Mr. Lim Hong HUAI
First Secretary
Spouse: Mrs. May Lim

Miss Lee LORING
First Secretary

Miss Jean TAN
First Secretary (Information)

Ms. Nor Azlina SULAIMAN
First Secretary (Economics)

Miss Yew Yin Eunice PECK
First Secretary (Admin. and Consular)
Spouse: Mr. Christopher Goh

Mr. Andy HO
Third Secretary (Defense Procurement)
Spouse: Ms. Sharon Goh

Slovak Republic

Embassy of the Slovak Republic
2201 Wisconsin Avenue, NW - Suite 250
Washington DC 20007
Phone: 202/965-5161
Fax: 202/965-5166

Dr. Branislav LICHARDUS
Ambassador

Date Credentials Presented: 6/23/94

Born: 12/1/30

Spouse: Dr. Eva Kellerova

Dr. Branislav Lichardus, (M.D., Ph.D., D.Sc.) a medical scientist, has lectured at many universities and research institutes around the world. In 1992, he became president of the Slovak Academy of Sciences. Between 1990 and 1993, he was the president of the Slovak Medical Society.

Lichardus obtained a degree in medicine, summa cum laude, from Comenius University in Bratislava in 1956. Since 1957, he has been a staff member of the Institute of Experimental Endocrimology of the Slovak Academy of Sciences. In 1963, he received his Ph.D. in physiology and pathophysiology at the Slovak Academy and became head of the Laboratory of Water and Electrolyte Metabolism. He continued his postdoctoral studies at the Department of Physiology at the University of Alberta in Canada.

Between 1968 and 1970, he was a visiting scientist at the Department of Physiology at the University of Toronto in Canada and later at the Department of Medicine at Hospital de Bavier, University de Leige, Belgium. In 1984, he was a visiting scientist at the Howard Florey Institute of Experimental Physiology and Medicine in Melbourne, Australia. His main field of study was renal, neural, and hormonal regulation of body fluid volumes.

Dr. Lichardus is the author of more than 400 papers and several books in his field. He was an invited lecturer at the Fourth International Congress of Endocrinology in Washington in 1972. He has been married to Eva Kellerova, M.D., D.Sc., since 1953, and they have two married daughters.

STAFF:

Mr. Jan GABOR
Counselor
Spouse: Mrs. Danka Gaborova

Dr. Miroslav MUSIL
Counselor (Cultural)
Spouse: Mrs. Margareta Musilova

Mr. Jaroslav SMIESNY
Counselor (Commercial, N.Y.)
Spouse: Mrs. Elena Benkova

Ms. Ingrid BROCKOVA
Second Secretary

Mr. Juraj SIVACEK
Second Secretary
Spouse: Mrs. Livia Sivackova

Mrs. Iveta HRICOVA
Third Secretary and Consul
Spouse: Mr. Lubos Hric

Mr. Jan ORLOVSKY
Third Secretary
Spouse: Mrs. Janet Livingstone

Mr. Richard GALBAVY
Attaché

Mr. Slavomir JAMRICH
Attaché (Communications)
Spouse: Mrs. Zofia Jamrichova

Colonel Stefan KRISTOF
Defense, Military, and Air Attaché
Spouse: Mrs. Daniela Kristofova

Major Vendelin LEITNER
Asst. Defense, Military, and Air Attaché
Spouse: Mrs. Zuzana Leitnerova

Commercial Section, Branch Office
10 East 40th Street, Suite 3606
New York NY 10016
Phone: 212/679-7044 Fax: 212/679-7045

Slovenia

Embassy of the Republic of Slovenia
1525 New Hampshire Avenue, NW
Washington DC 20036
Phone: 202/667-5363
Fax: 202/667-4563
Email: JURE.RIFEL@MZZ-DKP.SIGOV.SI
Url: http://www.sigov.si/m22/ang/index.htm

Dr. Dimitrij RUPEL
Ambassador

Date Credentials Presented: 11/12/97

Born: 4/7/46

Spouse: Mrs. Marjetica-Ana Rudolf Rupel

A University professor, writer, and politician, Dr. Dimitrij Rupel is the Republic of Slovenia's ambassador not only to the U.S. but to Mexico as well.

Between 1995 and 1997, Rupel served as mayor of the city of Ljubljana, the capital of Slovenia. Before that, he was a member of the National Assembly of Slovenia between 1993 and 1995. He served as minister of foreign affairs for Slovenia from 1990 to 1993.

Rupel began teaching in 1970 at the faculty of social sciences at the University of Ljubljana, becoming a full professor in 1992. In 1976-77, he was a visiting professor at Queen's University in Kingston, Ont. He also was a professor at the New School for Social Research in New York City in 1985 and at Cleveland State University in Cleveland, Ohio, in 1989.

The ambassador graduated from the University of Ljubljana (faculty of philosophy) in comparative literature and sociology in 1970. He received a Ph.D. in sociology from Brandeis University in Waltham, Mass., in 1976.

Rupel is proficient in five foreign languages---English, French, German, Italian, and Latin.

STAFF:

Mr. Igor KERSTEIN
Minister
Spouse: Mrs. Manja Kerstein

Mr. Marjan SMONIG
Counselor
Spouse: Mrs. Natasa Smonig

Ms. Andreja PURKART
Second Secretary

Mr. Jurij RIFELJ
Second Secretary

Lt. Colonel Mitja MIKLAVEC
Defense, Military, Naval and Air Attaché
Spouse: Mrs. Dolores Miklavec

Consular Office
1525 New Hampshire Avenue, NW
Washington DC 20036
Phone: 202/332-9332

Solomon Islands

Embassy of the Solomon Islands
820 Second Avenue, Suite 800
New York, NY 10017
Phone: 212/599-6193
Fax: 212/661-8925
Email: simny@solomons.com

Rex Stephen HOROI
Ambassador

Date Credentials Presented: 2/11/97

Born: 9/8/52

Spouse: Mrs. Mary O'Dea Horoi

Rex Stephen Horoi, the Solomon Islands' ambassador to the U.S., has been his nation's ambassador/permanent representative to the U.N. in New York since 1992. He is also the Solomon Islands' high commissioner to Canada.

Horoi has represented the Solomon Islands government at a number of United Nations global conferences including the Conference for Small Island Development States in Barbados in 1994; the first conference of the parties to the U.N. framework council on climate change in Berlin in 1995; and the World Food Summit in Rome in 1996.

An expert in language planning and literacy development, particularly of the Melanesian region of the Pacific, and in the development and preservation of Melanesian languages, Horoi's interests also extend to South Pacific politics, particularly that of the Melanesian Spearhead Group of countries.

From 1989 to 1992, he was director of the Solomon Islands College of Higher Education. He was senior lecturer in English at that institution from 1987, also serving as head of the English department in 1987 and as diploma course coordinator (1989).

He began his career in 1978 as a teacher at St. Joseph Catholic Secondary School. From 1979 to 1980, he was employed at the University of Hawaii as consultant and co-author of the Peace Corps Language Handbook Series. In 1983, he became deputy principal at St. Joseph's National Secondary School.

Horoi attended the University of the South Pacific from 1975 to 1977, where he earned a diploma in education. He received his bachelor of education degree from the University of Papua New Guinea in 1982. He also attended the University of Sydney, Australia, from 1984 to 1986, where he received a post-graduate diploma in teaching English as a foreign language, and a master's degree in applied linguistics.

He earned a post-graduate certificate in educational planning for technical education and vocational training (1988) from the University of London, and another in curriculum innovation in technical education (1990) from the Centre for International Education, also in the United Kingdom.

In addition to the Peace Corps Language Handbook, Horoi has authored handbooks on grammar, communications, and culture, and special skills; articles and papers on grammar; and a publication about tourism and Solomon Islands handicrafts.

The ambassador and his wife have two boys, Theodore Taki Rex and Damien J. Rex, and a girl, Francesca Mary Rex. Francesca and Damien are twins.

South Africa

Embassy of the Republic of South Africa
3051 Massachusetts Avenue, NW
Washington DC 20008
Phone: 202/232-4400
Fax: 202/265-1607
Email: safrica@southafrica.net
Url: http://www.southafrica.net

Franklin SONN
Ambassador

Date Credentials Presented: 3/20/95

*Born: 10/11/39 in Vosburg district of
    Victoria West*

Spouse: Mrs. Joan Sonn

In South Africa, Franklin Abraham Sonn was rector (president) of Peninsula Technikon, a degree-granting College of Technology of 8,000 students. At the time of his appointment to Washington, he was chief executive officer of New Africa Investments Limited, the largest black-led company listed on the Johannesburg Stock Exchange.

In 1992, Sonn was a member of the group that monitored the Zambian elections, along with ex-President Jimmy Carter, for whom he was a personal advisor.

Sonn is a graduate of the University of Western Cape and the University of South Africa - a Doctor's Degree (h.c.) inter alia Notre Dame University and the University of Cape Town. He has received the Young South African of the Year Award from the Jaycees, the Paul Harris Award for Exceptional Service from Rotary, a Special Award for Service from the Association of Black Accountants of South Africa, and the Human Resources Award of Excellence in 1993.

Sonn has been active in a number of organizations, including the National Education and Training Forum, of which he was chairman. He was president of the Union of Teachers' Associations of South Africa, and of the Western Cape Foundation of Community Work. He has served on a commission investigating education and one investigation training of artisans. He was chairman of the U.S. South Africa Leadership Exchange Program and governor of the University of Cape Town Foundation.

Sonn, who grew up near Queenstown and Cape Town, is married to Joan Heather Gelderbloem, and they have two adult children, Crispin and Heather.

STAFF:

Mr. Ronald SHARDELOW
Minister

Mr. Mohamed Ahmed CASSIMJEE
Counselor (Political)

Mr. Hendrik DU TOIT
Counselor (Political)
Spouse: Mrs. Magdalena Du Toit

Mr. Rean DU TOIT
Counselor (Administrative)
Spouse: Mrs. Sannetta Du Toit

Mr. Ezram MTSHONTSHI
Counselor
Spouse: Mrs. Jane K. Mtshontshi

Mr. Ndumiso NTSHINGA
Counselor
Spouse: Mrs. Ntshinga

Mrs. Marianna PURNELL
Counselor (Agriculture and Science)

Mr. Basil J. VAN DER MERWE
Counselor (Economic)
Spouse: Mrs. Sherreen van der Merwe

Mr. Phakamile GONGO
First Secretary
Spouse: Mrs. Pumelela Gongo

Mr. Victor MAKGALE
First Secretary

Mrs. Maria MARITZ
Second Secretary (Political)
Spouse: Mr. Carl Maritz

Mr. Johannes VAN VOLLENHOVEN
First Secretary

Ms. Lorraine Felicity WILKINSON
First Secretary (Political)

Mr. Monwabisi Morgan DLOKOVA
Third Secretary (Administration)
Spouse: Mrs. Nomabhele Diokova

Mr. Carl Benjamin MARITZ
Third Secretary
Spouse: Mrs. Marlene Maritz

Mr. Daniel NGWEPE

Third Secretary

Miss Alicia C. PETERS
Third Secretary (Political)

Ms. Debra STEINER
Third Secretary

Miss Tania STOTESBURY
Third Secretary

Ms. Albie MULDER
Attaché

Mr. Lucas Cornelius NEL
Attaché

Mr. Ryan SPARROW
Attaché
Spouse: Mrs. Petronella Sparrow

Colonel Frans LABUSCHAGNE
Attaché & Asst. Defense &
   Military Attaché
Spouse: Mrs. Irene Labuschagne

Colonel Christiaan GILDENHUYS
Military Attaché and Asst. Naval Attaché
Spouse: Mrs. Ruanda Gildenhuys

Captain Robert W. HIGGS
Naval Attaché and Asst. Air Attaché
Spouse: Mrs. Diana Higgs

Chancery Annex
3201 New Mexico Ave., NW
Washington DC 20016
Phone: 202/966-1650

Spain

Embassy of Spain
2375 Pennsylvania Avenue, NW
Washington DC 20037
Phone: 202/452-0100
Fax: 202/833-5670

Antonio OYARZÁBAL
Ambassador

Date Credentials Presented: 10/9/96

Born: 10/12/35 in Stockholm, Sweden

Spouse: Mrs. Beatrix Lodge Oyarzábal

Spain's ambassador to the U.S., Antonio Oyarzábal has previously served as Spain's ambassador to Ecuador, Japan, Denmark, and Lithuania. He joined the Spanish diplomatic service in 1961 with the grade of secretary.

Oyarzábal graduated from the law school of the Complutense University in Madrid, Spain, in 1957. In preparation for his diplomatic career, he entered the Spanish Diplomatic School in 1959.

From 1967 until February 1970, he worked in the executive office of the ministry of foreign affairs. He was then transferred to the embassy of Spain in the United Kingdom, where he remained until 1974. Returning to Madrid, he was promoted to the grade of counselor and served in the executive office of the prime minister until July 1976.

After a few months as a member of the foreign affairs high level council, the council of ministers appointed him as governor in Santa Cruz de Tenerife (Canary Islands) in 1976 and in 1977 as governor of Guipúzcoa (Basque region). In 1979, he became assistant secretary of state for public information, and in 1981, he was appointed Spain's ambassador to Ecuador.

Upon returning to Madrid in 1983, he served as secretary of the Joint Spanish-American committee for scientific and technological cooperation and director of bilateral scientific cooperation at the ministry of foreign affairs. In 1986, he was named assistant secretary of state for international cooperation.

From 1990 to 1994, he served as ambassador to Japan. He was then appointed ambassador to Denmark. In 1995, he also became ambassador to the Republic of Lithuania with residence in Copenhagen. His appointment as ambassador to the U.S. came in June 1996.

Oyarzábal has received numerous Spanish and foreign honors and awards.

He and his wife, the former Beatrix Lodge, have six children: Matilde, Marta, Juan, Gloria, Iñigo, and Borja.

STAFF:

Mr. Rafail CONDE
Minister (Deputy Chief of Mission)

Mr. Juan M. R. DE TERREROS
Minister (Cultural)
Spouse: Mrs. Carmen Fuente

Mr. Mariano BAQUEDANO
Counselor (Labor & Social Affairs)
Spouse: Mrs. Maria-Angeles Yanez

Ms. Maria BASSOLS
Counselor
Spouse: Mr. Alfonso Tena

Mr. David BELTRAN
Counselor (Juridical)
Spouse: Mrs. Maria del Carmen Arguelles

Mr. Javier CARBAJOSA
Counselor
Spouse: Mrs. Maria Jesus Murciego

Mr. Victor ECHEVARRIA UGARTE
Counselor (Economic and Commercial)
Spouse: Mrs. Amparo Icaza-Barrena

Mr. Luis Maria ESTERUELAS
Counselor (Agricultural, Fisheries & Food)
Spouse: Mrs. Juliana Burke

Mr. Luis FONT DE MORA
Counselor (Commercial)

Spouse: Mrs. Maria-Rosario Sainz
   de Mingo

Mr. Amado GIMENEZ
Counselor (Information)
Spouse: Mrs. Molinero

Mr. Gonzalo GOMEZ DACAL
Counselor (Education)
Spouse: Mrs. Maria Del Carmen
   Cid Fernandez

Mr. Miguel Angel GONZALEZ
Counselor
Spouse: Mrs. Susana Lara

Mr. Rafael JOVER
Counselor and General Consul
Spouse: Mrs. Maria Dolores de Villanueva

Mr. Pedro MEJIA
Counselor (Economic & Commercial)
Spouse: Mrs. Paloma Gonzalez-Cid

Mr. Agustin NUNEZ
Counselor
Spouse: Mrs. Maria Isabel Vicandi Plaza

Mr. Dario POLO
Counselor (Economic and Administrative)

Mr. Jose SEVILLA
Counselor (Financial)
Spouse: Mrs. Gladys Bendo Angulo

Mr. Alfonso TENA
Counselor
Spouse: Mrs. Maria Bassols

Mr. Julio VINUELA
Counselor (Economic and Commercial)
Spouse: Mrs. Paulina Beato

Mr. Cesar M. BALGUERIAS
Attaché
Spouse: Mrs. Pilar Amian

Mr. Javier CANOVAS
Attaché
Spouse: Mrs. Elena M. Gonzalez

Mr. Jose M. GONZALEZ
Attaché
Spouse: Mrs. Maria Jose Llop Garcia

Mr. Juan HIDALGO CUESTA
Attaché
Spouse: Mrs. Maria Dolores Martin
   Moreno

Mr. Candido MONTALVO
Attaché (Consular)
Spouse: Mrs. Christine Marin

Mr. Francisco PEREZ
Attaché ' (Commercial)
Spouse: Mrs. Antonio Garcia

Mr. Alfonso PINO
Attaché (Agricultural)

Mr. Jose A. RIERA
Attaché (Administrative)

Mr. Alberto BARCIELA
Asst. Attaché (Information)

Major General Francisco CARRETERO
Defense Attaché
Spouse: Mrs. Carmen Davila

Lt. Colonel Jose Luis CEBALLOS
Defense Cooperation Attaché
Spouse: Mrs. Maria Pilar de Diego
  Zurbano

Colonel Rafael BARBUDO
Military Attaché

Captain Fermin MOSCOSO DEL PRADO
Naval Attaché
Spouse: Mrs. Matilde Marten Romero

Colonel Luis REY
Air Attaché
Spouse: Mrs. Maria Cristina Villazon
  Lozano

Major Ignacio BARRASA
Asst. Defense Cooperation Attaché
Spouse: Mrs. Gomez

Commander Carlos Luis CORTEJOSO
Asst. Defense Attaché
Spouse: Mrs. Margarita Lino

Major Rafael DE LUCAS
Asst. Defense Cooperation Attaché
Spouse: Mrs. Estilia Gomez-Rodriquez

Major Victor GALAN
Asst. Defense Corporation Attaché
Spouse: Mrs. Rosa Cortini

Major Fernando ALEJANDRE
Asst. Military Attaché
Spouse: Mrs. Eva Mancebo

Agricultural Office
2375 Pennsylvania Avenue, NW
Washington DC 20037
Phone: 202/728-2339 Fax: 202/728-2320

Office of the Air Attaché
4801 Wisconsin Ave., NW, 3rd Floor
Washington DC 20016
Phone: 202/244-8843

Consular Office
2375 Pennsylvania Avenue, NW
Washington DC 20037
Phone: 202/728-2330 Fax: 202/728-2302

Cultural Office
2375 Pennsylvania Avenue, NW
Washington DC 20037
Phone: 202/728-2334 Fax: 202/728-2312

Office of the Defense Attaché
4801 Wisconsin Ave., NW, 4th Floor
Washington DC 20016
Phone: 202/244-0093

**Office of the Defense
  Cooperation Attaché**
4801 Wisconsin Ave., NW, 4th Floor
Washington DC 20016

Phone: 202/364-2257

**Office for Economic and
  Commercial Affairs**
2558 Massachusetts Ave., NW
Washington DC 20008
Phone: 202/265-8600

Education Office
2375 Pennsylvania Avenue, NW
Washington DC 20037
Phone: 202/728-2335 Fax: 202/728-2313

Financial Office
2375 Pennsylvania Avenue, NW
Washington DC 20037
Phone: 202/728-2338 Fax: 202/728-2318

Information Office
2375 Pennsylvania Avenue, NW
Washington DC 20037
Phone: 202/728-2332 Fax: 202/728-2308

Office of Labor and Social Affairs
2375 Pennsylvania Avenue, NW
Washington DC 20037
Phone: 202/728-2331 Fax: 202/728-2304

Office of the Military Attaché
4801 Wisconsin Ave., NW, 3rd Floor
Washington DC 20016
Phone: 202/244-6161

Office of the Naval Attaché
4801 Wisconsin Ave., NW, 3rd Floor
Washington DC 20016
Phone: 202/244-2166

Sri Lanka

Embassy of the Democratic Socialist
  Republic of Sri Lanka
2148 Wyoming Avenue, NW
Washington DC 20008
Phone: 202/483-4025
Fax: 202/232-7181
Email: slembassy@clark.net
Url: http://www.slembassy.org

Warnasena RASAPUTRAM
Ambassador

Date Credentials Presented: 11/12/97

Warnasena Rasaputram came to his post as
Sri Lanka's ambassador to the U.S. from

Malaysia, where he served as high
commissioner for Sri Lanka between 1995
and 1997. He was Sri Lanka's permanent
representative to United Nations offices in
Geneva and Vienna and ambassador to the
Holy See between 1990 and 1992. In 1989,
he served as ambassador to France.

Between 1979 and 1989, Rasaputram was
the governor of the Central Bank of Sri Lanka
after serving as the bank's deputy governor
from 1975 to 1979.

He has worked for the following international
organizations: alternative executive director
of the International Monetary Fund, 1976-
79; expert in Manpower Planning Asian
Regional Team for Employment Promotion,
International Labor Organization, in
Bangkok, 1970-71; and expert in national
accounts to the government of Iraq, United
Nations, from 1965 to 1967. He also has
served as a consultant to an International
Labor Organization Team for employment
promotion in Sri Lanka, the World Bank, and
other international organizations.

The ambassador was a visiting lecturer at
the University of Ceylon in 1951; the
University of Peradeniya in 1952; the
University of Vidyalankara in 1953-56; and
a tutor at the University of Wisconsin in
1958. He had guest lectureships at the
University of North Carolina in 1978 and at
the University of California in Fresno in
1993.

Among the international conferences
Rasaputram has attended are: the United
Nations General Assembly, meetings of the
International Monetary Fund and the World
Bank, and seminars on population and
statistics, income distribution, employment,
and trade and disarmament. More than 50
of his articles have been published in local
and international journals.

In 1991 in Geneva, Rasaputram was
president of a Disarmament Conference, as
well as chairman of the Asian Group of
Countries. He was president of Sri Lanka
Association of Economists between 1983 and
1987; a member of the South Asia Poverty
Commission in 1992; and a member of the
South Asia Development Fund in 1992. In
1977, he received the Kheimer Award for
International Understanding from the
Kheimer Institute of Washington, D.C.

The Ambassador received a B.A. in
economics from the University of Ceylon in
1950; an M.A. degree in statistics from the
University of Wisconsin in 1957; and a Ph.D.
from the University of Wisconsin in 1959.
He is married.

STAFF:

Mr. Asoka G. DHARMAWARDHANE
Minister (Commercial)
Spouse: Mrs. Dharmawardhane

Mr. Prasad A. KARIYAWASAM

Minister
Spouse: Mrs. Kariyawasam

Mr. M. Neeth G. DE SILVA
Minister
Spouse: Mrs. W. A. Dhanasiri de Silva

Mr. Sumanasena ABEYWARNA
Counselor and Consul
Spouse: Mrs. Abeywarna

Sudan

Embassy of the Republic of the Sudan
2210 Massachusetts Avenue, NW
Washington DC 20008
Phone: 202/338-8565
Fax: 202/667-2406

Mahdi Ibrahim MOHAMED
Ambassador

Date Credentials Presented: 4/30/96

Born: 1946 in Karkoug, Sudan

Spouse: Mrs. Wahbia Abdalla Ahmed

Mahdi Ibrahim Mohamed began his government service in 1986 when he was elected to the Constituent Assembly (Parliament) in Khartoum. Since then, he has held several high-level government positions.

In 1990, he chaired the Arab Solidarity Committee at the International Popular Friendship Council in Khartoum, after which he was appointed to the position of ambassador at the Ministry of Foreign Affairs in 1991. In 1992, he became Sudan Permanent Representative at the United Nations in Geneva, Switzerland. In 1993, he became director general of the Directorate for Political Affairs at the Ministry of Foreign Affairs. He was appointed state minister at the Presidency for Political Affairs in Khartoum in 1995.

After graduating with a B.A. (with honors) from the Faculty of Arts, University of Khartoum, Mohamed joined Sudan National Television, then went on to join the Ministry of Education as a teacher for secondary schools in Khartoum. In 1970, he joined the Saudi Ministry of Education in Jeddah, Saudi

Arabia, where he stayed for four years as a teacher. In 1981, he obtained his M.A. in public communications from California State University at Chico, Calif. For the next several years, he worked at El-Raya, a newspaper in Khartoum, for which he became editor-in-chief in 1985.

Mohamed, who speaks fluent Arabic and English, is married to Wahbia Abdalla Ahmed. They have one daughter and four sons.

STAFF:

Mr. Mirghani Mohamed SALIH
Deputy Chief of Mission
Spouse: Mrs. Nadia Awad Ahmed Salih

Mr. Eltayeb Ali AHMED
Counselor
Spouse: Mrs. Buthayna

Mr. Mahmoud Y. AHMED
First Secretary
Spouse: Mrs. Rahamt Ella

Mr. Azhari ELAMIN
Attaché (Administrative)

Office of the Cultural Counselor
2210 Massachusetts Avenue, NW
Washington DC 20008
Phone: 202/338-8565

Office of the Information Attaché
2210 Massachusetts Avenue, NW
Washington DC 20008
Phone: 202/797-8863 Fax: 202/745-2615

Suriname

Embassy of the Republic of Suriname
4301 Connecticut Ave., NW - Suite 460
Washington DC 20008
Phone: 202/244-7488
Fax: 202/244-5878
Email: embsur@erols.com

Arnold Theodoor HALFHIDE
Ambassador

Date Credentials Presented: 9/8/97

Born: 12/30/39

Spouse: Mrs. Carla Josephine Ooosterlen Halfhide

Arnold Theodoor Halfhide returned to Washington, D.C., in 1997 as Suriname's ambassador to the U.S., a post he had held between 1986 and 1989. For the past 30 years, he has divided his time between diplomacy and business.

Between 1994 and 1997, he was managing director of a firm that he co-founded, Selective Auto Imports N.V., in Paramaribo. He was president of another firm that he co-founded, Scala Holding International N.V.

between 1992 and 1994. During that period, he also was a member of the board of director of Cariana Gallery of Art Styles, Fashion, and Gifts in Paramaribo.

Halfhide was a member of the board of directors of the Central Bank of Suriname between 1989 and 1992. He also was president of the Joint Commission of Suriname and Brazil; president of the negotiating committee for the nationalization of Bruynzeel Suriname Houtmaatschappij B.V.; a member of the Joint Commission of Suriname and Venezuela; a member of the board of directors of Suriname Timbers; and co-founder of "ASFA", the Suriname Manufacturers Association.

Earlier in his business career, he was general manager of Varossieau Suriname Paint Industries in Paramaribo. Between 1968 and 1979, he was associated with Bruynzeel Suriname Houtmatschappij, rising to the position of vice president and director of marketing and sales.

During his first ambassadorship to the U.S., Halfhide also was ambassador and permanent representative to the Organization of American States and non-resident ambassador to Canada. He was ambassador to Venezuela from 1984 to 1986; in 1985 he also was non-resident ambassador to Nicaragua. He was minister-counselor at the ministry of foreign affairs in Suriname in 1983-84. From 1981 to 1983, he was consul-general with jurisdiction over the U.S. in New York, N.Y.

Halfhide has participated in many international meetings including the 43rd regular session of the General Assembly of the United Nations and several regular sessions of the general assembly of the Organization for American States.

The ambassador attended Commercial College, in The Netherlands; Ashridge Management College at Berkhemstead in the United Kingdom; and the International Marketing Management Centre Bruxelles in Brussels, Belgium. He has a fluent command of Dutch, English, French, German, Portuguese, Spanish, and Swedish.

STAFF:

Mr. Rudie M.J. ALIHUSAIN
Counselor

Ms. Georgine E. VAN DILLENBURG
Attaché (Administrative)

Swaziland

Embassy of the Kingdom of Swaziland
3400 International Drive, NW
Washington DC 20008-3006
Phone: 202/362-6683
Fax: 202/244-8059
Email: 73451.2752@compuserve.com

Mary Madzandza KANYA
Ambassador

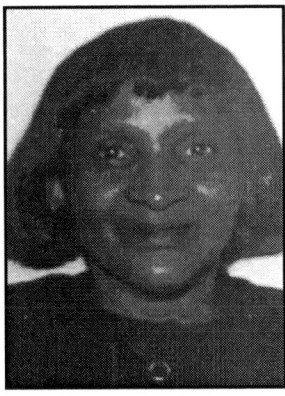

Date Credentials Presented: 11/21/94

Spouse: Mr. Leo L. Kanya

In the four years preceding assumption of her duties as ambassador to the U.S., Mary M. Kanya served as the Kingdom of Swaziland's High Commissioner to Canada and Jamaica. In 1993-94, she was dean of the Commonwealth Diplomatic Corps in Canada and dean of the Southern African Development Community (SADC) countries in Canada.

Between 1984 and 1990, Kanya was senior lecturer and curriculum director and consultant in computer education at the Institute of Development Management of Botswana, Lesotho, and Swaziland. Her previous positions were as senior inspector of schools for science in the Ministry of Education; as headteacher and tutor at Lozitha Royal Palace; and as lecturer, science curriculum designer, and writer at William Pitcher Training College. She began her career between 1972 and 1974 as an assistant teacher in various schools in Swaziland.

Kanya received a bachelor of science degree in education from U.B.L.S. Roma in Lesotho and a master of science degree in systems development in Dublin, Ireland. She took an education leadership course in 1977 at Eastern Michigan University and a management information system course in London in 1986. She served as organizing secretary of the Swaziland Science Teachers' Association.

Kanya is married and has four daughters.

STAFF:

Mr. Philemon M. DLAMINI
Counselor
Spouse: Mrs. B.S. Dlamini

Miss Naomalungelo MAGAGULA
First Secretary

Mr. Robinson MKHALIPHI
Third Secretary

Mr. Boy MDLULI
Attaché (Education)

Spouse: Mrs. Thembie Mdluli

Sweden

Embassy of Sweden
1501 M Street, NW
Washington DC 20005
Phone: 202/467-2600
Fax: 202/467-2699
Url: http://www.swedenemb.org/

Rolf EKÉUS
Ambassador

Date Credentials Presented: 9/8/97

Born: in Kristinehamn, Sweden

Spouse: Mrs. Christina Oldfelt

Before his appointment as Sweden's ambassador to the U.S. in September 1997, Rolf Ekéus held the post of executive chairman of the United Nations Special Commission for Iraq for six years.

He served as ambassador and head of the Swedish delegation to the Conference on Security and Cooperation in Vienna, where he was chairman of the committee on principles charter of Paris in 1990-91. Between 1983 and 1988, he was ambassador and permanent representative of Sweden to the conference on disarmament in Geneva. He was chairman of the committee on chemical weapons in 1984 and 1987.

Ekéus served as chief delegate to a number of disarmament review conferences, including the Biological Weapons Convention and Nuclear Proliferation Treaty (he chaired the drafting committee in 1985). He also was chief delegate to the First Committee and the Disarmament Commission of the United Nations between 1983 and 1988.

He joined the Swedish foreign service in 1962 and served in Bonn, West Germany, 1963-65; Nairobi, Kenya, 1965-67; New York (United Nations), 1973-78); The Hague, Netherlands, 1978-83; and special assistant to the minister for foreign affairs in Stockholm, 1967-1973.

The ambassador was a member of the Canberra Commission on the Elimination of Nuclear Weapons in 1995-96; and a member of the advisory board of the Nuclear Non-Proliferation Center at Monterey Institute. He was the recipient of various awards including the Wateler Peace Prize from the Carnegie Foundation in 1997.

Ekéus has published several articles and essays on foreign policy, the international economy, nuclear non-proliferation, disarmament and arms control, chemical weapons, European security, Iraq, and weapons of mass destruction.

He received a law degree from Stockholm

University in 1959 and practiced law at the country court of Karlstad, Sweden, between 1959 and 1962.

The ambassador, married to Christina Oldfelt, has three daughters and three sons.

STAFF:

Mr. Peter TEJLER
Minister (Deputy Chief of Mission)
Spouse: Mrs. Lillemor Tejler

Mr. Andreas Eric EKMAN
Minister (Economic Affairs)
Spouse: Mrs. Anita Siv Nasstrom-Ekman

Mr. Lars Eric Rolf MATHLEIN
Minister (Economic and Financial)
Spouse: Mrs. Eleonore Susanne Lori
  Mathlein

Mr. Lars F.V. BJERDE
Counselor (Defense Procurement)
Spouse: Mrs. Anita L. Bjerde

Ms. Katarina ERSMAN
Counselor (Press)

Mr. Bo Erik HEDBERG
Counselor (Science and Technology)

Mr. Olof HULDTGREN
Counselor

Mr. Lars Ove JOHANSSON
Counselor (Cultural)
Spouse: Mrs. Loth Eva Eriksson

Mr. Jan KNUTSSON
Counselor
Spouse: Mrs. Eva Berquist

Ms. Birgitta MOBERG
Counselor (Administrative and Consular)

Mr. Roland Gunnar SPANT
Counselor (Labor)

Ms. Louise E. BERGHOLM
Second Secretary

Ms. Signe BURGSTALLER
Second Secretary

Mrs. Ingrid Gunilla FIEBER-AKANDER
Third Secretary
Spouse: Mr. Sven Goran Akander

Major General Sven-Olof HOKBORG
Defense Attaché
Spouse: Mrs. Ingalill Hokborg

Brig. General Nils Ivan ROSENQVIST
Military Attaché & Asst. Defense Attaché
Spouse: Mrs. Eva Maria Gun B. Muhr
  Rosenqvist

Captain Kurt Robert Olaf JOSSON
Naval Attaché & Asst. Defense Attaché

Major Hans Rolf ROSEN
Asst. Air Attaché

Spouse: Mrs. Anna Karin Rosen

Office of Science and Technology
1501 M Street, NW
Washington DC 20005
Phone: 202/467-2600 Fax: 202/467-2678

Switzerland

Embassy of Switzerland
2900 Cathedral Avenue, NW
Washington DC 20008
Phone: 202/745-7900
Fax: 202/387-2564
Email: embassy@was.rep.admin.ch
Url: http://www.swissemb.org/

Alfred DEFAGO
Ambassador

Date Credentials Presented: 5/14/97

Spouse: Mrs. Maria T. Defago

Alfred Defago was appointed as Switzerland's ambassador to the U.S. in April 1997, having served as consul general of Switzerland in New York since 1994. Prior to his transfer to the U.S., he served as secretary general of the federal department of foreign affairs in Bern.

From 1986 to 1993, Defago was director of the federal office of culture, overseeing all cultural activities of the Swiss Confederation including (after a restructuring in 1989), the National Library, the National Museum, and all other federal museums and art collections. His tenure witnessed the foundation of the Swiss Literary Archives, made possible through the donation of the manuscripts of Friedrich Dürrenmatt, the most famous Swiss author of the postwar generation.

Defago's public serve began when he joined the Swiss Broadcasting Corporation, the public radio network in 1971. Having earned his Ph.D. in history and German literature from the University of Bern, he rose through the ranks of the German-language national radio service, first as a member of the foreign affairs department, then as head of the national and economic affairs department, finally becoming editor-in-chief of the network in 1984. In 1983, he spent a sabbatical year in Berkeley, Calif.

The ambassador and his wife, Maria, reside in Washington, D.C.

STAFF:

Mr. Pierre COMBERNOUS
Minister (Deputy Chief of Mission)
Spouse: Mrs. Dilbar Combernous

Mr. Christian ETTER
Minister (Economic)
Spouse: Mrs. Dorothee Etter

Mr. Jenoe C. A. STAEHELIN
Minister

Mr. Christoph BUBB
Counselor (Legal)
Spouse: Mrs. Regula Bubb

Mr. Xavier L. COMTESSE
Counselor (Scientific and Technology)
Spouse: Mrs. Michele Comtesse

Mr. Walter HAFFNER
Counselor (Cultural)
Spouse: Mrs. Sabine Haffner

Mr. Werner KAELIN
Counselor (Defense Procurement)
Spouse: Mrs. Carol A. Rowland Kaelin

Mr. Markus SAUTER
Counselor

Mr. Roberto BALZARETTI
First Secretary (Political)
Spouse: Mrs. Christina Ferrari Balzaretti

Mr. Roland Peter FISCHER
First Secretary and Consul
Spouse: Mrs. Iris Fischer

Mr. Bernard Jules JAGGY
First Secretary (Economic)

Mr. Thomas KOLLY
First Secretary (Economic)
Spouse: Mrs. Adelheid Kolly

Mr. Wolfgang MEYER
First Secretary
Spouse: Mrs. Ruth Gschwend Meyer

Mr. Eric PFANDLER
Second Secretary and Consul
Spouse: Mrs. Isabelle C. Pfandler

Mr. Markus BICHSEL
Attaché (Science and Technology)
Spouse: Mrs. Anne Christine
  Bichsel-Stettler

Mr. Christian BRUELHART
Attaché

Ms. Marianne GERBER
Attaché (Commercial) and Consul

Mr. Georges Etienne MALBOIS
Attaché

Ms. Florence NICOLE
Attaché (Cultural)

Mr. Denis NIEDERHAUSER
Attaché & Vice Consul
Spouse: Mrs. Chantal Niederhauser

Mr. Georg STEINER
Attaché

Mr. Hubert Franz STEINHAUSER
Attaché (Defense Engineering)
Spouse: Mrs. Johanna E. Steinhauser

Captain Patrik ANLIKER

Asst. Attaché
Spouse: Mrs. Astrid Anliker Stocker

Major General Markus RUSCH
Asst. Defense, Military, and Air Attaché
Spouse: Mrs. Alice Rusch Fuchs

Colonel Jurg H. WALSER
Asst. Defense, Military, and Air Attaché
Spouse: Mrs. Rosmarie Walser

Syria

Embassy of the Syrian Arab Republic
2215 Wyoming Avenue, NW
Washington DC 20008
Phone: 202/232-6313
Fax: 202/234-9548

Walid AL-MOUALEM
Ambassador

Date Credentials Presented: 8/7/90

Born: 7/17/41 in Damascus, Syria

Spouse: Mrs. Sawsan Al-Khayat

A career foreign service officer, Walid Al-Moualem has worked throughout Europe. Having entered the Ministry of Foreign Affairs in 1965, his first posting was as attaché at Syria's embassy in Dar Es Salam. He subsequently served with the Syrian missions in Jeddah and in Madrid. Returning to Syria in 1971, Al-Moualem worked as director of the office of Foreign Minister Abd-Al-Halim Khaddam for two years, before being posted to London as chargé d'affaires.

Receiving his first ambassadorial posting in 1975, Al-Moualem was his country's representative in Romania, returning in 1981 to work in the Ministry's Department of Authentication and Translation. Immediately prior to his Washington posting, he served from 1985 to 1990 as director of the Foreign Ministry's Department of Special Bureau. Al-Moualem is head of the Syrian delegation for the peace talks with Israel.

He has authored Palestine and Armed Peace, 1970; History of Syria: 1946-1958; 1983; Syria: The Road to Freedom, 1916-1946; 1986. Syria in the Days of Al-Zaim: The First Coup; The World and the Middle East in the American Perspective, 1987.

Al-Moualem holds a B.A. in economics from Cairo University. In addition to his native Arabic, he speaks English. He is married to Sawsan Al-Khayat and they have three children.

STAFF:

Mr. Mhd Badi KHATTAB
Minister-Counselor
Spouse: Mrs. Najwa Muijkan

Mr. Ali MUHRA
Third Secretary (Economic)

Mr. Mansour AZZAM
Attaché
Spouse: Mrs. Aseel Azzam

Mr. Ahmad Feda EL AMOUD
Attaché (Accounts)
Spouse: Mrs. Hanadi Al Khatib

Mr. Bassam SABAGH
Attaché (Consular)

Mr. Latif SABAGH
Attaché (Consular)

Taiwan

Taipei Economic and Cultural
  Representative Office in the U.S.
4201 Wisconsin Avenue, NW
Washington DC 20016-2137
Phone: 202/895-1850
Fax: 202/364-0416

NOTE: In the absence of diplomatic ties between the U.S. and Taiwan, the Taipei Economic and Cultural Representative Office in the United States and the American Institute in Taiwan, a non-governmental entity, facilitate commercial and cultural ties between the U.S. and Taiwan under the Taiwan Relations Act of 1979.

Stephen S.F. CHEN
Representative

Born: 2/11/34 in Nanking, China

Spouse: Mrs. Rosa Te Chen

Before coming to Washington, D.C., in 1997, as the representative of the Taipei Economic and Cultural Representative Office in the U.S., Stephen S. F. Chen (Si-Fang Chen) served as deputy secretary-general in the office of the president of Taiwan (the Republic of China---ROC) in 1996-97.

Chen began his diplomatic career in 1953 when he joined Taiwan's embassy in Manila, The Phillippines. He passed the foreign service exam of the ROC in 1960, after which he served as special assistant in the ministry of foreign affairs until 1963. He then was posted to Taiwan's embassy in Rio de Janéiro, Brazil, as second and then first secretary between 1963 and 1969. In 1967, he served as advisor to the ROC delegation to the annual meetings of the International Monetary Fund and the World Bank.

Between 1969 and 1971, Chen was chief of the second section of the Latin American affairs department in the ministry of foreign affairs in Taipei. He went to Buenos Aires, Argentina, in 1971 to serve for a year as counsellor at Taiwan's embassy after which he was chargé d'affaires at Taiwan's embassy in La Paz, Bolivia in 1972-73. Then, he went to Atlanta, Ga., to take the position of consul general of the ROC from 1973 to 1979. In 1979-80, he was director of the CCNAA office in Atlanta, then was assigned as director of the CCNAA office in Chicago, Ill

Back in Taipei, he served as consul general attached to the secretariat of the ministry of foreign affairs between 1982 and 1984 after which he took the ministry positions of director of the department of treaty and legal affairs and director of the department of international organizations between 1984 and 1988. In 1988-89, he served as director general of the CCNAA office in Los Angeles. Then, from 1989 to 1993, he was assigned as deputy representative of the CCNAA office in the U.S. From 1993 to 1996; he was vice minister of foreign affairs in Taipei before taking the deputy secretary-general post in the office of the president.

Chen received a B.A. degree in 1957 and an M.A. degree in 1959 from the University of Santo Tomas, where he also did Ph.D. studies in 1959-60. He has a D.B.A., honoris causa, from Kensington University in Los Angeles, Calif.

He is married and has two sons and a daughter. Chen speaks Chinese, English, and Portuguese as well as six Chinese dialects.

Tanzania

Embassy of the United Republic of Tanzania
2139 R Street, NW
Washington DC 20008
Phone: 202/939-6125
Fax: 202/797-7408
Email: tanz-us@clark.net

Mustafa Salim NYANG'ANYI
Ambassador

Date Credentials Presented: 9/15/95

Born: 10/20/42 in Kondoa, Tanzania

Spouse: Mrs. Mariam Nyang'Anyi

Mustafa Salim Nyang'anyi started his career as a news reporter and broadcaster for Radio Tanzania in 1964, but he soon ran for political office and was a member of the Tanzanian Parliament for 25 years, from 1970 to 1996.

He served as minister of state, office of the prime minister and first vice president in 1993-94. Before that, he was the regional commissioner for the Dar es Salaam region and, earlier, regional commissioner for the Morogoro region. From 1985 to 1989, he was minister for works, communication and transport.

Nyang'anyi was minister of state, office of the President, in the area of international and regional economic cooperation in 1984-85; a member of the National Executive Committee of the ruling party (CCM) and member of the central committee of the CCM continuously from 1984; minister of trade, 1983-84; and minister for lands, housing, and urban development, 1980-83. Earlier, he was deputy minister, Ministry of Water, Energy and Minerals; deputy minister, Ministry of Health; and deputy press secretary to the President.

He worked for Radio Tanzania from 1964-66, then became a research and information attaché for the Ministry of Foreign Affairs. He went on to be secretary of the Tanzania Basketball Association and Secretary of the Tanzania Olympic Committee.

Nyang'anyi has attended numerous international conferences. He was the leader of Tanzanian delegations to: the World Conference on Natural Disaster Reduction in Yokohama, Japan, in 1994; to the Conference on LDCs in Tripoli, Libya, in 1989; and from 1986 to 1988, to the Executive Council of United Nations International Civil Aviation Organization in Montreal, Canada.

Nyang'anyi has a master's degree in public administration and management from

Harvard University, and was an Edward Mason Fellow in Public Policy and Management at the Kennedy School of Government in 1992. He and his wife, Mariam, have a son and two daughters.

STAFF:

Mr. Anastase Rwekaza RWEGAYURA
Minister (Economic & Head of Chancery)
Spouse: Mrs. Symphorose K. Rwegayura

Ms. Diana KANTABULA
Counselor (Administrative)

Mrs. Justa Matari NYANGE
Counselor (Political)
Spouse: Mr. Herbert Horme Nyange

Thailand

Royal Thai Embassy
1024 Wisconsin Avenue, NW
Washington DC 20007
Phone: 202/944-3600
Fax: 202/944-3611
Email: thai.wsn@ari.net
Url: http://www.thaiembdc.org

Nitya PIBULSONGGRAM
Ambassador

Date Credentials Presented: 2/6/96

Spouse: Mrs. Pacharin Pibulsonggram

Before coming to Washington as ambassador, Nitya Pibulsonggram had served as Thailand's Permanent Representative to the United Nations for eight years.

From 1983-87, he was director-general of the Department of International Organizations at the Ministry of Foreign Affairs of Thailand. His other appointments at the ministry included ambassador-at-large in charge of political issues, 1982; deputy-director general of the political department, 1981; and deputy director-general of the information department, 1980.

Pibulsonggram began his career in Thailand's Foreign Service in 1968 in the foreign news division of the information department. From 1969 to 1972, he was a member of the Thai delegation to the South East Asia Treaty

Organization (SEATO). In 1973 and 1974, he served in the office of the Permanent Secretary of the ministry and in its policy/planning division. He also served in the office of the secretary to the foreign minister. He headed the political department's Southeast Asian division in 1975-76.

Pibulsonggram's first foreign posting was in 1976 at the Permanent Mission of Thailand to the United Nations, where he was appointed deputy permanent representative. He returned to the Ministry of Foreign Affairs in 1980 and remained in various capacities until his appointment as Thailand's Permanent Representative to the United Nations in 1988.

He received his B.A. degree from Dartmouth College and his M.A. from Brown University. He is married.

STAFF:

Mr. Akrasid AMATAYAKUL
Minister (Deputy Chief of Mission)

Mr. Kanissorn NAVANUGRAHA
Minister (Commercial)
Spouse: Mrs. Navanugraha

Lt. Nophadol BHANDHUGRAVI
Minister-Counselor (Economic and Financial)
Spouse: Mrs. Orathai Bhandhugravi

Mr. Somchai CHEEVAKRIANGGRAI
Minister-Counselor (Commercial)
Spouse: Mrs. Somchai Cheevakrianggrai

Mr. Kriangsak KITTICHAISAREE
Minister-Counselor
Spouse: Mrs. Sarapee Kittichaisaree

Ms. Malinda MANOONCHAI
Minister-Counselor

Mr. Soodsakorn PUTHO
Minister-Counselor (Industry)
Spouse: Mrs. Samnieng Putho

Mr. Chamnong SANGMAHACHAI
Minister-Counselor (Educational)
Spouse: Mrs. Chanpaka Sangmahachai

Mr. Boonlert SUPADHILOKE
Minister-Counselor (Information)
Spouse: Mrs. Nawarat Aupadhiloke

Mr. Sonthi VANNASAENG
Minister-Counselor (Science & Techn.)

Mr. Prakarn VIRAKUL
Minister-Counselor (Agricultural)
Spouse: Mrs. Chintana Virakul

Ms. Panorsee CHAOVALIT
Counselor (Education)
Spouse: Mrs. Vajrabhaya

Mr. Preecha NISARAT
Counselor (Education)
Spouse: Mrs. Jutamas Nisarat

Mr. Phusit RATANAKULSEREROENGRIT
Counselor (Commercial)
Spouse: Mrs. Dusanee Ratanakulserroengrit

Mr. Achvin WICHAIDIT
Counselor
Spouse: Mrs. Supajee Wichaidit

Mr. Uthai CENPUKDEE
First Secretary (Agriculture)
Spouse: Mrs. Karuna Cenpukdee

Mrs. Pariyaka IAMSAARD
First Secretary (Education)

Mr. Vijanat ISARABHAKDI
First Secretary (Political)
Spouse: Mrs. Wannipa Isarabhakdi

Ms. Wilailuk PADUNGKITTIMAL
First Secretary (Industry)

Mr. Tada PHUTTHITADA
First Secretary (Economic and Financial)
Spouse: Mrs. Rujira Phutthitada

Mrs. Chutima SAWASDEE
First Secretary (Education)
Spouse: Mr. Walathep Sawasdee

Mrs. Chalermsri SONGPRASERT
First Secretary (Education)
Spouse: Mr. Punlop Songprasert

Mr. Krisada THARASOOKT
First Secretary

Mr. Pornpop UAMPIDHAYA
First Secretary

Mr. Sasiwat WONGSINSAWAT
First Secretary

Mr. Nibhon BUMRARB
Second Secretary
Spouse: Mrs. Penpimol Bumrarb

Ms. Nantawan POWTAVEE
Second Secretary

Ms. Kasama SUEBWISES
Second Secretary (Information)

Ms. Sasirit TANGULRAT
Second Secretary (Protocol)

Mrs. Chittimas IAMSUDHA
Third Secretary
Spouse: Mr. Ekarach Iamsudha

Ms. Suksri LUMPRASERT
Third Secretary

Mr. Prayad DITTANTE
Attaché
Spouse: Mrs. Sutisa Dittante

Lt. Commander Wichian RITWIROON
Attaché

Colonel Pirasak SIKANGWAN

Defense and Military Attaché
Spouse: Mrs. Krisna Sikangwan

Captain Yodchai RUGSUMRUAD
Naval Attaché
Spouse: Mrs. Pearl Rugsumruad

Group Captain Itthaporn SUBHAWONG
Air Attaché
Spouse: Mrs. Napaporn Subhawong

Colonel Krisda NORAPOOMPIPAT
Asst. Military Attaché
Spouse: Mrs. Kanchan Norapoompipat

Captain Kaneepol SONGJAROEN
Asst. Naval Attaché
Spouse: Mrs. Wilawan Songjaroen

Group Captain Surasit HOLASUT
Asst. Air Attaché
Spouse: Mrs. Ampan Holasut

Office of Agricultural Affairs
1024 Wisconsin Avenue, NW
Washington DC 20007
Phone: 202/338-1543

Office of the Air Attaché
5600 16th St., NW
Washington DC 20011
Phone: 202/882-8550

Office of Commercial Affairs
1024 Wisconsin Ave., NW - Suite 201
Washington DC 20007
Phone: 202/944-2111

**Office of the Economic and
  Financial Affairs**
1025 Wisconsin Ave., NW - Suite 202
Washington DC 20007
Phone: 202/467-6790

Office of the Education Affairs
1906 23rd Street, NW
Washington DC 20008
Phone: 202/667-9110

Office of Industrial Affairs
1024 Wisconsin Ave., NW - Suite 304
Washington DC 20007
Phone: 202/944-3620

Office of the Information Attaché
1024 Wisconsin Avenue, NW
Washington DC 20007

Office of Military Attaché
2440 Foxhall Road, NW - Suite 103
Washington DC 20007
Phone: 202/944-3625

Office of the Naval Attaché
1024 Wisconsin Avenue, NW
Washington DC 20007
Phone: 202/944-3629

**Office of the Science and
  Technology Counselor**
1024 Wisconsin Ave., NW - Suite 104
Washington DC 20007
Phone: 202/944-5203

Togo

Embassy of the Republic of Togo
2208 Massachusetts Avenue, NW
Washington DC 20008
Phone: 202/234-4212
Fax: 202/232-3190

Pascal Akoussouleou BODJONI
Ambassador

Date Credentials Presented: 5/27/98

Due to the recent arrival of the ambassador, the embassy did not have biographical information on the ambassador available for release before press date of this publication.

STAFF:

Mr. Edem Frederic HEGBE
Counselor
Spouse: Mrs. Ameyo Hegbe

Mr. Lorempo T. LANDJERGUE
First Secretary
Spouse: Mrs. Azouma Dollah Landjergue

Mr. Nakpane ALI-NAPO
Attaché (Consular)

Mr. Adje AMEGAVI
Attaché (Consular)
Spouse: Mrs. Akouele Amegavi

Ms. Beheza GNASSINGBE
Attaché (Cultural)

Mr. Akoussoulelou BODJONA
Attaché

Mrs. Essi Dometo AZIZBU
Asst. Attaché (Financial)

Tonga

Embassy of the Kingdom of Tonga
36 Molyneux Street
London ENGLAND W1H6AB
Phone: 44 171 724 5828
Fax: 44 171 723 9074

Akosita FINEANGANOFO
Ambassador

Date Credentials Presented: 2/11/97

Born: 2/11/36 in Ha'apai, Tonga

Spouse: Mr. Musese Fineanganofo

Like previous Tongan ambassadors to the United States, Mrs. Akosita Fineanganofo concurrently holds the position of high commissioner to the United Kingdom and lives in London.

Mrs. Fineanganofo, has held a number of posts with the government of Tonga. Between 1990 and 1996, she was deputy secretary for foreign affairs and chief of protocol in Nuku'alofa. She was an alternate representative to the annual U.N. ASCAP commission session in Bangkok, Thailand; point of contact and commonwealth desk officer; a member of the delegation to the Commonwealth Senior Officials Meeting and International Women's Conference; and an alternate director on Royal Tongan Airline, NUK.

Between 1986 and 1989, she was counsellor to the Tonga High Commission in London. Her other foreign affairs positions include assistant secretary, Ministry of Foreign Affairs, in 1982 and second secretary, Tonga High Commission, in London in 1982. She joined the Ministry of Foreign Affairs in 1980.

Fineanganofo was a nurse, who trained and practiced in Australia, London, and the United States (Massachusetts). She did post-graduate studies in nursing in Wellington, New Zealand, and London.

She was appointed maternal and child health care sister at the Ministry of Health in Nuku'alofa in 1964, then was appointed matron of Vaiola Hospital, Ministry of Health, in Nuku'alofa in 1970. Two years later, she was promoted to chief nursing officer in the ministry.

Trinidad & Tobago

Embassy of the Republic of
  Trinidad and Tobago
1708 Massachusetts Avenue, NW
Washington DC 20036
Phone: 202/467-6490
Fax: 202/785-3130
Email: embttgo@erols.com

Michael A. ARNEAUD
Ambassador

Date Credentials Presented: 12/12/97

Born: 12/15/39

Spouse: Mrs. Sharon De La Rosa Arneaud

Michael A. Arneaud, Trinidad and Tobago's ambassador to the U.S. and permanent representative to the Organization of

American States, has pursued a varied career in business.

Between 1981 and 1997, he was director of Neal and Massy Holdings Limited. From 1988 to 1997, he also was director of Neal and Massy Caribbean Limited and chairman of the Canning's Group of Companies. In 1997, he was chairman of Auto Rentals. Between 1986 and 1997, his other business affiliations included: director of Tobago Services Limited; managing director of Massy Enterprises Limited; director of Auto Rentals Limited, and chairman of National Fisheries Limited.

He was director of General Finance Corporation between 1984 and 1988 and chairman of Climate Control Limited between 1984 and 1986. Earlier, he was director of Industrial Gases Limited, as well as Liquid Carbonic (W.I.) Limited and Nealco Properties Limited; managing director and later chairman of Tractors and Machinery (Trinidad) Limited; and director of Prestige Holdings Limited.

In 1997, Arneaud served as a member of the National-Partite Commission of the prime minister of the Republic of Trinidad and Tobago, as well as head of a trade and investment mission of the Tobago Chamber of Industry and Commerce to India. He was director of the Tourism and Industrial Development Company of Trinidad and Tobago Limited (TIDCO) in 1996-97; president of the Trinidad and Tobago Chamber of Industry and Commerce from 1995 to 1997; executive vice president of the chamber from 1993 to 1995; and president of the Junior Chamber of Commerce of Port of Spain in 1972.

The ambassador was educated at Belmont Boys Intermediate School and St. Mary's College. He is married and has two children, Karen and Stephen. His hobbies are golf, power boating, and music.

STAFF:

Mr. Lennox WATTLEY
Counselor
Spouse: Mrs. Wattley

Mr. Carl A. FRANCIS
Counselor
Spouse: Mrs. Lystra Francis

Mrs. Sandra HONORE BRAITHWAITE
Counselor
Spouse: Mr. Peter Braithwaite

Mr. Keith AMEERALI
Attaché (Immigration)

Mr. Desmond CODRINGTON
Attaché (Financial)

Miss Patricia FRANCOIS
Attaché (Administrative)

Colonel John C.E. SANDY

Defense and Military Attaché
Spouse: Mrs. Jacqueline H. P. Sandy

Tunisia

Embassy of Tunisia
1515 Massachusetts Avenue, NW
Washington DC 20005
Phone: 202/862-1850
Fax: 202/862-1858
Email: tunisemb@access.digex.net
Url: http://www.tunisiaOnline.com

Dr. Noureddine MEJDOUB
Ambassador

Date Credentials Presented: 11/12/97

Born: 1/20/35 in Tunis, Tunisia

Spouse: Mrs. Karima Mejdoub

Dr. Noureddine Mejdoub, who was appointed Tunisia's ambassador to the U.S. in October 1997, previously served as ambassador to Austria, Czechoslovakia, Italy, and most recently, Japan.

Mejdoub began his diplomatic career in 1960 in the position of chargé de mission in the office of the minister of foreign affairs. He was spokesman of the ministry of foreign affairs in 1962-63, after which he was appointed to the Tunisian embassy in London from 1963 to 1965. He then went to Washington, D.C. for four years as counselor to the Tunisian embassy.

In 1970, Mejdoub was named deputy director of political affairs in the ministry of foreign affairs. Between 1971 and 1973, he served in the Tunisian embassy in Paris as minister plenipotentiary, deputy chief of mission. He then went to Vienna between 1973 and 1977 as chargé d'affaires before his promotion to ambassador to Austria.

Between 1977 and 1980, he was back in Tunisia in the post of director of political affairs for Europe and America in the ministry of foreign affairs. He was ambassador to Czechoslovakia from 1980 to 1986 and ambassador to Italy from 1985 to 1989. In December 1989, he was appointed diplomatic counselor and chairman of the National Committee on Tunisia's Relations

with the European Economic Community. In 1991-92, he served as secretary of state to the minister of foreign affairs. Then in 1992 he was appointed ambassador to Japan.

Mejdoub is a Grand Officer of the Republic Order. He is married and has four children.

STAFF:

Mr. Slaheddine BEN MAHMOUD
Counselor (Commercial)
Spouse: Mrs. Ben Mahmoud

Mr. Mhamed Ezzine CHLAIFA
Counselor
Spouse: Mrs. Leila Chelaifa

Mr. Faycal GOUIA
Counselor
Spouse: Mrs. Khaoula Gouia

Mr. Sahbi KHALFALLAH
First Secretary
Spouse: Mrs. Monia Khalfallah

Mr. Nejmeddine LAKHAL
First Secretary

Mr. Mohamed YAZIDI
First Secretary

Mr. Sadok KASSOUS
Attaché (Administration)
Spouse: Mrs. Naima Kassous

Colonel Mahmoud BEN MHAMED
Defense, Military, Naval, and Air Attaché
Spouse: Mrs. Saloua Ben Mhamed

Lt. Colonel Hassine GHARSALLAH
Asst. Def., Military, Naval, & Air Attaché

Lt. Colonel Abdesselem ZOUBEIDI
Asst. Def., Military, Naval, & Air Attaché

**Office of the Defense
Armed Forces Attaché**
1515 Massachusetts Avenue, NW
Washington DC 20005
Phone: 202/862-1850

Office of Tunisian Information
1515 Massachusetts Avenue, NW
Washington DC 20005
Phone: 202/466-2546

Tunisian Foreign Investment Agency
1515 Massachusetts Ave., NW - Suite 400
Washington DC 20005
Phone: 202/223-8580 Fax: 202/223-8005

Turkey

Embassy of the Republic of Turkey
1714 Massachusetts Avenue, NW
Washington DC 20036
Phone: 202/659-8200
Fax: 202/659-0744
Email: embassy@turkey.org
Url: http://www.turkey.org

Baki ILKIN
Ambassador

Date Credentials Presented: 5/27/98

Due to the recent arrival of the ambassador, the embassy did not have biographical information on the ambassador available for release before press date of this publication.

STAFF:

Mrs. Melek Sina BAYDUR
Minister-Counselor (Deputy Chief of
  Mission)
Spouse: Mr. Mehmet Eser Baydur

Mr. O. Sener AKKAYNAK
Counselor (Financial)
Spouse: Mrs. Hulya Akkaynak

Mrs. Dilek EMIL
Counselor (Economic)
Spouse: Mr. Mustafa Ferhat Emil

Mr. Osman Bulent ERDEMGIL
Counselor (Press)
Spouse: Mrs. Fatma Sirindilek Erdemgil

Mr. Mehmet EYMUR
Counselor (Legal)
Spouse: Mrs. Canset Eymur

Mr. Mehmet GUCUK
Counselor
Spouse: Mrs. Serife Gucuk

Mr. Abdulbaki KESKIN
Counselor (Social)
Spouse: Mrs. Hacer Keskin

Mr. Ali Rifat KOKSAL
Counselor
Spouse: Mrs. Mubeccel Koksal

Mrs. Aysen KULAKOGLU
Counselor (Economic)
Spouse: Mr. Fikri Kulakoglu

Ms. Sukran OGUN
Counselor (Commercial)

Mr. Bulent SAHINALP
Counselor (Commercial)
Spouse: Mrs. Fisun Sahinalp

Mr. Aykut SEZGIN
Counselor
Spouse: Mrs. Hulya Sezgin

Mr. Namik TAN
Counselor
Spouse: Mrs. Talia Fugen Tan

Mr. Riza Tuna TURAGAY
Counselor (Commercial)
Spouse: Mrs. Elvan Turagay

Ms. Serra ERARSLAN
First Secretary

Mr. Ahmet OKTAY

First Secretary

Mr. S. Inan OZYILDIZ
First Secretary
Spouse: Mrs. Muzaffer Ozyildiz

Mr. Hakki YUNT
First Secretary
Spouse: Mrs. Figen Yunt

Mr. Mustafa ACAR
Attaché
Spouse: Mrs. Filiz Acar

Major Halil ARDA
Attaché (Army Supply)
Spouse: Mrs. Handan Arda

Mr. Akgun BOR
Attaché (Administrative)

Mr. Talat CALP
Attaché
Spouse: Mrs. Nagihan Calp

Mr. Salih CANER
Attaché
Spouse: Mrs. Sema Caner

Mr. Hasan CELIK
Attaché
Spouse: Mrs. Nalar Celik

Mrs. Jale COLAKOGLU
Attaché (Education)
Spouse: Mr. Selalettin Colakoglu

Mr. Husrev EKINCI
Attaché

Mrs. Yasemin ERGIN
Attaché
Spouse: Mrs. Hamdi Tamer Ergin

Mr. Recep GURDAL
Attaché
Spouse: Mrs. Asuman Gurdal

Mr. Aslan KUSCUOGLU
Attaché
Spouse: Mrs. Pakize Kuscuoglu

Colonel A. Muhtesem KUT
Attaché (Air Supply)
Spouse: Mrs. Bilge Kut

Mr. Isa Mufit MUTLU
Attaché
Spouse: Mrs. Merel Mutlu

Mr. Seref NURCIN
Attaché
Spouse: Mrs. Nuran Nurcin

Mr. Sami Turker ORCUN
Attaché (Information)
Spouse: Mrs. Nuran Orcun

Ms. Betul OZ
Attaché

Mr. Kadir Ahmet PARLA
Attaché (Press)

Mr. Aziimet SAHIN
Attaché
Spouse: Mrs. Perihan Sahin

Mr. Metin TANRIVER
Attaché (Security)
Spouse: Mrs. Nurten Tanriver

Mr. Selim TEMEL
Attaché
Spouse: Mrs. Sehrinaz Temel

Mr. Bora TUNCKANAT
Attaché

Mr. Gulay TURKVAN
Attaché (Administrative)
Spouse: Mrs. Akif Bulent Turkvan

Mr. Sazi TUZLA
Attaché (Administrative)
Spouse: Mrs. Tuler Tuzla

Mr. Levent VURAL
Attaché
Spouse: Mrs. Ozge Vural

Lt. Commander Sebahattin GUZEL
Asst. Attaché (Naval Supply)
Spouse: Mrs. Kamile Gulden Guzel

Lt. Colonel Ahmet Aydin YILMAZ
Asst. Attaché (Air Supply)
Spouse: Mrs. Sehnaz Yilmaz

Major Muzaffer YUKSEL
Asst. Attaché (Army Supply)
Spouse: Mrs. Gulnaz Yuksel

Lt. Commander Ismail DIKMIN
Defense Cooperation Attaché
  (Naval Supply)
Spouse: Mrs. Hamide Dikmen

Brigadier General Volkan TIRYAKILER
Defense and Air Attaché (Naval Supply)
Spouse: Mrs. Volkan Tiryalkiler

Colonel Mehmet OZTURK
Military Attaché
Spouse: Mrs. Dursen Ozturk

Captain Omer Halit AKSU
Naval Attaché
Spouse: Mrs. Zehra Aksu

Major Can SOLAKOGLU
Asst. Military Attaché
Spouse: Mrs. Siren Solakoglu

Office of the Agricultural Counselor
3005 Massachusetts Ave., NW
Washington DC 20036
Phone: 202/797-8177

Commercial Counselor
3005 Massachusetts Avenue, NW
Washington DC 20036
Phone: 202/483-6366

Office of the Defense Attaché
2202 Massachusetts Ave., NW
Washington DC 20008

Phone: 202/265-7365

Office of the Economic Counselor
3005 Massachusetts Ave., NW
Washington DC 20036
Phone: 202/408-5366

Office of the Educational Counselor
3005 Massachusetts Ave., NW
Washington DC 20008
Phone: 202/588-5590

Office of the Financial and
  Customs Counselor
3005 Massachusetts Ave., NW
Washington DC 20036
Phone: 202/332-4242

Planning Office
3005 Massachusetts Avenue, NW
Washington DC 20036
Phone: 202/483-5345

Office of the Press Counselor
3005 Massachusetts Ave., NW
Washington DC 20036
Phone: 202/223-2337

Office of Social Affairs
3005 Massachusetts Ave., NW
Washington DC 20036
Phone: 202/265-0298

Office of the Tourism Counselor
1717 Massachusetts Ave., NW
Washington DC 20036
Phone: 202/429-9844

Turkmenistan

Embassy of Turkmenistan
2207 Massachusetts Avenue, NW
Washington DC 20008
Phone: 202/588-1500
Fax: 202/588-0697
Email: embassy@dc.infi.net
Url: http://www.infi.net/~embassy

Halil UGUR
Ambassador

Date Credentials Presented: 6/23/94

Born: 6/16/50 in Ankara, Turkey

Spouse: Mrs. Zuhal Ugur

Halil Ugur was an active businessman and entrepreneur in Turkey until 1991 when he was appointed counsel general of Turkmenistan in Istanbul when Turkmenistan became an independent nation.

Ugur is of Turkmen origin on both sides of his family but was raised in Turkey. In 1972, he earned a degree in electronics engineering from the Middle East Technical University and later completed post-graduate studies at Harvard Business School in 1984.

The Ambassador is married and has one daughter. He is an avid horseback rider and is interested in folk arts of all cultures.

STAFF:

Mr. Tcharnazar ANNABERDIEV
Minister-Counselor
Spouse: Mrs. Maia Annaberdyeva

Uganda

Embassy of the Republic of Uganda
5909 16th Street, NW
Washington DC 20011
Phone: 202/726-7100
Fax: 202/726-1727
Email: ugaembassy@rocketmail.com
Url: http://www.ugandaweb.com/
  ugaembassy

Edith Grace SSEMPALA
Ambassador

Date Credentials Presented: 10/9/96

Born: 12/28/53

Spouse: Mr. Patrick Ssempala

During 1997, Edith Grace Ssempala, Uganda's ambassador to the U.S., coordinated the visit of Ugandan President Musevini and his wife to the U.S. and accompanied First Lady Hillary Rodham Clinton on her visit to Uganda. She had initiated Mrs. Clinton's trip and helped arrange it.

Ssempala also initiated Secretary of State Madeline Albright's trip to Uganda in 1997. She coordinated and participated in the visit of the "Presidential Delegation on Economic Cooperation to Africa," to Uganda, led by U.S. Rep. Charles Rangel (D-N.Y.). The 42-person delegation included five members of Congress, members of the Clinton administration, congressional staffers, and corporate sector executives. She arranged a separate congressional delegation's visit to Uganda, led by U.S. Rep. James Kolbe (R-Ariz.)

In addition to her duties at the Ugandan embassy in Washington, D.C., Ssempala is her country's representative to the World Bank and the International Monetary Fund. She is a member of the advisory board of the Center for Strategic and International Studies---Africa Program.

Between 1986 and 1996, Ssempala, based in Copenhagen, Denmark, served as her country's ambassador to Denmark, Finland, Iceland, Norway, and Sweden. She was a quality controller with Rifa Electronics Company of Stockholm, Sweden, between 1981 and 1986.

In the U.S. and Europe, she has organized seminars and lectured on such subjects as "Democracy and Human Rights in Uganda," "Uganda-Nordic Private Sector Cooperation,"

and "The Ugandan Miracle." Among her publications are "The Road to Development in Africa in the 21st Century," and "Democracy---Uganda's Experience."

The ambassador attended Gayaza High School from 1967 to 1970, then received an advanced level certificate from Nabumali High School in 1971-72. She obtained a master's degree in civil engineering from Lumumba University in Moscow, which she attended from 1973 to 1979.

The ambassador is married and has three children. She enjoys reading, debating with her children, and listening to news programs. She likes listening to music, especially jazz; sports; and discussing economic and political issues and current events.

STAFF:

Mr. Ahmed SSENYOMO
Counselor
Spouse: Mrs. Fatuma Ssenyomo

Mrs. Nimisha J.
  MADHVANI-CHANDARIA
First Secretary (Public Relations and
  Commercial)
Spouse: Mr. Kapoor Chandaria

Mr. Juilius MAGEMBE
First Secretary
Spouse: Mrs. Florence Magembe

Mr. Richard Tumusiime KABONERO
Second Secretary
Spouse: Mrs. Grace Tumusiime Kabonero

Mrs. Dora Nunguri KUTESA
Second Secretary (Finance and Admin.)

Colonel John MATEEKA
Defense, Military, Naval and Air Attaché

Ukraine

Embassy of Ukraine
3350 M Street, NW
Washington DC 20007
Phone: 202/333-0606
Fax: 202/333-0817

Dr. Yuri M. SHCHERBAK
Ambassador

Date Credentials Presented: 11/21/94

Born: 10/12/34 in Kiev

Spouse: Mrs. Mariya Shcherbak

Dr. Yuri Shcherbak, a well known Ukrainian novelist, presented his credentials to President Clinton during the state visit of President Leonid Kuchma to Washington Nov. 21, 1994.

Shcherbak began his active political career in 1989 when he won a seat in the USSR Supreme Soviet, where he was a close associate of Dr. Andrey Sakharov. As an opposition leader and chairman of the subcommittee on energy and nuclear safety, he initiated and led the first parliamentary investigation of the Chornoybyl accident, the nuclear catastrophe in Semipalatinsk, and in the Urals.

Having never been affiliated with the Soviet Communist Party, Shcherbak founded and became the leader of the Ukrainian Green Movement (the Green Party since 1990) in 1988.

An eyewitness of the 1986 Chornobyl disaster, he wrote the documentary novel, Chornobyl, which was printed in most ex-Soviet countries and in the West. Shcherbak also wrote extensively on the Stalinist man-made famine in Ukraine in 1932-33. He is the author of 20 books of poetry, prose, plays, and essays. He is a member of Ukraine's Writers' Union and Cinematographers' Union and was on the Board of Writers' Union between 1987 and 1989.

In 1991, Shcherbak was appointed Minister of Environmental Protection of Ukraine and a member of the National Security Council. He served as Ukraine's ambassador to Israel between 1992 and 1994.

He graduated from Kiev Medical College in 1958 and has a Ph.D. and D.sc. degrees in epidemiology. He is a member of Ukraine's Academy of Environmental Sciences.

Shcherbak, who is married and has two children, speaks Ukrainian, English, Russian, and Polish.

STAFF:

Mr. Veleriy P. KUCHINSKY
Minister-Counselor
Spouse: Mrs. Alla B. Kuchinsky

Mr. Volodymyr BELASHOV
Counselor
Spouse: Mrs. Irina Belashova

Mr. Oleksii BEREZHNYI
Counselor
Spouse: Mrs. Violetta Berezhna

Mr. Petro DATSENKO
Counselor (Science and Technology)
Spouse: Mrs. Iryna Datsenko

Mr. Mykhayie REZNIK
Counselor
Spouse: Mrs. Irena Reznik

Mr. Volodymyr Ivanovich VLASSOV
Counselor
Spouse: Mrs. Kaleria Vlassova

Mrs. Natalia ZARUDNA
Counselor
Spouse: Mr. Sergiy M. Zarudnyy

Mr. Vasyl GOLOVENKO
First Secretary
Spouse: Mrs. Mariya-Olga Golovenko

Mr. Volodymyr H. KHRIEBET
First Secretary

Mr. Leonid Olexsandrovych KOZHARA
First Secretary (Political)
Spouse: Mrs. Lyudmyla Kozhara

Mr. Oleksandr VASHCHENKO
First Secretary
Spouse: Mrs. Galina Vashchenko

Mr. Oleksandr VYKHODTSEV
First Secretary (Economic)
Spouse: Mrs. Natalia Vykhodtseva

Mrs. Natalia RYLCHIK
Second Secretary and Consul
Spouse: Mr. Sergiy Rylchik

Mr. Oleg SHEVCHENKO
Second Secretary

Mr. Vadym V. YAROTSKIY
Second Secretary and Consul
Spouse: Mrs. Olesia Yarotsaka

Mr. Vasyl ZORYA
Second Secretary
Spouse: Mrs. Anne Zorya

Mr. Oleh BELOKOLOS
Third Secretary
Spouse: Mrs. Olena Belokolos

Mr. Olexander O. PECHERYTSYA
Third Secretary
Spouse: Mrs. Nataliya Pecherytsya

Mr. Sergey ROMANOV
Third Secretary
Spouse: Mrs. Nataliya Romanova

Mr. Sergey ZAGURSKIY
Third Secretary
Spouse: Mrs. Olena Zagurska

Colonel Olexander GALAKA
Asst. Defense and Military Attaché
Spouse: Mrs. Tetyana Galaka

Major Vadym YAKHNO
Asst. Defense Attaché
Spouse: Mrs. Liudmyla Yakhno

Lt. Colonel Igor S. YURLOV
Asst. Air Attaché
Spouse: Mrs. Liudmyla Yakhno

United Arab Emirates

Embassy of the United Arab Emirates
1255 22nd Street, NW - Suite 700
Washington DC 20037
Phone: 202/955-7999
Fax: 202/337-7029

Mohammad bin Hussein AL-SHAALI

Ambassador

Date Credentials Presented: 9/8/92

Born: 10/1/50 in Emirate of Ajman

Spouse: Mrs. Huda Mahmoud Al-Shaali

A career diplomat, Mohammad bin Hussein Al-Shaali has had extensive foreign affairs experience at both the bilateral and multilateral levels.

Immediately prior to his appointment to Washington, he served with the United Nations as the United Arab Emirates' permanent representative and as chairman of the Third Committee of the U.N. General Assembly, and as President of the Security Council. In addition to his present duties as Ambassador in Washington, Al-Shaali has served concurrently since 1993 as non-resident ambassador to Mexico.

Having begun his career in 1974, Al-Shaali remained in his country until 1977, rising to the position of deputy director of the General Department of Political Affairs. During 1977 and 1978, he served as charge d'affairs in Vienna and in Tunis, returning to the United Arab Emirates as acting director of the Department of Administration and Finance. Between 1978 and 1984, he held several senior positions in his home country, including the directorship of the Department of Arab Homeland. In 1984, he was posted to New York as head of the Permanent Mission to the United Nations. He remained at the U.N. until his move to Washington in 1992.

Al-Shaali holds a B.A. in commerce, administration, and economics from Beirut University and speaks Arabic and English. He is married to Huda Mahmoud Al-Shaali and has four children.

STAFF:

Mr. Ali Mohammed ALI
Minister
Spouse: Mrs. Ali

Mr. Abdulhamid A. KAZIM
Counselor
Spouse: Mrs. Nasim Mohd

Mr. Mohammed Hareb B.K.
   AL MEHAIRBI
Second Secretary and Vice Consul

Mr. Abdulla Ahmed M. AL-SALEH
Second Secretary (Political)
Spouse: Mrs. Al-Qassemi

Sargeant Ahmed ALALAWI
Attaché (Administrative)
Spouse: Mrs. Shaikha Belhoon

Sargeant Abdulla ALALI
Attaché (Administrative)
Spouse: Mrs. Maryam Alali

First Lt. Mohammed ALJUNAIBI
Attaché (Administrative)

Mr. Saeed Majed ALMANSOURI
Attaché (Administrative and Medical)
Spouse: Mrs. Fatima Mohammed
   Almansouri

Mr. Salem Ali ALMAZROOEI
Attaché (Administrative)
Spouse: Mrs. Mariam Almazrooei

First Lt. Ali ALNAQBI
Attaché (Administrative)
Spouse: Mrs. Khadija Alnaqbi

Captain Khalid HASSAN
Attaché (Administrative)

Warrant Officer Nasser Abdulla YUSEF
Attaché (Administrative)

First Sargeant Qusay K. ABU-SAHAM
Asst. Attaché

Mr. Rashed Mubarak AL-HAJERI
Asst. Attaché (Cultural)
Spouse: Mrs. Fadda

Mr. Abdulla Mohamed Rashed
   AL HAMEERI
Asst. Attaché (Administrative)
Spouse: Mrs. Maryam Abdulla
   Al Hameeri

Mr. Yousif J. ALSAIFI
Asst. Attaché (Cultural)
Spouse: Mrs. Mariam Abdulla Alsaifi

First Sargeant Ahmed IBRAHIM
Asst. Attaché (Administrative)

Brigadier General Obaid ABED
Defense, Military, Naval and Air Attaché
Spouse: Mrs. Nabila Biba

Major Ahmed M. R. ALSHAMSI

Asst. Defense, Military, Naval and
   Air Attaché
Spouse: Mrs. Huda A. Alshamsi

Cultural Office
1010 Wisconsin Avenue, NW, Suite 505
Washington DC 20007
Phone: 202/342-1111

**Office of the Defense, Military,
   Naval and Air Attaché**
2209 Massachusetts Avenue, NW
Washington DC 20008
Phone: 202/328-4536

Medical Office
1000 Thomas Jefferson St., Suite 508
Washington DC 20007
Phone: 202/337-0400

United Kingdom

British Embassy
3100 Massachusetts Avenue, NW
Washington DC 20008
Phone: 202/588-6513
Fax: 202/588-7860

Sir Christopher Meyer
Ambassador

Date Credentials Presented: 11/12/97

Born: 2/22/44 in Beaconsfield, England

Spouse: Mrs. Catherine Meyer

Sir Christopher Meyer, a 32-year veteran of the United Kingdom's diplomatic service, served as British ambassador to the Federal Republic of Germany from March to October 1997 before taking the post of ambassador to the U.S.

He joined the diplomatic service in 1966, spending the first two years in London after which he was posted to Moscow from 1968 to 1970 and then to Madrid from 1970 to 1973.

On returning to London, Sir Christopher worked as head of the Soviet section in the East European and Soviet department. In 1976, he was transferred to the policy planning staff as speechwriter to the foreign secretary. In this capacity he worked until

1978 for three foreign secretaries: James Callaghan, the late Anthony Crosland, and David Owen.

In 1978, he was posted to Brussels to the UK representation to the European Communities where he specialized in trade policy. From there he went in 1982 to Moscow as political counselor.

On returning to London in 1984, he spent four years as foreign office spokesman and press secretary of the then foreign secretary, Sir Geoffrey Howe.

In 1988-89, he spent a sabbatical year as a visiting fellow at Harvard University's Center for International Affairs, after which he was posted to Washington, D.C., as minister with responsibility for trade policy. In 1992, he was promoted to minister and deputy head of mission. On returning to London in 1994, he was appointed government spokesman and press secretary to the prime minister.

He was educated at Lancing College and Peterhouse, Cambridge, where he read history. After Cambridge, he spent a year at the Paul Nitze School of Advanced International Studies in Bologna, Italy.

Sir Christopher was made a Knight Commander, Order of St. Michael and St. George, in 1998. He enjoys playing squash and tennis, watching football, and listening to jazz. He and his wife, Catherine, have between them five sons from previous marriages.

STAFF:

Mr. Stephen John Leadbetter WRIGHT
Minister (Deputy Chief of Mission)
Spouse: Mrs. Georgina Susan Wright

Mr. Huw Prideaux EVANS
Minister (Economic)

Mr. Augustine T. O'DONNELL
Minister (Economic)
Spouse: Mrs. Melanie O'Donnell

Mr. John C. T. TAYLOR
Minister (Defense Material)
Spouse: Mrs. Sheelagh Marjorie Taylor

Mr. Anthony Joyce CARY
Counselor (Political and Public Affairs)
Spouse: Mrs. Clare Louise Katherine Cary

Mr. Robert Nicholas CULSHAW
Counselor (Trade)
Spouse: Mrs. Elaine Richie Culshaw

Mr. David Julian EVANS
Counselor (Cultural)
Spouse: Mrs. Lona M. Evans

Mr. Roger FRENCH
Counselor (Mgmt.) and Consul General
Spouse: Mrs. Angela Joyce French

Mr. R. Andrew FULTON
Counselor
Spouse: Mrs. Patricia Mary Fulton

Mr. Christopher David GLYN JONES
Counselor
Spouse: Mrs. Phillipa Mary Glyn Jones

Mr. Charles GRAY
Counselor
Spouse: Mrs. Anne Marie Gray

Mr. James S. HIBBERD
Counselor (Economic)
Spouse: Mrs. Annette Ruth Hibberd

Mr. Paul Anthony KENNEDY
Counselor (Defense Scientific & Equip.)
Spouse: Mrs. Ann Elizabeth Kennedy

Mr. Neil Andrew MACLEAN
Counselor (Defense)
Spouse: Mrs. Isobel Margaret MaClean

Mr. Geoffrey MAGNUS
Counselor (Defense Supply)
Spouse: Mrs. Jeanette Magnus

Mr. John SAWERS
Counselor
Spouse: Mrs. Shelley Sawers

Mr. James E. SMITH
Counselor
Spouse: Mrs. Karen M. Smith

Dr. Peter SMYTH
Counselor
Spouse: Mrs. Yvonne J. Smyth

Mr. Christopher WHALEY
Counselor
Spouse: Ms. Jean Whaley

Mr. James David BEVAN
First Secretary
Spouse: Mrs. Alison J. Purdie

Mr. Brian Michael BISCOE
First Secretary (Trade)
Spouse: Mrs. June Heather Biscoe

Mr. James Nicholas BOWDEN
First Secretary
Spouse: Mrs. Alison Michelle Bowden

Miss Patricia BUCKLAND
First Secretary (Defense Supply)

Mr. Nigel CASEY
First Secretary

Mr. Robert CHATTERTON DICKSON
First Secretary (Press and Public Affairs)
Spouse: Ms. Teresa Albor

Mr. Michael Roberson CHILD
First Secretary (Defense Supply Land
Systems)
Spouse: Mrs. Kay Child

Miss Stephanie Lynn DAMAN
First Secretary

Mr. Nicholas C. DAVIDSON
First Secretary (Trade Policy)
Spouse: Mrs. Pauline Davidson

Mr. Andrew J. DAWSON
First Secretary (Economic)
Spouse: Mrs. Sarah F. Dawson

Mr. D. Hugh EVANS
First Secretary (Political)
Spouse: Mrs. Nirmala V. Evans

Mr. Kevin John FINNERTY
First Secretary and Consul
Spouse: Mrs. Norma Mary Finnerty

Mr. Neil Eric GILES
First Secretary
Spouse: Mrs. Penelope Sylvia Giles

Mrs. Patricia HAYES
First Secretary (Transport)
Spouse: Mr. Andrew Hayes

Mr. David Barclay KEEGAN
First Secretary
Spouse: Mrs. Susan Amanda Keegan

Mr. Terence Ronald KNIGHT
First Secretary (Management)
Spouse: Mrs. Jane Clare Knight

Mr. Paul D. MADDEN
First Secretary (Trade Policy)
Spouse: Mrs. Sarah Madden

Mr. Philip MATTHEWS
First Secretary
Spouse: Mrs. Paula P. Matthews

Mr. Simon G. MCDONALD
First Secretary (Political)
Spouse: Mrs. Olivia M. McDonald

Mrs. Janet E. MCIVER
First Secretary
Spouse: Mr. Donald A. P. Bundy

Mr. Philip John PARHAM
First Secretary
Spouse: Mrs. Anna Catherine A. L. Parham

Miss Philippa Ann ROGERS
First Secretary (Science and Technology)

Mr. John RYAN
First Secretary
Spouse: Mrs. Gillian Jean Ryan

Mr. William SHAPCOTT
First Secretary
Spouse: Mrs. Shelley M. Shapcott

Mr. Andrew SOPER
First Secretary
Spouse: Mrs. Kathryn Soper

Mr. John SWEENEY
First Secretary
Spouse: Mrs. Mairead A. Sweeney

Mr. Patrick Gilmer TOPPING
First Secretary

Spouse: Mrs. Indira Annick
Coomaraswamy

Mr. Alastair Ian WILSON
First Secretary (Agriculture and Trade)
Spouse: Mrs. Amy Louise Wilson

Mr. Richard John FAULKNER
Second Secretary and Vice Consul
Spouse: Mrs. Francoise Marie C. A.
Faulkner

Mr. Clive Richard FOX
Second Secretary
Spouse: Mrs. Barbara Ann Fox

Mr. Peter JONES
Second Secretary
Spouse: Mrs. Elaine Jones

Mr. Peter MCCLYMONT
Second Secretary (Transportation)
Spouse: Ms. Lesley Jane Bainsfair

Mrs. Carol Ann PRIESTLEY
Second Secretary (Management)
Spouse: Mr. Lawrence Minton Priestley

Mr. Colin Michael RICHARDS
Second Secretary
Spouse: Mrs. Jill Richards

Mr. David B. ARKLEY
Third Secretary (Press and Public Affairs)
Spouse: Mrs. Melissa B. Arkley

Mr. Richard David HOMER
Third Secretary (Visits)

Ms. Victoria SLORAH
Third Secretary

Mr. John Leonard STEERS
Third Secretary
Spouse: Mrs. Claire Margaret Steers

Mrs. Pamela Kay BARRETT
Attaché (Education)

Mr. John Edward HOLMES
Attaché (Defense Equipment Sea)
Spouse: Mrs. Ann Christine Holmes

Mr. Terence Martin KENNEDY
Attaché (Defense Supply)
Spouse: Mrs. Valerie Anne Kennedy

Mr. Richard Barrie LUETCHFORD
Attaché (Defense Equip. & Property)
Spouse: Mrs. Barbara Joan Luetchford

Ms. Jane Frances PAXMAN
Attaché (Environment)

Mr. James PLATT
Attaché (Defense Equipment Land)
Spouse: Mrs. Heather Lynn Platt

Mr. Robert Andrew STERN
Attaché (Defense Equipment Air)
Spouse: Mrs. Francesca Mary Stern

Mr. Antony Robert VAUDREY

Attaché (Civil Aviation)
Spouse: Mrs. Helen Vaudrey

Major General Charles Gerard VYVYAN
Defense Attaché
Spouse: Mrs. Elizabeth Francis Vyvyan

Brigadier General Fenwick BALY
Military Attaché & Asst. Defense Attaché
Spouse: Mrs. Elspeth Baly

Commodore Dered ANTHONY
Naval Attaché and Asst. Defense Attaché
Spouse: Mrs. Denise Anthony

Air Commodore David Kenworthy
   NORRISS
Air Attaché and Asst. Defense Attaché
Spouse: Mrs. Nancie Mae Norriss

Colonel Fiona Anne WALTHALL
Asst. Defense Attaché

Colonel Martin Spencer VINE
Asst. Military Attaché
Spouse: Mrs. Miranda F. Vine

Colonel Andrew Robert PILLAR
Asst. Naval Attaché
Spouse: Mrs. Shirley Pillar

Group Captain Robert D. IVESON
Asst. Air Attaché
Spouse: Mrs. Shirley Pillar

Civil Aviation and Mission to the FAA
1730 Rhode Island Ave., NW - Suite 419
Washington DC 20036
Phone: 202/463-7529

Uruguay

Embassy of Uruguay
2715 M Street, NW
Washington DC 20007
Phone: 202/331-1313
Fax: 202/331-8142
Email: uruguay@embassy.org
Url: http://www.embassy.org/uruguay

Alvaro DIEZ DE MEDINA
Ambassador

Date Credentials Presented: 9/15/95

Born: 4/3/57 in La Paz, Bolivia

Spouse: Mrs. Beatriz Benejam Camacho

Alvaro Diez de Medina is a lawyer, banker, journalist and international consultant who has been involved in commercial and banking enterprises as well as academic pursuits.

Between 1993 and 1995, Diez de Medina represented Union Bancaire Privec of Geneva, Switzerland, in Montevideo, and in 1989-92, he was the marketing representative of Coutts & Co. (Uruguay), a subsidiary of the National Westminster Bank of U.K. From 1982 to 1985, he was administrative secretary to the Wood Chamber of Industry in Montevideo and from 1980 to 1985, administrative secretary to the Automobile Chamber of Industry in Montevideo.

In 1992-93, he was the international politics editor for El Observador, a daily newspaper in Montevideo. He was a commentator on international affairs for Radio Sarandi for four years; editor of publications for the Center of Studies of the Economic and Social Reality; editor-columnist for El Dia, a daily newspaper in Montevideo; assistant editor of a magazine, Punto y Aparte; and a columnist on international politics for Jaque, a weekly newspaper.

In 1992, Diez de Medina was a consultant to the ORT Institute in Montevideo for the creation of graduate studies in international affairs in cooperation with Reading University in the United Kingdom and was a member of the faculty in international affairs. He was a consultant to the United National Development Program for its urban development and municipal policies program in cooperation with the Mayor of Montevideo in 1989.

In 1987, he was a consultant to the U.S. Agency for International Development for one of its assistance programs in Uruguay. From 1982 to 1985, he was assistant professor and Political Sciences Chair at the School of Law and Social Sciences, at the University of Uruguay.

Diez de Medina is the author of a book, "El Voto que el Alma Pronuncia." He obtained the First Prize in Literary Competition organized by the Ministry of Education and Culture of Uruguay for the publication, "Introduction to the Uruguayan Electoral System (1810-1910)."

Diez de Medina is married and has two children. He speaks English, French, and Portuguese.

STAFF:

Mr. Carlos Antonio MORA
Minister-Counselor (Deputy Chief of
   Mission)
Spouse: Mrs. Odette Susanne Le Moyne
   de Mora

Mr. Carlos Cesar STENERI
Minister (Financial)

Spouse: Mrs. Marie de Steneri

Mr. Nelson CHABEN
Counselor
Spouse: Dr. Brenda Cabrera Sosa
   de Chaben

Dr. Eduardo ROSENBROCK
First Secretary

Dr. Ricardo DUARTE
Second Secretary and Consul
Spouse: Mrs. Patricia Ventos Diaz

Colonel Guillermo RAVEL
Asst. Attaché
Spouse: Mrs. Maria Graziela Machado

General Yelton Acilbier BAGNASCO
Defense and Military Attaché

Captain Sergio ESTELLANO
Naval Attaché
Spouse: Mrs. Graciela Pepe

Colonel Roberto Freddy AMORIN
Air Attaché
Spouse: Mrs. Rosa Castro Firpo

Captain Jose AMUZ
Asst. Military Attaché
Spouse: Mrs. Monica Rotillo Fernandez

Colonel Washington J. GARCIA
Asst. Military Attaché
Spouse: Mrs. Amelia E. Lolo

Office of Financial Affairs
2021 L Street, NW
Washington DC 20036
Phone: 202/223-9833

**Office of the Military, Naval and
   Air Attachés**
1825 K Street, NW
Washington DC 20006
Phone: 202/466-3177

Uzbekistan

Embassy of the Republic of Uzbekistan
1746 Massachusetts Ave., NW
Washington DC 20036
Phone: 202/887-5300
Fax: 202/293-6804
Email: kriddleb@aol.com
Url: http://www.uzebekistan.org

Sodiq S. SAFAEV
Ambassador

Date Credentials Presented: 10/9/96

Born: 2/3/54 in Tashkent, Uzbekistan

Spouse: Mrs. Rahima Safaeva

At the time of his appointment as ambassador to the U.S. in 1996, Sodiq S. Safaev was serving as counselor of state to the president of Uzbekistan. In that capacity he dealt with international political and economic issues.

In 1971, Safaev enrolled in the economics department of Tashkent University and graduated in 1976. In 1984, he completed his doctoral work on problems of labor productivity in Uzbek industry. From 1985 to 1987, he taught at Tashkent University.

He subsequently served in various governmental agencies dealing with science, education, and inter-ethnic relations.

In 1990, Safaev was assigned by his government to be a visiting scholar at the Harvard University Institute for International Development, where he studied modern methods of economic analysis and ways of transforming a command economy into a market economy. Some of his research papers were published by Harvard and are available at the institute.

On his return to Tashkent Safaev was appointed chief of the foreign economic relations department of the office of the president. In March 1992, he became first deputy minister of foreign economic relations in Uzbekistan.

In February 1993, he was appointed minister of foreign affairs of the Republic of Uzbekistan. In September of that year, he was named ambassador to Germany. During this assignment he also represented Uzbekistan in the Organization for Security and Cooperation in Europe in Germany, Austria, and the Netherlands.

The ambassador's wife, Rahima, was trained in philosophy and for some years taught at the Tashkent Politechnical Institute. The Safaevs have two daughters and one son. The son, Johangir, lives with them in Washington, D.C. Their daughters, Saida and Kamola, live in Tashkent; Saida attends college and Kamola is married with one son.

In addition to his native Uzbek language, the ambassador is fluent in Russian, English, and German. His wife speaks those languages and Turkish as well.

STAFF:

Mr. Turdiqul BUTAYAROV
Counselor (Political)
Spouse: Mrs. Odin Butayarova

Mr. Ismatulla FAIZULLAEV
First Secretary (Culture, Education and
  Science)
Spouse: Mrs. Motabar Faizullaeva

Mr. Bakhram SALAKHITDINOV
First Secretary
Spouse: Mrs. Nodira Salahiddinova

Mr. Hasan IKROMOV
Second Secretary and Consul
Spouse: Mrs. Marhamat Ikromova

Mr. Dilmurod MIRKAMILOV

Second Secretary
Spouse: Mrs. Nargiza Mirkamilov

Mrs. Munira NIZAMOVA
Attaché (Administrative)
Spouse: Mr. Dilshod Valiyevich
  Mukhamedov

Venezuela

Embassy of the Republic of Venezuela
1099 30th Street, NW
Washington DC 20007
Phone: 202/342-2214
Fax: 202/342-6820
Email: Embavene@dgsys.com

Dr. Pedro Luis ECHEVERRIA
Ambassador

Date Credentials Presented: 8/11/94

Born: 5/19/44 in Caracas, Venezuela

*Spouse: Mrs. Marisol Jordan de
  Echeverria*

Pedro Louis Echeverria, a professor of economics and theory of economic integration, has served in a number of posts in the Venezuelan government. He has been director of the Department of Promotion of Exports (1974-76), director of economic integration at the Institute of Foreign Trade (1976-77), ambassador to Bolivia (1978-81), ambassador to Jamaica (1981-84), and a member of the Council of the Cartagena Agreement (1985-89).

As a professor, Echeverria lectured at the Universidad Central de Venezuela in Caracas, at Universidad de San Marcos in Lima, Peru, and at the Universidad de San Andres in La Paz, Bolivia. He was a consultant and adviser to national and international institutions and corporations, such as the Inter-American Development Bank, the U.N. Economic Commission for Latin America, and the U.N. Development Program. He was also general secretary of the Inter-American Development Bank from 1989 to 1994.

Echeverria has a B.A. degree in economics from the Universidad Central de Venezuela. He successfully completed graduate courses in macroeconomics, economic integration and international trade in Caracas, Buenos Aires, Brussels, Geneva, and Brighton.

Echeverria is married and has one daughter. He is fluent in English and Portuguese.

STAFF:

Mr. Alejandro J. PERERA
Minister-Counselor (Deputy Chief of
  Mission)
Spouse: Mrs. Rosa R. Perera

Mr. Gonzalo PALACIOS

Minister-Counselor (Cultural)
Spouse: Mrs. Anne Palacios

Mr. Roberto PALACIOS
Minister-Counselor

Mrs. Elena CSIKY DE RODRIGUEZ
Counselor

Mr. Douglas Oswaldo GOUSSOT
Counselor
Spouse: Mrs. Robaina de Goussot

Mrs. Luisa PEREZ CONTRERAS
Counselor

Mrs. Maria PEREZ DE PLANCHART
Counselor

Mrs. Gertrudis GUEVARA
First Secretary

Mr. Edgar MORAS
First Secretary

Mrs. Ana PEREZ YEPEZ
First Secretary

Mr. Gregorio E. FLORES BLANCO
Second Secretary
Spouse: Mrs. Bibiana L. Atehortua
  de Flores

Ms. Margarita AYELLO-PIRETTO
Third Secretary

Mr. Jose Ignacio MORENO
Third Secretary
Spouse: Mrs. Juliber A. Oyon de Moreno

Mr. Francisco SUCRE CIFFONI
Third Secretary

Mr. Jose CASTELLANOS
Attaché (Press)

Mr. Manuel Lorenzo IRIBARREN
CALCANO
Attaché (Energy)

Mr. Cesar A. OLARTE RISQUEZ
Attaché (Labor)

Lt. Colonel Marcial P. RIVERO
Asst. Attaché
Spouse: Mrs. Luz M. Rivero

Major General A. PRATO NAVAS
Defense Attaché

Brigadier General Jose A. ROSALES
Military Attaché
Spouse: Mrs. Blanca Rosales

Rear Admiral Miguel ALVAREZ DIAZ
Naval Attaché
Spouse: Mrs. Raiza Hernandez de Alvarez

Brigadier General Alfredo CONTRERAS
Air Attaché
Spouse: Mrs. Eva Maria Contreras

Colonel Edgar ESCALANTE

Asst. Defense Attaché
Spouse: Mrs. Yoleida Escalante

Colonel Roberto CASTRO
Asst. Air Attaché

Office of the Air Attaché
2409 California St., NW
Washington DC 20008
Phone: 202/234-9132

Office of the Defense Attaché
2437 California St., NW
Washington DC 20008
Phone: 202/588-0384

Office of Information Service
1099 30th St., NW
Washington DC 20007
Phone: 202/342-2214

Office of the Military Attaché
2409 California St., NW
Washington DC 20008
Phone: 202/234-3633

Office of the Naval Attaché
2437 California St., NW
Washington DC 20008
Phone: 202/265-7323

Vietnam

Embassy of Vietnam
1233 20th St., NW - Suite 400
Washington DC 20036
Phone: 202/861-0737
Fax: 202/861-0917

Bang Van LE
Ambassador

Date Credentials Presented: 5/14/97

Born: 1947 in Ninh Binh, Vietnam

Spouse: Mrs. Bui Thi An Le

Bang Van Le served briefly as assistant minister of the Socialist Republic of Vietnam's ministry of foreign affairs in 1997 before taking the post of ambassador to the U.S. in Washington, D.C., in May 1997.

Le came to the U.S. in 1993 to serve at the United Nations as Vietnam's ambassador and permanent representative. In 1995, he became the chief of Vietnam's liaison office in the U.S., and in 1997 he took the position of chargé d'affaires of Vietnam to the U.S. Le came to Washington, D.C., as a visiting fellow at the International Center for Development Policy in 1991

The ambassador joined the ministry of foreign affairs in Vietnam in 1972 and worked there for nine years before receiving a posting in London as deputy chief of mission at Vietnam's embassy from 1982 to 1985. Between 1986 and 1989, he served as assistant director of the Americas

department in the ministry of foreign affairs in Vietnam. In 1990, he was promoted to deputy director of the Americas department.

Le holds degrees from the University of Havana, Cuba, and Australian National University, as well as a post-graduate degree from the Institute of International Relations from the ministry of foreign affairs of Vietnam. He participated in a Georgetown University leadership seminar in 1993 and a Stanford University leadership seminar in 1994.

The ambassador is married to Mrs. Bui Thi An and has two sons.

STAFF:

Mr. Que Van PHAM
Minister-Counselor (Deputy Chief of Mission)

Mr. Hung Xuan DOAN
Minister-Counselor

Mr. Tran Trong KHANH
Counselor

Mr. Trang Chien NGUYEN
Counselor (Commercial)

Dr. Thuan Tien NGUYEN
Counselor (Economic)
Spouse: Mrs. Ngan Kim Thach

Mr. Dung LE
First Secretary
Spouse: Mrs. Thuy Thi Kim Nguyen

Mr. Dang The NGUYEN
First Secretary
Spouse: Mrs. Linh Thi Cao

Mr. Chi Huu PHAM
First Secretary (Political)

Mr. Xuan Thanh TRUONG
First Secretary and Consul

Mr. Chinh DINH
Second Secretary (Protocol & Admin.)
Spouse: Mrs. Lan Thi Ngoc Tran

Mr. Tran Quoc LY
Second Secretary
Spouse: Mrs. Dan Thi Tam Vu

Mr. Van Quyen NGUYEN
Second Secretary
Spouse: Mrs. Thi Ha Bac Nguyen

Mr. Minh Dung TRAN
Second Secretary (Consular)

Mr. Quang Tuyen TRAN
Second Secretary

Mr. Viet Khac HOANG
Third Secretary

Mr. Nam Hoanh NGUYEN
Attaché

Colonel Quang Dinh VO
Defense, Military, Naval and Air Attaché

Major Nghi Van DO
Asst. Defense, Military, Naval and
  Air Attaché

Colonel Bon Dinh LUU
Asst. Defense and Naval Attaché

Defense Attaché
1233 20th Street, NW, Suite 201
Washington DC 20036
Phone: 202/293-1822

Yemen

Embassy of the Republic of Yemen
2600 Virginia Avenue, NW, Suite 705
Washington DC 20037
Phone: 202/965-4760
Fax: 202/337-2017

Abdulwahab Abdullah A. AL-HAJJRI
Ambassador

Date Credentials Presented: 9/8/97

Born: 11/15/58 in Sana'a, Yemen

Spouse: Mrs. Saburra H. Al-Mahfadi

Abdulwahab Abdullah A. Al-Hajjri, a 19-year veteran of Yemen's diplomatic corps, officially became Yemen's ambassador to the U.S. in September 1997. He had been acting in that capacity since September 1996.

Between August 1995 and September 1996, Al-Hajjri served as minister plenipotentiary at Yemen's embassy in Washington, D.C.

Al-Hajjri joined the ADM and finance department of Yemen's ministry of foreign affairs in 1979. He was promoted to the position of diplomatic attache of the Yemen Embassy in Washington in 1982. In 1987, he went to the Yemen Embassy in Cairo, Egypt, first as cultural attache and, in 1992, as political counselor.

The ambassador received a B.A. degree in the Sharia'h religious law at Sana'a University and an M.A. degree in international law from American University in Washington, D.C.

He is married and has three children.

STAFF:

Mr. Abdulmalik Hassan AL ERYANI
Minister

Mr. Ahmed Al Saleh AL-HAMDI
Minister
Spouse: Mrs. Al-Hamdi

Mr. Ahmed Y.A. AL-KIBSI
Minister
Spouse: Mrs. Al-Kibsi

Mr. Hassan AL SHAMI
Minister
Spouse: Mrs. Amat Alrazag Al Shami

Mr. Ahmed Abdo NASHER
Minister
Spouse: Mrs. Asa'ad

Mr. Jamal Adbulwahab NUMAN
Minister

Mrs. Balqis Abdulraman ABDULMAJID
Counselor

Mr. Abdullah Ali AL-ANESI
Counselor (Cultural)
Spouse: Mrs. Al-Anesi

Mr. Ahmed ATEF
Counselor

Mr. Abdulwahab AL-AMRANI
First Secretary
Spouse: Mrs. Khadigah Al-Hodid

Mr. Saeed Mosed SAROOR
First Secretary
Spouse: Mrs. Rehima Nasser Shaker

Mr. Nabil Ali ALDHOBEE
Attaché

Mr. Jamal Ali Nasser MOHAMED
Attaché

Yugoslavia

Embassy of the Federal
  Republic of Yugoslavia
2410 California Street, NW
Washington DC 20008
Phone: 202/462-6566
Fax: 202/797-9663
Email: 102447.3066@compuserve.com
Url: http://ourworld.compuserve.com/
  homepage/yuembassy

Nebojsa VUJOVIC

Charge d'Affaires, ad interim

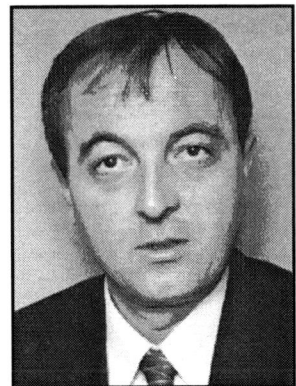

Date Credentials Presented: 9/2/96

Born: 1957 in Prizren, Serbia

Spouse: Mrs. Ivana Vujovic

Nebojsa Vujovic came to the embassy of the Federal Republic of Yugoslavia in Washington, D.C., in 1990 as counselor for political affairs and press. In 1994 he became head of the political and press department. Then, in 1996, he was appointed minister counselor, chief of mission, at the embassy.

Before that in Yugoslavia, he held several positions in the federal secretariat for foreign affairs. From 1981 to 1985, he was second secretary in the department for North America, Australia, and New Zealand; in that position, he was the desk officer for the United States.

From 1985-88, he was vice-consul in the consulate general of Yugoslavia in Sydney, Australia. In that capacity, he served as the Yugoslav representative at the World Trade Exhibition, EXPO 88, in Brisbane, Australia. From 1988 to 1990, he was counselor, first secretary, in the department of analysis and foreign policy planning.

Vujovic studied law at the University of Belgrade. He graduated in 1979. While a student, he worked in the Belgrade Students Union as vice president in charge of international affairs.

STAFF:

Mr. Zoran POPOVIC
Counselor (Consular and Political)
Spouse: Mrs. Biljana Popovic

Mrs. Ljiljana TOSKOVIC
First Secretary (Press, Info. and Cultural)

Mr. Miodrag MAKSIMOVIC
Counselor

Mr. Branimir BAJIC
Second Secretary

Mr. Igor VERGOVIC
Attaché

Colonel Dragan IVEZIC
Defense, Military, Naval and Air Attaché

Zambia

Embassy of the Republic of Zambia
2419 Massachusetts Avenue, NW
Washington DC 20008
Phone: 202/265-9717
Fax: 202/332-0826

Dunstan Weston KAMANA

Ambassador

Date Credentials Presented: 9/8/92

Born: 4/19/37 in Zambia

Spouse: Mrs. Bina Hilda Kamana

Dunstan Weston Kamana brings with him to Washington extensive experience as a diplomat and as a private businessman. Having joined the Northern Rhodesia Government Service as an information officer, he worked at home and in London for six years.

When a new government was formed in 1965, Kamana became press secretary to the first President of the new republic. Subsequently, he served the young nation as assistant secretary of the Ministry of Defence and as director of the Zambia Information and Broadcasting Service.

In 1968, Kamana became editor-in-chief of Times Newspapers Ltd., which publishes The Times of Zambia and the Sunday Times of Zambia. After four years, he left to enter the diplomatic service. Between 1972 and 1977, he served as Zambia's ambassador to the U.S.S.R, the U.N., and Canada, with concurrent accreditation to a dozen smaller nations, before going into private enterprise in 1977. During the subsequent 15 years, Kamana held upper executive positions in a number of industries, including agriculture, shipping, and metal fabrication.

Following Zambia's first free elections in 1991, the newly-elected President Chiluba appointed Kamana as ambassador to the U.S. to represent Zambia's commitment to a new era of democracy, free enterprise, and full accountability to its citizens.

Since Zambia is one of the first African nations to undergo a peaceful transition from a one-party system to a multi-party democracy, the ambassador believes that the success of democracy in Zambia is crucial to the future of democracy in all of Africa. He also believes economic development and diversification are crucial to success.

Kamana is attempting to interest U.S. investors in bidding for the numerous parastatal companies the government is empowered to dispose as part of the 1992 Privatization Act. He is particularly interested in alerting investors to the opportunities available in the mining, tourism, agriculture, and manufacturing industries in Zambia.

Further, because past fragmentation of the African market has deterred foreign investment, Zambia and 17 other nations have created a Preferential Trade Area encompassing 200 million people. Kamana considers Zambia, bordered by eight countries, to be the hub of the region.

Kamana was educated in Zambia and holds a professional diploma in journalism and mass communication.

Kamana is married to Bina Hilda Kamana and has six children.

STAFF:

Mr. Walubita IMAKANDO
Counselor

Mr. George R. NZALA
Counselor (Head of Chancery)
Spouse: Mrs. Rose C. Nzala

Mr. Mike Kundfa CHANGWE
First Secretary (Political)
Spouse: Mrs. Changwe

Mr. Longa John MULUTULA
First Secretary

Mr. Paul MULENGA
Second Secretary

Ms. Teresa TEMBO
Third Secretary

Brigadier General Gilbert C. CHILESHE
Defense, Military and Air Attaché
Spouse: Mrs. Upendo M. Chileshe

Zimbabwe

Embassy of the Republic of Zimbabwe
1608 New Hampshire Avenue, NW
Washington DC 20009
Phone: 202/332-7100
Fax: 202/483-9326

Amos Bernard Muvengwa MIDZI
Ambassador

Date Credentials Presented: 6/11/93

Born: 7/4/52 in Zimbiru Village, Chinamhora, Zimbabwe

Spouse: Mrs. Alice Hildah Midzi

An activist for the welfare of disadvantaged citizens of his country, Amos Bernard Muvengwa Midzi was placed under political detention from 1975 to 1978 during his country's struggle for independence. Since 1978, he has been active in politics and as a diplomat.

Since his university years were interrupted by his detainment, Midzi returned in 1978 for his final year of education after which he joined the civil service as the Harare branch official for the Citizens Advice Bureau. In 1981, Midzi was elected a member of Parliament. He remained in Parliament until 1987, also serving as deputy minister of transport from 1982 until 1984 and as deputy minister of youth, sport, and culture. Beginning in 1987 and ending with his appointment to Washington, Midzi was his nation's ambassador to Cuba and held concurrent accreditation as High Commission to Guyana.

Midzi holds a B.Sc. in sociology from the University of Rhodesia and speaks English, Spanish, and Shona.

Midzi is married to Alice Hilda Midzi and has three children.

STAFF:

Mrs. Elita Tinoenda Tandi SAKUPWANYA
Minister-Counselor

Mr. Claudius Deny Farai NHEMA
Counselor (Political)
Spouse: Mrs. Susan Nhema

Mr. Seigfred Temba SAMKANGE
Counselor (Political)
Spouse: Mrs. Samkange

Ms. Henry MUKONOWESHURO
First Secretary (Political)
Spouse: Mrs. Mary Mukonoweshuro

Mr. Lloyd SITHOLE
First Secretary (Consular)

Mr. Pedzisai JAKARASI
Attaché
Spouse: Mrs. Mary Jakarasi

Warrant Officer Godfrey MLAMBO
Asst. Attaché
Spouse: Mrs. Rozina Mlambo

Lt. Colonel Leonard MASINA
Defense, Military and Air Attaché
Spouse: Mrs. Regina Masina

Albania

Mr. Mustafa XHEPHA
Second Secretary
Embassy of the Republic of Albania
2100 S Street, NW
Washington DC 20008
Phone: 202/223-4942   Fax: 202/628-7342

Algeria

Mr. Ali ALAOUI
Counselor
Emb. of the Democratic & Popular Rep. of Algeria
2118 Kalorama Road, NW
Washington DC 20008
Phone: 202/265-2800   Fax: 202/667-2174

Angola

Mr. Agostinho A. FERNANDES
Commercial Attache
Embassy of the Republic of Angola
1615 M St., NW - Suite 900
Washington DC 20036
Phone: 202/785-1156   Fax: 202/785-1258

Antigua and Barbuda

Ms. Debbie PROSPER
First Secretary (Commercial)
Embassy of Antigua and Barbuda
3216 New Mexico Avenue, NW
Washington DC 20016
Phone: 202/362-5211   Fax: 202/362-5225

Argentina

Mr. Ruben Eduardo CARO
Commercial Minister
Embassy of the Argentine Republic
1600 New Hampshire Ave., NW
Washington DC 20009
Phone: 202/939-6400   Fax: 202/332-3171

Armenia

Mr. Tatoul MARKARIAN
Counselor
Embassy of the Republic of Armenia
2225 R Street, NW
Washington DC 20008
Phone: 202/319-1976   Fax: 202/319-2982

Australia

Mr. Bruce GOSPER
Commercial Minister
Embassy of Australia
1601 Massachusetts Ave., NW
Washington DC 20036
Phone: 202/797-3000   Fax: 202/797-3168

Austria

Mr. Helmut A. WAGNER
Commercial Counselor
Embassy of Austria
3524 International Ct., NW
Washington DC 20008
Phone: 202/895-6700   Fax: 202/895-6750

Azerbaijan

Mr. Hafiz Mir Jalal Oglu PASHAYEV
Ambassador
Embassy of the Republic of Azerbaijan
927 15th Street, NW, Suite 700
Washington DC 20005
Phone: 202/842-0001   Fax: 202/842-0004

Bahamas

Ms. Sheila G. CAREY
Minister-Counselor
Embassy of The Commonwealth of The Bahamas
2220 Massachusetts Avenue, NW
Washington DC 20008
Phone: 202/319-2660   Fax: 202/319-2668

Bahrain

Mr. Jaber Fahad ALROMAIHI
First Secretary
Embassy of the State of Bahrain
3502 International Drive, NW
Washington DC 20008
Phone: 202/342-0741   Fax: 202/362-2192

Bangladesh

Mr. Mizanur RAHMAN
Commercial Counsellor
Embassy of the People's Republic of Bangladesh
2201 Wisconsin Avenue, NW, Suite 300
Washington DC 20007
Phone: 202/342-8372   Fax: 202/333-4971

Barbados

Ms. Myrtle D. BISHOP
Commercial Counselor
Embassy of Barbados
2144 Wyoming Avenue, NW
Washington DC 20008
Phone: 202/939-9200   Fax: 202/332-7467

Belarus

Mr. Yevgeniy G. BOGOMAZOV
Counselor
Embassy of the Republic of Belarus
1619 New Hampshire Avenue, NW
Washington DC 20009
Phone: 202/986-1604   Fax: 202/986-1805

Belgium

Mr. Raoul DELCORDE
Minister-Counselor (Economic)
Embassy of Belgium
3330 Garfield Street, NW
Washington DC 20008
Phone: 202/333-6900   Fax: 202/333-3079

Belize

Mr. Claude Bromwell Fitzgeral HAYLOCK
Minister-Counselor
Embassy of Belize
2535 Massachusetts Avenue, NW
Washington DC 20008
Phone: 202/332-9636   Fax: 202/332-6888

Benin

Mrs. Haolatou Assani PIO
Counselor
Embassy of the Republic of Benin
2737 Cathedral Avenue, NW
Washington DC 20008
Phone: 202/232-6656   Fax: 202/265-1996

Bolivia

Mr. Carlos Javier IBARGUEN
First Secretary (Commercial)
Embassy of the Republic of Bolivia
3014 Massachusetts Avenue, NW
Washington DC 20008
Phone: 202/483-4410   Fax: 202/328-3712

Bosnia & Herzegovina

Mr. Malik SKALJIC
Counselor
Embassy of the Rep. of Bosnia & Herzegovina
2109 E St., NW
Washington DC 20037
Phone: 202/337-1500   Fax: 202/337-1502

Botswana

Mr. Peloeritle Shakie KEBASWELE
Commercial Attache
Embassy of the Republic of Botswana
3400 International Drive, NW, Suite 7M
Washington DC 20008
Phone: 202/244-4990   Fax: 202/244-4164

Brazil

Mr. Bernardo VELLOSO
Attache (Trade)
Brazilian Embassy

3006 Massachusetts Avenue, NW
Washington DC 20008
Phone: 202/238-2700   Fax: 202/238-2827

Brunei

Mr. Shofry ABDUL-GHAFOR
First Secretary
Embassy of the State of Brunei Darussalam
2600 Virginia Avenue, NW, Suite 300
Washington DC 20037
Phone: 202/342-0159   Fax: 202/342-0158

Bulgaria

Mr. Panteley A. PENEV
Commercial Counselor
Embassy of the Republic of Bulgaria
1621 22nd Street, NW
Washington DC 20008
Phone: 202/387-7969   Fax: 202/234-7973

Burkina Faso

Mr. Souleymanea OUEDRAOGO
Economic Counselor
Embassy of Burkina Faso
2340 Massachusetts Avenue, NW
Washington DC 20008
Phone: 202/332-5577   Fax: 202/667-1882

Burundi

Mr. Thomas NDIKUMANA
Charge d'Affaires ad interim
Embassy of the Republic of Burundi
2233 Wisconsin Avenue, NW, Suite 212
Washington DC 20007
Phone: 202/342-2574   Fax: 202/342-2578

Cambodia

Mr. Samnom MAO CHAN
Economic Counselor
Royal Embassy of Cambodia
4500 16th Street, NW
Washington DC 20011
Phone: 202/726-7742   Fax: 202/726-8381

Cameroon

Mr. Andre-Blaise KESSENG A MBASSA
Economic Counselor
Embassy of the Republic of Cameroon
2349 Massachusetts Avenue, NW
Washington DC 20008
Phone: 202/265-8790   Fax: 202/387-3826

Canada

Ms. Astrid-Yolanda PREGEL
Minister-Counselor (Commercial)
Embassy of Canada
501 Pennsylvania Avenue, NW
Washington DC 20001
Phone: 202/682-1740   Fax: 202/682-7726

Cape Verde

Mr. Alexandre GUILHERME
Commercial Attache
Embassy of the Republic of Cape Verde
3415 Massachusetts Avenue, NW
Washington DC 20007
Phone: 202/965-6820   Fax: 202/965-1207

Central African Republic

Ms. Lucienne PERRIERE
Economic Counselor
Embassy of Central African Republic
1618 22nd Street, NW
Washington DC 20008
Phone: 202/483-7800   Fax: 202/332-9893

Chad

Mr. Lemaye FAVITSOU-BOULANDI
Counselor
Embassy of the Republic of Chad
2002 R Street, NW
Washington DC 20009
Phone: 202/462-4009   Fax: 202/265-1937

Chile

Mr. Mario C. MATUS
Economic Counselor
Embassy of Chile
1732 Massachusetts Avenue, NW
Washington DC 20036
Phone: 202/785-1746   Fax: 202/887-5579

China

Mr. JIAN Xin Shi
Minister-Counselor
Embassy of the People's Republic of China
2300 Connecticut Ave., NW
Washington DC 20008
Phone: 202/328-2500   Fax: 202/588-0032

Colombia

Mr. Miguel FADUL
Commercial Counselor
Embassy of Colombia
2118 Leroy Place, NW
Washington DC 20008
Phone: 202/387-8338   Fax: 202/232-8643

Congo (Republic of)

Second Sec Andre TENTOKOLO
Ambassador
Embassy of the Republic of Congo
4891 Colorado Avenue, NW
Washington DC 20011
Phone: 202/726-5500   Fax: 202/726-1860

Costa Rica

Mr. Carlos SILVA
Minister-Counselor (Commercial)
Embassy of Costa Rica

2114 S Street, NW
Washington DC 20008
Phone: 202/234-2945   Fax: 202/265-4795

Cote D'Ivoire

Mr. Yalle AGBRE
Commercial Counselor
Embassy of the Republic of Cote d'Ivoire
2424 Massachusetts Avenue, NW
Washington DC 20008
Phone: 202/797-0300   Fax: 202/462-9444

Croatia

Mr. Aleksander HEINA
Economic Counselor
Embassy of the Republic of Croatia
2343 Massachusetts Avenue, NW
Washington DC 20008
Phone: 202/588-5899   Fax: 202/588-8937

Cyprus

Mr. Dennis DROUSHIOTIS
Commercial Counselor
Cyprus Trade Center
13 East 40th Street
New York NY 10016
Phone: 212/213-9100   Fax: 212/213-2918

Czech Republic

Mr. Miroslav TOMAN
Counselor, Economic & Commercial
Embassy of the Czech Republic
3900 Spring of Freedom Street, NW
Washington DC 20008
Phone: 202/274-9100   Fax: 202/966-8540

Denmark

Mr. Pernille HAUBROE
Commercial Attache and Consul
Royal Danish Embassy
3200 Whitehaven Street, NW
Washington DC 20008-3683
Phone: 202/234-4300   Fax: 202/328-1470

Djibouti

Mr. Issa D. BOURALEH
Second Secretary
Embassy of the Republic of Djibouti
1156 15th Street, NW, Suite 515
Washington DC 20005
Phone: 202/331-0270   Fax: 202/331-0302

Dominica

H.E. Nicholas J. O. LIVERPOOL
Ambassador
Embassy of the Commonwealth of Dominica
3216 New Mexico Ave., NW
Washington DC 20016
Phone: 202/364-6781   Fax: 202/364-6791

Dominican Republic

Mr. Virgilio MOTA
Commercial Attache
Embassy of the Dominican Republic
1715 22nd Street, NW
Washington DC 20008
Phone: 202/332-6280   Fax: 202/265-8057

Ecuador

Mr. Eduardo BRITO
Counselor, Economic and Commercial
Embassy of Ecuador
2535 15th Street, NW
Washington DC 20009
Phone: 202/234-7200   Fax: 202/667-3482

Egypt

Mr. Alaa Eldin SHALABY
Minister, Economic and Commercial
Embassy of the Arab Republic of Egypt
3521 International Court, NW
Washington DC 20008
Phone: 202/895-5400   Fax: 202/244-4319

El Salvador

Mr. Francisco Javier CALLEJA
Commercial Attache
Embassy of El Salvador
2308 California Street, NW
Washington DC 20008
Phone: 202/265-9671   Fax: 202/234-3834

Equatorial Guinea

Ms. Mari Cruz EVUNA ANDEME
Administrative Attache
Embassy of Equatorial Guinea
1511 K Street, NW - Suite 405
Washington DC 20005
Phone: 202/393-0525   Fax: 202/393-0348

Eritrea

Mr. Goitom Sium GHEBREZGHABIHER
Third Secretary
Embassy of the State of Eritrea
1708 New Hampshire Avenue, NW
Washington DC 20009
Phone: 202/319-1991   Fax: 202/319-1304

Estonia

Mr. Mait MARTINSON
First Secretary (Commercial)
Embassy of Estonia
2131 Massachusetts Ave., NW
Washington DC 20008
Phone: 202/588-0101   Fax: 202/588-0108

Ethiopia

Mr. Mohammed Y. GARAD
Counselor (Trade)
Embassy of Ethiopia

2134 Kalorama Road, NW
Washington DC 20008
Phone: 202/234-2281   Fax: 202/328-7950

European Union

Mr. Bernd LENGEHEIM
Trade Counselor
Delegation of the European Commission
2300 M Street, NW
Washington DC 20037
Phone: 202/862-9500   Fax: 202/429-1766

Fiji

Ms. Salaseini Lelevawalu VOSAILAGI
Second Secretary
Embassy of the Republic of Fiji
2233 Wisconsin Avenue, NW, Suite 240
Washington DC 20007
Phone: 202/337-8320   Fax: 202/337-1996

Finland

Mr. Jorma KORHONEN
Economic Counselor
Embassy of Finland
3301 Massachusetts Avenue, NW
Washington DC 20008
Phone: 202/298-5820   Fax: 202/298-0450

France

Mr. Bruno JACTEL
Counselor, Economic and Commercial
Embassy of France
4101 Reservoir Road, NW
Washington DC 20007
Phone: 202/944-6000   Fax: 202/944-6166

Gabon

Mr. Alba BIFFOT
Economic Counselor
Embassy of the Gabonese Republic
2034 20th Street, NW, Suite 200
Washington DC 20009
Phone: 202/797-1000   Fax: 202/332-0668

Gambia, The

Ms. Juliana G. BALDEH
First Secretary
Embassy of The Gambia
1155 15th Street, NW, Suite 1000
Washington DC 20005
Phone: 202/785-1399   Fax: 202/785-1430

Georgia

VACANT
Minister
Embassy of the Republic of Georgia
1511 K Street, NW, Suite 424
Washington DC 20005
Phone: 202/393-5959   Fax: 202/393-6060

Germany

Mr. Volker Hermann SCHLEGEL
Economic Minister
Embassy of the Federal Republic of Germany
4645 Reservoir Road, NW
Washington DC 20007
Phone: 202/298-4000   Fax: 202/298-4249

Ghana

Mr. Daniel Kwesi Ofori HAGAN
Commercial Counselor
Embassy of Ghana
3512 International Drive, NW
Washington DC 20008
Phone: 202/686-4520   Fax: 202/686-4527

Greece

Mr. Leonides ANANIADIS
Minister-Counselor, Economic and Commercial
Embassy of Greece
2221 Massachusetts Avenue, NW
Washington DC 20008
Phone: 202/939-5800   Fax: 202/939-5824

Grenada

Ms. Sibyl ALEXANDER
First Secretary and Consul
Embassy of Grenada
1701 New Hampshire Avenue, NW
Washington DC 20009
Phone: 202/265-2561   Fax: 202/265-2468

Guatemala

Mr. Robert E. ROSENBERG
Commercial Attache
Embassy of Guatemala
2220 R Street, NW
Washington DC 20008
Phone: 202/745-4952   Fax: 202/745-1908

Guinea

Mr. Frederick BANGOURA
Counselor (Economic, Financial, and Consular)
Embassy of the Republic of Guinea
2112 Leroy Place, NW
Washington DC 20008
Phone: 202/483-9420   Fax: 202/483-8688

Guinea-Bissau

Ms. Rdilia DA SILVA
Commercial Attache
Embassy of the Republic of Guinea-Bissau
1511 K St., NW, Suite 519
Washington DC 20005
Phone: 202/347-3950   Fax: 202/347-3954

Guyana

Ms. Gillian ROWE
First Secretary
Embassy of Guyana

2490 Tracy Place, NW
Washington DC 20008
Phone: 202/265-6900   Fax: 202/232-1297

Haiti

Ms. Marie-Claude MALEBRANCHE
First Secretary, Commercial
Embassy of the Republic of Haiti
2311 Massachusetts Avenue, NW
Washington DC 20008
Phone: 202/332-4090   Fax: 202/745-7215

Honduras

Mr. Jose Benjamin ZAPATA
Minister Counselor, Economic
Embassy of Honduras
3007 Tilden Street, NW,
Washington DC 20008
Phone: 202/966-7702   Fax: 202/966-9751

Hungary

Mr. Jozsef TOTH
Economic and Trade Counselor
Embassy of the Republic of Hungary
3910 Shoemaker St., NW
Washington DC 20008
Phone: 202/362-6730   Fax: 202/966-8135

Iceland

Mr. Magnus BJARNASON
Commercial Counselor
Embassy of the Republic of Iceland
1156 15th St., NW, Suite 1200
Washington DC 20005
Phone: 202/265-6653   Fax: 202/265-6656

India

Mr. Govind Singh KHAMPA
Second Secretary, Commerce
Embassy of India
2107 Massachusetts Avenue, NW
Washington DC 20008
Phone: 202/939-7000   Fax: 202/939-7027

Indonesia

Mr. Harmen SEMBIRING
Commercial Attache
Embassy of the Republic of Indonesia
2020 Massachusetts Avenue, NW
Washington DC 20036
Phone: 202/775-5200   Fax: 202/775-5365

Ireland

Mr. Kenneth THOMPSON
Economic Counselor
Embassy of Ireland
2234 Massachusetts Avenue, NW
Washington DC 20008
Phone: 202/462-3939   Fax: 202/232-5993

Israel

Mr. Ohad MARANI
Economic Minister
Embassy of Israel
3514 International Drive, NW
Washington DC 20008
Phone: 202/364-5500   Fax: 202/364-5560

Italy

Mr. Vittorio TEDESCHI
Economic Minister
Embassy of Italy
1601 Fuller St., NW
Washington DC 20009
Phone: 202/328-5500   Fax: 202/483-2187

Jamaica

Ms. Pamela Rosemarie COKE
Minister/Counselor
Embassy of Jamaica
1520 New Hampshire Avenue, NW
Washington DC 20036
Phone: 202/452-0660   Fax: 202/452-0081

Japan

Mr. Kazuo KANEKO
Minister
Embassy of Japan
2520 Massachusetts Ave., NW
Washington DC 20008
Phone: 202/238-6700   Fax: 202/328-2187

Jordan

Mr. Elias Samir Gh. MANSOUR
Commercial Counselor
Embassy of the Hashemite Kingdom of Jordan
3504 International Drive, NW
Washington DC 20008
Phone: 202/966-2664   Fax: 202/966-3110

Kazakhstan

Mr. Askar S. TAZHIYEV
First Secretary
Embassy of the Republic of Kazakhstan
3421 Massachusetts Avenue, NW
Washington DC 20007
Phone: 202/333-4504   Fax: 202/333-4509

Kenya

Mr. Peter Khamala NYIKULI
Commercial Attache
Embassy of Kenya
2249 R Street, NW
Washington DC 20008
Phone: 202/387-6101   Fax: 202/462-3829

Korea (Republic of)

Mr. Doug Young JOO
Commercial Counselor
Embassy of Korea

2450 Massachusetts Avenue, NW
Washington DC 20008
Phone: 202/939-5600   Fax: 202/232-0117

Kuwait

Mr. Bassam AL-TESA
Commercial Attache
Embassy of the State of Kuwait
2940 Tilden Street, NW
Washington DC 20008
Phone: 202/966-0705   Fax: 202/966-0517

Kyrgyzstan

Mr. Azamat KERIMBAEV
First Secretary
Embassy of the Kyrgyz Republic
1732 Wisconsin Ave., NW
Washington DC 20007
Phone: 202/338-5141   Fax: 202/338-5139

Laos

Ms. Mai SAYAVONGS
Third Secretary, Economics
Embassy of the Lao People's Democratic Republic
2222 S St., NW
Washington DC 20008
Phone: 202/332-6416   Fax: 202/332-4923

Latvia

Mr. Peteris VINKELIS
Counselor
Embassy of Latvia
4325 17th Street, NW
Washington DC 20011
Phone: 202/726-8213   Fax: 202/726-6785

Lebanon

Mr. Houssam DIAB
First Secretary and Consul
Embassy of Lebanon
2560 28th Street, NW
Washington DC 20008
Phone: 202/939-6300   Fax: 202/939-6324

Lesotho

Ms. Itumeleng Gladys RAFUTHO
First Secretary
Embassy of the Kingdom of Lesotho
2511 Massachusetts Avenue, NW
Washington DC 20008
Phone: 202/797-5533   Fax: 202/234-6815

Liberia

Mr. Alexander H.N. WALLACE III
Economic and Trade Counselor
Embassy of the Republic of Liberia
5201 16th St., NW
Washington DC 20011
Phone: 202/723-0437   Fax: 202/723-0436

Lithuania

Mr. Dalia GRYBAUSKAITE
Minister
Embassy of the Republic of Lithuania
2622 16th Street, NW
Washington DC 20009
Phone: 202/234-5860   Fax: 202/328-0466

Luxembourg

Mr. Carlo KRIEGER
Minister/Deputy Chief of Mission
Embassy of Luxembourg
2200 Massachusetts Avenue, NW
Washington DC 20008
Phone: 202/265-4171   Fax: 202/328-8270

Macedonia

Mr. Igor POPOV
Second Secretary, Economic and Consular Affairs
Embassy of the Republic of Macedonia
3050 K Street, NW - Suite 210
Washington DC 20007
Phone: 202/337-3063   Fax: 202/337-3093

Madagascar

Mr. Biclair Henri ANDRIANANTOANDRO
Charge d'Affaires ad interim
Embassy of the Democratic Republic of
Madagascar
2374 Massachusetts Avenue, NW
Washington DC 20008
Phone: 202/265-5525   Fax: 202/265-3034

Malawi

Mr. MacKenzie M. KUMBATIRA
Counselor and Head of Chancery
Embassy of Malawi
2408 Massachusetts Avenue, NW
Washington DC 20008
Phone: 202/797-1007   Fax: 202/265-0976

Malaysia

Mr. Mohd. Sidek HASSAN
Minister/Counselor, Economics
Embassy of Malaysia
2401 Massachusetts Avenue, NW
Washington DC 20008
Phone: 202/328-2700   Fax: 202/483-7661

Mali

Mr. Mahamane Banie TOURE
Counselor
Embassy of the Republic of Mali
2130 R Street, NW
Washington DC 20008
Phone: 202/332-2249   Fax: 202/332-6603

Malta

Mr. Alfred A. FARRUGIA
Counselor and Consul General

Embassy of Malta
2017 Connecticut Avenue, NW
Washington DC 20008
Phone: 202/462-3611   Fax: 202/387-5470

Marshall Islands

H.E. Banny DE BRUM
Ambassador
Embassy of the Republic of the Marshall Islands
2433 Massachusetts Avenue, NW
Washington DC 20008
Phone: 202/234-5414   Fax: 202/232-3236

Mauritania

Mr. Abdellahi OULD KEBD
Counselor
Embassy of the Islamic Republic of Mauritania
2129 Leroy Place, NW
Washington DC 20008
Phone: 202/232-5700   Fax: 202/319-2623

Mauritius

Mr. Peter CRAIG
First Secretary, Commercial
Embassy of Republic of Mauritius
4301 Connecticut Avenue, NW, Suite 441
Washington DC 20008
Phone: 202/244-1491   Fax: 202/966-0983

Mexico

Mr. Luis Fernando DE LA CALLE PARDI
Trade Minister
Embassy of Mexico
1911 Pennsylvania Avenue, NW
Washington DC 20006
Phone: 202/728-1600   Fax: 202/728-1698

Micronesia

Mr. Samson E. PRETRICK
First Secretary, Political and Economic
Embassy of the Federated States of Micronesia
1725 N St., NW
Washington DC 20036
Phone: 202/223-4383   Fax: 202/223-4391

Moldova

Mr. Andrei BOBOC
First Secretary, Commercial and Economic
Embassy of the Republic of Moldova
2102 S St., NW
Washington DC 20008
Phone: 202/667-1130   Fax: 202/667-1204

Mongolia

Mr. Khalkhuu NARANKUU
Economic Counselor
Embassy of Mongolia
2833 M Street, NW
Washington DC 20007
Phone: 202/333-7117   Fax: 202/298-9227

Morocco

Mr. Rachid Ismaili ALAOUI
First Secretary
Embassy of the Kingdom of Morocco
1601 21st Street, NW
Washington DC 20009
Phone: 202/462-7979   Fax: 202/462-7643

Mozambique

Mr. Salvador NAMBURETE
Economic Counselor
Embassy of the Republic of Mozambique
1990 M Street, NW, Suite 570
Washington DC 20036
Phone: 202/293-7146   Fax: 202/835-0245

Myanmar (Burma)

Mr. Linn WAI
Commercial Attache
Embassy of the Union of Myanmar
2300 S Street, NW
Washington DC 20008
Phone: 202/332-9044   Fax: 202/332-9046

Namibia

Mr. Gerry Wilson MUNYAMA
Commercial Counselor
Embassy of the Republic of Namibia
1605 New Hampshire Avenue, NW
Washington DC 20009
Phone: 202/986-0540   Fax: 202/986-0443

Nepal

Mr. Lekha Nath BHATTARAI
Attache
Royal Nepalese Embassy
2131 Leroy Place, NW
Washington DC 20008
Phone: 202/667-4550   Fax: 202/667-5534

Netherlands

Mr. Laurentius WESTHOFF
First Secretary, Economic
Embassy of the Netherlands
4200 Linnean Avenue, NW
Washington DC 20008
Phone: 202/244-5300   Fax: 202/362-3430

New Zealand

Mr. Alwyn Evan MOORES
Counselor, Commercial and Trade Commissioner
Embassy of New Zealand
37 Observatory Circle, NW
Washington DC 20008
Phone: 202/328-4800   Fax: 202/667-5227

Nicaragua

Mr. Mauricio RIVAS
Commercial Attache
Embassy of Nicaragua

1627 New Hampshire Avenue, NW
Washington DC 20009
Phone: 202/939-6570   Fax: 202/939-6542

Niger

Mr. Aboubacar KABO
Attache
Embassy of the Republic of Niger
2204 R Street, NW
Washington DC 20008
Phone: 202/483-4224   Fax: 202/483-3169

Nigeria

Mr. Fungbe Ralf ADERELE
Minister-Counselor
Embassy of the Federal Republic of Nigeria
1333 16th Street, NW
Washington DC 20036
Phone: 202/986-8400   Fax: 202/775-1385

Norway

Mr. Knut RINGSTAD
Commercial Counselor
Royal Norwegian Embassy
2720 34th Street, NW
Washington DC 20008-2714
Phone: 202/333-6000   Fax: 202/337-0870

Oman

Mr. Munther Mahfoodh AL-MANTHERI
First Secretary
Embassy of the Sultanate of Oman
2535 Belmont Road, NW
Washington DC 20008
Phone: 202/387-1980   Fax: 202/745-4933

Pakistan

Mr. Syed Abdul RAZZAQ
Third Secretary, Commercial
Embassy of Pakistan
2315 Massachusetts Ave., NW
Washington DC 20008
Phone: 202/939-6200   Fax: 202/387-0484

Panama

Mrs. Angela VELASQUEZ
Commercial Attache
Embassy of the Republic of Panama
2862 McGill Terrace, NW
Washington DC 20008
Phone: 202/483-1407   Fax: 202/483-8413

Papua New Guinea

Mr. Michael GRAHAM
Counselor
Embassy of Papua New Guinea
1615 New Hampshire Ave., NW, 3rd Floor
Washington DC 20009
Phone: 202/745-3680   Fax: 202/745-3679

Paraguay

Mr. Enrique RAMIREZ
Second Secretary
Embassy of Paraguay
2400 Massachusetts Avenue, NW
Washington DC 20008
Phone: 202/483-6960   Fax: 202/234-4508

Peru

Mr. Eduardo RIVOLDI
Counselor, Commercial Section
Embassy of Peru
1700 Massachusetts Avenue, NW
Washington DC 20036
Phone: 202/833-9860   Fax: 202/659-8124

Philippines

Ms. Josefa M. DIZON
Commercial Officer
Embassy of the Philippines
1600 Massachusetts Avenue, NW
Washington DC 20036
Phone: 202/467-9418   Fax: 202/467-9428

Poland

Mr. Andrzej ILCZUK
Counselor
Emb. of the Rep. of Poland, Commercial Office
1503 21st St. NW.
Washington DC 20036
Phone: 202/467-6690   Fax: 202/833-8343

Portugal

Mr. Diogo Jose VILAS-BOAS
Economic Counselor
Embassy of Portugal
2125 Kalorama Road, NW
Washington DC 20008
Phone: 202/328-8610   Fax: 202/462-3726

Qatar

Dr. Abraham ABRAHAM
Economic Counselor
Embassy of the State of Qatar
4200 Wisconsin Avenue, NW, Suite 200
Washington DC 20016
Phone: 202/274-1600   Fax: 202/237-0061

Romania

Mr. Adrian CONSTANTINESCU
Minister/Counselor, Economic
Embassy of Romania
1607 23rd Street, NW
Washington DC 20008
Phone: 202/332-4846   Fax: 202/232-4748

Russia

Mr. Sergey Y. CHESTNOY
Economic Counselor
Embassy of the Russian Federation

2650 Wisconsin Avenue, NW
Washington DC 20007
Phone: 202/298-5700   Fax: 202/298-5735

Rwanda

Mr. Joseph W. MUTABOBA
Counselor
Embassy of the Republic of Rwanda
1714 New Hampshire Avenue, NW
Washington DC 20009
Phone: 202/232-2882   Fax: 202/232-4544

Saint Kitts and Nevis

Mr. Kutayba Y. ALGHANIM
Minister/Counselor, Economic
Embassy of St. Kitts and Nevis
3216 New Mexico Avenue, NW
Washington DC 20016
Phone: 202/686-2636   Fax: 202/686-5740

Saint Lucia

Ms. Juliet MALLET PHILLIP
Counselor
Embassy of Saint Lucia
3216 New Mexico Avenue, NW
Washington DC 20016
Phone: 202/364-6792   Fax: 202/364-6723

Saint Vincent and the Grenadines

H.E. Kingsley C.A. LAYNE
Ambassador
Embassy of Saint Vincent and the Grenadines
3216 New Mexico Avenue, NW
Washington DC 20016
Phone: 202/364-6730   Fax: 202/364-6736

Saudi Arabia

Mr. Abdullah M.N. AL-ATHEL
Commercial Attache
Embassy of Saudi Arabia
601 New Hampshire Avenue, NW
Washington DC 20037
Phone: 202/342-3800   Fax: 202/944-5983

Senegal

Mrs. Seynabou Diop LY
Economic and Financial Counselor
Embassy of the Republic of Senegal
2112 Wyoming Avenue, NW
Washington DC 20008
Phone: 202/234-0540   Fax: 202/332-6315

Sierra Leone

Mr. James George CAULKER
First Secretary
Embassy of Sierra Leone
1701 19th Street, NW
Washington DC 20009
Phone: 202/939-9261   Fax: 202/483-1793

Singapore

Ms. Kathy Sou Tien LAI
Economic Counselor
Embassy of the Republic of Singapore
3501 International Place, NW
Washington DC 20008
Phone: 202/537-3100   Fax: 202/537-0876

Slovak Republic

Ms. Ingrid BROCKOVA
Second Secretary
  (Economic & Commercial Section)
Embassy of the Slovak Republic
2201 Wisconsin Avenue, NW, Suite 250
Washington DC 20007
Phone: 202/965-5161   Fax: 202/965-5166

Slovenia

Mr. Marjan SMONIG
Counselor
Embassy of the Republic of Slovenia
1525 New Hampshire Avenue, NW
Washington DC 20036
Phone: 202/667-5363   Fax: 202/667-4563

South Africa

Mr. Basil J. VAN DER MERWE
Economic Counselor
Embassy of the Republic of South Africa
3051 Massachusetts Ave., NW
Washington DC 20008
Phone: 202/232-4400   Fax: 202/265-1607

Spain

Mr. Julio VINUELA
Counselor, Commercial and Economic
Embassy of Spain - Office for Economic and
Commercial Affairs
2558 Massachusetts Avenue NW
Washington DC 20008
Phone: 202/265-8600   Fax: 202/265-9478

Sri Lanka

Mr. Asoka G. DHARMAWARDHANE
Commercial Minister
Embassy of the Democratic Socialist Republic
  of Sri Lanka
2148 Wyoming Avenue, NW
Washington DC 20008
Phone: 202/483-4025   Fax: 202/232-7181

Sudan

Mr. Mirghani Mohamed SALIH
Deputy Chief of Mission
Embassy of the Republic of the Sudan
2210 Massachusetts Avenue, NW
Washington DC 20008
Phone: 202/338-8565   Fax: 202/667-2406

Suriname

Mr. Rudie M.J. ALIHUSAIN
Counselor
Embassy of the Republic of Suriname
4301 Connecticut Avenue, NW, Suite 460
Washington DC 20008
Phone: 202/244-7488   Fax: 202/244-5878

Swaziland

Mr. Philemon M. DLAMINI
Counselor
Embassy of the Kingdom of Swaziland
3400 International Drive, NW
Washington DC 20008-3006
Phone: 202/362-6683   Fax: 202/244-8059

Sweden

Mr. Andreas Eric EKMAN
Economic Minister
Embassy of Sweden
1501 M St., NW
Washington DC 20005-7594
Phone: 202/467-2600   Fax: 202/467-2699

Switzerland

Mr. Christian ETTER
Minister of Economic Affairs
Embassy of Switzerland
2900 Cathedral Avenue, NW
Washington DC 20008
Phone: 202/745-7900   Fax: 202/387-2564

Syria

Mr. Ali MUHRA
Third Secretary, Economic
Embassy of the Syrian Arab Republic
2215 Wyoming Avenue, NW
Washington DC 20008
Phone: 202/232-6313   Fax: 202/234-9548

Taiwan

Mr. Stephen S.F. CHEN
Representative
Taipei Economic and Cultural Representative
Office
4201 Wisconsin Avenue, NW
Washington DC 20016-2137
Phone: 202/895-1850   Fax: 202/364-0416

Tanzania

Mr. Anastase R. RWEGAYURA
Economic Minister and Head of Chancery
Embassy of the United Republic of Tanzania
2139 R Street, NW
Washington DC 20008
Phone: 202/939-6125   Fax: 202/797-7408

Thailand

Mr. Kanissorn NAVANUGRAHA
Commercial Minister

Royal Thai Embassy
1024 Wisconsin Ave., NW
Washington DC 20007
Phone: 202/944-2111   Fax: 202/944-3611

Togo

Mr. Edem Frederic HEGBE
Counselor
Embassy of the Republic of Togo
2208 Massachusetts Avenue, NW
Washington DC 20008
Phone: 202/234-4212   Fax: 202/232-3190

Tonga

Ms. Emeline Uheina TUITA
Consul General
Consulate General, Kingdom of Tonga
360 Post Street, Suite 604
San Francisco California 94108
Phone: 415/781-0365   Fax: 415/781-3964

Trinidad and Tobago

Mr. Carl A. FRANCIS
Counselor
Embassy of the Republic of Trinidad and Tobago
1708 Massachusetts Avenue, NW
Washington DC 20036
Phone: 202/467-6490   Fax: 202/785-3130

Tunisia

Mr. Slaheddine BEN-MAHMOUD
Commercial Counselor
Embassy of Tunisia
1515 Massachusetts Avenue, NW
Washington DC 20005
Phone: 202/862-1850   Fax: 202/862-1858

Turkey

Mr. Sukran OGUN
Commercial Counselor
Embassy of the Republic of Turkey
1714 Massachusetts Avenue, NW
Washington DC 20036
Phone: 202/659-8200   Fax: 202/659-0744

Turkmenistan

Mr. Tcharnazar ANNABERDIEV
Minister-Counselor
Embassy of Turkmenistan
2207 Massachusetts Avenue, NW
Washington DC 20008
Phone: 202/588-1500   Fax: 202/588-0697

Uganda

Mr. Nimisha MADHVANI-CHANDARIA
First Secretary, Public Relations and Commercial
Embassy of the Republic of Uganda
5909 16th Street, NW
Washington DC 20011-2816
Phone: 202/726-7100   Fax: 202/726-1727

Ukraine

Mr. Mykhayie REZNIK
Counselor
Embassy of Ukraine
3350 M Street, NW
Washington DC 20007
Phone: 202/333-0606   Fax: 202/333-0817

United Arab Emirates

Mr. Amina AMER
Commercial Attache
Embassy of the United Arab Emirates
1255 22nd St., NW, Suite 700
Washington DC 20037
Phone: 202/955-7999   Fax: 202/337-7029

United Kingdom

Mr. Robert Nicholas CULSHAW
Counselor (Trade)
British Embassy
3100 Massachusetts Avenue, NW
Washington DC 20008
Phone: 202/588-6513   Fax: 202/588-7860

Uruguay

Dr. Ricardo DUARTE
Second Secretary and Consul
Embassy of Uruguay
2715 M St., NW
Washington DC 20007
Phone: 202/331-1313   Fax: 202/331-8142

Uzbekistan

VACANT
Embassy of the Republic of Uzbekistan
1746 Massachusetts Ave., NW
Washington DC 20036
Phone: 202/887-5300   Fax: 202/293-6804

Venezuela

Mr. Alejandro PERERA
Minister-Counselor, Deputy Chief of Mission
Embassy of the Republic of Venezuela
1099 30th Street, NW
Washington DC 20007
Phone: 202/342-2214   Fax: 202/342-6820

Vietnam

Mr. Trang Chien NGUYEN
Commercial Counselor
Embassy of Vietnam
1233 20th Street, NW, Suite 501
Washington DC 20036
Phone: 202/861-0737   Fax: 202/861-0917

Yemen

Mr. Saisal ABO-RASS
Counselor, Head of Commercial and Trade Office
Embassy of the Republic of Yemen
2600 Virginia Avenue, NW, Suite 705

Washington DC 20037
Phone: 202/965-4760   Fax: 202/337-2017

Yugoslavia

Ms. Arada DROBNJAK
Commercial Attache
Embassy of the Federal Republic of Yugoslavia
2410 California Street, NW
Washington DC 20008
Phone: 202/462-6566   Fax: 202/797-9663

Zambia

Mr. Mike Kundfa CHANGWE
First Secretary (Political & Consular Affairs)
Embassy of the Republic of Zambia
2419 Massachusetts Avenue, NW
Washington DC 20008
Phone: 202/265-9717   Fax: 202/332-0826

Zimbabwe

Mr. Claudius Deny Farai NHEMA
Counselor
Embassy of the Republic of Zimbabwe
1608 New Hampshire Avenue, NW
Washington DC 20009
Phone: 202/332-7100   Fax: 202/483-9326

INTRODUCTION

The consular offices that foreign governments maintain in cities throughout the U.S. can be of tremendous help to U.S. businesses engaged in international trade. Trade with other regions of the world has become an increasingly vital element in the economy of the United States. The machinery of this essential commerce is complicated by numerous restrictions, license requirements, quotas, and other measures adopted by the individual countries. Because the regulations affecting both trade and travel are the particular province of the consular service of the nations involved, they are well equipped to provide reliable information as to entrance requirements, consignment of goods, details of transshipment, and, in many instances, suggestions as to consumer needs and preferences.

The list of foreign consular offices in the U.S. that follows was compiled by the U.S. Department of State, with the full cooperation of the foreign missions in Washington. It was updated and confirmed by Almanac Publishing in the spring of 1998. Changes occur daily and the status of persons listed in this section can be confirmed by contacting several sources: the consular office, the embassy in Washington, the appropriate country desk officer at the State Department, or the State Department's Office of Protocol (202/647-2663).

Depending on the size of a particular consular office, various trade and export contacts may or may not be on staff. When contacting a consular office, be sure to clearly express your interest/problems. The office will direct you accordingly.

IMMUNITIES ACCORDED TO CONSULAR OFFICERS

Consular officers should be accorded their respective privileges, rights, and immunities as directed by international and domestic law. These foreign officials should be treated with the courtesy and respect befitting their positions. At the same time, it is a well established principle of international law that, without prejudice to their privileges and immunities, it is the duty of all persons enjoying such privileges and immunities to respect local laws and regulations. Unless otherwise provided under specific bilateral agreements, they are entitled to the limited immunities described in the Vienna Convention on Consular Relations (VCCR), which contains the current expression of international law on the subject of the rights, privileges, and immunities of consular personnel. Furthermore, recognized consular officers who also are accredited as diplomatic agents at certain diplomatic missions enjoy full immunity under the provisions of the Vienna Convention on Diplomatic Relations (VCDR).

Career Consular Officers

Article 43 of the VCCR states that the immunity to which consular officers are entitled relates only to acts arising in the exercise of consular functions. This limited form of immunity, generally referred to as "official acts immunity" or "functional immunity", must be asserted in court as an affirmative defense and is subject to court determination. It should be noted that civil action relating to private contacts and damage arising from accidents caused by automobiles, vessels, or aircraft are specifically excepted from a claim of "official acts immunity" as are those based on private contracts. Although career consular officers enjoy only limited immunity from jurisdiction,

Article 41 of the VCCR does grant them personal inviolability. Therefore, such individuals may not be arrested or detained pending trial, except in the case of a grave crime and pursuant to a decision of a competent judicial authority. Career consular officers can be identified by credentials issued by the U.S. Department of State, which bear its seal, the name of the officer, and title.

Families of Consular Officers

Family members of consular officers do not enjoy the same privileges and immunities with respect to the civil and criminal jurisdiction of the receiving state as do consular officers. However, they should be accorded appropriate courtesy and respect.

Consular Employees

Although foreign career consular employees are not listed in this section, these individuals with whom you may come into contact are entitled to immunity from the civil and criminal jurisdiction of the receiving state as to official acts performed in the exercise of their consular functions, subject to court determination. They do not, however, enjoy personal inviolability and, thus, are not immune from arrest or detention.

Honorary Consular Officers

As a matter of U.S. policy, honorary consular officers recognized by the U.S. Government are American citizens or permanent resident aliens who perform consular services on a part-time basis. The limited immunity afforded honorary consular officers is specified in Article 71 of the VCCR. Such individuals do not enjoy personal inviolability and may be arrested pending trial if circumstances should otherwise warrant. However, appropriate steps must be provided to accord such officers the protection required by virtue of their official position. In addition, the consular archives and documents of a consular post headed by an honorary consular officer are inviolable at all times and wherever they may be, provided they are kept separate from other papers and documents of a private or commercial nature relating to other activities of an honorary consular officer or persons working with that consular officer.

Countries with Specific Bilateral Agreements

The United States and the following countries have entered into bilateral agreements, which, in certain cases, may provide greater privileges and immunities to consular officers, family members, and employees:

The People's Republic of China
The Republic of Hungary
The Philippines
The Republic of Poland
The Former Soviet Republic

Details of these specific cases can be obtained from the State Department's Office of Protocol.

CONSULAR PREMISES

Consular premises used exclusively for the work of the consular post cannot be entered without explicit permission of the head of the consular post or his designee or by the head of the diplomatic mission. This permission may be assumed in the case of fire or other disaster requiring prompt protective action.

CONSULAR ARCHIVES, DOCUMENTS, RECORDS, & CORRESPONDENCE

The consular archives and documents are inviolable at all times and wherever they may be. The official correspondence of the consular post, which means all correspondences relating to the consular post and its functions, is likewise inviolable.

Afghanistan

New York

Mr. Abdul Habib SERAJ
Consul
Consulate General of Afghanistan
369 Lexington Ave., 19th Floor
New York 10017
Phone: 212/972-2276   Fax: 212/972-1216

Albania

Massachusetts

Mr. Anthony S. ATHANAS
Honorary Consul
Honorary Consulate of Albania
140 Northern Ave.
Boston 02210
Phone: 617/482-6262

Texas

Dr. Pedro A. RUBIO
Honorary Consul
Honorary Consulate of Albania
10738 Villa Lea
Houston 77071
Phone: 713/790-1341   Fax: 713/790-0114

Antigua and Barbuda

Florida

Dr. Norman B. ATHILL
Consul General
Consulate General of Antigua and Barbuda
Ingraham Bldg., 25 SE 2nd Ave. - Suite 300
Miami 33131
Phone: 305/381-6762   Fax: 305/381-7908

Argentina

California

Mr. Luis RICCHERI
Consul General
Consulate General of Argentina
5055 Wilshire Blvd., Suite 210 & 208
Los Angeles 90036
Phone: 213/954-9155   Fax: 213/937-3841

Argentine Trade Office
3580 Wilshire Blvd., Suite 1412
Los Angeles 90010
Phone: 213/623-3230

Mr. Luis Fernanado DEL SOLAR DORREGO
Deputy Consul
Consulate General of Argentina
870 Market St., Suite 1083
San Francisco 94102

Florida

Mr. Eduardo A. PIVA
Consular Agent
Tourism Office of Argentina
2655 Lejeune Rd., Suite F
Coral Gables 33134
Phone: 305/442-1366

Mr. Juan Carlos KRECKLER
Consul General
Consulate General of Argentina
Penthouse 1, 800 Brickell Ave.
Miami 33131
Phone: 305/373-7794   Fax: 305/371-7108

Georgia

Mr. Ruben Nestor PATTO
Consul General
Consulate General of Argentina
245 Peachtree Street, Suite 1401
Atlanta 30303
Phone: 404/880-0805   Fax: 404/880-0806

Illinois

Mr. Ricardo Augusto GAUTHIER
Consul General
Consulate General of Argentina
205 North Michigan Ave., Suite 4208
Chicago 60601
Phone: 312/819-2610   Fax: 312/819-2612

Argentine Trade Office
233 N. Michigan Ave., Suite 1408
Chicago 60601
Phone: 312/565-2466

New York

Mr. Guillermo Jorge MCGOUGH
Consul General
Consulate General of Argentina
12 W. 56th St.
New York 10019
Phone: 212/603-0400   Fax: 212/541-7746

Mrs. Liliana Elena SERSALE DI SERISANO
Deputy Consul General
Argentine Trade Office
900 Third Ave., 4th Floor
New York 10022
Phone: 212/759-6477

Texas

Mr. Juan Luis GARIBALDI
Consul General
Consulate General of Argentina
1990 Post Oak Blvd., Suite 770
Houston 77056
Phone: 713/871-8935   Fax: 713/871-0639

Argentine Trade Office
2000 S. Post Oak Rd., Suite 1810
Houston 77056
Phone: 713/871-8890

Armenia

California

Mr. Armen Vahan BAIBOURTIAN
Consul General
Consulate General of Armenia
50 N. La Cienega Bl., Suite 210
Beverly Hills 90211
Phone: 310/657-6102   Fax: 310/657-7419

Australia

California

Consul General
Consulate General of Australia

611 N. Larchmont Blvd.
Los Angeles 90004
Phone: 213/469-4300   Fax: 213/469-9176

Mr. Robert John O'DONOVAN
Consul General
Consulate General of Australia
Century Plaza Towers
2049 Century Pk., E., 19th Fl.
Los Angeles 90067
Phone: 310/229-4800   Fax: 310/277-2258

Mr. Stephen BULLOCK
Vice Consul
Senior Trade Commission - Australia
2049 Century Pk., E., 19th Fl.
Century Plaza Towers
Los Angeles 90067

Dr. Joseph Raymond HLUBUCEK
Consul General
Consulate General of Australia
1 Bush St., 7th Floor
San Francisco 94104
Phone: 415/362-6160   Fax: 415/956-9729

Colorado

Mr. Mark O'REGAN
Honorary Consul
Honorary Consulate of Australia
999 18th St., Suite 1370
Denver 80202
Phone: 303/297-1200   Fax: 303/297-1280

Georgia

Mr. Geoffrey Roy GRAY
Consul General
Consulate General of Australia
One Peachtree Center
303 Peachtree St., Suite 2920
Atlanta 30308
Phone: 404/880-1702   Fax: 404/880-1701

Hawaii

Mr. Colin Edward MCDONALD
Consul General
Consulate General of Australia
1000 Bishop Street, Penthouse
Honolulu 96813
Phone: 808/524-5050   Fax: 808/531-5142

Massachusetts

Mrs. Margaret STANZLER
Honorary Consul
Honorary Consulate of Australia
20 Park Plaza, Suite 457
Boston 02116
Phone: 617/542-8655   Fax: 617/426-9236

New York

Mr. Michael Ehrenfried BAUME
Consul General
Consulate General of Australia
630 5th Ave., Suite 420
New York 10111
Phone: 212/408-8400   Fax: 212/408-8401

Senior Trade Commission - Australia
630/636 5th. Ave.
New York 10111

Texas

Consul General

Consulate General of Australia
3 Post Oak Central A.H., Suite 800
Houston 77056-9998
Phone: 713/629-9131   Fax: 713/622-6924

Austria

California

Mr. Werner Eduard BRANDSTETTER
Consul General
Consulate General of Austria
11859 Wilshire Blvd., Suite 501
Los Angeles 90025
Phone: 310/444-9310   Fax: 310/477-9897

Mr. Johann KAUSL
Consul
Austrian Trade Commission
11601 Wilshire Blvd., Suite 2420
Los Angeles 90025
Phone: 310/477-9988   Fax: 310/477-1643

Mr. Donald C. BURNS
Honorary Consul General
Honorary Consulate General of Austria
41 Sutter St., Suite 207
San Francisco 94104
Phone: 415/951-8911   Fax: 415/444-7835

Colorado

Mr. Arnold C. WEGHER
Honorary Consul General
Honorary Consulate General of Austria
First Interstate Tower South
621 17th St., Suite 2455
Denver 80293-2450
Phone: 303/292-9000   Fax: 303/292-5445

Florida

Mr. Arthur W. KARLICK
Honorary Consul General
Honorary Consulate General of Austria
Republic Bldg.
1454 N.W. 17th Ave., Suite 200
Miami 33125
Phone: 305/325-1561   Fax: 305/325-1563

Georgia

Mr. Ferdinand C. SEEFRIED
Honorary Consul General
Honorary Consulate of Austria
10 N. Parkway Square
4200 Northside Pkwy., N.W.
Atlanta 30327
Phone: 404/264-9858   Fax: 404/266-3864

Hawaii

Mr. Hans J. STRASSER
Honorary Consul General
Honorary Consulate General of Austria
1314 S. King St., Suite 1260
Honolulu 96814
Phone: 808/923-8585   Fax: 808/528-2800

Illinois

Mr. Christian KREPELA
Consul General
Consulate General of Austria
400 N. Michigan Ave., Suite 707
Chicago 60611
Phone: 312/222-1515   Fax: 312/222-4113

Mr. Peter K. ATHANASIADIS
Consul (Comm.)
Austrian Trade Commission
500 N. Michigan Ave., Suite 1950
Chicago 60611
Phone: 312/644-5556   Fax: 312/644-6526

Louisiana

Mr. Philip D. LORIO
Honorary Consul
Honorary Consulate of Austria
755 Magazine St.
New Orleans 70130
Phone: 504/581-5141   Fax: 504/566-1201

Massachusetts

Mr. Ira A. KORFF
Honorary Consul
Honorary Consulate of Austria
15 School St., 3rd Floor
Boston 02108
Phone: 617/227-3131   Fax: 617/227-8420

Michigan

Mr. Aloys K. SCHWARZ
Honorary Consul General
Honorary Consulate of Austria
300 E. Long Lake Rd., Suite 365
Bloomfield Hills 48304
Phone: 313/645-1444   Fax: 248/645-1482

Minnesota

Mr. Ronald M. BOSROCK
Honorary Consul General
Honorary Consulate General of Austria
International Education Systems
26 E. Exchange St., Suite 313
St. Paul 55101-0448
Phone: 612/227-2052   Fax: 612/223-8383

Missouri

Mr. Dieter Karl UNGERBOECK
Honorary Consul
Honorary Consulate of Austria
1350 Elbridge Payne Rd.
Chesterfield 63017-8531
Phone: 314/537-0350   Fax: 314/537-3720

Mr. Dennis James OWENS
Honorary Consul General
Honorary Consulate General of Austria
Harzfold Bldg., 1111 Main St., 7th Fl.
Town Pavilion
Kansas City 64105
Phone: 816/474-3000   Fax: 816/474-5533

New York

Mr. Thomas M. DEAN
Honorary Consul
Honorary Consulate of Austria
Statler Bldg., 107 Delaware Ave., Suite 500
Buffalo 14202
Phone: 716/852-7000   Fax: 716/852-7001

Mr. Harold MILTNER
Consul General
Consulate General of Austria
31 E. 69th St.
New York 10021
Phone: 212/737-6400   Fax: 212/772-8926

Mr. Wolfgang Arnold WALDNER
Consul

Cultural Affairs Section - Austria
950 3rd Ave., 20th Floor
New York 10022
Phone: 212/759-5165

Mr. Benno KOCH
Consul
Austrian Trade Commission
150 E. 52nd St., 32nd Floor
New York 10022
Phone: 212/421-5250   Fax: 212/751-4675

Ohio

Mr. Friedrich K. BOEHM
Honorary Consul
Honorary Consulate of Austria
1555 Lake Shore Dr.
Columbus 43204
Phone: 614/224-5464   Fax: 614/224-6603

Pennsylvania

Mr. Harry C. SCHAUB
Honorary Consul General
Honorary Consulate General of Austria
123 S. Broad St., 24th Fl.
Philadelphia 19109-1029
Phone: 215/772-7630   Fax: 215/772-7620

Puerto Rico

Ms. Marie Helene MORROW
Honorary Consul
Honorary Consulate of Austria
Loca #24, Plaza Las Americas, 1st Fl.
Hato Rey
San Juan 00902
Phone: 787/767-1381

Texas

Mr. Otmar KOLBER
Honorary Consul General
Honorary Consulate General of Austria
1717 Bissonet St., Suite 306
Houston 77005
Phone: 713/723-9979   Fax: 713/526-9819

Washington

Mr. Walter R. WEBER
Honorary Consul General
Honorary Consulate General of Austria
1111 3rd Ave., Suite 2626
Seattle 98101-3210
Phone: 206/624-9887   Fax: 206/684-6831

Bahamas

Florida

Mr. Franklyn O. ROLLE
Consul General
Consulate General of the Bahamas
Ingraham Bldg. 25 S.E. 2nd Ave.
Miami 33131
Phone: 305/373-6295   Fax: 395/373-6312

New York

Dr. Doswell Clifton COAKLEY
Consul General
Consulate General of the Bahamas
231 E. 46th St., 2nd Floor
New York 10017
Phone: 212/421-6420   Fax: 212/759-2135

Bahrain

California

Mr. Charles W. HOSTLER
Honorary Consul General
Honorary Consulate General of Bahrain
1101 First St., Suite 302
Coronado 92118
Phone: 619/437-0044   Fax: 619/437-0066

New York

Mr. Tawfeeq Ahmed AL MANSOOR
Consul General
Consulate General of Bahrain
2 United Nations Plaza, 25th Floor
New York 10017
Phone: 212/223-6200   Fax: 212/319-0687

Bangladesh

California

Mr. Mohammad AL HAROON
Consul General
Consulate General of Bangladesh
10850 Wilshire Blvd., Suite 1250
Los Angeles 90024
Phone: 310/441-9399   Fax: 310/441-4458

Hawaii

Mr. Raymond Y. HO
Honorary Consul General
Honorary Consulate General of Bangladesh
3785 Old Pali Rd.
Honolulu 96817
Phone: 808/521-5353

Louisiana

Mr. Thomas Blaise COLEMAN
Honorary Consul General
Honorary Consulate General of Bangladesh
321 St. Charles Ave.
New Orleans 70130
Phone: 504/586-8300

New York

Mr. Kamrul Hasan SHEIKH
Consul General
Consulate General of Bangladesh
211 E. 43rd St., Suite 502
New York 10017
Phone: 212/599-6767   Fax: 212/682-9211

Texas

Mr. Edward Joseph HUDSON
Honorary Consul General
Honorary Consulate General of Bangladesh
35 N. Wynden Dr.
Houston 77056
Phone: 713/621-8462   Fax: 713/622-3964

Barbados

California

Mr. Don R. MCCARTHY
Vice Consul

Consulate of Barbados
3440 Wilshire Blvd., Suite 1215
Los Angeles 90010
Phone: 213/380-2198

Mr. Gerald B. LEVINE
Honorary Consul
Honorary Consulate of Barbados
Mentor International
442 Post St., Suite 800
San Francisco 94102
Phone: 415/421-8789

Colorado

Mr. Peter KELLEY
Honorary Consul
Honorary Consulate of Barbados
150 Fairplay Ave.
Bloomfield 80020

Florida

Mr. Euclid Patrick GOODMAN
Consul
Consulate General of Barbados
150 Alhambra Cir., Suite 1270
Coral Gables 33134
Phone: 305/442-1994

Mr. Benjamin MARTINEZ
Consul General
Consulate General of Barbados
7220 N.W. 36th St., Suite 105
Miami 33166
Phone: 305/599-1310

Georgia

Dr. Edward A. LAYNE
Honorary Consul
Honorary Consulate of Barbados
100 Colony Square
1175 Peachtree St., Suite 890
Atlanta 30309
Phone: 404/681-0000

Illinois

Mr. Andre Richardson KING
Honorary Consul
Honorary Consulate of Barbados
6700 S. Oglesby, Suite 1603
Chicago 60649
Phone: 312/922-7757

Kentucky

Mr. Bernard James STRENECKY
Honorary Consul
Honorary Consulate of Barbados
3518 Sorrento Ave.
Louisville 40241
Phone: 502/852-0574   Fax: 502/852-1497

Louisiana

Mr. Peter Dee COLEMAN
Honorary Consul
Honorary Consulate of Barbados
321 St. Charles Ave., 10th Floor
New Orleans 70130
Phone: 504/586-1979

Massachusetts

Mr. John W. LICORISH
Honorary Consul
Honorary Consulate of Barbados

794 Cummins Hwy.
Boston 02126
Phone: 617/296-3360

Michigan

Dr. Lacey WALKE
Honorary Consul
Honorary Consulate of Barbados
11012 E. 13 Mile Rd., Suite 208
Warren 48093
Phone: 313/751-8840

New York

Mr. Ricardo Antonio CRAIG
Consul General
Consulate General of Barbados
800 2nd Ave., 2nd Floor
New York 10017
Phone: 212/867-8435   Fax: 212/986-1030

Ohio

Dr. Ian D. MURPHY
Honorary Consul
Honorary Consulate of Barbados
723 Phillips Ave.
Toledo 43612
Phone: 419/478-5533

Oregon

Mr. Harold Desmond JOHNSON
Honorary Consul
Honorary Consulate of Barbados
10202 S.E. 32nd Ave., Suite 601
Milwaukee 97222
Phone: 503/659-0283

Texas

Mr. Robert Henry RUSSELL
Honorary Consul
Honorary Consulate of Barbados
25226 Sandi Lane
Katy 77494
Phone: 713/392-9794

Belarus

New York

Consul General
Consulate General of Belarus
708 3rd Ave., Suite 2101
New York 10017
Phone: 212/682-5392   Fax: 212/682-5491

Belgium

Alaska

Mr. Carl F. BRADY
Honorary Consul
Honorary Consulate of Belgium
1031 W. 4th Ave., Suite 400
Anchorage 99510-7502
Phone: 907/276-5617   Fax: 907/257-6394

Arizona

Mr. Reginald WINSSINGER
Honorary Consul

Honorary Consulate of Belgium
2999 N. 44th St., Suite 450
Phoenix 85018
Phone: 602/852-3870   Fax: 602/852-3878

California

Mr. Leopold MERCKX
Consul General
Consulate General of Belgium
6100 Wilshire Blvd., Suite 1200
Los Angeles 90048
Phone: 213/857-1244   Fax: 213/936-2564

Mr. Patrick John SEBRECHTS
Honorary Consul
Honorary Consulate of Belgium
5572 Trinity Wa.
San Diego 92120
Phone: 619/943-9121

Mrs. Rita M. BRAL
Honorary Consul
Honorary Consulate of Belgium
625 3rd St., Suite 400
San Francisco 94107
Phone: 415/882-4648   Fax: 415/957-0730

Colorado

Mr. Lothar G. ESTENFELDER
Honorary Consul
Honorary Consulate of Belgium
999 S. Broadway
Denver 80209
Phone: 303/744-4051   Fax: 303/744-5494

Florida

Mr. Gui Leopold GOVAERT
Honorary Consul
Honorary Consulate of Belgium
4100 North Miami Ave., Suite 2
Miami 33127
Phone: 305/573-0784   Fax: 305/573-0787

Georgia

Ms. Rita DE BRUYNE
Consul General
Consulate General of Belgium
Peachtree Ctr., No. Tower, Suite 850
235 Peachtree St., NE
Atlanta 30303
Phone: 404/659-2150   Fax: 404/659-8474

Hawaii

Mr. Roger A. ULVELING
Honorary Consul
Honorary Consulate of Belgium
749 Fort St. Mall, Suite 1800
Honolulu 96813
Phone: 808/533-6900   Fax: 808/527-8399

Illinois

Mr. Robert Roger VANDEMEULEBROUCKE
Consul General
Consulate General of Belgium
333 N. Michigan Ave., Room 2000
Chicago 60601
Phone: 312/263-6624   Fax: 312/263-4805

Ms. Dolores Helen BULTINCK
Honorary Consul
Honorary Consulate of Belgium
740 18th Ave.
Moline 61265

Phone: 309/762-7847   Fax: 309/762-1606

Kentucky

Mr. Alfred John WELSH
Honorary Consul
Consulate of Belgium
1009 S. 4th St.
Louisville 40203
Phone: 502/584-8583   Fax: 502/584-1826

Louisiana

Mr. Roland Hector TIMMERMAN
Honorary Consul
Honorary Consulate of Belgium
110 Veterans Memorial Bl.
Metairie 70005
Phone: 504/837-5880   Fax: 504/849-2302

Maryland

Mr. Louis G. CONNOR
Honorary Consul
Honorary Consulate of Belgium
401 E. Pratt St., Suite 700
Baltimore 21202
Phone: 301/332-4815   Fax: 410/547-6865

Massachusetts

Mr. Philippe T. CAPIAU
Honorary Consul
Honorary Consulate of Belgium
300 Commercial St., Suite 29
Malden 02148
Phone: 617/397-8566   Fax: 617/397-6752

Michigan

Ms. Elizabeth A. STEVENS
Honorary Consul
Honorary Consulate of Belgium
21777 Hoover St.
Warren 48089
Phone: 810/497-7567   Fax: 810/497-7007

Minnesota

Mr. Patrick H. O'NEILL
Honorary Consul
Honorary Consulate of Belgium
501 West Lawson St.
St. Paul 55117
Phone: 612/487-7262   Fax: 612/487-7279

Missouri

Mr. Stephen Franklin BRAUER
Honorary Consul
Honorary Consulate of Belgium
11250 Hunter Dr.
Bridgeton 63044
Phone: 314/731-3020   Fax: 314/731-7133

New York

Mr. Lu Marie DARRAS
Consul General
Consulate General of Belgium
1330 Avenue of the Americas
26th Floor
New York 10019-5422
Phone: 212/586-5110   Fax: 212/582-9657

Ohio

Mr. Paul Aime ALLAER FUGITT

Honorary Consul
Honorary Consulate of Belgium
312 Walnut St., Suite 1400
Cincinnati 45202
Phone: 513/352-6627   Fax: 513/241-4771

Mr. Jon E. DENNEY
Honorary Consul
Honorary Consulate of Belgium
25825 Science Park Dr., Suite 100
Cleveland 44122
Phone: 216/766-5780   Fax: 216/766-5796

Oregon

Mr. John Henry HERMAN
Honorary Consul
Honorary Consulate of Belgium
Duffel Sportswear
1870 N.W. 173rd. Ave.
Beaverton 97006
Phone: 503/228-0465

Pennsylvania

Mr. Joseph Howard HENNESSY
Honorary Consul
Honorary Consulate of Belgium
Curtis Center
6th & Walnut St., Suite 1150
Philadelphia 19106
Phone: 215/925-5645   Fax: 212/963-5289

Ms. Anne B. LACKNER
Honorary Consul
Honorary Consulate of Belgium
700 N. Bell Ave., Suite 290
Pittsburgh 15106
Phone: 412/279-2121   Fax: 412/279-6429

Puerto Rico

Mr. Richard Claiborne DURHAM
Honorary Consul
Honorary Consulate of Belgium
1250 Ponce De Leon, Suite 713
Santurce 00907
Phone: 809/725-3179

Texas

Mr. Ronald W. HADDOCK
Honorary Consul
Honorary Consulate of Belgium
8350 N. Central Expressway, Suite 2000
Dallas 75206
Phone: 214/987-4391   Fax: 214/750-2570

Mr. Andre Arthur CRISPIN
Honorary Consul General
Honorary Consulate General of Belgium
The Crispin Co.
2929 Allen Parkway, Suite 2222
Houston 77019
Phone: 713/529-0775   Fax: 713/224-1120

Mr. Robert P. BRAUBACH
Honorary Consul
Honorary Consulate of Belgium
105 S. Mary's St.
San Antonio 78205
Phone: 210/271-8820   Fax: 210/225-1951

Utah

Mr. Charles DIDIER
Honorary Consul
Honorary Consulate of Belgium
615 Northcrest Dr.
Salt Lake City 84103

Phone: 801/363-9806   Fax: 801/240-2033

Virginia

Mrs. Mia S. LANESE
Honorary Consul
Honorary Consulate of Belgium
1023-K Laskin Rd.
Virginia Beach 23451
Phone: 804/422-5571   Fax: 804/491-1845

Washington

Mr. Herbert Ronald MASNIK
Honorary Consul
Honorary Consulate of Belgium
3214 West Mcgraw, Suite 301
Seattle 98199
Phone: 206/285-4486   Fax: 206/282-9544

Wisconsin

Mr. Charles C. MULCAHY
Honorary Consul
Honorary Consulate of Belgium
Whyte Hirschboeck Dudek S.C.
111 E. Wisconsin Ave., Suite 2100
Milwaukee 53202
Phone: 414/273-2100   Fax: 414/223-5000

Belize

California

Mrs. Pearl Ann WARREN
Consul General
Consulate General of Belize
5825 W. Sunset Blvd., Suite 203
Hollywood 90028
Phone: 213/469-7343

Mr. Francis F. COPPOLA
Honorary Consul
Honorary Consulate of Belize
916 Kearny St.
San Francisco 94123
Phone: 415/788-7500

Florida

Ms. Araceli G. ACOSTA
Honorary Consul
Honorary Consulate of Belize
8620 NE 2nd Ave.
Miami 33138
Phone: 305/751-5655

Illinois

Mr. Eugene Michael VERDU
Honorary Consul
Honorary Consulate of Belize
1229 N. 17th St., Unit 23
Belleville 62223
Phone: 618/235-7143

Mr. Edwin T. SMILING
Honorary Consul
Honorary Consulate of Belize
1200 Howard Dr.
Chicago 60185
Phone: 708/943-0010

Louisiana

Mr. Teodosio Tito STAINES
Honorary Consul

Honorary Consulate of Belize
3601 Kent Ave.
Metairie 70006
Phone: 504/885-7704

Michigan

Dr. Lennox A. PIKE
Honorary Consul
Honorary Consulate of Belize
24984 Glen Orchard Dr.
Farmington Hills 48336-1732
Phone: 810/477-8768

Puerto Rico

Mr. William Vincent BURN
Honorary Consul
Honorary Consulate of Belize
567 Ramon Gandia St.
Hato Rey 00918
Phone: 809/766-7709

Texas

Mr. Hugh D. MCCAIN
Honorary Consul General
Honorary Consulate General of Belize
7101 Breen St.
Houston 77086
Phone: 713/999-4484

Mr. Arthur C. ELLIS
Honorary Consul
Honorary Consulate of Belize
1315 19th St., Suite 2A
Plano 75074
Phone: 214/579-0070

Benin

California

Mr. Mervyn M. DYMALLY
Honorary Consul
Honorary Consulate of Benin
9111 S. La Cienega Blvd., Suite 204
Inglewood 90301
Phone: 310/641-3688   Fax: 310/641-6980

Bhutan

California

Mr. Rudolph A. PETERSON
Honorary Consul
Honorary Consulate of Bhutan
555 California St., Suite 500
San Francisco 94104
Phone: 415/622-6011   Fax: 415/622-5388

District of Columbia

Mr. William David HOPPER
Honorary Consul
Honorary Consulate of Bhutan
1325 18th St., N.W., Suite 806
Washington 20036
Phone: 202/783-0112

New York

Mr. Kesang WANGDI
Consul General
Consulate General of Bhutan

2 United Nations Plaza
27th Floor
New York 10017
Phone: 212/826-1919   Fax: 212/826-2998

Bolivia

Arizona

Mr. Eduardo A. CASTILLO
Honorary Consul
Honorary Consulate of Bolivia
The Castillo Co., 2345 E. University Dr.
Phoenix 85034
Phone: 602/231-9000   Fax: 602/275-8593

California

Consul General
Consulate General of Bolivia
483 S. Spring St., Suite 1212
Los Angeles 90013
Phone: 213/680-0190

Mrs. Mabel RODRIGUEZ ZAMBRANA
Consul General
Consulate General of Bolivia
870 Market St., Suite 575
San Francisco 94102
Phone: 415/495-5173   Fax: 415/399-8958

Colorado

Mr. James J. RAAF
Honorary Consul
Honorary Consulate of Bolivia
21 Lemond Cir.
Snowmass Village 81615
Phone: 303/923-2668   Fax: 970/923-6716

Florida

Mr. Fernando CACERES DIAZ
Consul General
Consulate General of Bolivia
700 Ingraham Bldg.
25 E. 2nd Ave., Suite 545
Miami 33131
Phone: 305/358-3450   Fax: 305/374-8636

Georgia

Mr. S. George HANDELSMAN
Honorary Consul General
Honorary Consulate General of Bolivia
1375 Peachtree St., NW, Suite 180
Atlanta 30309
Phone: 404/522-0777   Fax: 404/873-3335

Illinois

Mr. Jaime ESCOBAR
Honorary Consul
Honorary Consulate of Bolivia
1200 W. Superior
Melrose Park 60160
Phone: 708/343-1234   Fax: 708/343-4290

Louisiana

Mr. David BALL
Honorary Consul
Honorary Consulate of Bolivia
643 Magazine St.
New Orleans 70130
Phone: 504/596-2720   Fax: 504/596-2800

Massachusetts

Mr. Russell D. LEBLANG
Honorary Consul General
Honorary Consulate General of Bolivia
85 Devonshire St., Suite 1000
Boston 02109
Phone: 617/742-1500   Fax: 617/742-9130

Minnesota

Mrs. Gloria STEIN
Honorary Consul
Honorary Consulate of Bolivia
20550 Hackamore Rd.
Hamel 55340

Missouri

Mrs. Beatriz E. CALVIN
Honorary Consul
Honorary Consulate of Bolivia
7710 Carondelet Ave., Suite 404
St. Louis 63105
Phone: 314/725-9466   Fax: 314/725-9103

New York

Mr. Julio Armando FORTUN SALMON
Consul General
Consulate General of Bolivia
211 E. 43rd St., Suite 702
New York 10017
Phone: 212/687-0530   Fax: 212/687-0532

Ohio

Mr. David C. MITCHELL
Honorary Consul
Honorary Consulate of Bolivia
5500 Mapleridge Dr.
Cincinnati 45227
Phone: 513/271-5381   Fax: 513/271-8189

Texas

Ms. Maria URIOSTE
Honorary Consul
Honorary Consulate of Bolivia
611 Singleton
Dallas 75212
Phone: 214/571-6131   Fax: 214/651-9514

Mr. Jorge GALATOIRE
Honorary Consul General
Honorary Consulate of Bolivia
1880 Dairy Ashford, Suite 691
Houston 77077
Phone: 713/497-4068   Fax: 713/789-8124

Washington

Mr. Rene Ricardo ANTEZANA MONTANO
Honorary Consul
Honorary Consulate of Bolivia
5200 Southcenter Blvd., Suite 5
Seattle 98188
Phone: 206/244-6696   Fax: 206/243-3795

Bosnia & Herzegovina

New York

Mr. Asim CEMALOVIC
Consul General
Consulate General of Bosnia and Herzegovina
866 U.N. Plaza, Suite 580
New York 10017
Phone: 212/751-9018   Fax: 212/751-9135

Botswana

California

Mr. William Barnum RUDELL
Honorary Consul
Honorary Consulate of Botswana
333 S. Hope St., 38th Floor
Los Angeles 90071
Phone: 213/626-8484

Texas

Mr. Stephen V. VALLONE
Honorary Consul
Honorary Consulate of Botswana
4615 Post Oak Pl., Suite 104
Houston 77027
Phone: 713/622-1900   Fax: 713/680-8055

Brazil

Alabama

Mr. Michael Hugh JOHNSON
Honorary Consul
Honorary Consulate of Brazil
1500 Resource Dr.
Birmingham 35342
Phone: 205/250-4731

Arizona

Mr. K. Charles OELFKE
Honorary Consul
Honorary Consulate of Brazil
7036 North 69th Place
Paradise Valley 85253
Phone: 602/948-4402   Fax: 602/948-4402

California

Consul General
Consulate General of Brazil
8484 Wilshire Blvd., Suite 730
Beverly Hills 90211
Phone: 213/651-4911   Fax: 213/651-1274

Mr. Jorio Salgado GAMA FILHO
Consul General
Consulate General Brazil
8484 Wilshire Blvd.
Suite 730, 711 and 260
Los Angeles 90211
Phone: 213/651-2644   Fax: 213/651-1274

Mr. Jose Augusto ALVES
Consul General
Consulate General of Brazil
300 Montgomery St., Suite 1160
San Francisco 94104
Phone: 415/981-8170   Fax: 415/981-3628

Florida

Mr. Luiz BENEDINI
Consul General
Consulate General of Brazil
2601 South Bayshore Dr., Suite 800
Miami 33133
Phone: 305/285-6225   Fax: 305/285-6232

Georgia

Mr. Mario Da ROITER
Consul General
Consulate General of Brazil
Cain Tower
229 Peachtree St., NE - Suite 2306
Atlanta 30303
Phone: 404/521-0061   Fax: 404/521-3449

Hawaii

Mr. John E. POAST
Honorary Consul
Honorary Consulate of Brazil
44-166 Nanamoana St.
Kaneohe 96744
Phone: 808/536-5105

Illinois

Mr. Fernando Jose Moura FAGUNDES
Consul General
Consulate General of Brazil
401 N. Michigan Ave., 30th Floor
Chicago 60611
Phone: 312/464-0244   Fax: 312/464-0299

Louisiana

Mr. Joseph Simon BROWN
Honorary Consul
Honorary Consulate of Brazil
1465 Ted Dunham Ave.
Baton Rouge 70802
Phone: 504/336-4143   Fax: 504/343-1806

Massachusetts

Mr. Mario VILALVA
Consul General
Consulate General of Brazil
The Statler Bldg.
20 Park Plaza, Suite 810
Boston 02116
Phone: 617/542-4000   Fax: 617/542-4318

New York

Mr. Marcus Camacho DE VINCENZI
Consul General
Consulate General of Brazil
630 Fifth Ave., Suite 2720
New York 10111
Phone: 212/757-3080

Puerto Rico

Mr. Jose NOGUEIRA FILHO
Consul General
Consulate General of Brazil
Banco De Ponce Bldg.
268 Munoz Rivera Ave.
Hato Rey 00919-2507

Texas

Ms. Maria Lucia SANTOS POMPEAU BRASIL
Consul General
Consulate General of Brazil
1700 W. Loop South, Suite 1450
Houston 77027
Phone: 713/961-0551   Fax: 713/961-3070

Virginia

Mr. James Earnest THOMPSON

Honorary Consul
Honorary Consulate of Brazil
625 Chesopeian Trail
Virginia Beach 23452
Phone: 804/340-5820

Washington

Mr. William Allan ELLIS
Honorary Consul
Honorary Consulate of Brazil
546 Alder St., Apt. 102
Edmonds 98020
Phone: 425/778-8358   Fax: 425/778-8358

Bulgaria

New York

Mr. Latchezar Y. PETKOV
Consul
Consulate of Bulgaria
121 E. 62nd St.
New York 10021
Phone: 212/935-4646

Burkino Faso

California

Mr. Allen I. NEIMAN
Honorary Consul General
Honorary Consulate General of Burkino Faso
11111 Santa Monica Bl., Suite 1840
Los Angeles 90025
Phone: 213/575-5567

Georgia

Mr. Gary R. GUNDERSON
Honorary Consul
Honorary Consulate of Burkino Faso
128 Candler Oaks Ln.
Decatur 30030
Phone: 404/378-7278

Louisiana

Mr. John William ORMOND
Honorary Consul
Honorary Consulate of Burkino Faso
1557 Calhoun St.
New Orleans 70118
Phone: 504/945-3152

Burundi

Illinois

Mr. Jay Herman SCHMIDT
Honorary Consul
Honorary Consulate of Burundi
854 Castlewood Terr.
Chicago 60640
Phone: 312/271-2530

Cameroon

California

Mr. Donald LOW

Honorary Consul
Honorary Consulate of Cameroon
147 Terra Vista
San Francisco 94115
Phone: 415/921-5372

Texas

Mr. Charles R. GREENE
Honorary Consul
Honorary Consulate of Cameroon
2711 Weslayan
Houston 77027
Phone: 713/499-3502   Fax: 713/774-7319

Canada

California

Ms. Avril P. CAMPBELL
Consul General
Consulate General of Canada
550 S. Hope St., 9th Floor
Los Angeles 90071
Phone: 213/346-2711   Fax: 213/620-8827

Mr. Michael Graham STINSON
Consul
Consulate Trade Office - Canada
4827 Tarantella Lane
San Diego 92130
Phone: 619/597-7050

Consul
Consulate Trade Office - Canada
50 Fremont Street, Suite 1825
San Francisco 94105
Phone: 415/543-2550

Mr. Brian Edward COX
Consul
Consulate - Trade Office of Canada
333 W. San Carlos St., Suite 945
San Jose 95110
Phone: 408/289-1157

Florida

Ms. Janis Ann LAWSON
Consul
Consulate of Canada
200 S. Biscayne Blvd., Suite 1600
Miami 33131
Phone: 305/579-1600   Fax: 305/374-6774

Georgia

Mr. Allan Joseph STEWART
Consul General
Consulate General of Canada
100 Colony Sq.
1175 Peachtree St., Suite 1700
Atlanta 30361
Phone: 404/532-2000   Fax: 404/532-2050

Illinois

Mr. Allan Norman LEVER
Consul General
Consulate General of Canada
2 Prudential Plaza
180 N. Stetson Ave., Suite 2400
Chicago 60601
Phone: 312/616-1860   Fax: 312/616-1877

Massachusetts

Mr. Paul DESBIENS

Deputy Consul General
Consulate General of Canada
3 Copley Pl., Suite 400
Boston 02116
Phone: 617/262-3760   Fax: 617/262-3415

Michigan

Mr. Donald Terry WISMER
Consul General
Consulate General of Canada
600 Renaissance Ctr., Suite 1100
Detroit 48283
Phone: 313/567-2340   Fax: 313/567-2164

Minnesota

Mr. Robert DERY
Consul General
Consulate General of Canada
701 4th Ave., South, 9th Floor
Minneapolis 55415-1899
Phone: 612/333-4641   Fax: 612/332-4061

New Jersey

Consul
Consulate Trade Office - Canada
90 Westcott Rd.
Princeton 08540
Phone: 609/252-0777   Fax: 609/252-0792

New York

Mr. Mark ROMOFF
Consul General
Consulate General of Canada
3000 Marine Midland Ctr.
Buffalo 14203-2884
Phone: 716/596-1600   Fax: 716/852-4340

Mr. George Leslie HAYNAL
Consul General
Consulate General of Canada
1251 Ave. of the Americas
16th Floor
New York 10020
Phone: 212/596-1600   Fax: 212/596-1790

Texas

Mr. Jon Lemasurier SWANSON
Consul General
Consulate General of Canada
750 N. Saint Paul St., Suite 1700
Dallas 75201
Phone: 214/922-9806   Fax: 214/922-9815

Washington

Mr. John Thomas BOEHM
Consul General
Consulate General of Canada
412 Plaza 600
6th and Stewart Sts.
Seattle 98101
Phone: 206/443-1777   Fax: 206/443-9662

Cape Verde

Massachusetts

Mr. Benjamin P. MONTIERO
Consul General
Consulate General of Cape Verde
535 Boylston St.
Boston 02116

Phone: 617/353-0014

Rhode Island

Mr. Francisco F. BARBOSA
Honorary Consul
Honorary Consulate of Cape Verde
387 Lonsdale Ave.
Pawtucket 02860
Phone: 401/729-1790   Fax: 401/729-1792

Central African Rep.

California

Mr. Bernard William KINSEY
Honorary Consul General
Hon. Consulate Gen. of the Central African Rep.
301 Mt. Holyoke Ave.
Pacific Palisades 90272
Phone: 310/454-9505   Fax: 310/454-4634

New York

Mr. Howard A. HIRSCHFELD
Honorary Consul
Hon. Consulate Gen. of the Central African Rep.
51 E. 42nd St.
New York 10117
Phone: 212/983-0330   Fax: 212/983-0472

Chile

California

Mr. Gonzalo MENDOZA NEGRI
Consul General
Consulate General of Chile
1900 Avenue of the Stars, Suite 2450
Los Angeles 90067
Phone: 310/785-0113   Fax: 310/785-0132

Mr. George L. GILDRED
Honorary Consul
Honorary Consulate of Chile
667 San Elijo St.
San Diego 92106
Phone: 619/222-0080   Fax: 619/222-6210

Mr. Alberto Manuel YOACHAM SOFFIA
Consul General
Consulate General of Chile
870 Market St., Suite 1062
San Francisco 94102
Phone: 415/982-7662   Fax: 415/982-2384

Mr. Carlos LOPEZ
Honorary Consular Agent
Honorary Consulate of Chile
1376 Johnson St.
P.O. Box 9054
Santa Clara 94025
Phone: 415/688-3847   Fax: 415/322-6403

Florida

Mr. Luis Gabriel LARRAIN CRUZ
Consul General
Consulate General of Chile
800 Brickell Ave., Suite 1230
Miami 33131
Phone: 305/371-3219   Fax: 305/374-4270

Hawaii

Mr. Keith E. ADAMSON

Honorary Consul
Honorary Consulate of Chile
1860 Ala Moana Blvd., Suite 1900
Honolulu 96815
Phone: 808/949-2850

Illinois

Mr. Luis AYALA
Consul
Consulate of Chile
875 N. Michigan Ave., Suite 3352
Chicago 60611
Phone: 312/654-8780   Fax: 312/654-8948

Louisiana

Mr. Angel Pelayo CARRERAS
Honorary Consul
Honorary Consulate of Chile
World Trade Center, 2 Canal St., 26th Fl.
P.O. Box 60046
New Orleans 70130
Phone: 504/528-3364

Massachusetts

Mr. Paul William GARBER
Honorary Consul
Honorary Consulate of Chile
79 Milk St., Suite 600
Boston 02109
Phone: 617/426-1678   Fax: 617/426-6925

New York

Mr. Ovid Alejandro HARASICH MISERDA
Consul General
Consulate General of Chile
866 United Nations Plaza, Suite 302
New York 10017
Phone: 212/980-3366   Fax: 212/688-5879

Pennsylvania

Mrs. Lucia AVETIKIAN DERENART
Consul General
Consulate General of Chile
Public Ledger Bldg., 446 6th and Chestnut
Philadelphia 19106
Phone: 215/829-9520   Fax: 215/829-0594

Puerto Rico

Mr. Ricardo Enrique PLAZA DUCO
Consul General
Consulate General of Chile
1509 Lopez Landron, Suite 800
Santurce 00911
Phone: 809/725-6365

South Carolina

Mr. Carlos SALINAS
Honorary Consul
Honorary Consulate of Chile
948 Equestrian Dr.
Mount Pleasant 29464
Phone: 803/881-6224

Texas

Ms. Dorothy J. REID
Honorary Consul
Honorary Consulate of Chile
3500 Oak Lawn Ave.
Suite 110
Dallas 75219-4343

Phone: 214/528-2731   Fax: 214/522-7167

Mr. Luis WINTER YGUALT
Consul General
Consulate General of Chile
1360 Post Oak Blvd., Suite 2330
Houston 77056
Phone: 713/621-5853   Fax: 713/961-3910

Utah

Mr. Mario MELENDEZ
Honorary Consul
Honorary Consulate of Chile
130 S. 500th E., Suite 510
Salt Lake City 84102
Phone: 801/531-1292

Washington

Mr. Jorge D. GILBERT
Honorary Consul
Honorary Consulate of Chile
700 Sleater-Kinney Rd., SE - Suite B261
Olympia 98503
Phone: 360/754-8747

China

California

Mr. FENG Shu Sen
Consul General
Consulate General of China
443 Shatto Place
Los Angeles 90020
Phone: 213/807-8088   Fax: 213/380-1961

Mr. WANG Yu Shang
Consul General
Consulate General of China
1450 Laguna St.
San Francisco 94115
Phone: 415/563-4857   Fax: 415/563-0494

Illinois

Mr. HUANG Dong Bi
Consul General
Consulate General of China
100 W. Erie St.
Chicago 60610
Phone: 312/803-0095   Fax: 312/803-0105

Mr. YOU Shao Zhong
Consul
Education Office - China
3322 W. Peterson Ave.
Chicago 60659
Phone: 312/463-9187

New York

Mr. QUI Sheng Yun
Consul General
Consulate General of China
520 12th Ave.
New York 10036
Phone: 212/330-7409   Fax: 212/502-0245

Texas

Mr. WU Zu Rong
Consul General
Consulate General of China
3417 Montrose Blvd.
Houston 77006

Phone: 713/524-4311   Fax: 713/524-7656

Colombia

California

Ms. Consuelo PEDRAZA
Consul General
Consulate General of Colombia
8383 Wilshire Blvd., Suite 420
Beverly Hills 90211
Phone: 213/653-4299   Fax: 213/653-2964

Mr. Roberto MARINO GARCIA
Deputy Consul General
Deputy Consul Gen. of Colombia - Trade Office
6100 Wilshire Blvd., Suite 1170
Los Angeles 90048

Mr. Luis Felipe SUAREZ
Consul General
Consulate General of Colombia
595 Market St., Suite 2130
San Francisco 94105
Phone: 415/495-7195   Fax: 415/777-3731

District of Columbia

Mrs. Consuelo SANCHEZ-DURAN
Consul
Consulate General of Colombia
1825 Connecticut Ave., NW
Washington 20009
Phone: 202/332-7476

Florida

Mr. Camilo CANO
Consul General
Consulate General of Colombia
280 Aragon Ave.
Coral Gables 33134
Phone: 305/448-5558   Fax: 305/441-9537

Mr. Luis G. ECHEVERRI
Deputy Consul General
Trade Office Colombia
1001 South Bay Shore Dr., Suite 1904
Miami 33131
Phone: 305/374-3144

Consulate of Colombia
A.D.P. Bldg., 1211 N. Westshore Blvd.
Suite 411
Tampa 33607
Phone: 813/875-1499

Georgia

Ms. Rocio OSORIO DE BARRERA
Consul
Consulate of Colombia
3379 Peachtree Rd., Suite 555
Atlanta 30326
Phone: 404/237-1045   Fax: 404/237-7957

Illinois

Dr. Carlos Alfonso NEGRET
Consul General
Consulate General of Colombia
500 N. Michigan Ave., Suite 2040
Chicago 60611
Phone: 312/923-1196   Fax: 312/923-1197

Louisiana

Mr. Gabriel DE VEGA

Consul General
Consulate General of Colombia
2 Canal Street, Suite 1844
World Trade Center
New Orleans 70130
Phone: 504/525-5580   Fax: 504/525-4903

Massachusetts

Mr. Felipe ZULETA LLERAS
Consul
Consulate General of Colombia
535 Boylston St., 11th Floor
Boston 02116
Phone: 617/536-6222   Fax: 617/536-9372

New York

Mr. Carlos Julio GAITAN
Consul General
Consulate General of Colombia
10 E. 46th St.
New York 10017
Phone: 212/370-0004   Fax: 212/972-1725

Mr. Feranando Eduardo URDANETA WIESNER
Deputy Consul General
Trade Office - Colombia
277 Park Ave., 47th Floor
New York 10172-4797
Phone: 212/223-1120

Puerto Rico

Mr. David SIMMONDS VALENCIA
Consul
Trade Office - Colombia
Banco Bilbao Vizcaya Plaza
1510 Esq. San Patricio
Caparra 00968
Phone: 787/273-1444   Fax: 787/273-7006

Ms. Ligia LONDONO
Consul General
Consulate General of Colombia
Edificio Mercantil Plaza 818
Ponce De Leon Avenue
Hato Rey 00918
Phone: 787/754-6885   Fax: 787/754-1675

Texas

Mr. Roberto SERRANO
Consul General
Consulate General of Colombia
2990 Richmond Ave., Suite 544
Houston 77098
Phone: 713/527-8919   Fax: 713/529-3395

Cook Islands

California

Mr. Metua NGARUPE
Honorary Consul
Honorary Consulate of Cook Islands
6033 W. Century Blvd., Suite 690
Los Angeles 90045
Phone: 310/216-2872

Hawaii

Mr. Robert E. WORTHINGTON
Honorary Consul
Honorary Consulate of the Cook Islands
144 Ke Ala Ola Rd.
Honolulu 96817

Phone: 808/847-6377

Costa Rica

California

Mrs. Ruth Susy GARCIA ULATE
Consul General
Consulate General of Costa Rica
1605 W. Olympic Blvd., Suite 400
Los Angeles 90015
Phone: 213/380-7791

Ms. Anna V. PARIS CHAVERRI
Consul General
Consulate General of Costa Rica
4007 S. Camino Del Rio, Suite 107
San Diego 92108
Phone: 619/563-6441

Mr. Eduardo CORDERO ANGULO
Consul General
Consulate General of Costa Rica
870 Market St., Room 546-548
San Francisco 94102
Phone: 415/392-8488

Colorado

Mr. Tito CHAVERRI
Honorary Consul
Honorary Consulate General of Costa Rica
3356 Xenia St.
Denver 80231-4542
Phone: 303/696-8211   Fax: 303/696-1110

Florida

Mr. Carlos Eduardo ODIO SOTO
Consul General
Consulate General of Costa Rica
Mission Hills Plaza
2907 SR 590, Suite 12
Clearwater 33759
Phone: 813/248-6741

Ms. Maria Eugenia SOTO VILLEGAS
Consul General
Consulate General of Costa Rica
1600 NW Le Jeune Rd., Suite 102
Miami 33126
Phone: 305/871-7485   Fax: 305/871-0860

Georgia

Mrs. Sheylla J. BINGHAM WANCHOPE
Consul General
Consulate General of Costa Rica
1870 The Exchange, Suite 100
Atlanta 30339
Phone: 404/951-7025   Fax: 770/951-7025

Illinois

Mr. Daniel Francisco BOLANOS ZAMORA
Consul General
Consulate General of Costa Rica
185 N. Wabash Ave., Suite 1123
Chicago 60601
Phone: 312/263-2772   Fax: 312/263-5807

Louisiana

Mrs. Victoria Eugenia ECHEVERRIA
GUTIERREZ
Consul General
Consulate General of Costa Rica
4532 W. Napoleon Ave., Suite 112

Metairie 70001
Phone: 504/887-8131

Massachusetts

Dr. Sherman Edward FEIN
Honorary Consul
Honorary Consulate of Costa Rica
52 Mulberry St.
Springfield 01105
Phone: 413/781-5400   Fax: 413/739-0801

Minnesota

Mr. Anthony L. ANDERSEN
Honorary Consul
Honorary Consulate of Costa Rica
2424 Territorial Rd.
St. Paul 55114
Phone: 612/236-4318   Fax: 612/645-4684

New Mexico

Consulate of Costa Rica
7033 Luella Anne Dr., NE
Albuquerque 87109
Phone: 505/822-1420

New York

Ms. Maria Elena VEGA-BESDANSKY
Consul
Consulate General of Costa Rica
80 Wall St., Suite 718
New York 10005
Phone: 212/425-2620   Fax: 212/785-6818

North Carolina

Consulate General of Costa Rica
3516 University Dr., Suite A
Durham 27707

Pennsylvania

Consulate General of Costa Rica
1411 Walnut St., Suite 200
Philadelphia 19102
Phone: 215/564-4415

Puerto Rico

Mr. Carlos PANIAGUA VALVERDE
Consul General
Consulate General of Costa Rica
Urb. Rio Piedras Heights, 1732 Yenisey St.
Rio Piedras 00926
Phone: 809/282-6747

Texas

Consulate of Costa Rica
1730 E. O Horf, Unit 320
Austin 78741
Phone: 512/445-0023

Mr. Carlos Arturo TERAN PARIS
Consul General
Consulate General of Costa Rica
2901 Wilcrest Dr., Suite 275
Houston 77042
Phone: 713/266-0484   Fax: 713/266-1527

Ms. Marta Celcilia ROJAS OROZCO
Consul
Consulate of Costa Rica
6836 San Pedro, Suite 206-B
San Antonio 78216

Phone: 210/308-8623

Cote d'Ivoire

California

Mr. Edgar De Pue OSGOOD
Honorary Consul General
Honorary Consulate General of Cote d'Ivoire
Pier 23
San Francisco 94111
Phone: 415/391-0176

Michigan

Mr. Harold Richard VARNER
Honorary Consul
Honorary Consulate of Cote d'Ivoire
1101 Washington Blvd.
Detroit 48226

Croatia

California

Mr. Miso MUNIVRANA
Consul General
Consulate General of Croatia
11766 Wilshire Blvd., Suite 710
Los Angeles 90025
Phone: 310/477-1009   Fax: 310/477-1866

Minnesota

Mr. Boris A. MISKIC
Honorary Consul General
Honorary Consulate General of Croatia
4119 White Bear Pw. - Suite 210
St. Paul 55110
Phone: 612/429-6183   Fax: 612/429-6079

New Jersey

Croatian National Tourist Office
300 Lanidex Plaza
Parsippany 07054
Phone: 973/428-0707   Fax: 973/428-3386

New York

Mr. Vjekoslav KARLOVCAN
Consul General
Consulate General of Croatia
369 Lexington Ave., 11th Floor
New York 10017
Phone: 212/599-3066   Fax: 212/599-3106

Ohio

Mr. Domagoj SOLA
Consul General
Consulate General of Croatia
34900 Lakeshore Blvd.
Eastlake 44094
Phone: 440/951-4246   Fax: 440/951-4268

Cyprus

Arizona

Mr. Stanley J. DRU
Honorary Consul
Honorary Consulate of Cyprus

1277 E. Missouri, Unit 214
Phoenix 85014
Phone: 602/264-9701   Fax: 602/274-8373

California

Mr. Andreas C. KYPRIANIDES
Honorary Consul General
Honorary Consulate General of Cyprus
4219 Coolidge Ave.
Los Angeles 90066
Phone: 310/397-0771   Fax: 310/398-6775

Dr. Anastassios Kyriako SIMONIDIS
Honorary Consul General
Honorary Consulate of Cyprus
205 Crocker Ave.
Piedmont 94610-1214
Phone: 510/547-5689   Fax: 510/547-4177

Georgia

Mr. Kyriakos M. MICHAELIDES
Honorary Consul
Honorary Consulate of Cyprus
895 Somerset Dr.
Atlanta 30327
Phone: 770/941-3764   Fax: 770/941-2109

Illinois

Dr. Charles KANAKIS
Honorary Consul
Honorary Consulate of Cyprus
9301 Golf Rd., Suite 303
Des Plaines 60016
Phone: 708/296-0064   Fax: 847/296-4857

Indiana

Mr. Evangelos COUFOUDAKIS
Honorary Consul
Honorary Consulate of Cyprus
2402 Oakridge Rd.
Fort Wayne 46805
Phone: 219/481-6897   Fax: 219/481-6985

Louisiana

Mr. Symeon C. SYMEONIDES
Honorary Consul
Honorary Consulate of Cyprus
410 LSU Law Center
Baton Rouge 70803-1000
Phone: 504/388-8701   Fax: 504/388-5935

Massachusetts

Mr. John C. PAPAJOHN
Honorary Consul
Honorary Consulate of Cyprus
70-7 Kirkland St.
Cambridge 02138
Phone: 617/497-0219   Fax: 617/497-2002

Michigan

Mr. Steve G. STYLIANOU
Honorary Consul
Honorary Consulate of Cyprus
15706 Michigan Ave.
Dearborn 48126
Phone: 513/582-1411   Fax: 313/582-6791

New York

Mr. Pantelakis ELIADES
Consul General

Consulate General of Cyprus
13 E. 40th St., 5th Floor
New York 10016
Phone: 212/213-9100   Fax: 212/685-7316

Tourist Office   Cyprus
13 E. 40th St.
New York 10016
Phone: 212/683-5280

Mr. Michael A. MICHAELIDES
Consul
Maritime Office - Cyprus
13 E. 40th St., 5th Floor
New York 10016
Phone: 212/447-1790   Fax: 212/685-7316

North Carolina

Dr. Takey Harry CRIST
Honorary Consul
Honorary Consulate of Cyprus
200 Memorial Dr., Suite 1974
Jacksonville 28546
Phone: 910/353-1389

Oregon

Mr. Alexander CHRISTY
Honorary Consul
Honorary Consulate of Cyprus
Mayer Bldg.
1130 Morrison St., SW - Suite 510
Portland 97205
Phone: 503/227-1411

Pennsylvania

Mr. James ORATIS
Honorary Consul
Honorary Consulate of Cyprus
7714 Langdon Street
Philadelphia 19111
Phone: 215/728-6980

Texas

Mr. William C. CRASSAS
Honorary Consul General
Honorary Consulate General of Cyprus
320 S. 66th St. - P.O. Box 9049
Houston 77071
Phone: 713/928-2264   Fax: 713/928-2093

Virginia

Mr. Thomas KYRUS
Honorary Consul
Honorary Consulate of Cyprus
2973 Shore Dr., Suite 102
Virginia Beach 23451
Phone: 804/481-3583   Fax: 804/481-6068

Washington

Mr. Vassos Michael DEMETRIOU
Honorary Consul
Honorary Consulate of Cyprus
205 North Lake St., South - Suite 100
Kirkland 98033
Phone: 425/827-1700   Fax: 425/889-0308

Czech Republic

California

Mrs. Ivana HLAVSOVA

Consul General
Consulate General of the Czech Republic
10990 Wilshire Blvd., Suite 1100
Los Angeles 90024
Phone: 310/473-0889   Fax: 310/473-9813

Mr. Richard PIVNICKA
Honorary Consul
Honorary Consulate of the Czech Republic
201 Filbert St., Suite 700
San Francisco 94133
Phone: 415/391-1313   Fax: 415/391-1313

Florida

Mr. Alan S. BECKER
Honorary Consul
Honorary Consulate of the Czech Republic
3111 Stirling Rd.
Ft. Lauderdale 33312
Phone: 954/987-7550   Fax: 954/985-4176

Georgia

Mr. George Alois NOVAK
Honorary Consul
Honorary Consulate of the Czech Republic
2110 Powers Ferry Rd., Suite 220
Atlanta 30339
Phone: 770/951-2922   Fax: 770/951-0751

New York

Mr. Bohuslav John ZAVREL
Honorary Consul
Honorary Consulate of the Czech Republic
10545 Main St.
Clarence 14031
Phone: 716/759-6078   Fax: 716/759-7925

Mr. Petr GANDALOVIC
Consul General
Consulate General of Czech Republic
1109-1111 Madison Ave., First Floor
New York 10028
Phone: 212/535-8814   Fax: 212/717-5064

Oregon

Mrs. Marie Rose AMICCI
Honorary Consul
Honorary Consulate of the Czech Republic
Lincoln Ctr., Five
10200 S.W. Greenburg Rd., Suite 350
Portland 97223
Phone: 503/293-9547   Fax: 503/293-9546

Pennsylvania

Mr. Peter A. RAFAELI
Honorary Consul
Honorary Consulate of the Czech Republic
417 Bethlehem Park
Fort Washington 19034
Phone: 215/646-7777   Fax: 215/646-7770

Texas

Mr. Jerry Garland BARTOS
Honorary Consul
Honorary Consulate of the Czech Republic
3239 Oradell Lane
Dallas 75220
Phone: 214/350-6871   Fax: 214/350-9611

Mr. Raymond Joseph SNOKHOUS
Honorary Consul
Honorary Consulate of the Czech Republic
4544 Post Oak Place, Suite 378

Houston 77027
Phone: 713/629-6963   Fax: 713/523-8694

Denmark

Alabama

Mr. Martin Horst CUNNINGHAM
Honorary Consul
Honorary Consulate of Denmark
1350 Dauphin St.
Mobile 36604
Phone: 205/432-4633   Fax: 334/432-8675

Alaska

Mr. Frank A. DANNER
Honorary Consul
Honorary Consulate of Denmark
3111 C St., Suite 100
Anchorage 99503
Phone: 907/261-7600   Fax: 907/261-7670

Arizona

Mr. Duane Morse ANDERSON
Honorary Consul
Honorary Consulate of Denmark
Valley Ctr., 241 N. Central Ave.
26th Floor
Phoenix 85001
Phone: 602/221-1254   Fax: 602/221-1517

California

Mr. Therkild Strunge THERKILDSEN
Deputy Consul General
Consulate General of Denmark
10877 Wilshire Blvd., Suite 1105
Los Angeles 90024
Phone: 310/443-2090   Fax: 310/443-2099

Mr. William LARSEN
Honorary Consul
Honorary Consulate of Denmark
1405 Savoy Cir.
P.O. Box 80456
San Diego 92107
Phone: 619/224-7640   Fax: 619/223-2376

Mr. Paul E. BACH
Honorary Consul
Honorary Consulate of Denmark
601 Montgomery St., Suite 440
San Francisco 94111
Phone: 415/391-0100   Fax: 415/391-0181

Colorado

Mrs. Nanna Marie SMITH
Honorary Consul
Honorary Consulate of Denmark
5353 W. Dartmouth Ave., Suite 508
Denver 80227
Phone: 303/980-9100   Fax: 303/985-9697

Florida

Mr. Larry Joe WARREN
Honorary Consul
Honorary Consulate of Denmark
9620 Dave Rawis Blvd.
P.O. Box 8689
Blount Island 32226
Phone: 904/696-7750   Fax: 904/696-7760

Mrs. Anne-Lise Dirks GUSTAFSON

Honorary Consul
Honorary Consulate of Denmark
Gables Int'l Plaza, 2655 Le Jeune Rd.
Penthouse 1-D
Coral Gables 33134
Phone: 305/446-0020   Fax: 305/448-4151

Mrs. Shirley KNIGHT
Honorary Consul
Honorary Consulate of Denmark
1701 Maritime Blvd.
Tampa 33605
Phone: 813/247-4550   Fax: 813/247-5420

Georgia

Mr. William T. BROWN
Honorary Consul
Honorary Consulate of Denmark
550 E. York St.
P.O. Box 9267
Savannah 31412
Phone: 912/236-0226   Fax: 912/236-6571

Hawaii

Mr. Laurence VOGEL
Honorary Consul
Honorary Consulate of Denmark
2626 Pauahi Tower, 1001 Bishop St.
Honolulu 96813
Phone: 808/545-2028   Fax: 808/545-5025

Illinois

Mr. Bent KIILERICH
Consul General
Consulate General of Denmark
875 N. Michigan Ave., Suite 3430
Chicago 60611
Phone: 312/787-8780   Fax: 312/787-8744

Iowa

Mr. Lowell Bernard KRAMME
Honorary Consul
Honorary Consulate of Denmark
Grand View College
1200 Grandview Ave.
Des Moines 50316-1599
Phone: 515/263-2802

Louisiana

Mr. Thomas Kendall WININGDER
Honorary Consul
Honorary Consulate of Denmark
321 St. Charles Ave.
New Orleans 70130
Phone: 504/586-8300   Fax: 504/523-1967

Maryland

Mr. Timothy Connor MCNAMARA
Honorary Consul
Honorary Consulate of Denmark
Sun Life Bldg., 20 S. Charles St.
Baltimore 21201-3220
Phone: 410/783-7575   Fax: 410/625-3848

Massachusetts

Mr. Christian Georg HALBY
Honorary Consul
Honorary Consulate of Denmark
Statler Bldg., 20 Park Plaza
Suite 436
Boston 02116
Phone: 617/542-1415   Fax: 617/426-9236

Michigan

Mr. David W. CHRISTENSEN
Honorary Consul
Honorary Consulate of Denmark
5510 N. Woodward Ave.
Detroit 48202
Phone: 313/875-9856   Fax: 313/875-8522

Minnesota

Ms. Anelise SAWKINS
Honorary Consul
Honorary Consulate of Denmark
60 S. 6th St., 17th Fl.
Minneapolis 55402
Phone: 612/371-7229   Fax: 612/371-2843

Missouri

Mr. Elcar A. NIELSEN
Honorary Consul
Honorary Consulate of Denmark
1700 W. 12th St.
P.O. Box 4046
Kansas City 64101
Phone: 800/821-2702   Fax: 816/421-0626

Mr. Martin John TOFT
Honorary Consul
Honorary Consulate of Denmark
100 S. 4th St., Suite 700
St. Louis 63102
Phone: 314/259-4500   Fax: 314/259-4599

Nebraska

Mr. Bruce Ronnow LAURITZEN
Honorary Consul
Honorary Consulate of Denmark
1620 Dodge St.
Omaha 68102
Phone: 402/633-3033   Fax: 402/342-4332

New York

Mr. Hans Torben GRUNNET
Consul General
Consulate General of Denmark
885 Second Ave., 18th Floor
New York 10017
Phone: 212/223-4545   Fax: 212/754-1904

Ohio

Mr. H. Stephen MADSEN
Honorary Consul
Honorary Consulate of Denmark
3200 National City Center
Cleveland 44114
Phone: 216/621-0200   Fax: 216/696-0740

Oklahoma

Mr. William W. TALLEY
Honorary Consul
Honorary Consulate of Denmark
9400 Broadway Ext., Suite 130
Oklahoma City 73114-7499
Phone: 405/478-0600   Fax: 405/475-0306

Oregon

Mr. Ingolf NOTO
Honorary Consul
Honorary Consulate of Denmark
900 S.W. Fifth Ave., Suite 2300
Portland 97204

Phone: 503/294-9307   Fax: 503/220-2480

Pennsylvania

Mr. Alfred J. KUFFLER
Honorary Consul
Honorary Consulate of Denmark
Public Ledger Bldg.
965 Independence Sq., 9th Floor
Philadelphia 19106
Phone: 215/625-9900   Fax: 215/625-0185

Mr. George Robert KNAPP
Honorary Consul
Honorary Consulate of Denmark
Tippins Industries
435 Butler St.
Pittsburgh 15223
Phone: 412/782-7253   Fax: 412/782-7210

Puerto Rico

Mr. Jose O. INIGUEZ BUSTO
Honorary Consul
Honorary Consulate of Denmark
360 San Francisco St.
San Juan 00901
Phone: 809/725-2532

South Carolina

Mr. George Lamb RIVERS
Honorary Consul
Honorary Consulate of Denmark
28 Broad St.
P.O. Box 993
Charleston 29402
Phone: 803/577-4000   Fax: 803/724-6600

Tennessee

Mr. Richard HELLER
Honorary Consul
Honorary Consulate of Denmark
Vanderbilt University Hospital
D 1120 Medical Ctr., N.
Nashville 37232
Phone: 615/322-3288   Fax: 615/322-3764

Texas

Mr. Ib Michael GERSMANN
Honorary Consul
Honorary Consulate of Denmark
22 Townhouse Ln.
P.O. Box 4585
Corpus Christi 78408
Phone: 512/991-3012

Mr. Harlan R. CROW
Honorary Consul
Honorary Consulate of Denmark
3200 Trammel Crow Center, 2001 Ross Ave.
Dallas 75201
Phone: 214/863-4221   Fax: 214/863-4249

Mr. Ray Jens DAUGBJERG
Honorary Consul
Honorary Consulate of Denmark
5 Post Oak Park, Suite 2370
Houston 77027
Phone: 713/622-9018   Fax: 713/622-7512

Utah

Mr. Niels Erik VALENTINER
Honorary Consul
Honorary Consulate of Denmark
524 S. 600 E.

Salt Lake City 84102
Phone: 801/531-7061   Fax: 801/531-9850

Virgin Islands

Mr. Soren BLAK
Honorary Consul
Honorary Consulate of Denmark
Havensight Mall, Scandinavian Ctr., Bldg. 3
Charlotte Amalie 00804
Phone: 809/776-0656

Virginia

Mr. William Edward RACHELS
Honorary Consul
Honorary Consulate of Denmark
1800 Nations Bank
Norfolk 23510-2197
Phone: 804/628-5568   Fax: 804/628-5566

Washington

Mr. Erik D. LAURSEN
Honorary Consul
Honorary Consulate of Denmark
6204 Mercer Way
Mercer Island 98040
Phone: 206/230-0888   Fax: 206/230-0888

Wisconsin

Mr. Barry N. JAMES
Honorary Consul
Honorary Consulate of Denmark
2095 Le Jardin Ct.
Brookfield 53005
Phone: 414/792-0799   Fax: 414/253-2277

Dominica

New York

Mrs. Edna Justina MURPHY
Consul General
Consulate General of Dominica
820 2nd Ave., Suite 900B
New York 10017
Phone: 212/949-0853   Fax: 212/808-4975

Dominican Republic

Alabama

Mrs. Maria Teresa DE DIAZ
Consul
Consulate of the Dominican Republic
4009 Old Shell Rd., Apt. E-16
Mobile 36608
Phone: 205/342-5648

California

Consulate General of Dominican Republic
548 South Spring St., Suite 309
Los Angeles 90013

Mr. Carmen Olga DE PERALTA
Honorary Consul
Honorary Consulate of the Dominican Republic
2490 Paloma
Pasadena 91104

Mr. Manlio DORREJO JIMENEZ
Consul General

Consulate General of the Dominican Republic
870 Market St., Suite 982
San Francisco 94103
Phone: 415/982-5144   Fax: 415/982-0237

Colorado

Mr. Jose Luis RODRIGUEZ VALLE
Honorary Consul
Honorary Consulate of the Dominican Republic
Applewood Knolls Dr.
Lakewood 80215

Florida

Mr. Alcibiades PEREZ FRIAS
Consul
Consulate of the Dominican Republic
1919 Beach Way Rd., Suite 6-0
Jacksonville 32207
Phone: 904/398-1118

Dr. Ramon S. PITTALUGA
Honorary Consul General
Hon. Consulate Gen. of the Dominican Republic
1038 Brickell Ave.
Miami 33131
Phone: 305/358-3221   Fax: 305/358-2318

Mr. Don Ray SPIVEY
Honorary Consul
Honorary Consulate of the Dominican Republic
2901 W. Tamiami Circle
Sarasota 33580

Georgia

Mr. Horace Holden SIBLEY
Honorary Counsel
Consulate General of Dominican Republic
191 Peachtree St., Suite 4600
Atlanta 30303
Phone: 404/572-4814   Fax: 404/215-3996

Illinois

Mr. Osvaldo C. MENA Y ARISTY
Honorary Vice Consul
Consulate General of the Dominican Republic
3228 W. North Ave.
Chicago 60647
Phone: 312/772-6363

Louisiana

Mrs. Nelly Mariana AGUILAR
Honorary Consul
Honorary Consulate of the Dominican Republic
4866 Whitehaven St.
Baton Rouge 70808

Mr. Glenn BROUSSARD
Honorary Consul
Honorary Consulate of the Dominican Republic
3566 Monroe St.
Lake Charles 70605
Phone: 318/477-4506

Mr. Joaquin A. BALAGUER RICARDO
Consul General
Consulate General of the Dominican Republic
611 Gravier St., Suite 1647
New Orleans 70130
Phone: 504/522-1843   Fax: 504/522-1007

Massachusetts

Consul General
Consulate General of the Dominican Republic

The Statler Bldg..
20 Park Plaza, Suite 601
Boston 02116
Phone: 617/267-4630   Fax: 617/482-8133

Michigan

Mr. Ramon SOUFFRONT
Honorary Consul
Consulate of the Dominican Republic
2171 Babcock
Troy 48084
Phone: 313/643-7022

Minnesota

Mr. Ralph S. PARKER
Honorary Consul General
Hon. Consulate Gen. of the Dominican Republic
One Financial Plaza, 120 S. 6th St., Suite 1910
Minneapolis 55402
Phone: 312/339-7566   Fax: 612/339-9055

Missouri

Mr. Fernando Emilio PEGUERO
Honorary Consul
Honorary Consulate of the Dominican Republic
1173 Rico Dr.
St. Louis 63126
Phone: 314/454-0266

New York

Ms. Delia Josefina FELIZ PENA
Consul General
Consulate General of the Dominican Republic
1501 Broadway, Suite 410
New York 10036
Phone: 212/768-2480   Fax: 212/768-2677

Ohio

Dr. Bolivar ALBAINY
Honorary Consul
Honorary Consulate of the Dominican Republic
6363 York Rd.
Parma Heights 44130
Phone: 216/932-7489

Pennsylvania

Mrs. Caperuza DE ALMONTE
Vice Consul
Consulate General of the Dominican Republic
5th and Chestnut Sts., Room 422
Philadelphia 19106
Phone: 215/923-3006   Fax: 215/923-3007

Puerto Rico

Mr. Antonio ROIG
Honorary Consul
Honorary Consulate of the Dominican Republic
Minerva 19
Humacao 00661
Phone: 809/852-0677

Mr. Eddy E. BERGES DREYFOUS
Honorary Consul
Honorary Consulate of the Dominican Republic
Calle 4, Suite H-18
Manati 00612

Mr. Rafael Diaz MARTINEZ
Consul
Consulate General of the Dominican Republic
30 Calle McKinley, Box 3067
2nd Floor

Mayaguez 00708
Phone: 809/833-0007

Mr. Usino GUZMAN LIRIANO
Consul
Consulate of the Dominican Republic
Marginal, Unit 303
Ponce 00731
Phone: 809/842-9004

Mr. Juan Felipe PENA
Vice Consul
Consulate General of the Dominican Republic
1612 Ponce De Leon Ave., Room 7
Santurce 00909
Phone: 809/725-9550

Texas

Mr. James Lynn ROBERTS
Honorary Vice Consul
Honorary Consulate of the Dominican Republic
12127 Ridgelake Dr.
Dallas 75218
Phone: 214/341-3250

Mr. Angel Plinio ROMERO BELTRE
Honorary Consul
Honorary Consulate of the Dominican Republic
6977 Granero Dr.
El Paso 79912

Mr. Modesto Lucas DIAZ MONTANO
Consul
Consulate of the Dominican Republic
3300 Gessner Rd., Suite 113
Houston 77024
Phone: 713/467-4372   Fax: 713/780-1543

Virgin Islands

Consulate of the Dominican Republic
5 & 6 Curacao Gage, Suite 1
Charlotte Amalie 00804

Ecuador

California

Dr. Homero A. LARREA
Consul General
Consulate General of Ecuador
548 S. Spring St., Suite 602
Los Angeles 90013
Phone: 213/628-3014   Fax: 213/689-8418

Mrs. Martha Celcilia ACOSTA DE ANDERSON
Consul
Consulate General of Ecuador
455 Market St., Suite 980
San Francisco 94105
Phone: 415/957-5921   Fax: 415/957-5923

Florida

Ms. Teresita De MENDENDEZ URAGA
Consul General
Consulate General of Ecuador
B.I.V. Tower
1101 Brickell Ave., Suite M102
Miami 33131
Phone: 305/539-8214   Fax: 305/539-8313

Mr. Emilio Gonzalo RUPERTI VELEZ
Consul - Executive Director
Ecuador Trade Center
3785 N.W. 82nd Ave., Suite 317
Miami 33166

Phone: 305/716-5252   Fax: 305/716-9296

Illinois

Mr. Franklin DE LA TORRE JARIN
Consul General
Consulate General of Ecuador
500 N. Michigan Ave., Suite 1510
Chicago 60611
Phone: 312/329-0266   Fax: 312/329-0359

Louisiana

Mr. Mario Rene ALEMAN SALVADOR
Consul General
Consulate General of Ecuador
1312 Int. Trade Mart Bldg., 2 Canal St.
New Orleans 70130
Phone: 504/523-3229   Fax: 504/522-9675

Maryland

Mr. Manuel L. JARAMILLO
Honorary Consul
Honorary Consulate of Ecuador
2925 N. Charles St.
Baltimore 21218
Phone: 301/889-4422   Fax: 410/889-0806

Massachusetts

Ms. Ivonnne A-BAKI
Honorary Consul General
Honorary Consulate General of Ecuador
32 Garrison St., Suite 4-302
Boston 02116
Phone: 617/859-0028

Michigan

Mr. Hector A. BUENO
Honorary Consul
Honorary Consulate of Ecuador
136 State St.
Pontiac 48341-1450
Phone: 313/332-7356   Fax: 313/332-7881

Nevada

Mr. Peter Gustav JARAMILLO
Honorary Consul
Honorary Consulate of Ecuador
3500 Paradise Rd.
Las Vegas 89109
Phone: 313/332-7356   Fax: 313/332-7881

New Jersey

Ms. Maria Azucena CABALLERO MEIER
Consular Agent
Consulate of Ecuador
1180 Raymond Blvd., Suite 611
Newark 07102

New York

Ecuador Commercial Office
399 Park Ave., Suite 28B
New York 10022

Mr. Jose Luis MORENA GUERRA
Consul General
Consulate General of Ecuador
800 Second Ave., Suite 501
New York 10017
Phone: 212/808-0170   Fax: 212/808-0188

Pennsylvania

Mr. Luis Fernando ROBERT ANDINO
Consul
Consulate General of Ecuador
Public Ledger Bldg., Independence Sq.
Suite 1015-1017
Philadelphia 19106
Phone: 215/925-9060   Fax: 215/676-3481

Puerto Rico

Mr. Carlos ARCOS-MOSCOSO
Honorary Consul
Honorary Consulate of Ecuador
301 Calle Recinto Sur, Suite 401A
San Juan 00901
Phone: 809/724-2356

Texas

Mr. Victor Eduardo GOMEZJURADO CASTRO
Consul General
Consulate General of Ecuador
4200 Westheimer, Suite 218
Houston 77027
Phone: 713/622-1787   Fax: 713/622-8105

Egypt

California

Mr. Abdel Monein AHMAD
Vice Consul
Commercial Office of Egypt
1255 Post St., Suite 910
San Francisco 94109
Phone: 415/771-1995   Fax: 415/771-1293

Ms. Hagar Abdel EL ISLAMBOULY
Consul General
Consulate General of Egypt
3001 Pacific Ave.
San Francisco 94115
Phone: 415/346-9700   Fax: 415/346-9480

Mr. Mohammed Ibrahim AGAMI
Consul
Egyptian Press Office
Cathedral Hill Office Bldg.
1255 Post St., Suite 1034
San Francisco 94109
Phone: 415/346-3427   Fax: 415/346-3430

Illinois

Mr. Atef Anwar ALI
Consul General
Consulate General of Egypt
500 N. Michigan Ave.
Chicago 60611
Phone: 312/828-9162   Fax: 312/828-9167

Ms. Mahy Abbas KOTB
Consul
Egyptian Tourist Office
645 N. Michigan Ave., Suite 829
Chicago 60611
Phone: 312/280-4666   Fax: 312/280-4788

New York

Ms. Soheir Salah ZAKI
Consul General
Consulate General of Egypt
1110 2nd Ave.
New York 10022
Phone: 212/759-7120   Fax: 212/308-7643

Mr. Abdel-Moneim Rashad MOHAMED

Consul
Egyptian Tourist Office
630 5th Ave.
New York 10022
Phone: 212/246-6960

Mr. Alaa Abdel KHALIL
Consul
Egyptian Economic and Commercial Office
45 Rockefeller Plaza, Suite 1507
New York 10111
Phone: 212/399-9898

Texas

Mr. Fouad Mahmoud CHERIF
Consul General
Consulate General of Egypt
2000 West Loop South
Houston 77027
Phone: 713/961-4915   Fax: 713/961-3868

El Salvador

Arizona

Mr. Tracy R. THOMAS
Honorary Consul
Honorary Consulate of El Salvador
4521 E. Charles Dr.
P.O. Box 2979
Paradise Valley 85253
Phone: 602/948-4899   Fax: 602/443-4838

California

Mr. Gerardo Antonio SOL MIXCO
Consul General
Consulate General of El Salvador
3450 Wilshire Blvd., Suite 250
Los Angeles 90010
Phone: 213/383-8580   Fax: 212/383-8599

Mr. Carlos E. GONZALEZ
Consul General
Consulate General of El Salvador
870 Market St., Suite 508
San Francisco 94102
Phone: 415/781-7924

Florida

Mr. Fernando Ernesto QUINONEZ MEZA
Consul General
Consulate General of El Salvador
300 Biscayne Blvd. Way, Suite 1020
Miami 33131
Phone: 305/371-8850   Fax: 305/371-7820

Mr. Fernando Ernesto QUINONEZ MEZA
Consul General
Consulate General of El Salvador
300 Biscayne Blvd. Way, Suite 1020
Miami 33131
Phone: 305/371-8850   Fax: 305/371-7820

Illinois

Consulate General of El Salvador
104 S. Michigan Ave., Suite 423
Chicago 60603
Phone: 312/332-1393

Louisiana

Mr. Emilio R. GARCIA PRIETO
Consul General

Consulate General of El Salvador
1136 Int. Trade Mart
New Orleans 70130
Phone: 504/522-4266   Fax: 504/523-5237

Massachusetts

Ms. Lorena SOL DE POOL
Consul
Consulate of El Salvador
222 3rd St., Suite 1221
Cambridge 02139

Missouri

Mr. Michael Jay BOBROFF
Honorary Consul
Honorary Consulate of El Salvador
7730 Forsyth, Suite 150
St. Louis 63105
Phone: 314/862-0300

New York

Ms. Marta Patricia MAZA DE PITTSFORD
Consul General
Consulate General of El Salvador
46 Park Ave.
New York 10016
Phone: 212/889-3608   Fax: 212/679-2835

Pennsylvania

Mrs. Ana Maria KEENE
Honorary Consul
Honorary Consulate of El Salvador
119 Bleddyn Rd.
Ardmore 19003

Puerto Rico

Ms. Maria Teresa DE ESTEVEZ
Honorary Consul General
Honorary Consulate General of El Salvador
Villa Caparra
Calle K-19
Bayamon 00619

Texas

Mrs. Rosanna C. SALAVERRIA DE
GUTIERREZ
Consul General
Consulate General of El Salvador
Oakbrook Plaza
1555 W. Mockingbird Lane, Suite 216
Dallas 75235
Phone: 214/637-0732

Ms. Astrid Maria SALAZAR DE ARIZ
Consul General
Consulate General of El Salvador
6420 Hillcroft St., Suite 100
Houston 77081
Phone: 713/270-6239   Fax: 713/270-9683

Equatorial Guinea

Florida

Mr. Viktor JIMENO
Honorary Consul General
Honorary Consulate General of Equatorial Guinea
5399 Northwest 36th St., Second Floor
Miami 33133
Phone: 305/871-2094

Estonia

California

Mr. Jaak TREIMAN
Honorary Consul
Honorary Consulate of Estonia
21515 Vanowen St., Suite 211
Canoga Park 91303
Phone: 818/884-5850   Fax: 818/593-2973

New York

Mr. H.E. Ernst Rudolf JAAKSON
Consul General
Consulate General of Estonia
600 Third Ave., 26th Floor
New York 10016
Phone: 212/883-0636   Fax: 212/883-0648

Washington

Mr. Mart KASK
Honorary Consul
Consulate of Estonia
500 Union St., Suite 930
Seattle 98101
Phone: 206/467-6314   Fax: 206/467-8129

Fiji

California

Dr. Narayan Rao RAJU
Honorary Consul
Honorary Consulate of Fiji
1171 Compass Ln., Suite 109
Foster City 94404
Phone: 650/358-4031

Dr. Donald Elbert VINSON
Honorary Consul
Honorary Consulate of Fiji
2050 West 190th St., Suite 102
Torrance 90504
Phone: 310/544-5800   Fax: 310/544-5801

New York

Hon. Brian Brijan SIN
Consul General
Consulate General of Fiji
One United Nations Plaza, 26th Floor
New York 10017
Phone: 212/355-7316

Oregon

Mr. James Willard BOSLEY
Honorary Consul
Honorary Consulate of Fiji
2153 NE Sandy Blvd.
Portland 97232
Phone: 503/231-4649   Fax: 503/231-4626

Finland

Alabama

Mr. Theodore C. KENNEDY
Honorary Consul
Honorary Consulate of Finland
2000 International Park Dr.

Birmingham 35243
Phone: 205/972-6000   Fax: 205/972-6300

Alaska

Mr. Wayne Allan STOLT
Honorary Consul
Honorary Consulate of Finland
1529 P St.
Anchorage 99501-4923
Phone: 907/274-6607   Fax: 907/279-2060

Arizona

Mr. Frank Reid SMITH
Honorary Consul
Honorary Consulate of Finland
Merrill Lynch Bldg., 9744 West Bell Rd.
Sun City 85351
Phone: 602/876-2718   Fax: 602/876-2747

California

Mr. Bert J. SALONEN
Honorary Consul
Honorary Consulate of Finland
1734 Caminito Ardiente
La Jolla 92037
Phone: 619/459-9202   Fax: 619/454-6602

Mrs. Maria Elisabeth SERENIUS
Consul General
Consulate General of Finland
1900 Avenue of the Stars, Suite 1025
Los Angeles 90067
Phone: 310/203-9903   Fax: 310/203-9186

Office for Industry and Technology - Finland
1900 Avenue of the Stars, Suite 1060
Los Angeles 90067
Phone: 213/203-9903

Mr. Richard J. GUGGENHIME
Honorary Consul General
Honorary Consulate General of Finland
333 Bush St., Suite 3012
San Francisco 94104
Phone: 415/772-6649   Fax: 415/772-6268

Colorado

Mr. Daniel L. KAMUNEN
Honorary Consul
Honorary Consulate of Finland
11002 Main Range Trail
Littleton 80127
Phone: 303/972-3790   Fax: 303/972-3790

Connecticut

Mr. Carl Dennis ANDERSON
Honorary Consul
Honorary Consulate of Finland
101 Water St.
Norwich 06360
Phone: 203/886-8845   Fax: 203/886-7376

Florida

Mr. Bill F. SPOHRER
Honorary Consul
Honorary Consulate of Finland
116 Alhambra Circle
Coral Gables 33134
Phone: 305/871-3212   Fax: 305/871-3078

Georgia

Mr. John Devaughn SAUNDERS

Honorary Consul
Honorary Consulate of Finland
1230 Peachtree St., Suite 3100, Promenade 2
Atlanta 30309
Phone: 404/264-2682   Fax: 404/685-6982

Hawaii

Mr. Erkki E. INKINEN
Honorary Consul
Honorary Consulate of Finland
1650 Alamoona Blvd., Apt. 1
Honolulu 96816
Phone: 808/944-8674   Fax: 808/596-0940

Illinois

Mr. Frederick Charles NIEMI
Honorary Consul
Honorary Consulate of Finland
15 Long Common Rd.
Riverside 60546
Phone: 708/442-0635   Fax: 708/442-0466

Louisiana

Mr. James L. SCHUPP
Honorary Consul
Honorary Consulate of Finland
3100 Energy Ctre., 1100 Poydras St.
New Orleans 70163-3100
Phone: 504/523-6451   Fax: 504/524-3257

Maryland

Mr. Edmond J. MORAN
Honorary Consul
Honorary Consulate of Finland
Building "B", 1615 Thames St.
P.O. Box 38400
Baltimore 21231-8400
Phone: 410/732-9600   Fax: 410/732-9622

Massachusetts

Mr. Leonard KOPELMAN
Honorary Consul General
Consulate General of Finland
31 St. James Ave., Suite 700
Boston 02116
Phone: 617/654-1800   Fax: 617/654-1735

Mr. Edwin Eino KAARELA
Honorary Consul
Honorary Consulate of Finland
56 Elm St.
P.O. Box 2226
Fitchburg 01420-2226
Phone: 508/342-6053   Fax: 978/343-6977

Michigan

Mr. Ruben H. NAYBACK
Honorary Consul
Honorary Consulate of Finland
7127 Edinborough Dr.
West Bloomfield 48322
Phone: 313/626-3618

Minnesota

Mr. David J. SPEER
Honorary Consul
Honorary Consulate of Finland
900 Am. Ctr. Bldg., 224 W. Franklin Ave.
Minneapolis 55404-2394
Phone: 612/871-8877

Montana

Mr. Keith Parmelee JOHNSON
Honorary Consul
Honorary Consulate of Finland
1 North-west Bank Bldg.
Butte 59701
Phone: 406/723-5411   Fax: 406/723-6667

New Mexico

Mr. Alan B. CLARK
Honorary Consul
Honorary Consulate of Finland
501 Copper Ave., NW
Albuquerque 87102
Phone: 505/768-5100   Fax: 505/768-5182

New York

Ms. Maija Kaarin LAHTEENMAKI
Consul General
Consulate General of Finland
866 United Nations Plaza, Suite 250
New York 10017
Phone: 212/750-4400   Fax: 212/750-4418

Finland Office for Trade
866 United Nations Plaza, Suite 249
New York 10017
Phone: 212/750-4411

Oregon

Mr. Paul Dennis THOMPSON
Honorary Consul
Honorary Consulate of Finland
108 Franklin St.
Astoria 97103
Phone: 503/325-1700

Mr. Paul Mccord NISKANEN
Honorary Consul
Honorary Consulate of Finland
2730 SW Cedar Hills Blvd.
Beaverton 97005
Phone: 503/526-0391   Fax: 503/526-0902

Pennsylvania

Mr. Bengt Olof JANSSON
Honorary Consul
Honorary Consulate of Finland
112 Christian St.
Philadelphia 19147
Phone: 215/465-5565   Fax: 215/336-3389

Puerto Rico

Mr. Gustavo Adolfo BENITEZ BADRENA
Honorary Consul
Honorary Consulate of Finland
Torremolinos, Guaynabo D St., Room G6
San Juan 00657
Phone: 809/257-1144

Texas

Mr. Edward Fahey WALKER
Honorary Consul
Honorary Consulate of Finland
1445 Ross Ave., Suite 3200
Dallas 75202
Phone: 214/855-4715   Fax: 214/855-4300

Mr. Ronald A. KAPCHE
Honorary Consul
Honorary Consulate of Finland
2190 N. Loop, W., Suite 410
Houston 77018
Phone: 713/680-2727   Fax: 713/552-1676

Utah

Mr. Spencer F. ECCLES
Honorary Consul
Honorary Consulate of Finland
79 S. Main, 2nd Floor
Salt Lake City 84111
Phone: 801/350-5287   Fax: 801/359-6928

Virgin Islands

Mrs. Inga I. HIILIVIRTA
Honorary Consul
Honorary Consulate of Finland
1823 Enighed
PO Box 56
Cruz Bay 00831
Phone: 809/776-6666   Fax: 809/693-8499

Virginia

Mr. David Findlay HOST
Honorary Consul
Honorary Consulate of Finland
World Trade Center, Main St., Suite 820
Norfolk 23510
Phone: 804/627-6286   Fax: 804/627-3948

Washington

Mr. E. Norman WESTERBERG
Honorary Consul
Honorary Consulate of Finland
11045 SE 28th Pl.
Bellevue 98004
Phone: 206/451-3983   Fax: 425/451-8864

France

Alabama

Mr. Philippe W. LATHROP
Honorary Consul
Honorary Consulate of France
31 Inverness Central Pkwy., Suite 100
Birmingham 35243
Phone: 205/995-0733

Alaska

Mrs. Colette G. LA ROSE
Honorary Consular Agent
Honorary Consular Agency for France
3931 Locarno Dr.
Anchorage 99504
Phone: 907/562-5713

Arizona

Mr. Claude A. PROSNIER
Honorary Consul
Honorary Consulate of France
8610 E. Hazelwood
Scottsdale 85251
Phone: 602/946-4185

Arkansas

Mr. Winthrop Paul ROCKEFELLER
Honorary Consul
Honorary Consulate of France
1 Union National Plaza, Suite 1590
Little Rock 72201
Phone: 501/224-1300

California

Mr. Guy YELDA
Consul General
Consulate General of France
10990 Wilshire Blvd., Suite 300
Los Angeles 90024
Phone: 310/235-3200   Fax: 310/312-0704

Commercial Office (Trade Commission) - France
1801 Avenue of the Stars, Suite 921
Los Angeles 90067
Phone: 310/843-1700   Fax: 310/843-1701

French Tourism Office
9454 Wilshire Blvd., Suite 715
Los Angeles 90212
Phone: 310/271-6665

Mrs. Juliette A. SALZMANN
Consul
French Cultural Division
10990 Wilshire Blvd., Suite 300
Los Angeles 90024
Phone: 310/235-3200

Mrs. Jane R. WHEATON
Honorary Consular Agent
Honorary Consular Agency for France
1831 Rockwood Drive
Sacramento 95864
Phone: 916/486-7228

Mr. Jean-Pierre PARIS
Honorary Consular Agent
Honorary Consular Agency for France
2230 4th Ave., Suite B
San Diego 92109
Phone: 619/239-4814

French Tourism Office
1 Hallidie Plaza, Suite 250
San Francisco 94014
Phone: 415/986-4161

Mr. Andre PARANT
Consul General
Consulate General of France
540 Bush St.
San Francisco 94108
Phone: 415/397-4330   Fax: 415/433-8357

French Cultural and Scientific Offices
540 Bush St.
San Francisco 94108

Mr. Philippe COSTE
Consul
Commercial Office (Trade Commission) - France
88 Kearny St., Suite 1510
San Francisco 94108
Phone: 415/781-0986

Mr. Herve LE MANSEC
Honorary Consul
Honorary Consulate of France
50 W. San Fernando, 2nd Floor
San Jose 95113
Phone: 408/429-2198

Colorado

Ms. Frieda SANIDAS
Honorary Consul
Consular Agency of France
1420 Ogden St., 1st Floor
Denver 80218-1910
Phone: 303/831-8616   Fax: 303/831-4871

Connecticut

Mrs. Yloland Dianne BOSMAN
Honorary Consul

Honorary Consulate of France
250 Shadduck Rd.
Middlebury 06762
Phone: 203/758-2042

Delaware

Mr. Raymond Fadio EID
Honorary Consul
Honorary Consulate of France
718 Princeton Rd.
Wilmington 19807
Phone: 302/654-5240

District of Columbia

Consul General
Consulate General of France
4101 Reservoir Road, NW
Washington 20007
Phone: 202/944-6195   Fax: 202/944-6148

Florida

Mr. Paul FONSAT
Vice Consul
Consulate General of France
1 Biscayne Tower
17th Floor, So. Biscayne Blvd.
Miami 33131
Phone: 305/372-9799   Fax: 305/372-9549

French Commercial Office
1 Biscayne Tower
2 S. Biscayne Blvd., Suite 1750
Miami 33131

Ms. Brigitte Marthe BROWN DAGOT
Honorary Consul
Honorary Consulate of France
7144 Somerworth Dr.
Orlando 32835
Phone: 407/292-1142

Georgia

Mr. Jean Paul MONCHAU
Consul General
Consulate General of France
285 Peachtree Center Ave., Suite 2800
Atlanta 30303
Phone: 404/522-4226   Fax: 404/880-9408

Commercial Office (Trade Commission) - France
285 Peachtree St., NW - Suite 2801
Atlanta 30303
Phone: 404/522-4803

Guam

Mr. Gerard J. GUEDON
Honorary Consular Agent
Honorary Consulate General of France
118 Governor Skinner
Tamuning 96931
Phone: 671/649-8882   Fax: 671/646-8878

Hawaii

Mrs. Patricia Sai LEE
Honorary Consul
Honorary Consulate of France
Alii Place, 1099 Alakea St. - Suite 1800
Honolulu 96813
Phone: 808/547-5625

Illinois

Mr. Gerard DUMONT

Consul General
Consulate General of France
737 N. Michigan Ave., Suite 2020
Chicago 60611
Phone: 312/787-5359   Fax: 312/664-4196

Mr. Daniel GAGNEUX
Consul
Commercial Office (Trade Commission) - France
1 E. Wacker Dr., Suite 3730
Chicago 60601
Phone: 312/661-1880

Ms. Danielle BRUGUERA
Consul
French Cultural and Scientific Offices
737 N. Michigan Ave., Suite 1170
Chicago 60611
Phone: 312/664-3525

Indiana

Mr. Thomas J. BECZKIEWICZ
Honorary Consul
Honorary Consulate of France
47 S. Pennsylvania, Suite 401
Indianapolis 40204
Phone: 317/637-4574

Iowa

Mr. Julian P. ARCHER
Honorary Consular Agent
Honorary Consular Agency for France
402 29th St.
Des Moines 50312
Phone: 515/243-4089

Kansas

Mr. Octave Camille MERVEILLE
Honorary Consul
Honorary Consulate of France
6500 Aberdeen
Kansas City 66208
Phone: 913/384-0834

Kentucky

Mr. David R. HERSHBERG
Honorary Consul
Honorary Consulate of France
Brodschi Hall, University of Louisville
Room 101
Louisville 40292
Phone: 502/588-6602

Louisiana

Mrs. Nicole Lenoir BERTRAND
Consul General
Consulate General of France
Lykes Bldg., 300 Poydras St. - Suite 2105
New Orleans 70130
Phone: 504/523-5772   Fax: 504/523-5725

Maine

Mr. Severin M. BELIVEAU
Honorary Consul
Honorary Consulate of France
443 Congress St.
Portland 04101-3590
Phone: 207/775-5831

Maryland

Ms. Claude EDELINE
Honorary Consul

Honorary Consulate of France
616 W. University Pkwy.
Baltimore 21210
Phone: 301/467-4367

Massachusetts

Mr. Maurice PORTICHE
Consul General
Consulate General of France
3 Commonwealth Avenue
Boston 02116
Phone: 617/266-1680   Fax: 617/437-1090

French Visa Section
20 Park Plaza
Boston 02116
Phone: 617/482-3650

French Cultural and Scientific Section
Park Square Bldg., 31 St. James Ave. - Suite 750
Boston 02116
Phone: 617/292-0064

Mr. Bernard Gilles THEROUX
Honorary Consular Agent
Honorary Consular Agency for France
1317 S. Main St.
Falls River 02721
Phone: 617/672-1295

Michigan

Honorary Consulate of France
1600 First Federal Bldg., 1001 Woodward Ave.
Detroit 48226-1962
Phone: 313/965-8300

Minnesota

Mr. Alain Jean-Christian FRECON
Honorary Consul
Honorary Consulate of France
Foshyay Tower, 821 Market Ave. - Suite 902
Minneapolis 55402
Phone: 612/338-6868

Mississippi

Mr. Silas Wood MCCHAREN
Honorary Consul
Honorary Consulate of France
111 E. Capitol St., Suite 600
Jackson 39201
Phone: 601/969-7607

Missouri

Mr. James F. MAUZE
Honorary Consul
Honorary Consulate of France
112 S. Hanley Rd.
St. Louis 63105
Phone: 314/726-2800

Montana

Ms. Susan WELLS TALBOT
Honorary Consular Agent
Honorary Consular Agency for France
11 Greenbrier Dr.
Missoula 59801
Phone: 406/549-8438

New Hampshire

Mr. Robert E. RAICHE
Honorary Consul
Honorary Consulate of France

694 Pine St.
Manchester 03104
Phone: 603/669-8080

New Mexico

Mr. Gilles J. MILINAIRE
Honorary Consul
Honorary Consulate of France
145 Brownell Howland Rd., Suite 2
Sante Fe 87501
Phone: 505/989-8929

New York

Mr. Patrick Henri GAUTRAT
Consul General
Consulate General of France
934 Fifth Ave.
New York 10021
Phone: 212/606-3689   Fax: 212/606-3620

French Tourism Office
444 Madison Ave., 16th Fl.
New York 10022
Phone: 212/838-7800   Fax: 212/838-7855

Mr. Louis Michel MORRIS
Deputy Consul General
Commercial Office (Trade Commission) - France
810 7th Ave., 38th Floor
New York 10019
Phone: 212/307-8800

Mr. Patrice BUREL
Deputy Consul General
French Cultural Services
972 5th Ave.
New York 10021
Phone: 212/606-3680

French Visa Section
10 E. 74th St.
New York 10021
Phone: 212/606-3644

French Press Section
10 E. 74th St.
New York 10021
Phone: 212/606-3685

Mr. Antoine MERIEUS
Deputy Consul General
Financial Office (Financial Agency) French
1 World Trade Center, Suite 5305
New York 10048
Phone: 212/432-1820

French Social Service
10 E. 74th St.
New York 10021
Phone: 212/606-3605

Mr. William Ignatius JAMES
Honorary Consul
Honorary Consulate of France
319 N. Forest Rd.
Williamsville 14221
Phone: 716/633-4766

North Carolina

Mrs. Mildred D. COX
Honorary Consul
Honorary Consulate of France
1440 Carmel Rd.
Charlotte 28226
Phone: 704/366-1241

Ohio

Mr. Stephen John KNERLY
Honorary Consul
Honorary Consulate of France
200 Public Sq., 3300 BP America Bldg.
Cleveland 44114
Phone: 216/621-0150

Mr. Jacques RIBONI
Honorary Consul
Honorary Consulate of France
Executive Ctr. 111, 25 Merchant St.
Springdale 45246
Phone: 513/552-3371

Oklahoma

Mr. Burt B. HOLMES
Honorary Consul
Honorary Consulate of France
7666 E. 61st
Tulsa 74105
Phone: 918/254-0471

Oregon

Mr. Serge D. D'ROVENCOURT
Honorary Consul
Honorary Consulate of France
921 SW 6th Ave.
Portland 97204
Phone: 503/226-1611

Pennsylvania

Mrs. Danielle Lucienne THOMAS EASTON
Honorary Consul
Honorary Consulate of France
2500 1 Liberty Place, 1650 Market St.
Philadelphia 19103-7301
Phone: 215/851-8100

Mr. Jean-Pierre COLLET
Honorary Consul
Honorary Consulate of France
800 Presque Isle Dr.
Pittsburgh 15239
Phone: 412/327-2911

Puerto Rico

Consulate General of France
Ponce De Leon Ave., Suite 720
Hato Rey 00918
Phone: 809/753-1700

South Carolina

Mr. Philippe Gerard FELSENHARDT
Honorary Consul
Honorary Consulate of France
1004 Rockwood Rd.
Columbia 29209
Phone: 803/783-3708

Tennessee

Mr. Charles Metcalf CRUMP
Honorary Consul
Honorary Consulate of France
81 Monroe Bldg.
Memphis 38103
Phone: 901/525-7744

Texas

Mr. John M. HARMON
Honorary Consul
Honorary Consulate of France
2300 Interfirst Tower, Suite 976

Austin 78701
Phone: 512/480-5605

Mr. John Franklin CRAWFORD
Honorary Consul
Honorary Consulate of France
750 N. Paul St., Suite 220
Dallas 75201
Phone: 214/855-5495

Mr. Roland GAYER
Consul
Consulate General of France
2777 Allen Parkway, Suite 650
Houston 77019
Phone: 713/528-2181   Fax: 713/528-1933

French Cultural and Scientific Offices
2777 Allen Pkwy., Suite 685
Houston 77019
Phone: 713/528-2231

Mr. Louis N. BONAPARTE-WYSE
Consular Agent
Commercial Office (Trade Commission) - France
5847 San Felipe, Suite 1600
Houston 77057
Phone: 713/266-7595

Mr. John L. COLLET
Honorary Consul
Honorary Consulate of France
Route 1, Box 229
San Antonio 78109
Phone: 210/659-3101

Utah

Mr. Carl W. BARTON
Honorary Consul
Honorary Consulate of France
175 E. 400 S., Suite 900
Salt Lake City 84111
Phone: 801/524-1000

Vermont

Mr. Frederick BATAILLE
Honorary Consul
Honorary Consulate of France
Main St.
Montgomery Center 05471
Phone: 802/326-4814

Virgin Islands

Mr. Aimery P. CARON
Honorary Consular Agent
Honorary Consular Agency for France
P.O. Box 3688
St. Thomas 00801
Phone: 809/774-5794

Virginia

Ms. Nicole YANCEY
Honorary Consul
Honorary Consulate of France
417 Pin Oak Rd.
Newport News 23601
Phone: 804/596-2754

Washington

Ms. Marguerite H. BAILLY
Honorary Consul
Honorary Consulate of France
1402 Third Ave., Suite 1313
Seattle 98104
Phone: 206/323-6870

Wisconsin

Mr. David A. ERNE
Honorary Consul
Honorary Consulate of France
1000 N. Water St., Suite 2100
Milwaukee 53202
Phone: 414/298-1000

Gabon

New York

Mrs. Yvonne WALKER
Consular Agent
Consulate of Gabon
18 E. 41st St., 9th Floor
New York 10017
Phone: 212/686-9720   Fax: 212/689-5769

Gambia

California

Ms. Aimee KLAUS
Honorary Consul General
Honorary Consulate General of Gambia
10777 Bellagio Rd.
Los Angeles 90077
Phone: 310/476-0532   Fax: 310/471-7424

Georgia

Massachusetts

Mr. Richard E. PIPES
Honorary Consul
Honorary Consulate of Georgia
17 Berkley St.
Boston 02138
Phone: 617/492-0727

Texas

Mr. Land Chase BENTSEN
Honorary Consul
Honorary Consulate of Georgia
3040 Post Oak Blvd., Suite 700
Houston 77056

Germany

Alabama

Dr. Sven Peter MANNSFLED
Honorary Consul
Honorary Consulate of Germany
c/o The Degussa Corporation, Degussa Rd.
P.O. Box 606
Theodore 36590
Phone: 205/443-4000   Fax: 205/443-1609

Alaska

Mr. Bernd Carl GUETSCHOW
Honorary Consul
Honorary Consulate of Germany
425 G St., Suite 650
Anchorage 99501
Phone: 907/274-6537   Fax: 907/274-8798

American Samoa

Mr. Eberhard NOLDEKE
Consul
Consulate of Germany
Williams City Centre
9092 Hobson St., 23rd Floor
Wellington

Arizona

Mr. William F. BEHRENS
Honorary Consul
Honorary Consulate of Germany
1130 E. Missouri, Suite 200
Phoenix 85014
Phone: 602/264-2545   Fax: 602/285-0296

California

Mr. Hans-Alard Alfred VON ROHR
Consul General
Consulate General of Germany
6222 Wilshire Blvd., Suite 500
Los Angeles 90048
Phone: 213/930-2703   Fax: 213/930-2805

Mr. Hermann J. ZILLGENS
Honorary Consul
Honorary Consulate of Germany
6215 Ferris Sq., Suite 125
San Diego 92121-3251
Phone: 619/455-1423   Fax: 619/452-0609

Mr. Ruprecht HENATSCH
Consul General
Consulate General of Germany
1960 Jackson St.
San Francisco 94109
Phone: 415/775-1061   Fax: 415/775-0187

Colorado

Mr. Hans Wiprecht VON BARBY
Honorary Consul
Honorary Consulate of Germany
350 Indiana St., Suite 400
Denver 80401
Phone: 303/279-1551   Fax: 303/278-4302

Florida

Mr. Gerd Ewald SCHROEDER
Honorary Consul
Honorary Consulate of Germany
5081 Sorrento Ct.
Cape Coral 33904
Phone: 941/945-6729

Mr. John Girvin MCGIFFIN
Honorary Consul
Honorary Consulate of Germany
1510 Talleyrand Ave.
Jacksonville 32201
Phone: 904/353-1741   Fax: 904/632-1319

Mr. Claus Hermann SOENKSEN
Consul General
Consulate General of Germany
100 N. Biscayne Blvd., Suite 2200
Miami 33132
Phone: 305/358-0290   Fax: 305/358-0307

Georgia

Mr. Klaus E. ZEHENTNER
Consul General
Consulate General of Germany
Marquis Two Twr., Suite 901

285 Peachtree Center Ave., NE
Atlanta 30303-1221
Phone: 404/659-4760   Fax: 404/659-1280

Mr. Frank Kohler PEEPLES
Honorary Consul
Honorary Consulate of Germany
Orleans Bldg.
6001 Chatham Center, 3rd Floor
Savannah 31401
Phone: 912/232-5581   Fax: 912/238-5524

Hawaii

Mr. Peter Heinrich SCHALL
Honorary Consul
Honorary Consulate of Germany
2005 Kalia Rd.
Honolulu 96815
Phone: 808/949-4321

Illinois

Mr. Klaus Deiter KOEPKE
Deputy Consul General
Consulate General of Germany
676 No. Michigan Ave., Suite 3200
Chicago 60611
Phone: 312/580-1199   Fax: 312/580-0099

Indiana

Mr. Horst Felix WINKLER
Honorary Consul
Honorary Consulate of Germany
2314 N. Meridian St.
Indianapolis 46208
Phone: 317/924-5321   Fax: 317/920-3208

Iowa

Mr. Mark Frederick SCHLENKER
Honorary Consul
Honorary Consulate of Germany
115 S. Howard
Indianola 50125
Phone: 515/961-2509   Fax: 515/961-5970

Kansas

Mr. Willard Breidenthal SNYDER
Honorary Consul
Honorary Consulate of Germany
8014 State Line
Leawood 66208
Phone: 913/642-5134   Fax: 913/642-5348

Kentucky

Mr. Eberhard Frederick ZOPP
Honorary Consul
Honorary Consulate of Germany
The Starks Bldg., 455 S. 4th Ave., Suite 546
Louisville 40202-2509
Phone: 502/561-7911   Fax: 502/561-7912

Louisiana

Mr. Edwin A. LUPBERGER
Honorary Consul
Honorary Consulate of Germany
Poydras Plaza
639 Loyola Ave., 8th Floor
New Orleans 70113
Phone: 504/576-4289   Fax: 504/576-4269

Massachusetts

Dr. Peter Christian HAUSWEDELL

Consul General
Consulate General of Germany
3 Copley Place
Boston 02116
Phone: 617/536-4414   Fax: 617/536-8573

Michigan

Mr. Juergen Guenter MEWS
Consul
Consulate General of Germany
Edison Plaza
660 Plaza Dr., Suite 2100
Detroit 48226-1849
Phone: 313/962-6526   Fax: 313/962-7345

Minnesota

Dr. Heino A. BECKMANN
Honorary Consul
Honorary Consulate of Germany
1000 LaSalle Ave.
Minneapolis 55403-2205
Phone: 612/962-4000

Mississippi

Mr. Emerson Barney ROBINSON
Honorary Consul
Honorary Consulate of Germany
Deposit Guaranty Nat'l Bank
210 East Capitol
Jackson 39205
Phone: 601/354-8281   Fax: 601/354-8192

Missouri

Mrs. Anna Mayer BECK
Honorary Consul
Honorary Consulate of Germany
49 Orange Hills Dr.
Chesterfield 63017
Phone: 314/576-4786   Fax: 314/576-9683

Nevada

Ms. Sigrid SOMMER
Honorary Consul
Honorary Consulate of Germany
925 E. Desert Inn Rd., Suite C
Las Vegas 89109
Phone: 702/734-9700   Fax: 702/737-6900

New Mexico

Mr. Lanny Dee MESSERSMITH
Honorary Consul
Honorary Consulate of Germany
5700 Harper, NE - Suite 430
Albuquerque 87109
Phone: 505/822-8826   Fax: 505/828-2682

New York

Mr. Michael Alexander BARRELL
Honorary Consul
Honorary Consulate of Germany
135 Delaware Ave., Suite 501
Buffalo 14202
Phone: 716/854-4010   Fax: 716/854-7860

Dr. Cornelius Alexander METTERNICH
Consul General
Consulate General of Germany
460 Park Ave.
New York 10022
Phone: 212/572-5622   Fax: 212/308-3422

North Carolina

Mr. Eskart E. GOETTE
Honorary Consul
Honorary Consulate of Germany
330 Eastover Rd.
Charlotte 28207
Phone: 704/373-0774   Fax: 704/333 6446

Ohio

Dr. Richard Erich SCHADE
Honorary Consul
Honorary Consulate of Germany
University of Cincinnati
733 Old Chemistry Bldg., Rm. ML0372
Cincinnati 45221-0372
Phone: 513/556-2752

Ms. Diana Marie THIMMIG
Honorary Consul
Honorary Consulate of Germany
1100 Huntington Bldg., 925 Euclid St.
Cleveland 44115-1475
Phone: 216/696-1100   Fax: 216/696-2645

Mr. Frank Georg WOBST
Honorary Consul
Honorary Consulate of Germany
Huntington Bank, 41 S. High St.
Columbus 43287
Phone: 614/463-3623   Fax: 614/463-5485

Oklahoma

Mr. Charles Everett WIGGIN
Honorary Consul
Honorary Consulate of Germany
5801 N. Broadway, Suite 510
Oklahoma City 73118
Phone: 405/842-0100   Fax: 405/848-8248

Oregon

Mr. Guenther Heinz HOFFMANN
Honorary Consul
Honorary Consulate of Germany
200 SW Market St., Suite 1695
Portland 97201
Phone: 503/222-0490

Pennsylvania

Mr. Charles M. TAYLOR
Honorary Consul General
Honorary Consulate General of Germany
1 Penn Ctr., 1617 John F. Kennedy Blvd.
19th Floor
Philadelphia 19103-1895
Phone: 215/665-3263   Fax: 215/665-3165

Mr. Michael Edmund GERLACH
Honorary Consul
Honorary Consulate of Germany
100 Sandusky St.
Pittsburgh 15212-5852
Phone: 412/237-8500   Fax: 412/321-7634

Puerto Rico

Mr. Otto Egon SCHULZ
Honorary Consul
Honorary Consulate of Germany
1618 Bibiana St.
San Juan 00936
Phone: 809/755-8228

South Carolina

Mr. Paul F. FOERSTER
Honorary Consul

Honorary Consulate of Germany
29 Montgomery Dr.
Spartanburg 29302
Phone: 803/579-5206   Fax: 803/579-5930

Tennessee

Mr. Edwin Warner BASS
Honorary Consul
Honorary Consulate of Germany
2700 First American Ctr.
Nashville 37238
Phone: 615/244-5370   Fax: 615/742-2710

Texas

Mr. Erich E. WENDL
Honorary Consul
Honorary Consulate of Germany
5440 Old Brownsville Rd.
Corpus Christi 78469
Phone: 512/289-2416   Fax: 512/289-7824

Mr. Daniel O. TOMLIN
Honorary Consul
Honorary Consulate of Germany
5580 Peterson Ln., Suite 150
Dallas 75240
Phone: 214/239-0788   Fax: 972/788-4247

Dr. Wolfgang Klaus MOSER
Consul General
Consulate General of Germany
1330 Post Oak Blvd., Suite 1850
Houston 77056-3818
Phone: 713/627-7771   Fax: 713/627-0506

Mr. Thomas Ernst PAWEL
Honorary Consul
Honorary Consulate of Germany
1500 Alomo Bldg.
105 S. St. Mary's St.
San Antonio 78205
Phone: 210/224-4455   Fax: 210/224-6430

Utah

Dr. Herwig GLANDER
Honorary Consul
Honorary Consulate of Germany
254 West 4th S., Suite 305
Salt Lake City 84101
Phone: 801/364-9573   Fax: 801/322-0930

Virginia

Mr. Manfred Wolfgang SCHWARZ
Honorary Consul
Honorary Consulate of Germany
536 Viking Dr.
Virginia Beach 23452
Phone: 757/486-8444   Fax: 757/486-9249

Washington

Dr. Manfred Lothar BIRMELIN
Consul General
Consulate General of Germany
One Union Square, Suite 2500
600 University St.
Seattle 98101
Phone: 206/682-4313   Fax: 206/682-3724

Mr. Hubertus P. GUENTHER
Honorary Consul
Honorary Consulate of Germany
S. 123rd Post
Spokane 99204
Phone: 509/624-5242   Fax: 509/624-7732

Ghana

Illinois

Mr. Robert Eugene BENNETT
Honorary Consul
Honorary Consulate of Ghana
19 S. La Salle St., Suite 301
Chicago 60603
Phone: 312/236-3309   Fax: 312/236-3310

New York

Mr. Samuel Adotey ANUM
Consul General
Consulate General of Ghana
19 E. 47th St.
New York 10017
Phone: 212/832-1300   Fax: 212/751-6743

Texas

Mr. Jack M. WEBB
Honorary Consul
Honorary Consulate of Ghana
3434 Locke Lane
Houston 77027-8806
Phone: 713/960-8806   Fax: 713/960-8833

Greece

California

Consul General
Consulate General of Greece
12424 Wilshire Blvd., Suite 800
Los Angeles 90025
Phone: 310/826-5555   Fax: 310/826-8670

Greek Tourist Office
611 W. 6th St., Suite 2198
Los Angeles 90017
Phone: 213/626-6696

Mr. Christos P. PANAGOPOULOS
Consulate General
Greek Commercial and Economic Office
12424 Wilshire Blvd., Suite 800
Los Angeles 90025
Phone: 310/826-5555   Fax: 310/826-8670

Mr. Constantin D. TRITARIS
Consul General
Consulate General of Greece
2441 Gough St.
San Francisco 94123
Phone: 415/775-2102   Fax: 415/776-6815

Georgia

Mr. Dimitris MACRYMIKOLAS
Consul
Consulate of Greece
Tower Place
3340 Peachtree Rd., NE - Suite 1670
Atlanta 30326
Phone: 404/261-3313   Fax: 404/262-2798

Illinois

Mr. Nicholas ZAFIROPOULOS
Consul General
Consulate General of Greece
650 N. Clair St.
Chicago 60611
Phone: 312/335-3915   Fax: 312/335-3958

Mr. Athanassios MAKRANDREOU
Consul
Greek Office of Tourism
168 N. Michigan Ave.
Chicago 60601
Phone: 312/782-1084   Fax: 312/782-1091

Louisiana

Mr. Georges DOGORITIS
Consul
Consulate of Greece
World Trade Center
2 Canal St., Suite 2318
New Orleans 70130
Phone: 504/523-1167   Fax: 504/524-5610

Mr. Evangelos MAZARAKIS
Vice Consul
Greek Office of Mercantile Marine
2335 Int'l Trade Mart, 2 Canal St.
New Orleans 70130
Phone: 504/529-5288

Massachusetts

Mr. John ECONOMIDES
Consul General
Consulate General of Greece
86 Beacon St.
Boston 02108
Phone: 617/523-0100   Fax: 617/523-0511

New York

Mrs. Ekaterini LOUPAS
Consul
Consulate General of Greece
69 E. 79th St.
New York 10021
Phone: 212/988-5500   Fax: 212/734-8492

Mr. Alexandros MOURKOYANNIS
Consul
Greek Office of Tourism
Olympic Tower, 645 5th Ave.
New York 10022
Phone: 212/421-5777   Fax: 212/826-6940

Mr. Ioannis K. PAPADIMITRIOU
Consul
Greek Office of the Commercial Counselor
150 E. 58th St.
New York 10155
Phone: 212/751-2404   Fax: 212/593-2278

Capt. Pelopidas ANGELOPOULOS
Consul
Greek Mercantile Marine Department
29 Broadway, Suite 2300
New York 10006
Phone: 212/425-5764   Fax: 212/425-3795

Texas

Mr. Panayotis STOURNARAS
Consul
Consulate of Greece
1360 Post Oak Blvd., Suite 2480
Houston 77056
Phone: 713/840-7522   Fax: 713/840-0614

Grenada

Florida

Mr. Richard A. NIXON
Honorary Consul
Honorary Consulate of Grenada
80 SW 8th St., Suite 1800
Miami 33130
Phone: 305/377-1110   Fax: 305/379-5007

Illinois

Dr. Alvin J. SCHONFELD
Honorary Consul
Honorary Consulate of Grenada
905 W. Castlewood Te.
Chicago 60640-4128
Phone: 312/878-7777   Fax: 312/878-9400

New York

Mr. Ronald CHARLES
Consulate General
Consulate of Grenada
820 Second Avenue, Suite 1100
New York 10017
Phone: 212/599-0301   Fax: 212/599-1540

Guatemala

Alabama

Mr. Jose Roberto ORTEGA-LOPEZ
Honorary Consul
Honorary Consulate of Guatemala
2153 Meadow Lane Dr.
Montgomery 36106
Phone: 205/269-2756

California

Mr. Rafael Antonio SALAZAR GALVEZ
Consul General
Consulate General of Guatemala
2975 Wilshire Blvd., Ground Floor
Los Angeles 90010
Phone: 213/365-9251

Mr. Eugene Herbert SAPPER
Honorary Consul
Honorary Consulate of Guatemala
10405 San Diego Mission Rd., Suite 205
San Diego 92108
Phone: 619/282-8127

Ms. Nora Eugenia CIFUENTES PAIZ
Consul General
Consulate General of Guatemala
870 Market St., Suite 667
San Francisco 94102
Phone: 415/788-5651

Florida

Mr. Maximo Augusto SANTA CRUZ ANCHISSI
Consul General
Consulate General of Guatemala
300 Sevilla Ave., Suite 210
Coral Gables 33134

Phone: 305/443-4828

Mr. John P. BAUER
Honorary Consul
Honorary Consulate of Guatemala
2200 S. Ocean Ln., Apt. 1705
Ft. Lauderdale 33316
Phone: 305/467-1700

Georgia

Mrs. Maria Teresa FRASER
Honorary Consul
Honorary Consulate of Guatemala
4772 E. Conway Dr., NW
Atlanta 30327
Phone: 404/255-7019

Illinois

Mrs. Rosa Carmina DE MALDONADO
Vice Consul
Consulate General of Guatemala
230 N. Michigan Ave., Suite 1000
Chicago 60601
Phone: 312/332-1587

Kansas

Mr. Ralph E. DIX
Honorary Consul
Honorary Consulate of Guatemala
419 Delaware St.
Leavenworth 66048
Phone: 913/682-0342

Louisiana

Mr. Enrique Leonardo HERRERA
Honorary Consul
Honorary Consulate of Guatemala
735 Rue Jefferson
Lafayette 70501
Phone: 318/291-5474   Fax: 318/291-5480

Mr. Mario JEREZ ZACHRISSON
Honorary Consul
Honorary Consulate of Guatemala
1532 World Trade Center
2 Canal St.
New Orleans 70130
Phone: 504/525-0013

New York

Ms. Fabiola FUENTES ORELLANA
Consul General
Consulate General of Guatemala
57 Park Ave.
New York 10016
Phone: 212/686-3837   Fax: 212/447-6947

Pennsylvania

Dr. Roberto RENDON MALDONADO
Honorary Consul
Honorary Consulate of Guatemala
1245 Highland Ave., Suite 301
Abington 19001
Phone: 215/885-5551

Mrs. Margarita WINIKOFF
Honorary Consul
Honorary Consulate of Guatemala
709 Washington Dr.
Pittsburgh 15229
Phone: 412/366-7715

Puerto Rico

Mr. Alberto M. PEREZ NEGRONI
Honorary Consul
Honorary Consulate of Guatemala
Garden Hills, A-22 Serrania St.
Guaynabo 00966
Phone: 809/782-7409

Rhode Island

Mrs. Zoila R. GUERRA
Honorary Consul
Honorary Consulate of Guatemala
11 Lancashire St.
Providence 02908

Tennessee

Mr. George E. WHITWORTH
Honorary Consul
Honorary Consulate of Guatemala
147 Jefferson Ave., Unit 900
Memphis 38103
Phone: 901/527-8466

Texas

Mr. Oscar Alfredo AGUILAR GALVEZ
Consul General
Consulate General of Guatemala
3600 S. Gessner Rd., Suite 200
Houston 77063
Phone: 713/953-9531

Mr. Carlose FERREYRO LUCERO
Honorary Vice Consul
Honorary Consulate of Guatemala
4840 Whirlwind
San Antonio 78217

Washington

Mrs. Elsa Osborne SMITH
Honorary Consul
Honorary Consulate of Guatemala
2100 5th Ave.
Seattle 98121
Phone: 206/728-5920

Guinea

Florida

Mr. Arnett E. GIRARDEAU
Honorary Consul
Consulate of Guinea
24 E. 6th St.
Jacksonville 32206

Ohio

Mr. Robert Michael CARTER
Honorary Consul
Honorary Consulate of Guinea
1104 Hanna Bldg., 1422 Euclid Ave.
Cleveland 44115
Phone: 216/621-2227   Fax: 216/621-2250

Pennsylvania

Mr. Stanley L. STRAUGHTER
Honorary Consul
Honorary Consulate of Guinea
1528 Walnut St.
Philadelphia 19102
Phone: 215/790-3220

Guyana

California

Mr. Joseph Gabriel D'OLIVEIRA
Honorary Consul
Honorary Consulate of Guyana
9111 S. La Cienega Blvd., Suite 201
Inglewood 90301
Phone: 213/222-0899   Fax: 213/222-0899

Florida

Mr. Hilton Narine RAMCHARITAR
Honorary Consul
Honorary Consulate of Guyana
1837 S. State Road 7
Ft. Lauderdale 33317
Phone: 954/797-6844   Fax: 954/797-7603

New York

Mr. Brentnold Fitzpatrick EVANS
Consul General
Consulate General of Guyana
866 United Nations Plaza, 3rd Floor
New York 10017
Phone: 212/527-3215   Fax: 212/935-7548

Ohio

Dr. Festus Lysas BROTHERSON
Honorary Consul
Honorary Consulate of Guyana
733 Merrimak Dr.
Berea 44017
Phone: 440/891-6828   Fax: 440/891-6864

Texas

Ms. Terri A. REIS
Honorary Consul
Honorary Consulate of Guyana
1810 Woodland Pk. Drive
Houston 77077
Phone: 281/497-4466   Fax: 713/497-4476

Haiti

California

Mr. Oscar Eduardo CARCELEN
Honorary Consul
Honorary Consulate of Haiti
100 Brannan St.
San Francisco 94107
Phone: 415/957-1189

Colorado

Mr. Paul VRANESIC
Honorary Consul
Honorary Consulate of Haiti
621 17th St., Suite 1741
Denver 80293
Phone: 303/298-7392

Florida

Mr. Jean Gabriel AUGUSTIN
Consul General
Consulate General of Haiti
Ingraham Bldg., 259 SW 13th St.
Miami 33131
Phone: 305/377-3547

Georgia

Mr. William G. BROWNING
Honorary Consul
Honorary Consulate of Haiti
P.O. Box 80340
Atlanta 30366
Phone: 404/455-3434

Illinois

Mr. Jean C. ROSEMBERT
Consul
Consulate General of Haiti
220 South State St., Suite 2110
Chicago 60601
Phone: 312/922-4004   Fax: 312/922-7122

Indiana

Mr. Alfred Decalb VANHOOSE
Honorary Consul
Honorary Consulate of Haiti
P.O. Box 4200
Evansville 47711
Phone: 812/423-8000

Louisiana

Mr. Pierre Benjamin CLEMENCEAU
Honorary Consul
Honorary Consulate of Haiti
416 Common St.
New Orleans 70130
Phone: 504/586-8309

Massachusetts

Mr. Jean Victor GENEUS
Consul General
Consulate General of Haiti
262 Washington St.
Boston 02108
Phone: 617/723-5211

Michigan

Mr. Ralph Jenkins OSBORNE
Honorary Consul
Honorary Consulate of Haiti
1st National Bldg., Suite 2121
Detroit 48226
Phone: 313/965-7962

Missouri

Mr. Norman Bradford WEST
Honorary Consul
Honorary Consulate of Haiti
441 Cloisters Walk
Kirkwood 63122
Phone: 314/966-5280

New Jersey

Ms. Jean-Claude Serge LEVY
Honorary Consul
Honorary Consulate of Haiti
667 Main Ave.
Passaic 07055
Phone: 201/777-2121

New York

Mr. Francel SAINT HILLIEN
Consul
Consulate General of Haiti
271 Madison Ave., 17th Floor

New York 10016
Phone: 212/697-9767

Ohio

Mr. Henry P. KOSLING
Honorary Consul
Consulate of Haiti
Standard Bldg., Suite 1016
Cleveland 44113
Phone: 216/771-0280

Pennsylvania

Mr. Albert MOMJIAN
Honorary Consul
Honorary Consulate of Haiti
Land Title Bldg., Suite 1430
Philadelphia 19110

Mr. John Joseph CURRAN
Honorary Consul
Honorary Consulate of Haiti
200 Mahatongo St.
Pottsville 17901

Puerto Rico

Mr. Jean Rameau YORK
Consul
Consulate General of Haiti
654 Nunos Rivera Ave., Suite 909
Hato Rey 00918

Texas

Mr. Renato F. PEREIRA
Honorary Vice Consul
Honorary Consulate of Haiti
3535 Sage Rd.
Houston 77027

Honduras

California

Ms. Ana Ruth ZUNIGA IZAGUIRRE
Honorary Consul
Consulate General of Honduras
3450 Wilshire Blvd., Suite 230
Los Angeles 90010
Phone: 213/383-9244

Ms. Ella Isabel FLORES-PARIS
Honorary Consul
Honorary Consulate of Honduras
Union Bank Bldg.
525 B St., Suite 2002
San Diego 92101
Phone: 619/533-4515

Mr. Mario Alfredo MALDONADO ZEPEDA
Consul General
Consulate General of Honduras
Flood Bldg., 870 Market St.
Room 451-453
San Francisco 94102
Phone: 415/392-0076

Florida

Mr. Raul Felipe TORRES MCDONOUGH
Consul General
Consulate General of Honduras
300 Sevilla Ave.
Coral Gables 33134
Phone: 305/447-8927

Mr Antonio J. VALLADARES
Consul
Consulate of Honduras
1914 Beachway Rd., Suite 3-0
Jacksonville 33207
Phone: 904/348-3550

Hawaii

Mrs. Lesby Perez BILLAM-WALKER
Honorary Consul
Honorary Consulate of Honduras
1734 Malanai St., Apt. B
Honolulu 96826
Phone: 808/944-2811

Illinois

Mr. Carlos Ruben CALLEJAS ESPINO
Consul General
Consulate General of Honduras
2000 N. Racine, Suite 2110
Chicago 60614
Phone: 773/472-8726   Fax: 773/472-8958

Louisiana

Ms. Vilma Cabrera CALHOUN
Honorary Consul
Honorary Consulate of Honduras
11017 N. Oak Hills Pw.
Baton Rouge 70810

Mr. Carlos Eduardo REINA GARCIA
Consul General
Consulate General of Honduras
World Trade Center
2 Canal St., Suite 1641
New Orleans 70130
Phone: 504/522-3118

Maryland

Mr. Rene LICONA DUARTE
Honorary Consul General
Honorary Consulate General of Honduras
5803 Loch Raven Blvd.
Baltimore 21239
Phone: 410/435-6233

Massachusetts

Ms. Graciela SUAREZ
Consul
Consulate of Honduras
486 Beacon St., Suite 2
Newton 02115
Phone: 617/247-2007

Michigan

Consulate of Honduras
3620 Shady Ln.
Detroit 48216

Minnesota

Mr. Harold PANUSKA
Honorary Consul
Honorary Consulate of Honduras
20 Cygnet Pl.
Long Lake 55356
Phone: 612/473-5376

Missouri

Mr. Francis DOLL
Honorary Consul General
Honorary Consulate General of Honduras

P.O. Box 158
St. Louis 63655
Phone: 314/783-2886

New York

Mr. Julio E. SANDOVAL DUARTE
Consul General
Consulate General of Honduras
80 Wall St., Suite 915
New York 10005
Phone: 212/269-3611

Puerto Rico

Mrs. Ruth PAZ AGUILAR
Consul General
Consulate General of Honduras
Mercantil Plaza Bldg.
Ponce De Leon Ave., Suite 604
Hato Rey 00918

Texas

Mrs. Leslie Carol CHINCHILLA MONCADA
Consul General
Consulate General of Honduras
4151 SW Freeway, Suite 700
Houston 77027
Phone: 713/622-4572

Hungary

Arizona

Dr. Omer K. REED
Honorary Consul
Honorary Consulate of Hungary
2999 N. 44th St., Suite 650
Phoenix 85018
Phone: 602/952-1200   Fax: 602/840-4561

California

Dr. Marta HORVATHNE FEKSZI
Consul General
Consulate General of Hungary
11766 Wilshire Blvd., Suite 410
Los Angeles 90025
Phone: 310/473-9344   Fax: 310/479-0456

Mrs. Eva E. VOISIN
Honorary Consul
Honorary Consulate of Hungary
10 Twin Dolphin Drive, Suite B500
Redwood City 94065-1404
Phone: 415/595-1448   Fax: 415/591-8884

Colorado

Mr. Eugene FELEGYHAZY-MEGYESY
Honorary Consul
Honorary Consulate of Hungary
1700 Broadway, Suite 1700
Denver 80290
Phone: 303/861-8013   Fax: 303/832-3804

Florida

Mr. Alexander S. TAR
Honorary Consul General
Honorary Consulate General of Hungary
1929 Ponce De Leon Blvd.
Coral Gables 33134
Phone: 305/448-4989   Fax: 305/448-3224

Hawaii

Mrs. Emese Rozalia PRING KOMJATHY
Honorary Consul
Honorary Consulate of Hungary
631 Puuikena Dr.
Honolulu 96821
Phone: 808/377-3637   Fax: 808/377-7188

Louisiana

Mr. Peter William BORDEAUX
Honorary Consul
Honorary Consulate of Hungary
1 Galleria Blvd., Suite 1714
Metairie 70001
Phone: 504/849-2749   Fax: 504/849-2740

Massachusetts

Consul General
Consulate General of Hungary
The Esplanade, #E1104
75 Cambridge Parkway
Cambridge 02142
Phone: 617/621-0886   Fax: 617/621-0961

New York

Mr. Istvan KOVACS
Consul General
Consulate General of Hungary
223 E. 52nd St.
New York 10022
Phone: 212/752-0661   Fax: 212/755-5986

Ohio

Mr. Laszlo BOJTOS
Honorary Consul
Honorary Consulate of Hungary
140 Public Sq., Suite 708
Cleveland 44114
Phone: 216/861-6091

Puerto Rico

Mr. Dennis BECHARA
Honorary Consul
Honorary Consulate of Hungary
637 South Post St.
Mayaguez 00681
Phone: 787/831-2010   Fax: 787/834-8380

Texas

Mr. Edmond S. SOLYMOSY
Honorary Consul
Honorary Consulate of Hungary
P.O. Box 27253
Houston 77227
Phone: 713/529-2727   Fax: 713/529-2870

Washington

Mrs. Helen M. SZABLYA
Honorary Consul
Honorary Consulate of Hungary
4416 134th Pl., SE.
Bellevue 98006
Phone: 425/643-0563   Fax: 425/562-6381

Iceland

Alaska

Mr. Philip W. BENEDIKTSSON

Honorary Consul General
Honorary Consulate General of Iceland
3915 Locarno Drive
Anchorage 99508
Phone: 907/561-1492   Fax: 907/562-4263

California

Mrs. Halla LINKER
Honorary Consul General
Honorary Consulate General of Iceland
1551 Westwood Blvd., Suite 108
Los Angeles 90024
Phone: 310/474-8485   Fax: 310/474-8728

Mr. Robert E. CARTWRIGHT
Honorary Consul
Honorary Consulate of Iceland
The Cartwright & Alexander Law Firm
222 Front Street, Fifth Floor
San Francisco 94111
Phone: 415/433-0444   Fax: 415/433-0449

Florida

Mr. Thorir S. GRONDAL
Honorary Consul
Honorary Consulate of Iceland
5220 North Ocean Drive
Hollywood 33019
Phone: 954/920-7977   Fax: 954/920-6977

Mr. Hilmar S. SKAGFIELD
Honorary Consul General
Honorary Consulate General of Iceland
270 Crossway Road
P.O. Box 753
Tallahassee 32302
Phone: 904/878-1144   Fax: 904/878-6093

Georgia

Mr. Maurice K. HOROWITZ
Honorary Consul General
Honorary Consulate General of Iceland
1677 Tullie Circle, NE
Suite 118
Atlanta 30329
Phone: 404/321-0777   Fax: 404/634-9640

Illinois

Mr. Edward DERWINSKI
Honorary Consul General
Honorary Consulate General of Iceland
Inter-Continental Real Estate & Development
15750 S. Harlem Ave., Suite 28
Orland Park 60611
Phone: 708/429-1126   Fax: 708/429-9972

Kentucky

Mr. Jon S. GUDMUNDSSON
Honorary Consul
Honorary Consulate of Iceland
2600 Highway 146 East
La Grange 40031
Phone: 502/222-1441   Fax: 502/222-1445

Louisiana

Mr. Greg J. BEUERMAN
Honorary Consul
Honorary Consulate of Iceland
210 Baronne St., Suite 1022
New Orleans 70112
Phone: 504/524-3342   Fax: 504/524-3344

Massachusetts

Mr. Elisha Flagg LEE
Honorary Consul
Honorary Consulate of Iceland
Winslow, Evans & Crocker
33 Broad Street
Boston 02210
Phone: 617/227-4300   Fax: 617/227-5505

Michigan

Mr. Edward K. CHRISTIAN
Honorary Consul
Honorary Consulate of Iceland
Saga Communications, Inc.
73 Kercheval Avenue
Gross Pointe Farms 48236
Phone: 313/886-2596   Fax: 313/886-7150

Minnesota

Dr. Orn ARNAR
Honorary Vice Consul
Honorary Consulate General of Iceland
6428 Nordic Circle
Edina 55439
Phone: 612/942-5745   Fax: 612/863-3784

Missouri

Mrs. Vigdis Adalsteinsdottir TAYLOR
Honorary Consul
Honorary Consulate of Iceland
7100 E. 131st St.
Grandview 64030
Phone: 816/763-2046

New York

Mr. Stefan Larus STEFANSSON
Consul General
Consulate General of Iceland
800 Third Avenue
36th Floor
New York 10022-7691
Phone: 212/593-2700   Fax: 212/593-6296

Pennsylvania

Mr. Hubert Jonas GEORGES
Honorary Consul
Honorary Consulate of Iceland
2015 D, South Point Drive
Hummelstown 17036
Phone: 717/566-7791   Fax: 717/566-7792

Puerto Rico

Mr. Antonio RUIZ OCHOS
Honorary Consul
Honorary Consulate of Iceland
Islandia St.#2, Flamboyant Gardens
Bayamon 00959
Phone: 809/786-7171   Fax: 809/740-2888

Texas

Ms. Pamela Kay BAUER
Honorary Consul
Honorary Consulate of Iceland
3205 Seaside
Irving 75062
Phone: 972/699-5417

Mr. Olafur A. ASGEIRSSON
Honorary Consul
Honorary Consulate of Iceland
2348 W. Settler's Way
The Woodlands 77380
Phone: 281/367-2777   Fax: 281/362-4385

Utah

Mr. J. Brent HAYMOND
Vice Consul
Honorary Consulate of Iceland
164 West 200 South
Springville 84663
Phone: 801/489-8046

Virginia

Mr. Gerald Lee PARKS
Honorary Consul
Honorary Consulate of Iceland
Capes Shipping Agencies, Inc.
1128 West Olney Road
Norfolk 23507
Phone: 804/625-3658   Fax: 804/625-6942

Washington

Mr. Jon M. JONSSON
Honorary Consul General
Honorary Consulate General of Iceland
5610-20th Ave. NW
Seattle 98107
Phone: 206/783-4100   Fax: 206/784-8916

India

California

Mr. C.R. BALACHANDRA
Consul General
Consulate General of India
540 Arguello Blvd.
San Francisco 94118
Phone: 415/668-0683   Fax: 415/668-7968

Hawaii

Mrs. Sheila Hessian WATUMULL
Honorary Consul General
Honorary Consulate General of India
2051 Young St.
Honolulu 96826
Phone: 808/947-2618   Fax: 808/262-7512

Illinois

Mr. Jagdish Chandra SHARMA
Consul General
Consulate General of India
455 N. Cityfront Plaza Dr., Suite 850
Chicago 60611
Phone: 312/595-0405   Fax: 312/595-0416

Louisiana

Mr. George DENEGRE
Honorary Consul
Consulate of India
1525 Webster St.
New Orleans 70188

New York

Mr. Harsh Kumar BHASIN
Consul General
Consulate General of India
3 East 64th St.
New York 10021-7097
Phone: 212/774-0600   Fax: 212/861-3788

India Tourist Office
30 Rockefeller Plaza

New York 10112

Ohio

Mr. George P. BICKFORD
Honorary Consul
Honorary Consulate of India
Union Commerce Blvd., Suite 1444
Cleveland 44115
Phone: 216/696-1144

Texas

Mr. Swashpawan SINGH
Consul General
Consulate General of India
1990 Post Oak Blvd., Suite 600
Houston 77056
Phone: 713/626-2148

Indonesia

California

Mr. Bambang Indro YUWONO
Consul General
Consulate General of Indonesia
3457 Wilshire Blvd.
Los Angeles 90010
Phone: 213/383-5126   Fax: 213/487-3871

Mr. Marah Hannief DJOHAN
Consul General
Consulate General of Indonesia
1111 Columbus Ave.
San Francisco 94133
Phone: 415/474-9571   Fax: 415/441-4320

Hawaii

Mr. John KIZIRIAN
Honorary Consul
Honorary Consulate of Indonesia
98-1032 Alania St.
Aiea 96701
Phone: 808/527-6291

Illinois

Mr. Soejono SOERJOATMODJO
Consul General
Consulate General of Indonesia
Two Illinois Ctr.
233 No. Michigan Ave.
Suite 1422
Chicago 60601
Phone: 312/938-0101   Fax: 312/938-3148

New York

Trade Promotion Center - Indonesia
1328 Broadway, Suite 510
New York 10001

Mr. Is ISNAEDI
Consul General
Consulate General of Indonesia
5 East 68th St.
New York 10021
Phone: 212/879-0600   Fax: 212/570-6206

Texas

Mr. Siswadi HARJOWIJOYO
Consul General
Consulate General of Indonesia

10900 Richmond Ave.
Houston 77057
Phone: 713/785-1691   Fax: 713/780-9644

Ireland

California

Mr. Declan M. KELLY
Consul General
Consulate General of Ireland
44 Montgomery St., Suite 3830
San Francisco 94104
Phone: 415/392-4214   Fax: 415/392-0885

Florida

Mr. Patrick J. BYRNE
Honorary Consul
Honorary Consulate of Ireland
2511 NE 31st Ct.
Lighthouse Point 33064
Phone: 305/785-0428

Georgia

Mr Thomas R. WILLIAMS
Honorary Consul
Honorary Consulate of Ireland
191 Peachtree St., Suite 1320
Atlanta 30303

Illinois

Mr. Frank SHERIDAN
Consul General
Consulate General of Ireland
400 N. Michigan Ave.
Chicago 60611
Phone: 312/337-1868   Fax: 312/337-1954

Massachusetts

Mrs. Orla Marie O'HANRAHAN
Consul General
Consulate General of Ireland
535 Boylston St.
Boston 02116
Phone: 617/267-9330   Fax: 617/267-6375

Missouri

Mr. Joseph B. MCGLYNN
Honorary Consul
Honorary Consulate of Ireland
65 Broadview
Clayton 63105
Phone: 617/274-0886

New York

Mr. Peter Barrie ROBINSON
Consul General
Consulate General of Ireland
345 Park Ave., 17th Floor
New York 10154-0037
Phone: 212/319-2555   Fax: 212/980-9475

Texas

Mr. John B. KANE
Honorary Consul
Honorary Consulate of Ireland
1331 Lamar St., Suite 600
Houston 77010
Phone: 793/654-8115

Israel

California

Mr. Yoram BEN ZEEV
Consul General
Consulate General of Israel
6380 Wilshire Blvd., Suite 1700
Los Angeles 90048
Phone: 212/852-5500   Fax: 213/852-5551

Mrs. Linda BEN SHOSHAN
Consul
Israel Economic Office
6300 Wilshire Blvd., #814
Los Angeles 90048
Phone: 213/658-7924   Fax: 213/651-0572

Mr. Daniel SHEK
Consul General
Consulate General of Israel
456 Montgomery St., Suite 2100
San Francisco 94104
Phone: 415/398-8885   Fax: 415/398-8589

Mr. Yishai LAKS
Consul
Israel Economic Office
2350 Mission College Blvd., Suite 365
Santa Clara 95054

Florida

Mrs. Rivka MANOR
Consul
Consulate General of Israel
100 N. Biscayne Blvd., Suite 1800
Miami 33132
Phone: 305/358-8111   Fax: 305/371-5034

Georgia

Ms. Limor NAKAR
Economic Consul, SE USA
Govt. of Israel Economic Mission
1100 Spring St., Rm. 330
Atlanta 30309-2823
Phone: 404/724-0830   Fax: 404/724-9030

Israel Economic Office
1100 Spring St., Suite 440
Atlanta 30309-2823
Phone: 404/875-9924   Fax: 404/875-9924

Mr. Arye MEKEL
Consul General
Israel Tourist Office
1100 Spring St., Suite 440
Atlanta 30309-2823
Phone: 404/875-7851   Fax: 404/874-5364

Illinois

Consul General
Consulate General of Israel
111 E. Wacker Dr., Suite 1308
Chicago 60601
Phone: 312/565-3300   Fax: 312/565-2063

Ms. Tzipora RIMON
Consul General
Consulate General of Israel
111 E. Wacker Dr., Suite 1308
Chicago 60601
Phone: 312/565-3300   Fax: 312/565-2063

Israel Office of Tourism
5 S. Wabash St., Suite 1402
Chicago 60603
Phone: 312/782-4306

Israel Investment and Export Authority
230 N. Michigan Ave., Suite 1620
Chicago 60601
Phone: 312/332-2160

Massachusetts

Mr. Itzhak LEVANON
Consul General
Consulate General of Israel
20 Park Plaza, Suite 1020
Boston 02116
Phone: 617/542-0041   Fax: 617/338-4995

New York

Mr. Shmuel SISSO
Consul General
Consulate General of Israel
800 Second Avenue
New York 10017
Phone: 212/499-5450   Fax: 212/499-5455

Mr. Abraham OREN
Consul
Israel Defense Procurement Mission
800 2nd Ave., 10,11,12 Floor
New York 10017
Phone: 212/551-0444   Fax: 212/551-0482

Mr. Arie Yehiel SOMMER
Consul
Israel Office of Tourism
800 2nd Ave., 16th Fl.
New York 10017
Phone: 212/499-5716   Fax: 212/499-5715

Mr. Shlomo RON
Consul
Israel Economic and Trade Mission
800 2nd Ave., 16 & 17 Fl.
New York 10017
Phone: 212/499-5716   Fax: 212/499-5715

Pennsylvania

Mr. Dan ASHBEL
Consul General
Consulate General of Israel
230 S. 15th St.
Philadelphia 19102
Phone: 215/546-5556   Fax: 215/545-3986

Texas

Mr. Amir ABILEAH
Director of Trade and Investment
Govt. of Israel Economic Mission, Western Region
24 Greenway Plaza, Suite 1500
Houston 77046
Phone: 713/627-3780   Fax: 713/622-1083

Italy

Alabama

Mr. Italo Manfredo FRANCALANCIA
Honorary Vice Consul
Honorary Vice Consulate of Italy
4160 E. Shan Drive
Mobile 36693
Phone: 205/661-1389

Alaska

Mr. Vittorio M. MONTEMEZZANI
Honorary Consular Agent
Honorary Consular Agency of Italy
12840 Silver Spruce Dr.
Anchorage 99516
Phone: 907/726-7664

Arizona

Mr. Joseph Peter MARTORI
Honorary Vice Consul
Honorary Vice Consulate of Italy
2901 N. Central Ave., Suite 2000
Phoenix 85001
Phone: 602/351-8099

California

Mr. Bernard SACCO
Honorary Vice Consul
Honorary Vice Consulate of Italy
1620 E. Brundage Ln.
Bakersfield 93302
Phone: 805/327-9386

Mr. Edward L. FANUCCHI
Honorary Vice Consul
Honorary Vice Consulate of Italy
2409 Merced St.
Fresno 93721
Phone: 209/268-8776

Mr. Folco DE LUCA GABRIELLI
Consul General
Consulate General of Italy
12400 Wilshire Blvd., Suite 300
Los Angeles 90025
Phone: 310/820-0622   Fax: 310/820-0727

Mr. Anthony Umberto VIRGADAMO
Honorary Vice Consul
Honorary Vice Consulate of Italy
1420 54th St., Suite 4
Sacramento 95819
Phone: 916/456-1950

Mrs. Maurizia M. CANTONI
Honorary Vice Consul
Honorary Vice Consulate of Italy
3945 Camino Del Rio South, Suite E
San Diego 92108
Phone: 619/281-3397   Fax: 619/528-0026

Mr. Giulio PRIGIONI
Consul General
Consulate General of Italy
2590 Webster St.
San Francisco 94115
Phone: 415/931-4924   Fax: 415/931-7205

Ms. Silvia RAVIOLA
Honorary Vice Consul
Honorary Vice Consulate of Italy
95 S. Market St., Suite 300
San Jose 95113
Phone: 408/971-9170

Colorado

Mrs. Caterina Gilda SCORDO
Honorary Vice Consul
Honorary Vice Consulate of Italy
8820 W. 84th St.
Denver 80005
Phone: 303/431-1683

Florida

Mr. Anthony F. MARINUCCI
Honorary Consular Agent

Honorary Consular Agency of Italy
7406 Fullerton St., Suite 106
Jacksonville 32256
Phone: 904/363-8811

Ms. Carmela Loredana CICCHETTI
Honorary Vice Consul
Honorary Vice Consulate of Italy
109 Weeping Elm Lane
Longwood 32779
Phone: 407/823-3078

Mr. Giovan Battista CAMPAGNOLA
Consul General
Consulate General of Italy
1200 Brickell Ave., 8th Floor
Miami 33131
Phone: 305/374-6322   Fax: 305/374-7945

Mr. Richard H. STORM
Honorary Consul
Honorary Consulate of Italy
Rivolta Development, Inc.
2833 Main St., Suite 104
Sarasota 34236
Phone: 813/365-6233

Georgia

Mr. John C. MUNNA
Honorary Consul
Honorary Consulate of Italy
755 Mt. Vernon Highway
Atlanta 30328
Phone: 404/303-0503

Mr. Joseph Mose CAFIERO
Honorary Consular Agent
Honorary Consular Agency of Italy
235 Kensington Dr.
Savannah 31405
Phone: 912/232-1276

Hawaii

Mrs. Carmen Theresa DI AMORE-SIAH
Honorary Vice Consul
Honorary Vice Consulate of Italy
735 Bishop St., Suite 419
Honolulu 96813

Illinois

Mr. Pasqauale D'AVINO
Consul General
Consulate General of Italy
500 N. Michigan Ave., Suite 1850
Chicago 60611
Phone: 312/467-1550   Fax: 312/467-1335

Indiana

Mr. Pietro AGOSTINO
Honorary Consular Agent
Honorary Consular Agency of Italy
720 Van Buren St.
South Bend 46616
Phone: 219/233-4021

Kansas

Mr. Roberto Leopoldo SERRA
Honorary Vice Consul
Honorary Vice Consulate of Italy
206 Brotherhood Blvd.
Kansas City 66101
Phone: 913/281-2222

Louisiana

Consul General
Consulate General of Italy
630 Camp St.
New Orleans 70130
Phone: 504/524-2271

Maryland

Mr. Francesco Luigi LEGALUPPI
Honorary Consul
Honorary Consulate of Italy
5 Light St., Suite 600
Baltimore 21202-1219
Phone: 301/727-6550   Fax: 301/727-6563

Massachusetts

Mr. Giovanni GERMANO
Consul General
Consulate General of Italy
100 Boylston St., Suite 900
Boston 02116
Phone: 617/542-0483   Fax: 617/542-3998

Mr. Giuseppe POLIMENI
Honorary Consular Agent
Honorary Consular Agency of Italy
11 Acushnet Ave.
Springfield 01105
Phone: 413/734-0575

Mr. Aspreno Pietro CICCARELLI
Honorary Consular Agent
Honorary Consular Agency of Italy
172 Shrewsbury St.
Worcester 01604
Phone: 508/755-5990

Michigan

Mr. Michele QUARONI
Consul
Consulate of Italy
1840 Buhl Bldg.
535 Griswold
Detroit 48226
Phone: 313/963-8560   Fax: 313/963-8180

Minnesota

Ms. Sarah ROCKLER
Honorary Consul
Honorary Consulate of Italy
24 Circle W.
Edina 55436
Phone: 612/920-3330

Mississippi

Mr. Gino B SCIALDONE
Honorary Consular Agent
Honorary Consular Agency of Italy
E. Pier. P.O. Box 1689
Gulfport 39502
Phone: 601/864-8282

Missouri

Mr. Joseph Alfred COLAGIOVANNI
Honorary Vice Consul
Honorary Vice Consulate of Italy
1 Metropolitan Square, Suite 3400
St. Louis 63102
Phone: 314/259-2008

Nevada

Mr. Paul V. CARELLI
Honorary Consular Agent

Honorary Consular Agency of Italy
302 E. Carson, Unit 830
Las Vegas 89101
Phone: 702/385-6843

New Jersey

Dr. Antonio GIANDOMENICO
Vice Consul
Vice Consulate of Italy
744 Broad St., Suite 2800
Newark 07102
Phone: 201/643-1448   Fax: 973/643-3043

Mr. Guido LUCCARELLI
Honorary Vice Consul
Honorary Vice Consulate of Italy
359 Hamilton Ave.
Trenton 08609
Phone: 609/393-7852

New Mexico

Ms. Paola B. QUARGNALI
Honorary Vice Consul
Honorary Vice Consulate of Italy
1712 Old Town Rd., NW
Albuquerque 87104
Phone: 505/897-0110

New York

Mr. Joseph C. MUSCA
Honorary Vice Consul
Honorary Vice Consulate of Italy
1366 Hertel Ave.
Buffalo 14216
Phone: 716/874-0912   Fax: 716/874-0911

Mr. Franco MISTRETTA
Consul General
Consulate General of Italy
690 Park Ave.
New York 10021-5044
Phone: 212/737-9100   Fax: 212/249-4945

Mr. Arthur ANZALONE
Honorary Vice Consul
Honorary Vice Consulate of Italy
185 Empire Blvd.
Rochester 14609
Phone: 716/482-2803

Ohio

Mr. Biagio PARENTE
Honorary Vice Consul
Honorary Vice Consulate of Italy
Statler Office Tower
1127 Euclid Ave., Room 319
Cleveland 44115
Phone: 216/861-1585

Pennsylvania

Dr. Anna DELLA CROCE DI DOJOLA
BRICANTE
Consul General
Consulate General of Italy
1026 Public Ledger Bldg.
100 South 6th St.
Philadelphia 19106-3470
Phone: 215/592-7329   Fax: 215/592-9808

Mr. Joseph F. D'ANDREA
Honorary Vice Consul
Honorary Vice Consulate of Italy
419 Wood St.
Pittsburgh 15222
Phone: 412/391-7669

Puerto Rico

Mr. Angelo Pio SANFILIPPO
Honorary Consul
Honorary Consulate of Italy
Urban Golden Gate, Calle Amatista 93
Guaynabo 00968
Phone: 809/793-5284

Texas

Mr. Vincenzo Enrico DE NARDO
Honorary Vice Consul
Honorary Vice Consulate of Italy
6255 W. Northwest Hwy., Apt. 304
Dallas 75225
Phone: 214/368-4113

Mr. Sebastiano SALVATORI
Consul General
Consulate General of Italy
1300 Post Oak Blvd., Suite 660
Houston 77056
Phone: 713/850-7520   Fax: 713/850-9113

Utah

Mr. Giovanni G. MASCHERO
Honorary Vice Consul
Honorary Vice Consulate of Italy
1784 W. 9585, S.
South Jordan 84065-9301
Phone: 801/254-7500

Virginia

Mr. Vito PIRAINO
Honorary Consul
Honorary Consulate of Italy
555 Main St.
Norfolk 23510
Phone: 804/622-4898   Fax: 804/625-1631

Washington

Mr. Quinto DE VITIS
Honorary Vice Consul
Honorary Vice Consulate of Italy
10939 NE 49th St.
Kirkland 98033
Phone: 206/885-3332

Jamaica

California

Dr. Horace A. PENSO
Honorary Consul
Honorary Consulate of Jamaica
Rose Hospital Med. Arts Bldg.
27206 Calaroga Ave., Suite 203
Hayward 94545-4300
Phone: 510/266-0060

Mr. Cleveland O. NEIL
Honorary Consul
Honorary Consulate of Jamaica
8703 Venice Blvd.
Los Angeles 90034
Phone: 310/559-3822   Fax: 310/559-3824

Florida

Mr. John P. ATKINS
Consul General
Consulate General of Jamaica
842 Ingraham Bldg., 25 2nd Ave., SE
Miami 33131
Phone: 305/374-8431   Fax: 305/577-4970

Georgia

Mr. Vin Newton MARTON
Honorary Consul
Honorary Consulate of Jamaica
1823 Chedworth Lane
Stone Mountain 30087
Phone: 404/398-6168   Fax: 770/270-0771

Illinois

Mr. Lloyd L. HYDE
Honorary Consul
Honorary Consulate of Jamaica
28 E. Jackson St., Suite 1009
Chicago 60604
Phone: 213/663-0023   Fax: 312/662-4247

Massachusetts

Mr. Kenneth I. GUSCOTT
Honorary Consul General
Honorary Consulate General of Jamaica
351 Massachusetts Ave.
Boston 02115
Phone: 617/266-8604   Fax: 617/266-0185

New York

Ms. Kay Andrea BAXTER
Consul General
Consulate General of Jamaica
767 Third Avenue, 2nd Floor
New York 10017
Phone: 212/935-9000   Fax: 212/935-7507

Texas

Mrs. Mary Beverly FORD
Honorary Consul
Honorary Consulate of Jamaica
7737 SW FW, Suite 580
Houston 77074
Phone: 713/541-3333   Fax: 713/774-4277

Washington

Mrs. Enid Lovida DWYER
Honorary Consul
Honorary Consulate of Jamaica
8223 S. 222nd St.
Kent 98032
Phone: 253/872-8950   Fax: 253/872-8953

Japan

Alabama

Mr. Marrion B. RAMBEAU
Honorary Consul General
Honorary Consulate General of Japan
358 Byron Ave.
Mobile 36609
Phone: 205/342-6654

Alaska

Mr. Takashi SHINOMIYA
Consul General
Consulate General of Japan
550 W. 7th Ave., Suite 701
Anchorage 99501
Phone: 907/279-8428   Fax: 907/279-9271

Arizona

Mr. Thomas S. KADOMOTO
Honorary Consul General
Honorary Consulate General of Japan
7635 N. 46th Ave.
Glendale 85301
Phone: 602/272-2112

California

Mr. Shotaro YACHI
Consul General
Consulate General of Japan
350 So. Grand Ave., Suite 1700
Los Angeles 90071
Phone: 213/617-6700   Fax: 213/617-6727

Dr. Randall Clinger PHILLIPS
Honorary Consul General
Honorary Consulate General of Japan
10455 Pomerado Rd.
San Diego 92131
Phone: 619/635-4537   Fax: 619/693-8562

Mr. Kiyohiko NANAO
Consul General
Consulate General of Japan
50 Fremont St., Suite 2300
San Francisco 94105
Phone: 415/777-3533   Fax: 415/974-3660

Colorado

Mr. William K. HOSOKAWA
Honorary Consul General
Honorary Consulate General of Japan
140 S. Upham Ct.
Denver 80226
Phone: 303/238-9872   Fax: 303/238-8310

Florida

Mr. Hiromu NITTA
Consul General
Consulate General of Japan
World Trade Center Building
80 SW 8th St., Suite 3200
Miami 33130
Phone: 305/530-9090   Fax: 305/530-0950

Georgia

Mr. Yoshiaki NAKAGAWA
Consul
Consulate General of Japan
100 Colony Sq. Bldg.
1175 Peachtree St., NE
Suite 2000
Atlanta 30361
Phone: 404/892-2700   Fax: 404/881-6321

Guam

Mr. Susumu YAMAGISHI
Consul General
Consulate General of Japan
Guam Int'l Trade Center Bldg.
590 S. Marine Dr., Suite 604
Tamuning 96911

Hawaii

Mr. Kishichiro AMAE
Consul General
Consulate General of Japan
1742 Nuuanu Ave.
Honolulu 96817-3294
Phone: 808/536-2226   Fax: 808/537-3276

Illinois

Mr. Tomoyuki ABE
Consul General
Consulate General of Japan
Olympia Ctr.
737 No. Michigan Ave., Suite 1100
Chicago 60611
Phone: 312/280-0400   Fax: 312/280-9568

Mr. Joji MIYAMORI
Consul
Japan Information Center
737 N. Michigan Ave., Suite 1000
Chicago 60611
Phone: 312/280-0430   Fax: 312/280-9568

Louisiana

Mr. Natsuo AMEMIYA
Consul General
Consulate General of Japan
One Poydras Plaza
639 Loyola Ave., Suite 2050
New Orleans 70113
Phone: 504/529-2101   Fax: 504/568-9847

Massachusetts

Mr. Akio KAWATO
Consul General
Consulate General of Japan
Federal Reserve Plaza
600 Atlantic Ave., 14th Floor
Boston 02210
Phone: 617/973-9772   Fax: 617/542-1329

Michigan

Mr. Hirotaka KAMA
Consul
Consulate General of Japan
200 Renaissance Center, Suite 3450
Detroit 48243
Phone: 313/567-0120   Fax: 313/567-0274

Minnesota

Mr. Evan B. WILLIAMS
Honorary Consul General
Honorary Consulate General of Japan
603 E. Lake St.
Wayzata 55391
Phone: 612/473-5347

Missouri

Mr. Tatsuo TANAKA
Consul General
Consulate General of Japan
2519 Commerce Tower
911 Main St.
Kansas City 64105-2706
Phone: 816/471-0111   Fax: 816/472-4248

Mr. Bruce S. BUCKLAND
Honorary Consul General
Honorary Consulate General of Japan
12647 Olive Blvd., Suite 550
St. Louis 63141
Phone: 314/994-1133   Fax: 314/994-1133

New York

Mr. Appleton FRYER
Honorary Consul General
Honorary Consulate General of Japan
85 Windsor St.
Buffalo 14209

Phone: 716/884-2376

Mr. Seiichiro OTSUKA
Consul General
Consulate General of Japan
299 Park Ave.
New York 10171
Phone: 212/371-8222   Fax: 212/319-6357

Oregon

Mr. Gunkatsu KANO
Consul General
Consulate General of Japan
2400 First Interstate Tower
1300 SW 5th Ave.
Portland 97201
Phone: 503/221-1811   Fax: 503/224-8936

Pennsylvania

Mr. William B. EAGLESON
Honorary Consul General
Honorary Consulate General of Japan
140 Jaffrey Rd.
Malvern 19355
Phone: 610/644-4507

Puerto Rico

Mr. Manuel MORALES
Honorary Consul General
Honorary Consulate General of Japan
530 Ponce De Leon Ave.
San Juan 00902
Phone: 787/722-0483

Tennessee

Mr. Edward Gage NELSON
Honorary Consul General
Honorary Consulate General of Japan
3401 West End Bldg., Suite 300
Nashville 37203
Phone: 615/292-8787   Fax: 615/385-3150

Texas

Mr. Theodore H. STRAUSS
Honorary Consul General
Honorary Consulate General of Japan
300 Crescent Court, Suite 200
Dallas 75201
Phone: 214/979-7731   Fax: 214/979-7956

Mr. Hitoshi HONDA
Consul General
Consulate General of Japan
First Interstate Bank Plaza
1000 Louisiana St., Suite 5300
Houston 77002
Phone: 713/652-2977   Fax: 713/651-7822

Washington

Mr. Yoshio NOMOTO
Consul General
Consulate General of Japan
601 Union St., Suite 500
Seattle 98101
Phone: 206/682-9107   Fax: 206/624-9097

Wyoming

Mrs. Mariko Terasaki MILLER
Honorary Consul General
Honorary Consulate General of Japan
111 West 14th St.
Casper 82601

Phone: 307/234-2317   Fax: 307/234-2317

Jordan

Illinois

Mr. Rafiq SWEIS
Honorary Consul General
Honorary Consulate General of Jordan
5423 W. 95th Street
Oaklawn 60453
Phone: 708/233-9988   Fax: 708/233-9911

Michigan

Mr. Habib Issa FAKHOUI
Honorary Consul
Honorary Consulate of Jordan
28551 South Field Rd., Suite 203
Lathrup 48076
Phone: 248/557-4377   Fax: 248/557-4517

New York

Hon. Hussein KHEIR
Consul General
Consulate General of Jordan
866 United Nations Plaza
New York 10017
Phone: 212/752-0135   Fax: 212/826-0830

Texas

Mr. Saber Muhammad AMAWI
Honorary Consul General
Honorary Consulate General of Japan
P.O. Box 3727
Houston 77253
Phone: 713/224-2911   Fax: 713/224-2301

Kazakstan

New York

Mr. Marat Khasenuly TASMAGAMBETOV
Consul
Consulate of Kazakstan
866 United Nations Place
Suite 586A
New York 10017
Phone: 212/888-3024   Fax: 212/230-1172

Kenya

California

Mr. Alfred Kyalo KASINGA
Consul General
Consulate General of Kenya
9150 Wilshire Blvd.
Suite 160
Beverly Hills 90212
Phone: 310/274-6635   Fax: 310/859-7010

New York

Ms. Mary M. MKIMBO
Consul General
Consulate General of Kenya
424 Madison Ave.
New York 10017-1106
Phone: 212/468-1300   Fax: 212/688-0911

Kiribati

Hawaii

Mr. William E. PAUPE
Honorary Consul
Honorary Consulate of Kiribati
850 Richards St., Suite 503
Honolulu 96813
Phone: 808/521-7703

Korea

Alabama

Mr. Lee Roe SEIFERT
Honorary Consul
Honorary Consulate of Korea
63 S. Royal St.
Mobile 36629
Phone: 334/438-8375   Fax: 334/438-8597

Alaska

Mr. Joon Kil CHA
Consul General
Consulate General of Korea
101 Benson Blvd., Suite 304
Anchorage 99503
Phone: 907/561-5488   Fax: 907/563-0313

California

Amb. Hyung-Ki MIN
Consul General
Consulate General of Korea
3243 Wilshire Blvd.
Los Angeles 90010
Phone: 213/385-9300   Fax: 213/384-5139

Mr. Ri Hoon HUR
Consul General
Consulate General of Korea
3500 Clay St.
San Francisco 94118
Phone: 415/921-2251   Fax: 415/921-5946

Korean Education Office
3500 Clay St.
San Francisco 94118

Colorado

Mr. Dwight Alan HAMILTON
Honorary Consul
Honorary Consulate of Korea
1600 Broadway, Suite 600
Denver 80202
Phone: 303/830-0500   Fax: 303/860-7855

Florida

Mr. Burton A. LANDY
Honorary Consul
Honorary Consulate of Korea
2601 E. Oakland Blvd., Suite 602
Ft. Lauderdale 33306
Phone: 305/467-1704   Fax: 305/577-7001

Mr. Boo Yul PARK
Consul General
Consulate General of Korea
201 So. Biscayne Blvd., Suite 800
Miami 33131
Phone: 305/372-1555   Fax: 305/371-6559

Georgia

Mr. Hoon CHANG
Consul General
Consulate General of Korea
229 Peachtree St., Suite 500
Atlanta 30303
Phone: 404/522-1611   Fax: 404/521-3169

Guam

Mr. Joong Yol AUN
Consul General
Consulate General of Korea
GCIC Bldg.
411 W. Soledad Ave., Suite 305
Agana 96910
Phone: 671/472-6488   Fax: 671/477-6391

Hawaii

Mr. Shin Sung KANG
Consul General
Consulate General of Korea
2756 Pali Hwy.
Honolulu 96817
Phone: 808/595-6109   Fax: 808/595-3046

Illinois

Amb. Jong Kyou BYUN
Consul General
Consulate General of Korea
455 No. City Front Plaza Dr.
27th Floor
Chicago 60611
Phone: 312/822-9485   Fax: 312/822-9849

Louisiana

Mr. James Julian COLEMAN
Honorary Consul General
Honorary Consulate General of Korea
321 St. Charles Ave.
New Orleans 70130
Phone: 504/586-1979   Fax: 504/525-9464

Massachusetts

Mr. Yang LEE
Consul General
Consulate General of Korea
One Financial Center, 15th Floor
Boston 02111
Phone: 617/348-3660   Fax: 617/348-3670

Michigan

Mr. Alphonse V. TABAKA
Honorary Consul
Honorary Consulate of Korea
40400 E. Ann Arbor Rd.
Plymouth 48170

Minnesota

Ms. Allison R. MERCER
Honorary Consul
Honorary Consulate of Korea
2222 Park Ave.
Minneapolis 55404
Phone: 612/870-4400   Fax: 612/871-1522

New York

Mr. Noh Soo PARK
Consul General

Consulate General of Korea
460 Park Ave., 5th Floor
New York 10022
Phone: 212/752-1700   Fax: 212/308-1756

Oklahoma

Mr. John KIRKPATRICK
Honorary Consul
Honorary Consulate of Korea
1200 Northwest 63rd., Suite 500
Oklahoma City 73116
Phone: 405/840-2882   Fax: 405/840-2946

Oregon

Mr. Ralph E. WEHINGER
Honorary Consul
Honorary Consulate of Korea
104 Royal Ave., N.
Eagle Point 97524
Phone: 503/826-6800

Mr. Robert William DONALDSON
Honorary Consul General
Honorary Consulate General of Korea
707 SW Washington St.
Suite 1200
Portland 97205
Phone: 503/248-1941   Fax: 503/224-5560

Puerto Rico

Mr. Hector REICHARD
Honorary Consul General
Honorary Consulate of Korea
255 Ponce de Leon Ave.
10th Floor
San Juan 00917
Phone: 787/758-8888   Fax: 787/765-4225

Texas

Mr. Kenneth R. MARVEL
Honorary Consul
Honorary Consulate of Korea
13111 N. Central Expressway
Dallas 75243
Phone: 214/454-1112   Fax: 214/454-1212

Mr. Haeng Kyeom OH
Consul General
Consulate General of Korea
1990 Post Oak Blvd., Suite 1250
Houston 77056
Phone: 713/961-0186   Fax: 713/961-3340

Washington

Mr. Hoon SOHN
Consul General
Consulate General of Korea
United Airlines Bldg.
2033 Sixth Ave., Suite 1128
Seattle 98121
Phone: 206/441-1011   Fax: 206/441-7912

Kuwait

New York

Consul General
Consulate General of Kuwait
321 E. 44th St.
New York 10017
Phone: 212/973-4318   Fax: 212/370-1733

Kyrgyzstan

California

Mr. Seymour Chic WOLK
Honorary Consul
Honorary Consulate of Kyrgyzstan
333 S. Grand Ave., Suite 3550
Los Angeles 90071
Phone: 213/626-7738   Fax: 213/626-7739

Latvia

California

Dr. Alfred RAISTERS
Honorary Consul
Honorary Consulate of Latvia
3013 Palos Verdes Dr., W.
Palos Verdes Estates 90274
Phone: 310/377-1784   Fax: 310/377-5235

Illinois

Mr. Norbert KLAUCENS
Honorary Consul
Honorary Consulate of Latvia
3239 Arnold Lane
Northbrook 60062
Phone: 847/498-5950   Fax: 847/498-6880

Ohio

Mr. Peteris JURJANS
Honorary Consul
Honorary Consulate of Korea
38021 Euclid Ave.
Willoughby 44094
Phone: 216/951-6665   Fax: 216/951-4797

Lebanon

California

Mr. Gebran Michel SOUFAN
Consul General
Consulate General of Lebanon
7060 Hollywood Blvd., Suite 510
Los Angeles 90028
Phone: 213/467-1253   Fax: 213/467-2935

Michigan

Mr. Hassan MUSLIMANI
Consul General
Consulate General of Lebanon
1959 E. Jefferson, Suite 4-A
Detroit 48207
Phone: 313/567-0233   Fax: 313/567-8797

New York

Mr. Antoine CHEDID
Consul General
Consulate General of Lebanon
9 East 76th St.
New York 10021
Phone: 212/744-7905   Fax: 212/794-1510

Lesotho

Louisiana

Mr. Morris W. REED
Honorary Consul
Honorary Consulate of Lesotho
4 Grand Teton Ct.
New Orleans 70131
Phone: 504/391-0452

Texas

Ms. Bertha E. MEANS
Honorary Consul
Honorary Consulate of Lesotho
7400 Valburn Dr.
Austin 78731
Phone: 512/478-2222

Liberia

California

Mr. Andrew V. IPPOLITO
Honorary Consul General
Honorary Consulate General of Liberia
6127 Ramirez Cyn Rd.
Malibu 90265
Phone: 310/457-1967   Fax: 310/454-9122

Mr. Gary SCHNITZER
Honorary Consul General
Honorary Consulate General of Liberia
3560 Jackson St.
San Francisco 94118
Phone: 415/673-5020

Georgia

Dr. Walter F. YOUNG
Honorary Consul General
Honorary Consulate General of Liberia
2717 Cascade Rd., SW
Atlanta 30311
Phone: 404/753-4754   Fax: 404/755-4466

Illinois

Mr. Alexander GBAYEE
Honorary Consul General
Honorary Consulate General of Liberia
423 E. 60th St.
Chicago 60637
Phone: 312/643-8635

Louisiana

Ms. Joyce DURLING-JONES
Honorary Consul
Honorary Consulate of Liberia
Vayou St. John, 1219 N. Rendon St.
New Orleans 70119
Phone: 504/486-7800   Fax: 504/486-3200

Michigan

Mr. Michael M. BAYDOUN
Honorary Consul General
Honorary Consulate General of Liberia
9602 Greenfield Rd.
Detroit 48227
Phone: 313/836-1000

New York

Mr. Charles H. WILSON
Consul General
Consulate General of Liberia
820 Second Ave.
New York 10017

Phone: 212/687-1027   Fax: 212/687-1035

Pennsylvania

Ms. Teta V. BANKS
Honorary Consul
Honorary Consulate of Liberia
204 Garnet Lane
Bala Cynwyd 19004
Phone: 610/668-1873   Fax: 215/751-9300

Texas

Mr. Fred RODELL
Honorary Consul General
Honorary Consulate General of Liberia
3300 S. Gessner
Houston 77063
Phone: 713/952-5959

Lithuania

California

Mr. Wheelock R. BINGHAM
Honorary Consul
Honorary Consulate of Lithuania
1 Maritime Pz., Suite 2525
San Francisco 94111
Phone: 415/788-7354   Fax: 415/788-5302

Mr. Vytautas CEKANAUSKAS
Honorary Consul General
Honorary Consulate General of Lithuania
3236 N. Sawtooth Ct.
Westlake Village 91362
Phone: 805/496-5324   Fax: 805/496-7435

Illinois

Mr. Vaclovas D. KLEIZA
Honorary Consul General
Honorary Consulate General of Lithuania
6500 S. Pulaski Rd.
Chicago 60629
Phone: 312/582-5478   Fax: 312/582-0961

New York

Mr. Petras ANUSAS
Consul General
Consulate General of Lithuania
420 Fifth Ave.
New York 10018
Phone: 212/354-7840   Fax: 212/354-7911

Ohio

Mrs. Ingrida Gertrude BUBLYS
Honorary Consul
Honorary Consulate of Lithuania
1801 Marcella Rd., Suite 101
Cleveland 44119
Phone: 216/486-8692   Fax: 216/486-8612

Luxembourg

California

Mr. Frank P. ANGEL
Honorary Consul
Honorary Consulate of Luxembourg
2961 Valmere Dr.
Malibu 90265
Phone: 310/456-8547   Fax: 310/277-7853

Mr. Pierre E. GRAMEGNA
Consul General
Consulate General of Luxembourg
1 Sansome St., Suite 830
San Francisco 94104
Phone: 415/788-0816   Fax: 415/788-0985

Florida

Mr. Jacques E. TURNER
Honorary Consul
Honorary Consulate of Luxembourg
200 S. Biscayne Blvd., Suite 3240
Miami 33131
Phone: 305/373-1300   Fax: 305/373-1303

Georgia

Mr. Georges A. HOFFMAN
Honorary Consul
Honorary Consulate of Luxembourg
Promenade II
1230 Peachtree St., NE - Suite 3100
Atlanta 30326
Phone: 404/815-3762   Fax: 404/685-7062

Illinois

Mr. Donald John HANSEN
Honorary Consul
Honorary Consulate of Luxembourg
180 N. La Salle St., Suite 1400
Chicago 60601
Phone: 312/726-0355   Fax: 312/263-9042

Indiana

Mr. James B. STEICHEN
Honorary Consul
Honorary Consulate of Luxembourg
8501 Harcourt Rd.
Indianapolis 46260
Phone: 317/257-9197   Fax: 317/875-8638

Louisiana

Mr. Gary J. MANNINIA
Honorary Vice Consul
Honorary Vice Consulate of Luxembourg
8012 Oak St.
New Orleans 70118
Phone: 504/861-3743   Fax: 504/861-3973

Michigan

Mr. William DAVIDSON
Honorary Consul
Honorary Consulate of Luxembourg
2300 Harmon Rd.
Detroit 48326
Phone: 810/340-2200   Fax: 810/340-2308

Minnesota

Mr. Paul R. HEINERSCHEID
Honorary Consul
Honorary Consulate of Luxembourg
2375 University Ave., W.
St. Paul 55114
Phone: 612/644-0942   Fax: 612/644-8025

Missouri

Mr. Robert F. SCHAEFFER
Honorary Consul General
Honorary Consulate General of Luxembourg
325 Westwoods Circle
Liberty 64068
Phone: 816/792-0841   Fax: 816/792-4999

New York

Mr. Jean GRAFF
Consul General
Consulate General of Luxembourg
17 Beekman Pl.
New York 10022
Phone: 212/888-6664   Fax: 212/888-6116

Ohio

Mr. James Robert BRIGHT
Honorary Consul
Honorary Consulate of Luxembourg
925 Euclid Ave., Suite 2000
Cleveland 44115
Phone: 216/696-4700   Fax: 216/696-2706

Texas

Mr. Clark Allen JOHNSON
Honorary Consul
Honorary Consulate of Luxembourg
301 Commerce St., Suite 600
Fort Worth 76102
Phone: 817/878-8000   Fax: 817/878-7861

Washington

Mr. Fred R. CERF
Honorary Consul
Honorary Consulate of Luxembourg
725 1st Ave., S.
Kirkland 98033
Phone: 206/266-0100   Fax: 206/266-0002

Macedonia

New York

Mr. Zvonko E. MUCUNSKI
Acting Consul General
Consulate General of Macedonia
866 United Nations Plaza, Suite 4018
New York 10017
Phone: 212/317-1727   Fax: 212/317-1484

Madagascar

California

Mr. Jean-Marie DE LA BEAUJARDIERE
Honorary Consul
Honorary Consulate of Madagascar
867 Garland Dr.
Palo Alto 94303
Phone: 415/323-7113

New York

Consulate of Madagascar
801 2nd Ave., Room 404
New York 10017
Phone: 212/986-9491   Fax: 212/986-6271

Pennsylvania

Mr. John HUFFAKER
Honorary Consul
Honorary Consulate of Madagascar
1235 Westlakes Dr., Suite 400
Berwyn 19312
Phone: 610/640-7832   Fax: 610/640-7835

Texas

Mr. Paul Aloysius O'BRYAN
Honorary Consul
Honorary Consulate of Madagascar
18010 Widcombe Dr.
Houston 77084
Phone: 713/550-2559   Fax: 713/550-1340

Malawi

California

Dr. James F. CLEMENTS
Honorary Consul
Honorary Consulate of Malawi
3420 Fredas Hill Rd.
Vista 92084
Phone: 619/598-1836   Fax: 619/598-0066

Malaysia

California

Mr. Ahmad Anuar ABDUL HAMID
Consul General
Consulate General of Malaysia
550 S. Hope St., Suite 400
Los Angeles 90071
Phone: 213/892-1238   Fax: 213/892-9031

Hawaii

Mr. Herbert E. WOLFF
Honorary Consul
Honorary Consulate of Malaysia
First Hawaiian Bank, P.O. Box 3200
Honolulu 96847
Phone: 808/525-8144

New York

Mr. Ching Hong SAW
Consul General
Consulate General of Malaysia
313 East 43rd St.
New York 10017
Phone: 212/490-2722   Fax: 212/867-2865

Mr. Noharuddin NORDIN
Trade Commissioner
Malaysia Trade Office
313 E. 43rd St., 3rd Floor
New York 10017
Phone: 212/682-0232   Fax: 212/983-1987

Oregon

Mr. Jay A. KILLEEN
Honorary Consul
Honorary Consulate of Malaysia
6144 SW 37th Ave.
Portland 97221
Phone: 503/246-0707

Mali

California

Mr. William A. BURKE
Honorary Consul
Honorary Consulate of Mali
1894 Westbridge Rd.
Los Angeles 90049
Phone: 213/476-9369

Florida

Mr. Mayer SHIRAZIPOUR
Honorary Consul
Honorary Consulate of Mali
1624 E. Sunrise Blvd.
Ft. Lauderdale 33304
Phone: 305/463-1700   Fax: 305/771-3281

Massachusetts

Mr. Warren J. SCHJOLDEN
Honorary Consul
Honorary Consulate of Mali
339 Union St.
Boston 02370

New Mexico

Mr. Oliver C. REESE
Honorary Consul
Honorary Consulate of Mali
7600 American Heritage Dr., NE
Albuquerque 87109

Malta

California

Mr. Charles J. VASSALLO
Honorary Consul General
Honorary Consulate General of Malta
2562 San Bruno Ave.
San Francisco 94134
Phone: 415/468-4321   Fax: 415/468-1461

Florida

Mr. John F. GALEA
Honorary Consul
Honorary Consulate of Malta
150 S. Golf Blvd.
Pompano Beach 33064
Phone: 305/942-2491

Michigan

Mr. Larry J. ZAHRA
Honorary Consul General
Honorary Consulate General of Malta
6755 Middlebelt Rd.
Garden City 48135
Phone: 313/565-5916   Fax: 313/525-9782

Minnesota

Mr. Joseph Stephen MICALLEF
Honorary Consul General
Honorary Consulate General of Malta
332 Minnesota St., Suite 3090
St. Paul 55101
Phone: 612/224-1844   Fax: 612/228-0776

Missouri

Dr. Marcel Vincent DINGLI ATTARD
INGUANEZ
Honorary Consul
Honorary Consulate of Malta
301 W. Lexington St., Room 201-201A
Independence 64050
Phone: 816/833-0033   Fax: 816/833-2125

New York

Malta National Tourist Office
Empire State Bldg.

350 Firth Ave., Suite 4412
New York 10118
Phone: 212/695-9520

Mr. Victor PACE
Consul
Consulate General of Malta
249 E. 35th St.
New York 10016
Phone: 212/725-2345   Fax: 212/779-7097

Pennsylvania

Mrs. Sheila Gail PARISH
Honorary Consul
Honorary Consulate of Malta
941 Bryn Mawr Ave.
Penn Valley 19072
Phone: 610/664-7475   Fax: 610/664-2835

Texas

Mr. Eugene LOVELAND
Honorary Consul General
Honorary Consulate General of Malta
910 Travis St., Suite 800
Houston 77002
Phone: 713/428-7800   Fax: 713/428-3044

Marshall Islands

Hawaii

Mr. Philip ANUNGAR
Consul
Consulate General of the Marshall Islands
1888 Lusitana St., Suite 301
Honolulu 96813
Phone: 808/545-7767   Fax: 808/545-7211

Mauritius

California

Mr. Bruce E. DIZENFELD
Honorary Consul
Consulate of Mauritius
10100 Santa Monica Blvd., 8th Floor
Los Angeles 90067
Phone: 310/557-2009   Fax: 310/551-0283

Georgia

Mr. Robert L. REARDEN
Honorary Consul
Honorary Consulate of Mauritius
3333 Peachtree Rd., N.E., Suite 500
Atlanta 30326-1043
Phone: 404/239-6471   Fax: 404/264-7100

Mexico

Alaska

Dr. Evelia M. EHRENBARD
Honorary Consul
Honorary Consulate of Mexico
4141 B St., Suite 308
Anchorage 99503
Phone: 907/345-6780

Arizona

Mr. Ecce lei MENDOZA MACHADO

Consul
Consulate of Mexico
541 10th St.
Douglas 85607
Phone: 520/364-3107   Fax: 520/364-1379

Mr. Roberto RODRIGUEZ HERNANDEZ
Consul
Consulate of Mexico
480 Grand Ave. & Terminal St.
Nogales 85621
Phone: 602/287-2521   Fax: 520/287-3175

Mr. Luis CABRERA CUARON
Consul General
Consulate General of Mexico
1990 West Camelback Plaza, Suite 110
Phoenix 85015
Phone: 602/242-7398   Fax: 602/242-2957

Mr. Carlos Angel TORRES GARCIA
Consul
Consulate Agent of Mexico
553 S. Stone Ave.
Tucson 85705
Phone: 602/882-5595   Fax: 602/882-8959

California

Mr. Hugo Rene OLIVA ROMERO
Deputy Consul
Consulate of Mexico
331-333 W. 2nd St.
Calexico 92231
Phone: 619/357-3863   Fax: 619/357-6284

Mr. Guillermo RAMOS URIARTE
Consul
Consulate of Mexico
830 Van Ness Ave.
Fresno 93721
Phone: 209/233-4219   Fax: 209/233-6156

Mr. Carlos CASAS-GUERRERO
Vice Consul
Mexico Commercial Office
350 S. Figueroa St., 2nd Floor
Los Angeles 90211

Mr. Jose Angel PESCADOR OSUNA
Consul General
Consulate General of Mexico
2401 W. 6th St.
Los Angeles 90057
Phone: 213/624-3261   Fax: 213/389-9186

Mr. Jorge A. GAMBOA PATRON
Vice Consul
Mexico Tourism Office
1801 Century Park, E., Suite 1080
Los Angeles 90067
Phone: 310/203-8328

Mrs. Luz Elena BUENO ZIRION
Consul
Consulate of Mexico
201 E. 4th St.
Oxnard 93030
Phone: 805/483-4684   Fax: 805/385-3527

Mr. Carlos Ignacio GIRALT CABRALES
Deputy Consul General
Consulate General of Mexico
9812 Old Winery Place, Suite 10
Sacramento 95827
Phone: 916/363-0403   Fax: 916/363-0625

Ms. Rosa Clementina CURTO-PEREZ
Consul
Consulate of Mexico
532 North D St.

San Bernardino 92401
Phone: 909/889-8936   Fax: 909/889-8285

Mr. Luis HERRERA LASSO MIJARES
Consul General
Consulate General of Mexico
1549 India St.
San Diego 92101
Phone: 619/231-8414   Fax: 619/231-4802

Office of Agriculture & Forestry Affairs - Mexico
12625 High Bluff Dr.
San Diego 92130

Mr. Santiago Ignacio GOMEZ AGUILAR
Vice Consul
Office of Mexican Fisheries
2550 Fifth Ave., E., Suite 101
San Diego 92101

Mr. Cesar A. LAJUD DESENTIS
Consul General
Consulate General of Mexico
870 Market St., Suite 528
San Francisco 94102
Phone: 415/392-6576   Fax: 415/392-3233

Mr. Sergio Ernesto CASANUEVA REGUART
Consul
Consulate of Mexico
380 N. 1st St., Suite 102
San Jose 95113
Phone: 408/294-3414   Fax: 408/294-4506

Ms. Maria De Lourdes URBINA-PAREDES
Consul
Consulate of Mexico
828 N. Broadway St.
Santa Ana 92701
Phone: 714/835-3069   Fax: 714/835-3472

Colorado

Mr. Carlos Antonio BARROS HORCASITAS
Consul General
Consulate General of Mexico
48 Steele Street
Denver 80206
Phone: 303/331-1110   Fax: 303/331-0169

Florida

Mr. Angel Luis ORTIZ MONASTERIO
CASTELLANOS
Consul General
Consulate General of Mexico
1200 N.W. 78th Ave., Suite 200
Miami 33126
Phone: 305/716-4953   Fax: 305/593-2758

Mexico Commercial Office
New World Tower
100 N. Biscayne Blvd., Suite 1601
Miami 33132
Phone: 305/372-9929

Mr. Benito ECHEVERRIA ZUNO
Vice Consul
Mexican Tourism Office
128 Aragon Ave.
Miami 33156
Phone: 305/443-9160

Mr. Martin TORRES GUTIERREZ RUBIO
Consul
Consulate of Mexico
823 E. Colonial Dr.
Orlando 32803
Phone: 407/895-5106   Fax: 407/895-6140

Georgia

Mr. Teodoro MAUS REISBAUM
Consul General
Consulate General of Mexico
3220 Peachtree Rd., NE
Atlanta 30305
Phone: 404/688-3258   Fax: 404/266-2302

Mexican Commercial Office
229 Peachtree St., NE
Suite 907
Atlanta 30303

Hawaii

Mrs. Martha Elia SILVERMAN
Honorary Consul
Honorary Consulate of Mexico
677 Ala Moana Blvd., Suite 501
Honolulu 96813
Phone: 808/524-4390   Fax: 808/531-7223

Illinois

Mr. Leonardo FRENCH IDUARTE
Consul General
Consulate General of Mexico
300 N. Michigan Ave., Suite 200
Chicago 60601
Phone: 312/833-6331   Fax: 312/855-9257

Mexican National Tourism Office
70 E. Lake St., Suite 1413
Chicago 60601
Phone: 312/565-2778

Mr. Miguel Angel LEAMAN RIVAS
Consul
Mexican Commercial Office
225 N. Michigan Ave., Suite 708
Chicago 60601
Phone: 312/856-0316

Louisiana

Mr. Agustin GARCIA LOPEZ SANTAOLALLA
Consul General
Consulate General of Mexico
1140 World Trade Center
2 Canal St., Suite 840
New Orleans 70130
Phone: 504/522-3596   Fax: 504/525-2332

Massachusetts

Mrs. Eugenia Estela MURILLO DE VILLEGAS
Consul
Consulate of Mexico
20 Park Plaza, Suite 506
Boston 02109
Phone: 617/426-4942   Fax: 617/695-1957

Michigan

Mr. Vicente MONTEMAYOR CANTU
Consul
Consulate of Mexico
600 Renaissance Center, Suite 1510
Detroit 48243
Phone: 313/965-1868   Fax: 313/567-7543

Commercial Office of Mexico
2000 Town Ctr., Suite 1900
Southfield 48075

Missouri

Mr. Humberto ZAMORA TREVINO
Consul General
Consulate of Mexico
1015 Locust St., Suite 922

St. Louis 63101
Phone: 314/436-3233   Fax: 314/436-2695

New Mexico

Mr. Jaime PAZ Y PUENTE GUTIERREZ
Consul
Consulate of Mexico
400 Gold Ave., SW., Suite 100
Albuquerque 87102
Phone: 505/247-2139   Fax: 505/842-9490

New York

Mr. Jorge PINTO MAZAL
Consul General
Consulate General of Mexico
8 E. 41st St.
New York 10017
Phone: 212/689-0456   Fax: 212/545-8197

Mr. Jose Luis SAMANO ROO
Vice Consul
Mexican Commercial Office
150 E. 58th St., 17th Floor
New York 10155

Mrs. Matilde GARCIA VERASTEGUI
Consul
Mexican Tourism Office
405 Park Ave.
New York 10022

Mexican Foreign Trade Institute
375 Park Ave., Suite 1905
New York 10152
Phone: 212/826-2916

North Carolina

Mr. Wayne P. COOPER
Honorary Consul
Honorary Consulate of Mexico
4101 West Blvd.
Charlotte 28219
Phone: 919/394-2198

Oregon

Mr. Gustavo MAZA PADILLA
Consul
Consulate of Mexico
1234 SW Morrison St.
Portland 97205
Phone: 503/274-1442

Pennsylvania

Mr. Juan Manuel LOMBERA LOPEZ
COLLADA
Consul
Consulate of Mexico
21 S. 5th Street, Suite 1010
Philadelphia 19106
Phone: 215/922-4262   Fax: 215/923-7281

Puerto Rico

Mr. Hugo Jesus GUTIERREZ VEGA
Consul General
Consulate General of Mexico
654 Avenida Munoz Rivera, Suite 1837
Hato Rey 00918
Phone: 809/764-0258

Tennessee

Mr. Eloy GUERRA
Honorary Consul

Honorary Consulate of Mexico
316 Philfre Ct.
Nashville 37217
Phone: 615/399-2127

Texas

Mr. Eusebio Augusto ROMERO ESQUIVEL
Deputy Consul General
Consulate General of Mexico
Little Field Bldg.
200 E. 6th St., Suite 200
Austin 78701
Phone: 512/478-2866   Fax: 512/478-8008

Ms. Berenice RENDON TALAVERA
Consul
Consulate of Mexico
724 E. Elizabeth & 7th St.
Brownsville 78520
Phone: 512/542-4431   Fax: 956/542-7267

Mr. Armando Federico BETETA MONSALVE
Consul
Consulate of Mexico
800 Shoreline Blvd., Suite 410
Corpus Christi 78401
Phone: 512/887-7366   Fax: 512/882-9324

Mr. Ramon XILOTL RAMIREZ
Consul General
Consulate General of Mexico
8855 Stemmons Freeway
Dallas 75247
Phone: 214/522-9740   Fax: 214/630-3511

Mr. Carlos Jose BELLO ROCH
Vice Consul
Office of the Commercial Counselor - Mexico
2777 Stemmons Freeway, Suite 1632
Dallas 52158

Mr. Leonardo AYALA TORRES
Consul
Consulate of Mexico
300 E. Losoya
Del Rio 78840
Phone: 512/775-2352   Fax: 210/774-6497

Mr. Jose Luis SUAREZ Y COELLO
Consul
Consulate of Mexico
140 Adams St.
Eagle Pass 78852
Phone: 512/773-9255   Fax: 210/773-9397

Mr. Armando ORTIZ-ROCHA
Consul General
Consulate General of Mexico
910 E. San Antonio St.
El Paso 79901
Phone: 915/533-3644   Fax: 915/532-7163

Mr. Jerry MURAD
Honorary Consul
Honorary Consulate of Mexico
108 N. Commerce St.
Fort Worth 76102
Phone: 817/870-2270

Mr. Manuel PEREZ CARDENAS
Consul General
Consulate General of Mexico
3015 Richmond Ave., Suite 100
Houston 77098
Phone: 713/524-2300   Fax: 713/523-6244

Mr. Leopoldo Octavio VIAL TORRES
Vice Consul
Mexican Tourism Office
2707 N. Loop, Suite 450

Houston 77008

Mr. Luis Humberto RAMIREZ
Consul
Consulate General of Mexico
1612 Farragut St.
Laredo 78040
Phone: 512/723-6369   Fax: 956/723-1741

Mrs. Martha Maria ORTIZ DE ROSAS DE
CARVAJAL
Consul
Consulate of Mexico
600 S. Broadway
Mc Allen 78501
Phone: 512/686-0243   Fax: 956/686-4901

Mrs. Juana Maria RUIZ MARTINEZ
Consul
Consulate of Mexico
511 W. Ohio St., Suite 121
Midland 79701
Phone: 915/687-2334   Fax: 915/687-2334

Mr. Carlos Manuel SADA SOLANA
Consul General
Consulate General of Mexico
127 Navarro St.
San Antonio 78205
Phone: 512/227-9145   Fax: 210/227-1817

Mr. Luis Felipe SANTANDER RODRIGUEZ
Consul
Mexican Cultural Institute
600 Hemisfair Plaza Way.
San Antonio 78205

Ms. Maria I. CASTANON CASTANON
Vice Consul
Mexican Commercial Affairs Office
1100 NW Loop 410, Suite 754
San Antonio 78213

Mr. Carlos Cecilio LANDEROS HIJAR
Consul
Office of the Mexican Attorney General
Frost Bank Bldg.
100 West Houston St., Suite 1441
San Antonio 78205

Utah

Mrs. Anacelia PEREZ DE MEYER
Consul
Consulate of Mexico
458 East Ave., Suite 110
Salt Lake City 84111
Phone: 801/521-8502   Fax: 801/521-0534

Virginia

Mr. Roberto RODRIGUEZ ITURRALDE
Honorary Consul
Honorary Consulate of Mexico
51 E. Virginia Beach Blvd.
Norfolk 23502
Phone: 804/461-4933

Mr. Walter W. REGIRER
Honorary Consul
Honorary Consulate of Mexico
University Park Bldg., 2420 Pemberton Rd.
Richmond 23233
Phone: 804/747-9200

Washington

Mr. Hugo Abel CASTRO BOJORQUEZ
Consul
Consulate of Mexico

2132 Third Ave.
Seattle 98121
Phone: 206/448-3526   Fax: 206/448-4771

Wisconsin

Dr. Rudolph Caro HECHT
Honorary Consul
Honorary Consulate of Mexico
141 North Hancock St.
Madison 53703
Phone: 608/283-6000

Micronesia

Guam

Mr. Wilton Jaboar MACKWELUNG
Consul General
Consulate General of Micronesia
Old Hakubotan Bldg.
973 S. Marine Dr., Suite 201
Tamuning 96911
Phone: 671/646-9154

Hawaii

Mr. Kasio Emil MIDA
Consul General
Consulate General of Micronesia
3049 Ualena St., Suite 408
Honolulu 96819
Phone: 808/836-4775   Fax: 808/836-6869

Monaco

California

Mr. Theodore M. ROOSENDAHL
Honorary Consul General
Honorary Consulate General of Monaco
7449 Melrose Ave.
Los Angeles 90046
Phone: 213/655-8970

Mrs. Paula Sullivan ESCHER
Honorary Consul General
Honorary Consulate General of Monaco
21 Presidio Ave.
San Francisco 94115
Phone: 415/346-7766

District of Columbia

Mr. Myles Joseph AMBROSE
Honorary Consul
Honorary Consulate of Monaco
888 16th St., NW, Suite 400
Washington 20006
Phone: 202/296-8600   Fax: 202/296-8791

Florida

Mr. Alfred J. LAUPHEIMER
Honorary Consul
Honorary Consulate of Monaco
Coastal House
2200 S. Ocean Blvd., Apt. 308
Palm Beach 33444
Phone: 305/278-8051

Louisiana

Mr. Carl Fredrick DAHLBERG
Honorary Consul General

Honorary Consulate General of Monaco
601 Poydras St., Suite 2415
New Orleans 70130
Phone: 504/522-5700

Massachusetts

Mrs. Helene Ravera DAY
Honorary Consul
Honorary Consulate General of Monaco
251 Payson Rd.
Belmont 02178
Phone: 617/489-1240

New York

Mrs. Maguy Jane DOYLE
Consul
Consulate of Monaco
845 Third Ave., 2nd Floor
New York 10022
Phone: 212/759-5227   Fax: 212/754-9320

Pennsylvania

Mr. Curtis P. LAUPHEIMER
Honorary Consul
Honorary Consulate of Monaco
Suburban Station Blvd., Suite 250
Philadelphia 19103
Phone: 215/665-0152

Puerto Rico

Mr. Guillermo MOSCOSO
Honorary Consul General
Honorary Consulate General of Monaco
GPO Box 4113
San Juan 00936
Phone: 809/721-4215

Texas

Mrs. Doris CANAAN
Honorary Consul
Honorary Consulate of Monaco
4700 St. John's Dr.
Dallas 75205
Phone: 214/521-1058

Mongolia

New York

Mr. Jagir SUHEE
Consular Agent
Consulate General of Mongolia
6 East 77th St.
New York 10021
Phone: 212/861-9460   Fax: 212/861-9464

Texas

Mr. Edward T. STORY
Honorary Consular Agent
Honorary Consular Agency of Mongolia
1221 Lamar, Suite 1201
Houston 77010
Phone: 713/759-1922   Fax: 713/951-9145

Morocco

California

Mr. Abdelhak SAOUD

Honorary Consul
Honorary Consulate of Morocco
521 N. Daroca
Los Angeles 91775
Phone: 213/570-0318

Kansas

Mr. Harry MCLEAR
Honorary Consul
Honorary Consulate of Morocco
1900 W. 47th Pl., Suite 208
Westwood 66205
Phone: 913/432-3883

New York

Mr. Abdeslam JAIDI
Consul General
Consulate General of Morocco
10 East 40th St., 23rd Floor
New York 10016
Phone: 212/758-2625

Texas

Mrs. Joanne J. DAVIS
Honorary Consul
Honorary Consulate of Morocco
5555 Del Monte, Apt. 2405
Houston 77056
Phone: 713/963-9110

Myanmar

New York

Mr. Tint DEIR
Consul General
Consulate General of Myanmar
10 E. 77th St.
New York 10021
Phone: 212/535-1310   Fax: 212/737-2421

Namibia

Michigan

Mr. Don Hamilton BARDEN
Honorary Consul
Honorary Consulate of Namibia
400 Renaissance Ctr., Suite 2400
Detroit 48243
Phone: 313/259-0050   Fax: 313/259-0154

Nauru

Guam

Mr. Manfred R. DEPAUNE
Consul
Consulate of Nauru
Ada Professional Bldg.
Marine Dr., 1st Floor
Agana 96910

Hawaii

Mr. Alfred H. STEPHEN
Honorary Consul
Honorary Consulate of Nauru
841 Bishop St., Suite 506
Honolulu 96813
Phone: 808/523-7821

Nepal

California

Mr. Richard C. BLUM
Honorary Consul General
Honorary Consulate General of Nepal
909 Montgomery St., Suite 400
San Francisco 94133
Phone: 415/434-1111

Mr. George Mark PAPPAS
Honorary Consul General
Honorary Consulate General of Nepal
1448 15th St., Suite 205
Santa Monica 90404
Phone: 310/319-3559

Massachusetts

Ms. Julian M. SOBIN
Honorary Consul General
Honorary Consulate of Nepal
790 Boylston St., Suite 25I
Boston 02199
Phone: 617/353-1994   Fax: 617/437-9638

New York

Mr. Niranjan Man BASNYAT
Consul
Consulate General of Nepal
820 2nd Ave., Suite 202
New York 10017
Phone: 212/370-4188   Fax: 212/953-2038

Ohio

Dr. William C. CASSELL
Honorary Consul General
Honorary Consulate General of Nepal
310 E. Market St.
Cleveland 44883
Phone: 419/447-7977

Netherlands

Arizona

Mr. Siebe K. VAN DER ZEE
Honorary Consul
Honorary Consulate of the Netherlands
2111 East Highland, Suite 145
Phoenix 85016
Phone: 602/957-8848   Fax: 602/224-0620

California

Mr. Jan P. WEVER
Consul General
Consulate General of the Netherlands
11766 Wilshire Blvd., Suite 1150
Los Angeles 90025
Phone: 310/268-1598   Fax: 310/312-0989

Netherlands Foreign Investment Agency
11755 Wilshire Blvd., Suite 1660
Los Angeles 90025
Phone: 213/477-8288

Mr. Fernand W. HERMANS
Honorary Consul
Honorary Consulate of the Netherlands
First Interstate Bldg.
530 Broadway, Suite 908
San Diego 92101

Phone: 619/696-7941   Fax: 619/452-8770

Mr. Ralph M. PAIS
Honorary Consul
Honorary Consulate of the Netherlands
1 Maritime Plaza, Suite 316
San Francisco 94111
Phone: 415/981-6454   Fax: 415/391-2493

Colorado

Mr. Ronald J. LUBBERS
Honorary Consul
Honorary Consulate of the Netherlands
5560 S. Chester Ct.
Greenwood Village 80111
Phone: 303/770-7747   Fax: 303/771-8224

Florida

Mr. M. Frederick WHELAN
Honorary Consul
Honorary Consulate of the Netherlands
900 University Blvd., N., Suite 500
Jacksonville 32211
Phone: 904/744-0275   Fax: 904/744-3547

Mr. Pieter N. GEMKE
Honorary Consul
Honorary Consulate of the Netherlands
801 Brickell Ave., Suite 918
Miami 33131
Phone: 305/789-6646   Fax: 305/372-0189

Mr. Gerardus VAN DER MADE
Honorary Consul
Honorary Consulate of the Netherlands
One City Commons
400 S. Orange Ave., 9th Floor
Orlando 32801-3302
Phone: 407/425-8000   Fax: 407/843-6161

Georgia

Mr. Johannes W. BEERKENS
Honorary Consul
Honorary Consulate of the Netherlands
The Randstad Bldg., 2015 South Park Place
Atlanta 30339
Phone: 770/937-7123   Fax: 770/937-7178

Hawaii

Mr. Gaylord G. TOM
Honorary Consul
Honorary Consulate of the Netherlands
345 Queen St., Suite 600
Honolulu 96813
Phone: 808/537-1100   Fax: 808/536-2647

Illinois

Mr. Gilbert Henri MONOD DE FROIDEVILLE
Consul General
Consulate General of the Netherlands
303 E. Wacker Dr., Suite 410
Chicago 60601
Phone: 312/856-0110   Fax: 312/856-9218

Louisiana

Mrs. Constance Charles WILLEMS
Honorary Consul
Honorary Consulate of the Netherlands
643 Magazine St.
New Orleans 70160
Phone: 504/596-2838   Fax: 504/596-2800

Maryland

Mr. William C. TRIMBLE
Honorary Consul
Honorary Consulate of the Netherlands
250 W. Pratt St., 15th Floor
Baltimore 21201
Phone: 410/539-5040   Fax: 410/539-5223

Michigan

Mr. Henry I. WITTE
Honorary Consul
Honorary Consulate of the Netherlands
3250 28th St., SE - Suite 301
Grand Rapids 49512
Phone: 616/285-9998   Fax: 616/957-9716

Mr. Paulus F. VAN DEN MUYSENBERG
Honorary Consul
Honorary Consulate of the Netherlands
2000 Town Center, Suite 1200
Southfield 48075
Phone: 313/353-0620   Fax: 248/357-8943

Minnesota

Mr. Lyle Dean DELWICHE
Honorary Consul
Honorary Consulate of the Netherlands
307 Ridgewood Ave.
Minneapolis 55403
Phone: 612/474-1475   Fax: 612/593-2748

Missouri

Mr. Robertus GODDIJN
Honorary Consul
Honorary Consulate of the Netherlands
5775 NW 64th Te.
Kansas City 64151-2382
Phone: 816/746-0078   Fax: 816/746-1965

Mr. Richard W. LODGE
Honorary Consul
Honorary Consulate of the Netherlands
562 N. Woodlawn
St. Louis 63112
Phone: 314/965-3533   Fax: 314/965-3533

New York

Mr. Bob Henry HIENSCH
Consul General
Consulate General of the Netherlands
1 Rockefeller Plaza, 11th Floor
New York 10020-2094
Phone: 212/246-1429   Fax: 212/333-3603

Ohio

Mr. Charles Arnout ANDRE DE LA PORTE
Honorary Consul
Honorary Consulate of the Netherlands
2100 One Cleveland Center
1375 E. 9th St., Suite 1724
Cleveland 44114
Phone: 216/365-8223   Fax: 440/365-8326

Oregon

Mr. Ted E. RUNSTEIN
Honorary Consul
Honorary Consulate of the Netherlands
4555 N. Channel Ave.
Portland 97217
Phone: 503/240-8848   Fax: 503/227-2980

Pennsylvania

Ms. Yvonne J. OROVA

Honorary Consul
Honorary Consulate of the Netherlands
45 Brennan Dr.
Bryn Mawr 19010
Phone: 610/520-9591

Puerto Rico

Mr. Frank F. HAACKE
Honorary Consul
Honorary Consulate of the Netherlands
P.O. Box 378
6616 Isla Verde Ave.
Carolina 00979
Phone: 809/759-9400   Fax: 809/726-7356

Texas

Mr. Alexander C.H. VAN SCHELLE
Consul General
Consulate General of the Netherlands
2200 Post Oak Blvd., Suite 610
Houston 77056
Phone: 713/622-8000   Fax: 716/622-3581

Utah

Mr. Legrande STEENBLIK
Honorary Consul
Honorary Consulate of the Netherlands
230 W. 700 S.
Salt Lake City 84101
Phone: 801/364-1981   Fax: 801/355-2119

Virgin Islands

Mrs. Ruddie GEORGE
Honorary Consul
Honorary Consulate of the Netherlands
5 Company Street
Christiansted 00820
Phone: 809/773-1048   Fax: 809/773-1917

Virginia

Mr. Gerald Lee PARKS
Honorary Consul
Honorary Consulate of the Netherlands
1128 W. Olney Rd.
Norfolk 23507
Phone: 804/625-3658   Fax: 804/625-6942

Washington

Mr. Stephen C. SIEBERSON
Honorary Consul
Honorary Consulate of the Netherlands
701 5th Ave., Suite 2200
Seattle 98104
Phone: 206/622-8020   Fax: 206/467-8215

New Zealand

California

Mr. James Alexander HOWELL
Consul General
Consulate General of New Zealand
12400 Wilshire Blvd., Suite 1150
Los Angeles 90025
Phone: 310/207-1605   Fax: 310/207-3605

Mr. Robert AYLING
Honorary Consul
Honorary Consulate of New Zealand
c/o Gray, Ware & Fridenrich
401 B Street, Suite 1700

San Diego 92101
Phone: 619/699-2993   Fax: 619/236-1048

Mr. Richard SEARS
Honorary Consul
Honorary Consulate of New Zealand
One Maritime Plaza, Suite 700
San Francisco 94111
Phone: 415/399-1255   Fax: 415/399-9775

Mr. Matthew E. BRADY
Vice Consul
New Zealand Tourism Board
501 Santa Monica Blvd., Suite 300
Santa Monica 90401
Phone: 310/395-7480   Fax: 310/395-5453

Georgia

Mr. Ian Ross LATHAM
Honorary Consul
Honorary Consulate of New Zealand
75 14th St., Suite 3000
Atlanta 30309
Phone: 404/888-5123   Fax: 404/888-5200

Guam

Mr. John W. SCRAGG
Honorary Consul
Honorary Consulate of New Zealand
POB 8196, 290 Sallas St.
Tamuning 96931
Phone: 671/646-7662

Illinois

Mr. Edward Arnold BURKHARDT
Honorary Consul
Honorary Consulate of New Zealand
c/o Wisconsin Central, Ltd.
6250 N River Road, Suite 900
Rosemont 60018
Phone: 708/384-5400   Fax: 708/318-4628

New York

Ms. Rebecca Jane CUNLIFFE
Consul General
Consulate General of New Zealand
780 3rd Ave., Suite 1904
New York 10017
Phone: 212/832-4038   Fax: 212/832-7602

Texas

Consul General
Consulate General of New Zealand
2503 Robinhood St., Suite 160
Houston 77005
Phone: 713/526-9325   Fax: 713/521-1484

Mrs. Kathleen L. KELLY
Honorary Consul
Honorary Consulate of New Zealand
2248 Robinhood St.
Houston 77005
Phone: 281/366-5497   Fax: 281/366-3693

Utah

Mr. Iain B. MCKAY
Honorary Consul
Honorary Consulate of New Zealand
1379 North Brookhurst Circle
Centerville 84014
Phone: 801/296-2494   Fax: 801/296-1523

Washington

Mr. John R. BOLLARD
Honorary Consul
Honorary Consulate of New Zealand
6810 51st Ave., NE
Seattle 98115
Phone: 206/525-9881   Fax: 206/525-0271

Nicaragua

California

Mr. Adolfo Jose JARQUIN ORTEL
Consul General
Consulate General of Nicaragua
3303 Wilshire Blvd., Suite 410
Los Angeles 90010
Phone: 213/252-1170

Consulate General of Nicaragua
James Flood Bldg.
870 Market St., Suite 1050/1052
San Francisco 94102
Phone: 415/765-6823

Florida

Ms. Josefina VANNINI PERETTI
Consul General
Consulate General of Nicaragua
8370 W. Flager St., Suite 220
Miami 33144
Phone: 305/220-6900

Georgia

Mrs. Carolina S. DORN DE CASTILLO
Honorary Consul
Honorary Consulate of Nicaragua
3004 Greyfield Trace
Marietta 30067

Louisiana

Mrs. Mayra Lacayp GRIMALDI
Consul General
Consulate General of Nicaragua
World Trade Center
2 Canal St., Suite 1937
New Orleans 70130
Phone: 504/523-1507

New York

Mr. Eliseo Fabio NUNEZ MORALES
Consul General
Consulate General of Nicaragua
820 Second Ave., Suite 802
New York 10017
Phone: 212/344-4491   Fax: 212/983-2646

Pennsylvania

Dr. Richard L. WHITE
Honorary Consul
Honorary Consulate of Nicaragua
Miles, Inc. Bldg. 4, Mobay Rd.
Pittsburgh 15205
Phone: 412/777-2000

Puerto Rico

Ms. Annabella RODRIGUEZ DE MORALES
Honorary Consul
Honorary Consulate of Nicaragua
1205 Ponce De Leon Ave.
Santurce 00907

Texas

Consul General
Consulate General of Nicaragua
6300 Hillcroft, Suite 312
Houston 77081
Phone: 713/272-9628

Wisconsin

Mr. Alvaro ALEMAN
Honorary Consul
Honorary Consulate of Nicaragua
Hispanic Medical Ctr., 3521 W. National Ave.
Milwaukee 53215

Nigeria

New York

Mr. Charles O. AWANI
Consul General
Consulate General of Nigeria
828 Second Ave.
New York 10017
Phone: 212/850-2200   Fax: 212/687-1476

Norway

Alabama

Mr. Leslie Harold STUART
Honorary Consul
Honorary Consulate of Norway
6204 Brandy Run Rd., N.
Mobile 36608
Phone: 334/342-2151   Fax: 334/344-6414

Alaska

Mr. Anton J. MEYER
Honorary Consul
Honorary Consulate of Norway
203 W. 15th Ave., Suite 105
Anchorage 99501
Phone: 907/279-6942   Fax: 907/279-4912

Arizona

Mr. Allan D. SOLHEIM
Honorary Consul
Honorary Consulate of Norway
2201 W. Desert Cove
Phoenix 85029
Phone: 602/870-5672   Fax: 602/870-5015

California

Mr. Richard Isaac FINE
Honorary Consul General
Honorary Consulate of Norway
10100 Santa Monica Blvd., Suite 1000
Los Angeles 90067
Phone: 310/277-1293   Fax: 310/788-0858

Mr. Oswald GILBERTSON
Honorary Consul
Honorary Consulate of Norway
6240 Brynwood Ct.
San Diego 92120
Phone: 619/582-5586   Fax: 619/582-6570

Mr. Hans Ola URSTAD
Consul General
Consulate General of Norway

20 California St., 6th Floor
San Francisco 94111
Phone: 412/968-0766   Fax: 415/986-3318

Colorado

Ms. Rita I. EHRMAN
Honorary Consul
Honorary Consulate of Norway
3220 Republic Plaza, 370 17th St.
Denver 80202
Phone: 303/592-5930   Fax: 303/592-5929

Florida

Mr. George D. GABEL
Honorary Consul
Honorary Consulate of Norway
76 S. Laura St., Suite 1600
Jacksonville 32202
Phone: 904/353-7329   Fax: 904/358-1637

Mr. Aage OS
Consul General
Consulate of Norway
1001 N. America Way, Suite 205
Miami 33132
Phone: 305/358-4386   Fax: 305/374-4369

Mr. Edward P. NICKINSON
Honorary Consul
Honorary Consulate of Norway
1960 Seville Dr.
Pensacola 32503-4222
Phone: 904/433-8259

Mrs. Shirley KNIGHT
Honorary Consul
Honorary Consulate of Norway
1701 Maritime Blvd.
Tampa 33605
Phone: 813/247-4438   Fax: 813/247-5420

Georgia

Mr. John R. MCDONALD
Honorary Consul
Honorary Consulate of Norway
Bldg. 300
3715 Northside Pkwy., Suite 650
Atlanta 30327
Phone: 404/239-0885   Fax: 404/239-0877

Hawaii

Ms. Ruth RITTMEISTER
Honorary Consul
Honorary Consulate of Norway
1001 Bishop St., Suite 1010
Honolulu 96813
Phone: 808/531-4811   Fax: 808/536-2308

Illinois

Consul General
Consulate General of Norway
P.O. Box 964
Arlington Heights 60006
Phone: 847/956-6969   Fax: 847/364-7374

Mr. Per Bye OHRSTROM
Honorary Consul General
Honorary Consulate General of Norway
900 Lively Blvd.
Elk Grove Village 60007
Phone: 847/956-6969   Fax: 847/364-7374

Iowa

Mr. Quentin BOYKEN

Honorary Consul
Honorary Consulate of Norway
2000 Financial Center
Des Moines 50309
Phone: 515/243-7100   Fax: 515/282-7615

Louisiana

Mr. Erik F. JOHNSEN
Honorary Consul
Honorary Consulate of Norway
650 Poydras St., Suite 1700
New Orleans 70130
Phone: 504/522-3526   Fax: 504/593-8376

Maryland

Mr. Hans J. HJELDE
Honorary Consul
Honorary Consulate of Norway
1522 World Trade Center
Baltimore 21202
Phone: 410/783-2330

Massachusetts

Mr. Terje KORSNES
Honorary Consul
Honorary Consulate of Norway
286 Congress St., 7th Floor
Boston 02210
Phone: 617/423-2515   Fax: 617/423-2057

Michigan

Mr. Norval Eide ENGELSEN
Honorary Consul
Honorary Consulate of Norway
46350 Grand River
Novi 48374
Phone: 248/347-6600   Fax: 248/347-7600

Minnesota

Mr. Ulf Sverre CHRISTIANSEN
Consul General
Consulate General of Norway
800 Foshay Tower
821 Marquette Ave.
Minneapolis 55402-2961
Phone: 612/332-3338   Fax: 612/332-1386

Missouri

Mr. Don L. WOLFSBERGER
Honorary Consul
Honorary Consulate of Norway
34 N. Brentwood Blvd., Suite 3
St. Louis 36105
Phone: 314/721-7776   Fax: 314/721-7484

Montana

Mr. James P. SITES
Honorary Consul
Honorary Consulate of Norway
500 Transwestern Plaza, 490 N. 31st St.
Billings 59103
Phone: 406/252-3441   Fax: 406/256-8526

Nebraska

Mr. Virgil K. JOHNSON
Honorary Consul
Honorary Consulate of Norway
1 Merril Lynch Plaza, 10330 Regency Pkwy. Dr.
Omaha 68114
Phone: 402/397-2200   Fax: 402/390-7137

New York

Mr. Jan FLATLA
Consul General
Consulate General of Norway
825 3rd Ave., 38th Floor
New York 10022
Phone: 212/421-7333   Fax: 212/754-0583

North Dakota

Mr. Armond G. ERICKSON
Honorary Consul
Honorary Consulate of Norway
10 Roberts St.
Fargo 58108
Phone: 701/232-8957   Fax: 701/237-4049

Ohio

Mr. Henry F. LUKAS
Honorary Consul
Honorary Consulate of Norway
739 National City Bank Bldg., 629 Euclid Ave.
Cleveland 44114
Phone: 216/241-6171   Fax: 216/241-6173

Oklahoma

Mr. Jon Rolf STUART
Honorary Consul
Honorary Consulate of Norway
4590 E. 29th St.
Tulsa 74114-6205
Phone: 918/744-5222   Fax: 918/742-5273

Oregon

Mr. Lorentz Kelly BRUUN
Honorary Consul
Honorary Consulate of Norway
5441 SW McAdam Ave., Suite 300
Portland 97201
Phone: 503/221-0870   Fax: 503/221-0515

Pennsylvania

Mr. Bengt Olof JANSSON
Honorary Consul
Honorary Consulate of Norway
112-124 Christian St.
Philadelphia 19147
Phone: 215/462-2502   Fax: 215/336-3389

Puerto Rico

Mr. Luis A. AYALA-PARSI
Honorary Consul
Honorary Consulate of Norway
3091 Santiago De Los Caballerosa Ave.
Ponce 00731
Phone: 787/848-9000

Mr. Jose O. INIGUEZ BUSTO
Honorary Consul
Honorary Consulate of Norway
360 San Francisco St.
San Juan 00901
Phone: 787/725-2532

South Carolina

Mr. James Doar LUCAS
Honorary Consul
Honorary Consulate of Norway
198 E. Bay St., Suite 101
Charleston 29402
Phone: 803/577-5782

South Dakota

Mr. Howard W. PAULSON
Honorary Consul
Honorary Consulate of Norway
509 S. Dakota Ave.
Sioux Falls 57102
Phone: 605/336-1030   Fax: 605/336-1027

Texas

Mr. Edward Merlin FJORDBAK
Honorary Consul
Honorary Consulate of Norway
4605 Live Oak St.
Dallas 75204
Phone: 214/826-5231   Fax: 214/823-7737

Mr. Odvar MOSNESSET
Consul General
Consulate General of Norway
2777 Allen Pkwy., Suite 1185
Houston 77019
Phone: 713/521-2900   Fax: 713/521-9473

Utah

Mr. Leif W. ANDERSEN
Honorary Consul
Honorary Consulate of Norway
958 W. 3265th St.
Salt Lake City 84119
Phone: 801/978-9325

Virgin Islands

Mr. Paul Edgar DRINKWINE
Honorary Consul
Honorary Consulate of Norway
Aquamarine Tours
5306 Long Bay Rd.
St. Thomas 00802
Phone: 809/774-1112   Fax: 809/774-9987

Virginia

Mr. Rolf Anders WILLIAMS
Honorary Consul
Honorary Consulate of Norway
201 E. City Hall Ave.
Norfolk 23514
Phone: 804/446-7300   Fax: 757/625-7854

Washington

Mr. Thomas A. STANG
Honorary Consul
Honorary Consulate of Norway
806 Joseph Vance Blvd.
1402 3rd. Ave.
Seattle 98101
Phone: 206/623-3957   Fax: 206/622-9552

Wisconsin

Mr. Trygve LONNEBOTN
Honorary Consul
Honorary Consulate of Norway
601 Rayovac Dr.
Madison 53711
Phone: 608/275-4430   Fax: 608/275-4577

Oman

California

Mr. William F. MANCINI

Honorary Consul
Honorary Consulate of Oman
10940 Wilshire Blvd., Suite 1600
Los Angeles 90024
Phone: 310/443-4175

New York

Mr. Salim AL-BATTASHI
Consul General
Consulate General of Oman
866 United Nations Plaza, Room 540
New York 10017
Phone: 212/355-3505   Fax: 212/644-0070

Pakistan

California

Trade Office of Pakistan
10850 Wilshire Blvd., Suite 510
Los Angeles 90024

Miss Asma ANISA
Consul General
Consulate General of Pakistan
10850 Wilshire Blvd., Suite 1100
Los Angeles 90024
Phone: 310/441-5114

Kentucky

Mr. William Howard DENHARD
Honorary Consul General
Honorary Consulate General of Pakistan
1056 Country Side Trace
Louisville 40223
Phone: 502/244-8594

Massachusetts

Mr. Barry D. HOFFMAN
Honorary Consul General
Honorary Consulate General of Pakistan
393 Commonwealth Ave.
Boston 02115
Phone: 617/267-9000   Fax: 617/266-6666

New York

Mr. Javaiduq ASLAM
Consul
Consulate General of Pakistan
12 E. 65th St.
New York 10021
Phone: 212/879-5800   Fax: 212/517-6987

Panama

California

Mrs. Elsa Alvarez DE CANO DEL CASTILLO
Honorary Consul
Honorary Consulate General of Panama
17341 E. Hurley St., Apt. 66
La Puente 91744

Mrs. Carolina Teran MOURITZEN
Honorary Consul
Honorary Consulate of Panama
2552 Chatsworth Blvd.
San Diego 92106
Phone: 619/225-8144

Mr. Rolando A. PAREDES ROBLES
Consul General

Consulate General of Panama
870 Market St., Suites 551-553
San Francisco 94102
Phone: 415/391-4268   Fax: 415/391-4269

Florida

Ms. Rosalinda PINILLA VALDES
Consul
Panama Trade Development Institute
1477 S. Miami Ave., 2nd Floor
Miami 33130
Phone: 305/374-8823   Fax: 305/374-7822

Mr. Rodrigo GONZALEZ JURADO
Consul General
Consulate General of Panama
444 Brickell Ave., Suite 729
Miami 33131
Phone: 305/371-7031   Fax: 305/371-2907

Mr. Jose B. ROBINSON HOOKER
Consul General
Consulate General of Panama
4326 El Prado Blvd., Suite 4
Tampa 33629
Phone: 813/831-6685

Georgia

Mr. Eric A. BRYAN
Honorary Vice Consul
Honorary Vice Consulate of Panama
Cain Tower - Peachtree Ctr.
229 Peachtree St., NE, Suite 1209
Atlanta 30303
Phone: 404/522-4114   Fax: 404/522-4120

Hawaii

Mrs. Armenia Adames DE WHITE
Honorary Consul General
Honorary Consulate General of Panama
1568 Uluhaku Pl.
Kailua 96734
Phone: 808/262-4949

Illinois

Mrs. Irma L. BLATCHFORD
Honorary Consul
Honorary Consulate of Panama
1310 N. Ritchie Ct.Dr., Apt. 11-C
Chicago 60610
Phone: 312/266-2770   Fax: 312/266-2447

Louisiana

Ms. Lizca BOMBET
Honorary Consul General
Honorary Consulate General of Panama
12077 Old Hammond Highway
Baton Rouge 70816
Phone: 504/275-0796   Fax: 504/272-3631

Mrs. Elizabeth Del Carmen MARTINEZ ARAYA
Consul General
Consulate General of Panama
1324 World Trade Center
2 Canal St., 13th Floor
New Orleans 70130
Phone: 504/525-3458   Fax: 504/524-8960

New York

Mfr. Francisco H. IGLESIAS
Consul General
Consulate General of Panama
1212 Avenue of the Americas, 10th Floor

New York 10036
Phone: 212/840-2450   Fax: 212/840-2469

Ms. Patricia Carolina MARTIN
Consul
Panama Office of Maritime Safety
6 W. 48th St., 10th Floor
New York 10036
Phone: 212/869-6440   Fax: 212/575-2285

Pennsylvania

Mrs. Georgia ATHANASOPULOS KONTU
Consul General
Consulate General of Panama
124 Chestnut St.
Philadelphia 19106
Phone: 215/574-2994   Fax: 215/625-4876

Puerto Rico

Honorary Vice Consulate of Panama
Reparto Metropolitano, Avenida San Patricio
Rio Piedras 00926

Texas

Mr. Julio SOSA
Consul General
Consulate General of Panama
24 Greenway Plaza, Suite 1307
Houston 77046
Phone: 713/622-4451   Fax: 713/622-4468

Papua New Guinea

California

Mr. Charles CHEATHEM
Honorary Consul
Honorary Consulate of Papua New Guinea
19203 S. Cliveden Ave.
Carson 90746
Phone: 310/639-9733   Fax: 310/639-9734

Hawaii

Mr. Harris Leland OLSEN
Honorary Consul General
Honorary Consulate Gen. of Papua New Guinea
1357 Kapiolani Blvd., Suite 1440
Honolulu 96814
Phone: 808/625-0175   Fax: 808/599-5004

Paraguay

California

Mr. Carlos Roberto CHAMORRO AUAD
Consul General
Consulate General of Paraguay
8322 Seaport Drive
Huntington Beach 92648
Phone: 714/848-3168   Fax: 714/841-4739

Florida

Mr. Juan A. DELLAVEDOVA
Consul General
Consulate General of Paraguay
300 Biscayne Blvd., Suite 907
Miami 33131
Phone: 305/374-9090   Fax: 305/374-5522

Louisiana

Consulate General of Paraguay
611 Gravier St., Suite 903
New Orleans 70130

Michigan

Mrs. Alice ROJAS
Honorary Consul
Honorary Consulate of Paraguay
27387 Parkview, Unit 8301
Detroit 48092

New York

Mr. Jose A. DOS SANTOS
Consul General
Consulate General of Paraguay
675 3rd Ave., Suite 1604
New York 10017
Phone: 212/682-9441   Fax: 212/682-9443

Puerto Rico

Mrs. Maria Elena DE HASZARD
Honorary Consul
Honorary Consulate of Paraguay
San Jorge 267, Apt. 5-C
San Juan 00903

Peru

California

Mr. Fernando MONTERO MONTALVA
Consul General
Consulate General of Peru
3460 Wilshire Blvd., Suite 1005
Los Angeles 90036
Phone: 213/651-0296

Mr. Jorge Eduardo ROMAN MOREY
Consul General
Consulate General of Peru
870 Market St., Suite 579
San Francisco 94102
Phone: 415/362-7136

Florida

Mr. Carlos J. CORNEJO
Consul General
Consulate General of Peru
444 Brickell Ave., Suite M-135
Miami 33131
Phone: 305/374-8935

Georgia

Dr. Thomas Lee SMITH
Honorary Consul
Honorary Consulate of Peru
4211 Erskine Rd., Apt. C-2
Clarkston 30021
Phone: 404/299-8234

Hawaii

Mr. Luis Ricardo CORONADO
Honorary Consul
Honorary Consulate of Peru
225 Queen St., Suite 18-E
Honolulu 96813
Phone: 808/737-0223   Fax: 808/535-7278

Illinois

Mr. Julian TORRES FLORES

Consul General
Consulate General of Peru
180 N. Michigan Ave., Suite 1830
Chicago 60601
Phone: 312/853-6173

Louisiana

Mr. Raffaele G. BELTRAM DEBEUZ-
MILLONIG
Honorary Consul
Honorary Consulate of Peru
333 St. Charles Ave., Suite 1705
New Orleans 70130
Phone: 504/861-7827

Massachusetts

Mr. Vincent Joseph RYAN
Honorary Consul
Honorary Consulate of Peru
535 Boylston St.
Boston 02116
Phone: 617/338-1144   Fax: 617/880-4401

Missouri

Mrs. Rosa Ana SCHWARZ
Honorary Consul
Honorary Consulate of Peru
1034 S. Brentwood Blvd., Suite 520
St. Louis 63117
Phone: 314/726-6610

New Jersey

Mr. Carlos M. GAMARRA MUJICA
Consul General
Consulate General of Peru
100 Hamilton Plaza, Suite 1221
Paterson 07505
Phone: 201/278-3324   Fax: 973/278-0254

New York

Mr. Fernando ROJAS SAMANEZ
Consul General
Consulate General of Peru
215 Lexington Ave., 21st Floor
New York 10016
Phone: 212/481-7410   Fax: 212/481-8606

Oklahoma

Dr. Luis Alberto REINOSE
Honorary Consul
Honorary Consulate of Peru
2430 E. 41st St.
Tulsa 74105
Phone: 918/245-5911

Puerto Rico

Mr. Luis E. VIVANCO BISBAL
Consul General
Consulate General of Peru
268 Avenue Ponce De Leon, Suite 1009
Hato Rey 00918
Phone: 809/250-0391

Texas

Mr. Jorge Antonio SALAS REZKALH
Consul General
Consulate General of Peru
5847 San Felipe Ave.
Suite 1481
Houston 77057
Phone: 713/781-5000   Fax: 713/781-1739

Mrs. Carmela Russell GILL
Honorary Consul
Honorary Consulate of Peru
28055 Ruffian Dr.
San Antonio 78006

Washington

Mr. Victor SCHIANTARELLI
Honorary Consul General
Honorary Consulate General of Peru
7209 NE 149th Pl.
Seattle 98011
Phone: 206/488-4705

Philippines

California

Mr. Josue Lucas VILLA
Consul General
Consulate General of the Philippines
4322 Wilshire Blvd., 3rd Floor
Los Angeles 90010
Phone: 213/930-3220   Fax: 213/930-3232

Philippines Tourism Office
3660 Wilshire Blvd., Suite 216
Los Angeles 90010

Philippines Commercial Office
3660 Wilshire Blvd.
Suite 216 & 218
Los Angeles 90010

Mrs. Teresita Vasquez MARZAN
Consul General
Consulate General of the Philippines
447 Sutter St., 6th Floor
San Francisco 94108
Phone: 415/433-6666   Fax: 415/421-2641

Georgia

Mr. Raoul R. DONATO
Honorary Consul General
Honorary Consulate General of the Philippines
950 E. Paces Ferry Rd., NE
Atlanta 30326
Phone: 404/233-9916   Fax: 404/231-7916

Guam

Mr. Antonio Pascual VILLAMOR
Consul General
Consulate General of the Philippines
Guam International Center
Marine Dr., Suite 406
Tamuning 96931
Phone: 671/646-4620

Hawaii

Ms. Minerva Jean FALCON
Consul General
Consulate General of the Philippines
2433 Pali Hwy.
Honolulu 96817
Phone: 808/595-6316   Fax: 808/595-2581

Illinois

Mr. Adelio Angelito CRUZ
Vice Consul
Consulate General of the Philippines
30 N. Michigan Ave., Suite 2100
Chicago 60602
Phone: 312/332-6458   Fax: 312/332-3657

Michigan

Mr. Renato S. ROXAS
Consul General
Consulate General of the Philippines
45 Woodland Shore
Grosse Pointe Shore 48236
Phone: 313/885-4642   Fax: 313/745-5448

New York

Mr. Willy C. GAA
Consul General
Consulate General of the Philippines
Philippine Ctr., 556 5th Ave.
New York 10036-5095
Phone: 212/764-1330   Fax: 212/382-1146

Ohio

Mr. Victor C. VICTUG
Honorary Consul
Honorary Consulate of the Philippines
378 Balmoral Dr.
Richmond Heights 44143
Phone: 216/692-0797   Fax: 216/397-4256

Poland

California

Mr. Maciej KRYCH
Consul General
Consulate General of Poland
12400 Wilshire Blvd., Suite 555
Los Angeles 90025
Phone: 310/442-8500   Fax: 310/442-8515

Illinois

Mr. Ryszard SARKOWICZ
Consul General
Consulate General of Poland
1530 Lake Shore Dr.
Chicago 60610-1695
Phone: 312/337-8166   Fax: 312/337-7841

Mr. Zbigniew KUBACKI
Consul
Commercial Division - Poland
333 E. Ontario St., Suite 3906B
Chicago 60611
Phone: 312/642-4102

Massachusetts

Mr. Marek LESNIEWSKI-LAAS
Honorary Consul
Honorary Consulate of Poland
31 Milk St.
Boston 02108
Phone: 617/357-1980   Fax: 617/542-7770

New York

Mr. Herakliusz ZWIRELLO
Consul
Consulate General of Poland
233 Madison Ave.
New York 10016
Phone: 212/889-9360   Fax: 212/779-3062

Puerto Rico

Mr. Bohdan Chester HRYNIEWICZ
Honorary Consul
Honorary Consulate of Poland

Hotel Pierre
105 De Diego Ave., Suite 103
San Juan 00911
Phone: 809/721-0495   Fax: 809/721-0495

Portugal

California

Mr. Edmundo DE MACEDO
Consul
Consulate of Portugal
1801 Avenue of the Stars, Suite 400
Los Angeles 90067
Phone: 213/277-1491

Mr. Joaqauim J. FERREIRA DA FONSECA
Consul General
Consulate General of Portugal
3298 Washington St.
San Francisco 94115
Phone: 415/346-3400

Connecticut

Dr. Adriano Seabra VEIGA
Honorary Consul
Honorary Consulate of Portugal
20 E. Main St., Suite 220
Waterbury 06702
Phone: 203/755-4111

Florida

Mr. Joseph T. THERIAGA
Honorary Consul
Honorary Consulate of Portugal
1901 Ponce De Leon Blvd., 2nd Floor
Coral Gables 33134
Phone: 305/444-6311

Hawaii

Mr. John Henry FELIX
Honorary Consul
Honorary Consulate of Portugal
1585 Kapiolani Blvd., Suite 728
Honolulu 96814
Phone: 808/949-6565

Illinois

Mr. Albano D. COELHO
Honorary Consul
Honorary Consulate of Portugal
1955 New England Ave.
Chicago 60635
Phone: 312/889-7405

Massachusetts

Mr. Luis Jose BARREIROS
Consul General
Consulate General of Portugal
899 Boylston St.
Boston 02115
Phone: 617/536-8740

Ms. Maria Gabriela SOARES DE ALBERGARIA
Consul
Consulate of Portugal
628 Pleasant St., Room 201
New Bedford 02740
Phone: 617/997-6151

New Jersey

Ms. Natercia Viana TEIXEIRA

Consul General
Consulate General of Portugal
The Legal Ctr., 1 Riverfront Plaza
Main Floor
Newark 07102
Phone: 973/643-4200

New York

Mr. Nuno Da Cunha TAVORA LORENA
Consul General
Consulate General of Portugal
630 Fifth Avenue, Suite 378
New York 10111
Phone: 212/246-4581   Fax: 212/459-0190

Pennsylvania

Mr. Baldomiro Nunes SOARES
Honorary Consul
Honorary Consulate of Portugal
2001 Welsh Rd.
Philadelphia 19115
Phone: 215/925-3222

Puerto Rico

Mr. Jose C. DUARTE DA SILVEIRA
Honorary Consul
Honorary Consulate of Portugal
Urb Sag Corazon, 416 San Leandro
Rio Piedras 00926
Phone: 809/755-8556

Rhode Island

Mr. Mario Rui DUARTE
Consul
Consulate of Portugal
56 Pine St., 6th Floor
Providence 02903
Phone: 401/272-2003

Texas

Mr. James H. WESTMORELAND
Honorary Consul
Honorary Consulate of Portugal
700 Louisiana Ave., Suite 4800
Houston 77002
Phone: 713/759-1188

Qatar

New York

Hon. Nassir AL-NASSER
Consul General
Consulate General of Qatar
747 3rd. Ave., 22nd Floor
New York 10017
Phone: 212/486-9368   Fax: 212/758-4952

Texas

Mr. Sultan Saad AL-MORAIKHI
Consul General
Consulate General of Qatar
4265 San Felipe St., Suite 1100
Houston 77027
Phone: 713/968-9840   Fax: 713/968-9841

Romania

California

Mr. Mihai Bujor SION
Consul General
Consulate General of Romania
11766 Wilshire Blvd., Suite 1230
Los Angeles 90025
Phone: 310/444-0043   Fax: 310/445-0043

Massachusetts

Dr. Radu R. FLORESCU
Honorary Consul
Honorary Consulate of Romania
48 Ladd's Way
Scituate 02026
Phone: 781/544-1326   Fax: 781/544-1326

New York

Mr. Gheorghe LUPES
Consul General
Consulate General of Romania
200 E. 38th St., 3rd Floor
New York 10016
Phone: 212/682-9120   Fax: 212/972-8463

Russia

Alaska

Mr. Steve Ross SMIRNOFF
Honorary Consul General
Honorary Consulate General of Russia
3581 Kachemak Ci.
Anchorage 99515
Phone: 907/349-5481   Fax: 907/522-1489

California

Mr. Vladimir S. KUZNETSOV
Consul General
Consulate General of Russia
2790 Green St.
San Francisco 94123
Phone: 415/922-6642   Fax: 415/929-0306

New York

Mr. Nikolay Ivanovich SADCHIKOV
Consul General
Consulate General of Russia
9 E. 91st St.
New York 10128
Phone: 212/348-0926   Fax: 212/831-9162

Washington

Mr. Georgiy Borisovich VLASKIN
Consul General
Consulate General of Russia
2001 6th Ave.
23rd Floor
Seattle 98121
Phone: 206/728-1879   Fax: 206/728-1871

Rwanda

Illinois

Mr. Glenn L. FELNER
Honorary Consul
Honorary Consulate of Rwanda
666 Dundee Rd., Suite 1401
Northbrook 60062
Phone: 708/205-1188

Saint Kitts and Nevis

Georgia

Mr. Bernard M. PORCHE
Honorary Consul
Honorary Consulate of Saint Kitts and Nevis
644 Atone St., NW
Atlanta 30318

Texas

Mr. William R. EWING
Honorary Consul
Honorary Consulate of Saint Kitts and Nevis
6336 Greenville Ave.
Dallas 75206

Saint Lucia

New York

Ms. Germain Patricia LOUIS
Deputy Vice Consul
Consulate General of Saint Lucia
820 2nd Ave., Suite 900E
New York 10017
Phone: 212/697-9360   Fax: 212/697-4993

Texas

Mrs. Annette STRAUSS
Honorary Consul
Honorary Consulate of Saint Lucia
Dallas City Hall
1500 Marilla
Dallas 75201
Phone: 214/670-3319

Virgin Islands

Mr. Luther F. RENEE
Honorary Consul
Honorary Consulate of Saint Lucia
67 Mahogany
St. Croix 00850

Samoa

Hawaii

Mr. Fitu TAFAOA
Honorary Consul General
Honorary Consulate General of Samoa
300 Ala Moana Blvd., Suite 4315A
Honolulu 96850

San Marino

District of Columbia

Mrs. Sheila WEIDENFELD
Honorary Consul General
Honorary Consulate General of San Marino
1899 L St., NW - Suite 500
Washington 20036
Phone: 202/223-3517   Fax: 202/452-8938

Michigan

Mr. Giuseppe PUTTI
Honorary Consul

Honorary Consulate of San Marino
1685 Big Beaver Rd.
Troy 48083
Phone: 313/528-1190   Fax: 303/528-0357

New York

Mr. Roberto L. BALSIMELLI
Honorary Consul General
Honorary Consulate General of San Marino
186 Lehrer Ave.
Elmont 11033
Phone: 516/242-2212   Fax: 516/775-5897

Sao Tome & Principe

Florida

Mr. William S. STEVENS
Honorary Consul
Honorary Consulate of Sao Tome and Principe
2125 Biscayne Blvd., Suite 350
Miami 33137
Phone: 305/587-5049

Illinois

Mr. James Yih KAO
Honorary Consul
Honorary Consulate of Sao Tome and Principe
1320 Valley Ct.
Libertyville 60048
Phone: 847/362-5615   Fax: 847/362-1637

Saudi Arabia

California

Mr. Mohammed A. AL SALLOUM
Consul General
Consulate General of Saudi Arabia
Sawtelle Courtyard Bldg., 2045 Sawtelle Blvd.
Los Angeles 90025
Phone: 310/479-6000

New York

Mr. Badr Othman BAKHSH
Consul General
Consulate General of Saudi Arabia
866 United Nations Plaza, Suite 480
New York 10017
Phone: 212/752-2740

Texas

Dr. Abdulaziz H. AL SOWAYEGH
Consul General
Consulate General of Saudi Arabia
5718 Westheimer
Suite 1500
Houston 77057
Phone: 713/785-5577

Senegal

Florida

Mr. Michael S. HACKER
Honorary Consul
Honorary Consulate of Senegal
14 1st Ave., NE - Suite 1400
Miami 33132
Phone: 305/371-4286   Fax: 305/371-4288

Louisiana

Mr. William Manchester AYERS
Honorary Consul General
Honorary Consulate General of Senegal
International Trade, Suite 1803
New Orleans 70561
Phone: 504/529-7561   Fax: 504/529-7562

Massachusetts

Dr. Michel ROSEN
Honorary Consul
Honorary Consulate of Senegal
381 Dudley Rd.
Newton 02159
Phone: 617/964-9641   Fax: 617/244-3605

Texas

Mrs. Cynthia SHEPARD PERRY
Honorary Consul General
Honorary Consulate General of Senegal
Stone Crest International
3602 S. Mcgregor Wa.
Houston 77021
Phone: 713/748-5016   Fax: 713/748-8108

Seychelles

Washington

Mrs. Anne Lise CHURCH
Honorary Consul
Honorary Consulate of Seychelles
3620 SW 309th St.
Federal Way 98023
Phone: 206/874-4579   Fax: 206/874-5483

Sierra Leone

New York

Consul General
Consulate General of Sierra Leone
245 E. 49th St.
New York 10017
Phone: 212/688-1656   Fax: 212/688-4924

Singapore

California

Mr. Chek Feng TAN
Honorary Consul
Honorary Consulate of Singapore
1670 Pine St.
San Francisco 94109
Phone: 415/673-8573   Fax: 415/673-0883

Mr. Daryl ARNOLD
Honorary Consul General
Honorary Consulate General of Singapore
2424 S. East Bristol, Suite 320
Santa Ana Heights 72707
Phone: 714/476-2330   Fax: 714/476-8301

New York

Mrs. Amanda Pinn YANG
Consul
Consulate of Singapore
231 E. 51st. St.
New York 10022

Phone: 212/826-0840   Fax: 212/826-5028

Slovak Republic

Colorado

Mr. Gregory FASING
Honorary Consul
Honorary Consulate of Slovak Republic
1325 S. Colorado Blvd., Suite 302
Denver 80222
Phone: 303/692-8833

Illinois

Mr. Thomas K. WARD
Honorary Consul
Honorary Consulate of Slovak Republic
131 West Jefferson Ave.
Naperville 60540
Phone: 603/548-1944

New York

Mr. Jaroslav SMIESNY
Consul General
Consulate General of Slovak Republic
10 East 40th St., Suite 3606
New York 10016
Phone: 212/679-7044   Fax: 212/679-7045

Pennsylvania

Mr. Joseph Thomas SENKO
Honorary Consul
Honorary Consulate of Slovak Republic
275 Curry Hollow Rd., Suite 203
Pittsburgh 15236
Phone: 888/756-8257   Fax: 412/892-2906

Puerto Rico

Mr. Jozef Gogol ABEL
Honorary Consul
Honorary Consulate of Slovak Republic
6 Clemenceau, Suite 805
San Juan 00907
Phone: 809/721-0183

Slovenia

California

Mr. Mark Ernest RYAVEC
Honorary Consul
Honorary Consulate of Slovenia
453 Rialto Ave.
Venice 90291
Phone: 310/392-5820   Fax: 310/396-3574

New York

Mr. Vojislav SUC
Consul General
Consulate General of Slovenia
600 Third Ave., 24th Floor
New York 10016
Phone: 212/370-3006   Fax: 212/370-3581

Ohio

Honorary Consulate of Slovenia
1111 Chester Ave., Suite 520
Cleveland 44114
Phone: 216/589-9220   Fax: 216/589-9210

Texas

Mr. Richard B. WILKENS
Honorary Consul
Honorary Consulate of Slovenia
2925 Briarpark, 7th Floor
Houston 77042
Phone: 713/430-7350   Fax: 713/430-7077

Somalia

New York

Consul General
Consulate General of Somalia
425 E. 61st St.
New York 10022
Phone: 212/688-9410

South Africa

Alabama

Mr. John H. VAN AKEN
Honorary Consul General
Honorary Consulate General of South Africa
2308 1st National Bank Bldg.
Mobile 36602
Phone: 205/438-2145

California

Mr. Johannes DE KLERK
Consul General
Consulate General of South Africa
50 La Cienega Blvd., Suite 300
Beverly Hills 90211
Phone: 310/657-9200   Fax: 310/657-9215

Illinois

Ms. Bella HARRISON
Consul General
Consulate General of South Africa
200 S. Michigan Ave., 6th Floor
Chicago 60604
Phone: 312/939-7929   Fax: 312/939-0344

New York

Mrs. Makate Shiela SISULU
Consul General
Consulate General of South Africa
333 E. 38th St., 9th Floor
New York 10016
Phone: 212/213-4880   Fax: 212/213-0102

Utah

Mr. Robert Paul THORN
Honorary Consul
Honorary Consulate of South Africa
2272 Ridgewood Way., S.
Bountiful 84010
Phone: 801/298-0824

Spain

California

Mr. Florentino SOTOMAYOR BASABE
Consul
Spanish National Tourist Office

8383 Wilshire Blvd., Suite 960
Beverly Hills 90211
Phone: 213/658-7188

Mr. Herminio MORALES FERNANDEZ
Consul General
Consulate General of Spain
5055 Wilshire Blvd., Suite 960
Los Angeles 90036
Phone: 213/938-0158   Fax: 213/938-2502

Mr. Ricardo FERNANDEZ CALVO
Consul
Spanish Commercial Office
660 S. Figueroa St., Suite 1050
Los Angeles 90017
Phone: 213/627-5284   Fax: 213/627-0883

Spanish Education Office
6300 Wilshire Blvd., Suite 1740
Los Angeles 90048
Phone: 213/852-6997

Mr. Camilo ALONSO VEGA SANCHEZ
Consul General
Consulate General of Spain
1405 Sutter St.
San Francisco 94123
Phone: 415/922-2995   Fax: 415/931-9706

Florida

Mr. Joaquin DE LA HERRAN MENDIVIL
Consul
Commercial Office of Spain
Gables International Plaza
2655 Le Jeune Rd., Suite 1114
Coral Gables 33134
Phone: 305/446-4387   Fax: 305/446-2602

Mr. Miguel Carlos DIAZ PACHE PUMAREDA
Consul General
Consulate General of Spain
Gables International Plaza
2655 Le Jeune Rd., Suite 203
Coral Gables 33134
Phone: 305/446-5511   Fax: 305/446-0585

Mr. Ignacio MORENO GOZALVEZ
Consul
Spanish Education Office
2655 Lejeune Rd., Suite 1008
Coral Gables 33134
Phone: 305/448-2146   Fax: 305/445-0508

Mr. Miguel Carlos DIAZ PACHE PUMAREDA
Consul General
Consulate General of Spain
2655 Le Jeune Rd., Suite 203
Coral Gables 33134
Phone: 305/446-5511   Fax: 305/446-0585

Mr. Cecilio OVIEDO
Consul
Commercial Office of Spain
2655 Le Jeune Rd., Suite 203
Coral Gables 33134
Phone: 305/466-5511

Mr. Manuel BUTLER HALTER
Consul
Spanish Tourist Office
1221 Brickell Ave., Suite 1850
Miami 33134
Phone: 305/358-1992

Ms. Maria Dolores DAVIS
Honorary Vice Consul
Honorary Vice Consulate of Spain
100 Ingalls Dr.
Pensacola 32506-5259

Phone: 850/455-5360   Fax: 850/455-9283

Georgia

Mr. Ignacio Luis TABOADA
Honorary Vice Consul
Honorary Vice Consulate of Spain
1010 Huntcliff, Suite 2315
Atlanta 30350
Phone: 404/993-4883

Hawaii

Mr. John Henry FELIX
Honorary Vice Consul
Honorary Vice Consulate of Spain
1441 Kapiolani Blvd., Suite 2020
Honolulu 96814
Phone: 808/946-8080   Fax: 808/545-2024

Illinois

Mr. Antonio SOLER ALGABA
Consul General
Consulate General of Spain
180 N. Michigan Ave., Suite 1500
Chicago 60601
Phone: 312/782-4588   Fax: 312/782-1635

Ms. Beatriz MARCO ARCE
Vice Consul
National Spanish Tourist Office
845 N. Michigan Ave., E., Suite 915
Chicago 60611
Phone: 312/642-1992

Mr. Rafael DE ANDRES DE ANDRES
Consul
Spanish Commercial Office
500 N. Michigan Ave., Suite 1500
Chicago 60611
Phone: 312/642-1154

Louisiana

Mr. Julio ALBI DE LA CUESTA
Consul General
Consulate General of Spain
2102 World Trade Center, 2 Canal St.
New Orleans 70130
Phone: 504/525-4951   Fax: 504/525-4955

Maryland

Mr. Conrado FERRERO
Honorary Vice Consul
Honorary Vice Consulate of Spain
8117 Forest Hill Dr.
Baltimore 21043
Phone: 410/465-5115

Massachusetts

Mr. Carlos SANCHEZ DE BOADO Y DE LA
   VALCG
Consul General
Consulate General of Spain
545 Boylston St., Suite 803
Boston 02116
Phone: 617/536-2506   Fax: 617/536-8512

Michigan

Mr. Louis BETANZOS
Honorary Vice Consul
Honorary Vice Consulate of Spain
2890 Lakewoods Ct.
Orchard Lake 48324
Phone: 810/683-9104

Missouri

Mr. Eugene F. GRAY
Honorary Vice Consul
Honorary Vice Consulate of Spain
1156 W. 103rd St., Suite 215
Kansas City 64114
Phone: 816/942-2649   Fax: 816/942-2649

Mr. Jose L. MOLINA
Honorary Vice Consul
Honorary Vice Consulate of Spain
5715 Manchester Ave.
St. Louis 63110

New Jersey

Mr. Arturo LOPEZ
Honorary Consul
Honorary Consulate of Spain
249 University Ave., Rutgers Univ.
Newark 07102

New Mexico

Mr. Tom Rey BENAVIDES
Honorary Consul
Honorary Consulate of Spain
2821 Gun Club Rd., SW
Albuquerque 87501
Phone: 505/873-2078

New York

Spanish Education Office
150 Fifth Ave., Suite 918
New York 10011

Mr. Jose M. ALLENDESALAZAR
Consul General
Consulate General of Spain
150 E. 58th St., 30th Floor
New York 10155
Phone: 212/355-4080   Fax: 212/644-3751

Mr. Juan Ignacio VASALLO TOME
Deputy Consul
National Spanish Tourist Office
666 5th Ave., 35th Floor
New York 10130
Phone: 212/265-8822

Mr. Agustin Maria MAINAR ALFONSO
Consul
Spanish Commercial Office
405 Lexington Ave., 44th Floor
New York 10174
Phone: 212/661-4959

Ohio

Mr. Sidney L. KAUFMAN
Honorary Vice Consul
Honorary Vice Consulate of Spain
2605 Burnet Ave.
Cincinnati 45219
Phone: 513/961-3737   Fax: 513/961-3737

Pennsylvania

Mr. Herminio MUNIZ
Honorary Vice Consul
Honorary Vice Consulate of Spain
3410 Warden Dr.
Philadelphia 19129

Puerto Rico

Mr. Mariano DE URIARTE Y LLODRA

Consul General
Consulate General of Spain
Edificio Mercantil Plaza, Suite 1101
Hato Rey 00918
Phone: 787/758-6090   Fax: 787/758-0190

Mr. Joaquin JAVALOYAS GARCIA
Consul
Spanish Commercial Office
239 Arterial Hostos Ave., Suite 705
Puerto Rico 00918
Phone: 787/758-6345   Fax: 787/758-6948

Texas

Ms. Janet POLLMAN KAFKA
Honorary Consul
Honorary Consulate of Spain
5499 Glen Lakes Dr., Suite 209
Dallas 75231
Phone: 214/373-1200

Mr. Arthur Sheldon HALL
Honorary Consul
Honorary Consulate of Spain
420 Golden Springs Dr.
El Paso 79912
Phone: 915/534-0677   Fax: 915/585-2537

Mr. Leopoldo STAMPA PINEIRO
Consul General
Consulate General of Spain
1800 Bering Drive, Suite 660
Houston 77057
Phone: 713/783-6200   Fax: 713/783-6166

Mrs. Isabel DE PEDRO MARIN
Honorary Consul
Honorary Consulate of Spain
8350 Delphian
San Antonio 78148

Washington

Mr. Luis F. ESTEBAN BERNALDEZ
Honorary Vice Consul
Honorary Vice Consulate of Spain
8th & Park, N.
Renton 98055
Phone: 425/237-9373   Fax: 425/228-6239

Sri Lanka

Hawaii

Mr. Gajaba O. WICKRAMARATNE
Honorary Consul
Honorary Consulate of Sri Lanka
957-A 15th Ave.
Honolulu 96816
Phone: 808/735-1622   Fax: 808/735-6920

Louisiana

Mr. David R. BURRUS
Honorary Consul
Honorary Consulate of Sri Lanka
4241 Veterans Blvd., Suite 200
Metairie 70006
Phone: 504/455-7600   Fax: 504/455-7605

New York

Mr. Wijesiri HETTIARACHCHI
Consul
Consulate of Sri Lanka
630 3rd Ave., 20th Floor
New York 10017

Phone: 212/986-7040   Fax: 212/986-1838

St. Vincent and the Grenadines

Louisiana

Mr. James Ray SUTTERFIELD
Honorary Consul General
Honorary Consulate General of
    St. Vincent and the Grenadines
650 Poydras St., 21st Floor
New Orleans 70130

Suriname

Florida

Mr. Frederik L. BOEKSTAAF
Consul General
Consulate General of Suriname
7235 NW 19th St., Suite A
Miami 33126
Phone: 305/593-2163   Fax: 305/599-1034

Indiana

Dr. Christopher Randy DAFOE
Honorary Consul
Honorary Consulate of Suriname
RR#3 Box 275
Cloverdale 46120

Sweden

Alabama

Mr. Richard W. OVERBEY
Honorary Consul
Honorary Consulate of Sweden
2256 Ashland Place Ave.
Mobile 36601
Phone: 334/478-1624   Fax: 334/433-0437

Alaska

Mr. Edward Bernard RASMUSON
Honorary Consul
Honorary Consulate of Sweden
301 W. Northern Lights Blvd.
Anchorage 99503
Phone: 907/265-2930   Fax: 907/265-2068

Arizona

Mr. Lars O. LAGERMAN
Honorary Consul
Honorary Consulate of Sweden
2800 N. Central Ave., 21st Fl.
Phoenix 85004-1098
Phone: 602/280-9317   Fax: 602/280-8448

California

Mr. Andreas EKMAN
Consul General
Consulate General of Sweden
10960 Wilshire Blvd., Suite 820
Los Angeles 90024
Phone: 310/445-4008   Fax: 310/473-2229

Mr. John NORTON

Honorary Consul
Honorary Consulate of Sweden
750 B. St., Suite 1020
San Diego 92101
Phone: 619/233-1106   Fax: 619/233-9890

Ms. Siri M. ELIASON
Honorary Consul General
Honorary Consulate General of Sweden
120 Montgomery St., Suite 2175
San Francisco 94104
Phone: 415/788-2631   Fax: 415/788-6841

Colorado

Mr. Glenn Donald PETERSON
Honorary Consul
Honorary Consulate of Sweden
4242 E. Amherst Avenue
Denver 80222
Phone: 303/758-0999   Fax: 303/758-1091

Florida

Mr. Howard L. HILL
Honorary Consul
Honorary Consulate of Sweden
Prudential Sec., Inc.
28100 U.S. Hwy. 19 N. - Suite 100
Clearwater 34261
Phone: 813/799-5540   Fax: 813/796-7952

Mr. David D. NORTH
Honorary Consul
Honorary Consulate of Sweden
Howard Amman Bldg.
611 Eisenhower Blvd., Suite 310
Ft. Lauderdale 33316
Phone: 305/467-3507   Fax: 305/467-1731

Mr. Lennart B. JANSSON
Honorary Consul
Honorary Consulate of Sweden
c/o: Sandwell, Inc.
6621 South Point Dr., N. - Suite 200
Jacksonville 33216
Phone: 904/296-2288   Fax: 904/281-2233

Georgia

Mr. Bruce Robert LARSON
Honorary Consul
Honorary Consulate of Sweden
Littler, Mendelson, Fastiff, Tichy & Mathiason
1100 Peachtree Street, NE, Suite 2000
Atlanta 30309
Phone: 404/817-7797   Fax: 404/817-9898

Hawaii

Mr. James M. CRIBLEY
Honorary Consul
Honorary Consulate of Sweden
Case, Myrdal, Bigelow & Lombardi
Ste. 2600 Mauka Twr., Grosvenor Ctr.
737 Bishop St.
Honolulu 96813
Phone: 808/528-4777   Fax: 808/523-1920

Illinois

Mr. Thomas R. BOLLING
Honorary Consul General
Honorary Consulate General of Sweden
150 N. Michigan Ave.
Chicago 60601
Phone: 312/781-6262   Fax: 312/781-1816

Louisiana

Mr. William B. FORSYTH
Honorary Consul
Honorary Consulate of Sweden
2640 Canal St.
New Orleans 70119
Phone: 504/827-8600   Fax: 504/827-8792

Massachusetts

Mr. Franklin B. MEAD
Honorary Consul
Honorary Consulate of Sweden
286 Congress St.
Boston 02210
Phone: 617/350-0111   Fax: 617/451-0746

Minnesota

Mr. Wendell R. ANDERSON
Honorary Consul General
Honorary Consulate General of Sweden
720 Baker Bldg., 706 2nd Ave., S.
Minneapolis 55402
Phone: 612/332-6897   Fax: 612/332-6340

Missouri

Mr. Grant R. OSCARSON
Honorary Consul
Honorary Consulate of Sweden
625 Packford Drive
St. Louis 63017
Phone: 314/227-4660   Fax: 314/453-0959

Nebraska

Mr. Thomas Joseph LUND
Honorary Consul
Honorary Consulate of Sweden
1904 Farnam St., 700 Service Life Bldg.
Omaha 68102
Phone: 402/341-3333   Fax: 402/341-3434

New York

Mr. John L. SELLSTROM
Honorary Consul
Honorary Consulate of Sweden
9-11 E. 4th St.
Jamestown 14701
Phone: 716/484-7195   Fax: 716/484-2133

Mr. Dag Sebastian AHLANDER
Consul General
Consulate General of Sweden
One Dag Hammarskjold Plaza
45th Street
New York 10017-2201
Phone: 212/751-5900   Fax: 212/755-2732

Mrs. Gorel Ingegerd BOGARDE
Consul General
Swedish Information Service
One Dag Hammarskjold Plaza
885 Second Ave., 45th Floor
New York 10017
Phone: 212/583-2550   Fax: 212/755-2732

Swedish Trade Council
599 Lexington Ave.
New York 10022
Phone: 212/838-5530

Ohio

Mr. Michael Lee MILLER
Honorary Consul
Honorary Consulate of Sweden
800 E. Superior Ave., Suite 1200

Cleveland 44114-2688
Phone: 216/621-4995   Fax: 216/241-0816

Oregon

Mr. Rolf FASTH
Honorary Consul
Honorary Consulate of Sweden
One World Trade Center
121 SW Salmon St., Suite 1100
Portland 97204
Phone: 503/221-7017   Fax: 503/646-0768

Pennsylvania

Mr. Bengt Olof JANSSON
Honorary Consul
Honorary Consulate of Sweden
112 Christian St.
Philadelphia 19147
Phone: 215/465-5565   Fax: 215/336-3389

Puerto Rico

Mr. David R. SEGARRA
Honorary Consul
Consulate of Sweden
Pier 11, INTERSHIP Fernandez Juncos Ave.
Puerta De Tierra 00902
Phone: 787/721-4355   Fax: 787/721-4343

Texas

Mr. Joseph R. ALPERT
Honorary Consul
Honorary Consulate of Sweden
1341 W. Mockingbird Lane, Suite 500W
Dallas 75247
Phone: 214/630-9112   Fax: 214/630-9111

Mr. Robert A. FOWLER
Honorary Consul General
Honorary Consulate General of Sweden
2401 Fountainview Dr., Suite 510
Houston 77057
Phone: 713/953-1417   Fax: 713/953-7776

Virgin Islands

Ms. Maria HODGE
Honorary Consul
Honorary Consulate of Sweden
Hodge and Francois
1340 Taarneberg
St. Thomas 00802
Phone: 340/774-6845   Fax: 340/776-8900

Virginia

Mr. Rolf Anders WILLIAMS
Honorary Consul
Honorary Consulate of Sweden
201 E. City Hall Ave.
Norfolk 23510
Phone: 804/446-7300   Fax: 804/625-7794

Washington

Mr. Jahn R. HEDBERG
Honorary Consul
Honorary Consulate of Sweden
1215 4th Ave., Suite 1019
Seattle 98161-1001
Phone: 206/622-5640   Fax: 206/622-1756

Wisconsin

Mr. Johan C. SEGERDAHL
Honorary Consul

Honorary Consulate of Sweden
205 E. Wisconsin Ave.
Milwaukee 53202
Phone: 414/291-7835   Fax: 414/291-7838

Switzerland

Arizona

Mr. Max HAECHLER
Honorary Consul
Honorary Consulate of Switzerland
3019 N. Scottsdale Rd., Suite A
Scottsdale 85251
Phone: 602/947-0020   Fax: 602/945-0351

California

Mr. Hans Peter EGGER
Consul General
Consulate General of Switzerland
11766 Wilshire Blvd., Suite 1400
Los Angeles 90025
Phone: 310/575-1145   Fax: 310/575-1982

Mr. Alfred U. BAEHLER
Consul General
Consulate General of Switzerland
456 Montgomery St., Suite 1500
San Francisco 94104
Phone: 415/768-2272   Fax: 415/788-1402

Colorado

Mr. Walter WYSS
Honorary Consul
Honorary Consulate of Switzerland
2810 Iliff
Boulder 80303
Phone: 303/499-5641   Fax: 303/499-9977

Florida

Dr. Urs LINDENMANN
Honorary Consul
Honorary Consulate of Switzerland
825 Brickell Bay Dr., Suite 1450
Miami 33131
Phone: 305/377-6700   Fax: 305/377-9936

Georgia

Mr. Fred JENNY
Consul General
Consulate General of Switzerland
1275 Peachtree St., NE
Suite 425
Atlanta 30309-3555
Phone: 404/870-2000   Fax: 404/870-2011

Hawaii

Mr. Niklaus SCHWEIZER
Honorary Consul
Honorary Consulate of Switzerland
4231 Papu Cir.
Honolulu 96816
Phone: 808/737-5297   Fax: 808/734-3996

Illinois

Mr. Eduard JUAN
Consul General
Consulate General of Switzerland
737 N. Michigan Ave., Suite 2301
Chicago 60611
Phone: 312/915-0061   Fax: 312/915-0388

Indiana

Mrs. Freida NYHART
Honorary Consul
Honorary Consulate of Switzerland
3515 Washington Blvd.
Indianapolis 46205
Phone: 317/925-7138   Fax: 317/926-3303

Louisiana

Mr. John GEISER
Honorary Consul
Honorary Consulate of Switzerland
1620 8th St.
New Orleans 70115
Phone: 504/897-6510

Massachusetts

Mr. Ernest M. JOST
Honorary Consul
Honorary Consulate of Switzerland
20 Park Plaza, Suite 1207
Boston 02116
Phone: 617/357-1617   Fax: 617/357-1618

Michigan

Mr. Karl A. PFISTER
Honorary Consul
Honorary Consulate of Switzerland
2129 Austin Ave.
Rochester Hills 48309
Phone: 313/852-0040   Fax: 810/853-5665

Minnesota

Mr. Rudolf F. GUTMANN
Honorary Consul
Honorary Consulate of Switzerland
1100 Xenium Lane
Minneapolis 55441
Phone: 612/540-8535   Fax: 612/540-8535

Missouri

Mr. Marcel BOLLIER
Honorary Consul
Honorary Consulate of Switzerland
5018 Main St.
Kansas City 64112
Phone: 816/561-3441   Fax: 816/561-2922

New York

Mr. Jean M. KUEBLER
Honorary Consul
Honorary Consulate of Switzerland
75 John Glenn Dr.
Amherst 14228
Phone: 716/691-8806   Fax: 716/691-5226

Mr. Jacques REVERDIN
Consul General
Consulate General of Switzerland
633 3rd Ave., 30th Floor
New York 10017-6706
Phone: 212/758-2560   Fax: 212/207-8024

Ohio

Mr. Peter Hans BRODER
Honorary Consul
Honorary Consulate of Switzerland
6000 S. Marginal Rd.
Cleveland 44103
Phone: 216/881-2772   Fax: 216/361-6374

Pennsylvania

Mr. Franz J. PORTMANN
Honorary Consul
Honorary Consulate of Switzerland
635 Public Ledger Bldg., Independence Sq.
Philadelphia 19106
Phone: 215/922-2215   Fax: 302/652-2316

Mr. Heinz W. KUNZ
Honorary Consul
Honorary Consulate of Switzerland
4677 Bayard St., P.O. Box 7379
Pittsburgh 15213
Phone: 412/612-8804   Fax: 412/621-9611

Puerto Rico

Mr. Christian B. GUEX
Honorary Consul
Honorary Consulate of Switzerland
1505 Loiza St.
San Juan 00911
Phone: 809/727-2978   Fax: 809/883-6288

South Carolina

Mr. Hans Jurg BALMER
Honorary Consul
Honorary Consulate of Switzerland
1-85 Business and Bryant Rd.
100 Sunbeam Road
Spartanburg 29304
Phone: 864/578-7101   Fax: 864/578-7107

Texas

Mr. Jean BARBIER MUELLER
Honorary Consul
Honorary Consulate of Switzerland
Harwood Pacific Corp.
2651 N. Harwood, Suite 455
Dallas 75201
Phone: 214/965-1025   Fax: 214/871-0879

Mr. Alphons N. MUEGGLER
Consul General
Consulate General of Switzerland
Wells Fargo Plaza
1000 Louisiana, Suite 5670
Houston 77002
Phone: 713/650-0000   Fax: 713/650-1321

Utah

Mr. Wilford LIEBER
Honorary Consul
Honorary Consulate of Switzerland
1455 S. 11th E.
Salt Lake City 84105
Phone: 801/487-0450   Fax: 801/467-7711

Syria

California

Dr. Hazem Hikmat CHEHABI
Honorary Consul General
Honorary Consulate General of Syria
1605 Avocado Ave.
Newport Beach 92660
Phone: 714/760-3025

Texas

Mr. Ayman M. MIDANI
Honorary Consul General

Honorary Consulate General of Syria
5443 Westheimer Rd., Suite 1020
Houston 77056
Phone: 713/622-8860   Fax: 713/965-9632

Taiwan

New York

Hon. Martin FENG
Consul General
Consulate General of Taiwan
801 2nd Ave., 9th Floor
New York 10017
Phone: 212/697-1250

Thailand

Alabama

Mr. Robert F. HENRY
Honorary Consul General
Honorary Consulate General of Thailand
1201 Union Band Bldg., 60 Commerce St.
Montgomery 36104
Phone: 205/269-2518   Fax: 334/269-4678

California

Mr. Suphot DHIRAKAOSAL
Consul General
Consulate General of Thailand
801 N. La Brea Ave.
Los Angeles 90038
Phone: 213/937-1894   Fax: 213/937-5987

Mr. Kunyaphan RAENGKHUM
Consul
Thai Trade Office
3660 Wilshire Blvd., Suite 230
Los Angeles 90010

Colorado

Mr. Donald W. RINGSBY
Honorary Consul General
Honorary Consulate General of Thailand
3980 Quebec St., Suite 214
Denver 80207
Phone: 303/320-4029   Fax: 303/355-2451

Florida

Mr. Frank HALL
Honorary Consul General
Honorary Consulate General of Thailand
2801 Ponce De Leon Blvd., Suite 1170
Coral Gables 33134
Phone: 305/445-7577   Fax: 305/446-9944

Georgia

Mr. Robert M. HOLDER
Honorary Consul General
Honorary Consulate General of Thailand
900 Ashwood Pkwy., Suite 300
Atlanta 30338
Phone: 404/399-4245   Fax: 404/399-4012

Hawaii

Mr. Colin T. MIYABARA
Honorary Consul General
Honorary Consulate General of Thailand
287-J Kalihi St.
Honolulu 96819

Phone: 808/845-7332   Fax: 808/845-7332

Illinois

Mr. Pichai PONGPAET
Consul General
Consulate General of Thailand
35 E. Wacker Dr., Suite 1834
Chicago 60601
Phone: 312/236-2447

Mrs. Kanchana TEMRUTRYNIT
Consul
Thai Trade Center
401 N. Michigan Ave., Suite 544
Chicago 60611

Louisiana

Mr. Arthur Q. DAVIS
Honorary Consul General
Honorary Consulate General of Thailand
335 Julia St.
New Orleans 70130
Phone: 504/566-0888   Fax: 504/522-3434

Massachusetts

Mr. Vernon R. ALDEN
Honorary Consul General
Honorary Consulate General of Thailand
420 Boylston St., Room 403
Boston 02116
Phone: 617/536-6552   Fax: 617/536-7927

Michigan

Mr. Thomas B. STEVENS
Honorary Vice Consul
Honorary Vice Consulate of Thailand
280 Moross Rd.
Gross Pointe 48236
Phone: 313/884-7075

Missouri

Ms. Mary Frances TAYLOR
Honorary Consul
Honorary Consulate General of Thailand
3 Dunford Cir.
Kansas City 64112
Phone: 816/361-8788

New York

Ms. Nualpan MAHAKUN
Consul General
Consulate General of Thailand
351 E. 52nd St.
New York 10022
Phone: 212/754-1770   Fax: 212/754-1907

Mr. Vittaya PRAISUWAN
Consul
Thai Commercial/Economic Office
5 World Trade Center, Suite 3443
New York 10048
Phone: 212/466-1777

Oklahoma

Mr. Richard H. HUGHES
Honorary Consul General
Honorary Consulate General of Thailand
72325 Atlanta Pl.
Tulsa 94136
Phone: 918/494-0992   Fax: 918/742-0037

Oregon

Mr. Nicholas John STANLEY
Honorary Consul
Honorary Consulate of Thailand
One Wold Trade Ctr., 121 SW Salmon, Ste. 1430
Portland 97204
Phone: 503/221-0440   Fax: 503/221-0550

Puerto Rico

Mr. Rolando J. PIERNES ALFONSO
Honorary Consul General
Honorary Consulate General of Thailand
159 Costa Rica St., Suite 11-F
Hato Rey 00917

Texas

Mr. W. Forrest SMITH
Honorary Consul General
Honorary Consulate General of Thailand
1717 Main St., Suite 4100
Dallas 75201
Phone: 214/740-1498   Fax: 214/740-1499

Mrs. Mary Lee PINKERTON
Honorary Consul General
Honorary Consulate General of Thailand
4401 N. Mesa, Suite 204
El Paso 79902
Phone: 915/533-5757   Fax: 915/532-1995

Mr. Charles Crawford FOSTER
Honorary Consul General
Honorary Consulate General of Thailand
600 Travis St., Suite 2800
Houston 77002-3094
Phone: 713/229-8733   Fax: 713/228-1303

Togo

Florida

Mr. Michael S. HACKER
Honorary Consul
Honorary Consulate of Togo
200 S. Biscayne Blvd., Suite 3520
Miami 33131
Phone: 305/371-4286

Tonga

California

Mr. Siosaia Ma'ulupekotofa TUITA
Consul General
Consulate General of Tonga
360 Post St., Unit 604
San Francisco 94108
Phone: 415/781-0365   Fax: 415/781-3964

Hawaii

Ms. Annie Megumi KANESHIRO
Honorary Consular Agent
Honorary Consular Agency of Tonga
220 South King St., Suite 1230
Honolulu 96813
Phone: 808/521-5149   Fax: 808/521-5264

Trinidad and Tobago

Florida

Mr. Chandradath SINGH

Consul General
Consulate General of Trinidad and Tobago
1000 Brickell Ave., Suite 800
Miami 33131
Phone: 305/374-2199   Fax: 305/374-3199

New York

Mr. George W. MCKENZIE
Consul General
Consulate General of Trinidad and Tobago
733 3rd Ave., Suite 1716
New York 10017-3204
Phone: 212/682-7272   Fax: 212/986-2146

Tunisia

California

Mr. Proctor P. JONES
Honorary Consul General
Honorary Consulate General of Tunisia
3401 Sacramento St.
San Francisco 94118
Phone: 415/922-9222   Fax: 415/922-8837

Florida

Ms. Deborah B. JACOBSON
Honorary Consul
Honorary Consulate of Tunisia
7480 Fairway Dr., Suite 206
Miami 33014
Phone: 305/576-5049   Fax: 305/573-2916

New York

Mr. Andre BACKAR
Honorary Consul
Honorary Consulate of Tunisia
781 5th Ave., Suite 1205
New York 10022
Phone: 212/272-6962   Fax: 212/272-5957

Turkey

California

Mr. Hayri Hayret YALAV
Consul General
Consulate General of Turkey
4801 Wilshire Blvd.
Los Angeles 90010
Phone: 213/937-0118

Mrs. Bonnie J. KASLAN
Honorary Consul General
Honorary Consulate General of Turkey
41 Sutter St., Suite 1581
Oakland 94102
Phone: 415/362-0912   Fax: 707/939-1433

Florida

Mr. Michael S. HACKER
Honorary Consul General
Honorary Consulate General of Turkey
200 Biscayne Blvd., Suite 3800
Miami 33131
Phone: 305/371-4286

Georgia

Dr. Yavuz A. TARCAN
Honorary Consul General
Honorary Consulate General of Turkey

7155 Brandon Mill Rd.
Atlanta 30328
Phone: 404/913-0900   Fax: 404/671-0265

Illinois

Mr. Ahmet Altay CENGIZER
Consul General
Consulate General of Turkey
360 N. Michigan Ave
Chicago 60601
Phone: 312/263-0644

Kansas

Mr. Jeffrey P. HILLELSON
Honorary Consul General
Honorary Consulate General of Turkey
8436 Somerset Dr.
Shawnee Mission 66207
Phone: 913/385-0119   Fax: 913/385-0120

Maryland

Mr. Cenap R. KIRATLI
Honorary Consul General
Honorary Consulate General of Turkey
313 Wendover Rd.
Baltimore 21218
Phone: 410/889-0697

New York

Mr. Fuat TANLAY
Consul General
Consulate General of Turkey
821 United Nations Plaza, 5th Floor
New York 10017
Phone: 212/949-0160   Fax: 212/983-1293

Office of Education - Turkey
821 United Nations Plaza, 7th Floor
New York 10017

Mr. Mehmet Selami KARAIBRAHIMGIL
Consular Agent
Turkish Culture and Information Office
821 United Nations Plaza, 4th Floor
New York 10017

Texas

Mr. Vakur GOKDENIZLER
Consul General
Consulate General of Turkey
1990 Post Oak Central
Houston 77056
Phone: 713/622-5849   Fax: 713/623-6639

Uganda

Illinois

Mr. Theodore KASTAR
Honorary Consular Agent
Honorary Consulate of Uganda
327 Shawnee
Park Forest 60466
Phone: 708/481-5501   Fax: 708/481-4519

Ukraine

Illinois

Mr. Victor A. KYRYK
Consul General

Consulate General of the Ukraine
10 E. Huron St.
Chicago 60611
Phone: 312/642-4388

New York

Mr. Victor A. KRYZHANIVSKY
Consul General
Consulate General of the Ukraine
240 E. 49th St.
New York 10017
Phone: 212/371-5690   Fax: 212/371-5547

United Kingdom

Alaska

Ms. Diddy R. HITCHINS
Honorary Consul
Honorary Consulate of the United Kingdom
3211 Providence Dr.
Anchorage 99508
Phone: 907/786-4848   Fax: 907/786-4647

Ms. Kiddy R. HITCHINS
Honorary Consul
Honorary Consulate of the United Kingdom
3211 Providence Dr.
Anchorage 99508
Phone: 907/786-4848   Fax: 907/786-4647

Arizona

Dr. Roy Alphonse HERBERGER
Honorary Consul
Honorary Consulate of United Kingdom
15249 N. 59th Ave.
Glendale 85306
Phone: 602/978-7200   Fax: 602/978-9663

California

Mr. William F. BLACK
Honorary Consul
Honorary Consulate of United Kingdom
7979 Ivanhoe Ave., Suite 5550
La Jolla 92037
Phone: 619/459-8231   Fax: 619/459-9250

Mr. Merrick S. BAKER-BATES
Consul General
Consulate General of the United Kingdom
Landmark II, Suite 400
11766 Wilshire Blvd.
Los Angeles 90025
Phone: 310/477-3322   Fax: 310/575-1450

Mr. Michael FROST
Consul General
Consulate General of the United Kingdom
1 Sansome St., Suite 850
San Francisco 94104
Phone: 415/981-3030   Fax: 415/434-2018

Colorado

Mr. Neil PECK
Honorary Consul
Honorary Consulate of the United Kingdom
370 Seventeenth St., Suite 4700
Denver 80202
Phone: 303/892-7300   Fax: 303/893-1379

Florida

Mr. Robin Grenville BAYLIS
Consul

Consulate of the United Kingdom
1001 S. Bayshore Dr., Suite 2110
Miami 33131
Phone: 305/374-1522   Fax: 305/374-8196

Mrs. Linda NASSAR
Honorary Vice Consul
Honorary Vice Consulate of the United Kingdom
200 S. Orange Ave., Suite 2110
Orlando 32801
Phone: 407/426-7855   Fax: 407/426-9343

Georgia

Mr. Peter James MARSHALL
Consul General
Consulate General of the United Kingdom
Marquis 1 Tower, Suite 2700
245 Peachtree Center Ave.
Atlanta 30303
Phone: 404/524-8823   Fax: 404/524-3153

Illinois

Mr. Michael HODGE
Consul General
Consulate General of the United Kingdom
33 North Dearborn St.
Chicago 60602
Phone: 312/346-1810   Fax: 312/346-7021

Louisiana

Mr. James J. COLEMAN
Honorary Consul
Honorary Consulate of the United Kingdom
321 St. Charles Ave., 10th Floor
New Orleans 70130
Phone: 504/586-1979   Fax: 504/568-9911

Massachusetts

Mr. James POSTON
Consul General
Consulate General of the United Kingdom
600 Atlantic Ave., 25th Floor
Boston 02199
Phone: 617/248-9555   Fax: 617/248-9578

Minnesota

Mr. William R. MCGRANN
Honorary Consul
Honorary Consulate of the United Kingdom
2200 Lasalle Plaza, 800 Lasalle Ave.
Minneapolis 55402-2041
Phone: 612/338-2525   Fax: 612/339-2386

Missouri

Mr. Val W. LAMMERT
Honorary Consul
Honorary Consulate of the United Kingdom
14904 Manor Lake Dr.
Chesterfield 63017

New York

Mr. Jeffrey LING
Vice Consul
Consulate General of the United Kingdom
845 3rd Ave., 11th Floor
New York 10022
Phone: 212/745-0202   Fax: 212/745-0456

Mr. Peter Ernest REID
Consul
British Information Services

845 Third Ave.
New York 10022

North Carolina

Mr. Trevor T. GATTY
Honorary Consul
Honorary Consulate of the United Kingdom
229 Poplar St., Apt. 15
Charlotte 28203
Phone: 704/333-2636   Fax: 704/333-3226

Ohio

Mr. Robert CALDER
Consul
Consulate General of the United Kingdom
650 Illuminating Blvd., 55 Public Sq.
Cleveland 44113
Phone: 216/621-7674   Fax: 216/621-2615

Oregon

Mr. W. Lain LEVIE
Honorary Consul
Honorary Consulate of the United Kingdom
520 SW Yamhill St., Suite 800
Portland 97204
Phone: 503/227-5669   Fax: 503/778-5299

Pennsylvania

Mr. Charles E. MATHER
Honorary Consul
Honorary Consulate of the United Kingdom
226 Walnut St.
Philadelphia 19106
Phone: 215/925-0118

Mr. William R. NEWLIN
Honorary Consul
Honorary Consulate of United Kingdom
One Oxford Center
301 Grant St.
Pittsburgh 15219
Phone: 412/562-8872   Fax: 412/391-0910

Puerto Rico

Dr. Ian COURT
Honorary Consul
Honorary Consulate of the United Kingdom
1509 Lopez Landron, Suite 1100
San Juan 00911
Phone: 809/728-6715

Texas

Mrs. Violet BROWN O'HARA
Consul
Consulate of the United Kingdom
2911 Turtle Creek, Suite 940
Dallas 75219
Phone: 214/637-3600   Fax: 214/521-4807

Mr. Peter J. BACON
Consul General
Consulate General of the United Kingdom
1000 Louisiana St., Suite 1900
Houston 77002
Phone: 713/659-6270   Fax: 713/659-7094

Utah

Mr. Gunther Franz JOKLIK
Honorary Consul
Honorary Consulate of the United Kingdom
Eagle Gate Tower

60 E. South Temple, Suite 700
Salt Lake City 84111
Phone: 801/237-1723   Fax: 801/297-6940

Washington

Mr. Michael J. UPTON
Consul
Consulate of the United Kingdom
820 1st Interstate C, 999 3rd Ave.
Seattle 98104
Phone: 206/622-9255   Fax: 206/622-4728

Uruguay

California

Mr. Julio V. GIAMBRUNO
Consul General
Consulate General of Uruguay
429 Santa Monica Blvd., Suite 400
Los Angeles 90401
Phone: 310/394-5777

Mr. Mark H. RITCHIE
Honorary Consul
Honorary Consulate of Uruguay
41 Sutter St., Suite 200
San Francisco 94104
Phone: 415/981-1115

Florida

Mr. Antonio Luis CAMPS VALGOI
Consul General
Consulate General of Uruguay
1077 Ponce De Leon Blvd.
Coral Gables 33134
Phone: 305/443-9764   Fax: 305/443-7802

Hawaii

Mr. Luis Enrique ZANOTTA
Honorary Consul
Honorary Consulate of Uruguay
1833 Kalakaua Ave., Suite 710
Honolulu 96815
Phone: 808/947-2889

Illinois

Mr. Carlos G. RIZOWY
Honorary Consul
Honorary Consulate of Uruguay
8000 Sears Tower
Chicago 60606
Phone: 312/876-7934

Louisiana

Mr. Julio E. RIOS PENA
Honorary Consul
Honorary Consulate of Uruguay
2 Canal St., Suite 2002
New Orleans 70130
Phone: 504/525-8354

Massachusetts

Mr. Paul LAGUARDA
Honorary Consul
Honorary Consulate of Uruguay
Medical Bldg., 67 Union St.
Natick 01760
Phone: 617/650-7936

New York

Mr. Carlos Ernesto ORLANDO BONET
Consul General
Consulate General of Uruguay
747 3rd Ave., 21st Floor
New York 10017
Phone: 212/753-8191   Fax: 212/753-1603

Puerto Rico

Ms. Josefina DE HILLYER
Honorary Consul
Honorary Consulate of Uruguay
Hamalaya 254, Monterrey Urb.
San Juan 00926

Washington

Mr. Hartley PAUL
Honorary Consul
Honorary Consulate of Uruguay
420 Fifth Ave., Suite 4100
Seattle 99101
Phone: 804/625-3658

Uzbekistan

New York

Mr. Iidar F. MUHAMEDOV
Consul
Consulate General of Uzbekistan
866 U.N. Plaza, Suite 326
New York 10017
Phone: 212/754-6178   Fax: 212/486-7998

Venezuela

California

Dr. Alonso Rafael PEREZ MARCHELLO
Consul General
Consulate General of Venezuela
455 Market St., Suite 220
San Francisco 94102
Phone: 415/421-5172   Fax: 415/512-7693

Florida

Mr. Gustavo A. RODRIGUEZ AMENGUAL
Consul General
Consulate General of Venezuela
1101 Brickell Ave., Unit 901
Miami 33131
Phone: 305/577-4301   Fax: 305/372-5167

Illinois

Mr. Ramon AYALA TROCONIS
Consul General
Consulate General of Venezuela
20 N. Wacker Dr., Suite 750
Chicago 60606
Phone: 312/236-9658   Fax: 312/580-1010

Louisiana

Mr. Jose L. SILVA-MENDEZ
Consul General
Consulate General of Venezuela
World Trade Center, Suite 1908
New Orleans 70130

Phone: 504/522-3284   Fax: 504/522-7092

Massachusetts

Mrs. Cynthia H. MORALES IZQUIERDO
Consul General
Consulate General of Venezuela
545 Boylston St., 6th Floor
Boston 02159
Phone: 617/266-9355   Fax: 617/266-2350

New York

Mr. Vicente L. CARRILLO BATALLA LUCAS
Consul General
Consulate General of Venezuela
7 E. 51st St.
New York 10022
Phone: 212/826-1675   Fax: 212/644-7471

Puerto Rico

Mr. Luis Miguel FAJARDO ARAUJO
Consul General
Consulate General of Venezuela
Edificio Mercantil Plaza
Ponce De Leon Ave., Suite 601
Hato Rey 00907
Phone: 809/725-4055

Texas

Mr. Mauricio Antonio PULIDO LEON
Consul
Consulate General of Venezuela
2700 Post Oak Blvd., Suite 1500
Houston 77056
Phone: 713/961-5141

Vietnam

California

Mr. Phong Xuan NGUYEN
Consul General
Consulate General of Vietnam
1700 California St., 4th Floor
San Francisco 94109

Yemen

Mr. Ismael A. MANSOOR
Honorary Consul
Honorary Consulate of Yemen
1255 Post St., Suite 1030
San Francisco 94109
Phone: 415/567-3036

Michigan

Mr. Abdulhakem Ahmed ALSADAH
Honorary Consul General
Honorary Consulate General of Yemen
10415 Div Ave.
Dearborn 48120
Phone: 313/842-8402

New York

Consul General
Consulate General of Yemen
866 United Nations Plaza, Room 435
New York 10017
Phone: 212/355-1730   Fax: 212/750-9613

Currency

Country	Monetary Unit
Afghanistan	Afghani
Albania	Lek
Algeria	Dinar
Angola	Kwanza
Antigua and Barbuda	EC Dollar
Argentina	Peso
Armenia	Dram
Australia	Dollar
Austria	Schilling
Azerbaijan	Manat
Bahamas	Dollar
Bahrain	Dinar
Bangladesh	Taka
Barbados	Dollar
Belarus	Ruble
Belgium	Franc
Belize	Dollar
Benin	CFA Franc
Bermuda	Dollar
Bolivia	Boliviano
Bosnia & Herzegovina	Croatian dinar and Yugoslav dinar
Botswana	Pula
Brazil	Real
Brunei Darussalam	Dollar
Bulgaria	Lev
Burkina Faso	CFA Franc
Burma	Kyat
Burundi	Franc
Cambodia	Riel
Cameroon	CFA Franc
Canada	Dollar
Cape Verde	Escudo
Central African Republic	CFA Franc
Chad	CFA Franc
Chile	Peso
China	Renminbi
Colombia	Peso
Comoros	CFA Franc
Congo	CFA Franc
Costa Rica	Colon
Côte d'Ivoire	CFA Franc
Croatia	Kuna
Cuba	Peso
Cyprus	Pound
Czech Republic	Koruna
Denmark	Krone
Djibouti	Franc
Dominica	EC Dollar
Dominican Republic	Peso
Ecuador	Sucre
Egypt	Pound
El Salvador	Colon
Equatorial Guinea	CFA Franc
Eritrea	Birr
Estonia	Kroon
Ethiopia	Birr
Faroe Islands	Krone
Fiji	Dollar
Finland	Markka
France	Franc
Fyrom (Macedonia)	Denar
Gabon	CFA Franc
Gambia	Dalasi
Georgia	Lavi
Germany	Mark
Ghana	Cedi
Greece	Drachma

Country	Monetary Unit
Grenada	EC Dollar
Guatemala	Quetzal
Guinea	Franc
Guinea-Bissau	CFA Franc
Guyana	Dollar
Haiti	Gourde
Holy See	Lira
Honduras	Lempira
Hong Kong	Dollar
Hungary	Forint
Iceland	Krona
India	Rupee
Indonesia	Rupiah
Iraq	Dinar
Ireland	Pound
Israel	Shekel
Italy	Lira
Jamaica	Dollar
Japan	Yen
Jordan	Dina
Kazakhstan	Tenge
Kenya	Shilling
Korea, South	Won
Korea	Won
Kuwait	Dinar
Kyrgyzstan	Som
Laos	Kip
Latvia	Lats
Lebanon	Pound
Lesotho	SA Rand
Liberia	Dollar
Lithuania	Litas
Luxembourg	Franc
Madagascar	Franc
Malawi	Kwacha
Malaysia	Ringgit
Mali	CFA Franc
Malta	Lira
Marshall Islands	Dollar
Martinique	French Franc
Mauritania	Ouguiya
Mauritius	Rupee
Mexico	New Peso
Micronesia	Dollar
Moldova	Leu
Mongolia	Tugrik
Morocco	Dirham
Mozambique	Metical
Namibia	Namibian Dol
Nepal	Rupee
Netherlands	Guilder
Netherlands Antilles	Guilder
New Zealand	Dollar
Nicaragua	Cordoba
Niger	CFA Franc
Nigeria	Naira
Norway	Krone
Oman	Rial
Pakistan	Rupee
Palu	Dollar
Panama	Balboa
Papua New Guinea	Kina
Paraguay	Guarani
Peru	Nuevo Sol
Philippines	Peso
Poland	Zloty
Portugal	Escudo
Qatar	Riyal
Romania	Leu
Russia	Ruble
Rwanda	Franc

Saint Lucia	EC Dollar
Saint Kitts and Nevis	EC Dollar
Saint Vincent and the Grenadines	EC Dollar
Saudi Arabia	Riyal
Senegal	CFA Franc
Seychelles	Rupee
Sierra Leone	Leone
Singapore	Dollar
Slovak Republic	Koruna
Slovenia	Tolar
Solomon Islands	Dollar
Somalia	Shilling
South Africa	Rand
Spain	Peseta
Sri Lanka	Rupee
Sudan	Pound
Suriname	Guilder
Swaziland	Lilangeni
Sweden	Krona
Switzerland	Franc
Syria	Pound
Taiwan	Dollar
Tajikistan	Ruble
Tanzania	Shilling
Thailand	Baht
Togo	CFA Franct
Tonga	Pa'Anga
Trinidad and Tobago	Dollar
Tunisia	Dinar
Turkey	Lira
Turkmenistan	Manat
Uganda	Shilling
Ukraine	Karbov
United Arab Emirates	Dirham
United Kingdom	Pound
Uruguay	Peso
Uzbekistan	Som
Vanuatu	Vatu
Venezuela	Bolivar
Vietnam	Dong
Western Samoa	Tala
Yemen	Rial
Yugoslavia	Dinar
Zambia	Kwacha
Zimbabwe	Dollar

Local & U.S. Holidays

INTRODUCTION

Many holidays change annually because they are determined by the position and sighting of the moon in accordance with Christian, Muslim, Hindu, Hebrew, or Chinese calendars. Hebrew and Islamic holy days actually begin at sundown on the day before the date given. Diplomatic missions are often closed on official holidays of their country as are U.S. missions in that country. U.S. holidays are also listed here. The dates shown are for 1998. If your communication with a diplomatic mission involves sensitive timing, it would make sense to contact the embassy or consular office to confirm their holiday schedule.

Afghanistan

Id al-Fitr	Jan. 29-31
Id al-Adha	Apr. 7-9
Anniversary of Revolution	Apr. 29

Workers' Day	May 1
Tenth of Moharram	May 6
Mawlid al Nabi	July 7
Independence Day	Aug. 19

Albania

New Year's Day	Jan. 1,2
Martin Luther King, Jr.'s Birthday	Jan. 18
Big Bajram	Jan. 29
President's Day	Feb. 17
Nevruz	Mar. 24
Easter	Apr. 12
Small Bajram	Apr. 7
Orthodox Easter	Apr. 19
May Day	May 1
Memorial Day	May 25
Independence Day	July 4*
Labor Day	Sep. 7
Columbus Day	Oct. 12
Veterans Day	Nov. 11
Thanksgiving Day	Nov. 26
Christmas Day	Dec. 25

*Observed Friday, July 3

Algeria

Aid al-Fitr	Mar. 3
Labor Day	May 2
Aid-al-AdHa	May 9
Awwel Mouharam	May 31
Revolution Recovery Day	June 19
Achoura	July 22
El Mawlid-en Nabaoui	Aug. 9
Revolution Day	Nov. 1

Argentina

New Year's Day	Jan. 1
Martin Luther King, Jr.'s Birthday	Jan. 20
President's Day	Feb, 27
Good Friday	Mar. 28
Labor Day (A)	May 1
Revolution Day	May 25
Memorial Day	May 26
Sovereignty Day	June 9
Flag Day	June 16
Independence Day (U.S.)	July 4*
Independence Day (A)	July 9
Death of San Martin	Aug. 18
Labor Day (U.S.)	Sept. 1
Columbus Day (A)	Oct. 12
Columbus Day (U.S.)	Oct. 13
Veterans Day	Nov. 11
Thanksgiving Day	Nov. 27
Immaculate Conception	Dec. 8
Christmas Day	Dec. 25

*Observed Friday, July 3

Austrailia

New Year's Day	Jan. 1
Australia Day	Jan. 26
Labor Day (Perth)*	1st Mon. in Mar.
Labor Day (Melbourne)*	2d Mon. in Mar.
Canberra Day (Canberra)	3d Mon. in Mar.

Good Friday	Apr. 5
Easter Saturday	Apr. 6
Easter Monday	Apr. 8
ANZAC Day	Apr. 25
Labor Day (Brisbane)*	1st Mon. in May
Foundation Day (Perth)*	1st Mon. in June
Queen's Birthday (except Perth)*	2d Mon. in June
Royal Nat'l Show Day (Brisbane)*	2nd Wed. in Aug.
Queen's Birthday (Perth)*	1st Mon. in Oct.
Labor Day (Canberra and Sydney)*	1st Mon. in Oct.
Melbourne Cup Day (Melbourne)*	1st Tues. in Nov.
Christmas Day	Dec. 25
Boxing Day	Dec. 26

*Regional holidays celebrated locally.

Austria

Epiphany	Jan. 6
Easter Monday	Apr. 8
Labor Day	May 1
Ascension Day	May 16
Whitmonday	May 27
Corpus Christi	June 6
Assumption Day	Aug. 15
National Day	Oct. 26
All Saints' Day	Nov. 1
Immaculate Conception	Dec. 8
Christmas	Dec. 25
St. Stephen's Day	Dec. 26
New Year's Eve	Dec. 31
New Year's Day	Jan. 1
Good Friday	Apr. 10
Easter Monday	Apr. 17
Whitmonday	June 1
Labour Day	June 5
Independence Day	July 10
Emancipation Day	Aug. 3
Discovery Day	Oct. 12
Christmas Day	Dec. 25
Boxing Day	Dec. 26

Bahrain

New Year's Day	Jan. 1
Martin Luther King, Jr.'s Birthday	Jan. 15
Eid al Fitr	Mar. 3
Memorial Day	May 27
Eid al Adha	May 9
Islamic New Year	May 31
Ashura	June 9
Independence Day	July 4*
Labor Day	Sept. 2
Prophet's Birthday	Aug. 9
Columbus Day	Oct. 14
Veterans Day	Nov. 11
Thanksgiving Day	Nov. 24
National Day	Dec. 16
Christmas Day	Dec. 25
*Observed Friday,	July 3

Bangladesh

New Years Day	Jan. 1
Martin Luther King, Jr.'s Birthday	Jan. 15
Shab-e-Quadr	Jan. 26
Eid-ul-Fitr	Jan. 29
President's Day	Feb. 16
Independence Day	Mar. 26

Eid-ul-Azha	April
Bangla New Year	April 14
Muharram	May 7
Buddha Purnima	May 21
Memorial Day	May 25
Independence Day (U.S.)	July 4*
Eid Miladunnabi	July 7
Janmasthami	Aug. 24
Labor Day	Sept. 7
Columbus Day	Oct. 12
Veterans Day	Nov. 11
Thanksgiving Day	Nov. 28
Victory Day	Dec. 16
Christmas Day	Dec. 25

* Observed Friday, July 3

Barbados

New Year's Day	Jan. 1
Errol Barrow's Birthday	Jan. 21
Good Friday	Apr. 10
Easter Sunday	Apr. 16
Labor Day	May 1
Whitmonday	June 1
Emancipation Day	Aug. 1
Kadooment Day	Aug. 3
United Nations Day	Oct. 5
Independence Day	Nov. 30
Christmas Day	Dec. 25
Boxing Day	Dec. 26

Belarus

New Year's Day	Jan. 1
Christmas Day (Orthodox)	Jan. 8
All Women's Day	Mar. 8
Easter Sunday	Apr. 7
Easter Monday (Orthodox)	Apr. 14
Radaunitsa	Apr.. 23
Labor Day	May 1
Victory Day	May 9
Independence Day	July 27
Memorial Day	Nov. 2
Christmas Day	Dec. 25

Belgium

New Year's Day	Jan. 1
Easter Monday	Apr. 8
Belgium Labor Day	May 1
Ascension Day	May 16
Whitmonday	May 27
Independence Day	July 4*
Assumption Day	Aug. 15
Labor Day	Sept. 2
All Saints' Day	Nov. 1
Veterans Day	Nov. 11
Christmas Day	Dec. 25

* Observed Friday, July 3

Belize

New Year's Day	Jan. 1
Baron Bliss Day	Mar. 11
Good Friday	Apr. 14
Easter Monday	Apr.17

Labor Day	May 1
St. George's Caye Day	Sept.10
Independence Day	Sept. 23
Pan American Day	Oct.14
Garifuna Day	Nov. 18
Christmas Day	Dec. 25
Boxing Day	Dec. 26

Benin

New Year's Day	Jan. 1
Easter Monday	Apr. 17
Beginning of Ramadan	Feb. 1
End of Ramadan	Mar. 2
Beninese Labor Day	May 1
Tabaski	May 9
Ascension Day	June 1
Pentecost Monday	June 5
Independence Day	Aug. 1
Assumption Day	Aug. 15
Id el Mouloud Day	Aug. 9
All Saints' Day	Nov. 1
Christmas Day	Dec. 25

Bermuda

New Year's Day	Jan. 1
Good Friday	Mar. 28
Bermuda Day	May 26
Queen's Birthday	June 16
Cup Match	July 31
Somers Day	Aug. 1
Labour Day	Sept. 1
Remembrance Day	Nov. 11
Christmas Day	Dec. 25
Boxing Day	Dec. 26

Bolivia

New Year's Day	Jan. 1
Martin Luther King, Jr.'s Birthday	Jan. 19
President's Day	Feb. 16
Carnival	Feb. 23-24
Good Friday	Apr. 10
Bolivian Labor Day	May 1
Memorial Day	May 25
Corpus Christi	June 11
Independence Day (U.S.)	July 4*
La Paz Day	July 16
Bolivian Independence Day	Aug. 6
Labor Day (U.S.)	Sept. 7
Columbus Day	Oct. 12
All Saints' Day	Nov. 2
Veterans Day	Nov. 11
Thanksgiving Day	Nov. 26
Christmas Day	Dec. 25

*Observed Friday, July 3

Bosnia-Herzegovina

New Year's Day	Jan. 1/2
Independence Day	March 1
Labor Day	May 1
Victory Day	May 9
Day of the Republic	November 25

Botswana

New Year's Day	Jan. 1
Public Holiday	Jan. 2—3
Martin Luther King, Jr.'s Birthday	Jan. 15
President's Day	Feb. 19
Public Holiday	Apr. 2
Good Friday	Apr. 14
Holy Saturday	Apr. 15
Easter Monday	Apr. 17
Memorial Day	May 27
Ascension Day	June 1
Sir Seretse Khama Day	July 1
Independence Day	July 4
President's Day	July 18
Public Holiday	July 19
Labor Day	Sept. 2
Botswana Day	Sept. 30
Public Holiday	Oct.1
Columbus Day	Oct. 14
Veterans Day	Nov. 11
Thanksgiving Day	Nov. 23
Christmas Day	Dec. 25
Boxing Day	Dec. 26
Public Holiday	Dec. 27

Brazil

New Year's Day	Jan. 1
Carnival	Feb. 28
Good Friday	Apr. 14
Tiradentes Day	Apr. 21
Labor Day	May 1
Corpus Christi	June 18
Independence Day	Sept. 7
Our Lady of "Aparecida"	Oct. 12
All Souls' Day	Nov. 2
Proclamation of the Republic	Nov. 15
Christmas Day	Dec. 25

Brunei

New Year's Day	Jan. 1
First Day of Ramadan	Jan. 22
Anniversary of Revelation Koran	Feb. 27
President's Day	Feb. 19
Chinese New Year	Feb. 19
Hari Raya Aidil Fitri	Feb. 21
Brunei National Day	Feb. 23
Hari Raya Aidil Adha	Apr. 29
Islamic New Year	May 20
Memorial Day	May 27
Brunei Armed Forces Day	May 31
Independence Day	July 4*
HM The Sultan's Birthday	July 15
Prophet Mohammad's Birthday	July 29
Labor Day	Sept. 2
Columbus Day	Oct. 14
Veterans Day	Nov. 11
Thanksgiving Day	Nov. 28
Israk Mikraj	Dec. 9
Christmas Day	Dec. 25

* Observed Friday, July 3

Bulgaria

New Year's Day	Jan. 1

Martin Luther King, Jr.'s Birthday	Jan. 19
President's Day	Feb. 16
National Day	Mar. 3
Easter Monday	April 20
Labor Day	May 1
Saints Cyril and Methodius Day	May 24
Memorial Day	May 25
Independence Day	July4*
Labor Day	Sept. 7
Columbus Day	Oct. 12
Veterans Day	Nov. 11
Thanksgiving Day	Nov. 26
Christmas Eve	Dec. 24
Christmas Day	Dec. 25
Day After Christmas	Dec. 26

*Observed Friday, July 3

Burkina Faso

New Year's Day	Jan. 1
National Day	Jan. 3
Ramadan	Feb.
International Women's Day	Mar. 8
Easter Monday	Apr. 8
Tabaski	Apr.
Labor Day	May 1
Ascension Day	May 16
Memorial Day	May 27
Independence Day	July 4
Mouloud	July 4
Revolution Day	Aug. 4
Independence Day	August 5
Assumption Day	Aug. 15
Labor Day	Sept. 7
Columbus Day	Oct. 12
Rectification Day	Oct. 15
All Saints' Day	Nov. 1
Proclamation of Independence	Dec. 11
Christmas Day	Dec. 25

*Observed Friday, July 3

Burma

New Year's Day	Jan. 1
Independence Day	Jan. 4
Martin Luther King, Jr.'s Birthday	Jan. 19
Union Day	Feb. 12
President's Day	Feb. 16
Armed Forces Day	Mar. 27
Thingyan (Bur Water Festival)	Apr.13-16
Burmese New Year	Apr. 17
Full Moon of Kason	May 10
Memorial Day	May 25
Independence Day	July 3
Full Moon of Waso	July 8
Martyrs' Day	July 19
Labor Day	Sept. 7
Full Moon of Thadingyut	Oct. 5
Columbus Day	Oct. 12
Veterans Day	Nov. 11
National Day	Nov. 13
Thanksgiving Day	Nov. 26
Christmas Day	Dec. 25

Burundi

New Year's Day	Jan. 1

Unity Day	February 5
Ascension Day	a Thursday, 40 days after Easter (movable)
Labor Day	May 1
Independence Day	July 1
Assumption Day	Aug. 15
Prince Louis Rwagasore Day	Oct. 13
President Ndadaye's Day	Oct. 21
All Saints' Day	Nov. 1
Christmas Day	Dec. 25

Cambodia

New Year's Day	Jan. 1
International Women's Day	Mar. 8
Cambodian New Year's Days	Apr. 13-15
—Embassy Observes	Apr. 14
Royal Ploughing Day	May 6
Pchum Ben Day	Oct. 11-13
—Embassy Observes Oct. 11	
Paris Peace Agreement Day	Oct. 23
King's Birthday	Oct. 30-Nov. 1
—Embassy Observes Oct. 31-Nov. 1	
Cambodian Independence Day	Nov. 8
Water Festival	Nov. 24-26
—Embassy observes Nov. 25	

Cameroon

New Year's Day	Jan. 1,2
Youth Day	Feb. 11
End of Ramadan	Varies
Good Friday	April 14
Labor Day	May 1
National Day	May 20
Ascension Day	May 25
70 days after Ramadan	Varies
Assumption Day	Aug. 15
Christmas Day	Dec. 25

Canada

New Year's Day	Jan. 1
New Year's Day (Quebec only)	Jan. 2
Martin Luther King, Jr.'s Birthday	Jan. 20
President's Day	Feb. 17
Family Day (Alberta only)	Feb. 17
Good Friday	Mar. 28
Easter Monday	Mar. 31
Victoria Day	May 19
Memorial Day	May 26
St. Jean Baptiste Day (Quebec)	June 24
Canada Day	July 1
Independence Day (U.S.)	July 4
Civic Holiday (Ottawa, Calgary, Toronto, and Vancouver; observed as Natal Day in Halifax)	Aug. 4
Labor Day	Sept. 1
Thanksgiving Day (Canada)	Oct. 13
Columbus Day	Oct. 13
Veterans Day	Nov. 11
Thanksgiving Day (U.S.)	Nov. 27
Christmas Day	Dec. 25
Boxing Day	Dec

* Observed Friday, July 3

Cape Verde

New Year's Day	Jan. 1
Martin Luther King, Jr.'s Birthday	Jan. 15
National Heroes' Day	Jan. 23
Ash Wednesday	Feb. 14
President's Day	Feb 19
Ash Wednesday	Mar. 1
Good Friday	Apr. 5
Labor Day (C.V.)	May 1
Municipal Day	May 19
Memorial Day	May 27
Independence Day (U.S.)	July 4*
Independence Day (C.V.)	July 5
Assumption Day	Aug. 15
Labor Day (U.S.)	Sept. 2
Columbus Day	Oct. 14
All Saints' Day	Nov. 1
Veterans Day	Nov. 11
Thanksgiving Day	Nov. 28
Christmas Day	Dec. 25

*Observed Friday, July 3

Central African Republic

Anniversary of Boganda's Death	Mar. 29
Easter Monday	Apr. 8
Labor Day	May 1
Ascension Day	May 16
Pentecost Monday	May 27
Independence Day	Aug. 13
All Saints' Day	Nov. 1
Proclamation of the Republic	Dec. 1

Chad

New Year's Day	Jan.1
Easter Monday	Apr. 17
Aid-El-Fitr	Mar. 3
Labor Day	May 1
Aid-El-Adha	May 9
African Liberation Day	May 25
Maouloud el Nebi	Aug. 9
Independence Day	Aug.11-12
All Saints' Day	Nov.1
Proclamation of the Republic	Nov. 28
Christmas Day	Dec. 25

Chile

New Year's Day	Jan. 1
Good Friday	Apr. 15
Labor Day	May 1
Battle of Iquique	May 21
Corpus Christi	June 6
Assumption Day	Aug. 15
Official Holiday	Sept. 11
Independence Day	Sept. 18
Day of the Army	Sept. 19
All Saint's Day	Nov. 1
Christmas Day	Dec. 25

China

New Year's Day	Jan.1-2

Martin Luther King. Jr.'s Birthday	Jan. 19
Spring Festival	Jan . 28-30
President's Day	Feb. 16
International Labor Day	May 1
Memorial Day	May 25
Independence Day	July 4*
Labor Day	Sept. 7
Chinese National Day	Oct. 2
Columbus Day	Oct. 12
Veteran's Day	Nov. 11
Thanksgiving Day	Nov. 26
Christmas Day	Dec. 25

*Observed Friday, July 3

Colombia

New Year's Day	Jan.1
Epiphany	Jan. 6
St. Joseph's Day	Mar. 24
Holy Thursday	Mar. 27
Good Friday	Mar. 28
Labor Day	May 1
Ascension Day	May 12
Feast of the Sacred Heart	June 9
Saints Peter and Paul	June 30
Assumption Day	Aug. 15
Columbus Day	Oct. 12
Feast of the Immaculate Conception	Dec. 8
Christmas Day	Dec. 25

Comoros

New Year's Day	Jan 1
Id-al-Fitr	Mar. 3
27th Djoumadi II	Mar. 8
Anniversary of Death of Said (Mohammed Cheikh)	Mar. 16
Day of Miiradji	Apr. 6.
Labor Day	May 1
Comoran Liberation Day	May 13
Muharram	May 31
National Day	July 6
Mouwlid	Aug. 9

Conogo, Republic of

New Year's Day	Jan. 1
Labor Day	May 1
Three Glorious Days Celebration	Aug. 15
All Souls' Day	Nov.1
Children's Day	Dec. 25

Costa Rica

New Year's Day	Jan. 1
St. Joseph's Day	Mar. 19
Juan Santamaria	Apr. 11
Holy Thursday	Apr. 13
Good Friday	Apr. 14
Labor Day	May 1
Corpus Christi	June 18
Annexation of Guancaste	July 25
Our Lady of the Angels	Aug. 2
Assumption Day (Mother's Day)	Aug. 15
Independence Day	Sept.15
Christmas Day	Dec. 25

Cote d'Ivoire

New Year's Day	Jan. 1
Id al-Fitr (End of Ramadan)	Mar. 3
Easter Monday	Apr. 4
Cote d'Ivoire Labor Day	May 1
Tabaski	May 9
Ascension Day	June 1
Pentecost Monday	June 12
All Saints' Day	Nov. 1
Cote d'Ivoire Independence Day	Dec. 7
Christmas Day	Dec. 25

Croatia

New Year's Day	Jan. 1
Epiphany	Jan. 6
Martin Luther King, Jr.'s Birthday	Jan. 19
President's Day	Feb. 16
Easter Monday	Apr. 13
Labor Day	May 1
Memorial Day	May 25
Croatian State Day	May 30
Croatian Uprising Day	June 22
Independence Day	July 4*
Patriotic Gratitude Day	Aug. 5
Assumption Day	Aug. 15
Labor Day	Sept. 7
Columbus Day	Oct. 1
All Saints' Day	Nov. 1
Veterans Day	Nov. 11
Thanksgiving	Nov 28
Christmas Day	Dec 25
St. Stephen's Day	Dec: 26

*Observed Friday, July 3

Cuba

National Liberation Day	Jan. 1
Labor Day	May 1
Cuban Nat'l Revolutionary Festival	July 25-27
Independence Day	Oct. 10

Cyprus

Greek Community Holidays

New Year's Day	Jan.1
Epiphany Day	Jan 6
Green Monday (Beginning of Greek Orthodox Lent)	Mar. 6
Greek Independence Day	Mar. 25
Eoka Day	Apr.1
Good Friday	Apr. 12
Holy Saturday	Apr. 13
Easter Monday	Apr. 15
Labor Day	May 1
Holy Spirit Day	June 3
Assumption Day	Aug. 15
Cyprus Independence Day	Oct. 1
Ohi Day	Oct. 28
Christmas Eve	Dec. 24
Christmas Day	Dec. 25
Boxing Day	Dec. 26

Turkish Cypriot Community Holidays

New Year's Day	Jan. 1
Ramazan Bayram*	Feb. 21
Opening of the Grand National Assembly	Apr. 23
Kurban Bairam*	Apr. 30
Labor Day	May 1
Turkish Youth Day	May 19
Peace and Freedom Day	July 20
Birthday of the Prophet	July 31
Victory Day	Aug. 30
Turkish Republic Day	Oct. 29
Rep. Day of Northern Cyprus	Nov. 15

— Several additional days around these holidays are often declared holidays each year.

Czech Republic

New Year's Day	Jan.1
Easter Monday	Apr. 17
May Day	May 1
Liberation Day	May 8
Saints Cyril and Methodius Day	July 5
Jan Hus Day	July 6
Czech Founding Day	Oct. 28
Christmas Eve	Dec. 24
St. Stephen's Day	Dec. 26

Denmark

New Year's Day	Jan. 1
Maundy Thursday	Apr. 9
Good Friday	Apr. 10
Easter Monday	Apr. 13
Prayer Day	May 8
Ascension Day	May 21
Whitmonday	June 1
Constitution Day	June 5
Christmas Eve	Dec. 24
Christmas Day	Dec. 25
Second Christmas Day	Dec. 26
New Year's Eve	Dec. 31

Djibouti

Eid al-Fitr	Feb. 20 & 21
Eid al-Adha	Apr. 27 & 28
Labor Day	May 1
Islamic New Year	May 18
Independence Day	June 27-28
Mohamed's Birthday	July 27
AI-Israh and AI-Miraj	Dec. 5

(Ascension of the Prophet Mohamed)

Dominican Republic

New Year's Day	Jan. 1
Epiphany	Jan. 6
Our Lady of Altagracia	Jan. 21
Duarte's Day	Jan. 26
Dominican Independence Day	Feb. 27
Good Friday	Apr. 10
Dominican Labor Day	May 1
Corpus Christi	June 11
Dominican Restoration Day	Aug. 16
Our Lady of las Mercedes	Sept. 24
Dominican Constitution	Nov. 6
Christmas Day	Dec. 25

Ecuador

Carnival	Feb. 20
Holy Thursday	Apr. 4
Good Friday	Apr. 5
Labor Day	May 1
Battle of Pichincha	May 24
Founding of Guayaquil (Guayaquil only)	July 25
Independence of Guayaquil	Oct. 9
Souls' Day	Nov. 1
Founding of Quito (Quito only)	Dec. 6

Egypt

Ramadan	Feb. 1
Id al-Fitr	Mar. 3
Revolution of Mar. 8	Mar. 8
Sinai Liberation Day	Apr. 26
Labor Day	May 1
Id al-Adha	May 9
Muharram	May 31
Evacuation Day	June 18
National Revolution Day	July 23
Mawlid al Nabi	Aug. 9
Sham El Nessi (Armed Forces Day)	Oct. 6
Popular Resistance Day	Oct. 24

El Salvador

Holy Thursday	Apr. 13
Good Friday	Apr. 14
Salvadoran Labor Day	May 1
Employee's Day	Aug. 3
Feasts of San Salvador	Aug. 5-6
Salvadoran Independence	Sept. 15
Columbus Day	Oct. 14
Revolution Day	Oct. 15
All Souls' Day	Nov. 1
Day of First Cry of Independence	Nov. 5
Christmas Day	Dec. 25

Equatorial Guinea

New Year's Day	Jan. 1
Good Friday	Apr. 14
Easter Sunday	Apr. 16
International Labor Day	May 1
OAU Day	May 25
Corpus Christi	May 30
President Obiang's Birthday	June 5
Armed Forces Day	Aug. 3
Constitution Day	Aug 15
Independence Day	Oct. 12
Feast of Santa Isabel	Nov. 17
Immaculate Conception	Dec. 8
Christmas Day	Dec. 25

Eritrea

Christmas	Jan. 7
Martin Luther King, Jr.'s Birthday	Jan. 15
Timket	Jan. 19
George Washington's Birthday	Feb. 19
International Women's Day	Mar. 8
Id Al Fetir	Apr. 24

Good Friday	Apr. 29
Liberation Day	May 24
Memorial Day	May 27
Martyrs Day and Id Al Adha Arafaf	June 20
Independence Day	July 4*
Start of Armed Struggle	Sept. 1
Labor Day	Sept. 2
Meskel & Mawlid (Birth of Prophet)	Sept. 27
Columbus Day	Oct. 14
Veterans Day	Nov. 11
Thanksgiving Day	Nov. 24
Christmas Day	Dec. 25

*Observed Friday, July 3.

Estonia

New Year's Day	Jan. 1
Independence Day	Feb. 24
Good Friday	Apr. 5
Easter	Apr. 7
May Day	May 1
Whitsunday	May 26
Victory Day	June 23
Midsummer	June 24
Christmas	Dec. 25-26

Ethiopia

New Year's Day	Jan. 1
Christmas	Jan. 7
Epiphany	Jan. 19
Martin Luther King, Jr.'s Birthday	Jan. 20
Id Al Fetir (Ramadan)	Feb. 8
President's Day	Feb. 17
Victory of Adwa	Mar. 2
Id Al Adaha (AREFA)	Apr. 17*
Good Friday	Apr. 25
Easter Sunday	Apr. 27
May Day	May 1
Patriot's Victory Day	May 5
Memorial Day	May 26
Downfall of the Dergue	May 28
Independence Day	July 4**
Birthday of Mohammed (Moulid)	July 16*
Labor Day	Sept. 1
New Year	Sept. 11
Meskal	Sept. 27
Columbus Day	Oct. 13
Veterans Day	Nov. 11
Thanksgiving Day	Nov. 27
Christmas Day	Dec. 25

*Dates are subject to change.

**Observed Friday, July 3

Fiji Islands

New Year's Day	Jan. 1
Good Friday	Apr. 14
Holy Saturday	Apr. 15
Easter Monday	Apr. 17
Queen's Birthday	June 17
Bank Holiday	Aug. 5
Prophet Mohammed's Birthday	Aug. 9
Fiji Day	Oct. 7
Diwali	Nov. 6
Prince Charles' Birthday	Nov. 11

Christmas Day	Dec. 25
Boxing Day	Dec. 26

Finland

New Year's Day	Jan. 1
Epiphany	Jan. 1
Good Friday	Apr. 14
Easter Monday	Apr. 17
May Day	May 1
Ascension Day	June 1
Whitsun Eve	June 4
Midsummer's Eve	June 21
Midsummer's Day	June 22
All Saints' Day	Nov. 1
Independence Day	Dec.6
Christmas Eve	Dec. 24
Christmas Day	Dec. 25
2nd Christmas Day	Dec. 26

France

New Year's Day	Jan.1
Martin Luther King, Jr.'s Birthday	Jan. 15
President's Day	Feb. 19
Easter Monday	Apr. 17
French Labor Day	May 1
Ascension Day	June 1
French Veterans Day (WW II)	May 8
Pentecost Monday	June 5
Memorial Day	May 27
Independence Day	July 4*
Bastille Day (Fr. National Day)	July 14
Assumption Day	Aug. 15
Labor Day	Sept. 2
Columbus Day	Oct. 14
All Saints' Day	Nov.1
Veterans Day	Nov. 11
Thanksgiving Day	Nov. 23
Christmas Day	Dec. 25

*Observed Friday, July 3

Gabon

New Year's Day	Jan.1
Aid EI-Fitr	Feb. 20
Easter Monday	Apr. 17
Labor Day	May 1
Aid EI-Adha	May 9
Pentecost	June 4
Assumption	Aug. 15
Independence Day	Aug. 16-18
All Saints' Day	Nov.1
Christmas Day	Dec. 2

The Gambia

New Year's Day	Jan.1
Martin Luther King, Jr.'s Birthday	Jan 15
Gambian Independence Day	Feb. 18
Eid EI-Fitri	Mar. 3
Labor Day	May 1
Tabaski	May 10
Yaamal-Assora	July 19
St. Mary's Day	Aug. 15
Muwlud-al-Nabi	Lunar Calendar

Georgia

Christmas	Jan. 7
Baptism Day (Orth. Church)	Jan. 19
Mother's Day	Mar 3
Memorial Day	Apr. 9
Recollection of Deceased	Apr. 15
Victory Day	May 9
Independence Day	May 26
Day of the Virgin (Orth.)	Aug. 28
Svetiskhovloba	Oct. 14
St. George's Day	Nov. 23

Germany

New Year's Day	Jan. 1
Epiphany	Jan. 6
Martin Luther King, Jr.'s Birthday	Jan. 20
President's Day	Feb. 17
Good Friday	Mar. 28
Easter Sunday	Mar. 30
Easter Monday	Mar 31
Labor Day	May 1
Ascension Day	May 8
Whitsunday	May 18
Whitmonday	May 19
Memorial Day	May 26
Corpus Christi Day	May 29
Independence Day	July 4*
Assumption Day	Aug. 15
Labor Day	Sept. 1
Day of German Unity	Oct. 3
Columbus Day	Oct. 13
All Saints' Day	Nov. 1
Veterans Day	Nov. 11
Thanksgiving Day	Nov. 27
Christmas Day	Dec. 25
Second Christmas Day	Dec. 26

*Observed Friday, July 3

Ghana

New Year's Day	Jan. 1
Martin Luther King, Jr.'s Birthday	Jan. 20
President's Day	Feb.17
Id-ul-Fitr	TBA
Independence Day	Mar. 6
Good Friday	Mar. 28
Easter Monday	Mar. 31
Labor Day	May 1
Memorial Day	May 26
Republic Day	July 1
Independence Day	July 4*
Labor Day	Sept. 1
Columbus Day	Oct. 13
Veterans Day	Nov. 11
Thanksgiving Day	Nov. 27
Farmers Day	Dec. 5
Christmas Day	Dec. 25
Boxing Day	Dec. 26

*Observed Friday, July 3

Greece

New Year's Day	Jan.1
Epiphany	Jan. 6

Martin Luther King, Jr.'s Birthday	Jan. 15
President's Day	Feb. 19
Kathara Deftera	Feb. 26
Dodecanese Accession Day (observed in Rhodes only)	Mar. 7
Good Friday	Apr. 12
Holy Saturday	Apr. 13
Easter Sunday	Apr. 14
Easter Monday	Apr. 15
May Day	May 1
Assumption Day	Aug 15
Liberation of Xanthi (observed in Xanthi only)	Oct. 4
St. Dimitrios Day (observed in Thessaloniki only)	Oct. 26
Ohi Day	Oct. 28
Christmas Day	Dec. 25
Boxing Day	Dec. 26

Grenada

New Year's Day	Jan. 1
Martin Luther King, Jr.'s Birthday	Jan. 19
Independence Day	Feb. 7
President's Day	Feb. 16
Good Friday	Apr. 10
Easter Monday	Apr. 13
Memorial Day	May 2
Whitmonday	June 1
Corpus Christi	June 11
Idependence Day	July 4*
Emancipation Day	Aug. 3
Day After Emancipation Day	Aug. 4
Carnival Monday	Aug. 10
Carnival Tuesday	Aug. 11
Labor Day	Sept. 7
Columbus Day	Oct. 12
Thanksgiving Day	Oct. 26
Veterans Day	Nov. 11
Thanksgiving Day	Nov. 26
Christmas Day	Dec. 25
Boxing Day	Dec. 26

*Observed Friday, July 3

Guatemala

Martin Luther King, Jr.'s Birthday	Jan. 15
President's Day	Feb. 19
Holy Thursday	Apr. 4
Good Friday	Apr. 5
Holy Saturday	Apr. 6
Easter Sunday	Apr. 7
Labor Day(G)	May 1
Memorial Day	May 27
Army Day	June 30
Independence Day (U.S.)	July 4*
Feast of the Assumption	Aug. 15
Labor Day (U.S.)	Sept. 2
Independence Day (G)	Sept. 15
Columbus Day	Oct. 14
Revolution Day	Oct. 20
All Saints' Day	Nov. 1
Veterans Day	Nov. 11
Thanksgiving Day	Nov. 28
Christmas Eve	Dec. 24
Christmas Day	Dec. 25
New Year's Eve	Dec. 31

*Observed Friday, July 3

Guinea

New Year's Day	Jan. 1
End of Ramadan (varies)	February
Declaration 2nd Republic	Apr. 3
Easter Monday	Apr. 8
Labor Day	May 1
Tabaski (varies)	mid-May
Maouloud (varies)	mid-Aug.
Assumption Day	Aug. 15
Independence Day	Oct. 2
Christmas Day	Dec. 25

Guinea-Bissau

New Year's Day	Jan.1
National Heroes' Day (varies)	Jan.
Veterans Day (varies)	Jan.
International Women's Day	Mar. 8
Ramadan (varies)	Mar.
Good Friday	Apr. 5
Easter Sunday	Apr. 7
Labor Day	May 1
Tabaski (varies)	June
Martyrs of Colonialism Day	Aug. 3
Independence Day	Sept. 24
Readjustment Movement Day	Nov.14
Christmas Eve	Dec. 24
Christmas Day	Dec. 25

Guyana

New Year's Day	Jan. 1
Republic Day	Feb. 23
Pagwah	Mar. 13
Good Friday	Apr. 10
Easter Monday	Apr. 13
Eid-Ul-Azah*	Apr 18
Labor Day	May 1
Caribbean Day	July 6
Youm-Un-Nabi*	July 11
Freedom Day	Aug. 1
Deepavali	Oct. 30
Christmas Day	Dec. 25
Boxing Day	Dec. 26

*Dates are dependent on sighting of the moon.

Haiti

Independence Day	Jan. 1
New Year's Day	Jan. 1
Ancestor's Day	Jan. 2
Martin Luther King, Jr.'s Birthday	Jan. 19
President's Day	Feb. 16
Carnival Mardi Gras	Feb. 24
Good Friday	Apr. 10
Labor Day	May 1
Memorial Day	May 25
Corpus Christi	June 1
Independence Day	July 4*
Labor Day	Sept. 7
Columbus Day	Oct. 12
All Souls' Day	Nov. 2
Veterans Day	Nov. 11
Anniversary of the Battle of Vertieres	Nov. 18
Thanksgiving Day	Nov. 26
Christmas Day	Dec. 25

*Observed Friday, July 3

The Holy See

New Year's Day	Jan. 1
Holy Thursday	Apr. 13
Good Friday	Apr. 14
Holy Saturday	Apr. 15
Easter Sunday	Apr. 16
Easter Monday	Apr. 17
Ascension	June 1
Pentecost	June 4
Assumption	Aug. 15
National Day	Oct. 22
All Saints' Day	Nov. 1
All Souls' Day	Nov. 2
Immaculate Conception	Dec. 8
Christmas Day	Dec. 25

Honduras

New Year's Day	Jan.1
Martin Luther King, Jr.'s Birthday	Jan. 15
President's Day	Feb. 19
Holy Thursday	Apr. 4
Good Friday	Apr. 5
Holy Saturday	Apr. 6
Day of the Americas	Apr. 14
Honduran Labor Day	May 1
Labor Day (H)	May 1
Memorial Day	May 27
Independence Day	July 4*
Labor Day (U.S.)	Sept. 2
Independence Day of Central America	Sept. 15
Birthday of General Francisco Morazan	Oct. 3
Discovery of America	Oct. 12
Columbus Day	Oct. 14
Honduran Armed Forces Day	Oct. 21
Veterans Day	Nov. 11
Thanksgiving Day	Nov. 28
Christmas Day	Dec. 25

*Observed Friday, July 3

Hong Kong

New Year's Day	Jan. 1
Martin Luther King, Jr.'s Birthday	Jan. 19
Lunar New Year (3 days)	Jan. 28-30
President's Day	Feb. 16
Day Following Ching Ming Festival	Apr. 6
Good Friday	Apr. 10
Memorial Day	May 25
Hong Kong Special Administrative Region Establishment Day	July 1
Independence Day	July 4*
Labor Day	Sept. 7
National Day	Oct. 1
Following National Day	Oct. 2
Day Following Mid-Autumn Festival	Oct. 6
Columbus Day	Oct. 12
Chung Yeung Festival	Oct. 28
Veterans Day	Nov. 11
Thanksgiving Day	Nov. 26
Christmas Day	Dec. 25

*Observed Friday, July 3

Hungary

New Year's Day	Jan.1
Martin Luther King, Jr.'s Birthday	Jan. 19
President's Day	Feb. 16
1848 March 15 Revolution Day	Mar. 15
Easter Monday	Apr. 13
Labor Day	May 1
Memorial Day	May 25
Whitmonday	June 1
Independence Day	July 4*
National Day	Aug. 20
Labor Day	Sept. 7
Columbus Day	Oct. 12
Republic Day	Oct. 23
Veterans Day	Nov. 11
Thanksgiving Day	Nov. 26
Christmas Day	Dec. 25
Boxing Day	Dec. 26

*Observed Friday, July 3

Iceland

New Year's Day	Jan. 1
Martin Luther King, Jr.'s Birthday	Jan. 19
President's Day	Feb 16
Maundy Thursday	Apr. 9
Good Friday	Apr. 10
Easter Monday	Apr. 13
First Day of Summer	Apr. 23
International Labor Day	May 1
Ascension Day	May 21
Memorial Day	May 25
Whitmonday	June 1
Icelandic National Day	June 17
Independence Day	July 4*
Bank Holiday	Aug. 3
U.S. Labor Day	Sept. 7
Columbus Day	Oct. 12
Veterans Day	Nov. 11
Thanksgiving Day	Nov. 26
Christmas Eve	Dec. 24
Christmas Day	Dec. 25
New Year's Eve	Dec. 31

*Observed Friday, July 3

India

Netaji's Birthday	Jan. 23
Sree Panchami	Jan. 25
Republic Day	Jan. 26
Id-Ul-Fitr	Feb 21
Doljatra	Mar. 5
Yearly Closing of Bank's Accounts	Apr. 1
Good Friday	Apr. 5
Id-Uz-Zoha	Apr. 29
May Day	May 1
Muharram	May 28
Milad-Un-Nabi	July 29
Independence Day	Aug. 15
Janmastami	Sept. 4
Half-yearly Closing of Bank's Accounts	Sept. 30
Gandhiji's Birthday	Oct. 2
Mahalaya	Oct. 12
Durga Puja (Saptami)	Oct. 19
Durga Puja (Dashami)	Oct. 21

Lakshmi Puja	Oct. 26
Parswanath's Rathajatra, and Guru Nanak's Birthday	Nov. 25
Christmas Day	Dec. 25

Indonesia

New Year's Day	Jan. 1
Idul Fitri	Mar. 3
Saka New Year	Mar. 17
Good Friday	Apr. 14
Waisak	May 3
Idul Adha	May 9
Ascension of Christ	June 1
Moslem New Year	June 10
Mohammad's Birthday	Aug. 9
Independence Day	Aug. 17
Christmas Day	Dec. 25

Iraq

Ascension of Mohammad	Varies
New Year's Day	Jan.1
Iraqi Army Day	Jan.6
Id al-Fitr	Mar. 3
Id al-Adha	May 9
Muharram	May 31
1958 Revolution	July 14
1968 Revolution	July 17
Ashura	Aug. 3
Mawlid al Nabi	Aug. 9

Ireland

New Year's Day	Jan.1
St. Patrick's Day	Mar. 17
Good Friday	Apr. 5
Easter Monday	Apr. 8
May Bank Holiday	May 6
June Bank Holiday	June 3
August Bank Holiday	Aug. 5
October Bank Holiday	Oct. 28
Christmas Day	Dec. 25
St. Stephen's Day	Dec. 26

*Observed Friday, July 3

Israel

New Year's Day	Jan. 1
Martin Luther King, Jr.'s Birthday	Jan. 19
President's Day	Feb. 16
Passover—First Day	Apr. 11
Passover—Last Day	Apr. 18
Israeli Independence Day	May 1
Memorial Day	May 25
Pentecost (Shavuot)	May 31
Independence Day	July 4*
Labor Day	Sep. 7
New Year (Rosh Hashana-1st Day)	Sept. 21
New Year (Rosh Hashana- 2d Day)	Sept.22
Day of Atonement (Yom Kippur)	Sept. 30
Succot (Feast of Tabernacles)	Oct. 5
Columbus Day	Oct. 12
Simhat Tora (Rejoicing of the Law)	Oct. 12
Columbus Day	Oct. 12
Veterans Day	Nov. 11

Thanksgiving Day	Nov. 28
Christmas Day	Dec. 25

Dates vary each year in accordance with the Hebrew and Islamic calendars.

*Observed Friday, July 3

Italy

New Year's Day	Jan. 1
Epiphany	Jan. 6
Easter Monday	Apr. 8
Anniversary of the Liberation	Apr. 25
Labor Day	May 1
St. John's Day (Florence)	June 24
St. Peter and St. Paul's Day	June 29
Assumption Day	Aug. 15
St. Gennaros Day (Naples)	Sept. 19
All Saints' Day	Nov. 1
St. Ambrogio's Day (Milan)	Dec. 7
Immaculate Conception	Dec. 8
Christmas Day	Dec. 25
St. Stephen's Day	Dec. 26

In addition, each city observes the local patron saint's day. When an Italian holiday falls on a Saturday, all Italian Government offices and stores are closed to the public.

Jamaica

New Year's Day	Jan. 1
Ash Wednesday	Feb. 25
Good Friday	Apr. 10
Easter Monday	Apr. 13
National Labor Day	May 23
Emancipation Day	Aug.
Independence Day	Aug. 6
National Heroes' Day	Oct. 19
Christmas Day	Dec. 25
Boxing Day	Dec. 26

Japan

New Year's Day	Jan. 1
Adult's Day	Jan. 15
National Foundation Day	Feb. 11
Vernal Equinox Day	Mar. 20
Greenery Day	Apr. 29
Constitution Memorial Day	May 3
Children's Day	May 5
Marine Day	July 20
Respect for the Aged Day	Sept. 15
Autumnal Equinox Day	Sept. 23
Health-Sports Day	Oct. 10
Culture Day	Nov. 3
Labor Thanksgiving Day	Nov. 23
Emperor's Birthday	Dec. 23

Jerusalem (City of)

New Year's Day	Jan. 1
Martin Luther King, Jr.'s Birthday	Jan. 19
President's Day	Feb. 16
Passover—First Day	Apr. 11
Passover—Last Day	Apr. 18
Israeli Independence Day	Apr. 24

Pentecost (Shavuot)	May 31
Memorial Day	May 25
Independence Day	July 4*
Labor Day	Sept. 7
New Year (Rosh Hashana)	Sept. 21
Rosh Hashana—2nd Day	Sept. 22
Day of Atonement (Yom Kippur)	Sept. 30
Feast of Tabernacles (Succot)	Oct. 5
Rejoicing of the Law (Simhat Tora)	Oct. 12
Columbus Day	Oct. 12
Veterans Day	Nov. 11
Thanksgiving Day	Nov. 28
Christmas Day	Dec. 25

Dates vary each year in accordance with the Hebrew calendars.

*Observed Friday, July 3

Jordan

New Year's Day	Jan. 1
Arbor Day	Jan. 15
Id al-Fitr	Mar. 3
Id al-Adha	May 9
Jordanian Independence Day	May 25
Muharram	May 31
Great Arab Revolt & Army Day	June 10
Mawlid al Nabi	Aug. 9
King Hussein's Accession to the Throne	Aug. 11
King Hussein's Birthday	Nov. 14
Christmas Day	Dec. 25

Kazakhstan

New Year's Day	Jan. 1-2
Martin Luther King, Jr.'s Birthday	Jan 19
Id-Ul-Fitr	February
President's Day	Feb. 16
Women's Day	Mar. 8
Muslim New Year - Nauryz	Mar. 22
Good Friday	Apr. 5
Easter Monday	Apr. 8
Day of the Unity of the People of Kazakhstan	May 1
Victory Day	May 9
Memorial Day	May 25
Independence Day	July 4*
Labor Day	Sep. 7
Columbus Day	Oct. 12
Veterans Day	Nov. 11
Thanksgiving Day	Nov. 26
Independence Day	Dec. 16
Christmas Day	Dec. 25

*Observed Friday, July 3

Kenya

New Year's Day	Jan. 1
Good Friday	Apr. 5
Easter Monday	Apr. 8
Id-U I-Fitr	February
Labor Day	May 1
Id-Ul-Adha	May 9
Madaraka Day	June 1
Moi Day	Oct. 10
Kenyatta Day	Oct. 20

Independence Day	Dec. 12
Christmas Day	Dec. 25
Boxing Day	Dec. 26

Korea

New Year's Day	Jan. 1, 2
Martin Luther King, Jr.'s Birthday	Jan. 19
Lunar New Year	Jan. 27-29
President's Day	Feb. 16
Children's Day	May 5
Memorial Day	May 25
Independence Day	July 4*
Constitution Day	July 17
Labor Day	Sep. 7
Thanksgiving Days	Oct. 5 & 6
Columbus Day	Oct. 12
Veterans Day	Nov. 11
Thanksgiving Day	Nov. 26
Christmas Day	Dec. 26

*Observed Friday, July 3

Kuwait

New Year's Day	Jan. 1
Kuwait National Day	Feb. 25
Id al-Fitr	Mar. 3
Id al-Adha	May 9
Muharram	May 31
Mawlid al-Nabi	Oct. 3

Kyrgyzstan

New Year's Day	Jan. 1
Orthodox Christmas	Jan. 7
Martin Luther King, Jr.'s Birthday	Jan. 19
Orozo Ait (end of the Lent)	Jan. 29
President's Day	Feb. 16
Women's Day	Mar. 8
Muslim New Year Holiday	Mar. 21
Kurman Ait (Sacrifice Day)	Apr. 7
Labor Day	May 1
Constitution Day	May 5
Victory Day	May 9
Memorial Day	May 25
Independence Day	July 4*
Independence Day of the Kyrgyz Republic	Aug. 31
Labor Day	Sept. 7
Columbus Day	Oct. 12
Veteran's Day	Nov. 11
Thanksgiving Day	Nov. 28
Christmas Day	Dec. 25

*Observed Friday, July 3

Laos

New Year's Day	Jan. 1
Martin Luther King, Jr.,'s Birthday	Jan. 19
President's Day	Feb. 16
Lao New Year	Apr. 14-16
Lao Labor Day	May 1
Memorial Day	May 25
Independence Day	July 3
Labor Day	Sep. 7
Buddhist Lent	Oct. 6

Boat Racing Festival	Oct. 7
Columbus Day	Oct. 12
That Luang Festival	Nov. 4
Veterans Day	Nov.11
Thanksgiving Day	Nov. 26
Lao National Day	Dec. 2
Christmas Day	Dec. 25

Latvia

New Year's Day	Jan. 1
Good Friday	Apr. 12
Labor Day/Constitution Day	May 1
Midsummer's Eve	June 23
Summer Solstice	June 24
LR Proclamation Day	Nov. 18
Christmas	Dec. 25
Boxing Day	Dec. 26
New Year's Eve	Dec. 31

Lebanon

End of Ramadan	Mar. 3
Good Friday	Apr. 14
Lebanese Labor Day	May 1
Id al-Adha	May 9
Al Hejra Mawlid al-Nabi	Aug. 9
Assumption Day	Aug. 15
Lebanese Independence Day	Nov. 22

Lesotho

New Year's Day	Jan. 1
Moshoeshoe's Day	Mar. 12
National Tree Planting Day	Mar. 21
Good Friday	Apr. 5
Easter Monday	Apr. 8
King's Birthday	May 2
Ascension Day	May 16
Family Day	July 1
Independence Day	Oct. 4
National Sports Day	Oct. 7
Christmas Day	Dec. 25
Boxing Day	Dec. 26

Liberia

New Year's Day	Jan. 1
Armed Forces Day	Feb. 11
Decoration Day	Mar. 8
J.J. Robert's Birthday	Mar. 15
National Redemption Day	Apr. 12
Fast and Prayer Day	Apr. 14
Unification Day	May 14
Independence Day	July 26
Flag Day	Aug. 24
Thanksgiving Day	Nov. 2
William V.S.Tubman's Day	Nov. 29
Christmas Day	Dec. 25

Lithuania

New Year's Day	Jan. 1
Martin Luther King, Jr.'s Birthday	Jan. 19
Lithuanian Statehood Day	Feb. 16
President's Day	Feb. 16

Independence Day	Feb. 16
Independence Day / Statehood Day	Mar. 11
Good Friday	Apr. 10
Easter Monday	Apr. 13
International Labor Day	May 1
Memorial Day	May 25
Independence Day	July 4*
Mindaugas Coronation Day	July 6
Labor Day	Sep. 7
Columbus Day	Oct. 12
All Saints Day	Nov. 1
Veterans Day	Nov. 11
Thanksgiving Day	Nov. 26
Christmas Day	Dec. 25
Boxing Day	Dec. 26

*Observed Friday, July 3

Luxembourg

New Year's Day	Jan. 1
Shrove Monday	Feb. 10
Easter Monday	Mar. 31
Luxembourg Labor Day	May 1
Ascension Day	May 8
Whitmonday	May 19
Grand Duke's Birthday	June 23
Assumption Day	Aug. 15
All Saints' Day	Nov. 1
All Souls' Day	Nov. 2
Christmas Day	Dec. 25
Second Day of Christmas	Dec. 26

Macedonia

New Year's Day	Jan. 1-2
Orthodox Christmas	Jan. 7
Orthodox Easter	April 19
Labor Day	May 1-2
Ilinden	Aug. 2
Independence Day	Sept. 8
People's Uprising	Oct. 11

Madagascar

New Year's Day	Jan. 1
Day Commemorating Martyrs	Mar. 29
Easter Monday	Apr. 8
Malagasy Labor Day	May 1
Ascension Day	May 16
African Liberation Day	May 25
Pentecost Day	May 26
Pentecost Monday	May 27
Malagasy Independence Day	June 26
Assumption Day	August 15
All Saints' Day	Nov. 1
Christmas Day	Dec. 25

Malawi

New Year's Day	Jan.1
Martyr's Day	Mar. 3-4
Good Friday	Apr. 14
Easter Monday	Apr. 17
Kamuzu Day	May 1
Republic Day	July 6-8
Mother's Day	Oct. 17
Tree-Planting Holiday	Dec. 21-23

©Almanac Publishing, Inc. 1998 - The Washington Almanac of International Trade & Business

Christmas Day	Dec. 25

Malaysia

New Year's Day	Jan. 1
Kuala Lumpur City Day	Feb. 1
Chinese New Year (2 days)	Feb. 15-16
Han Raya Puasa (2 days)	Mar. 3
Malaysia Labor Day	May 1
Wesak Day	May 3
Han Raya Haji	May 19
Birthday of the Yang Dipertuan Agun	June 5
Awal Muharram	June 10
Prophet Muhammad's Birthday	Aug. 9
Malaysian National Day	Aug. 31
Christmas Day	Dec. 25

Mali

New Year's Day	Jan. 1
Army Day	Jan. 20
End of Ramadan	Mar. 2
Easter Monday	Apr. 17
Labor Day	May 1
Tabaski	May 9
Day of Africa	May 25
Mawloud	Aug. 9
Independence Day	Sept. 22
Liberation Day	Nov. 19
Christmas Day	Dec. 25

Malta

St. Paul's Shipwreck	Feb. 10
St. Joseph's Day	Mar. 19
Freedom Day	Mar. 31
Good Friday	Varies
Malta Labor Day	May 1
Anniversary of 1919 Riots	June 7
St. Peter and St. Paul	June 29
Feast of the Assumption	Aug.15
Our Lady of Victories	Sept. 8
Independence Day	Sept. 21
Immaculate Conception	Dec. 8
Republic Day	Dec. 13
Christmas Day	Dec. 25

Marshall Islands

New Year's Day	Jan. 1
Memorial Day	Mar. 1
Constitution Day	May 1
Labor Day	Sept. 2
Independence Day	Oct. 21
President's Day	Nov. 17
Thanksgiving Day	Nov. 4
Christmas Day	Dec. 25

Martinique

New Year's Day	Jan. 1
Carnival	Feb.11-12
Good Friday	Apr. 14
Easter Monday	Apr. 17
Labor Day	May 1
Veterans Day	May 8

Emancipation Day	May 22
Ascension Day	June 1
Pentecost Monday	June 5
Assumption Day	Aug. 15
All Saints' Day	Nov. 1
Christmas Day	Dec. 25

Mauritania

New Year's Day	Jan. 1
Id el-Fitr (end of Ramadan)	Mar. 2
Mauritanian Labor Day	May 1
Id el-Adha or Tabaski	May 10
Africa Day	May 25
First Muharram	May 30
Id el-Maouloud Nebewi	Aug. 9
Mauritanian Independence Day	Nov. 28

Mauritius

New Year's Day	Jan. 1, 2
Thaipoosam Cavadee	Jan. 23
Chinese Spring Festival	Feb. 7
Id-el-Fitr	Feb. 9
Maha Shivaratree	Mar. 7
National Day	Mar. 12
Ougadi	Apr. 8
Labor Day	May 1
Ganesh Chaturthi	Sept. 6
Divali	Oct. 30
All Saints' Day	Nov. 1
Christmas Day	Dec. 25

Mexico

New Year's Day	Jan. 1
Martin Luther King, Jr.'s Birthday	Jan. 19
Anniversary of Mexican Constitution	Feb. 5
President's Day	Feb. 16
Benito Juarez's Birthday	Mar. 21
Holy Thursday	Apr. 9
Good Friday	Apr. 10
Mexican Labor Day	May 1
Anniversary of the Battle of Puebla	May 5
Memorial Day	May 25
Independence Day	July 4*
Labor Day	Sept. 7
Independence Day S	Sept. 16
Dia de Ia Raza and Columbus Day	Oct. 12
All Souls' Day	Nov. 2
Veterans Day	Nov. 11
Anniversary of the Mexican Revolution	Nov. 20
Thanksgiving Day	Nov. 26
Christmas Day	Dec. 25

*Observed Friday, July 3

Micronesia

New Year's Day Jan. 1	
Martin Luther King, Jr.'s Birthday	Jan. 15
President's Day	Feb. 19
Constitution Day	May 10
Memorial Day	May 27
Independence Day (U.S.)	July 4*
Labor Day	Sept. 2
Columbus Day	Oct. 14

United Nations' Day	Oct. 24
Independence Day (M)	Nov. 4
Veterans Day	Nov. 11
Thanksgiving Day	Nov. 26
Christmas Day	Dec. 25

*Observed Friday, July 3

Mongolia

New Year's Day	Jan. 1
Martin Luther King, Jr.'s Birthday	Jan. 19
President's Day	Feb. 16
Lunar New Year (Tsagan Tsar)	Feb. 27-28
Memorial Day	May 25
Mother /Child Day	June 1
Independence Day	July 3
Naadam	July 11-13
Labor Day	Sept. 7
Columbus Day	Oct. 12
Veterans Day	Nov. 11
Mongolian Independence Day and Thanksgiving Day	Nov. 26
Christmas Day	Dec. 25

Morocco

New Year's Day	Jan. 1
Martin Luther King, Jr.'s Birthday	Jan 15
Presidents Day	Feb. 19
Aid al-Fitr (end of Ramadan)	Feb. 20, 21
Aid al-Ahda (Feast of Pilgrimage)	Apr. 28, 29
Moroccan Labor Day	May 1
First Moharram (Moslem New Year)	May19
Moroccan National Day	May 23
Memorial Day	May 27
Independence Day	July 4
Youth Day (King's Birthday)	July 9
Aid al-Moulid (Prophet's Birthday)	July 28, 29
Labor Day	Sept. 2
Columbus Day	Oct. 14
Veterans Day	Nov. 11
Moroccan Independence Day	Nov. 18
Thanksgiving Day	Nov. 28
Christmas Day	Dec. 25

*Observed Friday, July 3

Mozambique

New Year's Day	Jan. 1
Anniversary of President Mondlane's Death	Feb. 3
Mozambican Women's Day	Apr. 7
Worker's Day	May 1
Independence Day	June 25
Lusaka Agreement	Sept. 7
Revolution Day	Sept. 25
Maputo City Day	Nov. 10
Christmas Day	Dec. 25

Namibia

New Year's Day	Jan. 1
Independence Day	Mar. 21
Good Friday	Apr. 5
Easter Monday	Apr. 8
Worker's Day	May 1

Cassingda Day	May 4
Ascension Day	May 16
African Freedom Day	May 25
Heroes' Day	Aug. 26
Christmas Day	Dec. 25
Family Day	Dec. 26

Nepal

King Tribhuvan Memorial and National Democracy Day	Feb. 19
Buddha Jayanti	May 28
Ghatasthapna	Oct. 8
Dasain	Oct. 15-17
Laxmi Puja	Nov. 5
Goverdhan Puja	Nov. 6
Bhai Tika	Nov. 7

Netherlands

New Year's Day	Jan. 1
Good Friday	Apr. 14
Easter Monday	Apr. 17
Queen's Birthday	Apr. 30
Liberation Day	May 5
Ascension Day	June 1
Whitmonday	June 5
2nd Christmas Day	Dec. 26

Netherlands Antilles

New Year's Day	Jan. 1
Betico Day (Aruba)	Jan. 25
Carnival Monday	Feb. 23
Aruba Flag Day	March 18
Good Friday	Apr. 10
Easter Monday	Apr. 13
Queen's Birthday	Apr. 30
Labor Day	May 1
Ascension Day	May 21
Flag Day (Curacao)	July 2
Flag Day (Bonaire)	Sept. 6
Antilles Day	Oct. 21
Flag Day (St. Maarten)	Nov. 11
Flag Day (St. Eustatius)	Nov. 16
Flag Day (Saba)	Dec. 5
Christmas Day	Dec. 25
Boxing Day	Dec. 26

New Zealand

New Year's	Jan. 1, 2
Anniversary Day (Wellington)	Jan. 21
Anniversary Day (Auckland)	Jan. 28
Waitangi Day	Feb. 6
Good Friday	Apr. 14
Easter Monday	Apr. 17
ANZAC Day	Apr. 25
Queen's Birthday	June 3
Labor Day	Oct. 28
Christmas Day	Dec. 25
Boxing Day	Dec. 26

Nicaragua

New Year's Day	Jan. 1

Holy Thursday	Apr. 4
Good Friday	Apr. 5
Labor Day	May 1
Holy Saturday	Apr. 15
Easter Sunday	Apr. 16
Anniversary of the Revolution	July 19
Battle of San Jacinto	Sept. 14
Independence Day	Sept. 15
Immaculate Conception	Dec. 8
Christmas Day	Dec. 25

Niger

New Year's Day	Jan. 1
Easter Monday	Apr. 17
End of Ramadan	Mar. 13
Niger Labor Day	May 1
Id al Adha	May 9
Niger Independence Day	Aug. 3
Mouloud	Sept. 22
Republic Day	Dec. 18
Christmas Day	Dec. 25

Nigeria

New Year's Day	Jan. 1
Good Friday	Apr. 1
Easter Monday	Apr. 4
Id al-Fitr	Mar. 3
May Day	May 1
Id al-Adha	May 9
Mawlid al-Nabi	Aug. 9
National Day	Oct. 1
Christmas Day	Dec. 25
Boxing Day	Dec. 26

Norway

New Year's Day	Jan. 1
Holy Thursday	Apr.4
Good Friday	Apr. 5
Easter Monday	Apr. 8
Norwegian Labor Day	May 1
Ascension Day	May 16
Independence Day	May 17
Whitsunday	May 26
Whitmonday	May 27
Christmas Day	Dec. 25
2d Christmas Day	Dec. 26

Oman

New Year's Day	Jan. 1
Martin Luther King Jr.'s Birthday	Jan. 18
Eid-AI-Fitr	Feb. 10, 11
President's Day	Feb. 15
Eid AI-Adha	Apr. 16, 17, 18
Islamic New Year	May 8
Memorial Day	May 24
Independence Day	July 4*
Birth of the Prophet	July 17
Labor Day	Aug. 30
Columbus Day	Oct. 11
Veterans Day	Nov 9
Oman National Day	Nov 17, 18
Thanksgiving Day	Nov 29
Christmas Day	Dec 25
Ascension Day	Dec 27

*Observed Friday, July 3

Pakistan

Eid-ul-Fitr	Jan. 29-31
Pakistan Day	Mar. 23
Eid-ul-Azha	7-9
May Day	May 1
9th & 10th day of Muharram	May 6-7
Eid-I-Milad-Un-Nabi	July 7
Independence Day	Aug. 14
Mawlid al Nabi	Aug. 9
Defense of Pakistan Day S	ept. 6
Death Anniversary of Quaid-l-Azam	Sept. 11
Iqbal Day	Nov. 9
Birthday of Quaid-l-Azam	Dec. 25
Christmas Day	Dec. 25

Palau

New Year's Day	Jan. 1
Martin Luther King, Jr.'s Birthday	Jan 15
President's Day	Feb. 19
Youth Day	Mar. 15
Senior Citizen's Day	May 6
Memorial Day	May 27
President's Day	May 31
Independence Day (U.S.)	July 4
Constitution Day	July 10
Labor Day	Sept. 2
Independence Day (P)	Oct. 1
Columbus Day	Oct. 14
Veterans Day	Nov. 11
Thanksgiving Day	Nov. 21
Christmas Day	Dec. 25

Panama

New Year's Day	Jan. 1
Mourning Day	Jan. 9
Martin Luther King, Jr.'s Day	Jan. 19
President's Day	Feb. 16
Carnival	Feb. 24
Good Friday	Apr. 10
Labor Day	May 1
Memorial Day	May 25
Independence Day	July 4*
Labor Day	Sept. 7
Columbus Day	Oct. 12
Independence Day	Nov. 3
Flag Day	Nov. 4
The Uprising of Los Santos	Nov. 10
Veterans Day	Nov. 11
Thanksgiving Day	Nov. 26
Independence Day From Spain	Nov. 28
Mother's Day*	Dec. 8
Christmas Day	Dec. 25

**Observed Friday, July 3

The Government of Panama Decree Law No. 8, dated July 12, 1997, modifies Article 46 of the Panamanian Labor Code concerning mandatory rest days (holidays) effective July 15, 1997. The modification establishes that January 9, May 1, November 10 and 28, and December 8 will br transferred to the next Monday. If the holiday falls on a Thursday or Friday and if the holiday falls on a Tuesday or Wednesday, the holiday will be celebrated the previous Monday. If the holiday falls on a Saturday, there is no substitute Friday. If a holiday falls on a Sunday, it will be transferred to Monday.

Papua New Guinea

New Year's Day	Jan.1
Good Friday	Apr. 14
Easter Monday	Apr. 17
Queen's Birthday	June 10
Remembrance Day (ANZAC)	July 23
Independence Day	Sept. 16
Christmas Day	Dec. 25
Boxing Day	Dec. 26

Paraguay

New Year's Day	Jan. 1
Heroes Day	Mar. 1
Holy Thursday	Apr. 13
Good Friday	Apr. 14
Labor Day	May 1
Independence Day	May 15
Chaco Armistice	June 12
Founding of the City of Asuncion	Aug. 15
Virgin of Caacupe	Dec. 8
Christmas Day	Dec. 25

Peru

New Year's Day	Jan. 1
Martin Luther King, Jr.'s Birthday	Jan. 19
President's Day	Feb. 16
Holy Thursday	Apr. 9
Good Friday	Apr. 10
Labor Day	May 1
Memorial Day	May 25
St. Peter and St. Paul	June 29
Independence Day (U.S.)	July 4
Independence Day (P)	July 28-29
St. Rose of Lima	Aug. 30
Labor Day	Sept. 2
Battle of Angamos	Oct. 8
Columbus Day	Oct. 12
All Saints' Day	Nov. 1
Veterans Day	Nov. 11
Thanksgiving Day	Nov. 26
Immaculate Conception	Dec. 8
Christmas Day	Dec. 25

*Observed Friday, July 3

Philippines

New Year's Day	Jan. 1
Martin Luther King, Jr.s Birthday	Jan. 20
President's Day	Feb. 17
Maundy Thursday	Mar. 27
Good Friday	Mar. 28
Araw Ng Kagitingan	Apr. 9
Batan & Corregidor Day (Heroism Day) Labor Day	May 1
Memorial Day	May 26
Independence Day	June 12

Poland

New Year's Day	Jan. 1
Martin Luther King, Jr.'s Birthday	Jan. 20
President's Day	Feb. 16

Easter Sunday	April 12
Easter Monday	Apr. 13
Labor Day	May 1
Constitution Day	May 3
Memorial Day	May 25
Corpus Christi Day	June 11
Independence Day	July 4*
Assumption of the Virgin Mary	Aug. 15
Labor Day	Sept. 7
Columbus Day	Oct. 12
All Saints' Day	Nov. 1
Veterans Day	Nov. 11
Independence Day	Nov. 11
Thanksgiving Day	Nov. 26
Christmas Day	Dec. 25
Boxing Day	Dec. 26

*Observed Friday, July 3

Portugal

New Year's Day	Jan.1
Carnival	Feb. 20
Good Friday	Apr. 5
Freedom Day	Apr 25
May Day	May 1
Corpus Christi Day	June 6
Portugal Day	June 10
St. Anthony's Day	June 13
Assumption Day	Aug. 15
Proclamation of the Portuguese Republic	Oct. 5
All Saints' Day	Nov. 1
Restoration of Portuguese Independence	Dec. 1
Immaculate Conception	Dec. 8
Christmas Day	Dec. 25

Qatar

Eid Al- Fitr	Mar. 3
Eid Al-Adha	May 9
Qatari National Day	Sept. 3

Romania

New Year's Day	Jan. 1
Day after New Year's Day	Jan. 2
Orthodox Easter	Apr. 14
Day after Orthodox Easter	Apr. 15
Romanian Labor Day	May 1
Romanian National Day	Dec. 1
Christmas Day	Dec. 25

Russia

New Year's Day	Jan. 1,2
Orthodox Christmas	Jan. 7
Martin Luther King, Jr.'s Birthday	Jan. 20
President's Day	Feb. 17
International Women's Day	Mar. 8
International Labor Day	May 1
Spring Day	May 2
Victory Day	May 9
Memorial Day	May 26
Independence Day (R)	June 12
Independence Day (U.S.)	July 4*

Labor Day	Sept. 1
Columbus Day	Oct. 12
Revolution Day	Nov. 7
Veterans Day	Nov. 11
Thanksgiving Day	Nov .27
Constitution Day	Dec. 12
Christmas Day	Dec. 25

*Observed Friday, July 3

Rwanda

New Year's Day	Jan. 1
Democracy Day	Jan. 28
Easter Monday	Apr. 4
Labor Day	May 1
Ascension Day	May 9
Pentecost Monday	June 5
National Day	July 1
Peace and National Unity Day	July 5
Assumption Day	Aug. 15
Culture Day	Sept. 8
Referendum Day	Sept. 25
Armed Forces Day	Oct. 26
All Saints' Day	Nov. 1
Christmas Day	Dec. 25

Samoa

New Year's Day	Jan. 1
Good Friday	Apr. 14
Easter Monday	Apr. 17
ANZAC Independence	June 1-3
Whitmonday	June 5
Arbor Day	Nov. 7
Christmas Day	Dec. 25
Boxing Day	Dec. 26
New Year's Eve	Dec. 31

Saudi Arabia

Id al-Fitr—Ramadan	Feb. 19
Id al-Adha—Hajj	Apr. 26

Senegal

New Year's Day	Jan. 1
Martin Luther King's Birthday	Jan. 15
National Heroes' Day	Jan. 20
Ash Wednesday	February 14
George Washington's Birthday	Feb. 19
Good Friday	Apr. 5
Labor Day (5)	May 1
Municipal Day	May 19
Memorial Day	May 27
Independence Day (U.S.)	July 4*
Independence Day (5)	July 5
Assumption Day	Aug. 15
Labor Day (U.S.)	Sept. 2
Columbus Day	Oct. 14
All Saints' Day	Nov. 1
Veterans Day	Nov. 11
Thanksgiving Day	Nov. 28
Christmas	Dec. 25

*Observed Friday, July 3

Serbia-Montenegro

New Year's Day	Jan. 1,2
Orthodox Christmas	Jan. 7
Martin Luther King, Jr.'s Birthday	Jan. 20
President's Day	Feb. 17
State Day	Mar. 28
Constitution Day	Apr. 27
Easter Monday	Apr. 28
May Day	May 1,2
Memorial Day	May 26
Independence Day	July 4*
Serbian Uprising Day (Serbia only)	July 7
Labor Day	Sept. 1
Columbus Day	Oct. 13
Veterans Day	Nov. 11
Thanksgiving Day	Nov. 27
Christmas Day	Dec. 25

*Observed Friday, July 3

Seychelles

New Year's Day	Jan.1
Bank Holiday	Jan. 2&3
Good Friday	Apr. 14
Labor Day	May 1
Corpus Christi	June 15
National Day	June 18
Independence Day	June 29
Feast of the Assumption	Aug. 15
All Saints' Day	Nov. 1
Immaculate Conception	Dec. 8
Christmas Day	Dec. 25

Sierra Leone

New Year's Day	Jan. 1
Good Friday	Apr. 1
Easter Monday	Apr. 4
Republic Day	Apr. 19
National Day	Apr. 27
Id al-Fitr	Mar. 3
Id al-Adha	May 9
Mawlid al Nabi	Aug. 9
Christmas Day	Dec. 25
Boxing Day	Dec. 26

Singapore

New Year's Day	Jan. 1
Chinese New Year	Feb. 15-16
Good Friday	Apr. 1
Han Raya Puasa	Apr. 16
Labor Day	May 1
Vesak Day	May 3
Hari Raya Ha]	June 24
Singapore National Day	Aug. 9
Deepavali	Nov. 5
Christmas Day	Dec. 25

Slovak Republic

New Year's Day	Jan. 1
Epiphany	Jan. 6
Good Friday	April 10

Easter Monday	April 13
Labor Day	May 1
St. Cyril and St. Methodius	July 5
Slovak National Uprising Day	Aug. 29
Constitution Day	Sept. 1
Virgin Mary of 7 Sorrows	Sept. 15
All Saints' Day	Nov. 1
Christmas Eve	Dec. 24
Christmas	Dec. 25
St. Stephen's Day	Dec. 26

Slovenia

New Year's Day	Jan. 1,2
Martin Luther King, Jr.'s Birthday	Jan 15
Slovenian Cultural Holiday	Feb. 8
President's Day	Feb. 23
Easter Sunday and Monday	Apr. 12&1 3
Resistance Day	Apr. 27
Labor Day	May 1,2
Memorial Day Whitsunday	May 25
Independence Day	June 25
Independence Day (U.S.)	July4
Assumption Day	Aug.15
Labor Day	Sept. 7
Columbus Day	Oct. 12
Reformation Day	Oct. 31
All Saints Day	Nov. 1
Veterans Day	Nov. 11
Thanksgiving Day	Nov. 26
Christmas Day	Dec. 25
National Day	Dec. 26

*Observed Friday, July 3

Solomon Islands

New Year's Day	Jan.1
Good Friday	Apr. 14
Easter Sunday	Apr. 16
Whitmonday	June 5
Queen's Birthday	June 14
Independence Day	July 7
Thanksgiving Day	Nov. 24
Christmas Day	Dec. 25

Somalia

Id al-Fitr	Mar. 3
Labor Day	May 1
Id al-Adha	May 9
Independence Day (Northern Region)	June 26
Independence Day	July 1
Mawlid al Nabi	Aug. 9
Revolution Days	Oct. 21,22

South Africa

New Year's Day	Jan. 1
Human Rights Day	Mar. 21
Good Friday	Friday before Easter Sun.
Family Day	Monday after Easter Sun.
Easter Monday	Apr. 17
Family Day	Monday after Easter
Freedom Day	April 27
Worker's Day	May 1

Youth Day	June 16
National Women's Day	Aug. 9
Heritage Day	Sept. 24
Day of Reconciliation	Dec. 16
Christmas Day	Dec. 25
Day of Goodwill	Dec. 26

Spain

New Year's Day	Jan. 1
Epiphany	Jan. 6
Holy Thursday	Mar. 27
Good Friday	Mar. 28
Labor Day	May 1
Community Day	May 2
St. Isidor	May 15
St. James	July 25
Assumption Day	Aug. 15
Labor Day	Sept. 1
Columbus Day	Oct. 13
National Day	Oct. 12
All Saints' Day	Nov. 1
La Almudena	Nov. 10
Veterans Day	Nov. 11
Thanksgiving Day	Nov. 27
Constitution Day	Dec. 6
Immaculate Conception Day	Dec. 8
Christmas Day	Dec. 25

Sri Lanka

New Year	Jan. 1
Tamil Thai Pongal Day	Jan. 14
Martin Luther King, Jr.'s Birthday	Jan. 20
Duruthu Full Moon Poya Day	Jan. 23
National Day	Feb. 4
President's Day	Feb. 17
Good Friday	March 28
Sinhala and Tamil New Year	Apr. 14
Bak Full Moon Poya Day	Apr. 22
May Day	May 1
Wesak Full Moon Poya Day	May 21
Memorial Day	May 26
Poson Full Moon Poya Day	June 20
Independence Day	July 4*
Milad-un-Nabi (Holy Prophet's Birth Day)	July 18
Labor Day	Sept. 1
Columbus Day	Oct. 13
Veterans Day	Nov. 11
Thanksgiving Day	Nov. 27
Christmas	Dec. 25

*Observed Friday, July 3

Sudan

Independence Day	Jan. 1
Id al-Fitr	Mar. 3
Id al-Fitr	Mar. 6
Ramadan	Mar. 29
Anniversary of Rajab Revolution	Apr. 6
Eastern Easter	Apr. 23
Sham El Nasim	Apr. 24
Id al-Adha	May 10, 11
Higra New Year	May 31
Proph. Mohamed's Birth	Aug. 9
Israa and Mirag	Dec. 9

Suriname

New Year's Day	Jan. 1
led u-Fitr	Jan. 29
Holi Phagwa	Mar. 13
Good Friday	Apr. 10
Easter Monday	Apr. 13
Labor Day	May 1
Emancipation Day	July 1
Independence Day	Nov. 25
Christmas Day	Dec. 25
Boxing Day	Dec. 26

Swaziland

New Year's Day	Jan.1
Commonwealth Day	Mar. 9
Good Friday	Apr. 14
Easter Monday	Apr. 17
King Mswati's Birthday	Apr. 19
National Flag Day— King Mswati's Coronation	Apr. 25
Public Holiday	July 22
Reed Dance Day	
Independence Day	Sept. 6
Christmas Day	Dec. 25
Boxing Day	Dec. 26

Sweden

New Year's Day	Jan. 1
13th Day of Christmas	Jan. 6
Good Friday	Apr. 10
Easter Monday	Apr. 13
Swedish Labor Day	May 1
Ascension Day	May 21
Whitmonday	June 1
Midsummer Eve	June 19
Christmas Eve	Dec. 24
Christmas Day	Dec. 25
2d Day of Christmas	Dec. 26
New Year's Eve	Dec. 31

Switzerland

New Year's Day	Jan.1
Martin Luther King, Jr.'s Birthday	Jan. 19
President's Day	Feb. 16
Good Friday	Apr. 10
Easter Monday	Apr. 13
Ascension Day	May 21
Memorial Day	May 25
Whitmonday	June 1
Independence Day	July 4*
Labor Day	Sept. 7
Columbus Day	Oct. 12
Veterans Day	Nov. 11
Thanksgiving Day	Nov. 26
Christmas Day	Dec. 25

*Observed Friday, July 3

Syria

New Year's Day	Jan.1
Eid Al Fitr	Mar. 3

Revolution Day	Mar. 8
Evacuation Day (Anniversary of French Departure From Syria)	Apr. 17
Eid al-Adha	May 9
Mawlid al Nabi	Aug. 9
Christmas Day	Dec. 25

Tajikistan

New Year's Day	Jan.1
Martin Luther King, Jr.'s Birthday	Jan. 19
President's Day	Feb. 16
Idi Rarazon	Feb. 20
Navruz	March 21-22
Idi Kurbon-Bairam	April 30
Solidarity of Working People Day	May 1
Victory Day	May 9
Memorial Day	May 27
Independence Day	July 4*
Labor Day	Sept. 7
Independence Day	Sept. 9
Columbus Day	Oct. 14
Constitution Day	Nov. 6
Veterans Day	Nov. 11
Thanksgiving	Nov. 26
Christmas	Dec. 25

*Observed Friday, July 3

Tanzania

New Year's Day	Jan. 1
Zanzibar Revolutionary Day	Jan. 12
Birth of Chama Cha Mapinduzi	Feb. 5
ldd el Fitr	Mar. 3
Good Friday	Apr. 14
Easter Monday	Apr. 17
Union Day	Apr. 26
International Workers' Day	May 1
ldd El Hajj	May 9
Peasants' Day	July 7
Maulid Day	Aug. 9
Independence Day	Dec. 9
Christmas Day	Dec. 25

Thailand

New Year's Day	Jan. 1
Martin Luther King, Jr.'s Birthday	Jan. 19
President's Day	Feb. 16
King Rama I Memorial/Chakri Day	Apr. 6
Songkran Day	Apr. 13-15
Coronation Day	May 5
Memorial Day	May 25
Independence Day	July 4*
Her Majesty the Queen's Birthday	Aug. 12
Labor Day	Sept. 7
Columbus Day	Oct. 12
Chulalongkorn Day	Oct. 23
Veterans Day	Nov. 11
Thanksgiving Day	Nov. 26
Substitute Day for His Majesty the King's Birthday & National Day	Dec.7
Constitution Day	Dec. 10
Christmas Day	Dec. 25
New Year's Day	Dec. 31

Togo

New Year's Day	Jan. 1
Togo National Liberation Day	Jan. 13
End of Ramadan	Varies
Easter Monday	Varies
Independence Day	Apr. 27
Labor Day	May 1
Tabaski	Varies
Ascension Day	Varies
Pentecost Monday	Varies
Martyrs Day	June 21
Assumption	Aug. 15
All Saints' Day	Nov. 1

Trinidad & Tobago

New Year's Day	Jan.1
Baptist Day	Mar. 30
Good Friday	Apr. 10
Easter Monday	Apr. 13
Indian Arrival Day	May 30
Corpus Christi	June 11
Labor Day	June 19
Emancipation Day	Aug. 1
Independence Day	Aug. 31
Christmas Day	Dec. 25
Boxing Day	Dec. 26
Divali & Eid-ul-Fitr*	

*Date is dependent upon sighting of moon.

Tunisia

Aid Esseghir (EI-Fitr)	Feb. 19-20
Independence Day	Mar. 20
Aid El Kebir (EI-Idha)	Apr. 29-30
Labor Day	May 1
Ras El Am El Hijri	May 2
Republic Day	July 25
Mouled	July 29
Women's Day	Aug. 13
Commemoration Day	Nov. 7

Turkey

New Year's Day	Jan.1
Seker Bayrami	Apr. 15-18
Milli Egemenlik ye Cocuk Bayrami	Apr. 23
Ataturk 'u Anma Genclik ye Spor Bayrami	May 19
Kurban Bayrami	June 22-26
Zafer Bayrami	Aug. 30
Turkish Independence Day	Oct. 28-29

All Muslim religious holidays are observed.

Turkmenistan

New Year's Day	Jan.1
Memorial Day	Jan. 12
Martin Luther King, Jr.'s, Birthday	Jan. 19
President's Day	Feb. 16
National Flag Day	Feb. 19
International Women's Day	Mar. 8
Novruz Bairam	Mar. 21

Victory Day	May 9
Revival and Unity Day	May 18
Memorial Day	May 25
Independence Day	July 4*
Labor Day	Sep.7
Remembrance Day	Oct. 6
Columbus Day	Oct. 12
Independence Day	Oct. 27-28
Veteran's Day	Nov. 11
Thanksgiving Day	Nov. 26
Day of Neutrality	Dec. 12
Christmas Day	Dec. 25
Kurban Bairam	Lunar calendar

*Observed Friday, July 3

Uganda

New Year's Day	Jan.1
Liberation Day	Jan. 26
Id el Fitr	Mar. 3
Good Friday	Apr. 14
Easter Monday	Apr. 17
Labor Day	May 1
Martyrs Day	June 3
Independence Day	Oct. 9
Christmas Day	Dec. 25
Boxing Day	Dec. 26

United Arab Emirates

New Year's Day	Jan.1
Id al-Fitr	Mar. 3
Waqfa	May 8
Id al-Adha	May 9
Muharram	May 31
Sheikh Zayed Accession Day	Aug. 6
Prophet's Birthday	Aug. 9
U.A.E. National Day	Dec. 2, 3

United Kingdom

London

New Year's Day	Jan. 1
Good Friday	Apr. 5
Easter Monday	Apr. 8
May Day	May 6
Spring Holiday	May 27
Summer Bank Holiday	Aug. 26
Christmas Day	Dec. 25
Boxing Day	Dec. 26

*Observed Friday, July 3

Belfast

New Year's Day	Jan. 1
St. Patrick's Day	Mar. 17
Good Friday	Apr. 5
Easter Monday	Apr. 8
Easter Tuesday	Apr. 9
May Day	May 6
Spring Holiday	May 27
Orangemen's Day	July 12
Summer Bank Holiday	Aug. 26
Christmas	Dec. 25
Boxing Day	Dec. 26

Edinburgh

New Year's Day	Jan. 1

Bank Holiday	Jan. 2
Good Friday	Apr. 5
Easter Monday	Apr. 8
Spring Holiday	April 15
May Day	May 6
Victoria Day	May 28
Bank Holiday	Aug. 4
Autumn Holiday	Sept. 16
Christmas	Dec. 25
Boxing Day	Dec. 26

USUN—New York

New Year's Day	Jan 1
Martin Luther King, Jr.'s Birthday	Jan 15
Memorial Day	May 27
Independence Day	July 4
Labor Day	Sept. 2
Columbus Day	Oct. 14
Veterans Day	Nov. 11
Thanksgiving Day	Nov. 28
Christmas Day	Dec. 25

Uzbekistan

New Year's Day	Jan 1
Martin Luther King, Jr.'s Birthday	Jan 19
Ruza Hayit (Yid-ul-Fitr)	Jan. 30
President's Day	Feb. 16
Kurban Hayit	Apr. 7
Memorial Day	May 25
Independence Day	July 4*
Independence Day	Sept. 1
Labor Day	Sept. 7
Teacher's Day	Oct. 1
Columbus Day	Oct. 12
Veterans Day	Nov. 11
Thanksgiving Day	Nov. 28
Constitution Day	Dec. 8
Christmas Day	Dec. 25

*Observed Friday, July 3

Uruguay

New Year's Day	Jan. 1
Martin Luther King, Jr.'s Birthday	Jan. 15
President's Day	Feb. 19
Carnival	Feb. 19-20
Holy Week	Apr. 4-5
Landing of the 33 Orientales	Apr. 19
Uruguayan Labor Day	May 1
Memorial Day	May 27
Natalicio De Artigas	June 19
Independence Day	July 4*
Constitution Day	July 18
Labor Day	Sept. 2
Columbus Day	Oct. 14
Veterans Day	Nov. 11
Thanksgiving Day	Nov. 28
Christmas Day	Dec. 25

*Observed Friday, July 3

Venezuela

New Year's Day	Jan. 1
Martin Luther King, Jr.'s Birthday	Jan. 15

President's Birthday	Feb. 19
Cam ival	Feb. 19-20
Holy Thursday	Apr. 4
Good Friday	Apr. 5
Declaration of Independence	Apr. 19
Labor Day	May 1
Memorial Day	May 27
Battle of Carabobo	June 24
Independence Day	July4*
Venezuelan Independence Day	July 5
Simon Bolivar's Birthday	July 24
Labor Day	Sept. 2
Dia De La Raza	Oct. 12
Columbus Day	Oct. 14
Veterans Day	Nov. 11
Thanksgiving Day	Nov. 28
Christmas Day	Dec. 25

*Observed Friday, July 3

Vietnam

New Year's Day	Jan. 1
Martin Luther King, Jr.'s Birthday	Jan. 19
Lunar New Year Festival	Jan. 27-30
President's Birthday	Feb. 16
Victory Day	Apr. 30
International Labor Day	May 1
Memorial Day	May 25
Independence Day	July 4*
Vietnamese National Day	Sep. 2
Labor Day	Sep. 7
Columbus Day	Oct. 12
Veterans Day	Nov. 11
Thanksgiving Day	Nov. 26
Christmas Day	Dec. 25

*Observed Friday, July 3

Yemen Arab Republic

Id al-Fitr	Mar. 3
Id al-Adha	May 9
Yemeni National Day	May 22
Muharram	May 31
Prophet's Birthday	Aug. 9

Zaire (Democratic Rep. of Congo)

New Year's Day	Jan. 1
Day of the Martyrs for Independence	Jan. 4
Labor Day	May 1
MPR Day	May 20
Anniversary of New Constitution	June 24
Independence Day	June 30
Parent's Day	Aug. 1
Youth Day/President's Birthday	Oct. 14
Trois Z Day	Oct. 27
Armed Forces Day	Nov. 17
Anniversary of the New Regime	Nov. 24
Christmas Day	Dec. 25

Zambia

New Year's Day	Jan.1
Youth Day	Mar. 12
Good Friday	Apr. 14
Holy Saturday	Apr. 15

Labor Day	May 1
Africa Freedom Day	May 25
Heroes Day	July 1
Unity Day	July 2
Farmer's Day	Aug. 5
Independence Day	Oct. 24
Christmas Day	Dec. 25

Zimbabwe

New Year's Day	Jan.1
Public Holiday	Dec. 31
Martin Luther King, Jr.'s Birthday	Jan. 15
President's Day	Feb. 19
Good Friday	Apr. 14
Easter Saturday	Apr. 15
Easter Monday	Apr. 17
Independence Day	Apr. 18
Worker's Day	May 1
Public Holiday	May 2
Africa Day	May 25
Memorial Day	May 27
Independence Day	July 4*
Heroes' Day	Aug. 11
Defense Forces Day	Aug. 12
Labor Day	Sept. 2
Columbus Day	Oct. 14
Veterans Day	Nov. 11
Thanksgiving Day	Nov. 23
Christmas Day	Dec. 25
Boxing Day	Dec. 26

*Observed Friday, July 3

World Time Table

INTRODUCTION

When its noon, eastern standard time, in Washington D.C., the time in other cities around the world is shown below. (An Asterisk (*) indicates the next day.)

Afghanistan	9:30 pm
Albania	6:00 pm
Algeria	6:00 pm
Andorra	6:00 pm
Angola	6:00 pm
Antigua and Barbuda	1:00 pm
Argentina	2:00 pm
Armenia	8:00 pm
Australia:	
Perth	1:00 pm*
Adelaide	2:30 am*
Brisbane	3:00 am*
Austria	6:00 pm
Azerbaijan	9:00 pm
Bahamas	noon
Bahrain	8:00 pm
Bangladesh	11:00 pm
Barbados	1:00 pm
Belarus	7:00 pm
Belgium	6:00 pm
Belize	11:00 am
Benin	6:00 pm
Bermuda	1:00 pm
Bhutan	11:00 pm
Bolivia	1:00 pm
Bosnia & Herzegovina	6:00 pm
Botswana	7:00 pm
Brazil	2:00 pm
Brasilia	2:00 pm
Manaus	1:00 pm
Brunei Darussalam	1:00 am*
Bulgaria	7:00 pm
Burkina Faso	5:00 pm
Burma	11:30 pm
Burundi	7:00 pm
Cambodia	midnight*
Cameroon	6:00 pm
Canada:	
Vancouver	9:00 am
Calgary	10:00 am
Winnepeg	11:00 am
Ottawa	noon
Halifax	1:00 pm
Cape Verde	4:00 pm
Cayman Islands	noon
Central African Republic	6:00 pm
Chad	6:00 pm
Chile	1:00 pm
China	1:00 am*
Colombia	noon
Comoros	8:00 pm
Congo	6:00 pm
Cook Islands	7:00 am
Costa Rica	11:00 am
Côte d'Ivoire	5:00 pm
Croatia	6:00 pm
Cuba	noon
Cyprus	7:00 pm
Czech Republic	6:00 pm
Denmark	6:00 pm
Djibouti	8:00 pm
Dominica	1:00 pm
Dominican Republic	1:00 pm
Ecuador	noon
Egypt	7:00 pm
El Salvador	11:00 am
Equatorial Guinea	6:00 pm
Eritrea	8:00 pm
Estonia	7:00 pm
Ethiopia	8:00 pm
Faroe Islands	5:00 pm
Fiji	5:00 am*
Finland	7:00 pm
France	6:00 pm
French Guiana	2:00 pm
French Polynesia	7:00 am
Gabon	6:00 pm
The Gambia	5:00 pm
Georgia	8:00 pm
Germany	6:00 pm
Ghana	5:00 pm
Gibralter	6:00 pm
Greece	7:00 pm
Grenada	1:00 pm
Guadaloupe	1:00 pm
Guam	3:00 am*
Guatemala	11:00 am
Guinea-Bissau	5:00 pm
Guinea	5:00 pm
Guyana	1:00 pm
Haiti	noon
Honduras	11:00 am
Hong Kong	1:00 am*
Hungary	6:00 pm
Iceland	5:00 pm
India	10:30 pm
Indonesia	midnight*
Iran	8:30 pm
Iraq	8:00 pm
Ireland	5:00 pm

©Almanac Publishing, Inc. 1998 - The Washington Almanac of International Trade & Business

Israel	7:00 pm	Qatar	8:00 pm
Italy	6:00 pm	Reunion	9:00 pm
Jamaica	noon	Romania	7:00 pm
Japan	2:00 am*	Russia:	
Jordan	7:00 pm	Moscow	8:00 pm
Kazakhstan	11:00 pm	St. Petersburg	8:00 pm
Kenya	8:00 pm	Vladivostok	3:00 am*
Kirbati	5:00 am	Rwanda	7:00 pm
Korea, North	2:00 am	Saint Kitts and Nevis	1:00 pm
Korea, South	2:00 am	Saint Lucia	1:00 pm
Kuwait	8:00 pm	Saint Vincent and the Grenadines	1:00 pm
Kyrgyzstan	11:00 pm	San Marino	6:00 pm
Laos	midnight*	Sao Tomé & Principé	5:00 pm
Latvia	7:00 pm	Saudi Arabia	8:00 pm
Lebanon	7:00 pm	Senegal	5:00 pm
Lesotho	7:00 pm	Serbia	6:00 pm
Liberia	5:00 pm	Seychelles	9:00 pm
Libya	6:00 pm	Sierra Leone	5:00 pm
Liechtenstein	6:00 pm	Singapore	midnight
Lithuania	7:00 pm	Slovakia	6:00 pm
Luxembourg	6:00 pm	Slovenia	6:00 pm
Macedonia	6:00 pm	Solomon Islands	4:00 am
Madagascar	8:00 pm	Somalia	8:00 pm
Malawi	7:00 pm	South Africa	7:00 pm
Malaysia	1:00 am*	Spain	6:00 pm
Maldives	10:00 pm	Sri Lanka	10:30 pm
Mali	5:00 pm	Sudan	7:00 pm
Malta	6:00 pm	Suriname	2:00 pm
Marshall Islands	5:00 am*	Swaziland	7:00 pm
Martinique	1:00 pm	Sweden	6:00 pm
Mauritania	5:00 pm	Switzerland	6:00 pm
Mauritius	9:00 pm	Syria	7:00 pm
Mexico:		Tajikistan	11:00 pm
Hermosillo	10:00 am	Taiwan	1:00 am
Mexico City	11:00 am	Tanzania	8:00 pm
Tijuana	9:00 am	Thailand	midnight*
Micronesia	4:00 am*	Togo	5:00 pm
Moldova	7:00 pm	Tonga	6:00 am
Monaco	6:00 pm	Trinidad and Tobago	1:00 pm
Mongolia	1:00 am*	Tunisia	6:00 pm
Montenegro	6:00 pm	Turkey	7:00 pm
Montserrat	1:00 pm	Tuvalu	5:00 am*
Morocco	5:00 pm	Turkmenistan	10:00 pm
Mozambique	7:00 pm	Turks & Caicos Islands	noon
Myanmar	11:30pm	Uganda	8:00 pm
Namibia	7:00 pm	Ukraine	7:00 pm
Nauru	5:00 am*	United Arab Emirates	9:00 pm
Nepal	10:45 pm	United Kingdom of Great Britain	
Netherlands	6:00 pm	and Northern Ireland	6:00 pm
Netherlands Antilles	1:00 pm	United States:	
New Caledonia	4:00 a.m.	Honolulu	7:00 am
New Zealand	5:00 am*	Anchorage	8:00 am
Nicaragua	11:00 am	Los Angeles	9:00 am
Niger	6:00 pm	Denver	10:00 am
Nigeria	6:00 pm	Houston	11:00 am
Northern Mariana Islands	3:00 am	Washington D.C.	noon
Norway	6:00 pm	Uruguay	2:00 pm
Oman	9:00 pm	Uzbekistan	11:00 pm
Pakistan	10:00 pm	Vanuatu	4:00 am*
Pacific Islands, Trust Territory		Vatican City	6:00 pm
of the (Palau)	2:00 am*	Venezuela	1:00 pm
Panama	noon	Vietnam	midnight
Papua New Guinea	3:00 am*	Virgin Islands	1:00 pm
Paraguay	1:00 pm	Western Samoa	6:00 am
Peru	noon	Yemen	8:00 pm
Philippines	1:00 am*	Yugoslavia	6:00 pm
Poland	6:00 pm	Zaire:	
Portugal:		Kinshasa	6:00 pm
Azores	4:00 pm	Lubumbashi	7:00 pm
Mainland	5:00 pm	Zambia	7:00 pm
Madeira	5:00 pm	Zimbabwe	7:00 pm
Puerto Rico	1:00 pm		

HILL & KNOWLTON

Your guide to communicating with the world's political capitals, media and consumer markets – all-at-once or one-by-one.

Today, more and more companies are competing in the international marketplace and are being affected by foreign and trade policies drafted in the world's capitals, commentaries issued by the world's media and decisions made by the international consumer.

The increasing number of these new players in the global marketplace has changed the dynamics and raised the requirements for devising and implementing integrated, multinational communications strategies that positively impact the bottom line.

Hill and Knowlton, with its 52 offices in 28 countries and 41 affiliated offices in 15 more countries, provides companies both the global consistency and local expertise they need to meet their most pressing international communications objectives.

HILL & KNOWLTON

Counseling the world's leading companies in

- Advanced Technologies
- Environment
- Financial Services
- Food and Nutrition

- Health Care
- International Trade
- Telecommunications
- Transportation

Atlanta.Chicago.Detroit.Honolulu.Houston.Irvine.Los Angeles.New York.Pittsburgh.San Franciso.San Juan.Tampa.
Washington, DC.Mexico City.Sao Paulo.Edmonton.Montreal.Ottawa.Toronto.Vancouver.Amsterdam.Athens.Barcelona.
Brussels.Budapest.Frankfurt.Helsinki.London.Madrid.Manchester.Milan.Paris.Prague.Riga.Stockholm.Tallinn.Tampere.
Dubai.Jeddah.Manama.Beijing.Hong Kong.Kuala Lumpur.Shanghai.Singapore.Taipei.Tokyo.Canberra.Melbourne.Sydney.
Auckland.Wellington

600 New Hampshire Avenue, NW   Washington, D.C. 20037   USA   (202) 333-7400

SECTION II

THE U.S. GOVERNMENT: WHO DOES WHAT?

The U.S. Government is an excellent source of free or inexpensive assistance for any firm seeking to enter foreign markets or to expand its international operations. It also is a fountain of information for any individual desiring to know more about foreign countries and about the ways our government interacts with them in various fields of endeavor from foreign trade to diplomatic relations to joint scientific/health research.

■   Company A might want to test the international market before making a major commitment. Perhaps it should buy a low-cost advertisement in <u>Commercial News USA</u>, the Commerce Department's catalog-magazine, which is circulated overseas.

■   Company B may be stumped on how to obtain export financing. It should check out the loan and loan-guarantee programs of the Small Business Administration and the U.S. Export-Import Bank.

■ Company C may want some actual hands-on help in setting up an international sales program. Such assistance is available from the Commerce Department's international trade specialists in offices throughout the U.S. and from the Service Corps of Retired Executives (SCORE), a private organization affiliated with the Small Business Administration.

■ Company D might sense a market for its products in the developing countries but not know how to find out about specific opportunities. It should contact the Agency for International Development (AID), which, through loans and grants, enables public- and private-sector importers in developing countries to purchase U.S. products and services. Although AID does no direct buying itself, it can direct firms to specific sources of information about export opportunities that arise from AID loans and grants.

These types of assistance, and much more, are there for the asking. The only problem is where to start and who to call. This section of *The Washington Almanac of International Trade and Business* will serve as your guide.

The section begins with General Export Information, compiled by the Commerce Department's Trade Information Center on behalf of the Trade Promotion Coordinating Committee, which represents 19 federal agencies with trade responsibilities. The services are listed by function so readers can easily locate the specific program of greatest interest to them.

The second segment covers the Federal Legislative Branch — the Congressional committees with jurisdiction over international trade and foreign policy issues. Over 50 key staff members were interviewed and are profiled in this section. Also included in this section are foreign trade and foreign policy contacts in each member's office.

The final segment covers the Federal Executive Branch entities with international responsibilities, including Cabinet agencies, offices in the Executive Office of the President, independent establishments, and government corporations. The entities are listed in alphabetical order. Each entry begins with the address of the agency and its telephone and fax numbers, followed by a short description of its international responsibilities. Officials who exercise those responsibilities are listed by name, together with their telephone and fax numbers. We have profiled many of the key officials and included their photographs.

Export Programs:

A Business Guide to Federal Export

Assistance Programs

1998 Edition produced by the Trade Information Center U.S. Department of Commerce Washington, DC 20230

Table of Contents:

INTRODUCTION

The material in this section helps businesses develop an export strategy, locate economic market research, ship overseas, complete export documentation, respond to overseas inquiries, and take advantage of U.S. Government export assistance programs.

General Export Counseling

International Trade Administration (ITA) - U.S. Department of Commerce-The International Trade Administration is dedicated to opening markets for U.S. products and providing assistance and information to exporters. ITA units include: 1) 100 domestic Export Assistance Centers and 141 overseas commercial offices in the U.S. & Foreign Commercial Service network, 2) industry experts and market and economic analysts in its Trade Development unit, and 3) country and regional experts in its Market Access and Compliance offices. Each unit promotes products and offers services and programs for the U.S. exporting community, including export promotion, counseling, and information programs listed elsewhere in this booklet.

Contact: Phone 1-800-USA-TRAD(E) (1-800-872-8723)
Internet home page: http://www.ita.doc.gov

Trade Information Center (TIC) - ITA/U.S. Department of Commerce-The Trade Information Center is the first stop for companies seeking export assistance from the government and comprehensive export counseling programs. TIC trade specialists: 1) advise exporters on how to find and use government programs; 2) guide businesses through the export process; 3) direct businesses to market research and trade leads; 4) provide information on overseas and domestic trade events and activities; and 5) supply sources of public and private export financing. The TIC trade specialists also inform callers on how to access reports and statistics from the computerized National Trade Data Bank (NTDB), and direct businesses to state and local trade organizations that provide additional

assistance. Country information is also available on Western Europe, Asia, Western Hemisphere, Africa, and the Near East.

The Trade Information Center's Fax Retrieval System, an automated fax information delivery system, provides hundreds of documents available to U.S. businesses 24-hours a day. These documents include a directory of international contacts listed by state; state export statistics; trade items containing key government speeches and announcements on trade; locations of National Trade Data Bank libraries; alternative export finance options; regional and country specific information; and the most recent version of *Export Programs Guide: A Business Guide to Federal Export Assistance.*

The Trade Information Center web site provides a variety of information, including the most frequently asked questions and answers on exporting, international trade contacts for each state, foreign trade offices in the United States, an alternative finance guide, an Internet guide to export trade leads, and the most up-to-date *Export Programs Guide.*

In addition, the Trade Information Center runs TRADEBASE, an electronic trade center for trade multiplier organizations to exchange information. It also provides information on export education events around the country and other export data. TRADEBASE is accessible on the Internet through the TIC home page.

Contact: Phone 1-800-USA-TRAD(E) (1-800-872-8723)
Fax (202) 482-4473
A special line is available for those who are deaf or hearing impaired using a TDD machine, 1-800-TDD-TRADE (1-800-833-8723)
E-mail: tic@ita.doc.gov
Internet home page: http://www.ita.doc.gov/tic

The U.S. and Foreign Commercial Service (US&FCS) - ITA/U.S. Department of Commerce-The mission of the U.S. and Foreign Commercial Service is to support U.S. firms-especially small- and medium-sized companies in their efforts to increase exports. The U.S. and Foreign Commercial Service maintains a worldwide service delivery network with offices in 141 cities in the United States and 76 countries overseas. The global capabilities of US&FCS provide seamless service to U.S. firms interested in exporting, from basic market research to arranging meetings with potential foreign buyers.

Contact: For the address and phone number of the Export Assistance Center nearest you, please see the appendix, call 1-800-USA- TRAD(E) (1-800-872-8723).
Internet home page: http://www.ita.doc.gov/uscs/

The Export Assistance Center Network (USEACs/EACs)-The U.S. Department of Commerce, the U.S. Small Business Administration (SBA), and the Export-Import (Eximbank) have formed a unique partnership to establish U.S. Export Assistance Centers. The U.S. Export Assistance Centers (USEACs), located at major metropolitan areas throughout the United States, are one-stop shops that provide small- and medium-sized businesses with hands-on export marketing and trade finance support. In addition, there are Export Assistance Centers (EACs), which provide small- and medium- sized businesses with export promotion assistance and refer them to a nearby SBA district office or to a local Eximbank representative for trade finance assistance. Trade specialists at the USEACs/EACs assist U.S. exporters in their locale to expand their international activities and other businesses that are new-to-export. USEAC/EAC trade specialists help firms: 1) identify the best markets for their products; 2) develop an effective market entry strategy based on information generated from overseas commercial offices; 3) facilitate the implementation of these strategies by advising clients on distribution channels, key factors to consider in pricing, and relevant trade shows and missions; and 4) assist with trade finance programs available through federal, state, and local public sources and private sector entities.

Contact: For the address and phone number of the USEAC/EAC nearest you, please see the appendix, call 1-800-USA-

TRAD(E) (1-800-872-8723).
Internet home page: http://www.ita.doc.gov/uscs/

District Export Councils (DECs) - ITA/U.S. Department of Commerce-DECs are organizations of leaders from local business communities whose knowledge of international business provides a source of professional advice for local firms. Closely affiliated with the Export Assistance Centers, the 51 DECs nationwide combine the energies of over 1,500 volunteers to supply specialized expertise to small- and medium-sized businesses in their local community who are interested in exporting. For example, DECs organize seminars that make trade finance both understandable and accessible to small exporters, host international buyer delegations, design guides to help firms export, put exporters on the Internet, and help build export assistance partnerships to strengthen the support given to local businesses interested in exporting.

Contact: Please contact your local Export Assistance Center for more information. For the address and phone number of the Export Assistance Center nearest you, please see the appendix, call, 1-800-USA-TRAD(E) (1-800-872-8723). Internet home page: http://www.ita.doc.gov/uscs/

Export Legal Assistance Network (ELAN) - Small Business Administration (SBA)-The Export Legal Assistance Network is a nationwide group of attorneys experienced in international trade that provides free initial consultations to new-to-export businesses on export-related matters.

Contact: The ELAN service is available through SBA district offices, Service Corps of Retired Executives (SCORE) offices, and Small Business Development Centers. For the address and phone number of your nearest SBA office call 1-800-U-ASK-SBA, or Judd Kessler, National Coordinator, ELAN, (202) 778-3080; fax (202) 778-3063 E-mail: jkessler@porterwright.com

Office of International Trade (OIT) - Small Business Administration (SBA)-The Office of International Trade works in coordination with other federal agencies and public and private sector organizations to encourage small businesses to expand their export activities and to assist small businesses seeking to export. OIT directs and coordinates SBA's export finance and export development assistance. OIT's outreach efforts include regional initiatives with Russia and Ireland, sponsoring or supporting export training conferences, and developing how to and market-specific publications for exporters. OIT actively markets the SBA's loan guarantee programs to small business exporters, including the Export Working Capital Program, which is available to exporters through the U.S. Export Assistance Centers (USEACs) and SBA field offices across the country. The office also spearheads a program, through the USEAC network, called E-TAP (Export Trade Assistance Partnership), which focuses on a small group of export-ready companies and gives them the assistance they need to develop export markets, acquire orders or contracts, and use export financing.

Contact: Phone (202) 205-6720
             Fax (202) 205-7272
             Internet home page: http://www.sbaonline.sba.gov/oit

Small Business Development Centers (SBDC) - Small Business Administration-The Small Business Development Centers, located throughout the United States, provide a full range of export assistance services to small businesses, particularly new-to-export companies, and offer counseling, training, and managerial assistance. They provide counseling services at no cost to the small business exporter, but they generally charge fees for export training seminars and other SBDC-sponsored export events.

Contact: Phone (202) 205-7303, Jorge F. Cardona
             Fax (202) 205-7727
             Internet home page: http://www.sba.gov/SBDC/
             For the location of the SBDC nearest you, please contact

the Trade Information Center at 1-800-USA-TRAD(E) (1-800-872-8723).

Service Corps of Retired Executives (SCORE)-Members of the SCORE program, many of whom have years of practical experience in international trade, provide one-on-one counseling and training seminars. Specialists assist small firms in evaluating export potential and in strengthening domestic operations by identifying financial, managerial, or technical problems.

Contact: Phone 1-800-634-0245, National SCORE office
             Fax (202) 205-7636
             Internet home page: http://www.score.org

Minority Business Development Agency - ITA/U.S. Department of Commerce - The Minority Business Development Agency (MBDA) provides management and technical assistance, as well as access to domestic and international markets. MBDA's mission is to promote the establishment and growth of minority-owned business enterprises in the United States; consequently, it is constantly seeking to create new and innovative ways to engage U.S. minority firms in the international business arena. MBDA assists minority firms in gaining international access in many ways, including: trade missions, matchmaker programs, one-on-one client counseling, seminars, and special international program events.

Contact: Phone (202) 482-1017, MBDA International Trade Office
             Fax (202) 219-8826
             Internet home page: http://www.mbda.gov/

Industry-Specific Export Counseling

Trade Development (TD) Industry Officers - ITA/U.S. Department of Commerce-Trade Development's industry and international trade specialists work directly with individual firms and with manufacturing and service industry associations to identify trade opportunities and obstacles by product or service, industry sector, and market. Trade Development analysts participate in trade policy development and negotiations, identify market barriers, and provide advocacy (see Advocacy Center below) on behalf of U.S. companies. Trade Development's statistical data and analyses are useful in export development (see Office of Trade and Economic Analysis). TD staff also develop export marketing programs and obtain industry advice on trade matters (see Office of Export Promotion Coordination below). To assist U.S. businesses in their export efforts, TD's industry and international experts conduct executive trade missions, trade fairs, product literature centers, marketing seminars, and business counseling. Experts are organized into six major industry sectors:

- Technology and Aerospace Industries
- Basic Industries
- Textiles, Apparel, and Consumer Goods Industries
- Service Industries
- Environmental Technology Exports
- Tourism Industries

Contact: For a list of TD industry and international trade officers, call 1-800-USA-TRAD(E) (1-800-872-8723). For TD industry information: http://www.ita.doc.gov/ For trade statistics: http://www.ita.doc.gov/tradestats/

Office of Export Promotion Coordination (OEPC) - ITA/U.S. Department of Commerce-The Office of Export Promotion Coordination serves as Trade Development's management and information dissemination arm for cross-sectoral programs that deal directly with the private sector. OEPC coordinates Trade Development's export promotion programs, plans high profile export promotion trade missions, identifies small business export needs, and provides analyses of the export potential of U.S. products in specific overseas markets. OEPC activities include identifying top targets for trade promotion, developing programs that target women-owned businesses in international trade, and providing information on all of the U.S. Government export assistance programs and services. OEPC also operates the Trade Information Center, the Tradebase program, and manages the Industry Consultations Program to seek industry input into trade policy development.

Contact: For more information on all OEPC programs and services call (202) 482-4501 or the Trade Information Center 1-800-USA-TRAD(E) (1-800-872-8723).

Infrastructure Division - ITA/U.S. Department of Commerce-The infrastructure project managers 1) coordinate government assistance and help U.S. firms to compete for major infrastructure and industrial projects overseas; 2) identify upcoming projects and develop specific information about them; 3) monitor worldwide infrastructure developments; 4) provide one-on-one business counseling to contractors, engineers, constructors, and engineered systems providers; and 5) offer guidance on appropriate market business contacts, contract bidding procedures, and strategies.

Contact: Project managers (202) 482-4436
Fax (202) 482-3954
Internet home page: http://www.ita.doc.gov/infrastructure

National Marine Fisheries Service (NMFS) - National Oceanic and Atmospheric Administration/U.S. Department of Commerce-The NMFS Inspection Services Division (ISD) consumer safety officers and trade specialists offer a range of services to assist U.S. fishing industry businesses engaged in the exports of fish and fishery products. Besides inspecting and certifying products for export, NMFS also advises seafood marketers about foreign regulations and maintains contacts with foreign government regulatory agencies to resolve sanitary-hygienic issues. ISD is an active participant in international activities that promote and facilitate the trade of fishery products.

Contact: Phone (301) 713-2355, Inspection Services Division, Richard V. Cano
Fax (301) 713-1081
Internet home page: http://kingfish.ssp.nmfs.gov/

Global Technology Network (GTN) - U.S. Agency for International Development (USAID)-Operated by USAID's Business Development office, the Global Technology Network receives technology requests from Asia, Latin America, Sub-Saharan Africa, Central and Eastern Europe, the Newly Independent States, and the Near East in areas of agriculture, communications and information, environment, and health technologies. GTN distributes these trade leads, via fax and e-mail, to appropriate U.S. businesses, service firms, and trade associations which are registered with GTN. GTN representatives are located in ten Latin American countries, five Sub-Saharan countries and ten Asian nations. GTN transmits these leads to U.S. firms within 48 hours from receipt from GTN offices.

Contact: Phone 1-800-872-4348, (202) 712-1624
Fax (202) 216-3526
Internet home page: http://www.usgtn.org

United States-Asia Environmental Partnership (US-AEP) - Environmental Technology Network for Asia (ETNA)-Established in 1993, the Environmental Technology Network for Asia (ETNA) is a partner in the United States-Asia Environmental Partnership (US-AEP) Program. US-AEP, led by the United States Agency for International Development (USAID), promotes environmental protection and sustainable development in Asia by using U.S. environmental technology, experience, and services. ETNA assists the U.S. business community in gaining access to the Asian environmental market through the provision of trade leads and market information. Business opportunities for U.S. companies are identified by environmental specialists in Asia and are sent by fax to U.S. companies registered with the ETNA system. Any U.S. based environmental firm is eligible to receive trade leads.

Contact: Phone 1-800-818-9911 or (202) 835-0333
Fax (202) 835-8358
Internet home page: http://www.usaep.org

Export Assistance Initiative - U.S. Department of Energy-Department of Energy export-related activities help U.S. energy sector exporters to: 1) identify overseas opportunities and discriminatory trade barriers; 2) evaluate U.S. laws and regulations that may restrict trade; 3) identify financing alternatives; and 4) work with other U.S. Government agencies in export promotion.

Contact: Phone (202) 586-7997, Kay Thompson, Office of Export Assistance
Fax (202) 586-0823

Committee on Renewable Energy Commerce and Trade (CORECT) - U.S. Department of Energy-CORECT is an interagency working group of 14 federal agencies, administered by the Department of Energy, which coordinates federal programs to assist export efforts of renewable energy industries. CORECT assistance to industry deals primarily with technical competitiveness, market development, and federal financing assistance.

Contact: Phone (202) 586-5517, Thomas W. Sacco, Office of Energy Efficiency and Renewable Energy
Fax (202) 586-1605

Committee on Energy Efficiency Commerce and Trade (COEECT) - U.S. Department of Energy-COEECT is an interagency working group of 15 federal agencies that: 1) coordinates federal programs supporting and affecting the export of energy efficiency products and services; 2) works with international banks to increase lending for energy efficiency and facilitate project loans; and 3) works with the energy efficiency industry on project endorsement, trade missions, and market assessments.

Contact: Phone (202) 586-9346, Roger Meyer, Office of Energy Efficiency and Renewable Energy
Fax (202) 586-1605

Office of Fossil Energy - International Program Coordination - U.S. Department of Energy-This program enhances the competitiveness of U.S. industry by support of domestic fossil energy (coal, oil, and gas) project developers and exporters trying to expand the international sales of fossil energy technology, resources, and services.

Contact: Coal Technologies: Barbara McKee, Director - Coal & Power Export & Import
Phone (301) 903-3820
Fax (301) 903-1591
E-mail: barbara.mckee@hq.doe.gov

Oil & Gas Technologies: Donald Juckett, Director - Oil & Gas Import & Export
Phone (202) 586-5600
Fax (202) 586-6221
E-mail: donald.juckett@hq.doe.gov
Internet home page: http://www.fe.doe.gov

Country-Specific Export Counseling

Trade Information Center - ITA/Department of Commerce-The Trade Information Center is available for counseling on Asia, Western Europe, Western Hemisphere, Africa, and the Near East. Through the latest in electronic information distribution systems, individual consultations, and cooperation with private trade groups, the Trade Information Center's trade specialists will provide information and assistance in the following areas: economic and commercial assessments; trade regulations; best prospects for U.S. manufacturers and service providers; trade promotion events; and organizations and other contacts for additional information and assistance.

Contact: Phone (800) 872-8723; Fax retrieval 1-800-USA-TRAD(E), press 1
Fax (202) 482-4473
Internet home page: http://www.ita.doc.gov

Business Information Service for the Newly Independent States (BISNIS) - ITA/U.S. Department of Commerce-BISNIS is the U.S. Government clearinghouse for business information on the Newly Independent States (NIS) of the former Soviet Union. BISNIS taps the extensive information resources of the U.S. Government, private sector, and other sources, to keep U.S. companies up-to-date on NIS commercial developments. BISNIS provides trade leads, market data, information on commercial law and regulation, finance, transportation, promotional events, and other practical information. BISNIS trade specialists are also available by phone and appointment to assist U.S. companies.

BISNIS publishes the monthly *BISNIS Bulletin*, which informs readers about finance, transportation, legal issues, and major product markets. *Search for Partners*, which appears both in print and electronic form, publicizes NIS companies interested in long-term cooperation with U.S. companies, and *Trades and Tenders*, a biweekly electronic publication, lists sales and procurement opportunities.

BISNIS makes thousands of documents available via *BISNIS Online*, an Internet home page, while e-mail subscription service from BISNIS trade specialists provides the most time-sensitive trade leads in specific industries and countries. The *BISNIS Fax Retrieval System*, an automated fax information delivery system, provides hundreds of documents available to U.S.-based businesses 24-hours a day.

Contact: Phone (202) 482-4655
Fax (202) 482-2293
E-mail: bisnis@usita.gov
Internet home page: http://www.mac.doc.gov/bisnis/bisnis.html

Central and Eastern Europe Business Information Center (CEEBIC) - ITA/U.S. Department of Commerce-CEEBIC is a business facilitation program for U.S. firms interested in expanding into the Central and Eastern European markets. CEEBIC combines high-technology information dissemination and individualized business counseling provided by its Washington-based trade specialists and staff in 14 countries. CEEBIC's extensive Internet home page and automated fax-on-demand systems provide the most recent economic and commercial information, including cables from U.S. embassies in the region, trade leads, and contacts. CEEBIC also publishes the monthly *Central and Eastern Europe Commercial Update* and bimonthly *Poland Looks for Partners*. Responding to political changes in Bosnia and the Balkans, CEEBIC has developed its Bosnia/Balkan Reconstruction Initiative, which includes a hotline staffed by CEEBIC's Bosnia trade specialists, new overseas employees in Bosnia and Croatia, and a weekly e-mail service, *Southeastern Europe Business Brief*.

Contact: Phone (202) 482-2645
Fax (202) 501-0787
CEEBIC Bosnia/Balkan Reconstruction Hotline, (202) 482-5418
CEEBIC fax retrieval: 1-800-USA-TRAD(E) (1-800-872-8723)
E-mail: ceebic@usita.gov
Internet home page: http://www.mac.doc.gov/eebic/ceebic.html

Regional Bureaus - U.S. Department of State-Country desk officers in regional bureaus maintain regular contact with overseas diplomatic missions and provide country specific economic and political analysis for U.S. companies. There are the bureaus of African, Inter-American, European, Near East, South Asian, and East Asian and Pacific Affairs. Each bureau has a commercial coordinator to assist U.S. businesses.

Contact: Africa (202) 647-3502
East Asia and Pacific (202) 647-6594
Europe (202) 647-3207
Russia and Newly Independent States (202) 647-6747
Inter-America (202) 647-2079
Near East (202) 647-1552
South Asia (202) 736-4328
Internet home page: http://www.state.gov

Country and Export Information Available by Fax

Several offices now offer documents on demand, delivered directly to your fax machine 24 hours a day. These automated systems each have a menu of available documents which can be sent to a fax machine by dialing from a touch-tone phone and following the instructions. The fax-on-demand system is accessible by calling 1-800-USA-TRAD(E) (1-800-872-8723)

Central and Eastern Europe

- Export and financing information
- Current trade and business opportunities
- Trade events
- Country information
- Current issues of both *Eastern Europe Business Bulletin* and *Eastern Europe Looks for Partners*

Newly Independent States (NIS)

- NIS country overviews
- Specific industry information
- Trade statistics
- Contact information
- Publications from the Business Information Service for the Newly Independent States (BISNIS)

The Americas: Mexico, Canada, Latin America, and the Caribbean

- Country information on Mexico and Canada, and the NAFTA
- Information on making the NAFTA Rules of Origin Determination
- Mexican and Canadian tariff schedules
- Country and market information on Latin American and Caribbean countries

Asia

- Country and market information on Asia, including South Asia, Australia, and New Zealand
- Trade events
- Trade statistics

Japan

- Market opening initiatives (listed by industry)
- Commercial programs
- Economic, trade, investment, and market structure information
- Useful contacts
- Publications

Africa and the Near East

- Country and market information on countries in Africa and the Middle East
- Trade statistics

Northern Ireland and the Border Counties (NIBC)

- Country and market information on Northern Ireland and the border counties
- NIBC White House Conference materials

Specialized Market Access and Technical Assistance

Advocacy Center - ITA/U.S. Department of Commerce-For a U.S. company bidding for a foreign government procurement contract, exporting today can mean more than just selling a good product at a competitive price. It can also mean dealing with foreign governments and complex rules. If you feel the bidding process is not open and transparent, or may be tilted in favor of your foreign competition, then you need to contact the Advocacy Center. The Advocacy Center coordinates the actions of 20 U.S. Government agencies involved in international trade, to level the playing field overseas for U.S. exporters and ensure that sales of U.S. products and services have the best possible chance abroad. Advocacy assistance can include a visit to a key foreign official by a high-ranking U.S. government official, direct support by U.S. officials stationed overseas, letters to foreign decision makers, and coordinated action by U.S. Government agencies to businesses of all types and sizes.

Contact: Phone (202) 482-3896
Fax (202) 482-3508
Internet home page: http://www.ita.doc.gov/advocacy

Office of Export Trading Company Affairs (OETCA) - ITA/U.S. Department of Commerce-OETCA works with individual companies, trade associations, U.S. joint venture partners, and business consortia to promote the use of export trading companies and export management companies (ETCs and EMCs). OETCA encourages the formation of ETCs (including the formation of U.S. export joint ventures and U.S. export consortia) through Commerce's Export Trade Certificate of Review program. This program provides significant antitrust protection to U.S. firms interested in conducting joint export activities so that they can coordinate their export activities and achieve economies of scale with virtual immunity from antitrust liability at the state and federal levels. Such export activities might include: allocation of export markets and sales to avoid rivalry; joint bidding to obtain large volume and long-term contracts; coordination of export prices; cost sharing on developing distribution networks, marketing, and promotion; consolidation of export shipments to reduce transportation costs; sharing commercial intelligence; and other joint activities. Approximately 5,000 firms are operating under the program's antitrust protection.

The OETCA-coordinated *Export Yellow Pages* directory has information on more than 17,000 U.S. companies, including ETCs, manufacturers, and business service providers that are interested in exporting.

Contact: Phone (202) 482-5131
Fax (202) 482-1790
Internet home page: http://www.ita.doc.gov/
export_admin/sox3.html

Market Development Cooperator Program (MDCP) - ITA/U.S. Department of Commerce-The MDCP is a competitive matching grants program providing federal assistance to states, trade associations, Chambers of Commerce, world trade centers, and other nonprofit industry groups to help underwrite the start-up costs of creative export marketing ventures. MDCP applications may be targeted for any market in the world and any industry covered by ITA's industry units.

Projects that concentrate on the following priorities also present opportunities to develop, maintain, and expand overseas markets and create/support U.S. jobs: 1) advocacy; 2) monitoring of foreign compliance with our trade agreements; 3) facilitating the involvement in exporting of small- and medium-sized U.S. businesses; 4) working cooperatively to support ITA export marketing initiatives and facilities. Examples of activities which applicants might propose include: 1)opening an overseas representative office; 2)commissioning overseas market research, participating in overseas trade exhibitions and trade missions and hosting reverse trade missions; 3) overseas U.S. product demonstrations; 4) export seminars; 5) technical trade servicing; 6) joint promotions of U.S. goods or services with foreign customers; 7) training of foreign nationals; 8) working with organizations in the foreign marketplace responsible for setting standards and for product testing; 9) publishing an export resource guide or an export product directory; and 10) establishing an electronic business information system.

Contact: Phone (202) 482-3197, Greg O'Connor, MDCP Program Manager
Internet home page: http://www.ita.doc.gov/industry/
opcrm/mdcp.html

Consortia of American Businesses in the Newly Independent States (CABNIS) - ITA/U.S. Department of Commerce-The Commerce Department initiated the CABNIS program to help U.S. firms do business in the evolving and complex markets of Russia and the Newly Independent States (NIS). Through CABNIS, Commerce has provided matching grant funding to several nonprofit organizations. The organizations manage business consortia (trade groups) composed of U.S. firms that are interested in doing business in the NIS. Federal funding has been used to help defray the costs of opening, staffing, and operating consortia trade offices in the NIS. On-site industry specialists help U.S. firms identify and pursue new business opportunities. The CABNIS consortia represent the commercial interests of firms involved in agribusiness and food processing equipment, biotechnology, coal production, utilization technologies, semiconductor production equipment, telecommunications, and other industry sectors.

Contact: Phone (202) 482-5004, Office of Export Trading Company Affairs (OETCA)

American Business Centers (ABCs) in the Newly Independent States (NIS)-ABCs in the states of the former Soviet Union provide American companies with a professional office and support services essential to doing business in these markets. Five ABCs are at Commercial Service posts in Vladivostok, St. Petersburg, Tashkent, Almaty, and Kiev. Eight solo ABCs are established and operated by nonfederal entities through cooperative agreements with the Department of Commerce. Centers provide services, including short-term office and exhibit space, market research and counseling, interpretation and translation services, telecommunications and computer equipment, and assistance in making NIS contacts.

Contact: Phone (202) 482-4655 option 2, Business Information Service for the Newly Independent States
Fax (202) 482-2293
Internet home page: http://www.iep.doc.gov/bisnis/abc/
abc.htm

Market Access and Compliance (MAC) Officers - ITA/U.S. Department of Commerce-Market Access and Compliance (MAC) works to open foreign markets for American goods and services, country-by-country and region-by-region, by concentrating on market access issues and developing strategies to overcome obstacles faced by U.S. business. MAC specialists maintain in-depth knowledge of trade policies and practices of our trading partners. Working hand-in-hand with U.S. business, trade associations, Trade Development's industry and technical specialists, and U.S. and Foreign Commercial Service offices, MAC country and regional experts develop information needed to conduct trade negotiations, monitor foreign country compliance with trade agreements, and ensure that U.S. firms know how to use market opening agreements.

Contact: Phone 1-800-USA-TRAD(E) (1-800-872-8723) to locate a MAC officer
Internet home page: http://www.itaiep.doc.gov

Trade Compliance Center (TCC) - ITA/U.S. Department of Commerce-The TCC, established in July 1996, is designed to ensure vigorous enforcement of existing U.S. international trade agreements and standards of behavior. The center serves as a key contact point for U.S. businesses and industry concerned with foreign compliance with their trade obligations. The TCC plays a major role in this effort by monitoring, investigating, and evaluating foreign compliance with multilateral and bilateral trade agreements and other standards of conduct. In addition, the TCC is developing the U.S. Government's first comprehensive computerized database and information retrieval system that will contain trade agreements, analyses, and other associated documents. They are designing the system to help U.S. companies more readily understand what their rights are-and what foreign obligations exist-under the wide variety of existing trade agreements.

The Trade Compliance Center fax retrieval system, an automated fax information delivery system, provides documents available to U.S.-based businesses 24-hours a day. These documents include state opportunity reports, topical and special reports, tariff 0/0 and harmonization decisions, and an explanation of the Uruguay Round.

Contact: Phone (202) 482-1191
Fax (202) 482-6097
Fax retrieval 1-800-USA-TRAD(E) (1-800-872-8723)
Internet homepage: http://www.mac.doc.gov/tcc

Office of Multilateral Affairs (OMA) - ITA/U.S. Department of Commerce-OMA serves as a contact point for nonsectoral international trade and investment policy issues related to the World Trade Organization (WTO), the Organization for Economic Cooperation and Development (OECD), and other international organizations. OMA is involved in the following trade policy areas: accessions to the WTO and WTO negotiations, concessions, and rules; OECD investment negotiations, bilateral investment treaties, expropriation; the Generalized System of Preferences; trade and environment, and related trade policy initiatives.

Contact: Phone (202) 482-0603
Fax (202) 482-5939

Japanese Untied Aid Program - ITA/U.S. Department of Commerce-This program is a central source for information on how to access Japan's foreign aid program to finance U.S. export sales in infrastructure and other sectors. In 1994, developing countries benefited from approximately $17.1 billion in Japanese Official Development Assistance, which includes grant aid, "soft loans," and technical cooperation. According to the Organization for Economic Cooperation and Development (OECD) data, approximately $11 billion of these funds were "untied" (i.e., not contingent upon the purchase of goods and services from the donor country) and therefore potentially available to finance procurement from U.S. and other non-Japanese suppliers and consultants. Information is provided via the ITA Internet home page.

Contact: Office of Finance, Michael Fuchs, (202) 482-4002, fax (202) 482-5702
E-mail: michael_fuchs@ita.doc.gov

Office of Japan Trade Policy, Nicole Melcher, (202) 482-2515, fax (202) 482-0469
E-mail: melcher@usita.gov
Internet home page: http://www.ita.doc.gov

European Union Single Internal Market 1992 Information Service (SIMIS) - ITA/U.S. Department of Commerce-SIMIS serves as the major contact point within the U.S. Government for U.S. business questions on commercial and trade implications of the Single Market program of the European Union (EU). SIMIS maintains a comprehensive database of EU directives and regulations plus specialized documentation published by the EU Commission, the U.S. Government, and the private sector. Services provided by SIMIS include a basic information packet on EC 1992, sectoral guides to EU legislation, copies of EU directories and regulations, informational seminars, and business counseling.

Contact: Phone (202) 482-5276
Fax (202) 482-2155

WTO/GATT Hotline and EU Hotline - National Institute of Standards and Technology (NIST)/Technology Administration/ U.S. Department of Commerce-NIST provides information about foreign standards, technical regulations, and certification requirements. In addition, NIST maintains a World Trade Organization hotline with the latest notifications of proposed foreign technical regulations that may affect trade. NIST also assists U.S. exporters in identifying European Union (EU) standards and directives for products to be marketed to the EU. An EU hotline provides information on draft standards of the European Committee for Standardization (CEN) and the European Committee for Electrotechnical Standardization (CENELEC).

Contact: National Center for Standards and Certification Information, (301) 975-4040
Fax (301) 926-1559
WTO/GATT hotline, (301) 975-4041
EU Hotline, (301) 921-4164
Internet home page: http://ts.nist.gov/ts/htdocs/210/217/217.htm

Metric Program - National Institute of Standards and Technology - Technology Administration/U.S. Department of Commerce-The Metric Program seeks to accelerate the national transition to the metric system of measurement, the preferred system of weights and measures for U.S. trade and commerce. Implementing the 1988 amendments to the Metric Conversion Act of 1975, the Metric Program coordinates the metric transition activities of all federal agencies. The program provides leadership and assistance on metric usage and conversion to businesses, state and local governments, standards organizations, trade associations, and the educational community. Current initiatives focus on education and public awareness to gain broad-based support for national metrication from industry and the general public.

Contact: Phone (301) 975-3690, Gerard C. Iannelli, Director, Metric Program
Fax (301) 948-1416
E-mail: metric_prg@nist.gov
Internet home page: http://www.nist.gov/metric

Coordinator for Business Affairs - U.S. Department of State-The Office of the Coordinator for Business Affairs, an ombudsman for business in the State Department, was created as part of the "America Desk" commitment. The coordinator reports to the under secretary for economic, Business, and Agricultural Affairs. The office works closely with U.S. embassies abroad and with State Department bureau coordinators in Washington to promote U.S. economic and commercial interests and to ensure that the department provides consistent and effective support to U.S. businesses. The coordinator is the primary point of contact for business concerns within the Department of State.

Contact: Phone (202) 647-1625
Fax (202) 647-3953
Internet home page: http://www.state.gov

Bureau of Economic and Business Affairs - U.S. Department of State-The bureau formulates and carries out U.S. foreign economic policy in cooperation with other U.S. Government agencies in Washington and with U.S. embassies abroad. The bureau is divided into five units along functional lines: communications, energy-resources-sanctions, finance and investment, trade, and transportation (aviation and maritime).

Contact: Phone (202) 647-5991
Internet home page: http://www.state.gov

Office of the U.S. Trade Representative (USTR)-USTR staff can provide information to exporters confronted with foreign barriers to trade and unfair trade practices. Offices are organized according to sectoral responsibilities.

Contact: Agricultural Affairs, James Murphy, (202) 395-6127
Office of Industry, Don Eiss, (202) 395-5656
Investment, Services and Intellectual Property Rights, and Technology, Donald Abelson, (202) 395-4510
Services, Peter Collins, (202) 395-7271
Office of Textiles, Rita Hayes, (202) 395-3026
Monitoring and Enforcement,Jane Bradley, (202) 395-3582
Fax for all offices (202) 395-3911
Internet home page: http://www.ustr.gov/

Office of the General Counsel - Office of the U.S. Trade Representative-USTR is responsible for administering trade cases that provide relief from unfair trade practices under Section 301 of the Trade Act of 1974. Individual exporters should contact USTR concerning procedures for filing a complaint.

Contact: Phone (202) 395-3432, Irving Williamson, Deputy General Counsel
Fax (202) 395-3639

ATA Carnet - U.S. Customs Service/U.S. Department of the Treasury-The ATA Carnet is a special international customs document which may be used for temporary imports/exports, particularly professional equipment and commercial samples that are out of the country for less than one year. The carnet is issued in lieu of the usual customs documents and eliminates value-added taxes, duties, and temporary import bonds. Forty-seven participating countries accept the carnet as a guarantee against the payment of customs duties that may become due on goods temporarily imported under a carnet and not reexported.

Contact: Phone (202) 927-0440, Jerrald Worley, Office of International Programs
Fax (202) 927-6892
Internet home page: http://www.imex.com/uscib/frame5a.htm

Office of Small and Disadvantaged Business Utilization/Minority Resource Center (OSDBU/MRC) - Agency for International Development (USAID)-An advocate for U.S. small businesses and disadvantaged enterprises (including women-owned businesses), OSDBU/MRC ensures their consideration as sources for the procurement of goods and services financed through USAID development assistance activities. The office maintains the USAID Consultant Registry Information System (ACRIS) and publishes *The Guide to Doing Business with the Agency for International Development*.

Contact: Phone (703) 875-1551, Ivan R. Ashley, Office of Small and Disadvantaged Business
Fax (703) 875-1862
Internet home page: http://www.info.usaid.gov/procurement_bus_opp/osbdu/index.html

Office of Minority Enterprise Development - Small Business Administration (SBA)-Through this office's 7(j) Management and Technical Assistance Program, SBA contracts for the services of professional management firms and others, as appropriate, to provide management and technical assistance to 8(a) and other eligible firms in the areas of accounting, marketing, proposal preparation, and industry-specific issues.

Contact: Phone 1-800-U-ASK-SBA (1-800-872-5722) for your nearest SBA district office
Internet home page: http://www.sba.gov/med/

Technical Assistance - U.S. Department of Transportation (DOT)-The department has an active program to promote U.S. transportation technology and products abroad. At various multilateral fora, DOT vigorously pursues harmonization of safety and construction standards to ensure that U.S. companies are not put at a competitive disadvantage. Under bilateral and multilateral agreements, the

Department also participates, through its operating administrations, in cooperative programs and technology sharing initiatives with partners worldwide.

Contact: International Transportation and Trade,
Tami Fields, (202) 366-4398, fax (202) 366-7417
Federal Aviation Administration,
Marci Kenney, (202) 267-8157, fax (202) 267-5032
Federal Highway Administration,
King Gee, (202) 366-0111, fax (202) 366-9626
Federal Railroad Administration,
Ted Krohn, (202) 632-3133, fax (202) 632-3705
Maritime Administration,
James Treichel, (202) 366-5773, fax (202) 366-3746

Computerized and Published Market Information

Business America - ITA/U.S. Department of Commerce-This is the principal Commerce Department international trade publication. Each monthly issue includes discussions of U.S. trade policies, news of government actions affecting trade, and a calendar of upcoming trade shows, exhibitions, fairs, and seminars. An annual subscription is $63.

Contact: Phone (202) 482-3251, Doug Carroll, ITA Office of Public Affairs
Fax (202) 482-5819
Subscriptions: U.S. Government Printing Office (stock #703-011-00000-4-W), (202) 512-1800
Internet home page: http://www.ita.doc.gov/bizam/

Office of Trade and Economic Analysis (OTEA) - ITA/U.S. Department of Commerce-OTEA provides a broad range of U.S. foreign trade data useful in evaluating trends in U.S. export performance by major export categories and foreign markets. Among its major publications are the *U.S. Industrial Outlook* and its successor publications and the annual *U.S. Foreign Trade Highlights*. The OTEA web site includes state and metropolitan area trade data as well as national statistics.

Contact: Phone (202) 482-5145, Jeffrey Lins
Fax (202) 482-4614
E-mail jeffrey_lins@ita.doc.gov
Internet home page: http://www.ita.doc.gov/tradestats

National Trade Data Bank (NTDB) - U.S. Department of Commerce-The NTDB is a one-stop source for export promotion and international trade data collected by more than 40 U.S. Government agencies. The NTDB is accessible on the Internet or on two CD-Rom discs (see ordering information below), and enables the user to view more than 200,000 trade-related documents. The NTDB contains: 1) the latest Census data on U.S. imports and exports by commodity and country, 2) the complete set of Country Commercial Guides, 3) current market research reports compiled by the Commercial Service, 4) the complete Country Directory of International Contacts (CDICs), which contains hundreds of names and addresses of primary sources that each U.S. Commercial Service post identified as useful, 5) State Department country reports on economic policy and trade practices, 6) the publications: *Export Yellow Pages, A Basic Guide to Exporting*, and the *National Trade Estimates Report on Foreign Trade Barriers*, 7) the Export Promotion Calendar, and many other data series.

The NTDB is available as part of STAT-USA/Internet. The cost is $50 for three months and $150 for one year. The Internet address is http://www.STAT-USA.gov

The NTDB can be purchased in the form of CD-ROM discs for $59 per monthly issue or $575 for a 12-month subscription. Non-U.S.

shipments will be charged $75 monthly or $775 for an annual subscription. Additional charges apply for network or redistribution use. For ordering and other specific information, call (202) 482-1986 or 1-800-STAT-USA (1-800-782-8872), fax (202) 482-2164

Contact: The NTDB is also available at over 1,100 federal depository libraries nationwide.
Call 1-800-USA-TRAD(E) (1-800-872-8723) for a list of these libraries.

The Economic Bulletin Board (EBB) - U.S. Department of Commerce-The EBB system comprises two personal computer-based, electronic bulletin boards, which are updated daily.

"GLOBUS" provides businesses with agricultural and nonagricultural sales opportunities in foreign markets, and U.S. Government procurement opportunities, as well as late-breaking international news and in-depth market studies produced by the Commercial Service of the Department of Commerce.

State of the Nation provides businesses with the economic news, statistics, and indicators necessary to gauge the direction of the American economy.

Subscribers to each individual system may obtain 24 hour access or may choose to have only off-peak hour access (before 8:00 a.m. and after 12:00 noon EST) for a reduced fee. Subscriptions to both systems are also available. The EBB systems are available as a part of STAT-USA/Fax7 and STAT-USA/Internet7.

Contact: Phone (202) 482-1986 or 800-STAT-USA (800-782-8872)
Fax (202) 482-2164
Try the EBB as a guest user by dialing (202) 482-3870 with your personal computer and modem (8 bit words, no parity, 1 stop bit).

STAT-USA/Fax - U.S. Department of Commerce-Use your fax machine to receive trade leads, procurement opportunities, and the latest trade and economic information from the federal government. Subscriptions are $29.95 per quarter or $100 per year for unlimited access. Try using the system for free as a guest user by dialing 202-482-0005 from your fax machine and enter "800" for a list of available information.

Contact: Phone (202) 482-1986 or 800-STAT-USA (800-782-8872)
Fax (202) 482-2164

STAT-USA/Internet - U.S. Department of Commerce-Trade, economic, and business information is available on the Internet at one worldwide web address. The contents of the National Trade Data Bank (NTDB) CD-ROM and the best of the Economic Bulletin Board (EBB) can all be found at: http://www.stat-usa.gov. Subscriptions are $50 for three months or $150 a year for unlimited access.

Contact: Phone (202) 482-1986 or 800-STAT-USA (800-782-8872)
Fax (202) 482-2164

International Data Base - Bureau of the Census/U.S. Department of Commerce-The International Programs Center compiles and maintains up-to-date global demographic and social information for all countries in its International Data Base (IDB), which is available to U.S. companies seeking to identify potential markets overseas.

Contact: Phone (301) 457-1403, Peter Johnson, Information Resources Branch
Fax (301) 457-1539
E-mail: peterj@census.gov
Information about the IDB, including online access and free download, is available on the Internet at:
http://www.census.gov/ipc/www/idbnew.html

Export and Import Trade Data Base - Bureau of the Census/U.S. Department of Commerce-This database contains U.S. export and import statistics tracked by mode of transportation and port of entry or exit. Various levels of classification, including the Harmonized System of Commodity Classification, Standard International Trade Classification (SITC), Standard Industrial Classification (SIC) based codes, and End-Use Classification are available. Customized tabulations and reports can be prepared to user specifications. Prices begin at $25 and vary depending upon user requirements and job size. Export and import databases can also be purchased individually on CD-ROM at a price of $1,200 a year, $500 a quarter, or $150 a month.

Contact: Phone (301) 457-2311, Trade Data Services Branch
Fax (301) 457-4615 for reports; (301) 457-4100 for CD-ROM
Internet home page: http://www.census.gov/foreign_trade/www/

SBA Online BBS - Small Business Administration (SBA)-SBA Online is an electronic bulletin board developed to expedite dissemination of information to the small business community on starting, expanding, and financing a business. The system operates 23 hours a day and 365 days a year. All you need is a computer, modem, phone line, and communications software. Data parameters are 14.4, N, 8, 1. You can access different SBA Online services by calling the following numbers on your modem:

1-800-697-4636 (This line provides SBA and other government agency information and some downloadable text files.)

1-900-463-4636 (This number allows you to access, for $.14 a minute, SBA and other government information, a wide range of downloadable files, including application and software files, the gateway, mail, interact mail, news groups and on-line searchable data banks.)

This information can also be obtained by calling (202) 401-9600.

Contact: Technical support for this service is available by calling (202) 205-6400.
The TDD line is (202) 205-7333.

SBA Internet Home Page - Small Business Administration (SBA)-The SBA Home Page provides SBA services, downloadable files, plus services from agency resource partners, links to other federal and state governments, and direct connections to additional outside resources. Special areas of interest focus on assisting U.S. companies that are setting up an operation, seeking financing, looking to expand, and beginning to engage in exporting. SBA Online also contains information on SBA programs that assist minority- and women-owned businesses. In addition, large libraries of business-focused shareware, downloadable SBA loan forms, and agency publications are available. A wide variety of services listed by state are provided, including calendars of local training courses sponsored by SBA. On-line workshops are offered for individuals to work through self-paced activities that help them start and expand their business. In addition, the home page links directly to the White House home page and the U.S. Business Advisor, which houses a large volume of regulatory information for small businesses. SBA provides full text search capabilities as well as an area for user comments and suggestions.

Contact: Phone (202) 205-6400, SBA Help Desk, or (202) 205-6253, Dianne Gannon
E-mail: diane.gannon@sba.gov
Internet: http://www.sba.gov/

Overseas Security Advisory Council (OSAC) - U.S. Department of State-OSAC is the point of contact between the Department of State and the U.S. private sector on all overseas security-related matters such as political unrest, terrorism, and the protection of information. OSAC manages an on-line bulletin board system available to U.S. businesses with overseas interests. The bulletin board provides comprehensive, timely security-related and country specific information. OSAC also works closely with U.S. embassies and consulates worldwide to expedite contacts between U.S. business representatives and State Department security officers.

Contact: Phone (202) 663-0533, Nickolas W. Proctor, Executive Director, OSAC
Fax (202) 663-0868

Foreign Labor Trends **- U.S. Department of Labor-***Foreign Labor Trends*** is a series of annual reports that describe and analyze labor trends in some 75 foreign countries. The reports cover labor-management relations, labor and government, international labor activities, and other significant developments. A list of key labor indicators is also included. The U.S. Department of Labor's Office of Foreign Relations publishes additional reports on four foreign countries each year.

Contact: Phone (202) 219-6234 ext. 168, Sudha Haley, Office of Foreign Relations
Fax (202) 219-5613

International Trade Contacts

Computerized and Published Trade Contacts

The Economic Bulletin Board/Fax - U.S. Department of Commerce-Use your fax machine to receive trade leads, procurement opportunities, and the latest trade and economic information from the federal government. Subscriptions are $29.95 a quarter or $100 a year for unlimited access. Try using the system for free as a guest user: dial 202-482-0005 from your fax machine and enter "800" for a list of available information.

Contact: Phone (202) 482-1986 or 800-STAT-USA (800-782-8872), STAT-USA HelpLine
Fax (202) 482-2164

Trade Opportunity Program (TOP) - ITA/U.S. Department of Commerce-TOP provides companies with current sales leads from international firms seeking to buy or represent their products or services. TOP leads are distributed electronically via the Department of Commerce's Economic Bulletin Board (EBB), STAT-USA/FAX, and STAT-USA/Internet (http://www.stat-usa.gov/). There is a nominal annual fee to access these services. TOP leads are also printed daily in leading commercial newspapers.

Contact: For information on the TOP program, contact the Trade Information Center at 1-800-USA-TRAD(E).

To subscribe to the Department of Commerce Economic Bulletin Board, STAT-USA/Fax, or STAT-USA/Internet, call 1-800-STAT-USA (1-800-782-8872) or (202) 482-1986, fax (202) 482-2164.

Country Directories of International Contacts (CDIC) - ITA/U.S. Department of Commerce-CDIC provides the names and contact information for directories of importers, agents, trade associations, government agencies, etc., on a country-by-country basis. Both are available on the National Trade Data Bank (NTDB).

Contact: For information on accessing the National Trade Data Bank, see previous section or contact the Trade Information Center at 1-800-USA-TRAD(E) (1-800-872-8723).

The Export Yellow Pages **- ITA/U.S. Department of Commerce-**Coordinated by the Office of Export Trading Company Affairs, *The Export Yellow Pages* is a free directory that includes information on more than 17,000 U.S. companies interested in exporting. This popular directory includes trade contact data on U.S. manufacturers, export trading companies, and business service providers. *The Export Yellow Pages* directory is distributed nationwide though U.S. Department of Commerce Export Assistance Centers and worldwide through U.S.

embassies and consulates. The directory is also accessible on the National Trade Data Bank, and other outlets. A company's basic listing in the directory is free. Display advertising is available for a small fee.

Contact: To register your company or to obtain a free copy of *The Export Yellow Pages*, contact your local U.S. Department of Commerce Export Assistance Center or call 1-800-USA-TRAD(E) (1-800-872-8723).

To learn more about the activities of the Office of Export Trading Company Affairs, call (202) 482-5131 to receive an information kit.

United States Agency for International Development (USAID)/ Environmental Technology Network for Asia and the Americas (ETNA)-Operated by USAID's Global Technology Network (GTN), ETNA matches environmental technology opportunity notices sent from US-AEP technology representatives from regions around the world, with appropriate U.S. environmental product manufacturers, service firms, and trade associations that are registered with ETNA's environmental trade opportunity database. The technology representatives are located in ten Latin American countries, five Sub-Saharan African countries, and ten Asian nations. U.S. environmental firms receive trade leads via a broadcast fax system within 48 hours of leads being identified and entered electronically from these regions.

Contact: USAID/ETNA, 1-800-818-9911
Latin America region, 1-800-872-4348
Asia region, (202) 835-8358
Internet homepage: http://www.usgtn.org

Customized Trading Partner Programs

Agent/Distributor Service (ADS) - ITA/U.S. Department of Commerce-Provides a customized search that helps identify agents, distributors, and foreign representatives for U.S. firms based on the foreign companies' examination of U.S. product literature. A fee of $250 per country is charged.

Contact: For more information on the ADS, contact your local Department of Commerce Export Assistance Center (EAC).
For the address and phone number of the EAC nearest you call 1-800-USA-TRAD(E) (1-800-872-8723).
Internet home page: http://www.ita.doc.gov/uscs/ uscshelp.html

Customized Market Analysis (CMA) - Department of Commerce-A custom-tailored research service provides firms with specific information on marketing and foreign representation for their individual products in one overseas market. Foreign commercial posts conduct interviews or surveys to determine overall marketability of the product, key competitors, price of comparable products, customary distribution and promotion practices, trade barriers, possible business partners, and applicable trade events. Fees for the CMA vary from $1,000 to $5,100 per country.

Contact: For more information on the CMA, contact your local Department of Commerce Export Assistance Center (EAC).
For the address and phone number of the EAC nearest you call 1-800-USA-TRAD(E) (1-800-872-8723).
Internet home page: http://www.ita.doc.gov/uscs/ uscshelp.html

International Company Profile (ICP) - ITA/U.S. Department of Commerce-A service for checking the reputation, reliability, and financial status of a prospective trading partner. An exporter can obtain this information in a confidential report, along with a recommendation from commercial officers at the U.S. embassy as to the suitability of the company as a trading partner. A fee of $100 per company is charged. This service is offered in approximately 40 countries, where reliable, private sector providers are not available.

Contact: For more information on the ICP, contact your local Department of Commerce Export Assistance Center (EAC).
For the address and phone number of the EAC nearest you call 1-800-USA-TRAD(E) (1-800-872-8723).
Internet home page: http://www.ita.doc.gov/uscs/uscshelp.html

Commercial News USA - **ITA/U.S. Department of Commerce**-*Commercial News USA*, a catalog-magazine containing advertisements of U.S. products, is published twelve times per year by the Commercial Service through its private sector partner, Associated Business Publications International, to promote U.S. products and services to overseas markets.

Contact: For information and costs on advertising in *Commercial News USA*, call 1-800-USA-TRAD(E) (1-800-872-8723), or call Associated Business Publications International at (212) 490-3999, fax (212) 822-2028.
Internet home page: http://www.cnewsusa.com

Gold Key Service - **ITA/U.S. Department of Commerce**-Offered by many Commercial Service overseas posts, the Gold Key Service is a custom-tailored service for U.S. firms planning to visit a country. This service provides assistance in developing a sound market strategy, orientation briefings, introductions to potential partners, interpreters for meetings, and effective follow-up planning. The fees range from $150 to $1,300 (for the first day) per country.

Contact: For more information on the Gold Key Service, contact your local Department of Commerce Export Assistance Center (EAC).
For the address and phone number of the EAC nearest you call 1-800-USA-TRAD(E) (1-800-872-8723).
Internet home page: http://www.ita.doc.gov/uscs/uscshelp.html

Domestic Trade Promotion Events

International Buyer Program (IBP) - **ITA/U.S. Department of Commerce**-IBP supports major domestic trade shows featuring products and services of U.S. industries with high export potential. Commercial Service officers worldwide recruit qualified foreign buyers to attend the shows. The shows are extensively publicized through embassy and regional commercial newsletters, catalog magazines, foreign trade associations, chambers of commerce, travel agents, government agencies, corporations, import agents, and equipment distributors in targeted markets. An international business center at each international buyer show provides interpreters, multilingual brochures, counseling, and private meeting rooms.

Contact: Phone (202) 482-0146, Jim Boney, Export Promotion Services
Fax (202) 482-0872
Internet home page: http://www.ita.doc.gov/uscs/uscshelp.html

Industry Outreach Program - **ITA/U.S. Department of Commerce**-Trade Development's Office of Export Promotion Coordination (OEPC) provides on-the-spot export assistance to attendees and exhibitors at 10 to 20 domestic industry exhibitions and conferences per year. This assistance is provided through OEPC's traveling Trade Information Center exhibit. The mix of industry exhibitions covered varies from year to year.

Contact: Phone (202) 482-4501, Office of Export Promotion Coordination
Fax (202) 482-1889

Domestic Trade Fair Certification - **ITA/U.S. Department of Commerce**-The Tourism Industries unit of Trade Development is responsible for certification and promotion of domestic trade fairs. The Trade Fairs Act of 1959 permits the Secretary of Commerce to extend the privileges provided in the act to any trade fair held in the United States that serves the public interest in promoting trade. Items to be exhibited at these domestic shows are allowed into the United States duty free.

Contact: Phone (202) 482-2404, Linda Harbaugh, Tourism Industries
Fax (202) 482-2887
Internet: http://tinet.ita.doc.gov

Business Briefings and Technical Symposia - **U.S. Trade and Development Agency**-The U.S. Trade and Development Agency sponsors a variety of business briefings and technical symposia geared to meet the development needs of foreign countries. Conducted in cooperation with and co-funded by industry and other U.S. Government agencies, these symposia and briefings are intended to familiarize foreign governments and industry with U.S. products and services and to encourage U.S. firms to export.

Contact: Phone (703) 875-4357, TDA Information Resource Center
Fax (703) 875-4009
Internet home page: http://www.tda.gov

Reverse Trade Missions - **U.S. Trade and Development Agency**-The U.S. Trade and Development Agency funds visits to the United States by high-level foreign government officials to meet with U.S. industry and government representatives. These foreign officials represent procurement authorities of specific projects interested in purchasing U.S. equipment and services. U.S. industry has usually co-funded the missions.

Contact: Phone (703) 875-4357, TDA Information Resource Center
Fax (703) 875-4009
E-mail:info@tda.gov
Internet home page: http://www.tda.gov

Visitors Program - **U.S. Department of Transportation**-The department maintains a visitors program for foreign officials interested in U.S. transportation policy and facilities.

Contact: International Transportation and Trade, Tami Fields, (202) 366-4398, fax (202) 366-7417
Federal Aviation Administration, Nancy Angelo, (202) 267-8186, fax (202) 267-5306
Internet home page: http://www.usia.gov/education/ivp/usintiv.htm

Foreign Trade Promotion Events

Trade Fairs and Exhibitions - **ITA/U.S. Department of Commerce**-The Department of Commerce selects between 80 and 100 worldwide trade fairs each year for recruitment of a USA pavilion. They give selection priority to events in good markets that are suitable for new-to-export or new-to-market, "export ready" firms. Fees depend upon the country, and exhibitors receive pre- and post-event logistical and transportation support, design and management of the USA pavilion, and extensive overseas market promotional campaigns to attract appropriate business audiences. In addition, each firm is asked to identify its goals in participating in the event, and the U.S. embassy makes every effort to assure that these goals are met.

Contact: For information on Department of Commerce recruited trade shows and a listing of trade events call the Trade Information Center at 1-800-USA-TRAD(E) (1-800-872-8723).

Overseas Trade Fair Certification - **ITA/U.S. Department of Commerce**-Each year the Commerce Department certifies a variety of trade show organizers to recruit and manage U.S. pavilions at approximately 90 fairs worldwide. These private-public cooperative arrangements allow the organizer and the Department of Commerce to combine and focus their resources and expertise for each event. Certification ensures participation standards, provides a high visibility U.S. pavilion at each exhibit, signals U.S. firms that the event is a carefully developed opportunity to promote their export sales, provides exhibitors with complete Commercial Service support from U.S. embassies, and encourages new-to-export and new-to-market participation.

Contact: Don Huber, Export Promotion Services, (202) 482-2525, fax (202) 482-0115
Internet home page: http://www.ita.doc.gov/uscs/uscshelp.html

Trade Missions - ITA/U.S. Department of Commerce-Trade missions are an essential element of a broad-based public policy designed to increase job opportunities for all Americans. Trade missions may be undertaken for a variety of purposes:

■ Commercial missions, which seek to produce near-term export sales of U.S. goods and services. These missions may include a broad range of U.S. companies or be focused on assisting small and mid-size businesses, minority businesses, or women-owned/managed businesses, which may be less familiar with exporting. The United States' National Export Strategy had adopted the policy of concentrating our resources on Big Emerging Markets, or large trading partners, and particular sectors that hold the greatest promise of increased exports. Commercial missions focus on these targets.

■ Market access missions, which seek to create market and investment opportunities through the removal of barriers to trade and investment. Market entry for U.S. businesses that have been closed out of such opportunities is another goal of these missions.

■ Policy missions, which seek to advance the U.S. bilateral or multilateral objectives across a range of issues with the objective of enhancing overall bilateral or multilateral economic and political relations. This category includes missions designed to promote political stability in a foreign country or region by fostering U.S. investment and trade.

■ Combined missions, which embody aspects of two or more of the above types.

Contact: Don Huber, Export Promotion Services, (202) 482-2525, fax (202) 482-0115
Internet home page: http://www.ita.doc.gov/uscs/uscshelp.html

Women-in-Trade Business Development Missions - ITA/U.S. Department of Commerce-Organized by Trade Development, Office of Export Promotion Coordination, Women-in-Trade Business Development Missions fall into the category of commercial missions. These missions, which emphasize small-to-medium sized women-owned or women-managed firms, are typically comprised of ten to twelve companies representing a mixture of product and service industries. These missions follow the same format as those described above in trade missions.

Contact: Phone (202) 482-5479, Loretta Allison, Project Manager, Office of Export Promotion Coordination
Fax (202) 482-1999
E-mail: loretta_allison@ita.doc.gov

Multi-State/Catalog Exhibitions Program - ITA/U.S. Department of Commerce-This program showcases U.S. company product literature in fast-growing markets within a geographic region. The U.S. Department of Commerce and representatives from state development agencies present product literature to hundreds of interested business prospects abroad and send the trade leads directly to U.S. participants.

Contact: Phone (202) 482-3973, Nancy Hesser, Export Promotion Services
Fax (202) 482-2718
Internet home page: http://www.ita.doc.gov/uscs/uscsmsc.html

Matchmaker Trade Delegations - ITA/U.S. Department of Commerce-The Matchmaker Trade Delegation Program, a variant of commercial missions, is designed to match small- to medium-sized new-to-market or new-to-export U.S. firms with qualified business contacts abroad. Each mission targets major markets in two or three countries that have strong potential for U.S. goods and services. Delegation members travel to each country and benefit from export counseling, interpreter service and logistics support, market research, in-depth market briefings, and a personalized itinerary of business appointments screened by commercial specialists at U.S. embassies and consulates.

Contact: Phone (202) 482-0692, Molly Costa, Export Promotion Services
Fax (202) 482-0178
Internet home page: http://www.ita.doc.gov/exportmatch/

Product Literature Centers - ITA/U.S. Department of Commerce-This program showcases U.S. company product literature through exhibits in international trade shows held in both mature and emerging markets. The Product Literature Center is a low cost, efficient way for small- and medium-sized firms to get worldwide sales leads in their particular industry. A Trade Development industry/international specialist operates the Product Literature Center. Visitors to the Product Literature Center are required to register, and may take company literature with them. All sales leads are sent directly to the Product Literature Center participant.

Contact: For more information on product literature centers, contact the Trade Information Center at 1-800-USA-TRAD(E) (1-800-872-8723), which will refer you to the appropriate Trade Development industry specialist.

Other Trade Contact Services

U.S. Embassies and Consulates - U.S. and Foreign Commercial Service (Department of Commerce); Department of State; Foreign Agricultural Service (FAS); U.S. Information Service (USIS)-The Commerce Department's U.S. and Foreign Commercial Service officers are present in U.S. embassies in 70 leading export markets. They collect information about trends and barriers to trade in their representative countries. Commercial Service officers also identify trade and investment opportunities, which are then transmitted to U.S. businesses.

Department of State commercial and economic staffs provide political and economic briefings and advice on the business culture and practices of the host country to U.S. firms. Their Foreign Service officers are responsible for commercial work in 96 embassies and 36 consulates not covered by the Commercial Service, and they work closely with their Commercial Service colleagues worldwide.

The Foreign Agricultural Service maintains more than 60 overseas offices to represent the interests of U.S. agriculture, carry out market promotion, and collect information pertaining to agricultural trade. Most of these offices are located in U.S. embassies. In addition, the Foreign Agricultural Service maintains 20 overseas agricultural trade offices to assist exporters of U.S. farm and forest products in key overseas markets. The office facilities vary depending on local conditions, but may include a trade library, conference rooms, office space, and kitchens for preparing product samples.

The U.S. Information Service (USIS) is the overseas arm of the U.S. Information Agency (USIA). USIS posts overseas work closely with their colleagues in other mission elements to provide business assistance though policy advocacy, trade fairs, trade missions, and business information centers. The USIA's Foreign Press Centers in Washington, New York, and Los Angeles provide frequent briefings for resident foreign journalists with U.S. officials on trade policy and trade promotion. USIA has also sent out over 100 U.S. speakers on trade and business in the last two years to lecture and give seminars abroad under U.S. embassy auspices. USIS-organized press events abroad result in frequent coverage in major foreign media of U.S. positions on trade. USIS officers in embassies generally initiate programs.

Contact: State Department operator, (202) 647-4000; AgExport Services Division, (202) 720-7420; or call 1-800-USA-TRAD(E) (1-800-872-8723).

USIA programs and contacts can be found on the Internet at: http://www.usia.gov

Office of Citizen Exchange - U.S. Information Agency (USIA)- The U.S. Information Agency designs and develops exchange programs to encourage market-based economic development. It funds programs conducted by U.S. nonprofit organizations that work with international leaders, including young professionals. All grants are made to American nonprofit organizations. One program, Community Connections brings young entrepreneurs from the Newly Independent States, local government officials, and legal professionals to the United States for practical internships.

Contact: Phone (202) 619-5348
Fax (202) 619-4350
E-mail: citex@usia.gov
Internet home page: http://www.usia.gov/education/citizens/citizens.htm

U.S. Commercial Centers - ITA/U.S. Department of Commerce- A model of public-private partnerships, overseas Commercial Centers house state export development agencies, industry associations, government agencies, and other strategic partners. The U.S. Commercial Centers represent highly integrated business networks that leverage resources and extend the range of public-private support available in one location.

Commercial Centers provide an ideal base for U.S. companies to track down business leads, close deals with the full support of hands-on U.S. government advocacy, gain a first-hand perspective on market conditions and local business practices, find and assess reliable business partners, host a reception of potential business partners, stage technical seminars, launch new products/services, or even set up a permanent office. The direct access to both Commercial Service trade promotion staff and programs as well as business facilities (including fully-equipped offices, meeting rooms, exhibit space, etc.) in one location makes the Commercial Centers particularly useful to small and medium-size companies, for whom cost constraints or availability of export counseling pose the biggest hurdles to exporting.

To maximize their ability to help U.S. exporters, Commercial Centers are located in Big Emerging Markets that offer the most promising business opportunities, and in cities that represent an existing or emerging commercial hub for the entire economic region. They are strategically found outside U.S. chanceries or consulates in the heart of primary business districts, where U.S. companies need to be, closer to prospective business partners.

U.S. Commercial Center - Sao Paulo, Brazil - The first U.S. Commercial Center, Sao Paulo has built a strong base for expanding public-private partnerships and fostering interagency cooperation.

Contact: Phone (011) 55-11-853-2811, Alan Long, Director, U.S. Commercial Center, Sao Paulo, Brazil
Fax (011) 55-11-3068-0323
E-mail: ALong@doc.gov
Internet homepage: http://www.ita.doc.gov/uscs/ccsnpaul.html

U.S. Commercial Center - Jakarta, Indonesia - The Jakarta Commercial Center houses the California Trade and Commerce Agency, the Foreign Agricultural Service's Agricultural Trade Office, and the U.S.-Asia Environmental Partnership.

Contact: Phone (011) 62-21-344-2211, Laron Jensen, Director
Fax (011) 62-21-385-1632
E-mail: LJensen1@doc.gov
Internet homepage: http://www.ita.doc.gov/uscs/ccjakrta.html

U.S. Commercial Center - Shanghai, China - Placing the Commercial Center in Shanghai, the financial hub of all of China, positions U.S. companies to compete in the entire Chinese economic area. The U.S. Commercial Center in Shanghai houses state development economic offices from Maryland, Michigan, and Washington.

Contact: Phone 86-21-6279-7630, Will Center, Director
Fax 86-21-6279-7639
Portman Shanghai Centre, Suite 631, 1369 Nanjing Road West, Shanghai 200040, China
Internet homepage: http://www.ita.doc.gov/uscs/ccshnghi.html

***Doing Business* Television Program - U.S. Information Agency-** The half-hour long monthly televised business program is sent by satellite in several languages to more than 100 countries, highlighting innovation and excellence in U.S. business. The program consists of segments on new products, services, and processes of interest to overseas buyers.

Contact: Phone (202) 401-8173, Patrick Hayden, Worldnet TV
Fax (202) 401-8270

Financing, Insurance & Tax Programs

Export Financing Hotline - Export-Import Bank of the United States (Eximbank)-Through its special toll-free number, the Export-Import Bank provides information on its export credit insurance and pre-export financing through working capital guaranteed loans, and medium and long-term loans and guarantees to overseas buyers. Information is accessible through e-mail, from a fax system, on the Eximbank Internet home page, and on a bulletin board service. Eximbank offers briefing programs to the business community, including regular seminars and group briefings offered both at Eximbank and at locations around the country.

Contact: Phone 1-800-565-3946, (202) 565-3946 (Alaska, Hawaii, and District of Columbia)
Fax retrieval: 1-800-565-EXIM, press 1, press 2
E-mail: bdg@exim.gov
Internet: http://www.exim.gov

City-State Program - Export-Import Bank-Eximbank works with state and local government agencies to offer export counseling and financial assistance to businesses in their jurisdictions. Cooperative programs currently operate in more than 30 states and regions and in Puerto Rico.

Contact: Phone (202) 565-3935, Joyce Papes, Marketing Officer
Fax (202) 565-3932

Regional Offices - Export-Import Bank-Eximbank regional offices provide services to businesses interested in Eximbank programs. Regional offices are in New York, Miami, Chicago, Houston, and Los Angeles. Eximbank is also represented at each of the U.S. Export Assistance Centers (USEACs).

Contact: New York:
6 World Trade Center, Suite 635
New York, NY 10048
Phone (212) 466-2950
Fax (212) 466-2959

Miami:
5600 NW 36th Street, Suite 617
Miami, FL 33159
Phone (305) 526-7425
Fax (305) 526-7435

Chicago:
55 W. Monroe St., Suite 2440
Chicago, IL 60603
Phone (312) 353-8040
Fax (312) 353-8098

Houston:
1880 South Dairy Ashford, Suite 585
Houston, TX 77077
Phone (713) 589-8182
Fax (713) 589-8184

Los Angeles:
1 World Trade Center, Suite 1670
Los Angeles, CA 90831
Phone (310) 980-4580
Fax (310) 980-4590

For the addresses and telephone numbers of the USEACs call 1-800-USA-TRAD(E) (1-800-872-8723).

Working Capital Guarantee Program - Export-Import Bank-The Working Capital Guarantee Program helps small and medium-size businesses obtain critical pre-export financing from commercial lenders. Eximbank will guarantee 90 percent of the principal and interest on loans or revolving lines of credit that are extended to eligible exporters. The funds may be used for pre-export activities, which include the purchase of raw materials and foreign marketing.

Contact: Phone (202) 565-3900, International Business
Development, or Regional Offices
Fax (202) 565-3931
Internet: http://www.exim.gov

Export Credit Insurance - Export-Import Bank-Eximbank offers insurance that covers political and commercial risks on export receivables:

The Small Business Policy is available to firms just beginning to export or with average annual export credit sales of less than $2 million for the past two years. These businesses must also meet SBA guidelines for the definition of a small business. The policy offers enhanced coverage and a lower premium than usually found in regular insurance policies.

The Umbrella Policy is available to commercial lenders, state agencies, export trading companies, and similar organizations to insure export receivables of their small-business clients.

The Bank Letter of Credit Policy insures commercial banks against loss on irrevocable letters of credit issued by foreign banks for U.S. exporters.

The Multi-Buyer Policy insures all or a reasonable spread of an exporters short- or medium-term export credit sales.

The Financial Institution Buyer Credit Policy insures individual short-term export credits extended by financial institutions to foreign buyers.

The Short-Term Single-Buyer Policy and the Medium-Term Single-Buyer Policy allow exporters to insure their receivables against loss due to commercial and specified political risks on a selective basis.

Lease Insurance Policies offer a leasor the opportunity to expand its overseas leasing program by providing comprehensive insurance for both the stream of lease payments and the fair market value of the leased products.

Contact: Phone (202) 565-3900, International Business
Development, or Regional Offices
Fax (202) 565-3931
Internet: http://www.exim.gov

Direct Loans and Guarantees - Export-Import Bank-This program extends direct loans to foreign buyers or guarantees to financing intermediaries for creditworthy entities who purchase capital goods or services. The loans and guarantees offered are for up to 85 percent of the U.S. export value. Direct loans provide competitive fixed-rate financing to the foreign buyer. The guarantee coverage provides protection to the finance source against payment default for either political or commercial reasons. Interest rates for the guarantees are negotiated between the finance source and the seller and are typically floating rates. Political only guarantee coverage is available. In addition, Eximbank is willing to provide support for a broad range of environmental exports. There are specialized transaction structures for certain lease transactions, industrial design, architectural or engineering services, and overseas operations and maintenance contracts.

Contact: Phone (202) 565-3900, International Business
Development, or Regional Offices
Fax (202) 565-3931
Internet: http://www.exim.gov

Limited Resource Project Finance Program - Export-Import Bank-The Limited Resource Project Finance Program provides financing for projects that are dependent on the cash flows of the project for repayment rather than on the credit strength of a purchaser. Combinations of either direct loans or guarantees for commercial bank loans with political risk only or comprehensive coverage is available for a given project. During the construction period, Eximbank will provide guarantees to cover only political risk, and will finance up to 85 percent of the export value. Eximbank offerings also include: financing of interest accrued during construction, financing of host country local costs of up to 15 percent of the U.S. contract value, and maximum repayment terms under OECD guidelines.

Contact: Phone (202) 565-3900, International Business
Development, or Regional Offices
Fax (202) 565-3931
Internet: http://www.exim.gov

7(a) Business Loan Guarantee Program - Small Business Administration (SBA)-SBA's 7(a) Program assists qualified small businesses to obtain financial assistance from banks. The Business Loan Guarantee Program provides the lender with a guarantee that if the borrower cannot repay the loan, the federal government will repay the loan up to the percentage of the SBA guarantee. Therefore, when a business applies for an SBA loan, they are applying for a commercial loan with an SBA guarantee.

SBA can make 7(a) loans to businesses engaged in manufacturing, construction, wholesale, retail, or service industries, and the proceeds may be used to acquire equipment, facilities, machinery, supplies or materials; to obtain working capital; to finance construction, conversion, or expansion; and to refinance most existing debt.

There are no limits on the total dollar amount of an SBA guaranteed loan, but the maximum dollar amount that SBA will guarantee is $750,000. The maximum maturity is 25 years; however, SBA expects all loans to be repaid as soon as possible. Therefore, maturity is based on the ability of the business to pay without hardship. Interest rates on SBA guarantee loans are negotiated between the applicant and the lender based on the credit merits of the request, subject to a maximum of prime plus 2.75 percent.

Contact: 1-800-U-ASK-SBA for the nearest SBA district office or
             U.S. Export Assistance Center
             Internet: http://www.sbaonline.sba.gov/oit

Export Working Capital Program (EWCP) - Small Business Administration (SBA)-The Export Working Capital Program provides short-term, transaction-specific financing for small business exporters. Exporters may use this program for pre-export financing of labor and materials, financing receivables generated from these sales, and standby letters of credit used as performance bonds or payment guarantees to foreign buyers. The EWCP provides repayment guarantees up to $750,000 to commercial lenders and offers exporters preliminary commitments (PCs) that encourage lenders to provide credit to small business exporters. The small business must be established for at least one year, though not necessarily engaged in exporting, to quality for the EWCP. Interest rates and fees are negotiable between the lender and the small business exporter.

Contact: 1-800-U-ASK-SBA for the nearest SBA district office or
             U.S. Export Assistance Center
             Internet: http://www.sbaonline.sba.gov/oit

International Trade Loan Guarantee Program - Small Business Administration (SBA)-The International Trade Loan Guarantee Program helps small businesses that are either new-to-export, already engaged in exporting and seeking to expand their operation, or adversely affected by competition from imports. SBA guarantees up to $1.25 million, less the amount of SBA's guaranteed portion of other loans outstanding, to the borrower under SBA's regular lending program. Loans are made by lending institutions with the SBA guaranteeing a portion of the loan. Proceeds may be used for working capital and facilities or equipment. Maturities of loans for facilities or equipment may extend to the 25-year maximum.

Contact: 1-800-U-ASK-SBA for the nearest SBA district office or
             U.S. Export Assistance Center
             Internet: http://www.sbaonline.sba.gov/oit

Small Business Investment Companies - Small Business Administration (SBA)-Licensed by SBA, firms whose investment strategies include export activities may receive equity capital or term working capital in excess of SBA's $750,000 statutory limit.

Contact: Phone (202) 205-6510, Investment Division
             Internet: http://www.sba.gov/inv/

Multilateral Development Bank Operations (MDBO) - ITA/U.S. Department of Commerce-MDBO counsels U.S. firms about opportunities associated with funding by the World Bank, Asian, African, and Inter-American development banks, and the European Bank for Reconstruction and Development; ensures project information is available on a timely basis; and organizes and develops outreach programs throughout the United States. The development banks assist in financing social and economic infrastructure and privatization projects in developing countries. The liaison officers in each of these institutions are dedicated to the identification of these projects at the earliest possible stage. They provide in-depth counseling to U.S. firms on bank opportunities and advocate on behalf of U.S. firms.

Contact: MDBO (ITA)
             Janet Thomas, (202) 482-3399, fax (202) 273-0927

             World Bank
             Charles Kestenbaum (202) 458-0120, fax (202) 477-2967

             Inter-American Development Bank (IADB)
             Eric Weaver, (202) 623-3821, fax (202) 623-2039

African Development Bank
Mark Herrling, (225)-21-46-16, fax (225)-22-24-37
(Cote D'Ivoire)

Asian Development Bank
Cantwell Walsh, (632)-890-9364, fax (632)-890-9713
(Philippines)

European Bank for Reconstruction and Development
Dean Peterson, (44)-171-338-6569, fax (44)-171-338-6487 (United Kingdom)

Training Grants - U.S. Trade and Development Agency-The U.S. Trade and Development Agency has authority to offer training grants in support of short-listed companies on a transaction-specific basis. These grants frequently enable a company to cover the cost of training local personnel on the installation, operation, and maintenance of equipment specific to its bid proposal.

Contact: Phone (703) 875-4357, TDA Information Resource Center
             Fax (703) 875-4009
             Internet: http://www.tda.gov

Tax Programs

Foreign Sales Corporation (FSC) - U.S. Department of the Treasury-The Foreign Sales Corporation (FSC) rules of the Internal Revenue Code (26 U.S.C. 921-927) exempt from federal income taxes a portion of the export income channeled through corporations that qualify as FSCs. To satisfy these rules, U.S. tax law provides that a FSC must be a foreign corporation that has a foreign presence and meets foreign management requirements. Also, a FSC must satisfy certain foreign economic process requirements in order to earn the type of foreign income that is eligible for a partial tax exemption. If a U.S. corporation uses a FSC in selling products abroad, a portion of the foreign trade income of the FSC will be exempt from U.S. tax. The FSC program is generally available only for income from the sale or lease outside of the United States of goods manufactured in the United States.

Contact: Ann Fisher, Office of Tax Policy
             phone (202) 622-1755
             fax (202) 622-8784

             Jack Feldman, Office of the Associate Chief Counsel
             (International), Internal Revenue Service
             phone (202) 622-3830
             fax (202) 622-4408

Investment & Feasibility Studies

Automated Information Line - Overseas Private Investment Corporation (OPIC)-OPIC supports U.S. businesses that invest in developing countries and emerging market economies, creating U.S. jobs, exports, and promoting economic growth at home and abroad. In addition to fostering American global competitiveness, OPIC considers an investment=s impact on the U.S. economy, the environment, and rights of workers in the host country. The OPIC hotline responds to all preliminary inquiries or initial requests for information regarding OPIC programs and services. OPIC maintains a fax retrieval system with information on OPIC programs, project finance, and political risk insurance.

Contact: Phone (202) 336-8799
             Fax (202) 408-5155
             Fax retrieval (202) 336-8700
             Internet home page: http://www.opic.gov

Investment Insurance - Overseas Private Investment Corporation-
OPIC offers several programs to insure U.S. investments in emerging markets and developing countries against the risks of: 1) currency inconvertibility-the inability to convert profits, debt service, and other investment remittances from local currency into U.S. dollars, 2) expropriation-loss of an investment due to expropriation, nationalization, or confiscation by a foreign government, and 3) political violence-loss of assets or income due to war, revolution, insurrection, or civil strife. Coverage is available for new investments and for investments to expand or modernize existing operations. Equity, debt, loan guarantees, leases, and most other forms of long-term investment can be insured. Special programs are also available for contractors, exporters, and oil and gas projects.

Contact: Phone (202) 336-8799
Fax (202) 408-5155
Fax retrieval (202) 336-8700
Internet home page: http://www.opic.gov

Finance Programs - Overseas Private Investment Corporation-
Medium- to long-term financing for sound overseas investment projects is made available through loan guarantees and direct loans. Direct loans generally range from $2 million to $30 million and are reserved exclusively for projects significantly involving U.S. "small businesses" or cooperatives. Loan guarantees generally range from $10 million to $200 million. OPIC's financing commitment may range from 50 percent of total project costs for new ventures and up to 75 percent for expansion of existing successful operations, with final maturities of five to 12 years or more. Additionally, OPIC supports a family of privately managed direct investment funds in various regions and business sectors.

Contact: Phone (202) 336-8799
Fax (202) 408-5155
Fax retrieval (202) 336-8700
Internet home page: http://www.opic.gov

Feasibility Studies - U.S. Trade and Development Agency (TDA)-
A primary activity of the agency is the grant funding of feasibility studies, consultancies, and other project planning services for major projects in developing countries. The studies are conducted by U.S. private sector firms and represent a wide range of host government high priority sectors, including: agribusiness, educational technology, electronics, energy, minerals development, telecommunications, transportation, and waste management. Feasibility studies assess the economic, financial, and technical viability of a potential project. The host countries must hire U.S. firms to undertake the detailed studies of the technical and economic feasibility of the proposed projects. Applications for feasibility studies are accepted with host government endorsement.

Contact: Phone (703) 875-4357, TDA Information Resource Center
Fax (703) 875-4009
Internet home page: http://www.tda.gov

Technical Assistance Grants - U.S. Trade and Development Agency-The agency funds activities designed to bring U.S. technical assistance to bear on a variety of projects.

Contact: Phone (703) 875-4357, TDA Information Resource Center
Fax (703) 875-4009
Internet home page: http://www.tda.gov

Definitional Missions (DM) - U.S. Trade and Development Agency-After receiving a request to fund a major study for a new project, the agency hires a technically qualified U.S. consultant to visit the country and discuss the plan with the project sponsors. In addition to making recommendations as to whether the project should be funded, the definitional missions consultant works with the project sponsor to define the work program for the proposed feasibility study.

Contact: For a listing of current opportunities, contact the TDA Definitional Mission hotline, (703) 875-7447.

To be included in TDA's DM consultant list, contact Della Glenn, (703) 875-4357, fax (703) 875-4009.
E-mail: info@tda.gov
Internet home page: http://www.tda.gov

Trust Funds for U.S. Firms at the Multilateral Development Banks - U.S. Trade and Development Agency-The U.S. Trade and Development Agency maintains trust funds at six multilateral development banks (MDBs): the World Bank, the International Finance Corporation, the European Bank for Reconstruction and Development, the Inter-American Development Bank, and its private sector arm, the Inter-American Investment Corporation, and the African Development Bank. These funds can be used for technical assistance and for feasibility studies. Most are known as Evergreen Funds. TDA maintains a minimum balance that is readily available to fund project opportunities for U.S. firms or to help U.S. businesses take advantage of time-sensitive projects.

Since MDBs finance many of the capital projects in the developing world, TDA's close relationship with them is advantageous for the U.S. business community. In addition to the valuable project information gained through the MDBs, which TDA passes on to American firms, working with bank projects ensures that a potential funding source has been identified-a plus toward successful implementation.

Contact: Phone (703) 875-4357
Fax (703) 875-4009, Barbara Bradford
Internet home page: http://www.tda.gov

Agriculture Export Programs

U.S. Trade Assistance and Promotion Office (TAPO) - U.S. Department of Agriculture (USDA)-The Trade Assistance and Promotion Office of the Foreign Agricultural Service (FAS) serves as the first point of contact for businesses who need information on foreign markets for agricultural products. The TAPO staff provides basic export counseling and directs you to the appropriate USDA offices to answer your export-related questions. In addition, the staff supplies country and commodity specific Foreign Market Information Reports, which focus on best market prospects and contain contact information on distributors and importers. Extensive information on the Foreign Agricultural Service is also available through the FAS home page on the Internet.

Contact: Phone (202) 720-7420
Fax (202) 690-4374
Internet home page: http://www.fas.usda.gov

Agriculture Trade and Marketing Information Center (ATMIC) - U.S. Department of Agriculture-The Agriculture Trade and Marketing Information Center, part of the National Agricultural Library (NAL) of the Agricultural Research Service, serves as a clearinghouse of informational resources on agricultural marketing and trade. The staff responds to inquiries with customized assistance by combining subject expertise, state-of-the-art technology and networking. The National Agricultural Library staff also assists users in accessing the library's online systems and web sites: ISIS (Integrated System for Information Services), AGRICOLA (Agricultural Online Access database). To access ISIS via the Internet-telnet to: opac.nal.usda.gov. Enter ISIS (all caps) at the OPAC login prompt. National Agricultural Library web site: http://www.nal.usda.gov

Contact: Phone (301) 504-5509, Mary Lassanyi, Coordinator
Fax (301) 504-6409
E-mail: mlassany@nal.usda.gov
Reference Branch, 301-504-5204
Reference Desk, 301-504-5479
e-mail: agref@nal.usda.gov
Internet home page: http://www.usda.gov/atmic/

Economic Research Service (ERS) - U.S. Department of Agriculture-The Economic Research Service provides in-depth economic analysis on agricultural economies, trade policies of foreign countries, world agricultural trade and development issues, and on their linkages with the U.S. food and fiber economy. ERS analyzes how factors influencing demand (population, income, and tastes), production variables (inputs and technology), foreign governments' domestic and trade policies and programs (price controls, environmental and food safety laws, and tariffs), macroeconomic conditions (exchange rates and debt), and major events (breakup of the former Soviet Union), affect countries' agricultural production, consumption, and trade; international food and fiber prices; and U.S. food and fiber competitiveness. ERS widely disseminates information and analyses on international agricultural trade, and food aid and development through regional and commodity reports, bulletins and updates, periodicals, and electronic databases.

Contact: Phone (202) 219-0700, John Dunmore, Deputy Director,
             Commercial Agriculture Division
             Fax (202) 219-0759
             Internet home page: http://www.econ.ag.gov/

AgExport Connections - U.S. Department of Agriculture-The AgExport Action Kit provides information to U.S. businesses on the export programs available from AgExport Connections. The information is designed to put exporters of food, farm, forest, and seafood products in contact with foreign buyers. To receive a free copy of the Action Kit, call (202) 720-7103 or (202) 720-7420.

AgExport Connections manages four basic services that are available to exporters of U.S. food, farm, forest, and seafood products:

Trade Leads are foreign trade inquiries that the overseas offices of the Foreign Agricultural Service transmit electronically to the USDA. They are made available to U.S. exporters on a daily basis through the FAS Internet home page and the Department of Commerce's Electronic Bulletin Board. *Trade Leads* are also available through a Trade Leads Fax Polling System, various trade publications, and the various state departments of agriculture and trade development centers.

Buyer Alert is a biweekly newsletter, which can introduce your food, farm, forest, and seafood products to foreign buyers at only $15 per announcement. Advertisements for up to five products may be submitted for each announcement. *Buyer Alert* announcements are transmitted electronically to overseas offices of the Foreign Agricultural Service, which distributes the newsletter to more than 18,000 potential buyers in 65 countries.

Foreign Buyer Lists contain detailed contact information on more than 20,000 importers of food, farm, forest, and seafood products in 85 countries. Lists may be ordered by product or country at a cost of $15 each.

U.S. Supplier Lists may be used to source U.S. food, farm, forest, and seafood products for export. Nearly 4,000 firms are included in this database, which is also made available to foreign buyers through the overseas offices of the Foreign Agricultural Service. Lists may be ordered by product at a cost of $15 each.

Contact: Phone (202) 690-4172, Wendell Dennis,
             AgExport Connections
             Fax (202) 690-4374
             Internet home page: http://www.fas.usda.gov

Foreign Agricultural Service (FAS) - U.S. Department of Agriculture-The Foreign Agricultural Service maintains 15 overseas agricultural trade offices, in key overseas markets, to assist U.S. businesses engaged in the export of farm and forest products. The facilities vary depending on local conditions, but may include a trade library, conference rooms, office space, and kitchens for preparing product samples.

Contact: Phone (202) 720-6343, Agricultural Trade Office
             Coordinator
             Fax (202) 690-4374
             Internet home page: http://www.fas.usda.gov

Trade Shows - U.S. Department of Agriculture-The USDA Trade Show Office offers U.S. food and beverage exporters a choice of programs to satisfy their marketing needs. Programs include fully sponsored trade shows, sales missions, and endorsed shows in both leading markets and emerging markets worldwide. Fully sponsored trade shows consist of a package of services, which include a fully appointed booth, shipping of product samples, and educational programs. Sales missions include guaranteed appointments with interested buyers, orientation to the market, and translation services. In addition, the USDA Trade Show Office provides information on the promoters of other international food and beverage shows.

Contact: Phone (202) 690-1182, USDA Trade Show Office
             Fax (202) 690-4374
             Internet home page: http://www.fas.usda.gov

Market Access Program (MAP) - FAS/U.S. Department of Agriculture-The Market Access Program, formerly the Market Promotion Program, promotes a variety of U.S. agricultural commodities in almost every region of the world. Funds from the Commodity Credit Corporation are used to partially reimburse agricultural trade organizations conducting specific foreign market development projects on eligible products in specified countries. Applications for MAP programs are developed by agricultural trade organizations and private firms, and submitted to the Department of Agriculture by a deadline date specified in the program announcement. The deadline date is published annually in the *Federal Register*.

Contact: Phone (202) 720-4327, Marketing Operations Staff
             Fax (202) 720-9361
             Internet home page: http://fas.usda.gov/ffas/expprog.html

Commodity Credit Corporation Supplier Credit Guarantee Program (SCGP) - U.S. Department of Agriculture-The Commodity Credit Corporation's Supplier Credit Guarantee Program provides a guarantee, in the event of an importer's default, on a portion (currently 50 percent) of a U.S. exporter's open account receivable. U.S. exporters can purchase coverage for agricultural commodity or product sales where short-term (up to 180 days) credit has been extended directly to the importer. The payment obligation of the importer must be evidenced by a signed promissory note as prescribed by CCC. The SCGP emphasizes high-value or value-added agricultural commodities and consumer oriented products. Information regarding country and product eligibility and additional program details are available on the Foreign Agricultural Service's Internet home page.

Contact: CCC Operations Division, William Hawkins, (202) 720-
             3241 or Penny Stevenson, (202) 720-8639
             Fax (202) 720-0938
             Internet home page: http://www.fas.usda.gov

Rural Business-Cooperative Service - U.S. Department of Agriculture-Researches cooperative involvement in international trade and provides trade-related technical assistance to U.S. farmer-owned cooperatives.

Contact: Phone (202) 690-1428, Tracey Kennedy, International
             Trade Program
             Fax (202) 690-2723
             E-mail: tkennedy@rdasun2.rurdev.usda.gov

Food Safety and Technical Services - U.S. Department of Agriculture-Food Safety and Technical Services coordinates the Department of Agriculture activities that focus on food safety regulations and other technical issues, which may serve as barriers to international trade of U.S. agricultural products and commodities. The office also serves as the U.S. Sanitary and Phytosanitary Agreement (SPS) Enquiry Point for the World Trade Organization.

Contact: Phone (202) 720-1301, Office of Food Safety and
Technical Services
Fax (202) 690-0677
E-mail: ofsts@fas.usda.gov
Internet home page: http://www.fas.usda.gov

Transportation Publications and Resource Guidance - U.S. Department of Agriculture-The Transportation Publications and Resource Guidance Center provides publications and guidance to help agricultural exporters efficiently use transportation resources and maintain product quality in transit. A weekly grain transportation newsletter, monthly ocean container freight rate bulletin, a 10-year database of ocean freight costs for international grain shipments, and special reports are also available.

Contact: Phone (202) 690-1304, Jim Caron or SEA staff, Shipper
and Exporter Assistance Program
Fax (202) 690-1340
E-mail: jcaron@usda.gov
Internet home page: http://www.usda.gov/ams/
titlepag.htm

Inspection Certificates for Food and Agricultural Exports - U.S. Department of Agriculture-Several agencies within the Agriculture Department provide inspection services when certificates are required to clear imported products through overseas customs:

The Animal and Plant Health Inspection Service (APHIS) offers exporters information concerning health and sanitation standards for animals, plants, and agricultural products both entering and exiting the United States

Contact: Documents Management Branch, (301) 734-5524,
fax (301) 734-8455.

The Federal Grain Inspection Service (FGIS) provides inspections under the U.S. Grain Standards Act and the Agricultural Marketing Act. FGI also conducts mandatory inspections for all exported grain. Products examined by FGIS include rice, peas, beans, lentils, all grains, and grain-based processed products.

Contact: John Giler, Standards and Procedures Branch, (202)
720-0252, fax (202) 720-1015

The Food Safety and Inspection Service (FSIS) guarantees that meat and poultry products are properly labeled and U.S. inspected and approved.

Contact: Food Safety and Inspection Service, (202) 690-3752,
fax (202) 690-4633

Voluntary Food Quality Certification Service - U.S. Department of Agriculture-USDA's Agricultural Marketing Service, in cooperation with state agencies, offers official grading or inspection for quality of manufactured dairy products, poultry and eggs, meat, and fresh and processed fruits and vegetables. Grading is based on U.S. grade standards developed by the Department of Agriculture for these products.

Contact: Kenneth C. Clayton, Agricultural Marketing Service,
(202) 720-4276, fax (202) 720-8477, e-mail:
kyclayton@usda.gov Internet home page: http://
www.ams.usda.gov/index.htm

Food Quality Assurance Program - U.S. Department of Agriculture-This program manages and approves federal food product descriptions and establishes quality assurance policies and procedures applicable to food procurement by the U.S. Government.

Contact: Roger L. Luttrell, Food Quality Assurance Staff,
(202) 690-4938, fax (202) 690-0102, e-mail:
rluttrel@usda.gov Internet home page: http://
www.ams.usda.gov/index.htm

Inspection and Certification Services for Seafood Exports - National Oceanic and Atmospheric Administration/U.S. Department of Commerce-The National Marine Fisheries Service (NMFS), Inspection Services Division (ISD) is the primary U.S. federal agency that inspects and certifies fish and fishery products for export and issues official U.S. Government certificates attesting to the findings. These official sanitary certificates are recognized worldwide. In addition to inspection and certification of products, NMFS also provides consultative, laboratory, analytical, and training services, sanitation assessments of establishments, product grading, and a voluntary HACCP-based inspection program. The HACCP-based system has been recognized as equivalent to European Union requirements, and ISD also attempts to maintain the current hygienic-sanitary regulatory requirements of importing countries, thereby facilitating the importing country clearance of the exported shipments. The service also maintains liaison with the federal inspection counterparts in the foreign country to resolve sanitary-hygienic product issues that may occur. Additionally, ISD is an active participant in international agencies, such as Codex Alimentarius, that promote trade of foodstuffs and harmonization of international standards.

Contact: Phone (301) 713-2355, Richard V. Cano, National
Seafood Inspection Program
Fax (301) 713-1081
Internet home page: http://www.nmfs.gov/iss/
services.html

Office of Shipper and Exporter Assistance (SEA) - U.S. Department of Agriculture-SEA provides new and experienced agricultural exporters with the information they need to get their products overseas, on time, in good condition, and at the lowest cost. The center conducts export transportation seminars to teach new or prospective agricultural exporters how to transport their high-value or value-added food products overseas. These seminars cover an array of transportation issues such as finding a freight forwarder, selecting transportation options, packaging, container loading, and temperature management, and are held throughout the country.

Contact: Phone (202) 690-1304, Jim Caron or SEA staff, Shipper
and Exporter Assistance Program
Fax (202) 690-1340
E-mail: jcaron@usda.gov
Internet home page: http://www.ams.usda.gov/index.htm

Export Licenses & Controls

Bureau of Export Administration (BXA) - U.S. Department of Commerce-The Bureau of Export Administration provides export assistance on export licensing requirements through its Exporter Counseling Division (ECD). ECD interprets the Export Administration Regulations (EAR) and provides assistance such as: detailed and up-to-date status information on pending license applications; advice on a broad range of export issues, licensing requirements, required documentation for export transactions, special policy concerns for specific countries; assistance in selecting the appropriate license; and answers to inquiries regarding the Bureau of Export Administration policy issues and processing time frames.

ECD counselors can be an intermediary and arrange meetings between the exporters and BXA licensing officials. ECD also authorizes emergency processing on export applications. Cases meeting specific criteria are expedited through the licensing system. These cases are often approved within a few days of receipt of the application.

Throughout the year BXA provides introductory and advanced seminars across the United States.

Contact: Export Counseling Division, (202) 482-4811,
Room 1099C, Washington, D.C. 20230

Export Seminar Staff, (202) 482-6031,
Room 1099C, Washington, D.C. 20230
BXA Western Regional Office, (714) 660-0144,
3300 Irvin Ave., Suite 345, Newport Beach, CA 92660
Internet homepage: http://www.bxa.doc.gov

Office of Foreign Assets Control (OFAC) - U.S. Department of the Treasury-OFAC administers and enforces economic and trade sanctions against targeted foreign countries, terrorism-sponsoring organizations, and international narcotics traffickers based on U.S. foreign policy and national security goals. OFAC publishes an extensive list of "Specially Designated Nationals and Blocked Persons" with whom U.S. persons may not deal. Also available are fact sheets for each of the sanctions programs ("What You Need to Know About the U.S. Embargo"), and a booklet, "Foreign Assets Control Regulations for Exporters and Importers." OFAC publications are available through several programs of the U.S. Department of Commerce discussed elsewhere in this brochure, including: the Economic Bulletin Board (EBB), the STAT-USA/Internet web site, the National Trade Data Bank CD-ROM service, and the STAT-USA/FAX automated fax-on-demand service. Exporters should contact OFAC's compliance staff to obtain hard copies of OFAC publications or get answers to specific questions about export restrictions.

Contact: Phone (202) 622-2490, Judith Klock, Lorraine Lawlor, or Dennis Wood, Compliance Programs Division
Fax (202) 622-1657
24 hour fax retrieval service, (202) 622-0077
Internet home page: http://www.ustreas.gov/services/fac/fac.html

Office of Defense Trade Controls - U.S. Department of State-The Office of Defense Trade Controls implements the International Traffic in Arms Regulations (ITAR) and the U.S. Munitions List (USML) regulating the export of U.S. defense articles, services, and related technical data. The Arms Licensing Division receives, evaluates, and adjudicates export license applications for items regulated under the ITAR and USML.

Contact: Phone (703) 875-6644, Arms Licensing Division
Fax (703) 875-6647
24 hour fax retrieval service, (202) 622-0077

Questions regarding compliance with the ITAR maybe addressed to the Compliance and Enforcement Branch:

(703) 875-6650
fax (703) 875-5663.
Internet home page: http://www.pmdtc.org

Export regulations

Although export licensing is a basic part of exporting, it is one of the most widely misunderstood aspects of government regulations for exporting. The export licensing procedure may appear complex at first, but in most cases it is a rather straightforward process. Exporters should remember, however, that violations of the Export Administration Regulations (EAR) carry both civil and criminal penalties. Export controls are administered by the Bureau of Export Administration (BXA) in the U.S. Department of Commerce. Whenever there is any doubt about how to comply with export regulations, Department of Commerce officials or qualified professional consultants should be contacted for assistance.

The EAR are available by subscription from the Superintendent of Documents, U.S. Government Printing Office, Washington, D.C. 20401; telephone 202/512-1800. Subscription forms may be obtained from local Commerce Department district offices or from the Office of Export Licensing, Exporter Counseling Division, Room 1099D, U.S. Department of Commerce, Washington, D.C. 20230; telephone 202/482-2000.

Types of license

Export License

For reasons of national security, foreign policy, or short supply, the United States controls the export and reexport of goods and technical data through the granting of two types of export license: general licenses and individually validated licenses (IVLs). There are also special licenses that are used if certain criteria are met, for example, distribution, project, and service supply. Except for U.S. territories and possessions and, in most cases, Canada, all items exported from the United States require an export license. Several agencies of the U.S. government are involved in the export license procedure.

General License

A general license is a broad grant of authority by the government to all exporters for certain categories of products. Individual exporters do not need to apply for general licenses, since such authorization is already granted through the EAR; they only need to know the authorization is available.

Individually Validated License

An IVL is a specific grant of authority from the government to a particular exporter to export a specific product to a specific destination if a general license is not available. The licenses are granted on a case-by-case basis for either a single transaction or for many transactions within a specified period of time. An exporter must apply to the Department of Commerce for an IVL. One exception is munitions, which require a Department of State application and license. Other exceptions are listed in the EAR.

Determining which license to use

The first step in complying with the export licensing regulations is to determine whether a product requires a general license or an IVL. The determination is based on what is being exported and its destination. The determination is a three-step procedure:

1. *Determine the destination.* Check the schedule of country groups in the EAR (15 CFR Part 770, Supp. 1) to see under which country group the export destination falls.

2. *Determine the export control commodity number (ECCN).* All dual-use items (items used for both military and civilian purposes) are in one of several categories of commodities controlled by the Department of Commerce. To determine what ECCN applies to a particular commodity, see the Commodity Control List in the EAR (15 CFR Part 799.1, Supp. 1).

3. *Determine what destinations require an IVL.* Refer to the specified ECCN in Part 799.1 of the EAR. Look under the paragraph "Validated License Required" to check which country groups require an IVL. If the country group in question is not listed there, no IVL is required. If it is listed there, an IVL is required unless the commodity meets one of the technical exceptions cited under the ECCN.

To avoid confusion, the exporter is strongly advised to seek assistance in determining the proper license. The best source is the Department of Commerce's Exporter Counseling Division. Telephone or write to Exporter Counseling Division, Room 1099D, U.S. Department of Commerce, Washington, D.C. 20230; telephone 202/482-2000. Or the exporter may check with the local Commerce district office. An exporter can also request a preliminary, written commodity classification opinion from the Office of Technology and Policy Analysis, U.S. Department of Commerce, P.O. Box 273, Washington, D.C. 20044.

Shipments under a general license

If, after reviewing the EAR or after consulting with the Department of Commerce, it is determined that an IVL is not required, an exporter may ship its product under a general license.

A general license does not require a specific application. Exporters who are exporting under a general license must determine whether a *destination control statement* is required. (See the "Antidiversion, Antiboycott, and Antitrust Requirements" subdivision of this section.)

Finally, if the shipment is destined for a free-world destination and is valued at more than $2,500 or requires a validated export license, the exporter must complete a shipper's export declaration (SED). SEDs are used by Customs to indicate the type of export license being used and to keep track of what is exported. They are also used by the Bureau of Census to compile statistics on U.S. trade patterns.

Shipments under an individually validated license

If an IVL is required, the U.S. exporter must prepare a Form BXA-622P, "Application for Export License," and submit it to BXA. The applicant must be certain to follow the instructions on the form carefully. In some instances, technical manuals and support documentation must also be included.

If the application is approved, a Validated Export License is mailed to the applicant. The license contains an export authorization number that must be place on the SED. Unlike some goods exported under a general license, all goods exported under an IVL must be accompanied by an SED.

The final step in complying with the IVL procedure is recordkeeping. The exporter must keep records of all shipments against an IVL. All documents related to an export application should be retained for five years. Section 787.13 of the EAR covers recordkeeping requirements.

Avoiding Delays in Receiving an Individually Validated License

In filling out license applications, exporters commonly make four errors that account for most delays in processing applications:

1. Failing to sign the application.

2. Handwriting, rather than typing, the application.

3. Responding inadequately to section 9b of the application, "Description of Commodity or Technical Data," which calls for a description of the item or items to be exported. The applicant must be specific and is encouraged to attach additional material to explain the product fully.

4. Responding inadequately to section 12 of the application, where the specific end use of the products or technical data is to be described. Again, the applicant must be specific. Answering vaguely or entering "Unknown" is likely to delay the application process.

In an emergency, the Department of Commerce may consider expediting the processing of an IVL application, but this procedure cannot be used as a substitute for the timely filing of an application. An exporting firm that feels it qualifies for emergency handling should contact the Exporter Counseling Division.

Additional Documentation

Certain applications for an IVL must be accompanied by supporting documents supplied by the prospective purchaser or the government of the country of ultimate destination. By reviewing Part 775 of the EAR, the exporter can determine whether any supporting documents are required.

The most common supporting documents are the *international import certificate* and the *statement of ultimate consignee and purchaser*. The international import certificate (Form ITA-645P/ATF-4522/DSP-53) is a statement issued by the government of the country of destination that certifies that the imported products will be disposed of responsibly in the designated country. It is the responsibility of the exporter to notify the consignee to obtain the certificate. The import certificate should be retained in the U.S. exporter's files, and a copy should be submitted with the IVL application.

The statement of ultimate consignee and purchaser (BXA Form 629P) is a written assurance that the foreign purchaser of the goods will not resell or dispose of goods in a manner contrary to the export license under which the goods were originally exported. The exporter must send the statement to the foreign consignee and purchaser for completion. The exporter then submits this form along with the export license application.

In addition to obtaining the appropriate export license, U.S. exporters should be careful to meet all other international trade regulations established by specific legislation or other authority of the U.S. government. The import regulations of foreign countries must also be taken into account. The exporter should keep in mind that even if help is received with the license and documentation from others, such as banks, freight forwarders or consultants, the exporter remains responsible for ensuring that all statements are true and accurate.

Antidiversion, antiboycott, & antitrust requirements

Antidiversion clause

To help ensure that U.S. exports go only to legally authorized destinations, the U.S. government requires a destination control statement on shipping documents. Under this requirement, the commercial invoice and bill of lading (or air waybill) for nearly all commercial shipments leaving the United States must display a statement notifying the carrier and all foreign parties (the ultimate and intermediate consignees and purchaser) that the U.S. material has been licensed for export only to certain destinations and may not be diverted contrary to U.S. law. Exceptions to the use of the destination control statement are (1) shipments to Canada and intended for consumption in Canada and (2) shipments being made under certain general license. Advice on the appropriate statement to be used can be provided by the Department of Commerce, the Commerce district office, an attorney, or the freight forwarder.

Antiboycott regulations

The United States has an established policy of opposing restrictive trade practices or boycotts fostered or imposed by foreign countries against other countries friendly to the United States. This policy is implemented through the antiboycott provisions of the Export Administration Act enforced by the Department of Commerce and through the Tax Reform Act of 1977 enforced by the Department of the Treasury.

In general, these laws prohibit U.S. persons from participating in foreign boycotts or taking actions that further or support such boycotts. The antiboycott regulations carry out this general purpose by

• prohibiting U.S. persons from refusing to do business with blacklisted firms and boycotted friendly countries pursuant to foreign boycott demands;

• prohibiting U.S. persons from discriminating against other U.S. persons on the basis of race, religion, sex, or national origin in order to comply with a foreign boycott;

• prohibiting U.S. persons from furnishing information about their business relationships with blacklisted friendly foreign countries or blacklisted companies in response to boycott requirements;

• prohibiting U.S. persons from appearing to perform any of these prohibited acts;

• providing for public disclosure of requests to comply with foreign boycotts; and

• requiring U.S. persons who receive requests to comply with foreign boycotts to disclose publicly whether they have complied with such requests.

The antiboycott provisions of the Export Administration Act apply to all U.S. persons, including intermediaries in the export process, as well as foreign subsidiaries that are "controlled in fact" by U.S. companies and U.S. officials.

The Department of Commerce's Office of Antiboycott Compliance (OAC) administers the program through ongoing investigations of corporate activities. OAC operates an automated boycott-reporting system providing statistical and enforcement data to Congress and to the public, issuing interpretations of the regulations for the affected public, and offering nonbinding informal guidance to the private sector on specific compliance concerns. U.S. firms with questions about complying with antiboycott regulations should call OAC at 202/482-2381 or write to Office of Antiboycott Compliance, Bureau of Export

Administration, Room 6098, U.S. Department of Commerce, Washington, D.C. 20230.

Antitrust laws

The U.S. antitrust laws reflect this nation's commitment to an economy based on competition. They are intended to foster the efficient allocation of resources by providing consumers with goods and services at the lowest price that efficient business operations can profitably offer. Various foreign countries - including the EC, Canada, the United Kingdom, Federal Republic of Germany, Japan, and Australia - also have their own antitrust laws that U.S. firms must comply with when exporting to such nations.

The U.S. antitrust statutes do not provide a checklist of specific requirements. Instead they set forth broad principles that are applied to the specific facts and circumstances of a business transaction. Under the U.S. antitrust laws, some types of trade restraints, known as per se violations, are regarded as conclusively illegal. Per se violations include price-fixing agreements and conspiracies, divisions of markets by competitors, and certain group boycotts and tying arrangements.

Most restraints of trade in the United States are judged under a second legal standard known as the *rule of reason*. The rule of reason requires a showing that (1) certain acts occurred and (2) such acts had an anticompetitive effect. Under the rule of reason, various factors are considered, including business justification, impact on prices and output in the market, barriers to entry, and market shares of the parties.

In the case of exports by U.S. firms, there are special limitations on the application of the per se and rule of reason tests by U.S. courts. Under Title IV of the Export Trading Company Act (also known as the Foreign Trade Antitrust Improvements Act), there must be a "direct, substantial and reasonably foreseeable" effect on the domestic or import commerce of the United States or on the export commerce of a U.S. person before an activity may be challenged under the Sherman Antitrust Act or the Federal Trade Commission Act (two of the primary federal antitrust statutes). This provision clarifies the particular circumstances under which the overseas activities of U.S. exporters may be challenged under these two antitrust statutes. Under Title III of the Export Trading Company Act, the Department of Commerce, with the concurrence of the U.S. Department of Justice, can issue an export trade certificate of review that provides certain limited immunity from the federal and state antitrust laws.

Although the great majority of international business transactions do not pose antitrust problems, antitrust issues may be raised in various types of transactions, among which are

•overseas distribution arrangements;

•overseas joint ventures for research, manufacturing, construction, and distribution;

•patent, trademark, copyright, and know-how licenses;

•mergers and acquisitions involving foreign firms; and

•raw material procurement agreements and concessions.

Where potential U.S. or foreign antitrust issues are raised, it is advisable to obtain the advice and assistance of qualified antitrust counsel.

For particular transactions that pose difficult antitrust issues, and for which an export trade certificate of review is not desired, the Antitrust Division of the Department of Justice can be asked to state its enforcement views in a *business review letter*. The business review procedure is initiated by writing a letter to the Antitrust Division describing the particular business transaction that is contemplated and requesting the department's views on the antitrust legality of the transaction.

Certain aspects of the federal antitrust laws and the Antitrust Division's enforcement policies regarding international transactions are explored in the Department of Justice's *Antitrust Enforcement Guidelines for International Operations* (1988).

Foreign Corrupt Practices Act (FCPA)

The FCPA makes it unlawful for any person or firm (as well as persons acting on behalf of the firm) to offer, pay, or promise to pay (or to authorize any such payment or promise) money or anything of value to any foreign official (or foreign political party or candidate for foreign political office) for the purpose of obtaining or retaining business. *Knowing* includes the concepts of *conscious disregard* and *willful blindness*. The FCPA also contains provisions applicable to publicly held companies concerning financial recordkeeping and internal accounting controls.

The Department of Justice enforces the criminal provisions of the FCPA and the civil provisions against "domestic concerns." The Securities and Exchange Commission (SEC) is responsible for civil enforcement against "issuers." The Department of Commerce supplies general information to U.S. exporters who have questions about the FCPA and about international developments concerning the FCPA.

There is an exception to the antibribery provisions for "facilitating payments for routine governmental action." Actions "similar" to the examples listed in the statute are also covered by this exception. A person charged with violating the FCPA's antibribery provisions may assert as a defense that the payment was lawful under the written laws and regulations of the foreign country or that the payment was associated with demonstrating a product or performing a contractual obligation.

Firms are subject to a fine of up to $2 million. Officers, directors, employees, agents, and stockholders are subject to a fine of up to $100,000 and imprisonment for up to five years. The U.S. attorney general can bring a civil action against a domestic concern (and the SEC against an issuer) for a fine of up to $10,000 as well as against any officer, director, employee, or agent of a firm or stockholder acting on behalf of the firm, who willfully violates the antibribery provisions. Under federal criminal law other than the FCPA, individuals may be fined up to $250,000 or up to twice the amount of gross gain or gross loss if the defendant derives pecuniary gain from the offense or causes a pecuniary loss to another person.

The attorney general (and the SEC, where appropriate) may also bring a civil action to enjoin any act or practice whenever it appears that the person or firm (or a person acting on behalf of a firm) is in violation or about to be in violation of the antibribery provisions.

A person or firm found in violation of the FCPA may be barred from doing business with the federal government. Indictment alone can lead to a suspension of the right to do business with the government.

Conduct that constitutes a violation of the FCPA may give rise to a private cause of action under the Racketeer-Influenced and Corrupt Organizations Act.

The Department of Justice has established an FCPA opinion procedure to replace the former FCPA review procedure. The details of the opinion procedure are provided in 28 CFR Part 77 (1991). Under the opinion procedure, any party is able to request a statement of the Department of Justice's present enforcement intentions under the antibribery provisions of the FCPA regarding any proposed business conduct. Conduct for which Justice has issued an opinion stating that the conduct conforms with current enforcement policy is entitled in any enforcement action to a presumption of conformity with the FCPA.

Food and Drug Administration (FDA) & Environmental Protection Agency (EPA) restrictions

In addition to the various export regulations that have been discussed, rules and regulations enforced by the FDA and EPA also affect a limited number of exporters.

Food and Drug Administration

FDA enforces U.S. laws intended to assure the consumer that foods are pure and wholesome, that drugs and devices are safe and effective, and that cosmetics are safe. FDA has promulgated a wide range of regulation to enforce these goals. Exporters of products covered by FDA's regulations are affected as follows:

•If the item is intended for export only, meets the specifications of the foreign purchaser, is not in conflict with the laws of the country to which it is to be shipped, and is properly labeled, it is exempt from the adulteration and misbranding provisions of the Federal Food, Drug, and Cosmetic Act (see 801(e)). This exemption does not apply to "new drugs" or "new animal drugs" that have not been approved as safe and effective or to certain devices.

•If the exporter thinks the export product may be covered by FDA, it is important to contact the nearest FDA field office or the Public Health Service, Food and Drug Administration, 5600 Fishers Lane, Rockville, MD 20857.

Environmental Protection Agency

EPA's involvement in exports is limited to hazardous waste, pesticides, and toxic chemicals. Although EPA has no authority to prohibit the export of these substances, it has an established notification system designed to inform receiving foreign governments that materials of possible human health concern will be entering their country.

Under the Resource Conservation and Recovery Act, generators of waste who wish to export waste considered hazardous are required to notify EPA before shipping a given hazardous waste to a given foreign consignee. EPA then notifies the government of the foreign consignee. Export cannot occur until written approval is received from the foreign government.

As for pesticides and other toxic chemicals, neither the Federal Insecticide, Fungicide, and Rodenticide Act nor the Toxic Substances Control Act requires exporters of banned or severely restricted chemicals to obtain written consent before shipping. However, exporters of unregistered pesticides or other chemicals subject to regulatory control actions must comply with certain notification requirements.

An exporter of hazardous waste, unregistered pesticides, or toxic chemicals should contact the Office of International Activities, U.S. Environmental Protection Agency, 401 M Street, S.W., Washington, D.C. 20460; telephone 202/260-4870.

Import regulations of foreign governments

Import documentation requirements and other regulations imposed by foreign governments vary from country to country. It is vital that exporters be aware of the regulations that apply to their own operations and transactions. Many governments, for instance, require consular invoices, certificates of inspection, health certification, and various other documents.

Customs benefits for exporters

Drawback of customs duties

Drawback is a form of tax relief in which a lawfully collected customs duty is refunded or remitted wholly or in part because of the particular use made of the commodity on which the duty was collected. U.S. firms that import materials or components that they process or assemble for reexport may obtain drawback refunds of all duties paid on the imported merchandise, less 1 percent to cover customs costs. This practice encourages U.S. exporters by permitting them to compete in foreign markets without the handicap of including in their sales prices the duties paid on imported components.

The Trade and Tariff Act of 1984 revised and expanded drawbacks. Regulations implementing the act have been promulgated in 19 CFR Part 191. Under existing regulations several types of drawback have been authorized, but only three are of interest to most manufacturers:

1. If articles manufactured in the United Sates with the use of imported merchandise are exported, then the duties paid on the imported merchandise that was used may be refunded as drawback (less 1 percent).

2. If both imported merchandise and domestic merchandise of the same kind and quality are used to manufacture articles, some of which are exported, then duties that were paid on the imported merchandise are refundable as drawback, regardless of whether that merchandise was used in the exported articles.

3. If articles of foreign origin imported for consumption after December 28, 1980, are exported from the United States or are destroyed under the supervision of U.S. Customs within three years of the date of importation, in the same condition as when imported and without being "used" in the United States, then duties that were paid on the imported merchandise (less 1 percent) are refundable as drawback. Incidental operations on the merchandise (such as testing, cleaning, repacking, or inspection) are not considered to be "uses" of the article.

To obtain drawback, the U.S. firm must file a proposal with a regional commissioner of customs (for the first type of drawback) or with the Entry Rulings Branch, U.S. Customs Headquarters, at the address in the following paragraph (for other types of drawback). These offices may also provide a model drawback proposal for the U.S. company.

Drawback claimants must establish that the articles on which drawback is being claimed were exported within five years after the merchandise in question was imported. Once the request for drawback is approved, the proposal and approval together constitute the manufacturer's drawback rate. For more information contact Entry Rulings Branch, Room 2107, U.S. Customs Headquarters, 1301 Constitution Avenue, N.W., Washington, D.C. 20229; telephone 202/927-0380.

U.S. foreign-trade zones

Exporters should also consider the customs privileges of U.S. foreign-trade zones. These zones are domestic U.S. sites that are considered outside U.S. customs territory and are available for activities that might otherwise be carried on overseas for customs reasons. For export operations, the zones provide accelerated export status for purposes of excise tax rebates and customs drawback. For import and reexport activities, no customs duties, federal excise taxes, or state and local ad valorem taxes are charged on foreign goods moved into zones unless and until the goods, or products made from them, are moved into customs territory. This means that the use of zones can be profitable for operations involving foreign dutiable materials and components being assembled or produced here for reexport. Also, no quota restrictions ordinarily apply.

There are now 214 approved foreign-trade zones in port communities throughout the United States. Associated with these projects are some 324 subzones. These facilities are available for operations involving storage, repacking, inspection, exhibition, assembly, manufacturing, and other processing.

More than 2,700 business firms used foreign-trade zones in fiscal year 1994. The value of merchandise moved to and from the zones during that year exceeded $80 billion. Export shipments from zones and subzones amounted to some $119.8 billion.

Information about the zones is available from the zone manager, from local Commerce district offices, or from the Executive Secretary, Foreign-Trade Zones Board, International Trade Administration, U.S. Department of Commerce, Washington, D.C. 20230.

Foreign free port and free trade zones

To encourage and facilitate international trade, more than 300 free ports, free trade zones, and similar customs-privileged facilities are now in operation in some 75 foreign countries, usually in or near seaports or airports. Many U.S. manufacturers and their distributors use free ports or free trade zones for receiving shipments of goods that are reshipped in smaller lots to customers throughout the surrounding areas. Information about free trade zones, free ports, and similar facilities abroad may be found in *Tax-Free Trade Zones of the World*, published by Matthew Bender & Co., International Division, 1275 Broadway, Albany, NY 12204; telephone 800/424-4200.

Bonded warehouses

Bonded warehouses can also be found in many locations. Here, goods can be warehoused without duties being assessed. Once goods are released, they are subject to duties.

Foreign sales corporations

One of the most important steps a U.S. exporter can take to reduce federal income tax on export-related income is to set up a foreign sales corporation (FSC). This tax incentive for U.S. exporters replaced the domestic international sales corporation (DISC), except the interest charge DISC. While the interest charge DISC allows exporters to defer paying taxes on export sales, the tax incentive provided by the FSC legislation is in the form of a permanent exemption from federal income tax for a portion of the export income attributable to the offshore activities of FSCs (26 U.S.C., sections 921-927). The tax exemption can be as great as 15 percent on gross income from exporting, and the expenses can be kept low through the use of intermediaries who are familiar with and able to carry out the formal requirements. A firm that is exporting or thinking of exporting can optimize available tax benefits with proper planning, evaluation, and assistance from an accountant or lawyer.

An FSC is a corporation set up in certain foreign countries or in U.S. possessions (other than Puerto Rico) to obtain a corporate tax exemption on a portion of its earnings generated by the sale or lease of export property and the performance of some services. A corporation initially qualifies as an FSC by meeting certain basic formation tests. An FSC (unless it is a small FSC) must also meet several foreign management tests throughout the year. If it complies with those requirements, the FSC is entitled to an exemption on qualified export transactions in which it performs the required foreign economic processes.

FSCs can be formed by manufacturers, nonmanufacturers, or groups of exporters, such as export trading companies. An FSC can function as a principal, buying and selling for its own account, or as a commission agent. It can be related to a manufacturing parent or it can be an independent merchant or broker.

An FSC must be incorporated and have its main office (a shared office is acceptable) in the U.S. Virgin Islands, American Samoa, Guam, the Northern Mariana Islands, or a qualified foreign country. In general, a firm must file for incorporation by following the normal procedures of the host nation or U.S. possession. Taxes paid by an FSC to a foreign country do not qualify for the foreign U.S. tax credit. Some nations, however, offer tax incentives to attract FSCs; to qualify, a company must identify itself as an FSC to the host government. Consult the government tax authorities in the country or U.S. possession of interest for specific information.

A country qualifies as an FSC host if it has an exchange of information agreement with the United States approved by the U.S. Department of the Treasury. As of February 20, 1991, the qualified countries were Australia, Austria, Barbados, Belgium, Bermuda, Canada, Costa Rica, Cyprus, Denmark, Dominican Republic, Egypt, Finland, France, Germany, Grenada, Iceland, Ireland, Jamaica, Korea, Malta, Mexico, Morocco, Netherlands, New Zealand, Norway, Pakistan, Philippines, Sweden, and Trinidad and Tobago. Since the Internal Revenue Service (IRS) does not allow foreign tax credits for foreign taxes imposed on the FSC's qualified income, it is generally advantageous to locate an FSC only in a country where local income taxes are minimized. Most FSCs are incorporated in the U.S. Virgin Islands or Guam.

The FSC must have at least one director who is not a U.S. resident, must keep one set of its books of account (including copies or summaries of invoices) at its main offshore office, cannot have more than 25 shareholders, cannot have any preferred stock, and must file an election to become an FSC with the IRS. Also, a group may not own both an FSC and an interest charge DISC.

The portion of the FSC gross income from exporting that is exempt from U.S. corporate taxation is 32 percent for a corporate-held FSC if it buys from independent suppliers or contracts with related suppliers at an "arm's-length" price - a price equivalent to that which would have been paid by an unrelated purchaser to an unrelated seller. An FSC supplied by a related entity can also use the special administrative pricing rules to compute its tax exemption. Although an FSC does not have to use the two special administrative pricing rules, these rules may provide additional tax savings for certain FSCs.

Small FSCs and interest charge DISCs are designed to give export incentives to smaller businesses. The tax benefits of a small FSC or an interest charge DISC are limited by ceilings on the amount of gross income that is eligible for the benefits.

The small FSC is generally the same as an FSC, except that a small FSC must file an election with the IRS designating itself as a small FSC - which means it does not have to meet foreign management or foreign economic process requirements. A small FSC tax exemption is limited to the income generated by $5 million or less in gross export revenues.

An exporter can still set up a DISC in the form of an interest charge DISC to defer the imposition of taxes for up to $10 million in export sales. A corporate shareholder of an interest charge DISC may defer the imposition of taxes on approximately 94 percent of its income up to the $10 million ceiling if the income is reinvested by the DISC in qualified export assets. An individual who is the sole shareholder of an interest charge DISC can defer 100 percent of the DISC income up to the $10 million ceiling. An interest charge DISC must meet the following requirements: the taxpayer must make a new election; the tax year of the new DISC must match the tax year of its majority stockholder; and the DISC shareholders must pay interest annually at U.S. Treasury bill rates on their proportionate share of the accumulated taxes deferred.

A *shared FSC* is an FSC that is shared by 25 or fewer unrelated exporter-shareholders to reduce the costs while obtaining the full tax benefit of an FSC. Each exporter-shareholder owns a separate class of stock and each runs its own business as usual. Typically, exporters pay a commission on export sales to the FSC, which distributes the commission back to the exporter.

States, regional authorities, trade associations, or private businesses can sponsor a shared FSC for their state's companies, their association's members, or their business clients or customers, or for U.S. companies in general. A shared FSC is a means of sharing the cost of the FSC. However, the benefits and proprietary information are not shared. The sponsor and the other exporter-shareholders do not participate in the exporter's profits, do not participate in the exporter's tax benefits, and are not a risk for another exporter's debts.

For more information about FSCs, U.S. companies may contact the assistant secretary for trade development (phone 202/482-1461); the Office of the Chief Counsel for International Commerce, U.S. Department of Commerce (202/482-5301); or a local office of the IRS.

Commerce assistance related to multilateral trade negotiations

The Tokyo Round Trade Agreements, completed in 1979 under General Agreement on Tariff and Trade (GATT) auspices, produced significant tariff reductions and established several nontariff trade barrier (NTB) agreements or codes. The codes currently in effect address the following NTBs:

- Countervailing measures to offset trade-distortive subsidies.

- Antidumping duties used to counter injurious price discrimination.

- Discriminatory government procurement.

- Technical barriers to trade (e.g., product standards).

- Uniform and equitable customs valuation for duty purposes.

- Import licensing procedures.

- Trade in civil aircraft (both tariff and nontariff issues).

An important benefit for U.S. exporters stemming from the Tokyo Round is the GATT Government Procurement Agreement opening many foreign government procurement orders to U.S. suppliers. Commerce's TOP has been designated the primary clearing point for tenders generated under this agreement. Information on the TOP can be obtained by contacting the local Commerce district office or Trade Opportunity Program, U.S. Department of Commerce, Export Promotion Services, Washington, D.C. 20230; phone 202/482-4203.

Users can also access TOP leads by tapping in directly to the EBB, a data base service of the Department of Commerce. Subscriptions to this service can be obtained by mail from U.S. Department of Commerce, National Technical Information Service, 5285 Port Royal Road, Springfield, VA 22161.

Other data base information on foreign tenders can be obtained from the *Commerce Business Daily*, available from the U.S. Government Printing Office, Washington, D.C. 20402; phone 202/512-1800. Brief summaries of leads also appear in the *Journal of Commerce.*

In 1991, negotiators were engaged in achieving a successful conclusion of the Uruguay Round of multilateral trade negotiations. U.S. objectives included (1) a substantial market access agreement covering tariffs and nontariff measures and (2) improvement in GATT to cover trade in such new areas as services, intellectual property rights, and trade-related investment measures. General information on the

Uruguay Round can be obtained from the Office of Multilateral Affairs, H3513, U.S. Department of Commerce/ITA, Washington, D.C. 20230.

Bilateral trade agreements

The United States has concluded bilateral trade agreements with several Eastern European countries and Mongolia. These congressionally approved agreements are required by the Trade Act of 1974 for these countries to receive most-favored nation (MFN) treatment. In addition to an article providing for reciprocal MFN status, the agreements contain guarantees on intellectual property rights and business facilitation. Such guarantees as the right to establish commercial representation offices in a country by no more than a simple registration process, the right to serve as and hire agents, the right to deal directly with customers and end users of products and services, and the right to hire employees of a company's choice are all included in the agreements. The intellectual property rights provisions include protection for computer software and trade secrets. Trade agreements are in effect with Hungary, Czechoslovakia, and Romania (the MFN provisions of this agreement have been suspended). As of August 14, 1991, the trade agreements with the then Soviet Union, Mongolia, and Bulgaria had been signed and submitted to the Congress for approval.

Intellectual property rights considerations

The United States provides a wide range of protection for intellectual property (i.e., patents, trademarks, service marks, copyrights, trade secrets, and semiconductor mask works). Many businesses - particularly high-technology firms, the publishing industry, chemical and pharmaceutical firms, the recording industry, and computer software companies - depend heavily on the protection afforded their creative products and processes.

In the United States, there are five major forms of intellectual property protection. A U.S. patent confers on its owner the exclusive right for 17 years from the date the patent is granted to manufacture, use, and sell the patented product or process within the United States. The United States and the Philippines are the only two countries that award patents on a first-to-invent basis; all other countries award patents to the first to file a patent application. As of November 16, 1989, a trademark or service mark registered with the U.S. Patent and Trademark Office remains in force for 10 years from the date of registration and may be renewed for successive periods of 10 years, provided the mark continues to be used in interstate commerce and has not been previously canceled or surrendered.

A work created (fixed in tangible form for the first time) in the United States on or after January 1, 1978, is automatically protected by a U.S. copyright from the moment of its creation. Such a copyright, as a general rule, has a term that endures for the author's life plus an additional 50 years after the author's death. In the case of works made for hire and for anonymous and pseudonymous works (unless the author's identity is revealed in records of the U.S. Copyright Office of the Library of Congress), the duration of the copyright is 75 years from publication or 100 years from creation, whichever is shorter. Other, more detailed provisions of the Copyright Act of 1976 govern the term of works created before January 1, 1978.

Trade secrets are protected by state unfair competition and contract law. Unlike a U.S. patent, a trade secret does not entitle its owner to a government-sanctioned monopoly of the discovered technology for a particular length of time. Nevertheless, trade secrets can be a valuable and marketable form of technology. Trade secrets are typically protected by confidentiality agreements between a firm and its employees and by trade secret licensing agreement provisions that prohibit disclosures of the trade secret by the licensee or its employees.

Semiconductor mask work registrations protect the mask works embodied in semiconductor chip products. In many other countries, mask works are referred to as integrated circuit layout designs. The Semiconductor Chip Protection Act of 1984 provides the owner of a mask work with the exclusive right to reproduce, import, and distribute such mask works for a period of 10 years from the earlier of two dates: the date on which the mask work is registered with the U.S. Copyright Office or the date on which the mask work is first commercially exploited anywhere in the world.

The rights granted under U.S. patent, trademark, or copyright law can be enforced only in the United States, its territories, and its possessions; they confer no protection in a foreign country. The protection available in each country depends on that country's national laws, administrative practices, and treaty obligations. The relevant international treaties set certain minimum standards for protection, but individual country laws and practices can and do differ significantly.

To secure patent and trademark right outside the United States a company must apply for a patent or register a trademark on a country-by-country basis. However, U.S. individuals and corporations are entitled to a "right of priority" and to "national treatment" in the 100 countries that, along with the United States, are parties to the Paris Convention for the Protection of Industrial Property.

The right of priority gives an inventor 12 months from the date of the first application filed in a Paris Convention country (6 months for a trademark) in which to file in other Paris Convention countries - to relieve companies of the burden of filing applications in many countries simultaneously. A later treaty to which the United States adheres, the Patent Cooperation Treaty, allows companies to file an international application for protection in other member states. Individual national applications, however, must follow within 18 months.

National treatment means that a member country will not discriminate against foreigners in granting patent or trademark protection. Rights conferred may be greater or less than provided under U.S. law, but they must be the same as the country provides its own nationals.

The level and scope of copyright protection available within a country also depends on that country's domestic laws and treaty obligations. In most countries, the place of first publication is an important criterion for determining whether foreign works are eligible for copyright protection. Works first published in the United States on or after March 1, 1989 - the date on which U.S. adherence to the Berne Convention for the Protection of Literary and Artistic Works became effective - are, with few exceptions, automatically protected in the more than 80 countries that comprise the Berne Union. Exporters of goods embodying works protected by copyright in the United States should find out how individual Berne Union countries deal with older U.S. works, including those first published (but not first or simultaneously published in a Berne Union country) before March 1, 1989.

The United States maintains copyright relations with a number of countries under a second international agreement called the Universal Copyright Convention (UCC). UCC countries that do not also adhere to Berne often require compliance with certain formalities to maintain copyright protection. Those formalities can be either or both of the following: (1) registration and (2) the requirement that published copies of a work bear copyright notice, the name of the author, and the date of first publication. The United States has bilateral copyright agreements with a number of countries, and the laws of these countries may or may not be consistent with either of the copyright conventions. Before first publication of a work anywhere, it is advisable to investigate the scope of and requirements for maintaining copyright protection for those countries in which copyright protection is desired.

Intellectual property rights owners should be aware that after valuable intellectual property rights have been secured in foreign markets, enforcement must be accomplished through local law. As a general matter, intellectual property rights are private rights to be enforced by the rights owner. Ease of enforcement varies from country to country and depends on such factors as the attitude of local officials, substantive requirements of the law, and court procedures. U.S. law affords a civil remedy for infringement (with money damages to a successful plaintiff) and criminal penalties (including fines and jail terms) for more serious offenses. The availability of criminal penalties for infringement, either as the exclusive remedy or in addition to private suits, also varies among countries.

A number of countries are parties to only some, or even none, of the treaties that have been discussed here. Therefore, would-be U.S. exporters should carefully evaluate the intellectual property laws of their potential foreign markets, as well as applicable multilateral and bilateral treaties and agreements (including bilateral trade agreements), *before* making a decision to do business there. The intellectual property considerations that arise can be quite complex and, if possible, should be explored in detail with an attorney.

In summary, U.S. exporters with intellectual property concerns should consider taking the following steps:

1. Obtaining protection under all applicable U.S. laws for their inventions, trademarks, service marks, copyrights, and semiconductor mask works.

2. Researching the intellectual property laws of countries where they may conduct business. The US&FCS has information about intellectual property laws and practices of particular countries, although it does not provide legal advice.

3. Securing the services of competent local counsel to file appropriate patent, trademark, or copyright applications within priority periods.

4. Adequately protecting their trade secrets through appropriate confidentiality provisions in employment, licensing, marketing, distribution, and joint venture agreements.

Arbitration of disputes in international transactions

The parties to a commercial transaction may provide in their contract that any disputes over interpretation or performance of the agreement will be resolved through arbitration. In the domestic context, arbitration may be appealing for a variety of reasons. Frequently cited advantages over conventional courtroom litigation include potential savings in time and expense, confidentiality of the proceedings, and expertise of the arbitrators.

For export transactions, in which the parties to the agreement are from different countries, additional important advantages are neutrality (international arbitration allows each party to avoid the domestic courts of the other should a dispute arise) and ease of enforcement (foreign arbitral awards can be easier to enforce than foreign court decisions).

In an agreement to arbitrate (usually just inserted as a term in the contract governing the transaction as a whole), the parties also have broad power to agree on many significant aspects of the arbitration. The arbitration clause may do the following:

•Specify the location (a "neutral site") where the arbitration will be conducted, although care must be taken to select a country that has adopted the UN Convention on the Recognition and Enforcement of Foreign Awards (or another convention providing for the enforcement of arbitral awards).

•Establish the rules that will govern the arbitration, usually by incorporating a set of existing arbitration rules such as the UN Commission on International Trade Law (UNCITRAL) Model Rules.

•Appoint an arbitration institute to administer the arbitration. The International Chamber of Commerce based in Paris, the American Arbitration Association in New York, and the Arbitration Institute of the Stockholm Chamber of Commerce in Sweden are three such prominent institutions.

•Choose the law that will govern procedural issues or the merits of the dispute, for example, the law of the State of New York.

•Place certain limitations on the selection of arbitrators, for example, by agreeing to exclude nationals of the parties to the dispute or by requiring certain qualifications or expertise.

•Designate the language in which the arbitral proceedings will be conducted.

For international arbitration to work effectively, the national courts in the countries of both parties to the dispute must recognize and support arbitration as a legitimate alternative means for resolving disputes. This support is particularly crucial at two stages in the arbitration process. First, should one party attempt to avoid arbitration after a dispute has arisen, the other party must be able to rely on the judicial system in either country to enforce the agreement to arbitrate by compelling arbitration. Second, the party that wins in the arbitration proceeding must be confident that the national courts will enforce the decision of the arbitrators. This will ensure that the arbitration process is not ultimately frustrated at the enforcement stage if the losing party refuses to pay or otherwise satisfy the arbitral award.

The strong policy of U.S. federal law is to approve and support resolution of disputes by arbitration. Through the UN Convention on the Recognition and Enforcement of Foreign Arbitral Awards (popularly known as the New York Convention), which the United States ratified in 1970, more than 80 countries have undertaken international legal obligations to recognize and enforce arbitral awards. While several other arbitration treaties have been concluded, the New York Convention is by far the most important international agreement on commercial arbitration and may be credited for much of the explosive growth of arbitration of international disputes in recent decades.

Providing for arbitration of disputes makes good sense in many international commercial transactions. Because of the complexity of the subject, however, legal advice should be obtained for specific export transactions.

The United Nations sales convention

The UN Convention on Contracts for the International Sale of Goods (CISG) became the law of the United States on January 1, 1988. It establishes uniform legal rules to govern the formation of international sales contracts and the rights and obligations of the buyer and seller. The CISG is expected to facilitate and stimulate international trade.

The CISG applies automatically to all contracts for the sale of goods between traders from two different countries that have both ratified the CISG. This automatic application takes place unless the parties to the contract expressly exclude all or part of the CISG or expressly stipulate to law other than the CISG. Parties can also expressly choose to apply the CISG when it would not automatically apply.

At present, the following nations apply the CISG: Argentina, Australia, Austria, Bulgaria, Byelorussian Socialist Republic, Chile, China, Czechoslovakia, Denmark, Egypt, Finland, France, Germany, Hungary, Iraq, Italy, Lesotho, Mexico, Norway, Russia, Spain, Sweden, Switzerland, Syria, Ukraine, United States, Yugoslavia, and Zambia. The CISG entered the force in the Netherlands on January 1, 1992, and in Guinea on February 1, 1992.

The United States made a reservation, the effect of which is that the CISG will apply only when the other party to the transaction also has its place of business in a country that applies the CISG.

Convention provisions

The provisions and scope of the CISG are similar to Article 2 of the Uniform Commercial Code (effective in the United States except Louisiana). The CISG comprises four parts:

•Part I, Sphere of Application and General Provisions (Articles 1-13), provides that the CISG covers the international sale of most commercial goods.

•Part II, Formation of the Contract (Articles 14-24), provides rules on offer and acceptance.

•Part III, Sale of Goods (Articles 25-88), covers obligations and remedies of the seller and buyer and rules governing the passing of risk and damages.

•Part IV, Final Provisions (Articles 89-101), covers the right of a country to disclaim certain parts of the convention.

Applying (or excluding) the CISG

U.S. businesses can avoid the difficulties of reaching agreement with foreign parties on choice-of-law issues because the CISG text is available as a compromise. Using the CISG may decrease the time and legal costs otherwise involved in research of different unfamiliar foreign laws. Further, the CISG may reduce the problems of proof and foreign law in domestic and foreign courts.

Application of the CISG may especially make sense for smaller firms and for American firms contracting with companies in countries where the legal systems are obscure, unfamiliar, or not suited for international sales transaction of goods. However, some larger, more experienced firms may want to continue their current practices, at least with regard to parties with whom they have been doing business regularly.

When a firm chooses to exclude the CISG, it is not sufficient to simply say "the laws of New York apply," because the CISG would be the law of the State of New York under certain circumstances. Rather, one would say "the provisions of the Uniform Commercial Code as adopted by the State of New York, and not the UN Convention on Contracts for the International Sale of Goods, apply."

After it is determined whether or not the CISG governs a particular transaction, the related documentation should be reviewed to ensure consistency with the CISG or other governing law. For agreements about to expire, companies should make sure renewals take into account the applicability (or nonapplicability) of the CISG.

The CISG can be found in the *Federal Register* (Vol. 52, p. 6262, 1987) along with a notice by the U.S. Department of State, and in the pocket part to 15 U.S.C.A. app. at 29. To obtain an up-to-date listing of ratifying or acceding countries and their reservations call the UN at 212/963-3918 or 212/963-7958. For further information contact the Office of the Assistant Legal Adviser for Private International Law, U.S. Department of State (202/776-8420), or the Office of the Chief Counsel for International Commerce, U.S. Department of Commerce (202/482-0937).

TEN KEYS TO EXPORT SUCCESS

There is profit to be made by U.S. firms in exports. The international market is more than four times larger than the U.S. market. Growth rates in many overseas markets far outpace domestic market growth. Meeting and beating innovative competitors abroad can help companies keep the edge they need at home.

There are also real costs and risks associated with exporting. It is up to each company to weigh the necessary commitment against the potential benefit.

Ten important recommendations for successful exporting should be kept in mind:

1. Obtain qualified export counseling and develop a master international marketing plan before starting an export business. The plan should clearly define goals, objectives, and problems encountered.

2. Secure a commitment from top management to overcome initial difficulties and financial requirements of exporting. Although the early delays and costs involved in exporting may seem difficult to justify in comparison with established domestic sales, the exporter should take a long-range view of this process and carefully monitor international marketing efforts.

3. Take sufficient care in selecting overseas distributors. The complications involved in overseas communications and transportation require international distributors to act more independently than their domestic counterparts.

4. Establish a basis for profitable operations and orderly growth. Although no overseas inquiry should be ignored, the firm that acts mainly in response to unsolicited trade leads is trusting success to the element of chance.

5. Devote continuing attention to export business when the U.S. market booms. Too many companies turn to exporting when business falls off in the United States. When domestic business starts to boom again, they neglect their export trade or relegate it to a secondary position.

6. Treat international distributors on an equal basis with domestic counterparts. Companies often carry out institutional advertising campaigns, special discount offers, sales incentive programs, special credit term programs, warranty offers, and so in the U.S. market, but fail to make similar offers to their international distributors.

7. Do not assume that a given market technique and product will automatically be successful in all countries. What works in Japan may fall flat in Saudi Arabia. Each market has to be treated separately to ensure maximum success.

8. Be willing to modify products to meet regulations or cultural preferences of other countries. Local safety and security codes as well as import restrictions cannot be ignored by foreign distributors.

9. Print service, sale, and warranty messages in locally understood languages. Although a distributor's top management may speak English, it is unlikely that all sales and services personnel have this capability.

10. Provide readily available servicing for the product. A product without the necessary service support can acquire a bad reputation quickly

EXPORT GLOSSARY

Acceptance - This term has several related meanings: (1) A time draft (or bill of exchange) that the drawee has accepted and is unconditionally obligated to pay at maturity. The draft must be presented first for acceptance - the drawee becomes the "acceptor" - then for payment. The word "accepted" and the date and place of payment must be written on the face of the draft. (2) The drawee's act in receiving a draft and thus entering into the obligation to pay its value at maturity. (3) Broadly speaking, any agreement to purchase goods under specified terms. An agreement to purchase goods at a stated price and under stated terms.

Ad valorem - According to value. See Duty.

Advance against documents - A loan made on the security of the documents covering the shipment.

Advising bank - A bank, operating in the exporter's country, that handles letters of credit for a foreign bank by the export firm that the credit has been opened in its favor. The advising bank fully informs the exporter of the conditions of the letter of credit without necessarily bearing responsibility for payment.

Advising capacity - A term indicating that a shipper's agent or representative is not empowered to make definitive decisions or adjustments without approval of the group or individual represented.

Agent - See Foreign sales agent.

Air waybill - A bill of lading that covers both domestic and international flights transporting goods to a specified destination. This is a nonnegotiable instrument of air transport that serves as a receipt for the shipper, indicating that the carrier has accepted the goods listed and obligates itself to carry the consignment to the airport of destination according to specified conditions. Compare **Inland bill of lading**, **Ocean bill of lading**, and **Through bill of lading.**

Alongside - The side of a ship. Goods to be delivered "alongside" are to be placed on the dock or barge within reach of the transport ships's tackle so that they can be loaded aboard the ship.

Antidiversion clause - See Destination control statement.

Arbitrage - The process of buying foreign exchange, stocks, bonds, and other commodities in one market and immediately selling them in another market at higher prices.

Asian dollars - U.S. dollars deposited in Asia and the Pacific Basin. Compare Eurodollars.

ATA Carnet - See **Carnet**

Balance of trade - The differences between a country's total imports and exports. If exports exceed imports, favorable balance of trade exists; if not, a trade deficit is said to exist.

Barter - Trade in which merchandise is exchanged directly for other merchandise without use of money. Barter is an important means of trade with countries using currency that is not readily convertible.

Beneficiary - The person in whose favor a letter of credit is issued or a draft is drawn.

Bill of exchange - See **Draft.**

Bill of lading - A document that establishes the terms of a contract between a shipper and a transport company under which freight is to be moved between specified points for a specified charge. Usually prepared by the shipper on forms issued by the carrier, it serves as a document of title, a contract of carriage, and a receipt for goods. Also see **Air waybill, Inland bill of lading, Ocean bill of lading**, and **Through bill of lading.**

Bonded warehouse - A warehouse authorized by customs authorities for storage of goods on which payment of duties is deferred until the goods are removed.

Booking - An arrangement with a steamship company for the acceptance and carriage of freight.

Buying agent - See **Purchasing agent**.

Carnet - A customs document permitting the holder to carry or send merchandise temporarily into certain foreign countries (for display, demonstration, or similar purposes) without paying duties or posting bonds.

Cash against documents (CAD) - Payment for goods in which a commission house or other intermediary transfers title documents to the buyer upon payments in cash.

Cash in advance - Payment for goods in which the price is paid in full before shipment is made. This method is usually used only for small purchases or when the goods are built to order.

Cash with order - Payment for goods in which the buyer pays when ordering and in which the transaction is binding on both parties.

Certificate of inspection - A document certifying that merchandise (such as perishable goods) was in good condition immediately prior to its shipment.

Certificate of manufacture - A statement (often notarized) in which a producer of goods certifies that manufacture has been completed and that the goods are now at the disposal of the buyer.

Certificate of origin - A document, required by certain foreign countries for tariff purposes, certifying the country of origin of specified goods.

CFR - Cost and freight. A pricing term indicating that the cost of the goods and the freight charges are included in the quoted price; the buyer arranges for and pays insurance.

Charter party - A written contract, usually on a special form, between the owner of a vessel or a part of its freight space. The contract generally includes the freight rates and the ports involved in the transportation.

CIF - Cost, insurance, freight. A pricing term, indicating that the cost of the goods, insurance, and freight are included in the quoted price.

Clean bill of lading - A receipt for goods issued by a carrier that indicates that the goods were received in "apparent good order and condition", without damages or other irregularities. Compare **foul bill of lading**.

Clean draft - A draft to which no documents have been attached.

Collection papers - All documents (commercial invoices, bills of lading, etc.) submitted to a buyer for the purpose of receiving payment for a shipment.

Commercial attache - The commerce expert on the diplomatic staff of his or her country's embassy or large consulate.

Commercial invoice - An itemized list of goods shipped, usually among an exporter's collection papers.

Commission agent - See Purchasing agent.

Common carrier - An individual, partnership, or corporation that transports persons or goods for compensation.

Confirmed letter of credit - A letter of credit, issued by a foreign bank, the validity of which has been confirmed by a U.S. bank. An exporter whose payment terms are a confirmed letter of credit is assured of payment by the U.S. bank even if the buyer or foreign bank defaults. See **Letter of credit**.

Consignment - Delivery of merchandise from an exporter (the consignor) to an agent (the consignee) under agreement that the agent sell the merchandise for the account of the exporter. The consignor retains title to the goods until the consignee has sold them. The consignee sells the goods for commission and remits the net proceeds to the consignor.

Consular declaration - A formal statement, made to the consul of a foreign country, describing goods to be shipped.

Consular invoice - A document, required by some foreign countries, describing a shipment of goods and showing information such as the consignor, consignee, and value of the shipment. Certified by a consular official of the foreign country, it is used by the country's customs officials to verify the value, quantity, and nature of the shipment.

Convertible currency - A currency that can be bought and sold for other currencies at will.

Correspondent bank - A bank that, in its own country, handles the business of a foreign bank.

Countertrade - The sale of goods or services that are paid for in whole or in part by the transfer of goods and services from a foreign country. See **Barter**.

Countervailing duty - A duty imposed to counter unfairly subsidized products.

CPT (carriage paid to) and **CIP (carriage and insurance paid to)** - Pricing terms indicating that carriage, or carriage and insurance, are paid to the named place of destination. They apply in place of CFR and CIF, respectively, for shipment by modes other than water.

Credit risk insurance - Insurance designed to cover risks of nonpayment for delivered goods. Compare **Marine insurance**.

Customhouse broker - An individual or firm licensed to enter and clear goods through customs.

Customs - The authorities designated to collect duties levied by a country on imports and exports. The term also applies to the procedures involved in such a collection.

Date draft - A draft that matures in a specified number of days after the date is issued, without regard to the date of acceptance. See **Draft, Sight draft**, and **Time draft**.

Deferred payment credit - Type of letter of credit providing for payment some time after presentation of shipping documents by exporter.

Demand draft - See **sight draft**.

Destination control statement - Any of various statements that the U.S. government requires to be displayed on export shipments and that specify the destinations for which export of the shipment has been authorized.

Devaluation - The official lowering of the value of one country's currency in terms of one or more foreign currencies. For example, if the U.S. dollar is devalued in relation to the French franc, one dollar will "buy" fewer francs than before.

DISC - Domestic international sales corporation.

Discrepancy - Letter of credit - When documents presented do not conform to the letter of credit it is referred to as a discrepancy.

Dispatch - An amount paid by a vessel's operator to a charterer if loading or unloading is completed in less time than stipulated in the charter party.

Distributor - A foreign agent who sells for a supplier directly and maintains an inventory of the supplier's products.

Dock receipt - A receipt issued by an ocean carrier to acknowledge receipt of a shipment at the carrier's dock or warehouse facilities. Also see **Warehouse receipt**.

Documentary draft - A draft to which documents are attached.

Documents against acceptance (D/A) - Instructions given by a shipper to a bank indicating that documents transferring title to goods should be delivered to the buyer (or drawee) only upon the buyer's acceptance of the attached draft.

Draft (or Bill of exchange) - An unconditional order in writing from one person (the drawer) to another (the drawee) only upon the buyer's acceptance of the attached draft.

Drawback - Articles manufactured or produced in the United States with the use of imported components or raw materials and later exported are entitled to a refund of up to 99 percent of the duty charged on the imported components. The refund of duty is known as a drawback.

Drawee - The individual or firm on whom a draft is drawn and who owes the stated amount. Compare **Drawer**. Also see **Draft**.

Drawer - The individual or firm that issues or signs a draft and thus stands to receive payment of the stated amount from the drawee. Compare **Drawee**. Also see **Draft**.

Dumping - Selling merchandise in another country at a price below the price at which the same merchandise is sold in the home market or selling such merchandise below the costs incurred in production and shipment.

Duty - A tax imposed on imports by the customs authority of a country. Duties are generally based on the value of the goods (ad valorem duties), some other factor such as weight or quantity (specific duties), or a combination of value and other factors (compound duties)

EMC - See **Export management company**.

ETC - See **Export trading company**.

Eurodollars - U.S. dollars placed on deposit in banks outside the United States; usually refers to deposits in Europe.

Ex - From. When used in pricing terms such as "ex factory" or "ex dock", it signifies that the price quoted applies only at the point of origin (in the two examples, at the seller's factory or a dock at the import point). In practice, this kind of quotation indicates that the seller agrees to place the goods at the disposal of the buyer at the specified place within a fixed period of time.

Exchange permit - A government permit sometimes required by the importer's government to enable the import firm to convert its own country's currency into foreign currency with which to pay a seller in another country.

Exchange rate - The price of one currency in terms of another, that is, the number of units of one currency that may be exchanged for one unit of another currency.

Eximbank - Export-Import Bank of the United States.

Export broker - An individual or firm that brings together buyers and sellers for a fee but does not take part in actual sale transactions.

Export commission house - An organization which, for a commission, acts as a purchasing agent for a foreign buyer.

Export declaration - See **Shipper's export declaration**.

Export license - A government document that permits the licensee to export designated goods to certain destinations. See **General export license** and **Individually validated export license**.

Export management company - A private firm that serves as the export department for several producers of goods or services, either by taking title or by soliciting and transacting export business on behalf of its clients in return for a commission, salary, or retainer plus commission.

Export trading company - A firm similar or identical to an export management company.

FAS - Free alongside ship - A pricing term indicating that the quoted price includes the cost of delivering the goods alongside a designated vessel.

FCA - "Free carrier" to named place. Replaces the former term "FOB named inland port" to designate the seller's responsibility for the cost of loading goods at the named shipping point. May be used for multimodal transport, container stations, and any mode of transport, including air.

FCIA - Foreign Credit Insurance Association.

FI - Free in. A pricing term indicating that the charterer of a vessel is responsible for the cost of loading and unloading goods from the vessel.

Floating policy - See **Open policy**.

FO - Free out. A pricing term indicating that the charterer of a vessel is responsible for the cost of loading goods from the vessel.

FOB - "Free on board" at named port of export. A pricing term indicating that the quoted price covers all expenses up to and including delivery of goods upon an overseas vessel provided by or for the buyer.

Force majeure - The title of a standard clause in marine contracts exempting the parties for nonfulfillment of their obligations as a result of conditions beyond their control, such as earthquakes, floods, or war.

Foreign exchange - The currency or credit instruments of a foreign country. Also, transactions involving purchase or sale of currencies.

Foreign freight forwarder - See **Freight forwarder**.

Foreign sales agent - An individual or firm that serves as the foreign representative of a domestic supplier and seeks sales abroad for the supplier.

Foreign trade zone - See **Free-trade zone**.

Foul bill of lading - A receipt for goods issued by a carrier with an indication that the goods were damaged when received. Compare **Clean bill of lading**.

Free port - An area such as a port city into which merchandise may legally be moved without payment of duties.

Free-trade zone - A port designated by the government of a country for duty-free entry of any nonprohibited goods. Merchandise may be stored, displayed, used for manufacturing etc., within the zone and reexported without duties being paid. Duties are imposed on the merchandise (or items manufactured from the merchandise) only when the goods pass from the zone into an area of the country subject to the customs authority.

Freight forwarder - An independent business that handles export shipments for compensation. (A freight forwarder is among the best sources of information and assistance on U.S. export regulations and documentation, shipping methods, and foreign import regulations.)

GATT - General Agreement on Tariffs and Trade. A multilateral treaty intended to help reduce trade barriers between signatory countries and to promote trade through tariff concessions.

General export license - Any of various export licenses covering export commodities for which **Individually validated export licenses** are not required. No formal application or written authorization is needed to ship exports under a general export license.

Gross weight - The full weight of a shipment, including goods and packaging. Compare **Tare weight**.

Import license - A document required and issued by some national governments authorizing the importation of goods into their individual countries.

Individually validated export license - A required document issued by the U.S. Government authorizing the export of specific commodities. This license is for a specific transaction or time period in which the exporting is to take place. Compare **General export license**.

Inland bill of lading - A bill of lading used in transporting goods overland to the exporter's international carrier. Although a through bill of lading can sometimes be used, it is usually necessary to prepare both an inland bill of lading and an ocean bill of lading for export shipments. Compare **Air waybill**, **Ocean bill of lading**, and **Through bill of lading**.

International freight forwarder - See **Freight forwarder**.

Irrevocable letter of credit - A letter of credit in which the specified payment is guaranteed by the bank if all terms and conditions are met by the drawee.

Letter of credit (L/C) - A document, issued by a bank per instructions by a buyer of goods, authorizing the seller to draw a specified sum of money under specified terms, usually the receipt by the bank of certain documents within a given time.

Licensing - A business arrangement in which the manufacturer of a product (or a firm with proprietary rights over certain technology, trademarks, etc.) grants permission to some other group or individual to manufacture that product (or make use of that proprietary material) in return for specified royalties or other payment.

Manifest - See **Ship's manifest**.

Marine insurance - Insurance that compensates the owners of goods transported overseas in the event of loss that cannot be legally recovered from the carrier. Also covers air shipments. Compare **Credit risk insurance**.

Marking (or marks) - Letters, numbers, and other symbols placed on cargo packages to facilitate identification.

Ocean bill of lading - A bill of lading (B/L) indicating that the exporter consigns a shipment to an international carrier for transportation to a specified foreign market. Unlike an inland B/L, the ocean B/L also serves as a collection document. If it is a "straight" B/L, the foreign buyer can obtain the shipment from the carrier by simply showing proof of identity. If a "negotiable" B/L is used, the buyer must first pay for the goods, post a bond, or meet other conditions agreeable to the seller. Compare **Air waybill, Inland bill of lading,** and **Through bill of lading.**

On board bill of lading - A bill of lading in which a carrier certifies that goods have been placed on board a certain vessel.

Open account - A trade arrangement in which goods are shipped to a foreign buyer without guarantee of payment. The obvious risk this method poses to the supplier makes it essential that the buyer's integrity be unquestionable.

Open insurance policy - A marine insurance policy that applies to all shipments made by an exporter over a period of time rather than to one shipment only.

Order bill of lading - A negotiable bill of lading made out to the order of the shipper.

Packing list - A list showing the number and kinds of items being shipped, as well as other information needed for transportation purposes.

Parcel post receipt - The postal authorities' signed acknowledgment of delivery to receiver of a shipment made by parcel post.

PEFCO - Private Export Funding Corporation. A corporation that lends to foreign buyers to finance exports from the United States.

Perils of the sea - A marine insurance term used to designate heavy weather, stranding, lightning, collision, and sea water damage.

Phytosanitary inspection certificate - A certificate, issued by the U.S. Department of Agriculture to satisfy import regulations for foreign countries, indicating that a U.S. shipment has been inspected and is free from harmful pests and plant disease.

Political risk - In export financing, the risk of loss due to such causes as currency inconvertibility, government action preventing entry of goods, expropriation or confiscation, and war.

Pro forma invoice - An invoice provided by a supplier prior to the shipment of merchandise, informing the buyer of the kinds and quantities of goods to be sent, their value, and important specifications (weight, size, etc.)

Purchasing agent - An agent who purchase goods in his or her own country on behalf of foreign importers such as government agencies and large private concerns.

Quota - The quantity of goods of a specific kind that a country permits to be imported without restriction or imposition of additional duties.

Quotation - An offer to sell goods at a stated price and under specified conditions.

Remitting bank - The bank that sends the draft to the overseas bank for collection.

Representative - See **Foreign sales agent.**

Revocable letter of credit - A letter of credit that can be canceled or altered by the drawee (buyer) after it has been issued by the drawee's bank. Compare **Irrevocable letter of credit.**

Schedule B - Refers to Schedule B, Statistical Classification of Domestic and Foreign Commodities Exported from the United States. All commodities exported from the United States must be assigned a seven-digit Schedule B number.

Shipper's export declaration - A form required for all shipments by the U.S. Treasury Department and prepared by a shipper, indicating the value, weight, destination, and other basic information about an export shipment.

Ship's manifest - An instrument in writing, signed by the captain of a ship, that lists the individual shipments constituting the ship's cargo.

Sight draft (S/D) - A draft that is payable upon presentation to the drawee. Compare **Date draft** and **Time draft.**

Spot exchange - The purchase or sale of foreign exchange for immediate delivery.

Standard industrial classification (SIC) - A standard numerical code system used by the U.S. government to classify products and services.

Standard international trade classification (SITC) - A standard numerical code system developed by the United Nations to classify commodities used in international trade.

Steamship conference - A group of steamship operators that operate under mutually agreed-upon freight rates.

Straight bill of lading - A nonnegotiable bill of lading in which the goods are consigned directly to a named consignee.

Tare weight - The weight of a container and packing materials without the weight of the goods it contains. Compare **Gross weight.**

Tenor (of a draft) - Designation of a payment as being due at sight, a given number of days after sight, or a given number of days after date.

Through bill of lading - A single bill of lading converting both the domestic and international carriage of an export shipment. An air waybill, for instance, is essentially a through bill of lading used for air shipments. Ocean shipments, on the other hand, usually require two separate documents - an inland bill of lading for domestic carriage and an ocean bill of lading for international carriage. Through bills of lading are insufficient for ocean shipments. Compare **Air waybill, Inland bill of lading,** and **Ocean bill of lading.**

Time draft - A draft that matures either a certain number of days after acceptance or a certain number of days after the date of the draft. Compare **Date draft** and **Sight draft.**

Tramp steamer - A ship not operating on regular routes or schedules.

Transaction statement - A document that delineates the terms and conditions agreed upon between the importer and exporter.

Trust receipt - Release of merchandise by a bank to a buyer in which the bank retains title to the merchandise. The buyer, who obtains the goods for manufacturing or sales purposes, is obligated to maintain the goods (or the proceeds from their sale) distinct from the remainder of his or her assets and to hold them ready for repossession by the bank.

Warehouse receipt - A receipt issued by a warehouse listing goods received for storage.

Wharfage - A charge assessed by a pier or dock owner for handling incoming or outgoing cargo.

Without reserve - A term indicating that a shipper's agent or representative is empowered to make definitive decisions and adjustment abroad without approval of the group or individual represented. Compare **Advisory capacity.**

U.S. HOUSE--The following is a list of individuals within each U.S. Representative's office who deal with Foreign Trade and Foreign Policy issues. The abbreviation "FT" stands for Foreign Trade and is the person in the office responsible for foreign trade policy issues. The abbreviation "FP" stands for Foreign Policy and is the person in the office responsible for foreign policy issues. In some cases, the same individual handles both issue areas. When that occurs, the name is repeated for consistency. The area code for all numbers is 202.

Mailing address:

Contact Person
U.S. House of Representatives
Room #
Washington, DC 20515

Neil **ABERCROMBIE** (D-HI-01)
FP: Michael Slackman
FT: Tom Wanley
1233 Longworth House Office Building
Phone: 202-225-2726   Fax: 202-225-4580

Gary L. **ACKERMAN** (D-NY-05)
FP: David Adams - Professional Staff,
Subcmte. on Western Hemisphere
FT: Johnathan Berger
2243 Rayburn House Office Building
Phone: 202-225-2601   Fax: 202-225-1589

Robert **ADERHOLT** (R-AL-04)
FP: Mark Dawson - Legislative Assistant
FT: Mark Dawson - Legislative Assistant
1007 Longworth House Office Building
Phone: 202-225-4876   Fax: 202-225-5587

Thomas H. **ALLEN** (D-ME-01)
FP: Todd Stein - Legislative Assistant
FT: Todd Stein - Legislative Assistant
1630 Longworth House Office Building
Phone: 202-225-6116   Fax: 202-225-5590

Robert **ANDREWS** (D-NJ-01)
FP: Maureen Doherty - Legislative Assistant
FT: Maureen Doherty - Legislative Assistant
2439 Rayburn House Office Building
Phone: 202-225-6501   Fax: 202-225-6583

Bill **ARCHER** (R-TX-07)
FP: Gary Bartlett
FT: Don Carlson
1236 Longworth House Office Building
Phone: 202-225-2571   Fax: 202-225-4381

Richard K. **ARMEY** (R-TX-26)
FP: Lisa Vogt - Legislative Assistant
FT: Lisa Vogt - Legislative Assistant
301 Cannon House Office Building
Phone: 202-225-7772

Spencer **BACHUS** (R-AL-06)
FP: Terry Campbell - Legislative Assistant
FT: Terry Campbell - Legislative Assistant
442 Cannon House Office Building
Phone: 202-225-4921   Fax: 202-225-2082

Scotty **BAESLER** (D-KY-06)
FP: John Townsend
FT: John Townsend
2463 Rayburn House Office Building
Phone: 202-225-4706   Fax: 202-225-2122

Richard H. **BAKER** (R-LA-06)
FP: Thomas Wilson - Legislative Assistant
FT: Fraser Verrusio - Sr. Legislative Assistant
434 Cannon House Office Building
Phone: 202-225-3901   Fax: 202-225-7313

John E. **BALDACCI** (D-ME-02)
FP: Mike Rabasco
FT: Mike Rabasco
1740 Longworth House Office Building
Phone: 202-225-6306   Fax: 202-225-2943

Cass **BALLENGER** (R-NC-10)
FP: George Southworth - Legislative Assistant
FT: George Southworth - Legislative Assistant
2182 Rayburn House Office Building
Phone: 202-225-2576   Fax: 202-225-0316

James **BARCIA** (D-MI-05)
FP: John Ferrrera - Legislative Director
FT: John Ferrera - Legislative Director
2419 Rayburn House Office Building
Phone: 202-225-8171   Fax: 202-225-2168

Robert L. **BARR** (R-GA-07)
FP: Bob Herriott - Legislative Director
FT: Bob Herriott - Legislative Director
1130 Longworth House Office Building
Phone: 202-225-2931   Fax: 202-225-2944

Bill **BARRETT** (R-NE-03)
FP: Mark Whitacre - Legislative Director
FT: Mark Whitacre - Legislative Director
2458 Rayburn House Office Building
Phone: 202-225-6435

Tom **BARRETT** (D-WI-05)
FP: Murat Gokcigdem - Legislative Assistant
FT: Murat Gokcigdem - Legislative Assistant
1224 Longworth House Office Building
Phone: 202-225-3571   Fax: 202-225-2185

Roscoe **BARTLETT** (R-MD-06)
FP: Randall Stephens
FT: Randall Stephens
322 Cannon House Office Building
Phone: 202-225-2721   Fax: 202-225-2193

Joe **BARTON** (R-TX-06)
FP: Brandon Steinmann - Legislative Assistant
FT: Brandon Steinmann - Legislative Assistant
2264 Rayburn House Office Building
Phone: 202-225-2002   Fax: 202-225-3052

Charles F. **BASS** (R-NH-02)
FP: James Martin - Legislative Assistant
FT: Annette O'Connor - Legislative Assistant
218 Cannon House Office Building
Phone: 202-225-5206   Fax: 202-225-2946

Herbert H. **BATEMAN** (R-VA-01)
FP: Steve Stombres
FT: Paul McClung
2350 Rayburn House Office Building
Phone: 202-225-4261   Fax: 202-225-4382

Xavier **BECERRA** (D-CA-30)
FP: Luis Ayala - Legislative Fellow
FT: Kim Richan
1119 Longworth House Office Building
Phone: 202-225-6235   Fax: 202-225-2202

Kenneth E. **BENTSEN** (D-TX-25)
FP: Gary Palmquist - Legislative Assistant
FT: Gary Palmquist - Legislative Assistant
128 Cannon House Office Building
Phone: 202-225-7508   Fax: 202-225-2947

Doug **BEREUTER** (R-NE-01)
FP: Mike Ennis - Legislative Director
FT: Mike Ennis - Legislative Director
2184 Rayburn House Office Building
Phone: 202-225-4806   Fax: 202-226-1148

Howard L. **BERMAN** (D-CA-26)
FP: Rick Kessler
FT: Rick Kessler
2330 Rayburn House Office Building
Phone: 202-225-4695   Fax: 202-225-5279

Marion **BERRY** (D-AR-01)
FP: Paul Charton - Legislative Assistant
FT: Paul Charton - Legislative Assistant
1407 Longworth House Office Building
Phone: 202-225-4076   Fax: 202-225-5602

Brian P. **BILBRAY** (R-CA-49)
FP: Paige Anderson - Legislative Assistant
FT: Paige Anderson - Legislative Assistant
1530 Longworth House Office Building
Phone: 202-225-2040   Fax: 202-225-2948

Michael **BILIRAKIS** (R-FL-09)
FP: Rebecca Hyder
FT: Rebecca Hyder
2369 Rayburn House Office Building
Phone: 202-225-5755   Fax: 202-225-4085

Sanford **BISHOP** (D-GA-02)
FP: Roxanne Burnham - Legislative Assistant
FT: Ken Keck - Legislative Assistant
1433 Longworth House Office Building
Phone: 202-225-3631   Fax: 202-225-2203

Rod R. **BLAGOJEVICH** (D-IL-05)
FP: Greg Adams - Legislative Assistant
FT: Sarah Wills - Legislative Assistant
501 Cannon House Office Building
Phone: 202-225-4061   Fax: 202-225-5603

Thomas J. **BLILEY** (R-VA-07)
FP: Cary Justice - Legislative Assistant
FT: Cary Justice - Legislative Assistant
2409 Rayburn House Office Building
Phone: 202-225-2815   Fax: 202-225-0011

Earl **BLUMENAUER** (D-OR-03)
FP: Adam Carstens - Legislative Assistant
FT: Adam Carstens - Legislative Assistant
1113 Longworth House Office Building
Phone: 202-225-4811   Fax: 202-225-8941

Roy **BLUNT** (R-MO-07)
FP: Duncan Haggart - Special Asst. for Policy
FT: Duncan Haggart - Special Asst. for Policy
508 Cannon House Office Building
Phone: 202-225-6536   Fax: 202-225-5604

Sherwood L. **BOCHLERT** (R-NY-23)
FP: Sara Gray - Legislative Assistant
FT: Sara Gray - Legislative Assistant
2246 Rayburn House Office Building
Phone: 202-225-3665   Fax: 202-225-1891

John A. **BOEHNER** (R-OH-08)
FP: Mason Wiggins
FT: Mason Wiggins

1011 Longworth House Office Building
Phone: 202-225-6205   Fax: 202-225-0704

Henry **BONILLA** (R-TX-23)
FP: Marcus Lubin - Legislative Director
FT: Leslie Sanchez - Legislative Assistant
1427 Longworth House Office Building
Phone: 202-225-4511   Fax: 202-225-2237

David E. **BONIOR** (D-MI-10)
FP: Scott Paul - Legislative Assistant
FT: Scott Paul - Legislative Assistant
2207 Rayburn House Office Building
Phone: 202-225-2106   Fax: 202-226-1169

Robert A. **BORSKI** (D-PA-03)
FP: Mark Vieth - Chief of Staff
FT: Mark Vieth - Chief of Staff
2267 Rayburn House Office Building
Phone: 202-225-8251   Fax: 202-225-4628

Leonard L. **BOSWELL** (D-IA-03)
FP: E.H. "Ned" Michalek - Legislative Dir.
FT: Alex Fischer - Legislative Assistant
1029 Longworth House Office Building
Phone: 202-225-3806   Fax: 202-225-5608

Rick **BOUCHER** (D-VA-09)
FP: Sharon Ringley - Deputy Chief of Staff
FT: Sharon Ringley - Deputy Chief of Staff
2329 Rayburn House Office Building
Phone: 202-225-3861   Fax: 202-225-0442

F. Allen **BOYD** (D-FL-02)
FP: Eve Yosing - Legislative Director
FT: Jason Quaranto - Legislative Assistant
1237 Longworth House Office Building
Phone: 202-225-5235   Fax: 202-225-5615

Kevin P. **BRADY** (R-TX-08)
FP: David Malech - Legislative Assistant
FT: Barry Brown - Legislative Director
1531 Longworth House Office Building
Phone: 202-225-4901   Fax: 202-225-5524

Robert **BRADY** (D-PA-01)
FP: Adam Witkonis - Legislative Assistant
FT: Adam Witkonis - Legislative Assistant
242 Cannon House Office Building
Phone: 202-225-4731   Fax: 202-225-0088

Corrine **BROWN** (D-FL-03)
FP: Patricia Taylor - Legislative Assistant
FT: Patricia Taylor - Legislative Assistant
1610 Longworth House Office Building
Phone: 202-225-0123   Fax: 202-225-2256

George E. **BROWN** (D-CA-42)
FP: Dana Dubose - Legislative Assistant
FT: Dana Dubose - Legislative Assistant
2300 Rayburn House Office Building
Phone: 202-225-6161   Fax: 202-225-8671

Sherrod **BROWN** (D-OH-13)
FP: Joel Cliff
FT: Steve Fought - Senior Advisor
328 Cannon House Office Building
Phone: 202-225-3401   Fax: 202-225-2266

Edward G. **BRYANT** (R-TN-07)
FP: Mark Johnson - Legislative Assistant
FT: Mark Johnson - Legislative Assistant
408 Cannon House Office Building
Phone: 202-225-2811   Fax: 202-225-2989

Jim **BUNNING** (R-KY-04)
FP: Mike Haywood - Legislative Assistant
FT: Mike Haywood - Legislative Assistant
2437 Rayburn House Office Building
Phone: 202-225-3465   Fax: 202-225-0003

Richard M. **BURR** (R-NC-05)

FP: John Versaggi - Legislative Assistant
FT: John Versaggi - Legislative Assistant
1513 Longworth House Office Building
Phone: 202-225-2071   Fax: 202-225-2995

Dan **BURTON** (R-IN-06)
FP: Mike Delph - Legislative Assistant
FT: Jason Lovell - Legislative Assistant
2185 Rayburn House Office Building
Phone: 202-225-2276   Fax: 202-225-0016

Steve **BUYER** (R-IN-05)
FP: Jim Lariviere - Legislative Assistant
FT: Amy Staton - Legislative Assistant
326 Cannon House Office Building
Phone: 202-225-5037

Sonny **CALLAHAN** (R-AL-01)
FP: Nancy Tippins - Legislative Director
FT: Michael J. Sharp - Legislative Assistant
2418 Rayburn House Office Building
Phone: 202-225-4931   Fax: 202-225-0562

Ken **CALVERT** (R-CA-43)
FP: Nelson Garcia
FT: Nelson Garcia
1034 Longworth House Office Building
Phone: 202-225-1986   Fax: 202-225-2004

Dave **CAMP** (R-MI-04)
FP: Tim Wineland - Legislative Assistant
FT: Tim Wineland - Legislative Assistant
137 Cannon House Office Building
Phone: 202-225-3561   Fax: 202-225-9679

Tom **CAMPBELL** (R-CA-15)
FP: Jackie Benditt
FT: Jackie Benditt - Legislative Asst./Attorney
2442 Rayburn House Office Building
Phone: 202-225-2631   Fax: 202-225-6788

Charles T. **CANADY** (R-FL-12)
FP: Zack Moore - Legislative Director
FT: David Lindsay - Legislative Assistant
2432 Rayburn House Office Building
Phone: 202-225-1252   Fax: 202-225-2279

Christopher B. **CANNON** (R-UT-03)
FP: Meredith Rasmussen - Legislative Asst.
FT: Claudia Hrvatin - Legislative Director
118 Cannon House Office Building
Phone: 202-225-7751   Fax: 202-225-5629

Lois **CAPPS** (D-CA-22)
FP: Clare Dowling - Legislative Assistant
FT: Randolph Harrison - Legislative Director
1118 Longworth House Office Building
Phone: 202-225-3601   Fax: 202-225-5632

Benjamin L. **CARDIN** (D-MD-03)
FP: Michelle Ash - Legislative Assistant
FT: Christopher Lynch - Legislative Director
104 Cannon House Office Building
Phone: 202-225-4016   Fax: 202-225-9219

Julia M. **CARSON** (D-IN-10)
FP: Susan Eads Role - Sr. Legislative Assistant
FT: Susan Eads Role - Sr. Legislative Assistant
1541 Longworth House Office Building
Phone: 202-225-4011   Fax: 202-225-5633

Michael **CASTLE** (R-DE-AL)
FP: Booth Jameson - Legislative Director
FT: Booth Jameson - Legislative Director
1227 Longworth House Office Building
Phone: 202-225-4165   Fax: 202-225-2291

Steven J. **CHABOT** (R-OH-01)
FP: Kevin Fitzpatrick - Legislative Director
FT: Kevin Fitzpatrick - Legislative Director
129 Cannon House Office Building
Phone: 202-225-2216   Fax: 202-225-3012

C. Saxby **CHAMBLISS** (R-GA-08)
FP: Matt Echols - Legislative Assistant
FT: Matt Echols - Legislative Assistant
1019 Longworth House Office Building
Phone: 202-225-6531   Fax: 202-225-3013

Helen P. **CHENOWETH** (R-ID-01)
FP: Joe Mertz - Legislative Assistant
FT: Joe Mertz - Legislative Assistant
1727 Longworth House Office Building
Phone: 202-225-6611   Fax: 202-225-3029

Jon L. **CHRISTENSEN** (R-NE-02)
FP: Eric Winterbauer - Legislative Director
FT: Eric Winterbauer - Legislative Director
413 Cannon House Office Building
Phone: 202-225-4155   Fax: 202-225-3032

Donna M. **CHRISTIAN-GREEN** (D-VI-DL)
FP: Brian Modeste - Legislative Director
FT: Brian Modeste - Legislative Director
1711 Longworth House Office Building
Phone: 202-225-1790   Fax: 202-225-5517

William **CLAY** (D-MO-01)
FP: Michele Bogdanovich
FT: Michele Bogdanovich
2306 Rayburn House Office Building
Phone: 202-225-2406   Fax: 202-225-1725

Eva **CLAYTON** (D-NC-01)
FP: Arshi Siddiqui - Legislative Assistant
FT: Arshi Siddiqui - Legislative Assistant
2440 Rayburn House Office Building
Phone: 202-225-3101   Fax: 202-225-3354

Bob **CLEMENT** (D-TN-05)
FP: Caroline Nielson - Legislative Assistant
FT: Caroline Nielson - Legislative Assistant
2229 Rayburn House Office Building
Phone: 202-225-4311   Fax: 202-226-1035

James **CLYBURN** (D-SC-06)
FP: Lisa Toporek - Legislative Assistant
FT: Lisa Toporek - Legislative Assistant
319 Cannon House Office Building
Phone: 202-225-3315   Fax: 202-225-2313

Howard **COBLE** (R-NC-06)
FP: Missy Branson - Legislative Director
FT: Missy Branson - Legislative Director
2239 Rayburn House Office Building
Phone: 202-225-3065   Fax: 202-225-8611

Thomas A. **COBURN** (R-OK-02)
FP: Neil Bradley - Legislative Assistant
FT: Neil Bradley - Legislative Assistant
429 Cannon House Office Building
Phone: 202-225-2701   Fax: 202-225-3038

Michael **COLLINS** (R-GA-03)
FP: Christopher Ptomey - Legislative Assistant
FT: Bo Bryant - Legislative Director
1131 Longworth House Office Building
Phone: 202-225-5901   Fax: 202-225-2515

Larry **COMBEST** (R-TX-19)
FP: Tom Sell - Legislative Assistant
FT: Tom Sell - Legislative Assistant
1026 Longworth House Office Building
Phone: 202-225-4005   Fax: 202-225-9615

Gary **CONDIT** (D-CA-18)
FP: Randy Groves - Legislative Assistant
FT: Randy Groves - Legislative Assistant
2245 Rayburn House Office Building
Phone: 202-225-6131   Fax: 202-225-0819

John **CONYERS** (D-MI-14)
FP: Carl LeVan - Legislative Director
FT: Carl LeVan - Legislative Director
B351C Rayburn House Office Building

Phone: 202-225-6906   Fax: 202-225-7680

Merrill COOK (R-UT-02)
FP: Connie Humphrey - Legislative Director
FT: Connie Humphrey - Legislative Director
1431 Longworth House Office Building
Phone: 202-225-3011   Fax: 202-225-5638

John C. COOKSEY (R-LA-05)
FP: Baird Webel - Legislative Assistant
FT: Baird Webel - Legislative Assistant
317 Cannon House Office Building
Phone: 202-225-8490   Fax: 202-225-5639

Jerry F. COSTELLO (D-IL-12)
FP: Elizabeth Pile - Legislative Director
FT: Heidi Zoerb - Legislative Assistant
2454 Rayburn House Office Building
Phone: 202-225-5661   Fax: 202-225-0285

C. Christopher COX (R-CA-47)
FP: Brad Campbell - Legislative Assistant
FT: Brad Campbell - Legislative Assistant
2402 Rayburn House Office Building
Phone: 202-225-5611   Fax: 202-225-9177

William J. COYNE (D-PA-14)
FP: Matt Dinkle - Press Secretary
FT: Matt Dinkle - Press Secretary
2455 Rayburn House Office Building
Phone: 202-225-2301   Fax: 202-225-1844

Bud CRAMER (D-AL-05)
FP: Dana Gresham - Legislative Assistant
FT: Dana Gresham - Legislative Assistant
2416 Rayburn House Office Building
Phone: 202-225-4801   Fax: 202-225-4392

Philip M. CRANE (R-IL-08)
FP: Robert Mueller - Legislative Assistant
FT: Donna Swanson - Legislative Assistant
233 Cannon House Office Building
Phone: 202-225-3711   Fax: 202-225-7830

Mike CRAPO (R-ID-02)
FP: Shannon McMurtrey - Legislative Asst.
FT: Shannon McMurtrey - Legislative Asst.
437 Cannon House Office Building
Phone: 202-225-5531   Fax: 202-225-8216

Barbara L. CUBIN (R-WY-AL)
FP: Michael Hubbard - Legislative Assistant
FT: Marian Marshall - Legislative Director
1114 Longworth House Office Building
Phone: 202-225-2311   Fax: 202-225-3057

Elijah E. CUMMINGS (D-MD-07)
FP: Neil Rochkind - Legislative Assistant
FT: Neil Rochkind - Legislative Assistant
1632 Longworth House Office Building
Phone: 202-225-4741   Fax: 202-225-3178

Randy CUNNINGHAM (R-CA-51)
FP: Bill Berl - Legislative Assistant
FT: Bill Berl - Legislative Assistant
2238 Rayburn House Office Building
Phone: 202-225-5452   Fax: 202-225-2558

Pat DANNER (D-MO-06)
FP: Amy Perlik - Legislative Director
FT: Amy Perlik - Legislative Director
1207 Longworth House Office Building
Phone: 202-225-7041   Fax: 202-225-8221

Danny K. DAVIS (D-IL-07)
FP: Brian Sims - Legislative Assistant
FT: Brian Sims - Legislative Assistant
1218 Longworth House Office Building
Phone: 202-225-5006   Fax: 202-225-5641

James DAVIS (D-FL-11)
FP: Tricia Borrentine - Legislative Director

FT: John S. Hill - Budget Assoc./Leg. Asst.
327 Cannon House Office Building
Phone: 202-225-3376   Fax: 202-225-5652

Thomas M. DAVIS (R-VA-11)
FP: Uyen Dinn - Legislative Assistant
FT: Amy Heerink - Sr. Legislative Assistant
224 Cannon House Office Building
Phone: 202-225-1492   Fax: 202-225-3071

Nathan DEAL (R-GA-09)
FP: Pamela Nix - Legislative Assistant
FT: Frank Tillotson - Legal Counsel
1406 Longworth House Office Building
Phone: 202-225-5211   Fax: 202-225-8272

Peter A. DEFAZIO (D-OR-04)
FP: Carrie Lynch - Legislative Assistant
FT: Carrie Lynch - Legislative Assistant
2134 Rayburn House Office Building
Phone: 202-225-6416   Fax: 202-225-0373

Diana L. DEGETTE (D-CO-01)
FP: Shannon Good - Legislative Assistant
FT: Shannon Good - Legislative Assistant
1404 Longworth House Office Building
Phone: 202-225-4431   Fax: 202-225-5657

William D. DELAHUNT (D-MA-10)
FP: Mark Agrast - Legislative Director
FT: Mark Agrast - Legislative Director
1517 Longworth House Office Building
Phone: 202-225-3111   Fax: 202-225-5658

Rosa DELAURO (D-CT-03)
FP: Sarah Walkling - Legislative Assistant
FT: Sarah Walkling - Legislative Assistant
436 Cannon House Office Building
Phone: 202-225-3661   Fax: 202-225-4890

Tom DELAY (R-TX-22)
FP: Jim Morrell
FT: Jim Morrell
341 Cannon House Office Building
Phone: 202-225-5951   Fax: 202-225-5241

Ronald V. DELLUMS (D-CA-09)
FP: Ying Lee - Senior Legislative Assistant
FT: Ying Lee - Senior Legislative Assistant
2108 Rayburn House Office Building
Phone: 202-225-2661   Fax: 202-225-9817

Peter DEUTSCH (D-FL-20)
FP: Joshua Shapiro
FT: Joshua Shapiro
204 Cannon House Office Building
Phone: 202-225-7931   Fax: 202-225-8456

Lincoln DIAZ-BALART (R-FL-21)
FP: John Barsa - Sr. Legislative Assistant
FT: John Barsa - Sr. Legislative Assistan/
   Press Secretary
404 Cannon House Office Building
Phone: 202-225-4211   Fax: 202-225-8576

Jay DICKEY (R-AR-04)
FP: Jim McGuire - Legislative Assistant
FT: Brain Casal - Legislative Director
2453 Rayburn House Office Building
Phone: 202-225-3772   Fax: 202-225-1314

Norman D. DICKS (D-WA-06)
FP: Colin Sheldon
FT: Colin Sheldon
2467 Rayburn House Office Building
Phone: 202-225-5916   Fax: 202-226-1176

John D. DINGELL (D-MI-16)
FP: Peter Casey - Legislative Assistant
FT: Michael Scholl - Legislative Assistant
2328 Rayburn House Office Building
Phone: 202-225-4071   Fax: 202-226-0371

Julian C. DIXON (D-CA-32)
FP: J. Chris Thompson - Legislative Assistant
FT: J. Chris Thompson - Legislative Assistant
2252 Rayburn House Office Building
Phone: 202-225-7084   Fax: 202-225-4091

Lloyd DOGGETT (D-TX-10)
FP: Patrick Marotta
FT: Michael Harrison
126 Cannon House Office Building
Phone: 202-225-4865   Fax: 202-225-3073

Cal DOOLEY (D-CA-20)
FP: Port Telles - Legislative Assistant
FT: Emily Beizer
1201 Longworth House Office Building
Phone: 202-225-3341   Fax: 202-225-9308

John DOOLITTLE (R-CA-04)
FP: John Willis - Legislative Assistant
FT: John Willis - Legislative Assistant
1526 Longworth House Office Building
Phone: 202-225-2511   Fax: 202-225-5444

Michael F. DOYLE (D-PA-18)
FP: Peter Cohen - Legislative Director
FT: Peter Cohen - Legislative Director
133 Cannon House Office Building
Phone: 202-225-2135   Fax: 202-225-3084

David DREIER (R-CA-28)
FP: Brian Bieron
FT: Brian Bieron
237 Cannon House Office Building
Phone: 202-225-2305   Fax: 202-225-7018

John J. DUNCAN (R-TN-02)
FP: David Balloff
FT: David Balloff
2400 Rayburn House Office Building
Phone: 202-225-5435   Fax: 202-225-6440

Jennifer DUNN (R-WA-08)
FP: Scott Lindsay - Legislative Assistant
FT: Doug Badger - Legislative Director
432 Cannon House Office Building
Phone: 202-225-7761   Fax: 202-225-8673

Chet EDWARDS (D-TX-11)
FP: Timothy Bromelkamp - Legislative Asst.
FT: Timothy Bromelkamp - Legislative Asst.
2459 Rayburn House Office Building
Phone: 202-225-6105   Fax: 202-225-0350

Vernon J. EHLERS (R-MI-03)
FP: Will Plaster
FT: Will Plaster
1717 Longworth House Office Building
Phone: 202-225-3831   Fax: 202-225-5144

Robert L. EHRLICH (R-MD-02)
FP: John Meiers - Legislative Fellow
FT: John Meiers - Legislative Fellow
315 Cannon House Office Building
Phone: 202-225-3061   Fax: 202-225-3094

Jo Ann H. EMERSON (R-MO-08)
FP: Jordan Bernstein - Legislative Assistant
FT: Glenn Kelly - Legislative Assistant
132 Cannon House Office Building
Phone: 202-225-4404   Fax: 202-226-0326

Eliot L. ENGEL (D-NY-17)
FP: Jason Steinbaum - Legislative Director
FT: Jason Steinbaum - Legislative Director
2303 Rayburn House Office Building
Phone: 202-225-2464

Philip S. ENGLISH (R-PA-21)
FP: Jeff Woodland - Legislative Assistant
FT: Karin Johns - Legislative Director
1721 Longworth House Office Building

Phone: 202-225-5406   Fax: 202-225-3103

John E. **ENSIGN** (R-NV-01)
FP: Brocke Allmon - Legislative Assistant
FT: Brocke Allmon - Legislative Assistant
414 Cannon House Office Building
Phone: 202-225-5965   Fax: 202-225-3119

Anna **ESHOO** (D-CA-14)
FP: Ryan Trapani - Legislative Assistant
FT: Ryan Trapani - Legislative Assistant
308 Cannon House Office Building
Phone: 202-225-8104   Fax: 202-225-8890

Bob **ETHERIDGE** (D-NC-02)
FP: Zeke Creech - Legislative Assistant
FT: Zeke Creech - Legislative Assistant
1641 Longworth House Office Building
Phone: 202-225-4531   Fax: 202-225-5662

Lane **EVANS** (D-IL-17)
FP: Cori Shropshire - Legislative Assistant
FT: Cori Shropshire - Legislative Assistant
2335 Rayburn House Office Building
Phone: 202-225-5905   Fax: 202-225-5396

Terry **EVERETT** (R-AL-02)
FP: Wade Heck - Legislative Director
FT: Wade Heck - Legislative Director
208 Cannon House Office Building
Phone: 202-225-2901

Thomas W. **EWING** (R-IL-15)
FP: Justin McCarthy - Legislative Assistant
FT: Justin McCarthy - Legislative Assistant
2417 Rayburn House Office Building
Phone: 202-225-2371   Fax: 202-225-8071

Eni F.H. **FALEOMAVAEGA** (D-AS-DL)
FP: Enere Levi - Legislative Assistant
FT: Enere Levi - Legislative Assistant
2422 Rayburn House Office Building
Phone: 202-225-8577   Fax: 202-225-8757

Sam **FARR** (D-CA-17)
FP: Matthew Green
FT: Matthew Green
1117 Longworth House Office Building
Phone: 202-225-2861   Fax: 202-225-6791

Chaka **FATTAH** (D-PA-02)
FP: Craig Galloway - Legislative Assistant
FT: Craig Galloway - Legislative Assistant
1205 Longworth House Office Building
Phone: 202-225-4001   Fax: 202-225-3127

Harris W. **FAWELL** (R-IL-13)
FP: Chuck Clampton
FT: Pat McCurry
2368 Rayburn House Office Building
Phone: 202-225-3515   Fax: 202-225-9420

Vic **FAZIO** (D-CA-03)
FP: Angela Melton
FT: Maria Petersen
2113 Rayburn House Office Building
Phone: 202-225-5716   Fax: 202-225-5141

Bob **FILNER** (D-CA-50)
FP: Richard Patrick - Legislative Director
FT: Richard Patrick - Legislative Director
330 Cannon House Office Building
Phone: 202-225-8045   Fax: 202-225-9073

Mark A. **FOLEY** (R-FL-16)
FP: Shawn Gallagher - Legislative Assistant
FT: Liz Nicolson - Legislative Director
113 Cannon House Office Building
Phone: 202-225-5792   Fax: 202-225-3132

Michael P. **FORBES** (R-NY-01)
FP: Gary Burns - Legislative Director

FT: Gary Burns - Legislative Director
416 Cannon House Office Building
Phone: 202-225-3826   Fax: 202-225-3143

Harold **FORD** (D-TN-09)
FP: Marland Buckner - Sr. Policy Advisor
FT: Marland Buckner - Sr. Policy Advisor
1523 Longworth House Office Building
Phone: 202-225-3265   Fax: 202-225-5663

Tillie **FOWLER** (R-FL-04)
FP: Bill Klein - Legislative Director
FT: Bill Klein - Legislative Director
109 Cannon House Office Building
Phone: 202-225-2501   Fax: 202-225-9318

Jon D. **FOX** (R-PA-13)
FP: Kristen McSwain - Legislative Director
FT: Kristen McSwain - Legislative Director
435 Cannon House Office Building
Phone: 202-225-6111   Fax: 202-225-3155

Barney **FRANK** (D-MA-04)
FP: Daniel McGlinchey - Legislative Assistant
FT: Daniel McGlinchey - Legislative Assistant
2210 Rayburn House Office Building
Phone: 202-225-5931   Fax: 202-225-0182

Bob **FRANKS** (R-NJ-07)
FP: Doug Tansey - Legislative Director
FT: Robin Countee - Legislative Assistant
225 Cannon House Office Building
Phone: 202-225-5361   Fax: 202-225-9460

Rodney P. **FRELINGHUYSEN** (R-NJ-11)
FP: Ed Krenik
FT: Ed Krenik
228 Cannon House Office Building
Phone: 202-225-5034   Fax: 202-225-3186

Martin D. **FROST** (D-TX-24)
FP: Justin Kasmir - Legislative Assistant
FT: Justin Kasmir - Legislative Assistant
2256 Rayburn House Office Building
Phone: 202-225-3605   Fax: 202-225-4951

Elizabeth **FURSE** (D-OR-01)
FP: Amy Burgess
FT: Jennie Kugel
316 Cannon House Office Building
Phone: 202-225-0855   Fax: 202-225-9497

Elton **GALLEGLY** (R-CA-23)
FP: Vince Morelli - Legislative Director
FT: Vince Morelli - Legislative Director
2427 Rayburn House Office Building
Phone: 202-225-5811   Fax: 202-225-1100

John Gregory **GANSKE** (R-IA-04)
FP: Shellane Quinn
FT: Catherine Willis
1108 Longworth House Office Building
Phone: 202-225-4426   Fax: 202-225-3193

Sam **GEJDENSON** (D-CT-02)
FP: Jason Gross - Legislative Assistant
FT: Amos Hockstein
1401 Longworth House Office Building
Phone: 202-225-2076   Fax: 202-225-4977

George W. **GEKAS** (R-PA-17)
FP: Lou Roth - Legislative Assistant
2410 Rayburn House Office Building
Phone: 202-225-4315   Fax: 202-225-8440

Richard A. **GEPHARDT** (D-MO-03)
FP: Joy Drucker - Legislative Assistant
FT: Joy Drucker - Legislative Assistant
1226 Longworth House Office Building
Phone: 202-225-2671   Fax: 202-225-7452

James A. **GIBBONS** (R-NV-02)

FP: Greg King - Legislative Assistant
FT: Greg King - Legislative Assistant
100 Cannon House Office Building
Phone: 202-225-6155   Fax: 202-225-5679

Wayne T. **GILCHREST** (R-MD-01)
FP: Eric Webster - Legislative Director
FT: Eric Webster - Legislative Director
332 Cannon House Office Building
Phone: 202-225-5311   Fax: 202-225-0254

Paul E. **GILLMOR** (R-OH-05)
FP: Chris Bremer - Legislative Assistant
FT: Chris Bremer - Legislative Assistant
1203 Longworth House Office Building
Phone: 202-225-6405   Fax: 202-225-1985

Benjamin A. **GILMAN** (R-NY-20)
FP: Richard Garon - Chief of Staff/
    Intl. Relations Cmte.
FT: Frank Record - Intn'l. Relations Specialist
2449 Rayburn House Office Building
Phone: 202-225-3776   Fax: 202-225-2541

Newt **GINGRICH** (R-GA-06)
FP: Krister Holliday
FT: Krister Holliday
2428 Rayburn House Office Building
Phone: 202-225-4501   Fax: 202-225-4656

Henry B. **GONZALEZ** (D-TX-20)
FP: Tod Wells - Legislative Director
FT: Tod Wells - Legislative Director
2413 Rayburn House Office Building
Phone: 202-225-3236

Virgil H. **GOODE** (D-VA-05)
FP: Jim Severt - Chief of Staff
FT: Jim Severt - Chief of Staff
1520 Longworth House Office Building
Phone: 202-225-4711   Fax: 202-225-5681

Bob **GOODLATTE** (R-VA-06)
FP: Brett Shogren - Legislative Assistant
FT: Brett Shogren - Legislative Assistant
123 Cannon House Office Building
Phone: 202-225-5431   Fax: 202-225-9681

William F. **GOODLING** (R-PA-19)
FP: Christine O'Connor - Legislative Director
FT: Christine O'Connor - Legislative Director
2263 Rayburn House Office Building
Phone: 202-225-5836   Fax: 202-226-1000

Bart **GORDON** (D-TN-06)
FP: Patton Lane - Legislative Assistant
FT: Lee Hammer - Legislative Assistant
2201 Rayburn House Office Building
Phone: 202-225-4231   Fax: 202-225-6887

Porter J. **GOSS** (R-FL-14)
FP: Jim Boxold - Legislative Assistant
FT: Jim Boxold - Legislative Assistant
108 Cannon House Office Building
Phone: 202-225-2536   Fax: 202-225-6820

Lindsey O. **GRAHAM** (R-SC-03)
FP: Aleix Jarvis - Legislative Director
FT: Aleix Jarvis - Legislative Director
1429 Longworth House Office Building
Phone: 202-225-5301   Fax: 202-225-3216

Kay **GRANGER** (R-TX-12)
FP: Lisa Helfman - Legislative Assistant
FT: Kasey Pipes - Legislative Assistant
515 Cannon House Office Building
Phone: 202-225-5071   Fax: 202-225-5683

Gene **GREEN** (D-TX-29)
FP: Michael Hollon - Sr. Legislative Assistant
FT: Michael Hollon - Sr. Legislative Assistant
2429 Rayburn House Office Building

Phone: 202-225-1688   Fax: 202-225-9903

James **GREENWOOD** (R-PA-08)
FP: Sara Michelone - Legislative Assistant
FT: Mara Guarducci - Legislative Assistant
2436 Rayburn House Office Building
Phone: 202-225-4276   Fax: 202-225-9511

Luis **GUTIERREZ** (D-IL-04)
FP: Mark Fine
FT: Mark Fine
2438 Rayburn House Office Building
Phone: 202-225-8203   Fax: 202-225-7810

Gilbert W. **GUTKNECHT** (R-MN-01)
FP: John Boling - Legislative Assistant
FT: John Boling - Legislative Assistant
425 Cannon House Office Building
Phone: 202-225-2472   Fax: 202-225-3246

Ralph M. **HALL** (D-TX-04)
FP: Marcha Shasteen - Legislative Counsel
FT: Elizabeth Kowal - Exec./Legislative Asst.
2221 Rayburn House Office Building
Phone: 202-225-6673   Fax: 202-225-3332

Tony P. **HALL** (D-OH-03)
FP: Bob Zachritz - Legislative Assistant
FT: Bob Zachritz - Legislative Assistant
1432 Longworth House Office Building
Phone: 202-225-6465

Lee H. **HAMILTON** (D-IN-09)
FP: Mike VanDusen
FT: David Weiner
2314 Rayburn House Office Building
Phone: 202-225-5315   Fax: 202-225-1101

James V. **HANSEN** (R-UT-01)
FP: Bill Johnson - Legislative Director
FT: Kimo Kaloi - Legislative Assistant
2466 Rayburn House Office Building
Phone: 202-225-0453   Fax: 202-225-5857

Jane **HARMAN** (D-CA-36)
FT: Maria Alongi - Legislative Assistant
325 Cannon House Office Building
Phone: 202-225-8220   Fax: 202-226-0684

J. Dennis **HASTERT** (R-IL-14)
FP: Tim Kurth - Legislative Assistant
FT: Tim Kurth - Legislative Assistant
2241 Rayburn House Office Building
Phone: 202-225-2976   Fax: 202-225-0697

Alcee **HASTINGS** (D-FL-23)
FP: Ann Jacobs - Legislative Director
FT: Ann Jacobs - Legislative Director
1039 Longworth House Office Building
Phone: 202-225-1313   Fax: 202-226-0690

Richard **HASTINGS** (R-WA-04)
FP: Jon Devaney - Legislative Assistant
FT: Doug Riggs - Legislative Director
1323 Longworth House Office Building
Phone: 202-225-5816   Fax: 202-225-3251

John David **HAYWORTH** (R-AZ-06)
FP: Cameron Sellers - Legislative Assistant
FT: Katharine Mottley - Legislative Director
1023 Longworth House Office Building
Phone: 202-225-2190   Fax: 202-225-3263

Joel **HEFLEY** (R-CO-05)
FP: Jennifer Johnson Calvert - Leg. Asst.
FT: Rob Smith - Legislative Assistant
2230 Rayburn House Office Building
Phone: 202-225-4422   Fax: 202-225-1942

W.G. **HEFNER** (D-NC-08)
FP: Sandra Latta
FT: Sandra Latta

2470 Rayburn House Office Building
Phone: 202-225-3715   Fax: 202-225-4036

Wally **HERGER** (R-CA-02)
FP: Ron Shinn - Press Secretary/Leg. Dir.
FT: Dave Olander - Legislative Assistant
2433 Rayburn House Office Building
Phone: 202-225-3076

Rick **HILL** (R-MT-AL)
FP: Warren Tryon - Legislative Assistant
FT: Warren Tryon - Legislative Assistant
1037 Longworth House Office Building
Phone: 202-225-3211   Fax: 202-225-5687

Van **HILLEARY** (R-TN-04)
FP: Joby Fortson - Legislative Assistant
FT: Roger Morse - Legislative Director
114 Cannon House Office Building
Phone: 202-225-6831   Fax: 202-225-3272

Earl **HILLIARD** (D-AL-07)
FP: Matthew Lyons
FT: Tunstall Wilson
1314 Longworth House Office Building
Phone: 202-225-2665   Fax: 202-226-0772

Maurice **HINCHEY** (D-NY-26)
FP: Dan Ahouse
FT: Diane Millererg - Legislative Director
2431 Rayburn House Office Building
Phone: 202-225-6335   Fax: 202-226-0774

Ruben E. **HINOJOSA** (D-TX-15)
FP: Lee Murphy - Legislative Assistant
FT: Lee Murphy - Legislative Assistant
1032 Longworth House Office Building
Phone: 202-225-2531   Fax: 202-225-5688

David L. **HOBSON** (R-OH-07)
FP: Kenny Kraft
FT: Kenny Kraft
1514 Longworth House Office Building
Phone: 202-225-4324

Peter **HOEKSTRA** (R-MI-02)
FP: Karen Spoelman - Legislative Assistant
FT: Todd Sutton - Legislative Assistant
1122 Longworth House Office Building
Phone: 202-225-4401   Fax: 202-226-0779

Tim **HOLDEN** (D-PA-06)
FP: Jennifer Saraeeno
FT: Jennifer Saraeeno
1421 Longworth House Office Building
Phone: 202-225-5546   Fax: 202-226-0996

Darlene **HOOLEY** (D-OR-05)
FP: Grey Gardner - Legislative Assistant
FT: Steve Giuli - Legislative Director
1419 Longworth House Office Building
Phone: 202-225-5711   Fax: 202-225-5699

Steve **HORN** (R-CA-38)
FP: Eric Swedlund - Legislative Director
FT: Eric Swedlund - Legislative Director
438 Cannon House Office Building
Phone: 202-225-6676   Fax: 202-226-1012

John N. **HOSTETTLER** (R-IN-08)
FP: Robert Ziegler - Sr. Legislative Assistant
FT: Robert Ziegler - Sr. Legislative Assistant
431 Cannon House Office Building
Phone: 202-225-4636   Fax: 202-225-3284

Amo **HOUGHTON** (R-NY-31)
FP: Bob VanWicklin
FT: David Pearce
1110 Longworth House Office Building
Phone: 202-225-3161   Fax: 202-225-5574

Steny H. **HOYER** (D-MD-05)

FP: Dana Lewis - Legislative Assistant
FT: Cory Alexander - Legislative Director
1705 Longworth House Office Building
Phone: 202-225-4131   Fax: 202-225-4300

Kenny C. **HULSHOF** (R-MO-09)
FP: Rob Monsees - Legislative Assistant
FT: Manning Feraci - Legislative Director
1728 Longworth House Office Building
Phone: 202-225-2956   Fax: 202-225-5712

Duncan **HUNTER** (R-CA-52)
FP: Vicki Middleton
FT: Lorissa Bounds - Legislative Assistant
2265 Rayburn House Office Building
Phone: 202-225-5672   Fax: 202-225-0235

Asa **HUTCHINSON** (R-AR-03)
FP: Sametta Klinetob - Legislative Assistant
FT: Lisa Vogt - Legislative Assistant
1535 Longworth House Office Building
Phone: 202-225-4301   Fax: 202-225-5713

Henry J. **HYDE** (R-IL-06)
FT: Nancy Short
2110 Rayburn House Office Building
Phone: 202-225-4561   Fax: 202-225-1166

Bob **INGLIS** (R-SC-04)
FP: Stovall Witte
FT: Stovall Witte
320 Cannon House Office Building
Phone: 202-225-6030   Fax: 202-226-1177

Ernest **ISTOOK** (R-OK-05)
FP: Nancy Nowak - Legislative Assistant
FT: Nancy Nowak - Legislative Assistant
119 Cannon House Office Building
Phone: 202-225-2132   Fax: 202-226-1463

Jesse **JACKSON** (D-IL-02)
FP: Kenneth Edmonds - Legislative Director
FT: Charles Dujon - Legislative Assistant
313 Cannon House Office Building
Phone: 202-225-0773   Fax: 202-225-0899

Sheila **JACKSON-LEE** (D-TX-18)
FP: Leon Buck - Chief of Staff/Leg. Dir.
FT: Leon Buck - Chief of Staff/Leg. Dir.
410 Cannon House Office Building
Phone: 202-225-3816   Fax: 202-225-3317

William J. **JEFFERSON** (D-LA-02)
FP: Atonte Diete-Spiff - Legislative Assistant
FT: Rory Verrett - Trade Counsel
240 Cannon House Office Building
Phone: 202-225-6636   Fax: 202-225-1988

William **JENKINS** (R-TN-01)
FP: Brenda J. Otterson/Richard Vaughn -
     Legislative Director/Legislative Assistant
FT: Brenda J. Otterson/Richard Vaughn -
     Legislative Director/Legislative Assistant
1708 Longworth House Office Building
Phone: 202-225-6356   Fax: 202-225-5714

Christopher **JOHN** (D-LA-07)
FP: David Kay - Legislative Assistant
FT: Gordon Taylor - Legislative Director
1504 Longworth House Office Building
Phone: 202-225-2031   Fax: 202-225-5724

Eddie Bernice **JOHNSON** (D-TX-30)
FP: Horace Jennings - Chief of Staff
FT: Horace Jennings - Chief of Staff
1123 Longworth House Office Building
Phone: 202-225-8885   Fax: 202-226-1477

Jay W. **JOHNSON** (D-WI-08)
FP: Jesse Sevcik - Legislative Assistant
FT: George Shevlin - Legislative Assistant
1313 Longworth House Office Building

Phone: 202-225-5665   Fax: 202-225-5729

Nancy **JOHNSON** (R-CT-06)
FP: Todd Funk
FT: Kathy Havey
343 Cannon House Office Building
Phone: 202-225-4476   Fax: 202-225-4488

Sam **JOHNSON** (R-TX-03)
FP: Kristan Mack - Deputy Legislative Dir.
FT: Kristan Mack - Deputy Legislative Dir.
1030 Longworth House Office Building
Phone: 202-225-4201   Fax: 202-225-1485

Walter B. **JONES** (R-NC-03)
FP: Mia Zur - Military Legislative Assistant
FT: Mia Zur - Military Legislative Assistant
422 Cannon House Office Building
Phone: 202-225-3415   Fax: 202-225-3286

Paul E. **KANJORSKI** (D-PA-11)
FP: Alan Pentz - Legislative Assistant
FT: Alan Pentz - Legislative Assistant
2353 Rayburn House Office Building
Phone: 202-225-6511   Fax: 202-225-9024

Marcy **KAPTUR** (D-OH-09)
FP: Bobbi Jean Qunat
FT: George Wilson
2311 Rayburn House Office Building
Phone: 202-225-4146   Fax: 202-225-7711

John R. **KASICH** (R-OH-12)
FP: Ron Christie - Legislative Director
FT: Jason McKitrick - Legislative Assistant
1111 Longworth House Office Building
Phone: 202-225-5355

Sue **KELLY** (R-NY-19)
FP: Al Garesche'
FT: Al Garesche'
1222 Longworth House Office Building
Phone: 202-225-5441   Fax: 202-225-3289

Joseph P. **KENNEDY** (D-MA-08)
FP: Robert Gerber - Professional Staff
FT: Robert Gerber - Professional Staff
2242 Rayburn House Office Building
Phone: 202-225-5111   Fax: 202-225-9322

Patrick J. **KENNEDY** (D-RI-01)
FP: Kimber Colton - Legislative Assistant
FT: Kimber Colton - Legislative Assistant
312 Cannon House Office Building
Phone: 202-225-4911   Fax: 202-225-3290

Barbara B. **KENNELLY** (D-CT-01)
FP: Adam Rak - Legislative Assistant
FT: Nick Gwyn - Legislative Assistant
201 Cannon House Office Building
Phone: 202-225-2265   Fax: 202-225-1031

Dale E. **KILDEE** (D-MI-09)
FP: Christopher Mansour - Chief of Staff
FT: Christopher Mansour - Chief of Staff
2187 Rayburn House Office Building
Phone: 202-225-3611   Fax: 202-225-6393

Carolyn Cheeks **KILPATRICK** (D-MI-15)
FP: Deborah Willig - Leg. Correspondent
FT: Deborah Willig - Leg. Correspondent
503 Cannon House Office Building
Phone: 202-225-2261   Fax: 202-225-5730

Jay **KIM** (R-CA-41)
FP: John Mechem
FT: John Mechem
227 Cannon House Office Building
Phone: 202-225-3201   Fax: 202-226-1485

Ron J. **KIND** (D-WI-03)
FP: Brad Logsdon - Legislative Counsel

FT: Brad Logsdon - Legislative Counsel
1713 Longworth House Office Building
Phone: 202-225-5506   Fax: 202-225-5739

Peter **KING** (R-NY-03)
FP: Kerry O'Hare - Legislative Director
FT: Dan Michaelis - Communications Director
403 Cannon House Office Building
Phone: 202-225-7896   Fax: 202-226-2279

Jack **KINGSTON** (R-GA-01)
FP: Adam Sullivan - Senior Legislative Asst.
FT: Adam Sullivan - Senior Legislative Asst.
1507 Longworth House Office Building
Phone: 202-225-5831   Fax: 202-226-2269

Gerald D. **KLECZKA** (D-WI-04)
FP: Dana Trytten - Legislative Assistant
FT: Vacant
2301 Rayburn House Office Building
Phone: 202-225-4572   Fax: 202-225-8135

Ron **KLINK** (D-PA-04)
FP: Beth Osborne - Legislative Assistant
FT: Peter Madaus
125 Cannon House Office Building
Phone: 202-225-2565   Fax: 202-226-2274

Scott **KLUG** (R-WI-02)
FP: Peter Bietozero - Legislative Assistant
FT: Peter Bietozero - Legislative Assistant
2331 Rayburn House Office Building
Phone: 202-225-2906   Fax: 202-225-6942

Joseph **KNOLLENBERG** (R-MI-11)
FP: Amanda Barnett - Legislative Assistant
FT: Amanda Barnett - Legislative Assistant
1511 Longworth House Office Building
Phone: 202-225-5802   Fax: 202-226-2356

Jim **KOLBE** (R-AZ-05)
FP: Everett Eissenstat
FT: Everett Eissenstat
205 Cannon House Office Building
Phone: 202-225-2542   Fax: 202-225-0378

Dennis J. **KUCINICH** (D-OH-10)
FP: Lisa Chamberlain - Legislative Assistant
FT: Jaron Bourke - Legislative Assistant
1730 Longworth House Office Building
Phone: 202-225-5871

John J. **LAFALCE** (D-NY-29)
FP: Ralph Posner - Legislative Assistant
FT: Marilyn Seiber
2310 Rayburn House Office Building
Phone: 202-225-3231   Fax: 202-225-8693

Ray **LAHOOD** (R-IL-18)
FP: David Kunz - Sr. Legislative Asst./
    Counsel
FT: Chris Guidry - Legislative Director
329 Cannon House Office Building
Phone: 202-225-6201   Fax: 202-225-9249

Nick **LAMPSON** (D-TX-09)
FP: Stanley Allen - Legislative Assistant
FT: Stanley Allen - Legislative Assistant
417 Cannon House Office Building
Phone: 202-225-6565   Fax: 202-225-5547

Tom **LANTOS** (D-CA-12)
FP: David Lee
FT: Chris Walker
2217 Rayburn House Office Building
Phone: 202-225-3531   Fax: 202-225-7900

Stephen M. **LARGENT** (R-OK-01)
FP: Bob Bolster - Legislative Assistant
FT: Bob Bolster - Legislative Assistant
426 Cannon House Office Building
Phone: 202-225-2211   Fax: 202-225-9187

Tom **LATHAM** (R-IA-05)
FP: Scott McCoy
FT: Scott McCoy
516 Cannon House Office Building
Phone: 202-225-5476   Fax: 202-225-3301

Steven C. **LATOURETTE** (R-OH-19)
FP: Christine Garsice - Legislative Assistant
FT: Brian Niceswanger - Sr. Legislative Asst.
1239 Longworth House Office Building
Phone: 202-225-5731   Fax: 202-225-3307

Rick **LAZIO** (R-NY-02)
FP: Mary Angelini
2444 Rayburn House Office Building
Phone: 202-225-3335   Fax: 202-225-4669

Jim **LEACH** (R-IA-01)
FP: Amy Butler - Legislative Assistant
FT: Amy Butler - Legislative Assistant
2186 Rayburn House Office Building
Phone: 202-225-6576   Fax: 202-226-1278

Sander M. **LEVIN** (D-MI-12)
FP: Don Jourdan
FT: Craig Kramer - Deputy Chief of Staff
2209 Rayburn House Office Building
Phone: 202-225-4961   Fax: 202-226-1033

Jerry **LEWIS** (R-CA-40)
FP: Alex Heslop - Legislative Assistant
FT: Alex Heslop - Legislative Assistant
2112 Rayburn House Office Building
Phone: 202-225-5861   Fax: 202-225-6498

John **LEWIS** (D-GA-05)
FP: Debbie Spielberg - Legislative Director
FT: Debbie Spielberg - Legislative Director
229 Cannon House Office Building
Phone: 202-225-3801   Fax: 202-225-0351

Ron **LEWIS** (R-KY-02)
FP: Sam Willett - Legislative Assistant
FT: Sam Willett - Legislative Assistant
223 Cannon House Office Building
Phone: 202-225-3501   Fax: 202-226-2019

John **LINDER** (R-GA-04)
FP: Rob Woodall - Legislative Director
FT: Rob Woodall - Legislative Director
1005 Longworth House Office Building
Phone: 202-225-4272   Fax: 202-225-4696

William O. **LIPINSKI** (D-IL-03)
FP: Jason Tai
FT: Jason Tai
1501 Longworth House Office Building
Phone: 202-225-5701   Fax: 202-225-1012

Bob **LIVINGSTON** (R-LA-01)
FP: Stan Skocki
FT: Stan Skocki
2406 Rayburn House Office Building
Phone: 202-225-3015   Fax: 202-225-0739

Frank A. **LOBIONDO** (R-NJ-02)
FP: Craig Montesano - Sr. Legislative Aide
FT: Carl Thorsen - Counsel
222 Cannon House Office Building
Phone: 202-225-6572   Fax: 202-225-3318

Zoe **LOFGREN** (D-CA-16)
FP: Sue Ramanathan - Legislative Assistant
FT: Sue Ramanathan - Legislative Assistant
318 Cannon House Office Building
Phone: 202-225-3072   Fax: 202-225-3336

Nita M. **LOWEY** (D-NY-18)
FP: Matthew Traub - Legislative Assistant
FT: Matthew Traub - Legislative Assistant
2421 Rayburn House Office Building
Phone: 202-225-6506   Fax: 202-225-0506

Frank **LUCAS** (R-OK-06)
FP: Amy Blair
FT: Mike Bertman
107 Cannon House Office Building
Phone: 202-225-5565   Fax: 202-225-8698

William P. **LUTHER** (D-MN-06)
FP: Steven Heuer - Legislative Assistant
FT: Steven Heuer - Legislative Assistant
117 Cannon House Office Building
Phone: 202-225-2271   Fax: 202-225-3368

Carolyn **MALONEY** (D-NY-14)
FP: Maggie McDow - Legislative Assistant
FT: Ian Fried - Legislative Assistant
1330 Longworth House Office Building
Phone: 202-225-7944   Fax: 202-225-4709

James H. **MALONEY** (D-CT-05)
FP: Brian Miller - Legislative Assistant
FT: Brian Miller - Legislative Assistant
1213 Longworth House Office Building
Phone: 202-225-3822   Fax: 202-225-5746

Thomas J. **MANTON** (D-NY-07)
FP: Lizzy O'Hara - Legislative Assistant
FT: Matt Socknat - Legislative Assistant
2235 Rayburn House Office Building
Phone: 202-225-3965   Fax: 202-225-1909

Donald **MANZULLO** (R-IL-16)
FP: Kevin Opstrup
FT: Phil Eskeland
409 Cannon House Office Building
Phone: 202-225-5676   Fax: 202-225-5284

Edward J. **MARKEY** (D-MA-07)
FP: Jeff Duncan - Legislative Director
FT: Naomi Freeman - Legislative Assistant
2133 Rayburn House Office Building
Phone: 202-225-2836

Matthew G. **MARTINEZ** (D-CA-31)
FP: Jamie Jones - Legislative Assistant
FT: Mary Ellen Sprenkel - Legislative Asst.
2234 Rayburn House Office Building
Phone: 202-225-5464   Fax: 202-225-5467

Frank R. **MASCARA** (D-PA-20)
FP: Lee Footer
FT: Jonathan Godfrey - Legislative Assistant
314 Cannon House Office Building
Phone: 202-225-4665   Fax: 202-225-3377

Robert T. **MATSUI** (D-CA-05)
FP: Steve Mastorakos - Legislative Assistant
FT: Frances Grab - Tax and Trade Counsel
2308 Rayburn House Office Building
Phone: 202-225-7163   Fax: 202-225-0566

Carolyn **MCCARTHY** (D-NY-04)
FP: Sean McDonough - Legislative Director
FT: Sean McDonough - Legislative Director
1725 Longworth House Office Building
Phone: 202-225-5516   Fax: 202-225-5758

Karen **MCCARTHY** (D-MO-05)
FP: Andy Walker - Legislative Assistant
FT: Andy Walker - Legislative Assistant
1232 Longworth House Office Building
Phone: 202-225-4535   Fax: 202-225-4403

Bill **MCCOLLUM** (R-FL-08)
FP: Jennifer Hargon - Legislative Assistant
FT: Jennifer Hargon - Legislative Assistant
2266 Rayburn House Office Building
Phone: 202-225-2176   Fax: 202-225-0999

Jim **MCCRERY** (R-LA-04)
FP: Chris King - Legislative Assistant
FT: Anel Vallillo - Legislative Director
2104 Rayburn House Office Building

Phone: 202-225-2777   Fax: 202-225-8039

Joseph M. **MCDADE** (R-PA-10)
FP: Teresa Baker
FT: Teresa Baker
2107 Rayburn House Office Building
Phone: 202-225-3731   Fax: 202-225-9594

James A. **MCDERMOTT** (D-WA-07)
FP: Michael Shannon - Legislative Assistant
FT: Peter Rubin - Legislative Assistant
2349 Rayburn House Office Building
Phone: 202-225-3106   Fax: 202-225-9212

James P. **MCGOVERN** (D-MA-03)
FP: Cindy Buhl - Legislative Director
FT: Karl Moeller - Legislative Assistant
512 Cannon House Office Building
Phone: 202-225-6101   Fax: 202-225-5759

Paul **MCHALE** (D-PA-15)
FP: Geoffrey Plague
FT: Geoffrey Plague
217 Cannon House Office Building
Phone: 202-225-6411   Fax: 202-225-5320

John **MCHUGH** (R-NY-24)
FP: Anne LeMay - Legislative Assistant
FT: Anne LeMay - Legislative Assistant
2441 Rayburn House Office Building
Phone: 202-225-4611   Fax: 202-226-0621

Scott **MCINNIS** (R-CO-03)
FP: Jon Hrobsky
FT: Jon Hrobsky
215 Cannon House Office Building
Phone: 202-225-4761   Fax: 202-226-0622

David M. **MCINTOSH** (R-IN-02)
FP: John Steele - Legislative Assistant
FT: John Steele - Legislative Assistant
1208 Longworth House Office Building
Phone: 202-225-3021   Fax: 202-225-3382

Mike **MCINTYRE** (D-NC-07)
FP: James Norment - Legislative Assistant
FT: John Hayes - Legislative Assistant
1605 Longworth House Office Building
Phone: 202-225-2731   Fax: 202-225-5773

Howard **MCKEON** (R-CA-25)
FP: Greg Campbell - Sr. Legislative Aide
FT: Karen Weiss - Legislative Aide
307 Cannon House Office Building
Phone: 202-225-1956   Fax: 202-226-0683

Cynthia **MCKINNEY** (D-GA-11)
FP: Ada Loo - Legislative Assistant
FT: Jayme Roth - Legislative Assistant
124 Cannon House Office Building
Phone: 202-225-1605   Fax: 202-226-0691

Michael R. **MCNULTY** (D-NY-21)
FP: Charles Segel - Press Secretary/
     Legislative Assistant
FT: David Torian - Legislative Counsel
2161 Rayburn House Office Building
Phone: 202-225-5076   Fax: 202-225-5077

Martin **MEEHAN** (D-MA-05)
FP: Amy Rosenbaum
FT: Amy Rosenbaum
2434 Rayburn House Office Building
Phone: 202-225-3411   Fax: 202-226-0771

Carrie **MEEK** (D-FL-17)
FP: Cheryl Parker Rose
FT: Cheryl Parker Rose
401 Cannon House Office Building
Phone: 202-225-4506   Fax: 202-226-0777

Robert **MENENDEZ** (D-NJ-13)

FP: Jody B. Christiansen
FT: Jody B. Christiansen
405 Cannon House Office Building
Phone: 202-225-7919   Fax: 202-226-0792

Jack **METCALF** (R-WA-02)
FP: Jeffrey Markey
FT: Jeffrey Markey
1510 Longworth House Office Building
Phone: 202-225-2605   Fax: 202-225-4420

John **MICA** (R-FL-07)
FP: Wiley Dick
FT: Sharon Pinkerton
106 Cannon House Office Building
Phone: 202-225-4035   Fax: 202-226-0821

Juanita **MILLENDER-MCDONALD**
     (D-CA-37)
FP: Vincent Harris - Legislative Assistant
FT: Alex Hanson - Legislative Assistant
419 Cannon House Office Building
Phone: 202-225-7924   Fax: 202-225-7926

Dan **MILLER** (R-FL-13)
FP: Amy Steinmann
FT: Todd Irons
102 Cannon House Office Building
Phone: 202-225-5015   Fax: 202-226-0828

George **MILLER** (D-CA-07)
FP: vacant
FT: vacant
2205 Rayburn House Office Building
Phone: 202-225-2095   Fax: 202-225-5609

David **MINGE** (D-MN-02)
FP: Curt Yukum - Legislative Assistant
FT: Curt Yukum - Legislative Assistant
1415 Longworth House Office Building
Phone: 202-225-2331   Fax: 202-226-0836

Patsy T. **MINK** (D-HI-02)
FP: Russell Kudo
FT: Russell Kudo
2135 Rayburn House Office Building
Phone: 202-225-4906   Fax: 202-225-4987

Joe **MOAKLEY** (D-MA-09)
FP: Steve LaRose - Office Manager
FT: Steve LaRose - Office Manager
235 Cannon House Office Building
Phone: 202-225-8273   Fax: 202-225-3984

Alan B. **MOLLOHAN** (D-WV-01)
FP: Sally A. Gaines - Legislative Director
FT: Sally A. Gaines - Legislative Director
2346 Rayburn House Office Building
Phone: 202-225-4172   Fax: 202-225-7564

James P. **MORAN** (D-VA-08)
FP: Mike Eastman - Legislative Assistant
FT: Tim Aiken - Sr. Legislative Assistant
1214 Longworth House Office Building
Phone: 202-225-4376   Fax: 202-225-0017

Jerry **MORAN** (R-KS-01)
FP: Tyler Sherer - Legislative Assistant
FT: Tyler Sherer - Legislative Assistant
1217 Longworth House Office Building
Phone: 202-225-2715   Fax: 202-225-5124

Constance A. **MORELLA** (R-MD-08)
FP: Craig Powers
FT: Craig Powers
2228 Rayburn House Office Building
Phone: 202-225-5341   Fax: 202-225-1389

John P. **MURTHA** (D-PA-12)
FP: Debbie Tekavec - Legislative Director
FT: Debbie Tekavec - Legislative Director
2423 Rayburn House Office Building

Phone: 202-225-2065   Fax: 202-225-5709

Sue **MYRICK** (R-NC-09)
FP: Nina Owcharenko - Legislative Assistant
FT: Gil Murdock - Legislative Assistant
230 Cannon House Office Building
Phone: 202-225-1976   Fax: 202-225-3389

Jerrold **NADLER** (D-NY-08)
FP: David Lachmann - Counsel
FT: Brett Heimov - Legislative Director
2448 Rayburn House Office Building
Phone: 202-225-5635   Fax: 202-225-6923

Richard E. **NEAL** (D-MA-02)
FP: Bill Tranghese - Press Secretary
FT: Kathleen Sullivan - Legislative Assistant
2236 Rayburn House Office Building
Phone: 202-225-5601   Fax: 202-225-8112

George R. **NETHERCUTT** (R-WA-05)
FP: Rob Neal
FT: Rob Neal
1527 Longworth House Office Building
Phone: 202-225-2006   Fax: 202-225-3392

Mark **NEUMANN** (R-WI-01)
FP: John Richardson
FT: John Richardson
415 Cannon House Office Building
Phone: 202-225-3031   Fax: 202-225-3393

Robert W. **NEY** (R-OH-18)
FP: Maria Robinson
FT: Maria Robinson
1024 Longworth House Office Building
Phone: 202-225-6265   Fax: 202-225-3394

Anne Meagher **NORTHUP** (R-KY-03)
FP: Thomas Hewitt - Legislative Assistant
FT: Thomas Hewitt - Legislative Assistant
1004 Longworth House Office Building
Phone: 202-225-5401   Fax: 202-225-5776

Eleanor Holmes **NORTON** (D-DC-DL)
FP: Bing Yee - Legislative Assistant
FT: Bing Yee - Legislative Assistant
1424 Longworth House Office Building
Phone: 202-225-8050   Fax: 202-225-3002

Charles W. **NORWOOD** (R-GA-10)
FP: Dan LaPre - Legislative Assistant
FT: Dan LaPre - Legislative Assistant
1707 Longworth House Office Building
Phone: 202-225-4101   Fax: 202-225-0279

Jim **NUSSLE** (R-IA-02)
FP: Steven Berry - Legislative Assistant
FT: Steven Berry - Legislative Assistant
303 Cannon House Office Building
Phone: 202-225-2911   Fax: 202-225-9129

James L. **OBERSTAR** (D-MN-08)
FP: Chip Gardiner - Legislative Director
FT: Neil Weinstein - Legislative Assistant
2366 Rayburn House Office Building
Phone: 202-225-6211   Fax: 202-225-0699

David R. **OBEY** (D-WI-07)
FP: William Painter - Legislative Assistant
FT: Paul Carver - Legislative Assistant
2462 Rayburn House Office Building
Phone: 202-225-3365   Fax: 202-225-3240

John **OLVER** (D-MA-01)
FP: Kelly Bovio - Legislative Assistant
FT: David Oliveira - Legislative Assistant
1027 Longworth House Office Building
Phone: 202-225-5335   Fax: 202-226-1224

Solomon P. **ORTIZ** (D-TX-27)
FP: Luther Jones - Legislative Fellow

FT: Luther Jones - Legislative Fellow
2136 Rayburn House Office Building
Phone: 202-225-7742   Fax: 202-226-1134

Major R. **OWENS** (D-NY-11)
FP: Jacqui Ellis - Chief of Staff
FT: Jacqui Ellis - Chief of Staff
2305 Rayburn House Office Building
Phone: 202-225-6231   Fax: 202-226-0112

Michael G. **OXLEY** (R-OH-04)
FP: Robert Foster - Legislative Director
FT: Robert Foster - Legislative Director
2233 Rayburn House Office Building
Phone: 202-225-2676

Ron **PACKARD** (R-CA-48)
FP: Eric Mondero - Legislative Director
FT: Nora Bomar - Legislative Assistant
2372 Rayburn House Office Building
Phone: 202-225-3906   Fax: 202-225-0134

Frank **PALLONE** (D-NJ-06)
FP: Ted Loud
FT: Kap Sharma
420 Cannon House Office Building
Phone: 202-225-4671   Fax: 202-225-9665

Mike **PAPPAS** (R-NJ-12)
FP: William Burlew - Legislative Assistant
FT: William Burlew - Legislative Assistant
1710 Longworth House Office Building
Phone: 202-225-5801   Fax: 202-225-6025

Mike **PARKER** (R-MS-04)
FP: Scott Malvaney - Chief of Staff
FT: Scott Malvaney - Chief of Staff
2445 Rayburn House Office Building
Phone: 202-225-5865   Fax: 202-225-5886

William J. **PASCRELL** (D-NJ-08)
FP: Chris Blanda - Legislative Assistant
FT: Chris Blanda - Legislative Assistant
1722 Longworth House Office Building
Phone: 202-225-5751   Fax: 202-225-5782

Ed **PASTOR** (D-AZ-02)
FP: Blake Gable
FT: Don Medley
2465 Rayburn House Office Building
Phone: 202-225-4065   Fax: 202-225-1655

Ron E. **PAUL** (R-TX-14)
FP: Joseph Becker - Legislative Director
FT: Joseph Becker - Legislative Director
203 Cannon House Office Building
Phone: 202-225-2831   Fax: 202-226-4871

Bill **PAXON** (R-NY-27)
FP: Chris Downing - Legislative Assistant
FT: Mary G. Mitschow - Legislative Assistant
2412 Rayburn House Office Building
Phone: 202-225-5265   Fax: 202-225-5910

Donald M. **PAYNE** (D-NJ-10)
FP: Charisse Glassman - Foreign Affairs
    Adviser
FT: Charisse Glassman - Foreign Affairs
    Adviser
2244 Rayburn House Office Building
Phone: 202-225-3436   Fax: 202-225-4160

Edward A. **PEASE** (R-IN-07)
FP: Greg Goode - Legislative Assistant
FT: Greg Goode - Legislative Assistant
226 Cannon House Office Building
Phone: 202-225-5805

Nancy **PELOSI** (D-CA-08)
FP: Carolyn Bartholomew
FT: Carolyn Bartholomew
2457 Rayburn House Office Building

Phone: 202-225-4965   Fax: 202-225-8259

Collin **PETERSON** (D-MN-07)
FP: Joanna Barrett - Exec./Legislative Asst.
FT: Rob Lareu - Senior Policy Advisor
2159 Rayburn House Office Building
Phone: 202-225-2165   Fax: 202-225-1593

John E. **PETERSON** (R-PA-05)
FP: Ian Pilling - Legislative Assistant
FT: Ian Pilling - Legislative Assistant
1020 Longworth House Office Building
Phone: 202-225-5121   Fax: 202-225-5796

Thomas E. **PETRI** (R-WI-06)
FP: John Broehm - Legislative Assistant
FT: Paul Trampe - Legislative Assistant
2262 Rayburn House Office Building
Phone: 202-225-2476   Fax: 202-225-2356

Charles W. **PICKERING** (R-MS-03)
FP: John Rothrock - Legislative Director
FT: John Rothrock - Legislative Director
427 Cannon House Office Building
Phone: 202-225-5031   Fax: 202-225-5797

Owen B. **PICKETT** (D-VA-02)
FP: Jennifer Bering - Legislative Assistant
FT: Jennifer Bering - Legislative Assistant
2430 Rayburn House Office Building
Phone: 202-225-4215   Fax: 202-225-4218

Joseph R. **PITTS** (R-PA-16)
FP: Julie Hershey - Legislative Assistant
FT: Julie Hershey - Legislative Assistant
504 Cannon House Office Building
Phone: 202-225-2411   Fax: 202-225-2013

Richard W. **POMBO** (R-CA-11)
FP: Paul Kavinoky
FT: Paul Kavinoky
1519 Longworth House Office Building
Phone: 202-225-1947   Fax: 202-226-0861

Earl **POMEROY** (D-ND-AL)
FP: Michael Smart
FT: Michael Smart
1533 Longworth House Office Building
Phone: 202-225-2611   Fax: 202-226-0893

John Edward **PORTER** (R-IL-10)
FP: Kelley Currie
FT: Kelley Currie
2373 Rayburn House Office Building
Phone: 202-225-4835   Fax: 202-225-0837

Rob **PORTMAN** (R-OH-02)
FP: Seth Webb - Legislative Assistant
FT: Seth Webb - Legislative Assistant
238 Cannon House Office Building
Phone: 202-225-3164   Fax: 202-225-1992

Glenn **POSHARD** (D-IL-19)
FP: David Gillies - Acting Chief of Staff
FT: Kristin Nicholson - Legislative Director
2334 Rayburn House Office Building
Phone: 202-225-5201   Fax: 202-225-1541

David E. **PRICE** (D-NC-04)
FP: Chuck Cushman - Legislative Assistant
FT: Chuck Cushman - Legislative Assistant
2162 Rayburn House Office Building
Phone: 202-225-1784   Fax: 202-225-2014

Deborah **PRYCE** (R-OH-15)
FP: John Lendak - Legislative Assistant
FT: John Lendak - Legislative Assistant
221 Cannon House Office Building
Phone: 202-225-2015   Fax: 202-226-0986

Jack **QUINN** (R-NY-30)
FP: Dan Skopec - Legislative Assistant

FT: Dan Skopec - Legislative Assistant
331 Cannon House Office Building
Phone: 202-225-3306   Fax: 202-226-0347

George P. **RADANOVICH** (R-CA-19)
FP: Ian M. Houston
FT: Ian M. Houston
213 Cannon House Office Building
Phone: 202-225-4540   Fax: 202-225-3402

Nick Joe **RAHALL** (D-WV-03)
FP: Birdie Kyle - Legislative Director
FT: Craig Clapper - Legislative Assistant
2307 Rayburn House Office Building
Phone: 202-225-3452   Fax: 202-225-9061

Jim **RAMSTAD** (R-MN-03)
FP: Michael Hagenson
FT: Megan Ivory
103 Cannon House Office Building
Phone: 202-225-2871   Fax: 202-225-6351

Charles B. **RANGEL** (D-NY-15)
FP: Emile Mille - Legislative Director
FT: Emile Mille - Legislative Director
2354 Rayburn House Office Building
Phone: 202-225-4365   Fax: 202-225-0816

Bill **REDMOND** (R-NM-03)
FP: Troy Tidwell - Legislative Assistant
FT: Ashlie Warnick - Legislative Assistant
2268 Rayburn House Office Building
Phone: 202-225-6190   Fax: 202-226-1331

Ralph **REGULA** (R-OH-16)
FP: Connie Veillette - Chief of Staff
FT: Karen Buttato - Legislative Council
2309 Rayburn House Office Building
Phone: 202-225-3876   Fax: 202-225-3059

Silvestre **REYES** (D-TX-16)
FP: Maurice Kurland - Legislative Assistant
FT: Maurice Kurland - Legislative Assistant
514 Cannon House Office Building
Phone: 202-225-4831   Fax: 202-225-2016

Frank D. **RIGGS** (R-CA-01)
FP: Jim Tobin - Legislative Assistant
FT: Mark Davis - Legislative Director
1714 Longworth House Office Building
Phone: 202-225-3311   Fax: 202-225-3403

Bob **RILEY** (R-AL-03)
FP: Sandler Passman - Legislative Director
FT: Dan Ganes - Legislative Director
510 Cannon House Office Building
Phone: 202-225-3261   Fax: 202-225-5827

Lynn Nancy **RIVERS** (D-MI-13)
FP: Rebecca Hoisington
FT: Rebecca Hoisington
1724 Longworth House Office Building
Phone: 202-225-6261   Fax: 202-225-3404

Ciro **RODRIGUEZ** (D-TX-28)
FP: Asim Ghapoor - Legislative Assistant
FT: Diego DeLagarea - Legislative Assistant
323 Cannon House Office Building
Phone: 202-225-1640   Fax: 202-225-1641

Tim **ROEMER** (D-IN-03)
FP: Pete Spiro - Sr. Legislative Assistant
FT: Pete Spiro - Sr. Legislative Assistant
2348 Rayburn House Office Building
Phone: 202-225-3915   Fax: 202-225-6798

James E. **ROGAN** (R-CA-27)
FP: Myron Jacobson
FT: Dave Joergenson
502 Cannon House Office Building
Phone: 202-225-4176   Fax: 202-225-5828

Harold **ROGERS** (R-KY-05)
FP: Will Smith - Sr. Legislative Assistant
FT: Will Smith - Sr. Legislative Assistant
2468 Rayburn House Office Building
Phone: 202-225-4601   Fax: 202-225-0940

Dana **ROHRABACHER** (R-CA-45)
FP: Al Santoli
FT: Al Santoli
2338 Rayburn House Office Building
Phone: 202-225-2415   Fax: 202-225-0145

Carlos A. **ROMERO-BARCELO** (D-PR-RC)
FP: Yvonne E. R. Benner - Legislative Director
FT: Yvonne E.R. Benner - Legislative Director
2443 Rayburn House Office Building
Phone: 202-225-5029   Fax: 202-225-2154

Ileana **ROS-LEHTINEN** (R-FL-18)
FP: Jay O'Callaghan - Legislative Assistant
FT: Catheryn Castillo - Legislative Assistant
2240 Rayburn House Office Building
Phone: 202-225-3931   Fax: 202-225-5620

Steven R. **ROTHMAN** (D-NJ-09)
FP: Raffi Hamparian - Legislative Assistant
FT: Raffi Hamparian - Legislative Assistant
1607 Longworth House Office Building
Phone: 202-225-5061   Fax: 202-225-5851

Marge **ROUKEMA** (R-NJ-05)
FP: Christopher Brinson - Legislative Assistant
FT: Chistopher Brinson - Legislative Assistant
2469 Rayburn House Office Building
Phone: 202-225-4465   Fax: 202-225-9048

Lucille **ROYBAL-ALLARD** (D-CA-33)
FP: Kathleen Sengstock - Legislative Assistant
FT: Kathleen Sengstock - Legislative Assistant
2435 Rayburn House Office Building
Phone: 202-225-1766   Fax: 202-226-0350

Ed **ROYCE** (R-CA-39)
FP: Thomas Sheehy
FT: Thomas Sheehy
1133 Longworth House Office Building
Phone: 202-225-4111   Fax: 202-226-0335

Bobby **RUSH** (D-IL-01)
FP: Megan Griffin - Staff Assistant
FT: Megan Griffin - Staff Assistant
131 Cannon House Office Building
Phone: 202-225-4372   Fax: 202-226-0333

Jim **RYUN** (R-KS-02)
FP: Valerie Shank
FT: Jim Dolbow
511 Cannon House Office Building
Phone: 202-225-6601   Fax: 202-225-7986

Martin Olav **SABO** (D-MN-05)
FP: Eileen Baumgartner
FT: Eileen Baumgartner
2336 Rayburn House Office Building
Phone: 202-225-4755   Fax: 202-225-4886

Matthew J. **SALMON** (R-AZ-01)
FP: Mike Paranzino/Steve Chucri - Legislative Assistant
FT: Kelly Surrick
115 Cannon House Office Building
Phone: 202-225-2635   Fax: 202-225-3405

Loretta **SANCHEZ** (D-CA-46)
FP: Laura Rodriguez - Legislative Staff
FT: Laura Rodriguez - Legislative Staff
1529 Longworth House Office Building
Phone: 202-225-2965   Fax: 202-225-5859

Bernard **SANDERS** (I-VT-AL)
FP: Bill Goold

FT: Bill Goold
2202 Rayburn House Office Building
Phone: 202-225-4115   Fax: 202-225-6790

Max A. **SANDLIN** (D-TX-01)
FP: Dean Aguiller - Legislative Assistant
FT: Jason Richardson - Legislative Assistant
214 Cannon House Office Building
Phone: 202-225-3035   Fax: 202-225-5866

Marshall **SANFORD** (R-SC-01)
FP: Holly Swanson - Legislative Assistant
FT: Holly Swanson - Legislative Assistant
1223 Longworth House Office Building
Phone: 202-225-3176   Fax: 202-225-3407

Thomas C. **SAWYER** (D-OH-14)
FP: Derrick Owens - Sr. Legislative Assistant
FT: Heather Stephens - Legislative Assistant
1414 Longworth House Office Building
Phone: 202-225-5231   Fax: 202-225-5278

Jim **SAXTON** (R-NJ-03)
FP: Ethan Cooper - Legislative Assistant
FT: Ethan Cooper - Legislative Assistant
339 Cannon House Office Building
Phone: 202-225-4765   Fax: 202-225-0778

Joe **SCARBOROUGH** (R-FL-01)
FP: Bart Roper
FT: James Griffin
127 Cannon House Office Building
Phone: 202-225-4136   Fax: 202-225-3414

Dan **SCHAEFER** (R-CO-06)
FP: Luke Rose - Legislative Assistant
FT: Luke Rose - Legislative Assistant
2160 Rayburn House Office Building
Phone: 202-225-7882   Fax: 202-225-7885

Bob **SCHAFFER** (R-CO-04)
FP: Cory J. Flohr - Legislative Assistant
FT: Cory J. Flohr - Legislative Assistant
212 Cannon House Office Building
Phone: 202-225-4676   Fax: 202-225-5870

VACANT (R-NM-01)
FP: Pamela Kirbey
FT: Pamela Kirbey
2404 Rayburn House Office Building
Phone: 202-225-6316   Fax: 202-225-4975

Charles E. **SCHUMER** (D-NY-09)
FP: Brett DeResta - Legislative Assistant
FT: Jim Kessler - Legislative Director
2211 Rayburn House Office Building
Phone: 202-225-6616   Fax: 202-225-4183

Bobby **SCOTT** (D-VA-03)
FP: Bob Ramsey - Legislative Assistant
FT: Bob Ramsey - Legislative Assistant
2464 Rayburn House Office Building
Phone: 202-225-8351   Fax: 202-225-8354

F. James **SENSENBRENNER** (R-WI-09)
FP: Steve Pinkos - Legislative Director
FT: Steve Pinkos - Legislative Director
2332 Rayburn House Office Building
Phone: 202-225-5101   Fax: 202-225-3190

Jose **SERRANO** (D-NY-16)
FP: Nadine Berg - Legislative Assistant
FT: Nadine Berg - Legislative Assistant
2342 Rayburn House Office Building
Phone: 202-225-4361   Fax: 202-225-6001

Pete A. **SESSIONS** (R-TX-05)
FP: Bill Cotton - Legislative Assistant
FT: Bill Cotton - Legislative Assistant
1318 Longworth House Office Building
Phone: 202-225-2231   Fax: 202-225-5878

John B. **SHADEGG** (R-AZ-04)
FP: Eric Schlecht - Legislative Assistant
FT: Eric Schlecht - Legislative Assistant
430 Cannon House Office Building
Phone: 202-225-3361   Fax: 202-225-3462

E. Clay **SHAW** (R-FL-22)
FP: VACANT
FT: Michael Harrington - Legislative Director
2408 Rayburn House Office Building
Phone: 202-225-3026   Fax: 202-225-8398

Christopher **SHAYS** (R-CT-04)
FP: Len Wolsson - Legislative Assistant
FT: Len Wolsson - Legislative Assistant
1502 Longworth House Office Building
Phone: 202-225-5541   Fax: 202-225-9629

Brad **SHERMAN** (D-CA-24)
FP: Demetra Pappas - Legislative Assistant
FT: Erzic Edwards - General Counsel
1524 Longworth House Office Building
Phone: 202-225-5911   Fax: 202-225-5879

John M. **SHIMKUS** (R-IL-20)
FP: Morna Gibbons - Legislative Assistant
FT: Morna Gibbons - Legislative Assistant
513 Cannon House Office Building
Phone: 202-225-5271   Fax: 202-225-5880

Bud **SHUSTER** (R-PA-09)
FP: John McAllister
FT: John Murphy
2188 Rayburn House Office Building
Phone: 202-225-2431   Fax: 202-225-2486

Norman **SISISKY** (D-VA-04)
FP: Perry Floyd - Military Assistant
FT: Perry Floyd - Military Assistant
2371 Rayburn House Office Building
Phone: 202-225-6365   Fax: 202-226-1170

David E. **SKAGGS** (D-CO-02)
FP: Sue Hardesty - Legislative Assistant
FT: Sue Hardesty - Legislative Assistant
1124 Longworth House Office Building
Phone: 202-225-2161   Fax: 202-226-3806

Joe **SKEEN** (R-NM-02)
FP: Bruce Donisthorpe - Legislative Director
FT: Bruce Donisthorpe - Legislative Director
2302 Rayburn House Office Building
Phone: 202-225-2365   Fax: 202-225-9599

Ike **SKELTON** (D-MO-04)
FP: Bill Natter - Legislative Assistant
FT: Lara Battles
2227 Rayburn House Office Building
Phone: 202-225-2876   Fax: 202-225-2695

Louise McIntosh **SLAUGHTER** (D-NY-28)
FP: Tom Bantle - Legislative Director
FT: Stuart Spencer - Legislative Assistant
2347 Rayburn House Office Building
Phone: 202-225-3615   Fax: 202-225-7822

Adam **SMITH** (D-WA-09)
FP: Max Chyrmovitz - Staff Assistant
FT: Shannon Ashpole - Legislative Assistant
1505 Longworth House Office Building
Phone: 202-225-8901   Fax: 202-225-5893

Christopher H. **SMITH** (R-NJ-04)
FP: Joseph Rees/Stan DeBoe - Subcommittee
   Director/Legislative Assistant
FT: Andrew Napoli - Legislative Assistant
2370 Rayburn House Office Building
Phone: 202-225-3765   Fax: 202-225-7768

Lamar S. **SMITH** (R-TX-21)
FP: Johnnie Kaserle - Legislative Assistant
FT: Johnnie Kaserle - Legislative Assistant

2231 Rayburn House Office Building
Phone: 202-225-4236   Fax: 202-225-8628

Linda A. **SMITH** (R-WA-03)
FP: Jocelyn Rowe - Sr. Legislative Assistant
FT: Jocelyn Rowe - Sr. Legislative Assistant
1317 Longworth House Office Building
Phone: 202-225-3536   Fax: 202-225-3478

Nick **SMITH** (R-MI-07)
FP: Dena Plummer - Legislative Assistant
FT: Dena Plummer - Legislative Assistant
306 Cannon House Office Building
Phone: 202-225-6276   Fax: 202-225-6281

Robert F. **SMITH** (R-OR-02)
FP: John Luddy - Sr. Legislative Assistant
FT: John Luddy - Sr. Legislative Assistant
1126 Longworth House Office Building
Phone: 202-225-6730   Fax: 202-225-5774

Vincent K. **SNOWBARGER** (R-KS-03)
FP: Jonathan Fellows - Legislative Director
FT: Jonathan Fellows - Legislative Director
509 Cannon House Office Building
Phone: 202-225-2865   Fax: 202-225-5897

Vic F. **SNYDER** (D-AR-02)
FP: Mike Casey - Legislative Assistant
FT: Mike Casey - Legislative Assistant
1319 Longworth House Office Building
Phone: 202-225-2506   Fax: 202-225-5903

Gerald B.H. **SOLOMON** (R-NY-22)
FP: Jim Doran - Legislative Assistant
FT: Jim Doran - Legislative Assistant
2206 Rayburn House Office Building
Phone: 202-225-5614   Fax: 202-225-6234

Mark Edward **SOUDER** (R-IN-04)
FP: Amy Adair
FT: Amy Adair
418 Cannon House Office Building
Phone: 202-225-4436   Fax: 202-225-3479

Floyd **SPENCE** (R-SC-02)
FP: Miriam Wolff - Legislative Director
FT: Miriam Wolff - Legislative Director
2405 Rayburn House Office Building
Phone: 202-225-2452   Fax: 202-225-2455

John M. **SPRATT** (D-SC-05)
FP: David Talbot - Legislative Assistant
FT: Andrew Hunter - Legislative Assistant
1536 Longworth House Office Building
Phone: 202-225-5501   Fax: 202-225-0464

Debbie **STABENOW** (D-MI-08)
FP: Libbie Ward - Congressional Aide
FT: Kimberly Love - Legislative Assistant
1516 Longworth House Office Building
Phone: 202-225-4872   Fax: 202-225-5820

Fortney H. **STARK** (D-CA-13)
FP: Andrea Salinas
FT: Ann Raffaelli
239 Cannon House Office Building
Phone: 202-225-5065   Fax: 202-226-3805

Cliff **STEARNS** (R-FL-06)
FP: Peter Krug
FT: Peter Krug
2352 Rayburn House Office Building
Phone: 202-225-5744   Fax: 202-225-3973

Charles W. **STENHOLM** (D-TX-17)
FP: Julie Turner - Legislative Assistant
FT: Edward Lorenzen - Legislative Assistant
1211 Longworth House Office Building
Phone: 202-225-6605   Fax: 202-225-2234

Louis **STOKES** (D-OH-11)

FP: Vacant
FT: Vacant
2365 Rayburn House Office Building
Phone: 202-225-7032   Fax: 202-225-1339

Ted **STRICKLAND** (D-OH-06)
FP: Mary Huttlinger - Legislative Assistant
FT: Mary Huttlinger - Legislative Assistant
336 Cannon House Office Building
Phone: 202-225-5705   Fax: 202-225-5907

Bob **STUMP** (R-AZ-03)
FP: Tina Guziak - Legislative Assistant
FT: Dolores Dunn - LA/Scheduler
211 Cannon House Office Building
Phone: 202-225-4576   Fax: 202-225-6328

Bart **STUPAK** (D-MI-01)
FP: Jen Pihlaja - Legislative Assistant
FT: Matt Berzok - Sr. Legislative Assistant
1410 Longworth House Office Building
Phone: 202-225-4735   Fax: 202-225-4744

John E. **SUNUNU** (R-NH-01)
FP: John Richardson - Legislative Assistant
FT: John Richardson - Legislative Assistant
1229 Longworth House Office Building
Phone: 202-225-5456   Fax: 202-225-5822

Jim **TALENT** (R-MO-02)
FP: Lindsey R. Neas
FT: Katherine Kless
1022 Longworth House Office Building
Phone: 202-225-2561   Fax: 202-225-2563

John S. **TANNER** (D-TN-08)
FP: Joe Dickson
FT: Chad Jenkins - Sr. Legislative Assistant
1127 Longworth House Office Building
Phone: 202-225-4714   Fax: 202-225-1765

Ellen O. **TAUSCHER** (D-CA-10)
FP: Ken Kero - Legislative Assistant
FT: Ken Kero - Legislative Assistant
1440 Longworth House Office Building
Phone: 202-225-1880   Fax: 202-225-5914

W.J. **TAUZIN** (R-LA-03)
FP: Garret Graves - Deputy Chief of Staff
FT: Monica Azare - Legislative Director
2183 Rayburn House Office Building
Phone: 202-225-4031   Fax: 202-225-0563

Charles H. **TAYLOR** (R-NC-11)
FP: Ken Moffit - Legislative Director
FT: Ken Moffit - Legislative Director
231 Cannon House Office Building
Phone: 202-225-6401

Gene **TAYLOR** (D-MS-05)
FP: Randy Jennings
FT: Stacy Ballow
2447 Rayburn House Office Building
Phone: 202-225-5772   Fax: 202-225-7074

William M. **THOMAS** (R-CA-21)
FP: David Kavanaugh - Legislative Assistant
FT: Bob Winters - Legislative Assistant
2208 Rayburn House Office Building
Phone: 202-225-2915   Fax: 202-225-2878

Bennie G. **THOMPSON** (D-MS-02)
FP: Walter Vinson
FT: Walter Vinson
1408 Longworth House Office Building
Phone: 202-225-5876   Fax: 202-225-5898

William M. **THORNBERRY** (R-TX-13)
FP: Kyle Ruckert - Legislative Assistant
FT: Brian Thomas - Sr. Legislative Assistant
412 Cannon House Office Building
Phone: 202-225-3706   Fax: 202-225-3486

John R. **THUNE** (R-SD-AL)
FP: John Weaver - Legislative Assistant
FT: John Weaver - Legislative Assistant
506 Cannon House Office Building
Phone: 202-225-2801   Fax: 202-225-5823

Karen **THURMAN** (D-FL-05)
FP: Bob Dobek - Legislative Director
FT: Nora Matus - Administrative Assistant
440 Cannon House Office Building
Phone: 202-225-1002   Fax: 202-226-0329

Todd **TIAHRT** (R-KS-04)
FP: Jeff Kahrs
FT: Joe Cramer
428 Cannon House Office Building
Phone: 202-225-6216   Fax: 202-225-3489

John F. **TIERNEY** (D-MA-06)
FP: Elliot Kaye - Legislative Director
FT: Toni Cooper - Legislative Assistant
120 Cannon House Office Building
Phone: 202-225-8020   Fax: 202-225-5915

Esteban Edward **TORRES** (D-CA-34)
FP: Eric Reuther - Legislative Assistant
FT: Nancy Alcalde - Legislative Assistant
2269 Rayburn House Office Building
Phone: 202-225-5256   Fax: 202-225-9711

Edolphus **TOWNS** (D-NY-10)
FP: Alex Beckles
FT: Alex Beckles
2232 Rayburn House Office Building
Phone: 202-225-5936   Fax: 202-225-1018

James A. **TRAFICANT** (D-OH-17)
FP: Kim Harris - Sr. Legislative Assistant
FT: Kim Harris - Sr. Legislative Assistant
2446 Rayburn House Office Building
Phone: 202-225-5261   Fax: 202-225-3719

Jim **TURNER** (D-TX-02)
FP: Keith Langston - Legislative Assistant
FT: Trey Henderson - Legislative Assistant
1508 Longworth House Office Building
Phone: 202-225-2401   Fax: 202-225-5955

Robert **UNDERWOOD** (D-GU-DL)
FP: Mariel Loriega - Legislative Assistant
FT: Mariel Loriega - Legislative Assistant
424 Cannon House Office Building
Phone: 202-225-1188   Fax: 202-226-0341

Frederick S. **UPTON** (R-MI-06)
FP: Scott Aliferis - Legislative Director
FT: Scott Aliferis - Legislative Director
2333 Rayburn House Office Building
Phone: 202-225-3761   Fax: 202-225-4986

Nydia **VELAZQUEZ** (D-NY-12)
FP: Luis Rosaro - Legislative Assistant
FT: Salomon Torres - Legislative Assistant
1221 Longworth House Office Building
Phone: 202-225-2361   Fax: 202-226-0327

Bruce F. **VENTO** (D-MN-04)
FP: Jennifer Cless - Legislative Assistant
FT: Jennifer Cless - Legislative Assistant
2304 Rayburn House Office Building
Phone: 202-225-6631   Fax: 202-225-1968

Peter J. **VISCLOSKY** (D-IN-01)
FP: Geoff Gerhart - Legislative Manager
FT: Geoff Gerhart - Legislative Manager
2313 Rayburn House Office Building
Phone: 202-225-2461   Fax: 202-225-2493

James T. **WALSH** (R-NY-25)
FP: John Simmons
FT: John Simmons/Ron Anderson
2351 Rayburn House Office Building

Phone: 202-225-3701   Fax: 202-225-4042

Zachary P. **WAMP** (R-TN-03)
FP: Jack Turner - Senior Legislative Assistant
FT: Jack Turner - Senior Legislative Assistant
423 Cannon House Office Building
Phone: 202-225-3271   Fax: 202-225-3494

Maxine **WATERS** (D-CA-35)
FP: Mike Schmitz - Legislative Assistant
FT: Mike Schmitz - Legislative Assistant
2344 Rayburn House Office Building
Phone: 202-225-2201   Fax: 202-225-7854

Wes **WATKINS** (R-OK-03)
FP: Scott Raab - Legislative Director
FT: Scott Raab - Legislative Director
2312 Rayburn House Office Building
Phone: 202-225-4565   Fax: 202-225-5966

Mel **WATT** (D-NC-12)
FP: Dominique McCoy
FT: Dominique McCoy
1230 Longworth House Office Building
Phone: 202-225-1510   Fax: 202-225-1512

J.C. **WATTS** (R-OK-04)
FP: Dave Silverstein - Legislative Assistant
FT: Sandy Campbell - Legislative Assistant
1210 Longworth House Office Building
Phone: 202-225-6165   Fax: 202-225-3512

Henry A. **WAXMAN** (D-CA-29)
FT: Patricia Delgado
2204 Rayburn House Office Building
Phone: 202-225-3976   Fax: 202-225-4099

Curt **WELDON** (R-PA-07)
FP: Brian Taylor - Legislative Assistant
FT: Terri Fish - Legislative Assistant
2452 Rayburn House Office Building
Phone: 202-225-2011   Fax: 202-225-8137

David J. **WELDON** (R-FL-15)
FP: Michael Bishop - Legislative Assistant
FT: Michael Bishop - Legislative Assistant
216 Cannon House Office Building
Phone: 202-225-3671   Fax: 202-225-3516

Gerald C. **WELLER** (R-IL-11)
FP: Chris Rogers
FT: Chris Rogers
130 Cannon House Office Building
Phone: 202-225-3635   Fax: 202-225-3521

Robert **WEXLER** (D-FL-19)
FP: Jonathan Katz - Legislative Assistant
FT: Jonathan Katz - Legislative Assistant
1609 Longworth House Office Building
Phone: 202-225-3001   Fax: 202-225-5974

Robert A. **WEYGAND** (D-RI-02)
FP: Tom Santos - Legislative Assistant
FT: Tom Santos - Legislative Assistant
507 Cannon House Office Building
Phone: 202-225-2735

Richard A. **WHITE** (R-WA-01)
FP: Dan Horowitz - Legislative Assistant
FT: Josh Mathis - Legislative Assistant
116 Cannon House Office Building
Phone: 202-225-6311   Fax: 202-225-3524

Edward **WHITFIELD** (R-KY-01)
FP: Rob Freeman - Legislative Director
FT: Beth McAree - Legislative Assistant
236 Cannon House Office Building
Phone: 202-225-3115   Fax: 202-225-3547

Roger F. **WICKER** (R-MS-01)
FP: Bret Loper
FT: Bret Loper

206 Cannon House Office Building
Phone: 202-225-4306   Fax: 202-225-3549

Robert E. **WISE** (D-WV-02)
FP: Gael Sullivan
FT: Casey DeShong
2367 Rayburn House Office Building
Phone: 202-225-2711   Fax: 202-225-7856

Frank R. **WOLF** (R-VA-10)
FP: Anne Huiskes
FT: Anne Huiskes
241 Cannon House Office Building
Phone: 202-225-5136   Fax: 202-225-0437

Lynn **WOOLSEY** (D-CA-06)
FP: Mark Dooley - Legislative Assistant
FT: Mark Dooley - Legislative Assistant
439 Cannon House Office Building
Phone: 202-225-5161   Fax: 202-225-5163

Albert **WYNN** (D-MD-04)
FP: Claudia Arko - Legislative Director
FT: Claudia Arko - Legislative Director
407 Cannon House Office Building
Phone: 202-225-8699   Fax: 202-225-8714

Sidney R. **YATES** (D-IL-09)
FP: Steve Marchese
FT: Steve Marchese
2109 Rayburn House Office Building
Phone: 202-225-2111   Fax: 202-225-3493

C.W. **YOUNG** (R-FL-10)
FP: David Jolly - Legislative Assistant
FT: David Jolly - Legislative Assistant
2407 Rayburn House Office Building
Phone: 202-225-5961   Fax: 202-225-9764

Don **YOUNG** (R-AK-AL)
FP: Gregory Thom
FT: Dan Logan
2111 Rayburn House Office Building
Phone: 202-225-5765   Fax: 202-225-0425

Mary Bino(R-CA-44)
FP: Chris J. Katopis
FT: Chris J. Katopis
324 Cannon House Office Building
Phone: 202-225-5330   Fax: 202-225-2961

U.S. SENATE--*The following is a list of individuals within each U.S. Senator's office who deal with Foreign Trade and Foreign Policy issues. The abbreviation "FT" stands for Foreign Trade and is the person in the office responsible for foreign trade policy issues. The abbreviation "FP" stands for Foreign Policy and is the person in the office responsible for foreign policy issues. In some cases, the same individual handles both issue areas. When that occurs, the name is repeated for consistency.*

Mailing address:

Contact Person
U.S. Senate
Room #
Washington, DC 20510

Spencer ABRAHAM (R-MI)
FP: Randa Hudome - Counsellor
FT: Gregg Willhauck
329 Dirksen Senate Office Building
Phone: 202-224-4822   Fax: 202-224-8834

Daniel K. AKAKA (D-HI)
FP: Ed Thompson - Legislative Assistant
FT: Ed Thompson - Legislative Assistant
720 Hart Senate Office Building
Phone: 202-224-6361   Fax: 202-224-2126

Wayne A. ALLARD (R-CO)
FP: Doug Flanders - Legislative Assistant
FT: Doug Flanders - Legislative Assistant
513 Hart Senate Office Building
Phone: 202-224-5941   Fax: 202-224-6471

John D. ASHCROFT (R-MO)
FP: James Odom
FT: Taunya Mclarty
316 Hart Senate Office Building
Phone: 202-224-6154   Fax: 202-228-0998

Max BAUCUS (D-MT)
FP: Art Grant
FT: Ed Gresser
511 Hart Senate Office Building
Phone: 202-224-2651

Robert F. BENNETT (R-UT)
FP: Bill Triplett
FT: Lisa Norton
431 Dirksen Senate Office Building
Phone: 202-224-5444   Fax: 202-224-4908

Joseph R. BIDEN (D-DE)
FP: Ed Hall - Minority Chief of Staff,
   Foreign Relations Comm.
FT: Jim Greene - Economic Advisor
221 Russell Senate Office Building
Phone: 202-224-5042   Fax: 202-224-0139

Jeff BINGAMAN (D-NM)
FP: R.J. Soderquist
FT: R.J. Soderquist
703 Hart Senate Office Building
Phone: 202-224-5521   Fax: 202-224-2852

Christopher S. BOND (R-MO)
FP: Jeff Kuhnreich
FT: Jack Bartling
274 Russell Senate Office Building
Phone: 202-224-5721   Fax: 202-224-8149

Barbara BOXER (D-CA)
FP: Matt Kagan
FT: Karen Day
112 Hart Senate Office Building
Phone: 202-224-3553

John B. BREAUX (D-LA)
FP: Mark Ashby/Jeff Lewis - Leg. Counsel
FT: Mark Ashby - Legislative Counsel
516 Hart Senate Office Building
Phone: 202-224-4623   Fax: 202-228-2577

Sam D. BROWNBACK (R-KS)
FP: Christina Rocca - Professional Staff
FT: Howard Waltzman - General Counsel/
   Legislative Assistant
303 Hart Senate Office Building
Phone: 202-224-6521   Fax: 202-228-1265

Richard H. BRYAN (D-NV)
FP: Polly Synk
FT: Andy Vermilye - Legislative Director
269 Russell Senate Office Building
Phone: 202-224-6244   Fax: 202-224-1867

Dale BUMPERS (D-AR)
FP: Brian Moran
FT: Stan Fendley
229 Dirksen Senate Office Building
Phone: 202-224-4843   Fax: 202-224-6435

Conrad BURNS (R-MT)
FP: Jennifer Chartrand
FT: Jennifer Chartrand
187 Dirksen Senate Office Building
Phone: 202-224-2644   Fax: 202-224-8594

Robert C. BYRD (D-WV)
FP: Martin McBroom - Legislative Aide
FT: Maritn McBroom - Legislative Aide
311 Hart Senate Office Building
Phone: 202-224-3954   Fax: 202-228-0002

Ben Nighthorse CAMPBELL (R-CO-)
FP: Vacant
FT: Vacant
380 Russell Senate Office Building
Phone: 202-224-5852   Fax: 202-224-1933

John H. CHAFEE (R-RI)
FP: John Seggerman
FT: Amy Dunathan
505 Dirksen Senate Office Building
Phone: 202-224-2921   Fax: 202-228-2853

Max CLELAND (D-GA)
FP: Bill Johnstone - Senior Policy Advisor
FT: Bill Johnstone - Senior Policy Advisor
461 Dirksen Senate Office Building
Phone: 202-224-3521   Fax: 202-224-0072

Dan COATS (R-IN)
FP: Pam Sellars
FT: Michael O'Brien - Legislative Assistant
404 Russell Senate Office Building
Phone: 202-224-5623   Fax: 202-228-4745

Thad COCHRAN (R-MS)
FP: Hunt Shipman - Legislative Assistant
FT: Clayton Heil - Legislative Assistant
326 Russell Senate Office Building
Phone: 202-224-5054   Fax: 202-224-9450

Susan M. COLLINS (R-ME)
FP: Christopher Ford - Nat'l. Security Advisor
FT: Christopher Ford - Nat'l. Security Advisor
172 Russell Senate Office Building
Phone: 202-224-2523   Fax: 202-224-2693

Kent CONRAD (D-ND)
FP: Bob Faust
FT: Bob Faust
530 Hart Senate Office Building
Phone: 202-224-2043   Fax: 202-224-7776

Paul COVERDELL (R-GA)
FP: Steve Schrage
FT: Dan McGirt
200 Russell Senate Office Building
Phone: 202-224-3643   Fax: 202-228-3783

Larry CRAIG (R-ID)
FP: Lori Otto - Legislative Assistant
FT: Damon Tobias - Special Counsel/LA
313 Hart Senate Office Building
Phone: 202-224-2752   Fax: 202-228-1067

Alfonse M. D'AMATO (R-NY)
FP: Kraig M. Siracuse - Legislative Assistant
FT: Kraig M. Siracuse - Legislative Assistant
520 Hart Senate Office Building
Phone: 202-224-6542   Fax: 202-224-5871

Thomas A. DASCHLE (D-SD)
FP: Sheila Murphy - Legislative Assistant
FT: Rick Samans
509 Hart Senate Office Building
Phone: 202-224-2321   Fax: 202-224-2321

Mike DEWINE (R-OH)
FP: Gina Marie Hathaway - Legislative Asst.
FT: Gina Marie Hathaway - Legislative Asst.
140 Russell Senate Office Building
Phone: 202-224-2315   Fax: 202-224-6519

Christopher J. DODD (D-CT)
FP: Janice O'Connell
FT: Janice O'Connell
444 Russell Senate Office Building
Phone: 202-224-2823

Pete V. DOMENICI (R-NM)
FP: Marco Gonzales
FT: Denise Ramonas
328 Hart Senate Office Building
Phone: 202-224-6621   Fax: 202-224-7371

Byron L. DORGAN (D-ND)
FP: Jeremy Bates - Legislative Assistant
FT: Carl Limvere - Legislative Assistant
713 Hart Senate Office Building
Phone: 202-224-2551   Fax: 202-224-1193

Richard J. DURBIN (D-IL)
FP: Christopher Midura - Legislative Fellow
FT: Dan O'Grady - Legislative Assistant
364 Russell Senate Office Building
Phone: 202-224-2152   Fax: 202-228-0400

Michael B. ENZI (R-WY)
FP: Joel Oswald - Legislative Assistant
FT: Chad Calvert - Legislative Assistant
290 Russell Senate Office Building
Phone: 202-224-3424   Fax: 202-228-0359

Lauch FAIRCLOTH (R-NC)
FP: Alex Mistri - Legislative Aide
FT: Kimrey Woodard - Legislative

Correspondent
317 Hart Senate Office Building
Phone: 202-224-3154   Fax: 202-224-7406

Russ **FEINGOLD** (D-WI)
FP: Linda Rotblatt - Legislative Assistant
FT: Sumner Slichter - Policy Analyst
716 Hart Senate Office Building
Phone: 202-224-5323   Fax: 202-224-2725

Dianne **FEINSTEIN** (D-CA)
FP: Dan Shapiro - Legislative Assistant
FT: Kevin Cronin - Legislative Assistant
331 Hart Senate Office Building
Phone: 202-224-3841   Fax: 202-228-3954

Wendell H. **FORD** (D-KY)
FP: Charlie Smith
FT: Jim Low
173A Russell Senate Office Building
Phone: 202-224-4343   Fax: 202-224-0046

Bill **FRIST** (R-TN)
FP: Michael Miller - Legislative Assistant
FT: Katie Braden - Legislative Assistant
567 Dirksen Senate Office Building
Phone: 202-224-3344   Fax: 202-228-1264

John **GLENN** (D-OH)
FP: Pat Buckheit - Legislative Assistant
FT: Pat Buckheit - Legislative Assistant
503 Hart Senate Office Building
Phone: 202-224-3353   Fax: 202-224-7983

Slade **GORTON** (R-WA)
FP: Susan Wunderly - Legislative Assistant
FT: Susan Wunderly - Legislative Assistant
730 Hart Senate Office Building
Phone: 202-224-3441   Fax: 202-224-9393

Bob **GRAHAM** (D-FL)
FP: Bob Filippone - Legislative Assistant
FT: Jason Macnamara - Legislative Assistant
524 Hart Senate Office Building
Phone: 202-224-3041   Fax: 202-224-2237

Phil **GRAMM** (R-TX)
FP: Wayne Abernathy
FT: Wayne Abernathy
370 Russell Senate Office Building
Phone: 202-224-2934   Fax: 202-228-2856

Rod **GRAMS** (R-MN)
FP: Pam Weimann
FT: Pat Eveland
257 Dirksen Senate Office Building
Phone: 202-224-3244   Fax: 202-228-0956

Charles E. **GRASSLEY** (R-IA)
FP: Sarah Gesiriech - Legislative Assistant
FT: Jim Jochum - Legislative Director
135 Hart Senate Office Building
Phone: 202-224-3744   Fax: 202-224-6020

Judd **GREGG** (R-NH)
FP: Vas Alexopoulos - Legislative Assistant
FT: Vas Alexopoulos - Legislative Assistant
393 Russell Senate Office Building
Phone: 202-224-3324   Fax: 202-224-4952

Chuck **HAGEL** (R-NE)
FP: Ken Peel - Foreign Policy Counsel
FT: Ken Peel - Foreign Policy Counsel
346 Russell Senate Office Building
Phone: 202-224-4224   Fax: 202-224-5213

Tom **HARKIN** (D-IA)
FP: Rosemary Gutierrez
FT: Mark Halverson
731 Hart Senate Office Building
Phone: 202-224-3254   Fax: 202-224-9369

Orrin G. **HATCH** (R-UT)
FP: Paul Matulic - Legislative Assistant
FT: Bob Lockwood - Senior Counsel
  (Trade & Defense)
131 Russell Senate Office Building
Phone: 202-224-5251   Fax: 202-224-6331

Jesse **HELMS** (R-NC)
FP: James W. Nance
FT: John Folmar
403 Dirksen Senate Office Building
Phone: 202-224-6342   Fax: 202-228-1339

Ernest F. **HOLLINGS** (D-SC)
FP: Dan McGill
FT: Gregg Elias
125 Russell Senate Office Building
Phone: 202-224-6121   Fax: 202-224-4293

Tim **HUTCHINSON** (R-AR)
FP: Todd Weiss - Legislative Assistant
FT: Todd Weiss - Legislative Assistant
245 Dirksen Senate Office Building
Phone: 202-224-2353   Fax: 202-228-3973

Kay Bailey **HUTCHISON** (R-TX)
FP: Dave Davis - Legislative Assistant
FT: Mike Gerber - Legislative Assistant
284 Russell Senate Office Building
Phone: 202-224-5922   Fax: 202-224-0776

James M. **INHOFE** (R-OK)
FP: Greg McCarthy - Military Legislative Asst.
FT: Greg McCarthy - Military Legislative Asst.
453 Russell Senate Office Building
Phone: 202-224-4721   Fax: 202-228-0380

Daniel K. **INOUYE** (D-HI)
FP: Keith Gouveia - Legislative Assistant
FT: Keith Gouveia - Legislative Assistant
722 Hart Senate Office Building
Phone: 202-224-3934   Fax: 202-224-6747

James M. **JEFFORDS** (R-VT)
FP: Laurie Schultzheim - Legislative Assistant
FT: Laurie Schultzheim - Legislative Assistant
728 Hart Senate Office Building
Phone: 202-224-5141

Tim P. **JOHNSON** (D-SD)
FP: Stephanie Helfrich - Legislative Assistant
FT: Bret Healy - Legislative Assistant
502 Hart Senate Office Building
Phone: 202-224-5842   Fax: 202-228-5765

Dirk **KEMPTHORNE** (R-ID)
FP: Glen Tait - Legislative Assistant
FT: Glen Tait - Legislative Assistant
304 Russell Senate Office Building
Phone: 202-224-6142   Fax: 202-224-5893

Edward M. **KENNEDY** (D-MA)
FP: Trina Vargo - Legislative Assistant
FT: Kathleen Glonz - Legislative Assistant
315 Russell Senate Office Building
Phone: 202-224-4543   Fax: 202-224-2417

J. Robert **KERREY** (D-NE)
FP: Todd Stubbendeek - Legislative Assistant
FT: Reginal Leichty - Legislative Assistant
141 Hart Senate Office Building
Phone: 202-224-6551   Fax: 202-224-7645

John F. **KERRY** (D-MA)
FP: Whitney Harrelson - Leg. Correspondent
FT: Whitney Harrelson - Leg. Correspondent
421 Russell Senate Office Building
Phone: 202-224-2742   Fax: 202-224-8525

Herbert H. **KOHL** (D-WI)
FP: Naomi Baum - Legislative Assistant

FT: Chad Metzler - Legislative Assistant
330 Hart Senate Office Building
Phone: 202-224-5653   Fax: 202-224-9787

Jon L. **KYL** (R-AZ)
FP: Jeanine Esperne - Legislative Assistant
FT: Elizabeth Maier - Legislative Assistant
724 Hart Senate Office Building
Phone: 202-224-4521   Fax: 202-228-1239

Mary L. **LANDRIEU** (D-LA)
FP: Jason Matthews
FT: Jason Matthews
702 Hart Senate Office Building
Phone: 202-224-5824   Fax: 202-224-9735

Frank R. **LAUTENBERG** (D-NJ)
FP: Sharon Waxman - Legislative Assistant
FT: Cathy Carpino - Legislative Assistant
506 Hart Senate Office Building
Phone: 202-224-4744   Fax: 202-224-9707

Patrick J. **LEAHY** (D-VT)
FP: Tim Rieser - Minority Clerk
FT: Ed Pagano - Counsel
433 Russell Senate Office Building
Phone: 202-224-4242   Fax: 202-224-3595

Carl **LEVIN** (D-MI)
FP: Kane Burns - Legislative Assistant
FT: Alison Pascale - Legislative Assistant
459 Russell Senate Office Building
Phone: 202-224-6221   Fax: 202-224-1388

Joe **LIEBERMAN** (D-CT)
FP: Frederick Downey
FT: Nao Matsukita
706 Hart Senate Office Building
Phone: 202-224-4041   Fax: 202-224-9750

Trent **LOTT** (R-MS)
FP: Randy Scheunemann - Legislative Asst.
FT: Robert Wilkie - Legislative Assistant
487 Russell Senate Office Building
Phone: 202-224-3135   Fax: 202-224-2262

Richard G. **LUGAR** (R-IN)
FP: Andy Semmel - Legislative Assistant
FT: Andy Semmel - Legislative Assistant
306 Hart Senate Office Building
Phone: 202-224-4814   Fax: 202-228-0360

Connie **MACK** (R-FL)
FP: Gary Shiffman - Legislative Assistant
FT: Patrick Kearney - Legislative Assistant
517 Hart Senate Office Building
Phone: 202-224-5274   Fax: 202-224-8022

John **MCCAIN** (R-AZ)
FP: Walker "Skip" Fischer
FT: Walter "Skip" Fischer
241 Russell Senate Office Building
Phone: 202-224-2235   Fax: 202-228-2862

Mitch **MCCONNELL** (R-KY)
FP: Billy Piper - Legislative Assistant
FT: Tamara Somerville - Legislative Assistant
361A Russell Senate Office Building
Phone: 202-224-2541   Fax: 202-224-2499

Barbara A. **MIKULSKI** (D-MD)
FP: Julia Frifield - Legislative Assistant
FT: Julia Frifield - Legislative Assistant
709 Hart Senate Office Building
Phone: 202-224-4654   Fax: 202-224-8858

Carol **MOSELEY-BRAUN** (D-IL)
FP: Anne Collett - Legislative Assistant
FT: Anne Collett - Legislative Assistant
324 Hart Senate Office Building
Phone: 202-224-2854   Fax: 202-228-1318

Daniel Patrick **MOYNIHAN** (D-NY)
FP: Mike Lostumbo
FT: Mike Lostumbo
464 Russell Senate Office Building
Phone: 202-224-4451   Fax: 202-228-0406

Frank H. **MURKOWSKI** (R-AK)
FP: Dianna Tanner Okun - Counsel for
    International Affairs
FT: Dianna Tanner Okun - Counsel for
    International Affairs
322 Hart Senate Office Building
Phone: 202-224-6665   Fax: 202-224-5301

Patty **MURRAY** (D-WA)
FP: Ben McMakin - Legislative Assistant
FT: Ben McMakin - Legislative Assistant
111 Russell Senate Office Building
Phone: 202-224-2621   Fax: 202-224-0238

Don **NICKLES** (R-OK)
FP: Steve Moffitt - Legislative Assistant
FT: Steve Moffitt - Legislative Assistant
133 Hart Senate Office Building
Phone: 202-224-5754   Fax: 202-224-6008

John F. **REED** (D-RI)
FP: Elizabeth King - Legislative Assistant
FT: Kevin Davis - Legislative Assistant
320 Hart Senate Office Building
Phone: 202-224-4642   Fax: 202-224-4680

Harry **REID** (D-NV)
FP: Matthew Urbanek - Legislative Fellow
FT: James Ryan - Legislative Assistant
528 Hart Senate Office Building
Phone: 202-224-3542   Fax: 202-224-7327

Charles S. **ROBB** (D-VA)
FP: Peter Cleveland - Legislative Assistant
FT: Peter Cleveland - Legislative Assistant
154 Russell Senate Office Building
Phone: 202-224-4024   Fax: 202-224-8689

Pat **ROBERTS** (R-KS)
FP: Alan McCurry - Military Legislative Asst.
FT: Bryan Edwardson - Legislative Assistant
302 Hart Senate Office Building
Phone: 202-224-4774   Fax: 202-224-3514

Jay **ROCKEFELLER** (D-WV)
FP: Ellen Doneski
FT: Ellen Doneski
531 Hart Senate Office Building
Phone: 202-224-6472   Fax: 202-224-7665

William V. **ROTH** (R-DE)
FP: Ian Brzezinski - Legislative Assistant
FT: Grant Aladonas - Legislative Assistant
104 Hart Senate Office Building
Phone: 202-224-2441   Fax: 202-228-0354

Richard J. **SANTORUM** (R-PA)
FP: George Bernier - Legislative Assistant
FT: David French - Legislative Assistant
120 Russell Senate Office Building
Phone: 202-224-6324   Fax: 202-228-0604

Paul S. **SARBANES** (D-MD)
FP: Vince Sanfuentes - Legislative Assistant
FT: Marty Gruenberg - Professional Staff
Member
309 Hart Senate Office Building
Phone: 202-224-4524   Fax: 202-224-1651

Jeff **SESSIONS** (R-AL)
FP: Jim Hirni - Legislative Assistant
FT: Arch Galloway - Legislative Assistant
495 Russell Senate Office Building

Phone: 202-224-4124   Fax: 202-224-3149

Richard C. **SHELBY** (R-AL)
FP: Kathy Casey
FT: Geoff Gradler
110 Hart Senate Office Building
Phone: 202-224-5744   Fax: 202-224-3416

Gordon H. **SMITH** (R-OR)
FP: Rob Epplin - Legislative Assistant
FT: Rob Eppline - Legislative Assistant
359 Dirksen Senate Office Building
Phone: 202-224-3753   Fax: 202-228-3997

Robert C. **SMITH** (R-NH)
FP: John Luddy - Legislative Assistant
FT: John Luddy - Legislative Assistant
307 Dirksen Senate Office Building
Phone: 202-224-2841   Fax: 202-224-1353

Olympia J. **SNOWE** (R-ME)
FP: Eric Scheinkopf - Legislative Assistant
FT: Eric Scheinkopf - Legislative Assistant
250 Russell Senate Office Building
Phone: 202-224-5344   Fax: 202-224-1946

Arlen **SPECTER** (R-PA)
FP: Molly Birmingham
FT: Jeff Gabriel
711 Hart Senate Office Building
Phone: 202-224-4254   Fax: 202-228-1229

Ted **STEVENS** (R-AK)
FP: Brian Utter - Legislative Assistant
FT: Brian Utter - Legislative Assistant
522 Hart Senate Office Building
Phone: 202-224-3004   Fax: 202-224-2354

Craig **THOMAS** (R-WY)
FP: Rich Houghton - General Counsel
FT: Rich Houghton - General Counsel
109 Hart Senate Office Building
Phone: 202-224-6441   Fax: 202-224-1724

Fred D. **THOMPSON** (R-TN)
FP: Curt Silvers - Legislative Assistant
FT: Curt Silvers - Legislative Assistant
523 Dirksen Senate Office Building
Phone: 202-224-4944   Fax: 202-228-3679

Strom **THURMOND** (R-SC)
FP: Ms. Mele Williams
FT: Ms. Mele Williams
217 Russell Senate Office Building
Phone: 202-224-5972   Fax: 202-224-1300

Robert G. **TORRICELLI** (D-NJ)
FP: Josh Shapiro - Legislative Assistant
FT: Josh Shapiro - Legislative Assistant
113 Dirksen Senate Office Building
Phone: 202-224-3224   Fax: 202-224-8567

John William **WARNER** (R-VA)
FP: Ed Edens, Judy Ansley
FT: Chas Phillips
225 Russell Senate Office Building
Phone: 202-224-2023   Fax: 202-224-6295

Paul **WELLSTONE** (D-MN)
FP: Charlotte Oldham-Moore - Leg. Assistant
FT: Brian Ahlberg - Legislative Assistant
136 Hart Senate Office Building
Phone: 202-224-5641   Fax: 202-224-8438

Ron **WYDEN** (D-OR)
FP: Jim Sheire - Legislative Assistant
FT: Carole Grunberg - Legislative Director
717 Hart Senate Office Building
Phone: 202-224-5244   Fax: 202-228-2717

Committee on Agriculture

Subcommittee on General Farm Commodities

1301 Longworth House Office Building
Washington, D.C. 20515-6001
202/225-2171   Fax: 202/225-0917

MAJORITY MEMBERS:

Bill Barrett, NE
Chairman
Larry Combest, TX
Vice Chairman
John A. Boehner, OH
Frank D. Lucas, OK
Saxby Chambliss, GA
Jo Ann Emerson, MO
Jerry Moran, KS
John R. Thune, SD
John Cooksey, LA

MINORITY MEMBERS:

David Minge, MN
Ranking Minority Member
Bennie G. Thompson, MS
Mike McIntyre, NC
Debbie Stabenow, MI
Bob Etheridge, NC
Christopher John, LA
Jay W. Johnson, WI

Jurisdiction: Wheat, feed grains, soybeans, oilseeds, cotton, cottonseed, rice, dry beans, peas and lentils, Commodity Credit Corporation, and trade matters related to such commodities, generally.

KEY MAJORITY STAFF:

Mike Neruda
Staff Director
Subcommittee on General Farm Commodities
1430 Longworth House Office Bldg.
225-0171

Personal: born 3/13/46 in Lincoln, Neb.

Education: B.S., Univ. of Nebraska, 1968. M.A., Univ. of Oklahoma, 1971.

Professional: 1979-92, U.S. Navy. 1992-97, U.S. Dept. of Agriculture. 1997-present, staff dir., subc. on general farm commodities, House Cmte. on Agriculture.

Expertise: Farm commodities

Trade and its many side issues will highlight Mike Neruda's work in 1998 as staff director for the Subcommittee on General Farm Commodities. Among the first matter explored was the effect Asian economic troubles could have on U.S. farm products flowing into that region.

"We've already had one hearing on the Asian situation, and I'm sure it won't be the last," he said. Lawmakers have been considering how the United States can make sure Asian nations do not cut back on purchases of U.S. commodities as they weather their economic crisis. Credit guarantees are one of the options proposed.

Neruda said he also will be working on proposals to reduce artificial barriers to U.S. products overseas, particularly those involving genetically modified organisms. On that and other issues, he said, hearings and briefings are in the works. "We've had our plate full at the subcommittee," he said.

Trade is a major focus for many subcommittees and the full panel as well this year. The United States will enter world trade talks in 1999 at which agriculture issues will be the focus.

In addition, Neruda said he will be working on a bill known as the Warehouse Accounting Act, which has not been reauthorized by Congress since 1916. The cotton industry has switched over to a system of electronic receipts when farmers sell their products, he said, but all others still use paper. The bill would help other commodity markets make the conversion where feasible.

Neruda said he also will monitor the market situation for wheat and corn prices, part of continued oversight of implementation of the 1996 Farm Bill. That was the major effort of 1997 for the subcommittee, which had a huge role in shaping the legislation that allowed farmers more control over their own production.

The subcommittee also kept track last year of changes implemented in the Conservation Reserve Program, a voluntary program that makes annual rental payments over a 10-year period to participating farmers.

Neruda joined the subcommittee during last year's oversight process. He has worked on agricultural issues in Washington since 1979 on the staffs of both agriculture committees and for panel members. He also has worked at the U.S. Department of Agriculture.

KEY MINORITY STAFF:

Andrew W. Baker
Deputy Minority Counsel
1002 Longworth House Office Bldg.
225-3069

Personal: born 3/16/61 in Shreveport, La.

Education: B.A., Univ. of Virginia, 1983. J.D., Univ. of Georgia, 1986.

Professional: 1986-88, attorney-adviser, office of administrative law judges, U.S. Dept. of Labor. 1988-90, trial attorney, office of the general counsel, U.S. Dept. of Agriculture. 1990-97, minority professional staff/associate counsel; 1998-present, deputy minority counsel, House Cmte. on Agriculture.

Expertise: Trade, international development, legal issues

International issues, from upcoming World Trade Organization talks to the Asian economic crisis, will occupy much of Andy Baker's time in 1998. As the House agriculture committee looks at ways to improve U.S. access to foreign markets where barriers now exist for American agricultural products, it also will be looking at ways agriculture can help economically struggling parts of the world.

"The committee will be looking at issues of how the Asian crisis affects agricultural interests," said Baker, the committee's deputy minority counsel. "Agriculture is dependent on the Asian economies for a significant portion of its exports."

In anticipation of global trade talks on agriculture during 1999, the committee also will look at ways nations try to block those exports. Hearings will not delve into U.S. strategy for the talks, "That would be showing our hand," Baker said, but they will look at market access barriers, internal subsidies, and export subsidies that either block or hinder U.S. farm products abroad. "The more you can do on all three fronts the better for agriculture," he said. "We'll look at issues that are important to U.S. agriculture and look at the problems of the (predecessor) Uruguay Round. Look at those and learn from them."

Among other barriers that will get closer study are biotechnology and sanitary rules that U.S. exporters complain are based more on economic than scientific concerns. The United States would like a uniform set of standards worldwide.

Baker is hoping for more success in 1998 than the committee saw on last year's biggest trade issue. Agriculture committee leaders were solidly behind President Clinton's request for continued authority on fast track trade negotiations, by which Congress is given the chance to approve or reject but not to alter U.S. trade agreements. The administration pulled its request, though, when it became clear there was not enough support for the measure to prevail in Congress.

Baker is one of two attorneys on the House agriculture committee's minority staff. In addition to drafting legislation and reviewing committee reports, he specializes in trade issues and serves as minority consultant to the panel's subcommittee on general farm commodities.

Baker amassed 11 years of legal experience at the Department of Labor, the Department of Agriculture, and on the House Agriculture Committee. He served as a committee counsel during both the 1990 and 1996 farm bills.

Subcommittee on Livestock, Dairy & Poultry

1301 Longworth House Office Building
Washington, D.C. 20515-6001
202/225-2171   Fax: 202/225-0917

MAJORITY MEMBERS:

Richard W. Pombo, CA
Chairman
John A. Boehner, OH
Vice Chairman
Bob Goodlatte, VA
Nick Smith, MI
Frank D. Lucas, OK
Ron Lewis, KY
John N. Hostettler, IN
Roy Blunt, MO
Charles W. "Chip" Pickering, MS
William L. Jenkins, TN

MINORITY MEMBERS:

Collin C. Peterson, MN
Ranking Minority Member
Earl F. Hilliard, AL
Tim Holden, PA
Jay W. Johnson, WI
Gary A. Condit, CA
Calvin M. Dooley, CA
Sam Farr, CA
Leonard L. Boswell, IA

Jurisdiction: General livestock, dairy, poultry, meat, seafood, and seafood products, and the inspection of those commodities,

aquaculture, animal welfare, and domestic and foreign marketing related to assigned commodities.

KEY MAJORITY STAFF:

Christopher D'Arcy
Staff Director
Subcommittee on Livestock, Dairy and Poultry
1301 Longworth House Office Bldg.
225-1564

Personal: born 2/12/66 in Tampa, Fla.

Education: B.A., Villanova University, 1988. M.A., Villanova University, 1989.

Professional: 1990-92, leg. corresp. and leg. asst., Rep. Ron Marlenee, R-Mont. 1993-97, leg. asst. and leg. dir., Rep. Richard Pombo, R-Calif. 1997-present, staff dir., subc. on livestock, dairy and poultry, House Cmte. on Agriculture.

Expertise: Agriculture issues

When Congress reshaped federal agriculture programs in the 1996 Farm Bill, it sidestepped deep divisions in the U.S. dairy industry by ordering Agriculture Secretary Dan Glickman to make recommendations on reforms in the nation's milk-pricing setup. Glickman's final decision, which marks the biggest overhaul in the federal dairy program since it began in the 1930s, will be made by the end of 1998 and implemented by April 1999.

Christopher D'Arcy says the subcommittee on livestock, dairy and poultry will be watching the process closely. "We will provide a forum for the industry and the department to comment on the reforms of both milk marketing orders and pricing," said D'Arcy, the panel's staff director. "It's somewhat of a parallel track to USDA's own hearing process. We do want to give everyone an opportunity to have their say."

While the industry remains divided over the exact shape of dairy reforms, which will consolidate a system of 31 milk marketing orders and usher in a new formula for setting milk prices paid to farmers nationwide, most agree with the goal they bring: helping U.S. farmers gain a bigger share of the market for their products worldwide. Last year, the subcommittee conducted hearings looking at new technologies that can help the industry become more competitive globally. D'Arcy said the subject will receive further study throughout 1998.

Dairy will not be the only issue occupying the subcommittee's time. Highly publicized 1997 outbreaks of illness from contaminated food and the biggest meat recall in U.S. history have put food safety high on the subcommittee's agenda, D'Arcy said.

In January, USDA began implementation of a new meat and poultry inspection program called Hazard Analysis and Critical Control Points, which D'Arcy called a "pretty serious change in the way meat inspection is done." Under the concept, meat and poultry plants look at their own operations, determine where safety problems might occur and take the steps they determine are necessary to prevent them. The program begins with the largest processors this year and will extend to smaller and smaller operations until all are covered by January 2000.

It's something the subcommittee will be keeping an eye on, D'Arcy said. "The oversight is to see how the industry interprets it and how USDA interprets it," he said. In addition to oversight of new inspection rules, the subcommittee will conduct hearings on other ways to make food safer.

"We are looking very closely at promising new technology," he said. "This subcommittee wants to marshal all the tools it can to make food safer. Inspection only finds the problems. It doesn't prevent the problems."

KEY MINORITY STAFF:

Danelle Farmer
Minority Consultant
Subcommittee on Livestock, Dairy, and Poultry
1002-A Longworth House Office Bldg.
225-4453

Personal: born 10/22/66 in East Moline, Ill.

Education: B.S., Texas Tech. Univ., 1987.

Professional: 1991-97, leg. asst., Rep. Charles Stenholm, D-Texas. 1997-present, minority consultant, subc. on livestock, dairy, and poultry, House Cmte. on Agriculture.

Expertise: Food safety, agriculture labor

Danelle Farmer, one of several House Agriculture Committee staff members who formerly served on the staff of its ranking Democrat, works today as the minority contact person for the subcommittee on livestock, dairy, and poultry. She also follows other issues on a day-to-day basis.

One of Farmer's projects is food safety. Although a House bill has yet to be introduced on the issue, lawmakers have been looking at the federal response to last year's outbreaks of illness caused by contaminated beef and strawberries. In the Senate, one proposal would strengthen the U.S. Department of Agriculture's authority to respond to problems, allowing the secretary to order product recalls and levy penalties against companies with repeated safety violations. Others have proposed using technology to reduce potential health risks.

Farmer also has followed implementation of 1996 revisions to the Federal Insecticide, Fungicide and Rodenticide Act (FIFRA). The law sets the allowable pesticide levels for the nation's food supply and for the first time since the 1950s amended the Delaney Clause, which prohibited the use of any additive shown to cause cancer.

Agriculture labor is another of Farmer's issues. Agriculture Committee Chairman Bob Smith, R-Ore., has introduced legislation that would change rules governing the process farmers must follow to hire migrant workers. Farmers currently must make requests at least 60 days in advance, but many contend they are unable to predict their needs that far in advance.

Smith also has introduced legislation in another of Farmer's specialty areas. A plan proposed by the Oregon Republican would direct the U.S. Forest Service to set priorities for dealing with dead and decaying areas of federal forest lands, something he has said would introduce more scientific policy to forest health.

In the subcommittee, dairy program reforms pending at the U.S. Department of Agriculture will be followed throughout the year. The 1996 Farm Bill sidestepped the commodity, instead ordering USDA to make a proposal and have it in place by April 1999.

Early this year, Secretary Dan Glickman proposed a consolidation in the number of federal milk marketing orders, and also unveiled two options for changing the way federal officials set the formula price for milk.

Farmer joined the committee staff in 1997, the year Rep. Charles Stenholm, D-Texas, took over as ranking member. She had worked as a legislative assistant for Stenholm since 1991.

Subcommittee on Risk Mgmt. & Specialty Crops

1301 Longworth House Office Building
Washington, D.C. 20515-6001
202/225-2171   Fax: 202/225-0917

MAJORITY MEMBERS:

Thomas W. Ewing, IL
Chairman
Larry Combest, TX
Vice Chairman
John T. Doolittle, CA
Richard W. Pombo, CA
Nick Smith, MI
Terry Everett, AL
Ron Lewis, KY
Ed Bryant, TN
Mark Foley, FL
Saxby Chambliss, GA
Jerry Moran, KS

MINORITY MEMBERS:

Gary A. Condit
Ranking Minority Member
Scotty Baesler, KY
Sanford D. Bishop, Jr., GA
Earl Pomeroy, ND
John Elias Baldacci, ME
Virgil H. Goode, Jr., VA
Mike McIntyre, NC
Bob Etheridge, NC
Leonard L. Boswell, IA

Jurisdiction: Commodity futures, crop insurance, peanuts, tobacco, sugar, honey and bees, family farming, fruits and vegetables, domestic and foreign marketing related to assigned commodities, and related marketing orders, generally.

KEY MAJORITY STAFF:

Stacy Carey
Staff Director
Subcommittee on Risk Management and Specialty Crops
1741-P Longworth House Office Bldg.
225-4652

Personal: born 12/15/65 in Neptune City, N.J.

Education: B.A., The American Univ., 1987.

Professional: 1984-93, leg. asst., Rep. Tom Lewis, R-Fla. 1993-94, minority consultant, subc. on specialty crops and natural resources, House Cmte. on Agriculture. 1994-95, public affairs, Cargill Inc. 1995-present, staff dir., subc. on risk management and specialty crops, House Cmte. on Agriculture.

Expertise: Rural crops

The 1996 Farm Bill that pushed American agriculture toward greater market orientation also directed the U.S. Department of Agriculture and the Commodity Futures Trading Commission to help educate farmers about the new way of doing business. Congressional hearings and a national risk management summit in Kansas City began an oversight process in 1997 that Stacy Carey said will continue throughout 1998.

This year, she said, lawmakers will look at whether the proper information is being made available to farmers and whether the $5 million earmarked for education efforts is being used efficiently by the federal agencies. The subcommittee also will follow up, possibly through legislation, on concerns about the federal crop insurance program. "There's a lot of discussion about a funding problem in the program," Carey said.

As always, Agriculture Committee members expect to find themselves fending off a number of floor amendments during the appropriations process from lawmakers who want to kill federal programs for sugar, peanut, and tobacco farmers. "We addressed many of these issues in the Farm Bill," Carey said. "It's not appropriate to address them in the appropriations process."

She said the subcommittee will also monitor a potential financial settlement between government and the tobacco industry. Legislation is a possibility to address growers' concerns because the settlement currently makes no mention of the impact it could have on farmers.

Like most of the other subcommittees and the full Agriculture Committee itself, the panel will spend considerable time during 1998 looking toward next year's scheduled agriculture trade talks in the next round of World Trade Organization negotiations. The specialty crops subcommittee will address trade issues for fruits, vegetables, sugar, tobacco, and peanuts.

A major concern in the trade arena is sanitary and phytosanitary issues, which some countries raise as a reason for placing restrictions on U.S. crops. Carey said they're simply trade barriers. "A lot of times they're not based in science,'" she said.

Oversight hearings are also planned by the subcommittee on the Commodity Futures Trading Commission's 1997 proposed rule lifting a ban on agriculture trade options outside an official exchange. After a hearing last July, the commission proposed allowing trading on a three-year pilot basis. Carey said lawmakers also will build upon hearings conducted last year on reforming the Commodity Exchange Act. The CFTC reauthorization expires in 2000.

Carey began working on Capitol Hill as a legislative assistant to Rep. Tom Lewis, R-Fla., while she was still a student at The American University in Washington. She joined the Agriculture Committee in 1993, left briefly to work in the private sector and returned in 1995 to take her current position.

KEY MINORITY STAFF:

John Riley
Minority Senior Professional Staff Member
1305 Longworth House Office Bldg.
225-7987

Personal: born 12/1/58 in Orange County, Calif.

Education: B.A. in government, The College of William and Mary, 1981. M.A. in economics, Virginia Polytechnic Institute and State University, 1991.

Professional: 1981-83, legislative assistant, Rep. Claude Pepper, D-Fla. 1983-89, senior professional staff member, House Cmte. on the Rules. 1989-present, senior professional staff member, House Cmte. on Agriculture.

Expertise: Crop insurance reform, futures markets

John Riley's focus this year remains fixed on the issues of crop insurance, dairy policy, and futures markets. He will be working on policy analysis and strategic planning projects in the areas of futures market regulation, tax policy, and agricultural and rural economic development.

Riley says 1998 "will be a crucial year for administrative decisions regarding federal milk marketing regulations. Agriculture Committee oversight of implementation of the 1996 farm bill may be significant," he added. The committee may also be active in reforming the federal crop insurance program.

Issues from the 1996 farm bill Riley will be tracking include dairy farming. The dairy title of the farm bill expires in 2000 and ends price supports for milk. The Department of Agriculture will also be required to consolidate the nation's system of milk marketing orders this year.

Riley said the committee may review commodity futures regulatory policy as part of risk management strategy. The committee will be overseeing changes to the commodity programs to assure international competitiveness for U.S. farmers. Another part of the risk management strategy is the crop insurance program.

Other top priorities include assuring a safety net for farmers, and evaluating several new crop insurance products, including crop revenue coverage and income protection.

The 1996 farm bill created an independent Office of Risk Management to coordinate multi-peril crop insurance, underwrite new crop revenue insurance, and assist farmers in using futures, options, and risk management savings accounts. The bill also removed a mandate that all farmers carry crop insurance even when they did not need it.

The crop insurance program that has been in place provided farmers with a government-subsidized insurance policy that protected them in the event of a natural disaster, Riley said. The administration has proposed a nation-wide revenue insurance plan. The committee is particularly interested in improving farm income protection aspects of the farm bill, which includes crop and revenue insurance programs.

As farmers come to grips with the new farm bill, which changes the 60-year-old relationship on which the farm program was based, the committee will be carefully monitor its effects. Fluctuations in market prices could have a significant impact on farmers in this new market environment, Riley said.

Subcommittee on Department Operations, Nutrition & Foreign Agriculture

1301 Longworth House Office Building
Washington, D.C. 20515-6001
202/225-2171   Fax: 202/225-0917

MAJORITY MEMBERS:

Bob Goodlatte, VA
Chairman
Thomas W. Ewing, IL
Vice Chairman
Charles T. Canady, FL
Nick Smith, MI
Mark Foley, FL
Ray LaHood, IL
John R. Thune, SD

MINORITY MEMBERS:

Eva M. Clayton, NC
Ranking Minority Member
Bennie G. Thompson, MS
Marion Berry, AR
George E. Brown, Jr., CA
Sanford D. Bishop, Jr., GA

Jurisdiction: Agency review and analysis, special investigations, pesticides, nutrition, food stamps, hunger, consumer programs, and trade matters not otherwise assigned, including foreign agriculture assistance programs, generally.

KEY MAJORITY STAFF:

Kevin Kramp
Staff Director
Subcommittee on Dept. Operations, Nutrition & Foreign Agriculture
1430 Longworth House Office Bldg.
225-0171

Personal: born 2/9/69 in Chicago, Ill.

Education: B.A., Cornell College (Mount Vernon, Iowa), 1991.

Professional: 1991-93, staff asst., Rep. Jim Nussle, R-Iowa. 1993-94, systems mgr.; 1994-96, agriculture leg. asst., Rep. Bob Goodlatte, R-Va. 1997-present, staff dir., subc. on dept. operations, nutrition, and foreign agriculture, House Cmte. on Agriculture.

Expertise: Operations, nutrition, foreign agriculture

The subcommittee on department operations, nutrition, and foreign

agriculture is turning its attention both near and far in 1998, looking at issues within the halls of USDA to those affecting the troubled economies of Asia, says staff director Kevin Kramp.

Of course, it also will be looking at issues on the farm as well. Kramp said "a big target for us" will be the Environmental Protection Agency's implementation of the 1996 Food Quality Protection Act, which regulates pesticides. Complaints that EPA has not set specific processes for reviewing pesticides means growers have been unable to use some products temporarily even if they are not thought to be harmful to the environment.

"We hear some horror stories from industry," Kramp said. "We have a sympathetic subcommittee chair (Rep. Bob Goodlatte, R-Va.), and he hopes to hold hearings on it this year."

Close to home, the subcommittee will work on legislation to establish clearer guidelines for the Department of Agriculture's procurement of information technology, a process General Accounting Office reports have criticized as fraught with problems. Kramp said estimates are that $10 billion has been wasted in years past because of poor inventory management and purchases of new equipment that is too expensive, unneeded, or not compatible with equipment already in use.

Another area of USDA oversight, a reorganization of the Farm Service Agency to reflect an estimated 35 percent cut in the workload because of 1996 Farm Bill reforms, was put on hold in 1997 pending a consultant's report. The Coopers & Lybrand report on field office restructuring is due in August, Kramp said.

On international issues, the committee will study the economic crisis in Asia. Kramp said members will look at ways agricultural programs might be used to alleviate problems on the continent. He said he is unsure whether the U.S. Food for Progress program will be a solution, because it has just $65 million in unobligated funds.

The committee also will monitor continued implementation of provisions from 1996 welfare reforms that called for states to begin electronic benefit transfers for food stamp recipients. So far, 35 percent to 40 percent of recipients are receiving benefits electronically instead of by paper coupons. Congress has mandated that the program use transfers exclusively by 2002.

The new method of distributing food-stamp assistance is "going pretty well," Kramp said. USDA's inspector general told the subcommittee last year that electronic benefit transfers make it much easier to find fraud and abuse.

KEY MINORITY STAFF:

Russell Middleton
Minority Professional Staff Member
1002-B Longworth House Office Bldg.
225-1496

Personal: born 3/31/60 in Abilene, Texas.

Education: B.S., Hardin Simmons Univ., 1987.

Professional: 1987-97, staff and legis. asst., Rep. Charles Stenholm, D-Texas. 1997-present, min. prof. staff member, House Cmte. on Ag.

Expertise: Rural development

In a Congress where representation is skewed toward the cities and suburbs due to their population increases, Russell Middleton is one of the people looking out for rural America. A product of rural Texas and a specialist in rural development, he says it is important for small towns and farming communities to get the help they need in development, utilities, housing, and other areas.

"That will be something I'll be trying to keep an eye on for the minority side," Middleton said. "We'd like to continue to fund programs that people are using to keep small-town America alive."

President Clinton devoted considerable time in his State of the Union message this year to the problems of urban America, and his fiscal 1999 budget proposal contained money for enterprise zones, anti-drug efforts, and other programs to help the nation's cities. Middleton said it also contained plans for development, distance learning, and other projects to help rural residents. Outside the Agriculture Committee, though, he acknowledged such proposals are not always an easy sell with lawmakers. "In just the sheer numbers, rural America is at a disadvantage," he said. "Sometimes these proposals are at a disadvantage."

In addition to rural issues, Middleton follows the domestic biotechnology industry for the committee's minority members and serves as minority consultant to the Subcommittee on Department Operations, Nutrition and Foreign Agriculture.

In the latter role, Middleton said he will follow the Department of Agriculture's "administrative convergence" initiative, which is designed to consolidate administrative functions within the field offices of the Farm Service Agency, the Natural Resources Conservation Service, and the Rural Utility Service. The Clinton administration in 1997 proposed reductions in the number of field personnel within USDA. Middleton said the department's program is trying to eliminate duplication of administrative functions at the federal, regional, and state levels. "We're trying to find the most efficient way to deliver the programs and hopefully with as few staff reductions as possible, but certainly that is part of what's driving these efforts," he said.

While others on the Agriculture Committee staff will spend time this year focusing on ways to boost biotechnology internationally, Middleton said his focus will be on how the industry is treated domestically.

"So far biotech has really been looked at as a benefit to farmers in that they use less pesticides or have a higher quality of seed," he said. "The most exciting thing about biotech and the domestic side is that companies are creating products that have a consumer benefit to them - less fat or more nutritious."

Middleton joined the Agriculture Committee staff in 1997 after 10 years as a staff assistant and legislative assistant for Rep. Charles Stenholm, D-Texas, who became the panel's ranking Democrat.

Committee on Appropriations

Subcommittee on Commerce, Justice, State, the Judiciary, & Related Agencies

H-309, The Capitol
Washington, D.C. 20515-6017
202/225-3351

MAJORITY MEMBERS:

Harold Rogers, KY
Chairman
Jim Kolbe, AZ
Charles H. Taylor, NC
Ralph Regula, OH
Michael P. Forbes, NY
Tom Latham, IA

MINORITY MEMBERS:

Alan B. Mollohan, WV
Ranking Minority Member
David E. Skaggs, CO
Julian C. Dixon, CA

Jurisdiction: (1) Department of Commerce; (2) Department of Justice; (3) Department of State (except Anti-terrorism Assistance; International Narcotics Control; International Organizations and Programs; Migration and Refugee Assistance; Peacekeeping Operations; U.S. Emergency Refugee and Migration Assistance Fund); (4) The Judiciary; (5) Department of Transportation (Maritime vAdministration). Related Agencies; (6) Arms Control and Disarmament Agency; (7) Board for International Broadcasting; (8) Commission on Civil Rights; (9) Commission on Immigration Reform; (10) Commission on Security and Cooperation in Europe; (11) Commission for the Preservation of America's Heritage Abroad; (12) Competitiveness Policy Council; (13) Equal Employment Opportunity Commission; (14) Federal Communications Commission; (15) Federal Maritime Commission; (16) Federal Trade Commission; (17) International Trade Commission; (18) Japan-United States Friendship Commission; (19) Legal Services Corporation; (20) Marine Mammal Commission; (21) National Commission to Support Law Enforcement; (22) Office of the U.S. Trade Representative; (23) Securities and Exchange Commission; (24) Small Business Administration; (25) State Justice Institute; (26) Martin Luther King, Jr., Federal Holiday Commission; (27) Thomas Jefferson Commemoration Commission; (28) U.S. Information Agency.

KEY MAJORITY STAFF:

James Kulikowski
Clerk
Subcommittee on Commerce, Justice and State
H-309, The Capitol
225-3351

Personal: born 3/14/54 in Northampton, Mass.

Education: B.A. (summa cum laude, Phi Beta Kappa), Harvard Coll., 1976. J.D. (cum laude), Harvard Univ., 1979. M.P.H., Harvard Univ., 1988.

Professional: 1979-81, attorney, Fried, Frank, Harris, Shriver and Jacobson. 1981-82, staff member, House Cmte. on Small Business. 1982-86, staff asst., subc. on Labor, HHS, and Education; 1988-95, minority staff director; 1995-present, clerk, subc. on Commerce, Justice and State, House Cmte. on Appropriations.

Expertise: Appropriations

The subcommittee on Commerce, Justice and State deals with a variety of issues, including crime, Voice of America, the many components of the Justice Department's budget, and a range of issues associated with the Commerce Department. For the fourth year now, the job of defending Republican budget-cutting initiatives while trying to reach compromise with Democrats falls to subcommittee clerk Jim Kulikowski.

Kulikowski is described by colleagues as one who concentrates on making the political system work, smoothing disagreements and clearing roadblocks thrown up from both sides of the aisle. But

Kulikowski downplays his role. "I deal with funding issues for those departments. The challenge is to continue to make progress on spending reductions," he said. "The primary issue facing the subcommittee involves the need for continued fiscal restraint, though the administration's budget requests significant increases, while addressing needs in such areas as juvenile crime and the cyclical increase in census funding with all of its attendant issues."

President Clinton's fiscal 1999 spending plan calls for a 5 percent increase in the Commerce Department's budget, except for the 2000 Census, which would see its budget almost double, Kulikowski said. Census spending is expected to total $927 million in 1999, up from $487 million in the current fiscal year and $198 million in 1997. Staffing for the Census Bureau also jumps sharply as the 2000 Census approaches. The bureau is expected grow from 2,166 workers in 1997 to 6,237 this year and 12,108 in 1999.

Clinton's plan also calls for increasing the Justice Department's budget to $18.3 billion. Under the plan, the FBI would add 75 agents to set up computer crime squads in Atlanta, Boston, Charlotte, Miami, Minneapolis, and Seattle. Programs to combat drug trafficking, illegal immigration, juvenile crime, and terrorism would also get increases. One proposal seeks $28 million and 160 new agents for the Bureau of Alcohol, Tobacco and Firearms in an effort to take guns out of the hands of youth gangs in 27 cities.

The administration's proposed budget for the State Department under the subcommittee's jurisdiction allocates $4.2 billion for operations, foreign aid, peacekeeping, and international lending institutions.

Subcommittee on Foreign Operations, Export Financing, & Related Programs

H-150, The Capitol
Washington, D.C. 20515-6021
202/225-2041

MAJORITY MEMBERS:

Sonny Callahan, AL
Chairman
John Edward Porter, IL
Frank R. Wolf, VA
Ron Packard, CA
Joe Knollenberg, MI
Michael P. Forbes, NY
Jack Kingston, GA
Rodney P. Frelinghuysen, NJ

MINORITY MEMBERS:

Nancy Pelosi, CA
Ranking Minority Member
Sidney R. Yates, IL
Nita M. Lowey, NY
Esteban Edward Torres, CA
Marcy Kaptur, OH

Jurisdiction: (1) Agency for International Development; (2) African Development Foundation; (3) African Development Fund and Bank; (4) Asian Development Fund and Bank; (5) Department of State (Anti-terrorism Assistance, International Narcotics Control, International Organizations and Programs, Migration and Refugee Assistance, Peacekeeping Operations, U.S. Emergency Refugee and Migration Assistance Fund); (6) Enterprise for the Americas Initiative; (7) Export-Import Bank; (8) European Bank for Reconstruction and Development; (9) Foreign Military Financing Program; (10) Guarantee Reserve Fund; (11) Inter-American Development Bank; (12) Inter-American Foundation; (13) International Bank for Reconstruction and Development (World Bank); (14) International Development Association; (15) International Development Cooperation Agency; (16) International Finance Corporation; (17) International Fund for Agricultural Development; (18) International Military Education and Training; (19) International Monetary Fund Programs; (20) Military Assistance Program; (21) Military to Military Contact Program (DOD-Military); (22) Multilateral Investment Guarantee Agency; (23) Overseas Private Investment Corporation; (24) Peace Corps; (25) Special Defense Acquisition Fund; (26) Special Assistance for Central America (Assistance for Democratic Nicaraguan Resistance; Central American Reconciliation Assistance); (27) Trade & Develop. Program.

KEY MAJORITY STAFF:

Charles O. Flickner Jr.
Clerk
Subcommittee on Foreign Operations
H-150, The Capitol
225-2041

Personal: born 9/26/46 in Biloxi, Miss.

Education: B.S., Loyola Univ., 1969. 1970-74, graduate studies, Univ. of Va.

Professional: 1969-70, Mechanized Infantry Unit, U.S. Army. 1974, majority staff member; 1975-81, junior analyst, defense and international affairs; 1982-87, group leader, international security and credit; 1988-95, senior analyst for international affairs, Senate Cmte. on the Budget. 1995-present, clerk, subc. on foreign operations, House Cmte. on Appropriations.

Expertise: Foreign affairs, military budgets, international security

As usual, dealing with the appropriations bill for foreign operations will take up much of Charles O. Flickner's time during the second half of the 105th Congress. However, the clerk of the subcommittee on foreign operations says the spending measure is not the year's overriding issue.

"The budget is not the biggest issue this year, frankly," Flickner said. "The IMF (International Monetary Fund) is the biggest single issue for this subcommittee." About $18 billion has been requested for the IMF this year. Flickner said the request will be dealt with in a supplemental bill for 1998.

Flickner has worked on Capitol Hill for 24 years and is in his fourth year as clerk of the Subcommittee on Foreign Operations, the panel responsible for deciding how much money goes to foreign aid, international development projects, and other programs that further U.S. interests overseas.

About $14 billion has been requested for Foreign Operations in the proposed fiscal 1999 budget, nearly $1 billion above the 1998 funding level, Flickner said.

Rep. Sonny Callahan, R-Ala., is subcommittee chairman and Flickner's boss. Nancy Pelosi, D-Calif., is the panel's ranking member. At the staff level, the majority team is made up of seasoned professionals like Flickner. "We have a very comfortable fit," he said.

Flickner worked for the Senate Budget Committee from 1974 until 1995 when he moved to the House Appropriations Committee. He said he was drawn by the quality of the staff, the reputation of committee staff director Jim Dyer, and by the committee itself.

"The new majority was elected for a purpose," Flickner said. "And this is the place that is really prepared to carry out that change."

Flickner graduated from Loyola University in 1969 and then served in the U.S. Army's Mechanized Infantry Unit for a year. He did graduate studies at the University of Virginia from 1970 to 1974. He and his wife adopted two children from a Russian orphanage in 1993.

Committee on
Banking & Financial Services

Subcommittee on Domestic & International Monetary Policy

B-304 Rayburn House Office Building
Washington, D.C. 20515-6058
202/226-0473   Fax: 202/226-0537

MAJORITY MEMBERS:

Michael Castle, DE
Chairman
Jon Fox, PA
Vice Chairman
Steven LaTourette, OH
Frank Lucas, OK
Jack Metcalf, WA
Robert Ney, OH
Bob Barr, GA
Ron Paul, TX
Dave Weldon, FL
Marge Roukema, NJ
Doug Bereuter, NE
Merrill Cook, UT
Donald Manzullo, IL
Mark Foley, FL

MINORITY MEMBERS:

Maxine Waters, CA
Ranking Minority Member
Barney Frank, MA
Joseph Kennedy, MA
Bernard Sanders, VT
Carolyn Maloney, NY
Maurice Hinchey, NY
Jesse Jackson, Jr., IL
Melvin Watt, NC
Darlene Hooley, OR
Julia Carson, IN
Gregory Meeks, NY
Barbara Lee, CA

Jurisdiction: (1) All matters relating to all multilateral development lending institutions, including activities of the National Advisory Council on International Monetary and Financial Policies as related thereto, and monetary and financial developments as they relate to the activities and objectives of such institutions; (2) All matters within the jurisdiction of the Committee relating to international trade, including but not limited to the activities of the Export-Import Bank; (3) The International Monetary Fund, its permanent and temporary agencies and all matters related thereto; (4) International investment policies, both as they relate to United States investments for trade purposes by citizens of the United States and investments made by

all foreign entities in the United States; (5) All matters relating to financial aid to all sectors and elements within the economy, all matters relating to economic growth and stabilization, and all defense production matters as contained in the Defense Production Act of 1950, as amended, and all related matters thereto; (6) All matters relating to domestic monetary policy and agencies which directly or indirectly affect domestic monetary policy, including the effect of such policy and other financial actions on interest rates, the allocation of credit, and the structure and functioning of domestic and foreign financial institutions; (7) All matters relating to coins, coinage, currency and medals, proof and mint sets and other special coins, the Coinage Act of 1965, gold and silver, including coinage thereof (but not the par value of gold), gold medals, counterfeiting, currency denominations and design, the distribution of coins, and the operations and activities of the Bureau of the Mint and the Bureau of Engraving and Printing.

KEY MAJORITY STAFF:

James McCormick
Assistant Staff Director
Subcommittee on Domestic and International Monetary Policy
B-303 Rayburn House Office Bldg.
226-0473

Education: B.A. in history, Univ. of Iowa, 1983. J.D., Univ. of Iowa, 1988. M.A. in history, Univ. of Iowa, 1991.

Professional: Nov. 1988-March 1989, leg. asst., Rep. Jim Leach, R-Iowa. 1989-94, minority staff; subc. on Asia and the Pacific, House Cmte. on Foreign Affairs. 1995- present, asst. staff director, subc. on domestic and international monetary policy, House Cmte. on Banking and Financial Services.

Expertise: International banking/financial issues

James McCormick is Banking Committee Chairman Jim Leach's, R-Iowa, lead staffer at the subcommittee on domestic and international monetary policy. McCormick works closely with the panel's senior counsel, John Lopez.

The subcommittee began the year with a Feb. 24 hearing on the Federal Reserve's semi-annual reports on the nation's monetary policy. The subcommittee will hold a second hearing no later than July 20 pursuant to the Humphrey-Hawkins Act, which requires the reports to Congress.

Subcommittee Chairman Michael Castle's, R-Del., 1998 agenda includes hearings into the need for reform of the International Monetary Fund (IMF) "with the goal of encouraging countries to embrace transparent, market-based economic policies, and to better protect U.S. taxpayers from future international financial crises." In a Jan. 29 speech, Leach said he wants to ensure that "the IMF's role is not expanded from being a last resort stabilizer of currencies and economies to a last-resort lender to banking systems."

Other items on Castle's agenda are hearings into "the future of money," the European Monetary Union (EMU), foreign counterfeiting of U.S.

Treasury instruments, on-line computer fraud, and the impact of the year 2000 computer problem.

The currency hearing will look at new technologies such as biometric identification to secure electronic financial transactions. The hearing on the EMU will examine the potential impact that a common European currency could have on the international monetary system, the U.S. dollar, and American businesses and travelers. Another hearing will investigate reports of foreign counterfeiting of U.S. financial instruments abroad. The Treasury Department's plans to redesign U.S. paper currency to avoid this problem will be explored as well.

The problems and potential solutions of fraud for consumers who use the internet will be the subject of another hearing this year. The subcommittee is concerned with on-line casinos, fraudulent banking, insurance, and investment scams. Finally, the subcommittee will look at potential year 2000 computer problems on the International Payments System and the U.S. payments system.

McCormick's political career began as a campaign volunteer for George Bush in the fall of 1988, and as a campaign assistant to Leach. McCormick went on to work as a legislative assistant for Leach from November 1988 to March 1989. His next stop was the House Foreign Affairs subcommittee on Asia and the Pacific, where he worked from 1989-1994.

Committee on Commerce

2125 Rayburn House Office Building
Washington, D.C. 20515-6115
202/225-2927   Fax: 202/225-0654

MAJORITY MEMBERS:

Tom Bliley, VA
Chairman
W.J. "Billy" Tauzin, LA
Michael G. Oxley, OH
Michael Bilirakis, FL
Dan Schaefer, CO
Joe Barton, TX
J. Dennis Hastert, IL
Fred Upton, MI
Cliff Stearns, FL
Bill Paxon, NY
Paul E. Gillmor, OH
Vice Chairman
Scott L. Klug, WI
James C. Greenwood, PA
Michael D. Crapo, ID
Christopher Cox, CA
Nathan Deal, GA
Steve Largent, OK
Richard Burr, NC
Brian P. Bilbray, CA
Ed Whitfield, KY
Greg Ganske, IA
Charlie Norwood, GA
Rick White, WA
Tom Coburn, OK
Rick Lazio, NY
Barbara Cubin, WY
James Rogan, CA
John Shimkus, IL

MINORITY MEMBERS:

John D. Dingell, MI
Ranking Minority Member
Henry A. Waxman, CA

Edward J. Markey, MA
Ralph M. Hall, TX
Rick Boucher, VA
Thomas J. Manton, NY
Edolphus Towns, NY
Frank Pallone, Jr., NJ
Sherrod Brown, OH
Bart Gordon, TN
Elizabeth Furse, OR
Peter Deutsch, FL
Bobby L. Rush, IL
Anna G. Eshoo, CA
Ron Klink, PA
Bart Stupak, MI
Eliot L. Engel, NY
Thomas C. Sawyer, OH
Albert R. Wynn, MD
Gene Green, TX
Karen McCarthy, MO
Ted Strickland, OH
Diana DeGette, CO

Jurisdiction: (1) Biomedical research and development; (2) Consumer Affairs and consumer protection; (3) Health and health facilities, except health care supported by payroll deductions; (4) Interstate energy compacts; (5) Interstate and foreign commerce generally; (6) Measures relating to the exploration, production, storage, supply, marketing, pricing, and regulation of energy resources, and other unconventional or renewable energy resources; (7) Measures relating to the conservation of energy resources; (8) Measures relating to energy information generally; (9) Measures relating to (A) the generation and marketing of power (except by federally chartered or Federal regional power marketing authorities), (B) the reliability and interstate transmission of, and ratemaking for, all power, and (C) the siting of generation facilities; except the installation of interconnection between Government waterpower projects; (10) Measures relating to general management of the Department of Energy, and the management and all functions of the Federal Energy Regulatory Commission; (11) National energy policy generally; (12) Public health and quarantine; (13) Regulation of the domestic nuclear energy industry, including regulation of research and development reactors and nuclear regulatory research; (14) Regulation of interstate and foreign communications; (15) Securities and exchanges; (16) Travel and tourism.

KEY MAJORITY STAFF:

James E. Derderian
Staff Director
2125 Rayburn House Office Bldg.
225-2927

Personal: born 2/12/63 in Morristown, N.J.

Education: B.A. (cum laude, Phi Beta Kappa), Univ. of Richmond, 1985.

Professional: 1985, assistant policy director, Durrette for Governor.

1986-87, legislative asst., Virginia Senate Republican Leader. 1987-94, legislative director, Rep. Thomas Bliley, R-Va. 1995-present, staff director, House Cmte. on Commerce.

Expertise: Commerce, economic issues

James Derderian, staff director for Chairman Thomas Bliley, R-Va., on the Commerce Committee, will be working for much of the second session on legislation providing for the deregulation of the electric utility industry in the United States. He will also work on the Communications Satellite Competition and Privatization Act, and H.R. 10, the Financial Services Reform Act, expected to be on the House floor before summer.

Utility deregulation and satellite privatization are major concerns of the chairman who has long pushed for their passage. The Financial Services Reform Act looked derailed at the end of the first session, but now is back on track.

Much of Derderian's effort in the first session was centered on the hearings, mark-up, floor passage, and final action on the Food and Drug Administration Modernization Act of 1997 which was approved in November. Derderian notes that one of Bliley's greatest skills is "working with members on the other side of the aisle", and that ability helped to speed the passage of this landmark bill.

Derderian has lead the committee staff since 1995 when the Republicans won control of the Congress and Bliley became chairman of the Commerce Committee. That first session of the 104th Congress saw the passage of a major securities litigation reform bill and the second session dealt with safe drinking water and telecommunications reform. Bliley runs the committee with what is called a unified staff. This eliminates subcommittee staffs and all Commerce Committee majority staffers now report directly to the chairman through Derderian.

Derderian enjoys Bliley's confidence. He served as the congressman's legislative director for seven years before assuming his current role on the committee staff. Derderian is a graduate of the University of Richmond where he earned his Phi Beta Kappa key and was a member of Omicron Delta Kappa. He came to Bliley's staff after working in Virginia state Republican politics.

He is married to Mary Fitzgerald Bannon and is interested in football and racquet sports.

KEY MINORITY STAFF:

Howard P. Bauleke
Minority Counsel
564 Ford House Office Bldg.
226-3400

Personal: born 4/16/59 in Lawrence, Kan.

Education: B.A., Univ. of Kan., 1981. J.D., Georgetown Univ., 1984.

Professional: 1980, campaign coordinator, State Rep. John Solbach,

D-Kan. 1984-87, leg. asst.; 1987-91, staff director; 1991-94, admin. asst., Rep. Jim Slattery, D-Kan. Jan. 1995-March 1995, admin. asst., Rep. Karen McCarthy, D-Mo. June 1995-97, associate counsel, House Democratic Policy Committee. 1997-present, minority counsel, House Cmte. on Commerce.

Expertise: Energy issues, trade regulation

Howard Bauleke, a lawyer and Kansas native, joined the House Committee on Commerce last year as Democratic counsel. Previously, he served as associate counsel for the House Democratic Policy Committee, tracking issues as diverse as telecommunications, securities, small business, labor, veterans, product liability, and international trade.

In the second session, Bauleke is working on electricity industry restructuring, which encompasses several complicated issues including the pre-emption of state regulation, ensuring reliability of the electricity grid, ensuring continuation of consumer protection, energy efficiency and environmental programs, resolving how utilities can satisfy current mandated regulations in a competitive marketplace, and whether the Public Utility Holding Company Act (PUHCA) should be repealed. Bauleke will also be involved as the committee looks at how public utilities, rural electric cooperatives, federal power marketing administrations, and the Tennessee Valley Authority would function in a deregulated marketplace.

"Despite attempts by the Republican committee leadership to make it so, electricity restructuring is not a partisan issue," Bauleke said. "The widely divergent interests of both Democratic and Republican committee members are driven primarily by cost and available conditions in their local energy markets."

Bauleke this year will also be handling issues, and possibly hearings, involving federal standards for the relicensing of hydroelectric projects, global climate change, and implementation of Government Performance and Results Act (GPRA), the statute that requires that all agencies, as part of their 1999 budget proposals, submit performance plans.

In 1997, energy issues, including proposals to restructure the electricity industry, took up much of Bauleke's time. Other priorities included the GPRA and legislation that would establish a high-level nuclear waste repository in Nevada.

Bauleke was among those Democratic staffers who felt the sting of the Republican landslide in 1994. Bauleke's former boss, Rep. Jim Slattery, D-Kan., was swamped in a bid for the Kansas governorship, a loss that ended their long-time professional relationship. Bauleke started in January 1984 as a legislative assistant for the Kansas congressman, eventually moving up to become staff director and later administrative assistant. Many of the issues he is currently involved with are ones Bauleke began tracking while working for Slattery, who was an active member of the then-House Committee on Energy and Commerce.

Bauleke describes himself as a libertarian on social issues, a conservative on fiscal policy, and a supporter of a strong federal government to ensure fairness in the marketplace and to protect public health and safety.

Committee on International Relations

2170 Rayburn House Office Building
Washington, D.C. 20515
202/225-5021

MAJORITY MEMBERS:

Benjamin A. Gilman, NY
Chairman

William F. Goodling, PA
James A. Leach, IA
Henry J. Hyde, IL
Doug Bereuter, NE
Christopher H. Smith, NJ
Dan Burton, IN
Elton Gallegly, CA
Ileana Ros-Lehtinen, FL
Cass Ballenger, NC
Dana Rohrabacher, CA
Donald A. Manzullo, IL
Edward R. Royce, CA
Peter T. King, NY
Jay Kim, CA
Steven J. Chabot, OH
Marshall "Mark" Sanford, SC
Matt Salmon, AZ
Amo Houghton, NY
Tom Campbell, CA
Jon Fox, PA
John M. McHugh, NY
Lindsey O. Graham, SC
Roy Blunt, MO
Kevin Brady, TX

MINORITY MEMBERS:

Lee H. Hamilton, IN
Ranking Minority Member
Sam Gejdenson, CT
Tom Lantos, CA
Howard L. Berman, CA
Gary L. Ackerman, NY
Eni F.H. Faleomavaega, AS
Matthew G. Martinez, CA
Donald M. Payne, NJ
Robert E. Andrews, NJ
Robert Menendez, NJ
Sherrod Brown, OH
Cynthia A. McKinney, GA
Alcee L. Hastings, FL
Pat Danner, MO
Earl F. Hilliard, AL
Brad Sherman, CA
Robert Wexler, FL
Steven R. Rothman, NJ
Bob Clement, TN
Bill Luther, MN
Jim Davis, FL

Jurisdiction: (1) Relations of the United States with foreign nations generally; (2) Acquisition of land and buildings for embassies and legations in foreign countries; (3) Establishment of boundary lines between the United States and foreign nations; (4) Export controls, including nonproliferation of nuclear technology and nuclear hardware; (5) Foreign loans; (6) International commodity agreements (other than those involving sugar), including all agreements for cooperation in the export of nuclear technology and nuclear hardware; (7) International conferences and congresses; (8) International education; (9) Intervention abroad and declarations of war; (10) Measures relating to the diplomatic service; (11) Measures to foster commercial intercourse with foreign nations to safeguard American business interests abroad; (12) Measures relating to international economic policy; (13) Neutrality; (14) Protection of American citizens abroad and expatriation; (15) The American National Red Cross; (16) Trading with the enemy; (17) United Nations Organizations.

In addition to its legislative jurisdiction under the preceding provisions of this paragraph (and its general oversight function under clause 2(b)(1)), the committee shall have the special oversight function provided for in clause 3(d) with respect to customs administration, intelligence activities relating to foreign policy, international financial and monetary organization, and international fishing agreements.

KEY MAJORITY STAFF:

Richard J. Garon
Chief of Staff
2170 Rayburn House Office Bldg.
225-5021

Personal: born 9/9/48 in Bronxville, N.Y.

Education: B.A., Hartwick Coll., 1972. M.A., New York Univ., 1975. Ph.D., New York Univ., 1983.

Professional: 1977-79, leg. asst., Rep. Benjamin Gilman, R-N.Y. 1979-83, minority staff asst., House Cmte. on Post Office and Civil Service. 1983-85, minority staff consultant, subc. on Europe and the Middle East, House Cmte. on Foreign Affairs. 1985-89, administrative asst., Rep. Gilman. 1989-93, dep. staff dir. for the minority, House Cmte. on Post Office and Civil Service. 1993-95, minority chief of staff, House Cmte. on Foreign Affairs. 1995-present, majority chief of staff, House Cmte. on International Relations.

Expertise: Foreign affairs

In 1998, the House International Relations Committee is looking extensively at U.S. drug policy, said Rich Garon, the committee's chief of staff. Members are concerned about the large amount of narcotics that enter the U.S. each year. Hearings will focus on what policies have been effective and how to improve those that are not working.

Another committee priority this year is the issue of U.S. troop involvement overseas, Garon said. Specifically, the committee is looking at deployments in Haiti and Bosnia. In Haiti, U.S. troops were successful initially in reducing killings. However, the troops have been there for several years, and their presence must be reassessed.

Garon coordinates committee activities and promotes the legislative agenda of Chairman Benjamin Gilman, R-N.Y. In 1998, the committee is focusing on U.S. policy toward Iraq, an on-going issue. Hearings on sanctions legislation are also scheduled. These include continued oversight of the Helms-Burton Act, which deals with Cuba, and the Iran-Libya Sanctions Act, which deals with companies investing in foreign oil in these countries. Another committee priority for this year is the conference on the State Department authorization bill, which includes foreign agency reorganization and the payment of U.S. arrears to the United Nations.

In 1997, the committee addressed NATO expansion and United Nations reform, two issues that occupied much of Garon's time in 1996. Early in 1997, Garon worked on legislation to decertify Mexico as a country that is fully cooperating with U.S. anti-drug efforts. When President Clinton certified Mexico as a cooperating country, the House, led by Rep. Clay Shaw, R-Fla., and Gilman, swiftly passed a joint resolution to overturn the certification.

In the 104th Congress, Garon worked on the controversial National Security Revitalization Act, which deals with the United States's relationship with the United Nations and the future of U.N. peacekeeping efforts.

Garon has spent all 21 of his years on Capitol Hill working for Gilman. At the beginning of the 103rd Congress, when Gilman became ranking Republican on what was then the Foreign Affairs Committee, he brought Garon over from the Post Office and Civil Service Committee. Garon was happy to return to the panel, where he served for two years in the 1980s as a minority staff consultant for the Subcommittee on Europe and the Middle East.

Stephen G. Rademaker
Majority Chief Counsel
2170 Rayburn House Office Bldg.
225-5021

Personal: born 7/18/59 in Baltimore, Md.

Education: B.A., Univ. of Va., 1981. J.D., Univ. of Va., 1984. M.A., Univ. of Va., 1985.

Professional: 1984-86, associate, Covington & Burling. 1986, clerk to Judge James L. Buckley, U.S. Court of Appeals for D.C. 1986-87, counsel to vice chairman, U.S. International Trade Commission. 1987-89, special asst. to asst. secretary for inter-American affairs, U.S. Dept. of State. 1989-92, associate counsel to the president and deputy legal advisor, National Security Council. 1992-93, general counsel, Peace Corps. 1993-95, minority chief counsel; 1995-present, majority chief counsel, House Cmte. on International Relations.

Expertise: National security law

In 1998, the Committee on International Relations will spend considerable time on the Asian financial crisis, oversight of NATO enlargement, and the narcotics certification process. A high priority is enactment of a bill to reorganize foreign affairs agencies and to address U.S. debt to the United Nations. A bill to accomplish these objectives is in conference committee, but passage has been held-up by a controversial provision on international family planning.

As the committee's majority chief counsel, Steve Rademaker is responsible for drafting legislation and shepherding it to enactment. He also reviews all legal issues that come before the panel.

The Asian financial crisis has dire implications for North Korea, Rademaker said. In question is the viability of a plan to construct two nuclear reactors at an estimated cost of $5 billion. Most of the funds for the reactors are supposed to come from Japan and South Korea, and the U.S. will closely watch this situation as it develops.

The committee has also scheduled hearings on a religious persecution bill co-sponsored by Sen. Arlen Specter, R-Pa., and Rep. Frank Wolf, R-Va. The committee will also address arms control matters in 1998. With respect to NATO enlargement, members are looking at the inclusion of Poland, Hungary, and the Czech Republic. The second round of NATO enlargement, another top priority, involves the admission of Romania and the Baltic states.

The panel remains interested in U.N. reform, Rademaker said. In 1997, the House passed legislation expanding funding for Radio Free Asia broadcasts and for human rights monitoring. These bills are now being considered by the Senate. Another House bill which passed in 1997 and is being considered by the Senate is the Iran Missile Proliferation Sanctions Act. The bill sanctions companies that send missile technology to Iran. Despite strong Senate support, a veto threat imperils enactment of the measure, Rademaker said.

In 1997, the committee spent considerable time on the State Department authorization bill, United Nations reform, NATO expansion, and Sino-American relations. Rademaker counts 1996 as a very successful year for the committee. He worked on three bills that were enacted: the Helms-Burton Act, the Iran-Libya Sanctions Act, and the NATO Enlargement Act.

Before moving to the Hill, Rademaker worked two years at the State Department, where he helped develop and implement U.S. policy toward Central America. During that time, he made more than 20 trips to the region and served as an advisor to the Nicaraguan contras on diplomatic strategy. In his next job, with the National Security Council, Rademaker handled legal issues surrounding foreign aid, arms control, the military, and trade.

Frank C. Record
Senior Professional Staff Member
2170 Rayburn House Office Bldg.
225-5021

Personal: born 7/29/50 in Boston, Mass.

Education: B.A., Harvard Coll., 1972. M.A., School of Advanced International Studies, Johns Hopkins Univ., 1975.

Professional: 1972-73, VISTA volunteer, Riker's Island Project. 1974-75, research asst., economic projections dept., World Bank. 1975-77, researcher, Worldwatch Institute. 1978-83, staff consultant, Arms Control and Foreign Policy Caucus. 1983-88, minority staff counsel, subc. on intl. development, House Cmte. on Banking. 1988-90, deputy vice president for congressional and external affairs, Export-Import Bank. 1990-present, senior professional staff member, House Cmte. on International Relations.

Expertise: United Nations and International Economic and Trade Issues

Many of the issues that senior professional staffer Frank Record worked on in 1997 have returned in the second session of the 105th Congress. Oversight of economic sanctions issues in general, and the Iran-Libya Sanctions Act in particular, will receive special attention. He is working with colleagues on the committee to prepare a hearing relating to the work of the United Nations Sanctions Committee (UNSCOM) inside Iraq.

United Nations reform is also still at the top of the agenda, with the payment of U.S. arrears to the UN in the supplemental appropriations bill conditioned on a satisfactory resolution to the family planning dispute between the Congress and the Clinton administration. Record says that once the administration unveils its new benchmark requirements on the UN reform package, the bargaining will start in earnest between the House, Senate, and the administration.

Record's responsibilities include international trade, export control, international organizations, and peacekeeping issues. He is expected to take a leading role in advising chairman Benjamin A. Gilman on the Asian financial crisis and the pending supplemental request for the quota increase for the International Monetary Fund. Oversight of trade issues, the Overseas Private Investment Corporation, and the export of high performance computers will get priority attention as well.

Record earned a bachelor's degree from Harvard College in 1972. He spent his junior year abroad, studying at the Institute of Political Studies in Paris. Before he began work on Capitol Hill, Record worked as a VISTA volunteer for the Riker's Island Project, a research assistant at the World Bank, and as a researcher for the Worldwatch Institute. He came to the Washington area when he started graduate school.

"I decided I wanted to do more policy-related things, so I got a job on the Hill," Record said. From 1978 to 1983, he worked as a staff consultant for the bipartisan Arms Control and Foreign Policy Caucus, which was made up of House and Senate members. He then went to the House Banking Committee's International Development Subcommittee, where he was minority staff counsel from 1983 to 1988.

Record's next job was as deputy vice president for congressional and external affairs at the Export-Import Bank, where he was responsible for developing and carrying out the bank's legislative program until 1990. At that point, he joined the staff of the House International Relations Committee.

John Walker Roberts
Senior Professional Staff Member
2170 Rayburn House Office Bldg.
225-7705

Personal: born 3/24/60 in Indianapolis, Ind.

Education: B.A. in history (with honors), Denison Univ., 1982. M.A., School of Advanced International Studies, Johns Hopkins Univ., 1985.

Professional: 1985-87, staff assistant, Senate Cmte. on Foreign Relations. 1987-88, office of congressional correspondence; 1988-89, special assistant to President Reagan, office of legislative affairs, The White House. 1989-93, professional staff member; 1993-present, senior professional staff member, House Cmte. on Inter'l. Relations.

Expertise: Arms transfers and Security assistance

The House International Relations Committee has scheduled hearings this year on U.S. drug policy, U.S. troop involvement overseas, and U.S. policy towards Iraq. It continues oversight of sanctions legislation

(Helms-Burton and Iran-Libya Sanctions Act).

Another committee priority in 1998 is a conference on the State Department authorization bill, which includes foreign agency reorganization and the payment of U.S. arrears to the United Nations. Members are still trying to work out a compromise on a provision involving family planning.

John Roberts serves as the committee's principal adviser in a number of areas, including arms transfers, proliferation and arms control issues, security assistance, Department of Defense-related issues, and NATO. "In addition to my substantive responsibilities, I also spend a great deal of time helping to ensure that the committee runs smoothly, as liaison to the minority, Republican leadership, and the executive branch, principally on scheduling hearings, markups, and in negotiating what witnesses will be provided for hearings," Roberts said.

Roberts expects a continuing emphasis on maintaining strong congressional oversight on the Clinton administration's foreign policy, particularly with respect to Bosnia, Haiti, and North Korea.

In 1997, Roberts spent much of his time working on the issue of NATO enlargement. Early in this session, the ratification debate on expanding NATO to include Poland, the Czech Republic, and Hungary was held in the Senate.

Roberts also worked last year on U.S. policy on conventional arms transfers to Latin America and on Greece-Turkey arms transfers. "We need an overall policy, of which arms transfers is an element, that is sustainable over the long haul with respect to these countries," Roberts said. "We don't have one now and it is leading to a tit-for-tat fight over each proposed arms sale to each country."

Roberts is a native of Indianapolis who earned a B.A. in history from Denison University and a master's from Johns Hopkins University's School of Advanced International Studies. He has been in his current position since 1993.

Hillel Weinberg
Senior Professional Staff Member/Counsel
2170 Rayburn House Office Bldg.
225-5021

Personal: born 6/7/52 in the Bronx, N.Y.

Education: B.A. in political science, State Univ. of New York at Buffalo, 1973. M.A., Yale Univ., 1974. M. Phil. Yale Univ., 1975. Ph.D., Yale Univ., 1981. J.D., Univ. of Virginia, 1985.

Professional: 1978-79, legislative assistant, Rep. Don Young, R-Ala. 1979-82, legislative director, Rep. Benjamin Gilman, R-N.Y. 1985-88, minority staff consultant and counsel, subc. on Europe and the Middle East, House Cmte. on Foreign Affairs. 1988-89, attorney, Mayer, Brown & Platt. 1989-91, legislative director and chief counsel, Sen. Rudy Boschwitz, R-Minn. 1991-93, special assistant to the assistant secretary for human rights and humanitarian affairs, U.S. Department of State. 1993-94, tax counsel, Sen. David Durenberger,

R-Minn. 1994-present, senior professional staff member/counsel, House Cmte. on International Relations.

Expertise: Policy development, budget issues, oversight, procedural matters, Europe and the Middle East

In 1997, Hillel Weinberg, a senior professional staff member and counsel to the House Committee on International Relations, worked on State Department reauthorization, reorganization of foreign policy agencies, and reauthorization of foreign assistance programs. The House passed the State Department authorization bill last year and the legislation is currently in conference. "We expect the family planning issue to be resolved (in conference) and hope to see the bill enacted this year," Weinberg said.

As a senior professional staff member, Weinberg has both oversight and legislative responsibilities. Weinberg drafts a formal oversight plan for the committee, which must be done every two years in accordance with House Rules. The committee's oversight duties include working with relevant federal agencies to ensure that they meet the requirements of the Government Performance & Results Act.

Weinberg's extensive background puts him in the middle of a variety of issues that come before the committee. "I work with other staffers and help plan things and provide assistance," he said.

In the second session of the 105th Congress, Weinberg will work on NATO enlargement and U.S.- European relations. According to Weinberg, the committee will conduct oversight of the "new transatlantic agenda." Lawmakers want to assess how Congress can support U.S. businesses and the private sector to break down trade barriers and increase cooperation with European allies. Making sure that U.S. interests are protected in Europe is a priority, he added.

Weinberg has traveled to Brussels twice during the 105th Congress as part of a member/staff delegation to meet with representatives of the European Union Parliament and the European Commission. During those talks, some progress was made in urging the Europeans to change some of their political and trade policies, Weinberg said. For example, the European Union agreed to lift a former ban on the use of beef tallow in pharmaceuticals and cosmetics, he said.

In 1998, the committee will also conduct oversight of narcotics, the spread of weapons of mass destruction, and the U.S. military presence overseas.

In addition to his other duties, Weinberg is the committee's parliamentary advisor."Because of that, I work on almost all of our legislation. I advise the chairman and staff on how documents should be drafted and how motions should be made in committee," he said.

KEY MINORITY STAFF:

Michael H. Van Dusen
Minority Chief of Staff
B-360 Rayburn House Office Bldg.
225-6735

Personal: born 10/13/42 in Philadelphia, Pa.

Education: B.A., Princeton Univ., 1966. M.A., Johns Hopkins Univ. School of Advanced International Studies, 1968. Ph.D., Johns Hopkins Univ., 1971.

Professional: 1964-65 and summers of 1963 and 1966, studied in the Middle East. 1967, research associate, Brookings Institution. 1967-71, editorial assistant, Middle East Journal. 1971-93, staff director, subc. on Europe and the Middle East; 1993-95, majority chief of staff; 1995-present, minority chief of staff, House Cmte. on International Relations.

Expertise: Congress and foreign policy, Middle East, Europe and the former Soviet states

As minority chief of staff to the Committee on International Relations, Michael Van Dusen works with ranking member Rep. Lee Hamilton, D-Ind., to advance the Democrats' foreign policy agenda. The two major pieces of legislation on which Van Dusen worked in 1996, the foreign aid and the State Department reauthorization bills, were vetoed.

When the first session of the 105th Congress ended, "We had the State Department authorization bill in conference," Van Dusen said. "It contains important provisions that address our arrears to the United Nations while pressing for reform of the organization ... " The measure, along with legislation involving China, a bill that sanctions Russian entities for selling missile technology to Iran, and another dealing with religious persecution are high on the priority list for Van Dusen and the committee in 1998.

In the first session, "The committee sponsored some 40 resolutions on the floor during the year," Van Dusen said. "We also worked on a foreign aid and State Department authorization bill, as well as legislation on China and Russia. Little was enacted, and much remains uncompleted as the second session starts."

Van Dusen expects to work on these issues again this year. There must be bipartisan consensus in Congress and agreement with the administration on four key issues for the State Department bill to be enacted. They are resource allocation for foreign policy agencies, reorganization of foreign policy agencies, United Nations reform and payment of U.S. arrears to the U.N., and population concerns.

In 1996, Van Dusen worked on the Helms-Burton law, which attempts to promote political change in Cuba. A bill applying sanctions against Libya and Iran was also enacted in 1996. The law places restrictions on investment in the oil and gas industries in both countries. It is unclear how successful the sanctions will be in promoting change in Libya and Iran, Van Dusen said.

Van Dusen worked as majority chief of staff for the committee in the 103rd Congress when Hamilton was chair. He had previously served as staff director for the Subcommittee on Europe and the Middle East for 21 years when Hamilton led the panel.

Van Dusen is an expert on the Middle East and Southern Europe and studied in the region while earning his B.A. from Princeton and his masters and doctorate from the Johns Hopkins University School of Advanced International Studies.

Christopher Kojm
Coordinator, Regional Issues
B-360 Rayburn House Office Bldg.
225-6735

Personal: born 8/12/55 in Buffalo, N.Y.

Education: A.B., Harvard College, 1977. M.P.A., Woodrow Wilson School, Princeton Univ. 1979.

Professional: 1984-92, staff, subc. on Europe and the Middle East; 1993-94, full cmte. staff, House Cmte. on Foreign Affairs. 1995-present, coordinator of regional issues, House Cmte. on International Relations.

Expertise: Regional and security issues, Europe and Middle East

The key priorities for the Committee on International Relations in 1998 are the U.S. peacekeeping mission in Bosnia and dealing with the payment of United Nations arrears, according to Christopher Kojm, the minority staff's regional issues coordinator. Committee members are also concerned about the situation in Iraq and are grappling with the possible use of U.S. forces to compel compliance with U.N. resolutions regarding weapons inspections.

Committee members are also addressing the proliferation of missile technology in Iran. In addition, Kojm is working on the Middle East peace process and tracking the NATO enlargement ratification debate. Although the Banking Committee has primary jurisdiction over the Asian financial crisis, committee members are keenly interested in the issue. Kojm said he hopes that 1998 will be a more fruitful year than 1997 with respect to enacting legislation.

Kojm's duties include working with the committee's professional staff members who have regional responsibilities and coordinating their work. "I make sure we work together and not at cross purposes, and that we meet the ranking member's needs," he said. "We'll seek to keep the committee and the Democrats on the committee in the process of a thoughtful exchange with the administration."

As in the past, Kojm will supervise committee consultants as they handle military and political matters involving other countries. His responsibilities extend to issues such as arms control, nonproliferation, and U.S. alliances.

Kojm moved to the full committee staff in 1993 after working since 1984 on the Europe and Middle East Subcommittee. In 1994, when Democrats were in the majority and Rep. Lee Hamilton, D-Ind., was chairman, Kojm was the director for regional and security affairs. As such, he spent more of the second session of the 103rd Congress on policy issues than on specific legislation. When Republicans gained the majority for the 104th Congress, Hamilton became ranking minority member and Kojm moved into his current position.

F. (Frances) Marian Chambers
Minority Professional Staff Member
B-350C Rayburn House Office Bldg.
226-0670

Personal: born 8/25/54 in Wichita, Kan.

Education: B.A. (Phi Beta Kappa, summa cum laude), Dartmouth College, 1975. M.S., London School of Economics, 1976.

Professional: 1977, sr. foreign policy analyst, Rep. Joe Skubitz, R-Kan. 1978-94, prof. staff member, House Cmte. on Foreign Affairs. 1995-present, prof. staff member, House Cmte. on Intern'l. Relations.

Expertise: Peacekeeping and collective security, United Nations, foreign affairs, budget matters, international criminal organizations and administration of justice programs, and Micronesia

In 1998, Marian Chambers anticipates spending much of her time on United Nations reform and efforts to pay $1 billion in U.S. arrears to the U.N. Congress has been reluctant to pay until certain reforms are implemented. Such conditions present "a complicated set of issues because the U.N. has many budgets and specialized agencies, including the World Health Organization, the Food and Agriculture Agency, and the International Labor Organization," Chambers said.

Also this year, Chambers anticipates that U.S. contributions to the International Monetary Fund will be a key issue. She said it is "hard to see how the impasse over Mexico City will be resolved in a manner which allows IMF and U.N. funding to go forward."

In the first session of the 105th Congress, Chambers focused on the State Department/foreign aid authorization bill, which was not enacted. "There were many reasons, including differences between the administration and Republicans over the so-called `Mexico City' policy on population planning funds," Chambers said. "This disagreement ultimately derailed efforts to solve unrelated issues, such as U.S. arrears to the U.N. and the reorganization of the foreign affairs agencies."

In the 104th Congress, Chambers also spent a considerable amount of time trying to identify areas for reform in the multi-billion dollar U.N. system.

Chambers also will work on the State Department reauthorization and foreign aid bills this year, but sees little hope for passage. These bills were not enacted last year due in part to partisan disagreements.

In February 1996, Chambers traveled overseas to examine food agencies based in Rome. In 1997, she also traveled to New York for meetings at U.N. headquarters and to travel in conjunction with an examination of U.N. peacekeeping operations.

In the 104th Congress, Chambers attended a Stanley Foundation conference on U.N. in Oregon. She also traveled to Croatia, Bosnia, and Eastern Slovenia to review U.N. peacekeeping operations.

During her career, Chambers has handled issues ranging from international refugee problems to the National Endowment for Democracy. When the panel reorganized in 1993, she shed her 10-year responsibility for international narcotics matters and took on peacekeeping and collective security matters, as well as oversight of the multi-lateral development banks.

Chambers, whose hobbies include reading, traveling, and collecting unusual art objects. She speaks Spanish, French, and Rumanian, and is president general of a somewhat unusual group, the Associated Daughters of Early America Witches, comprised of descendants of women tried for witchcraft.

Subcommittee on Africa

705 O'Neill House Office Building
Washington, D.C. 20515
202/226-7812

MAJORITY MEMBERS:

Ed Royce, CA
Chairman
Amo Houghton, NY
Steve Chabot, OH
Mark Sanford, SC
Tom Campbell, CA
John McHugh, NY

MINORITY MEMBERS:

Robert Menendez, NJ
Ranking Minority Member
Donald Payne, NJ
Cynthia A. McKinney, GA
Alcee Hastings, FL

Jurisdiction: Designated by title.

KEY MAJORITY STAFF:

Thomas P. Sheehy
Staff Director
Subcommittee on Africa
705 O'Neill House Office Bldg.
226-7812

Personal: born 7/20/63 in Boston, Mass.

Education: B.A., Trinity College, 1986. M.A. in government and foreign affairs, Univ. of Virginia, 1989.

Professional: 1991-94, policy analyst for African affairs; 1994-96, Jay Kingham Fellow in International Regulatory Affairs, Heritage Foundation. 1996, legislative director, Rep. Ed Royce, R-Calif. 1997-present, staff dir., subc. on Africa, House Cmte. on Intern'l. Relations.

Expertise: U.S. foreign and defense policy, economic development.

In 1997, the subcommittee on Africa marked up H.R. 1432, the Africa Growth and Opportunity Act. This major piece of legislation is currently in the Ways and Means Committee and will be acted upon in this session, according to subcommittee staff director Tom Sheehy.

Before assuming his current post, Sheehy worked for subcommittee Chairman Ed Royce, R-Calif., as his legislative director. Although he oversaw the congressman's entire legislative agenda, Sheehy paid particular attention to international relations issues. Royce is very interested in U.S. foreign policy and wants the subcommittee to help guide U.S. policy in Africa, Sheehy said.

In the second session, the subcommittee continues to support H.R. 1432. Legislation to increase public broadcasting in Africa is also anticipated. In addition, members will continue to focus on Angola and hope to see a successful completion of the peace process currently underway in that country.

Royce believes that the U.S. has tremendous amount of influence in Africa and that what happens on the continent affects American interests, Sheehy said. In the coming year, the chairman would like the U.S. to promote democracy in the region and weigh-in on the civil conflicts in Liberia and Angola, he added. Royce is also interested in addressing traditional humanitarian concerns.

The subcommittee has both opportunities and challenges for guiding U.S. policy in Africa, Sheehy said. Many African economies are enjoying renewed growth and American businesses see investment

potential in the region, especially in South Africa and Ghana, he added.

Sheehy has considerable experience on Africa issues. Before arriving on Capitol Hill, he spent five years at the Heritage Foundation covering African affairs. While there, he co-authored the Index of Economic Freedom, which analyzes economic policy in 142 countries around the world, including most African countries. This index is in its fourth edition, and is co-published by the Wall Street Journal.

KEY MINORITY STAFF:

Jodi Christiansen
Minority Professional Staff Member
Subcommittee on Africa
405 Cannon House Office Bldg.
225-7919

Personal: born 2/5/71 in Minneapolis, Minn.

Education: B.A., American Univ., 1993. Johns Hopkins Univ. School of Advanced International Studies (graduate work on international finance), 1993.

Professional: 1993-97, legislative asst., Rep. Robert Menendez, D-N.J. 1997-present, minority professional staff member, subcommittee on Africa, House Committee on International Relations.

Expertise: Africa issues, foreign policy, transition governments

Professional staff member Jodi Christiansen began handling international relations issues for Rep. Robert Menendez, D-N.J., in 1995. She began her current position with Menendez, who is the ranking member of the subcommittee on Africa, in 1997.

According to Christiansen, on-going priorities for Menendez include the Angolan peace process, economic development in Africa, and protection of intellectual property rights in Africa. This year, the subcommittee is dealing with an upcoming referendum in the Western Sahara involving a territorial dispute with Morocco. In 1997, the United Nations negotiated the terms of the referendum with the assistance of former Secretary of State James Baker. Hearings on the issue culminated in a House resolution to support the outcome of the referendum.

The subcommittee will also deal with an on-going conflict in the Great Lakes region of Africa. Hearings are being held on the political stability, democratization, and cessation of violence in the area, which comprises the new Democratic Republic of Congo (formerly Zaire), the Republic of Congo, Burundi, Rwanda, and Uganda.

The subcommittee also will hold hearings on the continuing internal turmoil in Algeria. The turbulence involves a religious-based conflict between the secular government and military and fundamental Muslims who are trying to create a Muslim state.

In 1997, Christiansen participated in a fact-finding mission to South Africa, Zimbabwe, Angola, and the new Democratic Republic of

Congo. Specifically, Christiansen looked at economic development issues and the peace process in Angola.

Christiansen first joined Menendez as a legislative assistant in 1993. Prior to that time, she worked at the National Democratic Institute for International Affairs. In 1992 she interned at the International Foundation for Electoral Systems.

Christiansen is fluent in Spanish and has traveled extensively. She earned her undergraduate degree at American University and has taken graduate courses in international finance at Johns Hopkins University's School of Advanced International Studies.

Subcommittee on Asia & the Pacific

B-358 Rayburn House Office Building
Washington, D.C. 20515
202/226-7825

MAJORITY MEMBERS:

Doug Bereuter, NE
Chairman
Jim Leach, IA
Dana Rohrabacher, CA
Peter King, NY
Jay Kim, CA
Matt Salmon, AZ
Jon Fox, PA
John McHugh, NY
Donald Manzullo, IL
Ed Royce, CA

MINORITY MEMBERS:

Howard Berman, CA
Ranking Minority Member
Eni F.H. Faleomavaega, AS
Robert Andrews, NJ
Sherrod Brown, OH
Matthew Martinez, CA
Alcee Hastings, FL
Robert Wexler, FL
Lois Capps, CA

Jurisdiction: Designated by title.

KEY MAJORITY STAFF:

Mike Ennis
Staff Director
Subcommittee on Asia and the Pacific
B-358 Rayburn House Office Bldg.
226-7825

Personal: born 4/26/52 in Pensacola, Fla.

Education: B.A., Randolph-Macon Coll., 1974. M.A., Catholic Univ., 1978. Doctoral candidate, Catholic Univ.

Professional: 1979-80, professor, Randolph-Macon Coll. 1982-89, National Institute for Public Policy. 1989-93, subc. on human rights and intern'l. organizations; 1993-95, subc. on intern'l. security, intern'l. organizations and human rights; 1995-present, staff director, subc. on Asia and the Pacific, House Cmte. on Intern'l. Relations.

Expertise: Security, defense issues, arms control and proliferation

The reversion of Hong Kong to the People's Republic of China in July 1997 was a major issue for the subcommittee on Asia and the Pacific. Last summer, House Speaker Newt Gingrich, R-Ga., appointed subcommittee Chairman Doug Bereuter, R-Neb., as the chair of a task force to observe and report on changes resulting from the reversion. Mike Ennis has worked for Bereuter on the International Relations Committee since 1989 and became staff director of the subcommittee in 1995.

The Asia and Pacific subcommittee covers everything from agriculture to civil wars, taking in a geographic region that extends from Afghanistan to northeast Asia, the Central Asian republics of the former Soviet Union, and the Pacific islands.

According to Ennis, a major priority for the subcommittee in 1998 is the "economic contagion that has affected all of Asia." In addition to watching the Asian financial crisis closely, members are also focusing on events in the Korean peninsula. Specifically, members are interested in the continuing downward spiral of the government in North Korea, and in watching the new South Korean government take shape. How South Korea addresses the Asian financial crisis will also be a priority for the subcommittee. Maintaining the U.S. military presence in Asia, advancing U.S. economic interests, and promoting democratic values in the region are objectives for the 105th Congress, Ennis said.

The subcommittee has a continuing interest in the People's Republic of China and events there will be followed most closely in the coming year, Ennis said. U.S. relations with Vietnam are also very important to subcommittee members, he added. Specifically, members are awaiting President Clinton's announcement on lifting trade limitations with Vietnam.

In addition to preparing the subcommittee for hearings and dealing with legislation, Ennis's job is to help carry out Bereuter's agenda. That itinerary is headed by combating any efforts to decrease the U.S. military and economic presence in Asia. Bereuter also wants to make sure the U.S. has a cultural presence in Asia, and advances trade and economic interests in the region.

KEY MINORITY STAFF:

Richard J. Kessler
Democratic Professional Staff Member
Subcommittee on Asia and the Pacific
B-359 Rayburn House Office Bldg.
226-7875

Personal: born 4/11/48 in Oneida, N.Y.

Education: B.A., Colgate Univ., 1970. M.A. in law and diplomacy, and Ph.D., Fletcher School of Law and Diplomacy, Tufts Univ., 1974-86.

Professional: 1970-73, U.S. Army Sgt.. 1985-88, senior associate, Carnegie Endowment for International Peace. 1988, professor, School of International Service, American Univ. 1989-93, professional staff member, subc. on East Asian and Pacific affairs; 1993-94, professional staff member, full Senate Cmte. on Foreign Relations. 1995-present, Democratic professional staff member, subcommittee on Asia and the Pacific, House Cmte. on International Relations.

Expertise: Asia policy, foreign policy, U.N. peacekeeping

In 1998, Democratic professional staff member Richard Kessler expects the subcommittee on Asia and the Pacific to consider the new International Monetary Fund borrowing arrangements, U.S. arrears to the United Nations, and State Department reorganization. U.S. policy toward Iran, as well as a look at pending European business deals in Iran, will also be evaluated.

In his current position, Kessler handles all subcommittee work and foreign policy issues for ranking member Rep. Howard Berman, D-Calif. In the 105th Congress, the subcommittee has new jurisdictional responsibilities covering some of the Central Asian Republics which were formerly part of the Soviet Union, including Kazakhstan.

In 1997, the House passed legislation to implement sanctions unless Russia cuts off aid to the Iranian missile program. Last summer, Berman became the ranking member on a task force to study the reversion of Hong Kong to China. The task force has released several reports and continues to study the issue and how it affects U.S. policy.

A new issue for the subcommittee in the second session of the 105th is the U.S.-China Nuclear Cooperation Agreement. The Clinton administration has submitted the pact to Congress for review; Kessler expects the subcommittee to study the agreement early this year.

Subcommittee hearings on the Asian financial crisis will focus on how the instability affects U.S. policy and what the United States can do to help. According to Kessler, Berman is interested in all facets of Asia policy. His other priorities include the Middle East and proliferation policy. The subcommittee will also address U.S. relations with North and South Korea this year.

Last year, Kessler assisted Berman in an effort to generate a higher budget for U.S. aid programs overseas. He also worked on the State Department reauthorization bill. In the 104th Congress, Kessler spent a considerable amount of time dealing with issues related to China, assistance to North Korea in exchange for freezing its nuclear weapons program, and immigration rights for Vietnamese refugees.

Subcommittee on International Economic Policy & Trade

702 O'Neill House Office Building
Washington, D.C. 20515
202/225-3345

MAJORITY MEMBERS:

Ileana Ros-Lehtinen, FL
Chairman
Don Manzullo, IL
Steve Chabot, OH
Tom Campbell, CA
Lindsey Graham, SC
Roy Blunt, MO
Kevin Brady, TX

Doug Bereuter, NE
Dana Rohrabacher, CA

MINORITY MEMBERS:

Sam Gejdenson, CT
Ranking Minority Member
Pat Danner, MO
Earl Hilliard, AL
Brad Sherman, CA
Steve Rothman, NJ
Bob Clement, TN
Tom Lantos, CA
Bill Luther, MN

Jurisdiction: To deal with measures relating to international economic and trade policy; measures to foster commercial intercourse with foreign countries; export administration; international investment policy; trade and economic aspects of nuclear technology and materials and of international communication and information policy; licenses and licensing policy for the export of dual use equipment and technology; legislation pertaining to and oversight of the Overseas Private Investment Corporation; scientific developments affecting foreign policy; commodity agreements; international environmental policy and oversight of international fishing agreements; and special oversight of international financial and monetary institutions, and the Export-Import Bank, and customs.

KEY MAJORITY STAFF:

Mauricio J. Tamargo
Staff Director
Subcommittee on International Economic Policy and Trade
702 O'Neill House Office Bldg.
226-7814

Personal: born 10/22/57 in Havana, Cuba.

Education: B.A., Univ. of Miami, 1985. J.D., Cumberland School of Law, Samford Univ., 1989.

Professional: 1982-86, legislative asst., Florida State Rep. Ileana Ros-Lehtinen. 1989-92, legislative director; 1992-95, chief of staff and legal counsel, Rep. Ileana Ros-Lehtinen, R-Fla. 1995-96, staff director, subc. on Africa; 1997-present, staff director, subc. on intl. economic policy and trade, House Cmte. on International Relations.

Expertise: Foreign policy, international relations, administrative law

International Economic Policy and Trade Subcommittee Staff Director Mauricio Tamargo is responsible for ensuring that "the meetings, hearings, and other functions of the subcommittee are conducted in an orderly manner." He also makes sure subcommittee Chairman Ileana Ros-Lehtinen, R-Fla., and other members have all the information they need on the various topics and issues that come before the panel.

According to Tamargo, a subcommittee priority for 1998 is to study reauthorization of the Export Administration Act. The bill, H.R. 1942, was introduced by Ros-Lehtinen last year. Subcommittee members also consider encryption legislation to be a priority. In 1997 the panel favorably reported H.R. 695, an encryption bill sponsored by Rep. Bob Goodlatte, R-Va. Tamargo believes that prospects for enactment of this legislation are good.

In 1998, the subcommittee will hold hearings on the Multilateral Agreement on Investments. Subcommittee members are interested in this Agreement, which would equalize and raise standards to an acceptable level on goods sold throughout the world. Currently, members are discussing their concerns about this issue with Clinton administration officials, who have on-going negotiations with the European Union.

Tamargo became staff director for the subcommittee on at the beginning of the 105th Congress. He took this new post after serving as staff director for the subcommittee on Africa during the 104th Congress. "In this Congress, I approach my subcommittee assignment somewhat familiar with the subject matter due to the fact that much of my work in [the Subcommittee on Africa] involved U.S. trade and investment overseas," Tamargo said.

In addition to his job with the subcommittee, Tamargo also works directly for Ros-Lehtinen. "She is the chairwoman of the subcommittee, but I continue to have responsibilities in her personal office," Tamargo said. "I am her chief of staff and legal counsel. I advise the congresswoman on legislative and administrative matters."

Tamargo said that during his tenure on the Africa subcommittee, the panel helped maintain strong congressional support for many developmental and relief programs in the region. The subcommittee also persuaded Congress "to remain strongly engaged in U.S.-African relations," he said. During the 104th Congress, the subcommittee hosted numerous meetings between African ambassadors and congressional leaders, including a May 1996 meeting between Speaker Newt Gingrich, R-Ga., and more than 50 ambassadors.

KEY MINORITY STAFF:

Amos Hochstein
Democratic Professional Staff Member
Subcommittee on International Economic Policy and Trade
703 O'Neill House Office Bldg.
225-3358

Personal: born 1/4/71 in Jerusalem, Israel.

Education: Certificate, Hartman Institute (Jerusalem), 1991.

Professional: 1992-93, assistant, Bankers Trust Financial News Services. 1994, public affairs freelance work, international press and public relations in Jerusalem. 1995-96, legislative assistant, Rep. Sam Gejdenson, D-Conn. 1996-present, Democratic professional staff member, subc. on international economic policy and trade, House Cmte. on International Relations.

Expertise: Foreign policy, Middle Eastern affairs, international trade

One of the biggest priorities for Rep. Sam Gejdenson, D-Conn., ranking member of the Subcommittee on International Economic Policy and Trade, is enactment of encryption legislation. In 1997, the Committee on International Relations passed an encryption bill that liberalizes export controls over high technology encryption products. Subcommittee members will be crucial in moving this bill forward in the House, said Amos Hochstein, the panel's Democratic professional staff member.

According to Hochstein, Gejdenson and other subcommittee members believe the bill is necessary to protect U..S. national security and preserve the commercial and technological edge held by American companies. However, the bill is opposed by the Clinton administration. Efforts to defeat the measure are being led by FBI Director Louis Freeh.

In 1998, the subcommittee is holding hearings on the upcoming summit on Free Trade For the Americas. The summit will be held in Chile in April. This year the subcommittee will also review practices of the World Trade Organization's dispute settlement body. Specifically, the panel is examining whether changes should be made to the dispute resolution process.

According to Hochstein, the subcommittee has "shied away from modernizing trade legislation that needs to be updated." He expects members to be busy reviewing and monitoring policy, rather than proactively attempting to change policy through legislation.

In 1997, Hochstein worked on several reauthorization bills involving the Overseas Private Investment Corporation, the Export-Import Bank, and the Trade Development Agency. All of the reauthorizations were enacted during the first session of the 105th Congress.

In 1996, Hochstein worked on foreign policy, energy, and immigration issues for Gejdenson in the congressman's personal office. Gejdenson, who supports retaining current levels of legal immigration, was born in 1948 in a German displaced persons' camp to Holocaust survivors.

Hochstein, who is fluent in English and Hebrew, grew up in Jerusalem and New York City.

Subcommittee on International Operations & Human Rights

B-358 Rayburn House Office Building
Washington, D.C. 20515
202/225-5748

MAJORITY MEMBERS:

Christopher H. Smith, NJ
Chairman
William Goodling, PA
Henry Hyde, IL
Dan Burton, IN
Cass Ballenger, NC
Peter King, NY
Matt Salmon, AZ
Lindsey Graham, SC
Ileana Ros-Lehtinen, FL

MINORITY MEMBERS:

Tom Lantos, CA
Ranking Minority Member
Cynthia McKinney, GA
Gary Ackerman, NY
Eni F.H. Faleomavaega, AS
Donald Payne, NJ
Earl Hilliard, AL
Robert Wexler, FL

Jurisdiction: To deal with Department of State, U.S. Information Agency, and related agency operations and legislation; the diplomatic service; international education and cultural affairs; foreign buildings; programs; activities and the operating budget of the Arms Control and Disarmament Agency; oversight of, and legislation pertaining to, the United Nations, its affiliated agencies, and other international organizations including assessed and voluntary contributions to such agencies and organizations; parliamentary conferences and exchanges; protection of American citizens abroad; international broadcasting international communication and information policy; the American Red Cross; implementation of the Universal Declaration of Human Rights and other matters relating to internationally recognized human rights generally; and oversight of international population planning and child survival activities.

KEY MAJORITY STAFF:

Grover Joseph Rees
Staff Director and Chief Counsel
Subcommittee on International Operations and Human Rights
B-358 Rayburn House Office Bldg.
225-5748

Personal: born 10/11/51 in New Orleans, La.

Education: B.A., Yale Univ., 1975. J.D., Louisiana State Univ., 1978.

Professional: 1978-79, law clerk, Justice Albert Tate, La. Supreme Court. 1979-86, law professor, Univ. of Texas. 1981-82, counsel, Senate Cmte. on the Judiciary. 1985-86, special counsel, U.S. Attorney General Ed Meese. 1986-88, chief justice; 1988-91, associate justice, High Court of American Samoa. 1991-93, general counsel, U.S. Immigration and Naturalization Service. 1994, visiting faculty member, Yale Law School, St. Mary's Univ., and Univ. of Detroit. 1995-present, staff director and chief counsel, subc. on international operations and human rights, House Cmte. on International Relations.

Expertise: International law

Leadership by subcommittee Chairman Chris Smith, R-N.J., and full committee Chairman Benjamin Gilman, R-N.Y., has resulted in a strong focus on human rights, according to Grover Joseph Rees, lead staffer on the subcommittee on international operations and human rights.

In the first session of the 105th Congress, the subcommittee looked at issues such as refugee protection, the integration of human rights promotion into U.S. foreign policy, and building support for Smith's efforts to end U.S. foreign aid from supporting the international abortion industry, Rees said. The panel also worked on H.R. 1757, the Foreign Relations Authorization Act, which is pending in a House-Senate conference.

The subcommittee last year also reported the Freedom from Religious Persecution Act (H.R. 2431), and the Justice for Victims of Communism Act, which extends and clarifies the eligibility of children of long-time re-education camp survivors to be admitted to the U.S. as refugees. The measure, which passed the House on the last day of the first session, is pending in the Senate.

This session, Rees says the subcommittee will revisit many of the same issues, and also work on the Torture Victims Relief Act and the Child Labor Elimination Act.

"We have everything that's not trade or economics related," said Rees, the subcommittee's staff director and chief counsel. "Our subcommittee is in charge of legislation and oversight concerning the State Department, the U.N., and other international organizations, as well as human rights violations around the world."

Rees spent most of his career teaching law. He taught at the University of Texas from 1979 to 1986 and has been a visiting faculty member at Yale Law School, St. Mary's University, and the University of Detroit.

While on leave from Yale, Rees also worked as counsel to the Senate Judiciary Committee and later as special counsel to U.S. Attorney General Ed Meese. He also served on the High Court of American Samoa and was general counsel to the INS.

KEY MINORITY STAFF:

Robert R. King
Minority Staff Director
Subcommittee on International Operations and Human Rights
Chief of Staff, Rep. Tom Lantos, D-Calif.
B-360 Rayburn House Office Bldg.
225-3531

Personal: born 6/6/42 in Rock Springs, Wyo.

Education: B.A., Brigham Young Univ., 1966. M.A., Fletcher School of Law and Diplomacy, Tufts Univ., 1967. M.A.L.D., Fletcher, 1968. Ph.D., Fletcher, 1970.

Professional: 1970-77, asst. director of research and senior analyst, Radio Free Europe. 1971-77, college lecturer. 1977-78, staff member, National Security Council. 1979, private consultant. 1980-81, special asst. to federal co-chairman, Appalachian Regional Commission. 1981-83, private business. 1983-93, admin. asst., Rep. Tom Lantos, D-Calif. 1993-94, staff dir., subc. on int'l. security, int'l. organizations and human rights, House Cmte. on Foreign Affairs. 1995-present, minority staff director, subc. on int'l. operations and human rights, House Cmte. on Int'l. Relations and chief of staff, Rep. Tom Lantos, D-Calif.

Expertise: Foreign affairs

In 1998, the major issue for the subcommittee on international operations and human rights will be to complete work on the international relations authorization legislation. The House and Senate adopted different versions of the legislation last year. Efforts of the House-Senate conference committee to resolve differences broke down over the international family planning issue (the Mexico City Policy). The authorization legislation includes provisions relating to the payment of the U.S. debt to the U.N., and reform and consolidation of foreign affairs agencies. Several matters require congressional action, so pressure to compromise is increasing.

The conference committee may be revived in an effort to work out differences so that the legislation can be adopted. If necessary, provisions where there is agreement may be enacted in a piece-meal fashion.

As majority staff director, Robert King ensures that Democratic subcommittee members are fully informed on all issues that come before the panel, especially with respect to legislative matters and oversight hearings. The jurisdiction of the subcommittee covers the activities and programs of the State Department and the diplomatic service, the U.S. Information Agency, including international exchange and education programs, U.S. participation in the U.N., and human rights issues.

Human rights has been an important area of subcommittee activity, and King said he expects that to continue in 1998. There will be active oversight of State Department human rights reporting and policies. As the annual debate over extending most-favored nation status trade privileges to China comes before Congress in late spring and summer, the committee will likely focus on Chinese human rights practices.

Religious persecution is an issue of continuing concern to subcommittee members. The panel will likely continue its series of hearings on specific instances of the violation of freedom of worship, with particular focus on Chinese restrictions on Christian and Buddhist believers. Legislation on religious persecution (H.R. 2431, a revised version of H.R. 1685) was approved by the subcommittee last year, but the bill has been controversial. Efforts are underway to develop a compromise version of the bill that will win House support.

In addition to his activities with the subcommittee, King is also the Democratic staff member for the congressional delegation which meets semi-annually with a delegation of members of the European Parliament. The two groups discuss political, trade, and economic issues between the United States and European Union.

King is the author of a number of books and articles on Central and East European politics and the problems of ethnic nationalism. He has taught as an adjunct professor for university programs in both Europe and the U.S.

Subcommittee on Western Hemisphere

2401-A Rayburn House Office Building
Washington, D.C. 20515
202/226-7820

MAJORITY MEMBERS:

Elton Gallegly, CA
Chairman
Cass Ballenger, NC
Mark Sanford, SC
Christopher Smith, NJ
Dan Burton, IN
Ileana Ros-Lehtinen, FL
Jay Kim, CA
Roy Blunt, MO
Kevin Brady, TX

MINORITY MEMBERS:

Gary Ackerman, NY
Ranking Minority Member
Matthew Martinez, CA
Robert Andrews, NJ
Robert Menendez, NJ

Robert Wexler, FL
Steven R. Rothman, NJ
Jim Davis, FL

Jurisdiction: Designated by title.

KEY MAJORITY STAFF:

Vincent L. Morelli
Staff Director
Subcommittee on the Western Hemisphere
2401-A Rayburn House Office Bldg.
226-7820

Personal: born 3/22/48 in Philadelphia, Pa.

Education: B.A., Canisius College, 1970. M.S. Ed., Canisius College, 1974. M.A., American Univ., 1980.

Professional: 1971-75, high school teacher, Buffalo, N.Y. 1976, research assistant, Rep. Jack Kemp, R-N.Y. 1977-78, leg. asst., Rep. Richard Schulze, R-Pa. 1978-80, leg. asst., Rep. David Emery, R-Maine. 1980-86, lobbyist, Bath Iron Works Corp. 1986-87, lobbyist, Lockheed Corp. 1987-95, leg. dir., Rep. Marge Roukema, R-N.J. 1995-97, leg. dir., Rep. Elton Gallegly, R-Calif. 1997-present, staff director, subc. on the western hemisphere, House International Relations Committee.

Expertise: International relations, Central America policy

During the second session of the 105th Congress, the subcommittee on the western hemisphere is continuing its oversight of Democratic and economic reform in the region, according to staff director Vincent Morelli. The panel will also keep a close eye on Haiti, Cuba, and Colombia, as well as continue its review of trade developments and anti-narcotics efforts.

In the first session, the subcommittee completed a broad set of hearings on the Western hemisphere, concentrating on political stability, democratization of the region, and economic development. "Drugs and trade were also reviewed," he said.

Morelli, who assumed his current post last year, has always been interested in international affairs. After a series of jobs both on and off Capitol Hill, the Philadelphia native is exactly where he wants to be. So is Chairman Elton Gallegly, R-Calif., who in 1997 led the subcommittee in an overview of regional events beginning with hearings on democracy movements in Central America.

The subcommittee also looked at democratic movements in Nicaragua, El Salvador, and Guatemala, and followed developments in Haiti.

U.S. relations with Mexico are another priority for the subcommittee. Morelli expects members to focus on Mexico's anti-narcotics efforts and attempts to control the tide of illegal immigration. The impact of NAFTA on Mexico will also be considered. In July, administration officials issued a three-year study on the impact of NAFTA on the U.S. and Mexico.

Another subcommittee priority is examining the question of expanding NAFTA to other Latin American countries or creating a free trade zone in the region. According to Morelli, Chile's economic progress makes it the most likely candidate for inclusion in NAFTA.

In 1996, Morelli was Gallegly's International Relations committee advisor. He also coordinated and supervised the work of the congressman's legislative assistants. According to Morelli, the biggest accomplishment in Gallegly's office last year was enactment of the 1996 illegal immigration act.

KEY MINORITY STAFF:

David S. Adams
Professional Staff Member
2401-A Rayburn House Office Building
Washington, D.C. 20515
202/226-7820

Committee on the Judiciary

Subcommittee on Immigration & Claims

B-370-B Rayburn House Office Building
Washington, D.C. 20515-6217
202/225-5727

MAJORITY MEMBERS:

Lamar Smith, TX
  Chairman
Elton Gallegly, CA
Bill Jenkins, TN
Edward Pease, IN
Christopher Cannon, UT
Ed Bryant, TN
James Rogan, CA

MINORITY MEMBERS:

Melvin Watt, NC
  Ranking Minority Member
Charles Schumer, NY
Howard Berman, CA
Zoe Lofgren, CA
Robert Wexler, FL

Jurisdiction: Immigration and naturalization; admission of refugees; treaties; conventions and international agreements; claims against the United States; Federal charters of incorporation; private immigration and claims bills; other appropriate matters as referred by the Chairman; relevant oversight.

KEY MAJORITY STAFF:

VACANT
Chief Counsel
Subcommittee on Immigration & Claims
B-370B Rayburn House Office Bldg.
225-5727

KEY MINORITY STAFF:

Martina A. Hone
Minority Counsel
Subcommittee on Immigration and Claims
B-336, Rayburn House Office Bldg.
225-2329

Personal: born 10/21/62 in Chicago, Ill.

Education: B.A. in political science, Univ. of Chicago, 1984. J.D., Univ. of Calif. at Berkeley, 1989.

Professional: 1989-90, litigation assoc., Katten Muchin & Zavis (Chicago). 1991-92, litigation assoc., Kamensky & Rubinstein (Chicago). 1992-94, corp member, Teach for America (Oakland, Calif.). 1995-96, leg. aide, Rep. Melvin L. Watt, D-N.C. 1996-97, special asst., U.S. Dept. of Commerce. 1997-present, minority counsel, subc. on immigration and claims, House Cmte. on the Judiciary.

Expertise: Immigration

Martina Hone became minority counsel in early 1997 after eight months at the U.S. Department of Commerce, where she was a special assistant in the office of legislative and intergovernmental affairs. At Commerce, Hone monitored and reported on legislative activities related to the U.S. Census Bureau, the Minority Business Development Administration, the Economic Development Agency, and the Patent and Trademark Office.

In joining the subcommittee staff, Hone returns to the Hill, where she worked for two years as a legislative aide to ranking member Rep. Melvin L. Watt, D-N.C. In 1996, Hone worked on the Illegal Immigration Reform and Immigrant Responsibility Act. She also was responsible for legislative activities in the subcommittee on the constitution and the subcommittee on crime.

This session, Hone expects to be focusing on improvements to the naturalization process, exit controls, and reviews of visa decisions. "We want better customer service at the Immigration and Naturalization Service," Hone said. "We want to make it faster." Hone said the subcommittee also would be looking at ways to improve integrity in light of reports of cheating on the naturalization exams.

The subcommittee in 1998 likely will be debating whether special immigration consideration should be given to skilled technology workers. Congress is under pressure from high-tech industries to ease entry for skilled workers because of a growing shortage of those workers. Hone said the subcommittee also would be looking at the controversial subject of exit controls. New INS regulations are scheduled to take effect in September requiring visitors to get exit papers from the INS when they leave. Canada is strongly opposed to the new requirement, Hone said.

Hone said that Watt and others would be pushing to increase the number of immigrants permitted from Africa. The subcommittee also will consider legislation introduced by Rep. Barney Frank, D-Mass., to establish a review process for consular decisions on whether to grant visas. Currently, there is no appeal of those decisions, Hone said, which means that persons who are denied visas at overseas consular offices have no option to protest.

Hone said her interest in public policy was sparked by teaching at some of the toughest and neediest middle schools in the San Francisco area. After three years practicing law in Chicago, Hone moved to

San Francisco, where she taught language arts and social studies for two years with Teach for America. One of her schools primarily served immigrant children. "I have always been interested in the rights of the dispossessed and unempowered," she said.

Committee on Resources

Subcommittee on Fisheries, Conservation, Wildlife & Oceans

805 O'Neill House Office Building
Washington, D.C. 20515
202/226-0200   Fax: 202/225-1542

MAJORITY MEMBERS:

Jim Saxton, NJ
Chairman
Billy Tauzin, LA
Wayne Gilchrest, MD
Walter Jones, NC
John Peterson, PA
Michael Crapo, ID

MINORITY MEMBERS:

Frank Pallone, NJ
Ranking Minority Member
Neil Abercrombie, HI
Solomon Ortiz, TX
Mr. Sam Farr, CA
Patrick Kennedy, RI

Jurisdiction: (1) Fisheries mgmt. and fisheries research generally, including the mgmt. of all commercial and recreational fisheries, the Magnuson Fishery Conservation and Mgmt. Act, interjurisdictional fisheries, intern'l. fisheries agreements, aquaculture, seafood safety, and fisheries promotion; (2) Wildlife resources, including research, restoration, refuges and conservation; (3) All matters pertaining to the protection of coastal and marine environments, including estuarine protection; (4) Coastal barriers; (5) Oceanography; (6) Marine science and research generally; (7) Ocean engineering, including materials, technology, and systems; (8) Coastal zone mgmt.; (9) Marine sanctuaries; (10) U.N. Convention on the Law of the Sea; (11) Sea Grant programs and marine extension services; (12) General and continuing oversight and investigative authority over activities, policies and programs within the jurisdiction of the subcommittee.

KEY MAJORITY STAFF:

Harry F. Burroughs III
Staff Director
Subcommittee on Fisheries Conservation, Wildlife, and Oceans
805 O'Neill House Office Bldg.
226-0200

Personal: born 5/28/52 in Riverhead, N.Y.

Education: B.A., Baker Univ. (Kansas), 1974. M.A., Kansas State Univ., 1975.

Professional: 1977-80, legislative director, Rep. Richard T. Schulze, R-Pa. 1981-85, legislative director, Rep. Jack Fields, R-Texas. 1985-92, counsel; 1993-94, minority staff director, House Committee on Merchant Marine and Fisheries. 1995-present, staff director, subc. on fisheries conservation, wildlife and oceans, House Resources Committee.

Expertise: Endangered Species Act, Migratory Bird Treaty Act, National Wildlife Refuge System, wildlife issues

The Rhino and Tiger Labeling Act, reauthorization of the Federal Aid in Fish Restoration Act, the Oceans Act of 1998, the Disabled Sportsmen's Access Act, and legislation to extend a number of fishery laws are among the items topping Harry Burroughs' activities in the second session of the 105th Congress. As well, Burroughs, staff director of the subcommittee on fisheries conservation, wildlife and oceans, says the panel intends to hold oversight hearings on the destruction of the Arctic tundra by snow geese, implementation of the Magnuson-Stevens Fishery Conservation Act, and ways to improve the nation's fishery conservation laws as administered by the National Marine Fishery Service. "The subcommittee will also work for final action on legislation to extend the important National Sea Grant College Program Act," Burroughs said.

During the first session of the 105th, Burroughs says the subcommittee "was extremely successful in moving its legislative priorities forward ... for instance, after three years of hard work, the president signed into law an historic act, authored by Chairman Don Young, R-Alaska, that established for the first time an organic statute for the nation's 92 million-acre National Wildlife Refuge System," he said.

In addition, Congress completed action on the International Dolphin Conservation Program Act, reauthorized the Sikes Act, which affects wildlife on 29 million acres of military lands, and extended the Atlantic Striped Bass Conservation Act. "Finally, the president signed into law the Asian Elephant Conservation Act," Burroughs said. "This new act will allow Congress to appropriate up to $5 million per year for the conservation of highly endangered wild populations of Asian elephants."

In the second session of the 104th Congress, the subcommittee was successful in obtaining final action on a number of important measures, including legislation to extend and improve the Coastal Zone Management Act, the National Marine Sanctuaries Act, and the Magnuson Fishery Conservation and Management Act. In addition, several federal fish hatcheries were transferred to the states, improvements were made to several federal wildlife refuges, and certain Coastal Barrier Resource System maps were corrected.

Burroughs took his current position in the first session of the 104th Congress. Supervising a staff of seven, he oversees the fish and wildlife issues taken over by the panel when the Committee on Merchant Marine and Fisheries was abolished in January 1995.

A bipartisan task force was appointed in the opening days of the last Congress to study the endangered species issue. The task force has no legislative authority, but developed a record through public hearings which was used to produce legislation.

Burroughs was also involved in a review of international trade quotas on fish and several bilateral and multi-lateral fishery agreements. Also remaining on the agenda is oversight of the National Wildlife Refuge System, with an eye toward making certain scarce federal dollars are allocated fairly.

Committee on Small Business

Subcommittee on Tax, Finance and Exports

B-363 Rayburn House Office Building
Washington, D.C. 20515-6320
202/226-2630   Fax: 202/225-8950

MAJORITY MEMBERS:

Donald Manzullo, IL
Chairman
Linda Smith, WA
Vice Chairman
Vince Snowbarger, KS
Mike Pappas, NJ
Phil English, PA
Joseph Pitts, PA

MINORITY MEMBERS:

John Baldacci, ME
Ranking Minority Member
Rubén Hinojosa, TX
Marion Berry, AR
(TWO VACANCIES)

Jurisdiction: (1) Tax policy and its impact on small business; (2) Access to capital and finance issues generally; (3) Export opportunities and promotion.

KEY MAJORITY STAFF:

Philip Eskeland
Majority Staff Director
Subcommittee on Tax, Finance, and Exports
B-363 Rayburn House Office Bldg.
226-2630

Personal: born 12/19/62 in Brooklyn, N.Y.

Education: B.A. in political science, Wheaton College (Ill.), 1983. M.A., American Univ., School of International Service, 1986.

Professional: 1986-88, writer, office of correspondence, The White House. 1988-89, leg. asst.; 1989-93, leg. director, Rep. Ron Marlenee, R-Mont. 1993-95, leg. director, Rep. Don Manzullo, R-Ill. 1995-present, staff director, subcommittee on tax, finance, and exports, House Committee on Small Business.

Expertise: Trade issues

As staff director of the subcommittee on tax, finance, and exports, Phil Eskeland focuses on retaining federal funding for export promotion for small businesses. That will entail protecting appropriations for the U.S. and Foreign Commercial Service, the Export-Import Bank, and the Overseas Private Investment Corp. He also expects to continue assisting committee members in their goal of expanding Export-Import Bank programs that benefit small businesses.

In the second session of the 105th Congress, the subcommittee will focus on fast-track and the impact of sanctions on small business exporters, he says.

Because the panel now includes tax issues, Eskeland also expects to be working on tax reform that favors small businesses and hopefully influencing any further tax cuts that emerge from the 105th Congress. He will also work, as part of a coalition, to help pass fast-track legislation by demonstrating how open markets help small exporters, and analyze the impact of unilateral economic sanctions on American small business exporters.

Committee Chairman Jim Talent, R-Mo., has given subcommittees more discretion in their agendas, and that is expected to translate into more intensive work on a variety of topics instead of major efforts on just a few. Last session, Eskeland helped reverse a narrow 1996 decision to kill OPIC, secure overwhelming passage of the Export-Import Bank reauthorization bill, and roll-back a proposal by the Federal Trade Commission "to weaken the 'Made in the USA' label by highlighting the impact this proposed rule could have on small manufacturers."

Because the subcommittee does not have legislative authority, Eskeland says his task is to "raise the voice of small business" in other committees. In the past, for instance, he has worked extensively with the House committees on Ways and Means and International Relations.

Before coming to Capitol Hill in 1988, Eskeland worked in the Reagan White House as a writer in the Office of Correspondence. He moved to the staff of Rep. Ron Marlenee, R-Mont., in 1988, where he focused on foreign affairs, defense, veterans affairs, health care, senior citizens, retirement, and education issues.

In addition, Eskeland wrote speeches for the congressman and was responsible for the legislative activities of Marlenee's personal office. He also graduated from the Congressional Research Service and House Republican Parliamentary law schools.

Eskeland joined Manzullo's staff in 1993 and was the point person for the congressman on foreign affairs and House floor action. In addition, he has traveled extensively abroad and speaks French.

Committee on Ways and Means

Subcommittee on Trade

1104 Longworth House Office Building
Washington, D.C. 20515-6354
202/225-6649

MAJORITY MEMBERS:

Philip M. Crane, IL
Chairman
Bill Thomas, CA
E. Clay Shaw, Jr., FL
Amo Houghton, NY
Dave Camp, MI
Jim Ramstad, MN
Jennifer Dunn, WA
Wally Herger, CA
Jim Nussle, IA

MINORITY MEMBERS:

Robert T. Matsui, CA
Ranking Minority Member
Charles B. Rangel, NY
Richard E. Neal, MA
Jim McDermott, WA
Michael R. McNulty, NY
William J. Jefferson, LA

Jurisdiction: Proposed legislation and oversight activities involving: (1) Customs and customs administration including tariff and import fee structure, classification, valuation of and special rules applying to imports, and special tariff provisions and procedures relating to customs operation affecting exports and imports; import trade matters, including import impact, industry relief from injurious imports, adjustment assistance and programs to encourage competitive responses to imports, unfair import practices including antidumping and countervailing duty provisions, and import policy relating to dependence on foreign sources of supply; (2) Commodity agreements and reciprocal trade agreements including multilateral and bilateral trade negotiations and implementation of agreements involving tariff and non-tariff trade barriers to and distortions of international trade; (3) International rules, organizations and institutional aspects of international trade agreements; (4) Budget authorizations for the U.S. Customs Service, the U.S. International Trade Commission, and U.S. Trade Representative; (5) Special trade-related problems involving market access, competitive conditions of specific industries; export policy and promotion, access to materials in short supply, bilateral trade relations, including trade with developing countries, operations of multinational corporations, and trade with non-market economies.

KEY MAJORITY STAFF:

Thelma Askey
Staff Director
Subcommittee on Trade
1104 Longworth House Office Bldg.
225-6649

Personal: born in Lakehurst, N.J.

Education: B.A., Tenn. Technological Univ., 1970. Graduate work in history and economics at George Wash. Univ. and American Univ.

Professional: 1972-74, press asst., Rep. John Duncan, R-Tenn. 1974-76, editor, The National Research Council Marine Board. 1976-79, asst. minority counsel for trade; 1979-94, minority trade counsel, House Cmte. on Ways and Means. 1995-present, staff director, subcommittee on trade, House Cmte. on Ways and Means.

Expertise: Trade laws and issues

Since becoming staff director of the House Ways and Means Committee's subcommittee on trade in the 104th Congress, Thelma Askey has been the point person on major trade initiatives before Congress. This final session of the 105th Congress promises to be as hectic as the first, when Congress considered the perennial issue of renewing China's most-favored-nation trade status and negotiated an agreement with the Clinton White House on a plan that would grant the president negotiating authority to pursue trade liberalization across the globe.

Dubbed fast-track authority, the agreement reached last year was significant because it marked the first time that Hill Republicans and the Democratic White House found common ground. Despite broad Republican support, including that of the leaders of the House Ways and Means Committee, the White House withdrew the bill from consideration when it could not muster enough Democratic support for passage.

House Trade Subcommittee Chairman Phil Crane, R-Ill., along with Ways and Means chairman Bill Archer, R-Texas, have vowed to put fast-track back on their agendas this year, but have cautioned the White House that it will lose critical Republican backing if it seeks to appease Democratic opposition by adding labor and environmental standards as negotiating principles.

Also on the agenda this year is a bill that would grant free-trade privileges to qualifying Sub-Saharan Africa states based on liberalized textile trade. Crane, along with Rep. Jim McDermott, D- Wash., has sponsored the bill, which enjoys broad bipartisan support. Critics in the textile industry fear that Africa could become a platform for Far Eastern countries to illicitly ship textiles and apparel to the U.S.

Askey also is expected to assist the panel as it again takes up the question of whether to renew China's most-favored-nation trade status, which grants the low tariffs now enjoyed by most U.S. trading partners. In an attempt to diffuse some of the conflict over the matter, Archer has said he wants to change the name of the trade program from "most-favored" to "normal" trade status.

In her years on the panel, Askey has helped shape major trade initiatives, including the North American Free Trade Agreement and the GATT Uruguay Round. There are few Capitol Hill staffers with Askey's historical memory, understanding of the impact of U.S. trade policy, and vision for potential trade opening possibilities.

Askey, who began her Hill career in 1972 as an assistant to former Rep. John Duncan, R-Tenn., joined the committee in 1976 and became minority trade counsel in 1979. She held that job continuously until Republicans won control of the House in 1994, and Rep. Phil Crane, R-Ill., became chairman of the subcommittee.

Angela P. Ellard
Trade Counsel
Subcommittee on Trade
1104 Longworth House Office Bldg.
225-6659

Personal: born 3/19/61.

Education: B.A. (summa cum laude), Newcomb Coll. of Tulane Univ., 1982. M.A. in public policy, Tulane Univ., 1983. J.D. (cum laude), Tulane Univ., 1986.

Professional: 1986-90, atty., Akin, Gump, Strauss, Hauer & Feld. 1990-95, attorney, Weil, Gotshal & Manges. 1995-present, trade counsel, subc. on trade, House Cmte. on Ways and Means.

Expertise: Trade litigation and policy

Angela Ellard, who came to Capitol Hill at the beginning of the 104th Congress, is the chief trade attorney for the subcommittee on trade of the House Committee on Ways and Means. Ellard has extensive experience in the private sector and a comprehensive knowledge of trade policy.

Ellard specializes in dumping cases, fast track, dispute resolution, and application of trade statutes intended to address concerns about unfair practices. She also reviews all legislation produced by the subcommittee, according to a colleague, and "acts as our in-house legislative counsel."

In the second session of the 105th Congress, Ellard has resumed work on fast track legislation that would permit the president to negotiate trade agreements and bring them to Congress for implementation under special procedures. It is an issue she worked on last year, when legislation passed the Committee on Ways and Means.

Last year, Ellard also worked on most-favored-nation (MFN) status for China, an issue that will also be contentious in 1998. She was involved as well in legislation to implement an international agreement on shipbuilding to end global shipbuilding subsidies and establish a mechanism to prevent unfair pricing by foreign shipyards. The measure passed the House with an amendment that potentially violates the agreement, and it was not considered by the Senate.

Legislation to amend the anti-dumping law, which establishes penalties for unfair pricing in the U.S. market by foreign suppliers, has also been a priority for the last several years. The committee intends to continue its oversight of the implementation of this law, Ellard said.

In the first session of the 105th, Ellard will again be working on fast track, MFN status for China, anti-dumping legislation, the shipbuilding measure, the World Trade Organization, and on oversight of various trade agreements, including the North America Free Trade Agreement.

Ellard came to Capitol Hill after several years in private practice. From 1986 to 1990, she worked at Akin, Gump, and from 1990 to 1995, she worked at Weil, Gotshal & Manges. Ellard earned a law degree and a master's degree in public policy from Tulane University.

KEY MINORITY STAFF:

S. Bruce Wilson
Minority Trade Counsel
Subcommittee on Trade
1106 Longworth House Office Bldg.
225-4021

Personal: born 8/27/48 in Salina, Kan.

Education: B.A., Stanford Univ., 1970. M.A., Johns Hopkins School of Advanced International Studies, 1972. M.B.A., George Washington Univ., 1979. J.D., George Washington Univ., 1986.

Professional: 1972-74, business and economic consultant, Center for Industrial Development, Peace Corps (Bahia, Brazil). 1975-91, Office of the U.S. Trade Representative. 1991-95, full cmte. professional staff member; 1995-present, minority trade counsel, subc. on Trade, House Cmte. on Ways and Means.

Expertise: Trade

This year's trade agenda is topped by a bipartisan effort to grant free trade privileges to qualifying Sub-Sahara African states, and it will be minority trade counsel Bruce Wilson who will direct Democratic efforts. The measure enjoys broad bipartisan support and is expected to easily pass the House, Wilson predicts, noting that possible amendments could occur when it reaches the Senate.

A repeat item on the trade front is the president's request to get fast-track negotiating authority, which allows him to pursue trade pacts free from fear that Congress will amend them. Agreements negotiated under fast-track may only be approved or denied by Congress under a strict timetable. While Clinton failed to muster enough Democrats last year to secure fast track, this year's effort will be complicated by the administration's quest to secure an additional $18 billion for the International Monetary Fund.

Wilson predicts that fast-track will not advance until Congress has considered IMF funding. He also predicts that a broad bill, such as one presented last year to Congress, will not be considered. Instead, Wilson sees a much narrower fast-track proposal being drafted. "It's unlikely there will be a comprehensive fast-track this year," he said.

Wilson also expects that Congress will take up another extension of China's most-favored-nation trading status, a contentious matter that has been a perennial debate on Capitol Hill since the Tiananmen Square massacres in 1989. The chairman of the Ways and Means Committee, Rep. Bill Archer, R-Texas, has vowed to change the name of the status to "normal trade relations" in an effort to appease opponents.

In previous sessions, Wilson worked on the development of the North American Free Trade Agreement and the Uruguay Round of the General Agreement on Tariffs and Trade. Both trade pacts received attention in 1996. A particular focus was given to the administration's efforts to shore up the Mexican economy. The subcommittee's legislative agenda also included action on renewal of the GSP, a program through which the U.S. creates export markets in developing countries.

A one-time aide to former Rep. Sam Gibbons, D-Fla., Wilson moved into his post as minority trade counsel in 1995 when Rep. Charles Rangel, R-N.Y., became the ranking member on the trade subcommittee. He joined the panel's professional staff in 1991, moving up to staff director in 1993.

Wilson brings to his job impressive credentials and extensive experience in trade matters. He has worked in the Peace Corps as a business and economic consultant, and spent 16 years at the Office of the U.S. Trade Representative.

Committee on Agriculture, Nutrition, & Forestry

Subcommittee on Marketing, Inspection, & Product Promotion

328-A Russell Senate Office Building
Washington, D.C. 20510-6000
202/224-2035   Fax: 202/224-1725

MAJORITY MEMBERS:

Paul Coverdell, GA
 Chairman
Jesse Helms, NC
Thad Cochran, MS
Mitch McConnell, KY

MINORITY MEMBERS:

Max Baucus, MT
 Ranking Minority Member
Robert Kerrey, NE
Mary Landrieu, LA

Jurisdiction: Legislation on foreign agricultural trade; foreign market development; agriculture product promotion and domestic marketing programs; oversight of international commodity agreements and export controls on agricultural commodities; foreign assistance programs and Food for Peace; marketing orders; inspection and certification of meat, flowers, fruit, vegetables, and livestock.

KEY MAJORITY STAFF:

Terri Snow
Professional Staff Member
647 Dirksen Senate Office Bldg.
224-5207

Personal: born 6/14/70 in Indianapolis, Ind.

Education: B.A., Indiana Univ., 1992. M.A., George Mason Univ., 1997.

Professional: 1992, intern, Sen. Dan Coats, R-Ind. 1992-95, leg. staff asst.; 1995-present, prof. staff member, Senate Cmte. on Ag.

Expertise: Trade issues, marketing orders and promotion, milk marketing orders

Like others who handle agricultural trade issues, Terri Snow is planning on a busy 1998. As the United States gears up for next year's World Trade Organization talks that will focus on international agriculture agreements, she will be helping to set the stage and exploring possible directions for U.S. strategy.

In May, she will travel to Geneva for WTO ministerial meetings. She will also work throughout the year on preparations with commodity groups, agribusiness, government agencies, and House and Senate Agriculture Committee staff. "Part of my job also is to coordinate with the U.S. Trade Representative and USDA on what is our strategy for agriculture, especially if we don't have fast-track," she said. One of the people she will work with is a new agriculture trade ambassador at the U.S. Trade Representative's office.

Despite last year's failure to reauthorize fast-track trade negotiating authority for the executive branch, Snow said Agriculture Committee Chairman Richard Lugar, R-Ind., remains hopeful it can be accomplished in 1998. Lugar has identified two other trade issues as priorities as well, she said.

The first is the African Growth and Opportunity Act, which encourages trade and investment in 48 sub-Saharan nations on the continent. The bill would help the countries gain access to U.S. markets in return for lower trade barriers abroad. Snow said it also contains a small earmark for agricultural technical assistance through the U.S. Agency for International Development.

The bill has the backing of a diverse group of lawmakers, she said, ranging from House Speaker Newt Gingrich, R-Ga., to Rep. Charles Rangel, D-N.Y. President Clinton included a push for the measure as well in his State of the Union address. "It's based on a trade, not aid sort of principle," Snow said. "You look at countries like Uganda and you can easily see advantages in their economies just by having democracy."

Lugar's other trade priority is the Sanctions Policy Reform Act, which would require economic impact statements when economic sanctions are proposed against other countries. It also would demand that sunset provisions be included in all sanctions plans. "Right now, sanctions go into perpetuity, basically," Snow said.

Snow also handles non-farm trade issues for Lugar. She has been a member of the committee staff since 1992, coming over after an internship with Sen. Dan Coats, R-Ind.

KEY MINORITY STAFF:

Mark Halverson
Minority Chief Counsel
639 Dirksen Senate Office Bldg.
224-6901

Personal: born 8/26/55 in Marshalltown, Iowa.

Education: A.S., Marshalltown Community College, 1975. B.S., Iowa State Univ., 1977. J.D., Univ. of Iowa, 1981.

Professional: 1981-82, private law practice, Des Moines, Iowa. 1982-84, law clerk, U.S. Court of Appeals, Eighth Circuit, Judge George Fagg. 1984-88, private law practice, Bryan Case (Wash., D.C.). 1988-96, leg. asst., Sen. Tom Harkin, D-Iowa. 1996-present, minority chief counsel, Senate Cmte. on Agriculture, Nutrition and Forestry.

Expertise: Agriculture trade, nutrition programs

A reauthorization bill for expiring child nutrition programs will be one of the priorities this year for minority chief counsel Mark Halverson. The Senate Agriculture Committee's ranking member, Sen. Tom Harkin, D-Iowa, joined committee Chairman Richard Lugar, R-Ind., in introducing a bare-bones reauthorization bill in January. Hearings throughout the spring are likely to result in provisions being added to the legislation.

The reauthorization bill would extend the Supplemental Nutrition Program for Women, Infants and Children (WIC) through 2003. It also would extend programs such as the WIC Farmers' Market, which allows states and Indian tribes to offer vouchers so participants can buy fresh produce. A summer nutrition program and another that helps states cover general administrative costs associated with running federal child nutrition programs are also included in the bill.

While there have been huge differences between Democrats and Republicans over the past three years over the scope and cost of other federal assistance programs, the child nutrition reauthorization has produced none so far. Lugar has long voiced his support for child nutrition programs and has said he is not interested in block-granting them to states. He sided with Democrats in 1995 when his own party sought to turn federal school lunch programs over to the states.

Halverson also has responsibility for another bipartisan piece of committee legislation, this one to amend the Commodity Exchange Act. Introduced last year by Lugar, Harkin and Sen. Patrick Leahy, D-Vt., the bill would modernize futures trading laws and streamline regulatory processes at the Commodity Futures Trading Commission.

The minority chief counsel has also taken up foreign trade issues. Last year, the committee reviewed barriers to U.S. products erected by the European Union and Pacific Rim nations. This year, it will help lay the groundwork for 1999 World Trade Organization talks on agriculture.

Agriculture has long been part of Halverson's life. He grew up on an Iowa farm and travels frequently to his home state to manage a 240-acre family farm that produces corn and soybeans. He earned a bachelor's degree in animal science from Iowa State University, and after law school and seven years in the legal profession, moved to Washington for a job on Harkin's staff.

Committee on Appropriations

Subcommittee on Agriculture, Rural Development, & Related Agencies

136 Dirksen Senate Office Building
Washington, D.C. 20510-6026
202/224-5270

MAJORITY MEMBERS:

Thad Cochran, MS
Chairman
Arlen Specter, PA
Christopher Bond, MO
Slade Gorton, WA
Mitch McConnell, KY
Conrad Burns, MT

MINORITY MEMBERS:

Dale Bumpers, AR
Ranking Minority Member
Tom Harkin, IA
Herb Kohl, WI
Robert Byrd, WV
Patrick Leahy, VT

Jurisdiction: (1) Department of Agriculture (except Forest Service); (2) Farm Credit Administration; (3) Commodity Futures Trading Commission; (4) Food and Drug Administration (HHS).

KEY MAJORITY STAFF:

Rebecca Davies
Clerk
Subcommittee on Agriculture

136 Dirksen Senate Office Bldg.
224-5270

Professional: minority clerk, subc. on treasury, postal service, and general government; 1993-94, minority clerk; 1995-present, majority clerk, subc. on agriculture, Senate Cmte. on Appropriations.

Expertise: Appropriations

The Subcommittee on Agriculture could be the scene of a battle between nutrition interests and farm groups this year. In 1996, Congress made fundamental changes in crop subsidy programs, changes that many commodity groups say were only the beginning of deep cuts made in farm programs. The law boosted the subsidies in 1996-97 but gradually decreased fixed payments to growers. The commodity groups claim their programs were cut while food stamp programs were increased.

This is the background Rebecca Davies and her boss, Sen. Thad Cochran, R-Miss., will be working against in the second session of the 105th Congress. President Clinton has asked for an increase in outlays from $1.6 billion to $24 billion for food stamps. The increase will make it possible for the Agriculture Department to restore food stamp eligibility status to 730,000 legal immigrants at a cost of $535 million. The administration notes that the food stamp program still costs less than it did five years ago.

Clinton has also requested an increase of $114 million for the Women, Infants and Children (WIC) program. The objective is to help about 7.5 million low-income women and children receive nutrition education and food supplements.

The president has also requested full funding for the crop subsidy program. Cochran is a defender of soil and seed programs, as well as price supports for important Mississippi crops such as cotton and rice. Cochran is especially supportive of federal aid for agriculture research and the Warmwater Aguaculture Research Center at Stoneville, Miss.

Davies is in her sixth year handling the agriculture appropriations bill, and her fourth as the majority clerk with responsibility for helping the subcommittee schedule testimony by farm agencies and interest groups. Davies moved to the subcommittee in 1993 after serving as minority clerk on the Treasury, Postal Service, and General Government Subcommittee.

Besides chairing the ag panel, Cochran is a veteran member of the Senate Agriculture Committee. The combination makes the Mississippi senator a key voice in Congress on farm issues.

KEY MINORITY STAFF:

Galen Fountain
Minority Clerk
Subc. on Agriculture, Rural Development, & Related Agencies
123 Hart Senate Office Bldg.
224-7202

Personal: born 9/3/51 in Hutchinson, Kan.

Education: B.A., Wichita State Univ., 1977. J.D., Univ. of Ark. Law School, 1989.

Professional: 1980-84, district office manager, Rep. Dan Glickman, D-Kan. 1984-90, district office manager, Rep. Beryl Anthony, D-Ark. 1990-95, chief agriculture counsel, Senate Cmte. on Small Business. 1995-present, minority clerk, subc. on agriculture, rural develop. and related agencies, Senate Cmte. on Appropriations.

Expertise: Appropriations, agriculture

As a result of the consensus reached on the farm bill last year, Galen Fountain, minority clerk for the subcommittee on agriculture, rural development, and related agencies, believes that the road that leads to an agriculture appropriations bill in 1998 will be less rocky. Fountain, in his fourth year working for Sen. Dale Bumpers, D-Ark., the subcommittee's ranking member, believes a new and better relationship was established between the House and Senate appropriations committees and the Department of Agriculture last year. Because of that, he is hopeful that the agriculture appropriations bill will be less contentious in the second session.

The subcommittee is watching how recently consolidated rural programs are working out. Last year, Congress gave the states and the Agriculture Department discretion over how to spend the money within each fund. However, Fountain says there's a limit on how much discretion the subcommittee is willing to permit.

Subcommittee Democrats are concerned about "user fees" that have not been authorized by the appropriate committee. Fountain says that these user fees could jeopardize the subcommittee's ability to meet its program levels as proscribed in the budget. They are also looking at any new proposed initiatives the president puts forth and are continuing to protect agricultural and rural base programs for research, food safety, and farm programs, Fountain said.

In addition to writing the check for farm and conservation programs, the subcommittee handles nutrition programs run by the Agriculture Department. Last year, an initiative was included to help eliminate teenage smoking. The subcommittee is following up on this directive to ensure it works and is cost-effective.

The administration is requesting an increase in funding for the Women, Infants, and Children nutrition program. For the past few years, funding for the program has been growing incrementally, Fountain said, adding that at the end of each year, WIC showed a surplus. The directors of the program claim that it is hard to accurately project the precise amount of money they need. The subcommittee wants to make sure that the money appropriated is cost-effective and fully utilized.

Fountain says that the subcommittee will also help correct a civil rights problem at the Department of Agriculture that pre-dates the Clinton administration. He believes the president will propose a remedy for minority farmers who have been discriminated against when applying for Department of Agriculture loans.

On another front, Bumpers has a home-state interest in policies that deal with soybeans, rice, cotton, and catfish. About 40 percent of all U.S. rice is grown in Arkansas. Bumpers also has a strong interest in rural development and research. Last year's spending bill contained money for rural housing, farm credit, enterprise grants, and other economic development programs that are beneficial to rural Arkansas.

Subcommittee on Commerce, Justice, & State, the Judiciary, and Related Agencies

S-146A The Capitol
Washington, D.C. 20510-6027
202/224-7277

MAJORITY MEMBERS:

Judd Gregg, NH
Chairman
Ted Stevens, AK
Pete Domenici, NM
Mitch McConnell, KY
Kay Bailey Hutchinson, TX
Ben Nighthorse Campbell, CO

MINORITY MEMBERS:

Ernest Hollings, SC
Ranking Minority Member
Daniel Inouye, HI
Dale Bumpers, AR
Frank Lautenberg, NJ
Barbara Mikulski, MD

Jurisdiction: (1) Department of Commerce; (2) Department of Justice; (3) Department of State (except Migration and Refugee Assistance); (4) Department of the Treasury (Fishermen's Protective Fund); (5) Department of Transportation (Maritime Administration); (6) The Judiciary. Related Agencies; (7) Arms Control and Disarmament Agency; (8) Board for International Broadcasting; (9) Commission on Civil Rights; (10) Commission on Security and Cooperation in Europe; (11) Equal Employment Opportunity Commission; (12) Federal Communications Commission; (13) Federal Maritime Commission; (14) Federal Trade Commission; (15) United States Information Agency; (16) International Trade Commission; (17) Japan-United States Friendship Commission; (18) Legal Services Corporation; (19) Marine Mammal Commission; (20) Office of the United States Trade Representative; (21) Securities and Exchange Commission; (22) Small Business Administration.

KEY MAJORITY STAFF:

Jim Morhard
Clerk
Subcommittee on Commerce, Justice and State
S-146A The Capitol
224-7277

Personal: born 9/20/56 in Arlington, Va.

Education: B.S. in accounting, St. Francis College (Pa.), 1978. M.B.A., George Washington Univ., 1984. J.D., Georgetown Univ., 1993.

Professional: 1978-85, office of the comptroller and secretary, U.S. Navy. 1984, leg. fellow, Sen. Pete Wilson, R-Calif. 1985-91, leg. assistant and leg. director, Sen. Robert Kasten, R-Wis. 1991-94, minority clerk; 1995-97, clerk, subc. on military construction; prof. staff member, subc. on defense; 1997-present, clerk, subc. on Commerce, Justice and State, Senate Cmte. on Appropriations.

Expertise: Appropriations

Majority clerk Jim Morhard and the Subcommittee on Commerce, Justice and State are looking closely in 1998 at a new Clinton administration proposal to combat drug trafficking, illegal immigration, juvenile crime, and terrorism.

Morhard, who focuses on the priorities of subcommittee Chairman Judd Gregg, R-N.H., said that two of Gregg's priorities are preventing crimes against children and older Americans. The subcommittee's goals this year are include legislation to combat marketing scams used against older adults and to address the issue of child pornography on the Internet. The panel is also monitoring Clinton administration progress against potential terrorist attacks.

The subcommittee also has jurisdiction over the budget for the State and Commerce departments, the Census Bureau, and the Legal Services Corporation.

Last year, as the panel's new chairman, Gregg was able to break tradition and push his appropriations bill through the legislative process. Moreover, Gregg shepherded the Senate version of the Commerce, Justice, State and Judiciary bill to passage by a vote of 99-0. Morhard is hopeful that the subcommittee's funding bill will be as well received on the Senate floor in 1998.

This is Morhard's second year as clerk. His appropriations experience was built during previous stints with the defense and military construction subcommittees.

Morhard came to his current assignment after working seven years for Sen. Robert Kasten, D-Wis. He spent two years as Kasten's legislative director, and before that was legislative assistant for national security issues.

His first job in Washington was in the office of the comptroller of the Navy, where he helped implement financial directives from Congress.

KEY MINORITY STAFF:

Scott Gudes
Minority Clerk
Subcommittee on Commerce, Justice, State,
  the Judiciary, and Related Agencies
160 Dirksen Senate Office Bldg.
224-7270

Personal: born 8/16/56 in Los Angeles, Calif.

Education: B.A. (Phi Beta Kappa), San Diego State Univ. and Univ. of Liverpool (United Kingdom), 1976. Masters of Public Admin., California State Univ. at Fullerton, 1978. John C. Stennis Fellow, 1997-98.

Professional: 1977-78, administrative intern, city manager's office, City of Costa Mesa, Calif. 1978-80, presidential management intern, office of the secretary, U.S. Dept. of Defense. 1980-83, economic adjustment project manager, office of economic adjustment, U.S. Dept. of Defense. 1983-86, budget examiner, Office of Management and Budget. 1986-90, professional staff member, subc. on defense; 1990-

94, clerk, subc. on Commerce, Justice, State, the Judiciary, and related agencies; 1995-present, minority clerk, subc. on Commerce, Justice, State, the Judiciary, and related agencies, Senate Cmte. on Appropriations.

Expertise: Appropriations

Scott Gudes, the minority clerk for the Subcommittee on Commerce, Justice, State, the Judiciary, and Related Agencies, says that his appropriations bill used to be one of the more contentious bills in the Senate. Bipartisanship has been restored to both the subcommittee and full Appropriations Committee, however, under the chairmanship of Sen. Ted Stevens, R-Alaska, Gudes says.

While the bill last year was passed on a bipartisan basis in the Senate, several legislative issues ended up bogging it down in conference, Gudes said. "Due to the negotiations on census sampling, we were the last bill enacted for FY 1998," he said.

Gudes thinks that the census will remain a major issue in his subcommittee's appropriations measure in the second session of the 105th Congress. The administration has proposed $1.4 billion for the census, an increase of $480 million from last year.

The president's budget request this year is predicated on receiving some revenue from the tobacco settlement. Critics say that without the money, the administration's budget does not really live within the appropriations caps mandated by the balanced budget agreement signed last year. Thus, Gudes speculates, if the money does not materialize, many of last year's problem areas could again become controversial.

The fiscal 1997 legislation also included funding for legal services for the poor and federal technology programs. "The jury is still out," Gudes says with regard to whether these issues could again become controversial. The hottest item within the census debate is whether statistical sampling should be used to account for residents who are difficult to contact.

The subcommittee also handles budgets for the federal court system and the marine fishery programs, making Gudes a generalist on a variety of issues. Gudes says there is a continued trend toward funding new law enforcement grant programs for state and local communities that will remain an issue this year. On another front, both sides of the aisle in the Senate subcommittee favor programs funding the National Oceanic Atmospheric Administration. This covers the weather, global warming, hurricane tracking, and coastal and oceanic research. The House is not as supportive of NOAA, however, and the debate could become heated in conference.

Gudes has worked the Commerce, Justice, State appropriations bill for seven years. For five years before that, he worked on the Appropriations Defense Subcommittee, where he handled various accounts, including operation and maintenance for the Army, Navy, Air Force, and defense agencies.

Gudes arrived on the Hill in 1986 from OMB. There, he served as a budget examiner reviewing commerce accounts and the Panama Canal Commission.

Subcommittee on Defense

122 Dirksen Senate Office Building
Washington, D.C. 20510-6028
202/224-7255

MAJORITY MEMBERS:

Ted Stevens, AK
  Chairman
Thad Cochran, MS

Arlen Specter, PA
Pete Domenici, NM
Christopher Bond, MO
Mitch McConnell, KY
Richard Shelby, AL
Judd Gregg, NH
Kay Bailey Hutchinson, TX

MINORITY MEMBERS:

Daniel Inouye, HI
   Ranking Minority Member
Ernest Hollings, SC
Robert Byrd, WV
Patrick Leahy, VT
Dale Bumpers, AR
Frank Lautenberg, NJ
Tom Harkin, IA
Byron Dorgan, ND

Jurisdiction: (1) Department of Defense-Military: Departments of Army, Navy (including Marine Corps), Air Force, and Office of Secretary of Defense (except Military Construction); (2) The Central Intelligence Agency; (3) Intelligence Community Oversight.

KEY MAJORITY STAFF:

Steven J. Cortese
Staff Director
S-128, The Capitol
224-7255

Professional: 1984-85, budget analyst, GAO. 1991-95, minority clerk for defense, subcommittee on defense; 1995-96, majority clerk, subcommittee on defense; 1996-present, staff director, Senate Cmte. on Appropriations.

Expertise: Defense, appropriations

Steven Cortese, staff director for the Senate Committee on Appropriations, has been working for Sen. Ted Stevens, R-Alaska, since 1986. He has worked on the Appropriations Committee since 1991, first as minority clerk for the Defense Subcommittee, then as a majority staffer. He was promoted to staff director of the full committee in 1996.

Cortese said Steven's number-one priority in the second session of the 105th Congress is working with his House counterpart, Rep. Robert Livingston, R-La., to get the 13 appropriations bills through both chambers. Stevens hopes to build on the productive working relationship the two forged last year that resulted in passage of all the appropriations bills by the scheduled adjournment date of Nov. 14. This is a shorter legislative year, but the precedent is set and lawmakers hope the process will run smoothly.

It is a "zero-sum process this year integrating the president's priorities and Congress' priorities and all the appropriations bills by Oct. 9," Cortese said. The budget resolution is right at the levels proscribed

in the agreement last year. As such, the appropriations process could be completed by the August recess.

Cortese said that a national missile defense system remains the key priority for his boss. Support for the National Guard and military medical care are high priorities as well. While spending for defense was increased last year, events in Bosnia and the Middle East remain possible areas of contention.

This year's appropriation only funded the U.S. mission in Bosnia through June 30. Many expect a supplemental appropriations bill to be dropped for Bosnia in late March. Cortese predicts the matter will touch off disagreements since additional funding for Bosnia was not provided in the balanced budget agreement.

Congress will also be watching to see how President Clinton uses a new enhanced rescission authority to veto provisions he doesn't like within the appropriations bills.

Cortese said last year was a learning process for both the executive and legislative branch. Stevens, who supported the line-item veto, has said he believes the president' will exercise his authority sparingly this year. "His view is, if the work of the committee is done well, the committee has nothing to fear from the line-item veto," Cortese said.

KEY MINORITY STAFF:

Charles J. Houy
Minority Clerk
Subcommittee on Defense
117 Dirksen Senate Office Bldg.
224-7293

Professional: 1995-present, minority clerk, subc. on defense, Senate Cmte. on Appropriations.

Expertise: Defense issues

President Clinton has proposed spending $2.4 billion more on defense in next year's budget than in 1998. Some Pentagon officials claim, however, that the figure when adjusted for inflation will be 1.1 percent less than last year. The minority clerk who will be handling the defense appropriations bill is Charles Houy. Beginning as a staff assistant, Houy has been the clerk for the subcommittee for three years.

Houy's boss, Sen. Daniel Inouye, D-Hawaii, has maintained a hawkish voting record and generally supports most Pentagon projects. Inouye tends to use his seat on the appropriations panel to back the Defense Department and projects and programs important to Hawaii.

Inouye has used his post to push the transfer of the unpopulated island of Kahoolawe from the federal government to the state of Hawaii. He also pushed through $455 million for environmental clean-up there. He earmarked another $60 million to clean up an island that was used by the military for years as a bombing practice target.

Inouye's home state also has the Pacific Missile Range Facility, a processing center that supports the Air Force Maui Space Surveillance Site and the Maui High Performance Computing Center. The family housing construction budget also has contained millions of dollars for construction on Navy-owned land in Hawaii.

In last year's defense budget battle, Inouye made sure no funds earmarked for Hawaii were vetoed by the White House. Some of those programs included the U.S. Flag Cruise Ship/Troop pilot program and the National Defense Center of Excellence for Research in Ocean Sciences. Inouye also added an amendment to the defense bill that prohibited expenditures to maintain vintage battleships. The USS Missouri, the battleship that hosted the formal Japanese surrender that ended World War II is one of these battleships. Inouye wants the vessel sent to Hawaii. Since the amendment effectively forces the Navy to give the ships away, it is likely that Hawaii will get its museum piece.

As in past years, the panel will debate financing missile defense systems. Inouye has previously fought to preserve funding for the Strategic Defense Initiative and the B-2 bomber. Another issue that could prove controversial is funding to continue the deployment of U.S. troops in Bosnia. The administration will submit a supplemental appropriations request of about $600 million to fund the Bosnia operation from July 1 through Sept. 30. The request will also have money in it to fund a recent surge of activity in the Persian Gulf region.

Subcommittee on Foreign Operations

142 Dirksen Senate Office Bldg.
Washington, D.C. 20510-6031
202/224-2104

MAJORITY MEMBERS:

Mitch McConnell, KY
Chairman
Arlen Specter, PA
Judd Gregg, NH
Richard Shelby, AL
Robert Bennett, UT
Ben Nighthorse Campbell, CO
Ted Stevens, AK

MINORITY MEMBERS:

Patrick Leahy, VT
Ranking Minority Member
Daniel Inouye, HI
Frank Lautenberg, NJ
Tom Harkin, IA
Barbara Mikulski, MD
Patty Murray, WA

Jurisdiction: (1) Agency for International Development; (2) African Development Foundation; (3) African Development Fund; (4) Asian Development Fund and Bank; (5) Department of State; (6) Anti-terrorism assistance; International narcotics control; (7) Migration and Refugee Assistance; (8) U.S. Emergency Refugee and Migration Assistance Fund; (9) Export-Import Bank; (10) Foreign military credit sales; (11) Inter-American Development Bank; (12) Inter-American Foundation; (13) International Bank for Reconstruction and Development (World Bank); (14) International Development Association; International Development Cooperation Agency; (15) International Finance Corporation; (16) International Fund for Agricultural Development; (17) International Military Education and Training; (18) International Monetary Fund; (19) International organizations and programs; (20) Military Assistance Program; (21) Overseas Private Investment Corporation; (22) Peace Corps; (23) Special Defense Acquisition Fund.

KEY MAJORITY STAFF:

Robin Cleveland
Clerk
Subcommittee on Foreign Operations
142 Dirksen Senate Office Bldg.
224-2104

Personal: born in Munich, West Germany.

Education: B.A. (cum laude), Wesleyan Univ., 1977.

Professional: 1977-78, legal researcher. 1978-86, professional staff member, Senate Select Cmte. on Intelligence. 1986-96, foreign policy and defense leg. asst., Sen. Mitch McConnell, R-Ky. 1997-present, clerk, subc. on foreign operations, Senate Cmte. on Appropriations.

Expertise: Defense, foreign policy

Robin Cleveland has been clerk on the subcommittee on foreign operations, chaired by Sen. Mitch McConnell, R-Ky, for two years. Previously, Cleveland served for a decade on McConnell's personal staff.

Although known these days more for his stance on campaign finance reform and as former chairman of the Senate Ethics Committee, McConnell has carved out a niche in the foreign policy arena as well. The subcommittee which McConnell heads funds America's foreign aid programs as well as special programs such as the Peace Corps and activities in anti-terrorism assistance and international narcotics control.

McConnell has staked two out two priorities since taking over the subcommittee. First, he wants to support countries willing to accept the responsibilities of NATO membership and, second, to expand U.S. aid to the new, non-Russian states of the former Soviet Union. McConnell believes the two goals directly impact the stability of Europe and the U.S.

McConnell is skeptical about helping Russia until officials understand explicitly the importance of NATO expansion and unless they stop helping Iran advance that nation's nuclear agenda. Last year's foreign aid bill stipulates that the president will have to prove that the Russians have curtailed their activities in the latter area. McConnell also feels that legislation cannot be ambiguous with regard to whether Russia has a voice or a veto power in NATO matters.

Another issue important to McConnell when it comes to assisting Russia is the protection of religious freedom. Last year's bill included a provision conditioning assistance on protecting such rights. McConnell will remain a key participant in future debates about Russian aid.

McConnell supports continuing aid to Israel. He also believes Egypt should receive assistance as long as Egypt continues to work toward peace in the Middle East. McConnell is supportive of the financial assistance in last year's bill for Jordan, and feels King Hussein should be recognized for his contribution to regional security.

Other important items for McConnell include providing aid to supporters of democracy in Burma, restricting assistance to the Hun Sen government in Cambodia, and funding for the Korean Energy Development Organization. McConnell believes that aid to governments in the Balkans that refuse to cooperate in the extradition of war criminals should be halted. As chairman of the foreign operations subcommittee, he also will be facing a supplemental appropriations bill this year for the U.S. mission in Bosnia.

KEY MINORITY STAFF:

Timothy S. Rieser
Minority Clerk
Subcommittee on Foreign Operations
123 Hart Senate Office Bldg.
224-7284

Personal: born 1/3/52 in Palo Alto, Calif.

Education: B.A. (summa cum laude), Dartmouth College, 1976. J.D., Antioch Law School, 1979.

Professional: 1995-present, minority clerk, subc. on foreign operations, Senate Cmte. on Appropriations.

Expertise: Foreign operations

Subcommittee on foreign operations minority clerk Tim Rieser works for ranking member Sen. Patrick J. Leahy, D-Vt., who has a wide range of foreign policy interests in the second session of the 105th Congress.

The biggest challenge for the panel this year is to simply maintain current funding levels and provide additional money where it is most needed in foreign assistance programs. Among the programs important to Leahy are contributions the U.S. makes to the United Nations and the World Health Organization, programs to support democracy in the former Soviet Union, and plans to address humanitarian and development needs in Africa and Latin America.

Leahy continues to be at the forefront of an issue that recently received international attention, disarming millions of land mines in war-torn areas. Problems tied to the matter include assisting victims of mine explosions, removing unexploded mines, and convincing the U.S. government to sign a treaty to ban land mines.

Funds also need to be allocated to combat other obvious threats to the U.S. such as organized crime, drug trafficking, and the smuggling of nuclear material. Rieser also pointed out that international environmental and health problems, regardless of where they occur in the world, are sure to affect the U.S. The subcommittee will consider these matters as well in 1998.

Family planning will again affect foreign policy discussions. "As has been the case in recent years, Congress will undoubtedly have to face the controversial issue of funding for international family planning," Rieser said. At issue is whether the U.S. will fund private organizations that use their own money to perform abortions.

Leahy will continue to be a strong advocate for human rights throughout the world. Rieser says his boss is working to ensure that the foreign aid bill contains key human rights provisions. He also wants to make sure that funding to fight infectious diseases is in the foreign aid bill.

Last year, Leahy was instrumental in adding $50 million to the program. He would like to see the amount maintained or increased for fiscal 1999.

Committee on Banking, Housing, & Urban Affairs

Subcommittee on International Finance

534 Dirksen Senate Office Bldg.
Washington, D.C. 20510-6075
202/224-7391   Fax: 202/224-5137

MAJORITY MEMBERS:

Rod Grams, MN
Chairman
Chuck Hagel, NE
Phil Gramm, TX
Robert Bennett, UT

MINORITY MEMBERS:

Carol Moseley-Braun, IL
Ranking Minority Member
Barbara Boxer, CA
Jack Reed, RI

KEY MAJORITY STAFF:

Dave Berson
Staff Director
Subc. on International Finance
534 Dirksen Senate Office Bldg.
224-7391

KEY MINORITY STAFF:

Patrick A. Mulloy
Chief International Counsel, Minority
544 Dirksen Senate Office Bldg.
224-7391

Personal: born 9/14/41 in Wilkes-Barre, Pa.

Education: B.A., Kings Coll., 1963. M.A., Univ. of Notre Dame, 1965. J.D., George Washington Univ., 1971. L.L.M., Harvard Law School, 1978.

Professional: 1965-72, U.S. Foreign Service. 1973-77, lands division; 1978-82, antitrust division, U.S. Dept. of Justice. 1983, American Political Science Association Congressional Fellow from Justice Dept., House Cmte. on Ways and Means and Senate Cmte. on Banking. 1984, minority general counsel; 1987-89, general counsel; 1989-92, senior counsel and international affairs adviser; 1993-94, chief international counsel; 1995-present, chief minority international counsel, Senate Cmte. on Banking.

Expertise: International trade, finance, banking

Reauthorization of the Export-Import Bank was the major legislation that Pat Mulloy oversaw last year for the Senate Banking Committee. Mulloy staffs the Democrats on the International Finance Subcommittee. This year, he is concentrating on the International Monetary Fund (IMF), Defense Production Act, Exchange Stabilization Fund, and the Convention on Bribery.

The instability in Asian currency markets will be a subject of Banking Committee hearings, Mulloy adds. Although the Foreign Relations Committee has lead jurisdiction on IMF, Mulloy expects the banking panel to play a role in developing legislation to strengthen international capital markets and in the IMF New Arrangements to Borrow and quota increase. His boss, Sen. Paul S. Sarbanes, D-Md., also serves on the Foreign Relations Committee and is a strong supporter of Clinton administration effort to refund the IMF. A non-controversial reauthorization of the Defense Production Act is also up this year.

A controversial bill that could surface, however, involves the Treasury Department's Exchange Stabilization Fund. The $30 billion fund is available to the secretary of the treasury to temporarily shore-up foreign currencies. It was used, for example, to halt the Mexican peso crisis. Banking Committee Sen. Lauch Faircloth, R-N.C., has sponsored a bill that would require Treasury to seek congressional approval if the agency wants to use more than $100 million for any single purpose. Mulloy foresees Democratic resistance to the proposal.

Another issue is ratification and implementation of the multilateral Convention on Bribery, which was adopted by the Organization for Economic Cooperation and Development. The pact will not take effect until it is ratified by a sufficient number of countries. The Foreign Relations Committee has jurisdiction over ratification of the treaty; the Banking Committee has jurisdiction over implementing legislation, which will come as amendments to the Foreign Corrupt

Practices Act. Mulloy sees both issues, ratification and implementation, proceeding down parallel tracks this session.

In February, President Clinton announced his intention to nominate Mulloy to be assistant secretary of commerce for market access and compliance. In that position, he will have a major role in improving access by U.S. companies to overseas markets and in strengthening the nation's international competitive position. The nomination will be considered by the Senate Finance Committee.

Committee on Commerce, Science & Transportation

Subcommittee on Consumer Affairs, Foreign Commerce, & Tourism

425 Hart Senate Office Building
Washington, D.C. 20510
202/224-5183   Fax: 202/228-0326

MAJORITY MEMBERS:

John Ashcroft, MO
Chairman
Slade Gorton, WA
Spencer Abraham, MI
Conrad Burns, MT
Sam Brownback, KS

MINORITY MEMBERS:

John Breaux, LA
Ranking Minority Member
Wendell Ford, KY
Richard Bryan, NV

Jurisdiction: (1) U.S. Dept. of Commerce; (2) Federal Trade Commission; (3) Consumer Product Safety Commission; (4) National Highway Traffic Safety Administration; (6) Insurance; (7) Domestic industries; (8) Foreign commerce; (9) Tourism; (10) Olympics and sports.

KEY MAJORITY STAFF:

Lance Bultena
Counsel
Subcommittee on Consumer Affairs, Foreign Commerce, & Tourism
425 Hart Senate Office Bldg.
224-5183

Personal: born 5/18/63, in Lennox, S.D.

Education: B.S. in political science and economics, Univ. of South Dakota, 1985. M.Phil. in economics, Oxford Univ., 1987. D.Phil. in

political science, Oxford Univ., 1990. J.D., Harvard Law School, 1991.

Professional: 1991-95, attorney, Winthrop, Stimson, Putnam & Roberts. 1995-present, counsel, subc. on consumer affairs, foreign commerce, and tourism, Senate Cmte. on Commerce, Science and Transportation.

Expertise: Consumer issues

The Senate Commerce, Science, and Transportation Committee has jurisdiction over most key portions of the proposed settlement between the government and American tobacco companies. This means a very busy year for Lance Bultena, counsel to the consumer affairs subcommittee.

At the outset of the session, Bultena helped organize seven hearings on the proposed deal, and more are likely to follow. In setting out on a steady work schedule on the matter, committee Chairman John McCain, R-Ariz., has expressed hope that some version of tobacco legislation might reach the Senate floor during the 1998 session. "The Senate takes its role in this matter very seriously," the chairman said when he introduced in legislative form the settlement reached by the tobacco industry and state attorneys general late in 1997. McCain has said the settlement will serve as a basis for discussion and amendment.

Besides tobacco, Bultena is assisting senators trying to work out a compromise among themselves and with the Clinton administration on product liability reform. The Senate Commerce Committee passed a version early in 1997 that has served as a base for the latest attempts to find consensus on the matter. Congress passed product liability reform bill during the 104th Congress, but it was vetoed by the president. Clinton signaled he might accept a narrower bill to revamp the ground rules for product liability lawsuits. Since then, Sens. Jay Rockefeller, D-W.Va., and Slade Gorton, R-Wash., have led efforts to find a way through the issue and get it settled this year.

Bultena also is among committee staffers working on sections of the Intermodal Surface Transportation Efficiency Act that deal with traffic safety, such as air bag provisions and incentive grants to states that enforce traffic safety laws. The Commerce Committee completed work on its jurisdictional portion of the highway bill in 1997.

Mixed in with these issues, Bultena expects the committee at some point to begin work on reauthorization bills dealing with the Federal Trade Commission, the Consumer Product Safety Commission, and the National Highway Traffic Safety Administration.

Bultena was recruited to the committee staff when Sen. Larry Pressler, R-S.D., became chairman in 1995. Bultena is a native South Dakotan who served two stints on Pressler's personal staff over the years.

KEY MINORITY STAFF:

Gregg Elias
Minority Professional Staff Member
516 Dirksen Senate Office Bldg.
224-0415

Personal: born 8/26/64 in New York City, N.Y.

Education: B.A. in American history and political science, Univ. of Pa., 1986. J.D., Georgetown Univ., 1992.

Professional: 1987-89, special assistant, Rep. Steny Hoyer, D-Md. 1989-92, special assistant to chairman, House Democratic Caucus. 1992-97, international trade lawyer, Wiley, Rein and Fielding (Wash., D.C.). 1997-present, minority professional staff member, Senate Cmte. on Commerce, Science and Transportation.

Expertise: Trade

Gregg Elias is the chief adviser to committee Democrats on matters of trade. He also handles issues developed by the Manufacturing/ Foreign Commerce Subcommittee, which was formed at the outset of the 105th Congress to examine how the nation's industrial base is being affected by rapid changes in the economy, education, and other segments of society.

Elias works most closely with the Commerce Committee's ranking Democrat, Sen. Ernest Hollings, D-S.C., long one of the more active voices on Capitol Hill in matters of international trade and particularly its impact on domestic jobs. Elias also is the contact point for other senators and committee staff on anything having to do with trade. He organizes briefings, develops issue papers and option memos, and serves as a contact with the Office of the U.S. Trade Representative and other administration agencies with a voice on the topic.

Early in the 1998 session, he was advising senators on President Clinton's request to boost the International Monetary Fund with $18 billion to bolster threatened economies in the Far East. As the session progresses, he expects to have a hand in whatever response the Senate committee develops to administration efforts to revive the president's request for fast-track trade authority. He also keeps a watchful eye on issues involving the World Trade Organization, the General Agreement on Tariffs and Trade, most-favored-nation trade status for U.S. trading partners, the North American Free Trade Agreement, the Caribbean Basin Initiative, and other issues better known to the public by their headline acronyms.

Elias developed trade expertise during a five-year stint as an international trade attorney at Wiley, Fein and Fielding, a Washington, D.C. firm. He developed expertise on the Hill through earlier positions in the House. He began his career as a special assistant to Rep. Steny Hoyer, D-Md., and moved to the Democratic Caucus staff when Hoyer became caucus chairman. His responsibilities were to help Hoyer monitor House Democratic politics.

On the manufacturing subcommittee, Elias notes the panel has been conducting a thorough review of the sector. During the 1997 session, it examined environmental regulations, workforce issues and the impact that high tech is having on traditional manufacturing. The panel was created at the outset of the 105th Congress at the urging of Sen. Spencer Abraham, R-Mich., who became its chairman. Among items on the agenda for 1998, the subcommittee will examine advanced manufacturing issues, the impact of technology on manufacturing processes and perhaps take a look at the workings of the Silicon Valley. Elias works most closely with the subcommittee's ranking Democrat, Sen. Richard Bryan, D-Nev., who is interested in ensuring a proper balance between the needs of manufacturers and the needs of the thousands of people they employ.

Committee on Finance

Subcommittee on International Trade

219 Dirksen Senate Office Building
Washington, D.C. 20510-6200
202/224-4515   Fax: 202/224-5920

MAJORITY MEMBERS:

Charles Grassley, IA
Chairman
William Roth, DE
John Chafee, RI
Orrin Hatch, UT
Alfonse D'Amato, NY
Frank Murkowski, AK
Phil Gramm, TX
Trent Lott, MS
Connie Mack, FL

MINORITY MEMBERS:

Daniel Moynihan, NY
Ranking Minority Member
Max Baucus, MT
John Rockefeller, WV
John Breaux, LA
Kent Conrad, ND
Bob Graham, FL
Carol Moseley-Braun, IL
J. Robert Kerrey, NE

KEY MAJORITY STAFF:

Grant Aldonas
Chief International Trade Counsel
219 Dirksen Senate Office Bldg.
224-4515

Personal: born 2/6/55 in Minneapolis, Minn.

Education: B.A., Univ. of Minn., 1975. J.D., Univ. of Minn. Law School, 1979.

Professional: Foreign service officer. special asst. to the under sec. of state for economic affairs, U.S. Dept. of State. partner, Miller & Chevalier. 1997-present, chief international trade counsel, Senate Cmte. on Finance.

Expertise: International trade

As the chief international trade counsel for the Senate Finance Committee, Grant Aldonas is responsible for overseeing a multitude of trade issues. This year, he is helping the panel craft its version of a free trade bill with Africa based on liberalized textile trade. To reach his goal, Aldonas must strike a compromise between the domestic industry, which fears it will lose its share of the domestic market if quotas and duties in Africa are eliminated and Asian textile and apparel powerhouses ship illicitly to the U.S. through Africa, and those who want to open Africa to trade instead of aid.

Aldonas is also working on a bill that would broaden trade privileges to Caribbean Basin countries through benefits similar to those given Mexico under the North American Free Trade Agreement. A version of Caribbean parity was defeated last November by the House, but advocates of the plan in the Senate, including Majority Leader Trent Lott, R-Miss., are insistent it become law this year.

Also on the 1998 agenda is a plan to extend duty-free treatment to exports from developing countries under the Generalized System of Preferences. Aldonas predicts the three initiatives could be packaged as one trade bill this year.

Aldonas also is responsible for the committee's oversight of the Office of the U.S. Trade Representative, the Department of Commerce's Bureau of Import Administration, the U.S. Customs Service, and the International Trade Commission.

Aldonas came to the Finance Committee with a wealth of experience. While a partner with the Washington, D.C. law firm, Miller &

Chevalier, he specialized in international trade, investment, and litigation. During that tenure he served concurrently as counsel to the bipartisan Commission on Entitlement and Tax Reform and as an advisor to the commission on U.S. Pacific Trade and Investment Policy. Until joining the committee, Aldonas chaired the American Bar Association's Task Force on Multilateral Investment Agreements, and previously served as vice chair of the ABA international section's trade committee and its committee on foreign investment in the U.S.

Aldonas also served in government as a foreign service officer. His assignments included stints as a special assistant to the under secretary of state for economic affairs, where he was responsible for trade and monetary issues, and as director for South American and Caribbean affairs in the office of the U.S. Trade Representative. There, he was responsible for implementation of the Caribbean Basin Initiative and negotiation of trade and investment agreements with Latin America.

He has authored numerous articles on international trade, investment, and related topics.

Faryaz Shirzad
International Trade Counsel
219 Dirksen Senate Office Bldg.
224-4515

KEY MINORITY STAFF:

Deborah Lamb
Chief Minority Trade Counsel
203 Hart Senate Office Bldg.
224-5315

Personal: born 5/31/53 in Missoula, Mont.

Education: B.A., Lewis and Clark Coll. (Portland, Ore.), 1975. M.A., Johns Hopkins School of Advanced Intl. Studies, 1977. J.D., Georgetown Univ., 1988.

Professional: 1978-88, International Trade Administration, U.S. Dept. of Commerce. 1988-90, associate, Steptoe and Johnson. 1990-94, trade counsel; 1995-96, minority trade counsel; 1996-present, chief minority trade counsel, Senate Cmte. on Finance Committee.

Expertise: Trade

A variety of trade issues confronts the Senate Finance Committee this year. Chief minority trade counsel Deborah Lamb predicts she will assist the committee in what has become an annual extension of China's most-favored-nation trade status. In addition, she will work on an extension of the generalized system of preferences (GSP), which gives duty-free treatment to exports from third world countries with the exception of textiles and apparel. GSP is favored by U.S. importers, and because of budget constraints, has joined the ranks of benefits requiring annual review.

In addition, some Senate Finance Committee members are anxious to expand trade benefits to Caribbean Basin countries equivalent to

those given Mexico under the North American Free Trade Agreement. The House failed to pass such an expansion last year, but Senate backers of the plan remain undeterred.

A bill to grant qualifying Sub-Saharan Africa countries free trade privileges also is expected to come before the committee, and could become the vehicle for the other trade initiatives, Lamp said. It also could provide a ride to an expansion of trade adjustment assistance programs set to expire Sept. 30. The programs provide job training for workers displaced by U.S. trade policies. While President Clinton has proposed tripling funding, Lamb doubts the additional money can be delivered before the programs are reauthorized.

While prospects for the administration's fast-track negotiating authority are not good this year, Lamb said the committee could offer a forum for critics to air their grievances in an attempt to build consensus. Many congressional Democrats criticized the negotiating authority plan offered by the administration last year because it did not include labor and environmental standards as negotiating requirements. Republicans insisted they be omitted because they are considered trade barriers.

The Asian economic crisis does not fall under the committee's jurisdiction, but could be considered if the Asian economies of Thailand, South Korea, and Indonesia close their markets to U.S. exports as they attempt to increase their exports to the U.S. Lamb said committee Democrats want to ensure that the International Monetary Fund bailout does not end up benefitting foreign manufacturers who compete with U.S. makers.

Lamb is a veteran trade analyst with a particular understanding of Asian issues. She joined the committee in 1990 after stints in the private sector and executive branch. Lamb spent 10 years at the Commerce Department, holding a number of positions. She was regional economist in the agency's International Trade Administration's Bureau of East-West Trade from 1978-82, and bureau director for Korea and Taiwan from 1982-88. Lamb's tenure on the Hill includes contributions to NAFTA and GATT.

Committee on Foreign Relations

450 Dirksen Senate Office Building / Washington, D.C. 20510
202/224-4651   Fax: 202/224-0836

MAJORITY MEMBERS:

Jesse Helms, NC
Chairman
Richard Lugar, IN
Paul Coverdell, GA
Chuck Hagel, NE
Gordon Smith, OR
Craig Thomas, WY
Rod Grams, MN
John Ashcroft, MO
Bill Frist, TN
Sam Brownback, KS

MINORITY MEMBERS:

Joseph Biden, DE
Ranking Minority Member
Paul Sarbanes, MD
Christopher Dodd, CT
John Kerry, MA
Charles Robb, VA
Russell Feingold, WI
Dianne Feinstein, CA
Paul Wellstone, MN

Jurisdiction: (1) Acquisitions of land and buildings for embassies and legations of foreign countries. (2) Boundaries of the United States. (3) Diplomatic service. (4) Foreign economic, military, technical, and humanitarian assistance. (5) Foreign loans. (6) International activities of the American National Red Cross and the International Committee on the Red Cross. (7) International aspects of nuclear energy, including nuclear transfer policy. (8) International conferences and congresses. (9) International law as it relates to foreign policy. (10) International Monetary Fund and other international organizations established primarily for international monetary purposes (except that, at the request of the Committee on Banking, Housing, and Urban Affairs). (11) Intervention abroad and declarations of war. (12) Measures to foster commercial intercourse with foreign nations and to safeguard American business interests abroad. (13) National security and international aspects of trusteeships of the United States. (14) Oceans and international environmental and scientific affairs as they relate to foreign policy. (15) Protection of United States citizens abroad and expatriation. (16) Relations of the United States with foreign nations generally. (17) Treaties and executive agreements, except reciprocal trade agreements. (18) United Nations and its affiliated organizations. (19) World Bank group, the regional development banks, and other international organizations established primarily for development assistance purposes.

Such committee shall also study and review, on a comprehensive basis, matters relating to the national security policy, foreign policy, and international economic policy as it relates to foreign policy of the United States, and matters relating to food, hunger, and nutrition in foreign countries, and report thereon from time to time.

KEY MAJORITY STAFF:

James "Bud" Nance
Staff Director
447 Dirksen Senate Office Bldg.
224-4651

Personal: born 10/20/21 in Monroe, N.C.

Education: B.S., U.S. Naval Academy, 1944. Postgraduate: Naval War Coll., 1958; Nat'l War Coll., 1967. M.S., George Washington Univ., 1967.

Professional: 1944, commanding ensign, U.S. Navy. 1967-69, commanding officer, U.S.S. Raleigh, U.S.S. Forrestal. 1970-72, dep. dir., Nat. Mil. Command Center, Joint Chiefs of Staff. 1972-73, dep. chief of staff, Supreme Allied Comdr., Atlantic. 1973-75, dep. chief of staff to cmdr. in chief, U.S. European Command. 1975-79, asst. vice chief of naval ops.; dir, naval admin., U.S. Dept. of Navy (Wash., D.C.). 1979-81, special counsel for SALT, Senate Cmte. on Foreign Relations. 1981-83, deputy assistant to the President, National Security Council. 1992-95, minority staff director; 1995-present, staff director, Senate Cmte. on Foreign Relations.

Expertise: Foreign affairs, military

James "Bud" Nance came back to the Senate Foreign Relations Committee during the summer of 1997 after recuperating from an auto accident, which occurred in late 1996. Nance has been majority staff director of the committee since 1995.

This year, Nance is coordinating committee activities on NATO treaty expansion, U.S. dependence on foreign oil, the Asian financial crisis, and the on-going issue of U.N. arrears. Another committee priority is whether to authorize $18 billion to replenish funding for the International Monetary Fund. According to Nance, the committee will probably authorize about $3.5 billion and "we'll fight about the rest."

Early this year, the committee addressed the land mine issue. Chairman Jesse Helms, R-N.C., opposes efforts to prohibit the U.S. from using "smart mines," which automatically deactivate after 20 hours. Nance said that these mines are essential to preserve American lives. Helms opposes the land mines used by China and North Korea, which do kill civilians because they do not deactivate automatically, according to Nance.

Last year was a busy one for the committee, which cleared 127 ambassadors and at least 25 treaties, including tax and criminal extradition treaties. According to Nance, the committee will probably consider nominations for 60 ambassadorships in 1998. In addition, the committee will also deal with 20 mutual legal assistance and extradition treaties.

Nance is an Annapolis graduate and had a career as a naval aviator. After retiring form the Navy with the rank of rear admiral in 1979, he served as a special consultant to the Senate Foreign Relations Committee during the SALT II deliberations. In the early 1980s, he served in the Reagan White House as deputy assistant for national security affairs. From 1983 to 1990, he worked for Boeing Military Airplanes as head of the company's Naval Systems Division. He returned to the Foreign Relations Committee as Republican staff director in 1991.

Nance joined the foreign relations staff in 1991 as a favor to long-time friend Helms. The 76-year-old Nance has known Helms since their childhood together in the small town of Monroe, N.C. Nance, at the request of Helms, "cleaned the place out" and rebuilt the entire staff. As a result, nine of 22 staffers were dismissed, including the staff director and chief counsel.

Christopher J. Walker
Professional Staff Member
451 Dirksen Senate Office Bldg.
224-4651

Personal: born 1/24/64 in Boston, Mass.

Education: B.A. in political science, Texas Christian Univ., 1986.

Professional: 1986-88, leg. asst., Rep. Mickey Edwards, R-Okla. 1988-92, associate staff for Rep. Edwards, subc. on foreign operations; 1992-93, associate staff for Rep. Frank Wolf, R-Va., House Cmte. on Appropriations. 1993-94, minority professional staff member; 1995-present, professional staff member, Senate Cmte. on Foreign Relations.

Expertise: Foreign affairs, international operations

In 1997, professional staff member Christopher Walker focused on foreign aid issues. In the second session, he is covering international operations for the committee.

A committee priority in this session is enactment of a bill to reorganize U.S. foreign affairs agencies and comprehensive reform of the United Nations. This bill is in conference and is likely to be enacted, pending agreement on a international family planning provision.

"Passage of this legislation is at the top of Chairman (Jesse) Helms' (R-N.C.) agenda for the 105th Congress," Walker said. "We are optimistic that under the leadership of Secretary Albright, the administration will take a fresh look at reorganization and that a bipartisan consensus can be reached."

In the 104th Congress, Walker was deeply involved in the committee's efforts to enact legislation to streamline and reorganize the nation's foreign policy apparatus. The bill, ultimately vetoed by President Clinton, sought to consolidate the foreign policy bureaucracy and achieve significant cost savings, Walker said.

"There has been much debate in Washington about the budget constraints on foreign affairs spending," Walker said, "but when Congress presented the president with legislation that would have achieved nearly $2 billion in bureaucratic savings, money that could have been redirected to payment of U.N. arrears or for security assistance, the president's advisers convinced him to veto it."

As delicate negotiations for Middle East peace continue, U.S. aid to Israel and Egypt will likely remain under scrutiny. Walker has said previously that Helms is reluctant to reduce aid to Israel, the biggest recipient of American assistance, because doing so may make the nation appear weak. Cutting aid could be seen by terrorists as a way to "blow the peace process apart," Walker said.

Walker is no stranger to foreign aid battles. In 1988, he staffed Rep. Mickey Edwards, R-Okla., on the subcommittee on foreign operations of the House Appropriations Committee. At that time, Egyptian debt relief and Israeli loan guarantees were the subjects of repeated legislative skirmishes between Edwards and Rep. David R. Obey, D-Wis., the subcommittee's liberal chairman.

Andrew K. Semmel
Legislative Assistant
Sen. Richard Lugar, R-Ind.
306 Hart Senate Office Bldg.
224-7441

Personal: born in Palmerton, Pa.

Education: B.A., Moravian Coll. M.A., Ohio Univ. Ph.D., Univ. of Mich.

Professional: 1971-79, associate professor of political science, Univ. of Cincinnati. 1979-81, faculty fellow under Intergovernmental

Personnel Act at International Security Affairs, U.S. Dept. of Defense. 1981-84, foreign affairs specialist; 1984-85, chief, analysis division, plans directorate, Defense Security Assistance Agency, U.S. Dept. of Defense. 1985-87, professional staff member, Senate Cmte. on Foreign Relations. 1987-present, leg. asst., Sen. Richard G. Lugar, R-Ind.

Expertise: Foreign affairs, national security

During the first session of the 105th Congress, Andrew Semmel, legislative assistant for foreign policy to Sen. Richard Lugar, R-Ind., worked on issues involving the Bosnian peace process, U.N. arrears and reform, international exchange and public diplomacy, the international affairs budget and appropriations, Central Asia, and the Persian Gulf.

Lugar pays close attention to the problems in Bosnia, Semmel said. Specifically, he advocates programs to promote economic growth in the region and regularly makes speeches and writes letters to President Clinton regarding Bosnia. Last year a Lugar amendment to appropriations legislation restored $30 million in funding for the National Endowment for Democracy, which provides action grants to groups abroad working to promote open markets and pluralism around the world. In 1997, Semmel also concentrated on foreign assistance legislation and the foreign relations authorization bill.

A big priority for Lugar in 1998 is sanctions reform. He has a sanctions policy reform bill, which establishes procedures to make U.S. consideration of the use of unilateral sanctions more deliberative. Lugar is also the principal sponsor of the Africa Growth and Opportunity Act, which promotes trade in Sub-Saharan Africa.

Bilateral relations with China and Japan are also important to Lugar. He also believes the U.S. can play a role in preventing nuclear proliferation on the Korean peninsula. In 1998, the committee will hold hearings on this issue. The committee will also closely watch the Asian financial crisis, according to Semmel. Lugar strongly supports free trade for the Americas and fast-track negotiating authority for the president on trade issues.

As foreign policy advisor to Lugar, Semmel gives many speeches in both the U.S. and abroad. On a 1996 speaking tour in China, he addressed groups on U.S. foreign policy, the U.S. presidential election, and U.S.-Sino policy.

Semmel, a former associate professor of political science at the University of Cincinnati, has served on Lugar's personal staff since 1987. He also worked two years as a professional staff member on the Foreign Relations Committee. As a committee staff member, his credits include coordinating the world-wide security assistance and arms export program.

Danielle M. Pletka
Sr. Professional Staff Member
450 Dirksen Senate Office Bldg.
224-4651

Personal: born 6/12/63 in Melbourne, Australia.

Education: B.A., Smith College, 1984. M.A., Johns Hopkins University School of Advanced International Studies, 1987.

Professional: 1984-85, editorial asst., Los Angeles Times. 1987-92, staff writer, Insight magazine. 1992-95, minority professional staff member; 1995-present, majority professional staff member, Senate Cmte. on Foreign Relations.

Expertise: Near Eastern and South Asian affairs

Professional staff member Danielle Pletka hit the ground running in 1998, working on Iraq and Iran issues. Specifically, she dealt with congressional attempts to pressure the Clinton administration to find "medium to long-term" solutions to the Iraqi problem. She is also working on issues related to potential military action against Iraq.

Iran elected a new president in 1997, which changed the Iranian political landscape. Pletka is studying this situation to see whether any changes for U.S. policy develop. Specifically, the bottom line is whether the Iranians continue to support terrorism, pursue development of weapons of mass destruction, and demonstrate hatred for Israel, according to Pletka. How the administration approaches the question of European and Russian investment in Iranian oil is also an important issue for committee members.

Although many in Congress believe that companies investing in Iranian oil should be sanctioned, the administration has not taken a firm position, Pletka said. In 1998, the issue will come up in talks with the Europeans; Russia and France are "particular problems," she added.

Foreign Relations Committee Chairman Jesse Helms, R-N.C., believes that it is important to persuade the administration not to pressure the Israelis and the Palestinians in the Middle East peace process. Because peace will be between Israel and other parties, and not the U.S., Helms believes the U.S. cannot force the countries involved to do things they are not prepared to do, Pletka said.

The committee will be working on foreign aid issues this year. In 1998, Israel approached the U.S. with a request for a 50 percent reduction in the amount of economic assistance they receive each year.

In 1997, committee members worked on issues including sanctioning terrorist states, the Middle East peace process, Palestinian aid, and the proliferation of weapons of mass destruction.

Pletka, a native of Melbourne, Australia, has served on the committee staff since 1992. She is married to Stephen Rademaker, majority chief counsel to the House International Relations Committee.

Steve Biegun
Professional Staff Member
450 Dirksen Senate Office Bldg.
224-4651

Personal: born 3/30/63 in Detroit, Mich.

Education: B.A., Univ. of Mich., 1986.

Professional: 1986-92, professional staff member, House Cmte. on Foreign Affairs. 1992-94, resident program officer, International Republican Institute (Moscow, Russia). 1995-present, professional staff member, Senate Cmte. on Foreign Relations.

Expertise: Europe, Central Asia, and the South Caucasus

Steve Biegun has a dual role in his position as professional staff member. He serves Republican members of the Senate Foreign Relations Committee and also members of the Subcommittee on European Affairs. In 1997, Biegun organized seven hearings for the full committee on the issue of NATO expansion.

"The goal was to review all elements and implications [of NATO expansion] and we wanted to be thorough," Biegun said. A ratification debate on NATO expansion should occur this spring.

A priority for Chairman Jesse Helms, R-NC, is to accept Poland, Hungary, and the Czech Republic into the NATO alliance, while limiting Russia's ability to interfere with NATO decision making, Biegun said. The chairman's other priority with respect to NATO is to ensure that it remains "a strong militarily defensive alliance with an evenly shared cost burden among members," he added.

As the year unfolds, Helms intends to keep pressure on the Clinton administration to ensure that U.S. troops are withdrawn from Bosnia as rapidly as possible. According to Biegun, the situation is relatively stable and U.S. troops cannot be tied down to one region of the world. Helms wants to ensure that the U.S. security commitment to Europe, which has stable democracies, does not come at the expense of U.S. security interests in Asia and the Persian Gulf.

In 1998, Helms intends to press the European Union "to pursue a foreign policy based, first and foremost, on shared principles of democracy and human rights, rather than responding to the mainly economic interests of its membership," Biegun said.

In his tenure as senior professional staff member for European Affairs, Biegun has visited nearly every country in Europe and the former Soviet Union. He is responsible for all matters pertaining to U.S. foreign policy in this region.

Biegun meets with foreign embassy representatives and attends briefings with administration officials who are responsible for foreign policy. These briefings enable Biegun to assist the committee in its oversight function of U.S. foreign policy. He also serves as the liaison between congressional and embassy staffers to ensure that policy initiatives are properly understood.

G. Garrett Grigsby
Senior Professional Staff Member
450 Dirksen Senate Office Bldg.
224-4651

Personal: born 9/1/63 in Nashville, Tenn.

Education: B.A., Hanover College, 1985. Graduate work at the School of International Service, American Univ., 1988-90

Professional: 1985-88, account executive, Miami Systems Corporation (Nashville, Tenn.). 1988-91, purchasing mgr./ account assistant, Bruce W. Eberle and Associates (Vienna, Va.). 1991-96, prof. staff member; 1996-97, professional staff member, subc. on Africa; Aug. 1997-present, senior professional staff member, Senate Cmte. on Foreign Relations.

Expertise: Foreign aid, international population and abortion issues, religious persecution, international trade promotion

After serving in various positions with the Senate Foreign Relations Committee over the last six years, G. Garrett Grigsby was promoted to senior professional staff member in August 1997. In this capacity, he is directly responsible to Chairman Jesse Helms, R-N.C., for committee initiatives and oversight of U.S. foreign aid programs, including the World Bank and the International Monetary Fund (IMF), international population control policy and abortion, international trade promotion programs, international petroleum issues, and religious persecution abroad.

In 1998, the committee will conduct oversight hearings of U.S. bilateral foreign aid programs. Another priority this year is the Clinton administration's plan to deal with the Asian financial crisis.

Specifically, the committee will examine the use of the IMF's New Arrangements to Borrow facility, bilateral U.S. assistance, and the $14.5 billion IMF quota increase. The committee expects to be an important forum to consider reform at the IMF and will examine whether reform should be a condition of congressional approval of the proposed quota increase.

After six years in the private sector, Grigsby joined the committee in 1991. Initially, his committee responsibilities included arms control, Latin America, and protecting U.S. citizens' rights abroad. Grigsby drafted speeches, legislation, amendments, and reports.

Several reports that he wrote or co-wrote for the committee include "Nicaragua Today" (August 1992), "The Haiti Crisis" (December 1993), "Issues Regarding Senate Ratification of the Chemical Weapons Convention" (December 1994), and "Sudan Today: Prospects for Peace and Democracy" (February 1998).

In 1996, Grigsby was promoted to professional staff member for the subcommittee on Africa. During his tenure with the panel, Grigsby has traveled extensively to Europe, Africa, and Latin America on fact-finding missions.

Grigsby was educated at Hanover College and American University. He has been in his current post since 1991.

KEY MINORITY STAFF:

Edwin K. Hall
Minority Staff Director
439 Dirksen Senate Office Bldg.
224-3953

Personal: born 6/8/41 in Providence, R.I.

Education: B.A., Harvard Coll., 1964. J.D., Univ. of Mich. Law School, 1967.

Professional: 1967-69, associate, Boston law firm. 1969-72, U.S. Attorney's Office (Wash., D.C.). 1972-75, partner, Providence law firm. 1975-78, chief counsel, subc. on privileges and elections, Senate Cmte. on Rules. 1978-82, general counsel, Senate Cmte. on Commerce. 1982-84, dir. of public affairs and congressional relations, Office of Technology Assessment. 1984-86, partner, law firm (Salmon,

Idaho). 1986-91, vice president, government relations, MCI Communications Corp. 1991-95, chief counsel; 1995-97, minority staff director/chief counsel; 1997-present, minority staff director, Senate Cmte. on Foreign Relations.

Expertise: Foreign affairs

Senator Joseph Biden, D-Del., is now in his second session as the ranking member of the Senate Foreign Relations Committee. Ed Hall, minority staff director of the committee, is primarily responsible for overseeing the minority agenda.

In 1998, one of Biden's priorities for the committee is to enlarge NATO to include the Czech Republic, Hungary, and Poland. Legislation to implement the Chemicals Weapons Convention, a nuclear safety convention, protocols to the Conventional Weapons Convention, and ratification of the Comprehensive Test Ban Treaty are also priorities, according to Hall.

The highest committee priorities are IMF funding, repaying the U.S. back dues to the U.N., U.N. reform, and authorizing legislation for the State Department, the U.S. Information Agency, the Arms Control and Disarmament Agency, and the Agency for International Development. Legislation to restructure U.S. foreign affairs agencies is also a focus in this session. U.S. efforts to combat international narcotics and terrorism will also be major issues for Biden.

Hall, a native of Providence, R.I., has been back and forth to Washington many times throughout his professional career. He first came to the nation's capital in 1969 as an assistant to the U.S. Attorney for the District of Columbia. He later returned to Rhode Island, but returned to Washington in 1975 to serve as chief counsel to the subcommittee on privileges and elections of the Senate Rules Committee.

Nine years later, Hall left Capitol Hill again, this time to work as a rural lawyer and county prosecutor in Salmon, Idaho, a town with a population of 3,000. In 1986, the lure to come back to Washington was too great to resist when MCI Communications Corp. offered him a job as vice president for government relations. Five years later, he returned as staff director and chief counsel of the Foreign Relations Committee.

Hall is an alumnus of the University of Michigan Law School and Harvard College.

Dr. Michael H. Haltzel
Minority Professional Staff Member
439 Dirksen Senate Office Bldg.
224-3953

Personal: born 3/28/41 in New York, N.Y.

Education: B.A. (magna cum laude), Yale Univ., 1963. M.A., Ph.D., Harvard Univ., 1966, 1971.

Professional: 1971-75, professor., Hamilton College (N.Y.). 1975-

78, deputy director, Aspen Institute (West Berlin, Germany). 1980-82, associate, Russell Reynolds Associates (New York City). 1982-84, vice president for academic affairs, Longwood College (Va.). 1985-92, director of West European Studies, Woodrow Wilson International Center for Scholars, Smithsonian Institution. 1992-94, chief of the European division, Library of Congress. 1994-present, minority professional staff member, Senate Cmte. on Foreign Relations.

Expertise: Foreign affairs, Western Europe and Eastern Europe, territories of the former Soviet Union

As a minority professional staff member for the Foreign Relations Committee, Michael Haltzel assists ranking member Sen. Joseph R. Biden, Jr., D- Del., on a variety of legislative initiatives. Haltzel is also Biden's senior foreign policy advisor. His responsibilities include drafting foreign affairs legislation, preparing for hearings and mark-ups, and representing the committee in the U.S. and abroad.

Haltzel, who has held his position since 1994, is an historian who has published extensive works on the Baltic provinces of tsarist Russia and on international affairs. He joined the committee staff after holding senior positions at the Library of Congress and the Woodrow Wilson International Center for Scholars at the Smithsonian Institution.

With a reputation for bipartisanship, Haltzel collaborated last year with the Republicans on two important vehicles for NATO enlargement. Beginning in the spring of 1997, he worked with Ian Brzezinski, Sen. William Roth's, R-Del., European foreign policy aide, on organizing the Senate NATO Observer Group, which is co-chaired by Roth and Biden. The group carried out a wide variety of briefings and meetings for its 28 senators and their European affairs staffers, including meetings with President Clinton and a delegation to the NATO summit in Madrid in July.

Last fall, the Foreign Relations Committee also held a widely acclaimed series of hearings on NATO enlargement, which Haltzel helped plan and direct.

In the second session, the committee is expected to give quick consideration to the Protocols of Accession of the Czech Republic, Hungary, and Poland to NATO, in the form of an amendment to the Treaty of Washington of April 4, 1949. Haltzel, a strong supporter of enlargement, predicts the amendment would clear the committee by a large majority and be debated on the floor.

Haltzel, who has focused on Bosnia for several years, accompanied Biden on a trip throughout the Muslim-Croat Federation and the Republika Srpska during the 1997 summer recess. Biden has been a highly visible advocate of continued U.S. participation in the international peacekeeping force in Bosnia. This session, Haltzel will continue to help the senator on NATO enlargement and a supplemental appropriation for U.S. forces in Bosnia and Herzegovina after June 1998.

In September 1996, Haltzel served as an official international monitor for the elections in Bosnia and Herzegovina, carried out by the Organization for Security and Cooperation in Europe. In 1990, he was a member of the U.S. delegation to the Copenhagen Conference on the Human Dimension of the Conference on Security and Cooperation in Europe.

Haltzel is fluent in German and has a good working knowledge of Russian. Although he has had many diverse professional experiences, Haltzel considers his current post "the most interesting job in Washington."

Subcommittee on African Affairs

450 Dirksen Senate Office Building
Washington, D.C. 20510-6225
202/224-4651

MAJORITY MEMBERS:

John Ashcroft, MO
Chairman
Rod Grams, MN
Bill Frist, TN

MINORITY MEMBERS:

Russell Feingold, WI
Ranking Minority Member
Paul Sarbanes, MD

Jurisdiction: (1) Geographic responsibilities corresponding to those of the Bureau of in the Department of State; (2) All matters and problems relating to all of Africa, with the exception of the countries bordering on the Mediterranean Sea from Egypt to Morocco, which are under the purview of the Subcommittee on Near Eastern and South Asian Affairs; (3) The subcommittee's responsibilities include all matters, problems, and policies involving promotion of U.S. trade and export; terrorism, crime, and the flow of illegal drugs; and oversight over U.S. foreign assistance programs that fall within the subcommittee's regional jurisdiction.

Subcommittee on European Affairs

450 Dirksen Senate Office Building
Washington, D.C. 20510-6225
202/224-4651

MAJORITY MEMBERS:

Gordon Smith, OR
Chairman
Richard Lugar, IN
John Ashcroft, MO
Chuck Hagel, NE
Craig Thomas, WY

MINORITY MEMBERS:

Joseph Biden, DE
Ranking Minority Member
Paul Wellstone, MN
Paul Sarbanes, MD
Christopher Dodd, CT

Jurisdiction: Matters concerning: (1) The continent of Europe, including the Soviet Union, Greece and Turkey; (2) The United Kingdom, Greenland, Iceland, and the north polar region; (3) The subcommittee's responsibilities include all matters, problems, and policies involving promotion of U.S. trade and export; terrorism, crime, and the flow of illegal drugs; and oversight over U.S. foreign assistance programs that fall within the subcommittee's regional jurisdiction.

Subcommittee on East Asian & Pacific Affairs

450 Dirksen Senate Office Building
Washington, D.C. 20510-6225
202/224-4651

MAJORITY MEMBERS:

Craig Thomas, WY
Chairman
Bill Frist, TN
Richard Lugar, IN
Paul Coverdell, GA
Chuck Hagel, NE

©Almanac Publishing, Inc. 1998 - The Washington Almanac of International Trade & Business

MINORITY MEMBERS:

John Kerry, MA
Ranking Minority Member
Charles Robb, VA
Russell Feingold, WI
Dianne Feinstein, CA

Jurisdiction: (1) Matters extending geographically from China and Mongolia to Burma, inclusive, on the mainland of Asia; and to Hong Kong, Japan, the Philippines, Malaysia, Indonesia, Australia and New Zealand, Oceania, and the South Pacific Islands; (2) Trusteeship matters in the Pacific region. (3) The subcommittee's responsibilities include all matters, problems, and policies involving promotion of U.S. trade and export; terrorism, crime, and the flow of illegal drugs; and oversight over U.S. foreign assistance programs that fall within the subcommittee's regional jurisdiction.

Subcommittee on International Economic Policy, Export & Trade Promotion

450 Dirksen Senate Office Building
Washington, D.C. 20510-6225
202/224-4651

MAJORITY MEMBERS:

Chuck Hagel, NE
Chairman
Craig Thomas, WY
Bill Frist, TN
Paul Coverdell, GA

MINORITY MEMBERS:

Paul Sarbanes, MD
Ranking Minority Member
Joseph Biden, DE
Paul Wellstone, MN

Jurisdiction: Responsibilities relating directly to U.S. foreign economic policy and encompassing these primary areas: (1) Intern'l. monetary policy, including U.S. participation in the Intern'l. Monetary Fund and other intern'l. economic organizations; (2) Intern'l. trade policy, including intern'l. energy policy, raw material supply policy, and economic relations with Communist countries; (3) U.S. policies, programs, and participation in intern'l.institutions and organizations concerned with economic growth and development, or the transfer of economic resources, directly or indirectly, to less developed countries; (4) Intern'l. investment, management and technological transfer and general commercial policies to include the overseas operations of U.S. business firms; (5) Measures to foster commercial intercourse with foreign nations and to safeguard American business interests abroad; (6) Matters involving the use, development and exploitation of oceans, space and the intern'l. environment, as well as intern'l. marine affairs generally, including the Antarctic and Arctic areas.

Subcommittee on International Operations

450 Dirksen Senate Office Building
Washington, D.C. 20510-6225
202/224-4651

MAJORITY MEMBERS:

Rod Grams, MN
Chairman
Jesse Helms, NC
Sam Brownback, KS
Gordon Smith, OR

MINORITY MEMBERS:

Dianne Feinstein, CA
Ranking Minority Member
Christopher Dodd, CT
John Kerry, MA

Jurisdiction: All matters, problems and policies involving international operations, terrorism, and the international flow of illegal drugs, including: (1) The oversight of all U.S. foreign policy, programs and international cooperative efforts to combat international terrorism; (2) The oversight of all U.S. foreign policy, programs, and international cooperative efforts to combat the illegal flow of illegal drugs or substances; (3) The general oversight responsibility for the Department of State, the United States Information Agency, the Foreign Service, international educational and cultural affairs, foreign broadcasting activities, foreign buildings, U.S. participation in the United Nations, and other international organizations not under the jurisdiction of other subcommittees. In addition, the subcommittee has jurisdiction over general matters of international law, law enforcement, and illegal activities.

Subc. on Near Eastern & South Asian Affairs

450 Dirksen Senate Office Building
Washington, D.C. 20510-6225
202/224-4651

MAJORITY MEMBERS:

Sam Brownback, KS
Chairman
Gordon Smith, OR
Rod Grams, MN
Jesse Helms, NC
John Ashcroft, MO

MINORITY MEMBERS:

Charles Robb, VA
Ranking Minority Member
Dianne Feinstein, CA
Paul Wellstone, MN
Paul Sarbanes, MD

Jurisdiction: (1) All matters and problems relating to the Middle East and Arab North Africa including Arab-Israeli and inter-Arab issues, economic relations, and general security in the Persian Gulf, Mediterranean, the Middle East and North Africa; (2) Matters and problems relating to Afghanistan, Bangladesh, Bhutan, India, the Maldives, Nepal, Pakistan, and Sri Lanka; (3) The subcommittee's responsibilities include all matters, problems, and policies involving promotion of U.S. trade and export; terrorism, crime, and the flow of illegal drugs; and oversight over U.S. foreign assistance programs that fall within the subcommittee's regional jurisdiction.

Subcommittee on Western Hemisphere, Peace Corps, Narcotics & Terrorism

450 Dirksen Senate Office Building
Washington, D.C. 20510-6225
202/224-4651

MAJORITY MEMBERS:

Paul Coverdell, GA
Chairman
Jesse Helms, NC
Richard Lugar, IN
Sam Brownback, KS

MINORITY MEMBERS:

Christopher Dodd, CT
Ranking Minority Member
John Kerry, MA
Charles Robb, VA

Jurisdiction: (1) Matters extending geographically from the Arctic Ocean to Tierra del Fuego, including the Caribbean. Problems which are of concern to the subcommittee include relations between the American nations, U.S.-Canadian affairs, boundary matters, the implementation of various treaties and conventions, economic relations and security matters affecting the Western Hemisphere, and the Organization of American States; (2) The subcommittee's responsibilities include all matters, problems, and policies involving promotion of U.S. trade and export; crime; and oversight of U.S. foreign assistance programs that fall within the subcommittee's regional jurisdiction; (3) The subcommittee also exercises general oversight over all activities of the Peace Corps; all U.S. foreign policy, programs, and international cooperative efforts to combat the flow of illegal drugs or substances; and all U.S. foreign policy, programs, and cooperative efforts to combat international terrorism.

Committee on the Judiciary

Subcommittee on Immigration

323 Dirksen Senate Office Building
Washington, D.C. 20510
202/224-6098

MAJORITY MEMBERS:

Spencer Abraham, MI
Chairman
Charles Grassley, IA
Jon Kyl, AZ
Arlen Specter, PA

MINORITY MEMBERS:

Edward Kennedy, MA
Ranking Minority Member
Dianne Feinstein, CA
Richard Durbin, IL

KEY MAJORITY STAFF:

Lee Liberman Otis
Chief Counsel and Staff Director
Subcommittee on Immigration
323 Dirksen Senate Office Bldg.
224-6098

Personal: born 8/19/56 in New York City, N.Y.

Education: B.A., Yale College, 1979. J.D., University of Chicago, 1983.

Professional: 1983-84, law clerk, Judge Antonin Scalia, U.S. Court of Appeals for the District of Columbia. 1984-85, special assistant to the assistant attorney general, civil division, U.S. Department of Justice. 1985-86, associate deputy attorney general, U.S. Department of Justice. 1986-87, law clerk to Justice Antonin Scalia, U.S. Supreme Court. 1987-89, assistant professor of law, George Mason Univ. School of Law. 1989-93, associate counsel, President George Bush. 1993-94, associate, Jones, Day, Reavis and Pogue. 1995-96, chief judiciary counsel, Sen. Spencer Abraham, R-Mich. 1997- present, chief counsel and staff director, subc. on immigration, Senate Cmte. on the Judiciary.

Expertise: Immigration issues, constitutional law, federal courts

Lee Liberman Otis expects the subcommittee to hold oversight hearings on the Immigration and Naturalization Service this session. Specifically, the subcommittee will focus on reforming naturalization processes and will be examining citizenship testing fraud, she said.

Subcommittee Chairman Spencer Abraham, R-Mich., also wants to hold hearings on INS detention facilities to find out how asylum applicants held in the facilities are being treated, Otis said. Additionally, Abraham wants to look at the apparent failure of the INS to obtain sufficient detention space to hold deportable criminal aliens.

The subcommittee will consider legislation introduced by Abraham to amend Section 110 of the 1996 Illegal Immigration and Immigrant Responsibility Act. The section calls for INS to implement automated entry-exit control systems along the country's land borders. The systems are untested, Otis said, and "likely to wreak havoc" on the borders by interrupting the free flow of goods and services that enter the U.S. from Canada and Mexico. Abraham's bill would exclude land borders from any automated entry-exit system and require the INS to do a feasibility study of such systems.

In 1997, Otis worked on several provisions of the 1996 Immigration Act, including immigration relief for certain Central Americans who fled from civil wars in the 1980s. She also helped get permanent authority for a program that provides religious workers with special religious worker visas for entry to the U.S.

In 1996, Otis worked on several provisions in the 1996 Immigration Act, including establishing a penalty for people who overstay their visas and facilitating the deportation of those aliens who commit serious crimes in the U.S. She also oversaw all other Judiciary Committee issues for Abraham. She worked on several Abraham initiatives that became law. One such enactment blocked the U.S. Sentencing Commission's crack cocaine proposal to lower penalties for possession of the drug. Otis also worked on an amendment to the appropriations bill that placed limits on litigation brought by prisoners.

An attorney, Otis clerked for Judge Antonin Scalia during his service on the U.S. Court of Appeals and in the U.S. Supreme Court. She also worked in the civil division at the Department of Justice and as an associate counsel in the Bush White House. Prior to her work with Abraham in 1995, Otis worked at the law firm of Jones, Day, Reavis & Pogue in Washington, D.C.

KEY MINORITY STAFF:

J. Michael Myers
Minority Staff Director
Subcommittee on Immigration
520 Dirksen Senate Office Bldg.
224-7878

Personal: born 4/17/55 in Cleveland, Miss.

Education: B.A., Columbia Univ., 1979. M.A., Columbia Univ., 1981.

Professional: 1979-80, staff, U.N. High Commissioner for Refugees. 1980-86, Washington representative, Church World Service. 1987-93, counsel, subcommittee on immigration and refugee affairs and foreign policy advisor to Sen. Edward Kennedy, D-Mass. 1993-95, director of policy, office of humanitarian and refugee affairs, U.S. Dept. of Defense. 1995-96, minority special counsel on immigration; 1997-present, minority staff director, subcmte. on immigration, Senate Cmte. on the Judiciary.

Expertise: Immigration issues, international humanitarian affairs

In 1998, Michael Myers is working on several immigration bills and issues as well as civil rights legislation and the juvenile justice crime bill as minority staff director for Sen. Edward M. Kennedy, D-Mass., the subcommittee's ranking member.

Among the immigration measures Myers will be handling are a bill to promote naturalization and a bill to restore benefits, especially food stamps, to legal immigrants. Those benefits were taken away in the 1996 welfare reform legislation. Last year, Myers worked on legislation enacted and that restored SSI and Medicaid benefits to legal immigrants. He also worked on legislation in 1997 that prevented the deportation of about 300,000 Central American refugees.

The subcommittee also will be debating this session whether immigration rules should be relaxed for high technology workers, Myers said. The government is under pressure to let in more high-tech workers because of a growing shortage.

Kennedy is co-sponsoring a hate crimes bill with Sen. Arlen Specter, R-Pa., that expands the scope of hate crimes covered by federal law to include the disabled, gays, lesbians, and others. Myers said he also will be pushing for more resources for the EEOC and other civil rights agencies that have seen their caseloads increase faster than their budgets.

Kennedy expects to continue to fight for Bill Lan Lee's controversial nomination to head the civil rights post at the Justice Department, Myers said. Myers will also be helping Kennedy to make changes to the Republican leadership's juvenile crime bill. Myers said the senator wants to strengthen crime prevention measures and is particularly concerned about provisions that would permit juvenile offenders to be housed with adults. "The bills needs to be changed so it's a balance of enforcement and prevention," Myers said.

Myers rejoined the subcommittee as special counsel in 1995 at Kennedy's urging. He had been counsel to the subcommittee and a foreign policy advisor to Kennedy from 1987 to 1993. He left to become policy director for the Defense Department's Office of Humanitarian and Refugee Affairs. Kennedy convinced him to relinquish that post and return to Capitol Hill at a particularly divisive time and help him with the 1996 Illegal Immigration Act. Myers,

credited with a talent for bridging the aisle between Democrats and Republicans, became minority staff director last year.

Myers described his successes on the immigration bill as "preventive." Minority members were able to remove provisions that would have made things worse for legal immigrants and refugees. Efforts to reduce legal immigration were thwarted. Minority members also got some protections for refugees at ports of entry.

Myers grew up in Vietnam where his parents served as missionaries. He is fluent in Vietnamese.

Committee on Small Business

428A Russell Senate Office Building
Washington, D.C. 20510-6350
202/224-5175   Fax: 202/224-4885

MAJORITY MEMBERS:

Christopher Bond, MO
 Chairman
Conrad Burns, MT
Paul Coverdell, GA
Dirk Kempthorne, ID
Robert Bennett, UT
John Warner, VA
Bill Frist, TN
Olympia Snowe, ME
Lauch Faircloth, NC
Mike Enzi, WY

MINORITY MEMBERS:

John Kerry, MA
 Ranking Minority Member
Dale Bumpers, AR
Carl Levin, MI
Tom Harkin, IA
Joe Lieberman, CT
Paul Wellstone, MN
Max Cleland, GA
Mary Landrieu, LA

Jurisdiction: (1) All legislation referred to the committee; (2) Jurisdiction over all matters related to the Small Business Administration; (3) Study and survey, through research and investigation, of all problems of American small business enterprises.

KEY MAJORITY STAFF:

Louis Taylor
Staff Director and Chief Counsel
428-A Russell Senate Office Bldg.
224-5175

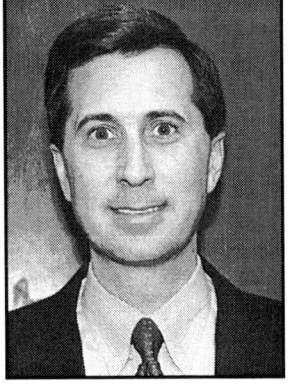

Personal: born 9/25/57 in Enid, Okla.

Education: B.A. (cum laude), Westminster College, 1979. J.D. (with honors), Univ. of Texas at Austin, 1982.

Professional: 1982-91, attorney, Locke Purnell Rain Harrell (Dallas, Texas). 1991-94, asst. general counsel/dir. government affairs and international trade, Leggett and Platt (Carthage, Mo.). 1995-present, staff director and chief counsel, Senate Cmte. on Small Business.

Expertise: Small business regulation and finance

Staff Director and Chief Counsel Louis Taylor expects to spend much of the second session of the 105th Congress on efforts to restructure the Internal Revenue Service and providing relief to small businesses on federal regulatory enforcement matters.

Republicans began targeting the IRS last year through hearings that detailed agency abuses. At the start of the second session, IRS Commissioner Charles O. Rossotti promised a "new day" for the agency, saying he will revamp the agency and peel away unnecessary management layers. Republicans remain skeptical, saying it takes too long for the agency to catch mistakes and that the current income tax system is too complex.

Taylor will be honing in on how restructuring changes affect small businesses. He said the committee will examine a bill approved by the House in the first session that restricts the agency and invests taxpayers with more power. The Senate Finance Committee is considering even more restrictive legislation.

Taylor will also work for "the full and effective" implementation of the committee's 1996 legislation that provided significant relief to small business on federal regulatory enforcement matters. Among other things, the law gives teeth to the 1980 Regulatory Flexibility Act so that small businesses can take federal agencies to court if they continue to ignore the act's requirement to consider ways to reduce the economic impact of new regulations. It also requires agencies to prepare clearly written compliance guides that will allow small business owners to comply with federal regulations without legal assistance.

The most significant accomplishment of the first session was reauthorization of the Small Business Administration for the next three years, with two major enhancements sought by committee Chairman Christopher "Kit" Bond, R-Mo.

Under the SBA act, a new program centering on HUBZones, which stands for Historically Unidentified Business Zones, was created. The program gives government contracting benefits to small businesses located in areas of high poverty and high unemployment if the businesses hire a significant percentage of local residents. The second part of the bill put limits on the practice of "bundling" contracts, which created contracts too large for small businesses to bid on.

Now in his fourth year as staff director, Taylor will continue to lead committee staffers in their broad mandate to study, investigate, and report on all problems of American small business enterprises. Taylor came to the committee's top staff post directly from the business world. After nearly a decade as an attorney in Dallas, he became assistant general counsel and director of governmental affairs and international trade for Leggett and Platt, a Missouri manufacturer of supplies and component parts for the furniture and bedding industries.

Paul Cooksey
Deputy Chief Counsel
428-A Russell Senate Office Bldg.
224-5175

Personal: born 8/13/48 in Tokyo, Japan.

Education: B.A., Hampden-Sydney College, 1970. J.D., George Mason Univ., 1981.

Professional: 1970-80, leg. asst., Sen. Richard S. Schweiker, R-Pa. 1980-81, v.p., government affairs, Cooksey Corp. 1981-83, congressional affairs, National Aeronautics and Space Administration. 1984, v.p. and gen. counsel, Dutko & Assoc. 1985-86, dep. asst. sec., U.S. Dept. of the Treasury. 1986-88, v.p. and gen. manager, Robinson, Lake, Lerer and Montgomery. 1988-91, v.p., Oliver Carr Co. 1991-92, deputy administrator, U.S. Small Business Administration. 1993-94, attorney, Goldman, Marshall & Muszynski. 1995-present, deputy chief counsel, Senate Cmte. on Small Business.

Expertise: Small Business Administration and related issues

Paul Cooksey, a former administrator at the Small Business Administration, provides a critical view of the SBA's mission and structure to Sen. Christopher Bond, R-Mo., chairman of the Senate Small Business Committee.

The focus of SBA has shifted with the reauthorization of the agency in the first session of the 105th Congress. The panel will monitor the progress of a new program aimed at replacing the less-than-successful federal enterprise zone program that gave tax breaks to businesses located in depressed areas. The HUBZones program, which stands for Historically Underutilized Business Zones, gives government contracting benefits to small businesses located in neighborhoods where there is high poverty, high unemployment, and where businesses hire many of their employees from local neighborhoods.

Another change brought about in the reauthorization of the SBA is limiting the practice of "bundling" contracts, a practice federal agencies used in the past to create large contracts that inadvertently shut out small businesses from bidding.

The committee is expecting big strides by the SBA after changing some of its loan programs and enhancing others. For instance, in 1999, the SBA will be expected to guarantee more than 56,000 long-term, low-interest loans, a 7 percent increase over 1998 levels. As an SBA expert, Cooksey will assist in the oversight of these changes at the agency.

During the 104th Congress, the committee passed two major pieces of legislative relief for small businesses, the Paperwork Reduction Act and the Small Business Regulatory Enforcement Fairness Act. Cooksey was involved as deputy counsel in the oversight of the two acts during the current session.

Cooksey has experience in both governmental bureaucracies and the private sector. He began his Hill career as a legislative assistant for former Sen. Richard S. Schweiker, R-Pa., in 1970. Later, he served in the congressional liaison office of the National Aeronautics and Space Administration. He was appointed deputy assistant secretary of the Treasury Department by President Bush and also served as deputy administrator of the SBA. Cooksey has also managed a strategic communications company and served as a vice president of a major real estate concern in the Washington D.C. area.

Jack Bartling
Majority Counsel
428-A Russell Senate Office Bldg.
224-5175

Education: B.A., University of Mo., 1988. J.D., St. Louis University, 1993.

Professional: 1988-90, account executive, Kerlick, Switzer & Johnson. 1995-present, majority counsel, Senate Cmte. on Small Business.

Expertise: Trade, product liability, economics

Majority Counsel Jack Bartling continues in 1998 to advise committee Chairman Christopher "Kit" Bond, R-Mo., on a number of key issues that affect small business. Legislation affecting intellectual property rights, product liability reform and copyright reform will all be part of Bartling's work in this short second session of the 105th Congress. Bartling also tracks economic and trade issues for Bond, as well as innovations that can help small business.

The chairman will focus much of his attention this year on economic issues that affect small businesses. Earlier this year, he introduced legislation to reform the Internal Revenue Service. Called the "Putting the Taxpayer First Act of 1998," the bill provides structural changes to the IRS, including reorganization of the agency to serve distinct groups such as individuals and small businesses. It also would establish an independent, full-time board of governors to oversee the agency.

In addition, the bill expands protections of taxpayers' rights and reforms the tax penalty rules. The bill also addresses the increased use of electronic filing by taking steps to ensure that electronic filing of tax returns will be voluntary and not impose extra expenses and burdens on individuals and small businesses.

Last year, a three-year re-authorization of the Small Business Administration was passed resulting in new programs to help spur growth and development of small businesses. A central feature of the reauthorization is the HUBZones program, for Historically Underutilized Business Zones. The program gives government contracting benefits to small businesses located in neighborhoods where there is high poverty, high unemployment, and where businesses hire employees from local neighborhoods. The reauthorization bill also limited the practice of "bundling," which federal agencies used in the past to create large contracts that in turn, shut out small businesses from bidding.

Bartling grew up in the St. Louis area and moved to Washington shortly after graduating from law school. He joined Bond's staff because it was an opportunity to do policy as well as legal work.

Before attending law school, Bartling worked as an account executive at the advertising agency of Kerlick, Switzer & Johnson in Chicago. He has a degree in history and business from the University of Missouri and a law degree from St. Louis University.

KEY MINORITY STAFF:

Patricia R. Forbes
Minority Staff Director and Chief Counsel
428-A Russell Senate Office Bldg.
224-8496

Personal: born 3/28/54 in Plainfield, N.J.

Education: B.A., Middlebury College (Middlebury, Vt.), 1976. J.D., Univ. of Southern Calif., Los Angeles, (third year visiting student, Georgetown Univ. Law Center, Wash., D.C.), 1981.

Professional: 1982-86, attorney advisor; 1986-91, chief counsel for legislation and regulations, office of general counsel, U.S. Small Business Administration. 1991-92, majority counsel; 1993-94, deputy majority staff director and counsel, Senate Cmte. on Small Business. 1995-97, acting associate dep. admin. for economic development, U.S. Small Business Administration. 1997-present, minority staff director and chief counsel, Senate Cmte. on Small Business.

Expertise: Business and finance law, economic development

Patty Forbes joined the Senate Committee on Small Business in 1997 as minority staff director after serving as acting associate deputy administrator for economic development at the U.S. Small Business Administration (SBA).

Issues that Forbes will be working on during the second session of the 105th Congress include oversight of SBA programs that provide financial, procurement and business education assistance to the nation's small businesses, and expansion of the agency's microloan program.

Forbes's extensive background with the SBA includes senior management of nine major programs including Financial Assistance, the Small Business Investment Business Company Program, International Trade (Export Working Capital Loans), Business Education and Training, Women's Business Ownership, Veterans Affairs, Native American Affairs, Small Business Development Centers, and the Surety Bond Guarantee Program.

In her final post with the agency, Forbes provided overall leadership and direction to SBA economic development programs that render access to capital and business education and training to more than one million small businesses per year.

Forbes also served on the Finance Committee of the North American Development Bank (Domestic Window), the Advisory Board for the Community Development Financial Institutions Fund, and on the selection committee for the president's first Excellence in Microenterprise Development Awards.

Before going to the agency, Forbes served on the Senate Committee on Small Business as deputy staff director and counsel. Preceding her service on the Senate committee, Forbes was chief counsel for legislation and attorney advisor for SBA's Office of General Counsel.

Major legislative achievements Forbes worked on include SBA's 1997 three-year Reauthorization Act, changes to P.L. 103-81, which reduced the cost of SBA's 7(a) guaranteed business loan program by half, SBA's 1994 three-year reauthorization act (P.L. 103-403), authorizing legislation for the Small Business Innovation Research Program, and authorizing legislation for the Microloan Demonstration program.

Forbes, a native of Plainfield, N.J., has resided in Virginia for nearly 20 years and is licensed to practice law in Washington, D.C.

Albanian Issues Caucus

An informal group, the caucus seeks to turn congressional attention to the concerns of Albania, ethnic Albanians in Kosova and ethnic Albanians in other regions of the former Yugoslavia.

STAFF CONTACTS

Jason Steinbaum
Legislative Director to Rep. Engel
2303 RHOB
Washington, D.C. 20515
202/225-2464

Kerry O'Hare
Legislative Director to Rep. King
403C CHOB
Washington, D.C. 20515
202/225-7896

African Trade and Investment Caucus

A group of Representatives who have the common goal of developing policies and legislation that support the growth of the African private sector.

STAFF CONTACTS

Donna Thiessen
Legislative Assistant/Sr. Trade Policy Adviser to Rep. Crane
233 CHOB
Washington, D.C. 20515
202/225-6649

Charles Williams
Admin. Asst. to Rep. McDermott
2349 RHOB
Washington, D.C. 20515
202/225-3106

Congressional Automotive Caucus

2187 Rayburn House Office Building
Washington, D.C. 20515
202/225-3611

An informal bipartisan organization that focuses attention on the problems of the U.S. automobile industry. The purposes of the caucus include determining the effects of the automobile industry on various groups, and seeking legislative solutions to the problems within the industry.

STAFF CONTACTS

Michele Arnold
Caucus Coordinator/Legislative Director to Rep. Kildee
2187 RHOB
Washington, D.C. 20515
202/225-3611

Scott Aliferis
Legislative Director to Rep. Upton
Transportation/Infrastructure Committee for Rep. Shuster
2333 RHOB
Washington, D.C. 20515
202/225-3761

Congressional Boating Caucus

2408 Rayburn House Office Building
Washington, D.C. 20515
202/225-3026   Fax: 202/225-8398

An informal, bipartisan organization of Members of Congress concerned with bringing attention to issues affecting boating, recreation and industry. Protection of the environment, opposition to new taxes and development of novel trade opportunities for the boating industry are positions held by the caucus.

STAFF CONTACT

Michael Harrington
Legislative Director/Counsel to Rep. Shaw
2408 RHOB
202/225-3026

Congressional Border Caucus

A bipartisan group with congressional districts next to or near the U.S.-Mexican border. Its members represent California, Arizona, New Mexico and Texas. The caucus, established in 1983, deals with matters of mutual concern related to the proximity of the Members' districts to the border.

STAFF CONTACTS

Marcus Lubin
Leg. Assistant to Rep. Bonilla
1427 LHOB
Washington, D.C. 20515
202/225-4511

Luther Jones
Legislative Assistant to Rep. Ortiz
2136 RHOB
Washington, D.C. 20515
202/225-7742

Congressional Caucus on Armenian Issues

An informal, bipartisan group of legislators dedicated to maintaining and strengthening the U.S.-Armenia relationship.

STAFF CONTACTS

Ted Loud
Press Secretary to Rep. Pallone
420 CHOB
Washington, D.C. 20515
202/225-4671

Kelley Currie
Legislative Assistant to Rep. Porter
2373 RHOB
Washington, D.C. 20515
202/225-4835

Congressional Caucus on Hellenic Issues

A bipartisan group of Members whose goal is to foster and improve relations between the U.S. and Greece by focusing on diplomatic, military, and human rights issues that affect the relationship.

STAFF CONTACTS

Jerry White
Press Secretary to Rep. Bilirakis
2369 RHOB
Washington, D.C. 20515
202/225-5755

Margaret McDow
Legislative Asst. to Rep. Maloney
1330 LHOB
Washington, D.C. 20515
202/225-7944

Congressional Caucus on India and Indian-Americans

An informal, bipartisan group of legislators committed to better representing the more than one million Asian Indians living in America. The caucus is dedicated to strengthening Indo-U.S. ties, particularly in the area of trade.

STAFF CONTACTS

Ted Loud
Press Secretary to Rep. Pallone
420 CHOB
Washington, D.C. 20515
202/225-4671

Jenn Hargon
Legislative Assistant to Rep. McCollum
2266 RHOB
Washington, D.C. 20515
202/225-2176

Congressional Coalition on Population and Development

A bipartisan coalition established in 1985 to raise awareness and knowledge of domestic and international population concerns. The coalition seeks to keep family planning and population issues high on the nation's agenda.

STAFF CONTACTS

Craig Powers
Legislative Assistant to Rep. Morella
2228 RHOB
Washington, D.C. 20515
202/225-5341

Denise Metzger
Legislative Assistant to Rep. Sawyer
1414 LHOB
Washington, D.C. 20515
202/225-5231

Congressional Footwear Caucus

235 Cannon House Office Building
Washington, D.C. 20515
202/225-8273
Fax: 202/225-3984

The caucus focuses attention on the domestic footwear industry and proposes legislative initiatives to solve problems such as unemployment and foreign competition in the domestic market.

STAFF CONTACT

Kevin Ryan
Chief of Staff to Rep. Moakley
235 CHOB
Washington, D.C. 20515
202/225-8273

Congressional Human Rights Caucus

A 160 member bipartisan organization represented by all political perspectives united by the belief that the violation of one person's rights is a threat to free people all over the world. Formed at the start of the 98th Congress the caucus continues to coordinate congressional activity relating to human rights issues.

STAFF CONTACTS

Kellie Currie
Legislative Assistant to Rep. Porter
2373 RHOB
Washington, D.C. 20515
202/225-4835

Hans Hoegreffe
Legislative Assistant to Rep. Lantos
2217 RHOB
Washington, D.C. 20515
202/225-3531

Congressional Jobs & Fair Trade Caucus

A bipartisan group of 120 Members of Congress whose goal is to raise the visibility of trade issues through briefings and seminars.

STAFF CONTACTS

William Hawkins
Senior Research Analyst for Rep. Hunter
2265 RHOB
Washington, D.C. 20515
202/225-5672

George Wilson
Sr. Legislative Assistant to Rep. Kaptur
2311 RHOB
Washington, D.C. 20515
202/225-4146

Congressional Steel Caucus

A bipartisan organization of 88 House Members that works to ensure the stability of the American steel industry and its workers.

STAFF CONTACTS

Karen Buttaro
Legislative Counsel to Rep. Regula
2309 RHOB
Washington, D.C. 20515
202/225-3876

Debbie Tekavec
Legislative Director to Rep. Murtha
2423 RHOB
Washington, D.C. 20515
202/225-2065

Congressional Task Force Against Anti-Semitism

An organization of Members of Congress whose purpose is to provide a framework in which to exchange information and coordinate efforts with their counterparts worldwide to counter anti-Semitism.

STAFF CONTACTS

Deborah Bodlander
Professional Staff Member for Rep. Gilman
Cmte. on International Relations
2170 RHOB
Washington, D.C. 20515
202/225-5021

Kay King
Sr. Policy Adviser to Rep. Lantos
2217 RHOB
Washington, D.C. 20515
202/225-3531

Congressional Task Force on International HIV/AIDS

2349 Rayburn House Office Building
Washington, DC 20515
202/225-3106

A bipartisan group of 60 Senators and Representatives that is concerned with the spread of the AIDS epidemic in the world. The Task Force wishes to provide more education about the spread of HIV/AIDS in the world as well as examining the economic implications of the epidemic and possible legislative action that could be taken as a result.

STAFF CONTACT

Rita Patel
Legislative Assistant to Rep. McDermott
2349 RHOB
Washington, D.C. 20515
202/225-3106

Congressional Task Force to end the Arab Boycott

An informal group interested in ending the boycott against Israel and companies that do business with Israel. The task force acts to provide information on the boycott and promote initiatives to end it.

STAFF CONTACTS

Brett DiResta
Legislative Assistant to Rep. Schumer
2211 RHOB
Washington, D.C. 20515
202/225-6616

Catherine Castillo
Counsel to Rep. Ros-Lehtinen
2240 RHOB
Washington, D.C. 20515
202/225-3931

Congressional Travel & Tourism Caucus

An informal House organization seeking to provide a forum for Members of Congress to voice their ideas and views on travel and tourism issues. Members work to initiate and develop national policies that enhance an understanding of tourism's economic importance.

STAFF CONTACTS

Elizabeth Nicolson
Legislative Director to Rep. Foley
113 CHOB
Washington, D.C. 20515
202/225-5792

Sandy Heutges
Legislative Correspondent to Rep. Farr
1117 LHOB
Washington, D.C. 20515
202/225-2861

Congressional Ukrainian Caucus

A bipartisan group of Members of Congress organized to strengthen U.S.-Ukrainian relations and to offer support as the Ukraine converts to a democracy.

STAFF CONTACTS

Tom Bantle
Counsel/LD to Rep. Slaughter
2347 RHOB
Washington, D.C. 20515
202/225-3615   Fax: 202/225-7822

Kristen McSwain
Legislative Director to Rep. Fox
435 CHOB
Washington, D.C. 20515
202/225-6111   Fax: 202/225-3155

Congressional U.S.-Former Soviet Union Energy Caucus

A bipartisan group of Members of Congress that seeks to bring attention to oil production as a means to help restructure and stabilize the collapsing economy of the Former Soviet Union.

STAFF CONTACTS

Doug Ritter
Admin. Asst. to Rep. Weldon
2452 RHOB
Washington, D.C. 20515
202/225-2011

Cory Alexander
Associate Appropriations Staff for Rep. Hoyer
1705 LHOB
Washington, D.C. 20515
202/225-4131

Congressional Working Group on China

An informal, bipartisan group of Members of Congress who meet to discuss U.S./China policy including issues like human rights, proliferation, and trade.

STAFF CONTACTS

Carolyn Bartholomew
Legislative Director to Rep. Pelosi
2457 RHOB
Washington, D.C. 20515
202/225-4965

Anne Huiskes
Legislative Assistant to Rep. Wolf
241 CHOB
Washington, D.C. 20515
202/225-5136

Export Task Force

343 Cannon House Office Building
Washington, DC 20515
202/225-4476   Fax: 202/225-4488

A bipartisan group of Members of Congress representing almost every geographic region in the U.S. and a variety of economic interests and philosophical viewpoints. It serves to inform Members on export issues both within Congress and the business community and to advocate trade legislation that aids and supports American business and promotes American export trade.

STAFF CONTACT

Todd Funk
Legislative Assistant to Rep. Johnson
343 CHOB
Washington, D.C. 20515
202/225-4476

House Beef Caucus

An informal, bipartisan forum created to promote and protect the interests of beef producers. The caucus has supported the Japanese Agreement on Beef and Citrus and worked with the Administration on the EC Hormone Ban and on the ongoing efforts to liberalize beef imports in numerous foreign markets.

STAFF CONTACTS

Emily Beizer
Legislative Director to Rep. Dooley
1201 LHOB
Washington, D.C. 20515
202/225-3341

Ken Flanz
Administrative Assistant to Rep. Crapo
437 CHOB
Washington, D.C. 20515
202/225-5531

House Portuguese American Caucus

A bipartisan group that provides a forum for discussing and advancing issues and proposals of interest to the Portuguese American community including trade, economic development, cultural ties, and immigration.

STAFF CONTACTS

Kimber Colton
Senior Legislative Assistant to Rep. Kennedy
312 CHOB

Washington, D.C. 20515
202/225-4911

Paul Kavinoky
Legislative Director to Rep. Pombo
1519 LHOB
Washington, D.C. 20515
202/225-1947

House Republican Israel Caucus

An informal group of Members of Congress who meet to educate Members on the importance of U.S./Israel relations and to act as a clearinghouse for information on the Middle East peace process.

STAFF CONTACTS

Kristen McSwain
Legislative Director to Rep. Fox
453 CHOB
Washington, D.C. 20515
202/225-6111

Jeanette Forcash
Press Secretary to Rep. Weller
130 CHOB
Washington, D.C. 20515
202/225-3635

Information Technology Caucus

An informal, bipartisan group interested in the issues affecting the information technology industry. The caucus seeks to create an educational forum that focuses attention on areas of concern to the industry through panel discussions, briefings, and technology demonstrations on software, hardware, and telecommunications. Issues which the caucus addresses include international trade, patent and copyright protection, Internet and information highway restrictions, tax and financial policy, encryption, piracy, and government's role in the regulation of the information technology industry.

STAFF CONTACTS

Mike Hettinger
Legislative Director to Rep. Davis
224 CHOB
Washington, D.C. 20515
202/225-1492

Bill McBride
Legislative Director to Rep. Ehlers
1717 LHOB
Washington, D.C. 20515
202/225-3831

Northern Border Caucus

A group of Members whose states border Canada organized to examine issues including customs, transportation, immigration, and implementation of NAFTA.

STAFF CONTACT

Marilyn Seiber
Chief Minority Economist, Rep. LaFalce
Cmte. on Small Business
559 FHOB
Washington, D.C. 20515
202/226-3420

United Nations Working Group

A bipartisan group of Members organized to ensure the U.S. leadership role in the UN, secure reforms within the organization, and honor U.S. financial commitments to the UN.

STAFF CONTACTS

Jason Steinbaum
Legislative Director to Rep. Engel
2303 RHOB
Washington, D.C. 20515
202/225-2464

Amy Butler
Legislative Assistant to Rep. Leach
2186 RHOB
Washington, D.C. 20515
202/225-6576

©Almanac Publishing, Inc. 1998 - The Washington Almanac of International Trade & Business

Friends of Portugal

A bipartisan group of Senators organized to strengthen relations between the U.S. and Portugal.

STAFF CONTACTS

Mike Russell
Deputy Chief of Staff to Sen. Campbell
SR-380
Washington, D.C. 20510
202/224-5852

Elizabeth King
Legislative Assistant to Sen. Reed
SH-320
Washington, D.C. 20510
202/224-4642

Senate Anti-Terrorism Caucus

A bipartisan group of Senators formed in 1985 whose chief concern is to prevent terrorism. In order to accomplish its goal, the caucus works with the Administration and the Senate Foreign Relations, Select Intelligence, and Judiciary Committees to formulate effective unilateral and multilateral policy.

STAFF CONTACTS

Gregg Rickman
Legislative Director to Sen. D'Amato
SH-520
Washington, D.C. 20510
202/224-6542

Paul Matulic
Legislative Assistant to Sen. Hatch
SR-131
Washington, D.C. 20510
202/224-5251

Senate Auto Caucus

A bipartisan group of 25 Senators who provide a forum for members to exchange ideas on issues affecting the auto industry.

STAFF CONTACTS

Lori Sharpe
Legislative Director to Sen. Ashcroft
SH-316
Washington, D.C. 20510
202/224-6154

Alison Pascale
Legislative Assistant to Sen. Levin
SR-459
Washington, D.C. 20510
202/224-6221

Senate Beef Caucus

A bipartisan group of Senators concerned with increasing the competitiveness of the domestic beef industry.

STAFF CONTACTS

Brian Cavey
Legislative Director to Sen. Baucus
SH-511
Washington, D.C. 20510
202/224-2651

Brian Klippenstein
Legislative Assistant to Sen. Bond
SR-274
Washington, D.C. 20510
202/224-5721

Senate Drug Enforcement Caucus

The caucus serves as a clearinghouse for legislative and administrative proposals to stop the spread of illegal narcotics. Its goal is to focus national attention on the need for improved drug enforcement and to promote legislative solutions to the national narcotics crisis.

STAFF CONTACT

Gail Zawadzki
Legislative Assistant to Sen. D'Amato
SH-520
Washington, D.C. 20510
202/224-6542

Senate NATO Observer Group

A group of nearly 30 Senators organized to aid in the Senate's consideration of enlargement of NATO in the post-Cold War era.

STAFF CONTACTS

Ian Brzezinski
Legislative Assistant to Sen. Roth
SH-104
Washington, D.C. 20510
202/224-2441

Michael Haltzel
Professional Staff Member for Sen. Biden
Committee on Foreign Relations
SD-439
Washington, D.C. 20510
202/224-3953

Senate Steel Caucus

An informal, bipartisan group of Senators concerned with the steel industry and jobs. They meet informally with administration officials and representatives of the steel industry and labor to review issues affecting the steel industry. Caucus business is handled through Sen. Specter's office.

STAFF CONTACTS

Kristin Bodenstedt
Legislative Counsel to Sen. Specter
SH-711
Washington, D.C. 20510
202/224-4254

Ellen Doneski
Policy Director to Sen. Rockefeller
SH-531
Washington, D.C. 20510
202/224-6472

Senate Textile Steering Committee

SR-217 Russell Senate Office Bdg.
Washington, D.C. 20510
202/224-5972

An informal group of senators who meet occasionally to discuss mutual concerns about the textile industry. The group has no officers or operating committees.

STAFF CONTACT

Alfred Bundrick
Legislative Director to Sen. Thurmond
SR-217
Washington, D.C. 20510
202/224-5972

Senate Tourism Caucus

An informal, bipartisan group of more than 70 senators whose pupose is to communicate information to Senators on the issues relating to travel and tourism.

STAFF CONTACTS

Randall Popelka
Legislative Assistant to Sen. Burns
SD-187
Washington, D.C. 20510
202/224-2644

Jean Toal
Professional Staff for Sen. Hollings
SD-566
Washington, D.C. 20515
202/224-4912

AD HOC Congressional Committee for Irish Affairs

A bipartisan, bicameral committee, established in 1977 to advocate a positive U.S. role in Northern Ireland, specifically advancing peace and justice and ending the widespread violence in this area.

STAFF CONTACTS

Elizabeth O'Hara
Legislative Asst. to Rep. Manton
2235 RHOB
Washington, D.C. 20515
202/225-3965

John P. Mackey
Investigative Counsel, Intern'l. Relations Cmte. for Rep. Gilman
2170 RHOB
Washington, D.C. 20515
202/225-5021

Dan Michaelis
Press Secretary to Rep. King
403 CHOB
Washington, D.C. 20515
202/225-7896

William Tranghese
Press Secretary to Rep. Neal
2236 RHOB
Washington, D.C. 20515
202/225-5601

Commission on Security and Cooperation in Europe

234 Ford House Office Building
Washington, DC 20515
202/225-1901   Fax: 202/226-4199

The Commission on Security and Cooperation in Europe, also known as the Helsinki Commission, is a U.S. Government agency created in 1976 by Public Law 94-304 with the mandate to monitor and encourage compliance with the Final Act of the Conference on Security and Cooperation in Europe, which was signed in Helsinki, Finland, on August 1, 1975, by the leaders of 33 European countries, the United States and Canada. The Conference was renamed the Organization for Security and Cooperation in Europe (OSCE) in 1994. The addition of Albania, the Baltic States, the newly independent states of the former Soviet Union, and several of the former Yugoslav republics has increased the number of participating OSCE countries to 53.

The Commission consists of nine members of the U.S. House of Representatives, nine members from the U.S. Senate, and one member each from the Departments of State, Defense and Commerce. The positions of Chairman and Co-Chairman are shared by the House and Senate and rotate every 2 years, when a new Congress convenes. A professional staff of approximately 15 persons assists the Commissioners in their work.

The Helsinki Commission carries out its mandate in a variety of ways. First, it gathers and disseminates to the U.S. Congress, non-governmental organizations and public information on Helsinki-related topics. Public hearings and briefings with expert witnesses focusing on these topics are held frequently. Similarly, the Commission issues reports on the implementation of OSCE commitments by the countries of Central and Eastern Europe and the

former Soviet Union, and the United States. Reports on specific OSCE meetings are also published. The Commission plays a unique role in assisting the planning and execution of U.S. policy in the OSCE, including through member and staff participation on U.S. delegations to OSCE meetings, and in certain OSCE institutions. Finally, members of the Commission have regular contact with parliamentarians, government officials and private individuals from OSCE participating States.

Chairman: Alfonse M. D'Amato, R-NY

Co-Chairman: Christopher H. Smith, R-NJ

STAFF CONTACTS

Michael R. Hathaway
Chief of Staff
202/225-1901

Dorothy Douglas Taft
Deputy Chief of Staff
202/225-1901

Chadwick R. Gore
Communications Director
202/225-1901

Congressional Asian Pacific Caucus

2135 Rayburn House Office Building
Washington, DC 20515
202/225-4906
Fax: 202/225-4987

An informal, bipartisan group of Members of Congress who share an interest in establishing policies on legislation and issues relating to persons of Asian and Pacific Islands ancestry. The caucus plans to ensure that legislation passed by the Congress provides for the full participation of Asian Pacific Americans and reflects the concerns and needs of the Asian Pacific American communities to the greatest extent possible.

STAFF CONTACTS

Laura Efurd
Legislative Director to Rep. Mink
2135 RHOB
Washington, D.C. 20515
202/225-4906

Mariel Luriega
Legislative Assistant to Rep. Underwood
424 CHOB
Washington, D.C. 20515
202/225-1188

Congressional Caucus on Hong Kong

A bicameral, bipartisan group of Members of Congress who want to ensure that Hong Kong's democratic institutions, economy, and way of life are preserved given the Chinese assumption of Hong Kong from the British in 1997.

STAFF CONTACTS

Kellie Currie
Legislative Assistant to Rep. Porter
2373 RHOB
Washington, D.C. 20515
202/225-4835

Jason Gross
Legislative Assistant to Rep. Gejdenson
1401 LHOB
Washington, D.C. 20515
202/225-2076

Fred Downey
Legislative Fellow to Sen. Lieberman
SH-706
Washington, D.C. 20510
202/224-4041

Gary Shiffman
Foreign Policy Advisor to Sen. Mack
SH-517
Washington, D.C. 20510
202/224-5274

Congressional Competitiveness Caucus

A bipartisan, bicameral organization that seeks to stress the importance of U.S. economic competitiveness and design and implement a long-term agenda of activity that would enable the nation to market more competitive goods and services.

STAFF CONTACTS

Ed Gresser
Policy Director to Sen. Baucus
SH-511
Washington, D.C. 20510
202/224-2651

Ken Cunningham
Chief of Staff to Sen. Grassley
SH-135
Washington, D.C. 20510
202/224-3744

George Wilson
Chief of Staff to Rep. Kaptur
2311 RHOB
Washington, D.C. 20515
202/225-4146

Frances McNaught
Chief of Staff to Rep. Kolbe
205 CHOB
Washington, D.C. 20515
202/225-2542

Congressional Friends of Human Rights Monitors

1432 Longworth House Office Building
Washington, DC 20515
202/225-6465

An informal, bipartisan, bicameral group that was established in 1983 to protest abuses of Human Rights Monitors around the world. The group consists of 100 Representatives and 25 Senators.

STAFF CONTACT

Robert Zachritz
Sr. Legislative Assistant to Rep. Hall
1432 LHOB
Washington, D.C. 20515
202/226-6465

Congressional Hispanic Caucus

1119 Longworth House Office Building
Washington, D.C. 20515
202/225-2410
Fax: 202/225-2202

An organization dedicated to improving the condition of Hispanics through the legislative process. The caucus monitors policies of the executive and judicial branches of government and seeks to strengthen the roles of Hispanics at all levels of government. The caucus also has issue task forces to coordinate their legislative agenda including: immigration, citizenship, education, welfare reform, language promotion, housing and community development, corporate and community cooperation, military and veterans affairs, civil rights (affirmative action/voting rights), health and environment, and international relations.

STAFF CONTACT

Esther Aguilera
Caucus Executive Director
1119 LHOB
Washington, D.C. 20515
202/225-2410

Friends of Ireland

This 160-member informal bipartisan group is interested in advancing a better understanding of the problems in Ireland. It supports a peaceful solution to the conflict in Northern Ireland with consent of the involved parties.

STAFF CONTACTS

John Simmons
Legislative Assistant to Rep. Walsh
2351 RHOB
Washington, D.C. 20515
202/225-3701   Fax: 202/225-4042

Trina Vargo
Foreign Policy Adviser to Sen. Kennedy
SR-315
Washington, D.C. 20510
202/224-2638

House/Senate International Education Study Group

SR-444 Russell Senate Office Building
Washington, DC 20515
Phone: 202/224-2823

Organized to increase congressional and national awareness of the importance of both foreign language and international education to the national security and economic prosperity of the United States. It is a 65 bipartisan and bicameral group that consists of 65 members.

STAFF CONTACT

Suzanne Day
Prof. Staff Member, Labor Committee
SH-404
Washington, D.C. 20510
202/224-5630

National Security Caucus

A bipartisan group of Senators and Representatives who subscribe to the principles and goals of a national strategy for peace through strength. The key principles of the caucus are maintaining a strong national defense; providing for effective security and intelligence capabilities; accepting no agreements which in any way jeopardize the security of the U.S. and its allies; maintaining a strong economy; and protecting our overseas sources of energy and other vital raw materials.

STAFF CONTACT

Bill Berl
Senior Legislative Assistant to Rep. Cunningham
2238 RHOB
Washington, D.C. 20515
202/225-5452

©Almanac Publishing, Inc. 1998 - The Washington Almanac of International Trade & Business

Council of Economic Advisers

Old Executive Office Building
17th Street & Pennsylvania, NW / Washington DC 20502
202/395-5042

INTRODUCTION

The Council of Economic Advisers performs an analysis and appraisal of the national economy for the purpose of providing policy recommendations. It recommends to the President policies for economic growth and stability and assists in the preparation of the economic reports of the President to Congress. The Council analyzes interrelationships between the U.S. economy and the international economy.

Chair
Dr. Janet L. Yellen
202/395-5042   FAX 202/395-6958
OEOB 314

Personal: born 8/13/46 in Brooklyn, N.Y.

Education: B.A. in economics (summa cum laude), Brown Univ., 1967. Ph.D. in economics, Yale Univ., 1971.

Professional: 1971-76, asst. professor of economics, Harvard Univ. 1974, research fellow, Mass. Institute of Technology. 1974-75, consultant, div. of intl. finance, Board of Governors, Federal Reserve System. 1975-76, consultant, Congressional Budget Office. 1976, research affiliate, Yale Univ. 1977-78, economist, div. of intl. finance, trade and financial studies section, Board of Governors, Federal Reserve System. 1978-80, lecturer, London School of Economics and Political Science. 1980-82, asst. professor; 1982-85, assoc. professor and professor; 1992, Bernard T. Rocca, Jr. professor of intl. business and trade, Haas School of Business Administration, Univ. of Calif. at Berkeley. 1994-1997, member, Board of Governors, Federal Reserve System. Feb. 1997-present, chair, Council of Economic Advisers, The White House.

Dr. Janet Yellen replaced Joseph Stiglitz as chair of the Council of Economic Advisers in early 1997. She came over to this White House position from a seat on the Board of Governors of the Federal Reserve System which she had held since confirmation in 1994. Dr. Stiglitz resigned to take a position at the World Bank.

The Council of Economic Advisers was created by the Full Employment Act of 1946 and consists of three members appointed by the President and confirmed by the Senate. The council analyzes and appraises the national economy and advises the President. The council annually publishes "The Economic Report of the President," an important document outlining where the administration thinks the economy is and where it is going.

Published reports indicate Dr. Yellen got quickly into the decision-making swim at the White House, regularly attending the chief of staff's budget strategy sessions and offering recommendations on new air pollution rules and proposals to mix banking and commerce. (*Wall Street Journal*, June 20, 1997).

In July of 1997, Dr. Yellen took to the bully pulpit of the op-ed page of the *New York Times*, to argue strongly for the continuation of the federal budget-cutting efforts then underway between the Administration and the Congress. (July 18, 1997)

Yellen had previously served on the seven-member Board of Governors of the Federal Reserve System. The Board decides the nation's general monetary and credit policies and monitors credit conditions. It also oversees the implementation of certain consumer credit protection laws.

Yellen came to the Board after 14 years on the faculty of the University of California at Berkeley as a professor of international business and trade. She had earlier served as an assistant professor at Harvard University from 1971 to 1976 and lectured at the London School of Economics from 1978 to 1980.

She graduated from Brown University in 1967 and received her doctorate in economics from Yale University in 1971. In addition to being a recognized scholar on international economics, she has written on a variety of macroeconomic issues, specializing in the causes, mechanisms and implications of unemployment.

Yellen is married to Professor George Akerlof, a fellow economist. They have one son.

Member
Dr. Jeffrey A. Frankel
202/395-5046   FAX 202/395-6947
OEOB 314

Personal: born 1952 in San Francisco, Calif.

Education: B.A., Swarthmore College, 1974. Ph.D., Massachusetts Institute of Technology, 1978.

Professional: 1983-84, senior staff economist for international economic policy, Council of Economic Advisers. 1988-89, visiting professor for public policy, Harvard University. Director, International Finance and Macroeconomics, National Bureau of Economic Research (Cambridge, Mass.). Senior Fellow, Institute for International Economics (Washington, D.C.). Visiting Scholar, International Monetary Fund, the Federal Reserve Board, the University of Michigan, Yale University, the World Bank, and the Federal Reserve Bank of San Francisco. 1979-97, professor of economics, University of California, Berkeley. February 1997-present, member, Council of Economic Advisers, The White House.

Jeffrey A. Frankel appeared before the Senate Banking Committee in March of 1997 during its consideration of his nomination to be a member of the Council of Economic Advisers and promised the

Senators that he would continue to specialize in international economics and macroeconomics if confirmed. He was confirmed in April and in speeches since then has been an active promoter of the "internationalist" aspects of the Clinton Administration, pointing out their success in passing NAFTA and the Uruguay Round of trade talks and advocating for fast track trade authority for the President.

Frankel's research interests include the globalization of financial markets, the workings of the foreign exchange market, targets and indicators for monetary policy, the term structure of interest rates, monetary determinants of agricultural prices, international macroeconomic policy coordination, regional trading blocs, financial issues in Japan and the Pacific, emerging markets, and trade and growth in East Asia. He has pursued these interests as a professor or economics at the University of California at Berkeley for almost 20 years. He has also been a visiting professor at a number of other academic and financial institutions.

His publications include *The Internationalization of Equity Markets* (University of Chicago Press, 1994), *Financial Markets and Monetary Policy* (MIT Press, 1995), and *The Microstructure of Foreign Exchange Markets* (University of Chicago Press, 1996). In 1991, he won first place in the AMEX Bank Review Awards for his essay, "Is a Yen Bloc Forming in Pacific Asia?"

Member
VACANT
202/395-5036   FAX 202/395-6958
OEOB, Rm. 314

Alicia Munnell departed as a member of the Council of Economic Advisers in August of 1997. At press time, a new Member had not been confirmed by the Senate.

Council on Environmental Quality

Old Executive Office Building
17th St. & Pennsylvania Ave., NW / Washington, DC 20501
202/456-6224   FAX 202/456-2710

INTRODUCTION

Environmental issues have taken center stage in the Clinton Administration. The Council on Environmental Quality plays a direct role in the planning and coordination of the Administration's environmental policy in both the domestic and international arenas.

Chair
Ms. Kathleen Alana "Katie" McGinty
202/456-6224   FAX 202/456-2710
OEOB Rm. 360

Personal: born 1963 in Philadelphia, Pa.

Education: B.S. in chemistry, Saint Joseph's University, 1985. J.D., Columbia University School of Law, 1988.

Professional: 1984-85, research asst., Atlantic Richfield Chemical Co. 1986-88, law clerk for several firms including: Cooper and Dunham (New York); Skadden, Arps, Slate, Meagher & Flom (New York); Morgan, Lewis & Bockius (Philadelphia); and Thelen, Marrin, Johnson & Bridges. 1988-89, law clerk, Hon. H. Robert Mayer, Court of Appeals for the Federal Circuit (Wash., D.C.). 1990, congressional fellow, American Chemical Society. 1991-92, senior leg. asst. on environment and energy issues, Sen. Albert Gore, (D-Tenn.). 1992, congressional staff coordinator, Senate Delegation to U.S. Conference on Environment and Development. 1993-95, director, Office of Environmental Policy, The White House. 1996-present, chair, Council on Environmental Quality, The White House.

Katie McGinty was confirmed by the Senate on December 22, 1995, as chair of the Council on Environmental Quality and was sworn in January 25, 1996. The Council on Environmental Quality was set up under the National Environmental Policy Act of 1969 with additional responsibilities provided by the Environmental Quality Improvements Act of 1970.

The council consists of thee members appointed by the President with the advice and consent of the Senate. The council develops and recommends to the President national policies that further environmental quality; performs continuing analysis of changes or trends in the national environment; and appraises programs of the Federal Government to determine their contributions to sound environmental policy.

McGinty's office also conducts studies, research, and analysis relating to ecological systems and environmental quality; assists the President in the preparation of the annual environmental quality report to the Congress; and oversees implementation of the National Environmental Policy Act. She also serves as chair of the President's Commission on Environmental Quality.

McGinty was brought into the Clinton Administration by Vice President Albert Gore. McGinty met Gore when she was assigned to his staff while a congressional fellow at the American Chemical Society. There, she worked on the Clean Air Act Amendments of 1990 and issues involving science education and scientific research funding.

She went to work in 1991 as a legislative assistant for Senator Gore, working on global warming, ozone depletion, deforestation and other global environmental issues; World Bank and third world development policy questions; and environmental aspects of international trade policy. She also participated in efforts to pass the National Energy Security Act. She served as an official member of the U.S. delegation to the Antarctica Environmental Protection Protocol and the Framework Convention on Climate Change treaty negotiations.

McGinty was an official member of the U.S. delegation to the UN Conference on Environment and Development (UNCED) preparatory sessions and represented the Senate at the UNCED conference in Rio de Janeiro in June 1992.

Chief of Staff
Shelly N. Fidler
202/456-6224
OEOB, Rm. 360

Associate Director for the Global Environment
Mr. David Sandalow
202/456-6543   FAX 202/456-2710
OEOB Rm. 361A

Education: B.A. in philosophy, Yale College, 1978. J.D., Univ. of

Michigan Law School, 1982.
Professional: private practice. office of general counsel, Environmental Protection Agency. Current: senior director for environmental affairs, National Security Council and associate director for the global environment, Council on Environmental Quality.

David Sandalow is concurrently director for environmental affairs at the National Security Council and associate director for the global environment at the Council on Environmental Quality.

In these jobs, he helps advise the president and vice president on a broad range of international environmental issues. Included in his portfolio are climate change, ozone depletion, biodiversity, oceans, trade and environment, forests, chemicals, regional environmental issues, and U.S. policy toward the multilateral development banks.

Sandalow is a member of the Standing Committee on Environmental Law of the American Bar Association. He is co-chair of the ABA's Annual Conference on Environmental Law, and is a past member of the Steering Committee of the DC Bar's Committee on Environmental and Natural Resources Law. He is a co-author of the ABA's *Clean Water Act Deskbook.*

Prior to coming to the White House, Sandalow was with the office of general counsel at EPA. Before that, he was in the private practice of law.

He is a graduate of the University of Michigan Law School and of Yale College.

National Economic Council

The White House
1600 Pennsylvania Ave., NW / Washington DC 20500
202/456-2620

INTRODUCTION

The National Economic Council was established in 1993 to coordinate the economic policy making of the Clinton Administration. It integrates policies to increase the nation's economic security in the same way the National Security Council integrates domestic, foreign, and military policies relating to the national security.

Asst. to the President for Economic Policy & Director of the NEC
Mr. Gene B. Sperling
202/456-2174   FAX 202/456-2878
Rm. 2/WW

Education: B.A., Univ. of Minnesota. J.D., Yale Law School.

Professional: 1988, economic/domestic policy staff, Dukakis for President Committee. 1989, consulting attorney with Laurence H. Tribe. 1989-90, attorney and consultant, National Abortion Rights Action League (NARAL). 1990-92, asst. to Governor Mario Cuomo, (D-N.Y.). 1992, economic policy dir., Clinton for President Committee. 1992-93, dep. transition director, Presidential Transition. 1993-97, dep. asst. to the President for economic policy, The White House. 1997-present, asst. to the President and dir., National Economic Council, The White House.

Gene Sperling was promoted by President Clinton to direct the National Economic Council (NEC) in December 1996. Sperling had previously served as deputy director for the Council under both Laura D'Andrea Tyson and Robert Rubin. The National Economic Council was established by President Clinton in his first term to coordinate economic policy across the government much as the National Security Council does for international policy.

Former NEC director Tyson praised Sperling for his "encyclopedic

knowledge of budgetary issues." (*National Journal*, June 14, 1997). He needed that knowledge throughout the spring and summer of 1997 as part of the White House team negotiating with congressional leaders over the terms of a balanced budget and tax cut proposal.

Sperling entered politics kind of sideways. After graduating from Yale Law School, he began to pursue an MBA at the Wharton School at the University of Pennsylvania. He was attracted by the candidacy of Michael Dukakis for the Democratic Presidential nomination in 1988 and interrupted his schooling to work on economic issues during that campaign. He then served as an attorney for the National Abortion Rights Action League for two years before joining the staff of New York Governor Mario Cuomo in 1990.

After being approached by George Stephanopoulos about joining the Clinton campaign, Sperling made another change and became a Clinton disciple, working on issues for Clinton's campaign platform such as urban enterprise zones, health care reform, economic stimulus, and a tax plan. Since 1993, he has continued his work on economic policy areas for the administration first as staff, and now as director of, the National Economic Council.

While at Yale Law School, Sperling worked summers for the NAACP Legal Defense Fund and for Professor Robert B. Reich. He has also worked with Harvard Law professor, Laurence H. Tribe.

Chief of Staff
Mr. Jonathan Kaplan
202/456-2023   FAX 202/456-2878
OEOB Rm. 235

Special Asst. to the President for Intl. Trade and Economics
Mr. Robert D. Kyle
202/456-9281   FAX 202/456-9280
Rm. 2/WW

Personal: born 3/20/55 in Evanston, Ill.

Education: B.A., Cornell Univ., 1977. M.A., Oxford Univ. (Marshall Scholar), 1979. J.D. (with honors), Harvard Law School, 1982.

Professional: 1982-85, attorney, Hogan and Hartson (Wash., D.C.). 1985-87, legis. counsel for international trade, Sen. Max Baucus (D-Mont.). 1988-90, vice pres., Shearson Lehman Hutton, Inc. 1990-93, counsel, Senate Finance Committee. 1993-present, special assistant to the President for international trade and economics, National Economic Council/National Security Council.

Robert Kyle is the special assistant to the President for international trade and economics at The White House. He has a joint appointment to both the National Security Council and the National Economic Council.

In that capacity, he has responsibility for all international economic matters. He has been a key player on such issues as NAFTA, the Uruguay Round, US-Japan trade issues, the Mexican peso crisis, China policy, regional trade initiatives in Asia and Latin America, and issues involving the World Bank and the International Monetary Fund.

From 1990 to February 1993, Kyle was chief international trade counsel for the Senate Committee on Finance under the chairmanship of Senator Lloyd Bentsen (D-Texas). In that capacity, he was active on all trade issues to come before the committee, including the early work on the Uruguay Round and the NAFTA structure.

From 1988 to 1990, Kyle was in the private sector, serving as a vice president at Shearson Lehman and Hutton, an investment banking firm. While there, he worked with former budget director Richard Darman, former Mondale campaign aide James Johnson, and former cabinet secretary James Schlesinger.

From 1985 to 1987, Kyle served as trade counsel to Senator Max Baucus (D-Mont.) where he worked on a wide variety of trade issues including the Omnibus Trade and Competitiveness Act of 1988.

Kyle was an associate with the Washington, D.C. law firm of Hogan and Hartson from 1982 to 1985. During the 1984 presidential campaign, he served as a senior domestic issues advisor to vice-presidential nominee Geraldine Ferraro.

Kyle received his B.A. from Cornell University and then attended Oxford University on a Marshall Scholarship. He graduated from Harvard Law School with honors.

Assistant to the President for International
 Economic Policy and Economic Affairs
Mr. Daniel K. Tarullo
202/456-5353   FAX 202/456-1605
OEOB, Rm. 231

Personal: born in Boston, Mass.

Education: B.A., Georgetown Univ., 1973. M.A., Duke Univ., 1974. J.D. (summa cum laude), Univ. of Michigan Law School, 1977.

Professional: 1978-79, antitrust division, U.S. Dept. of Justice. 1980-81, exec. asst. to the under secretary for international trade, U.S. Dept. of Commerce. 1981-87, asst. professor, Harvard Law School. 1987-89, chief counsel, Sen. Edward M. Kennedy (D-Mass.). 1989-93, international counsel, Shearman & Sterling. 1993-March 1996, asst. sec. for economic and business affairs, U.S. Dept. of State. March 1996-December 1996, dep. asst. to the President for economic policy; 1997-present, assistant to the President for international economic policy, National Economic Council, The White House.

Dan Tarullo is assistant to the President for international economic policy. He is responsible for the international economic policymaking process, for shaping international economic policy issues, and for advising the president on these matters. He participates as a principal on both the National Security Council and the National Economic Council. He had previously served as deputy assistant to the president for economic policy at the National Economic Council, with particular responsibility for international and regulatory issues.

From July 1993 to March 1996, Tarullo served as assistant secretary of State for economic and business affairs. He headed the bureau of economic and business affairs, which represents the State Department on international trade, finance, and economic matters both internationally and in the formulation of administration policies. The bureau also leads negotiations for the U.S. government in the areas of aviation, energy, and telecommunications. In March 1995, President Clinton appointed Tarullo as his personal representatives for the G-7 group of industrialized nations to lead the preparatory work for this groups' annual summit meetings.

Tarullo has experience as a government official, law professor, and private practitioner. Prior to joining the State Department, he was counsel to the law firm of Shearman & Sterling, where he concentrated on antitrust, securities, and international transactions. From 1981 to 1987, he taught international economic regulation, antitrust, and corporation law at the Harvard Law School.

His earlier government service includes positions at the antitrust division of the U.S. Department of Justice, as executive assistant to the under secretary of Commerce for international trade, and as chief counsel to Sen. Edward M. Kennedy (D-Mass.) from 1987 to 1989.

Tarullo is a graduate of the law school at the University of Michigan where he was articles editor of the *Law Review*.

Special Asst. to the President for International Economic Policy
Ms. S. Lael Brainard
202/395-5104   FAX 202/395-6853
OEOB, Rm. 330

Director to the NEC/NSC for International Economic Policy
Mr. Malcolm R. Lee
202/456-9291   FAX 202/456-9290
OEOB Rm. 389

National Security Council

Old Executive Office Building
17th St. & Pennsylvania Ave., NW / Washington, D.C. 20506
Public Affairs: 202/456-9271

> ### INTRODUCTION
>
> *The National Security Council, chaired by the President, advises and assists the President in integrating all aspects of national security policy as it affects the U.S. --- domestic, foreign, military, intelligence, and economic --- in conjunction with the National Economic Council.*

National Security Council Staff

The NSC staff, headed by the Executive Secretary, serves as the President's national security and foreign policy staff within the White House. The staff receives its direction from the President, through the National Security Advisor. The Executive Secretary assists the President and the Assistant to the President for National Security Affairs in preparing for meetings with foreign leaders and in connection with the President's foreign travel. The staff performs a variety of activities in advising and assisting the President and the Assistant to the President for National Security Affairs, including participating in Presidential briefings, assisting the President in responding to Congressional inquiries and preparing public remarks. The NSC staff serves as an initial point of contact for departments and agencies who wish to bring a national security issue to the President's attention.

The NSC staff also prepares briefing materials for the President and the Assistant to the President for National Security Affairs to assist them in making decisions regarding national security policy and operations, including preparation of meeting agendas, decision and discussion papers. Staff members participate in inter-agency working groups organized to assess policy issues in a coordinated fashion among several agencies at an initial staff level; they prepare analysis and recommendations for the Deputy Assistants to the President for National Security Affairs, the Assistant to the President for National Security Affairs and the President.

Assistant to the President for National Security Affairs
Mr. Samuel R. (Sandy) Berger
202/456-9481   FAX 202/456-2883
Rm. 1/WW

Personal: born 10/28/45 in Sharon, Conn.

Education: B.A., Cornell Univ., 1967. J.D. (cum laude), Harvard Law School, 1971.

Professional: 1971, leg. asst., Sen. Harold E. Hughes (D-Iowa). 1972, spec. asst. to New York City Mayor John Lindsay and leg. asst. to U.S. Rep. Joseph Resnick (D-N.Y.). 1973-77, 1981-92, attorney and partner, Hogan and Hartson. 1977-80, deputy director, policy planning staff, U.S. Dept. of State. 1992-93, senior foreign policy advisor, Clinton presidential campaign. 1993, asst. transition director for national security, Clinton-Gore transition. 1993-97, deputy assistant to the President for national security affairs, National Security Council. 1997-present, assistant to the President and director, National Security Council, The White House.

After serving for four years as deputy assistant to the President for national security affairs, Sandy Berger became national security advisor at the start of President Clinton's second term, succeeding Anthony Lake.

Almost from the beginning of his tenure at the top, Berger was thrown into controversies developing from the 1996 Presidential election year. Allegations were made that the NSC staff had improperly given briefings to contributors after urgings from the Democratic National Committee (DNC). In another matter, two NSC staffers did not relay FBI warnings about foreign campaign contributions up the chain of command. Finally, it was alleged that some questionable foreign figures were cleared into the White House for Presidential visits.

In April of 1997, Berger instituted new measures to limit DNC contact with his staff and to screen foreign visitors to the White House. He also directed his staff not to attend briefings from outside agencies which are given with the proviso that information cannot be shared with superiors. (*New York Times*, April 21, 1997).

Berger is considered a more public NSC advisor than his predecessor Anthony Lake. He appears frequently on the Sunday morning public affairs shows. A *Washington Post* headline described his activities, "Berger Combines Stagecraft with Statecraft" (July 7, 1997).

An early policy effort in 1997 was securing Senate passage of the Chemical Weapons Ban and winning passage of Most Favored Nation

status for China in the U.S. House of Representatives.

Berger has known the President since the 1972 McGovern for President campaign and stayed in touch with him over the years.

Before signing on with President Clinton during the 1992 campaign as an advisor on national security issues, Berger practiced law at the Washington firm of Hogan and Hartson, where he directed the firm's international trade group.

Berger's Democratic credentials include writing speeches for secretaries of State Cyrus R. Vance and Edmund S. Muskie during the Carter Administration and writing for the late Ambassador to France Pamela Harriman.

Berger and his wife Susan, a real estate agent, have two grown daughters and a son in high school.

Deputy Assistant to the President for National Security Affairs
Mr. James B. Steinberg
202/456-9491   FAX 202/456-2883
Rm. 1/WW

Personal: born 5/7/53 in Boston, Mass.

Education: B.A., Harvard Univ., 1973. J.D., Yale Law School, 1977.

Professional: special asst. to the asst. sec. for planning and evaluation, U.S. Dept. of Health, Education and Welfare. law clerk, Judge David L. Bazelon, U.S. Court of Appeals. special asst. to the U.S. asst. attorney general, civil division, U.S. Dept. of Justice. minority counsel, U.S. Senate Labor and Human Resources Cmte. principal aide for Sen. Edward Kennedy (D-Mass.), Senate Armed Services Cmte. senior fellow, U.S. strategic policy, Intern'l. Institute for Strategic Studies (London). senior dep. issues dir. for foreign policy and national defense, Dukakis for President Committee. senior analyst, RAND Corp. (Santa Monica, Calif.). 1993-94, dep. asst. sec. for analysis, bureau of intelligence and research, U.S. Dept. of State. 3/ 94-12/96, dir., policy planning staff, U.S. Dept. of State. 1997-present, dep. natl. security adviser and dep. asst. to the President for National Security Affairs, National Security Council, The White House.

James Steinberg was named deputy national security adviser and deputy assistant to the President for national security affairs on December 18, 1996. He had previously served as director of the State Department's policy planning staff since 1994. He had served as deputy assistant secretary for analysis at the bureau of intelligence and research at State from 1993 to 1994.

In his current position, Steinberg serves as one of two deputies to National Security Council Director Sandy Berger. As part of the solution to one of the controversies dogging the Clinton White House as a result of the 1996 campaign, Berger has designated Steinberg as "the only person on the national security staff allowed to have contact with the Democratic National Committee." (*New York Times*, April 21, 1997).

Steinberg has previously served as a senior analyst for the RAND Corporation, and as issues director for foreign policy and national defense for the presidential campaign of Michael Dukakis. He has also been a senior fellow in U.S. strategic policy at the International Institute for Strategic Studies in London. Steinberg worked as principal aide to Senator Edward Kennedy (D-Mass.) on the Senate Armed Services Committee.

In previous legal work, he served as minority counsel to the U.S. Senate Labor and Human Resources Committee and as special assistant to the U.S. assistant attorney general in the civil division of the Justice Department. He clerked for Judge David L. Bazelon at the U.S. Court of Appeals and worked as a special assistant to the assistant secretary for planning and evaluation at the U.S. Department of Health, Education and Welfare.

Steinberg is married and resides in the District of Columbia. He is a member of the D.C. Bar and has authored a number of books and articles on foreign and domestic policy.

Deputy Assistant to the President for National Security Affairs
MG Donald L. Kerrick
202/456-9471   FAX 202/456-9460
Rm. G/WW

Education: B.A., Florida Southern College. M.S., Univ. of Southern Calif. Military Education: Armor Officer Basic Course; Military Intelligence Officer Advance Course; U.S. Army Command and General Staff College; and National War College.

Professional: 2nd Lieutenant, U.S. Army: combat experience in Southeast Asia and Desert Storm; commander: military intelligence company, aviation company, military intelligence battalion, & a military intelligence brigade. Staff: U.S. Army, Berlin; U.S. Army Intelligence & Security Command; the Third Army; the Army Staff; & the Joint Staff. 1994-95, director of European affairs, National Security Council, The White House. 1995-96, director for operations, Defense Intelligence Agency. January 1997-present, deputy assistant to the President for national security affairs, National Security Council.

Major General Donald Kerrick became the deputy assistant to the President for national security affairs on the National Security Council in January of 1997. Prior to that position, Kerrick had served as director for operations at the Defense Intelligence Agency.

In 1994 and 1995, Kerrick served on the White House's National Security Council as director of European affairs, where he was responsible for developing and managing U.S. policy in Europe, including the former Yugoslavia and the North Atlantic Treaty Organization. He also served, by presidential appointment, as the White House and National Security Council representative on the United States' Balkans Peacekeeping Delegation that concluded a peace accord ending the Balkan conflict.

Kerrick has extensive foreign service with two tours in Germany in Berlin and Augsburg, two in the Republic of Korea both at Camp Humphreys, and one in Thailand at Ramasun Station, and in Saudi Arabia while assigned to Third Army, the Army component of the U.S. Central Command.

His combat experience includes service in Southeast Asia and Desert Storm. Kerrick has commanded a military intelligence company, an aviation company, a military intelligence battalion, and a military intelligence brigade. Staff assignments include service with the U.S. Army Berlin, the U.S. Army Intelligence and Security Command, the Third Army, the Army Staff, the Joint Staff, and the National Security Council.

Kerrick was commissioned a second lieutenant in the U.S. Army upon graduation from Florida Southern College and was promoted form brigadier general to major general in 1997. He holds a master of science degree from the University of Southern California. His military education includes the Armor Officer Basic course, the

Military Intelligence Officer Advance Course, the U.S. Army Command and General Staff College, and the National War College.

Among the military awards and decorations received by Kerrick are the Defense Distinguished Service Medal, the Defense Superior Service Medal with one Oak Leaf Cluster, the Legion of Merit with two Oak Leaf Clusters, the Bronze Staff Medal, the Meritorious Service Medal with three Oak Leaf Clusters, the Air Medal, and the Army Commendation Medal. Additionally, he is a Master Army Aviator and is authorized to wear the Army General Staff, Joint Staff identification, and Presidential Service Badges. He also received the Defense Intelligence Agency Director's Award in 1997. His civilian awards include the Secretary of State's Distinguished Service Award, the Distinguished Alumni Achievement Citation for Distinguished Career Achievement from Florida Southern College, and an honorary Doctor of Diplomacy conferred by Florida Southern College.

Kerrick is married to Thayne W. Kerrick.

Assistant to the President for National Security Affairs and
    National Security Adviser to Vice President Al Gore
Mr. Leon Fuerth
202/456-9501   FAX 202/456-9500
Rm. 294

Personal: born 1939 in New York City.

Education: B.A., M.A., New York Univ. M.A., John F. Kennedy School of Government, Harvard University.

Professional: 1969, entered the Foreign Service, U.S. State Department. 1969-79: served in bureau of intelligence and research; U.S. Consulate General (Zagreb, Yugoslavia); special assistant to the counselor of the department; special assistant to the director, political-military bureau; special assistant for policy planning to the assistant secretary for European affairs; desk officer, NATO Nuclear and Arms Control Affairs. 1979-85, senior staff member, U.S. House Select Committee on Intelligence. 1985-92, senior staff aide for national security affairs, Senator Al Gore, Jr. (D-Tenn.) 1993-present, national security adviser for the vice president and subsequently asst. to the President for national security affairs, Office of the Vice President.

Leon Fuerth continues as national security adviser for Vice President Gore during the Clinton/Gore Administration's second term. He also serves as assistant the President for National Security Affairs on the National Security Council.

Fuerth has worked with Gore on national security affairs since the late-70's when Gore served on the U.S. House Select Committee on Intelligence.

Fuerth has been a key player in administration decision-making on arms control, foreign policy, and national security. Fuerth was chosen to sit on the White House Deputies Committee, a group of officials from each of the national security departments that meets several times weekly to hammer out foreign policy options in the White House Situation Room. Among the Deputies Committee's responsibilities was the management of U.S. responses on Bosnia.

Fuerth was a 10-year veteran of the foreign service before he first went to work on Capitol Hill. In 1979 he became a senior staff member for the House Select Committee on Intelligence and worked with then-US Representative Gore. He served on that select committee until joining Gore's Senate staff in 1985 as senior staff aide for national security affairs.

While in the foreign service, Fuerth served in the US consulate in Zagreb, Yugoslavia and acquired expertise in Eastern Europe and US-NATO relations. In April 1993, the President sent Fuerth to Europe to work with US allies on toughening sanctions against the Serbs in

Yugoslavia. A few months later, Fuerth traveled to Moscow to oppose Russian export of rocket technology to India.

Fuerth is a native of New York City and holds bachelors and masters degrees from New York University and a masters in public administration from Harvard's Kennedy School of Government. He was in the foreign service from 1969 to 1979, developing expertise in arms control and US relations with the Soviet Union, Eastern Europe, and NATO.

Fuerth and his wife have four children.

Executive Secretary

Ms. Glyn T. Davies
202/456-9461
Rm. G/WW

The Executive Secretary serves as the chief manager and administrative officer of the NSC. It is the job of the Executive Secretary to assist in directing the activities of the NSC staff on the broad range of defense, intelligence and foreign policy matters. The office tasks, reviews and insures proper coordination of all information and action memoranda submitted by the NSC staff to the National Security Advisor and the President. The Executive Secretary is the principal point of contact between the National Security Council and other government agencies and with the Executive Offices of the President.

African Affairs

Special Assistant to the President and Senior Director
Mr. Joseph C. Wilson, IV
202/456-9261   FAX 202/456-9260
OEOB Rm. 499

Personal: born in Bridgeport, Conn.

Education: B.A., Univ. of Calif. at Santa Barbara.

Professional: 1988-91, deputy chief of mission, U.S. Embassy, Baghdad, Iraq. 1992-95, U.S. Ambassador to Gabon and to Sao Tome and Principe. 1995-97, political advisor to the commander-in-chief, U.S. Armed Forces in Europe. Aug. 1997-present, special assistant to the President and senior director for African affairs, National Security Council.

In August of 1997, National Security Advisor Samuel Berger announced the appointment of Ambassador Joseph Wilson as special assistant to the President and senior director for African affairs at the National Security Council. The office advises and assists the President and National Security Advisor on all aspects of U.S. foreign policy with respect to Sub-Saharan Africa's economy, politics and security concerns. Wilson succeeded Dr. Susan Rice who became assistant secretary for African affairs at the State Department.

A career member of the Foreign Service, Ambassador Wilson has served in various positions including deputy chief of mission in Bujumbura, Burundi and Brazzaville, Congo. His other assignments include tours in Niger, Togo, and South Africa.

At the time of his appointment, Wilson was serving as political advisor to the commander-in-chief of the U.S. Armed Forces in Europe. From 1992 to 1995, he was U.S. Ambassador to Gabon and Sao Tome and Principe. From 1988 to 1991, Wilson served as deputy chief of the U.S. mission in Baghdad, Iraq. Prior to the launching of Operation Desert Storm, he was responsible for negotiating the release of several hundred American hostages held by the Iraqi government.

As an American Political Science Association Congressional Fellow, Wilson worked in the offices of then-Sen. Albert Gore (D-Tenn.) and then-House Majority Whip, Rep. Thomas Foley (D-Wash.).

Wilson has a daughter and a son.

Asian Affairs

Special Assistant to the President and Senior Director
Ms. Sandra J. Kristoff
202/456-9251   FAX 202/456-9250
OEOB Rm. 493

Personal: born 1949 in Washington, Pa.

Education: B.A., M.A., The American Univ. J.D., George Washington University Law School.

Professional: 1985-92, deputy asst. U.S. trade representative, then asst. U.S. trade representative for Asia and the Pacific, Office of the U.S. Trade Representative (USTR). 1992-93, deputy asst. sec. for East Asia and Pacific affairs, U.S. Dept. of State. 1993-94, director for Asian affairs, National Security Council. 1994-95, special assistant to the President and senior director for Asia Pacific Economic Affairs with joint appointment to the National Security Council and the National Economic Council. 1995, U.S. Ambassador for Asia Pacific Economic Cooperation, U.S. Dept, of State. 1996-present, special asst. to the President for Asian affairs, National Security Council.

Sandra Kristoff is a career senior executive service officer with more than 20 years of government service. She currently serves as senior director for Asian affairs at the National Security Council.

The Asian Affairs Office of the National Security Council advises and assists the President and the National Security Advisor on all aspects of U.S. foreign policy with respect to the Asia-Pacific region, including Northeast Asia, Southeast Asia(including Indochina) and Oceania.

In addition to focusing on U.S. policy for the many bilateral relationships in the region, the Asian Affairs Office also advises the President on regional security and institutions (APEC, the ASEAN Regional Forum), the North Korean nuclear problem (together with the Nonproliferation Directorate) and the promotion of human rights and democracy in the region.

Kristoff served for seven years at the US Trade Representative's Office as deputy assistant for Asia and the Pacific. She went to the State Department in 1992, serving as deputy assistant secretary for East Asia and Pacific affairs. She became director for Asian affairs at the National Security Council in 1993 and then served as special assistant to the President and senior director for Asia Pacific Economic Affairs with joint appointments to both the National Security Council and the National Economic Council. In 1995, she served as U.S. Ambassador for Asia Pacific Economic Cooperation (APEC) and as deputy assistant secretary of State for East Asia and Pacific affairs.

Central and Eastern Europe

Special Assistant to the President and Senior Director
Mr. Steve Flanagan
202/456-9151   FAX 202/456-9100
OEOB Rm. 372

Steve Flanagan was named to succeed Daniel Fried as special assistant to the President for national security affairs and senior director for Central and Eastern Europe in the fall of 1997.

In his role as head of the office, Flanagan advises and assists the President and National Security Advisor on all aspects of U.S. foreign policy with respect to the eleven countries of the region, including Estonia, Latvia, Lithuania, Poland, the Czech Republic, Slovakia, Hungary, Slovenia, Romania, Bulgaria and Albania.

Flanagan and his staff advise and assist the President in carrying out his policies of support for democracy, free market-based economic prosperity and security in CEE. Among the issues on which the office provides advise and assistance to the President are: the enlargement of NATO and related aspects of European security; CEE integration with other key Euroatlantic institutions; promotion of intra-CEE cooperation and friendship, for example, between Romania and Hungary; support for U.S. trade and investment with CEE; the development of military relations between the U.S. and CEE democracies; U.S. economic assistance priorities with CEE; and support for the strengthening of democratic institutions and practices within the region.

Defense Policy and Arms Control

Special Assistant to the President and Senior Director
Mr. Robert G. Bell
202/456-9191   FAX 202/456-9190
OEOB Rm. 386

Personal: born 8/26/47 in Birmingham, Ala.

Education: B.S. (with honors), U.S. Air Force Academy, 1969. M.A. in international security studies, Fletcher School of Law and Diplomacy, Tufts University, 1970.

Professional: 1970-75, squadron commander in air traffic control and communications field, U.S. Air Force (Delaware, Florida, and Greenland). 1975-78 and 1980, defense analyst, Congressional Research Service (CRS), Library of Congress. 1979, staff director, Military Committee at the North Atlantic Assembly (Brussels, Belgium). 1981-84, principal staff aide for defense policy and arms control issues, Senator Charles H. Percy, (R-Ill.) chairman of the Senate Committee on Foreign Relations. 1984-93, principal staff assistant for arms control issues, Senator Sam Nunn,(D-Ga.) chairman of the Senate Committee on Armed Services. 1993-present, senior director for defense policy and arms control and special assistant to the President for national security affairs, National Security Council (NSC).

Robert Bell serves the President as special assistant and senior director for defense policy and arms control at the National Security Council. He has held this position since 1993. Bell advises President Clinton on a wide range of defense and arms control issues such as national security strategy, defense budgets and programs, defense conversion, weapons acquisition, and strategic nuclear and conventional arms control.

Bell began his public service career as a squadron commander in air traffic control and communication in the U.S. Air Force serving in Delaware, Florida, and Greenland. In the mid 70's, he served as a defense analyst for the Congressional Research Service of the Library of Congress.   At CRS, Bell authored studies for Members and congressional committees on strategic weapons and doctrine, NATO, arms control, and arms sales policy. He directed a staff of 50 in studies of foreign and defense policy issues.

In 1979, Bell served as staff director for the Military Committee at the North Atlantic Assembly in Brussels, and returned to Capitol Hill in 1981 to serve as principal staff aide for defense policy and arms control issues for Chairman Charles H. Percy (R-Ill.) on the Foreign Relations Committee. From 1984 to 1993, Bell worked as principal staff assistant for arms control issues for Chairman Sam Nunn (D-Ga.) on the Senate Committee on Armed Services.

Democracy, Human Rights & Humanitarian Affairs

Special Assistant the President and Senior Director
Mr. Eric Schwartz
202/456-9141   FAX 202/456-9140
OEOB, Rm. 365

Education: B.A. in political science (with honors), State Univ. of N.Y. at Binghamton. M.P.A., Woodrow Wilson School of Public and International Affairs, Princeton Univ. J.D., N.Y. Univ. School of Law.

Professional: Washington director, Asia Watch Committee, Human Rights Watch. staff consultant, House Foreign Affairs subcommittee on Asian and Pacific affairs. director, office of global affairs and multilateral programs; March, 1996-present, special asst. to the President and sr. dir. for democracy, human rights and humanitarian affairs, National Security Council, The White House.

Eric Schwartz was named as special assistant to the President and senior director for democracy, human rights and humanitarian affairs at the National Security Council by then-National Security Adviser Anthony Lake in February of 1996. The appointment expanded the responsibilities of the NSC Office of Democracy to include all aspects of U.S. foreign policy with respect to democratic governance, human rights and humanitarian affairs (including refugee issues and migration).

Schwartz had previously served on the NSC staff as director of the office of global affairs and multilateral programs. He joined the White House staff after serving as a staff consultant for the U.S. House Foreign Affairs subcommittee on Asian and Pacific affairs. Before going to Capitol Hill, Schwartz had served as Washington Director of the Asia Watch Committee for Human Rights Watch, a humanitarian advocacy organization.

Schwartz earned his B.A. in political science with honors from the State University of New York at Binghamton. He received a master's in public administration from the Woodrow Wilson School of Public and International Affairs at Princeton University and a J.D. from New York University School of Law.

European Affairs

Special Assistant to the President and Senior Director
Mr. Donald K. Bandler
202/456-9151   FAX 202/456-9150
OEOB Rm. 368

Personal: born in Pennsylvania.

Education: B.A. in political philosophy, Kenyon College (Ohio). Master's Degree in classics, St. Johns College (Santa Fe, N.M.). J.D., George Washington University's National Law Center.

Professional: career Foreign Service: Africa, Bonn, France and Washington. director, office of Israel and Arab-Israeli affairs, U.S. State Dept. 1995-97, deputy chief of mission, U.S. Embassy, France. August 1997-present, special assistant to the President and senior director for European affairs, National Security Council, The White House.

National Security Advisor Samuel Berger announced on August 26, 1997 that Donald Bandler had been appointed as special assistant to the President and senior director for European affairs succeeding Alexander Vershbow.

The Office for European Affairs advises and assists the President and the National Security Advisor on all aspects of U.S. foreign policy with respect to all the countries of Western and Southern Europe, Canada, the North Atlantic Treaty Organization (NATO), the Organization for Security and Cooperation in Europe (OSCE), the European Union (EU), and other European regional organizations.

Among the issues that the office provides advice and assistance to the President on are: the evolution and future enlargement of NATO; development of close political and economic cooperation between the U.S. and the EU; supporting the peace process in Northern Ireland; implementing the Dayton peace agreements in Bosnia; promoting long-term stability in the Balkans; promoting a negotiated settlement on Cyprus and reducing tensions between Greece and Turkey; and the conduct of bilateral relations with the United Kingdom, Germany, France, Canada and other close friends and allies of the U.S. in Europe.

Bandler, a career foreign service officer, had been deputy chief of mission as the U.S. Embassy in France since 1995. During the last eight months of that tenure, he was chargé d'Affaires and U.S. Observer to the Council of Europe. Prior to that, he served as director of the State Department's office of Israel and Arab-Israeli affairs, and represented the U.S. in the Middle East Peace Process environmental negotiations.

Bandler had earlier European assignments in Bonn during German reunification, in France, and in Washington as coordinator for the Conference on Security and Cooperation in Europe. He is a frequent speaker on US-European and security affairs.

A native of Pennsylvania, Bandler received his BA from Kenyon College and a J.D. from the George Washington University. Following his marriage in 1972, he and his wife went to Nigeria, where he worked in the ministry of education. According to Bandler, "I really caught the international bug then and it was then I took the Foreign Service Exam". He worked in the Foreign Service while attending law school at night and much of that work was done in and about Africa (*Jewish Exponent,* December 2, 1994).

He and his wife, Jane Goldwin Bandler, a psychological counselor, have two daughters and a son.

Global Issues and Multilateral Affairs

Special Assistant to the President and Senior Director
Mr. Richard A. Clarke
202/456-9351   FAX 202/456-9360
OEOB Rm. 302

Personal: born in Cambridge, Mass.

Education: B.A., Univ. of Pennsylvania, 1972. S.M., Massachusetts

Institute of Technology, 1978.

Professional: 1973-77, policy analyst, U.S. Dept. of Defense. 1978-79, senior analyst, Pacific Sierra Research Corp. 1979-85, Bureau of Politico-Military Affairs; 1985-89, dep. asst. sec. for intelligence analysis; 1989-93, asst. sec. for political-military affairs, U.S. Dept. of State. 1993-present, spec. asst. to the President and senior director, office of global issues and multilateral affairs, National Security Council.

A career member of the Senior Executive Service, Richard Clarke joined the White House staff during the Bush Administration in 1992 and was asked to remain when the Clinton team came on in 1993.

Clarke chairs administration committees on issues such as peacekeeping, terrorism, and international crime. The office of global issues, which he directs, performs both a planning and a crisis coordination function for the National Security Council. It also serves as a focal point for issues such as international resources, UN affairs, international narcotics control, and arms transfers.

Since joining the government nearly 25 years ago, Clarke has served in Washington in national security positions at the Defense Department, the State Department, the intelligence community and the White House.

Intelligence

Special Assistant to the President and
    Senior Director for Intelligence Programs
Mr. Rand R. Beers
202/456-9341   FAX 202/456-9340
OEOB, Rm. 300

Professional: career CIA official. director, Center for Defense Trade, U.S. Department of State. 1993-present, special assistant to the President and senior director for intelligence programs, National Security Council.

Rand Beers, a career Central Intelligence Agency professional, is currently serving as special assistant to the President and senior director for intelligence programs at the National Security Council. The office advises and assists the President and the National Security Advisor on all aspects of U.S. foreign policy with respect to all issues relating to intelligence.

Inter-American Affairs

Special Assistant to the President and Senior Director
Mr. James Dobbins
202/456-9131   FAX 202/456-9130
OEOB Rm. 361

Personal: born 1942 in New York City.

Education: B.A., Georgetown Univ. School of Foreign Service, 1963.

Professional: 1964-67, officer, U.S. Navy. 1967, U.S. Foreign Service: policy planning staff, the European Bureau, and the office of the counselor, U.S. Department of State. Member: U.S. Delegation to the Vietnam Peace Talks; U.S. Delegation to the OECD; and U.S. Mission to the United Nations. Assignments in London, Paris and Strasbourg. 1985-89, deputy chief of mission, Bonn.; 1989-91, acting assistant secretary of state for European affairs.; 1991-93, U.S. Representative to the European Community; 1995-96, State Department Fellow, Council on Foreign Relations. October 1993-March 1996, coordinator and senior adviser to Secretary of State Warren Christopher, on Somalia, then on Haiti. March 1996-present, special assistant to the president and senior director for Inter-American affairs, National Security Council.

Ambassador James F. Dobbins was appointed special assistant to the President and senior director for Inter-American affairs at the National Security Council in March of 1996. In that role, he advises the President and the National Security Advisor on foreign, defense, intelligence, economic, and other policy issues involving the Western Hemisphere. In this capacity, he manages both country-specific issues covering Haiti, Cuba, Mexico, and Columbia, and regional trade, security, and counternarcotics policy for Latin America.

Prior to joining the National Security Council, Dobbins had served from 1993 to 1996 at the Department of State as the coordinator and senior adviser to Secretary of State Warren Christopher, first on Somalia and then on Haiti.

Ambassador Dobbins was the U.S. Representative to the European Community with the rank of ambassador from 1991 to 1993. He worked on the December 1992 US-EC accord on agricultural trade, which laid the essential bases for the 1994 GATT World Trade Agreement.

From 1989 to 1991, Dobbins served as principal deputy assistant secretary and then acting assistant secretary for European and Canadian affairs, in which capacities he managed American diplomacy through the unification of Germany, the liberation of Eastern Europe, and the break up of the Soviet Union.

The European Bureau was then the largest policy arm of the Department of State, with an annual budget of nearly $400 million. With the end of the Cold War, Dobbins instigated a major shift in the bureau's resources, initiating a move of hundreds of positions and tens of millions of dollars from West to East in order to staff new posts and expand old ones in the former Warsaw Pact and Soviet Union. Dobbins had spent the previous four years as minister and deputy chief of the U.S. Mission in Bonn, Germany.

Dobbins has received two Superior Honor Awards, two Presidential Awards, five Senior Performance Awards, the Department of the Army Decoration for Distinguished Civilian Service, the Armed Forces Expeditionary Medal, the National Defense Service Medal, and the Expeditionary Medal of the Republic of Vietnam.

Dobbins is married and has two sons. He speaks German and French.

International Economic Affairs

Special Assistant to the President and Senior Director
Mr. Sherman Boone
202/456-9297
OEOB Rm. 365

The International Economic Affairs office advises and assists the President and the National Security Advisor on all aspects of U.S. foreign policy with respect to U.S. international economic policies.

Among the issues the office provides advice and assistance to the President on are the World Trade Organization, regional trade initiatives in Asia and Latin America and bilateral trade and investment issues.

Special Asst. to the President for Intl. Trade and Finance
Mr. Robert D. Kyle
202/456-9281   FAX 202/456-9280
Rm. 2/WW

See profile under the National Economic Council

Legal Adviser

Special Assistant to the President and Legal Adviser
Mr. James E. Baker
202/456-9111
OEOB Rm. 348

In coordination with the White House Counsel, the Legal Office of the NSC advises and assists the President and the National Security Advisor on legal issues relevant to national security. The Office also provides legal advice to NSC staff members on matters arising in the course of their official responsibilities.

Among the issues on which the office provides advice and assistance to the President are the interpretation of U.S. domestic law, international treaties, and customary international law arising in the consideration of national security issues. In providing this advice, the Legal Office works closely with the General Counsel of relevant agencies, the Justice Department, and the White House Counsel's office. The Office also reviews legislative proposals, particularly for implications for the President's foreign policy and commander-in-chief prerogatives. The Office reviews official documents going to the President for approval (e.g. reports to Congress, Presidential Determinations and certifications).

Legislative Affairs

Special Assistant to the President and Senior Director
Ms. Mara Rudman
202/456-9171   FAX   202/456-9170
OEOB Rm. 375

Personal: born 8/23/62 in San Antonio, Texas.

Education: A.B. (summa cum laude), Dartmouth College, 1984. J.D. (cum laude), Harvard Law School, 1990.

Professional: 1984-87, leg. asst., Rep. Gerry Studds, D-Mass. 1990-91, law clerk, Judge Stanley Marcus, U.S. District Court, Southern District of Fla. 1991-93, assoc., Hogan & Hartson. 1993-95, legal counsel, majority; 1995-97, Democratic counsel, House International Relations Committee. 1997-present, special asst. to the President and senior director for legislative affairs, National Security Council.

Mara Rudman, a veteran Hill staffer, replaced William Danvers in 1997 as Senior Director of Legislative Affairs at the NSC. The legislative affairs office advises and assists the President and the National Security Advisor on all aspects of U.S. foreign policy with respect to all legislation on National Security matters.

Rudman's first job after college in the mid-1980s was as a foreign affairs legislative assistant for Rep. Gerry Studds, D-Mass. After law school and a stint at the law firm of Hogan & Hartson, she returned to Capitol Hill at the beginning of the 103rd Congress and served on the House International Relations Committee until assuming her current responsibilities at the NSC.

Near East and South Asian Affairs

Special Assistant to the President and Senior Director
Mr. Bruce O. Riedel
202/456-9121   FAX 202/456-9120

OEOB Rm. 351

Education: B.A., Brown Univ. M.A. in history, Harvard Univ., 1976.

Professional: 1977-91, intelligence analyst, Central Intelligence Agency with Middle East assignments from 1984 to 1986 and Persian Gulf Task Force in 1990-91. 1991-93, director, Near East and South Asian affairs, National Security Council. 1993-95, national intelligence officer for Near East and South Asia for the director, Central Intelligence Agency. 1995-97, dep. asst. sec. of defense for Near Eastern and South Asian affairs, U.S. Dept. of Defense. April 1997-present, special asst. to the President and senior dir. for Near East and South Asian affairs, National Security Council, The White House.

Bruce Riedel is the special assistant to the President and senior director for Near East and South Asian affairs of the National Security Council. He replaced Mark Parris in April, 1997.

Riedel serves as the principal advisor to the President on all foreign policy and defense matters regarding four distinct areas abroad: North Africa, the Levant, the Persian Gulf and South Asia.

Among the issues the office provides advice and assistance to the President on are the Middle East peace process; the continued containment of rogue states such as Iraq, Iran, and Libya; the maintenance of good relations with several important U.S. allies; and the challenges for U.S. policy posed by political and economic reform, regional development, ethnic conflict, proliferation of weapons of mass destruction and the rise of political Islam.

Prior to his current White House post, Riedel served as the deputy assistant secretary of Defense for Near Eastern and South Asian Affairs from July 1995 to April 1997. In this position he was the principal advisor to the Secretary of Defense on Middle East and South Asian issues. In January of 1997, Defense Secretary William Perry awarded Riedel the Secretary of Defense Medal for Meritorious Civilian Service.

Before his Defense role, Riedel served as the national intelligence officer (NIO) for Near East and South Asia for the director of central intelligence. In this position he was responsible for preparing the national intelligence estimates on the region and presenting intelligence community judgments to the policy making community.

Before joining the National Intelligence Council in the summer of 1993, Riedel served for over two years as director for Near East and South Asian affairs on the staff of the National Security Council at the White House. At the NSC, his duties included responsibility for Persian Gulf and South Asian affairs. He served in this capacity for both President Bush and President Clinton.

A career intelligence analyst, Riedel joined the CIA in 1977. From 1984 through 1986, he was assigned overseas in the Middle East. Riedel served as deputy chief, Persian Gulf Task Force at the CIA during the 1990-91 Iraq-Kuwait crisis. He was awarded the Intelligence Medal of Merit for his contribution to CIA analysis during this assignment.

Riedel has traveled widely in the Near East and has met with numerous regional leaders. He is a graduate of Brown University and received a master's degree in history from Harvard in 1976.

Nonproliferation and Export Controls

Special Assistant to the President and Senior Director
Mr. Gary S. Samore
202/456-9181   FAX   202/456-9180
OEOB Rm. 380

Personal: born 3/31/53 in Brookline, Mass.

Education: Ph.D. in government, Harvard Univ., 1984.

Professional: 1984-86, Lawrence Livermore National Laboratory. 1987-92, spec. asst. to the ambassador-at-large for nonproliferation and nuclear energy policy; 1992-93, dir., office of regional nonproliferation affairs, bureau of political military affairs; 1994-95, dep. to the ambassador-at-large for Korean affairs, U.S. Dept. of State. 1995-96, dir. for nonproliferation and export controls; Nov. 1996-present, special asst. to the President and sr. dir. for nonproliferation and export controls, National Security Council.

Dr. Gary Samore was appointed special assistant to the President and senior director for nonproliferation and export controls at the National Security Council on November 8, 1996. He had previously served as director.

The Nonproliferation and Export Controls Office advises and assists the President and the National Security Advisor on all aspects of U.S. foreign policy with respect to all issues relating to nonproliferation and arms control. Among the issues are: diplomatic efforts with respect to North Korea, China, Japan, the former Soviet Union, South Asia, the Middle East, South Africa and Latin America; fissile material initiatives and controls including the US-Russia Agreement on Highly-Enriched Uranium and efforts to combat nuclear smuggling; multilateral regimes such as the Nuclear Non-Proliferation Treaty, Biological and Toxic Weapons Convention, Chemical Weapons Convention, Australia Group, Missile Technology Control Regime, Nuclear Suppliers Group and the Wassenaar Arrangements; export controls for specific economic sectors as well as the Export Administration Act; and conventional arms transfer policy.

Prior to joining the National Security Council, Dr. Samore held various positions at the Department of State working on nonproliferation issues. From 1994 to 1995, he was deputy to the Ambassador-at-Large for Korean Affairs, Robert Gallucci. He led several U.S. delegations to expert level talks with North Korea to negotiate the US-DPRK Agreed Framework of October 21, 1994, and the subsequent agreement between North Korea and the Korean Peninsula Energy Development Organization (KEDO) for a light water reactor project. For his role in the North Korea nuclear negotiations, he received the Secretary of Defense Medal for Meritorious Civilian Service in October of 1995.

From 1992 to 1993, Samore headed the office of regional

nonproliferation affairs in the bureau of political military affairs at State. He was special assistant to the Ambassador-at-large for Nonproliferation and Nuclear Energy Policy, Richard T. Kennedy, from 1987 to 1992. He is the author of numerous publications on nonproliferation issues.

Samore worked at the Lawrence Livermore National Laboratory from 1984 to 1986. He was a National Science Foundation and Olin Fellow at Harvard University, where he received his Ph.D. in government in 1984. He is a member of Phi Beta Kappa.

Samore and his wife Paula have a daughter.

Public Affairs/Press Office

Special Asst. to the President, Dep. Press Sec. and Senior Director
Ms. Anne Luzzatto
202/456-9271   FAX 202/456-9270
OEOB Rm. 489

Personal: born 7/25/41 in Washington, DC.

Education: B.A., Univ. of Wisconsin at Madison, 1963. J.D., American Univ. Law School, 1978. M.A. in international economics, Johns Hopkins School of Advanced International Studies, 1984.

Professional: 1984, deputy press secretary, Mondale-Ferraro presidential campaign. 1985-87, vice president, corporate external relations, CBS Inc. 1987-92, vice president, public affairs, Citibank. 1992, The Investigative Group, Inc. 1992-93, Clinton-Gore Transition Team. 1993-95, assistant U.S. trade representative for public affairs. 1995-96, director, office of public affairs, U.S. Department of Commerce. 1997-present, special assistant to the president and senior director for public affairs, National Security Council, The White House.

Anne Luzzatto began her service in the Clinton administration working as the U.S. Trade Representative for public affairs for Mickey Kantor, when he served as the United States Trade Representative. When Kantor moved over to head the Commerce Department following the 1995 death of former Secretary Ron Brown, Luzzatto moved to Commerce to direct the office of public affairs. In Clinton's second term, Luzzatto serves as senior director for public affairs at the National Security Council as well as deputy press secretary.

Luzzatto and her staff serve the President, National Security Advisor and White House Press Secretary on all press-related matters involving national security and foreign policy issues. The press secretaries also coordinate all contacts between the NSC staff and the press. Responsibilities include coordinating press affairs with U.S. Government agencies responsible for foreign, defense and intelligence policy. The NSC press secretaries provide briefings the White House press corps on foreign policy matters. The press secretaries accompany the President on all foreign trips where they brief the President, the National Security Advisor and the Press Secretary on breaking foreign news stories and brief the press corps traveling with the President.

Luzzatto brings a background of political and press work to her position. She served as deputy press secretary in 1984 for the Mondale-Ferraro campaign and then joined CBS as vice president for corporate external relations. From 1987 to 1992, she worked as vice president for public affairs at Citibank. In the election year of 1992, she worked for the Investigative Group and the Clinton-Gore Transition Team.

Born in Washington, D.C. and raised in Northern California, Luzzatto graduated from the University of Wisconsin at Madison in 1963 and received her law degree from American University Law School in 1978. She earned a master's in international economics from Johns Hopkins School of Advanced International Studies in 1984.

Russia/Ukraine/Eurasia Affairs

Special Assistant to the President and Senior Director
Mr. William Harrison Courtney
202/456-9161   FAX 202/456-9160
OEOB Rm. 374

Personal: born in West Virginia.

Education: B.A., West Virginia Univ. Ph.D. in economics, Brown Univ.

Professional: international affairs fellow, Council of Foreign Relations. 1972-present, career foreign service officer: service at the Nuclear and Space Talks (Geneva); American Embassy (Moscow); American Embassy (Brasilia); Ambassador to Kazakstan; co-chair of the US delegation on Safety, Security and Dismantlement of Nuclear Weapons; head of U.S. delegation to the implementing commissions for the Threshold Test Ban and the Peaceful Nuclear Explosions Treaties. 1995-97, ambassador to Georgia. August 25, 1997-present, special assistant to the President and senior director for Russia, Ukraine and Eurasian affairs, National Security Council, The White House.

National Security Advisor Samuel Berger announced on July 25, 1997 that William Harrison Courtney would become a special assistant to the President and senior director for Russia, Ukraine and Eurasian affairs, effective August 25, 1997, succeeding Steve Pifer.

The Russia, Ukraine and Eurasian affairs office advises the President and the National Security Advisor on all aspects of U.S. foreign and security policy regarding Russia, Ukraine and the other New Independent States (NIS) of the former Soviet Union (Armenia, Azerbaijan, Belarus, Georgia, Kazakhstan, Kyrgyzstan, Moldova, Tajikstan, Turkmenistan and Uzbekistan).

The United States wants the NIS to develop as stable, democratic, market-oriented and outward-looking states, secure in their borders and at peace with their neighbors. In addition to advising the President and the National Security Advisor on U.S. bilateral relationships with these countries, the office focuses on reducing former Soviet nuclear and other weapons of mass destruction and supporting the political and legal reforms necessary for democratic systems and the macroeconomic and structural reforms critical to competitive market economies.

William Courtney had been U.S. ambassador to Georgia since 1995. Prior to his service at our Embassy in Tbilisi, he was ambassador to Kazakstan, co-chair of the U.S. delegation on Safety, Security and Dismantlement of Nuclear Weapons, and head of the US delegation, with the rank of ambassador, to the implementing commissions established by the Threshold Test Ban and Peaceful Nuclear Explosions Treaties.

Earlier, Courtney had served at the Nuclear and Space Talks in Geneva and at the American Embassies in Moscow and Brasilia. He was an international affairs fellow at the Council on Foreign Relations and has been a career Foreign Service Officer since 1972.

A native of West Virginia, Ambassador Courtney is a graduate of West Virginia University and received a Ph.D. in economics from Brown University. He is married and has two children.

White House Situation Room

1600 Pennsylvania Ave., NW / Washington DC 20500

Director
Mr. Kevin Cosgriff
202/456-9433
Rm. SR

The White House Situation Room is a 24-hour watch and alert center. Its mission is to provide the President, the National Security Advisor and the members of the NSC staff with current intelligence and open-source information in support of the formulation and implementation of national security policy.

Office of Management and Budget

17th Street & Pennsylvania Avenue, NW
Washington, D.C. 20503
202/395-7524

INTRODUCTION

In carrying out its responsibilities to prepare the Administration's budget and evaluate, formulate, and coordinate management procedures and program objectives, the Office of Management and Budget has a section that focuses on national security and international affairs.

The primary activity of the Office of Management and Budget (OMB) in the interagency Trade Promotion Coordinating Committee (TPCC), is in the TPCC Budget Committee for which OMB is the chair. The TPCC Budget Committee was responsible for the creation and compilation of the first unified trade promotion budget published in the 1994 TPCC Annual Report and updated in the President's 1996 budget. The unified budget provides a comprehensive analysis of where the Federal Government spends resources to assist U.S. companies by agency, types of trade promotion activities, industrial sectors, geographic export markets, and firm size. OMB and the TPCC Budget Committee are also leading the effort to develop a comprehensive and consistent set of trade promotion performance measures designed to help assess where federal trade promotion can best serve U.S. businesses.

Director
Mr. Franklin Raines
202/395-4840   FAX 202/395-3888
OEOB Rm. 252

Personal: born 1/14/49 in Seattle, Wash.

Education: B.A. (magna cum laude), Harvard Univ. Rhodes Scholar, Oxford Univ. J.D. (cum laude), Harvard Univ. Law School, 1976.

Professional: 1972-73, assoc. dir., Model Cities Program (Seattle, Wash.). 1976-77, associate, Preston, Thorgrimson, Ellis, Holman and Fletcher (Seattle). 1977-78, asst. dir., domestic policy staff, The White House. 1978-79, assoc. dir., Office of Management and Budget. 1979-82, vice president; 1982-84, senior vice president; 1984-91, general partner, Lazard, Freres and Co. (New York). 1991-96, vice chair, Federal National Mortgage Corporation (Fannie Mae). 1996-present, director, Office of Management and Budget.

Franklin Raines was confirmed as director of the Office of Management Budget by the U.S. Senate on September 6, 1996, and succeeded Alice Rivlin who became a member of the Board of Governors of the Federal Reserve System.

Prior to becoming Director of OMB, Raines was vice chairman of Fannie Mae, headquartered in Washington, D.C. He joined Fannie Mae in July 1991. As vice chairman, he was in charge of Fannie Mae's legal, credit policy, finance, and corporate development functions.

Raines came to Fannie Mae from a general partnership in municipal finance at the investment banking firm of Lazard Freres & Company in New York City. He began at Lazard Freres as a vice president in 1979. At Lazard Freres, he spent much of his time on the fiscal woes of cities such as Cleveland and Chicago. That helped him in 1997 when one of his assignments was to put together a rescue package for the troubled capital city of Washington, D.C.

During the Carter Administration, Raines had served from 1977 to 1978 as assistant director of the White House domestic policy staff and from 1978 to 1979 as associate director for economics and government at the Office of Management and Budget.

Raines received a B.A. in government from Harvard College and a J.D. from Harvard Law School. He also attended Magdalen College at Oxford University as a Rhodes Scholar.

Raines has served as a member of the board of directors of several major corporations, foundations, and public service organizations. He presently serves as chairman of the Visiting Committee of the Harvard Kennedy School of Government, and was formerly president of the Board of Overseers for Harvard University.

Raines was a member of the congressionally-mandated Commission on Roles and Missions of the Armed Forces and served as economics and trade cluster coordinator for the Clinton Presidential Transition. He has also served on a number of federal and state public policy advisory groups regarding tax equity, education, poverty, and welfare reform.

Raines is an elected Fellow of the American Academy of Arts and Sciences, a member of the National Academy for Social Insurance, and of the Council on Foreign Relations. He and his wife, the former Wendy Farrow, have three children.

Communications

Associate Director
Mr. Lawrence J. Haas
202/395-7254
OEOB Rm. 253

Legislative Reference

Chief, Resources-Defense-International Branch
Mr. Ronald K. Peterson
202/395-7302
NEOB Rm. 7228

National Security and International Affairs

Associate Director
VACANT
202/395-4657   FAX 202/395-3513
OEOB Rm. 238

Following the departure of Dr. Gordon Adams as associate director of the Office of National Security and International Affairs, the position was left vacant. The office is responsible for both defense and foreign policy budgets.

International Affairs Division

Deputy Associate Director
Mr. Philip A. DuSault
202/395-4770
NEOB Rm. 10002

Chief, Economic Affairs Branch

Mr. Rodney Bent
202/395-6854
NEOB Rm. 10025

Fiscal Economist
Mr. Ronald L. Silberman
202/395-4595
NEOB Rm. 10025

Chief, State-U.S. Information Agency Branch
Mr. Bruce Sasser
202/395-4580
NEOB Rm. 10026

Office of Science & Technology Policy

Old Executive Office Building
17th St. & Pennsylvania Avenue, NW / Washington DC 20502
202/456-7116   FAX 202/456-6021

INTRODUCTION

The Office of Science and Technology Policy, established in 1976, serves as a source of scientific, engineering, and technological analysis and judgment for the President. It advises the President of scientific and technological considerations involved in areas of national concern, including the economy, national security, health, foreign relations, and the environment.

Assistant to the President for Science and Technology and
  Director, Office of Science and Technology Policy
Dr. John H. (Jack) Gibbons, Ph.D.
202/456-7116   FAX 202/456-6021
Rm. 424

Personal: born 1/15/29, in Harrisonburg, Va.

Education: B.S. in mathematics and chemistry, Randolph-Macon Coll., (Ashland, Va.), 1949. Ph.D. in physics, Duke University, 1954.

Professional: 1954-69, physicist and group leader, nuclear geophysics, Oak Ridge National Laboratory. 1969-73, director, environmental program, Oak Ridge National Laboratory. 1973-74, director, office of energy conservation, Federal Energy Admin. (Wash., D.C.). 1974-79, director, Energy, Environment, and Resources Center, and professor of physics, Univ. of Tennessee. 1979-93, director, office of technology assessment, U.S. Congress. 1993-present, assistant to the President and director, Office of Science and Technology.

John Gibbons is assistant to the President for science and technology, and director of the office of science and technology of The White House. He is the most senior adviser to the president and the vice president on matters of science and technology policy, one of six Cabinet-level, policy-level assistants to the President.

As science adviser, Gibbons also co-chairs the President's Committee of Advisers on Science and Technology; is a member of the Domestic Policy Council, the National Economic Council, the National Security Council; and is a member of and oversees the National Science and Technology Council. In general, the president's science adviser is responsible for coordinating science and technology policy and budgets throughout the federal government.

Gibbons also represents the U.S. in major multilateral and bilateral forums. Multilateral meetings of ministers for science and technology occur in the Organization for Economic Cooperation and Development (OECD), the Asia Pacific Economic Cooperation Forum (APEC), the Summit of the Americas, and among the G-7 nations. High level bilateral meetings require the science adviser's participation in the US-Russia Joint Commission on economic and technological cooperation, the US-South Africa Binational Commission, the US-Japan Joint High Level Committee, and the US-China Joint Commission.

Dr. Gibbons is an internationally recognized scientist who has a deep interest and concern about the support of science and the impacts of technology on society. Following his formal training in physics, he spent 15 years at the Oak Ridge National Laboratory. Beginning in 1970, he pioneered studies on how to use technology to conserve energy and to minimize environmental impacts. In 1973, at the start of the nation's first major energy crisis, he was appointed the first director of the Federal Office of Energy Conservation. Two years later, he returned to Tennessee to the University of Tennessee's Energy, Environment and Resources Center. In 1979, he returned to Washington to direct the office of technology assessment for the U.S. Congress.

Gibbons is a fellow of the American Physical Society and the American Association for the Advancement of Science and is a member of the National Academy of Engineering. He is also a member of the Council on Foreign Relations. He has received the Federation of American Scientists Public Service award, the Leo Szilard Award for Physics in the Public Interest, and medals from the German and French governments for fostering scientific cooperation. In 1995, his home state of Virginia presented him its Life Achievement in Science award.

National Security and International Affairs

Associate Director
Dr. Keri-Ann Jones
202/456-2894   FAX 202/456-6028
OEOB Rm. 494

Education: A.B. in chemistry, Barnard Coll., Columbia Univ., 1975. M.Ph., Dept. of Molecular Biophysics and Biochemistry, Yale Univ., 1981. Ph.D., Dept. of Molecular Biophysics and Biochemistry, Yale Univ., 1985.

Professional: 1985-86, science, engineering and diplomacy fellow, American Association for the Advancement of Science. 1986-89, independent consultant. 1989-program officer, Near East and South Asia, NIH Fogarty International Center for International Health. 1989-

95, various positions, U.S. Agency for International Development. July 1995-March 1996, dep. to the assoc. dir., natl. security and intl. affairs; March 1996-May 1997, acting assoc. dir.; May 1997-present, assoc. dir. for natl. sec. and intl. affairs, Office of Science and Technology Policy, The White House.

Dr. Kerri-Ann Jones is the associate director for national security and international affairs in the Office of Science and Technology Policy (OSTP). She also serves on the National Security Council as senior director for science and technology affairs. She joined OSTP in 1995 as deputy to the associate director for national security and international affairs. OSTP's national security and international affairs office provides leadership and oversight to the White House effort to use science and technology in the service of our national security.

Before joining OSTP, Jones directed the management and coordination function in U.S. AID's Asia and Near East bureau. During her service with USAID (1989-95), she headed the division of technical resources for the Asia bureau where she was responsible for a portfolio that included technology and policy programs in the areas of agriculture, health, education, and environment. She designed and managed the US-Asia Pacific Economic Cooperation (APEC) Partnership for Education, the first major U.S. contribution to APEC. She was also involved in the initial design of the US-Asia Environmental Partnership.

Before going to U.S. AID, Dr. Jones worked at NIH's Fogarty International Center, where she was the program manager for biomedical programs in the Near East and South Asia regions. She is a graduate of the Office of Personnel Management's Executive Potential Program, a one-year, in-service management training program.

Before beginning her work with the U.S. government, Jones worked as an independent consultant in international development and science and technology. Her principal areas of expertise are biotechnology, health, and technology commercialization. She lived for a year in New Delhi, India, serving as the biotechnology advisor to the U.S. AID mission. In 1985, she was the recipient of a Science, Engineering and Diplomacy Fellowship from the American Association for the Advancement of Science.

Dr. Jones obtained her Ph.D. from the department of molecular biophysics and biochemistry at Yale University, where she studied the effects of stress on protein expression and metabolism, using nuclear magnetic resonance. Before her graduate studies, she worked as an assistant for research at the Rockefeller University in immunology and developmental biology.

Assistant Director, National Security
Mr. Bruce MacDonald
202/456-6068
Rm. 490

Assistant Director, International Affairs
Ms. Deanna Behring
202/456-6058
Rm. 490

Office of the U.S. Trade Representative

600 17th St., NW / Washington DC 20506
Public Affairs: 202/395-3230
Fax Retrieval: 202/395-4809 (press releases, etc.)

Office in Geneva

1-3 Avenue de la Paix
1202 Geneva, Switzerland
Phone: 011-41-22-749-5112

INTRODUCTION

The Office of the U.S. Trade Representative (USTR) is responsible for developing and coordinating U.S. international trade, commodity, and direct investment policy, and leading or directing negotiations with other countries on such matters. The office was established as an agency of the Executive Office of the President.

The USTR is a Cabinet-level official who acts as the principal trade advisor, negotiator, and spokesperson for the President on trade and related investment matters. Through the interagency structure, the USTR coordinates trade policy, resolves agency disagreements, and frames issues for Presidential decision.

The agency provides trade policy leadership and negotiating expertise in its major areas of responsibility. Among these are the following: all matters with the General Agreement of Tariffs and Trade (GATT); trade, commodity, and direct investment matters dealt with by international institutions such as the Organization for Economic Cooperation and Development (OECD) and the United Nations Conference on Trade Development (UNCTAD); export expansion policy; East-West trade; industrial and services trade policy; international commodity agreements and policy; bilateral and multilateral trade and investment issues; and import policy. The agency is organized to accommodate sectoral, regional, and functional policy perspectives which are integrated into the decision-making process and coordinated externally with government agencies, the private sector, and foreign entities.

The agency has administrative responsibility for the Generalized System of Preferences (GSP) and Section 301 complaints against foreign unfair trade practices. It coordinates the Presidential review phase in intellectual property cases under Section 337 and import relief cases under Section 201. The Omnibus Trade & Competitiveness Act of 1988 transferred authority to the USTR to take action under Section 301, subject to the direction of the President.

The USTR also has primary responsibility for administering and implementing obligation undertaken by the U.S. by virtue of the U.S.-Canada Free Trade Agreement that went into effect Jan. 1, 1989.

The USTR has an office in Geneva, Switzerland, to cover general GATT Affairs, Non-Tariff Agreements, and Agricultural Policy and Commodity Policy and the Harmonized Code System.

U.S. Trade Representative
Ambassador Charlene Barshefsky
202/395-6890   FAX 202/395-4549
Rm. 209A

Personal: born 8/11/50 in Chicago, Ill.

Education: B.A. (with honors), Univ. of Wisconsin, 1972. J.D., Catholic Univ. School of Law, 1975.

Professional: 1975-93, partner, Steptoe & Johnson. 1993-95. dep. U.S. trade rep.; 1996-97, acting USTR, and USTR-designate. March 1997-present, U.S. Trade Rep., Office of the U.S. Trade Rep.

Charlene Barshefsky was confirmed by the U.S. Senate and sworn in on March 17, 1997 as the twelfth U.S. Trade Representative. She holds the rank of Ambassador Extraordinary and Plenipotentiary. She had served as acting USTR since April 1996, when Mickey Kantor went to head the U.S. Department of Commerce following the death of Ron Brown. She served as deputy U.S. trade representative since 1993.

Barshefsky has been a leading architect of the Clinton administration's trade policy over the past four years. Her tenure at USTR demonstrates a consistent focus to open global markets through bilateral and multilateral trade agreements that increase export opportunities for U.S. businesses and workers, a central principle in President Clinton's economic strategy to build domestic prosperity.

As the President's chief trade negotiator and trade policy maker, Barshefsky has overseen an unprecedented period of trade expansion. Since 1993, the Clinton administration has negotiated over 220 trade agreements, including the NAFTA and Uruguay Round which launched the World Trade Organization (WTO), in addition to an ambitious bilateral trade agenda with Japan which features 30 market opening agreements.

With regard to Japan, Barshefsky has served as a key policy maker and was a negotiator of the comprehensive 1994 Japan Framework Agreement. In August of 1996, Barshefsky secured a new US/Japan agreement on semiconductor trade that retains key features of previous agreements while encouraging other nations to eliminate tariffs on semiconductors, an area where the U.S. is the world leader in production and exports. In December of 1996, she negotiated a market access agreement that builds on the 1994 Framework Agreement by providing for substantial deregulation of the Japanese insurance market while securing concrete opportunities for foreign companies to sell insurance in Japan on a competitive basis.

On a global basis, Barshefsky marshaled support for an Information Technology Agreement (ITA) to boost world technology trade and the February 1997 Global Agreement on Basic Telecommunications. Together these agreements open more than a trillion dollar sector of global trade for U.S. companies. She also negotiated the landmark 1995 and 1996 China Intellectual Property Rights Enforcement Agreements which require closure of illegal CD and software factories and open the Chinese market for the legitimate sale of U.S. software, music, and film products.

Prior to her tenure at USTR, Barshefsky was a partner in the Washington, D.C. law firm of Steptoe & Johnson where she specialized in international trade law and policy for 18 years and co-chaired the firm's substantial international practice group. Both during her tenure at USTR and at Steptoe & Johnson, she had published, lectured, and testified extensively on U.S. and international trade policy and laws.

Barshefsky has been on the editorial advisory boards of the *European Business Law Review* and the *International Trade Corporate Counsel Advisor* and is on the board of the International Legal Studies Program of The American University School of Law. In addition, Barshefsky chaired the U.S. Court of International Trade Advisory Committee and served as an initial roster member of the Chapter 19 Canada-U.S. Dispute Resolution Panels under the Canada-U.S. Free Trade Agreement.

She is married to Edward B. Cohen. The couple resides in Washington, D.C. with their two daughters.

Chief of Staff
Ms. Nancy LeaMond
202/395-6850   FAX 202/395-3911
Rm. 209

Personal: born in Millburn, N.J.

Education: A.B., Smith College, 1972. M.A., John F. Kennedy School of Government, Harvard Univ., 1974.

Professional: 1974-75, program analyst, office of the asst. sec. for health; 1975-76, program analyst, Medical Services Admin., U.S. Dept. of Health, Education and Welfare. 1976-77, policy analyst, office of the sec., U.S. Dept. of Commerce. 1977-80, member, President's Reorganization Project, Office of Management and Budget. 1977-79, senior health analyst, the Reorganization Project concerning proposed reorganizations of federal health agencies. 1978-79, staff dir., U.S. Dept. of Education Reorganization Study. 1979, exec. sec., U.S. Dept. of Education Transition. 1980-81, spec. asst. to the sec., U.S. Dept. of Education. 1982, consultant, Northern Calif. Grantmakers. 1983-87, admin. asst., Rep. Mary Rose Oakar (D-Ohio). 1987-93, president, Congressional Economic Leadership Institute. 1993-96, asst. U.S. trade rep. for congressional affairs; 1997-present, chief of staff, Office of the U.S. Trade Representative.

Nancy LeaMond moved into the chief of staff's office at the office of the U.S. trade representative to work for Ambassador Charlene Barshefsky who was confirmed as the new USTR in March of 1997. LeaMond had previously served as assistant U.S. trade representative for congressional affairs since the start of the Clinton administration.

Prior to joining the trade office, LeaMond had been president of the Congressional Economic Leadership Institute, a private, non-profit, non-partisan public policy group founded in 1987 to identify and conduct research on emerging international economic, trade, tax, and labor issues. The institute provides a forum for dialogue among members of Congress and leaders from business, labor, and education.

LeaMond's experience as president of the group included major discussions involving US-Japan trade, NAFTA, the European Community, GATT and U.S. manufacturing. LeaMond was able to use her experience with leaders of Congress to help the Clinton Administration win passage of NAFTA. LeaMond had also served with former Rep. Mary Rose Oakar of Ohio when she was a member of the House Democratic Leadership, developing other Hill ties that were useful in her congressional liaison position.

LeaMond served as student government president at Smith College and served for four years on the college's board of trustees following her graduation. She received the Professional Achievement Award from the Department of Education in 1980 and has served as a parent volunteer for pre-schools and elementary schools since 1982. She has also been a keynote speaker and panelist before business, foundation, public interest, and women's groups.

LeaMond is married to Stephen E. Finan. They live in Bethesda, Md., with their two sons.

Deputy USTR (Washington)
Ambassador Jeffrey M. Lang
202/395-5114   FAX 202/395-4549
Rm. 201

Personal: born in 1942.

Professional: 1979-90, trade policy adviser, Senate Finance Committee. 1990-94, attorney, Winthrop, Stimson, Putnam & Roberts (New York). 1995-97, deputy U.S. Trade Representative, Geneva; 1997-present, deputy USTR, Washington, Office of the U.S. Trade Representative.

Since the fall of 1997, Jeffrey Lang has been the deputy USTR in Washington. Prior to this posting, he was the Deputy U.S. Trade Representative in Geneva since January 1995.

Before joining USTR, Lang was an attorney with Winthrop, Stimson, Putnam & Roberts in New York, specializing in international trade law.

As chief international counsel for the Senate Finance Committee, Lang participated at the staff level in every major piece of U.S. trade legislation in the 1980s. He is putting that knowledge to good use in his new position as deputy U.S. trade representative.

On the Senate Finance Committee, Lang worked on the landmark Omnibus Trade and Competitiveness Act of 1988, the legislation to implement free trade agreements with Israel and Canada, and other U.S. legislation related to international trade. He also traveled throughout Asia, Europe, and North America in connection with the Committee's work, attending many of the most important international trade negotiations that occurred over the last 15 years in an oversight capacity.

Lang was chosen for the Senate Finance Committee staff in 1979 on the strength of his advice to the committee on the impact of the Tokyo Round of Multilateral Trade Negotiations upon American statutory law. Before going to the committee, he was deputy general counsel of the U.S. International Trade Commission.

Following his Finance Committee service, Lang joined the law firm of Winthrop, Stimson, Putnam & Roberts, a Wall Street-based international law firm. At Winthrop, he divided his time between the Brussels and Washington offices of the firm, concentrating on international trade and trade policy matters.

Lang has experience in federal court litigation and has served on the advisory committee that prepared the initial set of rules for the Court of International Trade in New York. He is frequently called upon to speak on trade questions to business, academic, and public interest groups in the U.S., Europe, and Asia. In 1994, he was the Co-Chairman of the annual meeting of the American Society of International Law.

Lang is married to Dr. Lynn Z. Lang, an educator.

Deputy USTR (Washington)
Ambassador Richard W. Fisher
202/395-6890
Rm. 200A

Nominated by President Clinton in October, 1997, and subsequently confirmed by the Senate, Richard Fisher is the new Deputy U.S. Trade Representative in Washington. Fisher is responsible for conducting trade negotiations and assisting the U.S. Trade Representative in developing and implementing international trade policy.

Fisher, of Texas, was most recently managing partner of Fisher Capital Management and Fisher Ewing partners. He is an adjunct professor at the University of Texas at Austin, LBJ School. Fisher also serves as chairman of the Dallas Committee on Foreign Relations, as director of the United States-Russia Investment Fund, as a member of the executive committee of the Inter-American Dialogue, and as a member of the Council on Foreign Relations.

In 1994, Fisher was the Democratic nominee for the U.S. Senate from his home state of Texas. He held several positions during the Carter administration, including executive assistant to the Secretary of the Treasury, assistant to President Carter at the Tokyo Economic Summit in 1979, advisor at the Bonn Economic Summit in 1978, and as a member of the team that negotiated the historic Claims and Asset Settlement between the U.S. and the People's Republic of China.

He graduated with honors from Harvard University with an economics degree and received an MBA from Stanford University.

Special Trade Negotiator
Mr. Peter Scher
202/395-5057   FAX 202/395-3390
Rm. 200A

Personal: born 4/12/61 in New York.

Education: B.A. in political science, American Univ., 1983. J.D., Washington College of Law, American Univ., 1987.

Professional: 1987-88, Dukakis-Bentsen presidential campaign. 1989-91, attorney, Keck, Mahin, and Cate. 1991-93, chief of staff to Sen. Max Baucus (D-Mont.). 1992, Clinton-Gore presidential campaign. 1993-94, staff director, Senate Cmte. on Environment and Public Works. 1995-96, chief of staff, Office of the U.S. Trade Representative. 1996-97, chief of staff, U.S. Dept. of Commerce. 1997-present, special trade negotiator, Office of the U.S. Trade Representative.

Peter Scher returned to the U.S. Trade Representative's office in 1997 to serve as special trade negotiator. He had served in 1995 and 1996 as chief of staff to former U.S. Trade Representative Mickey Kantor. When Kantor replaced the late Ron Brown as Secretary of the U.S. Department of Commerce, Scher became his chief of staff.

As special trade negotiator, Scher has responsibility for all bilateral and multilateral agricultural trade negotiations on behalf of the United States. In the next several years, the U.S. faces a number of critical challenges in opening international markets to agriculture products, including ensuring further opening of the world's largest market, China, to U.S. agricultural exports, the elimination of trade barriers which use sanitary and phytosanitary standards to discriminate against our products, and new barriers to products developed through biotechnology. Scher will also direct the negotiations for the next round of multilateral agriculture negotiations scheduled to begin in the World Trade Organization in 1999.

While working for Kantor at the Commerce Department, Scher served as chief operating officer with responsibility for coordinating all Department activities with the White House and other federal agencies. He served as a member of the President's Management Council and was a principal policy advisor to the Secretary, representing Kantor in meetings of the National Economic Council regarding trade policy and other Administration issues. Scher oversaw the development and preparation for the 1996 Joint Committee on Commerce and Trade meetings between the United States and China.

Prior to joining the Clinton Administration, Scher served as chief of staff for U.S. Sen. Max Baucus (D-Mont.), chairman of the US Senate subcommittee on international trade and as staff director for the Senate

Committee on Environment and Public Works. In those positions he work on Most Favored Nation (MFN) status for China and advised on the environmental impacts of the North American Free Trade Agreement (NAFTA) and the General Agreement on Tariffs and Trade (GATT).

Scher is a member of the Bar Associations of New York State and Washington, D.C. He is married to Kimberly H. Tilley.

Counselor to the USTR
Mr. Robert T. Novick
202/395-9494
Rm. 213

Robert Novick joined USTR as counselor to the United States Trade Representative in April 1997. He is advising Ambassador Barshefsky on key policy and legal issues, and has responsibility within USTR for the Administration's "fast track" initiative.

Before joining USTR, Novick was a partner with the Washington, D.C. firm of Steptoe & Johnson LLP, where he practiced law for 14 years. At Steptoe & Johnson, he specialized in international law, trade and trade policy matters. His practice included assisting U.S. companies and trade associations to obtain greater market access; counseling clients with respect to WTO dispute settlement; and advising a member of the President's Export Council on policies and priorities for U.S. export promotion. In addition, Novick represented multinationals in international arbitration matters and handled import relief cases under U.S. and foreign trade laws.

Novick received his law degree cum laude in 1983 from the American University, Washington College of Law, where he was the executive editor of the American University Law Review. He received his Bachelor of Arts degree in political science from Bucknell University in 1980.

Chief Negotiator for Communications and Information
Mr. Donald Abelson
202/395-5740
Rm. 314

Personal: born 4/6/50 in New York, N.Y.

Education: B.A., Sarah Lawrence Coll., 1972. M.A., School of Advanced International Studies, Johns Hopkins Univ., 1975.

Professional: 1975-76, international economic consultant, office of international finance and investment, U.S. Department of Commerce. 1975-77, economic consultant, division of marketing practices, Federal Trade Commission. 1977-79, international economist, Office of the Special Representative for Trade Negotiations. 1980-88, director, Technical Trade Barriers; 1988-91, deputy assistant U.S. Trade representative for North American Affairs; 1991-93, deputy assistant U.S. Trade Representative for Inter-American & African Affairs; 6/93-9/93, acting assistant U.S. Trade representative for intellectual property & the environment; Sept. 1993-97, assistant U.S. Trade Representative for intellectual property, investment & services; 1997-present, chief negotiator for communications and information, Office of the USTR.

After five years serving as assistant U.S. trade representative for intellectual property, investment and services, Don Abelson was appointed Chief Negotiator for Communications and Information in the fall of 1997.

Abelson first joined USTR as director of technical trade barriers in 1977, and for the next eleven years, was the chief U.S. negotiator on regulatory trade issues. During this time, Abelson was the leader of several important bilateral standards discussions. These included Japanese regulatory negotiations, telecommunications equipment and animal hormone regulations with the Commission of the European

Communities, and medical device equipment with the Federal Republic of Germany. Abelson also served as U.S. representative to the General Agreement on Tariffs and Trade (GATT) Committee on Technical Barriers to Trade, as principal policy counselor for regulatory trade issues, and as chairman of the trade policy staff committee's Subcommittee on Standards and Bilateral Issues.

In 1988, Abelson was appointed deputy assistant U.S. trade representative for North American affairs. In this position, he served as the associate U.S. trade negotiator for U.S.-Mexican affairs and as policy coordinator for U.S.-Mexican bilateral trade and investment policy issues. During this pre-NAFTA period, he served as chief policy advisor on Mexican trade and investment issues, including acting as the principal USTR contact with business leaders and corporate executives. Abelson was also the primary advocate for U.S. trade and investment interests in bilateral agriculture and industrial discussions.

From 1991 until 1993, Abelson was deputy assistant U.S. trade representative for inter-American and African Affairs where he was chief negotiator of the Uruguay Round "Services Market Access" bilateral talks with Latin American and African nations.

Abelson's career is marked by accomplishments such as acting as chief U.S. negotiator with Latin American and African governments on bilateral services market access issues including professional services, telecommunications and insurance. He also served as senior policy coordinator for investment trade talks under the "Enterprise for the Americas Initiative." As U.S. chairman of the "FTA Working Group" established under the U.S.-Chilean Framework Agreement, Abelson led development of interagency reports on Chilean trade and investment practices for use in policy debates on a possible free trade agreement.

Deputy USTR (Geneva)
Ambassador Rita D. Hayes
1-3 Avenue de law Paix 1202 Geneva, Switzerland
Phone: 011-41-22-749-5112

Office of the U.S. Trade Representative
Old Executive Office Building
17th St. & Pennsylvania Ave., NW
Washington, D.C. 20506
202/395-5114   FAX 202/395-3390

Education: B.A. in education, University of Georgia. Graduate Studies, Winthrop College, South Carolina.

Professional: member, Governor Richard Riley's Special Review Committee, South Carolina. chair, Governor's Nuclear Advisory Committee for the State of South Carolina. 1982-87, district administrator and chief of staff, Congressman John M. Spratt, Jr. (D-S.C.). 1987-93, chief of staff, Congresswoman Elizabeth J. Patterson (D-S.C.). 1992-93, staff for energy and natural resources, Clinton-Gore Transition Team. 1993-95, deputy assistant secretary for textiles, apparel and consumer goods industries, U.S. Department of Commerce. October 1995-97, chief textile negotiator; 1997-present, Deputy USTR, Geneva, Office of the U.S. Trade Representative.

In July 1997, Rita Hayes was nominated by the President to replace Jeffrey Lang as deputy U.S. trade representative in Geneva. Hayes was subsequently confirmed by the Senate and replaced Lang in Geneva. Immediately prior to assuming her new responsibilities, Hayes served as chief textile negotiator at USTR since October, 1995. In that capacity, she served as the chief advisor to the U.S. Trade Representative on international trade policies and negotiations concerning textile and apparel.

Hayes had previously served in the Clinton administration as the deputy assistant secretary for textiles, apparel and consumer goods industries for the U.S. Department of Commerce. As deputy assistant secretary, she was responsible for policy initiatives, domestic and international, that encourage U.S. businesses and companies to expand their horizons. In this role, she had responsibility for developing programs to improve the domestic and international competitiveness of American fiber, textile, apparel, and consumer products.

Prior to her work at the Department of Commerce, Hayes served on the Clinton-Gore Transition Team in the area of energy and natural resources. From 1987 until 1993, she was chief of staff for Congresswoman Elizabeth J. Patterson of South Carolina. From 1982 until 1987, she was the district administrator and chief of staff to Congressman John M. Spratt, Jr.. She had previously served as chair of then-Governor Richard Riley's Nuclear Advisory Committee for the State of South Carolina and as a member of Riley's Special Review Committee.

Hayes resides in Bethesda, Md. with her three children.

Deputy Chief of Mission
Office of the United States Trade Representative - Geneva
United States Mission to the World Trade Organization
Mr. Andrew L. Stoler
1-3 Avenue de law Paix 1202 Geneva, Switzerland
Phone: 011-41-22-749-5112

Andrew L. Stoler has been Deputy Chief of Mission at the Geneva, Switzerland office of the United States Trade Representative (USTR), Executive Office of the President, since September, 1989. In this capacity, he serves as the Deputy Permanent Representative of the United States to the World Trade Organization (WTO) where, with the Ambassador, he is charged with the local day-to-day coordination and execution of the multilateral trade policies of the United States.

During the Uruguay Round of Multilateral Trade Negotiations, Stoler was principal U.S. negotiator for the Agreement Establishing the WTO. Stoler is Chairman of the Working Party on the Accession to the WTO of Ukraine.

From January, 1988 through August, 1989, Stoler served as Deputy Assistant U.S. Trade Representative for Europe and the Mediterranean in the Washington office of USTR. In that position, he was charged with bilateral trade relations with the European Union, non-EU Europe and countries in the Near East and North Africa. During this period, Stoler organized and chaired the U.S. Government's Interagency Task Force on the EC's "Internal Market" program.

Stoler served as MTN Codes Coordinator in the Geneva USTR office from January, 1982 through December, 1987. In this capacity, he represented the United States in the Committees and Councils established for the Non-tariff Measure "Codes" negotiated during the Tokyo Round of multilateral trade negotiations.

Joining USTR in early 1980, Stoler's first assignment in the office was as Director for Canada, Australia and New Zealand — a position he occupied until his departure for Geneva. Prior to working at USTR, Stoler served in the Office of International Trade Policy at the U.S. Department of Commerce from 1975 through 1979.

Stoler holds an M.B.A. in international business from George Washington University and a B.S. in international economic affairs from Georgetown University's School of Foreign Service. He and his wife, Christine Elstob, reside in Geneva, Switzerland with their daughter Angela.

Administration

Asst. USTR
Mr. John Hopkins
202/395-5797
Rm. 125

As Assistant U.S. Trade Representative for Administration, John Hopkins is responsible for directing the agency's management and administrative support programs, including budget and personnel services, computer and communications systems, facility support, administrative services and security.

These programs are organized under USTR's Office of Administration, which includes an Office of Computer Operations, and units for Financial Management, Human Resources Management and Administrative Services. The Office of Administration also provides support for USTR's strategic planning activities.

Prior to his 1991 appointment at USTR, Mr. Hopkins served in a number of management positions at the U.S. Department of Health and Human Services, and prior to that worked in municipal government. Mr. Hopkins is a native of Concord, Massachusetts, a graduate of Colby College and a resident of Virginia.

Agricultural Affairs

Asst. USTR
Dr. James M. Murphy
202/395-6127   FAX 202/395-4579
Rm. 415

Education: B.A., Williams College. M.A., Ph.D., Claremont Graduate School (Claremont, Calif.).

Professional: 1974-78, asst. dir., Council on International Economic Policy, The White House. 1978-79, deputy dir., office of international trade, U.S. Dept. of the Treasury. 1980-97, office of U.S. Trade Rep.: asst. USTR for Japan; asst. USTR for Europe and the Mediterranean; asst. USTR for Latin America, The Caribbean and Africa; leader, U.S. delegation to OECD Trade Cmte. June 1997-present, asst. USTR for agricultural affairs, Office of the U.S. Trade Rep.

Dr. James Murphy has worked with the Office of the US Trade Representative for 17 years. He began as assistant U.S. trade representative for Japan, then for Europe and the Mediterranean, and then for Latin America, the Caribbean, and Africa. Murphy also led the U.S. delegation to the OECD Trade Committee.

From 1978 to 1979, Murphy served as deputy director of the office of international trade, at the U.S. Department of Treasury. He had previously served as assistant director of the Council on International Economic Policy at the White House during both the Ford and Carter Administrations.

In June of 1997, Murphy assumed his current position as assistant USTR for agricultural affairs. His office has the lead responsibility for the coordination of agricultural trade policy within the administration and the negotiation of trade agreements with foreign governments.

Dr. Murphy holds a B.A. from Williams College and an M.A. and Ph.D. from Claremont Graduate School in Claremont, California. He resides in Washington, D.C. with his wife and daughter.

Senior Policy Adviser
Ms. Kathryn Early
202/395-6127
Rm. 417

Asia, Pacific, and APEC Affairs

Asst. USTR
Mr. Donald M. Phillips
202/395-3430   FAX 202/395-3512
Rm. 400

Personal: born 3/21/43 in Baltimore, Md.

Education: B.A., Univ. of Maryland, 1963. M.A. (Phi Kappa Phi), Univ. of Maryland, 1972.

Professional: 1964-66, U.S. Army. 1967-69, intl. economist, trade policy div.; 1969-75, project leader, foreign demand and competition div., Economic Research Service. 1975-79, asst. agricultural attaché, U.S. mission to the European Communities; 1979-80, agricultural economist, grain and feed div., Foreign Agriculture Service, U.S. Dept. of Agriculture. 1980-85, dir., commodity policy; 1985-88, asst. USTR for trade policy coordination; 1988-97, asst. USTR for industry; May 1997-present, asst. USTR for Asia Pacific, and APEC, Office of the USTR.

Don Phillips has worked in the field of international trade for more than 25 years. As assistant U.S. trade representative for Asia Pacific and Asia Pacific Economic Cooperation (APEC) since May, 1997, Phillips develops and implements trade policy for this region. This involves negotiation of a wide range of bilateral trade issues with Asian countries (except Japan and China) as well as the pursuit of trade initiatives and representation of U.S. trade interests in the multilateral APEC forum.

As assistant USTR for industry from 1988 until assuming his present post, Phillips developed trade policy issues involving manufactured and other industrial goods. His work was geared toward the support of USTR bilateral and multilateral initiatives on industrial trade issues as well as the conduct of trade negotiations affecting sectors such as aircraft, steel, telecommunications, and semiconductors.

Phillips started at USTR as director of commodity policy, developing policy on international commodity agreements as well as working on agricultural trade policy issues. In 1985, he became Assistant USTR for trade policy coordination, where he managed the government's decision-making process for trade policy. One of the hallmarks of his tenure was the start of negotiations for the GATT Uruguay Round, which led to an agreement in 1994.

Except for Army service after college, Phillips has always worked in the international trade area. As an international economist for the Agriculture Department, he provided analyses, briefs and background papers on agricultural trade problems. As a project leader for the Department's Economic Research Service, Phillips planned and directed a research program for Western Europe, analyzing trends in major U.S. markets and the impact of trade and financial policies.

This experience prepared Phillips for his assignment as assistant agricultural attaché in Brussels, where he analyzed and reported on European Community (EC) policies affecting agriculture, and recommended U.S. actions as needed. He also represented U.S. positions to EC officials and provided support and advice to U.S. agricultural groups, private companies, and government officials visiting Brussels. As an agricultural economist within the grain and feed division of the Foreign Agriculture Service, Phillips directed work on demand analysis and trade policy problems. He also led U.S. delegations to meetings of the International Wheat Council.

Phillips is married and has one daughter. He enjoys tennis, squash, swimming, and reading.

Deputy Asst, USTR for India and Asian Affairs
Mr. Francis Ruzicka
202/395-3430
Rm. 405

Director for South Asia and Oceania
Ms. Betsy Stillman
202/395-6813
Rm. 405

Director, Southeast Asia Affairs

Mr. Joseph Damond
202/395-6813
Rm. 405

Director, Office of APEC Affairs
Ms. Mary Latimer
202/395-6813
Rm. 407

Director for OECD Portfolio
Ms. Jane Earley
202/395-6813
Rm. 400

Office of Chief Textile Negotiator

Chief Textile Negotiator
Mr. Don Johnson
202/395-3026   FAX 202/395-5639
Rm. 300A

Don Johnson was named Chief Textile Negotiator by U.S. Trade Representative Charlene Barshefsky on March 9, 1998, replacing Ambassador Rita Hayes who is now the Deputy USTR in Geneva. In this capacity, Johnson serves as the principal advisor to the United States Trade Representative (USTR) and the President on all textile and apparel trade matters and negotiates all trade agreements covering trade in textiles and apparel. Trade in textiles and apparel between the U.S. and its trading partners amounted to over $70 billion last year.

Johnson previously served in the United States Congress, representing the 10th District of Georgia. After leaving Washington in January 1995, Johnson served as President of an international trade and investment consulting company, and acted as corporate counsel to a group of companies engaged international trade. He taught part time at the University of Georgia, and was an advisor to the Dean Rusk Center for International and Comparative Law and the European Center in Atlanta. Additionally, he worked with USIS and the Former Members of Congress Association to assist new democratic legislative bodies in South Asia and Eastern Europe in the area of parliamentary reform. He also served on the board of directors of Sector Communications, Inc.

Johnson received his Bachelor of Arts degree from the University of Georgia where he majored in modern European history. He earned his Juris Doctorate degree from the University of Georgia Law School with a concentration in international law, under former Secretary of State Dean Rusk. He was articles editor of the Georgia Journal of International and Comparative Law. He received a Master of Laws degree in international economic law and European law from The London School of Economics, and attended The Hague Academy of International Law on a Loridans Foundation scholarship.

He served as legislative counsel to the Ways and Means Committee of the United States House of Representatives, where he assisted in drafting foreign trade legislation, principally the Trade Act of 1974. Johnson also served as a judge advocate in the U.S. Air Force, and following his military service, he was employed by Continental Bank in Chicago, specializing in international finance law. In 1980, he began private law practice first with the law firm of Powell, Goldstein, Frazer, and Murphy in Atlanta and later his own firm in northeast Georgia.

In 1987, he was elected to serve in the Georgia Senate. During the six years he was in the state Senate, he was selected as one of the Governor's Floor Leaders, Vice Chairman of the Judiciary Committee, and in his last term in office, as Chairman of the Appropriations Committee. He was the original author of major legislation enacted to reform the state budget process, the ethical standards of public officials, sovereign immunity and rural telecommunications. He also chaired a study committee on export promotion, spurring reforms in

Georgia's export promotion programs.

During his service in the U.S. House of Representatives, Johnson served on the Armed Services and Science, Space and Technology Committees. He was also selected as a member of the Speaker's Working Group on Policy and as a delegate to the North Atlantic Assembly. In the latter capacity, he was a member of a team of NATO country legislators that monitored the first Russian parliamentary elections in December 1993. He was an active member of the Textile Caucus and assisted in the whip organizations promoting GATT and NAFTA.

Johnson and his wife Suzanne currently maintain their residence on a farm in Hart County, Georgia. They have three children.

Deputy Chief Textile Negotiator
Ms. Carol Miller
202/395-3026
Rm. 309

China, Hong Kong, Taiwan and Mongolia

Asst. USTR
Mr. Robert B. Cassidy
202/395-3900   FAX 202/395-3597
Rm. 401A

Personal: born in 1944.

Education: B.A. in economics, St. Anselm's College, 1966. M.A. in economics, Boston College, 1968.

Professional: 1980-84, office of development policy; 1984-86, office of trade finance, U.S. Dept. of the Treasury. 1986-93, deputy assistant USTR for industry; 1993-97, assistant USTR for Asia and the Pacific; 1997-present, assistant USTR for China, Hong Kong, Taiwan and Mongolia, Office of the U.S. Trade Representative.

Robert Cassidy took over the China portfolio at the Office of the U.S. Trade Representative in 1997. He succeeds Lee Sands. As such, Cassidy manages and supervises U.S. government trade negotiations with China, Taiwan, Hong Kong, and Mongolia, including development of negotiating positions, intra-government coordination, and coordination with the Congress and private industry.

Cassidy had previously served, from 1993 to 1997, as assistant USTR for Asia and the Pacific where he was responsible for developing and implementing U.S. bilateral and multilateral trade policies and negotiating strategies in Asia and the Pacific region. He brings to both positions many years of experience in economic and international policy matters.

As assistant USTR for Asia and the Pacific, Cassidy played a key role in several recent trade negotiations in Asia. He negotiated with a Taiwanese delegation seeking to stave off U.S. trade sanctions by promising to beef up protection of intellectual property rights. He participated in U.S. talks with South Korea which led to pledges that the South Korean government would work to deregulate business and facilitate foreign investment.

From 1986 to 1993, Cassidy served as deputy assistant USTR for industry. In that position, he developed and coordinated trade policies which affected U.S. industry, particularly steel and shipbuilding.

Cassidy, who holds bachelor's and master's degrees in economics, had previously worked at the U.S. Treasury Department in the office of the assistant secretary for international affairs. In addition, he worked in the office of development policy and the office of trade finance at Treasury.

Cassidy and his wife have three children.

Deputy Asst. USTR for China and Mongolia
Ms. Christine Lund
202/395-6813
Rm. 405

Senior Adviser for China
Mr. David Burns
202/395-5050
Rm. 322A

Director of Policy Planning for China
Ms. Barbara Weisel
202/395-5070
Rm. 318

Director for China, Hong Kong, Mongolia and Macao
Ms. Martha Cheng
202/395-5050   FAX 202/395-4579
Rm. 316

Office of Congressional Affairs

Asst. USTR
Ms. Liz Arky
202/395-6951   FAX 202/395-4656
Rm. 113

Education: B.A. (cum laude), Newcomb College, Tulane Univ. (Louisiana), 1983. J.D. (with honors), National Law Center, George Washington Univ. (Wash., D.C.).

Professional: 1986-92, attorney, Winthrop, Stimson, Putnam and Roberts. 1992-93, staff member, Clinton-Gore Presidential Transition Team. 1993-94, spec. asst. to the sec., then 1994-95, dep. asst. sec. for plans and policy, office of congressional and intergovernmental affairs, U.S. Dept. of Housing and Urban Development. 1995, dep. asst. USTR, office of congressional affairs, Office of the U.S. Trade Representative. 1995-96, dep. asst. sec. for plans and policy, office of congressional and intergovernmental relations, U.S. Dept. of Housing and Urban Development. 1996-present, asst. USTR for congressional affairs, Office of the U.S. Trade Representative.

Elizabeth Arky has served as the assistant U.S. trade representative for congressional affairs at the Office of the U.S. Trade Representative since 1996. She had previously served as deputy assistant U.S. Trade Representative in the congressional affairs shop in 1995.

Arky has also served two stints in the Clinton administration at the US Department of Housing and Urban Development. She served as special assistant to former Secretary Henry Cisneros in 1993 and 1994 and then served as deputy assistant secretary for plans and policy in HUD's congressional and intergovernmental affairs shop in 1995/96.

Arky worked as an attorney from 1986 to 1992 for the law firm of Winthrop, Stimson, Putnam and Roberts in Washington, D.C. before joining the Clinton-Gore Presidential Transition Team. She is a member of the New York and D.C. Bars and is the founding director in 1992 of First Book.

Economic Affairs

Asst. USTR for Economic Affairs
Mr. David A. Walters
202/395-5636   FAX 202/395-7226
Rm. 216

Personal: born in Providence, R.I.

Education: B.A., Brown Univ. Graduate degrees from the Fletcher School of Law and Diplomacy and in economics from the Graduate

Institute of International Studies (Geneva, Switzerland).

Professional: U.S. Army, Vietnam. economics teacher, Graduate Institute of International Studies (Geneva). staff, American Paper Institute (New York). staff, National Science Foundation (Wash., D.C.). 1979-94, various positions; 1994-present, asst. U.S. trade representative for economic affairs and chief economist, Office of the USTR.

David Walters has been serving as assistant USTR for economic affairs and chief economist at USTR since 1994. He is responsible for trade and related economic analyses. He has served at the trade representative's office in various capacities since 1979.

After serving in the U.S. Army during the Vietnam era, Walters taught economics at the Graduate Institute of International Studies in Geneva and was then employed by the American Paper Institute in New York and at the National Science Foundation in Washington, D.C.

He holds degrees from Brown University, the Fletcher School of Law and Diplomacy, and the Graduate Institute of International Studies in Geneva, Switzerland, where he taught economics.

Deputy Asst. USTR
Mr. William Shpiece
202/395-3583
Rm. 516

International Economist
Mr. Michael Anderson
202/395-3583
Rm. 516

Environment and Natural Resources

Asst. USTR
Ms. Jennifer Haverkamp
202/395-7320   FAX   202/395-4579
Rm. 415

Education: B.A. in biology, Coll. of Wooster. M.A. (Rhodes Scholar) in politics and philosophy, Oxford Univ. J.D., Yale Law School.

Professional: 1981-84, associate, The Conservation Foundation. 1987-88, law clerk, U.S. Court of Appeals for the Ninth Circuit. 1988-91, attorney, Environment and Natural Resources Division, U.S. department of Justice. 1992, special assistant to the assistant administrator for enforcement, U.S. Environmental Protection Agency. 1993-94, offices of North American affairs and intellectual property and environment; 1994-95, deputy assistant USTR for environment and natural resources; 1995-present, assistant USTR, environment and natural resources, Office of the U.S. Trade Representative.

Jennifer Haverkamp assumed the position of assistant U.S. trade representative for the environment and natural resources in July 1995. Her office deals with issues involving U.S. trade and international environmental policies. She had served as deputy assistant for the office in 1994.

Haverkamp has participated in the negotiation of the North American Free Trade Agreement environmental and labor side agreements and the OECD trade and environmental guidelines for members. She also headed the U.S. delegation that renegotiated the International Tropical Timber Agreement.

Haverkamp joined the office of U.S. Trade Representative in 1993 in the offices of North American affairs and intellectual property and the environment. She had previously served as a special assistant to the assistant administrator for enforcement at the U.S. Environmental Protection Agency. She began her executive branch service as an attorney in the environmental and natural resources division at the

U.S. Department of Justice.

Haverkamp earned her B.A. in biology from the College of Wooster in Ohio. She was a Rhodes Scholar at Oxford University where she received a master's degree in politics and philosophy. Her law degree is from Yale Law School.

Deputy Asst. USTR for Intellectual Property
Mr. David Shark
202/395-9590
Rm. 411

Director of Environment
Ms. Laura Anderson
202/395-9590
Rm. 411

Director for Intl. Trade and Development
VACANT
202/395-7320
Rm. 409

Director for Multilateral Trade and Environmental Policy
Ms. Jan McAlpine
202/395-9590
Rm. 409

Europe and the Mediterranean

Acting Asst. USTR
Ms. Catherine Novelli
202/395-4620
Rm. 321

Catherine Novelli assumed the position of acting assistant USTR for Europe and the Mediterranean upon the departure of Jim Murphy. Until the appointment and confirmation of a successor, Novelli is responsible for trade and technology issues along with the broader issues affecting the region. Novelli concurrently holds the position of deputy assistant USTR for Central Europe and Eurasia.

Dep. Asst. USTR for Western Europe and the Middle East
Mr. Ralph Ives
202/395-3320
Rm. 323A

Dep. Asst. USTR for Central Europe and Eurasia
Ms. Catherine Novelli
202/395-3074
Rm. 317

Director, European Union Affairs
Mr. Mark Mowrey
202/395-4620
Rm. 323

Director, Middle East and the Mediterranean
Mr. Daniel Cluhe
202/395-3320
Rm. 323A

Director, Central and Eastern Europe and Eurasia
Mr. Robert Bloehme
202/395-4620
Rm. 317

Director, European Services and Agriculture
Mr. Roland de Marcellus
202/395-3320
Rm. 323A

Office of the General Counsel

General Counsel
Ms. Susan G. Esserman
202/395-3150   FAX 202/395-3639
Rm. 221

Education: B.A. (with honors) Wellesley College, 1974. J.D., University of Michigan Law School, 1977.

Professional: 1977-78, law clerk, Honorable Oliver Gasch, U.S. District Court for the District of Columbia. 1978-84, associate; 1985-93, partner, Steptoe & Johnson (Washington, D.C.). 1994-96, assistant secretary for import administration; August 1996-April 1997, acting general counsel, U.S. Department of Commerce. April 1997-present, general counsel, Office of the U.S. Trade Representative.

Susan Esserman was appointed to serve as general counsel to the office of the U.S. Trade Representative in April 1997. The U.S. Trade Representative's office is responsible for the development and coordination of United States trade policy and for the negotiation of trade agreements on behalf of the United States.

Prior to assuming this position, Esserman held two posts at the U.S. Department of Commerce. In the previous year, she served as acting general counsel at the Department of Commerce. Between March 1994 and April 1996, she served as assistant secretary for import administration. In that position, she was responsible for enforcement and development of policy in connection with the antidumping and countervailing duty laws, which protect U.S. industry against unfair trade practices. She played a lead role on behalf of the administration in connection with the GATT legislation relating to these two areas. She was also responsible for administration of the foreign trade zone program as well as other statutory import programs.

Prior to joining the Clinton Administration in 1994, Esserman was a partner at the Washington law firm of Steptoe & Johnson, where she specialized in international trade law and handled a wide range of policy and litigation matters, including antidumping and countervailing duty cases. She also worked with American industry to reduce barriers in Japanese markets.

Esserman chaired the International Law Section Steering Committee of the D.C. Bar in 1985 and from 1985 to 1987, she edited the ABA International Trade Committee Newsletter. More recently, she was editor-in-chief of the ABA International Law Section's *International Law News*. Esserman served as administrative editor of the *Michigan Law Review*, while earning her J.D. at the University of Michigan Law School.

Deputy General Counsel
Irving Williamson
202/395-3432   FAX   202/ 395-3639
Room 219

Education: A.B., Brown University. M.A., Johns Hopkins School of Advanced International Studies. J.D., George Washington University.

Professional: economic officer, Brazil Desk, U.S. State Department. deputy chief, office of aviation policy, U.S. State Department. attorney, office of the assistant general counsel for international affairs, U.S. Department of Treasury. 1980-83, general counsel, Office of the U.S. Trade Representative. 1985-93, manager of trade policy, Port Authority of New York and New Jersey. executive secretary, trade policy committee, World Trade Centers Association. 1993-present, deputy general counsel, Office of the U. S. Trade Representative.

Irving Williamson serves as deputy general counsel at the Office of the United States Trade Representative and also serves as chair of the Section 301 Committee. Before joining the USTR in June 1993, he was manager of trade policy for the Port Authority of New York and New Jersey and also served as executive secretary of the trade policy committee of the World Trade Centers Association.

For eighteen years prior to joining the Port Authority in 1985, Williamson was a foreign service officer with the U.S. Department of State. From 1980-83 he was an associate general counsel in the USTR where he authored the Caribbean Basin Initiative legislation. He has also been an attorney in the office of the assistant general counsel for international affairs at the Treasury Department. Williamson has served in several positions with the State Department, including as an economic officer on the Brazil desk and deputy chief in the office of aviation policy. His overseas assignments included the U.S. mission to the International Organizations in Geneva, Switzerland, where he worked on GATT matters, and the U.S. embassies in Antannarivo, Madagascar, and Port Louis, Mauritius.

Williamson is the author of articles on the GATT Uruguay Round, the U.S.-Canada Free Trade Agreement, the North American Free Trade Agreement, and on removing foreign trade barriers.

Industry

Acting Asst. USTR
Mr. Donald Eiss
202/395-5656   FAX 202/395-9674
Rm. 420

Donald Eiss serves as the acting assistant U.S. Trade Representative for industry in the office of the USTR. He concurrently serves as the Deputy Assistant USTR for Industry and Labor. Until a nominee is confirmed, Eiss fills the position vacated by Donald Phillips in 1997.

As acting assistant U.S. trade representative for industry, Eiss develops trade policy issues involving manufactured and other industrial goods. His work is geared toward the support of USTR bilateral and multilateral initiatives on industrial trade issues as well as for the conduct of trade negotiations affecting sectors such as aircraft, steel, telecommunications, and semiconductors.

Deputy Asst. USTR for Industry and Labor
Mr. Donald Eiss
202/395-9603
Rm. 418

Deputy Asst. USTR for Industry
Ms. Gordana Earp
202/395-6160
Rm. 422A

Director, Aerospace and Automotive Trade Policy
Mr. Steven Falken
202/395-4946
Rm. 423A

Director for Information Industry Trade Policy
Ms. Barbara Norton
202/395-6160
Rm. 416

Director, Capital Goods and Small Minority Business
Mr. Lawrence Hiram
202/395-5656
Rm. 423A

Director Telecommunications
Mr. William Corbett
202/395-6160
Rm. 416

Director, Intl. Commodity Policy and Non-Ferrous Metals
Mr. Jonathan McHale
202/395-5656
Rm. 418

Intergovernmental Affairs and Public Liaison

Asst. USTR
Mr. John Pate Felts
202/395-6120   FAX 202/395-3692
Rm. 101A

Education: B.S. and B.A. in accounting, Univ. of Richmond, 1974. M.B.A. in finance and management, The College of William and Mary, 1978.

Professional: 1974-76, tax & audit specialist, Peak & Drescher, CPAs. 1978-79, tax & audit specialist, Peat Marwick Mitchell & Co. 1979-81, partner, Simmermacher & Felts, CPAs. 1981-86, CFO and director, Gray & Company Public Communications International, Inc. 1986-87, regional financial officer, Hill & Knowlton, Inc. 1987-91, financial consultant. 1991-95, deputy chief of staff; January 1996-November 1996, chief of staff, U.S. Sen. David Pryor (D-Ark.). December 1996-97, special counsel for investment and financial policy; 1997-present, asst. USTR for intergovernmental affairs and public liaison, Office of the U.S. Trade Representative, Executive Office of the President.

John Pate Felts was appointed as the assistant U.S. trade representative for intergovernmental affairs and public liaison in 1997 and as such, is the administration's main liaison on trade issues to the private sector and state and local governments. He replaced Phyllis Jones.

Prior to assuming his current post, Felts was the special counsel for investment and financial policy since December 1996. The special counsel for finance and investment policy is responsible for coordinating U.S. trade policy with U.S. government financial initiatives and monetary policy, and for developing and evaluating trade-related U.S. government investment initiatives and policies. Felts had negotiating responsibilities for cross border banking and securities issues, and interagency responsibility for U.S. inward direct investment policy and approval under the Committee on Federal Investment in the United States (CFIUS) review procedures.

Felts was licensed as a Certified Public Accountant in Virginia and worked as a tax and audit specialist after receiving his B.S. and B.A. in accounting from the University of Richmond in 1974. He received his MBA in finance and management from The College of William and Mary in 1978 and then worked as a tax and audit specialist for Peat Marwick & Mitchell.

Felts was a partner in his own CPA firm from 1979 to 1981 and then joined Gray & Company Public Communications International as chief financial officer in 1981. He was with this Washington DC public relations firm until 1986 when he joined Hill & Knowlton, another PR firm, as regional financial officer for the Southeast Region in November of 1986.

Felts worked as a self-employed financial consultant from 1987 to 1991 when he became deputy chief of staff for U.S. Senator David Pryor (D-Ark.). He served as Pryor's chief of staff from January 1996 to November of 1996 when he joined the Executive Office of the President at the Office of the U.S. Trade Representative.

Deputy Director of Intergovernmental Affairs and Public Liaison
Mr. Clayton Parker
202/395-9505
Rm. 101A

Japan

Asst. USTR for Japan
Ms. Wendy Cutler
202/395-5070
Rm. 320

Education: B.A. in international relations, George Washington University, 1979. MSFS, Georgetown University, 1983.

Professional: 1983-88, GATT issues, U.S. Department of Commerce. 1988-present, various positions at USTR including, director of non-tariff measures in the GATT Affairs office; the Office of Industry; 1993-96, deputy assistant USTR for Japan; May 1996-July 1997, assistant USTR for services, investment and intellectual property; July 1997-present, asst. USTR for Japan, Office of the U.S. Trade Representative.

Wendy Cutler became the Assistant U.S. Trade Representative for Japan at the Office of the U.S. Trade Representative in July 1997. In this capacity, she is responsible for the development and implementation of the United States' overall trade policy towards Japan. She is also responsible for the negotiation and implementation of bilateral trade agreements with Japan on a wide range of issues, including telecommunications, autos, and deregulation. In addition, she is also the lead USTR negotiator for the ongoing financial services negotiations in the World Trade Organization.

Cutler joined USTR in 1988. Since that time she has held a number of positions including Assistant U.S. Trade Representative for Services, Investment and Intellectual Property, and Deputy Assistant U.S. Trade Representative for Japan. Major negotiations include U.S.-Japan Framework agreements on telecommunications and insurance, U.S.-Japan Semiconductor Arrangement, bilateral investment treaties, WTO services negotiations, the OECD Multilateral Agreement on Investment, and the Uruguay Round Agreements on Rules of Origin and Preshipment Inspection.

Prior to joining USTR, Cutler worked at the Commerce Department from 1983-1988. She received her master's degree in foreign service from Georgetown University and her B.A. from the George Washington University.

Policy Analyst for Trade
Mr. Ralph Sigel
202/395-5070
Rm. 322A

Monitoring and Enforcement Unit

Asst. USTR for and Director of Monitoring and Enforcement
Ms. Jane A. Bradley
202/395-3582   FAX 202/395-3640
Rm. 501

Professional: attorney, Cohen, Vitt and Annand (Alexandria, Virginia). 1980-81, White House Fellow. 1981-94, various positions, office of the U.S. Trade Representative. 1994-95, director, global environmental affairs, National Security Council and associate director for international trade and development, Council on Environmental Quality, The White House. 1995-present, assistant U.S. trade representative for monitoring and enforcement, Office of the U.S. Trade Representative.

Jane Bradley is assistant U.S. trade representative for monitoring and enforcement. In that capacity she heads the office at USTR devoted to monitoring all trade agreements to which the United States is a party, determining compliance of foreign governments, and pursuing actions necessary to enforce U.S. rights under those agreements.

In 1994 and 1995, Bradley served jointly as director for global environmental affairs at the national security council and as associate director for international trade and development at the Council on Environmental Quality, where she provided policy advice on international environmental issues including trade and the environment.

Prior to joining the White House staff in early 1994, Bradley served at USTR for 13 years, including almost four years as the legal advisor in USTR's Geneva, Switzerland office. Her previous posts at USTR include that of assistant USTR for dispute resolution and senior deputy general counsel.

Bradley was the chief U.S. lawyer for the Uruguay Round trade negotiations under the General Agreements on Tariffs and Trade (GATT), and was the lead U.S. negotiator on dispute settlement procedures and the agreement establishing the World Trade Organizations. As deputy general counsel, she supervised litigation of trade disputes under GATT and other international trade agreements, and was responsible for running the "Section 301" and "Super 301" programs, involving investigations of foreign government unfair trade practices.

Bradley was a White House Fellow in 1980 and 1981 and prior to that fellowship, practiced law in Alexandria, Virginia with the law firm of Cohen, Vitt and Annand.

Policy Coordination

Asst. USTR for Policy Coordination
Mr. Frederick Montgomery
202/395-3582   FAX 202/395-3640
Rm. 501

Education: B.A. in political science, Univ. of Arizona. M.A. in government, and J.D., the George Washington University.

Professional: 1963-80, staff economist and then director (1976) office of trade policy, U.S. Dept. of Commerce. 1981-84, deputy assistant USTR, policy coordination; 1985-87, chief U.S. negotiator for the Harmonized System; 1987-89, deputy chief of mission in the US Mission to the GATT; 1989-91, private sector coordinator for multilateral trade negotiations; 1992-present, assistant USTR for policy coordination, Office of the U.S. Trade Representative.

Frederick Montgomery is the assistant U.S. trade representative for policy coordination in the office of the U.S. Trade Representative (USTR). In this capacity, he directs the office of policy coordination, and serves as the chairman of the Interagency Trade Policy Staff Committee (TPSC) and as the executive secretary of the agency.

In his capacity as chairman of the TPSC, Montgomery is responsible for coordinating the positions of 17 federal agencies involved in trade policy, reaching financial decisions, and bumping up unresolved issues to the sub-cabinet level. The scope for the committee's action range across the entire spectrum of U.S. trade policy, whether conducted bilaterally, regionally (e.g., NAFTA, APEC, and the European Union) or multilaterally (e.g., the GATT/WTO, UNCTAD and the OECD).

Policy decisions cover agriculture, industry, services, and specific trade-related areas such as import restraints, standards, government procurement, subsidies, intellectual property, investment, and the environment.

As executive secretary for USTR, Montgomery is the main point of contact for other federal agencies, including substantive communications and taskings, legislative referrals, investigations by the General Accounting Office, and a range of other activities. He edits and supervises the production of USTR's annual report, the annual National Trade Estimate report on trade barriers, and various other reports to the Congress and the President.

Montgomery previously served as USTR's private sector coordinator for multilateral trade negotiations from 1989 to 1991. Before that he was assigned to the USTR office in Geneva, Switzerland as the deputy chief of mission in the U.S. mission to the GATT talks (1987-89) and as chief U.S. negotiator for the Harmonized System (1985-87). He was the deputy assistant USTR for policy coordination in Washington from 1981 to 1984.

Prior to coming to the USTR office, Montgomery served at the U.S. Department of Commerce as director of the office of trade policy from 1976 until 1980. Within that office, Montgomery also directed the Trade Negotiations and Agreements Division (1975-76) and the Industrialized Nations Division (1973-74). He began his professional career in 1963 serving as staff economist within the office of trade policy. He was assigned to Geneva for the Kennedy Round of Negotiations from 1965 to 1967.

Public Affairs

Asst. USTR Public and Media Affairs
Mr. Jay Ziegler
202/395-3230   FAX 202/395-6121
Rm. 103A

Education: B.A. in political science-public service, Univ. of Calif. at Davis, 1984.

Professional: 1984-89, press sec., admin. asst., Calif. State Sen. John Garamendi (D). July-Nov. 1988, dep. press sec., Calif. Coordinated Democratic Campaign. Nov. 1989-Sept. 1990, Nov. 1990-June 1992, deputy controller, director of communications, Calif. State Controller's Office (Sacramento). Oct.-Nov. 1990, press secretary, "No To Propositions 131 & 140". July-Nov. 1992, Calif. press sec., Clinton-Gore Campaign (Los Angeles). Nov. 1992-Jan. 1993, network television coordinator, dep. press sec., Presidential Inaugural Committee. Jan. 1993-Jan. 1995, dep. dir., office of communications; Jan. 1995-April 1996, special asst. to the Secretary of the Interior for intergovernmental affairs, U.S. Dept. of the Interior. May 1996-present, asst. USTR for public affairs, Office of the U.S. Trade Representative.

Jay Ziegler came to the office of the U.S. trade representative as assistant USTR for public affairs in May of 1996. He is responsible for the overall direction of all aspects of the USTR's public affairs, including outreach to international and national news media, liaison with business constituencies, public outreach, interagency policy coordination. He has an advisory role in trade negotiations, participates on the senior management team, and supervises agency reports, speeches, news releases and internet communications.

Ziegler came to Washington following the election of the Clinton/Gore ticket in November of 1992 to serve as network television coordinator and deputy press secretary for the Presidential Inaugural Committee, where he directed overall planning with national television networks and news magazine shows on the behalf of the committee. He joined the U.S. Department of the Interior in January of 1993 as deputy director of its office of communications where he handled the public affairs responsibilities for special initiatives such as the restoration of the Florida Everglades, implementation of the

Endangered Species Act, and National Park Service initiatives.

In January of 1995, Ziegler moved up to become a special assistant to Secretary of the Interior Bruce Babbitt for intergovernmental affairs and was responsible for policy coordination with other federal agencies, state and local governments, conservation organizations and private land owners. He also served as the Secretary's representative in addressing resource management issues.

Before coming to Washington, Ziegler had been active in California Democratic politics. He served as California press secretary for the Clinton/Gore Campaign and as deputy controller and director of communications of the California State Controller's Office in Sacramento. He earlier had worked for five years as press secretary and administrative assistant for then-State Senator John Garamendi. Garamendi is now the deputy secretary of the Department of the Interior. In addition to his work for the Clinton/Gore campaign, Ziegler served on the Dukakis/Bentsen National Advance staff in 1988 and was active on several ballot proposition campaigns in California.

Ziegler received his B.A. from the University of California at Davis in 1984, winning an Ewing C. Kelly Broadcasting Scholarship for 1983.

Deputy Asst. USTR
Ms. Kirsten Powers
202/395-3230
Rm. 101A

Senior Counsel and Negotiator

Senior Counsel and Negotiator
VACANT
202/395-3150
Rm. 223A

Services, Investment, & Intellectual Property

Asst. USTR
Mr. Joseph Papovich
202/395-4510
Rm. 301A

Joe Papovich succeeds Donald Abelson as the Assistant U.S. Trade Representative for Services, Investment and Intellectual Property.

In this capacity, he is responsible for U.S. trade and investment policy concerning these activities. This includes overseeing such activities as implementation of, and further negotiations regarding, the General Agreement on Trade in Services ("GATS") and the Agreement on Trade-related Aspects of Intellectual Property ("TRIPS") in the World Trade Organization. Papovich's responsibilities also involve preparation of the annual "Special 301" report regarding the degree to which other countries provide adequate and effective protection of intellectual property, the negotiation of bilateral investment treaties, and U.S. participation in the negotiation of the services, investment and intellectual property provisions in the FTAA and APEC.

Papovich has worked at USTR since 1982, negotiating trade agreements and resolving trade problems in many areas. Over this period, he has served as Acting Assistant USTR for Industry, Deputy Assistant USTR for Intellectual Property, and Deputy Assistant USTR for Industry, Senior Agricultural Trade Policy Advisor, chief U.S. negotiator on "safeguards" in the Uruguay Round trade negotiations, Director of Steel Trade Policy and Director of Middle Eastern Affairs. His first responsibility at USTR, in 1982, was to serve as USTR's liaison to organized labor. Prior to 1982, he was employed by the U.S. Department of Labor.

Deputy Asst. USTR for Intellectual Property
VACANT
202/395-4510
Rm. 311

Deputy Asst. USTR for Services
Mr. Peter H. Collins
202/395-4510
Rm. 311

Director, Regional Services and Investments
Mr. Bernard Ascher
202/395-4510
Rm. 313

Director, Investment Affairs
Ms. Lisa Kubiske
202/395-9587
Rm. 303

Director, Telecommunications Services Trade Policy
Ms. Carol Balassa
202/395-4510
Rm. 313

Director of Bilateral Investment Affairs
Ms. Mary Ryckman
202/395-4510
Rm. 303

Director, Intellectual Property Rights
Mr. Claude Burcky
202/395-6864
Rm. 303

Director of Services
Mr. William Corbett
202/395-9586
Rm. 303

Trade and Development

Asst. USTR for Trade and Development
Dr. H. Jon Rosenbaum
202/395-6971   FAX 202/395-9481
Rm. 515

Education: B.A., Univ. of Pa. M.A., M.A. Law and Diplomacy, and Ph.D., Fletcher School of Law and Diplomacy (Tufts/Harvard Univ.).

Professional: asst. professor, Wellesley College. assoc. professor, City Univ. of N.Y. (Graduate School and City College.) adjunct professor, American Univ. special asst., late Sen. Jacob Javits (R-N.Y.), U.S. Senate Foreign Relations Cmte. 1977-present: asst. USTR for the Americas; asst. USTR for Latin America; asst. USTR for Africa; asst. USTR for commodity policy; senior policy advisor; and asst. USTR for trade and development, Office of the U.S. Trade Rep.

Dr. H. Jon Rosenbaum is currently serving as assistant U.S. trade representative for trade and development at the Office of the U.S. Trade Representative. Among his current responsibilities are supervision of the U.S. Generalized System of Preferences, representation at the UN Committee on Trade and Development (UNCTAD), and worker rights issues.

Rosenbaum joined USTR in 1977. In recent years he has been assistant USTR for the Americas, for Latin America, for Africa, for commodity policy, and has served as senior policy advisor. He began his Washington career as a special assistant to the late Senator Jacob Javits (R-N.Y.) assigned to the U.S. Senate Foreign Relations Committee.

Rosenbaum received an M.A., an M.A. in law and diplomacy, and a Ph.D. from the Fletcher School of Law and Diplomacy at Tufts/ Harvard University. Upon graduation he taught for a decade as an assistant professor at Wellesley College and later as an associate professor at the City University of New York, both at the graduate school and at city college. He also held adjunct teaching positions at American University and at several institutions in Mexico and Brazil.

Senior Economist
Mr. David Morrisey
202/395-6971
Rm. 515

Secretary
Ms. Regina Teeter
202/395-6971
Rm. 513

Western Hemisphere

Associate USTR
Mr. Peter F. Allgeier
202/395-6135   FAX 202/395-9675
Rm. 521

Personal: born 4/17/47 in Orange, New Jersey.

Education: A.B. (cum laude), Brown University, 1969. Rockefeller Fellow, Harvard Divinity School, 1969-70. M.A., School of Advanced International Studies, Johns Hopkins University, 1972. Ph.D., University of North Carolina at Chapel Hill, 1977.

Professional: 1976, visiting instructor of economics, Duke University. 1977-80, economist, U.S. Agency for International Development, U.S. Department of State. 1980-81, economist; 1981, director for Japanese affairs; 1981-85, deputy assistant USTR for Asia and the Pacific; 1985-89, assistant USTR for Asia and the Pacific; 1989-96, assistant USTR for Europe and the Mediterranean; 1996-present, associate USTR, Western Hemisphere, Office of the U.S. Trade Representative.

As associate U.S. Trade Representative for the Western Hemisphere, Peter Allgeier conducts negotiations and supervises U.S. trade negotiators dealing with the countries of the Western Hemisphere, NAFTA, and the Free Trade Agreement for the Americas (FTAA). He also helps coordinate U.S. government inter-agency decision-making on trade issues involving this region.

Allgeier has been with the U.S. Trade Representative's office since 1980. He started as an economist, became director for Japanese affairs in 1981, served as deputy assistant USTR for Asia and the Pacific from 1981 to 1985, and was promoted to assistant USTR for that region in 1985. In 1989, he served as assistant USTR for Europe and the Mediterranean dealing with Western and Eastern Europe, the former Soviet Union, the Middle East, and North Africa.

Allgeier's career at USTR has covered a range of trade negotiations, including those affecting the elimination and reduction of foreign tariffs and non-tariff barriers on U.S. goods and services; liberalization of investment regulations; establishment of orderly marketing arrangements; removal of foreign export subsidies; and improvement in foreign laws covering patents, trademarks and copyrights. In addition, he has negotiated trade and investment agreements with countries in Central and Eastern Europe and the former Soviet Union and international resolutions in the UN. In August of 1993, Allgeier unveiled a final agreement with Russia to address international competition in satellite launch services to alleviate the concerns of U.S. companies.

Asst. USTR for North American Affairs
Mr. Jon Huenemann
202/395-5190
Rm. 519

Jon Huenemann was appointed by the U.S. Trade Representative as Assistant U.S. Trade Representative for North American Affairs in November of 1997. As such, he is the agency's chief strategist, coordinator and negotiator in regards to Canada, Mexico, the North American Free Trade Agreement and its supplemental agreements. He is the U.S. NAFTA Coordinator and oversees the team that represents the U.S. in over 20 trilateral Working Groups and Committees as well as USTR's North American Affairs staff. He is also the chief agency strategist and negotiator in regards a free trade agreement with Chile and has responsibilities in regards agency work on "fast track" trade agreement authority.

Huenemann has 17 years of professional experience in international economic affairs, including 12 years at USTR. Prior to his current position he was: Deputy Assistant U.S. Trade Representative for the Western Hemisphere (1995-97); Deputy Assistant U.S. Trade Representative for Latin America and the Caribbean (1993-95); Director for Brazil and Southern Cone Affairs (1988 - 1993); Chief of the Advance Team and Coordinator of the U.S. Delegation to the Mid-Term Trade Ministerial Review of the Uruguay Round in Montreal (1988); and Deputy Director of the U.S. Generalized System of Preferences (1985-88).

Prior to his service at USTR, Huenemann was: an International Economist at the Department of Treasury (1984-85); assisting in U.S. Senator Bill Bradley's office on economic/trade issues (1983-84); assisting the Coordinator of a United Nations/non-governmental organization project monitoring global economic development issues(1981-82); and assisting in research at the Center for Strategic and International Studies in Washington, D.C. (1980).

Huenemann has a master's degree from The American University, Washington, D.C. in International Development and Economics and a Bachelor of Arts Degree from Richard Stockton College in New Jersey in political science with studies in economics.

Director for Canadian Affairs
Ms. Megan Waters
202/395-3412
Rm. 522

Director for Mexican Affairs
Mr. John Melle and Mr. Michael Koplovsky
202/395-3412
Rm. 522

Director for Central America and The Carribean
Mr. Sue Cronin
202/395-5190
Rm. 523

Deputy Asst. USTR for Latin America
Mr. Bennett Harman
202/395-6135
Rm. 523

Director for Brazil and Southern Cone Market
Ms. Kellie Meiman
202/395-5190
Rm. 519

World Trade Organization & Multilateral Affairs

Asst. USTR
Ms. Dorothy Dwoskin
202/395-6843   FAX 202/395-5674
Rm. 509

Education: B.A., School of International Service, American University, 1978.

Professional: 1978-93, office of trade policy development and then assistant director, office of the private sector liaison; deputy director, U.S. Generalized System of Preferences; chairman, Committee on Import Licensing; and dep. asst. USTR for multilateral trade negotiations; 1993-95 assistant USTR for GATT affairs; 1995-present, assistant USTR for World Trade Organization and multilateral affairs, Office of the U.S. Trade Representative.

Dorothy Dwoskin serves as assistant U.S. trade representative for the World Trade Organization and multilateral affairs in the office of the U.S. trade representative. She had previously served as assistant U.S. trade representative for GATT affairs when the negotiations on the General Agreement on Tariffs and Trade (GATT) were completed in December of 1993. That major agreement followed seven years of negotiations and covered, for the first time, areas such as textiles, banking, and software.

Previously, as deputy assistant U.S. Trade Representative for multilateral trade negotiations, Dwoskin oversaw activities on the GATT Uruguay Round. She developed negotiating instructions through the inter-agency process, directed coordinators and negotiators, and served as a liaison to the private sector and Congress. She also handled operations at the office, including management of the section's budget and administrative matters.

Dwoskin was a member of the staff at the USTR's office in Geneva, which represented the United States at the GATT talks. From 1985-88, she was the principal officer in Geneva dealing with negotiations on trade in services, the agreements on trade in civil aircraft and import licensing, and developing country issues raised at GATT. Dwoskin chaired the GATT Committee on Import Licensing in Geneva and represented the United States at the U.N. Conference on Trade and Development.

Before her assignment in Geneva, Dwoskin was the deputy director for the U.S. Generalized System of Preferences, a program of temporary tariff preferences to benefit beneficiary developing countries. Her work focused on seeking an extension of the program which expired at the end of 1984 and implementing the renewal authority.

Dwoskin has also served as assistant director in the office of private sector liaison at USTR. USTR maintains an extensive program of private sector advisory committees mandated by Congress. These committees were active in the completion of the Tokyo Round of Multilateral Trade Negotiations.

Director, WTO Affairs
Ms. Cecilia Klein
202/395-3063
Rm. 503

Director for Technical Trade Barriers
Ms. Suzanne Troje
202/395-3063
Rm. 513

Director for Tariff Affairs
Ms. Barbara Chattin
202/395-5097
Rm. 505

Director for Market Access
Ms. Elena Bryan
202/395-5097
Rm. 505

Policy Analyst
Mr. Richard Lorentzen
202/395-6843
Rm. 509

Director of Customs Affairs
Mr. Matthew Rhode
202/395-3063
Rm. 513

Advisory Board for Cuba Broadcasting

5325 NW 77th Avenue / Miami FL 33166

Chair
Mr. Jorge Mas
305/599-1800

Executive Director
Ms. Yvonne F. Soler-McKinley
305/994-1720

Assistant
Ms. Angela Washington
305/994-1720

Advisory Committee for Trade Policy and Negotiations

801 N. First St. / San Jose CA 95110

Chair
Ms. Susan Hammer
408/277-4237
Rm. 600

O'Melveny & Myers
555 13th St., NW / Washington DC 20004

Staff Assistant to Chair
Mr. Kermit Almstedt
202/383-5310
Rm. 500W

600 17th St., NW / Washington DC 20508

USTR
Ms. Charlene Barshefsky
202/395-3204
Rm. 209

Asst. USTR for Intergovt. Affairs and Public Liaison
Mr. John Pate Felts
202/395-6120
Rm. 100

President's Foreign Intelligence Advisory Board

OEOB RM. 340 / Washington DC 20500

INTRODUCTION

The Foreign Intelligence Advisory Board advises the President on national security issues and reviews the activities of the intelligence gathering services.

Acting Chair
Mr. Warren B. Rudman
202/456-2352

Acting Vice Chair
Mr. Anthony S. Harrington
202/456-2352

Acting Executive Director
Mr. Randy W. Deitering
202/456-5075

U. S. Department of Agriculture

14th St. & Independence Ave., SW / Washington DC 20250
202/720 8732
http://www.usda.gov

INTRODUCTION

Through a variety of programs, the U.S. Department of Agriculture assists U.S. farmers and businesses interested in exporting their products overseas. The agency offers information about all facets of exporting agriculture commodities from credit to forecasting to information about emerging markets.

Office of the Secretary of Agriculture

14th St. & Independence Ave., SW / Washington DC 20250

Secretary Daniel R. Glickman
202/720-3631   FAX 202/720-5437
Rm. 200A

Personal: born 11/24/44 in Wichita, Kansas.

Education: B.A. in history, Univ. of Michigan. L.L.B., The George Washington Univ.

Professional: 1977-95, member, U.S. House of Representatives (4th Congressional District, Kansas). 1995-present, secretary, U.S. Dept. of Agriculture.

Dan Glickman was sworn in as the 26th U.S. Secretary of Agriculture on March 30, 1995. Prior to his confirmation, Glickman served in the U.S. House of Representatives for 18 years, representing the 4th Congressional District of Kansas. USDA's 90,000 employees implement federal agriculture policy from the distribution of farm subsidies and food stamps to the promotion of agricultural exports and the management of the nation's forests.

Widely recognized as a leading spokesman for American agriculture, Glickman brought to his cabinet post the experience gained from nearly two decades on the House Agriculture Committee, including six years as chairman of the subcommittee on general farm commodities and its predecessor, the subcommittee on wheat, soybeans, and feed grains. In addition to his work on four farm bills, he led the way in such areas as expanding trade in agriculture goods and food safety. Glickman's career in the House also encompassed a two-year term as chairman of the House Permanent Select Committee on Intelligence.

Glickman was the original author of the House legislation to reorganize the USDA, and after becoming Secretary, he helped to downsize and streamline the department to a level not seen since 1966. During his tenure, he has focused on such areas as food safety, expanding export opportunities, rural development, protecting natural resources, and maintaining a nutritional safety net for those in need.

Glickman is spearheading an administration initiative to promote gleaning and food recovery, efforts to help feed the hungry by saving and providing food that otherwise would be wasted.

In December 1996, black farmers picketed the White House, claiming that USDA's white-dominated bureaucracy was conspiring to push them off their farms. Glickman responded by setting up a civil rights task force to handle their complaints and the complaints of the department's minority workers. "Civil rights," he said, "is going to be my legacy to this place."

Since becoming secretary, Glickman has enjoyed widespread popularity among farmers. Although Glickman credits much of that popularity to high grain prices, he is regarded by the agricultural community as a plain speaking man who is not afraid to take on the hard issues. Small wonder that Glickman was, in 1996, the cabinet officer most often requested by Democratic congressional candidates to make campaign appearances on their behalf.

Glickman and his wife Rhoda have two children.

Chief of Staff
Mr. Greg M. Frazier
202/720-3631   FAX 202/720-2119
Rm. 200A

Personal: born 9/17/53 in Abilene, Kansas.

Education: B.S., Kansas State Univ., 1975. M.A., Univ. of Connecticut, 1976.

Professional: 1977-85, staff and legislative assistant; 1985-86, legislative director, Rep. Dan Glickman (D-Kan.). 1987-93, staff director, subcommittee on wheat, soybeans and feed grains, House Committee on Agriculture. 1993-94, staff member, Permanent Select Committee on Intelligence, U.S. House of Representatives. 1995-present, chief of staff, U.S. Dept. of Agriculture.

Greg Frazier followed his boss, former Kansas Congressman Dan Glickman, to the Department of Agriculture in 1995 after Glickman, who lost his re-election bid in the 1994 Republican sweep of Congress, was nominated to replace former Agriculture Secretary Mike Espy. As chief of staff, Frazier directs the Department's overall policy agenda, consisting of issues as diverse as welfare reform to forestry to civil rights, as well as overseeing operations of USDA, which has 100,000 employees and an annual budget of $60 billion.

With 18 years of Hill experience, including work on four farm bills, Frazier is very familiar with the policies and issues included in USDA's jurisdiction. During his tenure as staff director of the subcommittee on wheat, soybeans and feed grains, he witnessed extensive hearings on the structure of American agriculture policy

---

and export programs. In addition, he was deeply involved in the writing of the 1990 farm bill and several key farm trade bills.

Frazier's involvement in the 1996 farm bill came from a different perspective, directing the development of the administration's position on the proposed legislation, negotiating with Congress, and speaking for the department during congressional debate on the legislation. Since its passage, he has overseen the implementation of the bill, particularly many of its basic commodity program and natural resource provisions.

Office of the Deputy Secretary

14th St. & Independence Ave., SW / Washington DC 20250

Deputy Secretary
Mr. Richard E. Rominger
202/720-6158   FAX   202/720-5437
Rm. 202B-A

Personal: born 7/1/27 in Woodland, Calif.

Education: B.S. in plant sciences (summa cum laude), Univ. of Calif. at Davis, 1949.

Professional: 1949-93, partner in family farming corp., A.H. Rominger & Sons (Winters, Calif.). 1977-82, director, State of Calif. Dept. of Food and Ag. 1993-present, deputy secretary, U.S. Dept. of Ag.

Richard Rominger became deputy secretary at USDA in 1993, bringing a lifetime of farming and agriculture policy experience to the Department. He is a fourth-generation family farmer and has been a farmer all of his life, with the exception of a six-year stint as director of the California Department of Food and Agriculture. Rominger's three sons, brother, and two nephews and their families continue to operate the 6,000-acre family farm.

As deputy secretary, Rominger supervises the activities of USDA, one of the largest and most diverse departments in the federal government. USDA's mission includes management of traditional farm programs, conservation programs, domestic food assistance, research and education, agricultural marketing, international trade, meat and poultry inspection, forestry and rural development. Rominger has also had responsibility for USDA's budget, reorganization, and downsizing.

In his four decades as a farmer, Rominger has been associated with numerous agricultural groups, including the Agricultural Council of California, the Council for Agricultural Research, Extension, and Teaching, Farm Bureau, and the Rice Research Board. Rominger also has served as president of the Yolo Land Trust, and a board member of the American Farmland Trust. He served in the U.S. Navy, 1945-46.

Office of Budget and Program Analysis

Supervisor International Affairs and Commodity Staff

Mr. Lynn Maish
202/720-3396
Rm. 126W
Office of the General Counsel

Associate General Counsel, Intl. Affairs, Commodity Programs and Food Assistance
Mr. Thomas V. Conway
202/720-6883
Rm. 2043

Asst. Gen. Counsel, Intl. Affairs & Commodity Programs Div.
Mr. Ralph Linden
202/720-2432
Rm. 2013

Asst. Gen. Counsel, Trade Practices Division
Ms. Mary Hobbie
202/720-5293
Rm. 2446

Asst. Gen. Counsel, Marketing Division
Mr. Kenneth H. Vail
202/720-5935
Rm. 2014

Office of Communications

Director
Mr. Tom Amontree
202/720-4623
Rm. 402A

Under Secretary for Farm and Foreign Agricultural Services

14th St. & Independence Ave., SW / Washington DC 20250

> ### INTRODUCTION
>
> *The Farm and Foreign Agricultural Services mission area is responsible for numerous agricultural price and income support programs, production adjustment programs. Among them are programs that support exports of agricultural products including initiatives to combat unfair competition, that develop new markets for U.S. suppliers, and that provide food assistance to food-deficit countries.*

Under Secretary
Mr. August J. Schumacher, Jr.
202/720-3111   FAX 202/720-8254
Rm. 205E

Personal: born in Lexington, Mass.

Education: B.S. in economics, Harvard College.

Professional: 1985-90, commissioner of food and agriculture, Massachusetts. 1990-94, agricultural lending official, World Bank. 1994-97, administrator, Foreign Agricultural Service; 1997-present, under secretary for farm and foreign agricultural services, U.S. Dept. of Agriculture.

Following his nomination as under secretary by President Clinton and confirmation by the Senate, Gus Schumacher was sworn in on August 5, 1997. He also serves as a member of the board of the Commodity Credit Corporation.

As under secretary of agriculture for farm and foreign agricultural services, Schumacher oversees the Farm Service Agency, the Foreign Agricultural Service, and the Risk Management Agency. These agencies administer farm commodity programs, farm operating and emergency loans, conservation and environmental programs, emergency assistance, domestic and international food assistance, multi-peril crop and revenue insurance programs, and a variety of export financing, market development, trade policy, and market-related technical assistance programs.

Prior to his appointment, Schumacher served as administrator of USDA's Foreign Agricultural Service, overseeing programs designed to foster exports of American agricultural, fish, and forest products. During his three years as administrator, Schumacher worked to educate America's farmers, ranchers, and food processors about the importance of the export market and to increase the number of small businesses and farmer cooperatives involved in exporting.

Before coming to USDA, Schumacher worked for the World Bank's agricultural lending group on a series of projects on agricultural policy adjustment, forestry, and biodiversity protection in Central Europe, Belarus, and Ukraine. Earlier, he worked on farm projects in China, Latin America, the Middle East, and Africa for the World Bank.

Schumacher also served as commissioner of food and agriculture for the Commonwealth of Massachusetts from 1985 to 1990. During his tenure there, Schumacher was heavily involved in the joint efforts of USDA and the National Association of State Departments of Agriculture to promote agricultural trade. As commissioner, he also fostered several state market development initiatives including the Women, Infants, and Children (WIC) farmers' market coupon program.

Schumacher is from a farm family in Lexington, Massachusetts. He has a degree in economics from Harvard College and attended the London School of Economics. He was also a research associate with the Agribusiness Department of the Harvard Business School.

Counsel to the Under Secretary
Mr. John Winski
202/690-4653
Rm. 205E

Counsel to the Under Secretary
Ms. Teresa Stuber
202/720-2797
Rm. 205E

Deputy Under Secretary
Mr. Dallas R. Smith
202/720-7107
Rm. 205E

Personal: born 10/1/42 in Bolton, N.C.

Education: B.S. in agricultural engineering, North Carolina Agricultural and Technical Univ., 1965.

Professional: 1965-68, agricultural extension agent, N.C. Extension Service; 1969-75, cotton marketing specialist; 1976-77, chief of peanut branch; 1977-85, deputy director; tobacco and peanuts division; 1985-93, director, tobacco and peanuts division, Agricultural Stabilization and Conservation Service; 1993-present, deputy under secretary, Farm and Foreign Agricultural Service, U.S. Dept. of Agriculture.

Dallas Smith was appointed deputy under secretary at the Farm and Foreign Agricultural Service, in 1993. In the first half of 1997, he served as acting under secretary of the agency until the confirmation of August Schumacher.

Smith has been a career senior executive at USDA, serving eight years as the director of the tobacco and peanuts division of the Agricultural Stabilization and Conservation Service, where he had responsibility for administration of price support and production adjustment programs for the two commodities.

He comes from a farm background, having been born and raised on a tobacco farm in Columbus County, North Carolina. He attended public schools in Columbus County and earned a B.S. in agricultural engineering at North Carolina A&T in 1965.

Smith has participated in several fellowship programs. As an undergraduate, he was the agricultural participant in a U.S.-U.S.S.R. cultural exchange program. As an extension agent in North Carolina, he was chosen as once of six agents nationwide to participate in the 1968 National 4-H Fellowship Program. The experience led to a three-month internship with the U.S. House of Representatives Committee on Agriculture the following summer.

Smith is married to the former Shirley Turner of Columbus, Texas. They have two adult children and three grandchildren.

Deputy Under Secretary
Mr. James W. Schroeder
202/720-8297   FAX 202/720-8254
Rm. 205E

Personal: born 4/19/36 in Elmhurst, Ill.

Education: B.A., Woodrow Wilson School of International and Public Affairs, Princeton Univ., 1958. J.D., Harvard Law School, 1964.

Professional: 1958-61, active duty, U.S. Navy. 1965-72, attorney, Mosley, Wells & Schroeder (Denver, Colorado). 1973-92, attorney, Kaplan, Russin, Vecchi (Washington, D.C.) and attorney, Whitman and Ransom (Washington, D.C.). 1993-present, deputy under secretary for farm and foreign agricultural services, U.S. Dept. of Agriculture.

James Schroeder is the deputy under secretary of agriculture for farm and foreign agricultural services. His office administers the nation's massive commodity programs, including the Farm Services Agency (FSA), the Commodity Credit Corporation, and the Risk Management Agency (RMA). It also oversees the Foreign Agricultural Service and USDA's international assistance programs.

Since joining USDA, Schroeder has headed up the department's NAFTA Task Force. He is actively engaged in departmental reorganization efforts and is the department's representative on China trade matters.

Schroeder spent twenty years practicing law in Washington, most recently at the Washington office of New York's Whitman and Ransom. He specialized in international trade, commercial, and administrative law. Before moving to Washington, he practiced in Denver for 8 years, primarily in the areas of natural resources and resort development.

A native of Illinois, Schroeder spent many summers on a family farm. He is married to former Colorado Congresswoman Pat Schroeder.

Commodity Credit Corporation

INTRODUCTION

The Commodity Credit Corporation (CCC) supports the prices of some agricultural commodities through loans and purchases. CCC loan rates are designed to keep crops competitive in the marketplace. CCC commodities fill the need for hunger relief both in the United States and in foreign countries. The agency purchases and delivers foods for domestic feeding programs and donates to "Food for Peace" and other programs administered by voluntary organizations which help USDA fight hunger worldwide.

Chair of the Board
Secretary Daniel R. Glickman
202/720-3631
Rm. 200A

Vice Chair of the Board
Mr. Richard E. Rominger
202/720-6158
Rm. 200A

President
Mr. August Schumacher
202/720-3111
Rm. 205E

Executive Vice President
Mr. Keith Kelly
202/720-3467
Rm. 3086

Foreign Agricultural Service

MISSION

The Foreign Agricultural Service (FAS) of the USDA is the U.S. farm and food industry's link to world markets. Crops from nearly one-third of U.S. farm acreage go to overseas consumers. Farm exports generate employment, income, and purchasing power in both farm and non-farm sectors.

FAS promotes U.S. agricultural sales by supporting cooperative market development activities with U.S. exporters and overseas importers of American farm products, negotiating increased market access abroad, working with our trading partners to reduce and eliminate unfair trade practices, supporting international agricultural cooperation and development, and engaging in global information collection and analysis of world commodity markets.

Cont'd.

It also collects, analyzes, and disseminates information about global supply and demand, trade trends, and emerging market opportunities. FAS seeks improved market access for U.S. products and implements programs designed to build new markets and to maintain the competitive position of U.S. products in the global marketplace.

FAS also carries out food aid and market-related technical assistance programs, as well as operates a variety of Congressionally mandated import and export programs. FAS helps USDA and other federal agencies, U.S. universities, and others enhance the global competitiveness of U.S. agriculture, and helps increase income and food availability in developing nations by mobilizing expertise for agriculturally led economic growth.

Formed in 1953 by executive reorganization, FAS is one of the smaller USDA agencies, with a personnel strength of 1,090. FAS operates worldwide with personnel located in more than 80 posts covering more than 100 countries. Additional countries are covered by Washington, D.C.-based officers with regional responsibilities. The FAS overseas staff is backed up by a team of analysts, negotiators, and marketing specialists located in Washington, D.C.

Annually, roughly 40 percent of the FAS budget is devoted to building markets overseas for U.S. farm products. This includes the funding for all of FAS' trade and attache offices overseas, as well as its work with U.S. commodity associations on cooperative promotion projects. The remaining funds cover other trade functions, including the gathering and dissemination of market information and trade policy efforts.

Trade offices in 10 key market countries function as service centers for U.S. exporters and foreign buyers seeking market information. U.S. Agricultural Trade Offices and attache offices provide foreign buyers with up-to-the-minute communication with potential suppliers in the United States. They also assist U.S. exporters in launching products in overseas markets characterized by different food preferences, social customs, and marketing systems.

Statistics and Market Information

FAS collects global crop and livestock production data and import/export information provided by the attache service, U.S. agricultural traders, remote sensing systems, and other sources. FAS uses this information to prepare production forecasts and assess export marketing opportunities, as well as to track changes in policies affecting U.S. agricultural exports and imports. These analyses are used by policymakers, program administrators, farmers, exporters, and others.

A series of reports are prepared by FAS attaches overseas. Overseas offices prepare reports on:

- the agriculture production situation
- trade trends and forecasts
- foreign government legislation and regulations
- trade policies affecting U.S. agricultural trade

The offices submit about 3500 reports each year. They include scheduled, special request and voluntary reports. Scheduled reports are those required by the Washington office on a periodic basis. Special request reports are those submitted in response to a one-time request by the Washington office. Voluntary reports are those initiated by the officers to report unusual or changing situations. These reports contain individual office estimates of the situation in a country, but the information is not official USDA data. Official USDA production, supply and distribution data are determined after analyzing all overseas reports, and drawing upon sources not available to our overseas offices.

Import Responsibilities

Through a licensing system, FAS controls imports of about 85 percent of all cheese and most other dairy products coming into the United States. FAS also administers the tariff rate quota for sugar and sugar syrups, as well as several programs to permit domestic refineries to utilize foreign sugar without disrupting the U.S. market.

Trade Assistance and Promotion Office
202/720-7420
Fax: 202/690-4374
TDD: 202/690-4837

The Trade Assistance and Promotion Office (TAPO) of the Foreign Agricultural Service (FAS) serves as the first point of contact for persons who need information on foreign markets for agricultural products or assistance in accessing government programs. TAPO can:

— Provide country and commodity specific Foreign Market Information Reports which focus on best market prospects, and contain contact information on distributors and importers.

— Put you in touch with several low-cost services that help U.S. exporters make direct contact with foreign buyers such as the Trade Leads, Foreign Buyer Lists, and Buyer Alert programs.

— Provide basic export counseling, and direct you to the appropriate USDA offices to answer your specific technical questions on exporting.

— Connect exporters with the appropriate export programs operated by the FAS such as the Export Enhancement Program, the Market Promotion Program, or our credit guarantee programs.

— Help in getting information on export-related programs managed by other Federal agencies, such as the Export-Import Bank, the Department of Commerce and the Small Business Administration.

Administrator
Mr. Lon S. Hatamiya
202/720-3935   FAX 202/690-2159
Rm. 5071

Personal: born in Marysville, Calif.

Education: A.B. in economics, Harvard Univ., 1981. M.B.A. (with honors), UCLA Graduate School of Management, 1987. J.D., UCLA School of Law, 1987.

Professional: 1981-83, purchasing manager, The Procter and Gamble Co. (Cincinnati, Ohio). 1985, international marketing analyst, Sony Corp. (Tokyo and Atsugi, Japan). 1987-89, associate attorney, Orrick, Herrington, and Sutcliffe (Sacramento, Calif.). 1991-92, founder and president, BHP Associates, Inc. (Sacramento, Calif.). 1992-93, public

member, State of California Rural Economic Development Infrastructure Program. 1989-93, inspection station general manager, H.B. Orchards Co., Inc. (Marysville, Calif.). 1993-97, administrator, Agricultural Marketing Service; 1997-present, administrator, Foreign Agricultural Service, U.S. Dept. of Agriculture.

After the confirmation of August Schumacher as under secretary for farm and foreign agricultural services, Lon Hatamiya, who had been administrator of USDA's Agricultural Marketing Service (AMS) since 1993, was nominated and subsequently confirmed to head up the Department's Foreign Agricultural Service.

Hatamiya was born and raised in Marysville, California, where his family has been farming for the past 90 years. He has had various administrative, legal, and management responsibilities in operation of the family's 1,200-acre prune, peach, almond, and walnut orchards. He was also a founder and president of BHP Associates, Inc., an economic development, education, and agribusiness consulting firm in Sacramento.

In 1991, he was selected for the California Agricultural Leadership Program of the California Agricultural Education Foundation, comprising top leaders of California agriculture. He was appointed by the California State Assembly in 1992 to serve on the Rural Economic Development Infrastructure Panel. As president of the Sacramento Chapter of the Japanese American Citizens League, he was recognized for his longtime work on obtaining reparations for Japanese Americans interned during World War II. Hatamiya was the Democratic nominee and first Japanese American in the previous 10 years to run for the California State Legislature from Northern California's vast 3rd Assembly District.

Hatamiya's wife Nancy is chief of staff of the President's Crime Prevention Council. They have two sons.

Associate Administrator
Mr. Timothy J. Galvin
202/720-5691   FAX 202/690-2159
Rm. 5081

Associate Administrator and General Sales Manager
Mr. Christopher E. Goldthwait
202/720-5173   FAX 202/690-1595
Rm. 5071

Director, Legislative Affairs
Ms. Paula Thomasson
202/720-6829
Rm. 5065

Export Credits

Export Financing

FAS provides U.S. agricultural exporters with short- and intermediate-term financing support through the CCC credit guarantee programs. These programs protect U.S. exporters or U.S. financial institutions against risk if the importer's foreign bank fails to make payment. These programs are designed to help developing nations make the transition from concessional financing to cash purchases.

Concessional Sales

The United States is the world's largest food aid donor. Over the years, donated U.S. food has often meant a life-or-death difference to victims of earthquakes, floods, droughts, and civil strife. The administration of U.S. food aid programs is shared by the U.S. Department of Agriculture (USDA) and the Agency for International Development (A.I.D.) in providing assistance to needy people around the world.

Cont'd.

USDA currently provides food aid through three channels: the Public Law 480 Title I program; Section 416(b) program, and the Food for Progress program. Both programs are administered through this office.

The Title I program provides for government-to-government sales of agricultural commodities to developing countries. Agreements signed under Title I provide for payment terms of up to 30 years, low interest rates, and grace periods up to seven years. Section 416(b) programs provide for overseas donations of food and feed commodities owned by USDA's Commodity Credit Corporation. Food for Progress programs provide commodities to support countries that have made commitments to expand free enterprise in their agricultural economies.

A.I.D. administers Titles II and III of the Public Law 480 program. Title II provides for the donation of agricultural commodities to meet emergency and non-emergency food needs. Title III provides for government-to-government grants to support long-term growth in the least developed countries.

Deputy Administrator, Export Credits
Ms. Mary T. Chambliss
202/720-6301
Rm. 4077

Asst. Deputy Administrator, Export Credits
Mr. Glenn D. Whiteman
202/720-4274   FAX 202/690-5727
Rm. 4079

Director, Emerging Markets Office
Mr. James O'Meara
202/720-0368   FAX 202/690-4369
Rm. 6506

Deputy Director, Emerging Markets Office
Mr. Douglas Freeman
202/720-0367
Rm. 6512

Director, Program Development Division
Mr. Kerry E. Reynolds
202/720-4221   FAX 202/690-0251
Rm. 4506

Area Mgr., Eastern Europe and the Former Soviet Union
Mr. Grant Pettrie
202/720-5319
Rm. 4524

Area Mgr., Asia, Africa and the Middle East
Ms. Lynne Reich
202/720-4216
Rm. 4514

Area Mgr., Latin America and the Caribbean
Mr. Roger Wentzel
202/720-0625
Rm. 4516

Director, Commodity Credit Corporation Operations Division
Mr. Lawrence T. McElvain
202/720-6211   FAX 202/720-0938
Rm. 4521

Deputy Director
Mr. Robert Simpson
202/720-6211
Rm. 4519

Chief, Credit Sales Registration Branch

Mr. Richard L. Godsey
202/720-0576
Rm. 4517

Chief, Export Programs Administration and Reports Branch
VACANT
202/720-2150
Rm. 4536

Chief Negotiator, Export Sales & Program Operations Branch
Mr. Mark Rowse
202/720-5540
Rm. 4525

Chief, Export Program Survey and Review Branch
Mr. William Hawkins
202/690-1635
Rm. 4535

Director, Public Law 480 Operations Division
Ms. Constance B. Delaplane
202/720-3664   FAX 202/720-6208
Rm. 4549

Chief, Vessel Approval Branch
Ms. Judith Dementriades
202/720-6711
Rm. 4549

Chief, Title 1 Commodities Branch
Mr. Patrick A. Lyons
202/720-5780
Rm. 4554

Director, Commodity Credit Corp. Program Support Division
Mr. Ira Branson
202/720-3573   FAX 202/690-0727
Rm. 4077

Chief, Planning and Funding Branch
Ms. Dee Linse
202/720-9846
Rm. 4085

Chief, Program Evaluation Branch
Mr. Bill Cammack
202/720-2465
Rm. 4528

Foreign Agricultural Affairs

INTRODUCTION

Within the Foreign Agricultural Service, the Office of Foreign Agricultural Affairs (FAA) has administrative oversight of the agency's overseas offices as well as any contact with the Secretary of Agriculture by foreign government and business officials.

FAA is administratively organized around area officers with direct responsibility for specific regions of the world in which FAS maintains offices. Operational responsibilities of the area officers within the Foreign Agricultural Affairs office are, for the most part, confined to managing the day-to-day administrative operations of the agencys overseas offices.

Inquiries about a particular country's commodity or trade situation, trade policy issues, trade promotion activities and export credit programs are handled by other FAS program areas.

Cont'd.

Among the resources available from FAA is an Overseas Directory listing the foreign agricultural posts maintained by FAS. The directory includes mailing addresses for inquiries originating from either within the United States or abroad; as well as telephone, telex and facsimile (fax) numbers; normal business hours; and both American and foreign national personnel currently assigned to these overseas offices. A copy can be obtained by calling: (202) 720-6138

Deputy Administrator
Ms. Mary Revelt
202/720-6138   FAX 202/720-6063
Rm. 5092

Asst. Deputy Administrator
Mr. Ted Horoschak
202/720-3253
Rm. 5092

Asst. to the Deputy Administrator
Mr. Ron Verdonk
202/720-6878
Rm. 5084

FAS Area Officers

Africa and Middle East
Mr. Paul Hoffman
202/720-7053   FAX 202/720-8316
Rm. 5953

Country coverage:
Algeria, Angola, Azerbaijan, Bahrain, Botswana, Côte d'Ivoire, Egypt, Ghana, Jordan, Kenya, Kuwait, Kyrgystan, Lesotho, Liberia, Morocco, Mozambique, Namibia, Nigeria, Oman, Qatar, Saudi Arabia, Senegal, South Africa, Swaziland, Syria, Tajikistan, Tunisia, Turkey, Turkmenistan, United Arab Emirates, Uzbekistan, the Republic of Yemen and Zimbabwe.

Europe
Mr. Philip Letarte
202/720-6727   FAX 202/720-8316
Rm. 5080

Country coverage:
Armenia, Austria, Belarus, Belgium, Bosnia-Herzegovina, Bulgaria, Croatia, Czech Republic, Denmark, Estonia, Finland, France, Georgia, Germany, Greece, Hungary, Ireland, Israel, Italy, Kazakhstan, Latvia, Lithuania, Macedonia, Moldova, Netherlands, Norway, Portugal, Romania, Serbia-Montenegro, Slovak Republic, Slovenia, Spain, Sweden, Switzerland, Ukraine, and the United Kingdom.

North Asia
Mr. Wayne Molstad
202/720-3080   FAX 202/720-8316
Rm. 5098

Country coverage:
China, Hong Kong, Japan, Korea and Taiwan.

South, Southeast Asia, Russia and Poland
Mr. Weyland Beeghly
202/720-2690   FAX 202/720-8316
Rm. 5098

Country coverage:
Australia, Bangladesh, Brunei, Burma, India, Indonesia, Papua New Guinea, Poland, Malaysia, New Zealand, Pakistan, Philippines, Russia, Singapore, Sri Lanka and Thailand.

Western Hemisphere
Mr. Bill Westman
202/720-3221   FAX 202/720-8316
Rm. 5951

Country coverage:
Argentina, Aruba, Barbados, Belize, Bolivia, Brazil, Canada, Chile, Colombia, Costa Rica, Dominican Republic, Ecuador, El Salvador, Grenada, Guadeloupe, Guatemala, Guyana, Haiti, Honduras, Jamaica, Martinique, Mexico, Netherlands Antilles, Nicaragua, Paraguay, Peru, St. Vincent, St. Lucia, Suriname, Trinidad & Tobago, Uruguay, and Venezuela.

Reports Officer
Mr. Kent Sisson
202/720-0924
Rm. 6072

Representation and Foreign Visitors Staff
Mr. Allen Alexander
202/720-6725
Rm. 5604

Foreign Visitor Program Coordinator
Ms. Sue Murphy
202/720-6725
Rm. 5604

Program Assistant
Mr. Jesse Mitchell
202/720-6725
Rm. 5604

Commodity and Marketing Programs

INTRODUCTION

Virtually every U.S. farm product entering world trade is promoted by market development activities. FAS programs help U.S. exporters develop and maintain markets overseas for hundreds of food and agricultural products, ranging from bulk commodities to brand-name grocery items.

Promotional activities are carried out chiefly in cooperation with non-profit agricultural trade associations and firms which agree to plan, manage, and contribute staff resources and funds to support these activities. The largest of FAS' promotional programs are the Market Development Cooperator and Market Promotion (MPP) programs. In addition, FAS sponsors U.S. participation in several major trade shows and a number of single-industry exhibitions overseas each year.

Deputy Administrator
Mr. James Parker
202/720-4761   FAX 202/690-3606
Rm. 5089A

Asst. Deputy Administrator
Ms. Beth Callanan
202/720-7791
Rm. 5089A

Asst. Deputy Administrator (Analysis)
Mr. Frank Tarrant
202/720-1595
Rm. 5087

Director, Marketing Operations Staff

Mr. Kent Sisson
202/720-4327   FAX 202/720-8461
Rm. 4932

Deputy Director
Ms. Denise Fetters
202/720-5521
Rm. 4932

Director, Production Estimates and Crop Assessment Division
Mr. Edwin I. Cissel
202/720-0888   FAX 202/720-8880
Rm. 6053

Chief, Grains, Oilseeds, and Cotton Branch
Mr. Allen L. Vandergriff
202/720-0873
Rm. 6053

Director, Dairy, Livestock and Poultry Division
Mr. John Reddington
202/720-8031   FAX 202/720-0617
Rm. 6616

Deputy Director, Marketing
Mr. Robert Wicks
202/720-3899
Rm. 6616

Deputy Director, Analysis
Mr. Max Browser
202/720-1350
Rm. 6621

Director, Grain and Feed Division
Mr. Robert A. Riemenschneider
202/720-6219   FAX 202/720-0340
Rm. 5603

Deputy Director, Marketing
Ms. Francine Radler
202/720-4168
Rm. 5603

Deputy Director, Analysis
Mr. Henry Lee Schatz
202/720-4935
Rm. 5615

Director, Cotton, Oilseeds, Tobacco and Seeds Division
Mr. Larry Blum
202/720-9516   FAX 202/720-7670
Rm. 5932

Deputy Director, Marketing
Mr. W. Lynn Abbott
202/720-8809
Rm. 5638

Deputy Director, Analysis
Mr. Frank Coolidge
202/720-9518
Rm. 5646

Director, Horticultural and Tropical Products Division
Mr. Frank J. Piason
202/720-6590   FAX 202/720-3799
Rm. 5647

Deputy Director, Marketing
Mr. Robert Tisch
202/720-7931
Rm. 5644

Deputy Director, Analysis
Mr. Howard Wetzel
202/720-3423
Rm. 5647

Director, Forest Products Division
Mr. Mark Dries
202/720-0638   FAX 202/720-8461
Rm. 4647

Deputy Director, Marketing
VACANT
202/720-0638
Rm. 4647

Deputy Director, Analysis
Mr. David B. Young
202/720-1296
Rm. 4651

Director, Agriculture Export Services Division
Mr. Charles Alexander
202/720-6343   FAX 202/720-9509
Rm. 4939

Deputy Director
Mr. James Warden
202/690-1148
Rm. 4646

Deputy Director, Outreach and Exporter Assistance
Mr. Dale Miller
202/690-0752
Rm. 4941

Chief, Agriculture Export Connections Branch
Mr. Dennis Wendell
202/690-4172
Rm. 4640

Trade Assistance and Planning Officer
VACANT
202/690-0188
Rm. 4951

Chief, Trade Shows and Missions
Ms. M. Maria Nemeth-Ek
202/720-9423
Rm. 4944

International Trade Policy

INTRODUCTION

FAS coordinates and directs USDA's responsibilities in international trade agreement programs and negotiations, working closely with the U.S. Trade Representative's office in this effort. International trade policy experts within FAS help identify—and work to reduce—foreign trade barriers and practices that discourage the export of U.S. farm products.

In virtually every foreign market, U.S. agricultural exports are subject to import duties and non-tariff trade restrictions. Trade information sent to Washington from FAS personnel overseas is used to map strategies for improving market access, pursuing U.S. rights under trade agreements, and developing programs and policies to make U.S. farm products more competitive.

FAS has certain responsibilities with respect to imports of agricultural products. The agency acts to prevent imports from interfering with the operation of U.S. price support programs.

Acting Deputy Administrator
Ms. Patricia Sheikh
202/720-6887   FAX 202/720-0069
Rm. 5057

Assistant Deputy Administrator
Mr. Randolph Zeitner
202/720-4055
Rm. 5055

Assistant to the Deputy Administrator
Ms. Beverly Simmons
202/720-4433
Rm. 5053

Director, Multilateral Trade Negotiations Division
Mr. Geoffrey Wiggins
202/720-1312   FAX 202/720-6139
Rm. 5549

WTO Monitoring Team Leader
Mr. Allen Harapsky
202/720-6278
Rm. 5538

Trade Negotiations Coordination Team Leader
Ms. Cathy McKinnell
202/720-6064
Rm. 5536

Director, Europe, Africa, and the Middle East
Ms. Craig Thorn
202/720-1340   FAX 202/720-3799
Rm. 5514

Eastern Europe, Africa, and the Middle East Team Leader
Mr. Jeff Hesse
202/720-2258
Rm. 5513

Europe Team Leader
Ms. Merritt Chesley
202/720-1322
Rm. 5517

Director, Asia, Americas Division
Mr. Larry Deaton
202/720-1289   FAX 202/720-0069
Rm. 5509

Deputy Director
VACANT
202/720-1289
Rm. 5504

Americas Team Leader
Ms. Carol Goodloe
202/720-1325
Rm. 55508

Asia Team Leader
Mr. David Salmon
202/720-4376
Rm. 5501

Director, Import Policies and Programs Division
Mr. Steve Hammond
202/720-2916   FAX 202/720-0876
Rm. 5533

Import Quota Team Leader
Mr. William Huth
202/720-1061

Rm. 5527

Import Policies Team Leader
Ms. Diana C. Wanamaker
202/720-1330
Rm. 5535

Acting Director, Trade and Economic Analysis Division
Mr. Randy Zeitner
202/720-1294   FAX 202/720-7772
Rm. 3059

Chief, International Economic and Financial Analysis Branch
VACANT
202/720-1293
Rm. 3055

Chief, Export Sales Reporting Branch
Mr. Thomas B. McDonald
202/720-3273
Rm. 5959

Director, Office of Food Safety and Technical Services
Mr. Lloyd S. Harbert
202/720-1301   FAX 202/690-0677
Rm. 5547

Marketing Specialist
Mr. Leroy Barrett
202/720-7054
Rm. 5543

Marketing Specialist
Mr. Gregg Young
202/690-3334
Rm. 5549

International Cooperation and Development

INTRODUCTION

The Foreign Agricultural Service's International Cooperation and Development (ICD) program area enhances U.S. agriculture's competitiveness by providing linkages to world resources and international organizations and building a spirit of cooperation. These linkages produce new technologies that are vital to improving the agricultural base and producing new and alternative products. ICD helps scientists and leaders from other agencies within USDA, the university community, and elsewhere to establish relationships.

ICD also serves as a link between the technical expertise of the U.S. agricultural community and counterparts in Africa, Asia, Latin America, and the Newly Independent States of the Former Soviet Union.

Deputy Administrator
Ms. Mary Ann Keefe
202/690-0776   FAX 202/720-6103
Rm. 3008

Assistant Deputy Administrator
Mr. John A. Miranda
202/690-0775
Rm. 3010

Director, International Organizations Division
Mr. Rick Helm
202/690-1801   FAX 202/690-1841
Rm. 3123

Director, Food Industries Division
Dr. Frank A. Fender
202/690-3737   FAX 202/690-0349
Rm. 3245

Leader, Cochran Fellowship Program
Mr. Gary L. Laidig
202/690-1734
Rm. 3844

Leader, Trade and Investment Program
Mr. Richard H. Rortvedt
202/690-3985
Rm. 3250

Acting Leader, Professional Development Program
Ms. Margaret L. Hively
202/690-1141
Rm. 3247

Director, Research and Scientific Exchanges Division
Mr. L. Whetten Reed
202/690-4872   FAX 202/690-0892
Rm. 3222

Deputy Director
Ms. Linda Lynch
202/690-4872
Rm. 3226

Acting Leader, Scientific Exchange Program
Mr. L. Whetten Reed
202/690-4872
Rm. 3222

Acting Leader, Binational Research Program
Mr. L. Whetten Reed
202/690-4872
Rm. 3222

Acting Leader, Foreign Currency Research Program
Mr. L. Whetten Reed
202/690-4872
Rm. 3226

Leader, Reimbursable Research Program
Mr. Richard S. Afflick
202/720-2589
Rm. 3202

Director, Development Resources Division
Mr. Howard Anderson
202/690-1924   FAX 202/690-0952
Rm. 3219

Deputy Director
VACANT
202/690-1924
Rm. 3219

Chief, Africa, Asia and Europe Branch
Mr. Robert J. Wilson
202/690-1945
Rm. 3225

Chief, Natural Resources and the Environment Branch
Mr. John Sutton
202/690-1918
Rm. 3211

Chief, Inter-American and International Programs Branch
Mr. Andres Delgado
202/690-2946

Rm. 3239

World Agricultural Outlook Board
1400 Independence Ave., SW / Washington DC 20250

INTRODUCTION

The World Agricultural Outlook Board (WAOB) coordinates the Department's commodity forecasting program; monitors global weather and analyzes its impact on agriculture; and coordinates USDA's weather, climate and remote sensing work.

The Secretary of Agriculture established the (WAOB) as an agency of the U.S. Department of Agriculture on June 4, 1977, under authority of the Reorganization Plan No. 2 of 1953. Under the reorganization plan of October 20, 1994, the Board became part of a newly created Office of the Chief Economist.

The mission of the Board is to improve the consistency, objectivity, and reliability of USDA forecasts. Under the Board's direction, interagency committees of experts develop official forecasts of supply, utilization, and prices for commodities. The Board also reviews agricultural outlook and situation reports released by other USDA agencies and provides direction in estimating methods and quality improvement.

The Board coordinates weather, climate, and remote sensing work among USDA agencies. It also monitors and analyzes the impact of global weather on agriculture. This activity is conducted jointly by the Board and the National Weather Service of the U.S. Department of Commerce.

Chair
Mr. Gerald A. Bange
202/720-6030   FAX 202/690-1850
Rm. 5143

Under Secretary for Food, Nutrition, and Consumer Services

Animal and Plant Health Inspection Service
14th St. & Independence Ave., SW / Washington DC 20250

International Services

Deputy Administrator
Dr. Angel Cielo
202/720-7021
Rm. 324E

Associate Deputy Administrator
Mr. Dan J. Sheesley
202/720-7593
Rm. 324E

Acting Director, Trade Support Team
Mr. John Greifer
202/720-7677
Rm. 1128

4700 River Road - Rm. 5C04 / Riverdale MD 20737

Associate Deputy Administrator
Mr. Carl W. Castleton
301/734-8892

Liaison Officer, Region III
Mr. Robert T. Tanaka
301/734-8292

Assistant Director, Import/Export
Mr. Rick Yoshimitsu
301/734-8892

Assistant Director, Foreign Pest Programs
Mr. Wilmer Snell
301/734-8892

Assistant Director, Foreign Animal Diseases
Ms. Cheryl French
301/734-8892

Assistant Director, International Organizations
Mr. Douglas Barnett
301/734-8892

Assistant Director, Epidemiology
Mr. Richard Pacer
301/734-8892

Food Safety and Inspection Service
14th St. & Independence Ave., SW / Washington DC 20250

Associate Deputy Administrator, Intl. and Domestic Policy
Dr. John C. Prucha
202/720-3521
Rm. 350

1099 14th St., NW / Washington, DC 20005

Intl. Policy Development Division
Director
Mr. Mark Manis
202/501-7500
Rm. 3702

Under Secretary for
Natural Resources and Environment

International Forestry
201 14th St., SW / Washington DC 20090

Deputy Chief
Mr. Val Mezainis
202/205-1650
4th Floor

1099 14th St., NW / Washington, DC 20005

Director, Disaster Assistance Support Program
Mr. Gregory Garbinsky
202/273-4724
5th Floor

Natural Resources Conservation Service
14th St. & Independence Ave., SW / Washington DC 20250

Programs

Director, International Conservation Division
Mr. Jerry Hammond
202/690-0333   FAX 202/720-0668
Rm. 4840

Program Specialist
Mr. Clifford G. Doke
202/690-2212
Rm. 4237

Program Management Specialist
Ms. Helen Huntington
202/720-0373
Rm. 4237

Under Secretary for Research,
Education and Economics

Agricultural Research Service
*Bldg. 005 Beltsville Agricultural Research Center-West
Beltsville MD 20705*

Assistant Administrator, Office of Intl. Research Programs
Mr. Rick Bennett
301/504-5605
Rm. 107

Economic Research Service
1800 M Street, NW / Washington DC 20036

Deputy Director/International Programs Coordinator
Ms. Cheryl Christensen
202/694-5203   FAX 202/694-5792

Chief, Europe, Africa and Middle East Branch
Ms. Mary Bohman
202/694-5150   FAX 202/694-5795

Chief, Asia and Western Hemisphere Branch
Mr. Praveen Dixit
202/694-5220   FAX 202/694-5793

Chief, Trade Analysis Branch
Mr. Ronald Trostle
202/694-5270   FAX 202/694-5822

National Agricultural Statistics Service
14th St. & Independence Ave., SW / Washington DC 20250

Director, International Programs Office
Mr. Larry A. Sivers
202/720-4505   FAX 202/720-0506
Rm. 4114

Cooperative State Research,
Education and Extension Service
14th St. & Independence Ave., SW / Washington DC 20250

International Programs

Director
Mr. Earl Teeter
202/720-3801
Rm. 338A

U. S. Department of Commerce

14th St. & Constitution Ave., NW / Washington DC 20230

Central: 202/482-2000
Business Liaison: 202/482-3942
Media Affairs: 202/482-4901
Public Affairs: 202/482-3263
http://www.doc.gov/

INTRODUCTION

The U.S. Department of Commerce operates more programs than any other federal agency to assist U.S. exporters, most of which are handled by the Department's International Trade Administration. The Secretary of Commerce chairs the Trade Promotion Coordinating Committee, which is comprised of representatives of 20 federal agencies. The committee seeks a more focused U.S. Government approach to trade promotion.

Office of the Secretary

14th St. & Constitution Ave., NW / Washington DC 20230

Secretary of Commerce
Chairman of the Trade Promotion Coordinating Committee
Secretary William M. Daley
202/482-2112
Rm. 5854

Personal: born 8/9/48 in Chicago, Ill.

Education: B.S., Loyola Univ. (Chicago), 1970. LL.B., John Marshall Law School (Chicago), 1975.

Professional: 1975-85, partner, Daley and George (Chicago). 1985-90, partner, Mayer, Brown and Platt. 1989-90, vice chair, then president and chief operating officer, Amalgamated Bank of Chicago. 1992, chair, Illinois Clinton/Gore campaign. 1993, special counsel to the president for the North America Free Trade Agreement. 1993-97, partner, Mayer, Brown and Platt. Jan. 1997-present, secretary of commerce, U.S. Dept. of Commerce.

William Daley was confirmed by the Senate on Jan. 30, 1997, as the nation's 32nd secretary of commerce. Described by President Clinton as a man of "rare effectiveness," Daley served as special counsel to the president for the North American Free Trade Agreement, coordinating the campaign to guide passage of the trade accord through Congress.

In accepting the nomination, Daley said he was committed to working "in partnership with American businesses from Fortune 500

companies to small enterprises, in our inner cities and rural America, to help our nation face the challenges and seize the opportunities that lie ahead."

Daley said, "The Commerce Department is where America's potential and promise come together, where our future jobs are created and our economic growth in nurtured through trade, technology, and information." The new secretary has set a broad agenda that ranges from doubling the number of small business exporters to modernizing the weather service to making the 2000 census the best in U.S. history to maintaining U.S. leadership in advanced technologies.

A long-time Chicago civic and business leader, Daley was a partner in the law firm of Mayer, Brown & Platt. He was president and chief operating officer of Amalgamated Bank of Chicago from 1990 to 1993, after joining the bank as vice chairman in 1989. He also practiced law with the firm of Daley and George in Chicago.

Daley has served on corporate boards and been active in many Chicago community and civil projects. His professional honors include the St. Ignatius Award for excellence in the practice of law in 1994 and the 1994 World Trade Award presented by the World Trade Center of Chicago.

Daley was admitted to the Illinois bar in 1975. He holds an LL.B. from John Marshall Law School of Chicago; a B.A. from Loyola University; and an honorary degree of Doctor of Laws from John Marshall Law School.

The secretary is the son of the late mayor of Chicago, Richard J. Daley, and the brother of the current Chicago mayor, Richard M. Daley. He and his wife Loretta have two daughters and a son.

Executive Assistant to the Secretary
Ms. Shirley Rothlisberger
202/482-2112
Rm. 5854

Chief of Staff
Mr. Paul M. Donovan
202/482-4246
Rm. 5858

Personal: born 3/24/55 in Cohasset, Mass.

Education: B.A. in government, Dartmouth College, 1977.

Professional: 1978-84, journalist, various newspapers in Colorado. 1985-87, deputy press secretary (Boston, Mass.), Sen. John F. Kerry (D-Mass.). 1987-89, press secretary, Senate Committee on Labor and Human Resources. 1989-93, press secretary; 1993-96, chief of staff, Sen. Edward M. Kennedy (D-Mass.). 1997-present, chief of staff to the secretary, U.S. Dept. of Commerce.

After more than a decade of service as a staff member in the legislative branch, Paul Donovan moved to the executive branch in 1997 to serve as chief of staff to Secretary of Commerce William Daley.

Most recently, Donovan served as Sen. Edward Kennedy's (D-Mass.) chief of staff. As such, he managed Kennedy's staff of over 100 and handled legislative, press, political, fundraising, and personnel issues. Donovan served as Kennedy's press secretary and spokesman from 1989 until he became his chief of staff in 1993. As press secretary, he developed and implemented media, political, and legislative strategies.

Donovan first began working for Kennedy in 1987 as press secretary for the Senate Committee on Labor and Human Resources which Kennedy chaired. There, he created and executed media strategy to advance the committee's legislative agenda primarily in the areas of employment, health care, and education policy.

U.S. DEPARTMENT OF COMMERCE

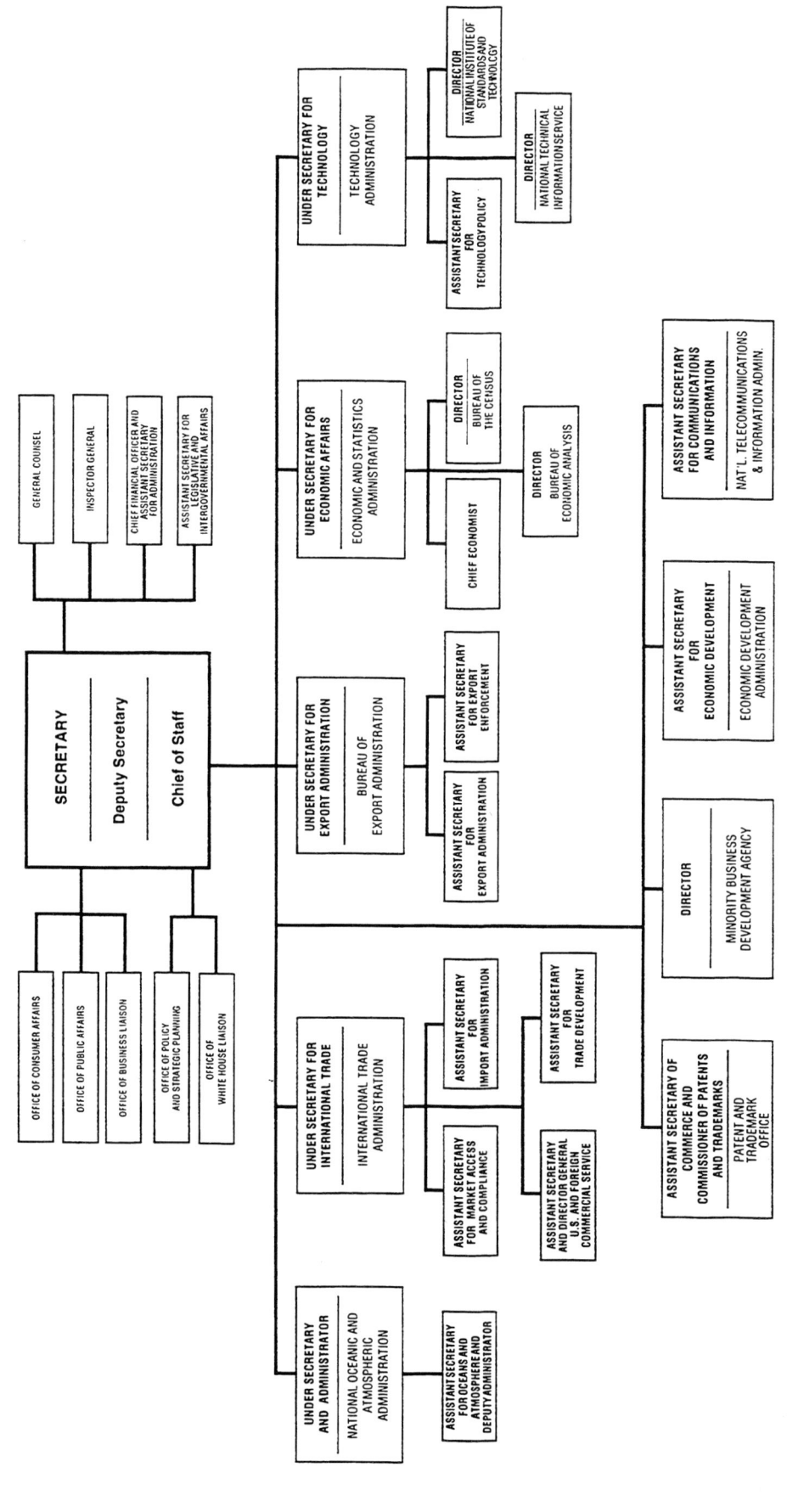

A graduate of Dartmouth College in 1977, Donovan began his professional career as a journalist. He worked as an editor, reporter, and correspondent for a number of newspapers in Colorado from 1978 to 1984 including the *Rocky Mountain News*, the *Glenwood Post*, the *Avon-Beaver Creek Times*, and the *Vail Trail*. In 1985, he made his move to government serving as deputy press secretary to Sen. John Kerry (D-Mass.) working in Boston as the senator's in-state press secretary.

Deputy Chief of Staff
VACANT
202/482-4246
Rm. 5858

Counselor to the Department

Mr. Jan H. Kalicki
202/482-3500   Fax: 202/482-6330
Rm. 3427

Personal: born 1948 in London, England.

Education: B.A., Columbia Coll., 1968. Ph.D., London School of Economics and Political Science, 1971.

Professional: 1972-74, U.S. foreign service officer. 1974-77, policy planning staff, U.S. State Dept. 1977-84, chief foreign policy advisor, Sen. Edward Kennedy (D-Mass.). 1985-88, executive director, Center for Foreign Policy Development and assistant to the president, Brown Univ. (R.I.). 1984-93, senior vice president, Lehman Brothers (New York). 1984-93, senior advisor and adjunct professor, Brown Univ. 1993-present, counselor, U.S. Dept. of Commerce.

As counselor to the U.S. Department of Commerce, Jan Kalicki specializes in international trade and investment, and is responsible for the New Independent States, the Middle East, and other emerging markets.

In addition, Kalicki is the Clinton administration's ombudsman for energy and commercial cooperation with the Newly Independent States. In this capacity, he is the administration's central point of contact in promoting the development of oil and gas and other commercial projects with Russia, working under the auspices of the Joint Commission for Economic and Technological Cooperation (the Gore-Chernomyrdin Commission), and with the other New Independent States.

Before joining the Commerce Department in 1993, Kalicki was senior vice president at Lehman Brothers in New York, where he managed the firm's New Independent States and Middle East business, and senior adviser and adjunct professor at Brown University in Rhode Island. He also has served as executive director of the Center for Foreign Policy Development and assistant to the president of Brown University (1985-88). He had taught previously at Harvard, Georgetown, and Princeton Universities.

Kalicki was chief foreign policy advisor to Sen. Edward Kennedy (D-Mass.) between 1977 and 1984; a member of the U.S. State Department's policy planning staff under Secretary Henry Kissinger and Secretary Cyrus Vance (1974-77); and a U.S. foreign service officer from 1972 to 1974.

Kalicki received his B.A. in 1968 from Columbia College and his Ph.D. in 1971 from the London School of Economics and Political Science. He is the author of a book and numerous publications on China, Russia, and U.S., foreign, national security, and international economic policies. He is a member of the Council on Foreign Relations, the Royal Institute of International Affairs, and the International Institute for Strategic Studies.

Chief of Protocol
Ms. Wilma Greefield
202/482-3225
Rm. 5847

INTRODUCTION

The Office of Policy and Strategic Planning *advises the Secretary on policy issues and directs issue-based and departmental strategic planning initiatives.*

Director, Policy & Strategic Planning
Mr. David J. Lane
202/482-4127
Rm. 5385

Personal: born 1/4/60 in Miami, Fla.

Education: B.A., Univ. of Virginia, 1982. Rotary Scholar, Univ. of Auckland, New Zealand, 1983. M.P.A., Princeton, Univ., 1988.

Professional: legislative assistant, U.S. Sen. Gary Hart (D-Colo.). 1988-93, management consultant, strategic management services group, Coopers & Lybrand. 1992-93, Clinton-Gore presidential transition (Dept. of Treasury transition team). 1993-96, exec. director, National Economic Council, The White House. 1996-present, assistant to the secretary of commerce and director of office of policy and strategic planning, U.S. Dept. of Commerce.

David Lane came to the U.S. Department of Commerce in April 1996 from the White House, where he served for three years as executive director of the National Economic Council (NEC).

As assistant to the secretary of commerce and director of the office of policy and strategic planning, Lane advises the secretary of commerce on a wide range of policy matters. He manages policy coordination among the Commerce Department's bureaus, emphasizing interagency integration and support of key department and administration goals.

In his White House post, Lane coordinated NEC policy staff responsibilities. In addition to his management duties, he focused on development and coordination of defense reinvestment and defense community economic adjustment policies. He played a key role on numerous special projects, including the Summit of the Americas held in Miami in December 1994. He was responsible for coordinating the G-7 Jobs Conference in Detroit in March 1994 and for managing the planning and execution of the president's Regional Economic Conferences in 1995.

During the 1992-93 Clinton-Gore presidential transition, Lane managed the Department of Treasury transition team, reporting to the incoming Treasury leadership team on department operations and key issues.

Before joining the Clinton administration, Lane spent five years as a management consultant with the strategic management services group of Coopers & Lybrand, where he assisted companies and not-for-profit and government organizations with strategic planning and other management public policy issues, including economic development and privatization policies. Earlier, he worked as a legislative assistant to U.S. Sen. Gary Hart (D-Colo.) for defense and foreign policy.

Office of the Deputy Secretary

14th St. & Constitution Ave., NW / Washington DC 20230

Deputy Secretary
Mr. Robert L. Mallett
202/482-8376
Rm. 5838

Personal: born 4/1/57 in Houston, Texas.

Education: London School of Economics, 1978. B.A. in political science and English (magna cum laude), Morehouse Coll., Atlanta, Ga., 1979. J.D., Harvard Law School, 1982.

Professional: 1983-87, associate attorney, Kaye, Scholer, Fierman, Hays & Handler (Wash., D.C.). 1987-91, legal counsel, Senator Lloyd Bentsen (D-Texas). 1991, principal corporation counsel, office of the corp. counsel; 1991-95, city administrator and deputy mayor for operations, District of Columbia government. 1995-97, Verner, Liipfert, Bernhard, McPherson & Hand (D.C.). Sept. 1997-present, deputy assistant secretary, U.S. Dept. of Commerce.

President Clinton nominated Robert Mallett, a Washington, D.C., lawyer and a former deputy mayor for the District of Columbia, to the post of deputy secretary of commerce on June 11, 1997. His predecessor was David Barram, who left the department in 1996. Mallett was subsequently confirmed by the Senate on September 26, 1997, and assumed his post.

As deputy secretary, Mallett is responsible for the day-to-day management of the department as well as the implementation of policy direction for the general supervision of organizational units and personnel. He will also perform duties and responsibilities of the Secretary of Commerce as acting secretary in the absence of the Secretary.

Since 1995, Mallett had been affiliated with the D.C. law firm of Verner, Liipfert, Bernhard, McPherson & Hand. He was a member of the firm's legislative and energy and environmental practice groups. He served as director of marketing for the 1997 presidential inaugural committee.

Between 1991 and 1995, Mallett served as city administrator and deputy mayor for operations for the District of Columbia. He was the chief administrative officer for the government of the District of Columbia which then had an annual operating budget in excess of $3.5 billion and more than 40,000 employees. Before taking the city administrator post, he served in the D.C. government for nine months as principal deputy corporation counsel for the office of the corporation counsel.

Between 1987 and 1991, Mallett was legal counsel to former Senator Lloyd Bentsen (D-Texas). He worked on the Clean Air Act, the Clean Water Act, cable legislation, aviation-related work, phone company monopoly issues, and nuclear waste disposal initiatives. In staffing the House Commerce Committee for Bentsen, he handled the authorizations for the Commerce and Transportation Departments.

Mallett began his career as an attorney with the D.C. law firm of Kaye, Scholer, Fierman, Hays & Handler between 1983 and 1987. In 1982-83, Mallett was a law clerk to Judge John R. Brown of the U.S. Court of Appeals for the Fifth Circuit.

At Harvard Law School, Mallett he was project editor for the Harvard Civil Right-Civil Liberties Law Review. He has been adjunct professor of law at the Georgetown Law Center and the Georgetown Graduate Public Policy Program.

Mallett's other activities include: secretary, board of directors, National Capital Area Kidney Foundation; chairman, board of trustees, Asbury United Methodist Church; president of Washington Metropolitan Council of Governments, 1994-95; member of board of trustees, Wesley Theological Seminary; member of board of directors for the Legal Aid Society of the District of Columbia; and member of the board of directors for Asbury Dwellings, a 147-unit senior citizen complex.

Associate Deputy Secretary
Mr. Kent Hughes
202/482-6315
Rm. 5027

Senior Advisor
Mr. Elias Hyman
202/482-8376
Rm. 5838

Office of Public Affairs

14th St. & Constitution Ave., NW / Washington DC 20230

Director of Public Affairs and Press Secretary
Ms. Mary F. Hanley
202/482-8920
Rm. 5411

Personal: native of Endicott, N.Y.

Education: B.A. in intern'l. affairs, George Wash. Univ., 1970. Political science scholar, Europa Inst. (Amsterdam, The Netherlands), 1971.

Professional: 1973-75, Washington bureau, United Press Intern'l. 1976, press asst., presidential campaign of U.S. Rep. Morris Udall (D-Ariz). 1976, national campaign staff for Carter-Mondale. 1977-81, special asst. to then-Deputy Sec. of State Warren Christopher and as press officer to the bureau of human rights, U.S. Dept. of State. 1991-84, dir. of ceremonial and special events for Philadelphia's dept. of commerce, co-dir. of city's tricentennial celebration. 1984-97, vice president of communications, The Wilderness Society. June 1997-present, director of public affairs, U.S. Dept. of Commerce.

Mary Hanley took over the post of director of public affairs for the U.S. Department of Commerce on June 3, 1997, bringing more than 20 years of experience in the communications field, the last 13 with the Wilderness Society. At Commerce, she oversees public affairs activities and plans department-wide efforts.

In announcing the appointment, Secretary of Commerce William Daley said that Hanley's "vast experience will serve the department well as she works with me and with the bureaus of the Commerce Department to communicate our mission and our goals in the years ahead."

For the past 13 years, Hanley has been with the Wilderness Society where she served as vice president of communications, directing media and public education activities for the national conservation organization.

Hanley worked for Philadelphia's department of commerce as the director of ceremonial and special events from 1981 to 1984, co-directing the city's tricentennial celebration. Between 1977 and 1981, she served in the State Department as special assistant to then-Deputy Secretary of State Warren Christopher and as press officer to the bureau of human rights.

In 1976, Hanley was on the national campaign staff for Carter-Mondale and served previously as a press assistant on the presidential campaign of U.S. Rep. Morris Udall (D-Ariz.). From 1973 until 1975, she worked in the Washington bureau of United Press International.

She received a B.A. in international Affairs from George Washington University in Washington, D.C., and studied the European Common Market at the Europa Institute in Amsterdam, The Netherlands, as a political science scholar.

Office of Business Liaison

14th St. & Constitution Ave., NW / Washington DC 20230

Outreach Program: 202/482-1360
Business Assistance Program: 202/482-3176
FAX 202/482-4054
E-MAIL: obl@doc.gov

INTRODUCTION

The Office of Business Liaison serves as the primary point of contact between the Department of Commerce and the business community.

Director, Office of Business Liaison
Ms. Cheryl Burner
202/482-3942
Rm. 5062

Office of Consumer Affairs

14th St. & Constitution Ave., NW / Washington DC 20230
202-482-5001   Fax 202-482-6007
E-mail: caffairs@doc.gov

INTRODUCTION

The Office of Consumer Affairs seeks to promote a better understanding between businesses and consumers, to help businesses improve the quality of their services, to educate consumers to make wise purchasing decisions, and to provide the consumer viewpoint in the development of economic policy. Through a variety of programs, OCA works with businesses, consumers, government agencies, and international organizations to develop innovative ways to encourage American businesses to become more competitive both in the U.S. and in the global marketplace. Issue areas covered by OCA include:

1. Global Outreach
2. Technology
3. Consumer Services
4. Business Education.

Available Information from OCA:

1. Consumer Tips — Available in English and Spanish, this series of fact sheets helps consumers avoid problems with businesses, know their rights, and resolve any complaints that may happen.

2. Business Education — The office offers a unique series of Consumer Affairs Guides for Business which define and encourage exemplary standards of business conduct and seek to heighten business sensitivity to consumer needs and preferences. Although the Guides are suitable and appropriate for any size organization, the target audience is primarily small- and medium-sized business.

3. Special Reports — A Resource Guide of Distance Selling Codes of Conduct/Ethics in Organization for Economic Cooperation and Development Nations. The resource guide examines voluntary direct marketing and selling codes of conduct/ethics from 16 countries in the OECD and four international organizations. They include voluntary codes from Australia, Belgium, Canada, Finland, France, Germany, Ireland, Japan, Mexico, the Netherlands, New Zealand, Norway, Portugal, Switzerland, the United Kingdom, and the United States. The four international codes examined include the European Mail Order Traders Association, the European Union, International Chamber of Commerce, and World Federation of Direct Selling Associations. There are no voluntary codes for distance selling in Austria, Denmark, and Turkey.

4. Consumer Bulletins — Published to inform consumers about Department of Commerce programs and issues.

Director of Consumer Affairs
Mr. Lajuan M. Johnson
202/482-5001
Rm. 5718

Personal: born 3/15/45 in Washington, D.C.

Professional: 1988-89, city administrator's office, D.C. govt. 1989-92, Democratic National Committee. 1992-93, staff, presidential inaugural committee. 1993-present, dir. of consumer affairs, U.S. Dept. of Commerce.

Lajuan Johnson, who has been director of the office of consumer affairs in the U.S. Department of Commerce since May 1993, has sought to promote a better understanding between consumers and business, to educate consumers to make wise purchasing decisions, and to provide the consumer viewpoint in the development of economic policy.

Johnson examines how international trade agreements affect

consumers and what protections are necessary for consumers in cross-border transactions. She has initiated several partnerships with government agencies and the private sector, including a conference to educate U.S. consumers about the North American Free Trade Agreement and a mini-conference focusing on foreign consumers who visit the United States.

Through a set of Consumer Tips and Consumer Bulletins, Johnson has sought to educate the public on the consumer impact of issues and to increase the breadth of outreach to consumers. Consumer Tips, published in English and Spanish, help consumers avoid problems with businesses, understand their rights, and resolve any complaints they may have. The Consumer Bulletins, written in a plain English format, tell consumers about Department of Commerce programs and issues on such topics as trade agreements and the information superhighway. Through a series of Consumers Affairs Guides for Business, Johnson defines and encourages exemplary standards of conduct in the business community and seeks to heighten business sensitivity to consumer needs and preferences.

Johnson represents the Commerce Department on the U.S. Consumer Affairs Council, an interagency body established to provide leadership and coordination of federal programs for consumers. She also serves as a member of the U.S. delegation to the committee on consumer policy of the Organization for Economic Cooperation and Development (OECD), a multi-national organization that seeks to foster sound economic policies among developed nations.

Before joining the Commerce Department, Johnson worked for the Democratic National Committee between 1989 and 1992 and served on the staff of the 1992 Democratic National Convention, and the 1993 Presidential Inaugural Committee. She worked in the city administrator's office in the District of Columbia government in 1988-89.

Chief Financial Officer and Assistant Secretary for Administration

14th St. & Constitution Ave., NW / Washington DC 20230

W. Scott Gould
Assistant Secretary for Administration and Chief Financial Officer
202/482-4951
Rm. 5830

Education: A.B. in philosophy, Cornell University MBA, University of Rochester. Ed.D. in administration and finance, University of Rochester.

Professional: active duty officer, U.S. Navy. managing associate, Theodore Barry and Associates (New York). assistant receiver and director of operations, city of Chelsea, Mass. 1993-94, White House Fellow. 1995-97, deputy assistant secretary of the treasury in departmental finance and management, U.S. Dept. of Treasury. Sept. 1997-present, assistant secretary for administration and chief financial officer, U.S. Department of Commerce.

President Clinton nominated W. Scott Gould to be assistant secretary for administration and chief financial officer at the Department of Commerce in April, 1997. The previous assistant secretary, Thomas Bloom, left the Commerce Department in 1996 to take the post of inspector general at the U.S. Department of Education. On September 26, 1997, the Senate confirmed Gould as assistant secretary and chief financial officer.

In his positions, Gould serves as the principal adviser to the secretary and deputy secretary of commerce on financial, administrative, and budget management. His responsibilities include program planning, budget management, personnel, finance, automated data processing management, contracting and procurement, administrative services, and equal employment activities.

Gould, from Topsfield, Massachusetts, most recently served as deputy assistant secretary of the treasury in departmental finance and management where he oversaw a $10.5 billion budget, and was instrumental in downsizing the department's 11 bureaus and workforce of 165,000. From 1993 to 1994, Gould served as a White House Fellow. As special assistant to the chairman of the Export-Import Bank, he conducted a diagnostic review of the agency's reinventing government effort.

Before that, Gould was appointed by the governor of Massachusetts to assist in the financial operations of the city of Chelsea, serving as assistant receiver and director of operations. Prior to that assignment, he was managing associate at Theodore Barry and Associates, a management consulting firm based in New York. He also served as an active duty officer in the U.S. Navy for eight years.

He holds an A.B. degree in philosophy from Cornell University, an MBA degree from the University of Rochester, and an Ed.D. degree in administration and finance from the University of Rochester.

Office of Small and Disadvantaged Business Utilization

Director
VACANT
202/482-1472
Rm. 6411

General Counsel

14th St. & Constitution Ave., NW / Washington DC 20230

> The General Counsel is the chief legal officer of the U.S. Department of Commerce.

General Counsel
Andrew J. Pincus
202/482-4772
Rm. 5870

Personal: born 4/17/57 in Hempstead, N.Y.

Education: B.A. (cum laude), Yale College, 1977. J.D., Columbia Univ. School of Law, 1981.

Professional: 1981-82, law clerk, Hon. Harold H. Greene, U.S. District Court for the District of Columbia. 1982-84, associate, Hughes, Hubbard & Reed. 1984-88, asst. to the solicitor general, U.S. Dept. of Justice. 1988-97, partner, Mayer, Brown & Platt. May 1997-present, general counsel, U.S. Department of Commerce.

Andrew Pincus, confirmed by the Senate on May 23, 1997, as general counsel of the U.S. Department of Commerce, cites regulatory activities as one of the general counsel's important responsibilities.

During confirmation hearings before the Senate Commerce Committee, Pincus said, "As a lawyer representing private companies I learned that it is critical to focus on the real-world impact of government regulations, and not legal abstractions. I will work hard to assure that regulations issued by the Commerce Department effectively implement the relevant public policy without imposing unnecessary burdens upon regulated entities." Pincus told the committee, "The government lawyer has an independent duty to the American people to ensure that the government's actions comply with the Constitution and the relevant statues and regulations, including ethical standards."

As general counsel of the Commerce Department, Pincus is the chief legal officer and adviser to the secretary of commerce, the under secretaries, the assistant secretaries, and other officers. He is responsible for the legislative program, as well as for developing and articulating the view of the department on pending legislation, and fulfilling the department's legislative clearance responsibilities with other government agencies. He oversees regulatory policy within the department.

Pincus himself had been a government lawyer as assistant to the solicitor general in the U.S. Department of Justice between 1984 and 1988. He also served as a law clerk to Judge Harold H. Greene of the U.S. District Court for the District of Columbia in 1981-82.

From 1988 until 1997, Pincus was a partner in the law firm of Mayer, Brown & Platt where he focused on Supreme Court and appellate litigation and legislative policy. Between 1982 and 1984, he was an associate with Hughes, Hubbard & Reed.

Pincus has filed briefs in more than 50 cases before the U.S. Supreme Court and presented oral argument in 13 cases. He has briefed and argued cases in the U.S. Court of Appeals and other lower courts. He did pro bono work in the Supreme Court for the American Civil Liberties Union and has given speeches on Supreme Court practice before varied groups.

In 1981, Pincus received his J.D. degree from the Columbia University of Law, where he was a James Kent Scholar, a Harlan Fiske Stone Scholar, and notes and comments editor for the Columbia Law Review. He obtained a B.A. from Yale College in 1977.

He is married to Laura Wertheimer, and they have two children.

INTRODUCTION

The Office of the Chief Counsel for International Commerce (OCC-IC) is responsible for legal matters related to the promotion of U.S. trade and investment and the competitiveness of domestic firms abroad. OCC-IC provides legal advice to the Under Secretary for International Trade Administration (ITA) and the following components of ITA: U.S. & Foreign Commercial Service, Trade Development, and Market Access and Compliance.

Chief, Cousel for International Commerce
Ms. Eleanor Roberts Lewis
202/482-0937   Fax: 202/482-4076
Rm. 5624

INTRODUCTION

The Office of the Chief Counsel for Import Administration provides legal support to the International Trade Administration, specifically the Assistant Secretary for Import Administration, in connection with the administration of the laws regulating unfairly-traded imports into the United States, primarily the antidumping law (which deals with exports to the United States priced below their price in the home market or below their cost of production) and the countervailing duty law (which deals with exports to the United States from foreign industries that receive government subsidies).

Chief Counsel, Import Administration
Mr. Stephen J. Powell
202/482-0916   Fax: 202/482-4912
Rm. 3624

INTRODUCTION

*The mission of the **Office of Chief Counsel for Export Administration** ("OCC") is to provide legal counsel to the Bureau of Export Administration ("BXA"). BXA protects U.S. national security and foreign policy interests by controlling exports and protecting the U.S industrial base while minimizing negative impact to our economic prosperity. The office is managed by a politically appointed Chief Counsel who is assisted by a career Deputy Chief Counsel and two senior career attorneys who serve as division chiefs.*

Chief Counsel, Export Administration
Mr. Hoyt H. Zia
202/482-5301
Rm. 3839

Director, Office of Commercial Law Development
  for C. & E. Europe
Ms. Linda A. Wells
202/482-5382
Rm. 6708

Inspector General

14th St. & Constitution Ave., NW / Washington DC 20230

Director, International Audits Division
Mr. William E. Todd
202/482-4176
Rm. 7721

Assistant Secretary for
Legislative & Intergovernmental Affairs

Acting Assistant Secretary
Ms. Ellen Bloom
202/482-3663
Rm. 5421

The office of the assistant secretary for legislative and intergovernmental affairs serves as a liaison between the Department of Commerce and the U.S. Congress. It is responsible for developing and maintaining a relationship with members of Congress and their staff, as well as legislative committees in efforts to gain their support for the department's legislative program.

The previous assistant secretary, S. Jane Bobbitt, left the department in August 1997. The deputy assistant secretary for legislative and intergovernmental affairs, Ellen Bloom, was acting as assistant secretary pending the administration's selection of a nominee for the post. At press time, no nominee had been put forward by The White House.

National Telecommunications and Information Administration

14th St & Constitution Ave., NW / Washington DC 20230

INTRODUCTION

In the 21st Century, telecommunications and information-related industries will account for approximately 20 percent of the U.S. economy. As global competition increases, it is imperative that the U.S. continue its leadership role in telecommunications by vigorously pursuing policies to open foreign markets to U.S. businesses and by encouraging greater competition among domestic telecommunications services and products.

The National Telecommunications and Information Administration (NTIA), an agency of the U.S. Department of Commerce, is headed by Larry Irving, assistant secretary for communications and information, and is the President's principal voice on domestic and international telecommunications and information policy-making. NTIA aggressively works to spur innovation, encourage competition, create job growth, and provide consumers with more choices and better quality telecommunications and information services and products at lower prices.

NTIA missions include:

• Developing and advocating pro-investment and pro-competitive policies before the Congress and the Federal Communications Commission and in bilateral and multilateral international conferences and negotiations.

• Managing and allocating all Federal use of the electromagnetic spectrum and promoting efficient use of spectrum. NTIA played a leadership role in developing and promoting policies to auction radio spectrum. This effort resulted in the awarding of licenses for Personal Communications Services (PCS) within one year and added approximately $9 billion to the National Treasury.

• Leading the development of a national and global information infrastructure through initiatives that seek to ensure that all people can take advantage of the opportunities provided by advanced technologies and services. In addition to policy development, NTIA coordinates the activities of the Clinton Administration's Information Infrastructure Task Force (IITF), chaired by Commerce Secretary Mickey Kantor, and the National Information Infrastructure Advisory Council (NIIAC).

• Assisting U.S. communities and non-profit institutions with their telecommunications needs through the Telecommunications and Information Infrastructure Assistance Program (TIIAP), the Public Telecommunications Facilities Program (PTFP), and the National Endowment for Children's Educational Television (NECET).

• Conducting cutting-edge technology research and telecommunication standards development in partnership with private industry.

Assistant Secretary for Communications & Information

Asst. Secretary for Communications and Information
Mr. Clarence "Larry" Irving, Jr.
202/482-1841   Fax 202/482-1635
Rm. 4898

Personal: born 7/7/55 in Queens, N.Y.

Education: B.A., Northwestern Univ., 1976. J.D., Stanford Univ., 1979.

Professional: 1979-83, associate, Hogan & Hartson. 1983-87, legislative director and counsel, U.S. Rep. Mickey Leland, (D-Texas). 1978-93, senior counsel, subc. on telecommunications and finance, House Commerce and Energy Cmte. 1993-present, asst. secretary for communications and information, National Telecommunications and Information Administration (NTIS), U.S. Dept. of Commerce.

Helping keep the United States on the cutting edge of economic and technological advances in the communications field is the stated goal of Larry Irving, assistant secretary for communications and information and administrator of the National Telecommunications and Information Administration (NTIA) at the U.S. Department of Commerce.

"For the first time in memory, the White House has elevated technology to the top of its agenda," says Irving. "The NTIA will play a lead role in assisting the private sector to develop and deploy telecommunications technologies." Irving reports directly to the secretary of commerce and President Clinton on domestic and international communica-tions issues.

Issues at the NTIA include personal communications services (PCS), spectrum allocation, international telecommun-ications and liberalization of markets, standards, and inter-operability.

Irving came to the Clinton administration in 1993 from Capitol Hill, where he was senior counsel on the House Commerce and Energy subcommittee on telecommun-ications and finance. His governmental experience began in 1983 when he served as legislative director and counsel to the late U.S. Rep. Mickey Leland (D-Tex.). He also served two years as Leland's chief of staff.

On the House Commerce and Energy subcommittee on telecommu-nications and finance, Irving was heavily involved in enactment of the Cable Television Consumer Protection Act of 1992. He is also credited with helping put together the Children's Television Act of 1990 and the Television Decoder Circuitry Act of 1990.

<u>Office of Congressional Affairs</u>

Acting Director
Mr. James Wasilewski
202/482-1551
Rm. 4899A

Office of Public Affairs

Director
Ms. Paige Darden
202/482-7002
Rm. 4897

Office of the Chief Counsel

Acting Chief Counsel
Ms. Kathy Smith
202/482-1816
Rm. 4713

Spectrum Management

INTRODUCTION

OSM is responsible for managing the Federal Government's use of the radio frequency spectrum. To achieve this, OSM receives assistance and advice from the Interdepartment Radio Advisory Committee (IRAC). OSM carries out this responsibility by:

• Establishing and issuing policy regarding allocations and regulations governing the Federal spectrum use;
• developing plans for the peacetime and wartime use of the spectrum;
• preparing for, participating in, and implementing the results of international radio conferences;
• assigning frequencies;
• maintaining spectrum use databases;
• reviewing Federal agencies' new telecommunications systems and certifying that spectrum will be available;
• providing the technical engineering expertise needed to perform specific spectrum resources assessments and automated computer capabilities needed to carry out these investigations;
• participating in all aspects of the Fed. Government's communications related emergency readiness activities;
• and, participating in Fed. Government telecommunications and automated info. systems security activities.

Associate Administrator
Mr. Richard D. Parlow
202/482-1850   Fax: 202/482-4396
Rm. 4099

Program Manager for International Spectrum Policy & Mgmt.
VACANT
202/482-1138
Rm. 4076

Policy Analysis and Development

INTRODUCTION

NTIA's Office of Policy Analysis and Development supports NTIA's role as principal adviser to the President on telecommunications and information policies. Its goal is to enhance the public interest by generating, articulating, and advocating creative and influential policies and programs in the telecommunications and information sectors that enhance service, competition, consumer welfare, and economic and social opportunities for all, and that remove impediments to the growth and vitality of these sectors.

Associate Administrator
Ms. Kathy Brown
202/482-1880   FAX 202/482-6173
Rm. 4725

International Affairs

INTRODUCTION

The goal of NTIA's Office of International Affairs is to provide policy analyses, technical guidance, and representation in international fora, so as to advance the strategic interests and the international competitiveness of the United States before a diverse, world-wide audience. OIA's wide variety of activities are designed to further advance and promote these U.S. interests by advocating:

1)telecommunications and information standards consistent with U.S. objectives;

2)regulations governing the international use of the radio frequency spectrum;

3)regulatory policies pertaining to the provision of information and telecommunications services both within and between U.S. and foreign markets; and,

4)the deployment of new technologies in these markets, to improve global communications and expand trade opportunities for our citizens.

OIA advocates Executive Branch policy perspectives in bilateral and multilateral consultations with foreign governments, in international regulatory conferences, and in other forums dealing with Global Information Infrastructure issues. Specific oversight responsibilities include, in cooperation with the State Department and with the FCC, the Communications Satellite Corporation (COMSAT) its activities in the International Telecommunications Satellite Organization (Intelsat) and the International Mobile Satellite Organization (Inmarsat).

To improve U.S. competitiveness in international markets, OIA provides policy and technical counsel to diverse U.S. interests. To support its representational and counseling activities, OIA tracks market development opportunities by maintaining a database on regulatory, technical, and commercial information for foreign telecommunications and information markets. This information is collected in a timely manner and distributed as requested throughout the world.

Acting Associate Adminstrator
Mr. J. Beckwith Burr
202/482-1304   Fax: 202/482-1865
Rm. 4701

Director, International Telecommunications Policy Division
Ms. Helen A. Shaw
202/482-2333
Rm. 4701

Director, International Policy Division
Mr. Jack A. Gleason
202/482-1874
Rm. 4720

Telecommunications and Information Applications

> **INTRODUCTION**
>
> *OTIA funds the following federal assistance programs: TIIAP, PTFP, NECET, and the Pan-Pacific Education and Communications Experiments by Satellite (PEACESAT) program.*

Associate Administrator
Dr. Bernadette McGuire-Rivera
202/482-5802   FAX 202/501-8009
Rm. 4096

Program Manager, PEACESAT
Mr. William O. Cooperman
202/482-5802
Rm. 4625

Policy Coordination and Management

Chief Policy Coordinations Division
Ms. Sarah Maloney
202/482-1835
Rm. 4892

Institute for Telecommunication Sciences
325 Broadway / Boulder CO 80303

> **INTRODUCTION**
>
> *ITS serves as the Federal government's principal research laboratory for telecommunications science & engineering.*

Director
Mr. William F. Utlaut
303/497-3500   Fax: 303/497-5993
Bldg. 30

Technology Administration

14th St. & Constitution Ave., NW / Washington DC 20230

> **INTRODUCTION**
>
> *The Technology Administration is the only Federal agency charged with the explicit mission of working with industry to maximize technology's contribution to U.S. economic growth.*
>
> *Directed by the Under Secretary for Technology, the Technology Admin. consists of three agencies: the National Institute of Standards and Technology, Office of Technology Policy, and the National Technical Information Service.*
>
> *The Office of the Under Secretary also provides advice and assistance to the Secretary of Commerce for the formulation of new policies and program initiatives for science and technology policy matters. In this capacity, the Federal Administration assists in the development and promotion of Federal technology policies to increase U.S. commercial and industrial innovation, productivity, and economic growth.*
>
> *Con'td.*

> *The Under Secretary:*
>
> *• chairs the President's Civilian Industrial Technology Committee, linking industry's needs and government technology efforts in electronics, manufacturing, materials, environmental technologies, and building & construction.*
>
> *• leads the Federal government's participation with U.S. automobile manufacturers in the Partnership for a New Generation of Vehicles, a ten-year technical collaboration aimed at achieving ground breaking improvements in fuel efficiency, emissions and safety.*
>
> *• directs the administration's efforts to follow up on recommendations made by the State-Federal Task Force led by former Governors Celeste and Thornburg.*

Acting Under Secretary for Technology
Mr. Gary R. Bachula
202/482-1575   Fax: 202/501-2492
Rm. 4824

Personal: born 1/1/47 in Saginaw, Mich.

Education: A.B. (cum laude), Harvard College, 1968. J.D. (cum laude), Harvard Law School, 1973.

Professional: 1975-86, chief of staff, U.S. Rep. Bob Traxler (D-Mich.). 1987-90, chair, Governor's Cabinet Council on Human Investment, state of Mich. 1991-93, vice president, Consortium for International Earth Science Information Network. 1993-present, deputy under secretary of commerce for technology; June 1997-present, acting under secretary of commerce for technology, U.S. Department of Commerce.

When Dr. Mary L. Good resigned as under secretary for technology June 3, 1997, her chief deputy, Gary Bachula, moved up the ladder to the post of acting under secretary. At press time, no nominee had been named.

In announcing the designation of Bachula as acting under secretary, Secretary of Commerce William M. Daley said, "Since joining the department in 1993, Gary has served as the deputy under secretary for technology and has been a key player in the department's tech team. He has been instrumental in developing the U.S. Innovation Partnership with the National Governors Association. Gary brings not only his experience managing the strategic and day-to-day aspects of the Technology Administration, but over 20 years of experience in technology and economic development in the state, federal, and non-profit sectors," the secretary stated.

As deputy under secretary, Bachula has helped to oversee the work of the office of technology policy, the National Institute of Standards and Technology, and the National Technical Information Service.

The office of the under secretary also provides advice and assistance to the secretary of commerce for the formulation of new policies and program initiatives for science and technology policy matters. The Technology Administration assists in the development and promotion of federal technology policies to increase U.S. commercial and industrial innovation, productivity, and economic growth.

Bachula also serves as the department's representative to the Committee on Education and Training of the National Science and Technology Council.

Bachula served as chief of staff to U.S. Rep. Bob Traxler (D-Mich.) from 1974 to 1986. He advised the congressman on appropriations for NASA, the Environmental Protection Agency, the National Science Foundation, and other federal agencies.

From 1986 to 1990, he worked for Michigan Governor James J. Blanchard, serving as chairman of the Governor's Cabinet Council. The focus of the council was to "reinvent" Michigan's job training and education programs.

Bachula also served as vice president for planning and program development for the Consortium for International Earth Science Information Network (CIESIN). CIESIN is a federally funded project to integrate and extend the value of current and future U.S. environmental data collection efforts (satellite and on the ground) to a broad array of applied users.

Bachula served at the Pentagon in the U.S. Army during the Vietnam War.

Counselor to the Under Secretary
Mr. Mark F. Bohannon
202/482-1984
Rm. 4835

Director, Congressional Affairs
VACANT
202/482-2123
Rm. 4822

Director, Public Affairs
VACANT
202/482-6030
Rm. 4845

Office of Technology Policy

INTRODUCTION

The Office of Technology Policy (OTP) develops and advocates national policies that foster technological innovation.

Assistant Secretary
VACANT
202/482-1581
Rm. 4814C

Deputy Assistant Secretary
Ms. Kelly H. Carnes
202/482-1403
Rm. 4814C

Director, Strategic Planning
Ms. Cheryl Mendonsa
202/482-8321
Rm. 4814C

Acting Director, International Technology Policy Staff
Mr. Phyllis G. Yoshida
202/482-1287
Rm. 4411

Director, International Science & Technology Initiatives
Mr. Lee E. Bailey
202/482-6264
Rm. 4821

Director, Manufacturing Competitiveness Staff
Mr. Cary Gravatt
202/482-6260
Rm. 4841

Director, Technology Competitiveness Staff
Mr. R. Jon Paugh
202/482-6101
Rm. 4418

Director, Air & Space Commercialization
Mr. Keith Calhoun-Senghor
202/482-6125
Rm. 4821

National Institute of Standards and Technology (NIST)
Gaithersburg MD 20899-001

INTRODUCTION

The National Institute of Standards and Technology (NIST) addresses basic technology needs, delivering broadly useful results shared among companies, industries, and consumers. Results of NIST's four programs underpin the technical efforts of U.S. industry. Industry drives NIST's programs and priorities.

Director
Mr. Raymond G. Kammer
301/975-2300   Fax: 301/869-8972
Rm. A1134

Kammer, of Maryland, began his career with the Commerce Department in 1969 as a program analyst. Prior to being detailed to the position of acting assistant secretary for administration, Kammer was the deputy director of NIST since 1993. He also served as deputy director of NIST from 1980 to 1991. During the period from 1991 until 1993, Kammer was deputy under secretary of Commerce for oceans and atmosphere. Kammer received a B.A. from the University of Maryland.

Office of International and Academic Affairs

Chief Director, Office of International and Academic Affairs
Dr. B. Stephen Carpenter
301/975-4119
Rm. A500

Chief, International Affairs
Dr. Claire M. Saundry
301/975-2386
Rm. A513

International Relations Officer
Dr. Marian F. McCurley

301/975-2624
Rm. A507

International Specialist
Ms. Cathy A. Smith
301/975-3082
Rm. A511

International Specialist
Ms. Aija Roess
301/975-3072
Rm. A511

International Specialist
Ms. Bonnie J. DeBord
301/975-3079
Rm. A511

National Technical Information Service
8001 Forbes Place / Springfield VA 22161

> ### INTRODUCTION
>
> *The National Technical Information Service (NTIS) collects and disseminates scientific, technical, engineering and related business information produced by the U.S. government and foreign sources.*

Director
Dr. Donald R. Johnson
703/605-6400
Rm. 200

Personal: native of Tacoma, Wash.

Education: B.S. in physics, Univ. of Puget Sound, 1960. M.S. in physics, Univ. of Idaho, 1962. Ph.D. in physics, Univ. of Oklahoma, 1967.

Professional: 1967-93, various assignments with National Technical Information Service (NTIS) and National Bureau of Standards (before its name change to National Institute of Standards and Technology) including bench-level researcher to laboratory dir., concluding with the post of dir. of technology services, NIST. 1993-present, director, NTIS.

As the director of the National Technical Information Service (NTIS) in the Technology Administration of the U.S. Department of Commerce, Dr. Donald Johnson presides over an agency that offers access to the largest and most comprehensive collection of scientific, technical, and related business information offered anywhere in government. The agency is self-sustaining, supported only by customer fees.

NTIS, which has been in operation since 1945, acquires its material from U.S. governmental agencies and their contractors or grantees, as well as from foreign government sources. The NTIS core collection includes 2.7 million titles, reports, computer software, CD-ROMs, and audiovisual products. It maintains this permanent repository and adds about 100,000 new titles to the collection each year.

In the 1996 fiscal year, NTIS achieved record gross receipts of $77 million and a record earned revenue of $50 million. It began the 1997 fiscal year with almost six months of future revenue assured.

At the beginning of 1996, FedWorld, NTIS' online information network received the Federal Technology Leadership Award. In 1996, NTIS launched two new online subscription services, the World News Connection and NTIS Order Now, and it established a world wide web site.

Before he was named director of NTIS in 1993, Johnson served as the director of technology services at the National Institute for Standards and Technology (NIST), where he was responsible for NIST's business and industrial services program. Up to 1993, his combined service at NTIS and at the National Bureau of Standards (before the name change to NIST), also in the Commerce Department, spanned more than 26 years and included assignments ranging from bench-level researcher to laboratory director.

Johnson has authored more than 60 scientific papers and has given many lectures by invitation. His professional recognition includes silver and gold meals from the Commerce Department, the Arthur S. Flemming Award, the Senior Executive Service Meritorious Award, the Presidential Rank Award for Distinguished Executives, and the Commerce Department Outstanding Volunteer Award.

In 1996, Johnson was a winner of the "Federal 100" awards from Federal Computer Week. The prestigious award is given to individuals both inside and outside the government in recognition of their impact on federal computing.

Johnson, a native of Tacoma, Wash., received a B.S. in physics from the University of Puget Sound in 1960, an M.S. in physics from the University of Idaho in 1972, and a Ph.D. in physics from the University of Oklahoma in 1967. He has been active in civic affairs and has served as an adviser to state and local governments in Maryland.

Associate Director for Business Development

Associate Director
Mr. Walter L. Finch
703/605-6407
Rm. 302

Economics and Statistics Administration

14th St. & Constitution Ave., NW / Washington DC 20230
Main Phone: 202/482-2235

> ### INTRODUCTION
>
> *Much of the statistical, economic, and demographic information collected by the Federal Government is made available to the public through the bureaus and offices of the Department of Commerce that are known collectively as the Economics and Statistics Administration (ESA).*

Under Secretary for Economic Affairs

Acting Under Secretary
Mr. James L. Price
202/482-3727   Fax: 202/482-0432
Rm. 4848

Personal: raised in Gonzalez, Texas.

Education: B.A. in economics, Stanford Univ., 1972. M.A. in economics, Univ. of Mich., 1976. J.D., joint program in law and economics, Univ. of Mich., 1977.

Professional: 1978-85, economist for United Auto Workers International. 1985-86, economist, subcommittee on economic stabilization, Housing Banking, Finance and Urban Affairs Committee. 1986-87, economist, Senate Democratic Policy Committee. 1987-94, chief economist then deputy director and senior economist; 1995-96, director of the Democratic staff, Joint Economic Committee of Congress. 1996-present, chief economist, Economics and Statistics Administration; May 1997-present, acting under secretary of commerce for economic affairs, U.S. Dept. of Commerce.

Lee Price came to the Commerce Department in 1996 to the post of chief economist from the Joint Economic Committee of Congress. In May 1997, he was designated as acting under secretary for economic affairs after the resignation of Under Secretary Everett M. Ehrlich, who left to start up his own consulting practice in business economics. Price continues to also serve as chief economist and will remain as such upon the nomination and confirmation of an appointee to the under secretary position. At press time, no nominee had been named.

As acting under secretary, Price manages the Economics and Statistics Administration, including its two principal agencies, the Bureau of Economic Analysis and the Bureau of the Census. Much of the statistical, economic, and demographic information collected by the federal government is made available to the public through the bureaus and offices of the Economics and Statistics Administration. Price also serves as the principal adviser to the secretary of commerce on economic trends and policy.

As chief economist, Price monitors and analyzes domestic and international economic developments as well as statistical policy issues concerning the production of economic data.

Price served nine years on the staff of the Joint Economic Committee of Congress (JEC). From January 1995 to September 1996, he was director of the Democratic staff of the JEC. Before that he served as chief economist, deputy director, and senior economist on the JEC staff. At the Joint Economic Committee, Price worked on a variety of issues, including monetary and fiscal policy, labor and income distribution, and international trade and finance.

Price's earlier experience as a congressional staffer included positions as economist for the Senate Democratic Policy Committee and the House Banking Committee. He also worked as an economist for the United Auto Workers.

Price grew up in the rural Texas town of Gonzalez. After receiving a B.A. in economics from Stanford University, he entered the joint program in law and economics at the University of Michigan, where he obtained a J.D. in law and an M.A. in economics.

He has published research on a variety of economic topics, including

trends in work and income distribution, Japan's trade imbalance, and the internationalization of the U.S. economy. In his studies at the Joint Economic Committee, he co-authored "Men at Work: Signs of Trouble," a 1992 publication which traced a two-decade collapse in the trajectory of men's career earnings. Also in 1992, he co-authored "Families on a Treadmill: Work and Income in the 1980s," which studied rising hours and earnings gains for middle-income two-parent families. While working for the Democratic Policy Committee, he authored several reports including "Trade Deficit Slows U.S. Growth," "Reagan Recovery: Best or Worst?" and "Trade Problems for U.S. Industries."

Price and his wife live in Falls Church, Va., where he enjoys gardening, swimming, and doing math puzzles with his two sons.

Office of the Chief Economist

Director, Office of International Macroeconomic Analysis
Dr. Sumiye O. Okubo
202/482-1675
Rm. 4868

Bureau of Economic Analysis
1441 L Street, NW / Washington DC 20230

> ### INTRODUCTION
>
> *BEA is the Nation's accountant, integrating and interpreting a tremendous volume of data to draw a complete and consistent picture of the U.S. economy. BEA's economic accounts (national, regional, and international) provide information on such key issues as economic growth, regional development, and the Nation's position in the world economy.*

Director
Mr. J. Steven Landefeld
202/606-9600
Rm. 6005

Office of the Associate Director for International Economics

Associate Director
Mr. Gerald A. Pollack
202/606-9604
Rm. 6004

Assistant to the Associate Director
VACANT
202/606-9635
Rm. 6059

Chief, Balance of Payments Division
Mr. Christopher L. Bach
202/606-9545
Rm. 8024

Assistant Division Chief
Mr. Anthony J. DiLullo
202/606-9558
Rm. 8023

Chief, Merchandise Trade Branch
Mr. Kwok Y. Lee
202/606-9572
Rm. 8017

Chief, Current Account Services Branch

Mr. Michael A. Mann
202/606-9573
Rm. 8018

Chief, Private Capital Branch
Mr. Russell B. Scholl, Jr.
202/606-9579
Rm. 8019

Chief, Government Grants and Capital Branch
Mr. William McCormick
202/606-9574
Rm. 8042

Chief, Analysis, Projections, and Special Studies Branch
Mr. John Rutter
202/606-9587
Rm. 8026

Chief, International Investment Division
Mr. R. David Belli
202/606-9807
Rm. 7005

Assistant Division Chief
Mr. Obie G. Whichard
202/606-9890
Rm. 7002

Chief, Direct Investment in the U.S. Branch
Mr. James L. Bomkamp
202/606-9809
Rm. 7051

Acting Chief, Research Branch
Mr. Obie G. Whichard
202/606-9890
Rm. 7002

Chief, Data Retrieval and Analysis Branch
Mr. Smith W. Allnutt, III
202/606-9803
Rm. 7069

Chief, Direct Investment Abroad Branch
Ms. Patricia C. Walker
202/606-9889
Rm. 7029

Acting Chief, Special Surveys Branch
Mr. R. David Belli
202/606-9807
Rm. 7005

Bureau of the Census
8903 Presidential Pkwy. / Upper Marlboro MD 20772

INTRODUCTION

The Bureau of the Census conducts most surveys for other departments as well as the Department of Commerce. Most of the data in its periodic economic indicators is derived from surveys of businesses and most of the demographic information comes from surveys of households or the decennial census.

Office of the Associate Director for Demographic Programs

Chief, International Programs Center
VACANT
301/457-1390
Rm. 308

Chief, Eurasia Branch
Mr. Marc Rubin
301/457-1362
Rm. 114

Office of the Associate Director for Economic Programs

Chief, Foreign Trade Division
Mr. C. Harvey Monk, Jr.
301/457-2255
Rm. 2104

Asst. Division Chief, Trade Analysis and Dissemination
Mr. Haydn R. Mearkle
301/457-2246
Rm. 2102

Subject-Specific Census Telephone Contacts

Bus. Econ/Ag. P.R., Virgin Is., Guam, N. Marianas & Amer. Samoa
Mr. Kent Hoover
301/763-8564

Bus. Economics/Foreign Trade/Data Services (FTD)
Ms. Reba Higbee
301/457-3041

Bus. Economics/Foreign Trade/Shipper's Declaration (FTD)
Mr. Hal Blyweiss
301/457-1086

Bus. Economics/Manufacturing/Exports
  from Manufacturing Establishments
Mr. Philippe Morris
301/457-4623

Bus. Economics/Manufacturing/Foreign Direct Investment
Ms. Sharon K. Boyer
301/457-1313

Demographics and Pop./Immigration and Emigration
Mr. Edward Farnandez
301/457-2103

Intl. Statistics/Africa, Asia, Latin Amer., N. Amer., and Oceania
Ms. Patricia M. Rowe
301/457-1358

Intl. Statistics/Aging Population
Mr. Kevin Kinsella
301/457-1371

Intl. Statistics/China, People's Republic
Ms. Loraine West
301/457-1360

Intl. Statistics/Europe, Former Soviet Union
Mr. Marc Rubin
301/457-1362

Intl. Statistics/Health
Ms. Karen Stanecki
301/457-1406

Intl. Statistics/Intl. Data Base
Mr. Peter Johnson
301/457-1403

Intl. Statistics/Technical Assistance and Training
Mr. Robert Bush
301/457-1444

Intl. Statistics/Women in Development

Ms. Patricia M. Rowe
301/457-1358

Economic Development Administration

14th St. & Constitution Ave., NW / Washington DC 20230

INTRODUCTION

The Economic Development Administration (EDA) was established under the Public Works and Economic Development Act of 1965 (42 U.S.C. 3121), as amended, to generate new jobs, help retain existing jobs, and stimulate industrial and commercial growth in economically-distressed areas of the United States. EDA assistance is available to rural and urban areas of the Nation experiencing high unemployment, low income, or sudden and severe economic distress.

In fulfilling its mission, EDA is guided by the basic principle that distressed communities must be empowered to develop and implement their own economic development and revitalization strategies. Based on these locally- and regionally-developed priorities, EDA works in partnership with state and local governments, regional economic development districts, public and private nonprofit organizations, and Indian tribes. EDA helps distressed communities address problems associated with long-term economic distress, as well as sudden and severe economic dislocations including recovering from the economic impacts of natural disasters, and the closure of military installations and other Federal facilities.

Assistant Secretary for Economic Development

Assistant Secretary
Mr. Phillip A. Singerman
202/482-5081
Rm. 7800B

Personal: born 8/23/44 in Dade County, Fla.

Education: B.A., Oberlin College, 1965. M.A. in political science, Yale Univ., 1968. Ph.D, Yale Univ., 1980.

Professional: 1975-76, instructor in political science, Barnard College. 1976-77, city plan dept.; 1977-80, exec. asst. to the development administrator, city of New Haven, Conn. 1980-82, director, policy development, Conn. Conference of Municipalities. 1982-83, director, mayor's office of policy develop., city of Philadelphia. 1983-95,

president/CEO, Ben Franklin Technology Center of Southeastern Pa. 1995-present, assistant secretary of commerce for economic development, U.S. Dept. of Commerce.

Assistant Secretary of Commerce for Economic Development Phillip Singerman serves as administrator of the Economic Development Administration (EDA), which provides assistance to distressed communities for infrastructure development, technical assistance, planning and economic adjustment projects. In fiscal year 1996, EDA had an overall budget of $350 million.

Singerman served from 1983 to 1995 as president/CEO of the Ben Franklin Technology Center of Southeastern Pennsylvania, a public-private partnership that promotes regional economic competitiveness through innovation and technology. While at the center, he managed a $10 million annual program with $20 million in matching funds, which funded projects involving economic development, educational, and research organizations, and private companies.

Singerman also served as a planning consultant for the city of Philadelphia, coordinating technology and business development re-use strategies for the Philadelphia Naval Base Complex. Before that, he served on the board of the Philadelphia Commercial Development Corporation, the Philadelphia-Israel Chamber of Commerce, the West Philadelphia Empowerment Zone Community Trust Board, and the Governor's Task Force on Technology Transfer. He is currently a member of the board of the Ben Franklin Technology Center.

Singerman's 20 years of experience in economic development includes the following positions: director, mayor's office of policy development, city of Philadelphia; director, policy development, Connecticut Conference of Municipalities; and executive assistant to the development administrator, city of New Haven, Conn.

Singerman received his Ph.D. and M.A. in political science from Yale University and his B.A. from Oberlin College. He has taught urban policy and regional development at Barnard College (Columbia University), the University of Pennsylvania, and Yale University.

From 1965 to 1967, he served as a Peace Corps volunteer in Colombia, South America, working in programs of rural community development.

Trade Adjustment Assistance Program

14th St. & Constitution Ave., NW / Washington DC 20230
202/482-4031   FAX 202/482-0466

INTRODUCTION

The Trade Adjustment Assistance Program offers technical assistance to domestic manufacturers that have been adversely affected by import competition. The program is authorized under the Trade Act of 1974 and administered by the U.S. Department of Commerce, which provides services to eligible firms through a network of Trade Adjustment Assistance Centers located around the U.S.

The Department of Labor administers a Trade Adjustment Assistance Program for workers. For information, call (202) 219-5555.

Coordinator, Trade Adjustment Assistance Division
Mr. Anthony Meyer
202/482-2127   Fax: 202/482-0466
Rm. 7315

Trade Adjustment Assistance Centers

There are 12 Trade Adjustment Centers (TAAC) providing services to producing firms throughout the 50 states. The Centers are staffed with professionals who have extensive private-sector experience, including specialized expertise in engineering, marketing, and finance.

Manufacturers that have experienced (1) a decline in sales in either units or dollars, or (2) a decline in production, and (3) a decline, or impending decline, in employment as a direct result of increased import competition, may be certified as eligible for Trade Adjustment Assistance.

Under the TAA Program, the cost of these technical consulting services is shared between the client firm and the U.S. Government. The TAACs may also help clients obtain financing from alternative sources, such as commercial banks or the Small Business Administration.

Great Lakes Trade Adjustment Assistance Center

Ms. Maureen Burns
Director
School of Business Administration
506 East Liberty Street
Ann Arbor, Michigan 48104-2210
734/998-6213   Fax: 734/998-6224
E-mail: moburns@umich.edu
Area: MI, OH, IN

Mid-America Trade Adjustment Assistance Center

Mr. Paul Schmid
Director
University of Missouri
University Place - Suite 1700
Columbia, Missouri 65211
573/882-6162   Fax: 573/882-6156
E-mail: schmidp@ext.missouri.edu
Area: MO, KS, AR

Mid-Atlantic Trade Adjustment Assistance Center

Mr. Tom Papp
Manager, Marketing
P.O. Box 833
Valley Forge, Pennsylvania 19482
610/666-7800   Fax: 610/666-5871
Area: PA, DE, MD, VA, WV, DC

Midwest Trade Adjustment Assistance Center

Mr. Howard Yefsky
Director
150 N. Wacker Drive - Suite 2240
Chicago, Illinois 60606
312/368-4600   Fax: 312/368-9043
E-mail: HYASI@aol.com
Area: IL, MN, IA, WI

New England Trade Adjustment Assistance Center

Mr. Richard McLaughlin
Executive Director
120 Boylston Street
Boston, Massachusetts 02116
617/542-2395   Fax: 617/542-8457

E-mail: Richard@netaac.org
Area: CT, RI, VT, NH, MA, ME

New Jersey Trade Adjustment Assistance Center

Mr. John F. Walsh
Director
Capital Place One - CN990
200 South Warren Street
Trenton, New Jersey 08625
609/292-0348   Fax: 609/984-4301
E-mail: taac@njeda.com
Area: NJ

New York State Trade Adjustment Assistance Center

Mr. John Lacey
Executive Director
117 Hawley Street - Suite 102
Binghamton, New York 13901
607/771-0875   Fax: 607/724-2404
E-mail: jllacey@binghamton.edu
Area: NY

Northwest Trade Adjustment Assistance Center

Mr. Gary Kuher
Executive Director
900 4th Avenue - Suite 2430
Seattle,Washington 98164
206/622-2730   Fax: 206/622-1105
E-mail: nwtaac@sprynet.com
Area: AK, ID, MT, OR, WA

Rocky Mountain Trade Adjustment Assistance Center

Mr Edvard M. Hag
Director
5353 Manhattan Circle - Suite 200
Boulder, Colorado 80303
303/499-8222   Fax: 303/499-8298
E-mail: EdvardH@aol.com
Area: CO, UT, NE, SD, ND, WY, NM

Southeastern Trade Adjustment Assistance Center

Mr. Paul Lewis
Director
151 6th Street
O'Keefe Building - Rm. 145
Atlanta, Georgia 30332
404/894-6789   Fax: 404/894-0291
E-mail: Paul.lewis@edi.gatech.edu
Area: AL, TN, KY, MS, GA, NC, SC, FL

Southwest Trade Adjustment Assistance Center

Mr. Robert Velasquez
Director
1222 N. Main - Suite 740
San Antonio, Texas 78212
210/458-2490   Fax: 210/458-2491
Area: TX, LA, OK

Western Trade Adjustment Assistance Center

Mr. George F. Evans
Executive Director
3716 S. Hope - Suite 200
Los Angeles, California 90007
213/743-2788   Fax: 213/746-9043
E-mail: gfevans@mizar.usc.edu
Area: AZ, CA, NV, HI

International Trade Administration (ITA)

14th St. & Constitution Ave., NW / Washington DC 20230

202/482-5091   FAX 202/482-4821
http://www.ita.doc.gov/

INTRODUCTION

The International Trade Administration was established in 1980 to promote world trade and to strengthen the international trade and investment position of the U.S.

ITA is headed by the Under Secretary for International Trade, who coordinates all issues concerning import administration, international economic policy and programs, and trade development. It is responsible for nonagricultural trade operations of the U.S. Government and supports the trade policy negotiation efforts of the U.S. Trade Representative. The under secretary is assisted by a deputy under secretary, a deputy under secretary for international trade policy development, and four assistant secretaries, one of whom is the Director General of The U.S. and Foreign Commercial Service.

Market Access and Compliance

The assistant secretary for market access and compliance advises on the analysis, formulation, and implementation of international economic policies of a bilateral, multilateral, or regional nature. Reporting to the assistant secretary are five deputy assistant secretaries (for Europe; the Western Hemisphere; East Asia and the Pacific; Africa, the Near East and South Asia; and Japan) who have responsibility for trade and investment issues with particular countries and regions of the world. These officials, assisted by desk officers for every country in the world maintain in-depth commercial and economic information on the countries and regions for which they are responsible. In addition, there is a deputy assistant secretary for market access and compliance who has responsibility for multilateral affairs and for overall policy coordination.

Import Administration

The assistant secretary for the import administration defends American industry against injurious and unfair trade practices by administering the antidumping and countervailing duty laws of the U.S., the machine tool arrangements with Japan and Taiwan under the President's Machine Tool Program, and the U.S.-Japan Semiconductor Arrangement. The administration plays a leading role in federal efforts to improve functioning of the GATT antidumping code. The assistant secretary also ensures the proper administration of foreign trade zones and advises the secretary on establishment of new zones, administers programs governing watch assemblies, and administers other statutory import programs.

Trade Development

The assistant secretary for trade development advises on international trade and investment policies pertaining to U.S. industrial sectors, carries out programs to strengthen domestic export competitiveness, and promotes U.S. industry's increased participation in international markets. The assistant secretary manages an integrated trade development Program that includes industry analysis and trade promotion organized by industry sectors. Deputy assistant secretaries for technology and aerospace industries; basic industries; service industries and finance; textiles, apparel and consumer goods industries; and environmental technologies exports report to the assistant secretary. They are assisted by industry specialists. Among other functions, the assistant secretary gathers, analyzes, and disseminates trade information; reports on foreign investment in the U.S.; and promotes the formation of export trading companies and issues certificates of review providing them with limited exemption from liability under the antitrust laws.

The U.S. and Foreign Commercial Service

The assistant secretary and director general of The U.S. and Foreign Commercial Service develops, produces, markets, and manages an effective line of high-quality products and services geared to the marketing information needs of the U.S. exporting and international business community and manages the delivery of ITA programs through 83 district and branch offices located in the U.S. and 134 posts located in 69 countries throughout the world. The assistant secretary and director general supports overseas trade promotion events; manages a variety of export promotion services and products; promotes U.S. products and services throughout the world market; conducts conferences and seminars in the U.S.; assists state and private-sector organizations on export financing; and promotes the export of U.S. fish by working with the domestic fishing industry and the National Oceanic and Atmospheric Administration.

Under Secretary for International Trade

14th St. & Constitution Ave., NW / Washington DC 20230

Under Secretary
Mr. David L. Aaron
202/482-2867   Fax: 202/482-4821
Rm. 3850

Personal: born 8/21/38 in Chicago, Ill.

Education: B.A., Occidental Col. M.A., Princeton University.

Professional: 1962-74, U.S. Foreign Service: political and economic officer, Guayaquil, Ecuador; international relations officer, Dept. of State (1964-66); political officer, NATO, Paris (1966); Arms Control and Disarmament Agency; senior staff member, National Security Council (1972-74). 1974-75, legis. asst., U.S. Sen. Walter Mondale (D-Minn.) 1975-76, task force leader, Senate Select Cmte. on Intelligence. 1977-81, dep. asst. to the president for national security, The White House. 1981-85, v.p. for mergers and acquisitions, Oppenheimer and Company. 1984, senior adviser, Mondale presidential campaign. 1985-93, writer, lecturer, Lantz-Harris Agency. 1993-present, special envoy for cryptography and U.S.

Permanent Representative to the Organization for Economic Cooperation and Development, U.S. Dept. of State. Sept. 1997-present, under sec. for intn'l. trade, U.S. Dept. of Commerce.

At the time of his nomination to be under secretary of commerce for international trade, David Aaron was serving at the State Department with the rank of ambassador as special envoy for cryptography and as U.S. Permanent Representative to the Organization for Economic Cooperation and Development (OECD).

OECD is a group of 29 of the most advanced industrialized countries, and is dedicated to fostering economic growth by a more open global economy. In this connection, OECD is developing guidelines for cryptography in international communications and commerce.

Aaron has served in the U.S. Foreign Service and in the Carter White House and has held top positions in the private sector. He is also the author of three novels that have been translated and published in ten languages.

A graduate of Occidental College and Princeton University, Aaron entered the Foreign Service in 1962 where he had a variety of posts including NATO and the strategic arms limitations talks. After leaving the Foreign Service, he continued in government in several positions, including legislative assistant to Senator Walter F. Mondale (D-Minn.) and deputy national security adviser to President Jimmy Carter. In the latter capacity, he served as a confidential presidential emissary to Europe, the Middle East, Africa, Latin America, and Asia. He was awarded the National Defense Medal in 1981.

Upon leaving government, Aaron became vice president for mergers and acquisitions at Oppenheimer and Company, a member of the board of Oppenheimer International, and subsequently, a member of the board of Oppenheimer's Quest for Value Dual Purpose Fund.

Aaron has also been a senior fellow at the Twentieth Century Funds, served on the board of the National Democratic Institute, and the International League for Human Rights, and is a member of the Council on Foreign Relations.

He is married to Chloe W. Aaron, a television producer.

Executive Assistant to the Under Secretary
VACANT
202/482-2867   Fax: 202/482-4821
Rm. 3850

Deputy Under Secretary for International Trade
Mr. Timothy J. Hauser
202/482-3917   Fax: 202/482-2925
Rm. 3842

Timothy J. Hauser was appointed deputy under secretary for international trade in the U.S. Commerce Department's International Trade Administration (ITA) in July 1991. From June 1992 until November 1993, and for the second half of 1997, he also served as acting under secretary. Hauser manages the day-to-day operations of the more than 2,300 person, $260 million agency and serves as principal deputy to the under secretary, advising him on trade policy, promotion and management issues.

A 16-year Commerce employee, Hauser served from 1987-1991 as deputy assistant secretary for planning, responsible for the department's participation in interagency trade policy development activities. In 1986-87, he was detailed to the White House as deputy executive secretary of the Economic Policy Council, where he developed recommendations on international trade issues for the President, Cabinet and senior white House staff.

From 1982-86, Hauser directed ITA's office of multilateral affairs. There, he managed Commerce's work on trade and investment issues in the General Agreement on Tariffs and Trade (GATT), the Organization for Economic Cooperation and Development (OECD) and the United Nations. He frequently represented the department in international negotiations.

Hauser joined Commerce in 1979 on the staff of the assistant secretary for policy. From 1971 to 1979, he worked as an economist with the Bureau of Labor Statistics' International Price Competitiveness Program.

A 1970 graduate of Georgetown University's School of Foreign Service, Hauser received a master's degree in international relations (1972) and did additional graduate work at the Johns Hopkins School of Advanced International Studies in Washington, D.C. and Bologna, Italy.

In 1988, Hauser received the Presidential Meritorious Executive Award. In 1993, he received the Senior Executive Association's Distinguished Executive Service Award, and in 1992 he received the Presidential Distinguished Executive Award.

A native of Pittsburgh, Hauser is married and has one son.

Executive Assistant to the Deputy Under Secretary
Ms. Sherry Lewis-Khanna
202/482-3917   Fax: 202/482-2925
Rm. 3842

Program Coordinator
Ms. Patricia Corken
202/482-3917
Rm. 3842

Office of Legislative and Intergovernmental Affairs

Director
Mr. Jerry Bonham
202/482-3015   Fax: 202/482-5819
Rm. 3424

Office of Public/Media Affairs

Acting Director
Ms. Patricia Woodward
202/482-3809   Fax: 202/482-5819
Rm. 3414

Publications Division

Director
Mr. Thomas C. Witherspoon
202/482-5487
Rm. 3420

Editor, Business America
Mr. Douglas F. Carroll
202/482-3251
Rm. 4019

Trade Promotion Coordinating Committee Secretariat

INTRODUCTION

The Secretary of Commerce serves as chairman of the Trade Promotion Coordinating Committee (TPCC), which provides a means for all federal agencies to coordinate their trade promotion activities and provide a more focused U.S. Government approach to trade promotion. The TPCC was established by Executive Order of the President in May 1990. The Export Enhancement Act of 1992 codified the committee.

Committee members include 20 federal agencies: the Departments of State, Commerce, Treasury, Defense, Interior, Agriculture, Labor, Transportation, and Energy; the Office of Management and Budget, the Office of the U.S. Trade Representative, the Council of Economic Advisers; the Environmental Protection Agency; the Small Business Administration; the Agency for International Development; the Export-Import Bank of the United States, the Overseas Private Investment Corporation; the U.S. Trade and Development Agency; and the U.S. Information Agency.

Director
Ms. Jeri Jensen-Moran
202/482-5455   Fax: 202/482-4137
Rm. 3051

As director of the TPCC Secretariat, Jeri Jensen-Moran coordinates the network to develop and implement the National Export Strategy. In 1996, the strategy encompassed government-wide efforts on foreign competitive practices including bribery, trade promotion and finance, advocacy, standards, offsets, technical assistance, increasing small business exports and the development of a unified trade promotion budget.

With the exception of a one-year stint at the National Security Council where she coordinated economic and trade policy issues related to the Summit of the Americas, Jensen-Moran has served at the Department of Commerce since 1987. Most recently she directed review and coordination of the ITA policy process in the Office of the Under Secretary for ITA. She also coordinated and developed positions on trade policy issues affecting U.S. industry regarding market access and U.S. trade law in the Office of Industrial Trade.

Prior to her Commerce Department experience, Jensen-Moran was senior economist to the chairwoman of the International Trade Commission. She has worked as a consultant to IBM, The Business Roundtable, and Royal Dutch/Shell and as an analyst for Asia Investor Services and International Reporting and Information Systems.

Jensen-Moran holds a Master of Science in foreign service from Georgetown University and a Bachelor of Arts in political science from Northwestern University and was awarded a Council on Foreign Relations International Affairs Fellowship in 1994. She has published "Trade Battles as Investment Wars: The Coming Rules of Origin Debate," in the Washington Quarterly (Winter 1996), reprinted in Brad Roberts, New Issues in the World Economy, 1996.

President's Export Council

14th St. & Constitution Ave., NW / Washington DC 20230

202/482-1124   FAX 202/482-4452

INTRODUCTION

The President's Export Council (PEC), is the premier national advisory committee on international trade. The Council advises the President on government policies and programs that affect U.S. trade performance; it promotes export expansion and provides a forum for discussing and resolving trade-related problems among the business, industrial, agricultural, labor, and government sectors.

Early in 1995, President Clinton appointed 28 private sector members of the Council, including the Chairman--- Michael Armstrong, who is Chairman of the Board & Chief Executive Officer of Hughes Electronic Corporation.

Executive Director

Under Secretary for International Trade
Mr. David L. Aaron
202-482-2867   Fax: 202-482-4821
Rm. 3850

Staff and Executive Secretary

Staff Director and Executive Secretary
Mr. J. Marc Chittum
202-482-1124   Fax: 202-482-4452
Rm. 2015B

Private Sector Members

Chairman
C. Michael Armstrong
Chairman of the Board & C.E.O.
Hughes Electronics Corporation

J. Joe Adorjan
President & C.O.O
Borg-Warner Security Corp

John J. Barry
International President
International Brotherhood of Electrical Workers

Carol Bartz
Chairman & C.E.O.
Autodesk, Inc.

George F. Becker
President
United Steelworkers of America

Frank Biondi
President & C.E.O.
Viacom Inc.

Susan Corrales-Diaz
President & C.E.O.
Systems Integrated

Ellen R. Gordon
President
Tootsie Roll Industries, Inc.

Joseph Gorman
Chairman & C.E.O.
TRW, Inc.

Ray R. Irani
Chairman, President, & C.E.O.
Occidental Petroleum Corp.

Michael H. Jordan
Chairman & C.E.O.
CBS Corp.

Dennis J. Picard
Chairman & C.E.O.
Raytheon Company

Frank Savage
Chairman
Alliance Capital Mgmt. Int'l.

Kathryn C. Turner
Chairman & C.E.O.
Standard Technology, Inc.

Asst. Secretary for Import Administration

14th St. & Constitution Ave., NW / Washington DC 20230

> ### WHAT IS IMPORT ADMINISTRATION?
>
> *Who ensures a level playing field for America's industries in the competitive global market? The Import Administration (IA) enforces laws and agreements to prevent unfairly traded imports and to safeguard jobs and the competitive strength of American industry.*
>
> ### HOW IMPORT ADMINISTRATION BENEFITS AMERICAN INDUSTRY:
>
> • *Administers the U.S. antidumping and countervailing duty laws to provide a remedy to domestic industries injured by unfairly traded imports;*
>
> • *Assists domestic industries — especially small businesses — to decide whether there is sufficient evidence to petition for antidumping and countervailing duty investigations;*
>
> • *Participates — with the U. S. Trade Representative — in negotiating fair and transparent international rules for antidumping and countervailing duty investigations. This involves working to safeguard the interests of U.S. producing industries adversely affected by unfairly traded imports and those of U.S. exporters facing the antidumping and anti-subsidy regimes of our trading partners;*
>
> • *Participates in negotiations to promote fair trade in specific sectors, such as steel, aircraft and shipbuilding; and*
>
> • *Implements the laws concerning foreign trade zones to enhance the international competitiveness of U.S. exporters.*

Assistant Secretary
Mr. Robert S. LaRussa
202/482-1780   Fax: 202/482-0947
Rm. 3099B

Personal: born in New York City, N.Y.

Education: B.A., Univ. of Massachusetts, 1976. J.D., State Univ. of N.Y. at Buffalo Law School, 1980.

Professional: 1980-82, attny., Appalachian Research and Defense Fund (Columbia, Ky.). 1980-82, reporter, Valley Advocate (Springfield, Mass.). 1982-86, managing editor, Advocate Newspapers (New Haven, Conn.). 1986-89, reporter covering international trade and the Supreme Court, Capital Cities/ABC, Inc. 1989-93, intern'l. trade asst., Rep. Sander Levin (D-Mich.). 1993, deputy director, manufacturing and technology, Clinton presidential transition team. 1993-96, principal deputy asst. sec., U.S. and Foreign Commercial Service; 6/96-7/31/97, acting asst. secretary of commerce for import administration; 7/31/97-present, asst. secretary of commerce for import administration, U.S. Dept. of Commerce.

In his second post in the International Trade Administration (ITA) of the U.S. Department of Commerce since 1993, Robert LaRussa administers the U.S. foreign trade laws as the assistant secretary of commerce for import administration. After serving in the job in an acting capacity for more than a year, he was confirmed for the assistant secretary position July 31, 1997. The previous assistant secretary was Susan G. Esserman.

The import administration unit of ITA administers the U.S. antidumping and countervailing duty laws to provide a remedy to domestic industries injured by unfairly traded imports. It participates in negotiating fair and transparent international rules for antidumping and countervailing duty investigations. It takes part in negotiations to promote trade in specific sectors, such as steel, aircraft, and shipbuilding. It implements the laws concerning foreign trade zones.

In his previous Commerce Department position, that of principal deputy assistant secretary for the U.S. and Foreign Commercial Service, LaRussa designed the "Export Mexico" program that won for him the department's highest decoration, the Gold Medal. He spearheaded ITA's Southeast Asia and ASEAN commercial agenda, including the orchestration of the highly successful U.S. presence at the Asian Pacific Economic Cooperation (APEC) summit in Jakarta, Indonesia. He has since launched the innovative "Destination ASEAN" market awareness program, which has helped hundreds of small-to-medium-sized U.S. firms gain entry into the lucrative Southeast Asian markets.

LaRussa played the key role in developing the "Commercial Center" concept which provides a home-away-from home business environment for small-to-medium-sized U.S. firms in key overseas markets. Thus far, commercial centers have opened in Sao Paulo (Brazil), Jakarta (Indonesia), and Shanghai.

Before joining the Commerce Department, LaRussa worked as an international trade counsel to a senior member of the House Ways and Means Committee. He advised on international trade and manufacturing issues during the Clinton presidential transition as deputy to Dr. Laura D'Andrea Tyson, former chair of the White House National Economic Council.

LaRussa has also worked as an editor and correspondent for several newspapers and magazines; he covered the U.S. Supreme Court and international trade issues as a reporter. He practiced law in Appalachia for a legal services organization. LaRussa describes himself as an attorney by training and a journalist by profession.

Director, Statutory Import Programs Staff
Mr. Frank W. Creel
202/482-1660   Fax: 202/482-0949
Rm. 4211

Director, Office of Policy & Analysis
Mr. Richard Moreland
202/482-1768
Rm. 3093

Director, Central Recording Unit/Foreign Subsidy Library
Mr. Andrew Lee Beller
202/482-1248
Rm. B-099

Director, Office of Accounting
Mr. Christian Marsh
202/482-2210
Rm. 3087B

Director, Office of Policy
Mr. David Mueller
202/482-4412
Rm. 3713

Foreign Trade Zones Board

INTRODUCTION

Foreign-Trade Zones are designated sites licensed by the Foreign-Trade Zones (FTZ) Board (the Secretary of Commerce is Chairman) at which special Customs procedures may be used. FTZ procedures allow domestic activity involving foreign items to take place as if it were outside U.S. Customs territory, thus offsetting Customs advantages available to overseas producers who export in competition with products made here. Subzones are special-purpose zones, usually at manufacturing plants.

For a complete list of Foreign-Trade Zones see Section III

Director, Foreign Trade Zones Staff & Executive Secretary
Mr. John J. DaPonte
202/482-2862   FAX 202/482-0002
Rm. 3716

Antidumping Countervailing Duty Enforcement I

Acting Deputy Assistant Secretary
Mr. Richard Moreland
202/482-5497   Fax: 202/482-1059
Rm. 3099

Director, Office of ACDE I
Ms. Susan Kuhbach
202/482-0112   Fax: 202/482-4776
Rm. 3707

Director, Office of ACDE II
Mr. Gary Taverman
202/482-0161
Rm. 3709

Director, Office of ACDE III
Ms. Laurie Parkhill
202/482-4733
Rm. 4203

Antidumping Countervailing Duty Enforcement II

Acting Deputy Assistant Secretary
Mr. Richard Moreland
202/482-1780
Rm. 3099B

Director, Office of ACDE IV
Ms. Holly Kuga
202/482-4737   Fax: 202/482-5105
Rm. 3064

Director, Office of ACDE V
Mr. Louis Apple
202/482-1779
Rm. 3086

Director, Office of ACDE VI
Ms. Barbara Tillman
202/482-2786   Fax: 202/482-4001
Rm. 4012

Antidumping Countervailing Duty Enforcement III

Deputy Assistant Secretary
Mr. Joseph A. Spetrini
202/482-2104   Fax: 202/482-5105
Rm. 3069A

Joseph A. Spetrini oversees the office that conducts annual reviews of all outstanding countervailing and antidumping orders and certain suspension agreements. His office also administers the President's program for the steel industry and Voluntary Restraint Agreements (VRAs) regulating imports of machine tools from Japan and Taiwan. Previously, he was deputy to the deputy assistant secretary for import administration.

From 1981-86, Spetrini worked intensively on the import problems of the U.S. steel industry in import administration. As the director of the office of agreements compliance, he played a key role in the negotiation and implementation of the President's program for the steel industry. During 1978-80, he worked in U.S. Customs, participating in various import programs, including the steel trigger price mechanism. Before that, Spetrini worked in Commerce's office of international trade policy on the Tokyo Round of Multilateral Trade negotiations. From 1975-76, he handled trade adjustment assistance cases at the Labor Department.

Spetrini has a B.A. in English from Manhattan College, an M.A. in English from Rhode Island College and an M.A. in economics from the University of Rhode Island.

Director, Office of ACDE VII
Mr. Roland MacDonald
202/482-3793   Fax: 202/482-1388
Rm. 7866

Director, Office of ACDE VIII
Mr. Richard Weible
202/482-1103
Rm. 7856

Director, Office of ACDE IX
Mr. Edward Yang
202/482-0406
Rm. 7860

Assistant Secretary for Trade Development

14th St. & Constitution Ave., NW / Washington DC 20230

WHAT IS TRADE DEVELOPMENT?
From AEROSPACE to ZINC, where do people turn when they need advocacy or in-depth information on industry sectors, markets and trends around the world?

Trade Development experts monitor, analyze, and provide information on hundreds of industries — from basic industries to new emerging high technology industries. This collection of expertise is found nowhere else either inside or outside the Government.

HOW TRADE DEVELOPMENT HELPS U.S. BUSINESSES:

ADVOCACY: The heart of the National Export Strategy is a coordinated, government-wide Advocacy Program. To counter the practices of foreign governments, the United States puts its full weight behind the efforts of U.S. businesses, both small and large, to compete effectively in foreign countries. Through its Advocacy Center, Trade Development leads the Government-wide Advocacy Network in fighting for an international level playing field. Thus, Trade Development:

• Marshals the full resources of the U.S. Government to support U.S. companies' bids abroad, from the White House to U.S. embassies to the regulatory agencies and beyond.

• Fights for projects from multibillion dollar infrastructure initiatives to small strategic contracts where the deals would otherwise fall prey to lobbying from other governments, particularly in the Big Emerging Markets.

• Provides essential advocacy in foreign government procurements where there are no adequate mechanisms to ensure American companies have a fair chance.

BREAKING BARRIERS and PROTECTING U.S. INDUSTRIES:

Trade Development provides much of the ammunition for the President, USTR, State, Treasury, and the Secretary of Commerce to conduct trade negotiations. USTR relies on Trade Development's industry experts in negotiations from GATT to NAFTA [Mexico & Canada]. Trade Development draws up retaliation lists which provide U.S. Government leverage to remove non-market barriers to U.S. exports. It uses bilateral trade committees in Russia, China, and elsewhere to seek equity for American businesses, large and small. In addition, Trade Development helps administer key trade agreements like the Multilateral Fiber Agreement, which prevents disruption of the U.S. textile and apparel market; the Aircraft Agreement with the European Union; the successful Japan Semiconductor Agreement; and numerous other such agreements.

WORKING WITH U.S. BUSINESS:

Trade Development experts work with U.S. industry to develop and implement sectoral, market-opening missions throughout the world where trade missions and sectoral events cannot be privatized or governments have important influence over industry decisions. In one year alone, Trade Development led 86 international events that involved some 3,500 small, medium and large American businesses.

Trade Development houses the nerve center for information for small and mid-sized businesses exporting abroad. The TRADE INFORMATION CENTER-TIC provides a single point of contact in the U.S. Government for export counseling and assistance. The TIC provides information on Government-wide assistance programs through a toll-free number: 1-800-USA-TRADE. In one year, the TIC counsels over 60,000 firms and individuals.

Acting Assistant Secretary
Mr. Ellis R. Mottur
202/482-1461   Fax: 202/482-5697
Rm. 3832

Personal: born 11/17/30 in New York City, New York.

Education: B.A. (with honors), Swarthmore Coll., 1952. M.B.A. (with distinction), Harvard Graduate School of Business Admin., 1954. Guest scholar, Woodrow Wilson Intern'l. Ctr. for Scholars, 1978-79.

Professional: 1962-67, dir. of mgmt. analysis office, Nat'l. Science Foundation. 1967-71, director of high tech policy research, George Washington Univ. 1971-78 and 1989-92, sr. adviser to Sen. Edward M. Kennedy (D-Mass.). 1992, deputy political director for business and high tech, Clinton presidential campaign and transition. 1993-97, deputy asst. sec. for tech. and aerospace industries; May 1997-present, acting asst. sec. for trade develop., U.S. Dept. of Commerce.

Ellis Mottur was named acting assistant secretary for trade development in the U.S. Department of Commerce's International Trade Administration (ITA) by Secretary of Commerce William Daley in May 1997. Until a replacement is named by President Clinton and confirmed by the Senate, Mottur fills the position most recently held by Raymond Vickery. Since 1993, Mottur has served as deputy assistant secretary for technology and aerospace industries in ITA.

The assistant secretary for trade development is responsible for enhancing the international competitiveness of American industry. The mission entails research and analysis of industry and trade patterns, policy formulation and negotiations to increase U.S. access to foreign markets, and specific steps to expand U.S. exports, such as sponsoring trade missions and shows in foreign markets and advocacy for American companies in foreign competition.

In his deputy assistant secretary post, Mottur's responsibilities included aerospace, telecommunications, computers, software, microelectronics, instrumentation, medical equipment, and advanced materials.

Before he joined the Commerce Department in 1993, Mottur served in the presidential transition as deputy political director for business and high tech, the same position he held throughout the 1992 Clinton presidential campaign. During the campaign he was responsible for drafting the defense conversion plan and the national technology strategy and for enlisting the support of hundreds of CEOs throughout the nation.

Before the campaign, as a long-time aide and adviser to Sen. Edward Kennedy (D-Mass.), Mottur was instrumental in the creation of the White House office of science and technology policy and the congressional office of technology assessment. He authored many other legislative initiatives such as the "Excellence in Mathematics, Science, and Engineering Education Act of 1990." His publications include National Strategy for Technological Innovation and Implementing Technology Assessments.

Earlier in his career, Mottur directed the management analysis office of the National Science Foundation and high tech policy research at George Washington University and served as a consultant to government and industry on high technology issues.

Office of Planning, Coordination and Resource Mgmt.

Director
Mr. Robert W. Pearson
202/482-4921   Fax: 202/482-4462
Rm. 3223

Director, Policy and Coordination Staff
Ms. Elizabeth W. King
202/482-4921
Rm. 3221

Director, Resource Management and Planning Staff
Mr. Jerome Morse
202/482-3197
Rm. 3209

Office of Export Promotion Coordination

Director
Mr. Gary Enright
202/482-4501   Fax: 202/482-1999
Rm. 2003

Deputy Director
VACANT
202/482-4501
Rm. 2003

Director, Advisory Committee Support Division
VACANT
202/482-1124
Rm. 2015

Director, Promotion Planning, Coordination and Support Div.
Mr. Thomas J. Nisbet
202/482-2474
Rm. 2013

Director, Trade Information Center
Ms. Wendy H. Smith
202/482-0543   Fax: 202/482-4473
Rm. 7424

Office of Trade and Economic Analysis

INTRODUCTION

The Office of Trade and Economic Analysis (OTEA) conducts a comprehensive program of data development, dissemination, and research and analysis on international and domestic trade and investment issues to support trade promotion and trade policy responsibilities of Trade Development, ITA, Department of Commerce and U.S. Government organizations and officials. The OTEA Director manages a staff of approximately 50 individuals who collect, analyze and interpret trade, investment and industry statistics that are disseminated to private sector clients and U.S. Government officials and analysts.

Director
Mr. Jonathan C. Menes
202/482-5145   Fax: 202/482-4614
Rm. 2815

Director, Industrial Trade Staff
Mr. Bruce Jon Miller

202/482-3703
Rm. 1211

Advocacy Center

INTRODUCTION

The Advocacy Center puts the resources and authority of the U.S. government behind your team to help you resolve problems like these:
•Contracts pursued by foreign firms that receive assistance from their home governments to pressure a customer into a buying decision;
•Unfair treatment by government decision-makers, preventing you from a chance to compete; •Tenders tied up in bureaucratic red type, resulting in lost opportunities and unfair advantage to a competitor.

If these or any similar export issues are affecting your company, it's time to call the Advocacy Center.

Director, Advocacy Center
Mr. T.S. Chung
202/482-3896   Fax: 202/482-3508
Rm. 3814-A

Director, Trade Data Systems Division
VACANT
202/482-5994
Rm. 2815

Director, Industry Publications Division
Mr. John J. Bistay
202/482-4356
Rm. 1211

Director, International Economics Division
Mr. William F. Kolarik
202/482-4691
Rm. 2221

Director, Trade and Industry Analysis Division
Mr. Kemble Stokes
202/482-2056
Rm. 2223

Director, Investment Analysis Division
Mr. Richard A. Eberhart
202/482-2311
Rm. 2805

Office of Basic Industries

INTRODUCTION

Basic Industries (BI) encompasses a broad range of U.S. industries that include motor vehicles, auto parts and accessories, machine tools, chemicals and pharmaceuticals, construction and mining equipment, forest products, metals and materials, energy (including equipment) and biotechnology. The Basic Industries sectors of the U.S. economy account for total annual shipments exceeding $2 trillion. Their exports constitute approximately 52% of the manufacturing sector's international shipments.

The Office of Basic Industries is separated into three divisions: Energy, Infrastructure and Machinery; Automotive Affairs; and Metals, Materials and Chemicals.

Deputy Assistant Secretary for Basic Industries

Mr. Michael J. Copps
202/482-0614   Fax: 202/482-5666
Rm. 4043

As the deputy assistant secretary for basic industries Michael Copps is the director of a staff of 100 industry analysts, economists, and international trade specialists dedicated to improving market access and competitiveness of American industry sectors including: capital goods, automotive, metals, energy, chemicals, pharmaceuticals, wood products and machinery, environmental technologies, metalworking, food processing and packaging, international engineering and domestic and international mining construction.

Previously, Copps was the senior vice president for legislative affairs with the American Meat Institute, a national trade association, where he was responsible for the operation of the association's legislative affairs department, including policy development, and presentation of the association's positions to the Congress and federal government agencies. He also managed international trade issues for the Institute. From 1985 to 1989, Copps was the director of government affairs for Collins & Aikman Corporation, a Fortune 500 company. He was responsible for directing the firm's legislative program, managing its regulatory agency activities, and overseeing international trade policies affecting the company.

Formerly, Copps was the administrative assistant to Senator Ernest F. Hollings (D-S.C.) from 1970 to 1985. He directed a 35 member staff that covered a wide variety of issues including national security and international trade. Copps also coordinated the Senator's Washington office activities with those of his district offices and was the liaison with the Senator's committees.

Copps has a bachelor of arts degree from Wofford College, with a major in U.S. history and a minor in philosophy. He holds a doctorate in U.S. history from the University of North Carolina.

Office of Energy, Infrastructure and Machinery

INTRODUCTION

The Office of Energy, Infrastructure, and Machinery (OEIM) works to assist U.S. companies through a range of Trade Development initiatives. The Office continually tracks markets for U.S. goods and services in its industry sectors and strives to promote these industries' products via numerous different forums (such as through trade shows and U.S. embassy posts around the world). OEIM Trade Specialists work directly with industry to help determine industry trade priorities, to locate possible barriers for trade, and to alert industry of future trade opportunities. OEIM, furthermore, works to ensure a level field of competition for U.S. businesses by acting as a conduit between industry and other government agencies and through its assistance of U.S. government advocacy. The Divisions of OEIM are organized around its three industry areas:

The Energy Division monitors overseas trade and investment opportunities and informs U.S. industry of these opportunities; advocates on behalf of U.S. energy firms; monitors trade policy issues and develops appropriate, interagency strategies to remove foreign trade barriers; offers trade promotion services and extensive export counseling; and provides policy support for other units within the U.S. Government.

Cont'd.

The Infrastructure Division helps U.S. firms compete for contracts to study, plan, design, construct and equip major foreign infrastructure and industrial projects overseas. The Division works with architectural, engineering and construction companies and with manufacturers of major components for infrastructure projects. Its Project Managers provide U.S. firms with information on project opportunities in the transportation, power, water, commercial and industrial infrastructure sectors. They support individual companies competing for projects, working closely with the other U.S. government agencies, including the Trade Development Administration and Eximbank along with America's diplomatic and consular posts worldwide.

The Industrial Machinery Division assists U.S. businesses in the export of production machinery and general components. Its analysts provide input on trade policy through their development of industry sector analysis and forecasts, and are actively involved in the Department's trade promotion programs. The Division's coverage includes the machinery used in the food processing, packaging, agricultural, material handling, metalworking, welding, printing, pulp and paper, and textile. The Division is also responsible for the bearing, pump, industrial fastener, screw machine product, tool, pipe fitting, gear, gasket and industrial valve industries. To further its goal of aiding U.S. businesses competing abroad, the Division's trade specialists work closely with other Commerce offices, other government agencies, industry trade associations and individual companies in developing and expanding export markets.

Acting Director, OIEM
Mr. Damon Greer
202/482-0169   Fax: 202/482-5666
Rm. 4411

Director, Energy Division
Ms. Helen Burroughs
202/482-4931   FAX 202/482-5361

Director, Infrastructure Division
Mr. Jay Smith
Rm. 4314
202/482-4642   Fax: 202/482-3954

Director, Industrial Machinery Division
Mr. John A. Mearman
202/482-0315
Rm. 4035

Office of Automotive Affairs

Director
Mr. Henry P. Misisco
202/482-0554   Fax: 202/482-0784
Rm. 4036

Director, Parts and Suppliers Division
Mr. Robert O. Reck
202/482-1418
Rm. 4044

Director, Motor Vehicle Division
Mr. Albert T. Warner
202/482-0669
Rm. 4036

Office of Metals, Materials, and Chemicals

> ### INTRODUCTION
>
> *The Office of Metals, Materials and Chemicals consists of three divisions covering all metal producing and fabricating industries, chemicals, pharmaceuticals, biotechnology, paper, wood and wood products and domestic construction. The office provides expertise on these industries to the Department of Commerce as well as to numerous other government agencies and industry. The office is involved in the major policy, environmental and trade issues affecting these industries. In addition, the office is responsible for international organizations, negotiations, agreements specific to these industries. The office has an active export promotion program which includes trade missions and catalogue shows.*

Director
Mr. Robert C. Reiley
202/482-0575   Fax: 202/482-1436
Rm. 4039

Director, Chemical and Allied Products Division
Mr. Stuart S. Keitz
202/482-0120
Rm. 4033

Dir., Forest Products, Bldg. Materials, & Ind. Machinery Div.
Mr. Christian Kristensen
202/482-0384
Rm. 4020

Director, Metals and Metalworking Equipment Division
Mr. John A. Mearman
202/482-5157
Rm. 4059

Deputy Assistant Secretary for Environmental Technologies Exports

> ### INTRODUCTION
>
> *Created in April, 1994, the Office for Environmental Technologies Exports (ETE), serves as a liaison to the private sector to assist U.S. environmental technology firms export their goods, services and equipment abroad.*
>
> *The ETE office helps foster public-private partnerships by coordinating interagency cooperation to facilitate U.S. exports, including improving business access to financing and fostering grants. U.S. environmental technology export efforts concentrate on specific emerging markets in the global arena, with a particular focus on Latin America, targeting Argentina, Brazil, Chile and Mexico.*
>
> *In addition to providing key information to the environmental technologies industry, ETE takes a leadership role in fostering public-private partnerships in this sector. For example, ETE leads the private-sector Environmental Technologies Trade Advisory Committee (ETTAC). ETE also administers grants under the Market Development Cooperator Program (MDCP) and works closely with grantees in the private sector to foster greater U.S. environmental technologies exports through outreach, trade promotion, business counseling, and training workshops. ETE also works closely with the district offices and foreign posts of the U.S. and Foreign Commercial Service.*

Deputy Assistant Secretary
Ms. Anne L. Alonzo
202/482-5225   FAX 202/482-5665
Rm. 1001

Prior to assuming her present position as the first deputy assistant secretary for environmental technology exports, Anne Alonzo, served for three years as the Environmental Protection Agency's first attaché to a U.S. diplomatic mission, the American Embassy in Mexico City. In this capacity her mandate was primarily one of assistance and counseling to the government of Mexico, to the U.S. and Mexican public and private sectors, and as advisor to the U.S. Ambassador and Embassy staff on environmental matters.

During this posting she worked extensively with the environmental communities in Mexico and the U.S. promoting the exchange of environmental business opportunities between the two countries. Alonzo's tenure in Mexico coincided with a particularly critical and dynamic period in U.S.-Mexican relations as an emerging prominence of Environmental concerns during the Salinas administration climaxed in the successful launching and culmination of the NAFTA negotiations in November, 1993.

Alonzo's expertise in environmental affairs developed during her seven-year tenure as an enforcement attorney at EPA's Region V office in Chicago, where she was a specialist in hazardous waste issues under the federal statutes of RCRA and Superfund. Her working relationship with the Mexican government commenced in October, 1988, when she received a special assignment through EPA to provide environmental-related counseling to the legal division of SEDUE, now SEDESOL, Mexico's counterpart to EPA.

Deputy Assistant Secretary for Service Industries & Finance

> ### INTRODUCTION
>
> *Service Industries and Finance (SIF) is one of the industry clusters within the International Trade Administration, U.S. Department of Commere.*
>
> *SIF works with other agencies and the private sector to improve market access to, and penetration of, foreign markets for trade finance and services. To this end, SIF develops relevant policy, supports and participates in international trade negotiations, and promotes exports through foreign trade missions and domestic industry outreach conferences.*
>
> *In addition, SIF is responsible for a broad area of trade finance, developing the Commerce Department's policy positions on international financial and monetary affairs. SIF works with exporters, banks and other financial firms and Federal export financing programs (such as the Export Import Bank of the U.S.)& multilateral development banks to improve trade finance availability and usage. Other areas of responsibility include insurance, private banking, and specialized financing techniques such as leasing. SIF implements a statutory mandate to monitor countertrade trends, disseminates information on the subject and counsels U.S. firms seeking such trade opportunities.*
>
> *SIF also coordinates Commerce/Government-wide efforts to promote the establishment of export trading companies and export intermediaries, to provide assistance for their operations and to publicize their export capabilities. SIF administers the antitrust exemption certificate program for joint export activity under the Export Trading Company Act.*

Deputy Assistant Secretary
Mr. A. Everett James
202/482-5261   Fax: 202/482-4775
Rm. 1128

Office of Service Industries

> *INTRODUCTION*
>
> *As an advocate for the development of U.S. service industries international trade, the of Office Service Industries specialists work closely with the private sector to provide export assistance and participate with other agencies to improve foreign market access for U.S. companies. The office coordinates the Services Working Group of the Trade Promotion Coordinating Committee (TPCC), in addition to the following:*
>
> *Trade Policy*
> *Supports and participates in multilateral and bilateral negotiations on services trade. Works with other U.S. agencies on implementation of services trade agreements, e.g. the Uruguay Round and NAFTA. Works with two Congressionally mandated Industry Sector Advisory Committees—Service Industries, and Wholesaling and Retailing— to ensure industry input in policy development.*
>
> *Export Development*
> *Provides U.S. companies export development assistance and information. Manages a trade promotion program of trade missions and industry conferences. Helps exporters identify opportunities in specific overseas markets.*
>
> *Industry Analysis*
> *Prepares analyses on key service industries. Provides policy makers information and analysis on international trade and competitiveness in services.*

Director
Ms. Josephine H. Ludolph
202/482-3575   Fax: 202/482-2669
Rm. 1124

Director, Transportation and Health Care Division
VACANT
Rm. 2217

Director, Info., Entertainment and Professional Svcs. Division
Mr. Wray O. Candilis
202/482-0339
Rm. 1110

Office of Export Trading Company Affairs

> *INTRODUCTION*
>
> *The Office of Export Trading Company Affairs (OETCA) coordinates Commerce/Government-wide efforts to promote the establishment of export trading companies and export intermediaries, to provide assistance for their operations and to publicize their export capabilities. This office also administers the antitrust exemption certificate program for joint export activity under the Export Trading Company Act.*

Director
VACANT
202/482-5131   Fax: 202/482-1790
Rm. 1800

Office of Finance

> *INTRODUCTION*
>
> *Within the broad area of trade finance, the Office of Finance (OF) has responsibility for developing the Commerce Department's policy positions on international financial and monetary affairs. The office works with exporters, banks and other financial firms and Federal export financing programs (such as the Export Import Bank of the United States) to improve trade finance availability and usage. The office also works with the multilateral development banks on the international major projects program and general export promotions efforts. The office implements a statutory mandate to monitor countertrade trends, disseminate information on the subject and counsel some U.S. firms seeking such trade opportunities.*

Director
Mr. David Bowie
202/482-3277   Fax: 202/482-5702
Rm. 1104

Director, Financial Services and Countertrade Division
Mr. Pompiliu Verzariu
202/482-4434
Rm. 1104

Director, Trade & Project Finance/Multilateral
  Development Banks Division
Mr. Robert Y. Lee
202/482-3277
Rm. 4004

Deputy Assistant Secretary for Technology and Aerospace Industries

Deputy Assistant Secretary
Mr. Ellis R. Mottur
202/482-1872   Fax: 202/482-0856
Rm. 2800-A

Note: See profile under Assistant Secretary for Trade Development

Office of Aerospace

> *INTRODUCTION*
>
> *The primary mission of the Office of Aerospace is to promote American commercial and economic interests related to international trade and investment in aerospace products. The office:*
>
> * *analyzes aerospace market trends abroad;*
> * *identifies export opportunities for American aerospace companies;*
> * *disseminates trade leads to aerospace businesses;*
> * *counsels aerospace manufacturers and suppliers on their export strategies;*
> * *conducts a range of trade promotion activities;*
> * *develops trade policy positions aimed at increasing free and fair trade in the aerospace sector;*
> * *participates in trade negotiations and consultations;*
> * *advocates on behalf of U.S. exporters in particular transactions.*

The industries covered by this office include civil transport aircraft, general aviation aircraft, helicopters, aircraft engines, other aircraft parts, air traffic control equipment, and commercial spacecraft.

Within the office are the Aerospace Market Development Division and the Aerospace Policy and Analysis Division.

Director
Ms. Sally H. Bath
202/482-1229   Fax: 202/482-0856
Rm. 2128

Aerospace Market Development Division

The Aerospace Market Development Division (AMD) identifies market opportunities overseas and conducts trade promotion activities to help U.S. aerospace companies increase their exports. Among other things, AMD organizes trade missions to foreign markets and operates Aerospace Product Literature Centers (APLC) at selected international aerospace trade shows. Other responsibilities include organizing U.S. Government and U.S. company participation at the Paris Air Show.

Director, Market Development Division
Mr. Anthony M. Largay
202/482-2835   Fax: 202/482-3113
Rm. 2128

Aerospace Policy and Analysis Division

The Aerospace Policy and Analysis Division (APA) is responsible for describing the industry and its competitive environment. APA generates data on aerospace markets overseas and analyzes trends as they relate to U.S. export interests. It develops policy positions related to international trade in aerospace and represents the Commerce Department in aerospace trade negotiations. Issues covered by this division include commercial space launch services, aircraft financing, and advocacy for individual exporters.

Director, Policy and Analysis Division
Mr. Fred Elliot
202/482-1233   Fax: 202/482-3383
Rm. 2124

Office of Computers and Business Equipment

INTRODUCTION

OCBE covers particular industries: computers systems, computer software, and business equipment. For each of these industries, OCBE provides three primary functions:

• Industry Analysis: OCBE provides numerous publications, including market analyses, write-ups on upcoming events and policy issues, and other trade-related information.

• Trade Promotion: To promote U.S. exports, the DOC conducts trade shows and trade missions in many countries.

• Trade Policy: OCBE also aims to increase exports by helping to formulate positions on policy issues and to negotiate agreements with foreign governments on trade policy issues, such as market access and intellectual property rights.

Director
Mr. John McPhee
202/482-0572   Fax: 202/482-0652
Rm. 2806

Director, Software Division
Ms. Heidi Hijikata
202/482-0569
Rm. 2806

Director, Systems Division
Mr. Timothy Miles
202/482-2990
Rm. 2806

Office of Microelectronics,
**   Medical Equipment and Instrumentation**

INTRODUCTION

OMMI is responsible for collecting and disseminating information on industry products and international markets. OMMI engages in activities which develop export opportunities for U.S. companies, through providing market research, organizing international trade events, and facilitating market access through U.S. Commercial policy initiatives.

Within OMMI there are three primary product areas: Microelectronics, Medical Equipment and Instrumentation. Each product area is covered individually by international trade specialists, whose primary purpose is to provide information to U.S. exporters.

Director
Mr. Jeffrey L. Gren
202/482-2587   FAX 202/482-0975
Rm. 1015

Director, Instrumentation, Medical Equipment and
    Advanced Materials Division
Mr. Joseph J. Burke
202/482-5014
Rm. 1015

Director, Microelectronics Division
Ms. Margaret T. Donnelly
202/482-5466
Rm. 1015

Office of Telecommunications

Director
Ms. Robin Layton
202/482-4466   Fax: 202/482-5834
Rm. 4324

Director, Wireline Equipment and Services Division
Mr. John R. Henry
202/482-4466
Rm. 4327-C

Director, Wireless Equipment and Services Division
Ms. Linda Gossack
202/482-4466
Rm. 4327-C

Deputy Assistant Secretary for
Textiles, Apparel & Consumer Goods

> **INTRODUCTION**
>
> *The Deputy Assistant Secretary (DAS) for Textiles, Apparel and Consumer Goods Industries oversees programs and strategies to improve the domestic and international competitiveness of the U.S. fiber, textile, and apparel industries, as well as industries which manufacture a wide range of consumer products. The DAS also serves as chairman of the Committee for the Implementation of Textile Agreements (CITA), which determines when market disrupting factors exist in the domestic fiber, textile, and apparel marketplace. The DAS also administers U.S. textile quota agreements, formulates trade policy, performs research and analysis, complies industry data, and promotes U.S. trade events for a whole spectrum of textile, apparel, and consumer goods.*

Deputy Assistant Secretary
Ms. Troy H. Cribb
202/482-3737   Fax: 202/482-2331
Rm. 3001

Office of Textiles and Apparel
Director
Mr. D. Michael Hutchinson
202/482-5078   Fax: 202/482-2331
Rm. 3100A

Industry Assessment Division

> *The Industry Assessment Division evaluates the current state of the domestic fiber, textile and apparel industries; recommends the establishment of quotas to prevent market disruption; analyzes the economic impact of fiber, textile and apparel imports, import policies, regulations, and legislation on the fiber, textile and apparel industries and recommends appropriate action; assesses the impact of changes in trade policy and the U.S. textile and apparel program on the domestic industry; collects, develops, monitors, maintains, and disseminates economic data and information concerning fiber, textile and apparel markets and industries; and prepares data and economic analyses on these industries for publications, studies, briefing papers, speeches and reports.*

Director, Industry Assessment Division
Mr. William J. Dulka
202/482-4058
Rm. 3121

International Agreements Division

> *The Agreements Division is principally responsible for implementing textile and clothing agreements. Country Analysts instruct Customs to limit imports, require visas and make charges to limits for transshipments, and otherwise undertake specific provisions of the agreements. In most cases, and always if the directive affects current year charges, the directives are published in the Federal Register.*
>
> *Analysts also prepare Federal Register Notices announcing a "call". A call is a consultation request to a foreign Government for a discussion of U.S. imports from that country which are contributing to serious damage or actual threat thereof to the domestic industry, with a view to reaching a mutually agreed limit.*
>
> *The Agreements Division represents the Commerce Department in negotiations with the foreign Governments and provides briefing materials to the other CITA representatives assigned to negotiations. The negotiation positions are confidential. After signing of an agreement, the State Department makes a public release available.*
>
> *The analysts review the monthly "Performance Report" and make necessary adjustments and footnotes. In addition the analysts exchange data and information with local embassy officials of textile and apparel suppliers to the U.S. to ensure an open forum on issues.*

Director, International Agreements Division
Mr. Donald R. Foote
202/482-4212
Rm. 3104

Market Expansion Division

> *The objective of the Market Expansion Division (MED) is to improve exports of U.S. textile and apparel companies in overseas markets. To expand export sales of U.S. made products, the MED sponsors U.S. companies' participation in international exhibitions abroad, U.S. Solo Exhibitions, Trade Missions, and Export Seminars. MED offers event-related market research and provides export counseling. MED identifies barriers to trade and maintains an inventory of foreign regulations affecting U.S. textile/ apparel exports. MED solicits textile and apparel exporters to advise us of any barriers or problems they encounter.*

Director, Market Expansion Division
Mr. Ferenc Molnar
202/482-5153
Rm. 3107

Trade Data Division

The Trade and Data Division recommends and implements trade classification schemes to implement the WTO Agreement on Textiles and Clothing and bilateral agreements; initiates and participates in fraud and transshipment investigations and participates in negotiations and consultations on matters of transshipment, classification and investigation; presents classification and investigation issues to the Office Director and Chairman of CITA; participates in GATT and Free Trade Agreement negotiations; assures import data quality by reviewing import data, identifying problems, by working with the Census Bureau and the U.S. Customs Service; conducts data investigations and reconciliations with foreign governments; conducts classification and categorization seminars for foreign governments; reviews and implements visa agreements; processes visa waivers; obtains descriptions and samples of imported textile and apparel products; plans and operates the Textile Information Management System; and provides ADP, product identification and trade classification support for the International Agreements Division and Industry Assessment Division, including identifying need for support.

Director, Trade Data Division
Mr. Philip J. Martello
202/482-3400
Rm. 3001-A

Office of Consumer Goods

Director
Mr. J. Hayden Boyd
202/482-0337   Fax: 202/482-3981
Rm. 3013

Director, Durable Goods Division
Mr. Kevin M. Ellis
202/482-1176
Rm. 3004

Director, Nondurable Goods Division
Ms. Leslie B. Simon
202/482-0341
Rm. 3015

Deputy Assistant Secretary for Tourism Industries

INTRODUCTION

The newest office at ITA, created after the demise of the U.S. Travel and Tourism Administration, the DAS for tourism industries is charged with fostering tourism trade development and representing the United States in tourism-related meetings with foreign government officials. The office also serves as the principal point-of-contact for the U.S. tourism industry on policy and tourism trade development issues. The office is responsible for organizing a follow-up meeting to the White House new Conference on Travel and Tourism (WHCTT) regarding the public/private partnership and to further the recommendations in the national tourism strategy from the WHCTT. The office interacts with the U.S. & Foreign Commercial Service to advise and assist the tourism trade development officers on matters of policy, technical assistance and research.

Through the Tourism Industries office, the government will look to increase the number of tourism exporters by providing research and technical assistance to communities and businesses interested in tapping international markets, as well as to coordinate tourism-related activities and policies within the government itself. The office will interact with the newly formed U.S.A. National Tourism Organization, Inc., formed (after Congress cut the USTTA) to market the United States to potential international visitors and increase the number of international travelers to the U.S.

The Tourism Office is headed by a DAS and includes the DAS office, the Tourism Policy Council, and the Tourism Development Group. The office is staffed by 12 employees.

Deputy Assistant Secretary
Ms. Leslie R. Doggett
202/482-0140   Fax: 202/482-4279
Rm. 1860

The Tourism Policy Council

The Tourism Policy Council (TPC) serves as the administrative arm of the Secretary's TPC, composed of the Secretaries and heads of thirteen federal agencies and Amtrak. The TPC was created to coordinate federal tourism policies and to ensure that the national interest in tourism is fully considered in federal decisions that affect tourism development. This group also is responsible for representing the U.S. government in trade and investment negotiations, for conferences that stimulate an open trade environment for international tourism trade, such as the OECD, APEC, and Western Hemispheric Conferences.

Director
Ms. Terry K. Smith-Labet
202/482-4746   Fax: 202/482-4279
Rm. 1860

The Tourism Development Group

The Tourism Development Group is responsible for economic policy and technical assistance for tourism development. This includes collection, analysis, and dissemination of baseline data for the U.S. on international travelers to and from the United States. The data collected by this group serves as the foundation for the Department of Commerce's Bureau of Economic Analysis (BEA) in configuring the National Travel Account for the Balance of Trade figures. This Tourism Development Group is the only source of international travel data for the public and private sectors of the travel and tourism industry. The staff serves as the national and international statistical experts for consultation, presentation, and guidance on international travel for the U.S. industry and intergovernmental statistical efforts, such as the OECD and the WTO. The Tourism Development group is responsible for responding to thousands of requests from the public sector and private industry clients through an electronic customer inquiry system and establishment of an electronic database of international statistics. Another key responsibility of this group is to generate sales throughout the industry to help offset the actual cost of the programs.

The Research component of the Tourism Industry office scrutinizes the patterns of international tourism on a worldwide basis for the benefit of the agency as well as the industry. The responsibilities of the Office of Research include: Gathering, analyzing, and publishing international travel research information; Providing statistics to define the size and characteristics of existing and emerging markets; Assessing changes in travel demand and international travel market potential; and Guiding the development of marketing efforts and evaluating their effectiveness.

In addition, the Office manages three broad research programs/data bases which form the nucleus of subsequent reports, programs, and statistical information. These are:

1) Basic Data on International Visitor Arrival Statistics to the United States;

2) In-Flight Survey of International Air Travelers; and

3) Pleasure Travel Markets to North America.

Director
Ms. Helen Marano
202/482-4752   Fax: 202/482-4279
Rm. 1860

Trade Development (TD) Industry Officers

INTRODUCTION

Industry specialists work with manufacturing and service industry associations and firms to identify trade opportunities and obstacles by product or service, industry sector, and market. They also develop export marketing plans and programs. To assist U.S. businesses in their export efforts, industry experts conduct executive trade missions, trade fairs, product literature centers, marketing seminars, and business counseling. Industry officers are organized into five major sectors:

- *Technology and Aerospace Industries*
- *Basic Industries*
- *Textiles, Apparel, and Consumer Goods Industries*
- *Service Industries and Finance*
- *Environmental Technology Exports*

A list of the nearly 500 subject areas with contact information follows. If mailing to any of the individuals shown, use this format:

Contact
Dept. of Commerce/ITA
14th Street & Constitution Ave., NW
Rm. (Room #)
Washington, DC 20230

Abrasive Products
Mr. Graylin Presbury
Phone: 202/482-5158
Room: 4035

Accounting
Mr. J. Marc Chittum
Phone: 202/482-0345
Room: 1118

Adhesives/Sealants
Mr. Raimundo Prat
Phone: 202/482-0810
Room: 4059

Advanced Materials
Mr. Lauren Brosler
Phone: 202/482-4431
Room: 2128

Advertising
Mr. Bruce Harsh
Phone: 202/482-4582
Room: 1120

Aerospace Financing Issues
Mr. Jon Montgomery
Phone: 202/482-6234
Room: 2104

Aerospace Industry Analysis
Mr. Frederick Elliot
Phone: 202/482-1233
Room: 2104

Aerospace Industry Data
Mr. Ronald Green
Phone: 202/482-3068
Room: 2104

Aerospace Info. & Analysis
Mr. Ronald Green
Phone: 202/482-3068
Room: 2104

Aerospace Market Develop.
Mr. Tony Largay
Phone: 202/482-6236
Room: 2128

Aerospace Market Promo
Mr. Tony Largay
Phone: 202/482-6236
Room: 2128

Aerospace Mktg. Support
Ms. Heather Pederson
Phone: 202/482-6239
Room: 2128

Aerospace Trade Policy
Mr. Fred Elliot
Phone: 202/482-1233
Room: 2104

Aerospace Trade Promo
Mr. Tony Largay
Phone: 202/482-6236
Room: 2128

Aerospace, Office of
Ms. Sally H. Bath
Phone: 202/482-1229
Room: 2128

Aerospace-Space Mkt. Support
Ms. Kim Farner
Phone: 202/482-2232
Room: 2104

Aerospace-Space Programs
Ms. Kim Farner
Phone: 202/482-2232
Room: 2104

Agricultural Chemicals
Mr. Michael Kelly
Phone: 202/482-0811
Room: 4053

Agricultural Machinery
Ms. Mary Wiening
Phone: 202/482-4708
Room: 4327

Air Conditioning Equipment
Mr. Eugene Shaw
Phone: 202/482-3494

Air Couriers
Mr. Eugene Alford
Phone: 202/482-5071
Room: 1120

Air Pollution Control Eqmt
Mr. Eric Fredell
Phone: 202/482-0343
Room: 4321

Air Traffic Control Eqmt
Ms. Shannon Ballard
Phone: 202/482-3786
Room: 2128

Air Transport Services
Mr. Eugene Alford
Phone: 202/482-5071
Room: 1116

Air, Gas Compressors
Mr. Leonard Heimowitz
Phone: 202/482-0552
Room: 4025

Air, Gas Compressors (Trade Promo)
Mr. George Zanetakos
Phone: 202/482-0558
Room: 4324

Aircraft & Aircraft Engines (Market Support)
Ms. Heather Pederson
Phone: 202/482-6239
Room: 2128

Aircraft Auxiliary Equipment
Ms. Heather Pederson
Phone: 202/482-6239
Room: 2128

Aircraft Parts (Market Support)
Ms. Shannon Ballard
Phone: 202/482-3786
Room: 2128

Airlines
Mr. Eugene Alford
Phone: 202/482-5071
Room: 1116

Airport (Major Proj)
Mr. Mike Thompson
Phone: 202/482-5126
Room: 4314

Airport Equipment
Ms. Shannon Ballard

Phone: 202/482-3786
Room: 2128

Alcoholic Beverages
Mr. Donald Hodgen
Phone: 202/482-3346
Room: 3008

Aluminum
Mr. David Cammarota
Phone: 202/482-5157
Room: 4035

Aluminum Oxide
Mr. Graylin Presbury
Phone: 202/482-5158
Room: 4035

Analytical & Scientific Instruments (Trade Promo)
Mr. Franc Manzolillo
Phone: 202/482-2991
Room: 1008

Analytical Instrument
Mr. George Litman
Phone: 202/482-3411
Room: 1010

Apparel
Ms. Joanne Tucker
Phone: 202/482-4058
Room: 3119

Apparel (Trade Promotion)
Mr. Ferenc Molnar
Phone: 202/482-5153
Room: 3109

Artificial Intelligence
Mr. Mike Diaz
Phone: 202/482-0397
Room: 2807

Asbestos/Cement Prod.
Mr. Charles B. Pitcher
Phone: 202/482-0385
Room: 4022

Audio Visual Services
Mr. John E. Siegmund
Phone: 202/482-4781
Room: 1120

Auto Industry (Trade Promo)
Mr. John C. White
Phone: 202/482-0671
Room: 4028

Auto Industry Affairs
Mr. Henry Misisco
Phone: 202/482-0554
Room: 4036

Auto Parts & Suppliers
Mr. Robert O. Reck
Phone: 202/482-1418
Room: 4044

Aviation Services
Mr. Eugene Alford
Phone: 202/482-5071
Room: 1116

Avionics Marketing
Ms. Heather Pederson
Phone: 202/482-2835

Room: 2128

Bakery Products
Mr. Donald Hodgen
Phone: 202/482-3346
Room: 3008

Ball Bearings
Mr. Richard Reise
Phone: 202/482-3489
Room: 4025

Banking Services
Mr. John Shuman
Phone: 202/482-3050
Room: 1004

Basic Paper & Board Mfg
Mr. Gary Stanley
Phone: 202/482-0375
Room: 4016A

Bauxite, Alumina, Prim Alum
Mr. David Cammarota
Phone: 202/482-5157
Room: 4035

Beer
Mr. Donald Hodgen
Phone: 202/482-3346
Room: 3008

Belting & Hose
Mr. Raimundo Prat
Phone: 202/482-0128
Room: 4059

Beryllium
Ms. Barbara Males
Phone: 202/482-0606

Beverages
Mr. Donald Hodgen
Phone: 202/482-3346
Room: 3008

Bicycles
Mr. John Vanderwolf
Phone: 202/482-0348
Room: 3006

Biomass Energy Equipment
Mr. Les Garden
Phone: 202/482-0556
Room: 4312

Biotechnology
Ms. Emily Arakaki
Phone: 202/482-0130
Room: 4051

Boats, Pleasure
Mr. John Vanderwolf
Phone: 202/482-0348
Room: 3006

Books
Mr. William S. Lofquist
Phone: 202/482-0379
Room: 3015B

Breakfast Cereal
Mr. Donald Hodgen
Phone: 202/482-3346
Room: 3008

Bridges (Major Proj)

Mr. Michael Thompson
Phone: 202/482-5126
Room: 4314

Broadcasting Equipment
Ms. Krysten Jenci
Phone: 202/482-2952
Room: 1009

Brooms & Brushes
Mr. John M. Harris
Phone: 202/482-1178
Room: 3006

Building Materials & Construction
Mr. Charles B. Pitcher
Phone: 202/482-0385
Room: 4022

Business Eqmt (Trade Promo)
Ms. Judy A. Fogg
Phone: 202/482-4936
Room: 2132

Business Forms
Ms. Rose Marie Bratland
Phone: 202/482-0380
Room: 3008

Canned Food Products
Mr. Donald Hodgen
Phone: 202/482-3346
Room: 3015A

Carbon Black
Mr. Raimundo Prat
Phone: 202/482-0128
Room: 4059

CAD/CAM/CAE Software
Ms. Vera A. Swann
Phone: 202/482-0396
Room: 2807

Cellular Radio Telephone Equipment
Mr. Richard Paddock
Phone: 202/482-5235
Room: 1009

Cement
Mr. Charles B. Pitcher
Phone: 202/482-0385
Room: 4022

Cement Plants (Major Proj)
Mr. Wally Haraguchi
Phone: 202/482-4877
Room: 4329

**Chemical Industries Machinery
(Trade Promo)**
Mr. Eugene Shaw
Phone: 202/482-3494

Chemical Plants (Major Proj)
Mr. Wally Haraguchi
Phone: 202/482-4877
Room: 4329

Chemicals & Allied Products
Mr. Michael J. Kelly
Phone: 202/482-0128
Room: 4057

Chinaware
Ms. Rose Marie Bratland
Phone: 202/482-0380

Room: 3008

Chromium
Mr. Graylin Presbury
Phone: 202/482-5158
Room: 4035

Civil Aircraft Agreement
Mr. Fred Elliott
Phone: 202/482-5158

Civil Aviation Policy
Mr. Eugene Alford
Phone: 202/482-5071
Room: 1116

Coal Exports
Mr. John Rasmussen
Phone: 202/482-1466
Room: 4413

Cobalt
Mr. Graylin Presbury
Phone: 202/482-5158
Room: 4035

Columbium
Mr. Graylin Presbury
Phone: 202/482-5158
Room: 4035

Commercial Lighting Fixtures
Mr. Tony Vandermuhll
Phone: 202/482-2390

Commercial Printing
Mr. William S. Lofquist
Phone: 202/482-0379
Room: 3015B

Commercial/Indus Refrig Eqmt
Mr. Eugene Shaw
Phone: 202/482-3494

Commercialization of Space (Market)
Ms. Kim Farner
Phone: 202/482-4222
Room: 2104

Computer and DP Services
Ms. Jennifer Tallarico
Phone: 202/482-5820
Room: 1118

Computer Consulting
Ms. Jennifer Tallarico
Phone: 202/482-5820
Room: 1118

Computer Software
Ms. Heidi C. Hijikata
Phone: 202/482-0571
Room: 2806

Computer Systems (Hardware)
Mr. Timothy Miles
Phone: 202/482-2990
Room: 2806

Computers (Workstations)
Mr. R. Clay Woods
Phone: 202/482-3013
Room: 2806

Computers (Trade Promo)
Ms. Judy A. Fogg
Phone: 202/482-4936

Room: 2132

Computers, Large Scale
Mr. Wayne Ebenfeld
Phone: 202/482-1987
Room: 2808

Computers, Personal/Portable
Mr. Clay R. Woods
Phone: 202/482-3013
Room: 2805

Confectionery Products
Mr. Donald Hodgen
Phone: 202/482-3346
Room: 3008

**Construction Machinery,
Large Off Road**
Mr. Leonard Heimowitz
Phone: 202/482-0558
Room: 4325

Construction Services
Mr. Wally Haraguchi
Phone: 202/482-4877

Construction Statistics
Mr. Patrick Macauley
Phone: 202/482-0132
Room: 4026

Consumer Electronics
Ms. Laureen Daly
Phone: 202/482-3360
Room: 1015

Consumer Goods
Phone: 202/482-0338
Room: 3013

Containers & Packaging
Phone: 202/482-0132
Room: 4024

Conveyors/Conveying Equipment
Ms. Mary Wiening
Phone: 202/482-4708
Room: 4327

Copper
Ms. Barbara Males
Phone: 202/482-0606
Room: 4024

**Cosmetics (Overseas Trade Show
Recruitment)**
Mr. Edward K. Kimmel
Phone: 202/482-3640
Room: 2107

Countertrade Services
Mr. Pompiliu Verzariu
Phone: 202/482-4434
Room: 1106

Countertrade Services
Ms. Paula Mitchell
Phone: 202/482-4471
Room: 1106

Cutlery
Ms. Rose Marie Bratland
Phone: 202/482-0380
Room: 3008

Dairy Products

Mr. Donald Hodgen
Phone: 202/482-3346

Data Base Services
Ms. Jennifer Tallarico
Phone: 202/482-5820
Room: 1118

Data Processing Services
Ms. Jennifer Tallarico
Phone: 202/482-5820
Room: 1118

Dental Equipment (Devices & Supplies)
Mr. Duaine Priestly
Phone: 202/482-2410
Room: 1008

Dental Equipment (Trade Promo)
Mr. George B. Keen
Phone: 202/482-2010
Room: 1006

Desalination (Major Proj)
Mr. William Holroyd
Phone: 202/482-6168
Room: 4314

Desalination/Water Reuse
Ms. Frederica Wheeler
Phone: 202/482-3509
Room: 1009

Diamond Industrial
Mr. Graylin Presbury
Phone: 202/482-5158
Room: 4035

Direct Marketing
Mr. Bruce Harsh
Phone: 202/482-4582
Room: 1120

Disk Storage
Mr. Daniel Valverde
Phone: 202/482-0573
Room: 2803

Distilled Spirits
Mr. Donald Hodgen
Phone: 202/482-3346
Room: 3015A

Dolls
Mr. Jonathan Freilich
Phone: 202/482-5783
Room: 3008

Drugs
Mr. William Hurt
Phone: 202/482-0128
Room: 4057

Durable Consumer Goods
Mr. Kevin M. Ellis
Phone: 202/482-1176
Room: 3004

Education Services/Manpower Training (Trade Promo)
Mr. J. Marc Chittum
Phone: 202/482-0345
Room: 1118

Electric Industrial Apparatus Nec
Ms. Julie Fouque
Phone: 202/482-2390

Room: 4029

Electrical Power Plants (Major Proj)
Mr. Andy Collier
Phone: 202/482-0680
Room: 4329

Electrical Test & Measuring Instruments
Mr. Michael Andrews
Phone: 202/482-2795

Electricity
Mr. Andy Collier
Phone: 202/482-0680
Room: 4329

Electronic Components
Ms. Marleen Ruffin
Phone: 202/482-0570

Electronic Components (Director)
Ms. Margaret Donnelly
Phone: 202/482-5466

Electronic Database Services
Ms. Jennifer Tallarico
Phone: 202/482-5820
Room: 1118

Electronic Power Gen. Transmission & Dist. Eqmt (Trade Promo)
Mr. Andy Collier
Phone: 202/482-0680
Room: 4329

Electronics (Printed Circuit Boards)
Ms. Jodee Mussehl-Aziz
Phone: 202/482-3360

ElectroOptical Instruments (Trade Promo)
Mr. Franc Manzolillo
Phone: 202/482-2991
Room: 1008

Elevators, Moving Stairways
Ms. Mary Wiening
Phone: 202/482-4708
Room: 4327

Employment Services (Trade Promo)
Mr. J. Marc Chittum
Phone: 202/482-0345
Room: 1118

Energy
Ms. Helen Bourroughs
Phone: 202/482-1466
Room: 4413

Energy, Renewable
Mr. Les Garden
Phone: 202/482-0556
Room: 4413

Energy, Renewable (Tech & Eqmt)
Mr. Les Garden
Phone: 202/482-0556
Room: 4312

Engineering/Construction Services
Mr. Jay Smith
Phone: 202/482-4642
Room: 1118

Entertainment Industries
Mr. John E. Siegmund

Phone: 202/482-4781
Room: 1120

Entertainment Services
Mr. Wray O. Candilis
Phone: 202/482-0339

Environmental Technologies
Main Number
Phone: 202/482-5225
Room: 1002

Equipment, Used
Mr. John Bodson
Phone: 202/482-0681

Explosives
Mr. Mike Kelly
Phone: 202/482-0811
Room: 4053

Export Trading Companies
Ms. W. Dawn Busby
Phone: 202/482-5131
Room: 1800

Fabricated Metal Construction Materials
Mr. Franklin Williams
Phone: 202/482-0132
Room: 4026

Farm Machinery
Ms. Mary Weining
Phone: 202/482-4708
Room: 4327

Fasteners (Industrial)
Mr. Richard Reise
Phone: 202/482-3489
Room: 4025

Fats and Oils
Mr. Donald Hodgen
Phone: 202/482-3346
Room: 3008

Fencing (Metal)
Mr. Franklin Williams
Phone: 202/482-0132
Room: 4026

Ferroalloys Products
Mr. Graylin Presbury
Phone: 202/482-5158
Room: 4035

Ferrous Scrap
Mr. Charles Bell
Phone: 202/482-0608

Fertilizers
Mr. Mike Kelly
Phone: 202/482-0811
Room: 4053

Fiber Optics
Mr. Stuart Sandall
Phone: 202/482-2006

Filters/Purifying Eqmt
Mr. Eric Fredell
Phone: 202/482-0343
Room: 4411

Financial Services
S. Cassin Muir

Phone: 202/482-0349
Room: 1110

Fisheries
National Marine Fisheries Service
Phone: 301/713-2379

Flexible Mftg Systems
Ms. Megan Pilaroscia
Phone: 202/482-0609

Flour
Mr. Donald Hodgen
Phone: 202/482-3346
Room: 3008

Flowers
Mr. Donald Hodgen
Phone: 202/482-3346
Room: 3008

Food Processing/Packaging Machinery (Trade Promo)
Mr. Eugene Shaw
Phone: 202/482-3494

Food Products Machinery
Mr. Eugene Shaw
Phone: 202/482-3494

Food Retailing
Mr. Donald Hodgen
Phone: 202/482-3346
Room: 3008

Footwear
Mr. James E. Byron
Phone: 202/482-4034
Room: 3015B

Forest Products
Mr. Gary Stanley
Phone: 202/482-0375
Room: 4016A

Forest Products, Building Materials
Mr. Chris Kristensen
Phone: 202/482-0384

Forestry/Woodworking Eqmt (Trade Promo)
Mr. Edward Abrahams
Phone: 202/482-0312
Room: 4025

Forgings Semifinished Steel
Mr. Charles Bell
Phone: 202/482-0608
Room: 4029B

Fossil Fuels
Mr. John Rasmussen
Phone: 202/482-1889
Room: 4329

Foundry Industry
Mr. Charles Bell
Phone: 202/482-0608

Frozen Food Products
Mr. Donald Hodgen
Phone: 202/482-3346
Room: 3008

Fruits
Mr. Donald Hodgen

Phone: 202/482-3346
Room: 3008

Fur Goods
Mr James E. Byron
Phone: 202/482-4034
Room: 3015B

Furniture
Mr. Jonathan Freilich
Phone: 202/482-5783

Gallium
Mr. David Cammarota
Phone: 202/482-5157
Room: 4035

Games & Children's Vehicles
Mr. Jonathan Freilich
Phone: 202/482-5783

Gaskets/Gasketing Materials
Mr. Richard Reise
Phone: 202/482-3489
Room: 4025

Gen Indus Mach Nec, Exc 35691
Mr. Raymond Robinson
Phone: 202/482-0610

General Aviation Aircraft
Mr. Eugene Alford
Phone: 202/482-5071

Generator Sets/Turbines (Major Proj)
Mr. Andy Collier
Phone: 202/482-0680
Room: 4329

Germanium
Mr. David Cammarota
Phone: 202/482-5171
Room: 4035

Giftware (Trade Promo)
Mr. Les Simon
Phone: 202/482-0341
Room: 3015

Glass, Flat
Mr. Franklin Williams
Phone: 202/482-0132
Room: 4026

Glassware (household)
Ms. Rose Marie Bratland
Phone: 202/482-0380
Room: 3006

Gloves (Work)
Mr. James E. Byron
Phone: 202/482-4034
Room: 3015B

Grain Mill Products
Mr. Donald Hodgen
Phone: 202/482-3346
Room: 3008

Greeting Cards
Ms. Rose Marie Bratland
Phone: 202/482-0380
Room: 3008

Grocery Retailing
Mr. Donald Hodgen
Phone: 202/482-3346

Room: 3008

Hand Saws, Saw Blades
Mr. Edward Abrahams
Phone: 202/482-0312
Room: 4025

Hand/Edge Tools Ex Mach TI/Saws
Mr. Edward Abrahams
Phone: 202/482-0312
Room: 4025

Handbags
Mr. James E. Byron
Phone: 202/482-4034
Room: 3015B

Hard Surfaced Floor Coverings
Mr. Franklin Williams
Phone: 202/482-0132

Hardware (Export Promo)
Mr. Edward Kimmel
Phone: 202/482-3640
Room: 2107

Hazardous Waste
Ms. Loretta Jonkers
Phone: 202/482-0564

Health Care Services
Mr. Francis Simon
Phone: 202/482-2697

Heating Eqmt Ex Furnaces
Mr. John Manger
Phone: 202/482-2732

Helicopters
Mr. Ronald Green
Phone: 202/482-3068

High Tech Trade, U.S. Competitiveness
Ms. Victoria L. Hatter
Phone: 202/482-3895
Room: 2225

Hoists, Overhead Cranes
Ms. Mary Wiening
Phone: 202/482-4708
Room: 4327

Home Video
Mr. Wray O. Candilis
Phone: 202/482-0339

Hose & Belting
Mr. Raimundo Prat
Phone: 202/482-0128
Room: 4059

Hotel and Restaurant Equipment
Mr. Edward K. Kimmel
Phone: 202/482-3640
Room: 2107

Household Appliances
Mr. John M. Harris
Phone: 202/482-1178
Room: 3006

Household Appliances (Trade Promo)
Mr. Les Simon
Phone: 202/482-0341

Household Furniture
Mr. Jonathan Freilich

Phone: 202/482-5783
Room: 3008

Housewares (Export Promo)
Mr. Les Simon
Phone: 202/482-0341
Room: 2107

Housing (Manufactured)
Mr. Charles Pitcher
Phone: 202/482-0385

Housing Construction
Mr. Charles Pitcher
Phone: 202/482-0385

Hydro Power, Plants (Major Proj)
Mr. Andrew Collier
Phone: 202/482-0680

Industrial Chemicals
Mr. William Hurt
Phone: 202/482-0128
Room: 4057

Industrial Controls
Mr. John Bodson
Phone: 202/482-0681
Room: 4029

Industrial Drives/Gears
Mr. Richard Reise
Phone: 202/482-3489
Room: 4025

Industrial Eqmt (Trade Promo)
Mr. Eugene Shaw
Phone: 202/482-3494

Industrial Gases
Mr. Antonio Kostalas
Phone: 202/482-2390

Industrial Organic Chemicals
Mr. William Hurt
Phone: 202/482-0128
Room: 4057

Industrial Robots
Ms. Megan Pilaroscia
Phone: 202/482-0609

Industrial Trucks
Ms. Mary Weining
Phone: 202/482-4708
Room: 4327

Information Industries
Ms. Jennifer Tallarico
Phone: 202/482-5820
Room: 1118

Information Services
Mr. Wray O. Candilis
Phone: 202/482-0339

Infrastructure (Main Number)
Mr. Jay Smith
Phone: 202/482-4642

Infrastructure/Water
Mr. Bill Holroyd
Phone: 202/482-6168

Inorganic Chemicals
Mr. Vincent Kamenicky
Phone: 202/482-0812

Inorganic Pigments
Mr. Vincent Kamenicky
Phone: 202/482-0812

Insulation
Mr. Patrick Macauley
Phone: 202/482-0134
Room: 4026

Insurance
Mr. Bruce McAdam
Phone: 202/482-0346
Room: 1110

Intellectual Property Rights (Services)
Mr. John E. Siegmund
Phone: 202/482-4781
Room: 1120

Investment Management
S. Cassin Muir
Phone: 202/482-0349
Room: 1110

Iron
Mr. Charles Bell
Phone: 202/482-0608

Irrigation (Major Proj)
Mr. Jay Smith
Phone: 202/482-4642
Room: 4327

Irrigation Equipment
Ms. Mary Weining
Phone: 202/482-4708
Room: 4327

Jams & Jellies
Mr. Donald Hodgen
Phone: 202/482-3346
Room: 3008

Jewelry
Mr. John M. Harris
Phone: 202/482-1178
Room: 3006

Jewelry (Trade Promo)
Ms. Ludene Capone
Phone: 202/482-2087
Room: 2107

Jute Products
Ms. Maria Corey
Phone: 202/482-4058
Room: 3119

Kitchen Cabinets
Ms. Suzanne Willis
Phone: 202/482-0577
Room: 4018

Laboratory Instruments
Mr. George Litman
Phone: 202/482-3411
Room: 1010

Laboratory Instruments (Trade Promo)
Mr. Franc Manzolillo
Phone: 202/482-2991
Room: 1008

Lasers/ElectroOptics (Trade Promo)
Mr. Franc Manzolillo
Phone: 202/482-2991
Room: 1008

Lawn & Garden Equipment
Mr. John Vanderwolf
Phone: 202/482-0348

Lead Products
Mr. David Larrabee
Phone: 202/482-0607

Leasing: Equip, Vehicles, Services
Ms. Elnora Uzzelle
Phone: 202/482-0351

Leather Apparel
Mr. James E. Byron
Phone: 202/482-4034
Room: 3015B

Leather Products
Mr. James E. Byron
Phone: 202/482-4034
Room: 3015B

Leather Tanning
Mr. James E. Byron
Phone: 202/482-4034
Room: 3015B

Legal Services
Mr. J. Marc Chittum
Phone: 202/482-0345
Room: 1118

LNG Plants (Major Proj)
Mr. Wally Haraguchi
Phone: 202/482-4877

Local Area Networks
Phone: 202/482-0572

Logs, Wood
Mr. Gary Stanley
Phone: 202/482-0375
Room: 4018

Luggage
Mr. James E. Byron
Phone: 202/482-4034
Room: 3015B

Lumber
Mr. Gary Stanley
Phone: 202/482-0375
Room: 4018

Machine Tool Accessories
Ms. Megan Pilaroscia
Phone: 202/482-0609

Magazines
Ms. Rose Marie Bratland
Phone: 202/482-0380
Room: 3008

Magnesium
Mr. David Cammarota
Phone: 202/482-5157
Room: 4035

Major Projects
Mr. Jay Smith
Phone: 202/482-4642

Management and Research Services (Trade Promo)
Mr. J. Marc Chittum
Phone: 202/482-0345
Room: 1118

Management Consulting
Mr. J. Marc Chittum
Phone: 202/482-0345
Room: 1118

Manifold Business Forms
Ms. Rose Marie Bratland
Phone: 202/482-0380
Room: 3008

Manmade Fiber
Ms. Joanne Tucker
Phone: 202/482-4058
Room: 3119

Margarine
Mr. Donald Hodgen
Phone: 202/482-3346
Room: 3008

Marine Insurance
Mr. C. William Johnson
Phone: 202/482-5012
Room: 1112

Marine Port/Shipbuilding (Major Proj.)
Mr. Mike Thompson
Phone: 202/482-5126

**Marine Port/Shipbuilding Equipment
(Trade Promo)**
Ms. Ludene Capone
Phone: 202/482-2087

**Marine Recreational Equipment
(Trade Promo)**
Ms. Ludene Capone
Phone: 202/482-2087
Room: 3015

Maritime Shipping
Mr. C. William Johnson
Phone: 202/482-5012

**Materials Handling Machinery
(Trade Promo)**
Ms. Mary Wiening
Phone: 202/482-4708
Room: 4327

Materials, Advanced
Mr. David Cammarota
Phone: 202/482-5157
Room: 4035

Meat Products
Mr. Donald Hodgen
Phone: 202/482-3346
Room: 3008

Mech Power Transmission Equipment
Mr. Richard Reise
Phone: 202/482-3489
Room: 4025

Medical Instruments
Ms. Victoria Kader
Phone: 202/482-4073

**Medical Instruments & Equipment
(Trade Promo)**
Mr. George B. Keen
Phone: 202/482-2010
Room: 1008

Medical Services
Mr. Simon Francis

Phone: 202/482-2697

Mercury
Mr. David Larrabee
Phone: 202/482-0607

Metal Building Products
Mr. Franklin Williams
Phone: 202/482-0132
Room: 4026

Metal Cutting Machine Tools
Ms. Megan Pilaroscia
Phone: 202/482-0609

Metal Forming Machine Tools
Ms. Megan Pilaroscia
Phone: 202/482-0609

Metal Powders
Mr. David Cammarota
Phone: 202/482-5157
Room: 4035

Metals, Secondary
Mr. Charles Bell
Phone: 202/482-0608
Room: 4029B

Metalworking
Mr. John Mearman
Phone: 202/482-0315
Room: 4027

Metalworking Eqmt. Nec
Ms. Megan Pilaroscia
Phone: 202/482-0609

Millwork
Mr. Gary Stanley
Phone: 202/482-0375
Room: 4018

**Mineral Based Const Mtrls (Clay/
Concrete/Gypsum/Asphalt/Stone)**
Mr. Charles B. Pitcher
Phone: 202/482-0385
Room: 4022

Mining Machinery
Mr. Len Heimowitz
Phone: 202/482-0558

Mining Machinery (Trade Promo)
Mr. George Zanetakos
Phone: 202/482-0552
Room: 4324

Mobile Homes
Phone: 202/482-0132

Molybdenum
Mr. David Cammarota
Phone: 202/482-5157
Room: 4035

Monorails (Trade Promo)
Ms. Mary Wiening
Phone: 202/482-4708
Room: 4327

Motion Pictures
Mr. John E. Siegmund
Phone: 202/482-4781
Room: 1120

Motor Vehicles

Mr. Albert T. Warner
Phone: 202/482-0669
Room: 4317

Motorcycles
Mr. John Vanderwolf
Phone: 202/482-0348
Room: 3006

Motors, Electric
Mr. John Mearman
Phone: 202/482-0315

Multichip Modules
Mr. Duaine Priestly
Phone: 202/482-2410

Music (pre-recorded)
Mr. John E. Siegmund
Phone: 202/482-4781
Room: 1120

Musical Instruments (Trade Promo)
Mr. John M. Harris
Phone: 202/482-1178
Room: 3006

Mutual Funds
S. Cassin Muir
Phone: 202/482-0349
Room: 1110

Natural Gas
Mr. John Rasmussen
Phone: 202/482-1889
Room: 4413

Natural, Synthetic Rubber
Mr. Raimundo Prat
Phone: 202/482-0128
Room: 4059

Newspapers
Ms. Rose Marie Bratland
Phone: 202/482-0380
Room: 3008

Nickel Products
Mr. Graylin Presbury
Phone: 202/482-0575
Room: 4035

Non-alcoholic Beverages
Mr. Donald Hodgen
Phone: 202/482-3346
Room: 3008

Noncurrent Carrying Wiring Devices
Mr. John Bodson
Phone: 202/482-0681
Room: 4029

Nondurable Goods
Mr. Les Simon
Phone: 202/482-0341
Room: 3015

Nonferrous Foundries
Mr. David Cammarota
Phone: 202/482-5157

Nonferrous Metals
Mr. David Larrabee
Phone: 202/482-0607
Room: 4035

Nonmetallic Minerals Nec

Mr. Robert Shaw
Phone: 202/482-5124

Nonresidential Constr.
Mr. Patrick Macauley
Phone: 202/482-0132
Room: 4026

**Nuclear Power Plants
(Major Projects)**
Mr. Andrew Collier
Phone: 202/482-0680
Room: 4329

Nuclear Power Plants/Machinery
Mr. Andrew Collier
Phone: 202/482-0680

Numerical Controls for Mach Tools
Ms. Megan Pilaroscia
Phone: 202/482-0609

Nuts, Bolts, Washers
Mr. Richard Reise
Phone: 202/482-3489
Room: 4025

Ocean Shipping
Mr. C. William Johnson
Phone: 202/482-5012
Room: 1112

Oil & Gas (Fuels Only)
Mr. John Rasmussen
Phone: 202/482-1889

Oil Field Machinery
Mr. John Rasmussen
Phone: 202/482-1889
Room: 4413

Oil Shale (Major Proj)
Mr. Wally Haraguchi
Phone: 202/482-4877

Operations & Maintenance
Mr. J. Marc Chittum
Phone: 202/482-0345
Room: 1118

Organic Chemicals
Mr. William Hurt
Phone: 202/482-0128
Room: 4057

Outdoor Lighting Fixtures
Mr. John Bodson
Phone: 202/482-0681
Room: 4029

Outdoor Power Eqmt (Trade Promo)
Mr. Les Simon
Phone: 202/486-0341

Overseas Export Promotion
Mr. Edward Kimmel
Phone: 202/482-3640

Packaging & Containers
Mr. John Bodson
Phone: 202/482-0681

Packaging Machinery
Mr. Eugene Shaw
Phone: 202/482-3494

Paints/Coatings

Mr. Raimundo Prat
Phone: 202/482-0128
Room: 4059

Paper
Mr. Gary Stanley
Phone: 202/482-0375
Room: 4016A

Paper & Board Packaging
Mr. Gary Stanley
Phone: 202/482-0375
Room: 4016A

Paper Industries Machinery
Mr. Edward Abrahams
Phone: 202/482-0312
Room: 4025

Pasta
Mr. Donald Hodgen
Phone: 202/482-3346
Room: 3008

**Paving Materials
(Asphalt & Concrete)**
Mr. Charles B. Pitcher
Phone: 202/482-0385
Room: 4022

Pectin
Mr. Donald Hodgen
Phone: 202/482-3346
Room: 3008

Periodicals
Ms. Rose Marie Bratland
Phone: 202/482-0380
Room: 3008

Pet Food
Mr. Donald Hodgen
Phone: 202/482-3346
Room: 3008

Pet Products (Trade Promo)
Mr. Edward K. Kimmel
Phone: 202/482-3640
Room: 2107

Petrochem, Cyclic Crudes
Mr. William Hurt
Phone: 202/482-0128
Room: 4057

Petrochemicals
Mr. William Hurt
Phone: 202/482-0128
Room: 4057

Petrochemicals Plants (Major Projects)
Mr. Wally Haraguchi
Phone: 202/482-4877

Petroleum, Crude & Refined Products
Mr. John Rasmussen
Phone: 202/482-1889
Room: 4413

Pharmaceuticals
Mr. William Hurt
Phone: 202/482-0128
Room: 4057

Photographic Eqmt & Supplies
Ms. Joyce Watson
Phone: 202/482-0574

Room: 2805

Pipelines (Major Projects)
Mr. Wally Haraguchi
Phone: 202/482-4877

Plastic Construction Products (Most)
Mr. Franklin Williams
Phone: 202/482-0132
Room: 4026

Plastic Materials/Resins
Mr. Raimundo Prat
Phone: 202/482-0128
Room: 4059

Plastic Products
Mr. Raimundo Prat
Phone: 202/482-0128
Room: 4059

Plastic Products Machinery
Mr. Eugene Shaw
Phone: 202/482-3494

Plumbing Fixtures & Fittings
Mr. Charles Pitcher
Phone: 202/482-0385
Room: 4026

Plywood/Panel Products
Mr. Gary Stanley
Phone: 202/482-0377
Room: 4018

Pollution Control Equip
Ms. Loretta Jonkers
Phone: 202/482-0564
Room: 4321

Porcelain Electrical Supplies
Ms. Helen Burroughs
Phone: 202/482-4931
Room: 4029

Ports
Mr. Michael Thompson
Phone: 202/482-5126

Potato Chips
Mr. Donald Hodgen
Phone: 202/482-3346
Room: 3008

Poultry Products
Mr. Donald Hodgen
Phone: 202/482-3346
Room: 3008

Power Generation
Mr. Andy Collier
Phone: 202/482-0680
Room: 4329

Power Hand Tools
Mr. Edward Abrahams
Phone: 202/482-0312
Room: 4025

Precious Metal Jewelry
Mr. John M. Harris
Phone: 202/482-1178
Room: 3006

Prefabricated Buildings (Metal)
Mr. Franklin Williams
Phone: 202/482-0132

Room: 4026

Prefabricated Housing (Wood)
Phone: 202/482-0132
Room: 4024

Prepared Meats
Mr. Donald Hodgen
Phone: 202/482-3346
Room: 3008

Pretzels
Mr. Donald Hodgen
Phone: 202/482-3346
Room: 3008

Primary Commodities
Mr. Fred Siesseger
Phone: 202/482-5124

Printed Circuit Boards
Ms. Judee Mussehl
Phone: 202/482-0429

Printing & Publishing
Mr. William S. Lofquist
Phone: 202/482-0379
Room: 3015B

Printing Trade Services
Ms. Rose Marie Bratland
Phone: 202/482-0380
Room: 3008

Printing Trades Mach/Eqmt
Mr. Raymond Robinson
Phone: 202/482-0610
Room: 4049

Process Control Instruments
Mr. George Litman
Phone: 202/482-3411
Room: 1010

Process Control Instruments
(Trade Promo)
Mr. Franc Manzolillo
Phone: 202/482-2991
Room: 1008

Pulp & Paper Machinery
(Trade Promo)
Mr. Edward Abrahams
Phone: 202/482-0312
Room: 4025

Pulp and Paper Mills
(Construction & Major Projects)
Mr. Wallace Haraguchi
Phone: 202/482-4877
Room: 4016

Pumps, Pumping Eqmt
Mr. John Manger
Phone: 202/482-2732
Room: 4025

Pumps, Valves, Compressors
(Trade Promo)
Mr. George Zanetakos
Phone: 202/482-0552
Room: 4324

Radio & T.V. Broadcasting
Mr. John E. Siegmund
Phone: 202/482-4781
Room: 1120

Radio & TV Communications Eqmt
Ms. Linda Gossack
Phone: 202/482-4523

Railroad Eqmt (Trade Promo)
Mr. Len Heimowitz
Phone: 202/482-0558

Recorded Music
Mr. John E. Siegmund
Phone: 202/482-4781
Room: 1120

Recreational Eqmt (Trade Promo)
Mr. John Vanderwolf
Phone: 202/482-0348
Room: 3015

Refractory Products
Mr. David Cammarota
Phone: 202/482-5157

Refrigeration Eqmt (Industrial Only)
Mr. Charles Pitcher
Phone: 202/482-0385
Room: 4024

Renewable Energy Eqmt
Mr. Les Garden
Phone: 202/482-0556
Room: 4312

Residential Lighting Fixtures
Mr. John Bodson
Phone: 202/482-0681
Room: 4029

Retail Trade
Mr. Aaron Schavey
Phone: 202/482-4117

Rice Milling
Mr. Donald Hodgen
Phone: 202/482-3346
Room: 3008

Roads, Railroads, Mass Trans
(Major Projects)
Mr. Mike Thompson
Phone: 202/482-5126
Room: 4314

Robots/Factory Automation
Ms. Megan Pilaroscia
Phone: 202/482-0609

Roller Bearings
Mr. Richard Reise
Phone: 202/482-3489
Room: 4025

Rolling Mill Machinery
Mr. Edward Abrahams
Phone: 202/482-0312
Room: 4025

Roofing, Asphalt
Mr. Charles B. Pitcher
Phone: 202/482-0385
Room: 4022

Rubber & Rubber Products
Mr. Raimundo Prat
Phone: 202/482-0128
Room: 4059

Saddlery & Harness Products

Mr. James E. Byron
Phone: 202/482-4034
Room: 3015B

Safety & Security Equip (Trade Promo)
Ms. Laureen Daly
Phone: 202/482-3360

Satellites & Space Vehicles (Marketing)
Ms. Kim Farner
Phone: 202/482-2232
Room: 2104

Satellites, Communications
Ms. Krysten Jenci
Phone: 202/482-2952
Room: 1003

Science & Electronics (Trade Promo)
Mr. Bart Maroni
Phone: 202/482-4125
Room: 2800A

Scientific Instruments (Trade Promo)
Mr. Franc Manzolillo
Phone: 202/482-2991
Room: 1008

Scientific Measurement/Control Equip
Mr. George Litman
Phone: 202/482-3411
Room: 1010

Screw Machine Products
Mr. Richard Reise
Phone: 202/482-3489
Room: 4025

Screws, Washers
Mr. Richard Reise
Phone: 202/482-3489
Room: 4025

Security Management Svcs.
Mr. J. Marc Chittum
Phone: 202/482-0345
Room: 1118

Security/Safety Equip. (Trade Promo)
Ms. Laureen Daly
Phone: 202/482-3360

Semiconductor Manufacturing Equip.
Mr. Mike Andrews
Phone: 202/482-2795

Semiconductors (except Japan)
Ms. Robin Roark
Phone: 202/482-3090
Room: 1012

Semiconductors (Japan)
Ms. Laureen Daly
Phone: 202/482-3360
Room: 1015C

Services Data Base Development
Ms. Jennifer Tallarico
Phone: 202/482-5820
Room: 1118

Shingles (Wood)
Mr. Gary Stanley
Phone: 202/482-0377
Room: 4018

Shipbuilding (Projects)

Mr. Mike Thompson
Phone: 202/482-5126

Shipping
Mr. C. William Johnson
Phone: 202/482-5012
Room: 1112

Shoes
Mr. James E. Byron
Phone: 202/482-4034
Room: 3015B

Silverware
Mr. John M. Harris
Phone: 202/482-1178
Room: 3006

Sisal Products
Mr. John Manger
Phone: 202/482-2732

Small Arms, Ammunition
Mr. John Vanderwolf
Phone: 202/482-0348
Room: 3006

Small Business
Ms. Millie Sjoberg
Phone: 202/482-4792

Snackfood
Mr. Donald Hodgen
Phone: 202/482-3346
Room: 3008

Soaps, Detergent, Cleaners
Mr. William Hurt
Phone: 202/482-0128
Room: 4057

Software
Ms. Heidi C. Hyikata
Phone: 202/482-0571
Room: 2806

Software (Trade Promo)
Ms. Judy A. Fogg
Phone: 202/482-4936
Room: 2132

Solar Cells/Photovoltaic Devices
Mr. Les Garden
Phone: 202/482-0556
Room: 4312

Solar Equip/Ocean/Biomass/Geothermal
Mr. Les Garden
Phone: 202/482-0556
Room: 4312

Soy Products
Mr. Donald Hodgen
Phone: 202/482-3346
Room: 3008

Space Commercialization Eqmt.
Ms. Kim Farner
Phone: 202/482-2232
Room: 2104

Space Policy Development
Ms. Kim Farner
Phone: 202/482-2232
Room: 2104

Space Services

Mr. Ernest Plock
Phone: 202/482-5620

Special Industry Machinery
Mr. Eugene Shaw
Phone: 202/482-3494

Speed Changers
Mr. Richard Reise
Phone: 202/482-3489
Room: 4025

Sporting & Athletic Goods
Mr. John Vanderwolf
Phone: 202/482-0348
Room: 3006

Sporting Goods (Trade Promo)
Ms. Ludene Capone
Phone: 202/482-2087
Room: 3015

Steel Industry
Mr. Charles Bell
Phone: 202/482-0608
Room: 4029B

Steel Markets
Mr. Charles Bell
Phone: 202/482-0608
Room: 4029B

Storage Batteries
Mr. David Larrabee
Phone: 202/482-0607
Room: 4029B

Sugar Products
Mr. Donald Hodgen
Phone: 202/482-3346

Supercomputers
Mr. Wayne Ebenfeld
Phone: 202/482-1987

Switching
Mr. Jason Leuck
Phone: 202/482-4202
Room: 4029

Tea
Mr. Donald Hodgen
Phone: 202/482-3346
Room: 3008

Technology Affairs
Mr. Edwin B. Shykind
Phone: 202/482-4694
Room: 2800A

Telecommunication Services
Ms. Jennifer Tallarico
Phone: 202/482-5820
Room: 1118

Telecommunications
Ms. Krysten Jenci
Phone: 202/482-2952
Room: 1009

**Telecommunications
(Cellular Technology)**
Mr. Richard Paddock
Phone: 202/482-5235
Room: 1009

Telecommunications (Major Proj)

Mr. Richard Paddock
Phone: 202/482-5235
Room: 1009

Telecommunications (Network Eqmt)
Mr. Richard Paddock
Phone: 202/482-5235
Room: 1009

Telecommunications (Terminal Eqmt)
Mr. Nathaniel Cadwell
Phone: 202/482-0399
Room: 1009

Telecommunications (Trade Promo)
Ms. Alexis Kemper
Phone: 202/482-1512

Telecommunications (Wireless)
Ms. Linda Gossack
Phone: 202/482-4523

Teletext Services
Ms. Jennifer Tallarico
Phone: 202/482-5820
Room: 1118

Textile Machinery
Mr. Jon Manger
Phone: 202/482-2732
Room: 4310

Textiles
Ms. Joanne Tucker
Phone: 202/482-4058
Room: 3119

Textiles (Trade Promo)
Mr. Ferenc Molnar
Phone: 202/482-5153
Room: 3109

Timber Products Tropical
Ms. Sue Willis
Phone: 202/482-0577

Tin Products
Mr. John Manger
Phone: 202/482-2732
Room: 4310

Tires
Mr. Raimundo Prat
Phone: 202/482-0128
Room: 4059

Tools/Dies/Jigs/Fixtures
Ms. Megan Pilaroscia
Phone: 202/482-0609

Tourism Services
Mr. Scott Johnson
Phone: 202/482-0140

Toys & Games (Trade Promo)
Mr. Jonathan Freilich
Phone: 202/482-5783
Room: 3015

Transborder Data Flows
Ms. Jennifer Tallarico
Phone: 202/482-5820
Room: 1118

Transformers
Ms. Julie Fouque
Phone: 202/482-2390

Transportation Industries
Mr. C. William Johnson
Phone: 202/482-5012

Transportation Services (Trade Promo)
Mr. C. William Johnson
Phone: 202/482-5012
Room: 1112

Travel Services
Mr. Scott Johnson
Phone: 202/482-0140

Tropical Commodities
Ms. Sue Willis
Phone: 202/482-0577

Trucking Services
Ms. Claudia Wolfe
Phone: 202/482-5086

Trucks, Trailers. Buses, (Trade Promo.)
Mr. John C. White
Phone: 202/482-0671
Room: 4028

Tungsten Products
Mr. John Manger
Phone: 202/482-2732

Turbines, Steam
Mr. John Mearman
Phone: 202/482-0315

Uranium
Mr. Andy Collier
Phone: 202/482-0680
Room: 4329

Used Reconditioned Equipment (Trade Promo)
Mr. John Bodson
Phone: 202/482-0681
Room: 4029

Value Added Telecommunication Svcs.
Ms. Jennifer Tallarico
Phone: 202/482-5820
Room: 1118

Valves, Pipe Fittings (Except Brass)
Mr. Richard Reise
Phone: 202/482-3489
Room: 4025

Vegetables
Mr. Donald Hodgen
Phone: 202/482-3346
Room: 3008

Video Services
Mr. John Siegmund
Phone: 202/482-4781

Videotext Services
Ms. Jennifer Tallarico
Phone: 202/482-5820
Room: 118

Wallets, Billfolds, Flatgoods
Mr. James E. Byron
Phone: 202/482-4034
Room: 3015B

Wastepaper
Mr. Gary Stanley
Phone: 202/482-0375

Room: 4016A

Watches
Mr. John M. Harris
Phone: 202/482-1178
Room: 3006

Water and Sewage Treatment Plants (Major Projects)
Mr. Jay Smith
Phone: 202/482-4642

Water Resource Eqmt
Ms. Denise Carpenter
Phone: 202/482-1500

Water Supply & Distribution
Ms. Denise Carpenter
Phone: 202/482-1500

Welding/Cutting Apparatus
Mr. Edward Abrahams
Phone: 202/482-0312

Windmill Components
Mr. Les Garden
Phone: 202/482-0556
Room: 4312

Wine
Mr. Donald Hodgen
Phone: 202/482-3346
Room: 3008

Wire & Wire Products
Mr. Charles Bell
Phone: 202/482-0608
Room: 4029B

Wire Cloth
Mr. Franklin Williams
Phone: 202/482-0132
Room: 4026

Wire Cloth, Industrial
Mr. Richard Reise
Phone: 202/482-3489
Room: 4025

Wood Containers
Mr. Gary Stanley
Phone: 202/482-0375
Room: 4018

Wood Preserving
Mr. Gary Stanley
Phone: 202/482-0375

Wood Products
Mr. Gary Stanley
Phone: 202/482-0375
Room: 4016

Wood Working Machinery
Mr. Edward Abrahams
Phone: 202/482-0312
Room: 4025

Yarns (Trade Promo)
Mr. Ferenc Molnar
Phone: 202/482-5153
Room: 3109

Yeast
Mr. Donald Hodgen
Phone: 202/482-3346
Room: 3008

©Almanac Publishing, Inc. 1998 - The Washington Almanac of International Trade & Business

Assistant Secretary for
Market Access and Compliance

14th St. & Constitution Ave., NW / Washington DC 20230

WHAT IS MARKET ACCESS AND COMPLIANCE?

From AFGHANISTAN to ZIMBABWE, Market Access and Compliance (MAC) desk officers with expertise in nearly 200 countries provide U.S. businesses, policy makers and legislators with critical, in-depth country-by-country expertise.

MAC works to expand access to overseas markets for U.S. goods and services, increase U.S. exports, enhance worldwide protection of intellectual property rights and U.S. investment, and promote U.S. commercial policy. To remove international commercial barriers, MAC develops policy positions to benefit United States business interests in multilateral negotiations and bilateral consultations.

HOW Market Access and Compliance ASSISTS AMERICAN BUSINESSES:

• Maintains comprehensive, up-to-the-minute information, profiles and analyses on commercial markets worldwide to benefit American businesses and policy makers;

• Provides export counseling;

• Develops international trade and investment policies to reduce trade barriers;

• Monitors foreign compliance with U.S. trade agreements and intellectual property rights and international agreements; and

• Seeks prompt, aggressive action when foreign violations occur.

Acting Assistant Secretary
Mr. Franklin J. Vargo
202/482-3022   Fax: 202/482-5444
Rm. 3868-A

Personal: born 3/11/42 in Pittsburgh, Pa.

Education: MBA, Indiana Univ., 1965.

Professional: 1965-82, career international economist, U.S. Dept. of Commerce: assignments included deputy asst. secretary for policy planning; director of economic research; director of export promotion planning; and deputy director for export strategy. 1982-present, deputy asst. secretary of commerce for Europe; 4/22/97-present, acting asst. secretary of commerce, market access and compliance, U.S. Dept. of Commerce.

A career economist with the U.S. Department of Commerce since 1965, Frank Vargo was named acting assistant secretary of commerce for market access and compliance in the department's International Trade Administration on April 22, 1997. Since 1982, he has held the post of deputy assistant secretary of commerce for Europe. At press time, no nominee for the position had been announced.

The assistant secretary for market access and compliance is responsible for directing the U.S. Department of Commerce's activities aimed at opening foreign markets globally and ensuring that U.S. companies have access to both country and regional markets.

The assistant secretary manages the department's market access and compliance offices for the various regions of the world and the Trade Compliance Center.

As deputy assistant secretary for Europe, Vargo has been responsible for implementing the department's market access and commercial policy activities with Western Europe, Eastern Europe, and the former Soviet Union. Vargo has initiated a variety of innovative programs for the Commerce Department, including the Transatlantic Business Dialogue.

Among the other positions he has held during his career in the International Trade Administration are: deputy assistant secretary for policy planning, director of economic research, director of export promotion planning, and deputy director for export strategy. In addition, Vargo had served as the senior international economist in the office of the secretary of commerce.

Vargo has received the Commerce Department's silver medal and gold medal and has twice received the president's Meritorious Executive Award. He has also been awarded the president's Distinguished Executive award, the highest award that can be received by a career government executive.

Vargo received an MBA degree from Indiana University in 1965. He is married, has four children, and is a resident of McLean, Virginia.

Office of Policy Coordination

Director
Mr. Peter Hale
202/482-5341   Fax: 202/482-5445
Rm. 386AA

Agreements Compliance

Deputy Assistant Secretary
Mr. Douglas C. Olin
202/482-5767
Rm. 3413

Acting Director, Office of Multilateral Affairs
Ms. Judith A. Sever
202/482-0603   Fax: 202/482-5939
Rm. 3513

Director, NAFTA Secretariat
Mr. James Holbein
202/482-5438   FAX 202/482-0148
Rm. 2061

Acting Director, Trade Compliance Center
Ms. Nancy Morgan
202/482-1191
Rm. 3415

Deputy Assistant Secretary for Europe

Acting Deputy Assistant Secretary
Mr. Charles Ludolph
202/482-5638   Fax: 202/482-4098
Rm. 3863

Office of Eastern Europe, Russia and the Newly Independent States

Director
Ms. Suzanne Lotarski
202/482-1104   Fax: 202/482-4505
Rm. 3319

As director of the Office of Eastern Europe, Russia, and the NIS, Susanne Lotarski is responsible for economic information, business assistance, trade policy, and commercial negotiations for the region.

A specialist on communist political and economic systems, Dr. Lotarski has been with the Commerce Department since 1973, where she has served as director of the Eastern European Affairs Division, and deputy and acting director of the People's Republic of China Division during the opening of diplomatic and trade relations with China. She has accompanied seven Secretaries of Commerce to Eastern Europe, the Soviet Union, and China for commercial negotiations.

Prior to joining the Department of Commerce, she taught political science at Vassar College and was a fellow of the Research Institute on communist affairs, directed by Dr. Zbigniew Brzezinski, at Columbia University. She received the Ph.D. degree from Columbia University and B.A. from Vassar college.

Dr. Lotarski has written numerous articles and contributed to books on East-West trade, Eastern European politics, and Chinese foreign policy, including chapters in Anatomy of Communist Revolutions and Gierek's Poland. She is fluent in Russian and Polish.

Business Info. Service for the Newly Independent States
Ms. Anne Grey
202/482-4655
Rm. 7411

Central and Eastern Europe Business Information Center
Mr. Jay Burgess
202/482-5324
Rm. 7412

Special American Business Internship Training Program
Ms. Liesel Duhon
202/482-0073
Rm. 2062

Office of European Union and Regional Affairs

Director
Mr. Charles Ludolph
202/482-5276   Fax: 202/482-2155
Rm. 3036

Charles Ludolph is director of the U.S. Commerce Department's Office of European Union and Regional Affairs. In this position, Ludolph is responsible for developing the Department's trade and investment activities with the European Union. Ludolph's office routinely counsels more than 15,000 U.S. exporters a year on such matters as ISO 9000, labeling of hazardous substances, merger regulations, worker and tax rules and the thousands of EC rules that affect U.S. business and takes U.S. businesses part with the EC Commission to assure market access.

Since 1988, Ludolph has chaired the U.S. government committee on EC1992 standards, testing and certification charges with developing policy toward European standards initiatives. He also chairs the Standards Working Group for the National Export Strategy.

A career international economist with the Department of Commerce since 1971, Ludolph has served in every international program administered by the Department from export promotion to U.S. trade law administration. In 1980, Ludolph was chief economist for the Import Administration which implements U.S. antidumping and countervailing duty laws. In 1983, he took over Commerce programs concerning the European Union and has served in this capacity to date.

Ludolph was born in Waterbury, Connecticut in 1946. He hold an undergraduate degree from Georgetown University as well as an M.B.A. and D.B.A. in international business from the George Washington University. He is on the Dean's Council at the George Washington Business School.

Ludolph is married to the painter-artist Josephine Haden and resides in Arlington, Virginia.

Deputy Asst. Secretary for the Western Hemisphere

Deputy Assistant Secretary
Ms. Regina Vargo
202/482-5324   FAX 202/482-4736
Rm. 3826

Regina K. Vargo is the deputy assistant secretary for the Western Hemisphere. In this capacity, she directs the department's activities on trade and investment policy and on commercial and economic relations with the countries of the region. She is responsible within the department for the implementation of the U.S.-Canada Free Trade Agreement and the North American Free Trade Agreement. She formulates departmental policy on economic integration in Latin America and the Caribbean, including potential NAFTA accession. Her programs provide support to such important departmental initiatives as advocacy, the Big Emerging Markets, and several bilateral Business Development Councils.

Prior to this position, Vargo served as the director of the NAFTA Office where she was instrumental in the negotiation and implementation of the NAFTA. During her tenure, she earned two Gold Medals, the department's highest award. The first medal was for her contribution to the NAFTA negotiations, and the second for her role in developing the Export Mexico program.

Vargo is a graduate of Georgetown University's School of Foreign Service with a major in international economics, who joined the Commerce Department in 1971. She has been involved in numerous trade initiatives, including the Uruguay Round, the U.S.-Canada Free Trade Agreement, trade sanctions under Section 301 and the commercial implications of EC 1992 for U.S. business.

Office of NAFTA and Inter-American Affairs

Acting Director
Mr. Stephen Jacobs
202/482-2314   Fax: 202/482-5865
Rm. 3022

Office of Latin America and the Caribbean

Director
Mr. Walter M. Bastian
202/482-2436   Fax: 202/482-4726
Rm. 3025

Director, Andean and Caribbean Division
Ms. Janice M. Bruce
202/482-4673
Rm. 3033

Deputy Asst. Secretary for Africa and the Near East

Deputy Assistant Secretary
Mr. Judith Barnett
202/482-4925   Fax: 202/482-6083
Rm. 3819

Office of Africa

Director
Ms. Sally K. Miller
202/482-4227   Fax: 202/482-5198
Rm. 2037

Office of the Near East

Director
Mr. Thomas Parker
202/482-1860   Fax: 202/482-0878
Rm. 2029-B

Deputy Asst. Secretary for Asia and the Pacific

Deputy Assistant Secretary
VACANT
202/482-5251   Fax: 202/482-4760
Rm. 3203

Office of China Economic Area

Director
Mr. Donald R. Forest
202/482-5527   Fax: 202/482-1576
Rm. 2317

Office of Korea and Southeast Asia

Director
Ms. Susan Blackman
202/482-1695   Fax: 202/482-4760
Rm. 3203

Director, Korea, Vietnam, Laos and Cambodia Division
Ms. Linda Droker
202/482-3876
Rm. 2308

Office of South Asia and Oceania

Director
Mr. Richard Harding
202/482-2955   Fax: 202/482-5330
Rm. 2308

Policy Director
Mr. Kent Stauffer
202/482-3875
Rm. 2308

Deputy Assistant Secretary for Japan

Acting Deputy Assistant Secretary
Mr. Philip Agress
202/482-4527   Fax: 202/482-0469
Rm. 2318

Office of Japan Trade Policy

Director
Mr. Philip Agress
202/482-1820   FAX: 202/482-0469
Rm. 2320

Office of Japan Commercial Programs/Japan Export Info. Ctr.

Director
Mr. Robert Francis
202/482-2425   FAX: 202/482-0469
Rm. 2328

U.S. and Foreign Commercial Service

14th St. & Constitution Ave., NW / Washington DC 20230

WHAT IS THE U.S. and FOREIGN COMMERCIAL SERVICE?

From ATHENS, Greece to ATHENS, Georgia, the 1,300 men and women of the U.S. and Foreign Commercial Service (US&FCS) promote and protect U.S. business interests abroad. US&FCS is committed to increasing the number of U.S. firms, particularly small- and medium-sized firms, involved in international trade.

US&FCS is a global network — unique among Federal agencies — strategically located in more than 200 cities worldwide to assist U.S. exporters. Overseas, US&FCS is present in 69 countries, which represent more than 95 percent of the world market for U.S. exports. In the United States, US&FCS operates a hub-and-spoke network of 73 District Offices, which offer companies a comprehensive range of export facilitation services in one location.

Many US&FCS export promotion products are designed specifically for small-and medium- sized companies, including our Matchmaker program, which links U.S. firms with a worldwide network of agents and distributors to help U.S. business expand sales to markets around the globe.

HOW THE US&FCS HELPS AMERICAN BUSINESS:

• *Provides advocacy support for U.S. business through government-to-government representation on behalf of U.S. firms vying for contracts abroad.*

• *Supports the National Export Strategy's emphasis on Big Emerging Markets through specialized export counseling and facilitation services including customized market research covering specific industry sectors and current business trends, and location of potential overseas representatives and distributors. These key markets include ten countries — Mexico, Argentina, Brazil, the Chinese Economic Area, India, Indonesia, South Korea, Poland, Turkey and South Africa — which are expected to account for over 40 percent of total global imports over the next 20 years.*

• *Provides export promotion assistance in key industries, including environmental technologies exports and defense conversion assistance.*

US&FCS also provides many essential exporter assistance services, including:

• *Export counseling via a global network;*
• *Trade finance information/support and liaison with Multilateral Development Banks;*
• *Organization and management of trade missions and events;*
• *Hosting and leading U.S. Government and business delegations overseas;*
• *Customized market research for specific business sectors and current business trends;*
• *Credit checks of potential overseas business partners;*
• *Identification of trade leads; and*
• *Certification of organized trade events*

Acting Assistant Secretary of Commerce and Director General
Ms. Marjory E. Searing
202/482-5777   Fax: 202/482-5013
Rm. 3802

Personal: born 3/29/45 in New York, N.Y.

Education: B.A. (Regents Scholarship), Harpur College, 1966. M.A., Georgetown University, 1969. Ph.D. (with distinction), Georgetown University Fellowship, 1972.

Professional: 1968-74, economist, U.S. Dept. of Commerce. 1974-76, international economist; 1976-79, director, office of East-West economic policy, U.S. Department of the Treasury. 1980-82, director of international sector policy; director, office of industry assessment; director, office of multilateral affairs; 1990-present, deputy assistant secretary for Japan; April 1997-present, acting assistant secretary and director general of the U.S. and Foreign Commercial Service, International Trade Administration, U.S. Department of Commerce. Marjory Searing was designated by Secretary of Commerce William Daley as acting assistant secretary of commerce and director general of the U.S. and Foreign Commercial Service in the department's International Trade Administration (ITA) on April 29, 1997. Since 1990, Searing has served as deputy assistant secretary for Japan in ITA. Her predecessor, Lauri Fitz-Pegado, re-joined the private sector in the spring of 1997. At press time, no nominee had been named by The White House.

The office's mission is to promote exports, support U.S. international commercial interests in the United States and abroad, and to assist the U.S. business community in identifying new markets, expanding sales and market share around the globe.

As the Commerce Department's only deputy assistant secretary assigned to one country, Searing's appointment in December 1990 signified the importance of U.S.-Japan trade relations. As the department's principal policy adviser on U.S.-Japan trade issues, she directed the development of economic, commercial, and trade policy, as well as other programs related to Japan. Her office was also responsible for analyzing Japanese economic and political developments.

Searing was a key player in the U.S.-Japan Framework Agreement reached by the Clinton administration and the government of Japan in 1993. She was a lead negotiator in the talks that led to the 1994 construction and medical equipment agreements, and the automotive agreement signed by the two countries in June 1995. She also was re-sponsible for across-the-board monitoring of other sections of the Framework Agreement, including flat glass, telecommunications, pharmaceuticals, and semiconductors.

Since joining the Commerce Department in 1967, Searing has held various positions. Before her appointment as deputy assistant secretary, she was the director of the office of multilateral affairs, where she was responsible for managing the department's participation in the Uruguay Round of GATT negotiations. She also was director of the office of industrial assessment and director of international sector policy.

Executive Assistant
Mr. Noel Nigretti
202/482-5777
Rm. 3802

Director, Human Resources Development Staff
Mr. Scott Bozek
202/482-2392   Fax: 202/482-1629
Rm. 3813

Acting Director, Office of Foreign Service Personnel
Ms. Nancy Kripner
202/482-2368   Fax: 202/482-1629
Rm. 3226

Acting Director, Office of Information Systems
Mr. Thomas Kelsey
202/482-5291   Fax: 202/482-0251
Rm. 1848

Director, Office of Planning
Mr. Scott Bozek
202/482-4996   Fax: 202/482-2391
Rm. 3809

Deputy Asst. Secretary for International Operations

Deputy Assistant Secretary
Ms. Dolores F. Harrod
202/482-6228   Fax: 202/482-3159
Rm. 3130

Director, Western Hemisphere
Mr. Richard Lenahan
202/482-2736   Fax: 202/482-3159
Rm. 3130

Director, Europe
Mr. James Wilson
202/482-1599   Fax: 202/482-3159
Rm. 3130

Acting Director, Africa/Near East/South Asia
Ms. Jenelle Matheson
202/482-4836   Fax: 202/482-5179
Rm. 1223

Director, East Asia and the Pacific
Ms. Alice Davenport
202/482-2422   Fax: 202/482-5179
Rm. 1229

Director, Multilateral Development Bank Operations
Ms. Janet Thomas
202/482-3399   Fax: 202/273-0927
Rm. 1107

Director, World Bank Liaison
Mr. Charles Kestenbaum
202/458-0120   Fax: 202/477-2967

U.S. and Foreign Commercial Service Posts Abroad

INTRODUCTION

Administered by the USFCS, Commercial Officers are located at U.S. embassies around the globe. These officers advise U.S. businesses on local trade and tariff laws, government procurement procedures, and business practices; identify potential importers, agents, distributors, and joint venture partners; provide information on local government tenders; and assist with resolution of trade and investment disputes.

NOTE: Changes occur frequently. When contacting address inquiries to the senior commercial officer.

Algeria

Post: American Embassy Algiers
Phone: 011-213-2-60-39-73
Fax: 011-213-2-69-39-79
Workweek: Saturday-Wednesday
Street Address: 4 Chemin Cheich Bachir Brahimi
Mailing Address:
U.S. Dept. of State (Algiers)
Washington, DC 20521-6030

Armenia

Post: American Embassy Yerevan
Phone: 011-3742-151-144
Fax: 011-3742-151-138
Street Address: 18 Gen Bagramian
Mailing Address:
U.S. Dept. of State (Yerevan)
Washington, DC 20521-7020

Argentina

Post: American Embassy Buenos Aires
Phone: 011-54-1-777-4533 ext. 2226
Fax: 011-54-1-777-0673
Street Address: 4300 Colombia 1425
Mailing Address:
Unit 4334 APO AA 34034

Australia

Post: American Consulate General Sydney
Phone: 011-612-9373-9200
Fax: 011-612-9221-0573
Street Address:
Hyde Park Tower—36th Fl., Park & Elizabeth Streets
Mailing Address:
Unit 11024 APO AP 96554-0002
E-mail: OSydney@doc.gov

Post: American Consulate Brisbane
Phone: 011-61-7-831-3330
Fax: 011-61-7-832-6247
Street Address: 383 Wickham Terrace
Mailing Address:
Unit 11018 APO AP 96553-0002

Post: American Consulate General Melbourne
Phone: 011-613-9526-5925 Fax: 011-613-9510-4660
Street Address: 553 St. Kilda Road
Mailing Address:
Unit 11011 APO AP 96551-0002
E-mail: OMelbour@doc.gov

Post: American Consulate Gen. Perth
Phone: 011-61-9-231-9410
Fax: 011-61-9-231-9444
Street Address: 16 St. George's Terrace, 13th Floor
Mailing Address:
Unit 11021 APO AP 96553-0002

Austria

Post: American Embassy Vienna
Phone: 011-431-313-39-2296
Fax: 011-431-310-6917
Street Address:
Boltzmanngasse 16, A-1091

Azerbaijan

Post: American Embassy Baku
Phone: 011-9-9412-98-03-35
Fax: 011-9-9412-96-04-69
Street Address: Azadliq Prospetati 83
Mailing Address:
U.S. Dept. of State (Baku)
Washington, D.C. 20521-7050

Belarus

Post: American Embassy Minsk
Phone: 011-375-172-31-50-00
Fax: 011-375-172-34-78-53
Street Address:
Starivilenskaya 346-220002
Mailing Address:
U.S. Dept. of State (Minsk)
Washington, D.C. 20521-7010

Belgium

Post: American Embassy Brussels
Phone: 011-32-2-508-2425
Fax: 011-32-2-512-6653
Street Address: 27 Boulevard du Regent
Mailing Address:
PSC 82, Box 002
APO AE 09724-1015

Post: US Mission to the European Community (Brussels)
Phone: 011-32-2-513-2746
Fax: 011-32-2-513-1228
Street Address: 40 Blvd du Regent, B-1000
Mailing Address:
PSC 82, Box 002
APO AE 09724

Bosnia

Post: American Embassy Sarajevo
Phone: 011-387-71-445-700
Fax: 011-387-71-659-722
Street Address: 43 ul. Dure, Dakovica
Mailing Address:
U.S. Dept. of State (Sarajevo)
Washington, D.C. 20521-7030

Brazil

Post: American Consulate General Sao Paulo
Phone: 011-55-11-853-2811
Fax: 011-55-11-853-2744
Street Address: Rua Estados Unidos 1812
Mailing Address:
APO AA 34030-0002

Post: American Consular Agency Belem
Phone: 011-55-91-223-0800
Fax: 011-55-91-223-0413
Mailing Address:
APO AA 34030

Post: American Consular Agency Belo Horizonte
Phone: 011-55-31-213-1571
Fax: 011-55-31-213-1575
Street Address: Minas Trade Center Rua Timbiras, 1200, 7th Floor
Mailing Address:
APO AA 34030-3505

Post: American Embassy Brasilia
Phone: 011-55-61-321-7272
Fax: 011-55-61-225-3981
Street Address:
Avenida das Nocoes, Lote 3
Mailing Address:
Unit 3500 APO AA 34030

Post: American Consulate General Rio de Janeiro
Phone: 011-55-21-292-7117
Fax: 011-55-21-240-9738
Street Address: Avenida Presidente Wilson, 147 Castelo
Mailing Address:
APO AA 34030

Bulgaria

Post: American Embassy Sofia
Phone: 011-359-2-980-5241
Fax: 011-359-2-980-68-50
Street Address: 1 Saborna Street
Mailing Address:
Unit 1335
APO AE 09213-1335

Canada

Post: American Embassy Ottawa
Phone: 1-613-238-5335
Fax: 1-613-238-5999
Street Address:
World Exchange Plaza, 45 O'Connor, Suite 1140 - Postal Code K1P-1A4
Mailing Address:
P.O. Box 5000
Ogdensburg, NY 13669-0430

Post: American Consulate General Calgary
Phone: 1-403-266-8962
Fax: 1-403-266-6630
Street Address:
615 MacLeod Trail S.E. Room 1050
Mailing Address:
c/o AmEmbassy Ottawa
P.O. Box 5000
Ogdensburg, NY 13669

Post: American Consulate General Halifax
Phone: 1-902-429-2480
Fax: 1-902-429-7690
Street Address:
Suite 910, Cogswell
Tower Scotia Square
Halifax Nova Scotia B3J 3K1
Mailing Address:

c/o AmEmbassy Ottawa
P.O. Box 5000
Ogdensburg, NY 13669

**Post: American Consulate General
Montreal**
Phone: 1-514-398-9695
Fax: 1-514-398-0711
Street Address:
455 Rene Levesque Blvd., 19th Floor
Montreal, Quebec, H2Z-1Z2
Mailing Address:
P.O. Box 847
Champlain, NY 12919-0847

**Post: American Consulate General
Toronto**
Phone: 1-416-595-1700
Fax: 1-416-595-0051
Street Address:
360 University Avenue, Suite 602
Toronto, Ontario, M5G-1S4
Mailing Address:
P.O. Box 135
Lewiston, NY 14092

**Post: American Consulate General
Vancouver**
Phone: 1-604-685-4311
Fax: 1-604-687-6095
Street Address:
1095 West Pender Street, 20th Floor
Vancouver, British Columbia, V6E-2M6
Mailing Address:
P.O. Box 5002
Point Roberts, Washington 98281-5002

Chile

Post: American Embassy Santiago
Phone: 011-56-2-330-3310
Fax: 011-56-2-330-3172
Street Address:
Andres Bello 2800, Los Condes
Mailing Address:
Unit 4111, APO AA 34033

China

Post: American Embassy Beijing
Phone: 011-86-10-6532-6924
Fax: 011-86-10-6532-3297
Street Address: Xiu Shui Bei Jie 3
Mailing Address:
PSC 461 Box 50
FPO AP 96521-0002
E-mail: OBeijing@doc.gov

**Post: American Consulate General
Chengdu**
Phone: 011-86-28-558-9642
Fax: 011-86-28-558-9221
Street Address:
No. 1 South Shamian
St. Shamian Island
Mailing Address:
PSC 461 Box 100
FPO AP 96521-0002
E-mail: uscscd@public.cd.sc.cn

**Post: American Consulate General
Guangzhou**
Phone: 011-86-20-8667-4011
Fax: 011-86-20-8666-6409

Street Address:
China Hotel 14/F
Liu Hua Road
Mailing Address:
PSC 461 Box 100
FPO AP 96521-0002
E-mail: OGuangzh@doc.gov

**Post: American Consulate General
Shanghai**
Phone: 011-86-21-6279-7630
Fax: 011-86-21-6279-7639
Street Address:
1469 Huai Hai Middle Road
Mailing Address:
PSC 461 Box 200
FPO AP 96521-0002
E-mail: OShangha@doc.gov

Post: U.S. Commercial Center Shanghai
Phone: 011-86-21-6279-7640
Fax: 011-86-21-6279-7639
Street Address:
Shanghai Centre Suite 631, East Tower
1376 Nanjing Xi Lu
E-mail: AChang1@doc.gov

**Post: American Consulate General
Shenyang**
Phone: 011-86-21-6279-7640
Fax: 011-86-21-6279-7649
Street Address:
40 Lane 4, Section 5
Sanjing Street, Heping District
Mailing Address:
PSC 461 Box 45
FPO AP 96521-0002

Colombia

Post: American Embassy Bogota
Phone: 011-57-1-315-2126 ext. 2684
Fax: 011-57-1-315-2171
Street Address:
Calle 22 D bis No. 47-51
Santa Fe de Bogota
Mailing Address:
Unit 5120
APO AA 34038

Costa Rica

Post: American Embassy San Jose
Phone: 011-506-220-2454/3939
Fax: 011-506-231-4783
Street Address:
Embajada de los Estados Unidos,
Frente al Centro, Commercial del Oeste,
Unit 2508, Pavas,
San Jose, Costa Rica
Mailing Address: APO AA 34020

Cote d'Ivoire

Post: American Embassy Abidjan
Phone: 011-225-21-4616
Fax: 011-225-22-2437
Street Address: 0 I.B.P. 1712
Mailing Address:
U.S. Dept of State (Abidjan)
Washington DC 20521-2010

Croatia

Post: American Embassy Zagreb
Phone: 011-359-2-980-5241
Fax: 011-359-2-981-8977
Street Address: Andrije Hebranga 2
Mailing Address:
Unit 345
APO AE 09213-1345

Czech Republic

Post: American Embassy Prague
Phone: 011-422-2421-9844
Fax: 011-422-2421-9965
Street Address:
Hybernska 7a 117
16 Praha 1
Mailing Address:
U.S. Dept. of State (Prague)
Washington, D.C. 20521-5630

Denmark

Post: American Embassy Copenhagen
Phone: 011-45-3142-3144
Fax: 011-45-3142-0175
Street Address:
Dag Hammarskjolds Alle 24
Mailing Address: APO AE 09176

Dominican Republic

Post: American Embassy Santo Domingo
Phone: 1-809-221-2171
Fax: 1-809-688-4838
Street Address:
Corner of Calle Cesar Nicolas
Penson & Calle
Leopoldo Navarro
Mailing Address:
Unit 5515
APO AA 34041-0008

Ecuador

Post: American Embassy Quito
Phone: 011-593-2-561-404
Fax: 011-593-2-504-550
Street Address: Avenida 12 de Octubre y
Avenida Patria
Mailing Address:
Unit 5334
APO AA 34039-3420

**Post: American Consulate General
Guayaquil**
Phone: 011-593-4-323-570
Fax: 011-593-4-325-286
Street Address: 9 de Octubre y
Garcia Moreno
Mailing Address: APO AA 34039

Egypt

Post: American Embassy Cairo
Phone: 011-20-2-357-2340
Fax: 011-20-2-355-8368

Workweek: Sunday-Thursday
Street Address:
   3 Lazougi Street Garden City, Cairo
Mailing Address:
   Unit 64900 Box 11
   APO AE 09839-4900

**Post: American Consulate General
   Alexandria**
Phone: 011-20-3-482-5607
Fax: 011-20-3-482-9199
Street Address: 3 El Faranna Street
Mailing Address:
   Unit 64900, Box 24
   FPO AE 09839-4900

Finland

Post: American Embassy Helsinki
Phone: 011-358-9-171-931
Fax: 011-358-9-635-332
Street Address: Itainen Puistotie 14ASF
Mailing Address: APO AE 09723

France

Post: American Embassy Paris
Phone: 011-33-1-4312-2370
Fax: 011-33-1-4312-2172
Street Address: 2 Avenue Gabriel
Mailing Address: APO AE 09777

Post: US Mission to the OECD (Paris)
Phone: 011-33-1-4524-7437
Fax: 011-33-1-4524-7410
Street Address:
   19 Rue de Franqueville
   75016 Paris
Mailing Address: APO AE 09777

Post: American Consulate General Lyon
Phone: 011-33-472-407-220
Fax: 011-33-478-391-409
Street Address: 7 Quai General Sarrail
Mailing Address:
   c/o American Embassy Paris
   APO AE 09777

**Post: American Consulate General
   Marseille**
Phone: 011-33-491-549-200
Fax: 011-33-491-550-947
Street Address: 12 Boulevard Paul Peytral
Mailing Address:
   c/o American Embassy Paris
   APO AE 09777

**Post: American Consulate General
   Strasbourg**
Phone: 011-33-88-35-31-04
Fax: 011-33-88-24-06-95
Street Address: 15 Avenue d'Alsace
Mailing Address:
   c/o American Embassy Paris
   Unit 21551
   APO AE 09777

Georgia

Post: American Embassy Tbilisi
Phone: 011-995-32-989-967
Fax: 011-995-32-933-759
Street Address: 25 Atoneli

Mailing Address:
   U.S. Dept. of State (Tbilisi)
   Washington, D.C. 20521-7060

Germany

Post: American Embassy Bonn
Phone: 011-49-228-339-2895
Fax: 011-49-228-334-649
Street Address: Deichmanns Ave 29
Mailing Address:
   Unit 21701 Box 53170
   Bonn APO AE 09080

Post: American Embassy Office Berlin
Phone: 011-49-30-238-5174
Fax: 011-49-30-238-6290
Street Address:
   Neustaedtische Kirchstrasse 4-5
   10117 Berlin
Mailing Address:
   Unit 10117
   APO AE 09235-5500

**Post: U.S. Commercial Office
   Dusseldorf**
Phone: 011-49-211-431-744
Fax: 011-49-211-431-431
Street Address: Emmanual Lutz Str. 1B
Mailing Address:
   Unit 21701 Box 30
   APO AE 09080

**Post: American Consulate General
   Frankfurt**
Phone: 011-49-69-956-79-013
Fax: 011-49-69-561-114
Street Address:
   Platenstrasse 1 60320
   Frankfurt/Main
Mailing Address:
   PSC 115
   APO AE 09213-0115

**Post: American Consulate General
   Hamburg**
Phone: 011-49-40-4117-1304
Fax: 011-49-40-410-6598
Street Address: Alsterufer 27/28, 20354
Mailing Address:
   U.S. Dept. of State (Hamburg)
   Washington, D.C. 20521-5180

**Post: American Consulate General
   Leipzig**
Phone: 011-49-341-213-8421
Fax: 011-49-341-213-8441
Street Address:
   Wilhelm-Seyfferth-Strasse 4
   04107 Leipzig
Mailing Address:
   PSC 120, Box 1000
   APO AE 09265

**Post: American Consulate General
   Munich**
Phone: 011-49-89-2888-748
Fax: 011-49-89-285-261
Street Address: Koeniginstrasse 5
Mailing Address: APO AE 09178

Greece

Post: American Embassy Athens

Phone: 011-30-1-729-4302
Fax: 011-30-1-721-8660
Street Address: 91 Vasilissia Sophias Blvd.
Mailing Address: PSC 108 APO AE 09482

Guatemala

Post: American Embassy Guatemala
Phone: 011-502-3-31-1541 ext. 259
Fax: 011-502-3-31-7373
Street Address:
   7-01 Avenida de la Reforma, Zona 10
Mailing Address: Unit 3306, APO AA
34024

Honduras

Post: American Embassy Tegucigalpa
Phone: 011-504-36-9230/38-5114
Fax: 011-504-38-2888
Street Address: Avenido La Paz
Mailing Address: APO AA 34022

Hong Kong

**Post: American Consulate General
   Hong Kong**
Phone: 011-85-22-521-1467
Fax: 011-85-22-845-9800
Street Address: 26 Garden Road 17th Floor
Mailing Address:
   PSC 464 Box 30
   FPO AP 96522-0002
E-mail: OHongKon@doc.gov

Hungary

Post: American Embassy Budapest
Phone: 011-36-1-302-6100
Fax: 011-36-1-302-0089 or 0091
Street Address: V. Szabadsag Ter 7
Mailing Address:
   U.S. Dept. of State (Budapest)
   Washington, D.C. 20521-5270

India

Post: American Embassy New Delhi
Phone: 011-91-11-611-3033
Fax: 011-91-11-419-0025
Street Address:
   Shanti Path, Chanakyapuri 110021
Mailing Address:
   U.S. Dept. of State (New Delhi)
   Washington, DC 20521-9000

**Post: Commercial Office, US&FCS
   Bangalore**
Phone: 011-91-80-558-1452
Fax: 011-91-80-558-3630
Mailing Address:
   W-202, 2nd Floor, West Wing, Sunrise
Chambers
   22 Ulsoor Road
   Bangalore 560 042

**Post: American Consulate General
   Calcutta**
Phone: 011-91-33-242-1074
Fax: 011-91-33-242-2335

Street Address:
  5/1 Ho Chi Minh Sarani
  Calcutta 700071
Mailing Address:
  U.S. Dept. of State (Calcutta)
  Washington, DC 20521-6250

Post: American Consulate Gen. Chennai
Phone: 011-91-44-827-7542
Fax: 011-91-44-827-0240
Street Address:
  220 Mount Road, Chennai 600006
Mailing Address:
  U.S. Dept. of State (Chennai)
  Washington, DC 20521-6260

**Post: American Consulate General
  Mumbai (Formerly Bombay)**
Phone: 011-91-22-265-2511
Fax: 011-91-22-262-3851/3850
Street Address:
  4, New Marine Lines
  Mumbai 400020
Mailing Address:
  U.S. Dept. of State (Bombay)
  Washington, DC 20521-6240

Indonesia

Post: American Embassy Jakarta
Phone: 011-62-21-344-2211
Fax: 011-62-21-385-1632
Street Address: Medan Merdeka Selatan 5
Mailing Address: Box 1, APO AP 96520
E-mail: OJakarta@doc.gov

Post: U.S. Commercial Center Jakarta
Phone: 011-62-21-526-2850
Fax: 011-62-21-526-2855
Street Address:
  World Trade Center Wisma
  Metropolital II,
  3rd Floor Jalan Jenral Sudiman 29-31
  Jakarta 12920
E-mail: OJakart1@doc.gov

**Post: American Consulate General
  Surabaya**
Phone: 011-62-31-561923/5676880
Fax: 011-62-31-5677748/5674492
Street Address:
  Jalan Raya Dr.
  Sutomo 33 Box 18131
Mailing Address: APO AP 96520
Email: OSurabay@doc.gov

Ireland

Post: American Embassy Dublin
Phone: 011-353-1-667-4755

Fax: 011-353-1-667-4754
Street Address: 42 Elgin Rd., Ballsbridge
Mailing Address:
  U.S. Dept. of State (Dublin)
  Washington, DC 20521-5290

Israel

Post: American Embassy Tel Aviv
Phone: 011-972-3-519-7327
Fax: 011-972-3-510-7215
Street Address: 71 Rehov, Tel Aviv 63432
Mailing Address:
  PSC 98, Box 100
  APO AE 09830

Italy

Post: American Embassy Rome
Phone: 011-39-6-46741
Fax: 011-4674-2113
Street Address: Via Veneto 119/A
Mailing Address: PSC 59, APO AE 09624

**Post: American Consulate General
  Florence**
Phone: 011-39-55-211-676
Fax: 011-39-55-283-780
Street Address: Lungarno Amerigo
Vespucci 38
Mailing Address: APO AE 09624

Post: American Consulate Gen. Genoa
Phone: 011-39-10-247-1412
Fax: 011-39-10-290-027
Street Address:
  Banca d'Americae d'Italia Building
  Piazza Portello
Mailing Address:
  PSC 59 Box G
  APO AE 09624

Post: American Consulate Gen. Milan
Phone: 011-39-2-6592-260
Fax: 011-39-2-6592-561
Street Address:
  Via Principe Amerdeo 2/10
  20121 Miliano
Mailing Address:
  PSC 59 Box M
  APO AE 09624

Post: American Consulate Gen. Naples
Phone: 011-39-81-761-1592
Fax: 011-39-81-761-1869
Street Address: Piazza della Repubblica
Mailing Address:
  PSC 810 Box 18
  FPO AE 09619-0002

Jamaica

Post: American Embassy Kingston
Phone: 1-876-926-8115
Fax: 1-809-920-2580
Street Address:
  Jamaica Mutual Life Center
  2 Oxford Road 3rd Floor
  Kingston 5
Mailing Address:
  U.S. Dept. of State (Kingston)
  Washington DC 20521-3210

Japan

Post: American Embassy Tokyo
Phone: 011-81-3-3224-5060
Fax: 011-81-3-3589-4235
Street Address:
  1-10-5 Akasaka
  1-chome Minato-ku (107)
Mailing Address:
  Unit 45004 Box 204
  APO AP 96337-5004
E-mail: OTokyo@doc.gov

Post: U.S. Trade Center Tokyo
Phone: 011-81-3-3987-2441
Fax: 011-81-3-3987-2447
Street Address:
  7th Fl., World Import Mart
  1-3 Higoshi Ikebukuro
  3-chome Toshima-ku
  Tokyo 170
Mailing Address:
  Unit 45004 Box 258
  APO AP 96337-0001
E-mail: OTokyo1@doc.gov

Post: American Consulate Fukuoka
Phone: 011-81-92-751-9331
Fax: 011-81-92-713-9222
Street Address:
  5-26 Ohori 2-chome Chuo-ku
  Fukuoka-810
Mailing Address:
  Box 10
  FPO AP 98766

Post: American Consulate Nagoya
Phone: 011-81-52-203-4277
Fax: 011-81-52-201-4612
Street Address:
  10-33 Nishiki 3-chome Naka-ku
  Nagoya 460, Japan
Mailing Address:
  c/o AmEmbassy Tokyo
  Unit 45004, Box 280
  APO AP 96337-0001
E-mail: ONagoya@doc.gov

**Post: American Consulate General
  Osaka-Kobe**
Phone: 011-81-6-315-5957
Fax: 011-81-6-315-5963
Street Address:
  11-5, Nishitnma 2-Chrome Kita-Ku
  Osaka (530)
Mailing Address:
  Unit 45004 Box 239
  APO AP 96337-0002
E-mail: OOsakaKo@doc.gov

Post: American Consulate Sapporo
Phone: 011-81-11-641-1115
Fax: 011-81-11-643-1283
Street Address:
  Kita 1-Jo Nishi 28-chome Chuoku
  Sapporo 064
Mailing Address: APO AP 96337-0003

Kazakhstan

Post: American Embassy Almaty
Phone: 011-7-3275-81-15-77
Fax: 011-7-3275-81-15-76
Street Address:

99/97 Furmanova Street
Almaty, 480012
Mailing Address:
  U.S. Dept. of State (Almaty)
  Washington, D.C. 20521-7030

Kenya

Post: American Embassy Nairobi
Phone: 011-254-2-212-354
Fax: 011-254-2-216-648
Street Address: Moi/Haile Selassie Ave.
Mailing Address:
  P.O. Box 30137, Unit 64100
  APO AE 09831

Korea

Post: American Embassy Seoul
Phone: 011-82-2-397-4535
Fax: 011-82-2-739-1628
Street Address: 82 Sejong-Ro Chongro-Ku
Mailing Address:
  Unit 15550
  APO AP 96205-0001
E-mail: OSeoul@doc.gov

Kuwait

Post: American Embassy Kuwait
Phone: 011-965-539-6362/5307
Fax: 011-965-538-0281
Workweek: Saturday-Wednesday
Street Address:
  Al Masjeed Al Aqsa
  Street Plot 14, Block 14
  Bayan Plan 3602
Mailing Address:
  Unit 6900 Box 10
  APO AE 09880-9000

Macedonia

Post: American Embassy Skopje
Phone: 011-389-91-116-180
Fax: 011-389-91-117-103
Street Address:
  Bul Linden BB
  9100 Skopje
Mailing Address:
  U.S. Dept. of State (Skopje)
  Washington, D.C. 20521-7120

Malaysia

Post: American Embassy Kuala Lumpur
Phone: 011-603-457-2724
Fax: 011-603-242-1866
Street Address: 376 Jalan Tun Razak
Mailing Address: APO AP 96535-5000

Mexico

Post: American Embassy Mexico
Phone: 011-52-5-209-9100
Fax: 011-52-5-207-8837
Street Address:
  Paseo de la Reforma 305

Colonia Cuauhtemoc
06500 Mexico, D.F. Mexico
Mailing Address:
  P.O. Box 3087
  Laredo, TX 78044-3087

Post: U.S. Trade Center Mexico
Phone: 011-52-5-591-0155
Fax: 011-52-5-566-1115
Street Address:
  Liverpool 31, Co. Juarez,
  06600 Mexico, D.F. Mexico
Mailing Address:
  P.O. Box 3087
  Laredo, TX 78044-3087

**Post: American Consulate General
  Guadalajara**
Phone: 011-52-3-825-2700, ext. 371
Fax: 011-52-3-826-3576
Street Address: Jal. Progreso 175
Mailing Address:
  P.O. Box 3088
  Laredo, TX 78044-3098

**Post: American Consulate General
  Monterrey**
Phone: 011-52-83-45-2120
Fax: 011-52-83-45-5172/343-4440
Street Address:
  N.L. Avenida Constitucion
  411 Poniente
Mailing Address:
  P.O. Box 3098
  Laredo, TX 78044-3098

Morocco

**Post: American Consulate General
  Casablanca**
Phone: 011-212-2-26-45-50
Fax: 011-212-2-22-02-59
Street Address: 8 Blvd. Moulay Youssef
Mailing Address:
  PSC 74, Box 24
  APO AE 09718

Post: American Embassy Rabat
Phone: 011-212-7-622-65
Fax: 011-212-7-656-61
Street Address: 2 Ave de Marrakech
Mailing Address:
  PSC 74 Box 003
  APO AE 09718

Netherlands

Post: American Embassy The Hague
Phone: 011-31-70-310-9417
Fax: 011-31-70-363-2985
Street Address: Lange Voorhout 102
Mailing Address:
  PSC 71 Box 1000
  APO AE 09715

**Post: American Consulate General
  Amsterdam**
Phone: 011-31-20-575-5351
Fax: 011-31-20-575-5350
Street Address: Museumplein 19
Mailing Address:
  Box 1000 APO AE 09715

New Zealand

**Post: American Consulate General
  Auckland**
Phone: 011-649-303-2038
Fax: 011-649-302-3156
Street Address:
  4th Floor Yorkshire General Bldg.
  Shortland and O'Connell Streets
Mailing Address:
  PSC 467 Box 99
  FPO AP 96531-1099
E-mail: OAucklan@doc.gov

Post: American Embassy Wellington
Phone: 011-644-472-2068
Fax: 011-644-471-2380
Street Address:
  29 Fitzherbert Terr., Thorndon
Mailing Address:
  PSC 467 Box 1
  FPO AP 96531-1001

Nigeria

Post: American Embassy Lagos
Phone: 011-234-1-261-0078 ext. 383
Fax: 011-234-1-261-9856
Street Address:
  2 Eleke Crescent, Victoria Island
Mailing Address:
  U.S. Dept. of State (Lagos)
  Washington DC 20521-8300

Norway

Post: American Embassy Oslo
Phone: 011-47-22-44-8550
Fax: 011-47-22-55-8803
Street Address: Drammensveien 18
Mailing Address:
  PSC 69 Box 1000
  APO AE 09707

Pakistan

Post: American Embassy Islamabad
Phone: 011-92-51-826-161
Fax: 011-92-51-823-981
Workweek: Sunday-Thursday
Street Address:
  Diplomatic Enclave, Ramna 5
Mailing Address:
  P.O. Box 1048, Unit 6220
  APO AE 09812-2200

Post: American Consulate Gen. Lahore
Phone: 011-92-42-636-5530
Fax: 011-92-42-636-5177
Workweek: Sunday-Thursday
Street Address: 50 Shahrah-E-Bin Badees
Mailing Address:
  Unit 62216
  APO AE 09812-2216

Panama

Post: American Embassy Panama
Phone: 011-507-227-1777
Fax: 011-507-227-1713

Street Address:
' Avenida Balboa Y Calle 38
Apartado 6959
Mailing Address:
Unit 0945
APO AA 34002

Peru

Post: American Embassy Lima
Phone: 011-51-1-434-3040
Fax: 011-51-1-434-3041
Street Address:
Avenida la Encalada Cuadro 17
Lima 33
Mailing Address:
Unit 3780
APO AA 34031

Philippines

Post: American Embassy Manila
Phone: 011-632-890-9362
Fax: 011-632-895-3028
Street Address:
395 Senator Gil Puyat Ave.
Extension Makati
Mailing Address: APO AP 96440
E-mail: OManila@doc.gov

Poland

Post: American Embassy Warsaw
Phone: 011-48-2-628-3041
Fax: 011-48-2-628-8298
Street Address: Aleje Ujazdowskle 29/31
Mailing Address:
c/o AmConGen (WAW) Unit 1340
APO AE 09213-1340

Post: U.S. Trade Center Warsaw
Phone: 011-48-2-621-4515
Fax: 011-48-2-621-6327
Street Address:
Aleje Jerozolimski 56C
IKEA Building, 2nd Floor
00-803 Warsaw

Portugal

Post: American Embassy Lisbon
Phone: 011-351-1-727-5086
Fax: 011-351-1-726-8914
Street Address:
Avenida das Forcas Armadas
Mailing Address:
PSC 83 Box FCS
APO AE 09726

Post: American Business Center Oporto
Phone: 011-351-2-606-3094
Fax: 011-351-2-600-2737
Street Address:
Apartado No. 88
Rua Julio Dinis 826 3rd Floor
Mailing Address:
c/o AmEmbassy Lisbon
APO AE 09726

Romania

Post: American Embassy Bucharest
Phone: 011-40-1-210-4042
Fax: 011-40-1-210-0690
Street Address: Strada Tudor Arghezi 7-9
Mailing Address:
The Commercial Service
U.S. Embassy (Bucharest-5260)
C/O U.S. Department of State
Washington, D.C. 20521-5260

Russia

Post: American Embassy Moscow
Phone: 011-7-502-224-1105
Fax: 011-7-402-224-1106
Street Address: Novinsky Bulvar 19/23
Mailing Address: APO AE 09721

**Post: American Consulate General
St. Petersburg**
Phone: 011-7-812-850-1902
Fax: 011-7-812-850-1903
Street Address: Furshatskaya 15
Mailing Address: Box L APO AE 09723

**Post: American Consulate General
Vladivostok**
Phone: 011-7-4232-268-458
Fax: 011-7-4232-268-445
Street Address: Ulitsa Mordovtseva 12
Mailing Address: APO AE 09721

Saudi Arabia

Post: American Embassy Riyadh
Phone: 011-966-1-488-3800
Fax: 011-966-1-488-3237
Workweek: Saturday-Wednesday
Street Address:
Collector Road M, Diplomatic Quarter
Mailing Address:
Unit 61307
APO AE 09803-1307

Post: American Consulate Gen. Dhahran
Phone: 011-966-3-891-3200
Fax: 011-966-3-891-8332
Workweek: Saturday-Wednesday
Street Address:
P.O. Box 81
Dhahran Airport, 31932
Mailing Address:
Unit 66803
APO AE 09858-6803

Post: American Consulate Gen. Jeddah
Phone: 011-966-2-667-0040
Fax: 011-966-2-665-8106
Workweek: Saturday-Wednesday
Street Address:
Palestine Road Ruwais
P.O. Box 149
Mailing Address:
Unit 62112
APO AE 09811-2112

Singapore

Post: American Embassy Singapore

Phone: 011-65-476-9037
Fax: 011-65-476-9080
Street Address: 27 Napier Road
Mailing Address: FPO AP 96534-0001
E-mail: OSingapo@doc.gov

Slovak Republic

Post: American Embassy Bratislava
Phone: 011-421-7-533-0861
Fax: 011-421-7-335-096
Street Address:
Hviezdoslavovo Namestie 4
81102 Bratislava
Mailing Address:
U.S. Dept. of State (Bratislava)
Washington, D.C. 20521-5840

**Post: American Business Center
Bratislava**
Phone: 011-421-7-361-079
Fax: 011-421-7-361-085
Street Address:
Grosslingova 35
81109 Bratislava

South Africa

**Post: American Consulate General
Johannesburg**
Phone: 011-27-11-442-3571
Fax: 011-27-11-442-3770
Street Address:
1 Commercial Service Office
15 Chaplin Road
Illovo 2196
Mailing Address:
U.S. Dept. of State (Johannesburg)
Washington DC 20521-2500
Mailing Address (Int'l):
P.O. Box 2155
Johannesburg 2000, South Africa

**Post: American Consulate General
Cape Town**
Phone: 011-27-21-214-269
Fax: 011-27-21-254-151
Street Address:
Broadway Industries Center
Herrengracht, Foreshore
Mailing Address:
U.S. Dept. of State (Cape Town)
Washington DC 20521-2480

Spain

Post: American Embassy Madrid
Phone: 011-34-91-564-8976
Fax: 011-34-91-563-0859
Street Address: Serrano 75
Mailing Address:
PSC 61 Box 0021
APO AE 09642

American Consulate General Barcelona
Phone: 011-34-93-280-2227
Fax: 011-34-93-205-7705
Street Address:
Paseo Leina Elisenda, 23
08034 Barcelona, Spain
Mailing Address:
PSC 61, Box 0005
APO AE 09642

Sweden

Post: American Embassy Stockholm
Phone: 011-46-8-783-5346
Fax: 011-46-8-660-9181
Street Address: Strandvagen 101
Mailing Address:
    U.S. Dept. of State (Stockholm)
    Washington DC 20521-5750

Switzerland

Post: American Embassy Bern
Phone: 011-41-31-357-7270
Fax: 011-41-31-357-7336
Street Address: Jubilaeumstrasse 93
Mailing Address:
    U.S. Dept. of State (Bern)
    Washington DC 20521-5110

Post: US Mission to the GATT (Geneva)
Phone: 011-41-22-749-5281
Fax: 011-41-22-749-4885
Street Address:
    Botanic Building
    1-3 Avenue de la Paix
Mailing Address:
    U.S. Dept. of State (Geneva)
    Washington, DC 20521-5130

Post: American Consulate General Zurich
Phone: 011-41-1-552-070
Fax: 011-41-1-382-2655
Street Address: Zolliikerstrasse 141
Mailing Address:
    U.S. Dept. of State (Zurich)
    Washington DC 20521-5130

Taiwan

The American Institute in Taiwan: Taipei Office
Phone: 011-886-2-720-1550
Fax: 011-886-2-757-7162
Street Address:
    600 Min Chuan East Road, Taipei
Mailing Address:
    American Institute in Taiwan
    Commercial Unit
    Dept. of State (Taipei)
    Washington DC 20521
E-mail: OTaipei@doc.gov

Location: Kaohsiung Office
Phone: 011-886-7-224-0154
Fax: 011-886-7-223-8237
Street Address:
    3d Fl., #2 Chung Cheng 3d Road,
    Kaohsiung
Mailing Address:
    American Institute in Taiwan
    Commercial Unit
    Dept. of State (Kaohsiung)
    Washington DC 20521
E-mail: OKaohsiu@doc.gov

Thailand

Post: American Embassy Bangkok
Phone: 011-662-255-4365
Fax: 011-662-255-2915
Street Address:
    Diethelm 93/1 Wireless Road,
    Towers Bldg.
Mailing Address: APO AP 96546
E-mail: OBangkok@doc.gov

Turkey

Post: American Embassy Ankara
Phone: 011-90-312-467-0949
Fax: 011-90-312-467-1366
Street Address: 110 Ataturk Blvd
Mailing Address:
    PSC 93 Box 5000
    APO AE 09823

Post: American Consulate Gen. Istanbul
Phone: 011-90-1-251-1651
Fax: 011-90-1-252-2417
Street Address:
    104-108 Mesrutiyet Caddesi, Tepebasi
Mailing Address:
    PSC 97 Box 0002
    APO AE 09827-0002

Post: American Consulate Gen. Izmir
Phone: 011-90-232-421-3643
Fax: 011-90-232-463-5040
Street Address: 92 Ataturk Caddesi (3rd Fl)
Mailing Address:
    PSC 88, Box 5000
    APO AE 09821

Turkmenistan

Post: American Embassy Ashgabat
Phone: 011-9-7-3632-35-00-45
Fax: 011-9-7-3632-51-13-05
Street Address: 9 Pushkin Street
Mailing Address:
    U.S. Dept. of State (Ashgabat)
    Washington, D.C. 20521-7070

Ukraine

Post: American Embassy Kiev
Phone: 011-380-44-417-2669
Fax: 011-380-44-417-1419
Street Address: 10 Yuria Kotsyubinskono
Mailing Address:
    U.S. Dept. of State (Kiev)
    Washington DC 20521-5850

United Arab Emirates

Post: American Consulate Gen. Dubai
Phone: 011-971-4-313-584
Fax: 011-971-4-313-121
Workweek: Saturday-Wednesday
Street Address:
    Dubai International Trade Center
    21st Floor
Mailing Address:
    U.S. Dept. of State (Dubai)
    Washington DC 20521-6020

Post: American Embassy Abu Dhabi
Phone: 011-971-2-273-666
Fax: 011-971-2-271-377
Workweek: Saturday-Wednesday
Street Address:
    8th Floor, Blue Tower Building
    Shaikh Khalifa Bin Zayed St.
Mailing Address:
    U.S. Dept. of State (Abu Dhabi)
    Washington DC 20521-6010

United Kingdom

Post: American Embassy London
Phone: 011-44-71-408-8019
Fax: 011-44-71-408-8020
Street Address: 24-31 Grosvenor Square
Mailing Address:
    PSC 801 Box 40
    FPO AE 09498-4040

Uzbekistan

Post: American Embassy Tashkent
Phone: 011-7-3712-771-407
Fax: 011-7-3712-776-953
Street Address: 82 Chelanzanskaya
Mailing Address:
    U.S. Dept. of State (Tashkent)
    Washington, D.C. 20521-7110

Venezuela

Post: American Embassy Caracas
Phone: 011-58-2-977-2792
Fax: 011-58-2-977-2177
Street Address:
    Calle F con Calle Suapure
    Colinas de Valle
    Arriba Codigo Postal 1060
Mailing Address:
    Unit 4958
    APO AA 34037

Vietnam

Post: Commercial Service Hanoi
Phone: 011-844-824-2422
Fax: 011-844-824-2421
Street Address:
    U.S. Commercial Center
    31 Hai Ba Trung 4th Floor
    Hanoi, Vietnam
E-mail: 10313.3220@compuserve.com

Deputy Asst. Sec. for Export Promotion Services

Deputy Assistant Secretary
Ms. Mary Fran Kirchner
202/482-6220   Fax: 202/482-2526
Rm. 2810

Office of Export Information and Marketing Services

Director
Mr. J. Laurence Eisenberg
202/482-4909   Fax: 202/482-0973
Rm. 2202

Office of Public/Private Initiatives

Director
Mr. John Klingelhut
202/482-4231
Rm. 2116

Office of Trade Events Management

Director
VACANT
202/482-4705   Fax: 202/482-5398
Rm. 2107

Deputy Assistant Secretary for Domestic Operations

Deputy Assistant Secretary
Mr. Daniel J. McLaughlin
202/482-4767   Fax: 202/482-0687
Rm. 3810

Daniel J. McLaughlin is the deputy assistant secretary of domestic operations in the U.S. & Foreign Commercial Service of the International Trade Administration. In this capacity, he oversees the export promotion of the U.S. Department of Commerce in 92 offices in the United States and a headquarters staff in Washington, D.C.

In April of 1994, the office won the Vice-President's Hammer Award for developing a government that "works better and costs less." In October of 1994, the office won the Secretary of Commerce's Silver Award for achieving the critical departmental goal of consolidating all export promotion and trade finance services of the U.S. Government. The office worked relentlessly in spearheading and designing the implementation of the U.S. Export Assistance Centers, which offers effective and responsive trade facilitation.

As a result, the Office of Domestic Operations received the 1995 Public Service Excellence Award sponsored by the Public Employees Roundtable and the President's Council on Management Improvement. Most recently, the office was selected as a finalist for the 1996 Innovations in American Government Award co-sponsored by the Ford Foundation and Harvard University's Kennedy School of Government.

As deputy assistant secretary, McLaughlin has demonstrated that government can be a source of creative solutions to critical social problems. Under his leadership, the Office of Domestic Operations has increased cooperation between public and private export service organizations to leverage international trade resources for exporters. By establishing strategic alliances, or partnerships, Domestic Operations has improved the quality of services available to a greater number of U.S. firms in an environment of ever-shrinking resources.

McLaughlin came to US&FCS with nearly twenty years experience as a senior manager in public administration in state and local governments, and as a strategic consultant in the private sector. He has also participated in some of the earliest international commercial

and cultural exchanges between U.S. cities and their overseas counterparts. His most recent position before joining the government was as a private consultant to an international organization of chief executive officers.

McLaughlin's educational credentials include a bachelors degree from the University of Massachusetts, a masters degree in public administration, (with a concentration in international political economy) from Harvard University's Kennedy School of Government with further directed studies at Tufts University's Fletcher School of Law and Diplomacy, and at Ecole Nationale D'Administration (ENA) in Paris.

Office of Operations

Director
Ms. Anita Blackman
202/482-2975   Fax: 202/482-0687
Rm. 3811

Director, Field Support Staff
Mr. David Miller
202/482-2683   Fax: 202/482-0687
Rm. 3810

U.S. Export Assistance Center Network

Note: The following list includes all offices that are part of the EAC network. For more information contact the Deputy Assistant Secretary for Domestic Operations at 202/482-4767.

INTRODUCTION

As one of the key export promotion agencies of the federal government, the Commercial Service's Office of Domestic Operations continually strives to assist American businesses expand their exports to markets around the globe. ODO provides export counseling and marketing assistance to the U.S. business community through its Export Assistance Centers (EACs). The EACs work closely with the Office of International Operations' overseas posts to facilitate export transactions by linking U.S. suppliers with international buyers. The two field networks work in unison to provide U.S. exporters with the best international trade support that the U.S. government can offer.

EXPORT ASSISTANCE CENTERS (EACs)

The Office of Domestic Operations operates the Export Assistance Center Network with 19 U.S. Export Assistance Centers (USEACs) connecting 100 EACs, including 51 offices that are part of the District Export Council network, in a "hub and spoke" network. The mission of the EAC network is to deliver a comprehensive array of export counseling and trade finance services to U.S. firms, particularly small and medium-sized enterprises. As client-driven, bottom-line oriented offices that integrate the export marketing know-how of the Department of Commerce with the trade finance expertise of the Small Business Administration (SBA) and Export-Import Bank, EACs have the look and feel of private sector export consulting firms. They have gone beyond being simply a federal partnership by also incorporating the resources of state and local export promotion organizations.

EACs focus on service to U.S. business clients. They provide in-depth, value-added counseling to U.S. firms seeking to expand their international activities and to those companies that are just beginning to venture overseas. EAC trade specialists help firms enter new markets and increase market share by:

- *identifying the best markets for their products,*
- *developing an effective market entry strategy aided by information generated from our overseas offices,*
- *facilitating the implementation of these plans by advising clients on distribution channels, market entry strategies and exporting operational procedures, Export Promotion Services (EPS) programs and services, relevant trade shows and missions, etc., and*
- *assisting with trade finance programs that are available through federal, state and local (public and private sector) entities.*

EAC trade professionals counsel clients on relevant program information and market research as a standard part of their operations. Additionally, they facilitate communication between clients and overseas contacts through the most expedient technologies available, such as the Internet and e-mail, phone and fax. The trade specialists are mobile, equipped with laptops, modems and cell phones that allow them to deliver export services at the client's place of business wherever and whenever is most convenient for the client.

REGIONAL OFFICES

Eastern Region

Mr. Thomas Cox
Regional Director
Regional EAC Office
World Trade Ctr., Suite 2450
401 East Pratt St.
Baltimore MD 21202
Phone: 410/962-2805   Fax: 410-962-2799
E-mail: OBaltimo@doc.gov

Mid-Eastern Region

Mr. Gordon B. Thomas
Regional Director
Regional EAC Office
36 East 7th St., Suite 2025
Cincinnati OH 45202
Phone: 513/684-2947   Fax: 513-684-3200

Mid-Western Region

Ms. Sandra Gerley
Regional Director
Regional EAC Office
8182 Maryland Ave., Suite 1011
St. Louis MO 63105
Phone: 314/425-3300   Fax: 314-425-3375

Western Region

Mr. Keith Bovetti
Regional Director
Regional EAC Office
250 Montgomery St., 14th Floor
San Francisco CA 94104
Phone: 415/705-2310   Fax: 415-705-2299

STATE OFFICES

Alabama

Mr. George Norton
Director
Birmingham Export Assistance Center
950 22nd Street North, Room 707
Birmingham AL 35203
Phone: 205/731-1331   Fax: 205-731-0076
E-mail: OBirming@doc.gov

Alaska

Mr. Charles Becker
Director
Anchorage Export Assistance Center
3601 C Street, Suite 700
Anchorage AK 99503
Phone: 907/271-6237   Fax: 907-271-6242
E-mail: OAnchora@doc.gov

Arizona

Mr. Frank Woods
Director
Phoenix Export Assistance Center
2901 N. Central Ave., Suite 970
Phoenix AZ 85012
Phone: 602/640-2513   Fax: 602-640-2518
E-mail: OPhoenix@doc.gov

Arkansas

Mr. Lon J. Hardin
Director
Little Rock Export Assistance Center
425 W. Capitol Avenue, Suite 700
Little Rock AR 72201
Phone: 501/324-5794   Fax: 501-324-7380
E-mail: OLittleR@doc.gov

California

Ms. Arlene Mayeda
Manager
Fresno Export Assistance Center
390-B Fir Avenue
Clovis CA 93611
Phone: 209/325-1619   Fax: 209-325-1647
E-mail: OFresno@doc.gov

Mr. Joe Sachs
Director
Long Beach U.S. Export Assistance Center
One World Trade Center, Suite 1670
Long Beach CA 90831
Phone: 562/980-4550   Fax: 562-980-4561
E-mail: OLongBea@doc.gov

Mr. Sherwin Chen
Manager
West Los Angeles Export Assistance Center
1150 Olympic Blvd., Suite 975
Los Angeles CA 90064
Phone: 310/235-7104   Fax: 310-235-7220
E-mail: OLosAnge@doc.gov

Mr. Jim Cunningham
Acting Director
Downtown Los Angeles Export Assistance Center
350 South Figueroa Street, Suite 172
Los Angeles CA 90071
Phone: 213/894-8784   Fax: 213-894-8790
E-mail: jcunning@doc.gov

Mr. Dao Le
Manager
Monterey Export Assistance Center
411 Pacific St., Suite 200
Monterey CA 93940
Phone: 408/641-9850   Fax: 408-641-9849
E-mail: OMontere@doc.gov

Mr. Paul Tambakis
Director
Orange County Export Assistance Center
3300 Irvine Avenue, Suite 305
Newport Beach CA 92660
Phone: 714/660-1688   Fax: 714-660-8039
E-mail: ONewport@doc.gov

Ms. Elizabeth Krauth
Manager

Novato Export Assistance Center
330 Ignacio Blvd., Suite 102
Novato CA 94949
Phone: 415/883-1996   Fax: 415-883-2711
E-mail: ONorthBa@doc.gov

Mr. Raj Shea
Manager
Oakland Export Assistance Center
530 Water Street, Suite 740
Oakland CA 94607
Phone: 510/273-7350   Fax: 510-251-7352
E-mail: OOakland@doc.gov

Mr. Fred Latuperissa
Director
Inland Empire Export Assistance Center
2940 Inland Empire Blvd., Suite 121
Ontario CA 91764
Phone: 909/466-4134   Fax: 909-466-4140
E-mail: OOntario@doc.gov

Mr. Gerald Vaughn
Manager
Oxnard Export Assistance Center
300 Esplanade Drive, Suite 2090
Oxnard CA 93030
Phone: 805/981-8150   Fax: 805-981-1855
E-mail: OOxnard@doc.gov

Mr. Brooks Ohlson
Manager
Sacramento Export Assistance Center
917 7th Street, 2nd Floor
Sacramento CA 95814
Phone: 916/498-5155   Fax: 916-498-5923
E-mail: OSacrame@doc.gov

Mr. Matt Andersen
Director
San Diego Export Assistance Center
6363 Greenwich Drive, Suite 230
San Diego CA 92122
Phone: 619/557-5395   Fax: 619-557-6176
E-mail: OSanDieg@doc.gov

Mr. Stephan Crawford
Director
San Francisco/World Trade Center Export Assistance Center
345 California Street, 7th Floor
San Francisco CA 94104
Phone: 415/705-1053   Fax: 415-705-1054
E-mail: OWTCente@doc.gov

Vacant
Manager
San Francisco Export Assistance Center
250 Montgomery Street, 14th Floor
San Francisco CA 94104
Phone: 415/705-2300   Fax: 415-705-2297
E-mail: OSanFran@doc.gov

Mr. James S. Kennedy
Director
San Jose U.S. Export Assistance Center
101 Park Center Plaza, Suite 1001
San Jose CA 95113
Phone: 408/271-7300   Fax: 408-271-7307
E-mail: OSanJosx@doc.gov

Mr. James C. Rigassio
Director
Santa Clara Export Assistance Center
5201 Great American Parkway, Suite 456
Santa Clara CA 95054
Phone: 408/970-4610   Fax: 408-970-4618
E-mail: OSantaCl@doc.gov

Colorado

Ms. Nancy Charles-Parker
Director
Denver U.S. Export Assistance Center
1625 Broadway, Suite 680
Denver CO 80202
Phone: 303/844-6622   Fax: 303-844-5651
E-mail: ODenver@doc.gov

Connecticut

Mr. Carl R. Jacobsen
Director
Middletown Export Assistance Center
213 Court St., Suite 903
Middletown CT 06457-3346
Phone: 860/638-6950   Fax: 860-638-6970
E-mail: OHartfor@doc.gov

Delaware

District Export Assistance Center
Served by Philadelphia, Pennsylvania EAC
E-mail: OPhilade@doc.gov

District of Columbia

District Export Assistance Center
Serviced by Baltimore, Md. Branch Office

Florida

Mr. George Martinez
Manager
Clearwater Export Assistance Center
1130 Cleveland Street
Clearwater FL 34615
Phone: 813/461-0011   Fax: 813-449-2889
E-mail: OClearwa@doc.gov

Mr. John McCartney
Director
Miami U.S. Export Assistance Center
5600 Northwest 36th Street, Suite 617
Miami FL 33166
Phone: 305/526-7425   Fax: 305-526-7434
E-mail: OMiami@doc.gov

Mr. Philip A. Ouzts
Manager
Orlando Export Assistance Center
200 E. Robinson Street, Suite 1270
Orlando FL 32801
Phone: 407/648-6235   Fax: 407-648-6756
E-mail: OOrlando@doc.gov

Mr. Michael Higgins
Manager
Tallahassee Export Assistance Center
The Capitol, Suite 2001
Tallahassee FL 32399-0001
Phone: 850/488-6469   Fax: 850-487-3014
E-mail: OTallaha@doc.gov

Georgia

Mr. Samuel Troy
Director

Atlanta U.S. Export Assistance Center
285 Peachtree Center Ave., NE, Suite 200
Atlanta GA 30303-1229
Phone: 404/657-1900   Fax: 404-657-1970
E-mail: OAtlanta@doc.gov

Ms. Barbara Prieto
Director
Savannah Export Assistance Center
6001 Chatham Center Drive, Suite 100
Savannah GA 31405
Phone: 912/652-4204   Fax: 912-652-4241
E-mail: OSavanna@doc.gov

Hawaii

Mr. Amer Kayani
Manager
Honolulu Export Assistance Center
P.O. Box 50026
300 Ala Moana Boulevard, Room 4106
Honolulu HI 96850
Phone: 808/541-1782   Fax: 808-541-3435
E-mail: OHonolul@doc.gov

Idaho

Mr. Steve Thompson
Manager
Boise Export Assistance Center
700 W. State Street, 2nd Floor
Boise ID 83720
Phone: 208/334-3857   Fax: 208-334-2783
E-mail: OBoise@doc.gov

Illinois

Ms. Mary Joyce
Director
Chicago U.S. Export Assistance Center
55 West Monroe Street, Suite 2440
Chicago IL 60603
Phone: 312/353-8045   Fax: 312-353-8120
E-mail: OChicago@doc.gov

Ms. Robin F. Mugford
Manager
Highland Park Export Assistance Center
610 Central Ave., Suite 150
Highland Park IL 60035
Phone: 847/681-8010   Fax: 847-681-8012
E-mail: OHighlan@doc.gov

Mr. James Mied
Manager
Rockford Export Assistance Center
515 North Court Street
P.O. Box 1747
Rockford IL 61103
Phone: 815/987-8123   Fax: 815-963-7943
E-mail: ORockfor@doc.gov

VACANT
Manager
Wheaton Export Assistance Center
Illinois Institute of Technology
201 East Loop Road
Wheaton IL 60187
Phone: 312/353-4332   Fax: 312-353-4336
E-mail: OWheaton@doc.gov

Indiana

Mr. Dan Swart
Manager
Indianapolis Export Assistance Center
11405 N. Pennsylvania St., Suite 106
Carmel IN 46032
Phone: 317/582-2300   Fax: 317-582-2301
E-mail: OIndiana@doc.gov

Iowa

Mr. Allen Patch
Director
Des Moines Export Assistance Center
210 Walnut St., Rm. 817
Des Moines IA 50309
Phone: 515/284-4222   Fax: 515-284-4021
E-mail: ODesMoin@doc.gov

Kansas

Mr. George D. Lavid
Manager
Wichita Export Assistance Center
151 N. Volutsia
Wichita KS 67214
Phone: 316/269-6160   Fax: 316-683-7326
E-mail: OWichita@doc.gov

Kentucky

Mr. John Autin
Director
Louisville Export Assistance Center
601 W. Broadway, 634B
Louisville KY 40202
Phone: 502/582-5066   Fax: 502-582-6573
E-mail: OLouisvi@doc.gov

Ms. Sara Melton
Manager
Somerset Export Assistance Center
2292 S. Highway 27, Suite 320
Somerset KY 42501
Phone: 606/677-6160   Fax: 606-677-6161
E-mail: OSomerse@doc.gov

Louisiana

Mr. David Spann
Director
Delta U.S. Export Assistance Center
365 Canal St., Suite 2150
New Orleans LA 70130
Phone: 504/589-6546   Fax: 504-589-2337
E-mail: ONewOrle@doc.gov

Mr. Norbert O. Gannon
Manager
Shreveport Export Assistance Center
5210 Hollywood Ave. - Annex
Shreveport LA 71109
Phone: 318/676-3064   Fax: 318-676-3063
E-mail: OShrevep@doc.gov

Maine

Mr. Jeffrey Porter

Manager
Portland, Maine Export Assistance Center
511 Congress Street
Portland ME 04101
Phone: 207/541-7400   Fax: 207-541-7420
E-mail: JPorter1@doc.gov

Maryland

Mr. Michael Keavney
Director
Baltimore U.S. Export Assistance Center
World Trade Center
401 East Pratt Street, Suite 2432
Baltimore MD 21202
Phone: 410/962-4539   Fax: 410-962-4529
E-mail: OBaltimo@doc.gov

Massachusetts

Mr. Frank J. O'Connor
Director
Boston U.S. Export Assistance Center
World Trade Center
164 Northern Avenue, Suite 307
Boston MA 02210
Phone: 617/424-5990   Fax: 617-424-5992
E-mail: OBoston@doc.gov

Mr. William Davis
Manager
Marlborough Export Assistance Center
100 Granger Blvd., Unit 102
Marlborough MA 01752
Phone: 508/624-6000   Fax: 508-624-7145
E-mail: OMarlbor@doc.gov

Michigan

Mr. Paul Litton
Manager
Ann Arbor Export Assistance Center
425 S. Main St., Suite 103
Ann Arbor MI 48104
Phone: 313/741-2430   Fax: 313-741-2432
E-mail: OAnnArbo@doc.gov

Mr. Neil Hesse
Director
Detroit U.S. Export Assistance Center
211 W. Fort St., Suite 2220
Detroit MI 48226
Phone: 313/226-3650   Fax: 313-226-3657
E-mail: ODetroit@doc.gov

Mr. Thomas F. Maguire
Manager
Grand Rapids Export Assistance Center
301 W. Fulton St., Suite 718-S
Grand Rapids MI 49504
Phone: 616/458-3564   Fax: 616-458-3872
E-mail: OGrandRa@doc.gov

Mr. Richard Corson
Director
Pontiac Export Assistance Center
250 Elizabeth Lake Rd.
Pontiac MI 48341
Phone: 810/975-9600   Fax: 810-975-9606
E-mail: OPontiac@doc.gov

E-mail: OReno@doc.gov

Minnesota

Ms. Nancy Libersky
Director
SBA District Office/USEAC
100 North 6th Street - Suite 610
Minneapolis MN 55403
Phone: 617/370-2306   Fax: 617-370-2303

Mr. Ronald E. Kramer
Director
Minneapolis U.S. Export Assistance Center
110 S. 4th Street, Rm. 108
Minneapolis MN 55401
Phone: 612/348-1638   Fax: 612-348-1650
E-mail: OMinneap@doc.gov

Mississippi

Mr. Harrison Ford
Director
Mississippi Export Assistance Center
704 East Main Street
Raymond MS 39164
Phone: 601/857-0126   Fax: 601-857-0026
E-mail: OJackson@doc.gov

Missouri

Mr. Thomas Strauss
Director
Kansas City Export Assistance Center
235 Grand, Suite 650
Kansas City MO 64106
Phone: 816/410-9201   Fax: 816-410-9208
E-mail: OKansasC@doc.gov

Mr. Randall J. LaBounty
Director
St. Louis U.S. Export Assistance Center
8182 Maryland Avenue, Suite 303
St. Louis MO 63105
Phone: 314/425-3302   Fax: 314-425-3381
E-mail: OStLouis@doc.gov

Montana

District Export Assistance Center
Serviced by Boise Branch Office
E-mail: OBoise@doc.gov

Nebraska

Ms. Meredith Bond
Manager
Omaha Export Assistance Center
11135 "O" Street
Omaha NE 68137
Phone: 402/221-3664   Fax: 402-221-3668
E-mail: OOmaha@doc.gov

Nevada

Ms. Jere Dabbs
Manager
Reno Export Assistance Center
1755 E. Plumb Lane, Suite 152
Reno NV 89502
Phone: 702/784-5203   Fax: 702-784-5343

New Hampshire

Ms. Susan Berry
Manager
Portsmouth Export Assistance Center
17 New Hampshire Ave.
Portsmouth NH 03801-2838
Phone: 603/334-6074   Fax: 603-334-6110
E-mail: OPortsmo@doc.gov

New Jersey

Mr. William Spitler
Director
Newark Export Assistance Center
One Gateway Center, 9th Floor
Newark NJ 07102
Phone: 201/645-4682   Fax: 201-645-4783
E-mail: ONewark@doc.gov

Mr. Rod Stuart
Director
Trenton Export Assistance Center
3131 Princeton Pike, Building 6
Suite 100
Trenton NJ 08648
Phone: 609/989-2100   Fax: 609-989-2395
E-mail: OTrenton@doc.gov

New Mexico

Ms. Sandra Necessary
Manager
Santa Fe Export Assistance Center
c/o New Mexico Dept. of Economic Development
P.O. Box 20003
Santa Fe NM 87504-5003
Phone: 505/827-0350   Fax: 505-827-0263
E-mail: OSantaFe@doc.gov

New York

Mr. George Buchanan
Director
Buffalo Export Assistance Center
111 West Huron St., Room 1304
Buffalo NY 14202
Phone: 716/551-4191   Fax: 716-551-5290
E-mail: OBuffalo@doc.gov

Mr. George Soteros
Manager
Long Island Export Assistance Center
1550 Franklin Ave., Room 207
Mineola NY 11501
Phone: 516/739-1765   Fax: 516-739-3310
E-mail: OLongIsl@doc.gov

Mr. K.L. Fredericks
Manager
Harlem Export Assistance Center
163 West 125th Street, Suite 904
New York NY 10027
Phone: 212/860-6200   Fax: 212-860-6203
E-mail: OHarlem@doc.gov

Mr. Joel W. Barkan
Acting Director
New York, NY U.S. Export Assistance Center
6 World Trade Center, Rm. 635

New York NY 10048
Phone: 212/466-5222   Fax: 212-264-1356
E-mail: ONewYork@doc.gov

Ms. Joan Kanlian
Manager
Westchester Export Assistance Center
707 West Chester Ave.
White Plains NY 10604
Phone: 914/682-6218   Fax: 914-682-6698
E-mail: OWestche@doc.gov

North Carolina

Mr. Roger Fortner
Director
Carolinas U.S. Export Assistance Center
521 East Morehead Street, Suite 435
Charlotte NC 28202
Phone: 704/333-4886   Fax: 704-332-2681
E-mail: OCharlot@doc.gov

Ms. Linda Jones
Acting Manager
Greensboro Export Assistance Center
400 West Market Street, Suite 400
Greensboro NC 27401
Phone: 910/333-5345   Fax: 910-333-5158
E-mail: OGreensb@doc.gov

North Dakota

District Export Assistance Center
Serviced by Minneapolis District Office
E-mail: OMinneap@doc.gov

Ohio

Mr. Michael Miller
Director
Cincinnati Export Assistance Center
36 East 7th St., Suite 2650
Cincinnati OH 45202
Phone: 513/684-2944   Fax: 513-684-3227
E-mail: OCincinn@doc.gov

Mr. Clem Von Koschembahr
Acting Director
Cleveland U.S. Export Assistance Center
600 Superior Ave., East, Suite 700
Cleveland OH 44114
Phone: 216/522-4750   Fax: 216-522-2235
E-mail: OClevela@doc.gov

Ms. Mary Beth Double
Manager
Columbus Export Assistance Center
37 North High St., 4th Floor
Columbus OH 43215
Phone: 614/365-9510   Fax: 614-365-9598
E-mail: OColumbu@doc.gov

Mr. Robert Abrahams
Manager
Toledo Export Assistance Center
300 Madison Ave.
Toledo OH 43604
Phone: 419/241-0683   Fax: 419-241-0684
E-mail: OToledo@doc.gov

Oklahoma

Mr. Ronald L. Wilson
Director
Oklahoma City Export Assistance Center
301 Northwest 63rd Street, Suite 330
Oklahoma City OK 73116
Phone: 405/231-5302   Fax: 405-231-4211
E-mail: OOklahom@doc.gov

VACANT
Manager
Tulsa Export Assistance Center
700 N. Greenwood Ave., Suite 1400
Tulsa OK 74106
Phone: 918/581-7650   Fax: 918-594-8413
E-mail: OTulsa@doc.gov

Oregon

Ms. Pamela Ward
Manager
Eugene Export Assistance Center
1445 Willamette Street, Suite 13
Eugene OR 97401-4003
Phone: 541/465-6575   Fax: 541-465-6704
E-mail: OEugene@doc.gov

Mr. Scott Goddin
Director
Portland, Oregon Export Assistance Center
One World Trade Center
121 S.W. Salmon Street, Suite 242
Portland OR 97204
Phone: 503/326-3001   Fax: 503-326-6351
E-mail: OPortlan@doc.gov

Pennsylvania

Ms. Deborah Doherty
Manager
Harrisburg Export Assistance Center
One Commerce Sq.
417 Walnut St., 3rd. Floor
Harrisburg PA 17101
Phone: 717/232-0051   Fax: 717-232-0054
E-mail: OHarrisb@doc.gov

Mr. Henry LeBlanc
Manager
Scranton Export Assistance Center
One Montage Mountain Road, Suite B
Moosic PA 18507
Phone: 717/969-2530   Fax: 717-969-2539
E-mail: OScranto@doc.gov

Ms. Maria Galindo
Director
Philadelphia U.S. Export Assistance Center
615 Chestnut St., Suite 1501
Philadelphia PA 19106
Phone: 215/597-6101   Fax: 215-597-6123
E-mail: OPhilade@doc.gov

Mr. Ted Arnn
Manager
Pittsburgh Export Assistance Center
2002 Federal Building
1000 Liberty Avenue
Pittsburgh PA 15222
Phone: 412/395-5050   Fax: 412-395-4875
E-mail: OPittsbu@doc.gov

Puerto Rico

Mr. J. Enrique Vilella
Director
San Juan Export Assistance Center
525 F.D. Roosevelt Ave., Suite 905
San Juan PR 00918
Phone: 787/766-5555   Fax: 787-766-5692
E-mail: OSanJuan@doc.gov

Rhode Island

Mr. Raimond Meerbach
Manager
Providence Export Assistance Center
One West Exchange St.
Providence RI 02903
Phone: 401/528-5104   Fax: 401-528-5067
E-mail: OProvide@doc.gov

South Carolina

Mr. David Kuhlmeier
Director
Charleston Export Assistance Center
81 Mary Street
Charleston SC 29403
Phone: 803/727-4051   Fax: 803-727-4052
E-mail: OCharlSC@doc.gov

Ms. Ann Watts
Director
Columbia Export Assistance Center
1835 Assembly Street, Suite 172
Columbia SC 29201
Phone: 803/765-5345   Fax: 803-253-3614
E-mail: OColumbi@doc.gov

Mr. Denis Csizmadia
Director
Upstate, SC Export Assistance Center
Park Central Office Pk., Bldg. 1, Ste. 109
555 N. Pleasantburg Dr.
Greenville SC 29607
Phone: 864/271-1976   Fax: 864-271-4171
E-mail: OGreenvi@doc.gov

South Dakota

VACANT
Manager
Siouxland Export Assistance Center
Augustana College
2001 S. Summit Ave., Room SS-29A
Sioux Falls SD 57197
Phone: 605-330-4264   Fax: 605-330-4266
E-mail: OSiouxFa@doc.gov

Tennessee

Mr. Thomas McGinty
Manager
Knoxville Export Assistance Center
301 E. Church Avenue
Knoxville TN 37915
Phone: 423/545-4637   Fax: 423-545-4435
E-mail: OKnoxvil@doc.gov

Ms. Ree Russell
Manager

Memphis Export Assistance Center
22 North Front Street, Suite 200
Memphis TN 38103
Phone: 901/544-4137   Fax: 901-544-3646
E-mail: OMemphis@doc.gov

Mr. Michael Speck
Director
Nashville Export Assistance Center
404 James Robertson Parkway, Suite 114
Nashville TN 37219
Phone: 615/736-5161   Fax: 615-736-2454
E-mail: ONashvil@doc.gov

Texas

Ms. Karen Parker
Manager
Austin Export Assistance Center
1700 Congress, 2nd Floor
Austin TX 78701
Phone: 512/916-5939   Fax: 512-916-5940
E-mail: OAustin@doc.gov

Mr. William Schrage
Director
Dallas U.S. Export Assistance Center
2050 N. Stemmons Frwy., Suite 170
Dallas TX 75207
Phone: 214/767-0542   Fax: 214-767-8240
E-mail: ODallas@doc.gov

Ms. Vavie Sellschopp
Manager
Fort Worth Export Assistance Center
711 Houston Street
Fort Worth TX 76102
Phone: 817/212-2673   Fax: 817-978-0178
E-mail: OFortWor@doc.gov

Mr. James D. Cook
Director
Houston Export Assistance Center
500 Dallas, Suite 1160
Houston TX 77002
Phone: 713/718-3062   Fax: 713-718-3060
E-mail: OHouston@doc.gov

Mr. Mitchel Auerbach
Manager
San Antonio Export Assistance Center
1222 N. Main, Suite 450
San Antonio TX 78212
Phone: 210/228-9878   Fax: 210-228-9874
E-mail: OSanAnto@doc.gov

Utah

Mr. Stephen P. Smoot
Director
Salt Lake City Export Assistance Center
324 South State Street, Suite 221
Salt Lake City UT 84111
Phone: 801/524-5116   Fax: 801-524-5886
E-mail: OSaltLak@doc.gov

Vermont

Mr. James Cox
Manager
Montpelier Export Assistance Center
National Life Building, Drawer 20

Montpelier VT 05620-0501
Phone: 802/828-4508   Fax: 802-828-3258
E-mail: OMontpel@doc.gov

Virginia

Ms. Sylvia Burns
Director
Northern Virginia Export Assistance Center
1616 N. Ft. Myer Dr., Suite 1300
Arlington VA 22209
Phone: 703/524-2885   Fax: 703-524-2649

Mr. William Davis Coale, Jr.
Director
Richmond Export Assistance Center
704 East Franklin Street, Suite 550
Richmond VA 23219
Phone: 804/771-2246   Fax: 804-771-2390
E-mail: ORichmon@doc.gov

Washington

Ms. Lisa Kjaer-Schade
Director
Seattle U.S. Export Assistance Center
2001 6th Avenue, Suite 650
Seattle WA 98121
Phone: 206/553-5615   Fax: 206-553-7253
E-mail: OSeattle@doc.gov

Mr. James K. Hellwig
Manager
Spokane Export Assistance Center
801 W. Riverside Ave., Suite 400
Spokane WA 99201
Phone: 509/353-2625   Fax: 509-353-2449
E-mail: OSpokane@doc.gov

West Virginia

Mr. Harvey Timberlake
Director
Charleston, WV Export Assistance Center
405 Capitol Street, Suite 807
Charleston WV 25301
Phone: 304/347-5123   Fax: 304-347-5408
E-mail: OCharlWV@doc.gov

Ms. Martha Butwin
Manager
Wheeling Export Assistance Center
1310 Market St., 2nd Floor
Wheeling WV 26003
Phone: 304/233-7472   Fax: 304-233-7492
E-mail: OWheelin@doc.gov

Wisconsin

Mr. Paul D. Churchill
Director
Milwaukee Export Assistance Center
517 E. Wisconsin Ave., Room 596
Milwaukee WI 53202
Phone: 414/297-3473   Fax: 414-297-3470
E-mail: OMilwauk@doc.gov

Wyoming
District Export Assistance Center
Served by Denver EAC
E-mail: ODenver@doc.gov

Bureau of Export Administration

14th St. & Constitution Ave., NW / Washington DC 20230

INTRODUCTION

The Bureau of Export Administration directs the nation's export control policy. Major functions include processing license applications, conducting foreign availability studies to determine when products should be decontrolled, and enforcing U.S. export control laws.

BXA plays a key role in challenging issues involving national security and nonproliferation, export growth, and high technology. The Bureau's continuing major challenge is combating the proliferation of weapons of mass destruction while furthering the growth of U.S. exports, which are critical to maintaining our leadership in an increasingly competitive global economy.

There is an assistant secretary for each of BXA's two principal operating units, Export Administration and Export Enforcement, as well as its Office of Administration, have undergone significant reorganization and downsizing in recent years in order to meet the goals of reforming and streamlining the export control system, as recommended by the National Performance Review (NPR) and the Trade Promotion Coordinating Committee (TPCC). BXA is also an NPR Reinvention Laboratory.

Major Programs and Activities

• Implementing the Export Administration Act (EAA) through the Export Administration Regulations (EAR): The EAA, which has lapsed, and needs to be re-authorized, provides for export controls on dual use goods and technology (primarily commercial goods which have potential military applications) not only to fight proliferation, but also to pursue other national security, short supply, and foreign policy goals (such as combating terrorism). Simplifying and updating these controls in light of the end of the Cold War has been a major accomplishment of BXA.

• Enforcing the export control and antiboycott provisions of the EAA, as well as other statutes such as the Fastener Quality Act. The EAA is enforced through a variety of administrative, civil, and criminal sanctions.

• Analyzing and protecting the defense industrial and technology base, pursuant to the Defense Production Act and other laws: As the Defense Department increases its reliance on dual-use high technology goods as part of its cost-cutting efforts, ensuring that we remain competitive in those sectors and sub-sectors is critical to our national security.

• Helping Ukraine, Kazakstan, Belarus, Russia, and other newly emerging countries develop effective export control systems: The effectiveness of U.S. export controls can be severely undercut if "rogue states" or terrorists gain access to sensitive goods and technology from other supplier countries.

• Working with former defense plants in the Newly Independent States (NIS) to help make a successful transition to profitable and peaceful civilian endeavors: This involves helping remove unnecessary obstacles to trade and investment and identifying opportunities for joint ventures with U.S. companies.

• Assisting U.S. defense enterprises to meet the challenge of the reduction in defense spending by converting to civilian production and by developing export markets: This work assists in maintaining our defense industrial base as well as preserving jobs for U.S. workers.

Under Secretary for Export Administration

Under Secretary
Mr. William A. Reinsch
202/482-1455   Fax: 202/482-2387
Rm. 3898

Education: B.A. in intern'l. relations, Johns Hopkins Univ., 1968. M.A., Johns Hopkins School of Advanced Intern'l. Studies, 1969.

Professional: 1968-73, teacher, Bethesda, Md. 1973-76, legislative asst., Rep. Gilbert Gude (R-Md.). 2/76, acting director, Environmental Study Conference. 1976-77, legislative asst. Rep. Richard Ottinger (D-N.Y.). 1977-91, chief legislative asst., Sen. John Heinz (R-Pa.). 1990-present, adjunct professor, Univ. of Maryland, Univ. Coll. Graduate School of Management and Technology. 1991-93, senior leg. asst., Sen. John D. Rockefeller IV (D-W.Va.). 1994-present, under sec. of commerce for export administration, U.S. Dept. of Commerce.

"One of the most formidable portfolios in town," said the National Journal of William Reinsch, under secretary of commerce for export administration, in naming him one of the 100 most influential men and women in Washington, D.C., in the magazine's June 14, 1997, issue.

The National Journal said that Reinsch has "one of the most difficult duties of anyone in the Clinton administration." As head of the bureau of export administration (BXA), he is responsible for administering and enforcing the export control policies of the federal government, as well as its antiboycott laws.

Through its office of industrial resource administration, BXA is responsible for monitoring and protecting the health of American industries critical to our national security and defense industrial base and assisting in domestic defense conversion efforts. The BXA is also part of an interagency team helping Russia and other newly emerging nations to develop effective export control systems and to convert their defense industries to civilian production.

Reinsch and the BXA are continuing the reform and streamlining of the export control systems through further administrative actions and enactment of a new Export Administration Act, increasing export enforcement efforts, enhancing efforts to identify and correct weaknesses in the defense industrial base, and continuing the bureau's work to facilitate defense conversion, both in the United States and in the former Soviet Union. BXA is also continuing to administer export controls on encryption products, which were transferred to the Commerce Department at the beginning of 1997, and it has begun its work to implement the Chemical Weapons Convention.

Reinsch brings political and academic experience to the post. He served as legislative assistant to Rep. Gilbert Gude (R-Md.) and later to Rep. Richard Ottinger (D-N.Y.) before spending 14 years in the office of the late Senator John Heinz (R-Pa.). He served as Heinz's chief legislative assistant, focusing on foreign trade and competitiveness policy issues. Reinsch also provided staff support to Heinz for the banking subcommittee on international finance and the international trade subcommittee of the Senate Finance Committee. In this role, he worked on several revisions of the Export Administration Act and other major trade bills.

From 1991-93, Reinsch served as senior legislative assistant to Senator John D. Rockefeller IV (D-W.Va.), and worked for the senator on trade, international economic policy, foreign affairs, and defense issues. He also provided staff support for Rockefeller's related efforts on the Finance Committee and the Commerce, Science, and Transportation Committee.

Reinsch has served as an adjunct associate professor at the University of Maryland University College Graduate School of Management and Technology since 1990, teaching a course in international trade and trade policy.

Reinsch's publications include, "The Legislative Agenda and Its Impact Upon the Court of International Trade," panel discussion in Proceedings of the Seventh Annual Judicial Conference of the United States Court of International Trade (Oct. 15, 1990), and "Building a New Economic Relationship with Japan," in Destler and Yankelovich's Beyond the Beltway: Engaging the Public in U.S. Foreign Policy (W.W. Norton, Apr. 1994.).

Reinsch, his wife, and their two sons live in Bethesda, Md. He is president of the Saint Mark Elderly Housing Corporation, a non-profit corporation that runs Saint Mark House, a home for the frail elderly in Rockville, Maryland.

Confidential Assistant
Ms. Amy Bellanca
202/482-1458
Rm. 3898B

Senior Policy Analyst
Mr. Anstruther Davidson
202/482-1149
Rm. 3898B

Executive Secretariat
Ms. Bonnie Mason
202/482-1460
Rm. 3898

Deputy Under Secretary, Export Administration

VACANT
202/482-1427
Rm. 3892

Director, Congressional and Public Affairs
Ms. Rosemary Warren
202/482-0097
Rm. 3897

Public Affairs Specialists
Mr. Eugene Cottilli & Ms. Sue Hofer
202/482-2721
Rm. 3897

Nonproliferation & Export Control Cooperation Team (NEC)

NEC coordinates Commerce's effort to help other countries develop or strengthen export controls and stop the proliferation of sensitive goods and technology to "rogue states" and terrorists.

Team Leader and Senior Policy Advisor
Mr. Daniel C. Hurley, Jr.
202/482-1427   Fax: 202/482-8224
Room 3894

Office of Chief Counsel for Export Administration

The attorneys in this unit of the Department's Office of General Counsel provide legal counsel and services for all BXA programs, including representing the agency in administrative enforcement proceedings.

Chief Counsel
Mr. Hoyt Zia
202/482-5301   Fax: 202/482-0085
Rm. 3839

Assistant Secretary for Export Administration

Assistant Secretary
Mr. R. Roger Majak
202/482-5491
Rm. 3886C

President Clinton nominated R. Roger Majak of Alexandria, Virginia, on September 4, 1997, to serve as assistant secretary of commerce for export administration and he was subsequently confirmed by the Senate.

The assistant secretary for export administration is responsible for overseeing the Commerce Department's export licensing system, and analyzes and develops policy relating to goods and technology subject to control for national security and foreign policy reasons. The assistant secretary also works with U.S. allies in implementing stronger and more uniform controls on strategic exports.

At the time of the White House announcement, Majak was a consultant with expertise in the areas of international and domestic trade promotion and regulation, international telecommunications, and government finance. Prior to becoming a consultant, he was the legislative director for the law firm of Powell, Goldstein, Frazer and Murphy from 1990-96 where his clients included Hewlett-Packard, INTELSAT, British Airways, and Dr. Pepper/7UP. Prior to this position, Majak was the federal government relations manager for TEKTRONIX Inc., a Fortune 500 electronic technology company.

From 1975-85, Majak was the chief of staff at the U.S. House of Representatives subcommittee on international economic policy and trade. He was responsible for legislation relating to foreign investment and export trade promotion and regulation, including authority for the use of economic sanctions. He was also chief of staff in the office of U.S. Rep. Jonathan Bingham (D-N.Y.), and served on the staff of the U.S. Commission on the Organization of Government for the Conduct of Foreign Policy.

Majak was born in Hammond, Ind., and was raised in Lansing, Ill. He received a B.S. in political science and journalism from Northwestern University and an M.A. in political science and international security policy from Ohio State University.

Senior Technical Adviser
Mr. Irwin Pikus
202/482-0074
Rm. 1089

Senior Policy Adviser
Ms. Maureen Tucker
202/482-5491
Rm. 3886C

Deputy Assistant Secretary
Mr. Iain S. Baird
202/482-5711
Rm. 3886C

Acting Director, Operating Committee
Ms. Carol Kalinoski
202/482-5863
Rm. 2639

Technical Advisory Committee
Ms. Lee Ann Carpenter
202/482-2583
Rm. 2621

Office of Export Services

This office is responsible for counseling exporters, conducting export control seminars, and drafting and publishing changes to the Export Administration Regulations. It is also responsible for licensing and compliance actions relating to the special comprehensive license, and for administering the processing of license applications and commodity classifications.

Director
Ms. Eileen Albanese
202/482-0436   Fax: 202/482-3322
Rm. 1091

Export Counseling Division
Ms. Laverne Smith
202/482-5247   Fax: 202/482-3617
Rm. 1099D

Export Seminar Staff
Mr. Rod Menas
202/482-6031
Rm. 1099D

Operations Support Division
Ms. Cheryl Suggs
202/482-3298
Rm. 2616

Regulatory Policy Division
Ms. Hillary Hess
202/482-2440
Rm. 1087

Acting Special Licensing and Compliance Division
Ms. Deborah Kappler
202/482-0062
Rm. 2627

<u>Western Regional Office</u>
3300 Irvine Avenue, Suite 345 / Newport Beach, CA 92660
Director
Mr. Michael Hoffman
714/ 660-0144   Fax: 714/ 660-9347

<u>Northern California Branch</u>
5201 Great America Pkwy., Suite 333 / Santa Clara, CA 95054
Director
Ms. Jo Allyn Scott
408/748-7450   Fax: 408/748-7470

Office of Nuclear and Missile Technology Controls

This office is responsible for all export control policy issues relating to the Nuclear Suppliers Group and Missile Technology Control Regime, and has a full range of responsibilities associated with the licensing of exports controlled for nuclear or missile technology reasons.

Acting Director
Mr. Steven Goldman
202/482-4188   Fax: 202/482-4145
Rm. 2631

Nuclear Technology Controls Division
Mr. Joseph Chuchla
202/482-1641
Rm. 2631

Missile Technology Controls Division
Mr. Raymond Jones
202/482-4244
Rm. 2631

Office of Chemical & Biological Controls & Treaty Compliance

This office has overall responsibility for administering export controls and policy development relating to the Australia Group (e.g. chemical precursors and biological agents). This office also acts as the principle point of contact for representing U.S. industrial interests in the development of a legally binding protocol to the Biological and Toxin Weapons Convention.

Director
Mr. Steven Goldman
202/482-3825   Fax: 202/482-0751
Rm. 2093

Treaty Compliance Division
Mr. Chuck Guernieri
202/501-7876
Rm. 2099

Chemical/Biological Controls Division
Mr. James Seevaratnam
202/482-3343
Rm. 2090

Office of Strategic Trade and Foreign Policy Controls

This office is responsible for implementing the multilateral export controls under the Wassenaar Arrangement, the successor regime to COCOM, which deals with conventional arms and related dual-use items. It also implements U.S. foreign policy controls such as crime control, antiterrorism, and regional stability, and is the Commerce office responsible for controls on exports to terrorist countries.

Director
Mr. James A. Lewis
202/482-4196
Rm. 2626

Strategic Trade Division
Ms. Tanya Motley
202/482-1837
Rm. 2089

Foreign Policy Controls Division
Ms. Joan Roberts
202/482-0171
Rm. 2620

Encryption Policy Division
Ms. Patricia Sefcik
202/482-0707
Rm. 2620

Office of Strategic Industries and Economic Security

This office is responsible for implementing programs to ensure the U.S. defense industries can meet national security requirements, for facilitating diversification of U.S. defense related industries into civilian markets, and for promoting the conversion of military enterprises in the Newly Independent States to civilian applications. It also analyzes the economic impact of U.S. export controls and other trade policies on U.S. industrial competitiveness.

Deputy Assistant Secretary
Mr. William V. Skidmore
202/482-4506   Fax: 202/482-5650
Rm. 3878

Economic Analysis Division
Ms. Karen Swasey
202/482-3795
Rm. 1608

Defense Programs Division
Mr. William Denk
202/482-3695
Rm. 3878

Strategic Analysis Division
Mr. Brad Botwin
202/482-4060
Rm. 3878

Assistant Secretary for Export Enforcement

Assistant Secretary
Ms. F. Amanda DeBusk
202/482-1561
Rm. 3727

At the time of her nomination in the fall of 1997, F. Amanda DeBusk, of Potomac, Md., was serving at Commerce as a senior advisor to Secretary Daley and the under secretary. She came to that post in June, 1997, from her position as a partner in the international trade department of the law firm of O'Melveny & Myers, where she worked for 11 years. DeBusk handled a variety of issues within the international arena and has had extensive experience with antidumping, countervailing duty, escape clause investigations, and obtaining export licenses.

DeBusk was an associate at Surrey & Morse from 1984 to 1986 and has represented clients in matters involving GATT, the World Trade Organization, NAFTA, and steel voluntary restraint agreements. In her law practice, she has dealt with the Commerce Department, the U.S. International Trade Commission, and other agencies. She has also served on the Investment and Services Policy Advisory Committee.

She received a B.A. from the University of Richmond and a J.D. from Harvard University.

Deputy Assistant Secretary
Mr. Frank W. Deliberti
202/482-3618
Rm. 3727

Personal: born 7/9/48 in Brooklyn, N.Y.

Professional: 1967-68, U.S. Postal Service. 1968-70, Social Security Administration, Dept. of Health and Human Services. 1970-76, U.S. Customs Service, U.S. Dept. of Treasury. 1976-1994, series of positions including: dir., office of export enforcement; special agent-in-charge of the office of export enforcement's field office in San Jose, Calif.; 1994-present, deputy asst. secretary of export enforcement; March 1997-present, acting asst. secretary for export enforcement, U.S. Dept. of Commerce.

Frank Deliberti has been deputy assistant secretary for export enforcement since 1994 after having served as the acting deputy assistant secretary for four months and as the acting assistant secretary in early 1993 and again for most of 1997. He is the first career employee and the first criminal investigator to hold these positions.

Deliberti formed and heads the interagency law enforcement "Business Executives' Enforcement Team," which creates a dialogue between government and industry. He overseas export enforcement's liaison with U.S. law enforcement and policy agencies, the intelligence community, and various international enforcement cooperation programs.

Previously, Deliberti served as director of the office of export enforcement, where he was responsible for managing eight regional offices, its intelligence division and headquarters as well as overseas export control attachés. Under his supervision, criminal investigators and intelligence analysts developed and helped to prosecute and sanction some of the most critical export control cases during the Cold War.

Between 1986 and 1991, Deliberti was the special agent-in-charge of the office of export enforcement's regional field offices in San Jose, Calif. Special agents in his office were responsible for enforcement of the dual-use export control laws in 10 states. During his time there, his office was among the most productive in the country, conducting major investigations into illegal shipments to Iran, Iraq, Libya, and other rogue countries.

In the late 1970s and early 1980s, Deliberti was a special agent and later team leader at the national headquarters and Washington field office of export enforcement. For his work, he was awarded the Commerce Department's bronze medal as outstanding employee of the year. In the 1970s, he held a number of positions with the U.S. Customs Service, including inspector and patrol officer.

In 1994, President Clinton honored Deliberti by designating him a "meritorious executive" within the senior executive service. He has received a number of commendations, including the Commerce Department's silver medal for his work on the Commerce-Customs Enforcement Memorandum of Understanding.

Sr. Adviser for Enforcement/International Issues
Mr. Stephen Leacy
202/482-3618
Rm. 3727

Office of Anti-Boycott Compliance (OAC)

OAC is responsible for implementing the antiboycott provisions of the Export Administration Regulations. This office performs three main functions:

(1) enforcing the regulations;
(2) assisting the public in antiboycott compliance; and
(3) compiling and analyzing information regarding international boycotts.

Acting Director
Mr. Dexter Price
202/482-5914
Rm. 6098

Office of Export Enforcement (OEE)

OEE is responsible for investigating violations to the Export Administration Regulations and violations of the Fastener Quality Act; apprehending violators; and working with BXA's Office of Chief Counsel, U.S. Attorneys, and other officials in the prosecution of violators. The special agents in Washington, D.C. and OEE's eight field offices (shown below) are staffed with Federal criminal investigators who are empowered to make arrests, carry firearms, execute search warrants, and seize goods about to be exported illegally.

Acting Director
Mr. Mark D. Menefee
202/482-2252   Fax: 202/482-5889
Rm. 4616

Regional Offices

Boston Field Office
Mr. Joseph Leone
Special Agent-in-Charge
New Boston Federal Building
Room 350, 10 Causeway Street
Boston, MA 02222
617/565-6030   Fax: 617/565-6039

New York Field Office
Ms. Josephine Fontana-Moran
Special Agent-in-Charge
2 Teleport Drive
Staten Island, NY 10311
718/370-0070   Fax: 718/370-0826

Washington Field Office
Mr. Richard Sherwood
Special Agent-in-Charge
381 Elden St. - #1125
Herndon, VA 20171
703/487-9300   Fax: 703/487-4955

Miami Field Office
Mr. Lyndon Berezowsky
Special Agent-in-Charge
200 E. Las Olas Boulevard, Suite 1260
Fort Lauderdale, FL 33301
954/356-7540   Fax: 954/356-7549

Chicago Field Office
Mr. Reid Pederson
Special Agent-in-Charge
2400 E. Devon, Suite 300
Des Plaines, IL 60018
312/353-6640   Fax: 312/353-8008

Dallas Field Office
Mr. Leonard Patak
Special Agent-in-Charge
525 Griffin Street, Room 622
Dallas, TX 75202
214/767-9294   Fax: 214/767-9299

San Jose Field Office
Mr. Randall Sike
Special Agent-in-Charge
96 North Third Street, Suite 250
San Jose, CA 95112-5572
408/291-4204   Fax: 408/291-4320

Los Angeles Field Office
Mr. Robert Schoonmaker
Special Agent-in-Charge
2601 Main Street, Suite 310
Irvine, CA 92714-6299
714/251-9001   Fax: 714-251-9103

Intelligence

Acting Assistant Director
Mr. Richard Sherwood
202/482-1208   Fax: 202/482-0964
Rm. 4520

Export Compliance Specialist
Ms. Sandra Ruf
202/482-1208
Rm. 4520

Intelligence Research
Ms. Elizabeth Rosenkrantz
202/482-1208
Rm. 4520

Field Support

Assistant Director
Mr. Mark D. Menefee
202/482-2252   Fax: 202/482-5889
Rm. 4616

Office of Enforcement Support (OES)

> *OES assists the OEE field offices and BXA's export licensing offices by receiving and disseminating export control information on problem end-users and end-uses. The office also makes licensing recommendations to BXA licensing officers based on intelligence information and input received from special agents in the field.*

Director
Mr. Thomas W. Andrukonis
202/482-4255   Fax: 202/482-0971
Rm. 4065

Deputy Director
Mr. Jay Hatfield
202/482-4255
Rm. 4065

Minority Business Development Agency

14th St. & Constitution Ave., NW / Washington DC 20230

> *MBDA is the only federal agency specifically created to encourage the growth of minority-owned businesses in the United States. The agency increases opportunities for racial and ethnic minorities to participate in the free enterprise system through the formation and development of competitive minority-owned and managed firms. MBDA was established in 1969 by executive order.*

Office of the Director

Acting Director
Mr. Courtland Cox
202/482-5061
Rm. 5053

Under Secretary for Oceans & Atmosphere and Administrator, NOAA

14th St. & Constitution Ave., NW / Washington DC 20230

Under Secretary for Oceans and Atmosphere and Administrator,
   National Oceanic and Atmospheric Administration
Dr. D. James Baker
202/482-3436   Fax: 202/408-9674
Rm. 5128

Personal: born 3/23/37 in Long Beach, Calif.

Education: B.S. in physics, Stanford Univ., 1958. Doctorate in experimental physics, Cornell Univ., 1962.

Professional: 1962-63, research associate, Graduate School of Oceanography, Univ. of Rhode Island. 1963-64, doctoral fellow, instant chemical biodynamics, University of Calif. at Berkeley. 1964-73, assistant and associate professor, Harvard University. 1979-86, chairman, professor, School of Oceanography, and dean, Coll. of Ocean and Fisheries Sciences, Univ. of Washington (Seattle). 1982-1993, distinguished visiting scientist, Jet Propulsion Lab, Calif. Inst. of Technology (Pasadena, Calif.). 1983-93, president, Joint Oceanographic Institutions. 1993-present, under sec. for oceans and atmosphere and administrator, National Oceanic and Atmospheric Administration (NOAA), U.S. Dept. of Commerce.

Dr. D. James Baker has been at the helm of the National Oceanic and Atmospheric Administration (NOAA) at the U.S. Department of Commerce since 1993. NOAA's mission is to warn of environmental change and to protect natural resources. NOAA describes, monitors, and predicts weather and climate change; issues warnings against impending destructive natural events; assesses and protects marine fisheries and other living resources and coastal regions; explores, maps, and charts the global ocean; and provides the reference base for navigation and positioning.

As under secretary for oceans and atmosphere and administrator of NOAA, Baker is responsible for the National Weather Service; the National Environmental Satellite, Data, and Information Service; the National Marine Fisheries Service; the National Oceanic Service; and NOAA's office of oceanic and atmospheric research. He is the U.S. commissioner to the International Whaling Commission.

Baker also serves as the co-chairman of the committee on environment and natural resources of the National Science and Technology Council and as an ex-officio member of the president's Council on Sustainable Development. He is the co-chair of the space committee of the U.S.-Russian Joint Commission on Economic and Technological Cooperation and the vice chair of the science and technology committee of the U.S./South Africa Binational Commission. From 1992 until early 1995, he served as chair of Coastal America, and from November 1993 to February 1994, as acting chair of the Council on Environmental Quality in 1993-94.

During the first Clinton term, Baker led a strategic planning effort for NOAA resulting in a plan that includes short-term warning and forecasts of weathers, floods, and coastal impacts including continued modernization of the weather services, prediction of seasonal climate change, and understanding and assessment of long-term change caused by human impact and natural changes. Also included are major efforts to build sustainable fisheries, recover protected species, preserve healthy coastal ecosystems, and support improvements in navigation and positioning.

Under Baker's leadership, NOAA has taken the lead in a newly converged system of civilian and defense meteorological satellites, and has developed new arrangements for the delivery of climate forecasts. In the area of fisheries, NOAA has developed new partnerships among the government, commercial fisheries, coastal communities, and environmental groups in order to provide economic assistance while it is enforcing much-needed enforcement rules.

Baker was previously president of Joint Oceanographic Institutions Inc., dean of the College of Ocean and Fishery Sciences at the University of Washington, and on the faculties of Harvard University and the University of Rhode Island.

Baker has published more than 80 papers and written the book Planet Earth - the View from Space. He has been a member of the editorial boards of Oceanus magazine, Marine Technology Society Journal, and Dynamics of Atmospheres and Oceans. He holds a joint patent for a deep-sea pressure gauge.

Baker is married to Emily Lind Baker.

Office of International Affairs

Deputy Assistant Secretary for International Affairs
Mr. William E. Martin
202/482-6076
Rm. 5809

Office of General Counsel

General Counsel
Ms. Monica Medina
202/482-4080
Rm. 5814A

Senior Counsel for International Law
Ms. Karen K. Davidson
202/482-2114
Rm. 7837

Office of Public and Constituent Affairs

Director
Ms. Lori A. Arguelles
202/482-5647
Rm. 6225

Office of Global Programs

Director
Dr. J. Michael Hall
301/427-2089
Rm. 1210 WAYNE

National Weather Service

8455 Colesville Road / Silver Spring MD 20910

International Affairs Officer
Mr. Martin Yerg
301/713-0645
Rm. 13426

National Marine Fisheries Service (NMFS)

1315 East-West Highway / Silver Spring MD 20910

NMFS administers NOAA's programs which support the domestic and international conservation and management of living marine resources. NMFS provides services and products to support domestic and international fisheries management operations, fisheries development, trade and industry assistance activities, enforcement, protected species and habitat conservation operations, and the scientific and technical aspects of NOAA's marine fisheries program.

Assistant Administrator for Fisheries
Mr. Rolland A. Schmitten
301/713-2239
Rm. 14555

Chief, International Fisheries Division
Mr. Dean Swanson
301/713-2276
Rm. 14141

Chief, Organization and Agreements Division
Mr. Dean E. Swanson
301/713-2276
Rm. 14141

Chief, Intl. Science, Coordination and Analysis Division
Mr. Frederick H. Beaudry
301/713-2288
Rm. 14117

Chief, Trade Services Division
Ms. Linda A. Chaves
301/713-2379
Rm. 12454

National Environmental Satellite, Data and Information Service

FOB 4, Suitland & Silver Hill Roads / Suitland MD 20233

Asst. Administrator for Natl. Envir. Satellite Data & Info. Services
Mr. Robert S. Winokur
301/457-5115
Rm. 2069

Chief, Intl. and Interagency Affairs Office
Mr. Brent D. Smith
301/713-2024
Rm. 3620

Office of Oceanic and Atmospheric Research

1315 East-West Hightway / Silver Spring MD 20910

Asst. Administrator for Oceanic and Atmospheric Research
Dr. Elbert W. Friday, Jr.
301/713-2458
Rm. 11627

Staff Director for Program Development and Coordination
Dr. William Hooke
301/713-2465
Rm. 11560

Patent and Trademark Office

2121 Crystal Drive / Arlington VA 22202

Asst. Secretary and Commissioner of Patents and Trademarks
Mr. Bruce A. Lehman
703/305-8600   Fax: 703/305-8664
Rm. 906

Personal: born 9/19/45 in Beloit, Wis.

Education: B.A., Univ. of Wisconsin, 1967. J.D., Wisconsin Law School, 1970.

Professional: 1974-83, counsel, Cmte. on the Judiciary, U.S. House of Representatives. 1984-93, attorney, Swidler and Berlin (Wash., D.C.). 1993-present, assistant secretary of commerce and commissioner of patents and trademarks, U.S. Department of Commerce. 9/97-present, acting chairman, National Endowment for the Humanities.

The National Journal (June 16, 1997) named Bruce Lehman among the 100 most influential men and women in Washington, D.C. "In today's Information Age, the issue of intellectual property rights is no longer an arcane concern, but a vital part of U.S. trade policy," the National Journal said. "Since taking over his current posts in 1993, Lehman has been the Clinton administration's outspoken voice on such matters here and abroad."

Confirmed by the Senate in 1993 as assistant secretary of commerce and commissioner of patents and trademarks, Lehman is responsible for administering laws relating to patents and trademarks, developing intellectual property policy, and advising the secretary of commerce and the president on copyright and trade-related matters.

In September, 1997, President Clinton appointed him acting chairman of the National Endowment for the Humanities on an interim basis until the White House nominates someone to replace retiring NEH Chairman Sheldon Hackney. The NEH is an independent federal agency which supports research, education, and public programs in the humanities.

Serving as the head of the U.S. delegation to the World Intellectual Property Organization's (WIPO) Diplomatic Conference on Certain Copyright and Neighboring Rights Questions, Lehman successfully concluded negotiations which resulted in the adoption of two treaties: the WIPO Copyright Treaty and the WIPO Performances and Phonograms Treaty. By updating international copyright law for the digital age, the treaties will facilitate the growth of on-line digital commerce over the global information infrastructure.

Lehman helped develop legislation implementing the intellectual property provisions of the Uruguay Round Agreement to enable American inventors to more easily commercialize their inventions in the highly lucrative Japanese market.

Lehman is streamlining the Patent and Trademark Office (PTO) to be more responsive and customer-focused. The effort has been recognized by Vice President Gore's National Performance Review as a success story for government reinvention. The commissioner held a series of public hearings throughout the country to solicit the views and concerns of PTO customers. Feedback has led PTO to develop new guidelines for patents in the biotechnology field and establish partnership libraries in Sunnyvale, Calif. and Detroit, Mich., to provide better access to PTO information and services.

Lehman chairs the working group on intellectual property rights of the National Information Infrastructure Task Force. In September 1995, the working group released Intellectual Property and the National Information Infrastructure, which examines the role of copyright law in cyberspace and makes recommendations to fortify copyright protection of intellectual property in the networked environment of the information highway.

Before coming to the Patent and Trademark Office, Lehman was a partner for ten years in the Washington, D.C., law firm of Swidler & Berlin, where he represented individuals, companies, and trade associations in the areas of intellectual property rights, and the interests of the motion picture, telecommunications, pharmaceutical, computer software, and broadcasting industries.

Before that, Lehman worked for nine years in the U.S. House of Representatives as counsel to the Judiciary Committee and chief counsel to the subcommittee on courts, civil liberties, and the administration of justice. He was the committee's principal legal adviser in the drafting of the 1976 Copyright Act, the 1980 Computer Software Amendments, and the 1982 Amendments to the patent laws.

Earlier in his career, Lehman served as legal counsel to the Wisconsin state legislature, as an attorney with the U.S. Department of Justice, and as an officer in the U.S. Army.

Office of Legislative and Intl. Affairs

Administrator
Mr. Robert L. Stoll
703/305-9300
Rm. 902

Intl. Trade Policy Analyst
Ms. JoEllen Urban
703/305-9300
Rm. 902

Deputy Asst. Commissioner for Patent Policy & Projects

Director, Office of Intl. Liaison
Mr. Robert Saifer
703/308-6851
Rm. 749

2221 Jefferson Davis Hwy. / Arlington VA 22202

Manager
Foreign Documents Division
Ms. Kathleen Dell'Orto
703/308-3278
Rm. 2C15

U. S. Department of Defense

1000 Defense Pentagon / Washington DC 20301-1000
703/545-6700

INTRODUCTION

The Defense Department operates internationally in carrying out its responsibility of providing the military forces needed to deter war and protect the security of the nation. The readiness function includes keeping a close eye on the industrial base and evaluating the U.S.'s dependence on off-shore suppliers. The Defense Technology Security Administration reviews the international transfer of defense-related technology, goods, services, and munitions consistent with U.S. foreign policy and national security objectives.

Office of the Secretary

1000 Defense Pentagon / Washington DC 20301-1000

Secretary of Defense
Secretary William S. Cohen
703/695-5261   FAX 703/695-1219
Rm. 3E880

Personal: born 8/28/40 in Bangor, Maine.

Education: B.A. (cum laude) in Latin, Bowdoin Coll., 1962. LL.B. (cum laude), Boston Univ. Law School, 1965.

Professional: 1965-66, assistant editor, Journal of American Trial Lawyers Association. 1967-72, practicing attorney, Paine, Cohen, Lynch, Weatherbee and Kobritz. 1966, instructor, Husson Coll. 1968-70, assistant county attorney, Penobscot County. 1968-72, instructor, Univ. of Maine. 1969-72, member, Bangor City Council. 1971-72, mayor, Bangor, Maine. 1971-72, member, Bangor School Board. 1973-79, member, U.S. House of Representatives. 1979-97, member, U.S. Senate (R-Maine). 1997-present, secretary, U.S. Department of Defense.

On Jan. 22, 1997, William S. Cohen became the 20th secretary of the Department of Defense. Prior to this position, Cohen had served as a senator and representative on Capitol Hill for 26 years.

As secretary of defense, Cohen is the principal defense adviser to the president and is responsible for the formulation of general defense policy and policy related to all matters of direct and primary concern to DOD, and for execution of approved policy. Under the direction of the president, the secretary exercises authority, direction, and control over DOD, its $250 billion budget, and 2.5 million employees.

Upon examination of the Quadrennial Defense Review, Cohen has focused on both strategy and management of DOD. In a speech before the Center for Strategic and International Studies in May 1997, Cohen articulated a new defense strategy that called for shaping the international security environment in ways favorable to the U.S., responding quickly and decisively to threats, and preparing for an uncertain future.

In terms of management, Cohen's priorities include re-engineering the department to make it more efficient. He has stated "the only way to pay for the continuing revolution in military affairs was to also have a revolution in the business affairs of DOD to slough off the excess weight we still carry from the long winter of the Cold War...We need to be like a decathlon athlete...fast, agile, and able to do many things well."

Since becoming secretary of defense, Cohen has recommended peripheral cuts in troop levels and weapons purchases, and continuation of efforts to privatize numerous defense support functions by contracting them out to civilian companies. Cohen supports active engagements for the U.S. military forces, rather than "myriad peacekeeping operations" (*National Journal* 6/14/97).

Upon graduation from law school, Cohen worked as an editor, lawyer, and educator between 1965 and 1972. His political career took flight following 1969, when he served as a member on the Bangor City Council and in 1971 when he was elected mayor of Bangor for two years. After his term as mayor, Cohen began his extended stay on Capitol Hill. After a six year stint in the House, Cohen served as a Maine senator between 1979 and 1997.

While in the Senate, Cohen gained valuable experience serving on the Armed Forces Committee. Cohen, an advocate for strong defense, worked to ensure the defense budget was not cut at the expense of current or long term readiness.

An influential voice on defense and international security issues, Cohen played a leading role in crafting the Goldwater-Nichols Defense Reorganization Act of 1986. He was the Senate sponsor of the GI Bill of 1984, and the subsequent enhancements to this landmark legislation. Cohen's efforts led to the creation of the Rapid Deployment Force, which later developed into the Central Command, and the maritime prepositioning program, both of which were key to the success of the Gulf War. He also co-authored the Intelligence Oversight Reform Act of 1991, as well as legislation designed to overhaul U.S. counterintelligence efforts and defend against foreign political and industrial espionage.

From the Competition in Contracting Act of 1984, which he authored, to the enactment of the Federal Acquisition Reform Act of 1996, which he played a key role in drafting, Cohen has been in the forefront of reforming the federal government's procurement process. Committed to bringing accountability and private sector practices to government agencies, he also authored the Information Technology Management Reform Act of 1996 to improve the way federal agencies manage information technology investments and streamline the acquisition process.

Cohen served on the board of directors of the Council on Foreign Relations from 1989 to 1997, and in 1996, he chaired the Council's Middle East Study Group. He also has chaired and served on numerous study groups and committees at the Center for Strategic and International Studies, School for Advanced International Studies, and Brookings Institution on issues ranging from DOD reorganization, to NATO enlargement, to chemical weapons arms control. Since 1985, Cohen has led the American delegation of senior executive branch officials and members of congress to the Munich conference on security policy, which brings together senior officials from NATO and Partnership for Peace countries. He also led American delegations to the American-Arab Dialogue in Cairo and the Pacific Dialogue in Kuala Lumpur, regional conferences on security and economic issues.

In 1974, Cohen was selected by TIME magazine as one of America's

DEPARTMENT OF DEFENSE

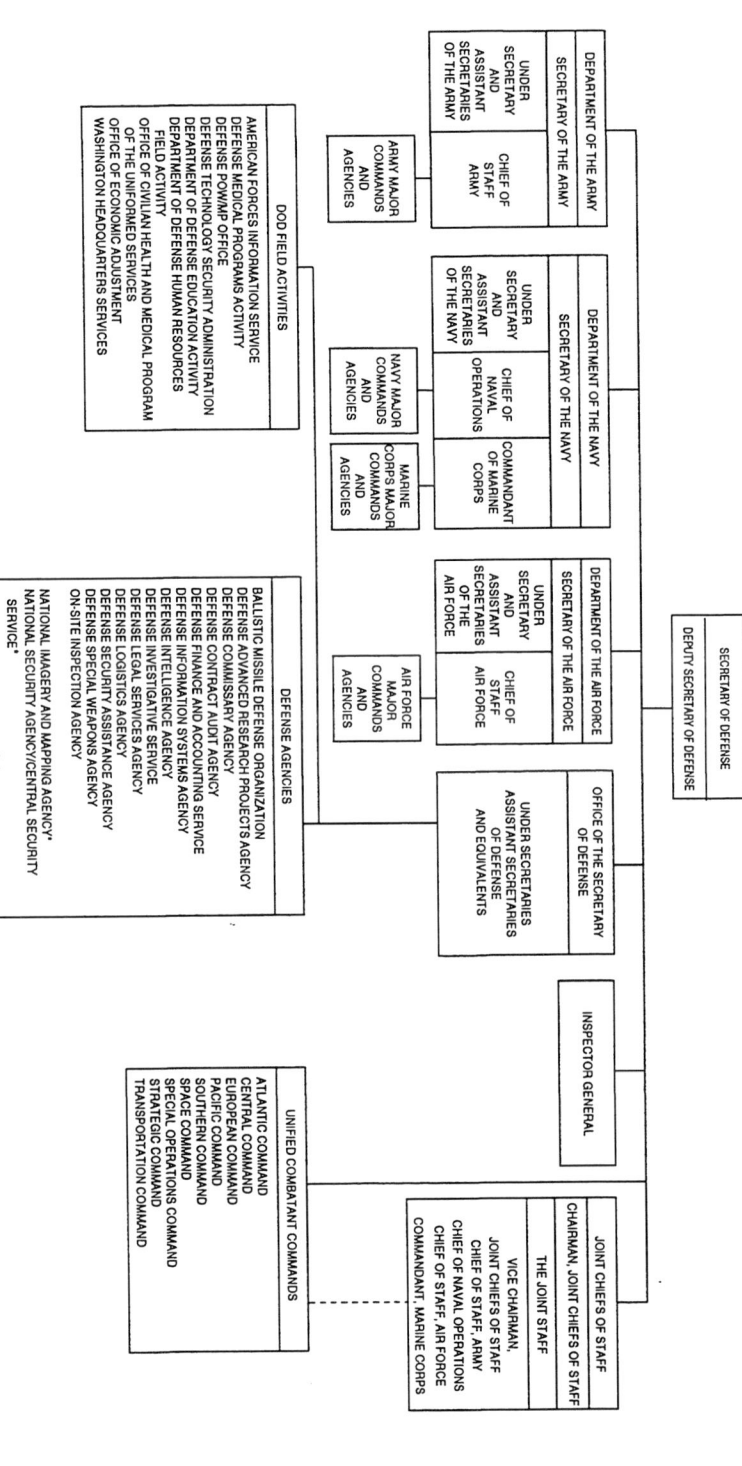

SECRETARY OF DEFENSE

DEPUTY SECRETARY OF DEFENSE

DEPARTMENT OF THE ARMY
SECRETARY OF THE ARMY

- UNDER SECRETARY AND ASSISTANT SECRETARIES OF THE ARMY
- CHIEF OF STAFF, ARMY
- ARMY MAJOR COMMANDS AND AGENCIES

DEPARTMENT OF THE NAVY
SECRETARY OF THE NAVY

- UNDER SECRETARY AND ASSISTANT SECRETARIES OF THE NAVY
- CHIEF OF NAVAL OPERATIONS
- COMMANDANT OF MARINE CORPS
- NAVY MAJOR COMMANDS AND AGENCIES
- MARINE CORPS MAJOR COMMANDS AND AGENCIES

DEPARTMENT OF THE AIR FORCE
SECRETARY OF THE AIR FORCE

- UNDER SECRETARY AND ASSISTANT SECRETARIES OF THE AIR FORCE
- CHIEF OF STAFF, AIR FORCE
- AIR FORCE MAJOR COMMANDS AND AGENCIES

OFFICE OF THE SECRETARY OF DEFENSE
- UNDER SECRETARIES ASSISTANT SECRETARIES OF DEFENSE AND EQUIVALENTS

INSPECTOR GENERAL

JOINT CHIEFS OF STAFF
- CHAIRMAN, JOINT CHIEFS OF STAFF
- THE JOINT STAFF
- VICE CHAIRMAN, JOINT CHIEFS OF STAFF
- CHIEF OF STAFF, ARMY
- CHIEF OF NAVAL OPERATIONS
- CHIEF OF STAFF, AIR FORCE
- COMMANDANT, MARINE CORPS

DOD FIELD ACTIVITIES
- AMERICAN FORCES INFORMATION SERVICE
- DEFENSE MEDICAL PROGRAMS ACTIVITY
- DEFENSE POW/MIP OFFICE
- DEFENSE TECHNOLOGY SECURITY ADMINISTRATION
- DEPARTMENT OF DEFENSE EDUCATION ACTIVITY
- DEPARTMENT OF DEFENSE HUMAN RESOURCES FIELD ACTIVITY
- OFFICE OF CIVILIAN HEALTH AND MEDICAL PROGRAM OF THE UNIFORMED SERVICES
- OFFICE OF ECONOMIC ADJUSTMENT
- WASHINGTON HEADQUARTERS SERVICES

DEFENSE AGENCIES
- BALLISTIC MISSILE DEFENSE ORGANIZATION
- DEFENSE ADVANCED RESEARCH PROJECTS AGENCY
- DEFENSE COMMISSARY AGENCY
- DEFENSE CONTRACT AUDIT AGENCY
- DEFENSE FINANCE AND ACCOUNTING SERVICE
- DEFENSE INFORMATION SYSTEMS AGENCY
- DEFENSE INTELLIGENCE AGENCY
- DEFENSE INVESTIGATIVE SERVICE
- DEFENSE LEGAL SERVICES AGENCY
- DEFENSE LOGISTICS AGENCY
- DEFENSE SECURITY ASSISTANCE AGENCY
- DEFENSE SPECIAL WEAPONS AGENCY
- ON-SITE INSPECTION AGENCY
- NATIONAL IMAGERY AND MAPPING AGENCY*
- NATIONAL SECURITY AGENCY/CENTRAL SECURITY SERVICE*

*Reports directly to the Secretary of Defense

UNIFIED COMBATANT COMMANDS
- ATLANTIC COMMAND
- CENTRAL COMMAND
- EUROPEAN COMMAND
- PACIFIC COMMAND
- SOUTHERN COMMAND
- SPACE COMMAND
- SPECIAL OPERATIONS COMMAND
- STRATEGIC COMMAND
- TRANSPORTATION COMMAND

200 future leaders. The U.S. Junior Chamber of Commerce named him one of the 10 Outstanding Young Men in America in 1975. In 1975, the Boston University Law School honored him with its prestigious "Young Lawyers Chair," and in 1976, the Boston University Alumni Association presented him with its Award for Distinguished Public Service. In 1980, he received the "Vanguard" award from the Non-Commissioned Officers Association for his work on behalf of military personnel and in 1983, the same association honored him with the L. Mendel Rivers Award. In 1996, he received the U.S. Special Operations Command Medal.

In addition to his public service career, Cohen is a novelist and poet, having written and co-written eight books, including two books of poetry, three novels, and three works of non-fiction.

Cohen is a 1962 graduate of Bowdoin University and received his LL.B. from Boston University Law School in 1965. He is married to Janet Langhart and they have two grown sons, Kevin and Chris.

Chief of Staff
Mr. Robert S. Tyrer
703/695-5261   FAX 703/697-9080

Personal: born 4/30/57 in Hamilton, Ohio.

Education: B.S., Univ. of Maine, 1987.

Professional: 1975-79, staff, Rep. William S. Cohen (R-Maine). 1979-87, staff, Sen. Cohen. 1987-88, reporter, *Sentinel-News* (Kentucky). 1989-97, administrative assistant, Sen. Cohen. 1997-present, chief of staff, Office of the secretary of Defense, U.S. Dept. of Defense.

Robert Tyrer is a familiar face on Secretary of Defense William Cohen's staff. Tyrer has served as Cohen's chief of staff since the secretary was sworn in on Jan. 24, 1997, but he first started working for Cohen more than 20 years ago.

Tyrer joined then-Congressman Cohen (R-Maine) in 1975 as a college intern and then became a staff assistant. After Cohen's election to the U.S. Senate in 1978, Tyrer held positions as director of the Bangor, Maine office, press secretary, campaign manager, and starting in 1989, chief of staff.

Between jobs on Cohen's staff, Tyrer worked from 1987 to 1988 as a reporter for the *Sentinel-News* in Kentucky.

Tyrer was born in Ohio in 1957 and is a 1987 graduate of the University of Maine.

Under Secretary for Acquistiion & Technology

Deputy Under Secretary of Defense, International and Commercial Programs

3070 Defense Pentagon / Washington DC 20301-3070

Deputy Under Secretary of Defense
Mr. Paul J. (Page) Hoeper
703/697-4172   FAX 703/693-2026

Education: B.S.E. in basic engineering, Princeton Univ., 1968. M.A.T. in mathematics, Harvard Univ., 1972.

Professional: president, Fortune Financial. 1996-present, deputy under secretary of defense for international and commercial programs, U.S. Department of Defense.

Page Hoeper's association with the Department of Defense and the defense industry dates back to the mid-1970s, but he didn't join the department until 1996 when he was appointed deputy under secretary of defense for international and commercial programs.

Hoeper advises the under secretary of defense for acquisition and technology, establishes policies for economic reinvestment, dual use technology programs, international cooperative programs, and the Defense Export Loan Guarantee program. He also reports to the deputy secretary of defense on all matters affecting small business and serves as the deputy secretary's principal adviser on small business matters.

Prior to joining DOD, Hoeper served as president of Fortune Financial, a private merchant bank, where he was responsible for directing and implementing investment strategy and for overseeing the management of several private companies the firm controlled.

In the mid-1970s, Hoeper consulted to the U.S. Navy on major missile and anti-submarine system procurement. He also has consulted to private companies in the aerospace industry on numerous defense programs, strategic issues, and corporate restructuring.

Hoeper was selected in 1993 to serve on the Defense Science Board Task Force on Acquisition Reform. As a member of the task force, he served on various panels including the Oversight Cost Panel and the Large-Scale R&D Commercial Practices Panel. He was the DSB representative to the Integrated Dual Use Commercial Companies Working Group sponsored by the deputy under secretary for acquisition reform.

Hoeper also served on the Stanford Law School faculty and as an adjunct professor at the University of Southern California Law Center. He developed "What Lawyers Should Know About Business" for the Stanford Law School in 1989 and has been teaching the course at USC since 1991.

Hoeper received the Secretary of Defense Medal for Outstanding Public Service in December 1996. He graduated from Princeton University in 1968 with a degree in basic engineering and earned his M.A.T. in mathematics form Harvard University in 1972.

When he's not working, Hoeper enjoys competitive tennis, fly fishing, and playing the piano. He and his wife, Barbara, have two children.

Asst. Deputy Under Sec. of Defense (Armaments Cooperation)
Mr. Alfred G. Volkman

703/697-4431
Rm. 3E1082

Asst. Deputy Under Secretary (Export Finance)
Mr. Tom Murtagh
703/697-6800
Rm. 2B329

International Liaison
Ms. Elaine Kalaidis
703/693-2472
Rm. 3E1082

Deputy Under Secretary for
Environmental Security

International Activities
Director
COL Mark Hamilton, USAF
703/695-3329
Rm. 3D765

Under Secretary of Defense for Policy

2000 Defense Pentagon / Washington DC 20301-2000

Under Secretary of Defense for Policy
Mr. Walter B. Slocombe
703/695-5136   FAX 703/697-6602
Rm. 4E808

Personal: born 1941; raised in Ann Arbor, Mich.

Education: B.A., Woodrow Wilson School of Public and International Affairs, Princeton Univ., 1963. Graduate studies on Soviet politics (Rhodes Scholar), Balliol College (Oxford, England), 1963-65. J.D. (summa cum laude, note editor, law review), Harvard Law School, 1968.

Professional: 1968-69, law clerk for Justice Abe Fortas, U.S. Supreme Court. 1969-70, staff member, program analysis office, National Security Council. 1970-71, research associate, International Institute for Strategic Studies (London, England). 1971-77, attorney (partner since 1974), Caplin & Drysdale (Wash., D.C.) 1977-79, principal deputy assistant secretary; 1979-81, deputy under secretary for policy planning, Department of Defense. 1981-93, attorney, Caplin & Drysdale. 1/93-6/93, consultant to the under secretary for policy; 6/93-9/94, principal deputy under secretary of defense for policy;. 9/94-present, under secretary for policy, DOD.

As under secretary of defense for policy since Sept. 14, 1994, Walter Slocombe is the principal staff assistant to the secretary of defense for policy matters relating to overall international security policy and political-military affairs. Functional areas include NATO affairs; net assessments; foreign military sales; arms limitation agreement; international trade and technology; regional security affairs; special operations and low-intensity conflict; integration of departmental plans and policies with overall national security objectives; drug control policy, requirements, priorities, systems, resources, and programs; and issuance of policy guidance affecting departmental programs. Slocombe previously was principal deputy under secretary of defense for policy from June 1993 until he took on his current job.

When Slocombe was brought into the Carter administration by Harold Brown, *The Economist* called him, "an accomplished young lawyer" and a "bright young liberal." The praise for Slocombe was a result of his academic studies at Oxford University as a Rhodes Scholar, and the term he spent working as a research associate at London's International Institute for Strategic Studies.

Slocombe became well respected by the arms community and by DOD for his performance as deputy under secretary for policy planning and as principal deputy assistant secretary for international security affairs. His service at DOD interrupted a career at the Washington D.C. law firm of Caplin & Drysdale where he had become a full partner in 1974.

Slocombe has written extensively on matters of defense strategy and national security. While working in London, he authored "The Political Implications of Strategic Parity", a paper for the International Institute for Strategic Studies. His contributions to the study of U.S. Cold War strategies include: "The Countervailing Strategy" (*International Security*, 1981); "Extended Deterrence" (*Washington Quarterly*, 1984); and, "Strategic Stability in a Restructured World" (*Survival*, 1990).

Slocombe has served as an advisor to several quasi-governmental organizations, such as RAND, the Strategic Air Command (SAC) Technical Advisory Committee, and the advisory panel for the Office of Technology Assessment studies of strategic command and controls. He has held memberships on the advisory councils of the Center for Strategic and International Studies at Princeton University's Woodrow Wilson School of Public and International Affairs, the National Security Archive, the Center for Naval Analyses Strategy and Forces Division, MIT's Lincoln National Laboratory, and the Center for National Security Studies at the Los Alamos National Laboratory. Slocombe also sits on the board of directors of the U.S. Committee for the International Institute for Strategic Studies.

Slocombe is married to another Clinton appointee, Ellen Seidman, who is a member of the National Economic Council staff. The couple has two grown daughters and a teen-age son.

Principal Deputy Under Secretary of Defense (Policy)
Mr. Jan Lodal
703/695-7114   FAX 703/697-8520

Education: B.A. in engineering, Rice Univ., 1965. M.S. in engineering and M.P.A., Princeton Univ., 1967.

Professional: division director, office of the secretary of defense. executive vice president, director and co-founder, American Management Systems. senior staff member, National Security Council. 1986-94, president, chairman, and founder, Intelus. 1994-present, principal deputy under secretary of defense for policy, U.S. Department of Defense.

Jan Lodal left a computer systems firm he founded to become the Department of Defense's principal deputy under secretary of defense for policy. He was sworn in on Oct. 3, 1994.

Lodal founded Intelus in 1986 and was the company's president and chairman. Prior to that, he was executive vice president, director, and co-founder of American Management Systems, a leading computer systems and software firm. In addition to his corporate responsibilities there, Lodal was responsible for the design and installation of New York City's integrated financial management system, which became the model for new financial systems in more than 150 major state and local governments.

During the Nixon and Ford administrations, Lodal was on the White House staff as deputy for program analysis to Henry A. Kissinger. He was the primary White House staff officer on arms control matters and defense program issues. Lodal has also been director of the NATO and General Purpose Forces analysis division in DOD's systems analysis office. Earlier, he worked in both the strategic forces division and the Southeast Asia programs division.

Lodal has served as chairman of the board of Group Health Association Inc. and as a director of The Atlantic Council and Republic Engineered Steels. He also has been a member and director of the Aspen Strategy Group and a member of the editorial board of Foreign Policy. Lodal is a member of the Council on Foreign Relations, the American Economic Association, the American Council on Germany, the International Institute for Strategic Studies, and the Council on Excellence in Government. He also is a trustee of the American Boychoir.

Lodal, who lives in McLean, Va., has written numerous articles and given many lectures on national security policy, arms control, and state and local government financial management.

Lodal earned a bachelor's degree in engineering from Rice University in 1965. He graduated from Princeton University in 1967 with and a master's of science degree in engineering and a masters of public affairs degree. Lodal and his wife, Elizabeth, have two children.

Assistant Director, International Security Programs
Ms. Susan Ludlow-MacMurray
703/695-6607
Rm. 2E812

Assistant for NATO Security
Ms. Christine Bromwell
703/697-9832
Rm. 3C277

Assistant Secretary for Strategy and Threat Reduction

2900 Defense Pentagon / Washington D.C. 20301-2900

Assistant Secretary of Defense for
  Strategy and Threat Reduction
Dr. Edward L. (Ted) Warner
703/697-7728   FAX 703/614-9281
Rm. 4E817

Personal: born 1940 in Okemos, Mich.

Education: B.S., U.S. Naval Academy, 1962. M.A., Ph.D., Princeton Univ., 1975.

Professional: 20 years in the U.S. Air Force. intelligence officer with the 93rd Bomb Wing; instructor, U.S. Air Force Academy. analyst, CIA Assistant Air Attaché, U.S. Embassy, Moscow. 1978-82, deputy, head of staff group, deputy chief of strategy division, USAF headquarters. 1982-93, senior defense analyst, RAND Corp. 1993-present, assistant secretary of defense for strategy and requirements (renamed strategy and threat reduction), U.S. Dept. of Defense.

Ted Warner became assistant secretary of defense for strategy and requirements in 1993 after more than 10 years as a senior defense analyst at RAND Corp., one of the nation's premier think tanks. The office and his position have since been renamed "Strategy and Threat Reduction" as of November, 1997, and assumed the responsibilities of the office of the assistant secretary of for international security policy.

Warner advises the secretary of defense and the under secretary of defense for policy on national security strategy; on the resources, forces and contingency plans necessary to implement that strategy; and on the DOD policy and planning for U.S. participation in international peacekeeping and humanitarian assistance activities.

Warner, a 20-year veteran of the Air Force, also provides policy input to the military requirements process and the Defense Acquisition Board, administers the National Security Education Program, and is the assistant chairman of the Defense Policy Board.

Until his retirement from the Air Force in 1982, Warner served for 20 years in various assignments, including positions on the USAF staff at the Pentagon. From 1982 to 1993, he was a senior defense analyst with the RAND Corp. in Washington, D.C., where he conducted studies on American national security policy and the defense and foreign policies of Russia and other successor states of the former Soviet Union, and East-West arms control issues.

Warner has taught graduate seminars on Soviet defense and arms control policy at The George Washington University, Johns Hopkins School of Advanced International Studies, Princeton University, and Columbia University. He also has been a member of two advisory panels for the Central Intelligence Agency.

He has published several books and numerous reports on defense issues and has testified numerous times before Congress. He is a 1962 graduate of the U.S. Naval Academy and earned his Ph.D. in politics from Princeton University in 1975.

Principal Deputy Asst. Secretary for
  Strategy and Threat Reduction
Mr. Franklin C. Miller
703/695-0942
Rm. 4E817

Personal: born 10/2/50 in New York, N.Y.

Education: A.B., Williams Coll., 1972. M.P.A., Woodrow Wilson School, Princeton Univ., 1977.

Professional: 1972-75, U.S. Navy. 1977-79, politico affairs officers, politico-military bureau, Department of State. 1979-81, assistant for theater nuclear forces policy; 1981-89, director, strategic forces policy; 1989-94, deputy assistant secretary for nuclear forces and arms control policy; 1994-present, principal deputy assistant secretary of defense for strategy and threat reduction, U.S. Department of Defense.

Department of Defense policy for countering the proliferation of weapons of mass destruction is one of Franklin Miller's responsibilities. Before joining DOD, Miller worked for two years at the State Department's politico-military bureau on a variety of nuclear policy and arms control issues. He was responsible for analyzing and recommending various aspects of naval support of U.S. diplomatic initiatives and was a principal State Department action officer on the nuclear weapons deployment plan.

Miller's career with DOD began in 1979 when he transferred from the State Department to become an assistant for theater nuclear policy in the office of the secretary of defense. In that position he was involved in NATO's decision to modernize its long-range nuclear forces and in many other nuclear policy issues relating to short-range, intermediate-range, and naval tactical systems.

In late 1981, Miller was appointed director of strategic forces policy. He was responsible for the formulation and review of U.S. nuclear deterrence policy and for ensuring the U.S. strategic force capabilities and nuclear targeting plans were consistent with national policy objectives.

Miller was promoted to deputy assistant secretary of defense for nuclear forces and arms control policy in December 1989. In that role he was responsible for directing the formulation and coordination of DOD policy on strategic offensive forces and strategic targeting, theater nuclear forces and arms control, and strategic nuclear arms control. He made major contributions to the START I and START II treaties, the September 1991 Presidential Nuclear Initiative, and to changes in NATO's nuclear posture. He also led DOD's 1989 through 1991 overhaul of the nuclear planning process and of the SIOP. Miller was promoted to principal deputy assistant secretary of defense for international security policy in May 1994.

Miller received his bachelor of arts degree with honors in history and highest honors in political science from Williams College in 1972. After graduation, Miller entered the Navy and served as communications officer and later as anti-submarine warfare officer on board the USS Joseph Hewes. Miller transferred to the U.S. Naval Reserve in 1975 in order to continue his education. He earned a master's in public affairs from the Woodrow Wilson School at Princeton University in 1977.

Miller was awarded the Defense Distinguished Civilian Service Medal, the Defense Department's highest civilian award, in 1985,

1988, 1989, and 1993. In January 1997, he was presented with the Department of Defense Medal for Distinguished Public Service. He also was presented with the Department of State's Meritorious Honor Medal in 1993 for his contributions to the START II Treaty. In September 1996, Miller was made an honorary graduate of the United Kingdom's Joint Services Defense College. He is the fourth American and the only U.S. civilian to have received this honor. A career member of the Senior Executive Service, Miller was awarded the rank of Meritorious Executive by the president in 1989. He is a member of the Council on Foreign Relations and the International Institute for Strategic Studies.

Miller and his wife, Alice, have two sons.

Deputy Assistant Secretary for Forces Policy

Deputy Assistant Secretary
Dr. John Harvey
703/695-5553
Rm. 4B868

Deputy Assistant Secretary for Requirements and Counterproliferation Policy

Deputy Assistant Secretary
Dr. James N. Miller
703/697-0209
Rm. 4B940

Deputy Assistant Secretary for Russia, Ukraine, and Eurasia

Deputy Assistant Secretary
Dr. Catherine Kelleher
703/697-7202
Rm. 4D825

Director, Slavic States Office
Mr. Ed Pusey
703/614-6721
Rm. 4D825

Deputy Director, Russia and Belarus
Ms. Patricia Jacubec
703/697-0809
Rm. 4D825

Deputy Director, European Section
Mr. Ralph Cacci
703/697-7202
Rm. 4D825

Deputy Assistant Secretary for Strategy

Deputy Assistant Secretary
Ms. Michele A. Flournoy
703/614-0421
Rm. 4B724

Deputy Assistant Secretary for Threat Reduction Policy

Deputy Assistant Secretary
Dr. Susan Koch
703/695-4503
Rm. 4C762

Director, Former Soviet Union Nuclear Affairs Office
Dr. Mark B. Schneider
703/697-0030
Rm. 5A670

Asst. Secretary for Intl. Security Affairs

2400 Defense Pentagon / Washington DC 20301-2400

Assistant Secretary of Defense for International Security Affairs
Mr. Franklin D. Kramer
703/695-4351   FAX 703/697-7230
Rm. 4E838

Education: B.A. (cum laude), Yale Univ., 1967. J.D. (magna cum laude), Harvard Law School, 1971.

Professional: 1971-72, law clerk, Hon. J. Edward Lumbard, Second Circuit U.S. Court of Appeals. 1972-77, associate, Shea & Gardner. 1977-79, special assistant to the assistant secretary of defense for international security affairs; 1979-81, principal deputy assistant secretary of defense for international security affairs, U.S. Department of Defense. 1982-96, partner, Shea & Gardner. 1/31/96-3/29/96, deputy assistant secretary of defense for European and NATO Affairs; 3/29/96-present assistant secretary of defense for international security affairs, U.S. Dept. of Defense.

Franklin Kramer was appointed assistant secretary of defense for international security affairs in March 1996 after serving about two months as deputy assistant secretary of defense for European and NATO affairs.

Kramer left the Washington, D.C., law firm of Shea & Gardner, where he had been a partner since 1982, to work for DOD. He was not a newcomer to the department in 1996, however. Kramer's career with DOD started in 1977 when he was special assistant to the assistant secretary of defense for international security affairs. From 1979 to 1981, he was principal deputy assistant secretary of defense for international security affairs.

While at Shea & Gardner, Kramer handled international transactions and trade, government contracts, acquisitions and finance, and antitrust. He previously worked as an associate at the firm from 1972 to 1977.

During the 1992 presidential campaign, Kramer advised the Democratic presidential campaign on defense and politico-military matters. He also has advised Senate and House members, prior Democratic presidential campaigns, and congressional candidates on national security issues.

Kramer has written and testified on various defense and foreign policy issues and served on a number of task forces and committees on matters ranging from the development and control of ballistic missiles to U.S. policy in China. His publications include articles ranging from the role of the secretary of defense in the national security process, to U.S. military strategy and force development, to the government's approach to security assistance, to the modernization of nuclear weapons.

Kramer is a member of the International Institute of Strategic Studies. He also has served as president of the World Affairs Council of Washington, D.C., a member of the advisory board for the Center for National Policy, a member of the Technical Advisory Committee for the Center for Naval Analyses' Strategic Policy Analysis Group, and a principal on the Council for Excellence in Government.

Kramer graduated from Yale University in 1967. He received his law degree from Harvard Law School in 1971. He was executive editor of the *Harvard Law Review* from 1970 to 1971.

Kramer is married and has two children.

Principal Deputy Assistant Secretary
Mr. Frederick C. Smith
703/693-0482
4E841

Director, Foreign Military Rights Affairs
Mr. Philip E. Barringer
703/695-6385
Rm. 4B661

Deputy Assistant Secretary for African Affairs

Deputy Assistant Secretary
Mr. Vincent D. Kern
703/697-8824
4B747

Country Director, Benin, Burkina Faso, Cape Verde, Côte d'Ivoire, Guinea, Guinea-Bissau, Mali, Mauritania, Niger, Senegal, Togo and Western Sahara

VACANT
703/697-8824
Rm. 4B747

Country Director, Burundi, Cameroon, Chad, Congo, Equatorial Guinea, Gabon, Rwanda, Sao Tome, Principe, Angola and Mozambique

Mr. Greg Saunders
703/697-9753
Rm. 4B746

Country Director, Lesotho, Namibia, South Africa, Swaziland,

Ms. Amanda Dory
703/697-9753
Rm. 4B746

Country Director, Botswana, Comoros, Djibouti, Eritrea, Ethiopia, Kenya, Madagascar, Malawi, Mauritius, Seychelles, Somalia, Sudan, Tanzania, Uganda, Zambia, and Zimbabwe

Mr. John Lellenberg
703/697-9753
Rm. 4B746

African Crisis Response Initiative Project Coordinator
Mr. Charles Ikins
703/697-9753
Rm. 4B746

Deputy Asst. Secretary for Asian and Pacific Affairs

Deputy Assistant Secretary
Dr. Kurt Campbell
703/695-4175
Rm. 4C839

Country Director, Australia, New Zealand & S. Pacific Islands
VACANT

703/695-6944
Rm. 4C840

Country Director, Philippines, Indonesia, Singapore, Malaysia and Brunei

Ms. Mary Tighe
703/697-0555
Rm. 4C840

Country Director, Thailand, Burma, Vietnam, Laos and Cambodia
Dr. Lewis M. Stern
703/695-0555
Rm. 4C840

Country Director, Japan
LTC Robin Sakoda, USA
703/695-7886
Rm. 4C840

Country Director, South Korea
Mr. Richard Finn
703/697-4689
Rm. 4C840

Country Director, North Korea
Mr. Thomas Harvey
703/697-5278
Rm. 4C840

Country Director, China, Mongolia, Hong Kong and Taiwan
Mr. Randy Schriver
703/697-7757
Rm. 4C840

Defense Prisoner of War/Missing in Action (POW/MIA) Office
1745 Jefferson Davis Hwy. / Arlington VA 22202

Executive Secretary, U.S.-Russia Joint Commission
Mr. Norm Kass
703/602-2202   FAX 703/602-1890
Rm. 800

Deputy Assistant Secretary for Near East and South Asian Affairs
1100 Defense Pentagon / Washington DC 20301-1100

Deputy Assistant Secretary
Ms. Alina Romanowski
703/697-5146
Rm. 4D765

Country Director, Egypt
COL Gerald Jeanes, USAF
703/697-4592
Rm. 4D765

Country Director, Israel
Mr. Danny Sebright
703/697-5173
Rm. 4D765

Country Director, Jordan, Lebanon, Syria and Palestinian Affairs
LTC Gary Taphorn, USA
703/697-4592
Rm. 4D765

Country Director, Algeria, Morocco, Libya and Tunisia
Mr. James Russell
703/697-9745
Rm. 4D765

Country Director, India, Sri Lanka, Nepal and Diego Garcia
COL Larry Smith, USAF
703/697-4592
Rm. 4D765

Country Director, Pakistan, Afghanistan, Bangladesh and Bhutan
COL Jay Greer, USA
703/695-3890   FAX 703/693-6795
Rm. 4D765

Country Director, Saudi Arabia and United Arab Emirates
Mr. Michael M. MacMurray
703/697-3890
Rm. 4D765

Country Director, Bahrain, Oman, Qatar and Yemen
CAPT Larry Salter, USN
703/697-8088
Rm. 4D765

Country Director, Iraq
CMDR Woody Short, USN
703/697-4592
Rm. 4D765

Country Director, for Iran and Kuwait
Ms. Leslie Ireland
703/697-9745
Rm. 4D765

Deputy Asst. Secretary for European & NATO Affairs
2400 Defense Pentagon / Washington DC 20301-2400

Acting Deputy Assistant Secretary
Mr. Tom Longstreth
703/697-7207
Rm. 4D800

Director, European Policy
Mr. John Berry
703/695-1512
Rm. 4D762

Director, NATO Policy
Ms. Lisa Bronson
703/697-1386
Rm. 4D820

Assistant Secretary for Special Operations and Low-Intensity Conflict

2500 Defense Pentagon / Washington DC 20301-2500

Assistant Secretary of Defense
Mr. Henry Allen Holmes
703/693-2895   FAX 703/693-6335

Personal: born 1/31/33 in Bucharest, Romania.

Education: B.A., Princeton Univ., 1954. Graduate Studies, Institut d'Etudes Politiques, Univ. of Paris.

Professional: 1954-57, infantry officer, U.S. Marine Corps. 1963-67, political officer, U.S. Foreign Service (Rome, Italy); 1972-74, counselor for political affairs, U.S. Foreign Service (Paris, France); 1974-75, senior seminar; 1975-77, director, office of NATO and Atlantic affairs; 1977-79, deputy chief of mission, U.S. Foreign Service (Rome, Italy); 1979-82, principal deputy assistant secretary of state for European and Canadian affairs; 1982-85, U.S. ambassador to Portugal; 1985-89, assistant secretary of state for politico-military affairs; 1989-92, ambassador at large for burdensharing; U.S. Department of State. 1993-present, assistant secretary of defense for special operations and low intensity conflict, U.S. Department of Defense.

Henry Allen Holmes, who spent about 30 years in the Foreign Service, is now serving as assistant secretary for special operations and low-intensity conflict at the Defense Department. He is responsible for the overall supervision, including oversight of policy and resources, of DOD's special operations and low-intensity conflict, drug enforcement policy, and humanitarian and refugee affairs activities. He also serves as the principal civilian advisor to the secretary of defense on those matters.

Prior to his appointment in 1993, Holmes served as the ambassador at large for burden-sharing. In that role, he worked with the DOD to ensure a more balanced sharing of security responsibilities and costs by NATO members and others, including Japan and the Republic of Korea. From 1982 to 1985, as the U.S. Ambassador to Portugal, Holmes negotiated a new Base Rights Agreement while simultaneously establishing a Portuguese/American Development Foundation capitalized by security assistance funds.

While at State from 1985 to 1989, Holmes served as the assistant secretary for politico-military affairs. During this period, he chaired interdepartmental groups on arms control negotiations, NATO's Special Consultative Group on U.S.-Soviet INF negotiations, and co-chaired working groups with the Soviets on the topics of chemical warfare and nuclear testing. He also was responsible for directing the negotiations of the Missile Technology Control Regime as well as supervising munitions and strategic high-technology export controls.

After Holmes graduated from Princeton in 1954, he joined the Marine Corps, serving as an infantry officer from 1954 to 1957. He then moved across the Atlantic to study at the Institut d'Etudes Politiques in Paris, France.

Holmes, who was born in Bucharest, Romania, and his wife, Marilyn, have two children. Holmes speaks French, Italian, and Portuguese.

Deputy Assistant Secretary for Policy and Missions

Deputy Assistant Secretary
BG Larry Dodgen, USA
703/693-2896
Rm. 2B535

Deputy Asst. Secretary for Inter-American Affairs

Deputy Assistant Secretary
Ms. Maria Fernandez
703/697-5884
Rm. 4C800

Director of Inter-American Affairs
BG Howard G. DeWolf, USA
703/697-7588
Rm. 4C800

Deputy Director of Inter-American Affairs
Mr. Ralph Novak
703/697-9302
Rm. 4C800

Country Director, Haiti
Mr. Paul Mikesh
703/697-9301
Rm. 4C800

Country Director, Mexico
Maj. Craig A. Deare, USA
703/697-9301
Rm. 4C800

Country Director, Bolivia, Colombia, Ecuador and Peru
LTC Stephen H. Harris, USAF
703/697-9302
Rm. 4C800

Country Director, El Salvador, Guatemala, Belize, Honduras and Nicaragua
Ms. Deborah Norden
703/697-9301
Rm. 4C800

Country Director, Panama and Southern Command Matters, Counternarcotic Policy
LTC John Williamson, USA
703/697-2520
Rm. 4C800

Country Director, Brazil, Guyana, Suriname, Venezuela, and French Guiana
Ms. Lorraine McMillan
703/697-2520
Rm. 4C800

Regional Policy and Country Director for the Dominican Republic Jamaica, the Bahamas, Cuba, the Caribbean Islands and Chile
Mr. William G. Mock
703/697-3607
Rm. 4C800

Country Director, Antarctic, Argentina, Uruguay and Paraguay
VACANT
703/697-9301
Rm. 4C800

Deputy Assistant Secretary for Forces and Resources

Deputy Assistant Secretary
Mr. Raymond Dominguez
703/693-5217
Rm. 1A674A

Deputy Assistant Secretary for Drug Enforcement Policy and Support
1510 Defense Pentagon / Washington D.C. 20301-1510

Deputy Assistant Secretary
Mr. Brian E. Sheridan
703/695-7996
Rm. 2E538

Defense Technology Security Administration
400 Army Navy Drive / Arlington VA 22202

Director
Mr. Dave Tarbell
703/604-5215
Rm. 300

Asst. Sec. of Defense for Legislative Affairs

1300 Defense Pentagon / Washington DC 20301-1300

Assistant for International Security Policy
Mr. Mark Tavlarides
703/614-8423

Assistant to the Secretary for Public Affairs

1400 Defense Pentagon / Washington DC 20301-1400

Assistant Secretary of Defense for Public Affairs
Mr. Kenneth H. Bacon
703/697-9312 FAX 703/695-4299
Rm. 2E800

Personal: born 11/21/44 in Bronxville, N.Y.

Education: B.A. in English, Amherst Coll., 1966. M.B.A. in journalism, Columbia Univ., 1969.

Professional: 1968-74, served in U.S. Army Reserve. 1968-69, legislative assistant, Sen. Thomas J. McIntyre (D-N.H.). 1969-94, writer/editor, the *Wall Street Journal*. 9/20/94-present, assistant secretary of defense for public affairs, U.S. Department of Defense.

Kenneth Bacon brings a strong journalism background to his job as assistant secretary of defense for public affairs. Since 1994, Bacon has served as the principal staff advisor and assistant to the secretary and deputy secretary of defense on Defense Department public information matters. He also is responsible for internal information, the Freedom of Information Act, mandatory declassification review and clearance of DOD information for public release, community relations, information training, and audiovisual matters. In addition, he provides the regular DOD press briefings.

Bacon was assistant news editor for the *Wall Street Journal* before his appointment on September 20, 1994, by then-Secretary of Defense William J. Perry. Bacon began his career at the *Journal* covering regulatory agencies, economics and the Nixon wage-price control program. He then spent four years covering the Pentagon, including the Iranian hostage crisis, the development of the cruise missile, and the beginning of the effort to rebuild the military.

From 1980 to 1983, Bacon was an economics reporter and an author of a weekly column, "Outlook" at the *Wall Street Journal*. He became an assistant news editor in 1983. In that position, he supervised economics and foreign policy coverage out of Washington. He later covered health, education, and the banking industry. Bacon also served as a global financial correspondent covering banking, the IMF and World Bank, and U.S. dollar policy in 1993. From June 1993 until his appointment, he was assistant news editor supervising health, crime, and other coverage.

Aside from his broad journalism experience, Bacon also has ventured into military and political realms. He served in a civil affairs unit of the U.S. Army Reserve from 1968 to 1974. He also served as the legislative assistant to Senator Thomas J. McIntyre of New Hampshire for two years.

Bacon received his B.A. in English in 1966 from Amherst College and an M.B.A. in journalism from Columbia University in 1969. He and his wife, Darcy, have two daughters.

Programs and Community Relations Directorate

International Visitor Program Officer
Mr. Clint Wright
703/697-2113
Rm. 1E776

Office of the General Counsel

1600 Defense Pentagon / Washington DC 20301-1600

Senior Deputy Gen. Counsel, International Affairs and Intelligence
Mr. David Koplow
703/695-2604
Rm. 3E963

Joint Chiefs of Staff

Office of the Chairman
9999 Defense Pentagon / Washington DC 20301-9999

Chairman
GEN Henry Shelton, USA
703/697-9121 FAX 703/697-8758
Room 2E872

Personal: born 1/2/42 in Tarboro, N.C..

Education: B.S. in textile engineering, North Carolina State Univ. M.S. in political science, Auburn Univ. National and International Security Program, Harvard Univ. Infantry Officer Basic (1964) and Advanced (1970) courses. Air Command and Staff Coll., 1973. National War Coll., 1983.

Professional: 1963-64, platoon leader, Headquarters Company, 1st Battalion, 38th Infantry, 2nd Infantry Division, Fort Benning, Ga. 1964-65, platoon leader, Company D, 1st Battalion, 5th Cavalry, 1st Cavalry Division, Fort Benning. 1965-66, U.S. Army Reserve. 1966-67, platoon leader, Detachment B52, 5th Special Forces Group, 1st Special Forces, U.S. Army, Vietnam. 7/67-12/67, commander, Detachment A-104, Company C, 5th Special Forces Group, U.S. Army Pacific. 1/68-3/68, executive officer, 11th Battalion, 3rd Training Brigade, U.S. Army Training Center, Fort Jackson, S.C. 3/68-12/68, S-4 (Logistics), 3rd Advanced Individual Training Brigade Fort Jackson. 1969-70, S-2 (Intelligence), later commander, Company C, later acting S-3 (Operations), 4th Battalion, 503rd Infantry, 173rd

Airborne Brigade, U.S. Army, Vietnam. 1970-72, instructor, later operations officer, Ranger Department, U.S. Army Infantry School, Fort Benning. 1973-75, S-1 (Personnel), later S-3 (Operations), 2nd Brigade, 25th Infantry Division, Schofield Barracks, Hawaii. 1975-76, chief, officer management branch, later deputy G-1 (Personnel), 25th Infantry Division, Schofield Barracks. 1976-77, executive officer, 1st Battalion, 14th Infantry, 2nd Brigade, 25th Infantry Division, Schofield Barracks. 1977-79, professional development officer, Combat Arms Branch, later chief, Assignments Branch, Majors Division, Officer Personnel Management Directorate, U.S. Army Military Personnel Center (Alexandria, Va.). 1979-81, commander, 3rd Battalion, 60th Infantry, 2nd Brigade, 9th Infantry Division, Fort Lewis, Washington. 1981-82, assistant chief of staff, G-3 (Operations), 9th Infantry Division, Fort Lewis. 6/83-10/83, chairman, reserve components study group, office of the deputy chief of staff for personnel, U.S. Army (Washington, D.C.). 1983-85, commander, 1st Brigade, 82nd Airborne Division, Fort Bragg, N.C. 1985-87, chief of staff, 10th Mountain Division(Light Infantry), Fort Drum, N.Y. 1987-88, deputy director for operations, National Military Command Center, J-3; 1988-89, deputy director for operations (current operations), J-3, Organization of the Joint Chiefs of Staff (Washington, D.C.). 1989-90, assistant division commander, 101st Airborne Division (Air Assault), Fort Campbell, Ky. 1990-91, assistant division commander, 101st Airborne Division (Air Assault) Desert Storm, Saudi Arabia. 3/91-5/91, assistant division commander, 101st Airborne Division (Air Assault), Fort Campbell, Ky. 1991-93, commanding general, 82nd Airborne Division, Fort Bragg, N.C. 1993-96, commanding general, XVIII Airborne Corps and Fort Bragg, Fort Bragg. 1996-8/97, commander in chief, U.S. Special Operations Command, MacDill Air Force Base, Fla. 9/97-present, chairman, Joint Chiefs of Staff, U.S. Dept. of Defense.

Gen. Harry Hugh Shelton was confirmed in September, 1997 by the Senate to become the new chairman of the Joint Chiefs of Staff. He replaces Gen. John Shalikashvili, who retired after serving in the position since 1993.

The chairman of the Joint Chiefs of Staff is the nation's top soldier and is the principal adviser to the president, the secretary of defense, and the National Security Council. "Gen. Hugh Shelton is the right officer to lead the U.S. Armed Forces into the 21st Century. He is a consummate military professional, a decorated combat veteran and a superb leader," said Shalikashvili of Shelton's nomination. "Gen. Shelton has the proven skills, the broad experience and, most importantly, the dynamic vision required to ensure our military forces remain the best in the world. Gen. Shelton is superbly qualified to provide sound, forthright military advice to the president and the secretary of defense."

Secretary of Defense William Cohen called Shelton a "superb leader." He said warfighting experience, diplomatic skill, global perspective, and the human touch were important factors in his recommendation of Shelton. "I'm confident that Gen. Shelton's leadership, experience and skill will serve him well as he meets this new challenge," Cohen said.

Shelton had served as commander in chief of the United States Special Operations Command headquartered at MacDill Air Force Base in Florida since February 1996. He was responsible for the readiness of all special operations forces of the Army, Navy, and Air Force, both on active duty and reserve. Previously, Shelton served as commanding general of the XVIII Airborne Corps at Fort Bragg, N.C. His past assignments also include: commander, 82nd Airborne Division at Fort Bragg; assistant division commander for operations, 101st Airborne Division (Air Assault), Fort Campbell, Ky.; and commander of Company C, 4th Battalion, 503rd Infantry, 173rd Airborne Brigade in the Republic of Vietnam.

Shelton also has commanded the 3rd Battalion, 60th Infantry, 9th Division at Fort Lewis, Wash., and the 1st Brigade, 82nd Airborne Division at Fort Bragg. He has served as deputy director for operations, J-3, Organization of the Joint Chiefs of Staff in Washington, D.C.; chief of staff, 10th Mountain Division (Light), Fort Drum, N.Y.;

Division G-3 (Operations), 9th Infantry Division, Fort Lewis; brigade S-1 and S-3 officer, Deputy Division G-1, and infantry battalion executive officer, while assigned to the 25th Infantry Division in Hawaii.

Shelton completed two tours in Vietnam. He also deployed to Saudi Arabia and participated in Operations Desert Shield and Desert Storm. Most recently, he served as the Joint Task Force commander during Operation Uphold Democracy in Haiti.

The North Carolina native has more than 32 years of active commissioned service and has received numerous awards and decorations. They include the Defense Distinguished Service Medal with oak leaf cluster, Distinguished Service Medal, Legion of Merit with oak leaf cluster, Bronze Star Medal with "V" device and three oak leaf clusters, and the Purple Heart.

Shelton and his wife, Carolyn, have three sons.

Operations Directorate (J-3)

Current Operations (J-33)
3000 Defense Pentagon / Washington DC 20301-5000

Chief, Pacific Command Division
CAPT. T.J. Wilson, USN
703/695-3248   FAX 703/695-3792

Chief, Western Hemisphere Division
COL Thomas Stewart, USA
703/695-1854   FAX 703/695-3792

Chief, European Command Division
COL Ralph Jodice, USAF
703/695-2541   FAX 703/695-3792

Chief, Central Command Division
COL Leif Hendrickson, USMC
703/695-2538   FAX 703/695-3792

Logistics Directorate (J-4)
4000 Defense Pentagon / Washington DC 20318-4000

Chief, International Logistics Division
COL Ronald Hawthorn, USA
703/697-5469

Strategic Plans and Policy Directorate (J-5)

Politico-Military Affairs
5101 Defense Pentagon / Washington DC 20318-5101

Deputy Director, Western Hemisphere and Global Issues
BG Gary Parks, USMC
703/614-0243

Deputy Director, Asia Pacific and Middle East
BG T. Michael Moseley, USAF
703/695-6585

Deputy Director, Europe
BG George Casey, USAF
703/697-8591

International Negotiations
5101 Defense Pentagon / Washington DC 20318-5101

Deputy Director
BG Robert Dierker, USAF
703/695-5904   FAX 703/614-0727

Russia, Ukraine, and Eurasia Division
COL Douglas Dovey, USAF
703/693-5181

Department of Defense Field Activities

Armed Forces Sports Committee Secretariat and Conseil International Du Sport Militaire (CISM) U.S. Executive Office

2461 Eisenhower Ave. / Alexandria VA 22331-0522

Director, Executive Office
Mr. William G. Begel
703/325-2512
Rm. 400

Defense Agencies and Related Organizations

Defense Intelligence Agency

7400 Defense Pentagon / Washington DC 20301-7400

Director
LTG Patrick M. Hughs, USA
703/695-7353
Rm. 3E258

Personal: born 9/19/42 in Great Falls, Mont.

Education: B.S. in commerce, Montana State Univ., 1968. Infantry Officer Basic Course, 1968. Military Intelligence Officer Advanced Course, 1973. U.S. Army Command and Staff Coll., 1978. M.A. in business management, Central Michigan Univ., 1978. Senior Service College Fellow, School of Advanced Military Studies, 1987.

Professional: 6/68-9/68, platoon leader; then 11/68-1/69, battalion S-1, 82nd Airborne Div.n, Ft. Bragg, N.C. 1/69-7/69, platoon leader, 9th Infantry Div., Vietnam. 7/69-9/70, Battalion S-1, 25th Infantry Division, Hawaii. 1971-72, adviser, Military Assistance Command, Vietnam. 1973-74, strategic intelligence officer; 1974-77, field detachment commander, Camp Zama, Japan. 1978-79, foreign liaison officer, Pentagon. 1979-80, intelligence doctrine staff officer, Pentagon. 1980-81, asst. to dir. of Army staff, office of the chief of staff, pentagon. 1981-82, exec. officer, 109th MI Battalion, 9th Infantry Div., Fort Lewis, Washington. 1982-83, commander, Ops Support Detachment, 9th Infantry Div. 1983-84, asst. chief of staff, G-2, 9th Infantry Div. 1984-86, commander, 109th MI Battalion. 1987-88, professor, School of Advanced Military Studies. 1988-90, commander, 501st MI Brigade, Korea. 7/90-12/90, exec. officer to the commander in chief, Combined Forces Command, Korea. 1991-92, commander, U.S. Army Intelligence Agency (Wash., D.C.). 1992-94, J2, U.S. Central Command, MacDill AFB, Fla. 1994-96, J2, The Joint Staff (Wash., D.C.). 1996-present, director, Defense Intelligence Agency.

Lt. Gen. Patrick M. Hughes is director of the Defense Intelligence Agency and is the senior uniformed intelligence officer in the Department of Defense. He became the twelfth person to head the DIA, a combat support agency with military and civilian personnel stationed worldwide, on Feb. 16, 1996. Hughes is also the director of the General Defense Intelligence Program, managing selected intelligence resources for all services as part of the National Foreign Intelligence Program.

Established in 1961, the DIA is the senior military component of the U.S. Intelligence Community. It provides intelligence in support of: 1) joint military operations in peacetime, crisis, contingency, and combat; 2) weapons system acquisition; and 3) defense policy-making. The agency's main objectives are to maintain a high degree of capability and readiness to address all military contingencies and to provide reliable operational intelligence and force protection information in support of U.S. deployed military forces.

In addition, Hughes has established three broad goals for the DIA to prepare it for the challenges of the 21st century. They are the recapitalization of people, facilities, and leveraging of new technology into the intelligence cycle. Hughes has embarked on an effort to revitalize the DIA work force by attracting, training, and retaining the best people. He has endeavored to capitalize upon the information and technology revolution by leveraging new innovations into the collaborative virtual environment. By using imaginative concepts, aggressive organizational processes and new technologies, Hughes also aims to provide the best possible work environment for intelligence professionals. Consolidating and improving DIA facilities constitutes a major step toward achieving that goal.

Hughes believes the intelligence community must collaborate and cooperate closely both internally and with allies, other branches of the U.S. government and with the private sector to provide effective intelligence. He has continued the transition to a centralized Defense HUMINT (human intelligence) Service that emphasizes the close cooperation with allies, sister services, and other agencies. He also is working to strengthen measurement and signals intelligence (MASINT) collection and exploitation to benefit the entire intelligence community. By seizing upon established regional and functional expertise throughout the government, the private sector and our allies, Hughes wants to improve both the quality and timeliness of intelligence in an effective and efficient manner.

Prior to taking on his current assignment, Hughes was director for intelligence, J2, with the Joint Staff, DIA. He first enlisted in the Army in 1962 and served until 1965. He then attended Montana State University where he obtained his bachelor's degree in 1968 and was commissioned in the U.S. Army infantry. Hughes transferred to Military Intelligence in 1970. During his career, Hughes served two tours in Vietnam, and commanded several MI detachments, an MI battalion, an MI brigade and the Army Intelligence Agency. He also served in senior staff positions, including a tour as the J2 of the U.S. Central Command.

Hughes and his wife, Karlene, have two sons.

Policy Support

Foreign Liaison
Mr. Edward L. Stephens
703/695-5373
Rm. 5C323

Defense Special Weapons Agency

6801 Telegraph Rd. / Alexandria VA 22310-3398

Director
MG Gary L. Curtin, USAF
703/325-7004   FAX 703/325-2960

Personal: born 4/24/43 in Washington, D.C.

Education: B.S. in aerospace engineering, Univ. of Maryland, 1965. M.S. in economics, Air Force Institute of Technology's Minuteman education program, South Dakota State Univ. 1970. Squadron Officer School, 1970. Armed Forces Staff Coll., 1976. National War Coll., 1983. Program for senior executives in National and International Security, Harvard Univ., 1992. Seminar XXI, Massachusetts Institute of Technology, 1993.

Professional: 1965-70, missile launch officer, 44th Strategic Missile Wing, Ellsworth Air Force Base, S.D. 1971-72, air targets officer, 7th Airborne Command and Control Squadron, Udorn Royal Thai AFB, Thailand. 1972-76, air targets officer and intelligence plans officer, headquarters, Pacific Air Forces, Hickam AFB, Hawaii. 1976-80, Korea desk officer, then Pacific Command branch chief, Pacific-East Asia Division, Directorate of Plans, headquarters, USAF (Washington, D.C.). 1980-82, commander, 400th Strategic Missile Squadron; 1981-82, assistant deputy commander for operations, 90th Strategic Missile Wing, F.E. Warren AFB, Wyo. 1983-86, chief, Advanced Missile Development Division, and special assistant to the commander in chief for Peacekeeper Intercontinental Ballistic Missile, then director of ICBM requirements, Strategic Air Command, Offutt AFB, Neb. 1986-88, vice commander, then wing commander, 90th Strategic Missile Wing, F.E. Warren AFB. 1988-89, director of command control, office of the deputy chief of staff, operations, then assistant deputy chief of staff for plans and programs, Strategic Air Command, Offutt AFB. 1990-91, Joint Chiefs of Staff representative to Strategic Arms Reduction Talks, Geneva, Switzerland. 1991-92, assistant deputy director, international negotiations, J-5; 1992-93, deputy director, international negotiations, the Joint Staff (Pentagon). 1993-95, director for intelligence, U.S. Strategic Command, Offutt AFB. 1995-present, director, Defense Special Weapons Agency.

Maj. Gen. Gary Curtin has been director of the Defense Special Weapons Agency since 1995. The agency supports the Department of Defense and other federal agencies on matters concerning nuclear weapons, including their effects on weapons systems and forces, their safety and security, and nuclear weapons system acquisitions.

Curtin, who was born in Washington, D.C., and grew up in the area, has been in the Air Force since 1965. Prior to his current position he had been director for intelligence at the U.S. Strategic Command, Offutt Air Force Base in Nebraska since 1993. Previously, Curtin worked for the Joint Staff.

He was the Joint Chiefs of Staff representative to the Strategic Arms Reduction Talks (START) in January 1990. Working with his Soviet Union military counterparts, he helped conclude the START negotiations in Geneva that led to signing of the treaty in July 1991. The general became assistant deputy director for international negotiations at the Joint Staff in August 1991, focusing on nuclear issues including START Treaty ratification and the presidential nuclear initiatives of September 1991 and January 1992. In February 1992, Curtin became the deputy director of international negotiations responsible for completion of the Chemical Weapons Convention, Open Skies Treaty, START II, and a variety of counterproliferation initiatives.

Curtin's first assignment was as a deputy missile combat crew commander for the 44th Strategic Missile Wing at Ellsworth Air Force Base in South Dakota. In 1971, he was stationed at Udorn Royal Thai Air Force Base in Thailand as an air targets officer with the 7th Airborne Command and Control Squadron. While there he flew 105 combat missions over Laos and acted as the squadron's chief of intelligence. From 1972 to 1976, he was assigned to Pacific Air Forces headquarters in Hawaii as an air targets officer and later as an intelligence plans officer.

After graduating from the Armed Forces Staff College in 1976, Curtin was assigned to the Directorate of Plans at Air Force headquarters in Washington, D.C., as an international politico-military affairs staff officer in the Pacific-East Asia Division. He served as Korean desk officer until August 1979, when he became Pacific Command branch chief. He then was transferred to Francis E. Warren AFB in Wyoming as commander of the 400th Strategic Missile Squadron. From 1981 to 1982, he was the 90th Strategic Missile Wing's assistant deputy commander for operations.

In 1983, he was assigned to the office of the deputy chief of staff, plans, Headquarters Strategic Air Command at Offutt AFB. He served simultaneously as chief of the Advanced Missile Development Division and as special assistant to the commander in chief for the Peacekeeper Intercontinental Ballistic Missile. He later became director of ICBM requirements. In 1986, he returned to F.E. Warren AFB as vice commander, 90th Strategic Missile Wing, and later became wing commander. He returned to SAC headquarters in 1988 as director of command control in the office of the deputy chief of staff, operations. In 1989, he became SAC's assistant deputy chief of staff for plans and programs.

Curtin's military awards and decorations include the Defense Distinguished Service Medal, Defense Superior Service Medal, the Legion of Merit, Bronze Star Medal, Meritorious Service Medal with two oak leaf clusters, Air Medal with two oak leaf clusters, Aerial Achievement Medal, and Air Force Commendation Medal.

Curtin and his wife, Karen, have two children.

Chief, Counterproliferation Program Office
Mr. Vayl S. Oxford
703/325-4899

Defense Security Assistance Agency

1111 Jefferson Davis Highway / Arlington VA 22202-4306

Director for Europe, Russia, Americas and Subsaharan Africa
Ms. Diana Blundell
703/604-6593

Chief of Middle East, Asia and North Africa
Mr. Edward Ross
703/604-6640

National Security Agency (NSA) Central Security Service (NSA/CSS)

9800 Savage Road / Fort George G. Meade, MD 20755-6000

Director, Natl. Security Agency and Chief, Central Security Service
LTG Kenneth A. Minihan, USAF
301/688-6524   FAX 301/497-2844

Education: B.A. in political science, Florida State Univ., 1966. Squadron Officer School, 1972. M.A. in national security affairs, Naval Postgraduate School, 1979. Air Command and Staff Coll., 1979.

Air War Coll., 1984. Program for Senior Executives in National and International Security, Harvard Univ., 1993.

Professional: 1966-69, target intelligence officer, Headquarters 7th Air Force, Tan Son Nhut Air Base, South Vietnam. 1970-74, chief, Current Intelligence and Presentations Branch, Headquarters U.S. Southern Command, Howard AFB, Panama. 1974-78, program element monitor, assistant executive, assistant chief of staff, intelligence, and special assistant for external affairs, Headquarters U.S. Air Force (Washington, D.C.). 1980-81, legislative liaison officer, Defense Intelligence Agency. 1981-82, chief, office of support to military operations, National Security Agency (Fort Meade, Md.). 1982-83, commander, 6941st Electronic Security Squadron, Fort Meade. 1984-85, commander, 12th Tactical Intelligence Squadron, Bergstrom AFB, Texas. 1985-87, commander, 6917th Electronic Security Group, San Vito dei Normanni Air Station, Italy. 1987-89, deputy chief of staff, plans, Headquarters Electronic Security Command, Kelly AFB, Texas. 1989-91, deputy chief of staff, intelligence, Headquarters Tactical Air Command, Langley AFB, Va. 1991-93, director of plans and requirements, assistant chief of staff, intelligence, Headquarters U.S. Air Force. 6/93-10/93, commander, Air Force Intelligence Command, and director, Joint Electronic Warfare Center, Kelly AFB. 1993-94, commander, Air Intelligence Agency, and director, Joint Command and Control Warfare Center, Kelly AFB. 1994-95, assistant chief of staff, intelligence, Headquarters U.S. Air Force. 1995-96, director, Defense Intelligence Agency. 1996-present, director, National Security Agency/Central Security Service (Fort Meade, Md.).

Lt. Gen. Kenneth A. Minihan is the senior uniformed intelligence officer in the Department of Defense and is head of a super secret federal organization that gathers electronic intelligence. He is the director of the National Security Agency/Central Security Service, a DOD combat support agency with almost 20,000 military and civilian employees stationed worldwide.

Minihan, a former director of the Defense Intelligence Agency, was appointed NSA director in February 1996. Since then, the agency, which has some of the most advanced computers in the federal government, has played a major role in formulating Clinton administration policies on computer data security. Those policies could determine how Americans communicate with each other and the rest of the world in the 21st century. In an interview with the *National Journal*, Minihan said he believes interlocking computer networks such as the internet will become the foundation for communications in the near future. "I think (computer networks) might one day be as important as electricity is to us today," he said. "They'll be sort of ever-present. Given that context, we (at NSA) want to understand what are the security services a democratic society would need."

Minihan, a Texas native, graduated from Florida State University and joined the Air Force in 1966. He served in Vietnam in 1970 and has since held a variety of intelligence posts, including that of commander of the Air Force Intelligence Agency at Kelly Air Force Base in Texas. He also has served in other senior staff officer positions in the Pentagon; Headquarters Tactical Air Command, Langley Air Force Base; Electronic Security Command, Kelly Air Force Base; and the National Security Agency at Fort Meade. He has commanded squadrons, groups, and a major air command both in the United States and overseas. He has been the assistant chief of staff, intelligence, at U.S. Air Force headquarters in Washington, D.C., and most recently was the director of the Defense Intelligence Agency.

Minihan and his wife, Barbara, have three children.

ON-Site Inspection Agency (OSIA)

Rhein-Mein AB / Frankfurt Germany 011-49-6969-9-6213

Commander, European Operations
COL Kenneth D. Guillory, USA

Ballistic Missile Defense Organization

7100 Defense Pentagon / Washington DC 20301-7100

Director, International Affairs
Ms. Deborah Vinson
703/693-1779

Joint Service Schools

National Defense University

Industrial College of the Armed Forces
Fort McNair, Bldg. 59 / Washington DC 20319-6000

International Affairs Adviser
Ambassador Roman Popadiuk
202/685-3984

Related International Organizations

Canada-U.S. Military Cooperation Committee

The Pentagon / Washington D.C. 20318

Chair
BG Garry L. Parks, USMC
703/614-0243
Rm. 2E980

Canada-U.S. Permanent Joint Board on Defense

1111 Jefferson Davis Highway / Arlington VA 22202

Chair
Mr. Dwight N. Mason
703/604-0487   FAX 703/604-0486
Suite 511

Canada-U.S. Regional Planning Group/NATO

9999 Defense Pentagon / Washington D.C. 20318-9999

Chair
BG Garry L. Parks, USMC
703/697-8591
Rm. 2E980

Inter-American Defense Board

2600 16th St., NW / Washington DC 20441

Chair
Mg. John C. Thompson, USA
202/939-6600

Inter-American Defense College

4th and P Streets, SW / Fort McNair 20319-6000

Director
Mg. John C. Thompson, USA
202/646-1337
Bldg 52

Joint Mexican-U.S. Defense Commission

1911 Pennsylvania Ave., NW / Washington DC 20006

Chair and Army-Air Member, Mexican Section
BG Eduardo Martinez
202/728-1740
6th Floor

*Crystal Gateway North, 1111 Jefferson Davis Hwy
Arlington, VA 22202*

Chair, U.S. Section
MG David S. Weisman, USA
703/604-0482
Rm. 509

Department of the Air Force

1080 Air Force Pentagon / Washington DC 20330-1080

Deputy Under Secretary, International Affairs

Deputy Under Secretary
Mr. Robert D. Bauerlein
703/614-8475
Personal: born 4/1/45 in Erie, Pa.

Education: B.S. (cum laude) in political science, Case Western Reserve Univ., 1967. Attended graduate school, Univ. of Virginia, 1968. Master's degree, Case Western Reserve Univ., 1969.

Professional: 1969-71, assistant to the mayor, Cleveland, Ohio. 1972-76, assistant to the city manager, Alexandria, Va. 1976-83, budget analyst, Office of Management and Budget, Executive Office of the President. 1983-87, special assistant to under secretary of state for security assistance, science and technology; 1987-90, adviser on policy and resources, office of the deputy secretary of state; 1990-92, director, office of policy and resources, office of deputy secretary of State, U.S. Department of State. 1992-present, deputy under secretary of the Air Force for international affairs, Department of the Air Force.

Robert Bauerlein's entire professional career has been in public service. He currently is serving as deputy under secretary of the Air Force for international affairs, a position he has held since February 1992. He is responsible for the direction, guidance, and supervision of the international activities of the Department of the Air Force.

From 1969 until 1971, Bauerlein was an assistant to the mayor of Cleveland. He then moved to Alexandria, Va., and was an assistant to the city manager from 1972 until 1976. Bauerlein began his career with the federal government in 1976 as a budget analyst in the Office of Management and Budget. While at OMB, Bauerlein reviewed programs of the Interior and State departments. He participated in several negotiations related to both domestic and international issues, including settlement of eastern Indian land claims, law of the sea matters, and Micronesian political status talks.

Bauerlein joined the State Department in 1983 as a special assistant to the under secretary of state for security assistance, science, and technology. From 1983 to 1987, he helped coordinate U.S. foreign assistance programs with an emphasis on military sales financing and arms transfer issues. He was a principal point of contact with the Department of Defense on military assistance issues and coordinated efforts to allow countries to refinance their high interest foreign military sales debt.

In 1987, Bauerlein moved to the office of the deputy secretary of State as an adviser on policy and resources. While there, he counseled the deputy secretary and secretary of state on a range of international affairs issues. In 1990, he was appointed director of the deputy secretary's office of policy and resources and became the department's principal adviser on how to match national security and foreign policy objectives with the resources necessary to achieve them. He also participated in the formulation and execution of several foreign policy initiatives including the successful effort to forgive Egypt's foreign military debt to the United States, collection of contributions from other nations to support U.S. efforts during Operation Desert Storm, and bases' negotiations with Philippine government.

Bauerlein earned a bachelor's degree in political science from Case Western Reserve University in 1967, attended graduate school at the University of Virginia in 1968, and received a master's degree from Case Western Reserve in 1969.

Bauerlein and his wife, Joan, have two children.

Principal Assistant Deputy Under Secretary
MG Clinton V. Horn
703/695-7261
Rm. 4E334

Assistant Deputy Under Secretary
BG William E. Stevens
703/697-9851
Rm. 5D518

Military Assistant
COL Marc J. Neifert
703/695-7261
Rm. 4E334

Executive Officer
Major Paul Thomson
703/695-7261
Rm 4E334

The Vice Chief of Staff

1670 Air Force Pentagon / Washington D.C. 20330-1670

Chief, Foreign Liaison
COL John B. Longenecker
703/695-2251
Rm. 4A916

Chief, National Guard Bureau (Army & Air Force)

Park Center 4, 4501 Ford Avenue / Alexandria, VA 22302

International Affairs
COL Robert B. James, USA
703/681-3097

Office of the General Counsel

1740 Air Force Pentagon / Washington DC 20330-1740

Asst. General Counsel, International Affairs
Mr. Michael W. Zehner
703/697-5196

United States Air Forces in Europe (USAFE)

Unit 3050, Box 1 / APO AE 09094-0501
Ramstein Air Base / Germany 09094-5001

Commander, U.S. Air Forces in Europe
GEN John Jumper

Department of the Army

101 Army Pentagon / Washington DC 20310-0101

Deputy Under Secretary, International Affairs

Deputy Under Secretary
LTG Claude M. Kicklighter
703/697-5075   FAX 703/697-3145

Personal: born 8/22/33 in Glennville, Ga.

Education: B.A. in biology, Mercer Univ., 1955. M.A. in management of national resources, George Washington Univ. Graduate of U.S. Army Command and General Staff Coll. and Industrial Coll. of the Armed Forces.

Professional: 1976-78, commander, 24th Infantry Division, Artillery, Fort Stewart, Ga. 1978-79, assistant division commander. 1979-81, assistant chief of staff for logistics, Allied Forces Central Europe, the Netherlands. 1981-83, commander, Security Assistance Command (Alexandria, Va.). 1983-84, chief of staff, Army Material Development and Readiness Command (Alexandria, Va.). 1984-86, commanding general, 25th Infantry Division. 1986-87, assistant deputy chief of staff for logistics; 1987-89, director of the Army Staff, Department of the Army. 1989-91, commanding general, U.S. Army Pacific, Fort Shafter, Hawaii. 1991-95, executive director, World War II Commemoration Committee. 1995-present, deputy under secretary of the Army for international affairs, Department of the Army.

LTG Claude M. Kicklighter's responsibilities as deputy under secretary of the Army for international affairs are numerous. He acts on behalf of the secretary of the Army on all international activities and affairs, including coordination, integration, and oversight.

From August 1991 until he was named deputy under secretary in July 1995, Kicklighter served as the executive director of the Department of Defense 50th anniversary of World War II Commemoration Committee. He was responsible for managing a program designed to thank and honor the veterans of WWII, their families and those who served on the home front and for developing a program to promote a greater understanding of the lessons and history of the war.

Kicklighter, who was commissioned as a second lieutenant in 1955, advanced to the rank of lieutenant general in 1987. Kicklighter has served at numerous locations in the United States and overseas. His assignments included duty with three Army schools and service in Vietnam, Iran, Europe, and Washington, D.C.

Kicklighter commanded at every level from company through division. He commanded the 25th Infantry Division (Light) at Schofield Barracks from 1984 until 1986. He commanded the U.S. Army Security Assistance Center in Alexandria, Va., and served in staff assignments from battalion to headquarters, Department of the Army,

the Joint Staff, and the Office of the Secretary of Defense. He served as director of the Army Staff from 1987 to 1989 and was commanding general of the U.S. Army in the Pacific from 1989 to 1991.

Kicklighter graduated from Mercer University in 1955 with a bachelor's degree in biology and earned a master's degree in management of national resources from George Washington University. He is a graduate of the U.S. Army Command and General Staff College and the Industrial College of the Armed Forces. He also has completed two Harvard University courses, the National and International Security Program and Senior Managers in Government.

Kicklighter's many awards include the Distinguished Service Medal with two oak leaf clusters, the Defense Superior Service Medal, the Legion of Merit with three oak leaf clusters, the Bronze Star, the Meritorious Service Medal with oak leaf cluster, and the Army Commendation Medal with four oak leaf clusters. He received the Eisenhower Liberation Medal, presented by the U.S. Holocaust Memorial Council, in 1994. In 1995, Kicklighter was awarded the Presidential Citizen Medal and the Department of Defense Medal for Distinguished Public Service.

Kicklighter and his wife, Elizabeth, have three adult children.

Chief of Staff
COL Kevin T. Hanretta
703/697-5075
Rm. 3E412

Chief, Foreign Liaison
COL Michael VanBuskirk
703/697-4762
Rm. 2E484

Director, International Development and Security Assistance
Mr. Robert Keltz
703/694-4872
Rm. 3E522

Henderson Hall, Southgate Rd. & Orne St. / Arlington, VA 20380

Director, Treaty Implementation Planning Agency (TIPA)
Mr. Richard P. McSeveney
703/693-6328
Rm. 2057

The U.S. Army General Staff

Deputy Chief of Staff for Intelligence
1000 Army Pentagon / Washington DC 20310-1000

Foreign Intelligence Directorate
Director
COL William Speer
703/614-9897

Deputy Chief of Staff for Operations and Plans

Strategy, Plans and Policy Directorate
400 Army Pentagon / Washington DC 203140-0400

Chief, Foreign Area Officer Proponent Office
COL C.F. Doroski
703/697-3600

Chief, European Regional Desk
LTC Fred L. Schwein
703/697-9553

Chief, Middle East, Africa and South Asia Regional Desk
LTC John E. Sterling
703/614-5859

Chief, Asia and Pacific Regional Desk
Major Albert Wilner
703/695-3197

Chief, Western Hemisphere Regional Desk
Major Richard Kennedy
703/695-8290

Panama Canal Treaty Implementation Plan Agency
Columbia Pike & Southgate Rd. / Arlington VA 20370-5001

Director
Mr. Richard A. McSeveney
703/693-6326
Rm. 2057

U.S. Army War College
122 Forbes Ave. / Carlisle PA 17013-5213

Deputy Commandant for International Affairs
Ambassador Theodore Russell
717/245-3505   FAX 717/245-3412

The Judge Advocate General
2200 Army Pentagon / Washington DC 20310-2200

International and Operational Law Division
COL David E. Graham
703/695-3170

Chief of Engineers
20 Mass., Ave., NW / Washington DC 20314

Civil Works Directorate

Chief, Office of Interagency and International Activities
Mr. Donald R. Kisicki
202/761-4273
Rm. 7116

Office of the Chief Counsel

Senior Counsel for Military Programs and International Law
Mr. Rupert J. Jennings
202/761-8524
Rm. 8212

Office of Security and Law Enforcement

Foreign Disclosure Officer
Ms. Lori Herrington
202/761-8724
Rm. 4127

U.S. Army Intelligence & Security Command
8825 Beulah St., Bldg. 2444 / Fort Belvoir VA 22060-5246

Commanding General
MG John Thomas
703/706-1603
Rm. 2-F

5001 Eisenhower Avenue / Alexandria VA 22333-0001

Deputy Chief of Staff for Security Assistance

Headquarters U.S. Army Security Assistance Command

International Industrial Cooperation Office
Mr. Doug Leach
703/617-9394
Rm. 5S10

Mideast, Africa Directorate
COL R. Pitts
703/617-8451
Rm. 5S54

Europe Directorate
COL Glenn Harrold
703/617-8399
Rm. 5N14

Asia, Pacific, Americas Directorate
COL D. Wayne
703/617-8097
Rm. 5N40

Saudi Arabia National Guard (SANG) Modernization Program

Chief of Washington Office
Mr. D. Walker
703/617-9126
Rm. 5S42

Foreign Liaison Office

Liaison Officer, Australia
LTC D. McGahey
703/617-9676   FAX 703/617-2958
Rm. 10S44

Liaison Officer, United Kingdom
LTC S. Lloyd Williams
703/617-9675   FAX 703/617-2958
Rm. 10S44

Liaison Officer, Canada
LTC R. Bassarab
703/617-9679
Rm. 10S44

Liaison Officer, Germany
Mr. Hans Thuenemann
703/617-9684   FAX 703/617-0824
Rm. 10S38

Department of the Navy

5000 Navy Pentagon / Washington DC 20350-5000

Assistant Secretary for Research, Development and Acquisition

1111 Jefferson Davis Hwy. Rm. 701 / Arlington VA 22202

International Programs Office

Director
RADM Robert Sutton
703/604-0228

The Judge Advocate General

2400 Navy Pentagon / Washington DC 20350-2400

Deputy Assistant Judge Advocate General, International Law
Capt. Charles Allen
703/697-9161

Chief of Naval Operations

Office of the Oceanographer of the Navy
Mass. Ave. at 34th St., NW / Washington DC 20392-5101

Director, International and Interagency Affairs
Ms. Linda K. Glover
202/762-1008

Deputy Chief of Naval Operations for Plans, Policy and Operations
2000 Navy Pentagon / Washington DC 20350-2000

Politico-Military Affairs Division

Director
RADM Ronald A. Route
703/697-2453

Africa, Middle East and South Asia Plans and Policy Branch
Capt. Dirk Deverill
703/695-9411

East Asia and Pacific Plans and Policy Branch
Capt. Richard Kikla
703/697-1192

Western Hemisphere Plans and Policy Branch
Capt. Gordon G. Stewart
703/695-3882

Ocean Policy Branch
VACANT
703/697-0837

International Programs Branch
Mr. William A. Wither
703/695-3835

Europe, NATO, and Russia Plans and Policy Branch
Capt. Bill Farawell
703/695-4901

U. S. Department of Education

600 Independence Ave., SW / Washington DC 20202

Central: 202/708-5366
Press: 202/401-1576
http://www.ed.gov

INTRODUCTION

The Department of Education administers two programs to improve international business education. The first provides matching grants to institutions of higher education for enhancing their international academic programs. The second provides three-year grants to colleges and universities to operate Centers for International Business Education. The Department has international outreach programs in other areas of responsibility as well.

Office of the Secretary

600 Independence Ave., SW / Washington DC 20202

Secretary of Education
Mr. Richard W. Riley
202/401-3000   FAX 202/401-0596
E-mail: richardriley@ed.gov
Rm. 6161

Personal: born 1/2/33 in Greenville County, South Carolina.

Education: B.A. in political science (cum laude), Furman University, 1954. J.D., University of South Carolina School of Law, 1959.

Professional: 1959, legal counsel, Judiciary Committee, United States Senate. 1960-63, joined family's law firm. 1963-67, South Carolina state representative. 1967-77, state senator, South Carolina. 1978-86, governor, South Carolina. 1990, institute fellow, John F. Kennedy School of Government, Harvard University. Prior to 1993, senior partner, Nelson, Mullins, Riley & Scarborough (South Carolina). 1993-present, secretary, U.S. Department of Education.

Education Secretary Richard Riley has stayed on in the second Clinton term to continue the work in education reform that he began in the first term. Included are tax credits and deductions for college tuition, some of which were included in the 1997 tax package that has been signed into law.

As governor of South Carolina, Riley gained a national reputation as a leader in the area of quality education reform. He achieved a major overhaul of education in a state ranked near the bottom in educational achievement. He initiated and led the fight for the Education Improvement Act (1984), which, according to a Rand study, was the most comprehensive education reform measure in the country. A 1986 *Newsweek* poll of the nation's governors ranked Riley the third most effective by his colleagues. It was during those years that he worked closely with a fellow southern governor, Bill Clinton of Arkansas, on the National Governor's Association education reform agenda.

In the first Clinton term, Riley successfully shepherded no fewer than seven groundbreaking education initiatives through Congress, a cohesive set of programs that span from kindergarten through college, all of which passed with bipartisan support and were signed into law by the President. Not since the 1960s has so much significant education legislation been enacted.

The Clinton lifelong learning package includes the Goals 2000: Education America Act, the School-to-Work Opportunities Act, the Student Loan Reform Act, the Safe Schools Act, the National Service Trust Act, the Technology for Education Act, the overhauled Elementary and Secondary Education Act of 1965, reauthorization of the Office of Education Research and Improvement, and Head Start. The package promotes safer schools, better discipline, higher academic standards, improved teaching and learning, greater family involvement, improved access to college, expanded availability of technology for classroom use, and community-based solutions to educational improvement.

In response to Vice President Gore's National Performance Review, Riley instituted reforms to transform the department into an agency that can carry out an ambitious policy agenda. Riley established the department's first formal management structure and put into place the agency's first strategic plan, setting goals and priorities to guide policy implementation and identifying key performance indicators to track progress.

Riley was elected governor in 1978 and re-elected in 1982 after the voters amended the state constitution to enable him to be the first person in modern South Carolina history to run for a second term.

Riley is married to Ann Osteen Yarborough. They have four children and six grandchildren.

Office of Postsecondary Education

Deputy Asst. Secretary for Higher Education Programs

International Education and Graduate Program Services
1250 Maryland Ave., SW / Washington DC 20202-6132

Director
Mr. Richard D. Scarfo
202/401-9798   FAX 202/205-9489
Rm. 600B

Team Leader, International Studies
Mr. Ralph Hines
202/401-9798   FAX 202/205-9489
Rm. 600B

Business and International Education Program
Ms. Sarah T. Beaton
202/401-9778

Under the Business and International Education Program, the Secretary of Education awards grants to institutions of higher education to provide suitable international education and training for business personnel in various stages of professional development. To qualify for federal funds, a college or university must develop a program that will enhance the international academic program of the institution and provide appropriate services to the business community that will expand its capacity to engage in commerce

abroad. Institutional matching of 50 percent of the total cost of the program is required by law. Eligible activities might include export education programs; improvement of the business and international education curriculum of institutions; and the establishment of internships overseas to enable foreign language studies to develop their foreign language skills and knowledge of foreign cultures and societies.

Centers for International Business Education Program
Ms. Susanna Easton
202/401-9780

INTRODUCTION

The Centers for International Business Education Program provides grants to institutions of higher education to pay the federal share of the cost of planning, establishing, and operating Centers for International Education. The program requires that such Centers will:

• Be national resources for the teaching of improved business techniques, strategies, and methodologies that emphasize the international context in which business is transacted;
• Provide instruction for critical foreign languages and international fields needed to provide an understanding of the cultures and customs of U.S. trading partners;
• Provide research and training in the international aspects of trade, commerce, and other fields of study;
• Provide training to students enrolled in the institution or institutions in which a center is located;
• Serve as regional resources to local businesses by offering programs and providing research designed to meet the international training needs of such businesses; and
• Serve other faculty, students, and institutions of higher education located within their region.

Arizona

Mr. Robert E. Grosse
Director
CIBER-Thunderbird
The American Graduate School of Intl. Mgmt.
15249 North 59th Avenue
Glendale AZ 85306
Phone: 602/978-7250

California

Mr. Jose de la Torre
Director
CIBER- U.C.L.A.
John F. Anderson Grad. School of Mgmt.
405 Hilgard Avenue
Los Angeles CA 90024
Phone: 310/825-4507   Fax: 310/825-8098

Mr. Richard Drobnik
Director
CIBER-University of Southern California
School of Business
Los Angeles CA 90089-1421
Phone: 213/740-7135

Mr. Al Branon
Co-Director

CIBER-San Diego State University
College of Arts & Letters & Business Administration
5178 College Avenue
San Diego CA 92182-1900
Phone: 619/594-3008

Colorado

Mr. Donald L. Stevens
CIBER-University of Colorado-Denver
Institute for International Business
P.O. Box 173364, Campus Box 165
Denver CO 80217
Phone: 303/556-6392

Connecticut

Mr. Subhash Jain
Director
CIBER-University of Connecticut
School of Business Administration
368 Fairfield Road, U-41C
Stoors CT 06269-2041
Phone: 203/486-2317

Florida

Mr. Antonio Prados
Co-director
CIBER-Florida Int'l University
College of Business
University Park
Miami FL 33199
Phone: 305/348-3279

Georgia

Mr. John R. McIntyre
Director
CIBER-Georgia Institute of Technology
School of Management and Economics
755 Ferft Drive
Atlanta GA 30332-0520
Phone: 404/894-4379

Hawaii

Ms. Shirley Daniel
Director
CIBER-University of Hawaii at Manoa
College of Business Administration
2404 Maile Way, C202
Honolulu HA 96822
Phone: 808/956-7232

Illinois

Mr. Lee J. Alston
Director
CIBER-University of Illinois
College of Business Administration
428 Commerce West Bldg., 1206 Sixth St.
Champaign IL 61820
Phone: 217/333-7664

Mr. Albert Madansky
Director
CIBER-University of Chicago
Graduate School of Business
970 E Street
Chicago IL 60637
Phone: 312/702-7288

Indiana

Mr. Roger Schmenner
Director
CIBER-Indiana University
School of Business
P.O. Box 1
Bloomington IN 47402
Phone: 317/274-2544

Ms. Marie Thursby
Director
CIBER-Purdue University
School of Business
Hovde Hall
West Lafayette IN 60637
Phone: 317/494-4463

Maryland

CIBER-University of Maryland-College Park
4305 Van Munching Hall
College of Business and Management
College Park MD 20742-1815
Phone: 301/405-7579

Michigan

Mr. Brad Farnsworth
Director
CIBER-University of Michigan
School of Business Administration
474 East Jefferson St., Room 1322
Ann Arbor MI 48109-1248
Phone: 313/936-3917

Mr. Tamer Cavusgil
Director
CIBER-Michigan State University
School of Business
205 International Center
East Lansing MI 48824
Phone: 517/355-8377

New Jersey

Mr. Hugo Kinje
Director
CIBER-Rutgers, State University of New Jersey
Graduate School of Management
University Heights NJ 07102-1895
Phone: 973/353-5533

New York

Mr. Jace Schindeman
Associate Deans
CIBER-Columbia University
Columbia Business School

101 Uris Hall, 3022 Broadway
New York NY 10027
Phone: 212/854-6085

North Carolina

Mr. Ari Lewin
Director
CIBER-Duke University
Fuqua School of Business
Towerview Drive
Durham NC 27706
Phone: 919/660-7836

Ohio

Mr. Joseph Alutto
Co-Director
CIBER-Ohio State University
College of Business
Columbus OH 43210
Phone: 614/292-2666

Pennsylvania

Ms. Linda Blair
Director
CIBER-University of Pittsburgh
Joseph M. Katz Graduate School of Business
Pittsburgh PA 15260
Phone: 412/648-1570

South Carolina

CIBER-University of South Carolina
College of Business Administration
Columbia SC 29208
Phone: 803/777-4400   Fax: 803/777-3609

Tennessee

Mr. Ben Kedia
Director
CIBER-University of Memphis
Robert Wang Center for International Business
220 Fogelman Executive Center
Memphis TN 38152
Phone: 901/678-2038

Texas

Mr. Robert T. Green
Director
CIBER-University of Texas at Austin
School of Business
Austin TX 78712
Phone: 512/471-1128

Mr. Kerry Cooper
Executive Director
CIBER-Texas A&M University
College of Business Administration
College Station TX 77843-4113
Phone: 409/845-7082

Utah

CIBER-University of Utah
1645 East Campus Center Drive
School of Business
Salt Lake City UT 84112
Phone: 801/585-3360

Washington

Mr. Douglas MacLachlan
Senior Associate Dean
CIBER-University of Washington
School of Business Administration, Box 353200
Seattle WA 98195
Phone: 206/543-4750

Office of Bilingual Education and Minority Languages Affairs

330 C St., SW / Washington DC 20202

Director
Ms. Delia Pompa
202/205-5463   FAX 202/205-8737
Rm. 5094

Established in 1974, the office assists school districts in providing equal access for children whose primary language is not English.

Education Boards, Commissions, & Councils

1250 Maryland Ave., SW / Washington DC 20202

Exchange Visitor Waiver Review Board

Chair
Mr. Richard Scarfo
202/401-9798   FAX 202/205-9489
Rm. 600

President's Advisory Commission of Educational Excellence for Hispanic Americans

Chair
Ms. Ana Guzman
202/401-1411   FAX 202/401-8377
Rm. 2115

National Committee on Foreign Medical Education and Accreditation
Seventh and D Streets, SW / Washington DC 20202-7563

Chair
Mr. William Deal
202/260-3636   FAX 202/358-4200
Rm. 3905

U. S. Department of Energy

1000 Independence Ave., SW / Washington DC 20585

Central: 202/586-5000
Press: 202/586-5806
Public Affairs: 202/586-4940

INTRODUCTION

The Department of Energy monitors foreign energy markets and assesses their potential impact on U.S. energy industries. It promotes the international trade and investment interests of all facets of U.S. energy industries, including electric power and conservation, oil and gas, environmental technologies and alternative fuel technologies. In trade policy, the Department represents the interests of the U.S. energy sector in interagency

---

Office of the Secretary

1000 Independence Ave., SW / Washington DC 20585

Secretary of Energy
Secretary Designate - Ambassador Bill Richardson (May, 1997)
202/586-6210   FAX 202/586-4403
Rm. 7A-257

General Counsel

1000 Independence Ave., SW / Washington DC 20585

Deputy General Counsel for Energy Policy

Acting Assistant General Counsel for Intl. and Legal Policy
Mr. Samuel M. Bradley
202/586-6738   FAX 202/586-7396
Rm. 6H-064

Assistant Secretary for Policy and International Affairs

1000 Independence Ave., SW / Washington DC 20585

Assistant Secretary
Mr. Robert Gee
202/586-5800   FAX 202/586-0861
Rm. 7C-016

Robert Gee was confirmed in the fall of 1997 as the assistant secretary for policy and international affairs at the Department of Energy. Gee had been of counsel to the law firm of Akin, Gump, Strauss, Hauer & Feld, as well as an attorney specializing in natural gas litigation in Texas for Tenneco Oil Company and the law firm of Reynolds, Shannon, Miller, Blinn, White & Cook. He previously served as an attorney for the Federal Energy Regulatory Commission.

The assistant secretary for policy and international affairs is the principal advisor to the secretary, deputy secretary, and the under secretary on all domestic and international policy issues. The assistant secretary has primary responsibility for the formulation and development of domestic and international energy policy. The assistant secretary also deals with departmental strategic planning as well as integration of departmental policy, program, and budget goals in coordination with the chief financial officer and the office of the director of administration and human resources management. The

assistant secretary also analyzes, develops, and coordinates departmental technology, environmental, and economic policies.

Gee of Austin, Texas, was appointed a member of the Texas Public Utility Commission in October 1991 by Governor Ann Richards and served as chairman of the commission from 1991 until 1995. Gee also has served as the chairman of the National Association of Regulatory Utility Commissioners' committee on electricity, representing the interests of state public utility commissions before the U.S. Congress, the U.S. Department of Energy, trade associations, and various public interest associations at the local and national level.

He holds a B.A., with honors, and a J.D. from the University of Texas.

Deputy Asst. Secretary for International Energy Policy, Trade and Investment

Deputy Asst. Secretary
Mr. David J. Jhirad
202/586-5493   FAX 202/586-3047
Rm. 7C-034

Associate Deputy Secretary
Mr. John R. Brodman
202/586-5915
Rm. 7C-034

Director, Policy Analysis, Trade and Investment for
the Americas, Asia and Africa

Mr. David L. Pumphrey
202/586-6832   FAX 202/586-6148
Rm. 7G-076

Director, Policy Analysis, Trade and Investment for
Europe, the NIS, and the Middle East

Mr. Leonard Coburn
202/586-6383   FAX 202/586-6148
Rm. 7G-090

Deputy Asst. Secretary for Science, Technology Policy and Cooperation

Director, Office of International Science and
Technology Cooperation

Mr. Robert S. Price
202/586-6777   FAX 202/586-1180
Rm. 1E-218

Energy Information Administration

1000 Independence Ave., SW / Washington DC 20585

Office of Energy Markets and End Use

Chief, International Statistics Branch
Mr. Louis D. DeMouy
202/586-6557
Rm. 2G-053

Office of Integrated Analysis and Forecasting

Chief, Intl. Economic & Integrated Forecasting Branch
Mr. Gerald E. Peabody
202/586-1142
Rm. 2H-070

Assistant Secretary for Fossil Energy

1000 Independence Ave., SW / Washington DC 20585

Sr. Adviser for Intl. Activities
Mr. Sun Chun
202/586-6660   FAX 202/586-7847
Rm. 4G-084

Office of Nuclear Energy, Science & Technology

1000 Independence Ave., SW / Washington DC 20585

Office of International Nuclear Safety

Associate Director
Ms. Kristen L. Suokko
202/586-7313   FAX 202/586-8353

Office of Energy Research

19901 Germantown Rd. / Germantown MD 20874

Office of Fusion Energy Sciences

Director, International Programs Staff
Dr. Michael Roberts
301/903-3068   FAX 301/903-1233
Rm. L-225

Nuclear Weapons Council

The Pentagon / Washington DC 20301

Chair
Mr. Jacques Gansler
703/695-2381
Rm. 3E933

Office of Nonproliferation & National Security

1000 Independence Ave., SW / Washington DC 20585

Principal Deputy Director
Mr. Kenneth E. Baker
202/586-0645
Rm. 7A-049

Office of Arms Control and Nonproliferation

Director
Mr. Leonard Spector
202/586-2102
Rm. 4C-014

Acting Director, International Policy and Analysis Division
Mr. Anthony F. Czajkowski
202/586-5553
Rm. 4C-024

Director, Nuclear Transfer and Supplier Policy
Ms. Patricia Dedik
202/586-2331
Rm. 6A-030

Director, International Safeguards Division
Mr. Kenneth E. Sanders
202/586-8460   FAX 202/586-0936
Rm. 6A-045

U. S. Department of Health & Human Services

200 Independence Ave., SW / Washington DC 20201

Information: 202/619-0257

> ### INTRODUCTION
>
> *The Health and Human Services Department is involved in international matters, because disease and other problems affecting people do not respect national boundaries.*

Office of the Secretary

200 Independence Ave., SW / Washington DC 20201

Secretary of Health and Human Services
Secretary Donna E. Shalala
202/690-7000   FAX 202/690-7023
RM. 615F

Personal: born 2/14/41 in Cleveland, Ohio.

Education: A.B., Western College for Women (Oxford, Ohio), 1962. Ph.D., Maxwell School of Citizenship and Public Affairs, Syracuse University, 1970.

Professional: 1962-64, volunteer, U.S. Peace Corps (Iran). 1966-70, professor of political science, Bernard Baruch Coll. 1972-73, Spencer Fellow, National Academy of Education. 1972-79, prof. of politics and education, Teachers Coll., Columbia Univ. 1975-76, John Simon Guggenheim Fellow. 1976, visiting professor, Yale Law School. 1975-77, director and treasurer, Municipal Assistance Corp. (N.Y.). 1977-80, assistant secretary for policy development and research, U.S. Department of Housing and Urban Development. 1980-88, professor of political science and president, Hunter Coll., City Univ. of New York. 1987, Leadership Fellow, Japan Society. 1988-92, professor of political science and chancellor, Univ. of Wisconsin at Madison. 1993-present, secretary, U.S. Dept. of Health and Human Services.

In January, 1993, Donna Shalala became secretary of the largest department of the federal government. As secretary of Health and Human Services, Shalala oversees the agency that touches most directly on the lives of Americans. She has been a scholar, educational administrator, and public servant for her entire career. In announcing her appointment, then-President-elect Clinton noted her "astonishing leadership abilities--and her love of mountain climbing. Of all the mountains Donna Shalala has scaled, HHS may be the highest."

HHS is the federal government's principal agency for protecting the health of Americans and providing essential human services. With a

1997 budget of approximately $354 billion and 59,000 employees, HHS administers a wide variety of programs, including Medicaid and Medicare, the Food and Drug Administration, the National Institutes of Health, the Centers for Disease Control and Prevention, and nearly all of the federal welfare and children's programs. Its programs represent 40 percent of the federal budget and provide direct services or income support to more than 20 percent of all Americans.

Shalala advises the president on health, welfare, and income security. She directs the operation of all department programs and reports to the Congress and the public regarding HHS actions. President Clinton's interest in health care and welfare reform make Shalala a key player in the administration.

A recipient of more than 20 honorary degrees, Shalala has lectured and written extensively on education, political science, urban and social policy, and government finance. She has also served as a Peace Corps volunteer, and as a member of the Committee for Economic Development, reporting on ways to better meet the health and educational needs of disadvantaged children.

In the Carter administration, Shalala worked to fund battered women's shelters and to study the housing needs of families headed by women. She helped orchestrate the reversal of New York City's financial collapse in her role as director of the Municipal Assistance Corporation. In addition, she served on the board of the Children's Defense Fund for more than a decade and chaired the organization in 1992.

Since taking the helm at HHS, Shalala has shifted the focus of the department to the everyday needs of Americans. She is a leader in the administration's efforts to reform the nation's welfare system and improve health care while containing health costs. She is also carrying out management restructuring and reform at HHS, under Vice President Gore's initiative to "reinvent government," aimed at improving efficiency and service to constituents.

Office of the Chief of Staff

200 Independence Ave., SW / Washington DC 20201

Director, Office of Intl. Affairs and Exchange Visitor
Waiver Review Board
Mr. David Hohman
202/690-6174
RM. 639H

Administration for Children and Families

Office of the Assistant Secretary

Office of Refugee Resettlement
370 L'Enfant Promenade, SW / Washington DC 20447

The Department's Office of Refugee Resettlement advises the Secretary of Health and Human Services on policies and programs regarding refugee resettlement, legalized aliens, and repatriation matters.

Director
Ms. Lavinia M. Limon
202/401-9246
6th Floor

Office of Public Health and Science

Office of International and Refugee Health
5600 Fishers Lane / Rockville MD 20857

Director, Office of International Health
Ms. Linda A. Vogel
301/443-1774
Rm. 18-75

Centers for Disease Control and Prevention

Epidemiology Program Office
1600 Clifton Rd,. NE, Bldg. 11 / Atlanta GA 30333

Chief, International Branch
Mr. Mark White
404/639-2231
Rm. 5421

Global Health Office
2858 Woodcock Blvd. / Atlanta GA 30341

Director
Dr. Stephen Blount
770/488-1085
Rm. 1075

National Center for Health Statistics
6525 Belcrest Rd. / Hyattsville MD 20782

Acting Associate Director, Office of Intl. Statistics
Mr. Jack Anderson
301/436-7016
Rm. 1140

Food and Drug Administration

5600 Fishers Lane / Rockville MD 20857

Acting Director, International Policy Staff
Ms. Linda R. Horton
301/827-3344
Rm. 15-74

Associate Commissioner for Regulatory Affairs

Office of Regional Operations

International and Technical Operations Branch
VACANT
301/443-1855
Rm. 12-18

15800 Crabbs Branch Way / Rockville, MD 20855

Director, Division of Import Operations and Policy
Mr. Thomas Gardine
301/443-6553
Rm. 118

Associate Commissioner for Health Affairs
5600 Fishers Lane / Rockville MD 20857

Executive Director for International Harmonization
Ms. Janet Showalter
301/827-0865
Rm. 15-22

Associate Director for International & Domestic Drug Control
Mr. Nicholas P. Reuter
301/827-1696
Rm. 15-22

Director, International Affairs Staff

Mr. Walter M. Batts
301/827-4480
Rm. 15A-30

Associate Director for Africa and the Middle East
Ms. Mary Doug Tyson
301/827-4480
Rm. 15A-30

Associate Director for Asia and the Pacific
Ms. Julia Ho
301/827-4480
Rm. 15A-30

Associate Director for Europe
Mr. Donald Aronson
301/827-4480
Rm. 15A-30

Associate Director for Trade Policy and Related Activities
Dr. Merton V. Smith
301/827-4480
Rm. 15A-30

Associate Director for Intl. Standards and Related Issues
Ms. Roberta Dresser
301/827-4480
Rm. 15A-30

Associate Director for the Americas
Ms. Marilyn Veek
301/827-4480
Rm. 15A-30

Associate Director for International Organizations
Ms. Lois A. Beaver
301/827-4480
Rm. 15A-30

International Visitor Coordinator
Ms. Anne Marie Dromerick
301/827-4480
Rm. 15A-30

International Travel Coordinator
Ms. Cristen DiLallo
301/827-4480
Rm. 15A-30

Center for Biologics Evaluation and Research
8800 Rockville Pike, Bld. 29B / Rockville MD 20205

Associate Director for Medical and International Affairs
Dr. Elaine C. Esber
301/827-0641   FAX 301/827-0644
RM 1NN06

Center for Food Safety and Applied Nutrition

Office of Constituent Operations
200 C-Street, SW / Washington DC 20204

International Activities Staff
Mr. Charles W. Cooper
202/205-5042
Rm. 5823

Office of Field Programs
200 C-Street, SW / Washington DC 20204

Import Programs Branch
Mr. Leonard Nessen
202/205-4726

Rm. 5413

Center for Devices and Radiological Health

Office of Health and Industry Programs
2094 Oakgrove Bldg., Gaither Rd. / Rockville MD 20850

International Relations and External Affairs Staff
301/594-7491 Ext. 127
Rm. 1305

Health Resources & Services Administration

Office of the Administrator

International Health Affairs
5600 Fishers Lane / Rockville MD 20857

Senior Adviser
Mr. George B. Dines
301/443-6152   FAX 202/443-7834
Rm. 14-12

National Institutes of Health

National Institute on Aging
7201 Wisconsin Ave. / Bethesda MD 20892

International Coordinator
Dr. Leslie Stenull
301/496-0767
Rm. 2C227

Dir., Special Program for Research on Aging, World Health Org.
VACANT
301/496-4692   FAX 301/402=0260
Rm. 2C227

National Institute of Allergy and Infectious Diseases
6003 Executive Blvd. / Rockville MD 20852

Assistant Director for International Research
Dr. Karl A. Western
301/496-5643
Rm. 1B01

National Cancer Institute

Office of International Affairs
6130 Executive Blvd. / Rockville MD 20852

Associate Director for International Affairs
Dr. Federico Welsch
301/496-4761   FAX 301/496-3954
Rm. 100

International Cancer Information Center
9000 Rockville Pike, Bldg. 82 / Bethesda MD 20892

Director
Ms. Susan Hubbard
301/496-9096
Rm. 102

Chief, International Cancer Research Data Bank Branch
Dr. Gisele Sarosy
301/496-7406
Rm. 113

National Institute of Dental Research
45 Center Drive / Bethesda MD 20892

Assistant Director for International Health
Dr. Lois K. Cohen
301/594-7710
Rm. 4AN12C

National Institute of Diabetes
Digestive and Kidney Diseases
45 Center Drive / Bethesda MD 20892

Digestive Diseases and Nutrition Division
Director, U.S.-Japan Malnutrition Panel Program
Dr. Michael K. May
301/594-8884
Rm. 6AN18J

National Institute of Environmental Health Sciences
9000 Rockville Pike, Bldg. 31 / Bethesda MD 20892

Office of Intl. Programs and Public Health
Director
Dr. Gerald Poje
301/496-3511
Rm. B1C02

National Eye Institute
9000 Rockville Pike, Bldg. 31 / Bethesda MD 20892

Assistant Director, Office of Intl. Program Activities
Mr. Terrence Gillen
301/496-4876   FAX 301/496-3246
Rm. 6A06

National Heart, Lung and Blood Institute

Office of International Programs
9000 Rockville Pike, Bldg. 31 / Bethesda MD 20892

Associate Director
Dr. Ruth Hegyeli
301/496-5375   FAX 301/496-2734
Rm. 4A07

National Library of Medicine
8600 Rockville Pike, Bldg. 38 / Bethesda MD 20894

Director for Intl. Programs
Dr. Elliot R. Siegel
301/496-2311
Rm. 2S20

Fogarty International Center
16 Center Drive, MSC 2220 / Bethesda MD 20892-2220

Administers a number of programs for advanced study in health sciences.

Director
Dr. Philip E. Schambra
301/496-1415   FAX 301/402-2173

Director, Office of Intl. Science Policy and Analysis
Mr. Robert Eiss
301/496-1491

Acting Asst. Dir. for Intl. Relations & Dir. Division of Intl. Rel.
Ms. Linda Staheli
301/496-5903

Program Officer for Africa and the Middle East
Dr. Charles Gardner
301/496-4784

Program Officer for Americas, World Health Org. and PAHO
Dr. Arlene Fanaroff
301/496-4784

Program Officer for Europe
Dr. Amar Bhat
301/496-4784

Program Officer for Russia and the NIS
Ms. Natalie Tomitch
301/496-4784

Program Officer for East Asia and the Pacific
Dr. Allen Holt
301/496-4784

Special Foreign Currency Program
Mr. Chris Keenan
301/496-4784

Director, Division of Intl. Training and Research
Dr. Kenneth Bridbord
301/496-2516

Program Officer
Dr. Jean Flagg-Newton
301/496-1653   FAX 301/402-0779

Director, Division of Intl. Advanced Studies
Dr. Richard Krause
301/496-4161   FAX 301/496-8496

Exec. Off. & Dir., Office of Administrative Mgmt. & Intl. Services
Mr. Richard Miller
301/496-4625

U. S. Department of Housing & Urban Development

451 Seventh Street, SW / Washington, DC 20410

202/708-1420

INTRODUCTION

The Department of Housing and Urban Development coordinates international contacts and exchanges with foreign governments in the industrial world and with international organizations such as the United Nations and the Organization for Economic Cooperation and Development (OECD) on matters dealing with housing financing and urban development policy.

Assistant Secretary for Policy Development and Research

Deputy Assistant Secretary for Policy Development

Senior Officer, International Affairs Staff
Mr. John M. Geraghty
202/708-0770, ext. 237   FAX 202/708-5536
Rm. 8118

U. S. Department of the Interior

18th and C Streets, NW / Washington, DC 20240

Locator: 202/208-3100
Communications: 202/208-6416

INTRODUCTION

Despite its name, the Interior Department engages in a number of activities that extend beyond U.S. borders: in doing research and gathering information on the world's supply of minerals; in identifying and protecting fish, wildlife, and plants; and in overseeing U.S. insular areas in the Caribbean and the Pacific and small independent states in the Pacific.

The Interior Department's U.S. Geological Survey keeps track of minerals all over the world - of who produces them and where they are exported. It provides authoritative information on their supply and demand and assists U.S. trade negotiators. The U.S. Geological Survey absorbed these functions of the Bureau of Mines, which was abolished.

The Department's Fish and Wildlife Service provides both national and international leadership in the area of identifying, protecting, and restoring endangered species of fish, wildlife, and plants. This program includes: development of the Federal Endangered and Threatened Species List, conduct of status surveys, preparation of recovery plans, and coordination of efforts nationally and internationally. It includes foreign importation enforcement and consultation with foreign countries.

The National Park Service provides technical assistance to foreign governments for the preservation of natural sites and historic/cultural properties worldwide.

The Interior Department --- in consultation with the assistant secretary of State for East Asian and Pacific Affairs --- is responsible for general oversight of all federal programs provided to the Freely Associated States of the Republic of the Marshall Islands and the Federated States of Micronesia under the Compact of Free Association. The Department also is responsible for building mutually beneficial partnerships to facilitate locally determined economic, social, and political development in the U.S. insular areas of Guam, American Samoa, the Virgin Islands, the Commonwealth of the Northern Mariana Islands, and the Trust Territory of the Pacific Islands (Republic of Papua).

Office of the Secretary

1849 C Street, NW / Washington, DC 20240

Secretary of the Interior
Mr. Bruce Babbitt
202/208-735   FAX 202/208-7545
Rm. 6156

Personal: born 6/27/38 in Los Angeles, Calif.; raised in Flagstaff, Ariz.

Education: B.A. in geology, Univ. of Notre Dame, 1960. M.S. in geophysics, Univ. of Newcastle (England), 1963. L.L.B., Harvard Law School, 1965.

Professional: 1965-67, field representative, Office of Economic Development (Austin, Texas). 1967-75, attorney, Brown & Bain (Phoenix, Ariz.). 1975-78, attorney general; 1978-87, governor, State of Ariz. 1988, candidate for the Democratic nomination for president. 1988-93, attorney, Steptoe & Johnson (Phoenix, Ariz. and Wash., D.C.). 1993-present, secretary, U.S. Department of the Interior.

Bruce Babbitt was appointed secretary of the Interior Department by President Clinton in January 1993. He had served as governor of Arizona from 1978-87 and was the state's attorney general from 1975 to 1978.

The U.S. Department of Interior was established in 1849 and oversees the nation's parks, federal lands, mineral resources, and Indian reservations. The appointment of Babbitt signaled a change in the management of federal lands and natural resources from the business-leaning policies of his politically conservative predecessors toward the development of large scale, consensus-based environmental restoration projects.

An unsuccessful 1988 presidential candidate, Babbitt is a long-time friend of Clinton who served as chairman of the Democratic Governors Association in 1985. Babbitt was also a founding member, along with then-Governor Clinton, of the moderate Democratic Leadership Council. Because of his diverse background, Babbitt has been considered for a number of positions in the administration, including a top trade post and a seat on the U.S. Supreme Court.

Babbitt and his wife Harriet, who is U.S. Ambassador to the Organization of American States, have two sons.

Office of Communications

Assistant to the Secretary and Director, Office of Communications
Mr. Michael G. Gauldin
202/208-6416   FAX 202/208-5133
Rm. 6213

Asst. Secretary for Policy, Mgmt. & Budget

1849 C St., NW / Washington DC 20240

Office of Insular Affairs

Desk Officer, Commonwealth of the Northern Mariana Islands
Ms. Debbie Subera-Wiggins
202/208-6816
Rm. 4327

Desk Officer, Virgin Islands
Mr. Edgar Johnson
202/208-6816
Rm. 4325

Desk Officer, American Samoa
Mr. Nik Pula
202/208-6816
Rm. 4324

Desk Officer, Federated States of Micronesia
  and the Marshall Islands
Mr. Joseph H. McDermott
202/208-6816
Rm. 4322

Deputy Assistant Secretary for Policy and International Affairs

Deputy Assistant Secretary
Ms. Brooks Yeager
202/208-6182
Rm. 6122

Office of Policy Analysis

International Programs Officer
Ms. Katherine C. Washburn
202/208-3048
Rm. 4429

Asst. Secretary for Fish & Wildlife and Parks

National Park Service
1849 C St., NW / Washington DC 20240

Chief, Office of International Affairs
Ms. Sharon Cleary
202/565-1001
Rm. 2256

U.S. Fish and Wildlife Service

International Affairs
1849 C St., NW / Washington DC 20240

Assistant Director
Mr. Marshall P. Jones
202/208-6393
Rm. 3247

4401 N. Fairfax Drive / Arlington VA 22203

Chief, Office of Intl. Affairs
Mr. Herbert A. Raffaele
703/358-1754
Rm. 860

Asst. Secretary for Land & Minerals Mgmt.

Minerals Management Service
381 Elden St. / Herndon VA 22070-4817

Offshore Minerals Management

Program Director, Intl. Activities and
  Marine Minerals Division
Ms. Carol Hartgen
703/787-1300
Rm. 2327

Deputy Program Director, Intl. Activities
Mr. John W. Padan
703/787-1300
Rm. 2327

Assistant Secretary for Water and Science

Bureau of Reclamation
1849 C St., NW / Washington DC 20240

Chief, Intl. Affairs Group
Mr. Richard Ives
202/208-5235
Rm. 7445

Advisory Councils and Independent Offices

United States Board on Geographic Names
4600 Sangamore Rd. / Bethesda MD 20816-5003

Executive Secretary for Foreign Names Committee
Mr. Randall E. Flynn
301/227-3050
Rm. 2N158

U. S. Department of Justice

950 Pennsylvania Avenue, NW / Washington, D.C. 20530

Locator: 202/514-2000
Press and Public Affairs: 202/514-2007
http://www.usdoj.gov

INTRODUCTION

The Justice Department impacts on international business through its responsibilities to ensure healthy competition; to protect the public against criminals and subversion; and to enforce drug, immigration, and naturalization laws.

Office of the Attorney General

Attorney General
Ms. Janet Reno
202/514-2001   FAX 202/514-4371
Rm. 5111

Personal: born 7/21/38 in Miami, Fla.

Education: A.B., Cornell Univ., 1960. LL.B., Harvard Law School, 1963.

Professional: 1960, intern, Dade County Sheriff's office, Board of County Commissioners. 1962 and 1963-67, attorney, Brigham and Brigham. 1967-71, junior partner, Lewis and Reno. 1971-72, staff director, Judiciary Comm., Florida House of Reps. 1972-73, counsel, Criminal Justice Committee for the Revision of Florida's Criminal Code, Florida state senate. 1973-76, asst. state attorney, 11th Judicial Circuit of Florida. 1976-78, partner, Steel, Hector & Davis. 1978-93, state attorney, 11th Judicial Circuit. 1993-present, attorney general, U.S. Dept. of Justice.

Janet Reno is among the more recognized members of President Clinton's cabinet, but her recognition was hard earned during a tumultuous opening six months as the nation's top justice official. Reno joined the Cabinet in the wake of a controversy that undermined Clinton's first two nominees for attorney general. Even before her Senate confirmation, it became clear, as former colleague Donald Nelson put it, that "she won't try to fit in with Washington; Washington is going to have to fit in with her."

The attorney general represents the U.S. in legal matters, gives advice and opinions to the president upon request, and appears before the U.S. Supreme Court "in cases of exceptional gravity and importance."

Reno, the nation's first female attorney general, was instrumental in the enactment of anti-terrorism legislation in the wake of the Oklahoma City bombing. That year the department led efforts for a peaceful resolution to the Freeman standoff in Montana.

A native of western Dade County, Reno earned her battle scars, and a reputation as a tough but judicious prosecutor, during a 14-year tour of duty as state attorney in Miami. She won re-election five times in a heavily Republican district and survived controversial court cases that threatened to derail her career.

Chief of Staff
Mr. John M. Hogan
202-514-3892   FAX 202/616-5117
Rm. 5113

Personal: born 3/8/50 in St. Louis, Mo.

Education: B.A., Univ. of Mass., 1972. J.D. Univ. of Miami, 1977.

Professional: 1977-79, associate, Shutts and Bowen (Miami, Fla.). 1979-87, assistant state attorney (Miami). 1987-89, state prosecutor and regional director for South Florida, office of Florida Attorney General. 1989-93, chief assistant state attorney, felony division, office of Florida's State's Attorney. 6/93-1/94, special asst. to the attorney general of the U.S.; 6/93-1/95, acting U.S. attorney, Northern District of Ga.; 1995- present, chief of staff to the attorney general, U.S. Dept. of Justice.

As chief of staff to the attorney general, John Hogan assists Janet Reno in managing all aspects of the Department of Justice. When Reno came to Justice, she brought Hogan with her as counselor to the attorney general. They had worked together since the late 1970's in Florida and have "a wonderful working relationship," according to one member on his staff. Hogan had distinguished himself as an outstanding state prosecutor in Florida, and was awarded the Trial Lawyer of the Year in 1993 by the Association of Government Attorneys in Capital Litigation.

As chief assistant state attorney in Miami in the early 1990's, Hogan supervised all felony prosecutors and handled several high profile cases including State v. Fuster et al. (1985). This case, labeled the "Country Walk" case, involved the prosecution of Frank and Ileana Fuster, who ran a babysitting service in an affluent Dade suburb. The case was the nation's first successfully prosecuted mass sex abuse case involving preschool aged children. It was the subject of a best selling book entitled "Unspeakable Acts" by Jan Hollingsworth. The case is a model for prosecutors on methods for dealing with child witnesses and child sex abuse.

From 1987 to 1989, Hogan served as statewide prosecutor in the Florida attorney general's office, and as regional director for South Florida. The office of statewide prosecutor was created under the Florida Constitution to investigate and prosecute organized crime that affect more than one section of Florida. Hogan was Florida's first statewide prosecutor. As regional director for South Florida, Hogan supervised the attorney general's consumer protection unit and the criminal appeals section. He was also Florida's representative at various National Association of Attorneys' General meetings.

Hogan previously served as associate deputy attorney general of the U.S. and then special assistant to the attorney general from June 1993

to January 1994. From June 1993 to January 1995 he also served as the acting U.S. Attorney for the Northern District of Georgia and the director of the Justice Department's BNL Task Force, where he supervised the largest bank fraud case in U.S. history.

Deputy Attorney General

Mr. Eric Holder
202/514-2101   FAX 202/514-0467
Rm. 4111

Personal: born 1/21/51 in New York City, N.Y.

Education: B.A., Columbia College, 1973. J.D. , Columbia Law School, 1976.

Professional: 1976-88, public integrity section, U.S. Justice Department. 1988-93, associate judge, Superior Court of the District of Columbia. 1993-97, U.S. Attorney for the District of Columbia. July 1997-present, deputy attorney general, U.S. Dept. of Justice.

On April 14, 1997, President Clinton nominated Eric Holder to be the deputy attorney general of the United States. Holder received unanimous confirmation from the Senate and was sworn in on July 18, 1997. As deputy attorney general, Holder is responsible for the supervision of the day-to-day operation of the Department of Justice. He is the highest ranking African-American in law enforcement in the history of the United States.

The deputy attorney general oversees the work of the civil rights, antitrust, tax, and environment and natural resources divisions within the Justice Department. Holder also has oversight responsibility for the Immigration and Naturalization Service, the Executive Office for Immigration Review, the office of legal counsel, the office of legislative affairs, the office of information and privacy, the Community Relations Service, and the Foreign Claims Settlement Commission.

After law school, Holder joined the Department of Justice as part of the Attorney General's Honors Program. He was assigned to the newly formed public integrity section in 1976 and was tasked to investigate and prosecute official corruption on the local, state, and federal levels. While at the public integrity section, Holder participated in a number of prosecutions and appeals involving such defendants as the Florida state treasurer, the ambassador to the Dominican Republic, a local judge in Philadelphia, an assistant U.S. Attorney in New York City, FBI agents, and a "capo" in an organized crime family.

In 1988, President Reagan nominated Holder to become an associate judge of the Superior Court of the District of Columbia. His investiture occurred in October of that year. Over the next five years, Judge Holder presided over hundreds of criminal trials, many of which involved homicides and other crimes of violence.

In 1993, President Clinton nominated Holder to become the U. S. Attorney for the District of Columbia. He served as the head of the largest U.S. Attorney's office in the nation for nearly four years. As U.S. Attorney, Holder created a new domestic violence unit to more effectively handle those types of tragic cases, implemented a community prosecution pilot project to work hand-in-hand with residents and local government agencies to make neighborhoods safer, supported a renewed enforcement emphasis on hate crimes so that criminal acts of intolerance will be severely punished, developed a comprehensive strategy to improve the manner in which agencies handle cases involving child abuse, launched a new community outreach program to reconnect the U.S. Attorney's office with the citizens it serves, revitalized the victim/witness assistance program to better serve those individuals who are directly affected by crime, and developed Operation Ceasefire, an initiative designed to reduce violent crime by getting guns out of the hands of criminals.

Holder graduated from Columbia Law School in 1976. While in law school, he clerked at the N.A.A.C.P. Legal Defense Fund and the Department of Justice's criminal division. He has been active in the organization Concerned Black Men, a group that seeks to help District of Columbia youth with many of the problems they face, ranging from teenage pregnancy to sub-par academic achievement. Holder lives in Northwest Washington with his wife, Sharon Malone, who is a doctor in obstetrics and gynecology, and has two daughters.

Executive Office for National Security
Director
Mr. Daniel S. Seikaly
202/514-6753
Rm. 4119

Office of Public Affairs

Director
Mr. Burt Brandenberg
202/616-2777   FAX 202/514-5331
Rm. 1228

Antitrust Division

> The antitrust division of the Justice Department represents the U.S. on the Committee on Competition Law and Policy of the Organization for Economic Cooperation and Development, and participates in the United Nations Conference on Trade and Development. Through the State Department, the division maintains liaison with foreign governments on antimonopoly laws and policies.

Assistant Attorney General
Mr. Joel I. Klein
202/514-2401   FAX 202/616-2645
Rm. 3109

Personal: born 10/25/46 in New York City, N.Y.

Education: B.A. (magna cum laude), Columbia College, 1967. J.D.(magna cum laude), Harvard Law School, 1971.

Professional: 1973-74, law clerk, Chief Judge David Bazelon, U.S. Court of Appeals. 1974-75, law clerk, Justice Lewis Powell, U.S. Supreme Court. 1975-76, attorney, The Mental Health Law Project. 1976-81, associate and partner, Rogovin, Stern & Huge. 1981-93, partner, Klein, Farr, Smith & Taranto. 1993-95, deputy counsel to the President, The White House. 1995-96, principal deputy assistant attorney general; 1996-97, acting assistant attorney general; 1997-present, assistant attorney general, antitrust division, U.S. Dept. of Justice.

Joel Klein left his law practice in 1993 to become deputy counsel to President Clinton at the White House. In 1995 Clinton appointed Klein as the principal deputy assistant attorney general of the antitrust division at the Justice Department. After serving for nine months as acting assistant attorney general, the Senate confirmed his nomination to head the division in 1997.

Klein, who believes strongly in antitrust enforcement, cited several factors that make his job a challenging one: the fact that antitrust enforcement is an international enterprise, that new technology has many implications for antitrust enforcement, and that deregulation is considered to be the best way to protect consumers today. At his confirmation hearing, Klein noted that the antitrust division should "play a major role in ... deregulatory efforts by helping to design as well as implement them ... and that it should be prepared to commit the resources necessary to do this job well."

As chief of the antitrust division, Klein is responsible for leadership and oversight of all of the division's programs and policies. The division is charged with investigating possible antitrust violations, conducting grand jury proceedings, preparing and trying antitrust cases, prosecuting appeals, and negotiating and enforcing final judgments.

Klein began his legal career as a law clerk to Chief Judge David Bazelon on the U.S. Court of Appeals for the D.C. Circuit in 1973. Subsequently, he clerked for Justice Lewis Powell on the U.S. Supreme Court. Klein then worked for the Mental Health Law Project where he litigated law reform cases on behalf of persons with mental illness. From 1976 to 1993 he served in various volunteer positions at the Green Door, a D.C. community-based, non-government center for the mentally ill. Klein litigated cases in private practice for five years before starting his own firm with several partners. Klein, Farr, Smith & Taranto specialized in Supreme Court and appellate litigation. Klein focused on health care, constitutional litigation, and in appellate advocacy.

Klein has also taught courses in civil procedure, federal jurisdiction, and constitutional litigation at Georgetown University Law Center. Klein, who lives in Washington, D.C., is married to Harriet Howard Davis, and has two daughters.

Section Chiefs
601 D Street, NW / Washington DC 20530

Chief, Foreign Commerce Section
Mr. Charles S. Stark
202/514-2464   FAX 202/514-4508
Rm. 10024

Civil Division

Commercial Litigation Branch
1100 L Street NW / Washington DC 20530

Director, Office of Foreign Litigation

Mr. David Epstein
202/514-7455
Rm. 11006

26 Federal Plaza / New York NY 10278-0140

Attorney in Charge, Intl. Trade Field Office
Mr. Joseph I. Liebman
212/264-9232
Rm. 339

Office of Immigration Litigation
950 Pennsylvania Avenue, NW / Washington, D.C. 20530

Deputy Asst. Attorney General, Office of Immigration Litigation
Mr. Philip D. Bartz
202/514-5421
Rm. 3607

Civil Rights Division

Office of Special Counsel for
Immigration Related Unfair Employment Practices

1425 New York Ave., NW / Washington DC 20005

> **INTRODUCTION**
>
> *The Immigration Reform and Control Act of 1986 (IRCA) prohibits employment discrimination on the basis of national origin and citizenship status against citizens and certain classes of aliens. The Office of Special Counsel for Immigration Related Unfair Employment Practices was established to ensure that protected individuals and aliens authorized to work in the United States are not discriminated against with respect to hiring, firing or recruitment or referral for a fee based on their citizenship status or national origin.*
>
> ---
>
> **IRCA's** prohibition against citizenship status discrimination covers the following protected individuals: citizens and nationals of the United States; those lawfully admitted for permanent residence; those granted temporary resident status under IRCA's amnesty program who resided unlawfully in the United States since January 1982; those granted temporary resident status through the Special Agricultural Worker program or the Replenishment Agricultural Worker program; those admitted as refugees; and those granted asylum.
>
> It is also illegal under IRCA for employers with four to 14 employees to discriminate with respect to hiring, firing, or recruitment or referral for a fee against any work-authorized individual on the basis of his or her national origin. Employers with 15 or more employees are covered under the Civil Rights Act of 1964 and complaints for these companies are handled by the Equal Employment Opportunity Commission.
>
> The Office of Special Counsel for Immigration Related Unfair Employment Practices handles all charges of "citizenship status" discrimination against employers with four or more employees. It is also responsible for protecting legally authorized workers against document abuse by employers in the employment eligibility verification process.
>
> In April of 1994 the Office of Special Counsel merged with the Civil Rights Division as part of a reorganization intended to centralize all civil rights enforcement activities within the Department of Justice and to promote cost effectiveness through the consolidation of programmatic and administrative functions.
>
> In investigating charges and filing complaints, the office has continued to vigorously prosecute cases involving national origin
>
> *Cont'd.*

> and citizenship status discrimination, and to seek civil penalties and equitable relief in cases involving employers who violated the document abuse provisions of IRCA.
>
> The office has also continued its long term effort to provide public education to both employers and employees about their rights and responsibilities. This outreach mission was carried out through grants to community based organizations and employers groups to conduct education activities, the dissemination of information through the media, and the participation by staff attorneys at activities attended by appropriate target groups.

Acting Special Counsel
Mr. P.A. Marmolejos
202/616-1950
Rm. 9030

Criminal Division

1400 New York Ave., NW / Washington DC 20530

> **INTRODUCTION**
>
> *The Office of International Affairs in the Criminal Division supports the Department's legal divisions, the U.S. Attorneys, and local prosecutors regarding questions of foreign and international law, including issues related to extradition and mutual legal assistance treaties. The office also coordinates all international evidence gathering. In conjunction with the State Department, the office engages in the negotiations of new extradition and mutual legal assistance treaties and executive agreements throughout the world. Office attorneys also participate on a number of committees established under the auspices of the United Nations and other international organizations to resolve a variety of international law enforcement problems, such as narcotics trafficking and money laundering. The office maintains a permanent office in Rome.*

Acting Director, Office of Intl. Affairs
Mr. Thomas G. Snow
202/514-0000
Rm. 5100

1331 F Street, NW / Washington DC 20530

Director, Intl. Criminal Investigative Training Assistance Program
Ms. Janice M. Stromsen
202/514-1323
Rm. 540

Registration Unit, Internal Security Section
1400 New York Ave., NW / Washington DC 20530

> **INTRODUCTION**
>
> *The Registration Unit is the initial point of contact for registering as a foreign agent and collects and provides to the public complete information on all entities registered as foreign agents. The public office (202/514-1145) of the registration unit is located at 1400 New York Ave., NW - on the Ninth Floor. It is open for inquiries from 11 am to 3 pm Monday-Friday. A photo ID is required for entry. A complete list of all entities registered as foreign agents under the 1938 FARA act can be found in the Foreign Agents section of this book.*

Chief, Registration Unit, Internal Security Section
Frederick J. Close, Jr.
202/514-1216   FAX: 202/514-2836
Rm. 9300

Drug Enforcement Administration

700 Army Navy Drive / Washington DC 20537

INTRODUCTION

The Drug Enforcement Agency maintains liaison with INTERPOL and other organizations on matters relating to international narcotics control programs.

Administrator
Mr. Thomas A. Constantine
202/307-8000   FAX   202/307-7335
Rm. 12060

Personal: born 1939 in Buffalo, N.Y.

Education: B.A., State Univ. of N.Y. at Buffalo. M.A. in criminal justice, State Univ. of N.Y. at Albany, 1986. Graduate (first in class), N.Y. State Police Academy, 1962.

Professional: 1962-66, state trooper (Batavia, N.Y.); 1966-71, sergeant; 1971-78, lieutenant in charge of recruit training; 1978-80, major; 1980-83, staff inspector; 1983-86, deputy superintendent; December 1986-94, superintendent, N.Y. State Police. 3/94-present, administrator, Drug Enforcement Agency, U.S. Department of Justice.

Career law enforcement officer Thomas Constantine was nominated to become administrator of the Drug Enforcement Administration (DEA) in January of 1994 and took office in March of that year. The DEA was created in 1973 from four separate drug law enforcement agencies under a Government Reorganization Plan.

DEA's mission is to enforce, on a worldwide basis, the provisions of the Controlled Substances Act. The DEA presents cases to U.S. criminal and civil courts on organizations and their members involved in cultivating, producing, smuggling, distributing, or diverting controlled substances appearing in or destined for illegal trafficking in the U.S. DEA special agents immobilize these organizations by arresting their members, confiscating their drugs, and seizing their assets.

To accomplish this, the DEA also creates, manages, and supports enforcement-related programs, domestically and internationally, aimed at reducing the availability of and demand for controlled substances. In addition, the DEA manages the El Paso Intelligence Center (EPIC), a 24-hour tactical drug intelligence center, which utilizes DEA and federal personnel from 13 other participating agencies. The agency also maintains an active training program for narcotics officers from state and local domestic agencies, as well providing training for such officers from other countries.

During FY 96, DEA seized 79,000 pounds of cocaine, 1,000 pounds of heroin, 411,000 pounds of marijuana, and arrested more than 26,000 suspects. For FY 97, DEA was authorized 7799 employees and a budget of $1.05 billion.

Since assuming the position of administrator, Constantine has implemented significant changes in DEA's internal, domestic, and foreign policies. Internally, he has instituted changes in DEA's integrity program to improve the timeliness of decisions and ensure thorough investigations. He directed a reorganization of the DEA offices of inspection and professional responsibility to ensure proper adherence to professional standards and codes of conduct. On the domestic front he has greatly enhanced cooperative efforts with state and local police in violent drug trafficking cases. In the international arena, DEA continues to target the major international drug trafficking organizations that have become the most serious organized crime problem facing the international community. The DEA works cooperatively with host country law enforcement to dismantle these organizations and arrest and incarcerate their leaders.

During 1997, Constantine's priorities have been to reduce violent drug trafficking, renewing an emphasis on emerging threats of illegal heroin and methamphetamine trafficking, and continued enforcement pressure on international drug trafficking organizations that target the U.S. for distributing their illicit product.

Former Governor Mario Cuomo presented Constantine with the New York State Law Enforcement Executive of the Year award in October, 1994.

Operations Division
700 Army Navy Drive / Washington DC 20537

Chief, Office of Intl. Operations
Mr. Michael T. Horn
202/307-4233
Rm. 11024

Chief, Europe and Middle East Section
Mr. Mark Lloyd
202/307-4252
Rm. 11104

Chief, Far East Section
Mr. John E. Driscoll
202/307-4262
Rm. 11200

Chief, Central America and Caribbean Section
Mr. Michael Ferguson
202/307-4266
Rm. 2116

Chief, South America Section
Mr. Ronald Lard
202/307-4300
Rm. 2122

Chief, Mexico Section
Mr. Richard Barrett
202/307-5527
Rm. 2116

Special Operations Division
8199 Backlick Road / Newington, VA 22079

Special Agent in Charge
Mr. Richard Hano
703/541-6701

Chief, Latin America Section
Mr. William T. Healy
703/541-6715

Chief, Europe and Asia Section
Ms. Barbara J. Barclay
703/541-6725

Human Resources Division
Adm. Bldg. 1, DEA/FBI Academy / Quantico VA 22135

Asst. Special Agent in Charge, Intl. Training Section
Mr. James E. Cappola
703/640-7419

Intelligence Division
700 Army Navy Drive / Washington DC 20537

Acting Chief of Intelligence
Mr. John Barrett
202/307-3607
Rm. 12036

Chief, International Section
Ms. Joan Zolak
202/307-8431
Rm. 10348

Federal Bureau of Investigation

935 Pennsylvania Ave., NW / Washington DC 20535

INTRODUCTION

The FBI's role in international investigations has expanded with the growth in international criminal activity. FBI investigations abroad require the approval of the host country and coordination with the U.S. Department of State and any other involved agency through the FBI's legal attache program. There are 23 legal attache offices around the world. They are located in the U.S. embassies in the countries to which they are accredited.

Director
Mr. Louis J. Freeh
202/324-3444   FAX 202/324-4705
Rm. 7176

Personal: born in Jersey City, N.J.

Education: B.A. (Phi Beta Kappa), Rutgers Coll., 1971. J.D., Rutgers Law School, 1974. LL.M. in criminal law, New York Univ. Law School, 1984.

Professional: 1975-81, special agent, Federal Bureau of Investigation (New York, Wash., D.C.). 1981-91, assistant U.S. attorney; chief of organized crime unit; deputy U.S. attorney, U.S. Attorney's Office, Southern District of New York. 1991-93, federal judge, U.S. District Court of Southern New York. 1993-present, director, Federal Bureau of Investigation.

Louis Freeh took over the position of director of the Federal Bureau of Investigations (FBI) in 1993, replacing controversial Director William Sessions. His initial experience with the bureau came in the mid 1970's when he worked as a special agent for six years in New York City and Washington. In 1981, he joined the U.S. Attorney's Office for the Southern District of New York as an assistant U.S. attorney.

Over the next 11 years, Freeh worked to combat organized crime in America. His biggest triumph came during a 14-month trial, the "Pizza Connection" case, during which he successfully convicted 16 out of 17 co-defendants accused of smuggling heroin into the U.S. Freeh has also served as a district court judge in New York City.

The FBI was established in 1908 to serve as the principal investigative arm of the Department of Justice. Responsible for all types of investigations, the FBI's jurisdiction includes criminal, civil, and security violations of federal law. The bureau's investigations are conducted through 56 field offices worldwide that are staffed by more than 10,000 special agents. At headquarters in Washington, the director oversees a staff of more than 7,500 employees.

In recent years, Freeh and the bureau have earned accolades for the World Trade Center bombing case. However, he has taken the heat for FBI crime lab problems and the investigation of Richard Jewell for the 1996 Olympic Bombing in Atlanta.

In 1994, Freeh made changes in the bureau, ranging from tightening employment requirements to cracking down on employee misconduct. Freeh has pledged himself to diversity by appointing members of minority groups and women to high-level positions, and wants to ensure they are treated with respect and fairness.

Freeh claims that "More changes are coming, changes for the better. We've only just begun." One of these changes is the adoption of new drug-use policies. A new policy requires that all applicants submit to a polygraph on answering drug-use questions.

Freeh has continued to downsize the bureau, and says that the successful implementation of his plan, "coupled with retirements and career development transfers, made it unnecessary to have a formal reduction-in-force program to reach the important goal of reducing the headquarters staff and adding resources to the field divisions." Freeh also reassigned 600 FBI special agents from supervisory and administrative positions to investigating priority criminal and national security cases in Washington, D.C., and other high crime areas.

Freeh and his wife Marilyn have five sons.

Deputy Asst. Director, Intl. Relations, Operational Support
VACANT
202/324-5904
Rm. 7443

Immigration and Naturalization Service

425 Eye St., NW / Washington DC 20536

INTRODUCTION

The Immigration and Naturalization Service (INS) was created by act of March 3, 1891 (8 U.S.C. 1551 note), and its purpose and responsibilities were further specified by the Immigration And Nationality Act, as amended (8 U.S.C. 1101 note), which charges the Attorney General with the Administration and enforcement of its provisions.

Cont'd.

INS is headed by a commissioner, who reports to the Attorney General. The structure of INS is divided into operational and management functions. Operations includes both Enforcement and Examinations programs; Management covers information resources, finance, human resources, administration, and equal employment opportunity. Overall, policy and executive direction flows from the Washington, DC, headquarters to 33 districts and 21 border patrol sectors throughout the United States. In addition, four regional offices provide administrative support to the field offices.

Unique to the Service is the dual mission of providing information and service to the general public, while concurrently exercising its enforcement responsibilities. Its mission is divided into four major areas of responsibility:

■ facilitating the entry of person legally admissible as visitors or as immigrants to the United States;

■ granting benefits under the Immigration and Nationality Act, as amended, including providing assistance to those seeking permanent resident status or naturalization;

■ preventing unlawful entry, employment, or receipt of benefits by those who are not entitled to them.; and

■ apprehending or removing those aliens who enter or remain illegally in the United States and/or whose stay is not in the public interest.

The Service also has a firm commitment to strengthen criminal investigations and seek the most effective deterrents to illegal immigration.

The Attorney General has delegated authority to the Commissioner of the Immigration and Naturalization Service to carry out a national immigration policy that will administer and enforce the immigration laws and promote the public health and safety, economic welfare, national security, and humanitarian interests of this country.

The Immigration Act of 1990 (8 U.S.C. 1101 note) represents a major overhaul of immigration law, amending the Immigration and Nationality Act. Changes include revisions to the numerical limits and preference system regulating immigration, administrative naturalization empowering the Attorney General to issue final determinations on applications for U.S. citizenship, and issuing certificates of naturalization.

Commissioner
Ms. Doris M. Meissner
202/514-1900   FAX 202/307-9911
Rm. 7100

Personal: born 1941 in Milwaukee, Wis.

Education: B.A., Univ. of Wis. at Madison, 1963. M.A., Univ. of Wis. at Madison, 1969.

Professional: 1964-68, assistant director, student financial aid, University of Wisconsin at Madison. 1971-73, executive director, National Women's Political Caucus (Washington, D.C.). 1973-74, White House Fellow, special assistant to the attorney general, U.S. Department of Justice. 1976, assistant director, office of policy and planning; 1976, executive director, Cabinet Committee on Illegal Aliens; 1977-80, deputy associate attorney general, U.S. Justice Department. 1981, acting commissioner; 1982-85, executive associate commissioner, Immigration and Naturalization Services. 1986-93, senior associate and director, Immigration Policy Project, the Carnegie Endowment for International peace. 1993-present, commissioner, Immigration and Naturalization Service, U.S. Department of Justice.

Doris Meissner's long relationship with the Department of Justice began in 1973 when she was selected as a White House Fellow and assigned to work as a special assistant to the attorney general. Since then, she has worked within the department in a number of positions, developing expertise in the area of immigration.

She left Justice in 1986 to become immigration policy program director for the Carnegie Endowment for International Peace. She returned to Justice in October of 1993 to become commissioner of the Immigration and Naturalization Service.

Meissner works closely with Attorney General Janet Reno in developing plans to carry out the Clinton administration's initiatives for improving border security and controlling illegal immigration. These initiatives are focused on strengthening border enforcement, removing criminal aliens, reforming the asylum process, improving workplace enforcement, and promoting naturalization.

A *New York Times* editorial in August 1997 stated that the "[INS] has improved under the leadership of Doris Meissner. Since her appointment in 1993, the budget has doubled to $3.1 billion, with most of the increase going to enforcement. The border is tighter, and the INS is deporting record numbers of criminal aliens. On the service side, naturalizations are moving faster and so is the asylum process."

The daughter of German immigrants, Meissner grew up with a sensitivity to the issues affecting foreign born residents of the United States. She accepted the appointment as commissioner with the goal of molding the INS into a more professional agency which exercises "control with compassion" while enforcing immigration laws and administering various immigration programs to regulate the admissions of foreign born persons to the United States.

The programs Meissner directs include patrolling U.S. borders; inspecting arriving travelers; investigating violations of immigration law; detaining and deporting criminal aliens and other lawbreakers; adjudicating petitions for various benefits such as immigrant status, naturalization, asylum, or work authorization; and working with other agencies and the United Nations on issues affecting refugees and international relations.

Office of the Deputy Commissioner
425 I Street, NW / Washington D.C. 20536

Deputy Commissioner
Ms. Mary Ann Wyrsch
202/514-1900
Rm. 7100

Naturalization Office
801 I Street, NW / Washington D.C. 20536

Acting Executive Director for Naturalization
Mr. Robert K. Bratt
202/574-6442
9th Floor

Congressional and Intergovernmental Relations Office
425 I Street, NW / Washington D.C. 20536

Acting Director
Mr. Allen M. Erenbaum
202/514-5231
Rm. 7030

Communications Office

Director
Ms. Julie H. Anbender
202/514-4817   FAX 202/514-1776
Rm. 7021

Office of the Executive Associate Commissioner for Policy & Planning

Executive Associate Commissioner, Policy and Planning
Mr. Robert L. Bach
202/514-3242
Rm. 6038

Office of the Executive Associate Commissioner for Field Operations
425 I Street, NW / Washington D.C. 20536

Executive Associate Commissioner, Field Operations
COL Michael A. Pearson
202/514-0078
Rm. 7114

U.S. Border Patrol
Assistant Commissioner
Mr. Douglas M. Kruhm
202/514-3073
Rm. 4226

Office of International Affairs
1111 Mass., Ave. NW / Washington DC 20536

Director, Intl. Affairs
Ms. Phyllis A. Coven
202/305-2798   FAX 202/305-2911
3rd Floor

Deputy Director
Mr. John W. Cummings
202/305-2798
3rd Floor

Director, Asylum Division
Mr. Jeffrey L. Weiss
202/305-2769
3rd Floor

Director, Resource Information Center
Mr. John D. Evans
202/305-2672   FAX 202/305-2796
3rd Floor

Director, Refugee Branch
Ms. Kathleen A. Thompson
202/305-2756
3rd Floor

Director, Desk Unit
Ms. Marianne Kilgannon-Martz
202/305-2658   FAX 202/305-2915
3rd Floor

Asian Desk Officer
Mr. Thomas Simmons
202/305-2658

European Desk Officer
Mr. Robert Wiemann
202/305-2658

Latin American Desk Officer
Ms. Carol Ballew
202/305-2658

Enforcement Coordinator
Mr. Neville Cramer
202/305-2790
3rd Floor

Humanitarian Affairs Coordinator
Mr. Kenneth Leutbecker
202/305-2790
1st Floor

Office of the Executive Associate Commissioner for Programs
425 I Street, NW / Washington D.C. 20536

Executive Associate Commissioner, Programs
Mr. Paul W. Virtue
202/514-8223   FAX 202/616-7612
Rm. 7309

Associate Commissioner, Enforcement
VACANT
202/514-8223   FAX 202/514-9262
Rm. 5300

Assistant Commissioner, Detention and Deportation
Ms. Joan C. Higgins
202/514-2543
Rm. 3008

Acting Assistant Commissioner, Investigations
Mr. Gregory Bednarz
202/514-1189
Rm. 1000

Acting Assistant Commissioner, Intelligence
Mr. Clifford T. Landsman
202/514-4402
Rm. 5300

Director, Asset Forfeiture Office
Mr. John F. Shaw
202/616-2737   FAX 202/616-2281
Rm. 1040

INS Regional Offices:

<u>Eastern Region</u>

Regional Director
Mr. William Yates
70 Kimball Ave.
S. Burlington VT 05403-6813
802/660-5000   FAX 802/660-5114

<u>Central Region</u>

Regional Director
Mr. Mark Reed
7701 North Stemmins Freeway, Rm. 2300
Dallas TX 75247

214/767-7020   FAX 214/767-7477

Western Region

Regional Director
Mr. Johnny Williams
24000 Avila Road, PO Box 30080
Laguna Nuguel CA 92677
714/306-2995   FAX 714/360-3081

INS District Offices:

Alaska

District Director
Mr. Robert. C. Eddy
620 E Tenth Ave. Suite 102
Anchorage AK 99501
907/271-3524

Arizona

District Director
Ms. Roseanne Sonchik
2035 N. Central Ave.
Phoenix AZ 85004
602/379-3114

California

District Director
Mr. Richard K. Rogers
300 N. Los Angeles St.
Los Angeles CA 90012
213/894-2780

Acting District Director
Ms. Adele Fusano
880 Front St.
San Diego CA 92188
619/557-5645

District Director
Mr. Thomas H. Schiltgen
630 Sansome St.,
Appraisers Bldg.
San Francisco CA 94111
415/705-4411

Colorado

District Director
Mr. Joseph R. Greene
4730 Paris St.
Denver CO 80209
303/371-0986

Florida

District Director
Mr. Robert Wallis
7880 Biscayne Blvd.
Miami FL 33138
305/530-7657

Georgia

District Director
Mr. Thomas Fischer
77 Forsythe St., SW
Rm. G-85
Atlanta GA 30303

404/331-0253

Hawaii

District Director
Mr. Donald A. Radcliffe
595 Ala Moana Blvd.
Honolulu HI 96813
808/532-3746

Illinois

District Director
Mr. Brian R. Perryman
10 W. Jackson Blvd. Rm. 600
Chicago IL 60604
312/886-6770

Louisiana

District Director
VACANT
701 Loyola Ave. Rm. T-8005
New Orleans LA 70113
504/589-6521

Maine

District Director
Mr. Eugene Fitzpatrick
739 Warren Ave.
Portland ME 04103
207/780-3399

Maryland

District Director
Mr. Benedict J. Ferro
100 S. Charles St.
Baltimore MD 21201
410/962-2010

Massachusetts

District Director
Mr. Steven Farquharsen
Government Center
JFK Federal Bldg. Rm. 700
Boston MA 02203
617/565-4214

Michigan

District Director
Ms. Carol Jenifer
333 Mt. Elliott St., Fed. Bldg.
Detroit MI 48207
313/568-6000

Minnesota

District Director
Mr. Curtis Aljets
2901 Metro Drive
Bloomington MN 55425
612/335-2211

Montana

District Director
Mr. Donald M. Whitney
2800 Skyway Drive
Helena MT 59601

406/449-5220

Missouri

District Director
Mr. Ronald Sanders
9747 N. Conant Ave.
Kansas City MO 64153
816/891-0684

Nebraska

District Director
Mr. Frank Heinhauer
3736 S. 132nd St.
Omaha NE 68144
402/697-9155

New Jersey

District Director
Ms. Andrea Quarantillo
970 Broad St., Federal Bldg.
Newark NJ 07102
201/645-2269

New York

District Director
Mr. John J. Ingham
68 Court St.
Buffalo NY 14202
716/551-4741

District Director
Mr. Edward McElroy
26 Federal Plaza
New York NY 10278
212/206-6500

Ohio

District Director
Mr. Robert L. Brown
1240 E. Ninth Street
Rm. 1917
Cleveland OH 44199
216/522-4766

Oregon

District Director
Mr. David V. Beebe
511 NW Broadway
Federal Bldg.
Portland OR 97209
503/326-3962

Pennsylvania

District Director
Mr. Scott Blackman
1600 Callowhill St.
Philadelphia PA 19130
215/656-7150

Puerto Rico

District Director
Mr. Charles A. Kirk
Carlos Chardon St. Rm. 359
Hato Rey PR 00918
809/766-5380

Texas

District Director
Mr. Arthur E. Strapp
8101 N. Stemmons Fwy.
Dallas TX 75247
214/655-3011

District Director
Mr. Luis Garcia
1545 Hawking Blvd.,
Ste. 167
El Paso TX 79901
915/540-7341

District Director
Mr. E.M. Trominski
2102 Teege Ave.
Harlingen TX 78550
210/427-8592

Acting District Director
Mr. Richard B. Cravener
509 N. Belt Drive

Houston TX 77060
713/847-7950

District Director
Mr. Kenneth Pasquarell
727 E. Durango Drive
San Antonio TX 78206
210/871-7000

Virginia

District Director
Mr. William J. Carroll
4420 N. Fairfax Drive
Arlington VA 22203
202/307-1642

Washington

District Director
Mr. Richard C. Smith
815 Airport Way S.
Seattle WA 98134
206/553-0070

Intl. Criminal Police Organization (INTERPOL) U.S. National Central Bureau

INTERPOL-USNCB / 600 E Street, NW / Washington, DC 20530

> **INTRODUCTION**
>
> *The U.S. National Central Bureau represents the U.S. in INTERPOL, the International Criminal Police Organization, an association of 169 countries dedicated to promoting mutual assistance among law enforcement authorities in the prevention and suppression of international crime.*

Chief
Mr. John J. Imhoff
202/616-9000   FAX 202/ 616-1048
Rm. 600

Personal: born 10/24/52.

Education: B.A. Loyola College, 1974 . M.B.A., Loyola Coll., 1978.

Professional: 1974-75, auditor, Arthur Andersen & Company. 1976-78, investigator, Detroit division; 1981-84, auditor, inspection division; 1984-89, supervisor, organized crime/drug and white collar crime squads, Baltimore division; 1989-95, finance division; 1996, international relations branch, Federal Bureau of Investigation. 1997-present, chief, INTERPOL, U.S. National Central Bureau.

John Imhoff began his career with the FBI in 1976 and served in a variety of investigative and managerial positions. He successfully conducted and/or supervised investigations in virtually every criminal program. Through administrative positions at FBI headquarters, he gained valuable insight into every facet of FBI operations.

On January 13, 1997 Imhoff assumed the role of chief at the United States National Central Bureau of the International Criminal Police Organization (INTERPOL-USNCB). In that capacity, he represents the United States through criminal investigation cooperation and related matters with the other 176 INTERPOL NCBs and the organization's secretary general in Lyon, France.

On June 7, 1996, Imhoff completed the 38th Senior Seminar. This Department of State course, considered the most prestigious executive training opportunity in government, studied significant issues facing government, and built crucial executive skills. During 1996, Imhoff held a variety of positions in the FBI's international relations branch. After managing an FBI headquarters unit overseeing legal attache (Legat) operations in the Americas and the Pacific Rim, he initiated the FBI's new Legat operations in Tallinn, Estonia. He also served temporarily in the Rome, Italy Legat.

From 1989 to 1995 Imhoff served in the finance division representing the FBI's long term fiscal planning interests to the Department of Justice, Office of Management and Budget, and Congress. From 1984 to 1989 he supervised the organized crime (OC)/drug and white-collar crime (WCC) squads in the Baltimore division. His WCC Squad was among the first in the FBI to successfully prosecute corrupt executives for crimes leading to failed Savings and Loans. From 1981 to 1984 Imhoff served in the FBI's inspection division, conducting studies and audits of various investigative programs. From 1976 to 1981 he served as an investigator in the FBI Detroit division, recognizing achievements in the WCC and OC programs.

Imhoff holds an MBA and is a Certified Public Accountant. He is married and has two sons.

Asst. Chief, Alien and Fugitive Investigations
Mr. Matt Quinn
202/616-9000

Executive Office for Immigration Review

5107 Leesburg Pike, Skyline Twr. / Falls Church VA 22041

Director
Mr. Anthony C. Moscato
703/305-0169
Rm. 2400

Board of Immigration Appeals

Chair
Mr. Paul W. Schmidt
703/305-1193
Rm. 2400

Office of the Chief Immigration Judge

Chief Immigration Judge
Mr. Michael J. Creppy
703/305-1247
Rm. 2545

Office of the Chief Administrative Hearing Officer

Chief Administrative Hearing Officer
Mr. Jack E. Perkins
703/305-0864
Rm. 2519

Foreign Claims Settlement Commission

600 E St., NW / Washington DC 20579

INTRODUCTION

The Foreign Claims Settlement Commission of the United States is an independent, quasi-judicial agency within the U.S. Department of Justice. The primary mission of the Commission is the adjudication of the claims of U.S. nationals (corporations and individuals) against foreign governments under special claims programs. The decisions of the tribunal are final and are not reviewable under any standard by any court or other authority in the world.

Chair
Ms. Delissa A. Ridgway
202/616-6985   FAX 202/616-6993
Rm. 6002

Education: B.A. (honors), Univ. of Missouri-Columbia, 1975. J.D., Northeastern Univ. School of Law, 1979.

Professional: adjunct professor, American Univ. consultant, international commercial law, United Nations Centre on Transnational Corporations. attorney, international practice group, Shaw, Pittman, Potts & Trowbridge (Washington, D.C.) September 1994-present, chair, Foreign Claims Settlement Commission.

In her capacity as Chairman of the Commission, Delissa Ridgway is both the administrative head of the agency and the president of the three-member international tribunal.

The unique mission of the Foreign Claims Settlement Commission puts it on the cutting edge of international law and foreign policy. The commission recently completed an Albanian Claims Program, adjudicating the expropriation claims of U.S. nationals against the Communist regime which took power in that country at the end of World War II. Another ongoing program involves claims of U.S. survivors of the Holocaust. That program implements a September 1995 agreement between the U.S. and Germany arising out of the celebrated Hugo Princz case.

In February 1995, the commission completed the Iranian Claims Program, involving awards in excess of $88 million and the adjudication of 3100+ claims against the government of Iran arising out of the 1979 Islamic Revolution. In addition, the commission is presently engaged in planning for the Iraq Claims Program, which would include claims arising from the Persian Gulf War, pending the enactment of legislation by Congress conferring jurisdiction on the commission. Preliminary estimates value those claims in excess of $5.4 billion, which would make it the largest such claims program ever. Past programs have adjudicated claims against countries such as Cuba, Vietnam, Bulgaria, Rumania, Hungary, the Soviet Union, Czechoslovakia, Poland, China, East Germany, Ethiopia, and Egypt.

Before her appointment by President Clinton in June 1994 and her confirmation by the Senate in September 1994, Ridgway was a member of the international practice group at Shaw, Pittman, Potts & Trowbridge in Washington, D.C. She is a recognized authority in the areas of international commercial law, international transactions and international commercial arbitration and litigation, and has published and lectured widely.

Ridgway has been an adjunct professor of law teaching international business transactions and international commercial arbitration in the LL.M. program at The American University. She has also served as a consultant on international commercial law to the United Nations Centre on Transnational Corporations advising developing countries on matters of international law and commercial law reform. She is a member of the panels of both the ICC International Court of Arbitration (Paris) and the American Arbitration Association.

Ridgway has a working knowledge of both the common law and civil law legal systems, and substantive expertise in a wide spectrum of areas such as turnkey contracts, construction, commercial transactions, computers, energy, and defense technology. She also has cross-cultural experience in developing close working relationships with a broad range of parties from both the public and private sectors including developing nations and parastatal entities as well as multinational corporations.

Ridgway has traveled extensively in North America, South America, Scandinavia, Western Europe, Africa and Australia. She was a founder and initial Steering Committee member of the Federal Bar Association's innovative Democracy Development Initiative Program, which provides legal assistance to emerging democracies and free market economies in Eastern-Central Europe and the former Soviet Union.

She is a member of the American Law Institute, a fellow of the American Bar Foundation, and a member of the board of governors of the District of Columbia Bar. She also sits on the National Council of the Federal Bar Association and has held national office in both the International Law and Administrative Law Sections of the FBA. She was a founding member of the board of directors of the District of Columbia Conference on Opportunities for Minorities in the Legal Profession.

In addition to her undergraduate degree from the University of Missouri, she completed coursework there for an M.S. in community/international development before earning her law degree from Northeastern University School of Law in 1979.

Commissioner
Mr. Richard T. White
202/616-6975
Rm. 6002

Personal: born 1/14/45.

Education: A.B. (with honors), Morehouse College, 1967. J.D., Harvard Law School, 1970.

Professional: 1972-95, Lewis, White & Clay, PC. 1996, senior vice president, AAA Michigan. 1997-present, commissioner, Foreign Claims Settlement Commission, U.S. Department of Justice.

Since his appointment to the Foreign Claims Settlement Commission, Richard White has focused on the Iran Claims, Albanian Claims, and Holocaust Survivors Programs. Immediately before joining the commission, White served as senior vice president of corporate administration and secretary and general counsel of AAA Michigan. For 23 years before that he was associated with Lewis, White & Clay, PC where he was both a founder and the president of the firm.

White graduated from Morehouse College with honors and earned his law degree form Harvard Law School. White's term on the commission expires September 30, 1999.

Commissioner
Mr. John R. Lacey
202/616-6975   FAX 202/616-6993
Rm. 6002

Personal: born 6/28/45.

Education: B.S. in foreign service, Georgetown Univ., 1967. J.D., Univ. of Virginia, 1971. M.A., Fletcher School of Law & Diplomacy, 1975; MALD, 1976.

Professional: 1977-82, assistant attorney general, state of Connecticut. 1982-89, partner, Copp, Berall & Hempstead (Hartford, Conn.). 1983-84, 1986-93, adjunct professor of international law, Fletcher School of Law & Diplomacy. 1990-94, partner, Lacey, Meissel, Koven & Kaufmann (Hartford). 1994-present, commissioner, Foreign Claims Settlement Commission, U.S. Department of Justice.

John Lacey serves as one of the three members of the U.S. Foreign Claims Settlement Commission. In 1994, President Clinton nominated Lacey, who assumed his duties after being confirmed by the Senate later that year. He subsequently was nominated and confirmed to a full term expiring in September 1998.

Prior to his resignation in 1994, Lacey was a partner in the Hartford, Connecticut law firm of Lacey, Meissel, Koven & Kaufmann and, from 1982 to 1989, he was a partner in the firm of Copp, Berall & Hempstead. In addition to his law practice, he also served as an adjunct professor of international law, first at the Fletcher School of Law & Diplomacy and, later, at the University of Connecticut Graduate Business School.

From 1977 to 1982, Lacey served as an assistant attorney general in Connecticut. As a member of the antitrust unit and, eventually, its acting head, he was responsible for civil antitrust enforcement and was counsel in various appellate as well as constitutional litigation matters.

Lacey attended the School of Foreign Service at Georgetown University where he majored in international affairs and received his B.S. in 1967. Subsequently, he was a student at the University of

Virginia Law School where he was articles editor of the *Virginia Journal of International Law* and was granted a J.D. in January, 1971. Lacey continued graduate studies in law, economics, and history at the Fletcher School of Law and Diplomacy at Tufts University and was awarded an M.A. in 1975 and an MALD in 1976.

In addition to a number of book reviews, he was the editor of *Act of State and Extraterritorial Reach* (ABA, 1983), and the author of the article "Antitrust and Foreign Commerce: Reach and Grasp" (N.C. *Journal of International Law & Commercial Regulation,* 1980). Most recently he was editor of the book *The Law & Policy of International Business* (University Press, 1991).

Lacey is a member of the Connecticut, the District of Columbia, the U.S. District Court (Connecticut), the U.S. Courts of Appeal for the D.C. and Second Circuits, and the U.S. Supreme Court Bars. He is active in various professional organizations including the American and Connecticut Bar Associations. He is a past chair of the CBA section on international law and is a member of the executive committee of the antitrust section. He is also a member of the American Society of International Law and the International Bar Association. He was appointed by the Senate President Pro Tem as a member of the Connecticut General Assembly's Export Trade Panel in 1991. In 1993, he served as a member of President Clinton's Meritorious Executive Awards Board.

U. S. Department of Labor

200 Constitution Avenue, NW / Washington, D.C. 20210
Personnel Locator: 202/219-5000
Public Affairs: 202/219-7316

INTRODUCTION

The Labor Department has a Bureau of International Labor Affairs, which carries out the Department's international responsibilities under the direction of the Deputy Under Secretary for International Affairs and assists in formulating international economic, trade, and immigration policies affecting American workers. Another bureau, the Bureau of Labor Statistics, collects statistics on labor productivity and unit labor costs in other industrial nations and develops comparative levels of hourly compensation. The data is used to assess U.S. economic performance relative to other industrial countries and to provide insight into the changing competitive position of the U.S.

Office of the Secretary

200 Constitution Avenue, NW / Washington, D.C. 20210

Secretary of Labor
Ms. Alexis A. Herman
202/219-8271   FAX 202/219-8822
Room S2018

Personal: born in Mobile, Ala.

Education: B.A., Xavier Univ. (New Orleans, La.), 1969.

Professional: 1972-77, national director, Minority Women Employment Program. 1977-81, director, women's bureau, U.S. Dept. of Labor. 1980-91, president, A.M. Herman and Associates, Wash., D.C. 1990-93, deputy chairman, Democratic National Cmte. 1993-97, asst. to the president and dir. of public liaison, White House. May 1997-present, secretary, U.S. Dept. of Labor.

"A feather in her cap" is how the *Washington Post* described the role of Secretary of Labor Alexis Herman in ending the two-week strike of the Teamsters Union against the United Parcel Service in August 1997. She encouraged the two sides in the labor dispute to keep bargaining, and they reached an agreement after two weeks.

Herman said on NBC's "Today" show the morning after negotiators announced the agreement: "I wasn't trying to be subtle. I was trying to be very direct. I moved right in with them."

Herman's triumph, coming only three months after she took charge

of the Labor Department, was all the sweeter in light of a difficult confirmation process in the Senate and lukewarm support from the labor movement.

Gerry Shea, a top assistant to AFL-CIO President John J. Sweeney rated her performance in the negotiations "at least a 9, if not a 9.5," according to the *Washington Post*. Shea said that those who have watched Herman "both publicly and privately, as we have, are extremely impressed by her presence. There's a grace that she has. It's the key to why she is so good at the interpersonal stuff."

Shortly after her confirmation as the nation's 23rd secretary of labor, Herman outlined five goals she has set for the Department of Labor. Appearing before the House Appropriations subcommittee on labor, HHS, and education, she testified, "My goals are: First, to equip every working American with the skills to find and hold good jobs, with rising income through their lives; Second, to help people move from welfare to work; Third, to assure that working Americans enjoy secure pensions when they retire; Fourth, to guarantee every American a safe and healthy workplace; and Fifth, to help working people balance work and family."

Herman brings more than two decades of leadership to the position of labor secretary. She has spent her career on the front lines of the changing workforce, as a business woman, a government executive, and a community leader, developing, promoting, and implementing policies to benefit workers and to increase opportunities and skills for the hard-to-employ.

Most recently, she served as assistant to President Clinton and director of the White House public liaison office. In 1992, she served as the deputy director of the presidential transition office.

As founder and president of A.M. Herman & Associates, Herman advised state and local governments, as well as private corporations during the 1980s. An expert on reducing and eliminating formal and informal labor market barriers, she guided corporations on human resource issues related to training, mentoring, and reducing turnover. She also helped state governments link economic development activities to job creation and training strategies.

During the Carter administration, Herman served as director of the women's bureau at the U.S. Department of Labor, where she advised the administration and Labor Secretary Ray Marshall on workplace policy. She mounted new programs to help low-income and younger women with employment-related problems, and strengthened cooperation on women's concerns among private business, labor unions, and government agencies. Before that, Herman was national director of the Minority Women Employment Program of R-T-P, Inc., in Atlanta, where she established programs to place minority women in white-collar and non-traditional jobs.

In 1991, Herman was named chief executive officer of the 1992 Democratic National Convention Committee.

Herman began her career in 1969 as a social worker for Catholic Charities developing training opportunities for unemployed youth, unskilled workers, and new entrants to the Mobile labor force at Ingall's Shipbuilding, Inc., in Pascagoula, Miss. She graduated from Xavier University in New Orleans in 1969.

Office of Public Affairs (OPA)

200 Constitution Avenue, NW / Washington, D.C. 20210

Agency Public Affairs Officers

International Labor Affairs
Mr. Bob Zachariasiewicz
202/219-6373

Employment and Training Administration

200 Constitution Avenue, NW / Washington, D.C. 20210

Office of Trade Adjustment Assistance
Acting Director
Mr. Grant D. Beale
202/219-4820

Bureau of International Labor Affairs

200 Constitution Avenue, NW / Washington, D.C. 20210

INTRODUCTION

The Bureau of International Labor Affairs represents the U.S. on delegations to multilateral and bilateral trade negotiations and on such international bodies as General Agreement on Tariffs and Trade (GATT), now the World Trade Organization; the International Labor Organization (ILO); the Organization for Economic Cooperation and Development; and other U.N. organizations. It also helps administer the U.S. labor attaché program at embassies abroad, carries out overseas technical assistance projects, monitors internationally recognized worker rights, and conducts labor study programs for foreign visitors to the U.S.

The deputy under secretary for international affairs serves as the U.S. representative to the ILO governing body, and as head of the tripartite U.S. delegation to the annual ILO conference. The Labor Department is the lead agency on ILO matters in cooperation with the Departments of State and Commerce. The AFL-CIO represents American workers, and American employers are represented by the U.S. Council for International Business. The President's Committee on the ILO, a federal advisory committee chaired by the Secretary of Labor, was established to formulate and coordinate U.S. policy toward the ILO in order to promote continued reform and progress in the organization. Its other members are the secretaries of State and Commerce, the assistant to the president for national security affairs, and the presidents of the AFL-CIO and the U.S. Council for International Business. The deputy under secretary serves as counselor to the committee, and the bureau provides support, as necessary.

Deputy Under Secretary for International Affairs
Mr. Andrew Samet
202/219-6043   FAX 202/219-5980
Rm. S2235

Personal: born 6/29/57 in Boston, Mass.

Education: B.A., Yale Univ., 1978. M.A., Carleton Univ. (Ottawa, Ontario, Canada), 1981. J.D., Georgetown Univ. Law Center, 1983.

Professional: 1978-79, staff member, Senate Appropriations Cmte. 1983-85, associate, Chapman, Duff & Paul. 1985-87, associate, Mudge, Rose, Guthrie, Alexander & Ferdon. 1987-93, legislative staff, Sen. Daniel P. Moynihan (D-N.Y.). 1993-96, associate deputy under secretary, bureau of international labor affairs; 1996-present, acting deputy under secretary for international labor affairs, U.S. Dept. of Labor.

Andrew Samet is the senior U.S. Department of Labor official responsible for international matters. He was designated acting deputy

under secretary for international labor affairs in August 1996 until his confirmation in the fall of 1997 by the Senate. He had previously served for three years as associate deputy under secretary in the bureau of international labor affairs.

In his current role, Samet is responsible for U.S. government participation in the International Labor Organization (ILO) and represents the U.S. government on the governing body of the ILO. He coordinates policy on issues related to worker rights and international labor standards, and is responsible for labor department studies and programs on international child labor issues. His bureau also implements the North American Agreement on Labor Cooperation, the labor side agreement to the North American Free Trade Agreement (NAFTA).

Samet represents the Labor Department at such international bodies as the World Trade Organization (WTO) and the Organization for Economic Cooperation and Development (OECD) and coordinates U.S. government participation in the human resources working groups of the Asia-Pacific Economic Cooperation Forum (APEC). Samet represents the Labor Department on the U.S. government Trade Promotion Coordination Committee and the President's Export Council. His bureau jointly administers the labor attaché program with the State Department, and Samet serves on the board of foreign service. His bureau also operates a large number of foreign technical assistance programs.

Samet was a member of the U.S. delegation to the G-7 Jobs Conference in Detroit, the Marrakech Ministerial to conclude the World Trade Organization (WTO) Uruguay Round, the Miami Summit of the Americas, the G-7 Jobs Conference in Lille, and the Singapore WTO Ministerial. He headed the U.S. delegation to the Amsterdam Child Labor Conference.

Prior to joining the Clinton administration in 1993, Samet served as legislative counsel and later as legislative director for Sen. Daniel P. Moynihan (D-N.Y.). His responsibilities on Moynihan's staff, which he joined in 1987, included international trade, transportation, environment, labor and welfare policy.

Before his government service, Samet was in private law practice. He has a B.A. from Yale University, an M.A. from Carleton University in Ottawa, and a J.D. from Georgetown University. He has written numerous articles and edited two books on international trade and human rights issues.

Office of International Economic Affairs

Director
Mr. Jorge Perez-Lopez
202/219-7597

Chief, Trade Policy Division
Ms. Betsy White
202/219-6096

Acting Chief, International Commodities Division
Ms. Janie Hester
202/219-6227

Chief, Foreign Economic Research Division
Mr. Gregory Schoepfle
202/219-7610

Chief, Immigration Policy and Research Division
Mr. Roger Kramer
202/219-9098

Office of International Organizations

Director
Mr. H. Charles Spring

202/219-7682

Coordinator, Organization for Economic Cooperation and Develop.
Mr. Melvin Brodsky
202/219-6244

Office of Foreign Relations

Director
Mr. John Ferch
202/219-7631

Development Assistance Group
Mr. James Perlmutter
202/219-7633

Bureau of Labor Statistics (BLS)
Two Massachusetts Ave., NE / Washington DC 20212

Commissioner
Ms. Katharine G. Abraham
202/606-7800
Rm. 4040

Directorate of Survey Processing

Chief, International Price Systems Division
Mr. D. Michael Share
202/606-7200
Rm. 5045

Office of Prices and Living Conditions

Chief, International Prices Division
Ms. Katrina W. Reut
202/606-7100
Rm. 3955

Office of Productivity and Technology

Chief, International Prices Division
Ms. Katrina Reat
202/606-7100
Rm. 3955

Office of the Solicitor (SOL)

200 Constitution Ave., NW / Washington DC 20210

Employment and Training Legal Services Division

Counsel for Employment and Immigration Programs
Mr. Bruce W. Alter
202/219-7857

Labor-Management Laws Division

Counsel for International Affairs and Opinions
Ms. Susan M. Webman
202/219-8627

U. S. Department of State

2201 C Street, NW / Washington, DC 20520

Personnel Locator: 202/647-4000
Press: 202/647-2492
Public Affairs: 202/647-6575
Passport Information: 202/647-0518
Freedom of Information Office: 202/647-8484

INTRODUCTION

The Department of State is the lead U.S. foreign affairs agency. It advances U.S. objectives and interests through formulating, representing, and implementing the President's foreign policy. The Secretary of State, the ranking member of the Cabinet and fourth in line of presidential succession, is the President's principal adviser on foreign policy and the person chiefly responsible for U.S. representation abroad.

There are 190 countries in the world and the United States maintains diplomatic relations with about 180 of them and also maintains relations with many international organizations. The State Department operates more than 250 diplomatic and consular posts around the world, including embassies, consulates, and delegations and missions to international organizations.

The Clinton Administration's "New State Department" includes diplomacy aimed at creating American jobs by opening markets abroad. In the first term of the Clinton Administration, more than 200 trade agreements helped exports grow by 34% creating an estimated 16 million new jobs.

Among other recent policy initiatives, the Department is intensifying efforts to confront the transnational security challenges of terrorism, proliferation of weapons of mass destruction, international crime and narcotics, and environmental degradation.

In addition to appointed positions and Foreign Service officers, the State Department in Washington, D.C. is staffed by some 5,000 Civil Service employees working in a variety of professional, technical, and administrative capacities.

A BRIEF HISTORY OF THE DEPARTMENT

Congress created the Department of State in 1789 to assist the President in carrying out foreign policy responsibilities under the Constitution to conclude treaties and appoint diplomatic and consular officials, receive foreign emissaries, and exercise other authority provided by legislation. As head of the new Department, the Secretary of State was made the President's principal adviser on foreign affairs and the person chiefly responsible for U.S. representation abroad. The first Secretary was Thomas Jefferson.

After World War II, U.S. global responsibilities expanded greatly. The Departments of Agriculture, Commerce, and the Treasury acquired new duties in world economic affairs. The Department of Defense, established in 1947, assumed duties for military aid and cooperation. These—and other U.S. Government departments—operate out of embassies overseas.

The 1947 National Security Act created the National Security Council, which assists the President on foreign policy and coordinates the work of the many agencies involved in foreign relations.

UNITED STATES DEPARTMENT OF STATE

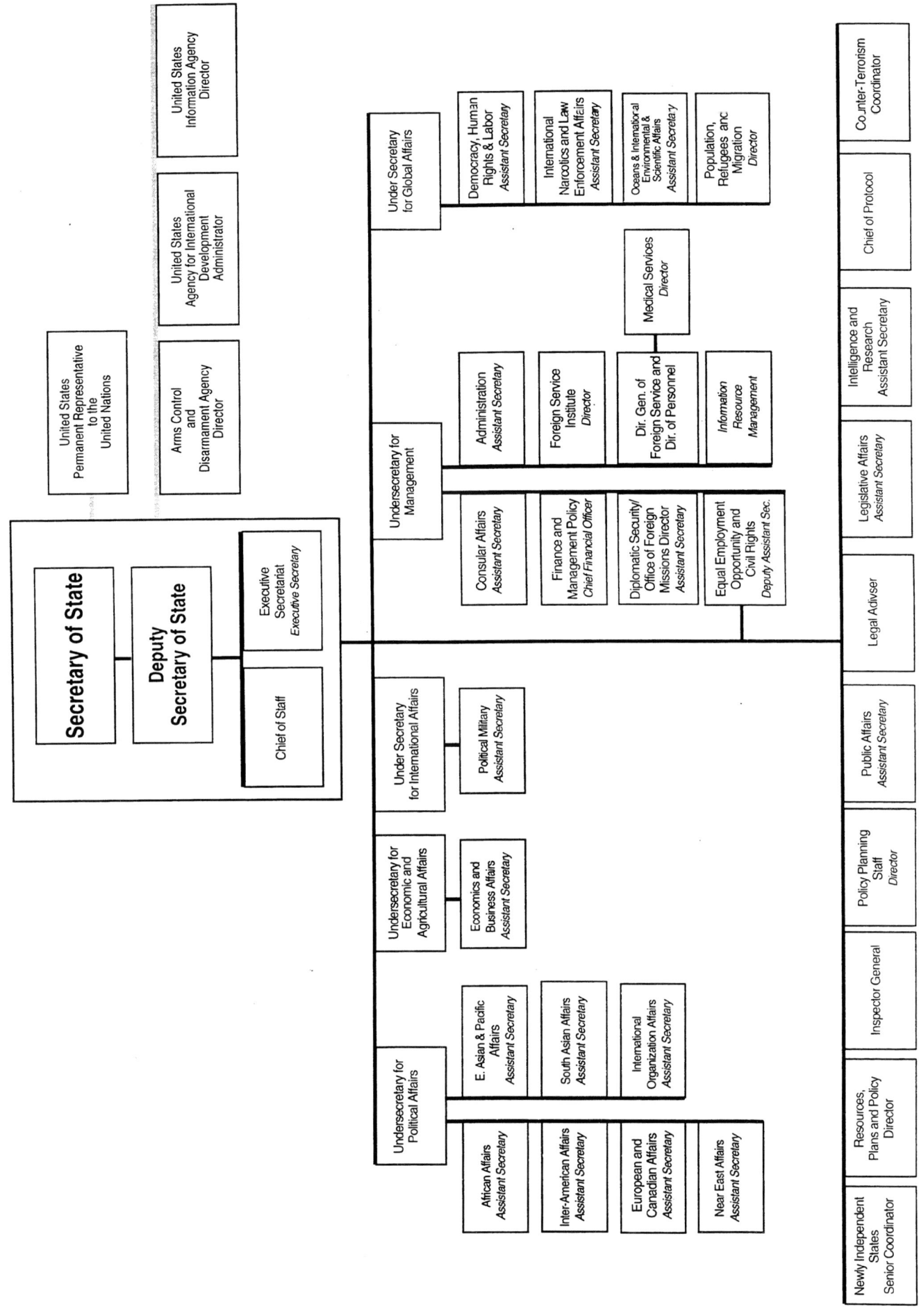

Secretary of State

Deputy Secretary of State

Chief of Staff

Executive Secretariat
Executive Secretary

United States Permanent Representative to the United Nations

Arms Control and Disarmament Agency
Director

United States Agency for International Development
Administrator

United States Information Agency
Director

Undersecretary for Political Affairs

African Affairs
Assistant Secretary

Inter-American Affairs
Assistant Secretary

European and Canadian Affairs
Assistant Secretary

Near East Affairs
Assistant Secretary

E. Asian & Pacific Affairs
Assistant Secretary

South Asian Affairs
Assistant Secretary

International Organization Affairs
Assistant Secretary

Undersecretary for Economic and Agricultural Affairs

Economics and Business Affairs
Assistant Secretary

Under Secretary for International Affairs

Political Military
Assistant Secretary

Undersecretary for Management

Consular Affairs
Assistant Secretary

Finance and Management Policy
Chief Financial Officer

Diplomatic Security/ Office of Foreign Missions Director
Assistant Secretary

Equal Employment Opportunity and Civil Rights
Deputy Assistant Sec.

Administration
Assistant Secretary

Foreign Service Institute
Director

Dir. Gen. of Foreign Service and Dir. of Personnel

Information Resource Management

Medical Services
Director

Under Secretary for Global Affairs

Democracy, Human Rights & Labor
Assistant Secretary

International Narcotics and Law Enforcement Affairs
Assistant Secretary

Oceans & International Environmental & Scientific Affairs
Assistant Secretary

Population, Refugees and Migration
Director

Newly Independent States Senior Coordinator

Resources, Plans and Policy
Director

Inspector General

Policy Planning Staff
Director

Public Affairs
Assistant Secretary

Legal Adviser

Legislative Affairs
Assistant Secretary

Intelligence and Research
Assistant Secretary

Chief of Protocol

Counter-Terrorism Coordinator

During the Cold War, new foreign affairs agencies were placed under the general policy direction of the Secretary of State: the United States Information Agency, the Arms Control and Disarmament Agency, and the U.S. Agency for International Development.

CURRENT STRUCTURE

The Department of State is headed by the Secretary (S) aided by a Deputy Secretary (D), five Under Secretaries, and 19 Assistant Secretaries. The Chief of Staff (S/COS) and Executive Secretariat (S/S) closely support the Secretary and Deputy Secretary. Several specialized offices and bureaus—headed by top aides and key advisers to the Secretary—help the Department focus on certain critical foreign policy areas and on important management issues.

The Department's Under Secretaries act as the "corporate board" of key advisers to the Secretary. They oversee the activities of most of the Department's bureaus and offices—which are organized under them to support their policy planning, coordination, and implementation activities. The Under Secretaries are those for Political Affairs (P); Economic, Business, and Agricultural Affairs (E); Arms Control and International Security Affairs (T); Management (M); and Global Affairs (G).

An Assistant Secretary or the equivalent runs each of the Department's regional, functional, and management bureaus; most bureaus comprise several offices headed by directors.

KEY BUSINESS CONTACTS

Office of the Coordinator for Business Affairs:
Coordinates State Department resources for U.S. business.
202/647-1625   FAX: 202/647-3953

Bureau of Economic and Business Affairs:
Coordinates international economic policies, with a lead role in civil aviation and telecommunications sectors.
202/647-7950   FAX: 202/647-5713

Bureau of Oceans & Intl. Environmental & Scientific Affairs:
Promotes trade and in environmental science and technology industries.
202/647-2801   FAX: 202/736-7336

Bureau of Consular Affairs:
Issues travel advisories, passports, and visas, and manages American citizen services abroad. Information is available on the World Wide Web (http://travel.state.gov.); computer bulletin board: 301/946-4400; automated fax: 202-647-3000; and telephone: 202-647-1488.

Bureau of Public Affairs:
Provides publications and foreign policy info. in print and on the WWW (http://www.state.gov.); coordinates regional town meetings, briefings and speakers; and answers foreign policy questions: call 202-647-6575. Fax-on-demand for publications: 202-738-7720.

Bureau for International Organizations:
Promotes procurement opportunities with agencies of the U.N.
202/647-1155   FAX: 202/647-4628.

Bureau of Political and Military Affairs:
Helps U.S. firms self defense and sensitive dual-use articles and services overseas, consistent with U.S. nonproliferation policies.
202/647-4231   FAX: 202/647-4232.

Bureau of Diplomatic Security (Overseas Security Advisory Council):
Provides international security updates.
202/663-0533   FAX: 202-663-0868.

Office of Small and Disadvantaged Business Utilization:
Promotes diversity in procurement.
703/875-6822

REGIONAL CONTACTS

Regional bureaus facilitate business assistance and arrange country economic and political briefings through the regional American outreach offices listed below:

Bureau of African Affairs (Sub-Sahara):
202/647-6476   FAX: 202/647-4583

Bureau of East Asian and Pacific Affairs:
202/647-6594   FAX: 202/647-7350

Bureau of European and Canadian Affairs:
202-647-2469   FAX: 202/647-9959.

New Independent States of the Former U.S.S.R.:
202/647-6729   FAX: 202/647-2699

Bureau of Inter-American Affairs (Mexico, Caribbean, Central and South America):
202/647-6754   FAX: 202/647-0791.

Bureau of Near Eastern Affairs (N. Africa & the Middle East):
202-647-1552   FAX: 202/736-4465.

Bureau of South Asian Affairs (Indian sub-continent):
202/736-4331   FAX: 202/736-4333

SERVICE TO BUSINESS

The U.S. Department of State works with other federal agencies in the Trade Promotion Coordinating Committee to ensure that the U.S. government provides steady and effective support to U.S. business overseas.

The department and its U.S. embassies around the world are working harder than ever to level the playing field for American businesses. In many overseas markets, our officers are the on-call eyes, ears, and in-country negotiators for the entire spectrum of U.S. businesses and government agencies. They play an important role in negotiating a myriad of global, regional, and bilateral international economic agreements- on trade, investment, intellectual property rights, taxation, civil aviation, telecommunications, and debt-- and in making sure that agreements are honored.

Due to their close interaction with host government officials on policy issues, embassy officers have well-established contacts, ranging from trade and industry to finance and customs. They help U.S. businesses resolve trade and investment disputes with foreign governments and help them overcome business problems relating to local rules, laws, taxation, and import restrictions. They analyze political and economic developments in a country and brief U.S. business executives on the local political climate. As experts on host country economies and business practices, State department officers work with the U.S. Foreign Commercial Service to identify opportunities for U.S. companies and advocate on their behalf.

U.S. business representatives are now making the Department of State or a U.S. embassy their first port of call when they do business abroad. U.S. economic diplomacy-and the presence of U.S. companies on the global scene -is not only essential to advancing U.S. commercial interests but is also a powerful tool for promoting peace, stability and progress toward democracy around the world.

U.S. BUSINESS BILL OF RIGHTS

American businesses operating or expanding abroad can expect assistance from the U.S. government team. As outlined in the State Department's Bill of Rights for American Business, these services include:

• Having your views heard and considered on foreign policy issues that affect your interests;

• Being assured that the ground rules for the conduct of international trade are fair and nondiscriminatory;

• Receiving assistance from well-trained and knowledgeable trade specialists in each overseas mission;

• Benefitting from sound professional advice and analysis on the local political and business environment;

• Gaining unique insight through networking assistance with contacts in key public and private sector positions;

• Obtaining active support and promotion in international bids and, where more than one U.S. firm is involved, evenhanded support for all interested firms; and

• Achieving amicable settlement of investment and trade disputes and, in cases of expropriation or similar action, to obtain prompt, adequate and effective compensation.

WWW AND PUBLICATIONS

Country Commercial Guides (CCGs) and other publications are available on the U.S. Department of State Home Page on the World Wide Web at http://www.state.gov under *Business Services*, along with economic policy updates, country analyses, congressional reports, briefings, and speeches, plus *Background Notes* and *Dispatch Magazine*. For print or CD-ROM publications, contact the Government Printing Office, 202-512-1800.

Office of the Secretary

2201 C Street, NW / Washington, DC 20520

Secretary Madeleine K. Albright
202/647-5291   FAX 202/647-1533
7th Floor

Personal: born 5/15/37 in Prague, Czechoslovakia.

Education: B.A. in political science (with honors), Wellesley College, 1959. M.A., Columbia University, 1968. Ph.D., Columbia University (Department of Public Law and Government), 1976. Certificate, Russian Institute, Columbia University.

Professional: 1976-78, chief legislative assistant, Senator Edmund S. Muskie (D-Maine). 1978-81, staff member, National Security Council and White House. 1981-82, fellowship, Woodrow Wilson International Center for Scholars (Smithsonian Institution). 1981-91, adjunct fellow, Center for Strategic and International Studies. 1982-93, research professor of international affairs and director of Women in Foreign Service Affairs, Georgetown University; president, Center for National Policy. 1993-97, U.S. Permanent Representative to the United Nations. 1997-present, Secretary of State, U.S. Dept. of State.

President Clinton nominated Madeleine Korbel Albright as Secretary

of State on December 5, 1996. After being unanimously confirmed by the Senate, she was sworn in as the 64th Secretary of State on January 23, 1997. Secretary Albright is the first female Secretary of State and the highest ranking woman in the U.S. government.

As Clinton's principal advisor on U.S. foreign policy, Albright conducts negotiations relating to foreign affairs, advises the president on diplomatic appointments, supervises the U.S. Foreign Service, and negotiates, interprets, and terminates treaties and agreements.

Since her appointment, Albright has been busy overseeing a reorganization of the State Department, which includes integrating the U.S. Information Agency, the Arms Control and Disarmament Agency, and the Agency for International Development with the department. She also has focused on the problems in Bosnia and NATO expansion and traveled to China in her first year as Secretary of State. Albright made headlines early on in her tenure when she learned that her grandparents had died in the Holocaust and that she had been born Jewish.

Prior to her appointment, Albright served as the United States Permanent Representative to the United Nations (presenting her credentials at the UN on February 6, 1993) and as a member of President Clinton's Cabinet and National Security Council.

Albright formerly was president of the Center for National Policy, a non-profit research organization formed in 1981 by government, industry, labor, and education representatives. Its mandate is to promote the study and discussion of domestic and international issues. As a research professor of international affairs and director of the Women in Foreign Service Program at Georgetown University's School of Foreign Service, she taught undergraduate and graduate courses in international affairs, U.S. foreign policy, Russian foreign policy, and Central and Eastern European politics, and was responsible for developing and implementing programs designed to enhance women's professional opportunities in international affairs.

From 1981 to 1982, Albright was awarded a fellowship at the Woodrow Wilson International Center for Scholars at the Smithsonian following an international competition in which she wrote about the role of the press in political changes in Poland during the early 1980's. She also served as a senior fellow in Soviet and Eastern European affairs at the Center for Strategic and International Studies, conducting research in developments and trends in the Soviet Union and Eastern Europe.

From 1978-1981, Albright was a staff member on the National Security Council, as well as a White House staff member, where she was responsible for foreign policy legislation. From 1976-1978, she served as chief legislative assistant to Senator Edmund S. Muskie (D-Maine).

Albright has written on issues related to Czechoslovakia, Poland and the former Soviet Union. Her work includes *Poland, the Role of the Press in Political Change*, published in 1983. Her dissertation at Columbia University was on *The Role of the Press in Political Change: Czechoslovakia 1968*, and her master's thesis was on *The Soviet Diplomatic Service: Profile of an Elite*.

Awarded a B.A. from Wellesley College with honors in political science, she studied at the School of Advanced International Studies at Johns Hopkins University, received a certificate from the Russian Institute at Columbia University, and her master's and doctorate from Columbia University's Department of Public Law and Government.

Secretary Albright is fluent in French and Czech, with good speaking and reading abilities in Russian and Polish. She has three daughters.

Senior Adviser
Mr. James C. O'Brien
202/647-7190
Rm. 7246

Executive Assistant
Mr. David Hale
202/647-9572   FAX 202/647-1533
Rm. 7226 (S)

Special Assistant
Ms. Colombia Barrosse
202/647-9573
Rm. 7226

Special Assistant
Mr. Richard Denniston
202/647-6822
Rm. 7226

Personal Assistant
Ms. Elizabeth Lineberry
202/647-5291
Rm. 7226

Scheduling Assistant
Ms. Linda Dewan
202/647-5733
Rm. 7226

Office of the Chief of Staff

Chief of Staff
Ms. Elaine Shocas
202/647-5548   FAX 202/647-5939
Rm. 7234A (S)

Education: B.A., Anna Maria College, 1970. J.D., Univ. School.

Professional: 1980, director of congressional affairs, Kennedy for President campaign. 1984-88, counsel to the treasurer, Democratic National Party. 1993-97, chief of staff to the U.S. Permanent Representative to the United Nations. 1997-present, chief of staff to the secretary, U.S. Dept. of State.

Elaine Shocas replaced Thomas Donilon as chief of staff to the Secretary of State. As such, Shocas directs and coordinates the agenda and activities of Secretary Albright.

Prior to assuming this position, Shocas had worked closely with Secretary Albright as her chief of staff in her previous job, that of U.S. Permanent Representative to the United Nations. Shocas had served in that position from 1993 until 1997, when Secretary Albright was confirmed.

Deputy Chief of Staff
Ms. Suzanne George
202/647-9574
Rm. 7226

Executive Secretariat (S/S)

**Special Assistant to the Secretary and
Executive Secretary of the Department**

Ms. Kristie A. Kenney
202/647-5301
Rm. 7224

Director, Secretariat Staff
Mr. Jim Bean
202/647-9938
Rm. 7241

Office of the Deputy Secretary (D)

Deputy Secretary of State
Mr. Strobe Talbott
202/647-9641   FAX 202/647-6047
Rm. 7220 (D)

Personal: born 4/25/46 in Ohio.

Education: B.A./M.A. (summa cum laude and Phi Beta Kappa), Yale Univ., 1968. M.Litt., Oxford Univ. (Rhodes Scholar), 1971.

Professional: 1971-73, East European correspondent. 1973-75, State Department correspondent; 1975-77, White House correspondent; 1977-84, diplomatic correspondent; 1984-89, Washington Bureau Chief; 1989, editor at large/foreign affairs columnist, *Time* magazine. 1993, ambassador-at-large/special adviser on the Newly Independent States; 1994-present, deputy secretary, U.S. Dept. of State.

Strobe Talbott was sworn in as deputy secretary of State on February 22, 1994. He moved into the number two position at the department after serving as ambassador at large and special adviser on the Newly Independent States of the former Soviet Union. As deputy secretary, Talbott has strongly advocated continued support for democratization and economic reform in Russia and the other Newly Independent States.

Prior to joining the State Department, Talbott had spent his entire career with *Time* magazine. He has been a European correspondent, state department correspondent, White House correspondent, diplomatic correspondent, Washington bureau chief, and editor at large/foreign affairs columnist.

Talbott has written extensively on foreign affairs. His publications include: *At the Highest Levels: The Inside Story of the End of the Cold War*, with Michael Beschloss; *The Master of the Game: Paul Nitze and the Nuclear Peace* (1988); *Reagan and Gorbachev*, with Michael Mandelbaum (1987); *Deadly Gambits; The Reagan Administration and the Stalemate in Nuclear Arms Control* (1984); and *Endgame: the Inside Story of Salt II*, (1970). Several of his articles were also published in *Foreign Affairs*, including "Why START Stopped" (1988); "Reykjavik and Beyond," with Michael

Mandelbaum (Winter 1986-87); and "Buildup and Breakdown," (1979).

Talbott's list of awards include the Edward Weintal Prize for Distinguished Diplomatic Reporting in 1980 and 1985 and the Overseas Press Club awards in 1979, 1981, 1987, and 1988. He has served on the boards on the Carnegie Endowment for International Peace and the Council of Foreign Relations and the advisory board of the Stanford Center on Arms Control and Disarmament. He was also active in the International Free Press Development Foundation and the Aspen Strategy Group.

Talbott's interest in Russian politics and culture can be traced to his days at Yale where he wrote his thesis on Russian poetry. Along with others in the administration, Talbott holds the distinction of being a "Friend of Bill."

Talbott is married to Brooke Shearer and they have two sons.

Executive Assistant
Mr. Philip Goldberg
202/647-8931   FAX 202/647-6047
Rm. 7220 (D)

Special Assistants:

Mr. Gregory Fukutomi
202/647-6237

Mr. John Bass
202/647-8930

Ms. Margot Sullivan
202/647-8930

Mr. Kent Pekel
202/647-8198

Office of the Counselor (C)

Counselor
Ms. Wendy R. Sherman
202/647-5529   FAX 202/647-0247
Rm. 7509

Personal: born 6/7/49 in Baltimore, Md.

Education: Attended Smith College, 1967-1969. B.A. (with honors), Boston Univ., 1971. M.S.W., Univ. of Maryland, School of Social and Community Planning, 1976.

Professional: 1977-80, center associate, Univ. of Southern Calif. and the Washington Public Affairs Center (Wash., D.C.) 1980-82, dir., office of child welfare social services admin., Maryland Dept. of Human Resources. 1982-85, admin. asst. (chief of staff), Rep. Barbara Mikulski (D-Md.), U.S. House of Representatives. 1985, dir. of

resource development, The Enterprise Foundation (Md.). 1985-87, campaign manager, Mikulski for Senate. 1987, special sec. for children and youth, State of Md. 1987-88, dir. of Washington operations, Dukakis for President. 1988, dir., Campaign '88, Democratic National Committee. 1988-91, political and public policy consultant, Center for National Policy, Foreman and Heidepriem. 1989-91, exec. dir., Emily's List (Wash., D.C.). 1991-93, partner, Doak, Shrum, Harris, Sherman. 1993-97, asst. sec., bureau of legislative affairs; 1997-present, counselor, U.S. Dept. of State.

Wendy Sherman became counselor to Secretary Albright in August 1997. She had served as assistant secretary for legislative affairs at the U.S. State Department for four years before assuming this position. In her previous position, she was responsible for supervising and coordinating all legislative activities at the department.

Sherman has worked as a specialist in strategic communications, managing Emily's List, the largest financial and political resource for pro-choice Democratic women candidates. As director of Emily's List (Early Money Is Like Yeast), Sherman is credited with the strategic development of the organization which led to groundbreaking numbers of women candidates in 1992.

In 1988, while director of Campaign '88 for the Democratic National Committee, Sherman was responsible for political and field operations, communications, congressional relations, constituency operations, issue development and coordination with all federal, state, and local campaigns and state parties. In 1991, Sherman became a partner in Doak, Shrum, Harris & Sherman, a political and media consulting firm. She has also managed numerous political campaigns and has a solid grounding in communications, management, and congressional relations.

Office of the Chief of Protocol

INTRODUCTION

The Office of the Chief of Protocol (S/CPR) advises the President, Vice President, Secretary of State, and others on matters of national and international protocol; supports ceremonial events and functions in the U.S. and abroad; manages Blair House—the President's guest house; and is responsible for accreditation activities.

Chief of Protocol
Ambassador Mary Mel French
202/647-4543   FAX 202/647-3980
Rm. 1232 (S/CPR)

President Clinton nominated Mary Mel French as chief of protocol to replace Molly Raiser at the State Department on October 10, 1997. French had been serving as acting chief of protocol.

French, of Arkansas, was appointed by the White House in 1993 to serve as the assistant chief of protocol in charge of the Visits Division, U.S. Department of State. She later was promoted to deputy chief of protocol. She began her career as a businesswoman and volunteer activist in the State of Arkansas. She served on several appointed volunteer boards. For many years, she has been a member of the Arkansas Arts Center and Fine Arts Club.

The chief of protocol is responsible for coordinating visits of heads of state, heads of government, and other high officials. She also helps plan the president's trips abroad. Additionally, the chief of protocol is responsible for the operation of Blair House, the President's guest house.

In addition to high profile social and political responsibilities, the chief of protocol is responsible for the accreditation of over 100,000 embassy, consular, and other international personnel and families in the United States; for determining the entitlement to diplomatic immunity and resolving legal and policy matters involving immunity questions; and approving the opening of consular offices in the United States.

French earned an Associate of Arts degree at Stephens College in Missouri before completing her undergraduate degree at the University of Arkansas in Little Rock with a Bachelor of Arts in International Studies.

Deputy Chief of Protocol
Mr. David H. Pryor, Jr.
202/647-4120
Rm. 1232

Office of the Policy Planning Staff (S/P)

INTRODUCTION

The Policy Planning Staff (S/P) is responsible for developing and proposing to the Secretary of State strategic political and economic policies.

Director
Mr. Gregory B. Craig
202/647-2372   FAX   202/647-4147
Rm. 7311 (S/P)

Personal: born 3/4/45 in Norfolk, Va.

Education: A.B.(magna cum laude), Harvard College, 1967. Diploma in Historical Studies, Cambridge University, Emmanuel College (John Harvard Scholar), 1968. J.D., Yale Law School, 1972.

Professional: 1972-74, associate, Williams, Connolly & Califano. 1974-76, assistant federal public defender, Federal District Courts of Connecticut. 1976-84, associate and partner, Williams & Connolly. 1984-88, senior advisor for foreign policy, defense and national security affairs, Sen. Edward M. Kennedy (D-Mass.). 1989-97, partner, Williams & Connolly. 1997-present, director, policy planning staff, U.S. Department of State.

Gregory Craig was appointed director of the State Department's policy planning staff in 1997. As such, he plays a broad role in formulating and coordinating U.S. foreign policy, and works closely with the Secretary of State and other senior government officials.

Craig brings a varied background and foreign policy experience to his new post. From 1984 to 1988 he was senior advisor for foreign policy, defense and national security affairs to Senator Edward Kennedy (D-Mass.).

Although he has spent most of his career in private legal practice with Williams & Connolly, Craig has been actively involved in foreign

affairs through his associations with many organizations. From 1990 to 1997 Craig was a member of the board of trustees of the Carnegie Endowment for International Peace and, in 1997, he served as a member of the board of directors of the U.S. Committee to Expand NATO. Craig also served as chairman of the board of the International Human Rights Law Group from 1992 to 1996. From 1994 to 1996, he was a member of the board of trustees of the Overseas Development Council.

Craig is a member of the District of Columbia Bar Association and the bars of the U.S. Supreme Court and U.S. Courts of Appeals for Second, Fourth, Sixth, Seventh and D.C. Circuits. He is also a member of the American Bar Association's sections on international law, criminal justice, and human rights and is a member of the American Society on International Law.

Craig is married to Margaret Davenport Noyes, and they have five children.

Principal Deputy Director
Mr. Alan D. Romberg
202/647-2972
Rm. 7311

Deputy Director
Mr. William Woodward
202/647-9943

Associate Director
Mr. Daniel Hamilton
202/647-4735
Rm. 7312

Office of Resources, Plans, and Policy (S/RPP)

INTRODUCTION

The Office of Resources, Plans, and Policy (S/RPP) is responsible for coordinating policy formulation with resource planning activities. The office develops for the Secretary's decision recommendations on international affairs resource issues, allocates funds in accordance with the Secretary's decisions, and conducts periodic program reviews.

Director
Ambassador L. Craig Johnstone
202/647-4427   FAX 202/647-1681
Rm. 7417A (S/RPP)

Personal: born 9/1/42 in Seattle, Wash.

Education: B.A., Univ. of Maryland, 1964. Graduate studies, Univ.

of Maryland, 1965. Graduate studies, Harvard Univ., 1971.

Professional: 1965, intern, International Institute for Education, Agency for International Development. 1966-70, with Dept. of State on detail to Agency for International Development in Vietnam. 1970-71, Council on Foreign Relations and faculty, Institute of Politics at Harvard University. 1971-73, political/military officer in Ottawa, Canada; 1974-76, deputy director of the Secretariat Staff; 1976, U.S. Sinai Support Mission; 1976-77, chief. economic section, Jamaica; 1978, French language training; 1978-81, political/military officer, France; 1981-83, chief, office of Central American affairs; 1983-85, deputy asst. secy. for Inter-American affairs; 1985-88, U.S. Ambassador to Algeria, U.S. Dept. of State. 1988-89, international vice president, Cabot Corp. 1989-93, president, Cabot Plastics International. 1994-present, director, office of resources, plans and policy, U.S. Department of State.

Craig Johnstone is the director for resources, plans and policy in the office of secretary of State Madeleine Albright. In this capacity, he has oversight of the Function 150 Account and the Department's budget and resource planning.

Ambassador Johnstone was vice president for international operations for the Cabot Corporation of Boston from 1989 until he returned to the Department of State in 1997. He was the U.S. Ambassador to Algeria from 1985 to 1989 and was deputy assistant secretary of State and regional director in the Bureau of Inter-American Affairs from 1981 to 1984. Johnstone has also served at American embassies in France, Jamaica, and Vietnam. He was part of the team that established the Sinai Field Mission in 1975 and also went on a refugee rescue mission to Vietnam in that same year. He served on the secretariat staff under Henry Kissinger and was the recipient of Council on Foreign Relations and Kennedy Institute of Politics Fellowships.

Johnstone graduated from the University of Maryland in 1964 and attended graduate school at the University of Maryland and at the Kennedy School of Government. He is married to Janet G. Buechel, a foreign service officer, and they have three children.

Deputy Director
Ms. Deborah Dawson
202/647-4734   FAX 202/647-1681
Rm. 7328 (S/RPP)

Coordinator for Counterterrorism (S/CT)

INTRODUCTION

The office of the coordinator for counterterrorism has primary responsibility within the U.S. Government for developing, coordinating, and implementing American counterterrorism policy. The office plays this role as chairman of the Policy Coordinating Committee on Terrorism (to develop and coordinate policy) and as chairman of the Department of State's task force (to coordinate responses to international terrorist incidents).

The office coordinates all U.S. Government efforts to improve counterterrorism cooperation with foreign governments, including the policy and planning of the department's Anti-terrorism Training Assistance Program. The office also coordinates all other U.S. counterterrorism assistance programs and the inter-agency research and development program for counterterrorism.

Acting Coordinator
Mr. Kenneth R. McKune
202/647-9892   FAX 202/647-0221
Room 2507

Kenneth McKune, a career foreign service officer, became acting coordinator for counterterrorism in June 1997. He has been the associate coordinator for this office since August 1995.

Prior to enlisting in the Foreign Service in 1973, McKune served from 1970-72 as a Peace Corps volunteer in Morocco. From 1967-69, he served in the U.S. Army including a 12 month Infantry tour in Vietnam. His career in the Foreign Service includes:

Aug. 1995-present: associate coordinator for counterterrorism; 1992-95: counselor for political affairs, American Embassy Riyadh; 1991-92: deputy director, Office of Arabian Peninsula Affairs, Department of State; 1989-91: deputy director, Office of Israeli and Arab-Israeli Affairs, Department of State; 1988-89: graduate of the 1989 class at the National War College/National Defense University; 1986-88: counselor for political affairs, Embassy Beirut; 1982-86: political officer, Embassy Cairo; 1980-82: Arabic Language Training at Foreign Service Institute in Washington and Tunis; 1978-80: international relations officer, Office of Mexican Affairs, Department of State; 1974-78: rotational tour at American Embassy Tel Aviv: political officer, economic officer, personnel officer; 1973-74: vice consul, American Embassy Kuwait.

McKune received a B.A. degree in philosophy in 1966 from Bellarmine College in Louisville, Kentucky. He speaks Arabic and French and is married to Elizabeth Davenport McKune.

Associate Coordinator
VACANT
202/647-9892
Rm. 2507

Director for Counterterrorism Operations
Col. Paul Barton, USA
202/647-7264
Rm. 2507

Director for Regional Affairs
Mr. Gordon Gray
202/647-8485
Rm. 2407

Office of Equal Opportunity and Civil Rights (S/EEOCR)

Deputy Assistant Secretary
Ms. Deidre Davis
202/647-9294
Rm. 4216

Office of Global Humanitarian De-mining (S/GHD)

Special Representative
Amb. Karl F. Inderfurth
202/647-0562
Rm. 6484

Executive Director
Ms. Stacy B. Davis
202/647-0595
Rm. 6484

Office of the Special Middle East Coordinator

Special Middle East Coordinator
Ambassador Dennis B. Ross
202/647-1494   FAX 202/647-4808
Rm. 7527 (S/MEC)

Personal: born in San Francisco, Calif.

Education: B.A., Univ. of Calif. at Los Angeles. M.A., Univ. of Calif. at Los Angeles.

Professional: 1980-82, member, policy planning staff for Middle Eastern issues, U.S. Dept. of State. 1982-84, deputy dir., office of net assessment, U.S. Dept. of Defense. 1984-86, executive director, Berkeley-Stanford program on Soviet International Behavior. 1986-88, director, Near East and South Asian affairs, National Security Council. 1988-89, senior foreign policy adviser, Bush Campaign and head of national security affairs during presidential transition. 1989-92, director, policy planning staff, U.S. Dept. of State. 1992, asst. to the President for policy planning. 1993-present, special Middle East coordinator, U.S. Dept. of State.

Dennis Ross became the special Middle East coordinator for the State Department in 1993. In this position, Ross advises Secretary Albright on Middle Eastern affairs and represents the U.S. in dealing with issues in this contentious region. He is a troubleshooter, diplomat, and skillful envoy, all qualities that are necessary in dealing with recent terrorist attacks in the Middle East and forging an alliance between leaders in the region with the goal of achieving peaceful coexistence.

Deputy Special Middle East Coordinator
Mr. Aaron D. Miller
202/647-2946
Rm. 7527

Office of the Special Adviser to the President and the Secretary for NATO Enlargement Ratification (S/NERO)

Special Adviser
Mr. Jeremy D. Rosner
202/647-003
Rm. 6317

Office of the Special Adviser to the Secretary for the New Independent States (S/NIS)

Ambassador at Large
Ambassador Steven R. Sestanovich
202/647-3112   FAX 202/647-2699
Rm. 7531 (S/NIS)

Education: B.A., Cornell Univ., 1972. Ph.D., Harvard Univ., 1978.

Professional: 1980-81, senior leg. asst. for foreign policy, Sen. Daniel P. Moynihan (D-N.Y.). 1981-84, member, policy planning staff, U.S. Department of State. 1984-87, senior director for policy development, Natl. Security Council. 1987-94, director of Russia and Eurasian studies, Center for Strategic and International Studies. 1994-97, vice president of Russian and foreign affairs, Carnegie Endowment for Intern'l. Peace. Sept. 1997-present, amb. at large and special adviser to the Secretary on the New Independent States, U.S. Dept. of State.

President Clinton nominated Stephen Sestanovich as ambassador at large and special adviser to the Secretary of State on the New Independent States (NIS) on May 22, 1997. He was confirmed for the position by the Senate on September 16.

As the principal adviser to the secretary on the NIS, Sestanovich brings overall operational coordination to U.S. relations with and assistance to the NIS of the former Soviet Union; implements proposals on NIS policy; coordinates NIS policy both in the department and with other government entities; and serves as the principal spokesman for the administration and the Department of State before Congress and the public on policy toward the NIS.

Immediately prior to assuming his new responsibilities, Sestanovich was vice president for Russian and foreign affairs at the Carnegie Endowment for International Peace, where he oversaw the endowment's new policy research effort in Moscow and its program of post-Soviet studies in Washington. Prior to joining the endowment in 1994, Sestanovich was director of Russian and Eurasian studies at the Center for Strategic and International Studies from 1987 to 1994. He was the senior director for policy development at the National Security Council from 1984 to 1987. Sestanovich was a member of the policy planning staff at the Department of State from 1981 to 1984 and the senior legislative assistant for foreign policy to Sen. Daniel Patrick Moynihan (D-N.Y.) from 1980 to 1981.

He received a B.A. degree from Cornell University in 1972, and a Ph.D. in government from Harvard University in 1978.

Principal Deputy
Mr. Ross Wilson
202/647-3566
Rm. 7531

Office of the Special Adviser to the President and Secretary of State on Assistance to the New Independent States (S/NIS/C)

Coordinator
Ambassador Richard L. Morningstar
202/647-4670   FAX 202/647-2636
Rm. 4419 (S/NIS/C)

Education: B.A. (with high honors), Harvard College. J.D., Stanford Law School.

Professional: 1970-75, associate; 1976-81, partner and administrator of litigation dept., Peabody & Brown (Boston). 1981-92, chairman and CEO, Costar Corporation. 1993-95, senior vice president for policy and investment development, Overseas Private Investment Corporation. 1995-present, special adviser to the President and Secretary of State on Assistance to the New Independent States, U.S. Dept. of State.

On April 4, 1995, President Clinton appointed Richard Morningstar to be special adviser to the President and Secretary of State on assistance to the Newly Independent States (NIS) of the former Soviet Union and coordinator of U.S. Assistance to the NIS. On June 11, 1996, the Senate confirmed him with the rank of ambassador. According to his charter signed by the President, Ambassador Morningstar oversees all bilateral assistance and trade and investment activities of the 16 U.S. government agencies engaged in technical assistance, trade and investment, exchange, weapons dismantlement and other programs in the NIS.

From June 1993 to April 1995, Morningstar served as senior vice president for policy and investment development at the Overseas Private Investment Corporation (OPIC). In that position, he was responsible for development and implementation of strategies for the opening of new investment programs in Russia and the other New Independent States as well as new programs in Eastern Europe, Gaza/West Bank, and South Africa. He coordinated OPIC's seven-fold increase in NIS finance and insurance programs in 1994.

Before OPIC, Morningstar had 20 years of business, policy, and legal experience. For over ten years, he served as chairman and CEO at Costar Corporation, which was listed by *Forbes* magazine as one of the top 200 small companies in the country and recognized as one of the nation's fastest growing exporters. He has advised the Department of Commerce on international trade and technology issues, served on the economics and international trade cluster, and prepared analysis of the Trade and Development Agency for the 1992 Presidential Transition.

From 1970 to 1981, Morningstar practiced law with the firm of Peabody & Brown in Boston, Massachusetts, and from 1976 was a partner and administrator of the litigation department. He has been adjunct professor of law at the Boston College Law School and commissioner of the National Conference of Commissioners on Uniform State Laws.

Morningstar graduated from Harvard College and received a law degree from Stanford Law School. A baseball enthusiast, he was part-owner of the Lowell Spinners, a minor league baseball team in Lowell, Massachusetts. Morningstar is married with four children.

Deputy Coordinator
Mr. Bill Taylor
202/647-2180
Rm. 4419

Director for Humanitarian Programs
Mr. Russ Hardesty
202/647-1224   FAX 202/647-2636
Rm. 4423

Director for Democracy Programs
Mr. Margo Squiers
202/647-1239   FAX 202/647-2636
Rm. 4419

Director for Technical Assistance
Ms. Kathy Kavalec
202/647-3099
Rm. 4419

Office of the Special Negotiator for Nagorno-Karabakh and NIS Regional Conflicts (S/NIS/RA)

Special Negotiator
Ambassador B. Lynn Pascoe
202/647-8741
Rm. 4234

Deputy
Mr. Philip Remler
202/647-8741
Rm. 4234

Office of the Special Adviser to the Secretary of State (S/SAS)

Special Adviser
Ambassador Richard Schifter
202/647-3032
Rm. 5314A

Office of the Special Representative to the President and Secretary of State for Implementation of the Dayton Peace Accords (S/SR)

Special Representative
Ambassador Robert S. Gelbard
202/647-3774
Rm. 6219

Ambassador-at-Large for War Crime Issues (S/WCI)

Ambassador-at-Large David Scheffer
202/647-5074
Rm. 7421

Deputy
Mr. Tom Warrick
202/647-5093
Rm. 7421

Office of the Special Coordinator for Tibet (S/STC)

Mr. Greg Craig
202/647-3007
Rm. 7528A

Office of the Under Secretary for Political Affairs (P)

2201 C Street, NW / Washington DC 20520

INTRODUCTION

The Under Secretary for Political Affairs is the Department's crisis manager and also is responsible for integrating political, economic, global, and security issues into the United States' bilateral relationships.

The geographic bureaus coordinate the conduct of U.S. foreign relations in six world regions. They are:

—The Bureau of African Affairs (AF);
—The Bureau of East Asian and Pacific Affairs (EAP);
—The Bureau of European and Canadian Affairs (EUR);
—The Bureau of Inter-American Affairs (for Latin America and the Caribbean—ARA);
—The Bureau of Near Eastern Affairs (NEA); and
—The Bureau of South Asian Affairs (SA).

The Assistant Secretaries of these bureaus advise the Secretary and guide the operation of the U.S. diplomatic establishments within their regional jurisdiction. They are assisted by Deputy Assistant Secretaries, office directors, post management officers, and country desk officers to ensure interdepartmental coordination. These officials work closely with U.S. embassies and consulates overseas and with foreign embassies in Washington, DC.

Under Secretary
Ambassador Thomas Pickering
202/647-2471   FAX 202/647-4780
Rm. 7240 (P)

Personal: born 11/5/31 in Orange, N.J.

Education: B.A. (cum laude), Bowdoin College., 1953. M.A., Tufts University, 1954. M.A., Melbourne Univ. 1956.

Professional: 1956-59, active duty, U.S. Navy. 1959, entered the Foreign Service. 1961-64, political officer, U.S. Arms Control and Disarmament Agency in Geneva. 1965-67, principal officer in Zanzibar, Tanzania; 1969-73, deputy director, bureau of political-military affairs; 1973-74, executive secretary of the Department of State and spec. asst. to Secretaries of State Rogers and Kissinger; 1974-78, U.S. ambassador to Hashemite Kingdom of Jordan; 1978-81, asst. sec. for oceans and intl. development; 1981-83, U.S. ambassador to Nigeria; 1983-85, U.S. ambassador to El Salvador; 1985-88, U.S. ambassador to Israel; 1988-92, U.S. representative to the UN; 1992-93, U.S. ambassador to India; 1993-96, U.S. ambassador to Russia, U.S. Dept. of State. 1996-97, president, Eurasia Foundation. 1997-present, under secretary for political affairs, Department of State.

On May 27, 1997, Thomas R. Pickering was sworn in as under secretary of State for political affairs. He holds the personal rank of career ambassador, the highest in the United States Foreign Service. As under secretary, Pickering is the number three person at the department. He assists the secretary and the deputy secretary in the formulation and conduct of foreign policy and in the overall direction of the bureau of political affairs and serves as acting secretary in the absence of them. Pickering also coordinates relations with other departments and agencies as well as interdepartmental activities of the U.S. government overseas.

Prior to becoming under secretary, Pickering served as president of the Eurasia Foundation, a Washington-based organization which makes small grants and loans in the states of the former Soviet Union to support democracy and economic reform. He previously served as ambassador to the Russian Federation from May 1993 until November 1996. He also served as ambassador to India from 1992 to 1993, permanent representative to the UN from 1989-92, and as ambassador to Israel from 1985-88, to El Salvador from 1983-85, and to Nigeria from 1981-83. He was assistant secretary for oceans and international environmental and scientific affairs from 1978 to 1981. From 1974 until 1978, Pickering was ambassador to the Hashemite Kingdom of Jordan.

Pickering received a bachelor's degree in 1953 from Bowdoin College in Brunswick, Maine, with high honors in history. In 1954 he attended the Fletcher School of Law and Diplomacy at Tufts University and received a master's degree. He was awarded a Fulbright Scholarship to the University of Melbourne and received a second master's degree in 1956. From 1956 to 1959, he was on active duty in the U.S. Navy and later served in the Naval Reserve with the grade of lieutenant commander. Between 1959 and 1961, Pickering served in the bureau of intelligence and research of the State Department, in the Arms Control and Disarmament Agency, and from 1962 to 1964, in Geneva as a political officer at the 18-National Disarmament Conference.

Following his assignment to Geneva, Pickering studied Swahili at the Foreign Service Institute in Washington and was assigned in 1965

to Zanzibar. In 1967 he became deputy chief of mission in Dar es Salaam, Tanzania, and, in 1969, he returned to Washington to become deputy director of the bureau of political-military affairs. From 1973 to 1974 he was executive secretary of the Department of State and special assistant to Secretary Rogers and Secretary Kissinger.

In 1983, and in 1986, Pickering won the Distinguished Presidential Award and, in 1996, the Department's Distinguished Service Award. He is a member of the International Institute of Strategic Studies and the Council on Foreign Relations. His speaks French, Spanish, Swahili, Arabic, and Hebrew.

Pickering is married to Alice Stover Pickering and they have a son, Timothy, and a daughter, Margaret.

Executive Assistant
Mr. Daniel Russell
202/647-1598   FAX 202/647-4780
Rm. 7240 (P)

Office of the Under Secretary for Economic, Business, and Agricultural Affairs (E)

2201 C Street, NW / Washington DC 20520

> ### INTRODUCTION
> *Economics and trade are assuming greater importance in U.S. foreign policy. There is increasing demand for the "E" Group's services as more and more countries — including emerging democracies — move to open their markets to international trade and investment.*

Under Secretary
Mr. Stuart E. Eizenstat
202/647-7575   FAX 202/647-9763
Rm. 7256 (E)

Personal: born 1943 in Chicago, Ill.

Education: B.A. (Phi Beta Kappa), Univ. of North Carolina, 1964. J.D., Harvard Law School, 1967.

Professional: 1968-70, law clerk, Hon. Newell Edenfield, Northern District of Ga. 1970-76, attorney and partner, Powell, Goldstein, Frazer & Murphy (Atlanta). 1977-81, assistant to the president for domestic affairs and policy and executive director of the domestic policy staff, The White House. 1981-93, head of Washington office and vice chairman, Powell, Goldstein, Frazer & Murphy. 1993-96, U.S. Ambassador to the European Union. 1996-97, under secretary for international trade, U.S. Dept. of Commerce. 1997-present, under secretary for economic, business, and agricultural affairs, U.S. Dept. of State.

Stuart Eizenstat was sworn in as under secretary of State for economic, business and agricultural affairs on June 6, 1997. As under secretary, Eizenstat serves as the senior economic official at the Department of State. He advises the secretary on international economic policy and leads the work of the department on issues ranging from trade and aviation negotiations to bilateral relations with major partners such as Japan and the European Union. Ambassador Eizenstat retains his title and responsibilities as Special Envoy for Property Claims in Central and Eastern Europe. He is a leader within the administration in promoting democracy and human rights in Cuba.

From April 1996 until his confirmation at State, Eizenstat was under secretary of commerce for international trade. At Commerce, he led the International Trade Administration, which has responsibility for promoting U.S. exports, assisting American business efforts abroad, enforcing laws against unfair foreign trade practices, and developing trade policy. He established the new Compliance Center, which gives the U.S. government the capacity to monitor foreign government compliance with trade agreements they have reached with the U.S. This provides U.S. businesses and workers greater assurance that they are reaping the full benefits of the trade agreements negotiated by the U.S.

Eizenstat served as U.S. Ambassador to the European Union in Brussels, Belgium, from September 1993 until April 1996. He was one of the initiators of the New Transatlantic Agenda, signed by President Clinton and European leaders in 1995, to develop closer ties between the U.S. and the European Union in the post-Cold War era. He also helped to develop the highly successful Transatlantic Business Dialogue, which brings together European and American business leaders to provide advice on removing impediments to transatlantic trade and investment. In 1996, at the conclusion of his service to the European Union, Eizenstat received the Foreign Affairs Award for Public Service, the highest award which can be given to a non-career ambassador.

Prior to becoming ambassador to the EU, Eizenstat was partner and vice chairman of the law firm and chairman of the Washington office of Powell, Goldstein, Frazer & Murphy, where he had been since 1981. He concurrently served as adjunct lecturer at the John F. Kennedy School of Government at Harvard University from 1981 to 1992, teaching a course on presidential decision making. He had also been a guest scholar at the Brookings Institution in Washington, D.C.

From 1977 to 1981, Eizenstat served as President Carter's chief domestic policy adviser in the White House. In 1976, he served on the Carter presidential campaign as director of issues and policy. After the election, he became the Carter-Mondale Transition Planning Group's director for policy, planning and analysis.

Eizenstat has written extensively in leading newspapers in the U.S. and abroad and co-edited a book, *The American Agenda*, a bipartisan project he co-directed to provide advice to the President-elect in 1988.

Eizenstat has served on the boards of such non-profit organizations as the Weizmann Institute of Science, The Jerusalem Foundation, Brandeis University, Council on Foreign Relations, Council for Excellence in Government, Center for National Policy, the Overseas Development Council, International Management and Development Institute (Jerusalem), American Jewish Committee, and the UJA Federation of Greater Washington, and was chairman of the Feinberg Graduate School of the Weizmann Institute. He was president of the Greater Washington Jewish Community Center from 1989 to 1991. He also was on the board of directors of Hercules Incorporated, PSI Energy, Inc., and the Israel Discount Bank of New York.

Eizenstat was born in Chicago and raised in Atlanta. He is an honors graduate in political science of the University of North Carolina at Chapel Hill and received his law degree from Harvard University in 1967. During his university years, Eizenstat spent three summers working as an intern for both the legislative and the executive branches of the federal government. In 1967 and 1968, he served as a staff aide in the Johnson White House and in 1968 as research director for

Vice President Hubert Humphrey's presidential campaign.

Eizenstat is married to Frances Carol Eizenstat and is the father of two sons, Jay and Brian.

Executive Assistant
Mr. Peter Bass
202/647-7449
Rm. 7256 (E)

Senior Adviser
Mr. Bennett Freeman
202/647-7572
Rm. 7256

Office of Business Affairs (E/CBA)

INTRODUCTION

The office of the coordinator for business affairs (CBA) is a good point of contact for firms seeking State Department support and assistance. CBA works directly with American companies to help them tap the worldwide resources of the department when they need advocacy or help in solving problems. As a business ombudsman and adviser to the secretary of state and senior officials, the coordinator ensures that U.S. business concerns are at the forefront of the foreign policy process.

Established as part of the Department's emphasis on being America's Desk, CBA:

• Coordinates State Department advocacy on behalf of U.S. businesses;

• Provides problem-solving assistance to U.S. companies in opening markets, leveling playing fields, and resolving trade and investment disputes;

• Ensures that appropriate U.S. business interests are taken into account in the foreign policy process;

• Develops and implements internal policies, procedures, and training to improve the Department's support for U.S. businesses; and

• Coordinates support with the Commerce Department's U.S. and Foreign Commercial Service for posts where the State Department is directly responsible for trade promotion and commercial services.

Acting Senior Coordinator
Mr. Marshall Adair
202/647-1625   FAX 202/647-3953
Rm. 2318 (E/CBA)

Deputy Coordinator
Mr. Marshall Adair
202/647-1625   FAX 202/647-3953
Rm. 2318 (E/CBA)

Special Assistant
Mr. K. Jeffrey Donald
202/647-0079   FAX 202/647-3953
Rm. 2318 (E/CBA)

Special Assistant
Ms. Barbara R. Pace
202/647-4103   FAX 202/647-3953
Rm. 2318 (E/CBA)

Special Assistant
Mr. A. David Miller
202/647-1682   FAX 202/647-3953
Rm. 2318 (E/CBA)

Office of the Under Secretary for Arms Control and International Security Affairs (T)

2201 C Street, NW / Washington DC 20520

INTRODUCTION

The under secretary for international security affairs is responsible for international scientific and technological issues, communications and information policy, and technology transfers.

Under Secretary for Arms Control and Intl. Security Affairs
Mr. John D. Holum
202/647-1049   FAX 202/647-4920
Rm. 7208 (T)

Personal: born 12/4/40 in Highmore, S.D.

Education: B.A., Northern State Teachers College (Aberdeen, S.D.). J.D., (with honors), George Washington Univ., 1970.

Professional: 1965-79, staff and then legislative dir., Sen. George McGovern (D-S.D.). 1979-81, policy planning staff, U.S. Dept. of State. 1981-93, attorney, O'Melveny & Myers. 1993-present, dir., Arms Control & Disarmament Agency (ACDA). 1997-present, under sec. of State for arms controls and intern'l. security affairs, U.S. Dept. of State.

John Holum has served as director of the U.S. Arms Control and Disarmament Agency since 1993. ACDA was established by 1961 legislation in response to congressional feeling that the nation's national security efforts could be most effectively executed by centralizing arms control and disarmament responsibilities. Until 1997, the agency operated as an autonomous governmental unit.

In April of 1997, the Clinton administration announced a reorganization plan for the U.S. State Department which would fold both the ACDA and the United States Information Agency into the U.S. Department of State. Officials of all the agencies involved are currently working on implementation plans for the reorganization which should be complete by 1999.

Holum will be "dual-hatted" for the integration period as ACDA director and as under secretary of State for arms control and international security affairs. He will serve as the principal advisor to the Secretary of State and the President on the full range of arms control, nonproliferation, and international security matters.

Holum brings to the executive branch a mix of experience drawn from the worlds of foreign policy, international law and negotiation, and political and public affairs. From 1981 until his swearing in, he practiced law in the Washington office of O'Melveny & Myers, concentrating on regulatory and international matters. Former Secretary of State Warren Christopher was a partner at the firm. Holum concentrated on regulatory proceedings and enforcement.

Holum served as a defense and foreign policy adviser in the 1992 Clinton Presidential Campaign and assisted in the Clinton Presidential Transition. He also served as executive director of the Democratic Platform drafting committee and the Platform committee for the 1992 Democratic National Convention.

From 1979 to 1981, Holum served on the policy planning staff at the Department of State. Working on arms control and legal issues with Samuel Berger and under-secretary Anthony Lake, he drafted speeches and testimony for Secretary Vance, Secretary Muskie, and Deputy Secretary Christopher.

From 1965 to 1979, Holum was a member of the staff of US Senator George McGovern (D-SD), where he served as legislative director and managed the Senator's work on the Foreign Relations Committee. He was McGovern's issues director in the 1972 presidential primaries and served as his chief speechwriter in the general election.

Holum grew up on a family farm in the northeastern part of South Dakota. His undergraduate education at Northern State Teachers College was in mathematics and physical sciences. Holum attended law school at George Washington University, where he earned his J.D. with honors in 1970.

Holum is married and has a daughter. He enjoys sailing, flying, scuba diving, and playing bluegrass/country music.

Executive Assistant
Ms. Barbara F. Starr
202/647-1749
Rm. 7210 (T)

Senior Adviser
Mr. James P. Timbie
202/647-4404
Rm. 7210

Office of the Under Sec. for Management (M)

2201 C Street, NW / Washington DC 20520

INTRODUCTION

In addition to overseeing the State Department's traditional management issues, the Under Secretary for Management is responsible for the Department's recent management improvement initiatives, including the SMI process. The Office of Management Policy and Planning (M/P), reporting directly to the Under Secretary, serves as the focal point for these initiatives. It provides dedicated policy, planning, and analytical support to the Under Secretary on management issues in the three broad areas of M responsibility—human resources, financial management and operations, and support services—and supports Department-wide strategic planning activities as well as the implementation of initiatives arising from the National Performance Review. It also performs the functions associated with National Security Decision Directive 38 and chiefs of mission authority, implements the Government Performance and Results Act, and provides other staff support for the Under Secretary.

Under Secretary
Ms. Bonnie R. Cohen
202/647-1500   FAX 202/647-0168
Rm. 7207 (M)

Personal: born 12/11/42 in Brockton, Mass.

Education: B.A., Smith College, 1964. M.A., Harvard, 1965. MBA, Harvard Graduate School of Business Admin., 1967.

Professional: 1967-72, consultant, Resource Management Corp. 1972-75, asst. vice president of schools, D.C. Public School System. 1977-80, consultant, Lewin and Associates. 1976-81, chief financial officer and treasurer, United Mine Workers Health and Retirement Funds. 1981, consultant, Stanford Management Co. (Stanford Univ. Endowment). 1982-present, private investment consultant (self-employed, part-time). 1983-87, trustee investment chair, D. C. Retirement Board. 1985-present, trustee, American Red Cross Retirement Board. 1987-89, consultant, National Corp. for Housing Partnerships. 1981-89, vice-president for finance; 1990-93, senior vice president, National Trust for Historic Preservation. 1993-97, asst. secretary for policy, management and budget, U.S. Dept. of the Interior. 1997-present, under secretary for mgmt., U. S. Dept. of State.

Bonnie Cohen was sworn in as the State Department's under secretary for management, on August 20, 1997. Cohen comes to the department after serving for four years as the assistant secretary for policy management and budget at the Interior Department. She assumed the position at State previously held by Richard Moose.

While at Interior, Cohen oversaw the financial management and administrative activities of all Interior Department bureaus and acted as the department's chief financial officer. She will have similar duties in her new post at the State Department. Her former boss, Interior Secretary Bruce Babbitt calls Cohen "a superb financial manager."

One of the first women to graduate from the Harvard Graduate School of Business Administration, Cohen has used her financial acumen and investment skills to help organizations and individuals optimize their resources. Her clients have included the Stanford University Endowment and the National Housing Partnership, and she has served on numerous organizational boards including the Environmental Defense Fund, the Center for Marine Conservation, the American Red Cross Retirement Fund, and the D.C. Retirement Board. Cohen is a founding member of the Council of Institutional Investors.

Cohen came to the Interior Department with no government experience, a fact that proved of little consequence given her history of success. She worked at the National Trust for Historic Preservation, the largest national non-profit devoted to historic and cultural preservation. Until 1989, she served as the trust's vice president for finance. From 1989 to 1993, she was senior vice president and acted as the organization's chief financial and administrative officer.

Cohen's husband, Louis Richard Cohen, is a partner at the law firm of Wilmer, Cutler and Pickering. Their daughter, Amanda, is at Harvard Law School. Their son, Eli, is attending Harvard College.

Executive Assistant
Mr. Theodore Strickler
202/647-1501
Rm. 7207

Office of Congressional Relations

Director
Mr. Will Davis
202/647-2135
Rm. 7261

Office of Management, Policy and Planning (M/P)

Director
Ms. Eliza McClenaghan
202/647-0093
Rm. 5214

Office of the Under Sec. for Global Affairs (G)

2201 C Street, NW / Washington DC 20520

> ### INTRODUCTION
> *The office of the Under Secretary for Global Affairs is responsible for coordinating a broad group of global programs including population, environment, science, counternarcotics, terrorism, democracy, human rights and refugees.*

Under Secretary
VACANT
202/647-6240   FAX 202/647-0753
Rm. 7250 (G)

This office was most recently headed by former Colorado Senator Timothy Wirth. At press time, a new appointee had not been confirmed.

Executive Assistant
Ms. Carol Thompson
202/647-6240   FAX 202/647-0753
Rm. 7250 (G)

Senior Coordinator for International Women's Issues
Ms. Theresa Loar
202/647-5440
Rm. 2906 (G)

Bureau of Public Affairs (PA)

2201 C Street, NW / Washington DC 20520

Public Information Service: 202/647-6575
Fax-on-Demand Service: 202/736-7720

> ### INTRODUCTION
> *The Bureau of Public Affairs (PA) interaction with the American public is key to the Secretary's America's Desk concept — the Department's commitment to relating foreign policy goals to the American people and keeping the public involved in the foreign policy process.*

The bureau does this in a variety of ways:

— Conducting daily press briefings and arranging interviews for the Secretary and other Department principals with television, radio, and print media;

— Drafting speeches and testimonies for the Secretary of State;

— Releasing material on current and historical U.S. foreign policy in hard copy and electronically;

— Promoting Department relations with state and local elected officials;

— Holding briefing programs in the Department and throughout the Washington metropolitan area;

— Conducting regional town meetings;

— Sending speakers around the country; and

— Answering the public's phone calls and mail to the Secretary and Deputy Secretary.

Assistant Secretary for Public Affairs and Department Spokesman
Mr. James Rubin
202/647-7191
Rm. 7246 (PA)

Education: B.A., Columbia Univ., 1982. M.A. in international affairs, Columbia Univ., 1984.

Professional: 1985-89, research director, Arms Control Association (Wash., D.C.). 1990-93, staff member, U.S. Senate Foreign Relations Cmte. and senior foreign policy advisor, Sen. Joseph Biden, Jr. (D-Del.). 1993-96, senior advisor to the U.S. Permanent Representative and press spokesman for the United States at the U.N. 1996-97, senior advisor to Secretary of State, Madeleine Albright; July 1997-present, asst. secretary for public affairs, U.S. Dept. of State.

James Rubin was confirmed as assistant secretary of State for public affairs on July 31, 1997. In this capacity, he directs the development and execution of department-wide public information policies and oversees public outreach efforts to the American public on foreign policy issues. He acts as the principal advisor to the Secretary of State, other department officials and other government agencies on the department's responsibilities to the American public.

Prior to his confirmation, Rubin served as senior advisor to Secretary of State Madeleine Albright. From May 1993 until August 1996, Rubin was the senior advisor to the U.S. Permanent Representative and press spokesman for the United States at the United Nations. Prior to joining the Department of State, he was a professional staff member of the U.S. Committee on Foreign Relations and senior policy advisor to Senator Joseph Biden, Jr. From 1985 to 1989, Rubin was the research director for the Arms Control Association in Washington, D.C.

Deputy Assistant Secretary/Spokesman
Mr. James Foley
202/647-6607   FAX 202/647-5939
Rm. 6800

Deputy Assistant Secretary for Public Liaison
Ms. Lula Rodriguez
202/647-6088   FAX 202/647-5939
Rm. 6800 (PA)

Deputy Assistant Secretary for Public Communication
Ms. Danielle Paris
202/647-5760   FAX 202/647-5939
Rm. 6805 (PA)

Deputy Assistant Secretary for Strategic Planning
Mr. Jonathan Prince
202/647-6088   FAX 202/647-5939
Rm. 6800 (PA)

Executive Assistant
Ms. Susan Povenmire
202/647-6088   FAX 202/647-5939
Rm. 6800 (PA)

Director of Communications
Ms. Carrie Goux
202/647-5078   FAX 202/647-5939
Rm. 6800 (PA)

Office of Press Relations

Director
Mr. Lee McClenny
202/647-2492
Rm. 2109

Office of the Historian (PA/HO)
2401 E St., NW - Rm. L-409 / Washington DC 20520

Historian
Mr. William Z. Slany
202/663-1123   FAX 202/663-1289

Deputy Historian
Mr. David Patterson
202/663-1127   FAX 202/663-1289

General and European Division
Chief
Mr. David C. Humphrey
202/663-1142   FAX 202/663-1289

Arms Control and Economics Division
Chief
Mr. David Herschler
202/663-1145   FAX 202/663-1289

Asian and American Division
Chief
Mr. Edward Keefer
202/663-1131   FAX 202/663-1289

Declassification Coordination Division
Acting Chief
Ms. Rita Baker
202/663-1139   FAX 202/663-1289

Editing Division
Chief

Ms. Rita Baker
202/663-1139   FAX 202/663-1289

Middle Eastern and African Division
Chief
Ms. Harriet Schwar
202/663-1130   FAX 202/663-1289

Special Projects Division
Chief
Mr. Paul Claussen
202/663-1126   FAX 202/663-1289

Office of Public Communications (PA/PC)
2201 C Street, NW / Washington DC 20520

Director
Ms. Colleen Hope
202/647-6265   FAX 202/647-6738
Rm. 6805

Deputy Director
Mr. Peter Knecht
202/647-3512   FAX 202/647-6738
Rm. 6805

Office of Public and Intergovernmental Liaison (PA/PIL)

Director
Ms. Joan Colbert
202/647-5171
Rm. 5827 (PA/PIL)

Office of the Inspector General (OIG)

2201 C Street, NW / Washington DC 20520

INTRODUCTION

The Office of Inspector General (OIG) is an independent office that audits, inspects, and investigates the activities of all elements of the Department. The Inspector General reports directly to the Secretary and the Congress on the results of this work and makes recommendations to promote economy and efficiency and to prevent fraud, waste, and abuse in Department programs and operations.

Inspector General
Ms. Jacquelyn L. Williams-Bridgers
202/647-9450   FAX 202/647-7660
Rm. 6817 (OIG)

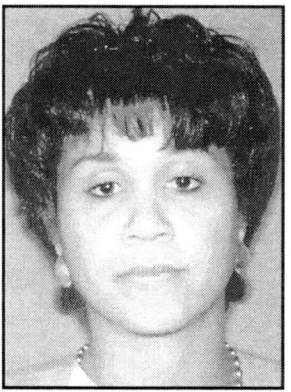

Personal: born 2/27/56 in Washington, D.C.

Education: B.A., and master's in public administration, Syracuse Univ.

Professional: 1983-84, staff, fraud control unit, U.S. Department of Housing and Urban Development. 1978-83 and 1984-94, evaluator, public housing programs and federal highway and bridge programs, U.S. General Accounting Office. 1995-present, inspector general, U.S. Department of State, U.S. Arms Control and Disarmament Agency (USACDA), and U.S. Information Agency (USIA).

As inspector general for the Department of State, USACDA, and USIA, Jacquelyn Williams-Bridgers directs and conducts inspections, investigations, and audits of the offices and bureaus of these three organizations.

Williams-Bridgers brings more than sixteen years of experience at the General Accounting Office and at the office of inspector general for the U.S. Department of Housing and Urban Development to her position.

At the General Accounting Office, she directed the design and reporting strategies for GAO evaluations of HUD's public housing programs and conceived and implemented a strategic plan for delivery of over 30 highway and bridge evaluations/analyses. She also was involved with congressional and intergovernmental relations, testifying at more than 15 congressional hearings.

Williams-Bridgers has received the Arthur S. Fleming Award and the General Accounting Office Meritorious Service Award in recognition of her skills and accomplishments.

Personal Assistant
Ms. Carol Johnson
202/647-9450
Rm. 6817

Counsel
Mr. John Duncan, Jr.
202/647-5059
Rm. 6817

Office of Audits
Assistant Inspector General
Mr. Mac MacDonald
202/6479567
Rm. 6817 (OIG/AUD)

Office of Inspections
Assistant Inspector General
Ms. Marilyn McAfee
202/647-9567
Rm. 6817 (OIG/ISP)

Office of Investigations
Assistant Inspector General
Mr. Robert S. Terjesen
202/647-9450
Rm. 6817 (OIG/INV)

Office of Security and Intelligence Oversight
Assistant Inspector General
Mr. Jon Wiant
202/647-9450
Rm. 6817 (OIG/SIO)

Office of Policy, Panning and Management
Assistant Inspector General
Mr. James K. Blubaugh
202/647-9450
Rm. 6817 (OIG/PPM)

Bureau of Administration (A)

2201 C Street, NW / Washington DC 20520

> ### INTRODUCTION
>
> *The Bureau of Administration (A) provides administrative support for the Department and overseas posts. Its responsibilities include both domestic and foreign building operations; acquisition management; supply and transportation; travel support for the White House; overseas schools assistance; establishing allowance rates; and providing translation, safety, and occupational health services.*
>
> *Other services include maintaining the Department's library, overseeing the printing of Department publications, and responding to requests under privacy acts and the Freedom of Information Act. The bureau also provides domestic and worldwide information services for the Department, which includes managing a secure global communications network and maintaining the Department's central automated data processing system.*

Assistant Secretary
Mr. Patrick F. Kennedy
202/647-1492   FAX 202/647-1558
Rm. 6330 (A)

Personal: born 6/22/49 in Chicago, Ill.

Education: B.A., Georgetown Univ., 1971.

Professional: entered the Foreign Service in 1973: 1973-74, regional admin. officer, Africa; 1975-76, personnel officer, bureau of African affairs; 1977-81, spec. asst., office of the under secretary for management; 1981-85, general services officer, U.S. Embassy in Paris; 1989-91, deputy exec. sec. to the Executive Secretariat; 1991-93, counselor for admin. affairs, U.S. Embassy in Cairo; 1993-present, asst. sec., bureau of administration; 1996-97, acting under secretary for management, Dept. of State.

Pat Kennedy entered the foreign service in 1973. Since then, he has served at posts in Europe and in Africa. He brings a broad range of knowledge and experience in international affairs and management to his current assignment as assistant secretary for the department's bureau of administration. The bureau manages the department's buildings and embassies and oversees administrative, publishing and technical services.

Kennedy has served in his current post since 1993 with one interruption. He served as acting under secretary for management for one year. While in that position, Secretary Albright appointed Kennedy to develop a plan to reorganize and integrate the U.S. Information Agency and the Arms Control and Disarmament Agency with the State Department. This plan was completed in 1997, and shortly after, Kennedy resumed his position as assistant secretary for the bureau of administration.

Kennedy's list of accolades includes the Distinguished Honor Award in 1988, the Group Superior Honor Award in 1989, and the award of Senior Performance pay since 1989.

Personal Assistant
Ms. Judith K. Adams
202/647-1492
Rm. 6330

CHINA 2000
Mr. Patrick Hayes
202/647-5630
Rm. 2906

Office of the Executive Director

Executive Director
Mr. Robert B. Dickson
202/647-8883   FAX 202/647-1302
Rm. 3800 (A/EX)

Office of the Procurement Executive
1700 North Ft. Myer Dr. / Arlington VA 20520

Procurement Executive
Mr. Lloyd W. Pratsch
703/516-1680
Rm. 603 (A/OPE)

Competition Advocate
Ms. Mary Ackerman
703/516-1697
Rm. 603 (A/OPE)

Office of Small and Disadvantaged Business Utilization
1700 North Ft. Myer Dr. / Arlington VA 20520

Operations Director
Mr. Durie N. White
703/875-6824   FAX 709/875-6825
Rm. 633 (A/SDBU)

Deputy Asst. Secretary for Foreign Buildings Operations
1700 North Ft. Myer Dr. / Arlington VA 20520

Deputy Assistant Secretary
Ms. Patsy L. Thomasson
703/875-6361   FAX 703/875-5043
Rm. 1309 (A/FBO)

Acquisitions and Planning Office
Director
Mr. Ronald B. Rabens
703/875-6358   FAX 703/875-5043
Rm. 1307 (A/FBO/AP)

Operations and Post Support Office
Director
Mr. Timothy E. Roddy
703/875-6350   FAX 703/875-5043
Rm. 1310 (A/FBO/OPS)

Art in Embassies Program

Ms. Gwen E. Berlin
202/647-5723   FAX 202/647-4080
Rm. B-258 (A/FBO/OPS/ART)

Deputy Assistant Secretary for Logistics

Deputy Assistant Secretary
VACANT
202/663-1990

Deputy Assistant Secretary for Operations
2201 C Street, NW / Washington DC 20520

Deputy Assistant Secretary
Mr. Vincent Chavirini
202/647-1638   FAX 202/647-7509
Rm. 1417 (A/OPR)

Office of Acquisitions
Acting Director
Ms. Betsy Murphy
703/875-6060   FAX 703/875-6085
Rm. 528 (A/OPR/ACQ)

Office of Language Services
Director
Ms. Brenda Sprague
202/647-1528   FAX 202/647-0749
Rm. 2214 (A/OPR/LS)

Office of Overseas Schools
3100 Clarendon Blvd. / Arlington VA

Director
Dr. Keith D. Miller
703/875-7800   FAX 703/875-7979
Rm. 245 (A/OPR/OS)

Africa
Dr. Joseph Carney
703/875-7975   FAX 703/875-7979
Rm. 245 (A/OPR/OS)

East Asia and Pacific
Dr. Beatrice Cameron
703/875-7975   FAX 703/875-7979
Rm. 245 (A/OPR/OS)

Canada, Near East and South Asia
Dr. Beatrice Cameron
703/875-7921   FAX 703/875-7979
Rm. 245 (A/OPR/OS)

Europe
Dr. Robert Spillane
703/875-7921   FAX 703/875-7979
Rm. 245 (A/OPR/OS)

Central America, Caribbean and Mexico
Dr. Salvatore J. Rinaldi
703/875-7977   FAX 703/875-7979
Rm. 245 (A/OPR/OS)

South America
Dr. William Scotti
703/875-7977   FAX 703/875-7979
Rm. 245 (A/OPR/OS)

Bureau of African Affairs (AF)

2201 C Street, NW / Washington DC 20520

> ### INTRODUCTION
> *The Bureau of African Affairs advises the Secretary and guides the operation of the U.S. diplomatic establishment in the countries of Sub-Saharan Africa.*

Assistant Secretary
Ms. Susan E. Rice
202/647-4440   FAX 202/647-6301
Rm. 6234A (AF)

Personal: born in Washington, DC.

Education: B.A. in history, Stanford Univ. M.A., and D.Phil., International Relations, Oxford Univ., England.

Professional: management consultant, McKinsey and Company (Toronto, Ontario). director for intl. organization affairs and peacekeeping, office of global issues and multilateral affairs, National Security Council. March 1995-August, 1997, special assistant to the President and sr. dir. for African affairs, National Security Council. August 1997-present, asst. sec. designate for African affairs, U.S. Dept. of State.

Dr. Susan E. Rice began her work for the Clinton National Security Council as director for international organization and peacekeeping with the office of global issues and multilateral affairs. In March of 1995, she became special assistant to the President and senior director for African affairs, replacing Donald K. Steinberg who accepted an African Ambassadorship.

In May of 1997, President Clinton nominated Rice to become assistant secretary of state for African affairs. She was replaced at the NSC in August by Ambassador Joseph C. Wilson. Rice was confirmed by the Senate on October 9, 1997.

The assistant secretary of State for African affairs is responsible for American foreign policy throughout the African region. He is the primary adviser to the secretary on developing and implementing U.S. policy toward sub-Saharan Africa. He also supervises interdepartmental and interagency matters dealing with the African region and chairs an interdepartmental group on the area in the National Security Council system.

Rice received her B.A. in history from Stanford University and attended Oxford University in England on a Rhodes scholarship. She received her M.A. and D.Phil. (Ph.D.) in international relations from Oxford, specializing in peacekeeping and conflict resolution in Africa. She then became a management consultant for McKinsey and Company in Toronto, Ontario.

Dr. Rice is a native of Washington, D.C. and attended the National Cathedral School for Girls.

Executive Secretary
Ms. Annette Bushelle
202/647-2530   FAX 202/647-6301
Rm. 6234A (AF)

Principal Deputy Assistant Secretary
Mr. Johnnie Carson
202/647-4493   FAX 202/647-6301
Rm. 6234A (AF)

478

Deputy Assistant Secretary
Ms. Vicki Huddleston
202/647-4485
Rm. 6234A

Office of the Executive Director

Executive Director
Mr. Steven A. Browning
202/647-1298   FAX 202/647-6805
Rm. 3517 (AF/EX)

Economic Policy Staff

Director
VACANT
202/647-3503   FAX 202/736-4583
Rm. 5242A (AF/EPS)

Commercial Coordinator
Ms. Ada S. Adler
202/647-3502
Rm. 5242A

International Economist
Mr. Anthony Woods
202/647-3503   FAX 202/736-4583
Rm. 5242A (AF/EPS)

International Economist
Mr. Aubrey Verdun
202/647-3502   FAX 202/763-4583
Rm. 5242A (AF/EPS)

Office of Regional Affairs

Director
Mr. Charles Snyder
202/647-6476   FAX 202/736-4872
Rm. 5232 (AF/RA)

Office of Central African Affairs
[Burundi, Cameroon, Central African Republic, Chad, Congo
(Brazzaville), Equatorial Guinea, Gabon, Rwanda, Sao Tome and
Principe, Zaire]

Director
Mr. Marc Baas
202/647-2080   FAX 202/647-1726
Rm. 4246 (AF/C)

Office of East African Affairs
[Ethiopia, Somalia, Djibouti, Kenya, Tanzania, Uganda, Eritrea,
Seychelles, Mauritius, Republic of Madagascar, Sudan, Comoros,
British Indian Ocean Territory, Diego Garcia]

Director
Mr. David Dunn
202/647-9742   FAX 202/647-0810
Rm. 5240 (AF/E)

Office of Southern African Affairs
[Angola, Botswana, Lesotho, Malawi, Mozambique, Namibia, South
Africa, Swaziland, Zambia, Zimbabwe]

Director
Mr. John Blaney
202/647-9836   FAX 202/647-5007
Rm. 4238 (AF/S)

Office of Francophone West African Affairs
[Benin, Burkina Faso, Côte D'Ivoire, Guinea, Mail, Cape Verde, The
Gambia, Ghana, Guinea-Bissau, Liberia, Nigeria, Sierra Leone,
Mauritania, Niger, Senegal, Togo, Western Sahara]

Director
Mr. Howard F. Jeter
202/647-2637   FAX 202/647-4855
Rm. 4250 (AF/W)

American Crisis Response
Initiative Interagency Working Group

Special Coordinator
Mr. Marshall F. McCallie
202/647-0111
Rm. 1802A

Bureau of Consular Affairs (CA)

2201 C Street, NW / Washington DC 20520

> **INTRODUCTION**
>
> *The Bureau of Consular Affairs (CA) assists American
> citizens traveling or living abroad and issues visas to
> foreign nationals who wish to visit or reside in the United
> States. The 13 passport agencies and one processing
> center—in the United States—and the U.S. posts overseas
> issue about 4 million passports each year. Annually, the
> Office of Overseas Citizens Services in the State
> Department monitors the cases of an estimated 2,500
> Americans arrested in other countries, responds to 21,000
> welfare and whereabouts inquiries, repatriates about 1,000
> U.S. citizens, assists about 3,000 returnees with family/
> friend prepaid trust funds, and deals with crises—such as
> hostage-taking and natural disasters.*

Assistant Secretary
Ms. Mary A. Ryan
202/647-9576   FAX 202/647-0341
Rm. 6811 (CA)

Personal: born in New York City, N.Y.

Education: B.A./M.A., St. John's Univ. (New York).

Professional: 1966-80, various positions at Dept. of State: rotational
officer (Naples, Italy); personnel officer (Tegucigalpa, Honduras);
consular officer, consulate general (Monterey, Mexico); roving
administrative officer for Africa and post management officer, bureau
of African affairs (Wash., D.C.); career development officer, bureau
of personnel (Wash., D.C.). 1980, administrative counselor, U.S.
Embassies at Abidjan and Khartoum; 1980-85, foreign service
inspector and the exec. dir., bureau of European and Canadian affairs;

1985-88, exec. asst. to the under secretary for management; 1988-90, U.S. Ambassador to Swaziland; 1990-92, principal dep. asst. sec., bureau of consular affairs and later, director, Kuwait Task Force; director of operations, United Nations Special Commission on the Elimination of Iraqi Weapons of Mass Destruction; dep. asst. sec. for European and Canadian affairs; 1993-present, asst. sec. for consular affairs, U.S. Dept. of State.

Mary Ryan was appointed assistant secretary of State for consular affairs on May 12, 1993. Ryan is responsible for the protection and welfare of American citizens and interests abroad, for the administration and enforcement of the provisions of the Immigration and Nationality Act, and for the issuance of passports for U.S. citizens and visas for foreigners overseas who desire to visit or emigrate to the United States.

Consular services are provided at more than two hundred and seventy embassies, consulates, and missions around the world to American citizens traveling or residing abroad and to foreigners who wish to visit this country. The bureau issues five million passports each year to U.S. citizens at home and abroad through its fourteen regional passport agencies and embassies and consulates abroad.

The consular officers overseas provide information on absentee voting, selective service registration, acquisition and loss of U.S. citizenship, recording the birth of more than 40,000 Americans born abroad each year, and arranging for the transfer of federal benefit payments. They also provide U.S. tax forms, notarize document and monitor child custody disputes. Annually, consular officers issue about seven million visas to foreign nationals coming to the United States.

Ryan is a career foreign service officer and one year prior to her appointment was promoted to career minister. Her career in the Foreign Service has taken her to Africa, Italy, Mexico, and to posts at the United Nations, the bureau of African affairs, the U.S. embassies in Abidjan and Khartoum, and the bureau of European and Canadian Affairs.

In 1992, Ryan received the Presidential Distinguished Service Award.

Personal Assistant
Ms. Laurie Major
202/647-9576
Rm. 6811

Principal Deputy Assistant Secretary
Ms. Donna Hamilton
202/647-9577
Rm. 6811

Office of the Executive Director

Executive Director
Mr. George Lannon
202/647-3118   FAX 202/647-3677
Rm. 4820A (CA/EX)

Deputy Assistant Secretary for Passport Services

Deputy Assistant Secretary
Mr. Kenneth Hunter
202/647-5366   FAX 202/647-0341
Rm. 6811 (CA/PPT)

Office of Passport Policy and Advisory Services
Acting Director
Mr. John M. Hotchner
202/955-0231

Recorded Passport Information
202/647-0518

Deputy Assistant Secretary for Visa Services

Deputy Assistant Secretary
Ms. Nancy Sambaiew
202/647-9584   FAX 202/647-0341
Rm. 6811 (CA/VO)

Office of Public and Diplomatic Liaison
2401 E Street. NW / Washington DC 20037
Mr. Pablo Barreyro
202/663-1213   FAX 202/663-3899
Rm. 7030 (CA/VO/P)

Recorded Visa Information
202/663-1225

Deputy Asst. Secretary for Overseas Citizens Services

Deputy Assistant Secretary
Ms. Donna Hamilton
202/647-9577   FAX 202/647-3732
Rm. 6811 (CA/OCS)

Citizens Emergency Center (Recorded Information)
202/647-5225
Managing Director
Ms. Katherine Peterson
202/647-9018   FAX 202/647-3632
Rm. 4811A (CA/OCS/EMR)

American Citizens Services Crisis Management
Director
Ms. Georgia Rogers
202/647-5225
Rm. 4811

Latin American and Caribbean Division
202/647-5118
Rm. 4811

European and Canadian Division
202/647-6178
Rm. 4800

Near East and South Asia Division
202/647-7899
Rm. 4811

African Division
202/647-6060
Rm. 4811

Office of Citizen Consular Services
Director
Mr. Carmen A. DiPlacido
202/647-3666   FAX 202/647-0103
Rm. 4817 (CA/OCS/CCS)

Recorded Information
202/736-7000
(CA/OCS/CCS)

African Services Division
202/647-4994
(CA/OCS/CCS/AF)

Inter-American Services Division
202/647-3712

(CA/OCS/CCS/ARA)

East Asian and Pacific Services Division
202/647-3675
(CA/OCS/CCS/EAP)

European Services Division
202/647-3445
(CA/OCS/CCS/EUR)

Near Eastern and South Asian Services Division
202/647-3926
(CA/OCS/CCS/NEA)

Bureau of Democracy, Human Rights & Labor (DRL)

2201 C Street, NW / Washington DC 20520

INTRODUCTION

The Bureau of Democracy, Human Rights, and Labor (DRL) oversees initiatives and policies to promote and strengthen democratic institutions, civil society, and respect for human and worker rights. The bureau ensures that human rights and labor conditions in foreign countries are taken into account in the U.S. policy-making process and submits an annual report to the Congress extensively reviewing human rights practices in each country. DRL's responsibilities include promoting democracy worldwide, formulating U.S. human rights policies and coordinating policy in human rights-related labor issues. It also provides in-country security briefings and threat assessments to business executives.

Assistant Secretary
Mr. John Shattuck
202/647-2126   FAX 202/647-5283
Rm. 7802 (DRL)

Education: B.A. (magna cum laude), Yale College, 1965. M.A. in international law and jurisprudence, Cambridge Univ., 1967. LL.B., Yale Law School, 1970.

Professional: 1970-71, law clerk, U.S. District Judge. 1971-76, national counsel, American Civil Liberties Union (Washington, D.C.). 1972, lecturer, Woodrow Wilson School, Princeton University. 1976-84, executive director, American Civil Liberties Union. 1984, vice president, Harvard Univ. 1986, lecturer, Harvard Law School. Later: senior associate for programs on science, technology and public policy, Kennedy School of Government, Harvard Univ. 1993-present, asst. sec. for democracy, human rights and labor, U.S. Dept. of State.

John Shattuck was sworn in as assistant secretary of the bureau of democracy, human rights and labor on June 2, 1993. As such, Shattuck is responsible for the development and implementation of U.S. policy relating to the observance of human rights throughout the world.

The bureau provides advice to the Immigration and Naturalization Service regarding applications for political asylum by foreign nationals. In addition, the bureau maintains liaison with nongovernmental organizations active in the human rights field and is principally responsible for the preparation of the annual department report on human rights practices in countries abroad.

Shattuck has spent most of his career as an administrator and academic. While at Harvard University, he was responsible for management, governmental relations, media relations, communications and public and community service activities for the university. He lectured on legislative and administrative process,

privacy law, and civil liberties. At the ACLU, Shattuck was in charge of directing relations with the U.S. Congress and executive branch agencies. As the ACLU's national counsel he was in charge of litigating in areas of privacy, government secrecy, and political surveillance.

Over the years, Shattuck has won a number of prestigious awards for his contributions to civil liberties and human rights, and for his commitment to public service. He won the H.L. Mencken Award from the Free Press Association in 1989, the Yale Law School Public Service Award in 1988, and the Roger Baldwin Award in 1984.

Shattuck is married to Ellen Hume and has four children.

Principal Deputy Assistant Secretary
Mr. Steven Coffey
202/647-2570
Rm. 7802 (DRL)

Deputy Assistant Secretary
Mr. Gare Smith
202/647-1780   FAX 202/647-5283
Rm. 7802 (DRL)

Sr. Coordinator for Democracy Promotion
Mr. David Yang
202/647-1180
Rm. 7802 (DRL)

Office of Bilateral Affairs

Director
Mr. Susan Keogh-Fisher
202/647-1716
Rm. 7802 (DRL/BA)

Office of Multilateral Affairs

Director
Mr. John Bargeron
202/647-1385   FAX 202/647-9519
Rm. 7802 (DRL/MLA)

Office of Labor and External Affairs

Director
Mr. James Ehrman
202/647-3663
Rm. 4827A (DRL/LEA)

Special Coordinator
Director
Ms. Alexandra Arriaga
202/647-1422
Rm. 7802

Office of Asylum Affairs
2430 E Street, NW / Washington DC 20520

Director
Mr. William M. Bartlett
202/776-8515   FAX 202/776-8528
Rm 104

Bureau of Diplomatic Security (DS)

2201 C Street, NW / Washington DC 20520

> ### INTRODUCTION
>
> *The Bureau of Diplomatic Security's (DS) regional security officers and engineers protect U.S. personnel and missions overseas, advising U.S. ambassadors on all security matters and establishing and maintaining an effective security program against terrorist, espionage, and criminal threats at U.S. diplomatic facilities. In the U.S., the bureau's special agents investigate passport and visa fraud, conduct personnel security investigations, issue security clearances, and provide protection for the Secretary of State and many visiting foreign dignitaries .*
>
> *The bureau helps foreign embassies and consulates in the U.S. protect their diplomats and facilities, manages the Counter-terrorism Rewards Program, and trains foreign civilian police under the Anti-Terrorism Assistance Program. It also chairs the Overseas Security Advisory Council, a joint venture between the Department and the U.S. private sector to exchange timely information on security problems with U.S. businesses.*

Assistant Secretary for Diplomatic Security

Acting Assistant Secretary
Mr. Patrick F. Kennedy
202/647-6290   FAX 202/647-0953
Rm. 6316 (DS)

Executive Assistant
Mr. Bob Brand
202/647-1496
Rm. 6316

Senior Policy Adviser
Mr. Gary Russell
202/647-0147
Rm. 6316

Principal Deputy Assistant Secretary for Diplomatic Security and Director for the Diplomatic Security Service

2121 Virginia Ave. NW / Washington DC 20037

Acting Deputy Assistant Secretary and Director
Mr. Peter Bergin
202/663-0473   FAX 202/663-0831
8th Fl.

Office of the Antiterrorism Assistance Program
Director
Mr. Burley P. Fuselier
202/663-0261
3rd Fl. (DS/DSS/ATA)

Office of Field Office Management
Director
Mr. Bernard J. Dougherty
202/663-0111
4th Floor

Office for Investigations and Counterintelligence
Acting Director
Mr. Thomas McKeever
202/663-0110
4th Floor

Office of Intelligence and Threat Analysis
Director
Mr. William D. Armor
202/663-0786
7th Floor

Office of Overseas Operations
Director
Mr. Robert P. O'Brien
202/663-0489
8th Fl. (DS/DSS/OP)

African Affairs Division
Division Chief
Mr. Alan Nathanson
202/663-0504   FAX 202/663-0565
8th Fl. (DS/OP/AF)

Inter-American Affairs Division
Division Chief
VACANT
202/663-0501   FAX 202/663-0565
8th Fl. (DS/OP/ARA)

East Asian And Pacific Affairs Division
Division Chief
Mr. Frank Juni
202/663-0527   FAX 202/663-0565
8th Fl. (DS/OP/EAP)

European and Canadian Affairs Division
Division Chief
Mr. Chris Leibengood
202/663-0508   FAX 202/663-0565
8th Fl. (DS/OP/EUR)

Near Eastern and South Asian Affairs Division
Division Chief
Mr. William L. Adams
202/663-0525
8th Fl. (DS/OP/NEA)

Office for Protection
Director
Mr. Robert Franks
202/663-0107

Overseas Security Advisory Council

> *The Overseas Security Advisory Council (OSAC) was established by the U.S. Department of State in 1985 to foster the exchange of information between American companies with overseas operations and the U.S. Government. Since that time, OSAC had developed into a successful joint venture and a dynamic vehicle for effective security cooperation.*
>
> *OSAC consists of 21 organizations from the private sector and four U.S. Government departments and agencies. There are 1,400-plus private sector organizations that participate in the Council's activities and are recipients of the information and guidance it provides.*
>
> *As part of its security program, OSAC has prepared publications containing suggested security and emergency planning guidelines for American private sector personnel and organizations abroad.*
>
> *Vice Chairman of OSAC and Manager of security is James A. Brooke of Exxon Company, International.*

Executive Director
Mr. Nicholas Proctor
202/663-0869   FAX 202/663-0868
8th Fl. (DS/DSS/OSAC)

Deputy Assistant Secretary for Countermeasures and Information Security

2121 Virginia Ave. NW / Washington DC 20037

Deputy Assistant Secretary
Mr. Wayne R. Rychak
202/663-0538   FAX 202/663-0653
8th Fl. (DS/CIS)

Office of the Diplomatic Courier Service
Director
Mr. Jerome M. Lafluer
202/663-0562   FAX 202/663-0653
3rd Fl. (DS/CIS/DC)

Office of Domestic Operations
2401 E Street, NW / Washington DC 20037
Acting Director
Mr. Donald E. Blake
202/663-1347
Rm. L309

Office of Information Security Technology
2121 Virginia Ave., NW / Washington DC 20037
Director
Mr. John Bainbridge
202/663-0561
8th Floor

Office of Physical Security Programs
1701 N. Ft. Myer Drive / Rosslyn VA 22209
Acting Director
Mr. Cliff Flowers
703/875-6525
8th Floor

Deputy Assistant Secretary for Foreign Missions
2201 C Street, NW / Washington DC 20520

INTRODUCTION

The Office of Foreign Missions (M/OFM) is responsible for oversight of foreign missions in the United States. It employs reciprocity to ensure equitable treatment for U.S. diplomatic and consular missions abroad and regulates selected activities of foreign missions in the United States to protect foreign policy and national security interests and to protect the public from abuses of diplomatic privileges and immunities by foreign mission members. It has regional offices in Chicago, San Francisco, New York, and Los Angeles.

Deputy Assistant Secretary
Mr. Thomas E. Burns, Jr.
202/647-3417
Rm. 2238

Office of Motor Vehicles, Tax and Customs
3507 International Place, NW / Washington DC 20008

Director
Ms. Kathleen Austin
202/895-3500
Rm. 216

Property and Travel Office
2201 C Street, NW / Washington DC 20520
Director
Mr. Richard C. Massey
202/647-4554
Rm. 2238

Executive Director for Diplomatic Security
2121 Virginia Ave. NW / Washington DC 20037
Executive Director
Mr. Robert Spencer
202/663-0660   FAX 202/663-0831
8th Fl. (DS/EX)

Office of Administration
Director
Ms. Joan A. Lewis
202/663-0031
3rd Floor

Office of Professional Development
2216 Gallows Road / Dunn Loring VA 22027
Director
Mr. Michael Beckner
703/204-6205
Rm. 340C

Office of Policy, Planning and Budget
2121 Virginia Ave. NW / Washington DC 20037
Director
Mr. Thomas G. McGrath
202/663-0478
8th Floor

Bureau of East Asian And Pacific Affairs (EAP)

2201 C Street, NW / Washington DC 20520

INTRODUCTION

The Bureau of East Asian and Pacific Affairs deals with U.S. foreign policy and U.S. relations with the countries in the Asia-Pacific region.

Assistant Secretary
Ambassador Stanley Owen Roth
202/647-9596   FAX 202/647-7350
Rm. 6205 (EAP)

Education: B.A., 1959. M.A., Fletcher School of Law and Diplomacy, 1960. Honorary Doctorates: Williams College, Tufts Univ., Dominican College, Bryant College.

Professional: 1979-82, leg. asst., Rep. Stephen Solarz. 1983-85, staff consultant, House Foreign Affairs Cmte. 1985-92, staff dir., subcommittee on Asian and Pacific affairs; 1993, director of committee liaison, House Committee on Foreign Affairs. 1993-94, deputy asst. sec. of defense for East Asia and Pacific affairs, U.S. Dept. of Defense. 1994-95, special assistant to the President and senior director for Asian affairs, National Security Council. 1996-97, director of research and studies, U.S. Institute of Peace. 1997-present, asst. sec. of state for East Asian and Pacific affairs, U.S. Dept. of State.

As assistant secretary of East-Asian and Pacific affairs, Stanley Owen Roth is responsible for advising the secretary on all countries in the region. He is also responsible for directing, coordinating and supervising interdepartmental and interagency matters involving these regions. He serves as chairman of interdepartmental groups in the National Security Council system where, along with other group members, he discusses, recommends, and implements National Security Council decisions.

Roth comes to his position with 20 years of foreign affairs experience, beginning as a staffer dealing with these issues in the House of Representatives. He began working on Asian and Pacific affairs specifically in the mid-1980s as the staff director for the House Subcommittee on Asian and Pacific Affairs. In 1993 and 1994 he was deputy assistant secretary of Defense for East Asia and Pacific affairs. Roth then was a special advisor to President Clinton and senior director for Asian affairs at the National Security Council. He left government service for one year before assuming his current position.

Personal Assistant
Ms. Debra Boyer
202/647-9596
Rm. 6205

Principal Deputy Assistant Secretary
Mr. Charles Kartman
202/736-4393   FAX 202/647-7350
Rm. 6205 (EAP)

Deputy Assistant Secretary
Ms. Aurelia E. Brazeal
202/647-6094   FAX 202/647-7350
Rm. 6205 (EAP)

Deputy Assistant Secretary
Ms. Susan L. Shirk
202/736-6910   FAX 202/647-7350
Rm. 6205 (EAP)

Coordinator for APEC
Mr. John S. Wolf
202/647-7266   FAX 202/647-7350
Rm. 6205 (EAP)

Sr. Adviser and Commercial Coordinator
Mr. Philip Yun
202/647-6904
Rm. 6205

Office of the Executive Director

Executive Director
Mr. Herbert W. Schulz
202/647-9054   FAX 202/647-6142
Rm. 4313A (EAP/EX)

Office of Australia, New Zealand, and Pacific Island Affairs

Director
Ms. Suzanne Butcher
202/736-4741   FAX 202/647-4402
Rm. 4313 A (EAP/ANP)

Office of Chinese and Mongolian Affairs

Director
Mr. Howard Lange
202/647-6803   FAX 202/647-6820
Rm. 4318 (EAP/CM)

Office of Economic Policy

Director
Mr. Jack Andre
202/647-4835   FAX 202/647-0136
Rm. 4210 (EAP/EP)

Office of Japanese Affairs

Director
Mr. Robert C. Reis
202/647-2913   FAX 202/647-4402
Rm. 4206 (EAP/J)

Office of Korean Affairs

Director
Mr. Mark Minton
202/647-7717   FAX 202/647-7388
Rm. 5313 (EAP/K)

Office of Public Affairs

Director
Mr. Kenneth Bailes
202/647-2538   FAX 202/647-0996
Rm. 5209 (EAP/P)

Office of Philippine, Indonesia, Malaysia, Brunei, and Singapore Affairs

Director
Mr. Douglas Hartwick
202/647-3276   FAX 202/736-4559
Rm. 5206 (EAP/PIMBS)

Office of Regional and Security Policy Affairs

Director
Ms. Pamela Slutz
202/647-1260
Rm. 4312 (EAP/RSP)

United Nations Adviser
Mr. Bruce Malkin
202/647-2722   FAX 202/647-0076
Rm. 4312 (EAP/RSP)

Political-Military Adviser
Mr. Alan G. Young
202/647-2399   FAX 202/647-0076
Rm. 4312 (EAP/RSP)

Office of Taiwan Coordination

Taiwan Coordination Adviser
Ms. Sylvia Stanfield
202/647-7711   FAX 202/647-0076
Rm. 4312 (EAP/RSP/TC)

Office of Burma, Cambodia, Laos, Thailand and Vietnam Affairs

Director
Ms. Marie Huntala
202/647-3132
Rm. 5210 (EAP/BCLTV)

Bureau of Economic and Business Affairs (EB)

2201 C Street, NW / Washington DC 20520

> **INTRODUCTION**
>
> *The Bureau of Economic and Business Affairs (EB) deals with issues of trade, international finance and development, energy, commodities, transportation, economic sanctions, and telecommunications policy. It also promotes U.S. business opportunities overseas.*

Assistant Secretary
Ambassador Alan P. Larson
202/647-7971   FAX 202/647-5713
Rm. 6828 (EB)

Education: B.A., Univ. of Iowa. M.A.,Univ. of Iowa. Ph.D., Univ. of Iowa.

Professional: 1973-75, economic officer, U.S. Embassy, Sierra Leone; 1975-77, economic officer, U.S. Embassy, Zaire; 1978-80, international economist, energy policy office; 1980-82, deputy director, energy policy office; 1982-84, counselor for economic and commercial affairs, U.S. Embassy, Jamaica; 1984-86, executive assistant to the under secretary of state for economic affairs;. 1986-87, deputy assistant secretary of state for international energy and resources policy; 1987-90, principal deputy assistant secretary of state for economic and business affairs; 1990-93, ambassador to the Organization for Economic Cooperation and Development, Paris; 1994-96, deputy assistant secretary for international finance and development; 1996-present, assistant secretary for economic and business affairs, U.S. Department of State.

Alan Larson became assistant secretary for economic and business affairs at the State Department in July of 1996. He is responsible for developing and implementing policy on the entire range of foreign economic matters, including trade, investment, telecommunications, aviation and maritime transport, energy, sanctions, finance, and development.

Prior to his appointment by President Clinton, Larson served as deputy assistant secretary for international finance and development for more than two years. In the early 1990's Larson served as American ambassador to the Organization for Economic Cooperation and Development in Paris. From 1987 until 1990, Larson was principal deputy assistant secretary of State for economic and business affairs. From 1986 to 1987 Larson served as deputy assistant secretary of State for international energy and resources policy. From 1984-86, he was the executive assistant to the under secretary of State for economic affairs.

Earlier in his career, Larson was counselor for economic and commercial affairs at the U.S. Embassy in Jamaica, an international economist in the State Department's energy policy office, and an economic officer in American embassies in Zaire and Sierra Leone.

Larson has B.A., M.A., and Ph.D. degrees from the University of Iowa. He has also attended Johns Hopkins School of Advanced International Studies. Larson is married and has three children.

Secretary
Ms. Ann Alexandrowicz
202/647-7727
Rm. 6828

Principal Deputy Assistant Secretary
Ms. Vonya McCann
202/647-5212
Rm. 4826 (EB)

Executive Staff

Executive Director
Mr. J. Scott Monier
202/647-2720   FAX 202/647-1888
Rm. 6820 (EB/EX)

International Finance and Development

Deputy Assistant Secretary
Ms. Barbara Griffiths
202/647-9496   FAX 202/647-0320
Rm. 3336 (EB/IFD)

Office of Development Finance
Director
Ms. Joyce Rabens
202/647-9426
Rm. 3245 (EB/IFD/ODF)

Office of Monetary Affairs
Director
Mr. Robert Deutsch
202/647-5935   FAX 202/647-7453
Rm. 3425 (EB/IFD/OMA)

Office of Investment Affairs
Director
Mr. Wesley Scholz
202/736-4247   FAX 202/647-0320
Rm. 3336 (EB/IFD/OIA)
Trade, Policy and Programs

Deputy Assistant Secretary
Mr. David Marchick
202/647-2532   FAX 202/647-1537
Rm. 3831A (EB/TPP)

Office of Bilateral Trade Affairs
Director
Ms. Robin White
202/647-4017
Rm. 3828 (EB/TPP/BTA)

Developed Country Trade Division
Chief
Mr. Chris Webster
202/647-1983   FAX 202/647-6540
Rm. 3822 (EB/TPP/BTA/DCT)

Developing Countries and Trade Organization Division
Chief
Mr. Anthony Interlandi
202/647-2324
Rm. 3829 (EB/TPP/BTA/ODC)

Office of Multilateral Trade Affairs
Director
Mr. William Craft
202/647-1310
Rm. 3831A (EB/TPP/MTA)

Special Trade Activities Division
Chief
Ms. Mary Jo Willis
202/647-8202
Rm. 3828 (EB/TPP/MTA/STA)

Intellectual Property and Competition Division
Chief
Mr. James McGlinchey
202/647-2777
Rm. 3828 (EB/TPP/MTA/IPC)

Office of Agricultural and Textile Trade Affairs

Director
Mr. Richard Miller
202/647-3090
Rm. 3526 (EB/TPP/ATT)

Deputy Director
Mr. Nicholas Riegg
202/647-1813   FAX 202/647-1894
Rm. 3526 (EB/TPP/ATT)

Textile Trade Policy and Agreements Division
Chief
Mr. Nicholas Riegg
202/647-1813
Rm. 3526 (EB/TPP/ATT/TEX)

Agricultural Trade Policy and Program Division
Chief
Ms. Amy Winton
202/647-1813
Rm. 3526 (EB/TPP/ATT/TPP)

Transportation Affairs

Deputy Assistant Secretary
Mr. Joel Spiro
202/647-4045   FAX 202/647-4324
Rm. 5830 (EB/TRA)

Office of Aviation Negotiations
Director
Mr. Richard Behrend
202/647-8350   FAX 202/647-8628
Rm. 5531 (EB/TRA/AN)

Office of Transportation Policy
Director
Mr. Russell LaMantia
202/647-5840   FAX 202/647-4324
Rm. 5828 (EB/TRA/AVP)

Energy, Sanctions, and Commodities

Deputy Assistant Secretary
Ambassador William Ramsay
202/647-1498   FAX 202/647-8758
Rm. 3529 (EB/ESC)

Office of International Energy and Commodity Policy
Director
Mr. William Weingarten
202/647-2875   FAX 202/647-4037
Rm. 3529 (EB/IEP)

Energy and Natural Resources Division
Chief
Mr. Stephen Mueller
202/647-3423   FAX 202/647-4037
Rm. 3535 (EB/IEP/ECC)

Energy Producer-Country Affairs Division

Chief
Mr. Stephen Gallogly
202/647-3036   FAX 202/647-4037
Rm. 3535 (EB/IEP/ECC)

Office of Economic Sanctions Policy
Director
Mr. David Moran
202/647-5673   FAX 202/647-4037
Rm. 3329 (EB/ESP)

International Communications and Information Policy

U.S. Coordinator and Deputy Assistant Secretary
Ms. Vonya McCann
202/647-5212   FAX 202/647-5957
Rm. 4826 (EB/CIP)

Senior Deputy U.S. Coordinator
Mr. Richard Beaird
202/647-5832   FAX 202/647-5957
Rm. 4826 (EB/CIP)

Bilateral and Regional Affairs
Deputy U.S. Coordinator
Mr. Edward Malloy
202/647-5220
Rm. 2529 (EB/CIP/TD)

Strategic Planning and Satellite Policy
Deputy U.S. Coordinator
Mr. Steven Lett
202/647-5832   FAX 202/647-5957
Rm. 4826 (EB/CIP)

Office of Multilateral Affairs
Deputy U.S. Coordinator
Mr. Richard Shrum
202/647-0050
Rm. 2529

Bureau of European and Canadian Affairs (EUR)

2201 C Street, NW / Washington DC 20520

INTRODUCTION

The Bureau of European and Canadian Affairs is responsible for developing coordinating, and implementing U.S. foreign policy on a variety of issues that deal with national security, economic prosperity, democracy, human rights, protection of the environment, halting the proliferation of weapons of mass destruction, and combating terrorism and international crime.

Assistant Secretary
Ambassador Marc Grossman
202/647-9626   FAX 202/647-0967
Rm. 6226 (EUR)

Personal: born 9/23/51.

Education: B.A., University of California. Msc., London School of Economics and Political Science.

Professional: 1976, joined Foreign Service. 1984-86, deputy director of the private office of the Secretary General of NATO. 1986-89, exec. asst. to dep. asst. sec. of state, bureau of political and military affairs; 1990-92, principal dep. asst. sec., bureau of political and military affairs; 1993-94, special asst. to the secretary of state and exec. sec.; 1994-97, U.S. Ambassador to Turkey; 1997-present, asst. sec. for European and Canadian affairs, U.S. Dept. of State.

Ambassador Marc Grossman was sworn in as assistant secretary of State for European and Canadian affairs on August 5, 1997. In this position, Grossman is responsible for formulating and implementing U.S. foreign policy over the broad range of political and economic issues affecting U.S. interests in Europe and Canada.

Grossman serves as the principal advisor to the secretary and under secretary of State for political affairs on these issues, including U.S. relations with NATO, the European Union, and the Conference on Security and Cooperation in Europe (CSCE). He supervises and manages the dozens of U.S. embassies and consulates in Europe and Canada and is responsible for coordinating with the Office of the Vice President, the National Security Council, the Department of Defense, and foreign governments.

Grossman has been a career foreign service officer since 1976. His most recent assignment, from November 1994 to June 1997, was as U.S. Ambassador to Turkey. Prior to this, he was special assistant to the secretary of State and executive secretary of the Department of State. Before assuming these duties, Grossman served as principal deputy assistant secretary of State for political military affairs. He was executive assistant to then deputy secretary of State John C. Whitehead from September 1986 to January 1989.

From 1984 to, 1986 Grossman was the deputy director of the private office of Lord Barrington, then secretary general of NATO. Other overseas assignments include tours as a political officer at the U.S. Mission to NATO and in Islamabad. In Washington he has also served as deputy special advisor to President Carter and in several capacities for the bureau of Near Eastern and South Asian affairs at State.

Grossman earned a B.A. from the University of California, Santa Barbara and an MSc. in International Relations from the London School of Economics and Political Science. He is married to Mildred Patterson, who is also a foreign service officer. They have a daughter, Anne.

Principal Deputy Assistant Secretary
Mr. E. Anthony Wayne
202/647-6402   FAX 202/647-0967
Rm. 6226 (EUR)

Deputy Assistant Secretary
Ms. Eileen Malloy
202/647-6415   FAX 202/647-0967
Rm. 6226 (EUR)

Deputy Assistant Secretary
Mr. James I. Gadsden
202/647-1126   FAX 202/647-0967
Rm. 6226 (EUR)

Deputy Assistant Secretary
Mr. Ronald D. Asmus
202/647-1622
Rm. 6226 (EUR)

Special Presidential Envoy
Amb. Richard C. Holbrooke

202/647-0684
Rm. 6226

Special Representative for Military Stabilization in the Balkans
Mr. James Pardew
202/647-2797
Rm. 5220

Special Coordinator for Cyprus
Mr. Thomas J. Miller
202/647-0684
Rm. 6511A

Coordinator for Eastern European Assistance
Mr. James Holmes
202/647-0853
Rm. 1420

Special Adviser to the President and Secretary of State
  for Economic Initiatives in Ireland
Mr. James M. Lyons
20/647-7721
Rm. 3240

Education: B.A., College of the Holy Cross. J.D., DePaul University College of Law.

Professional: 1971-97, attorney and then partner, Rothgerber, Appel, Powers & Johnson (Denver, Colo.). Sept. 1997-present, U.S. Special Advisor to the President and to the Secretary of State for Economic Initiatives for Ireland, U.S. Dept. of State.

In late September 1997, President Clinton named James Lyons to be the U.S. Special Advisor to the President and to the Secretary of State for Economic Initiatives for Ireland. In his new capacity, Lyons will coordinate the efforts of U.S. government agencies to further the President's and the Secretary of State's economic initiatives to support the peace process in Northern Ireland. Former Senate Majority Leader George Mitchell (D-Maine) held this post since 1995 until earlier this year when he joined the Washington, D.C. lobbying/law firm of Verner, Liipfert, McPherson and Hand.

At the time of the announcement, Lyons was a senior trial partner with the Colorado law firm of Rothgerber, Appel, Powers & Johnson. He joined the firm in 1971, concentrating his practice in complex business matters and litigation. His practice also involved international trade. He was named by the President in 1993 to be the U.S. Observer to the International Fund for Ireland (IFI). He worked actively to further the fund's objectives for the promotion of economic redevelopment and reconciliation in Ireland.

Listed in the *Best Lawyers in America,* Lyons is a fellow of the American College of Trial Lawyers and the International Academy of Trial Lawyers. He has been honored for his public service in Colorado by the Governor and the Colorado Supreme Court. Since 1995, he has served as a trustee of the University of Northern Colorado.

Lyons received a B.A. from the College of the Holy Cross and his law degree from DePaul University College of Law in Chicago.

American Outreach Staff

Special Adviser on Consular Policy for the NIS
Ms. Gladys Blouda
202/647-8956   FAX 202/647-3506
Rm. 4223 (EUR/AO)

Office of the Special Adviser, Bosnia Implementation

Special Adviser
Mr. David Dlouhy
202/647-1880
Rm. 6219

Office of Canadian Affairs

Director
Mr. Eric Kunsman
202/647-2170   FAX 202/647-4088
Rm. 5227 (EUR/CAN)

Office of Caucasus and Central Asian Affairs

Director
Mr. Stephen M. Young
202/647-9370   FAX 202/736-4710
Rm. 4217 (EUR/CASA)

Office of Eastern European Assistance

Coordinator
Mr. James Holmes
202/647-0853   FAX 202/647-0414
Rm. 1420 (EUR/EEA)

Office of European and Political Affairs

Director
Ms. Barbra Owens-Kirkpatrick
202/647-1626   FAX 202/647-1369
Rm. 6227 (EUR/RPM)

Office of European Union and Regional Affairs

Director
Mr. William Primosch
202/647-3932   FAX 202/647-9959
Rm. 6519 (EUR/ERA)

Office of the Executive Director

Executive Director
Mr. Donald S. Hays
202/647-5954   FAX 202/647-3507
Rm. 5428 (EUR/EX)

Office of German, Austrian and Swiss Affairs

Director
Ms. Ruth van Heuven
202/647-1484   FAX 202/647-5117
Rm. 4228 (EUR/AGS)

NIS Bilateral Commission and Global Issues

Senior Adviser
Ms. Neriss J. Cook
202/647-5728
Rm. 4219

Office of Nordic and Baltic Affairs

Director

Mr. Gillian Milovanovic
202/647-5669   FAX 202/736-4170
Rm. 5229 (EUR/NB)

Office of North Central European Affairs

Director
Mr. Jonathan Rickert
202/647-4136   FAX 202/736-4853
Rm. 5220 (EUR/NCE)

Office of Policy and Public Affairs

Director
Mr. Jeffrey C. Murray
202/647-6925   FAX 202/647-5116
Rm. 4513 (EUR/P)

Office of Policy and Regional Affairs

Director
VACANT
202/647-6729   FAX 202/647-3506
Rm. 4227 (EUR/CEN)

Office of Russian Affairs

Director
Mr. George Krol
202/647-9806   FAX 202/647-3506
Rm. 4223 (EUR/RUS)

Office of South Central European Affairs

Director
Mr. Jim Swigert
202/647-0608   FAX 202/647-0555
Rm. 5221 (EUR/SCE)

Office of Southeast European Cooperative Initiative

Director
Mr. Victor Jackovich
202/647-4114
Rm. 5314A

Office of Southern European Affairs

Director
Mr. Stephen Mull
202/647-6112   FAX 202/647-5087
Rm. 5511 (EUR/RPM)

Office of UK, Benelux, and Ireland Affairs

Director
Mr. Randy Bell
202/647-5687   FAX 202/647-3463
Rm. 4513 (EUR/UBI)

Office of Western European Affairs

Director
Ms. Shirley E. Barnes

202/647-3072   FAX 202/647-3459
Rm. 5226 (EUR/WE)

Office of Western Slavic and Moldovan Affairs

Director
Mr. Jack Segal
202/647-8671
Rm. 4227 (EUR/WST)

Bureau of Finance and Management Policy (FMP)

2201 C Street, NW / Washington DC 20520

INTRODUCTION

The Bureau of Finance and Management Policy (FMP) oversees the Department's worldwide financial and asset management activities. This includes establishing, maintaining, and enhancing management control policies, standards, and compliance guidelines as well as developing and operating an integrated system for accounting and financial management. The bureau develops annual budget requests to the Office of Management and Budget and Congress; monitors financial execution of the budget; and reviews, on a biennial basis, the fees, royalties, rents, and other charges imposed by the Department for goods and services it provides.

In addition to administering the Department's financial accounting and disbursement program, the bureau performs payroll services—such as foreign currency management and accounting, payroll, and fiscal records monitoring—and provides pension services for Foreign Service employees.

Chief Financial Officer
Mr. Richard L. Greene
202/647-7490   FAX 202/647-8194
Rm. 7427 (FMP)

Education: B.A. in economics, North Carolina State University, 1975. M.A. in public administration, George Washington University, 1978.

Professional: 1975-82, economic analyst, Department of Labor. 1983-89, financial management; 1989-93, associate comptroller, budget and planning; 1993-94, acting chief financial officer; August 1994-present, chief financial officer, U.S. Department of State.

Richard Greene became the chief financial officer (CFO) for the Department of State in August 1994. He had been acting CFO since July 1993. The CFO directs the activities of the bureau of finance

and management and serves as the department's budget officer and management control officer and assists in managing the department and its posts.

Greene is responsible for establishing effective management policies and internal controls; ensuring adequate systems to produce useful, reliable, and timely financial and related programmatic information; developing financial analysis and performance reports; and integrating budget execution and accounting functions.

Greene's government career began at the Department of Labor in 1975 as an economic analyst. He was responsible for the analysis of industry and business related information for economic significance at the state and local level and directed the compilation and analysis of labor market information for a major federal-state employment statistics program.

He moved to the Department of State in 1983. As a financial manager, he was responsible for all facets of the resource management process including financial planning, budget formulation, Congressional presentations, Congressional liaison and economic analyses. As associate comptroller with rank equivalent of deputy assistant secretary, Greene was responsible for the formulation, presentation, justification and execution of the Department's total budget of approximately $6 billion.

He has contributed articles to the Monthly Labor Review and his work has been cited in Business Week, the New York Times and the Wall Street Journal.

He was nominated by the Department of State for the 1992 and 1993 Presidential Rank Awards, SES Performance Awards, and the Meritorious Honor Awards.

Deputy Assistant Secretary for Budget and Planning
Ms. Kathleen J. Charles
202/647-8517
Rm. 1332

Deputy Assistant Secretary for Financial Services and Deputy CFO
Mr. Larry J. Eisenhart
202/875-6920
Rm. 4316

Office of the Executive Director
Mr. Ruben Torres
202/647-8675
Rm. 1802

Foreign Service Institute (M/FSI)
4020 Arlington Blvd. / Arlington VA 22204-1500

INTRODUCTION

The Foreign Service Institute (M/FSI) is the federal government's primary foreign affairs training institution. In addition to Department of State and foreign affairs community personnel, the Institute provides professional and job-related training to the employees of more than 40 other government agencies in more than 300 courses, including some 60 foreign languages, at its National Foreign Affairs Training Center.

Director
Ms. Ruth A. Davis
703/302-6703   FAX 703/302-7461
Rm. F2102 (M/FSI)

Office of the Executive Director
Executive Director
Ms. Catherine J. Russell
703/302-6729   FAX 703/302-7121
Rm. F2205 (M/FSI/EX)

Overseas Briefing Center
Director
Mr. Ray S. Leki
703/302-7266   FAX 703/302-7452
Rm. E2122 (M/FSI/OBC)

School of Language Studies
Dean
Ms. Carol Kay Stocker
703/302-7242   FAX 703/302-7254
Rm. F4415 (M/FSI/SLS)

School of Professional and Area Studies
Dean
Ms. Mary Virginia Kennedy
703/302-6940   FAX 703/302-6949
Rm. F4101 (M/FSI/SPS)

Bureau of Intelligence and Research (INR)

2201 C Street, NW / Washington DC 20520

INTRODUCTION

The Bureau of Intelligence and Research (INR), drawing on all-source intelligence, provides value-added independent analysis of events to Department policymakers; ensures that intelligence activities support foreign policy and national security purposes; and coordinates issues involving intelligence, security, and counterintelligence. INR's primary mission is to harness intelligence to serve U.S. diplomacy.

Assistant Secretary
Ambassador Phyllis E. Oakley
202/647-9177   FAX 202/736-4688
Rm. 6531 (INR)

Personal: born 1934 in Omaha, Neb.

Education: B.A. in political science (Phi Beta Kappa), Northwestern, Univ. Master's in international relations/affairs, Fletcher School of International Law and Diplomacy, Tufts Univ.

Professional: 1957-58, Foreign Service Officer. 1974, rejoined the Foreign Service: served in the bureau of international organization affairs; special assistant on the Middle East to Mr. Philip Habib, under secretary for political affairs; congressional and public affairs, Latin American bureau. 1979-82, assistant cultural affairs officer, Kinshasa, Zaire. 1982-85, Afghanistan desk officer, State Dept.

legislative management officer for the Near East and South Asia, bureau of legislative affairs. 9/85-6/86, Pearson Exchange Fellow, office of Sen. Charles Mathias.   11/86-1/89, deputy spokesperson, State Dept. 1989-91, Afghanistan Cross-Border Humanitarian Assistance Program, Islamabad, Pakistan. 1991-93, deputy assistant for regional analysis, bureau of intelligence research; 1993-94, senior dep. asst. sec. and acting dir., bureau for refugee programs; 1994-fall 1997, asst. sec. of state, Bureau of Population, Refugees, and Migration, U.S. Dept. of State. Fall 1997-present, asst. sec. of state, Bureau of Intelligence and Research, U.S. Dept. of State.

Phyllis Oakley, a career member of the Senior Foreign Service, was nominated by President Clinton in the summer of 1997 to a new post at state, head of the Bureau of Intelligence and Research. Until confirmed by the Senate in the fall, Oakley remained in her position of assistant secretary for the Bureau of Population, Refugees, and Migration, a post that she held since 1994.

Oakley first joined the State Department in 1957, but resigned a year later. Upon marrying fellow Foreign Service Officer, now-retired Ambassador Robert B. Oakley, Phyllis Oakley had to leave the department in accordance with regulations prohibiting married female officers in the Foreign Service. She was able to rejoin in 1974, and has worked at the State Department ever since.

Her distinguished career includes service in the bureau of international organization affairs, with the congressional and public affairs office in the Latin American bureau, as assistant cultural affairs officer in Kinshasa, Zaire, and in the bureau of legislative affairs as the legislative management officer for the Near East and South Asia. She has also been the State Department's Afghanistan desk officer and served as the department's deputy spokesperson from 1986 to 1989, the first woman to hold that position. She was on loan to AID for two years, working with the Afghanistan Cross-Border Humanitarian Assistance Program in Islamabad, Pakistan.

Oakley has received two Departmental Superior Honor Awards and the Intelligence Community's National Intelligence Medal of Achievement. She is a member of the Council on Foreign Relations. She and her husband have two grown children.

Principal Deputy Assistant Secretary
Mr. Edward G. Abington
202/647-7826
Rm. 6531

Deputy Assistant Secretary for Analysis
Mr. C. Thomas Finger
202/647-9633
Rm. 6531

Deputy Assistant Secretary for Intelligence Policy and Coordination
Ms. Jennifer E. Sims
202/647-7754
Rm. 6531

Office of the Executive Director

Director
Mr. Warrington E. Brown
202/647-1080   FAX 202/647-4296
Rm. 6639 (INR/EX)

Office of Analysis for Strategic and Military Issues

Director
Mr. Allen W. Locke
202/647-8216   FAX 202/647-4296
Rm. 6526 (INR/SPM)

Office of Analysis for Africa

Director
Mr. David Kaeuper
202/647-7331   FAX 202/647-4296
Rm. 4534 (INR/AA)

Central and East Africa Division
Chief
Mr. Dennis Linskey
202/647-7698
Rm. 4534

West and Southern Africa Division
Chief
Mr. Stanley Shaloff
202/647-7150
Rm. 4534

Office of Analysis for East Asia and the Pacific

Director
Ms. Paula Causey
202/647-1338   FAX 202/647-5286
Rm. 8840 (INR/EAP)

China Division
Chief
Mr. Robert Sutter
202/647-8082   FAX 202/647-5286
Rm. 8840 (INR/EAP/CH)

NE Asia Division
Chief
Mr. Robert L. Carlin
202/647-4766   FAX 202/647-5286
Rm. 8840 (INR/EAP/NA)

SE Asia Division
Chief
Ms. Paula Causey
202/647-1338   FAX 202/647-5286
Rm. 8647 (INR/EAP/SEA)

Office of Economic Analysis

Director
Mr. Stephen Ecton
202/647-2215   FAX 202/647-4296
Rm. 8722 (INR/EC)

Economic Security and Trade Division
Chief
Mr. David R. Konkel
202/647-4803
Rm. 8442

Economies in Transition Division
Chief
Mr. John T. Danylyk
202/647-8082   FAX 202/647-4296
Rm. 8442 (INR/EC/MT)

Office of Analysis for Europe and Canada

Director
Mr. Bowman H. Miller
202/647-9214
Rm. 4644 (INR/EUC)

Northern Europe and Regional Analysis Division

Chief
Mr. James Schollaert
202/647-5322   FAX 202/647-5334
Rm. 4741 (INR/EUC/NE)

Southern Europe Division
Chief
Mr. Robert W. Hansen
202/647-9289
Rm. 4743 (INR/EUC/SE)

Office of the Geographer and Global Issues

Director
Mr. William B. Wood
202/647-2021
Rm. 8742 (INR/GGI)

Cartography Support Staff
Acting Chief
Mr. Dan Kiser
202/647-2250
Rm. 8742 (INR/GGI/CBA)

Global Issues Division
Chief
Mr. Lee Schwartz
202/647-1988   FAX 202/647-5286
Rm. 8749 (INR/GGI/UNHC)

Office of Analysis for Inter-American Affairs

Director
Mr. Robert Homme
202/647-2229
Rm. 8727 (INR/IAA)

Middle America-Caribbean Division
Chief
Mr. David G. Smith
202/647-2229
Rm. 8666 (INR/IAA/MAC)

South America Division
Chief
Mr. James E. Buchanan
202/647-2229
Rm. 8727 (INR/IAA/SA)

Office of Analysis for Near East and South Asia

Director
Mr. Stephen Grumman
202/647-8661
Rm. 4634 (INR/NESA)

Arab-Israeli States Division
Chief
Mr. Tom Dowling
202/647-9446   FAX 202/647-5334
Rm. 4634 (INR/NESA/AI)

North Africa and Arabian Peninsula Division
Chief
Mr. Wayne White
202/647-9520   FAX 202/467-4269
Rm. 4634 (INR/NESA/NA)

South Asia Division
Acting Chief
Mr. Walter Andersen
202/647-5345   FAX 202/647-4296
Rm. 4634 (INR/NESA/SOA)

Office of Analysis for Russia and Eurasia

Director
Mr. Louis D. Sell
202/647-5642
Rm. 4758 (INR/REA)

Regional Analysis and Eastern Republics Division
Chief
Mr. John Parker
202/647-8034   FAX 202/647-1464
Rm. 4846 (INR/REA/REA)

Russia Domestic Affairs Division
Chief
Mr. Jack Sontag
202/647-9204
Rm. 4843 (INR/REA/RD)

Foreign Policy and Western Republics Division
Chief
Mr. Wayne Limberg
202/647-9201
Rm. 4754 (INR/REA/WR)

Office of Intelligence Liaison

Director
Mr. Allen Keiswetter
202/647-1505
Rm. 6635 (INR/IL)

Office of Intelligence Coordination

Director
Mr. Kenneth A. Ducan
202/647-7679
Rm. 6751 (INR/IC)

Office of Intelligence Resources

Director
Ms. Joan H. Downs
202/647-1344
Rm. 2737A (INR/IRE)

Office of Analysis for Terrorism, Narcotics and Crime

Director
Mr. Mark Steinitz
202/647-6812   FAX 202/647-5062
Rm. 6510 (INR/TNC)

Bureau of Inter-American Affairs (ARA)

2201 C Street, NW / Washington DC 20520

> ### INTRODUCTION
> *The Bureau of Inter-American Affairs advises the Secretary and guides the operation of the U.S. diplomatic establishment in Latin America and the Caribbean.*

Mr. Jeffrey Davidow
202/647-5780   FAX 202/647-0791
Rm. 6263 (ARA)

Personal: born 1/26/44 in Boston, Mass..

Education: B.A., Univ. of Mass., 1965. M.A., Univ. of Minnesota, 1967.

Professional: 1969, entered the foreign service. 1972-74, political officer, Foreign Service in Santiago, Chile. 1974-76, political officer in Capetown and Pretoria, South Africa; 1976-78, South African desk officer, Dept. of State. 1978-79, congressional fellow. 1979-82, head, U.S. liaison office, U.S. Embassy in Harare, Zimbabwe. 1982-83, fellow, Center for International Affairs, Harvard Univ. 1983-85, director, office of regional affairs; 1985-86, director, office of South African affairs; 1986-88, deputy chief of mission, Caracas, Venezuela; 1988-90, ambassador to Zambia; 1990-93, principal deputy asst., African bureau; 1993-96, ambassador to Venezuela; 1996-present, assistant secretary for inter-American affairs, U.S. Dept. of State.

Jeffrey Davidow was sworn in as assistant secretary for inter-American affairs on August 7, 1996. Ambassador Davidow has spent much of his 27-year career focusing on Latin America. He has served in American embassies in Guatemala and Chile and was the deputy chief of mission of the U.S. Embassy in Caracas from 1986 to 1988. He returned to Venezuela as ambassador in September 1993, and became acting assistant secretary for inter-American affairs in May 1996 as which he served until his confirmation.

As assistant secretary for inter-American affairs, Davidow is responsible for keeping Secretary Albright abreast of developments as well as directing U.S. diplomatic establishments in this region. He also chairs an interdepartmental group in the National Security Council. He works closely with representatives in his region to strengthen social, economic, and political relations. In addition to his responsibilities as assistant secretary, President Clinton nominated Davidow on September, 1997 to be a member of the board of directors of the Inter-American Foundation for a term expiring September 20, 2002.

Davidow was ambassador to Zambia from 1988 to 1990 and principal deputy assistant secretary in the State Department's African bureau from 1990 to 1993. He participated in peace negotiations in southern Africa and is the author of a number of articles and a book on the process of negotiations.

Davidow graduated from the University of Massachusetts in 1965, the University of Minnesota in 1967, and studied at Osmania University in Hyderabad, India, in 1968 and 1969. While in the Foreign Service, he spent one year as a fellow of the American Political Science Association working as a congressional staff aide in 1979 and another year as a fellow at the Center for International Affairs at Harvard University in 1982.

Davidow is married to the former Joan Labuzoski.

Secretary
Ms. Celestina Renteria
202/647-5780
Rm. 6263

Principal Deputy Assistant Secretary for South America
Mr. Peter F. Romero
202/647-8387   FAX 202/647-0791
Rm. 6263 (ARA)

Deputy Assistant Secretary for Regional Economic
   and Summit Coordination, and Mexican Affairs
Mr. Bryan Samuel
202/647-6754   FAX 202/647-0791
Rm. 6263 (ARA)

Deputy Assistant Secretary for Central America, Caribbean and Cuba
Mr. John Hamilton
202/647-8562   FAX 202/647-0791
Rm. 6263 (ARA)

Special Haiti Coordinator
Mr. David N. Greenlee
202/647-8369
Rm. 6263

Office of the Executive Director

Executive Director
Mr. Robert B. Nolan
202/647-3318   FAX 202/647-0949
Rm. 3909 (ARA/EX)

Permanent Mission of the United States of America to the Organization of American States

U.S. Permanent Representative
Ambassador Victor Marrerro
202/647-9376   FAX 202/647-0911
Rm. 6494 (ARA)

NOTE: See profile under the OAS entry in the Quasi-Official &
Intergovernmental, Section of this book.

Deputy United States Permanent Representative
Ms. Sarah Horsey-Barr
202/647-9422   FAX 202/647-0911
Rm 6494 (ARA)

Office of Policy Planning Coordination and Press

Director
Ms. Roberta Jacobson
202/647-9492
Rm. 6913 (ARA/PPC/P)

Office of Press and Public Affairs

Press and Public Affairs Officer
Mr. Michael Hahn
202/647-4252   FAX 202/647-4551
Rm. 6914 (ARA/P)

Office of Summit Coordinating Economic Policy

Director
Ambassador Richard Brown

202/736-7531
Rm. 3250 (ARA/EPSC)

Deputy Director, Summit Coordinating

Mr. Christian Kennedy
202/647-0746
Rm. 3250 (ARA/SCO)

Office of Andean Affairs

Director
Mr. David Passage
202/647-1715   FAX 202/647-2628
Rm. 5906 (ARA/AND)

Office of Brazilian and Southern Cone Affairs

Director
Mr. David F. Rogus
202/647-2407   FAX 202/736-4475
Rm. 5911 (ARA/BSC)

Office of Caribbean Affairs

Director
Mr Peter Reams
202/647-5088
Rm. 4906 (ARA/CAR)

Office of Cuban Affairs

Director
Mr. Michael Ranneberger
202/647-9273   FAX 202/736-4476
Rm. 3250 (ARA/CCA)

Office of Central American Affairs and Panamanian Affairs

Director
Mr. Don McConville
202/647-4010   FAX 202/647-2597
Rm. 4915 (ARA/CEN/PAN)

Belize
Desk Officer
Ms. Mary Sue Conaway
202/647-3482
Rm. 4915 (ARA/CEN/PAN)

Costa Rica
Desk Officer
Mr. Brad Johnson
202/647-3518   FAX 202/647-2597
Rm. 4915 (ARA/CEN/PAN)

El Salvador
Desk Officer
Mr. John Feeley

202/647-3505
Rm. 4915 (ARA/CEN/PAN)

Guatemala
Desk Officer
Ms. Elie Kleinwaks
202/647-3559
Rm. 4915 (ARA/CEN/PAN)

Honduras
Desk Officer
Mr. Bill Meara
202/647-0087
Rm. 4915 (ARA/CEN/PAN)

Nicaragua
Desk Officer
Mr. David Alarich
202/647-3727   FAX 202/647-2597
Rm. 4915 (ARA/CEN/PAN)

Desk Officer
Ms. Debra Heviah
202/647-1510   FAX 202/647-2597
Rm. 4915 (ARA/CEN/PAN)

Panama
Desk Officer
Mr. David Noble
202/647-3549   FAX 202/647-2597
Rm. 4915 (ARA/CEN/PAN)

Desk Officer
Ms. Mary Burnicle
202/647-4984   FAX 202/647-2597
Rm. 4915 (ARA/CEN/PAN)

Desk Officer
Ms. Karen Gallegos
202/647-3519   FAX 202/647-2597
Rm. 4915 (ARA/CEN/PAN)

Office of Mexican Affairs

Director
Amb. John P. Leonard
202/647-9894   FAX 202/647-5752
Rm. 4258 (ARA/MEX)

U.S.-Mexico Border Affairs Unit

Border Coordinator
Ms. M. Elizabeth Swope
202/647-8529   FAX 202/647-5752
Rm. 4258

Border Liaison Officer
Mr. Sean Murphy
202/647-8529   FAX 202/647-5752
Rm. 4258

International Boundary and Water Commission (IBWC)

Officer in Charge
Mr. Paul E. Storing
202/647-8529   FAX 202/647-5752
Rm. 4258

Bureau of International Narcotics and Law Enforcement Affairs (INL)

2201 C Street, NW / Washington DC 20520

INTRODUCTION

The Bureau for International Narcotics and Law Enforcement Affairs (INL) works with foreign governments to increase awareness of the importance of global narcotics control. It coordinates efforts with other governments and international organizations to halt the flow of illegal drugs into the United States by providing assistance to foreign governments to: eradicate narcotics crops, destroy illicit laboratories, train interdiction personnel, and develop education programs to counter drug abuse by their populations.

The bureau also has an international criminal justice office, dedicated to development and coordination of U.S. policy on: combating international organized crime's involvement in financial crime and illicit drug trafficking, strengthening judicial institutions and assisting foreign law enforcement agencies, and coordination with the UN. The office is the principal point of contact and source of advice for the Office of Management and Budget, the National Security Council, and the White House Office of National Drug Control Policy on international narcotics matters.

Assistant Secretary
VACANT
202/647-8464   FAX 202/736-4885
Rm. 7333 (INL)

Personal Assistant
Ms. Kay A. Burrell
202/647-8464
Rm. 7333

Principal Deputy Assistant Secretary
Mr. R. Rand Beers
202/647-6642   FAX 202/736-4885
Rm. 7333 (INL)

Acting Deputy Assistant Secretary
Ms. Jane Becker
202/647-6642   FAX 202/736-4885
Rm. 7333 (INL)

Deputy Assistant Secretary
Mr. Jonathan M. Winer
202/647-6643   FAX 202/736-4885
Rm. 7333 (INL)

Office of the Controller/Executive Director
2430 E Street, NW / Washington DC 20520

VACANT
202/776-8750
1st Floor (INL/RM)

Office of Latin America Programs
2201 C Street, NW / Washington DC 20520

Director
Ms. Patricia Hall

202/647-9090
Rm. 7811 (INL/LP)

Deputy Director
Mr. William McGlynn
202/647-8727
Rm. 7811 (INL/LP)

Office of AS/AF/EUR and Multilateral Programs
2430 E Street, NW / Washington DC 20520

Director
Mr. Daniel Fantozzi
202/776-8746   FAX 202/776-6780
Rm. 144 (INL/LP)

Deputy Director
Ms. Judith Strotz
202/647-5092   FAX 202/766-6870
Rm 144 (INL/LP)

Office of Policy, Planning and Coordination
2201 C Street, NW / Washington DC 20520

Director
Mr. Charles L. English
202/647-0457
Rm. 7334 (INL/PC)

Office of EUR/NIS Programs
2201 C Street, NW / Washington DC 20520

Director
Mr. Gary Alexander
202/736-4551   FAX 202/736-4515
Rm. 5819 (INL/ENT)

Bureau of International Organization Affairs (IO)

2201 C Street, NW / Washington DC 20520

INTRODUCTION

The bureau of international organization affairs provides guidance and support for U.S. participation in international organizations and conferences. It leads in the development, coordination, and implementation of U.S. multilateral policy. The bureau formulates and implements U.S. policy toward international organizations, with particular emphasis on those organizations which make up the United Nations system.

Assistant Secretary
Mr. Princeton Lyman
202/647-9600   FAX 202/736-4116
Rm. 6323 (IO)

Personal: born 11/20/35.

Education: B.A., Univ. of California, Berkeley, 1957. Ph.D., Harvard Univ., 1961.

Professional: 1961, entered government service. 1976-78, director, Agency for International Development in Ethiopia. 1981-86, deputy asst. secretary, Africa bureau; 1986-89, U.S. Ambassador to Nigeria; 1989-92, director, bureau of refugee programs; 1992-95, U.S. Ambassador to South Africa; 1996-present, asst. secretary for international organization affairs, U.S. Dept. of State.

As assistant secretary for international organization affairs, Princeton Lyman is responsible for formulating and implementing U.S. policies with respect to the UN and other international organizations. On UN issues, he works with the U.S. mission to the UN. The bureau provides guidance and support for U.S. participation in international organizations and conferences. It is also charged with developing policies and programs, and administering U.S. contributions to more than 40 international organizations to which the U.S. belongs.

Lyman also recommends the U.S. annual contributions for these organizations, both assessed and voluntary, and testifies before Congress on these recommendations and other program issues. The top priority for the current year is to reach agreement with Congress on the payment of approximately $1 billion in U.S. arrears to these organizations, to agree on what reforms need to be pursued within those organizations, and to negotiate agreement on these matters with the other member states. Within the UN, Lyman and others charged with responsibility for these matters, pursue greater efficiency, budget discipline, and more effective program delivery in the areas of economic development, human rights, the environment, and the control of international crime and drug trafficking.

In the specialized agencies, Lyman and his colleagues also seek to assure a fair and level playing field for U.S. exports, to establish humane standards for child labor and living wages through the International Labor Organization, and to establish standards for trade within Europe by the Economic Commission for Europe.

Lyman has published several foreign policy articles and received the President's Distinguished Service Award. He is married to Helen Ermann and has three daughters.

Special Assistant
Ms. R.P. Eddy
202/736-4348
Rm. 6323 (IO)

Principal Deputy Assistant Secretary
Ms. Molly K. Williamson
202/647-9602
Rm. 6323 (IO)

Deputy Assistant Secretary
Mr. E. Michael Southwick

202/647-9604   FAX 202/736-4116
Rm. 6323 (IO)

Deputy Assistant Secretary
Mr. Michael A. Sheehan
202/647-9431   FAX 202/736-4116
Rm. 6323 (IO)

Office of the Executive Director

Executive Director
Ms. Julee A. Brand
202/647-9326
Rm. 1509

Office of UN Political Affairs

Director
Mr. William Imbrie, III
202/647-2392   FAX 202/647-0039
Rm. 6334 (IO/UNP)

Office of Peacekeeping and Humanitarian Operations

Director
Mr. Edmund J. Hull
202/736-7733   FAX 202/647-0046
Rm. 5323 (IO/PHO)

Office of Economic and Social Affairs

Acting Director
Mr. John P. McGuinness
202/647-3886   FAX 202/647-4628
Rm. 5333 (IO/ESA)

Officer-in-Charge of Human Rights Affairs
Ms. Beverly Zweiben
202/647-1155
Rm. 5331 (IO/ESA)

Officer-in-Charge of UNCTAD
Mr. Frank John Kerber
202/647-1654
Rm. 5331 (IO/ESA)

Officer-in-Charge of International Women's Affairs
Ms. Sharon B. Kotok
202/647-3901   FAX 202/647-4628
Rm. 5333 (IO/ESA)

Officer-in-Charge of Social Issues
Ms. Jocelyn Gilbert Breeland
202/647-1155
Rm. 5331 (IO/ESA)

Office of Technical Specialized Agencies

Director
Mr. John S. Blodgett
202/647-1044
Rm. 5336 (IO/T)

Office of International Development Assistance

Director
Mr. Ralph E. Bresler
202/647-1269   FAX 202/736-7467
Rm. 5328 (IO/D)

Office of Policy, Public and Congressional Affairs

Director
Mr. Geoffrey W. Chapman
202/647-7857
Rm. 4334A (IO/PPC)

Office of UN System Administration

Director
Ambassador John Sprott
202/647-6424   FAX 202/736-7320
Rm. 4808 (IO/S)

Office of International Conferences

Director
Mr. Frank R. Provyn
202/647-6875   FAX 202/647-1301
Rm. 1517 (IO/OIC)

Office of the Legal Adviser
2201 C Street, NW / Washington DC 20520

> ### INTRODUCTION
>
> *The legal adviser at the Department of State, is the principal adviser to the secretary and through the secretary, to President Clinton, on all matters of international law arising in the conduct of U.S. foreign relations. The legal adviser also provides general legal advice and services to the secretary and other officials of the Department of State on matters with which the department and overseas posts are concerned.*

Legal Adviser
Mr. David R. Andrews
202/647-9598   FAX 202/647-1037
Rm. 6423 (L)

Personal: born 1/4/42 in Oakland, Calif.

Education: B.A. in economics, University of California, Berkeley, 1968. J.D., University of California, Berkeley, 1971.

Professional: 1971-75, associate, McCutchen, Doyle, Brown & Enersen. 1975-77, regional counsel, Region IX, (San Francisco, Calif.); 1977-80, legal counsel & special asst. for policy, U.S. Environmental Protection Agency (Wash., D.C.). 1980-81, principal deputy general counsel, U.S. Dept. of Health and Human Services. 1981-84, associate; 1985-91, managing partner of Wash., D.C. office and chairman of environmental and natural resources practice group; 1991-94, chairman; 1995-97, partner and chairman of environmental, natural resources and land use practice group, McCutchen, Doyle, Brown & Enersen. 1997-present, legal adviser, U.S. Dept. of State.

The Senate confirmed David Andrews as the State Department's legal adviser on July 31, 1997. Andrews brings a wealth of legal experience from both the public and private sectors to his post. He comes to the State Department directly from private practice as partner and chairman of the environmental, natural resources and land use practice group at McCutchen, Doyle, Brown & Enersen. During the 1970's and early 1980's he served in various positions at the U.S. Environmental Protection Agency and the Department of Health and Human Services.

The legal adviser is the principal adviser on all legal matters domestic and international to the Department of State, including the Foreign Service and diplomatic and consular posts abroad. The legal adviser is also the principal adviser on legal matters relating to the conduct of foreign relations to other agencies and, through the Secretary of State, to the President and the National Security Council.

The legal adviser's responsibilities encompass all domestic legal aspects of the operations of the State Department, including compliance with statutory and administrative requirements, as well as all domestic and international affairs which pose important legal questions, such as relations with foreign countries, economic affairs, legislative and administrative matters, international organization affairs, problems in connections with the use of force and laws of armed conflict, international adjudication, human rights, law enforcement and intelligence, oceans and environmental matters, treaty matters, and international obligations regarding the personal and private rights of aliens in the United States and of American citizens in foreign countries.

Andrews was the first African-American to chair a major U.S. law firm. He was also founder and chairman of his firm's environmental practice group and had an active international practice that involved counseling several Asian countries on the structure of their environmental laws.

In addition to the number of educational and civil rights boards and advisory groups that he served on, Andrews was also a member of the board of directors of Kaiser Permanente, the largest non-profit health maintenance organization in the world; a member of the board of trustees of the Marin Community Foundation, the fourth largest community foundation in the country; and a member of the board of directors of the San Francisco Museum of Modern Art.

Principal Deputy Legal Adviser
Mr. Michael J. Matheson
202/647-8460
Rm. 6423

Deputy Legal Adviser
Mr. James H. Thessin
202/647-8460
Rm. 6423

Deputy Legal Adviser
Ms. Jamison M. Borek Selby

202/647-7942
Rm. 6423

Deputy Legal Adviser
Mr. Jonathan B. Schwartz
202/647-5036
Rm. 6423

Counselor on International Law
VACANT
202/647-7990
Rm. 6423

Office of the Executive Director

Executive Director
Mr. Robert J. McCannell
202/647-8323
Rm. 5519

Assistant Legal Advisers
2201 C Street, NW / Washington DC 20520

African Affairs
Mr. Ted A. Borek
202/647-4110   FAX 202/736-7115
Rm. 6420 (L/AF)

Buildings and Acquisitions
1701 N. Ft. Myer Dr. / Rosslyn VA 22209
Mr. Dennis J. Gallagher
703/516-1535   FAX 703/516-1547
Rm. 610 (L/BA)

Consular Affairs
2201 C Street, NW / Washington DC 20520
Ms. Catherine Brown
202/647-4415
Rm. 5527A (L/CA)

International Claims and Investment Disputes
2430 E Street, NW / Washington DC 20520
Mr. Ronald J. Bettauer
202/776-8360   FAX 202/776-8389
Rm. 205 (L/CID)

Diplomatic Law and Litigation
Ms. Linda Jacobson
202/647-1074
Rm. 5420 (L/DL)

East Asian and Pacific Affairs
Mr. James G. Hergen
202/647-3044   FAX 202/736-7559
Rm. 5527A (L/EAP)

Economic and Business Affairs
Ms. Joan E. Donoghue
202/647-5242   FAX 202/736-7115
Rm. 6420 (L/EBC)

Employment Law
Ms. Melinda P. Chandler
202/647-4646
Rm. 3422 (L/EMP)

Ethics
VACANT
202/647-6668
Rm. 5425 (L/Ethics)

European and Canadian Affairs
Mr. Timothy E. Ramis
202/647-6295   FAX 202/736-7784
Rm. 5515A (L/EUR)

Human Rights and Refugees
Mr. David P. Stewart
202/647-4065   FAX 202/736-7116
Rm. 3422 (L/HRR)

Inter-American Affairs
Mr. T. Michael Peay
202/647-6328   FAX 202/736-7784
Rm. 5515A (L/ARA)

Law Enforcement and Intelligence
Mr. Samuel M. Whitten
202/647-7324   FAX 202/647-4802
Rm. 5419A (L/LEI)

Legislation and General Management
Mr. D. Stephen Mathias
202/647-5154
Rm. 5425 (L/LM)

Near Eastern and South Asian Affairs
Ms. JoAnn Dolan (ACTING)
202/647-4446   FAX 202/736-7116
Rm. 3422 (L/NEA)

Oceans, International Environmental and Scientific Affairs
Ms. Susan Biniaz and Mr. Robert K. Harris
202/647-1370
Rm. 6420 (L/OES)

Private International Law
2430 E Street, NW / Washington DC 20520
Mr. Jeffrey D. Kovar
202/776-8420   FAX 202/776-8482
Rm. 356 (L/PIL)

Political-Military Affairs
2201 C Street, NW / Washington DC 20520
Mr. Todd F. Buchwald
202/647-7838 (L/PM)
Rm. 6429

Treaty Affairs
Assistant Legal Adviser
Mr. Robert E. Dalton
202/647-2044   FAX 202/736-7541
Rm. 5420 (L/T)

United Nations Affairs
Assistant Legal Adviser
Mr. John R. Crook
202/647-2767   FAX 202/736-7028
Rm. 3422 (L/UNA)

Bureau of Legislative Affairs (H)

2201 C Street, NW / Washington DC 20520

INTRODUCTION

The Bureau of Legislative Affairs (H) serves as liaison between the State Department and the Congress. The bureau performs a critical role in advancing the President's and the Department's legislative agenda in the area of foreign policy.

Assistant Secretary
Ms. Barbara M. Larkin
202/647-4204   FAX 202/647-2762
Rm. 7261 (H)

Personal: born 7/26/51 in Dubuque, Iowa.

Education: B.A. (magna cum laude), Clarke College, 1973. J.D., Univ. of Iowa, 1977.

Professional: 1973, legislative aide, Iowa State Senate. 1974, campaign coordinator, Blouin for Congress. 1974-76, legislative assistant, Congressman Michael T. Blouin (D-Iowa). 1977-78, staff attorney, N.C. Dept. of Insurance. 1978-83, associate, Sanford, Adams, McCullough & Beard. 1986-92, leg. asst. and counsel, Senator Terry Sanford (D-N.C.). 1992-93, leg. dir. and counsel, Senator Diane Feinstein (D-Calif.). 1993-97, dep. asst. sec. for leg. affairs; 1997-present, asst. sec., bureau of legislative affairs, U.S. Dept. of State.

After serving for four years as deputy assistant secretary for legislative affairs, Barbara Larkin became assistant secretary for legislative affairs at the U.S. State Department in 1997. In this capacity Larkin is responsible for supervising and coordinating legislative activities at the department. Her office monitors all correspondence from the department to Congress and serves as the initial point of contact for legislative affairs. Under Larkin's direction, the office also monitors legislation that affects the foreign affairs agencies and coordinates the confirmation process for ambassadors and other nominees requiring Senate confirmations.

Larkin brings a wealth of legislative experience to this demanding job. She worked on Capitol Hill on both the House and Senate sides and understands the political process because she worked on successful House and Senate campaigns. Larkin's four years in the legislative bureau have prepared her to spearhead the State Department's Capitol Hill efforts.

Between positions on Capitol Hill, Larkin practiced law for nine years at Sanford, Adams McCullough & Beard in Raleigh, North Carolina. She was one of the first women to be made a partner in a major firm in that state. Larkin graduated from the University of Iowa Law School in 1977.

Deputy Assistant Secretary
Mr. Michael Klosson
202/647-1050
Rm. 7261

Deputy Assistant Secretary
Ms. Meg Donovon
202/647-1048
Rm. 7261

Deputy Assistant Secretary (House)
Ms. Shirley Cooks
202/647-1050
Rm. 7261

Deputy Assistant Secretary (Senate)
Mr. Peter Yeo
202/647-1050
Rm. 7261

Foreign Operations (House)
Mr. Carl Raether
202/647-2135   FAX 202/647-2762
Rm. 7261

Foreign Operations (Senate)
Mr. Chip Walgren
202/647-2135   FAX 202/647-2762
Rm. 7261

Office of Legislative Management

African Affairs
Mr. Jerry Lanier
202/647-8732
Rm. 7251 (H)

Consular Affairs and Refugees
Ms. Burnadette Allen
202/647-8728   FAX 202/647-9667
Rm. 7251 (H)

East Asian and Pacific Affairs
Mr. H. Dean Pittman
202/647-8722   FAX 202/647-2762
Rm. 7251 (H)

Economics and Trade
Ms. Jaci Wilson
202/647-8732   FAX 202/647-2762
Rm. 7251 (H)

European Affairs
Mr. James Hamilton
202/647-8732   FAX 202/647-2762
Rm. 7251 (H)

European and NIS Affairs
Mr. Francisco Palmieri
202/647-8722   FAX 202/647-2762
Rm. 7251 (H)

Human Rights
Mr. David Killion
202/647-8722   FAX 202/647-2762
Rm. 7251 (H)

Inter-American Affairs
Ms. Maria Trejo
202/647-8732   FAX 202/647-2762
Rm. 7251 (H)

Intelligence and Political-Military
Mr. James Lande
202/647-8728   FAX 202/647-2762
Rm. 7251 (H)

International Operations
Ms. Beth Pousson
202/647-8802   FAX 202/647-2762
Rm. 7251 (H)

Counter Narcotics, Crime, and Legal
Mr. Wayne Miele
202/647-8722   FAX 202/647-2762
Rm. 7251 (H)

Near East and South Asia
Ms. Lowry Teller
202/647-8732   FAX 202/647-2762
Rm. 7251 (H)

New Independent States Affairs
Mr. Randy LeCocq
202/647-8802   FAX 202/647-2762
Rm. 7251 (H)

Ocean and Environmental Affairs
Ms. Julia Norton
202/647-8728
Rm. 7251 (H)

Political-Military and Arms Control

Ms. Terri Lodge
202/647-8728   FAX 202/647-2762
Rm. 7251 (H)

Office of Congressional and Interagency Services

Director
Mr. Carlos Perez
202/647-1714
Rm. 7260

Congressional Inquiries
Ms. Roxanne Reed
202/647-2163
Rm. 5917

Nominations
Ms. Loretta Oliver
202/647-3436
Rm. 5917

Office of Medical Services
2401 E Street, NW / Washington DC 20520

Medical Director
Dr. Cedric E. Dumont, M.D.
202/663-1649
Rm. 209 (M/DGP/MED)

Foreign Service Nurse Programs
Ms. Susan P. Smith
202/663-1647
(M/DGP/MED)

Foreign Programs
Dr. Lawrence Hill
202/663-1662
Rm. 209 (M/DGP/MED)

Bureau of Near Eastern Affairs (NEA)

2201 C Street, NW / Washington DC 20520

INTRODUCTION

The Bureau of Near Eastern Affairs deals with U.S. foreign policy and U.S. diplomatic relations with the countries in the Near East and North Africa region. These include: Algeria, Bahrain, Egypt, Iran, Iraq, Israel, Jordan, Kuwait, Lebanon, Libya, Morocco, Oman, United Arab Emirates, Palestine, Saudi Arabia, Syria, Tunisia, Yemen, and Qatar. The assistant secretary is also responsible for directing, coordinating, and supervising interdepartmental and interagency matters involving these countries.

Assistant Secretary
Ambassador Martin S. Indyk
202/647-7209   FAX 202/736-4462
Rm. 6242 (NEA)

Personal: born 7/1/51 in England; raised in Australia.

Education: Bachelor of Economics, Univ. of Sydney, 1972. Ph.D. in international relations, Australian National Univ., 1977.

Professional: 1985-92, exec. dir., Washington Institute for Near East Policy. 1993-March 1995, special asst. to the President and senior director for Near East and South Asian affairs, National Security Council, The White House. March 1995-present, U.S. ambassador to Israel. May 1997-present, assistant secretary designate for Near Eastern affairs, U.S. Dept. of State.

Martin Indyk, the U.S. Ambassador to Israel since March 1995, was confirmed by the Senate on October 9, 1997 to be the assistant secretary of State for Near Eastern affairs succeeding of Robert H. Pelletreau who retired in January, 1997.

Indyk joined the Clinton administration in January 1993 as special assistant to the President and senior director for Near East and South Asian affairs at the National Security Council. During that period, he served as principal advisor to the President and National Security Advisor on Arab-Israeli issues, Iraq, Iran, and South Asia. He also served as a member of Secretary Warren Christopher's Peace Team.

Prior to entering the government, Ambassador Indyk served for eight years as the executive director of the Washington Institute for Near East Policy, a research institute that specializes in Arab-Israeli relations. He was also an adjunct professor at the Johns Hopkins School of Advanced International Studies where he taught Israeli politics and foreign policy.

Indyk has published widely on U.S. policy towards the Arab-Israeli peace process. In 1991, Indyk attended the Madrid Middle Eat Peace Conference as a commentator for CNN.

Indyk has also been a visiting fellow at Columbia University's Middle East Institute and Tel Aviv University's Dayan Center for Middle East Studies. He is a member of the International Institute for Strategic Studies, has served on the editorial board of *Orbis*, and was a contributing editor to the *Jerusalem Report*.

Indyk was raised and educated in Australia where he received a Bachelor of Economics degree from the University of Sydney in 1972, and a Ph.D. from the Australian National University in 1977. He resides in Washington with his wife and son.

Principal Deputy Assistant Secretary
Mr. David Welch
202/647-7207
Rm. 6242 (NEA)

Deputy Assistant Secretary
Mr. Ronald E. Neumann
202/647-7166
Rm. 6244 (NEA)

Deputy Assistant Secretary
Ms. Toni G. Verstandig
202/647-7170
Rm. 6244 (NEA)

Office of the Executive Director

Executive Director
Mr. Charles R. Allegrone
202/647-3269
Rm. 4253 (NEA/SA/EX)

Lebanon, Jordan, Syria Affairs

Director
Ms. Elizabeth McKune
202/647-1031
Rm. 6250 (NEA/ARN)

Deputy Director
Mr. Robert Mustain
202/647-4453
Rm. 6250 (NEA/ARN)

Saudi Arabia, Kuwait, Bahrain, Qatar, Oman, UAE, Yemen Affairs

Director
Mr. John Craig
202/647-6184
Rm. 4224 (NEA/ARP)

Deputy Director
Ms. Marguerita Ragsdale
202/647-6563
Rm. 4224 (NEA/ARP)

Egyptian and North African Affairs

Director
Mr. Ronald Schlicher
202/647-4679
Rm. 5250 (NEA/ENA)

Deputy Director
Mr. Philo Dibble
202/647-4675
Rm. 5250 (NEA/ENA)

Israel and Arab-Israeli Affairs

Director
Mr. David M. Satterfield
202/647-3672
Rm. 6247 (NEA/NGA)

Deputy Director
Mr. Richard Olson
202/647-4580
Rm. 6247 (NEA/NGA)

Iran and Iraq Affairs

Director
Ms. Ann Korky
202/647-5692
Rm. 4515 (NEA/NGA)

Deputy Director
Mr. Joseph LeBaron
202/647-6111
Rm. 4515 (NEA/NGA)

Peace Process and Regional Affairs

Director
Mr. Paul Simons
202/647-4589
Rm. 5256 (NEA/PPR)

Deputy Director

Ms. Kathleen Allegrone
202/647-4589
Rm. 5256 (NEA/PPR)

Bureau of Oceans and International Environmental Scientific Affairs (OES)

2201 C Street, NW / Washington DC 20520

INTRODUCTION

The Bureau of Oceans and International Environmental and Scientific Affairs (OES) melds an emphasis on environmental issues and science and technology with traditional diplomacy. The bureau and the environment, science, and technology officers at embassies overseas deal with such global issues as trade and environment; biodiversity; global climate change; environmental pollution; oceans policy, fisheries, and marine conservation; international civil and commercial space cooperation; technology; and health.

Acting Assistant Secretary for Oceans and International
    Environmental and Scientific Affairs
Ms. Melinda Kimble
202/647-1554   FAX 202/647-0217
Rm. 7831 (OES)

Melinda Kimble was named Principal Deputy Assistant Secretary for Oceans and International Environmental and Scientific Affairs (OES) in August 1997. As there was no Assistant Secretary at that time, she also became Acting Assistant Secretary.

Previously, Kimble served as Deputy Assistant Secretary in the Bureau of International Organization Affairs (IO), where she oversaw U.S. policy toward a wide range of economic and social issues in the United Nations. In this capacity, she developed the U.S. negotiating strategies for recent UN conferences, including Cairo, Copenhagen, and Beijing.

Kimble is a career Foreign Service Officer, joining the Department of State in January 1971. She was promoted to the Senior Foreign Service in 1989, and promoted to the rank of Minister Counselor in 1993. Before assuming her IO position, Kimble was the Director of the Office of Egyptian Affairs in the Near East and South Asia Bureau. From 1987 to 1989 she served as the Deputy and Acting Director of the Office of Monetary Affairs in the Economic and Business Bureau. She has also served in Tunisia, Egypt, and Cote d'Ivoire as well as in the Africa Bureau in Washington.

Kimble has bachelor's and master's degrees in economics from the University of Denver and a master's from Harvard. She is a recipient of the Department of State's Meritorious, Superior, and Distinguished Honor Awards, senior performance pay, a Presidential Performance Award, an award from the Global Alliance for Women's Health, and an International Honor Award from the U.S. Department of Agriculture. Her foreign languages are Arabic and French. She is married to James R. Phippard, a former career AID official, and has four grown stepchildren.

Special Rep. to the UN Commission on Sustainable Development
Mr. Mark G. Hambley
202/647-1555
Rm. 7831 (OES)

Special Assistant for Congressional Relations
Ms. Linda A. Strachan
202/647-3550
Rm. 7831

Office of the Executive Director

Executive Director
Ms. Stephanie Kinney
202/647-3622
Rm. 7821 (OES/EX)

Office of Regional Policy Initiatives

Acting Director
Mr. Jonathan Margolis
202/647-2958
Rm. 7831

Environment

Deputy Assistant Secretary
Mr. Rafe Pomerance
202/647-2232
Rm. 7831 (OES/E)

Office of Environmental Policy
Director
Mr. Michael Metelits
202/647-9266
Rm. 4325 (OES/ENV)

Office of Ecology and Terrestrial Conservation
Director
Ms. Mary McLeod
202/647-2418
Rm. 4333 (OES/ETC)

Office of Global Change
Director
Mr. Daniel A. Reifsnyder
202/647-4069
Rm. 4330 (OES/EGC)

Office of Oceans, Science and Technology

Deputy Assistant Secretary
Ms. Mary Beth West
202/647-2396
Rm. 7831 (OES/O)

Oceans
Director
Mr. Richard T. Scully
202/647-3262
Rm. 5805

Office of Marine Conservation
Director
Mr. Larry Snead
202/647-2335
Rm. 7820

Space and Advanced Technology Staff
Director
Mr. Ralph Braibanti
202/647-2433
Rm. 5806

Bureau of Personnel (M/DGP)

2201 C Street, NW / Washington DC 20520

> ### INTRODUCTION
>
> *The Director General of the Foreign Service and Director of Personnel (M/DGP) oversees the medical services office; the family liaison office; and the Bureau of Personnel (PER), which determines employment requirements and administers recruitment, evaluation, assignment, career development, and retirement policies and programs for the Department's employees.*

Director General of the Foreign Service and Director of Personnel
Amb. Edward W. Gnehm, Jr.
202/647-9898   FAX 202/647-5080
Rm. 6218 (M/DGP)

Personal: born 11/10/44 in Carrolton, Ga.

Education: B.A., The George Washington University, 1966. Rotary Fellow, American University in Cairo, Egypt, 1966-67.

Professional: 1968-69, management intern, U.S. Department of the Navy. 1969-74, Foreign Service with tours in Saigon and Katmandu; then in Washington as public affairs and desk officer for Nepal. 1974, appointed deputy principal officer in the U.S. interest section, Damascus, Syria; 1976-78, officer in charge, U.S. Liaison Office in Riyadh, Saudi Arabia; 1978-81, deputy chief of mission, Sanaa, Yemen Arab Republic; 1981-84, served as Pearson Fellow on Capitol Hill and as chief of the junior officer division, bureau of personnel and as director of the secretariat staff in the office of the secretary (Washington, D.C.); 1984-87, deputy chief of mission, Amman, Jordan; 1987-89, deputy assistant secretary for Near Eastern and South Asian affairs; 1990-93, U.S. Ambassador to Kuwait; 1994-97, dep. U.S. representative to the United Nations; 1997-present, director general of the Foreign Service and director or personnel, U.S. Dept. of State.

After serving as deputy U.S. representative to the United Nations for three years, Edward Gnehm assumed the position of director general of the Foreign Service and director of personnel on August 25, 1997. In this role, he develops and implements recruitment and training strategies for the Foreign Service. Gnehm replaces Anthony C.E. Quainton.

Gnehm has been a public servant in the Foreign Service for almost three decades. In his prior position, Gnehm served as the deputy U.S. representative to the UN with the rank and status of ambassador extraordinary and plenipotentiary. Before his posting at the UN, Gnehm obtained an interesting mix of Far East and Middle Eastern foreign service experience. During the Gulf War, Gnehm was U.S. Ambassador to Kuwait. He served as the department's deputy assistant secretary for Near Eastern and South Asian affairs from 1987 to 1989. Gnehm has represented the U.S. in Saigon, Katmandu, and Nepal. Since 1976, he has become a Middle East expert, serving in Syria, Saudi Arabia, Yemen, and Jordan.

Gnehm speaks Arabic and French. He is married and has two children.

Secretary
Ms. Penny O'Brien
202/647-9898
Rm. 6218

Principal Deputy Assistant Secretary
Ms. Janice F. Bay
202/647-9438
Rm. 6218

Deputy Assistant Secretary
Mr. Alex de la Garza
202/647-5152
Rm. 6216

Deputy Assistant Secretary
Ms. Gretchen D. Welch
202/647-5942
Rm. 6218

Policy Coordination Staff

Director
Ms. Janet M. Weber
202/647-2675
Rm. 6217 (M/DGP/PC)

Executive Office

Executive Director
Ms. Patricia A. Popovich
202/647-8118
Rm. 3811 (PER/EX)

Office of Career Development and Assignments

Director
Mr. James A. Williams
202/647-1692
Rm. 2328 (PER/CDA)

Office of Overseas Employment
1550 Wilson Blvd. / Rosslyn VA 22209

Director
Mr. Robert Morris
703/235-4661
Rm. 510 (PER/OE)

Office of Recruitment, Examination and Employment
1800 N. Kent Street / Rosslyn VA 22209

Director
Mr. Nicholas N. Williams
703/875-7252
Rm. 7314

Bureau of Political-Military Affairs (PM)

2201 C Street, NW / Washington DC 20520

INTRODUCTION

The Bureau of Political-Military Affairs (PM) which reports to the Under Secretary for Arms Control and International Security Affairs, advises the Secretary and other Department principals on security and defense issues worldwide, including arms control negotiations; non-proliferation of weapons of mass destruction and the means to deliver them; regional security arrangements; programs for selected foreign security assistance; conventional arms sales; peaceful uses of nuclear energy and nuclear reactor safety; dual use and technology transfers; and international space issues involving military systems and controlled technologies. The bureau also is responsible for licensing and regulating commercial exports of military equipment and services.

Acting Assistant Secretary of State for Political-Military Affairs
Mr. Eric D. Newsom
202/647-9022   FAX 202/647-1346
Rm. 7325 (PM)

At press time, Eric Newsom, the Principal Deputy Assistant Secretary and Deputy Assistant Secretary for Arms Control served as Acting Assistant Secretary until the confirmation of a replacement for former Assistant Secretary Thomas McNamara.

Special Assistant
Ms. Joan S. Wadelton
202/647-5039
Rm. 7325

Deputy Assistant Secretary for Nonproliferation
Mr. Robert J. Einhorn
202/647-8699
Rm. 7325 (PM)

Deputy Assistant Secretary For Export Controls
Mr. John Baker
202/647-6977
Rm. 7325 (PM)

Deputy Assistant Secretary for Regional Security
Mr. Michael C. Lemmon
202/647-8698
Rm. 7325 (PM)

Deputy Assistant Secretary for Burdensharing
Mr. Ray L. Caldwell
202/647-0187
Rm. 4831 (PM)

Negotiator & Presidential Rep. for
  Nuclear Security and Dismantlement
VACANT
202/647-0806
Rm. 7815 (PM)

U.S. Representative to the International
  Atomic Energy Agency
VACANT
202/647-0845
Rm. 1480

Director, Congressional and Public Affairs
Mr. J. Christian Kessler

202/647-6968
Rm. 7319

Manager, Nonproliferation and Disarmament Fund Program
Mr. Steven A. Saboe
202/647-0094
Rm. 7815

Office of the Executive Director

Acting Executive Director
Mr. Craig M. White
202/736-7366
Rm. 3817 (PM/EX)

Office of Strategic Policy and Negotiations

Director
Mr. Richard A. Davis
202/647-7775
Rm. 7424 (PM/SPN)

Nuclear Risk Reduction Center

Staff Director
Mr. Harold W. Kowalski
202/647-0027
Rm. 7635 (PM/NRRC)

Office of Arms Transfer and Export Control Policy

Director
Mr. Gregory Suchan
202/647-4231
Rm. 2422 (PM/ATEC)

Office of Security Relations, Policy and Resources

Director
Ms. Pamela I. Frazier
202/647-8111
Rm. 7424 (PM/SRP)

Office of Defense Trade Controls
1701 N. Ft. Myer Drive / Rosslyn VA 22209

Director
Mr. William J. Lowell
703/812-2564
Rm. 200 (PM/DTC)

Arms Licensing Division
Chief
Ms. Rose Biancaniello
703/812-2566
Rm. 200 (PM/DTC)

Office of Chemical, Biological and Missile Technology
2201 C Street, NW / Washington DC 20520

Director
Mr. Vann H. Van Diepen
202/647-1142
Rm. 7319 (PM/CBM)

Office of Regional Nonproliferation

Director
Mr. Steven Aoki
202/736-7141
Rm. 1480 (PM/RNP)

Office of Nuclear Energy Affairs

Director
Mr. Richard J.K. Stratford
202/647-3310
Rm. 7828 (PM/NE)

Nonproliferation and Export Policy
Ms. Eleanor Busick
202/647-4812
Rm. 7828 (PM/NE)

Safeguards and Technology
Mr. Alex R. Burkart
202/647-4413
Rm. 7828 (PM/NE)

Senior Coordinator for Nuclear Reactor Safety
Ms. Carol Kessler
202/647-6425
Rm. 2835 (PM/NE)

Office of Intl. Security & Peacekeeping Operations

Director
Col. Victor Raphael
202/647-3136
Rm. 7430 (PM/ISP)

Bureau of Population, Refugees and Migration (PRM)

2201 C Street, NW / Washington DC 20520

INTRODUCTION

The Bureau of Population, Refugees, and Migration (PRM) is responsible for coordinating the Department's policy on global population, refugees, and migration issues and for managing Migration and Refugee Assistance appropriations. As part of its work, the bureau is at the center of a cooperative effort among the State Department, other U.S. Government agencies, private voluntary organizations, and international agencies to: implement a more comprehensive international population policy, including broadening of population assistance programs to cover a wider range of reproductive health services; provide assistance to refugees in first-asylum countries and admit refugees to the United States for permanent resettlement; and develop bilateral and multilateral approaches to international migration issues.

Assistant Secretary
Ms. Julia V. Taft
202/647-7360   FAX 202/647-8162
Rm. 5824 (PRM)

President Clinton nominated Julia Vadala Taft to serve as assistant secretary of the Bureau of Population, Refugees, and Migration on September 2, 1997. She was confirmed by the Senate on November 6 and took office on November 10.

Taft, a leading authority on refugee and humanitarian affairs, has held senior positions in both government and the private sector throughout her career. Before assuming her current post, for four years Taft was President and CEO of InterAction (American Council for Voluntary International Action), a coalition of 156 U.S.-based private, voluntary organizations working on international development, refugee assistance, and humanitarian relief around the world.

Her first exposure to refugee issues came in 1975 with the collapse of Vietnam, when President Ford named her Director of the Interagency Task Force for Indochina Refugees. The refugee resettlement program which Taft directed brought more than 130,000 Indochinese into the United States.

From 1992-93, Taft was a consultant with the State Department's Office of Coordinator/CIS Affairs, where she was responsible for developing projects to assist families of Russian military personnel. She was also director of the Office of U.S. Foreign Disaster Assistance at the Agency for International Development from 1986-89, where she managed all U.S. relief responses to foreign disasters such as earthquakes, hurricanes, famines, civil unrest, and toxic chemical incidents.

Taft was born in New York City. As the daughter of a U.S. Army surgeon, she lived in Germany, Colorado, and Texas. She graduated from the University of Colorado with a B.A. in political science, and also received an M.A. in political science from the same institution.

From 1970-71 she was a White House Fellow, serving in the Office of the Vice President. Other positions she has held include: Special Assistant to the Secretary of Health, Education and Welfare (1971-73); Deputy Assistant Secretary for Human Development, HEW (1973-77); Consultant to the White House Drug Abuse Prevention Office (1977-78); Consultant to the State Department, in which she helped design the Office of Coordinator of Refugee Affairs (1978); Project Director, New TransCentury Foundation (1978-79); and Public Policy Consultant (1982-85). She accompanied her husband to Brussels, Belgium, where he served as U.S. Ambassador to NATO (1989-92).

During her career she has received several awards, including: the Presidential End Hunger Award (1989); the AID Distinguished Service Award (1989); the USSR Supreme Award for Personal Courage, presented for relief efforts in the Armenian earthquake (1990); and the Flemming Award as "One of the Ten Outstanding Men and Women in Federal Service" (1975). She also served as Alumni President of the White House Fellows Association (1977).

Senior Deputy Assistant Secretary
Mr. Allan Kreczko
202/647-5767
Rm. 5824 (PRM)

Deputy Assistant Secretary
Ms. Marguerite Rivera
202/647-5822
Rm. 5824 (PRM)

Special Assistant
Mr. Nick Miscione
202/736-4449
Rm. 5824

*Bureau of Population, Refugees and Migration offices located at:
2401 E Street, NW / Washington DC 20037*

Office of the Executive Director

Acting Director
Mr. James P. Kelley
202/663-1520

Rm. L505 (PRM)

Office of Refugee Admissions

Director
Ms. Theresa L Rusch
202/663-1047
Rm. L505 (PRM)

Office of Refugee Assistance for Africa, The Americas, and Southeast Asia

Director
Ms. Margaret J. McKelvey
202/663-1027
Rm. L505 (PRM)

Office of Refugee Assistance for Europe, the Near East and South Asia

Director
Mr. Allan Jury
202/663-1024
Rm. L505 (PRM)

Office of Population

Director
Ms. Margaret Pollack
202/663-3029
Rm. L505

Office of Policy

Director
Mr. Douglas R. Hunter
202/663-1077
Rm. L505

Bureau of South Asian Affairs (SA)

2201 C Street, NW / Washington DC 20520

Assistant Secretary
Mr. Karl F. (Rick) Inderfurth
202/736-4325   FAX 202/736-4333
Rm. 6254 (SA)

Personal: born 9/29/46 in Charlotte, N.C.

Education: A.B., Univ. of North Carolina, 1968. M.A., Princeton

University, 1975. Duke Univ. Divinity School, 1969-70. Fulbright Scholar, Strathclyde Univ. (Glasgow, Scotland), 1972-73.

Professional: 1970-71, intern and staff assistant, Sen. William Proxmire (D-Wis.). 1971-72, field organizer, McGovern for President Campaign (Wash., D.C.). 1975-76, professional staff for the Senate Intelligence Committee and representative of Sen. Gary Hart (D-Colo.). 1977-79, special asst. to the National Security Advisor, Zbigniew Brzezinski. 1979-81, dep. staff dir., Senate Foreign Relations Cmte. 1981-91, national security correspondent and Moscow correspondent, ABC News. 1991-92, consultant, Citizens' Democracy Corps, Eurasia Foundation (Wash., D.C.). 1992, project dir., Center for National Policy (Wash., D.C.). 1993-97, U.S. representative for special political affairs, Office of the Permanent Representative to the UN. 1997-present, asst. sec., bureau of South Asian affairs, U.S. Department of State.

Rick Inderfurth has been shaping international affairs for the last twenty-five years. He has held powerful security positions in two of the three branches of our government, and has also been a member of the fourth estate, reporting on issues of national security. On July 31, 1997, the Senate confirmed Inderfurth for a new seat at the international affairs table, that of assistant secretary of State for South Asian affairs.

As assistant secretary of the bureau of South Asian affairs at the Department of State, Inderfurth will be responsible for advising Secretary Albright regarding the countries within his regional jurisdiction and for guiding the operation of the U.S. diplomatic establishments in those countries. Inderfurth also directs, coordinates, and supervises interdepartmental and interagency matters involving the South Asian region.

In 1993, Inderfurth was enticed away from humanitarian work aimed at rebuilding the economy of the former Soviet Union to assume the position of U.S. Ambassador to the UN for Special Political Affairs. Inderfurth assumed that sensitive position during a defining moment in its history. In the wake of the Cold War, he says, "the international climate ... exists for the United Nations to become a major force on the world's stage."

Inderfurth has been a vocal advocate of transforming the National Security Council (NSC) into a "Global Policy Council" which would advise the president on economics and trade, as well as military and diplomatic issues. He bases his argument on the premise that the post-Cold War world order turns more frequently on economic than on military issues.

Inderfurth's career began in politics, serving on the staff of Senator William Proxmire (D-Wis.) and on the campaign trail for George McGovern. In 1975, he became Senator Gary Hart's (D-Colo.) representative on the Senate Select Committee on Intelligence. By 1977, when Jimmy Carter held the White House, he had moved across town to the Executive Branch, where he was serving as a special assistant to National Security Adviser Zbigniew Brzezinski. Before Ronald Reagan took office, Inderfurth returned to the Hill to become deputy staff director of the Senate Foreign Relations Committee.

Two years later, Inderfurth made a dramatic career change. He went to work for ABC News, as a national security correspondent. Inderfurth's security background came in handy, and he soon distinguished himself as an award-winning journalist. In 1984, he won an Emmy Award for a piece he did on the balance of power between the bipolar superpowers: the U.S. and the Soviet Union. In the same year, he won Columbia University's award for excellence in broadcast journalism. The following year, his reporting of the Geneva arms talks earned him another Emmy nomination. During Inderfurth's ten years at ABC, he covered the Pentagon, the State Department, and national security affairs. Eventually, he was assigned to be ABC's Moscow Correspondent.

In 1992, Inderfurth left journalism to become a *pro bono* project director at the Center for National Policy and also worked to stimulate economic and democratic reform in the former Soviet Union. He is a member of the Council on Foreign Relations, the International Institute for Strategic Studies, and the Fulbright Association. He has published a book on the National Security Council, and has written articles regarding international organizations.

Inderfurth married Meredith Roosa Inderfurth in 1977. They have three children.

Deputy Assistant Secretary
Mr. E. Gibson Lanpher
202/736-4328
Rm. 6254 (SA)

Senior Adviser
Mr. George Pickart
202/736-4331
Rm. 6254

Office of the Executive Director

Executive Director
Mr. Charles R. Allegrone
202/647-3269
Rm. 4253 (NEA/SA/EX)

India, Nepal, Sri Lanka, Bhutan, Maldives Affairs

Director
Mr. Steven Mann
202/647-2141
Rm. 5251 (SA/INS)

Pakistan, Afghanistan, Bangladesh Affairs

Director
Mr. Michael Malinowski
202/647-7593
Rm. 5247 (SA/PAB)

Office of South Asian Regional Affairs

Director
Mr. Robert K. Boggs
202/736-4256
Rm. 5246 (SA/RA)

American Foreign Service Association

2101 E St., NW / Washington DC 20520

President
Mr. Daniel Geisler
202/338-4045

Office of the US. Permanent Representative to the United Nations, Washington Office

2201 C Street, NW / Washington DC 20520

UN Permanent Mission to the United Nations in New York:

799 United Nations Plaza
New York, NY 10017
212/415-4402   FAX 212/415-4303

INTRODUCTION

The Office of the Permanent Representative to the United Nations (USUN/W) is headed by the Permanent Representative, a Cabinet member who represents the United States at the UN. This office shapes U.S. policy at the UN, working for multilateral policy formulation and implementation where possible and seeking to make the UN and its agencies more effective instruments for advancing U.S. interests and addressing global needs.

U.S. Permanent Representative
Ambassador Bill Richardson
202/736-7555   FAX 202/736-7551
Rm. 6333 (USUN/W)

NOTE: At press time, President Clinton had recently announced the nomination of Ambassador Richardson to be the Secretary of Energy replacing Federico Peña. At the same time, President Clinton announced the nomination of Ambassador Richard Holbrooke who was serving as a Special Presidential Envoy to replace Richardson at the UN.

Personal: born 11/15/47 in Pasadena, Calif.

Education: B.A., Tufts Univ., 1970. M.A., Fletcher School of International Relations, 1971.

Professional: 1971-72, professional staff member, U.S. House. 1973-75, congressional relations office, U.S. State Dept. 1975-78, professional staff member, Senate Foreign Relations Committee. 1978-82, executive director, New Mexico Democratic Party. 1980, democratic nominee for U.S. House. 1982-96, member, U.S. House of Representatives (3rd District of New Mexico). 1997-present, U.S. Permanent Representative to the United Nations.

President Clinton nominated Bill Richardson to be U.S. Ambassador to the United Nations on December 13, 1996. Richardson was sworn into office on February 13, 1997. As Ambassador, he is a member of the President's Cabinet and the National Security Council. Richardson is the first Hispanic to serve in a foreign policy cabinet level position.

As U.S. Representative to the United Nations, Richardson serves as spokesperson for the U.S. and confronts contentious issues such as Bosnia, Iraq, Israeli-Palestinian relations and the former Soviet Union.

Prior to becoming the U.S. Representative to the UN, Richardson served New Mexico's 3rd congressional district, one of the largest and most ethnically diverse in the country, and was elected eight times. As a member of the U.S. Congress, Richardson held one of the highest ranking posts in the House Democratic leadership, serving as chief deputy whip. He was a member of the Resources Committee, the Commerce Committee, the Permanent Select Committee on Intelligence, the Helsinki Commission on Human Rights, and also chaired the Congressional Hispanic Caucus. He also served as vice-chairman of the Democratic National Committee.

Admired for his work as President Clinton's special envoy on many sensitive diplomatic missions, Richardson was nominated for the Nobel Peace Prize a second time in January 1997. As a diplomatic "trouble shooter," he has worked to free hostages and prisoners in several countries including, Burma, Cuba, Iraq, North Korea, and the Sudan. Most recently, President Clinton dispatched Richardson to Central Africa, where he successfully brought together former Zairian President Mobutu and Alliance leader Kabila for their first meeting. Richardson's shuttle diplomacy helped avert a looming crisis and lead to a relatively peaceful transfer of power in the now Democratic Republic of Congo.

Richardson received a B.A. from Tufts University in 1970 and an M.A. from The Fletcher School of Law and Diplomacy in 1971. He has also received a number of honorary degrees and has been presented with many honors and awards during his career.

Ambassador Richardson is fluent in Spanish, with good speaking and reading abilities in French.

Chief of Staff
Ms. Rebecca Cooper
202/736-7555   FAX 202/736-7551
Rm. 6333 (USUN/W)

Senior Adviser and Counsel
Mr. David Goldwyn
202/736-7555
Rm. 6333

Senior Adviser
Mr. Burgess Laird
202/736-7555
Rm. 6333

U.S. Deputy Representative to the United Nations
799 United Nations Plaza
New York, NY 10017

Ambassador A. Peter Burleigh
212/415-4410   FAX 212/415-4443

Personal: born 3/7/42 in Los Angeles, Calif.

Education: B.A., Colgate University, 1963. Fulbright Scholar, Katmandu, Nepal, 1966.

Professional: 1963-65, member, Peace Corps, Nepalganj, Nepal. 1967-87, Foreign Service with tours in Sri Lanka, Nepal, Bahrain. 1987-89, deputy assistant secretary, Near Eastern and South Asian affairs; 1989-91, principal deputy assistant secretary for intelligence and research; 1991-92, coordinator, office of counter-terrorism; 1992-95, principal deputy assistant secretary for personnel; 1995-97, U.S. Ambassador to Sri Lanka and to the Republic of Maldives; 1997-present, U.S. deputy representative to the United Nations, U.S. Dept. of State.

President Clinton nominated A. Peter Burleigh to serve as deputy representative of the United States to the United Nations, with ambassadorial rank, on May 20, 1997. He was confirmed by the Senate on July 31, 1997 and sworn into office by Ambassador Bill Richardson, Permanent Representative of the United States to the UN, on August 5, 1997.

In his capacity as U.S. deputy representative to the UN, Burleigh will represent the U.S. in the Security Council and at other major UN bodies. He will head U.S. delegations to international meetings in New York and deal directly with the Secretary-General and other ranking United Nations officials.

Immediately prior to serving as the deputy representative to the UN, Burleigh served as the U.S. Ambassador to Sri Lanka and to the Republic of Maldives. He has held many high level positions at the State Department including principal deputy assistant secretary of State for Personnel (1992-95); coordinator of the office of counter-terrorism (1991-92); principal deputy assistant secretary of State for intelligence and research (1989-91); and deputy assistant secretary of State, bureau of Near Eastern and South Asian affairs (1987-89). Burleigh also served in various capacities in U.S. embassies in Nepal, Bahrain, and India.

Upon graduation from Colgate University in 1963, Burleigh joined the Peace Corps and served in Nepaiganj, Nepal for two years. Following his tour with the Peace Corps, Burleigh was a teaching fellow at the Wharton School of the University of Pennsylvania. In 1966, he returned to Nepal as a Fulbright Scholar to study in Katmandu. Burleigh's first posting after joining the Foreign Service in 1967 was as a political officer at the U.S. Embassy in Colombo, Sri Lanka. He is fluent in Bengali, Hindi, Nepali, and Sinhalese.

In recognition of his public service, Burleigh received the Department of State Superior Honor Awards in 1985, 1987, 1991 and 1995, as well as the Senior Foreign Service Presidential Awards, Meritorious Service Award in 1990 and 1993, and the Senior Foreign Service - Pay Award, in 1987-1992. He has also received numerous academic honors including a teaching fellowship at the Wharton School of the University of Pennsylvania (1965-66), a fellowship for the study of Hindi under the National Defense Education Act (1966) and also at the University of Pennsylvania, and the Alfred P. Sloan Foundation Scholarship at Colgate University in Hamilton, New York (1959-63).

Burleigh is a member of the Middle East Institute, the Walters Art Gallery in Baltimore, Maryland, the Asia Society, and the American Foreign Service Association.

U. S. Representative to the Economic and Social Council
Ms. Betty King
212/415-4278   FAX 212/415-4299

Betty King joined the Clinton administration as U.S. Representative to the United Nations Economic and Social Council (UNESCO) in 1997. This position, which carries the rank of ambassador, is part of the United States Mission to the United Nations.

At the time of her nomination in September 1997, King was a vice president of the Annie E. Casey Foundation, an independent philanthropic organization dedicated to the welfare of disadvantaged children and families. She has been an assistant professor at the University of Arkansas at Pine Bluff; the director of the Arkansas Office on Aging; the executive director of the Southwest Society on Aging; and the deputy commissioner of the Commission on Mental Health Services in the District of Columbia.

King earned her B.A. in psychology from the University of Windsor, Ontario, Canada, her M.A. in sociology from the State University of New York at Stony Brook, and studied gerontology at the University of Michigan. She was also a National Endowment for the Humanities fellow at Harvard University.

U.S. Representative for Special Political Affairs
VACANT
212/415-4016   FAX 212/415-4443

Karl F. Inderfurth, the most recent U.S. Ambassador to the United Nations for special political affairs, left that position in the summer of 1997 to take a new seat at the international affairs table, that of assistant secretary of State for the bureau of South Asian affairs. No one has yet been nominated to replace him.

U.S. Representative for UN Reform and Management
Amb. Richard Sklar
212/415-4402   FAX 212/415-4303

Personal: born 11/18/34 in Baltimore, Md.

Education: B.M.E., Cornell Univ., 1957.

Professional: 1958, officer, U.S. Army. 1958-76, president, Allied Steel and Tractor Company. 1983-96, president, O'Brien Kreitzberg and Associates. 1985-89, president, Recyclene Products, Inc. 1996-97, special representative of the President and the Secretary of State for Civilian Implementation in Bosnia. 1997-present, U.S. Representative for UN Reform and Management, Office of the Permanent Representative to the United Nations.

Richard Sklar was nominated by President Bill Clinton to serve as the United States Representative to the United Nations for UN Reform and Management, with ambassadorial rank, on May 6, 1997. He was confirmed by the Senate on July 31, 1997 and sworn into office by Ambassador Bill Richardson, US Permanent Representative to the UN, on August 5, 1997.

As the Representative for UN Reform and Management, Ambassador Sklar will spearhead the United States' efforts to implement UN reform, oversee the US mission's role within the UN on management and reform issues, and work with the UN on its interaction with US businesses.

Sklar has established a distinguished career in private and public sector management. Prior to serving as the U.S. Representative to the UN for Reform and Management, he was the special representative of the President and the Secretary of State for civilian implementation in Bosnia. Before his presidential appointment, Sklar was president of O'Brien Kreitzberg and Associates, a construction management firm from 1983 to 1996 and president of Recyclene Products, Inc., from 1985 to 1989. He also served as general manager of the public utilities commission and project manager for construction in San Francisco.

After serving in the US Army in 1958 as an officer, Sklar began a steady climb through the ranks at Allied Steel and Tractor Company in Ohio, where after nearly 20 years he left as President in 1976.

A resident of California, Sklar received a bachelor's degree of mechanical engineering from Cornell University in 1957.

Sklar and his wife, Barbara, have four children and four grandchildren. From 1993 to 1996, Sklar served on the board of directors of the Russian American Enterprise Fund.

U.S. Representative to the U.N. Human Rights Commission
U.S. Department of State
IO/ESA, Rm. 5333
Washington, D.C. 20520

Ambassador Nancy Rubin
202/647-1155   FAX 202/686-9058
E-mail: NHRubin@aol.com

Personal: born in New York City, N.Y.

Education: B.A., Univ, of Calif., Los Angeles.

As U.S. Head of Delegation to the UN Commission on Human Rights, Nancy Rubin serves as the U.S. spokesperson at the commission's meetings and reports to the Department of State on its activities. She maintains liaison with counterpart representatives of other member governments to exchange views and information. The commission is the premier international forum of discussion and debate of human rights issues and meets annually in New York or Geneva.

Rubin has spent the last 25 years in public service and related public policy arenas. Her broad experience includes many domestic and international activities with a focus on human rights. Her service in government includes both the Clinton and Carter White House. She attended the 4th UN World Conference on Women in Beijing in 1995, representing the NGO Community in consultative status with the UN. In 1993, she was a U.S. delegate the UN Economic and Social Council in Vienna. Rubin also attended the Forum of the 1985 UN Conference on Women in Kenya.

In the international arena, Rubin has served as an officer of the Overseas Education Fund Int'l., and was chair of the Committee on Women, Law, and Development. Rubin also served in the past on the executive committee of the International Human Rights Law Group and the leadership council of Amnesty International. She now serves on the steering committee for the Women's Leadership Conference of the Americas and the planning committee for Women, Law, and Development Int'l. Rubin has been on fact-finding missions and presidential delegations to all parts of the world. She has been an election observer to countries in transition, including Chile, Gaza, the West Bank, and Bosnia.

Rubin currently serves on The Council on Foreign Relations, the Bretton Woods Committee, Women's Commission on Refugee Women and Children, Women's Foreign Policy Group, A.S.H.A., Congressional Oversight Committee to evaluate American Schools, and Hospitals Abroad, and as a director of the Overseas Development Council. She also serves as co-chair of the Women's Campaign Research Fund and formerly served on the National Red Cross Board of Governors Public Support Committee.

Rubin was coordinator of The White House National Consumer-Education Project. She has also worked as a teacher with the L.A. Unified school district and served on the Mayor's Education Advisory Committee in Los Angeles and the Mayor's Education Summit in Washington, D.C.

U.S. Rep. to the U.N. Commission on the Status of Women
2201 C Street, NW- Rm. 5331 / Washington, D.C. 20520

Ambassador Linda Tarr-Whelan
202/647-3901   FAX 202/647-4628

Personal: born in Springfield, Mass.

Education: B.S., John Hopkins Univ. M.S., Univ. of Maryland.

Professional: director, program development, American Federation of State, County, and Municipal Employees. administrative director, N.Y. State Department of Labor. director government relations, National Education Association. deputy assistant to President Carter for Women's Concerns. 1986-present, president and CEO, Center for Policy Alternatives. 1996-present, U.S. representative to the U.N. Commission on the Status of Women.

Linda Tarr-Whelan has more than 25 years of experience in shaping public policy as an advocate and government official. In 1996, she was appointed by President Clinton to serve as U. S. Representative to the United Nations Commission on the Status of Women. In 1997, President Clinton nominated Tarr-Whelan to the rank of ambassador. Tarr-Whelan continues her role as the president and chief executive officer of the Center for Policy Alternatives. CPA is a 21-year-old nonpartisan non-profit progressive public policy and leadership center focusing on innovative people and ideas across the 50 states.

Prior to joining CPA in 1986, she served as deputy assistant to the President for Women's Concerns in the Carter White House, director of government relations for the National Education Association, administrative director of the New York State Department of Labor, and director of public policy for the American Federation of State, County and Municipal Employees.

She is the editor of three books, including *A Matter of simple Justice: Women's Rights are Human Rights,* and has published numerous articles. She speaks on public policy in the national media, with a special expertise on women and the economy.

Her current board positions include the State Issues Forum, the Advocacy Institute, the Benton Foundation, Freddie Mac Affordable Housing Advisory Board, Independent Sector, the National Conference of State Legislatures Foundation for State Legislatures, the Council for Excellence in Government, and "Renew America." Tarr-Whelan is a founder of the Coalition of Labor Union Women and the Center for Women in Government.

As a public member of the U.S. Delegation to the United Nations Fourth World Conference on Women in Beijing, China, Tarr-Whelan was also a delegate to the U.N. preparatory meetings in 1994 and 1995. She has received the Women Executives in State Government 1996 "Breaking the Glass Ceiling" Award for service in the public sector, and was recognized in 1996 by the *Ladies Home Journal* as one of the 50 most powerful women in American politics.

Tarr-Whelan is a nurse with a B.S.N. from the Johns Hopkins University and M.S. from the University of Maryland. She is married to Keith Tarr-Whelan, and has two adult children and one grandson.

Country Desk Officers

2201 C Street, NW / Washington DC 20520

INTRODUCTION

Country desk officers at the Department of State listed here by country maintain regular contact with overseas diplomatic missions and can provide country-specific economic and political analysis for U.S. companies. The numbers listed below take you directly to the desk officer for the country shown. The main number for the country desk officer section at State is 202/647-4000.

Afghanistan - 202/647-9552

Albania (Tirana) - 202/647-3747

Algeria (Algiers) - 202/647-4680

Andorra - 202/647-1412

Angola (Luanda) - 202/647-8434

Antigua and Barbuda (St. John's) - 202/647-2621

Argentina (Buenos Aires) - 202/647-2401

Armenia (Yerevan) - 202/647-6758

Australia (Canberra) - 202/647-9691

Austria (Vienna) - 202/647-2005

Azerbaijan (Baku) - 202/647-6048

Bahamas, The (Nassau) - 202/647-2621

Bahrain (Manama) - 202/647-6572

Baltic States - 202/647-3187

Bangladesh (Dhaka) - 202/647-9552

Barbados (Bridgetown) - 202/647-2130

Belarus (Minsk) - 202/647-6764

Belgium (Brussels) - 202/647-6664

Belize (Belize City) - 202/647-3381

Benin (Cotonou) - 202/647-1540

Bermuda (Hamilton) - 202/647-8027

Bhutan - 202/647-2141

Bolivia (La Paz) - 202/647-3076

Bosnia - Herzegovina (Sarajevo) - 202/736-7024

Botswana (Gaborone) - 202/647-8433

Brazil (Brasilia) - 202/647-9407

British Indian Ocean Territory (BIOT) - 202/647-5684

Brunei (Bandar Seri Begawan) - 202/647-3276

Bulgaria (Sofia) - 202/647-0310

Burkina Faso (Ouagadougou) - 202/647-2791

Burundi (Bujumbura) - 202/647-3139

Cambodia (Phnom Penh) - 202/647-3133

Cameroon (Yaounde) - 202/647-1707

Canada (Ottawa) - 202/647-3135

Cape Verde (Praia) - 202/647-1596

Central African Republic (Bangui) - 202/647-1707

CENTAM Regional Affairs - 202/647-3381

Chad (N'Djamena) - 202/647-1707

Chile (Santiago) - 202/647-2401

China (Beijing) - 202/647-6300

Colombia (Bogota) - 202/647-3023

Commonwealth of Independent States - 202/647-9559

Comoros - 202/647-6473

Congo (Brazzaville) - 202/647-3139

Congo (Kinshasa) - 202/647-2080

Cook Islands - 202/647-3546

Costa Rica (San Jose) - 202/647-3518

Cote D'Ivoire (Abidjan) - 202/647-1540

Council of Europe - 202/647-1708

Croatia (Zagreb) - 202/736-7361

Cuba (Havana) - 202/647-9272

Cyprus (Nicosia) - 202/647-6113

Czech Republic (Prague) - 202/647-1457

Denmark (Copenhagen) - 202/647-5669

Diego Garcia - 202/647-6453

Djibouti (Djibouti) - 202/647-5684

Dominica - 202/647-2130

Dominican Republic (Santo Domingo) - 202/647-2620

Ecuador (Quito) - 202/647-3338

Egypt (Cairo) - 202/647-1228

El Salvador (San Salvador) - 202/647-3681

Equatorial Guinea (Malabo) - 202/647-1707

Eritrea (Asmara) - 202/647-6485

Estonia (Tallin) - 202/647-5669

Ethiopia (Addis Ababa) - 202/647-6485

European Atomic Energy Commission - 202/647-1626

European Coal & Steel Community (ECSC) - 202/647-3932

European Communities - 202/647-3932

European Economic Community (EEC) - 202/647-1708

European Free Trade Association (EFTA) - 202/647-2395

European Space Agency (ESA) - 202/647-2395

Fiji (Suva) - 202/647-3546

Finland (Helsinki) - 202/647-5669

France (Paris) - 202/647-1412

French Antilles (Martinique, Guadeloupe,

and French Guyana) - 202/647-2620

French Polynesia - 202/647-3546

Gabon (Libreville) - 202/647-3139

Gambia, The (Banjul) - 202/647-4567

GCC Affairs (Gulf Cooperation Council) - 202/647-6562

Georgia (Tbilisi) - 202/647-6795

Germany (Bonn) - 202/647-2155

Ghana (Accra) - 202/647-1596

Gibraltar - 202/647-8027

Greece (Athens) - 202/647-6113

Greenland - 202/647-5669

Grenada (St. George) - 202/647-2621

Guadeloupe - 202/647-2620

Guatemala (Guatemala City) - 202/647-3559

Guinea (Conakry) - 202/647-3407

Guinea-Bissau (Bissau) - 202/647-1596

Guyana (Georgetown) - 202/647-2621

Haiti (Port-au-Prince) - 202/736-4707

Honduras (Tegucigalpa) - 202/647-4980

Hungary (Budapest) - 202/647-3238

Iceland (Reykjavik) - 202/647-5669

India (New Delhi) - 202/647-2141

Indonesia (Jakarta) - 202/647-3276

Iran - 202/647-6111

Iraq - 202/647-5692

Ireland (Dublin) - 202/647-8027

Israel (Tel Aviv) - 202/647-3672

Italy (Rome) - 202/647-3746

Jamaica (Kingston) - 202/647-2620

Japan (Tokyo) - 202/647-3152

Jordan (Amman) - 202/647-1022

Kazakhstan (Almaty) - 202/647-6859

Kenya (Nairobi) - 202/647-6479

Kiribati - 202/647-3546

Korea, North - 202/647-7717

Korea, South (Seoul) - 202/647-7717

Kuwait (Kuwait) - 202/647-6562

Kyrgyzstan (Bishkek) - 202/647-6740

Laos (Vientiane) - 202/647-3133

Latvia (Riga) - 202/647-5669

Lebanon (Beirut) - 202/647-6148

Lesotho (Maseru) - 202/647-8434

Liberia (Monrovia) - 202/647-1658

Libya - 202/647-4674

Liechtenstein - 202/647-2155

Lithuania (Vilnius) - 202/647-5669

Luxembourg (Luxembourg) - 202/647-6664

Macau - 202/647-6300

Macedonia (Skopje) - 202/647-0757

Madagascar (Antananarivo) - 202/647-6473

Malawi (Lilongwe) - 202/647-8432

Malaysia (Kuala Lumpur) - 202/647-3276

Maldives - 202/647-2351

Mali (Bamako) - 202/647-2791

Malta (Valletta) - 202/647-3746

Marshall Islands (Majuro) - 202/647-0108

Martinique - 202/647-2620

Mauritania (Nouakchott) - 202/647-3407

Mauritius (Port Louis) - 202/647-6473

Mexico (Mexico, D.F.) - 202/647-9894

Micronesia, Federated States of (Kolonia) - 202/647-0108

Moldova (Chisinau) - 202/647-6733

Monaco - 202/647-1412

Mongolia (Ulaanbaatar) - 202/647-6300

Morocco (Rabat) - 202/647-4249

Mozambique (Maputo) - 202/647-8433

Namibia (Windhoek) - 202/647-9429

Nauru - 202/647-3546

NATO - 202/736-7299

Nepal (Kathmandu) - 202/647-1450

Netherlands (The Hague) - 202/647-6664

Netherlands Antilles (Curacao) - 202/647-2620

New Caledonia - 202/647-3546

New Zealand (Wellington) - 202/647-9691

Nicaragua (Managua) - 202/647-2205

Niger (Niamey) - 202/647-2791

Nigeria (Abuja) - 202/647-1597

Norway (Oslo) - 202/647-5669

OECD - 202/647-2469

Oman (Muscat) - 202/647-6571

OSCE - 202/736-7299

Pacific Islands (General) - 202/647-3546

Pakistan (Islamabad) - 202/647-9823

Palau (Koror) - 202/647-0108

Panama (Panama City) - 202/647-4986

Papua New Guinea (Port Moresby) - 202/647-3546

Paraguay (Asuncion) - 202/647-2296

Peru (Lima) - 202/647-3360

Philippines (Manila) - 202/647-1221

Poland (Warsaw) - 202/647-4139

Portugal (Lisbon) - 202/647-1412

Qatar (Doha) - 202/647-6572

Reunion - 202/647-2453

Romania (Bucharest) - 202/647-4272

Russia (Moscow) - 202/647-9806

Rwanda (Kigali) - 202/647-3139

Samoa (Apia) - 202/647-3546

San Marino - 202/647-2453

Sao Tome and Principe - 202/647-3139

Saudi Arabia (Riyadh) - 202/647-7550

Senegal (Dakar) - 202/647-2865

Serbia (inc. Serbia and Montenegro) - 202/736-7480

Sierra Leone (Freetown) - 202/647-4567

Singapore (Singapore) - 202/647-3278

Slovakia (Bratislava) - 202/647-3191

Slovenia (Ljubljana) - 202/736-7152

Solomon Islands - 202/647-3546

Somalia - 202/647-6453

South Africa (Pretoria) - 202/647-8252

South Pacific Commission - 202/647-3546

Spain (Madrid) - 202/647-1412

Sri Lanka (Colombo) - 202/647-2351

Sudan (Khartoum) - 202/647-6475

Suriname (Paramaribo) - 202/647-2620

Swaziland (Mbabane) - 202/647-8434

Sweden (Stockholm) - 202/647-5669

Switzerland (Bern) - 202/647-2155

Syria (Damascus) - 202/647-1131

Taiwan Coordination Staff - 202/647-7711

Tajikistan (Dushanbe) - 202/647-6757

Tanzania (Dar es Salaam) - 202/647-6473

Thailand (Bangkok) - 202/647-7108

Togo (Lome) - 202/647-1540

Tonga - 202/647-3546

Trinidad and Tobago (Port-of-Spain) - 202/647-2621

Tunisia (Tunis) - 202/647-3614

Turkey (Ankara) - 202/647-6114

Turkmenistan (Ashgabat) - 202/647-6831

Tuvalu - 202/647-3546

Uganda (Kampala) - 202/647-6479

Ukraine (Kiev) - 202/647-8696

United Arab Emirates (Abu Dhabi) - 202/647-6558

United Kingdom (London) - 202/647-8027

Uruguay (Montevideo) - 202/647-2296

Uzbekistan - 202/647-6765

Vanuatu - 202/647-3546

Vatican - 202/647-3746

Venezuela (Caracas) - 202/647-3023

Vietnam (Hanoi) - 202/647-3132

Western European Union (WEU) - 202/736-7299

Western Sahara - 202/647-3407

Yemen (Sanaa) - 202/647-6572

Zambia (Lusaka) - 202/647-8432

Zimbabwe (Harare) - 202/647-9429

U.S. Ambassadors Abroad

INTRODUCTION

U.S. Missions Abroad

To support its relations with other countries and international organizations, the United States maintains diplomatic and consular posts around the world. Under the President's direction, the Secretary of State is responsible for the overall coordination and supervision of U.S. Government activities abroad. Country missions and missions to international organizations are headed by Chiefs of Mission. Chiefs of Mission are considered the President's personal representatives and, with the Secretary of State, assist in implementing the President's constitutional responsibilities for the conduct of U.S. foreign relations.

Most missions have personnel assigned from other executive branch agencies in addition to those from the Department of State; in some cases, State Department employees may account for less than one-half of the mission staff. Department of State employees at missions comprise U.S.-based political appointees and career diplomats; and Foreign Service nationals. The last are local residents, who provide continuity for the transient American staff and have language and cultural expertise; they also are employed at post by other agencies.

Other executive branch agencies represented may include the Departments of Commerce, Agriculture, Defense, and Justice (the Immigration and Naturalization Service, the Drug Enforcement Administration, and the Federal Bureau of Investigation); the U.S. Agency for International Development; and the U.S. Information Agency. Other U.S. Government agencies also make vital contributions to the success of U.S. foreign relations and in promoting U.S. interests.

Country Missions

In most countries with which it has diplomatic relations, the U.S. maintains an embassy, which usually is located in the host country capital. The U.S. also may have consulates in other large commercial centers or in dependencies of the country. Several countries have U.S. ambassadors accredited to them who are not resident in the country. In a few special cases—such as when it does not have full diplomatic relations with a country—the U.S. may be represented by only a U.S. Liaison Office or U.S. Interests Section, which may be headed by a Principal Officer rather than a Chief of Mission.

The Chief of Mission —with the title of Ambassador, Minister, or Charge d'Affaires—and the Deputy Chief of Mission are responsible for and head the mission's "country team" of U.S. Government personnel.

Chiefs of Mission—Authorities And Responsibilities

Authorities and responsibilities of Chiefs of Mission at post include:

— Following, articulating, and speaking with one voice to others on U.S. policy—and ensuring mission staff do likewise—while also providing to the President and Secretary of State expert guidance and frank counsel and seeking the same from mission staff;

— Directing, coordinating, and supervising all executive branch offices and personnel, except for personnel under the command of a U.S. area military commander, under another chief of mission, or on the staff of an international organization;

— Cooperating with U.S. legislative and judicial branch personnel so that U.S. foreign policy goals are advanced, security is maintained, and executive, legislative, and judicial responsibilities are carried out;

— Reviewing all communications to or from mission elements, however transmitted, except those specifically exempted by law or executive decision;

— Taking direct responsibility for the security of the mission—including security from terrorism—and protecting all U.S. Government personnel on official duty (other than those personnel under the command of a U.S. area military commander) and their accompanying dependents;

— Viewing budgetary stringency as an incentive to innovate and to exercise careful stewardship of mission resources, including carrying out regular reviews of programs, personnel, and funding levels and cooperating with other departments and agencies in downsizing efforts;

— Using given Chief-of-Mission authorities to reshape the mission in ways that directly serve American interests and values and ensuring that all executive branch agencies attached to the mission do likewise by obtaining Chief-of-Mission approval to change the size, composition, or mandate of their staffs within the mission;

— Serving the people of the U.S. with professional excellence, the highest standards of ethical conduct, and diplomatic discretion and ensuring that mission staff adhere to the same strict standards and maintain a shared commitment to equal opportunity and against discrimination and harassment.

Albania

The Honorable Marisa R. Lino
Ambassador
American Embassy Tirana
PSC 59, Box 100 (A)
APO AE 09624
Phone: [355] (42) 32875
Fax: [355] (42) 32222
Appointed - 07/02/96
Oath - 07/15/96

Algeria

The Honorable Cameron R. Hume
Ambassador
American Embassy Algiers
4 Chemin Cheich Bachir El Ibrahimi
B.P. Box 549 (Alger-Gare)
16000 Algiers, Algeria
Phone: [213] (2) 69-11-86
Fax: [213] (2) 69-39-79
Appointed - 11/10/97
Oath - 12/05/97

Angola

The Honorable Donald K. Steinberg
Ambassador
American Embassy Luanda
Department of State
Washington DC 20521-2550
Phone: [244] (2) 346-418
Fax: [244] (2) 346-924
Appointed - 06/27/95
Oath - 07/24/95

Antigua and Barbuda

Vacant
Ambassador
RESIDENT IN BARBADOS

Argentina

Vacant
Ambassador
American Embassy Buenos Aires
Unit 4334, APO AA 34034
Phone: [54] (1) 777-4533
Fax: [54] (1) 777-0197

Armenia

The Honorable Peter Tomsen
Ambassador
American Embassy Yerevan
18 Gen Bagramian
Yerevan, Armenia
Phone: 3742-151-144
Fax: 3742-151-138
Appointed - 06/27/95
Oath - 07/17/95

Australia

The Honorable Genta Hawkins Holmes

Ambassador
American Embassy Canberra
APO AP 96549
Phone: [61] (6) 270-5000
Fax: [61] (6) 270-5970
Appointed - 02/10/97

Austria

The Honorable Kathryn Walt Hall
Ambassador
American Embassy Vienna
Boltzmanngasse 16
A-1091 Vienna, Austria
Phone: [43] (1) 313-39
Fax: [43] (1) 310-0682
Appointed - 11/10/97
Oath - 11/21/97

Azerbaijan

The Honorable Stanley Tuemler Escudero
Ambassador
American Embassy Baku
Azadliq Prospekti 83
Baku, Azerbaijan
Phone: (9) (9412) 98-03-36
Fax: (9) (9412) 96-04-69
Appointed - 11/10/97
Oath - 11/17/97

Bahamas

The Honorable Sidney Williams
Ambassador
American Embassy Nassau
Department of State
Washington DC 20521-3370
Phone: (809) 322-1181
Fax: (809) 356-0222
Appointed - 02/09/94
Oath - 03/04/94

Bahrain

The Honorable Johnny Young
Ambassador
American Embassy Manama
FPO AE 09834-5100
Phone: (973) 273-300
Fax: (973) 275-418
Appointed - 11/10/97
Oath - 12/05/97

Bangladesh

The Honorable John C. Holzman
Ambassador
American Embassy Dhaka
G.P.O. Box 323
1000 Dhaka, Bangladesh
Phone: [880] (2) 884700-22
Fax: [880] (2) 883-744
Appointed - 08/01/97
Oath - 08/14/97

Barbados

Vacant

Ambassador
American Embassy Bridgetown
P.O. Box 302
FPO AA 34055
Phone: (246) 436-4950
Fax: (246) 429-5246

Belarus

The Honorable Daniel W. Speckhard
Ambassador
American Embassy Minsk
Starovilenskaya #46-220002
Minsk, Belarus
Phone: (375) (172) 31-50-00
Fax: (375) (172) 34-78-53
Appointed - 08/01/97
Oath - 08/28/97

Belgium

The Honorable Alan John Blinken
Ambassador
American Embassy Brussels
PSC 82, Box 002
APO AE 09724
Phone: [32] (2) 508-2111
Fax: [32] (2) 511-2725
Appointed - 11/04/93
Oath - 11/12/93

Belize

The Honorable Carolyn Curiel
Ambassador
American Embassy Belize City
P.O. Box 286, Unit 7401
APO AA 34025
Phone: [501] (2) 77161
Fax: [501] (2) 30802
Appointed - 11/12/97
Oath - 11/14/97

Benin

The Honorable John M. Yates
Ambassador
American Embassy Cotonou
Rue Caporal Bernard Anani, B.P. 2012
Cotonou, Benin
Phone: [229] 30-06-50
Fax: [229] 30-14-39
Appointed - 10/03/95
Oath - 11/03/95

Bolivia

The Honorable Donna Jean Hrinak
Ambassador
American Embassy La Pez
P.O. Box 425
APO AA 34032
Phone: [591] (2) 430251
Fax: [591] (2) 433900
Appointed - 11/12/97
Oath - 12/10/97

Bosnia & Herzegovina

The Honorable Richard Dale Kauzlarich
Ambassador
American Embassy Sarajevo
43 Ul. Dure Dakovica
Sarajevo, Bosnia-Herzegovina
Phone: [387] (71) 645-992
Fax: [387] (71) 659-722
Appointed - 08/01/97
Oath - 08/22/97

Botswana

The Honorable Robert Krueger
Ambassador
American Embassy Gaborone
P.O. Box 90
Gaborone, Botswana
Phone: [267] 353-982
Fax: [267] 356-947
Appointed - 06/06/96
Oath - 06/14/96

Brazil

The Honorable Melvyn Levitsky
Ambassador
American Embassy Brasilia
Unit 3500
APO AA 34030
Phone: [55] (61) 321-7272
Fax: [55] (61) 225-9136
Appointed - 05/09/94
Oath - 05/16/94

Brunei Darussalam

The Honorable Glen Robert Rase
Ambassador
American Embassy Bandar Seri Begawan
AMEMB Box B
APO AP 96440
Phone: [673] (2) 229-670
Fax: [673] (2) 225-293
Appointed - 07/02/96
Oath - 07/26/96

Bulgaria

The Honorable Avis T. Bohlen
Ambassador
American Embassy Sofia
Unit 1335,
APO AE 09213-1335
Phone: [359] (2) 980-5241
Fax: [359] (2) 981-8977
Appointed - 07/02/96
Oath - 07/22/96

Burkina Faso

The Honorable Sharon P. Wilkinson
Ambassador
American Embassy Ouagadougou
01 B.P.35
Ouagadougou, Burkina Faso
Phone: [226] 30-67-23
Fax: [226] 31-23-68
Appointed - 06/11/96
Oath - 07/16/96

Burundi

The Honorable Morris N. Hughes, Jr.
Ambassador
American Embassy Bujumbura
B.P. 1720 Avenue de Etats-Unis
Bujumbura, Burundi
Phone: [257] 22-34-54
Fax: [257] 22-29-26
Appointed - 06/11/96
Oath - 06/14/96

Cambodia

The Honorable Kenneth M. Quinn
Ambassador
American Embassy Phnom Penh
Box P
APO AP 96546
Phone: (855) 23-426-436
Fax: (855) 234-26437
Appointed - 12/19/95
Oath - 01/31/96

Cameroon

The Honorable Charles H. Twining
Ambassador
American Embassy Yaounde
Department of State
Washington DC 20521-2520
Phone: (237) 23-40-14
Fax: (237) 23-07-53
Appointed - 12/19/95
Oath - 01/05/96

Canada

The Honorable Gordon Giffin
Ambassador
American Embassy Ottawa
P.O. Box 5000
Ogdensburg NY 13669-0430
Phone: (613) 238-5335
Fax: (613) 238-5720
Appointed - 08/01/97
Oath - 08/13/97

Cape Verde

The Honorable Lawrence Neal Benedict
Ambassador
American Embassy Praia
Rua Abilio Macedo 81
Praia
Phone: [238] 61-56-16
Fax: [238] 61-13-55
Appointed - 06/06/96
Oath - 06/17/96

Central African Republic

Vacant
Ambassador
American Embassy Bangui
Avenue David Dacko, B.P. 924
Bangui, Central African Republic
Phone: [236] 61-02-00
Fax: [236] 61-44-94

Chad

The Honorable David C. Halsted
Ambassador
American Embassy N'Djamena
Avenue Felix Eboue, B.P. 413
N'Djamena, Chad
Phone: [235] 51-70-09
Fax: [235] 51-56-54
Appointed - 06/11/96
Oath - 07/31/96

Chile

The Honorable Gabriel Guerra-Mondragon
Ambassador
American Embassy Santiago
Av. Anderes Bello 2800
APO AA 34033
Phone: [56] (2) 232-2600
Fax: [56] (2) 330-3710
Appointed - 10/05/94
Oath - 10/25/94

China

The Honorable James R. Sasser
Ambassador
American Embassy Beijing
PSC 461, Box 50
FPO AP 96521-0002
Phone: [86] (10) 6532-3831
Fax: [86] (10) 6532-6422
Appointed - 12/19/95
Oath - 01/10/96

Colombia

The Honorable Curtis Warren Kamman
Ambassador
American Embassy Bogota
P.O. Box AA 3831
APO AA 34038
Phone: [57] (1) 315-0811
Fax: [57] (1) 315-2197
Appointed - 11/07/97
Oath - 12/10/97

Comoros

The Honorable Harold Walter Geisel
Ambassador
RESIDENT IN MAURITIUS
Appointed - 06/06/96
Oath - 07/08/96

Congo

The Honorable Daniel Howard Simpson
Ambassador
American Embassy Kinshasa
Unit 31550
APO 09828
Phone: 011-243-12-21533
Fax: 011-243-88-43805
Appointed - 10/03/95
Oath - 10/30/95

Congo

The Honorable Aubrey Hooks
Ambassador
American Embassy Brazzaville
Avenue Amilcar Cabral, B.P. 1015
Brazzaville, Congo
Phone: (242) 83-20-70
Fax: (242) 83-63-38
Appointed - 06/06/96
Oath - 06/10/96

Costa Rica

The Honorable Thomas J. Dodd
Ambassador
American Embassy San Jose
APO AA 34020
Phone: [506] 220-3939
Fax: [506] 220-2305
Appointed - 10/14/97
Oath - 10/20/97

Cote d'Ivoire

The Honorable Lannon Walker
Ambassador
American Embassy Abidjan
5 Rue Jesse Owens, 01 B.P. 1712
Abidjan, Cote D'Ivoire
Phone: (225) 21-09-79
Fax: (225) 22-32-59
Appointed - 06/27/95
Oath - 06/30/95

Croatia

The Honorable William Dale Montgomery
Ambassador
American Embassy Zagreb
Andrije Hebranga 2
Zagreb, Croatia
Phone: [385] (1) 455-55-00
Fax: [385] (1) 458-8585
Appointed - 11/18/97
Oath - 11/25/97

Cuba

Mr. Michael G. Kozak
Principal Officer
Swiss Embassy, Calzada
Vedado
Havana, Cuba
Phone: [53] (7) 33-3551
Fax: [53] (7) 33-3700
Appointed - 7/01/96

Cyprus

The Honorable Kenneth C. Brill
Ambassador
American Embassy Nicosia
P.O. Box 4536
FPO AE 09836
Phone: [357] (2) 776-400
Fax: [357] (2) 780-944
Appointed - 06/11/96
Oath - 06/26/96

Czech Republic

The Honorable Jenonne R. Walker
Ambassador
American Embassy Prague
Unit 1330
APO AE 09213-1330
Phone: [42] (2) 5732-0663
Fax: [42] (2) 5732-0614
Appointed - 06/27/95
Oath - 06/30/95

Denmark

The Honorable Edward Elliott Elson
Ambassador
American Embassy Copenhagen
PSC 73
APO AE 09716
Phone: [45] 3555-3144
Fax: [45] 3543-0223
Appointed - 11/22/93
Oath - 11/23/93

Djibouti

The Honorable Lange Schermerhorn
Ambassador
American Embassy Djibouti
Plateau du Serpent Blvd. Marechal Joffre
BP 185 Djibouti
Phone: [253] 35-39-95
Fax: [253] 35-39-40
Appointed - 11/10/97
Oath - 12/04/97

Dominica

Vacant
Ambassador
RESIDENT IN BARBADOS

Dominican Republic

Vacant
Ambassador
American Embassy Santo Domingo
Unit 5500
APO AA 34041
Phone: (809) 221-2171
Fax: (809) 686-7437

Ecuador

The Honorable Leslie M. Alexander
Ambassador
American Embassy Quito
APO AA 34039
Phone: [593] (2) 562-890
Fax: [593] (2) 502-052
Appointed - 07/02/96
Oath - 07/17/96

Egypt

The Honorable Daniel Charles Kurtzer
Ambassador
American Embassy Cairo
Unit 64900
APO AE 09839-4900
Phone: [20] (2) 355-7371
Fax: [20] (2) 357-3200
Appointed - 11/10/97
Oath - 12/02/97

El Salvador

The Honorable Anne W. Patterson
Ambassador
American Embassy San Salvador
Unit 3116
APO AA 34023
Phone: [503] 278-4444
Fax: [503] 278-6011
Appointed - 02/10/97
Oath - 03/07/97

Equatorial Guinea

The Honorable Charles H. Twining
Ambassador
RESIDENT IN CAMEROON
Appointed - 12/19/95
Oath - 01/05/96

Eritrea

Vacant
Ambassador
American Embassy Asmara
P.O. Box 211
Asmara, Eritrea
Phone: [291] (1) 12-00-04
Fax: [291] (1) 12-75-84

Estonia

Vacant
Ambassador
American Embassy Tallinn
Kentmanni 20
EE 0001 Tallinn, Estonia
Phone: [372] (6) 312-021
Fax: [321] (6) 312-025

Ethiopia

The Honorable David H. Shinn
Ambassador
American Embassy Addis Ababa
P.O. Box 1014
Addis Ababa, Ethiopia
Phone: [251] (1) 550-666
Fax: [251] (1) 552-191
Appointed - 06/06/96
Oath - 06/17/96

Fiji

Vacant
Ambassador
American Embassy Suva
P.O. Box 218
Suva, Fiji
Phone: [679] 314-466
Fax: [679] 300-081

Finland

Vacant
Ambassador
American Embassy Helsinki
APO AE 09723
Phone: [358] (0) 171-931
Fax: [358] (0) 174-681

France

The Honorable Felix Rohatyn
Ambassador
American Embassy Paris
PSC 116
APO AE 09777
Phone: [33] (1) 4312-2222
Fax: [33] (1) 4266-9783
Appointed - 08/01/97
Oath - 08/12/97

Gabon

The Honorable Elizabeth Raspolic
Ambassador
American Embassy Libreville
Blvd. de la Mer B.P. 4000
Libreville, Gabon
Phone: [241] 762003/4
Fax: [241] 745-507
Appointed - 10/03/95
Oath - 10/11/95

Gambia

The Honorable Gerald Wesley Scott
Ambassador
American Embassy Banjul
Fajara, Kairaba Ave., P.M.B. No. 19
Banjul, Gambia
Phone: (220) 392-856
Fax: (220) 392-475
Appointed - 12/19/95
Oath - 01/10/96

Georgia

The Honorable William Harrison Courtney
Ambassador
American Embassy Tbilisi
#25 Antoneli
Tbilisi, Georgia
Phone: 995-32-989-967
Fax: 995-32-933-803
Appointed - 08/14/95
Oath - 09/06/95

Germany

The Honorable John Christian Kornblum
Ambassador
American Embassy Bonn
PSC 117
APO AE 09080
Phone: [49] 228-3391
Fax: [49] 228-339-2663
Appointed - 08/01/97
Oath - 08/11/97

Ghana

The Honorable Edward Brynn
Ambassador
American Embassy Accra
P.O. Box 194
Accra, Ghana
Phone: [233] (21) 775348
Fax: [233] (21) 776008
Appointed - 10/03/95
Oath - 11/09/95

Greece

The Honorable R. Nicholas Burns
Ambassador
American Embassy Athens
PSC 108
APO AE 09842
Phone: [30] (1) 721-2951
Fax: [30] (1) 645-6282
Appointed - 11/04/97
Oath - 11/10/97

Grenada

Vacant
Ambassador
American Embassy St. George's
P.O. Box 54
St. George's, Grenada
Phone: (809) 444-1173/8
Fax: (809) 444-4820

Guatemala

The Honorable Donald J. Planty
Ambassador
American Embassy Guatemala
APO AA 34024
Phone: [502] (2) 31-15-41
Fax: [502] (2) 31-88-85
Appointed - 07/02/96
Oath - 07/18/96

Guinea

The Honorable Tibor P. Nagy, Jr.
Ambassador
American Embassy Conakry
Rue KA 038, B.P. 603
Conakry, Guinea
Phone: (224) 41-15-20
Fax: (224) 44-15-22
Appointed - 07/02/96
Oath - 07/05/96

Guinea-Bissau

The Honorable Peggay Blackford
Ambassador
American Embassy Bissau
Bairro de Penha, 1067 Bissau Codex
Bissau, Guinea-Bissau
Phone: [245] 25-2273
Fax: [245] 25-2282
Appointed - 10/03/95
Oath - 10/27/95

Guyana

The Honorable James F. Mack
Ambassador
American Embassy Georgetown
P.O. Box 10507
Georgetown, Guyana
Phone: [592] (2) 54900-9
Fax: [592] (2) 58497
Appointed - 08/01/97
Oath - 09/12/97

Haiti

The Honorable Timothy Michael Carney
Ambassador
American Embassy Port-au-Prince
P.O. Box 1761
Port-au-Prince, Haiti
Phone: [509] 22-0354
Fax: [509] 23-1641
Appointed - 11/12/97
Oath - 12/18/97

Holy See

The Honorable Corinne Claiborne Boggs
Ambassador
American Embassy Vatican City
PSC 59, Box F
APO AE 09624
Phone: [396] 46741
Fax: [396] 575-8346
Appointed - 10/14/97
Oath - 10/17/97

Honduras

The Honorable James Francis Creagan
Ambassador
American Embassy Tegucigalpa
AP No. 3453
APO AA 34022
Phone: [504] 36-9320
Fax: [504] 36-9037
Appointed - 07/02/96
Oath - 07/29/96

Hungary

The Honorable Peter Francis Tufo
Ambassador
American Embassy Budapest
V. 1054 Szabadsag Ter 12
Budapest, Hungary
Phone: [36] (1) 267-4400
Fax: [36] (1) 269-9326
Appointed - 11/10/97
Oath - 11/12/97

Iceland

The Honorable Day Olin Mount
Ambassador
American Embassy Reykjavik
PSC 1003, Box 40
FPO AE 09728-0340
Phone: [354] 562-9100
Fax: [354] 562-9139

Appointed - 06/11/96
Oath - 08/22/96

India

The Honorable Richard Frank Celeste
Ambassador
American Embassy New Delhi
Shanti Path, Chanakyapuri 110021
New Delhi, India
Phone: [91] (11) 688-9033
Fax: [91] (11) 687-2391
Appointed - 11/10/97
Oath - 11/10/97

Indonesia

The Honorable J. Stapleton Roy
Ambassador
American Embassy Jakarta
Box 1
APO AP 96520
Phone: [62] (21) 344-2211
Fax: [62] (21) 386-2259
Appointed - 12/19/95
Oath - 12/19/95

Ireland

The Honorable Jean Kennedy Smith
Ambassador
American Embassy Dublin
42 Elgin Rd., Ballsbridge
Dublin, Ireland
Phone: [353] (1) 44-1232-328239
Fax: [353] (1) 6689946
Appointed - 06/17/93
Oath - 06/18/93

Israel

The Honorable Edward S. Walker, Jr.
Ambassador
American Embassy Tel Aviv
PSC 98, Box 100
APO AE 09830
Phone: [972] (3) 519-7575
Fax: [972] (3) 517-3227
Appointed - 11/10/97
Oath - 12/22/97

Italy

The Honorable Thomas M. Foglietta
Ambassador
American Embassy Rome
PSC 59, Box F
APO AE 09624
Phone: [39] (6) 46741
Fax: [39] (6) 488-2672
Appointed - 11/12/97
Oath - 11/12/97

Jamaica

The Honorable Stanley Louis McLelland
Ambassador
American Embassy Kingston
Jamaica Mutual Life Center

2 Oxford Rd., 3rd Floor
Kingston, Jamaica
Phone: (809) 929-4850
Fax: (809) 926-6743
Appointed - 11/12/97
Oath - 01/28/98

Japan

The Honorable Thomas S. Foley
Ambassador
American Embassy Tokyo
Unit 45004, Box 258
APO AP 96337-0001
Phone: [81] (3) 3224-5000
Fax: [81] (3) 3505-1862
Appointed - 10/31/97
Oath - 11/06/97

Jordan

The Honorable Wesley William Egan
Ambassador
American Embassy Amman
P.O. Box 354
APO AE 09892-0200
Phone: [962] (6) 820-101
Fax: [962] (6) 820-159
Appointed - 02/11/94
Oath - 02/26/94

Kazakhstan

The Honorable A. Elizabeth Jones
Ambassador
American Embassy Almaty
99/97 Furmanova St.
480012 Almaty, Kazakhstan
Phone: [7] (3272) 63-24-26
Fax: [7] (3272) 63-38-83
Appointed - 10/03/95
Oath - 10/11/95

Kenya

The Honorable Prudence Bushnell
Ambassador
American Embassy Nairobi
P.O. Box 30137, Unit 64100
APO AE 09831
Phone: [254] (2) 334141
Fax: [254] (2) 340838
Appointed - 06/11/96
Oath - 07/17/96

Kiribati

The Honorable Joan M. Plaisted
Ambassador
RESIDENT IN MARSHALL ISLANDS
Appointed - 12/19/95
Oath - 01/18/96

Korea, Republic of

The Honorable Steven W. Bosworth
Ambassador
American Embassy Seoul
Unit 15550

APO AP 96205-0001
Phone: [82] (2) 397-4114
Fax: [82] (2) 738-8845
Appointed - 10/24/97
Oath - 11/07/97

Kuwait

The Honorable James A. Larocco
Ambassador
American Embassy Kuwait
Unit 69000
APO AE 09880-9000
Phone: [965] 539-5307
Fax: [965] 538-0282
Appointed - 11/10/97
Oath - 12/09/97

Kyrgyz Republic

The Honorable Anne Marie Sigmund
Ambassador
American Embassy Bishkek
Erkindik Prospect #66
Bishkek 720002 Kyrgyzstan
Phone: [996] (3312) 22-29-20
Fax: [996] (3312) 22-35-51
Appointed - 08/01/97
Oath - 09/04/97

Laos

The Honorable Wendy Jean Chamberlin
Ambassador
American Embassy Vientiane
Box V
APO AP 96546
Phone: [856] (21) 212581
Fax: [856] (21) 212854
Appointed - 07/02/96
Oath - 08/01/96

Latvia

The Honorable Larry C. Napper
Ambassador
American Embassy Riga
PSC 78, Box R
APO AE 09723
Phone: [371] 721-0005
Fax: [371] 722-2764
Appointed - 06/27/95
Oath - 07/18/95

Lebanon

The Honorable Richard Henry Jones
Ambassador
American Embassy Beirut
PSC 815, Box 2
FPO AE 09836-0002
Phone: [961] (1) 402-200
Fax: [961] (1) 407-112
Appointed - 12/19/95
Oath - 02/02/96

Lesotho

The Honorable Bismarck Myrick

Ambassador
American Embassy Maseru
P.O. Box 333
100 Maseru, Lesotho
Phone: [266] 312-666
Fax: [266] 310-116
Appointed - 03/04/95
Oath - 03/24/95

Liberia

The Honorable William B. Milam
Charge d'Affaires
American Embassy Monrovia
P.O. Box 10-0098, Mamba Point
Monrovia, Liberia
Phone: [231] 226-370
Fax: [231] 226-148
Appointed - 11/08/95

Liechtenstein

The Honorable Madeleine May Kunin
Ambassador
RESIDENT IN SWITZERLAND
Appointed - 02/10/97
Oath - 02/20/97

Lithuania

The Honorable Keith C. Smith
Ambassador
American Embassy Vilnius
PSC 78, Box V
APO AE 09723
Phone: [370] (2) 223-031
Fax: [370] (6) 706-084
Appointed - 08/01/97
Oath - 08/19/97

Luxembourg

The Honorable Clay Constantinou
Ambassador
American Embassy Luxembourg
Unit 1410
APO AE 09126-1410
Phone: [352] 460123
Fax: [352] 461401
Appointed - 07/05/94
Oath - 07/21/94

Macedonia

The Honorable Christopher Robert Hill
Ambassador
American Embassy Skopje
Bul. Ilinden bb
91000 Skopje, Macedonia
Phone: [389] (91) 116-180
Fax: [389] (91) 117-103
Appointed - 07/02/96
Oath - 07/18/96

Madagascar

Vacant
Ambassador
American Embassy Antananarivo

14-16 Rue Rainitovo, Antsahavola
B.P. 620
Antananarivo, Madagascar
Phone: [261] (2) 212-57
Fax: [261] (2) 345-39

Malawi

The Honorable Amelia Ellen Shippy
Ambassador
American Embassy Lilongwe
P.O. Box 30016
Lilongwe 3, Malawi
Phone: [265] 783-166
Fax: [265] 780-471
Appointed - 11/07/97
Oath - 12/03/97

Malaysia

The Honorable John Raymond Malott
Ambassador
American Embassy Kuala Lumpur
P.O. Box 10035
APO AE 96535-8152
Phone: [60] (3) 248-9011
Fax: [60] (3) 242-2207
Appointed - 12/19/95
Oath - 12/27/95

Maldives

The Honorable Shaun Edward Donnelly
Ambassador
RESIDENT IN SRI LANKA
Appointed - 11/10/97
Oath - 11/25/97

Mali

The Honorable David P. Rawson
Ambassador
American Embassy Bamako
Rue Rochester NY and Rue Mohamed V.
B.P. 34 Bamako, Mali
Phone: [223] 225470
Fax: [223] 223712
Appointed - 12/19/95
Oath - 01/18/96

Malta

The Honorable Kathryn Linda Haycock
Proffitt
Ambassador
American Embassy Valletta
P.O. Box 535
Valletta, Malta
Phone: [356] 235960
Fax: [356] 243229
Appointed - 11/10/97
Oath - 12/17/97

Marshall Islands

The Honorable Joan M. Plaisted
Ambassador
American Embassy Majuro
P.O. Box 1379

Majuro, Marshall Islands 96960-1379
Phone: 692-247-4011
Fax: 692-247-4012
Appointed - 12/19/95
Oath - 01/18/96

Mauritania

The Honorable Timberlake Foster
Ambassador
American Embassy Nouakchott
B.P. 222
Nouakchott, Mauritania
Phone: [222] (2) 526-60
Fax: [222] (2) 515-92
Appointed - 10/24/97
Oath - 10/31/97

Mauritius

The Honorable Harold Walter Geisel
Ambassador
American Embassy Port Louis
P.O. Box 544
Port Louis, Mauritius
Phone: [230] 208-2347
Fax: [230] 208-9534
Appointed - 06/11/96
Oath - 07/08/96

Mexico

Vacant
Ambassador
American Embassy Mexico City
P.O. Box 3087
Laredo Texas 78044-3087
Phone: [52] (5) 209-9100
Fax: [52] (5) 208-3373

Micronesia

Vacant
Ambassador
American Embassy Kolonia
P.O. Box 1286, Pohnpei
96941 Kolonia, Micronesia
Phone: [691] 320-2187
Fax: [691] 320-2186

Moldova

The Honorable John Todd Stewart
Ambassador
American Embassy Chisinau
Strada Alexei Mateevicie, #103
277014 Chisinau, Moldova
Phone: 373 (2) 23-37-72
Fax: 373 (2) 23-30-44
Appointed - 10/03/95
Oath - 10/31/95

Mongolia

The Honorable Alphonse F. La Porta
Ambassador
American Embassy Ulaanbaatar
PSC 461, Box 300
FPO AP 96521-0002

Phone: [976] (1) 329095
Fax: [976] (1) 320-776
Appointed - 10/24/97
Oath - 11/13/97

Morocco

The Honorable Edward M. Gabriel
Ambassador
American Embassy Rabat
PSC 74, Box 003
APO AE 09718
Phone: [212] (7) 76-22-65
Fax: [212] (7) 76-56-61
Appointed - 11/10/97
Oath - 11/20/97

Mozambique

The Honorable Brian Dean Curran
Ambassador
American Embassy Maputo
Avenida Kaunda, P.O. Box 783
Maputo, Mozambique
Phone: [258] (1) 492797
Fax: [258] (1) 490114
Appointed - 10/24/97
Oath - 11/17/97

Myanmar

The Honorable Kent M. Wiedemann
Charge d'Affaires
American Embassy Rangoon
Box B
APO AP 96546
Phone: [95] (1) 282055
Fax: [95] (1) 280409
Appointed - 10/18/96

Namibia

The Honorable George F. Ward, Jr.
Ambassador
American Embassy Windhoek
14 Lossen St. P.B. 12029 Ausspannplatz
Windhoek, Namibia
Phone: [264] (61) 221-601
Fax: [264] (61) 229-792
Appointed - 06/11/96
Oath - 07/24/96

Nauru

Vacant
Ambassador
RESIDENT IN FIJI

Nepal

The Honorable Ralph Frank
Ambassador
American Embassy Kathmandu
Pani Pokhari
Kathmandu, Nepal
Phone: [977] (1) 411179
Fax: [977] (1) 419963
Appointed - 08/01/97
Oath - 09/15/97

Netherlands

The Honorable K. Terry Dornbush
Ambassador
American Embassy The Hague
PSC 71, Box 1000
APO AE 09715
Phone: [31] (70) 310-9209
Fax: [31] (70) 361-4688
Appointed - 02/09/94
Oath - 03/04/94

New Zealand

The Honorable Josiah Horton Beeman
Ambassador
American Embassy Wellington
PSC 467, Box 1
FPO AP 96531-1001
Phone: [64] (4) 472-2068
Fax: [64] (4) 472-3537
Appointed - 03/28/94
Oath - 04/13/94

Nicaragua

The Honorable Lino Gutierrez
Ambassador
American Embassy Managua
APO AA 34021
Phone: [505] (2) 666010
Fax: [505] (2) 669074
Appointed - 07/02/96
Oath - 11/26/96

Niger

The Honorable Charles O. Cecil
Ambassador
American Embassy Niamey
Rue Des Ambassades, B.P. 11201
Niamey, Niger
Phone: [227] 72-26-61
Fax: [227] 73-31-67
Appointed - 06/11/96
Oath - 08/20/96

Nigeria

The Honorable William H. Twaddell
Ambassador
American Embassy Abuja
2 Eleke Crescent, P.O. Box 554
Abuja, Nigeria
Phone: [234] (1) 261-0097
Fax: [234] (1) 261-0257
Appointed - 11/10/97
Oath - 11/28/97

Norway

The Honorable David B.. Hermelin
Ambassador
American Embassy Oslo
PSC 69, Box 1000
APO AE 09707
Phone: [47] (22) 44-85-50
Fax: [47] (22) 44-33-63
Appointed - 11/10/97

Oath - 12/03/97

Oman

The Honorable Frances D. Cook
Ambassador
American Embassy Muscat
P.O. Box 202, Code No. 115
Medinat Qaboos
Muscat, Oman
Phone: [968] 698-989
Fax: [968] 699-779
Appointed - 12/19/95
Oath - 12/28/95

OSCE (Organization for Security & Cooperation in Europe)

The Honorable David Timothy Johnson
Head of U.S. Delegation
Obersteinergasse 11/1,
A-1190 Vienna
Phone: [43] (1) 313-39
Fax: [43] (1) 368-6385
Appointed - 01/03/98

Pakistan

The Honorable Thomas W. Simons, Jr.
Ambassador
American Embassy Islamabad
P.O. Box 1048, Unit 62200
APO AE 09812-2200
Phone: [92] (51) 826161
Fax: [92] (51) 276427
Appointed - 12/19/95
Oath - 01/05/96

Palau

The Honorable Thomas C. Hubbard
Ambassador
RESIDENT IN PHILIPPINES
P.O. Box 6028
Palau 96940
Phone: (680) 488-2920
Fax: (680) 488-2911
Appointed - 07/02/96
Oath - 08/06/96

Panama

The Honorable William J. Hughes
Ambassador
American Embassy Panama
Unit 0945
APO AA 34002
Phone: [507] 227-1377
Fax: [507] 227-1964
Appointed - 10/03/95
Oath - 10/25/95

Papua New Guinea

The Honorable Arma Jane Karaer
Ambassador
American Embassy Port Moresby

Douglas St., P.O. Box 1492
Port Moresby, New Guinea
Phone: [675] 321-1455
Fax: [675] 321-3423
Appointed - 02/10/97
Oath - 02/28/97

Paraguay

The Honorable Maura Harty
Ambassador
American Embassy Asuncion
Unit 4711
APO AA 34036-0001
Phone: [595] (21) 213-715
Fax: [595] (21) 213-728
Appointed - 08/01/97
Oath - 09/23/97

Peru

The Honorable Dennis C. Jett
Ambassador
American Embassy Lima
P.O. Box 1995, Lima 1
APO AA 34031-5000
Phone: [51] (1) 434-3000
Fax: [51] (1) 434-3037
Appointed - 07/02/96
Oath - 10/04/96

Philippines

The Honorable Thomas C. Hubbard
Ambassador
American Embassy Manila
FPO AP 96515
Phone: [63] (2) 523-1001
Fax: [63] (2) 522-4361
Appointed - 07/02/96
Oath - 08/05/96

Poland

The Honorable Daniel Fried
Ambassador
American Embassy Warsaw
Aleje Ujazdowskie 29/31
00-054 Warsaw, Poland
Phone: [48] (2) 628-3041
Fax: [48] (2) 628-8298
Appointed - 11/10/97
Oath - 11/13/97

Portugal

The Honorable Gerald S. McGowan
Ambassador
American Embassy Lisbon
PSC 83
APO AE 09726
Phone: [351] (1) 727-3300
Fax: [351] (1) 726-9109
Appointed - 11/10/97
Oath - 01/08/98

Qatar

The Honorable Patrick Nickolas Theros

Ambassador
American Embassy Doha
P.O. Box 2399
Doho, Qatar
Phone: (974) 864701
Fax: (974) 877499
Appointed - 10/03/95
Oath - 10/19/95

Romania

The Honorable James Carew Rosapepe
Ambassador
American Embassy Bucharest
Strada Tudor Arghezi 7-9
Bucharest, Romania
Phone: [40] (1) 210-4042
Fax: [40] (1) 210-0395
Appointed - 11/10/97
Oath - 01/20/98

Russia

The Honorable James Franklin Collins
Ambassador
American Embassy Moscow
APO AE 09721
Phone: [7] (095) 252-2451
Fax: [7] (095) 956-4261
Appointed - 08/01/97
Oath - 09/02/97

Rwanda

The Honorable Robert E. Gribbin III
Ambassador
American Embassy Kigali
Blvd. de la Revolution, B.P. 28
Kigali, Rwanda
Phone: [250] 75601
Fax: [250] 72128
Appointed - 12/19/95
Oath - 12/22/95

Samoa

The Honorable Josiah Horton Beeman
Ambassador
American Embassy Apia
P.O. Box 3430
Apia, Samoa
Phone: (685) 21-631
Fax: (685) 22-030
Appointed - 03/28/94
Oath - 04/13/94

Sao Tome and Principe

The Honorable Elizabeth Raspolic
Ambassador
RESIDENT IN GABON
Appointed - 10/03/95
Oath - 10/11/95

Saudi Arabia

The Honorable Wyche Fowler, Jr.
Ambassador

American Embassy Riyadh
Unit 61307
APO AE 09803-1307
Phone: [966] (1) 488-3800
Fax: [966] (1) 488-3278
Appointed - 10/31/97
Oath - 11/18/97

Senegal

The Honorable Dane Farnsworth Smith, Jr.
Ambassador
American Embassy Dakar
Avenue Jean XXIII, B.P. 49
Dakar, Senegal
Phone: [221] 823-4296
Fax: [221] 822-2991
Appointed - 06/11/96
Oath - 08/05/96

Serbia-Montenegro

The Honorable Richard M. Miles
Charge d'Affaires
American Embassy Belgrade
U.S. Department of State
Washington DC 20521-5070
Phone: [381] (11) 645-655
Fax: [381] (11) 645-221
Appointed - 08/02/96

Seychelles

The Honorable Harold Walter Geisel
Ambassador
RESIDENT IN MAURITIUS
Appointed - 06/06/96
Oath - 07/08/96

Sierra Leone

The Honorable John L. Hirsch
Ambassador
American Embassy Freetown
Corner Walpole & Siaka Stevens St.
Freetown, Sierra Leone
Phone: [232] (22) 226481
Fax: [232] (22) 225471
Appointed - 08/14/95
Oath - 08/18/95

Singapore

The Honorable Steven J. Green
Ambassador
American Embassy Singapore
FPO AP 96534
Phone: [65] 338-0251
Fax: [65] 338-4550
Appointed - 11/10/97
Oath - 11/18/97

Slovak Republic

The Honorable Ralph R. Johnson
Ambassador
American Embassy Bratislava
Hviezdoslavovo Namestie 4
81102 Bratislava, Slovakia

Phone: [421] (7) 533-3597
Fax: [421] (7) 533-5439
Appointed - 01/18/96
Oath - 03/15/96

Slovenia

Vacant
Ambassador
American Embassy Ljubljana
Department of State
Washington DC 20521-7140
Phone: [386] (61) 301-427
Fax: [386] (61) 301-401

Solomon Islands

The Honorable Arma Jane Karaer
Ambassador
RESIDENT IN PAPUA NEW GUINEA
Appointed - 02/10/97
Oath - 02/28/97

South Africa

The Honorable James A. Joseph
Ambassador
American Embassy Pretoria
P.O. Box 9536
0001 Pretoria, South Africa
Phone: [27] (12) 342-1048
Fax: [27] (12) 342-2244
Appointed - 12/19/95
Oath - 01/03/96

Spain

Vacant
Ambassador
American Embassy Madrid
APO AE 09642
Phone: [34] (1) 587-2200
Fax: [34] (1) 587-2303

Sri Lanka

The Honorable Shaun Edward Donnelly
Ambassador
American Embassy Colombo
P.O. Box 106
Colombo, Sri Lanka
Phone: [94] (1) 448007
Fax: [94] (1) 437345
Appointed - 11/10/97
Oath - 11/25/97

St. Kitts and Nevis

Vacant
Ambassador
RESIDENT IN BARBADOS

St. Lucia

Vacant
Ambassador
RESIDENT IN BARBADOS

St. Vincent & the Grenadines

Vacant
Ambassador
RESIDENT IN BARBADOS

Sudan

Vacant
Ambassador
American Embassy Khartoum
P.O. Box 699
APO AE 09829
Phone: [249] (11) 774611
Fax: [249] (11) 774137

Suriname

The Honorable Dennis K. Hays
Ambassador
American Embassy Paramaribo
Department of State
Washington DC 20521-3390
Phone: [597] 472900
Fax: [597] 420800
Appointed - 02/10/97
Oath - 02/28/97

Swaziland

The Honorable Alan R. McKee
Ambassador
American Embassy Mbabane
P.O. Box 199
Mbabane, Swaziland
Phone: [268] 46441
Fax: [268] 45959
Appointed - 07/02/96
Oath - 08/19/96

Sweden

The Honorable Lyndon Lowell Olson, Jr.
Ambassador
American Embassy Stockholm
Strandvagen 101
S-115 89 Stockholm, Sweden
Phone: [46] (8) 783-5300
Fax: [46] (8) 661-1964
Appointed - 11/10/97
Oath - 01/12/98

Switzerland

The Honorable Madeleine May Kunin
Ambassador
American Embassy Bern
Jubilaeumstrasse 93
3005 Bern, Switzerland
Phone: [41] (31) 357-7011
Fax: [41] (31) 357-7344
Appointed - 08/08/96
Oath - 08/08/96

Syria

Vacant

Ambassador
American Embassy Damascus
P.O. Box 29
Damascus, Syria
Phone: [963] (11) 333-2814
Fax: [963] (11) 224-7938

Taiwan

Unofficial commercial and other relations with the people of Taiwan are conducted through an unofficial instrumentality, the American Institute in Taiwan, which has offices in Taipei and Kaohsiung. AIT Taipei operates an American Trade Center, located at the Taipei World Trade Center. The addresses of these offices are:

American Institute in Taiwan
#7 Lane 134, Hsin Yi Rd. - Section 3
Taipei, Taiwan
Phone: [886] (2) 709-2000
Fax: [886] (2) 702-7675

American Trade Center
Room 3207 International Trade Bldg.
Taipei World Trade Center
333 Keelung Road - Section 1
Taipei 10548 Taiwan
Phone: [886] (2) 720-1550
Fax: [886] (2) 757-7162

American Institute in Taiwan
5th Fl., #2 - Chung Cheng 3d Rd.
Kaohsiung, Taiwan
Phone: [886] (7) 224-0154/7
Fax: [886] (7) 223-8237

For further information, contact the Washington, D.C., office:
American Institute in Taiwan
1700 N. Moore St. Suite 1700
Arlington, VA 22209-1996
Phone: (703) 525-8474
Fax: (703) 841-1385

Tajikistan

The Honorable R. Grant Smith
Ambassador
American Embassy Dushanbe
Octyabrskaya Hotel, 105A Prospect
Rudaki, Dushanbe Tajikistan 734001
Phone: [7] (3772) 21-03-56
Fax: [7] (3772) 20-03-62
Appointed - 06/27/95
Oath - 06/14/95

Tanzania

Vacant
Ambassador
American Embassy Dar es Salaam
P.O. Box 9123
Dar es Salaam, Tanzania
Phone: [255] (51) 666010
Fax: [255] (51) 666701

Thailand

The Honorable William H. Itoh
Ambassador

American Embassy Bangkok
APO AP 96546
Phone: [66] (2) 205-4000
Fax: [66] (2) 254-2990
Appointed - 12/19/95
Oath - 12/28/95

Togo

The Honorable Brenda Schoonover
Ambassador
American Embassy Lome
Rue Pelletier Caventou & Rue Vauban,
B.P. 852
Lome, Togo
Phone: [228] 21-77-17
Fax: [228] 21-79-52
Appointed - 11/10/97
Oath - 12/18/97

Tonga

Vacant
Ambassador
RESIDENT IN FIJI

Trinidad and Tobago

The Honorable Edward E. Shumaker, III
Ambassador
American Embassy Port-of-Spain
P.O. Box 752
Port-of-Spain, Trinidad and Tobago
Phone: (809) 622-6372
Fax: (809) 628-5462
Appointed - 10/24/97
Oath - 12/04/97

Tunisia

The Honorable Robin Lynn Raphel
Ambassador
American Embassy Tunis
144 Ave. de la Liberte
1002 Tunis-Belvedere, Tunisia
Phone: [216] (1) 782-566
Fax: [216] (1) 789-719
Appointed - 11/07/97
Oath - 11/19/97

Turkey

The Honorable Mark Robert Parris
Ambassador
American Embassy Ankara
PSC 93, Box 5000
APO AE 09823
Phone: [90] (312) 468-6110
Fax: [90] (312) 467-0019
Appointed - 11/04/97
Oath - 11/10/97

Turkmenistan

The Honorable Michael William Cotter
Ambassador
American Embassy Ashgabat
9 Pushkin St.
Ashgabat, Turkmenistan

Phone: [9] (9312) 35-00-45
Fax: [9] (9312) 51-13-05
Appointed - 10/03/95
Oath - 10/13/95

Tuvalu

Vacant
Ambassador
RESIDENT IN FIJI

Uganda

The Honorable Nancy Jo Powell
Ambassador
American Embassy Kampala
P.O. Box 7007
Kampala, Uganda
Phone: [256] (41) 259792
Fax: [256] (41) 259794
Appointed - 11/07/97
Oath - 11/21/97

Ukraine

The Honorable Steven Karl Pifer
Ambassador
American Embassy Kiev
10 Yuria Kotsubynskoho
254053 Kiev 53, Ukraine
Phone: [380] (44) 244-73459
Fax: [380] (44) 244-7350
Appointed - 11/10/97
Oath - 01/05/98

United Arab Emirates

The Honorable David C. Litt
Ambassador
American Embassy Abu Dhabi
Department of State
Washington DC 20521-6010
Phone: [971] (2) 436-691
Fax: [971] (2) 434-771
Appointed - 10/03/95
Oath - 10/10/95

United Kingdom

The Honorable Philip Lader
Ambassador
American Embassy London
PSC 801, Box 40
FPO AE 09498-4040
Phone: [44] (171) 499-9000
Fax: [44] (171) 409-1637
Appointed - 08/01/97
Oath - 09/12/97

Uruguay

The Honorable Christopher C. Ashby
Ambassador
American Embassy Montevideo
APO AA 34035
Phone: [598] (2) 23-60-61
Fax: [598] (2) 48-86-11
Appointed - 11/10/97
Oath - 11/21/97

Uzbekistan

The Honorable Joseph A. Presel
Ambassador
American Embassy Tashkent
82 Chilanzarskaya
Tashkent, Uzbekistan
Phone: [7] (3712) 77-14-07
Fax: [7] (3712) 40-63-35
Appointed - 11/10/97
Oath - 11/24/97

Vanuatu

The Honorable Arma Jane Karaer
Ambassador
RESIDENT IN PAPUA NEW GUINEA
Appointed - 02/10/97
Oath - 02/28/97

Venezuela

The Honorable John Francis Maisto
Ambassador
American Embassy Caracas
Unit 4900
APO AA 34037
Phone: [58] (2) 977-2011
Fax: [58] (2) 977-0843
Appointed - 02/10/97
Oath - 02/28/97

Vietnam

The Honorable Pete Peterson
Ambassador
American Embassy Hanoi
PSC 461, Box 400
FPO AP 96521-0002
Phone: [84] (4) 843-1500
Fax: [84] (4) 835-0484
Appointed - 04/11/97
Oath - 04/14/97

Yemen

The Honorable Barbara K. Bodine
Ambassador
American Embassy Sanaa
P.O. Box 22347
Sanaa, Yemen
Phone: [967] (1) 238-843
Fax: [967] (1) 251-563
Appointed - 11/07/97
Oath - 12/10/97

Zambia

The Honorable Arlene Render
Ambassador
American Embassy Lusaka
P.O. Box 31617
Lusaka, Zambia
Phone: [260] (1) 250-955
Fax: [260] (1) 252-225
Appointed - 07/02/96
Oath - 10/18/96

Zimbabwe

The Honorable Tom McDonald
Ambassador
American Embassy Harare
P.O. Box 3340
Harare, Zimbabwe
Phone: [263] (4) 794-521
Fax: [263] (4) 796-488
Appointed - 11/04/97
Oath - 11/19/97

U.S. Consular Offices Abroad

INTRODUCTION

Consular Affairs. Whether in a U.S. embassy or a consulate, consular officers at post are the State Department employees that American citizens overseas are most likely to meet. Consular officers extend to U.S. citizens and their property abroad the protection of the U.S. Government. They are involved in protecting and assisting millions of Americans living and traveling abroad.

Consular officers help transfer personal funds to those in financial difficulty, search for missing Americans, issue Consular Information Sheets and Travel Warnings, visit Americans in prison, maintain lists of local attorneys, act as liaison with police and other officials, assist hospitalized Americans, re-issue lost or stolen passports, and assist next of kin in the United States when relatives die abroad.

They also perform non-emergency services—dispensing information on absentee voting, international parental kidnaping and child custody, selective service registration, and acquisition and loss of U.S. citizenship; providing U.S. tax forms; notarizing documents; issuing passports; and processing estate and property claims. U.S. consular officers also issue about 6 million visas annually to foreign nationals who wish to visit the United States and almost 500,000 immigrant visas to those who wish to reside here permanently.

Australia

The Honorable Ross L. Wilson
Consulate General
American Consulate - Melbourne
Unit 11011
APO AP 96551-0002
Phone: [61] (3) 9526-5900
Fax: [61] (3) 9510-4646

The Honorable Nicholas A. Sherwood
Consulate General
American Consulate - Perth
APO AP 96530
Phone: [61] (9) 231-9400
Fax: [61] (9) 231-9444

The Honorable Jerome F. Tolson, Jr.
Consulate General
American Consulate - Sydney
PSC 280, Unit 11026
APO AP 96554-0002
Phone: [61] (2) 373-9200
Fax: [61] (2) 373-9125

Bermuda

The Honorable Robert A. Farmer
Consulate General
American Consulate - Hamilton
Department of State
Washington DC 20521-5300
Phone: (441) 295-1342
Fax: (441) 295-1592

Brazil

The Honorable Earl Irving
Principal Officer
American Consulate - Recife
APO AA 34030
Phone: [55] (81) 421-2441
Fax: [55] (81) 231-1906

The Honorable Cristobal R Orozco
Consulate General
American Consulate - Rio de Janeiro
Unit 3501
APO AA 34030
Phone: [55] (21) 292-7117
Fax: [55] (21) 220-0439

The Honorable Melissa Wells
Consulate General
American Consulate - Sao Paulo
P.O. Box 8063
APO AA 34030
Phone: [55] (11) 881-6511
Fax: [55] (11) 852-5154

Canada

The Honorable Richard V. Fisher
Consulate General
American Consulate - Calgary, Alberta
Suite 1050, 615 Macleod Trail, S.E.
Calgary, Alberta, Canada T2G 4T8
Phone: (403) 266-8962
Fax: (403) 264-6630

The Honorable R. Bruce Ehrnman
Consulate General
American Consulate - Halifax, Nova Scotia
Suite 910, Cogswell Tower, Scotia Sq.
Halifax, NS, Canada B3J 3K1
Phone: (902) 429-2480
Fax: (902) 423-6861

The Honorable Eleanor W. Savage
Consulate General
American Consulate - Montreal, Quebec
P.O. Box 65, Postal Station Desjardins
H5B 1G1, Montreal, Quebec, Canada
Phone: (514) 398-9695
Fax: (514) 398-0973

The Honorable Stephen Kelly
Consulate General
American Consulate - Quebec, Quebec
2 Place Terrasse Dufferin, C.P. 939
G1R 4T9, Quebec, Canada
Phone: (418) 692-2095
Fax: (418) 692-4640

The Honorable Gregory L. Johnson
Consulate General
American Consulate - Toronto, Ontario
360 University Ave.
M5G 1S4, Toronto, Ontario, Canada
Phone: (416) 595-1700
Fax: (416) 595-0051

The Honorable Judson L. Bruns III
Consulate General
American Consulate - Vancouver,
  British Columbia
1095 West Pender St.
V6E 2M6, Vancouver, British Columbia,
Canada
Phone: (604) 685-4311
Fax: (604) 685-5285

China

The Honorable Cornelius M. Keur
Consulate General
American Consulate - Chengdu
PSC 461, Box 85
FPO AP 96521-0002
Phone: [86] (28) 558-3992
Fax: [86] (28) 558-3520

The Honorable Edward McKeon
Consulate General
American Consulate - Guangzhou
PSC 461, Box 100
FPO AP 96521-0002
Phone: [86] (20) 8188-8911
Fax: [86] (20) 8186-2341

The Honorable Richard A. Boucher
Consulate General

American Consulate - Hong Kong
PSC 464, Box 30
FPO AP 96522-0002
Phone: [852] 2523-9011
Fax: [852] 2845-4845

The Honorable Joseph J. Borich
Consulate General
American Consulate - Shanghai
PSC 461, Box 200
FPO AP 96521-0002
Phone: [86] (21) 6433-6880
Fax: [86] (21) 6433-4122

The Honorable Gerard R. Pascua
Consulate General
American Consulate - Shenyang
PSC 461, Box 45
FPO AP 96521-0002
Phone: [86] (24) 322-1198
Fax: [86] (24) 322-2374

Ecuador

The Honorable Daniel A. Johnson
Consulate General
American Consulate - Guayaquil
APO AA 34039
Phone: [593] (4) 323-570
Fax: [593] (4) 325-286

France

The Honorable Joyce E Leader
Consulate General
American Consulate - Marseille
PSC 116
APO AE 09777
Phone: [33] (4) 91-54-92-00
Fax: [33] (4) 91-55-09-47

The Honorable Steven Wagenseil
Consulate General
American Consulate - Strasbourg
PSC 116
APO AE 09777
Phone: [33] (3) 88-35-21-04
Fax: [33] (3) 88-24-06-95

Germany

The Honorable Thomas L. Boam
Consulate General
American Consulate - Dusseldorf
Kennedydamm 15-17
40476 Dusseldorf, Germany
Phone: [49] (211) 47061-0
Fax: [49] (211) 43-14-48

The Honorable Janet S. Andres
Consulate General
American Consulate - Frankfurt Am Main
PSC 115
APO AE 09213-0115
Phone: [49] (69) 7535-0
Fax: [49] (69) 748-938

The Honorable A. Daniel Weygandt
Consulate General
American Consulate - Hamburg
Alsterufer 27/28
20354 Hamburg, Germany
Phone: [49] (40) 41171-0

Fax: [49] (40) 41171-222

The Honorable J. Patrick Truhn
Consulate General
American Consulate - Leipzig
PSC 120, Box 1000
APO AE 09265
Phone: [49] (341) 213-840
Fax: [49] (341) 213-8417

The Honorable George A. Glass
Consulate General
American Consulate - Munich
Unit 24718
APO AE 09178
Phone: [49] (89) 28880
Fax: [49] (89) 283-047

Greece

The Honorable Miriam Hughes
Consulate General
American Consulate - Thessaloniki
PSC 108, Box 37
APO AE 09842-0108
Phone: [30] (31) 242905
Fax: [30] (31) 242927

India

The Honorable Cheryl J. Sim
Consulate General
American Consulate - Calcutta
5/1 Ho Chi Minh Sarani
Calcutta 700071, India
Phone: [91] (33) 282-3611
Fax: [91] (33) 282-2335

The Honorable Michele J. Sison
Consulate General
American Consulate - Madras
220 Mount Rd.
600006 Madras, India
Phone: [91] (44) 827-3040
Fax: [91] (44) 825-0240

The Honorable Franklin Huddle, Jr.
Consulate General
American Consulate - Mumbai
Lincoln House, 78 Bhulabhai Desai Rd.
400026 Mumbai, India
Phone: [91] (22) 363-3611
Fax: [91] (22) 363-0350

Indonesia

The Honorable William A. Pierce
Consulate General
American Consulate - Surabaya
Gen Box 1, Unit 8131
APO AP 96520-0002
Phone: [62] (31) 582287
Fax: [62] (31) 574492

Italy

The Honorable Louis McCall
Consulate General
American Consulate - Florence
PSC 59 Box F
APO AE 09624
Phone: [39] (55) 239-8276

Fax: [39] (55) 284-088

The Honorable George G.B. Griffin
Consulate General
American Consulate - Milan
PSC 59, (M)
APO AE 09624
Phone: [39] (2) 290-351
Fax: [39] (2) 2900-1165

The Honorable Clarke N. Ellis
Consulate General
American Consulate - Naples
Box 18, PSC 810
FPO AE 09619-0002
Phone: [39] (81) 583-8111
Fax: [39] (81) 761-1869

Japan

The Honorable Jason P. Hyland
Principal Officer
American Consulate - Fukuoka
Unit 45004, Box 242
APO AP 96337-0001
Phone: [81] (92) 751-9331
Fax: [81] (92) 713-9222

The Honorable Daniel L. Shields III
Principal Officer
American Consulate - Nagoya
Unit 45004, Box 280
APO AP 96337-0001
Phone: [81] (52) 203-4011
Fax: [81] (52) 201-4612

The Honorable Aloysius M. O'Neill III
Consulate General
American Consulate - Naha, Okinawa
PSC 556, Box 840, Unit 45
FPO AP 96386-0840
Phone: [81] (98) 876-4211
Fax: [81] (98) 876-4243

The Honorable Frederic W. Maerkle
Consulate General
American Consulate - Osaka-Kobe
Unit 45004, Box 239
APO AP 96337-45004
Phone: [81] (6) 315-5900
Fax: [81] (6) 315-5915

The Honorable Marlene J. Sakave
Consulate General
American Consulate - Sapporo
Unit 45004, Box 276
APO AP 96337-0003
Phone: [81] (11) 641-1115
Fax: [81] (11) 643-1283

Jerusalem

The Honorable John E. Herbst
Consulate General
American Consulate - Jerusalem
P.O. Box 290, PSC 98, Box 100
APO AE 09830
Phone: [9726] (2) 253288
Fax: [9726] (6) 259270

Korea

The Honorable Holcombe H. Thomas

Principal Officer
American Consulate - Pusan
24, 2-Ka, Daechung-Dong, Chung-ku
Pusan, Korea
Phone: [82] (51) 246-7791
Fax: [82] (51) 246-8859

Mexico

The Honorable Larry Colbert
Consulate General
American Consulate - Ciudad Juarez
Chihuahua, Avenue Lopez Mateos
924 Norte
32000 Ciudad Juarez
Chihuahua, Mexico
Phone: [52] (16) 113000
Fax: [52] (16) 169056

The Honorable Danny B. Root
Consulate General
American Consulate - Guadalajara
Progreso 175
44100 Guadalajara, Jalisco, Mexico
Phone: [52] (3) 825-2998
Fax: [52] (3) 826-6549

The Honorable Sandra Salmon
Principal Officer
American Consulate - Hermosillo
Son., Monterrey 141 Pre.
83260 Hermosillo, Sonora, Mexico
Phone: [52] (62) 17-2375
Fax: [52] (62) 17-2578

The Honorable George B. Kopf
Principal Officer
American Consulate - Matamoros
Tamps., Ave., Primera 2002
87330 Matamoros, Tamaulipas, Mexico
Phone: [52] (88) 12-44-02
Fax: [52] (88) 12-21-71

The Honorable David R. van Valkenburg
Principal Officer
American Consulate - Merida
Yuc., Paseo Montejo 453
97000 Merida, Yucatan, Mexico
Phone: [52] (99) 25-5011
Fax: [52] (99) 25-6219

The Honorable Eileen M. Heaphy
Consulate General
American Consulate - Monterrey
N.L. Ave., Constitucion 411 Poniente
64000 Monterrey, Mexico
Phone: [52] (8) 345-2120
Fax: [52] (8) 342-0177

The Honorable Isiah L. Parnell
Principal Officer
American Consulate - Nuevo Laredo
Tamps., Calle Allende 3330, Col. Jardin
88260 Nuevo Laredo, Tamaulipas, Mexico
Phone: [52] (87) 14-0512
Fax: [52] (87) 14-7984

The Honorable Norman A. Singer
Consulate General
American Consulate - Tijuana
B.C.N., Tapachula 96
22420 Tijuana, Baja California
Norte, Mexico
Phone: [52] (66) 81-7400
Fax: [52] (66) 81-8016

Morocco

The Honorable Marcia Bernicat
Consulate General
American Consulate - Casablanca
PSC 74, Box 24
APO AE 09718
Phone: [212] (2) 264-550
Fax: [212] (2) 204-127

Netherlands

The Honorable Diane M. Andruch
Consulate General
American Consulate - Amsterdam
PSC 71, Box 1000
APO AE 09715
Phone: [31] (20) 5755 309
Fax: [31] (20) 5755 310

Netherlands Antilles

The Honorable James L. Williams
Consulate General
American Consulate - Curacao
P.O. Box 158, Willemstad
Curacao, Netherlands Antilles
Phone: [599] (9) 461-3066
Fax: [599] (9) 461-6489

New Zealand

The Honorable Michael E. Thurston
Consulate
American Consulate - Auckland
PSC 467, Box 99
FPO AP 96531-1099
Phone: [64] (9) 303-2724
Fax: [64] (9) 366-0870

Pakistan

The Honorable Douglas B. Archard
Consulate General
American Consulate - Karachi
Unit 62400
APO AE 09814-2400
Phone: [92] (21) 568-5170
Fax: [92] (21) 568-0496

The Honorable Geoffrey Pyatt
Consulate General
American Consulate - Lahore
Unit 62216
APO AE 09812-2216
Phone: [92] (42) 636-5530
Fax: [92] (42) 636-5177

The Honorable Bradford E. Hanson
Principal Officer
American Consulate - Peshawar
Unit 62217
APO AE 09812-2217
Phone: [92] (091) 279801
Fax: [92] (091) 276712

Poland

The Honorable Francis Scanlan
Consulate General
American Consulate - Krakow
Ulica Stolarska 9
31043 Krakow, Poland
Phone: [48] (12) 422-9764
Fax: [48] (12) 421-8292

Portugal

The Honorable Bernice A. Powell
Principal Officer
American Consulate - Ponta Delgada, Sao
Miguel Azores
PSC 76, Box 3000
APO AE 09720-0002
Phone: [351] (96) 22216
Fax: [351] (96) 27216

Russia

Vacant
Consulate General
American Consulate - St. Petersburg
PSC 78, Box L
APO AE 09723
Phone: [7] (812) 275-1701
Fax: [7] (812) 110-7022

The Honorable Jane Miller Floyd
Consulate General
American Consulate - Vladivostok
Ulitsa Pushkinskaya 32
Vladivostok, Russia 690000
Phone: [7] (501-4232) 30-00-70
Fax: [7] (501-4232) 30-00-72

The Honorable Howard J.T. Steers
Consulate General
American Consulate - Yekaterinburg
Department of State
Washington DC 20521-5890
Phone: [7] (3432) 564-619
Fax: [7] (3432) 564-515

Saudia Arabia

The Honorable Douglas C. Greene
Consulate General
American Consulate - Dhahran
Unit 66803
APO AE 09858-6803
Phone: [966] (3) 891-3200
Fax: [966] (3) 891-7416

The Honorable Stephen W. Buck
Consulate General
American Consulate - Jeddah
Unit 62112
APO AE 09811
Phone: [966] (2) 667-0080
Fax: [966] (2) 669-2991

South Africa

The Honorable April C. Glaspie
Consulate General

American Consulate - Cape Town
Broadway Industries Centre
Heerengracht, Foreshore
Cape Town, South Africa
Phone: [27] (21) 21-4280
Fax: [27] (21) 25-4151

The Honorable Frederic C. Hassani
Consulate General
American Consulate - Durban
Durban Bay House, 29th Fl.
333 Smith St.
Durban, South Africa
Phone: [27] (31) 304-4737
Fax: [27] (31) 301-8206

The Honorable Gregory W. Engle
Consulate General
American Consulate - Johannesburg
Kine Centre 11th Fl.
Commissioner & Kruis Sts.
Johannesburg, South Africa
Phone: [27] (11) 331-1681
Fax: [27] (11) 331-1327

Spain

The Honorable Maurice S. Parker
Consulate General
American Consulate - Barcelona
PSC 61, Box 0005
APO AE 09642
Phone: [34] (3) 280-2227
Fax: [34] (3) 205-5206

Thailand

The Honorable Scott P. Bellard
Principal Officer
American Consulate - Chiang Mai
Box C
APO AP 96546
Phone: [66] (53) 252-629
Fax: [66] (53) 252-633

Turkey

The Honorable Elizabeth W. Shelton
Principal Officer
American Consulate - Adana
PSC 94
APO AE 09824
Phone: [90] (322) 454-3774
Fax: [90] (322) 457-6591

The Honorable Carolyn R. Huggins
Consulate General
American Consulate - Istanbul
PSC 97, Box 0002
APO AE 09827-0002
Phone: [90] (212) 251-3602
Fax: [90] (212) 251-2554

United Arab Emirates

Vacant
Consulate General
American Consulate - Dubai
Department of State
Washington DC 20521-6020

Phone: [971] (4) 313-115
Fax: [971] (4) 314-043

United Kingdom

The Honorable Kathleen Stephens
Consulate General
American Consulate - Belfast,
 Northern Ireland
PSC 801, Box 40
APO AE 09498-4040
Phone: [44] (1232) 328-239
Fax: [44] (1232) 248-482

The Honorable Julie Rethmeier Moyes
Consulate General
American Consulate - Edinburgh, Scotland
PSC 801, Box 40
FPO AE 09498-4040
Phone: [44] (131) 556-8315
Fax: [44] (131) 557-6023

U. S. Department of Transportation

400 Seventh St., SW / Washington DC 20590

Central: 202/366-4000
Public Information: 202/366-5580
http://www.dot.gov

INTRODUCTION

By focusing attention on American technology and expertise, the Transportation Department helps American companies in the competition for overseas priority projects and procurement contracts. The Department is an active participant in the interagency Trade Promotion Coordinating Committee Advocacy Network, which was established to develop an effective system of aggressive advocacy, in close coordination with the private sector and within the context of overall U.S. foreign policy. The Transportation Department's advocacy activities have resulted in the awarding of contracts to American businesses around the world on a variety of transportation-related projects, such as air traffic control systems, aircraft sales, passenger terminal design, and port-dredging equipment.

Office of the Secretary

400 Seventh St., SW / Washington DC 20590

Secretary of Transportation
Mr. Rodney E. Slater
202/366-1111   FAX 202/366-7202
Rm. 10200

Personal: born 2/23/55 in Tutwiler, Miss.

Education: B.A., Eastern Michigan Univ., 1977. J.D., Univ. of Arkansas School of Law, 1980.

Professional: 1980-82, assistant attorney general, state of Ark. 1982-83, deputy campaign manager, Clinton for Governor Campaign Committee. 1983-85, special asst.; 1985-87, exec. asst., Gov. Bill Clinton. 1987-92, director of govt. relations, Ark. State Univ. 1992-93, dep. camp. manager, Clinton for President Campaign. 1993, deputy to Transition Director Warren Christopher, Clinton-Gore Presidential Transition Team. 1993-97, administrator, Federal Highway Administration; 1997-present, Secretary, U.S. Department of Transportation.

Rodney Slater was named Secretary of Transportation on February

14, 1997. He is the 13th Secretary in the 30-year history of the department and only the third Arkansan in American history to ever hold a position in the Cabinet.

In nominating Slater, President Clinton said that "he has built bridges both of steel and of goodwill to bring people closer together." As secretary, Slater is working to build the nation's airports, highways, railroads, mass transit, and maritime resources. The department, which has 100,000 employees and a budget of almost $40 billion, also includes the United States Coast Guard.

After being sworn in, Slater made improving transportation safety, investing in infrastructure, and running a department that costs less and works better his guiding principles. Within his first few months on the job, he sent Congress a plan to invest more in building highways and transit systems than any Transportation Secretary in history. He is working to ensure former welfare recipients have public transportation to get to their new jobs. He also launched the Garrett A. Morgan Technology and Transportation Futures Program, aimed at attracting 1 million students into transportation careers and mentoring and tutoring them to make sure they have needed skills. In addition, he has signed a dozen agreements to open aviation services to Asian and Latin American countries and has focused the department's attention on increasing trade in Africa.

Prior to becoming secretary, Slater was administrator of the Federal Highway Administration, creating the 160,000-mile National Highway System, upsizing highway investment by 20 percent, while downsizing the staff by 10 percent. He also helped develop an innovative financing program that is allowing hundreds of transportation projects to be built two to three years sooner, on average, at no extra cost to the federal taxpayer.

From 1987 to 1992, Slater was a member of the Arkansas State Highway Commission, serving as its chairman in 1992. He held several other positions in Arkansas, including director of governmental relations at Arkansas State University; executive assistant for economic and community programs for then-Governor Clinton; the governor's special assistant for community and minority affairs; and assistant attorney general in the litigation division of the Arkansas State Attorney General's Office. He also was liaison for the Martin Luther King Jr. Federal Holiday Commission.

Slater grew up in Marianna, Ark., one of the poorest areas in America. His first job was at age six, when he worked in a cotton field with his mother to earn money to buy his first vehicle, a bicycle. Slater graduated from Eastern Michigan University and earned a law degree at the University of Arkansas. At Eastern Michigan, he was captain of the football team and a member of the school's National Championship Forensics team. Eastern Michigan University presented him its Black Alumni Achievement Award in 1994 and an honorary doctorate degree in 1996.

He has received numerous honors. *Ebony* named him one of the 100 Most Influential Black Americans. The National Bar Association gave him its coveted President's Award and the *Arkansas Times* named him "Arkansas Hero." He also was one of the Arkansas Jaycees' Ten Outstanding Young Arkansans. He received the Arkansas Public Transportation Award and the W. Harold Flowers Law Society Lawyer-Citizen Award.

Slater and his wife, Cassandra Wilkins, have a daughter.

Trade Promotion Coordinating Committee

Task Force Contact
Ms. LeeAnn Moore
202/366-1219
Rm. 10300

Assistant to the Secretary and
Director of Public Affairs

400 Seventh St., SW / Washington DC 20590

Assistant to the Secretary and Director of Public Affairs
Mr. Steven J. Akey
202/366-4570   FAX 202/366-6337
Rm. 10414

Office of the General Counsel

400 Seventh St., SW / Washington DC 20590

Assistant General Counsel, International Law
Mr. Donald H. Horn
202/366-2972
Rm. 10118

Assistant Secretary for Aviation
and International Affairs

400 Seventh St., SW / Washington DC 20590

Assistant Secretary
Mr. Charles A. Hunnicutt
202/366-8822   FAX 202/493-2005
Rm. 10232

Personal: born and raised in LaGrange, Ga.

Education: B.S., American Univ. (Washington DC), 1972. J.D., Univ. of Georgia, 1975. LL.M., Vrije Univ. (Brussels, Belgium), 1981.

Professional: 1977-79, asst. to the deputy sec.; 1979-80, exec. asst. to the under secretary, U.S. Dept. of Commerce. 1980-87, legal adviser to the chair, U.S. International Trade Commission. 1987-96, partner, Robins, Kaplan, Miller, and Ciresi. 1996-present, assistant secretary for aviation and international affairs, U.S. Department of Transportation.

Charles Hunnicutt was appointed assistant secretary of Transportation for aviation and international affairs in January 1996. Hunnicutt serves as the principal adviser to the Secretary of Transportation on commercial aviation policy, including economic and regulatory issues, as well as other international transportation and trade matters. Hunnicutt also directs DOT activities involving the negotiation and implementation of international aviation agreements and the development of international activities in maritime, highway, and rail transportation.

Before joining DOT, Hunnicutt was a partner in the Washington DC office of the law firm of Robins, Kaplan, Miller & Ciresi. His practice

included all aspects of international trade, with particular emphasis on government regulation of international trade, including representation in unfair trade actions such as countervailing and antidumping duty investigations. He assisted Ukraine in developing a legal system acceptable to World Trade Organization standards, including a new customs regime, product standards procedures, and intellectual property.

From 1980 to 1987 he was legal adviser to the chairwoman of the U.S. International Trade Commission. The commission is an independent, impartial, fact-finding government agency which deals with matters of international trade and tariffs. Hunnicutt also served as the executive assistant to the under secretary of commerce for international trade. Earlier, he was assistant to the deputy assistant secretary of commerce responsible for textile trade policy. In 1977, he worked in the White House presidential personnel office, following his work on the Carter-Mondale transition team.

Hunnicutt received a degree in international business from The American University, a J.D. from the University of Georgia, where he was editor in chief of the *Georgia Journal of International and Comparative Law*. He holds an L.L.M. in international and comparative law from the Vrije Universiteit Brussel in Brussels, Belgium, and received the certificate of the Hague Academy of International Law in 1975.

He served as president of the Washington Foreign Law Society and chairman of the ad hoc committee on the UNICTRAL Model Law on International Commercial Arbitration. He is a member of the American Society of International Law, serving on the budget committee, and the American Bar Association, serving on the steering committee for international trade. Hunnicutt is also a member of the Federal Bar Association and the International Bar Association.

Director, Aviation and International Economics
Mr. James Craun
202/366-1053
Rm. 6419E

Deputy Director
Mr. Randall Bennett
202/366-1054
Rm. 6401

International Transportation and Trade Office

Director
Mr. Bernard Gaillard
202/366-4368
Rm. 10300

Deputy Director
VACANT
202/366-2892
Rm. 10300

Senior Trade Policy Adviser
Ms. Florizelle Liser
202/366-9508
Rm. 10300

Chief, International Assistance Division
Mr. Roger Dean
202/366-9540
Rm. 9215

Chief, Maritime Surface and Facilitation Division
Mr. David DeCarme
202/366-2892
Rm. 10300

Chief, International Cooperation and Trade Division
Ms. Bernestine Allen
202/366-4398
Rm. 10302

Chief, International Secretariat
Ms. Melva Cunningham
202/366-9543
Rm. 10302

International Aviation Office

Director
Mr. Paul L. Gretch
202/366-2423
Rm. 6402

Deputy Director
Mr. Edward P. Oppler
202/366-2422
Rm. 6402

Assistant Director for Regulatory Affairs
Mr. Jeffrey B. Gayne
202/366-2424
Rm. 6402

Assistant Director for Negotiations
Ms. Susan E. McDermott
202/366-2361
Rm. 6402

Chief, Pricing and Multilateral Affairs Division
Mr. John Kiser
202/366-2435
Rm. 6420

Chief, U.S. Carrier Licensing Division
Ms. Teresa Bingham
202/366-2390
Rm. 6412

Chief, Foreign Carrier Licensing Division
Mr. George Wellington
202/366-2388
Rm. 6412

Chief, Europe Division
Ms. Mary Street
202/366-2379
Rm. 6402H

United States Coast Guard

2100 Second St., SW / Washington DC 20593-0001

International Affairs and Foreign Policy Adviser

Director
Mr. Gerard P. Yoest
202/267-2280
Rm. 2114

Deputy Director, International Affairs Staff
Capt. Domenico Dilulio
202/267-2280
Rm. 2114

Asst. Director, Technical Asst. and Intl. Organization
Mr. Gene F. Hammel
202/267-2280
Rm. 2114

Office of the Chief Counsel

Chief, Maritime and Intl. Law Division
Capt. Malcolm J. Williams, Jr.
202/267-1527
Rm. 3400

Office of Law Enforcement

Chief, Migrant Interdiction Division
Lt. Cdr. Mike Farrell
202/267-1178
Rm. 3110

Chief, Drug Interdiction Division
Cdr. George A. Russell
202/267-1771
Rm. 3110

Coast Guard Liaison to Dept. of State, Intl. Narcotics Matters
Capt. Bradley J. Niesen
202/647-7848
Rm. 7811

Coast Guard Liaison to Dept. of State, Law Enforcement
Cdr. Joseph Conroy
202/736-4377
Rm. 7811

Federal Aviation Administration

800 Independence Ave., SW / Washington DC 20591

Asst. Adm. for Policy, Planning and Intl. Aviation

Acting Assistant Administrator
Ms. Louise E. Maillett
202/267-3033
Rm. 1005D

International Aviation Office
Director
Ms. Joan W. Bauerlein
202/267-8112
Rm. 1027

United Kingdom Representative
Mr. Tony Vaudrey
202/463-7529

French Representative
Mr. Edmond Boullay
202/944-6054

Manager, Global Issues Division
Mr. Michael O'Neill
202/267-8124
Rm. 1025

Manager, Americas Division
Ms. Cecilia Capestany
202/267-3231
Rm. 1025

Manager, Europe, Africa, and Mideast Division
Ms. Marci Kenney
202/267-8157
Rm. 1026

Manager, Asia Pacific Division
Mr. Peter M. Keefe
202/267-8174
Rm. 1023

Associate Administrator for Civil Aviation Security

Manager, International Liaison Staff
Mr. David Leach
202/267-7200
Rm. 321

Manager, Foreign Operations Division
Mr. Joseph Teixera
202/267-7752
Rm. 315

Associate Administrator for Air Traffic Services

Manager, International
Mr. Charles R. Reavis
202/267-9313
Rm. 427

Associate Administrator for Regulation and Certification

Manager, International Liaison Staff
Ms. Lynn A. Jensen
202/267-3719
Rm. 821

Federal Highway Administration

Associate Administrator for Policy
400 Seventh St., SW / Washington DC 20590

Director, Office of Intl. Programs
Mr. King Gee
202/366-0111
Rm. 3325

Chief, Intl. Cooperation Division
Mr. Robert Ford
202/366-9636
Rm. 3327

National Highway Institute
901 Stuart Street / Arlington VA 22203

Chief, University, Industry and Intl. Programs Division
VACANT
103/235-0533
Rm. 300

Federal Railroad Administration

1120 Vermont Ave., NW / Washington DC 20005

Assoc. Administrator for Policy and Program Develop.

Director, International and Management Program Staff
Mr. Ted Krohn
202/632-3133
Rm. 7085

Maritime Administration

Associate Administrator for Policy, International Trade and Marketing
400 Seventh St., SW / Washington DC 20590

Associate Administrator
Mr. Bruce J. Carlton

202/366-5772
Rm. 7218

Director, Office of Intl. Activities
Mr. James A. Treichel
202/366-5773
Rm. 7119

National Highway Traffic Safety Administration

400 Seventh St., SW / Washington DC 20590

Director, Intl. Harmonization
Mr. Frank Turpin
202/366-2114
Rm. 5220

Saint Lawrence Seaway Development Corp.

400 Seventh St., SW / Washington DC 20590

Acting Administrator
Mr. David Sanders
202/366-0118   FAX 202/366-7147
Rm. 5424

As acting administrator, David Sanders serves as the chief operating officer of the Saint Lawrence Seaway Development Corporation, a wholly owned government corporation responsible for the operation and maintenance of the U.S. locks and channels on the St. Lawrence River. Sanders previously served as the corporation's acting administrator from April 1995 to January 1996, and has also held the position of chief of staff from 1992 to 1995, and deputy administrator from January 1996 to June 1997 until being named acting administrator.

Sanders is leading an effort to establish the corporation as a performance-based organization, the first of it's kind in the federal government. He is also a key member of a U.S.- Canadian Seaway Working Group that is examining new ways for improving the binational operation of the Seaway.

Sanders has developed a strong reputation for working to contain Seaway costs. In late 1993, he served as the chairman of the Seaway's Joint Tolls Advisory Board and was instrumental in negotiating the first Seaway toll freeze in almost a decade with the Canadian Seaway Authority for the 1994 navigation season. He also led the corporation during toll negotiations that resulted in a continuation of the freeze for the 1995 and 1996 seasons, and elimination of the Welland Canal lockage charges beginning in 1998.

Before joining the corporation, Sanders was the staff director of the subcommittee on international economic policy and trade of the U.S. House of Representatives Committee on Foreign Affairs.

Prior to undertaking graduate studies in business management and public administration in 1993 at the Atkinson School Of Management, Willamette University in Salem, Ore., Sanders graduated with a bachelor's degree in economics and philosophy from the College of William and Mary, in 1981. He also studied history and literature at Cambridge University in England in 1979 and shipping and international trade at the Seatrade Academy at the Cambridge Academy of Transport in 1992 and 1994.

U. S. Department of Treasury

1500 Pennsylvania Ave., NW / Washington DC 20220
Central: 202/622-2111
Public Affairs: 202/622-2960

INTRODUCTION

As a means of promoting U.S. export competitiveness, the Treasury Department participates in international negotiations to open new markets, lower trade barriers to existing markets, and reduce export subsidies abroad. Specifically, the Department leads export credit negotiations to reduce export-financing subsidies offered by other governments and to maintain a market-based trade finance environment. Treasury also leads financial services negotiations to reduce or remove barriers to the provision of U.S. financial services abroad. And the Department provides policy guidance on the negotiation, implementation, and enforcement of trade agreements, such as the North American Free Trade Agreement and Uruguay Round Agreement, from legislation drafting to dispute resolution.

Office of the Secretary

1500 Pennsylvania Ave., NW / Washington DC 20220

Secretary of the Treasury
The Hon. Robert E. Rubin
202/622-1100   FAX   202/622-0073
Rm. 3330

Personal: born 1938 in New York City, N.Y.

Education: A.B. in economics, Harvard Univ. Graduate in economics, London School of Economics. LL.B., Yale Law School.

Professional: 1964-66, attorney, Cleary, Gottlieb, Steen & Hamilton (New York). 1966-93: associate ('66-'69), general partner ('71), vice chairman and co-chief operating officer ('87-'90), and co-senior partner and co-chair ('90-'93), Goldman Sachs & Co. (New York). 1993-95, assistant to the President for economic policy and director, National Economic Council, The White House. 1995-present, Secretary of the Treasury.

Robert Rubin became Secretary of the Treasury in January of 1995, succeeding Lloyd Bentsen who resigned in December of 1994. Rubin had previously served President Clinton as the first director of the White House National Economic Council (NEC). The NEC was established by President Clinton to focus on the economic welfare of the country in a manner similar to the focus on the security interests of the country by the National Security Council.

Shortly after assuming office, Rubin was faced with an international financial crisis when Mexico devalued the peso and foreign investment started fleeing that country. Rubin's initial attempt to put together a long guarantee package to address the situation was blocked by the newly-Republican controlled Congress. Eventually the Exchange Stabilization Fund and an IMF loan were put together to handle the crisis.

At the beginning of the second Clinton term, it became clear to many in Washington that Rubin had become the principal economic policy force in the Administration. Indeed when the President was introducing his new economic team in December of 1996, he noted that Rubin would be "the captain of the team" (*New York Times,* December 15, 1996). *Time Magazine* named him one of the 25 most influential Americans in its April 1997 listing. Another Administration official referred to Rubin as "the most powerful but least pompous member of the Cabinet". (*National Journal,* June 14, 1997).

Rubin's clout was evident throughout the spring and summer of 1997 as the Congress and the Administration wrestled over the details of a balanced budget plan. During these negotiations, it was Rubin's job to define the President's position to the Republican leaders and point out the "deal breakers".

Within the Treasury Department itself, Rubin has delegated some sticky administrative problems to Deputy Secretary Lawrence Summers, particularly the management problems at the Internal Revenue Service and the costly over-runs on IRS' new computer plans. IRS officials were forced to disclose to Congress in March of 1997 that they had wasted about $400 million in an attempt to modernize its computer and telecommunications systems in the previous ten years.

Rubin had been associated with the investment banking firm of Goldman Sachs in New York City from 1966 until he took the White House position in 1993. He is rumored to be personally worth $100 million and during the 1997 budget negotiations, the President reportedly took delight in pointing out that his wealthy Treasury Secretary was the one fighting for the earned income tax credit for the working poor.

Rubin has also taken an interest in urban policy and helped to fight Republican efforts to cut a low income housing tax credit and blocked their efforts to limit the Community Reinvestment Act.

Office of the Chief of Staff

Chief of Staff
Mr. Michael B.G. Froman
202/622-1906   FAX 202/622-0073
Rm. 3408
E-Mail: Mike.Froman@Treas.sprint.com

Education: A.B. in public and international affairs (summa cum laude*),* Princeton Univ., 1985. D.Phil. in international relations, Oxford Univ., 1988. J.D. (magna cum laude*),* Harvard Law School, 1991.

Professional: 1987-88, research associate; 1988-91, research affiliate, Center for International Affairs, Harvard University. Spring 1989, teaching assistant, Harvard College. Summer 1989, summer associate, general counsel's office, U.S. Department of Defense. Summer 1990, summer associate, legal adviser's office, U.S. Department of State. Summer 1991, summer associate, Reichler & Soble (Wash., DC). 10/91-9/92, staff expert, Commission of the European Communities (Brussels, Belgium). Mar-Sept 1992, liaison, legal assistance program, ABA Central and East European Law Initiative (Tirana, Albania). 9/92-1/93, staff member, office of domestic and economic policy, The White House. l/93-12/95, director, international economic affairs, National Economic Council/National Security Council, The White House. 12/95-1/97, deputy assistant secretary, Eurasia and the Middle East; January 1997-present, chief of staff , U.S. Department of the Treasury.

Michael Froman was appointed chief of staff of the Department of the Treasury on January 6, 1997. As chief of staff, Froman serves as Treasury Secretary Robert E. Rubin's advisor on foreign and domestic economic policy, enforcement, tax policy, budget, management, and communications issues. He is responsible for coordinating and implementing the Secretary's priorities throughout the Department and its 12 operating bureaus. Froman also serves as the Secretary's liaison to the Department, the White House and other government agencies.

Froman had previously served as Treasury Deputy Assistant Secretary for Eurasia and the Middle East in 1996. His responsibilities included U.S. economic policy toward Russia, Bosnia, and the Middle East peace process. From January 1993 until December 1995, Froman was director for international economic affairs on the National Economic Council and the National Security Council at the White House. He served in the White House office of domestic and economic policy from September 1992 to January 1993.

Prior to assuming his position at the White House, Froman served as liaison for the American Bar Association's Central and East European Law initiative legislative assistance program in the Republic of Albania and as a member of the Forward Studies Unit of the European Commission in Brussels. He has practiced law with the firms of Covington & Burling and Reichler & Soble in Washington DC and Nishimura & Sanada in Tokyo. He served on the policy planning staff and in the legal adviser's office at the US Department of State. In addition, he worked in the office of the general counsel for the U.S. Department of Defense and at the USIA.

Among other fellowships and scholarships, Froman has received a White House Fellowship, a Council on Foreign Relations International Affairs Fellowship, a Fulbright, and a Harry S. Truman Scholarship. He is a member of the Council on Foreign Relations, the American Society of International Law, and the American Bar Association, as well as the bars of New York, Massachusetts, and the District of Columbia. He is the author of a book, *Coming to Terms -- The Development of the Idea of Detente* (Macmillan/St Martin's Press, 1991) and several articles on international relations, trade, and law.

Froman received a bachelor's degree in public and international affairs from Princeton University, a doctorate in international relations from Oxford University, and a law degree from Harvard Law School where he was an editor of the *Harvard Law Review* and a staff member of the *Harvard International Law Journal*. He and his wife, Nancy F. Goodman, live in Washington DC

Office of the Under Secretary for Intl. Affairs

1500 Pennsylvania Ave., NW / Washington DC 20220

Under Secretary
Mr. David A. Lipton
202/622-1270   FAX 202/622-0417
Rm. 3432

Personal: born 11/9/53 in Boston, Mass.

Education: B.A. in economics, Wesleyan Univ. M.A. and Ph.D. in economics, Harvard Univ.

Professional: 1981-89, economist, International Monetary Fund. 1989-92, economic advisor. UN Development Program & the World Institute for Development Economics Research. 1993-95, dep. asst. sec. for Eastern Europe and the former Soviet Union; December 1995-Aug. 1997, asst. sec. of Treasury for international affairs; Sept. 1997-present, under secretary for international affairs, U.S. Dept. of the Treasury.

President Clinton announced his nomination of assistant secretary of the Treasury for international affairs David Lipton to be under secretary of the Treasury for international affairs on June 27, 1997. On September 18, 1997, the Senate confirmed Lipton's nomination.

As under secretary, Lipton advises and assists the secretary and the deputy secretary on all aspects of international economic policy. Secretary Rubin welcomed Lipton's promotion, saying "David has been an important part of this Administration's international economic team. He has been a key contributor to our policy toward Russia and the Ukraine and has been instrumental in shaping the economic and financial aspects of our policy is Bosnia."

As assistant secretary of the Treasury for international affairs since December of 1995, Lipton focused on international and economic policy coordination, economic and financial relations with both industrialized and developing countries, foreign investment in the U.S. and U.S. policy with respect to the International Monetary Fund and the multilateral development banks.

Prior to becoming assistant secretary, Lipton had served as deputy assistant secretary for Eastern Europe and the former Soviet Union. During this time, he worked to design and implement a policy of U.S. leadership in support of comprehensive, market-oriented reform in the economies in transition and worked to engage the G-7 and the international financial institutions in pursuit of multilateral backing for that historic process.

Before joining the Clinton administration in the spring of 1993, Lipton was a Fellow at the Woodrow Wilson Center of Scholars. From 1989 to 1992, working under the auspices of the UN Development Program and the World Institute for Development Economics Research, he was an economic advisor to the governments of Russia, Poland, and Slovenia. Lipton served as an economist at the International Monetary Fund from 1981 to 1989.

Lipton is married to Susan Galbraith and they have three children.

Senior Policy Adviser
Mr. Michael Moynihan
202/622-0182
Rm. 3203

Office of the Asst. Secretary for Intl. Affairs

1500 Pennsylvania Ave., NW / Washington DC 20220

> ### INTRODUCTION
>
> *The Treasury Department helps formulate and execute U.S. international economic policy. It develops policies in international monetary affairs, trade and investment policy, international debt strategy, and directs U.S. participation in international financial institutions. The U.S. Customs collects revenue from imports and enforces customs and related laws.*

The Office of the Assistant Secretary for International Affairs divides its work into groups responsible for monetary affairs, developing nations, trade and investment policy, and Arabian Peninsula affairs. These functions are performed by supporting staff offices, which:

- conduct financial diplomacy with industrial and developing nations and regions;

- work toward improving the structure and operations of the international monetary system;

- monitor developments in foreign exchange and other markets and official operations affecting those markets;

- facilitate structural monetary cooperation through the International Monetary Fund and other channels;

- oversee U.S. participation in the multilateral development banks and coordinate U.S. policies and operations relating to bilateral and multilateral lending programs and institutions;

- formulate policy concerning the financing of trade;

- coordinate policies toward foreign investments in the U.S. and U.S. investments abroad; and analyze balance of payments and other basic financial and economic data, including data on petroleum affecting world payments patters and the world economic outlook.

As part of those functions, the office supports the Secretary of Treasury in his role as co-chairman of the U.S.-Saudi Arabian Joint Commission on Economic Cooperation, co-chairman of the U.S.-Israel Joint Committee for Investment and Trade; co-chairman of the U.S.-China Joint Economic Committee, and chairman of the National Advisory Council on International Monetary and Financial Policies.

Asst. Secretary
Mr. Timothy F. Geithner
202/622-0656   FAX 202/622-0081
Rm. 3430

Personal: born 8/18/61 in New York City, N.Y.

Education: B.A. in government and Asian studies, Dartmouth College, 1983. M.A. in international economics and East Asian studies, School of Advanced International Studies, Johns Hopkins Univ., 1985.

Professional: 1984-85, int'l. economist, development office, Overseas Private Investment Corporation. 1985-88, analyst for East Asia, Kissinger Associates. 1988-89, int'l economist; 1989-90, asst. to the U.S. negotiator for financial services in the Uruguay Round; 1990-92, asst. financial attache, U.S. Embassy, Tokyo; 1992-93, spec. asst. to the asst. sec. for int'l affairs; 1993-94, special asst. to the under secretary for international affairs; 1994-97, dep. asst. sec. for intl. monetary and financial policy; Sept. 1997-present, asst. sec. for international affairs, U.S. Dept. of Treasury.

President Clinton nominated senior deputy assistant secretary of the Treasury, Timothy Geithner, to be assistant secretary of the Treasury for international affairs on July 11, 1997. Geithner's nomination was confirmed by the Senate on September 18.

Geithner has served as a career civil servant at the Treasury Department since 1988 and "has made an important contribution to our international economic policy team by playing a key role in formulating our U.S. exchange rate policy and U.S. policy toward Japan," said Treasury Secretary Robert Rubin on the announcement of Geithner's nomination.

As assistant secretary for international affairs, Geithner advises and assists the secretary, the deputy secretary, and the under secretary for international affairs on the formulation and execution of U.S. international economic policy. Specifically, his office is responsible for developing and executing U.S. policy in the areas of international economic and financial diplomacy; international monetary policy issues including exchange rate policy; economic policy cooperation among industrial nations (G-7); U.S. participation in international financial institutions; financial services negotiations and policy issues affecting international financial markets; and international trade and investment policy.

Geithner is married to Carole Sonnenfeld Geithner and they have two children.

Deputy Asst. Secretary for International Monetary and Financial Policy

Deputy Asst. Secretary
Ms. Caroline Atkinson
202/622-0489
Rm. 3221

Director, Office of Foreign Exchange Operations
Mr. Timothy Dulaney
202/622-0454
Rm. 2409

Director, Office of Intl. Banking and Securities Markets
Mr. William Murden
202/622-1255
Rm. 1064

Director, Office of Industrial Nations and Global Analyses
Mr. Joseph Gagnon
202/622-0138
Rm. 5050

Director, Office of Intl. Monetary Policy
Mr. James M. Lister
202/622-0112
Rm. 5050

Deputy Asst. Secretary for Eurasia and the Middle East

Deputy Asst. Secretary
Mr. Mark Medish
202/622-0770
Rm. 3221

Director, Office of Central and Eastern European Nations
Ms. Nancy Lee
202/622-2916
Rm. 5323

Director, Office of Middle Eastern and Central Asian Nations
Ms. Karen Mathiasen
202/622-2916
Rm. 5037

Deputy Asst. Secretary for Technical Assistance Policy

Deputy Assistant Secretary
Mr. James H. Falls III
202/622-0667
Rm. 3209

Director, Technical Assistance Office
Riddell Building, 1730 K Street, NW / Washington DC 20006
Mr. Robert T. Banque
202/622-5787
Rm. 204

Director, Saudi Arabian Joint Commission Program Office
1401 New York Ave., NW / Washington DC 20220
Mr. Jon M. Gaaserud
202/879-4350
Rm. 700

Senior Adviser for Middle East Affairs
1401 New York Ave., NW / Washington DC 20220
VACANT
202/622-0667
Rm. 700

Deputy Asst. Sec. for International Development, Debt, and Environmental Policy
1500 Pa. Ave., NW / Washington DC 20220

Deputy Asst. Secretary
Mr. William E. Schuerch
202/622-0154
Rm. 3218

Director, Office of Multilateral Development Banks
Mr. Joseph Eichenberger
202/622-1231
Rm. 5400

Director, Office of Intl. Debt Policy
Ms. Mary E. Chaves
202/622-1850
Rm. 5218

Deputy Asst. Secretary for Asia, The Americas, and Africa

Deputy Asst. Secretary
Mr. Daniel M. Zelikow
202/622-7222
Rm. 3222

Director, Office of Latin American and Caribbean Nations
Mr. Wesley McGrew
202/622-2876
Rm. 5413

Director, Office of East and South Asian Nations
Mr. Todd W. Crawford
202/622-0359
Rm. 5221

Director, Office of African Nations
Mr. Edwin L. Barber
202/622-1730
Rm. 5205

Deputy Asst. Secretary for Trade and Investment Policy

Deputy Asst. Secretary
Ms. Margrethe Lundsager
202/622-0168
Rm. 3208

Director, Office of Intl. Trade
Mr. T. Whittier Warthin
202/622-1733
Rm. 4436

Director, Office of Intl. Investment
Ms. Gay Sills Hoar
202/622-9066
Rm. 1136

Director, Office of Trade Finance
Mr. Steven F. Tvardek
202/622-1749
Rm. 4448

Director, Office of Financial Services Negotiations
Mr. Matthew Hennesey
202/622-0151
Rm. 4430

Office of the Under Secretary for Enforcement

1500 Pennsylvania Ave., NW / Washington DC 20220

Deputy Assistant Secretary for Regulatory, Tariff and Trade Enforcement

Deputy Asst. Secretary
Mr. John P. Simpson
202/622-0230
Rm. 4308

Director, Office of Trade and Tariff Affairs
Mr. Dennis M. O'Connell
202/622-0220
Rm. 4004

Pa. Ave. & Madison Place, NW / Washington DC 20220

Director, Office of Foreign Assets Control
Mr. R. Richard Newcomb
202/622-2500
Rm. 2233

Intl. Programs
Mr. Robert McBrien
202/622-2420
Rm. 2023

Office of the Asst. Secretary for Economic Policy

1500 Pennsylvania Ave., NW / Washington DC 20220

Deputy Asst. Secretary for Policy Coordination

Director, Office of Intl. Financial Analysis
Mr. Thomas A. McCown, Jr.
202/622-2250
Rm. 5460

Director, Office of Foreign Investment Studies
Mr. William L. Griever
202/622-2240
Rm. 5466

Office of the General Counsel

1500 Pennsylvania Ave., NW / Washington DC 20220

Asst. General Counsel, Intl. Affairs
Mr. Russell L. Munk
202/622-1899
Rm. 2314

Pa. Ave. & Madison Place, NW / Washington DC 20220
Chief Counsel, Foreign Assets Control
Mr. William B. Hoffman
202/622-2410
Rm. 3123

Office of the Asst. Secretary for Public Affairs

1500 Pennsylvania Ave., NW / Washington DC 20220

Assistant Secretary for Public Affairs
Mr. Howard M. Schloss
202/622-2910
Rm. 3442

Prior to his confirmation as assistant Secretary for public affairs at the U.S. Department of the Treasury, Howard Schloss had been a deputy assistant secretary at the Department. Schloss directs all external communications initiatives for the Secretary and his staff with the media, the White House Press Office and other government agencies.

Schloss was a former newspaper editor and Democratic Congressional Campaign Committee aide who worked at a Washington public relations firm before joining the Administration.

Office of the Assistant Secretary for Tax Policy

Deputy Assistant Secretary for Tax Policy
1201 Constitution Ave., NW / Washington DC 20220

International Tax Counsel

Director
Mr. Joseph H. Guttentag
202/622-0130
Rm. 7114

Deputy Intl. Tax Counsel
Mr. Phillip West
202/622-1762
Rm. 7119

Associate Intl. Tax Counsel
Mr. David Sutherland
202/622-1754
Rm. 7116

Associate Intl. Tax Counsel
Ms. Patricia Brown
202/622-1781
Rm. 7122

Deputy Asst. Secretary for Tax Analysis

Acting Director, Intl. Taxation
Mr. William Randolph
202/622-0455
Rm. 7203

Comptroller of the Currency

250 E St., SW / Washington DC 20219-0001

International Affairs

Senior Deputy Comptroller
Ms. Susan F. Krause
202/874-5010
Rm. 9-13

Deputy Comptroller, Intl. Banking and Finance
Mr. John M. Abbott
202/874-4730
Rm. 3-6

Director, Intl. Banking and Finance
Mr. Jose A. Tuya
202/874-4730
Rm. 3-6

Chief Counsel

Counselor for Intl. Activities
Ms. Raija H. Bettauer
202/874-0680
7-6

U.S. Customs Service

1300 Pennsylvania Ave., NW / Washington DC 20229
202/927-6724

> *INTRODUCTION*
>
> *As the principal border enforcement agency, the U.S. Customs Service enforces the Tariff Act of 1930 and other customs statutes. It also:*
>
> - *enforces export control laws and intercepts illegal high-technology and weapons exports;*
>
> - *cooperates with other federal agencies and foreign governments in suppressing the traffic of illegal narcotics and pornography;*
>
> - *enforces reporting requirements of the Bank Secrecy Act; and*
>
> - *collects international trade statistics.*

Acting Commissioner
Mr. Samuel H. Banks
202/927-1000   FAX 202/927-1380
Rm. 4.4D

Personal: born 1/20/45 in Portland, Oregon.

Education: B.S., Georgetown Univ.

Professional: U.S. Army, Vietnam. 1971-85, entered Customs Service as uniformed inspector in the San Francisco District then held various positions; 1985, area director, JFK International Airport; 1986-90, asst. commissioner for inspection and control; 1990-94, asst. commissioner for commercial operations; 1994-9/96, asst. commissioner of field operations; 9/96-present, dep. commissioner; 8/97-present, acting commissioner, U.S. Customs Service.

George Weise, who had been commissioner of the U.S. Customs Service since May of 1993, retired from this position on August 14, 1997. At press time, no replacement had been nominated. Samuel H. Banks, the deputy commissioner, was named acting commissioner until a nominee is appointed by the President and confirmed by the Senate.

The commissioner of U.S. Customs directs 19,000 employees responsible for enforcing hundreds of laws and international agreements which protect the American public. Customs collects over $20 billion annually in revenue from U.S. imports; protects our borders against the illegal importations of narcotics and other contraband as well as other hazardous products; enforces laws intended to prevent illegal trade practices and laws to prevent the export of high-technology products and weapons; and processes over 450 million persons entering the United States each year.

Since September 1996, Banks has served the Customs Service as its deputy commissioner, the highest ranking career position in the organization. From 1994 to 1996, Banks served as assistant commissioner of field operations, leading the largest office within Customs, consisting of nearly 12,000 personnel. He oversaw the major restructuring and streamlining of field operations as part of the overall Customs reorganization in 1995. This effort helped to empower staff at over 300 ports of entry to improve their processes for drug enforcement; revenue collection; entry of imports valued at over $800 billion; inspection of persons, vehicles, vessels, and aircraft arriving in the United States. Banks was a key member of the Customs Executive Team which earned a Hammer Award from the Vice President under the National Performance Review.

Banks began his career at Customs in the front lines of law enforcement, starting as a uniformed inspector in the San Francisco District in 1971. He moved up through the ranks and, in 1985, was appointed area director of Customs at JFK International Airport in New York. He went on to serve as assistant commissioner for inspection and control from 1986 to 1990, directing the enforcement and compliance programs for the Customs inspectional force at the nation's ports. From 1990 to 1994, as assistant commissioner for commercial operations, he managed all Customs trade programs and led the negotiations for the successful passage of the Customs Modernization Act.

He holds a bachelor's degree from Georgetown University and attended the U.S. State Department Senior Seminar. He was awarded a bronze star in 1970 while serving with the Army in Vietnam. Banks lives in Virginia with his wife and daughter.

Trade Ombudsman
Mr. Walter Corley
202/927-1440
Rm. 4.2A

Office of Field Operations

Director, Trade Compliance Division
Mr. Philip Metzger
202/927-0300
Rm. 5.4C

Acting Director, Import Operations Branch
Mr. Paul Schwartz
202/927-0667
Rm. 5.2D

Office of Regulations and Rulings

Director, Intl. Agreements Staff
Mr. Myles A. Harmon
202/927-2256
Third Floor

Director, Tariff Classification Appeals
Mr. John Durant
202/927-1964
Third Floor

Director, Intl. Trade Compliance Division
VACANT
202/927-2244
Rm. 3.3D

Chief, Intellectual Property Rights Branch
Mr. John F. Atwood
202/927-2263
Third Floor

Office of Strategic Trade

Asst. Commissioner
Mr. Charles Winwood
202/927-0570
Rm. 5.4A

Director, Strategic Trade Operations Division
Ms. Elizabeth Durant
202/927-0200
Rm. 1106

Office of Foreign Operations

Director
Mr. Roger Urbanski
202/927-0640
Rm. 6.5D

Director, Europe Desk
Mr. Dave Palmatier
202/927-0640
Rm. 6.5D

Director, Americas Desk
Mr. Justo Diaz
202/927-0640
Rm. 6.5D

Director, Far East Desk
Ms. Jan Mallory
202/927-0640
Rm. 6.5D

Office of Intl. Affairs

Asst. Commissioner
Mr. Douglas Browning
202/927-0400
Rm. 8.5C

Office of Intl. Policy

Director
Mr. Jerrald Worley
202/927-0440
Rm. 8.2C

Director, Intl. Organization and Agreements Division
Mr. Dennis Sequeira
202/927-1480
Rm. 8.2B

Chief, Americas Branch
Ms. Denna Henry
202/927-0440

Chief, Asia Branch
Mr. Allen Kent
202/927-0440

Chief, Europe/Africa/Pacific Rim Branch
Mr. Thomas Adams
202/927-0440

Office of Intl. Training

Director
Mr. David H. Harrell
202/927-0430
Rm. 8.5B

Director, Intl. Assistance Division

Mr. Samuel Snyder
202/927-1490
Rm. 8.5B

U.S. Customs-Area Port of Washington DC
Customhouse, Dulles Intl. Apt.,
Gateway Bldg. 1 / Wash. DC 20041

Port Director
Mr. Robert M. Jacksta
703/318-5901
Rm. 225

Internal Revenue Service

Office of the Chief Compliance Officer

Office of the Asst. Commissioner for Intl.
490 L'Enfant Plaza East, SW / Washington DC 20219

Assistant Commissioner
Mr. John T. Lyons
202/874-1900
Rm. 4401

Director, Office of Intl. Programs
Mr. Elvin Hedgpath
202/874-1700
Rm. 4425

Office of the Chief Counsel

International Trade Litigation Staff
26 Federal Plaza / New York, NY 10278

Assistant Chief Counsel
Ms. Karen Binder
212/264-9271
Rm. 258

United States Mint

Office of Marketing
633 Third St., NW / Washington DC 20220

Asst. Director for Intl. Sales
Mr. David Anderson
202/874-6400
Rm. 300

U.S. Secret Service

U.S. Secret Service/Uniformed Division
3507 International Place, NW / Washington DC 20223

Deputy Chief, Foreign Missions Branch
Mr. Charles O'Malley
202/634-2555
Rm. 137

©Almanac Publishing, Inc. 1998 - The Washington Almanac of International Trade & Business

African Development Foundation

1400 I St., NW - 10th Floor / Washington DC 20005
202/673-3916   FAX 202/673-3810

INTRODUCTION

Established in 1980 by the U.S. Congress, the African Development Foundation is a nonprofit government corporation that works with groups and institutions in Africa on research and development at the local level where it is most needed. It seeks to involve the African poor in all phases of a given project. Unlike other development organizations, ADF funds go directly into the hands of local groups, both public and private. The Foundation is funded by the U.S. Government through Congressional appropriations.

For funding to be considered by ADF, an applicant must be able to exhibit its capacity to improve the life of a community and to show evidence of its independence from any external funding source. ADF awards go to endeavors that promote the growth of local development organizations and self-help initiatives that increase opportunities for Africans to engage in development research and the transfer of resources or expertise and that provide technical and other assistance promoting self-sufficiency. Areas for which funding is granted include agriculture and forestry; health and education; and economic and small business development. Awards of up to $250,000 are offered. Unlike many other development institutions, ADF funds almost invariably do not go to large-scale building or construction projects.

ADF fund recipients must hold legal status as a group authorized to carry out or facilitate projects for local development, must give evidence of project control by disadvantaged, indigenous Africans and must present a coherent, financially reasonable plan of action in line with ADF aims.

With a staff of experienced development professionals, ADF is governed by a seven-member Board of Directors and given guidance by its Advisory Council, which is made up in large part by African natives with hands-on experience in managing community development.

Green, Herman & Associates (consulting firm). 1984-87, president, Ernest Green & Associates (consulting firm). 1987-present, managing director of public finance, Lehman Brothers (Wash., D.C.). 1994-present, chairman, African Development Foundation.

The African Development Foundation was established as a nonprofit government corporation to support the self-help efforts of poor people in African countries. The foundation became operational in 1984. Ernest Green became chairman of its seven-member board of directors in 1994. In addition to its self-help development activities, the corporation tries to strengthen friendship and understanding between the people of Africa and the United States. It also works to stimulate and promote participation of Africans in the community development process. To carry out its purposes, the foundation makes grants, loans, and loan guarantees to private groups and organizations in Africa engaged in activities that allow the people there to develop more fully.

The foundation is governed by a seven-member board appointed by the President and confirmed by the Senate. Green, managing director of public finance for Lehman Brothers' Washington, D.C. office, was appointed to a six-year term on the board in 1994.

He has worked for Lehman Brothers since 1987 and has managed transactions for such clients as the cities of New York, Chicago, and Atlanta, the Port of Oakland, the Fresno Transportation Authority, the Denver Airport and the Washington Metropolitan Airport Authority. Prior to joining Lehman Brothers, Green was president of Ernest Green & Associates, a minority consulting firm that provided technical assistance in marketing, financial management, and economic forecasting. During the Carter administration, Green served as assistant secretary of labor for employment and training.

The Arkansas native graduated from Central High School in Little Rock, Arkansas where he and eight other black students were the first to integrate the school after the 1954 U.S. Supreme Court decision that declared segregation illegal. He went on to earn a B.S. in social science and a master's in sociology from Michigan State University.

Green serves on a number of boards, including those for Africare, the Winthrop Rockefeller Foundation, the National Association of Securities Professionals, Quality Education for Minorities, the Eisenhower World Affairs Institute, Advanced Technological Solutions Inc., and the March of Dimes Birth Defects Foundation. He also has been appointed by Secretary of Education Richard Riley to serve as chairman of the Historically Black Colleges and Universities Capital Financing Advisory Board.

Chair, Board of Directors
Mr. Ernest G. Green

Personal: born 9/22/41 in Arkansas.

Education: B.S. in social science, Michigan State Univ., 1962. Master's in sociology, Michigan State Univ., 1964.

Professional: 1964-77, executive director, New York Recruitment Training Program. 1977-81, asst. sec., U.S. Dept. of Labor. 1981-84,

Vice Chair, Board of Directors
Mr. Willie Grace Campbell

President, Chief Executive Officer
Mr. William R. Ford

William R. Ford came to the presidency of the African Development Foundation in 1995 with a strong background in human resource

development in the U.S. Agency for International Development (USAID), in the District of Columbia government, and in his home state of Michigan.

Ford joined USAID in 1971 as the Director of the USAID Mission to Nigeria. After breaks to serve as the chief executive officer of Delta Oil, Ltd., a Nigerian mini-conglomerate, and as Director of the District of Columbia's Department of Labor, he returned to USAID as an Office Director for Indonesia, South Pacific, and ASEAN Affairs. In 1989, he was named desk officer of Coastal and Central West Africa. Three years later, he was appointed deputy director of the USAID Mission to South Africa as preparations were being made for the April 1993 elections when Nelson Mandela was elected President.

He began his career in 1957 as a teacher of mathematics and science at a school for emotionally and socially disturbed youth, a service of the Michigan Department of Social Welfare. In 1965, he accepted a position as Director of the Lansing Job Training Center for the Michigan Catholic Conference, where he supervised literacy education and job training for the unemployed and the under-employed. He was named Director of Michigan's Economic Opportunity Office in 1966. He also served as director of Michigan's Employment Security Commission.

A native of Oakland Park, Mich., Ford earned a bachelor of science degree in physical science and a master of arts degree in administrative and educational service from Michigan State University in Lansing in 1957 and 1959. He studied economics at Johns Hopkins University, earning a second master's degree in international public policy.

General Counsel
Mr. Paul S. Magid

Public Affairs Officer
Ms. Teixeira Nash

Central Intelligence Agency

Physically located in Langley, Va.
703/482-1100
Washington DC 20505

INTRODUCTION

The Central Intelligence Agency collects, evaluates, and disseminates information on political, military, economic, scientific, and other developments abroad needed to safeguard national security.

Director
Mr. George J. Tenet
703/482-1100   FAX 703/482-1739

Personal: born 1/5/53 in Flushing, N.Y.

Education: B.S., School of Foreign Service, Georgetown University, 1976. M.A., Columbia University, 1978.

Professional: 1982-85, legislative assistant/legislative director, Sen. John Heinz (R-Pa.). 1985-87, committee staff, Sen. Patrick Leahy (D-Vt.); 1988-93, majority staff director, Senate Select Committee on Intelligence. 1993-95, senior director for intelligence, National Security Council. 1995-97, deputy director; July 10, 1997-present, director, Central Intelligence Agency.

George Tenet was unanimously confirmed as director of the Central Intelligence Agency by the U.S. Senate on July 10, 1997. The vote followed a rather rocky period for the agency. Former Director John M. Deutch left in December, 1996 and President Clinton nominated his National Security Adviser, Anthony Lake, to succeed Deutch. Lake withdrew in March with a public blast at the "nasty" nominating process. Clinton then nominated Tenet, who was serving as acting director, on March 19 to be the new director.

The Senate Committee on Intelligence held open hearings on the nomination during the first week of May and all seemed clear for Tenet, a former staff director of the committee, to be approved. A question arose, however, about some property and stock Tenet had been left by his late father and the Justice Department needed two additional months to conclude that Tenet's handling of the reporting of the inheritance did not require an independent counsel investigation. The Senate then promptly confirmed him as director.

Tenet is the second youngest director of the agency and the fifth in six years. He is the 18th director in the agency's 50-year history. In addition to the turnover at the top, published reports indicate that Tenet faces a serious morale problem within the agency. The agency has been publicly embarrassed by the exposure of two traitors in their top ranks, secret operations have been uncovered in both friendly and unfriendly countries, and there is continuing controversy about the sharing of information regarding chemical weapons at Iraqi munitions dumps.

While awaiting Senate confirmation, Tenet and the agency also faced severe criticism from the House Permanent Select Committee on Intelligence which released a report in June of 1997 charging that U.S. intelligence agencies had "limited analytical capabilities" and an "uncertain commitment and capability to collect human intelligence on a worldwide basis through espionage." (*Washington Post*, June 1997). The criticism was all the more stinging because the chair of the House Committee is a former CIA officer.

Tenet was named as deputy director of the CIA in May of 1995 by then-director John Deutch. He came to the agency after serving for two years as senior director of intelligence at the National Security Council under then-director Anthony Lake.

Perhaps most valuable for the agency's Hill relations in the future, Tenet had been majority staff director of the Senate Select Committee on Intelligence from 1988 to 1993 under then-Chairman David Boren (D-Okla.). He had previously worked for Democratic Sen. Patrick Leahy (D-Vt.) and a Republican, the late Sen. John Heinz (R-Pa.).

Tenet is married to A. Stephanie Glakas-Tenet and resides in Potomac, Maryland. They have a son, John Michael.

Deputy Director
Lt. Gen. John A. Gordon
703/482-6363   FAX 703/482-1739

Personal: born in Missouri.

Education: B.S. in physics, Univ. of Missouri (Columbia), 1968. M.S., Naval Postgraduate School (Monterey, Calif.). M.A. in business administration, Highlands University (Las Vegas, Nev.), 1972.

Professional: entered Air Force, 1968. defense and arms control, National Security Council. director of operations for the Air Force Space Command. special assistant to the Air Force chief of staff for long range planning. 9/96-1997, associate director of central intelligence for military support; 1997-present, deputy director, Central Intelligence Agency.

President Clinton nominated Air Force Lieutenant General John Gordon as deputy director of the Central Intelligence Agency on July 21, 1997, and he was subsequently confirmed to succeed George Tenet who is now the director of the CIA.

The director and the deputy director of central intelligence have overall responsibility for the direction of the CIA and of the intelligence community as a whole. The deputy director acts for and exercises the power of the director in his absence or disability or in the event of a vacancy in the position of director.

Gordon had been serving as associate director of central intelligence for military support at the agency since September, 1996. Prior to this tenure, General Gordon was special assistant to the Air Force Chief of Staff for long range planning. He also served as the director of operations for the Air Force Space Command, responsible for overseeing and developing policy and guidance for the command's operational missions.

Gordon previously worked with the National Security Council in the areas of defense and arms control including the oversight and completion of the Start II negotiations.

Gordon received his B.S. with honors in physics from the University of Missouri at Columbia and completed his M.S. at the Naval Postgraduate School. He then received his M.A. in business administration from the Highlands University.

Executive Director
Mr. David Carey
703/482-1100

Director, Congressional Affairs
Mr. John Moseman
703/482-1100

General Counsel
Mr. Robert McNamara
703/482-1100

Chief of Staff
Ms. Joan Dempsey
703/482-1100

Director, Public Affairs
Mr. William Harlow
703/482-7558   FAX 703/482-6790

Director, Agency Information Staff
VACANT
703/482-1100

Environmental Protection Agency

401 M St., SW / Washington DC 20460
202/260-4700

Locator: 202/260-2090
Public Affairs: 202/260-4355
Public Information: 202/260-7751
Procurement and Contracts: 202/260-5020

INTRODUCTION

The Environmental Protection Agency (EPA) assists other countries in implementing their environmental laws and standards. It provides grants and other specialized assistance to countries that are in the early stages of environmental planning. And it cooperates with other agencies in promoting the exports of U.S. environmental technology firms.

The Environmental Protection Agency cooperates with other federal agencies in the 19-agency Trade Promotion Coordinating Committee. EPA co-chairs the Environmental Trade Working Group, comprised of representatives from EPA, the Departments of Commerce, Energy, Defense, and Treasury, the Ex-Im Bank, Overseas Private Investment Corporation, Trade and Development Agency, the Agency for International Development, and the Small Business Administration.

The goal of the Working Group, as stated by President Clinton is to "assess the competitiveness of current environmental technologies and to develop a strategy to give U.S. companies the trade development, promotional efforts and technical assistance they need to increase exports, create U.S. jobs, and improve environmental quality. EPA's role is to coordinate its technical assistance and market development activities with the activities of other agencies. The intended result of these actions is to improve the global environment.

Office of the Administrator

Administrator
Ms. Carol M. Browner
202/260-4700   FAX 202/260-0279
Rm. W1200
E-Mail: Browner.carol@epamail.epa.gov

Personal: born 12/16/55 in Miami, Fla.

Education: A.A., Miami Dade Community College, 1974. B.A., Univeristy of Florida, 1977. J.D., Universityof Florida Law School, 1979.

Professional: 1977-81, clerk, Joint Committee on Administrative Procedures, Florida House of Representatives. 1981-82, deputy campaign manager, Sheldon for Congress (Tampa, Fla.). 1983, fundraising staff, Cranston for President (Washington, D.C.). 1983-84, senior staff, Clean Water Action Project (Wash., D.C.). 1984-86, associate director, Citizen Action (Wash., D.C.). 1986, independent consultant, PBS Frontline (Washington, D.C.). 1986-88, senior legislative aide, Sen. Lawton Chiles (D-Fla.). 1/89-2/89, counsel, Senate Government Affairs Committee. 2/89-6/89, counsel, Senate Energy Committee. 6/89-91, legislative director, Senator Al Gore,(D-Tenn.). 1991-93, secretary, Florida Department of Environmental Regulation. 1993-present, administrator, U.S. Environmental Protection Agency.

After back-to-back fights in 1995 and 1996 with the Republican Congress, Carol Browner found her agency embroiled in another regulatory battle in 1997. Browner had successfully fought cuts in her enforcement budget in 1995 and maintained the right to review wetlands permits issued by the Army Corps of Engineers. In 1997, the battle is over EPA regulations issued in July under the authority of the Clear Air Act which are aimed at improving air quality.

There was a fierce fight within the Clinton administration about the cost benefit ratio of the proposed rule, with Vice President Gore finally tipping the balance in favor of Browner's proposal. On the Hill, the big public attack on the proposed regulations came not from the Republicans, but from the powerful Michigan Democrat John Dingell. By August, two Republican Members of the House joined Democrat Henry Waxman in a bipartisan effort to ensure that the regulations were not weakened.

Browner was brought to the Environmental Protection Agency at the recommendation of her former boss, Vice President Al Gore and her appointment was warmly welcomed by the environmental community. As EPA administrator, she manages EPA programs that provide environmental guidelines in the areas of air and water pollution, hazardous waste disposal and clean-up, the handling of toxic substances, pesticides, drinking water, noise pollution, and radiation. She is also attempting to restructure the agency to make the most effective use of budget and staff resources.

An inherited problem for Browner has been the task of untangling the Superfund environmental clean-up program. She is working with the Department of Energy to tackle questions of liability and contractor accountability at Superfund sites. Browner also worked within the Administration on the environmental side agreements to the North American Free Trade Agreement.

Florida Governor Lawton Chiles (D) appointed Browner to head that state's troubled Department of Environmental Regulation in 1991. She won excellent reviews taking on tasks such as resolving a lawsuit against the state for its environmental neglect of the Everglades. The suit was spearheaded by Steven Herman, current EPA assistant administrator for enforcement.

Browner is married to Michael Podhorzer and they have one child.

Education: B.A. (with distinction), Univ. of Oklahoma, 1978. J.D. (cum laude), Georgetown Univ. Law Center, 1987.

Professional: staff, Rep. James R. Jones (D-Okla.). professional staff member, Committee on the Budget, U.S. House of Representatives. associate, Patton, Boggs & Blow (Wash., D.C.). deputy assistant administrator, solid waste and emergency response; January 1995-present, chief of staff, U.S. Environmental Protection Agency.

Peter Robertson was appointed chief of staff of the Environmental Protection Agency (EPA) in January 1995. He was previously deputy assistant administrator for solid waste and emergency response.

Robertson came to the EPA from the Washington, D.C. law firm of Patton, Boggs & Blow, where he specialized in both environmental and legislative law. He has administrative, legislative, and litigative experience on a number of environmental statutes, including CERCLA, RCRA, the Clear Air Act, the Safe Drinking Water Act, and the Oil Pollution Act of 1990. He has written several chapters on environmental law included in widely used environmental handbooks and has spoken at numerous conferences on environmental law and legislation.

Before entering private practice, Robertson was a professional staff member of the Committee on the Budget of the U.S. House of Representatives. His responsibilities at the committee included national security programs, transportation programs, administration of justice funding, and general government functions. He had earlier worked on Capitol Hill as a staff member to former Representative James R. Jones (D-Okla.).

A 1987 graduate of Georgetown University Law Center, Robertson graduated with a B.A. degree in 1978 from the University of Oklahoma, where he was a member of Phi Beta Kappa.

Office of Cooperative Environmental Management

499 South Capitol St., SW / Washington DC 20460

Team Leader, Global, Environment and Trade Staff
Mr. Robert L. Hardaker
202/260-2477
Rm. 115

Associate Administrator for Communications, Education and Public Affairs

Chief of Staff
Mr. Peter D. Robertson
202/260-4700   FAX 202/260-0279
E-Mail: Robertson.peter@epamail.epa.gov.

Associate Administrator
Ms. Loretta M. Ucelli
202/260-9828   FAX 202/260-3684
Rm. W1204

Assistant Administrator for Enforcement and Compliance Assurance

12th Street and Pa. Ave., NW / Wash. DC 20004

Office of Federal Activities

Director, Intl. Enforcement Program
Mr. Michael S. Alushin
202/564-7137   FAX 202/564-0073
Rm. NE1203

Assistant Administrator for International Activities

1300 Pennsylvania Ave., NW / Washington DC 20004

Asst. Administrator
Mr. William A. Nitze
202/564-6600   FAX 202/565-2407
Rm. 31207

Personal: born 9/27/42 in New York City, N.Y.

Education: B.A., Harvard College, 1964. B.A., Wadham College, Oxford Univ., 1966. J.D., Harvard Univ., 1969.

Professional: 1970-72, associate, Sullivan and Cromwell (New York City). 1972-73, vice-president, London Arts, Inc. (New York City). 1974-76, counsel, Mobil South, Inc. (New York City). 1976-80, general counsel, Mobil Oil Japan, (Tokyo, Japan). 1980-87, assistant general counsel, exploration and producing division, Mobil Oil Corporation (New York City). 1987-90, deputy assistant secretary for environment, health, and natural resources, U.S. Department of State. Feb-Aug 1990, visiting scholar, Environmental Law Institute (Washington, D.C.) 1990-94, president, Alliance to Save Energy. 1994-present, assistant administrator for international activities, U.S. Environmental Protection Agency.

William Nitze was confirmed by the Senate on August 25, 1994, to become EPA assistant administrator for international activities. Nitze, an internationally renowned expert on environmental issues, has held key positions in government, non-governmental organizations, and the private sector in the U.S. and abroad.

Prior to joining EPA, Nitze served since September of 1990 as president of the Alliance to Save Energy, a non-profit coalition of environmental, government, industry, and consumer leaders dedicated to promoting investment in energy efficiency. As a visiting scholar at the Environmental Law Institute in Washington, DC, he was at the forefront of the effort to develop international environmental policy.

Nitze's work at ELI was a natural follow-up to his position as deputy assistant secretary for State of environment, health and natural resources from 1987 to 1990, where he played a lead role in international negotiations on global issues such as climate change, ozone layer protection, trans boundary shipments of hazardous substances, biotechnology, and the conservation of tropical forests. He received the Superior Honor Award of the Department of State in 1988.

Nitze has served on the advisory committee of the School for Advanced International Studies since 1982, and is a director of the National Symphony Orchestra Association. He is also a trustee of the Aspen Institute and a member of the Council on Foreign Relations.

He lives in Washington, D.C., with his wife and two sons.

Executive Asst.
Ms. Carolyn Hicks
202/564-6600

Principal Deputy Assistant Administrator
Dr. Alan Hecht
202/564-6600
Rm. 31225

Director, Intl. Cooperation and Assistance Division
Mr. Jameson Koehler
202/564-6440   FAX 202/565-2411
Rm. 31134

Director, International Environmental Policy Office
Mr. Paul Cough
202/564-6455   FAX 202/565-2409
Rm. 31130

Director, Office of Western Hemisphere and Bilateral Affairs
Ms. Patricia Koshel
202/564-6400   FAX 202/565-2412
Rm. 31245

Director, Management Operations
Ms. Joan Fidler
202/564-6605   FAX 202/565-2408
Rm. 31245

Intl. Visitors Coordinator
Ms. Diana Gearhart
202/564-6617
Rm. 31234

Intl. Travel Coordinator
Mr. William Whitehouse
202/564-6632
Rm. 31215

Assistant Administrator for Policy Planning and Evaluation

Assistant Administrator
David M. Gardiner
202/260-4332   FAX 202/260-0275
Room WT1013
E-Mail: Gardiner.david@epamail.epa.gov

Personal: born 4/25/55 in Boston, Mass.

Education: B.A. in history, Harvard College, 1977.

Professional: 1978-80, field coordinator, Sierra Club, San Francisco. 1980, consultant, California League of Conservation Voters. 1981-83, Washington representative, Sierra Club. 1983-93, legislative director, Sierra Club. 1993-present, assistant administrator for policy, planning and evaluation, U.S. Environmental Protection Agency.

David Gardiner serves as assistant administrator for policy, planning and evaluation at the Environmental Protection Agency (EPA). He advises EPA Administrator Carol Browner on policy, and oversees the office of strategic planning and environmental data, the office of policy analysis, and the office of regulatory management. The office of policy, planning, and evaluation also conducts cost-benefit analyses of regulations proposed by the EPA, an area at the forefront of the policy debate in 1997 as Congress debates proposed EPA regulations on air quality.

Gardiner has endorsed the use of cost-benefit analysis for the evaluation of regulations but cautions that environmental regulation must meet multiple criteria. "Often, costs are easier to quantify than benefits," he says, adding that EPA "will continue to improve the usefulness of this methodology as a policy evaluation tool." Gardiner says the goals "of timely issuance of regulations and quality economic analysis are not incompatible, and I am committed to providing both."

Gardiner had previously served as legislative director of the Sierra Club and pursued that group's aggressive environmental protection policy, often taking on business to push his agenda on Capitol Hill. Gardiner says he shares Browner's desire to communicate and cooperate with business leaders and to forge alliances with the private sector to promote environmental protection.

Gardiner says that he learned during the debate and votes on the 1990 Clean Air Act, that many businesses can be friends of the environmental movement. "I also learned that the barriers between people who are in disagreement can only be broken down through sustained, patient dialogue," he says.

Gardiner's office emphasizes pollution prevention and the use of innovative technologies, which can help the nation's economic interests as America tries to capture a larger share of a global $200 billion-market for environmental engineering products.

Gardiner and his wife have three children.

Office of the General Counsel

Associate General Counsel, Intl. Environmental Law
Mr. Daniel B. McGraw
202/260-1810   FAX 202/260-3828
Rm. 641A

Assistant Administrator for Water

Intl. Activities Coordinator
Mr. Timothy Kasten
202/260-5700   FAX 202/260-5711
Rm. 1029A

Export-Import Bank of the United States

811 Vermont Ave., NW / Washington DC 20571

Central: 202/565-3946 or 800/565-3946
Business Development: 202/565-3900
Public Affairs: 202/565-3200
Export Financing Hotline: 800/565-5201
FAX 202/565-3380

INTRODUCTION

Established in 1934, the Export-Import Bank of the United States (Ex-Im Bank) is an independent federal agency mandated with financing U.S. goods and services exports. Since its inception, it has assisted with exports worth $300 billion, facilitating such exports by matching the effect of export subsidies from foreign governments and absorbing through insurance reasonable credit risks beyond the current reach of the private sector.

Specific Ex-Im Bank assistance programs help U.S. exporters obtain pre-export financing by guaranteeing export-related loans from commercial lenders, extending credit to creditworthy foreign buyers of U.S. exports when private financing is not available, and facilitating the participation of U.S. exporters in overseas development projects. While the Ex-Im Bank is not itself a development foreign aid agency, it does at times cooperate with other institutions in such activities, co-financing projects with the U.S. Agency for International Development, the World Bank, and regional development banks.

Working capital guarantees and export credit insurance - the two principal vehicles for Ex-Im Bank programs - focus, respectively, on alleviating export financing difficulties for the exporter and on protecting against political and commercial risks that a foreign buyer may default on credit purchases.

President and Chair
Mr. James A. Harmon
202/565-3500   FAX 202/565-3505
Rm. 1215

Education: B.A. in English literature, Brown Univ., 1957. M.B.A. in finance, Wharton Graduate School, Univ. of Pa., 1959.

Professional: senior chairman, Schroder Wertheim & Co. June 17, 1997-present, president and chairman, Export-Import Bank of the United States.

James Harmon was nominated on May 6, 1997 by President Clinton as president and chairman of the Export-Import Bank of the United States. His four-year appointment was confirmed by the U.S. Senate on June 12, 1997 and he was officially sworn in on June 17.

Vice President Al Gore presided at a formal White House swearing in ceremony on July 9, for Harmon and First Vice President Jackie M. Clegg. Gore said "The Export Import Bank plays a vital role in sustaining jobs and assisting U.S. businesses to compete in the global marketplace. Jim Harmon and Jackie Clegg have the knowledge, skills and ability to lead this vital agency into the next century."

Harmon welcomed the challenge of the new position, "I hope to enhance the important role this institution plays in helping American businesses meet the relentless international competition from the world marketplace. It is important for Congress, business leaders and the American public to recognize how Ex-Im Bank supports our economic growth and sustains US jobs. Our mission, to finance creditworthy transactions in challenging markets, is even more relevant today given the significant competition in the global economy."

Harmon is a successful businessman with extensive experience in international business operations. He served as senior chairman of Schroder Wertheim & Co. prior to accepting his current position at Ex-Im Bank. Harmon balances his professional life with a lifelong commitment to community service.

At Schroder Wertheim, Harmon oversaw the expansion of the firm's domestic and international investment banking activities. In 1986, he initiated a strategic and highly successful partnership between Schroder PLC (UK) and Wertheim that created a global investment bank with approximately 5,000 employees operating in 33 countries around the world. In 1987, Harmon became chairman and chief executive officer of Schroder Wertheim and assumed senior chairmanship of the firm in 1996.

In 1994, Harmon co-founded the Barnard-Columbia University Center for Public Policy with former New York City Mayor David Dinkins. In December 1995, he received the Gustave L. Levy award from the UJA-Federation of New York for his exceptional professional achievement and enduring commitment to Jewish philosophy.

Harmon received his undergraduate degree from Brown University and an MBA from Wharton at the University of Pennsylvania. Harmon has served two terms as a trustee at Brown University and now serves as trustee emeritus there, as well as a trustee of Barnard College.

Harmon lives in Connecticut and New York with his wife, Jane, a theatrical producer. Harmon has been active in the Weston, Connecticut community where their three children attended public school. Harmon's grandmother, Bessie Hamburger, was the first female assistant district attorney in New York City.

First Vice President & Vice-Chair
Jackie M. Clegg
202/565-3535   FAX 202/565-3505
Rm. 1210

Professional: leg. asst., U.S. Senator Jake Garn (R-Utah). professional staff, U.S. Senate Committee on Banking, Housing and Urban Affairs. 1993-97, vice president for congressional and external affairs and chief of staff; June 12, 1997-present, first vice president and vice-chair, U.S. Export-Import Bank.

Jackie Clegg was nominated as first vice president and vice-chair of the U.S. Export-Import Bank on May 6, 1997 by President Clinton and confirmed by the U.S. Senate on June 12. Along with James

Harmon, the new president and chairman of the bank, Clegg was formally sworn in by Vice President Al Gore on July 9.

Clegg said, "I am honored to have an opportunity to serve the Administration in this new and challenging capacity and to lead the Ex-im Bank's rechartering effort. I am also proud of the important work done by the staff at Ex-Im Bank, and its positive impact on communities across the country."

Clegg has served as vice president for Congressional and external affairs and as chief of staff of Ex-Im prior to her current appointment. Before joining Ex-Im in 1993, she served on the professional staff of the U.S. Senate Committee on Banking, Housing and Urban Affairs and as a legislative assistant to former Senator Jake Garn (R-Utah).

Ex-Im Bank is an independent federal agency that supports American jobs by financing the sales of U.S. goods and services to foreign markets and by matching export credit subsidies from foreign governments. Nationally, Ex-Im Bank has supported more than 2,000 communities throughout America by approving over 10,000 transactions worth $65.6 billion in authorized financing in the past five years. Ex-Im Bank annually sustains an estimated 200,000 jobs directly among exporters and suppliers and another one million jobs indirectly among sub-suppliers.

Chief of Staff
Ms. Andrea Adelman
202/565-3538
Rm. 1228

Director
Julie D. Belaga
202/565-3540   FAX 202/565-3548
Rm. 1257

Professional: 1976-86, member, deputy majority leader and asst. minority leader, Connecticut House of Representatives. 1986, Republican candidate for Connecticut governor. 1987-89, television commentator, WTNH-TV,(ABC), New Haven. fellow, Institute of Politics, adjunct lecturer in public policy, Kennedy School of Government, Harvard University. 1989-93, regional administrator (New England), U.S. Environmental Protection Agency. 1993-94, senior vice president, Makovsky and Company (New York). 1994-present, director, Export-Import Bank of the U.S.

Julie Belaga is a member of the board of the Export-Import Bank of the United States. Belaga, sworn in to the 5-member board in September 1994, leads Ex-Im's new efforts to increase financing for the U.S. firms that export products and services to benefit the global environment. Water treatment, hazardous waste clean-up, renewable energy, and pollution control are among the industry sectors included in the bank's initiatives. She will also oversee implementation of Ex-Im Bank's environmental procedures and guidelines.

Belaga has a long and distinguished career in government and private sector service. Prior to her appointment she was senior vice president at the New York consulting firm, Makovsky and Company, where she established an environmental services office. From 1989-93, she was regional administrator for the Environmental Protection Agency for New England. In that capacity she managed 760 employees with a budget of over $330 million. She was responsible for the implementation of all federal environmental laws in the New England States.

Belaga also has served on the board of directors of the Connecticut Development Authority(CDA). CDA provides financing and makes investment in businesses that present the greatest potential for Connecticut's job growth and economic base. Prior to her work with EPA, Belaga was a fellow at the Institute of Politics and an adjunct lecturer in public policy at the Kennedy School of Government at Harvard University.

From 1987 to 1989, she was a television commentator at WTNH-TV, the ABC affiliate in New Haven. In that capacity she commented on environmental and other governmental issues that impacted the citizens of Connecticut.

She was the Republican candidate for governor of Connecticut in 1986. Previously, she served for 10 years in the Connecticut House of Representatives. She was elected by her peers to be deputy majority leader (1984) and assistant minority leader (1978, 1980, and 1982). During her five terms in the legislature, she was a leader in the development of environmental legislation including Coastal Zone Management, solid and hazardous waste disposal, and drinking water delivery system improvements.

She has received numerous awards for outstanding public service, including the Governor John Davis Lodge Award, the Liberty Bell Bar Association Award, the YWCA Salute to Women Award, and the Women in Management Award.

Director
Maria Luisa M. Haley
202/565-353   FAX 202/565-3548
Rm. 1241

Professional: 1983-90, director of international development, State of Arkansas. 1993-94, special assistant to the President and associate director of presidential personnel, The White House. April 1994-present, director, Export-Import Bank of the United States.

Maria Luisa Haley is a member of the board of directors at the Export-Import Bank of the United States. The president nominated her to this position, and she was confirmed by the US Senate in April of 1994. Haley focuses on the promotion of US exports and more specifically she works to expand Small Business' role in exporting.

Before accepting her position at the Export-Import Bank, Haley worked at the White House as a special assistant to the President and associate director of presidential personnel for economics, commerce, and trade. She played an integral part in the selection and approval of political appointments in three Cabinet departments and twelve independent agencies.

Haley has worked in international business for the past twenty-five years in sales, marketing, and operations. From 1983 to 1990, Haley was in charge of International Development for the State of Arkansas focusing on export development and foreign investment programs.

Director
Rita M. Rodriguez, Ph.D.
202/565-3520   FAX 202/565-3505
Rm. 1229

Personal: born in Cuba.

Education: B.B.A., Univ. of Puerto Rico. M.B.A. (1968) and Ph.D. (1969), New York Univ. Graduate School of Business.

Professional: 1969-78, assistant and then associate professor of business administration, Harvard Business School. 1978-82, professor of finance, Univ. of Illinois (Chicago). 1982-present, director, Export-Import Bank of the United States.

Rita Rodriguez is a full-time member of the board of directors of the Export-Import Bank of the United States. She was first nominated by President Reagan and confirmed by the U.S. Senate in 1982.

In addition to her board duties, Dr. Rodriguez heads the Policy Groups comprised of the policy, planning and program development division and the country risk analysis division. She oversees Ex-m Bank policy development and coordination for countries and programs through these units. Rodriguez is also responsible for the formulation of Ex-Im Bank policy objectives and negotiating strategy with regard to international organizations such as the OECD, Berne Union, and the Paris Club. She also coordinates Ex-Im Bank's strategy and staff participation in U.S. government interagency groups and meetings with international organizations.

Rodriguez was professor of finance at the University of Illinois at Chicago from 1978 to 1982 and assistant and associate professor of business administration at Harvard Business School from 1969 to 1978. She has served as a consultant in international finance to U.S. multinational companies and to U.S. and foreign government agencies.

Rodriguez is the author of numerous books and articles on international finance, including *The Export-Import Bank at Fifty* (DC Heath and Company, 1987), and *Foreign Exchange Management in US Multinationals* (DC Heath, 1980). She is co-author, with E. Eugene Carter, of *International Financial Management* (Prentice-Hall, Inc. Third Edition, 1984), and co-author, with Heinz Riehl, of *Foreign Exchange and Money Markets* (McGraw Hill Inc., 1983) and *Foreign Currency Operation* (McGraw Hill Inc., 1977).

Born in Cuba, Dr. Rodriguez is an American citizen. She is married to E. Eugene Carter and they have one daughter.

Vice President, Aircraft Finance
VACANT
202/565-3551   FAX 202/565-3558
Rm. 933

Vice President, Communications
Mr. David Carter
202/565-3203   FAX 202/565-3210
Rm. 1203

Acting Vice President, Congressional and External Affairs
Mr. David Carter
202/565-3203   FAX 202/565-3236

Rm. 1228

Vice President, Country Risk Analysis
Mr. Daniel L. Bond
202/565-3731
Rm. 969

Vice President, Policy Planning and Program Development
Mr. James C. Cruse
202/565-3761   FAX 202/565-3770
Rm. 1243

Executive Vice President
Mr. Allen I. Mendelowitz
202/565-3220
Rm. 1115

Vice President, Small and New Business Development Group
VACANT
202/565-3925   FAX 202/565-3931
Rm. 919

Vice President, Marketing
Mr. Robert J. Kaiser
202/565-3902   FAX 202/565-3932
Rm. 911

Vice President, Americas
VACANT
202/565-3401   FAX 202/565-3420
Rm. 1157

Vice President, Asia and Africa
VACANT
202/565-3701   FAX 202/565-3717
Rm. 1129

Deputy Vice President, Asia and Africa
Ms. Deborah La Mar Thompson
202/565-3702
Rm. 1129

Vice President, NIS and Central Europe
Mr. Stephen Glazer
202/565-3801   FAX 202/565-3816
Rm. 1267

Deputy Vice President, Europe
Mr. LeRoy M. LaRoche
202/565-3431
Rm. 1275

Vice President, United States
Mr. Sam Zytcer
202/565-3782   FAX 202/565-3793
Rm. 905

Vice President, Engineering and Environment
Mr. James A. Mahoney
202/565-3573
Rm. 1167

Vice President, Credit Administration
Mr. Jeffrey Miller
202/565-3471   FAX 202/565-3486
Rm. 1135

Vice President, Export Credit Insurance
Mr. William Redway
202/565-3633
Rm. 719

Vice President, Project Finance Division

Ms. Barbara O'Boyle
202/565-3692   FAX 202/565-3695
Rm. 1005

General Counsel
Mr. Ken Hansen
202/565-3430   FAX 202/565-3462
Rm. 947

Librarian
Mr. Eugene Hardin Ferguson
202/565-3980   FAX 202/565-3985
Rm. 966

Chief Financial Officer
Mr. James K. Hess
202/565-3240   FAX 202/565-3294
Rm. 1055

Mgr., Portfolio Management and Review
Mr. Esteban de la Riva
202/565-3266
Rm. 1078

Portfolio Analyst, Portfolio Management and Review
Mr. J. Doug Gatenbee
202/565-3272

Vice President, Asset Management
Mr. Jeffrey Miller
202/565-3601   FAX 202/565-3625
Rm. 741

Regional Offices

Midwest
55 W. Monroe St. / Chicago IL 60603

Regional Mgr.
Mr. Bradley J. Dunderman
312/353-8081   FAX 312/353-8098
Suite 2440

Northeast
Six World Trade Center / New York NY 10048

Regional Mgr.
Mr. John Lavelle
212/466-2950   FAX 212/466-2954
Suite 635

Southeast
5600 N.W. 36th St. / Miami FL 33159-0570

Regional Mgr.
Mr. Peter B. Alois
305/526-7425   FAX 305/526-7435
Suite 617

Southwest
Ashford Crossing II, 1880 Dairy Ashford / Houston TX 77077

Regional Mgr.
Mr. Patrick Crilley
281/721-0465   FAX 281/679-0150
Suite 585

West
One World Trade / Long Breach CA 90831

Regional Mgr.
Mr. Jerri Slifer
562/980-4580   FAX 562/980-4590
Suite 1670

Ex-Im Bank - City/State Program

What is the City/State Program?

The City/State Program is a partnership between Ex-Im Bank and state and local entities around the country to bring the Bank's financing services to small and medium-sized U.S. companies that are ready to export. Small business represents the economic sector where the greatest potential for American job and export growth lies. But despite the competitiveness of their products, smaller businesses often cannot get commercial bank export financing. Frequently they are unaware of Ex-Im Bank's programs and how to use them, or cannot make the trip to Washington to apply for financing.

To bridge the gap, Ex-Im Bank has formed partnerships with 35 state and local government offices and private sector organizations to bring its programs to the exporter at the lowest cost to the American taxpayer. Ex-Im Bank has resources in the form of loans, guarantees and insurance programs. State and local representatives have the staff and the knowledge of the local market and how to reach it. By pooling their strengths in a local-federal partnership, they accomplish what neither could do alone — creating high-quality U.S. jobs and expanding the local tax base through exports.

How Does the Program Work?

Ex-Im Bank trains the staff of its City/State partners to market the Bank's programs to local businesses and commercial banks, teach seminars, counsel exporters and banks, and package transactions. The expense of packaging a small deal is often prohibitive for a bank. By packaging transactions for the banks, City/State partners facilitate many commercial loans that otherwise would not go forward.

To join the City/State Program, a state export finance or development agency must: 1) prepare a one-year budget and a marketing plan, and 2) send two qualified professionals to Washington, D.C. for a five-day seminar on Ex-Im Bank programs and an additional week of advanced training.

Where are programs operating?

City/State programs presently are operating in 32 states, one county, a Chamber of Commerce and the Commonwealth of Puerto Rico. The addresses of these programs are listed on the following pages. For further information contact:

Ms. Judith Katz Nath
Communication Officer

or

Ms. Joyce E. Papes
City/State Coordinator

Office of Communications
(202) 565-3906
(202) 565-3932 (Fax)

What Services Are Available Through the Program?

All Ex-Im Bank resources are available through its City/State partners, including two programs found particularly useful by smaller exporters: 1) the Working Capital Guarantee Program which provides guarantees of working capital loans to finance companies' export-related and pre-export activity, and 2) the Export Credit Insurance Program that insures companies against payment default by foreign customers. Ex-Im Bank also provides medium-term credits and guarantees.

Export Assistance Center Liaison

City/State partners also represent Ex-Im Bank in the U.S. Export Assistance Centers set up around the country by the Trade Promotion Coordinating Committee to bring a wide range of federal government trade promotion services to smaller exporters.

PROGRAMS LISTED BY STATE

Alaska

Mr. Jim McMillan
Deputy Director
Alaska Industrial Development & Export Authority (AIDEA)
480 West Tudor Road
Anchorage AK 99503
Phone: 907/269-3000   Fax: 907/269-3044
E-mail: jmcmillan@aldea.alaska.net

Arkansas

Ms. Nancy Mitchell
Trade Finance Manager
Arkansas Industrial Development Commission
One Capitol Mall
Little Rock AR 72201
Phone: 501/682-6103   Fax: 501/324-9856

California

Ms. Caroline V. Brown
Director
California Export Finance Office
6 Centerpointe Dr., Suite 760
La Palma CA 90623
Phone: 714/562-5519   Fax: 714/562-5530
E-mail: caroline-brown@worldnet.att.net

Mr. Peter Yap
Trade Manager
Bay Area Trade
345 California Street, 7th Floor
San Francisco CA 94104
Phone: 415/392-2705   Fax: 415/392-1710
E-mail: pyap@bawtc.buytrade.org

Florida

Mr. Steve Fancher
President
Florida Export Finance Corp.
5600 North West 36th St., Suite 615
P.O. Box 526524
Miami FL 33152-6524
Phone: 305/870-5027   Fax: 305/870-5017
E-mail: fefc@icanect.net

Georgia

Mr. Jean Prasher
Export Assistance Coordinator
Georgia Housing & Finance Authority
285 Peachtree Center Ave., NE, Suite 200
Atlanta GA 30303-1229
Phone: 404/657-1958   Fax: 404/657-1970
E-mail: jprasher@itt.state.ga.us

Indiana

Ms. Autumn Brooks Brown
Trade Finance Specialist
Indiana Dept. of Commerce/Indiana Finance Authority
Int'l Trade Division
One N. Capitol St., Suite 700
Indianapolis IN 46204-2288

Phone: 317/233-4337   Fax: 317/232-4146
E-mail: abrown@commerce.state.in.us

Louisiana

Mr. Michael Williams
Deputy Director
Louisiana Economic Development Corp.
101 France Street
Baton Rouge LA 70802
Phone: 504/342-5675   Fax: 504/342-5389

Mr. Felipe E. Martinez
Int'l Finance Manager
Lousiana Office of Financial Institutions
P.O. Box 44095
Baton Rouge LA 70804-9095
Phone: 504/589-6546   Fax: 504/589-2337

Ms. M. Carol Ward
Financing Manager
Jefferson Parish Economic Development Commission (JEDCO)
3445 N. Causeway Blvd., Suite 300
Metairie LA 70002
Phone: 504/833-1881   Fax: 504/833-7676
E-mail: jedco1@jedco.com

Ms. Gina Nadas
Manager Latin America Initiative
Jefferson Parish Economic Development Commission (JEDCO)
1221 Elmwood Park Blvd., Suite 405
New Orleans LA 70123
Phone: 504/736-6550   Fax: 504/736-6554

Maryland

Mr. William L. Green
Commercial Loan Officer
Maryland Industrial Development Bank Financing Authority (MIDFA)
Redwood Tower
217 E. Redwood, Rm. 1101
Baltimore MD 21202
Phone: 410/767-6383   Fax: 410/333-2065
E-mail: wgreen@mdbusiness.state.md.us

Massachusetts

Mr. Eric Hunter
Lending Officer
Massachusetts Industrial Finance Agency (MIFA)
75 Federal St.
Boston MA 02110
Phone: 617/451-2477   Fax: 617/451-3429
E-mail: ehunter@state.ma.us

Michigan

Mr. Don Keesee
President
Michigan Int'l Trade Authority (MITA)
Keesee & Associates
199 West Brown St., Suite 260
Birmingham MI 48009
Phone: 810/540-8476   Fax: 810/540-2250
E-mail: 102635.2211@compuserve.com

Minnesota

Mr. Noor Doja
Exec. Director
Minnesota Export Finance Authority
1000 World Trade Center
St. Paul MN 55101-4902
Phone: 612/297-4658   Fax: 612/296-3555

E-mail: NDOJA@DTED.STATE.MN.US

Mississippi

Ms. Allison G. Crews
Project Manager
Mississippi Dept. of Economic & Community Development
P.O. Box 849
Jackson MS 39205
Phone: 601/359-6672   Fax: 601/359-2832
E-mail: acrews%gw@decd.state.ms.us

Missouri

Ms. Ashley R. Weaver
Export Loan Officer
Missouri Development Finance Board
Harry S. Truman Bldg.
301 West High St., Rm. 680, P.O. Box 567
Jefferson City MO 65102
Phone: 314/751-8479   Fax: 314/526-4418
E-mail: aweaver@mail.state.mo.us

Mr. John Schneider
Trade Specialist
State of Missouri Int'l Trade & Development Office
8182 Maryland Ave., Suite 303
St. Louis MO 63105
Phone: 314/425-3310   Fax: 314/425-3381

Nevada

Mr. Peter S. Cunningham
Director of Intl. Trade
Commission on Economic Dev.
555 E. Washington Ave., Suite 5400
Las Vegas NV 89501
Phone: 702/486-2700   Fax: 702/486-2701
E-mail: pscexport@aol.com

Ms. Debra Swartz
Vice President
Nevada State Dev. Corp.
4800 Alpine Place, Suite 17
Las Vegas NV 89119
Phone: 702/877-9111   Fax: 702/877-2803

Ms. Bobbi Bennett
President
Nevada State Dev. Corp.
350 S. Center St., Suite 310
Reno NV 89501
Phone: 702/323-3625   Fax: 702/323-1997

New Hampshire

Mr. Daniel J. Hussey
Manager Export Finance
Office of Int'l Commerce
Int'l Trade Resource Center
17 New Hampshire Avenue
Portsmouth NH 03801-2838
Phone: 603/334-6074   Fax: 603/334-6110
E-mail: d_hussey@dred.state.nh.us

New York

Mr. Alfred Culliton
Chief Lending Officer
Erie County Industrial Development Agency
Suite 300 - Liberty Bldg., 424 Main St.
Buffalo NY 14202
Phone: 716/856-6525   Fax: 716/856-6754

E-mail: ecida@buffnet.net

Mr. Paul Hohensee
Business Dev. Analyst
Monroe County Planning and Development
2 State Street, Suite 500
Rochester NY 14614
Phone: 716/428-5347   Fax: 716/428-2148

North Carolina

Mr. Barry Phillips
Counselor
SBTDC — Chapel Hill
608 Airport Road, Suite B
Chapel Hill NC 27514
Phone: 919/962-0389   Fax: 919/962-3291

Ms. Annetta Brady
Director, Intl. Bus Dev.
Small Business and Tech. Dev. Center (SBTDC)
333 Fayetteville Street Mall, Suite 1150
Raleigh NC 27601-1742
Phone: 919/715-7272   Fax: 919/715-7777
E-mail: albrady.sbdc@mhs.unc.edu

Mr. Charles D. John
Intl. Trade Counselor
SBTDC — Winston-Salem
P.O. Box 13025
Winston-Salem NC 27110
Phone: 910/750-2030   Fax: 910/750-2031

Ohio

Mr. Tom LaPorte
Manager
Int'l Trade Division
Ohio Dept. of Dev.
P.O. Box 1001
Columbus OH 43216-1001
Phone: 614/466-5017   Fax: 614/463-1540
E-mail: TLAPORTEITD@odod.ohio.gov

Oklahoma

Ms. Karla Graham
Business Finance Specialist
Oklahoma Dept. of Commerce Export Finance Program
6601 Broadway/P.O. Box 26980
Oklahoma City OK 73126-0980
Phone: 405/841-5259   Fax: 405/841-5142

Pennsylvania

Ms. Mary McGlinchey
Export Finance Specialist
Pennsylvania Dept. of Community and Econ. Dev.
Office of Int'l Dev.
303 Forum Bldg.
Harrisburg PA 17120
Phone: 717/787-7190   Fax: 717/234-4560
E-mail: mmcglinc@doc.state.pa.us

Mr. Ray Devlin
Manager, Program Division
Philadelphia Industrial Dev. Corp. (PIDC)
2600 Centre Sq. West, 1500 Market St.
Philadelphia PA 19102-2126
Phone: 215/496-8112   Fax: 215/496-9618

Puerto Rico

Mr. Zayda Abadia

Trade Specialist
Economic Dev. Bank of Puerto Rico
Munoz Rivera Ave., 6th Fl.
Hato Rey Tower
Hato Rey Puerto Rico 00919
Phone: 809/765-2727   Fax: 809/765-4260
E-mail: PR51ST@aol.com

South Carolina

Mr. Wayne Trotter
Director
Export Financial Services Division, U. of South Carolina
Carolina Plaza Suite 1124
937 Assembly Street
Columbia SC 29208
Phone: 803/777-1924   Fax: 803/777-4575
E-mail: trotter@iopa.sc.edu

South Dakota

Mr. Joop Bollen
Director
South Dakota International Business Institute, Northern State U.
620 SE 15th Ave.
Aberdeen SD 57401
Phone: 605/626-3098   Fax: 605/626-3004
E-mail: bollenj@wolf.northern.edu

Texas

Mr. Philip Rocha III
Finance Specialist
Texas Dept. of Commerce, Finance Division
P.O. Box 12728
Austin TX 78711
Phone: 512/936-0279   Fax: 512/936-0520
E-mail: PhilR@mail.tdoc.texas.gov

Mr. Thierry Meyrat
Director of Trade Finance
Dallas Chamber of Commerce
World Trade Center, Suite 150
2050 Stemmons Freeway
Dallas TX 75258
Phone: 214/712-1934   Fax: 217/748-5774

Utah

Mr. Kent Vance
Portfolio Loan Officer
Utah Technology Finance Corp.
177 East 100 South
Salt Lake City UT 84111
Phone: 801/741-4220   Fax: 801/741-4249
E-mail: utfc.kvance@email.state.ut.us

Vermont

Ms. Marie Dussault
Loan Officer
Vermont Economic Dev. Authority
56 East State St.
Montpelier VT 05602
Phone: 802/223-7226   Fax: 802/223-4205

Virginia

Ms. Anna B. Mackley-Cobb
Finance Services Rep.
Virginia Small Business Finance Authority
901 East Byrd. St., Suite 1800

Richmond VA 23219
Phone: 804/371-8255   Fax: 804/225-3384
E-mail: AMackleyCobb@dba.state.va.us

Washington

Mr. Warren Gross
Managing Director and President
Export Finance Assistance Center of Washington
2001 6th Ave., Suite 650
Seattle WA 98121
Phone: 206/464-7152   Fax: 206/464-7230

Federal Communications Commission

1919 M St., NW / Washington DC 20554-0001
Public Affairs: 202/418-0500

INTRODUCTION

The Federal Communications Commission, created in 1934, regulates interstate and foreign communications including radio, television, wire, satellite, and cable. It has jurisdiction over the 50 states, the District of Columbia, Guam, Puerto Rico and the Virgin Islands. The duties of the FCC's five commissioners include processing applications for various broadcast construction permits; considering license assignments and transfers; licensing all classes of non-government stations; assigning frequencies, power and call signs; modifying and renewing licenses; authorizing communications circuits; and taking remedial action when necessary. Currently, 4 out of the 5 commissioner posts are filled. One is vacant.

Commissioners

Chair
Mr. William Kennard
202/418-1000   FAX 202/418-2801
Rm. 814

Education: A.B. in communications (with distinction), Stanford Univ., 1978. J.D., Yale Law School, 1981.

Professional: 1981-82, legal fellow, National Association of Broadcasters. Sept. 1982-July 1983, associate, Verner, Liipfert, Bernhard, McPherson & Hand (Wash., D.C.). July 1983-April 1984, asst. general counsel, National Association of Broadcasters. April 1984-Dec. 1993, associate, then partner, Verner, Liipfert, Bernhard, McPherson & Hand (Wash., D.C.). Dec. 1993-present, general counsel; May 1997-present, commissioner designate and August 1997-present, chair designate, Federal Communications Commission.

Confirmed by the Senate in the fall of 1997, William Kennard became the first African American to chair the FCC. Prior to his confirmation, Kennard was the general counsel to the FCC, a position he has held since December of 1993.

As chief legal officer, Kennard was responsible for advising the commission on all matters involving the interpretation and application of the Communications Act of 1934 as amended as well as other enacted or proposed legislation or regulations affecting the responsibilities and jurisdiction of the commission. The general counsel also serves as the commission's legal representative in all litigation involving the commission. During Kennard's tenure, the commission's win record in the U.S. Courts of Appeals has increased from 55% to 85%.

In recent years, the commission has been faced with the massive task of implementing the Telecommunications Act of 1996, which to date has entailed approximately 45 rulemakings and over 150 commission orders. Kennard has been credited with recruiting the most talented and diverse group of lawyers in OGC's history, attracting many former Supreme Court clerks and attorneys from major Washington D.C. communications firms.

For nine years before coming to the FCC, Kennard was with the Washington D.C. law firm of Verner, Liipfert, Bernhard, McPherson & Hand where he was a partner from January of 1990 to December 1993. He specialized in communications law with emphasis on regulatory and transactional matters for communications companies. This experience included representing clients in financings, acquisitions, and sales of broadcast, cable, cellular telephone, and public companies and representing clients in proceedings before the FCC and other federal agencies.

Prior to joining the law firm, Kennard had served as assistant general counsel for the National of Broadcasters (NAB) where his primary responsibility was representing this major trade association on legal issues involving its members. He served the previous year as an associate of Verner, Liipfert. Just after earning his J.D. at Yale, Kennard served a year at NAB on a one-year legal fellowship.

While earning his law degree, Kennard was a member of the Yale Moot Court Board of Directors, and a semi-finalist at the Yale Moot Court of Appeals. He chaired the admissions committee of the Black Law Students Union, served as student representative for the Admissions Committee, and was student recruiter for the office of admission. He earned his A.B. in communications from Stanford University in May of 1978 where he was Phi Beta Kappa.

Kennard is active in the Federal Communications Bar Association and is a member of the American Bar Association, the California Bar, the D.C. Bar, and the National Bar Association. He serves as a member of the board of directors of Sasha Bruce Youthworks, a nonprofit homeless shelter serving the youth of Washington, D.C.

Chief of Staff
Mr. John Nakata
202/418-1000
Rm. 814

Commissioner
Mr. Harold Furchtgott-Roth
202/418-2200   FAX 202/418-2809
Rm. 802

Personal: born 12/13/56 in Knoxville, Tenn.

Education: B.S. in economics, Mass. Institute of Technology, 1978.

Ph.D. in economics, Stanford Univ., 1986.

Professional: 1976-82, research assistant/intern, various federal agencies. 1983-84, research fellow, Brookings Institution. 1984-88, research staff, Center for Naval Analysis. 1988-95, senior economist, Economists Inc. 1995-present, chief economist, House Commerce Cmte. Fall 1997-present, commissioner, Federal Communications Commission.

Former Commissioner Andrew Barrett left the Federal Communications Commission in late 1996. In May of 1997, President Clinton named Harold W. Furchtgott-Roth to fill this Republican seat on the FCC and he was confirmed by the Senate Commerce Committee in October, 1997.

Furchtgott-Roth had been chief economist for the U.S. House Commerce Committee, a position he took when the Republicans won control of the House. In that position, he served as a generalist on issues such as health care, the environment, international trade, energy, telecommunications, and finance. Almost immediately after taking the job, he plunged into the telecommunication overhaul legislation which passed as the Telecommunications Act of 1996 and after its passage, was charged with scrutinizing how the new law is put into effect.

A strong proponent of deregulation and consumer choice, his nomination aroused some opposition in the Senate because of his support for changing "the 'universal service' subsidy program that ensures low telephone prices in rural areas. He wants more of a free market mechanism". (*Washington Post*, July 4, 1997).

Before joining the House Committee staff, Furchtgott-Roth was a senior economist with Economists Inc., specializing in antitrust, taxation, international trade, and telecommunications regulation. Before that, he was on the research staff of the Center for Naval Analysis.

He is the co-author of three books including *International Trade in Computer Software,* and *Economics of a Disaster,* which examines the Exxon Valdez oil spill. His most recent book, published in 1996, is *Cable TV: Regulation or Competition?* co-authored by Robert Crandall.

Furchtgott-Roth received a B.S. in economics from MIT and a Ph.D. in economics from Stanford University.

Commissioner
Mr. Michael Powell
202/418-2200   FAX 202/418-2804
Rm. 844

At the time of his nomination in 1997, Michael Powell, of Fairfax Station, Virginia, was the chief of staff of the antitrust division at the U.S. Department of Justice, where he served since December 1996.

Prior to this position, Powell served as an associate from 1994 to 1996 with O'Melveny & Myers where he practiced in the areas of telecommunications law, antitrust, regulatory affairs, and general litigation. He served as a judicial clerk to the Honorable Harry T. Edwards, Chief Judge of the U.S. Court of Appeals for the District of Columbia Circuit, from 1993 to 1994. From 1988 to 1990, Powell was a policy advisor to the assistant secretary of Defense for international security affairs.
Powell holds an A.B. from The College of William and Mary and a J.D. from Georgetown University Law Center. He served as a cavalry officer in the U.S. Army from 1985 to 1988. He is the son of retired General Colin Powell.

Commissioner
Ms. Gloria Tristani
202/418-2300
Rm. 826

Gloria Tristani, of Albuquerque, New Mexico, was the first woman elected to the New Mexico State Corporation Commission (SCC) where she held office since 1995. She served as commission chair in 1996. Tristani was confirmed as a commissioner of the FCC in October, 1997.

As a commissioner on the New Mexico SCC, Tristani was actively involved in the enactment of legislation authorizing the SCC to fine telecommunications companies for failure to comply with the law. Under her direction, the SCC issued expanded area service regulations which permit expanding the local calling area for certain toll calls.

Prior to serving on the SCC, Tristani was an attorney in private practice in Albuquerque. She holds memberships in numerous professional and community organizations and has received a number of awards for her outstanding achievements. She received her undergraduate degree from Barnard College of Columbia University and her law degree from the University of New Mexico School of Law.

Commissioner
Ms. Susan Ness
202/418-2100   FAX 202/418-2821
Rm. 832

Personal: born 8/11/48 in Elizabeth, N.J.

Education: B.A., Douglass College (Rutgers Univ.), 1970. Sarah Lawrence College, Geneva, Switzerland Program, 1968-69. J.D. (cum laude), Boston College Law School, 1974. M.B.A., Univ. of Pa., Wharton Graduate School, 1983.

Professional: 1974-75, attorney adviser, Consumer Product Safety Commission. 1975-77, asst. counsel, U.S. House Cmte. on Banking, Currency and Housing. 1977-82, consultant on consumer credit and government relations. 1978-81, dir., Judicial Appointments Project, National Women's Political Caucus. 1983-84, corporate banking representative; 1984, asst. treasurer; 1986-92, vice president; 1988-92, group head, communications industries division, American Security Bank. 1994-present, commissioner, Federal Communications Commission.

Susan Ness was nominated by President Clinton and confirmed by the Senate in 1994 to fill an unexpired term as commissioner of the Federal Communications Commission. She has subsequently been reappointed to a full five-year term which ends on June 30, 1999. Because of major upheavals on the commission in 1997, Ness is now the senior member of the five-member board.

Commission seats are considered partisan and a 3/2 split in favor of the incumbent administration is the norm. Ness' seat is considered a "Democratic" seat, and she was considered a voting ally of retiring

Chairman Reed Hundt, also a Clinton appointee. In July of 1997 Ness and Hundt voted to take up President Clinton's request to investigate the effects of hard liquor advertising on television. The two retiring Republican members, however, voted against the proposal and it was defeated. The issue is expected back on the agenda when the all the new members have been confirmed.

Ness had previously served as a senior lender and then group head in the communications industries division of American Security Bank in Washington, D.C., where she evaluated, structured, negotiated, and supervised more than a quarter billion dollars in loans to communications enterprises nationwide. Her career also has included working as an attorney adviser for the Consumer Products Safety Commission, as an assistant counsel to the U.S. House Committee on Banking, Currency and Housing and as a consultant on consumer credit and government relations. She also founded and directed the Judicial Appointments Project of the National Women's Political Caucus.

Ness earned her B.A. from the Douglass College at Rutgers University in 1970. Her involvement in communications began at Douglass where she served on the board of directors of WRSU Radio (Rutgers University) and produced public affairs and foreign language programming for the station. She earned her J.D. from Boston College Law School in 1974. She later returned to school earning an MBA from the Wharton Graduate School of the University of Pennsylvania in 1983.

Ness is married to Lawrence A. Schneider and they have two school-aged children.

Office of the Managing Director

Operations

Route 116 / Gettysburg PA 17326

Chief, Intl. Telecommunications Settlement Section
Ms. Edna S. Steinour
717/338-2685

Office of Public Affairs

1919 M St., NW / Washington DC 20554-0001

Director
Ms. Elizabeth Rose
202/418-0500
Rm. 202

Tariff Public Reference Room
202/418-1933
Rm. 250

Common Carrier Bureau

Tariff Division

Chief, Tariff Review Board
Ms. Judith A. Nitsche
202/418-1540
Rm. 518

International Bureau

2000 M St., NW / Washington DC 20554

Chief
Ms. Regina Keeney
202/418-0420
Rm. 800

Deputy Chief
Mr. Roderick K. Porter
202/418-0420

Associate Chief, Policy
Mr. James Ball
202/418-0420

Deputy Chief, Policy
Ms. Mindel De La Torre
202/418-1470

Chief, Telecommunications Division
Ms. Diane J. Cornell
202/418-1470

Deputy Chief, Operations
Mr. George Li
202/418-1470

Chief, Multilateral and Development Branch
Mr. Thomas Wasilewski
202/418-1470

Chief, Satellite and Radio Communications Branch
Mr. Thomas Tycz
202/418-0719

Chief, Satellite Engineering Branch
Mr. Steve Sharkey
202/418-7280

Chief, Radio Communications Policy Branch
Mr. William A. Luther
202/418-0729

Chief, Planning and Negotiations Division
Mr. Richard Engelman
202/418-2150
Rm. 868

Federal Maritime Commission

800 North Capitol St., NW / Washington DC 20573
202/523-5900

INTRODUCTION

The Federal Maritime Commission, established in 1961, regulates the waterborne foreign and domestic offshore commerce of the U.S., assures that U.S. international trade is open to all nations on fair and equitable terms, and protects against unauthorized, concerted activity in the waterborne commerce of the U.S. There is one vacancy on the commission.

Office of the Commissioners

Chair
Mr. Harold J. Creel
202/523-5911   FAX 202/523-4224
Rm. 1000

Personal: born in Florence, S.C.

Education: B.A. in political science, Wofford College (Spartanburg, S.C.), 1979. J.D., Univ. of S.C. School of Law, 1982.

Professional: 1982-83, assoc. attorney, Courtenay, Forstall, Grace and Hebert (New Orleans). 1983-89, attorney advisor, National Oceanic and Atmospheric Administration. 1989-94, senior counsel, merchant marine subcmte., U.S. Senate Cmte. on Commerce, Science and Transportation. Aug. 1994-present, commissioner, Federal Maritime Commission. Feb. 1996-present, chairman, Federal Maritime Commission.

Harold Creel has been chairman of the Federal Maritime Commission since February 5, 1996. He was nominated by President Clinton to a five year term on the commission on July 1, 1994 and was confirmed by the US Senate on August 17, 1994.

The Federal Maritime Commission is composed of five commissioners appointed for five-year terms by the President with the advice and consent of the Senate. Not more than three members of the commission may belong to the same political party. The President designates one of the commissioners to serve as chairman. The chairman is the chief executive and administrative officer of the agency. As such, the chair has exclusive authority over agency personnel matters, organization, and supervision and distribution of business.

Prior to his appointment to the commission, Creel was the senior counsel of the merchant marine subcommittee of the U.S. Senate Committee on Commerce, Science, and Transportation. He held that position from October 1989 to October 1994. As senior counsel of the subcommittee, he advised the committee chairman, the subcommittee chairman, and all Democratic Senators on issues pertaining to commercial shipping.

Before joining the Commerce Committee, Creel was an attorney with the National Oceanic and Atmospheric Administration (NOAA) of the Department of Commerce. In that capacity, he acted as the chief staff attorney on issues pertaining to endangered marine species. While at NOAA, he assisted the Department of Justice in administrative proceedings and litigation of cases involving endangered species issues. He also wrote, negotiated, and reviewed regulations implementing NOAA's legal authority.

A native of Florence, South Carolina, Creel graduated from James E. Byrnes Academy in 1975. He then attended Wofford College and graduated in 1979 with a B.A. in political science. He received his J.D. from the University of South Carolina School of Law in 1982 and moved to New Orleans to practice in a law firm specializing in admiralty law.

Commissioner
Ms. Ming Chen Hsu
202/523-5715   FAX 202/523-0298
Rm. 1044

Personal: born 9/14/24 in Beijing, China.

Education: B.A. (summa cum laude), George Washington University School of Government Affairs, 1949. LL.D., Ramapo College (N.J.), 1988. LL.D., Kean College, (N.J.), 1989.

Professional: vice-president, international trade relations, and director of international planning, RCA Corp. (N.Y. City). 1982-90, governor's special trade rep. and dir., division of intern'l. trade, State of New Jersey. 1990-present, commissioner, Federal Maritime Commission.

Ming Chen Hsu has been a member of the Federal Maritime Commission since 1990. She was originally appointed by President George Bush. She brings to the commission a long history in international trade. She served for many years as vice president for international trade relations and director of international planning for the RCA Corporation in New York City.

For eight years beginning in 1982, Hsu worked as the governor's special trade representatives for New Jersey Governor Thomas Kean and as director of the state's division of international trade. In her positions with RCA and the state of New Jersey, Commissioner Hsu led over 20 trade missions to different countries throughout the world, including Europe and Russia.

As a Federal Maritime commissioner, Hsu has addressed maritime industry groups in Brussels, London, Singapore, Hong Kong, Shanghai, Beijing, and many U.S. cities. As a writer and consultant on international business and trade, she is also a speaker and lecturer and has appeared on numerous network and local television programs.

Hsu has served on many government commissions including service on the Secretary of Defense's Advisory Commission on Women in the Services. She was appointed by President Gerald R. Ford to serve on the National Commission on Observance of International Women's Year, served on the Secretary of Commerce's Advisory Commission on East-West Trade, and served on the U.S. Trade Representative's Advisory Commission on Trade in Services.

Hsu has received many honors for her service including a special award by the Women's Equity Action League in 1978, a Woman of the Year Award in 1983 from the Asian-American Professional Women's Association and, in the same year, an Alumni Achievement Award from the George Washington University. She served as a delegate at large to the Republican National Conventions in 1984 and 1988.

A naturalized U.S. citizen, Hsu was born in Beijing, China and lived throughout Asia. She is a graduate of George Washington University and is a member of Phi Beta Kappa. At New York University, Commissioner Hsu was a Penfield Fellow for International Law.

Commissioner
Mr. Joe Scroggins, Jr.
202/523-5712   FAX 202/523-0298
Rm. 1032

Education: B.S. in marine transportation, Merchant Marine Academy, 1963. M.B.A., Harvard Univ., 1973.

Professional: 1967-71, asst. dean, U.S. Merchant Marine Academy. sr. transp. analyst, John J. McMullen Associates, Inc. economist, Conoco, Inc. 1982-90, dir. of planning, then dir. of facilities, Port of Houston Authority. 1990-94, sr. deputy port director, Tampa Port Authority. 1994-present, commissioner, Federal Maritime Commission.

Joe Scroggins was nominated by President Clinton in May of 1994 to be a commissioner at the FMC. He was confirmed by the U.S. Senate on June 13 and was sworn in on June 27, 1994.

Scroggins came to the commission after serving for four years as the senior deputy port director for the Port Authority of Tampa. Prior to working in Tampa, Scroggins served four years as the director of planning and then for five years as director of facilities for the Port of Houston Authority.

Commissioner Scroggins had earlier worked as a senior transportation analyst for John J. McMullen, Inc. in Houston and as an economist for Conoco, Inc., also in Houston.

Scroggins is a graduate of the U.S. Merchant Marine Academy at Kings Point. He sailed for the Military Sealift Command and United States Lines as a Third Mate and Second Mate. He currently holds a chiefmate license. Scroggins served as an assistant dean at the U.S. Merchant Marine Academy subsequent to leaving his shipboard employment.

Commissioner Scroggins holds an MBA from the Graduate School of Business Administration at Harvard University. He is the recipient of the U.S. Department of Commerce's Silver Medal Award for Meritorious Service as well as the Department of Commerce's Special Achievement Award.

Commissioner
Mr. Delmond J.H. Won
202/523-5721   FAX 202/523-0298
Rm. 1026

Personal: born in Honolulu, Hawaii.

Education: B.S., Univ. of Hawaii, School of Engineering. M.B.A., Univ. of Hawaii, Graduate School of Business.

Professional: 1977-90, various positions, Hawaiian Tug & Barge Corporation and Young Brothers, Limited. 1990-94, commissioner, Hawaii State Land Use Commission. 1990-93, vice president, Hawaii Pacific Industries. 1993-94, consultant, maritime related issues, Hawaii. August 1994-present, commissioner, Federal Maritime Commission.

Delmond Won became a commissioner of the Federal Maritime Commission in August of 1994. The commission regulates the waterborne foreign and domestic offshore commerce of the United States, assures that United States international trade is open to all nations on fair and equitable terms, and protects against unauthorized concerted activity in the waterborne commerce of the United States.

Won came to the commission after thirteen years with the Hawaiian Tug & Barge Corporation & Young Brothers. He held various positions including manager, government affairs and customer service; manager, planning and analysis; and marketing assistant and analyst. When he left the company in 1990, he was director for planning and regulatory affairs. Key responsibilities included development of strategic and operating plans, development of company cases before the Hawaii Public Utilities Commission, development of operating budgets, analysis of business opportunities, and financial analysis of operating methods and capital asset acquisition.

Won was commissioner for the Hawaii State Land Use Commission from 1990 to 1994. He was one of nine appointees of the governor of Hawaii responsible for the re-zoning of lands within the state. Also from 1990 to 1993, he served a vice president for Hawaii Pacific Industries where he was responsible for the operation of a dry bulk cargo unloading and loading facility located at Barbers Point Harbor, Oahu, Hawaii. He then served as a consultant on maritime related issues before taking the assignment as Federal Maritime Commissioner in August of 1994.

Office of the Managing Director

Managing Director
Mr. Edward Patrick Walsh
202/523-5800
Rm. 1038

Bureau of Tariffs, Certification and Licensing

Director
Mr. Bryant L. van Brakle
202/523-5796
Rm. 940

Deputy Director
Mr. Theodore Zook
202/523-5796

Chief, Office of Tariffs
Mr. James G. Cannon
202/523-5818

Chief, Office of Service Contract Operations &
    Passenger Vessel Operations
Mr. Theodore A. Zook
202/523-5856

Chief, Office of Freight Forwarders
Ms. Betty J. Bennett
202/523-5843

Chief, Tariff Control Center
VACANT
202/523-5828

Federal Mediation & Conciliation Service

2100 K Street, NW / Washington DC 20427
Central: 202/606-8100
Public Information: 202/606-8080
Personnel Office: 202/606-5460

INTRODUCTION

The Federal Mediation and Conciliation Service represents the public interest by promoting the development of sound and stable labor-management relations, preventing or minimizing work stoppages by assisting labor and management to settle their disputes through mediation. The Service assists foreign countries in methods of dispute mediation and preventive mediation that have proved successful in the U.S.

Office of the Director

Mgr. Intl. Relations
Mr. James F. Power
202/606-9143
Rm. 200

Federal Reserve System

20th and C Streets, NW / Washington DC 20551
General Information: 202/452-3000
Public Affairs: 202/452-3204
Publications: 202/452-3244

INTRODUCTION

The Federal Reserve System (FED), as the central bank of the U.S., helps to maintain the banking industry in sound condition, capable of responding to the nation's domestic and international needs and objectives.

The Federal Reserve System was established in 1913 as 12 separate financial institutions that collectively comprised the nation's central bank. Although this initial structure was designed in a decentralized fashion, since the Great Depression the FED has become more of a unified organization.

Today, the FED serves a unique role in the American economy. Its actions on interest rates have a direct impact on the economy, world markets, and the Federal budget. Yet it is considered "independent" of any administration. A natural tension results from this relationship and many administrations have telegraphed their displeasure as interest rate hikes have interfered with fiscal policy plans. The FED also has a responsibility for bank regulation and this role also often puts it at loggerheads with administration proposals in this area.

The Federal Reserve System is made up of seven parts: the board of governors; the 12 Federal Reserve Banks and their branches; the federal open market committee; the federal advisory council; the consumer advisory council; the thrift institutions advisory council; and financial institutions, including commercial banks, savings and loan associations and credit unions.

The FED has three financial tools that it uses to control the money supply: the use of Open Market Operations (the buying and selling of

Treasury Notes); the Discount Window (the rate at which the FED loans money to member banks); and the setting of the Reserve Requirement (the amount of money any one bank must have on hand at all times).

The Board of Governors

The board of governors, which has seven members (including a chairman and vice chairman) appointed by the president and confirmed by the Senate, decides the system's general monetary, credit and operating policies. The board monitors credit conditions and supervises the Federal Reserve Banks and other member banks. It also oversees the implementation of certain consumer credit protection laws.

The board's primary task is to formulate monetary policy. The board sets monetary reserve requirements and works with the Federal Reserve Banks to determine discount rate policy. The Federal Reserve Board also has regulatory power over banks which are members of the Federal Reserve System. The board sets limits for the use of credit for the purchasing of securities, and also administers those regulations which involve consumer lending, such as the Truth in Lending Act, the Home Mortgage Disclosure Act, the Equal Credit Opportunity Act, and the Truth in Savings Act.

To ensure fair representation of regional interests, the president is directed by law to select a "fair representation of the financial, agricultural and commercial and geographical divisions of the country." The chairman and vice chairman are also chosen by the President and confirmed by the Senate for four-year terms.

The Federal Open Market Committee

Comprised of seven members of the board of governors and five of the FED's regional banks, the federal open market committee (FOMC) is responsible for the buying and selling of Treasury notes. This action ultimately controls the amount of money that circulates in the American economy.

Senior Federal Reserve Officials

Chair
Mr. Alan Greenspan
202/452-3201   FAX 202/452-3819
Rm. B-2046

Personal: born 3/6/26 in New York City, N.Y.

Education: B.S. in economics *(summa cum laude)*, NYU, 1948. M.A. in economics, NYU, 1950. Ph.D. in economics, NYU, 1977.

Professional: 1954-74, chairman, president, Townsend-Greenspan and Co., Inc. 1974-77, chairman, Council of Economic Advisors. 1977-87, chairman, president, Townsend-Greenspan and Co., Inc. 1981-

83, chairman, National Commission on Social Security Reform. 1987-present, chairman, Board of Governors of the Federal Reserve System.

Alan Greenspan was originally appointed to the Federal Reserve System by Ronald Reagan in 1987. Currently, he is serving his third four-year term as chairman of the Fed's Board of Governors.

The board is comprised of seven members appointed by the president and confirmed by the Senate for 14-year terms. To a ensure a representation of regional interests, the president is directed by law to select a "fair representation of the financial, agricultural and commercial and geographical divisions of the country." The chairman and vice chairman are also chosen by the president and confirmed by the Senate for four-year terms.

Greenspan also serves as chairman of the Federal Open Market Committee (FOMC). The committee generally meets eight times a year to establish monetary policy. This policy can be affected through the use of the three tools afforded the Fed: open market operations, discount rate, and reserve requirements.

Greenspan caused some jitters in the stock market in early 1997 when he warned about "irrational exuberance" unduly escalating "stock prices". As the year went on, he appeared to back off from commenting about the stock market.

Prior to his Federal Reserve appointment, Greenspan worked at the economic consulting firm of Townsend-Greenspan, Inc. in New York City for almost 30 years. He took a break from the firm in 1974 to serve as chairman of President Ford's Council of Economic Advisors. He also chaired the National Commission on Social Security Reform from 1981 to 1983.

The Federal Reserve System serves a unique role in the American economy. Its actions on interest rates have a direct impact on the economy, world markets, and the federal budget. Yet it is considered "independent" of any administration. A natural tension results from this relationship and many administrations have telegraphed their displeasure as interest rate hikes have interfered with fiscal policy plans. The Fed also has a responsibility for bank regulation and this role often puts it at loggerheads with administration proposals in this area.

Vice Chair and Governor
Ms. Alice Rivlin
202/452-3271   FAX 202/452-3819
Rm. B-2052

Personal: born 3/4/31 in Philadelphia, Pa.

Education: B.A. in economics, Bryn Mawr College, 1952. M.A. in economics, 1955, and Ph.D. in economics, 1958, Radcliffe College.

Professional: 1966-68, dep. asst. sec. for program coordination; 1968-69, asst. sec. for planning and evaluation, U.S. Dept. of Health, Education and Welfare. 1975-83, director, Congressional Budget Office. 1983-87, director; 1987-93, senior fellow, economic studies

program, Brookings Institution. 1992-93, Hirst Professor of Public Policy, George Mason Univ. 1993-94, dep. dir.; 1994-96, dir., Office of Management and Budget. June 1996-present, vice chair and member, Board of Governors, Federal Reserve System.

Dr. Alice Rivlin took office June 24, 1996 as vice chair of the Board of Governors of the Federal Reserve System for a four-year term ending June 24, 2000. In addition to her position as vice chair, Rivlin is serving as a member of the Board with a full term ending January 31, 2010.

In October of 1996, Chairman Alan Greenspan appointed Rivlin to head a committee to conduct a fundamental review of the Fed's participation in payment services to banks and other financial institutions.   Rivlin is also chair of the board's budget committee and it committee on economic affairs.

Before becoming a member of the Board, Rivlin served as director of the White House Office of Management and Budget (1994-96) and deputy director (1993-94). She was the Hirst Professor of Public Policy at George Mason University during 1992.

Rivlin was the founding director of the Congressional Budget Office serving there from 1975 to 1983. She served as a member of the staff at the Brookings Institution (1957-66), (1969-75), (1983-93), and as director of economic studies at Brookings from 1983 to 1987. Rivlin also has served as assistant secretary for planning and evaluation at the U.S. Department of Health, Education and Welfare (1968-69) and as deputy assistant secretary for program coordination at HEW from 1966 to 1968.

She is the recipient of a MacArthur Foundation Prize Fellowship, has taught at Harvard University, served on the boards of directors of several corporations, and served as president of the American Economics Association. She has written numerous books, the most recent of which is *Reviving the American Dream,* and has contributed frequently to newspapers, magazines, and journals.

Rivlin was invited to deliver a guest lecture series on the issues involved in public policy analysis at the University of California at Berkeley in 1970. The series was published by the Brookings Institution in 1971. *Systematic Thinking for Social Action* has become a classic in the public policy and public administration disciplines. More than 75,000 copies of the text have been sold.

Dr. Rivlin received a B.A. in economics from Bryn Mawr College in 1952 and earned an M.A. in economics in 1955 and a Ph.D. in economics in 1958, both from Radcliffe College.

Rivlin grew up in Bloomington, Indiana. She is married to another economist, Professor Sidney G. Winter. She has three children.

Governor
Mr. Edward W. Kelley, Jr.
202/452-3285   FAX 202/452-3819
Rm. B-2004

Personal: born 1/27/32 in Eugene, Ore.

Education: B.A., Rice University, 1954. M.B.A., Harvard Business School, 1959.

Professional: 1959-81, president and CEO, Kelley Industries, Inc. 1961-72, director, Southern National Bank. 1974-82, director, Westwood Commerce Bank. 1982-84, director, West Belt National Bank. 1981-87, chairman of the board, Investment Advisors Incorporated. 1987-present, board member, Board of Governors of the Federal Reserve System.

Edward Kelley took office as a member of the Board of Governors of the Federal Reserve System on April 10, 1990 for a full term ending January 31, 2004. He had previously served from May of 1987, completing an unexpired term.

Before becoming a member of the board, Kelley had been chairman of the board of Investment Advisors Incorporated in Houston, Texas from 1981 to 1987. From 1959 to 1981, he was president and CEO of Kelley Industries, Inc., a Houston-based holding company with subsidiaries involved in manufacturing, distribution, and business services.

Kelley has been active as an executive or director in a number of industries including metals and plastics fabrication, industrial distribution, cement, steel, construction, trucking, terminaling, and computer services. He has also been a founding director of three banks in the Houston area. He has served with numerous business, academic, civic, and charitable organizations, including the Better Business Bureau; Rice University, Trustee; National Association of Independent Schools, Trustee Committee; St. John's School, Board of Trustees and Chair; Metropolitan YMCA; Harris County United Fund; the Houston Symphony; Young President's Organization; and the World Business Council.

Kelley received a B.A. in history from Rice University in 1954 and an MBA from Harvard Business School in 1959. He served in the U.S. Navy as a lieutenant.

Governor
Mr. Roger Ferguson
202/452-3213   FAX 202/452-5254
Rm. B-2010

Education: B.A.; Ph.D. in economics; J.D., Harvard Univ.

Professional: securities and banking lawyer, Davis Polk & Wardwell. partner, director of research and information systems, McKinsey & Company (N.Y. City). July 1997-present, governor designate, Federal Reserve System.

President Clinton nominated Roger Ferguson to serve on the Board of Governors of the Federal Reserve System in July, 1997. Confirmed by the Senate in the fall, Ferguson replaced Janet Yellen who now serves as chair of the Council of Economics Advisors at The White House.

At the time of his nomination, Ferguson was a partner and director of research and information systems at McKinsey & Company in New York. He holds a B.A., a J.D., and a Ph.D. in economics, all from Harvard University. After completing his formal education, Ferguson spent three years as a securities and banking lawyer at Davis Polk & Wardwell before joining McKinsey. At McKinsey, he has specialized in financial issues.

His consulting experiences have included designing a super-regional bank strategy for a money center bank, a post-acquisition strategy and consolidation for a California thrift, and an information technology strategy for a full-line brokerage house. As director of research and information systems at McKinsey, Ferguson has first-hand experience

applying information technology to improve productivity in a service organization.

Governor
Ms. Susan M. Phillips
202/452-3217   FAX 202/452-3819
Rm. B-2062

Personal: born 12/23/44 in Richmond, Va.

Education: B.A. in mathematics (Phi Beta Kappa), Agnes Scott College, 1967. M.S. in finance and insurance (Beta Gamma Sigma), Louisiana State Univ., 1971. Ph.D. in finance and economics, LSU, 1973.

Professional: 1973-74, asst. professor, LSU. 1974-76, asst. professor of business admin., University of Iowa. 1976-77, economic policy fellow, Brookings Institution (Wash., D.C.). 1977-78, economics fellow, Securities and Exchange Commission. 1978, associate professor, University of Iowa. 1979-80, asst. vice president for finance and university services; 1980-81, assoc. v.p. for finance and university services, Univ. of Iowa. 1981-87, member, Commodity Futures Trading Commission (1983-87, chairman). 1987-91, v.p. of finance and university services and professor of finance, Univ. of Iowa. 1991-present, member, Board of Governors of the Federal Reserve System.

Dr. Susan Phillips brings a range of academic and governmental experience to her position as a member of the Board of Governors of the Federal Reserve System. She was appointed to the Board in 1991 by President George Bush to fill an unexpired term which ends January 31, 1998. She continues on until a new nominee is put forward by the President.

Phillips is a well-known specialist in commodity futures, financial management, and the economic theory of regulation. Throughout her academic career, she has authored a number of publications and articles on finance and economic theory. She co-authored *The SEC and the Public Interest* along with J. Richard Zecher.

Her teaching career began at Louisiana State University. She began teaching at the University of Iowa in 1974 advancing through the ranks at Iowa to become vice president of finance and university services and professor of finance before joining the board of governors.

Phillips was a member of the Commodity Futures Trading Commission from 1981 to 1987 and served for part of that time as its chair. She has received a number of awards as a result of her academic and professional achievements. These include the Pomerance Prize Award from the Chicago Board Options Exchange, and the Outstanding Alumna Award from her alma mater, Agnes Scott College.

Governor
Dr. Edward M. Gramlich
202/452-3735   FAX 202/452-5254
Rm. B-2022

Education: B.A., Williams College. M.A. and Ph.D. in economics, Yale Univ.

Professional: staff, Federal Reserve Board, U.S. Office of Economic Opportunity; and Brookings Institution. 1986-87, deputy director and then acting director, Congressional Budget Office. 1994-96, chair, Quadrennial Advisory Council on Social Security. 1987-present, economics professor and dean, School of Public Policy, Univ. of Mich. July 1997-present, governor-designate, Federal Reserve System.

In July, 1997, President Clinton nominated Edward Gramlich to serve on the Board of Governors of the Federal Reserve System. Confirmed in the fall, Gramlich replaced Laurence Lindsey who resigned.

Most recently, Dr. Gramlich was an economics professor and dean of the School of Public Policy at the University of Michigan. He holds a B.A. from Williams College, and an M.A. and Ph.D. in economics from Yale University.

Gramlich has written nine books and numerous journal articles. He has previously worked at the Federal Reserve, the Office of Economic Opportunity, and the Brookings Institution. He served as the deputy director and then the acting director of the Congressional Budget Office in 1986 and 1987.

Governor
Laurence H. Meyer
202/452-3211   FAX 202/452-2271
Room B2064

Personal: born 3/8/44 in the Bronx, N.Y.

Education: B.A. (magna cum laude), Yale Univ., 1965. Ph.D. in economics, Mass. Institute of Technology, 1970.

Professional: economist, Federal Reserve Bank of New York. visiting scholar, Federal Reserve Bank of St. Louis. 1969-96, research associate and former chair, economics dept., Washington Univ. (St. Louis). 1982-96, co-founder and president, Laurence H. Meyer and Associates (St. Louis). 1996-present, member, Board of Governors, Federal Reserve System.

Laurence Meyer took office as a member of the Board of Governors of the Federal Reserve System on June 20, 1996, to fill an unexpired term ending January 31, 2002.

Prior to becoming a member of the board, Meyer was president of Laurence H. Meyer and Associates, a St. Louis-based economic consulting firm he helped found in 1982 specializing in macroeconomic forecasting and policy analysis. He was a professor of economics at Washington University from 1969 to 1996, where he was a research associate of the University's Center for the Study of American Business and a former chair of the economics department.

Meyer is widely recognized as one of the nation's leading economic forecasters. He was honored by *Business Week* in 1986 as the top forecaster for the year on its forecast panel. He was similarly honored in 1993 and 1996, receiving the prestigious Annual Forecast Award, presented to the most accurate forecaster on the panel for the Blue Chip Economic indicators.

Dr. Meyer has served as an economist at the Federal Reserve Bank of New York and as visiting scholar at the Federal Reserve Bank of St. Louis. He has had numerous articles published in the top professional journals, has authored a textbook on macroeconomic modeling, and has testified before Congress on macroeconomic policy issues.

He received his B.A. from Yale University in 1965 and his Ph.D. in economics from Massachusetts Institute of Technology in 1970.

Office of Board Members

Asst. to the Board, Public Affairs
Mr. Joseph R. Coyne
202/452-3204
Rm. B-2120A

Division of International Finance

Staff Director
Mr. Edwin M. Truman
202/452-3614
Rm. B-1242C

Senior Associate Director
VACANT
202/452-3533
Rm. B-1242A

Senior Associate Director
VACANT
202/452-3308
Rm. B-1228C

Senior Adviser
Mr. David H. Howard
202/452-3796
Rm. B-1202E

Associate Director
Mr. Dale W. Henderson
202/452-2343
Rm. B-1202C

Associate Director
Mr. Peter Hooper
202/452-3426
Rm. B-1228B

Associate Director
Ms. Karen H. Johnson
202/452-2345
Rm. B-1258B

Associate Director
Mr. Lewis Alexander
202/452-2375
Rm. B-1252B

Asst. Director
Mr. Donald B. Adams
202/452-2364
Rm. B-2266E

Asst. Director
Mr. Thomas A. Connors
202/452-3639
Rm. B-1226E

Education: B.A. (with honors) in English and history (Phi Beta Kappa), New York Univ., 1951. LL.B., Columbia School of Law, 1954.

Professional: 1956-67, attorney, U.S. Dept. of Justice (Wash., D.C.). 1957-63, attorney, Dewey, Ballantine, Bushby, Palmer & Wood (New York City). 1963-70, professor of law, New York University School of Law. 1970-73, director, Bureau of Consumer Protection, U.S. Federal Trade Commission. 1973-78, professor of law, Georgetown Univ. Law Center; of counsel, Arnold & Porter (Wash., D.C.). 1978-81, commissioner, Federal Trade Commission. July 1983-June 1989, dean and executive v.p. for Law Center affairs, Georgetown University Law Center. May 1981-June 1983, July 1989-1995, professor of law, Georgetown University Law Center; of counsel, Arnold & Porter (Wash., D.C.). 1995-present, chairman, Federal Trade Commission.

Federal Trade Commission

601 Pennsylvania Ave., NW / Washington DC 20580

Main: 202/326-2000
Congressional Relations: 202/326-2195
Public Affairs: 202/326-2180

INTRODUCTION

The FTC is an independent administrative agency with the authority to promote competition by preventing restraint of trade and other unfair trade practices and to protect customers from unfair and deceptive conduct. In carrying out its mission of keeping competition both free and fair, the five-member Federal Trade Commission reviews the effect of mergers and acquisitions of foreign firms, as well as domestic firms, on the U.S. market. It supervises the registration and operation of associations of American exporters engaged in export trade. And it works jointly with the Justice Department to enforce compliance with U.S. intellectual property laws.

Robert Pitofsky began his service as chairman of the Federal Trade Commission (FTC) in 1995. Pitofsky had previously served as a commissioner at FTC and as a director of its bureau of consumer protection. He has also spent more than three decades teaching and practicing law. He is co-author of a major case text on trade regulation and has written numerous books and articles on antitrust, advertising, and regulations. He has been a frequent witness before congressional committees considering antitrust matters.

In addition to his work as a law professor at New York University and Georgetown University law schools, he has been a visiting law professor at Harvard and was a faculty member at the Salzburg Seminar in American Studies in Salzburg, Austria. He has also been a guest scholar at the Brookings Institution in Washington, D.C. and a resident scholar at the Rockefeller Study and Conference Center in Bellagio, Italy in 1990.

Pitofsky received an honorary doctor of law degree from Georgetown University in 1989, has received the Distinguished Service Award from the Federal Trade Commission, and was selected by *Time* magazine as one of ten outstanding mid-career law professors.

Created in 1914 by an act of Congress, the Federal Trade Commission's primary objective was to supervise the emerging trusts in commerce and industry that were beginning to hinder the spirit of a free market. Over the years however, Congress has passed several laws, including the Wheeler-Lea Amendment in 1938 and the Magnuson-Moss Act of 1975, which have expanded the powers of the FTC to not only include supervisory authority, but also the ability to punish those who violate existing laws.

While earning his law degree at the Columbia Law School he served on the *Columbia Law Review*. He served as a member of the Board of Advisers to the Columbia University Center for Law and Economic Studies from 1975 to 1995. He has also served on numerous American Bar Association specialized committees and was a member of the Special Committee on Gender Bias in the Courts for the District of Columbia Bar Association.

Three bureaus of the commission support its mission: The bureau of consumer protection is responsible for protecting consumers against unfair, deceptive or fraudulent practices; the bureau of competition — the commission's antitrust arm -- seeks to prevent business practices that restrain competition; and the bureau of economics helps to ensure that the commission considers the economic impact of its actions.

Pitofsky chaired the Clinton Administration Transition Team reporting on the antitrust division of the Department of Justice. He also chaired the Defense Science Board Task Force on Antitrust Aspects of Defense Industry Downsizing in 1994. He is also a member of the Washington Advisory Committee to the Lawyers Committee on International Human Rights.

The FTC is made up of five commissioners, nominated by the President and confirmed by the Senate. Each member of the commission is appointed to a seven year term, and at no one time can the commission have more than three members from the same political party.

Chair
Mr. Robert Pitofsky
202/326-2100   FAX 202/326-2396
Rm. 440

Commissioner
Orson Swindle
202/326-2150
Rm. 540

Personal: born 3/8/37 in Thomasville, Georgia.

Orson Swindle was sworn in as a Commissioner on the Federal Trade Commission December 18, 1997. Swindle has had a distinguished military career and served in the Reagan Administration from 1981 to 1989 directing financial assistance programs to economically distressed rural and municipal areas of the country.

As Assistant Secretary of Commerce for Development he managed the Department of Commerce's national economic development efforts directing seven offices across the country. Swindle was State Director of the Farmers Home Administration for the U.S. Department of Agriculture financing rural housing, community infrastructure, businesses, and farming.

In 1992, Swindle became the first national leader of United We Stand America and in 1993 worked with Jack Kemp, Vin Weber, William Bennett and Ambassador Jeanne Kirkpatrick to form Empower America. In 1994 and in 1996 he was a Republican candidate for Congress in Hawaii's 1st Congressional District.

As a Marine aviator serving in South Vietnam on November 11, 1966, Swindle was shot down from the skies over North Vietnam while flying his 205th and last combat mission. He was captured by the North Vietnamese and held Prisoner of War in Hanoi for the next six years and four months. On March 4, 1973, Swindle was released from captivity.

Swindle retired from the U.S. Marine Corps in 1979 with the rank of Lieutenant Colonel. His 20 military decorations for valor in combat include two Silver Stars, two Bronze Stars, and two Purple Hearts.

Swindle earned a Bachelor of Science degree in Industrial Management from Georgia Tech in 1959 and a Master of Business Administration from Florida State University in 1975.

He and his wife, Angie have resided in Honolulu, Hawaii.

Commissioner
Ms. Mary L. Azcuenaga
202/326-2145   FAX 202/326-3446
Rm. 526

Personal: born 7/25/45 in McCall, Idaho.

Education: B.A. in English, Stanford Univ., 1967. J.D., Univ. of Chicago Law School, 1973.

Professional: 1973-present, various positions with the Federal Trade Commission, including: attorney, office of the general counsel; 1975-76, assistant to the general counsel; 1977-80, litigation attorney, San Francisco Regional Office; 1980-81, assistant regional director, San Francisco Regional Office; 1981-82, assistant to the executive director, FTC; 1982, litigation attorney, office of the general counsel; 1983-84, assistant general counsel for legal counsel; and 1984-present, commissioner, Federal Trade Commission.

Attorney Mary Azcuenaga has served her entire professional career at the Federal Trade Commission (FTC). She began her work at the FTC in 1973 after graduation from law school as an attorney in the office of general counsel and served in a variety of legal positions before her appointment as commissioner in 1984.

Azcuenaga is a career civil servant with experience in a broad range of legal issues, particularly in the areas of antitrust, administrative, and consumer protection law. She was the first member of the commission to have been appointed directly from a career staff position. While on the staff, she received the FTC Chairman's Award for her sustained contributions to the work of the commission. Azcuenaga, a political independent, first was appointed to the commission by President Reagan in 1984 and was reappointed by President Bush in 1991.

Azcuenaga and her colleagues on the Commission currently are engaged in continued efforts to eliminate deceptive advertising claims and fraudulent marketing practices and to study emerging areas and issues such as privacy on the internet. They also face complex issues relating to antitrust enforcement in the health, care, defense, and various high-tech industries, as well as questions involving the antitrust aspects of joint ventures and the treatment of intellectual property.

From her position as FTC commissioner, Azcuenaga has had the opportunity to speak on numerous timely issues including, most recently, an address to the American Law Institute-American Bar Association conference on Antitrust/Intellectual Property Claims in High Technology Markets entitled "Antitrust and Intellectual Property: Recent Highlights and Uncertainties"; an address to the Turkish Association of Advertising Agencies entitled, "The Role of Advertising and Advertising Regulation in the Free Market"; and remarks to the British-American Business Association and the French-American Chamber of Commerce entitled, "The Unintended Effects of Government Regulation: Lessons for the Future?"

Commissioner
Mr. Mozelle Thompson
202/326-3400
Rm. 340

Personal: born in Pittsburgh, Pennsylvania.

Mozelle Thompson was sworn in as a Commissioner on the Federal Trade Commission December 18, 1997.

Thompson most recently held the position of Principal Deputy Assistant Secretary of the Treasury, where he was responsible for overseeing domestic spending and credit policies, including the operations of the Federal Financing Bank and the Office of Government Financing. He was responsible for creating the Office of Privatization, which among its activities, provides guidance on the privatization of federal assets and operations. Appointed Deputy Assistant Secretary in August 1993, Thompson served as Principal Deputy Assistant Secretary since April 1996.

Prior to joining the Treasury Department, Thompson served as Senior Vice President and General Counsel to the New York State Finance Agency and its four sister corporations. In addition, he was an adjunct associate professor at the Fordham University School of Law where he taught courses in municipal law and finance. He also was an attorney with the New York firm of Skadden, Arps, Slate, Meagher and Flom.

Thompson is a graduate of Columbia College and Columbia Law School. He also holds an M.P.A. from Princeton University's Woodrow Wilson School of Public and International Affairs. After graduating law school, Thompson served as law clerk to U.S. District Court Judge William M. Hoeveler in Miami, Florida.

He has been active in a number of professional and civic organizations, including the Association of Black Princeton Alumni and the Executive Board of Practicing Attorneys for Law Students, a mentoring organization assisting African-American and Latino law students. He is a member of the bar in New York State and the District of Columbia.

Commissioner
Ms. Sheila Foster Anthony
202/326-2170
Rm. 440

Personal: born 1951 in Hope, Ark.

Education: B.A. in government, Univeristy of Arkansas, 1962. J.D., The American University, 1984.

Professional: teacher, Arkansas public schools. member, platform and executive committees, Arkansas Democratic Party. 1971, elected Justice of the Peace, Union County Quorum Court, Arkansas. 1980, elected delegate to the Democratic National Convention. 1985-93, senior associate, Dow, Lohnes and Albertson (Washington, D.C.). Early 1993, legislative affairs staff, U.S. Dept. of Commerce. 7/93-1995, assistant attorney general for legislative affairs, U.S. Department of Justice. 9/97-present, commissioner, Federal Trade Commission.

In January of 1997, President Clinton announced the nomination of Sheila Foster Anthony to replace Janet Steiger on the Federal Trade Commission. The Senate confirmed Anthony on September 24, 1997 to the term of seven years dating from September 26, 1995, the date of expiration of Steiger's term.

Anthony previously served as an assistant attorney general for legislative affairs at the U.S. Department of Justice during part of Clinton's first term. In that role, her duties included devising and implementing strategies that carried out the Attorney General's initiatives which required legislative support, as well as managing the Senate confirmation process for federal judges, assistant attorneys general, and U.S. attorneys.

From 1985 to 1993, Anthony was a senior associate with the law firm of Dow, Lohnes and Albertson, specializing in intellectual property law, including trademark, copyright, unfair competition, and licensing and technology transfer. She is a member of the bars of the District of Columbia and Supreme Court of Arkansas, and is admitted to practice before the local D.C. Courts, the U.S. Court of Appeals for D.C., and the U.S. Supreme Court.

She received her B.A. from the University of Arkansas and her J.D. from American University in 1984. She and her husband Beryl, a former Arkansas Congressman, reside in Washington, D.C. and have two children.

Office of Public Affairs (Press Office)

Director
Ms. Victoria Streitfeld
202/326-2718
Rm. 421

Office of the General Counsel

General Counsel
Ms. Debra Valentine
202/326-2481
Rm. 570

Bureau of Competition

Acting Asst. Director for Intl. Antitrust
Mr. John Parisi
202/326-2133
Rm. 382

Federal Trade Commission Regional Offices

60 Forsyth Street, SW / Atlanta GA 30303

Director
Mr. Anthony DiFesta
404/656-1355
Rm. 5M35

101 Merrimac St. / Boston MA 02114-4719

Acting Director
Mr. Andrew Caverly
617/424-5960
Suite 810

55 E. Monroe St. / Chicago IL 60603

Director
Mr. C. Steven Baker
312/353-8156
Suite 1860

1111 Superior Ave. / Cleveland OH 44114

Acting Director
Mr. John Mendenhall
216/263-3455
Rm. 200

1999 Bryan Street / Dallas TX 75201

Director
Mr. Thomas B. Carter
214/979-9372
Suite 2150

1961 Stout St. / Denver CO 80294

Acting Director
Ms. Janice Charter
303/844-2868
Suite 1523

11000 Wilshire Blvd. / Los Angeles CA 90024

Acting Director
Mr. Greg Staples
310/824-4320
Suite 13209

150 William St. / New York NY 10038

Director
Mr. Michael J. Bloom
212/264-1201
Suite 1300

901 Market St. / San Francisco CA 94103

Director
Mr. Jeffrey A. Klurfeld
415/356-5270
Suite 570

Federal Bldg., 915 Second Ave. / Seattle WA 98174

Director
Mr. Charles A. Harwood
206/220-4480
Rm. 2896

Inter-American Foundation

901 N. Stuart St. / Arlington VA 22203
703/841-3800   FAX 703/841-3595

INTRODUCTION

Created by Congress in 1969, The Inter-American Foundation is a public corporation whose mission is to support the self-help efforts of poor people in Latin America and the Caribbean. It makes grants annually to local and private, indigenous organizations that carry out projects helping the poor. It also makes a small number of grants to centers in Latin America and the Caribbean for research on the problems of poor people and grassroots development. Seventy-five percent of the foundation's funding comes from Congressional appropriations. The remainder comes from the Social Progress Trust Fund administered by the Inter-American Development Bank.

President
Mr. George A. Evans

Chair
Ms. Maria Otero

Vice Chair
Mr. Neil H. Offen

Board Member
Ms. Harriet C. Babbitt

Board Member
Mr. Mark L. Schneider

Board Member
Ms. Ann Brownell Sloane

Board Member
Ms. Patricia Hill Williams

Board Member
Mr. Frank D. Yturria

Board Member
Mr. Jeffrey Davidow

Board Member
Ms. Nancy Dorn

International Development Cooperation Agency

1300 Pa. Ave., NW / Washington, D.C. 20523
202/712-4040   FAX 202/216-3455

INTRODUCTION

The U.S. International Development Cooperation Agency's function is policy planning, policymaking, and policy coordination on international economic issues affecting developing countries. The Agency for International Development (AID), the Overseas Private Investment Corporation (OPIC) , and the Trade and Development Agency are components of IDCA. See separate entries in this section for those units.

Director
J. Brian Atwood   *(see profile under U.S. AID)*

National Aeronautics & Space Administration

Two Independence Sq., 300 E St., SW / Washington DC 20546
202/358-0000

INTRODUCTION

The National Aeronautics and Space Administration (NASA) conducts research for the solution of problems of flight within and outside the Earth's atmosphere and develops, constructs, tests, and operates aeronautical and space vehicles. It conducts and arranges for the most effective utilization of the scientific and engineering resources of the U.S. with other nations engaged in aeronautical and space activities for peaceful purposes.

Administrator
Mr. Daniel S. Goldin
202/358-1010   FAX 202/358-2810
Rm. 9F44

Office of External Relations

Associate Administrator
Mr. John D. Schumacher
202/358-0400   FAX 202/358-4329
Rm. 7V17

Mgr., Foreign Assessments
Mr. Anton J. Dorr

202/358-0102   FAX 202/358-4081
Rm. 6R61

Mgr., Intl. Tech. Transfer Policy & NASA Export Administrator
Mr. Robert L. Tucker
202/358-0330
Rm. 7G13

Director, Mission to Planet Earth Division
Dr. Lisa R. Shaffer
202/358-0793   FAX 202/358-2798
Rm. 7Z59

Office of Mission to Planet Earth

Acting Associate Administrator
Mr. William Townsend
202/358-2165   FAX 202/358-3092
Rm. 5A70

National Science Foundation

4201 Wilson Blvd. / Arlington VA 22230
703/306-1234

INTRODUCTION

The National Science Foundation supports major national and international science and engineering activities, including the U.S. Antarctic Program, the Ocean Drilling Program, global geoscience studies, and others. Cooperative scientific and engineering research activities support exchange programs for American and foreign scientists and engineers, execution of jointly designed research projects, participation in the activities of international science and engineering organizations, and travel to international conferences.

The National Science Foundation was established as an independent agency by the National Science Foundation Act of 1950. The Foundation consists of a National Science Board and a Director.

Director
Mr. Neal F. Lane
703/306-1000   FAX 703/306-0109
Rm. 1205

National Science Board

Chair
Dr. Richard Zare
703/306-2000
Rm. 1225

Directorate for Geosciences

Senior Science Associate, Global Change Research
VACANT
703/306-1514
Rm. 1070

Senior Scientist, Intl. Affairs
Mr. Louis B. Brown
703/306-1516   FAX 703/306-0095
Rm. 1070

400 Virginia Ave., SW / Washington DC 20024

Director, U.S. Global Change Research Program
Mr. Michael C. MacCracken
202/314-2233
Rm. 750

Directorate of Social, Behavioral & Economic Sciences

4201 Wilson Blvd. / Arlington VA 22230

Acting Director, Division of Intl. Programs
Mr. Pierre Perrolle
703/306-1710
Rm. 935

Deputy Director
Ms. Laura P. Bautz
703/306-1709

Nuclear Regulatory Commission

11555 Rockville Pike / Rockville MD 20852
Personnel: 301/415-7000
Public Affairs: 301/415-8200

INTRODUCTION

The NRC is the federal agency responsible for regulating all safety and environmental aspects of the civilian use of atomic energy. The five-member commission also is charged with licensing and regulation of the construction and operation of nuclear facilities, as well as inspecting those facilities and investigating nuclear incidents. The agency has a role in combating the proliferation of nuclear materials worldwide; licensing the possession, use, processing, handling and disposal of nuclear materials; conducting public hearings on such things as nuclear and radiological safety and environmental concerns; and developing relationships with the states concerning the regulation of nuclear materials.

Chair
Ms. Shirley Ann Jackson
301/415-1759   FAX 301/415-2275
Rm. 17D1

Personal: born 8/5/46 in Washington, D.C.

Education: B.S. in physics, 1968; Ph.D. in physics, 1973; Mass. Institute of Technology.

Professional: 1973-74 and 1975-76, research associate, theory department, Fermi National Accelerator Laboratory. 1974-75, visiting scientist, theoretical div., European Center for Nuclear Research (Geneva, Switzerland). 1976-91, theoretical physicist; 1991-95, consultant, AT&T Bell Laboratories. 1991-95, physics professor, Rutgers University. 1995-present, chairman, Nuclear Regulatory Commission.

Dr. Shirley Ann Jackson, chairman of the U.S. Nuclear Regulatory Commission, is a theoretical physicist. She was nominated to the commission and designated to become chair by President Bill Clinton. After confirmation by the Senate, she was sworn in as a commissioner on May 2, 1995 and assumed the chairmanship two months later, on July 1, 1995. Prior to joining the NRC, Dr. Jackson was a university professor, research scientist, consultant, and corporate director.

As chairman of the bipartisan commission, Jackson is the principal executive officer and official spokesperson for the NRC, the federal agency responsible for regulating all safety and environmental aspects of the civilian use of atomic energy. The five-member commission is also charged with licensing and regulation of the construction and operation of nuclear facilities, as well as inspecting those facilities and investigating nuclear incidents.

A native of Washington, D.C., Jackson graduated from Roosevelt High School in 1964 as class valedictorian. She earned a B.S. in physics in 1968 and a Ph.D. in the field of theoretical elementary particle physics in 1973 both from the Massachusetts Institute of Technology in Cambridge, Massachusetts.

For 15 years, Jackson conducted research in theoretical physics, solid state and quantum physics, and optical physics at AT&T Bell Laboratories in Murray Hill, New Jersey. From 1991 to 1995, Jackson was a professor of physics at Rutgers University and served concurrently as a consultant in semiconductor theory to AT&T Bell Labs.

Jackson has achieved a number of firsts in her career. She was the first African-American woman to receive a doctorate from M.I.T. and is the first African-American to become an NRC commissioner as well as the first woman and African-American to serve as NRC chairman.

With the May 1997 formation of the International Nuclear Regulator's Association, Jackson was elected as the group's first chairman. The association is made up of the most senior nuclear regulatory officials from Canada, France, Germany, Japan, Spain, Sweden, the United Kingdom, and the United States.

Jackson has served on the board of directors of Public Service Enterprise Group and its subsidiary Public Service Electric and Gas Co., Sealed Air Corp., CoreStates Financial Corp., CoreStates New Jersey National Bank, and New Jersey Resources Corp. She is a life member of the MIT Board of Trustees. She also served on an advisory panel to the Secretary of Energy on the future of the Department of Energy national laboratories, on research councils of the National Academy of Sciences, and on the Advisory Council of the Institute of Nuclear Power Operations.

Jackson is a fellow of the American Academy of Arts and Sciences and the American Physical Society. In 1993, she was awarded the New Jersey Governor's Award in Science, New Jersey's highest award to a state citizen.

Jackson is married to Dr. Morris A. Washington, also a physicist, and they have a son.

Senior Assistant, International Affairs
Ms. Janice Dunn Lee
301/415-1750
Rm. 1706

Office of International Programs

Director
Mr. Carlton R. Stoiber
301/415-1780   FAX 301/415-2400
Rm. 16E2

Director, Bilateral Cooperation and Assistance Division
Mr. James R. Shea
301/415-2336   FAX 301/415-2395
Rm. 4E2

Director, Non-Proliferation, Exports & Multilateral Relations Div.
Mr. Ronald D. Hauber
301/415-2344   FAX 301/415-2395
Rm. 4E8

Overseas Private Investment Corporation

1100 New York Avenue, N.W. / Washington, D.C. 20527
Central: 202/336-8400
Personnel: 202/336-8531
Media Relations: 202/336-8636

INTRODUCTION

An independent federal agency established in 1971, the Overseas Private Investment Corporation (OPIC) has supported investment projects abroad worth nearly $73 billion and generated $40 billion in exports. Established to encourage U.S. business investment in emerging market economies and developing countries, OPIC has - under the Clinton Administration - been given a broader role as an instrument of foreign policy. As a result, OPIC is expected to offer a record level of financial assistance and insurance for foreign investors in the coming years, with notably increased activity in the former Soviet Union, South Africa, and the Middle East.

OPIC financial services offered to investors include medium- and long-term project financing. They also include direct loans to small businesses and loan guarantees for larger projects, insurance against state expropriation, political violence, and currency inconvertibility, and a variety of investor services such as feasibility studies, database listings of investment opportunities, and OPIC-sponsored investment missions.

In addition, OPIC has become increasingly involved in equity investment and the leveraging of private capital through its several country and regional investment funds - the Africa, Asia-Pacific and Israel Growth Funds, the Russia Country Fund, and Poland Partners. Inroads have been made recently into projects in the Commonwealth of Independent States (CIS) countries other than Russia and into Third World environmental projects involving U.S. firms.

Because users of services pay premiums for OPIC's political risk insurance and fees for its investment and finance services, OPIC has turned a profit every year since 1971, building up more than $2.4 billion in reserves. Thus it costs taxpayers nothing.

Office of the President (OPIC/IP)

President and CEO
Mr. George Muñoz
202/336-8401   FAX 202/408-5133
12th Floor

Personal: born 5/2/51.

Education: B.B.A. in accounting, Univ. of Texas Coll. of Business, 1974. J.D., Harvard Law School, 1978. Master's in public policy, Harvard's Kennedy School of Govt., 1978. LL.M. (master's of law in taxation), DePaul Univ., 1984.

Professional: 1978-80, attorney, Gary, Thomasson, Hall & Marks (Corpus Christi, Texas). 1980-89, attorney (partner 1985), Mayer, Brown & Platt (Chicago). 1984-87, president, Chicago Board of Education. 1989-93, managing partner, George Muñoz & Associates, P.C. (Chicago). 1993-97, assistant secretary for management and chief financial officer, U.S. Dept. of the Treasury. July, 1997-president and CEO, Overseas Private Investment Corporation.

George Muñoz was confirmed by the U.S. Senate as president and chief executive officer of the Overseas Private Investment Corporation (OPIC) in July of 1997.

Muñoz had previously served as assistant secretary for management and chief financial officer at the Treasury Department since 1993, first under Secretary Lloyd Bentsen and then under Secretary Robert E. Rubin. He is credited with improving the internal and financial management of the Treasury Department. He is also credited for invigorating the CFO community. He was elected by his peers as executive vice chairman of the federal government-wide Chief Financial Officers' Council (1994-97). President Clinton appointed Muñoz to the National Partnership Council which fosters management-labor partnerships in federal agencies as a means of bringing about positive change.

Prior to joining Treasury, Muñoz worked in international law and business. He was well-known in Chicago as an international attorney especially in dealing with Mexico and Latin America. He is also viewed as a nationally recognized leader in the Hispanic community. Part of this reputation is attributable to his having served as the highly visible and effective president of the Chicago Board of Education from 1984 to 1986. Muñoz has also served on various civic and corporate boards, including the Illinois International Port Authority, the Chicago Council on Foreign Relations, the Chicago Symphony Orchestra, the Chicago Economic Development Commission, Catholic Charities, DePaul University, and the Northwest Memorial (Hospital) Corporation.

Administrative Assistant to the President
Ms. Jeanne P. Frederick
202/336-8403   FAX 202/408-5133

Confidential Assistant to the President
Ms. Susan M. Ohlenroth
202/336-8404   FAX 202/408-5133

Chief of Staff
Mr. David Wofford
202/336-8409   FAX 202/408-5133

Finance Department (OPIC/F)

Vice President
Mr. Frank L. Langhammer
202/336-8480   FAX 202/408-9866

Investment Funds Department (OPIC/IF)

Vice President
Mr. Robert D. Stillman
202/336-8762   FAX 202/842-5194

Insurance Department (OPIC/I)

Vice President
Ms. Julie A. Martin
202/336-8586   FAX 202/408-5142

Asia/Middle East

Regional Manager
Mr. James T. Brache
202/336-8585   FAX 202/408-5142

Central America, Caribbean, and Africa

Regional Manager
Ms. Edith P. Quintrell
202/336-8573   FAX 202/408-5142

Europe and the New Independent States

Regional Manager
Ms. Audrey Zuck
202/336-8589   FAX 202/408-5142

South America

Regional Manager
Ms. J. Lila Granda
202/336-8664   FAX 202/408-5142

Investment Development Department (OPIC/ID)

Vice President
Mr. Robert Schiffer
202/336-8610   FAX 202/408-5145

Managing Director of Business Development
Ms. Joan Edwards
202/336-8621   FAX 202/408-5145

Department of Legal Affairs (OPIC/LA)

Vice President and General Counsel
Mr. Charles D. Toy
202/336-8410   FAX 202/408-0297

Management Services Department (OPIC/MS)

Vice President
Mr. William C. Moss
202/336-8521   FAX 202/408-9859

Treasury Department (OPIC/T)

Vice President
Ms. Mildred O. Callear
202/336-8455   FAX 202/408-9862

Panama Canal Commission

Unit 2300 APO AA / 34011

INTRODUCTION

Established as an independent agency in 1979, the commission is supervised by a nine-member board and is charged with operating, maintaining, and improving the Panama Canal to provide efficient, safe, and economical transit service for the benefit of world commerce. The commission will perform these duties until it is terminated on December 31, 1999, at which the Republic of Panama assumes complete responsibility for the Panama Canal.

Administrator
Mr. Alberto Aleman Zubieta
507/272-3169   FAX 507/272-1660
E-Mail: ad@pancanal.com

Personal: born 5/26/51 in Panama.

Education: B.S. in industrial engineering, Texas A&M Univ., 1973. B.S. in civil engineering, Texas A&M Univ.

Professional: 1976-96, executive president, Constructora Urbana, SA. 1996-present, administrator, Panama Canal Commission.

Alberto Aleman was appointed administrator of the Panama Canal Commission on August 18, 1996 by the President of the United States and confirmed by the U.S. Senate to hold the highest-ranking position in the Canal agency. As head of the Canal Commission, Aleman is responsible for the management, operation of the waterway, and for preparations for its smooth transfer to Panamanian control on December 31, 1999.

In 1973, Aleman earned an industrial engineering degree from Texas A&M University. He subsequently obtained a degree in civil engineering from the same university. Upon graduation, he began work with a family-owned construction firm, Constructora Urbana, SA and served as executive president of that company before joining the Canal in 1996.

Major projects accomplished by Constructora Urbana, considered one of the largest heavy construction firms in the Republic, included work on the Construction for the Trans-Isthmian oil pipeline, construction of the highway between Fortuna and Chiriqui Grande, cleanup of the 1986 landslide at the Canal (removing nearly one million cubic meters of material), and performing excavation work in the Gaillard Cut-widening program.

Aleman is a member of various Panama civic and professional organizations. He has served on the boards of many organizations including the Panama Contractors Association (CAPAC), the Panama Architects and Engineers Association, the Panama Sur Rotary Club, and Young President's Organization both the Panama and International Chapters. In recognition of his outstanding leadership and loyal support of the Panama Contractors Association and lifetime career achievements, Aleman was awarded the William Ross Medal, CAPAC's most prestigious award, in 1992.

Deputy Administrator
Mr. Joseph W. Cornelison

1825 I St. Rm. 1050 / Washington DC 20006

Secretary of the Commission
Mr. John A. Mills
202/634-6441

Peace Corps

1990 K St., NW / Washington DC 20526
Personnel Locator: 202/606-3886
Public Affairs: 202/606-3010
Recruiting Info: 703/235-9191 or 800/424-8580

INTRODUCTION

The Peace Corps, an independent agency, prepares men and women to serve overseas as volunteers to promote world peace and friendship and to help other countries in meeting their needs for trained manpower. The volunteers are trained for a 9- to 14-week period in the appropriate local language, the technical skills necessary for their particular job, and the cross-cultural skills needed to adjust to a society with traditions and attitudes different from their own. Thousands of volunteers serve throughout Latin America, Africa, the Near East, and Central and Eastern Europe.

Director
Mr. Mark D. Gearan
202/606-3970   FAX 202/606-4458
Rm. 8114

Personal: born 9/19/56 in Gardner, Mass.

Education: B.A. in government (cum laude), Harvard College, 1978. J.D., Georgetown Univ. School of Law, 1991.

Professional: 1978, press secretary, re-election campaign of Congressman Robert F. Drinan (D-Mass.). 1978, press secretary for a Massachusetts ballot initiative. 1978-80, newspaper reporter, *Fitchburg-Leominster Sentinel and Enterprise.* 1980-83, press secretary/then chief of staff, Congressman Berkley Bedell (D-Iowa). 1982, campaign manager, Bedell congressional campaign. 1983-87, director, Massachusetts Office of Federal Relations for Governor Michael Dukakis. 1987-88, headquarters press secretary, Dukakis presidential campaign. 1988-89, director, Massachusetts Office of Federal Relations. 1989-92, executive director, Democratic Governors' Association. 1992-93, senior advisor, Clinton presidential campaign. Jan-Jun, 1993, deputy chief of staff; 1993-95, communications director, Office of the President, The White House. 1995-present, director, Peace Corps.

Mark Gearan was confirmed by the U.S. Senate and sworn in as the 14th director of the Peace Corps in September 1995. Since becoming director, Gearan has worked to prepare the Peace Corps for the 21st century by building on the agency's proud legacy of service over the last 36 years.

Gearan's highest priority is to support nearly 6,500 Peace Corps volunteers serving in more than 90 countries. He is also working to create new opportunities for Peace Corps service. Under Gearan's leadership, Peace Corps volunteers are serving for the first time in South Africa, and entered Jordan in April 1997. In addition, Gearan oversaw the return of Peace Corps Volunteers to Haiti in 1996 after a five-year absence. Gearan has also launched the Crisis Corps, a new program within the Peace Corps that allows volunteers and returned Peace Corps volunteers to provide short-term assistance to communities during humanitarian crises and natural disasters.

Gearan has visited volunteers in Poland, Ukraine, Swaziland, Botswana, Nepal, Haiti, the Dominican Republic, Nicaragua, Honduras, El Salvador, Guatemala and Paraguay. Domestically, Gearan has worked to strengthen the Peace Corps' ties to thousands of Americans who make up the returned Peace Corps volunteer community.

Gearan brings to the Peace Corps an extensive career in public service. From 1993 to 1995, he served as assistant to the President and director of communications, as well as White House deputy chief of staff. Gearan traveled extensively with President Clinton on overseas trips to Russia, Japan, the Middle East, Germany, Italy, and Ireland.

During the 1992 presidential campaign, Gearan was Vice President Gore's campaign manager and was appointed deputy director for President-elect Clinton's transition team. Gearan has also served as executive director of the Democratic Governors Association, director of the Massachusetts Office of Federal Relations, headquarters press secretary for Governor Michael Dukakis' presidential campaign, press secretary for U.S. Representative Robert F. Drinan of Massachusetts, and chief of the staff for former U.S. Representative Berkeley Bedell of Iowa.

Gearan earned a B.A. in government at Harvard College in 1978 and a J.D. from the Georgetown University Law Center in 1991. He met his wife, Mary Herlihy, while they were both working for Congressman Robert Drinan, a Roman Catholic priest, who married them in 1981. They have one daughter.

Deputy Director
Mr. Charles R. Baquet III
202/606-3970   FAX 202/606-4458
Rm. 8106

Education: B.A. in history and English literature, Xavier Univ. (New Orleans). M.S. in public administration, Maxwell School of Government, Syracuse Univ.

Professional: High school social studies teacher. 1965-67, Peace Corps volunteer, Somali Republic. program officer, VISTA. foreign service, U.S. State Dept.: 1988-91, U.S. Consul General, Cape Town, South Africa; Sept. 1991-Oct. 1993, U.S. Ambassador to Djibouti. March 1994-present, deputy director, Peace Corps.

Charles Baquet was unanimously confirmed by the U.S. Senate on March 26, 1994 as deputy director of the Peace Corps. Baquet brings to the Peace Corps a long and distinguished career as a foreign service officer. He also served as a Peace Corps volunteer in the Somali Republic from 1965 to 1967.

Prior to returning to the Peace Corps, Baquet was the US Ambassador to Djibouti in East Africa from September 1991 to October of 1993. He also was the U.S. Consul General in Cape Town, South Africa, from 1988 to 1991. As a foreign service officer, Baquet has worked at American embassies in Paris, Hong Kong, and Beirut

A former high school social studies teacher, Baquet was also a program officer for VISTA (Office of Economic Opportunity) between his Peace Corps service and entry to the foreign service.

Baquet received a B.A. in history and English literature from Xavier University in New Orleans. He also attended Chicago Teacher's College and earned his M.A. in public administration from the Maxwell School of Government at Syracuse University.

Baquet is a member of the American Foreign Service Association, the African-American Ambassador's Association, and Rotary International.

A native of New Orleans, Baquet and his wife have three children.

General Counsel
Ms. Nancy Hendry
202/606-3114
Rm. 8302

Acting Director, Planning and Policy Analysis Staff
Mr. Peter Loan
202/606-9470
Rm. 9324

Director, External Relations
Ms. Gloria Johnson
202/606-3210
Rm. 8424

Associate Director, Private Sector Cooperation and
    Intl. Volunteerism Office
Ms. Patricia Garamendi
202/606-3262

Rm. 9530

International Volunteer Coordinator
Ms. Janet Donaghy
202/606-3763
Rm. 7503

Management

Overseas Support Services Specialists

Mr. Morris Manley
202/606-3141
Rm. 5346

Ms. Joice Williams
202/606-3141
Rm. 5346

Ms. Jennifer Jacoby
202/606-3141
Rm. 5349

International Operations

Director
Mr. Thomas Tigue
202/606-3970   FAX 202/606-3627
Rm. 8714

Deputy Director
Ms. Kathy Rulon
202/606-9469
Rm. 8420

Director, Overseas Training and Development Division
Mr. Duane Karlen
202/606-9370
Rm. 7640

Regional Director, Office of Inter-American and Pacific Operations
Mr. Patrick Fn'Piere
202/606-3337   FAX 202/606-3524
Rm. 7316

Acting Regional Director, Office of Africa Operations
Ms. Maureen Carroll
202/606-3180   FAX 202/606-3491
Rm. 7518

Regional Director, Office of Europe, Asia and the Mediterranean
Mr. Donald Mooers
202/606-3862   FAX 202/606-2375
Rm. 7222

Volunteer Recruitment and Selection

Associate Director
Ms. Judy Harrington
202/606-3080
Rm. 9112

Volunteer Support

Associate Director
Mr. Mike Ward
202/606-3916
Rm. 6422

Securities and Exchange Commission

450 Fifth St., NW / Washington DC 20549
Information Line: 202/942-8088
Public Affairs: 202/942-0020

INTRODUCTION

When an overseas company registers to sell securities in the U.S., it becomes subject to U.S. securities laws, which are administered by the Securities and Exchange Commission (SEC). The SEC seeks to provide protection for investors; to ensure that securities markets are fair and honest; and when necessary, to provide the means to enforce securities laws through sanctions. Currently one out of the five commission posts is vacant.

The Commission

Chair
Mr. Arthur Levitt, Jr.
202/942-0100   FAX 202/942-9646
Rm. 6010

Education: B.A. (Phi Beta Kappa), Williams College, 1952.

Professional: 1952-54, U.S. Air Force. 1954-59, assistant promotion director, Time Inc. 1959-62, executive vice president and director, Oppenheimer Industries. 1962-69, partner, Shearson Hayden Stone, Inc. 1969-78, president and director, Shearson Hayden Stone, Inc. 1978-89, chairman, American Stock Exchange. 1990-93, president, Levitt Media Company. 1993-present, chairman, Securities and Exchange Commission.

Arthur Levitt became chairman of the Securities and Exchange Commission in 1993. Prior to his appointment, he had served on several presidential commissions, including the White House Small Business Task Force from 1978-80 and, most recently, as a member of the 1993 Base Closure and Realignment Commission.

Levitt spent almost 30 years on Wall Street, as director and then president, of Shearson Hayden Stone (today Smith Barney Shearson), before leaving to chair the American Stock Exchange. During his 12 years as chairman, Levitt also served on ten corporate and philanthropic boards, including the Equitable Life Assurance Society of the US, the East New York Savings Bank, First Empire State Corporation, the Revson Foundation, the Rockefeller Foundation, the Solomon R. Guggenheim Foundation, and the Williams College board of trustees.

Levitt founded the Levitt Media Company in 1990, the primary holding of which was the Capitol Hill newspaper *Roll Call.* Levitt served as company chairman for three years before joining the commission. He sold the newspaper before taking his present position.

Levitt identified several areas which need work to provide enhanced protection of individual investors and they include: reform of the municipal debt markets, improvement in investor education in mutual fund investing, higher standards for broker sales practices, and strengthening the international preeminence of the U.S. securities markets.

With regard to municipal debt market reforms, Levitt drew some flack in June of 1997 for a speech suggesting that "lawyers should end political contributions made to influence the award of municipal securities legal work, a practice known as 'pay-to-play'". (*Wall Street Journal,* July 11, 1997). For his efforts to improve investor knowledge of mutual funds, Levitt and the commission were praised by the General Accounting Office in the summer of 1997. (*Wall Street Journal,* July 1, 1997).

Chief of Staff
Ms. Jennifer Scardino
202/942-0120
Rm. 6010

Commissioner
Ms. Laura Unger
202/942-0800
Rm. 6300

Personal: born 1/8/61 in New York City, N.Y.

Education: B.A., Univ. of Calif. at Berkeley, 1983. J.D., New York Law School, 1987.

Professional: 1988-89, attorney, enforcement division, N.Y. regional office; 1989-92, attorney, Securities and Exchange Commission (Washington, D.C.). 1990-92, congressional fellow, Sen. Alphonse D'Amato (R-N.Y.). 1992-94 minority counsel; 1995-97, counsel, U.S. Senate Committee on Banking, Housing and Urban Affairs. 1997-present, commissioner-designate, Securities and Exchange Commission.

September of 1997, President Clinton sent the nomination of Laura Unger to the Senate for confirmation. Unger was subsequently confirmed for a term expiring June 5, 2001. She replaced J. Carter Beese who resigned in 1996.

At the time of her nomination, Unger was serving on the U.S. Senate Banking, Housing and Urban Affairs Committee as counsel for Chairman Alphonse D'Amato (R-N.Y.). Unger had been with the committee since 1992, specializing in securities litigation, including a major bill passed over a Presidential veto in late 1995.

In a story on her nomination, The *Wall Street Journal,* quoted a Washington securities lawyer as saying "She is a fair-minded person, who has good relationships with the SEC, the securities bar, and both aisles of Congress." (Aug. 15, 1997).

Before serving on the Banking Committee staff, Unger had been a

congressional fellow with the office of Senator D'Amato. She began her professional legal career in 1988 as an attorney with the enforcement division of the New York regional office of the SEC and then served as an attorney at the SEC office in Washington.

Unger received her B.A. from the University of California at Berkeley, and her J.D. from New York Law School.

Commissioner
Mr. Isaac C. Hunt, Jr.
202/942-0500   FAX 202/942-9647
Rm. 6193

Personal: born on 8/1/37 in Danville, Va.

Education: B.A., Fisk Univ. (Nashville, Tenn.), 1957. LL.B., Univ. of Virginia School of Law, 1962.

Professional: 1962-67, staff attorney, Securities and Exchange Commission. associate, Jones, Day, Reavis and Pogue. principal dep. general counsel, acting general counsel, U.S. Dept. of the Army. dean, Antioch School of Law (Wash., D.C.). 1987-95, dean and professor of law, Univ. of Akron School of Law. February 29, 1996-present, commissioner, Securities and Exchange Commission.

Issac Hunt was nominated to the Securities and Exchange Commission by President Bill Clinton in August 1995 and confirmed by the Senate on January 26, 1996. He was sworn in as a commissioner on February 29, 1996.

Prior to being nominated to the SEC, Hunt was dean and professor of law at the University of Akron School of Law, a position he held from 1987 to 1995. He taught securities law for seven of the eight years he served as dean.

Previously, Hunt was dean of the Antioch School of Law in Washington, D.C., where he also taught securities law. In addition, Hunt served during the Carter and Reagan administrations at the Department of the Army in the office of the general counsel as principal deputy general counsel and as acting general counsel.

As an associate with the law firm of Jones, Day, Reavis and Pogue, Hunt practiced in the fields of corporate and securities law, government procurement litigation, administrative law, and international trade. He commenced his career at the SEC as a staff attorney from 1962 to 1967.

Hunt earned his B.A. from Fisk University and his LL.B. from the University of Virginia School of Law. He was a member of the Kerner Commission in 1967 and 1968.

Commissioner
Mr. Norman S. Johnson
202/942-0500   FAX 202/942-9666
Rm. 6200

Professional: law clerk to the chief justice of the Utah Supreme Court. 1959-65, asst. attorney general, office of the Utah Attorney General. 1965-67, staff member, Securities and Exchange Commission. 1968-95, associate and then senior partner, Van Cott, Bagley, Cornwall & McCarthy (Salt Lake City, Utah). February 13, 1996, commissioner, Securities & Exchange Commission.

Following his appointment by President Clinton, and his confirmation by the Senate, Norman Johnson was sworn in as a commissioner of the Securities and Exchange Commission on February 13, 1996 in a ceremony presided over by the Chief Federal District Judge in Salt Lake City, Utah.

Prior to his nomination, Commissioner Johnson was senior partner in the firm of Van Cott, Bagley, Cornwall & McCarthy and had a long and illustrious legal career focusing on federal and state securities law. Johnson commenced his career in private practice after serving as a staff member for the SEC from 1965 through 1967. In addition Commissioner Johnson served as an assistant attorney general in the office of the Utah attorney general from 1959 to 1965. He had previously served as a law clerk to the chief justice of the Utah Supreme Court.

During his career, Johnson has served as president of the Utah State Bar Association, was chosen as a state delegate to the House of Delegates of the American Bar Association, and was named chair of the Governor's Advisory Board on Securities Matters for the state of Utah. In addition, he served on the Governor's Task Force on Officer and Director Liability and numerous other committees and groups concerned with the application of federal and state securities laws.

Johnson has received numerous honors and awards in recognition of his outstanding contributions to the practice of securities law in the Rocky Mountain area. He has authored several articles in legal periodicals, including the much-cited "The Dynamics of SEC Rule 2(E): A Crisis for the Bar."

Johnson has involved himself in many community groups including the Utah Supreme Court Committee on Gender and Justice. He has been married since 1956 to the former Carol Groshell and they have three grown daughters.

Commissioner
Mr. Paul R. Carey
202/942-0700
Rm. 6120

Personal: born in 1953.

Education: B.A. in economics, Colgate Univ.

Professional: municipal bond salesman & investment banker, First Albany Corporation and then with Donaldson, Lufkin & Jenrette. Northeast finance director, Clinton/Gore 1992 Presidential Campaign.

1993-97, special assistant to the President for legislative affairs. 1997-present, commissioner-designate, Securities and Exchange Commission.

Paul Carey was nominated by President Clinton and confirmed by the Senate in the fall of 1997 to assume the seat on the SEC left vacant when Stephen Wallman's term expired June 5, 1997. His term expires June 5, 2002.

Carey is the son of former Democratic New York State Governor Hugh Carey. At the time of his nomination, he was serving as a special assistant to President Clinton for legislative affairs on banking and securities matters, primarily working for administration positions on the Senate side of the Capitol.

Prior to joining the administration, Carey worked with Donaldson, Lufkin & Jenrette and at First Albany Corporation in their institutional equity divisions. Carey served as northeast finance director for the Clinton/Gore 1992 Presidential Campaign.

Carey received his B.A. in economics from Colgate University.

Division of Market Regulation

Assoc. Dir., Office of Trading Practices, Automation & Intl. Mkts
Mr. Larry E. Bergmann
202/942-0770

Asst. Director, Automation and Intl. Markets
Ms. Sheila Slevin
202/942-0796

Office of International Affairs

Director
Ms. Marissa Lago
202/942-2770
Rm. 11080

Secretary to the Director, Administrative Contact
Ms. Jacqueline Clay
202/942-2771
Rm. 11075

Deputy Director
Mr. Paul Leder
202/942-2770
Rm. 11078

Asst. Director
Ms. Felice Friedman
202/942-2770
Rm. 11087

Asst. Director
Ms. Elizabeth Jacobs
202/942-2770
Rm. 11076

Asst. Director
Mr. Robert D. Strahota
202/942-2770
Rm. 11103

Asst. Director
Ms. Ester Saverson
202/942-2770
Rm. 11088

Small Business Administration

409 Third St., SW / Washington DC 20416
Main: 202/205-6600
Answer Desk: 202/205-7701 or 800-U-ASK-SBA
Personnel Locator: 202/205-6600
http://www.sbaonline.sba.gov

INTRODUCTION

Created by the Small Business Act of 1953, the Small Business Administration (SBA) provides financial and business development assistance to help small businesses take advantage of export markets. The SBA assists firms in obtaining the capital needed to explore, establish, or expand international markets. Export loans are available under SBA's guaranty program. If a lender is unable or unwilling to make a loan directly, a firm should request that the lender seek SBA participation. The financing staff of each SBA district and branch office administers the financial assistance programs. SBA expands its reach through its network of Small Business Development Centers (SBDCs) and Small Business Institutes (SBIs) and by working with the Service Corps of Retired Executives (SCORE). The agency also collaborates with other federal agencies in helping exporters.

The SBA cooperates with the Export-Import Bank of the U.S. in administering the Export Working Capital Program, formerly the Export Revolving Line of Credit Program. SBA also administers the International Trade Loan Program, a guarantee program offering long-term financing to small businesses engaged, or preparing to, engage in international trade.

SBA runs the Reach Strategic Venture Partners Program (RSVP), a new computer database system designed to match U.S. companies with joint venture partners from around the world. The agency participates with the Commerce Department and the Federal Bar Association in the Export Legal Assistance Network (ELAN -- see listing at end of this section) to provide initial free legal consultations to small business exporters. And SBA helps other federal agencies in running U.S. Export Assistance Centers in several cities.

The agency operates an Automated Trade Locator Assistance Program, the SBAtlas, that provides market data to exporters — both product-specific and country-specific.

Contact information on these programs can be found in "Directory of U.S. Government Export Programs" section of this Almanac.

Administrator
Mr. Aida Alvarez
202/205-6605   FAX 202/205-6802
Rm. 7000

Personal: born in Aguadilla, Puerto Rico.

Education: B.A. (cum laude), Harvard College.

Professional: reporter, *New York Post.* news reporter, anchor, Metromedia Television (New York). commissioner, New York City Charter Revision Commission. vice president, NYC Health & Hospitals Corporation. investment banker, Bear Stearns then First Boston Corporation. June 1993-1997, director, Office of Federal Housing Enterprise Oversight, U.S. Dept. of Housing and Urban Development. 1997-present, administrator, Small Business Administration.

Aida Alvarez is the administrator of the U.S. Small Business Administration (SBA) and a member of the President's Cabinet. Alvarez, a former government financial regulator, investment banker, and journalist, was confirmed on February 14, 1997. She is the first Hispanic woman and the first person of Puerto Rican heritage to hold a position in the President's Cabinet.

As SBA administrator, Alvarez directs the delivery of a comprehensive set of financial and business development programs for U.S. small businesses. The agency provides financing worth about $11 billion a year to small businesses across the nation. The administrator's principal goals are to ensure access to capital and credit for all entrepreneurs and to transform the SBA into a leading edge financial institution.

Toward that goal, Alvarez released proposed new regulations for the SBA's 8(a) minority business program in August which would "greatly expand the number of white women entrepreneurs eligible for the government's largest program that aids minority businesses." (*Washington Post,* August 13, 1997).

Alvarez comes to the SBA after leading the government's first effort to regulate the nation's two largest housing finance companies, the Federal National Mortgage Association (Fannie Mae) and the Federal Home Loan Mortgage Corporation (Freddie Mac). As director of the Office of Federal Housing Enterprise Oversight (OFHEO), she created a financial safety and soundness oversight program for Fannie Mae and Freddie Mac. The two firms are government-chartered corporations whose operations form the core of the trillion-dollar secondary mortgage market.

Before her OFHEO appointment in June of 1993, Alvarez was an investment banker at the First Boston Corporation and at Bear Stearns. Her public service background includes two years as vice president at the NYC Health & Hospitals Corporation. She also served as a commissioner on the New York City Charter Revision Commission, as a member of the Governor's State Judicial Screening Committee, and as a member of the Mayor's Committee on Appointments.

During her career as a journalist, Alvarez won a Front Page award while at the *New York Post.* She also was an award winning television news reporter and anchor for Metromedia television in New York. In 1982, she won an Associated Press Award for Excellence and an Emmy nomination for her reporting on guerrilla activities in El Salvador.

Alvarez's past board memberships include the National Hispanic Leadership Agenda, the New York Community Trust, and the National Civic League. She is a former board chairman of the Municipal Assistance Corporation/Victim Services Agency in New York. In 1985, she was awarded an honorary Doctor of Laws from Iona College. In 1997, she received honorary Doctor of Law degrees from Bethany College in Kansas and from the Inter-American University in Puerto Rico.

Alvarez is married to Dr. Raymond J. Baxter and the couple has a daughter.

Office of International Trade

INTRODUCTION

The Office of International Trade develops new methods and techniques for assisting small businesses entering international markets; and plans, develops, and implements programs to encourage small business participation in international trade.

Acting Asst. Administrator for International Trade
Ms. Eileen Cassidy
202/205-6720
Rm. 8500

Education: B.A. in international studies, American University (Washington, D.C.), 1985. MBA, American University, 1990. Studied at Universidad Nacional Autonoma de Mexico, (Mexico City, Mex.), 1983-84.

Professional: 1985-90, former National Bank of Washington (Washington, D.C.), and Mercantile Safe Deposit & Trust Company (Baltimore, Md.). 1990-93, international public affairs division, Hill and Knowlton Public Affairs Worldwide, Inc. (Washington,DC). 1993-95, US and Foreign Commercial Service, then, office of public liaison, U.S. Dept. of Commerce. 1995-present, acting administrator for international trade and director of the office of international trade, U.S. Small Bus. Admin.

As the acting assistant administrator for international trade and director of the office of international trade at the Small Business Administration (SBA), Eileen Cassidy is responsible for managing the marketing of SBA's export assistance programs for small businesses.

She came into government in 1993 as part of the incoming Clinton administration. At the Commerce Department between 1993 and 1995, she was manager for major projects in the office of business liaison, and earlier, as special assistant to the assistant secretary and director general of the U.S. and Foreign Commercial Service in the International Trade Administration.

Before that, Cassidy served as senior account executive in the international public affairs division at Hill and Knowlton Public Affairs Worldwide, Inc., in Washington, D.C., from 1990 to 1993. In that job, she provided assistance to a broad range of clients, including U.S. and foreign corporations, as well as foreign governments. She assisted in managing the firm's Latin American and Caribbean office network.

From 1985 to 1990, Cassidy worked in the international and corporate banking fields in Washington, D.C., and Baltimore, Md. At the former National Bank of Washington, she was an international business representative and credit analyst, specializing in small business and real estate loans. At Mercantile Safe Deposit & Trust Co. in Baltimore, she was a senior credit analyst and assisted in managing the bank's credit division.

Cassidy is fluent in Spanish and has a working knowledge of Portuguese and French. She is a member of the World Affairs Council of Washington, D.C., Women in International Trade, and the Kogod School of Business' advisory council at American University. She is married to Ronald W. Imback, Jr., and resides in Arlington, Va.

Small Business Development Centers

INTRODUCTION

The U.S. Small Business Administration (SBA) administers the Small Business Development Center Program to provide management assistance to current and prospective small business owners. SBDCs offer one-stop assistance to small businesses by providing a wide variety of information and guidance in central and easily accessible branch locations.

The program is a cooperative effort of the private sector, the educational community and federal, state and local governments. It enhances economic development by providing small businesses with management and technical assistance.

There are now 56 small business development centers — one in every state (Texas has four), the District of Columbia, Guam, Puerto Rico and the U.S. Virgin Islands — with a network of nearly 1,000 service locations. In each state there is a lead organization which sponsors the SBDC and manages the program. The lead organization coordinates program services offered to small businesses through a network of subcenters and satellite locations in each state. Subcenters are located at colleges, universities, community colleges, vocational schools, chambers of commerce and economic development corporations.

SBDC assistance is tailored to the local community and the needs of individual clients. Each center develops services in cooperation with local SBA district offices to ensure statewide coordination with other available resources.

Each center has a director, staff members, volunteers and part-time personnel. Qualified individuals recruited from professional and trade associations, the legal and banking community, academia, chambers of commerce and SCORE (the Service Corps of Retired Executives) are among those who donate their services.

SBDCs also use paid consultants, consulting engineers and testing laboratories from the private sector to help clients who need specialized expertise.

Funding

The SBA provides 50 percent or less of the operating funds for each state SBDC; one or more sponsors provide the rest. These matching fund contributions are provided by state legislatures, private sector foundations and grants, state and local chambers of commerce, state-chartered economic development corporations, public and private universities, vocational and technical schools, community colleges, etc. Increasingly, sponsors contributions exceed the minimum 50 percent matching share.

What the Program Does

The SBDC Program is designed to deliver up-to-date counseling, training and technical assistance in all aspects of small business management. SBDC services include, but are not limited to, assisting small businesses with financial, marketing, production, organization, engineering and technical problems and feasibility studies. Special SBDC programs and economic development activities include international trade assistance, technical assistance, procurement assistance, venture capital formation and rural development.

The SBDCs also make special efforts to reach minority members of socially and economically disadvantaged groups, veterans, women and the disabled. Assistance is provided to both current or potential small business owners. They also provide assistance to small businesses applying for Small Business Innovation and Research (SBIR) grants from federal agencies.

Eligibility

Assistance from an SBDC is available to anyone interested in beginning a small business for the first time or improving or expanding an existing small business, who cannot afford the services of a private consultant.

Additional Information

In addition to the SBDC Program, the SBA has a variety of other programs and services available. They include training and educational programs, advisory services, publications, financial programs and contract assistance. The agency also offers specialized programs for women business owners, minorities, veterans, international trade and rural development.

The SBA has offices located throughout the country. For the one nearest you, consult the telephone directory under "U.S. Government", or call the Small Business Answer Desk at 1-800-8-ASK-SBA or (202) 205-7064 (fax). For the hearing impaired, the TDD number is (202) 205-7333.

Associate Administrator for Small Business Development Centers
Ms. Johnnie Albertson
202/205-6766
Rm. 4600

Johnnie Albertson joined the Small Business Administration in 1973 in SBA's Washington District Office as a Management Assistance Officer after a career in major newspapers - the Washington Post, New York Times and New York Herald Tribune. In 1976 she was selected to head the Office of Small Business Training and during that period received the Agency's Silver Medal for her work in designing and implementing a national training program for women entrepreneurs. Using the community college system, nation wide, the program trained more than 30,000 women in an 18 month period in business and marketing planning.

In 1980, Albertson was selected for the Agency's first Senior Executive Candidate program and in 1982 became SBA's first woman career Senior Executive. As a part of her Senior Executive Candidate's training, Albertson did a three month study of the role of SBA's District Director in the Agency's field office system. The result of her study was subsequently utilized as a basis for the Agency's widely acclaimed District Director's Training program.

In addition to her work with the Small Business Development Center Program, Albertson served for three years as the Deputy Associate Administrator with the Minority Enterprise Development program of SBA. During this period, the reform legislation for the 8(a) program was in process and, at the request of the House Small Business Committee staff, a policy recommendation from Albertson resulted in the establishing of a Minority Commission for the 8(a) Program which served for three years.

In 1992, Albertson served a one-year detail to the Office of Conservation and Renewable Energy at the Department of Energy, to design and implement a three part procurement program for the marketing and commercial utilization of developing technologies in energy conservation. Albertson received an Outstanding Rating for her work in designing and implementing this program. As an adjunct to these duties, Albertson was asked to review and evaluate the Senior Executive level of management in Conservation and Renewable Energy. The study, carried out in addition to her regular duties, earned a Special Achievement Award from the Deputy Assistant Secretary of Energy.

Albertson was selected in 1982 to be the first Associate Administrator for the Small Business Development Center program. Under her direction, the SBDC program has grown from 17 SBDCS, located primarily in the Northeast corridor, to 57 lead SBDCs and 940 service centers, providing services to small businesses in every state and in the territories of Guam, Puerto Rico and the Virgin Islands. Working closely with state governments and economic development organizations within the state, Albertson has developed the SBDC program into a key resource for state governments, other federal agencies and many private sector partners, capable of providing a wide range of assistance to small businesses nationwide.

Albertson has received numerous Outstanding Performance Awards from SBA, including the Administrator's Award in 1991, from state and local governments and from universities participating in the SBDC Program. In 1988, she received the Distinguished Service Award from the Association of SBDCS.

A resident of Washington, Albertson is active in her Capital Hill community, participating as a volunteer in the Area Neighborhood Commission and with the organization to preserve historic Eastern Market.

Small Business Development Centers

Alabama

Mr. John Sandefur
State Director
Alabama SBDC Consortium
Univ. of Alabama at Birmingham
1717 11th Ave., S - Suite 419
Birmingham AL 35294-4410
Phone: 205/934-7260
Fax: 205-934-7645
E-mail: asbd003@uabdpo.dpo.uab.edu

Alaska

Ms. Jan Fredericks
State Director
Small Business Development Center
University of Alaska/Anchorage
430 West 7th Ave., Suite 110
Anchorage AK 99501
Phone: 907/274-7232
Fax: 907-274-9524
E-mail: attac@artic.net

Arizona

Mr. Michael York
State Director
Small Business Development Center
Maricopa County Community College
2411 West 14th St., Suite 132
Tempe AZ 85281-6941
Phone: 602/230-7308
Fax: 602-230-7989
E-mail: york@maricopa.edu

Arkansas

Ms. Janet Nye
State Director
Small Business Dev. Center
Univ. of Arkansas- Little Rock
100 S. Main, Suite 401
Little Rock AR 72201
Phone: 501/324-9043
Fax: 501-324-9049
E-mail: jmnye@ualr.edu

California

Ms. Kim Neri
State Director
Small Business Development Center
California Trade & Commerce Agency
801 K Street, Suite 1700
Sacramento CA 95814
Phone: 916/324-5068
Fax: 916-322-5084
E-mail: http://commerce.ca.gov/small

Colorado

Mr. Cec Ortiz
State Director
Small Business Development Center
Office of Business Development
1625 Broadway, Suite 1710
Denver CO 80202
Phone: 303/892-3840
Fax: 303-892-3848
E-mail: sbdclc1@attmail.com

Connecticut

Mr. Dennis Gruell
State Director
Small Business Development Center
University of Connecticut, School of Bus. Admin.
2 Bourn Place, U-94
Storrs CT 06269-5094
Phone: 203/486-4135
Fax: 203-486-1576
E-mail: statedirect@ct.sbdc.uconn.edu

D.C.

Ms. Edith McCloud
Director
Small Business Development Center
Howard University
2600 6th St., NW, Rm. 128
Washington D.C. 20059
Phone: 202/806-1550
Fax: 202-806-1777

Delaware

Mr. Clinton Tymes
State Director
Small Business Development Center
University of Delaware
102 MBNA America Hall
Newark DE 19716-2711
Phone: 302/831-1555
Fax: 302-831-1423
E-mail: 43220@brahms.udel.edu

Florida

Mr. Jerry Cartwright
State Director
Small Business Development Center
University of West Florida
19 West Garden St., Third Floor
Pensacola FL 32501
Phone: 904/444-2060
Fax: 904-474-2070
E-mail: jcartwri@uwf.cc.uwf.edu

Georgia

Mr. Hank Logan
State Director
Small Business Development Center
University of Georgia
1180 East Broad Street
Athens GA 30602-5412
Phone: 706/542-6762
Fax: 706-542-6776
E-mail: sbdcath@uga.cc.uga.edu

Guam

Dr. Stephen L. Marder
Executive Director
Small Business Development Center
University of Guam
P.O. Box 5061-U.O.G. Station
Mangilao Guam 69623
Phone: 671/735-2590
Fax: 671-734-2002
E-mail: smarder@uog.edu

Hawaii

Mr. Darryll Mlyneck
State Director
Small Business Development Center
University of Hawaii at Hilo
200 West Kaili Street
Hilo HI 96720-4091
Phone: 808/974-7515
Fax: 808-974-7683
E-mail: darrylm@interpac.net

Idaho

Mr. James Hogge
State Director
Small Business Development Center
Boise State University
1910 University Drive
Boise ID 83725
Phone: 208/385-1640
Fax: 208-385-3877
E-mail: jhogge@bus.idbsu.edu

Illinois

Mr. Jeff Mitchell
State Director
Small Business Development Center
Department of Commerce and Community Affairs
620 East Adams St., Third Floor
Springfield IL 62701
Phone: 217/524-5856
Fax: 217-785-6328
E-mail: jeff.mitchell@asscessil.com

Iowa

Mr. Ronald Manning
State Director
Small Business Development Center
Iowa State University
137 Lynn Avenue
Ames IA 50014
Phone: 515/292-6351
Fax: 515-292-0020
E-mail: rmanning@iastate.edu

Kansas

Ms. Debbie Bishop
State Director
Small Business Development Center
Kansas SBDC State Office
214 S. W. 6th St., Suite 205
Topeka KS 66603
Phone: 785/296-6514
Fax: 785-291-3261
E-mail: ksbdc@cjnetworks.com

Kentucky

Ms. Janet Holloway
State Director
Small Business Development Center
University of Kentucky, College of Bus. & Econ.
225 Business and Economics Bldg.
Lexington KY 40506-0034
Phone: 606/257-7668
Fax: 606-258-1907
E-mail: cbejh@ukcc.uky.edu

Louisiana

Dr. John Baker
State Director
Louisiana SBDC
NE Louisiana University, College of Bus. Admin.
700 Univ. Ave., Adm. 2-57
Monroe LA 71209-6435
Phone: 318/342-5506
Fax: 318-342-5510
E-mail: brwall@merlin.nlu.edu

Maine

Mr. Charles Davis
Director
Small Business Development Center
University of Southern Maine
15 Surrenden St.
Portland ME 04103
Phone: 207/780-4420
Fax: 207-780-4810
E-mail: msbdc@portland.maine.edu

Maryland

Mr. James N. Graham
Director
Small Business Development Center
Lead Center
7100 Baltimore Ave., Suite 401
College Park MD 20740-3627
Phone: 301/403-8300

Massachusetts

Mr. John Ciccarelli
State Director
Small Business Development Center
University of Massachusetts
205 School of Management
Amherst MA 01003
Phone: 413/545-6301
Fax: 413-545-1273
E-mail: j.ciccarelli@umassp.edu

Michigan

Mr. Ronald R. Hall
State Director
Small Business Development Center
Wayne State University
2727 Second Ave.
Detroit MI 48201
Phone: 313/964-1798
Fax: 313-964-3648
E-mail: rhall@cms.cc.wayne.edu

Minnesota

Ms. Mary Kruger
State Director
Small Business Development Center
Dept. of Trade and Economic Dev.
500 Metro Square - 121 7th Place East
St. Paul MN 55101-2146
Phone: 612/297-5773
Fax: 612-296-1290
E-mail: mkruger@dted.state.mn.us

Mississippi

Mr. Walter D. Gurley
State Director
Small Business Development Center
University of Mississippi
Old Chemistry Bldg., Suite 216
University MS 38677
Phone: 601/232-5001
Fax: 601-232-5650
E-mail: msbcd@olemiss.edu

Missouri

Mr. Max E. Summers
State Director
Small Business Development Center
University of Missouri
Suite 300, University Place
Columbia MO 65211
Phone: 314/882-0344
Fax: 314-884-4297
E-mail: sbdc-mso@ext.missouri.edu

Montana

Mr. Ralph Kloser
State Director
Small Business Development Center
Department of Commerce
1424 Ninth Ave.
Helena MT 59620
Phone: 406/444-4780
Fax: 406-444-1872

Nebraska

Mr. Robert Bernier
State Director
Small Business Development Center
University of Nebraska at Omaha
60th & Dodge Streets, CBA Room 407
Omaha NE 68182
Phone: 402/554-2521
Fax: 402-554-3747
E-mail: rbernier@cbafaculty.unomaha.edu

Nevada

Mr. Sam Males
State Director
Small Business Development Center
University of Nevada, Reno
College of Business Administration, Room 411
Reno NV 89557-0100
Phone: 702/784-1717
Fax: 702-784-4337
E-mail: wmoore@scs.unr.edu

New Hampshire

Ms. Mary Collins
State Director
Small Business Development Center
University of New Hampshire
108 McConnell Hall
Durham NH 03824
Phone: 603/862-2200
Fax: 603-862-4876

New Jersey

Ms. Brenda Hopper
State Director
Small Business Development Center
Rutgers University
Third Floor, Ackerson Hall, 49 Bleeker Street
Newark NJ 07102
Phone: 201/648-5950
Fax: 201-648-1110
E-mail: bhopper@andromeda.rutgers.edu

New Mexico

Mr. J. Roy Miller
State Director
Small Fe Community College
6401 Richards Avenue
Santa Fe NM 87505
Phone: 505/438-1362
Fax: 505-471-9469

New York

Mr. James L. King
State Director
Small Business Development Center
State University of New York
SUNY Plaza, S-523
Albany NY 12246
Phone: 518/443-5398
Fax: 518-465-4992
E-mail: kingjl@sysadm.suny.edu

North Carolina

Mr. Scott Daugherty
Executive Director
Small Business Development Center
University of North Carolina
333 Fayetteville Street Mall, Suite 1150
Raleigh NC 27601-1742
Phone: 919/715-7272
Fax: 919-715-7777
E-mail: srdaughe.sbdc@mhs.unc.edu

North Dakota

Mr. Walter Kearns
State Director
Small Business Development Center
University of North Dakota
118 Gamble Hall, University Station
Grand Forks ND 58202-7308
Phone: 701/777-3700
Fax: 701-777-3225
E-mail: kearns@praire.nodak.edu

Ohio

Ms. Holly Schick
State Director
Small Business Development Center
Department of Development
77 South High Street, 28th Floor
Columbus OH 43215-6108
Phone: 614/466-2711
Fax: 614-466-0829
E-mail: hschick@odod.ohio.gov

Oklahoma

Dr. Grady Pennington
State Director
Small Business Development Center
Southeastern Oklahoma State University
517 West University - Station A, Box 2584
Durant OK 74701
Phone: 405/924-0277
Fax: 405-924-7471
E-mail: gpennington@sosu.edu

Oregon

Dr. Sandy Cutler
State Director
Small Business Development Center
Lane Community College
44 W. Broadway, Suite 501
Eugene OR 97401-3021
Phone: 503/726-2250
Fax: 503-345-6006
E-mail: ccutler@aol.com

Pennsylvania

Mr. Gregory Higgins
State Director
Small Business Development Center
University of Pennsylvania, The Wharton School
423 Vance Hall, 3733 Spruce Street
Philadelphia PA 19104-6374
Phone: 215/898-1219
Fax: 215-573-2135
E-mail: pasdc@wharton.upenn.edu

Rhode Island

Mr. Douglas Jobling
State Director
Small Business Development Center
State Administration Office, Bryant College
1150 Douglas Pike
Smithfield RI 02917-1284
Phone: 401/232-6111
Fax: 401-232-6933

South Carolina

Mr. John Lenti
State Director
Small Business Development Center
University of South Carolina
School of Bus. Admin.
1710 College Street
Columbia SC 29208
Phone: 803/777-4907
Fax: 803-777-4403
E-mail: lenti@darla.badm.scarolina.edu

South Dakota

Mr. Steve Tracy
Acting State Director
Small Business Development Center
University of South Dakota, School of Business
414 East Clark
Vermillion SD 57069-2390
Phone: 605/677-5287
Fax: 605-677-5427
E-mail: stracy@usd.edu

Tennessee

Dr. Kenneth J. Burns
State Director
Small Business Development Center
University of Memphis
South Campus - Getwell Rd., Bldg. 1
Memphis TN 38152-0001
Phone: 901/678-2500
Fax: 901-678-4072
E-mail: gmickle@adin1.memphis.edu

Texas

Ms. Elizabeth Klimback
Regional Director (North Texas)
Small Business Development Center
Dallas County Community College
1402 Corinth St.
Dallas TX 75215
Phone: 214/860-5833
Fax: 214-860-5813
E-mail: em9402@dcccd.edu

Dr. Elizabeth Gatewood
Region Director (South Texas)
Small Business Development Center
University of Houston
1100 Louisiana, Suite 500
Houston TX 77002
Phone: 713/752-8444
Fax: 713-756-1500
E-mail: ejg@uh.edu

Mr. Craig Bean
Region Director (NW Texas)

Small Business Development Center
Texas Tech University
2579 South Loop 289, Suite 114
Lubbock TX 79423-1637
Phone: 806/745-3973
Fax: 806-745-6207
E-mail: odaus@ttacs.ttu.edu

Mr. Robert McKinley
Regional Director
Small Business Development Center
University of Texas at San Antonio Downtown
1222 North Main, Suite 450
San Antonio TX 78212
Phone: 210/458-2450
Fax: 210-458-2464
E-mail: rmckinley@otsa.edu

Vermont

Mr. Donald Kelpinski
State Director
Small Business Development Center
Vermont Technical College
PO Box 422
Randolph VT 05060
Phone: 802/728-9101
Fax: 802-728-3026
E-mail: dkelpins@night.vtc.vsc.edu

Virgin Islands

Mr. Chester Williams
State Director
Small Business Development Center
University of the Virgin Islands
8000 Nisky Center, Suite 202
St. Thomas 00802-5804
Phone: 809/776-3206
Fax: 809-775-3756
E-mail: ihodge@uvi.edu

Virginia

Mr. Robert D. Wilburn
State Director
Small Business Development Center
Dept. of Economic Development
901 East Byrd St., Suite 1400
Richmond VA 23219
Phone: 804/371-8253
Fax: 804-225-3384
E-mail: rwilburn@dba.state.va.us

Washington

Ms. Carol Riesenberg
State Director
Small Business Development Center
Washington State University,
    College of Business & Economics
501 Johnson Tower
Pullman WA 99164-4851
Phone: 509/335-1576
Fax: 509-335-0949
E-mail: riesenbe@wsu.edu

West Virginia

Dr. Hazel Kroesser Palmer
State Director

Small Business Development Center
West Virginia Development Office
950 Kanawha Blvd., East, 2nd Floor
Charleston WV 25301
Phone: 304/558-2960
Fax: 304-558-0127
E-mail: palmeh@mail.wvnet.edu

Wyoming

Ms. Diane Wolverton
State Director
Small Business Development Center
University of Wyoming
P.O. Box 3622
Laramie WY 82071-3622
Phone: 307/766-3505
Fax: 307-766-3406
E-mail: ddw@uwyo.edu

SBA Field Offices

INTRODUCTION

Field offices of the Small Business Administration provide counseling, training, & seminars on establishing and managing a small business. They offer limited export counseling and financing assistance and are a source for information on the SBA's Export Working Capital Program.

REGION I

Mr. Patrick K. McGowan
Regional Administrator
SBA Field Office
10 Causeway St., Suite 812
Boston MA 02222-1093
Phone: 617/565-8415
Fax: 617-565-8420

District Offices:

Mr. Leroy G. Perry
District Director
SBA Field Office
40 Western Avenue, Room 512
Augusta ME 04330
Phone: 207/622-8378
Fax: 207-622-8277

Ms. Mary E. McAleney
District Director
SBA Field Office
10 Causeway Street, Room 265
Boston MA 02222-1093
Phone: 617/565-5560
Fax: 617-565-5597

Mr. William K. Phillips
District Director
SBA Field Office
143 North Main Street, Suite 202
Concord NH 03301
Phone: 603/225-1400
Fax: 603-225-1409

VACANT
District Director
SBA Field Office
330 Main Street, 2nd Floor
Hartford CT 06106
Phone: 203/240-4700
Fax: 203-240-4659

Mr. Kenneth Silvia
District Director
SBA Field Office
87 State Street, Room 205
Montpelier VT 05602
Phone: 802/828-4422
Fax: 802-828-4485

Mr. Joseph Loddo
District Director
SBA Field Office
380 Westminster Hall, 5th Floor
Providence RI 02903
Phone: 401/528-4561
Fax: 401-528-4539

Branch Offices:

Mr. Harold C. Webb
Branch Manager
SBA Field Office
1441 Main Street, Room 410
Springfield MA 01103
Phone: 413/785-0268
Fax: 413-785-9267

REGION II

Mr. Thomas M. Bettridge
Regional Administrator
SBA Field Office
26 Federal Plaza, Suite 3108
New York NY 10278
Phone: 212/264-1450
Fax: 212-264-0038

District Offices:

Mr. Franklin J. Sciortino
District Director
SBA Field Office
111 West Huron Street, Room 1311
Buffalo NY 14202
Phone: 716/551-4305
Fax: 716-551-4418

Mr. Ivan E. Irizary
District Director
SBA Field Office
252 Ponce De Leon Blvd., Suite 201
Hato Rey PR 00918
Phone: 787/766-5166
Fax: 787-766-5525

Mr. Francisco Marrero
District Director
SBA Field Office
Two Gateway Center, 4th FL.
Newark NJ 07102
Phone: 973/645-3580
Fax: 973-645-6265

Mr. Bernard J. Paprocki
District Director
SBA Field Office
100 South Clinton Street, Suite 1071
Syracuse NY 13260
Phone: 315/471-9932
Fax: 315-471-9272

Branch Offices:

Mr. James J. Cristofaro
Branch Manager
SBA Field Office
333 East Water Street, 4th Floor
Elmira NY 14901
Phone: 607/734-1571
Fax: 607-733-4656

Mr. Bert X. Haggerty
Branch Manager
SBA Field Office
35 Pinelawn Road, Suite 207W
Melville NY 11747
Phone: 516/454-0764
Fax: 516-454-0769

Mr. F. Peter Flihan
Branch Manager
SBA Field Office
100 State Street, Suite 410
Rochester NY 14614
Phone: 716/263-6700
Fax: 716-263-3146

Posts of Duty:

Mr. Carl Christensen
Officer in Charge
SBA Field Office
3013 Golden Rock, Suite 165
Christiansted/St.Croix VI 00820-4355
Phone: 340/778-5380
Fax: 340-778-1102

Mr. Aubrey A. Rogers
District Director
SBA Field Office
26 Federal Plaza, Room 3100
New York NY 10278
Phone: 212/264-2454
Fax: 212-264-7751

Mr. Calford Martin
Branch Manager
SBA Field Office
3800 Crown Bay
St. Thomas VI 00820
Phone: 340/774-8530
Fax: 340-776-2312

REGION III

Ms. Susan M. McCann
Regional Administrator
SBA Field Office
475 Allendale Road, Suite 201
King of Prussia PA 19406
Phone: 610/962-3710
Fax: 610-962-3743

District Offices:

Mr. Allan Stephenson
District Director
SBA Field Office
10 S. Howard Street, Suite 6220
Baltimore MD 21201-2525
Phone: 410/962-4392
Fax: 410-962-1805

Ms. Jayne Armstrong
District Director
SBA Field Office
168 West Main Street, 5th Floor
Clarksburg WV 26301
Phone: 304/623-5631
Fax: 304-623-0023

Mr. Clifton Toulson, Jr.
District Director
SBA Field Office
475 Allendale Road, Suite 201
King of Prussia PA 19406
Phone: 610/962-3800
Fax: 610-962-3795

Mr. Althier Jones
District Director
SBA Field Office
1000 Liberty Ave., Room 1128
Pittsburgh PA 15222
Phone: 412/395-6560
Fax: 412-395-6562

Mr. Charles J. Gaston

District Director
SBA Field Office
1504 Santa Rosa Rd., Suite 200
Richmond VA 23229
Phone: 804/771-2400
Fax: 804-771-8018

Mr. Daryl Hairston
District Director
SBA Field Office
1110 Vermont Avenue, NW, Suite 900
Washington DC 20005
Phone: 202/606-4000
Fax: 202-606-4225

Branch Offices:

Mr. Bill Durham
Economic Development Specialist
SBA Field Office
405 Capitol Street, Suite 412
Charleston WV 25301
Phone: 304/347-5220
Fax: 304-347-5350

Ms. Bonnie Gerhard
Program Assistant
SBA Field Office
100 Chestnut Street, Room 108
Harrisburg PA 17101
Phone: 717/782-3840
Fax: 717-782-4839

Mr. William Dougherty
Economic Development Specialist
SBA Field Office
7 N. Wilkes-Barre Boulevard, Suite 407
Wilkes-Barre PA 18702
Phone: 717/826-6497
Fax: 717-826-6287

Mr. Joseph M. Kopp
Branch Manager
SBA Field Office
824 North Market St., Suite 610
Wilmington DE 19801-3011
Phone: 302/573-6294
Fax: 302-573-6060

REGION IV

Mr. Billy Max Paul
Regional Administrator
SBA Field Office
1720 Peachtree Rd., NW, Suite 496
Atlanta GA 30309
Phone: 404/347-4999
Fax: 404-347-2355

District Offices:

Ms. Laura A. Brown
District Director
SBA Field Office
1720 Peachtree Road, NW, 6th Floor
Atlanta GA 30309
Phone: 404/347-4147
Fax: 404-347-4745

Mr. James C. Barksdale
District Director
SBA Field Office
2121 8th Avenue, North, Suite 200
Birmingham AL 35203-2398
Phone: 205/731-1341
Fax: 205-731-1404

Mr. Gary Cook
District Director

SBA Field Office
200 North College Street, Suite A2015
Charlotte NC 28202-2173
Phone: 704/344-6561
Fax: 704-344-6769

Mr. Elliott Cooper
District Director
SBA Field Office
1835 Assembly Street, Room 358
Columbia SC 29201
Phone: 803/765-5339
Fax: 803-765-5962

Mr. Charles E. Anderson
District Director
SBA Field Office
1320 South Dixie Highway, Suite 350
Coral Gables FL 33146-2911
Phone: 305/536-5521
Fax: 305-536-5058

Ms. Janita Stewart
District Director
SBA Field Office
101 West Capitol Street, Suite 400
Jackson MS 39201
Phone: 601/965-4378
Fax: 601-965-4294

Mr. Wilfredo Gonzalez
District Director
SBA Field Office
7825 Baymeadows Way, Suite 100-B
Jacksonville FL 32256-7504
Phone: 904/443-1970
Fax: 904-443-1980

Mr. William Federhofer
District Director
SBA Field Office
600 Dr. M.L. King Jr. Place, Room 188
Louisville KY 40202
Phone: 502/582-5971
Fax: 502-582-5009

Mr. W. Clinton Smith
District Director
SBA Field Office
50 Vantage Way, Suite 201
Nashville TN 37228-1500
Phone: 615/736-5039
Fax: 615-736-7232

Branch Offices:

Mr. Charles A. Gillis
Branch Manager
SBA Field Office
2909 13th Street, Suite 203
Gulfport MS 39501-1949
Phone: 228/863-4449
Fax: 228-864-0179

REGION V

Mr. Peter W. Barca
Regional Administrator
SBA Field Office
500 W. Madison Street, Suite 1240
Chicago IL 60661-2511
Phone: 312/353-0357
Fax: 312-353-3426

District Offices:

Mr. John L. Smith
District Director
SBA Field Office

500 West Madison Street, Suite 1250
Chicago IL 60661-2511
Phone: 312/353-4528
Fax: 312-886-5688

Mr. Gilbert B. Goldberg
District Director
SBA Field Office
1111 Superior Avenue, Suite 630
Cleveland OH 44114-2507
Phone: 216/522-4180
Fax: 216-522-2038

Mr. Frank D. Ray
District Director
SBA Field Office
2 Nationwide Plaza, Suite 1400
Columbus OH 43215-2592
Phone: 614/469-6860
Fax: 614-469-2391

Mr. Dwight G. Reynolds
District Director
SBA Field Office
477 Michigan Avenue, Room 515
Detroit MI 48226
Phone: 313/226-6075
Fax: 313-226-4769

Ms. Janice E. Wolfe
District Director
SBA Field Office
429 North Pennsylvania, Suite 100
Indianapolis IN 46204-1873
Phone: 317/226-7272
Fax: 317-226-7259

Mr. Michael W. Kiser
District Director
SBA Field Office
212 East Washington Avenue, Room 213
Madison WI 53703
Phone: 608/264-5261
Fax: 608-264-5541

Mr. Edward A. Daum
District Director
SBA Field Office
100 North 6th Street, Suite 610
Minneapolis MN 55403-1563
Phone: 612/370-2324
Fax: 612-370-2303

Branch Offices:

Mr. Ronald Carlson
Branch Manager
SBA Field Office
525 Vine Street, Suite 870
Cincinnati OH 45202
Phone: 513/684-2814
Fax: 513-684-3251

Mr. Paul Jacobson
Branch Manager
SBA Field Office
500 South Front St., Suite 11
Marquette MI 49855
Phone: 906/225-1108
Fax: 906-225-1109

Mr. Paul Roppuld
Acting Branch Manager
SBA Field Office
310 West Wisconsin Avenue, Suite 400
Milwaukee WI 53203
Phone: 414/297-3941
Fax: 414-297-1377

Mr. Curtis A. Charter
Branch Manager

SBA Field Office
511 West Capitol Avenue, Suite 302
Springfield IL 62704
Phone: 217/492-4416
Fax: 217-492-4867

REGION VI

Mr. James W. Breedlove
Regional Administrator
SBA Field Office
4300 Amon Carter Blvd., Suite 108
Ft. Worth TX 76155
Phone: 817/885-6581
Fax: 817-885-6588

District Offices:

Mr. Robert Blaney
District Director
SBA Field Office
625 Silver Avenue, SW, Suite 320
Albuquerque NM 87102
Phone: 505/766-1870
Fax: 505-766-1057

Mr. Carlos G. Mendoza
District Director
SBA Field Office
10737 Gateway West, Suite 320
El Paso TX 79935
Phone: 915/540-5586
Fax: 915-540-5636

VACANT
District Director
SBA Field Office
4300 Amon Carter Boulevard, Suite 114
Ft. Worth TX 76155
Phone: 817/885-6500
Fax: 817-885-6516

VACANT
District Director
SBA Field Office
222 East Van Buren Street, Room 500
Harlingen TX 78550-6855
Phone: 956/427-8625
Fax: 956-427-8537

Mr. Milton Wilson
District Director
SBA Field Office
9301 Southwest Freeway, Suite 550
Houston TX 77074-1591
Phone: 713/773-6500
Fax: 713-773-6550

Mr. Joseph T. Foglia
District Director
SBA Field Office
2120 Riverfront Drive, Suite 100
Little Rock AR 72202
Phone: 501/324-5871
Fax: 501-324-5199

Mr. Tommy W. Dowell
District Director
SBA Field Office
1205 Texas Ave., Room 408
Lubbock TX 79401
Phone: 806/472-7462
Fax: 806-472-7487

VACANT
District Director
SBA Field Office
365 Canal Street, Suite 2250
New Orleans LA 70130
Phone: 504/589-6685

Fax: 504-589-2339

Mr. Raymond L. Harshman
District Director
SBA Field Office
210 Park Avenue, Suite 1300
Oklahoma City OK 73102
Phone: 405/231-5521
Fax: 405-231-4876

Mr. Rodney Martin
District Director
SBA Field Office
727 E. Durango Boulevard, Room A-527
San Antonio TX 78206-1204
Phone: 210/472-5900
Fax: 210-472-5935

Branch Offices:

Mr. Jesse Sendijo
Branch Manager
SBA Field Office
606 N. Carancahua, Suite 1200
Corpus Christi TX 78476
Phone: 512/888-3331
Fax: 512-888-3418

REGION VII

Mr. Bruce W. Kent
Regional Administrator
SBA Field Office
323 West 8th Street, Suite 307
Kansas City MO 64105-1500
Phone: 816/374-6380
Fax: 816-374-6339

District Offices:

Mr. James Thomson
District Director
SBA Field Office
215 4th Avenue, SE, Suite 200
Cedar Rapids IA 52401-1806
Phone: 319/362-6405
Fax: 319-362-7861

Mr. Conrad E. Lawlor
District Director
SBA Field Office
210 Walnut Street, Room 749
Des Moines IA 50309-2186
Phone: 515/284-4580
Fax: 515-284-4572

Ms. Dorothy D. Kleeschulte
District Director
SBA Field Office
323 West 8th Street, Suite 501
Kansas City MO 64105-1500
Phone: 816/374-6708
Fax: 816-374-6759

Ms. Glenn E. Davis
District Director
SBA Field Office
11145 Mill Valley Road
Omaha NE 68154-3949
Phone: 402/221-4691
Fax: 402-221-3680

Mr. Robert Andrews
District Director
SBA Field Office
815 Olive Street, Room 242
St. Louis MO 63101
Phone: 314/539-6600
Fax: 314-539-3785

Ms. Elizabeth Auer
District Director
SBA Field Office
100 East English Street, Suite 510
Wichita KS 67202
Phone: 316/269-6616
Fax: 316-269-6499

Branch Offices:

Mr. James R. Combs
Branch Manager
SBA Field Office
620 South Glenstone Street, Suite 110
Springfield MO 65802-3200
Phone: 417/864-7670
Fax: 417-864-4108

REGION VIII

Ms. Joan Coplan
Regional Administrator
SBA Field Office
721 19th St., Suite 400
Denver CO 80202-2599
Phone: 303/844-0500
Fax: 303-844-0506

District Offices:

Mr. Stephen Despain
District Director
SBA Field Office
100 East B Street, Room 4001
Casper WY 82602-2839
Phone: 307/261-6500
Fax: 307-261-6535

Ms. Patricia Barela-Rivera
District Director
SBA Field Office
721 19th Street, Suite 426
Denver CO 80202-2599
Phone: 303/844-4028
Fax: 303-844-6468

Mr. James L. Stai
District Director
SBA Field Office
657 2nd Avenue, North, Room 219
Fargo ND 58108-3086
Phone: 701/239-5131
Fax: 701-239-5645

Ms. Jo Alice Mospan
District Director
SBA Field Office
301 South Park, Room 334
Helena MT 59626
Phone: 406/441-1081
Fax: 406-441-1090

Mr. Stanley Nakano
District Director
SBA Field Office
125 South State Street, Room 2229
Salt Lake City UT 84138-1195
Phone: 801/524-5804
Fax: 801-524-4160

Mr. Gene F. Van Arsdale
District Director
SBA Field Office
110 South Phillips Avenue, Suite 200
Sioux Falls SD 57102-1109
Phone: 605/330-4243
Fax: 605-330-4215

REGION IX

Ms. Viola I. Canales
Regional Administrator
SBA Field Office
455 Market Street, 6th Floor
San Francisco CA 94105-2445
Phone: 415/744-2118
Fax: 415-744-2119

District Offices:

Mr. Antonio Valdez
District Director
SBA Field Office
2719 North Air Fresno Drive
Suite 200
Fresno CA 93727-1547
Phone: 209/487-5791
Fax: 209-487-5636

Mr. Alberto G. Alvarado
District Director
SBA Field Office
330 North Brand Boulevard
Suite 1200
Glendale CA 91203-2304
Phone: 818/552-3210
Fax: 818-552-3260

Mr. Andrew Poepoe
District Director
SBA Field Office
300 Ala Moana Boulevard
Room 2-235
Honolulu HI 96850-4981
Phone: 808/541-2990
Fax: 808-541-2976

Mr. John E. Scott
District Director
SBA Field Office
301 East Stewart Street, Room 301
Las Vegas NV 89101
Phone: 702/388-6611
Fax: 702-388-6469

Mr. Philip D. Mahoney
Acting District Director
SBA Field Office
2828 North Central Avenue
Suite 800
Phoenix AZ 85004-1093
Phone: 602/640-2316
Fax: 602-640-2360

Mr. George P. Chandler, Jr.
District Director
SBA Field Office
550 West C Street, Suite 550
San Diego CA 92101
Phone: 619/557-7252
Fax: 619-557-5894

Mr. Mark Quinn
District Director
SBA Field Office
455 Market Street, Sixth Floor
San Francisco CA 94105-2420
Phone: 415/744-6820
Fax: 415-744-6812

Ms. Sandra V. Sutton
District Director
SBA Field Office
200 West Santa Ana Blvd., Suite 700
Santa Ana CA 92701
Phone: 714/550-7420
Fax: 714-550-0191

Branch Offices:

Mr. Ken Lujan
Branch Manager
SBA Field Office
400 Route 8, Suite 302
Mongmong GU 96927
Phone: 671/472-7277
Fax: 671-472-7365

Ms. Teresa Bellmore
Acting District Director
SBA Field Office
660 J Street, Suite 215
Sacramento CA 95814-2413
Phone: 916/498-6410
Fax: 916-498-6422

REGION X

Ms. Gretchen Sorensen
Regional Administrator
SBA Field Office
1200 Sixth Avenue, Suite 1805
Seattle WA 98101-1128
Phone: 206/553-0291
Fax: 206-553-4155

District Offices:

Mr. Frank Cox
District Director
SBA Field Office
222 West 8th Avenue, Room 67
Anchorage AK 99513-7559
Phone: 907/271-4022
Fax: 907-271-4545

Mr. Thomas Bergdoll
District Director
SBA Field Office
1020 Main Street, Suite 290
Boise ID 83702-5745
Phone: 208/334-1696
Fax: 208-334-9353

Mr. John L. Gilman
District Director
SBA Field Office
1515 SW Fifth Ave., Suite 1050
Portland OR 97201-5494
Phone: 503/326-5221
Fax: 503-326-2808

Mr. Robert Meredith
District Director
SBA Field Office
1200 Sixth Ave., Suite 1700
Seattle WA 98101-1128
Phone: 206/553-7310
Fax: 206-553-7099

Mr. Robert D. Wiebe
District Director
SBA Field Office
601 West First Avenue, 10th Floor East
Spokane WA 99201-3826
Phone: 509/353-2810
Fax: 509-353-2829

INTRODUCTION - Export Legal Assistant Network

The Export Legal Assistant Network (ELAN) is a nationwide group of attorneys experienced in international trade that provide free initial consultations to new-to-export businesses on export-related matters. Listed below are the Regional ELAN Coordinators. The national coordinator of the program is Judd Kessler: 202/778-3080; FAX 202/778-3063; e-mail jkessler@portwright.com.

Alabama

Mr. Joseph W. Blackburn
Regional Coordinator
Sirote & Permutt, PC
2222 Arlington Ave., South
P.O. Box 55727
Birmingham AL 35255
Phone: 205/933-7111   Fax: 205/930-5301

Alaska

Mr. John K. Norman
Regional Coordinator
Hartig, Rhodes et al.
717 K Street
Anchorage AK 99501-3397
Phone: 907/276-1592   Fax: 907/777-4352

Arizona

Mr. Frank G. Long
Regional Coordinator
Gust Rosenfeld
201 N. Central Avenue, Suite 3300
Phoenix AZ 85073-3300
Phone: 602/257-7961   Fax: 602/254-4878

California

Mr. Michael R. Doram
Regional Coordinator, Los Angeles
Michael R. Doram, Esquire
911 Wilshire Boulevard, Suite 2288
Los Angeles CA 90017
Phone: 213/627-0896   Fax: 213/622-1154

Mr. Mark F. Johannessen
Regional Coordinator, Northeastern
Mark F. Johannessen, Esquire
1909 Capitol Avenue, Suite 302
Sacramento CA 95814
Phone: 916/443-1200   Fax: 916/443-3740

Mr. Harold C. Pope
Regional Coordinator, San Diego
Pope & Dixson
5060 Shoreham Place, Suite 200
San Diego CA 92122
Phone: 619/622-8970   Fax: 619/458-5863

Lawyer Referral Service
Bar Association of San Francisco
685 Market Street, Suite 700
San Francisco CA 94105
Phone: 415/764-1616

Mr. Harry B. Endsley
Regional Coordinator, San Francisco
Harry B. Endsley & Associates
465 California Street, Suite 1225
San Francisco CA 94104
Phone: 415/296-1141   Fax: 415/296-7845

Colorado

Ms. Louise Aron
Regional Coordinator
1536 South Ingalls
Lakewood CO 80232-7016
Phone: 303/922-7687   Fax: 303/922-1370

Connecticut

Mr. William E. Huth
Regional Coordinator
Huth, Grinnell & Flaherty, LLC
1055 Washington Boulevard
Stamford CT 06901
Phone: 203/363-7104   Fax: 203/363-7108

Delaware

Mr. Gordon W. Stewart
Regional Coordinator
Stewart & Associates
Chemical Bank Plaza, Suite 1700
1201 Market Street
Wilmington DE 19801
Phone: 302/652-5200   Fax: 302/652-7211

District of Columbia

Mr. Judd L. Kessler
Regional Coordinator
Porter, Wright et al., Suite 400
1233 20th Street, NW
Washington DC 20036
Phone: 202/778-3080   Fax: 202/778-3063

Ms. Margaret Png
Regional Coordinator
Akin, Gump et al.
133 New Hampshire Avenue, NW
Suite 400
Washington DC 20036
Phone: 202/887-4000   Fax: 202/887-4288

Florida

Mr. Sidney W. Kilgore
Regional Coordinator, West Coast
Coton, Kilgore & Lavigne, PA
611 Druid Road, Suite 206
Clearwater FL 34616
Phone: 813/422-7684   Fax: 813/441-8048

Mr. Michael A. Pyle
Regional Coordinator,
   Central East Coast & NE
P.O. Box 3096
Daytona Beach FL 32118-0096
Phone: 904/252-1561   Fax: 904/254-8157

Mr. Thomas F. Morante
Regional Coordinator, Southeast

Cantor & Morante, PA
Sunbank Building, Suite 500
777 Brickell Avenue
Miami FL 33131
Phone: 305/374-3886   Fax: 305/371-4564

Mr. Stanley F. Rose
Regional Coordinator, West Coast
2110 Imperial Golf Course Blvd.
Naples FL 33942
Phone: 813/566-3511   Fax: 813/566-8523

Ms. Rosellen Kraus
Regional Coordinator, Central & NW
SBDC
College of Business Administration
Univ. of Central Fla., P.O. Box 25000
Orlando FL 32816-1513
Phone: 407/823-5554   Fax: 407/345-5554

Ms. Donna L. Draves
Regional Coordinator, Central & NW
Law Offices
120 East Concord Street
Orlando FL 32801
Phone: 407/423-1183   Fax: 407/841-6746

Mr. Christopher K. Caswell
Regional Coordinator, West Coast
Icard, Merrill et al.
2033 Main Street, Suite 600
Sarasota FL 34237
Phone: 813/366-8100   Fax: 813/366-6384

Mr. Lucius Dyal
Regional Coordinator, West Coast
Shackleford, Farrior et al.
P.O. Box 3323
Tampa FL 33601
Phone: 813/273-5000   Fax: 813/273-5145

Mr. George C.J. Moore
Regional Coordinator,
   Central East Coast & NE
Citizens Building
Suite 812, 105 So. Narcissus Avenue
West Palm Beach FL 33401
Phone: 407/833-9000   Fax: 407/833-0999

Georgia

Mr. William M. Poole
Regional Coordinator
Cofer, Beauchamp & Butler
99 West Paces Ferry Road, NW
Suite 200
Atlanta GA 30305
Phone: 404/233-6200   Fax: 404/364-0044

Hawaii

Mr. David L. Bourgoin
Regional Coordinator
1001 Bishop Street, Suite 1560
Honolulu HI 96813
Phone: 808/523-7779

Idaho

Mr. Charles D. Herrington
Regional Coordinator
Hawley, Troxell et al.
First Interstate Center, Suite 1000
877 Main St., P.O. Box 1617
Boise ID 83701-1617
Phone: 208/344-6000   Fax: 208/342-3829

Illinois

Mr. Paul H. Vishny
Regional Coordinator
D'Ancona & Pflaum, Suite 2900
30 North LaSalle Street
Chicago IL 60602
Phone: 312/580-2000   Fax: 312/580-0932

Indiana

Mr. Eugene L. Henderson
Regional Coordinator
Henderson, Daley et al.
2600 One Indiana Square
Indianapolis IN 46204
Phone: 317/639-4121   Fax: 317/639-0191

Iowa

Mr. A.J. Greffenius
Regional Coordinator
Davis, Hockenberg et al.
666 Walnut Street
2300 Financial Center
Des Moines IA 50309-3993
Phone: 515/288-2500   Fax: 515/243-0634

Kentucky

Mr. Stephen T. McMurtry
Regional Coordinator
McMurtry & Wolff
411 Garrard Street
Covington KY 41011
Phone: 606/581-4200   Fax: 606/581-2122

Mr. James H. Newberry, Jr.
Regional Coordinator
Newberry, Hargrove & Rambicure
2800 Lexington Financial Center
250 West Main Street
Lexington KY 40507-1743
Phone: 606/231-3700   Fax: 606/259-1092

Mr. Jay Middleton Tannon
Regional Coordinator
Brown, Todd & Heyburn, PLLC
3200 Providian Center
Louisville KY 40202-3363
Phone: 502/568-0332   Fax: 502/581-1087

Louisiana

Ms. Sharon A. Perlis
Regional Coordinator
Perlis & Hogg
3421 No. Causeway Boulevard
Metairie LA 70002-3751
Phone: 504/834-3700   Fax: 504/834-3745

Massachusetts

Mr. Michael A. Ugolini
Regional Coordinator
935 Main Street
Springfield MA 01103
Phone: 413/737-3972   Fax: 413/737-7849

Mr. Robert W. Chmielinski
Regional Coordinator
Chmielinski, Wilchins & Witman

36 Washington Street, Suite 70
Wellesley Hills MA 02181
Phone: 617/235-8815   Fax: 617/235-8563

Michigan

Mr. Roger H. Leemis
Regional Coordinator
29777 Telegraph Road, Suite 2500
Southfield MI 48034
Phone: 810/353-5060   Fax: 810/353-5661

Minnesota

Mr. Philip R. Sherwood
Regional Coordinator
Sherwood & McKenzie
1900 World Trade Center
St. Paul MN 55101
Phone: 612/297-6564   Fax: 612/297-6565

Mississippi

Mr. Stephen M. Roberts
Regional Coordinator
Watkins, Ludlam & Stennis
P.O. Box 427
633 No. State Street
Jackson MS 39205
Phone: 601/949-4900   Fax: 601/949-4804

Missouri

Mr. Robert S. Conway
Regional Coordinator, Western
Blackwell, Sanders, Matheny et al.
2300 Main Street, Suite 1100
Kansas City MO 64108
Phone: 816/274-6961   Fax: 816/274-6914

Mr. Jeffrey L. Michelman
Regional Coordinator, Eastern
Blumenfeld, Kaplan et al.
168 No. Meramec, Fourth Floor
St. Louis MO 63105
Phone: 314/863-0800   Fax: 314/863-9388

Montana

Ms. Mae Nan Ellingson
Regional Coordinator
Dorsey & Whitney, Suite 310
127 East Front Street
Missoula MT 59802
Phone: 406/721-6025   Fax: 406/543-0863

New Hampshire

Mr. Arthur W. Mudge
Regional Coordinator
13 South Park Street
P.O. Box 986
Hanover NH 03755
Phone: 603/795-4460

New Jersey

Mr. Stephen Vasak
Regional Coordinator, Northern
Two University Plaza

Hackensack NJ 07601
Phone: 201/488-3737   Fax: 201/343-8517

Mr. Richard L. Abbott
Regional Coordinator
43 Foxcroft Drive
Princeton NJ 08540
Phone: 609/924-9265   Fax: 609/924-3484

New Mexico

Ms. Alison K. Schuler
Regional Coordinator
Schuler, Mesersmith & McNeill
5700 Harper Drive, NE - Suite 430
Albuquerque NM 87199
Phone: 505/822-8826   Fax: 505/828-2682

New York

Mr. Paul A. Mitchell
District Coordinator, Buffalo
Lippes, Silverstein et al.
700 Guaranty Building
28 Church Street
Buffalo NY 14202-3950
Phone: 716/853-5100   Fax: 716/853-5199

Mr. Thomas M. Pitegoff
District Coordinator, Westchester
Halket & Pitegoff, LLP
1890 Palmer Avenue, Suite 405
Larchmont NY 10538
Phone: 914/833-0700   Fax: 914/834-0888

Mr. M. Barry Levy
Regional Coordinator, New York City
Sharetts, Paley et al.
67 Broad Street, 26th Floor
New York NY 10004
Phone: 212/425-0055   Fax: 212/425-1797

Mr. John Bermingham
District Coordinator, Long Island
34 Audrey Avenue
Oyster Bay NY 11771
Phone: 516/624-7171   Fax: 516/624-7195

Ms. Ellen G. Kulik
Regional Coordinator, Syracuse
Bond, Schoeneck & King, LLP
One Lincoln Center
Syracuse NY 13202-1355
Phone: 315/422-0121   Fax: 315/422-3598

North Carolina

Mr. E. Thomas Watson
Regional Coordinator
Parker, Poe et al.
2600 Charlotte Plaza
201 S. College Street
Charlotte NC 28244
Phone: 704/372-9000   Fax: 704/334-4706

Ohio

Mr. Thomas Talcott
Regional Coordinator, Cleveland
Porter, Wright et al.
Suite 1700, Huntington Bldg.
925 Euclid Avenue
Cleveland OH 44115
Phone: 216/443-9000   Fax: 216/443-9011

Mr. Dixon F. Miller
Regional Coordinator, Columbus
Porter, Wright et al.
Huntington Center
41 South High Street
Columbus OH 43215-3406
Phone: 614/227-2000   Fax: 614/227-2100

Mr. Gary W. Gottschlich
Regional Coordinator, Dayton
Porter, Wright et al.
One Dayton Centre, Suite 1600
One South Main St., P.O. Box. 1805
Dayton OH 45401-1805
Phone: 513/449-6740   Fax: 513/449-6820

Oklahoma

Mr. Charles S. Turpin
Regional Coordinator, Oklahoma City
6112 North Villa
Oklahoma City OK 73112
Phone: 405/848-4805

Mr. Jonathan C. Neff
Regional Coordinator, Tulsa
Brune & Neff
230 Mid-Continent Tower
401 So. Boston Avenue
Tulsa OK 74103-4032
Phone: 918/599-8600   Fax: 918/599-8673

Oregon

Ms. Carol Emory
Regional Coordinator
Emory & Associates
1 SW Columbia, Suite 1990
Portland OR 97258
Phone: 503/226-6499   Fax: 503/226-2201

Mr. Keith C. Jones
Regional Coordinator
Drummond, Woodsum et al.
245 Commercial Street
Portland OR 04101
Phone: 207/772-1941   Fax: 207/772-3627

Pennsylvania

Mr. Timothy D. Charlesworth
Regional Coordinator, Allentown
Fitzpatrick, Lentz & Bubba, P.C.
P.O. Box 219
Center Valley PA 18034-0219
Phone: 610/797-9000   Fax: 610/797-6633

Mr. Robert Jones
Regional Coordinator, Eastern
Drinker, Biddle & Reath
Suite 1100, Philadelphia Nat'l. Bank Bldg.
1345 Chestnut Street
Philadelphia PA 19107-3496
Phone: 215/988-2745   Fax: 215/988-2757

Mr. David P. Hanson
Regional Coordinator, Western
School of Business Administration
Duquesne University
Pittsburgh PA 15282
Phone: 412/434-6238

Puerto Rico

Lic. A. J. Bennazar Zequeira
Regional Coordinator
Gonzalez & Bennazar
Capital Center Building, Arterial Hostos Avenue
South Tower, 9th Floor
San Juan PR 00918
Phone: 809/754-9191   Fax: 809/754-9325

South Carolina

Mr. Timothy D. Scranton
Regional Coordinator
Ten State Street, LLP
10 State Street
Charleston SC 29401
Phone: 803/937-0110   Fax: 803/937-4310

Mr. James V. Dunbar, Jr.
Regional Coordinator
Berry, Dunbar et al.
1200 Main Street, 8th Floor
P.O. Box 11645, Capitol Station
Columbia SC 29211-1645
Phone: 803/765-1030   Fax: 803/799-5536

Tennessee

Mr. Thomas W. Bell, Jr.
Regional Coordinator, Memphis
Armstrong, Allen, Prewitt, et al.
Brinkley Plaza
80 Monroe Avenue, Suite 700
Memphis TN 38103-2467
Phone: 901/523-8211   Fax: 901/524-4936

Mr. Stephen K. Rush
Regional Coordinator, Nashville
Farris, Warfield & Kanaday
Third National Financial Center
424 Church Street, Suite 1900
Nashville TN 37219-2387
Phone: 615/244-5200   Fax: 615/726-3185

Texas

Mr. Jay M. Vogelson
Regional Coordinator, Dallas & Ft. Worth
Stutzman & Bromberg
2200 Allianz Financial Center
2323 Bryan
Dallas TX 75201
Phone: 214/969-4900   Fax: 214/960-4999

Mr. Mark C. Joye
Regional Coordinator, Houston
Baker & Hostetler
1000 Louisiana, Suite 200
Houston TX 77002-5009
Phone: 713/751-1600   Fax: 713/751-1717

Mr. Arturo Torres
Regional Coordinator, McAllen
Martin, Drought & Torres, Inc.
111 First City Bank Tower
McAllen TX 78501
Phone: 210/686-2348   Fax: 210/686-2610

Mr. Frank B. Burney
Regional Coordinator, San Antonio
Martin, Drought & Torres, Inc.
111 First City Bank 25th Floor
300 Covent Street
San Antonio TX 78205-3789
Phone: 210/227-7591   Fax: 210/227-7924

Utah

Mr. Lee Ford Hunter
Regional Coordinator
Kirton, McConkie & Bushnell
1800 Eagle Gate Tower
60 East South Temple
Salt Lake City UT 84111
Phone: 801/328-3600   Fax: 801/321-4893

Vermont

Ms. Virginia A. Goddard
Regional Coordinator
Attorney at Law
157 Main Street
P.O. Box 419
North Springfield VT 05150-0419
Phone: 802/886-2499   Fax: 802/886-2446

Virginia

Mr. Jeffrey M. Gallagher
Regional Coordinator, Richmond & Norfolk
Mezzullo & McCandlish
1111 East Main Street, Suite 1500
P.O. Box 796
Richmond VA 23218
Phone: 804/775-3100   Fax: 804/775-3800

Washington

Mr. E. Charles Routh
Regional Coordinator
Garvey, Schubert, Adams & Barer
1191 Second Ave.
18th Floor
Seattle WA 98101
Phone: 206/464-3939   Fax: 206/464-0125

Wisconsin

Mr. Thomas F. Clasen
Regional Coordinator
Foley & Lardner
777 East Wisconsin Ave.
Milwaukee WI 53202-5367
Phone: 414/271-2400   Fax: 414/289-3791

Social Security Administration

6401 Security Boulevard / Baltimore, MD 21235
410/965-7700

INTRODUCTION

The Social Security Administration, which became an independent agency April 1, 1995, cooperates with other federal agencies in handling matters involving federal benefits for Americans living abroad.

Office of Operations

Office of Disability and Intl. Operations

1500 Woodlawn Drive / Baltimore MD 21241

Director
Mr. W. Burnell Hurt
410/966-7000   FAX 410/966-6005
Rm. 7000

Deputy Director
Mr. Edward C. Podhajsky
410/966-7002
Rm. 7000

Executive Officer
Ms. Sharyn McQuid
410/966-7006
Rm. 7330

6401 Security Blvd. / Baltimore MD 21235

Acting Director, Office of Intl. Operations
Mr. Frank Zamostny
410/965-9321
Rm. 4-B-2

Office of Programs & Policy

Office of International Policy
6401 Security Blvd. / Baltimore MD 21235

Associate Commissioner
Mr. James A. Kissko
410/965-7388   FAX 410/966-9797
Rm. 142

Staff Asst.
Ms. Anne Zwagil
410/965-7385
Rm. 142

Program Adviser
Ms. Lois Copeland
410/965-7383
Rm. 142

Director, Intl. Program Policy and Agreements Division
Mr. Barry Powell
410/965-3545   FAX 410/966-7025
Rm. 1104

Intl. Agreements Branch
Mr. Jack Rice
410/965-3553
Rm. 1104

Foreign Program Policy Branch
Ms. Sally Zeller
410/965-3564
Rm. 1104

Director, Intl. Activities Staff
Mr. Dennis Frederick
410/965-3558   FAX 410/966-7025
Rm. 1104

Trade and Development Agency

Mailing Address: Rm. 309, SA-16 / Washington, DC 20523

Deliveries: 1621 North Kent St., Suite 300 / Arlington, VA 22209

703-875-4357   FAX 703-875-4009
Email: info@tda.gov
http://www.tda.gov

INTRODUCTION

The Trade and Development Agency (TDA) promotes economic development in, and at the same time, exports of U.S. goods and services to developing and middle-income nations in Africa/Middle East , Asia/Pacific, Central Europe, Latin America and the Caribbean, and the New Independent States.

The agency funds feasibility studies, orientation visits, training grants, conferences, symposia, and various forms of technical assistance that supports specific projects. This enables American businesses to become involved in the planning of infrastructure and industrial projects in developing and middle-income nations. TDA makes its funds available on the condition that the foreign entity contracts with a U.S. firm to perform the actual work on the project. This affords American firms market entry, exposure, and information, thus helping them to establish a position in markets that are otherwise difficult to penetrate.

TDA AT A GLANCE

—Since the U.S. Trade and Development Agency's inception in 1981, TDA has been associated with approximately $7 billion in exports — or nearly $30 in exports for every dollar invested in TDA activities.

—In Fiscal Year 1996, TDA obligated $43.5 million for U.S. firms in 39 strategically targeted developing and middle-income countries in the following regions: Africa/Middle East; Asia/Pacific; Central and Eastern Europe; Latin America and the Caribbean; and the New Independent States (NIS).

—TDA's focus is the planning and design engineering phase of major infrastructure and industrial projects.

—TDA primarily is involved in these sectors: agriculture; energy; environment; health care; manufacturing; mining and minerals development; telecommunications; transportation; & water resources.

—TDA, through the Trade Promotion Coordinating Committee (TPCC), works closely with the Department of Commerce, The Export-Import Bank, the Overseas Private Investment Corporation, and other export Promotion agencies to advance American business interests abroad.

WHICH PROJECTS DOES TDA SUPPORT?

Because of its focused mission, TDA only considers projects that have potential to mature into significant business opportunities for U.S. companies. To be considered for funding, projects must:

* Face strong competition from foreign companies that receive subsidies and other support from their governments;

* Be a development priority of the country where the project is located and have the endorsement of the U.S. embassy in that nation;

* Represent an opportunity for sales of U.S. goods or services that is many times greater than the cost of TDA assistance; and

* Be likely to receive implementation financing, and have a procurement process open to U.S. firms.

TDA learns of viable public and private sector projects from the U.S. business community and from other government agencies, such as the Commerce Department's U.S. and Foreign Commercial Service (US&FCS) and the State Department's economic officers. It also receives project information from the public and private sectors of foreign countries.

Official requests for assistance must be made directly to TDA by the sponsoring organization (government or private sector) of the host country. A description of the proposed project should accompany the official letter of request to expedite the review process.

WHAT ARE FEASIBILITY STUDIES?

Feasibility Studies — which evaluate the technical, legal, economic, and financial aspects of a development project in the concept stage, are TDA's most important funding activity. Since these project plans are required by financial institutions to assess the creditworthiness of a project before it can go forward, they provide American firms the opportunity to get in on the "ground floor" of a project. Feasibility studies typically include procurement plans, contact information, technical data, financial information, and market studies — essential information for investors, developers, as well as providers of goods and services (including small businesses).

TDA-funded feasibility studies also advise project sponsors about the availability of specific U.S. equipment and services — advice that leads to the use of U.S. goods and services in the project's implementation. For example, a recent TDA study on a wastewater treatment plant in South America resulted in the sponsor buying millions of dollars of U.S. pollution control equipment that was specified in the feasibility study.

WHAT OTHER ACTIVITIES DOES TDA FUND?

Definitional Missions — teams of technical specialists contracted for a short-term visit to a host country to gather additional information to analyze whether to proceed with a feasibility study. Carried out exclusively by small and minority-owned business, Definitional Missions also provide American small business with an opportunity to establish working relationships with foreign officials.

Desk Studies — used by TDA when there is sufficient project information available, and an overseas visit is not necessary. In these situations, TDA hires a technical specialist to perform a review of the proposed project and to answer specific questions — without leaving the U.S.

Both of these evaluations review the nature of the project, its priority to the host government, its expected total cost, the likelihood of project financing, the need for a feasibility study, the scope of work and budget for the study, its environmental impact, the U.S. export potential, the expected impact on U.S. jobs, and the U.S. companies which could compete for procurement of goods and services for the project.

Based on the recommendations contained in the Definitional Mission or Desk Study report, the advice of the U.S. embassy, our internal analysis, and budget capabilities, TDA makes decisions on funding requests for feasibility studies.

U. S. Trade and Development Agency

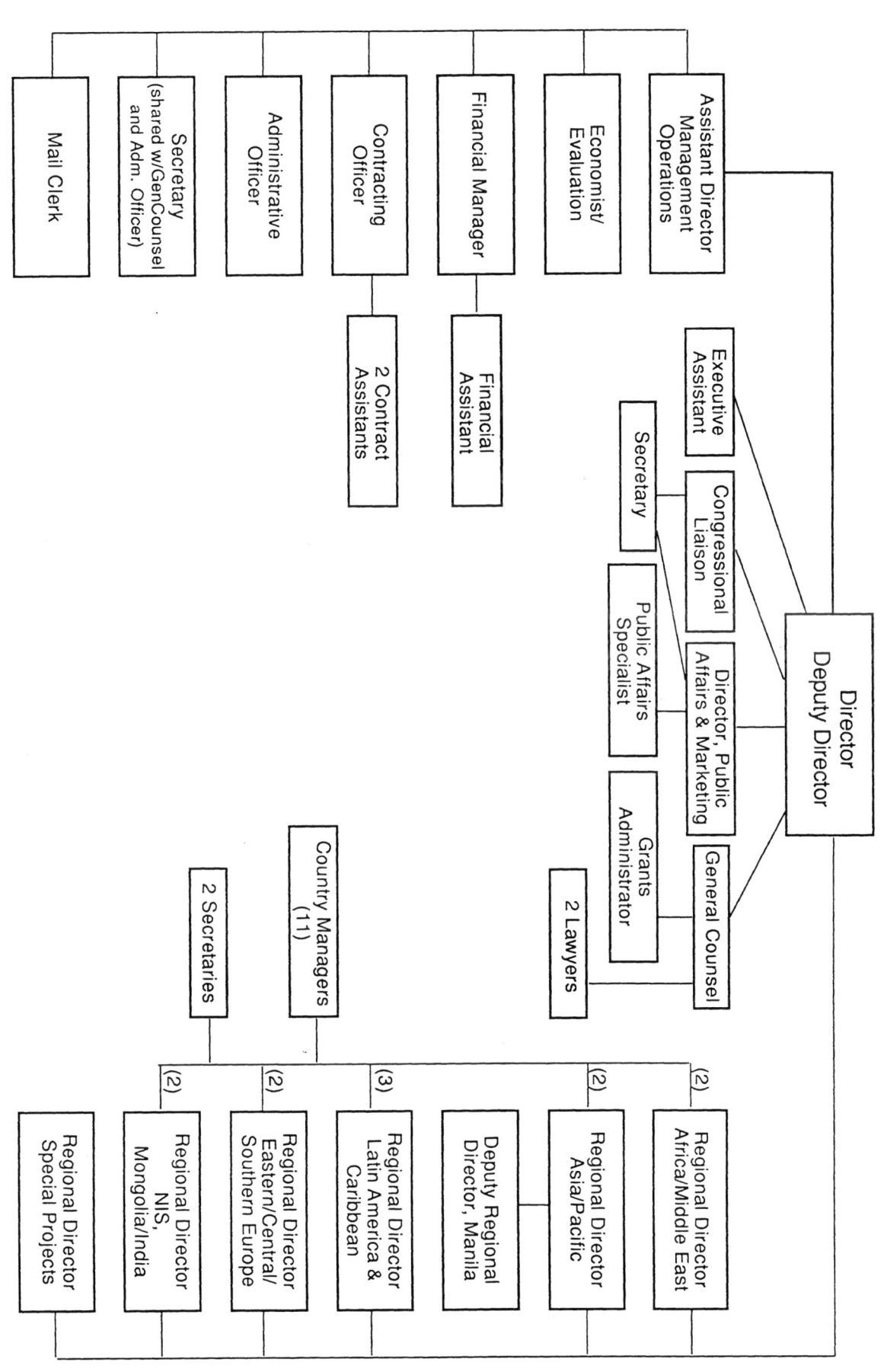

Director
Deputy Director

Executive Assistant

Congressional Liaison

Secretary

Director, Public Affairs & Marketing

Public Affairs Specialist

Grants Administrator

General Counsel

2 Lawyers

Assistant Director Management Operations

Economist/ Evaluation

Financial Manager

Financial Assistant

Contracting Officer

2 Contract Assistants

Administrative Officer

Secretary (shared w/GenCounsel and Adm. Officer)

Mail Clerk

Country Managers (11)

2 Secretaries

Regional Director Africa/Middle East (2)

Regional Director Asia/Pacific (2)

Deputy Regional Director, Manila

Regional Director Latin America & Caribbean (3)

Regional Director Eastern/Central/ Southern Europe (2)

Regional Director NIS, Mongolia/India (2)

Regional Director Special Projects

9/2/97

TDA sponsors *Technical Symposia*, reverse trade missions called *Orientation Visits*, and *Business Briefings*. These activities familiarize foreign decision-makers with U.S. goods and services and provide them an opportunity to meet with U.S. suppliers. At its conferences, U.S. companies hear the results of feasibility studies, learn the nature and type of procurements that will be associated with specific projects, and meet one-on-one with senior officials from the country or company sponsoring the project.

In certain regions, TDA also funds *Trade-Related Training*. This enables host country project personnel to receive necessary technical and managerial training when a U.S. firm is selected to implement the project. TDA also funds *Technical Assistance* to respond to the complex demands of a given project when required expertise is unavailable from the host country.

TDA also provides limited funds to Multilateral Development Banks (MDBs), including the World Bank, European Bank for Reconstruction and Development, Interamerican Development Bank, African Development Bank, and the International Finance Corporation. These TDA funds allow the MDBs to hire U.S. consultants to assist in planning or evaluating projects that they are considering. As a result, TDA gains valuable information about the projects' potential early in the process — information that we pass on to American businesses.

COST SHARING & SUCCESS FEES

Costs associated with feasibility studies in private investor projects are shared between TDA and the U.S. firm's willingness to share part of the cost of the study demonstrates its commitment to the project's overall success. Cost sharing is also required on certain public sector projects.

In private sector investor projects, coproduction arrangement, and other appropriate situations, TDA has adopted a policy that requires reimbursement of its contribution to a project. This "success fee" is collected when the project is implemented and the U.S. firm involved in the study obtains significant economic benefit related to the project for which the study was funded. to actual implementation.

INFORMATION RESOURCES

TDA offers a variety of services and information resources to help American firms win contracts for projects overseas.

General inquiries about TDA's services should be made through TDA's library, located at the agency's office in Rosslyn, Va. In addition to providing information about TDA services, the library maintains final reports on all TDA activities. The library also can provide details on purchasing copies of completed feasibility studies through the Department of Commerce's National Technical Information Service.

TDA has two regular publications: The TDA *Biweekly*, which is available by subscription, provides U.S. suppliers and manufacturers with timely information on agency-supported projects. The TDA *Update* contains current items of interest on a variety of program activities.

TDA information also is available via the Internet at http://www.tda.gov. The site features a catalog of TDA library holdings, agency news, information on TDA-sponsored studies, and more.

Requests for Proposals to conduct TDA-funded feasibility studies are listed in the *Commerce Business Daily*. Call 202-482-0632 for on-line computer related information and 202-783-3238 for subscription information.

Information on Definitional Mission opportunities can be obtained by calling TDA's Definitional Mission Hotline at 703-875-7447. Small and minority U.S. firms that wish to be included in TDA's consultant database and considered for future Definitional Mission solicitations should contact the Contracts Office.

Office of the Director

Director
Mr. J. Joseph Grandmaison
703/875-4311   FAX 703/875-4009

Personal: born 5/19/43 in Nashua, New Hampshire.

Education: B.A. in business administration, Burdett College, 1963.

Professional: 1977-81, federal co-chairman, New England Regional Commission, Boston. 1981-93, self-employed consultant, government and community relations. 1984-86, regional community relational director, Warner-AMEX Cable Communications. 1988-90, adjunct professor, College of Communications, Boston University. 1988-93, vice president, Weil and Howe (Augusta, Maine). 1990, democratic nominee for governor of New Hampshire. 1993-present, director, U.S. Trade & Development Agency.

A New Hampshire native, Joseph Grandmaison became director of the Trade and Development Agency in August, 1993.

Recently cited in The Wall Street Journal as "the most lean and efficient agency there is" by the Coalition for Employment through Exports, Grandmaison has made TDA a major player on the Clinton Administration's trade promotion team. During his tenure, the agency has broadened its outreach efforts, aggressively marketing its services to small- and medium-sized businesses, strategically expanding its range of activities, and actively participating in the Trade Promotion Coordinating Committee (TPCC).

Under Grandmaison's leadership, TDA organized the historic Jordan Rift Valley Development Symposium, bringing together U.S., Jordanian, and Israeli business and government leaders for the first time. It also sponsored a landmark business conference on the growing South American market that resulted in more than 700 deal-making meetings between U.S. and South American business leaders.

Grandmaison has extensive background in both business and government. Before coming to TDA, he was vice president of Weil & Howe, a management consulting and project development company specializing in energy and environmental matters. He also has served as a consultant to both public and private sector clients, specializing in community and government relations, politics, and economic development.

From 1977 to 1980, he served as the federal co-chairman of the New England Regional Commission. The Commission conducted programs in the areas of transportation, energy, economic development, international trade, tourism promotion, and hazardous waste management. Grandmaison also served as chairman of the Federal Regional Council, which is comprised of the major Federal officials in the region. The Council was responsible for streamlining and coordinating the delivery of Federal programs in New England.

Grandmaison was the Democratic nominee for Governor of New Hampshire in 1990. He served as chairman of the New Hampshire

Democratic Party from 1987 to 1990. He has taught at Boston University's School of Public Communication and served as a Fellow at Harvard University's John F. Kennedy School of Government.

Grandmaison is a graduate of the Burdett College School of Business Administration. He attended the Senior Management Program at Harvard's JFK School of Government.

Deputy Director
Ms. Nancy D. Frame
703/875-4311

General Counsel
Mr. Kenneth Fries
703/875-4357

Special Assistant for Public Affairs/Marketing
Mr. Donald Dunn
703/875-4357

Congressional Liaison
Mr. Ned Cabot
703/875-4357

Attorney Adviser
Mr. Cam Trowbridge & Ms. Deborah Forhan
703/875-4357

Executive Assistant
Ms. Eatrice A. James
703/875-4311

Office of Programs

Regional Directors

Africa and Middle East
Mr. John Richter
703/875-4357

East Asia and Pacific Islands
Mr. Geoffrey R. Jackson
703/875-4357

Central, Eastern and Southern Europe
Mr. Rodney Azama
703/875-4357

Latin America and the Caribbean
Mr. Albert W. Angulo
703/875-4357

New Independent States, South Asia and Mongolia
Mr. Daniel D. Stein
703/875-4357

Special Projects
Ms. Barbara Bradford
703/875-4357

Deputy Regional Director (Asia)
Mr. John Herrman
703/875-4357

Office of Management Operations

Assistant Director for Management Operations
Ms. Deirdre Curley
703/875-4159

U.S. Agency for International Development

1300 Pennsylvania Ave., NW / Washington, DC 20523-0001

Congressional Affairs: 202/647-8264
Contracting/Small Business Inquiries: 703/875-1551
Development Information: 703/875-4818
Foreign Disaster Assistance: 202/647-5916
Personnel: 202/647-4000
Press: 202/647-4274
Public Inquiries: 202/647-1850

http://www.info.usaid.gov/

INTRODUCTION

The U.S. Agency for International Development (AID) is the federal agency responsible for managing U.S. foreign economic and humanitarian assistance programs in more than 100 countries. AID routinely works with private U.S. business and non-profit organizations as partners in foreign development. AID operations are remarkably diverse, including health programs in Asia; assistance to farmers in Africa to increase productivity; and hurricane relief in the Caribbean. A central thrust of AID activities worldwide always includes the development of democratic governments and the encouragement of private business and free-market economies.

AID oversees operations across the developing world, Central and Eastern Europe, and the republics of the former Soviet Union. Programs are currently being implemented which improve delivery of cost-effective health care; reduce population growth rates; promote energy efficiency and the utilization of new environmental technologies; support economic policy reforms that stimulate growth; and facilitate private financing for housing and urban services for impoverished families.

Notable new programs aim at private sector development in the emerging economies of Eastern Europe and the former Soviet Union. AID technical assistance programs have augmented major privatization efforts in Russia, for example, and U.S.-financed investment advisers have helped secure significant U.S. investment in the Czech Republic and in Poland.

AID-sponsored organizations are located in all countries in which bilateral programs are being implemented, with in-country representatives subject to direction by the U.S. diplomatic mission to the particular country, and with the organizations reporting to the Agency's assistant administrators for the five regions - Africa, Asia, Europe, Latin America and the Caribbean, and the Near East.

The administrator of AID serves as the director of the U.S. International Development Cooperation Agency (IDCA). The IDCA, of which both AID and the Overseas Private Investment Corporation (OPIC) are a part, coordinates the Administration's overall political and economic policy toward developing countries.

Office of the Administrator (A/AID)

Administrator
Mr. J. Brian Atwood
202/712-4040
Rm. 6.09 - 010 (A/AID)

AGENCY FOR INTERNATIONAL DEVELOPMENT

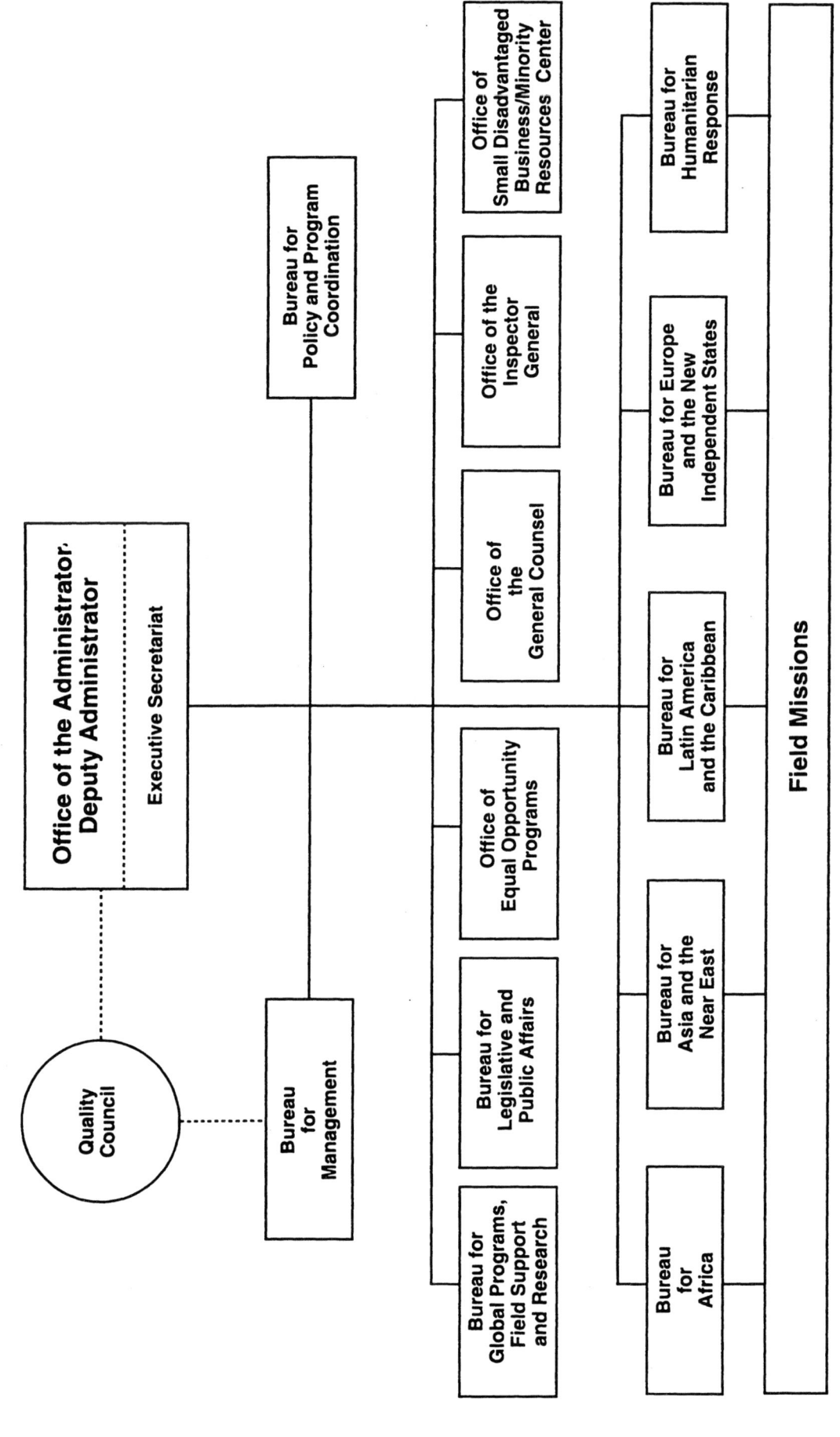

Personal: born 7/25/42 in Wareham, Mass.

Education: B.A. in history and government, Boston Univ., 1964.

Professional: 1964-66, management intern, National Security Agency. 1966-72, foreign service officer, U.S. Dept. of State (Ivory Coast, Spain). 1972-77, legislative assistant, U.S. Sen. Thomas Eagleton, (D-Mo.). 1977-79, deputy assistant secretary for congressional relations; 1979-81, assistant secretary for congressional relations, U.S. Dept. of State. 1981-82, dean of professional studies and academic affairs, Foreign Service Institute (Wash., DC). 1982-83, vice president, International Reporting and Information Systems (Wash., D.C.). 1983-84, executive director, Democratic Senatorial Campaign Committee. 1985-93, president, National Democratic Institute for International Affairs (Wash., DC). 1993, under secretary for management, U.S. Department of State. 1993-present, administrator, U.S. Agency for International Development.

J. Brian Atwood has served as administrator of the U.S. Agency for International Development (USAID) since 1993. His appointment followed years of service in the federal government at the National Security Agency, the State Department, and on the Hill. He has also been active in Democratic politics.

The administrator of the USAID plans, directs, and coordinates the operations of the agency. Atwood, a foreign affairs veteran with extensive contacts in many of the world's new democracies, formulates foreign assistance policy and oversees development programs. He also supervises the activities of 3,000 USAID employees overseas and in the U.S. In addition, he serves as the President's special coordinator for international disaster assistance. In the appropriations bill for the State Department's FY 1998 funding, USAID would come under the authority of the Secretary of State, while remaining a distinct agency.

Atwood entered government as a foreign service officer in 1966, serving in the Ivory Coast and in Spain. After working as a legislative assistant in the U.S. Senate, he returned to the State Department in the Carter Administration to handle congressional relations, first as a deputy, and later as an assistant secretary of State.

Atwood has been involved in Democratic politics since 1983, when he served under then-Senator Lloyd Bentsen (D-Texas) as executive director of the Democratic Senatorial Campaign Committee. He later became president of the National Democratic Institute for International Affairs, the democracy-building arm of the Democratic Party. He significantly expanded NDI's educational and election monitoring activities, notably in Chile, Panama, Nicaragua, Pakistan, the Philippines, Eastern Europe, and the nations of the former Soviet Union.

USAID provides a wide range of economic, technical, and humanitarian assistance worldwide. After becoming director, Atwood moved quickly to reorganize the agency, simplifying its structure and closing 26 missions. Atwood announced a new mission for the agency, sustainable development, and targeted its programs on five basic objectives: population and health, broad-based economic growth,

protecting the environment, democracy-building, and humanitarian aid.

Deputy Administrator
Ms. Harriet C. Babbitt
202/712-4070
Rm. 6.09-025 (A/AID)

Personal: born 11/13/47 in Charleston, W.Va.

Education: Univ. of Americas, Mexico City, 1965. Sweet Briar Coll., 1965-67. Univ. of Madrid (Spain), 1967-68. B.A. in Spanish (with honors), Ariz. State University, 1969. J.D. (with distinction), Ariz. State Univ. Coll. of Law, 1972.

Professional: 1972-73, law clerk, Ariz. Supreme Court Chief Justice Jack D. H. Hayes. 1973, legal writing instructor, Ariz. State Univ. Coll. of Law. 1974-93, attorney, Robbins and Green (Phoenix, Ariz.). 1982-85, judge pro tempore, Superior Court of Maricopa County. 1988-93, director, National Democratic Institute for International Affairs. 1993-97, permanent representative of the U.S., Organization of American States. 1998-present, deputy administrator, USAID.

On October 2, 1997, President Clinton nominated Ambassador Harriet Babbitt to be deputy administrator at the U.S. Agency for International Development (USAID). She was subsequently confirmed by the Senate and began work at AID in January, 1998.

The deputy administrator is responsible for the day-to-day management of USAID, including decision-making and implementation of agency policy. The deputy also assists the administrator in all responsibilities, serve as the acting administrator in his absence, and acting as the primary advisor to the administrator on policy and operations, particularly with respect to sustainable development.

Babbitt had served as the U.S. Permanent Representative to the Organization of American States since 1993. She came to the OAS from the National Democratic Institute for International Affairs, an organization sponsored by the Democratic Party that promotes democracy around the world. As a member of the board of directors, Babbitt represented the NDI at international electoral and human rights conferences in Angola, Czechoslovakia, and Venezuela. She also served as an election monitor in Chile, Paraguay, Guatemala, and Czechoslovakia.

Babbitt is fluent in Spanish and is married to U.S. Interior Secretary Bruce Babbitt. They have two sons.

Chief of Staff
Richard L. McCall Jr.
202/712-5090
Rm. 6.08-025

Personal: born 05/06/42 in Detroit, Michigan.

Education: B.A., Hastings College. Graduate study (2 years), University of Nebraska.

Professional: 1978-80, deputy staff director for international economic policy and foreign assistance, Senate Committee on Foreign Relations. 1980, assistant secretary of state for international organization affairs, Dept. Of State. 1981-82, legislative assistant for foreign policy; 1982-85, deputy staff director for foreign and defense policy, Senate Democratic Policy Committee. 1985-91, legislative assistant for foreign policy, Sen. John F. Kerry. 1991-93, professional staff member, Subcommittee on International Economic Policy, Oceans and the Environment, Senate Committee on Foreign Relations. 1993-present, chief of staff, U.S. Agency for International Development.

Richard L. McCall Jr. was appointed chief of staff at the USAID in May 1993. As such, McCall is the USAID administrator's chief political adviser. His responsibilities include acting as a liaison with the deputy secretary of state and as an interagency liaison with the departments of State, Treasury, and Agriculture and with the National Security Council, the Export-Import Bank, and the Overseas Private Investment Corporation. McCall also serves as the congressional liaison for implementing the reorganization of USAID.

Prior to joining USAID, from 1978 to 1980, McCall worked for the Senate Committee on Foreign Relations as deputy staff director for international economic policy and foreign assistance. In 1980 during the Carter administration, McCall was assistant secretary of state for international organization affairs. Before serving as deputy staff director for foreign and defense policy for the Senate Democratic Policy Committee in 1982, McCall worked for the committee as a legislative assistant for foreign policy from 1981-82. In 1985, McCall served as Senator John Kerry's legislative assistant for foreign policy.

McCall was a professional staff member from 1991 to 1993 on the Senate Committee on Foreign Relations and the Subcommittee on International Economic Policy, Oceans and the Environment. The subcommittee has legislative responsibility for bilateral and multilateral foreign assistance programs. In addition, McCall has been a foreign policy legislative assistant for Sens. Hubert H. Humphrey, Muriel Humphrey, and Gale McGee.

Born in Detroit, Michigan, McCall was raised in Nebraska and Wyoming. He has a bachelor's degree from Hastings College in Nebraska and completed two years of graduate study at the University of Nebraska.

McCall resides in Falls Church, Va., he is married and has two sons.

Counselor
Kelly C. Kammerer
202/712-0200
Rm. 4.09-034

See profile under Bureau for Asia and the Near East.

Office of the Executive Secretariat (ES)

Executive Secretary
Mr. Ryan Conroy
202/712-0700
Rm. 6.08-036 (ES)

Bureau for Policy & Program Coordination (PPC)

Office of the Assistant to the Administrator

Acting Assistant to the Administrator
Mr. Larry A. Garber
202/712-5820
Rm. 6.08-119 (AA/PPC)

Cross-Cutting Initiative

Senior Advisor/Participation
Ms. Diane E. Lavoy
202/712-5820
Rm. 6.08-073 (PPC/CCI)

Office of Humanitarian Response

Deputy Assistant to the Administrator
Mr. Larry A. Garber
202/647-8592
Rm. 3892 NS (PPC/HR)

Office of Health, Population & Human Development

Deputy Assistant to the Administrator
Mr. Nils M. Daulaire
202/647-8592
Rm. 3892 NS (PPC/PHD)

Office of Environment

Acting Director
Mr. James S. Hester
202/647-9012
Rm. 3947A NS (PPC/ENV)

Office of Democracy

Deputy Assistant to the Administrator
Mr. Larry A. Garber
202/712-5820
Rm. 6.08-119 (PPC/DEM)

Office of Development Partners

Director
Ms. Cathryn Thorup
202/712-5250
Rm. 6.08-075 (PPC/DP)

Office of Economics

Director
Mr. Michael J. Crosswell
202/712-5820
Rm. 6.07-005 (PPC/ECON)

Office of Program Coordination

Director
Mr. Karl J. Schwartz

202/712-4060
Rm. 6.07-014 (PPC/PC)

Center for Development Information & Evaluation

Director
Mr. Gerald M. Britan
202/712-5450
Rm. 6.07-1654 (PPC/CDIE)

Bureau for Africa (AFR)

Office of the Assistant Administrator

Acting Assistant Administrator
Ms. Carol A. Peasley
202/712-0500
Rm. 4.08-037 (AA/AFR)

Education: B.S. in economics, Univ. of Calif. at Santa Barbara, 1968. M.S. in development economics, Sussex Univ. (England), 1969. MBA in management, Stanford Graduate School of Business, 1982.

Professional: 1970-97, various positions with the U.S. Agency for International Development, including: 1970-75, international development intern, program economist, Nepal; 1976-78, program economist, Costa Rica; 1979-82, division chief, Central America, office of development resources in the Latin America and Caribbean bureau; 1982-84, dep. dir., Thailand; 1984-85, asst. dir for finance, Latin America and Caribbean bureau; 1985-88, deputy, then director, office of project development, Africa bureau; 1988-93, mission director, Malawi; 1993-96, senior deputy assistant administrator for the Africa bureau; August 1996-present, acting assistant administrator for Africa.

Since August of 1996, Carol Peasley, a career minister with the US Agency for International Development, has been the acting assistant administrator for Africa and therefore responsible for all USAID activities on the continent. In FY 1997, this included nearly $1 billion of USAID resources: $665 million of Development Assistance funds, $300 million of food aid, and $34 million of other resources. From Fall of 1993 to August of 1996, she was the senior deputy assistant administrator for the Africa bureau. At press time, no nominee had been named.

Immediately before returning to Washington, Peasley was the mission director for USAID/Malawi for five years. Her earlier positions included: service as an international development intern and then program economist in Nepal; program economist in Costa Rica; division chief for Central America in the office of development resources in the Latin America and Caribbean bureau, deputy director for USAID in Thailand; and assistant director for finance in the Latin America and Caribbean bureau of USAID.

Prior to joining USAID as an international development intern in 1970, Peasley worked as a research economist at the Export-Import Bank for about six months.

Peasley appeared before the subcommittee on Africa of the U.S. House International Relations Committee in May of 1997 and outlined the four basic principles which are framing AID's vision of Africa's future: Africa's success depends on Africans themselves, economic growth is imperative, crisis prevention on this fragile continent is critical, and strategic coordination is essential.

Disaster Response Coordination Staff

Chief Special Projects Officer
Mr. David Adams
202/712-0190
Rm. 4.07-105 (AFR/AA/DRC)

Office of East African Affairs

Director
Mr. Phillip-Michael Gary
202/712-0410
Rm. 4.07-014 (AFR/EA)

Deputy Director
Ms. Patricia Rader
202/712-0410
Rm. 4.07-012 (AFR/EA)

REDSO/Kenya/Djibouti/Rwanda - Ms. Gretchen Sierra-Zorita
202/712-4115
Rm. 4.07-103 (AFR/EA)

Uganda - Mr. Dulal Datta
202/712-1518
Rm. 4.07-076 (AFR/EA)

Madagascar/Tanzania - Mr. Rick Handler
202/712-0251
Rm. 4.07-082 (AFR/EA)

Burundi/Rwanda - Mr. Ron Ullrich
202/712-1073
Rm. 4.07-084 (AFR/EA)

Eritrea/Sudan - Ms. Antoinette Ferrara
202/712-5367
Rm. 4.07-104 (AFR/EA)

Somalia/Ethiopia - Ms. Jeanne Pryor
202/712-1504
Rm. 4.07-086 (AFR/EA)

Horn of Africa - Ms. Patricia Rader
202/712-0410
Rm. 4.07-012 (AFR/EA)

Office of Southern African Affairs

Director
Mr. William Jeffers
202/712-4790
Rm. 4.07-004 (AFR/SA)

Deputy Director
Ms. Maureen Dugan
202/712-4790
Rm. 4.07-005 (AFR/SA)

South Africa - Mr. Will Elliott
202/712-1484
Rm. 4.07-042 (AFR/SA)

Malawi - Mr. David Washburn
202/712-5162
Rm. 4.07-055 (AFR/SA)

Mozambique/Angola - Ms. Deborah Mendelson
202/712-1475
Rm. 4.07-053 (AFR/SA)

Namibia - Ms. Gail Spence
202/712-4877
Rm. 4.07-403 (AFR/SA)

Zambia - Ms. Meredith Scovill
202/712-5731
Rm. 4.07-052 (AFR/SA)

Zimbabwe - Mr. David Cohn

202/712-5029
Rm. 4.07-044 (AFR/SA)

RCSA - Ms. Patricia Jordan
202/712-0302
Rm. 4.07-063 (AFR/SA)

Office of West African Affairs

Director
Mr. Harry Lightfoot
202/712-0220
Rm. 4.06-001 (AFR/WA)

Deputy Director
Ms. Carol Grisby
202/712-0220
Rm. 4.06-002 (AFR/WA)

Club du Sahel/Regional Develop. Officer - Ms. Joan Atherton
202/712-4955
Rm. 4.07-094 (AFR/WA)

Eq. Guinea/Mauritana/Sao Tome & Principe - Mr. Bernard Lane
202/712-4153
Rm. 4.06-012 (AFR/WA)

Gambia/Ghana - Mr. Thomas Marr
202/712-0366
Rm. 4.06-014 (AFR/WA)

Liberia/Sierra Leone - Ms. Minnie S. Wright
202/712-4175
Rm. 4.06-081 (AFR/WA)

Niger/Cape Verde/Guinea - Ms. Louise Werlin
202/712-5441
Rm. 4.06-016 (AFR/WA)

Nigeria - Mr. Neil Woodruff
202/712-1824
Rm. 4.06-023 (AFR/WA)

Senegal/Car/Gabon - Mr. George Thompson
202/712-4128
Rm. 4.06-022 (AFR/WA)

Togo/REDSO/WCOBenin - Mr. Claude Reece
202/712-0958
Rm. 4.06-082 (AFR/WA)

Program Support/Economic Division
Chief
Mr. Leroy Jackson
202/712-0872
Rm. 4.07-015 (AFR/WA/PSEA)

Cameroon/Burkina Faso/Mali - Ms. Doral Watts
202/712-0585
Rm. 4.06-080 (AFR/WA)

Office of Development Planning

Director
Mr. James Govan
202/712-0230
Rm. 4.08-044 (AFR/DP)

Office of Sustainable Development

Director
Mr. Jerome Wolgin
202/712-1660
Rm. 4.06-119 (AFR/SD)

Bureau for Asia and the Near East (ANE)

Office of the Assistant Administrator

Acting Assistant Administrator
Mr. Kelly Kammerer
202/712-0200
Rm. 4.09-034 (ANE/AA)

Education: B.A., Univ. of Notre Dame. J.D., Univ. of Virginia Law School.

Professional: 1963-65, Peace Corps volunteer, Colombia. 1970-74, dep. gen. counsel, Peace Corps. 1975-present, asst. gen. counsel; sr. dep. general counsel; acting general counsel; director of congressional relations; mission director in Nepal; counselor; acting asst. administrator, Bureau for Asia and the Near East, U.S. Agency for International Development.

Kelly Kammerer is currently serving as acting assistant administrator of the Bureau for Asia and the Near East at the U.S. Agency for International Development (USAID).

Kammerer has been with USAID in a variety of roles since 1975. Before taking the acting assistantship for Asia and the Near East, he had served as counselor for USAID since January of 1994. As counselor, he provided advice to the administrator and other senior staff on a wide range of policy, operational, and management matters. The counselor holds the most senior career officer position in the agency and serves as an ombudsman for employees.

Prior to becoming counselor, Kammerer was USAID mission director in Nepal from 1989 to 1993. He served in Washington as director of congressional relations from 1982 to 1989, as acting general counsel and senior deputy general counsel from 1978 to 1982, and as assistant general counsel from 1975 to 1978.

Before joining USAID, Kammerer served as deputy general counsel for the Peace Corps from 1970 to 1974. He was a Reginald Heber Smith Fellow at the University of Pennsylvania Law School from 1968 to 1970. He served as a Peace Corps volunteer in Colombia from 1963 to 1965.

Kammerer has a B.A. from the University of Notre Dame and a J.D. from the University of Virginia Law School. He is a member of the New York, Florida, Virginia and DC bars.

Deputy Assistant Administrator for Asia
Mr. Dirk Dijkerman
202/712-0300
Rm. 4.08-037 (ANE/AA)

Deputy Assistant Administrator for Near East
Mr. Terrence Brown
202/712-0300
Rm. 4.09-036 (ANE/AA)

Secretariat for U.S. - Asia Environmental Partnership

Mr. Larry Crandall
202/712-0270
Rm. 4.10-001 (ANE/AA)

Office of East & South Asian Affairs

Director
Mr. Sidney Chernenkoff
202/712-1990
Rm. 4.10-007 (ANE/ESA)

Philippines - Ms. Paula Bryan (Acting)
202/712-1592
Rm. 4.10-054 (ANE/EA/PHIL)

Indonesia - Ms. Paula Bryan (Acting)
202/712-1592
Rm. 4.10-054 (ANE/EA/I)

Mongolia - Ms. Calista Downey
202/712-1002
Rm. 4.10-062 (ANE/EA/M)

Cambodia - Mr. Clinton Doggett
202/712-0409
Rm. 4.10-051 (ANE/EA/C)

Nepal/Sri Lanka/Maldives - Mr. Jerry Tarter
202/712-0678
Rm. 4.10-066 (ANE/SA/NS)

Pakistan - Ms. Carol Kiranbay
202/647-6967
Rm. 3318 (ANE/SA/P)

India - Mr. Jerry Tarter
202/712-0678
Rm. 4.10-066 (ANE/SA/I)

Bangladesh - Mr. Louie Kohn
202/712-0253
Rm. 4.10-061 (ANE/SA/B)

Office of Middle East Affairs

Director
Ms. Kimberly Finan
202/712-0050
Rm. 4.10-003 (ANE/MEA)

Egypt - Ms. Kay Freeman
202/712-0050
Rm. 4.10-021 (ANE/ENA/E)

Morocco/Yemen/Oman/Algeria - Ms. Maryanne Hoirup-Bacolod
202/712-0050
Rm. 4.10-023 (ANE/ENA/MYO)

West Bank/Gaza Strip - Ms. Dorothy Young
202/712-0050
Rm. 4.10-033 (ANE/ME/WB/G)

Israel/Lebanon - Ms. Pirie Gall
202/712-0050
Rm. 4.10-032 (ANE/ME/JIL)

Jordan - Ms. Pirie Gall (Acting)
202/712-0050
Rm. 4.10-032 (ANE/ME/J)

Office of Operations & Resource Allocation

Director
Ms. Mary Lewellen
202/712-4820
Rm. 4.09-057 (ANE/ORA)

Office of Strategic & Economic Analysis

Director
Ms. Carol Becker (Acting)
202/712-0040
Rm. 4.09-050 (ANE/SEA)

Bureau for Europe & the New Independent States (ENI)

Office of the Assistant Administrator

Acting Assistant Administrator
Mr. Donald L. Pressley
202/712-0290
Rm. 5.06-193 (ENI/AA)

Education: B.A., Univ. of S.C., 1967. M.B.A., Univ. of S.C., 1968. J.D., Georgetown Univ., 1975.

Professional: 1968-72, U.S. Army (retired as captain). 1975-86, regional legal advisor, USAID. 1986-90, president, Columbia Resources, Inc. (Wash., D.C.). 1990-92, director, office of European affairs; 1992-93, USAID Rep. to the UN Organizations in Geneva; 1993-95, USAID Rep. to Poland; July 1995 - July 1997, deputy asst. admin.; Aug. 1997-present, acting asst. admin., Bureau for Europe and the New Independent States, U.S. Agency for International Development.

In August of 1997, Thomas Dine left his position as assistant administrator for Europe and the New Independent States at USAID to join Radio Free Europe. At press time, no nominee had been named and Donald Pressley served in an acting capacity. The office is responsible for USAID's assistance programs to the 27 countries that today constitute the former Communist bloc, as well as to Ireland, Cyprus, and Turkey.

Pressley brings over 20 years of management experience to support his current function. A career foreign service officer, Pressley has served in six overseas posts in Europe, Asia, and the Middle East. Pressley's legal training, small business hands-on experience, and his successive management positions at USAID give him a unique combination of skills to head this large and complex assistance program.

Since 1990, Pressley has managed all aspects of the Central Europe and NIS assistance programs totaling over $7 billion. Immediately prior to being named acting assistant administrator he was the deputy assistant administrator at the bureau. He directed the U.S. assistance program to Poland during the height of its funding from 1993-1995. Earlier, he established the USAID office in Geneva and provided direct policy oversight for the $140 million per year of USAID funds going to UN organizations.

Between stints at USAID, Pressley, from 1986-1990, directed a successful private business specializing in international trade and investment. Pressley first joined USAID after law school in 1975 and served for the next ten years as a legal advisor and government attorney at USAID headquarters in Washington, D.C. and at field missions in Pakistan, Afghanistan, India, Nepal, Sri Lanka, Bangladesh, Thailand, Philippines, the South Pacific, and Egypt.

Pressley earned his B.A. and MBA from the University of South Carolina after which he enlisted in the Army. He later received his

J.D. from Georgetown University. He and his wife Sherry have two children.

Acting Deputy Assistant Administrator
Ms. Barbara Turner
202/712-0080
Rm. 5.06-191 (ENI/AA)

Deputy Assistant Administrator
Mr. Brian Kline
202/712-0260
Rm. 5.06-192 (ENI/AA)

Office of Program Coordination and Strategy

Director
Ms. Patricia Matheson
202/712-0367
Rm. 5.06-055 (ENI/PCS)

Office of New Independent States Country Affairs

Acting Director
Ms. Robin Phillips
202/712-0177
Rm. 5.06-157 (ENI/NCA)

OIC/Russia
Mr. Richard Steelman
202/712-0518
Rm. 5.06-154 (ENI/NCA/R)

Central Asian Republics Desk

(Almaty, Kazakstan; Bishkek, Kyrgyz Republic; Dushanbe, Tajikstan; Ashgabat, Turkmenistan; Tashkent , Uzbekistan)
Ms. Theresa Ware
202/712-0365
Rm. 5.06-155 (ENI/NCA/CAR)

West NIS Desk

(Kiev, Ukraine; Chisinau, Moldova; Minsk, Belarus)
Ms. Sherry Grossman
202/712-0542
Rm. 5.06-158 (ENI/NCA/WN)

Caucasus Desk

(Yerevan, Armenia; Tiblisi, Georgia; Baku, Azerbaijan)
Ms. Dagnija Kreslins
202/712-0762
Rm. 5.06-159 (ENI/NCA/C)

Office of European Country Affairs

Director
Mr. David Cowles
202/712-1751
Rm. 5.06-010 (ENI/ECA)

Deputy Director
Ms. Maria Mamlouk
202/712-5212
Rm. 5.06-012 (ENI/ECA)

Bosnia-Herzegovnia;Croatia Desk

Ms. Ellen Leddy
202/712-1898

Rm. 5.06-003 (ENI/ECA)

Northern Tier Division

(Chief and Czech Republic/Lithuania Desk)
Mr. William Duncan
202/712-1954
Rm. 5.06-015 (ENI/ECA/NT)

(Hungary, Slovenia Desk) - Mr. Brian Wickland
202/712-5248
Rm. 5.06-022 (ENI/ECA/NT)

(Slovak Republic/Estonia Desk) - Ms. Nan Newman
202/712-1934
Rm. 5.06-001 (ENI/ECA/NT)

(Poland Desk) - Mr. Brian Wickland (Acting)
202/712-5248
Rm. 5.06-022 (ENI/ECA/NT)

(Turkey/Latvia Desk) - Ms. Denise Lee
202/712-4916
Rm. 5.06-033 (ENI/ECA/NT)

Southern Tier Division

(Chief and Albania/Macedonia Desk)
Mr. Richard Hough
202/712-1601
Rm. 5.06-014 (ENI/ECA/ST)

(Bulgaria/Cyprus Desk) - Ms. Laura Libanti
202/712-5876
Rm. 5.06-024 (ENI/ECA/ST)

(Romania Desk) - Mr. James E. Watson
202/712-4843
Rm. 5.06-023 (ENI/ECA/ST)

Office of Enterprise Development

Director
Mr. Richard Johnson
202/712-1690
Rm. 5.08-101 (ENI/ED)

Small Business Division
Chief
Mr. Paul Novick
202/712-4812
Rm. 5.08-109 (ENI/ED/SB)

Agriculture and Agribusiness Division
Chief
Mr. Charles Uphaus
202/712-1172
Rm. 5.08-106 (ENI/ED/AG)

Enterprise Funds Division
Chief
Mr. Garry Imhoff
202/712-5966
Rm. 5.08-103 (ENI/ED/EF)

Office of Democracy, Governance and Social Reform

Director
Mr. Tom Nicastro
202/712-1490
Rm. 5.07-118 (ENI/DGSR)

Civil Society Division
Chief
Ms. Maryann Riegelman
202/712-1253
Rm. 5.07-115 (ENI/DGSR/CS)

Rule of Law and Governance Division
Chief
Mr. Howard Sumka
202/712-1415
Rm. 5.07-116 (ENI/DGSR/RLG)

Human Resources Development & Social Reform Division
Chief
Ms. Carolyn Coleman
202/712-1830
Rm. 5.07-062 (ENI/DGSR/HRDSR)

Health Reform and Humanitarian Assistance Division
Chief
Ms. Mary Ann Micka
202/712-4781
Rm. 5.07-004 (ENI/DGSR/HRHA)

Office of Privatization and Economic Restructuring

Acting Director
Mr. Richard Burns
202/712-1332
Rm. 2.06-012 (ENI/PER)

Capital Markets and Banking Division
Chief
Ms. Mitzi Likar
202/712-1399
Rm. 2.06-016 (ENI/PER/CMB)

Enterprise Restructuring & Privatization Division
Chief
Mr. Jim Watson
202/712-5998
Rm. 2.06-090 (ENI/PER/ERP)

Legal Regulatory and Tax Fiscal Division
Chief
Mr. Alexander Shapleigh
202/712-1535
Rm. 2.06-013 (ENI/PER/LRTF)

Program Operations Division
Chief
Mr. David Leong
202/712-5291
Rm. 2.06-055 (ENI/PER/PO)

Office of Environment, Energy and Urban Development

Director
Mr. James Bever
202/712-0070
Rm. 5.10-053 (ENI/EEUD)

Environment and Natural Resources Division
Acting Chief
Ms. Melodie Bacha
202/712-4673
Rm. 5.10-006 (ENI/EEUD/ENR)

Energy and Infrastructure Division
Chief
Mr. Robert Ichord

202/712-1352
Rm. 5.10-051 (ENI/EEUD/EI)

Urban Development and Housing Division
Acting Chief
Ms. Nancy Hooff
202/712-1609
Rm. 5.10-096 (ENI/EEUD/UDH)

Bureau for Latin America and the Caribbean (LAC)

Office of the Assistant Administrator

Assistant Administrator
Mr. Mark L. Schneider
202/712-4800
Rm. 5.09-12 (LAC/AA)

Personal: born 12/31/41 in Newark, N.J.

Education: B.A. in journalism, Univ. of Calif. at Berkeley. M.A. in political science, San Jose State College.

Professional: 1966-68, Peace Corps volunteer, El Salvador. Reporter: *Washington Daily News, San Francisco News Call Bulletin,* and United Press International. leg. asst., U.S. Senate Cmte. on Labor and Human Resources and U.S. Senate Judiciary Cmte. 1977-79, sr. dep. asst. sec. of State for human rights, U.S. Dept. of State. 1980-92, chief, office of analysis and strategic planning, Pan American Health Organization (Wash., D.C.). November 22, 1993-present, asst. administrator, Bureau of Latin America and the Caribbean, U.S. Agency for International Development.

Mark Schneider was sworn in as assistant administrator for Latin America and the Caribbean of the U.S. Agency for International Development (USAID) on November 22, 1993. President Clinton also appointed Schneider as a board member of the Inter-American Foundation.

Before joining USAID, Schneider, a Latin America specialist, served 12 years with the Pan American Health Organization (PAHO), a regional office of the World Health Organization, in Washington, D.C. as chief of its office of analysis and strategic planning. As such, Schneider coordinated programming and evaluation of PAHO's technical cooperation program and served as senior policy adviser to the director on PAHO's relations with the U.S., other Western Hemisphere countries, the Organization of American States, the United Nations, and other international organizations.

From 1977 to 1979, Schneider was senior deputy assistant secretary of State for human rights. In this capacity, he served as a member of the U.S. delegation to the UN Human Rights Commission in Geneva, the UN General Assembly, and the Organization of American States General Assembly.

Schneider also has served as legislative assistant and Senate committee staff member for Senator Edward M. Kennedy (D-Mass.), working on the Labor and Human Resources and the Judiciary Committees.

In the 1960's, Schneider was a reporter for the *Washington Daily News,* the *San Francisco News Call Bulletin* and United Press International. He was a Peace Corps volunteer in El Salvador from 1966 to 1968.

Schneider graduated from the University of California at Berkeley and has a master's degree in political science from San Jose State College. He lives in Washington, D.C. with his wife Susan and two children.

Deputy Assistant Administrator
Ms. Norma J. Parker
202/712-4800
Rm. 5.09-15 (LAC/AA)

Deputy Assistant Administrator
Mr. Carl H. Leonard
202/712-4760
Rm. 5.09-13 (LAC/AA)

Deputy Assistant Administrator
Mr. George A. Wachtenheim
202/712-4800
Rm. 5.09-16 (LAC/AA)

Office of Development Planning and Budget

Director
Mr. Michael Deal
202/712-5529
Rm. 5.08-002 (LAC/DPB)

Office of Strategy and Portfolio Management

Director
Mr. Vincent Cusumano
202/712-5363
Rm. 5.08-085 (LAC/SPM)

Deputy Director
Mr. Paul Thorn
202/712-4240
Rm. 5.08-030 (LAC/SPM)

Project Support Team
Team Leader
Ms. Susan Hill
202/712-1355
Rm. 5.08-024 (LAC/SPM/PS)

Central America/Caribbean Team
Team Leader
Mr. Paul Thorn
202/712-1067
Rm. 5.08-030 (LAC/SPM/CAC)

South America Team
Team Leader
VACANT
202/712-4240
Rm. 5.08-024 (LAC/SPM/SAM)

Office of Regional Sustainable Development

Director
Mr. Timothy Mahoney

202/712-1706
Rm. 5.09-056 (LAC/RSD)

Deputy Director
Ms. Judy Gilmore
202/712-5353
Rm. 5.09-056 (LAC/RSD)

Broad-Based Economic Growth Team
Team Leader
Mr. John A. Becker
202/712-0761
Rm. 5.09-122 (LAC/RSD/BEG)

Environment Team
Team Leader
Mr. Jeffrey Brokaw
202/712-5623
Rm. 5.09-055 (LAC/RSD/ENT)

Democracy and Human Rights Team
Team Leader
Ms. Margaret Sarles
202/712-1416
Rm. 5.09-073 (LAC/RSD/DHR)

Education and Human Resources Team
Team Leader
Mr. David Evans
202/712-1328
Rm. 5.09-071 (LAC/RSD/EHR)

Health/Population/Nutrition Team
Team Leader
Ms. Carol Dabbs
202/712-0473
Rm. 5.10-103 (LAC/RSD/HPN)

Office of South American and Mexican Affairs

Director
Mr. Wayne Tate
202/712-1738
Rm. 5.08-068 (LAC/SAM)

Deputy Director
Ms. Ann McDonald
202/712-0478
Rm. 5.08-066 (LAC/SAM)

Chile/Venezuela/Brazil/Paraguay/Argentina/Ecuador
Ms. Babette Prevot
202/712-0955
Rm. 5.08-057 (LAC/SAM)

Bolivia/Colombia - Mr. Kenneth Wiegand
202/712-4740
Rm. 5.08-072 (LAC/SAM)

Peru/Mexico - Mr. Ross Wherry
202/712-4716
Rm. 5.08-052 (LAC/SAM)

Narcotics Coordinator
Mr. Thomas Kellerman
202/712-4750
Rm. 5.08-052 (LAC/SAM)

Office of Caribbean Affairs

Director
Mr. Robert Dakan

202/712-1533
Rm. 5.08-093 (LAC/CAR)

Deputy Director
Mr. John Schneider
202/712-0490
Rm. 5.09-131B (LAC/CAR)

Haiti Task Force
Director
Mr. Douglas Chiriboga
202/712-1618
Rm. 5.08-092 (LAC/CAR)

Haiti - Mr. Daniel Riley
202/712-1641
Rm. 5.09-132B (LAC/CAR)

Eastern Caribbean/Guyana/Dominican Republic/Jamaica
   Ms. Robin Brinkley
202/712-1644
Rm. 5.09-134B (LAC/CAR)

Office of Central American Affairs

Director
Ms. Janice Weber
202/712-5308
Rm. 5.08-065 (LAC/CEN)

Deputy Director
Mr. Neil Levine
202/712-0121
Rm. 5.08-086 (LAC/CEN)

Guatemala/Honduras - VACANT

El Salvador - VACANT

Panama - Ms. Bernadette Bundy
202/712-5366
Rm. 5.08-075 (LAC/CEN)

Nicaragua - Mr. John Sullivan
202/712-1063
Rm. 5.08-065 (LAC/CEN)

Bureau for Humanitarian Response (BHR)

Office of the Assistant Administrator

Assistant Administrator
Mr. Leonard M. Rogers
202/712-0770
Rm. 8.06-086 (BHR/AA)

Office of Foreign Disaster Assistance

Director
Ms. Nan Borton
202/712-0400
Rm. 8.06-017 (BHR/OFDA)

Office of Food for Peace

Director
Mr. Tom Oliver
202/712-5340
Rm. 8.06-157 (BHR/FFP)

Office of Private and Voluntary Cooperation

Director
Mr. John P. Grant
202/712-4969
Rm. 7.06-062 (BHR/PVC)

Office of American Schools and Hospitals Abroad

Director (Acting)
Ms. Mable Meares
202/712-0643
Rm. 8.07-091 (BHR/ASHA)

Office of Transition Initiatives

Director
Mr. Frederick Barton
202/712-0962
Rm. 8.06-068 (BHR/TI)

Office of Program, Planning & Evaluation

Director (Acting)
Mr. Michael Korin
202/712-5952
Rm. 8.06-099 (BHR/PPE)

Bureau for Global Programs, Field Support and Research (G)

Office of the Assistant Administrator

Assistant Administrator
Ms. Sally Shelton
202/712-1190
Rm. 3.08-008 (G/AA)

Education: B.A. (Phi Beta Kappa, honors) in French, University of Missouri. M.A. in international relations, The Johns Hopkins School of Advanced International Studies. Fulbright scholar, Institut des Sciences Politiques (Paris).

Professional: vice president, Banker's Trust Company (New York). senior economic consultant, World Bank. legislative assistant for international affairs, Sen. Lloyd Bentsen. member, U.S. Mission to the United Nations. deputy assistant secretary of state, Inter-American Affairs. 1979-81, U.S. ambassador, Grenada, Barbados, other Eastern Caribbean nations. senior fellow and adjunct professor, Georgetown University's Center for Latin American Studies. 1994-present, assistant administrator for Global Programs, U.S. Agency for International Programs.

Sally A. Shelton's position as assistant administrator for Global Programs puts her in charge of the Global Bureau at USAID. Shelton manages the agency's repository of scientific and technical expertise. The bureau has five centers that address the agency's global strategic objectives: Population, Health and Nutrition; Environment; Economic Growth; Democracy and Governance; and Human Resource Development. Shelton also oversees the Office of Women in Development.

Shelton comes to USAID with many years of business and foreign relations experience. She was the director of two companies: Valero Energy Corporation, a Fortune 500 company involved in oil refining, and Baring Brothers & Co. Ltd.'s Puma Fund, a closed-ended investment fund traded on the London Stock Exchange. She has been a senior economic consultant to the World Bank and a vice president of Bankers Trust, New York where she was responsible for developing countries' debt.

She has served on the U.S. Mission to the United Nations and was legislative assistant for international affairs to then Sen. Lloyd Bentsen. She has been deputy assistant secretary of State for Inter-American Affairs. From 1979-81, Shelton was the U.S. ambassador to Grenada, Barbados, and several other Eastern Caribbean nations.

Before joining USAID, Shelton was an adviser to several multinational corporations on international trade and investment strategies. She was also a senior fellow and adjunct professor at Georgetown University's Center for Latin American Studies.

She has been a member of several nonprofit boards of directors and various organizations including the Council on Foreign Relations, International Planned Parenthood Federation, and the National Democratic Institute for International Affairs.

Shelton was a Fulbright Scholar at the Institut des Sciences Politiques in Paris and has a master's degree in international relations from The Johns Hopkins School of Advanced International studies in Bologna, Italy, and Washington, D.C. She has a bachelor's degree from the University of Missouri where she graduated Phi Beta Kappa with honors in French.

She has lectured at several universities, both in the United States and abroad. She has been a fellow at the Center for International Affairs at Harvard University and has taught U.S. foreign policy decision-making at the John F. Kennedy School of Government.

Assistant General Counsel for Global Programs
Mr. Michael G. Kitay
202/712-5019
Rm. 6.06-096 (GC/G)

Assistant General Counsel for Global Programs
Ms. Nina Nathani
202/712-4775
Rm. 6.06-057 (GC/G)

Office of Program Development & Strategic Planning

Director
Mr. Timothy Mahoney
202/712-1538
Rm. 3.09-035 (BHR/FFP)

Office of Women in Development

Director
Ms. Margaret Lycette
202/712-0570
Rm. 3.08-051 (G/WID)

Center for Democracy and Governance

Deputy Assistant Administrator
Mr. Charles Costello
202/712-1210
Rm. 3.10-008 (G/DG/DAA)

Center for Economic Growth

Deputy Assistant Administrator
Mr. Walter Bollinger
202/712-1140
Rm. 2.10-085 (G/EG/DAA)

Office of Microenterprise Development
Director
Ms. Elisabeth Rhyne
202/712-5578
Rm. 2.11-011 (G/EG/MD)

Office of Business Development
Director
Mr. Henry Merrill
202/712-4406
Rm. M.01-053 (G/EG/BD)

Office of Agriculture and Food Security
Director
Mr. John Lewis
202/712-5118
Rm. 2.11-003 (G/EG/AFS)

Office of Emerging Markets
Director
Mr. Russell Anderson
202/712-1050
Rm. 2.11-123 (G/EG/EM)

Center for Environment

Deputy Assistant Administrator
Mr. David Hales
202/712-1750
Rm. 3.08-095 (G/ENV/DAA)

Office of Environment and Urban Programs
Director
Ms. Viviann Gary
202/712-1770
Rm. 3.08-100 (G/ENV/UP)

Office of Environment and Natural Resources
Director
Mr. William Sugrue
202/712-1730
Rm. 3.08-099 (G/ENV/ENR)

Office of Energy, Environment and Technology
Director
Mr. Jeff Seabright
202/712-4370
Rm. 3.07-003 (G/ENV/EET)

Center for Population, Health and Nutrition

Deputy Assistant Administrator
Mr. Duff Gillespie
202/712-4120
Rm. 3.06-001 (G/PHN/DAA)

Office of Field and Program Support
Director
Ms. Joyce M. Holfeld
202/712-4638
Rm. 3.06-004 (G/PHN/FPS)

Office of Population
Director
Ms. Elizabeth Maguire
202/712-0540
Rm. 3.06-011 (G/PHN/POP)

Office of Health and Nutrition
Director
Ms. Joy Riggs-Perla
202/712-4150
Rm. 3.07-100 (G/PHN/HN)

Center for Human Capacity and Development

Deputy Assistant Administrator
Ms. Emily Vargas-Baron
202/712-0236

Rm. 3.06-036 (G/HCD/DAA)

Office of Basic Education and Learning Systems
Acting Director
Mr. Donald Foster-Gross
202/712-1573
Rm. 3.10-013 (G/HCD/BELS)

Office of Higher Education and Training Systems
Acting Director
Mr. John Jessup
202/712-0172
Rm. 3.09-080 (G/HCD/HETS)

Bureau for Management (M)

Assistant Administrator for Management
Mr. Terrance Brown
202/712-1200
Rm. 6.09-036 (M/AA)

Office of Procurement

Director, Procurement Executive
Mr. Marcus Stevenson
202/712-5130
Rm. 7.08-099 (M/OP)

Contracts Division A

Chief
Ms. Joyce Frame
202/712-5882
Rm. 7.10-075

Contracts Division B

Chief
Mr. Stephen Dean
202/712-5717
Rm. 7.09-118

Contract Division ENI

Chief
Ms. Judith Johnson
202/712-1794
Rm. 7.09-073 (M/OP/ENI)

Bureau for Legislative and Public Affairs (LPA)

Assistant Administrator
Ms. Jill Buckley
202/712-4360
Rm. 6.10-106 (LPA/AA)

Education: B.A. in English, Univ. of Oregon.

Professional: 1973-82, founding partner, Rothstein/Buckley, Inc. (consulting firm). 1983-88, founder, J. Buckley & Associates, Inc. (consulting and public relations). 1988-92, partner, FMR Group (public affairs). Jan.-May 1993, re-established Jill Buckley & Associates. May 1993-Feb. 1994, director for external affairs; Feb. 1994-present, asst. admin. for legislative and public affairs, U.S. Agency for International Development.

Jill Buckley was sworn in February 11, 1994 as assistant administrator for legislative and public affairs at the U.S. Agency for International Development (USAID). Buckley had previously served as director of external affairs at USAID since May 1993.

Before joining USAID, Buckley headed her own public affairs/ communications consulting firm, Jill Buckley & Associates, which she had re-established in January of 1993. Among her clients were the American Association of Retired Persons, the National Legal Aid and Defenders Association, and the Jefferson Center.

From 1988 to 1992, Buckley was a partner in the FMR Group, a full-service public affairs firm whose clients included the Sierra Club, the National Democratic Institute for International Affairs, the American Israel Public Affairs Committee, the American Nurses Association, the National Association of Social Workers, and the Planned Parenthood Federation of America.

Before joining the FMR Group, she headed her own organization, J. Buckley & Associates Inc., from January 1983 to November 1988 where she advised over 100 candidates for federal and statewide offices on campaign strategy and message and produced and placed campaign advertising. Other clients included the National Education Association, the American Trial Lawyers Association, and the National Clean Air Coalition.

From 1973 to 1982, Buckley was a founding partner in Rothstein/ Buckley Inc., one of the nation's first Democratic political consulting firms specializing in media. Rothstein/Buckley served political candidates in 40 states, including Senators Don Riegle (D-Mich.), Bob Kerrey (D-Neb.), Tom Daschle (D-S.D.) and many members of the US House of Representatives.

Buckley has frequently conducted training sessions for the Democratic Party, as well as environmental, international, and women's groups. In addition, she led sessions in the Czech and Slovak Republics, Romania, South Africa, and Northern Ireland for the National Democratic Institute for International Affairs. She also has lectured at the University of Chicago, Yale, Harvard, George Washington University and the American University.

Buckley has a bachelor's degree in English from the University of Oregon and has done graduate work at the University of Denver and Georgetown University.

Buckley resides in Washington, D.C. and has one daughter.

Congressional Liaison Division

Global (WID, Displaced Children, Pop., Health), Peace Corps
Ms. Dorothy Rayburn
202/712-4416
Rm. 6.10-064 (LPA/CL)

Europe and New Independent States - Ms. Kathleen Murphy
202/712-4422
Rm. 6.10-063 (LPA/CL)

Asia and Near East - Ms. Carol Kiranbay
202/712-4038
Rm. 6.10-052 (LPA/CL)

Latin America & the Caribbean, Narcotics
  Ms. Gladys Rodriquez
  202/712-4423
  Rm. 6.10-061 (LPA/CL)

Africa, OSDBU, Nyka - Mr. Jasper Feldman
  202/712-4423
  Rm. 6.10-061 (LPA/CL)

Press Relations Division

Chief (Acting)
Ms. Ann Kittlaus
202/712-0460
Rm. 6.10-108 (LPA/PR)

Office of the General Counsel (GC)

General Counsel
Ms. Singleton McAllister
202/712-0460
Rm. 6.06-125 (GC)

Education: B.A. in government and politics and African studies, University of Maryland. Graduate, Howard University School of Law.

Professional: teaching assistant, Howard University Law School. summer associate, Butler & Binion Law Firm (Washington office). judicial law clerk, Judge Jack E. Tanner, Federal District Court. legislative assistant, Rep. Parren J. Mitchell. legislative director, Rep. William H. Gray III. special asst., legislative dir., Rep. Mickey Leland. 1986-88, senior counsel, U.S. House of Representatives, Committee on the Budget. 1988-92, partner, Reed Smith, Shaw & McClay. 1990, special consultant, USAID. 1992-96, counsel, Shaw, Pittman, Potts & Towbridge (Wash., D.C.). 1996-present, general counsel, U.S. Agency of International Development.

Singleton B. McAllister comes to her new role as general counsel for USAID with an extensive background in government relations and legislative matters.

Before joining USAID, she was counsel to Shaw, Pittman, Potts & Towbridge of Washington, D.C. for four years. She specialized in government relations, contracts, health care, and corporate law. Prior to that, she was a partner at Reed, Smith, Shaw & McClay.

McAllister's government experience has spanned two decades. From January 1986 to January 1988, she was senior counsel to the U.S. House of Representatives, Committee on the Budget. In this capacity, she assisted senior staff in resolving legal issues and addressing budget matters for congressional committees including the Armed Services, Education and Labor, Foreign Affairs, House Administration, Small Business, and Select Committees. Prior to working with the House of Representatives, she was special assistant and legislative director to the late Rep. Mickey Leland.

In addition, McAllister's Capitol Hill positions have included serving as a legislative director for former Rep. William H. Gray III and as legislative assistant for former Rep. Parren J. Mitchell, past chairman of the House Small Business Committee. While working with Rep. Gray, she was responsible for initiating and drafting legislation to create the African Development Foundation, which in 1981 became Public Law 96-533. She also served as a special consultant to USAID in 1990 on regulations implementing the Gray Amendment set-aside for small and minority businesses.

McAllister has served as judicial law clerk to Judge Jack E. Tanner in the Federal District Court of Tacoma, Washington and was a summer associate for the Washington office of Butler & Binion Law Firm, a firm based in Houston. She has also been assistant director

of TransAfrica and a teaching assistant at Howard University Law School.

McAllister has been active in many civic affairs and has served as a member of the Board of Directors of the Greater Washington Board of Trade's Federal Affairs Committee and as a member of the Howard University Hospital Board of Directors. In addition, McAllister has served as general counsel, vice president, and president of Women in Government Relations Inc. and was a member of the Advisory Board of the Congressional Black Caucus Foundation and the African Development Foundation.

McAllister graduated from the Howard University Law School and has a bachelor's degree in government and politics, as well as African Studies, from the University of Maryland. She is a member of the District of Columbia and Pennsylvania bars.

Advisory Committees

USAID Malaria Vaccine Program Advisory Committee

Designated Federal Officer
Mr. Carter L. Diggs
202/712-5728
Rm. 3.07-013

Advisory Committee on Voluntary Foreign Aid

Chairman
Mr. Tom Fox
202/638-6300
(ACVFA)

Board for International Food & Agriculture Development

Designated Federal Officer
Ms. Tracy Atwood
202/712-5571

U.S. Arms Control & Disarmament Agency

320 21st Street, NW / Washington DC 20451
Personnel: 202/647-2034
Public Information: 202/647-8677

INTRODUCTION

The U.S. Arms Control and Disarmament Agency formulates and implements arms control and disarmament policies that promote the national security of the U.S. and its relations with other countries.

Office of the Director (ACDA/D)

Director
Mr. John D. Holum
202/647-9610   FAX 202/647-4920
Rm. 5930

UNITED STATES ARMS CONTROL AND DISARMAMENT AGENCY

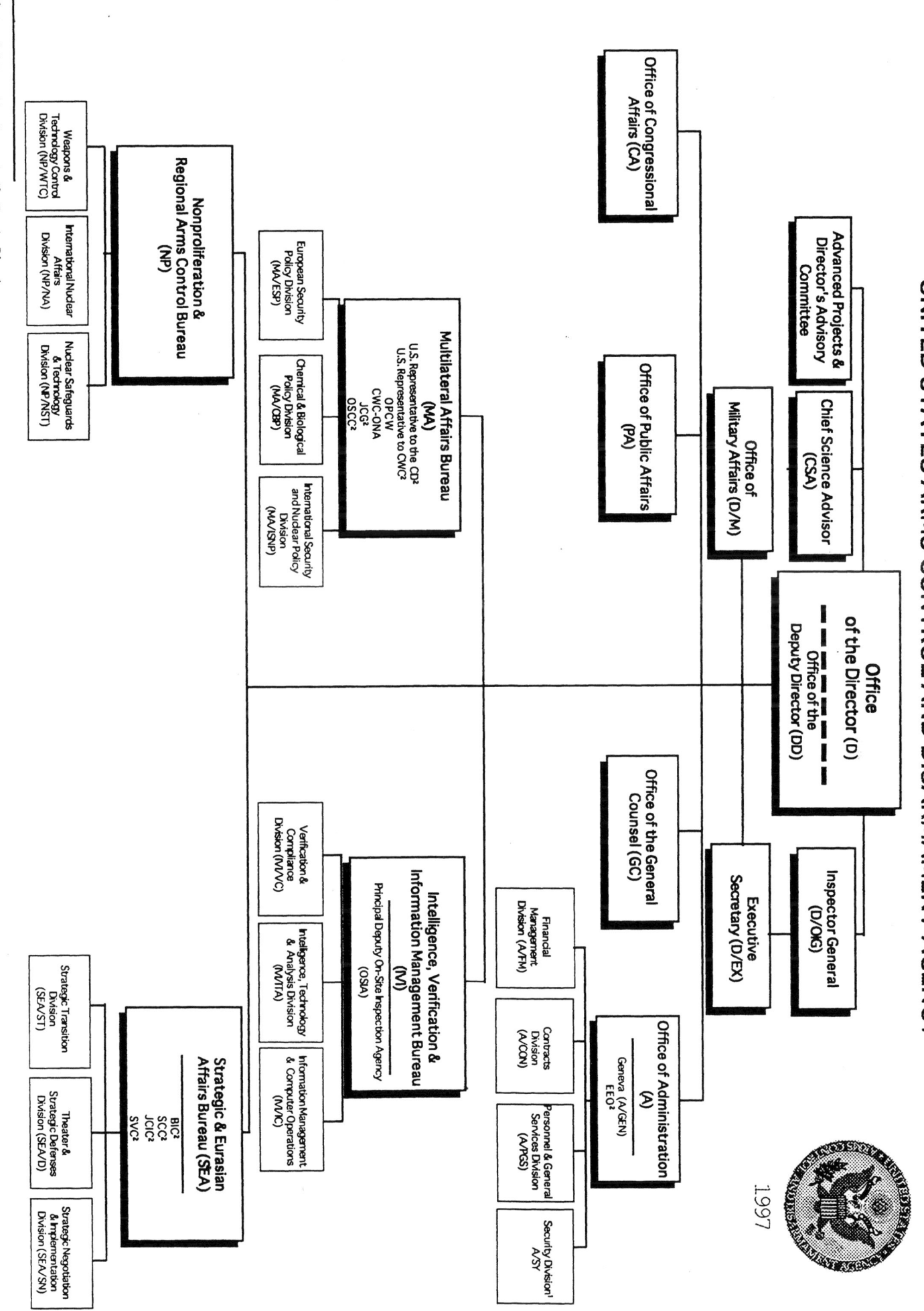

1997

1 Special Reporting Access to the Deputy Director
2 Direct Access to the Director

Office of the Director (D)
Office of the Deputy Director (DD)

Office of Congressional Affairs (CA)

Advanced Projects & Director's Advisory Committee

Chief Science Advisor (CSA)

Office of Public Affairs (PA)

Office of Military Affairs (D/M)

Inspector General (D/OIG)

Executive Secretary (D/EX)

Office of the General Counsel (GC)

Nonproliferation & Regional Arms Control Bureau (NP)
- Weapons & Technology Control Division (NP/WTC)
- International Nuclear Affairs Division (NP/NA)
- Nuclear Safeguards & Technology Division (NP/NST)

Multilateral Affairs Bureau (MA)
U.S. Representative to the CD²
U.S. Representative to CWC²
OPCW
CWC-ONA
JCG²
OSCC²
- European Security Policy Division (MA/ESP)
- Chemical & Biological Policy Division (MA/CBP)
- International Security and Nuclear Policy Division (MA/ISNP)

Intelligence, Verification & Information Management Bureau (IV)
Principal Deputy On-Site Inspection Agency (OSIA)
- Verification & Compliance Division (IV/VC)
- Intelligence, Technology & Analysis Division (IV/ITA)
- Information Management & Computer Operations (IV/IC)

Strategic & Eurasian Affairs Bureau (SEA)
BIC²
SCC²
JCIC²
SVC²
- Strategic Transition Division (SEA/ST)
- Theater & Strategic Defenses Division (SEA/D)
- Strategic Negotiation & Implementation Division (SEA/SN)

Office of Administration (A)
Geneva (A/GEN)
EEO²
- Financial Management Division (A/FM)
- Contracts Division (A/CON)
- Personnel & General Services Division (A/PGS)
- Security Division¹ A/SY

Personal: born 12/4/40 in Highmore, S.D.

Education: B.A., Northern State Teachers College (Aberdeen, S.D.). J.D., (with honors), George Washington Univ., 1970.

Professional: 1965-79, staff and then legislative dir., Sen. George McGovern (D-S.D.). 1979-81, policy planning staff, U.S. Dept, of State. 1981-93, attorney, O'Melveny & Myers. 1993-present, director, Arms Control and Disarmament Agency (ACDA). 1997-present, under secretary of State for arms controls, nonproliferation, and international security affairs, U.S. Dept. of State.

John Holum has served as director of the U.S. Arms Control and Disarmament Agency since 1993. ACDA was established by 1961 legislation in response to congressional feeling that the nation's national security efforts could be most effectively executed by centralizing arms control and disarmament responsibilities. Until 1997, the agency operated as an autonomous governmental unit.

In April of 1997, the Clinton administration announced a reorganization plan for the U.S. State Department which would fold both the ACDA and the United States Information Agency into the U.S. Department of State. Officials of all the agencies involved are currently working on implementation plans for the reorganization which should be complete by 1999.

Holum will be "dual-hatted" for the integration period as ACDA director and as under secretary of State for arms control, nonproliferation, and international security affairs. He will serve as the principal advisor to the Secretary of State and the President on the full range of arms control, nonproliferation, and international security matters.

Holum brings to the executive branch a mix of experience drawn from the worlds of foreign policy, international law and negotiation, and political and public affairs. From 1981 until his swearing in, he practiced law in the Washington office of O'Melveny & Myers, concentrating on regulatory and international matters. Former Secretary of State Warren Christopher was a partner at the firm. Holum concentrated on regulatory proceedings and enforcement.

Holum served as a defense and foreign policy adviser in the 1992 Clinton Presidential Campaign and assisted in the Clinton Presidential Transition. He also served as executive director of the Democratic Platform drafting committee and the Platform committee for the 1992 Democratic National Convention.

From 1979 to 1981, Holum served on the policy planning staff at the Department of State. Working on arms control and legal issues with Samuel Berger and under-secretary Anthony Lake, he drafted speeches and testimony for Secretary Vance, Secretary Muskie, and Deputy Secretary Christopher.

From 1965 to 1979, Holum was a member of the staff of US Senator George McGovern (D-SD), where he served as legislative director and managed the Senator's work on the Foreign Relations Committee. He was McGovern's issues director in the 1972 presidential primaries and served as his chief speechwriter in the general election.

Holum grew up on a family farm in the northeastern part of South Dakota. His undergraduate education at Northern State Teachers College was in mathematics and physical sciences. Holum attended law school at George Washington University, where he earned his J.D. with honors in 1970.

Holum is married to Barbara P. Holum, a Commissioner of the Commodity Futures Trading Commission, and has one daughter, Tracy Lynn. He enjoys sailing, flying, scuba diving, and playing bluegrass/country music.

Counselor
Mr. Donald Grossi
202/647-5553
Rm. 5930

Office of the Deputy Director (ACDA/DD)

Deputy Director
Ambassador Ralph Earle
202/647-8463
Rm. 5934

Education: B.A., Harvard College. J.D., Harvard Law School.

Professional: 1950-52, 1st and 2nd lieutenant, Corps of Engineers and Counter Intelligence Corps, U.S. Army. partner, Baker & Daniels (Wash., D.C.). partner, Morgan, Lewis & Bockius (Philadelphia). 1968-69, principal deputy assistant secretary of defense for international security affairs, U.S. Dept. of Defense. 1969-72, defense advisor, U.S. Mission to NATO. 1972-73, consultant to the Secretary of Defense on SALT-related issues. 1972-77, ACDA Representative on the US SALT Delegation. 1977-78, alternative chief U.S. negotiator; 1978-80, chief negotiator, SALT II Treaty. 1980-81, director, U.S. Arms Control and Disarmament Agency (ACDA). 1994-present, deputy director, U.S. Arms Control and Disarmament Agency.

Ambassador Ralph Earle II is the deputy director of the U.S. Arms Control and Disarmament Agency (ACDA). Earle, a Washington lawyer, was most recently chairman of the board of directors of the Lawyers Alliance for World Security (LAWS).

Since returning to the ACDA in 1994, Earle has concentrated on the extension of the Non-Proliferation of Nuclear Weapons Treaty, U.S. accession to the African Nuclear Weapon Free Zone, and negotiations on the Comprehensive Test Ban Treaty. In 1997, Ambassador Earle has worked to get Senate approval of the Chemical Weapons Convention and to seek implementation of the President's goal of a global ban on anti-personnel landmines. He is also heavily engaged in the reorganization of the U.S. foreign affairs agencies which will place ACDA in the Department of State in 1999.

From 1980 to 1981, Earle was the director of ACDA, where he served as the administration's principal advisor on all matters involving arms control and disarmament. Earle previously served (with the rank of Ambassador) as alternate chief U.S. negotiator (1977-78) and chief negotiator (1978-80) of the SALT II Treaty. During that period, he also served as ACDA's special representative for arms control and disarmament negotiations. Previously, he was the ACDA representative on the U.S. SALT Delegation (1973-77).

Ambassador Earle additionally served as a consultant to the secretary of defense on SALT-related issues, as defense advisor for the U.S. Mission to NATO, and as principal deputy assistant secretary of defense for international security affairs.

In addition to his government service, Earle, a graduate of Harvard College and Harvard Law School has practiced law as a partner of Morgan, Lewis & Bockius in Philadelphia and at Baker & Daniels in Washington. From 1950 to 1952, he served in the U.S. Army, as a 2nd and a 1st Lieutenant, in the Corps of Engineers, and in the Counter Intelligence Corps.

Earle is a member of the Council on Foreign Relations, the International Institute for Strategic Studies, the Council of American Ambassadors, and the American Law Institute. He has also served as a member of the boards of directors of a number of business corporations and non-profit organizations, including the Provident National Bank (Philadelphia), the Finance Company of Pennsylvania, the Arms Control Association, and the Committee for National Security. He is the author of numerous publications dealing with national security.

Ambassador Earle is married to the former Julie von Sternberg. They have five children and eight grandchildren.

Office of the General Counsel (ACDA/GC)

General Counsel
Ms. Mary Elizabeth Hoinkes
202/647-4621
Rm. 5635

Office of Congressional Affairs (ACDA/CA)

Director
Mr. Ivo Spalatin
202/647-3612
Rm. 5637

Bureau of Multilateral Affairs (ACDA/MA)

Assistant Director
VACANT
202/647-5999
Rm. 5499

Deputy Assistant Director
Mr. Donald Mahley
202/647-7450
Rm. 5499

U.S. Rep. to the Conference on Disarmament (MA/CD)
VACANT
202/647-5999

European Security Negotiations Division (MA/ESN)
Chief
Mr. Walter E. Dalch
202/647-7909
Rm. 5499

Chemical and Biological Policy Division (MA/CBP)
Chief
Mr. Robert Mikulak
202/647-5477
Rm. 5486

International Security and Nuclear Policy Division
Chief
Mr. Pierce Corden
202/647-7909
Rm. 5499 (MA/ISNP)

Bureau of Intelligence, Verification and Information Management (ACDA/IVI)

Assistant Director
VACANT
202/647-5315
Rm. 4953

Deputy Assistant Director
Mr. O. J. Sheaks
202/647-5315
Rm. 4953

Bureau of Strategic & Eurasian Affairs (ACDA/SEA)

Assistant Director
VACANT
202/647-9518
Rm. 4498

Deputy Assistant Director & Acting Assistant Director
Mr. R. Lucas Fischer
202/647-6567
Rm. 4498

Education: B.S. in aeronautics and astronautics, Massachusetts Institute of Technology (MIT), 1964. B.S. in political science, MIT, 1965.

Professional: 1972-present, U.S. Arms Control and Disarmament Agency: 1979-87, chief, theater affairs division; 1987-88, chief, strategic affairs division; present: deputy assistant director of the strategic and Eurasian affairs bureau.

Until the appointment of an assistant director, Robert Lucas Fischer is acting assistant director of the strategic and Eurasian affairs bureau at the U.S. Arms Control and Disarmament Agency (ACDA). Fischer's career posting is that of deputy assistant director of the bureau.

This bureau is responsible for ACDA's work on issues related to implementation of the START I, START II, and INF Treaties and for the study of possible further strategic arms reductions and limitations; the ABM Treaty and negotiations on strategic defense issues; the safe and secure dismantlement of nuclear weapons of the former Soviet Union; and defense conversion efforts in the former Soviet Union and elsewhere.

Fischer has been with ACDA since 1972. From February 1987 to November 1988, he was chief of the theater affairs division, responsible for ACDA's involvement in INF arms control issues and for support of the U.S. delegation to the INF negotiations. He additionally served as advisor to and a member of the U.S. Delegation to the CSCE Review Conference in Madrid in 1981 and the US INF Delegation in Geneva in 1980 and in 1981 to 1983.

Fischer graduated from the Massachusetts Institute of Technology in 1964 with a B.A. in aeronautics and astronautics. He also received a B.S. in political science at MIT in 1965. From 1965 to 1969, Fischer pursued graduate studies in political science, specializing in international relations and national security policy at MIT.

Fischer is married to Anne Mangan Fischer.

Bureau of Nonproliferation and Regional Arms Control (ACDA/NP)

Assistant Director
VACANT
202/647-3466
Rm. 4936

Deputy Assistant Director
Mr. Norman Wulf
202/647-2489
Rm. 4936

International Nuclear Affairs Divsision
Chief
Ms. Susan Burk
202/647-1300
Rm. 4953

Office of Public Affairs (ACDA/PA)

Director
Ms. Mary Dillon
202/647-8677
Rm. 5840

U.S. Information Agency

301 4th Street, SW / Washington DC 20547

Media Relations: 202/619-4355
Personnel: 202/619-4611
Public Affairs: 202/619-4355

INTRODUCTION

USIA uses its multilingual media --- Voice of America, Worldnet, and Wireless Field --- to promote and explain U.S. trade policy to foreign publics within their own cultural context. It directs its message at key host country media representatives, members of the academic community, government and other institutions and individuals. Known overseas as the U.S. Information Service, the agency conducts a variety of other activities including academic and cultural exchanges to press, radio, television, film, library, seminar, and cultural centers abroad. The agency is also charged with advising the President, the National Security Council, and other key government officials on the implications of foreign public opinion for present and contemplated U.S. policies, programs, and official statements.

Office of the Director (D)

Director
Mr. Joseph D. Duffey
202/619-4742   FAX 202/619-6705
Rm. 800 (D)

Personal: born 7/1/32 in Huntington, W.V.

Education: A.B., Marshall Univ., 1954. B.D., Andover Newton Theological School, 1957. S.T.M., Yale Univ., 1964. Ph.D., Hartford Seminary Foundation, 1969.

Professional: 1960-63, asst. professor; 1965-70, assoc. professor and director, Center for Urban Studies, Hartford Seminary. 1971-73, adjunct prof. and fellow, Calhoun College and Yale University. 1974-76, exec. officer, American Assn. of University Professors. 1977, asst. secretary for educational and cultural affairs, U.S. Department of State. 1977-81, chairman, National Endowment for the Humanities. 1982-91, chancellor, Amherst and Univ. of Massachusetts System. 1991-93, president, The American University. 1993-present, director, U.S. Information Agency.

Dr. Joseph D. Duffey has directed the United States Information Agency (USIA) since 1993. Since its creation in 1953, the USIA has had fourteen directors and two names. Throughout that time, USIA's

UNITED STATES INFORMATION AGENCY

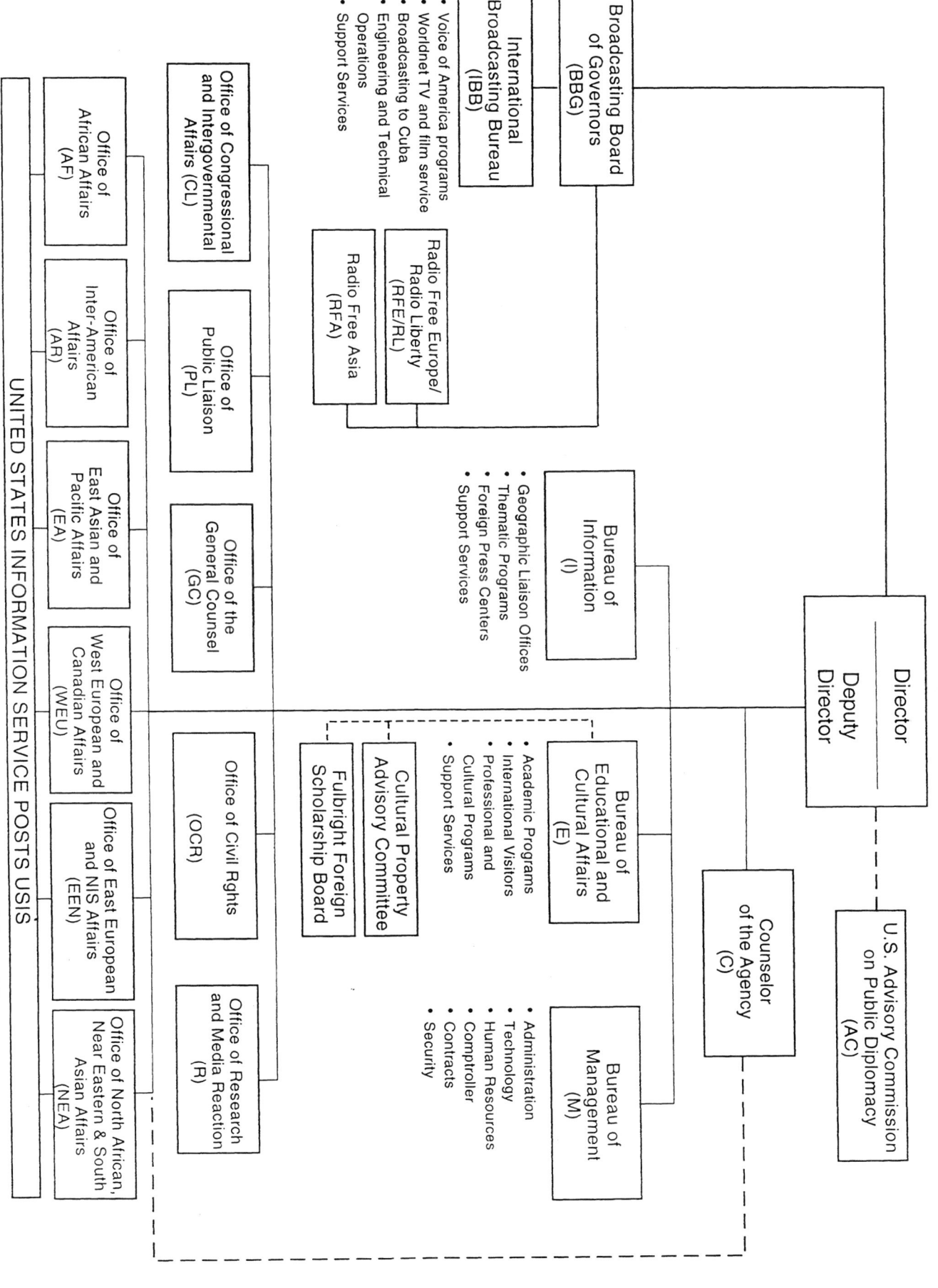

Director

Deputy Director

U.S. Advisory Commission on Public Diplomacy (AC)

Counselor of the Agency (C)

Broadcasting Board of Governors (BBG)

International Broadcasting Bureau (IBB)
- Voice of America programs
- Worldnet TV and film service
- Broadcasting to Cuba
- Engineering and Technical Operations
- Support Services

Radio Free Europe/ Radio Liberty (RFE/RL)

Radio Free Asia (RFA)

Bureau of Information (I)
- Geographic Liaison Offices
- Thematic Programs
- Foreign Press Centers
- Support Services

Bureau of Educational and Cultural Affairs (E)
- Academic Programs
- International Visitors
- Professional and Cultural Programs
- Support Services

Fulbright Foreign Scholarship Board

Cultural Property Advisory Committee

Bureau of Management (M)
- Administration
- Technology
- Human Resources
- Comptroller
- Contracts
- Security

Office of Congressional and Intergovernmental Affairs (CL)

Office of Public Liaison (PL)

Office of the General Counsel (GC)

Office of Civil Rights (OCR)

Office of Research and Media Reaction (R)

Office of African Affairs (AF)

Office of Inter-American Affairs (AR)

Office of East Asian and Pacific Affairs (EA)

Office of West European and Canadian Affairs (WEU)

Office of East European and NIS Affairs (EEN)

Office of North African, Near Eastern & South Asian Affairs (NEA)

UNITED STATES INFORMATION SERVICE POSTS USIS

NOTE: In 1996, the USIA IG was merged with the Department of State IG

mission has been to promote the national interest and national security of the U.S. through understanding, informing and influencing foreign publics, and broadening dialogue between American citizens and institutions and their counterparts abroad. In the upcoming century of faster and wider communication and contact between the U.S. and other countries and peoples, public diplomacy's contribution to safeguarding America's short, medium and long term national interests will grow every year.

On April 18, 1997, Vice President Gore announced "an historic opportunity to reinvent" the nation's foreign affairs agencies (Department of State, USIA, U.S. Arms Control and Disarmament Agency and the U.S. Agency for International Development) to ensure that they can effectively confront the challenges of the new century. These four federal agencies are currently preparing an implementation plan for the reorganization, which should be completed by 1999. At that time, USIA will become a part of the U.S. State Department.

As administrator of the U.S. Information Agency, Joseph Duffey directs its educational and cultural activities around the world. The agency's mission includes cultural exchange programs as well as the Voice of America, which broadcasts in more than 40 languages to audiences around the world; the wireless news division, which transmits stories and features about the United States for global dissemination; and Worldnet, which is the agency's television arm.

Before coming to USIA, Duffey served for two years as president of The American University in Washington, DC, and for nine years as chancellor of the Amherst campus at the University of Massachusetts.

Duffey's first political experience came under presidents Carter and Reagan when he served as assistant secretary of state for educational and cultural affairs and as chairman of the National Endowment for the Humanities. In 1991, he was joint head of the U.S. delegation observing national elections in Ethiopia.

In addition to his educational and political positions, Duffey has served as a director of the Baybank Valley Trust Company in Springfield, Massachusetts, and as chairman of the Governor's Commission on Mature Industries in Massachusetts. He is a member of the National Business-Higher Education Forum and the executive committee of the National Council on Competitiveness.

Duffey's wife, Ann Wexler, is a well-known Washington lobbyist.

Chief of Staff to the Director
Ms. Joyce Kravitz
202/619-4742 (D)

Deputy Director
Mr. Richard Penn Kemble
202/619-5747
Rm. 806 (D)

Education: B.A., Univ. of Colorado, 1962.

Professional: 1963-69, program director, League for Industrial Democracy. 1969-72, chairman, Frontlash, Inc. 1972-78, co-founder, Coalition for a Democratic Majority. 1978-79, special assistant, U.S. Senator Daniel Patrick Moynihan (D-N.Y.). 1979-81, producer/writer, WETA-TV (Wash., D.C.). 1981-88, president, Prodemca. 1988-present, senior associate, Freedom House. 1991-present, member, Board for International Broadcasting. June 29, 1993-present, deputy director, U.S. Information Agency.

Penn Kemble was nominated by President Bill Clinton to be deputy director of the U.S. Information Agency on May 4, 1993 and was confirmed by the U.S. Senate on June 29, 1993.

Since 1991, Kemble has served as a member of the Board for International Broadcasting and since 1988 as a senior associate with the Freedom House, a bipartisan human rights organization which supports democracy around the world. In 1972, Kemble co-founded the Coalition for a Democratic Majority, later moving on to co-edit *The Defense Democrat* and serve as chair of the coalition's executive committee.

Kemble was president of Prodemca, an organization supporting democratic development in the Americas, from 1981 to 1988. From 1979 to 1981, he worked in public broadcasting as a producer and writer for WETA-TV in Washington, D.C. From 1978 to 1979, he was a special assistant and speech writer for Senator Daniel Patrick Moynihan (D-N.Y.). From 1969 to 1972, he served as chair of Frontlash, Inc., an AFL-CIO-sponsored voter registration and political education campaign for working class and minority youth. Kemble also served as program director of the League for Industrial Democracy, with responsibility for youth and student affairs, from 1963 to 1969.

Kemble has had articles published in *Commentary, The New Republic,* and on the op-ed pages of *The New York Times,* and *The Washington Post.* He is a member of the board of directors of the National Democratic Institute for International Affairs and, in the early 1980s, served on USIA's Radio Programs Advisory Council.

In nominating Kemble, President Clinton said, "Penn Kemble has worked hard to promote the cause of freedom abroad. I am certain he and Joe Duffey will work well together to use the USIA's resources to continue pursuing that ideal."

Kemble's major priority in his first years at USIA were the consolidation of the US foreign broadcasting operations. He is currently working on the reorganization of U.S. foreign affairs agencies, which will see USIA consolidated into the State Department, and the creation of Civitas, an international movement for Education for Democracy.

Kemble is married to Marie-Louise Caravatti.

Office of Strategic Communications (D/C)

Director
Ms. Carol Doerflein
202/619-6554
Rm. 848 USIA

Global Issues
Ms. Barbara Scarlett
202/619-6818
Rm. 848 USIA

Counselor of the Agency (C)

Counselor
Ms. Harriet Elam
202/619-4618
Rm. 820 (C)

Office of Public Liaison (PL)

Director
Ms. Marthena S. Cowart
202/619-4355
Rm. 602 (PL)

Deputy Director
Mr. William Brent
202/619-4355 (PL)

Media Relations Section

Public Affairs Specialist
Ms. Catherine Stearns
202/401-1190

Public Affairs Specialist
Ms. Cheryl Irwin
202/619-4372

Public Affairs Specialist
Mr. William B. Reinkens
202/619-4370

Public Affairs Specialist
Ms. Lois M. Herrmann
202/619-4365

Office of the General Counsel (GC)

General Counsel
Mr. Les Jin
202/619-4979
Rm. 700 (GC)

Exchange Visitor Program Services
Program Director
Ms. Sally Lawrence
202/401-9810
Rm. 734 (GC/V)

Office of Congressional & Intergovernmental Affairs (CL)

Director
Ms. Ronna Freiberg
202/619-6828
Rm. 852 (CI)

Bureau of Information (I)

Acting Associate Director
Mr. Myron Hoffman
202/619-4545
Rm. 4 South (I)

Upon the departure in 1997 of R. Barry Fulton, Myron Hoffman assumed the duties of this office as acting associate director until the nomination and confirmation of a new appointee.

The Bureau of Information is USIA's primary source of information products for its posts and publics abroad. It is moving into new electronic communications media as fast as technology permits, while maintaining an extensive line of print products, operating a specialized wire service, facilitating the activities of foreign media in the U.S., and operating a worldwide speakers bureau on significant issues in foreign affairs.

Office of Geographic Liaison

Director
Mr. Dave Hamill
202/619-4136
Fourth Floor South (I/G)

American Republics
Team Leader
Mr. Tom Eichler
202/619-4154
Fourth Floor South (I/GAR)

Africa
Team Leader
Ms. Rosemary Crockett
202/619-4930
Fourth Floor South (I/GAF)

East Asia
Team Leader
Mr. Jonathan Silverman
202/619-4766
Fourth Floor South (I/GEA)

Near East-South Asia
Team Leader
Ms. Jane Gaffney
202/205-2726
Fourth Floor South (I/GNEA)

Europe
Team Leader
Ms. Lea Perez
202/619-4113
Fourth Floor South (I/GEU)

Office of Thematic Programs

Director
Ms. Judith Siegel
202/619-4210
Fourth Floor North (I/T)

Economic Security
Team Leader
Mr. Mark Taplin
202/619-4090
Fourth Floor South (I/TES)

Political Security
Team Leader
Ms. Patricia Kushlis
202/619-4144
Fourth Floor North (I/TPS)

Democracy and Human Rights
Team Leader
Mr. Mark Smith
202/619-4752
Fourth Floor North (I/TDHR)

Global Issues & Communications
Team Leader
Mr. John Walsh
202/619-6669
Fourth Floor North (I/TGIC)

Foreign Press Centers
National Press Building, Washington, DC 20045

Director
Ms. Marjorie Ransom

202/724-0032
Rm. 130 (I/F)

Office of Research and Media Reaction (R)

Director
Ms. Ann Pincus
202/619-4965
Rm. 352 (R)

Deputy Director
Mr. Stephen M. Shaffer
202/619-4965
Rm. 352 (R)

Senior Analyst
Mr. Alvin Richman
202/619-5140
Rm. 366 (R)

Asia, Pacific, and American Republics Branch

Chief
Mr. Dennis Gombert
202/619-4987
Rm. 356 (R/AA)

Near East/South Asia/Africa Branch

Acting Chief
Ms. Elaine Elassal
202/619-5122
Rm. 358 (R/NA)

Russia/Ukraine/Commonwealth Branch

Chief
Mr. Steven Grant
202/619-5130
Rm. 366 (R/RUC)

Europe Branch

Chief
Ms. Dina Smeltz
202/619-4490
Rm. 366 (R/EU)

Media Reaction Branch

Chief
Mr. William Ritchey
202/619-4969
Rm. 367 (R/MR)

Broadcasting Board of Governors (BBG)

300 Independence Ave., SW / Washington DC 20547

INTRODUCTION

Now part of the U.S. Information Agency, the Broadcasting Board of Governors & the International Broadcasting Bureau are responsible for overseeing the operations of the Voice of America, Radio Free Europe/Radio Liberty, Radio Marti, Television Marti, and the planned Asian-Pacific Network.

Chair
Mr. David W. Burke
202/401-3736
Suite 3360

Education: graduate of Tufts University in economics. B.A. from the University of Chicago.

Professional: 1960, worked on a study for Committee for Economic Development. 1960s, assistant to Secretary of Commerce Luther Hodges and later to Secretary of Labor Willard Wirtz; also, executive secretary of the President's advisory committee on labor management policy. 1965-66, legislative assistant; 1966-71, admin. asst., Senator Edward Kennedy (D-Mass.). 1971-75, vice president, Dreyfus Corporation. 1975, secretary to governor of New York. 1977-90, vice president and executive vice president of ABC News and later as president of CBS News. 1990, rejoined Dreyfus Corporation. 1995-present, chairman, Broadcasting Board of Governors.

In 1995, David W. Burke was named chairman of the Broadcasting Board of Governors, which has policy and oversight for all non-military international broadcasting services of the U.S. government.

Burke has had a long distinguished career in government, communication, and finance, including the Dreyfus Corporation, from 1971-75, where he served as vice president.

Burke began his professional career in 1960 working with George P. Shultz (later secretary of state) on a study for the Committee for Economic Development. He later served in the Kennedy administration as assistant to Secretary of Commerce Luther Hodges, as well as to Secretary of Labor Willard Wirtz. During that period, he also was executive secretary of the president's advisory committee on labor management policy.

In 1965, Burke was named legislative assistant to Senator Edward Kennedy (D-Mass.), and from 1966 to 1971, he was the senator's administrative assistant.

Upon leaving Dreyfus in 1975, Burke was appointed secretary to Governor Hugh Carey of New York. In that position, as chief of staff to the governor, Burke was responsible for the daily activities of the government of the state, oversight of all state agencies, and was especially associated with the Emergency Financial Control Board and the creation of the Municipal Assistance Corporation during the New York City fiscal crises.

For the following 13 years, Burke was involved in the management of national television news, as vice president and executive vice president of ABC News and later as president of CBS News. He rejoined The Dreyfus Corporation in 1990 as vice president and chief administrative officer.

Chief of Staff
Ms. Kathleen Harrington
202/401-3736
Rm. 3360

International Broadcasting Bureau (B)

300 Independence Avenue, SW / Washington DC 20547

Associate Director for Broadcasting
Mr. Kevin Klose
202/619-1088
Rm. 3300 (B)

Education: B.A., Harvard Univ., 1962.

Professional: 1967-92, news and management positions, The Washington Post. 1992-94, director, Radio Liberty. June 1994-January 1997, president, Radio Free Europe/Radio Liberty. January 14, 1997-present, director, International Broadcasting Bureau, U.S. Information Agency.

Kevin Klose was appointed director of the International Broadcasting Bureau on January 14, 1997. He is responsible for all non-military international broadcasting by the U.S. Information Agency, and is the chief operating officer of the International Broadcasting Bureau, which comprises the Voice of America, Radio and Television Marti, WORLDNET Television, engineering and technical operations, and all related support activities. Under the supervision of the Broadcasting Board of Governors, he will work closely with the presidents of the independent grantees, Radio Free Europe/Radio Liberty and Radio Free Asia.

Klose was president of Radio Free Europe/Radio Liberty, Inc. from June 1994 to January of 1997. He was previously director for Radio Liberty, which he joined in September 1992, after a 25-year career with *The Washington Post.* He has spearheaded reforms at RFE/RL that saved millions in U.S. tax dollars through corporate downsizing, technological transformation, and relocation of the broadcast service from high-cost Germany to Prague.

At *The Washington Post,* Klose served in key news and management positions under editor Ben Bradlee. These included deputy national editor (1987-90); Moscow bureau Chief (1977-81); and city editor (1974-76). He is author or co-author of five books, including *Russia and the Russians: Inside the Closed Society,* which won the Overseas Press Club's Cornelius Ryan award in 1985 for outstanding foreign policy reporting.

Raised on a farm in Dutchess County, New York, Klose graduated from Harvard University in 1962 and served with the U.S. Pacific Fleet for two years as a surface warfare officer. He and has wife, Eliza Darcy Kellogg, are the parents of three children.

Office of External Affairs

Director
Mr. Sidney Davis
202/619-2538
Rm. 3323   (B/K)

Office of Affiliate Relations and Audience Analysis

301 4th Street, SW / Washington DC 20547

Director
Ms. Myrna Whitworth
202/619-0055
Rm. 3666   (B/N)

Office of International Media Training
Chief
Mr. Louis T. Lantner
202/619-1982
Rm. 1437   (B/NI)

Office of Personnel & Administration

Director
Ms. Eva Jane Fritzman
202/619-3763
Rm. 1543   (B/PA)

Foreign Service Personnel Division
Chief
Ms. L. Karen Cooke
202/619-3732
Rm. 1543   (B/PA/PF)

Voice of America

300 Independence Avenue, SW / Washington DC 20547

Director
Ms. Evelyn S. Lieberman
202/619-3375
Rm. 3300   (B/VOA)

Professional: communications dir., National Urban Coalition. 1981-88, director of public affairs, Children's Defense Fund. 1988-93, press secretary, Senator Joseph Biden (D-Del.). 1993-94, executive asst. to the chief of staff, Office of the First Lady. 1994-95, deputy asst. to the President and deputy press secretary for operations; 1995-96, asst. to the President and deputy chief of staff for White House operations, Executive Office of the President. 1996-present, director, Voice of America.

Evelyn Lieberman was named by President Clinton to be the 23rd director of the Voice of America (VOA). Prior to her appointment, Lieberman was assistant to the President and deputy chief of staff for White House operations, the first woman to hold that position.

The Voice of America is the International Broadcasting Bureau's functional element for worldwide radio broadcasting. VOA is required to serve as a consistently reliable, authoritative, accurate, objective, and comprehensive news source presenting a balanced and complete projection of significant American thought and institutions. VOA produces and broadcasts radio programs in English and 46 foreign languages for overseas audiences, and to over 2000 affiliate stations worldwide. Its programming includes world and regional news, reports from correspondents on the scene, analyses of worldwide events, feature programs, music, and editorials.

Lieberman joined the administration in January 1993 as assistant to the chief of staff in the office of the First Lady, and in 1994, was named deputy assistant to the President and deputy press secretary for operations, serving under Mike McCurry.

From 1988 to 1993, she was press secretary to U.S. Senator Joseph R. Biden, Jr. (D-Del.). then chairman of the Senate Judiciary Committee. From 1981 to 1988, Lieberman was the director of public affairs for the Children's Defense Fund. Before that, she was communications director for the National Urban Coalition.

Lieberman is married to Edward H. Lieberman, a lawyer, and lives in Washington, D.C.

Worldwide English Division

Chief
Mr. John Stevenson
202/619-1222
Rm. 3025 (B/VOA/W)

News Division

Chief
Mr. Scott Bobb
202/619-1741
Rm. 3250 (B/VOA/X)

Broadcast Operations

Chief
Mr. Mike Ostergard
202/619-1899
Rm. 2054 (B/VOA/BA)

Africa Division

Chief
Mr. Steve Lucas
202/619-3657
Rm. 1728 (B/VOA/A)

European Division

Chief
Mr. Frank Shkreli
202/260-6447
Rm. 3075 (B/VOA/E)

East Asia and Pacific Division

Chief
Mr. Philip Harley
202/619-1405
Rm. 2709 (B/VOA/F)

Latin American Division

Chief
Mr. Richard Araujo
202/619-3961
Rm. 3041 (B/VOA/L)

Near East & North Africa Division

Chief
Mr. Ismail Dahiyat
202/401-7876
Rm. 1439 (B/VOA/NE)

South & Central Asia Division

Chief
Mr. Moazzam Siddiqi

202/619-0331
Rm. 1448E (B/VOA/SC)

Eurasian Division

Chief
Mr. Sherwood Demetz
202/619-3422
Rm. 2344 (B/VOA/U)

Office of Cuba Broadcasting

5325 NW 77th Ave.,   / Miami, FL 33166

Director
Mr. Hermino San Roman
305/994-1720
Rm. 103 (B/C)

Advisory Board for Cuba Broadcasting

Executive Director
Ms. Yvonne Soler
305/994-1720
Rm. 103 (B/CX)

Radio Marti

Director
VACANT
305/994-1720

Television Marti

Director
Mr. Antonio Dieguez
305/994-1772
Rm. 144 (B/CT)

Office of Worldnet Television and Film Service

Acting Director
Mr. John Lennon
202/205-5600
Rm. 5400 (B/TV)

Worldnet Programming Directorate

Director
Mr. Ken Sale
202/205-5610
Rm. 5029 (B/TVP)

Policy Coordination Division

Director
Mr. Lawrence Ewalt
202/401-8959
Rm. 5030 (B/TV)

Worldnet Production Directorate

Director
Ms. Lisa A. Keathley
202/401-8326
Rm. 4023 (B/TVW)

Interactives Division

ARNET/EANET Branch

Chief
Ms. Wendy Lyle
202/401-8337
Rm. 4412 (B/TVWPA)

European & Near East Asia Branch
Chief
Ms. Deborah Jones
202/690-4855
Rm. 4414 (B/TVWPF)

Africa Branch
Chief
Mr. Brian Padden
202/401-8332
Rm. 4410 (B/TVWPF)

Staff Production Division

Chief
Ms. Elizabeth van Etten
202/401-8265
Rm. 4049 (B/TVWS)

Bureau of Management (M)

301 4th Street, SW / Washington, DC 20547

Associate Director
Mr. Henry Howard
202/619-4626
Rm. 816 (M)

Office of Administration

Director
Ms. Eileen Keane Binns
202/619-4300
Rm. 618 (M/A)

Overseas Support Division
Chief
Ms. Cathy Chikes
202/619-4561
Rm. 618 (M/A)

Office of the Comptroller

Area Budget Staff

African
Ms. Valerie Reynolds
202/619-4542
Rm. 656 (M/CBA)

East Asian and Pacific
Mr. Charles T. Forrester
202/619-4516
Rm. 656 (M/CBA)

North African, Near Eastern, and South Asian
Ms. Carol F. Kieth
202/619-4527
Rm. 662 (M/CBA)

American Republics
Ms. Cathy L. Jackson
202/619-4530
Rm. 664 (M/CBA)

Eastern European
Ms. Susan D. Wood

202/619-4514
Rm. 668 (M/CBA)

Western European
Ms. Nellie Nelson
202/619-6079
Rm. 656 (M/CBA)

Office of Human Resources

Foreign Service Division
Chief
Mr. Robert Bemis
202/619-4695
Rm. 506 (M/HRF)

Overseas Development Team
Mr. Neil Klopfenstein
202/260-7014
Rm. 1086 (M/HRF)

Office of Contracts

Deputy Director
Mr. Edward Muller
202/205-5498
Rm. M-22 (M/K)

Bureau of Educational and Cultural Affairs (E)

Associate Director
Dr. John Peter (Jack) Loiello
202/619-4597
Rm. 849 (E)

Education: Ph.D. in African history, School of Oriental and African Studies, Univ. of London.

Professional: special assistant to the chairman, National Endowment for the Humanities. founding executive director, National Democratic Institute for International Affairs. president and CEO, Gowran International Ltd. May, 1994-present, associate director, bureau of educational and cultural affairs, U.S. Information Agency.

John Loiello was nominated by President Clinton and confirmed by the Senate as USIA associate director for educational and cultural affairs in May of 1994. Dr. Loiello is responsible for all of USIA's international education, professional, and cultural exchange and training activities. He oversees more than 60 discrete programs, supervising a staff in excess of 400 persons and a budget of more than $450 million.

Well-known activities of the bureau include the J. William Fulbright Program, the Hubert H. Humphrey Fellowships, the International Visitor Program, the Arts America program, binational and cultural centers overseas, student advising, English teaching programs, citizens and youth exchanges, as well as the special Freedom Support Act and SEED programs for Eastern and Central Europe and the states of the former Soviet Union.

Loiello comes to USIA from Gowran International Ltd., where he served as president and CEO for that international consulting firm, which specializes in providing services to overseas foundations and non-profit organizations in the realm of public diplomacy. Clients have included cultural, educational, corporate, and think tank foundations in Asia, Eastern and Western Europe, and West Africa.

Previously, Loiello played a major role in the development and legislative creation of the National Endowment for Democracy (NED), one of the few truly bipartisan U.S. foreign policy initiatives of the last twenty years. He subsequently served as founding executive director of the National Democratic Institute for International Affairs, a non-profit international organization designed to promote and support democratic institutions and pluralistic values overseas through joint planning, training, and exchanges. In these capacities, Loiello had the opportunity over a four-year period to work closely with foreign leaders and organizations in more than 40 countries.

Loiello also served for more than two years as special assistant to the Chairman of the National Endowment for the Humanities, with responsibility for special projects concerned with international and intercultural relations, urban affairs, the labor movement, and public issues.

Loiello received his doctorate of philosophy in African history from the School of Oriental and African Studies of the University of London and has taught at the State University of New York at Buffalo and the University of Maryland (European Division). He lived in Nigeria for more than six months in 1975, while completing doctoral dissertation research at the University of Ibadan and elsewhere.

While resident abroad (1973-79), Loiello was an active member and elected office holder of Democrats Abroad. He served as a delegate to the 1976 Democratic National Convention as well as to the Democratic Mid-Term Conference in 1978. As overseas campaign manager for Carter/Mondale, he established the first full-time campaign organization abroad. Subsequently, Loiello successfully worked for legislation granting Americans resident overseas the right to vote in federal elections and guaranteeing their ability to transmit United States citizenship to their children born abroad.

Loiello served on the 1980 Democratic Platform Committee and chaired the Platform's Foreign Policy Subcommittee that same year. He also sat on the Democratic Platform Accountability Commission from 1981 to 1984. He has been a foreign policy advisor and contributor to various presidential and senatorial campaigns, most recently the Clinton/Gore campaign of 1992.

Dr. Loiello is married to Elaine Margaret Robinson.

Deputy Associate Director
Mr. Robert Earle
202/619-6599
Rm. 849 (E)

J. William Fulbright Scholarship Board Staff

Staff Director
Mr. Ralph Vogel
202/619-4290
Rm. 247 (E/BFS)

Office of Academic Programs

Director
Mr. Keith Gieger
202/619-6409
Rm. 202 (E/A)

Academic Exchange Programs Division
Chief
Mr. Barry Ballow
202/619-4360
Rm. 234 (E/AE)

African Programs Branch
Chief
VACANT
202/619-5355
Rm. 232 (E/AEA)

American Republics Programs Branch
Chief
Mr. James O'Callaghan
202/619-5365
Rm. 314 (E/AEL)

East Asian Programs Branch
Chief
Ms. Ursula Williams
202/619-5402
Rm. 208 (E/AEF)

European Programs Branch
Chief
Mr. Craig Springer
202/619-4420
Rm. 246 (E/AEE)

Near Eastern/South Asian Programs Branch
Chief
Mr. Martin Quinn
202/619-5568
Rm. 212 (E/AEN)

Teacher Exchange Branch
Chief
Dr. Jochen Hoffman
202/619-4555
Rm. 353 (E/ASX)

English Language Programs Division

Chief
Mr. Thomas Miller
202/619-5869
Rm. 304 (E/AL)

Office of Citizen Exchanges

Director
VACANT
202/619-5348
Rm. 220 (E/P)

American Republic and East Asia Division
Chief
Mr. Raymond Harvey
202/619-5326
Rm. 216 (E/PL)

Europe Division
Acting Chief
Mr. Raymond Harvey
202/619-5319
Rm. 220 (E/PE)

Near East/South Asia and Africa Division
Chief
Mr. Curt Huff
202/619-5319
Rm. 224 (E/PS)

Russia/Eurasia Division
Chief
Ms. Molly Raymond
202/619-5326
Rm. 216 (E/PN)

NIS/Secondary School Initiative Division
Chief
Mr. Robert Persiko
202/619-6299
Rm. 320 (E/PY)

Office of International Visitors

Acting Director
Ms. Leslie Wiley
202/619-5217
Rm. 255 (E/V)

Grant Programs Division
Chief
VACANT
202/619-5239
Rm. 271 (E/VG)

Africa Division
Chief
Ms. Mary Jeffers
202/619-5243
Rm. 268 (E/VGA)

American Republics Branch
Chief
Ms. Sarah Dupree
202/619-5245
Rm. 267 (E/VGR)

East Asia Branch
Team Leader
Ms. Marta Pereyma
202/619-5241
Rm. 270 (E/VGF)

Europe Branch
Chief
Ms. Nan Bell
202/619-5247
Rm. 263 (E/VGE)

Near East/South Asia Branch
Chief
Mr. William Royer
202/619-5237
Rm. 265 (E/VGN)

Voluntary Visitors Division
Chief
Mr. Beth Rule
202/619-4582
Rm. 266 (E/VF)

Office of African Affairs (AF)

Director
Ms. Marilyn Hulbert
202/619-4894
Rm. 716 (AF)

West Africa-(Francophone) - Benin, Cape Verde, The Gambia, Guinea, Guinea Bissau, Ivory Coast, Mali, Niger, Senegal, Togo, Burkina Faso

Country Officer
Ms. Judith Mudd Kaula
202/619-5900

West Africa-(Anglophone) - Ghana, Liberia, Nigeria, Sierra Leone

Country Officer
Ms. Claudia Anyaso
202/619-5900

Central Africa - Cameroon, Central African Republic, Chad, Congo, Gabon, Equatorial Guinea, Sao Tome, Burundi, Rwanda, Zaire

Country Officer
Ms. Cynthia Caples
202/619-5900

Southern Africa - South Africa, Lesotho, Mozambique, Namibia, Zambia, Zimbabwe, Malawi, Botswana, Swaziland, Angola

Country Officer
Mr. Paul Patin
202/619-5900

East Africa - Comoros, Dijibouti, Eritrea, Ethiopia, Kenya, Madagascar, Mauritius, Seychelles, Somalia, Uganda, Tanzania

Country Officer
Mr. David Andresen
202/619-5900

Office of Inter-American Affairs (AR)

Director
Ms. Linda Jewell
202/619-6848
Rm. 750 (AR)

Cuba, Mexico, Panama

Country Officer
Ms. Marge Coffin
202/619-6879

Costa Rica, El Salvador, Guatemala, Honduras, Nicaragua

Country Officer
Mr. Gonzalo Gallegos
202/619-5185

Bolivia, Chile, Colombia, Ecuador, Peru

Country Officer
Ms. Elizabeth Davis
202/619-5090

Argentina, Brazil, Paraguay, Uruguay

Country Officer
Ms. Kathleen Davis
202/619-6877

English Speaking Caribbean, Dominican Republic, Venezuela

Country Officer

Mr. Peter Samson
202/619-6878

Office of East Asian and Pacific Affairs (EA)

Director
Mr. Frank Scotton
202/619-4829
Rm. 766 (EA)

China, Hong Kong, AIT-Taipei

Country Officer
Ms. Lisa Heller
202/619-5838

Japan, Korea

Country Officer
Mr. John Ohta
202/619-5838

Thailand, Burma (Myanmar), Cambodia, Laos, Vietnam

Country Officer
Ms. Elizabeth Kauffman
202/619-5837

Australia, New Zealand, Papua New Guinea, Mongolia, Pacific Nations

Country Officer
Mr. Leonard Korycki
202/619-5836

Philippines, Malaysia, Singapore, Indonesia

Country Officer
Ms. Patricia Garon
202/619-5836

Office of East European and NIS Affairs (EEN)

Director
Mr. Robert McCarthy
202/619-4563
Rm. 868 (EEN)

OSCE Vienna

Country Affairs Officer
Ms. Louise Taylor
202/619-5571

RPO Vienna

Country Affairs Officer
Ms. Nikita Grigorovich-Barsky
202/619-5571

Russia

Country Affairs Officer
Mr. Douglas Ebner
202/205-3558

Baltics (Estonia, Latvia, Lithuania), Belarus, Ukraine, Poland

Country Affairs Officer

Mr. Michael Boyle
202/619-5856

Bulgaria, Czech Republic, Hungary, Moldova, Romania, Slovak Republic, Slovenia

Country Affairs Officer
Ms. Carol Lynn MacCurdy
202/619-5942

Armenia, Azerbaijan, Georgia, Kazakhstan, Kyrgyzstan, Tajikistan, Turkmenistan, Uzbekistan

Country Affairs Officer
Ms. Susan Hovanec
202/619-5057

Albania, Bosnia-Herzegovina, Croatia, Macedonia, Serbia-Montenegro

Country Affairs Officer
Mr. Thomas Leary
202/619-5945

Central & Eastern European Assistance & Exchange

Coordinator
Ms. Allison Portnoy
202/619-5993

Russia & the New Independent States Assistance & Exchange

Coordinator
Ms. Lorraine Predham
202/619-6169

Office of West European & Canadian Affairs (WEU)

Director
Mr. Charles Miller Crouch
202/619-6565
Rm. 751 (WEU)

International Organizations (USIO Geneva, USNATO, USEU)

Multilateral Officer/Media Coordinator
Mr. Tom Casey
202/619-6565

Denmark, Finland, Iceland, Norway, Sweden, Ireland, Canada, United Kingdom

Country Affairs Officer
Ms. Honora Rankine Galloway
202/619-6570

Italy, Malta, Greece, Turkey, Cyprus

Country Affairs Officer
Ms. Valerie Crites
202/619-6853

Germany, Austria, Switzerland

Country Affairs Officer
Mr. Paul Denig
202/619-6582

France, Spain, Portugal, Belgium, Netherlands, Luxembourg

Country Affairs Officer
Mr. David Mees
202/619-6570

Office of North African, Near Eastern, and South Asian Affairs (NEA)

Director
Mr. David Good
202/619-4520
Rm. 866 (NEA)

Algeria, Libya, Mauritania, Morocco, Tunisia, Egypt, Sudan

Country Affairs Officer
Mr. Claud Young
202/619-6528

Iraq, Bahrain, Kuwait, Oman, Qatar, Saudi Arabia, U.A.E, Yemen

Country Affairs Officer
Mr. John Roney
202/619-6528

Afghanistan, Bangladesh, Iran, Nepal, Pakistan

Country Affairs Officer
Mr. Mark Larsen
202/619-6538

Bhutan, India, Maldive Islands, Sri Lanka

Country Affairs Officer
Mr. Tom Mesa
202/619-5529

Israel, Jerusalem (West Bank), Jordan, Lebanon, Syria

Country Affairs Officer
Mr. Chris Datta
202/619-4905

U.S. Advisory Commission on Public Diplomacy (AC)

Chairman
Mr. Lewis Manilow
202/619-4457

Vice Chairman
Mr. William J. Hybl
202/619-4457

Staff Director
Mr. Bruce Gregory
202/619-4457
Rm. 600 (AC)

U.S. International Trade Commission

500 E Street, SW / Washington DC 20436

Personnel: 202/205-2651
Public Affairs: 202/205-1819
http://www.usitc.gov

INTRODUCTION

The U.S. International Trade Commission has its special niche in the U.S. Government's trade apparatus. It decides whether U.S. industries are being injured by imports of products that are either being sold in this country at unfairly low prices or are being unfairly subsidized by foreign governments. If so, antidumping or countervailing duties can be imposed on the American importer of such products. To help U.S. firms that have a grievance under U.S. trade laws, the ITC has set up a Trade Remedy Assistance Office.

The U.S. International Trade Commission (ITC) is an independent, nonpartisan, federal agency. Established in 1916 as the U.S. Tariff Commission, the ITC was given its present name through the Trade Act of 1974. Although it deals with a broad range of international trade matters, the ITC is not a policymaking body nor a court of law, and it does not negotiate trade agreements.

In countervailing duty and antidumping investigations, which involve either subsidies provided to foreign companies by their governments or the selling of foreign products in the U.S. at less than fair value, the ITC works in concert with the U.S. Department of Commerce. The Commerce Department determines whether the alleged subsidies or dumping are actually occurring and, if so, at what levels (called the subsidy or dumping "margin"). The ITC determines whether the U.S. industry is injured by reason of the dumped or subsidized imports. If the Commerce Department's final subsidy or dumping determination and the ITC's final injury determination are both affirmative, the Commerce Department issues an order to the U.S. Customs Service to impose duties.

The ITC also assesses whether U.S. industries are being injured by fairly traded imports and can recommend to the President that relief be provided to those industries to facilitate positive adjustment to import competition. Relief could take the form of increased tariffs or quotas on import and/or adjustment assistance for the domestic industry.

The ITC functions as the U.S. government's think tank on international trade, conducting objective studies on myriad international trade matters, including nearly every commodity imported into or exported from the U.S., as well as any topic requested by the president, the Senate Finance Committee, or the House Ways and Means Committee. The ITC has an extensive library of international trade resources called the National Library of International Trade, which is open to the public.

The agency frequently holds hearings as part of its investigations and studies. The hearings are generally open to the public and the media.

The ITC makes determinations in investigations involving intellectual property rights matters, mainly involving allegations of infringement of U.S. patents and trademarks by imported goods. If it finds a violation of the law, the ITC may order the exclusion of the foreign production from the U.S.

The ITC is responsible for continually reviewing the Harmonized Tariff Schedule of the U.S., a list of specific items that are imported into and exported from the U.S., and for recommending modifications to the Schedule that it considers necessary or appropriate.

ITC ORGANIZATION

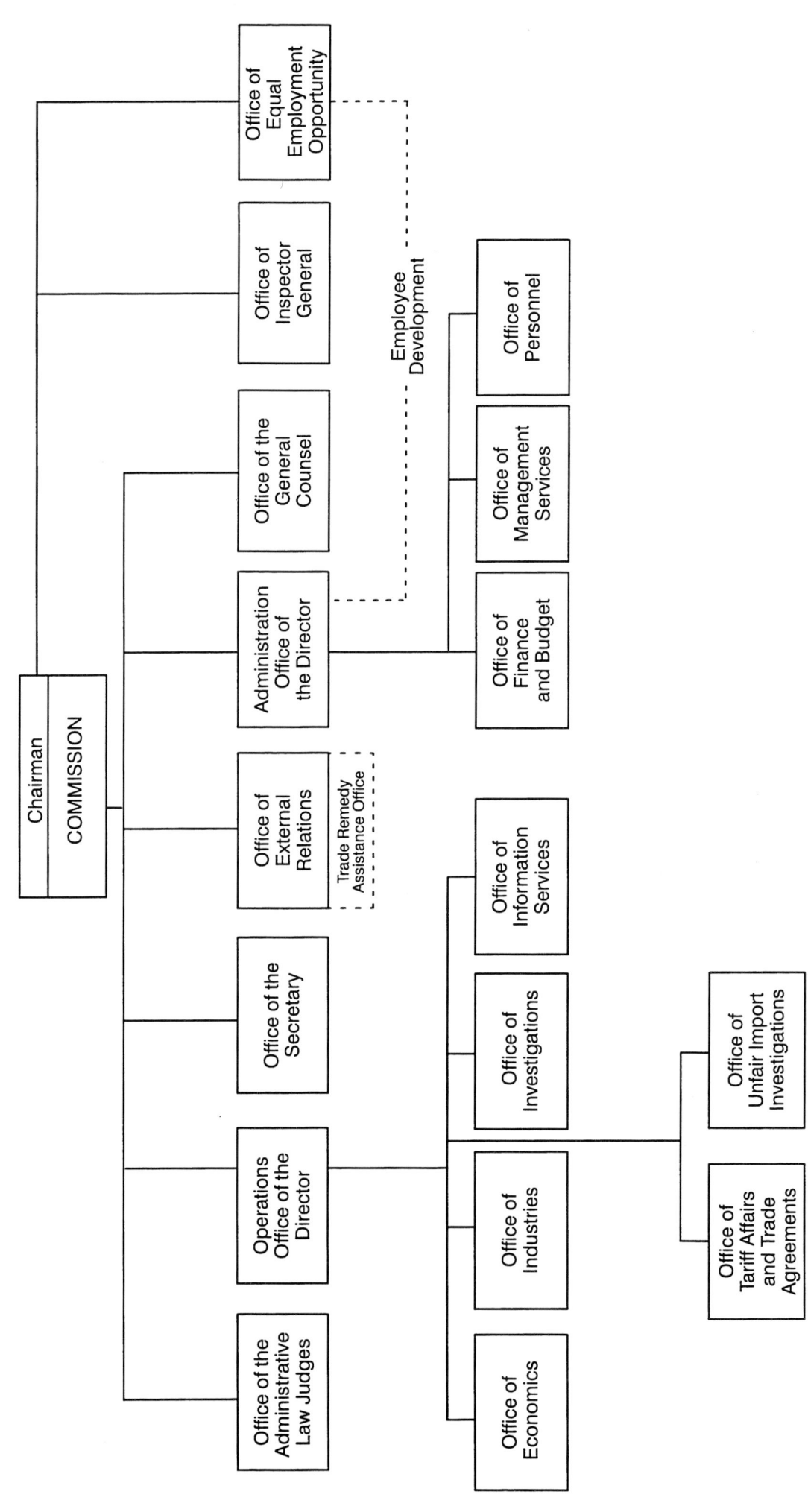

The ITC is headed by six commissioners who are nominated by the President and confirmed by the U.S. Senate. No more than three Commissioners may be of any one political party. Currently three Democrats and three Republicans serve as commissioners. The commissioners serve overlapping terms of nine years each, with a new term beginning every 18 months. The chairman and vice chairman are designated by the president from among the current commissioners for two-year terms.

The ITC staff of about 365 individuals includes international trade analysis (experts in particular industries), international economists, attorneys, and technical support personnel. The ITC publishes its studies and determinations. In most instances, these publications are available to the public free of charge upon request.

Public Reading Room:
The Office of the Secretary maintains a public reading room, open during agency hours, where researchers, journalists, and other interested parties may review public files containing non-confidential information for each USITC investigation. Photocopies of documents contained in the public files may be ordered for a fee from an outside duplicating firm (information available in the reading room). No on-site photocopying is available.

The National Library of International Trade & ITC Law Library:
The USITC maintains one of the most extensive libraries specializing in international trade in the United States. The National Library of International Trade houses over 100,000 volumes and approximately 2,000 periodical titles related to U.S. industry and international trade laws and practices as well as several CD-ROM and on-line information data bases. The library is located on the third floor of the USITC Building. It is open during agency hours.

The ITC Law Library is located on the sixth floor of the USITC Building. It is open to the public during agency hours. PHONE: 202/205-2630.

The Commissioners

Note: There are currently two vacancies on the six-member ITC.

Chairman
Marcia E. Miller
202/205-2021   FAX 202/205-2338
Rm. 700

Personal: born 8/15/55 in Indianapolis, Ind.

Education: B.A., Miami Univ. (Ohio), 1977. M.D., Advanced School of International Studies, Johns Hopkins Univ., 1981.

Professional: 1981-85, staff, American Textile Manufacturers Institute. 1985-87, international economist, law firm of Wilmer, Cutler and Pickering (Wash., DC). 1987-93, professional staff member; 1993-95, chief international trade counselor; 1995-96, international counselor, U.S. Senate Committee on Finance. Aug. 1996-present, member and then chair, U.S. International Trade

Commission.

Marcia Miller, a Democrat of Indiana, is chair of the U.S. International Trade Commission. She was nominated to the commission by President Clinton in May of 1996 and was confirmed by the Senate on June 16, 1996. She was sworn in as a member on August 5, 1996 for a term ending December 16, 2003 and was subsequently designated by President Clinton to serve as chairman for a term ending June 16, 1998.

Prior to her appointment, Miller was the minority chief international trade counselor with the U.S. Senate Committee on Finance. The committee has jurisdiction over U.S. foreign trade policy, customs, and import matters, and the budgets of several related agencies, as well as tax and other fiscal matters. Miller was named chief international trade counselor to the committee by then-Chairman Daniel Patrick Moynihan (D-N.Y.) in February 1993 following five years of service as a professional staff member with the committee.

Earlier in her career, Miller was an international economist with the law firm of Wilmer, Cutler and Pickering. Prior to that, she handled international trade issues for the American Textile Manufacturers Institute.

Miller holds a master's of arts degree from the School of Advanced International Studies at Johns Hopkins, and a bachelor of arts degree from Miami University in Oxford, Ohio.

She is married, has one son, and resides in Washington DC

Vice Chairman
Lynn M. Bragg
202/205-2250   FAX 202/205-2344
Rm. 706

Personal: born 6/15/54 at Fort Leonard Wood, Mo.

Education: B.A. in English (final honors), Mary Washington Coll. M.S. in public relations, Boston Univ.

Professional: 1978-80, various positions, corporate affairs department, Potomac Electric Power Company (Wash., DC). 1981-91, legislative assistant and legislative director, U.S. Senator Malcolm Wallop (R-Wyo.). 1991-94, director of government affairs, Edison Electric Institute. 1994-present, commissioner; Aug. 1996-present, vice chair, U.S. International Trade Commission.

Lynn Munroe Bragg, a Republican of Maryland, is the vice chairman of the U.S. International Trade Commission (ITC). Bragg was designated vice chair by President Clinton on August 5, 1996 for the term ending June 16, 2002. She has served as a commissioner since March 31, 1994. Bragg was appointed to the ITC by President Clinton for the term that will expire on June 16, 2002.

Prior to her appointment, Bragg served in a senior management position with the Edison Electric Institute, a trade association representing the investor-owned electric utility industry. As a director of government affairs, she advised member companies on legislative matters relating to fossil fuels and industry structure issues.

From 1981 to 1992, Vice Chair Bragg served on the staff of former Senator Malcolm Wallop (R-Wyo.). In that position, she worked extensively on energy, tax, and trade issues as the legislative director and a legislative assistant. Before joining Senator Wallop's staff, Bragg held several positions in the corporate affairs department of the Potomac Electric Power Company (PEPCO) in Washington DC

Bragg holds a master's degree in public relations from Boston University and a B.A. in English from Mary Washington College in Fredericksburg, Virginia. As a student, she lived in Germany and traveled extensively throughout Europe.

Bragg is married, has three children.

Commissioner
Mr. Don E. Newquist
202/205-2781   FAX 202/205-2342
Room 704

Personal: born 8/23/43 in Stamford, Texas.

Education: B.B.A., McMurry Univ., 1966.

Professional: 1967-69, officer, U.S. Navy. 1969-72, asst. general manager, Chamber of Commerce (Corpus Christi, Texas). 1972, general manager, Chamber of Commerce (Denver). 1974-78, asst. vice pres.; 1978-82, vice pres.; 1982-88, senior vice pres., Valero Energy Corp. 1988-present, member; 1991-94, chairman, U.S. International Trade Commission.

Don Newquist, a Democrat of Texas, was nominated to the ITC by President Reagan in January 1988 to fill a vacancy, and in July 1988 he was nominated to the nine-year term expiring December 16, 1997. The U.S. Senate confirmed both nominations, and Newquist was sworn in as a member on October 18, 1988. Newquist also served a two-and-one-half year term as chair of the Commission. He was first designated chair by President Bush on December 13, 1991 and was redesignated as chair on June 16, 1992 for the term ending June 16, 1994.

Newquist is the president for the United States for the North American Institute, a private-not-for-profit organization with a secretariat in Santa Fe, New Mexico. NAMI explores the emerging North American regional relationship between the United States, Canada, and Mexico through forums, seminars, and publications with trinational participants from academia and education, business and nonprofit institutions, government, labor, and the media.

Commissioner
Ms. Carol T. Crawford
202/205-3051   FAX 202/205-2186
Room 703

Personal: born 2/25/43 in Mt. Holly, N.J.

Education: B.A. in political science, Mt. Holyoke College, 1965. J.D. (magna cum laude), American Univ., Washing. College of Law, 1978.

Professional: 1967-68, departmental asst., U.S. Rep. Robert Denney (R-Neb.). 1969-75, leg. asst., Sen. Bob Packwood (R-Ore.). 1979-81, attorney, Collier, Channon, Rill & Scott. 1981-83, exec. assistant to the chairman; 1983-85, director, bureau of consumer protection, Federal Trade Commission. 1985-89, associate director, economics and government, U.S. Office of Management and Budget. 1989-90, assistant attorney general, legislative affairs, U.S. Department of Justice. 1991-present, commissioner, International Trade Commission.

Carol Crawford was appointed to the International Trade Commission by President Bush in 1991 for a term expiring in 1999.

Crawford is a veteran of the Reagan and Bush Administrations and of Capitol Hill. Prior to her appointment to the ITC, Crawford was an assistant attorney general in the U.S. Justice Department where she headed the office of legislative affairs and handled the department's liaison with Congress. From 1985 to 1989, Crawford served as associate director of the Office of Management and Budget and was responsible for overseeing the budgets of five cabinet level departments and related smaller agencies.

Crawford was director of the Federal Trade Commission's Bureau of Consumer Protection from 1983 to 1985 and served as executive assistant to the FTC's chairman from 1981 to 1983. She began her Capitol Hill career in 1967 as a departmental assistant to U.S. Representative Robert Denney (R-Neb.). She then served, from 1969 to 1975, as legislative assistant to Senator Robert Packwood (R-Ore.).

A 1978 graduate of American University's Washington College of Law, Crawford was in private practice at a Washington DC law firm from 1979 to 1981.

Crawford serves on the Dean's Advisory Council of Washington College of Law, is a member of the Advisory Board of the Law School 's International Law Program, and is an advisor to the Independent Women's Forum. She is a trustee of the Barry Goldwater Chair of American Institutions at Arizona State University.

Office of External Relations

The Office of External Relations is the USITC's primary liaison with the public, the news media, Congress and executive branch agencies, State and local agencies, as well as foreign governments and international organizations. The agency's Trade Remedy Assistance Office is also a component of the Office of External Relations. External Relations issues all USITC news releases, responds to inquiries, produces the agency's annual report, and offers a variety of brochures, pamphlets, and other materials to enhance public understanding of the ITC, its mission, and its role in U.S. international trade matters.

Director
Mr. Daniel Leahy
202/205-3141
Room 716A

Office of the General Counsel

General Counsel
Ms. Lyn M. Schlitt
202/205-3061
Room 707D

Asst. General Counsel, Antidumping & Countervailing Duties
Mr. Edwin J. Madaj
202/205-3100
Room 707J

Asst. General Counsel, Sec. 337 Investigations
Mr. N. Timor Yaworski
202/205-3096
Room 707F

Senior Counsel for Special Investigations
Mr. William W. Gearhart
202/205-3091
Room 707E

Office of Congressional Relations

Officer
Ms. Nancy Carman
202/205-3151
Room 718

Office of Investigations

Director
Ms. W. Lynn Featherstone
202/205-3160
Room 615AA

Office of Unfair Import Investigations

Director
Ms. Lynn I. Levine
202/205-2561
Room 401G

Trade Remedy Assistance Office

The Trade Remedy Assistance Office assists the public and small businesses seeking benefits or relief under U.S. trade laws. The office offers general information concerning remedies and benefits available under the trade laws of the United States, and it provides technical and legal assistance and advice to small businesses seeking those remedies and benefits.

Director
Ms. Elizabeth Seltzer
202/205-2200
Room 716B

Office of Economics

Acting Director
Mr. Robert A. Rogowsky
202/205-3216
Room 602F

Office of Tariff Affairs and Trade Agreements

Director
Mr. Eugene A. Rosengarden
202/205-2592
Room 404B

Office of Industries

Director
Mr. Vern Simpson
202/205-3296
Room 504D

Chief, Agriculture & Forest Products Division
Ms. Cathy Jabara
202/205-3309
Room 511-O

Chief, Energy, Chemicals & Textiles Division
Mr. John J. Gersic
202/205-3342
Room 513I

Chief, Minerals, Metals, Machinery & Misc. Manufacturers Div.
Mr. Larry L. Brookhart
202/205-3419
Room 511C

Chief, Services, Electronics & Transportation Division
Mr. Norman McLennan
202/205-3380
Room 501A

©Almanac Publishing, Inc. 1998 - The Washington Almanac of International Trade & Business

American Red Cross

17th and D Streets, NW / Washington DC 20006

Chair
Mr. Norman R. Augustine
202/639-3930

European Space Agency

955 L'Enfant Plaza, SW / Washington DC 20024

Head, Washington Office
Mr. I.W. Pryke
202/488-4158   FAX 202/488-4930
Rm. 7800

International Boundary & Water Commission, U.S. & Mexico

The IBWC was transformed from the International Boundary Commission (IBC), which dated from 1889, by the 1944 Water Treaty. The Commission has the status of an international body and is split into a Mexico section and a U.S. section. Its mission is to apply the rights and obligations of the U.S. and Mexico assumed under the numerous boundary and water treaties and related agreements.

2201 C Street, NW Rm. 4258 / Washington DC 20520

Special Assistant
Paul E. Storing
202/647-8529   FAX 915/534-6680
Rm. 4258

4171 North Mesa Street Rm. 310 / El Paso TX 79902-1442

Commissioner
Mr. John M. Bernal
915/832-4101
Rm. 301

International Boundary Commission, U.S. & Canada

1250 23rd St., NW Rm. 100 / Washington DC 20037

The International Boundary Commission, U.S. and Canada, defines and maintains the demarcation of the international boundary line between the U.S. and Canada.

U.S. Commissioner
Mr. Thomas Baldini
202/736-9100

Deputy Commissioner
Mr. Clyde R. Moore
202/736-9102   FAX 202/736-9015

Ottawa Office - Canadian Section
615 Booth St. Ottawa, Ontario, Canada K1AOE9

Canadian Commissioner
Mr. Michael O'Sullivan
613/995-4951

International Joint Commission, U.S. & Canada

1250 23rd St., NW / Washington DC 20440

The 1909 Boundary Waters Treaty established the Commission, which has six members. It assists governments in finding solutions to problems in the rivers and lakes which lie along, or flow across, the border between the U.S. and Canada. The IJC also investigates and monitors specific situations upon request by the government of the U.S. and Canada. It reports every two years on progress under the 1978 Great Lakes Water Quality Agreement.

Chair, U.S. Section
Mr. Thomas L. Baldini
202/736-9000   FAX 202/736-9015

Canadian Section
100 Metcalfe St. Ottawa, Ontario K1P 5M1 Canada

Chair, Canadian Section
Mr. Leonard Legault
613/995-2984

International Labor Organization

Washington Branch Office
1828 L St., N.W. - Suite 801, Washington DC 20036

The ILO was created in 1919 by the Treaty of Versailles to improve living and working conditions worldwide. It is made up of more than 160 member nations, all in pursuit of freedom and democracy.

Director
Anthony G. Freeman
202/653-7652   FAX 202/653-7687

Japan-U.S. Friendship Commission

1120 Vermont Ave., NW Rm. 925 / Washington DC 20005

Chair
Mr. Richard J. Wood
202/275-7712

National Research Council

2101 Constitution Ave., NW / Washington DC 20418

Although established by an Act of Congress in 1863, the National Research Council and its three organizations, the National Academy of Sciences, the National Academy of Engineering, and the Institute of Medicine, operate as private organizations and receive no federal funding. They do, however, advise the federal government on scientific and technical questions.

Chair, NRC / President, National Academy of Sciences
Dr. Bruce M. Alberts

202/334-2100

Executive Director, Office of Intl. Affairs
Mr. John Boright
202/334-2800

Institute of Medicine

1055 Thomas Jefferson St, NW / Washington DC 20007

Director, Intl. Health Division
Dr. Judith Bule
202/334-2427

Organization for Economic Cooperation & Development

2001 L St., NW Rm. 650 / Washington DC 20036-4910
202/785-6323 FAX 202/785-0350

An international, inter-governmental organization - and the successor of the Organization for European Economic Cooperation created in 1948 for the implementation of the Marshall Plan - OECD now boasts 24 member states from the industrialized world. The original 18 European states, the U.S. and Canada, have since been joined by Australia, Finland, Japan and New Zealand. Its mandate is to push for the highest level of sustainable economic growth, employment and living standards in member countries - while maintaining international financial stability - and to promote the expansion of world trade and assist economic development in non-member states.

OECD Washington Representative
Mr. William C. Danvers
202/822-3866

Organization of American States

17th Street and Constitution Ave., NW / Washington DC 20006
202/458-3000 FAX 202/458-3967

The Organization of American States (OAS) is a regional, intergovernmental organization whose primary purposes are to preserve peace and security and to promote, by cooperative action, the integral development of the member states. Organized in its present form in 1948, its roots date from 1890, making it the oldest regional, international organization in the world.

The OAS member states are Argentina, Antigua and Barbuda, Commonwealth of the Bahamas, Barbados, Belize, Bolivia, Brazil, Canada, Chile, Colombia, Costa Rica, Cuba, Commonwealth of Dominica, Dominican Republic, Ecuador, El Salvador, Grenada, Guatemala, Guyana, Haiti, Honduras, Jamaica, Mexico, Nicaragua, Panama, Paraguay, Peru, St. Kitts and Nevis, St. Lucia, St. Vincent and the Grenadines, Suriname, Trinidad and Tobago, the U.S., Uruguay, and Venezuela. The present Government of Cuba is excluded from participation by a decision of the Consultation of Ministers of Foreign Affairs in 1962. Twenty-nine non-American countries and the European Union are Permanent Observers.

Secretary General
Mr. Cesar Gaviria
202/458-6836

Chief of Staff of the Secretary General
Dr. Ricardo Avila
202/458-3841

Director, Department of Public Information
Mr. Canton Santiago
202/458-3760

Executive Secretary, Inter-American Drug Abuse Control Commission
Mr. David Beall
202/458-3178

Permanent Representative of the U.S. to the OAS

2201 C Street NW - Room 6494 / Washington DC 20520

Ambassador Victor Marrero
202/647-9376   FAX   202/647-0911

Personal: born in Santurce, Puerto Rico.

Education: B.A. in history (cum laude and Phi Beta Kappa), New York Univ., 1964. J.D., Yale Law School, 1968.

Professional: 1968-70, asst. to Mayor John Lindsay, N.Y. City. 1970-72, asst. admin., N.Y. City Model Cities Administration. 1973, exec. dir., dept. of city planning, N.Y. City. 1974-75, special counsel, N.Y. City Comptroller. 1975, first asst. counsel, Governor of New York. 1976-77, chairman, N.Y. City Planning Commission. 1978-79, commissioner, division of housing and community renewal, N.Y. State. 1979, under sec., U.S. Dept. of Housing and Urban Development. 1982-86, partner, Tufo & Zuccotti (New York). 1986-93, partner, Brown & Wood (New York). 1993-97, U.S. representative to the Economic and Social Council, United Nations. 1997-present, Permanent Representative of the U.S. to the OAS

Victor Marrero joined the Clinton administration as U.S. Representative to the United Nations Economic and Social Council (UNESCO) in 1993. He served in that position until the fall of 1997, when he replaced Harriet Babbitt as the U.S. Permanent Representative to the Organization of American States.

In the post-Cold War era, the OAS plays an increasing role in settling regional disputes and securing political and economic stability in the Western Hemisphere. As the U.S. representative, Marrero is responsible for the formulation of U.S. policy with respect to actions taken by the OAS, the world's oldest international membership organization. He is the principal liaison for the U.S. government in its relations with the organization, and coordinates the activities of other U.S. departments vis-a-vis the OAS.

In his former post as the U.S. Representative to UNESCO, Ambassador Marrero represented U.S. interests in the United Nations on issues such as human rights, population, environment and development, drug control, and the status of women and children. He also served as a senior member of the U.S. delegation to various United Nations agencies, conferences and other events dealing with these issues.

Marrero was appointed to the UN position in 1993 after serving for seven years as a partner in the New York law firm of Brown and

Wood. Prior to that he had served as a law partner at Tufo & Zuccotti in New York.

Prior to joining the private sector as a land use and environmental lawyer, Marrero had spent part of his professional career working for federal, state and city governments. He has served as commissioner of the New York State Division of Housing and Community Renewal and as vice chair for the New York State Housing Finance Agency. He also worked as the under secretary of the U.S. Department of Housing and Urban Development during the Carter Administration. Marrero worked as a first assistant counsel to the comptroller of New York from 1974 to 1975 and served as an assistant to Mayor John Lindsay of New York from 1968 to 1970.

Marrero has also served on various special public boards, committees, and commissions. These include the State University of New York, the New York State Committee to Improve the Availability of Legal Services, the New York Public Library, the New York Telephone Company, the Consolidated Edison Company, and the Association of the Bar of the City of New York.

Marrero was born in Santurce, Puerto Rico and is a long-time resident of New York City. He graduated cum laude and Phi Beta Kappa from New York University and went on to earn his law degree from Yale School in 1968. While at Yale, he was editor of the *Yale Law Journal.* Marrero was a Fulbright Scholar and studied in England at the Sheffield School of Law. He has also taught as a visiting lecturer at both the Yale and Columbia Law Schools.

Smithsonian Institution

1000 Jefferson Drive, SW / Washington DC 20560

Office of the Provost

Director, Office of Intl. Relations
Ms. Francine Berkowitz
202/357-4795
Rm. 3123

United Nations - Washington DC Office

1775 K St., NW - Suite 400 / Washington DC 20006

INTRODUCTION

With Member States currently numbering 185, U.N. Members commit themselves to cooperate in fulfilling the principles and purposes set out in the U.N. Charter. An international treaty, the Charter codifies at the international level, the major principles of international relations—from the sovereign equality of States, to the prohibition of the use of force in international relations to the basic human rights to which all women and men are entitled. The U.N. and its attendant bodies are to provide channels for all the peoples of the Member States to achieve the common goals and ideals reflected in the U.N. Charter.

The U.N. Charter, created during the Second World War at the United Nations Conference on International Organization in San Francisco, arose out of proposals from the now five permanent members of the U.N. Security Council. China, France, the Soviet Union (now the Russian Federation), the United Kingdom and the United States had met the previous year, from August to October of 1944, to agree on the founding principles. The U.N. Charter was signed on 26 June 1945 by the 50 states in attendance at the Conference. Poland, who had not been represented at the Conference, signed later and became one of the original 51 Member States.

The United Nations officially came into existence on 24 October 1945, when the Charter had been ratified by China, France, the Soviet Union, the United Kingdom, the United States and the 45 remaining signatory members. The Charter sets out the broad functions of the six primary organs of the U.N.:

The General Assembly

The primary deliberative organ of the U.N., the General Assembly is comprised of representatives from each member state, each with one vote. The GA is mandated to make decisions on important issues, including those related to security and peace, budgetary concerns and the admission of new U.N. members. Decisions on important issues, require two-thirds majority vote, while decisions on other matters are reached by a simple majority. The General Assembly's regular session commences annually on the third Tuesday of September and generally continues until the middle of December. The Presidency of the Assembly rotates each year among 5 member-state groups: African, Asian, Eastern European, Latin American, Western European and other states. Beyond its regular session, the GA may be summoned at the request of the Security Council, of a majority of Members of the U.N., or of one member if the majority concurs.

The Security Council

The Security Council has primary responsibility, under the Charter, for maintenance of international security and peace. In addition to the five permanent members of the Council, an additional 10 members are elected for 2-year terms by the General Assembly. Each Council Member has one vote. Decisions on procedural matters are made by an affirmative vote of at least 9 out of 15 members. Decisions on substantive issues also require 9 affirmative votes, including those of all 5 permanent members. Referred to as the veto, this stipulation has been utilized by each of the 5 permanent members. While other U.N. bodies may make recommendations to Member Governments, Security Council decisions are unique because member states are obligated to implement them, as stated in the Charter.

The Economic and Social Council

The Charter established the Economic and Social Council as the principal organ for the coordination of all economic and social work of the U.N. and its specialized agencies and institutions. The Council has 54 members, each serving for 3-year terms. Decisions are made by a simple majority. The Council generally holds one 5-week long substantive session each year, alternating between New York and Geneva, and at least 2 organizational sessions in New York. The Council's year round work is carried out by its subsidiary bodies, commissions and committees, which meet at regular intervals and report back to the Council.

The Trusteeship Council

In order to create an International Trusteeship System, the Charter established the Trusteeship Council as one of the main organs of the U.N. and assigned it the task of supervising the administration of Trust Territories placed under the Trusteeship System. Major goals of the System were to promote the advancement of the inhabitants of the 11 original Trust Territories and their progressive development towards self-government or independence. The Trusteeship Council is composed of the 5 permanent members of the Security Council.
The aims of the Trusteeship System have been fulfilled to the extent that all the Trust Territories have attained self-government of independence, either as separate states or by joining neighboring independent countries. In November 1994, the Security Council terminated the U.N. Trusteeship Agreement for the last of the original 11 Trustee Territories, the Trust Territory of the Pacific Islands (Palau).

The Trusteeship Council, by amendment of its rules of procedure, will now meet as and where the occasion requires.

The Trusteeship Council had been authorized to examine and discuss reports from the Administering Authority on the political, economic, social and educational advancement of the peoples of the Trust Territories, and to examine petitions from and undertake periodic and other special missions to the Trust Territories. On November 1994, the Security Council determined that the applicability of the Trusteeship Agreement had terminated with respect to Palau, the last remaining Trust Territory.

The International Court of Justice

The central judicial organ of the U.N., sitting in the Hague, Netherlands, the ICJ has 15 members who are elected by the General Assembly and the Security Council and who vote independently. Each member serves for a 9-year term. No two justices may represent the same state and care is taken to ensure that the world's major legal systems are represented on the Court. The Court is open to the parties to its Statute, which includes all U.N. members, and is open to non-members on conditions determined by the Security Council. Both the Security Council and the General Assembly may request an advisory opinion on any legal matter, as can specialized agents, if authorized by the General Assembly.

Court jurisdictions span all questions which States refer to it, as well as all matters provided for the U.N. Charter, treaties or conventions. As stipulated in its Statute, the Court is to apply the following in disputes arising before it: international conventions establishing rules accepted by contesting states, international custom as evidence of general practice accepted as law, general principles of law recognized by nations and written opinions of the most highly qualified scholars in the particular field of law.

The Secretariat

The Secretariat is an international staff working at UN Headquarters in New York and all over the world. This organ of the U.N. is responsible for carrying out the day-to-day operations of the Organization.

The Secretariat services the other major organs of the U.N. and administers the programs and policies laid down by them. At its head is the Secretary-General, who is appointed by the General Assembly on the Security Council recommendation, for a 5-year renewable term.

The Secretariat staff totals 13,288 women and men from some 170 countries, working in duty stations in New York, Geneva, Nairobi and Vienna, serving on peace keeping missions and working in information centers.

Director, UN Information Center
Mr. Joe Sills
202/331-8670   FAX 202/331-9191

U.N. Development Program (UNDP)
1775 K St., NW - Suite 420 / Washington DC 20006

Headquartered in New York and established in 1966, the UNDP is a technical assistance institution, providing pre-investment surveys, training and administrative development projects for encouraging Third World development.

Director
Mr. Roy D. Morey
202/331-9130   FAX 202/331-9363

U.N. Economic Commission for Latin America & the Caribbean
1825 K St., NW - Suite 1120 / Washington DC 20006

Established in 1948 and based in Santiago, Chile, the commission conducts surveys and analyzes Latin American and Caribbean economic and social developments, and offers development advice to governments.

Director
Mr. Isaac Cohen
202/955-5613   FAX 202/296-0826
Email: ECLAC@tmn.com

U.N. Food and Agriculture Organization
2175 K St., NW - Suite 300 / Washington DC 20437

http://www.fao.org

Based in Rome and founded in 1945, the FAO is the primary center for information on world food and agricultural issues, providing technical assistance to developing nations.

Director
Mr. Charles Riemenschneider
202/653-2402   FAX 202/653-5760
Email: FAO-LOWA@field.fao.org

U.N. High Commissioner for Refugees
1775 K St., NW - Suite 300 / Washington DC 20006

http://www.unicc.org/unhcr

A U.N. agency headquartered in Geneva, Switzerland and established in 1951, it provides worldwide assistance and protection to refugees.

Regional Representative
Mr. Anne Willem Bijleveld
202/296-5191   FAX 202/296-5660

U.S. Institute of Peace

1550 M St., NW Suite 700 / Washington DC 20005-1708

An independent, non-profit, federal institution corporation created and funded by Congress to develop and disseminate knowledge about international peace and conflict resolution. The institutes five central activities consist of grantmaking, fellowships, in-house, research projects, public education programs and information services. It has special initiatives on Middle-East peace, the Rule of Law and Religion, nationalism, and intolerance.

Chair of the Board
Mr. Chester A. Crocker
202/457-1700

Vice Chair of the Board
Mr. Max M. Kampelman
202/457-1700

President
Mr. Richard H. Solomon
202/457-1700   FAX 202/429-6063

Education: Ph.D. in political science & Chinese politics, Massachusetts Institute of Technology.

Professional: 1966-71, prof., political science, University of Michigan. 1971-76, senior staff member, Asian affairs, National Security Council. 1976-86, director, Political Science Department, RAND Corporation. 1986-89, director, policy planning staff, Department of State. 1989-92, assistant secretary of State for East Asian and Pacific affairs. 1992-93, U.S. Ambassador to the Philippines. 1993-present, president, U.S. Institute of Peace.

Richard H. Solomon heads the U.S. Institute of Peace. The Peace

Institute was established in 1984 to promote research, policy analysis, education and training on international peace and conflict resolution. An independent Federal agency, the Institute addresses this mission in three ways:

• It expands basic and applied knowledge about the origins, nature, and processes of peace and war, encompassing the widest spectrum of approaches and insights.

• It disseminates this knowledge to officials, policymakers, diplomats and others engaged in efforts to promote international peace.

• It supports education and training programs and provides information for secondary and university-level teachers and students and the general public.

The Institute's primary activities are grantmaking, fellowships, in-house research projects, public education and outreach activities, publications, and library services.

Solomon is a former ambassador to the Philippines and was in the State Department during the Bush Administration. Before joining the State Department, Dr. Solomon was head of the RAND Corporation's Political Science Department. He also directed RAND's research program on International Security Policy from 1977 to 1983.

Solomon has contributed articles to a variety of professional journals including Foreign Affairs and The China Quarterly, and has published six books, including: The Soviet Far East Military Buildup: Nuclear Dilemmas and Asian Security (1986); The China Factor (1981); Asian Security in the 1980s (1979); A Revolution is not a Dinner Party (1976); and Mao's Revolution and the Chinese Political Culture (1971).

Dr. Solomon has done research and consulting work for a variety of U.S. government offices and private sector corporations involved in international commerce. He served as a visiting professor at the Johns Hopkins School of Advanced International Studies in Washington from 1972 to 1974. He was an International Affairs Fellow of the Council on Foreign Relations in 1971, and served as a consultant to the President's Commission on Foreign Language and International Studies from 1978 to 1980. He has been a board member for the National Committee on U.S.-China Relations and the International Research and Exchanges Board (IREX); and has served on the Chief of Naval Operations' Executive Panel since 1983.

The Institute has been under the budgetary gun of late. The new chairman of the House Budget Committee, John Kasich (R., Ohio) had circulated a budget cut list in 1994 which targeted the Institute as one that "could be eliminated without directly affecting U.S. foreign policy." (Wall Street Journal, March 17, 1995).

Executive Vice President
Ms. Harriett Hentges
202/457-1700

Woodrow Wilson International Center for Scholars

1000 Jefferson Drive, SW / Washington DC 20560
202/357-2429

The mandate of the Woodrow Wilson International Center for Scholars is to integrate the world of learning with the world of public affairs. Through meetings and conferences, the Center brings scholars together with Members of Congress, Government officials, business leaders, and other policymakers. The Center awards approximately 40 residential fellowships annually to individuals with project proposals representing the entire range of superior scholarship, with a strong emphasis on the humanities and social sciences. Applications from any country are welcomed. Where appropriate, fellows may be associated with one of the Center's seven programs: the Asia Program; the East and West European Program; Historical, Cultural and Literary Studies Program; the International Studies Program; the Kennan Institute for Advanced Russian Studies Program; the Latin America Program; or the United States Studies Program.

Chair, Board of Trustees
Mr. Joseph H. Flom
202/357-2763
Rm. 337

Acting Director
Mr. Dean Anderson
202/357-2763
Rm. 336

Fellowship Office
Woodrow Wilson Center - Washington DC 20560

202/357-2429   FAX 202/357-4439
External Affairs 202/357-4335
Publications 202/287-3000

U.S.-Panama Joint Commission on the Environment of the Panama Canal

2201 C St., NW / Washington DC 20520

U.S. Commissioners
Mr. Gary Hartshorn and Mr. Philip Pillsbury
919/684-5774   or 202/647-4986

1998 International Exporters - Importers Conference

Orlando Centroplex
November 10, 11, 12, 1998
Orlando, Florida

IMPORT, EXPORT AND INTERNET SHOWCASE

International trade is the dominant force in the global economy, but the complexity of doing business overseas requires constant upgrading of skills, information and contacts. The 1998 International Exporters / Importers Conference is specifically geared towards helping you meet those requirements and helping you build your domestic and international business. World class speakers from the private and public sectors will provide the information and contacts you need to make your business more competitive and profitable.

On-site appointments will be facilitated with exhibiting and visiting buyers, vendors, distributors, potential joint venture partners, investors and other attendees who meet your interests and requirements. Complete turnkey exhibit packages are available for new-to-market companies interested in taking their first step in the global marketplace.

The Peoples Republic of China has committed to participate, as have Ecuador, the Dominican Republic, Italy, Malaysia, Mexico, Poland, the Russian Federation, Slovenia, Tunisia, Turkey and several Caribbean Countries.

Mail or fax this form with a copy of your business card to the address below:

Name _____

Title _____

Company _____

Address _____

City / State _____ Zip _____

Country _____

Phone _____ Fax _____

Please send me details about:

❏ Becoming a co-sponsor

❏ Exhibiting our product line

❏ Attending the conference and seminars

❏ Advertising in the show program

❏ Speaking at one of the seminars

❏ Hosting an event

❏ Holding a reception

❏ Hosting a hospitality suite

❏ Participating in a country Pavilion

❏ The Catalog showcase

Official Show Program of
EXIM
CONFERENCE
98
International Exporters - Importers Conference
April 22 - 24, 1997

PLEASE MAIL OR FAX REQUEST TO:
EXPORTERS-IMPORTERS CONFERENCE
242 South Military Trail
Deerfield Beach, Florida 33442
Phone: (954) 427-9717 • Fax: (954) 427-9178

————————— Co - Sponsored by: —————————

The Exporter Newspaper

SECTION III

OTHER ENTITIES DEALING WITH INTERNATIONAL TRADE

A number of independent and private organizations in Washington and across the country offer services, information, and assistance to exporters, investors, and others interested in international issues. They also are often key players affecting policy making in the international arena, from diplomatic relations to trade policy to human rights. This section of *The Washington Almanac on International Trade and Business* lists many of these groups with descriptions, addresses, key contacts, telephone and fax numbers.

The first segment covers the five Multilateral Development Banks: the African Development Group, the Asian Development Bank, the Inter-American Development Bank, the European Bank of Reconstruction and Development, and the World Bank. The segment explains how their activities can lead to U.S. business opportunities and tells how to find out about them.

The second segment describes the work of the International Monetary Fund (IMF).

The third segment lists nearly 500 international interest groups - both private and intergovernmental - including research oriented institutions with an international focus and trade associations with offices in Washington. We have provided a summary description of each entity's activities, the Washington address, key contact, and phone and fax numbers.

The fourth segment focuses on the organizations and individuals who represent foreign interests in the United States. It begins with a primer on the Foreign Agents Registration Act (FARA) and a summary of the registration process. It goes on to list the agents who have registered with the Justice Department under the Act first in order by Country origin of their client and then in alphabetical order by registered agent.

The fifth segment lists Washington's International Press in order by country.

The sixth segment lists World Trade Centers throughout the U.S. and abroad.

The seventh segment covers the international business education programs at major universities in the Washington, D.C. metro area.

The eighth segment lists the addresses and phone/fax numbers of Foreign Chambers of Commerce in the U.S. and U.S. Chambers of Commerce Abroad.

The ninth segment covers the state government offices that can help U.S. exporters develop overseas markets. These include state agriculture, trade finance, and trade offices.

The final sections list foreign trade zones, numerous international trade sites on the internet, port authorities throughout the U.S., and other trade centers throughout the U.S.

INTRODUCTION

Major contracts in developing markets financed by the five multilateral banks (MDBs) could lead to major long-term export opportunities for U.S. equipment suppliers, contractors, and consultants. Annual lending from the MDBs totals approximately $45 billion. The MDBs mobilize an additional $50 billion for projects in development markets, further enhancing these opportunities.

The five multilateral development banks are: African Development Bank, Asian Development Bank, European Bank for Reconstruction and Development, Inter-American Development Bank, and the World Bank Group.

MDBs are international lending institutions owned by member countries. The bank's objective is to promote economic and social progress in developing member nations by providing loans, technical assistance, capital investment, and help with economic development plans.

MDBs are active in supporting developing countries around the world. Since the U.S. is a shareholder in all five MDBs, U.S. firms and their subsidiaries are eligible to bid on procurement opportunities funded by each of the banks.

MDBs support clearly defined projects designed to foster economic and social progress within their specified geographic regions. Projects usually involve development of one or more of the following sectors: agribusiness, education and training, energy, investment, industry, municipal development, telecommunications, transportation, health, water and sewage, environment, housing, tourism, and power.

While all five of the MDBs are increasing their private sector investment activities, assistance with privatization and financial restructuring are top priorities for the World Bank affiliate, the International Finance Corporation, and the European Bank for Reconstruction and Development.

The primary sources of bank funds are capital subscriptions from member countries and borrowings on the international capital markets. Loans and grants are made directly to developing member governments, to public or private entities operating within these countries, and to international and regional enterprises concerned with economic development in the region.

U.S. companies seeking information and assistance on business opportunities available through MDB-supported projects should contact the U.S. Department of Commerce's Office of Multilateral Development Bank Operations. Information is facilitated through electronic media such as the Economic Bulletin Board, the National Trade Data Bank, and Internet. Companies interested in receiving early warning information regarding MDB projects can subscribe to these services.

Contact:

Multilateral Development Bank Operations
U.S. & Foreign Commercial Service Office of Intern'l. Operations
International Trade Administration
U.S. Department of Commerce
14th Street and Constitution Avenue, NW - Rm. 1806
Washington, D.C. 20230

Phone: 202/482-3399   Fax: 202/273-0927

Each bank also publishes a monthly or quarterly operational summary of projects under consideration. These are available by subscription

(see addresses, telephone, and fax numbers below).

Bank activities present many good opportunities for consultants, who may be hired by the borrowing country at any stage of a project. The MDBs themselves also hire consultants for sectoral studies, economic feasibility, preliminary engineering and design studies, government policy analysis, preparation of bid documents, and evaluation of bidders. Consulting firms may register with the World Bank's automated DACON (Data on Consultants) file. To be placed on the list, a consulting company must have a professional staff of at least five persons. Interested consultants should write or fax the World Bank requesting the DACON information package.

Contact:

Mail

The World Bank Group
DACON, Attention: Corinne de Jesus
1818 H Street, NW
Washington, D.C. 20433

Phone/Fax (Corinne de Jesus)

Phone: 202/458-4095   Fax: 202/334-0002

Firms may also submit a hard copy DACON form to each of the four regional development banks. Individual consultants may submit their credentials for review to any of the banks at any time. The banks use these rosters to provide borrowers and their own staff with descriptions of available consultants; therefore, it is important for a firm to keep its registration current.

The best prospects for the remainder of the decade appear to be projects in the environment, energy, social infrastructure, and financial sectors. Large companies frequently subcontract smaller suppliers for goods and services. Subscribing to the bank's project news bulletins or on-line information services will keep a firm advised of contract awards.

To subscribe, write each individual multilateral bank:

African Development Bank Group
01 BP 1387
Abidjan 01
Cote d'Ivoire
Phone: 011-225-20-44-44   Fax: 011-225-22-24-37

Asian Development Bank
No. 6 ADB Ave.
Mandaluyong City, 0410 Metro
Manila, Philippines
Phone: 011-632-711-3851   Fax: 011-632-890-9713

European Bank for Reconstruction and Development
One Exchange Square
London EC2A 2EH
United Kingdom
Phone: 011-44-171-338-6000   Fax: 011-44-171-338-6100

The Inter-American Development Bank
1300 New York Avenue, NW
Washington, D.C. 20577
Phone: 202/623-1000 (Central)   Fax: 202/623-3096 (Central)

World Bank
1818 H St., N.W.
Washington, D.C. 20433
Phone: 202/477-1234 (Central)   Fax: 202/522-2616 (Central)

Many of the MDB's projects involve the design, construction, rehabilitation, and maintenance of roads, bridges, ports, dams, irrigation systems, power plants, water treatment and health facilities, housing, and schools. Some services sought by the executing agencies of borrowing countries, as well as the banks are: design and feasibility studies, construction management, environmental assessment, monitoring of management activities, aerial photography and mapping, oil and gas exploration, financial services, and auditing.

Projects are initiated by (a) the government of the borrowing nation; (b) the banks themselves, through project identification missions; or (c) cofinancing proposals submitted by other financial institutions. New proposals are continually added to each bank's list of "pipeline" projects, which contains descriptive information on each project, program, or study under consideration. The banks analyze projects to determine (a) the borrower's capacity to finance and administer the project; (b) its economic, technical and environmental feasibility; and © its social and economic benefits to the recipient country.

For large-scale public sector projects, the banks' procurement policies require open international competitive bidding among companies from member countries. For private sector projects, the banks may authorize competitive bidding from selected sources. In either case, the MDBs encourage competition and attention to cost-benefit considerations on the part of the borrower. Pricing, quality, service, and the way a firm presents its bid can make the difference.

A company does not need to register with the banks in order to bid on projects. While the names of consultants maintained on automated bank files are often made available, without specific endorsement, to borrowers, most contracts for goods and services are awarded by the agency for the borrowing nation. When a firm learns that procurement is about to occur, it can request the bid tender specifications and carefully examine the guidelines and provisions before preparing its bids. Questions should be directed to the borrower up front.

The Multilateral Development Bank Operations [MDBO] staff within the Commerce Department's International Trade Administration, offers convenient counseling and referral—no fee is charged. The office gives firms the information they need to get started:

—Current projects worldwide. Information on approved projects and downstream financing plans.

—Expert guidance on how to pursue business at the MDBs.

—Advocacy. Assistance with pre-award support and procurement disputes.

—On-line information. A guide to electronic media providing up-to-date information relating to projects.

—Future opportunities. What's in the pipeline in terms of future project financing.

Firms can contact the Multilateral Development Bank Operations Office directly (202/482-3399) or through a local office of the Commerce Department's International Trade Administration (see list in Section under Commerce Department).

In addition, the Commerce Department has assigned commercial liaison officers to each of the MDBs. These officers work closely with the U.S. Executive Directors of the MDBs to support the efforts of U.S. companies pursuing MDB contracts. The MDB liaison officers and their addresses are listed with the information about each bank below.

African Development Bank Group

01 BP 1387
Abidjan 01
Cote d'Ivoire
Phone: 011-225-21-46-16   Fax: 011-225-22-24-37

U.S. Liaison Officer
Mark Herrling
Commercial Liaison to AFDB
(Internet address: Mherrling@doc.gov) - see mailing address below

Mr. Omar Kabbaj
President and Chairman of the Board of
**   Directors, African Development Bank Group**

The Washington, D.C., office of the African Development Bank was closed in 1994.

Ms. Alice Dear
U.S. Executive Director
01 B.P. 1387 Abidjan
01, Cote d'Ivoire
Phone: 011-225-20-40-15   Fax: 011-225-33-14-34

(for Herrling)

The U.S. Commercial Service
Ambassade des Etat Unis d'Amerique
6 Rue Jesse Owens
01 B.P. 1712 Abidjan O1, Cote d'Ivoire
Phone: 011-225-21-46-16   Fax: 011-225-22-24-37

Barbara White
U.S. Department of Commerce, Room 1107
Washington, D.C. 20230
Phone: 202/482-3399   Fax: 202/273-0927

> *The African Development Bank Group is made up of three distinct bodies: the African Development Bank (ADB), the African Development Fund (ADF), and the Nigeria Trust Fund (NTF).*

African Development Bank (ADB)

Established in 1963 and beginning operations in 1966, the African Development Bank (ADB) is comprised of 51 independent African states and, since the 1982 decision to open bank capital to non-African participation, to 26 non-African countries.

The Bank has a broad mandate to facilitate economic development and social progress in the region and to promote government and private investment. Its current strategic thrust involves the selection and implementation of macro-economic reforms, management of the environment, economic integration, and the promotion of trade and private sector growth.

Since its inception, the ADB has committed more than $25 billion in loans across all sectors of African economies and has accomplished a net transfer of resources of $9 billion to African states. It has implemented a good number of priority development projects in borrowing member countries and has aided in the establishment of institutions aimed at promoting development project coordination and financing, including the African Export-Import Bank, African Business Round Table, the Africa Reinsurance Corporation, and African Management Services Company.

The Board of Governors, comprised mostly of Ministers of Finance and Economy in the member states, directs general policies, while the 18-member Board of Directors carries out the day-to-day operations of the Bank. Each Director is elected by the Board of Governors for a three-year term; 12 Directors represent countries in the region and six are from countries outside the region in accordance with the 2-to-1 share holding structure of the Bank. The ADB staff numbers approximately 1,300. It maintains an office in London.

African Development Fund (ADF)

With a few exceptions, the membership of the African Development Fund (ADF) mirrors that of the ADB. Created in 1974 with an initial subscription of $244 million, ADF provides concessionary development financing to the poorer African member states - those with a per capita GNP of $510 or less. The fund is replenished every three years and has grown significantly since ADF inception. Dispersed funds are aimed at the financing of technical assistance and market and development studies.

The 12-member ADF Board of Directors is divided equally between appointees from non-African states and designees from among the regional Executive Directors of the ADB.

Nigeria Trust Fund (NTF)

Established by the Nigerian Government in 1976 to assist with economic development in the poorer ADB member states, the Nigeria Trust Fund (NTF) operates under ADB management and has a resource base of about $400 million. New initiatives have been passed by NTF aimed at financing intra-African trade and private sector development.

Asian Development Bank

No. 6 ADB Ave.
Mandaluyong City
Manila, Philippines
Phone: 011-632-890-9364 or 895-3020
Fax: 011-632-890-9713

U.S. Commercial Liaison Officer

Cantwell Walsh
Senior Commercial Officer/Commercial Liaison Office
American Embassy Manila
3rd Floor, Thomas Jefferson Cultural Center
395 Gil Puyat Avenue, Makati City, Philippines
(Internet address: CWalsh@doc.gov)

Phone: 011-632-890-9364 or 895-3020
Fax: 011/632/890/9713

Lisa Lumbao
AEP Representative
Commercial Liaison Office
U.S. Embassy, Manila
APO AP 96440
(Internet address: Llumbao@doc.gov)

Phone: 011-632-890-9364 or 895-3020
Fax: 011-632-890-9713

Established in 1966, the Asian Development Bank is an international development finance institution aimed at promoting the economic and social progress of its developing member countries (DMCs). The Bank has 56 member countries, of which 40 are in the Asia-Pacific region and 16 are in Europe and North America. Thirty-three are classified as developing nations.

The Bank's DMCs range from China, with a population exceeding one billion to small Pacific island-nations. The newest members are Kazakstan, the Kyrgyz Republic and Uzbekistan. Bank membership is open to countries that are members of the United Nations Economic and Social Commission for Asia and the Pacific (ESCAP) and all other developed nations within the U.N.

Primary Bank activities include loans and direct investment for

projects which benefit the DMCs; and loans and grants for technical assistance. The Asian Development Bank works with national governments and businesses, as well as the U.N. and other international development institutions on their development activities in the region. The Bank offers two species of loan: ordinary loans granted to more advanced developing countries and concessional loans to the poorest. In 1983, the Bank abandoned its policy of limiting its loans to governments, and it now makes loans to private companies, as well as equity investments in them. Since 1985, such loans have been granted without government guarantee and are provided only for companies that produce or provide essential products or services.

Bank loans fall within three categories: project, sector, and program loans. Whereas project loans are made specifically for a particular endeavor, sector loans service a number of individual sub-projects spread over a certain period of time or in a geographical area. Sector loans are especially useful for major infrastructure development and in the energy and sanitation sectors, as well as for health and education projects where several individual projects can be consolidated under a single loan.

Program lending, instituted in 1987, directs resources at sector development programs which include government policy reform, investment programs, or institutional improvements. These are made directly to DMC governments. The Bank has been traditionally an infrastructure bank with heavy emphasis on agriculture and energy. In recent years, the Bank has been gradually shifting towards social infrastructure lending. In 1995, 32.5 percent of total lending went to energy and 22 percent to social infrastructure.

The Bank's research and technical assistance activities support its development goals. Its research arm publishes annually a survey of the progress of development in the region - *Asian Development Outlook* - as well as *Asian Development Review,* a biannual journal. Particularly crucial for the region's least developed nations, the Bank's technical assistance identifies, formulates, implements, and operates development projects, formulates development strategies, promotes technological know-how and fosters regional development cooperation. Bank staff visit each DMC annually.

The day-to-day business of the Bank is directed by its 12-member Board of Directors—eight from countries in the region and four from nations outside the region. The Bank's President serves as Chairman of the Board, comprised of one representative from each member country.

Mitsuo Sato
President, Asian Development Bank

Personal: born 2/1/33 in Gumma, Japan.

Education: graduate of law department of Tokyo University, 1955. One-year special student course at Harvard Law School, 1966.

Professional: 1955, entered Japanese ministry of finance, rising to the posts of deputy director general of the international finance bureau and director-general of the customs and tariffs bureau. 1988-93, Tokyo Stock Exchange. 1993-present, president of Asian Development

Bank.

Mitsuo Sato, first elected president of the Asian Development Bank (ADB) in November 1993, has been recently re-elected to a new fiver-year term. Sato brought with him nearly four decades of financial experience in his native Japan and in the international arena.

Immediately prior to joining the ADB, he spent six years with the Tokyo Stock Exchange (TSE) serving first as a managing director and ultimately as deputy president. During his tenure there, he was responsible for policy planning and external representation, which included opening the TSE to foreign-firm members and representing the TSE at international organizations such as the OECD and the Group of Thirty.

Sato began his career in 1955, when he entered the ministry of finance. He held various posts in the ministry, rising to the posts of deputy director-general of the International Finance Bureau between 1983 and 1984 and director-general of the Customs and Tariffs Bureau in 1985-86. In the International Finance Bureau, he prepared rescue programs for Brazil, the Philippines, and other nations to solve their immediate payment difficulties. He also participated, as a chief negotiator, in the Japan-U.S. Yen/Dollar Working Committee talks, which led to comprehensive deregulation of Japan's financial and capital markets. In the Customs and Tariffs Bureau, he contributed to improving Japan's economic relations with other countries through tariff cuts, bilateral and multilateral consultations, and other measures.

Ambassador Linda Tsao Yang
U.S. Executive Director
Asian Development Bank
No. 6 ADB Avenue, Mandalluyong City
0401 Metro Manila
Phone: 011-632/632-6050
Fax: 011-632/636-2084

Personal: born in 1926.

Education: B.A. in economics, St. John's Univ. (Shanghai). M.Ph. in economics, Columbia Univ.

Professional: 1980-82, California savings and loan commissioner. member, board of admin., Public Employees Retirement System of the State of California (CalPERS). board member, Blue Cross of California. founding director, Mother Lode Savings Bank in Sacramento.

Ambassador Linda Tsao Yang was the first female executive director appointed to the board of a multilateral development bank and the first U.S. executive director of the Asian Development Bank appointed by President Clinton and confirmed by the U.S. Senate.

The first minority and the first woman appointed to serve as California's savings and loan commissioner, Yang was responsible for the regulation and supervision of the then $80 billion state-chartered savings and loan industry from 1980 to 1982. She was the first Asian American appointed to the board of administration of the

Public Employees' Retirement System of the State of California (CalPERS), and has served as vice chair for CalPERS' investment committee. She was also a board member of Blue Cross of California and an organizer and a founding director of Mother Lode Savings Bank in Sacramento.

Yang was a director of The 1990 Institute, a California-based non-profit think tank. She was also a member of the Advisory Committee on Real Estate and Urban Economics at the University of California at Berkeley, and the Dean's Advisory Committee of the College of Agricultural and Environmental Sciences at the University of California at Davis. She is a member of the Downtown Economists of New York, the National Economists Club of Washington, D.C., and the Trusteeship for the Betterment of Women in Los Angeles.

Yang is married to An Tzu Yang.

European Bank for Reconstruction and Development

European Bank for Reconstruction and Development
One Exchange Square
London EC2A 2EH
UNITED KINGDOM

Switchboard/central contact:
Phone: 44-171-338-6000
Fax: 44-171-338-6100
Telex: 8812161 EBRD L G

Project inquiries:
Phone: 44-171-338-6282
Fax: 44-171-338-6102

EBRD publications:
Phone: 44-171-338-7553
Fax: 44-171-338-6680

General inquiries about the EBRD:
Phone: 44-171-338-7931 or 7238
Fax: 44-171-338-6690

U.S. Liaison Officers

Dean A. Peterson
Senior Commercial Officer (US&FCS)
Office of the U.S. Executive Director
European Bank for Reconstruction and Development
One Exchange Square
London EC2A 2 EH
United Kingdom

Phone: 011-44-171-338-6569
Fax: 011-44-171-338-6487

Education: B.A. (cum laude), Augustana College. MBA and doctor of business administration, George Washington Univ.

Professional: 1961-68, commodity-industry analyst, U.S. International Trade Commission. 1968-70, senior economist, U.S. special trade representative. 1970-75, founding partner International Business and Economic Research Corporation (Washington, D.C.). 1975-89, director of economics and environmental analysis, RJR Nabisco (Nabisco Brands, 1982-86, and Nabisco, 1975-82). 1989-92, president, Global Market Strategies (Atlanta, Ga.). 1992-95, director, Detroit district office of the U.S. Department of Commerce's U.S. and Foreign Commercial Service (US&FCS). 1995-present, senior commercial officer in ofc. of the U.S. Exec. Dir. of the European Bank for Reconstruction and Development, US&FCS.

As senior commercial officer in the office of the U.S. executive director at the European Bank for Reconstruction and Development (EBRD), Dean A. Peterson acts as the advocate for U.S. firms in their dealings with the EBRD. Peterson is with the U.S. Department of Commerce's U.S. and Foreign Commercial Service (US&FCS).

Peterson's duties include advising firms on specific opportunities arising from current or prospective bank-financed projects, counseling them on the most effective means of competing for EBRD-financed business, and helping to match corporate capabilities with EBRD investment priorities. He also plays a major role in developing outreach initiatives to publicize the opportunities arising for U.S. companies as a result of EBRD-financed activities.

Before going with the US&FCS to London for the EBRD job, Peterson was the director of the US&FCS's district office in Detroit, Mich. He was with the Commerce Department from 1961-68, then spent two years as senior economist for the U.S. special trade representative. Between 1970 and 1992, he was in the private sector, as the founder of International Business and Economic Research Corporation in Washington, D.C., and as the president of Global Market Strategic in Atlanta Ga., and with RJR Nabisco.

Peterson is the author of Mainstay II - A New Account of the Critical Role of U.S. Multinational Companies in the U.S. Economy, published by the Emergency Committee for American Trade in 1993.

He has served as a director of the food and agricultural committee of the National Planning Association. He is a member of the economic research committee of the Business Roundtable and of the balance of payments and international trade committees of the National Foreign Trade Council.

Introduction to the EBRD

In 1981, the European Bank for Reconstruction and Development (EBRD) was established to foster the transition towards market-oriented economies and to promote private and entrepreneurial initiatives in the central and eastern European countries committed to and applying the fundamental principles of multiparty democracy, pluralism, and market economics.

The Bank aims to help its countries of operations to implement structural and sectoral economic reform, including demonopolization, decentralization, and privatization, taking into account the particular needs of countries at different stages of transition. Its activities include the promotion of private sector activity, the strengthening of financial institutions and legal systems, and the development of the infrastructure needed to support the private sector.

The EBRD encourages co-financing and foreign direct investment from the private sectors, helps to mobilize domestic capital, and provides technical cooperation in relevant areas. It works in close cooperation with international financial institutions and other international organizations. The Bank promotes environmentally sound and sustainable development in all its activities.

Membership and Capital

The EBRD has 80 members (58 countries, the European Community and the European Investment Bank), including 26 countries of operations in central and eastern Europe and the Commonwealth of Independent States (CIS).

The EBRD's initial subscribed capital is ECU 10 billion, of which 30 per cent is paid in. The Bank also borrows in various currencies on world capital markets.

Organization

The powers of the EBRD are vested in a Board of Governors, to which each member appoints a Governor and an Alternate. The Board of Governors has delegated powers to a Board of Directors with 23 members, who are elected by Governors for a 3-year term. The Board of Directors is responsible for the direction of the general operations of the Bank, including establishing policies, taking decisions concerning projects, and approving the budget. The President is elected by the Board of Governors for a 4-year term. Vice Presidents are appointed by the Board of Directors on the recommendation of the President.

Financing

One of the EBRD's strengths is that it can operate in both the private and public sectors. It merges the principles and practices of merchant and development banking, providing funding for private or privatizable enterprises and for physical and financial infrastructure projects needed to support the private sector.

The EBRD aims to be flexible by using a broad range of financing instruments, tailored to specific projects. The kinds of finance it offers include loans, equity investments and guarantee, in all of its operations, the Bank applies sound banking and investment principles.

The terms of the EBRD's funding are designed to enable it to cooperate both with other international financial institutions through co-financing arrangements.

By February 28, 1995, the Bank had approved 382 projects; these involved ECU 8.2 billion of the EBRD's own funds and were expected to mobilize an additional ECU 17.7 billion. Of the approved projects, 305 had been signed committing ECU 6.3 billion of the EBRD's own funds. Sixty-five per cent of total approved funding was for private sector projects.

Project-related technical cooperation is a major feature of the EBRD's activities. By the end of 1995, 43 cooperation fund agreements with bilateral donors, totaling ECU 388 million, had been made with the Bank for this purpose; 1,177 projects, with a total estimated cost of ECU 312 million, had been committed.

Operations

The EBRD's operations are carried out through its Banking department, which is composed of teams combing the Bank's private sector and public sector specialists. Country teams ensure consistent implementation of the Bank's country strategies; these are backed up by the specialist expertise of sector teams and operations support units.

The other departments are: Finance, Personnel and Administration, Project Evaluation, Office of the Secretary General, Office of the General Counsel, Office of the Chief Economist, Internal Audit and Communications.

The EBRD's headquarters are in London, with 18 Resident Offices or Regional Offices in 16 of its countries of operations.

Jacques de Larosiere de Champfeu
President

Education: attended Lycee Louis-le-Grand and the Faculties of Laws and Arts at the University of Paris. Graduate in arts and law. Post-graduate degree from the Institute d'Etudes Politiques of Paris.

Professional: 1967-71, chairman of the economic and development review committee of the Organization for Economic Cooperation and Development. 1976-78, chairman of the Group of Ten countries. 1978-87, managing director of the International Monetary Fund. 1990, named chairman of the governors of the central banks of the Group of Ten countries. Various positions with French government including inspector general of finance. 1993-present, president of the European Bank for Reconstruction and Development.

Bringing with him extensive experience in banking, finance, and government, Jacques de Larosiere de Champfeu took over as president of the European Bank for Reconstruction and Development in September 1993. Between 1978 and 1987, he was the managing director of the International Monetary Fund.

In 1990, Larosiere was named the chairman of the governors of the Central Banks of the Group of Ten Countries. He was the chairman of the Group of Ten between 1976 and 1978 and of the Economic and Development Review Committee of the Organization for Economic Cooperation and Development between 1967 and 1971.

Among positions he has held in the French government are inspector general of finance; treasury director; director of the cabinet of Valery Giscard d'Estaing, then (in 1974) minister of the economy and finance; and assistant director and later department head in the ministry of the economy and finance. He began his career as a student at the Ecole Nationale d'Administration in 1954.

Larosiere was censeur at Credit National, Comptoir des Entrepreneurs, and Credit Foncier de France, as well as at the General Council of the Bank of France. He was a director of Regie Nationale des Usines Renault, Banque Nationale de Paris, Compagnie Nationale Air France and SNCF, and Societe Nationale Industrielle Aerospatiale.

The Inter-American Development Bank

1300 New York Avenue, NW / Washington, D.C. 20577

Phone: 202/623-1000, Central
        202/623-1397, Public Information
        202/623-2096, Public Information Center (projects)

Fax :   202/623-3096, Central
        202/623-1403, Public Information
        202/623-1928, Public Information Center (projects)

U.S. Liaison Officers

L. Ronald Scheman
U.S. Executive Director
Inter-American Development Bank
1300 New York Avenue, NW
Washington, D.C. 20577
Phone: 202/623-103   Fax: 202/623-3612

Education: B.A., Dartmouth College. J.D., Yale Law School.

Professional: 1961-64, legal staff, Org. of American States (OAS). 1964, dir., Pan American Develop. Foundation. 1968-70, planning officer, OAS. 1970-75, president, Porter International Company. 1975-83, assistant secretary for management, OAS. founder, Inter-American Management Education Foundation. co-founder, Fund for Democracy and Development. 1983-93, senior partner, Heller, Rosenblatt and

Scheman. 1993-present, U.S. Executive Director, Inter-American Development Bank.

Ronald Scheman has been executive director of the Inter-American Development Bank (IADB)for the United States since 1993. He is also executive director of the Inter-American Investment Corporation, an IADB affiliate that supports small and medium-scale businesses in Latin America and the Caribbean.

Scheman has been active in inter-American affairs in finance, law, and academics for over 30 years. Most recently, he was senior partner at the law firm of Heller, Rosenblatt and Scheman. He had a long career in the Organization of American States (OAS), having served from 1975 to 1983 as assistant secretary for management; from 1968 to 1970 as planning officer; and from 1961 to 1964 as member of the department of legal affairs. He was the first U.S. staff member of the Inter-American Commission on Human Rights. In 1988, he was the principal adviser to the Latin American Integration Association on its restructuring.

Scheman has had extensive experience in the private sector, having served as President of Porter International Company between 1970 and 1975, and subsequently, in his law practice. In those capacities, he advised numerous Latin American governments and corporations on financial and public affairs.

He played a pioneering role in creating new patterns of financial and technical assistance to micro-enterprises when he founded the Pan American Development Foundation in the 1960s. He served as the first executive director of the foundation between 1964 and 1968, as a board member from 1968 to 1993, and as president of the board from 1977 to 1982.

Scheman has also had a distinguished career in academic affairs as adjunct professor in international relations at George Washington University. He also led efforts to create a Latin American Studies consortium in Washington and was the founding executive director of the Center of Advanced Studies of the Americas between 1984 and 1986, with the four major universities of the District of Columbia as members.

Scheman was one of the leaders organizing the efforts of U.S. private voluntary organizations in assisting the nations of the former Soviet Union in 1990, and served as president of the Fund for Democracy and Development. He was a former president of the Washington Foreign Law Society, and vice president of the American Foreign Law Association.

Scheman is the author of several books, including The Inter-American Dilemma (1988) which examines the future of inter-American cooperation, and The Alliance for Progress in Retrospect (1989) both published by Praeger. He is co-author of Foundations for Freedom (1965) on the theme of the interrelationship between democracy and human rights. He is the author of numerous other books, articles, and op-ed columns on international issues.

Scheman is fluent in Spanish and Portuguese and possesses a working knowledge of French and Russian.

Mr. Larry Harrington
U.S. Alternate Executive Direcor
1300 New York Ave., NW
Washington, D.C. 20577
Phone: 202/623-1033   Fax: 202/623-3612
E-mail: LarryH@iadb.org

Mr. Robert J. McEntire
U.S. Liaison to the IADB
1300 New York Ave., NW
Washington, D.C. 20577
Phone: 202/623-3822   Fax: 202/623-2039
E-mail: bobm@iadb.org

Mr. Eric Weaver, Director
Commerce Department Liaison Office
1300 New York Ave., NW
Washington, D.C. 20577
Phone: 202/623-3820   Fax: 202/623-2039

Mr. Robert J. McEntire
Procurement Liaison Officer
1300 New York Ave., NW
Washington, D.C. 20577
Phone: 202/623-3822   Fax: 202/623-2039
E-mail: bobm@iadb.org

Established in 1959, the Inter-American Development Bank (IDB) is an international financial institution aimed at accelerating economic and social development in Latin America and the Caribbean. For most countries in this region, the IDB is the principal source of external public financing for development. Using funds raised on financial markets and capital supplied by its member countries, the IDB finances development projects in its borrowing member countries; offers technical assistance; and promotes cofinancing of its projects by other institutions.

The IDB has proffered loans worth $70 billion, with loans spread across a broad array of areas, including agriculture and fisheries (19.1 percent), industry and mining (11.1 percent), energy (23 percent), transportation and communications (13.5 percent), environmental and public health (10.8 percent), education, science and technology (4.1 percent), urban development (4.6 percent), and planning and reform (8.3 percent). The IDB is thus focused on not only abetting the performance of individual economic sectors, but on building economic competitiveness and standards of living through improvements in infrastructure and economic planning.

The IDB's current President has specifically targeted the problem of poverty in Latin America and has stated that in the 1990s an increasing portion of the bank's funds will be put to use in areas (environment, health, education, urban development, etc.) intended to directly improve the productivity and social conditions of the poor.

Enrique V. Iglesias,
President, Inter-American Development Bank
Phone: 202/623-1100

Personal: born 1930 in Spain; naturalized citizen of Uruguay.

Education: graduate of University of the republic in economics and business administration.

Professional: Technical director of Uruguay's national planning office. Executive secretary of the Economic Commission of Latin America and the Caribbean. Professor of economic and economic development at the University of the Republic. President of Uruguay's central bank. Uruguay's minister of external relations. 1988-present, president of Inter-American Development Bank.

Enrique V. Iglesias, who acceded to the presidency of the Inter-

American Bank in 1988, is three years into his second five-year term.

Prior to joining the IDB, he served as Uruguay's minister of external relations. He has been president of Uruguay's Central Bank; a professor of economics and economic development at the University of the Republic; and technical director of Uruguay's National Planning Office, where he was responsible for developing and implementing the country's First National Economic and Social Development Plan. In 1972, he was named executive secretary of the Economic Commission for Latin America and the Caribbean, first holding the rank of United Nations assistant secretary general and subsequently that of under-secretary general. He remained at this post until taking the helm at the ministry of external relations.

Iglesias is a graduate of the University of the Republic in economic and business administration and has studied in the U.S. and in France. He is a member of the Latin American Executive Council of the International Society for Development and the North-South Round Table on Energy, and has authored numerous papers and articles on Latin American and Uruguayan economic issues.

During his first term of office as president of the IDB, Iglesias successfully concluded negotiations for the bank's Seventh General Increase of Resources and brought about a modernization of the IDB itself. During this period, the Inter-American Investment Corporation (IIC), the bank's affiliate for providing direct assistance to small- and medium-size enterprises, began operations.

World Bank Group

For all World Bank Group entities, mail to:

1818 H St., N.W.
Washington, D.C. 20433
(http://www.worldbank.org)

Phone: 202/477-1234 (Central)
          202/458-5041 (Media Division)
          202/458-5454 (Public Info.)
Fax: 202/522-2616 (Communication Unit)

Main European Office

66, avenue d'Iena
75116 Paris, France
Phone: 011-1-40-69-30-00
Fax: 011-1-40-69-30-66

Frankfurt Office

Bockenheimer Landstrasse 109
60325 Frankfurt a. M.
Germany
Phone: [49] 69-743-48230
Fax: [49] 69-743-48239

London Office

New Zealand House
15th Floor, Haymarket
London, SW1 Y4TE, England
Phone: 44-171-930-8511
Fax: 44-171-930-8515

Tokyo Office

Fukoku Seimei Building
10th Floor,
2-2-2, Uchisaiwai cho
Chiyoda-ku, Tokyo
Phone: 011-3-3597-6650
Fax: 011-3-3597-6695

U.S. Executive Director

Jan Piercy
U.S. Executive Director
International Bank for Reconstruction & Development
1818 H Street, NW - Rm. MC 13-525
Washington, D.C. 20433
202/458-0110   Fax: 202/477-2967
E-Mail: Jpiercy@worldbank.org

Education: B.A., Wellesley College. Graduate studies at the Woodrow Wilson School at Princeton Univ., and at Stanford Univ.

Professional: dir., public management program, Cornell Univ. director, public management program, Stanford University's Graduate School of Business. adviser, Southern Development Bancorporation, (Arkansas). senior vp, Shorebank Corp. (Chicago). 1994-present, U.S. Executive Dir., Intern'l. Bank for Reconstruction and Develop.

Jan Piercy was appointed by President Clinton and confirmed by the Senate as U.S. Executive Director to the International Bank for Reconstruction and Development, the World Bank, in 1994. She also serves as a commissioner of the White House Fellows Program, on the board of the Lewis T. Preston Fund (a private foundation) for the Education of Girls, and on the board of Jobs for the Future (a non-profit organization).

As executive director of the World Bank, Piercy has taken particular interest in financial sector reforms, including access to credit for the poor and the formation of CGAP, the Consultative Group to Assist the Poorest in the bank, and in increasing results in World Bank lending. She has visited Bank programs and resident missions in Asia and Africa.

Piercy was a U.S. delegate to the International Women's Conference in Beijing in 1995 and serves on the U.S. Inter-Agency Council on Women. Piercy was previously a senior White House official. Prior to joining the Clinton administration, she was senior vice president of Shorebank Corporation in Chicago, a bank holding company designed to promote economic development in disinvested urban and rural areas, and an advisor to the Southern Development Bancorporation in Arkansas, established on the ShoreBank model.

Earlier, Piercy worked in Bangladesh and Thailand and founded a student exchange program in South America. She served as director of the public management program at Stanford University's graduate school of business and in a similar capacity at Cornell University. Piercy was educated at Wellesley College, the Woodrow Wilson School at Princeton, and the senior management training program at Stanford University. She has been active throughout her career in promoting economic development, women's broader participation in public affairs, and democracy building. She has served in these areas as consultant, trustee, and board member to numerous organizations, including the John D. and Catherine T. MacArthur Foundation and the National Women's Education Fund.

U.S. Liaison Officers

Charles Kestenbaum
Director
Commerce Department Liaison Office
Office of the U.S. Executive Director
1818 H Street, NW
Washington, D.C. 20433
Phone: 202/458-0120   Fax: 202/477-2967
Internet address: Ckestenbaum@doc.gov

Janice Mazur
Procurement Liaison Officer
Office of the U.S. Executive Director
1818 H Street, NW
Washington, D.C. 20433
Phone: 202/458-0118   Fax: 202/477-2967
Internet address: Jmazur@doc.gov

Over its 50-year history, the World Bank has become a global partnership in 180 countries have joined together for a common purpose: to reduce poverty and improve living standards by promoting sustainable growth and investments in people. The Bank provides loans, technical assistance, and policy guidance to help its developing-country members achieve this objective. It does not make grants.

The term "World Bank" refers to two legally and financially distinct entities: the International Bank for Reconstruction and Development (IBRD) and the International Development Association (IDA). The IBRD and IDA have three related functions: to lend funds, to provide economic advice and technical assistance, and to serve as a catalyst to investment by others.

The International Finance Corporation (IFC), an affiliate of the World Bank, seeks to promote growth in the private sector of developing countries by mobilizing foreign and domestic capital to invest alongside its own funds in commercial enterprises. The Multilateral Investment Guarantee Agency (MIGA), also an affiliate of the World Bank, was established in 1988 to encourage direct foreign investment in developing countries by protecting investors from noncommercial risk, especially risk of war or repatriation.

James D. Wolfensohn
President, World Bank Group

Personal: born in 1933 in Australia; naturalized U.S. citizen.

Education: B.A. and LL.B. degrees from the University of Sydney. M.A. from the Harvard Graduate School of Business.

Professional: Associated with Darling & Co. in Australia. Executive deputy chairman and managing director of Schroder Ltd. in London. Head of investment banking department of Salomon Brothers in New York. President and chief executive of James D. Wolfensohn Incorporated. 1990-95, chairman of the board of trustees, The John F. Kennedy Center for Performing Arts (Wash., D.C.). June 1995-present, president and chief executive officer, The World Bank Group.

James D. Wolfensohn, an international investment banker who assumed the presidency of the World Bank June 1, 1995, has a long record of involvement in development and environmental issues and in the performing arts.

Wolfensohn was president and chief executive of James D. Wolfensohn Incorporated. The firm, created in 1981, provides high-level strategic and financial advice to more than 30 major U.S. and international corporations. The firm's practice covers Latin America, Europe, and Asia, as well as North America.

Wolfensohn has had extensive experience with other investment firms, including Solomon Brothers in New York, where he headed the investment banking department. While there, he steered the restructuring of the Chrysler Corporation. He was executive deputy chairman and managing director of Schroders Ltd in London and, before that, was at Darling & Co. in Australia.

Between 1990 and 1995, he was chairman of the board of trustees of the John F. Kennedy Center for the Performing Arts in Washington, D.C. He was previously associated with Carnegie Hall in New York for 20 years.

Wolfensohn served as director of both the Business Council for Sustainable Development and CBS Inc. He is chairman of the Institute for Advanced Study at Princeton University.

International Bank for Reconstruction and Development (IBRD)

Born at the 1944 United Nations monetary and financial conference at Bretton Woods, N.H., the International Bank for Reconstruction and Development was established to assist in the reconstruction and development of the territories of its members by facilitating the investment of capital for productive purposes. The IBRD now has 180 member countries

This goal is to be accomplished by promoting private foreign investment where possible. When private funds are not readily available on reasonable terms, they can be supplemented by IBRD funds, which come from the capital subscriptions of 180 member states. This capital is raised on world financial markets and from loan repayments.

The IBRD, also seeks the balanced growth of world trade and the maintenance of a balance-of-payments equilibrium among its members. To accomplish this, the IBRD encourages investment to develop the productive resources of its less developed members.

All IBRD loans are provided on an interest basis, with the interest rate charged to developing countries changing every six months. Bank loans generally come with a five-year grace period, with payments after that to be made over 15 to 20 years. The interest rate charged on IBRD loans, as of July 1, 1996 was 6.98 percent.

The IBRD charter sets out the basic rules governing its lending operations: that the bank must loan only for productive purposes such as agriculture and rural development, energy, education, health, roads and railways, telecommunications, and ports; that it must take due heed of repayment prospects; that each loan must have the guarantee of the government concerned; and that, except in special circumstances, the money must be channeled to specific projects. The Bank must convince itself that funds for the project are unavailable from other sources on reasonable terms. The money from loans may not be restricted to purchases from any particular country or countries. The Bank's lending decisions must be grounded on economic considerations.

The IBRD, in addition to its lending activities, provides a wide variety of technical assistance services.

All powers of the IBRD are vested in its Board of Governors, with one Governor and one alternate appointed by each member state. The Board of Governors normally meets once annually and delegates the day-to-day supervision of the Bank's operations to its 22 Executive Directors. Five directors are appointed by the five members with the largest capital subscriptions and the remainder by the Governors of the remaining members. The Bank's President is selected by the Board of Governors.

In the year ending June 30, 1996, the IBRD approved $14.5 billion in loans for 129 development projects.

International Development Association (IDA)

Established in 1960, the International Development Association (IDA) has 159 member states and provides loans without interest to the world's poorest countries. Only states with an annual per capita income lower than $1,395 are eligible for IDA loans. The majority of IDA funds, however, are dispersed to states in which that income does not exceed $865.

Referred to as credits, IDA loans carry with them a ten-year grace period and are repaid over 35 to 40 years depending on the credit-worthiness of the borrowing country. At present, approximately 70 of IDA's member are eligible for borrowing. Over the years, 21 have "graduated" from the roster of eligible nations. Two of those, Korea and Turkey, are now IDA contributors.

Because of the extremely concessional terms on which its loans are made, IDA - unlike the IBRD - is not able to raise funds on the world's capital markets. Rather, its lending capital is drawn from the contributions of wealthier nations, occasional contributions from IBRD profits, and from the repayment of its credits. In fiscal year 1995, IDA's approved credits totaled $5.7 billion, going to 45 countries. Although legally an independent entity, IDA shares both staff and facilities with the IBRD.

IDA approved $6.9 billion in credits to help pay for 127 development projects in the year that ended June 30, 1996.

International Finance Corporation (IFC)

As the World Bank Group's investment bank for developing countries, the International Finance Corporation (IFC) lends directly to private enterprises and makes equity investments in them. Founded in 1956, the IFC - unlike the IBRD - lends without government guarantees. The IFC has 170 member countries.

The IFC serves as a catalyst to attract investors from the private sector for projects. As such, it is the single largest source for direct financing of private sector projects in developing nations. Without government guarantees it shares a projects risks with other investors.

IFC focuses on expanding and modernizing established firms, as well financing new enterprises. It helps sectors ranging from agribusiness, to heavy industry, energy, and mining. Though the IFC does put itself on the line with such projects, it rarely finances more than a quarter of any given project and, though it may take up to a 35 percent stake in a given company, it never involves itself with the company's management and is never the largest shareholder.

Beyond its lending and investing activities, the IFC is active in providing technical assistance and advice. This takes many forms, from assisting a company in selecting a technology to use in its operations, to identifying markets for a company's products, to helping it reduce its debt.

Advisory services to governments are also a significant facet of IFC operations; it provides assistance with capital markets development and with privatization and restructuring of state enterprises. In conjunction with the IBRD and the Multilateral Investment Guarantee Agency, the IFC runs the Foreign Investment Advisory Service (FIAS), which it established. The FIAS advises governments of developing states on strategies for attracting foreign investment which may involve policy and institutional restructuring, financial inducements, or the restructuring of a state's legal system to provide investor protection.

The IFC approved $2.9 billion in financing for 213 private sector projects in 67 countries during the year that ended June 30, 1995.

Multilateral Investment Guarantee Agency (MIGA)

Established in 1988 and boasting 131 member states, the Multilateral Investment Guarantee Agency (MIGA) is mandated with promoting private investment in developing countries. Its importance is growing as developing countries increasingly realize the need for such investment.

MIGA's primary function in pursuing its goals is providing protection to investors from various non-commercial risks, such as war and the nationalization of property. During the 1960s and 1970s, politically motivated expropriations of foreign property were common. Guarantees by MIGA serve to lessen such concerns on the part of foreign investors, as well as concerns related to potential damage to property because of war or civil disturbance.

MIGA offers four basic types of protection against: currency inconvertibility, expropriation of property, losses due to war or civil disturbance and potential lack of remedy against breach of contract.

In addition to its insurance offerings, MIGA works - along with the IBRD and IFC - to educate developing countries on ways to increase private investment. It does so through the investment promotion services offered by its Policy and Advisory Services Department, as well as by various conferences and in-country executive development programs and through its participation in the Foreign Investment Advisory Service.

Since its inception, MIGA has approved 100 contracts valued at more than $1 billion.

International Centre for the Settlement of Investment Disputes (ICSID)

The International Centre for the Settle of Investment Disputes (ICSID), which has 123 member countries, does not receive as much attention as the other World Bank operations because of its small size and the markedly different nature of its work. Although it does not provide financing or direct development assistance, it plays a very important role in the development process by providing a common dispute-settlement mechanism and reference authority for private investors in developing countries.

International arbitration and conciliation—ICSID's focus points—provide an alternative to national court systems. Many foreign investors look for an alternative, because they are reluctant to submit to another nation's court jurisdiction and because they want to avoid the expenditure of time and money and the public scrutiny that is involved in going to court.

These considerations are often crucial to private investors as they make decisions about investing in the developing countries, which may be plagued by political, economic, or ethnic instability.

ICSID was established in response to this problem in 1965 through the "Convention on the Settlement of Investment Disputes Between States and Nationals of Other States."

ICSID serves two primary functions. First, it serves as a source for research, advice, and publications on foreign investment law; it maintains an extensive library of investment laws and treaties. ICSID is often called upon to work with the other World Bank bodies in providing foreign investment counsel to member-state governments.

Secondly, ICSID performs various functions aimed at facilitating foreign-investment dispute settlement. It offers administrative facilities for the conciliation and arbitration of foreign investment disputes; the decision by the involved parties to take part is always voluntary. Once the parties to an investment contract have consented to conciliation or arbitration, however, they are bound to let the process proceed, and, in the case of arbitration, they are bound to abide by the award. All contracting ICSID states are required to recognize the arbitration award resulting from the proceedings and to provide for enforcement.

In addition to its facilities for conciliation and arbitration under the Convention, ICSID offers assistance in disputes which fall outside the Convention's scope, such as investment-related disputes in which one of the parties is not an ICSID member. In certain instances, disputes may even be referred to ICSID which do not involve a pure "investment" dispute, yet which meet certain criteria.

Finally, the Secretary-General of ICSID - traditionally the World Bank's General Counsel - serves as an "appointing authority" for *ad hoc* arbitrations—that is, arbitrations in which the involved parties have not agreed to any specific international convention or rules. The Secretary-General will find appropriate arbitrators or conciliators for the case at hand. It is becoming increasingly common for foreign investment contracts to include specific reference to this procedure.

A tremendous rise in demand for ICSID's services has occurred since the agency was established. The trend is likely to continue, as additional national investment promotion legislation and bilateral investment treaties cite ICSID authority in disputes that may arise.

ICSID has handled more than 30 arbitration cases since it was established.

Questions and Answers about the World Bank (Prepared by the World Bank)

How does the Bank work?

The World Bank's goals are much the same as those of many governments' development assistance programs. But unlike such aid programs, it doesn't make grants. The Bank lends money to developing countries, and the loans are repaid. Developing countries borrow from the Bank because they need capital, technical assistance, and policy advice. There are basically two types of Bank lending. The first type is for developing countries that are able to pay near-market interest rates. The money for these loans comes from investors around the world. These investors buy bonds issued by the World Bank.

The second type of loan goes to the poorest countries, which are usually not creditworthy in the international financial markets and are therefore unable to pay near-market interest rates on the money they borrow. The World Bank, therefore cannot issue bonds to raise money that would finance lending to these countries. Lending to the poorest countries is done by the Bank's affiliate, the International Development Association. More than 30 member countries periodically contribute the money needed to finance "credits" to borrowers. IDA credits are free of interest, carry a 0.75 percent annual administrative charge, and are very long term—35 or 40 years including 10 years grace. Countries with per capita incomes of less than $1,305 (in 1992 dollars) are eligible for IDA credits. In practice, most IDA credits go to countries which are much poorer than this. But the credits are repaid. IDA lends about $6 billion a year to the poorest countries.

Who runs the Bank?

The Bank is comparable to a global cooperative, which is owned by member countries. The size of a country's shareholding is determined by the size of the country's economy relative to the world economy. Together, the largest industrial countries (the Group of Seven or G-7—Canada, France, Germany, Italy, Japan, the United Kingdom, and the U.S.) have about 45 percent of the share in the World Bank—and they carry great weight in international economic affairs generally. So it is true that the rich countries have a good deal of influence over the Bank's policies and practices. The U.S. has the largest shareholding—about 17 percent, which gives the U.S. the power to veto any changes in the Bank's capital base and Articles of Agreement (85 percent of the share are needed to effect such changes). However, virtually all other matters, including the approval of loans, are decided by a majority of the votes cast by all members of the Bank.

The Bank's Board of Executive Directors, which is resident at the Bank's headquarters in Washington, D.C., represents all the members. Policies and practices are regularly and frequently debated and decided upon by the Board, so every member's voice is heard. In fact, developing countries together have about half the votes in the Bank. And the Bank's cooperative spirit is reflected in the fact that voting is rare because consensus is the preferred way of making decisions.

Only developing countries can borrow from the Bank. But all members, including the richer nations, gain from economic growth in developing countries. A world increasingly divided between rich and poor is in no one's interest. We all benefit from higher incomes, fewer social tensions, better health and education, environmental protection, and increased trade and investment. The Bank's member countries, particularly the industrial countries, also benefit from procurement opportunities derived from World Bank-financed projects.

How open and accountable is the Bank?

The World Bank is an open partnership between more than 175 countries. It publishes a huge amount of information and is publicly accountable to its member countries.

The Bank recently expanded the range of documents prepared for operational purposes that are made available to the public, including a new Project Information Document, which describes projects at the early stages of development. The Bank operates a Public Information Center, which anyone can visit or access on-line by computer. The Bank also issues about 400 research, policy, and other publications a year, including a detailed *Annual Report*, and produces numerous newsletters, fact sheets, press releases, and video and audio materials. There are, of course, some constraints on the Bank's openness. It cannot, for example, divulge information supplied by members in confidence, but this is a very small portion of its material. Bank staff are encouraged to be open in their outside contacts. They frequently speak at conferences, address citizens' groups, and appear on radio and television.

At the same time, the Bank's staff and management are held directly accountable by its members, who in turn report to their parliaments and publics. Members are represented at the Bank's headquarters in Washington, D.C., by a resident Board of Executive Directors. The Bank also has an independent Operations Evaluation Department, which reviews Bank-financed projects and reports directly to the Board on the results of these evaluations.

How does the Bank follow-up on its lending?

Decisions to loan money for a project are but one part of an intensive dialogue between the Bank and the country on a wide range of development issues. In the end, the member countries themselves must decide whether a project (or program) is worthy of their support.

These are their projects, and if they are to work, the countries themselves must "own" them. Moreover, although lending is certainly a fundamental part of the World Bank's work, the Bank does a lot more than just lend money. The Bank also routinely includes technical assistance in projects. They might cover advice on issues such as the overall size of a country's budget and where the money should be allocated, or how to set up village health clinics, or what sort of equipment is needed to build a road. The Bank funds a few projects each year devoted exclusively to providing expert advice and training. In addition, the Bank's Economic Development Institute trains people from borrowing countries how to create and carry out development programs.

The Bank closely monitors its projects and tries to learn from its mistakes. A 1992 report concluded that, in a small number of cases, Bank-supported projects had run into difficulties. The report, which was written by an independent group headed by a former vice-president of the Bank said one source of these difficulties was a "culture" within the Bank that had placed too much value on approving loans and not enough on following up on the loans that had been approved. Since then, however, the Bank has taken steps to encourage staff to devote more time to supervising projects that are being implemented. The Bank is taking other steps to strengthen the impact of its lending on the poorest people, to involve non-governmental organizations and those most directly affected by a project in its planning, and to better monitor the performance of all projects in the Bank's portfolio.

How are Bank loans evaluated?

The majority of projects the Bank finances perform well. The Bank's criteria for "success" are exceptionally strict, however. For instance, before a project can be considered successful, it must have at least a 10 percent rate of economic return. This rate is far higher than the minimum demanded by many bilateral donors, which require that their investments in development projects show a rate of economic return of half that amount—between 5 percent and 6 percent.

What role does the environment play in the Bank's work?

Environmental protection is a key component of sustainable development. Without this, long-term development is undermined. Conversely, without development, it is difficult to generate the resources needed for environmental protection.

The World Bank seeks to build upon this linkage by supporting projects for reforestation, pollution control, and land management; by investing in water, sanitation, and agricultural extension to help combat the environmental problems which affect the poor; by promoting environmental action plans and economic policies which help to conserve natural resources; and by working with its partners, through the Global Environmental Facility, to help address international environmental issues such as ozone depletion and biodiversity loss. While environmental protect is a priority, the concept of "sustainability" also encompasses a concern for human well-being in the broadest sense. Consequently the Bank's approach to sustainable development includes support for:

—Programs for family planning to slow the rapid population growth which undermines economic growth and contributes to environmental degradation in many of the poorest countries.

—More participation by poor people, especially women, in economic decision making and in the design and implementation of development programs.

—The strengthening of institutions so that countries have the needed capacity to manage their own development program; and

—More transparent and open forms of governance.

The International Monetary Fund

700 19th Street, NW - Washington, D.C. 20431
202/623-7000   Fax: 202/623-4661
http://www.imf.org

General inquiries:
Phone: 202/623-7000   Fax: 202/623-6278
E-mail: publicaffairs@imf.org

Scholarship & external training program inquiries:
Phone: 202/623-6660   Fax: 202/623-6490
E-mail: insinfo@imf.org

Annual Meeting inquiries:
Phone: 202/473-7272   Fax: 202/623-4100

Inquiries from the media:
Phone: 202/623-7100   Fax: 202/623-6772
E-mail: info@imf.org

Copyright inquiries:
Phone: 202/623-7364   Fax: 202/623-6579
E-mail: copyright@imf.org

Joint Bank-Fund Library inquiries:
Phone: 202/623-7054   Fax: 202/623-6417

Employment & internship inquiries:
Phone: 202/623-7422   Fax: 202/623-7333
E-mail: recruit@imf.org

Publication inquiries:
202/623-7430   Fax: 202/623-7201
E-mail: publications@imf.org

Video series inquiries:
Phone: 202/623-7082   Fax: 202/623-4225
E-mail: videos@imf.org

Office in Europe
64-66, Avenue d'Iena
75116 Paris, France
Phone: (33-1) 40 69 30 70   Fax: (33-1) 47 23 40 89

Office in Geneva
58, Rue de Moillebeau
1209 Geneva, Switzerland
Phone: (41-22) 918 03 00   Fax: (41-22) 918 03 03

Regional Office for Asia & The Pacific
21F, Fukoku Seimei Bldg.
2-2-2 Uchisaiwai-cho
Chiyoda-Ku
Tokyo 100 Japan
Phone: (81-3) 3597 6700   Fax: (81-3) 3597 6705
E-mail: oap@imf.org

Fund Office United Nations
828 Second Ave., Fourth Floor
New York, NY 10017
Phone: 212/557-0894   Fax: 212/687-9123

INTRODUCTION

Established at the Bretton Woods Conference in New Hampshire in the wake of World War II and coming into existence Dec. 27, 1945, the International Monetary Fund (IMF) is an intergovernmental financial institution mandated with promoting monetary exchange stability and orderly exchange arrangements and long-term economic development.

With 182 member countries and a staff of 2,300 from some 110 countries, IMF has as goals the expansion and balanced growth of international trade and financial policy coordination between the major industrial countries. It accomplishes its aims by providing the machinery for international consultation and collaboration.

IMF serves as a monetary clearing house for current transactions between members, provides temporary credit to members to allow them to correct external payments problems, gives technical assistance in central banking and balance-of-payments accounting and taxation, and offers training for financial officials of member countries at the IMF Institute in Washington and the Vienna Institute in concert with other multilateral institutions.

Other services to low-income member states include concessional loans through its structural adjustment (SAF) and enhanced structural adjustment facilities (ESAF). As of April 1998, total credit and loans outstanding amounted to $145 billion in Special Drawing Rights (SDRs), an international reserve asset and the IMF unit of account, which equals $195 billion (US). IMF derives the majority of its lendable resources from its members' quotas, with required contributions based on each member state's relative economic size.

IMF is run by its Executive Board, composed of 24 Executive Directors meeting an average of three times weekly. The Articles of Agreement that instituted the IMF provide that the five member countries with the largest quotas (France, Germany, Japan, the U.K. and the U.S.) may appoint one Executive Director each. The remaining 19 are elected from the rest of the member countries. The Executive Board appoints IMF's Managing Director, who also serves as Chairman.

Michel Camdessus
Managing Director and Chairman, The IMF
Phone: 202/623-7759   Fax: 202/623-6278

IMF Organization Chart

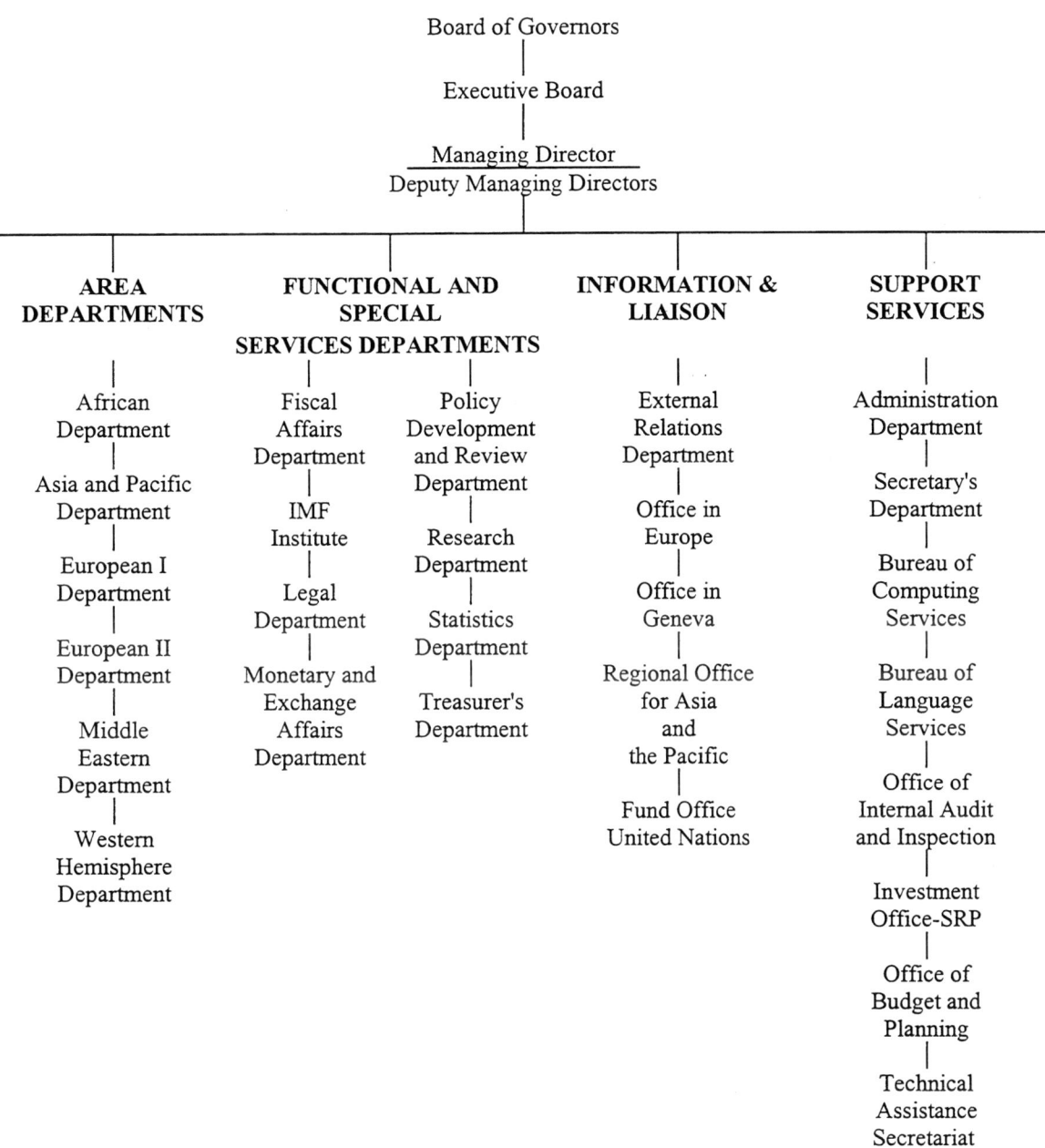

Board of Governors

Executive Board

Managing Director
Deputy Managing Directors

AREA DEPARTMENTS	FUNCTIONAL AND SPECIAL SERVICES DEPARTMENTS		INFORMATION & LIAISON	SUPPORT SERVICES
African Department	Fiscal Affairs Department	Policy Development and Review Department	External Relations Department	Administration Department
Asia and Pacific Department	IMF Institute	Research Department	Office in Europe	Secretary's Department
European I Department	Legal Department	Statistics Department	Office in Geneva	Bureau of Computing Services
European II Department	Monetary and Exchange Affairs Department	Treasurer's Department	Regional Office for Asia and the Pacific	Bureau of Language Services
Middle Eastern Department			Fund Office United Nations	Office of Internal Audit and Inspection
Western Hemisphere Department				Investment Office-SRP
				Office of Budget and Planning
				Technical Assistance Secretariat

Personal: born 5/1/33 in Paris, France.

Education: educated at University of Paris. Postgraduate degrees in economics at the Institute of Political Studies of Paris and at France's National School of Administration.

Professional: 1960-66, civil administrator, Ministry of Finance and Economic Policies. 1966-68, financial attaché to the French delegation of the European Economic Community. 1968-71, administrator, Ministry of Finance and Economic Policies. 1971-74, assistant director of the Treasury. 1974-82, deputy director of the Treasury. 1982-84, director of the Treasury. 1984-87, governor, the Bank of France. 1987-present, managing director and chairman of the executive board of the International Monetary Fund.

The executive board of the International Monetary Fund (IMF) in May 1996 unanimously selected Michel Camdessus to serve a third five-year term as managing director and chairman of the executive board of the IMF, beginning Jan. 16, 1997.

Camdessus noted that his appointment to a third term as managing director took place at the time of the celebration of the 50th anniversary of the first meeting of the executive board. Camdessus assumed his duties as the seventh managing director of the Fund on Jan. 16, 1987.

Before he was appointed managing director of the IMF, Camdessus was governor of the Bank of France between 1984 and 1987; director of the French Treasury between 1982 and 1984; chairman of the Paris Club between 1978 and 1984; and chairman of the monetary committee of the European Economic Community between 1982 and 1984. Camdessus was named governor of the IMF for France in 1984.

Camdessus was educated at the University of Paris and earned postgraduate degrees in economics at the Institute of Political Studies of Paris and at France's National School of Administration.

A French national, he is married to Brigitte d'Arcy. They have six children.

IMF Management and Senior Officers

Managing Director	Michel Camdessus
First Deputy Managing Director	Stanley Fischer
Deputy Managing Directors	Alassane D. Ouattara Shigemitsu Sugisaki
Economic Counsellor	Michael Mussa
Administration Department	K. Burke Dillon Director
African Department	Evangelos A. Calamitsis Director
Asia & Pacific Department	Hubert Neiss Director
European I Department	Michael C. Deppler Director
European II Department	John Odling-Smec Director
External Relations Dept.	Shailendra J. Anjaria Director
Fiscal Affairs Department	Vito Tanzi Director
IMF Institute	Mohsin S. Khan Director
Legal Department	Francois P. Gianviti General Counsel
Middle Eastern Dept.	Paul Chabrier Director
Monetary & Exchange Affairs	Manuel Guitián Director
Policy Development & Review	John T. Boorman Director
Research Department	Michael Mussa Director
Secretary's Department	Reinhard Munzberg Secretary
Statistics Department	Carol S. Carson Director
Treasurer's Department	David Williams Treasurer
Western Hemisphere Dept.	Claudio M. Loser Director
Special Advisor to the Managing Director	Massimo Russo
Bureau of Computing Services	Warren N. Minami Director
Bureau of Language Services	Patrice P. Guilmard Acting Director
Office at the United Nations	J.B. Zulu Director and Special Representative to the U.N.
Office in Europe (Paris)	Christian Brachet Director
Office in Geneva	Alan A. Tait Director and Special Trade Representative
Regional Office for Asia & The Pacific	Kunio Saito Director
Office of Budget and Planning	Lindsay A. Wolfe Director
Office of Internal Audit & Review	Eduard Brau Director

IMF Executive Board

General Department and Special Drawing Rights Department

Listed in Descending Voting Power Order

APPOINTED DIRECTORS:

Casting Votes of:	Executive Director (Alternate)	From	Percent of Fund Total
U.S.	Karin Lissakers (Barry S. Newman)	U.S.	17.78
Germany	Bernd Esdar (Wolf-Dieter Donecker)	Germany	5.53
Japan	Yukio Yoshimura (Hideaki Ono)	Japan	5.53
France	Jean-Claude Milleron (Ramon Fernandez)	France	4.98
U.K.	Gus O'Donnell (Jon Shields)	U.K.	5.00

ELECTED DIRECTORS:

Austria, Belarus, Belgium, Czech Republic, Hungary, Kazakhstan, Luxembourg, Slovak Republic, Slovenia, Turkey	Willy Kiekens (Johann Prader)	Belgium Austria	5.09
Armenia, Bosnia & Herzegovina, Bulgaria, Croatia, Cyprus, Georgia, Israel, Macedonia, Moldova, Netherlands, Romania, Ukraine	J. de Beaufort Wijnholds (Yuriy G. Yakusha)	Netherlands Ukraine	4.97
Costa Rica, El Salvador, Guatemala, Honduras, Mexico, Nicaragua, Spain, Venezuela	Juan Jose Toribio (Javier Guzman-Calafell)	Spain Mexico	4.30
Albania, Greece, Italy, Malta, Portugal, San Marino	Enzo R. Grilli (John Spraos)	Italy Greece	4.02
Antigua and Barbuda, The Bahamas, Barbados, Belize, Canada, Dominica, Grenada, Ireland, Jamaica, St. Kitts and Nevis, St. Lucia, St. Vincent and the Grenadines	Thomas A. Barnes (Charles X. O'Loghlin)	Canada Ireland	3.72
Denmark, Estonia, Finland, Iceland, Latvia, Lithuania, Norway, Sweden	Kai Aaen Hansen (Olli-Pekka Lehmussaari)	Denmark Finland	3.47
Saudi Arabia	Abdulrahman Al-Tuwaijri (Sulaiman M. Al-Turki)	Saudi Arabia Saudi Arabia	3.45
Angola, Botswana, Burundi, Eritrea, Ethiopia, The Gambia, Kenya, Lesotho, Liberia, Malawi, Mozambique, Namibia, Nigeria, Sierra Leone, South Africa, Swaziland, Tanzania, Uganda, Zambia, Zimbabwe	Dinah Z. Guti (Jose Pedro de Morais, Jr.)	Zimbabwe Angola	3.43
Australia, Kiribati, Korea, Marshall Islands, Micronesia, Mongolia, New Zealand, Papua New Guinea, Philippines, Seychelles, Solomon Islands, Vanuatu	Gregory Taylor (Okyu Kwon)	Australia Korea	3.29
Bahrain, Egypt, Iraq, Jordan, Kuwait, Lebanon, Libya, Maldives, Oman, Qatar, Syrian Arab Republic, United Arab Emirates, Yemen	A. Shakour Shaalan (Vacant)	Egypt	3.19

Casting Votes of:	Executive Director (Alternate)	From	Percent of Fund Total
Brunei Darussalam, Cambodia, Fiji, Indonesia, Lao People's Democratic Republic, Malaysia, Myanmar, Nepal, Singapore, Thailand, Tonga, Vietnam	ZAMANI Abdul Ghani (Subarjo Joyosumarto)	Malaysia *Indonesia*	2.91
Russia	Aleksei V. Mozhin (Andrei Vernikov)	Russia *Russia*	2.90
Azerbaijan, Kyrgyz Republic, Poland, Switzerland, Tajikistan, Turkmenistan, Uzbekistan	Roberto F. Cippa (Wieslaw Szczuka)	Switzerland *Poland*	2.76
Islamic State of Afghanistan, Algeria, Ghana, Islamic Republic of Iran, Morocco, Pakistan, Tunisia	Abbas Mirakhor (Mohammed Daïri)	Iran *Morocco*	2.65
Brazil, Colombia, Dominican Republic, Equador, Guyana, Haiti, Panama, Suriname, Trinidad and Tobago	Alexandre Kafka (Hamid O'Brien)	Brazil *Trinidad & Tobago*	2.63
Bangladesh, Bhutan, India, Sri Lanka	M.R. Sivaraman (A.G. Karunasena)	India *Sri Lanka*	2.58
China	ZHANG Zhixiang (HAN Mingzhi)	China *China*	2.28
Argentina, Bolivia, Chile, Paraguay, Peru, Uruguay	A. Guillermo Zoccali (Nicolas Eyzaguirre)	Argentina *Chile*	2.14
Benin, Burkina Faso, Cameroon, Cape Verde, Central African Republic, Chad, Comoros, Congo, Côte d'Ivoire, Djibouti, Equatorial Guinea, Gabon, Guinea, Guinea-Bissau, Madagascar, Mali, Mauritania, Mauritius, Niger, Rwanda, São Tomé and Príncipe, Senegal, Togo	Koffi Yao (Alexandre Barro Chambrier)	Côte d'Ivoire *Gabon*	1.33

ACCESS
Founded in 1985, ACCESS is a nonprofit, non-advocacy provider of information on international security, peace and world affairs.

1701 K St., NW - 11th Floor
Washington DC 20006
202/223-7949   FAX 202/223-7947
E-mail: access@4access.org   http://www.4access.org
Contact: Ms. Mary Lord
          Executive Director

Action Council for Peace in the Balkans
A group of prominent Americans dedicated to establishing democracy, political stability and economic development in the Balkan region. The organization focuses on persuading policy makers, foreign policy makers, the Congress, the media and the American public that the U.S. must exert its international leadership in opposing genocide and aggression against Bosnia. Members come from every ideological persuasion and a variety of disciplines.

P.O. Box 27974
Washington DC 20038-0268
202/737-1414   FAX 202/737-3005
Contact: Mr. James Hooper
          Executive Director

Adventist Development and Relief Agency Intl.
ADRA is an independent agency established by the Seventh-day Adventist church for the specific purposes of community development and disaster relief in developing countries. It focuses on the basic sources of poverty while seeking to build self reliance. ADRA works on the behalf of the poor, including agriculture, water, institutional, and mother/child health projects.

12501 Old Columbia Pike
Silver Spring MD 20904
301/680-6380   FAX 301/680-6370
E-mail: 74617.2255@compuserve.com
http://www.ADRA.org
Contact: Mr. Ralph S. Watts
          President

AFL-CIO Public Policy Dept.
815 16th St., NW

Washington DC 20006
202/637-3907   FAX 202/508-6967
E-mail: Tlee@aflcio.org   http://www.aflcio.org
Contact: Ms. Thea Lee
          Assistant Dir. for Intl. Economics

Africa Policy Information Center
The APIC was founded in 1972 as the Washington Office on Africa (WOA) by a coalition of religious denominations and trade unions. The Center monitors legislation and advocates for public policies in the U.S. that foster peace, justice, and economic development throughout the continent of Africa.

110 Maryland Avenue, NE - Suite 509
Washington DC 20002
202/546-7961   FAX 202/546-1545
Contact: Ms. Pearl Alice Marsh
          Executive Director

African-American Institute
Headquartered in New York and established in 1953, the institute is a private, nonprofit organization fostering African development, centering primarily on strengthening human resources and on trade, investment, and economic development.

1625 Massachusetts Avenue, NW - Suite 210
Washington DC 20036
202/667-5636   FAX 202/265-6332
E-mail: jdrew@aaionline.org
Contact: Mr. Jerry Drew
          Director

African Millers Assn.
Represents matters in West African nations, primarily for export programs.

3331 Dent Place, NW
Washington DC 20007
202/342-0007   FAX 202/342-7132
Contact: Mr. Simon Pinniger
          Vice President

African Wildlife Federation
Engaged in the financing and implementation of wildlife conservation efforts.

1400 16th St., NW - Suite 120
Washington DC 20036
202/939-3333   FAX 202/939-3332
E-mail: awfwash@iac.apc.org
http://www.awf.org
Contact: Mr. Michael R. Wright
          President

Africare
Established in 1971, Africare is a private, nonprofit institution that has assisted families and communities in 35 African countries to date. It administers projects in the areas of food, water, the environment, health, emergency humanitarian aid, governance training and enterprise development. Africare maintains field offices in 25 African countries. Currently, its 150 programs reach 28 countries Africawide.

440 R Street, NW
Washington DC 20001
202/462-3614   FAX 202/387-1034
E-mail: africare@fl104.n109.zl.fidonet.org
Contact: C. Payne Lucas
          President

Agri-Energy Roundtable

1312 18th St., NW - Suite 300
Washington DC 20036
202/296-4563   FAX 202/887-9178
Contact: Mr. Nicholas E. Hollis
          Executive Director

Agribusiness Council

Established in 1967 as a nonprofit institution, ABC serves to strengthen U.S. agricultural trade with less developed countries. It concentrates on the production, processing, and marketing of agro-food and related products. ABC coordinates networks of state agribusiness councils and links this informal federation to counterpart associations overseas.

1312 18th Street NW - Suite 300
Washington DC 20036
202/296-4563   FAX 202/887-9178
E-mail: agenergy@aol.com
Contact: Mr. Nick Hollis
          President

Agricultural Cooperative Development Intl.

ACDI works in developing countries and emerging economies under contract with the Agency for International Development as well as other funding agencies and donors. It specializes in agribusiness and trade development, rural banking and credit systems, food for development, and training/exchange.

50 F Street, NW, Suite 1100
Washington DC 20001
202/638-4661   FAX 202/626-8726
E-mail: info@acdi.org   http://www.acdi.org/acdi
Contact: Mr. Mike Deegan
          President

Air Line Pilots Assn. Intl.

A union representing 45,000 airline pilots at 36 U.S. airlines. Founded in 1931, it is chartered by the AFL-CIO. ALPA provides all of the traditional union representation services for its members including presenting its members' views to Congress and government agencies.

1625 Massachusetts Ave., NW
Washington DC 20036
202/797-4000   FAX 202/797-4052
Contact: Mr. J. Randolph Babbitt
          President

Airports Council Intl.- North America

The ACI-NA represents local, regional and state governing bodies that own and operate commercial airports in the US, Canada and Virgin Islands. Its member airports are responsible for more than 90 percent of the domestic and virtually all the international airline passenger and cargo traffic in North America. ACI-NA also encompasses Associates representing a wide variety of businesses that provide products and services to the air transportation industry.

1775 K St., NW, Suite 500
Washington DC 20006
202/293-8500   FAX 202/331-1362
E-mail: dpeterson@aci-na.org
Contact: Ms. Diane Petersen
          Vice President Intl. Affairs

American-Arab Anti-Discrimination Committee

The Committee, with 80 chapters and 25,000 members across the country, dedicates itself to fighting negative stereotyping of Arabs in media portrayals and political dialogue.

4201 Connecticut Ave., NW - Suite 300
Washington DC 20009
202/244-2990   FAX 202/244-3196
E-mail: adc@adc.org   http://www.adc.org
Contact: Dr. Hala Maksoud
          President

American Assn. of Retired Persons Headquarters

601 E St., NW
Washington DC 20049-0001
202/434-2277   FAX 202/434-6477
Contact: Ms. Bette Mullen
          Director of Intl. Activities

American Association for the Advancement of Science - Directorate for International Programs

The Directorate for International Programs, one of three directorates at AAAS, seeks to achieve the Association's goals through enhanced cooperation between scientists and engineers in the U.S. and those of other countries. The directorate's activities are designed to strengthen the role of scientists and engineers in developing countries and to increase the contribution of science and technology to the solution of regional and global problems.

1200 New York Ave., NW
Washington DC 20005
202/326-6400   FAX 202/371-0970
E-mail: rnichols@aaas.org
http://www.aaas.org
Contact: Dr. Richard Wander
          Nicholson

American Business Conference

The American Business Conference (ABC) is a Washington-based coalition of one hundred chief executive officers from America's fastest-growing, mid-size companies. ABC members advocate policies to promote economic growth and a higher standard of living for all Americans.

1730 K St., NW - Suite 1200
Washington DC 20006
202/822-9300   FAX 202/467-4070
Contact: Mr. Barry K. Rogstad
          President

American Business Council of the Gulf Countries

c/o Intercom 1101 30th St., NW - Suite 500
Washington DC 20007
202/887-1887   FAX 202/887-1888
E-mail: hamod@intercom-usa.com
Contact: Mr. David Hamod
          U.S. Representative

American Chemical Society

Founded in 1876, the society is a nonprofit organization and the world's largest scientific society with a membership of 155,000 chemists and chemical engineers. Chartered by a 1937 Act of the U.S. Congress, the Society is recognized for its scientific education and research and for promoting public understanding of science.

1155 16th St., NW
Washington DC 20036-4800
202/872-4449   FAX 202/872-6317
E-mail: j_malin@acs.org
http://www.acs.org
Contact: Mr. John M. Malin
          Administrator for Intl. Activities

American Citizens Abroad

The ACA seeks to protect and promote the welfare, rights and benefits of American citizens living abroad.

1051 North George Mason Dr.
Arlington VA 22205
703/276-0949   FAX 703/527-3269
E-mail: jacabr@aol.com   http://www.aca.ch/
Contact: Ms. Jacqueline M. Abrams
          Director

American Committee for Intl. Conservation

The committee is comprised of a group of nongovernmental organizations focused on international conservation.

1725 DeSales St., NW, Suite 500
Washington DC 20036
202/429-5609   FAX 202/872-0619
Contact: Mr. Roger McManus
          President

American Committee to Save Bosnia

The ACSB is a national grassroots network, formed by a conference of over 40 humanitarian, citizen advocacy, student, and religious organizations in December 1993 to coordinate and initiate grassroots political and humanitarian activities throughout the U.S. to influence U.S. policy on Bosnia.

P.O. Box 28265
Washington DC 20038-0265
202/737-1414   FAX 202/737-3005
Contact: Mr. Stephen Walker
          Director

American Cotton Shippers Assn.

1725 K St., NW, Suite 1404
Washington DC 20036
202/296-7116   FAX 202/659-5322
Contact: Mr. Neal P. Gillen
          Executive Vice President and General Counsel

American Council of Young Political Leaders

The ACYPL was founded in 1966 as a nonprofit bipartisan educational exchange organization to enhance foreign policy understanding and exposure among rising young American political leaders and their counterparts around the world.

1612 K St. NW, Suite 300
Washington DC 20006
202/857-0999   FAX 202/857-0027
E-mail: acypl@erols.com   http://www.acypl.org
Contact: Mr. Winston McGregor
          Executive Director

American Defense Institute

The ADI is a nonprofit, nonpartisan educational/public policy organization that promotes the value of freedom and our responsibility for protecting it with a strong national defense.

1055 N. Fairfax St., Suite 200
Alexandria VA 22314
703/519-7000   FAX 703/519-8627
E-mail: ebm1@americandefins.org
Contact: Mr. Eugene B. McDaniel
          President

American Educational Trust

P.O. Box 53062
Washington DC 20009
202/939-6050   FAX 202/232-6754
E-mail: wrmea@aol.com
Contact: Mr. Richard Curtiss
          Executive Editor and Director

American Electronics Assn.

AEA is the largest and most effective trade association of the technology industry. Founded in 1943 with 25 member companies, the organization now maintains a membership of 3000 firms.

601 Pennsylvania Ave., NW - North Bldg. - Suite 600
Washington DC 20004
202/682-9110   FAX 202/682-9111
E-mail: debra_waggoner@aeanet.org http://www.aeanet.org
Contact: Ms. Debra Waggoner
          Senior Vice President of International

American Foreign Policy Council

AFPC's mission is to bring information to those who make or influence the foreign policy of the U.S. and to assist leaders in the former USSR and other parts of the world in building democracies and market economies. It facilitates debate on foreign policy by providing primary-source information to policy-makers through fact-finding missions, dinner discussions, and congressional staff luncheons. Its publications include the Russia Reform Monitor and China Reform Monitor.

1521 16th St., NW
Washington DC 20036
202/462-6055   FAX 202/462-6045
E-mail: afpc@afpc.org   http://www.afpc.org
Contact: Mr. Herman Pirchner
          President

American Foreign Service Assn.

The objective of the AFSA corporate relations program is to cultivate a constituency for the Foreign Service and international affairs among business and corporate leaders. AFSA's International Associates programs bring together corporate and government leaders for open dialogues on vital global, economic and business issues.

2101 E St., NW
Washington DC 20037
202/944-5508   FAX 202/338-6820
E-mail: corp@afsa.org   http://www.afsa.org
Contact: Mr. Mark Lore
          Director, Corporate Relations

American Forest & Paper Assn.

1111 19th St., NW #800
Washington DC 20036-3603
202/463-2700   FAX 202/463-2785
E-mail: maureen_smith@afandpa.org   http://www.afandpa.org
Contact: Ms. Maureen H. Smith
          Vice President Intl.

American Frozen Food Institute

2000 Corporate Ridge - Suite 1000
McLean VA 22102
703/821-0770   FAX 703/821-1350
E-mail: affi@pop.dn.net
Contact: Ms. Heather Schroeder
          Mgr. of Intl. Affairs

American Hellenic Educational Progressive Assn. (AHEPA)

Focused on community service, AHEPA is the largest Greek-American association in North America.

1909 Q St., NW - Suite 500
Washington DC 20009
202/232-6300   FAX 202/232-2140
E-mail: ahepa@ix.netcom.com
Contact: Mr. Andrew Kaffes
            Director, Public & Governmental Affairs

American Hellenic Institute, Inc.

Founded in 1974, the institute works to strengthen trade and commerce between the U.S., Greece, and Cyprus.

1220 16th St., NW
Washington DC 20036
202/785-8430   FAX 202/785-5178
E-mail: ahi@interramp.com   http://www.hri.org/ahipac
Contact: Mr. Nicholas Larigakis
            Executive Director

American Institute for Cancer Research

AICR is a cancer charity focusing exclusively on diet, nutrition and cancer. It provides free consumer education publications and programs. Since 1983, AICR's grant program has committed money to more than 430 research studies in 41 states and six countries. AICR's international affiliates are the World Cancer Research Fund in the U.K. and the Verald Kanker Onderzoek Funds in the Netherlands.

1759 R St. NW
Washington DC 20009-2583
202/328-7744   FAX 202/328-7226
E-mail: jlough@aicr.org   http://www.aicr.org
Contact: Mr. John Lough
            Senior Vice President

American Institute of Aeronautics & Astronautics

The AIAA is a nonprofit organization with a membership of over 40,000 scientists and aerospace engineers.

1801 Alexander Bell Dr. - Suite 500
Reston VA 20191-4344
703/264-7500   FAX 703/264-7551
E-mail: mirielleg@aiaa.org
Contact: Ms. Mireille M. Gerard
            Business Developer/Intl. Focus

American Intl. Automobile Dealers Assn.

AIADA is the trade association for America's 10,000 international nameplate automobile dealerships and their 333,000 employees who sell and service world-class automobiles manufactured in the U.S. and abroad. AIADA works to preserve a free market for international automobiles in the U.S. and is dedicated to increasing public awareness of the benefits the industry provides. AIADA provides its members with representation before Congress and the Administration on issues of concern to international automobile dealers, with a special focus on tax and trade issues.

99 Canal Center Plaza, Suite 500
Alexandria VA 22314-1538
703/519-7800   FAX 703/519-7810
E-mail: goaiada@aiada.org http://www.aiada.org
Contact: Ms. Lori L. Weaver Barnes
            Director of Public Relations

American Israel Public Affairs Committee

A national committee of Americans established in 1954, the committee seeks to strengthen U.S. policy in the Middle East for the ensurance of regional security, to raise regional living standards and to promote Arab-Israeli Peace Settlement.

440 First Street, NW, Suite 600
Washington DC 20001
202/639-5200   FAX 202/347-4921
http://www.aipac.org
Contact: Mr. Howard Kohr
            Executive Director

American Jewish Committee

Founded in 1906, the committee seeks to protect the rights of Jews throughout the world; combats anti-Semitism and bigotry; works for the security of Israel; enhances human rights, democratic pluralism and intergroup understanding; and promotes the creative vitality of the Jewish people.

1156 15th St., NW, Suite 1201
Washington DC 20005
202/785-4200   FAX 202/785-4115
E-mail: ogia@ajc.org   http://www.ajc.org
Contact: Rabbi Andrew Baker
            Director, Office of European Affairs

American Jewish Congress

A national membership organization in the forefront of the struggle for social and economic justice, religious freedom, and human rights in the United States and throughout the world.

2027 Massachusetts Ave., NW
Washington DC 20036
202/332-4001   FAX 202/387-3434
E-mail: ajc-dc@clarkinet
Contact: Mr. David A. Harris
            Director, Washington Office

American League for Exports & Security Assistance

Lobbying organization founded in 1976 to affect regulations and legislation for the facilitation of
U.S. exports in the context of national security concerns.

122 C Street, NW, Suite 310
Washington DC 20001
202/783-0051   FAX 202/737-4727
E-mail: alesa@erols.com
Contact: Ms. Anna Stout
            Executive Vice President

American Muslim Council

The AMC is a nonprofit sociopolitical organization established in 1990 to serve the interests of the Muslim community in the U.S. The organization also sponsors the American Task Force for Bosnia.

1212 New York Ave., NW - Suite 400
Washington DC 20005
202/789-2262   FAX 202/789-2550
http://www.amermuslim.org
Contact: Mr. Khaled Saffuri
            Director of Governmental Affairs

American Near East Refugee Aid

Working in Lebanon, the West Bank, Gaza, Israel and Jordan, ANERA is a private organization founded in 1968 for the reduction of poverty and suffering in the Middle East. Its various activities include donating medical supplies, working on social and economic development projects and informing Americans about the Middle East.

1522 K Street, NW, Suite 202
Washington DC 20005
202/347-2558   FAX 202/682-1637
E-mail: anera@anera.org   http://www.anera.org
Contact: Dr. Peter Gubser
         President

American Petroleum Institute

Instituted in 1919 as a nonprofit foundation, API is the primary advocacy and trade association with more than 400 member companies, including the major U.S. oil industry actors.

1220 L Street, NW
Washington DC 20005
202/682-8500   FAX 202/682-8029
E-mail: canes@api.org   http://www.api.org
Contact: Dr. Michael Canes
         Vice President

American Physical Therapy Assn.

APTA is a national professional organization representing more than 75,000 members throughout the U.S. The association's efforts are directed toward serving its members and the public by increasing the understanding of the physical therapist's role in the nation's health care system and by fostering improvements in physical therapy education, practice and research.

1111 North Fairfax St.
Alexandria VA 22314-1436
703/706-3143   FAX 703/684-7343
E-mail: min-intl@apta.org http://www.apta.org
Contact: Ms. Johnette Meadows
         Director of Minority & Intl. Affairs

American Psychiatric Assn.

The oldest medical specialty society in the U.S., APA's 40,500 plus physician and medical student members throughout North America and in numerous foreign countries specialize in the diagnosis and treatment of mental and emotional disorders.

1400 K St., NW
Washington DC 20005-2403
202/682-6000   FAX 202/682-6114
E-mail: emercer@psych.org
Contact: Ms. Ellen Mercer
         Director of Intl. Affairs

American Security Foundation

Founded in 1990 as the Coalition for Desert Storm, the coalition is a bipartisan alliance of Congressional leaders, governors, national associations and individuals working to develop policy options for a broad-based national security strategy for the U.S. and the world. The strategy encompasses military, economic, and political considerations, as well as proposals for energy security, economic growth, the space program, human rights, and world trade.

5545 Security Circle
Ballston VA 22713
540/547-1776   FAX 540/547-9737
Contact: Mr. John Fisher
         Chairman/CEO

American Seed Trade Assn.

The ASTA seeks to promote and represent the general business interests, firms, and corporations engaged in the seed industry in the U.S., Canada and Mexico. Membership includes those who market products or services other than seed for use in agriculture or

horticulture.

601 13th St., NW - Suite 570 South
Washington DC 20005-3807
202/638-3128   FAX 202/638-3171
E-mail: lcahill@ixnetcom.com   http://www.amseed.com
Contact: Ms. Leslie C. Cahill
         Vice President, Govt. Affairs

American Society for Photogrammetry & Remote Sensing (ASPRS)

Founded in 1934, ASPRS is a nonprofit scientific and technical association dedicated to advancing knowledge and improving understanding of the mapping sciences to promote the responsible application of photogrammetry, remote sensing, geographic information systems and supporting technologies.

5410 Grosvenor Lane - Suite 210
Bethesda MD 20814-2160
301/493-0290   FAX 301/493-0208
E-mail: asprs@asprs.org   http://www.asprs.org/asprs
Contact: Mr. James R. Plasker
         Executive Director

American Society for Training & Development

PO Box 1443 1640 King St.
Alexandria VA 22313-2043
703/683-8100   FAX 703/683-8103
Contact: Mr. Fred E. Voss
         Director Intl. Programs

American Society of Assn. Executives - Intl. Section

The Section works to enhance the international perspective of the association management profession and the international competencies of ASAE members to help them thrive in a global marketplace. Over 700 members actively participate in the International Section. The Section publishes a bi-monthly newsletter called International News.

1575 I St., NW
Washington DC 20005
202/626-2828   FAX 202/408-9633
E-mail: epotter@asaenet.org
http://www.asaenet.org/sections/international/
Contact: Mr. Edward Potter
         Dir. of Intl. Activities

American Society of Intl. Law

Founded in 1906, the society's purpose is to educate and engage the public in international law, and to expand its frontiers as a vehicle for resolving disputes.

2223 Massachusetts Ave., NW
Washington DC 20008-2864
202/939-6000   FAX 202/797-7133
E-mail: dgross@asil1.mhs.compuserve.com
http://www.asil.org
Contact: Ms. Charlotte Ku
         Executive Director

American Sugarbeet Growers Association

1156 15th St., NW - Suite 1101
Washington DC 20005
202/833-2398   FAX 202/833-2962
E-mail: asga@aol.com
http://members.aol.com/asga/sugar.htm
Contact: Mr. Luther Markwart
         Executive Vice President

American Task Force for Lebanon

The ATFL was founded as part of the National Association of Arab Americans in 1987, becoming incorporated and fully independent in 1989. It is a nonprofit organization comprised primarily of dedicated Americans of Lebanese heritage who share a common interest in Lebanon and the goals of the ATFL. The organization is nonsectarian and nonpartisan.

2213 M St., NW - Suite 300
Washington DC 20037
202/223-9333   FAX 202/223-1399
http://www.atfl.org
Contact: Dr. George T. Cody, Ph.D.
          Executive Director

American Translators Association

Founded in 1959, ATA is the largest professional association of translators and interpreters in the U.S. with over 6,500 members. Its primary goals include fostering and supporting the professional development of translators and interpreters and promoting the translation and interpretation professions. ATA has nine chapters in the U.S. and 11 specialized divisions: Japanese, Literary, Portuguese, Slavic, Science and Technology, French, German, Nordic, Spanish, interpreters, and translation companies.

1800 Diagonal Rd. - Suite 220
Alexandria VA 22314
703/683-6100   FAX 703/683-6122
E-mail: ata@atanet.org   http://www.atanet.org
Contact: Mr. Walter Bacak
          Executive Director

American Trucking Associations

ATA's mission is to serve the united interests of the 7.8 million people and 265,000-plus companies involved in trucking, and to educate public officials at all levels of government about the nature of the business. The association provides: representation before Congress, the courts, the executive branch and independent regulatory agencies; current information to ensure compliance with laws and regulations at the federal, state and local levels; and programs and services designed to increase operating efficiency and productivity, improve highway safety, and promote environmental responsibility.

2200 Mill Rd.
Alexandria VA 22314-4677
703/838-1996   FAX 703/549-9570
http://www.trucking.org
Contact: Ms. Linda Darr
          Vice President for Intl. Affairs

American-Turkish Council

A business association dedicated to the promotion of U.S.-Turkish commercial, defense and cultural relations.

1010 Vermont Ave., NW, Suite 300
Washington DC 20005
202/783-0483   FAX 202/783-0511
E-mail: atcafot@aol.com
http://www.members.aol.com/atcafot/atc.htm
Contact: Mr. G. Lincoln McCurdy
          Executive Director

Americans for Free Intl. Trade (AFIT PAC)

AFIT PAC represents the interests of automobile import dealers.

112 S. West St. - Suite 310
Alexandria VA 22314
703/684-8880   FAX 703/836-5256
E-mail: afitpac@aol.com

Contact: Ms. Mary Dreape Hanagan
          Executive Director

Americans for Peace Now (APN)

1835 K St., NW - Suite 500
Washington DC 20006
202/728-1893   FAX 202/728-1895
Contact: Mr. Mark Bilsky
          Assistant Executive Director

AMIDEAST (America-Mideast Educational and Training Services, Inc.)

Founded in 1951, AMIDEAST is a private, nonprofit organization promoting cooperation and understanding between Americans and the people of the Middle East and North Africa through education, information, and development assistance programs. Headquartered in Washington, DC, AMIDEAST has a network of offices in Egypt, Jordan, Kuwait, Lebanon, Morocco, Syria, Tunisia, the United Arab Emirates, West Bank/Gaza Strip, and Yemen.

1730 M St., NW - Suite 1100
Washington DC 20036-4505
202/776-9600   FAX 202/776-7000
E-mail: inquiries@amideast.org   http://www.amideast.org
Contact: Mr. John R. Hayes
          Chair

Amnesty Intl. USA

A global, nongovernmental organization, established in 1961, working for the release of prisoners of conscience, the end of torture and execution and fair trials for all political prisoners.

304 Pennsylvania Avenue, SE
Washington DC 20003
202/544-0200   FAX 202/546-7142
Contact: Mr. Stephen Rickard
          Director, Washington Office

Antarctica Project

Works to preserve Antarctica by educating the public and governments on Antarctic issues. It monitors activities affecting Antarctica, conducts legal and policy research and analysis, produces educational materials, and works with the international scientific community to focus on globally and environmentally significant research. It also acts as the Secretariat to the Antarctic and Southern Ocean Coalition, which is comprised of 240 environmental groups in 49 nations, all working to protect Antarctica.

408 C St., NE
Washington DC 20002
202/544-0236   FAX 202/544-8483
E-mail: antarctica@igc.org http://www.asoc.org
Contact: Ms. Beth Clark
          Director

Anti-Defamation League of B'nai B'rith

Founded in 1913, the organization is committed to ending the defamation of Jews and to securing justice and fair treatment to all citizens alike. The Washington office represents the League in the nations capitol, on a range of international and domestic issues including: hate crimes, religious freedom, civil rights and international and domestic terrorism.

1100 Connecticut Ave., NW - Suite 1020
Washington DC 20036
202/452-8320   FAX 202/296-2371
http://www.adl.org
Contact: Ms. Stacy Burdett
          Assistant Director

Armenian Assembly of America
AAA serves as a forum and provides a national framework for the promotion of communication within the Armenian-American community. It fosters awareness and appreciation of Armenian cultural heritage and historical identity in the Armenian community. It also gathers and disseminates information to the Armenian-American community in order to promote greater Armenian-American participation in the American democratic process.

122 C St., NW - Suite 350
Washington DC 20001
202/393-3434   FAX 202/638-4904
E-mail: info@aaainc.org   http://www.aaainc.org
Contact: Ms. Joan Ablett
          Director, Public Affairs

Armenian Natl. Committee of America
Serves to foster U.S. public support in favor of a free, independent and united Armenia and to represent the views of Armenian-Americans on U.S. foreign policy issues.

888 17th St., NW - Suite 904
Washington DC 20006
202/775-1918   FAX 202/775-5648
E-mail: anca-dc@ix.netcom.com
Contact: Mr. Aram Hamparain
          Executive Director

Arms Control Assn.
A nonpartisan membership organization, founded in 1971, which promotes understanding of arms control and its role in national security.

1726 M. St., NW - Suite 201
Washington DC 20036
202/463-8270   FAX 202/463-8273
E-mail: aca@armscontrol.org   http://www.armscontrol.org
Contact: Mr. Spurgeon M. Keeny
          President and Executive Director

Asia Foundation, The
Founded in 1954 and headquartered in San Francisco, the foundation has 13 regional offices in the Asia-Pacific region and a Washington liaison office. It is a private, American grant making organization, promoting U.S.-Asian understanding and cooperation, and aimed at strengthening democratic processes and institutions, the rule of law, and market economies in the region. It gives more than 1500 grants annually to governmental and non-governmental organizations in 30 Asian and Pacific island nations. The foundation is funded by both public and private funds, receiving an annual appropriation from the U.S. Congress and competing for funding from the U.S. Agency for International Development.

1779 Massachusetts Ave., NW - Suite 815
Washington DC 20036
202/588-9420
http://www.asiafoundation.org/
Contact: Ms. Nancy Yuan
          Director

Asia Pacific Policy Center
Established in 1993 as a nonprofit institution, the APPC seeks closer ties between business and political leaders in the U.S. and their counterparts in Asia and the Pacific. The APPC aims at an engaged and creative U.S. role in the region, encompassing commercial, economic, political, and security issues. The Center does not engage in lobbying but promotes instead a bipartisan American commitment to the Asia-Pacific area, offering issue-by-issue analysis of U.S.-Asia trends.

1730 Rhode Island Ave., NW - Suite 1011
Washington DC 20036
202/223-7258   FAX 202/223-7280
E-mail: appcusa@aol.com   http://www.appcusa.org
Contact: Mr. Franklin L. Lavin
          Executive Director

Asia Society, The - Washington Center
The Asia Society Washington Center, a regional office of The Asia Society, provides a forum in the nation's capital to exchange views on a wide variety of subjects concerning Asia. The Asia Society is a national nonprofit, nonpartisan educational organization. Founded in 1956 by John D. Rockefeller III, its headquarters are in New York.

1800 K St., NW - Suite 1102
Washington DC 20006
202/833-2742   FAX 202/833-0189
http://www.asiasociety.org
Contact: Ms. Judith Sloan
          Director

Aspen Institute, The
1333 New Hampshire Ave., NW - Suite 1070
Washington DC 20036
202/736-5800   FAX 202/467-0790
E-mail: jriggs@aspeninst.org
Contact: Mr. Jack Riggs
          Director, Special Policy Programs

Assn. for Canadian Studies in the United States
Founded in 1971, the association promotes U.S. interest in the study of Canada at all educational levels.

1317 F Street, NW - Suite 920
Washington DC 20004-1105
202/393-2580   FAX 202/393-2582
E-mail: acsus@nicom.com http://canada-acsus.plattsburgh.edu/acsus/I_acsus.htm
Contact: Mr. David N. Biette
          Executive Director

Assn. for Childhood Education Intl.
Founded in 1982, ACEI is the oldest organization of its kind devoted to the development of the whole child from birth through early adolescence. The overall mission is to promote the inherent rights, education, and well-being of all children in their home, school, and community. The association has a dual commitment to the fulfillment of every child's potential and to the professional development of classroom teachers.

17904 Georgia Ave. - Suite 215
Olney MD 20832
301/570-2111   FAX 301/570-2212
E-mail: aceihq@aol.com   http://www.udel.edu/bateman/acei
Contact: Mr. Gerald C. Odland
          Executive Director

Assn. for Interactive Media
Since 1993, the Association for Interactive Media (AIM) has served businesses that use the Internet, including Intel, Citicorp, Disney, Price Waterhouse, and more than 300 others. The organization defends Internet industry against government regulation, promotes consumer confidence in Internet commerce, and provides business-to-business networking opportunities.

1019 19th St., NW - 10th Floor
Washington DC 20036
202/408-0008   FAX 202/408-0111
E-mail: info@interactivehq.org   http://www.interactivehq.org

Contact: Mr. Andrew L. Sernovitz
President

Assn. for the Advancement of Policy, Research and Development in the Third World
A professional, scholarly, private, nonprofit institution founded in 1981 to serve as a forum through which Third World professionals might become more substantially involved in the international development process.

1730 K Street, NW, Suite 304
Washington DC 20006
202/296-0947   FAX 202/331-3759
Contact: Mr. Mekki Mtewa
President

Assn. of American Chambers of Commerce in Latin America
Founded in 1967, AACCLA is the umbrella group for 23 American Chambers of Commerce in 21 Latin American/Caribbean nations. AACCLA advocates trade and investment between the U.S. and the countries of the region through free trade, free markets, and free enterprise.

1615 H St., NW
Washington DC 20062-2000
202/463-5485   FAX 202/463-3126
E-mail: inbox@aaccla.org   http://www.aacla.org
Contact: Mr. David Hirschmann
Executive Vice President

Assn. of Career Management Consulting Firms Intl.
An association of consulting firms from around the world who are engaged in the professional practice of outplacement. Its mission is to support the interests of the outplacement profession by providing those services and dealing with those interests best handled by the industry as a whole rather than any one member firm.

1200 19th St., NW - Suite 300
Washington DC 20036-2422
202/857-1185   FAX 202/857-1115
http://www.aocfi.org
Contact: Mr. Will Rijksen
Associate Manager

Assn. of Foreign Investors in U.S. Real Estate
Founded in 1988, AFIRE is the only organization in the U.S. dedicated to educating the American government and its citizens about the benefits and importance of foreign real estate investment to the U.S. economy. The Association provides a forum through which the foreign investment community may meet and discuss common issues and problems.

1300 Pennsylvania Ave., NW - Suite 880
Washington DC 20004
202/312-1400   FAX 202/312-1401
E-mail: jaf@afire.org   http://www.afire.org
Contact: Mr. James A. Fetgatter
Chief Executive

Assn. of Intl. Automobile Manufacturers, Inc. (AIAM)
AIAM is the trade association for U.S. subsidiaries of international automobile companies. It actively supports free market competition because it believes that it benefits both consumers and industry.

1001 19th Street North - Suite 1200
Arlington VA 22209
703/525-7788   FAX 703/525-8817
E-mail: mmarkowitz@aiam.org   http://www.aiam.org

Contact: Mr. Morry B. Markowitz
Vice President of Public Affairs

Assn. of Intl. Photography Art Dealers
Founded in 1979, AIPAD has members in the U.S., Australia, Canada, Europe and Japan and is dedicated to creating and maintaining high standards in the business of exhibiting, buying and selling photographs as art. It promotes communication within the photographic community, encourages public appreciation of photography as art, and concerns itself with the rights of photographers and collectors.

1609 Connecticut Avenue, NW
Washington DC 20009
202/986-0105   FAX 202/986-0448
Contact: Ms. Kathleen Ewing
Executive Director

Assn. of Junior Leagues Intl.
An organization of women committed to promoting volunteerism, developing the potential of women, and improving communities through the action and leadership of trained volunteers. Its purpose is exclusively educational and charitable.

1319 F Street, NW, Suite 604
Washington DC 20004
202/393-3364   FAX 202/393-4517
Contact: Ms. Mary Douglass
Senior Associate, Programs

Assn. of Professional Schools of Intl. Affairs
A nonprofit, institutional membership organization, comprised of 16 U.S. graduate schools of international affairs and two associate members. These schools are dedicated to advancing global understanding and cooperation by preparing men and women to assume positions of leadership in world affairs.

1779 Massachusetts Ave., NW
Washington DC 20036
202/939-2390   FAX 202/483-1542
E-mail: apsia@erols.com
Contact: Ms. Kay King
Executive Director

Assn. of School Business Officials Intl.
A professional association which provides programs and services to promote the highest standards of school business management practices and professional growth, and the effective use of educational resources. Representing over 6,000 members at the elementary, secondary, and junior and community college levels, members include non instructional employees at the local, state and national levels from specialized areas in school business management, as well as the generalized field of school business administration.

11401 North Shore Drive
Reston VA 20190-4200
703/478-0405   FAX 703/478-0205
E-mail: dithorpe@sprynet.com   http://www.asbointl.org
Contact: Dr. Don I. Tharpe
Executive Director

Assn. of TeleServices Intl.
The mission of the association is to enhance the value of members' businesses by: promoting fair competition through the pursuit of appropriate regulation and legislation; providing research into and development of the industry and its current and prospective markets; providing support services; providing educational opportunities and resources to address the challenges and trends affecting the operating environments; and encouraging and maintaining high standards of ethics and services.

1200 19th St., NW - Suite 300
Washington DC 20036-2422
202/429-5151   FAX 202/223-4579
http://www.atsi.org
Contact: Ms. Herta Tucker
          Executive Director

Assn. of the Wall & Ceiling Industries Intl.

Comprised of 1,200 members, primarily consisting of wall and ceiling contractors, product suppliers or product manufacturers, the association provides services and undertakes activities that enhance the members' ability to operate a successful business.

307 E. Annandale Rd. - Suite 200
Falls Church VA 22042-2433
703/534-8300   FAX 703/534-8307
E-mail: INFO@AWCI.ORG http://www.AWCI.org
Contact: Mr. Steven A. Etkin
          Executive Vice President

Assn. of Women in Intl. Trade, Inc.

Organized in 1987, WIIT is dedicated to enhancing the visibility of and opportunities for women in the field of international trade. WIIT provides educational and professional development seminars and many opportunities to meet with policy makers and network with other professionals. WIIT is the largest chapter of the Organization of Women in International Trade (OWIT).

P.O. Box 65962
Washington DC 20035
202/785-9842   FAX 202/358-9678
http://www.embassy.org/wiit
Contact: Ms. Loretta Dunn
          President

Assn. on Third World Affairs

A membership organization founded in 1967 and involved in research and public information projects concerning developing nations.

1629 K Street, NW - Suite 802
Washington DC 20006
202/331-8455   FAX 202/775-7465
Contact: Dr. Lorna Hahn
          Executive Director

Assn. to Unite the Democracies

Established in 1940, the association works toward a federation of the longstanding democracies for the ensurance of world peace and stability. It also works for the formation of a common market and common currency, and the building of a democratic world federation.

1506 Pennsylvania Avenue, SE
Washington DC 20003-3116
202/544-5150   FAX 202/544-3742
E-mail: atunite@aol.com   http://www.atunite.org
Contact: Capt. Tom Hudgens
          President

Atlantic Council of the U.S.

A nonprofit, bipartisan public policy research institution, the council addresses issues related to the advancement of U.S. global interests among the Atlantic and Pacific communities, focusing on U.S. foreign security and international economic policies.

910 17th St., NW - Suite 1000
Washington DC 20006
202/463-7226   FAX 202/463-7241
E-mail: info@acus.org   http://www.acus.org

Contacts:
Mr. Andrew J. Goodpaster
   Co-Chairman
Mr. David C. Acheson
   President
Mr. Peter B. Swiers
   Vice President, East-West Studies
Mr. Gayden Thompson
   Director, Program on NATO & European Comm.
Mr. Bill Dircks
   Director, Program on Nuclear Non-Proliferation

Australia America Association

P.O. Box 75195
Washington DC 20013-5195
202/672-5522
Contact: Mr. Samuel B. Sterrett
          President

B'nai B'rith Intl.

1640 Rhode Island Ave., NW
Washington DC 20036-3278
202/857-6545   FAX 202/857-6689
http://www.bnaibrith.org
Contact: Mr. Daniel S. Mariaschin
          Director, Center for Public Policy

Bakery, Confectionery & Tobacco Workers Intl. Union

10401 Connecticut Avenue
Kensington MD 20895
301/933-8600   FAX 301/946-8452
Contact: Mr. Frank Hurt
          President

Balkan Institute, The

Formed in May 1995 to educate the public on the nature of the crisis in the Balkans and its humanitarian, political, and military consequences. Through public education and discourse, it hopes to promote a greater understanding and higher level of awareness throughout the U.S.

P.O. Box 27974
Washington DC 20038-7974
202/737-5219   FAX 202/737-1940
Contact: Mr. Stephen Walker
          Co-Director

Bankers' Assn. for Foreign Trade

Founded in 1921, the BAFT is an association of banking institutions dedicated to fostering and promoting international trade, finance, and investment between the U.S. and its trading partners.

2121 K St., NW, Suite 701
Washington DC 20037
202/452-0952   FAX 202/452-0959
E-mail: baft@baft.org   http://www.baft.org
Contact: Ms. Mary Condeelis
          Executive Director

Beer Institute

Founded in 1986, the Beer Institute is the official trade association for the American brewing industry, whose 222 members include national, regional, local, and international brewers as well as suppliers of brewing goods, services, and agricultural products. Together, its members produce 93 percent of the beer brewed in America.

122 C St., NW - Suite 750
Washington DC 20001

202/737-2337   FAX 202/737-7004
http://www.beerinst.org
Contact: Mr. Raymond J. McGrath
               President

Brazil - U.S. Business Council

The Council is a bilateral trade organization that provides a high level private sector forum for the business communities of both countries. The Council's members engage in dialogue on trade and investment issues and communicate private sector priorities to both governments. The U.S. section of the council represents the majority of the largest American corporations invested in Brazil and operates under the administrative aegis of the U.S. Chamber of Commerce.

1615 H St., NW
Washington DC 20062
202/463-5485   FAX 202/463-3126
E-mail: host@brazilcouncil.org   http://www.brazilcouncil.org
Contact: Mr. Mark Smith
               Executive Director

Bread for the World

Religious based organization founded in 1974 to work toward greater government responsiveness to world hunger.

1100 Wayne Avenue, Suite 1000
Silver Spring MD 20910
301/608-2400   FAX 301/608-2401
E-mail: bread@bread.org   http://www.bread.org
Contact: Mr. David Beckmann
               President

British - American Business Assn.

P.O. Box 17482
Washington DC 20041
202/293-0010   FAX 202/296-3332
E-mail: dc-baba@ix.netcom.com   http://www.babc.org
Contact: Mr. Timothy C. Coughlin
               Chairman

British American Security Information Council (BASIC)

An independent research organization that analyzes international security policy in Europe and North America, BASIC works to promote public awareness of defense, disarmament, military strategy, and nuclear policies in order to foster informed debate on the issues.

1900 L St., NW - Suite 401-2
Washington DC 20036
202/785-1266   FAX 202/387-6298
E-mail: basicusa@basicint.org   http://www.basicint.org
Contact: Mr. Daniel T. Piesch
               Director

Brookings Institution

An independent, nonpartisan research organization, seeks to improve the performance of American institutions, the effectiveness of government programs, and the quality of U.S. public policies. It addresses current and emerging policy and challenges and offers practical recommendations for dealing with them, expressed in language that is accessible to policy makers and the general public alike. Brookings has attracted to its staff numerous senior government officials and notable scholars from both sides of the political aisle.

1775 Massachusetts Ave., NW
Washington DC 20036-2188
202/797-6000   FAX 202/797-6004
http://www.brook.edu/

Contacts:

Mr. Michael H. Armacost
     President
Mr. Bailey Morris-Eck
     Vice President of Communications
Mr. Robert E. Litan
     Director, Economic Studies
Mr. Richard N. Haass
     Director, Foreign Policy Studies

Building Owners & Managers Assn. Intl.

Founded in 1907, BOMA International is the oldest and largest trade association exclusively representing the office building industry. It is comprised of 100 federated associations across the U.S., Canada and around the world. Its over 16,000 members are office building owners, managers, developers, facility managers, leasing agents and brokers, investors, and companies who provide products and services to the industry. BOMA International is a source of information on office building management, development, leasing, building operating costs, energy consumption patterns, local and national building codes, legislation, occupancy statistics and technological advancements.

1201 New York Ave., NW, Suite 300
Washington DC 20005
202/408-2662   FAX 202/371-0181
E-mail: hchamber@boma.org   http://www.boma.org
Contact: Mr. Henry Chamberlain
               Senior Vice President

Building Service Contractors Assn. Intl.

Formed in 1965, BSCAI represents more than 2,500 member companies from across the U.S. and 39 other countries which provide cleaning, facility maintenance and other related services to building owners and managers. The association provides an annual convention and trade show, miscellaneous regional seminars, publications, video training programs, government lobbying, and networking opportunities developed specifically for the building service contracting industry.

10201 Lee Hwy., Suite 225
Fairfax VA 22030
703/359-7090   FAX 703/352-0493
http://www.bscai.org
Contact: Ms. Carol A. Dean
               Executive Vice President

Business Alliance for International Development

The Business Alliance for International Development is dedicated to informing the American public, elected officials, and the wider business community about the correlation between properly implemented foreign economic assistance and the expansion of U.S. exports and jobs. The Alliance believes there are development assistance roles that only the U.S. government and multi-lateral development banks can fulfill, and that sufficient resources must be made available to these institutions to accomplish this mission.

601 13th St., NW - Suite 900-S
Washington DC 20005
202/783-5588   FAX 202/783-5595
E-mail: Avenshire@aol.com
http://www.milcom.com/alliance
Contact: Mr. Terrence L. Bracy
               Executive Director

Business Executives for Natl. Security

Established in 1982 as a nonprofit, nonpartisan organization of business executives and entrepreneurs working for the application of sound business principles to government security policy, for the prevention of nuclear weapon usage, and for a strong economy as a base for security.

1717 Pennsylvania Ave., NW - Suite 350

Washington DC 20006
202/296-2125   FAX 202/296-2490
E-mail: tmcinerny@bens.org   http://www.bens.org
Contact: Mr. Thomas G. McInerny
          President and Chief Exec. Officer

Business Roundtable

The Business Roundtable is an association of chief executive officers who examine public issues that affect the economy and develop positions which seek to reflect sound economic and social principles. Established in 1972, the Roundtable was founded in the belief that business executives should take an increased role in the continuing debates about public policy.

1615 L St., NW - Suite 1100
Washington DC 20036-5610
202/872-1260   FAX 202/466-3509
http://www.brtable.org
Contact: Mr. Samuel L. Maury
          President

Business Software Alliance

Comprised of leading publishers of computer software, BSA promotes the continued growth of the software industry through its public policy, education, and enforcement programs in 65 countries throughout North America, Europe, Asia, Latin American, Africa and the Middle East.

1150 18th St., NW - Suite 700
Washington DC 20036
202/872-5500   FAX 202/872-5501
E-mail: software@bsa.org   http://www.bsa.org
Contact: Ms. Diane Smiroldo
          Vice President, Public Affairs

Campaign for U.N. Reform

A bipartisan citizen organization founded in 1975, its primary goal remains to gain support for an enhanced, reformed U.N. It advances this goal through public education, lobbying and electioneering.

4207 7th St., SE - Suite C
Washington DC 20003-0270
202/546-3956   FAX 202/546-8703
E-mail: cunr@aol.com
Contact: Mr. Don Kraus
          Executive Director

Canadian-American Business Council

1629 K St., NW, Suite 1100
Washington DC 20006
202/785-6717   FAX 202/331-4212
E-mail: stankrejci@aol.com
Contact: Mr. Stan Krejci
          President

Caribbean/Latin American Action

An independent, nongovernmental organization established in 1980 to promote private sector generated economic development in the nations of the Caribbean Basin by the stimulation of trade and investment and by assisting local private sector entities.

1818 N Street, NW, Suite 500
Washington DC 20036
202/466-7464   FAX 202/822-0075
http://www.claa.org
Contact: Mr. Antonio Colorado
          Executive Director

Carnegie Endowment for Intl. Peace

The Face-to-Face program is intended to broaden the perspectives and enrich the dialogue among foreign policy professionals through informal, invitation-only encounters with key international figures on a wide range of economic, political, military, and social topics. It provides world and national leaders the opportunity to present their views to a cross section of government, media, academia, and nongovernmental organizations.

1770 Massachusetts Ave., NW
Washington DC 20036
202/939-2310   FAX 202/483-1445
E-mail: RMarkowitz@ceip.org
Contact: Ms. Robin Markowitz
          Director, Face-to Face

Carrying Capacity Network

A national nonprofit organization, CNN's action-oriented initiatives focus on achieving national revitalization, population stabilization, immigration reduction, economic sustainability/fiscal integrity, and resource conservation.

2000 P Street, NW - Suite 240
Washington DC 20036
202/296-4548   FAX 202/296-4609
E-mail: ccn@igc.apc.org   http://www.carryingcapacity.org
Contact: Mr. Leon Kolankiewicz
          Network Coordinator

Cato Institute

A public policy research institute, favoring a market liberal approach to economic and political issues.

1000 Massachusetts Ave., NW
Washington DC 20001-5403
202/842-0200   FAX 202/842-3490
E-mail: cato@cato.org   http://www.cato.org

Contacts:
Mr. Edward H. Crane
     President
Mr. Roger Pilon
     Director, Center for Constitutional Studies
Mr. Stephen Moore
     Director, Fiscal Policy Studies
Mr. Ted Galen Carpenter
     Director, Foreign Policy Studies
Mr. Ian Vasquez
     Director, Project on Global Econ. Liberty
Mr. Michael Gough
     Director, Science and Risk Studies
Mr. Tom Bell
     Director, Telecommunications and Technology Studies

Center for Clean Air Policy

The Center believes that market-based approaches to environmental regulation are essential to achieving a balance in protecting both economic and environmental interests. The Center was formed in 1985 by a group of state governors, and focuses on acid rain, energy conservation, air toxins, and global warming policy. The Center conducts independent research and analysis, mediates dialogues between parties at odds over environmental issues, coordinates international exchange programs with top officials in other countries concerned with clean air, and works with political leaders and the press in the U.S. to advance the Center's policy recommendations.

750 First St., NE
Washington DC 20002
202/408-9260   FAX 202/408-8896
Contact: Mr. Edward A. Helme

Executive Director

Center for Defense Information
Founded in 1972 to serve as an independent monitor of the military, CDI is widely recognized as the foremost research organization in the country analyzing military spending, policies and weapons systems. It makes its military analysis available to Congress, the media, and the public through a variety of services and publications. CDI also provides assistance to the federal government upon request.

1779 Massachusetts Ave., NW - Suite 615
Washington DC 20036
202/332-0600   FAX 202/462-4559
E-mail: info@cdi.org   http://www.cdi.org
Contact: Mr. Dan Smith
        Associate Director

Center for Democracy
Founded in 1985, this nonprofit, nonpartisan center works to strengthen the democratic process internationally. Based in Washington DC, the center also has liaison staff in Moscow and Strasbourg (France). Its goals are to help facilitate and reinforce democratic institutions, encourage dialogue in conflict situations, and assist societies transitioning toward law-based democracies and market economies.

1101 15th St., NW, Suite 505
Washington DC 20005
202/429-9141   FAX 202/293-1768
E-mail: centdemoc@aol.com
Contact: Dr. Allen Weinstein
        President and CEO

Center for Intl. Environmental Law (CIEL)
CIEL was founded in 1989 to bring the energy and experience of the public interest and environmental law movement to the critical task of strengthening and developing international and environmental law, policy, and management throughout the world. CIEL works with non-governmental organizations, governments, and international agencies to promote sustainable societies through law, to incorporate fundamental principles of ecology and democracy into law, to support public interest movements around the world, and to educate and train public interest minded environmental lawyers.

1367 Connecticut Ave., NW - Suites 300
Washington DC 20036-1860
202/785-8700   FAX 202/785-8701
E-mail: cielus@igc.apc.org http://www.econet.apc.org/ciel/
Contact: Mr. Durwood J. Zaelke
        President

Center for Intl. Policy
A nonprofit research and education institution centering on the impact of U.S. foreign policy on Third World human rights and socioeconomic conditions.

1755 Massachusetts Avenue, NW - Suite 324
Washington DC 20036
202/232-3317   FAX 202/232-3440
E-mail: cip@igc.org   http://www.us.net/cip/index.htm
Contact: Mr. William C. Goodfellow
        Director

Center for Intl. Private Enterprise
Established in 1983 as an affiliate of the U.S. Chamber of Commerce, CIPE promotes private enterprise and market-oriented economic reform world-wide and supports strategies and techniques that address market-based democratic development.

1155 15th St., NW - Suite700
Washington DC 20005
202/721-9200   FAX 202/721-9250
E-mail: cipe@cipe.org   http://www.cipe.org
Contact: Mr. John D. Sullivan
        Executive Director

Center for Natl. Security Studies
Established in 1974, CNSS is a nonprofit public interest organization that uses research and analysis, public education, litigation, and other advocacy to ensure that civil liberties and human rights are not eroded in the name of national security. Through its international project, CNSS works with human rights activists, parliamentarians, and others to promote oversight and accountability of security services.

2130 H St., NW, Suite 701
Washington DC 20037
202/994-7060   FAX 202/994-7005
E-mail: cnss@gwu.edu
Contact: Ms. Kate Martin
        Director

Center for Security Policy
The center works with strategically significant developments relating to national and economic security while specializing in products created to supply policy makers with immediately usable information.

1250 24th St., NW - Suite 350
Washington DC 20037
202/466-0515   FAX 202/466-0518
E-mail: info@security-policy.org
http://www.security-policy.org
Contact: Mr. Frank J. Gaffney, Jr.
        Director

Center for Strategic and Budgetary Assessments
The CSBA is an independent, nonprofit public policy institute established to continue and expand upon the research and public education activities conducted by the Defense Budget Project since 1983. CSBA's research examines defense strategy options and provides data based assessment of defense budget and investment trends. It provides research on these issues to media, policy makers, and other interested individuals in the U.S. and abroad.

1730 Rhode Island Ave. - Suite 912
Washington DC 20036
202/331-7990   FAX 202/331-8019
E-mail: 102375.413@compuserve.com
http://www.csbahome.com
Contact: Dr. Andrew Krepinevich
        Director

Center for Strategic and Intl. Studies
Established in 1962, CSIS is a public policy research institution dedicated to analysis and policy impact. CSIS is the only institution that maintains resident experts on all the world's major geographic locations. The Center conducts research in the areas of: Africa, the Americas, Asia, U.S. policy issues, energy, national security, Europe, international business and economics, international communications, Middle East, political military studies, preventive diplomacy, Russian and Eurasia, global organized crime, new global economy, and the environment. Research findings and policy recommendations are disseminated through conferences and a variety of publications to policymakers, opinion leaders, and academic experts. CSIS has a history of being utilized by the government for decision making counsel. Several former government officials serve on its staff.

1800 K St., NW - Suite 400
Washington DC 20006
202/887-0200   FAX 202/775-3199

E-mail: info@csis.org   http://www.csis.org
Contact: Mr. Richard M. Fairbanks, III
         Managing Director, Domestic and Intl. Issues

Center for Taiwan International Relations

The CTIR is a private, non-profit, non-partisan research organization established in Washington, DC in 1988. It works with the international community to uphold the right of Taiwan's people to decide their future for themselves and to ensure that this decision is made freely without threat, coercion, or false information.

110 Maryland Ave., NE - Suite 206
Washington DC 20002
202/543-6287   FAX 202/543-2364
E-mail: ctirdwt@erols.com http://www.taiwandc.org
Contact: Mr. David Tsai
         President

Center for War, Peace and the News Media

The Center for War, Peace, and the News Media is a non-profit, non-partisan organization dedicated to supporting journalists and news organizations in their efforts to sustain an informed citizenry. The Center is headquartered at the New York University Department of Journalism and Mass Communication, where it was founded in 1985. The Centers chief goals are assisting American and other journalists in their coverage of international affairs, aiding Russian journalists and news organizations, and initiating projects that explore constructive roles for the media in ethnic, civil, and other intra- and international conflicts.

2450 Virginia Ave., NW - Suite E304
Washington DC 20037
301/320-9039   FAX 202/466-4344
E-mail: war.peace.news@nyu.edu
http://www.nyu.edu/globalbeat
Contact: Mr. Conrad Hohenlohe
         Washington Representative

Central & East European Working Groups of the U.S. Chamber of Commerce

The Bulgarian, Belarusian, and Ukrainian Working Groups of the U.S. Chamber of Commerce work toward improving trade and investment prospects for U.S. business in the respective markets.

PO Box 1200
Washington DC 20013-1200
202/463-5482   FAX 202/463-3114
E-mail: eurasia@uschamber.com
Contact: Mr. Gary Litman
         Executive Director

Central Eastern Europe and Eurasia, International, U.S. Chamber of Commerce

1615 H St., NW
Washington DC 20062-2000
202/463-5460   FAX 202/463-3114
E-mail: eurasia@uschamber.com
Contact: Mr. Gary Litman
         Director

Chemical Manufacturers Assn.

Represents more than 180 U.S. and Canadian chemical industry members.

1300 Wilson Blvd.
Arlington VA 22209
703/741-5920   FAX 703/741-6070
Contact: Ms. Kathleen A. Ambrose

Vice President, Intl. Affairs

Children's Hospice Intl.
The organization provides advocacy and outreach services, including referral and information services, to create public awareness of the needs of children with life-threatening conditions and their families. It also provides ongoing research, education, training and technical assistance programs to facilitate the inclusion of hospice perspectives in all areas of pediatric care and education.

2202 Mount Vernon Ave. - Suite 3C
Alexandria VA 22301
703/684-0330   FAX 703/684-0226
Contact: Mr. John Keeley
         Director

Chilean - American Chamber of Commerce

1913 Massachusetts Ave., NW - 2nd Fl.
Washington DC 20036
202/457-0349   FAX 202/835-8518
Contact: His Excellency Charles A. Gillespie
         President

China Chamber of Intl. Commerce/China Council for the Promotion of Intl. Trade

The China Council for the Promotion of International Trade was designated by the Chinese government as the liaison organization for China's non-governmental economic and trade relations with the U.S. in the early 1970s before the establishment of formal diplomatic ties between the two countries in 1979. In March, 1987, CCPIT opened its representative office in Washington DC the mission of which is to increase the awareness among the industrial and commercial circles of the two countries of each other's markets, trade regulations, economic policies, business practices, and investment environment. The office represents all the functions of CCPIT in the U.S. through organization and coordination of cross visits and trade shows, information service, patent application, trademark registration, and legal affairs advice. The office helps match up trade opportunities and business partners between Chinese and American corporations through forwarding trade leads to the headquarters in Beijing to circulate among CCPIT's membership enterprises. The office also helps locate companies and suppliers in China and provides China's market surveys and listings of trading companies and manufacturers of different industries.

4301 Connecticut Ave., NW #136
Washington DC 20008
202/244-3244   FAX 202/244-0478
E-mail: ccpitus@aol.com   http://www.ccpit.org
Contact: Mr. Ping Yu
         Chief U.S. Representative

Chocolate Mfrs. Assn. of the U.S.A.
7900 West Park Dr. #A320
McLean VA 22102-4297
703/790-5011   FAX 703/790-5752
E-mail: jjohnson@candyusa.org
Contact: Mr. James H. Johnson
         Intl. Marketing Services Mgr.

Citizens Democracy Corps

The CDC supports and develops small and medium sized businesses in Central and Eastern Europe and Russia, assists in the growth of market economies and a variety of stabilizing, democratic institutions, and provides new market opportunities and jobs for the region's companies and citizens. It was formed in 1990 by the American private sector to enlist American volunteers specifically in support of the transition to free market economies in the region. CDC volunteers have a minimum of ten years senior level management experience.

1400 I St., NW - Suite 1125
Washington DC 20005
202/872-0933   FAX 202/872-0923
E-mail: info@cdc.org   http://www.cdc.org
Contact: Mr. Michael Levett
          President

Citizens Network for Foreign Affairs

A nonprofit organization dedicated to stimulating international economic growth and development CNFA works with companies, entrepreneurs, farm groups, business alliances, and other groups to create opportunities in international markets.

1111 19th St., NW
Washington DC 20036
202/296-3920   FAX 202/296-3948
E-mail: cohen@cnfa.org   http://www.cnfa.com
Contact: Mr. David Cohen
          Director, Marketing and Public Outreach

Civicus: World Alliance for Citizen Participation

An international alliance of nonprofit, nongovernmental organizations dedicated to strengthening citizen action and civil society throughout the world. Founded in 1993, CIVICUS has over 400 members from 81 countries, committed to: strengthening the visibility and understanding of civil society; working to develop a more supportive environment of laws, policies and regulations; and developing self-sustaining, creative resource mechanisms.

919 18th St., NW - 3rd Fl.
Washington DC 20006-5503
202/331-8518   FAX 202/331-8774
E-mail: info@civicus.org   http://www.civicus.org
Contact: Mr. Miklos Marschall
          Executive Director

Coal Exporters Assn. of the U.S. (CEA)

CEA was established in 1945 to promote and encourage the reliable export of quality coals from the U.S. It is an affiliate of the National Mining Association and has the wide ranging resources of that organization available to assist in the implementation of policies and objectives of the Association.
1130 17th St., NW - 5th Floor
Washington DC 20036
202/463-2639   FAX 202/833-9636
Contact: Ms. Moya Phelleps
          Executive Director

Coalition for Employment through Exports, Inc. (CEE)

An organization of major U.S. exporters, CEE was established in 1981 to promote U.S. exports and to raise public awareness of the important link between exports and jobs for Americans. Support for aggressive U.S. export finance programs is the primary focus of CEE.

1100 Connecticut Ave., NW, Suite 910
Washington DC 20036
202/296-6107   FAX 202/296-9709
E-mail: CEE1100@worldnet.att.net
Contact: Mr. Edmund B. Rice
          Executive Director

Coalition of Service Industries, Inc. (CSI)

Established in 1982 to represent the interests of the service sector, CSI has directed its efforts toward increasing public awareness of the major role services play in the U.S. economy and to shaping domestic and foreign policy that affect the interests of that sector.

805 15th St., NW - Suite 1110
Washington DC 20005

202/289-7460   FAX 202/775-1726
E-mail: csi@uscsi.org   http://www.uscsi.org
Contact: Mr. Robert Vastine
          President

Committee for Natl. Security

Founded in 1980 to enhance public participation in the national security debate.

1901 Connecticut Avenue, NW, Suite 802
Washington DC 20006
202/745-2450   FAX 202/667-0444
E-mail: laws@earthlink.net http://www.home.earthlink.net/~laws/
Contact: Ms. Louise Walker
          President

Conservation Intl. Foundation

CI is a field-based, nonprofit organization that protects the Earth's biologically richest areas and helps the people who live there improve their quality of life. CI uses science, economics, policy, and community involvement to promote biodiversity conservation in tropical rain forests and other endangered ecosystems worldwide.

2501 M St., NW
Washington DC 20037
202/429-5660   FAX 202/887-0193
http://www.conservation.org
Contact: Mr. Russell A. Mittermeier
          President

Constituency for Africa (CFA)

CFA seeks to mobilize and foster increased cooperation and coordination among a broad based coalition of American, African, and international organizations, institutions, and individuals committed to the progress and empowerment of Africa and African peoples.

1030 15th St., NW - Suite 340
Washington DC 20005
202/371-0588   FAX 202/371-9017
E-mail: cfanet@cfanet   http://www.cfanet
Contact: Mr. Melvin P. Foote
          Executive Director

Consumer Electronics Manufacturers Assn.

CEMA is a sector of the Electronics Industries Alliance (EIA) which represents all facets of electronics manufacturing. CEMA represents U.S. manufacturers of audio, video, consumer information, accessories, mobile electronics, and multimedia products.

2500 Wilson Blvd.
Arlington VA 22201-3834
703/907-7600   FAX 703/907-7602
E-mail: cema-mktng@eia.org   http://www.cemacity.org
Contact:

Consumers for World Trade

Founded in 1978, CWT supports the expansion of world trade liberalization in the vein of promoting consumer interests.

2000 L Street, NW - Suite 200
Washington DC 20036-4907
202/785-4835   FAX 202/416-1734
E-mail: cwt@cwt.org   http://www.cwt.org
Contact: Mr. Doreen Brown
          President

Cooperative for American Relief Everywhere (CARE)

Established in 1980 and headquartered in Atlanta, Georgia, CARE is a private, nonsectarian organization which helps the developing world's poor and disadvantaged by providing disaster relief and technical assistance, training, management expertise, and materials. The Washington office analyzes public policy concerns related to world hunger and development and serves as a liaison to international development agencies located here in Washington.

1625 K St., NW - Suite 200
Washington DC 20006
202/296-5696　　　　　　FAX 202/296-8695
E-mail: rhodes@dc.care.org
Contact: Ms. Theresa Rhodes
　　　　　Major Gifts Officer

Cosmetic, Toiletry, and Fragrance Association

The CTFA provides a range of services supporting the personal care products industry's needs and interests in scientific, legal, regulatory, legislative, and international fields. The organization promotes voluntary industry self-regulation and reasonable governmental requirements to assure uniform national and international standards.

1101 17th St., NW - Suite 300
Washington DC 20036
202/331-1770　　　　　　FAX 202/331-1969
http://www.ctfa.org
Contact: Mr. Lou Santucci
　　　　　Vice President, International

Cotton Council Intl.

Established in 1956, CCI is the division of the National Cotton Council of America dedicated to U.S. exports of cotton, cottonseed, and their products. In overseas markets, CCI represents the seven segments of the U.S. raw cotton industry: farmers, ginners, warehousemen, merchants, cottonseed processors, cooperatives, and textile manufacturers.

1521 New Hampshire Avenue, NW
Washington DC 20036
202/745-7805　　　　　　FAX 202/483-4040
E-mail: cottonusa@cotton.org　　　　http://www.cottonusa.org
Contact: Ms. Vaughn Jordan
　　　　　Intl. Program Manager

Council for a Livable World

A political, lobbying and educational institution working for pragmatic means for securing a non-nuclear world.

110 Maryland Avenue, N.E. - Suite 409
Washington DC 20002
202/543-4100　　　　　　FAX 202/543-6297
E-mail: jdi@clw.org　　　　http://www.clw.org/pub/clw/
Contact: Mr. John D. Isaacs
　　　　　President

Council for Intl. Exchange of Scholars

Cooperates with the U.S. Information Agency in the administration of the Fulbright Scholar Program and provides information for U.S. and foreign scholars on international education exchange.

3007 Tilden Street, NW, Suite 5L
Washington DC 20008-3097
202/686-4000　　　　　　FAX 202/362-3442
E-mail: apprequest@cies.iie.org　　　　http://www.cies.org
Contact: Ms. Patii McGill Peterson
　　　　　Executive Director

Council for Social and Economic Studies

1133 13th St., NW - Suite C-2
Washington DC 20005
202/371-2700　　　　　　FAX 202/371-1523
Contact: Dr. Roger Pearson
　　　　　President

Council for the Defense of Freedom

A nonprofit educational organization existing to provide educational materials about issues of national security. It studies and tracks issues dealing with American foreign and military policy, strategic, and security issues. The council also follows the international and military news and the relations of other countries toward the U.S. and its allies.

4455 Connecticut Ave., NW, Suite 330
Washington DC 20008
202/364-2339　　　　　　FAX 202/364-4098
Contact: Col. Samuel T. Dickens
　　　　　Chairman

Council for the Natl. Interest

A nonprofit, membership organization seeking to promote even-handed U.S. foreign policy in the Middle East through seminars, publications, and direct contact with policy makers.

1511 K St., NW Suite 1043
Washington DC 20005
202/628-6962　　　　　　FAX 202/628-6958
E-mail: count@igc.apc.org　http://www.cni.mynet.net
Contact: Mr. Eugene Bird
　　　　　President

Council of the Americas - Washington Office

A business organization founded in 1965 and headquartered in New York City, the Council's aim is to promote regional economic integration, free trade, open markets and investment, and the rule of law throughout the Western Hemisphere.

1310 G St., NW Suite 690
Washington DC 20005
202/639-0724　　　　　　FAX 202/639-0794
E-mail: coa1310@aol.com　http://www.counciloftheamericas.org
Contact: Ambassador William T. Pryce
　　　　　Vice President, Washington Operations

Council on Competitiveness

A nonpartisan organization concerned with the position of U.S. industry in world trade. The council seeks to increase awareness of competitiveness issues and to work with business, labor and academics to formulate strategies for improving U.S. competitiveness. It serves as the proactive arm of the Foundation for American Economic Competitiveness.

1401 H St., NW - Suite 650
Washington DC 20005
202/682-4292　　　　　　FAX 202/682-5150
E-mail: council@compete.org
Contact: Mr. John N. Yochelson
　　　　　President

Council on Foreign Relations

Based in New York City, the Council is an influential public policy body which often contributes to government foreign policy formulation.

1779 Massachusetts Ave., NW

Washington DC 20036
202/518-3400
Contact: Mr. Daniel Fata
FAX 202/986-2984

Council on Hemispheric Affairs

A nonprofit research and information institution aimed at expanding public interest in, and U.S. and Canadian media coverage of Latin America.

1444 I St., NW - Suite 211
Washington DC 20005
202/216-9264   FAX 202/216-9193
E-mail: coha@the-hermes.net
http://www.the-hermes.net/coha
Contact: Mr. Larry Birns
         Director

Council on Intl. Non-Theatrical Events (CINE)

CINE recognizes outstanding achievement in film and video through a national competition. To promote worldwide recognition of these U.S. productions, CINE enters winners of its Golden Eagle Award in foreign festivals and competitions.

1001 Connecticut Ave., NW, Suite 625
Washington DC 20036
202/785-1136   FAX 202/785-4114
http://www.cine.org
Contact: Christine Reilly
         Executive Director

Cuban American National Foundation

The Cuban American National Foundation is an independent, non-profit organization dedicated to the re-establishment of freedom and democracy in Cuba. The Foundation supports the principles of: respect for human rights; freedom of thought and expression; freedom of religion; the right of the people to freely elect their government; the right to private property; free enterprise; and economic prosperity with social justice.

1000 Thomas Jefferson St., NW - Suite 505
Washington DC 20007
202/265-2822   FAX 202/338-0308
E-mail: canfnet@icanect.net   http://www.canfnet.org
Contact: Mr. Jose Cardenas
         Director, Washington Office

Czech Service Center (CSS)

CSS facilitates bilateral projects and project development in investments, trade, technology transfer, joint research, tourism, conventions and professional association meetings. The center provides language and other country-specific services.

8051 Nowell St. - P.O. Box 941
Silver Spring MD 20005
202/638-5505   FAX 202/638-5308
E-mail: czechslv@access.digex.net
http://www.clark.net/pub/czech/czechslv.html
Contact: Mr. Robert J. Miller
         Executive Director

DACOR (Diplomatic and Consular Officers, Rtd.) Bacon House Foundation

The foundation was established for the purpose of strengthening the ties between the people of the U.S. and other nations. To this end it pursues programs of a public and educational nature to enhance public awareness and foster educated leadership in international affairs.

1801 F St., NW
Washington DC 20006

202/682-0500   FAX 202/842-3295
E-mail: dacor@ix.netcom.com
Contact: Mr. William W. Lehfeldt
         Consul General Ret. - Executive Director

Dairy Export Incentive Program Coalition (DEIP)

1025 Thomas Jefferson St., NW - Suite 407
Washington DC 20007
202/342-1300   FAX 202/342-5880
Contact: Mr. John Whetten
         President

Demilitarzation for Democracy (DFD)

DFD promotes arms control efforts such as the campaign to ban land mines, the Code of Conduct of Arms Transfers and The Year 2000 Campaign to redirect world military spending to human development. There is a focus on the issue of militarization in the developing world and its impact on economic development and democracy.

2001 S St., NW - Suite 630
Washington DC 20007
202/319-7191   FAX 202/319-7194
E-mail: pdd@clark.net   http://www.dfe.net
Contact: Mr. Scott Nathanson
         Acting Director

Democracy Development Initiative

c/o McKenna & Cuneo LLP - 1900 K St., NW - Suite 100
Washington DC 20006
202/496-7599   FAX 202/496-7756
E-mail: philip_beauregard@mckennacuneo.com
Contact: Mr. Philip Beauregard
         Executive Director

Development Group for Alternative Policies

A nonprofit institution which aids Third World organizations in translating local development experience into policy-shaping analysis and advocacy.

927 15th Street, NW, 4th Floor
Washington DC 20005
202/898-1566   FAX 202/898-1612
E-mail: dgap@igc.apc.org   http://www.igc.apc.org/dgap/
Contact: Mr. Stephen Hellinger
         President

Dialogue Project, The

1555 Connecticut Avenue, NW - 3rd Floor
Washington DC 20036
202/797-8961   FAX 202/232-4963
Contact: Ms. Reena Bernards
         Co-Coordinator

Direct Selling Assn.

The DSA is a national trade association representing 151 companies that manufacture and distribute goods and services sold directly to consumers. DSA was founded in 1910 as the Agents Credit Association and adopted its present name in 1969. DSA's mission is to protect, serve and promote the effectiveness of member companies and the independent business people it represents, and to ensure that the marketing by member companies of products and or the direct sales opportunity is conducted with the highest level of business ethics and service to consumers.

1666 K St. NW #1010
Washington DC 20006-2803
202/293-5760   FAX 202/463-4569
E-mail: afernau@dsa.org   http://www.dsa.org

Contact: Ms. Anna Fernau
          International Project Mgr.

Eastern Caribbean Investment Promotion Service (ECIPS)

A joint economic development promotion effort of the Organization of Eastern Caribbean States: Anguilla, Antigua and Barbuda, Dominica, Grenada, Montserrat, St. Kitts and St. Nevis, St. Lucia, St. Vincent and the Grenadines, and the British Virgin Islands.

3216 New Mexico Ave., NW
Washington DC 20016
202/363-0229   FAX 202/363-4328
E-mail: ecipsdc1@aol.com http://www.ecips.com
Contact: Mr. John V. Arrindell
          Executive Director

Economic Policy Institute

EPI was founded in 1986 by a group of economic policy experts including economist Barry Bluestone and former Clinton secretary of labor Robert Reich.

1660 L Street, NW - Suite 1200
Washington DC 20036
202/775-8810   FAX 202/775-0819
E-mail: epi@epinet.org   http://epinet.org
Contact: Mr. Jeff Faux
          President

Economic Strategy Institute

1401 H St., NW - Suite 750
Washington DC 20005
202/289-1288   FAX 202/289-1319
E-mail: esidc@aol.com   http://www.ECONSTRAT.org
Contact: Mr. Robert A. Perkins
          Vice President, Washington Relations

Ecumenical Program on Central America and the Caribbean

Founded in 1968, the EPICA is an independent nonprofit organization serving a U.S. constituency of churches, grassroots organizations, and individual supporters. The EPICA provides resources toward building a movement of faith-based solidarity among the people of the Americas by combining theological reflection, political analysis, and social action. The EPICA has consultative status at the National Council of Churches and support from Catholic religious orders.

1470 Irving St., NW
Washington DC 20010
202/332-0292   FAX 202/332-1184
E-mail: epica@igc.org   http://www.center1.com/epica.html
Contact: Ms. Ann Butwell
          Coordinator

Eisenhower World Affairs Institute

1620 I Street, NW - Suite 7
Washington DC 20006
202/223-6710   FAX 202/452-1837
E-mail: jkravoti@saralink.net
Contact: Ms. Jane L. Kratovil
          Executive Director

Emergency Committee for American Trade (ECAT)

ECAT is an action-oriented organization of the CEO's of over 50 large U.S. multinational corporations. Its purpose is not to conduct research or to put on meetings or conferences, but to influence public policy in the direction of an open and equitable international trading, investment, and monetary system through working with the Congress and the Administration.

1211 Connecticut Ave., NW- Suite 801
Washington DC 20036
202/659-5147   FAX 202/659-1347
Contact: Mr. Calman J. Cohen
          President

Environmental Export Council (EEC)

With over 120 members principally including both large and small corporations from all sectors of the environmental industry, as well as several national laboratories, universities and trade associations, the EEC promotes the exports of U.S. environmental goods and services. Formed in 1994 as the result of a consolidation of the U.S. Environmental Technology Export Council and the Environmental Business Council of the U.S., it is an alliance between the U.S. environmental technology public and private sectors.

PO Box 77287
Washington DC 20013
202/466-6933   FAX 202/789-1623
E-mail: 73174.502@compuserve.com
http://solstice.crest.org/sustainable/eec
Contact: Mr. John Mizroch
          Executive Director

European-American Business Council

A transatlantic business organization supported by both European and American companies, the Council provides information and advocacy services on government policies that directly impact its members. It publishes a weekly newsletter, conducts research, issues white papers, and sponsors conferences and seminars that cover critical issues like taxes, trade liberalization, and economic sanctions.

1333 H St., NW - Suite 630
Washington DC 20005
202/347-9292   FAX 202/628-5498
E-mail: eabc@eabc.org   http://www.eabc.org
Contact: Mr. Willard M. Berry
          President

European Institute, The

Non lobbying and non profit, the institute is the only European-American public policy organization in Washington. It provides an independent forum for U.S. and European government and corporate decision makers, officials from multilateral organizations, academics, and expert journalists to exchange information, develop new policy options, and create new professional working relationships.

5225 Wisconsin Ave., NW - Suite 200
Washington DC 20015
202/895-1670   FAX 202/362-1088
http://www.europeaninstitute.org
Contact: Ms. Jacqueline Grapin
          President

European Space Agency (ESA) - Washington Office

A multinational, governmental, research and development organization, ESA seeks to provide for and promote cooperation on space research and technology for exclusively peaceful purposes. ESA works closely with other space powers in the world including the U.S., Russia, and Japan. ESA is operated by 14 European States: Austria, Belgium, Denmark, Finland, France, Germany, Ireland, Italy, Norway, Spain Sweden, Switzerland, The Netherlands, and The United Kingdom. There is also close cooperation with Canada on many matters.

955 L'Enfant Plaza, S.W. - Suite 7800
Washington DC 20024
202/488-4158   FAX 202/488-4930

E-mail: ipryke@euro.esa.int   http://www.esa.int
Contact: Mr. Ian W. Pryke
        Head, Washington Office

Executive Council on Foreign Diplomacy
818 Connecticut Ave., NW - 12th Fl.
Washington DC 20006
202/466-5052   FAX 202/872-8696
Contact: Ms. Solveig Spielmann
        Executive Director

Federation of Intl. Trade Assns.
Founded in 1984, FITA fosters international trade by strengthening the role of local, regional, and national associations throughout North America that have an international mission. FITA affiliates are 300 independent international associations with an aggregate membership of more than 150,000 U.S., Canadian, and Mexican businesses active in international trade.

1851 Alexander Bell Drive
Reston VA 20901
703/620-1588   FAX 703/391-0159
E-mail: info@fita.org   http://www.fita.org
Contact: Mr. Nelson T. Joyner
        Chairman

Financial Women Intl.
Formerly the National Association of Bank Women, Financial Women International was founded in 1921. It serves women in financial services who seek to expand their personal and professional capabilities through self-directed growth in a supportive environment.

200 N. Glebe Rd., Suite 820
Arlington VA 22203-3728
703/807-2007   FAX 703/807-0111
E-mail: fwistaff@erols.com http://www.fwi.org
Contact: Ms. Penny M. Dudley
        CAO

FINCA Intl., The Foundation for Intl. Community Assistance
A poverty lending organization which established village banks to loan money to poor entrepreneurs, mainly women, to start or improve small businesses. The village banks also provide a place to accumulate savings and group solidarity.

1101 14th St., NW - 11th Floor
Washington DC 20005-5601
202/682-1510   FAX 202/682-1535
E-mail: rscofield@villagebanking.org
Contact: Mr. Rupert Scofield
        Executive Director

FlightSafety Intl.
FlightSafety International is the factory authorized training organization for 23 aircraft manufacturers, offering pilot and maintenance technician training at 40 learning centers in the U.S., Canada and Europe. It has provided ab initio programs to international airlines for over 30 years. FlightSafety Simulation Systems Division is the world's principal supplier of flight simulators for civil aviation. Its Visual Systems Division provides Vital Visual systems for a wide range of advanced simulators. A major subsidiary, MarineSafety International provides maritime simulator, research and training services internationally.

1201 Pennsylvania Ave., NW - Suite 300
Washington DC 20004-2401
202/661-4700   FAX 202/638-2670
E-mail: 102503.3104@compuserve.com

Contact: Mr. Elmer G. Gleske
        Vice President, Governmental Affairs

Food Marketing Institute
Formed in 1977, the Food Marketing Institute is a nonprofit organization composed of food retailers and wholesalers. It conducts programs in education, research, and public affairs.

800 Connecticut Ave. NW #500
Washington DC 20006-2701
202/429-4580   FAX 202/429-4589
E-mail: fmi@fmi.org   http://www.fmi.org
Contact: Ms. Jeanine Gibson
        Coordinator Intl. Marketing

Food Processing Machinery & Supplies Assn.
Founded in 1885, FPMSA is an organization of suppliers to the global food and beverage industries whose goal is to assist its membership in the marketing of their products and services in ways that individual members could not do as economically and effectively on their own.

200 Daingerfield Rd.
Alexandria VA 22314-2884
703/684-1080   FAX 703/548-6563
E-mail: FPMSA@CLARK.NET   http://www.fpmsa.org
Contact: Ms. Sacha Helfand
        Director, Intl. Programs

Footwear Distributors and Retailers of America
FDRA is a Washington, DC-based trade association whose 100 member companies operate some 20,000 shoe retail outlets and account for nearly three-quarters of U.S. shoe sales. The organization's Footwear Retailers of America Shippers Association negotiates discounted ocean shipping rates for footwear firms, and the Footwear Open Trading Coalition services overseas manufacturing suppliers.

1319 F St., NW - Suite 700
Washington DC 20004
202/737-5660   FAX 202/638-2615
E-mail: fdra@fdra.org   http://www.fdra.org
Contact: Mr. Peter T. Mangione
        President

Footwear Industries of America
FIA is a nonprofit association that provides footwear businesses with the opportunity to share ideas from every aspect of the industry. As the industry representative in legislative and regulatory matters, FIA is responsible for lobbying activities needed to realize industry demands. The FIA is allied with the world's largest footwear research and development organization, the SATRA Footwear Technology Centre in Kettering, England.

1420 K St., NW - Suite 600
Washington DC 20005
202/789-1420   FAX 202/789-4058
E-mail: fawn@fia.org   http://www.fia.org
Contact: Ms. Fawn K. Evenson
        President

Foreign Services Research Institute
Established in 1974, the institute provides information on the U.S. to foreign embassies, foreign commercial enterprises, and overseas educational organizations. It also offers advice on the educational placement of foreign students.

P.O. Box 6317
Washington DC 20015-0317
202/362-1588

Contact: Mr. John Boyle
President

Formosan Association for Public Affairs

P.O. Box 15062
Washington DC 20003
202/547-3686   FAX 202/543-7891

Contact: Mr. Coen Blaauw
Director

Forum for Intl. Policy

The FORUM is a nonprofit, nonpartisan brain trust of nationally recognized foreign policy experts with extensive, senior-level policy experience who are committed to independence, integrity, and impact. It provides practical, real world policy options designed to further U.S. national interests in the new international environment.

900 17th Street, NW - #502
Washington DC 20006
202/296-9365   FAX 202/296-9395
E-mail: theforum@erols.com
Contact: Gen. Brent Scowcroft
President

Foundation for Intl. Community Assistance, Inc.

The FINCA, launched in 1985, now serves more than 70,000 poor families in 14 countries. Its mission is to support the economic and human development of families trapped in severe poverty through the creation of microenterprise programs called village banks. These consist of peer groups of 20 to 50 members, mostly women. Group members receive small loans, a safe means to accumulate savings, and a community based system of mutual support.

1101 14th St., NW - 11th Floor
Washington DC 20005-5601
202/682-1510   FAX 202/682-1535
E-mail: rscofield@villagebanking.org
http://www.villagebanking.org
Contact: Mr. Rupert Scofield
Executive Director

Foundation for Intl. Meetings

An organization comprised of various association and corporate executives who meet regularly outside of the U.S.

2111 Wilson Blvd. - Suite 350
Arlington VA 22201
703/908-0707   FAX 703/908-0709
Contact: Mr. Jack C. Sammis
President

Foundation for Middle East Peace

Established in 1958, the foundation serves to enhance understanding of Israeli-Palestinian problems and of the U.S. interests at stake, as it works for a peaceful resolution to the conflict.

1763 N St., NW
Washington DC 20036
202/835-3650   FAX 202/835-3651
Contact: Jean Nawsom
Executive Director

Freedom Forum, The

Formerly known as the Gannett Foundation until 1991, the Freedom Forum is a nonpartisan, international foundation dedicated to free press, free speech and free spirit for all people. It provides programs that support and encourage an independent, free press worldwide through exchanges, conferences and seminars involving international journalists and journalism educators and their U.S. counterparts.

1101 Wilson Blvd.
Arlington VA 22209-2248
703/528-0800   FAX 703/522-4831
E-mail: cwells@freedomforum.org   http://www.freedomforum.org

Contacts:
Ms. Lisa Ellis
    Executive Director/Intl. Programs
Ms. Christine Wells
    Senior Vice President Intl.

Freedom House/(National Forum Foundation)

Freedom House offers media, governance, and economic development training programs focusing on Central and Eastern Europe. It maintains an on-line database of and for Central and Eastern European NGOs.

1319 18th St., NW
Washington DC 20036
202/296-5101   FAX 202/296-5070
E-mail: nff@nff.org   http://www.nff.org
Contact: Mr. James S. Denton
    Executive Director

French American Chamber of Commerce

918 16th St., NW - Suite 406
Washington DC 20006
202/775-0256   FAX 202/785-4604
E-mail: FACCwdc@aol.comhttp://www.FACC-DC.org
Contact: Ms. Susan Shillinglaw
    Executive Director

Friedrich Ebert Foundation

Its mission is to contribute to a transatlantic dialogue by offering programs such as seminars, workshops and conferences on the following issues: overall political developments in Germany and Europe, including domestic policy issues and attitudes, as well as public studies; general social topics, including migration, minorities, multiculturalism, education, and gender issues; economic developments in Germany, Europe and the U.S., including labor market and trade union issues and problems of economic and political transformation in Eastern Europe; foreign policy and security issues such as NATO and European Union enlargement; ethnic conflicts, as well as arms control and disarmament; political and economic consequences of German unification; and historical and cultural issues.

1155 15th St., NW Suite 1100
Washington DC 20005
202/331-1819   FAX 202/331-1837
E-mail: FESDC@aol.com   http://www.fesdc.org/fesdc
Contact: Dr. Dieter Dettke
    Executive Director

Friends Committee on Natl. Legislation

A membership organization which works to: promote worldwide peace and justice, both by building the institutions and nonviolent processes that prevent and resolve conflicts, and by responding to particular conflicts; build a just, equitable, compassionate and safe society at home and abroad by shifting federal budget priorities away from massive military spending toward human needs; halt the production and global distribution of military weaponry to improve national and international security and advance the cause of peace.

245 2nd St., NE
Washington DC 20002-5795

202/547-6000   FAX 202/547-6019
E-mail: fcnl@igc.apc.org http://www.fcnl.org/pub/fcnl
Contact: Mr. E. Joe Volk
    Executive Secretary

Friends of Free China
A nonprofit organization founded in 1974 advocating U.S. support of Taiwan.

1629 K Street, NW
Washington DC 20006
202/296-5056   FAX 202/775-7465
http://www.fofc.org
Contact: Mr. Jack E. Buttram
    Director

Friends of the Earth
Founded in 1969, Friends of the Earth later merged with the Environmental Policy Institute. It works towards the preservation, restoration, and rational use of the ecosphere.

1025 Vermont Ave., NW - Third Fl.
Washington DC 20005-6303
202/783-7400   FAX 202/783-0444
Contact: Ms. Andrea Durbin
    Director Intl. Projects/MDB Trade

Fund for American Studies
Working together with Georgetown University, the fund sponsors educational programs in order to educate college students about the political, economic, and moral principles upon which the U.S. was founded.

1526 18th St., NW
Washington DC 20036
202/986-0384   FAX 202/986-0390
E-mail: sslattery@tfas.org http://www.tfas.org
Contact: Mr. Steve Slattery
    Director, Intl. Program

Fund for Peace, The
A nonprofit organization founded in 1966, the fund is dedicated to international engagement, public education toward an understanding of global problems that threaten human survival, and a search for solutions to those problems. The fund combines scholarship and activism working to eliminate conditions that cause war and conflict and for the attainment of a just, free and peaceful world. Currently there are seven projects and programs that are associated with the Fund for Peace: ACCESS: An international Affairs Information Service; The Center for National Security Studies; The Center for the Strategic Initiatives of Women (CSIW); The Institute for the Study of World Politics; The Media and Security Project; The National Security Archive; and The Human Rights Program in the Horn of Africa.

1701 K Street, NW, Suite 1100
Washington DC 20006
202/223-7940   FAX 202/223-7947
E-mail: Pbaker@fundforpeace.org http://www.fundforpeace.org
Contact: Dr. Pauline H. Baker
    President

Fund for Private Assistance in Intl. Development
Provides financial leveraging assistance to nonprofit charities working internationally and to corporations with overseas blocked assets.

8300 Boone Blvd., Suite 310
Vienna VA 22182
703/448-5701   FAX 703/448-5708

Contact: Dr. David Kline
    President

G7 Group
Founded in 1992, it works to provide the international financial community with a better understanding of the nexus between politics and economics. As a consulting service with advisers worldwide, the firm strives to predict how government decisions and political and economic events will impact global financial markets.

1015 18th St., NW - Suite 950
Washington DC 20036
202/496-9222   FAX 202/496-9234
E-mail: g7group@aol.com
Contact: Mr. Timothy D. Adams
    Managing Director

German American Business Assn.
Established in October 1990, as a not-for-profit business organization, GABA's purpose is to promote trade and investment between the U.S. and Germany. It aims to help the German and American business people develop a better understanding of each other's business environment and to help them meet others with whom they want to develop a business relationship.

103 Ross Alley
Alexandria VA 22314-3129
703/836-6120   FAX 703/836-6160
E-mail: info@gaba.org http://www.gaba.org
Contact: Mr. Charles W. Zschock
    Executive Director

German Marshall Fund of the United States
Established in 1972, aims to help Europeans and Americans learn from and apply practices which have proven effective elsewhere. It operates through projects, often utilizing cross-national comparisons involving both the U.S. and Europe, and is focused on economics, European-U.S. relations, the environment, and immigration.

11 Dupont Circle, NW, Suite 750
Washington DC 20036
202/745-3950   FAX 202/265-1662
Contact: Mr. Craig Kennedy
    President

Gibraltar Information Bureau
1156 15th St., NW - Suite 1100
Washington DC 20005
202/452-1108   FAX 202/452-1109
Contact: Mr. Perry J. Stieglitz
    Director

Global Climate Coalition
A coalition of trade associations and companies seeking to present the views of industry in the global climate debate.

1275 K Street, NW - Suite 890
Washington DC 20005
202/682-9161   FAX 202/638-1043
E-mail: gcc@igc.apc.org http://www.globalclimate.org
Contact: Ms. Gail C. McDonald
    Executive Director

Gold Institute
A Washington DC-based international trade association representing mining companies, refiners, banks, dealers, and suppliers. The Institute is a nonprofit association supported primarily by its membership comprised of 55 firms from 6 countries. Its mission is to promote the common business interests of the gold industry.

1112 16th St., NW - Suite 240
Washington DC 20036
202/835-0185   FAX 202/835-0155
E-mail: info@goldinstitute.org   http://www.goldinstitute.org
Contact: Mr. John Lutley
          President

Graphic Communications Intl. Union
1900 L St., NW, 9th Floor
Washington DC 20036
202/462-1400   FAX 202/331-9516
Contact: Mr. James J. Norton
          President

Greater Washington Board of Trade, The International Business Council
Serving as a regional chamber of commerce, the Board of Trade is the oldest business and professional association in the area, dating back to 1889, with nearly 1,000 corporate members. The International Business Council (IBC) was formed to strengthen the region's international competitiveness and to assist the Greater Washington business community in doing business with the international business community. The IBC has been developing a network of international businesses in the region through outreach programs, including linkages between area business leaders, embassies and other international institutions.

1129 20th St., NW
Washington DC 20036-3494
202/857-5992   FAX 202/223-2648
E-mail: AdrienneEdisis@bot.org   http://www.bot.org
Contact: Ms. Adrienne Edisis
          Director, International Business Council

Greenpeace
Environmental protection institution with worldwide operations and activities regarding diverse issues including acid rain, Antarctica, chemical and nuclear waste, endangered species of marine mammals, nuclear weapons testing, and ocean incineration of hazardous wastes.

1436 U Street, NW
Washington DC 20009
202/462-1177   FAX 202/462-4507
E-mail: grnpeace@aol.com http://www.greenpeace.org/~usa/
Contact: Ms. Kristen Engberg
          Executive Director

Group of 30, The
A think tank that aims to deepen understanding on international economic and financial issues, to explore the international repercussions of decisions taken in the public and private sectors, and to examine the choices available to market practitioners and to policy makers.

1990 M Street, NW - Suite 450
Washington DC 20036
202/331-2472   FAX 202/785-9423
E-mail: info@group30.org http://www.group30.org
Contact: Mr. John G. Walsh
          Executive Director

Guatemala Human Rights Commission/USA
Founded in 1982, the Commission supports survivors of human rights abuses in Guatemala and the relatives of victims; investigates human rights cases; documents cases for congressional investigations, political asylum claims, and media reports; and educates the public, the U.S. Congress, the INS, and other organizations whose policies affect Guatemalans. The goal of the Commission is to reduce the level of state sponsored repression in Guatemala and to mitigate the effects of political violence on those who have survived.

3321 12th St., NE
Washington DC 20017
202/529-6599   FAX 202/526-4611
E-mail: ghrc@igc.apc.org   http://www.center1.com/ghrc.html
Contact: Ms. Alice Zachmann
          Director

Hale Institute, The Nathan
An independent organization devoted to nonpartisan research in domestic and foreign intelligence, the institute has worked to increase public awareness and stimulate debate on important intelligence-related issues. It seeks a strong U.S. intelligence and security capability.

104 N. Carolina Ave., NW
Washington DC 20003-1803
202/546-2293   FAX 202/546-2293
E-mail: sulc@earthlink.net http://www.mtva.com/hale/
Contact: Mr. Lawrence B. Sulc
          President

Hazardous Materials Advisory Council
Aimed at ensuring safe domestic and international transport of hazardous materials, substances, and waste. Members include shippers, multi-model carriers, container manufacturers, and emergency response companies.

1101 Vermont Avenue, NW, Suite 301
Washington DC 20005
202/289-4550   FAX 202/289-4074
E-mail: jcollom@hmac.org http://www.hmac.org
Contact: Mr. Jonathon Collom
          President

Health Industry Manufacturers Assn.
A Washington, DC-based trade association and the largest medical technology association in the world, HIMA represents more than 800 manufacturers of medical devices, diagnostic products, and medical information systems. HIMA's members manufacture nearly 90% of the $55 billion of health care technology products purchased annually in the US and more than 50% of the $130 billion purchased annually around the world. Its stated mission is to be an effective advocate for a legal, regulatory, and economic climate that advances global health care by assuring worldwide patient access to the benefits of medical technology.

1200 G St., NW #400
Washington DC 20005-3814
202/783-8700   FAX 202/783-8750
http://www.himanet.com
Contact: Mr. Edward M. Rozynski
          Executive Vice President, Global Strategy/Analysis

Helicopter Assn. Intl.
The HAI represents a membership of civil helicopter operators domestically and abroad.

1635 Prince St.
Alexandria VA 22314-3406
703/683-4646   FAX 703/683-4745
http://www.rotor.com
Contact: Mr. Ray Rasavage
          President

Heritage Foundation
Established in 1973, Heritage is a public policy think tank and research institution, applying a conservative philosophy to current policy issues.

It focuses its research in the areas of domestic and economic policy, foreign policy, Asian studies, and the functioning of the United Nations.

214 Massachusetts Ave., NE
Washington DC 20002
202/546-4400   FAX 202/546-8321
E-mail: info@heritage.org   http://www.heritage.org

Contacts:
Mr. Edwin J. Feulner
    President Heritage Foundation
Mr. Herb B. Berkowitz
    Vice President, Public Relations
Dr. Stuart M. Butler
    VP & Director, Domestic & Economic Pol. Studies
Dr. Kim Holmes
    VP & Director, Foreign & Def. Pol. Studies
Mr. James Przystup
    Director, Asian Studies Center

Hong Kong Economic & Trade Office
The Washington office represents the Hong Kong government in conducting Hong Kong's economic and trade relations with the U.S. government and monitors U.S. initiatives which might affect Hong Kong's interests.

1520 18th Street, NW
Washington DC 20036
202/331-8947   FAX 202/331-8958
E-mail: hketo@hketowashington.org
Contact: Mr. Christopher Jackson
    Director General of Washington

Hospitality Sales and Marketing Assn. Intl.
Founded in 1927 as a hotel industry association, it now embraces all segments of the travel industry, serving over 4,500 members from hotels, inns, resorts, conference centers, airlines, cruise lines, car rental companies, railroads, convention and visitors bureaus, area attractions, and destinations.

1300 L St., NW, Suite 1020
Washington DC 20005
202/789-0089   FAX 202/789-1725
http://www.hsmai.org
Contact: Ms. Ilsa Whittemore
    Associate Executive Director

Hotel Employees & Restaurant Employees Intl. Union
1219 28th Street, NW
Washington DC 20007
202/393-4373   FAX 202/333-0468
Contact: Mr. Edward T. Hanley
    President

Hudson Institute
A diversified economic, security and foreign policy think tank based in Indianapolis, with offices in Washington.

1015 18th St., NW - Suite 200
Washington DC 20036
202/223-7770   FAX 202/223-8537
http://www.hudson.org

Contacts:
Mr. Herbert J. London
    President
Mr. Richard W. Judy
    Director, Ctr. for Central European & Eurasian Studies
Mr. Dennis T. Avery

Director, Ctr. for Global Food Issues
Mr. Alan Reynolds
    Director, Economic Research
Mr. William E. Odom
    Director, Natl. Security Studies
Mr. Michael J. Horowitz
    Director, Project on Civil Justice Reform
Mr. Thomas J. Duesterberg
    Director, Washington, DC Office
Mr. Mark Helprin
    Sr. Fellow, Strategic Issues & the Middle East

Human Rights Watch
A human rights institution headquartered in New York City whose operations include the following organizations: Americas Watch, Asia Watch, Helsinki Watch, and Middle East Watch.

1522 K Street, NW - Suite 910
Washington DC 20005
202/371-6592   FAX 202/371-0124
E-mail: rothk@hrw.org
Contact: Mr. Kenneth Roth
    Executive Director

IEEE Computer Society
Provided technical information and promotes technical cooperation and information exchange between its nearly 100,000 members. Other offices are located in Los Alamitos, (California), Brussels, and Tokyo.

1730 Massachusetts Avenue, NW
Washington DC 20036-1903
202/371-0101   FAX 202/728-9614
E-mail: csinfo@computer.org   http://www.computer.org
Contact: Dr. T. Michael Elliott
    Executive Director

Indonesian-American Business Council

c/o ITMC - 1819 H St., NW - Suite 550
Washington DC 20006
202/466-6068   FAX 202/338-4566
E-mail: tradestar@juno.com
Contact: Mr. Walter Koening
    President

Industrial Fabrics Assn. Intl. (IFAI)
IFAI serves its membership by facilitating the worldwide development, application, and promotion of products manufactured by the technical fabrics industry. Each year IFAI sponsors the Industrial Fabrics and Equipment Exposition, a 3-day trade show. It also offers an Information Central hotline for source-of-supply, technical and production questions, as well as a variety of publications.

2300 M St., NW - Suite 800
Washington DC 20037
202/861-0981   FAX 202/973-2881
E-mail: mtrifai@aol.com   http://www.ifai.com
Contact: Ms. Marcia Rounsaville
    Director, Government Affairs

Information Trust
Promotes freedom of expression in the U.S. and abroad, improvements in the quality of journalism, accountability in government through access to information, reforms of abuses of government secrecy, and protection of whistle blowers from retaliation. It also conducts investigations of complex factual disputes, publishes analytical reports, and provides expert witness testimony in litigation.

2620 Quebec St., NW

Washington DC 20008-1221
202/364-1100   FAX 202/364-2438
E-mail: sarmst@cni.org
Contact: Mr. R. Scott Armstrong
          Executive Director

Institute for Global Communications

The Institute for Global Communications is the U.S. member of the Association for Progressive Communications, a global partnership of computer networks that link activists around the world. Its mission is to expand and inspire movements for peace, economic and social justice, human rights, and environmental sustainability around the world by providing and developing accessible computer networking tools.

6741 Eastern Ave - Suite 200
Takoma Park MD 20912
202/588-5070   FAX 301/270-6416
E-mail: outreach@igc.org   http://www.igc.org
Contact: Ms. Debra Floyd
          Director, East Coast

Institute for Intl. Economics

Founded in 1981, the IIE is a private, nonprofit, nonpartisan research institution devoted to the study of international economic policy.

11 Dupont Circle, NW - Suite 620
Washington DC 20036
202/328-9000   FAX 202/328-5432
http://www.iie.com

Contacts:
Mr. C. Fred Bergsten
Director: Japan, the Administration; State of the Economy; Major Fiscal and Monetary   Changes
Mr. Morris Goldstein
   Dennis Weatherstone Senior Fellow: Intl. and Private Financial Questions
Ms. Ellen L. Frost
   Senior Fellow: Defense; U.S. Trade; Teaching Economics in High School
Mr. Marcus Noland
   Senior Fellow: Japan, Pacific Basin, Asia in general; Textiles
Mr. Jeffrey J. Schott
Senior Fellow: U.S. Trade Policy, NAFTA, Agriculture, European Union, Western   Hemisphere

Institute for Multi-Track Diplomacy

The IMTD promotes a systems approach to peacebuilding and facilitating the transformation of deep-rooted ethnic conflicts. IMTD maintains projects in areas such as Cyprus, Bosnia, Kashmir, and Tibet.

1819 H St., NW - Suite 1200
Washington DC 20006
202/466-4605   FAX 202/466-4607
E-mail: imtd@igc.apc.org   http://www.igc.apc.org/imtd
Contact: Dr. Louise Diamond
          Executive Director

Institute for Palestine Studies

Founded in 1963 for the study of the Palestine problem and its peaceful resolution.

3501 M Street, NW
Washington DC 20007
202/342-3990   FAX 202/342-3927
E-mail: ips-dc@cais.com   http://www.cais.com/ipsjps
Contact: Mr. Philip Mattar
          Executive Director

Institute for Policy Studies

Domestic, as well as international issues fall within the ambit of the mission of IPS, an independent, nonprofit research institution founded in 1963 and self described as a transnational center for research, education, and social invention. IPS scholars have been drawn from and have helped worldwide movements for civil liberties and civil rights. They have been strong advocates for women's liberation and environmental protection as well as for peace and economic justice.
Institute for Policy Studies

733 15th Street, NW - #1020
Washington DC 20005
202/234-9382   FAX 202/387-7915

Contacts:
Mr. John Cavanagh
   Director
Mr. Richard J. Barnet
   Dist. Fellow, Global Econ. & Co-Founder of IPS
Ms. Sarah Anderson
   Fellow, Global Economy Project
Mr. Saul Landau
   Fellow, Immig. & U.S. Pol. on Cuba & Lat. America
Ms. Martha Honey
   Fellow, Peace and Security
Mr. Marcus Raskin
   Fellow, Soc. Recon. & Co-Founder of IPS
Mr. Michael Shuman
   Fellow, Sustainable Communities

Institute for Science and International Security

236 Massachusetts Ave., NE - Suite 500
Washington DC 20002
202/547-3633   FAX 202/547-3634
E-mail: 73744.3675@compuserve.com
Contact: Mr. David H. Albright
          President

Institute for Soviet-American Relations, A Clearinghouse on Grassroots Cooperation in Eurasia

ISAR encourages democratic approaches to improving the conditions for the peoples of Eurasia. It promotes bilateral and multilateral cooperative activities to serve as a basis for solutions of the problems of the region. ISAR also collects and distributes information about the area and the democratic processes and efforts underway there.

1601 Connecticut Ave., NW - Suite 301
Washington DC 20009
202/387-3034   FAX 202/667-3291
E-mail: eliza@isar.org   http://www.isar.org/isar
Contact: Ms. Eliza K. Klose
          Executive Director

Institute for the Study of Diplomacy

School of Foreign Service - Georgetown Univ.
Washington DC 20057
202/687-8974   FAX 202/687-1159
Contact: Mr. Casimir Yost
          Director

Institute for Women, Law and Development

1350 Connecticut Ave., NW - Suite 407
Washington DC 20036
202/463-7477   FAX 202/463-7480
E-mail: iwld@iwld.org

Contact: Ms. Margaret A. Schuler
        Executive Director

Institute of Intl. Education
Established in 1919, IIE is a private, nonprofit institution promoting and facilitating international, educational and cultural exchange. IIE works with USIA, AID, and the Trade Development Agency on many of its projects.

1400 K Street, NW - 6th Floor
Washington DC 20005
202/898-0600   FAX 202/326-7696
http://www.iie.org
Contact: Mr. Robert Gordon
        Vice President

Institute of Intl. Finance
Established in 1983 to foster communication between the various participants in the international lending and development process, IIF provides information on developing countries and acts as a liaison for information between lenders and developing nations. Members include commercial banks from both developed and developing states and, as associate members, financial institutions such as investment banks, trading companies, export credit agencies and multinational corporations.

2000 Pennsylvania Avenue, NW, Suite 8500
Washington DC 20006
202/857-3600   FAX 202/775-1430
Contact: Mr. Charles Dallara
        Managing Director

Institute on Religion and Democracy (IRD)
The IRD organizes and leads efforts to challenge U.S. churches to be a responsible witness in the world. It promotes democracy-building around the world through direct involvement and support, and through education, analysis and publicity. It also trains religious leaders and others to be actively engaged in international ministries and programs on behalf of religious liberty and other fundamental rights.

1521 16th Street - Suite 300
Washington DC 20036
202/986-1440   FAX 202/986-3159
E-mail: 102676.56@compuserve.com
Contact: Ms. Diane L. Knippers
        President

Institutions and Governance Program
The IGP is a branch of the World Resources Program that acts on environmental and development issues.

1709 New York Avenue, NW, 7th Floor
Washington DC 20006
202/638-6300   FAX 202/638-0036
http://www.wri.org/wri
Contact: Ms. Frances Seymour
        Director

Intellectual Property Owners (IPO)
Founded in 1972 by individuals who were concerned about the lack of understanding of intellectual property rights in the U.S., IPO is the only organization that represents the interests of all owners of intellectual property before the U.S. Congress and other governmental bodies such as the Patent and Trademark Office.

1255 23rd St., NW - Suite 850
Washington DC 20037
202/466-2396   FAX 202/466-2893
E-mail: info@ipo.org   http://www.ipo.org

Contact: Mr. Herbert C. Wamsley
        Executive Director

Inter-American Bar Assn.
Founded in May 1940 by a group of distinguished lawyers and jurists representing 44 professional organizations and 17 countries of the western hemisphere, IABA offers a permanent forum for the exchange of professional views and information for lawyers to promote the Rule of Law and protect democratic institutions in the Americas.

1211 Connecticut Ave., NW - Suite 202
Washington DC 20036
202/393-1217   FAX 202/393-1241
E-mail: iaba@iaba.org   http://www.iaba.org
Contact: Ms. Patricia De La Riva
        Executive Director

Inter-American Commercial Arbitration Commission
Founded in 1934, the Commission maintains and administers a system for the settlement, by arbitration and conciliation, of commercial disputes throughout the Western Hemisphere.

19th & Constitution Ave., NW - Room 211
Washington DC 20006
202/458-3249   FAX 202/458-3293
Contact: Mr. Charles R. Norberg
        Honorary Director General

Inter-American Defense Board
Established in 1942, the Defense Board is an autonomous military organization within the Inter-American System which provides advice to the Organization of American States on security issues in the hemisphere.

2600 16th St., NW
Washington DC 20441
202/939-6041
http://www.jid.org
Contact: Maj. Gen. John C. Thompson
        President

Inter-American Dialogue
Founded in 1982, The Inter-American Dialogue is a U.S. center for policy analysis, communication, and exchange on Western Hemisphere affairs.

1211 Connecticut Ave., NW - Suite 510
Washington DC 20036
202/822-9002   FAX 202/822-9553
E-mail: iad@iadialog.org http://www.iadialog.org
Contact: Mr. Peter Hakim
        President

Inter-American Foundation
Created by the U.S. Congress in 1969, the foundation is a public corporation providing support to self-help efforts of disadvantaged peoples in Latin America and the Caribbean.

901 N. Stuart St.
Arlington VA 22203
703/841-3800   FAX 703/841-3884
E-mail: gevans@iaf.gov http://www.iaf.gov
Contact: Mr. George Evans
        President

Inter-American Institute for Cooperation on Agriculture (IICA)
Founded in 1942, the IICA seeks to encourage, facilitate, and support

cooperation among its Member States so as to promote agricultural development and rural well-being. The organization is currently composed of 33 Member States, creating a link between North, Central and South America, and the Caribbean.

1775 K Street, NW - Suite 320
Washington DC 20006
202/458-3767   FAX 202/458-6335
E-mail: kmcclana@aol.com
Contact: Ms. Kay McClanahan
          Representative in the USA

InterAction - The American Council for Voluntary International Action

The nation's largest coalition of international development, disaster relief, and refugee assistance agencies. InterAction's members include more than 150 US-based non-profit organizations, large and small, including secular and religious groups. Member organizations share the goals of easing human suffering and strengthening the ability of people to help themselves.

1717 Massachusetts Ave., NW, Suite 801
Washington DC 20036
202/667-8227   FAX 202/667-8236
E-mail: ia@interaction.org http://www.interaction.org
Contact: Mr. Jim Moody
          President and CEO

Intl. Air Transport Assn.

An international organization fostering cooperation between world airlines, aimed at ensuring safe and economical air transport and promoting international air commerce.

1001 Pennsylvania Avenue, NW, Suite 285
Washington DC 20004
202/624-2977   FAX 202/347-2366
http://www.iata.org
Contact: Mr. David M. O'Connor
          Director, External Affairs - United States

Intl. Anti-Counterfeiting Coalition, Inc.

IACC's mission is to combat counterfeiting and piracy by promoting laws, regulations and directives designed to render theft of intellectual property undesirable and unprofitable.

1620 L St. - Suite 1210
Washington DC 20036
202/223-5728   FAX 202/872-5848
E-mail: blissj@iacc.org   http://www.iacc.org/iacc
Contact: Mr. John Bliss
          President

Intl. Assn. for Continuing Education & Training (IACET)

IACET is an international recognition association for continuing education and training organizations focusing on research based standards and the Continuing Education Unit (CEU). It works to promote and enhance quality in continuing education and training through research, education, and the development and continuous improvement of criteria, principles and standards.
1200 19th St., NW, Suite 300
Washington DC 20036
202/857-1122   FAX 202/223-4579
E-mail: IACET@dc.sba.com   http://www.IACET.org
Contact: Dr. S. Jefferson McFarland III
          Executive Director

Intl. Assn. for Dental Research

The IADR has been established to promote in all aspects of oral and related sciences, to encourage development of improved methods for prevention and treatment of oral and dental diseases, and to facilitate cooperation among investigators and communication of research findings and their implications throughout the world.

1619 Duke St.
Alexandria VA 22314
703/548-0066   FAX 703/548-1883
E-mail: research@iadr.com http://www.iadr.com
Contact: Mr. Eli Schwartz
          Executive Director

Intl. Assn. for Document and Information Management Solutions (IBFI)

IBFI members are experts in providing solutions for paper-based systems to document and information management systems. IBFI has 650 corporate members in 51 countries.

100 Daingerfield Road
Alexandria VA 22314-2888
703/684-9606   FAX 703/684-9675
E-mail: info@ibfl.org   http://www.ibfi.org
Contact: Mr. Thomas C. Playford
          President

Intl. Assn. of Airport Duty Free Stores

In 1966, the IAADFS was formed to meet the needs of the airport duty free industry in the Western Hemisphere. Accompanying the recognition of the potential for duty free shopping in airport complexes came the need for a better understanding of the duty free business by government agencies and officials, as well as the need to provide a forum for the development of communication and business relationships between buyers and sellers of duty free products. Today, the IAADFS has evolved into an international trade association with approximately 500 company members. It sponsors the yearly Duty Free Show of the Americas.

1200 19th St., NW - Suite 300
Washington DC 20036
202/857-1184   FAX 202/429-5154
Contact: Mr. David Bernstein
          President

Intl. Assn. of Amusement Parks & Attractions

With more than 5000 members in 80 countries, IAAPA's membership includes amusement parks, family entertainment centers, waterparks, attractions and the manufacturers and suppliers that provide the goods and services that make the industry safe and fun. It hosts a convention and trade show and provides education and training programs as well as government representation.

1448 Duke St.
Alexandria VA 22314
703/836-4800   FAX 703/836-4801
E-mail: iaapa@iaapa.org   http://www.iaapa.org
Contact: Ms. Susan Mosedale
          Vice President of Membership and Mktng. Services

Intl. Assn. of Black Professional Fire Fighters

The IABPFF is dedicated to promoting interracial progress throughout the fire service through recruitment, employment, and advancement of black professional fire fighters.

8700 Central Ave. - Suite 306
Landover MD 20785
301/808-0804   FAX 301/808-0807
http://www.bin.org/assocorg/iabpff/iabpfinf.html
Contact: Mr. Romeo O. Spaulding
          President

Intl. Assn. of Boards of Examiners in Optometry

The mission of the association is to represent and assist member licensing agencies in regulating the practice of optometry for the public welfare.

4401 East-West Highway, Suite 205
Bethesda MD 20814-4521
301/913-0641   FAX 301/913-2034
E-mail: IAB@iabopt.org
Contact: Mr. James Vrac
             Executive Director

Intl. Assn. of Bridge, Structural, Ornamental, and Reinforcing Iron Workers

1750 New York Ave., NW - Suite 400
Washington DC 20006
202/383-4800   FAX 202/638-4856
Contact: Mr. Raymond J. Robertson
             Vice President

Intl. Assn. of Chiefs of Police

515 North Washington St.
Alexandria VA 22314
703/836-6767   FAX 703/836-4543
Contact: Mr. Daniel Rosenblatt
             Executive Director

Intl. Assn. of Color Manufacturers

1620 I St., NW - Suite 925
Washington DC 20005
202/293-5800   FAX 202/463-8998
Contact: Mr. Daniel R. Thompson
             Director

Intl. Assn. of Convention & Visitor Bureaus

Founded in 1914 to promote sound professional practices in the solicitation and servicing of meetings and conventions, IACVB represents over 420 member bureaus in 31 countries.

2000 L St., NW - Suite 702
Washington DC 20036-4990
202/296-7888   FAX 202/296-7889
E-mail: gwilson@iacvb.org http://www.iacvb.org
Contact: Mr. Greg Wilson
             Publications Coordinator

Intl. Assn. of Counseling Services

The IACS works to encourage and aid counseling services throughout the U.S. and internationally to meet high professional standards, to inform the public about those which are competent and reliable and to foster communication among counseling services operating in a variety of settings.   Membership is open to university and college counseling centers; and public and private counseling agencies.

101 South Whiting St. - Suite 211
Alexandria VA 22304
703/823-9840   FAX 703/823-9843
E-mail: iacs@vms1.gmu.edu
Contact: Ms. Nancy E. Roncketti
             Executive Officer

Intl. Assn. of Drilling Contractors

The IADC is the only organization to exclusively represent the worldwide drilling industry, encompassing the bulk of the upstream energy industry through its drilling-contractor membership and their associates in well servicing, oil and gas producing and, oilfield manufacturing and service.

1901 L St., NW, Suite 702
Washington DC 20036
202/293-0670   FAX 202/872-0047
Contact: Mr. Brian T. Petty
             Senior Vice President, Govt. Affrs.

Intl. Assn. of Fire Chiefs

Represents career and volunteer fire chiefs, chief fire officers, and managers of Emergency Services Organizations throughout the international community through vision, information, education, and services to enhance their professionalism and capabilities.

4025 Fair Ridge Dr.
Fairfax VA 22033-2868
703/273-0911   FAX 703/273-9363
E-mail: iafchq@iafc.org   http://www.iafc.org
Contact: Mr. Garry L. Briese
             Executive Director

Intl. Assn. of Fire Fighters

1750 New York Ave., NW
Washington DC 20006
202/737-8484   FAX 202/737-8418
Contact: Mr. Alfred K. Whitehead
             General President

Intl. Assn. of Fish & Wildlife Agencies

Founded in 1902, the association is a quasi-governmental organization of public agencies charged with the protection and management of North America's fish and wildlife resources. The association's governmental members include the fish and wildlife agencies of the states, provinces, and federal governments of the U.S., Canada and Mexico. All 50 states are members. It has been a key organization in promoting sound resource management and strengthening federal, state and private cooperation in protecting and managing fish and wildlife and their habitats in the public interest.

444 N. Capitol St., NW - Suite 544
Washington DC 20001
202/624-7890   FAX 202/624-7891
E-mail: iafish@aol.com
Contact: Mr. R. Max Peterson
             Executive Vice President

Intl. Assn. of Heat & Frost Insulators & Asbestos Wkrs.

1776 Massachusetts Ave., NW - Suite 301 Washington DC 20036
202/785-2388   FAX 202/429-0568
Contact: Mr. James Grogan
             General Secretary - Treasurer

Intl. Assn. of Machinists & Aerospace Workers

9000 Machinists Place
Upper Marlboro MD 20772-2687
301/967-4500   FAX 301/967-4588
Contact: Mr. Owen Herrnstadt
             Director, Intl. Affairs

Intl. Assn. of Official Human Rights Agencies

Established in 1947, IAOHRA seeks to enforce a variety of human and civil rights laws and represents statutory human rights and human relations agencies around the world. Its activities range from acting as a publisher and forum for the exchange of ideas, to liaison with international and national agencies, to providing technical legal assistance in the drafting of human rights legislation.
444 North Capitol Street, NW, Suite 408
Washington DC 20001
202/624-5410   FAX 202/624-8185

Contact: Mr. Kirk Baylor
Director

Intl. Assn. of Professional Security Consultants

The IAPSC is a nonprofit professional association of independent, non-product affiliated professional security consultants. The IAPSC was founded in 1984 as a professional society to recognize, as members, individual professional security consultants who meet Association standards, and to serve consumers of security consulting services.

1444 I St., NW - Suite 700
Washington DC 20005-2210
202/712-9043   FAX 202/216-9646
E-mail: IAPSC@IAPSC.org http://www.IAPSC.org
Contact: Ms. Claire Shanley
Executive Director

Intl. Assn. of Refrigerated Warehouses

Founded in 1891, the IARW represents 1,000 member warehouses in 34 countries. Its goals include: the promotion of a broader and more efficient warehousing service; the dissemination of statistical information and the exchange of ideas among its members; advising members of legislation, regulation, trade and international issues affecting their business; and promoting new technology in warehousing and product protection.

7315 Wisconsin Ave., Suite 1200N
Bethesda MD 20814
301/652-5674   FAX 301/652-7269
E-mail: email@iarw.org   http://www.iarw.org
Contact: Mr. J. William Hudson
President

Intl. Banana Assn.

1929 39th St., NW
Washington DC 20007
202/223-1183   FAX 202/223-1194
Contact: Mr. Robert M. Moore
President

Intl. Biometric Society

Founded in 1947, IBS is an international organization for the advancement of the biological and agricultural sciences through the development of quantitative theories and the development, application and dissemination of effective mathematical and statistical techniques. The Society has nearly 7,000 members in over 80 countries identified by location and affiliation with one of the 16 Regions of 16 National Groups in which membership is concurrent with the international society.

1444 I Street, NW - #700
Washington DC 20005
202/712-9049   FAX 202/216-9646
E-mail: ibs@bostromdc.com   http://www.tibs.org
Contact: Mr. Charles McGrath
Executive Director

Intl. Bottled Water Assn.

Founded in 1958 as the American Bottled Water Association (ABWA), the association merged with the Council of Natural Waters to become the International Bottled Water Association in 1982. It is a trade association representing all segments of the bottled water industry with approximately 1,000 member companies, including bottled products, distributors and manufacturers of bottled water supplies, and international bottlers who both sell and distribute imported waters in the U.S. as well as other countries. The mission of the IBWA is to increase the use of bottled water through expanded consumer

awareness, effective government relations and technical expertise and to provide association members with the appropriate services.

1700 Diagonal Rd. - Suite 650
Alexandria VA 22314-2973
703/683-5213   FAX 703/683-4074
Contact: Ms. Sylvia Swanson
President

Intl. Bridge, Tunnel and Turnpike Assn.

IBTTA represents the U.S. toll industry in legislative, regulatory, judicial forums, and the national media. The association also participates in a number of international transportation forums.

2120 L St., NW - Suite 305
Washington DC 20037
202/659-4620   FAX 202/659-0500
E-mail: ibtta@ibtta.org   http://www.ibtta.org
Contact: Mr. Neil D. Schuster
Executive Director

Intl. Brotherhood of Boilermakers, Iron Shipbuilders, Blacksmiths, Forgers, and Helpers

2722 Merrilee Dr. - Suite 360
Fairfax VA 22031
703/560-1493   FAX 703/560-2584
Contact: Mr. Ande M. Abbott
Intl. Representative and Legislative Director

Intl. Brotherhood of Electrical Workers (IBEW)

The objects of the union are: to organize all workers in the entire electrical industry in the U.S. and Canada, including all those in public utilities and electrical manufacturing, into local unions; to promote reasonable methods of work; to cultivate feelings of friendship among those of the industry; to settle all disputes between employers and employees by arbitration (if possible); to assist each other in sickness or distress; to secure employment; to reduce the hours of daily labor; to secure adequate pay; to seek a higher standard of living; and to seek security for the individual.

1125 15th St., NW
Washington DC 20005
202/833-7000   FAX 202/728-6056
http://www.ibew.org
Contact: Mr. Lawrence Liles
Intl. Representative

Intl. Brotherhood of Painters & Allied Trades

1750 New York Ave., NW
Washington DC 20006
202/637-0700   FAX 202/637-0771
http://www.ibpat.org
Contact: Mr. Mark L. Monroe
Executive Assistant to the General President

Intl. Brotherhood of Police Officers

The IBPO represents federal, state, and local officers nationwide. It is an affiliate of the Service Employees International Union and is the largest police union in the AFL-CIO. The IBPO is a full service public employee union representing 40,000 police officers nationwide. The union's headquarters are in Boston, Massachusetts, with regional offices in nine other states.

317 S. Patrick St.
Alexandria VA 22314
703/519-0300   FAX 703/519-0311
Contact: Mr. Chris Donnellan
Legislative Director

Intl. Brotherhood of Teamsters

25 Louisiana Ave., NW
Washington DC 20001-2198
202/624-6800   FAX 202/624-8973
Contact: Mr. Matt Witt
          Communications Director

Intl. Business Brokers Assn.

IBBA is an international non-profit organization operating exclusively for the benefit of people and firms engaged in the various aspects of business brokerage, and mergers and acquisitions.

11250 Roger Bacon Dr. - Suite 8
Reston VA 22090
703/525-1191   FAX 703/276-8196
E-mail: IBBAINC@aol.com http://www.IBBA.org
Contact: Ms. Yolande Nana Yakkara
          Administrator

Intl. Campaign for Tibet

A nonpartisan, public interest group dedicated to promoting human rights and democratic freedoms for the people of Tibet. ICT believes that Tibetans are a people under international law and have the right to self-determination; that Tibet is an occupied country which has a distinct language, culture and religion; and that dialogue between Tibetans and Chinese is integral towards finding a solution to the situation in Tibet.

1825 K Street NW - Suite 520
Washington DC 20006
202/785-1515   FAX 202/785-4343
E-mail: ict@peacenet.org   http://www.savetibet.org
Contact: Mr. John Ackerly
          President

Intl. CellularVision Assn.

ICVA was founded in 1993 to promote public industry professional and governmental awareness of the new local multi-point distribution system (LMDS). Its members include licensees of CellularVision Technology and Telecommunications (CT&T) and other interested parties.

2600 Virginia Ave., NW, Suite 508
Washington DC 20037
202/965-4282   FAX 202/965-762
Contact: Mr. Matthew J. Rinaldo
          President

Intl. Center

A private, non-profit organization providing independent analysis of U.S. foreign policy initiatives to government officials, interest groups, and the media.

731 8th Street, SE
Washington DC 20003
202/547-3800   FAX 202/546-4784
E-mail: icnfp@erols.com   http://www.internationalcenter.com
Contact: Ms. Lindsay Mattison
          Director

Intl. Center for Journalists

ICJ was founded in 1985 for the purpose of sharing advanced media skills and information with journalists and news organizations around the world. It seeks to help the news media attain the highest possible standards, fulfill their role as reliable servants of the public, strengthen the independence of the press, and broaden news coverage of both local and global issues.

1616 H Street, NW - 3rd floor
Washington DC 20006-4999
202/737-3700   FAX 202/737-0530
E-mail: anable@icfj.com
Contact: Mr. David Anable
          President

Intl. Center for Research on Women

Founded in 1976, the ICRW focuses principally on women in developing and transition countries. It is a private, nonprofit organization which advocates with governments and multilateral agencies, convenes experts, and provides information programs to advance women's rights and opportunities.

1717 Massachusetts Avenue, NW - Suite 302
Washington DC 20036
202/797-0007   FAX 202/797-0020
E-mail: icrw@igc.apc.org   http://www.icrw.org
Contact: Ms. Geeta Rao Gupta
          President

Intl. Chiropractors Assn.

1110 North Glebe Rd. - Suite 1000
Arlington VA 22201
703/528-5000   FAX 703/528-5023
E-mail: chiro@erols.com   http://www.chiropractic.org
Contact: Mr. Ron Hendrickson
          Executive Director

Intl. City/County Management Assn.

Founded in 1914, ICMA is a nonprofit professional association representing 8,500 local government officials and urban experts. ICMA's mission is to enhance the quality of local government and to support and assist professional local administrators worldwide.

777 N. Capitol St., NE, Suite 500
Washington DC 20002
202/289-4262   FAX 202/962-3500
E-mail: icmainfo@icma.org http://www.icma.org
Contact: Mr. William H. Hansell
          Executive Director

Intl. Climate Change Partnership

The ICCP addresses the issue of global climatic change from an industry perspective.

2111 Wilson Blvd. - Suite 850
Arlington VA 22201-3058
703/841-0626   FAX 703/243-2874
E-mail: ICCP@alcade-fay.com
Contact: Mr. Kevin J. Fay
          Executive Director

Intl. Commission for the Prevention of Alcoholism & Drug Dependancy

Specializes in the prevention of alcohol, tobacco, and other drug use through education.

12501 Old Columbia Pike
Silver Spring MD 20904-1600
301/680-6719   FAX 301/680-6090
E-mail: 74617.2242@compuserve.com
Contact: Mr. Thomas Neslund
          Executive Director

Intl. Communications Industries Assn.

Serves as the international trade association for the computer, video and audiovisual industries, with more than 1100 producers, manufacturers and distributors as members.

1242 Waples Hill Road - Suite 200
Fairfax VA 22030
703/273-7200   FAX 703/278-8082
E-mail: icia@icia.org   http://www.icia.org
Contact: Mr. Walter Blackwell
          Executive Director

Intl. Cotton Advisory Committee

Founded in 1939, the committee is a intergovernmental association of 42 member countries in the Americas, Europe, Africa, and Asia concerned with the international cotton market.

1629 K St., NW, Suite 702
Washington DC 20006
202/463-6660   FAX 202/463-6950
E-mail: secretariat@icac.org   http://www.icac.org
Contact: Mr. Lawrence H. Shaw
          Executive Director

Intl. Council of Cruise Lines

Represents the deep-sea, overnight, and foreign-flag passenger cruise ship industry.

1211 Connecticut Ave., NW - Suite 800
Washington DC 20036
202/296-8463   FAX 202/296-1676
Contact: Ms. Cynthia A. Colenda
          President

Intl. Council of Employers of Bricklayers & Allied Craftworkers

821 15th St., NW
Washington DC 20005
202/383-3907   FAX 202/383-3122
E-mail: wkardy@imiweb.org
Contact: Mr. Walter Kardy
          Executive Director

Intl. Council of Shopping Centers

Founded in 1957, the ICSC has 31,000 members in the U.S., Canada and more than 60 other countries including shopping center owners, developers, managers, marketing specialists, investors, lenders, retailers and other professionals as well as academics and public officials.

1033 N. Fairfax St. - Suite 404
Alexandria VA 22314
703/549-7404   FAX 703/549-8712
E-mail: govrel@icsc.org   http://www.icsc.org
Contact: Ms. Rebecca M. Sullivan
          Senior Director for Govt. Relations

Intl. Council on Education for Teaching

Established in 1953, ICET is an international, nongovernmental association of educational organizations, institutions, and individuals dedicated to the improvement of teacher education and all forms of education and training related to national development.

2009 N. 14th Street - Suite 609
Arlington VA 22201
703/525-5253   FAX 703/351-9381
Contact: Ms. Sandra J. Klassen
          Executive Director

Intl. Dairy Foods Assn.

The IDFA serves processors, manufacturers, distributors, and dairy industry suppliers across the U.S. and abroad. The IDFA consists of three separate associations: the Milk Industry Foundation; the National Cheese Institute; and the International Ice Cream Association. It is recognized as a legislative and policy advocate, an education resource, a crisis manager, a public affairs counselor, and an expert in the areas of marketing, economics, scientific, and regulatory affairs.

1250 H St., NW - Suite 900
Washington DC 20005
202/737-4332   FAX 202/331-7820
E-mail: adivjak@idfa.org
Contact: Ms. Anne Divjak
          Intl. Affairs Coordinator

Intl. District Energy Assn.

IDEA, previously known as the International District Heating and Cooling Association, was founded in 1909 to serve the needs of the district energy industry (steam, hot water, chilled water and cogeneration). IDEA organizes and sponsors several conferences during the year with topics including marketing, distribution, metering, physical plants, the environment, and district cooling concerns. The annual conference, which attracts over 400 attendees includes technical presentations, manufacturer supplier exhibits, and network opportunities.

1200 19th St., NW
Washington DC 20036
202/429-5111   FAX 202/429-5113
http://www.history.rochester.edu/idea
Contact: Mr. John Fiegel
          President

Intl. Downtown Assn.

Founded over 40 years ago, IDA is the catalyst for organizations committed to the revitalization of towns, cities and communities. It offers conferences, meetings and printed materials to foster the sharing of information about changes and improvements taking place in downtowns as well as working to gain positive local and national media exposure. IDA also represents downtowns to government leaders at the national and local levels.

910 17th St., NW - Suite 210
Washington DC 20006-2603
202/293-4505   FAX 202/293-4509
E-mail: question@ida-downtown.org
http://www.ida-downtown.org
Contact: Ms. Elizabeth Jackson
          President

Intl. Electronic Article Surveillance Manufacturers

1420 16th St., NW
Washington DC 20036
202/328-7460   FAX 202/332-2301
Contact: Mr. Randy Dyer
          President

Intl. Electronics Manufacturers & Consumers of America

A trade association composed of the U.S. manufacturing subsidiaries of 18 major overseas electronic companies.

601 13th St., NW - Suite 670 South
Washington DC 20005
202/783-7276   FAX 202/783-4345
Contact: Mr. Verrick O. French
          President

Intl. Energy Development Council

1050 Thomas Jefferson St., 7th Floor
Washington DC 20007
202/298-1800   FAX 202/338-2416
Contact: Mr. Howard Feldmen
          Managing Partner

Intl. Enterprise Group

3900 Huntington St., NW
Washington DC 20015
202/537-0201   FAX 202/537-0201
Contact: Mr. John Kerr
          Executive Director

Intl. Eye Foundation/Society of Eye Surgeons

7801 Norfolk Ave.
Bethesda MD 20814
301/986-1830   FAX 301/986-1876
E-mail: info@ief.permanet.org
Contact: Ms. Victoria Sheffield
          Executive Director

Intl. Fabricare Institute

12251 Tech Rd.
Silver Spring MD 20904
301/622-1900
http://www.ifi.org
Contact: Mr. David J. Uchic
          Vice President, Communications

Intl. Federation of Professional & Technical Engineers

8630 Fenton St. - Suite 400
Silver Spring MD 20910-3803
301/565-9016   FAX 301/565-0018
Contact: Mr. Paul E. Almeida
          President

Intl. Food Information Council

Provides nutritional and food safety information to the public dealing with such specific issues as child nutrition and food biotechnology.

1100 Connecticut Avenue, NW, Suite 430
Washington DC 20036
202/296-6540   FAX 202/296-6547
E-mail: rowe@ific.health.org   http://www.ificinfo.health.org
Contact: Ms. Sylvia Rowe
          President

Intl. Food Policy Research Institute

Analyzes global food problems and conducts policy research on sustainable ways of increasing food availability in developing countries.

1200 17th Street, NW
Washington DC 20036-3006
202/862-5600   FAX 202/467-4439
E-mail: ifpri@cgnet.com   http://www.cgiar/ifpri
Contact: Mr. Per Pinstrup-Anderson
          Director General

Intl. Foodservice Distribution Assn.

The partner organization of the National-American Wholesale Grocers' Assn., IFDA member companies sell food and related products to restaurants, hospitals and other institutional foodservice organizations.

201 Park Washington Court
Falls Church VA 22046-4621
703/532-9400   FAX 703/538-4673
E-mail: johnb@fdi.org   http://www.fdi.org
Contact: Mr. John R. Block
          President

Intl. Foundation for Election Systems (IFES)

A private, nonprofit foundation established in 1987 to support electoral, civic, and other democratic institutions and practices in emerging, evolving, and experienced democracies. Nonpartisan and technical in approach, IFES has conducted project, conference, and research activities in over 90 countries.

1101 15th St., NW - 3rd Floor
Washington DC 20005
202/828-8507   FAX 202/452-0804
E-mail: ray@ifes.org   http://www.ifes.org
Contact: Mr. J. Ray Kennedy
          Director of Information Resources

Intl. Franchise Assn.

Founded in 1960, IFA's mission is to enhance and safeguard the business environment for franchising worldwide. Its global membership consists of companies franchising the distribution of their goods and services, unit owners, and companies supplying products and services to franchise businesses.

1350 New York Ave., NW - Suite 900
Washington DC 20005-4709
202/628-8000   FAX 202/628-0812
E-mail: ifa@franchise.org   http://www.franchise.org
Contact: Ms. Katrina Schymik
          Director of Intl. Affairs and Information Services

Intl. Frozen Food Assn.

IFFA is an international organization comprised of such members as frozen food processing companies, associations, individuals, and suppliers. It desires to maintain open discussions on trade, technology, legislation, regulation, and communication.

2000 Corporate Ridge - Suite 1000
McLean VA 22102
703/821-0770   FAX 703/821-1350
Contact: Mr. Steven C. Anderson
          Director General

Intl. Fund for Renewable Energy & Energy Efficiency

IFREE was established to foster financially and environmentally sustainable energy projects in emerging markets and to facilitate partnerships between energy entrepreneurs in the U.S. and their counterparts in developing countries.

727 15th St., NW - 11th Floor
Washington DC 20005
202/408-7916   FAX 202/408-7916
E-mail: ifree@ifree.org
Contact: Ms. Dana Levy
          Vice President

Intl. Human Rights Law Group, The

A nonprofit organization of human rights and legal professionals engaged in human rights advocacy, litigation, and training around the world. The mission is to support and help empower advocates to expand the scope of human rights standards and procedures at the national, regional and international, levels. The Law Group, a network of experts and activists, lawyers and law firms, works together with local organizations in the developing world to place human rights, women, and development at the center of the international agenda.

1200 18th St., NW - Suite 602
Washington DC 20036
202/822-4600   FAX 202/822-4606
E-mail: ihrlg@aol.com
Contact: Ms. Gay McDougall
          Executive Director

Intl. Ice Cream Assn.
Representing manufacturers, distributors, and marketers of ice cream and related products in legislative, regulatory, marketing, production, and training activities, IICA works to promote the growth and profitability of the industry.

1250 H St., NW, Suite 900
Washington DC 20005
202/737-4332   FAX 202/331-7820
http://www.idfa.org
Contact: Mr. E. Linwood Tipton
          President and CEO

Intl. Institute for Energy Conservation
Devises and implements plans promoting sustainable development in developing countries, including East-Central and Eastern Europe, Asia, Latin America, and South Africa, through the conservation of energy.

750 1st Street, NE, Suite 940
Washington DC 20002
202/842-3388   FAX 202/842-1565
Contact: Mr. Russell Sturm
          President

Intl. Institute of Ammonia Refrigeration
Established in 1970 by a small, dedicated group of companies committed to the use of ammonia as a refrigerant, the IIAR has since grown in size and scope, now with a membership which includes contractors, manufacturers, representatives, end users, engineers, wholesalers, and manufacturers of ammonia refrigeration products.

1200 19th St., NW, Suite 300
Washington DC 20036
202/857-1110   FAX 202/223-4579
E-mail: iiar@dc.sba.com   http://www.iiar.org
Contact: Mr. Kent Anderson
          President

Intl. Institute of Business Technologies
8150 Leesburg Pike #1010
Vienna VA 22182-2714
703/821-1783   FAX 202/463-9368
Contact: Mr. Marshall D. Sokol
          President

Intl. Insurance Council
The International Insurance Council, based in Washington, DC, works to foster open markets for international insurance and to promote the interests of the international insurance industry.

900 19th St., NW - Suite 250
Washington DC 20006
202/682-2345   FAX 202/218-7730

Contact: Mr. Gordon Cloney
          President

Intl. Intellectual Property Alliance (IIPA)
Formed in 1984 to represent the U.S. copyright based industries (computer software, films, videos, music, recordings, and books), in a bilateral and multilateral effort to improve international protection of copyrighted works. IIPA is comprised of seven trade associations: the Association of American Publishers (AAP), the AFMA, the Business Software Alliance (BSA), the Interactive Digital Software Association (IDSA), the Motion Picture Association of America (MPAA), the National Music Publishers' Association (NMPA), and the Recording Industry Association of America (RIAA), each representing a significant segment of the U.S. copyright community.

1747 Pennsylvania Ave., NW, 12th Floor
Washington DC 20006-4604
202/833-4198   FAX 202/872-0546
E-mail: smimet@iipa.com   http://www.iipa.com
Contact: Mr. Eric H. Smith
          President

Intl. Kitchen Exhaust Cleaning Assn.
A not-for-profit trade association founded in 1988, IKECA has established Standards & Practices for contractors engaged in kitchen exhaust cleaning, conducted a variety of educational programs, and worked with code setting bodies to improve existing codes and regulations. Members meet twice yearly to keep abreast of the latest worker protection regulations, new products and chemicals, and local and national regulations.

1518 K St., NW - Suite 503
Washington DC 20005
202/737-0202   FAX 202/638-4833
E-mail: ikecahq@aol.com
Contact: Mr. Glenn Fellman
          Executive Director

Intl. Labor Organization (ILO)
Now a U.N. specialized agency, the ILO was created in 1919 by the Treaty of Versailles to improve living and working conditions worldwide. Consisting of 173 member states, it has a tripartite structure representing Governments, Workers and Employers. The ILO sets and monitors compliance with international labor standards called Conventions, provides technical cooperation, and conducts research on labor and employment issues. Its primary objectives are the promotion of democracy and human rights; the fight against unemployment and poverty; and the promotion of equality and protection of workers. The ILO is headquartered in Geneva, Switzerland. U.S. interests are represented by the Departments of State and Labor, the AFL-CIO and the U.S. Council for International Business.

1828 L St., NW - Suite 801
Washington DC 20036
202/653-7652   FAX 202/653-7687
E-mail: washilo@ilowbo.org   http://www.us.ilo.org
Contact: Mr. Anthony Freeman
          Director, Washington Branch Office

Intl. Labor Rights Fund
ILRF is a nonprofit organization dedicated to assuring that the human rights of workers are protected throughout the world. It works to draw various communities (human rights, labor, consumers, business, religious, academic and governmental) into consensus around policies that enhance and enforce international norms and standards to assure that adult working people are able to labor under conditions that respect their rights, dignity, economic needs, and their health and safety, and that children are not subject of exploitative, dangerous or unhealthy work.

733 15th St., NW - Suite 920
Washington DC 20005
202/347-4100   FAX 202/347-4885
E-mail: laborrights@igc.org   http://www.laborrights.org
Contact: Mr. Pharis J. Harvey
          Executive Director

Intl. Law Institute
Provides training and legal assistance programs in law, finance, and management to government officials from developing countries and publishes in the areas of international development, finance and commercial law.

1615 New Hampshire Avenue, NW
Washington DC 20009
202/483-3036   FAX 202/483-3029
E-mail: training@ili.org   http://www.ili.org
Contact: Mr. Stuart Kerr
          Executive Director

Intl. Legal Fraternity-Phi Delta Phi
An organization founded in 1869 to advance legal ethics, professionalism, and scholarship in the law schools.

1750 N Street, NW
Washington DC 20036
202/628-0148   FAX 202/296-7619
E-mail: phideltaphi@worldnet.att.net http://www.phideltaphi.org
Contact: Mr. Sam S. Crutchfield
          Executive Director

Intl. Longshore & Warehouse Union

1775 K St., NW, Suite 200
Washington DC 20006
202/463-6265   FAX 202/467-4875

Contact: Ms. Lindsay McLaughlin
          Legislative Director

Intl. Longshoremen's Assn.

1101 17th St., NW - Suite 400
Washington DC 20036
202/955-6304
Contact: Mr. John Bowers
          Legislative Director

Intl. Magnesium Assn.
Currently with 115 member companies from 22 countries, the association works to develop and promote in a responsible manner, the international use of magnesium metal and its alloys in all product forms.

1303 Vincent Place, Suite One
McLean VA 22101
703/442-8888   FAX 703/821-1824
E-mail: ima@bellatlantic.net   http://www.intlmag.org
Contact: Mr. Byron B. Clow
          Executive Vice President

Intl. Management and Development Institute
Provides informational programs to assist policy makers and business people in dealing with mutual problems.

1615 L St., NW, Suite 900
Washington DC 20037
202/337-1022   FAX 202/337-6678

E-mail: imdimail@aol.com
Contact: Mr. Don Bonker
          President

Intl. Masonry Institute
The IMI is a joint labor/management trust fund between the International Union of Bricklayers and Allied Craftsmen and contractors who employ the union's members in the U.S. and Canada. IMI's mission is to increase the union masonry industry's share of the construction market. IMI has four major programs: Apprenticeship and Training; Market Promotion; Research and Development; and Labor/Management Relations.

The James Brice House 42 East St.
Annapolis MD 21401
410/280-1305   FAX 301/261-2855
http://www.imiweb.org
Contact: Ms. Joan N. Baggett-Calambokidis
          President

Intl. Mass Retail Assn.
IMRA represents and promotes the mass retail industry through a wide variety of business services, including conferences, research studies, government relations, industry development, publications, and encouraging productive relations between retail and supplier members. IMRA's retail members, operating in the U.S. and internationally include full-line and specialty discount stores, membership warehouse clubs, home centers, off-price/outlet stores, catalog showrooms, deep-discount drugstores, dollar/variety stores, and others. IMRA's supplier members provide goods and services to the mass retail industry.

1700 N. Moore St. - Suite 2250
Arlington Va 22209-1903
703/841-2300   FAX 703/841-1184
E-mail: rwlanier@imra.com http://www.imra.org
Contact: Ms. Robin Lanier
          Senior Vice President, Industrial Affairs

Intl. Microwave Power Institute
Founded in 1966 to serve the information needs of specialists working with microwave heating systems, IMPI reorganized in 1977 to expand its industrial and scientific base to meet the information needs evolving in consumer microwave ovens and related products. Its two special interest sections include the Microwave Food Technology and Applications Section (MFTA) and the Industrial, Scientific, Medical and Instrumentation Section (ISMI).

10210 Leatherleaf Court
Manassas VA 20111
703/257-1415   FAX 703/257-0213
E-mail: AssnCtr@idsonline.com   http://www.impiweb.org
Contact: Mr. Robert Lagasse
          Executive Director

Intl. Military Community Executives Assn.
Established in 1972 as a nonprofit organization for Morale, Welfare, and Recreation Managers in all branches of the Armed Forces. The association works to improve the quality of life for service men, women, and their families through educational and training workshops, a certification program, tradeshows, awards, programs, and publications.

1800 Diagonal Rd. - Suite 285
Alexandria VA 22314
703/548-0093   FAX 703/548-0095
E-mail: dpavlik@erols.com
Contact: Mr. Donald Pavlik
          Executive Director

Intl. Military Community Executives Assn.
Established in 1972 as a nonprofit organization for Morale, Welfare, and Recreation Managers in all branches of the Armed Forces. The association works to improve the quality of life for service men, women, and their families through educational and training workshops, a certification program, tradeshows, awards, programs, and publications.

1800 Diagonal Rd. - Suite 285
Alexandria VA 22314
703/548-0093   FAX 703/548-0095
E-mail: dpavlik@erols.com
Contact: Mr. Donald C. Pavlik
          Executive Director

Intl. Mobile Telecommunications Association
The IMTA represents and serves the commercial trunked radio industry worldwide. It publishes a worldwide directory of commercial trunked radio operators as well as a directory of two-way radio dealers and distributors.

1150 18th St., NW - Suite 230
Washington DC 20036
202/331-7773   FAX 202/331-9062
E-mail: amta@aol.com   http://www.imta.org
Contact: Mr. Alan R. Shark
          President

Intl. Natural Sausage Casing Assn.

1518 K St., NW - Suite 503
Washington DC 20005
202/737-0202   FAX 202/638-4833
Contact: Mr. Glenn Fellmann
          Executive Director

Intl. Organization for Migration
An intergovernmental body, IOM is committed to the principle that humane and orderly migration benefits society. IOM acts with its partners in the international community to assist in meeting the operational challenges of migration; advance understanding of migration issues; encourage social and economic development through migration; and uphold the human dignity and well-being of migrants.

1750 K St., NW - Suite 1110
Washington DC 20006
202/862-1826   FAX 202/862-1879
E-mail: srowashington@iom.int   http://www.iom.int
Contact: Mr. Hans-Peter W. Boe
          Chief of Mission

Intl. Personnel Management Assn. (IPMA)
An organization of human resource professionals with over 50 chapters throughout the U.S. as well as in Pakistan and Germany.

1617 Duke St.
Alexandria VA 22314
703/549-7100   FAX 703/684-0948
E-mail: ipma@ipma-hr.org http://www.ipma-hr.org
Contact: Mr. Neil Reichenberg
          Executive Director

Intl. Policy Council on Agriculture, Food and Trade
Founded in 1987, the council's goal is to develop sensible and lasting solutions to global problems in the trade of agricultural and food products which may guide the actions of government, business, farm, and consumer leaders.

1616 P St., NW, Suite 100
Washington DC 20036
202/328-5056   FAX 202/328-5133
http://www.agritrade.org
Contact: Mr. Peter Lacy
          Executive Director

Intl. Religious Liberty Assn.

12501 Old Columbia Pike
Silver Spring MD 20904-6600
301/680-6680   FAX 301/680-6695
Contact: Mr. John Graz
          Secretary General

Intl. Republican Institute
IRI conducts programs outside the U.S. to promote and strengthen democratic ideals and institutions. The programs are tailored to the needs of pro-democracy activists in the host country and include campaign management, organization of political parties, training in civic responsibility, and conferences on procedures and processes for newly elected Parliamentarians. IRI has supported newly emerging democracies in all parts of the world: Africa, Eastern Europe, Russia and Ukraine, the Caribbean, the Middle East, and Asia.

1212 New York Ave., NW, Suite 900
Washington DC 20005
202/408-9450   FAX 202/408-9462
E-mail: iri@iri.org   http://www.iri.org
Contact: Mr. Lorne W. Craner
          President

Intl. Rescue Committee Inc.
Founded in 1933, the International Rescue Committee is a non-profit, nonsectarian voluntary organization providing relief, protection, and resettlement services for refugees and victims of oppression or violent conflict.

1612 K St., NW - Suite 700
Washington DC 20006
202/822-0043   FAX 202/822-0089
http://www.intrescom.org
Contact: Ms. Sheppie Abramowitz
          Vice President, Govt. Affairs

Intl. Road Federation
A not-for-profit, non-political service organization whose objective is to encourage better road and transportation systems worldwide and to help in the application of technology and management practices which will result in maximum economic and social returns from national road investments.

2600 Virginia Ave., NW - Suite 208
Washington DC 20037
202/338-4641   FAX 202/338-8104
http://www.irfnet.org
Contact: Mr. Richard Robertson
          Director, General

Intl. Service Agencies
A cooperative endeavor between various charitable organizations which provides health and welfare services to the needy overseas.

66 Canal Center Plaza, Suite 301
Alexandria VA 22314
703/548-2200   FAX 703/548-0786
E-mail: isa@charity.org   http://www.charity.org
Contact: Ms. Renee Acosta
          President

Intl. Sleep Products Assn.

333 Commerce St.
Alexandria VA 22314
703/683-8371   FAX 703/683-4503
Contact: Mr. Russ Abolt
          Executive Vice President

Intl. Slurry Surfacing Assn.

Founded in 1963, the ISSA is a nonprofit association dedicated to the interests, education, and success of slurry surfacing professionals and corporations around the world. It provides its members with information, technical assistance, and ongoing opportunities for networking and professional development.

1200 19th St., NW, - Suite 300
Washington DC 20036
202/857-1160   FAX 202/223-4579
E-mail: john__fiegel@dc.sba.com
http://www.history.rochester.edu/issa/
Contact: Mr. John Fiegel
          Executive Director

Intl. Society for Intercultural Educ., Training & Resources

SIETAR is an association of professionals from a variety of applied and academic disciplines who share a common interest in intercultural understanding. As an interdisciplinary professional and service organization, SIETAR promotes effective interaction and communication among people of diverse cultures, races, and ethnic groups. It is affiliated with the United Nations, has consultative status with the Council of Europe, and is recognized by UNESCO as a nongovernmental organization

1444 I St., NW, Suite 700
Washington DC 20005
202/712-9049   FAX 202/216-9646
E-mail: sietar@compuserve.com   http://www.aspin.asu.edu/~sietar/
Contact: Mr. Charles McGrath
          Executive Director

Intl. Society of Air Safety Investigators

The ISASI is a society formed to promote air safety by the exchange of ideas, experiences, and information about aircraft accident investigations, and to otherwise aid in the advancement of flight safety; to promote technical advancement by providing professional education through lectures, displays, and presentations and by the exchange of information for mutual development of improved investigations; to broaden professional relationships among members; to maintain and increase the prestige, standing and influence of the Air Safety Investigator in matters of air safety.

Technology Trading Pk., 5 Export Dr.
Sterling VA 20164-4421
703/430-9668   FAX 703/450-1745
E-mail: ISASI@Erols.com
Contact: Mr. Frank Del Gaudio
          Secretary

Intl. Society of Transport Aircraft Trading

Formed to promote improved communication among those involved in aviation and supporting industries who sell, purchase, finance, lease, appraise, insure or otherwise are engaged in activities related to the exchange of transport category aircraft.

5517 Talon Court
Fairfax VA 22032
703/978-8156   FAX 703/503-5964

http://www.istat.org
Contact: Ms. Dawn O'Day Foster
          Executive Director

Intl. Taxicab and Livery Assn.

Formed in 1917, it is a nonprofit trade association representing private, for-profit providers of for-hire ground transportation services. ITLA's mission is to enhance the ability of member organizations to serve effectively and profitably the local transportation needs of the public and to serve as the spokesperson for the for-hire ground transportation industry. It has five membership divisions: Contracted and Paratransit Services, Premium Services, Taxicab Services, International Operators, and Associates (suppliers). The nearly 900 members operate over 75,000 vehicles and are located in all 50 states and in 16 other countries.

3849 Farragut Ave.
Kensington MD 20895
301/946-5701   FAX 301/946-4641
E-mail: itla@itla-info.org   http://www.taxinetwork.com
Contact: Mr. Anthony Palmeri
          President

Intl. Technology Education Assn.

ITEA's mission is to advance everyone's technological capabilities and to nurture and promote the professionalism of those engaged in these pursuits. ITEA seeks to provide teaching and learning systems for developing technological literacy; foster research to advance technological literacy; serve as the catalyst in establishing technology education as the primary discipline for the advancement of technological literacy; and to increase the number and quality of people teaching technology.

1914 Association Drive - Suite 201
Reston VA 22091
703/860-2100   FAX 703/860-0353
E-mail: itea@iris.org   http://www.itea.org
Contact: Mr. Kendall Starkweather
          Executive Director

Intl. Telecommunications Satellite Organization (INTELSAT)

With 140 member countries, the organization provides global satellite voice, t.v. and data links.

3400 International Drive NW
Washington DC 20008-3098
202/944-6800   FAX 202/944-7898
http://www.intelsat.int
Contact: Ms. Diane Hinson
          Vice President and General Counsel

Intl. Thermographers Assn.

100 Daingerfield Road
Alexandria VA 22314
703/519-8122   FAX 703/548-3227
E-mail: ita@printing.org   http://www.printing.org
Contact: Ms. Alexandra Sharnoff
          Executive Director

Intl. Trade Commission Trial Lawyers Assn.

Since 1984, the association has been the primary organization informing attorneys around the world about Section 337 practice. It is a nonprofit, nonpartisan organization. Members and invited guests meet annually to review developments affecting Section 337 and to elect officers to lead the Association.

601 13th St., NW, Suite 500N

Washington DC 20005
202/626-6361   FAX 202/783-2331
E-mail: admin@itctla.org   http://www.itcla.org
Contact: Ms. Judith B. Oken
           Executive Director

Intl. Trade Council
A coalition of more than 800 commercial enterprises operating abroad, serving as liaison to the U.S. Congress and Administration, foreign embassies and international organizations in the interest of free trade and individual/corporate economic rights. Analyzes and provides information on trade and investment opportunities in over 200 countries.

3114 Circle Hill Road
Alexandria VA 22305-1606
703/684-1980   FAX 703/548-6216
E-mail: itctrade@erols.com
Contact: Dr. Peter T. Nelson
           President

Intl. Union for Conservation of Nature & Natural Resources - The World Conservation Union
IUCN brings together states, government agencies, and a range of nongovernmental organizations working to influence, encourage, and assist societies throughout the world to conserve the integrity and diversity of nature and to ensure that any use of natural resources is equitable and ecologically sustainable.

1400 16th Street, NW - Suite 502
Washington DC 20036
202/797-5454   FAX 202/797-5461
E-mail: postmaster@iucnus.org
Contact: Mr. Scott Hajost
           Executive Director

Intl. Union of Bricklayers & Allied Craftworkers
For past 150 years, the BAC has been the repository of all the trowel trades skills. The BAC represents its members and helps them improve their wages, hours, and working conditions, and provides a wide range of other benefits and services.

815 15th St., NW
Washington DC 20005
202/783-3788   FAX 202/393-0219
http://www.bacweb.org
Contact: Mr. John T. Joyce
           President

Intl. Union of Electronic, Electrical, Salaried, Machine, & Furniture Workers

1126 16th St., NW
Washington DC 20036
202/787-7207   FAX 202/785-7447
http://www.ive.org
Contact: Mr. Douglas Meyer
           Director, Research & Intl. Affairs

Intl. Union of Operating Engineers
The IUOE is a trade union representing heavy equipment operators and mechanics in the construction industry, as well as operations, maintenance and other workers, all referred to as stationary engineers, in building and industrial complexes and service industries throughout the U.S. and Canada.

1125 17th St., NW
Washington DC 20036

202/429-9100   FAX 202/778-2691
Contact: Mr. Frank Hanley
           General President

Intl. Union of Police Assns.

1421 Prince St. - Suite 330
Alexandria VA 22314
703/549-7473   FAX 703/683-9048
E-mail: IUPA@IUPA.org   http://www.sddi.com/iupa
Contact: Mr. Sam Cabral
           President

Intl. Voluntary Services
A voluntary development institution providing technical assistance primarily in rural areas and working with partner agencies in Bangladesh, Bolivia, Ecuador, Laos, Thailand, and Vietnam.

1901 Pennsylvania Ave., NW - Suite 501
Washington DC 20006
202/387-5533   FAX 202/466-5669
Contact: Ms. Anne Shirk
           Senior Associate, Program Development

Intl. Window Cleaning Assn.
Founded in 1989, the IWCA in a nonprofit trade association representing both commercial and residential window cleaning companies. It is committed to raising the standards of professionalism in the industry.

P.O. Box 10534
Rockville MD 20850
301/340-9560
E-mail: iwca@erols.com   http://www.iwca.org
Contact: Ms. Shannon M. Van Winter
           Executive Director

Intl. Women's Media Foundation
IWMF is a public, nonprofit organization dedicated to enhancing the role of women journalists in the media worldwide. The IWMF recognizes the enormous value of creating and strengthening networks among women dedicated to a brand of journalism that serves its community and the profession. It strives to create regional networks of professionals as well as a global organization. Founded in 1990, it promotes seminars, training sessions in the business of media, and forums for networking and professional exchange. The IWMF now has members in 100 countries who are predominantly women journalists, from both print and electronic media.

1001 Connecticut Ave., NW - Suite 1201
Washington DC 20036
202/496-1992   FAX 202/496-1977
E-mail: gloriaiwmf@aol.com
Contact: Ms. Gloria N. Kilburn
           Director of Outreach

Intl. Wood Products Assn. (IHPA)
An international trade association representing companies that handle imported wood products. IHPA advances responsible forest management and international trade in wood products through business, environmental and governmental affairs.

4214 King St. West
Alexandria VA 22302
703/820-6696   FAX 703/820-8550
E-mail: info@ihpa.org   http://www.ihpa.org
Contact: Ms. Wendy J. Baer
           Executive Vice President

Invest to Compete Alliance

The Alliance focuses on trade and taxation issues, emphasizing the need for American business to compete domestically and internationally.

1010 Pennsylvania Ave., SE
Washington DC 20003
202/546-4995   FAX 202/544-7926
Contact: Garland Miller
          Executive Director

Irish National Caucus

Self-described as an organization seeking a nonviolent solution to injustice and oppression in Northern Ireland, it aims to educate the U.S. public and policy makers on the situation in the six counties. The INC also initiated the MacBride Principles, a code of conduct for U.S. companies doing business in Northern Ireland.

413 E. Capitol Street, SE
Washington DC 20003
202/544-0568   FAX 202/543-2491
E-mail: inc@knight-hub.com   http://www.knight-hub.com/inc/
Contact: Fr. Sean McManus
          President

Israel Policy Forum

1225 15th St., NW
Washington DC 20005
202/462-4268   FAX 202/462-3892
E-mail: ipforum@aol.com   http://www.peacepulse.com
Contact: Mr. Thomas Smerling
          Executive Director

Italy - U.S. Business Conference of Washington DC

A member directed association dedicated to increasing the public's understanding of Italy's industrial, technological and financial capabilities.

801 Pennsylvania Ave., NW - Suite 350
Washington DC 20004
202/783-2261   FAX 202/783-1746
E-mail: bleblanc@nnsdc.com
Contact: Ms. Barbara LeBlanc
          Executive Director

Jamestown Foundation

The foundation seeks to monitor the evolution of the republics of the former Soviet Union; to provide information about, and analysis of, trends there which affect the vital interests of the U.S. and the West; and to encourage the development of democracy and free enterprise in that part of the world. Its publications include the Monitor and Prism.

1528 18th St., NW
Washington DC 20036
202/483-8888   FAX 202/483-8337
E-mail: Host@jamestown.org   http://www.jamestown.org
Contact: Mr. William W. Geimer
          Director

Japan Automobile Manufacturers Assn. (JAMA)

JAMA is a nonprofit trade association which was established in 1967. Because the automobile industry plays a major role both as employer and in Japan's overall manufacturing output, the association seeks to meet the diverse needs of consumers, at home and abroad.

1050 17th Street, NW, Suite 410
Washington DC 20036
202/296-8537   FAX 202/872-1212
http://www.japanauto.com
Contact: Dr. William C. Duncan
          General Director, Washington Office

Japan Economic Institute of America (JEI)

Founded in 1957, the institute is a nonprofit research organization supported in part by Japan's Ministry of Foreign Affairs and dedicated to promoting better understanding of U.S.-Japan issues. The institute has several publications and also sponsors seminars and informal talks featuring U.S. and Japanese government, business, and academic leaders.

1000 Connecticut Avenue, NW - Suite 211
Washington DC 20036
202/296-5633   FAX 202/296-8333
E-mail: aalexander@jei.org   http://www.jei.org
Contact: Mr. Arthur Alexander
          President

Japan Federation of Construction Contractors

Promoting the sound growth of the construction industry in Japan, JFCC has members from both Japanese and foreign construction companies.

1825 K Street, NW, Suite 1203
Washington DC 20006
202/466-3585   FAX 202/466-3586
Contact: Tetsuya Ishikawa
          Representative

Japan Information Access Project

Established in 1991, the Japan Information Access Project is a nonprofit. 501 (c) (3), research center that strengthens international understanding of Japanese information in science, technology, and public policy. The Project's goal is to teach professionals how to access, use, and evaluate Japanese information for research and planning.

2000 P St., NW - Suite 620
Washington DC 20036
202/822-6040   FAX 202/822-6044
E-mail: access@nmjc.org   http://www.nmjc.org/jiap
Contact: Ms. Mindy L. Kotler
          Director

Japan Iron and Steel Exporters Assn.

Conducts public relations activities to communicate the status of the Japanese steel industry and its position on current issues.

1155 21st Street, NW, Suite 600
Washington DC 20036
202/429-4766   FAX 202/463-9093
E-mail: dcjisea@msn.com
Contact: Mr. Yoshito Tamamura
          General Manager

Japan - U.S. Friendship Commission

Established by the U.S. Congress in 1976, the commission is a grant-making institution promoting educational and cultural exchange and policy research on the U.S. and Japan.

1120 Vermont Ave., NW - Suite 925
Washington DC 20005
202/275-7712   FAX 202/275-7413
E-mail: jusfc@compuserve.com

Contact: Dr. Eric Gangloff
Executive Director

Jewish Institute for Natl. Security Affairs

In favor of a strong U.S. defense posture, the institute provides information on defense matters to the American Jewish community and promotes security and defense cooperation between the U.S. and Israel.

1717 K Street, NW, Suite 800
Washington DC 20036
202/833-0020   FAX 202/296-6452
E-mail: info@jinsa.org   http://www.jinsa.org
Contact: Mr. Tom Neumann
Executive Director

Jewish Peace Lobby

With more than 3800 members, including over 250 rabbis, it seeks to influence U.S. foreign policy as to promote Middle-East peace.

8604 2nd Avenue - Suite 317
Silver Spring MD 20910
301/589-8764   FAX 301/589-2722
Contact: Dr. Jerome M. Segal
President

Joint Baltic American Natl. Committee

Founded in 1961 to support the restoration of independence and democracy to the Baltic republics by uniting the efforts of the Estonian American National Council, the American Latvian Association, and the Lithuanian American Council. The committee: acts as a liaison of the Baltic communities with Capitol Hill as well as the information agent to the parent organizations; assists the Estonian, Latvian, and Lithuanian people in strengthening democracy and free market economies in their countries; helps governmental and nongovernmental organizations formulate policies and programs that relate to the Baltic states by providing information and analysis on issues of importance to the Baltic communities; keeps the Baltic communities informed of U.S. government laws and policies pertaining to Estonia, Latvia, and Lithuania; and works to increase awareness of the languages, histories, and cultures of the Baltic people.

400 Hurley Ave.
Rockville MD 20850
301/340-1954   FAX 301/309-1406
E-mail: jbanc@jbanc.org   http://www.jbanc.org
Contact: Ms. Aija Straumanis
Director, Public Information

Joint Center for Political and Economic Studies

The Center aims to illuminate the nation's major public policy debates through research, analysis, and information dissemination. Areas of study for the Center, founded in 1970 by black intellectuals, professionals, and elected officials, include politics and elections, social issues, economic policy issues, and international affairs.

1090 Vermont Ave., NW - Suite 1100
Washington DC 20005-4961
202/789-3500   FAX 202/789-6390
http://www.jointctr.org
Contact: Mr. Eddie N. Williams
President

Joint Industry Group

Focusing on customs issues, the Joint Industry Group is a coalition of more than 100 trade associations, companies and professional firms with interests in international trade.

818 Connecticut Avenue, NW, 12th Floor
Washington DC 20006
202/466-5490   FAX 202/872-8696
E-mail: jig@moinc.com   http://www.moinc.com/jig
Contact: Mr. James B. Clawson
Secretariat

Juvenile Diabetes Foundation Intl.

1400 I St., NW - Suite 500
Washington DC 20005
202/371-9746   FAX 202/371-2760
Contact: Mr. William Schmidt
Director, Public Affairs

Kashmiri American Council

Seeks to foster Kashmiri's right to self determination through a free, fair and impartial plebiscite as assured under the U.N. Security Council resolutions of 1948 and 1949.

733 15th Street, NW, Suite 1100
Washington DC 20005
202/628-6789   FAX 202/393-0062
E-mail: kac@interserv.com
Contact: Dr. Ghulam Nabi Fai
Executive Director

Korea Economic Institute of America

Promotes U.S. - South Korean economic relations through research activities, seminars, conferences, and publications.

1101 Vermont Avenue, NW, Suite 401
Washington DC 20005
202/371-0690   FAX 202/371-0692
Contact: Mr. W. Robert Warne
President

Korea International Trade Assn. - DC Office

A private, member supported trade association representing the interests of South Korean exporters, importers, and overseas investors. It has offices across Asia, Europe, and the U.S.

1800 K St., NW, Suite 700
Washington DC 20006
202/828-4400   FAX 202/828-4404
E-mail: washing@kotis.net
Contact: Mr. Byoung-Joo Kim
Director, Public Relations and Research

Korea Trade Center

A South Korean government institution promoting the interests of Korean business overseas.

1129 20th Street, NW, Suite 410
Washington DC 20036
202/857-7919   FAX 202/857-7923
E-mail: dcktc@erols.com
Contact: Mr. Oh Nam Kwon
Director General

Laborers' Intl. Union of North America

905 16th St., NW
Washington DC 20006
202/737-8320   FAX 202/737-2754
http://www.liuna.org
Contact: Mr. Michael D. Boggs
Director, Intl. Affairs

Latin American Management Assn.

Founded in 1973, LAMA, formerly the Latin American Manufacturers Association, represents Hispanic small business owners involved in government contracting at the national level. It is involved in increasing the access of small businesses to government contracting opportunities, with the help of a number of minority organizations throughout the country. Its mission is to represent the Hispanic small business community at the federal level and promote avenues for small business development within that community.

419 New Jersey Ave., SE
Washington DC 20003-4007
202/546-3803   FAX 202/546-3807
Contact: Ms. Marina Laverdy
          Executive Director

Lawyers Alliance for World Security (LAWS/CNS)

LAWS is a nonprofit, nonpartisan membership organization of legal professionals dedicated to stopping unrestrained weapons proliferation and bringing the rule of law to the newly independent nations of the former Soviet Union.

1901 Pennsylvania Ave., NW Suite 802
Washington DC 20006
202/745-2450   FAX 202/667-0444
E-mail: disarmament@lawscns.org   http://www.lawscns.org
Contact: Ambassador Thomas Graham, Jr.
          President

Lawyers Committee for Human Rights

Since 1978, the LCHR has worked to protect and promote fundamental human rights. Its work is impartial, holding all governments accountable to the standards affirmed in the International Bill of Human Rights. Its programs focus on building the legal institutions and structures that will guarantee human rights in the long term. Strengthening independent human rights advocacy at the local level is a key feature of its work.

499 S. Capitol St., SW - Suite 508
Washington DC 20003
202/547-5692   FAX 202/543-5999
E-mail: wdc@Lchr.org   http://www.Lchr.org
Contact: Ms. Elisa Massimino
          Director, Washington Office

League of Arab States/Arab Information Center

The league was formally established on March 22, 1945, when seven founding member states, the only independent ones at the time, signed the constituent instrument, the Charter. The league is a national and regional organization that seeks to promote closer ties among member states and coordinate their policies and their economic, cultural, and security plans.

1100 17th St., NW, Suite 602
Washington DC 20036
202/265-3210   FAX 202/331-1525
Contact: Dr. Khalid Abdalla
          Chief Representative

Mail Advertising Service Assn. Intl.

MASA is a national trade association for the mailing services industry, comprised of 630 companies most of which are in the U.S. and Canada. For more than 75 years, it has worked to improve the business environment for mailing services companies and to provide opportunities for the learning and professional development of the management of these companies. MASA provides management education, employee training, business surveys, networking opportunities, postal information, other business news and individual help with technical, employment, and postal issues.

1421 Prince St., Suite 100
Alexandria VA 22314-2806
703/836-9200   FAX 703/548-8204
E-mail: masa@erols.com   http://www.masa.org
Contact: Mr. David A. Weaver
          President

Manufactured Imports Promotion Organization (MIPRO)

In 1978, the Japanese government joined with industry in establishing MIPRO, a new body to actively promote the import of manufactured products from countries all over the world. It also offers information on imported products, the Japanese market, and import procedures to Japanese consumers, Japanese businesses, and foreign businesses wishing to export to Japan.

2501 M St., NW - Suite 350
Washington DC 20037
202/659-3729   FAX 202/887-5159
Contact: Mr. Takeo Ijuin
          Director

Meridian Intl. Center

Formerly Meridian House International, the center was established in 1960 as a nonprofit institution dedicated to promoting intercultural understanding through the exchange of ideas, people, and the arts. The center is supported by both public contracts and private funds, and provides services to international diplomats and visitors, educational programs on global affairs, cultural events, and traveling art exhibitions.

1630 Crescent Place, NW
Washington DC 20009
202/667-6800   FAX 202/667-1475
E-mail: info@meridian.org http://www.meridian.org
Contact: Mr. Walter Cutler
          President

Mexico-U.S. Business Committee, U.S. Council

The U.S. Council is a standing committee of the Council of the Americas and is the oldest private-sector organization formed to increase trade and investment between Mexico and the U.S.

1310 G St., NW Suite 690
Washington DC 20005-3000
202/639-0724   FAX 202/639-0794
E-mail: coa1310@aol.com   http://www.counciloftheamericas.org
Contact: Ms. Lisa McLean
          Executive Director

Micronesia Institute

1275 K St., NW - Suite 360
Washington DC 20005-4006
202/842-1140   FAX 202/842-1150
Contact: Mr. Samuel Thomsen
          President

Mid-America Committee, The

An organization of U.S. CEOs based in Chicago, the committee presents its views on foreign policy, economics, trade, and investment issues to U.S. and foreign policy makers.

1025 Thomas Jefferson St., NW, Suite 700 E. Lobby
Washington DC 20007
202/625-3595   FAX 202/625-3599
Contact: Mr. Tom Miner
          President

Middle East Institute

Founded in 1946, the institute seeks to foster U.S. understanding of events in the Middle East. By charter, however, it may not seek to impact legislation or become a policy instrument.

1761 N Street, NW
Washington DC 20036-2882
202/785-1141   FAX 202/331-8861
E-mail: mei@mideasti.org http://www.mideasti.org/mei
Contact: Ambassador Roscoe Suddarth
          President

Middle East Policy Council

A nonprofit institution established in 1981 and aimed at expanding the public debate on the Middle East through conferences, teacher workshops, and the journal Middle East Policy.

1730 M Street, NW - Suite 512
Washington DC 20036
202/296-6767   FAX 202/296-5791
E-mail: ajoyce@mepc.org http://www.mepc.org
Contact: Ms. Anne Joyce
          Vice President

Middle East Research and Information Project

The MERIP was established 26 years ago to provide information and analysis on the Middle East that would be picked up by the existing media. The organization is nonprofit and independent, with no links to any religious, educational, or political organizations in the U.S. or elsewhere. Its magazine Middle East Report is published four times a year.

1500 Massachusetts Ave., NW - Suite 119
Washington DC 20005
202/223-3677   FAX 202/223-3604
E-mail: meripweb@igc.org http://www.merip.org
Contact: Mr. Joe Stork
          Editor

Mortgage Bankers Assn. of America

MBAA is a trade association representing some 2,000 members in the real estate finance industry

1125 15th St., NW
Washington DC 20005-2707
202/861-6568   FAX 202/861-0736
Contact: Ms. Debbie Erb
          International Division

Motor & Equipment Manufacturers Assn.

Founded in 1904, MEMA caters to the needs of manufacturers of products used in, on, or for the service of motor vehicles. MEMA provides services that are sharply focused responses to the specific needs and concerns of manufacturers.

1225 New York Ave., NW - Suite 300
Washington DC 20005
202/393-6362   FAX 202/737-3742
Contact: Mr. Christopher M. Bates
          President, International Operations

NAFSA: Assn. of Intl. Educators

NAFSA promotes the exchange of students and scholars to and from the U.S. The association sets and upholds standards of good practice, and provides professional education and training to strengthen the institutional programs and services related to international education exchange.

1875 Connecticut Ave., NW - Suite 1000
Washington DC 20009-5728
202/462-4811   FAX 202/667-3419
E-mail: inbox@nafsa.org   http://www.nafsa.org
Contact: Ms. Marlene M. Johnson
          Executive Director

Natl. Assn. of Arab Americans

A membership organization founded in 1972, NAAA lobbies the U.S. Congress and Administration for an evenhanded U.S. foreign policy based on justice and peace for all people of the region and is involved in a wide range of issues pertaining to U.S.-Arab bilateral relations.

1212 New York Ave., N.W - Suite 230
Washington DC 20005
202/842-1840   FAX 202/842-1614
E-mail: naaainc@aol.com   http://www.steele.com/naaa
Contact: Mr. Khalil E. Jahshan
          President

Natl. Assn. of Beverage Importers, Inc. (NABI)

Founded in 1934, NABI seeks to help the more than 2,000 U.S. importers of beverage alcohol operate more efficiently and profitably by providing timely information, aggressive representation, advice on technical and political matters, and a network of domestic and international contacts.

1025 Vermont Ave., NW - Suite 1066
Washington DC 20005
202/638-1617   FAX 202/638-3122
Contact: Mr. Robert J. Maxwell
          President

Natl. Assn. of Broadcasters

NAB represents the radio and television industries in Washington, before Congress, federal agencies, the courts, and on the expanding international front. It provides leadership and resources to its members through ongoing public service campaigns.

1771 N St., NW
Washington DC 20036-2805
202/429-5300   FAX 202/429-5410
http://www.nab.org
Contact: Ms. Terri Rabel
          Senior VP, Operations and Bus. Development

Natl. Assn. of Chain Drug Stores, Inc.

Founded in 1933, NACDS includes more than 135 chain companies ranging in size from four to over 2,500 pharmacies. Operating 30,000 retail community pharmacies, chain pharmacies comprise the largest component of pharmacy practice with over 86,000 pharmacists. NACDS membership includes more than 1,200 suppliers of goods and services to chain drug stores. Its international membership has grown to include 67 members from 22 foreign countries.

413 North Lee St. - P.O. Box 1417-D49
Alexandria VA 22313-1417
703/549-3001   FAX 703/836-4869
Contact: Mr. Frank Cummins
          Director of Intl. Trade Relations

Natl. Assn. of Foreign Trade Zones

Seeks to promote and improve the utilization of FTZs as tools for community economic development and abetting the global competitiveness of U.S. companies. Also works to enhance communication between U.S. government regulators and legislators and FTZ grantees, operators and users.

1000 Connecticut Avenue, NW - Suite 1001
Washington DC 20036
202/331-1950   FAX 202/331-1994
Contact: Ms. Brandi Hanback
          Executive Director

Natl. Assn. of Manufacturers
The mandate of NAM is to enhance the future competitiveness of
U.S. industry by helping to promote government policies fostering
U.S. industrial growth and global economic growth.

1331 Pennsylvania Ave., NW - Suite 600
Washington DC 20004-1790
202/637-3000   FAX 202/637-3182
E-mail: dsullivan@nam.org   http://www.nam.org
Contact: Ms. Dianne Sullivan
          Director, Trade Policy

Natl. Assn. of Realtors
700 11th St., NW
Washington DC 20001-4507
202/383-1000   FAX 202/383-7528
http://www.realtor.com

Contacts:
Ms. Therese Salmon
   Manager Intl. Operations
Mr. Scott Sherwood
   Intl. Operations Representative

Natl. Assn. of Secondary School Principals/Partnerships Intl.
SPI is a short term school-to-school pairing program designed to foster
long term academic and cultural partnerships between secondary
schools in the U.S. and other countries. Once schools are linked, a
group of 6-15 students, accompanied by a faculty member, visits their
partner school for approximately three weeks. During this time,
students live in the homes of host students, attend classes, participate
in school and community activities, learn about another way of life,
and discover local points of interest.

1904 Association Dr.
Reston VA 20191
703/860-7267   FAX 703/476-9319
E-mail: jacksonr@nassp.com
Contact: Mr. Randall Jackson
          Acting Director

Natl. Assn. of Social Workers
NASW is an organization of professional social workers with nearly
150,000 members representing approximately 50 percent of the
national social work labor force. There are 55 NASW chapters in the
U.S., Puerto Rico, the Virgin Islands, and abroad. NASW works to
protect consumers by working to improve state laws that license social
workers, setting social work practice standards, enforcing a Code of
Ethics, and publishing personnel standards for agencies.

750 First St. NE #700
Washington DC 20002-4241
202/408-8600   FAX 202/336-8310
E-mail: info@naswdc.org   http://www.socialworkers.org
Contact: Ms. Latisha Diaz
          Director Peace/Intl. Affairs

Natl. Assn. of State Development Agencies
750 First St., NE - Suite 710
Washington DC 20002
202/898-1302   FAX 202/898-1312

Contact: Mr. Miles Friedman
          Executive Director

Natl. Assn. of Wheat Growers (NAWG)
NAWG was founded in 1950 to be the voice of all U.S. wheat growers,
especially in matters relating to production and marketing of wheat.
NAWG is a lobbying organization and one of its main goals is to
keep its approximately 30,000 members aware of the legislative and
regulatory issues that can affect their farming operations.

415 2nd St., N.E. Suite 300
Washington DC 20002-4993
202/547-7800   FAX 202/546-2638
Contact: Ms. Wendy McDavid
          Information Director

Natl. Center for Economic and Security Alternatives
A non-profit corporation established in 1977 providing research,
education, and consultation on innovative solutions to problems that
face the American economy. Its work includes global issues from the
capacity of traditional reforms to alter destructive ecological and other
long-term trends, to international security concerns related to arms
control and disarmament. Since 1992, the Center has given increasing
emphasis to the relationship of affirmed values to system-wide
problems.

2000 P Street, NW - Suite 330
Washington DC 20036-6923
202/835-1150   FAX 202/835-1152
E-mail: ncesa1@igc.org
Contact: Mr. Ted Howard
          Executive Director

Natl. Chamber Foundation
A nonprofit public policy research institute affiliated with the Chamber
of Commerce of the U.S.A.

1615 II St., NW
Washington DC 20062-2000
202/463-5620   FAX 202/463-3174
Contact: Mr. Martin Regalia
          Executive Vice President

Natl. Conference on Soviet Jewry
Founded in 1964 as the major national coordinating agency for action
and policy on behalf of Jews in the Soviet Union, and now working
in the republics of the former Soviet Union.

1640 Rhode Island Ave., NW - 5th Floor
Washington DC 20036-3278
202/898-2500   FAX 202/898-0822
E-mail: NCSJ@erols.com
Contact: Mr. Mark Levin
          Executive Director

Natl. Council for Intl. Health
Nonprofit institution working to enhance the U.S. response to
international health issues, focusing heavily on the concerns of
developing nations.

1701 K St., NW - Suite 600
Washington DC 20006-1503
202/833-5900   FAX 202/833-0075
E-mail: ncih@ncih.org
Contact: Ms. Karen Sarrell
          Director, Communications

Natl. Council for Intl. Visitors

Coordinates a network of volunteer community organizations and national programming agencies which welcome and assist short-term visitors to the U.S. on international exchange and training programs.

1420 K Street, NW - Suite 800
Washington DC 20005
202/842-1414   FAX 202/289-4625
E-mail: jdenton@nciu.org   http://www.nciu.org
Contact: Ms. Julie Snyder Denton
          Director of Programs

Natl. Council for Languages and Intl. Studies

The Council is made up of 64 language and international studies organizations.

1118 22nd St., NW
Washington DC 20037
202/466-2666   FAX 202/466-2892
E-mail: info@languagepolicy.org
Contact: Dr. J. David Edwards
          Executive Director

Natl. Council on Intl. Trade Development (NCITD)

The council is a nonprofit, membership based organization focused on promoting global trade facilitation. It is comprised of over 100 major companies active in all areas associated with international trade including manufacturing, banking, transportation, brokering, freight forwarding, and consulting.

1200 19th St., NW - Suite 300
Washington DC 20036
202/828-6046   FAX 202/872-8696
Contact: Mr. Jim Wheeler
          Chairman of the Board

Natl. Council on U.S.-Arab Relations

Founded in 1983, the National Council on U.S.-Arab Relations is an American non-profit organization dedicated to improving American knowledge and understanding of the Arab world.

1140 Connecticut Ave., NW Suite 1210
Washington DC 20036
202/293-0801   FAX 202/293-0903
E-mail: info@ncusar.org   http://www.ncusar.org
Contact: Dr. John D. Anthony
          President and CEO

Natl. Customs Brokers & Forwarders Ass'n. of America

Founded in 1897, the NCBFAA is the trade association of customs brokers and international freight forwarders in the United States. Its membership includes brokers and forwarders in 33 affiliated associations.

1200 18th St., NW - Suite 901
Washington DC 20036
202/466-0222   FAX 202/466-0226
E-mail: staff@ncbfaa.org   http://www.tradecompass.com/ncbfaa/
Contact: Mr. Eric G. Scharf
          Executive Vice President

Natl. Democratic Institute for Intl. Affairs

1717 Massachusetts Ave., NW - Suite 503
Washington DC 20036
202/328-3136   FAX 202/939-3166
Contact: Ms. Jean B. Dunn
          Vice President, Development

Natl. Endowment for Democracy

The endowment is a private nonprofit organization created in 1983 to strengthen democratic institutions around the world through nongovernmental efforts. Through its worldwide grant program, it assists those abroad who are working for democratic goals.

1101 15th St., NW Suite 700
Washington DC 20005
202/293-9072   FAX 202/223-6042
E-mail: info@ned.org   http://www.ned.org
Contact: Mr. Carl Gershman
          President

Natl. Foreign Trade Council

The council was founded in 1914 by a group of U.S. industrial companies engaged in international trade and investment. The council has been a leading spokesman on behalf of the private sector for an open international trade and investment regime embodied in international agreements such as the World Trade Organization, formerly the General Agreement on Tariffs and Trade. The council has opposed government policies that constrain competitiveness, such as foreign policy sanctions, while encouraging a positive government role in such matters as export finance.

1625 K Street, NW, Suite 1090
Washington DC 20006
202/887-0278   FAX 202/452-8160
Contact: Mr. Frank Kittredge
          President

Natl. Grain Trade Council

Represents both domestic and international interests of the U.S. grain trade industry, focusing on futures trading, farm policy and agricultural trade programs. Its regular, policy making members are grain exchanges, boards of trade, and national grain marketing organizations, with associate members from grain and transportation companies, futures merchants, processing companies, banks and ports.

1300 L Street, NW, Suite 925
Washington DC 20005
202/842-0400   FAX 202/789-7223
Contact: Mr. Robert R. Petersen
          President

Natl. Institute for Public Policy

A nonprofit corporation founded in 1981 to promote public education on international issues, it provides wide-ranging analysis in the public interest, integrating political, military, historical, social, and economic perspectives.

3031 Wavier Rd. - Suite 300
Fairfax VA 22031
703/698-0563   FAX 703/698-0566
Contact: Dr. Keith B. Payne
          President

Natl. Institute of Oilseed Products

The National Institute of Oilseed Products (NIOP) is an international trade association with the principal objective of promoting the general business welfare of persons, firms, and corporations engaged in the buying, selling, processing, shipping, storage, and use of vegetable oils and raw materials. Over 60 years old, the organization has approximately 300 member firms in 25 countries.

1101 15th St., NW - Suite 202
Washington DC 20005-5008
202/785-3232   FAX 202/223-9741
E-mail: niop@assnhq.com   http://www.oilseed.org
Contact: Mr. Richard E. Cristol
          Washington Representative

Natl. League of Families of American Prisoners Missing in Southeast Asia

The league was incorporated in the District of Columbia in 1970. Membership is comprised solely of the wives, children, parents and other close relatives of Americans who were or are listed as prisoners of war, missing in action, killed in action/body not recovered in Southeast Asia, and returned POWs. It is a nonprofit, nonpartisan organization with the sole purpose of obtaining the release of all prisoners, the fullest account of the missing, and the repatriation of all recoverable remains of those who died serving the U.S. in Southeast Asia.

1001 Connecticut Ave., NW - Suite 919
Washington DC 20036-5504
202/223-6846   FAX 202/785-9410
E-mail: info@pow-miafamilies.org
Contact: Ms. Ann Mills Griffiths
          Executive Director

Natl. PAC, The

NatPAC was founded in 1982 and is the largest bipartisan, nonconnected PAC dedicated to promoting strong U.S. support for the survival and security of Israel.

600 Pennsylvania Ave., S.E.
Washington DC 20003
202/879-7710   FAX 202/879-7728
Contact: Mr. Charles D. Brooks
          Executive Director

Natl. Peace Foundation

The foundation is a private, nonpartisan, nonprofit organization with a membership nationwide of approximately 10,000 members. It seeks to promote peace building and conflict resolution on every level from the community, to the regional, to the national and international.

1835 K Street NW - Suite 610
Washington DC 20006
202/223-1770   FAX 202/223-1718
E-mail: npifnatl@igc.apc.org
Contact: Ms. Kathleen Lansing
          Deputy Director

Natl. Policy Association

The National Policy Association (formerly the National Planning Association) is a nonpartisan, nonprofit research institution founded in 1934 on the conviction that the private sector should participate actively in the making of public policy. The NPA provides a forum where business, labor, agricultural, and academic leaders come together in six policy committees to focus on economic and social issues of mutual concern and national significance.

1424 16th St., NW - Suite 700
Washington DC 20036
202/265-7685   FAX 202/797-5516
E-mail: npa@npa1.org   http://www.npa1.org
Contact: Mr. Malcom R. Lovell, Jr.
          President

Natl. Research Council

The NRC is the operating arm of the National Academy of Sciences, chartered by act of Congress on March 3, 1863 to advise the federal government on questions of science and technology.

2101 Constitution Ave., NW
Washington DC 20418
202/334-2000   FAX 202/334-1684
E-mail: news@nas.edu   http://www.nas.edu/nrc

Contact: Dr. Bruce M. Alberts
          President

Natl. Retail Federation

The NRF is the world's largest retail trade association with membership that includes department, specialty, discount, mass merchandise, and independent stores, as well as 32 national and 50 state associations. NRF members represent an industry that encompasses over 1.4 million U.S. retail establishments, employs more than 20 million people, and registered 1997 sales of $2.5 trillion. Its international members operate stores in more than 50 nations. NRF committees include the International Trade Advisory Committee, the Information Technology Council, the Small Stores Board of Directors, the Credit Management Advisory Council, and the Retail Privacy Council.

325 7th St., NW - Suite 1000
Washington DC 20004-2802
202/783-7971   FAX 202/737-2849
E-mail: nrf@mcimail.com   http://www.nrf.com
Contact: Ms. Tracy Mullin
          President

Natl. Security Archive

An independent nongovernmental research institute and library.

2130 H St., NW Suite 701
Washington DC 20037
202/994-7000   FAX 202/994-7005
E-mail: nsarchiv@gwu.edu http://www.seas.gwu.edu/nsarchive
Contact: Mr. Tom Blanton
          Executive Director

Natl. Strategy Information Center

A nonprofit education institution established in 1962 concerned with national security matters.

1730 Rhode Island Avenue, NW, Suite 500
Washington DC 20036
202/429-0129   FAX 202/659-5429
E-mail: nsic@ix.netcom.com
Contact: Dr. Roy Godson
          President

Natl. Telephone Cooperative Assn.

NTCA's International Division promotes the development of community-owned telephone systems in rural areas of the developing world and CEE countries that would otherwise go unserved or badly under served.

2626 Pennsylvania Ave. NW
Washington DC 20037-1695
202/298-2300   FAX 202/298-2320
E-mail: frs@ntca.org
Contact: Ms. Marlee R. Norton
          Director, International and Domestic Program Development

Natl. U.S. - Arab Chamber of Commerce

The mission of the NUSACC is to promote trade and commercial ties between the U.S. and the Arab world. It provides information products, services, and business contacts.

1100 New York Ave., NW - Suite 550 East Tower
Washington DC 20005-3934
202/289-5920   FAX 202/289-5938
E-mail: nusacc@aol.com   http://www.nusacc.org
Contact: Mr. Richard P. Holmes
          President

Netherlands Chamber of Commerce in the U.S.

Founded in 1903, the Netherlands Chamber is the largest and oldest Dutch American business group with some 500 members in the Netherlands and the U.S. The chamber's mission is to maintain and expand business relations between the two countries.

4200 Wisconsin Ave., NW - Suite 106-227
Washington DC 20016
202/393-1376   FAX 202/244-3325
E-mail: ncocdc@compuserve.com   http://www.netherlands.org
Contact: Mr. Simon De Jong
          Office Mgr.

Network in Solidarity with the People in Guatemala (NISGUA)

NISGUA is a network of 180 U.S. citizen's groups established to support grassroots movements in Guatemala in their struggle to build meaningful democracy there. Its publications include the quarterly news magazine, Report on Guatemala, and the bi-monthly Solidarity Update newsletter.

1830 Connecticut Ave., NW
Washington DC 20009
202/518-7638   FAX 202/223-8221
E-mail: nisgua@igc.apc.org
http://www.scruz.net/~goyo/nisgua/home.html/
Contact: Ms. Kathryn Irwin
          Coordinator

Network of East-West Women

1601 Connecticut Ave., NW - Suite 603
Washington DC 20009
202/265-3585   FAX 202/265-3508
Contact: Ms. Melissa Stone
          Acting Executive Director

New Directions for Policy

1015 18th St., NW - Suite 210
Washington DC 20036-5203
202/833-8877   FAX 202/833-8932
E-mail: jmesrindp@aol.com
Contact: Dr. Jack A. Meyer
          President

Nixon Center, The

A nonpartisan public policy institution founded in 1994 as an independent division of the Richard Nixon Library and Birthplace Foundation. The Center is committed to the analysis of policy challenges to the US through the prism of American national interest.

1615 L Street, NW - Suite 1250
Washington DC 20036
202/887-1000   FAX 202/887-5222
E-mail: nixonctr@erols.comhttp://www.nixonfoundation.org
Contact: Mr. Paul J. Saunders
          Director

Nonproliferation Policy Education Center

The NPEC, a project of the Institute for International Studies, is a nonpartisan, nonprofit, educational organization founded in 1994 to promote a better understanding of strategic weapons proliferation issues. NPEC educates policymakers, journalists, and university professors about proliferation threats and possible new policies and measures to meet them.

1718 M St., NW - Suite 244

Washington DC 20036
202/466-4406   FAX 202/659-5429
E-mail: npec@ix.netcom.com   http://www.wizard.net/~npec
Contact: Mr. Henry Sokolski
          Executive Director

North American Export Grain Assn. (NAEGA)

The association of grain and oil seed exporters and interested parties whose purpose is to promote and sustain the development of export grain, oil seed, and related agricultural products exports from the U.S.

1300 L Street, NW - Suite 900
Washington DC 20005
202/682-4030   FAX 202/682-4033
E-mail: naega@internetmci.com
Contact: Mr. Daniel G. Amstutz
          President/CEO

North American Free Trade Association

Trilateral business organization promoting investment and trade among the U.S., Canada, and Mexico. Assists member companies with the identification and pursuance of commercial opportunities through research, publications, trade missions, and conferences.

1150 18th St., NW - 9th Floor
Washington DC 20036
202/296-3019   FAX 202/296-3037
Contact: Mr. Brian Marshall
          Vice President, Public Affairs

Northern Ireland - U.S. Chamber of Commerce, Inc.

P.O. Box 17370
Washington DC 20041
703/471-1661   FAX 703/661-8251
Contact: Mr. Tony R. Culley-Foster
          Chairman

Nuclear Control Institute

Founded in 1981, the institute is a nonprofit educational organization seeking to stop proliferation of sensitive nuclear technology and facilities.

1000 Connecticut Avenue, NW, Suite 804
Washington DC 20036
202/822-8444   FAX 202/452-0892
http://www.nci.org/nci/
Contact: Mr. Paul Leventhal
          President

Of Human Rights

Of Human Rights is an independent, non-profit organization dedicated to the promotion of human rights in Cuba and to informing decision-makers about the dictatorial character of Fidel Castro's government. Founded in 1975 at Georgetown University by Cuban American students and professors, Of Human Rights has carried out numerous campaigns on behalf of Cuban political prisoners. The organization publishes occasional reports on the human rights situation in Cuba, and sponsors round-table discussions and other programs about Cuba. OHR seeks donations of medicines and antibiotics for pro-democracy organizations inside Cuba.

1319 18th St., NW
Washington DC 20036
202/296-8020
Contact: Msgr. Eduardo Boza-Masvidal
          Chairman

Office and Professional Employees Intl. Union

1660 L St., NW - Suite 801
Washington DC 20006
202/393-4464   FAX 202/347-0649
Contact: Mr. Gilles Beauregard
          Secretary-Treasurer

Oil, Chemical and Atomic Workers Intl. Union

2722 Merrilee Dr., Suite 250
Fairfax VA 22031
703/876-9300   FAX 703/876-8952
Contact: Mr. Pete Strader
          Intl. Representative

Organization for Economic Cooperation and Development (OECD)

An international, inter-governmental organization, and the successor of the Organization for European Economic Cooperation created in 1948 for the implementation of the Marshall Plan, OECD now boasts 29 member states from the industrialized world. The original 18 European states, the U.S. and Canada have since been joined by Australia, Finland, Japan, Korea, New Zealand, Mexico, Hungary, Poland and the Czech Republic. Its mandate is to push for the highest level of sustainable economic growth, employment and living standards in member countries, while maintaining international financial stability, and to promote the expansion of world trade and assist economic development in non-member states.

2001 L St., NW, Suite 650
Washington DC 20036-4910
202/785-6323   FAX 202/785-0350
E-mail: bill.danvers@oecd.org   http://www.oecdwash.org
Contact: Mr. Bill Danvers
          Head of OECD Wash. Ctr.

Organization for Intl. Investment

A Washington DC-based association representing the U.S. subsidiaries of foreign companies. OFII's member companies range from medium-sized enterprises to some of the largest firms in the U.S. OFII's mandate is to explain to policy makers and the public, the positive economic contributions its members make to the U.S. economy and to ensure that US subsidiaries receive nondiscriminatory treatment under U.S. federal and state law.

1901 Pennsylvania Avenue, NW - Suite 807
Washington DC 20006
202/659-1903   FAX 202/659-2293
http://www.ofii.org
Contact: Mr. Todd Malan
          Executive Director

Organization of American States (OAS)

The OAS is a regional, intergovernmental organization whose primary purposes are to preserve peace an security and to promote, by cooperative action, the integral development of the member states. Organized in its present form in 1948, its roots date from 1890, making it the oldest regional, international organization in the world.

The OAS member states are Argentina, Antigua and Barbuda, Commonwealth of the Bahamas, Barbados, Belize, Bolivia, Brazil, Canada, Chile, Colombia, Costa Rica, Cuba, Commonwealth of Dominica, Dominican Republic, Ecuador, El Salvador, Granada, Guatemala, Guyana, Haiti, Honduras, Jamaica, Mexico, Nicaragua, Panama, Paraguay, Peru, St. Kitts and Nevis, St. Lucia, St. Vincent and the Grenadines, Suriname, Trinidad and Tobago, the U.S., Uruguay, and Venezuela. The present Government of Cuba is excluded from participation by a decision of the Consultation of Ministers of Foreign Affairs in 1962. 29 non-American countries

and the European Union are Permanent Observers.

17th Street and Constitution Avenue, NW
Washington DC 20006
202/458-3841

Contacts:
Mr. Cesar Gaviria
    Secretary General
Mr. Thomas Bruce
    Director of Public Information

Organization of Women in Intl. Trade

A world wide network of international trade and business professionals, OWIT was founded in 1989 and currently has 20 chapters in the U.S., Bermuda and Mexico. The membership of 3,500 women and men are executives and entrepreneurs involved in all aspects of international business. OWIT works to enhance the roles of women in the global economy, providing an annual conference, professional forums, newsletters, member directory, and networking.

P.O. Box 65962
Washington DC 20035
301/785-9842
http://www.owit.org
Contact: Ms. June Dehlart
          DC Chapter President

Overseas Development Council

A private, independent organization, the ODC works to enhance the understanding of the U.S. public and policy makers of issues related to global economic and social development and how U.S. policy may impact these initiatives.

1875 Connecticut Avenue, NW, Suite 1012
Washington DC 20009
202/234-8701   FAX 202/745-0067
Contact: Mr. John W. Sewell
          President

Oxfam America

Oxfam America, a private international relief and development agency, works in partnership with disenfranchised communities to overcome global hunger and poverty. The organization emphasizes the elimination of the oppression of women as a necessary step toward true long-term development.

1511 K St., NW - Suite 640
Washington DC 20005
202/783-7302   FAX 202/783-8739
E-mail: gabrielac@igc.apc.org
http://www.charity.org/oxfam.html
Contact: Ms. Bernice Romero
          Advocacy Coordinator

Pacific Basin Economic Council - U.S. Member Cmte.

PBEC is a private regional multilateral association of business leaders dedicated to the expansion of trade and investment in the Pacific region. Founded in 1967, it works to achieve a business environment in the region that ensures open trade and investment and encourages competitiveness based on the capabilities of individual companies: to provide information, networking, and services to members that increase their business opportunities; and to support cooperative business efforts to address the economic well-being of its citizens in the region. The Council has also established working committees to develop PBEC policy on key issues to the region's business community.

Today, PBEC includes more than 1,000 firms in twenty Pacific Rim economies. There are Member Committees in the U.S., Australia,

Canada, Chile, China, Colombia, Fiji, Hong Kong, Indonesia, Japan, Korea, Malaysia, Mexico, New Zealand, Peru, the Philippines, Russia, Chinese Taipei, and Thailand. There is also a PBEC Applicant Member Committee in Ecuador.

1667 K St., NW - Suite 410
Washington DC 20006
202/293-5730   FAX 202/289-1940
E-mail: pbecus@p1.apfnet.org
http://www.econstrat.com/econstrat/pbec.htm
Contact: Ms. Ann R. Wise
          Director General

Pacific Economic Cooperation Council

Formed in 1980 at the behest of Pacific governments, the PECC combines the knowledge and resources of businesses, research institutions, and government agencies to develop new strategies for Asia-Pacific economic cooperation. Upon the founding of the intergovernmental organization on Asia-Pacific Economic Cooperation (APEC) in 1989, the PECC became the accredited private observer body to APEC, and has since worked in partnership with APEC.

1112 16th St., NW - Suite 520
Washington DC 20036
202/293-3995   FAX 202/293-1402
E-mail: uspecc@erols.com   http://www.pecc.org
Contact: Mr. Mark Borthwick
          Executive Director

Pakistani-American Business Assn.

PABA is a nonprofit bilateral trade association that seeks to promote business and commercial relations between Pakistan and the U.S. Founded in 1990, it works to assist the governments of both countries in establishing a dialogue and better understanding of the problems as well as opportunities in Pakistan for PABA members.

801 Pennsylvania Ave., NW, Suite 815
Washington DC 20004
202/508-3423   FAX 202/508-3402
E-mail: farrakh@aol.com
Contact: Mr. Farrakk Shah
          President

Palestine Affairs Center

Represents Palestinian interests at the League of Arab States in the U.S.

1730 K Street, NW, Suite 1004
Washington DC 20006
202/785-8394   FAX 202/887-5337
Contact: Mr. Hasan Abdel Rahman
          Director and Chief P.L.O. Representative

Pan American Development Foundation

PADF is a private nonprofit organization affiliated with the Organization of American States, with field offices in Haiti, El Salvador, and Bolivia. Founded in 1962, it works to strengthen the institutions of civil society which help the poor to help themselves.

2600 16th St., NW
Washington DC 20006
202/458-3970   FAX 202/458-6316
E-mail: pgarcia@gwis2.circ.gwu.edu
http://www.interaction.org/mb/padf.html
Contact: Mr. Peter Reitz
          Executive Director

Pan American Health Organization

PAHO is an international public health agency working to improve health and living standards of the countries of the Americas.

525 23rd Street, NW
Washington DC 20037
202/974-3178   FAX 202/974-3608
http://www.paho.org
Contact: Dr. David Brandling Bennett
          Deputy Director

Panos Institute, The

The Panos Institute disseminates information on sustainable development issues in the Americas through print media, radio productions, and book productions in Central America and the Caribbean. The organization also conducts training workshops for journalists.

1701 K St., NW - Suite 1100
Washington DC 20006
202/223-7949   FAX 202/223-7947
E-mail: panos@cais.com
Contact: Ms. Melanie Oliviero
          Executive Director

Partners of the Americas, Inc.

Established in 1964, the association is now the largest private, nonprofit, volunteer based organization for the promotion of economic, social, and human development centering on the Western hemisphere. Besides providing technical assistance and training to communities in Latin America, the Caribbean, and the U.S., Partners' network of volunteers promote collaboration in the region's social and economic development through working relationships among professionals and institutions across the hemisphere.

1424 K Street, NW, #700
Washington DC 20005
202/628-3300   FAX 202/628-3306
E-mail: info@partners.poa.com   http://www.partners.net
Contact: Mr. William S. Reese
          President

Pax World Service

Pax World Service's Sustainable Development Program works in partnership with community-based sustainable development organizations in Central America, the Caribbean, the Middle East, Eastern Europe, and Central Asia to support initiatives that benefit low-income producers and the environment. The Service also maintains the Pax World Fund mutual fund, which uses both financial and social criteria to select its holdings.

1111 16th St., NW - Suite 120
Washington DC 20036
202/293-7290   FAX 202/293-7023
E-mail: info@paxworld.org http://www.paxworld.org
Contact: Mr. Larry Ekin
          President

Peace Action

The organization works to develop public support for policies that will lead toward peace, including nuclear disarmament, reduced military spending, and a non-interventionist foreign policy. Formerly known as SANE/FREEZE: Campaign for Global Security, it also sponsors the Peace Action PAC.

1819 H St., NW - Suite 420
Washington DC 20006-3603
202/862-9740   FAX 202/862-9762
E-mail: paexec@igc.org   http://www.webcom.com/peaceact
Contact: Mr. William Sloane Coffin
          President, Advisory Board

Peace Links - Women Making a Difference!
A national, nonpartisan activist network of over 30,000 concerned citizens, including Congressional and Gubernatorial women, Peace Links primary mission is to promote violence prevention and non-violent conflict resolution at local and international levels.

729 8th St., SE - Suite 300
Washington DC 20003
202/544-0805   FAX 202/544-0809
E-mail: peacelinks@igc.apc.org
Contact: Ms. Donnan Beeson Runkel
          Director

Peace PAC
Peace PAC is a nonpartisan, grassroots political action committee that supports candidates for the U.S. House of Representatives who are committed to nuclear arms control, nuclear disarmament, the prevention of nuclear war, and significant reductions in military spending. It was founded in 1982 as an affiliate of the Council for a Livable World.

110 Maryland Ave., NE - Suite 409
Washington DC 20002
202/543-4100   FAX 202/543-6297
E-mail: skerr@clw.org   http://www.clw.org/pub/clw/
Contact: Ms. Suzanne S. Kerr
          Executive Director

Pharmaceutical Research and Manufacturers of America
Serves as the national representative for U.S. research-based pharmaceutical companies.

1100 15th Street, NW, Suite 900
Washington DC 20005
202/835-3400   FAX 202/728-3932
http://www.phrma.org
Contact: Mr. Shannon S.S. Herzfeld
          Senior Vice President, Intl.

Piedmont World Trade Council
The council works to encourage the growth of international trade in Central Virginia as well as in the U.S., with members including both large and small manufacturers; shippers; brokers; bankers; exporters and importers; college professors and students; and government planners for economic development.

Box 1374
Lynchburg VA 24505-1374
804/384-3454   FAX 804/525-2222
Contact: Ms. Barbara Wiley
          President

PlanEcon Research Associates, Inc.
A consulting firm specializing in Russian and Eastern European affairs.

1111 14th St., NW - Suite 801
Washington DC 20005
202/898-0471   FAX 202/898-0445
Contact: Dr. Keith Crane
          Research Director

Polish - U.S. Economic Council
Sponsored by the U.S. Chamber of Commerce, the council works to improve trade and investment prospects for U.S. business in the Polish market. For over 20 years the council has focused on bilateral relations between the U.S. and Poland, promoting a secure business environment that is hospitable to private sector development and free

enterprise.

1615 H St., NW
Washington DC 20062
202/463-5482   FAX 202/463-3114
E-mail: eurasia@uschamber.com   http://www.uschamber.org
Contact: Mr. Gary Litman
          Executive Director

Population Action Intl.
Established in 1965 and known formerly as the Population Crisis Committee/Draper World Population Fund, PAI is a nonprofit, independent research and advocacy institution for world population issues and for the promotion of global access to family planning services.

1120 19th Street, NW - Suite 550
Washington DC 20036
202/659-1833   FAX 202/293-1795
http://www.populationaction.org
Contact: Ms. Amy Coen
          President

Population Institute
An independent, nonprofit, grass-roots organization concerned with global population issues and stabilizing the world's population in line with available resources and environmental limitations.

107 2nd Street, N.E.
Washington DC 20002
202/544-3300   FAX 202/544-0068
E-mail: name@populationinstitute.org
http://www.populationinstitute.org
Contact: Mr. Werner H. Fornos
          President

Population Reference Bureau
Founded in 1929, the bureau is a nonprofit, nonadvocacy, educational organization working to increase the amount, accuracy and usefulness of information concerning changes in population and the impact those changes may have.

1875 Connecticut Avenue, NW - Suite 520
Washington DC 20009
202/483-1100   FAX 202/328-3937
E-mail: popref@prb.org   http://www.prb.org/prb/
Contact: Ms. Alene H. Gelbard
          Director, Intl. Programs

Privacy Intl.
Privacy Intl. promotes an international understanding of the importance of privacy and data protection. It is an independent, non-government organization with the primary role of advocacy and support in this area of human rights.

666 Penn. Ave., SE, Suite 301
Washington DC 20003
202/544-9240   FAX 202/547-5482
E-mail: pi@mail.privacy.org   http://www.privacy.org
Contact: Mr. Simon Davies
          Director General

Progressive Policy Institute
Founded in 1989 by the Democratic Leadership Council, at the helm of which President Clinton used to sit, PPI is a center for research and policy formulation, seeking to provide an alternative to the conventional left-right debate. By adapting the U.S. progressive tradition of individual liberty, equal opportunity, and civic obligation to the challenges of information, PPI seeks to fashion a public

philosophy for the twenty-first century. It focuses on both foreign and domestic issues.

518 C St., NE
Washington DC 20002
202/547-0001   FAX 202/544-5014
E-mail: info@dlcppi.org   http://www.dlcppi.org

Contacts:
Mr. Will Marshall
    President
Mr. Steven Nider
    Executive Director, Defense Working Group
Ms. Edith R. Wilson
    Director, Trade Project

Puebla Institute, The
Affiliated with the Freedom House, this international, nonprofit human rights organization focuses on religious persecution.

1319 18th St., NW - Second Floor
Washington DC 20036
202/296-8050   FAX 202/296-5078
E-mail:
Contact: Ms. Nina H. Shea
    Director

RAND Corporation
Based in Santa Monica, Calif., RAND is a major private, nonprofit institution engaged in research and analysis pertaining to national security and public welfare matters.

1333 H St., NW
Washington DC 20005-4707
202/296-5000   FAX 202/296-7960
Contact: Mr. David Chu
    Director, Washington Research Department

Refugee Policy Group
Founded in 1982, the group is an independent, nonprofit organization serving as a center for policy analysis and research on refugee matters.

PO Box 37
Kensington MD 20895-0037
301/588-6555
E-mail: refugeepg@worldnet.att.net
Contact: Mr. Dennis Gallagher
    Executive Director

Religious Task Force on Central America and Mexico
3053 4th St., NE
Washington DC 20017
202/529-0441
Contact: Ms. Margaret Swedish
    Director and Board Member

Richmond Export - Import Club
Founded in 1948, the membership organization serves the region's international trade professionals. Known for programs and speakers, the club provides a forum for the promotion of global commerce.
P.O. Box 12135
Richmond VA 23241
804/783-9307   FAX 804/780-0344
E-mail: mark@gwmail.grcc.com   http://www.grcc.com
Contact: Mr. Mark A. Herzog
    Club Secretary

Russian - American Chamber of Commerce (Wash., DC)

Founded in 1992, the RACC has offices in Washington, DC and Moscow. With over 300 members, the chamber works to create a direct, mutually beneficial relationship between U.S. businesses and an expanding private sector in 89 Russian regions.

P.O. Box 15343
Washington DC 20003
202/546-2103   FAX 202/546-3275
E-mail: rusric@erols.com   http://www.rusline.com
Contact: Dr. Igor S. Oleynik
    President & CEO

Satellite Broadcasting & Communications Assn. (SBCA)
The SBCA is the national trade organization representing all segments of the home satellite industry. It is committed to expanding the utilization of satellite technology for the broadcast delivery of entertainment news, information and educational programming. The SBCA is composed of satellite manufacturers, system operators, equipment manufacturers, distributors, retailers, DBS companies, mass merchandisers, encryption vendors, and programmers.

225 Reinekers Ln. #600
Alexandria VA 22314-2875
703/549-6990   FAX 703/549-7640
Contact: Ms. Marsha Saflin
    Mgr. of Foundation & Intl. Activities

Screenprinting & Graphic Imaging Assn. Intl.
Since 1948, SGIA is the international trade association representing the interests of screen printing and graphic imaging companies throughout the world, with over 3,500 corporate members, located in 126 countries.

10015 Main St.
Fairfax VA 22031-3489
703/385-1335   FAX 703/273-0456
E-mail: sgia@sgia.org   http://www.sgia.org
Contact: Mr. John M. Crawford
    President

Seafarers Intl. Union of North America

5201 Auth Way
Camp Springs MD 20746
301/899-0675   FAX 301/899-7355
Contact: Mr. Michael Sacco
    President

Search for Common Ground
A non-profit founded in 1982 with a vision of transforming how the world deals with conflict. In advocating cooperative solutions, SCG has developed seventeen operational methods utilizing conflict resolution techniques ranging from mediation and facilitiation to less traditional ones like TV production, radio soap opera, and community organizing. SCG has nine field offices and a partner organization, the European Centre for Common Ground, established in Brussels in 1995.

1601 Connecticut Ave., NW - Suite 200
Washington DC 20009
202/265-4300   FAX 202/232-6718
E-mail: search#sfcg.org   http://www.sfcg.org
Contact: Mr. John Marks
    President

Securities Industry Assn.
Established in 1972, the association is a proponent of capital markets, bringing together the shared interests of about 700 securities firms throughout North America to accomplish common goals. SIA

members, including investment banks, broker-dealers, specialists, and mutual fund companies, are active in all markets and in all phases of corporate and public finance.

1401 I St., NW, Suite 1000
Washington DC 20036
202/296-9410   FAX 202/296-9775
E-mail: dstrongin@sia.com http://www.sia.com
Contact: Mr. David Strongin
            Assistant Vice President & Director, Intl. Finance

Service Employees Intl. Union
SEIU represents public and private sector employees from industries such as education, social service, transportation, health, and building service. It has over one million members.

1313 L St., NW
Washington DC 20005
202/898-3200   FAX 202/898-3304
Contact: Mr. Andrew Stern
            Intl. President

Share Our Strength
Share Our Strength works nationally and internationally against poverty and hunger.

1511 K St., NW - Suite 940
Washington DC 20005
202/393-2925   FAX 202/347-5868
E-mail: sos@charitiesusa.com   http://www.strength.org
Contact: Mr. Bill Shore
            Executive Director

Sheet Metal Workers' Intl. Assn.
1750 New York Ave., NW, Sixth Floor
Washington DC 20006
202/783-5880   FAX 202/662-0890
Contact: Mr. John Brittle
            Intl. Representative

Sierra Club, Intl. Program
The Sierra Club's International Program, established in 1971, is composed of three campaigns: responsible trade, human rights and the environment, and international population and international financial institutions reform.

408 C St., N.E.
Washington DC 20002
202/547-1141   FAX 202/547-6009
E-mail: larry.williams@sierraclub.org
Contact: Mr. Larry Williams
            Director, Intl. Programs

Silver Institute
A nonprofit, intl. trade association representing leading silver mining houses, refiners, bullion suppliers, manufacturers of silver products, and wholesalers of silver investment products. Established in 1971, the Institute serves as the industry's voice in increasing public understanding of the many uses and values of silver and serves as a source of industry statistics through its publications.

1112 16th St., NW - Suite 240
Washington DC 20036
202/835-0185   FAX 202/835-0155
E-mail: info@silverinstitute.org   http://www.silverinstitute.org
Contact: Mr. Paul Bateman
            Executive Director

Sister Cities Intl.
Founded in 1956, SCI is the largest citizen diplomacy network creating and strengthening partnerships between 1,100 U.S. and 1,770 foreign cities in 123 countries. It is the national nonprofit volunteer membership organization of U.S. communities linked globally to promote lasting friendship through a variety of programs.

120 S. Payne Street
Alexandria VA 22314
703/836-3535   FAX 703/836-4815
E-mail: info @sister-cities.org   http://www.sister-cities.org
Contact: Ms. Juanita M. Crabb
            Executive Director

Small Business Exporters Association
SBEA is a nonprofit trade association now in its sixth year and is the only national advocacy organization representing small and mid-sized exporters (SME). It represents more than 200 SMEs, manufacturers, service providers, and trading companies. SBEA also compiles comparative studies on export finance, export promotion, and export controls.

4603 John Tyler Ct., - Suite 203
Annandale VA 22003
703/761-4140
E-mail: SBEA@freetrader.com   http://www.freetrader.com
Contact: Mr. E. Martin Duggan
            President/CEO

Society for Human Resource Management
SHRM represents the interests of more than 95,000 professional and student members from around the world It provides its membership with education and information services, conferences and new seminars, government and media representation and publications that equip human resource professionals for their roles as leaders and decision makers within their organizations. The society is a founding member and Secretariat of the World Federation of Personnel Management Associations (WFPMA) which links human resource associations in 55 nations.

1800 Duke St.
Alexandria VA 22314-3499
703/548-3440   FAX 703/836-0367
E-mail: shrm@shrm.org   http://www.shrm.org
Contact: Mr. Brian Glade
            Vice President Intl. Programs

Society for International Development
The SID was founded in Washington, DC, in 1957 to meet the professional needs of practitioners, policy-makers, and planners in the field of international development. The Society has over 7,000 members in 132 nations and territories around the world, including representatives of the Peace Corps and the World Bank. The Society's objectives are to promote international cooperation and dialog on global development issues, and encourage the expansion of skills and knowledge of development practitioners.

1875 Connecticut Ave., NW - Suite 1020
Washington DC 20009
202/884-8590   FAX 202/884-8499
http://www.aed.org/sid/
Contact: Ms. Andrea Camoens
            Executive Director

Solar Energy Industries Assn.
122 C St., NW - Suite 400
Washington DC 20001-2109
202/383-2600   FAX 202/383-2670

Contact: Mr. Scott Sklar
        Executive Director

South East Consortium for Intl. Develop. (SECID), The

A nonprofit organization formed in 1977 to provide research, training and extension to developing nations. Spanning over a dozen states, SECID encompasses 19 universities and one research institute. Such geographic diversity includes nearly every production, ecological, and environmental and cultural condition found in the U.S. Major project areas are: agriculture and rural development; environment; higher education; and human resource and institutional development.

1634 I St. NW #702
Washington DC 20006-4003
202/628-4551   FAX 202/628-4561
E-mail: secid@secid.com
Contact: Mr. Harry H. Wheeler
        Executive Director

Southeast Asia Resource Action Center (SEARAC)

SEARAC seeks to assist Southeast Asians in their transition from dependent refugees to a productive Asian American minority. It is a leading advocate, a source for technical assistance and training, and a clearinghouse for information.

1628 16th St., NW - 3rd Floor
Washington DC 20009
202/667-4690   FAX 202/667-6449
E-mail: searacdc@aol.com   http://www.searac.org
Contact: Mr. KaYing Yang
        Executive Director

Space Policy Institute

Established by the George Washington University in 1987, the Institute operates as a constituent element of the Center for International Science and Technology Policy of GWU's Elliott School of International Affairs. It focuses its activities on policy and historical issues related to space efforts of the U.S. and competitive and cooperative interactions in space between the U.S. and other countries. It is an affiliate of the International Space University.

2013 G Street, NW - Suite 201
Washington DC 20052
202/994-7292   FAX 202/994-1639
E-mail: cistp@gwis2.circ.gwu.edu   http://www.gwu.edu/~spi
Contact: Dr. John M. Logsdon
        Director

SRI International

A nonprofit research and consulting institution, SRI was founded in 1946 by the Trustees of Stanford University as Stanford Research Institute. Its name was changed in 1977 and it has been operating as an independent nonprofit entity since 1970. Headquartered in Menlo Park, California, SRI is one of the world's largest research technology development and consulting firms in the world, with five main business units: Policy Division, Science and Technology, Engineering Research Group, SRI Consulting, and the David Sarnoff Research Center.

1611 North Kent St.
Arlington VA 22209
703/524-2053   FAX 703/247-8569
Contact: Mr. John A. Mathieson
        Executive Director, Intl. Policy Center

Stimson Center, Henry L.

Founded in 1989 as a nonprofit, nonpartisan institution devoted to public policy research, the center focuses on difficult national and international security issues where policy, technology, and politics intersect. Projects at the Center deal with regional security, U.S. foreign and defense policies, arms control measures and their verification, and other building blocks of international security.

21 Dupont Circle, NW - 5th Floor
Washington DC 20036
202/223-5956   FAX 202/785-9034
E-mail: info@stimson.org   http://www.stimson.org
Contact: Mr. Michael Krepon
        President

Sugar Association

Established in 1943, the Sugar Association maintains an active role in informing the public about the role that sugar can play, in moderation, in a healthful diet. By creating public education programs with a variety of diet, health, nutrition, and fitness materials, the Association has worked to dispel misconceptions about sugar as well as provide opportunities for continued scientific research. Since 1984, the Sugar Promotion program has invested over $48 million in public education and promotion efforts.

1101 15th St., NW - Suite 600
Washington DC 20005
202/785-1122   FAX 202/785-5019
E-mail: sugar@sugar.org   http://www.sugar.org
Contact: Dr. Richard Keelor
        President

Swedish - American Chamber of Commerce of Washington, DC, Inc.

SACC is a membership organization with the objective of promoting trade between the U.S. and Sweden. Members in the Washington, DC chapter represent a diverse group of senior business executives, lawyers, and bankers dedicated to the development of good will and useful business relationship between the business communities of the Washington Metropolitan Area and Sweden.

1501 M St., NW - 9th floor
Washington DC 20005
202/467-2638   FAX 202/467-2656
E-mail: sten.graffman@foreign.ministry.se
Contact: Mr. Philip C. Gast
        Chairman

Taipei Economic and Cultural Representative Office in the United States

The Taipei Economic and Cultural Offices in the United States and Canada provide services to local Chinese residents and to Chinese scholars and students. The offices also expedite passport and visa applications and verification of documents. The offices aim to strengthen cultural exchanges and educational cooperation between the Republic of China on Taiwan and the U.S., and to enhance economic development and trade relationships with the U.S.

4201 Wisconsin Ave., NW
Washington DC 20016
202/895-1800   FAX 202/895-0825
http://www.houstoncul.org
Contact: Mr. Jason Hu
        Representative

Telecommunications Industry Assn.

A full-service trade organization of more than 550 companies which provide telecommunications materials, products, systems, distribution services, and professional services to the U.S. and countries around the world.

2500 Wilson Blvd., Suite 300
Arlington VA 22201
703/907-7700   FAX 703/907-7727

E-mail: enelson@tia.eia.org http://www.tiaonline.org
Contact: Mr. Eric Nelson
         Vice President, Intl. Affairs

TRAFFIC - World Wildlife Fund

Part of an international network monitoring international trade in wild animals and plants, TRAFFIC is the trade monitoring program of the World Wildlife Fund and stands for Trade Records Analysis of Flora and Fauna in Commerce.

1250 24th Street, NW
Washington DC 20037
202/293-4800   FAX 202/775-8287
Contact: Ms. Gina DeFerrari
         Director

TransAfrica

Founded in 1977, it was the first black foreign policy lobby in the U.S. and works for a more progressive foreign policy toward nations of Africa and the Caribbean.

1744 R Street, NW
Washington DC 20009
202/797-2301   FAX 202/797-2382
Contact: Mr. Randall Robinson
         President

Transnational Development Consortium

Advises both public and private sectors on foreign direct investment opportunities and on financing sources, as well as developing and implementing investment and marketing strategies.

3809 Warren Street, NW
Washington DC 20016-2234
202/362-7715   FAX 202/363-0958
Contact: Mr. Lane F. Miller
         Principal, International Inv./Trade/Venture Capital

Transportation-Communications Intl. Union

3 Research Place
Rockville MD 20850
301/948-4910   FAX 301/948-1369
Contact: Mr. Robert A. Scardelletti
         Intl. President

U.N. Assn. of the U.S. - Capital Area Division

Promotes public support for the U.N. and related agencies, and carries out U.N. oriented programs in the Washington area.

1319 18th Street, NW
Washington DC 20036-1802
202/785-2640   FAX 202/785-1940
Contact: Ms. Evelyn Falkowski
         Executive Director

U.S. - Africa Chamber of Commerce

An independent nonprofit organization comprised of U.S. based and overseas based businesses, trade associations, universities, foundations, and individuals with purposes of promoting the efficiency and integrity of trade and investment between the U.S. and Africa.

The National Chamber is a large umbrella agency that is the collective organization strength of various African embassies, numerous companies based in the U.S. and overseas, trade and professional associations, country, state and local chambers of commerce which are all committed to the development of free enterprise and economic, commercial and financial relations between the U.S. and Africa. The

National Chamber also seeks to promote an improved and conclusive policy environment within which trade and investment can benefit from broad-based and sustainable economic growth.

1899 L St., NW - Fifth Fl.
Washington DC 20036
202/331-7053   FAX 202/331-1809
Contact: Mr. Elias Belayneh
         President

U.S. - Angola Chamber of Commerce

An independent, nonpartisan membership organization dedicated to trade and investment within Angola. Established in 1990, and now with 65 members, it provides information and opportunities for members of the private sector interested in Angola to meet regularly with international and Angolan public officials and entrepreneurs.

1850 K St., NW #390
Washington DC 20006
202/223-0540   FAX 202/872-1521
E-mail: 75031.3361@compuserve.com
Contact: Mr. Paul J. Hare
         Ambassador

U.S. Apple Assn.

Membership includes both state and regional organizations representing growers, and individual companies in the apple industry.

P.O. Box 1137
McLean VA 22101
703/442-8850   FAX 703/790-0845
Contact: Ms. Julia Stewart Daly
         Director, Communications

U.S. - ASEAN Business Council Inc.

Promotes the expansion of U.S. business involvement in the member states of ASEAN - Brunei, Indonesia, Malaysia, the Philippines, Singapore, Thailand and Vietnam through support of policies which aid U.S. firms in identifying and competing for commercial opportunities in the area.

1400 L Street, NW - Suite 375
Washington DC 20005-3509
202/289-1911   FAX 202/289-0519
E-mail: mail@usasean.org
Contact: Mr. Ernest Z. Bower
         President

U.S. - Asia Institute

Founded in 1979, the institute is a nonprofit, nonpartisan organization aimed at enhancing economic cooperation and communication between the U.S. and Asia. Members include Asians and Asian-Americans, as well as interested parties from the government, academic and business sectors.

232 E. Capitol Street, NE
Washington DC 20003
202/544-3181   FAX 202/543-1748
Contact: Mr. Joji Konoshima
         President

U.S. - Baltic Foundation

The main goal of the Foundation is to assist educational and technical training programs in the Baltic States in order to strengthen democracy and free markets. The Foundation also promotes U.S.-Baltic relations by encouraging study of Baltic history and current events.

1100 17th St., NW - Suite 605
Washington DC 20036

202/986-0380   FAX 202/986-0306
E-mail: jnelson@usbf.org   http://www.usbf.org
Contact: Mr. Jeff Nelson
          Acting Executive Director

U.S. Business & Industrial Council

Founded in 1933, the council represents the views and voices the concerns of over 1,000 small and medium-sized American businesses before the U.S. Congress and Executive Branch. USBIC members own and operate their companies in 44 states. The council is principally concerned about issues related to the nation's business environment and America's ability to compete in international markets. The council lobbies and engages in educational campaigns on a variety of tax, labor, regulatory, and international trade issues.

122 C St., NW, Suite 815
Washington DC 20001
202/628-2211   FAX 202/628-3698
E-mail: USBIC@AOL.COM
Contact: Mr. Kevin L. Kearns
          President

U.S. Chamber of Commerce

The International Division of the chamber works to improve the ability of U.S. business to compete in the global marketplace. It is responsible for overall U.S. Chamber liaison with individual American Chambers of Commerce Abroad (AmChams). There are currently 76 AmChams accredited by the U.S. Chamber of Commerce in 67 different countries. The division also administers: the International Division Information Center; the International Business Exchange; the International Forum Breakfast Series; the U.S. Chamber Business Councils; and the U.S. Chamber Working Groups.

The IDIC provides technical assistance to U.S. Chamber members exploring foreign markets with a focus on greater outreach to small business. More information is available at (202)463-5483.

The IBEX features a menu-driven format electronic system that facilitates finding, qualifying and negotiating with business partners, both domestic and international, based on specific business needs. (800)537-IBEX.

The Forum series hosts the people who influence international trade and finance, including senior government officials and heads of state of American's trading partners, high level Administration officials, and business leaders in order to discuss trade, foreign affairs, and economic policy. (202)463-5443.

The U.S. Chamber Business Councils administers six business councils through which companies impact bilateral trade relations with Brazil, Canada, India, Poland, the Czech and Slovak Republics, and Hungary. The Working Groups serve to improve trade and investment relations with Romania, Bulgaria, and Ukraine. (202)463-5482.

1615 H St., NW
Washington DC 20062-2000
202/659-6000   FAX 202/463-5836
http://www.uschamber.org
Contact: Mr. Willard A. Workman
          Vice President, International Division

U.S. - China Business Council

Established with the encouragement of the U.S. and Chinese governments in 1979 to assist U.S. firms doing business in the PRC, the council is a private, nonprofit organization with more than 300 member companies.

1818 N Street, NW - Suite 200
Washington DC 20036
202/429-0340   FAX 202/775-2476

E-mail: info@uschina.org   http://www.uschina.org
Contact: Mr. Robert Kapp
          President

U. S. Committee for Refugees

Founded in 1958, the U.S. committee is a non-profit humanitarian organization that defends the rights of refugees and other displaced people around the world. USCR is dedicated to providing accurate information and analysis that the public and policy makers need to assist and protect refugees worldwide.

1717 Massachusetts Avenue, NW - Suite 701
Washington DC 20036
202/347-3507   FAX 202/374-3418
E-mail: mwyers@IRSIA-USCR.org   http://www.refugees.org
Contact: Mr. Roger Winter
          Executive Director

U.S. Committee for UNICEF - Office of Public Policy and Advocacy

A government relations office for the United Nations Children's Fund.

1775 K Street, NW - Suite 360
Washington DC 20006
202/296-4242   FAX 202/296-4060
Contact: Mr. Martin Rendon
          Vice President

U.S. Council for Intl. Business

Based in New York City, the council was established in 1945 to represent the interests and positions of U.S. business on international trade, finance, and investment issues. With members ranging from corporations and associations to law and consulting firms with interests abroad, the council is the principal private institution representing U.S. business with multilateral institutions including the Business and Industry Advisory Committee of OECD, the International Chamber of Commerce in Paris, U.N. agencies, and the International Labor Organization (as the U.S. member of the International Organization of Employers).

1015 15th Street, NW, Suite 975
Washington DC 20005
202/371-1316   FAX 202/371-8249
http://www.uscib.org
Contact: Mr. Timothy E. Deal
          Sr. Vice President, Washington Office

U.S. - Cuba Business Council

The council seeks to support current U.S. policy on Cuba designed to foster a democratic change with guarantees of freedom and human rights under the law. It promotes, on a strictly nonpartisan basis, cooperation among business, civic, and professional organizations which share the council's goals for democracy and a market economy in Cuba.

5313 Lee Highway, Suite B
Arlington VA 22207
703/241-0038   FAX 703/241-0548
E-mail: uscbc@mindspring.com
Contact: Mr. Tom Cox
          Executive Director

U.S. Energy Assn. Conference

USEA is an association of 180 public and private energy-related organizations, corporations, and government agencies. The association sponsors policy reports and conferences on global and domestic energy issues and trade and education exchange visits with other countries.

1620 Eye St., NW - Suite 1000

Washington DC 20006
202/331-0415   FAX 202/331-0418
E-mail: 76043.1425@compuserve.com
http://www.wec98congress.org/orgusea.htm
Contact: Mr. Barry K. Worthington
          Executive Director

U.S. Export Council for Renewable Energy
A coalition of seven national renewable energy associations, it provides trade promotion, export, and international trade coordination for the U.S. renewable energy industry.

122 C St., NW, 4th Floor
Washington DC 20001-2109
202/383-2550   FAX 202/383-2555
E-mail: usecre@usecre.org http://www.crest.org/renewables/usecre
Contact: Mr. Steve McNulty
          Acting President

U.S. Grains Council
A private, nonprofit institution working through 11 international offices and aimed at developing and expanding foreign markets for U.S. produced barley, corn, and grain sorghum and their related products.

1400 K Street, NW - Suite 1200
Washington DC 20005
202/789-0789   FAX 202/898-0522
E-mail: grains@grains.org http://www.grains.org
Contact: Mr. Kenneth Hobbie
          President and CEO

U.S. - Hispanic Chamber of Commerce
Founded in 1979, the chamber works to expand business opportunities; to encourage mutually beneficial ties with the public and private sectors; to serve as an active and visible advocate in Hispanic business arena; and to actively promote trade between the Hispanic American business community and their Latin American counterparts.

1019 19th St., NW - Suite 200
Washington DC 20036
202/842-1212   FAX 202/842-3221
E-mail: Ffarinetti@ushcc.com   http://www.ushcc.com
Contact: Mr. Ronald Montoya
          Chairman

U.S. - India Business Council
The U.S.-India Business Council was formed in 1975 at the request of the two governments to strengthen U.S.-India relations and to enable Indian and American business decision makers to conduct a continuing dialogue on bilateral economic relations.

U.S. Chamber of Commerce

1615 H Street., NW
Washington DC 20062
202/463-5492   FAX 202/463-3173
E-mail: usibc@uschamber.com   http://www.erols.com/askhan/usibc
Contact: Dr. Michael T. Clark
          Executive Director

U.S. - Indonesia Society
A nonprofit association founded in 1994 to meet the need for an organization focusing on the U.S.-Indonesia relationship and helping to develop better understanding between the two nations.
2000 L St., NW - Suite 200
Washington DC 20036

202/416-1611   FAX 202/416-1813
E-mail: usindo@aol.com
Contact: Mr. Edward Masters
          President

U.S. - Japan Business Council

1020 19th St., NW - Suite 130
Washington DC 20036
202/728-0068   FAX 202/728-0073
Contact: Mr. James Fatheree
          Executive Director

U.S. - Korea Business Council

1023 15th St., NW - Suite 700
Washington DC 20005
202/842-1381   FAX 202/842-3275
Contact: Mr. Nick van Nelson
          President

U.S.- Mexico Chamber of Commerce
A private, nonprofit organization of U.S. and Mexican businesses promoting trade and investment.
1726 M St., NW, Suite 704
Washington DC 20036
202/296-5198   FAX 202/728-0768
E-mail: zapantaz@usmcoc.org
http://www.usmcoc.org/usmcoc
Contact: Mr. Al Zapanta
          President and CEO

U.S. Mongolia Business Council
A nonprofit membership organization of American corporations and professionals founded in 1991. The Council's mission is to develop and strengthen economic ties between the U.S. and Mongolia and to help develop a policy framework which encourages strong bilateral trade, investment and partnership of benefit to both nations.

731 Eighth Street, SE
Washington DC 20003
202/547-3800   FAX 202/546-4784
E-mail: mongolia@clark.net
Contact: Mr. Lou Ivey
          Executive Director

U.S. Natl. Committee for Pacific Economic Cooperation
Established by then Secretary of State George Schultz in 1984, the committee advises the U.S. government of U.S.-Pacific Basin economic issues and is comprised of senior business, academic, and government officials.

1112 16th St., NW - Suite 520
Washington DC 20036
202/293-3995   FAX 202/293-1402
Contact: Mr. Mark Borthwick
          Executive Director

U.S. - New Zealand Council, The
A nonprofit organization founded in 1986 to strengthen relations between the two nations. While it deals primarily with large U.S. corporations investing in New Zealand, it also has a growing individual membership.

1801 F St., NW - 3rd Floor
Washington DC 20006
202/842-0772   FAX 202/842-0749
E-mail: usnzcounci@aol.com

Contact: Mr. Paul Cleveland
President

U.S. Olympic Committee
The committee is dedicated to providing opportunities for American Athletes at all age and skill levels, and to preparing and training those athletes for the challenges that range from domestic competitions to the Olympic Games themselves.

1150 18th Street, NW, Suite 300
Washington DC 20036
202/466-3399   FAX 202/466-5068
Contact: Mr. Steven Bull
          Director, Govt. Relations

U.S. Public Television Intl. Consortium
An organization of U.S. public television stations that frequently produce programs with foreign partners.

901 E St., NW
Washington DC 20001
202/879-9700   FAX 202/783-1019
Contact: Ms. Anita Klever
          Executive Director

U.S. - Russia Business Council
The largest nonprofit membership organization of American firms founded in 1993 which seeks to develop and expand U.S. private sector trade and investment in Russia.

1701 Pennsylvania Avenue, NW Suite 520
Washington DC 20006
202/739-9180   FAX 202/659-5920
E-mail: Lawson@usrbc.org
Contact: Mr. Eugene K. Lawson
          President

U.S. - Thailand Business Council
The council and its counterpart in Bangkok, the Thailand-U.S. Business Council, are nonprofit and nonpartisan organizations. The council works to advance the expansion of investment opportunities as well as commerce and business relations between the two nations through the organization of conferences, briefings, and trade missions to Thailand.

3050 K St., NW - Suite 105
Washington DC 20007
202/337-5973   FAX 202/337-0039
E-mail: USTBC@aol.com
Contact: Ms. Carol S. Armstrong
          Executive Director

U.S.-Ukraine Foundation
The U.S.-Ukraine Foundation creates and sustains channels of communication between the U.S. and Ukraine, in order to build peace and prosperity through an exchange of information that facilitates democratic development, encourages free market reform, and enhances human rights.

1511 K St., NW - Suite 110
Washington DC 20005
202/347-4264   FAX 202/347-4267
http://www.erols.com/usuf/ukrmain.htm
Contact: Ms. Nadia K. McConnell
          President

U.S. Wheat Associates
Mandated with developing foreign markets for the U.S. wheat industry, U.S. Wheat Associates has 15 offices abroad, in Asia, Africa, Europe, Central and South America, and Russia, as well as an office in Portland, Oregon.

1620 Eye Street, NW, Suite 801
Washington DC 20006
202/463-0999   FAX 202/785-1052
E-mail: info@uswheat.org   http://uswheat.org
Contact: Mr. Alan Tracey
          President

Ukrainian National Information Service
Since 1977, UNIS has provided information on issues of concern to the Ukrainian American community, informing policy makers, the academic community, and the media on current developments in Ukraine. The Service supports the democratic process in Ukraine by hosting Ukrainian dignitaries, working with other Ukrainian American organizations, and assisting the Ukrainian Embassy.

214 Massachusetts Ave., NE - Suite 225
Washington DC 20002
202/547-0018   FAX 202/543-5502
Contact: Mr. Askold S. Lozynskyj
          President

Union of Councils (UCSJ)
UCSJ was founded in 1970 and seeks to provide for the freedom, security, and welfare of the Jews of the former Soviet Union. UCSJ is an independent, grass roots organization with bureaus in Russia and Central Asia.

1819 H St., NW - Suite 230
Washington DC 20006
202/775-9770   FAX 202/775-9776
E-mail: ucsj@ucsj.com   http://www.ucsj.com
Contact: Mr. Gideon Aronoff
          Deputy Director

United Automobile, Aerospace, and Agricultural Implement Workers of America (UAW)
1757 N St., NW
Washington DC 20036
202/828-8500   FAX 202/293-3457
Contact: Mr. John Christensen
          Intl. Representative

United Brotherhood of Carpenters & Joiners of America
101 Constitution Ave., NW
Washington DC 20001
202/546-6206   FAX 202/543-5724
Contact: Mr. Douglas McCarron
          General President

United Food & Commercial Workers Intl. Union
1775 K St., NW
Washington DC 20006
202/223-3111   FAX 202/466-1562
Contact: Mr. Douglas H. Dority
          Intl. President

United Palestinian Appeal
Alleviates the suffering of Palestinians, especially those living in the West Bank, Gaza Strip, and Lebanon. Since its incorporation as a nonprofit, nonpolitical, independent, tax-exempt charity in 1978, UPA has developed extensive assistance programs in the areas of health care, education, community development and children's services. In 1985, UPA was registered with the U.S. Agency for International Development as a private voluntary organization and was accepted

in 1989 by the Combined Federal Campaign, which solicits contributions from government employees.

2100 M Street, NW - Suite 409
Washington DC 20037
202/659-5007   FAX 202/296-0224
E-mail: upa@cais.com   http://www.cais.net/upa
Contact: Makboula Yasin
           Financial Officer

USA-ROC (Taiwan) Economic Council
A nonprofit association formed in 1976 as the only nongovernmental American organization to foster trade and business relations with the Republic of China (ROC) and Taiwan.

1726 M St., NW - Suite 601
Washington DC 20036
202/331-8966   FAX 202/331-8985
E-mail: usaroc@aol.com   http://www.usaroc.org
Contact: Mr. David N. Laux
           President

Volunteers in Overseas Cooperative Assistance
Founded in 1970, VOCA is a nonprofit institution providing short term technical assistance to cooperatives and private sector agricultural enterprises in developing countries, Central and Eastern Europe, and the former Soviet Union. It does so through volunteer development specialists and is funded by the U.S. Agency for International Development, cooperative development institutions, and private sector donors.

50 F Street, NW, Suite 1075
Washington DC 20001
202/383-4961   FAX 202/783-7204
Contact: Yoo-Mi Lee
           Vice President, Business Development

Washington Center for China Studies
In order to answer the challenge of how to creatively and constructively conduct academic studies relating to China's future, a group of Chinese scholars in the U.S. founded the WCCS in January of 1990. The goals of WCCS are to organize, coordinate, and support Chinese scholars conducting studies on pressing Chinese issues, and to promote active exchange and better understanding between China and the world. It conducts research, consulting, and training, as well as information and scholarly exchange programs in the fields of social sciences and humanities.

1129 20th St., NW - Suite 400
Washington DC 20036
202/296-8071   FAX 202/296-8072
E-mail: wcpublic@asuvm.inre.asu.edu
http://www.wccs.org/wccs.htm
Contact: Mr. John Hao Jia
           President

Washington Customs Brokers & Freight Forwarders Association
Dulles Intl. Airport - P.O. Box 20202
Washington DC 20041
703/471-9824   FAX 703/661-6871
Contact: Mr. Wane Byer
           President

Washington Institute for Near East Policy
Founded in 1985, the institute works to promote understanding of developing issues impacting U.S. interests in the Middle East.

1828 L Street, NW - Suite 1050

Washington DC 20036
202/452-0650   FAX 202/223-5364
E-mail: info@washingtoninstitute.org
Contact: Dr. Robert Satloff
          Executive Director

Washington Institute of Foreign Affairs
Primarily through the forum of seminars and meetings, the institute, established in 1961, promotes understanding of international issues among its members, U.S. and foreign government officials, and influential visiting foreign nationals.

2121 Massachusetts Ave., NW - Suite 431
Washington DC 20008
301/469-7223   FAX 301/365-0859
Contact: Ms. Genevieve Weiler
          Executive Secretary

Washington Intl. Trade Association
WITA is a nonprofit private voluntary organization dedicated to providing a neutral forum in the nation's capital for the open discussion of international trade issues. Through an extensive series of informational programs, WITA keeps its members informed about the Administration's trade policies, changes in rules and regulations governing international trade, and foreign perspectives on U.S. trade policy.

2025 I Street, NW - Suite 822
Washington DC 20006
202/293-4193   FAX 202/293-4194
http://www.wita.org
Contact: Ms. Pamela Slater
          Executive Director

Washington Office on Latin America (WOLA)
WOLA was established in 1974 and monitors Central and South American political, economic, and social developments and provides information to Congress, Administration agencies, international organizations and the media.

400 C St., N.E.
Washington DC 20002
202/544-8045   FAX 202/546-5288
E-mail: wola@wola.org   http://www.wola.org
Contact: Mr. George Vickers
          Executive Director

Washington Peace Center
Founded in 1963, the center is a local, nonprofit, anti-racist, multi-issue, education, and action organization whose purpose is to be a constructive force for peace through nonviolent social change.

2025 I St., NW - Suite 804
Washington DC 20006
202/234-2000   FAX 202/887-5342
E-mail: peacecent@aol.com
Contact: Ms. Tammi L. Coles
          Coordinator

Water Environment Federation
An international 42,000 member professional society founded in 1928, WEF is a federation of independent local associations from the U.S. and 27 other countries. WEF publishes magazines, journals and design and operation manuals focusing on science, engineering, and policy aspects of water quality protection. Each year, WEF sponsors WEFTEC, North America's largest conference and exposition on water quality technologies, with over 15,000 attendees.

601 Wythe St.

Alexandria VA 22314-1994
703/684-2400   FAX 703/684-2492
E-mail: msc@wef.org   http://www.wef.org
Contact: Ms. Quincalee Brown
          Executive Director

Wheat Export Trade Education Committee

415 2nd St., N.E., Suite 300
Washington DC 20002
202/547-2004   FAX 202/546-2638
Contact: Ms. Karen Fegley
          Director

Wireless Communications Assn. Intl., Inc.

Formally called the Wireless Cable Assn., the WCA represents companies that deliver broad band video, voice, and data over a terrestrial microwave platform. The systems currently serve an estimated 8 million subscribers in 90 nations. Membership is comprised of system operators, program suppliers, equipment and service suppliers, academics, engineers, financial institutions and attorneys.

1140 Conn. Ave., NW, Suite 810
Washington DC 20036
202/452-7823   FAX 202/452-0041
E-mail: president@wcal.com
Contact: Mr. Andrew T. Kreig
          President

Women in Intl. Security

Established in 1987, WIIS is dedicated to enhancing opportunities for women working in foreign and defense policy. An international, nonprofit, nonpartisan network and educational program, WIIS includes women and men from academia, think tanks, the diplomatic corps, the intelligence community, the military, and the private sector. They are involved in issues affecting international security ranging from arms control, arms transfers in the Third World, and ethnic conflict resolution to democratization in Latin America and the development of international trade blocs.   It also aims to inform others about the roles and contributions women are making in the international security community.

WIIS/CISSM School of Public Affairs
University of Maryland - 4113F Van Munching Hall
College Park MD 20742
301/405-7612   FAX 301/403-8107
E-mail: WIIS@puafmail.umd.edu
Contact: Ms. Gayle Mattox
          President

Women Strike for Peace - Washington Office

Established in 1961, this women's movement is concerned with nuclear disarmament, dangers from radiation, and U.S. intervention in the Third World.

110 Maryland Ave., NE - Suite 102
Washington DC 20002
202/543-2660   FAX 202/544-1187
Contact: Ms. Edith Villastrigo
          National Legislative Director

Women's Foreign Policy Group, The

A nonprofit, educational organization dedicated to global engagement and the promotion of the leadership of women in international affairs professions. The WFPG conducts in-depth foreign policy programs with women experts and news makers, provides mentoring for international affairs graduate students, and is engaged in a research project on the leadership status of women in international affairs professions.

1875 Connecticut Avenue, NW - Suite 720
Washington DC 20009-5728
202/884-8597   FAX 202/884-8499
E-mail: wfpg@aed.org
Contact: Ms. Patricia Ellis
          Executive Director

Wood Machinery Manufacturers of America

7768 Woodmont Ave. #214
Bethesda MD 20814-6035
301/652-0693   FAX 301/986-1389
Contact: Mr. Harold Zassenhaus
          Export Director

Woodrow Wilson Intl. Center for Scholars

The mandate of the center is to integrate the world of learning with the world of public affairs. Through meetings and conferences, the center brings scholars together with Members of Congress, Government officials, business leaders and other policy makers. The center awards approximately 35 residential fellowships annually to individuals with project proposals representing the entire range of superior scholarship, with a strong emphasis on the humanities and social sciences. Applications from any country are welcome.

Fellowships Office
1000 Jefferson Dr., SW
Washington DC 20560
202/357-2429   FAX 202/357-4439
E-mail: WCfellow@sivm.si.edu   http://wwics.si.edu
Contact: Mr. Dean W. Anderson
          Acting Director

World Affairs Council of Washington, DC

A community based, nonprofit organization founded in 1980 which seeks to promote knowledge of international policy issues. It operates through seminars and monthly public forums.

1726 M Street, NW, Suite 800
Washington DC 20036-4502
202/293-1051   FAX 202/833-2369
Contact: July Chitwood
          Executive Director

World Federalist Assn.

Promotes a democratic world federation limited to achieving positive global goals that nations cannot accomplish alone.

418 7th Street, SE
Washington DC 20003
202/546-3950   FAX 202/546-3749
E-mail: wfa@wfa.org   http://www.wfa.org
Contact: Mr. Tim Barner
          Executive Director

World Government of World Citizens

Founded in 1953, the WGWC provides the means for individuals to civically, politically, and legally empower themselves at the global level by registering as world citizens and by participating in the evolution of world government, with the belief in the oneness of the human species, the sovereignty of every individual, and the planet as our common home.

1012 14th St., NW - Suite 1106
Washington DC 20005
202/638-2662   FAX 202/638-0638
E-mail: worldcitizen@compuserve.com

http://www.worldcitizen.org
Contact: Mr. Garry Davis
　　　　Founder/World Coordinator

World Hunger Education Service

Integrates and disseminates economic, social, political, and scientific information from many sources on questions of equitable and sustainable development as a solution to hunger.

P.O. Box 29056
Washington DC 20017
202/269-6322
Contact: Mr. Nickola A. Lagoudakis
　　　　Acting Executive Director

World Jurist Assn. of the World Peace Through Law Ctr.

Established in 1963, it is a nonprofit institution founded under the auspices of the American Bar Association that seeks to foster peace through the rule of law.

1000 Connecticut Avenue, NW, Suite 202
Washington DC 20036
202/466-5428　　　　　　FAX 202/452-8540
http://www.WJA-WPTLC.org
Contact: Ms. Margaret Henneberry
　　　　Executive Vice President

World Mercy Fund

Founded in 1974, the fund aims at alleviating the sufferings of the disadvantaged in the Third World, primarily in Africa, with particular emphasis on medical and water facilities, and the promotion of education and modern agricultural practices.

Market Hill P.O. Box 227
Waterford VA 20197
540/882-4425　　　　　　FAX 540/882-3226
Contact: Mr. Patrick Leonard
　　　　President

World Priorities, Inc.

A public interest research organization established in 1977 to assemble and analyze factual information on social policy issues of global importance, and to provide clear, brief and balanced reports for public dissemination and debate. A small organization, it carries out its program with the part-time help of university students and professionals. It publishes annually a research journal entitled World Military and Social Expenditures.

P.O. Box 25140
Washington DC 20007
202/965-1661　　　　　　FAX 202/965-1525
Contact: Ms. Fallon M. Moursund
　　　　Co-Director

World Resources Institute

The WRI is an independent research and policy institute created in 1982 with a mission of moving human society to live in ways that protect the Earth's environment and its capacity to provide for the needs and aspirations of current and future generations.

1709 New York Ave., NW
Washington DC 20006
202/638-6300　　　　　　FAX 202/638-0036
http://www.wri.org/wri
Contact: Mr. Jonathan Lash
　　　　President

World Service Authority

The WSA is the administrative branch of the World Government of World Citizens. The organization issues global human rights documents based on the Universal Declaration of Human Rights and provides legal education and legal services to individuals, throughout the world, who are suffering from human rights violations.

1012 14th Street, NW, Suite 1106
Washington DC 20005
202/638-2662　　　　　　FAX 202/638-0638
E-mail: worldcitizen@compuserve.com
http://www.worldcitizen.org
Contact: Mr. David Gallup
　　　　General Counsel

World Wildlife Fund

Known by its panda logo, the WWF is dedicated to protecting the world's wildlife and biological diversity as a privately supported international conservation organization. WWF has sponsored more than 2,000 projects in 116 countries and has more than 1 million members in the U.S.

1250 24th Street, NW
Washington DC 20037
202/293-4800　　　　　　FAX 202/293-9211
E-mail: sherwin+R%wwfus@mcimail.com
http://www.worldwildlife.org
Contact: Ms. Kathryn S. Fuller
　　　　President

Worldwatch Institute

The Worldwatch Institute is dedicated to fostering the evolution of an environmentally sustainable society. The Institute seeks to achieve this goal through the conduct of inter-disciplinary non-partisan research on emerging global environmental issues.

1776 Massachusetts Ave., NW
Washington DC 20036
202/452-1999　　　　　　FAX 202/296-7365
E-mail: worldwatch@worldwatch.org
http://www.worldwatch.org
Contact: Mr. Lester R. Brown
　　　　President

Youth for Understanding Intl. Exchange (YFU)

Established in 1951, YFU is a nonprofit educational organization dedicated to creating a more peaceful, cooperative world through greater understanding and friendship. As one of the oldest and largest exchange organizations in the world, YFU has arranged for more than 180,000 students to live with families overseas.

3501 Newark St., NW
Washington DC 20016-3199
202/966-6808　　　　　　FAX 202/895-1104
E-mail: cherylramp@yfu.org　　　http://www.yfu.org
Contact: Ms. Cheryl L. Ramp
　　　　Executive Vice President, External Affairs

Individuals and firms need to know the concerns and priorities of any foreign country they do business with. A good way to get a feel for these matters is to look at the interests in each country that retain U.S. agents to represent them in the U.S.

The Department of Justice registers U.S. firms that represent foreign governments, foreign political parties, and other foreign "principals" as required under the Foreign Agents Registration Act (FARA) of 1938. The list of foreign agents in this section was obtained from the U.S. Department of Justice and is current as of May, 1998.

The first section, Foreign Agents - By Country, lists each foreign agent in order of the country of origin of the client they represent along with the name of each client (italicized), the nature of the services (NS) provided for that client, and the registration date for work on behalf of that particular client (CRD).

The second section lists the foreign agents (bolded) in alphabetical order, each agent's foreign agent registration number (FARA#), their original registration date as a foreign agent (ORD), contact information, clients (italicized), country of origin of each client, and registration date for work on behalf of that particular client (CRD).

Information contained within this section is only as current as the list provided to us from the Department of Justice and from our subsequent confirmation. Further information including financial and work performed disclosures are available from the Department of Justice's Foreign Agents Registration Unit which maintains a computerized database of all agent filings (both initial filings and six-month supplemental filings). Contact them at 202/514-1145 or 202/514-1216.

The Foreign Agents Registration Act (FARA)

The Foreign Agents Registration Act (FARA) requires public disclosure by persons engaged in propaganda and other activities on behalf of foreign governments, foreign political parties, and other foreign entities. The law was enacted in 1938, revised in 1942, and amended further on several occasions, most recently in 1966.

The purpose of the act is to protect the national defense, internal security, and foreign relations of the U.S. by informing the U.S. Government and the American people of the identity of foreign agents so they will be able to appraise their statements and actions in light of their associations and activities.

The Justice Department, which administers the law, states that the law in no way places limitations on the activities in which foreign agents may engage and places no stigma on any person registering. It may be assumed, the Justice Department said, that persons who are legitimately engaged as foreign agents have nothing to fear from public disclosure of their activities.

The administration and enforcement of the act is under the general supervision of the Attorney General, who assigns the task to the Assistant Attorney General in charge of the Criminal Division.

A person desiring to serve as a foreign agent must file a registration statement and supplements with the Attorney General. Within 10 days of becoming an agent, the person must file a registration statement under oath on a form prescribed by the Attorney General. The Justice Department is required by statute to collect fees for registrations and other services to recover the operating costs.

Certain types of agents are exempt from the law, including duly accredited diplomatic or consular officers of a foreign government; persons engaging in religious, scholastic, academic, or scientific pursuits or of the fine arts; and individuals designated by foreign governments as their representatives in or to an international organization. The burden of establishing the availability from registration under the act is placed on the person who would benefit.

How Do I Obtain Additional Information On Registered Foreign Agents?

Where Do I Register As A Foreign Agent?

Registration Unit - Internal Security Section
U.S. Department of Justice
1400 New York Avenue, N.W. - 9th Floor
Washington, D.C. 20530.
202/514-1216
Public Affairs Office: 202/514-1145

The Registration Unit serves two purposes:

1) To collect and provide complete information on all entities registered as foreign agents. The information is accessible to the general public at the viewing room of DOJ's Foreign Agent Registration Unit. A state-of-the-art computer system makes accessing the information easy. The hours of operation for viewing are between 11 a.m and 3 p.m. Monday-Friday. For more information on viewing FARA files contact the Internal Security Section at 202/514-1216. A photo ID is required for admittance into the building.

2) The Registration Unit is also the initial point of contact for registering as a foreign agent. It has information packets on the 1938 FARA act including guidelines on how to begin the registration process.

Filing

The Registration Unit furnishes a copy of all official registration forms to each registrant to provide an original copy on color coded paper to be photocopied and filed in triplicate. The original must be returned to the office as the various forms have been printed on different colored paper purposely to facilitate processing by the Department.

Compliance is accomplished by filing an original official registration form and two legible photocopies.

Additional copies of all registration forms are provided upon request.

Senior Justice Department Officials Responsible for FARA Enforcement:

John C. Keeney
Acting Assistant Attorney General for the Criminal Division
U.S. Department of Justice, Suite 2107
10th St. and Constitution Avenue, N.W.
Washington, D.C. 20530
202/514-2601

Frederick J. Close, Jr.
Chief
Registration Unit, Internal Security Section
U.S. Department of Justice
1400 New York Avenue, N.W. - Room 9300
Washington, D.C. 20530
202/514-1216   FAX 202/514-2836

"Nature of Services"

The following is a list of the acronyms/abbreviations used in this section to describe the Nature of Services (NS) that the registered agent is providing for a particular client.

A	Advertising
AC	Aviation Consulting
API	Advertising/Promotion of Industry
APR	Advertising/Public Relations
C	Consultant
CAPEC	Consultant/Asia Pacific Economic Cooperative
CC	Consultant-Communications
CITS	Consultant/International Telecommunications and Satellite
CL	Consultant/Lobbying
CLS	Consultant/Legal Services
CMA	Consultant/Military Advisor
CPR	Consultant/Public Relations
DF	Distribution of Film
DPM	Distribution of Printed Material
DS	Diplomatic Service
DTC	Defense Trade Consultant
E	Editor
EP	Export Promotion
FR	Fund Raising
FRL	Fund Raising/Lobbying
GRL	Government Relations/Lobbying
IMP	Import Promotion
IP	Industrial Promotion
IPL	Industry Promotion/Lobbyist
ITP	Investment and Trade Promotion
L	Lobbying
LO	Legal and Other Services/Lobbying
LOC	Legal Other Services/Consultant
LOPC	Legal Other Services/Political Consultant
LPR	Lobbying/Public Relations
LTP	Lobbying/Trade Promotion
M	Marketing
MEPR	Media Public Relations
MMFSC	Marketing Malta's Financial Services Center
MNL	Monthly News Letter
MPR	Marketing/Public Relations
MPRC	Media Public Relations Consultant
MR	Media Relations
MRAPI	Media Relations Advertising/Promotion of Investment
MRC	Medial Relations Consultant
MREP	Marketing Representative
MRL	Media Relations/Lobbying
MRPT	Media Relations/Promotion of Trade
MSS	Maritime Support Services
P	Publicity
PA	Political Activities
PAL	Political Activities/Lobbyist
PCC	Political Campaign Consultant
PE	Promotion of Economy
PEC	Promotion of Economy/Consultant

PED	Promotion of Economic Development
PET	Promotion of Economy and Trade
PETEI	Promotion of Economy, Trade & Environmental Issues
PEX2000	Promotion of Expo 2000
PFFUS	Promotion of French Film in the U.S.
PI	Promotion of Investment
PINPRTR	Promotion of Investment/Public Relations & Trade
PIPTRADE	Promotion of Industry/Promotion of Trade
PITL	Promotion of Investment & Trade Lobbying
PJUSS	Planning Japan-U.S. Seminar
PMR	Public Media Relations
PPOS	Promote Palm Oil Sales
PR	Public Relations
PRC	Public Relations Consultant
PRDPM	Public Relations/Distribution of Printed Material
PRPE	Public Relations/Promotion of Economy
PRPED	Public Relations/Promotion of Economic Development
PRPI	Public Relations/Promotion of Investment
PRPTI	Public Relations/Promotion of Trade & Investments
PT	Promotion of Tourism
PTE	Promotion of Trade and Economy
PTI	Promotion of Trade & Investment
PTRADE	Promotion of Trade
PTRCT	Promotion of Trade/Culture/Tourism
RJRTV	Rebroadcast Japan Radio & T.V. Programs
RV	Registration of Vessels
TC	Trade Consultant
TEP	Trade Economic Promotion
TEP	Trade & Economic Promotion
TIP	Trade & Investment Promotion
TRNC	Transportation Consultant
TXCL	Tax Consultant/Lobbying
USGAL	U.S. Government Activities/Lobbying
USPC	U.S. Policy Consultant
USPCL	U.S. Policy Consultant/Lobbying
USPCL	U.S. Policy Consultant/Lobbying
USPCPR	U.S. Policy Consultant/Public Relations
USPOC	U.S. Public Opinion Consultant
USTPC	U.S. Trade Policy Consultant
VPM	Visit Prime Minister

Afghanistan

Embassy of the Islamic State of Afghanistan
Agent: Jaffe, Jordan A.
NS: PR   CRD: 8/11/97

Islamic State of Afghanistan/Mission in the U.S.
Agent: Jennings, John M.
NS: LPR   CRD: 12/4/96

Angola

Center for Democracy in Angola
Agent: Black, Kelly, Scruggs & Healey
NS: L   CRD: 10/16/85

Center for Democracy in Angola, Inc.
Agent: Schochet, Kenneth Barry
NS: L   CRD: 8/27/87

Commercial Section of the Embassy of Angola
Agent: Bristol Group, Inc.
NS: PTRADE   CRD: 3/25/98

Embassy of the Republic of Angola
Agent: C/R International, LLC
NS: PINPRTR   CRD: 7/2/96

Government of Angola
Agent: Samuels International Associates, Inc.
NS: PITL   CRD: 8/26/93

Government of the Republic of Angola
Agent: Cohen & Woods International, Inc.
NS: L   CRD: 10/2/96

National Shippers' Council of Angola
Agent: Oceans International Corporation
NS: C   CRD: 10/21/96

National Union for the Total Independence of Angola (UNITA)
Agent: National Union for the Total Independence of Angola (UNITA)
NS: L   CRD: 3/21/86

Anguilla

Department of Tourism, Government of Anguilla
Agent: Medhurst & Associates, Inc.
NS: PR   CRD: 6/19/87

Antigua and Barbuda

Antigua Ministry of Tourism
Agent: Trombone Associates, Inc.
NS: PT   CRD: 12/6/91

Argentina

Siderca Corporation
Agent: Chlopak, Leonard, Schechter & Associates, Inc.
NS: PR   CRD: 9/28/94

Aruba

Government of Aruba
Agent: Rendon Group, Inc.
NS: PR   CRD: 4/11/95

Government of Aruba
Agent: Mark A. Siegel & Associates, Inc.
NS: L   CRD: 1/9/95

Government of Aruba
Agent: Aruba Tourism Authority
NS: PT   CRD: 12/29/78

Government of Aruba
Agent: Winston & Strawn
NS: USPC   CRD: 5/18/95

Government of Aruba
Agent: Winston & Strawn
NS: L   CRD: 5/18/95

Government of Aruba, Tourism Authority in North America
Agent: Lou Hammond & Associates, Inc.
NS: PR   CRD: 12/24/86

Australia

Australia - U.S. Business Council
Agent: Collier, Shannon, Rill & Scott
NS: MNL   CRD: 1/24/96

Australian Broadcasting Corporation
Agent: Australian Broadcasting Corporation
NS: PR   CRD: 11/19/46

Australian Dairy Industry
Agent: Collier, Shannon, Rill & Scott
NS: L   CRD: 12/21/94

Australian Meat & Livestock Corporation
Agent: Australian Meat & Livestock Corporation
NS: PTRADE   CRD: 9/29/75

Australian National Travel Association
Agent: Australian Tourist Commission
NS: PT   CRD: 6/3/57

Australian Oat Exporters' Group
Agent: Collier, Shannon, Rill & Scott
NS: EP   CRD: 7/24/95

Australian Tourist Commission
Agent: Lou Hammond & Associates, Inc.
NS: PT   CRD: 6/23/95

New South Wales Tourism Commission
Agent: Tourism New South Wales
NS: PT   CRD: 12/18/90

Pacific Dunlop, Ltd./Pacific Brands
Agent: Crowell & Moring International, L.P.
NS: CL   CRD: 6/29/95

Queensland Tourist & Travel Corporation
Agent: Queensland Tourist & Travel Corporation
NS: PT   CRD: 5/31/88

Queensland Travel & Tourist Corporation
Agent: Fontayne Group, Inc.
NS: PT   CRD: 3/8/94

Austria

Alpine Tourist Commission
Agent: Alpine Tourist Commission
NS: PT   CRD: 12/4/67

Austrian Airlines
Agent: Global Aviation Associates, Ltd.
NS: AC   CRD: 3/14/94

Austrian National Tourist Office
Agent: Fontayne Group, Inc.
NS: PR   CRD: 10/14/86

Austrian National Tourist Office
Agent: Austrian National Tourist Office, N.Y.
NS: PT   CRD: 10/3/47

Austrian Press & Information Office
Agent: Modern Education Services, Inc.

NS: DF   CRD: 10/7/88

Federal Economic Chamber of Austria
Agent: Austrian Trade Commission in the U.S., Southern Region
NS: PTRADE   CRD: 8/17/95

Azerbaijan

Embassy of Azerbaijan
Agent: Ed Graves & Associates
NS: L   CRD: 12/10/93

P-NN Arkansas, Inc.
Agent: Catlett & Yancey, PLC
NS: PTRADE   CRD: 5/17/94

Republic of Azerbaijan
Agent: Piriev, Nizami
NS: L   CRD: 8/3/94

Bahamas

Bahamas Ministry of Tourism
Agent: Bahamas Tourist Office
NS: PT   CRD: 1/27/72

Government of the Bahamas
Agent: BSMG Worldwide
NS: LO   CRD: 12/4/95

Ministries of Foreign Affairs, Justice, Tourism & Economics
Agent: Hogan & Hartson, L.L.P.
NS: LO   CRD: 6/24/77

Sun International, Inc.
Agent: M. Silver Associates, Inc.
NS: PR   CRD: 5/15/95

Bahrain

Ministry of Information, Government House, State of Bahrain
Agent: DMRansom Associates, Inc.
NS: PI   CRD: 5/20/98

Barbados

Barbados Industrial Development Corporation
Agent: W.D.B. Advertising
NS: API   CRD: 5/17/90

Barbados Industrial Development Corporation
Agent: Peter Rothholz Associates, Inc.
NS: PR   CRD: 12/15/86

Barbados Industrial Development Corporation
Agent: Barbados Investment & Develop. Corp.
NS: PTRADE   CRD: 11/5/71

Barbados Tourism Authority
Agent: Ruder & Finn, Inc.
NS: PR   CRD: 4/29/98

Barbados Tourist Board
Agent: Barbados Investment & Develop. Corp.
NS: PTRADE   CRD: 11/5/71

The Government of Barbados
Agent: Cameron & Hornbostel
NS: USPC   CRD: 8/19/92

Belgium

Belgian National Tourist Office
Agent: Belgian National Tourist Office

NS: PT   CRD: 6/17/48

European Electronic Component
   Manufacturers' Association
Agent: Collier, Shannon, Rill & Scott
NS: CRD: 5/27/92

Fabrique Nationale Herstal, S.A.
Agent: FN Manufacturing, Inc.
NS: IP   CRD: 8/18/93

Belize

Caribbean Banana Growers' Association
Agent: Ross-Robinson & Associates
NS: EP   CRD: 5/8/96

Government of Belize
Agent: Lugano Group, Inc.
NS: FR   CRD: 9/8/97

Bermuda

Bermuda Department of Tourism
Agent: DDB Needham Worldwide, Inc.
NS: A   CRD: 4/17/90

Cambridge Beaches Resort
Agent: Whitmore, Judith M.
NS: MPR   CRD: 9/22/92

Government of Bermuda
Agent: Garvey, Schubert & Barer
NS: LO   CRD: 10/6/94

Government of Bermuda
Agent: Wunder, Knight, Levine, Thelen &
Forscey, PLLC
NS: LO   CRD: 7/25/89

Government of Bermuda, Department of Tourism
Agent: Bermuda Department of Tourism
NS: PT   CRD: 7/14/48

William Mulder/Stonington Beach Hotel
Agent: Pratt, Madigan
NS: PT   CRD: 8/9/93

XL Insurance Company, Ltd.
Agent: Bernstein Law Firm, PLLC
NS: L   CRD: 2/8/93

Bosnia & Herzegovina

Federation of Bosnia and Herzegovina
Agent: Barnes & Thornburg
NS: LO   CRD: 3/2/98

Government of Republika Srpska
Agent: Sremac, Danielle
NS: PR   CRD: 7/29/94

Brazil

*Associacao Industries de Calcados do
   Rio Grands do Sul*
Agent: L.A. Motley & Company
NS: L   CRD: 8/15/85

Banco do Nordeste do Brasil, S.A.
Agent: Zemi Communications, LLC
NS: PI   CRD: 2/25/97

Companhia de Navegacao Alianca, S.A.
Agent: L.A. Motley & Company
NS: USPC   CRD: 11/7/97

Instituto Brasiliero De turismo (Embratur)
Agent: Zemi Communications, LLC

NS: PT   CRD: 1/30/98

Varig Brazilian Airlines
Agent: Holland & Knight
NS: USPC   CRD: 9/7/89

British Virgin Islands

British Virgin Islands Government
Agent: Hyman, Lester S.
NS: L   CRD: 3/26/97

British Virgin Islands Tourist Board
Agent: FCB/Leber Katz Partners, Inc.
NS: PT   CRD: 11/7/90

British Virgin Islands Tourist Board
Agent: British Virgin Islands Tourist Board
NS: PT   CRD: 4/8/82

Government of the British Virgin Islands
Agent: GCI Group Inc.
NS: PR   CRD: 8/25/95

Brunei

Brunei Investment Agency
Agent: Kaye, Scholer, Fierman, Hays & Handler
NS: USPC   CRD: 2/7/94

Bulgaria

Republic of Bulgaria
Agent: White & Case
NS: C   CRD: 4/9/92

Cambodia

Cambodian People's Party
Agent: David Morey Group, Inc. (DMG)
NS: USPC   CRD: 5/4/98

Cambodian People's Party
Agent: Porter, Wright, Morris & Arthur
NS: LO   CRD: 4/22/98

Cambodian People's Party
Agent: Arnold & Porter
NS: LO   CRD: 4/22/98

Embassy of the Kingdom of Cambodia
Agent: Porter, Wright, Morris & Arthur
NS: CLS   CRD: 9/15/97

Kingdom of Cambodia
Agent: Shandwick
NS: PR   CRD: 2/12/95

Canada

Alcan Aluminum, Ltd.
Agent: Strategic Policy, Inc.
NS: CRD: 8/12/96

Algoma Steel, Inc.
Agent: Hogan & Hartson, L.L.P.
NS: PTRADE   CRD: 5/23/94

Atlantis Submarines International, Inc.
Agent: Leone & Leone, Ltd.
NS: P   CRD: 2/12/92

Canadair: a division of Bombardier, Inc.
Agent: Fleishman-Hillard, Inc.
NS: PR   CRD: 3/6/95

Canadian Broadcasting Corporation

Agent: Finkelstein, Thompson & Loughran
NS: L   CRD: 9/25/97

Canadian Life and Health Insurance Association
Agent: Harcar, Mary V.
NS: LO   CRD: 3/2/90

Canadian Pacific Hotels & Resorts
Agent: Leone & Leone, Ltd.
NS: P   CRD: 3/22/95

Canadian Pulp & Paper Association
Agent: Moresby Consulting, Ltd.
NS: L   CRD: 10/14/94

Canadian Pulp & Paper Association
Agent: Rogers & Wells
NS: LO   CRD: 7/17/92

Cominco, Ltd.
Agent: Keller & Heckman
NS: LO   CRD: 4/25/95

Dofasco, Inc.
Agent: Rogers & Wells
NS: LO   CRD: 3/18/92

Embassy of the Government of Canada
Agent: Steptoe & Johnson LLP
NS: LO   CRD: 2/28/90

Foothills Pipe Lines, Ltd.
Agent: Van Ness Feldman, A Professional
Corporation
NS: LO   CRD: 8/11/94

Government of British Columbia
Agent: Akin, Gump, Strauss, Hauer & Feld,
L.L.P.
NS: TC   CRD: 1/15/98

*Government of British Columbia, Ministry of
   Devel., Trade/Tourism*
Agent: Miller & Chevalier, Chartered
NS: LO   CRD: 9/27/91

Government of Canada
Agent: Paul, Hastings, Janofsky & Walker
NS: LO   CRD: 7/17/96

Government of Canada
Agent: Miller & Chevalier, Chartered
NS: LO   CRD: 3/23/87

*Government of Canada, Dept. of
   Foreign Affairs/Int. Trade*
Agent: Coudert Brothers
NS: LO   CRD: 4/23/98

Government of Canada, Embassy
Agent: Garvey, Schubert & Barer
NS: USPC   CRD: 3/9/89

Government of Newfoundland & Labrador
Agent: Development Counsellors International
NS: PT   CRD: 6/28/96

*Government of Ontario, Ministry of Economic
   Devel. & Trade/Tourism*
Agent: Hogan & Hartson, L.L.P.
NS: LO   CRD: 5/29/87

Grand Council of the Crees of Quebec
Agent: Keiner & Dumont, P.C.
NS: LO   CRD: 6/19/89

Her Majesty the Queen in Right of Canada
Agent: Boland & Madigan, Inc.
NS: USPC   CRD: 3/24/98

Hydro-Quebec
Agent: Morley Caskin
NS: LPR   CRD: 1/8/97

Hydro-Quebec
Agent: Nixon, Hargrave, Devans & Doyle, LLP
NS: CL   CRD: 11/20/91

Le Gouvernement du Quebec
Agent: Pepper, Hamilton & Scheetz
NS: LO   CRD: 10/20/94

Ministry of Economical Development,
* Trade and Tourism of Canada*
Agent: Hill & Knowlton, Inc.
NS: PT   CRD: 5/1/97

National Film Board of Canada
Agent: National Film Board of Canada
NS: Promotes & disseminates   CRD: 4/21/44

Nordion International, Inc.
Agent: Shandwick
NS: USPC   CRD: 1/3/94

Nova Scotia Department of Tourism
Agent: Nova Scotia Information Centre
NS: PT   CRD: 12/18/78

Pottawatomi National
Agent: Native American Rights Fund
NS: LO   CRD: 7/19/93

Quebec Government
Agent: Quebec Government House
NS: PTRADE   CRD: 9/2/64

Stentor Telecom Policy, Inc.
Agent: Kathleen Winn & Associates, Inc.
NS: CL   CRD: 6/29/93

The Great Canadian Railtour Company, Ltd.
Agent: Leone & Leone, Ltd.
NS: P   CRD: 2/12/92

The Manufacturers Life Insurance Company
Agent: Britt, Jr., Raymond L.
NS: PTRADE   CRD: 1/19/84

TransCanada PipeLines
Agent: Levine, Leonard B.
NS: USGAL   CRD: 6/3/91

Cayman Islands

Cayman Islands Department of Tourism
Agent: O'Leary Clarke & Partners, Inc.
NS: PT   CRD: 2/20/86

Government of the Cayman Islands
Agent: Patrice Tanaka & Company, Inc.
NS: PT   CRD: 3/11/97

Government of the Cayman Islands
Agent: Sidley & Austin
NS: L   CRD: 9/13/85

Government of the Cayman Islands
Agent: Cayman Island Department of Tourism
NS: PT   CRD: 3/4/74

Rudi Sezzer - Director of Tourism
Agent: Pratt, Madigan
NS: PT   CRD: 4/29/94

Chile

Government of Chile
Agent: Weil, Gotshal & Manges
NS: PT   CRD: 9/12/95

Government of Chile
Agent: Verner, Liipfert, Bernhard, McPherson &
Hand, Chartered
NS: L   CRD: 10/3/97

Government of Chile, Office of Communications
Agent: Edelman Public Relations Worldwide
NS: PTRADE   CRD: 11/15/94

China

Air China International Corp., Ltd.
Agent: Graham & James
NS: LO   CRD: 10/23/91

Beijing Review
Agent: China Books & Periodicals, Inc.
NS: PR   CRD: 6/11/87

China Daily of Beijing, China
Agent: China Daily Distribution Corporation
NS: PR   CRD: 4/19/83

China Eastern Airlines
Agent: Graham & James
NS: LO   CRD: 10/23/91

China International Travel Service
Agent: China International Travel Service, Inc.
NS: PT   CRD: 12/30/81

China National Textiles Import/Export Corp.
Agent: Powell, Goldstein, Frazer & Murphy
NS: PTRADE   CRD: 10/1/97

China Ocean Shipping Company
Agent: Garvey, Schubert & Barer
NS: LO   CRD: 2/12/85

China Today
Agent: China Books & Periodicals, Inc.
NS: PR   CRD: 4/6/60

Chinese Science New Overseas Edition
Agent: Hai Tian Development U.S.A., Inc.
NS: DPM   CRD: 6/5/97

Chinese Science News Overseas Edition
Agent: KMC Trading
NS: DPM   CRD: 8/24/93

Embassy of the People's Republic of China
Agent: Jones, Day, Reavis & Pogue
NS: L   CRD: 1/31/86

Guoji Shudian
Agent: China Books & Periodicals, Inc.
NS: PR   CRD: 4/6/60

Nanjing Ya dong International Corporation, Ltd.
Agent: Atlantic Gulf Communities Corporation
NS: TIP   CRD: 3/7/95

Outlook Weekly
Agent: KMC Trading
NS: DPM   CRD: 10/17/94

People's Daily Overseas Edition
Agent: Hai Tian Development U.S.A., Inc.
NS: DPM   CRD: 12/3/96

People's Daily Overseas Edition
Agent: KMC Trading
NS: DPM   CRD: 3/20/92

Republic of China (Taiwan)
Agent: Verner, Liipfert, Bernhard, McPherson &
Hand, Chartered
NS: LO   CRD: 1/6/98

Xin Min Evening Newspaper
Agent: Xin Min International, Inc.
NS: DPM   CRD: 11/7/94

Colombia

Aerovias Nacionales de Colombia, S.A.
* (AVIANCA)*
Agent: Holland & Knight
NS: LO   CRD: 12/12/85

Federacion Nacional de Cafeteros de Colombia

Agent: Colombian Coffee Federation, Inc.
NS: A   CRD: 4/6/94

Government of Colombia, Embassy
Agent: Edelman Public Relations Worldwide
NS: MR   CRD: 4/1/98

Government of the Republic of Colombia
Agent: Kelley, Swofford, Roy, Helmke, Inc.
NS: LPR   CRD: 6/4/97

National Federation of Coffee Growers
* of Colombia*
Agent: DDB Needham Worldwide, Inc.
NS: A   CRD: 10/22/71

Senate of the Republic of Colombia
Agent: Greenberg Traurig Consulting, Inc.
NS: PR   CRD: 7/11/97

Sociedad Aeronautica de Medellin
Agent: Holland & Knight
NS: LOC   CRD: 3/8/91

The Government of the Republic of Colombia
Agent: Kelley Swofford Roy, Inc.
NS: USPCPR   CRD: 4/4/96

Congo

Republic of the Congo
Agent: Barron-Birrell, Inc.
NS: LO   CRD: 12/9/97

Congo, Republic of

Office of the President of the Rep. of the Congo
Agent: Washington World Group, Ltd.
NS: LPR   CRD: 12/18/96

Pascal Lissouba, Brazzaville, Congo
Agent: Barron-Birrell, Inc.
NS: CRD: 12/9/97

Republic of the Congo
Agent: Barron-Birrell, Inc.
NS: PR   CRD: 12/9/97

Costa Rica

Camara de Azucareros
Agent: Costa Rican Board of Trade
NS: PTRADE   CRD: 8/21/72

Republic of Costa Rica
Agent: Holland & Knight
NS: PR   CRD: 4/15/98

Textile Association of Costa Rica (ASFAMEX)
Agent: Costa Rican Board of Trade
NS: PTRADE   CRD: 8/21/72

Croatia

Ministry of Defense, Republic of Croatia
Agent: Global Enterprises Group, Inc.
NS: LTP   CRD: 12/17/93

Republic of Croatia
Agent: White & Case
NS: C   CRD: 10/11/96

Republic of Croatia
Agent: Hunton & Williams
NS: LO   CRD: 8/11/95

Republic of Croatia, Office of the Presidency
Agent: Jefferson-Waterman International, LLC
NS: USPCL   CRD: 2/6/95

Curacao

Atlantic Gulf Asia Holding, N.V.
Agent: Atlantic Gulf Communities Corporation
NS: TIP   CRD: 3/7/95

Curacao Tourism Development Bureau
Agent: Marcella Martinez Associates, Inc.
NS: PT   CRD: 8/23/93

Government of the Island of Curacao
Agent: Curacao Tourist Board
NS: PT   CRD: 3/10/81

Cyprus

Embassy of Cyprus
Agent: Mullin Communications, Inc.
NS: E   CRD: 4/17/98

Embassy of the Republic of Cyprus
Agent: Hogan & Hartson, L.L.P.
NS: LO   CRD: 10/3/97

Government of the Republic of Cyprus
Agent: Derwinski, Edward
NS: L   CRD: 4/11/95

R.R. Denktash
Agent: Office of the Turkish Republic
   of Northern Cyprus
NS: USPC   CRD: 10/16/75

The Republic of Cyprus
Agent: Evans Group, Ltd. (The)
NS: L   CRD: 3/2/89

Czech Republic

Czech Ministry of Foreign Affairs
Agent: Czech Center, New York
NS: PTRCT   CRD: 6/21/96

Denmark

A.P. Moller-Maersk
Agent: Sher & Blackwell
NS: L   CRD: 11/7/94

Danish Bacon and Meat Council
Agent: Berry, Max N.
NS: L   CRD: 5/28/97

Danish Biscuit Alliance
Agent: Berry, Max N.
NS: USPC   CRD: 3/10/98

Danish Ministry of Business & Industry
Agent: Brady Company, Inc.
NS: IP   CRD: 11/8/96

Danish Tourist Board
Agent: Danish Tourist Board
NS: PT   CRD: 7/25/50

Dominican Republic

*Consejo Nacional de Zonas Francas de
   Exportacion'*
Agent: Sandler & Travis Trade Advisory
   Services, Inc.
NS: USTPCL   CRD: 3/1/94

*Consejo Nacionalde Zonas Francas de
   Exportacion*
Agent: Sandler & Travis Trade Advisory
   Services, Inc.
NS: LO   CRD: 3/1/94

Government of the Dominican Republic
Agent: Johnson II, Robert Winthrop
NS: LO   CRD: 1/9/85

Partido de la Liberacion Dominicana
Agent: Partido de la Liberacion Dominicana,
   New York
NS: FR   CRD: 4/17/74

Egypt

Arab Republic of Egypt
Agent: Bannerman & Associates, Inc.
NS: USPC   CRD: 3/22/90

Egyptian Tourist Authority
Agent: Herman Associates, Inc.
NS: A   CRD: 6/13/95

*Ministry of Foreign Affairs, Government
   of the Arab Rep. of Egypt*
Agent: Daniel J. Edelman, Inc.
NS: CRD: 5/20/95

El Salvador

Embassy of El Salvador
Agent: Rick Swartz & Associates, Inc.
NS: L   CRD: 6/17/98

Embassy of El Salvador
Agent: Hogan & Hartson, L.L.P.
NS: LO   CRD: 6/17/71

Embassy of El Salvador
Agent: Veve, Michael E.
NS: LO   CRD: 1/13/93

Embassy of El Salvador
Agent: Bannerman & Associates, Inc.
NS: L   CRD: 7/29/93

Government of El Salvador, Embassy
Agent: Phoenix Group
NS: L   CRD: 9/8/95

Equatorial Guinea

Government of Equatorial Guinea, Embassy
Agent: Black, Kelly, Scruggs & Healey
NS: C   CRD: 10/16/95

Ethiopia

Ethiopian Medhin Democratic Party
Agent: North American Medhin
   Democratic Association
NS: PA   CRD: 4/17/92

Ethiopian Peoples' Revolutionary Party
Agent: Ethiopian Peoples' Revolutionary Party,
   The
NS: LPR   CRD: 4/7/93

Oromo Liberation Front (OLF)
Agent: Oromo Liberation Front,
   North America Office
NS: PA   CRD: 1/29/92

Finland

City of Helsinki
Agent: Barbara Burns & Associates, Inc.
NS: MRC   CRD: 8/4/97

Consulate General of Finland
Agent: Alden Films, Business Education Films,
   Films of the Nations
NS: PR   CRD: 6/30/76

Investment in Finland Bureau
Agent: Burson-Marsteller, Inc.
NS: PI   CRD: 9/5/95

Ministry of Trade & Industry
Agent: Finnish Tourist Board, New York
NS: PT   CRD: 10/30/73

France

Aeroport de Paris
Agent: Marketing Challenges International, Inc.
NS: PR   CRD: 1/28/88

Agence de Developpement de l'Alsace
Agent: ALSACE/USA
NS: PI   CRD: 10/19/95

Airbus Industrie, G.I.E.
Agent: Hamilton, Charles A.
NS: USPCL   CRD: 1/25/91

Arianespace, S.A.
Agent: Arianespace, Inc.
NS: A   CRD: 4/30/85

*Avions de Transport Regional Groupement
   d'Interet Economique*
Agent: Powell Tate, Inc.
NS: PR   CRD: 12/30/96

*Cartre d'Arde au developpment des Entreprises
   de Bourgoque (CADEB)*
Agent: Levin Public Relations & Marketing, Inc.
NS: PR   CRD: 10/29/97

*Centre National Interprofessional d'Economie
   Laitiere*
Agent: Berry, Max N.
NS: LO   CRD: 6/3/80

*Compagnie Generale des Matieres Nucleaires,
   Subsidiary of*
Agent: COGEMA, Inc.
NS: PTRADE   CRD: 5/17/84

Credit Lyonnais
Agent: Shearman & Sterling
NS: LO   CRD: 5/7/98

Electricite de France
Agent: Fleishman-Hillard, Inc.
NS: PR   CRD: 3/5/92

GIAT Industries, S.A.
Agent: FN Manufacturing, Inc.
NS: IP   CRD: 8/18/93

*L'Association de Development du Bas-Phine
   (ADIRA)*
Agent: Alsace Development Agency
NS: PTRADE   CRD: 8/10/83

*Nociete National d'Etude et de Construction de
   Moteurs d'Aviation*
Agent: Meredith Concept Group, Inc.
NS: L   CRD: 3/20/96

Port Autonome du Havre
Agent: Barbara Burns & Associates, Inc.
NS: PR   CRD: 12/6/91

Rhone-Poulenc, S.A.
Agent: Baker & Botts, L.L.P.
NS: LO   CRD: 5/1/91

Thomson-CSF, S.A.
Agent: Thomson-CSF, Inc.
NS: LPR   CRD: 4/2/92

Unifrance File International
Agent: French Film Office
NS: PFFUS   CRD: 7/20/72

Gabon

Air Gabon
Agent: Legesse Travel & Tourism Consultants
NS: PT   CRD: 7/25/84

Gabon Ministry of Tourism
Agent: Legesse Travel & Tourism Consultants
NS: PT   CRD: 8/27/81

His Excellency El Hadj Omar Bongo
    (Gabonese President)
Agent: Salinger, Pierre
NS: PR   CRD: 12/30/97

Jean-Pierre Lemboumba
Agent: Eurostrategy Associates, Inc.
NS: PRC   CRD: 4/7/93

Republic of Gabon
Agent: Shandwick Public Affairs, Inc.
NS: PR   CRD: 12/30/97

Republic of Gabon
Agent: Barron-Birrell, Inc.
NS: PR   CRD: 3/2/98

Republic of Gabon
Agent: White & Case
NS: LO   CRD: 5/2/78

Gambia

Republic of the Gambia, Embassy
Agent: Washington World Group, Ltd.
NS: LPR   CRD: 12/18/97

Georgia

Embassy of Georgia
Agent: Capitol Advisors, Inc.
NS: IP   CRD: 3/25/98

Republic of Abkhazia
Agent: Kazan, Yanal
NS: LPR   CRD: 12/6/93

Republic of Georgia, Embassy
Agent: Skadden, Arps, Slate, Meagher & Flom
    LLP
NS: USPC   CRD: 7/29/97

Germany

AEG Electromcom GmbH
Agent: Civic Service, Inc.
NS: USPC   CRD: 7/28/92

Baden-Wuerttemburg Agency for International
    Economic Corp. GWZ
Agent: Moltzan, Gunter W.
NS: IP   CRD: 3/11/96

Bayer, Inc. Subsidiary of Bayer, A.G.
Agent: Barnes, Richardson & Colburn
NS: LO   CRD: 8/8/89

Berlin Tourismus Marketing GmbH
Agent: InterMarketing, Inc.
NS: PT   CRD: 8/29/94

Bundesverband der Deutschen Industrie
Agent: Rep. of German Industry & Trade
NS: PRPTI   CRD: 7/21/89

Business Location Germany
Agent: Fleishman-Hillard, Inc.
NS: PRPE   CRD: 5/5/97

Daimler-Benz Aerospace, A.G.
Agent: Pierson & Burnett, LLP
NS: LO   CRD: 8/7/96

Daimler-Benz Aerospace, A.G.
Agent: Daimler-Benz Aerospace of North
    America, Inc.
NS: CL   CRD: 10/9/92

Deutsche Telecom, A.G.
Agent: Deutsche Telekom, Inc.
NS: PIPTRADE   CRD: 10/9/90

Deutsche Zentrale fuer Tourismus (German
    National Tourist Board)
Agent: German National Tourist Office
NS: PT   CRD: 2/28/50

Deutscher Industrie - und Handelstag
Agent: Rep. of German Industry & Trade
NS: PRPTI   CRD: 7/21/89

Deutscher Industrie - und Handelstag
    (German National)
Agent: German-American Chamber of
    Commerce of Los Angeles, Inc.
NS: PTRADE   CRD: 3/14/75

Federal Republic of Germany
Agent: West Glen Communications
NS: DF   CRD: 11/23/88

German Convention Bureau
Agent: Trombone Associates, Inc.
NS: A   CRD: 12/6/91

German Information Center
Agent: West Glen Communications
NS: DF   CRD: 11/23/88

German Information Center
Agent: DDC Productions, Inc.
NS: MR   CRD: 12/20/84

German National Tourist Office
Agent: Trombone Associates, Inc.
NS: A   CRD: 12/6/91

Thyssen Rheinstahl Technik (TRT)
Agent: Gerich, Walter Raymond
NS: IP   CRD: 1/27/84

Greece

Greek National Tourist Organization
Agent: Berk, Peggy
NS: PT   CRD: 7/31/96

Hellenic Marine Environment Progrection
    Association (HELMEPA)
Agent: Sampson, Theodore James
NS: USPC   CRD: 3/30/98

Union of Greek Shipowners
Agent: Welch, Edmund Burt
NS: L   CRD: 10/15/97

Grenada

Grenada Board of Tourism
Agent: Trombone Associates, Inc.
NS: PT   CRD: 8/30/96

The Government of Grenada
Agent: Grenada Board of Tourism
NS: PT   CRD: 9/10/72

Guadeloupe & Martinique

Martinique & Guadeloupe Tourism
Agent: Clement-Petrocik Company, The
NS: PT   CRD: 3/18/71

Guatemala

CBI Sugar Group
Agent: Ed Graves & Associates
NS: GRL   CRD: 7/10/91

Guinea

Republic of Guinea
Agent: White & Case
NS: LO   CRD: 1/15/85

Guinea-Bissau

People of the Republic of Guinea Bissau
Agent: SACUR
NS: FR   CRD: 11/15/94

Guyana

Guyana Republican Party
Agent: Guyana Republican Party
NS: FR   CRD: 4/17/89

Republic of Guyana
Agent: Reichler, Milton & Medel
NS: LO   CRD: 3/3/93

Haiti

Embassy of Haiti
Agent: McKinney & McDowell Associates
NS: MR   CRD: 7/25/96

Government of Haiti
Agent: Ross-Robinson & Associates
NS: L   CRD: 2/7/95

Government of Haiti (Customs)
Agent: Sandler & Travis Trade Advisory
    Services, Inc.
NS: PTRADE   CRD: 7/19/97

Government of Haiti, Embassy
Agent: Trouillot, Mildred
NS: L   CRD: 2/8/93

Government of the Republic of Haiti
Agent: Arent Fox Kintner Plotkin & Kahn
NS: LO   CRD: 10/10/91

Republic of Haiti
Agent: Kurzban, Kurzban & Weinger, P.A.
NS: LO   CRD: 12/31/91

Honduras

Republic of Honduras
Agent: Reichler, Milton & Medel
NS: L   CRD: 4/26/96

Hong Kong

Better Hong Kong Foundation (BHKF)
Agent: Burson-Marsteller, Inc.

NS: PR   CRD: 6/4/96

Government of Hong Kong
Agent: Ketchum Communications
NS: MR   CRD: 4/12/96

Government of Hong Kong
Agent: Hong Kong Tourist Association
NS: PT   CRD: 10/29/68

*Government of Hong Kong Special
    Administrative Region*
Agent: Shandwick Public Affairs, Inc.
NS: PR   CRD: 4/10/98

Hong Kong Economic and Trade Office
Agent: Powell, Goldstein, Frazer & Murphy
NS: USPC   CRD: 11/21/97

Hong Kong Trade Development Council
Agent: Hong Kong Trade Develop. Council, Inc.
NS: PTRADE   CRD: 1/19/70

Hong Kong Trade Development Council
Agent: Arter & Hadden
NS: LO   CRD: 6/26/95

Hong Kong Trade Development Council
Agent: Powell, Goldstein, Frazer & Murphy
NS: PTRADE   CRD: 10/1/97

Physical Health Center of Hong Kong, Ltd.
Agent: GCI Group Inc.
NS: PR   CRD: 9/25/97

Hungary

Hungarian Broadcasting Corporation
Agent: Ruder & Finn, Inc.
NS: IP   CRD: 4/29/98

Iceland

Embassy of Iceland
Agent: Hall, Thomas Forrest
NS: CMA   CRD: 12/18/97

Government of Iceland
Agent: Kronmiller, Theodore George
NS: LO   CRD: 1/15/93

Iceland Tourist Board
Agent: Iceland Tourist Board
NS: PT   CRD: 2/15/78

India

Council of Khalistan
Agent: Council of Khalistan
NS: L   CRD: 5/11/88

Embassy of the Government of India
Agent: Washington Group
NS: LPR   CRD: 1/25/94

Government of India
Agent: American Continental Group
NS: L   CRD: 3/4/96

Government of India
Agent: Government of India Tourist Office,
    New York
NS: PT   CRD: 4/5/72

Government of India Tourist Office
Agent: Oasis International Group, Ltd.
NS: PT   CRD: 6/24/96

Nat'l Ass'n of Software & Service Companies
Agent: Washington Group
NS: LO   CRD: 12/1/95

Trade Development Authority
Agent: India Trade Promotion Organization
NS: PTRADE   CRD: 10/26/78

Indonesia

Government of Indonesia
Agent: Burson-Marsteller, Inc.
NS: C   CRD: 4/17/92

Indonesian Tourist Promotion Board
Agent: Indonesia Tourist Promotion
    Office for North America
NS: PT   CRD: 2/15/77

Lembaga Bantuan Perasaran & Managemen
Agent: Bogle & Gates
NS: USPC   CRD: 9/14/89

Mercurindo
Agent: BSMG Worldwide
NS: LO   CRD: 8/8/95

Ministry of Trade, Government of Indonesia
Agent: Crowell & Moring International, L.P.
NS: PTRADE   CRD: 1/13/94

Republic of Indonesia
Agent: White & Case
NS: LO   CRD: 3/9/77

International

Alexandre Sambat
Agent: McNeill, John
NS: PCC   CRD: 8/11/93

Allthane Technologies
Agent: TKC International, Inc.
NS: CRD: 1/9/94

Asatsu, Inc.
Agent: Asatsu America, Inc.
NS: DF   CRD: 3/6/98

*Asia Pacific Economic Cooperation of
    the Philippines*
Agent: Crowell & Moring International, L.P.
NS: C   CRD: 8/9/96

*Association des Amidonneries de Cereals
    de L.U.E.*
Agent: O'Mara, Charles J.
NS: CRD: 3/25/97

ASEA Brown Boveri
Agent: Ruder & Finn, Inc.
NS: PR   CRD: 10/30/90

ASEAN Permanent Committee on Tourism
Agent: ASEAN Promotional Chapter for
    Tourism - North America
NS: PTRADE   CRD: 1/4/77

Base Petroleum
Agent: C/R International, LLC
NS: PEC   CRD: 7/16/96

Caribbean Ispat, Ltd.
Agent: Steptoe & Johnson LLP
NS: LO   CRD: 8/11/97

Caribbean Tourism Organization
Agent: Caribbean Tourism Organization
NS: PT   CRD: 3/2/94

Cathay Pacific Airways Limited
Agent: Ruder & Finn, Inc.
NS: PR   CRD: 4/29/98

Cemex Central
Agent: Public Strategies, Inc.
NS: CC   CRD: 11/28/97

*Center for Information and Business
    Development (CIDEM)*
Agent: Burson-Marsteller, Inc.
NS: MPRC   CRD: 10/24/96

Chungchong Nam-Do Provincial Government
Agent: Chungchong Nam-Do Provincial
    Government, New York
NS: PTRADE   CRD: 6/23/97

Coalition for Safe Ceramicware
Agent: Collier, Shannon, Rill & Scott
NS: LO   CRD: 6/12/92

Coca Cola Femsa, S.A. de C.V.
Agent: Ruder & Finn, Inc.
NS: E   CRD: 8/22/97

Cominco, Ltd.
Agent: Cominco America, Inc.
NS: L   CRD: 3/17/98

*Comision Ejecutiva Hidroelectrica del
    Rio Lempa CEL*
Agent: Black, Kelly, Scruggs & Healey
NS: PR   CRD: 3/20/98

*Comision Ejecutive Hidroelectrica del
    Rio Lempa CEL*
Agent: Burson-Marsteller, Inc.
NS: PR   CRD: 3/20/98

Comsion Federal de Telecommunicaciones
Agent: Harris, Wiltshire & Grannis, LLP
NS: USPC   CRD: 2/27/98

Cruz Enverga & Raboca
Agent: Chlopak, Leonard, Schechter &
    Associates, Inc.
NS: LO   CRD: 4/14/98

Director General of Civil Aviation
Agent: Howie, Irene E.
NS: USPC   CRD: 2/27/98

East Asia Travel Association
Agent: East Asia Travel Association
NS: PT   CRD: 5/7/73

*Empresa Estatal de Telecommunicaciones
    (Emtel)*
Agent: Shaw, Pittman, Potts & Trowbridge
NS: LO   CRD: 7/31/97

European Community
Agent: Karol Media, Inc.
NS: DF   CRD: 1/15/98

European Travel Commission
Agent: European Travel Commission
NS: PT   CRD: 6/6/49

European Travel Commission
Agent: Donald N. Martin & Company, Inc.
NS: PT   CRD: 7/29/60

Expo 2000- General Kommissariat
Agent: Pordzik, Wolfgang G.
NS: PEX2000   CRD: 7/14/97

Exportadora De Sal, S.A. De C.V. (ESSA)
Agent: Ruder Finn, Inc.
NS: PR   CRD: 4/21/97

Federation of Electric Power Companies
Agent: Porter/Novelli
NS: MR   CRD: 6/30/97

Florida International Bankers Association
Agent: Holland & Knight
NS: LO   CRD: 12/19/91

Fouad Makhzoumi
Agent: Future Millennium Foundation, Inc.
NS: PED   CRD: 8/15/97

Four Seasons Hotels, Inc.

Agent: Ruder & Finn, Inc.
NS: PR   CRD: 4/29/98

Gilat Satellite Networks, Ltd.
Agent: Ruder & Finn, Inc.
NS: PRPI   CRD: 11/1/93

Government of Trinidad and Tobago
Agent: Steptoe & Johnson LLP
NS: LO   CRD: 9/4/97

Grupo Televisa, S.A.
Agent: Leventhal, Senter & Lerman
NS: LO   CRD: 3/4/97

Inkatha Freedom Party
Agent: Mzimela, Sipo Elijah
NS: PAL   CRD: 4/1/91

International Airline Coalition on
the Rule of Law
Agent: Steptoe & Johnson LLP
NS: L   CRD: 7/15/96

International Crystal Federation
Agent: Collier, Shannon, Rill & Scott
NS: LO   CRD: 6/1/92

Joint Stock Commercial Bank - UNIBEST
Agent: Hogan & Hartson, L.L.P.
NS: USPC   CRD: 10/27/97

League of Arab States
Agent: Arab Information Center
NS: PT   CRD: 8/15/66

Macronix International
Agent: GCI Group Inc.
NS: PR   CRD: 3/10/97

Manufactured Imports Promotion Org. (MIPRO)
Agent: Manufactured Imports Promotion
Organization (MIPRO)
NS: PTRADE   CRD: 2/5/81

Meat Industry Council
Agent: Nichols-Dezenhall Communications
Management Group, Inc.
NS: MR   CRD: 6/5/97

Meat Industry Council
Agent: Olsson, Frank & Weeds, P.C.
NS: CL   CRD: 4/21/97

MERHAV
Agent: Powell Tate, Inc.
NS: PE   CRD: 4/7/97

Middle East Airlines
Agent: Dickstein Shapiro Morin & Oshinsky
L.L.P.
NS: LO   CRD: 7/22/81

Ministerio del Interior Unidat Ejectiva
de Programas Especiales
Agent: Napolitano, Francisco
NS: PR   CRD: 12/15/97

Novartis, A.G.
Agent: Ruder & Finn, Inc.
NS: APR   CRD: 4/24/97

NOVA Gas International, Ltd.
Agent: Stuntz, Davis & Staffier, P.C.
NS: LO   CRD: 6/23/97

Organization of Eastern Caribbean States
Agent: Eastern Caribbean Investment
Promotion Service
NS: PI   CRD: 1/14/88

Orient Airlines Association
Agent: Global Aviation Associates, Ltd.
NS: L   CRD: 11/6/95

P.T. Teknojasa Sapta Utama (TSU)
Agent: KCM International, Inc.

NS: L   CRD: 4/11/97

Partido Reformista
Agent: Partido Reformista Social Cristiano
NS: FR   CRD: 2/5/64

Powerex
Agent: Brady & Berliner
NS: USPC   CRD: 4/2/97

President-Elect Kim Dae Jung/transition team
Agent: David Morey Group, Inc. (DMG)
NS: C   CRD: 2/19/98

Proexport
Agent: O'Connor & Hannan
NS: L   CRD: 5/22/95

ProExport
Agent: Powell, Goldstein, Frazer & Murphy
NS: TEP   CRD: 10/1/97

Rafael USA, Inc.
Agent: Yitzhaki, Eliyahu
NS: CL   CRD: 9/15/97

Ranbaxy Laboratories, Ltd.
Agent: Ruder & Finn, Inc.
NS: MRC   CRD: 10/28/94

RAO Gazprom
Agent: Hill & Knowlton, Inc.
NS: PR   CRD: 10/29/97

Republic of Cote d'Ivoire
Agent: Cohen & Woods International, Inc.
NS: PR   CRD: 7/18/95

Resource Group International
Agent: Rockey Company, Inc.
NS: DPM   CRD: 12/22/95

Russian-American Partnership Center
Agent: Russian-American Partnership Center,
Washington, DC
NS: L   CRD: 11/21/96

Sandline International
Agent: McCabe, Jr., Bernard J.
NS: IP   CRD: 1/29/97

Sandline International
Agent: Webster, Chamberlain & Bean
NS: C   CRD: 10/16/96

Sealand Housing Corporation
Agent: GCI Group Inc.
NS: PR   CRD: 9/25/97

Secretariat of the Common Market of
Eastern and Southern Africa
Agent: Pierson, Semmes and Bemis, LLP
NS: L   CRD: 4/16/98

SGS Government Programs, Inc.
Agent: Shea & Gardner
NS: LO   CRD: 11/30/87

SGS North America, Inc.
Agent: Shea & Gardner
NS: LO   CRD: 10/30/86

Sierra Rutile America, Inc.
Agent: Sierra Rutile America, Inc.
NS: L   CRD: 6/10/96

Societe General de Surveillance (SGS)
Agent: Powell Tate, Inc.
NS: PR   CRD: 12/8/97

Tilda Rice
Agent: O'Mara, Charles J.
NS: TRADE   CRD: 5/30/97

Trizec-Hahn Corporation
Agent: Baker & McKenzie
NS: LO   CRD: 11/12/91

Tyne & Wear Development Company
Agent: Hennessey, Timothy J.
NS: IP   CRD: 3/1/98

U Khin Shwe, Chairman & CEO of Zay
Kabar Company, Ltd.
Agent: Bain & Associates
NS: DPM   CRD: 9/4/97

Unicom Management Services, Ltd.
Agent: Brown Nelson & Associates, Inc.
NS: USPC   CRD: 3/30/98

Urenco, Ltd.
Agent: Urenco, Inc.
NS: LPR   CRD: 11/8/97

Virgin Atlantic Airways, Ltd.
Agent: CMG Communications, LLC
NS: A   CRD: 6/24/96

Vitro, Sociedad Anonima
Agent: Ruder & Finn, Inc.
NS: E   CRD: 8/22/97

Volgograd Administration
Agent: Hanna, Albert Rowell
NS: PTRADE   CRD: 7/19/96

Winnington, Ltd.
Agent: Cohen & Woods International, Inc.
NS: IP   CRD: 12/31/97

Xunta de Galicia
Agent: Instituto Galego de Promocion Economica
(IGAPE), New York
NS: PI   CRD: 9/12/97

Yorkshire & Humberside Develop. Association
Agent: YHDA International
NS: PI   CRD: 10/12/90

Iran

Press Office of the People's Mojahedin of Iran
Agent: People's Mojadehin of Iran,
Washington, D.C., Press Office
NS: MR   CRD: 11/20/87

Ireland

An Bord Trachtala/Irish Lrade Board
Agent: An Bord Trachtala/ Irish Trade Board
NS: PTRADE   CRD: 6/3/74

Bord Failte Eireann (Government of
Ireland Tourist Board)
Agent: Irish Tourist Board
NS: PT   CRD: 8/1/74

Fianna Fail
Agent: Friends of Fianna Fail, Inc.
NS: L   CRD: 6/8/84

Fine Gael
Agent: Friends of Fine Gael, Inc.
NS: FR   CRD: 11/8/95

Friends of Sinn Fein
Agent: McKinney & McDowell Associates
NS: MR   CRD: 7/25/96

Industrial Development Authority of Ireland
Agent: Horst & Frisch, Inc.
NS: C   CRD: 3/3/92

Irish Development Authority - Irish Govt. Body
Agent: IDA Ireland
NS: PTRADE   CRD: 7/10/64

Labour Party, Republic of Ireland
Agent: Friends of Irish Labour in America
NS: FR   CRD: 6/6/96

Northern Ireland Free Trade Initiative
Agent: Pathfinder Group, LLC
NS: L   CRD: 5/21/98

Shannon Free Airport Development Co., Ltd.
Agent: Shannon Free Airport Develop. Co., Ltd.
NS: IP   CRD: 10/23/73

Israel

Consulate General of Israel
Agent: Alden Films, Business Education Films,
   Films of the Nations
NS: CRD: 5/29/69

Government of Israel
Agent: Sidley & Austin
NS: LO   CRD: 7/27/92

*Government of Israel, Economic Mission to
   North America*
Agent: Burson-Marsteller, Inc.
NS: MPR   CRD: 8/13/97

Government of Israel, Ministry of Defense
Agent: Mintz, Victor K.
NS: L   CRD: 9/15/87

Government of Israel, Ministry of Defense
Agent: Dater, Elliott
NS: CL   CRD: 12/6/89

*Government of Israel/Ministry of Defense,
   Mission to the U.S.*
Agent: Forman, Jay
NS: LO   CRD: 8/25/88

Israel Lane Development Company
Agent: Ruder & Finn, Inc.
NS: PI   CRD: 4/29/94

Israeli Government Tourist Office
Agent: West Glen Communications
NS: DF   CRD: 11/23/88

Rafael Armament Development Authority
Agent: Rafiah, Zvi
NS: L   CRD: 12/1/92

State of Israel
Agent: Arnold & Porter
NS: L   CRD: 1/20/88

The Exec. of the World Zionist Org., Jerusalem
Agent: World Zionist Organization - American
Section, Inc.
NS: L   CRD: 9/21/71

Italy

Assicurazione Nazionale Imprese Assicuratrici
Agent: Hopkins & Sutter
NS: LO   CRD: 10/6/95

Ente Nazionale Italiano per il Turismo
Agent: Italian Government Tourist Board
   (ENIT), Chicago
NS: PT   CRD: 6/7/68

Ente Nazionale Italiano per il Turismo
Agent: Italian Government Tourist Board
   (ENIT), Los Angeles
NS: PT   CRD: 4/19/65

Ente Nazionale Italiano per il Turismo
Agent: Italian Government Tourist Board
   (ENIT), New York
NS: PT   CRD: 4/21/49

International Olive Oil Council, S.P.A.
Agent: Foodcom, Inc.
NS: IP   CRD: 2/21/89

M. Scott Vayer - Assicurazioni Generali, S.P.A.
Agent: Chlopak, Leonard, Schechter &
   Associates, Inc.
NS: CPR   CRD: 7/9/97

*Mr. Pier Francesco Guarguaglini,
   Managing Director*
Agent: Delta Tech, Inc.
NS: DTC   CRD: 5/20/94

Trentino Tourist Board (A.P.T.T.)
Agent: Hill & Knowlton, Inc.
NS: PR   CRD: 4/18/95

Jamaica

Government of Jamaica
Agent: JAMPRO
NS: IPL   CRD: 3/29/89

Government of Jamaica
Agent: Holland & Knight
NS: USPC   CRD: 8/15/96

Government of Jamaica
Agent: Holland & Knight
NS: LO   CRD: 8/15/96

Government of Jamaica
Agent: Jefferson-Waterman International, LLC
NS: LO   CRD: 2/6/95

Government of Jamaica
Agent: Ward, Curtis A.
NS: LO   CRD: 11/7/91

Jamaica Ministry of Tourism
Agent: Peter Martin Associates, Inc.
NS: PT   CRD: 4/5/89

Jamaica Tourist Board
Agent: Jamaica Tourist Board, New York
NS: PT   CRD: 5/3/61

Jamaica Tourist Board
Agent: Jamaica Tourist Board, Los Angeles
NS: PT   CRD: 11/18/81

Jamaica Tourist Board
Agent: Jamaica Tourist Board, Florida
NS: PT   CRD: 7/26/72

Jamaica Tourist Board
Agent: Jamaica Tourist Board, Chicago
NS: PT   CRD: 12/16/68

Jamaica Tourist Board
Agent: FCB/Leber Katz Partners, Inc.
NS: A   CRD: 6/20/90

Peoples' National Party
Agent: Jamaica Progressive League, Inc.
NS: L   CRD: 3/9/45

Japan

City of Osaka
Agent: JETRO, Chicago
NS: PTRADE   CRD: 5/28/74

Consulate General of Japan
Agent: Whitehouse Associates, Inc.
NS: PR   CRD: 2/24/70

Consulate General of Japan
Agent: Bernhagen & Associates
NS: PR   CRD: 6/15/87

Electronic Industries Association of Japan
Agent: Schmertz Company, Inc., The
NS: PR   CRD: 8/16/93

Electronic Industry Association of Japan

Agent: Powell Tate, Inc.
NS: PR   CRD: 12/30/96

Embassy of Japan
Agent: Mullin Communications, Inc.
NS: E   CRD: 4/17/98

Embassy of Japan
Agent: Smith, Dawson & Andrews, Inc.
NS: USPC   CRD: 10/27/97

Embassy of Japan
Agent: Hogan & Hartson, L.L.P.
NS: LO   CRD: 5/7/71

Embassy of Japan
Agent: Saunders & Company
NS: USPC   CRD: 3/8/83

Embassy of Japan
Agent: Dechert, Price & Rhoads
NS: LO   CRD: 4/27/77

Embassy of Japan
Agent: Larry C. Wallace & Associates, P.A.
NS: LTP   CRD: 11/7/95

Export-Import Bank of Japan
Agent: Dechert, Price & Rhoads
NS: LO   CRD: 4/27/77

*Fair Trade Center, Institute for
   International Trade & Investment*
Agent: Willkie Farr & Gallagher
NS: LOC   CRD: 2/20/91

*Federation of Electric Power
   Companies of Japan*
Agent: Washington Policy & Analysis, Inc.
NS: PR   CRD: 6/22/94

*Federation of Electric Power
   Companies of Japan*
Agent: Federation of Electric Power
   Companies of Japan
NS: PR   CRD: 6/22/94

*Federation of Electric Power
   Companies of Japan*
Agent: E. Bruce Harrison Company
NS: CPR   CRD: 8/4/94

*Federation of Electric Power
   Companies of Japan*
Agent: Denison, George H.
NS: L   CRD: 2/14/95

Fujitsu, Ltd.
Agent: Sitrick Krantz & Company, Inc.
NS: CPR   CRD: 10/14/94

Fujitsu, Ltd.
Agent: Michael Solomon Associates
NS: PR   CRD: 10/2/87

Fukui Prefectural Government
Agent: JETRO, New York
NS: PTRADE   CRD: 12/24/87

Government of Japan
Agent: Japan Economic Institute of America
NS: PT   CRD: 1/25/56

Government of Japan, Consulate
Agent: Keene & Associates
NS: LO   CRD: 5/14/91

Hitachi, Ltd.
Agent: Hill & Knowlton, Inc.
NS: PR   CRD: 3/30/87

Hokkaido Prefectural Government
Agent: JETRO, Los Angeles
NS: PTRADE   CRD: 5/28/74

International Business Organization of Osaka
Agent: Osaka Prefectual Government,

California Office
NS: PE   CRD: 4/21/97

International Public Relations Company, Ltd.
Agent: TKC International, Inc.
NS: USPC   CRD: 9/10/81

International Public Relations Company, Ltd.
Agent: Civic Service, Inc.
NS: USPC   CRD: 6/28/82

Japan Auto. Manufacturers Association (JAMA)
Agent: Jellinek, Schwartz & Connolly, Inc.
NS: C   CRD: 7/1/93

Japan Automobile Manufacturers' Association
Agent: Porter/Novelli
NS: PR   CRD: 5/18/92

Japan Auto. Manufacturers' Association, Inc.
Agent: Maseng Communications
NS: PR   CRD: 5/5/92

Japan Development Bank
Agent: U.S. Representative Office of the
    Japan Development Bank
NS: PE   CRD: 1/21/97

Japan Economic Foundation
Agent: Business Network Corporation
NS: DPM   CRD: 5/20/91

Japan External Trade Organization
Agent: Afridi & Angell
NS: PR   CRD: 2/4/98

Japan External Trade Organization
Agent: JETRO, New York
NS: PTRADE   CRD: 6/25/63

Japan External Trade Organization
Agent: Jefferson-Waterman International, LLC
NS: USPC   CRD: 3/24/95

Japan External Trade Organization
Agent: MS Research, Inc.
NS: PR   CRD: 8/10/92

Japan External Trade Organization (JETRO)
Agent: Business Network Corporation
NS: DPM   CRD: 11/24/97

Japan External Trade Organization (JETRO)
Agent: Smith McCabe, Ltd.
NS: USPOC   CRD: 12/5/97

Japan External Trade Organization (JETRO)
Agent: JETRO, San Francisco
NS: PTRADE   CRD: 11/5/64

Japan External Trade Organization (JETRO)
Agent: JETRO, Los Angeles
NS: PTRADE   CRD: 12/14/64

Japan External Trade Organization (JETRO)
Agent: JETRO, Denver
NS: PTRADE   CRD: 7/28/87

Japan External Trade Organization (JETRO)
Agent: JETRO, Chicago
NS: PTRADE   CRD: 2/2/65

Japan External Trade Organization (JETRO)
Agent: JETRO, Atlanta
NS: PTRADE   CRD: 12/1/87

Japan External Trade Organization (JETRO)
Agent: JETRO, Houston
NS: PTRADE   CRD: 9/20/71

Japan External Trade Organization (JETRO)
Agent: JETRO, Dallas
NS: PTRADE   CRD: 8/8/77

Japan External Trade Org. (JETRO, Chicago)
Agent: Mayeroff, Jerry M.
NS: MR   CRD: 11/7/95

Japan Federation of Construction Contractors
Agent: JFCC, Washington Office
NS: PR   CRD: 11/21/90

Japan Federation of Construction Contractors
Agent: Civic Service, Inc.
NS: USPC   CRD: 8/24/95

Japan Fisheries Association
Agent: Tele-Press Associates, Inc.
NS: L   CRD: 9/30/77

Japan Fisheries Association
Agent: Garvey, Schubert & Barer
NS: LO   CRD: 2/22/82

Japan Fisheries Association
Agent: Hastings, Jay Donald
NS: IP   CRD: 11/16/78

Japan Information Center (Consulate of Japan)
Agent: Modern Education Services, Inc.
NS: PR   CRD: 7/30/81

Japan International Agricultural Council (JIAC)
Agent: Donald G. Lerch & Company, Inc.
NS: MR   CRD: 7/19/93

Japan Iron & Steel Exporters' Association
Agent: Japan Iron & Steel Exporters' Association
NS: L   CRD: 10/9/80

Japan Iron & Steel Exporters' Association
Agent: Charles E. Butler & Associates
NS: PTRADE   CRD: 12/29/83

Japan Iron & Steel Exporters' Association
Agent: Willkie Farr & Gallagher
NS: LO   CRD: 12/26/85

Japan National Tourist Organization
Agent: Japan National Tourist Organization,
    San Francisco
NS: PT   CRD: 7/3/72

Japan National Tourist Organization
Agent: Japan National Tourist Organization,
    New York
NS: PT   CRD: 5/26/53

Japan National Tourist Organization
Agent: Japan National Tourist Organization,
    Los Angeles
NS: PT   CRD: 7/3/72

Japan National Tourist Organization
Agent: Japan National Tourist Organization,
    Chicago
NS: PT   CRD: 7/3/72

Japan Science and Technology Corporation
Agent: International Science & Technology
    Associates, Inc.
NS: USPC   CRD: 6/22/87

Japan Whaling Association
Agent: Tele-Press Associates, Inc.
NS: L   CRD: 11/14/79

Japan Wood-Products Info. and Research Center
Agent: Garvey, Schubert & Barer
NS: EP   CRD: 9/10/91

Japanese Government
Agent: Japan Center for Intercultural
    Communications (JCIC)
NS: MR   CRD: 3/1/95

JETRO New York
Agent: Rabin, Keith W.
NS: DPM   CRD: 7/2/96

JETRO, Houston
Agent: Fogarty, Klein & Partners Public Relations
NS: MR   CRD: 12/19/90

JETRO, New York

Agent: Modern Education Services, Inc.
NS: DF   CRD: 8/15/86

JETRO, New York
Agent: Michael Solomon Associates
NS: PTRADE   CRD: 1/6/87

JETRO, New York (Japan Trade Center)
Agent: Masaoka & Associates, Inc.
NS: USPC   CRD: 6/19/74

JETRO, San Francisco
Agent: TransPacific Communications
    Research Company
NS: PR   CRD: 8/26/88

JETRO-Houston
Agent: Baker & Botts, L.L.P.
NS: PI   CRD: 11/9/92

JNG Shareholders Group
Agent: Japan Network Group, Inc.
NS: RJRTV   CRD: 12/10/93

Kanagawa Prefectural Government
Agent: JETRO, Los Angeles
NS: PT   CRD: 5/28/74

Keizai Koho Center
Agent: Economic Information Center
NS: PRDPM   CRD: 1/4/95

Kobe Municipal Government
Agent: Kobe Trade Information Office
NS: PTRADE   CRD: 7/2/73

Kyoto Prefectural Government
Agent: JETRO, New York
NS: USPC   CRD: 5/9/89

*Manufactured Imports Promotion Organization
(MIPRO)*
Agent: Manufactured Imports Promotion
    Organization (MIPRO)
NS: CRD: 2/5/81

Marubeni America Corporation
Agent: Hill & Knowlton, Inc.
NS: PR   CRD: 2/24/88

Nagano Prefectural Government
Agent: JETRO, Los Angeles
NS: PTRADE   CRD: 5/28/74

Nintendo of America
Agent: Rockey Company, Inc.
NS: CRD: 12/30/92

Nippon Telegraph & Telephone Corporation
Agent: Hogan & Hartson, L.L.P.
NS: USPC   CRD: 1/24/94

*Nippon Telegraph & Telephone Public
Corporation (NTT)*
Agent: Civic Service, Inc.
NS: USPC   CRD: 6/15/83

Nissho Iwai Corporation
Agent: Richard Lewis Communications, Inc.
NS: DPM   CRD: 12/20/90

Office of the Japanese Consul General
Agent: Daniel J. Edelman, Inc.
NS: MR   CRD: 10/25/93

Osaka Prefectural Government
Agent: Osaka Prefectual Government,
    California Office
NS: PE   CRD: 4/21/97

Osaka Prefectural Government
Agent: JETRO, New York
NS: CRD: 5/26/74

Sanwa Bank, Ltd.
Agent: Civic Service, Inc.
NS: USPC   CRD: 7/25/88

Seiko Epson Corporation
Agent: Saunders & Company
NS: USPC   CRD: 6/14/89

Shizuoka Prefectural Government
Agent: JETRO, Los Angeles
NS: PTRADE   CRD: 5/28/74

Sony Corporation
Agent: Debevoise & Plimpton
NS: L   CRD: 10/5/93

Tohoku Electric Power Company, Inc.
Agent: Michael Solomon Associates
NS: PR   CRD: 8/11/89

Tokyo Electric Power Company
Agent: Washington Policy & Analysis, Inc.
NS: PJUSS   CRD: 1/31/92

Tokyo Metropolitan Government
Agent: JETRO, Los Angeles
NS: PTRADE   CRD: 5/28/74

Toyo Kogyo, Ltd. (Mazda Motor Corporation)
Agent: Hill & Knowlton, Inc.
NS: PR   CRD: 2/16/87

Jordan

Hashemite Kingdom of Jordan & the Higher Council
Agent: Owens, Wayne
NS: LO   CRD: 2/14/94

Kazakhstan

Office of the President of Kazakhstan
Agent: P/C Advisors, Inc.
NS: PRC   CRD: 8/31/93

Korea

Embassy of the Republic of Korea
Agent: Paul, Weiss, Rifkind, Wharton & Garrison
NS: LO   CRD: 2/28/95

Hyndai Electronics Industries, Co. & LG Semicon Co., Ltd.
Agent: Ogilvy Public Relations Worldwide
NS: MRC   CRD: 6/30/97

KBS Enterprises, Ltd.
Agent: Korean Television Enterprises, Ltd.
NS: PTRADE   CRD: 3/11/86

Kim Dae-Jung Peace Foundation, U.S.A.
Agent: Costello, Stephen
NS: PR   CRD: 10/27/95

Korea Economic Institute for International Economic Policy (KIEP)
Agent: Korea Economic Institute
NS: PTI   CRD: 2/28/90

Korea Local Authorities Foundation
Agent: Korea Local Government Center, New York
NS: PTRADE   CRD: 11/24/95

Korea National Tourism Corporation
Agent: Korea National Tourism Corporation, Chicago
NS: PT   CRD: 11/23/79

Korea National Tourism Corporation
Agent: Korea National Tourism Corporation, New Jersey
NS: PT   CRD: 10/1/75

Korea National Tourism Organization

Agent: Lord Group
NS: A   CRD: 8/21/96

Korea National Tourism Organization
Agent: Korea National Tourism Organization, Los Angeles
NS: PT   CRD: 10/25/74

Korea Telecom
Agent: Paul, Weiss, Rifkind, Wharton & Garrison
NS: LO   CRD: 3/6/95

Korea Trade Promotion Corporation
Agent: Korea Trade Center, New York
NS: PTRADE   CRD: 4/17/63

Korean International Trade Association
Agent: Crowell & Moring International, L.P.
NS: TC   CRD: 4/6/88

Korean Overseas Information Service
Agent: Jefferson-Waterman International, LLC
NS: LPR   CRD: 7/7/95

Korean Overseas Veterans Association (KOVA)
Agent: American Intern'l. Consulting Group, Inc.
NS: L   CRD: 8/8/94

Korean Traders' Association
Agent: Korea International Trade Association
NS: PTRADE   CRD: 12/21/84

Republic of Korea, Embassy
Agent: Jefferson-Waterman International, LLC
NS: LO   CRD: 2/6/95

Small & Medium Industry Promotion Corp.
Agent: Small & Medium Industry Promotion Corporation (SMIPC), USA
NS: PTRADE   CRD: 11/25/83

Kosova

Democratic League of Kosova
Agent: Shafiq, Nuri
NS: L   CRD: 4/9/93

Republic of Kosova
Agent: Tirana, Bardyl R.
NS: LO   CRD: 10/22/93

Kurdistan

Kurdistan Regional Government
Agent: Shemdin, Nijyar H.
NS: USPC   CRD: 7/22/97

Kuwait

Kuwait Airways
Agent: Dickstein Shapiro Morin & Oshinsky L.L.P.
NS: LO   CRD: 4/7/80

Kuwait Investment Authority
Agent: Price Waterhouse - International Tax Services Group
NS: TCL   CRD: 3/6/91

State of Kuwait
Agent: Cleary, Gottlieb, Steen & Hamilton
NS: LO   CRD: 8/13/90

Kyrgyzstan

Republic of Kyrgyzstan
Agent: White & Case
NS: CRD: 11/13/97

Lebanon

Lebanese Forces
Agent: Lebanese Information & Research Center
NS: L   CRD: 10/24/78

Liberia

Government of Republic of Liberia
Agent: Swidler & Berlin, Chartered
NS: L   CRD: 9/17/97

Office of Deputy Commissioner of Maritime Affairs
Agent: International Registries, Inc.
NS: MSS   CRD: 7/1/91

Republic of Liberia, Embassy
Agent: Hill & Knowlton, Inc.
NS: CRD: 11/24/97

Lithuania

Embassy of Lithuania
Agent: Smith, Anne Victoria
NS: L   CRD: 7/18/97

Luxembourg

Luxembourg Board of Economic Development
Agent: Luxcore, Ltd.
NS: MRAPI   CRD: 3/10/94

Macao

Civil Aviation Authority of Macau
Agent: Zuckert, Scoutt & Rasenberger, L.L.P.
NS: LO   CRD: 8/1/94

Malaysia

Malaysian Industrial Development Agency
Agent: Malaysian Industrial Develop. Authority
NS: PI   CRD: 4/17/72

Malaysian Palm Oil Promotion Council
Agent: Malaysian Palm Oil Council of America, Inc.
NS: PPOS   CRD: 10/4/91

Malaysian Palm Oil Promotion Council
Agent: Dickstein Shapiro Morin & Oshinsky L.L.P.
NS: LO   CRD: 4/18/91

Tourist Development Corporation
Agent: Malaysia Tourism Promotion Board
NS: PT   CRD: 4/17/79

Mali

Government of Mali
Agent: Barron-Birrell, Inc.
NS: PR   CRD: 12/9/97

Malta

Air Malta Company, Ltd.
Agent: Holland & Knight
NS: CRD: 1/29/98

Malta Development Corporation
Agent: Dechert, Price & Rhoads
NS: LO   CRD: 3/14/91

Malta Financial Services Centre
Agent: Dechert, Price & Rhoads
NS: MMFSC   CRD: 5/31/95

Marshall Islands

Embassy of the Republic of the Marshall Islands
Agent: Neas Group, LLC
NS: L   CRD: 1/24/97

Government of the Marshall Islands
Agent: Verner, Liipfert, Bernhard,
   McPherson & Hand, Chartered
NS: LO   CRD: 2/21/96

Government of the Marshall Islands (Embassy)
Agent: Kronmiller, Theodore George
NS: LOPC   CRD: 4/17/92

Republic of the Marshall Islands
Agent: International Registries, Inc.
NS: MSS   CRD: 7/1/91

Mauritania

Islamic Republic of Mauritania
Agent: Denison, George H.
NS: L   CRD: 10/3/96

Islamic Republic of Mauritania
Agent: Dymally International Group, Inc.
NS: PR   CRD: 4/27/93

Mexico

AFINOA
Agent: Equihua, Xavier
NS: IP   CRD: 4/30/97

ALFA Industries, S.A.
Agent: Scanlon, Thomas J.
NS: L   CRD: 2/25/86

Estafeta Mexicana, S.A. de C.V.
Agent: Smith, Dawson & Andrews, Inc.
NS: TRNC   CRD: 12/12/95

Fomento Economico Mexicano, S.A. de C.V.
Agent: Ruder & Finn, Inc.
NS: E   CRD: 8/22/97

Government of Mexico
Agent: McCutchen, Doyle, Brown & Enersen,
   LLP
NS: USPC   CRD: 11/18/97

Government of Mexico
Agent: Public Strategies Washington, Inc.
NS: GRL   CRD: 3/15/91

Government of Mexico
Agent: Public Strategies, Inc.
NS: MR   CRD: 9/18/95

*Government of Mexico, Ministry of
   Commerce & Industrial*
Agent: Burson-Marsteller, Inc.
NS: P   CRD: 12/12/90

Government of Mexico, Ministry of Tourism
Agent: Burson-Marsteller, Inc.
NS: PT   CRD: 9/5/95

Mexican Ministry of Tourism
Agent: Mexican Government Tourism Office,
   New York
NS: PT   CRD: 6/9/64

Mexican Ministry of Tourism
Agent: Mexican Government Tourism Office,
   Los Angeles
NS: PT   CRD: 9/8/70

Mexican National Tourist Office
Agent: Mexican Government Tourism Office,
   Chicago
NS: PT   CRD: 8/9/73

*Ministry of Communications & Transportation
   of Mexico*
Agent: Cleary, Gottlieb, Steen & Hamilton
NS: LO   CRD: 3/21/96

Ministry of Finance and Public Credit of Mexico
Agent: Cleary, Gottlieb, Steen & Hamilton
NS: LO   CRD: 4/4/91

Ministry of Foreign Relations of Mexico
Agent: Cleary, Gottlieb, Steen & Hamilton
NS: LO   CRD: 5/10/96

Presidente Hotels
Agent: M. Silver Associates, Inc.
NS: PR   CRD: 5/15/95

Pulsar International
Agent: Daniel J. Edelman, Inc.
NS: PR   CRD: 5/12/95

Secretaria de Comunicaciones y Transportes
Agent: Swidler & Berlin, Chartered
NS: CITS   CRD: 1/31/96

*Secretariat of Commerce & Industrial
   Development of Mexico*
Agent: Shearman & Sterling
NS: LOC   CRD: 2/26/91

*Secretary of Industrial & Commercial
   Development State of Ucatan*
Agent: MRB Group
NS: ITP   CRD: 1/26/93

Vitro Corporativo, S.A. de C.V.
Agent: Public Strategies, Inc.
NS: LO   CRD: 7/15/94

Micronesia

Federated States of Micronesia, Embassy
Agent: Staton, David Michael
NS: L   CRD: 3/10/95

*Government of the Federated States of
   Micronesia*
Agent: Stovall III, James T.
NS: L   CRD: 2/25/87

Moldova

Republic of Moldova
Agent: McCaffrey Braley, Inc.
NS: C   CRD: 5/9/98

Monaco

Direction de Tourisme et des Congres
Agent: Monaco Government Tourist Office
NS: PR   CRD: 4/25/72

Monaco Govt. Tourist & Convention Bureau
Agent: M. Silver Associates, Inc.
NS: PT   CRD: 9/10/93

Montenegro

Government of the Republic of Montenegro

Agent: Republic of Montenegro Trade Mission
   to the US
NS: PE   CRD: 8/4/97

Government of the Republic of Montenegro
Agent: Manatt, Phelps & Phillips
NS: L   CRD: 4/11/97

Morocco

Embassy of the Kingdom of Morocco
Agent: Powell Tate, Inc.
NS: PMR   CRD: 5/22/98

Embassy of the Kingdom of Morocco
Agent: Boland & Madigan, Inc.
NS: L   CRD: 5/26/98

Kingdom of Morocco, Embassy
Agent: Cassidy & Associates, Inc.
NS: L   CRD: 5/22/98

Moroccan National Tourist Office
Agent: Moroccan National Tourist Office
NS: PT   CRD: 9/21/64

The Kingdom of Morocco
Agent: White & Case
NS: LO   CRD: 5/16/85

Mozambique

Republic of Mozambique
Agent: Cameron, Bruce P.
NS: L   CRD: 10/13/87

Myanmar

Myanmar Resources Development, Ltd.
Agent: Jefferson-Waterman International, LLC
NS: CRD: 4/4/97

Netherlands

*Government of the Netherlands, Netherlands
   Foreign Investment Agency*
Agent: Ruder & Finn, Inc.
NS: PE   CRD: 4/24/97

Konimklijke Luchtvaart Maatschappij, N.V.
Agent: Hill & Knowlton, Inc.
NS: PR   CRD: 5/8/95

Nederlands Bureau voor Toerisme
Agent: Netherlands Board of Tourism
NS: PT   CRD: 3/20/50

Netherlands Foreign Investment Agency
Agent: Ogilvy Adams & Rinehart, Inc.
NS: PR   CRD: 12/28/90

Rotterdam Port Management Company
Agent: InterMarketing, Inc.
NS: PRPED   CRD: 8/29/94

Royal Netherlands Embassy
Agent: Hill & Knowlton, Inc.
NS: MR   CRD: 3/26/98

Netherlands Antilles

Government of the Netherlands/Antilles
Agent: O'Connor & Hannan
NS: L   CRD: 3/19/87

New Zealand

New Zealand Dairy Board
Agent: Wigman, Cohen, Leitner & Myers, P.C.
NS: PTRADE   CRD: 7/22/94

New Zealand Dairy Board
Agent: Bronz & Farrell
NS: PTRADE   CRD: 7/3/68

New Zealand Fishing Industry Board/Fishing
    Industry & Inspection
Agent: Crowell & Moring International, L.P.
NS: C   CRD: 4/8/93

New Zealand Meat Producers Board
Agent: Wigman, Cohen, Leitner & Myers, P.C.
NS: PTRADE   CRD: 7/22/94

New Zealand Meat Producers Board
Agent: Bronz & Farrell
NS: PTRADE   CRD: 5/22/64

New Zealand Meat Producers' Board
Agent: New Zealand Meat Producers' Board
NS: PTRADE   CRD: 7/8/74

Nigeria

Ambassador Ibrahim A. Gambarir
Agent: Ruder & Finn, Inc.
NS: MR   CRD: 8/22/97

Federal Government of Nigeria
Agent: J.H.S. Group, Inc.
NS: LPR   CRD: 8/16/93

Federal Republic of Nigeria
Agent: Davis, Manafort & Freedman, Inc.
NS: PR   CRD: 3/3/98

Federal Republic of Nigeria
Agent: White & Case
NS: USPC   CRD: 4/9/90

M.K.O. Biola (Nigerian President-Elect)
Agent: Echols, Sr., Randall Edwin
NS: L   CRD: 12/8/93

Nalicon - Nigeria
Agent: National Liberation Council of
    Nigeria - U.S.A. (Nalicon)
NS: FPR   CRD: 2/16/96

The Federal Republic of Nigeria
Agent: Barron-Birrell, Inc.
NS: LPR   CRD: 7/17/95

Norway

Norwegian Fisheries' Association
Agent: Bogle & Gates
NS: PTRADE   CRD: 5/24/83

Norwegian Seafood Export Council
Agent: Gilman, Bradley D.
NS: L   CRD: 7/15/94

Norwegian Tourist Board
Agent: Norwegian Tourist Board (NORTRA)
NS: PT   CRD: 5/13/48

Resource Group International
Agent: Rockey Company, Inc.
NS: CRD: 12/22/95

Royal Norwegian Consulate General New York
Agent: Burson-Marsteller, Inc.
NS: MPRC   CRD: 8/13/97

Royal Norwegian Government (Embassy)

Agent: Evans, Billy Lee
NS: USPC   CRD: 5/25/95

Thommessen Krefting Greve Lund, A.S.,
    Advokat Firma
Agent: Zapruder & Odell
NS: LO   CRD: 5/15/95

Oman

Government of the Sultanate of Oman
Agent: Jameson, Donald F.B.
NS: USPC   CRD: 10/6/94

Pakistan

Benazir Bhutto
Agent: Mark A. Siegel & Associates, Inc.
NS: L   CRD: 6/16/97

Embassy of Pakistan
Agent: Hooper, Hooper, Owen & Gould
NS: LO   CRD: 5/12/97

Government of Pakistan Embassy
Agent: Patton Boggs, L.L.P.
NS: LO   CRD: 1/30/94

Palestine

Arab Higher Committee for Palestine
Agent: Palestine Arab Delegation
NS: L   CRD: 6/26/91

Palestine Liberation Organization Office
Agent: Palestine Liberation Organization
NS: PR   CRD: 3/18/98

Palestinian National Authority
Agent: Stroock, Stroock, & Lavan
NS: LO   CRD: 4/23/96

Palestinian National Authority Gaza
Agent: Larry C. Wallace & Associates, P.A.
NS: LTP   CRD: 11/7/95

Paraguay

President of Paraguay, Juan Carlos Wasmosy
Agent: Foreign Policy Group
NS: PETEI   CRD: 4/7/97

Peru

PromPeru
Agent: Chlopak, Leonard, Schechter &
    Associates, Inc.
NS: MR   CRD: 5/17/96

Philippines

Department of Defense, Philippines
Agent: Winston & Strawn
NS: L   CRD: 4/24/97

Dept. of Trade & Industry, Republic of the
    Philippines Embassy
Agent: Patton Boggs, L.L.P.
NS: PI   CRD: 10/5/95

Government of the Philippines
Agent: Bannerman & Associates, Inc.
NS: L   CRD: 6/1/94

Government of the Philippines

Agent: International Business & Economic
Research Corporation
NS: L   CRD: 5/30/91

Government of the Republic of the Philippines
Agent: Icon Group
NS: PR   CRD: 7/8/94

Government of the Republic of the Philippines/
    Dept. of Trade & Ind.
Agent: Crowell & Moring International, L.P.
NS: CAPEC   CRD: 3/14/96

The Philippine Sugar Administration
Agent: L.A. Motley & Company
NS: LO   CRD: 3/15/89

Poland

Bank Polska Kasa Opieki, S.A.
Agent: Pekao Trading Corporation
NS: PT   CRD: 2/23/54

Lot Polish Airlines
Agent: Partners & Shevack, Inc.
NS: PT   CRD: 4/7/81

Ministry of Sports & Tourism of the
    Republic of Poland
Agent: Polish National Tourist Office, New York
NS: PT   CRD: 2/4/93

Polish People's Republic
Agent: White & Case
NS: LOC   CRD: 10/9/91

Portugal

Government of Portugal (Trade Commission)
Agent: Edelman Public Relations Worldwide
NS: PTRADE   CRD: 11/15/94

Government of Portugal, Embassy
Agent: Cameron, Bruce P.
NS: L   CRD: 2/18/97

ICEP - Investimentos
Agent: Heyward, Evelyn J.
NS: PT   CRD: 2/14/94

Qatar

Government of the State of Qatar
Agent: Patton Boggs, L.L.P.
NS: LO   CRD: 2/28/94

State of Qatar
Agent: Hill & Knowlton, Inc.
NS: PR   CRD: 9/6/96

Romania

National Bank of Romania
Agent: Cosmos, Inc.
NS: DPM   CRD: 5/31/91

Romanian Tourism Promotion Office
Agent: Romanian National Tourist Office
NS: PT   CRD: 6/3/68

Russia

Central Aerohydrodynamics Institute (TsAGI)
Agent: Redman, Eric
NS: LO   CRD: 8/22/94

Liberal Democratic Party of Russia

Agent: Reg'l. Org. of Liberal Democratic
    Party of Russia
NS: PR   CRD: 10/2/95

Most Group, Inc.
Agent: Rubenstein Associates, Inc.
NS: PR   CRD: 5/1/95

Promstroy Bank of Russia
Agent: Smith, Dawson & Andrews, Inc.
NS: LPR   CRD: 12/18/97

Republic of Bashkortostan
Agent: Bashkortostan Trade Mission
NS: PI   CRD: 11/5/92

*Trade Representation of the Russian
    Federation to the U.S.*
Agent: Samuels International Associates, Inc.
NS: L   CRD: 7/22/97

Saint Lucia

Caribbean Banana Exporters Association
Agent: Ross-Robinson & Associates
NS: CRD: 5/8/96

San Marino

Government of San Marino
Agent: San Marino, Republic of (Consulate Gen.)
NS: DS   CRD: 4/22/82

Saudi Arabia

Embassy of Saudi Arabia
Agent: Schmertz Company, Inc., The
NS: PR   CRD: 7/26/88

Embassy of Saudi Arabia
Agent: Dutton & Dutton, P.C.
NS: LO   CRD: 11/28/75

Embassy of the Kingdom of Saudi Arabia
Agent: Boland & Madigan, Inc.
NS: L   CRD: 12/30/96

Government of Kingdom of Saudi Arabia
Agent: Saudi Refining, Inc.
NS: L   CRD: 10/13/88

King Faisal Foundation
Agent: Burson-Marsteller, Inc.
NS: MPRC   CRD: 9/5/97

Kingdom of Saudi Arabia, Embassy
Agent: Mahoney, Maureen E.
NS: LO   CRD: 11/29/95

Royal Embassy of Saudi Arabia
Agent: Powell Tate, Inc.
NS: PR   CRD: 12/30/96

Royal Embassy of Saudi Arabia
Agent: Cassidy & Associates, Inc.
NS: MRL   CRD: 7/28/95

Saudi Arabian Oil Company
Agent: Saudi Refining, Inc.
NS: M   CRD: 5/12/89

Scotland

Locate in Scotland
Agent: Al Paul Lefton Company, Inc.
NS: A   CRD: 5/6/94

Scottish Enterprise
Agent: Scottish Enterprise

NS: PI   CRD: 4/17/79

Scottish National Party
Agent: Ackerman, Robert L.
NS: MEPR   CRD: 10/11/94

Scottish Trade International
Agent: Al Paul Lefton Company, Inc.
NS: MRPT   CRD: 10/24/95

Senegal

Government of the Republic of Senegal
Agent: Holland & Knight
NS: LO   CRD: 10/7/94

Seychelles

Rep. of the Seychelles Islands, President France
Agent: Norquist, Grover Glenn
NS: PR   CRD: 9/8/95

Sierra Leone

Mano River Union
Agent: James, John D.
NS: PI   CRD: 8/2/93

Singapore

Republic of Singapore
Agent: White & Case
NS: LO   CRD: 1/24/79

Republic of Singapore
Agent: Singapore Tourist Promotion Board
NS: PT   CRD: 3/27/73

Republic of Singapore, Embassy
Agent: APCO Associates, Inc.
NS: LPR   CRD: 6/28/95

Republic of Singapore, Embassy
Agent: Reed, T. Dean
NS: CPR   CRD: 9/13/95

Singapore Airlines
Agent: Global Aviation Associates, Ltd.
NS: AC   CRD: 3/14/94

Singapore Economic Development Board
Agent: Singapore Economic Development Board
NS: PI   CRD: 2/2/67

Singapore Tourism Promotion Board
Agent: Fontayne Group, Inc.
NS: PT   CRD: 7/19/88

Somalia

*Mohammed Farah Aidid, President of
    Somali Republic*
Agent: Gulaid, Ali Hasan
NS: L   CRD: 5/22/96

Somali National Movement
Agent: Somaliland Republic Office
NS: L   CRD: 1/18/85

South Africa

African National Congress of South Africa
Agent: African National Congress of
    South Africa, Washington
NS: PA   CRD: 5/23/91

Chamber of Mines of South Africa
Agent: C/R International, LLC
NS: ITP   CRD: 8/14/96

Embassy of the Republic of South Africa
Agent: C/R International, LLC
NS: PR   CRD: 7/16/96

South Africa Foundation
Agent: C/R International, LLC
NS: PR   CRD: 9/6/96

South African Airways, Div. of Transnet Limited
Agent: Ruder & Finn, Inc.
NS: PR   CRD: 4/29/98

South African Tourism Board
Agent: Development Counsellors International
NS: PT   CRD: 3/12/93

South African Tourist Corporation
Agent: South African Tourism Board
NS: PT   CRD: 1/4/50

Southern African Development Community
Agent: C/R International, LLC
NS: PI   CRD: 4/23/97

Spain

Spanish Ministry of Commerce
Agent: Camara Oficial Espanola de Comercio
NS: PTRADE   CRD: 12/27/72

Sri Lanka

Embassy of Sri Lanka
Agent: International Business &
    Economic Research Corporation
NS: IPL   CRD: 3/16/98

St. Eustatius & Saba

Governments of St. Eustatius & Saba
Agent: Medhurst & Associates, Inc.
NS: PR   CRD: 9/12/89

St. Kitts & Nevis

St. Kitts & Nevis Tourist Board
Agent: Benford Associates, Inc.
NS: PT   CRD: 3/13/89

St. Lucia

National Development Corporation
Agent: St. Lucia National Development Corp.
NS: PR   CRD: 6/24/77

St. Lucia Tourist Board
Agent: St. Lucia Tourist Board
NS: PT   CRD: 3/15/76

St. Vincent and the Grenadines

Government of St. Vincent & the Grenadines
Agent: William D. Harris & Associates, Inc.
NS: PTI   CRD: 11/9/95

Government of St. Vincent and the Grenadines
Agent: West Indies Communications Group, Ltd.
NS: PR   CRD: 8/4/97

Sudan

Embassy of the Republic of the Sudan
Agent: Dawkins, Dymally & Associates
NS: LPR   CRD: 7/7/97

Embassy of the Republic of the Sudan
Agent: McElligott Associates
NS: C   CRD: 1/15/97

Suriname

*Commander of the National Armed Forces
of Suriname*
Agent: Edward Shaw Productions
NS: PR   CRD: 7/17/90

Government of the Republic of Suriname
Agent: Hemisphere Key Consulting, LLC
NS: C   CRD: 8/28/97

Republic of Suriname
Agent: White & Case
NS: LO   CRD: 5/16/85

Sweden

Argonaut, A.B.
Agent: Brown, Nelson & Associates, Inc.
NS: USPC   CRD: 3/31/94

Most in Sweden Agency
Agent: Levin Public Relations & Marketing, Inc.
NS: PI   CRD: 10/22/97

Sveriges Radio Aktiebolag
Agent: Sveriges Television AB
(Swedish Broadcasting Corporation)
NS: PT   CRD: 6/14/89

Swedish Travel & Tourism Council AB
Agent: Swedish Travel & Tourism Council
NS: PT   CRD: 7/31/94

Switzerland

BEDA, Bernese Development Agency
Agent: H. Tschudin Associates, Inc., Dr.
NS: PTRADE   CRD: 7/10/85

Consulate General of Switzerland
Agent: Gibney, Anthony & Flaherty, LLP
NS: USPC   CRD: 5/19/93

*Council for Economic Development,
State of Vaud Switzerland*
Agent: Global Communicators/Harff
Communications, Inc.
NS: IP   CRD: 3/5/98

*Departement de l'economie publique,
Republic and Canton of Geneva*
Agent: Arter & Hadden
NS: PE   CRD: 7/18/96

Dr. Karl Dobler
Agent: Stearns, John Norton
NS: IP   CRD: 2/9/98

Dr. Karl Dobler
Agent: Ebert, Douglas Karl
NS: IP   CRD: 1/26/93

Dr. Karl Dobler, Industry Rep. Neuchatel
Agent: Pendred, Russell Jess
NS: IP   CRD: 2/24/95

Embassy of Switzerland
Agent: Barbour, Griffith & Rogers

NS: LO   CRD: 12/19/96

F. Hoffman-La Roche Ltd.
Agent: Kaiser, Dr. Donald
NS: USPC   CRD: 4/30/96

F. Hoffman-La Roche, Ltd.
Agent: Hilton, Susan Elaine
NS: L   CRD: 2/11/98

Geneva Departement de L'Economic Publique
Agent: Development Counsellors International
NS: PI   CRD: 5/11/93

Government of Switzerland, Embassy
Agent: Ruder & Finn, Inc.
NS: PR   CRD: 7/21/97

*Karl Dobler, Industry Representative,
Canton of Neuchatel*
Agent: Oestreicher, Michael R.
NS: PI   CRD: 12/8/82

Swedish Travel & Tourism Council
Agent: Development Counsellors International
NS: PT   CRD: 12/17/93

Swiss Federal Railroads
Agent: Switzerland Tourism
NS: PT   CRD: 3/1/43

Swiss National Tourist Office
Agent: Fontayne Group, Inc.
NS: PR   CRD: 10/14/86

Swiss National Tourist Office
Agent: Switzerland Tourism
NS: PT   CRD: 3/27/73

Swiss Ordnance Enterprise
Agent: GMD Solutions (A Division of
Defense Group, Inc.)
NS: USPC   CRD: 7/18/97

Swissair
Agent: Global Aviation Associates, Ltd.
NS: AC   CRD: 3/14/94

Winterthur Group
Agent: Barbour, Griffith & Rogers
NS: L   CRD: 4/6/98

Taiwan

Board of Foreign Trade (BOFT)
Agent: Ablondi, Foster, Sobin & Davidow, P.C.
NS: LO   CRD: 5/4/81

*Board of Foreign Trade, Ministry of
Economic Affairs*
Agent: Wasserman, Gary
NS: PTE   CRD: 12/14/94

*Board of Foreign Trade, Ministry of
Economic Affairs*
Agent: Rosenblatt, Peter R.
NS: LO   CRD: 9/13/83

Board of Foreign Trade, ROC
Agent: Crowell & Moring International, L.P.
NS: L   CRD: 6/23/87

*China External Trade Development Council
(CETDC)*
Agent: O'Connor & Hannan
NS: L   CRD: 6/17/87

*China External Trade Development Council
(CETDC)*
Agent: CETDC, Inc.
NS: PTRADE   CRD: 2/28/85

Directorate General of Telecommunications
Agent: Severance International, Inc.
NS: C   CRD: 4/13/98

Far East Trade Service, Inc.
Agent: Far East Trade Service, Inc.,
San Francisco
NS: EP   CRD: 12/6/78

Far East Trade Service, Inc.
Agent: Far East Trade Service, Inc., Chicago
NS: PT   CRD: 6/8/78

Institute of International Relations
Agent: Halpern Associates
NS: USPC   CRD: 3/7/86

Institute of International Relations
Agent: Gowran International, Ltd.
NS: PR   CRD: 8/15/94

Taipei Economic & Cultural Rep. Office, U.S.
Agent: Intern'l. Trade & Develop. Agency, Inc.
NS: PTRADE   CRD: 8/28/95

Taipei Economic & Cultural Rep. Office (ROC)
Agent: Asia Associates, Inc.
NS: PET   CRD: 8/14/97

Taipei Economic & Cultural Rep. Office
Agent: Holloman, Charlotte
NS: C   CRD: 10/4/96

*Taipei Economic & Cultural Representative
Office (TECRO)*
Agent: Bergner, Bockorny & Clough
NS: PTRADE   CRD: 5/9/86

*Taipei Economic & Cultural Representative
Office (TECRO)*
Agent: Jefferson-Waterman International, LLC
NS: L   CRD: 2/6/95

Taipei Economic and Cultural Rep. Office
Agent: MWW Group
NS: PR   CRD: 1/16/98

Taipei Economic and Cultural Rep. Office
Agent: Washington Group
NS: LTP   CRD: 2/2/94

Taiwain Textile Federation
Agent: International Business & Economic
Research Corporation
NS: IPL   CRD: 3/16/98

Taiwan Democratic Progressive Party
Agent: Taiwan Democratic Progressive Party
Mission in the US
NS: LPR   CRD: 4/12/95

*Taiwan Ministry of Foreign Affairs,
Board of Foreign Trade*
Agent: Weber Group
NS: PR   CRD: 3/24/98

Taiwan Research Institute
Agent: Savarese & Associates
NS: PR   CRD: 7/29/97

Taiwan Research Institute
Agent: Powell Tate, Inc.
NS: PR   CRD: 12/30/96

Taiwan Research Institute
Agent: Boland & Madigan, Inc.
NS: PR   CRD: 12/30/96

Taiwan Research Institute
Agent: Cassidy & Associates, Inc.
NS: MR   CRD: 7/18/94

TECRO, Taipei Economic & Cultural Rep. Office
Agent: Symms, Lehn & Associates, Inc.
NS: USTPC   CRD: 12/21/93

Tajikistan

Government of the Republic of Tajikistan

Agent: Foochs, Arkadiy I.
NS: USPCL   CRD: 3/29/94

Thailand

Kingdom of Thailand
Agent: White & Case
NS: LO   CRD: 10/10/89

Royal Thai Embassy
Agent: Intern'l. Trade & Develop. Agency, Inc.
NS: USPC   CRD: 3/5/87

Royal Thai Embassy
Agent: Dickstein Shapiro Morin & Oshinsky
   L.L.P.
NS: LO   CRD: 3/17/97

Tourism Authority of Thailand
Agent: Tourism Authority of Thailand, New York
NS: PT   CRD: 6/1/85

Tourism Authority of Thailand
Agent: Tourism Authority of Thailand,
   Los Angeles
NS: PT   CRD: 12/19/69

Tourism Authority of Thailand
Agent: Tourism Authority of Thailand, Chicago
NS: PT   CRD: 2/21/92

Tourism Authority of Thailand
Agent: M. Silver Associates, Inc.
NS: PT   CRD: 6/11/96

Tibet

Dalai Lama
Agent: Office of Tibet
NS: L   CRD: 3/12/64

Togo

Republic of Togo
Agent: David Apter & Associates, Inc.
NS: PR   CRD: 8/5/80

Tonga

Kingdom of Tonga
Agent: Eckert International, Inc.
NS: USPC   CRD: 9/29/89

Tongasat, Kingdom Of Tonga
Agent: Via/Net Companies
NS: CL   CRD: 10/4/93

Tunisia

Tunisian Agency for External Communications
Agent: Powell Tate, Inc.
NS: MR   CRD: 1/12/98

Turkey

Central Bank of the Republic of Turkey
Agent: White & Case
NS: LO   CRD: 11/9/78

Central Bank of Turkey
Agent: Hoffman & Hoffman Public Relations
NS: MR   CRD: 8/26/97

Embassy of the Republic of Turkey
Agent: Durak, Ahmet Unal

NS: USPCPR   CRD: 10/15/97

Embassy of the Republic of Turkey
Agent: Strauss, Joseph A.
NS: USPCPR   CRD: 10/15/97

Embassy of the Republic of Turkey
Agent: Patton Boggs, L.L.P.
NS: LO   CRD: 10/6/97

*Office of the Prime Minister Mesut Yilmaz -
   Republic of Turkey*
Agent: Varney, Kevin P.
NS: VPM   CRD: 12/29/97

Republic of Turkey
Agent: Shandwick Public Affairs, Inc.
NS: PR   CRD: 12/17/97

*Turkish Foreign Economic Relations Board
   (DEIK)*
Agent: IMPACT, LLC
NS: PR   CRD: 4/13/98

*Turkish Foreign Economic Relations Board
   (DEIK)*
Agent: C/R International, LLC
NS: L   CRD: 4/23/97

Turks & Caicos Islands

Turks & Caicos Tourist Board
Agent: Trombone Associates, Inc.
NS: PT   CRD: 3/2/94

Uganda

Embassy of the Republic of Uganda
Agent: Reichler, Milton & Medel
NS: L   CRD: 1/11/94

Ukraine

Embassy of the Ukraine to the U.S.A.
Agent: Foundation in Support of Diplomatic
   Missions of Ukraine, Inc.
NS: FR   CRD: 6/8/92

Government of the Ukraine
Agent: Aitken, Irvin, Lewin, Berlin,
   Vrooman & Cohn
NS: LO   CRD: 8/18/97

Government of Ukraine, Embassy
Agent: Ronald S. Winton & Associates
NS: L   CRD: 12/2/94

Kiev International Expansion Venture - K.I.E.V.
Agent: Stewart & Stewart
NS: PI   CRD: 12/15/92

Office of the President of the Ukraine
Agent: P/C Advisors, Inc.
NS: PR   CRD: 5/21/93

Permanent Mission of Ukraine to the U.N.
Agent: Foundation in Support of Diplomatic
   Missions of Ukraine, Inc.
NS: FR   CRD: 6/8/92

United Arab Emirates

Dubai Commerce & Tourism Promotion Board
Agent: McLaughlin & Morgan, Inc.
NS: PR   CRD: 12/15/95

Government of the United Arab Emirates
Agent: Bannerman & Associates, Inc.
NS: L   CRD: 8/9/91

Jebel Ali Free Zone Authority
Agent: Dubai Commerce & Tourism
   Promotion Board
NS: PR   CRD: 2/17/89

United Kingdom

AEA Technology
Agent: Lipsen, Zel E.
NS: L   CRD: 1/19/96

Association of British Insurers
Agent: Hopkins & Sutter
NS: LO   CRD: 8/16/91

British Broadcasting Corporation
Agent: Crane, Jonathan A.
NS: L   CRD: 10/7/93

British Ministry of Defense
Agent: Lipsen, Zel E.
NS: L   CRD: 1/19/96

British Tourist Authority
Agent: British Tourist Authority
NS: PT   CRD: 7/7/49

British Trade Development Office
Agent: Spring, O'Brien, Tolson & Company, Inc.
NS: PTRADE   CRD: 3/19/85

Brunswick, Ltd.
Agent: GCI Group Inc.
NS: PR   CRD: 8/25/95

Department of Economic Development
Agent: Industrial Development Board for
   Northern Ireland
NS: IP   CRD: 4/13/90

Devon & Cornwall Development Bureau
Agent: Spring, O'Brien, Tolson & Company, Inc.
NS: A   CRD: 4/21/88

Government of Gibraltar
Agent: Gibraltar Information Bureau
NS: PT   CRD: 10/5/88

Grand Metropolitan, PLC
Agent: Grand Metropolitan Consumer
   Services & Products, Inc.
NS: PI   CRD: 5/6/92

Institute of London Underwriters (ILU)
Agent: Hopkins & Sutter
NS: LO   CRD: 3/23/92

International Group of P&I Clubs
Agent: Robins, Kaplan, Miller & Ciresi
NS: LO   CRD: 4/16/90

International Group of P&I Clubs
Agent: International Group of P&I Clubs
NS: L   CRD: 11/5/91

Inward, Ltd.
Agent: Spring, O'Brien, Tolson & Company, Inc.
NS: A   CRD: 4/21/88

Inward, Ltd.
Agent: Inward, Ltd.
NS: PI   CRD: 6/16/86

*John Hume, MP and the Social Democratic
   Labour Party*
Agent: McDermott/O'Neill & Associates
NS: FR   CRD: 3/7/94

Lloyd's of London
Agent: Lloyd's of London Market Representatives
NS: L   CRD: 1/6/94

London Insurance & Reinsurance Market Ass'n.
Agent: Rossi, Marie-Louise
NS: L   CRD: 6/16/94

London Insurance & Reinsurance Market Ass'n.
Agent: Cane, Stephen Paul
NS: L   CRD: 9/11/95

Northern England Development
Agent: Northern Development Company (NDC)
NS: PI   CRD: 5/25/83

Plaid Cymru
Agent: Martin, Barbara Lefevre
NS: PR   CRD: 1/9/95

Republic of Zambia
Agent: Hill & Knowlton, Inc.
NS: MR   CRD: 3/26/98

S.I. Odogwu
Agent: Hill & Knowlton, Inc.
NS: L   CRD: 9/20/95

Sinn Fein
Agent: Friends of Sinn Fein, Inc.
NS: FRL   CRD: 4/3/95

Thomas De La Rue, PLC
Agent: Sack & Associates, Inc.
NS: PI   CRD: 9/15/95

Trafford Park Development Corporation
Agent: Oliver A. Dulle, Jr. & Company, Inc.
NS: MREP   CRD: 12/17/92

Ulster Unionist Council
Agent: AWS Services
NS: PR   CRD: 9/7/95

*United Kingdom of Great Britain & Northern
    Ireland, Govt. of the*
Agent: Morgan, Lewis & Bockius
NS: L   CRD: 3/12/86

Vickers Shipbuilding & Engineering, Ltd.
Agent: Lipsen, Zel E.
NS: L   CRD: 1/19/96

Welsh Development Agency (WINvest)
Agent: Welsh Development International
NS: PI   CRD: 4/24/86

West Midlands Development Agency
Agent: Tripp, Umbach & Associates, Inc.
NS: IP   CRD: 10/20/92

Uruguay

The Government of Uruguay
Agent: Verner, Liipfert, Bernhard, McPherson &
    Hand, Chartered
NS: LO   CRD: 11/16/95

Uzbekistan

Embassy of the Republic of Uzbekistan
Agent: Manatt, Phelps & Phillips
NS: MR   CRD: 10/15/97

Embassy of the Republic Uzbekistan
Agent: PBN Company
NS: PMR   CRD: 9/4/97

Ministry of Tourism of the Rep. of Uzbekistan
Agent: Uzbekistan Government Tourist Board
NS: PT   CRD: 12/12/96

Republic of Uzbekistan
Agent: White & Case
NS: CRD: 11/13/97

Vanuatu

Republic of Vanuatu

Agent: Office of the Deputy Commissioner of
    Maritime Affairs
NS: RV   CRD: 10/12/93

Venezuela

Petroleos de Venezuela, S.A.
Agent: Manning, Selvage & Lee
NS: PR   CRD: 6/10/92

*Petroleos de Venezuela, S.A. (Maraven,
    Lagoven, Corpoven)*
Agent: Collier, Shannon, Rill & Scott
NS: L   CRD: 6/24/85

Republic of Venezuela
Agent: Arnold & Porter
NS: L   CRD: 6/5/84

Vietnam

State Bank of Vietnam
Agent: White & Case
NS: CRD: 4/24/96

Wales

Welsh Development Agency
Agent: Hill & Knowlton, Inc.
NS: MR   CRD: 12/24/97

Yemen

Ministry of Foreign Affairs of the Rep. of Yemen
Agent: Baker & Botts, L.L.P.
NS: LO   CRD: 4/22/92

Zambia

Government of the Republic of Zambia
Agent: Carlington Sales Canada Corporation
NS: L   CRD: 3/31/98

*Zambia National Tourist Bureau,
    Ministry of Information*
Agent: Zambia National Tourist Board
NS: PT   CRD: 12/6/71

Ablondi, Foster, Sobin & Davidow, P.C.
1150 18th Street, NW - Ninth Floor
Washington DC 20036
Phone: 202/296-3355   Fax: 202/296-3922
E-mail: afsd@ablondifoster.com
URL: http://www.ablondifoster.com
FARA#: 3235   ORD: 5/4/81

Board of Foreign Trade (BOFT)
CRD: 5/4/81   Taiwan

Ackerman, Robert L.
870 West Centennial Boulevard
Springfield OR 97477-5298
FARA#: 4962   ORD: 10/11/94

Scottish National Party
CRD: 10/11/94   Scotland

**African National Congress of South Africa,
   Washington**
Post Office Box 15575
Washington DC 20003
FARA#: 4515   ORD: 5/23/91

African National Congress of South Africa
CRD: 5/23/91   South Africa

Afridi & Angell
230 Park Avenue, Suite 640
New York NY 10169-0639
FARA#: 5231   ORD: 2/4/98

Japan External Trade Organization
CRD: 2/4/98   Japan

Aitken, Irvin, Lewin, Berlin, Vrooman & Cohn
1709 N Street, NW
Washington DC 20036
Phone: 202/331-8045   Fax: 202/331-8191
E-mail: 75031.241@compuserve.com
FARA#: 5235   ORD: 8/18/97

Government of the Ukraine
CRD: 8/18/97   Ukraine

Akin, Gump, Strauss, Hauer & Feld, L.L.P.
ATT Warren E. Connelly
1333 New Hampshire Ave., NW - Suite 400
Washington DC 20036
Phone: 202/887-4000   Fax: 202/887-4288
FARA#: 3492   ORD: 6/24/83

Government of British Columbia
CRD: 1/15/98   Canada

Al Paul Lefton Company, Inc.
100 Independence Mall, West
Philadelphia PA 19106-2399
FARA#: 4912   ORD: 5/6/94

Locate in Scotland
CRD: 5/6/94   Scotland

Scottish Trade International
CRD: 10/24/95   Scotland

**Alden Films, Business Education Films,
   Films of the Nations**
Box 449
Clarksburg NJ 08510
Phone: 908/462-3522   Fax: 908/294-0330
FARA#: 2100   ORD: 8/12/68

Consulate General of Finland
CRD: 6/30/76   Finland

Consulate General of Israel
CRD: 5/29/69   Israel

Alpine Tourist Commission
c/o Austrian National Tourist Office

500 Fifth Avenue, Suite 800
New York NY 10110
FARA#: 2052   ORD: 9/27/67

Alpine Tourist Commission
CRD: 12/4/67   Austria

Alsace Development Agency
2029 Century Park East, Suite 1115
Los Angeles CA 90067
FARA#: 3506   ORD: 8/10/83

*L'Association de Development du Bas-Phine
   (ADIRA)*
CRD: 8/10/83   France

ALSACE/USA
Attn: Anne O'Neill
470 Riverside Dr.
Princeton NJ 08540-5421
FARA#: 5059   ORD: 10/19/95

Agence de Developpement de l'Alsace
CRD: 10/19/95   France

American Continental Group
701 Pennsylvania Avenue, NW, Suite 250
Washington DC 20004
Phone: 202/347-6443   Fax: 202/347-6268
URL: http://www.acgrep.com
FARA#: 5097   ORD: 3/4/96

Government of India
CRD: 3/4/96   India

American Intern'l. Consulting Group, Inc.
10033 9th Street, North, #300
St. Petersburg FL 33716-3804
FARA#: 4939   ORD: 8/8/94

Korean Overseas Veterans Association (KOVA)
CRD: 8/8/94   Korea

An Bord Trachtala/ Irish Trade Board
Ireland House
345 Park Avenue, 17th Floor
New York NY 10154-0037
FARA#: 2518   ORD: 6/8/74

An Bord Trachtala/Irish Lrade Board
CRD: 6/3/74   Ireland

APCO Associates, Inc.
1615 L Street, NW - Suite 900
Washington DC 20036
Phone: 202/778-1000   Fax: 202/466-6002
URL: http://www.apcoassoc.com
FARA#: 4561   ORD: 9/3/91

Republic of Singapore, Embassy
CRD: 6/28/95   Singapore

Arab Information Center
League of Arab States
1100 17th Street, NW - #602
Washington DC 20036
Phone: 202/265-3210   Fax: 202/331-1525
FARA#: 876   ORD: 3/3/55

League of Arab States
CRD: 8/15/66   International

Arent Fox Kintner Plotkin & Kahn
1050 Connecticut Avenue, NW - Suite 500
Washington DC 20036-5339
Phone: 202/857-6000   Fax: 202/857-6395
E-mail: infolaw@arentfox.com
URL: http://www.arentfox.com
FARA#: 2661   ORD: 2/18/76

Government of the Republic of Haiti
CRD: 10/10/91   Haiti

Arianespace, Inc.
601 13th Street, NW, Suite 710-North
Washington DC 20005
Phone: 202/628-3936   Fax: 202/628-3949
FARA#: 3673   ORD: 4/30/85

Arianespace, S.A.
CRD: 4/30/85   France

Arnold & Porter
ATT Lawrence Schneider, Esq.
555 12th Street, NW
Washington DC 20004-1202
Phone: 202/942-5000   Fax: 202/942-5999
FARA#: 1750   ORD: 6/4/64

Cambodian People's Party
CRD: 4/22/98   Cambodia

Republic of Venezuela
CRD: 6/5/84   Venezuela

State of Israel
CRD: 1/20/88   Israel

Arter & Hadden
1801 K Street, NW
Washington DC 20006-1301
Phone: 202/775-7100   Fax: 202/857-0172
FARA#: 5031   ORD: 6/26/95

*Departement de l'economie publique, Republic
   and Canton of Geneva*
CRD: 7/18/96   Switzerland

Hong Kong Trade Development Council
CRD: 6/26/95   Hong Kong

Aruba Tourism Authority
ATT Mr. Marcial F. Ibarra
1000 Harbor Boulevard, Ground Level
Weehawken NJ 07087
FARA#: 2987   ORD: 12/29/78

Government of Aruba
CRD: 12/29/78   Aruba

Asatsu America, Inc.
1411 West 190th Street
Gardena CA 90248
FARA#: 5242   ORD: 3/6/98

Asatsu, Inc.
CRD: 3/6/98   International

Asia Associates, Inc.
3486 Scotland Avenue
Chambersburg PA 17201
FARA#: 5201   ORD: 8/15/97

Taipei Economic & Cultural Rep. Office (ROC)
CRD: 8/14/97   Taiwan

**ASEAN Promotional Chapter for
   Tourism - North America**
2304 Meadow Valley Terrace
Los Angeles CA 90039
FARA#: 2744   ORD: 1/4/77

ASEAN Permanent Committee on Tourism
CRD: 1/4/77   International

Atlantic Gulf Communities Corporation
ATT Elliott I. Portnoy, Esquire
2602 South Bayshore Drive
Miami FL 33133-5461
FARA#: 5000   ORD: 3/7/95

Atlantic Gulf Asia Holding, N.V.
CRD: 3/7/95   Curacao

Nanjing Ya dong International Corporation, Ltd.

CRD: 3/7/95   China

Australian Broadcasting Corporation
529 14th St., NW, Suite 510
Washington DC 20045
Phone: 202/626-5160   Fax: 202/626-5188
FARA#: 394   ORD: 11/19/46

Australian Broadcasting Corporation
CRD: 11/19/46   Australia

Australian Meat & Livestock Corporation
750 Lexington Avenue, 17th Floor
New York NY 10022
FARA#: 2611   ORD: 9/29/75

Australian Meat & Livestock Corporation
CRD: 9/29/75   Australia

Australian Tourist Commission
2049 Century Park East
Suite 1920
Los Angeles CA 90067
FARA#: 1032   ORD: 6/3/57

Australian National Travel Association
CRD: 6/3/57   Australia

Austrian National Tourist Office, New York
c/o Austrian National Railways
500 5th Avenue, Suite 800
New York NY 10110
Phone: 212/575-7723   Fax: 212/730-4568
URL: http://.austria-info.at/
FARA#: 495   ORD: 10/3/47

Austrian National Tourist Office
CRD: 10/3/47   Austria

**Austrian Trade Commission in the U.S.,
Southern Region**
3030 Peachtree St., NE, Suite 4130
Atlanta GA 30308
FARA#: 5041   ORD: 8/17/95

Federal Economic Chamber of Austria
CRD: 8/17/95   Austria

AWS Services
600 West Service Rd., Suite 303
Dulles Airport
Washington DC 20166-7527
Phone: 703/260-3466
E-mail: uupna@ix.netcom.com
URL: http://www.uup.org/
FARA#: 5043   ORD: 9/7/95

Ulster Unionist Council
CRD: 9/7/95   United Kingdom

Bahamas Tourist Office
DBA Bahamas News Bureau, Ministry of Tourism
P.O. Box N-3701
Nassau BF FARA#: 2310   ORD: 1/27/72

Bahamas Ministry of Tourism
CRD: 1/27/72   Bahamas

Bain & Associates
913 King Street
Alexandria VA 22314
Phone: 703/549-9592   Fax: 703/549-9601
E-mail: bain@bainpr.com
URL: http://www.bainpr.com/bain
FARA#: 5205   ORD: 9/4/97

*U Khin Shwe, Chairman & CEO of Zay Kabar
    Company, Ltd.*
CRD: 9/4/97   International

Baker & Botts, L.L.P.
1299 Pennsylvania Ave., NW - Suite 1300 West

Washington DC 20004-2400
Phone: 202/639-7700   Fax: 202/639-7890
FARA#: 4293   ORD: 9/15/89

JETRO-Houston
CRD: 11/9/92   Japan

Ministry of Foreign Affairs of the Rep. of Yemen
CRD: 4/22/92   Yemen

Rhone-Poulenc, S.A.
CRD: 5/1/91   France

Baker & McKenzie
ATT Daniel Crosby
815 Connecticut Avenue, NW, Suite 900
Washington DC 20006-4078
Phone: 202/452-7000   Fax: 202/452-7073
FARA#: 4591   ORD: 11/12/91

Trizec-Hahn Corporation
CRD: 11/12/91   International

Bannerman & Associates, Inc.
FNA Bannerman, M. Graeme
888 16th Street, NW, Suite 606
Washington DC 20006
Phone: 202/835-8177   Fax: 202/835-8161
FARA#: 3964   ORD: 4/28/87

Arab Republic of Egypt
CRD: 3/22/90   Egypt

Embassy of El Salvador
CRD: 7/29/93   El Salvador

Government of the Philippines
CRD: 6/1/94   Philippines

Government of the United Arab Emirates
CRD: 8/9/91   United Arab Emirates

Barbados Investment & Development Corp.
800 Second Avenue, 17th Floor
New York NY 10017
Phone: 212/867-6420   Fax: 212/682-5496
E-mail: bidc@interport.net
URL: http://www.bidc.com
FARA#: 1995   ORD: 11/30/66

Barbados Industrial Development Corporation
CRD: 11/5/71   Barbados

Barbados Tourist Board
CRD: 11/5/71   Barbados

Barbara Burns & Associates, Inc.
DBA Consultants in Public Relations, S.A.
425 Madison Ave.
New York NY 10017
FARA#: 4600   ORD: 12/6/91

City of Helsinki
CRD: 8/4/97   Finland

Port Autonome du Havre
CRD: 12/6/91   France

Barbour, Griffith & Rogers
1275 Pennsylvania Avenue, NW, 10th Floor
Washington DC 20004
Phone: 202/333-4936   Fax: 202/833-9392
FARA#: 5146   ORD: 12/19/96

Embassy of Switzerland
CRD: 12/19/96   Switzerland

Winterthur Group
CRD: 4/6/98   Switzerland

Barnes & Thornburg
11 South Meridian Street

Indianapolis IN 46204
FARA#: 5239   ORD: 3/2/98

Federation of Bosnia and Herzegovina
CRD: 3/2/98   Bosnia & Herzegovina

Barnes, Richardson & Colburn
ATT Matthew McGrath
1225 I Street, NW, Suite 1150
Washington DC 20005
Phone: 202/457-0300   Fax: 202/331-8746
FARA#: 2751   ORD: 2/10/77

Bayer, Inc. Subsidiary of Bayer, A.G.
CRD: 8/8/89   Germany

Barron-Birrell, Inc.
1101 30th St., NW - Suite 500
Washington DC 20007-3646
Phone: 202/338-5393   Fax: 202/338-5391
FARA#: 4729   ORD: 11/2/92

Government of Mali
CRD: 12/9/97   Mali

Pascal Lissouba, Brazzaville, Congo
CRD: 12/9/97   Congo, Republic of

Republic of Gabon
CRD: 3/2/98   Gabon

Republic of the Congo
CRD: 12/9/97   Congo, Republic of

Republic of the Congo
CRD: 12/9/97   Congo

The Federal Republic of Nigeria
CRD: 7/17/95   Nigeria

Bashkortostan Trade Mission
ATT Michael Grundei, Esquire
2740 Coulter Lane
Gilette WY 82716
FARA#: 4731   ORD: 11/05/92

Republic of Bashkortostan
CRD: 11/5/92   Russia

Belgian National Tourist Office
780 Third Avenue, Suite 1501
New York NY 10017
FARA#: 529   ORD: 6/17/48

Belgian National Tourist Office
CRD: 6/17/48   Belgium

Benford Associates, Inc.
1464 Whippoorwill Way
Mountainside NJ 07092
FARA#: 4224   ORD: 3/13/89

St. Kitts & Nevis Tourist Board
CRD: 3/13/89   St. Kitts & Nevis

Bergner, Bockorny & Clough
1101 16th Street, NW - Suite 500
Washington DC 20036
Phone: 202/659-9111   Fax: 202/659-6387
FARA#: 3801   ORD: 3/20/86

*Taipei Economic & Cultural Representative
    Office (TECRO)*
CRD: 5/9/86   Taiwan

Berk, Peggy
276 Fifth Avenue, Suite 804
New York NY 10001
FARA#: 5124   ORD: 7/31/96

Greek National Tourist Organization
CRD: 7/31/96   Greece

Bermuda Department of Tourism
310 Madison Avenue
Suite 201
New York NY 10017
FARA#: 430   ORD: 1/3/47

Government of Bermuda, Department of Tourism
CRD: 7/14/48   Bermuda

Bernhagen & Associates
10233 - 26th Avenue, S.W.
Seattle WA 98146
Phone: 206/762-7945   Fax: 206/768-1113
FARA#: 3992   ORD: 6/15/87

Consulate General of Japan
CRD: 6/15/87   Japan

Bernstein Law Firm, PLLC
1730 K Street, NW, Suite 313
Washington DC 20006-3868
Phone: 202/452-8010   Fax: 202/296-2065
FARA#: 4764   ORD: 2/8/93

XL Insurance Company, Ltd.
CRD: 2/8/93   Bermuda

Berry, Max N.
3213 O Street, NW
Washington DC 20007
Phone: 202/298-6134   Fax: 202/333-3348
FARA#: 2216   ORD: 10/30/70

*Centre National Interprofessional d'Economie
   Laitiere*
CRD: 6/3/80   France

Danish Bacon and Meat Council
CRD: 5/28/97   Denmark

Danish Biscuit Alliance
CRD: 3/10/98   Denmark

Black, Kelly, Scruggs & Healey
1801 K Street, NW - Suite 901-L
Washington DC 20006
Phone: 202/530-0500   Fax: 202/530-4800
FARA#: 3600   ORD: 6/14/84

Center for Democracy in Angola
CRD: 10/16/85   Angola

*Comision Ejecutiva Hidroelectrica del Rio
   Lempa CEL*
CRD: 3/20/98   International

Government of Equatorial Guinea, Embassy
CRD: 10/16/95   Equatorial Guinea

Bogle & Gates
Two Union Square
601 Union Street
Seattle WA 98101-2346
Phone: 202/293-3600   Fax: 202/293-5825
FARA#: 3474   ORD: 5/24/83

Lembaga Bantuan Perasaran & Managemen
CRD: 9/14/89   Indonesia

Norwegian Fisheries' Association
CRD: 5/24/83   Norway

Boland & Madigan, Inc.
700 13th Street, NW - Suite 350
Washington DC 20005
Phone: 202/637-0040   Fax: 202/637-0041
E-mail: emial@bolandmadigan.com
FARA#: 5147   ORD: 12/30/96

Embassy of the Kingdom of Morocco
CRD: 5/26/98   Morocco

Embassy of the Kingdom of Saudi Arabia
CRD: 12/30/96   Saudi Arabia

Her Majesty the Queen in Right of Canada
CRD: 3/24/98   Canada

Taiwan Research Institute
CRD: 12/30/96   Taiwan

Brady & Berliner
1225 19th Street, NW
Washington DC 20036
Phone: 202/955-6067   Fax: 202/293-0307
FARA#: 5222   ORD: 4/2/97

Powerex
CRD: 4/2/97   International

Brady Company, Inc.
N80 W12878
Fond du Lac Avenue
Menomonee Falls WI 53051
FARA#: 5138   ORD: 11/8/96

Danish Ministry of Business & Industry
CRD: 11/8/96   Denmark

Bristol Group, Inc.
1900 L Street, NW - Suite 407
Washington DC 20036
Phone: 202/293-3454   FARA#: 5247
ORD: 3/25/98

Commercial Section of the Embassy of Angola
CRD: 3/25/98   Angola

British Tourist Authority
551 Fifth Avenue
Suite 701
New York NY 10176-0799
FARA#: 579   ORD: 7/7/49

British Tourist Authority
CRD: 7/7/49   United Kingdom

British Virgin Islands Tourist Board
370 Lexington Avenue
New York NY 10017
FARA#: 3354   ORD: 4/8/82

British Virgin Islands Tourist Board
CRD: 4/8/82   British Virgin Islands

Britt, Jr., Raymond L.
ManuLife Financial
73 Tremont Street
Boston MA 02108-3915
Phone: 617/854-4309   Fax: 617/854-4301
FARA#: 3549   ORD: 1/19/84

The Manufacturers Life Insurance Company
CRD: 1/19/84   Canada

Bronz & Farrell
ATT Edward J. Farrell
1735 Jefferson Davis Highway, Suite 200
Arlington VA 22202
FARA#: 1740   ORD: 5/22/64

New Zealand Dairy Board
CRD: 7/3/68   New Zealand

New Zealand Meat Producers Board
CRD: 5/22/64   New Zealand

Brown Nelson & Associates, Inc.
6200 Savoy Drive, Suite 350
Houston TX 77036
FARA#: 4615   ORD: 2/12/92

Unicom Management Services, Ltd.
CRD: 3/30/98   International

Brown, Nelson & Associates, Inc.
6200 Savoy Drive, Suite 350
Houston TX 77036
Phone: 713/784-6200   Fax: 713/784-6356
E-mail: BNPR@phoenix.net
URL: http://www.bnpr.com
FARA#: 4615   ORD: 2/12/92

Argonaut, A.B.
CRD: 3/31/94   Sweden

BSMG Worldwide
1501 M Street, NW - Suite 600
Washington DC 20005-1702
Phone: 202/739-0200   Fax: 202/659-8287
FARA#: 3911   ORD: 12/01/86

Government of the Bahamas
CRD: 12/4/95   Bahamas

Mercurindo
CRD: 8/8/95   Indonesia

Burson-Marsteller, Inc.
1801 K Street, NW - Suite 1000L
Washington DC 20006
Phone: 202/530-0400   FARA#: 2469
ORD: 10/23/73

Better Hong Kong Foundation (BHKF)
CRD: 6/4/96   Hong Kong

*Center for Information and Business
   Development (CIDEM)*
CRD: 10/24/96   International

*Comision Ejecutive Hidroelectrica del Rio
   Lempa CEL*
CRD: 3/20/98   International

Government of Indonesia
CRD: 4/17/92   Indonesia

*Government of Israel, Economic Mission to
   North America*
CRD: 8/13/97   Israel

*Government of Mexico, Ministry of
   Commerce & Industrial*
CRD: 12/12/90   Mexico

Government of Mexico, Ministry of Tourism
CRD: 9/5/95   Mexico

Investment in Finland Bureau
CRD: 9/5/95   Finland

King Faisal Foundation
CRD: 9/5/97   Saudi Arabia

Royal Norwegian Consulate General New York
CRD: 8/13/97   Norway

Business Network Corporation
245 Peachtree Center Avenue, Suite 2200
Atlanta GA 30303
Phone: 404/681-4279   Fax: 404/681-4175
FARA#: 4513   ORD: 5/20/91

Japan Economic Foundation
CRD: 5/20/91   Japan

Japan External Trade Organization (JETRO)
CRD: 11/24/97   Japan

C/R International, LLC
1150 17th Street, NW - Suite 406
Washington DC 20036
Phone: 202/861-4740   Fax: 202/861-6490
E-mail: consult@crinternational.c
FARA#: 5117   ORD: 7/2/96

Base Petroleum
CRD: 7/16/96   International

Chamber of Mines of South Africa
CRD: 8/14/96   South Africa

Embassy of the Republic of Angola
CRD: 7/2/96   Angola

Embassy of the Republic of South Africa
CRD: 7/16/96   South Africa

South Africa Foundation
CRD: 9/6/96   South Africa

Southern African Development Community
CRD: 4/23/97   South Africa

*Turkish Foreign Economic Relations Board
    (DEIK)*
CRD: 4/23/97   Turkey

Camara Oficial Espanola de Comercio
P.O. Box 9020894
San Juan PR 00902-0894
FARA#: 2400   ORD: 12/27/72

Spanish Ministry of Commerce
CRD: 12/27/72   Spain

Cameron & Hornbostel
818 Connecticut Avenue, NW, Suite 700
Washington DC 20006
Phone: 202/293-4690   Fax: 202/293-1877
E-mail: camhorn@erols.com
FARA#: 4705   ORD: 8/19/92

The Government of Barbados
CRD: 8/19/92   Barbados

Cameron, Bruce P.
1725 17th Street, NW, Suite 109
Washington DC 20009
Phone: 202/667-9563   Fax: 202/332-6544
FARA#: 4043   ORD: 9/28/87

Government of Portugal, Embassy
CRD: 2/18/97   Portugal

Republic of Mozambique
CRD: 10/13/87   Mozambique

Cane, Stephen Paul
Zurich Building
90 Fenchurch Street
London EN EC3M 4JX
FARA#: 5062   ORD: 9/11/95

*London Insurance & Reinsurance Market
    Association*
CRD: 9/11/95   United Kingdom

Capitol Advisors, Inc.
725 15th Street, NW - Suite 903
Washington DC 20005
FARA#: 5245   ORD: 3/25/98

Embassy of Georgia
CRD: 3/25/98   Georgia

Caribbean Tourism Organization
80 Broad Street, 32nd Floor
New York NY 10004
FARA#: 991   ORD: 12/31/56

Caribbean Tourism Organization
CRD: 3/2/94   International

Carlington Sales Canada Corporation
1260 Crescent, Suite 201
Montreal, Quebec CA H3G 2A9
FARA#: 5249   ORD: 3/31/98

Government of the Republic of Zambia
CRD: 3/31/98   Zambia

Cassidy & Associates, Inc.
700 13th Street, NW - Suite 400
Washington DC 20005
Phone: 202/347-0773   Fax: 202/347-0785
E-mail: cassidy@cassidy.com
FARA#: 4259   ORD: 5/25/89

Kingdom of Morocco, Embassy
CRD: 5/22/98   Morocco

Royal Embassy of Saudi Arabia
CRD: 7/28/95   Saudi Arabia

Taiwan Research Institute
CRD: 7/18/94   Taiwan

Catlett & Yancey, PLC
1800 Tower Building, 323 Center Street
Little Rock AR 72201
FARA#: 4914   ORD: 5/17/94

P-NN Arkansas, Inc.
CRD: 5/17/94   Azerbaijan

Cayman Island Department of Tourism
P.O. Box 67
Georgetown CJ
FARA#: 2500   ORD: 3/4/74

Government of the Cayman Islands
CRD: 3/4/74   Cayman Islands

CETDC, Inc.
420 Fifth Avenue, 28th Floor
New York NY 10018
FARA#: 3652   ORD: 2/28/85

China External Trade Develop. Council (CETDC)
CRD: 2/28/85   Taiwan

Charles E. Butler & Associates
DBA Japan Steel Information Center, New York
60 East 42nd Street, Room 541
New York NY 10165
FARA#: 3544   ORD: 12/29/83

Japan Iron & Steel Exporters' Association
CRD: 12/29/83   Japan

China Books & Periodicals, Inc.
2929 24th Street
San Francisco CA 94110
Phone: 415/282-2994   Fax: 415/282-0994
E-mail: chinabks@slip.net
URL: http://www.chinabooks.com
FARA#: 1350   ORD: 4/6/60

Beijing Review
CRD: 6/11/87   China

China Today
CRD: 4/6/60   China

Guoji Shudian
CRD: 4/6/60   China

China Daily Distribution Corporation
One World Trade Center, Suite 3369
New York NY 10048
Phone: 212/488-9677   Fax: 212/488-9493
FARA#: 3457   ORD: 4/19/83

China Daily of Beijing, China
CRD: 4/19/83   China

China International Travel Service, Inc.
ATT Stephen K. Seung, Esquire
350 Fifth Avenue
New York NY 10118

FARA#: 3318   ORD: 12/30/81

China International Travel Service
CRD: 12/30/81   China

Chlopak, Leonard, Schechter & Associates
1850 M Street, NW - Suite 550
Washington DC 20036
Phone: 202/289-5900   Fax: 202/289-4141
E-mail: info@clsdc.com
FARA#: 4953   ORD: 9/28/94

Cruz Enverga & Raboca
CRD: 4/14/98   International

M. Scott Vayer - Assicurazioni Generali, S.p.A.
CRD: 7/9/97   Italy

PromPeru
CRD: 5/17/96   Peru

Siderca Corporation
CRD: 9/28/94   Argentina

**Chungchong Nam-Do Provincial Government,
    New York**
Empire State Building
350 Fifth Avenue, Suite 1809
New York NY 10118
FARA#: 5187   ORD: 6/23/97

Chungchong Nam-Do Provincial Government
CRD: 6/23/97   International

Civic Service, Inc.
1050 Connecticut Ave., NW - Suite 870
Washington DC 20036
Phone: 202/785-2070   Fax: 202/785-1102
FARA#: 3385   ORD: 6/28/82

AEG Electromcom GmbH
CRD: 7/28/92   Germany

International Public Relations Company, Ltd.
CRD: 6/28/82   Japan

Japan Federation of Construction Contractors
CRD: 8/24/95   Japan

*Nippon Telegraph & Telephone Public
    Corporation (NTT)*
CRD: 6/15/83   Japan

Sanwa Bank, Ltd.
CRD: 7/25/88   Japan

Cleary, Gottlieb, Steen & Hamilton
2000 Pennsylvania Ave., NW
Washington DC 20006-1801
Phone: 202/974-1500   Fax: 202/974-1999
FARA#: 508   ORD: 1/19/48

*Ministry of Communications & Transportation
    of Mexico*
CRD: 3/21/96   Mexico

Ministry of Finance and Public Credit of Mexico
CRD: 4/4/91   Mexico

Ministry of Foreign Relations of Mexico
CRD: 5/10/96   Mexico

State of Kuwait
CRD: 8/13/90   Kuwait

Clement-Petrocik Company, The
14 East 60th Street
New York NY 10022
FARA#: 2249   ORD: 3/18/71

Martinique & Guadeloupe Tourism
CRD: 3/18/71   Guadeloupe & Martinique

CMG Communications, LLC
79 Fifth Avenue, 9th Floor
New York NY 10003
FARA#: 5129   ORD: 6/24/96

Virgin Atlantic Airways, Ltd.
CRD: 6/24/96   International

Cohen & Woods International, Inc.
2111 Wilson Boulevard - Suite 800
Arlington VA 22201
Phone: 703/875-8714   Fax: 703/243-3177
FARA#: 5003   ORD: 3/10/95

Government of the Republic of Angola
CRD: 10/2/96   Angola

Republic of Cote d'Ivoire
CRD: 7/18/95   International

Winnington, Ltd.
CRD: 12/31/97   International

Collier, Shannon, Rill & Scott
ATT John VillaFranco
3050 K St., NW, Suite 400
Washington DC 20007
Phone: 202/342-8400   Fax: 202/342-5534
E-mail: lawyers@colshan.com
FARA#: 3694   ORD: 6/24/85

Australia - U.S. Business Council
CRD: 1/24/96   Australia

Australian Dairy Industry
CRD: 12/21/94   Australia

Australian Oat Exporters' Group
CRD: 7/24/95   Australia

Coalition for Safe Ceramicware
CRD: 6/12/92   International

*European Electronic Component
    Manufacturers' Association*
CRD: 5/27/92   Belgium

International Crystal Federation
CRD: 6/1/92   International

*Petroleos de Venezuela, S.A.
    (Maraven, Lagoven, Corpoven)*
CRD: 6/24/85   Venezuela

Colombian Coffee Federation, Inc.
140 East 57th Street
New York NY 10022
FARA#: 4909   ORD: 4/6/94

Federacion Nacional de Cafeteros de Colombia
CRD: 4/6/94   Colombia

Cominco America, Inc.
601 West Riverside Avenue
Spokane WA 99201
FARA#: 5243   ORD: 3/17/98

Cominco, Ltd.
CRD: 3/17/98   International

Cosmos, Inc.
P.O. Box 30437
Bethesda MD 20824
Phone: 301/229-5875   Fax: 301/229-5876
FARA#: 4519   ORD: 5/31/91

National Bank of Romania
CRD: 5/31/91   Romania

Costa Rican Board of Trade
108 East 66th Street
New York NY 10021

FARA#: 2370   ORD: 8/21/72

Camara de Azucareros
CRD: 8/21/72   Costa Rica

Textile Association of Costa Rica (ASFAMEX)
CRD: 8/21/72   Costa Rica

Costello, Stephen
6110 Executive Blvd., Suite 1000
Rockville MD 20852
Phone: 301/231-5143   Fax: 301/231-5276
E-mail: kimdj@crosslink.net
FARA#: 5065   ORD: 10/27/95

Kim Dae-Jung Peace Foundation, U.S.A.
CRD: 10/27/95   Korea

Coudert Brothers
1627 I Street, NW - 12th Floor
Washington DC 20006
Phone: 202/775-5100   Fax: 202/775-1168
URL: http://www.coudert.com
FARA#: 5254   ORD: 4/23/98

*Government of Canada, Dept. of
    Foreign Affairs/Int. Trade*
CRD: 4/23/98   Canada

Council of Khalistan
FNA Gurmit Singh Aulakh
2025 I Street, NW, Suite 922
Washington DC 20006
FARA#: 4137   ORD: 5/11/88

Council of Khalistan
CRD: 5/11/88   India

COGEMA, Inc.
7401 Wisconsin Avenue
Bethesda MD 20814-3416
Phone: 301/986-8585   Fax: 301/652-5690
FARA#: 3587   ORD: 5/17/84

*Compagnie Generale des Matieres Nucleaires,
    Subsidiary of*
CRD: 5/17/84   France

Crane, Jonathan A.
355 Riverside Drive, #2W
New York NY 10025
FARA#: 4857   ORD: 10/07/93

British Broadcasting Corporation
CRD: 10/7/93   United Kingdom

Crowell & Moring International, L.P.
DBA C&M International, Ltd.
1001 Pennsylvania Ave., NW, Suite 1100
Washington DC 20004-2595
Phone: 202/624-2500   Fax: 202/628-5116
FARA#: 3988   ORD: 5/28/87

*Asia Pacific Economic Cooperation of
    the Philippines*
CRD: 8/9/96   International

Board of Foreign Trade, ROC
CRD: 6/23/87   Taiwan

*Government of the Republic of the Philippines/
    Dept. of Trade & Ind.*
CRD: 3/14/96   Philippines

Korean International Trade Association
CRD: 4/6/88   Korea

Ministry of Trade, Government of Indonesia
CRD: 1/13/94   Indonesia

*New Zealand Fishing Industry Board/Fishing
    Industry & Inspection*

CRD: 4/8/93   New Zealand

Pacific Dunlop, Ltd./Pacific Brands
CRD: 6/29/95   Australia

Curacao Tourist Board
475 Park Avenue South, Suite 2000
New York NY 10016
Phone: 212/683-7660   Fax: 212/683-9337
E-mail: Curacao@ix.netcom.com
URL: http://www.interknowledge.com.curacao
FARA#: 3209   ORD: 3/10/81

Government of the Island of Curacao
CRD: 3/10/81   Curacao

Czech Center, New York
1109 Madison Avenue
New York NY 10028
FARA#: 5115   ORD: 6/21/96

Czech Ministry of Foreign Affairs
CRD: 6/21/96   Czech Republic

Daimler-Benz Aerospace of N. America, Inc.
c/o Coudert Brothers
1350 I Street, N.W., Suite 800
Washington DC 20005
Phone: 202/408-4900   Fax: 202/408-4891
FARA#: 4719   ORD: 10/09/92

Daimler-Benz Aerospace, A.G.
CRD: 10/9/92   Germany

Daniel J. Edelman, Inc.
ATT Carol Fischer
1500 N. Broadway, 26th Floor
New York NY 10036
FARA#: 3657   ORD: 3/12/85

*Ministry of Foreign Affairs, Government of
    the Arab Rep. of Egypt*
CRD: 5/20/95   Egypt

Office of the Japanese Consul General
CRD: 10/25/93   Japan

Pulsar International
CRD: 5/12/95   Mexico

Danish Tourist Board
655 Third Avenue
Suite 1810
New York NY 10017
FARA#: 634   ORD: 7/25/50

Danish Tourist Board
CRD: 7/25/50   Denmark

Dater, Elliott
GOI-MOD Mission to the U.S.
800 Second Ave., 11th Floor
New York NY 10017
FARA#: 4322   ORD: 12/06/89

Government of Israel, Ministry of Defense
CRD: 12/6/89   Israel

David Apter & Associates, Inc.
1706 R Street, NW
Washington DC 20009
FARA#: 3133   ORD: 8/5/80

Republic of Togo
CRD: 8/5/80   Togo

David Morey Group, Inc. (DMG)
1701 K Street, NW, 11th Floor
Washington DC 20006
FARA#: 5236   ORD: 2/19/98

Cambodian People's Party

CRD: 5/4/98   Cambodia

President-Elect Kim Dae Jung/transition team
CRD: 2/19/98   International

Davis, Manafort & Freedman, Inc.
211 North Union Street - Suite 250
Alexandria VA 22314
Phone: 703/299-9100   Fax: 703/299-9110
FARA#: 5240   ORD: 3/3/98

Federal Republic of Nigeria
CRD: 3/3/98   Nigeria

Dawkins, Dymally & Associates
1825 I Street, NW, Suite 400
Washington DC 20006
FARA#: 5190   ORD: 7/7/97

Embassy of the Republic of the Sudan
CRD: 7/7/97   Sudan

DDB Needham Worldwide, Inc.
437 Madison Avenue
New York NY 10022
FARA#: 1066   ORD: 9/16/57

Bermuda Department of Tourism
CRD: 4/17/90   Bermuda

Nat'l. Federation of Coffee Growers of Colombia
CRD: 10/22/71   Colombia

DDC Productions, Inc.
301 East 22nd Street
New York NY 10010
FARA#: 2974   ORD: 11/01/78

German Information Center
CRD: 12/20/84   Germany

Debevoise & Plimpton
875 Third Avenue
New York NY 10022
Phone: 202/383-8000   Fax: 202/383-8118
FARA#: 3527   ORD: 10/05/83

Sony Corporation
CRD: 10/5/93   Japan

Dechert, Price & Rhoads
ATT Allan S. Mostoff
1500 K St., NW, Suite 500
Washington DC 20005-1208
Phone: 202/261-3300   Fax: 202/261-3333
FARA#: 2777   ORD: 11/21/77

Embassy of Japan
CRD: 4/27/77   Japan

Export-Import Bank of Japan
CRD: 4/27/77   Japan

Malta Development Corporation
CRD: 3/14/91   Malta

Malta Financial Services Centre
CRD: 5/31/95   Malta

Delta Tech, Inc.
9525 Clement Rd.
Silver Spring MD 20910
Phone: 301/588-4683   Fax: 301/587-9200
E-mail: deltaone@radix.net
FARA#: 4916   ORD: 5/20/94

Mr. Pier Francesco Guarguaglini, Managing Dir.
CRD: 5/20/94   Italy

Denison, George H.
5910 Woodacres Drive
Bethesda MD 20816

Phone: 202/229-5791   Fax: 202/229-5792
FARA#: 4991   ORD: 2/14/95

Federation of Electric Power Co's. of Japan
CRD: 2/14/95   Japan

Islamic Republic of Mauritania
CRD: 10/3/96   Mauritania

Derwinski, Edward
Derwinski & Associates
1800 Diagonal Road, Suite 600
Alexandria VA 22314
Phone: 703/684-4401   Fax: 703/548-9446
FARA#: 5011   ORD: 4/11/95

Government of the Republic of Cyprus
CRD: 4/11/95   Cyprus

Deutsche Telekom, Inc.
666 Fifth Avenue, 34th Floor
New York NY 10103
Phone: 202/452-9100   Fax: 202/452-9555
FARA#: 4419   ORD: 10/09/90

Deutsche Telecom, A.G.
CRD: 10/9/90   Germany

Development Counsellors International
461 Park Avenue South
12th Floor
New York NY 10016
FARA#: 4777   ORD: 3/12/93

Geneva Departement de L'Economic Publique
CRD: 5/11/93   Switzerland

Government of Newfoundland & Labrador
CRD: 6/28/96   Canada

South African Tourism Board
CRD: 3/12/93   South Africa

Swedish Travel & Tourism Council
CRD: 12/17/93   Switzerland

Dickstein Shapiro Morin & Oshinsky L.L.P.
2101 L Street, NW
Washington DC 20037
Phone: 202/785-9700   Fax: 202/887-0689
E-mail: ZausnerA@dsmo.com
URL: http://www.dsmo.com
FARA#: 3028   ORD: 6/7/79

Kuwait Airways
CRD: 4/7/80   Kuwait

Malaysian Palm Oil Promotion Council
CRD: 4/18/91   Malaysia

Middle East Airlines
CRD: 7/22/81   International

Royal Thai Embassy
CRD: 3/17/97   Thailand

DMRansom Associates, Inc.
1101 Connecticut Avenue, NW, Suite 310
Washington DC 20036
FARA#: 5256   ORD: 5/19/98

Ministry of Information, Government House,
   State of Bahrain
CRD: 5/20/98   Bahrain

Donald G. Lerch & Company, Inc.
1629 K Street, NW - Suite 1100
Washington DC 20006
Phone: 202/785-6705   Fax: 202/331-4212
FARA#: 4831   ORD: 7/19/93

Japan International Agricultural Council (JIAC)

CRD: 7/19/93   Japan

Donald N. Martin & Company, Inc.
One Rockefeller Plaza
Suite 214
New York NY 10020
FARA#: 1381   ORD: 7/29/60

European Travel Commission
CRD: 7/29/60   International

Dubai Commerce & Tourism Promo. Board
8 Penn Center, 19th Floor
Philadelphia PA 19103
FARA#: 4217   ORD: 2/17/89

Jebel Ali Free Zone Authority
CRD: 2/17/89   United Arab Emirates

Durak, Ahmet Unal
2550 M Street, NW
Washington DC 20037
Phone: 202/457-6421   FARA#: 5215
ORD: 10/15/97

Embassy of the Republic of Turkey
CRD: 10/15/97   Turkey

Dutton & Dutton, P.C.
5017 Tilden Street, NW
Washington DC 20016
Phone: 202/686-3500   Fax: 202/966-6621
FARA#: 2591   ORD: 6/12/75

Embassy of Saudi Arabia
CRD: 11/28/75   Saudi Arabia

Dymally International Group, Inc.
1602 Centinela Avenue, Suite 208
Inglewood CA 90302
Phone: 310/641-3688   Fax: 310/641-6980
FARA#: 4799   ORD: 4/27/93

Islamic Republic of Mauritania
CRD: 4/27/93   Mauritania

E. Bruce Harrison Company
808 17th Street, NW - Suite 600
Washington DC 20006-3910
FARA#: 4937   ORD: 8/4/94

Federation of Electric Power Co's. of Japan
CRD: 8/4/94   Japan

East Asia Travel Association
c/o Tourism Authority of Thailand
5 World Trade Center, Suite 3443
New York NY 10048
Phone: 212/924-0882   FARA#: 2423
ORD: 5/7/73

East Asia Travel Association
CRD: 5/7/73   International

Eastern Caribbean Investment Promo. Service
3216 New Mexico Avenue, NW
Washington DC 20016
Phone: 202/363-0229   Fax: 202/363-4328
FARA#: 4080   ORD: 1/14/88

Organization of Eastern Caribbean States
CRD: 1/14/88   International

Ebert, Douglas Karl
8347 Larch Court
Suite 100
Florence KY 41042
Phone: 606/282-8594   Fax: 606/282-0094
FARA#: 4757   ORD: 1/26/93

Dr. Karl Dobler
CRD: 1/26/93   Switzerland

Echols, Sr., Randall Edwin
601 James Ridge Road, Suite 612
Bowie MD 20721-7288
FARA#: 4873 ORD: 12/8/93

M.K.O. Biola (Nigerian President-Elect)
CRD: 12/8/93 Nigeria

Eckert International, Inc.
11201 Gray Fox Pointe
Spotsylvania VA 22553
FARA#: 4198 ORD: 12/16/88

Kingdom of Tonga
CRD: 9/29/89 Tonga

Economic Information Center
1900 K Street, NW, Suite 1075
Washington DC 20006
FARA#: 4983 ORD: 1/4/95

Keizai Koho Center
CRD: 1/4/95 Japan

Ed Graves & Associates
1615 L Street, NW, Suite 1150
Washington DC 20036
Phone: 202/467-3900 Fax: 202/833-1349
FARA#: 4541 ORD: 7/10/91

CBI Sugar Group
CRD: 7/10/91 Guatemala

Embassy of Azerbaijan
CRD: 12/10/93 Azerbaijan

Edelman Public Relations Worldwide
1420 K Street, NW - 10th Floor
Washington DC 20005
Phone: 202/371-0200 Fax: 202/371-2858
URL: http://www.edelman.com
FARA#: 3634 ORD: 11/15/84

Government of Chile, Office of Communications
CRD: 11/15/94 Chile

Government of Colombia, Embassy
CRD: 4/1/98 Colombia

Government of Portugal (Trade Commission)
CRD: 11/15/94 Portugal

Edward Shaw Productions
4740 NE, 22nd Ave.
Lighthouse Point FL 33064
FARA#: 4401 ORD: 7/17/90

*Commander of the National Armed Forces
of Suriname*
CRD: 7/17/90 Suriname

Equihua, Xavier
1000 Potomac Street, NW, Suite 300
Washington DC 20007
Phone: 202/625-0345 Fax: 202/393-5728
E-mail: xequihana@fedstrategies.c
FARA#: 5039 ORD: 8/7/95

AFINOA
CRD: 4/30/97 Mexico

Ethiopian Peoples' Revolutionary Party, The
P.O. Box 73337
Washington DC 20056-3337
FARA#: 4789 ORD: 4/7/93

Ethiopian Peoples' Revolutionary Party
CRD: 4/7/93 Ethiopia

European Travel Commission
One Rockefeller Plaza
Suite 214

New York NY 10020
Phone: 212/307-1200 Fax: 212/307-1205
FARA#: 574 ORD: 6/30/49

European Travel Commission
CRD: 6/6/49 International

Eurostrategy Associates, Inc.
1313 North Market Street, Suite 3410
Wilmington DE 19801-1150
FARA#: 4790 ORD: 4/7/93

Jean-Pierre Lemboumba
CRD: 4/7/93 Gabon

Evans Group, Ltd. (The)
c/o Thomas B. Evans, Jr.
700 13th Street, NW, Suite 950
Washington DC 20005
Phone: 202/333-8777 Fax: 202/333-8722
FARA#: 4222 ORD: 3/2/89

The Republic of Cyprus
CRD: 3/2/89 Cyprus

Evans, Billy Lee
ATT Benjamin L. Zelenko, Esquire
407 First Street, SE
Washington DC 20003
Phone: 202/659-0330 Fax: 202/296-6119
FARA#: 5021 ORD: 5/25/95

Royal Norwegian Government (Embassy)
CRD: 5/25/95 Norway

Far East Trade Service, Inc., Chicago
DBA Taiwan Trade Center-Chicago
225 North Michigan Ave., Suite 1888
Chicago IL 60601
FARA#: 2911 ORD: 6/8/78

Far East Trade Service, Inc.
CRD: 6/8/78 Taiwan

Far East Trade Service, Inc., San Francisco
555 Montgomery Street, Suite 603
San Francisco CA 94111-2564
FARA#: 2985 ORD: 12/06/78

Far East Trade Service, Inc.
CRD: 12/6/78 Taiwan

FCB/Leber Katz Partners, Inc.
150 East 42nd St., 11th Floor
New York NY 10017-5612
FARA#: 2415 ORD: 3/28/73

British Virgin Islands Tourist Board
CRD: 11/7/90 British Virgin Islands

Jamaica Tourist Board
CRD: 6/20/90 Jamaica

Federation of Electric Power Co's. of Japan
ATT John M. Stephens
Miller & Chevalier
1901 L St., NW - Suite 600
Washington DC 20036
Phone: 202/466-6781 Fax: 202/466-6758
FARA#: 4922 ORD: 6/22/94

Federation of Electric Power Co's. of Japan
CRD: 6/22/94 Japan

Finkelstein, Thompson & Loughran
1055 Thomas Jefferson Street, NW - Suite 601
Washington DC 20007
Phone: 202/337-8000 Fax: 202/265-9363
FARA#: 5213 ORD: 9/25/97

Canadian Broadcasting Corporation
CRD: 9/25/97 Canada

Finnish Tourist Board, New York
655 Third Avenue - Suite 1810
New York NY 10017-5617
Phone: 212/949-2333 Fax: 212/983-5260
FARA#: 573 ORD: 5/31/49

Ministry of Trade & Industry
CRD: 10/30/73 Finland

Fleishman-Hillard, Inc.
200 North Broadway
St. Louis MO 63102-2796
FARA#: 3774 ORD: 2/5/86

Business Location Germany
CRD: 5/5/97 Germany

Canadair: a division of Bombardier, Inc.
CRD: 3/6/95 Canada

Electricite de France
CRD: 3/5/92 France

FN Manufacturing, Inc.
ATT Jennie-Lynn Falk
797 Clemson Road, P.O. Box 24257
Columbia SC 48643
FARA#: 4864 ORD: 8/18/93

Fabrique Nationale Herstal, S.A.
CRD: 8/18/93 Belgium

GIAT Industries, S.A.
CRD: 8/18/93 France

Fogarty, Klein & Partners Public Relations
7155 Old Katy Road, Suite 100
Houston TX 77024
FARA#: 4504 ORD: 4/25/91

JETRO, Houston
CRD: 12/19/90 Japan

Fontayne Group, Inc.
430 Colorado Avenue, Penthouse
Santa Monica CA 90401
FARA#: 3752 ORD: 10/30/85

Austrian National Tourist Office
CRD: 10/14/86 Austria

Queensland Travel & Tourist Corporation
CRD: 3/8/94 Australia

Singapore Tourism Promotion Board
CRD: 7/19/88 Singapore

Swiss National Tourist Office
CRD: 10/14/86 Switzerland

Foochs, Arkadiy I.
4121 18th Ave.
Brooklyn NY 11218
FARA#: 4905 ORD: 3/29/94

Government of the Republic of Tajikistan
CRD: 3/29/94 Tajikistan

Foodcom, Inc.
708 Third Avenue, 18th Floor
New York NY 10017
FARA#: 4218 ORD: 2/21/89

International Olive Oil Council, S.p.A.
CRD: 2/21/89 Italy

Foreign Policy Group
1333 New Hampshire Avenue, NW, Suite 700
Washington DC 20036
FARA#: 5169 ORD: 4/7/97

President of Paraguay, Juan Carlos Wasmosy

CRD: 4/7/97   Paraguay

Forman, Jay
c/o GOI-MOD
800 Second Avenue
New York NY 10017
FARA#: 4171   ORD: 8/25/88

*Government of Israel/Ministry of Defense,
    Mission to the U.S.*
CRD: 8/25/88   Israel

**Foundation in Support of Diplomatic
    Missions of Ukraine, Inc.**
209 Grand Avenue - Apt. B
Rutherford NJ 07070
FARA#: 4683   ORD: 6/8/92

Embassy of the Ukraine to the U.S.A.
CRD: 6/8/92   Ukraine

Permanent Mission of Ukraine to the U.N.
CRD: 6/8/92   Ukraine

French Film Office
ATT Robert F. Jacobs, Esquire
Wormser, Kiely, Galef & Jacobs
745 Fifth Ave.
New York NY 10151
FARA#: 2358   ORD: 7/20/72

Unifrance File International
CRD: 7/20/72   France

Friends of Fianna Fail, Inc.
ATT Stanley Q. Casey, Esquire
Richardson Mahon & Casey, PC
1270 Ave. of The Americas - Suite 2911
New York NY 10020
FARA#: 3596   ORD: 6/8/84

Fianna Fail
CRD: 6/8/84   Ireland

Friends of Fine Gael, Inc.
c/o Joseph L. Hern, Esquire
10 Post Office Square
Boston MA 02109-4603
FARA#: 5068   ORD: 11/08/95

Fine Gael
CRD: 11/8/95   Ireland

Friends of Irish Labour in America
700 13th Street, NW, Suite 1000
Washington DC 20005
FARA#: 5110   ORD: 6/6/96

Labour Party, Republic of Ireland
CRD: 6/6/96   Ireland

Friends of Sinn Fein, Inc.
c/o Gilroy Downes Horowitz, et. al.
15 Park Row, 7th Floor
New York NY 10038
FARA#: 5006   ORD: 4/3/95

Sinn Fein
CRD: 4/3/95   United Kingdom

Future Millennium Foundation, Inc.
1111 Jefferson Davis Highway, Suite 602
Arlington VA 22202
FARA#: 5202   ORD: 8/15/97

Fouad Makhzoumi
CRD: 8/15/97   International

Garvey, Schubert & Barer
1191 Second Avenue
Seattle WA 98101-2939
Phone: 202/965-7880   Fax: 202/965-1729

E-mail: HBAILEY@gsblaw.com
URL: http://www.speakeasy.org/gsb/
FARA#: 3047   ORD: 8/9/79

China Ocean Shipping Company
CRD: 2/12/85   China

Government of Bermuda
CRD: 10/6/94   Bermuda

Government of Canada, Embassy
CRD: 3/9/89   Canada

Japan Fisheries Association
CRD: 2/22/82   Japan

*Japan Wood-Products Information and Research
Center*
CRD: 9/10/91   Japan

GCI Group Inc.
FNA GreyCom International
777 Third Avenue, 23rd Floor
New York NY 10017-1344
FARA#: 3856   ORD: 7/11/86

Brunswick, Ltd.
CRD: 8/25/95   United Kingdom

Government of the British Virgin Islands
CRD: 8/25/95   British Virgin Islands

Macronix International
CRD: 3/10/97   International

Physical Health Center of Hong Kong, Ltd.
CRD: 9/25/97   Hong Kong

Sealand Housing Corporation
CRD: 9/25/97   International

Gerich, Walter Raymond
1762 Old Annapolis Blvd.
Annapolis MD 21401
Phone: 410/974-0635   Fax: 410/757-3530
FARA#: 3495   ORD: 7/7/83

Thyssen Rheinstahl Technik (TRT)
CRD: 1/27/84   Germany

German National Tourist Office
122 East 42nd Street
52nd Floor
New York NY 10168
FARA#: 616   ORD: 2/28/50

*Deutsche Zentrale fuer Tourismus (German
National Tourist Board)*
CRD: 2/28/50   Germany

**German-American Chamber of Commerce of
    Los Angeles, Inc.**
c/o Coudert Brothers
5220 Pacific Concourse Drive, Suite 280
Los Angeles CA 90045
FARA#: 2563   ORD: 3/14/75

*Deutscher Industrie - und Handelstag
    (German National)*
CRD: 3/14/75   Germany

Gibney, Anthony & Flaherty, LLP
ATT Marc Rogovin
665 Fifth Ave., 2nd Floor
New York NY 10022
FARA#: 4805   ORD: 5/19/93

Consulate General of Switzerland
CRD: 5/19/93   Switzerland

Gibraltar Information Bureau
FNA Perry J. Stieglitz

1156 15th Street, NW, Suite 1100
Washington DC 20005
Phone: 202/452-1108   Fax: 202/452-1109
FARA#: 4182   ORD: 10/05/88

Government of Gibraltar
CRD: 10/5/88   United Kingdom

Gilman, Bradley D.
Robertson, Monagle & Eastaugh
2300 Clarendon Blvd. #1010
Arlington Va 22201
Phone: 703/527-4414   Fax: 703/527-0421
FARA#: 4973   ORD: 7/15/94

Norwegian Seafood Export Council
CRD: 7/15/94   Norway

Global Aviation Associates, Ltd.
1800 K St., NW, Suite 1104
Washington DC 20006
Phone: 202/457-0212   Fax: 202/833-3183
FARA#: 4902   ORD: 3/14/94

Austrian Airlines
CRD: 3/14/94   Austria

Orient Airlines Association
CRD: 11/6/95   International

Singapore Airlines
CRD: 3/14/94   Singapore

Swissair
CRD: 3/14/94   Switzerland

**Global Communicators/Harff
    Communications, Inc.**
1615 L Street, NW - Suite 1260
Washington DC 20036
Phone: 202/778-1486   FARA#: 5241
ORD: 3/5/98

*Council for Economic Development,
    State of Vaud Switzerland*
CRD: 3/5/98   Switzerland

Global Enterprises Group, Inc.
1415 Parker, Suite 370
Detroit MI 48214
FARA#: 4877   ORD: 12/17/93

Ministry of Defense, Republic of Croatia
CRD: 12/17/93   Croatia

GMD Solutions (A Div. of Defense Group, Inc.)
146 Hillwood Avenue, Suite B
Falls Church VA 22046
Phone: 703/538-5551   Fax: 703/532-0557
FARA#: 5195   ORD: 7/18/97

Swiss Ordnance Enterprise
CRD: 7/18/97   Switzerland

Government of India Tourist Office, New York
1270 Avenue of the Americas
Suite 1808
New York NY 10020
FARA#: 2329   ORD: 4/5/72

Government of India
CRD: 4/5/72   India

Gowran International, Ltd.
1661 Crescent Place, NW - Suite 608
Washington DC 20009
Phone: 202/387-1971   Fax: 202/387-1396
E-mail: gowran@erols.com
FARA#: 4417   ORD: 10/03/90

Institute of International Relations
CRD: 8/15/94   Taiwan

Graham & James
ATT Susan Gerson
2000 M Street, N.W., Suite 700
Washington DC 20036-3113
Phone: 202/463-0800   Fax: 202/463-0823
URL: http://www.gi.com
FARA#: 3275   ORD: 9/23/81

Air China International Corp., Ltd.
CRD: 10/23/91   China

China Eastern Airlines
CRD: 10/23/91   China

Grand Metropolitan Consumer
    Services & Products, Inc.
ATT Charles Mathias, Esquire
Pillsbury Centre, M.S. 39K5
200 South 6th Street
Minneapolis MN 55402
FARA#: 4661   ORD: 5/6/92

Grand Metropolitan, PLC
CRD: 5/6/92   United Kingdom

Greenberg Traurig Consulting, Inc.
1221 Brickell Avenue, Suite 2100
Miami FL 33131
FARA#: 5191   ORD: 7/11/97

Senate of the Republic of Colombia
CRD: 7/11/97   Colombia

Grenada Board of Tourism
820 Second Avenue, Suite 900-D
New York NY 10017
Phone: 800/927-9554   Fax: 212/573-9731
URL: http://www.interknowledge.com/grenada
FARA#: 2378   ORD: 9/10/72

The Government of Grenada
CRD: 9/10/72   Grenada

Gulaid, Ali Hasan
5423 Sheffield Court #212
Alexandria VA 22311
Phone: 703/820-4772   FARA#: 5113
ORD: 5/22/96

Mohammed Farah Aidid, President of
    Somali Republic
CRD: 5/22/96   Somalia

Guyana Republican Party
381 Broad Street, Suite A-617
Newark NJ 07104
FARA#: 4238   ORD: 4/17/89

Guyana Republican Party
CRD: 4/17/89   Guyana

H. Tschudin Associates, Inc., Dr.
215 RiverVale Road
River Vale NJ 07675
Phone: 201/666-3456   Fax: 201/666-8470
FARA#: 3702   ORD: 7/10/85

BEDA, Bernese Development Agency
CRD: 7/10/85   Switzerland

Hai Tian Development U.S.A., Inc.
136-40 39th Avenue, Suite 508
Flushing NY 11354
FARA#: 5143   ORD: 12/3/96

Chinese Science New Overseas Edition
CRD: 6/5/97   China

People's Daily Overseas Edition
CRD: 12/3/96   China

Hall, Thomas Forrest

1619 King Street
Alexandria VA 22314-2793
Phone: 703/548-5800   Fax: 703/683-3647
FARA#: 5221   ORD: 12/18/97

Embassy of Iceland
CRD: 12/18/97   Iceland

Halpern Associates
1730 K Street, NW - Suite 304
Washington DC 20006
Phone: 202/785-0075   Fax: 202/331-3759
FARA#: 3790   ORD: 3/7/86

Institute of International Relations
CRD: 3/7/86   Taiwan

Hamilton, Charles A.
5025 Overlook Road, NW
Washington DC 20016-1911
Phone: 202/237-8142   Fax: 202/237-8146
FARA#: 4467   ORD: 1/25/91

Airbus Industrie, G.I.E.
CRD: 1/25/91   France

Hanna, Albert Rowell
312 East Peach
El Dorado AR 71730
FARA#: 5122   ORD: 7/19/96

Volgograd Administration
CRD: 7/19/96   International

Harcar, Mary V.
5101 Wisconsin Avenue, NW, Suite 508
Washington DC 20016
Phone: 202/362-0840   Fax: 202/966-9409
FARA#: 3910   ORD: 11/21/86

Canadian Life and Health Insurance Association
CRD: 3/2/90   Canada

Harris, Wiltshire & Grannis, LLP
1025 Connecticut Avenue, NW
Suite 1012
Washington DC 20036
FARA#: 5238   ORD: 2/27/98

Comsion Federal de Telecommunicaciones
CRD: 2/27/98   International

Hastings, Jay Donald
1425 Western Ave., Suite 304
Seattle WA 98101-2036
Phone: 206/292-9792   Fax: 206/467-1043
FARA#: 2867   ORD: 3/14/78

Japan Fisheries Association
CRD: 11/16/78   Japan

Hemisphere Key Consulting, LLC
701 Brickell Avenue
Miami FL 33131
FARA#: 5204   ORD: 8/28/97

Government of the Republic of Suriname
CRD: 8/28/97   Suriname

Hennessey, Timothy J.
811 South Second Street
Springfield IL 62704
FARA#: 5246   ORD: 3/1/98

Tyne & Wear Development Company
CRD: 3/1/98   International

Herman Associates, Inc.
ATT Lester H. Hirsh
360 Lexington Avenue
New York NY 10017
FARA#: 2578   ORD: 4/22/75

Egyptian Tourist Authority
CRD: 6/13/95   Egypt

Heyward, Evelyn J.
DBA Heyward Marketing
205 West 57th Street
New York NY 10019
FARA#: 4893   ORD: 2/14/94

ICEP - Investimentos
CRD: 2/14/94   Portugal

Hill & Knowlton, Inc.
600 New Hampshire Avenue, NW - Suite 601
Washington DC 20037
Phone: 202/333-7400   Fax: 202/333-1638
FARA#: 3301   ORD: 11/10/81

Hitachi, Ltd.
CRD: 3/30/87   Japan

Konimklijke Luchtvaart Maatschappij, N.V.
CRD: 5/8/95   Netherlands

Marubeni America Corporation
CRD: 2/24/88   Japan

Ministry of Economical Development, Trade and
Tourism of Canada
CRD: 5/1/97   Canada

RAO Gazprom
CRD: 10/29/97   International

Republic of Liberia, Embassy
CRD: 11/24/97   Liberia

Republic of Zambia
CRD: 3/26/98   United Kingdom

Royal Netherlands Embassy
CRD: 3/26/98   Netherlands

S.I. Odogwu
CRD: 9/20/95   United Kingdom

State of Qatar
CRD: 9/6/96   Qatar

Toyo Kogyo, Ltd. (Mazda Motor Corporation)
CRD: 2/16/87   Japan

Trentino Tourist Board (A.P.T.T.)
CRD: 4/18/95   Italy

Welsh Development Agency
CRD: 12/24/97   Wales

Hilton, Susan Elaine
F. Hoffman - La Roche, Ltd.
CH 4070
Basel SZ FARA#: 5234   ORD: 2/11/98

F. Hoffman-La Roche, Ltd.
CRD: 2/11/98   Switzerland

Hoffman & Hoffman Public Relations
5683 Columbia Pike
Suite 200
Falls Church VA 22041
Phone: 703/820-2244   Fax: 703/820-2271
FARA#: 5203   ORD: 8/26/97

Central Bank of Turkey
CRD: 8/26/97   Turkey

Hogan & Hartson, L.L.P.
555 13th St., NW
Washington DC 20004-1109
Phone: 202/637-5600   Fax: 202/637-5910
E-mail: hhinfo@dc4.hhlaw.com
FARA#: 2244   ORD: 2/18/71

Algoma Steel, Inc.
CRD: 5/23/94   Canada

Embassy of El Salvador
CRD: 6/17/71   El Salvador

Embassy of Japan
CRD: 5/7/71   Japan

Embassy of the Republic of Cyprus
CRD: 10/3/97   Cyprus

*Government of Ontario, Ministry of Economic
   Development & Trade/Tourism*
CRD: 5/29/87   Canada

Joint Stock Commercial Bank - UNIBEST
CRD: 10/27/97   International

*Ministries of Foreign Affairs, Justice,
   Tourism & Economics*
CRD: 6/24/77   Bahamas

Nippon Telegraph & Telephone Corporation
CRD: 1/24/94   Japan

Holland & Knight
2100 Pa. Ave., NW - Suite 400
Washington DC 20037
Phone: 202/955-3000   Fax: 202/955-5564
URL: http://www.hklaw.com
FARA#: 3718   ORD: 8/7/85

*Aerovias Nacionales de Colombia, S.A.
   (AVIANCA)*
CRD: 12/12/85   Colombia

Air Malta Company, Ltd.
CRD: 1/29/98   Malta

Florida International Bankers Association
CRD: 12/19/91   International

Government of Jamaica
CRD: 8/15/96   Jamaica

Government of Jamaica
CRD: 8/15/96   Jamaica

Government of the Republic of Senegal
CRD: 10/7/94   Senegal

Republic of Costa Rica
CRD: 4/15/98   Costa Rica

Sociedad Aeronautica de Medellin
CRD: 3/8/91   Colombia

Varig Brazilian Airlines
CRD: 9/7/89   Brazil

Holloman, Charlotte
1625 1/2 19th Street, NW - Suite E
Washington DC 20009
Phone: 202/234-0180   FARA#: 5133
ORD: 10/4/96

Taipei Economic & Cultural Rep. Office
CRD: 10/4/96   Taiwan

Hong Kong Tourist Association
401 North Michigan Avenue, Suite 1640
Chicago IL 60611
Phone: 708/575-2828   Fax: 708/575-2829
URL: http://www.hkta.org
FARA#: 2110   ORD: 10/29/68

Government of Hong Kong
CRD: 10/29/68   Hong Kong

Hong Kong Trade Development Council, Inc.
219 East 46th Street

New York NY 10017
FARA#: 2181   ORD: 1/19/70

Hong Kong Trade Development Council
CRD: 1/19/70   Hong Kong

Hooper, Hooper, Owen & Gould
801 Pennsylvania Avenue, NW - Suite 730
Washington DC 20004
Phone: 202/638-7780   Fax: 202/638-7787
FARA#: 5179   ORD: 5/12/97

Embassy of Pakistan
CRD: 5/12/97   Pakistan

Hopkins & Sutter
888 16th St., NW
Washington DC 20006
Phone: 202/835-8000   Fax: 202/835-8136
URL: http://www.hopsut.com
FARA#: 4362   ORD: 4/11/90

Assicurazione Nazionale Imprese Assicuratrici
CRD: 10/6/95   Italy

Association of British Insurers
CRD: 8/16/91   United Kingdom

Institute of London Underwriters (ILU)
CRD: 3/23/92   United Kingdom

Horst & Frisch, Inc.
1133 Connecticut Avenue, NW, Suite 900
Washington DC 20036
FARA#: 4625   ORD: 3/3/92

Industrial Development Authority of Ireland
CRD: 3/3/92   Ireland

Howie, Irene E.
7321 Masonville Drive
Annandale VA 22003
FARA#: 5237   ORD: 2/27/98

Director General of Civil Aviation
CRD: 2/27/98   International

Hunton & Williams
1900 K Street, NW
Washington DC 20006
Phone: 202/955-1500   Fax: 202/778-2201
E-mail: info@hunton.com
URL: http://www.hunton.com
FARA#: 5040   ORD: 8/11/95

Republic of Croatia
CRD: 8/11/95   Croatia

Hyman, Lester S.
3000 K Street, NW - Suite 300
Washington DC 20007
Phone: 202/424-7500   Fax: 202/424-7643
FARA#: 5166   ORD: 3/26/97

British Virgin Islands Government
CRD: 3/26/97   British Virgin Islands

Iceland Tourist Board
655 Third Avenue, Suite 1810
New York NY 10017
FARA#: 2863   ORD: 2/15/78

Iceland Tourist Board
CRD: 2/15/78   Iceland

Icon Group
237 Park Ave., 21st Floor
New York NY 10017
FARA#: 4926   ORD: 7/8/94

Government of the Republic of the Philippines
CRD: 7/8/94   Philippines

IDA Ireland
345 Park Avenue
New York NY 10154
FARA#: 1770   ORD: 7/10/64

Irish Development Authority - Irish Gov't. Body
CRD: 7/10/64   Ireland

IMPACT, LLC
5446 Alta Vista Road
Bethesda MD 20814
FARA#: 5251   ORD: 4/13/98

*Turkish Foreign Economic Relations Board
   (DEIK)*
CRD: 4/13/98   Turkey

India Trade Promotion Organization
60 East 42nd Street, Suite 863
New York NY 10165
FARA#: 2975   ORD: 10/26/78

Trade Development Authority
CRD: 10/26/78   India

**Indonesia Tourist Promotion Office for
   North America**
ATT Sri Juniarti
3457 Wilshire Boulevard, Suite 104
Los Angeles CA 90010-2203
FARA#: 2757   ORD: 2/15/77

Indonesian Tourist Promotion Board
CRD: 2/15/77   Indonesia

**Industrial Development Board for
   Northern Ireland**
2201 Waukegan Road, Suite 150-South
Bannockburn IL 60015
FARA#: 4364   ORD: 4/13/90

Department of Economic Development
CRD: 4/13/90   United Kingdom

**Instituto Galego de Promocion Economica
   (IGAPE), New York**
950 Third Avenue, 18th Floor
New York NY 10022
FARA#: 5210   ORD: 9/12/97

Xunta de Galicia
CRD: 9/12/97   International

InterMarketing, Inc.
99 Park Avenue
New York NY 10016
FARA#: 4940   ORD: 8/29/94

Berlin Tourismus Marketing GmbH
CRD: 8/29/94   Germany

Rotterdam Port Management Company
CRD: 8/29/94   Netherlands

**International Business & Economic
   Research Corporation**
1001 Pennsylvania Avenue, NW, 6th Floor
Washington DC 20004
Phone: 202/955-6155   Fax: 202/955-5786
FARA#: 2944   ORD: 8/9/78

Embassy of Sri Lanka
CRD: 3/16/98   Sri Lanka

Government of the Philippines
CRD: 5/30/91   Philippines

Taiwain Textile Federation
CRD: 3/16/98   Taiwan

International Group of P&I Clubs
Manpower Building

78 Fenchurch Street, 3rd Floor
London ENGLAND EC3M 4BT
FARA#: 4584   ORD: 11/05/91

International Group of P&I Clubs
CRD: 11/5/91   United Kingdom

International Registries, Inc.
11495 Commerce Park Drive
Reston VA 22091-1507
FARA#: 4533   ORD: 7/1/91

*Office of Deputy Commissioner of
    Maritime Affairs*
CRD: 7/1/91   Liberia

Republic of the Marshall Islands
CRD: 7/1/91   Marshall Islands

**International Science & Technology
    Associates, Inc.**
551 West Lancaster Avenue, Suite 212
Haverford PA 19041
FARA#: 3998   ORD: 6/22/87

Japan Science and Technology Corporation
CRD: 6/22/87   Japan

Intern'l. Trade & Development Agency, Inc.
ATT Lester Wolff
2111 Jefferson Davis Highway
Arlington VA 22202
FARA#: 3690   ORD: 6/13/85

Royal Thai Embassy
CRD: 3/5/87   Thailand

*Taipei Economic & Cultural Rep.
    Office in the U.S.*
CRD: 8/28/95   Taiwan

Inward, Ltd.
1560 Sherman Avenue, Suite 307
Evanston IL 60201
FARA#: 3844   ORD: 6/16/86

Inward, Ltd.
CRD: 6/16/86   United Kingdom

Irish Tourist Board
345 Park Avenue, 17th Floor
New York NY 10154
Phone: 212/418-0800   Fax: 212/371-9052
FARA#: 536   ORD: 8/16/48

*Bord Failte Eireann (Government of Ireland
    Tourist Board)*
CRD: 8/1/74   Ireland

Italian Gov't. Tourist Board (ENIT), Chicago
500 North Michigan Ave., Suite 2240
Chicago IL 60611
Phone: 312/644-0990   Fax: 312/644-3019
FARA#: 1892   ORD: 6/7/68

Ente Nazionale Italiano per il Turismo
CRD: 6/7/68   Italy

**Italian Gov't. Tourist Board (ENIT),
    Los Angeles**
12400 Wilshire Boulevard, Suite 550
Los Angeles CA 90025
Phone: 310/820-0098   Fax: 310/820-6357
FARA#: 1884   ORD: 4/19/65

Ente Nazionale Italiano per il Turismo
CRD: 4/19/65   Italy

Italian Gov't. Tourist Board (ENIT), New York
630 Fifth Avenue, Suite 1565
New York NY 10111
Phone: 212/245-4822   Fax: 212/586-9249

FARA#: 568   ORD: 4/21/49

Ente Nazionale Italiano per il Turismo
CRD: 4/21/49   Italy

J.H.S. Group, Inc.
150 North Michigan Avenue, Suite 3300
Chicago IL 60601
FARA#: 4941   ORD: 8/16/93

Federal Government of Nigeria
CRD: 8/16/93   Nigeria

Jaffe, Jordan A.
2341 Wyoming Avenue
Washington DC 20008
FARA#: 5200   ORD: 8/11/97

Embassy of the Islamic State of Afghanistan
CRD: 8/11/97   Afghanistan

Jamaica Progressive League, Inc.
2230 Light Street
Bronx NY 10466
FARA#: 296   ORD: 3/12/45

Peoples' National Party
CRD: 3/9/45   Jamaica

Jamaica Tourist Board, Chicago
500 North Michigan Avenue, Suite 1030
Chicago IL 60611
FARA#: 2118   ORD: 12/16/68

Jamaica Tourist Board
CRD: 12/16/68   Jamaica

Jamaica Tourist Board, Florida
1320 South Dixie Highway, Suite 1101
Coral Gables FL 33146
FARA#: 2360   ORD: 7/26/72

Jamaica Tourist Board
CRD: 7/26/72   Jamaica

Jamaica Tourist Board, Los Angeles
3440 Wilshire Boulevard, Suite 805
Los Angeles CA 90010
FARA#: 3305   ORD: 11/18/81

Jamaica Tourist Board
CRD: 11/18/81   Jamaica

Jamaica Tourist Board, New York
801 Second Avenue, 20th Floor
New York NY 10017
FARA#: 1445   ORD: 5/3/61

Jamaica Tourist Board
CRD: 5/3/61   Jamaica

James, John D.
103 G Street, SW
Washington DC 20024
FARA#: 4836   ORD: 8/2/93

Mano River Union
CRD: 8/2/93   Sierra Leone

Jameson, Donald F.B.
DBA Jameson Associates
1009 Hariman Street
Great Falls VA 22066
FARA#: 4960   ORD: 10/06/94

Government of the Sultanate of Oman
CRD: 10/6/94   Oman

**Japan Center for Intercultural
    Communications (JCIC)**
ATT Michiko Ito, Esquire
2-7-7 Hirakawa-cho

Chiyoda-Ky
Tokyo, 102 JA FARA#: 4998   ORD: 3/1/95

Japanese Government
CRD: 3/1/95   Japan

Japan Economic Institute of America
1000 Connecticut Avenue, NW - Suite 211
Washington DC 20036
Phone: 202/296-5633   Fax: 202/296-8333
E-mail: jei@jei.org
FARA#: 929   ORD: 1/25/56

Government of Japan
CRD: 1/25/56   Japan

Japan Iron & Steel Exporters' Association
1155 - 21st Street, NW, Suite 600
Washington DC 20036
Phone: 202/429-4766   Fax: 202/463-9032
E-mail: dcjisea@man.com
FARA#: 3155   ORD: 10/09/80

Japan Iron & Steel Exporters' Association
CRD: 10/9/80   Japan

Japan National Tourist Organization, Chicago
ATT Francis Y. Sogi, Esquire
Kelley, Drye & Warren
401 N. Michigan
Chicago IL 60611
FARA#: 2347   ORD: 7/3/72

Japan National Tourist Organization
CRD: 7/3/72   Japan

Japan National Tourist Org., Los Angeles
ATT Francis Y. Sogi, Esquire
Kelley, Drye & Warren
624 South Grand Ave.
Los Angeles CA 90017
FARA#: 2350   ORD: 7/3/72

Japan National Tourist Organization
CRD: 7/3/72   Japan

Japan National Tourist Org., New York
One Rockefeller Plaza - Suite 1250
New York NY 10020
FARA#: 769   ORD: 5/26/53

Japan National Tourist Organization
CRD: 5/26/53   Japan

Japan National Tourist Org., San Francisco
ATT Francis Y. Sogi, Esquire
Kelley, Drye & Warren
360 Post Street
San Francisco CA 94108-4909
FARA#: 2349   ORD: 7/3/72

Japan National Tourist Organization
CRD: 7/3/72   Japan

Japan Network Group, Inc.
1325 Avenue of the Americas, 8th Floor
New York NY 10019
FARA#: 4490   ORD: 3/26/91

JNG Shareholders Group
CRD: 12/10/93   Japan

JAMPRO
25 Southeast 2nd Avenue, Suite 808
Miami FL 33131
FARA#: 4232   ORD: 3/29/89

Government of Jamaica
CRD: 3/29/89   Jamaica

Jefferson-Waterman International, LLC
1350 New York Ave., NW - 7th Fl.

Washington DC 20005
Phone: 202/626-8500   Fax: 202/626-8778
FARA#: 4990   ORD: 2/6/95

Government of Jamaica
CRD: 2/6/95   Jamaica

Japan External Trade Organization
CRD: 3/24/95   Japan

Korean Overseas Information Service
CRD: 7/7/95   Korea

Myanmar Resources Development, Ltd.
CRD: 4/4/97   Myanmar

Republic of Croatia, Office of the Presidency
CRD: 2/6/95   Croatia

Republic of Korea, Embassy
CRD: 2/6/95   Korea

*Taipei Economic & Cultural Representative
Office (TECRO)*
CRD: 2/6/95   Taiwan

Jellinek, Schwartz & Connolly, Inc.
1525 Wilson Boulevard, Suite 600
Arlington VA 22209
Phone: 703/527-1670   Fax: 703/527-5477
FARA#: 4345   ORD: 2/23/90

Japan Auto. Manufacturers Association (JAMA)
CRD: 7/1/93   Japan

Jennings, John M.
2341 Wyoming Avenue, NW
Washington DC 20008
FARA#: 5142   ORD: 12/4/96

Islamic State of Afghanistan/Mission in the U.S.
CRD: 12/4/96   Afghanistan

JETRO, Atlanta
ATT Carol Lyttle, Jr., Esquire
Whitman & Ransom
245 Peachtree Center Ave., NE
Suite 2208, Marquis One Tower
Atlanta GA 30303
FARA#: 4069   ORD: 12/01/87

Japan External Trade Organization (JETRO)
CRD: 12/1/87   Japan

JETRO, Chicago
ATT Carol Lyttle, Jr., Esquire
Whitman & Ransom
401 North Michigan
Chicago IL 60611
FARA#: 1850   ORD: 2/2/65

City of Osaka
CRD: 5/28/74   Japan

Japan External Trade Organization (JETRO)
CRD: 2/2/65   Japan

JETRO, Dallas
2050 Stemmons Freeway, Suite 152-1
P.O. Box 420370 - Suite 152-1
Dallas TX 75258-0370
FARA#: 2820   ORD: 8/8/77

Japan External Trade Organization (JETRO)
CRD: 8/8/77   Japan

JETRO, Denver
ATT Carol Lyttle, Jr., Esquire
Whitman & Ransom
1200-17th Street, Suite 1110
Denver CO 80202
FARA#: 4017   ORD: 7/28/87

Japan External Trade Organization (JETRO)
CRD: 7/28/87   Japan

JETRO, Houston
1221 McKinney, Suite 2360
Houston TX 77010
FARA#: 2277   ORD: 9/20/71

Japan External Trade Organization (JETRO)
CRD: 9/20/71   Japan

JETRO, Los Angeles
ATT Carol Lyttle, Jr., Esquire
Whitman & Ransom
777 S. Figueroa Street
Los Angeles CA 90017-2513
FARA#: 1833   ORD: 12/14/64

Hokkaido Prefectural Government
CRD: 5/28/74   Japan

Japan External Trade Organization (JETRO)
CRD: 12/14/64   Japan

Kanagawa Prefectural Government
CRD: 5/28/74   Japan

Nagano Prefectural Government
CRD: 5/28/74   Japan

Shizuoka Prefectural Government
CRD: 5/28/74   Japan

Tokyo Metropolitan Government
CRD: 5/28/74   Japan

JETRO, New York
ATT Carol Lyttle, Jr., Esquire
Whitman & Ransom
200 Park Ave.
New York NY 10166
FARA#: 1643   ORD: 6/25/63

Fukui Prefectural Government
CRD: 12/24/87   Japan

Japan External Trade Organization
CRD: 6/25/63   Japan

Kyoto Prefectural Government
CRD: 5/9/89   Japan

Osaka Prefectural Government
CRD: 5/26/74   Japan

JETRO, San Francisco
ATT Carol Lyttle, Jr., Esquire
Whitman & Ransom
235 Pine Street, Suite 1700
San Francisco CA 94104
FARA#: 1813   ORD: 11/05/64

Japan External Trade Organization (JETRO)
CRD: 11/5/64   Japan

JFCC, Washington Office
1825 K Street, NW, Suite 1203
Washington DC 20006
Phone: 202/466-3585   Fax: 202/466-3586
E-mail: 75663,474@compuserve.com
FARA#: 4440   ORD: 11/21/90

Japan Federation of Construction Contractors
CRD: 11/21/90   Japan

Johnson II, Robert Winthrop
1050 Potomac Street, NW
Washington DC 20007-3517
Phone: 202/337-6817   Fax: 202/337-3462
FARA#: 4460   ORD: 1/9/85

Government of the Dominican Republic

CRD: 1/9/85   Dominican Republic

Jones, Day, Reavis & Pogue
ATT Randy Davis
1450 G St., NW - Suite 700
Washington DC 20005-2088
Phone: 202/879-3939   Fax: 202/737-2832
FARA#: 3427   ORD: 12/10/82

Embassy of the People's Republic of China
CRD: 1/31/86   China

Kaiser, Dr. Donald
F. Hoffmann-La Roche, Ltd.
CH 4070
Basel SWITZERLAND FARA#: 5107
ORD: 4/30/96

F. Hoffman-La Roche Ltd.
CRD: 4/30/96   Switzerland

Karol Media, Inc.
350 North Pennsylvania Avenue
P.O. Box 7600
Wilkes-Barre PA 18773-7600
FARA#: 5228   ORD: 1/15/98

European Community
CRD: 1/15/98   International

Kathleen Winn & Associates, Inc.
911 Carlaw Ave.
Toronto, Ontario CA M4K 3L4 FARA#: 4480
ORD: 3/4/91

Stentor Telecom Policy, Inc.
CRD: 6/29/93   Canada

Kaye, Scholer, Fierman, Hays & Handler
425 Park Avenue
New York NY 10022-3598
FARA#: 4892   ORD: 2/7/94

Brunei Investment Agency
CRD: 2/7/94   Brunei

Kazan, Yanal
470 Chamberlain Avenue, Suite 1
Paterson NJ 07522
FARA#: 4875   ORD: 12/06/93

Republic of Abkhazia
CRD: 12/6/93   Georgia

KCM International, Inc.
1730 M Street, NW - Suite 911
Washington DC 20036
Phone: 202/785-9142   Fax: 202/659-5760
FARA#: 5170   ORD: 4/11/97

P.T. Teknojasa Sapta Utama (TSU)
CRD: 4/11/97   International

Keene & Associates
1228 N Street, Suite 4
Sacramento CA 95814
Phone: 916/448-1511   Fax: 916/446-5662
E-mail: keene@pacbell.net
FARA#: 4511   ORD: 5/14/91

Government of Japan, Consulate
CRD: 5/14/91   Japan

Keiner & Dumont, P.C.
72 Court Street
Middlebury VT 05753
FARA#: 4265   ORD: 6/19/89

Grand Council of the Crees of Quebec
CRD: 6/19/89   Canada

Keller & Heckman

Washington Center Building
1001 G Street, NW, Suite 500-West
Washington DC 20001
Phone: 202/434-4100   Fax: 202/434-4646
URL: http://www.khlaw.com
FARA#: 5017   ORD: 4/25/95

Cominco, Ltd.
CRD: 4/25/95   Canada

Kelley Swofford Roy, Inc.
355 Palermo Street
Coral Gables FL 33134
FARA#: 5104   ORD: 4/4/96

The Government of the Republic of Colombia
CRD: 4/4/96   Colombia

Kelley, Swofford, Roy, Helmke, Inc.
1002 King Street
Alexandria VA 22314
Phone: 703/684-6999   Fax: 703/549-3061
E-mail: ksrh@zmap.com
FARA#: 5182   ORD: 6/4/97

Government of the Republic of Colombia
CRD: 6/4/97   Colombia

Ketchum Communications
Six PPG Place
Pittsburgh PA 15222
FARA#: 5105   ORD: 4/12/96

Government of Hong Kong
CRD: 4/12/96   Hong Kong

KMC Trading
209 Post Street, Suite 1118
San Francisco CA 94108
Phone: 415/433-5231   Fax: 415/433-5743
FARA#: 4639   ORD: 3/20/92

Chinese Science News Overseas Edition
CRD: 8/24/93   China

Outlook Weekly
CRD: 10/17/94   China

People's Daily Overseas Edition
CRD: 3/20/92   China

Kobe Trade Information Office
1001 Fourth Avenue, Suite 2328
Seattle WA 98154
Phone: 206/622-7640   Fax: 206/682-6227
E-mail: kobe@pnw.com
FARA#: 2438   ORD: 7/2/73

Kobe Municipal Government
CRD: 7/2/73   Japan

Korea Economic Institute
1101 Vermont Avenue, NW, Suite 401
Washington DC 20005
Phone: 202/371-0690   Fax: 202/371-0692
FARA#: 3327   ORD: 2/1/82

Korea Economic Institute for International Economic Policy (KIEP)
CRD: 2/28/90   Korea

Korea International Trade Association
1800 K Street, NW, Suite 700
Washington DC 20006
Phone: 202/828-4400   Fax: 202/828-4404
E-mail: mfqn36a@prodigy.com
FARA#: 3636   ORD: 12/21/84

Korean Traders' Association
CRD: 12/21/84   Korea

Korea Local Government Center, New York

One World Trade Center, Suite 7835
New York NY 10048
FARA#: 5080   ORD: 11/24/95

Korea Local Authorities Foundation
CRD: 11/24/95   Korea

Korea National Tourism Corporation, Chicago
205 North Michigan Avenue, Suite 2212
Chicago IL 60601
FARA#: 3069   ORD: 11/23/79

Korea National Tourism Corporation
CRD: 11/23/79   Korea

Korea National Tourism Corp., New Jersey
Two Executive Drive, 7th Floor
Fort Lee NJ 07024
FARA#: 2614   ORD: 10/04/75

Korea National Tourism Corporation
CRD: 10/1/75   Korea

Korea National Tourism Org., Los Angeles
3435 Wilshire Boulevard, Suite 1110
Los Angeles CA 90010
Phone: 213/382-3435   Fax: 213/480-0483
E-mail: kntola@mail.wcis.com
FARA#: 2544   ORD: 10/25/74

Korea National Tourism Organization
CRD: 10/25/74   Korea

Korea Trade Center, New York
460 Park Avenue, Suite 402
New York NY 10022
FARA#: 1619   ORD: 4/17/63

Korea Trade Promotion Corporation
CRD: 4/17/63   Korea

Korean Television Enterprises, Ltd.
625 South Kingsley Drive
Los Angeles CA 90005
FARA#: 3792   ORD: 3/11/86

KBS Enterprises, Ltd.
CRD: 3/11/86   Korea

Kronmiller, Theodore George
9893 Georgetown Pike
Great Falls VA 22066
Phone: 703/757-6602   Fax: 703/757-6603
E-mail: kroncyber@msn.com
FARA#: 4649   ORD: 4/17/92

Government of Iceland
CRD: 1/15/93   Iceland

Government of the Marshall Islands (Embassy)
CRD: 4/17/92   Marshall Islands

Kurzban, Kurzban & Weinger, P.A.
2650 SW 27th Avenue, 2nd Floor
Miami FL 33133
FARA#: 4604   ORD: 12/31/91

Republic of Haiti
CRD: 12/31/91   Haiti

L.A. Motley & Company
1800 K St., NW, Suite 1000
Washington DC 20006
Phone: 202/223-8222   Fax: 202/775-8604
FARA#: 3723   ORD: 8/15/85

Associacao Industries de Calcados do Rio Grands do Sul
CRD: 8/15/85   Brazil

Companhia de Navegacao Alianca, S.A.
CRD: 11/7/97   Brazil

The Philippine Sugar Administration
CRD: 3/15/89   Philippines

Larry C. Wallace & Associates, P.A.
425 West Capitol, Suite 3801
Little Rock AR 72201
FARA#: 5070   ORD: 11/07/95

Embassy of Japan
CRD: 11/7/95   Japan

Palestinian National Authority Gaza
CRD: 11/7/95   Palestine

Lebanese Information & Research Center
1730 M Street, NW - Suite 807
Washington DC 20036
Phone: 202/785-6666   Fax: 202/785-6628
E-mail: lirc@erols.com
URL: http://www.lebanes-forces.org
FARA#: 2935   ORD: 7/27/78

Lebanese Forces
CRD: 10/24/78   Lebanon

Legesse Travel & Tourism Consultants, Ltd.
347 Fifth Ave., Suite 810
New York NY 10016
Phone: 212/447-6700   Fax: 212/447-1532
FARA#: 3240   ORD: 5/18/81

Air Gabon
CRD: 7/25/84   Gabon

Gabon Ministry of Tourism
CRD: 8/27/81   Gabon

Leone & Leone, Ltd.
27128-A Paseo Espada, Suite 1524
San Juan Capistrano CA 92675
FARA#: 4619   ORD: 2/12/92

Atlantis Submarines International, Inc.
CRD: 2/12/92   Canada

Canadian Pacific Hotels & Resorts
CRD: 3/22/95   Canada

The Great Canadian Railtour Company, Ltd.
CRD: 2/12/92   Canada

Leventhal, Senter & Lerman
2000 K Street, NW, Suite 600
Washington DC 20006-1809
FARA#: 5161   ORD: 3/4/97

Grupo Televisa, S.A.
CRD: 3/4/97   International

Levin Public Relations & Marketing, Inc.
30 Glenn Street
White Plains NY 10603
FARA#: 5217   ORD: 10/22/97

Cartre d'Arde au developpment des Entreprises de Bourgoque (CADEB)
CRD: 10/29/97   France

Most in Sweden Agency
CRD: 10/22/97   Sweden

Levine, Leonard B.
TransCanada PipeLines
601 13th Street, NW, Suite 350-S
Washington DC 20005
Phone: 202/393-2795   Fax: 202/393-2783
FARA#: 4520   ORD: 6/3/91

TransCanada PipeLines
CRD: 6/3/91   Canada

Lipsen, Zel E.

One Massachusetts Avenue, NW, Suite 330
Washington DC 20001
Phone: 202/289-6367   Fax: 202/289-6447
FARA#: 5092   ORD: 1/19/96

AEA Technology
CRD: 1/19/96   United Kingdom

British Ministry of Defense
CRD: 1/19/96   United Kingdom

Vickers Shipbuilding & Engineering, Ltd.
CRD: 1/19/96   United Kingdom

Lloyd's of London Market Representatives
One Lime Street
London EN EC3M 7HA
Phone: 202/986-8000   Fax: 202/986-8102
FARA#: 4883   ORD: 1/6/94

Lloyd's of London
CRD: 1/6/94   United Kingdom

Lord Group
4751 Wilshire Boulevard
Los Angeles CA 90010
FARA#: 4556   ORD: 8/14/91

Korea National Tourism Organization
CRD: 8/21/96   Korea

Lou Hammond & Associates, Inc.
39 East 51st Street
New York NY 10022-5916
FARA#: 3682   ORD: 5/23/85

Australian Tourist Commission
CRD: 6/23/95   Australia

*Government of Aruba, Tourism Authority in
    North America*
CRD: 12/24/86   Aruba

Lugano Group, Inc.
201 Charles Avenue, Suite 2544
New Orleans LA 70170-2500
FARA#: 5207   ORD: 9/8/97

Government of Belize
CRD: 9/8/97   Belize

Luxcore, Ltd.
ATT Jerrold S. Seeman, Esquire
5 East 67th Street
New York NY 10021
FARA#: 4901   ORD: 3/10/94

Luxembourg Board of Economic Development
CRD: 3/10/94   Luxembourg

M. Silver Associates, Inc.
747 Third Ave., 23rd Floor
New York NY 10017-2803
FARA#: 3131   ORD: 7/15/80

Monaco Gov't. Tourist & Convention Bureau
CRD: 9/10/93   Monaco

Presidente Hotels
CRD: 5/15/95   Mexico

Sun International, Inc.
CRD: 5/15/95   Bahamas

Tourism Authority of Thailand
CRD: 6/11/96   Thailand

Mahoney, Maureen E.
1001 Pennsylvania Ave., NW - Suite 1300
Washington DC 20004-2505
Phone: 202/637-2200   Fax: 202/637-2201
FARA#: 5082   ORD: 11/29/95

Kingdom of Saudi Arabia, Embassy
CRD: 11/29/95   Saudi Arabia

Malaysia Tourism Promotion Board
818 West Seventh Street
Los Angeles CA 90017-3432
FARA#: 2510   ORD: 4/17/74

Tourist Development Corporation
CRD: 4/17/79   Malaysia

Malaysian Industrial Development Authority
ATT Eh-oon
875 North Michigan Avenue, Suite 3350
Chicago IL 60611
FARA#: 2331   ORD: 4/17/72

Malaysian Industrial Development Agency
CRD: 4/17/72   Malaysia

Malaysian Palm Oil Council of America, Inc.
c/o Dickstein, Shapiro & Morin & Oshinsky LLP
2101 L Street, NW
Washington DC 20037-1526
Phone: 202/785-9700   Fax: 202/887-0689
E-mail: Peter_J._Kadzik@dsmllp.co
FARA#: 4575   ORD: 10/04/91

Malaysian Palm Oil Promotion Council
CRD: 10/4/91   Malaysia

Manatt, Phelps & Phillips
1501 M Street, NW, Suite 700
Washington DC 20005
Phone: 202/463-4300   Fax: 202/463-4394
E-mail: mpp@manatt.com
FARA#: 5171   ORD: 4/11/97

Embassy of the Republic of Uzbekistan
CRD: 10/15/97   Uzbekistan

Government of the Republic of Montenegro
CRD: 4/11/97   Montenegro

Manning, Selvage & Lee
79 Madison Ave.
New York NY 10016
FARA#: 4684   ORD: 6/10/92

Petroleos de Venezuela, S.A.
CRD: 6/10/92   Venezuela

**Manufactured Imports Promotion
    Organization (MIPRO)**
2501 M Street, NW, Suite 350
Washington DC 20037
Phone: 202/659-3729   Fax: 202/887-5159
FARA#: 3196   ORD: 2/5/81

Manufactured Imports Promotion Org. (MIPRO)
CRD: 2/5/81   International

Manufactured Imports Promotion Org. (MIPRO)
CRD: 2/5/81   Japan

Marcella Martinez Associates, Inc.
411 East 53rd Street, Apt. 4-D
New York NY 10022
FARA#: 4349   ORD: 3/9/90

Curacao Tourism Development Bureau
CRD: 8/23/93   Curacao

Mark A. Siegel & Associates, Inc.
FNA International Public Strategies, Inc.
2103 O Street, NW
Washington DC 20037
Phone: 202/371-5600   Fax: 202/371-5608
FARA#: 4200   ORD: 1/6/89

Benazir Bhutto
CRD: 6/16/97   Pakistan

Government of Aruba
CRD: 1/9/95   Aruba

Marketing Challenges International, Inc.
Ten East 21st Street, Suite 600
New York NY 10010
FARA#: 4084   ORD: 1/28/88

Aeroport de Paris
CRD: 1/28/88   France

Martin, Barbara Lefevre
6022 Pitt Street
New Orleans LA 70118
FARA#: 4986   ORD: 1/9/95

Plaid Cymru
CRD: 1/9/95   United Kingdom

Masaoka & Associates, Inc.
1000 Connecticut Avenue, NW, Suite 304
Washington DC 20036
Phone: 202/296-4484   Fax: 202/293-3060
FARA#: 2521   ORD: 6/19/74

JETRO, New York (Japan Trade Center)
CRD: 6/19/74   Japan

Maseng Communications
1501 M Street, NW, Suite 700
Washington DC 20005
Phone: 202/879-4109   Fax: 202/638-1976
E-mail: mailbox@masengcomm.com
FARA#: 4660   ORD: 5/5/92

Japan Auto. Manufacturers' Association, Inc.
CRD: 5/5/92   Japan

Mayeroff, Jerry M.
DBA Mayeroff & Associates
2724 West Coyle Ave.
Chicago IL 60645
FARA#: 5067   ORD: 11/07/95

Japan External Trade Org. (JETRO, Chicago)
CRD: 11/7/95   Japan

McCabe, Jr., Bernard J.
P.O. Box 30024
Alexandria VA 22310
FARA#: 5155   ORD: 1/29/97

Sandline International
CRD: 1/29/97   International

McCaffrey Braley, Inc.
814 Green Street
Alexandria VA 22314-4213
FARA#: 5255   ORD: 5/9/98

Republic of Moldova
CRD: 5/9/98   Moldova

McCutchen, Doyle, Brown & Enersen, LLP
3 Embarcadero Center
San Francisco CA 94111-4067
FARA#: 5218   ORD: 11/18/97

Government of Mexico
CRD: 11/18/97   Mexico

McDermott/O'Neill & Associates
1 Beacon Street, Suite 1600
Boston MA 02108
Phone: 617/227-2600   Fax: 617/742-4022
FARA#: 4898   ORD: 3/7/94

*John Hume, MP and the Social Democratic
    Labour Party*
CRD: 3/7/94   United Kingdom

McElligott Associates

1421 Foxhall Road, NW
Washington DC 20007
Phone: 202/797-9727   Fax: 202/986-5227
FARA#: 5151   ORD: 1/15/97

Embassy of the Republic of the Sudan
CRD: 1/15/97   Sudan

McKinney & McDowell Associates
1612 K Street, NW - Suite 904
Washington DC 20006
Phone: 202/833-9771   Fax: 202/833-9770
FARA#: 5139   ORD: 7/25/96

Embassy of Haiti
CRD: 7/25/96   Haiti

Friends of Sinn Fein
CRD: 7/25/96   Ireland

McLaughlin & Morgan, Inc.
146 North Bread St.
Philadelphia PA 19106
FARA#: 5088   ORD: 12/15/95

Dubai Commerce & Tourism Promotion Board
CRD: 12/15/95   United Arab Emirates

McNeill, John
P.O. Box 6194
1200 Pennsylvania Avenue, NW
Washington DC 20044
FARA#: 4845   ORD: 8/11/93

Alexandre Sambat
CRD: 8/11/93   International

Medhurst & Associates, Inc.
1208 Washington Drive
Centerport NY 11721-1815
FARA#: 3996   ORD: 6/19/87

Department of Tourism, Government of Anguilla
CRD: 6/19/87   Anguilla

Governments of St. Eustatius & Saba
CRD: 9/12/89   St. Eustatius & Saba

Meredith Concept Group, Inc.
110 N. Royal Street, Suite 300
Alexandria VA 22314
Phone: 202/364-8892   FARA#: 5101
ORD: 3/11/96

*Nociete National d'Etude et de Construction
    de Moteurs d'Aviation*
CRD: 3/20/96   France

Mexican Government Tourism Office, Chicago
70 East Lake Street, Suite 1413
Chicago IL 60601-5977
Phone: 312/606-9252   Fax: 312/606-9012
E-mail: MGTOCHI@CIS.CompuServe.co
URL: http://www.mexico-travel.com
FARA#: 2448   ORD: 8/9/73

Mexican National Tourist Office
CRD: 8/9/73   Mexico

Mexican Gov't. Tourism Office, Los Angeles
1801 Century Park East, Suite 1080
Los Angeles CA 90067
Phone: 310/203-8191   Fax: 310/203-8316
FARA#: 2209   ORD: 9/8/70

Mexican Ministry of Tourism
CRD: 9/8/70   Mexico

Mexican Gov't. Tourism Office, New York
405 Park Avenue, Suite 1401
New York NY 10022
FARA#: 1754   ORD: 6/9/64

Mexican Ministry of Tourism
CRD: 6/9/64   Mexico

Michael Solomon Associates
516 Fifth Avenue, Suite 801
New York NY 10036
FARA#: 3923   ORD: 1/6/87

Fujitsu, Ltd.
CRD: 10/2/87   Japan

JETRO, New York
CRD: 1/6/87   Japan

Tohoku Electric Power Company, Inc.
CRD: 8/11/89   Japan

Miller & Chevalier, Chartered
655 15th Street, NW, Suite 900
Washington DC 20005-5701
Phone: 202/626-5800   Fax: 202/628-0858
E-mail: inquiries@milchev.com
URL: http://www.millerchevalier.com
FARA#: 3626   ORD: 10/31/84

*Government of British Columbia, Ministry
    of Development, Trade/Tourism*
CRD: 9/27/91   Canada

Government of Canada
CRD: 3/23/87   Canada

Mintz, Victor K.
GOI - MOD Mission to the U.S.
800 Second Avenue, 11th Floor
New York NY 10017
FARA#: 4038   ORD: 9/15/87

Government of Israel, Ministry of Defense
CRD: 9/15/87   Israel

Modern Education Services, Inc.
ATT Sue Johnson
1015 18th St., NW, Suite 704
Washington DC 20036
FARA#: 1803   ORD: 10/19/94

Austrian Press & Information Office
CRD: 10/7/88   Austria

Japan Information Center (Consulate of Japan)
CRD: 7/30/81   Japan

JETRO, New York
CRD: 8/15/86   Japan

Moltzan, Gunter W.
14 Earth Star Court
Gaithersburg MD 20878-2777
FARA#: 5098   ORD: 3/11/96

*Baden-Wuerttemburg Agency for International
    Economic Corp. GWZ*
CRD: 3/11/96   Germany

Monaco Government Tourist Office
565 Fifth Avenue, 23rd Floor
New York NY 10017
Phone: 212/758-5227   Fax: 212/754-9320
E-mail: mgto.ny@ix.netcom.com
URL: http://www.monaco.mc/usa/
FARA#: 2327   ORD: 3/21/72

Direction de Tourisme et des Congres
CRD: 4/25/72   Monaco

Moresby Consulting, Ltd.
3259 Telescope Terrace
Nanaimo
British Columbia CA V9T 3V4
Phone: 604/758-8434   Fax: 604/758-4075
E-mail: parmstrong@island.net

FARA#: 4966   ORD: 10/14/94

Canadian Pulp & Paper Association
CRD: 10/14/94   Canada

Morgan, Lewis & Bockius
1800 M St., NW, Suite 600 North
Washington DC 20036-5869
Phone: 202/467-7000   Fax: 202/467-7176
FARA#: 3794   ORD: 3/12/86

*United Kingdom of Great Britain & Northern
    Ireland, Govt. of the*
CRD: 3/12/86   United Kingdom

Morley Caskin
1225 I Street, NW, Suite 402
Washington DC 20005
FARA#: 5150   ORD: 12/30/96

Hydro-Quebec
CRD: 1/8/97   Canada

Moroccan National Tourist Office
20 East 46th Street, Suite 1201
New York NY 10017
FARA#: 1793   ORD: 9/21/64

Moroccan National Tourist Office
CRD: 9/21/64   Morocco

MRB Group
12833 Atkinson Road
Lake Bluff IL 60044
FARA#: 4755   ORD: 1/26/93

*Secretary of Industrial & Commercial
    Development State of Ucatan*
CRD: 1/26/93   Mexico

MS Research, Inc.
626 Wilshire Boulevard, Suite 705
Los Angeles CA 90017
FARA#: 4697   ORD: 8/10/92

Japan External Trade Organization
CRD: 8/10/92   Japan

Mullin Communications, Inc.
1000 Thomas Jefferson Street, NW
Suite 305
Washington DC 20007
FARA#: 5253   ORD: 4/17/98

Embassy of Cyprus
CRD: 4/17/98   Cyprus

Embassy of Japan
CRD: 4/17/98   Japan

MWW Group
1747 Pennsylvania Ave., NW - Suite 1150
Washington DC 20006
Phone: 202/296-6222   Fax: 202/296-4507
URL: http://www.mwwpr.com
FARA#: 5230   ORD: 1/16/98

Taipei Economic and Cultural Rep. Office
CRD: 1/16/98   Taiwan

Mzimela, Sipo Elijah
1790 Lavista Road
Atlanta GA 30329
FARA#: 4493   ORD: 4/1/91

Inkatha Freedom Party
CRD: 4/1/91   International

Napolitano, Francisco
52 Temple Place
Boston MA 02111-1315
FARA#: 5219   ORD: 12/15/97

*Ministerio del Interior Unidat Ejectiva
de Programas Especiales*
CRD: 12/15/97   International

National Film Board of Canada
350 Fifth Avenue - Suite 4820
New York NY 10118
FARA#: 437   ORD: 4/21/44

National Film Board of Canada
CRD: 4/21/44   Canada

**National Liberation Council of
Nigeria - U.S.A. (Nalicon)**
7995 Old Montgomery Road
Ellicott City MD 21043
FARA#: 5095   ORD: 2/16/96

Nalicon - Nigeria
CRD: 2/16/96   Nigeria

**National Union for the Total Independence
of Angola (UNITA)**
DBA Free Angola Information Service, Inc.
1101 - 16th Street, NW, Suite 500
Washington DC 20036
FARA#: 3797   ORD: 3/21/86

*National Union for the Total Independence
of Angola (UNITA)*
CRD: 3/21/86   Angola

Native American Rights Fund
1712 N Street, NW
Washington DC 20036
Phone: 202/785-4166   Fax: 202/822-0068
FARA#: 4832   ORD: 7/19/93

Pottawatomi National
CRD: 7/19/93   Canada

Neas Group, LLC
750 17th Street, NW - Suite 1200
Washington DC 20006
Phone: 202/778-2340   Fax: 202/778-2330
E-mail: RNeas@fbt.com
FARA#: 5153   ORD: 1/24/97

Embassy of the Republic of the Marshall Islands
CRD: 1/24/97   Marshall Islands

Netherlands Board of Tourism
355 Lexington Avenue, 21st Floor
New York NY 10017
FARA#: 619   ORD: 3/20/50

Nederlands Bureau voor Toerisme
CRD: 3/20/50   Netherlands

Neuman & Company
1317 F Street, NW - Suite 900
Washington DC 20004
Phone: 202/628-2075   Fax: 202/628-2077
E-mail: Neumanco@erols.com
URL: http://www.wdcnet.com/neuman/
FARA#: 1686   ORD: 6/15/92

New Zealand Meat Producers' Board
ATT Barrie G. Saunders
8000 Towers Crescent Drive
Vienna VA 22182
Phone: 703/243-1295   Fax: 703/243-1497
FARA#: 2526   ORD: 7/8/74

New Zealand Meat Producers' Board
CRD: 7/8/74   New Zealand

**Nichols-Dezenhall Communications
Management Group, Ltd.**
1211 Connecticut Avenue, NW - Suite 812
Washington DC 20036
Phone: 202/296-0263   Fax: 202/452-9371

FARA#: 5184   ORD: 6/5/97

Meat Industry Council
CRD: 6/5/97   International

Nixon, Hargrave, Devans & Doyle, LLP
One KeyCorp Plaza, 9th Floor
Albany NY 12207
FARA#: 4596   ORD: 11/20/91

Hydro-Quebec
CRD: 11/20/91   Canada

Norquist, Grover Glenn
1320 18th Street, NW - Suite 200
Washington DC 20003
Phone: 202/785-0266   Fax: 202/785-0261
FARA#: 5061   ORD: 9/8/95

Rep. of the Seychelles Islands, President France
CRD: 9/8/95   Seychelles

**North American Medhin Democratic
Association**
ATT M. Yiman
P.O. Box 9380
Washington DC 20005
FARA#: 4650   ORD: 4/17/92

Ethiopian Medhin Democratic Party
CRD: 4/17/92   Ethiopia

Northern Development Company (NDC)
The Meadows Corporate Center
2850 Golf Road, Suite 717
Rolling Meadows IL 60008-4033
Phone: 847/593-6020   Fax: 847/593-7127
E-mail: ndc.newcastle@norder.co.u
URL: http://www.norder.co.uk
FARA#: 3476   ORD: 5/25/83

Northern England Development
CRD: 5/25/83   United Kingdom

Norwegian Tourist Board (NORTRA)
655 Third Avenue
18th Floor
New York NY 10017
Phone: 212/949-2333   Fax: 212/983-5260
E-mail: gonorway@Interport.net
URL: http://www.norway.org
FARA#: 526   ORD: 5/13/48

Norwegian Tourist Board
CRD: 5/13/48   Norway

Nova Scotia Information Centre
468 Commercial Street
Portland ME 04101
FARA#: 3078   ORD: 12/18/79

Nova Scotia Department of Tourism
CRD: 12/18/78   Canada

O'Connor & Hannan
1919 Pennsylvania Ave., NW, Suite 800
Washington DC 20006
Phone: 202/887-1400   Fax: 202/466-2198
FARA#: 2972   ORD: 10/25/78

*China External Trade Development Council
(CETDC)*
CRD: 6/17/87   Taiwan

Government of the Netherlands/Antilles
CRD: 3/19/87   Netherlands Antilles

Proexport
CRD: 5/22/95   International

O'Leary Clarke & Partners, Inc.
ATT John Koutsantanou, Vice Chairman

99 Madison Avenue, 17th Floor
New York NY 10016
FARA#: 3780   ORD: 2/20/86

Cayman Islands Department of Tourism
CRD: 2/20/86   Cayman Islands

O'Mara, Charles J.
1200 - 19th Street, NW, Suite 201
Washington DC 20036
FARA#: 5181   ORD: 5/30/97

*Association des Amidonneries de Cereals
de L.U.E.*
CRD: 3/25/97   International

Tilda Rice
CRD: 5/30/97   International

Oasis International Group, Ltd.
179 Franklin Street
New York NY 10013
FARA#: 5116   ORD: 6/24/96

Government of India Tourist Office
CRD: 6/24/96   India

Oceans International Corporation
5505 Mitchelldale, Suite 121
Houston TX 77092
FARA#: 5134   ORD: 10/26/96

National Shippers' Council of Angola
CRD: 10/21/96   Angola

Oestreicher, Michael R.
312 Walnut Street, Suite 1400
Cincinnati OH 45202
FARA#: 3426   ORD: 12/08/82

*Karl Dobler, Industry Representative,
Canton of Neuchatel*
CRD: 12/8/82   Switzerland

**Office of the Deputy Commissioner of
Maritime Affairs**
Vanuatu Maritime Services, Ltd.
90 Washington Street, 22nd Floor
New York NY 10006
FARA#: 4860   ORD: 10/12/93

Republic of Vanuatu
CRD: 10/12/93   Vanuatu

Office of the Turkish Rep. of Northern Cyprus
ATT Joseph P. Albanese, Esquire
821 United Nations Plaza
New York NY 10017
FARA#: 2619   ORD: 10/16/75

R.R. Denktash
CRD: 10/16/75   Cyprus

Office of Tibet
241 East 32nd Street, Ground Floor
New York NY 10016
FARA#: 1699   ORD: 3/14/64

Dalai Lama
CRD: 3/12/64   Tibet

Ogilvy Adams & Rinehart, Inc.
708 Third Avenue
New York NY 10017
FARA#: 4455   ORD: 12/28/90

Netherlands Foreign Investment Agency
CRD: 12/28/90   Netherlands

Ogilvy Public Relations Worldwide
1901 L Street, NW - Suite 300
Washington DC 20036

Phone: 202/466-7590   Fax: 202/466-7598
URL: http://www.ogilvypr.org
FARA#: 5189   ORD: 6/30/97

Hyndai Electronics Industries, Co. & LG Semicon Co., Ltd.
CRD: 6/30/97   Korea

Oliver A. Dulle, Jr. & Company, Inc.
7 North Brentwood Boulevard, Suite 202
St. Louis MO 63105
Phone: 314/721-2418   Fax: 314/721-5083
FARA#: 4739   ORD: 12/17/92

Trafford Park Development Corporation
CRD: 12/17/92   United Kingdom

Olsson, Frank & Weeds, P.C.
1400 16th Street, NW - Suite 400
Washington DC 20036-2220
Phone: 202/789-1212   Fax: 202/234-3537
E-mail: info@ofwlaw.com
URL: http://www.ofwlaw.com
FARA#: 5175   ORD: 4/21/97

Meat Industry Council
CRD: 4/21/97   International

Oromo Liberation Front, N. America Office
1810 9th Street, NW
Washington DC 20001
Phone: 202/462-5477   Fax: 202/332-7011
FARA#: 4610   ORD: 1/29/92

Oromo Liberation Front (OLF)
CRD: 1/29/92   Ethiopia

Osaka Prefectual Gov't., California Office
345 California Street, Suite 2575
San Francisco CA 94104
FARA#: 5174   ORD: 4/21/97

International Business Organization of Osaka
CRD: 4/21/97   Japan

Osaka Prefectural Government
CRD: 4/21/97   Japan

Owens, Wayne
c/o Weil, Gotshal & Manges
1615 L Street, N.W., Suite 700
Washington DC 20036
Phone: 202/682-7000   Fax: 202/857-0939
FARA#: 4907   ORD: 2/14/94

Hashemite Kingdom of Jordan & the Higher Council
CRD: 2/14/94   Jordan

P/C Advisors, Inc.
1575 I Street, N.W., #1050
Washington DC 20005
FARA#: 4806   ORD: 5/21/93

Office of the President of Kazakhstan
CRD: 8/31/93   Kazakhstan

Office of the President of the Ukraine
CRD: 5/21/93   Ukraine

Palestine Arab Delegation
Grand Central Station
P.O. Box 608
New York NY 10163
FARA#: 1459   ORD: 6/26/61

Arab Higher Committee for Palestine
CRD: 6/26/91   Palestine

Palestine Liberation Organization
1730 K Street, NW, Suite 1004
Washington DC 20006

FARA#: 5244   ORD: 3/18/98

Palestine Liberation Organization Office
CRD: 3/18/98   Palestine

Partido de la Liberacion Dominicana, N.Y.
ATT Jose Fernandez
2005 Amsterdam Avenue, #3-A
New York NY 10032
FARA#: 2509   ORD: 4/17/74

Partido de la Liberacion Dominicana
CRD: 4/17/74   Dominican Republic

Partido Reformista Social Cristiano
3736 - 10th Avenue, Apt. 9-A
New York NY 10034
FARA#: 1687   ORD: 2/5/89

Partido Reformista
CRD: 2/5/64   International

Partners & Shevack, Inc.
1211 Avenue of the Americas
New York NY 10036
FARA#: 1436   ORD: 3/28/61

Lot Polish Airlines
CRD: 4/7/81   Poland

Pathfinder Group, LLC
3000 South Randolph Street, Suite 517
Arlington VA 22206
FARA#: 5257   ORD: 5/21/98

Northern Ireland Free Trade Initiative
CRD: 5/21/98   Ireland

Patrice Tanaka & Company, Inc.
320 West 13th Street, 7th Floor
New York NY 10014
FARA#: 5162   ORD: 3/11/97

Government of the Cayman Islands
CRD: 3/11/97   Cayman Islands

Patton Boggs, L.L.P.
2550 M Street, NW - Suite 800
Washington DC 20037
Phone: 202/457-6000   Fax: 202/457-6315
E-mail: info@pattonboggs.com
FARA#: 2165   ORD: 10/09/69

Dept. of Trade & Industry, Republic of the Philippines Embassy
CRD: 10/5/95   Philippines

Embassy of the Republic of Turkey
CRD: 10/6/97   Turkey

Government of Pakistan Embassy
CRD: 1/30/94   Pakistan

Government of the State of Qatar
CRD: 2/28/94   Qatar

Paul, Hastings, Janofsky & Walker
1299 Pennsylvania Avenue, NW, 10th Floor
Washington DC 20004-2400
Phone: 202/508-9500   Fax: 202/508-9700
E-mail: info@phjw.com
URL: http://www.phjw.com
FARA#: 5121   ORD: 7/17/96

Government of Canada
CRD: 7/17/96   Canada

Paul, Weiss, Rifkind, Wharton & Garrison
ATT Terence J. Fortune
1285 Avenue of the Americas
New York NY 10019-6064
FARA#: 4539   ORD: 7/9/91

Embassy of the Republic of Korea
CRD: 2/28/95   Korea

Korea Telecom
CRD: 3/6/95   Korea

PBN Company
3 Embarcadero Center, Suite 2210
San Francisco CA 94111
FARA#: 5206   ORD: 9/4/97

Embassy of the Republic Uzbekistan
CRD: 9/4/97   Uzbekistan

Pekao Trading Corporation
Two Park Avenue, Suite 400
New York NY 10016
FARA#: 817   ORD: 2/23/54

Bank Polska Kasa Opieki, S.A.
CRD: 2/23/54   Poland

Pendred, Russell Jess
5829 Brookstone Walk, Suite 101-Q
Acworth GA 30101
FARA#: 4996   ORD: 2/24/95

Dr. Karl Dobler, Industry Rep. Neuchatel
CRD: 2/24/95   Switzerland

People's Mojadehin of Iran, Washington, D.C., Press Office
National Press Building - Suite 1065
P.O. Box 28087
Washington DC 20038
FARA#: 4061   ORD: 11/20/87

Press Office of the People's Mojahedin of Iran
CRD: 11/20/87   Iran

Pepper, Hamilton & Scheetz
1300 19th Street, NW
Washington DC 20036-1685
Phone: 202/828-1200   Fax: 202/828-1665
FARA#: 4968   ORD: 10/20/94

Le Gouvernement du Quebec
CRD: 10/20/94   Canada

Peter Martin Associates, Inc.
1200 High Ridge Road
Stamford CT 06905
FARA#: 4236   ORD: 4/5/89

Jamaica Ministry of Tourism
CRD: 4/5/89   Jamaica

Peter Rothholz Associates, Inc.
355 Lexington Avenue, 17th Floor
New York NY 10017
FARA#: 2830   ORD: 9/16/77

Barbados Industrial Development Corporation
CRD: 12/15/86   Barbados

Phoenix Group
2250 Clarendon Blvd, Suite 312
Arlington VA 22201
FARA#: 5060   ORD: 9/8/95

Government of El Salvador, Embassy
CRD: 9/8/95   El Salvador

Pierson & Burnett, LLP
1667 K Street, NW, Suite 801
Washington DC 20006
FARA#: 5127   ORD: 8/7/96

Daimler-Benz Aerospace, A.G.
CRD: 8/7/96   Germany

Pierson, Semmes and Bemis, LLP

1054 31st Street, NW - Suite 300
Washington DC 20007
Phone: 202/333-4000   Fax: 202/965-0100
FARA#: 5252   ORD: 4/16/98

*Secretariat of the Common Market of Eastern
and Southern Africa*
CRD: 4/16/98   International

Piriev, Nizami
#12 Bolshoi Kozlovsky
Pereulok, Suite #25
Moscow RU 107078
FARA#: 4936   ORD: 8/3/94

Republic of Azerbaijan
CRD: 8/3/94   Azerbaijan

Polish National Tourist Office, New York
488 Madison Avenue, 6th Floor
New York NY 10022
FARA#: 4762   ORD: 2/4/93

*Ministry of Sports & Tourism of the
Republic of Poland*
CRD: 2/4/93   Poland

Pordzik, Wolfgang G.
202 Old MacDonald Road, Apt. 337
Gaithersburg MD 20877
FARA#: 5192   ORD: 7/14/97

Expo 2000- General Kommissariat
CRD: 7/14/97   International

Porter, Wright, Morris & Arthur
1667 K Street, NW, Suite 1100
Washington DC 20006-1605
Phone: 202/778-3000   Fax: 202/778-3063
E-mail: dca@porterwright.com
FARA#: 5208   ORD: 9/15/97

Cambodian People's Party
CRD: 4/22/98   Cambodia

Embassy of the Kingdom of Cambodia
CRD: 9/15/97   Cambodia

Porter/Novelli
1120 Connecticut Ave., NW
Washington DC 20036-3902
Phone: 202/973-5800   Fax: 202/973-5858
E-mail: mpfeil@porternovelli.com
URL: http://www.pninternational.com
FARA#: 4671   ORD: 5/18/92

Federation of Electric Power Companies
CRD: 6/30/97   International

Japan Automobile Manufacturers' Association
CRD: 5/18/92   Japan

Powell Tate, Inc.
700 13th Street, NW - Suite 1000
Washington DC 20005
Phone: 202/347-6633   Fax: 202/347-8713
FARA#: 5148   ORD: 12/30/96

*Avions de Transport Regional Groupement
d'Interet Economique*
CRD: 12/30/96   France

Electronic Industry Association of Japan
CRD: 12/30/96   Japan

Embassy of the Kingdom of Morocco
CRD: 5/22/98   Morocco

MERHAV
CRD: 4/7/97   International

Royal Embassy of Saudi Arabia

CRD: 12/30/96   Saudi Arabia

Societe General de Surveillance (SGS)
CRD: 12/8/97   International

Taiwan Research Institute
CRD: 12/30/96   Taiwan

Tunisian Agency for External Communications
CRD: 1/12/98   Tunisia

Powell, Goldstein, Frazer & Murphy
ATT Richard Belanger
1001 Pennsylvania Ave., NW, 6th Floor South
Washington DC 20004
Phone: 202/347-0066   Fax: 202/624-7222
URL: http://www.pgfm.com
FARA#: 3274   ORD: 9/10/81

China National Textiles Import/Export Corp.
CRD: 10/1/97   China

Hong Kong Economic and Trade Office
CRD: 11/21/97   Hong Kong

Hong Kong Trade Development Council
CRD: 10/1/97   Hong Kong

ProExport
CRD: 10/1/97   International

Pratt, Madigan
220 Middlesex Road
Darien CT 06820
FARA#: 4651   ORD: 4/24/92

Rudi Sezzer - Director of Tourism
CRD: 4/29/94   Cayman Islands

William Mulder/Stonington Beach Hotel
CRD: 8/9/93   Bermuda

**Price Waterhouse - International Tax
Services Group**
1177 Avenue of the Americas
New York NY 10036
FARA#: 4481   ORD: 3/6/91

Kuwait Investment Authority
CRD: 3/6/91   Kuwait

Public Strategies Washington, Inc.
633 Pennsylvania Avenue, NW, 4th Floor
Washington DC 20004
Phone: 202/783-2596   Fax: 202/628-5379
FARA#: 4486   ORD: 3/15/91

Government of Mexico
CRD: 3/15/91   Mexico

Public Strategies, Inc.
98 Jacinot Boulevard, Suite 900
Austin TX 78701
FARA#: 4928   ORD: 7/15/94

Cemex Central
CRD: 11/28/97   International

Government of Mexico
CRD: 9/18/95   Mexico

Vitro Corporativo, S.A. de C.V.
CRD: 7/15/94   Mexico

Quebec Government House
ATT Kevin Drummond
One Rockefeller Plaza, 26th Floor
New York NY 10020
Phone: 212/397-0200   Fax: 212/757-4753
FARA#: 1787   ORD: 9/2/64

Quebec Government

CRD: 9/2/64   Canada

Queensland Tourist & Travel Corporation
Northrop Plaza
1800 Century Park Wast, Suite 330
Los Angeles CA 90067
FARA#: 4146   ORD: 5/31/88

Queensland Tourist & Travel Corporation
CRD: 5/31/88   Australia

Rabin, Keith W.
140 West End Ave.
New York NY 10023
FARA#: 5119   ORD: 7/2/96

JETRO New York
CRD: 7/2/96   Japan

Rafiah, Zvi
Asia House
4 Weizman Street
Tel Aviv IS 64239
FARA#: 4736   ORD: 12/01/92

Rafael Armament Development Authority
CRD: 12/1/92   Israel

Redman, Eric
Heller Ehrman White McAuliffe
701 Fifth Avenue, Suite 6100
Seattle WA 98104-7098
FARA#: 4852   ORD: 9/28/93

Central Aerohydrodynamics Institute (TsAGI)
CRD: 8/22/94   Russia

Reed, T. Dean
1155 15th St., NW, Suite 1003
Washington DC 20005
FARA#: 5044   ORD: 9/13/95

Republic of Singapore, Embassy
CRD: 9/13/95   Singapore

**Reg'l. Org. of Liberal Democratic Party
of Russia**
1380 North Ave., Unit 317
Elizabeth NJ 07208
FARA#: 5054   ORD: 10/02/95

Liberal Democratic Party of Russia
CRD: 10/2/95   Russia

Reichler, Milton & Medel
1747 Pennsylvania Avenue, N.W., Suite 1200
Washington DC 20006
Phone: 202/223-1200   Fax: 202/785-6687
FARA#: 4776   ORD: 3/2/93

Embassy of the Republic of Uganda
CRD: 1/11/94   Uganda

Republic of Guyana
CRD: 3/3/93   Guyana

Republic of Honduras
CRD: 4/26/96   Honduras

Rendon Group, Inc.
1875 Connecticut Avenue, NW, Suite 414
Washington DC 20009
Phone: 202/745-4900   Fax: 202/745-0215
E-mail: jrendon@rendon.com
URL: http://www.rendon.com
FARA#: 4449   ORD: 12/17/90

Government of Aruba
CRD: 4/11/95   Aruba

Representative of German Industry & Trade
1627 I Street, NW, Suite 550

Washington DC 20006
Phone: 202/659-4777   Fax: 202/659-4779
E-mail: 104075.1540@compuserve.co
FARA#: 4274   ORD: 7/21/89

Bundesverband der Deutschen Industrie
CRD: 7/21/89   Germany

Deutscher Industrie - und Handelstag
CRD: 7/21/89   Germany

Rep. of Montenegro Trade Mission to the US
1610 New Hampshire Avenue, NW
Washington DC 20009
FARA#: 5199   ORD: 8/4/97

Government of the Republic of Montenegro
CRD: 8/4/97   Montenegro

Richard Lewis Communications, Inc.
1211 Avenue of the Americas, 42nd Floor
New York NY 10036
FARA#: 4452   ORD: 12/20/90

Nissho Iwai Corporation
CRD: 12/20/90   Japan

Rick Swartz & Associates, Inc.
1869 Park Road, NW
Washington DC 20010
Phone: 202/328-1313   Fax: 202/797-9856
FARA#: 5185   ORD: 6/17/97

Embassy of El Salvador
CRD: 6/17/98   El Salvador

Robins, Kaplan, Miller & Ciresi
ATT Harold E. Mesirow, Esq.
1801 K Street, NW
Suite 1200
Washington DC 20006
Phone: 202/775-0725   Fax: 202/223-8604
FARA#: 4365   ORD: 4/16/90

International Group of P&I Clubs
CRD: 4/16/90   United Kingdom

Rockey Company, Inc.
2121 Fifth Ave.
Seattle WA 98121
Phone: 206/728-1100   Fax: 206/728-1106
FARA#: 4594   ORD: 11/14/91

Nintendo of America
CRD: 12/30/92   Japan

Resource Group International
CRD: 12/22/95   International

Resource Group International
CRD: 12/22/95   Norway

Rogers & Wells
607 14th Street, NW - Suite 900
Washington DC 20005-2011
Phone: 202/434-0700   Fax: 202/434-0800
FARA#: 3428   ORD: 12/10/82

Canadian Pulp & Paper Association
CRD: 7/17/92   Canada

Dofasco, Inc.
CRD: 3/18/92   Canada

Romanian National Tourist Office
14 East 38th Street, 12th Floor
New York NY 10016
Phone: 212/697-6971   Fax: 212/697-6972
FARA#: 2093   ORD: 6/3/68

Romanian Tourism Promotion Office
CRD: 6/3/68   Romania

Ronald S. Winton & Associates
1515 Jefferson Davis Highway, Suite 1007
Arlington VA 22202
FARA#: 4978   ORD: 12/02/94

Government of Ukraine, Embassy
CRD: 12/2/94   Ukraine

Rosenblatt, Peter R.
c/o Heller & Rosenblatt
1501 M Street, NW - Suite 1175
Washington DC 20005-1702
Phone: 202/466-4700   Fax: 202/223-4826
E-mail: ffddprosenblatt@erols.com
FARA#: 3518   ORD: 9/13/83

*Board of Foreign Trade, Ministry of
    Economic Affairs*
CRD: 9/13/83   Taiwan

Ross-Robinson & Associates
1090 Vermont Avenue, NW - Suite 801
Washington DC 20005
Phone: 202/408-7052   Fax: 202/682-3084
E-mail: hrr@rosro.com
FARA#: 4992   ORD: 2/7/95

Caribbean Banana Exporters Association
CRD: 5/8/96   Saint Lucia

Caribbean Banana Growers' Association
CRD: 5/8/96   Belize

Government of Haiti
CRD: 2/7/95   Haiti

Rossi, Marie-Louise
London Underwriting Centre
3 Minster Court, Mincing Lane
London EN EC3R 7DD
Phone: 202/986-8000   Fax: 202/986-8102
FARA#: 4919   ORD: 6/16/94

*London Insurance & Reinsurance
    Market Association*
CRD: 6/16/94   United Kingdom

Rubenstein Associates, Inc.
1345 Avenue of The Americas, 30th Floor
New York NY 10105
FARA#: 4778   ORD: 3/12/93

Most Group, Inc.
CRD: 5/1/95   Russia

Ruder & Finn, Inc.
301 East 57th Street
New York NY 10022
FARA#: 1481   ORD: 9/27/61

Ambassador Ibrahim A. Gambarir
CRD: 8/22/97   Nigeria

ASEA Brown Boveri
CRD: 10/30/90   International

Barbados Tourism Authority
CRD: 4/29/98   Barbados

Cathay Pacific Airways Limited
CRD: 4/29/98   International

Coca Cola Femsa, S.A. de C.V.
CRD: 8/22/97   International

Fomento Economico Mexicano, S.A. de C.V.
CRD: 8/22/97   Mexico

Four Seasons Hotels, Inc.
CRD: 4/29/98   International

Gilat Satellite Networks, Ltd.

CRD: 11/1/93   International

Government of Switzerland, Embassy
CRD: 7/21/97   Switzerland

*Government of the Netherlands, Netherlands
    Foreign Investment Agency*
CRD: 4/24/97   Netherlands

Hungarian Broadcasting Corporation
CRD: 4/29/98   Hungary

Israel Lane Development Company
CRD: 4/29/94   Israel

Novartis, A.G.
CRD: 4/24/97   International

Ranbaxy Laboratories, Ltd.
CRD: 10/28/94   International

South African Airways, Div. of Transnet Limited
CRD: 4/29/98   South Africa

Vitro, Sociedad Anonima
CRD: 8/22/97   International

Ruder Finn, Inc.
808 17th Street, NW, Suite 600
Washington DC 20006
Phone: 202/466-7800   Fax: 202/887-0905
E-mail: ruderfinn@juno.com
URL: http://www.ruderfinn.com
FARA#: 4315   ORD: 11/09/89

Exportadora De Sal, S.A. De C.V. (ESSA)
CRD: 4/21/97   International

**Russian-American Partnership Center,
    Washington, DC**
901 15th Street, NW - Suite 350
Washington DC 20005
FARA#: 5140   ORD: 11/21/96

Russian-American Partnership Center
CRD: 11/21/96   International

Sack & Associates, Inc.
8300 Greensboro Dr., Suite 1080
McLean VA 22102
Phone: 703/883-0102   Fax: 703/883-0108
FARA#: 5046   ORD: 9/15/95

Thomas De La Rue, PLC
CRD: 9/15/95   United Kingdom

Salinger, Pierre
3904 Hillandale Court, NW
Washington DC 20007
FARA#: 5224   ORD: 12/30/97

*His Excellency El Hadj Omar Bongo
    (Gabonese President)*
CRD: 12/30/97   Gabon

Sampson, Theodore James
c/o Helmepa
Five Pergamou Street, NEA SMYN
Athens GR 171 21
FARA#: 5248   ORD: 3/30/98

*Hellenic Marine Environment Progrection
    Association (HELMEPA)*
CRD: 3/30/98   Greece

Samuels International Associates, Inc.
1133 21st Street, NW
Suite 710
Washington DC 20036
Phone: 202/223-7683   Fax: 202/223-7687
E-mail: samuels@us.net
FARA#: 4848   ORD: 8/26/93

Government of Angola
CRD: 8/26/93   Angola

Trade Rep. of the Russian Federation to the U.S.
CRD: 7/22/97   Russia

San Marino, Republic of (Consulate General)
1899 L Street, NW, Suite 500
Washington DC 20036
Phone: 202/223-3517   Fax: 202/452-8938
FARA#: 3361   ORD: 4/22/82

Government of San Marino
CRD: 4/22/82   San Marino

Sandler & Travis Trade Advisory Services, Inc.
1300 Pennsylvania Ave., NW - Suite 400
Washington DC 20004
Phone: 202/638-2230   Fax: 202/638-2236
E-mail: info@strtrade.com
URL: http://www.strtrade.com
FARA#: 4699   ORD: 7/31/92

Consejo Nacional de Zonas Francas
de Exportacion'
CRD: 3/1/94   Dominican Republic

Consejo Nacionalde Zonas Francas
de Exportacion
CRD: 3/1/94   Dominican Republic

Government of Haiti (Customs)
CRD: 7/19/97   Haiti

Saudi Refining, Inc.
9009 West Loop, South, Suite 10158
Houston TX 77096
FARA#: 4184   ORD: 10/13/88

Government of Kingdom of Saudi Arabia
CRD: 10/13/88   Saudi Arabia

Saudi Arabian Oil Company
CRD: 5/12/89   Saudi Arabia

Saunders & Company
ATT Steven R. Saunders
1015 Duke Street
Alexandria VA 22314
Phone: 703/549-1555   Fax: 703/549-6526
FARA#: 3440   ORD: 2/8/83

Embassy of Japan
CRD: 3/8/83   Japan

Seiko Epson Corporation
CRD: 6/14/89   Japan

Savarese & Associates
700 13th Street, NW - Suite 1000
Washington DC 20005
Phone: 202/783-5600   FARA#: 5197
ORD: 7/29/97

Taiwan Research Institute
CRD: 7/29/97   Taiwan

SACUR
ATT Francine Del Vescovo, Esquire
C.P. 428
Rue Da Granja 95-1
Bissau GV FARA#: 4972   ORD: 11/15/94

People of the Republic of Guinea Bissau
CRD: 11/15/94   Guinea-Bissau

Scanlon, Thomas J.
Benchmarks, Inc.
3248 Prospect Street, NW
Washington DC 20007
Phone: 202/965-3983   Fax: 202/965-3987
FARA#: 3500   ORD: 7/12/83

ALFA Industries, S.A.
CRD: 2/25/86   Mexico

Schmertz Company, Inc., The
1185 Avenue of the Americas, 8th Floor
New York NY 10036
FARA#: 4161   ORD: 7/26/88

Electronic Industries Association of Japan
CRD: 8/16/93   Japan

Embassy of Saudi Arabia
CRD: 7/26/88   Saudi Arabia

Schochet, Kenneth Barry
1750 K Street, NW - 12th Floor
Washington DC 20006
Phone: 202/833-9664   Fax: 202/833-9712
FARA#: 4033   ORD: 8/27/87

Center for Democracy in Angola, Inc.
CRD: 8/27/87   Angola

Scottish Enterprise
4 Landmark Square, Suite 500
Stamford CT 06901
FARA#: 3013   ORD: 4/17/79

Scottish Enterprise
CRD: 4/17/79   Scotland

Severance International, Inc.
1120 C St., SE
Washington DC 20003-1402
Phone: 202/675-4585   FARA#: 5038
ORD: 7/26/95

Directorate General of Telecommunications,
Ministry of
CRD: 4/13/98   Taiwan

Shafiq, Nuri
American Trade & Investments
2000 L Street, NW, Suite 200
Washington DC 20036
Phone: 202/942-5000   Fax: 202/942-5999
FARA#: 4798   ORD: 4/9/93

Democratic League of Kosova
CRD: 4/9/93   Kosova

Shandwick
111 Fifth Avenue
New York NY 10003
FARA#: 4866   ORD: 11/05/93

Kingdom of Cambodia
CRD: 2/12/95   Cambodia

Nordion International, Inc.
CRD: 1/3/94   Canada

Shandwick Public Affairs, Inc.
655 15th Street, NW - Suite 475
Washington DC 20005
Phone: 202/383-9700   Fax: 202/383-0079
FARA#: 5220   ORD: 12/30/97

Government of Hong Kong Special
Administrative Region
CRD: 4/10/98   Hong Kong

Republic of Gabon
CRD: 12/30/97   Gabon

Republic of Turkey
CRD: 12/17/97   Turkey

Shannon Free Airport Development Co., Ltd.
345 Park Avenue
New York NY 10154-0037
FARA#: 2467   ORD: 10/23/73

Shannon Free Airport Development Co., Ltd.
CRD: 10/23/73   Ireland

Shaw, Pittman, Potts & Trowbridge
2300 N Street, NW
Washington DC 20037
Phone: 202/663-8000   Fax: 202/663-8007
E-mail: info@shawpittman.com
URL: http://www.shawpittman.com
FARA#: 5198   ORD: 7/31/97

Empresa Estatal de Telecommunicaciones (Emtel)
CRD: 7/31/97   International

Shea & Gardner
1800 Massachusetts Ave., N.W.
Washington DC 20036
Phone: 202/828-2000   Fax: 202/828-2195
FARA#: 3901   ORD: 10/30/86

SGS Government Programs, Inc.
CRD: 11/30/87   International

SGS North America, Inc.
CRD: 10/30/86   International

Shearman & Sterling
ATT Christopher F. Clarke
801 Pennsylvania Ave., NW, Suite 900
Washington DC 20004-2604
Phone: 202/508-8000   Fax: 202/508-8100
URL: http://www.shearman.com
FARA#: 4208   ORD: 7/23/89

Credit Lyonnais
CRD: 5/7/98   France

Secretariat of Commerce & Industrial
Development of Mexico
CRD: 2/26/91   Mexico

Shemdin, Nijyar H.
10903 Amherst Avenue, Suite 231
Silver Spring MD 20902
Phone: 301/946-1383
E-mail: nshemdin@erols.com
URL: http://www.krg.org
FARA#: 5196   ORD: 7/22/97

Kurdistan Regional Government
CRD: 7/22/97   Kurdistan

Sher & Blackwell
1850 M Street, NW - Suite 900
Washington DC 20036
Phone: 202/463-2500   Fax: 202/463-4950
E-mail: LMH@sher#@shebla.geis.com
FARA#: 4576   ORD: 8/1/91

A.P. Moller-Maersk
CRD: 11/7/94   Denmark

Sidley & Austin
1722 I Street, NW
Washington DC 20006
Phone: 202/736-8000   Fax: 202/736-8711
URL: www.sidley.com
FARA#: 3731   ORD: 9/13/85

Government of Israel
CRD: 7/27/92   Israel

Government of the Cayman Islands
CRD: 9/13/85   Cayman Islands

Sierra Rutile America, Inc.
P.O. Box 187
Center Valley PA 18034-0187
FARA#: 5128   ORD: 6/10/96

Sierra Rutile America, Inc.
CRD: 6/10/96   International

Singapore Economic Development Board
55 East 59th Street, 21st Floor
New York NY 10022
FARA#: 2003   ORD: 2/2/67

Singapore Economic Development Board
CRD: 2/2/67   Singapore

Singapore Tourist Promotion Board
8484 Wilshire Boulevard, Suite 510
Beverly Hills CA 90211
FARA#: 2414   ORD: 3/27/73

Republic of Singapore
CRD: 3/27/73   Singapore

Sitrick Krantz & Company, Inc.
ATT Nicholas J. Spiliotes, Esquire
Morrison & Foerster
2000 Pennsylvania Ave., NW - Suite 5500
Washington DC 20006-1812
Phone: 202/887-1500   Fax: 202/887-0763
E-mail: nspiliotes@mofo.com
FARA#: 4967   ORD: 10/14/94

Fujitsu, Ltd.
CRD: 10/14/94   Japan

Skadden, Arps, Slate, Meagher & Flom LLP
1440 New York Avenue, NW
Washington DC 20005-2107
Phone: 202/371-7000   Fax: 202/371-7956
FARA#: 4550   ORD: 7/29/91

Republic of Georgia, Embassy
CRD: 7/29/97   Georgia

**Small & Medium Industry Promotion
  Corporation (SMIPC), USA**
2360 East Devon Avenue, Suite 2010
Des Plaines IL 60018
Phone: 847/688-1080   Fax: 847/699-6866
FARA#: 3477   ORD: 5/25/83

Small & Medium Industry Promotion Corp.
CRD: 11/25/83   Korea

Smith McCabe, Ltd.
230 Park Avenue, Suite 1532
New York NY 10169
FARA#: 4687   ORD: 6/26/92

Japan External Trade Organization (JETRO)
CRD: 12/5/97   Japan

Smith, Anne Victoria
1100 17th Street, NW - Suite 605
Washington DC 20036
Phone: 202/955-6868   Fax: 202/955-6866
FARA#: 5177   ORD: 4/25/97

Embassy of Lithuania
CRD: 7/18/97   Lithuania

Smith, Dawson & Andrews, Inc.
1000 Connecticut Ave., NW, Suite 302
Washington DC 20036
Phone: 202/835-0740   Fax: 202/775-8526
URL: http://www.sda__inc.com
FARA#: 5085   ORD: 12/12/95

Embassy of Japan
CRD: 10/27/97   Japan

Estafeta Mexicana, S.A. de C.V.
CRD: 12/12/95   Mexico

Promstroy Bank of Russia
CRD: 12/18/97   Russia

Somaliland Republic Office
P.O. Box 90917

Washington DC 20009
Phone: 202/452-5545   FARA#: 3640
ORD: 1/18/85

Somali National Movement
CRD: 1/18/85   Somalia

South African Tourism Board
500 Fifth Avenue - Suite 2040
New York NY 10110-0002
Phone: 800/822-5368   Fax: 212/764-1980
FARA#: 603   ORD: 1/4/50

South African Tourist Corporation
CRD: 1/4/50   South Africa

Spring, O'Brien, Tolson & Company, Inc.
50 West 23rd Street - 11th Floor
New York NY 10100
FARA#: 3661   ORD: 3/19/85

British Trade Development Office
CRD: 3/19/85   United Kingdom

Devon & Cornwall Development Bureau
CRD: 4/21/88   United Kingdom

Inward, Ltd.
CRD: 4/21/88   United Kingdom

Sremac, Danielle
2500 Wisconsin Avenue, NW, Apt. 433
Washington DC 20007
FARA#: 4932   ORD: 7/29/94

Government of Republika Srpska
CRD: 7/29/94   Bosnia & Herzegovina

St. Lucia National Development Corporation
820 Second Avenue, Suite 900-E
New York NY 10017
Phone: 212/867-2952   Fax: 212/370-7867
E-mail: stluciadc@aol.com
URL: http://www.stluciadc.com
FARA#: 2796   ORD: 6/24/77

National Development Corporation
CRD: 6/24/77   St. Lucia

St. Lucia Tourist Board
820 Second Avenue, Suite 900-E
New York NY 10017
Phone: 212/867-2950   Fax: 212/867-2795
URL: http://www.interknowledge.com/St-Lucia.
FARA#: 2668   ORD: 3/15/76

St. Lucia Tourist Board
CRD: 3/15/76   St. Lucia

Staton, David Michael
Capitol Link
11490 Commerce Park Drive, Suite 130
Reston VA 20191
Phone: 703/758-1911   Fax: 703/758-1915
E-mail: mick@caplink.com
FARA#: 5002   ORD: 3/10/95

Federated States of Micronesia, Embassy
CRD: 3/10/95   Micronesia

Stearns, John Norton
48 South 14th Street
San Jose CA 95112
FARA#: 5232   ORD: 2/9/98

Dr. Karl Dobler
CRD: 2/9/98   Switzerland

Steptoe & Johnson LLP
1330 Connecticut Ave., NW
Washington DC 20036-1795
Phone: 202/429-3000   Fax: 202/429-3902

E-mail: WBatterton@steptoe.com
URL: http://www.steptoe.com
FARA#: 3975   ORD: 5/8/87

Caribbean Ispat, Ltd.
CRD: 8/11/97   International

Embassy of the Government of Canada
CRD: 2/28/90   Canada

Government of Trinidad and Tobago
CRD: 9/4/97   International

Intern'l. Airline Coalition on the Rule of Law
CRD: 7/15/96   International

Stewart & Stewart
2100 M Street, N.W., Suite 200
Washington DC 20037
Phone: 202/785-4185   Fax: 202/466-1286
E-mail: general@stewartlaw.com
FARA#: 4709   ORD: 9/21/92

Kiev International Expansion Venture - K.I.E.V.
CRD: 12/15/92   Ukraine

Stovall III, James T.
1725 N Street, NW
Washington DC 20036
FARA#: 3940   ORD: 2/25/87

Gov't. of the Federated States of Micronesia
CRD: 2/25/87   Micronesia

Strategic Policy, Inc.
FNA Strategic Planning. Inc.
1615 L Street, NW, Suite 650
Washington DC 20036
Phone: 202/659-0878   Fax: 202/659-3010
FARA#: 4206   ORD: 1/13/89

Alcan Aluminum, Ltd.
CRD: 8/12/96   Canada

Strauss, Joseph A.
2550 M Street, NW
Washington DC 20037
FARA#: 5214   ORD: 10/15/97

Embassy of the Republic of Turkey
CRD: 10/15/97   Turkey

Stroock, Stroock, & Lavan
180 Maiden Lane
New York NY 10038
FARA#: 5141   ORD: 4/23/96

Palestinian National Authority
CRD: 4/23/96   Palestine

Stuntz, Davis & Staffier, P.C.
1201 Pennsylvania Avenue, NW - Suite 819
Washington DC 20004
Phone: 202/662-6790   Fax: 202/624-0866
FARA#: 5194   ORD: 6/23/97

NOVA Gas International, Ltd.
CRD: 6/23/97   International

**Sveriges Television AB
  (Swedish Broadcasting Corporation)**
747 Third Avenue
New York NY 10017
FARA#: 1676   ORD: 1/2/64

Sveriges Radio Aktiebolag
CRD: 6/14/89   Sweden

Swedish Travel & Tourism Council
DBA "Next Stop Sweden"
Grand Central Station
PO Box 4649

New York NY 10163-4649
FARA#: 4885   ORD: 1/26/94

Swedish Travel & Tourism Council AB
CRD: 7/31/94   Sweden

Swidler & Berlin, Chartered
3000 K St., NW, Suite 300
Washington DC 20007-3841
Phone: 202/424-7500   Fax: 202/424-7643
FARA#: 4079   ORD: 1/7/88

Government of Republic of Liberia
CRD: 9/17/97   Liberia

Secretaria de Comunicaciones y Transportes
CRD: 1/31/96   Mexico

Switzerland Tourism
608 Fifth Avenue
New York NY 10020-2303
FARA#: 55   ORD: 3/1/43

Swiss Federal Railroads
CRD: 3/1/43   Switzerland

Swiss National Tourist Office
CRD: 3/27/73   Switzerland

Symms, Lehn & Associates, Inc.
210 Cameron St.
Alexandria VA 22314
Phone: 703/548-4205   Fax: 703/519-9212
FARA#: 4880   ORD: 12/21/93

*TECRO, Taipei Economic & Cultural
Representatives Office*
CRD: 12/21/93   Taiwan

**Taiwan Democratic Progressive Party Mission
in the US**
National Press Building
592 14th Street, NW - Suite 600
Washington DC 20045
Phone: 202/737-4443   Fax: 202/737-4411
FARA#: 5013   ORD: 4/12/95

Taiwan Democratic Progressive Party
CRD: 4/12/95   Taiwan

Tele-Press Associates, Inc.
321 East 53rd Street
New York NY 10022
FARA#: 2832   ORD: 9/30/77

Japan Fisheries Association
CRD: 9/30/77   Japan

Japan Whaling Association
CRD: 11/14/79   Japan

Thomson-CSF, Inc.
99 Canal Center Plaza, Suite 450
Alexandria VA 22314
Phone: 703/838-9685   Fax: 703/838-1688
URL: http://www.thomson-csf.com
FARA#: 4628   ORD: 4/2/92

Thomson-CSF, S.A.
CRD: 4/2/92   France

Tirana, Bardyl R.
4401 Connecticut Ave., NW, Suite 700
Washington DC 20008-2322
Phone: 202/244-0437   Fax: 202/363-8179
FARA#: 4863   ORD: 10/22/93

Republic of Kosova
CRD: 10/22/93   Kosova

TKC International, Inc.
444 North Capitol St., NW, Suite 841

Washington DC 20001
Phone: 202/638-7030   Fax: 202/638-6784
FARA#: 3075   ORD: 12/13/79

Allthane Technologies
CRD. 1/9/94   International

International Public Relations Company, Ltd.
CRD: 9/10/81   Japan

Tourism Authority of Thailand, Chicago
303 East Wacker Drive, Suite 400
Chicago IL 60601
FARA#: 4622   ORD: 2/21/92

Tourism Authority of Thailand
CRD: 2/21/92   Thailand

Tourism Authority of Thailand, Los Angeles
611 North Larchmont Boulevard, 1st Floor
Los Angeles CA 90004
FARA#: 2178   ORD: 12/19/69

Tourism Authority of Thailand
CRD: 12/19/69   Thailand

Tourism Authority of Thailand, New York
ATT Chalermsak Suranant
Five World Trade Center, Suite 3443
New York NY 10048
FARA#: 1897   ORD: 6/1/65

Tourism Authority of Thailand
CRD: 6/1/85   Thailand

Tourism New South Wales
13737 Fuji Way, Suite C-10
Marina Del Rey CA 90292
FARA#: 4450   ORD: 12/18/90

New South Wales Tourism Commission
CRD: 12/18/90   Australia

TransPacific Communications Research Co.
582 Market Street, Suite 516
San Francisco CA 94104
FARA#: 4173   ORD: 8/26/88

JETRO, San Francisco
CRD: 8/26/88   Japan

Tripp, Umbach & Associates, Inc.
Fort Pitt Commons
445 Fort Pitt Boulevard, Suite 220
Pittsburgh PA 15219
FARA#: 4724   ORD: 10/20/92

West Midlands Development Agency
CRD: 10/20/92   United Kingdom

Trombone Associates, Inc.
420 Madison Avenue
New York NY 10017
FARA#: 4601   ORD: 12/06/91

Antigua Ministry of Tourism
CRD: 12/6/91   Antigua and Barbuda

German Convention Bureau
CRD: 12/6/91   Germany

German National Tourist Office
CRD: 12/6/91   Germany

Grenada Board of Tourism
CRD: 8/30/96   Grenada

Turks & Caicos Tourist Board
CRD: 3/2/94   Turks and Caicos Islands

Trouillot, Mildred
168 John Brown Ave.

Port-au-Prince HA FARA#: 4763   ORD: 2/8/93

Government of Haiti, Embassy
CRD: 2/8/93   Haiti

**U.S. Representative Office of the Japan
Development Bank**
1101 17th Street, NW - Suite 1001
Washington DC 20036
Phone: 202/331-8696   Fax: 202/293-3932
FARA#: 5152   ORD: 1/21/97

Japan Development Bank
CRD: 1/21/97   Japan

Urenco, Inc.
2600 Virginia Avenue, NW, Suite 610
Washington DC 20037
Phone: 202/337-6644   Fax: 202/337-2421
FARA#: 5137   ORD: 11/8/96

Urenco, Ltd.
CRD: 11/8/97   International

Uzbekistan Government Tourist Board
60 East 42nd Street, Suite 2308
New York NY 10165
FARA#: 5145   ORD: 12/12/96

Ministry of Tourism of the Rep. of Uzbekistan
CRD: 12/12/96   Uzbekistan

Van Ness Feldman, A Professional Corp.
1050 Thomas Jefferson Street, N.W., 7th Floor
Washington DC 20007
Phone: 202/298-1800   Fax: 202/338-2416
E-mail: vnf@vnf.com
FARA#: 4696   ORD: 7/27/92

Foothills Pipe Lines, Ltd.
CRD: 8/11/94   Canada

Varney, Kevin P.
4526 Verplanck Place, NW
Washington DC 20016
FARA#: 5223   ORD: 12/27/97

*Office of the Prime Minister Mesut Yilmaz -
Republic of Turkey*
CRD: 12/29/97   Turkey

**Verner, Liipfert, Bernhard, McPherson &
Hand, Chartered**
901 15th Street, NW - Suite 700
Washington DC 20005-2301
Phone: 202/371-6000   Fax: 202/371-6279
URL: http://www.verner.com
FARA#: 3712   ORD: 8/5/85

Government of Chile
CRD: 10/3/97   Chile

Government of the Marshall Islands
CRD: 2/21/96   Marshall Islands

Republic of China (Taiwan)
CRD: 1/6/98   China

The Government of Uruguay
CRD: 11/16/95   Uruguay

Veve, Michael E.
2300 N Street, N.W., Suite 600
Washington DC 20037
Phone: 202/663-9087   Fax: 202/663-9013
FARA#: 4751   ORD: 1/13/93

Embassy of El Salvador
CRD: 1/13/93   El Salvador

Via/Net Companies
836 East Washington Street

San Diego CA 92103
FARA#: 4856   ORD: 10/04/93

Tongasat, Kingdom Of Tonga
CRD: 10/4/93   Tonga

W.D.B. Advertising
ATT Albert D. Van Brunt, President
419 East 57th St.
New York NY 10022
FARA#: 4376   ORD: 5/17/90

Barbados Industrial Development Corporation
CRD: 5/17/90   Barbados

Ward, Curtis A.
8121 Georgia Avenue, NW, Suite 801
Washington DC 20910-4933
FARA#: 4590   ORD: 11/07/91

Government of Jamaica
CRD: 11/7/91   Jamaica

Washington Group
1401 K Street, NW, Suite 400
Washington DC 20005
Phone: 202/789-2111   Fax: 202/789-4883
FARA#: 4332   ORD: 1/18/90

Embassy of the Government of India
CRD: 1/25/94   India

Nat'l Ass'n of Software & Service Companies
CRD: 12/1/95   India

Taipei Economic and Cultural Rep. Office
CRD: 2/2/94   Taiwan

Washington Policy & Analysis, Inc.
1025 Thomas Jefferson St., NW - Suite 411 West
Washington DC 20007
Phone: 202/965-1161   Fax: 202/965-1177
FARA#: 4611   ORD: 1/31/92

Federation of Electric Power Co's. of Japan
CRD: 6/22/94   Japan

Tokyo Electric Power Company
CRD: 1/31/92   Japan

Washington World Group, Ltd.
Law Offices of Robert W. Johnson II
2120 L Street, NW, Suite 210
Washington DC 20037
Phone: 202/463-7820   Fax: 202/223-3754
FARA#: 5016   ORD: 4/20/95

Office of the President of the Rep. of the Congo
CRD: 12/18/96   Congo, Republic of

Republic of the Gambia, Embassy
CRD: 12/18/97   Gambia

Wasserman, Gary
3626 Van Ness Street, NW
Washington DC 20008
Phone: 202/966-9199   Fax: 202/362-7222
E-mail: GWASSER115@aol.com
FARA#: 4981   ORD: 12/14/94

*Board of Foreign Trade, Ministry of
   Economic Affairs*
CRD: 12/14/94   Taiwan

Weber Group
101 Main Street, 8th Floor
Cambridge MA 02142
FARA#: 5250   ORD: 3/24/98

*Taiwan Ministry of Foreign Affairs,
   Board of Foreign Trade*
CRD: 3/24/98   Taiwan

Webster, Chamberlain & Bean
1747 Pennsylvania Avenue, NW, Suite 1000
Washington DC 20006
Phone: 202/785-9500   FARA#: 5136
ORD: 10/16/96

Sandline International
CRD: 10/16/96   International

Weil, Gotshal & Manges
ATT Bruce H. Turnbull
1615 L Street, NW - Suite 700
Washington DC 20036
Phone: 202/682-7000   Fax: 202/857-0939
FARA#: 3317   ORD: 12/29/81

Government of Chile
CRD: 9/12/95   Chile

Welch, Edmund Burt
1600 Wilson Boulevard - Suite 1000A
Arlington VA 22209
Phone: 703/807-0100   Fax: 703/807-0103
FARA#: 5216   ORD: 10/15/97

Union of Greek Shipowners
CRD: 10/15/97   Greece

Welsh Development International
85 Wells Avenue, Suite 200
Newton MA 02159
Phone: 617/928-3585   Fax: 617/928-3578
FARA#: 3819   ORD: 4/24/86

Welsh Development Agency (WINvest)
CRD: 4/24/86   United Kingdom

West Glen Communications
1430 Broadway
New York NY 10018
FARA#: 4191   ORD: 11/23/88

Federal Republic of Germany
CRD: 11/23/88   Germany

German Information Center
CRD: 11/23/88   Germany

Israeli Government Tourist Office
CRD: 11/23/88   Israel

West Indies Communications Group, Ltd.
18 Broad Street, Suite 405
Charleston SC 29401
FARA#: 5193   ORD: 8/4/97

Government of St. Vincent and the Grenadines
CRD: 8/4/97   St. Vincent and the Grenadines

White & Case
ATT Marvin J. Miller, Jr.
1155 Avenue of the Americas
New York NY 10036-2787
FARA#: 2759   ORD: 3/9/77

Central Bank of the Republic of Turkey
CRD: 11/9/78   Turkey

Federal Republic of Nigeria
CRD: 4/9/90   Nigeria

Kingdom of Thailand
CRD: 10/10/89   Thailand

Polish People's Republic
CRD: 10/9/91   Poland

Republic of Bulgaria
CRD: 4/9/92   Bulgaria

Republic of Croatia
CRD: 10/11/96   Croatia

Republic of Gabon
CRD: 5/2/78   Gabon

Republic of Guinea
CRD: 1/15/85   Guinea

Republic of Indonesia
CRD: 3/9/77   Indonesia

Republic of Kyrgyzstan
CRD: 11/13/97   Kyrgyzstan

Republic of Singapore
CRD: 1/24/79   Singapore

Republic of Suriname
CRD: 5/16/85   Suriname

Republic of Uzbekistan
CRD: 11/13/97   Uzbekistan

State Bank of Vietnam
CRD: 4/24/96   Vietnam

The Kingdom of Morocco
CRD: 5/16/85   Morocco

Whitehouse Associates, Inc.
DBA International Public Relations Co., Ltd.
523 West 6th Street, Suite 804
Los Angeles CA 90014-1222
FARA#: 2190   ORD: 2/24/70

Consulate General of Japan
CRD: 2/24/70   Japan

Whitmore, Judith M.
DBA International Communications Consulting
240 Old Silo Road
Ridgefield CT 06877
FARA#: 4336   ORD: 2/5/90

Cambridge Beaches Resort
CRD: 9/22/92   Bermuda

Wigman, Cohen, Leitner & Myers, P.C.
900 17th Street, NW - Suite 1000
Washington DC 20006
Phone: 202/463-7700   Fax: 202/463-6915
E-mail: iplaw@laser.net
FARA#: 4929   ORD: 7/22/94

New Zealand Dairy Board
CRD: 7/22/94   New Zealand

New Zealand Meat Producers Board
CRD: 7/22/94   New Zealand

William D. Harris & Associates, Inc.
1156 15th Street, NW - Suite 550
Washington DC 20005
Phone: 202/861-1922   Fax: 202/861-1947
FARA#: 5071   ORD: 11/09/95

Government of St. Vincent & the Grenadines
CRD: 11/9/95   St. Vincent and the Grenadines

Willkie Farr & Gallagher
Three Lafayette Center
1155 21st Street, NW
Washington DC 20036-3384
Phone: 202/328-8000   Fax: 202/887-8979
FARA#: 3765   ORD: 12/26/85

*Fair Trade Center, Institute for International
   Trade & Investment*
CRD: 2/20/91   Japan

Japan Iron & Steel Exporters' Association
CRD: 12/26/85   Japan

Winston & Strawn

1400 L St., NW
Washington DC 20005-3502
Phone: 202/371-5700   Fax: 202/371-5950
FARA#: 3869   ORD: 8/13/86

Department of Defense, Philippines
CRD: 4/24/97   Philippines

Government of Aruba
CRD: 5/18/95   Aruba

Government of Aruba
CRD: 5/18/95   Aruba

World Zionist Org. - American Section, Inc.
ATT Sam Zelig Chinitz
110 East 59th Street
New York NY 10022
FARA#: 2278   ORD: 9/21/71

The Exec. of the World Zionist Org., Jerusalem
CRD: 9/21/71   Israel

Wunder, Knight, Levine, Thelen & Forscey, PLLC
1615 L Street, NW, Suite 650
Washington DC 20036
Phone: 202/659-3005   Fax: 202/659-3010
FARA#: 3971   ORD: 4/29/87

Government of Bermuda
CRD: 7/25/89   Bermuda

Xin Min International, Inc.
1520 South Garfield Avenue
Alhambra CA 91801
FARA#: 4969   ORD: 11/07/94

Xin Min Evening Newspaper
CRD: 11/7/94   China

YHDA International
28 Junction Square
Concord MA 01742
FARA#: 4421   ORD: 10/12/90

Yorkshire & Humberside Development Association
CRD: 10/12/90   International

Yitzhaki, Eliyahu
4455 Connecticut Avenue, NW - Suite B-400
Washington DC 20008
Phone: 202/895-5290   Fax: 202/895-5298
FARA#: 5211   ORD: 9/15/97

Rafael USA, Inc.
CRD: 9/15/97   International

Zambia National Tourist Board
ATT E.P. Tembo
800 Second Avenue
New York NY 10017
FARA#: 2293   ORD: 12/06/71

*Zambia National Tourist Bureau,
   Ministry of Information*
CRD: 12/6/71   Zambia

Zapruder & Odell
601 13th Street, NW - Suite 720 North
Washington DC 20005
Phone: 202/508-9600   Fax: 202/508-9601
FARA#: 5019   ORD: 5/15/95

*Thommessen Krefting Greve Lund, A.S.,
   Advokat Firma*
CRD: 5/15/95   Norway

Zemi Communications, LLC
461 Fifth Avenue, 12th Floor
New York NY 10017

FARA#: 5120   ORD: 7/1/96

Banco do Nordeste do Brasil, S.A.
CRD: 2/25/97   Brazil

Instituto Brasiliero De turismo (Embratur)
CRD: 1/30/98   Brazil

Zuckert, Scoutt & Rasenberger, L.L.P.
888 17th Street, NW - Suite 600
Washington DC 20006-3959
Phone: 202/298-8660   Fax: 202/342-0683
E-mail: ZSR@tcmco.net
FARA#: 4933   ORD: 8/1/94

Civil Aviation Authority of Macau
CRD: 8/1/94   Macao

INTRODUCTION

The international media located in Washington, D.C., serve as the outposts for their home countries. They are the eyes and ears for millions of residents back home who are interested in what is happening in the United States.

Washington's international press corps is the largest in the world. It is safe to say that one can reach almost any corner of the globe through the Washington international press corps. For working with the media to communicate a message around the world, there is no more advantageous venue than Washington, D.C.

International reporters, just like U.S. reporters, are always looking for good stories and sources of information. An individual or organization which is credible and factual can build a good relationship with these reporters and help insure that reporting on a particular issue is more likely to include that individual or organization's point of view, assuming it is a legitimate one.

The following list of international media representatives in Washington, D.C. is in order by foreign country and organization.

Africa

West Africa
Mr. James Butty
Washington Correspondent
Post Office Box 29161
Washington DC 20017
Phone: 301/779-1382

Argentina

Editorial Atlantida
Ms. Ana Baron Supervielle
Washington Correspondent
3271 Prospect Street, NW
Washington DC 20007
Phone: 202/338-5703   Fax: 202/337-2242

La Nacion
Mr. Jorge Elias
Washington Correspondent
901 National Press Bldg.
Washington DC 20045
Phone: 202/628-7907   Fax: 202/333-1053

Asia

Asia Today Magazine International
Mr. Raghubir Goyal
Editor and Publisher
2020 National Press Building
Washington DC 20045
Phone: 202/271-1100   Fax: 703/978-7572

Asia TV Network News
Mr. Raghubir Goyal
Editor and Publisher
2020 National Press Building
Washington DC 20045
Phone: 202/271-1100   Fax: 703/978-7572

Washington Chinese Television
Mr. Michael Liu
President
8212-A Old Courthouse Road
Vienna VA 22182
Phone: 703/760-9091   Fax: 703/760-9093

Australia

2UE Radio Network
Ms. Connie Lawn
Washington Correspondent
3622 Stanford Circle
Falls Church VA 22041
Phone: 703/354-6795

Australian Broadcasting Corp. (Radio)
Ms. Agnes Cusack
Washington Correspondent
510 National Press Bldg., 529 14th Street
Washington DC 20045
Phone: 202/626-5160   Fax: 202/626-5188

Australian Broadcasting Corp. (TV)
Mr. Mark Bannerman
Washington Correspondent
510 National Press Bldg., 529 14th Street
Washington DC 20045
Phone: 202/626-5160   Fax: 202/626-5188

Australian Financial Review
Ms. Colleen Ryan
Washington Correspondent
1331 Pennsylvania Avenue, NW - Suite 904
Washington DC 20004
Phone: 202/639-8084   Fax: 202/639-8036

John Fairfax US Limited
Ms. Jennifer Hewett
Washington Correspondent
1331 Pennsylvania Avenue, NW - Suite 904
Washington DC 20004
Phone: 202/639-8084   Fax: 202/639-8036

Melbourne Age
Ms. Jennifer Hewett
Washington Correspondent
1331 Pennsylvania Avenue, NW - Suite 904
Washington DC 20004
Phone: 202/737-6360   Fax: 202/639-8036

Radio Pacific-New Zealand & Australian Radio Station
Ms. Connie Lawn
Washington Correspondent
3622 Stanford Circle
Falls Church VA 22041
Phone: 703/354-6795

Sydney Morning Herald
Ms. Jennifer Hewett
Washington Correspondent
1331 Pennsylvania Avenue, NW - Suite 904
Washington DC 20004
Phone: 202/737-6360   Fax: 202/639-8036

Austria

Deutsche Fernsehagentur (TV)
Mr. Roger Horne
Washington Correspondent
1199 National Press Bldg.
Washington DC 20045
Phone: 202/393-7571   Fax: 202/393-8554

Die Presse
Ms. Monica Riedler
Washington Correspondent
1703 Seaton Street, NW
Washington DC 20009
Phone: 202/986-7203   Fax: 202/986-0729
E-mail: mriedler@aol.com

ORF/Austrian Radio and Television
Mr. Eugen Freund
Bureau Chief
1206 Eton Court, NW
Washington DC 20007
Phone: 202/822-9570   Fax: 202/822-9569
E-mail: 10072,3554@compuserve.com

Vorarlberger Nachrichten
Ms. Dagmar Schroeder
Washington Correspondent
4100 Massachusetts Ave., NW
Washington DC 20016
Phone: 202/244-7013   Fax: 202/244-7069

Wirtschaftwoche (Daily)
Mr. Peter Schroeder
Washington Correspondent
4100 Massachusetts Ave., NW
Washington DC 20016
Phone: 202/244-7013   Fax: 202/244-7069

Belgium

L'Echo
Mr. Yve Janssens Laudy
Washington Correspondent
P.O. Box 6613
Arlington VA 22206
Phone: 202/667-8308   Fax: 202/667-3465

La Libre Belgique
Ms. Yve J. Laudy
Washington Correspondent
P.O. Box 6613
Arlington VA 22206
Phone: 202/667-8308
E-mail: laudyve@aol.com

Brazil

Jornal do Brasil
Ms. Flavia Sekles
Bureau Chief and Wash. Correspondent
5302 Albemarle Street
Bethesda MD 20816
Phone: 301/320-5296   Fax: 301/320-6734
E-mail: flavia.seles@pressroom.com

Jornal do Commercio
Mr. Jose Leme
Washington Correspondent
3522 King Arthur Rd.
Annandale VA 22003
Phone: 703/560-2232   Fax: 703/560-2232

O Estado de Sao Paulo
Mr. Paulo Sotero
Washington Correspondent
1225 Eye Street, NW - Suite 810
Washington DC 20005
Phone: 202/682-3752   Fax: 202/289-5475

TV Globo
Mr. Luis Fernando Silva-Pinto
Washington Correspondent
2141 Wisconsin Ave., NW - Suite L
Washington DC 20007
Phone: 202/429-2525   Fax: 202/429-1713

Canada

Broadcast News Limited
Mr. Robert Russo
Bureau Chief
1331 Pennsylvania Avenue, NW - Suite 524
Washington DC 20004
Phone: 202/638-3367   Fax: 202/638-3369

Canadian Broadcasting Corp./Societe Radio-Canada
Ms. Genevieve Ast
Manager, U.S. Operations
National Press Bldg. - Suite 500
Washington DC 20045
Phone: 202/383-2900   Fax: 202/383-2901

Canadian Press
Mr. Robert Russo
Bureau Chief
1331 Pennsylvania Avenue, NW
Washington DC 20004
Phone: 202/638-3367   Fax: 202/638-3369

CTV-Canadian Television
Mr. Alan Fryer
Washington Correspondent
2030 M Street, NW - Suite 602
Washington DC 20036
Phone: 202/466-3595   Fax: 202/296-2025
E-mail: 102676.1130@compuserve.com

Edmonton Sun
Mr. Patrick Harden
Washington Correspondent
8202 Excalibur Court
Annandale VA 22003-1343
Phone: 703/876-0594

Financial Post
Mr. Peter Morton
Bureau Chief
1225 I Street, NW - Suite 810
Washington DC 20005
Phone: 202/842-1190   Fax: 202/842-4441

Global TV
Mr. Carl Hanlon
Washington Correspondent
1333 H Street, NW - Suite 500
Washington DC 20005
Phone: 202/842-1254   Fax: 202/842-1424
E-mail: globtv@erols.com

Globe and Mail (Canada)

Mr. Andrew Cohen
Washington Correspondent
1331 Pennsylvania Avenue, NW - Suite 524
Washington DC 20004
Phone: 202/662-7165   Fax: 202/662-7112

Kipling News Service
Mr. Bogdan Kipling
Editor
12611 Farnell Drive
Silver Spring MD 20906
Phone: 301/929-0760   Fax: 301/949-8519

L'Actualite
Mr. Marc Gilbert
Correspondent
1516 33rd St. NW
Washington DC 20007
Phone: 202/337-4270

Maclean's
Mr. Andrew Phillips
Washington Correspondent
994 National Press Building
Washington DC 20045
Phone: 202/662-7321   Fax: 202/662-7341

Southam News Service
Mr. Julian Beltrame
Washington Correspondent
1206 National Press Building
Washington DC 20045
Phone: 202/662-7225   Fax: 202/662-7336

Telemedia
Mr. Standford Richardson
Washington Correspondent
2146 Georgia Avenue, NW
Washington DC 20001
Phone: 202/588-0666

Thomson Newspapers of Canada
Mr. Andrew Cohen
Washington Correspondent
1331 Pennsylvania Avenue, NW - Suite 524
Washington DC 20004
Phone: 202/628-2157   Fax: 202/662-7112
E-mail: globeandmail.wash@pressroom.com

Toronto Star
Ms. Kathleen Kenna
Washington Correspondent
982 National Press Building
Washington DC 20045
Phone: 202/662-7390   Fax: 202/662-7388

Toronto Sun Newspapers
Mr. Patrick Harden
Washington Columnist
8202 Excalibur Court
Annandale VA 22003
Phone: 703/876-0594   Fax: 703/849-9069

Chile

Channel 13
Ms. Cecilia Domeyko
Washington Correspondent
6731 Whittier Ave. - Suite 310
McLean VA 22101
Phone: 202/298-6839   Fax: 202/445-8534

China

China Medical Tribune

Mr. Curtis C. Cutter
Bureau Chief
1010 Wisconsin Avenue, NW - Suite 310
Washington DC 20007
Phone: 202/337-4442   Fax: 202/337-4498
E-mail: curtcutter@aol.com

China Radio International
Mr. Zhenbang Dong
Bureau Chief
2000 South Eads Street
Arlington VA 22202
Phone: 703/521-7556   Fax: 703/521-7560

China Youth Daily
Mr. Xiang Weng
Bureau Chief
1900 South Eads Street - Suite 1104
Arlington VA 22202
Phone: 703/271-4354   Fax: 703/271-8099

Guangming Daily
Mr. Fukang Xue
Bureau Chief
4816 Butterworth Place, NW
Washington DC 20016
Phone: 202/363-0628   Fax: 202/244-5956

The People's Daily
Mr. Li Yunfei
Bureau Chief
3706 Massachusetts Avenue, NW
Washington DC 20016
Phone: 202/966-2285   Fax: 202/966-8693

Wen Hui Bao Daily
Mr. Xingfu Zhu
Bureau Chief
1600 S. Eads Street - Suite 1134-N
Arlington VA 22202
Phone: 703/521-2371

Xinhua News Agency
Mr. Li Hong Qi
Bureau Chief
1740 N. 14th Street
Arlington VA 22209
Phone: 703/875-0082   Fax: 703/875-0086

Cyprus

Cyprus News Agency (CNA)
Mr. Dimitris Apokis
Bureau Chief
4201 Massachusetts Avenue, NW, #A249C
Washington DC 20016-4726
Phone: 202/686-2522   Fax: 202/686-0767
E-mail: apokis@email.msn.com

Czech Republic

Czech Radio
Mr. Jan Smid
Washington Correspondent
4849 Connecticut Avenue, NW, Apt. 204
Washington DC 20008
Phone: 202/244-6020   Fax: 202/362-3183

Denmark

Berlingske Tidende
Mr. Flemming Rose
U.S. Editor

1331 Pennsylvania Avenue, NW
Washington DC 20004
Phone: 202/347-1744   Fax: 202/347-2158
E-mail: rosefe@aol.com

Danish Broadcasting Corp. (Radio)
Mr. Torben Rasmussen
Radio Bureau Chief
2030 M Street, NW - Suite 700
Washington DC 20036
Phone: 202/785-1957   Fax: 202/785-5834

Danish Broadcasting Corp. (TV)
Mr. Torsten Jensen
Television Bureau Chief
2030 M Street, NW - Suite 700
Washington DC 20036
Phone: 202/785-1957   Fax: 202/785-5834

Jyllands-Posten
Mr. Michael Ulvemen
Bureau Chief and Wash. Correspondent
1934 35th Street, NW
Washington DC 20007
Phone: 202/965-4279
E-mail: ulveman@compuserv.com

TV2/Denmark
Mr. Allan Silberbrandt
Bureau Chief and Wash. Correspondent
2030 M Street, NW - Suite 510
Washington DC 20036
Phone: 202/828-4555   Fax: 202/828-8367

Egypt

Akhbaar-El-Yom
Mr. Maha Abdel Fattah
Bureau Chief
4701 Willard Avenue - Suite 1002
Chevy Chase MD 20815
Phone: 301/654-5610   Fax: 301/654-5675

Al Ahram
Mr. Atefi El-Ghamry
President and Bureau Chief
National Press Bldg. - Suite 1112
Washington DC 20045
Phone: 202/737-2121   Fax: 202/737-2122

Middle East News Agency
Mr. Khaled M. Khodeir
Bureau Chief
4530 Connecticut Avenue, NW - Suite 502
Washington DC 20008
Phone: 202/362-4995   Fax: 202/362-5001
E-mail: khaledk@erols.com

Finland

BBC Finnish Service
Ms. Marketta Kopinski
Washington Correspondent
3727 Albemarle Street, NW
Washington DC 20016
Phone: 202/966-0822   Fax: 202/364-8396
E-mail: 7353.3054@compuserve.com

Finnish Broadcasting Co.
Mr. Reijo Lindroos
Bureau Chief
2030 M Street, NW - Suite 700
Washington DC 20036
Phone: 202/785-2087   Fax: 202/785-5834
E-mail: risto@nmaa.org

Helsingin Sanomat
Mr. Tomi Ervamaa
Bureau Chief and Washington Correspondent
1726 M Street, NW - Suite 700
Washington DC 20036
Phone: 202/955-7956   Fax: 202/955-7958
E-mail: tomier@ix.netcom.com

France

Agence France-Presse
Mr. Pierre LeSourd
U. S. Bureau Chief
1015 15th Street, NW - Suite 500
Washington DC 20005
Phone: 202/289-0700   Fax: 202/414-0528

Dernieres Nouvelles D'Alsace
Mr. Yve J. Laudy
Washington Correspondent
Post Office Box 6613
Arlington VA 22206
Phone: 202/667-8308
E-mail: laudyve@aol.com

France 2 Television
Mr. Phillipe Gassot
Bureau Chief
2030 M Street, NW - Suite 502
Washington DC 20036
Phone: 202/833-1818   Fax: 202/833-2777

France Infos/France Inter
Mr. Philippe Reltien
Washington Correspondent
4940 Cathedral Avenue, NW
Washington DC 20016
Phone: 202/686-0963   Fax: 202/686-1485

International Herald Tribune
Mr. Brian Knowlton
Bureau Chief
1150 15th Street, NW
Washington DC 20071
Phone: 202/334-7418   Fax: 202/496-3928

Internews Media Services/
Internewsletter Inc.
Ms. Marie B. Allizon
Washington Bureau Chief
1063 National Press Bldg.
Washington DC 20045
Phone: 202/347-4575

Jacques Tiziou News Service
Mr. Jacques Tiziou
Editor
5152 Linnean Terrace, NW
Washington DC 20008
Phone: 202/966-6960   Fax: 202/537-3054
E-mail: j_tiziou@compuserve.com

Le Figaro
Mr. Jean-Jacques Mevel
Bureau Chief
1228 30th Street, NW
Washington DC 20007
Phone: 202/342-3199   Fax: 202/342-3194

Le Monde
Mr. Laurent Zecchini
Bureau Chief
6012 Kennedy Drive
Chevy Chase MD 20815
Phone: 301/986-8606   Fax: 301/986-8554

Liberation
Mr. Patrick Sabatier
Bureau Chief
1524 34th Street, NW
Washington DC 20007
Phone: 202/298-8580   Fax: 202/298-8581
E-mail: psabatier@aol.com

Radio France Internationale
Mr. Christian Billman
U.S. Representative and Bureau Chief
9519 East Stanhope Road
Kensington MD 20895
Phone: 301/929-6536   Fax: 301/929-6537

TF-1 Television Francaise
Mr. Ulysse Gosset
Bureau Chief
2100 M Street, NW - Suite 302
Washington DC 20037
Phone: 202/223-3642   Fax: 202/223-2196
E-mail: tflwash@worldnet.att.net

Germany

ARD German TV
Mr. Claus D. Kleber
Bureau Chief and TV Correspondent
3132 M Street, NW
Washington DC 20007
Phone: 202/298-6535   Fax: 202/342-9862

Bayerischer Rundfunk
Dr. Clemens Verenkotte
Washington Correspondent
1200 Eton Court, NW - Suite 200
Washington DC 20007-3239
Phone: 202/625-2503   Fax: 202/625-6814

Der Spiegel
Mr. Siegesmund Von Ilsemann
Bureau Chief
1202 National Press Building
Washington DC 20045
Phone: 202/347-5222   Fax: 202/347-3194
E-mail: 74431,736@compuserve.com

Deutsche Press-Agentur
Mr. Herbert Winkler
Bureau Chief
969 National Press Bldg.
Washington DC 20045
Phone: 202/783-5097   Fax: 202/783-4116

Deutsche Welle
Mr. Volker Strobel
Bureau Chief
2800 Shirlington Road - Suite 901
Arlington VA 22206
Phone: 703/931-6644   Fax: 703/931-6662

Die Welt
Mr. Gerd Grueggemann
Washington Correspondent
11148 Powder Horn Drive
Potomac MD 20854
Phone: 301/983-4177   Fax: 301/299-7928

Die Zeit
Mr. Michael Schwelien
Washington Correspondent
3421 Northampton Street, NW
Washington DC 20015
Phone: 202/244-3996   Fax: 202/244-3984
E-mail: schwelien@aol.com

EPD News Service
Mr. Konrad Ege
Washington Correspondent
4506 32nd Street
Mount Rainier MD 20712
Phone: 301/699-3908
E-mail: kege@compuserve.com

Frankfurter Allgemeine Zeitung
Mr. Leo Wieland
Bureau Chief
9413 Copenhaver Drive
Potomac MD 20854
Phone: 301/294-2345   Fax: 301/294-0102

Frankfurter Rundschau
Mr. Martin Winter
Bureau Chief
1624 19th Street, NW - Suite 301
Washington DC 20009
Phone: 202/265-7240   Fax: 202/265-7259

German Press Agency (DPA)
Mr. Herbert Winkler
Bureau Chief
969 Washington Press Building
Washington DC 20045
Phone: 202/783-8726   Fax: 202/783-4116

German Public Radio (ARD)
Mr. Clemens Verenkotte
Correspondent
1200 Eaton Ct., NW - Suite 200
Washington DC 20007
Phone: 202/625-2503   Fax: 202/625-6814

German Radio (NDR-WDR)
Mr. Udo Koelsch
Bureau Chief
3132 M St. NW
Washington DC 20007
Phone: 202/298-6535   Fax: 202/337-3889

German Television (ARD)
Mr. Claus Kleber
Washington Correspondent
3132 M Street, NW
Washington DC 20007
Phone: 202/298-6535   Fax: 202/298-5933

German TV News Agency
Mr. Roger Horne
Bureau Chief
1199 National Press Building
Washington DC 20045
Phone: 202/393-7571   Fax: 202/393-8554

Handelsblatt
Mr. Dietrich Zwaetz
Bureau Chief and Senior Editor
15321 Jones Ln. - North Potomac MD 20878
Phone: 301/926-2336   Fax: 301/926-2379

Mitteldeutscher Rundfunk
Mr. Ingolf Rackwitz
Washington Correspondent
1200 Eton Court, NW - Suite 200
Washington DC 20007-3239
Phone: 202/625-2503   Fax: 202/625-6814

Nachrichten fuer Aussenhandels info.
Dr. Rainer Lindberg
Washington Correspondent
412 National Press Building
Washington DC 20045
Phone: 202/662-7415   Fax: 202/662-7419

Rheinischer Merkur

Mr. Stephen-Gotz Richter
Washington Correspondent
927 15th Street, NW
Washington DC 20005
Phone: 202/898-4760   Fax: 202/898-4767
E-mail: srichter@tafnct.com

Sat. 1 German Television
Mr. Stephan Strothe
Bureau Chief and Wash. Correspondent
1620 I Street, NW - Suite 200
Washington DC 20006
Phone: 202/331-9400   Fax: 202/331-9508

Springer Foreign News Service
Mr. Cornel Faltin
Bureau Chief
4830 Brandywine Street, NW
Washington DC 20016
Phone: 202/342-3103   Fax: 202/342-3104

Sueddeutsche Zeitung
Mr. Peter de Thier
Washington Correspondent
905 Falls Bridge Lane, Post Office Box 977
Reston VA 20195
Phone: 703/406-4976   Fax: 703/406-4968

Sueddeutscher Rundfunk
Mr. Hans-Jurgen Maurus
Washington Correspondent
1200 Eton Court, NW - Suite 200
Washington DC 20007-3239
Phone: 202/625-2503   Fax: 202/625-6814

Suedwestfunk
Mr. Hans-Jurgen Maurus
Washington Correspondent
1200 Eton Court, NW - Suite 200
Washington DC 20007-3239
Phone: 202/625-2503   Fax: 202/625-6814

The Washington Journal
Mr. Gerald R. Kainz
Editor and Publisher
1113 National Press Building
Washington DC 20045
Phone: 202/628-0404   Fax: 703/938-2251

ZDF German Television
Mr. Klaus-Peter Siegloch
Bureau Chief
1077 31st Street, NW
Washington DC 20007
Phone: 202/333-3909   Fax: 202/333-9814

Greece

Agora Business Magazine
Mr. John Liveris
Bureau Chief
2500 Q Street, NW
Washington DC 20007
Phone: 202/965-1194

Eleftheri Ora
Mr. John Perdikis
Bureau Chief
6914 Selkirk Drive
Bethesda MD 20817
Phone: 301/907-3812   Fax: 301/907-3814

Flash Greek News Radio/Flash Mag.
Mr. John Liveris
Bureau Chief
2500 Q Street, NW

Washington DC 20007
Phone: 202/965-1194

Greece National TV
Mr. Dimitris Apokis
Bureau Chief
4201 Massachusetts Ave., NW, - Suite A249C
Washington DC 20016-4726
Phone: 202/686-2522   Fax: 202/686-0767
E-mail: apokis@email.msn.com

Greek Television (ERT)
Mr. Dimitris Y. Apokis
Bureau Chief
4201 Massachusetts Avenue, NW, A249C
Washington DC 20016-4726
Phone: 202/686-2522   Fax: 202/686-0767
E-mail: apokis@email.msn.com

Kathimerini
Mr. Alex Papachelas
U.S. Bureau Chief
3205 Cleveland Avenue, NW
Washington DC 20008
Phone: 202/234-1312   Fax: 202/337-3422

Makedonia
Mr. Elias P. Demetracopoulos
Washington Correspondent
1280 21st Street, NW - Suite 201
Washington DC 20036
Phone: 202/785-0912

MEGA Channel
Mr. Alex Papachelas
Washington Correspondent
3205 Cleveland Avenue, NW
Washington DC 20008
Phone: 202/234-1312   Fax: 202/337-3422

Ptisi Aerospace Magazine
Mr. John Liveris
Bureau Chief
2500 Q Street, NW
Washington DC 20007
Phone: 202/965-1194

Thessaloniki
Mr. Elias P. Demetracopoulos
Washington Correspondent
1280 21st Street, NW - Suite 201
Washington DC 20036
Phone: 202/785-0912

Guatemala

El Grafico of Guatemala
Mr. Cesar A. Orantes
Washington Correspondent
8907 Battery Road
Alexandria VA 22308
Phone: 703/360-2997   Fax: 703/360-3450
E-mail: orantes@pop.erols.com

El Imparcial
Mr. H. Hugo Perez
Washington Correspondent
2030 N. Clarendon Blvd. - Suite 309
Arlington VA 22201
Phone: 703/525-0177

Honduras

Channel 3 & 5 TV/Emisoras Unidas
  (HRN)

Mr. Jacobo Goldstein
Washington Correspondent
1069 National Press Bldg.
Washington DC 20045
Phone: 202/737-5349

La Tribuna
Mr. Jacobo Goldstein
Washington Correspondent
960A National Press Building
Washington DC 20045-2001
Phone: 202/737-5349

Hong Kong

Far Eastern Economic Review
Mr. Wong-Anan Nopporn
Interim Washington Bureau Chief
1025 Connecticut Avenue, NW - Suite 800
Washington DC 20036
Phone: 202/862-9286   Fax: 202/728-0624

Radio-Television Hong Kong
Mr. Simon Marks
Bureau Chief
1703 Rhode Island Ave. NW - Suite 405
Washington DC 20036
Phone: 202/269-9012   Fax: 202/269-9203

Hungary

Daily Nepszabasag
Mr. Oszkar Fuzes
U.S. Bureau Chief
4701 Willard Avenue - Suite 1603
Chevy Chase MD 20815
Phone: 301/986-5267   Fax: 301/986-5276
E-mail: 74143.1250@compuserve.com

Hungarian News Agency
Mr. Peter Racz
Washington Correspondent
8515 Farrell Drive
Chevy Chase MD 20815
Phone: 301/565-2221   Fax: 301/589-6907
E-mail: petrac@aol.com

Magyar Nemzet
Mr. Miklos Gabor
Washington Correspondent
750 Brewer House Road
Rockville MD 20852
Phone: 301/770-4601   Fax: 301/770-4603

India

Hindustan Times
Mr. N.C. Menon
Bureau Chief
5597 Seminary Road - Suite 2204 South
Falls Church VA 22041
Phone: 703/931-9038   Fax: 703/931-9087

India Globe
Mr. Raghubir Goyal
Editor and Publisher
2020 National Press Building
Washington DC 20045
Phone: 202/271-1100   Fax: 703/978-7572

Outlook
Ms. Ludwina A. Joseph
Washington Correspondent

1255 New Hampshire Avenue, NW - Suite 630
Washington DC 20036
Phone: 202/452-1462   Fax: 202/857-0619

Press Trust of India
Mr. T.V. Parasuram
Washington Correspondent
4450 South Park Avenue - Suite 1719
Chevy Chase MD 20815-3646
Phone: 301/951-8651

The Hindu
Dr. Sridhar Krishnaswami
Washington Correspondent
4701 Willard Avenue - Suite 1531
Chevy Chase MD 20815
Phone: 301/654-9038   Fax: 301/907-3493

United News of India
Mr. C.K. Arora
Washington Correspondent
1600 S. Eads Street - Suite 1126-N
Arlington VA 22202
Phone: 703/486-2696   Fax: 703/486-2963

Ireland

The Irish Times
Mr. Joe Carroll
Washington Bureau Chief
6221 Redwing Road
Bethesda MD 20817
Phone: 301/320-2308   Fax: 301/229-1036

Israel

Globes (Tel Aviv)
Mr. Yo'av Karny
Washington Correspondent
2120 16th St., NW - #404
Washington DC 20009
Phone: 202/265-8092

Israel Broadcasting Authority
Mr. Ehud Yaari
Bureau Chief
1620 I Street, NW
Washington DC 20006
Phone: 202/331-2859   Fax: 202/331-9064

Israeli TV
Mr. Jacob S. Ahimeir
Washington Correspondent
1620 Eye Street, NW - Suite 100
Washington DC 20006
Phone: 202/331-2859   Fax: 202/331-9064

The Jerusalem Report
Mr. Johnathan Broder
Washington Correspondent
6109 29th Street, NW
Washington DC 20015
Phone: 202/364-1913   Fax: 202/364-0366
E-mail: jdbroder@aol.com

Italy

ANSA Italian News Agency
Mr. Bruno Marolo
North American Bureau Chief
1285 National Press Bldg.
Washington DC 20045
Phone: 202/628-3317   Fax: 202/638-1792

Corriere Della Sera
Mr. Ennio Caretto
Bureau Chief
450 National Press Building
Washington DC 20045
Phone: 202/879-6733   Fax: 202/879-6735

Inter Press Service (IPS)
Mr. James Lobe
Bureau Chief
1293 National Press Building
Washington DC 20045
Phone: 202/662-7160   Fax: 202/662-7164

La Stampa
Mr. Andrea di Robilant
Bureau Chief and Wash. Correspondent
916/A National Press Building
Washington DC 20045
Phone: 202/347-5233   Fax: 202/347-5691

Japan

Akahata
Mr. Hiroshi Nishimura
Bureau Chief
978 National Press Bldg.
Washington DC 20045
Phone: 202/393-5238   Fax: 202/393-5239

Asahi Shimbun
Mr. Tatsuro Iwamura
Bureau Chief
1022 National Press Bldg.
Washington DC 20045
Phone: 202/783-0523   Fax: 202/783-0039

Chunichi Shimbun
Mr. Moriyoshi Sase
Bureau Chief
1012 National Press Building
Washington DC 20045
Phone: 202/783-9479   Fax: 202/628-9622

Fuji Television Network, Inc.
Mr. Makoto Wakamatsu
Bureau Chief
330 National Press Building
Washington DC 20045
Phone: 202/347-1600   Fax: 202/347-0724

Hokkaido Shimbun
Mr. Shinichiro Sakikawa
Bureau Chief
529 14th Street, NW - Suite 101
Washington DC 20045
Phone: 202/783-6033   Fax: 202/783-3944
E-mail: Sakikawa@pressroom.com

Jiji Press
Mr. Yasushi Tomiyama
Bureau Chief
550 National Press Building
Washington DC 20045
Phone: 202/783-4330   Fax: 202/783-1532

Kyodo News Service
Mr. Kazuyoshi Nishikura
Bureau Chief
400 National Press Building
Washington DC 20045
Phone: 202/347-5767   Fax: 202/393-2342

Mainichi Shimbun
Mr. Akiainori Takahata
Bureau Chief

340 National Press Building
Washington DC 20045
Phone: 202/737-2817   Fax: 202/638-5188

NHK
Mr. Ryuichi Teshima
Bureau Chief
2030 M Street, NW - Suite 706
Washington DC 20036
Phone: 202/828-5180   Fax: 202/828-4571

Nihon Shinbun Kyokai
Mr. Naoshi Hashimoto
Bureau Chief
1921 Gallows Rd., #600
Vienna VA 22182
Phone: 703/902-1870   Fax: 703/902-1936

Nippon TV International Corporation
Mr. Keisuke Yanaga
Bureau Chief
1036 National Press Building
Washington DC 20045
Phone: 202/638-0890   Fax: 202/638-0308

Nishi Nippon Shimbun
Mr. Megumi Kikuchi
Bureau Chief
1012 National Press Building
Washington DC 20045
Phone: 202/393-5812   Fax: 202/628-9622

NIKKEI Newspapers
Mr. Sigeru Komago
Bureau Chief
636 National Press Building
Washington DC 20045
Phone: 202/393-1388   Fax: 202/737-0170

Sankei Shimbun
Mr. Hiroshi Yuasa
Bureau Chief
330 National Press Building
Washington DC 20045
Phone: 202/347-2842   Fax: 202/628-7518

Sekai Nippo
Mr. Yuji Yokoyama
Bureau Chief
924 National Press Building
Washington DC 20045
Phone: 202/879-6785   Fax: 202/879-6789

Shakai Shimpo
Mr. Yasu Nakada
Washington Correspondent
Post Office Box 562
Garrett Park MD 20896
Phone: 301/942-0547   Fax: 301/949-9094
E-mail: ynakada102@aol.com

Television Tokyo 12
Mr. Tom Oki
Bureau Chief
803 National Press Bldg.
Washington DC 20045
Phone: 202/638-0441   Fax: 202/638-0443

Tokyo Broadcasting System Inc.
Mr. Jun Ogawa
Bureau Chief
1088 National Press Building
Washington DC 20045
Phone: 202/393-3800   Fax: 202/393-3809
E-mail: tbsdc@aol.com

Tokyo Shimbun
Mr. Moriyoshi Sase

Bureau Chief
1012 National Press Building
Washington DC 20045
Phone: 202/783-9479   Fax: 202/628-9622

TV Asahi
Mr. Junichi Kitasei
Bureau Chief
670 National Press Building
Washington DC 20045
Phone: 202/347-2933   Fax: 202/347-6558

TV Tokyo
Mr. Tom Oki
Bureau Chief
803 National Press Building
Washington DC 20045
Phone: 202/638-0441   Fax: 202/638-0443

Yomiuri Shimbun
Mr. Naomichi Fujimoto
Bureau Chief
802 National Press Building
Washington DC 20045
Phone: 202/783-0363   Fax: 202/737-2050

Korea, Republic of (South Korea)

Chosun Il Bo Daily News
Mr. Hyosang Khang
Bureau Chief
1171 National Press Building
Washington DC 20045
Phone: 202/783-4236   Fax: 202/783-5382

Dong-A Il Bo
Mr. Eun-Taek Hong
Washington Correspondent
974 National Press Building
Washington DC 20045
Phone: 202/347-4097   Fax: 202/273-0821

Han-Kyoreh Shinmun
Mr. Yun Joo Jung
Bureau Chief
1259 National Press Building
Washington DC 20045
Phone: 202/638-2141   Fax: 202/662-7186

Hankook Il Bo
Mr. Jaemine Shin
Bureau Chief and Washington Correspondent
961 National Press Building
Washington DC 20045
Phone: 202/783-2674   Fax: 202/783-0484

Joong-Ang Daily News
Mr. Nam-Kyu Han
Bureau Chief and Washington Correspondent
National Press Building - Suite 416
Washington DC 20045
Phone: 202/347-0121   Fax: 202/628-2719

Korean Broadcasting System
Mr. Choong Soo Lee
Bureau Chief and Chief Wash. Correspondent
National Press Bldg. - Suite 1076
Washington DC 20045
Phone: 202/662-7345   Fax: 202/662-7347

Kwangju Ilbo
Mr. Huney Kong
Bureau Chief
1115 National Press Building

Washington DC 20045
Phone: 202/638-1628   Fax: 202/638-5422
E-mail: huneyk@aol.com

Kwangju Ilbo
Mr. Huney Kong
Bureau Chief
1115 National Press Building
Washington DC 20045
Phone: 202/638-1628   Fax: 202/638-5422
E-mail: huneyk@aol.com

Kyung Hyang Daily News
Mr. Inkyu Park
Bureau Chief
839 National Press Building
Washington DC 20045
Phone: 202/737-3459   Fax: 202/737-5320
E-mail: nqinkyu@amsu.com

Maeil Business Newspaper
Mr. Sang Hyup Kim
Washington Bureau Chief
909 National Press Building
Washington DC 20045
Phone: 202/637-3258   Fax: 202/637-3259

MBC Television
Mr. Dong Jim Kim
Bureau Chief
414 National Press Building
Washington DC 20045
Phone: 202/347-4013   Fax: 202/347-1611

Segye Il Bo
Mr. Kiyon Kuk
Bureau Chief and Washington Correspondent
924 National Press Building
Washington DC 20045
Phone: 202/637-0587

Seoul Broadcasting System
Mr. Kumioul Ha
Bureau Chief
529 14th St., NW - Suite 979
Washington DC 20045
Phone: 202/637-9850   Fax: 202/662-1261

Seoul Shinmun
Mr. Yoo Dho Ra
Bureau Chief
1126 Naitonal Press Building
Washington DC 20045
Phone: 202/393-4061   Fax: 202/393-4064

Yonhap News Agency
Mr. Heesup Jun
Bureau Chief
1299 National Press Building
Washington DC 20045
Phone: 202/783-5539   Fax: 202/393-3460
E-mail: heesup@msn.com

Yonhap TV News
Mr. Jae-Chul Mun
Washington Bureau Chief
2030 M St. NW - Suite 504
Washington DC 20036
Phone: 202/463-4890   Fax: 202/463-4893

Kuwait

Kuwait News Agency (KUNA)
Mr. Faisal Alzaid
Bureau Chief
906 National Press Building

Washington DC 20045
Phone: 202/347-5554   Fax: 202/347-6837

Lebanon

Ad-Diyar
Mr. Samir Nader
Washington Correspondent
1410 N. Mckinley Rd.
Arlington VA 22205
Phone: 703/533-0541   Fax: 703/533-0556

Al-Hayat Newspaper
Mr. Rafic Maalouf
Bureau Chief
1185 National Press Bldg.
Washington DC 20045
Phone: 202/783-5544   Fax: 202/783-5525

Al-Kifah Al-Arabi
Mr. Samir F. Karam
Bureau Chief
3501 Stringfellow Court
Fairfax VA 22033
Phone: 703/471-5125   Fax: 703/471-4221

As-Safir
Mr. Hisham Melhem
Bureau Chief
5272 Dunleigh Drive
Burke VA 22015
Phone: 703/425-6017   Fax: 703/425-3879
E-mail: mhisham@aol.com

La Revue du Liban
Ms. Samia G. Abboud
Bureau Chief
2109 Greenery lane - Suite 301
Wheaton MD 20906
Phone: 301/933-4748

Lebanese Broadcasting Corp. Intl.
Mr. Samir Nader
Washington Correspondent
1410 North McKinley Road
Arlington VA 22205
Phone: 703/533-0541   Fax: 703/533-0556

Radio Free Lebanon
Mr. Robert Y. Farah
Bureau Chief
1730 M Street, NW - Suite 807
Washington DC 20036
Phone: 202/785-6666   Fax: 202/785-6628

Mexico

El Financiero
Mr. Dolia Estevez
Washington Correspondent
Post Office Box 65392
Washington DC 20035
Phone: 703/707-0236

El Universal
Mr. Jose Carreno
Washington Correspondent
801 National Press Building
Washington DC 20045
Phone: 202/662-7190   Fax: 202/662-7189
E-mail: carreno@wizard.net

Excelsior
Mr. Jose Manuel Nava
Bureau Chief

1639 Harvard Street, NW
Washington DC 20009-3702
Phone: 202/265-3400   Fax: 202/265-2066
E-mail: jmnava@erols.com

Mexico City News
Ms. Leigh Marjamaa
Washington Correspondent
1325 G Street, NW - Suite 730
Washington DC 20005
Phone: 202/661-0130   Fax: 202/347-1814

Notimex
Mr. Ignacio Basauri
Reg. Director, U.S. and Canada
495 National Press Building
Washington DC 20045
Phone: 202/347-5227   Fax: 202/347-5126

Proceso
Mr. Pascal Beltran-del-Rio
Washington Correspondent
986 Naitonal Press Building
Washington DC 20045
Phone: 202/393-1966   Fax: 202/393-1967
E-mail: 75374.2243@compuserve.com
proceso@msn.com

Televisa
Mr. Gregorio Miraz
Washington Bureau
1705 DeSales Street, NW - Suite 306
Washington DC 20045
Phone: 202/861-0626   Fax: 202/861-0936

Middle East

Contact Middle East
Mr. Adel Malek
Bureau Chief
529 14th Street, NW - Suite 1122
Washington DC 20045
Phone: 202/783-0368   Fax: 202/783-0326

Monaco

Radio Monte Carlo
Mr. Claude Porsella
Washington Correspondent
6071 Granite Knoll
Columbia MD 21045
Phone: 202/619-2175   Fax: 410/992-5779

Morocco

Maghreb Arabe Presse
Mr. Alem Assam
Bureau Chief
6226 Nelway Drive
McLean VA 22101
Phone: 703/790-3277   Fax: 703/790-3279

Netherlands

ANP-Dutch News Agency
Mr. Jaap Van Wesel
Bureau Chief
11903 Renwood Lane
Rockville MD 20852
Phone: 301/468-6863   Fax: 301/816-9173
E-mail: 76304,666@compuserve.com

Dutch TV News
Mr. Gerard Van der Wulp
Bureau Chief
2030 M Street, NW - Suite 500
Washington DC 20036
Phone: 202/466-8793   Fax: 202/828-4146
E-mail: pauls20255@aol.com

Netherlands Press Assocation
Mr. John Wanders
Washington Correspondent
520 Woodland Court, NW
Vienna VA 22180
Phone: 703/938-7715   Fax: 703/938-2846
E-mail: jwanders@gpd.nl

NOS Television
Mr. Gerard Van Der Wulp
Bureau Chief and Wash. Correspondent
2030 M Street, NW - Suite 400
Washington DC 20036
Phone: 202/466-8793   Fax: 202/828-4146
E-mail: vanderwal@compuserve.com

NRC Handelsblad
Mr. Juurd Eijsvoogel
Washington Correspondent
4219 Chesapeake St., NW
Washington DC 20016
Phone: 202/636-6944   Fax: 202/537-2959
E-mail: eijsvoogel@nrc.nl

Trouw Daily
Mr. Jaap Van Wesel
Bureau Chief
11903 Renwood Lane
Rockville MD 20852
Phone: 301/468-6863   Fax: 301/816-9173
E-mail: 76304,666@compuserve.com

New Zealand

Radio New Zealand
Ms. Connie Lawn
Washington Correspondent
3622 Stanford Circle
Falls Church VA 22041
Phone: 703/354-6795

Nigeria

Theweek
Ms. Jennifer Douglas
Bureau Chief
8811 Colesville Rd. - Suite 903
Silver Spring MD 20910
Phone: 301/585-2753   Fax: 301/589-4278
E-mail: theweek@afrika.com

Norway

Aftenposten
Mr. Uls Andenaes
Washington Correspondent
2030 M Street, NW - Suite 700
Washington DC 20036
Phone: 202/785-0658   Fax: 202/785-1546

Norwegian Broadcasting Corporation
Mr. Ingvild Bryn
Washington Correspondent
2030 M Street, NW - Suite 700
Washington DC 20036

Phone: 202/785-1460

Norwegian News Agency
Ms. Helge Ogrim
Washington Correspondent
5315 Westpath Way
Bethesda MD 20816
Phone: 301/229-3999   Fax: 301/229-8090

Pakistan

Information Times
Mr. Syed Adeeb
Editor
Post Office Box 7111
Washington DC 20044-7111
Phone: 703/660-6060   Fax: 703/660-6660
E-mail: adeeb@erols.com

Panama

La Prensa
Ms. Betty Brannan Jaen
Washington Correspondent
7729 Brookville Road
Chevy Chase MD 20815
Phone: 301/652-7645   Fax: 301/652-0629

Peru

Apoyo (consulting/publishing)
Mr. Edgar Triveri
Washington Correspondent
3333 University Blvd. West - Suite 811
Kensington MD 20895
Phone: 301/942-0614   Fax: 301/942-0614
E-mail: user100770@aol.com

Philippines

Business World (Manila)
Ms. Mercedes Tira Andrei
Washington Correspondent
3056 Seminole Road
Woodbridge VA 22192
Phone: 703/643-9716   Fax: 703/491-2516
E-mail: bizworld@erols.com

Poland

Polish Press Agency
Mr. Tomasz Zalewski
Bureau Chief
529 14th Street, NW - Suite 821
Bethesda MD 20045
Phone: 202/879-6780   Fax: 202/879-6779
E-mail: ppa@dgs.dgsys.com

Russia

Itar-Tass
Mr. Andrei Sitov
Bureau Chief
1004 National Press Building
Washington DC 20045
Phone: 202/662-7080   Fax: 202/393-6495
E-mail: borsc@aol.com

Izvestia

Mr. Vladimar Nadeine
Washington Correspondent
1860 Kirby Road
McLean VA 22101
Phone: 703/917-0517   Fax: 703/917-0518
E-mail: nadizv@aol.com

Russian Public TV
Mr. Sergei Goryachev
Bureau Chief
6237 Cheryl Drive
Falls Church VA 22044
Phone: 703/241-0530   Fax: 703/241-0649
E-mail: ortv@erols.com

Trud
Mr. Vissarion I. Sisnev
Washington Correspondent
4620 North Park Avenue - Suite 501W
Chevy Chase MD 20815
Phone: 301/656-3744

Saudi Arabia

Al Majalla
Mr. Mohammed Salih
Washington Correspondent
1310 G St. NW - Suite 750
Washington DC 20005
Phone: 202/638-7183   Fax: 202/683-1887

Al-Riyadh
Mr. Ahmed Al-Yami
Bureau Chief
1155 15th Street, NW - Suite 1108
Washington DC 20005
Phone: 202/822-0814   Fax: 202/822-0806

Arab News
Mr. Afshin Molavi
Washington Correspondent
1310 G St. NW - Suite 750
Washington DC 20005
Phone: 202/638-7182   Fax: 202/638-1887

Asharq Al-AWSAT/Arab News
Mr. Mohammed Sadeq
Bureau Chief
1310 G Street, NW - Suite 750
Washington DC 20005
Phone: 202/638-7183   Fax: 202/638-1887

Okaz Newspaper
Mr. Mohammed El-Maddeh
Bureau Chief
1145 National Press Building
Washington DC 20045
Phone: 202/393-0433   Fax: 202/393-0421

Saudi Gazette Newspaper
Ms. Barbara G.B. Ferguson
Bureau Chief
2027 North Utah Street
Arlington VA 22207-2350
Phone: 703/516-4837   Fax: 703/516-4887
E-mail: fergken@aol.com

Saudi Press Agency
Ms. Naila Al-Sowayel
Bureau Chief
1155 15th Street, NW - Suite 1111
Washington DC 20005
Phone: 202/861-0324   Fax: 202/872-1405

The Saudi Gazette
Ms. Barbara Ferguson
Bureau Chief

1145 National Press Bldg.
Washington DC 20045
Phone: 703/921-1478   Fax: 703/516-4887
E-mail: sgazettes@mcimail.com

Slovak Republic

News Agency of the Slovak Rep. (TASR)
Mr. Martin Douglas
Washington Correspondent
4501 Connecticut Avenue, NW, Apt. 713
Washington DC 20008
Phone: 202/686-4710   Fax: 202/537-0574

South Africa

Business Day
Mr. Simon Barber
Washington Correspondent
58 South Main Street, Box 300
Keedysville MD 21756
Phone: 301/432-2878
E-mail: sbarber@fred.net

Independent Newspapers Limited
Mr. Rich Mkhondo
Washington Bureau Chief
960C National Press Building
Washington DC 20045
Phone: 202/662-8722   Fax: 202/662-8723

Intro Communications, Inc.
Mr. Neil Lurssen
Editor
6908 Strata Street
McLean VA 22101
Phone: 703/847-6405   Fax: 703/356-4357
E-mail: editors@mainstreet.t5.com

National Media Limited
Mr. Johann Holzapfel
Bureau Chief, Politics
1263 D National Press Building
Washington DC 20045
Phone: 202/638-0399   Fax: 202/393-5647

South African Broadcasting Corp.
Mr. Simon Marks
Bureau Chief
1730 Rhode Island Ave. NW - Suite 205
Washington DC 20036
Phone: 202/296-9029   Fax: 202/296-9205

Spain

Catalan TV-3
Mr. Ramon Rovira
Washington Correspondent
1620 I Street, NW - Suite 150
Washington DC 20006
Phone: 202/785-0580   Fax: 202/296-7896
E-mail: tv3w@erols.com

EFE News Services, Inc.
Mr. Emiilio Sanchez
Bureau Chief
1252 National Press Building
Washington DC 20045
Phone: 202/745-7692   Fax: 202/393-4119

El Pais
Mr. Javier Valenzuela
Bureau Chief
1134 National Press Building

Washington DC 20045
Phone: 202/638-1533   Fax: 202/628-4788

Radio Nacional de Espana
Ms. Luz Rodriguez
Bureau Chief
1288 National Press Building
Washington DC 20045
Phone: 202/783-0768   Fax: 202/347-0147

SER (Sociedad Espanola de Radiodifusion)
Mr. Javier Del Pino
Washington Correspondent
1134 National Press Building
Washington DC 20045
Phone: 202/628-2522   Fax: 202/628-4788

Sweden

Dagens Nyheter
Mr. Kurt Malarstedt
Bureau Chief
1726 M Street, NW - Suite 700
Washington DC 20036
Phone: 202/429-0134   Fax: 202/429-0136

Svenska Dagbladet
Ms. Karin Henriksson
Washington Correspondent
Post Office Box 11816
Washington DC 20008-9016
Phone: 202/362-8253   Fax: 202/362-9338

Swedish Broadcasting Corporation
Mr. Bert Sundstrom
Washington Television Correspondent
2030 M Street, NW - Suite 700
Washington DC 20036
Phone: 202/785-1727

The Swedish News Agency - TT
Mr. Lennart Lundh
Washington Correspondent
3112 M Street, NW, 3rd Floor
Washington DC 20007
Phone: 202/333-5351   Fax: 202/333-5357

Switzerland

24 Heures
Mr. Pierre Ruetschi
Washington Correspondent
3711 Yuma Street, NW
Washington DC 20016
Phone: 202/237-5416   Fax: 202/237-5418
E-mail: ruetschi2worldnet.att.net

Le Matin
Mr. Yves Janssens Laudy
Washington Correspondent
P.O. Box 6613
Arlington VA 22206
Phone: 202/337-5557

Neue Zuercher Zeitung
Mr. Andreas Cleis
Political Correspondent
3007 P St. NW
Washington DC 20007
Phone: 202/298-7906   Fax: 202/298-8106

Swiss Broadcasting Corporation
Mr. Hans Peter Stalder
Bureau Chief

2030 M Street, NW - Suite 400
Washington DC 20036
Phone: 202/785-1727   Fax: 202/785-5834

Swiss News Agency
Mr. Steven Golob
Washington Correspondent
5235 Baltimore Avenue
Bethesda MD 20816-3003
Phone: 301/654-1009

Tribune de Geneve
Mr. Pierre Ruetschi
Washington Correspondent
3711 Yuma Street, NW
Washington DC 20016
Phone: 202/237-5416   Fax: 202/237-5418
E-mail: ruetschi@worldnet.att.net

Taiwan

Central News Agency, Inc.
Mr. Bill Wang
Bureau Chief
1173 National Press Bldg.
Washington DC 20045
Phone: 202/628-2738   Fax: 202/637-6788
E-mail: CNADC@aol.com

China Times Newspaper
Mr. Norman C. Fu
Bureau Chief
952 National Press Building
Washington DC 20045
Phone: 202/662-7570   Fax: 202/662-7573

Chinese Television System
Ms. Tina Chung
Bureau Chief
1273 National Press Building
Washington DC 20045
Phone: 202/662-8950   Fax: 202/662-8865

Commercial Times
Ms. Louise Ran Costich
Bureau Chief
10340 Zion Drive
Fairfax VA 22032
Phone: 703/764-1135   Fax: 703/764-1136

Taiwan TV Enterprise, Ltd. (TTV News)
Mr. Ernie Chuan-Yu Ko
Washington Correspondent
1705 DeSales Street, NW - Suite 302
Washington DC 20036
Phone: 202/223-6642   Fax: 202/452-8692
E-mail: erniettv@aol.com

United Daily News/Economic Daily News
Mr. James C. Wang
Washington Correspondent
1099 National Press Building
Washington DC 20045
Phone: 202/737-6426   Fax: 202/737-3732

Tunisia

Tunisian News Agency
Mr. Lotfi Ben Rejeb
Bureau Chief
1515 Massachusetts Avenue, NW
Washington DC 20005
Phone: 202/466-2546   Fax: 202/466-2553

Turkey

Anatolia News Agency
Mr. Kasim Cindemir
Bureau Chief
4450 South Park Avenue - Suite 1614
Chevy Chase MD 20815
Phone: 301/718-7966   Fax: 301/718-3691

Ihlas News Agency
Mr. Hasanz Hazar
Bureau Chief
495 National Press Bldg.
Springfield VA 20045
Phone: 202/737-7800   Fax: 202/737-5970

Turkish Daily News/Turkish Probe
Mr. Ugur Akinci
Washington Correspondent
4938 Hempdon Lane., #238
Bethesda MD 20814
Phone: 301/571-5204   Fax: 301/564-4318

Turkish Times
Mr. Ugur Akinci
Washington Editor
1601 Connecticut Avenue, NW - Suite 303
Washington DC 20009
Phone: 202/232-1833   Fax: 202/483-9092

Turkiye Daily News/Turkiye Gazetesi
Mr. Hasan Mesut Hazar
Bureau Chief
495 National Press Bldg.
Washington DC 20045
Phone: 202/737-7800   Fax: 202/737-7509

United Arab Emirates

Al-Ittihad
Mr. Hoda Tawfik
Bureau Chief
529 14th Street, NW - Suite 976
Washington DC 20045
Phone: 202/393-0546   Fax: 202/393-0547

United Arab Emirates News Agency
Mr. Fouzi El-Asmar
Bureau Chief
9216 Cedarcrest Drive
Bethesda MD 20814
Phone: 301/530-5019

United Kingdom

British Broadcasting Corporation
Mr. Andrew Roy
Bureau Chief, North America
2030 M Street, NW - Suite 607
Washington DC 20036
Phone: 202/223-2050   Fax: 202/775-1395

Daily Telegraph
Mr. Hugo Gurdon
Bureau Chief
1331 Pennsylvania Avenue, NW - Suite 904
Washington DC 20004-1718
Phone: 202/393-5195   Fax: 202/393-1335

Evening Standard
Mr. Jeremy Campbell
Washington Correspondent
4312 Fesseden Street, NW

Washington DC 20016
Phone: 202/966-9423   Fax: 202/362-2956

Financial Times
Ms. Patti Waldmeir
U.S. Editor and Bureau Chief
700 13th Street, NW - Suite 555
Washington DC 20005
Phone: 202/289-5474   Fax: 202/289-5475
E-mail: http://www.ft.com

Gancie Television, Inc.
Mr. Vincent Gancie
Director
4001 Nebraska Avenue, NW
Washington DC 20016
Phone: 202/885-4280   Fax: 202/885-4179

Independent
Ms. Mary Dejevsky
Bureau Chief
1726 M Street, NW - Suite 700
Washington DC 20036
Phone: 202/467-4460   Fax: 202/467-4458

Independent Television News
Mr. James Mates
Bureau Chief and Channel 1 Wash. Correspondent
400 N. Capitol St., NW - Suite 899
Washington DC 20001
Phone: 202/429-9080   Fax: 202/429-8948
E-mail: itnwash@worldnet.att.net

London Daily Telegraph
Mr. Hugo Gurdon
Bureau Chief
1331 Pennsylvania Avenue, NW - Suite 904
Washington DC 20004
Phone: 202/393-5195   Fax: 202/393-1335

London Evening Standard
Mr. Jeremy Campbell
Washington Correspondent
4312 Fessenden Street, NW
Washington DC 20016
Phone: 202/966-9423   Fax: 202/362-2956

London News Radio
Mr. Simon Marks
Bureau Chief
1730 Rhode Island Ave. NW - Suite 405
Washington DC 20036
Phone: 202/296-9012   Fax: 202/296-9205

London Observer
Mr. Ed Vulliamy
Bureau Chief and Washington Correspondent
1730 Rhode Island Avenue, NW - Suite 502
Washington DC 20036
Phone: 202/223-2486

Middle East Broadcasting Center
Mr. Aziz Fahmy Farag
Bureau Chief and Washington Correspondent
1510 H Street, NW - Suite 400
Washington DC 20005
Phone: 202/898-8222   Fax: 202/898-8088

Nature
Mr. Colin Macilwain
Sr. U.S. Correspondent
968 National Press Bldg., 529 14th St., NW
Washington DC 20045
Phone: 202/737-2355   Fax: 202/628-1609
E-mail: nature@naturedc.com
news@naturedc.com

New Scientist

Ms. Rachel Nowak
Bureau Chief
1150 8th Street, NW - Suite 725
Washington DC 20036
Phone: 202/331-2080   Fax: 202/331-2082
E-mail: rnowak@mail.idt.net

Reuters Television
Mr. Ralph Nicholson
Sr. Vice President
1333 H Street, NW, 5th Floor
Washington DC 20005
Phone: 202/898-0056   Fax: 202/898-1237

Sunday Telegraph
Mr. Ivorose Dawanay
Bureau Chief
1331 Pennsylvania Avenue, NW - Suite 904
Washington DC 20004-1718
Phone: 202/628-4823   Fax: 202/393-1335

Talk Radio UK
Mr. Simon Marks
Bureau Chief
1730 Rhode Island Ave. NW - Suite 405
Washington DC 20036
Phone: 202/296-9012   Fax: 202/296-9205

The Economist
Mr. Sebastian Mallaby
Bureau Chief
1331 Pennsylvania Avenue, NW - Suite 510
Washington DC 20004
Phone: 202/783-5753   Fax: 202/737-1035

The Guardian
Mr. Martin Kettle
U.S. Bureau Chief
1730 Rhode Island Avenue, NW - Suite 502
Washington DC 20036
Phone: 202/223-2486   Fax: 202/223-1764
E-mail: walke@gaurdian.co.uk

The Herald
Mr. Patrick Brogan
Bureau Chief and Washington Correspondent
1720 Rhode Island Avenue, NW - Suite 502
Washington DC 20036
Phone: 202/293-4729   Fax: 202/293-1764

The Independent
Mr. Andrew Marshall
Washington Bureau
1726 M Street, NW - Suite 700
Washington DC 20036
Phone: 202/467-4460   Fax: 202/467-4458

The London Sunday Times
Mr. Matthew Campbell
Washington Bureau Chief
4828 W. St., NW
Washington DC 20007
Phone: 202/333-9616   Fax: 202/333-9286
E-mail: 72360,3524@compuserve.com

The Times of London
Mr. Bronwen Maddox
Bureau Chief and U.S. Editor
1040 National Press Building
Washington DC 20045
Phone: 202/347-7659

Worldwide Television News
Mr. Paul C. Sisco
Bureau Chief
1705 DeSales Street, NW - Suite 300
Washington DC 20036
Phone: 202/835-0750   Fax: 202/222-7891

Venezuela

El Universal
Mr. Everett A. Bauman
Washington Correspondent
5519 Pollard Road
Bethesda MD 20816
Phone: 301/263-0277   Fax: 301/263-0385

Ven Pres
Ms. Delia Linares
Washington Correspondent
960-A National Press Bldg.
Washington DC 20045
Phone: 202/347-5505   Fax: 202/347-3327

INTRODUCTION

World Trade Centers Association (WTCA)

Established in 1970, the WTCA encourages mutual assistance and cooperation among members, promotes international business relationships, and fosters increased participation in world trade by industrializing nations. Headquartered in New York City, the WTCA, which is non-profit and non-political, represents several hundred member groups in over 80 countries.

The WTCA coordinates the administrative and financial activities of the organization. It also produces WTCA News, *membership directories and other publications, and disseminates a variety of materials and information to current and prospective World Trade Centers Association members. A primary goal of the WTCA is to encourage the establishment of new World Trade Centers and the development of improved services in those that now exist.*

Members of the association develop and maintain dedicated facilities, created to house the practitioners of trade and the services they need to conduct business. Creating a central focal point for a region's trade services and activities, a member facility is a "one-stop shopping center" for international business.

Among the services of World Trade Centers are World Trade Center Network access and support; trade research and information; educational programs and facilities; business clubs, exhibit facilities; consumer and business services (hotels, banks, restaurants, and shops); trade mission programs; and reciprocal privileges at all other operating member facilities worldwide.

What follows in this section is a list of the operating World Trade Centers located in the U.S. in alphabetical order by state and internationally in order by country.

For more information about the WTCA contact:

World Trade Centers Association, Inc.
One World Trade Center, Suite 7701
New York, NY 10048

Phone: 212/432-2640
Fax: 212/488-0064
Web: http://www.wtca.org
E-mail: wtca@wtca.org

Guy F. Tozzoli, President

Alaska

Ms. Robin Zerbel
Director
World Trade Center Alaska/Anchorage
421 West First Avenue, Suite 300
Anchorage AK 99501
Phone: 907/278-7233   Fax: 907-278-2982
E-mail: WTCAK@compuserv.com
URL: http://www.wtca.org/anchorage.html

Arizona

Mr. Jonathan Green
President
World Trade Center Phoenix
201 N. Central Avenue, Suite 2700
Phoenix AZ 85073
Phone: 602/495-6480   Fax: 602-253-9488
E-mail: wtcaz@mail.com

California

Mr. Donald A. Miller
President
World Trade Center Irvine
1 Park Plaza, Suite 150
Irvine CA 92614
Phone: 714/724-9822   Fax: 714-752-8723

Mr. Tom Teofilo
President
World Trade Center Association,
   Los Angeles/Long Beach
One World Trade Center, Suite 295
Long Beach CA 90831-0295
Phone: 562/495-7070   Fax: 562-495-7071
E-mail: infolb@wtcala-lb.com

Mr. Tom Teofilo
President
World Trade Center Association,
   Los Angeles/Long Beach
350 S, Figueroa Street - Suite 172
Los Angeles CA 90071
Phone: 213/680-1888   Fax: 213-680-1878
E-mail: enter@glawtca.latrade.org

Mr. Gary R. Snyder
Executive Director
World Trade Center of Oxnard
300 Esplanade Drive, Suite 2090
Oxnard CA 93030
Phone: 805/988-1406   Fax: 805-988-1862
E-mail: gnsyder@worldtradecenter.org
URL: http://www.worldtradecenter.org

Mr. Brooks Ohlson
Executive Director
World Trade Center Sacramento
917 7th Street
Sacramento CA 95814
Phone: 916/447-9827   Fax: 916-443-2672
E-mail: information@wtcsacramento.org
URL: http://www.tradeport.org

Ms. Kathy Ward
President
World Trade Center San Diego
1250 6th Avenue, Suite 100
San Diego CA 92101
Phone: 619/685-1450   Fax: 619-685-1460
E-mail: wtc@wtcsd.org
URL: http://www.wtcsd.org

Amb. Robert Pastorino
President
World Trade Center of San Francisco, Inc.
250 Montgomery Street, 14th Floor
San Francisco CA 94104
Phone: 415/392-2705   Fax: 415-392-1710
URL: http://www.wtcsf.org

Colorado

Mr. James F. Reis
President
World Trade Center Denver
1625 Broadway, Suite 680
Denver CO 80202-4706
Phone: 303/592-5760   Fax: 303-592-5228
E-mail: wtcdenver@worldnet.att.net
URL: http://www.wtcdn.com

Connecticut

Mr. James C. Nicholas
Executive Director
World Trade Center Bridgeport
Connecticut World Trade Association
330 Water Street, 2nd Floor
Bridgeport CT 06604
Phone: 203/336-5353   Fax: 203-331-9959
E-mail: nickcwta@aol.com
URL: http://www.imex.com/cwta.html

Delaware

Mr. Henry H. Beckler
Executive Director
World Trade Center Delaware, Inc.
802 West Street, Suite 303
Wilmington DE 19801
Phone: 302/656-7905   Fax: 302-428-1274
E-mail: wtcde@postoffice.dca.net

District of Columbia

Mr. Ronald Kendall
Director

The Ronald Reagan International Trade Center
1331 Pennsylvania Ave., NW - Suite 1220N
Washington DC 20004
Phone: 202/724-9091   Fax: 202-724-0246

Florida

Ms. Henrietta Frankel
Executive Vice President
World Trade Center Fort Lauderdale
200 East Las Olas Boulevard
Suite 100
Fort Lauderdale FL 33301
Phone: 954/761-9797   Fax: 954-761-9990
E-mail: wtcfl@gate.net
URL: http://www.worldtradefl.com

Ms. Joanne S. Emslie-Korn
Director of International Development
Jacksonville World Trade Center
3 Independent Drive
Jacksonville FL 32202
Phone: 904/366-6658   Fax: 904-353-6343

Ms. Charlotte Gallogly
President
World Trade Center Miami
5600 N.W. 36th Street, Suite 601
Miami FL 33166
Phone: 305/871-7910   Fax: 305-871-7904
E-mail: info@flatrade.org
URL: http://www.worldtrade.org

Mr. Byron Sutton
President
World Trade Center Orlando
105 E. Robinson Street, Suite 530
Orlando FL 32801
Phone: 407/649-1899   Fax: 407-649-1486
E-mail: wtcor@gdi.net
URL: http://www.gdi.net/wtcor

Mr. J. Kenneth Parker
President/CEO
World Trade Center Tampa Bay
800 Second Avenue South, Suite 340
St. Petersburg FL 33701
Phone: 813/822-2492   Fax: 813-823-8128
E-mail: wtctb@gate.net
URL: http://www.worldcommerce.org

Georgia

Mr. Mark Kitiyama
Interim Executive Director
World Trade Center Atlanta
SunTrust Plaza
303 Peachtree Street, NE, Suite LL100
Atlanta GA 30308-3235
Phone: 404/880-1550   Fax: 404-880-1555
E-mail: wtcatl@mindspring.com
URL: http://www.clubservices.com

Hawaii

Mr. Erlyne Lum
Economic Development Specialist(STB)
State of Hawaii World Trade Center Honolulu
c/o DBEDT
250 South Hotel Street, 5th Floor
Honolulu HI 96813
Phone: 808/587-2753   Fax: 808-586-2589
E-mail: elum@dbebt.hawaii.gov

Illinois

Hon. Neil F. Hartigan
Chairman
World Trade Center Chicago
Suite 929, The Merchandise Mart
200 World Trade Center
Chicago IL 60654
Phone: 312/467-0550   Fax: 312-467-0615
E-mail: wtcca@wtcca.com
URL: http://www.wtcca.com

Kansas

Ms. Pamela R. Doonan
Vice President and CEO
Kansas World Trade Center, Wichita
350 West Douglas Avenue
Wichita KS 67202-2970
Phone: 316/262-3232   Fax: 316-262-3585
E-mail: kwtc@wacc.org
URL: http://www.southwind.net/ict/kwtc

Kentucky

Ms. Holley Groshek
Executive Director
Kentucky World Trade Center Lexington
410 West Vine Street, Suite 290
Lexington KY 40507
Phone: 606/258-3139   Fax: 606-233-0658
E-mail: wtclex@uky.campus.mci.net
URL: http://www.kwtc.org

Louisiana

Mr. Eugene J. Schreiber
Managing Director
World Trade Center of New Orleans
2 Canal Street, Suite 2900
New Orleans LA 70130
Phone: 504/529-1601   Fax: 504-529-1691
E-mail: wtc-info@wtc-no.org
URL: http://www.wtc-no.org

Maryland

Ms. Penelope W. Menzies
Executive Director
The World Trade Center Baltimore
World Trade Institute
The World Trade Center, Suite 232
Baltimore MD 21202
Phone: 410/576-0022   Fax: 410-576-0751
E-mail: menzies@wtci.org
URL: http://www.wtci.org

Massachusetts

Mr. John E. Drew
President
World Trade Center Boston
164 Northern Avenue, Suite 50
Boston MA 02210-2004
Phone: 617/385-5000   Fax: 617-385-5033
E-mail: info@wtcb.com
URL: http://www.wtcb.com

Michigan

Mr. Sam Danou
President
World Trade Center Detroit/Windsor
1251 Fort Street
Trenton MI 48183
Phone: 313/479-2345   Fax: 313-479-5733
E-mail: wtcdw@sprintmail.com

Minnesota

Mr. Noor Doja
President & CEO
Minnesota World Trade Center St. Paul
30 East 7th Street, Suite 400
St. Paul MN 55101
Phone: 612/297-1580   Fax: 612-297-4812
URL: http://www.copycatdigital.com/wtc

Missouri

Mr. Peter S. Levi
President
Greater Kansas City World Trade Center
2600 Commerce Tower
911 Main Street
Kansas City MO 64105
Phone: 816/221-2424   Fax: 816-221-7440

Mr. Robert Frueh
Director
World Trade Center St. Louis
121 South Meramec, Suite 1111
St. Louis MO 63105
Phone: 314/854-6141   Fax: 314-862-0102
E-mail: wtcst@co.st-louis.mo.us
URL: http://www.st-louis.mo.us/st-louis/county/wtc/

Montana

Mr. Arnold E. Sherman
Executive Director
Montana World Trade Center Missoula
Gallagher Business Building, Suite 257
Missoula MT 59812-1216
Phone: 406/243-6982   Fax: 406-243-2086
E-mail: mwtc@selway.umt.edu

Nevada

Mr. Leonard S. Shoen
President
Nevada World Trade Center Las Vegas
901 East Desert Inn Road
Las Vegas NV 89109
Phone: 702/387-5581   Fax: 702-893-2339
E-mail: wtclucinda@earthlink.com
URL: http://www.wtcnevada.com

New York

Mr. Robert E. Catlin, Jr.
Director
World Trade Center New York
The Port Authority of New York and New Jersey
One World Trade Center, Suite 88W
New York NY 10048

Phone: 212/435-7168   Fax: 212-435-2810
E-mail: dmay@panynj.gov

Dr. Gabriel Basil
President
Capital Region World Trade Center, Schenectady
c/o Schenectady County Community College
78 Washington Avenue
Schenectady NY 12305
Phone: 518/381-1317   Fax: 518-346-7511
E-mail: crwtc@gw.sunysccc.edu
URL: http://www.crwtc.org

North Carolina

Ms. Ruth Turner Camp
President
North Carolina World Trade Center Raleigh-Durham
2 Hannover Square, Suite 1200
Raleigh NC 27601
Phone: 919/743-0177   Fax: 919-743-0188
E-mail: wtcnc@interpath.com
URL: http://www2.scsn.net/users/gen/wtcns1a.htm

Ohio

Mr. Russell A. Leach
Executive Director
World Trade Center Cleveland
200 Tower City Center
50 Public Square
Cleveland OH 44113-2291
Phone: 216/621-3300   Fax: 216-687-6788
E-mail: gcga@apk.net

Oregon

Mr. Lee Hodges
President
World Trade Center Portland
One World Trade Center
121 S.W. Salmon Street, Suite 250
Portland OR 97204
Phone: 503/464-8888   Fax: 503-464-8880
E-mail: wtcpd@pgn.com
URL: http://www.wtcpd.com

Pennsylvania

Mrs. Mame Bradley
Executive Director
World Trade Center Pittsburgh
Koppers Building, Suite 2312
436 Seventh Avenue
Pittsburgh PA 15219
Phone: 412/227-3180   Fax: 412-227-3188
E-mail: wtcp+@pitt.edu
URL: http://www.pitt.edu/wtcp

Rhode Island

Mr. Theodore J. Przybyla
Managing Director
World Trade Center Rhode Island Greater
Providence
One West Exchange Street
Providence RI 02903
Phone: 401/351-2701   Fax: 401-421-8510

South Carolina

Mr. John R. Kuhn
Executive Director
South Carolina World Trade Center Charleston
81 Mary Street
P.O. Box 975
Charleston SC 29402
Phone: 803/805-3081   Fax: 803-853-0444
E-mail: maddy@scwtc.org
URL: http://www.scwtc.org

Mr. R. Patrick Jenkins
President & CEO
The Greenville-Spartanburg World Trade Center
315 Old Boiling Springs Road
Greer SC 29650-4237
Phone: 864/297-8600   Fax: 864-297-8606

Tennessee

Mr. James W. Frierson
Chairman
Tennessee World Trade Center
535 Chestnut Street, Suite 212
Chattanooga TN 37402
Phone: 423/752-4316   Fax: 423-265-9751
E-mail: info@twtc.org
URL: http://www.twtc.org

Texas

Ms. Elia Mares Purdy
Executive Director
World Trade Center El Paso/Juarez
123 Pioneer Plaza
Suite 200 - Centre Building
El Paso TX 79901
Phone: 915/544-0022   Fax: 915-544-0030
E-mail: wtcepj@wtcepj.org
URL: http://www.wtcepj.org

Mr. Pat Foley
Manager, International Trade Development
Houston World Trade Association
1200 Smith, Suite 700
Houston TX 77002
Phone: 713/844-3637   Fax: 713-844-0200
E-mail: pfoley@houston.org
URL: http://www.houston.org

Mr. Ephraim Martinez
General Manager
World Trade Center Rio Grande Valley at
McAllen
Neuhaus Tower, Suite 410
200 South Tenth Street
McAllen TX 78501-4850
Phone: 956/686-1982   Fax: 956-618-1982
E-mail: wtcrgv@rgv.net
URL: http://www.rgv.net

Mr. Josef E. Seiterle
President
World Trade Center San Antonio
118 Broadway
San Antonio TX 78205
Phone: 210/978-7601   Fax: 210-978-7610
E-mail: wtcsa@newpro.net
URL: http://www.newpro.net/wtcsa

Virginia

Mr. J. Robert Bray
Executive Director
World Trade Center Norfolk
Virginia Port Authority
600 World Trade Center
Norfolk VA 23510
Phone: 757/683-8000   Fax: 757-683-8500

Washington

Mr. Steve Rosen
General Manager
World Trade Center Seattle
600 Stewart Street, Suite 1605
Seattle WA 98101-1220
Phone: 206/441-5144   Fax: 206-441-5144
E-mail: wtcseattle@crgnet.com

Mr. John A. Kennedy
Executive Director
World Trade Center Tacoma
3600 Port of Tacoma Road, Suite 309
Tacoma WA 98424
Phone: 253/383-9474   Fax: 253-926-0384
E-mail: info@wtcta.org
URL: http://www.wtca.org

Wisconsin

Ms. Mary Dermody
Director of Development
Wisconsin World Trade Center Milwaukee
424 E. Wisconsin Avenue
Milwaukee WI 53202
Phone: 414/274-3840   Fax: 414-274-3846
E-mail: wistrade@execpc.com
URL: http://www.wistrade.org

INTERNATIONAL

Argentina

Buenos Aires
Mr. Jorge E. Castex
President
World Trade Center Buenos Aires, S.A.
Moreno 584, 9th Floor
1091 Buenos Aires, Argentina

Aruba

Aruba
Ms. Lorraine C. de Souza
Executive Director
World Trade Center Aruba
Aruba World Trade Center Foundation
Zoutmanstraat #21
P.O. Box 140
Oranjestad, Aruba

Australia

Brisbane
Mr. Anthony Parkes
Senior Executive Officer
World Trade Centre Brisbane
375 Wickham Terrace
Brisbane, 4000 Australia

Melbourne
Ms. Jane Webb
Manager, Corporate Development
World Trade Center Association Melbourne
c/o Port of Melbourne Authority
P.O. Box 4721
Melbourne, Australia 3001

Sydney
Ms. Marianne Ash
Manager
World Trade Centre Sydney
Level 12, 83 Clarence St.
Sydney, NSW 2000
Australia

Austria

Salzburg
Mr. Georg Katcz
President, WTC Vienna, Austria
World Trade Center Salzburg
c/o WTC Development Ges.m.b.H.
Novotel Salzburg City
Franz Josef Strabe 26
A-5020 Salzburg, Austria

Vienna-Airport
Mr. Georg Katcz
President
World Trade Center Vienna-Airport
Vienna-Airport 1300 Austria

Bahamas

Nassau
Ms. Donna D. Smith
President

Bahamas World Trade Center, Nassau
c/o G.W. Smith Enterprises Limited
Crawford Street
P.O. Box N-9343
Nassau, N.P., Bahamas

Bahrain

Bahrain
Mr. Malik Helweh
Executive Director
World Trade Center Bahrain
Manama Center
Government Avenue
P.O. Box 669
Manama, Bahrain, Arabian Gulf

Belgium

Antwerp
Mr. Fabrice Goffin
Director
World Trade Center Association of Antwerp
Korte Sint Annastraat 11
2000 Antwerp, Belgium

Brussels
Ms. Merijn Kemps
World Trade Center Association Brussels A.S.B.L.
boulevard Emile Jacqmain 162 bte 5
1000 Brussels, Belgium

Brazil

Rio de Janeiro
Mr. Paulo Protasio
President
World Trade Center Rio de Janeiro
Rua da Candelaria, 9-11 andar, Centro
Rio de Janeiro, Brazil 20091-020

Sao Paulo
Mr. Carlos Aldan
Managing Director
World Trade Center de Sao Paulo
Av. das Nacoes Unidas
12551, Brooklyn Novo, Sao Paulo
Brazil 04578-903

Bulgaria

Sofia
Mr. Young-Sang Choe
Executive Director
Interpred-World Trade Center Sofia
36, Dragon Tzankov Blvd.
1040 Sofia, Bulgaria

Varna
Mr. Georgi Petkov
Managing Director
World Trade Center Varna
43 Osmi Primorski Polk Blvd.
Varna, Bulgaria 9000

Canada

Edmonton
Ms. Lorrine Hamdon
President
Alberta World Trade Centre, Edmonton

502 Metropolitan Place
10303 Jasper Avenue
Edmonton, Alberta, Canada T5J 3N6

Halifax
Mr. Dov Bercovici
General Manager
Atlantic-Canada World Trade Center Halifax
1800 Argyle Street, Suite 511
Halifax, Nova Scotia, Canada B3J 2V9

Montreal
Mr. Benoit Labonte
General Manager
World Trade Centre Montreal
380 St-Antoine Street West, Suite 2100
Montreal, Quebec
Canada H2Y 3X7

Ottawa
Mr. Gregory J. Gorman
President
World Trade Centre Ottawa
130 Slater Street, Suite 750
Ottawa, Ontario
K1P 6E2 Canada

Toronto
Mr. Doug Valentine
Director
World Trade Centre Toronto
The Board of Trade of Metro Toronto
P.O. Box 375
One First Canadian Place
Toronto, Ontario, Canada M5X 1E2

Vancouver
Mr. Robert Noon
Executive Director
World Trade Centre Vancouver
999 Canada Place, Suite 400
Vancouver, B.C. Canada V5C 3C1

Chile

Santiago
Mr. Carlos Sanchez
General Manager
World Trade Center Santiago
Avenida Nueva Tajamar 481
Oficina 101, Las Condes
Santiago - Chile

China

Beijing
Mr. Deng Peide
Chief, Vice Chairman
World Trade Centre Beijing
4/F, Hualong Bldg., Nanheyan
East City District
Beijing, 100006 P.R.C.

Beijing
Mr. Sun Yi Jun
Dept. Manager of General Office
China World Trade Center(Beijing)Ltd.
No. 1 Jian Guo Men Wai Avenue
Beijing, 100004 P.R.C.

Haikou
Mr. Jimmy J.M. Li
Chairman
World Trade Center Haikou
19/F, Huaxin Plaza, Huaxin St., Binhai Rd.

Haikou, Hainan, P.R.C. 570105

Hangzhou
Mr. Chen Rong
Chairman & President
Zhejiang World Trade Centre, Hangzhou
15 Shuguang Road
Hangzhou, P.R.C. 310007

Shanghai
Mr. Yang Zhihua
Chairman
World Trade Centre Shanghai
14F New Town Mansion
55 Lou Shan Guan Road
Shanghai, P.R.C. 200335

Shenzhen
Mr. Wang Xin Min
President
World Trade Centre Shenzhen
10/F Gonghui Bldg., No. 2
Shanghu Mid Road
Shenzhen, 518002, P.R.C.

Shijiazhuang
Mr. Zhang Yudong
Director General
World Trade Center Shijiazhuang
3, Zhonghua North Street
05000, Shijiazhuang, Hevei
P.R.C.

Tianjin
Mr. Ge Ziping
Chairman & President
World Trade Center Tianjin
Tianjin Leadar (Group) Co., Ltd.
3 Xinyuan, Kunming Rd.
300050 Tianjin, PRC

Wuhan
Mr. Cao Hengsheng
President
World Trade Center Wuhan
4 Fl. Zonghe Building
No. 1 Special, Changjian Ribao Road
Hankou, Wuhan, P.R.C. 430015

Colombia

Bogota
Mr. Carlos Ronderos
President
World Trade Center Bogota
Calle 98 No. 9-03 PH
Bogota, Colombia, S.A.

Cali
Mrs. Pilar Lozano
Director
World Trade Center Cali
Calle 8, #3-14 18 Floor
Cali, Colombia

Croatia

Rijeka
Mrs. Biserka Cerovic
World Trade Center Rijeka
Riva Boduli 1
51000 Rijeka, Croatia

Split
Mr. Zoran Milic

President
World Trade Center Split
Rudjera Boskovica 22
21000 SPLIT
Croatia

Zagreb
Mr. Nikola Jelincic
Director
World Trade Center Zagreb
Avenija Dubrovnik 15
10 020 Zagreb, Croatia

Cuba

Havana
Mr. Carlos Martinez Salsamendi
President
World Trade Center Havana
Chamber of Commerce of the Republic of Cuba
Calle 21 No. 661 Plaza
P.O. Box 4237
Havana, Cuba

Cyprus

Cyprus
Mr. Panayiotis Loizides
Secretary General
Cyprus World Trade Centre, Nicosia
Chamber Building
38, Grivas Dighenis Ave. & 3 Deligiorgis Street
P.O. Box 1455
Nicosia, CY-1509 Cyprus

Czech Republic

Brno
Mr. Jan Brazda
Managing Director
World Trade Center Brno
Vystaviste 1
60200 BRNO
Czech Republic

Prague
Mr. Lubomir Martinec
Executive Director
World Trade Center
Argentinska 38
Prague 7
170 05, Czech Republic

Ecuador

Quito
Dr. Diego Cordovez
President
World Trade Center Quito
Av. 12 de Octubre 1942 y Cordero
Quito - Ecuador, 17-12-964

Egypt

Cairo
Mr. Osama Ahmed Fouad
General Manager
World Trade Center Co., Cairo
1191 Corniche El Nil
P.O. Box 2007
Cairo, Egypt

Estonia

Tallinn
Mr. Mehis Pilv, Ph.D.
Director of Development
World Trade Center Tallinn
8 Ahtri Street
Tallinn EE0001, Estonia

Finland

Helsinki
Ms. Sirpa Rissa-Anttilainen Managing Director
World Trade Center Helsinki
Aleksanterinkatu 17
P.O. Box 800
00100 Helsinki, Finland

Turku
Dr. Sten-Olof Hansen
Managing Director
World Trade Center Turku
Veistamonaukis 1-3
20100 Turku
Finland

France

Bordeaux
Mr. Gilles Guyonnet Duperat
Executive Manager
World Trade Center Bordeaux Sud-Ouest
2, Place de la Bourse
33076 Bordeaux, France

Grenoble
Mrs. Odile Arnould
Executive Manager
World Trade Center Grenoble
Place Robert Schuman
P.O. Box 1509
38025 Grenoble, Cedex 1
France

Le Havre
Mr. Michel Prigent
Operational Manager
Le Havre World Trade Center
Quai George V
BP 1000
76061 Le Havre CEDEX

Lille
Mr. Alain van't Hoff
Manager
World Trade Center Lille
58 Rue de L'Hospital Militaire
BP 209
59029 Lille Cedex, France

Lyon
Mr. Pierre Helleputte
Director
World Trade Center Lyon/Lyon Commerce
International
16 re de la Republique
Lyon, France 69002

Marseille
Ms. Michele Uzel-Cazes
General Director
Mediterranean World Trade Center,
    Marseille/CMCI
CMCI-2 Rue Henri Barbusse

13241 Marseille Cedix 01, France

Metz
Mrs. Chantal Thiebaut
Executive Manager
World Trade Center Metz-Saarbrucken
2, rue Augustin Fresnel-Case 88248
57082 Metz Cedex 3, France

Montpellier
Mr. Patrick Geneste
President
World Trade Center Montpellier
La Coupole
275, Rue Leon Blum BP 9531
34045 Montpellier, Cedex 01
France

Nantes
Mrs. Catherine Lefaivre-Shah
Chief Executive
World Trade Center Nantes Atlantique
16 Quai Ernest Renaud
BP 90517
44105 Nantes Cedex 04
France

Paris
Ms. Genevieve Fournier
Director
World Trade Center Paris
Palais des Congres
2 place de la Porte Maillot
BP 18, Cedex 17
75853 Paris, France

Strasbourg
Mr. Patrick Schalck
Executive Director
World Trade Center Strasbourg
MCIS - 4 quai Kleber
67080 Strasbourg Cedex, France

French West Indies

Fort-De-France
Ms. Elizabeth Grant
Manager
World Trade Centre Martinique
Chamber of Commerce & Industry of Martinique
50 Rue Ernest Deproge
97200 Fort de France Cedex
Martinique, French West Indies

Pointe-A-Pitre
Mr. Claudy Alie
Secretary General
World Trade Center Pointe-a-Pitre
Zone de Commerce International
Pointe Jarry, Baie-Mahault
Gaudeloupe, F.W.I. 97122

Germany

Bremen
Mr. Fritz Reuter
General Manager
World Trade Center Bremen
Birkenstrasse 15
28195 Bremen, Germany

Dresden
Dr. Claus-Dieter Heinze
Gen. Mgr. & WTCA Reg. Coord.,
   Central/Eastern Europe
World Trade Center Dresden

Ammonstrasse 70
Dresden D-01067
Germany

Frankfurt (Oder)
Mr. Christian Plueschke
Executive Director
World Trade Center Frankfurt(Oder)GmbH
Im Technologiepark 1
15236 Frankfurt (Oder)
Germany

Hamburg
Mr. Peter Sackenheim
Managing Director
World Trade Center Hamburg
Neuer Wall 50
20354 Hamburg, Germany

Hannover
Ms. Reza-Rene Mertens
President
World Trade Center Hannover GmbH
Messegelande
30521 Hannover, Germany

Leipzig
Mr. Guenther Friedrich
Executive Director
World Trade Center Leipzig
Walter-Koehn-Strause 1C
D-04356 Leipzig
Germany

Rostock
Mr. Guenther Friedrich
Executive Director
World Trade Center Rostock
Parkstrasse 51
18119 Rostock
Germany

Ruhr Valley
Mr. Guenther Friedrich
Executive Director
World Trade Center Ruhr Valley
Sparkassenstrasse 1
45879 Gelsenkirchen
Germany

Hungary

Budapest
Mr. Jozsef Vasvari
C.E.O.
World Trade Center Budapest
Kecskemeti utca 14.
Budapest, Hungary H-1053

India

Calcutta
Mrs. Shanta Ghosh
Executive Director
World Trade Center Calcutta
24B Park Street
Calcutta 700 016, India

Mumbai
Mr. V.S. Gopalakrishnan
Director General
World Trade Center Mumbai
M. Visvesvaraya Industrial Research &
   Development Centre
Centre 1, 31st Floor, Cuffe Parade
Bombay 400 005, India

Indonesia

Jakarta
Dr. Erwin Ramedhan
Executive Director
World Trade Center Jakarta
World Trade Center Building, 2nd Floor
Jl. Jend. Sudirman Kav. 29-31
Jakarta 12920 Indonesia

Medan
Mr. Darwis Karim
President
World Trade Center Medan
BMW House, L.3
Jalan H. Adam Malik 161
Medan, Indonesia 20114

Surabaya
Mr. Alim Sutrisno
Director
World Trade Center Surabaya
Jalan Pemuda 27-31
Surabaya 60275 Indonesia

Israel

Tel-Aviv
Mr. Moshe Nahum
Director
World Trade Center Israel, Tel-Aviv
Industry House
29 Hamered Street
Tel-Aviv, 61825 Israel

Italy

Bari
Hon. Giuseppe De Gennaro
President
World Trade Center Bari
Il Baricentro
1st Floor - Tower B
S.S. 100 - Km. 18
70010 Casamassima, BariItaly

Genoa
Mr. Enrico Zanelli
Vice President and Managing Director
World Trade Center Genoa, S.p.A.
Via De Marini 1
16149 Genoa, Italy

Japan

Osaka
Mr. Hirofumi Kimba
Managing Director
World Trade Center Osaka
Osaka World Trade Center Building
50th Floor, Mail Box #1
1-14-16, Nanko-kita, Suminoe-ku
Osaka 559, Japan

Sapporo
Mr. Nobuo Sato
Managing Director
World Trade Center Sapporo
Sapporo International Communication
Plaza Foundation
MN Bldg., 3rd Floor, Kita 1 Nishi 3, Chuo-ku
Sapporo 060 Japan

Tokyo

Mr. Nubuo Nakaya
Secretary General
World Trade Center Tokyo, Inc.
P.O. Box 57
World Trade Center Building
4-1, Hamamatsu-cho 2-chome,
Minato-ku, Tokyo, 105 Japan

Jordan

Amman

Mr. Ousama G. Ghannoum
General Manager
Amman World Trade Center
Philadelphia International Hotel
Suite 121-122
Hussein Bin Ali Street
P.O. Box 962140Amman 11196, Jordan

Korea

Seoul

Mr. Bert H.B. Sheen
Director
Korea Int'l. Trade Assoc./Korea World Trade
Center, Seoul
159-1 Samsung-Dong
Kangnam-Ku
Seoul, Korea 135-729

Latvia

Riga

Mr. Normunds Bergs
Director General
World Trade Center Riga
2 Elizabetes Street
Riga LV-1340
Latvia

Luxembourg

Luxembourg

Dr. Rolphe L. Reding
President
World Trade Center Luxembourg
6-10, place de la Gare, 4th Fl.
L-1616 Luxembourg

Macau

Macau

Dr. Antonio Leca Da Veiga Paz
Managing Director
World Trade Center Macau SARL
Avenida de Amizade, No. 918
Edificio World Trade Center, 17th Floor
Macau

Malaysia

Kuala Lumpur

Mr. N.S. Pichoo
CEO
Putra World Trade Centre
Level 3, Convention Complex
41 Jalan Tun Ismail
50480 Kuala Lumpur, Malaysia

Mexico

Guadalajara

Ms. Aurelio Lopez Rocha
President
Guadalajara World Trade Center
Av. de las Rosas No. 2965
Rinconada del Bosque
Guadalajara, Jalisco 44540 Mexico

Mexico City

Mr. Diego Gutierrez
President of the Board
World Trade Center Mexico City
Montecito No.38
Col. Napoles
03810 Mexico, D.F.

Monterrey

Mrs. Ana Madero
Administrator
World Trade Center Monterrey
Edificio Cintermex, Oficina 99
Av. Fundidores 501
Colonia Abrera
Monterrey 64010Nuevo Leon, Mexico

Puebla

Mr. Gonzalo Bautista
President
World Trade Center Puebla
Calzada de los Fuertes #81
Col. los Fuertes CP 72290
Puebla Pue., Mexico

Veracruz

Mr. Enrique Rechy
Business Director
World Trade Center Veracruz
Boulevard Adolfo Ruiz Cortines No. 3497
Veracruz, 94290 Mexico

Netherlands

Amsterdam

Dr. Paul D. Kotvis
Managing Director
World Trade Center Amsterdam
Strawinskylaan 1
1077 XW Amsterdam
The Netherlands

Amsterdam Airport

Mrs. M.I.A.E. Mirck-Suren
Managing Director
World Trade Center Amsterdam Airport
Schiphol Boulevard 105
1118BG Schiphol Airport
The Netherlands

Eindhoven

Mr. Geert-Jan Nieveen
Managing Director
World Trade Center Eindhoven N.V.
Bogert 1
P.O. Box 2085
5600 CB Eindhoven, The Netherlands

Rotterdam

Mr. Henk J. Van Engelenburg
Managing Director & CEO
World Trade Center Rotterdam N.V.
Beursplein 37, P.O. Box 30055
3001 DB Rotterdam
The Netherlands

Netherlands Antilles

Curacao

Mr. Hugo de Franca
Managing Director
World Trade Center Curacao
Piscadera Bay
Curacao, Netherlands Antilles

New Zealand

Auckland

Mr. Michael Barneett
Chief Executive
World Trade Center Auckland
Auckland Regional Chamber of
  Commerce & Industry
100 Mayoral Drive
P.O. Box 47
Auckland, New Zealand

Nigeria

Lagos

Mr. John Adeyemi-Adeleke
Executive Director
World Trade Center of Nigeria Lagos
8th Floor, Western House
8-10 Broad Street
Lagos, Nigeria
P.O. Box 4466Lagos, Nigeria

Norway

Oslo

Mr. Arnt P. Sundli
President
World Trade Center Oslo
Pilestredet 17
0164 Oslo, Norway

Pakistan

Karachi

Mr. Qadeer A. Batlay
Director
World Trade Center Karachi
10 Khayaban-e-Roomi
KDA Scheme No. 5, Block-5
Clifton, Karachi, 75600 Pakistan

Palestinian Governing Authority

Gaza

Mr. Jihad Alwazir
Managing Director
World Trade Centre Gaza, Palestine
P.O. Box 5257
Gaza, Al Remal / Gaza Strip

Panama

Panama

Mr. Guillermo Ronderos
President & Managing Director
World Trade Center Panama
Calle 53, Urbanizacion Marbella

P.O. Box 6-2432
Panama City, Panama

Peru

Lima
Ms. Liliana Alvizuri
Director
World Trade Center Lima
2355 Av. de La Marina
San Miguel, Lima L-32
Peru

Philippines

Manila
Ms. Cecilia A. Sanchez
Managing Director
World Trade Center Metro Manila
WTCMM Complex, Financial Center Area
Roxas Blvd. along Sen. Gil Puyat Avenue Ext.
Pasay City, Philippines 1300

Poland

Gdynia
Mr. Peteris Gailitis
Chairman
World Trade Center Gdynia
Tadeusza Wendy 7/9
81-341 Gdynia, Poland

Warsaw
Mr. Jacques Tourel
Executive Director
World Trade Center Warsaw
The Palace of Culture & Science
1 Plac Defeilad (PKiN)
Warsaw 00-901, Poland

Portugal

Lisbon
Mr. Pedro Salazar Leite
President
World Trade Center Lisbon
Av. do Brasil
1700 Lisbon, Portugal

Porto
Mr. Micard Teixeira
Executive Director
World Trade Center Porto, S.A.
Av. Boavista 1277/81
4100 Porto, Portugal

Qatar

Doha
Mr. Majed Z. Jweihan
Managing Director
World Trade Center Doha Qatar
Al Asmaq
Doha, Qatar, Arabian Gulf

Romania

Bucharest
Dr. Doina Popa

President
World Trade Center Bucharest
2 Expozitiei Blvd. Sector 1
Bucharest, 78 334 Romania

Russia

Moscow
Mr. Sergey A. Tarachanov
Acting Director General
World Trade Center Moscow
12, Krasnopresnenskaya nab.
123610 Moscow, Russia

Novosibirsk
Mr. Sergei Yakushi
Managing Director
World Trade Center Novosibirsk
16, Gorky St.
630099 Novosibirsk
Siberia, Russia

St. Petersburg
Mr. Vladimir Lusin
World Trade Center St. Petersburg
Tambowskaya Str. 12 A
192007 St. Petersburg
Russia

Tyumen
Mr. Erjan N. Makash
General Director
World Trade Center Tyumen
Club WTC Tyumen "Janetta"
33 Respubliki Street
Tyumen 625000 Russia

Saudi Arabia

Riyadh
Mr. Andrew George
Chief Executive Officer
World Trade Center Riyadh
Olaya Street, Opposite Olaya Akariya
P.O. Box 57714
Riyadh, Saudi Arabia 11584

Singapore

Singapore
Mr. Ho Kiam Khiaw
Director
World Trade Centre Singapore
1 Maritime Square, #09-72
WTC Building
Singapore 099253
Republic of Singapore

Slovenia

Ljubljana
Mr. Gregor Simoniti
Secretary General
World Trade Center Ljubljana
Dunajska 156
1113 Ljubljana, Slovenia

South Africa

Johannesburg
Mr. C.P. Swart

Executive Chairman
World Trade Center Johannesburg
Jurgens Park
Jones Road, P.O. Box 500
Kempton Park, 1620 South Africa

Spain

Barcelona
Mr. Enric Garcia Castany
Managing Director
World Trade Center Barcelona
Urgell 240, 6 D
08036 Barcelona, Spain

Bilbao
Ms. Jose Maria Escondrillas
Chairman
Bilbao World Trade Center
Alameda de Urquijo 10, 1 D
48008 Bilbao, Spain

Madrid
Mr. Luis Larroque
Vice President & CEO
World Trade Center Madrid, S.A.
Paseo de la Habana, 26
3rd Floor, Suite #4
28036 Madrid, Spain

Sevilla
Mr. Pedro Bugallal
Trade Services Manager
World Trade Center Sevilla
Edificio World Trade Center
Isla de la Cartuja
41092 Sevilla, Spain

Sri Lanka

Colombo
Mr. Michel Saelen
Manager
World Trade Center Colombo
Hospitality International (Pvt) Ltd.
#36-00 & #37-00, West Tower
World Trade Center, Echelon Sq.
Colombo 01, Sri Lanka

Sweden

Gothenburg
Mr. Sture Perfjell
Managing Director
Scandinavian World Trade Center Gothenburg
Massans Gata 18, P.O. Box 5253
S-412 94 Gothenburg, Sweden

Jonkoping
Mr. Goran Kinnander
Managing Director
Jonkoping World Trade Center
Jonkoping Chamber of Commerce
Elmiavagen, S-554 54
Jonkoping, Sweden

Stockholm
Mr. Nils Forberg
Managing Director
World Trade Center Stockholm
Klarabergsviadukten 70
Box 70354
107 24 Stockholm, Sweden

Switzerland

Basel
Mr. Hans Hagenbuch
Chief Executive
World Trade Center Basel
Messeplatz 1
4021 Basel, Switzerland

Geneva
Mr. Philippe Doubre
President & Secretary General
World Trade Center Geneva
WTC II
29, Route de Pre-Bois
Switzerland

Lausanne
Mr. Robin Gordon
Managing Director & Secretary General
World Trade Center Lausanne
P.O. Box 476
Avenue de Gratta-Paille 1-2
1000 Lausanne 30 Grey
Switzerland

Lugano
Mr. Renato P. Dellea
Executive Director
World Trade Center Lugano
One World Trade Center
C.P. 317
6982 Lugano-Agno, Switzerland

Zurich
Mr. Roger Beier
Managing Director
World Trade Center Zurich
Leutschenbachstrasse 95
8050 Zurich, Switzerland

Taiwan

Kaohsiung
Mr. Min Chen
President
World Trade Center Kaohsiung
Southeast Building
21st Wu-Fu 3rd Road, 10th Floor
Kaohsiung, Taiwan

Taichung
Mr. Bormin Ting
President
World Trade Center Taichung
60 Tienpao St.
Taichung 407, Taiwan

Taipei
Mr. C.P. Hu
Exec. Director, Planning & Coordination Dept.
Taipei World Trade Center Co., Ltd.
3rd-8th Floor, CETRA TOWER
333 Keelung Rd., Section 1
Taipei 110, Taiwan

Thailand

Bangkok
Dr. Arun Panupong
Chairman of Executive Board
World Trade Center Bangkok
World Trade Center Complex, 7th Floor
4 Rajdamri Road
Bangkok, 10330, Thailand

Trinidad & Tobago

Trinidad and Tobago
Ms. Deborah Henville
Trade Info. & Sales Asst.
World Trade Center Trinidad and Tobago
Airports Administration Centre
Caroni North Bank Road
P.O. Box 1273
Piarco, Port of Spain, Trinidad W.I.

Tunisia

Tunis
Mr. Slaheddine El Goulli
President, Director General
Tunis World Trade Center
6, Avenue Mohamed Ali Akid 1003
Cite Olympique Tunis, Tunisia

Turkey

Ankara
Mr. Hasan Colak
Chairman
World Trade Center Ankara
Tahran Caddesi No:30
Kavaklidere 06700
Ankara, Turkey

Istanbul
Mr. Attila Pektas
Managing Director
World Trade Center Istanbul
Cobancesme Kavsagi
PK 40
34830 Havalimani, Istanbul
Turkey

United Arab Emirates

Dubai
Mr. Wahid Attalla
General Manager
Dubai World Trade Centre
Bur Dubai, Sheikh Zaid Road
Dubai, United Arab Emirates

United Kingdom

Bristol
Mr. Michael Langridge
Managing Director
World Trade Centre Bristol
c/o WTC Ltd.
University Gate
Park Row, Bristol BS1 5UB
United Kingdom

Cardiff
Ms. Debbie Monks
Facilities Coordinator
World Trade Center Wales Cardiff
Cardiff International Arena
Mary Ann Street
Cardiff, CF1 2EQ South Wales, U.K.

Uruguay

Montevideo
Mr. Nelson Pilosof
President
World Trade Center Montevideo
Hidalgos 527 Of. 802
11300 Montevideo, Uruguay

Venezuela

Caracas
Ms. Patricia Mosquera
General Director
World Trade Center Caracas
Torre Consolidada, Edificio Anexo
Mezzanina, Plaza La Castellana
Caracas, Venezuela 1060-A

Valencia
Mr. Manuel A. Schemke
Executive Director
World Trade Center Valencia
The Spiwak Knorpel Grp. of Co's./Dann Group
Constructora Henry Ford, Sede Asamblea Leg.
Av. Henry Ford, Blvd. Industrial Municipal Norte
Nave A, Mezzanina, Oficina la Zona Industrial
SurValencia, Venezuela

Yugoslavia

Belgrade
Mr. Sinisa Zaric
D. Sc, President
World Trade Center Belgrade
Bulevar Vojvode Misica 14
Yugoslavia, 11000 Belgrade

The American University - Washington, D.C.

Kogod College of Business Administration
4400 Massachusetts Avenue, N.W.
Washington, D.C. 20016-8044

The Kogod College of Business Administration offers a 54 credit MBA Program with a concentration in International Business. Part-time and evening classes are offered in addition to a full-time day program. Students choosing a concentration in international business choose from the following three tracks with the following electives:

International Finance
International Finance
International Banking
Legal Issues in Int'l & Investment & Trade

International Marketing
Culture & Int'l Markets
Int'l Marketing Strategies
Ex/Im Management
Int'l Market Research

International Management
Managing Hum. Res. in MNCs
Issues in International Training & Labor Relations
Comparative Mgmt. Systems

For more information call: (202) 885-1913

Office of Contract Programs
4400 Massachusetts Avenue, N.W.
Washington, D.C. 20016-8044

The Office of Contract Programs (OCP) provides on-site training and education for corporations, government agencies, and professional associations. These programs include Bachelor's Degrees, Master's Degrees, Professional Development Seminars and Certificate Programs. The areas of study covered by the OCP include International Business, International Communication, International Politics and various Language Study Programs.

For more information call: (202) 885-3990

George Mason University - Fairfax, Virginia

School of Business Administration
Fairfax, Virginia 22030-4444

The School of Business Administration offers both a full and part-time MBA. The curriculum consists of 12 required core courses and seven electives. Possible electives include International Taxation, International Finance, International Business Issues in Information Technology, Theory and Policies of International Business and an International Marketing Practicum. In addition, the business school

has implemented three new optional track programs for education and experience in a specific industry. The three track options are High Technology Management, Non- Profit/Public Policy, and Global Services.

The School of Business Administration also has a special program with the Virginia Department of Economic Development for second year MBA students that assists companies create business plans for development of their overseas activities.

For more information contact:

Office of the Dean,
  School of Business Administration, (703) 993-1807

Admissions Office, (703) 993-2136

The George Washington University - Washington, D.C.

School of Business and Public Management
710 21st Street, N.W.
Washington, D.C. 20052

The School of Business and Public Management offers both a full and part-time MBAProgram consisting of 20 courses (60 credit hours); the Office of Professional Development offers certificate programs in International Management.

The International Business Program is designed to prepare students for careers in international banking, exporting, multinational corporations, international strategic management, the federal government and international agencies.

The Institute for Brazilian Business and Public Management Issues offers special programs and seminars designed to provide interested parties with information and educational training regarding U.S.-Brazil relations.

For more information contact:

Mr. Paul Kolesa, Advisor
  (202) 944-5720, kolesa@gwis2.circ.gwu.edu

Dr. Hossein Askari, Chair,
  MBA Programs in International Business, (202) 994-0847

Dr. Davison Frame, Chair,
  MBA and The Management of International Science
  and Technology, (202) 994-5818

Ms. Barbara Maddox, Acting Director,
  Office of Professional Development, (202)994-5200

Dr. James Ferrer, Jr., Director,
  Institute of Brazilian Business and Public Management
  Issues, (202) 994-5205

Georgetown University - Washington, D.C.

Georgetown University School of Business
37th & O St., N.W.
Washington, D.C. 20057-1008

The School of Business offers a full-time 2 year MBA Program, an 18-month International Executive MBA (IEMBA), a 3 year joint MSFS/MBA Degree in conjunction with the School of Foreign Service, and a 4 year JD/MBA in conjunction with the Law Center.

MBA students can also get certificates in International Business Diplomacy or in Area Studies for the following regions: African Region; Asian Region; German/European Region; Latin American Region; Russian Region.

The International Executive MBA program takes place on alternate weekends and features an international study residency in Europe that addresses business-government issues with the European Community and Eastern Europe.

Georgetown and their Georgetown Executive Program also offer an Executive International Business (EIB) Certificate and a Global Business Leadership (GLB) Certificate. The EIB program consists of 7 courses, and the GLB consists of 4 courses. Each course meets for 22 hours, on Fridays and Saturdays. The EIB program lasts approximately 7 months while the GBL program lasts 4 months.

For more information contact:

School of Business,
    Graduate Programs for MBA, (202) 687-4200 and
    IEMBA (202) 944-3740

Georgetown Executive Program, (202) 687-6993

The School of Foreign Service
    (for the joint MSFS/MBA Degree), (202)687-5763

The Law Center (for joint JD/MBA Degree), (202) 662-9030

Howard University - Washington, D.C.

Howard University School of Business
2600 Sixth Street, N.W.
Washington, D.C. 20059

The School of Business offers day and evening classes for its 4 semester Masters in Business Administration Program.

The Howard University Small Business Development Center sponsors various programs and, workshops, such as "How to Be a Successful Exporter/Importer."

For more information contact:

School of Business, (202) 806-1657

Small Business Development Center, (202) 806-1550

Johns Hopkins University - Washington, D.C.

School of Continuing Studies
1625 Massachusetts Ave., NW
Washington, D.C. 20036
202/663-5600

Johns Hopkins University offers a 48 credit Masters of Science in business with a concentration in International Business at its Washington, D.C. campus.

For more information contact:

Judy Iredell
Johns Hopkins University D.C. Center, (202) 588-0597

Marymount University - Arlington, Virginia

School of Business Administration
1000 North Glebe Road
Arlington, Virginia 22201

Mail:

2807 North Glebe Road
Arlington, Virginia 22207-4299

Marymount University offers a part-time 63 credit Master of Business Administration. The program requires that one course in international business be taken and offers additional electives in International Finance, Global Marketing, Global Business Management, Global Operations Strategy and Global Markets and Economics.

Marymount also offers numerous certificate programs in International Business, Information Resources Management and Total Quality Management (TQM). The core courses for the international certificate program are:

—Global Markets and Economics
—International Finance
—Global Business Management
—Global Marketing
—Global Operations Strategy

For more information contact:

Tim McCrudden, Coordinator of Admissions,
    School of Business Administration, (703)284-5901

Art Meiners, Assoc. Dean for Graduate Programs, (703)284-5921

Mount Vernon College - Washington, D.C.

Mount Vernon College
2100 Foxhall Road, N.W.
Washington, D.C. 20007

Mount Vernon College offers a part-time 45 credit Masters in Business Administration with a specialization in Management or in Contracting and Procurement. Elective courses include International Financial Management, Marketing in Asian Nations, Marketing in Industrial Nations, International Management, and Import-Export Management. Students also have the option of pursuing a part-time 15 credit certificate in Management, Human Resources Management, or Procurement.

For more information contact:

The Division of Continuing Studies, (202)625-4500

Office of Admissions, (202)625-4636

University of the District of Columbia - Washington, D.C.

College of Business and Public Management
4200 Connecticut A venue, N.W .
Washington, D.C. 20006

The University of the District of Columbia offers a full and part-time MBA Degree which requires 45 credit hours, or 30 credits and a thesis. Students may declare International Business as their area of emphasis and may choose from electives such as International Marketing Management, International Business Management. and International Business Economics & Finance.

The International Business Center holds annual international business conferences and other special seminars and conferences.

For more information contact:

Graduate Admissions, (202) 274-5000

Dr. Falih Alsaaty,
Director of the International Business Center, (202) 274-7001

University of Maryland, College Park - College Park, MD

College of Business and Management
Van Munching Hall
University of Maryland
College Park, Maryland 20742-1815

The University of Maryland has a full and part-time MBA Program with day and evening classes being offered in College Park. Students can also take evening courses at the Shady Grove campus in Rockville.

Students can choose from a variety of electives in International Business, such as Management of the Multinational Firm, International Finance, International Marketing, International Accounting, International Logistics and Transportation Management, and International Marketing.

For more information contact:

Dr. Peter Marisi,
    Center for International Business (301) 405-2136

Masters Programs Office, (301) 405-2278

University of Maryland, University College - Graduate School of Management & Technology

University Boulevard at Adelphi Road
College Park, Maryland 20742-1614

University College offers a 36 semester hour Master of International Management. This program consists of 7 core courses, 4 electives and a capstone international management project. Students can choose from tracks in international finance, marketing, or commerce.

University College also offers an 18 semester hour professional certificate program. The certificate program consists of 3 required courses (Managing in a Competitive International Environment, Foreign Investment and Strategic Alliances, and International Trade and Trade Policy) and 3 electives from the fields of Marketing, Finance, Public Policy, and Taxation.

For more information contact:

Graduate School of Management and Technology, (301) 985-7200.

World Trade Center Institute (WTCI) - Baltimore, Maryland

World Trade Center Institute
World Trade Center Baltimore, Suite 1355
Baltimore, Maryland 21202

The WTCI is a public/private partnership which, through cooperation with the Maryland Department of Economic and Employment Development (DEED) and the Maryland International Division, assists Maryland companies expand their international business activities.

In addition to the numerous seminars given throughout the year, the WTCI offers two certificate programs, the Maryland International Trade Certificate and the World Trade Certificate.

Sample Core Courses:

—Introduction to World Trade
—Import/Export Letters of Credit
—Customs Brokerage
—Export Documentation
—Export Marketing and Promotion
—Importing Techniques

Sample Electives:

—Business Opportunities in Germany
—Russia: Selling, Distributing, and Getting Paid
—Technology Data/Software & Export Management Seminar
—Letter of Credit Symposium and UCP 500 Update
—Product Development for the Global Marketplace

For more information call: (410) 576-0022

INTRODUCTION - Foreign Chambers of Commerce

Like their U.S. counterparts, Foreign Chambers of Commerce are associations comprised of business executives concerned with foreign trade and investment between the U.S. and their respective countries. Located throughout the U.S., these chambers represent their members before the U.S. government, business communities, and general public. They often sponsor seminars and meetings and can be an excellent source of information about the economic climate and trade opportunities within their countries.

Africa

National Assn. of African-American
  Chambers of Commerce
750 St. Paul Place - #1920
Dallas TX 75201
Phone: 214/871-3060

Dr. Reuben JAJA
President
Africa-USA Chamber of Commerce & Industry
One World Trade Center - #800
Long Beach CA 90832
Phone: 310/983-8193   Fax: 310/983-8199

US Africa Chamber of Commerce
170 Broadway - Suite 1006
New York NY 10038
Phone: 212/732-6440   Fax: 212/608-0999

American - Southern Africa
  Chamber of Commerce
1080 Park Ave. - Suite 4W
New York NY 10128
Phone: 212/410-6560

Mr. Elias BELAYNEH
President
U.S.-Africa Chamber of Commerce
1899 L Street, NW - Fifth Floor
Washington DC 20036
Phone: 202/331-7053   Fax: 202/331-1809

Angola

Mr. Edmund DEJARATTE
Executive Director
US-Angola Chamber of Commerce
1850 K Street, NW - #390
Washington DC 20006
Phone: 202/223-0540   Fax: 202/872-1521
URL: http://ourworld.compuserve.com/
  homepages/usacc
E-mail: 75301.3361@compuserve.com

Argentina

Mr. Guillermo ORSELLI
Executive Director
Argentine-American Chamber of Commerce
10 Rockefeller Plaza - #1001
New York NY 10020
Phone: 212/698-2238   Fax: 212/698-2239

Australia

Australian-American Chamber of Commerce
611 Larchmont Blvd. - 2nd Fl.
Los Angeles CA 90004
Phone: 415/348-4825   Fax: 213/469-6419

Mr. Jim HUMPHREYS
Consulate General
Australian Consulate General
Dept. of Public Affairs 630 Fifth Avenue - #420
New York NY 10111
Phone: 212/408-8400   Fax: 212/408-8401

Austria

Mr. Hans KAUSL
Trade Commissioner
Austrian Trade Commission
11601 Wilshire Blvd. - #2420
Los Angeles CA 90025
Phone: 310/477-9988   Fax: 310/477-1643
URL: http://www.austriantrade.org
E-mail: atc-la@ix.netcom.com

Ms. Erika N. BOROZAN
Executive Director
US-Austrian Chamber of Commerce
165 W. 46th Street - #1112
New York NY 10036
Phone: 212/819-0117   Fax: 212/819-0117

Mr. Benno KOCH
Trade Commissioner
Austrian Trade Commission in New York
150 E. 52nd Street - 32nd Floor
New York NY 10022
Phone: 212/421-5250   Fax: 212/751-4675
URL: http://www.austriantrade.org
E-mail: atc-ny@ix.netcom.com

Azerbaijan

Mr. Galib MAMMAD
Executive Director
US-Azerbaijan Chamber of Commerce
1825 Eye Street, NW - #400
Washington DC 20006
Phone: 202/857-8069   Fax: 202/775-4188
URL: http://www.usacc.com
E-mail: gmammad@usacc.com

Bangladesh

Ms. Brenda J. CARTER
Director
BJ Marketing & Promotion
1392 Waterford Green Dr.
Marietta GA 30068
Phone: 770/518-7747   Fax: 770/643-0710

Belgium

Ms. Caroline LACOCQUE
Executive Director
Belgian-American Chamber of
  Commerce in the US

1330 Ave. of the Americas, 26th Floor
New York NY 10119
Phone: 212/969-9940   Fax: 212/969-9942
E-mail: bacc@ix.netcom.com

Bolivia

Mr. Robert COZZI
President
Bolivian Chamber of Commerce of Florida
7136 SW 47th St.
Miami FL 33155
Phone: 305/663-8821   Fax: 305/663-9560

Mr. Rene C. BARRIOS
Bolivian-American Chamber of Commerce
1290 Avenue of the Americas - 30th Fl.
New York NY 10104
Phone: 212/216-2539   Fax: 212/216-2598

Brazil

Ms. Gloria JOHNSON
Executive Director
Brazilian American Chamber of Commerce of FL.
1101 Brickell Ave.- #1102
Miami FL 33130
Phone: 305/579-9030   Fax: 305/579-9756
URL: http://www.brazilchamber.org
E-mail: baccf@brazilchamber.org

Ms. Sueli Cristina BONAPARTE
Executive Director
Brazilian-American Chamber of Commerce
22 West 58th Street - #404
New York NY 10036-1886
Phone: 212/575-9030   Fax: 212/921-1078

Mr. David HIRSCHMANN
Executive Vice President
Brazil-US Business Council
1615 H Street, NW
Washington DC 20062
Phone: 202/463-5485   Fax: 202/463-3126
URL: http://www.brazilcouncil.org
E-mail: host@brazilcouncil.org

Bulgaria

Bulgarian-American Chamber of Commerce
6464 Sunset Blvd. - Suite 850
Los Angeles CA 90028-8010
Phone: 213/962-2414   Fax: 213/962-2010

Central America

Ms. Ana B. HEDMAN
Executive Director
Central America-US Chamber of Commerce
2100 Ponce de Leon Blvd. - #1180
Miami FL 33134
Phone: 305/569-9113   Fax: 305/569-6477

Chile

Mr. Lester ZIFFREN
Executive Director
North American-Chilean Chamber of Commerce
220 E. 81st Street
New York NY 10028
Phone: 212/288-5691   Fax: 212/628-4978

H.E. Charles A. GILLESPIE

President
Chilean-American Chamber of Commerce
1913 Massachusetts Ave., NW - 2nd Floor
Washington DC 20036
Phone: 202/457-0349   Fax: 202/835-8518

China

American-Fukien Chamber of Commerce
8 Chatham Square
New York NY 10038
Phone: 212/233-2226   Fax: 212/608-9200

Mr. Ping YU
Chief Representative
US Office of China Chamber of Intn'l. Commerce
4301 Connecticut Avenue, NW - #136
Washington DC 20008
Phone: 202/244-3244   Fax: 202/244-0478
URL: http://www.ccpit-us.org
E-mail: ccpitus@aol.com

Colombia

Mr. Ernesto CUCALON
Executive Director
Colombian-American Chamber of Commerce
2355 S. Salzedo - #209
Coral Gables FL 33134
Phone: 305/446-2542   Fax: 305/448-5028

Mr. Roberto MARINO
Director
Colombian Government Trade Bureau
6100 Wilshire Blvd. - #1170
Los Angeles CA 90048
Phone: 213/965-9760   Fax: 213/965-5029

Cyprus

Mr. Dennis DROUSHIOTIS
Comm. Counselor
Cyprus Trade Center
13 E. 40th Street
New York NY 10016
Phone: 212/213-9100   Fax: 212/213-2918
URL: http://www.cyprustradeny.org
E-mail: ctcny@aol.com

Denmark

Mr. Werner VALEUR JENSEN
President
Danish-American Chamber of Commerce
825 Third Avenue - 32nd Floor
New York NY 10017
Phone: 212/980-6240   Fax: 212/754-1904

Mr. Gene POWELL
President
Danish-American Chamber of Commerce
P.O. Box 9412
Washington DC 20016
Phone: 202/775-8416

Ecuador

Mr. Raul VILLAVICENCIO
President
Ecuadorian-American Chamber of
   Commerce of Greater Miami
1390 Brickell Ave. - #220
Miami FL 33131

Phone: 305/539-0010   Fax: 305/539-8001
URL: http://www.ecuachamber.com
E-mail: ecuachamber@compuserve.com

Egypt

Mr. A. ZAKI
US-Egypt Chamber of Commerce
330 East 39th Street - Suite 32L
New York NY 10016
Phone: 212/867-2323   Fax: 212/490-1041

Europe

Mr. Sven C. OEHME
European-American Chamber of Commerce
40 W. 57th St. - 31st Fl.
New York NY 10019-4092
Phone: 212/315-2196   Fax: 212/315-2183

Mr. Willard BERRY
President
European-American Business Council
1333 H Street, NW - #630
Washington DC 20005
Phone: 202/347-9292   Fax: 202/628-5498
URL: http://www.eabc.org
E-mail: wberry@eabc.org

Finland

Mr. Robert KOLCZ
President
Finnish-American Chamber of
   Commerce of the Midwest
P.O. Box 11337
Chicago IL 60611-0337
Phone: 312/670-4700   Fax: 312/670-4777

Ms. Ava ANTTILA
President
Finnish American Chamber of Comm. - W. Coast
1900 Avenue of the Stars - #1060
Los Angeles CA 90067
Phone: 310/203-9903   Fax: 310/203-0301

Mr. George P. CARABERIS
President
Finnish-American Chamber of Commerce
866 UN Plaza - #249
New York NY 10017
Phone: 212/821-0225   Fax: 212/750-4417
URL: http://www.finlandtrade.com

France

Ms. Leslie PERRY
Executive Director
French-American Chamber of Commerce
999 Peachtree Street, NE - Suite 2095
Atlanta GA 30309
Phone: 404/874-2602   Fax: 404/875-9452

Ms. Betsy O'BRIEN
Executive Director
French-American Chamber of Commerce
15 Court Square - Suite 320
Boston MA 02108
Phone: 617/523-4438   Fax: 617/523-4461

Ms. Patrice CAVALLO
Managing Director
French-American Chamber of Commerce
55 East Monroe Street
Chicago IL 60603

Phone: 312/263-7668   Fax: 312/263-7860

Ms. Erin PETIT
Managing Director
French-American Chamber of Commerce
4835 LBJ Freeway
Dallas TX 75244
Phone: 214/991-4888   Fax: 214/991-4887

Mr. Howard B. HILL
Executive Director
French-American Chamber of Commerce
100 Renaissance Center - #2210
Detroit MI 48243-1100
Phone: 313/567-6010   Fax: 313/567-0142

Ms. Kathleen RIFFE
Managing Director
French-American Chamber of Commerce
1770 St. James - Suite 425
Houston TX 77056
Phone: 713/960-0575   Fax: 713/960-0495

Ms. Barbara HEARN
Executive Director
French-American Chamber of Commerce
6380 Wilshire Blvd. - #1608
Los Angeles CA 90048
Phone: 213/651-4741   Fax: 213/651-2547

Ms. N. Christine HEINERSCHEID
Executive Director
French-American Chamber of Commerce
821 Marquette Ave. - Suite 904 Foshay Tower
Minneapolis MN 55402
Phone: 612/338-7750

Mr. Lou JOHNSON
Executive Director
French-American Chamber of Commerce
World Trade Center - #2938 No. 2 Canal Street
New Orleans LA 70130-1135
Phone: 504/524-2042   Fax: 504/522-4003

Mr. Lenir DRAKE
President
French-American Chamber of Commerce
1350 Avenue of the Americas - 6th Floor
New York NY 10019
Phone: 212/765-4460   Fax: 212/765-4650

Ms. Susan L. SILVERSTEIN
Executive Director
French-American Chamber of Commerce
4000 Bell Atlantic Tower 1717 Arch Street
Philadelphia PA 19103-2713
Phone: 215/994-5373   Fax: 215/994-5366

Ms. Janet B. STIEHLER
Executive Director
French-American Chamber of Commerce
435 Sixth Ave.
Pittsburgh PA 15219
Phone: 412/288-4174   Fax: 412/288-3603

Ms. Jean Ward JACOTE
Executive Director
French-American Chamber of Commerce
425 Bush Street - Suite 401
San Francisco CA 94108
Phone: 415/395-2449   Fax: 415/398-8912

Mr. Jack COHAN
Executive Director
French-American Chamber of Commerce
2101 Fourth Ave., Suite 2330
Seattle WA 98121
Phone: 206/443-4703   Fax: 206/448-4218

Ms. Susan SHILLINGLAW
Executive Director
French-American Chamber of Commerce

918 16th Street, NW - Suite 406
Washington DC 20006
Phone: 202/785-0256   Fax: 202/785-4604
URL: http://www.facc-dc.org
E-mail: faccwdc@aol.com

Germany

Mr. Thomas BECK
President & CEO
German-American Chamber of
    Commerce of the Southern US
3340 Peachtree Road N.E. - #500
Atlanta GA 30326
Phone: 404/239-9494   Fax: 404/264-1761
URL: http://www.gaccsouth.com
E-mail: gaccsouth@mindspring.com

Mr. Christian J. ROEHR
Managing Director
German-American Chamber of
    Commerce of the Midwest
401 N. Michigan Avenue - #2525
Chicago IL 60611-4212
Phone: 312/644-2662   Fax: 312/644-0738
URL: http://www.gaccom.org
E-mail: 106025.402@compuserve.com

Mr. Friedrich W. KUHLMANN
Vice President and Managing Director
German-American Chamber of Commerce
5599 San Felipe - #510
Houston TX 77056
Phone: 713/877-1114   Fax: 713/877-1602
URL: http://www.gaccsouth.com
E-mail: gacchou@mindspring.com

Mr. Michael KRIEG
President and CEO
German-American Chamber of
    Commerce of the Western US
5220 Pacific Concourse Dr. - #280
Los Angeles CA 90045
Phone: 310/297-7979   Fax: 310/297-7966
URL: http://www.gaccwest.org
E-mail: gaccwest@compuserve.com

Mr. Werner WALBROEL
President
German-American Chamber of Commerce
40 W. 57th Street, 31st Floor
New York NY 10019-4092
Phone: 212/974-8830   Fax: 212/974-8867
E-mail: gaccny@compuserve.com

Mrs. Barbara AFANASSIEV
Managing Director
German-American Chamber of Commerce
1515 Market St. - #505
Philadelphia PA 19102
Phone: 215/665-1585   Fax: 215/665-0375
URL: http://www.ourworld.compuserve.com/
    homepages/gacc-ny/
E-mail: gaccphila@compuserve.com

Mr. Lawrence A. WALKER
Executive Vice President
German-American Chamber of Commerce
465 California St. - #506
San Francisco CA 94104
Phone: 415/392-2262   Fax: 415/392-1314
URL: http://www.gaccwest.org
E-mail: gaccwest_sfo@compuserve.com

Ghana

Ghanaian-American Chamber of Commerce
P.O. Box 1125

Monterey CA 93942
Phone: 408/648-3803

Ghanaian-American Chamber of Commerce
P.O. Box 12153
Oakland CA 94604
Phone: 510/653-7027

Greece

Mr. Andrew ATHENS
Chairman
Hellenic-American Chamber of Commerce
400 N. Franklin St. - #215
Chicago IL 60610
Phone: 312/822-0818   Fax: 312/822-0890

Hellenic-American Chamber of Commerce
P.O. Box 6053
Clearwater FL 34618
Phone: 813/593-1229   Fax: 813/593-1880

Mr. Stamatius GIKAS
Executive Secretary
Hellenic-American Chamber of Commerce
960 Avenue of the Americas - #1204
New York NY 10001
Phone: 212/629-6380   Fax: 212/564-9281

Haiti

Haitian Chamber of Commerce
P.O. Box 2374
Brooklyn NY 11202
Phone: 212/859-1002

Hungary

Hungarian-American Chamber of Commerce
355 South End Ave. - Suite 7N
New York NY 10280
Phone: 212/321-3310

Ms. Eva VOISIN
President
Hungarian-American Chamber of Commerce
250A Twin Dolphin Drive - #500
Redwood City CA 94065
Phone: 415/595-0444   Fax: 415/595-3976

Iceland

Mr. Magnus BJARNASON
Executive Director
Icelandic-American Chamber of Commerce
800 Third Ave., 36th Floor
New York NY 10022
Phone: 212/593-2700   Fax: 212/593-6269
URL: http://www.icelandtrade.com
E-mail: magnus.bjarnason@utn.stjr.is

India

Mr. Rajiv KHANNA
President
India American Chamber of Commerce
125 West 55th Street - 16th Floor
New York NY 10019-5389
Phone: 212/755-7181   Fax: 212/424-8500

Mr. Sri J. SRIDHARAN
Director, USA
Indian Chambers of Commerce and Industry

6241 Executive Vlvd.
Rockville MD 20852
Phone: 301/881-9091   Fax: 301/984-7053
E-mail: jayasri@worldnet.att.net

Indonesia

Mr. Wayne FORREST
Executive Director
American-Indonesian Chamber of Commerce
711 Third Ave. - 17th Floor
New York NY 10017
Phone: 212/687-4505   Fax: 212/867-9882

Ireland

Mr. Charles BOYLE
Executive Director
Ireland Chamber of Commerce in the US
1305 Post Road - #205
Fairfield CT 06430
Phone: 203/255-4774   Fax: 203/255-6752

Islam

Mr. Reza GHADIMI
Chairman
American Islamic Chamber of Commerce
P.O. Box 30807
Albuquerque NM 87190-0807
Phone: 505/881-3433   Fax: 505/881-3433
URL: http://www.americanislam.org/aicc
E-mail: aicc@americanislam.org

Israel

Mr. Tom GLASER
President
American-Israel Chamber of Commerce
1100 Spring Street - #410
Atlanta GA 30309
Phone: 404/874-6970   Fax: 404/874-7277
URL: http://www.mindspring.org/aiccse
E-mail: aiccse@mindspring.org

Ms. Marlene GREENBERG
Executive Vice President
American-Israel Chamber of Commerce and
    Industry of Metro Chicago
180 N. Michigan Avenue - #911
Chicago IL 60601
Phone: 312/641-2937   Fax: 312/641-2941
E-mail: aicci@interaccess.com

Mr. Milton LEVENFELD
President
America-Israel Chambers of Commerce
180 N. Michigan Ave.
Chicago IL 60601
Phone: 312/641-2944   Fax: 312/641-2941
E-mail: aicc@interaccess.com

Ms. Ronny BASSAN
Executive Vice President
American-Israel Chamber of Commerce & Ind.
310 Madison Ave. - #1103
New York NY 10017-6009
Phone: 212/661-4106   Fax: 212/661-7930

Italy

Italy-America Chamber of Commerce,
    South Regional

1050 Crown Pointe Pkwy. - Suite 310
Atlanta GA 30338
Phone: 404/913-9999   Fax: 404/671-8513

Italy-America Chamber of Commerce, New Eng.
100 Boylston Street
Boston MA 02116
Phone: 617/482-5949   Fax: 617/482-6434

Ms. Leonora LI PUMA
Executive Director
Italy-America Chamber of Comm. of Chicago
30 S. Michigan Avenue - #504
Chicago IL 60603
Phone: 312/553-9137   Fax: 312/553-9142
URL: http://www.italchambers.net/chicago
E-mail: info.chicago@italchambers.net

Italy-America Chamber of Commerce, Texas
4605 Post Oak Place - Suite 226
Houston TX 77002
Phone: 713/636-9303   Fax: 713/626-9309

Mrs. Piera KOULERMOS
Executive Director
Italy-America Chamber of Commerce, West
11520 San Vincente Blvd. - #203
Los Angeles CA 90049
Phone: 310/826-9898   Fax: 310/826-2876
URL: http://italy-america-chamber.com/iaccw/
    iaccw001.htm

Italy-America Chamber of Commerce, Southeast
1 SE 15th Road - Suite 150
Miami FL 33129
Phone: 305/577-9868   Fax: 305/577-3956

Mr. Franco DEANGELIS
Executive Secretary
Italy-America Chamber of Commerce
730 Fifth Avenue - #600
New York NY 10019
Phone: 212/459-0044   Fax: 212/459-0090
URL: http://www.italchambers.net/newyork
E-mail: info.newyork@italchambers.net

Italy-America Chamber of Comm., Mid-Atlantic
2411 Penn Center
Philadelphia PA 19103
Phone: 215/963-0998   Fax: 215/963-8821

Italy-America Chamber of Commerce
200 First Ave. - 4th Floor
Pittsburgh PA 15222
Phone: 412/261-2580   Fax: 412/261-2678

US-Italy Chamber of Commerce
1511 K Street, NW - Suite 1100
Washington DC 20005
Phone: 202/293-0633
URL: http://members.aol.com/USItaly
E-mail: usitaly@aol.com

Jamaica

Mr. Derryck E. COX
Jamaican-American Chamber of Commerce
PO Box 800
New York NY 10024
Phone: 212/877-8900   Fax: 212/877-1905

Japan

Mr. Hideo TOYOSHIMA
Executive Director
Japanese Chamber of Comm. & Ind. of Chicago
401 N. Michigan Avenue - #602
Chicago IL 60611

Phone: 312/332-6199   Fax: 312/822-9773

Honolulu-Japanese Chamber of Commerce
2454 S. Beretania Street
Honolulu HI 86826
Phone: 808/949-5531   Fax: 808/949-3020

Ms. Shoko KADOWAKI
Executive Director
Japan Business Association of Houston
14133 Memorial Drive - #3
Houston TX 77079
Phone: 713/493-1512   Fax: 713/493-2276

Mr. Sadao KITA
Executive Director
Japan Business Association of Southern California
345 S. Figueroa St.
Los Angeles CA 90071
Phone: 213/485-0160   Fax: 213/626-5526

Mr. SUZUKI
Executive Secretary
Japanese Chamber of Comm. of Southern Calif.
244 S. San Pedro Street - #504
Los Angeles CA 90012
Phone: 213/626-3067   Fax: 213/626-3070
URL: http://www.jccsc.com

Mr. Tsutomu KARINO
Executive Director
Japanese Chamber of Commerce and
    Industry of New York, Inc.
145 W. 57th Street - 6th Floor
New York NY 10019
Phone: 212/246-8001   Fax: 212/246-8002
URL: http://www.jcciny.org

Korea

Korean-American Chamber of Commerce
309 Fifth Avenue
New York NY 10016
Phone: 212/481-0042   Fax: 212/689-6608

Korea, Republic of

Mr. Jim CHOI
Executive Director
Korean American Chamber of Commerce of LA
3350 Wilshire Blvd. - #6600
Los Angeles CA 90010
Phone: 213/480-1115   Fax: 213/480-7521
E-mail: kaccla@wavenet.com

Mr. Kwang Rip BYUN
Executive Director
Korean Chamber of Commerce and Industry
460 Park Ave. - #1301
New York NY 10022
Phone: 212/644-0140   Fax: 212/644-9106

Latin America

Mr. Roy A. HASTICKS
Caribbean American Chamber of Commerce
Brooklyn Navy Yard Bldg. 5, Mezzanine A
Brooklyn NY 11205
Phone: 718/834-4544   Fax: 718/834-9774

Inter-American Chamber of Commerce
510 Bering Drive - Suite 300
Houston TX 77057-1400
Phone: 713/975-6171   Fax: 713/975-6610

Mr. Luis SABINES

President
Latin Chamber of Commerce
1417 W. Flagler Street
Miami FL 33135
Phone: 305/642-3870   Fax: 305/642-0653

Mr. Michael ROTHKIN
Senior Director, Admin. and Finance
Americas Society, Inc.
680 Park Avenue
New York NY 10021
Phone: 212/249-8950   Fax: 212/249-5868
URL: http://www.americas-society.org
E-mail: m.rothkin@as-coa.org

Council of the Americas
680 Park Ave.
New York NY 10021
Phone: 212/628-3200   Fax: 212/517-6247

Mr. David HIRSCHMANN
Executive Vice President
Assn. of American Chambers of
    Commerce in Latin America
1615 H Street, NW
Washington DC 20062-2000
Phone: 202/463-5485   Fax: 202/463-3126
URL: http://www.aacla.org
E-mail: inbox@aacla.org

Ms. Marina LAVERDY
Executive Director
Latin American Management Association
419 New Jersey Avenue, SE
Washington DC 20003
Phone: 202/546-3803   Fax: 202/546-3807

Mr. Ronald. MONTOYA
Chairman
US-Hispanic Chamber of Commerce
1019 19th Street, NW - # 200
Washington DC 20036
Phone: 202/842-1212   Fax: 202/842-3221
URL: http://www.ushcc.com
E-mail: ffarinetti@ushcc.com

Lithuania

US-Baltic Chamber of Commerce
13902 Fiji Way - #324
Marina del Rey CA 60292
Phone: 310/827-9590   Fax: 310/827-9590

Luxembourg

Mr. Fernand LAMESH
Executive Director
Luxembourg American Chamber of Commerce
350 Fifth Avenue - #1322
New York NY 10118
Phone: 212/967-9898   Fax: 212/629-0349

Mr. Patrick NICKLOS
Counsel General & Executive Director
Luxembourg Board of Economic Development
One Sansome Street - #830
San Francisco CA 94104
Phone: 415/788-0816   Fax: 415/788-0985
E-mail: luxcgsf@aol.com

Malaysia

Mr. Noharuddin NORDIN
Trade Commissioner
Malaysian Trade Commission
313 East 43rd St.

New York NY 10017
Phone: 212/682-0232   Fax: 212/983-1987

Mexico

US-Mexico Chamber of Commerce
150 N. Michigan Ave. - Suite 2910
Chicago IL 60601
Phone: 312/236-8745   Fax: 312/781-5925

US-Mexico Chamber of Commerce
3000 Carlisle Street - Suite 210
Dallas TX 75204
Phone: 214/754-8060   Fax: 214/871-9533

US-Mexico Chamber of Commerce
720 Kipling - Suite 201
Lakewood CO 80215
Phone: 303/237-7080   Fax: 303/237-5568

US-Mexico Chamber of Commerce
555 S. Flower Street - 25th Fl.
Los Angeles CA 90071-2236
Phone: 213/623-7725   Fax: 213/623-0032

Ms. Rosie BECK
US-Mexico Chamber of Commerce
400 East 59th Street - Suite 8B
New York NY 10022
Phone: 212/750-2638   Fax: 212/750-2149

Mr. Hector LEDESMA
President
Arizona Mexican Chamber of Commerce
6330 N. Central Avenue - #5 P.O. Box 626
Phoenix AZ 85021
Phone: 602/252-6448   Fax: 602/252-6448

Mr. Refugio Luis BARRAGAN
Director
Nuevo Leon Foreign Trade Center
100 W. Houston St. - #1400
San Antonio TX 78205
Phone: 210/225-0732   Fax: 210/225-0736

Mr. Fernando BARRUTIA
Chamber of Commerce of Mexico
1030 15th St., NW - #206
Washington DC 20005
Phone: 202/842-0729   Fax: 202/842-1212

Mr. Al ZAPANTA
President and CEO
US-Mexico Chamber of Commerce
1726 M St., NW - #704
Washington DC 20036
Phone: 202/296-5198   Fax: 202/728-0768
URL: http://www.usmcoc.org/usmcoc/
E-mail: zapantaz@usmcoc.org

Middle East

Mr. Abass ALI-DINAR
President & CEO
United Arab-American Chamber of Commerce
9461 Charleville Blvd. - #505
Beverly Hills CA 90212
Phone: 310/271-7396   Fax: 310/276-5086

Mr. Dirk D. SHARER
Regional Manager
National US-Arab Chamber of Commerce
208 S. LaSalle Street - #706
Chicago IL 60604
Phone: 312/782-0320   Fax: 312/782-7379

Mr. Maan AL-UBAIDI
Regional Director

Southwest US-Arab Chamber of Commerce
2915 LBJ Freeway - #260
Dallas TX 75234
Phone: 214/241-9992   Fax: 214/241-0114

Mr. Richard HOLMES
Executive Director
US-Arab Chamber of Commerce
420 Lexington Avenue - #2739
New York NY 10170
Phone: 212/986-8024   Fax: 212/986-0216

Mr. D.J. ASFOUR
Executive Director
US-Arab Chamber of Commerce (Pacific), Inc.
P.O. Box 422218
San Francisco CA 94142-2218
Phone: 415/398-9200   Fax: 415/398-7111
URL: http://www.usaccp.org
E-mail: ArabTrade@usaccp.org

Mr. Donald DEMARINO
Chairman
National US-Arab Chamber of Commerce
1100 New York Avenue, NW
East Tower - Suite 550
Washington DC 20005
Phone: 202/289-5920   Fax: 202/289-5938
URL: http://www.nusacc.org
E-mail: nusacc@aol.com

Netherlands

Mr. Ryan BARRAS
Executive Director
Netherlands Chamber of Commerce in the US
2015 S. Park Place - #110
Atlanta GA 30339
Phone: 770/933-9044   Fax: 770/933-9644
URL: http://www.netherlands.org
E-mail: ncocat@compuserve.com

Ms. Sandra VOGEL
Manager
Netherlands Chamber of Commerce in the US
303 E. Wacker Drive - #412
Chicago IL 60601
Phone: 312/938-9050   Fax: 312/938-8949
E-mail: 76746.2024@compuserve.com

Mr. Kersen DE JONG
Managing Director
Netherlands Chamber of Commerce in the US
One Rockefeller Plaza - #1420
New York NY 10020
Phone: 212/265-6460   Fax: 212/265-6402

Mr. Simon DE JONG
Office Manager
Netherlands Chamber of Commerce in the US
4200 Wisconsin Ave., NW - #106-227
Washington DC 20016
Phone: 202/393-1376   Fax: 202/244-3325
URL: http://www.netherlands.org
E-mail: ncocdc@compuserve.com

Nigeria

Nigerian-American Chamber of Commerce
828 Second Avenue
New York NY 10017
Phone: 212/808-0301

Northern Ireland

Mr. Tony R. CULLEY-FOSTER

Chairman
Northern Ireland - US Chamber of Commerce
P.O. Box 17370
Washington DC 20041
Phone: 703/471-1661   Fax: 703/661-8251

Norway

Dr. Sunny HANSEN
Norwegian-American Chamber of Commerce
821 Marquette Avenue 800 Foshay Tower
Minneapolis MN 55408-2961
Phone: 612/332-3338   Fax: 612/332-1386

Mr. Ingar M. TALLAKSEN
General Manager
Norwegian-American Chamber of Commerce
800 Third Avenue
New York NY 10022
Phone: 212/421-9210   Fax: 212/838-0374

Mr. Helge KROGENES
Trade Commissioner
Norwegian Trade Council
20 California Street, 6th Floor
San Francisco CA 94111-4803
Phone: 415/986-0770   Fax: 415/986-6025
URL: http://www.ntcusa.org
E-mail: helge.krogenes@ntc.org

Peru

Peruvian-American Chamber of Commerce
3460 Wilshire Blvd. - Suite 1006
Los Angeles CA 90010
Phone: 213/386-7378   Fax: 213/386-7376

Mr. Phelipe WOLL
President
Peruvian-US Chamber of Commerce
444 Brickell Avenue - #M-126
Miami FL 33131
Phone: 305/375-0885   Fax: 305/375-0884

Philippines

Philippino-American Chamber of Commerce
310 David Drive
Alamo CA 94507
Phone: 510/831-9257   Fax: 510/831-8728

Mr. Luis C. BAUTISTA
Executive Director
Philippine Chamber of Commerce-Chicago
2457 W. Peterson - #3
Chicago IL 60659
Phone: 312/271-8008   Fax: 312/271-8058

Mr. Paul CUNNION
Executive Director
Philippine-American Chamber of Commerce
711 Third Ave. - #1702
New York NY 10017-4046
Phone: 212/972-9326   Fax: 212/867-9882

Poland

US-Poland Chamber of Commerce
812 North Wood Ave. - Suite 214
Linden NJ 07036
Phone: 908/486-9311   Fax: 908/486-4084

Mr. Gary LITMAN
Executive Director

Polish-US Economic Council
1615 H St., NW
Washington DC 20062-2000
Phone: 202/463-5482   Fax: 202/463-3114

Portugal

Ms. Ana OSORIO
Executive Director
Portugal-US Chamber of Commerce
590 Fifth Avenue, 3rd Floor
New York NY 10036
Phone: 212/354-4627   Fax: 212/575-4737
URL: http://www.portugal-us.com
E-mail: anaosori@ix.netcom.com

Romania

Romanian-American Chamber of Commerce
909 Third Avenue, 27th Floor
New York NY 10022
Phone: 212/339-5453

Russia

Dr. Igor S. OLEYNIK
President and CEO
Russian-American Chamber of Commerce
P.O. Box 15343
Washington DC 20003
Phone: 202/546-2103   Fax: 202/546-3275
URL: http://www.rusline.com
E-mail: rusric@erols.com

Saudi Arabia

Mr. Abdullah ALATHEL
Attache
Royal Embassy of Saudi Arabia,
    Commercial Office
601 New Hampshire Ave., NW
Washington DC 20037
Phone: 202/337-4088   Fax: 202/342-0271
URL: http://www.saudicommercialoffice.com
E-mail: saco@resa.org

Singapore

Mr. Satvinder SINGH
Director
Singapore Trade Development Board
55 E. 59th St., FL 21 B
New York NY 10022-1122
Phone: 212/421-2207   Fax: 212/888-2897
E-mail: tbdny@compuserve.com

South Africa

American South African Chamber of
    Trade and Commerce
1080 Park Ave. - Suite 4W
New York NY 10128
Phone: 212/410-6560

Spain

Mr. David MARTI
Executive Director
Spain-US Chamber of Commerce

2655 Le Jeune Road - #906
Coral Gables FL 33134
Phone: 305/446-1992   Fax: 305/529-2854

Mr. Kevin KALLAHAN
Executive Director
Spain-US Chamber of Commerce
350 5th Avenue - #2029
New York NY 10118
Phone: 212/967-2170   Fax: 212/564-1415
E-mail: spuscha@aol.com

Sweden

Mr. Per KARLQUIST
Director
Swedish-American Chamber of Commerce
5118 S. Broadway
Englewood CO 80110
Phone: 303/761-3285   Fax: 303/761-3417
URL: http://www.sacc-usa.org/colorado

Mr. Marcus BOSSEM
General Manager
Swedish-American Chamber of Commerce
825 Third Avenue
New York NY 10022
Phone: 212/838-5530   Fax: 212/755-7953

Ms. Marie Louise ULNMARK
Executive Director
Swedish-American Chamber of Commerce
Northern California, Inc.
Market Street - #305
San Francisco CA 94104
Phone: 415/781-4188   Fax: 415/781-0491
URL: http://www.sacc-usa.org/sanfrans
E-mail: saccsf@ix.netcom.com

Mr. Philip C. GAST
Chairman
Swedish-American Chamber of
    Commerce of Washington, DC, Inc.
1501 M Street, NW - 9th Floor
Washington DC 20005
Phone: 202/467-2638   Fax: 202/467-2656
E-mail: sten.graffman@foreign.ministry.se

Switzerland

Swiss American Chamber of Commerce
1251 Bethlehem
Houston TX 77018
Phone: 713/682-8047   Fax: 713/682-6018

Swiss American Chamber of Commerce
800 Wilshire Blvd. - #800
Los Angeles CA 90017
Phone: 213/489-3167   Fax: 213/489-3336

Swiss-American Chamber of Commerce
347 Fifth Ave. - #1008
New York NY 10016
Phone: 212/213-0482   Fax: 212/481-7969

Mr. Eddie SENNHAUSER
Chairman
Swiss American Chamber of Commerce
P.O. Box 2269
San Francisco CA 94126-2269
Phone: 415/433-6679   Fax: 415/956-3882

Taiwan

Chinese Chamber of Commerce
33 Bowery

New York NY 10022
Phone: 212/226-2795

Thailand

Mr. Benjawan RATANAPRAYUL
Director
Thai Trade Center
5 World Trade Center - #3443
New York NY 10048
Phone: 212/466-1777   Fax: 212/524-0972
URL: http://www.thaitrade.com
E-mail: thtradny@ix.netcom.com

United Kingdom

Mr. Richard FURSLAND
Managing Director
British-American Chamber of Commerce
52 Vanderbilt Avenue, 20th Floor
New York NY 10017
Phone: 212/661-4060   Fax: 212/661-4074
URL: http://www.bacc.org
E-mail: info@bacc.org

Mr. Mostyn T. LLOYD
Executive Director
British-American Chamber of Commerce
41 Sutter Street - #303
San Francisco CA 94104
Phone: 415/296-8645   Fax: 415/296-9649

Mr. Dennis F. STORER
Executive Director
British-American Chamber of Commerce
1640 Fifth Street - #203
Santa Monica CA 90401
Phone: 310/394-4977   Fax: 310/394-0839

Uruguay

Uruguayan American Chamber of Commerce
401 E. 88th Street - Suite 12A
New York NY 10128
Phone: 212/713-5027   Fax: 212/996-2580

Uzbekistan

Mr. George J. CHALL
Uzbekistan Anerican Chamber of Commerce
c/o The Chall Group 237 Park Ave. - 21st Fl.
New York NY 10017
Phone: 212/580-0800   Fax: 212/580-0010

Venezuela

Venezuelan-American Chamber of Commerce
2199 Ponce de Leon, Mezz.
Coral Gables FL 33134
Phone: 305/461-8283   Fax: 305/443-4145

INTRODUCTION - American Chambers of Commerce Abroad

American Chambers of Commerce Abroad (AmChams) are voluntary associations comprised of business executives concerned with foreign trade and investment between the U.S. and their respective host countries. Affiliates of the U.S. Chamber of Commerce, the AmChams assert the U.S. business perspective in the host countries by representing their members before the governments, business communities, and general public of their respective countries. Through a wide variety of activities, AmChams work to:

- *develop mutually prosperous and amicable economic, social, and commercial relations between U.S. businesses and industrial interests and those of the host country;*

- *represent members' views on policy and regulatory matters to both U.S. and host country governments;*

- *interpret the point of view of other countries to the American business public;*

- *promote local economic and social contributions for the benefit of host countries.*

Argentina

Mr. Felix ZUMELZU
Executive Director
American Chamber of Commerce in Argentina
Viamonte 1133, Piso 8
Buenos Aires 1053
Phone: 54-1-371-4500   Fax: 541-1-371-8400
E-mail: amchamar@impsatl.com.ar

Asia

Mr. Douglas HENCK
Chairman
Asia-Pacific Council of American
    Chambers of Commerce
c/o AmCham Hong Kong
1904 Bank of America Tower 12 Harcourt Rd.
Hong Kong
Phone: 852-2-526-0165   Fax: 852-2-810-1289
E-mail: amcham@amcham.org.hk

Australia

Ms. Mareylene WILLIAMS
State Manager
American Chamber of Commerce in
    Australia - Adelaide Branch
Level 1, 300 Flinders Street
Adelaide SA 5000
Phone: 61-08-224-0761   Fax: 61-08-224-0628
URL: http://www.amcham.com.au
E-mail: sa@amcham.com.au

Ms. Marie SINCLAIR
General Manager
American Chamber of Commerce in
    Australia - Brisbane Branch
Level 23, Lennons Bldg.
68 Queen St.
Brisbane QLD 4000
Phone: 61-07-3221-8542

Fax: 61-07-3221-6313
URL: http://www.amcham.com.au
E-mail: qld@amcham.com.au

Ms. Robyn LARSON
State Manager
American Chamber of Commerce in
    Australia - Melbourne Branch
Level 21, 500 Collins Street
Melbourne VIC 3000
Phone: 61-03-9614-7744
Fax: 61-03-9614-8181
URL: http://www.amcham.com.au
E-mail: vic@amcham.com.au

Ms. Kate TUDOR
State Manager
American Chamber of Commerce in
    Australia - Perth Branch
Level 6, 231 Adelaide Terrace
Perth WA 6000
Phone: 61-09-325-9540   Fax: 61-09-221-3725
URL: http://www.amcham.com.au
E-mail: wa@amcham.com.au

Mr. Charles BLUNT
National Director
American Chamber of Commerce in
    Australia - National/NSW Office
Suite 4, Gloucester Walk
88 Cumberland Street
Sydney, NSW 2000
Phone: 61-02-9241-1907
Fax: 61-02-9251-5220
URL: http://www.amcham.com.au
E-mail: nsw@amcham.com.au

Austria

Dr. Patricia A. HELLETZGRUBER
Secretary General
American Chamber of Commerce in Austria
Porzellangasse 35
Vienna 1090
Phone: 43-1-319-5751   Fax: 43-1-319-5151

URL: http://www.amcham.or.at
E-mail: amcham@netway.at

Azerbaijan

Mr. Donald STEWART
Executive Director
American Chamber of Commerce in Azerbaijan
Rasul Tza Street 8, 15/26
Baku 37000
Phone: 99412-93-51-69   Fax: 99412-98-34-03

Belarus

Mr. Warren GRAWEMEYER
President
American Chamber of Commerce in Belarus
c/o Coca-Cola Amatil Belorussiya
Minsk District, Promuzel Kolyadichi
Minsk 223010
Phone: 375-172-100-210
Fax: 375-172-100-219
E-mail: ambusctr@minsk.sovam.com

Belgium

Ms. Jo Ann BROGER
General Manager
American Chamber of Commerce in Belgium
Avenue des Arts 50, Boite 5
Brussels 1000
Phone: 32-2-513-6770   Fax: 32-2-513-3590

Bolivia

Ms. Anna Maria GALINDO DE PAZ
General Manager
American Chamber of Commerce of Bolivia
P.O. Box 8268
La Paz
Phone: 591-2-432-573   Fax: 591-2-432-472
E-mail: amgal@utama.bolnet.bo

Brazil

Mr. Sergio RAPOSO
Executive Vice President
American Chamber of Commerce for
    Brazil - Rio De Janiero
C.P. 916, Praca Pio X-15
Fifth Floor
Rio de Janeiro 20040
Phone: 55-21-2032477   Fax: 55-21-2634477
E-mail: achambr@unisys.com.br

Mr. Laudilio Guimaraes MELLO
Executive Secretary
American Chamber of Commerce for
    Brazil - Salvador
Rua Torquato Bahia 69/705
Edif. Raimundo Magalhaes
Salvador, Bahia 40015-110
Phone: 55-71-242-0077   Fax: 55-71-243-9986

Mr. John Edwin MEIN
Executive Vice President
American Chamber of Commerce for
    Brazil - Sao Paulo
Rua da Paz 1431
Sao Paulo, SP 04713-001
Phone: 55-51-803-804   Fax: 55-51-803-777
URL: http://www.amcham.com.br
E-mail: evp@amcham.com.br

Bulgaria

Mr. Philip PHILIPOFF
Executive Director
American Chamber of Commerce in Bulgaria
19 Patriarh Evtimii Blvd.
Floor 5, Apt. 10
Sofia 1000
Phone: 359-2-981-5950   Fax: 359-2-980-4206
E-mail: amcham@lnd.internet-bg.bg

Chile

Mr. Francisco BERNALESSWETT
CEO/General Manager
Chilean-American Chamber of Commerce
Av Americo Vespucio sur 80-9 Piso
82 Correo 34
Santiago
Phone: 56-2-208-4140   Fax: 56-2-206-0911
E-mail: amcham@reuna.cl

China

Ms. Jane DRAKE
Executive Director
American Chamber of Commerce, PRC-Beijing
Great Wall Sheraton Hotel, Room 444
North Donghuan Avenue
Beijing 100026
Phone: 86-10-6500-5566 ext. 2271
Fax: 86-10-6501-8273
E-mail: amcham@public.bta.net.cn

Ms. Angie WILLIAMS
Director
American Chamber of Commerce in Shanghai
Shanghai Centre, Room 435
1376 Nanjing Road West
Shanghai 200040
Phone: 86-21-6279-7119
Fax: 86-21-6279-8802

Colombia

Mr. Joseph A. FINNIN
Manager
Colombian-American Chamber of Commerce
Apdo. Aereo 8008
Transversal 19 #12263
Bogota
Phone: 57-1-215-8859   Fax: 57-1-213-7071
E-mail: 73050.3127@compuserve.com

Ms. Leyda Lucia PEREZ B.
Executive Director
Colombian-American Chamber of
   Commerce - Cali
Av. 1N #3N-97
Cali
Phone: 57-2-661-0162   Fax: 57-2-667-2992

Ms. Patricia JARAMILLO
Executive Director
Colombian-American Chamber of
   Commerce - Cartagena
P.O. Box 15555
Cartagena
Phone: 57-56-657-724   Fax: 57-56-651-704

Mr. Nicolas DE ZUBIRIA
Executive Director
Colombian-American Chamber of
   Commerce - Medellin

P.O. Box 66655
Medellin
Phone: 57-4-268-7491   Fax: 57-4-268-3198

Costa Rica

Ms. Lynda SOLAR
Executive Director
Costa Rican-American Chamber of Commerce
P.O. Box 4946
San Jose 1000
Phone: 506-220-2200   Fax: 506-220-2300
URL: http://www.crica.com/amcham.html
E-mail: amchamcr@sol.racsa.co.cr

Cote D'Ivoire

American Chamber of Commerce
01 B.P. 3394
Abidjan 01
Phone: 225-21-46-16   Fax: 225-22-24-37

Czech Republic

Mr. Weston STACEY
Executive Director
American Chamber of Commerce in
   the Czech Republic
U Boziho Oka
Mala Stupartska 7
Praha 1 110 00
Phone: 420-2-2481-4280
Fax: 420-2-2481-8067
E-mail: amcham@mbox.vol.cz

Dominican Republic

Mr. Arthur E. VALDEZ
Executive Vice President
American Chamber of Commerce of the
Dominican Republic
P.O. Box 952
Santo Domingo
Phone: 809-544-2222   Fax: 809-544-0502
URL: http://www.codetel.net.do/amcham
E-mail: amcham@codetel.net.do

Ecuador

Dr. Maria Teresa PEREZ DE AYALA
Executive Director
Ecuadorian-American Chamber of
   Commerce - Guayaquil
G. Cordova 812, Piso 3, Officina 1
Edificio Torres de la Merced
Guayaquil
Phone: 593-4-566-481   Fax: 593-4-563-259
E-mail: caecanl@caecam.org.ec

Mr. Roque MINO
Executive Director
Ecuadorian-American Chamber of Commerce
Edificio Multicentro 4P
La Nina y Avda - 6 de Diciembre
Quito
Phone: 593-2-507-450   Fax: 593-2-504-571
URL: http://www.venweb.com/ec/ccea/ccea.htm
E-mail: cceal@ccea.org.ce

Egypt

Mr. El Motaz SONBOL
General Manager Operations
American Chamber of Commerce in Egypt
Cairo Marriott Hotel #1541
P.O. Box 33
Zamalek, Cairo
Phone: 20-2-340-8888   Fax: 20-2-340-9482

El Salvador

Ms. Patricia ALLWOOD
Executive Director
American Chamber of Commerce of El Salvador
87 Av. Norte #720,
Apto. A. Col. Escalon
San Salvador
Phone: 503-224-6003   Fax: 503-224-3646
E-mail: amcham@insatelsa.com

Estonia

Ms. Laura LEVENTIS
Executive Director
American Chamber of Commerce in Estonia
Vana Posti 7
Tallinn
Phone: 372-6-313-330   Fax: 372-6-314-012
E-mail: acce@datanet.ee

France

Mr. W. Barrett DOWER
Executive Director
American Chamber of Commerce in France
21 Avenue George V
Paris 75008
Phone: 33-1-4073-8990   Fax: 33-1-4720-1862

Germany

American Chamber of Commerce in
   Germany - Berlin Office
Budapesterstrasse 29
Berlin 10787
Phone: 49-30-261-5586   Fax: 49-30-262-2600

Dr. Dierk MUELLER
General Manager
American Chamber of Commerce in Germany
Rossmarkt 12
Postfach 100 162
Frankfurt 60311
Phone: 49-69-929-1040   Fax: 49-69-929-1041

Greece

Mr. Sotiris YANNOPOULOS
Executive Director
American-Hellenic Chamber of Commerce
16 Kanari Street, 3rd Floor
Athens 10674
Phone: 30-1-362-3231   Fax: 30-1-361-0170

Guatemala

Mr. Scott ROBERSON
Executive Director

American Chamber of Commerce in Guatemala
6a Avenida 14-77, Zona 10
Guatemala City 01010
Phone: 502-2-664-822   Fax: 502-2-683-106
URL: http://www.guatenet.com/amcham
E-mail: guamcham@ns.guatenet.com

Haiti

Ms. Josette NAZON
Executive Director
Haitian-American Chamber of Comm. & Industry
Complexe 384, Apt. 6
Delmas
Phone: 509-460-143   Fax: 509-460-143

Honduras

Ms. Maria de GRAY
Regional Manager
Honduran-American Chamber of Commerce
Centro Bella Aurora, 6 Avenida 13-14 Calles
San Pedro Sula
Phone: 504-580-164   Fax: 504-522-401

Mr. Hector CARCAMO
General Manager
Honduran-American Chamber of Commerce
Apdo. Postal 1838
Tegucigalpa
Phone: 504-32-70-43   Fax: 504-32-20-31

Hong Kong

Mr. Frank MARTIN
President
American Chamber of Commerce in Hong Kong
1904 Bank of America Tower
12 Harcourt Rd., Central
Hong Kong
Phone: 852-2526-0165   Fax: 852-2810-1289
URL: http://www.amcham.org.hk/
E-mail: amcham@hk.super.net

Hungary

Mr. Peter FATH
Executive Director
American Chamber of Commerce in Hungary
Deak Ferenc Utca 10
Budapest H-1052
Phone: 36-1-266-9880   Fax: 36-1-266-9888
E-mail: amcham@hungary.com

India

Mr. Ramesh BAJPAI
Executive Director
American Business Council-India
214 American Centre
24 Kasturba Gandhi Marg
New Delhi 110 001
Phone: 91-11-331-6841   Fax: 91-11-331-6556

Indonesia

Ms. Ruth CASSIDY
Executive Director
American Chamber of Commerce in Indonesia
World Trade Center, 11th Floor
Jendral Sudirman Kav. 29-31

Jakarta 12920
Phone: 62-21-526-2860   Fax: 62-21-526-2861

Ireland

Ms. Mary AINSCOUGH
CEO
American Chamber of Commerce of Ireland
Heritage House
23 St. Stephens
Dublin 2
Phone: 353-1-661-6201   Fax: 353-1-661-6217
E-mail: amcham@aol.ie

Israel

Ms. Nina ADMONI
Executive Director
Israel-America Chamber of Commerce
P.O. Box 33174
Tel Aviv 61333
Phone: 972-3-695-2341   Fax: 972-3-695-1272
URL: http://www.inter.net.il/~amchamil
E-mail: amchamil@inter.net.il

Italy

Mr. Sergio MINORETTI
Managing Director
American Chamber of Commerce in Italy
Via Cesare Cantu 1
Milano 20123
Phone: 39-2-869-0661   Fax: 39-2-805-7737

Jamaica

Dr. Ofe S. DUDLEY
CEO
American Chamber of Commerce of Jamaica
77 Knutsford Blvd.
Kingston 5
Phone: 809-929-7866   Fax: 809-929-8597
E-mail: odudley@mail/toj.com

Japan

Mr. Brian J. DUFFY
Executive Director
American Chamber of Commerce in Okinawa
P.O. Box 235
Okinawa 904
Phone: 81-9-8933-5146   Fax: 81-9-8933-7695
E-mail: acco@imicom.or.jp

Mr. Charles E. DUFFY
Executive Director
American Chamber of Commerce in Japan
Bridgestone Toranomon Bldg. 5F
3-25-2 Toranomon, Minato-ku
Tokyo 105
Phone: 81-33-433-5381   Fax: 81-33-436-1446
URL: http://www.accj.or.jp
E-mail: rfox@accj.or.jp

Korea

Ms. Tami OVERBY
Executive Director
American Chamber of Commerce in Korea
2nd Floor Westin Chosun Hotel
87 Sokong-dong Chung-Gu

Seoul
Phone: 82-2-753-6471   Fax: 82-2-755-6577
E-mail: 10053.1334@compuserve.com

Latvia

Ms. RueAnn ORMAND
Executive Director
American Chamber of Commerce in Latvia
Jauniela 24, Room 205
Riga
Phone: 371-721-2204   Fax: 371-782-0090
E-mail: amcham@mailbox.riga.lv

Lithuania

American Chamber of Commerce in Lithuania
P.O. Box 78
Vilnius 2000
Phone: 370-2-623-506   Fax: 370-2-608-604

Luxembourg

Mr. Guy HARLES
Executive Director
American Chamber of Commerce in Luxembourg
8-10 rue Mathias hardt, L-1717
Luxembourg
Phone: 352-400-218   Fax: 352-407-804
URL: http://www.aalux/amcham

Malaysia

Ms. Krystal E. ALLEY
Executive Director
American Malaysian Chamber of Commerce
22 Jalan Imbi
AMODA Bldg., Level 11
Kuala Lumpur 55100
Phone: 603-248-2407   Fax: 603-242-8540
URL: http://www.jaring.my/amcham
E-mail: excdir@amcham.po.my

Mexico

Ms. Claudia GROSSI
Executive Director
American Chamber of Commerce of
   Mexico - Guadalajara
Avda. Moctezuma #422
Zapopan
Guadalajara 45050
Phone: 52-3-634-6606   Fax: 52-3-634-7374
URL: http://www.amcham.com.mx
E-mail: amchamdgl@iserve.net.mx

Mr. John M. BRUTON
Executive Vice President
American Chamber of Commerce of Mexico, A.C.
Lucerna 78, Col. Juarez
Mexico, DF 06600
Phone: 52-5-724-3800   Fax: 52-5-703-2911
URL: http://www.amcham.com.mx
E-mail: amcham@amcham.com.mx

Mr. Santiago TREVINO
Manager
American Chamber of Commerce of
   Mexico - Monterrey
Rio Orinoco 307 Ote.
Col. del Valle San Pedro Garza Garcia
Nuevo Leon 66220
Phone: 528-335-6210   Fax: 528-335-6211

Netherlands

Mr. C.G. BURGERSDYJK
Executive Officer
American Chamber of Comm. in the Netherlands
Van Karnebeeklaan 14
2585 BB
The Hague
Phone: 31-70-365-9808   Fax: 31-70-364-6992
URL: http://www.unisys.nl/amcham
E-mail: amchamnl@worldaccess.nl

New Zealand

Mr. John W. LAVELLE
Executive Director
American Chamber of Commerce in New Zealand
P.O. Box 106-002, Downtown
Auckland 1001
Phone: 64-9-309-9140   Fax: 64-9-309-1090

Nicaragua

Ms. Desiree PEREIRA
Executive Director
American Chamber of Commerce in Nicaragua
P.O. Box 2720
Managua
Phone: 505-2-67-3099   Fax: 505-2-67-3098
E-mail: amcham@ns.tmx.com.ni

Norway

Ms. Kay Ellen VAN SCHEERS
Secretary
American Chamber of Commerce in Norway
P.O. Box 244
Hovik 1322
Phone: 47-67-54-6880   Fax: 47-67-54-6930
E-mail: scheeers@online.no

Pakistan

Mr. S. Rafat Ali HASHMI
Secretary
American Business Council of Pakistan
GPO Box 1322
Karachi 74400
Phone: 92-21-567-6436   Fax: 92-21-568-0135

Panama

Mr. Fred DENTON
Executive Director
American Chamber of Commerce &
   Industry of Panama
P.O. Box 168
Balboa, Ancon
Phone: 507-269-3881   Fax: 507-223-3508
URL: http://www.panamainfo.com
E-mail: amcham@pan.gbm.net

Paraguay

Mr. George C. MCCULLOCH
Executive Director
Paraguayan-American Chamber of Commerce
General Diaz 521, 4th Floor
Asuncion

Phone: 595-21-45-0747   Fax: 595-21-44-2135
E-mail: pamcham@isetec.com

Peru

Mr. James W. PLUNKETT, JR.
General Manager
American Chamber of Commerce of Peru
Ricardo Palma 836, Miraflores
Lima 18
Phone: 511-241-0708   Fax: 511-241-0709
URL: http://www.samerica.net/amcham
E-mail: postmaster@amcham.org.pe

Philippines

Mr. Robert W. SEARS
Executive Vice President
American Chamber of Comm. of the Philippines
P.O. Box 1578
Manila 3117
Phone: 63-2-818-7911   Fax: 63-2-811-3081

Poland

Mr. Tony HOUSH
Executive Director
American Chamber of Commerce in Poland
ul. Swietokrzyska 36 m 6, Ent. 1
Warsaw 00 116
Phone: 48-22-622-5525   Fax: 48-22-622-5525
URL: http://www.polishworld.com
E-mail: amcham@it.com.pl

Portugal

Dr. Henrique M. BRITO DO RIO
Executive Director
American Chamber of Commerce in Portugal
Rua De D. Estefania, 155, 5 ESQ
Lisbon 1000
Phone: 351-1-57-2561   Fax: 351-1-57-2580

Romania

Mr. Gabriel MIHAI
Executive Director
American Chamber of Commerce in Romania
Str. M. Eminescu nr. 105-107
Ap. 1, Sector 2
Bucharest
Phone: 40-1-210-9399   Fax: 40-1-210-9399

Russia

Mr. Peter CHAROW
Executive Director
American Chamber of Commerce in Russia
Kosmodamianskaya Nab. 52
Bldg. 1 - 8th Floor
Moscow 113054
Phone: 7095-961-2141   Fax: 7095-961-2142
E-mail: amchamru@online.ru

Saudi Arabia

Mr. John MCNAMARA
President
American Business Association, Eastern Province

P.O. Box 88
Dhahran 31932
Phone: 966-3-857-6464   Fax: 966-3-857-8883

Mr. Howard CAMPBELL
Chairman
American Business Council of the Gulf Countries
P.O. Box 88
Dhahran Airport 11471
Phone: 966-3-857-0595   Fax: 966-3-857-8130

Ms. Patricia A. SPATH
Office Manager
American Businessmen of Jeddah
P.O. Box 8483
Jeddah 21482
Phone: 966-2-652-1234 ext. 1759
Fax: 966-2-651-6260

Mr. Fred ERIKSON
Chairman
American Businessmen's Group of Riyadh
P.O. Box 8273
Riyadh 11482
Phone: 966-1-463-2796   Fax: 966-1-463-4150

Singapore

Mr. Donne PETITO
Executive Director
American Business Council of Singapore
1 Scotts Rd. #16-07 Shaw Centre
Singapore 228208
Phone: 65-235-0077   Fax: 65-732-5917
URL: http://www.amcham.org.sg
E-mail: amcham@pobox.org.sg

Slovak Republic

Mr. Patrick URAM
Executive Director
American Chamber of Commerce in
   the Slovak Republic
Hotel Danube, Rybne Namestie 1
Bratislava 811 02
Phone: 421-7-534-0508   Fax: 421-7-534-0556
E-mail: director@amcham.sanet.sk

South Africa

Ms. Luanne GRANT
Executive Director
American Chamber of Commerce in South Africa
P.O. Box 1132, Houghton
Johannesburg 2041
Phone: 27-11-788-0265   Fax: 27-11-880-1632

Spain

Mr. Jose A. MANRIQUE
Executive Director
American Chamber of Commerce in Spain
Avda. Diagonal 477
Barcelona 08036
Phone: 34-3-405-1266   Fax: 34-3-405-3124
E-mail: 101643.715@compuserve.com

Ms. Maria NIEVES HERMIDA
Assistant Executive Director
American Chamber of Commerce in Madrid
Lexington Intl. Business Center
Paseo de la Castellana, 141 200
Madrid 28046
Phone: 34-1-458-6559   Fax: 34-1458-6520

Sri Lanka

Ms. Susan K. SLOMBACK-KING
Executive Director
American Chamber of Commerce of Sri Lanka
P.O. Box 1000
Colombo Hilton, Third Floor
Colombo
Phone: 94-1-33-6074   Fax: 94-1-33-6072
URL: http://www.lanka.net/amcham

Sweden

Ms. Marianne RAIDNA WALI
Executive Director
American Chamber of Commerce in Sweden
Box 5512
Stockholm 114 85
Phone: 46-8-666-1100   Fax: 46-8-662-8884
E-mail: ara@gsh.se

Switzerland

Mr. Walter H. DIGGELMANN
Executive Director
Swiss-American Chamber of Commerce
Talacker 41
Zurich 8001
Phone: 41-1-211-2454   Fax: 41-1-211-9572
E-mail: info@amcham.ch

Taiwan, ROC

Mr. Les GUNBY
President
American Chamber of Commerce, Kaohsiung
15F, #123-7, Ta-Pei Road
NiaoSung Hsiang
Kaohsiung
Phone: 886-07-731-3712
Fax: 886-07-731-3712

Ms. Lynn MURRAY SIEN
Executive Director
American Chamber of Commerce, Taipei
N-1012, Chia Hsin Bldg., Annex
96 Chung Shan N. Road, Section 2
Taipei 10419SRI
Phone: 886-2-581-7089   Fax: 886-2-542-3376
URL: http://www.amcham.com.tw
E-mail: amcham@transend.com.tw

Thailand

Mr. Thomas A. SEALE
Executive Director
American Chamber of Commerce in Thailand
P.O. Box 1095
Bangkok 10330
Phone: 66-2-251-9266   Fax: 66-2-255-2454
E-mail: amcham@samart.co.th

Trinidad & Tobago

Ms. Debbie DE GANNES
Executive Director
American Chamber of Commerce
Upper Arcade, Trinidad Hilton
Lady Yound Rd.

Port of Spain
Phone: 809-627-8570   Fax: 809-627-7405
URL: http://www.trinidad.net/chambers/acchome/
   acchome.htm
E-mail: amcham@trinidad.net

Turkey

Mr. Seta USTA
Executive Director
Turkish-American Businessmen's Association
Barbaros Bulvari, Eer. Apt. #48
K.5 D.16
Balmumcu, Istanbul 80700
Phone: 90-212-274-2824
Fax: 90-212-275-9316
E-mail: 100732.2113@compuserve.com

Mr. Gures CARKOGLU
General Secretary
Turkish-American Businessmen's Association
Anadolu cad 37-39
Izmir 35250
Phone: 90-2324-614-660
Fax: 90-2324-350-549

Ukraine

Mr. Mark KALENAK
Executive Director
American Chamber of Commerce in Ukraine
7 Kudriavsky Uzviz, Rm. 212
Kiev 254053
Phone: 380-44-417-1015
Fax: 380-44-417-1015
E-mail: acc@chamber.ru.kiev.ua

United Arab Emirates

Ms. Alice D. GARDNER
Executive Director
American Business Council of Dubai-North
Emirates
P.O. Box 9281
Dubai
Phone: 97-1-431-4735   Fax: 97-1-431-4227
E-mail: amchamdx@emirates.net.ae

United Kingdom

Mr. Robert E. BRUNCK
Director General
American Chamber of Commerce of
   the United Kingdom
75 Brook St.
London England W1Y 2EB
Phone: 44-171-493-0381
Fax: 44-171-493-2394
URL: http://www.amcham.org.uk
E-mail: acc@amcham.demon.co.uk

Uruguay

Mr. Carlos BOUBET
Manager
Chamber of Commerce Uruguay-USA
Calle Bartolome Mitre 1337
Casilla de Correo 809
Montevideo
Phone: 598-2-95-9048   Fax: 598-2-95-9059
URL: http://www.zfm.com.amchamuru

E-mail: amcham@zfm.com

Venezuela

Dr. Antonio HERRERA-VAILLANT
General Manager
Venezuelan-American Chamber of
   Commerce & Industry
Campo Alegre, Apdo. 5181
Caracas 1010-A
Phone: 58-2-263-0833   Fax: 58-2-263-1829
URL: http://www.venamcham.org
E-mail: venam@ven.net

Vietnam

Ms. Rene DUGAN
Executive Director
American Chamber of Commerce in Vietnam
17 Ngo Quyen, Unite #01, First Floor
Hanoi
Phone: 84-4-825-1950   Fax: 84-4-824-3960

Ms. Amy EVERITT
Executive Director
American Chamber of Commerce in Vietnam
30 Le Thanh Ton, Room 112A
District 1
Ho Chi Minh City
Phone: 84-8-829-5829   Fax: 84-8-829-6078
E-mail: amcham@bdvn.vnd.net

INTRODUCTION

In the past decade, state governments have recognized that exporting is a key part of economic development and job creation. All states now have offices that focus on international trade and help companies that wish to develop overseas markets.

*The first part of this section lists **State Agriculture Offices** which primarily provide counseling and information on international agricultural trade, including trade shows and missions. Some also provide specific information on certificates of origin and federal export requirements.*

*The second part of this section lists **State Trade Finance Offices** which provide export financing information.*

*The third part of this section lists **State Trade Offices** which typically offer a number of export assistance resources including: in-state firm export counseling; resource directories; information on trade events; information on federal, state, and local export assistance programs; promotion of products overseas; public/private partnerships; matching buyer and seller programs; seminars and workshops; and trade leads.*

Some states also offer shared Foreign Sales Corporations (FSC) which are non-U.S. corporations organized to provide tax benefits to small- and medium-sized exporters who would not normally be able to establish an FSC by themselves. Ask the State Trade Office about this type of program.

State Trade Offices also will have information on that state's overseas offices. Most states have set up offices in key markets overseas to better assist exporters and to attract foreign investment to their state.

Two Washington-based organizations that keep track of the states' economic development and international activities are:

National Association of State Development Agencies
750 First Street, NE
Suite 710
Washington, D.C. 20002

Phone: 202/898-1302
Fax: 202/898-1312

National Association of Governors
Economic Development and Commerce Group
444 North Capitol Street, NE
Suite 267
Washington, D.C. 20001-1572

Phone: 202/624-5300
Fax: 202/624-5313

State Agriculture Offices

Alabama

Dr. John Gimble
Director
Alabama Dept. of Agriculture and Industries
Marketing and Economics Division
P.O. Box 3336
Montgomery AL 36109-0336
Phone: 334/240-7245   Fax: 334/240-7190

California

Ms. Cherie Watte
Agricultural Program Manager/Director of Intl.
Trade Policy
Marketing Export Branch
Calif. Dept. of Food and Agriculture
1220 N Street, Suite A-280
Sacramento CA 95814
Phone: 916/654-0389   Fax: 916/653-2604

Colorado

Mr. Tim Larson
International Marketing
Colorado Department of Agriculture
Markets Division
700 Kipling Street, Suite 4000
Lakewood CO 80215-5894
Phone: 303/239-4114   Fax: 303/239-4125

Connecticut

Mr. Ronald Olsen
Marketing Inspection Representative
Connecticut Department of Agriculture
Bureau of Marketing and Technology
165 Capitol Avenue, Room 263
Hartford CT 06106
Phone: 860/566-4845   Fax: 860/566-6094

Delaware

Mr. John A. Pastor
International Trade Market Specialist
Delaware Department of Agriculture
c/o: Delaware Development Office
2320 So. Dupont Highway
Dover DE 19901
Phone: 302/739-4271   Fax: 302/739-5749

Florida

Ms. Deborah Cox
Division of Marketing
Fla. Dept. of Agriculture and Consumer Svcs.
Mayo Building - Rm. 412, 407 So. Calhoun St.
Tallahassee FL 32399-0800
Phone: 850/488-4366   Fax: 850/922-0374

Georgia

Ms. Mary Ellen Lawson
Director
Georgia Department of Agriculture
Intl. Trade Div., Capitol Square
340 Agricultural Building
Atlanta GA 30334
Phone: 404/656-3740   Fax: 404/656-9380

Guam

Hon. Michael W. Kuhlmann
Director
Guam Department of Agriculture
192 Diary Road
Mangilao GU 96923
Phone: 671/734-3942   Fax: 671/734-6569

Hawaii

Mr. Calvin Lee
Manager
Hawaii Department of Agriculture
Market Development Branch
P.O. Box 22159
Honolulu HI 96823-2159
Phone: 808/973-9595   Fax: 808/973-9590

Idaho

Idaho Department of Agriculture
Agriculture Marketing
2270 Old Penitentiary Road
Boise ID 83712
Phone: 208/332-8535   Fax: 208/334-2879

Illinois

Ms. Sandra Rolando
Bureau Chief
Illinois Department of Agriculture
Intl. Trade and Marketing Division
P.O. Box 19281
Springfield IL 6294-9281
Phone: 217/782-6675   Fax: 217/524-5960

Indiana

Ms. Connie Beckworth
Assistant Commissioner
Indiana Office of the Commissioner of Ag.
ISTA Center
Suite 414, 150 West Market Street
Indianapolis IN 46204
Phone: 317/232-4459   Fax: 317/232-1362

Iowa

Mr. Michael Doyle
Division Administrator
Iowa Department of Economic Development
International Division
200 East Grand Avenue
Des Moines IA 50309
Phone: 515/242-4742   Fax: 515/242-4918

Kansas

Ms. Patti Clark
Director
Kansas State Board of Agriculture
Marketing Division
700 SW Harrison Street
Topeka KS 66603
Phone: 785/296-3736   Fax: 785/296-2247

Kentucky

Mr. Gene Royalty
Director of Marketing Services
Kentucky Department of Agriculture
Capitol Plaza Tower
7th Floor, 500 Metro Street
Frankfort KY 40601
Phone: 502/564-4696   Fax: 502/594-2133

Louisiana

Mr. Roy Johnson
Director of Market Development
Louisiana Department of Agriculture
P.O. Box 3334
Baton Rouge LA 70821-3334
Phone: 504/922-1280   Fax: 504/922-1289

Maine

Mr. Howard Jones
Director
Maine Department of Agriculture
Marketing and Production Development Division
Deering Bldg. (AMH), State House, Station 28
Augusta ME 04333
Phone: 207/287-3491   Fax: 207/287-7548

Maryland

Mr. Errol Small
Chief of Intl. Marketing
Maryland State Department of Agriculture
Marketing Division
50 Harry S Truman Parkway
Annapolis MD 21401
Phone: 410/841-5770   Fax: 410/841-5987

Massachusetts

Ms. Bonita Oehlke
Foreign Trade Specialist
Mass. Dept. of Food and Agriculture
100 Cambridge Street
21st Floor, Room 2103
Boston MA 02202
Phone: 617/727-3000   Fax: 617/727-7235

Michigan

Mr. Dale Posthumus
International Trade Specialist
Michigan Department of Agriculture
611 W. Ottawa
P.O. Box 30017
Lansing MI 48909
Phone: 517/373-1052   Fax: 517/335-1423

Minnesota

Mr. Gene Hugoson
Commissioner of Agriculture
Minnesota Department of Agriculture
90 West Plato Blvd.
St. Paul MN 55107-2094
Phone: 612/297-3210   Fax: 612/297-5522

Mississippi

Mr. Roger E. Barlow
Dir. of Marketing/Intl. Trade
Miss. Dept. of Agriculture and Commerce
P.O. Box 1609
Jackson MS 39215-1609
Phone: 601/354-1158   Fax: 601/354-6001

Missouri

Mr. Wayne Yokley
Director
Missouri Department of Agriculture
Marketing Development Division
P.O. Box 630, 1616 Missouri Blvd.
Jefferson City MO 65102
Phone: 573/751-2613   Fax: 573/751-2868

Montana

Mr. Ralph Peck
Director
Montana Department of Agriculture
Agriculture/Livestock Building
Capitol Station
Helena MT 59620-0201
Phone: 406/444-3144   Fax: 406/444-5409

Nebraska

Mr. Stan Garbacz
Administrator
Nebraska Department of Agriculture
Agriculture Promotion and Development Div.
301 Centennial Mall South, P.O. Box 94947
Lincoln NE 68509
Phone: 402/471-4876   Fax: 402/471-2759

Nevada

Mr. Robert Gronowski
Bureau Chief
Nevada Dept. of Agriculture
P.O. Box 11000
Reno NV 89510
Phone: 702/688-1180   Fax: 702/688-1178

New Hampshire

Ms. Gail McWilliams
Director
New Hampshire State Dept. of Agriculture
Market Development Division
25 Capitol Street, Caller Box 2042
Concord NH 03302-2042
Phone: 603/271-2505   Fax: 603/271-1109

New Jersey

Mr. Logan Brown
Agriculture Marketing Specialist
New Jersey Department of Agriculture
John Fitch Plaza, CN 330
Trenton NJ 08625
Phone: 609/292-8856   Fax: 609/984-2508

New Mexico

Mr. Edward Avalos
Director
New Mexico Department of Agriculture
Marketing and Development Division
P.O. Box 30005
Dept. 5600, NMSU
Las Cruces NM 88003
Phone: 505/646-4929   Fax: 505/646-3303

New York

Mr. William Kimball
N.Y. Dept. of Agriculture and Markets
Ag. Protection & Development Services
1 Winners Circle, Capitol Plaza
Albany NY 12235
Phone: 518/457-3880   Fax: 518/457-2716

North Carolina

Mr. Britt Cobb
Market Specialist/Exports
N.C. Dept. of Agriculture
P.O. Box 27647
Raleigh NC 27611
Phone: 919/733-7912   Fax: 919/733-0999

North Dakota

Ms. Shannon Bornson
Director
North Dakota Department of Agriculture
Division of Marketing

600 East Blvd., 6th Floor
Bismarck ND 58505-0020
Phone: 701/328-2231   Fax: 701/328-4567

Ohio

Ms. Mary Beth Cowardin
Division of Markets
Ohio Department of Agriculture
8995 E. Main
Reynoldsburg OH 43068
Phone: 614/466-6198   Fax: 614/466-6124

Oklahoma

Mr. Rick Maloney
Coordinator
Oklahoma Department of Agriculture
International Marketing
2800 North Lincoln
Oklahoma City OK 73105
Phone: 405/521-3864   Fax: 405/521-4912

Oregon

Mr. Jeff Jones
Director, International Marketing
Oregon Department of Agriculture
Agriculture Development and Mktng. Div.
121 SW Salmon Street, Suite 240
Portland OR 97204
Phone: 503/229-6734   Fax: 503/229-6113

Pennsylvania

Mr. Bradley R. Jones
Director
State Department of Agriculture
Bureau of Market Development
2301 N. Cameron Street
Harrisburg PA 17110-9408
Phone: 717/783-3181   Fax: 717/787-2387

Rhode Island

Mr. Stephen Volpe
Agricultural Specialist
R.I. Dept. of Environmental Mgmt.
235 Promenade Street
Providence RI 02908
Phone: 401/222-2781   Fax: 401/222-6047

South Carolina

Mr. Roy Copelan
Director of Intl. Mktg.
S.C. Department of Agriculture
Wade Hampton State Office Building
P.O. Box 11280
Columbia SC 29211
Phone: 803/734-2200   Fax: 803/734-2192

South Dakota

Ms. Cheri Rath
Marketing Specialist
South Dakota Dept. of Agriculture
Agricultural Development
523 East Capitol
Pierre SD 57501
Phone: 605/773-5436   Fax: 605/773-3481

Tennessee

Mr. Keith Harrison
Chief
Tennessee Dept. of Agriculture
Marketing Services
P.O. Box 40627, Melrose Station
Nashville TN 37204
Phone: 615/837-5160   Fax: 615/837-5194

Texas

VACANT
Director of International Marketing
Texas Department of Agriculture
Marketing Division
POB 12847, Capitol Station
Austin TX 78711
Phone: 512/463-7636   Fax: 512/463-9968

Utah

Mr. Randy Parker
Director, Marketing and Conservation
Utah Department of Agriculture
350 North Redwood Road
Salt Lake City UT 84116-3087
Phone: 801/538-7106   Fax: 801/538-9436

Vermont

Mr. Steven F. Justis
Marketing Specialist, International
Vermont Department of Agriculture
Agricultural Development
116 State Street, Drawer 20
Montpelier VT 05602-2901
Phone: 802/828-2416   Fax: 802/828-2361

Virgin Islands

Hon. Arthur C. Petersen
Commissioner
Virgin Islands Dept. of Agriculture
Estate Lower Love-Kings Hill
St. Croix VI 00850
Phone: 809/778-0991   Fax: 809/778-3101

Virginia

Mr. Robert P. Rich
Director of Intl. Mktng.
Va. Dept. of Agriculture and Consumer Srvcs.
International Marketing Division
1100 Bank Street, Suite 915
Richmond VA 23219
Phone: 804/786-3953   Fax: 804/225-4434

Washington

Ms. Janet Leister
Managing Director
Washington State Dept. of Agriculture
Market Development Division
406 General Admin. Bldg., AX-41
Olympia WA 98504-0641
Phone: 360/902-1931   Fax: 360/902-2089

West Virginia

Dr. Robert Williams
Marketing Director
West Virginia Dept. of Agriculture
Marketing and Development Division
1900 Kanawha Blvd. East
Charleston WV 25305
Phone: 304/558-2210   Fax: 304/558-2203

Wisconsin

Ms. Deborah Crave
Director
Wisconsin Intl. Agribusiness Center
2811 Agriculture Drive
Madison WI 53704-6777
Phone: 608/224-5117   Fax: 608/224-5111

Ms. Deborah Crave
Director
Wisconsin Department of Agriculture
Intl. Mktng. Division
801 Badger Road
Madison WI 53713
Phone: 608/224-5112   Fax: 608/224-5111

Wyoming

Mr. Bill Bunce
Manager of Marketing
Wyoming Department of Agriculture
2219 Carey Avenue
Cheyenne WY 82002
Phone: 307/777-6581   Fax: 307/777-6593

State Trade Finance Offices

Arkansas

Ms. Susan Thomas
Export Finance Manager
Arkansas Development Finance Authority
P.O. Box 8023
Little Rock AR 72203-8023
Phone: 501/682-5909   Fax: 501/682-5939

California

Ms. Caroline Brown
Director
Calif. Trade and Commerce Agency
Export Finance Office (CEFO)
One World Trade Center - Suite 900
Long Beach CA 90831
Phone: 562/499-6014   Fax: 562/499-6080
E-mail: CEFO@smtp.doc.ca.gov

Mr. Matthew Flynn
Director
California Office of Foreign Investment
801 K Street - Suite 1936
Sacramento CA 95814-3520
Phone: 916/322-3518   Fax: 916/322-3401
E-mail: OFI@smtp.doc.ca.gov

Florida

Mr. Steve Fancher
President and C.E.O.
Florida Export Finance Corporation
5600 NW 36th Street, 6th Floor
P.O. Box 526524

Miami FL 33152-6254
Phone: 305/870-5027   Fax: 305/870-5107
URL: http://www.dos.state.fl.us/fefc

Indiana

Ms. Autumn Brooks Brown
Trade Finance Specialist
State of Indiana Trade Finance Program
International Trade Division
One North Capitol, Suite 700
Indianapolis IN 46204-2288
Phone: 317/233-4337   Fax: 317/233-1680

Maryland

Mr. Greg Cole
Executive Director
Md. Industrial Devlpmt. Financing Authority
Dept. of Economic Employment Development
217 East Redwood Street, 22nd Floor
Baltimore MD 21202
Phone: 410/767-6383   Fax: 410/333-6931

Missouri

Ms. Ashley Weaver
Export Loan Officer
Missouri Development Finance Board
P.O. Box 567
Jefferson City MO 65102
Phone: 573/751-8479   Fax: 573/526-4418

New Jersey

Ms. Caren Franzini
Executive Director
N.J. Economic Development Authority
P.O. Box 990
Trenton NJ 08625
Phone: 609/292-1800
E-mail: www.njeda.com

Oklahoma

Ms. Rana Brown
Oklahoma Department of Commerce
Export Finance Program
P.O. Box 26980
Oklahoma City OK 73126
Phone: 405/815-5143   Fax: 405/815-5142

Virginia

Ms. Kathy Surface
Executive Director
Va. Small Business Financing Authority
707 E. Main Street, Suite 300
Richmond VA 23219
Phone: 804/371-8254   Fax: 804/225-3384

State Trade Offices

Alabama

Dr. Robert J. Lager
Executive Director
Alabama Foreign Trade Relations Commission
International Trade Center, Suite 131
250 N. Water Street

Mobile AL 36602
Phone: 334/433-1151   Fax: 334/438-2711

Ms. Cheryl Mullins
International Trade Specialist
Alabama Development Office
International Development
401 Adams Avenue, Suite 600
Montgomery AL 36130
Phone: 334/242-0400   Fax: 334/242-0486
URL: http://www.ado.state.al.us

Alaska

Ms. Priscilla Wohl
Trade Program Manager
State of Alaska
Office of Trade and Development
3601 C Street, Suite 798
Anchorage AK 99503
Phone: 907/269-8110   Fax: 907/269-8125

Arizona

Ms. Dorothy Bigg
Director
Arizona Department of Commerce
Int'l. Trade and Investment Division
3800 No. Central, Suite 1500
Phoenix AZ 85012
Phone: 602/280-1371   Fax: 602/280-1378
URL: http://www.commerce.state.az.us/
    fr_itrad.shtml

Mr. Eric Nielsen
City of Tucson
Office of Econ. Dev., Intl. Trade Program
P.O. Box 27210, 166 West Alameda
Tucson AZ 85726
Phone: 520/791-5093   Fax: 520/791-5413
E-mail: nielsen@econ.tucson.az.us
URL: http://www.tucson.com/oed/oed/.html

Arkansas

Mr. Robert Crum
Economic Development Officer
Arkansas Development Finance Authority
100 Main Street, Suite 200
Little Rock AR 72201
Phone: 501/682-5900   Fax: 501/682-5939

Mr. Robert J. Deane
Trade Specialist
Arkansas Economic Development Commission
Foreign Trade and Investment Division
One Capitol Mall
Little Rock AR 72201
Phone: 501/682-7690   Fax: 501/324-9856
E-mail: bdeane@aidc.state.ar.us
URL: http://www.state.ar.us/directory/
    detail.cgi?ID=28

California

Ms. Kimberly Rich
Acting Director
California Office of Export Development
One World Trade Center - Suite 990
Long Beach CA 90831-0990
Phone: 562/590-5965   Fax: 562/590-5985
E-mail: expdev@smtp.doc.ca.gov
URL: http://commerce.ca.gov

Mr. Tim Ogburn

Manager
Calif. Environmental Tech. Export Prog.
801 K Street, Suite 1926
Sacramento CA 95814-3520
Phone: 916/322-5298   Fax: 916/324-5791

Mr. Lloyd Day
Deputy Secretary
Calif. Trade and Commerce Agency
Office of Trade Policy and Research
801 K Street, Suite 1926
Sacramento CA 95814-3520
Phone: 916/324-5511   Fax: 916/324-5791
E-mail: ITI@smtp.doc.ca.gov
URL: http://www.ca.gov/commerce/home.html

Mr. Rudy Fernandez
Director
Office of California-Mexico Affairs
Symphony Towers
750 B Street, Suite 370
San Diego CA 92101
Phone: 619/645-2660   Fax: 619/645-2821
E-mail: rudyf@dmtp.dpc.ca.gov

Colorado

Mr. Morgan Smith
Director
Colorado Intl. Trade Office
Office of the Governor
1625 Broadway, Suite 900
Denver CO 80202
Phone: 303/892-3850   Fax: 303/892-3820
E-mail: sdotson@compuserve.com
URL: http://www.state.co.us/gov_dir/
    intl_trade_gov.html

Mr. Jake Danaher
International Programs Officer
Colorado Intl. Capital Corporation
1981 Blake Street - 4th Floor
Denver CO 80202-1272
Phone: 303/297-7327   Fax: 303/297-2615

Connecticut

Mr. Costas Lake
Intl. Director
Conn. Dept. of Economic Development
International Division
505 Hudson Street
Hartford CT 06106
Phone: 860/270-8060   Fax: 860/270-8070
URL: http://www.state.ct.us/ecd/international/
    index.html

Ms. Martha Hunt
President
Conn. Economic Resource Center, Inc.
805 Brook St., Bldg. 4
Rocky Hill CT 06067-3405
Phone: 800/392-2122   Fax: 860/574-7150
URL: http://www.cerc.com

Delaware

Mr. John A. Pastor
International Trade Specialist
Delaware Economic Development Office
820 French Street - 10th Floor
Wilmington DE 19801
Phone: 302/577-8464   Fax: 302/577-8499

District of Columbia

Ms. Dianne Page
District of Columbia
Office of International Affairs
441 4th St., NW, Suite 1140 North
Washington DC 20001
Phone: 202/727-6365   Fax: 202/727-6703

Florida

Mr. Mike Fitzgerald
President, Intl. Trade and Recruitment
Enterprise Florida
390 No. Orange Avenue
Orlando FL 32801
Phone: 407/316-4600   Fax: 407/316-4599

Ms. Beverly White
Intl. Trade Coordinator
Office of Tourism, Trade & Economic Develop.
The Capitol, Suite 2001
Tallahassee FL 32399-0001
Phone: 850/487-2568   Fax: 850/487-3014

Georgia

Mr. Kevin Langston
Director of International Trade
Georgia Dept. of Industry, Trade and Tourism
International Trade Division
285 Peachtree Ctr. Ave, NE, #1100
Atlanta GA 30303
Phone: 404/656-3571   Fax: 404/651-6505
E-mail: trade@itt.state.ga.us
URL: http://www.georgia.org

Hawaii

Ms. Debra Miyashiro
Hawaii Dept. of Bus., Econ. Develop. & Tourism
Business Resource Library
P.O. Box 2359
Honolulu HI 96804
Phone: 808/586-2424   Fax: 808/587-2790
URL: http://www.hawaii.gov/dbedt

Hawaii Dept. of Bus., Econ. Develop. & Tourism
Business Development & Marketing Division
P.O. Box 2359
Honolulu HI 96804
Phone: 808/587-2584   Fax: 808/587-3388
E-mail: hiprod@pixi.com
URL: http://www.hawaii.gov/dbedt/trade/
     greg4.html

Idaho

Ms. Vicki Thomas
Administrator
Idaho Department of Commerce
Division of International Business
700 W. State Street, P.O. Box 83720
Boise ID 83720-0093
Phone: 208/334-2470   Fax: 208/334-2783
URL: http://www.idoc.state.id.us/Pages/
     EXPORTPAGE.html

Illinois

Ms. Mary Anne Rogerio
Acting Manager
Illinois Dept. of Commerce & Community Affairs
Illinois International Business Division
100 West Randolph, Suite 3-400
Chicago IL 60601

Phone: 312/814-7164   Fax: 312/814-6581
URL: http://www.commerce.state.il.us/dcca/
     menus/int'l/int_home.htm

Indiana

Mr. Carlos Barbera
Director
Indiana Department of Commerce
International Trade Division
One North Capitol, Suite 700
Indianapolis IN 46204-2288
Phone: 317/233-3762   Fax: 317/232-4146
URL: http://www.ai.org/bdev/html/its.html

Iowa

Mr. Michael Doyle
Division Administrator
Iowa Department of Economic Development
International Division
200 East Grand Avenue
Des Moines IA 50309
Phone: 515/242-4743   Fax: 515/242-4918
URL: http://www.state.ia.us/international/
     program.htm

Kansas

Ms. Sheila Devine
Director
Trade Development Division
Kansas Department of Commerce
700 SW Harrison Street, 1300
Topeka KS 66603-3957
Phone: 785/296-4027   Fax: 785/296-5263
URL: http://www.kansascommerce.com/
     0306international.html

Mr. John Watson
Director
International Investment
Kansas Department of Commerce
700 SW Harrison Street, 1300
Topeka KS 66603-3957
Phone: 785/296-4027   Fax: 785/296-5263

Kentucky

Ms. Mary Beth Cordy
Director
Kentucky Cabinet for Economic Development
Office of International Trade
2300 Capitol Plaza Tower, 500 Metro Street
Frankfort KY 40601
Phone: 502/564-7140   Fax: 502/564-3256
E-mail: mcordy@mail.state.ky.us
URL: http://www.state.ky.us/edc/ito.htm

Louisiana

Mr. Lawrence Collins
International Trade Section
Louisiana Department of Economic Development
International Trade Division
P.O. Box 94185
Baton Rouge LA 70804-9185
Phone: 504/342-4320   Fax: 504/342-5389
E-mail: web-intltrade@lded.state.la.us
URL: http://www.lded.state.la.us/
     int_trade_assist.html

Maine

Mr. Keith Luke
Program Director
Maine International Trade Center
511 Congress Street
Portland ME 04101-3428
Phone: 207/541-7400   Fax: 207/541-7420
URL: http://www.mitc.com/

Maryland

Mr. James Hughes
Director
Maryland Department of Business & Economic
Devlpmt.
Maryland Office of International Trade
217 E. Redwood Street - 13th Floor
Baltimore MD 21202
Phone: 410/767-0695   Fax: 410/333-4302
URL: http://www.mdisglobal.com/

Mr. Robert Brennan
Assistant Secretary
Department of Economic Employment
Maryland Industrial Develop. Financing Authority
217 E. Redwood Street - 22nd Floor
Baltimore MD 21202
Phone: 410/767-6359   Fax: 410/333-8200

Massachusetts

Ms. Paula Murphy
Director
Massachusetts Export Center
Boston Fish Pier, Bldg. 2W
Suite 305
Boston MA 02210
Phone: 617/478-4133   Fax: 617/478-4135

Ms. Kathleen Maloney
Executive Director
Massachusetts Office of International Trade
100 Cambridge Street, Suite 1302
Boston MA 02202
Phone: 617/367-1830   Fax: 617/227-3488
E-mail: nrostow@staate.ma.us
URL: http://www.magnet.state.ma.us/moiti/

Michigan

Ms. Margaret Kavanagh
Research Analyst
Michigan Jobs Commission
Int'l. and Nat'l. Business Division
201 No. Washington Square, Suite 400
Lansing MI 48913
Phone: 517/335-5884   Fax: 517/335-1947
URL: http://www.state.mi.us/mjc/ceo/business/
     inbd.htm

Minnesota

Mr. Noor Doja
Executive Director
Minnesota Trade Office
1000 Minnesota World Trade Center
30 East 7th Street
St. Paul MN 55101-4902
Phone: 612/297-4222   Fax: 612/296-3000

Mississippi

Mr. Jay C. Moon
Director
Mississippi Dept. of Econ. and Community
Development
International Development Division
P.O. Box 849
Jackson MS 39205
Phone: 601/359-6672   Fax: 601/359-3605
E-mail: internatl@mississippi.org
URL: http://www.decd.state.ms.us/ecd/
    Assistance_International.htm

Missouri

Mr. Chris Gutierrez
Director
Missouri Department of Economic Development
International Trade Office
301 West High Street, Rm. 720C, P.O. Box 118
Jefferson City MO 65102
Phone: 573/751-4999   Fax: 573/751-1567
E-mail: cgutierr@mail.state.mo.us
URL: http://www.ecodev.state.mo.us/ded/

Montana

Mr. Mark Bison
Program Manager
Montana Department of Commerce
International Trade Office
1424 9th Avenue
Helena MT 59620
Phone: 406/444-4380   Fax: 406/444-2903
URL: http://commerce.mt.gov/economic/
    trade.htm

Nebraska

Ms. Susan R. Rouch
Director
Nebraska Department of Economic Development
Office of Int'l. Trade and Investment
301 Centennial Mall South, P.O. Box 94666
Lincoln NE 68509
Phone: 402/471-4668   Fax: 402/471-3778
URL: http://www.ded.state.ne.us/trade/tr-
    home.html

Nevada

Ms. Gayle Anderson
Acting Director, Intl. Trade,
    Diplomatic Relations, and Protocol Liaison
Nevada Commission on Economic Development
International Trade Program
555 East Washington, Suite 5400
Las Vegas NV 89101
Phone: 702/486-2700   Fax: 702/486-2701
URL: http://www.tpusa.com/nevada

New Hampshire

Ms. Dawn Wivell
Director
New Hampshire Dept. of Resources and Econ.
Development
International Trade Resource Center
17 New Hampshire Avenue
Portsmouth NH 03801-2838
Phone: 603/334-6074   Fax: 603/334-6110
E-mail: d_wivell@dred.state.nh.us
URL: http://www.ded.state.nh.us/oic/trade/

New Jersey

Mr. Carlos T. Kearns
Director
New Jersey Dept. of Commerce &
    Economic Development
Division of International Trade
20 West State Street, 8th Floor, CN 836
Trenton NJ 08625-0836
Phone: 609/633-3606   Fax: 609/633-3672

New Mexico

Mr. Alan Richardson
Deputy Secretary
Economic Development Division
New Mexico Economic Development and
    Tourism Department
1100 St. Francis Drive
Santa Fe NM 87503
Phone: 505/827-0300   Fax: 505/827-0328

Mr. Roberto Castillo
Director
State of New Mexico Trade Division
1100 St. Francis Drive
Santa Fe NM 87501
Phone: 505/827-0307   Fax: 505/827-0263
E-mail: trade2edd.state.nm.us
URL: http://www.edd.state.nm.us/TRADE/
    index.html

New York

Mr. Paulo Palumbo
Deputy Commissioner for Int'l. Trade
Empire State Development
633 Third Avenue
New York NY 10017
Phone: 212/803-2343   Fax: 212/803-2398
E-mail: esd@empire.state.ny.us
URL: http://www.empire.state.ny.us/

Mr. Lennox Ruiz
Deputy Director
International Division
N.Y. Department of Economic Development
1515 Broadway, 51st Floor
New York NY 10036
Phone: 212/803-2200   Fax: 212/803-2399

North Carolina

Mr. William Epps
Director, International Trade
North Carolina Department of Commerce
International Division
301 North Wilmington Street
Raleigh NC 27626-0571
Phone: 919/733-7193   Fax: 919/733-0110
E-mail: mepps@mail.commerce.state.nc.us
URL: http://www.commerce.state.nc.us/
    commerce/itd/

North Dakota

Ms. Rebecca Bosch
Intl. Trade Program Director
North Dakota Dept. of Economic
    Development and Finance
International Trade Division
1833 E. Bismarck Expressway
Bismarck ND 58504-6708

Phone: 701/328-5300   Fax: 701/328-5320
E-mail: bbosh@state.nd.us
URL: http://www.growingnd.com

Ohio

Mr. James E. P. Sisto
Deputy Director
International Trade Division
Ohio Department of Development
77 South High Street - 29th Floor
Columbus OH 43215
Phone: 614/466-5017   Fax: 614/463-1540
E-mail: itd@odod.ohio.gov
URL: http://ohiotrade.tpusa.com/

Mr. Tom LaPort
Trade Finance Specialist
International Trade Division
Ohio Department of Development
77 South High Street - 29th Floor
Columbus OH 43215
Phone: 614/466-5017   Fax: 614/463-1540

Oklahoma

Mr. Kevin Chambers
Director
International Trade and Investment
Oklahoma Department of Commerce
P.O. Box 26980
Oklahoma City OK 73126-0980
Phone: 405/815-5215   Fax: 405/815-5245

Mr. Kevin Chambers
Director
Oklahoma Department of Commerce
International Trade and Investment Division
700 No. Greenwood Ave., Suite 1400
Tulsa OK 74106-0703
Phone: 918/594-8116   Fax: 918/594-8413
URL: http://www.odoc.state.ok.us/

Oregon

Mr. Warren Banks
Manager, Portland Office
Oregon Economic Development Department
International Trade Division
One World Trade Ctr., Suite 300
Portland OR 97204
Phone: 503/229-5625   Fax: 503/222-5050
E-mail: craig.burk@state.or.us
URL: http://www.econ.state.or.us/INTL/IT.HTM

Mr. William C. Scott
Director
Oregon Economic Development Department
International Trade Division
775 Summer Street, NW
Salem OR 97310
Phone: 503/986-0123   Fax: 503/581-5115

Pennsylvania

Mr. Peter Cunningham
Director
Pennsylvania Dept. of Community and Econ.
Development
Office of International Business Development
303 Forum Building
Harrisburg PA 17120
Phone: 717/787-7190   Fax: 717/234-4560

Puerto Rico

Mr. Jaime Morgan
Administrator
Puerto Rico Econ. Devlpmt. Admin.
P.O. Box 362350
San Juan PR 00936-2350
Phone: 787/758-4747   Fax: 787/764-1415
URL: http://www.pr-eda.com/

Rhode Island

Ms. Maureen Mezei
International Trade Director
Rhode Island Economic Development Corporation
International Trade Office
1 West Exchange Street
Providence RI 02903
Phone: 401/222-2601   Fax: 401/222-2102
URL: http://www.riedc.com

South Carolina

Mr. Clarke Thompson
Director
South Carolina Department of Commerce
International Business Development
P.O. Box 927, 1201 Main Street - 16th Floor
Columbia SC 29202
Phone: 803/737-0400   Fax: 803/737-0818
E-mail: cthompso@commerce.state.sc.us
URL: http://www.state.sc.us/commerce/
    internat.htm

Mr. William H. Lacey, III
Manager of Trade
South Carolina Department of Commerce
P.O. Box 927, 1201 Main Street - 16th Floor
Columbia SC 29202
Phone: 803/737-0400   Fax: 803/737-0818

South Dakota

Mr. Joop Bollen
Director
Governor's Office of Economic Development
South Dakota Int'l. Business Institute
1200 South Jay Street
Aberdeen SD 57401-7198
Phone: 605/626-3149   Fax: 605/626-3004
E-mail: bollenj@wolf.northern.edu
URL: http://sdibi.northern.edu/sdibi.html

Tennessee

Ms. Lee Weiland
Director
Tennessee Dept. of Econ. and Comm.
Development
Tennessee Export Office
Rachel Jackson Bldg., 7th Floor
320 6th Ave., No.
Nashville TN 37243-0405
Phone: 615/741-5870   Fax: 615/532-8715
E-mail: apelych@mail.state.tn.us
URL: http://www.state.tn.us/ecd/export.htm

Texas

Mr. Rick Thrasher
Executive Director
Texas Department of Economic Development

Office of Trade and International Relations
1700 North Congress Ave., P.O. Box 12728
Austin TX 78711
Phone: 512/936-0249   Fax: 512/936-0445
URL: http://www.tded.state.tx.us/commerce/
    busdev/trade/trade.htm

Utah

Mr. Dan Mabey
Director
State of Utah Int'l. Bus. Development Office
324 So. State Street, Suite 500
Salt Lake City UT 84111
Phone: 801/538-8700   Fax: 801/538-8889
E-mail: dcobler@dced.state.ut.us
URL: http://www.dced.state.ut.us/international/
    welcome.htm

Vermont

Mr. Thomas Myers
Director of International Trade
Vermont Department of Economic Development
National Life Building, Drawer 20
Montpelier VT 05620-0501
Phone: 802/828-3211   Fax: 802/828-3258
E-mail: SGRAY@GATE.DCA.STATE.VT.US
URL: http://www.state.vt.us

Virgin Islands

Ms. Angela Ramos-Michael
Director
V.I. Dept. of Econ. Development and Agriculture
Bureau of Economic Research
1050 Norre Gade St., #5, Suite 301
St. Thomas VI 00802
Phone: 340/714-1700   Fax: 340/774-8106

Virginia

Ms. Nancy Vorona
International Marketing Manager
Virginia Economic Devlpmt. Partnership, Herndon
Division of International Trade and Investment
CIT Building, Suite 602, 2214 Rock Hill Road
Herndon VA 22070
Phone: 703/689-3059   Fax: 703/689-3056
URL: http://www.YesVirginia.com

Mr. Andrew Flores
International Trade Manager
Virginia Economic Devlpmt. Partnership,
Richmond
Division of International Trade and Investment
901 East Byrd Street
Richmond VA 23219
Phone: 804/371-0632   Fax: 804/371-8860
E-mail: ExportVA@vedp.state.va.us
URL: http://www.YesVirginia.com

Mr. Stewart Perkins
Senior Trade Manager
Division of Int'l Trade and Investment
Virginia Department of Economic Development
P.O. Box 798
Richmond VA 23206-0798
Phone: 804/371-8292   Fax: 804/371-8112

Mr. Joe Robinson
International Marketing Manager
Virginia Economic Devlpmt. Partnership, Roanoke
Division of International Trade and Investment
212 South Jefferson Street

Roanoke VA 24011-1938
Phone: 540/857-6028   Fax: 540/857-6161
URL: http://www.YesVirginia.com

Washington

Mr. John Savich
Director
International Trade
Department of Community,
    Trade and Economic Development
101 General Administration Building,
P.O. Box 42500
Olympia WA 98504
Phone: 360/753-5795   Fax: 360/753-4470

Mr. Robert Hamilton
Assistant Special Trade Representative
Washington State Dept. of Community,
    Trade & Economic Development
Special Trade Representative
2001 Sixth Avenue, Suite 2600, 26th Floor
Seattle WA 98121-2522
Phone: 206/464-7143   Fax: 206/464-7222
E-mail: roberth@cted.wa.gov
URL: http://www.wa.gov/wstr/

West Virginia

Mr. Stephen Spence
Director
West Virginia Development Office
International Division
1900 Kanawha Boulevard East
Charleston WV 25305-0311
Phone: 304/558-2234   Fax: 304/558-1957
E-mail: sspence@wvdo.org
URL: http://www.wvdo.org/international/
    index.htm

Wisconsin

Ms. Mary Regel
Director
Wisconsin Department of Commerce
Bureau of International Development
P.O. Box 7970, 123 West Washington Avenue
Madison WI 53707
Phone: 608/266-1767   Fax: 608/866-5551
URL: http://badger.state.wi.us/agencies/
    dodhtmlinttrade.html

Wyoming

Ms. Linda Norman
Protocol/Trade Offices
Wyoming Department of Commerce
Div. of Economic and Community Development
Herschler Bldg., First Floor East
Cheyenne WY 82002
Phone: 307/777-6199   Fax: 307/777-5840
E-mail: lnorma@missc.state.wy.us
URL: http://commerce.state.wy.us/decd/

Ms. Linda Norman
Acting Director
International Trade Office
Wyoming Department of Commerce
4th Floor North, Barrett Building
Cheyenne WY 82002
Phone: 307/777-7284   Fax: 307/777-5840

INTRODUCTION

Foreign-Trade Zones are designated sites licensed by the Foreign-Trade Zones (FTZ) Board (the Secretary of Commerce is Chairman) at which special Customs procedures may be used. FTZ procedures allow domestic activity involving foreign items to take place as if it were outside U.S. Customs territory, thus offsetting Customs advantages available to overseas producers who export in competition with products made here. Subzones are special-purpose zones, usually at manufacturing plants.

Alabama - *Birmingham*

FTZ: 98
Operator: Shaw Warehouse
Grantee: City of Birmingham
3000 Second Avenue South
Birmingham AL 35222
Contact: Mr. Warren Ceow
Phone: 205/251-7188

Alabama - *Huntsville*

FTZ: 211
Operator: FTZ Corp.
Grantee: Anniston Metropolitan
Airport Board of Commissioners
P.O. Box 6241
Huntsville AL 35824-0241
Contact: Mr. Greg Jones
Phone: 205/772-3105

Alabama - *Huntsville*

FTZ: 83
Operator: Huntsville-Madison County Airport Authority
Grantee: Huntsville-Madison County Airport Authority
1000 Glenn Hearn Blvd., Box 20008
Huntsville AL 35824
Contact: Mr. Craig Pool
Phone: 205/772-3105

Alabama - *Mobile*

FTZ: 82
Operator: Mobile Airport Authority
Grantee: City of Mobile
1840 South Broad, Brookley Complex
Mobile AL 36615
Contact: Mr. Greg Jones
Phone: 334/433-1222

Alaska - *Anchorage*

FTZ: 160
Grantee: Port of Anchorage
P.O. Box 196650
Anchorage AK 99519-6650
Contact: Mr. Thomas Jensen
Phone: 907/343-6209

Alaska - *Fairbanks*

FTZ: 195
Grantee: Fairbanks Industrial Dev. Corp.

515 7th Ave., Suite 320
Fairbanks AK 99701
Contact: Mr. Ronald Ricketts
Phone: 907/452-2185

Alaska - *St. Paul*

FTZ: 159
Grantee: City of St. Paul
P.O. Box 901
St. Paul Island AK 99660
Contact: Mr. John R. Merculies
Phone: 907/546-2331   Fax: 907/546-3199

Alaska - *Valdez*

FTZ: 108
Grantee: The City of Valdez, Alaska
P.O. Box 307
Valdez AK 99686
Contact: Mr. Tim Lopez
Phone: 907/835-4981

Arizona - *Nogales*

FTZ: 60
Grantee: Nogales-Santa Cruz County Economic
              Development Foundation, Inc.
P.O. Box 1688
Nogales AZ 85628
Contact: Mr. Steve Colontuoni
Phone: 602/761-7800

Arizona - *Phoenix*

FTZ: 75
Grantee: City of Phoenix
Community & Economic Development Dept.
200 West Washington St., 20th Floor
Phoenix AZ 85003-1611
Contact: Mr. Robert Wojtan
Phone: 602/262-5040

Arizona - *Pima County*

FTZ: 174
Grantee: City of Tucson Office of Economic Development
P.O. Box 27210
Tucson AZ 85276-7210
Contact: Mr. Kendal Bert
Phone: 520/791-5093

Arizona - *Sierra Vista*

FTZ: 139
Grantee: Sierra Vista Economic Development Foundation, Inc.
P.O. Box 2380
Sierra Vista AZ 85636
Contact: Mr. Barry Albrech
Phone: 520/458-6948   Fax: 520/458-7453

Arizona - *Tucson*

FTZ: 48
Grantee: Papago-Tucson FTZ Corp.
San Xavier Community Ctr.
P.O. Box 11246, Mission Station

Tucson AZ 85734
Contact: Mr. William Tatom
Phone: 602/746-3692

Arkansas - *Little Rock*

FTZ: 14
Operator: Little Rock Port Authority
Grantee: Arkansas Dept. of Industrial Development
7500 Lindsey Rd.
Little Rock AR 72206
Contact: Mr. Thomas Moore
Phone: 501/490-1468   Fax: 501/490-1800

California - *Long Beach*

FTZ: 50
Grantee: Board of Harbor Commissioners of
        the Port of Long Beach
P.O. Box 570
Long Beach CA 90801-0570
Contact: Mr. Fritz Bergman
Phone: 310/590-4162

California - *Los Angeles*

FTZ: 202
Grantee: Board of Harbor Commissioners of
        the City of Los Angeles
425 South Palos Verdes St.
San Pedro CA 90731
Contact: Ms. Karen Tozer
Phone: 310/732-3846

California - *Oakland*

FTZ: 56
Operator: Pacific American Warehousing & Trucking Co.
Grantee: City of Oakland
9401 San Leandro
Oakland CA 94603
Contact: Ms. Linda Childs
Phone: 415/568-8500

California - *Palmdale*

FTZ: 191
Grantee: City of Palmdale
38300 N. Sierra Highway
Palmdale CA 93550-4798
Contact: Mr. Al McCord
Phone: 805/267-5100

California - *Port Hueneme*

FTZ: 205
Grantee: Board of Harbor Commissioners,
        Oxnard Harbor District
Port of Hueneme, P.O. Box 608
105 East Port Hueneme Rd.
Port Hueneme CA 93044-0608
Contact: Ms. Kam Quarles
Phone: 805/488-3677   Fax: 805/488-2620

California - *San Diego*

FTZ: 153

Grantee: City of San Diego
Civic Center Plaza
1200 Third Ave., Suite 1620
San Diego CA 92101-4178
Contact: Ms. Lydia Moreno
Phone: 619/236-6550   Fax: 619/236-6512

California - *San Francisco*

FTZ: 3
Operator: Foreign Trade Services, Inc.
Grantee: San Francisco Port Commission
Pier 23
San Francisco CA 94111
Contact: Mr. Tom Faenzi
Phone: 415/391-0176   Fax: 415/391-0794

California - *San Jose*

FTZ: 18
Grantee: City of San Jose
50 West San Fernando St., Suite 900
San Jose CA 95113
Contact: Mr. Joe Hedges
Phone: 408/277-5880   Fax: 408/277-3615

California - *West Sacramento*

FTZ: 143
Operator: California Free Trade Zone
Grantee: Port of Sacramento
2650 Industrial Blvd.
W. Sacramento CA 95691
Contact: Mr. Tim O'Connor
Phone: 916/372-8322   Fax: 916/372-8389

Colorado - *Colorado Springs*

FTZ: 112
Grantee: Colorado Springs Foreign-Trade Zone, Inc.
90 South Cascade Ave., Suite 1050
Colorado Springs CO 80903
Contact: Mr. Robert K. Scott
Phone: 719/661-0955

Colorado - *Denver*

FTZ: 123
Grantee: City and County of Denver
216 16th St., Suite 1000
Denver CO 80202
Contact: Mr. Steve TeSelle
Phone: 303/640-7049

Connecticut - *Bridgeport*

FTZ: 76
Operator: City of Bridgeport
Grantee: City of Bridgeport
City Hall, 45 Lyon Terrace
Bridgeport CT 06604
Contact: Mr. Edward Lavernoich
Phone: 203/576-722   Fax: 203/332-5611

Connecticut - *New London*

FTZ: 208

Grantee: New London Foreign Trade Zone Commission
111 Union St.
New London CT 06320
Contact: Mr. Phil Biondo
Phone: 860/447-5203   Fax: 860/447-5247

Connecticut - *North Haven*

FTZ: 162
Grantee: Greater New Haven Chamber of Commerce
195 Church St.
New Haven CT 06510
Contact: Mr. Martin Tristine
Phone: 203/469-1391

Connecticut - *Windsor Locks*

FTZ: 71
Grantee: Economic & Industrial Development
Town Office Bldg., 50 Church St., P.O. Box L
Windsor Locks CT 06096
Contact: Mr. James E. Maitland
Phone: 860/627-1444   Fax: 860/592-1121

Delaware - *Wilmington*

FTZ: 99
Operator: State of Delaware
Grantee: State of Delaware
Delaware Development Office
99 Kings Highway
Dover DE 19903
Contact: Ms. Dorothy Sbriglia
Phone: 302/739-4271

District of Columbia - *Washington*

FTZ: 137
Grantee: Washington Dulles FTZ
P.O. Box 17349
Washington DC 20041
Contact: Mr. Joseph R. Trocino
Phone: 703/471-2120

Florida - *Brevard County*

FTZ: 136
Operator: Canaveral Port Authority
Grantee: Canaveral Port Authority
P.O. Box 267, Port Canaveral Station
Cape Canaveral FL 32920
Contact: Ms. Susan Cossey
Phone: 407/783-7831

Florida - *Fort Meyers*

FTZ: 213
Grantee: Lee County Port Authority
Southwest Florida International Airport
16000 Chamberlin Parkway, Suite 8671
Fort Meyers FL 33913
Contact: Mr. Donald L. Davenport
Phone: 941/768-4307

Florida - *Fort Pierce*

FTZ: 218
Grantee: Central Florida FTZ, Inc.

2300 Virginia Avenue
Fort Pierce FL 34982
Contact: Mr. T. Morris Adger
Phone: 407/462-1732

Florida - *Homestead*

FTZ: 166
Grantee: Vision Council, Inc.
43 North Krome Ave.
Homestead FL 33030
Contact: Mr. Richard H. Bauer
Phone: 305/247-7082

Florida - *Jacksonville*

FTZ: 64
Grantee: Jacksonville Port Authority
P.O. Box 3005, 2831 Talleyrand Ave.
Jacksonville FL 32206-0005
Contact: Ms. Deborah G. Claytor
Phone: 904/630-3053

Florida - *Manatee County*

FTZ: 169
Grantee: Manatee County Port Authority
13231 Eastern Ave.
Palmetto FL 34221-6608
Contact: Mr. Joseph Gontarski
Phone: 813/722-6621

Florida - *Miami*

FTZ: 32
Grantee: Greater Miami Foreign Trade Zone, Inc.
Omni International Complex, 1601 Biscayne Blvd.
Miami Florida 33132
Contact: Mr. Rodell Holzberg
Phone: 305/350-7700

Florida - *Miami (Wynwood)*

FTZ: 180
Operator: Wynwood Community Economic Development Corp.
Grantee: Wynwood Community Economic Devel. Corp.
3000 Biscayne Blvd., Suite 210
Miami FL 33137
Contact: Mr. William Rios
Phone: 305/576-0440

Florida - *Ocala*

FTZ: 217
Operator: Ocala Regional Airport
Grantee: Economic Development Council, Inc.
P.O. Box 1270
Ocala FL 34478-1270
Contact: Ms. Maritza R. Baker
Phone: 352/629-8401

Florida - *Orlando*

FTZ: 42
Operator: Orlando Aviation Authority
Grantee: Orlando Aviation Authority
9675 Tradeport Dr.
Orlando FL 32827

Contact: Ms. Linda Smith
Phone: 407/825-2213

Florida - *Palm Beach County*

FTZ: 135
Grantee: Port of Palm Beach District
P.O. Box 9935
Riviera Beach FL 33419
Contact: Mr. Henry McKay
Phone: 407/842-4201

Florida - *Palm Beach County*

FTZ: 209
Grantee: Palm Beach County Dept. of Airports
Palm Beach Int'l Airport, Bldg. 846
West Palm Beach FL 33406-1491
Contact: Mr. Bruce V. Pelly
Phone: 407/471-7412

Florida - *Panama City*

FTZ: 65
Operator: Panama City Port Authority
Grantee: Panama City Port Authority
P.O. Box 15095
Panama City FL 32406
Contact: Mr. Rudy Etheredge
Phone: 904/763-8471

Florida - *Pinellas County*

FTZ: 193
Grantee: Pinellas County Industry Council
c/o St. Petersburg/Clearwater Economic Development Council
Bldg. 1200, Suite 1, 7990 114th Ave. North
Largo FL 34643
Contact: Ms. Patsy Beyer
Phone: 813/541-8080

Florida - *Port Everglades*

FTZ: 25
Operator: Port Everglades Port Authority
Grantee: Port Everglades Port Authority
1850 Eller Dr.
Ft. Lauderdale FL 33316
Contact: Ms. Karen M. Varner
Phone: 305/523-3404

Florida - *Sebring*

FTZ: 215
Grantee: Sebring Regional Airport
128 Authority Lane
Sebring FL 33870
Contact: Mr. Mike Willingham
Phone: 941/655-6444

Florida - *Tampa*

FTZ: 79
Grantee: City of Tampa
Tampa Foreign-Trade Zones Board
2112 N. 15th St., Second Floor
Tampa FL 33601
Contact: Mr. John Darsey

Phone: 813/242-5442

Florida - *Volusia and Flagler Counties*

FTZ: 198
Grantee: County of Volusia, Florida
c/o Daytona Beach Int'l Airport
700 Catalina Dr., Suite 300
Daytona Beach FL 32114
Contact: Mr. Mike Ulrich
Phone: 904/248-8030

Georgia - *Atlanta*

FTZ: 26
Grantee: Georgia Foreign Trade Zone, Inc.
P.O. Box 95546, Suite 134
Atlanta GA 30347
Contact: Mr. Penn Worden
Phone: 404/636-7811

Georgia - *Brunswick*

FTZ: 144
Grantee: Brunswick Foreign-Trade Zone, Inc.
100 Shipyard Dr.
Brunswick GA 31520
Contact: Ms. Deborah G. Stubbs
Phone: 912/267-7181

Georgia - *Savannah*

FTZ: 104
Operator: Savannah Airport Commission
Grantee: Savannah Airport Commission
Savannah Int'l Airport
400 Airways Ave.
Savannah GA 31408
Contact: Mr. A. W. Barbee
Phone: 912/964-0904

Hawaii - *Honolulu*

FTZ: 9
Operator: State of Hawaii
Grantee: State of Hawaii
Pier 2, 521 Ala Moana
Honolulu HI 96813
Contact: Mr. Gordon Trimble
Phone: 808/586-2509   Fax: 808/586-2512

Idaho - *Meridian*

FTZ: 192
Operator: City of Meridian
Grantee: City of Meridian
33 East Idaho
Meridian ID 83642
Contact: Ms. Shari Stiles
Phone: 208/888-4433

Illinois - *Chicago*

FTZ: 22
Grantee: Illinois International Port Division
3600 East 95th St.
Chicago IL 60617-5193
Contact: Mr. Matt Dosen

Phone: 312/646-4400

Illinois - *Granite City*

FTZ: 31
Operator: Tri-City Regional Port District
Grantee: Tri-City Regional Port District
2801 Rock Rd.
Granite City IL 64040
Contact: Mr. Robert Wydra
Phone: 618/452-3337

Illinois - *Lawrence County*

FTZ: 146

Grantee: Bi-State Authority
Mid-America FTZ, Inc.
P.O. Box 514
Lawrenceville IL 62439
Contact: Mr. Terry L. Denison
Phone: 618/943-5219   Fax: 618/943-5205

Illinois - *Peoria*

FTZ: 114
Grantee: Economic Development Council, Inc.
124 S.W. Adams, Suite 300
Peoria IL 61602-1388
Contact: Mr. William Rigley
Phone: 309/676-7500

Illinois - *Rockford*

FTZ: 176
Grantee: Greater Rockford Airport Authority
60 Airport Dr., P.O. Box 5063
Rockford IL 61125-0063
Contact: Ms. Victoria Benson
Phone: 815/965-8639

Indiana - *Burns Harbor*

FTZ: 152
Grantee: The Indiana Port Commission
6600 U.S. Highway 12
Portage IN 46368
Contact: Mr. Don Miller
Phone: 317/232-9201

Indiana - *Clark County*

FTZ: 170
Grantee: Indiana Port Commission
5100 Post Rd.
Jefferson IN 47130
Contact: Mr. Don Miller
Phone: 317/232-9201

Indiana - *Evansville*

FTZ: 177
Operator: Morton Avenue Warehouse, Inc.
Grantee: Indian Port Commission
1700 Bluff Rd.
Evansville IN 47711
Contact: Mr. Owen Snodgrass
Phone: 812/464-3180   Fax: 812/465-0395

Indiana - *Fort Wayne*

FTZ: 182
Grantee: City of Fort Wayne, Economic Development
Redevelopment
One Main St., Room 840
Fort Wayne IN 46802
Contact: Ms. Trisha Gensic
Phone: 219/427-1127   Fax: 219/427-1375

Indiana - *Indianapolis*

FTZ: 72
Operator: Greater Indianapolis FTZ, Inc.
Grantee: Indianapolis Airport Authority
FTZ No. 72, P.O. Box 51681
Indianapolis IN 46251
Contact: Mr. William Herber
Phone: 317/487-7200   Fax: 317/487-7203

Indiana - *South Bend*

FTZ: 125
Operator: K.A.K. LLC
Grantee: St. Joseph County Airport Authority
1507 South Olive, P.O. Box 3559
South Bend IN 46619
Contact: Mr. Kenneth Kanczuzewski
Phone: 219/232-9357   Fax: 219/232-8283

Iowa - *Cedar Rapids*

FTZ: 175
Grantee: Cedar Rapids Airport Commission
2515 Wright Brothers Blvd. SW
Cedar Rapids IA 52404
Contact: Mr. Kurt Eilers
Phone: 319/362-3131

Iowa - *Des Moines*

FTZ: 107
Grantee: The Iowa Foreign Trade Zone Corp.
604 Locust St., Suite 309
Des Moines IA 50309-2577
Contact: Mr. James D. Polson
Phone: 515/284-1270

Iowa/Illinois - *Quad-City*

FTZ: 133
Grantee: Quad-City Foreign-Trade Zone, Inc.
1830 Second Ave., Suite 200
Rock Island IL 61201-8038
Contact: Mr. John Gardner
Phone: 309/788-7436   Fax: 309/788-4964

Kansas - *Kansas City*

FTZ: 15 & 17
Operator: Greater Kansas City FTZ, Inc.
Grantee: Greater Kansas City FTZ, Inc.
River Market Office Bldg.
20 East 5th Street, Suite 200
Kansas City Kansas 64106
Contact: Mr. Chris Vedros
Phone: 816/421-7666   Fax: 816/432-5500

Kansas - *Sedgwick County*

FTZ: 161
Grantee: Board of Commissioners of Sedgwick County
County Courthouse
525 N. Main, Suite 320
Wichita KS 67203-3759
Contact: Ms. Louanna Honeycutt-Burress
Phone: 316/268-7575   Fax: 316/268-7946

Kentucky - *Louisville*

FTZ: 29
Operator: Louisville & Jefferson County Riverport Auth.
Grantee: Louisville & Jefferson County Riverport Auth.
6900 Riverport Dr., P.O. Box 58010
Louisville KY 40268
Contact: Mr. C. Bruce Traughber
Phone: 502/935-6024

Louisiana - *Baton Rouge*

FTZ: 154
Grantee: Greater Baton Rouge Port Commission
P.O. Box 380
Port Allen LA 70767-0380
Contact: Ms. Karen St. Cyr
Phone: 504/342-1660

Louisiana - *Gramercy*

FTZ: 124
Grantee: South Louisiana Port Commission
P.O. Box 909
La Place LA 70069-0909
Contact: Ms. Glenda Jeansonne
Phone: 504/536-8300

Louisiana - *Lake Charles*

FTZ: 87
Operator: Lake Charles Harbor & Terminal District
P.O. Box 3753
Lake Charles LA 70602
Contact: Ms. Linda Manuel
Phone: 318/439-3661

Louisiana - *New Orleans*

FTZ: 2
Operator: Board of Commissioners of the Port of New Orleans
P.O. Box 60046
New Orleans LA 70160
Contact: Mr. Baldwin Van Benthuysen
Phone: 504/897-0189

Louisiana - *Shreveport*

FTZ: 145
Operator: Caddo-Bossier Parishes Port Commission
P.O. Box 52071
Shreveport LA 71135-2071
Contact: Mr. John W. Holt
Phone: 318/861-4981

Maine - *Bangor*

Maine - *Bangor* ...

FTZ: 58
Operator: City of Bangor
Grantee: City of Bangor
Economic Development Office, City Hall
73 Harlow St.
Bangor ME 04401
Contact: Mr. Stephen A. Bolduc
Phone: 207/945-4400

Maine - *Madawaska*

FTZ: 179
Operator: Northern Trading Co. Inc.
Grantee: Madawaska Foreign Trade Zone Corp.
P.O. Box 250, 190-202 East Main St.
Madawaska ME 04756
Contact: Ms. Jacqueline Clark
Phone: 207/728-4273

Maine - *Waterville*

FTZ: 186
Grantee: Maine International Foreign-Trade Zone, Inc.
P.O. Box 2611
Portland ME 04101
Contact: Mr. John Nale
Phone: 207/873-4304

Maryland - *Baltimore*

FTZ: 74
Operator: Baltimore City Development Corp.
Grantee: City of Baltimore
36 South Charles Street, Suite 1600
Baltimore MD 21201
Contact: Mr. Tom Buser
Phone: 410/837-9305

Maryland - *Baltimore/Washington Int'l Airport*

FTZ: 73
Grantee: Maryland Dept. of Transportation
Maryland Aviation Administration
P.O. Box 8766
BWI Airport MD 21240-0766
Contact: Mr. Gary Davies
Phone: 410/859-7002

Maryland - *Prince George's County*

FTZ: 63
Grantee: Prince George's County Government
14741 Governor Owen Bowie Dr.
Upper Marlboro MD 20772
Contact: Mr. Don Spicer
Phone: 301/985-5002

Massachusetts - *Boston*

FTZ: 27
Operator: Massachusetts Port Authority
Grantee: Massachusetts Port Authority
World Trade Center, Suite 321
Boston MA 02210
Contact: Mr. Andrew Bendheim
Phone: 617/478-4100

Massachusetts - *Holyoke*

FTZ: 201
Grantee: Holyoke Economic Development & Industrial Corp.
City Hall, Room 10
Holyoke MA 01040
Contact: Mr. Robert Bateman
Phone: 413/532-2200

Massachusetts - *New Bedford*

FTZ: 28
Operator: City of New Bedford
Grantee: City of New Bedford
Office of City Planning
133 William St., Rm. 211
New Bedford MA 02740-6172
Contact: Mr. Marc R. Rousseau
Phone: 508/979-1488

Michigan - *Battle Creek*

FTZ: 43
Operator: BC/CAL/KAL Inland Port Auth./South Central
          MI Development Corp.
Grantee: City of Battle Creek
P.O. Box 1438
Battle Creek MI 49016
Contact: Ms. Jan Burland
Phone: 616/962-7526

Michigan - *Detroit*

FTZ: 70
Grantee: Greater Detroit Foreign-Trade Zone, Inc.
8109 East Jefferson
Detroit MI 48214
Contact: Mr. W. Steven Olinek
Phone: 313/331-3842

Michigan - *Flint*

FTZ: 140
Grantee: City of Flint
City Hall, 1101 S. Saginaw St.
Flint MI 48502
Contact: Ms. Constance Scott
Phone: 810/766-7346

Michigan - *Kent/Ottawa/Muskegon Counties*

FTZ: 189
Grantee: KOM Foreign Trade Zone Authority
Seidman School of Business
301 West Fulton Ave., Eberhard Ctr. Rm. 718
Grand Rapids MI 49504-6495
Contact: Mr. Michael Michalski
Phone: 616/771-6653

Michigan - *Sault Ste. Marie*

FTZ: 16
Operator: Economic Dev. Corp. of Sault Ste. Marie
Grantee: Economic Dev. Corp. of Sault Ste. Marie
1301 W. Easterday
Sault Ste. Marie MI 49783
Contact: Mr. James F. Hendricks
Phone: 906/635-9131

Michigan - *St. Clair County*

FTZ: 210
Grantee: Port Huron-St. Clair County Industrial Develop. Corp.
800 Military St., Suite 320
Port Huron MI 48060
Contact: Mr. H. Thomas Rowland
Phone: 810/982-3510

Minnesota - *Deluth*

FTZ: 51
Operator: Seaway Port Authority of Duluth
1200 Port Terminal Dr., P.O. Box 16877
Deluth MN 55816-0877
Contact: Mr. Ray Skelton
Phone: 218/727-8525

Minnesota - *Minneapolis-St. Paul*

FTZ: 119
Grantee: Greater Metropolitan Area FTZ Commission
1000 Minnesota World Trade Center
30 E. Seventh St.
St. Paul MN 55101
Contact: Mr. Steven J. Anderson
Phone: 612/725-8361

Mississippi - *Harrison County*

FTZ: 92
Operator: Greater Gulfport/Biloxi FTZ, Inc.
Grantee: Greater Gulfport/Biloxi Foreign-Trade Zone, Inc.
P.O. Box 40
Jackson MS 39502
Contact: Mr. Bruce Frallic
Phone: 601/863-5951

Mississippi - *Vicksburg/Jackson*

FTZ: 158
Operator: Vicksburg/Jackson FTZ, Inc.
Grantee: Vicksburg/Jackson Foreign-Trade Zone, Inc.
P.O. Box 709
2020 Mission 66
Vicksburg MS 39180-0709
Contact: Mr. F.M. Biedenharn
Phone: 601/636-6914

Missouri - *Kansas City*

FTZ: 15
Operator: Greater Kansas City FTZ, Inc.
River Market Office Bldg.
20 East 5th St., Suite 200
Kansas City MO 64106
Contact: Mr. Chris N. Vedros
Phone: 816/421-7666

Missouri - *St. Louis*

FTZ: 102
Operator: St. Louis County Port Authority
Grantee: St. Louis County Port Authority
121 South Meramec, Suite 412
St. Louis MO 63105
Contact: Mr. Butch Miller
Phone: 314/889-7663

Montana - *Butte-Silver Bow*

FTZ: 190
Grantee: City and County of Butte-Silver Bow
P.O. Box 3641
Butte MT 59702
Contact: Mr. Bill Fogarty
Phone: 406/723-4321

Montana - *Great Falls*

FTZ: 88
Operator: Great Falls Int'l Airport Authority
Grantee: Great Falls Int'l Airport Authority
2800 Terminal Dr.
Great Falls MT 59404-5599
Contact: Mr. M.J. Attwood
Phone: 406/727-3404

Montana - *Toole County*

FTZ: 187
Operator: Northern Express Transportation, Inc.
Grantee: Northern Express Transportation, Inc.
301 First St., South, Suite 3
Shelby MT 59474
Contact: Mr. John Kavanagh
Phone: 406/434-5203

Nebraska - *Lincoln*

FTZ: 59
Operator: Lincoln Chamber of Commerce
Grantee: Lincoln Chamber of Commerce
1221 N St., Suite 606
Lincoln NE 68508
Contact: Mr. Duane S. Vicary
Phone: 402/476-7511

Nebraska - *Omaha*

FTZ: 19
Operator: Dock Board of the City of Omaha
Grantee: Dock Board of the City of Omaha
Omaha-Douglas Civic Ctr.
1819 Farnam St., Suite 300
Omaha NE 68183
Contact: Mr. Scott Knudsen
Phone: 402/444-5381

Nevada - *Clark County*

FTZ: 89
Operator: Nevada Int'l Trade Corp.
Grantee: Nevada Development Authority
1111 B Grier Dr.
Las Vegas NV 89119
Contact: Mr. Jerry Sandstrom
Phone: 702/791-0000

New Hampshire - *Portsmouth*

FTZ: 81
Operator: New Hampshire State Port Authority
Grantee: New Hampshire State Port Authority
555 Market St., Box 506
Portsmouth NH 03801
Contact: Mr. Thomas Orfe
Phone: 603/436-8500

New Jersey - *Mercer County*

FTZ: 200
Grantee: County of Mercer
Joyce McDade Admin. Bldg.
640 South Broad St.
Trenton NJ 08611
Contact: Mr. Robert D. Prunetti
Phone: 609/989-6518

New Jersey - *Morris County*

FTZ: 44
Operator: Division of International Trade
Grantee: NJ Dept. of Commerce & Economic Development
Division of Int'l Trade
P.O. Box 47024
Newark NJ 07102
Contact: Mr. H. Edward Burton
Phone: 609/633-3606

New Jersey - *Salem*

FTZ: 142
Grantee: South Jersey Port Corp.
P.O. Box 129, 2nd & Beckett Streets
Camden NJ 08103
Contact: Mr. John R. Maier
Phone: 609/757-4905

New Mexico - *Albuquerque*

FTZ: 110
Grantee: The City of Albuquerque
P.O. Box 1293
Albuquerque NM 87103
Contact: Mr. Simon Shima
Phone: 505/768-3269

New Mexico - *Dona Ana County*

FTZ: 197
Grantee: Board of County Commissioners, Economic Dev. Dept.
180 West Amador Ave.
Las Cruces NM 88001
Contact: Ms. Judy Price
Phone: 505/647-7248

New Mexico - *Rio Rancho*

FTZ: 194
Grantee: City of Rio Rancho
3900 Southern Blvd., P.O. Box 15550
Rio Rancho NM 87174
Contact: Mr. James Lewis
Phone: 505/891-7201

New York - *Albany*

FTZ: 121
Grantee: Capital District Regional Planning Commission
214 Canal Sq., 2nd Floor
Schenectady NY 12305
Contact: Mr. Chungchin Chen
Phone: 518/393-1715

New York - *Buffalo*

FTZ: 23
Grantee: County of Erie
424 Main St., Suite 300
Buffalo NY 14202
Contact: Mr. Paul R. Leone
Phone: 716/856-6525

New York - *Clinton County*

FTZ: 54
Operator: Clinton County Area Dev. Corp.
Grantee: Clinton County Area Dev. Corp.
61 Area Development Dr.
Plattsburgh NY 12901
Contact: Mr. Gerard E. Kelly
Phone: 518/563-3100   Fax: 518/562-2232

New York - *JFK Int'l Airport*

FTZ: 111
Grantee: The City of New York
110 William Street
New York NY 10038
Contact: Mr. Hugh Frasier
Phone: 212/312-3867

New York - *Monroe County*

FTZ: 141
Grantee: County of Monroe
Rochester Int'l Development Corp.
55 St., Paul St.
Rochester NY 14604
Contact: Mr. Charles Goodwin
Phone: 716/454-2220

New York - *New York City*

FTZ: 1
Operator: S & F Warehouse, Inc.
Grantee: City of New York
Brooklyn Navy Yard, Bldg. 77
Brooklyn NY 11205
Contact: Mr. Sol Braun
Phone: 718/834-0400

New York - *Newark/Elizabeth*

FTZ: 49
Operator: Port Authority of NY & NJ
Grantee: Port Authority of NY & NJ
One World Trade Center, Suite 34 South
New York NY 10048-0642
Contact: Ms. Lucy Ambrosino-Marchak
Phone: 212/435-6725   Fax: 212/435-6040

New York - *Niagara County*

FTZ: 34
Operator: North American Trading and Drayage
Grantee: County of Niagara
2221 Niagara Falls Blvd.
Niagara Falls NY 14304
Contact: Ms. Jodyne Murphy
Phone: 716/731-4900

New York - *Ogdensburg*

FTZ: 118
Grantee: Ogdensburg Bridge and Port Authority
One Bridge Plaza
Ogdensburg NY 13669
Contact: Mr. Doug McDonald
Phone: 315/393-4080

New York - *Oneida County*

FTZ: 172
Operator: Oneida County Industrial Development Corp.
Grantee: County of Oneida
153 Brooks Rd.
Rome NY 13441-4105
Contact: Mr. Joseph G. Karam
Phone: 315/338-0393

New York - *Onondaga*

FTZ: 90
Grantee: County of Onondaga
c/o Greater Syracuse FTZ, Ltd.
572 S. Salina St.
Syracuse NY 13202-3320
Contact: Ms. LouAnn Hood
Phone: 315/470-1884

New York - *Orange County*

FTZ: 37
Grantee: County of Orange
265 Main St.
Goshen NY 10924
Contact: Mr. Geoffrey Chanin
Phone: 914/294-5151   Fax: 914/294-1270

New York - *Watertown*

FTZ: 109
Grantee: The County of Jefferson
c/o Jefferson Industrial Development Agency
800 Starbuck Ave., Suite 800
Watertown NY 13601
Contact: Mr. Stephen Mitchell
Phone: 315/782-5865

North Carolina - *Lenoir County*

FTZ: 214
Grantee: North Carolina Global TransPark Authority
P.O. Box 27406
Raleigh NC 27611-7406
Contact: Ms. Stacey Burks
Phone: 919/733-1365

North Carolina - *Mecklenburg County*

FTZ: 57
Operator: Piedmont Distribution Center
Grantee: North Carolina Department of Commerce
P.O. Box 7123
Charlotte NC 28241-7123
Contact: Ms. Betty Robinson
Phone: 704/587-5573

Ohio - *Cincinnati*

FTZ: 47
Operator: Greater Cincinnati FTZ, Inc.
Grantee: Greater Cincinnati FTZ, Inc.
300 Carew Tower, 441 Vine St.
Cincinnati OH 45202-2812
Contact: Mr. Neil Hensley
Phone: 513/579-3122

Ohio - *Cleveland*

FTZ: 40
Grantee: Cleveland Port Authority
101 Erieside Ave.
Cleveland OH 44114
Contact: Mr. Steven L. Pfeiffer
Phone: 216/241-8004

Ohio - *Clinton County*

FTZ: 101
Operator: Airborne FTZ, Inc.
Grantee: Airborne FTZ, Inc.
145 Hunter Drive
Wilmington OH 45177
Contact: Mr. Mike Kuli
Phone: 513/382-5591

Ohio - *Dayton*

FTZ: 100
Operator: Greater Dayton Foreign-Trade Zone, Inc.
Grantee: Greater Dayton Foreign-Trade Zone, Inc.
c/o Dayton Area Chamber of Commerce
One Chamber Plaza
Dayton OH 45402-2400
Contact: Ms. Verity Snyder
Phone: 513/226-1444

Ohio - *Findlay*

FTZ: 151
Grantee: Community Dev. Foundation
Municipal Bldg., Room 310
Findlay OH 45840
Contact: Mr. John Kovach
Phone: 419/424-7095

Ohio - *Franklin County*

FTZ: 138
Grantee: Rickenbacker Port Authority
Rickenbacker International Airport
7400 Alum Creek Dr.
Columbus OH 43217-1232
Contact: Mr. Bruce Miller
Phone: 614/491-1401

Ohio - *Toledo*

FTZ: 8
Grantee: Toledo-Lucas County Port Authority
One Maritime Plaza
Toledo OH 43604-1866
Contact: Ms. Kelly Rivera
Phone: 419/243-8251

Oklahoma - *Muskogee*

FTZ: 164
Grantee: Muskogee City-County Port Authority
4901 Harold Scoggins Dr., Port 50
Muskogee OK 74401
Contact: Mr. Scott Robinson
Phone: 918/682-7886

Oklahoma - *Oklahoma City*

FTZ: 106
Operator: South Oklahoma City Chamber of Commerce
Grantee: Oklahoma City Office of FTZ No. 106
701 SW 74th St.
Oklahoma City OK 73139-4599
Contact: Ms. Alba Castillo
Phone: 405/634-1436

Oklahoma - *Rogers County*

FTZ: 53
Operator: City of Tulsa-Rogers County Port Auth.
Grantee: City of Tulsa-Rogers County Port Auth.
5350 Cimarron Rd.
Catoosa OK 74015-3027
Contact: Mr. Robert W. Portiss
Phone: 918/266-2291

Oregon - *Coos County*

FTZ: 132
Grantee: International Port of Coos Bay Commission
P.O. Box 1215
Coos Bay OR 97420
Contact: Mr. Martin Callery
Phone: 503/267-7678

Oregon - *Klamath Falls*

FTZ: 184
Grantee: City of Klamath Falls Dock Commission
P.O. Box 237
500 Klamath Avenue
Klamath Falls OR 97601-0361
Contact: Mr. Joseph Riker
Phone: 503/883-5361

Oregon - *Medford-Jackson County*

FTZ: 206
Grantee: Jackson County, Oregon
10 South Oakdale
Medford OR 97501
Contact: Mr. Burke M. Raymond
Phone: 503/776-7269

Oregon - *Porland*

FTZ: 45
Operator: Port of Portland
Grantee: Port of Portland
P.O. Box 3529
Portland OR 97208
Contact: Ms. Peggy J. Krause
Phone: 503/731-7537

Pennsylvania - *Philadelphia*

FTZ: 35
Grantee: Philadelphia Regional Port Authority
210 West Washington Sq.
Philadelphia PA 19106
Contact: Ms. Elizabeth Murphy
Phone: 215/426-6791

Pennsylvania - *Pittsburgh*

FTZ: 33
Grantee: Regional Industrial Dev. Corp. of Southwestern PA
Seventh Floor, 907 Penn Ave.
Pittsburgh PA 15222-3805
Contact: Mr. Frank Brooks Robinson
Phone: 412/471-3939

Pennsylvania - *Pittston*

FTZ: 24
Operator: Eastern Distribution Center, Inc.
Grantee: Eastern Distribution Center, Inc.
1151 Oak St.
Pittston PA 18640-3795
Contact: Mr. Michael J. Horvath
Phone: 717/655-5581

Pennsylvania - *Reading*

FTZ: 147
Grantee: FTZ Corp. of Southeastern Pennsylvania
645 Penn St.
Reading PA 19601
Contact: Mr. Anthony Grimm
Phone: 610/376-6766

Puerto Rico - *Mayaguez*

FTZ: 7
Operator: Puerto Rico Industrial Dev. Co.
Grantee: Puerto Rico Industrial Dev. Co.
P.O. Box 362350
Mayaguez PR 00936-2350
Contact: Mr. Gerardo Toro
Phone: 809/834-0620

Puerto Rico - *Ponce*

FTZ: 163
Grantee: CODEZOL C.D
Corporacion para el Desarrolo de la Zona Libre de Ponce
Apartado 384, Marginal 301-C La Rambla
Ponce PR 00731
Contact: Mr. Enrique Amy
Phone: 809/259-4445

Puerto Rico - *San Juan*

FTZ: 61
Operator: Commercial & Farm Credit & Development
　　　　　　Corp. of Puerto Rico
Grantee: Commercial & Farm Credit & Development
　　　　　　Corp. of Puerto Rico
Box 195009
San Juan PR 00919-5009
Contact: Mr. Lionel A. Lopez
Phone: 809/793-3090

Rhode Island - *Providence & North Kingstown*

FTZ: 105
Grantee: Rhode Island Economic Development Corp.
1330 Davisville Rd.
North Kingstown RI 02852
Contact: Mr. John Riendeau
Phone: 401/277-3134

South Carolina - *Dorchester County*

FTZ: 21
Grantee: South Carolina State Ports Authority
P.O. Box 22287
Charleston SC 29403-2287
Contact: Ms. Jacqueline B. Sassard
Phone: 803/577-8164

South Carolina - *Spartanburg County*

FTZ: 38
Operator: Carolina Trade Zone
Grantee: South Carolina State Ports Authority
P.O. Box 22287
Charleston SC 29413-2287
Contact: Ms. Jacqueline B. Sassard
Phone: 803/577-8164

South Carolina - *West Columbia*

FTZ: 127
Operator: Richland-Lexington Airport District
Grantee: Richland-Lexington Airport District
Columbia Metropolitan Airport
P.O. Box 280037
Columbia SC 29228-0037
Contact: Mr. Robert Waddle
Phone: 803/822-5010

Tennessee - *Chattanooga*

FTZ: 134
Grantee: Rivre Valley Partner, Inc.
835 Georgia Avenue, Suite 500
Chattanooga TN 37402
Contact: Mr. J. Steven Hiatt
Phone: 615/265-3711

Tennessee - *Knoxville*

FTZ: 148
Operator: Greater Knoxville FTZ
Grantee: Industrial Dev. Board of Blount County
c/o Tennessee Technology Foundation
P.O. Box 23184
Knoxville TN 37933-1184
Contact: Mr. Jeff Deardorff
Phone: 423/977-8704

Tennessee - *Memphis*

FTZ: 77
Grantee: The City of Memphis
Memphis & Shelby County, Div. of Planning & Develop.
City Hall, 125 N. Main St.
Memphis TN 38103-2084
Contact: Ms. Connie Binkowitz
Phone: 901/576-7107

Tennessee - *Nashville*

FTZ: 78
Grantee: Metropolitan Nashville Port Authority
214 Second Ave., North, Ste. 1
Nashville TN 37201
Contact: Mr. Robert Gowan
Phone: 615/862-6029

Tennessee/Virginia - *Tri-City*

FTZ: 204
Grantee: Tri-City Airport Commission
P.O. Box 1055
Blountville TN 37617-1055
Contact: Mr. Terry W. Barnes
Phone: 615/323-6288

Texas - *Austin*

FTZ: 183
Grantee: Foreign Trade Zone of Central Texas, Inc.
P.O. Box 142114
Austin TX 78714-2114
Contact: Mr. Lawrence Hart
Phone: 512/452-8848

Texas - *Beaumont*

FTZ: 115
Grantee: Foreign-Trade Zone of Southeast Texas, Inc.
2748 Viterbo Rd., Box 9
Beaumont TX 77705
Contact: Mr. Bill Kimbrough
Phone: 409/835-5367

Texas - *Brownsville*

FTZ: 62
Operator: Brownsville Navigation District
Grantee: Brownsville Navigation District
1000 Foust Road
Brownsville TX 78521
Contact: Ms. Jo Lynne Saban
Phone: 210/831-4592

Texas - *Calhoun/Victoria Counties*

FTZ: 155
Grantee: Calhoun-Victoria Foreign-Trade Zone, Inc.
P.O. Box 397
Point Comfort TX 77979
Contact: Mr. Robert Van Borssum
Phone: 512/987-2813

Texas - *Corpus Christi*

FTZ: 122
Operator: Port of Corpus Christi Authority
Grantee: Port of Corpus Christi Authority
222 Power St., P.O. Box 1541
Corpus Christi TX 78403
Contact: Mr. Larry Cunningham Moore
Phone: 512/882-5633

Texas - *Dallas/Fort Worth*

FTZ: 39
Operator: Dallas/Fort Worth Int'l Airport Board
P.O. Drawer 619428
DFW Airport TX 75261-9428
Contact: Ms. Tracy Kaplan
Phone: 214/574-3121

Texas - *Dallas/Fort Worth*

FTZ: 168
Operator: Foreign Trade Zone Operating Co. of Texas
Grantee: Dallas/Fort Worth Maquila Trade Development Corp.
P.O. Box 742916
Dallas TX 75374-2916
Contact: Mr. Dennis Konopatzke
Phone: 214/991-9955

Texas - *Del Rio*

FTZ: 97
Operator: City of Del Rio
Grantee: City of Del Rio
114 West Martin Street
Del Rio TX 78841
Contact: Mr. Juan Aguirre
Phone: 210/774-8553

Texas - *Eagle Pass*

FTZ: 96
Operator: Maverick Co. Dev. Corp.
Grantee: City of Eagle Pass
P.O. Box 3693
Eagle Pass TX 78853
Contact: Ms. Diane Galviz
Phone: 210/773-6166

Texas - *El Paso*

FTZ: 68
Grantee: City of El Paso
5B Butterfield Trail Blvd.
El Paso TX 79906-0616
Contact: Mr. Robert C. Jacob
Phone: 915/771-6016

Texas - *El Paso*

FTZ: 150
Grantee: Westport Economic Development Corp.
P.O. Box 9368
El Paso TX 79984
Contact: Ms. Patricia A. Minor
Phone: 915/533-1122

Texas - *Ellis County*

FTZ: 113
Operator: Trade Zone Operations, Inc.
Grantee: Midlothian Trade Zone Corp.
1500 North Service Rd., Highway 67, P.O. Box 788
Midlothian TX 76065
Contact: Mr. Lawrence A. White
Phone: 214/723-5522

Texas - *Fort Worth*

FTZ: 196

Grantee: Alliance Corridor, Inc.
2421 Westport Parkway, Suite 200
Fort Worth TX 76177
Contact: Mr. Timothy Ward
Phone: 817/890-1000

Texas - *Freeport*

FTZ: 149
Grantee: Port of Freeport
Brazos River Harbor Navigation District
P.O. Box 615
Freeport TX 77541
Contact: Ms. Phyllis Saathoff
Phone: 409/233-2667

Texas - *Galveston*

FTZ: 36
Operator: Port of Galveston
Grantee: City of Galveston
Galveston Wharves
P.O. Box 328
Galveston TX 77553
Contact: Mr. Jose Cavazos
Phone: 409/766-6121

Texas - *Harris County*

FTZ: 84
Grantee: Port of Houston Authority
111 East Loop North
Houston TX 77029
Contact: Mr. Jack Beasley
Phone: 713/670-2400   Fax: 713/670-2564

Texas - *Laredo*

FTZ: 94
Operator: Laredo International Airport
Grantee: City of Laredo
Operator of Foreign-Trade Zone No. 94
4719 Maher Avenue, Bldg. 132
Laredo TX 78041
Contact: Mr. Humberto Garza
Phone: 210/795-2000

Texas - *Liberty County*

FTZ: 171
Grantee: Liberty County Economic Development Corp.
P.O. Box 857
Cleveland TX 77575
Contact: Mr. John Herbert
Phone: 409/336-7311

Texas - *McAllen*

FTZ: 12
Operator: McAllen Economic Development Corp.
Grantee: McAllen Economic Development Corp.
6401 S. 33rd. St.
McAllen TX 78501
Contact: Ms. Joyce Dean
Phone: 210/682-4306

Texas - *Midland*

FTZ: 165
Grantee: City of Midland
c/o Midland Int'l Airport
P.O. Box 603053, 95066 La Force Blvd.
Midland TX 79711
Contact: Ms. Carroll Thomas
Phone: 915/560-2200

Texas - *Orange*

FTZ: 117
Grantee: Foreign-Trade Zone of Southeast Texas, Inc.
2748 Viterbo Rd., Box 9
Beaumont TX 77705
Contact: Mr. Bill Kimbrough
Phone: 409/835-5367

Texas - *Port Arthur*

FTZ: 116
Grantee: Foreign-Trade Zone of Southeast Texas, Inc.
2748 Viterbo Rd., Box 9
Beaumont TX 77705
Contact: Mr. Bill Kimbrough
Phone: 409/835-5367

Texas - *Presidio*

FTZ: 178
Operator: Presidio Economic Development Corp.
Grantee: Presidio Economic Development Corp.
P.O. Box 1414
Presidio TX 79845
Contact: Mr. Jose Leyva
Phone: 915/229-3724

Texas - *San Antonio*

FTZ: 80
Grantee: City of San Antonio
Economic Development Dept.
P.O. Box 839966
San Antonio TX 78283-3966
Contact: Ms. Margaret Anaglia
Phone: 210/207-8093

Texas - *Starr County*

FTZ: 95
Operator: Starr County Industrial Foundation
Grantee: Starr County Industrial Foundation
P.O. Box 502
Rio Grande City TX 78582
Contact: Mr. Chris Salinas
Phone: 210/487-2709

Texas - *Texas City*

FTZ: 199
Grantee: Texas City Foreign Trade Zone Corporation
P.O. Box 2608
Texas City TX 77592
Contact: Mr. Randy Dietel
Phone: 409/948-3111

Texas - *Weslaco*

FTZ: 156

Grantee: City of Weslaco
500 South Kansas
Weslaco TX 78596
Contact: Mr. Allan Romer
Phone: 210/968-3181

Utah - *Salt lake City*

FTZ: 30
Grantee: Redevelopment Agency of Salt Lake City
451 South State St., Room 404
Salt Lake City UT 84111
Contact: Ms. Allison Gregorson
Phone: 801/535-7320

Vermont - *Burlington*

FTZ: 55
Operator: Greater Burlington Industrial Corp.
Grantee: Greater Burlington Industrial Corp.
P.O. Box 786, 7 Burlington Sq.
Burlington VT 05402
Contact: Mr. C. Harry Behney
Phone: 802/862-5726   Fax: 802/860-1899

Vermont - *Newport*

FTZ: 91
Operator: Northeastern Vermont Dev. Assoc.
Grantee: Northeastern Vermont Dev. Assoc.
44 Main St., P.O. Box 630
St. Johnsbury VT 05819
Contact: Mr. Charles E. Carter
Phone: 802/748-5181

Virginia - *Culpeper County*

FTZ: 185
Grantee: Culpeper-County Chamber of Commerce, Inc.
133 West Davis St.
Culpeper VA 22701
Contact: Ms. Norma Dunwody
Phone: 540/825-8628

Virginia - *Richmond*

FTZ: 207
Grantee: Capital Region Airport Commission
Richmond Int'l Airport
Box A-3
Richmond VA 23231-5999
Contact: Mr. Timothy Doll
Phone: 804/236-2102

Virginia - *Suffolk*

FTZ: 20
Grantee: Virginia Port Authority
600 World Trade Ctr.
Norfolk VA 23510
Contact: Mr. Bob Merhige
Phone: 804/683-8000

Washington - *Bellingham*

FTZ: 129
Grantee: Port of Bellingham
625 Cornwall Ave.
Bellingham WA 98225-5017
Contact: Mr. Bob Hilpert
Phone: 206/676-2500   Fax: 206/671-6411

Washington - *Blaine*

FTZ: 130
Grantee: Port of Bellingham
625 Cornwall Ave.
Bellingham WA 98225-5017
Contact: Mr. Bob Hilpert
Phone: 206/676-2500   Fax: 206/676-6411

Washington - *Cowlitz County*

FTZ: 120
Grantee: Cowlitz Economic Development Council
1452 Hudson St., U.S. Bank Bldg., Suite 208
P.O. Box 1278
Longview WA 98632
Contact: Mr. Clint Page
Phone: 360/423-9921   Fax: 360/423-1923

Washington - *Everett*

FTZ: 85
Grantee: Port of Everett
P.O. Box 538
Everett WA 98206
Contact: Mr. Edward Paskovskis
Phone: 206/259-3164   Fax: 206/252-7366

Washington - *Grays Harbor*

FTZ: 173
Grantee: Port of Grays Harbor
P.O. Box 660
Aberdeen WA 98520-0141
Contact: Mr. Ron Popham
Phone: 360/533-9541

Washington - *Moses Lake*

FTZ: 203
Grantee: Moses Lake Public Corp.
Port of Moses Lake, Grant County Airport
Bldg. 1202, 7810 Andrews St. NE
Moses Lake WA 98837-3218
Contact: Mr. David M. Bailey
Phone: 509/762-5363

Washington - *Olympia*

FTZ: 216
Grantee: Port of Olympia
915 Washington Street NE
P.O. Box 827
Olympia WA 98507-0827
Contact: Mr. John M. Mohr
Phone: 360/586-6150

Washington - *Seattle*

FTZ: 5
Operator: Port of Seattle Commission
Grantee: Port of Seattle Commission
P.O. Box 1209
Seattle WA 98111

Contact: Mr. Scott Pattison
Phone: 206/728-3628

Washington - *Sumas*

FTZ: 131
Grantee: Port of Bellingham
625 Cornwall Ave.
Bellingham WA 982257-501
Contact: Mr. Bob Hilpert
Phone: 206/676-2500   Fax: 206/671-6411

Washington - *Tacoma*

FTZ: 212
Grantee: Puyallup Tribal FTZ Corp.
3702 Marine View Drive NE, Suite 200
Tacoma WA 98422
Contact: Mr. James May
Phone: 206/383-2820

Washington - *Tacoma*

FTZ: 86
Grantee: Port of Tacoma
One Sitcom Plaza
Tacoma WA 98421
Contact: Mr. Jerry Ahmann
Phone: 206/383-5841   Fax: 206/383-4534

Washington - *Whatcom County*

FTZ: 128
Grantee: Lummi Indian Business Council
2616 Kwina
Bellingham WA 98226
Contact: Mr. Clayton Finkbonner
Phone: 360/385-2374   Fax: 360/384-5521

Washington - *Yakima*

FTZ: 188
Grantee: Yakima Air Terminal Board
2400 West Washington Ave.
Yakima WA 98903
Contact: Mr. Bob Clem
Phone: 509/575-6149

Wisconsin - *Brown County*

FTZ: 167
Grantee: Brown County, Wisconsin
305 East Walnut, P.O. Box 23600
Green Bay WI 54305-3600
Contact: Mr. Jeff Finley
Phone: 414/448-4001

Wisconsin - *Milwaukee*

FTZ: 41
Grantee: Foreign Trade Zone of Wisconsin, Ltd.
P.O. Box 340046
Milwaukee WI 53224
Contact: Mr. Vincent J. Boever
Phone: 414/769-2956

Wyoming - *Casper*

FTZ: 157
Grantee: Natrona County International Airport
Airport Terminal Unit, Box 1
Casper WY 82604
Contact: Mr. Eddie F. Storer
Phone: 307/472-3521

This list was compiled by the Trade Information Center at the Department of Commerce's International Trade Administration and should not be considered a comprehensive guide of all international trade resources on the Internet.

The numeric codes assigned to each site stand for the following categories:

1 Comprehensive Sources of International Trade Information
2 Region Specific Information
3 Industry Specific Information
4 Trade Contacts and Leads
5 International Trade Services
6 Government Resources for Export Promotion
7 International Trade Law

For convenience the information is presented both in alphabetical order by the organization which hosts the site and by category.

Sites by Organization

A.R. Vogue Corporation
http://www.bekkoame.or.jp/~tomatell/business/vogue.htm
Trade leads and trade catalogues
CODE: 4

American Chamber of Commerce in Brazil
http://www.amcham.com.br
Regional info. (Brazil)
CODE: 2

American Material Resources, Inc.
http://www.commerce.com/placette
Export Trading Company
CODE: 3

American National Standards Institute
http://www.ansi.org/home.html
Info. on US Standards
CODE: 5,6

AmericasNet at Florida State Univ.
http://americas.fiu.edu/index.html
Americas Trade Forum
CODE: 2

ANANSE International Trade Law Project
http://itl.irv.uit.no/trade_law/
International organizations and conventions
CODE: 7

Asia Development Bank
http://www.asiandevbank.org/
ADB information, finance
CODE: 5

Asia in Cyberspace
http://silkroute.com/silkroute/asia/rsrc/country/index.html
Asian country information
CODE: 2

Asian Trade Links
http://asam.com.au/~atl-aust
Australian firm with Asian contacts
CODE: 2,5

Assist International
http://www.assist-intl.com
Comprehensive export information
CODE: 1

Atlanta International Magazine
http://www.aimlink.com/at/mag
Regional info. (SE US)
CODE: 2,4

Australian Embassy
http://www.aust.emb.nw.dc.us/intrade.htm
Regional info. (Australia and Asia)
CODE: 2

Big Dreams
http://www.wimsey.com/~duncans
Info. on starting a business
CODE: 1

BizPro
http://www.bizpro.com
Business listings on the Web
CODE: 4,5

BizWeb
http://www.bizweb.com
Index of commercial Web sites
CODE: 5

Bureau of National Affairs
http://www.bna.com
Legislative & regulatory information, publications
CODE: 5,7

Business Link
http://www.jsp.fi/
Finnish trading company (Russia)
CODE: 2,5

Business Publications
gopher://gopher.enews.com:70/11/magazines/category/business/
international
Business publications
CODE: 1

Business Researchers' Interests
http://www.pitt.edu/~malhotra/international.html
Net resources
CODE: 1,2

Canadiana
http://www.cs.cmu.edu/Web/Unofficial/Canadiana/
Info on Canada
CODE: 2

CBCC: Trade Leads
http://turnpike.net/emporium/I/icml/cbcc/czleads.html
Trade leads for Czech Republic
CODE: 2,4

Central Asia Information
http://coombs.anu.edu.au/WWWVL-AsianStudies.html
Links and info. on Central Asia
CODE: 2

Central Intelligence Agency
http://www.odci.gov/cia
Country background info.
CODE: 2,6

China News Digest
http://www.cnd.org:80
News and info. about China
CODE: 2

Chinese Business Journal
http://www.ncb.gov.sg:1080/news/cbj
Info. from daily Chinese Business Journal
CODE: 2

Circle International
http://circleintl.com
freight forwarder/customs broker
CODE: 5

Commerce Business Daily
gopher://counterpoint.com
Daily international business news
CODE: 1

CommerceNet
http://www.commerce.net
High-tech business resource
CODE: 3,4

Commercial List
http://www.directory.net
Index of commercial sites on the Web
CODE: 5

Commercial News Services
http://www.jou.ufl.edu/comres/webjou.htm.
Newspapers on-line
CODE: 5

Congressional Record for 104th Congress
http://thomas.loc.gov/
Congressional documents
CODE: 7

Consolidated Freightways
http://www.cnf.com/
Transportation info.
CODE: 5

Costa Rica Web Server
http://ns.cr/ecconeg.html
Links to sites in Costa Rica
CODE: 2

Daily International News
http://www.helsinki.fi/~Isaarine/news.html
Business and economic news
CODE: 1

Dharani Export Import Services, Inc.
http://www.webindia.com/cust/india/dharani/dharani.html
Indian trading company
CODE: 2

Dun & Bradstreet
http://www.dbisna.com/
Information services
CODE: 1,5

Electroni Embassy
http://www.embassy.org
Foreign Embassies in Washington DC
CODE: 1,2

Elvis Server
http://www.elvis.msk.su
Moscow service provider, Russian links
CODE: 2

Eniitco General Trading Europe, AB
http://www.pi.se/eniitco/index.html
Swedish trading company
CODE: 2

Entrepreneurs
http://sashimi.wwa.com/~notime/eotw/EOTW.html
Business info. for entrepreneurs
CODE: 1

EuroNet
http://www.euro.net
Info on the EU
CODE: 2

European Commission
http://www.cec.lu
Regional info. (Europe)
CODE: 2

European Community
http://echo.lu/home.html
Info. on the EU
CODE: 2

European Community
http://echo.lu
Regional info. (Europe)
CODE: 2

European Home Pages
http://s700.uminho.pt/cult-europ.html
Info. and links to Euro cities
CODE: 2

European News Library
http://www.meaddata.com
Information about Europe
CODE: 2

EUnet (Europe)
http://www.eu.net
EU service provider
CODE: 2

Experimental Stock Market Data
http://www.ai.mit.edu/stocks.html
Stock market Data
CODE: 5

Expo Guide
http://www.expoguide.com
Trade shows and exhibits
CODE: 5

Export Community of NY, NJ, and CT
http://www.exportcom.org
NY Distribution Export Council
CODE: 2

Export Leads
L.P.Export@mailback.com
BBS for export leads
CODE: 4

Export Legal Ass't Network (ELAN)
http://web.miep.org/elan
Legal assistance
CODE: 7

Export Price Indices and Percent Change
gopher://una.hh.lib.umich.edu/O/ebb/price/exim-4.bis
Pricing info.
CODE: 5

Export Today Magazine
http://www.enews.com/magazines/export/
Export Today Magazine
CODE: 1,5

Export USA
http://www.exportusa.com
Exec. resource for comprehensive info.
CODE: 1

EXECPC
http://www.execpc.com/bbsinfo.html
Extensive trade database
CODE: 1,5

Far East Business Directory
http://www.net-trade.com
Regional info. on the Far East
CODE: 2

Federal Government WWW Servers
http://www.fie.com/
Springboard to most Federal home pages
CODE: 1

Federation of International Trade Associations
http://www.webhead.com/FITA/home.html
Organization of trade associations (with links)
CODE: 5

FedWorld
http://www.fedworld.gov/
Information locator for US Government
CODE: 1

FINWeb
http://www.finweb.com/
Finance and economic information
CODE: 1,5

Fletcher School of Law & Diplomacy
http://www.tufts.edu/fletcher/multilaterals.html
Multilateral conventions
CODE: 7

Foreign Agricultural Service, USDA
http://www.usda.gov
Agricultural market info. and economic research
CODE: 2

Foreign Exchange Rates
gopher://una.hh.lib.umich.edu/O/ebb/monetary/noonfx.frb
Noon exchange rates daily
CODE: 5

Foreign Trade Zones
http://webvision.com/ftz
Information on foreign trade zones worldwide
CODE: 5

Free Advertise
http://www.freeadvertise.com
Web Advertising space
CODE: 5

Freylon Oy
http://clinet.fi/~frelon
Finnish trading company
CODE: 2

Global Access to Trade and Technology (GATT)
http://www.gatts.com/
Global trade information
CODE: 1

Global Business Forum Demo
http://www.pragmatix.com:80/gbf/gbf.html
Trade leads, marketing info.
CODE: 1,4

Global Connect, Inc.
http://www.gc.net/
Business newsletter
CODE: 1

Global Interact Network (GINLIST)
http://ciber.bus.msu.edu
International business and marketing
CODE: 1

Global Network Navigator Pers Finance Ctr.
http://gnn.com/wic/usics/persfin.new.html
Finance and economic information
CODE: 1,5

Global Recycling Network
http://grn.com/grn/
Trade Leads. Environmental industry
CODE: 1,3,4

Global Trade Point Network
http://www.unicc.org/untpdc/gtpnet/gtpnet.html
UNCTAD trade leads
CODE: 4

Global Ukraine
http://www.gu.kiev.ua/
Information on Ukraine and Kiev
CODE: 2

Glossary of International Trade Terms
http://circleintl.com
Trade terms
CODE: 2,5

GoldSite Europe
http://www.gold.net:80/
Info. and links to Europe
CODE: 2

Graduate Institute of International Studies
http://heiwww.unige.ch/gatt/final_act
GATT agreement (final text)
CODE: 7

Guide to Marketing on the Internet
http://www.industry.net/guide.html
Marketing guide
CODE: 5

Holt's Stock Market Reports
http://metro.turnpike.net/holt/index.html
Info. on international financial markets
CODE: 2

IBEX Exchange
http://www.ibex.com/
Listing of exporting companies
CODE: 1,4

IBEX Yellow Pages
http://www.cba.uh.edu/ylowpges/yi.html
Listing of exporting companies
CODE: 1,4,5

Impex Connect
http://www.aztec.co.za/impex
South African trading company
CODE: 2

Import/Export Connection
http://www.cam.org/~sailor/imexcon.htm/
Trade leads
CODE: 4

IMEX Exchange
http://www.imex.com/
Trade leads, general information
CODE: 1,4

Infomanage International
http://www.commerce.com/net2/business/business.html
Regional information globally; international business
CODE: 1

Institute for Ag and Trade Policy
http://wwww.igc.apc.org/iatp/
Trade news, strategies and fact sheet
CODE: 2,3

Intelligence Community
http://www.odci.gov/ic
Country background information
CODE: 2

Inter-American Development Bank
http://www.iadb.org/
IDB information, finance
CODE: 5

International Business Practices
gopher://umslvma.umsl.edu:70/11/library/govdocs/ibpa
Overview of 117 countries
CODE: 2

International Chamber of Commerce
http://www1.usa1.com/~ibnet/icchp.html
Extensive trade resources
CODE: 1

International Marketing Corp. (IMC)
http://www.internationalmarket.com
Business services and links
CODE: 1,5

International Standard Organization
http://www.iso.ch/
ISO standards
CODE: 1,5,6

International Trade Data Users, Inc.
http://www.itdu.org/itdu
Group for users of elec. business info.
CODE: 1

International Trade Desk
http://members.aol.com/tradedesk/
US Trade and Business
CODE: 1

International Trade Network
http://ds.internic.net/cgi-bin/enthtml/business/intltrade.b
Buyers and suppliers
CODE: 4

International Trade Organizations
http://www.yahoo.com/Economy/Organizations/
International_Trade/
Search engine
CODE: 5

International Trade Resources
http://infomanage.com/intltrade
CODE: 1

International TradeNET
http://intl-tradenet.com
Trade leads and information
CODE: 1,4

Internet Group
http://www.tig.com
Internet marketing group
CODE: 5

Internet Guide to Japan
http://fuji.stanford.edu/japan_information_guide.html
Information about Japan
CODE: 2

Internet Tradeline
http://www.intrade.com/
General information, trade leads
CODE: 4,5

Intertrade Mercantile Exchange
http://www.intergroup.com/mercantile
Trading forum
CODE: 4,5

J.J.L. Associates
http://www.cityscape.co.uk/users/dr39/
Customs & Freight (Europe)
CODE: 2,5

Japan Computer Science Co., Ltd.
http://www.jcsnet.or.jp/v-city/trade/guide-e/index-e.html
Japanese Market
CODE: 2

Japan External Trade Organization (JETRO)
http://www.jetro.go.jp/
Regional information (Japan)
CODE: 2

Japan-MITI
http://glocom.ac.jp/NEWS/MITI
MITI's programm for information infrastructure
CODE: 2

Japanese Ministry of Int'l Trade and Industry
http://www.glocom.ac/jp/NEWS/MITI-doc.html
Regional information (Japan)
CODE: 2

KEYMEXX
http://Jsasoc.com/keymexx.html
Regional information (Mexico)
CODE: 2

Knowledge Web
http://www.kweb.com
Trade show listings
CODE: 5

Koblas Currency Converter
http://hnn.com/cgi-bin/gnn/currency
Exchange rates for about 50 countries
CODE: 2

KoreaWeb Information Services
http://www.webcom.com/~koreaweb
Links to sites in South Korea
CODE: 2

Latin American Trade and Information Network
http://www.latinet.com/
Latin American Trade Information
CODE: 2

Latin American Trade Council of Oregon
http://www.teleport.com/~tmiles/latco.htm/
Regional Information (Oregon, Latin America)
CODE: 2

Latin American/Caribbean Bulletin
http://www.ita.doc.gov/region/latinam/
LAC business bulletin
CODE: 2

LatinoWeb Business
http://www.latinoweb.com/favision/business.htm
Trade leads. Regional Info. (Lat Am)
CODE: 2,4

Library of Commerce
http://www.loc.gov/
Information and research
CODE: 1

Mariner Systems, Inc.
http://msi.marsys.com/
Shipping rates, schedules, tariffs, etc.
CODE: 5

Market Link
http://m-link.com
Multilingual directories and resources
CODE: 2

Ministry of International Trade and Industry (MITI)
http://www.miti.go.jp/
Regional info. (Japan)
CODE: 2

National Technical Information Service
http://www.fedworld.gov/ntis/business/ibus.htm
Government international trade publications
CODE: 1

National Trade Data Bank
http://www.stat-usa.gov
Market information and research
CODE: 1

NAFTA
gopher://umslvma.umsl.edu:70/11/library/govdocs/naftaf
Text of agreement
CODE: 2,7

NAFTAnet Small Business Information
http://www.naftanet/smallbiz.htm
NAFTA
CODE: 2,5

Netherlands Contracts
http://www.euronet.nl/users/gandy/index.html
Info. on the Netherlands
CODE: 2

New York Library System
http://www.nysernet.org/
Information and research
CODE: 1

New York Times
http://www.nytimefax.com
New York Times Newspaper
CODE: 1

Nippon Telephone and Telegraph (NTT)
http://www.ntt.jp
Regional info. (Japan)
CODE: 2

North Carolina International Trade Notes
http://www.ces.ncsu.edu/itd/catalog.html
Trade info. and leads
CODE: 1,2,4

Notices of For Government Standards
gopher://gopher.counterpoint.com:2003/11/
Foreign%20Government%20Standards
CODE: 5,7

Online Manufacturers Network
http://www.mfrnet.com
Advertising/marketing
CODE: 5

Open Markets Commercial Sites
http://www.directory.net/
US Suppliers
CODE: 4

Organization of American States
http://www.sice.oas.org
Regional info. (Latin America)
CODE: 2

PangaeaNet Home Page
http://www.pangaea.net/homepage.htm
BBS trade leads and marketing information
CODE: 1,4

Pennsylvania International BusinessNet
http://www.pitt.edu/~wpaintl/
Market information, export assistance, Regional information (PA)
CODE: 1,2,5

Poppe Tyson Advertising and Public Relations
http://www.poppe.com:8400
Marketing and online services
CODE: 5

Port of Tacoma (Washington)
http://www.portoftacoma.com
Site of Tacoma Port
CODE: 3

ProTRADE Forum
http://www.cityscape.co.uk/users/bm22/pt.html
Info. on Comuserve's ProTrade forum
CODE: 1

Romanian Home Page (Burhala)
http://werple.apana.org.au/~florin/default.html
Romanian info.
CODE: 2

Russian Trade Connection
http://www.lh.com/rtc/
Russia
CODE: 2

Simon Fraser's David See-Chai Lan Centre Int'l Comm
http://hoshi.cic.sfu.ca/11/dlam/business/forum
Regional info. (Japan)
CODE: 2

Small Business Administration (SBA)
http://www.sbaonline.sba.gov
Info incl. finance for sm. exporter
CODE: 1,5,6

Small Business Foundation of America
http://web.miep.org/sbfa/
Information on starting a business
CODE: 1

Somers & Associates
http://ppp.jax-inter.net/ispy/
Business intelligence and investigation
CODE: 5

Starting Point
http://www.stpt.com
International & business news
CODE: 1,4

Stat-USA
http://www.stat-usa.gov
NTDB and EBB
CODE: 1

State Export Statistics
http://www.ita.doc.gov/industry/otea/state
State-by-state export statistics
CODE: 2,5,6

Taiwan Internet Gateway
http://pristine.com.tw/
Multi-lingual links to Taiwan and Asia
CODE: 2

Taiwan WWW Sites
http://peacock.tnjc.edu.tw/organ.html
Links to sites in Taiwan
CODE: 2

Texas-One Home Page (TX DOC)
http://www.texas-one.org
Regional Information (US)
CODE: 2

Thailand Information
http://www.nectec.or.th
Information on Thailand
CODE: 2

The Web in Slovenia
http://www.ijs.si/slo/country/
Links & Information on Slovenia
CODE: 2

Trade Compass
http://www.tradecompass.com/
General information, trade leads
CODE: 1,4,5

Trade Events, Shows and Exhibitions
http://www.expoguide.com/
Trade Show information
CODE: 5

Trade Law Home Page
http://itl.irv.uit.no/trade_law/
International trade laws
CODE: 7

Trade Point Fortaleiza
http://tpfort.sfiec.org.br/
UNCTAD's Trade Point homepage
CODE: 1,4

Trade Point USA
http://www.natp.iftea.com/
Trade leads, market info., UN info.
CODE: 1,4

Trade Scope
http://www.tradescope.com/
Insurance, credit reports
CODE: 1,4,5

Trade Show Central
http://www.tscentral.com
Trade Show listings
CODE: 5

Trade Trading (Taiwan)
http://trace.com.tw
Taiwanese trading company/Asian links
CODE: 2

Trade Zone
http://www.tradezone.com/tz/trdzone.html
Global trade information/mail order how to
CODE: 1,6

Tradefair International
http://www.tradefair.com/
Trade leads, financing
CODE: 4

TradeFair
http://www.tradefair.com/TradeFair.html
Trade leads, market information
CODE: 1,4

TradeNet
http://www.tradenet.org/
Trade leads
CODE: 4

TradePoint
http://www.tpusa.com
Trade leads and contacts
CODE: 4,5

TradePort
http://www.tradeport.org/
Comprehensive information for CA exporters
CODE: 1,5

Traders'Connection
http://www.trader.com
Member-based service; advertising
CODE: 5

Tradescope Home Page
http://www.tradescope.com/
Trade leads, marketing information
CODE: 1,4

Uniform Commercial Code (Cornell Univ)
http://www.law.cornell.edu/ucc/ucc.table.html
Uniform Commercial Code
CODE: 7

United Nations Development Program
http://www.undp.org/
UN information: UNDP and ECOSOC
CODE: 1

Univ of California at Fresno
http://caticsuf.csufresno.edu:70/1/atls
Trade leads & regional info. (Calif)
CODE: 2,4

Univ of Missouri at St. Louis
gopher://umslvma.umsl.edu:70/11/library/govdocs/naftaf
NAFTA agreement (final text)
CODE: 2,7

Univ of Pittsburgh Int'l Affairs Network
http://www.pitt.edu/~ian/ianres.html
International information and research
CODE: 1

UNCTAD Gopher
gopher://unicc.org/1/ITC
Extensive statistics and trade information
CODE: 1,5

UNISPHERE
http://www.nando.net/uni/
High tech industries
CODE: 3

US Agency for Int'l Development (USAID)
http://www.info.usaid.gov/
USAID procurement and opportunities
CODE: 2,5,6

US Census Bureau
http://www.census.gov/
Fact and statistics, data maps
CODE: 1,6

US Census Bureau
http://www.census.gov/ftp/pub/foreign-trade/www.schedule.b.html
HS (Schedule B) numbers
CODE: 5,6

US Commercial Service, The Netherlands
http://www.luna.nl/~attic
Info for US companies on Netherlands
CODE: 2,5

US Council for International Business
http://www.uscib.org
ATA Carnet and other documents
CODE: 5

US Department of Agriculture
http://www.usda.gov/
Ag Information, Market Research
CODE: 3,5,6

US Department of Commerce
http://www.doc.gov/
Home page for Department of Commerce
CODE: 1,5,6

US Department of State
http://www.stolaf.edu/network/travel-advisories.html
Political and Economic climate around the world
CODE: 2,6

US Government Printing Office
http://www.access.gpo.gov/
Directory of government documents
CODE: 6

US House of Representatives
http://www.house.gov/
Information from Capitol Hill
CODE: 6

US International Trade Commission
http://www.usitc.gov/
Industry, economic development, legal information
CODE: 1,6,7

US Trade Center Directory for Buffalo, NY
http://www.grasmick.com/ustrade.htm
International trade contacts in Buffalo, NY area
CODE: 2,5

USDA Foreign Agricultural Service
http://www.usda.gov/8000/fas//
Agriculture export information
CODE: 6

USDOC Bureau of Export Administration
http://www.doc.gov/resources/BXA_infor.html
Info. on BXA function and contacts
CODE: 5,6

USDOC, Big Emerging Markets
http://www.stat-usa.gov/itabems.html
Regional info. (BEMs)
CODE: 2,6

USDOC, Global Export Market Info System
http://www.itaiep.doc.gov/
BEMs, CEEBIC, BISNIS, NAFTA
CODE: 2,6

USDOC, Import Administration
http://www.ita.doc.gov/import_admin/records/
US import restrictions and regulations
CODE: 2,6

USDOC, International Trade Administration
http://www.ita.doc.gov/
General information, comprehensive
CODE: 2,6

USDOC, Japan Export Information Center
http://www.ita.doc.gov/regional/geo_region/japan
Regional info. (Japan)
CODE: 2,6

Venezuela's Web Server
http://venezuela.mit.edu
Information on Venezuela
CODE: 2

Virtual Africa
http://www.africa.com
Information on The Republic of South Africa
CODE: 2

Washington College of Law
http://sray.wcl.american.edu/pub/wcl.html
International legal information on the EU and UN
CODE: 7

Washington State Trade Center
http://mail.eskimo.com/~bwest/
Regional information (WA, Russia)
CODE: 2,5

Web India
http://www.webindia.com/india.html
Information and business contacts on India
CODE: 2

White Bear Trade International, Inc.
http://www.the-wire.com/whitebear/
Regional information (Russia, Ukraine)
CODE: 2

White House
http://www.whitehouse.gov/
Information from the White House
CODE: 6

WWW Servers for Former Soviet Union
http://www.w3.org/hypertext/DataSources/bySubject/
Overview.html
Links to all known sites in former USSR
CODE: 2

WWW Servers in Sweden
http://www.sunet.se/sweden
Links to Swedish sites
CODE: 2

Sites by Category

Comprehensive Sources of International Trade Information

Assist International
http://www.assist-intl.com
Comprehensive export information

Big Dreams
http://www.wimsey.com/~duncans
Info. on starting a business

Business Publications
gopher://gopher.enews.com:70/11/magazines/category/business/
international
Business publications

Business Researchers' Interests
http://www.pitt.edu/~malhotra/international.html
Net resources

Commerce Business Daily
gopher://counterpoint.com
Daily international business news

Daily International News
http://www.helsinki.fi/~Isaarine/news.html
Business and economic news

Dun & Bradstreet
http://www.dbisna.com/
Information services

Electroni Embassy
http://www.embassy.org
Foreign Embassies in Washington DC

Entrepreneurs
http://sashimi.wwa.com/~notime/eotw/EOTW.html
Business info. for entrepreneurs

Export Today Magazine
http://www.enews.com/magazines/export/
Export Today Magazine

Export USA
http://www.exportusa.com
Exec. resource for comprehensive info.

EXECPC
http://www.execpc.com/bbsinfo.html
Extensive trade database

Federal Government WWW Servers
http://www.fie.com/
Springboard to most Federal home pages

FedWorld
http://www.fedworld.gov/
Information locator for US Government

FINWeb
http://www.finweb.com/
Finance and economic information

Global Access to Trade and Technology (GATT)
http://www.gatts.com/
Global trade information

Global Business Forum Demo
http://www.pragmatix.com:80/gbf/gbf.html
Trade leads, marketing info.

Global Connect, Inc.
http://www.gc.net/
Business newsletter

Global Interact Network (GINLIST)
http://ciber.bus.msu.edu
International business and marketing

Global Network Navigator Pers Finance Ctr.
http://gnn.com/wic/usics/persfin.new.html
Finance and economic information

Global Recycling Network
http://grn.com/grn/
Trade Leads. Environmental industry

IBEX Exchange
http://www.ibex.com/
Listing of exporting companies

IBEX Yellow Pages
http://www.cba.uh.edu/ylowpges/yi.html
Listing of exporting companies

IMEX Exchange
http://www.imex.com/
Trade leads, general information

Infomanage International
http://www.commerce.com/net2/business/business.html
Regional information globally; international business

International Chamber of Commerce
http://www1.usa1.com/~ibnet/icchp.html
Extensive trade resources

International Marketing Corp. (IMC)
http://www.internationalmarket.com
Business services and links

International Standard Organization
http://www.iso.ch/
ISO standards

International Trade Data Users, Inc.
http://www.itdu.org/itdu
Group for users of elec. business info.

International Trade Desk
http://members.aol.com/tradedesk/
US Trade and Business

International Trade Resources
http://infomanage.com/intltrade

International TradeNET
http://intl-tradenet.com
Trade leads and information

Library of Commerce
http://www.loc.gov/
Information and research

National Technical Information Service
http://www.fedworld.gov/ntis/business/ibus.htm
Government international trade publications

National Trade Data Bank
http://www.stat-usa.gov
Market information and research

New York Library System
http://www.nysernet.org/
Information and research

New York Times
http://www.nytimefax.com
New York Times Newspaper

North Carolina International Trade Notes
http://www.ces.ncsu.edu/itd/catalog.html
Trade info. and leads

PangaeaNet Home Page
http://www.pangaea.net/homepage.htm
BBS trade leads and marketing information

Pennsylvania International BusinessNet
http://www.pitt.edu/~wpaintl/
Market information, export assistance, Regional information (PA)

ProTRADE Forum
http://www.cityscape.co.uk/users/bm22/pt.html
Info. on Comuserve's ProTrade forum

Small Business Administration (SBA)
http://www.sbaonline.sba.gov
Info incl. finance for sm. exporter

Small Business Foundation of America
http://web.miep.org/sbfa/
Information on starting a business

Starting Point
http://www.stpt.com
International & business news

Stat-USA
http://www.stat-usa.gov
NTDB and EBB

Trade Compass
http://www.tradecompass.com/
General information, trade leads

Trade Point Fortaleiza
http://tpfort.sfiec.org.br/
UNCTAD's Trade Point homepage

Trade Point USA
http://www.natp.iftea.com/
Trade leads, market info., UN info.

Trade Scope
http://www.tradescope.com/
Insurance, credit reports

Trade Zone
http://www.tradezone.com/tz/trdzone.html
Global trade information/mail order how to

TradeFair
http://www.tradefair.com/TradeFair.html
Trade leads, market information

TradePort
http://www.tradeport.org/
Comprehensive information for CA exporters

Tradescope Home Page
http://www.tradescope.com/
Trade leads, marketing information

United Nations Development Program
http://www.undp.org/
UN information: UNDP and ECOSOC

Univ of Pittsburgh Int'l Affairs Network
http://www.pitt.edu/~ian/ianres.html
International information and research

UNCTAD Gopher
gopher://unicc.org/1/ITC
Extensive statistics and trade information

US Census Bureau
http://www.census.gov/
Fact and statistics, data maps

US Department of Commerce
http://www.doc.gov/
Home page for Department of Commerce

US International Trade Commission
http://www.usitc.gov/
Industry, economic development, legal information

Region Specific Information

American Chamber of Commerce in Brazil
http://www.amcham.com.br
Regional info. (Brazil)

AmericasNet at Florida State Univ.
http://americas.fiu.edu/index.html
Americas Trade Forum

Asia in Cyberspace
http://silkroute.com/silkroute/asia/rsrc/country/index.html
Asian country information

Asian Trade Links
http://asam.com.au/~atl-aust
Australian firm with Asian contacts

Atlanta International Magazine
http://www.aimlink.com/at/mag
Regional info. (SE US)

Australian Embassy
http://www.aust.emb.nw.dc.us/intrade.htm
Regional info. (Australia and Asia)

Business Link
http://www.jsp.fi/
Finnish trading company (Russia)

Business Researchers' Interests
http://www.pitt.edu/~malhotra/international.html
Net resources

Canadiana
http://www.cs.cmu.edu/Web/Unofficial/Canadiana/
Info on Canada

CBCC: Trade Leads
http://turnpike.net/emporium/I/icml/cbcc/czleads.html
Trade leads for Czech Republic

Central Asia Information
http://coombs.anu.edu.au/WWWVL-AsianStudies.html
Links and info. on Central Asia

Central Intelligence Agency
http://www.odci.gov/cia
Country background info.

China News Digest
http://www.cnd.org:80
News and info. about China

Chinese Business Journal
http://www.ncb.gov.sg:1080/news/cbj
Info. from daily Chinese Business Journal

Costa Rica Web Server
http://ns.cr/ecconeg.html
Links to sites in Costa Rica

Dharani Export Import Services, Inc.
http://www.webindia.com/cust/india/dharani/dharani.html
Indian trading company

Electroni Embassy
http://www.embassy.org
Foreign Embassies in Washington DC

Elvis Server
http://www.elvis.msk.su
Moscow service provider, Russian links

Eniitco General Trading Europe, AB
http://www.pi.se/eniitco/index.html
Swedish trading company

EuroNet
http://www.euro.net
Info on the EU

European Commission
http://www.cec.lu
Regional info. (Europe)

European Community
http://echo.lu
Regional info. (Europe)

European Community
http://echo.lu/home.html
Info. on the EU

European Home Pages
http://s700.uminho.pt/cult-europ.html
Info. and links to Euro cities

European News Library
http://www.meaddata.com
Information about Europe

EUnet (Europe)
http://www.eu.net
EU service provider

Export Community of NY, NJ, and CT
http://www.exportcom.org
NY Distribution Export Council

Far East Business Directory
http://www.net-trade.com
Regional info. on the Far East

Foreign Agricultural Service, USDA
http://www.usda.gov
Agricultural market info. and economic research

Freylon Oy
http://clinet.fi/~frelon
Finnish trading company

Global Ukraine
http://www.gu.kiev.ua/
Information on Ukraine and Kiev

Glossary of International Trade Terms
http://circleintl.com
Trade terms

GoldSite Europe
http://www.gold.net:80/
Info. and links to Europe

Holt's Stock Market Reports
http://metro.turnpike.net/holt/index.html
Info. on international financial markets

Impex Connect
http://www.aztec.co.za/impex
South African trading company

Institute for Ag and Trade Policy
http://www.igc.apc.org/iatp/
Trade news, strategies and fact sheet

Intelligence Community
http://www.odci.gov/ic
Country background information

International Business Practices
gopher://umslvma.umsl.edu:70/11/library/govdocs/ibpa
Overview of 117 countries

Internet Guide to Japan
http://fuji.stanford.edu/japan_information_guide.html
Information about Japan

J.J.L. Associates
http://www.cityscape.co.uk/users/dr39/
Customs & Freight (Europe)

Japan Computer Science Co., Ltd.
http://www.jcsnet.or.jp/v-city/trade/guide-e/index-e.html
Japanese Market

Japan External Trade Organization (JETRO)
http://www.jetro.go.jp/
Regional information (Japan)

Japan-MITI
http://glocom.ac.jp/NEWS/MITI
MITI's programm for information infrastructure

Japanese Ministry of Int'l Trade and Industry
http://www.glocom/ac/jp/NEWS/MITI-doc.html
Regional information (Japan)

KEYMEXX
http://Jsasoc.com/keymexx.html
Regional information (Mexico)

Koblas Currency Converter
http://hnn.com/cgi-bin/gnn/currency
Exchange rates for about 50 countries

KoreaWeb Information Services
http://www.webcom.com/~koreaweb
Links to sites in South Korea

Latin American Trade and Information Network
http://www.latinet.com/
Latin American Trade Information

Latin American Trade Council of Oregon
http://www.teleport.com/~tmiles/latco.htm/
Regional Information (Oregon, Latin America)

Latin American/Caribbean Bulletin
http://www.ita.doc.gov/region/latinam/
LAC business bulletin

LatinoWeb Business
http://www.latinoweb.com/favision/business.htm
Trade leads. Regional Info. (Lat Am)

Market Link
http://m-link.com
Multilingual directories and resources

Ministry of International Trade and Industry (MITI)
http://www.miti.go.jp/
Regional info. (Japan)

NAFTA
gopher://umslvma.umsl.edu:70/11/library/govdocs/naftaf
Text of agreement

NAFTAnet Small Business Information
http://www.naftanet/smallbiz.htm
NAFTA

Netherlands Contracts
http://www.euronet.nl/users/gandy/index.html
Info. on the Netherlands

Nippon Telephone and Telegraph (NTT)
http://www.ntt.jp
Regional info. (Japan)

North Carolina International Trade Notes
http://www.ces.ncsu.edu/itd/catalog.html
Trade info. and leads

Organization of American States
http://www.sice.oas.org
Regional info. (Latin America)

Pennsylvania International BusinessNet
http://www.pitt.edu/~wpaintl/
Market information, export assistance, Regional information (PA)

Romanian Home Page (Burhala)
http://werple.apana.org.au/~florin/default.html
Romanian info.

Russian Trade Connection
http://www.lh.com/rtc/
Russia

Simon Fraser's David See-Chai Lan Centre Int'l Comm
http://hoshi.cic.sfu.ca/11/dlam/business/forum
Regional info. (Japan)

State Export Statistics
http://www.ita.doc.gov/industry/otea/state
State-by-state export statistics

Taiwan Internet Gateway
http://pristine.com.tw/
Multi-lingual links to Taiwan and Asia

Taiwan WWW Sites
http://peacock.tnjc.edu.tw/organ.html
Links to sites in Taiwan

Texas-One Home Page (TX DOC)
http://www.texas-one.org
Regional Information (US)

Thailand Information
http://www.nectec.or.th
Information on Thailand

The Web in Slovenia
http://www.ijs.si/slo/country/
Links & Information on Slovenia

Trade Trading (Taiwan)
http://trace.com.tw
Taiwanese trading company/Asian links

Univ of California at Fresno
http://caticsuf.csufresno.edu:70/1/atls
Trade leads & regional info. (Calif)

Univ of Missouri at St. Louis
gopher://umslvma.umsl.edu:70/11/library/govdocs/naftaf
NAFTA agreement (final text)

US Agency for Int'l Development (USAID)
http://www.info.usaid.gov/
USAID procurement and opportunities

US Commercial Service, The Netherlands
http://www.luna.nl/~attic
Info for US companies on Netherlands

US Department of State
http://www.stolaf.edu/network/travel-advisories.html
Political and Economic climate around the world

US Trade Center Directory for Buffalo, NY
http://www.grasmick.com/ustrade.htm
International trade contacts in Buffalo, NY area

USDOC, Big Emerging Markets
http://www.stat-usa.gov/itabems.html
Regional info. (BEMs)

USDOC, Global Export Market Info System
http://www.itaiep.doc.gov/
BEMs, CEEBIC, BISNIS, NAFTA

USDOC, Import Administration
http://www.ita.doc.gov/import_admin/records/
US import restrictions and regulations

USDOC, International Trade Administration
http://www.ita.doc.gov/
General information, comprehensive

USDOC, Japan Export Information Center
http://www.ita.doc.gov/regional/geo_region/japan
Regional info. (Japan)

Venezuela's Web Server
http://venezuela.mit.edu
Information on Venezuela

Virtual Africa
http://www.africa.com
Information on The Republic of South Africa

Washington State Trade Center
http://mail.eskimo.com/~bwest/
Regional information (WA, Russia)

Web India
http://www.webindia.com/india.html
Information and business contacts on India

White Bear Trade International, Inc.
http://www.the-wire.com/whitebear/
Regional information (Russia, Ukraine)

WWW Servers for Former Soviet Union
http://www.w3.org/hypertext/DataSources/bySubject/
Overview.html
Links to all known sites in former USSR

WWW Servers in Sweden
http://www.sunet.se/sweden
Links to Swedish sites

Industry Specific Information

American Material Resources, Inc.
http://www.commerce.com/placette
Export Trading Company

CommerceNet
http://www.commerce.net
High-tech business resource

Global Recycling Network
http://grn.com/grn/
Trade Leads. Environmental industry

Institute for Ag and Trade Policy
http://www.igc.apc.org/iatp/
Trade news, strategies and fact sheet

Port of Tacoma (Washington)
http://www.portoftacoma.com
Site of Tacoma Port

UNISPHERE
http://www.nando.net/uni/
High tech industries

US Department of Agriculture
http://www.usda.gov/
Ag Information, Market Research

Trade Contacts and Leads

A.R. Vogue Corporation
http://www.bekkoame.or.jp/~tomatell/business/vogue.htm
Trade leads and trade catalogues

Atlanta International Magazine
http://www.aimlink.com/at/mag
Regional info. (SE US)

BizPro
http://www.bizpro.com
Business listings on the Web

CBCC: Trade Leads
http://turnpike.net/emporium/I/icml/cbcc/czleads.html
Trade leads for Czech Republic

CommerceNet
http://www.commerce.net
High-tech business resource

Export Leads
L.P.Export@mailback.com
BBS for export leads

Global Business Forum Demo
http://www.pragmatix.com:80/gbf/gbf.html
Trade leads, marketing info.

Global Recycling Network
http://grn.com/grn/
Trade Leads. Environmental industry

Global Trade Point Network
http://www.unicc.org/untpdc/gtpnet/gtpnet.html
UNCTAD trade leads

IBEX Exchange
http://www.ibex.com/
Listing of exporting companies

IBEX Yellow Pages
http://www.cba.uh.edu/ylowpges/yi.html
Listing of exporting companies

Import/Export Connection
http://www.cam.org/~sailor/imexcon.htm/
Trade leads

IMEX Exchange
http://www.imex.com/
Trade leads, general information

International Trade Network
http://ds.internic.net/cgi-bin/enthtml/business/intltrade.b
Buyers and suppliers

International TradeNET
http://intl-tradenet.com
Trade leads and information

Internet Tradeline
http://www.intrade.com/
General information, trade leads

Intertrade Mercantile Exchange
http://www.intergroup.com/mercantile
Trading forum

LatinoWeb Business
http://www.latinoweb.com/favision/business.htm
Trade leads. Regional Info. (Lat Am)

North Carolina International Trade Notes
http://www.ces.ncsu.edu/itd/catalog.html
Trade info. and leads

Open Markets Commercial Sites
http://www.directory.net/
US Suppliers

PangaeaNet Home Page
http://www.pangaea.net/homepage.htm
BBS trade leads and marketing information

Starting Point
http://www.stpt.com
International & business news

Trade Compass
http://www.tradecompass.com/
General information, trade leads

Trade Point Fortaleiza
http://tpfort.sfiec.org.br/
UNCTAD's Trade Point homepage

Trade Point USA
http://www.natp.iftea.com/
Trade leads, market info., UN info.

Trade Scope
http://www.tradescope.com/
Insurance, credit reports

Tradefair International
http://www.tradefair.com/
Trade leads, financing

TradeFair
http://www.tradefair.com/TradeFair.html
Trade leads, market information

TradeNet
http://www.tradenet.org/
Trade leads

TradePoint
http://www.tpusa.com
Trade leads and contacts

Tradescope Home Page
http://www.tradescope.com/
Trade leads, marketing information

Univ of California at Fresno
http://caticsuf.csufresno.edu:70/1/atls
Trade leads & regional info. (Calif)

International Trade Services

American National Standards Institute
http://www.ansi.org/home.html
Info. on US Standards

Asia Development Bank
http://www.asiandevbank.org/
ADB information, finance

Asian Trade Links
http://asam.com.au/~atl-aust
Australian firm with Asian contacts

BizPro
http://www.bizpro.com
Business listings on the Web

BizWeb
http://www.bizweb.com
Index of commercial Web sites

Bureau of National Affairs
http://www.bna.com
Legislative & regulatory information, publications

Business Link
http://www.jsp.fi/
Finnish trading company (Russia)

Circle International
http://circleintl.com
freight forwarder/customs broker

Commercial List
http://www.directory.net
Index of commercial sites on the Web

Commercial News Services
http://www.jou.ufl.edu/comres/webjou.htm.
Newspapers on-line

Consolidated Freightways
http://www.cnf.com/
Transportation info.

Dun & Bradstreet
http://www.dbisna.com/
Information services

Experimental Stock Market Data
http://www.ai.mit.edu/stocks.html
Stock market Data

Expo Guide
http://www.expoguide.com
Trade shows and exhibits

Export Price Indices and Percent Change
gopher://una.hh.lib.umich.edu/O/ebb/price/exim-4.bis
Pricing info.

Export Today Magazine
http://www.enews.com/magazines/export/
Export Today Magazine

EXECPC
http://www.execpc.com/bbsinfo.html
Extensive trade database

Federation of International Trade Associations
http://www.webhead.com/FITA/home.html
Organization of trade associations (with links)

FINWeb
http://www.finweb.com/
Finance and economic information

Foreign Exchange Rates
gopher://una.hh.lib.umich.edu/O/ebb/monetary/noonfx.frb
Noon exchange rates daily

Foreign Trade Zones
http://webvision.com/ftz
Information on foreign trade zones worldwide

Free Advertise
http://www.freeadvertise.com
Web Advertising space

Global Network Navigator Pers Finance Ctr.
http://gnn.com/wic/usics/persfin.new.html
Finance and economic information

Glossary of International Trade Terms
http://circleintl.com
Trade terms

Guide to Marketing on the Internet
http://www.industry.net/guide.html
Marketing guide

IBEX Yellow Pages
http://www.cba.uh.edu/ylowpges/yi.html
Listing of exporting companies

Inter-American Development Bank
http://www.iadb.org/
IDB information, finance

International Marketing Corp. (IMC)
http://www.internationalmarket.com
Business services and links

International Standard Organization
http://www.iso.ch/
ISO standards

International Trade Organizations
http://www.yahoo.com/Economy/Organizations/
International_Trade/
Search engine

Internet Group
http://www.tig.com
Internet marketing group

Internet Tradeline
http://www.intrade.com/
General information, trade leads

Intertrade Mercantile Exchange
http://www.intergroup.com/mercantile
Trading forum

J.J.L. Associates
http://www.cityscape.co.uk/users/dr39/
Customs & Freight (Europe)

Knowledge Web
http://www.kweb.com
Trade show listings

Mariner Systems, Inc.
http://msi.marsys.com/
Shipping rates, schedules, tariffs, etc.

NAFTAnet Small Business Information
http://www.naftanet/smallbiz.htm
NAFTA

Notices of For Government Standards
gopher://gopher.counterpoint.com:2003/11/
Foreign%20Government%20Standards

Online Manufacturers Network
http://www.mfrnet.com
Advertising/marketing

Pennsylvania International BusinessNet
http://www.pitt.edu/~wpaintl/
Market information, export assistance, Regional information (PA)

Poppe Tyson Advertising and Public Relations
http://www.poppe.com:8400
Marketing and online services

Small Business Administration (SBA)
http://www.sbaonline.sba.gov
Info incl. finance for sm. exporter

Somers & Associates
http://ppp.jax-inter.net/ispy/
Business intellegence and investigation

State Export Statistics
http://www.ita.doc.gov/industry/otea/state
State-by-state export statistics

Trade Compass
http://www.tradecompass.com/
General information, trade leads

Trade Events, Shows and Exhibitions
http://www.expoguide.com/
Trade Show information

Trade Scope
http://www.tradescope.com/
Insurance, credit reports

Trade Show Central
http://www.tscentral.com
Trade Show listings

TradePoint
http://www.tpusa.com
Trade leads and contacts

TradePort
http://www.tradeport.org/
Comprehensive information for CA exporters

Traders'Connection
http://www.trader.com
Member-based service; advertising

UNCTAD Gopher
gopher://unicc.org/1/ITC
Extensive statistics and trade information

US Agency for Int'l Development (USAID)
http://www.info.usaid.gov/
USAID procurement and opportunities

US Census Bureau
http://www.census.gov/ftp/pub/foreign-trade/www.schedule.b.html
HS (Schedule B) numbers

US Commercial Service, The Netherlands
http://www.luna.nl/~attic
Info for US companies on Netherlands

US Council for International Business
http://www.uscib.org
ATA Carnet and other documents

US Department of Agriculture
http://www.usda.gov/
Ag Information, Market Research

US Department of Commerce
http://www.doc.gov/
Home page for Department of Commerce

US Trade Center Directory for Buffalo, NY
http://www.grasmick.com/ustrade.htm
International trade contacts in Buffalo, NY area

USDOC Bureau of Export Administration
http://www.doc.gov/resources/BXA_infor.html
Info. on BXA function and contacts

Washington State Trade Center
http://mail.eskimo.com/~bwest/
Regional information (WA, Russia)

Government Resources for Export Promotion

American National Standards Institute
http://www.ansi.org/home.html
Info. on US Standards

Central Intelligence Agency
http://www.odci.gov/cia
Country background info.

International Standard Organization
http://www.iso.ch/
ISO standards

Small Business Administration (SBA)
http://www.sbaonline.sba.gov
Info incl. finance for sm. exporter

State Export Statistics
http://www.ita.doc.gov/industry/otea/state
State-by-state export statistics

Trade Zone
http://www.tradezone.com/tz/trdzone.html
Global trade information/mail order how to

US Agency for Int'l Development (USAID)
http://www.info.usaid.gov/
USAID procurement and opportunities

US Census Bureau
http://www.census.gov/ftp/pub/foreign-trade/www.schedule.b.html
HS (Schedule B) numbers

US Census Bureau
http://www.census.gov/
Fact and statistics, data maps

US Department of Agriculture
http://www.usda.gov/
Ag Information, Market Research

US Department of Commerce
http://www.doc.gov/
Home page for Department of Commerce

US Department of State
http://www.stolaf.edu/network/travel-advisories.html
Political and Economic climate around the world

US Government Printing Office
http://www.access.gpo.gov/
Directory of government documents

US House of Representatives
http://www.house.gov/
Information from Capitol Hill

US International Trade Commission
http://www.usitc.gov/
Industry, economic development, legal information

USDA Foreign Agricultural Service
http://www.usda.gov/8000/fas//
Agriculture export information

USDOC Bureau of Export Administration
http://www.doc.gov/resources/BXA_infor.html
Info. on BXA function and contacts

USDOC, Big Emerging Markets
http://www.stat-usa.gov/itabems.html
Regional info. (BEMs)

USDOC, Global Export Market Info System
http://www.itaiep.doc.gov/
BEMs, CEEBIC, BISNIS, NAFTA

USDOC, Import Administration
http://www.ita.doc.gov/import_admin/records/
US import restrictions and regulations

USDOC, International Trade Administration
http://www.ita.doc.gov/
General information, comprehensive

USDOC, Japan Export Information Center
http://www.ita.doc.gov/regional/geo_region/japan
Regional info. (Japan)

White House
http://www.whitehouse.gov/
Information from the White House

Uniform Commercial Code (Cornell Univ)
http://www.law.cornell.edu/ucc/ucc.table.html
Uniform Commercial Code

Univ of Missouri at St. Louis
gopher://umslvma.umsl.edu:70/11/library/govdocs/naftaf
NAFTA agreement (final text)

US International Trade Commission
http://www.usitc.gov/
Industry, economic development, legal information

Washington College of Law
http://sray.wcl.american.edu/pub/wcl.html
International legal information on the EU and UN

International Trade Law

ANANSE International Trade Law Project
http://itl.irv.uit.no/trade_law/
International organizations and conventions

Bureau of National Affairs
http://www.bna.com
Legislative & regulatory information, publications

Congressional Record for 104th Congress
http://thomas.loc.gov/
Congressional documents

Export Legal Ass't Network (ELAN)
http://web.miep.org/elan
Legal assistance

Fletcher School of Law & Diplomacy
http://www.tufts.edu/fletcher/multilaterals.html
Multilateral conventions

Graduate Institute of International Studies
http://heiwww.unige.ch/gatt/final_act
GATT agreement (final text)

NAFTA
gopher://umslvma.umsl.edu:70/11/library/govdocs/naftaf
Text of agreement

Notices of For Government Standards
gopher://gopher.counterpoint.com:2003/11/
Foreign%20Government%20Standards

Trade Law Home Page
http://itl.irv.uit.no/trade_law/
International trade laws

> ## INTRODUCTION
>
> *A number of port authorities exist throughout the country. They are the physical locations where goods are shipped in and out of the U.S. Most also have offices of the U.S. Customs Service. This section provides a listing of the major port authorities throughout the U.S. as provided by the Trade Information Center of the U.S. Department of Commerce.*

Alaska

Mr. Donald L. Dietz
Port Director
Port of Anchorage
2000 Anchorage Port Road
Anchorage AK 99574
Phone: 907/272-1531   Fax: 907/235-3140

Mr. Dale R. Muma
Port Director
Port of Cordova
P.O. Box 1210
Cordova AK 99574
Phone: 907/581-1254   Fax: 907/424-6000

Mr. Spike Christopher
Port Director
Port of Homer
491 East Pioneer
Homer AK 99603-7624
Phone: 907/235-3160   Fax: 907/235-3140

Mr. Larry E. Munroe
Harbor Master
Port Juneau, City Dock & Alaska Steam Dock
155 South Seward
Juneau AK 99801
Phone: 907/586-5255

Mr. Larry E. Munroe
Harbor Master
Port of Kenai
210 Fidalgo
Kenai AK 99611
Phone: 907/586-5255

Mr. Doug Ensley
Director
City of Ketchikan Ports and Harbors Dept.
334 Front Street
Ketchikan AK 99901
Phone: 907/225-3610   Fax: 907/225-5075

Mr. G.V. McCorkle
Harbor Master/Port Administrator
City of Kodiak Harbor Department
P.O. Box 1397
Kodiak AK 99615
Phone: 907/486-5789   Fax: 907/486-4009

Mr. Gary K. Daily
Port Director
Matanuska-Susitna Borough Port
350 East Dahlia
Palmer AK 99645
Phone: 907/745-9831   Fax: 907/745-0886

Mr. Larry Merculiett
City Manager
Port of Nome
City of Saint Paul
Saint Paul AK 99762
Phone: 907/546-2331   Fax: 907/546-2365

Mr. Foster Singleton
Harbor Manager
Port of Seward

P.O. Box 167
Seward AK 99664
Phone: 907/224-3331   Fax: 907/224-7187

Mr. Brian Bergman
Harbor Master
City of Sitka Harbor Department
304 Lake Street
Sitka AK 99835
Phone: 907/747-3439

Mr. Ken Russo
Harbor Manager
Port of Skagway
City of Skagway P.O. Box 415
Skagway AK 99840
Phone: 907/983-2628   Fax: 907/983-2297

Mr. Jim Severns
Port Director
International Port of Dutch Harbor
P.O. Box 89
Unalaska AK 99685
Phone: 907/581-1254   Fax: 907/581-2519

Mr. Tom McAllister
Port Director
Port of Valdez
P.O. Box 307
Valdez AK 99686
Phone: 907/835-4313   Fax: 907/835-2992

Ms. Penny Mendenhall
Port Director
Whittier Port Authority Commission
P.O. Box 608
Whittier AK 99693
Phone: 907/472-2330   Fax: 907/472-2404

American Samoa

Mr. Leroy Ledoux
Port Director
Port of Pago Pago
Dept. of Port Admin.
Govt. of Amer. Samoa, P.O. Box 1539
Pago Pago AS 96799
Phone: 684/633-4251   Fax: 684/633-5281

California

Mr. David Hull
Chief Executive Director
Humboldt Bay Harbor District
P.O. Box 1030
Eureka CA 95502-1030
Phone: 707/443-0801   Fax: 707/443-0800

Mr. Steven R. Dillenbeck
Executive Director
Port of Long Beach
P.O. Box 570
Long Beach CA 90801
Phone: 562/447-0041   Fax: 562/437-3231

Mr. Charles W. Foster

Chief Executive Director
Port of Oakland
P.O. Box 2064
Oakland CA 94604
Phone: 510/272-1100   Fax: 510/272-1172

Mr. William J. Buenger
Executive Director
Port of Hueneme
P.O. Box 608
Port Hueneme CA 93044
Phone: 805/488-3677   Fax: 805/488-2620

Mr. Michael Giari
Executive Director
Port of Redwood City
675 Seaport Boulevard
Redwood City CA 94063-2794
Phone: 415/306-4150   Fax: 415/369-7636

Mr. Ronald W. Kennedy
Port Director
Port of Richmond
1411 Harbor Way South P.O. Box 4046
Richmond CA 94804
Phone: 510/214-4600   Fax: 510/233-3105

Mr. Lawrence M. Killeen
Port Director
San Diego Unified Port District
P.O. Box 448
San Diego CA 92112-0448
Phone: 619/291-3900   Fax: 619/291-0753

Mr. Douglas Wong
Acting Executive Director
Port of San Francisco
Ferry Building Room 3100
San Francisco CA 94111-4263
Phone: 415/274-0400   Fax: 415/398-1269

Mr. Charles W. Foster
Chief Executive Director
Port of Los Angeles
P.O. Box 151
San Pedro CA 94604
Phone: 510/272-1100   Fax: 510/272-1172

Port of Stockton
P.O. Box 2089
Stockton CA 95201-2089
Phone: 209/946-0246   Fax: 209/465-7244

Mr. John G. Sulpizio
Port Director
Port of Sacramento
P.O. Box 980070
West Sacramento CA 95798-0070
Phone: 916/371-8000   Fax: 916/372-4802

Connecticut

Mr. Joseph Riccio
Acting Executive Director
Bridgeport Port Authority
177 State Street
Bridgeport CT 06604
Phone: 203/384-9777   Fax: 203/384-9686

Mr. D. Douglas Brown
Director of Port Operations
Connecticut Dept. of Transportation
Bur. of Aviation & Ports
State Pier
New London CT 06320
Phone: 860/443-3856   Fax: 860/437-7251

Mr. Marty Toyen
Director

Connecticut Coastline Port Authority
2800 Berlin Turnpike P.O. Box 317546
Newington CT 06131-7546
Phone: 203/594-2542

Delaware

Mr. R. Adam McBride
Executive Director
Diamond State Port Corporation
Port of Wilmington P.O. Box 1191
Wilmington DE 19801
Phone: 302/571-4600   Fax: 302/571-4646

Florida

Mr. Charles M. Rowland
Executive Director
Canaveral Port Authority
P.O. Box 267 Port Canaveral Station
Cape Canaveral FL 32920
Phone: 407/783-7831   Fax: 407/784-6223

Mr. E.E. "Gene" Lasserre
Chairman
Nassau County Ocean Hwy. and Port Authority
P.O. Box 2
Fernandina Beach FL 32034
Phone: 904/261-0098

Mr. James J. O'Brien
Executive Director
Port Everglades
1850 Eller Drive
Fort Lauderdale FL 33316
Phone: 954/523-3404   Fax: 954/525-1910

Mr. Morris Adger
Port Director
Fort Pierce Port and Airport Authority
Route 5, Box 168
Fort Pierce FL 33450
Phone: 407/462-1732   Fax: 407/462-1718

Mr. Kenneth R. Krauter
Managing Director
Jacksonville Port Authority
P.O. Box 3005
Jacksonville FL 32206
Phone: 904/630-3000   Fax: 904/353-1611

Mr. Charles S. Hamilin
Executive Director
Key West Port & Transit Authority
P.O. Box 1078
Key West FL 33041
Phone: 305/292-8161   Fax: 305/292-8285

Mr. Carmen J. Lunetta
Port Director
Port of Miami
1015 North America Way
Miami FL 33132
Phone: 305/371-7678   Fax: 305/347-4843

Mr. David L. McDonald
Port Director
Manatee County Port Authority
13231 Eastern Avenue
Palmetto FL 34221-6608
Phone: 941/722-6621   Fax: 941/729-1463

Mr. H.R. "Rudy" Etheredge
Port Director
Panama City Port Authority
P.O. Box 15095
Panama City FL 32406
Phone: 904/763-8471   Fax: 904/769-5673

Mr. Tyler Jones
Port Director
Port of Pensacola
P.O. Box 889
Pensacola FL 32594
Phone: 904/435-1870   Fax: 904/435-1879

Mr. H.M. Hammock
Harbor Master
Port Authority of Port St. Joe
P.O. Box 280
Port St. Joe FL 32456
Phone: 904/227-1111

Mr. Edward R. Oppel
Executive Director
Port of Palm Beach
P.O. Box 9935
Riveria Beach FL 33419
Phone: 561/842-4201   Fax: 561/842-4240

Port of St. Petersburg
107 Eighth Avenue, SE
St. Petersburg FL 33701
Phone: 813/893-7654   Fax: 813/822-4767

Mr. Robert Steiner
Port Director
Tampa Port Authority
P.O. Box 2192
Tampa FL 33601
Phone: 813/272-0555   Fax: 813/272-0570

Georgia

Mr. Douglas Marchand
Executive Director
Georgia Ports Authority
P.O. Box 2406
Savannah GA 31402-2406
Phone: 912/964-3811   Fax: 912/964-3941

Guam

Capt. Eulogio C. Bermudez
General Manager
Port Authority of Guam
1026 Cabras Highway Suite 201
Piti GUAM 96910
Phone: 671/477-5931   Fax: 671/477-2689

Hawaii

Mr. Thomas T. Fujikawa
Chief, Harbors Division
Department of Transportation
Harbors Division 79 So. Nimitz Highway
Honolulu HI 96813
Phone: 808/587-1930   Fax: 808/587-1982

Illinois

Mr. Anthony G. Ianello, Jr.
Executive Director
Illinois International Port District
3600 E. 95th Street
Chicago IL 60617
Phone: 773/646-4400   Fax: 773/221-7678

Mr. Walter Jones
Executive Director
Waukegan Port District
P.O. Box 620
Waukegan IL 60079
Phone: 708/244-3133   Fax: 708/244-1348

Indiana

Mr. Frank G. Martin, Jr.
Executive Director
Indiana Port Commission
150 W. Market Street Suite 603
Indianapolis IN 46204
Phone: 317/232-9200   Fax: 317/232-0137

Louisiana

Mr. Bob Blais
Port Manager
Plaquemines Port, Harbor and Terminal District
Edna Lafrance Office Building 124 Edna
Lafrance Road
Braithwaite LA 70040-9715
Phone: 504/682-0081   Fax: 504/682-0081

Mr. Irwin A. Ruiz
Executive Director
St. Bernard Port, Harbor and Terminal
P.O. Box 1331
Chalmette LA 70044-1331
Phone: 504/277-8418   Fax: 504/277-8471

Mr. Ted M. Falgout
Executive Director
Greater Lafourche Port Commission
P.O. Box 3753
Lake Charles LA 70354
Phone: 504/632-6701   Fax: 504/632-6703

Mr. Glenwood "Willie" Wiseman
Executive Director
Port of Lake Charles
P.O. Box 3753
Lake Charles LA 70602
Phone: 318/439-3661   Fax: 318/493-3523

Mr. Gary P. LaGrange
Port Director
The Port of South Louisiana
P.O. Box 909
LaPlace LA 70069-0909
Phone: 504/652-9278   Fax: 504/652-9518

Mr. Roy C. Holleman
Interim Executive Director
Port of Iberia
P.O. Box 9986
New Iberia LA 70562
Phone: 318/364-1065   Fax: 318/364-3136

Mr. J. Ron Brinson
Port President and Chief Executive Officer
Port of New Orleans
P.O. Box 60046
New Orleans LA 70160-4156
Phone: 504/522-2551   Fax: 504/524-4156

Mr. Gary K. Pruitt
Executive Director
Greater Baton Rouge Port Commission
P.O. Box 380
Port Allen LA 70767
Phone: 504/342-1660   Fax: 504/342-1666

Maine

Mr. Robert D. Elder
Director
Department of Transportation
Division of Ports and Marine Transportation State
House - Station 16, Transp. Bldg.
Augusta ME 04333-0016

Phone: 207/287-2841   Fax: 207/287-8300

Massachusetts

Ms. Kelly Hedglin
Eastern Europe Trade Representative
Massachusetts Port Authority
International Marketing World Trade Center
Suite 321
Boston MA 02210
Phone: 617/478-4100   Fax: 617/478-4111

Mr. Andrew Bendheim
Director of Trade Development
Massachusetts Port Authority (MASSPORT)
Foreign Trade Unit World Trade Center
 Suite 321
Boston MA 02210
Phone: 617/478-4100   Fax: 617/478-4111

New Jersey

Mr. Donald Rainear
Delaware River Port Authority
One Port Center 2 Riverside Drive
Camden NJ 08101
Phone: 609/968-2000   Fax: 609/968-2216

New York

Mr. Lawrence Rosensheim
General Manager
New York/New Jersey Port Authority
One World Trade Center Office of Int'l. Business
Room 34 North
New York NY 10048
Phone: 212/435-7000   Fax: 212/435-4088

Ohio

Mr. Gary L. Sailor
Executive Director
Port of Cleveland-Cuyahoga County
   Port Authority
101 Erieside Avenue
Cleveland OH 44114
Phone: 216/241-8004   Fax: 216/241-8016

Puerto Rico

Mr. Herman Sulsona
Executive Director
Puerto Rico Ports Authority
P.O. Box 362829
San Juan PR 00936-2829
Phone: 787/729-8804   Fax: 787/722-7867

Rhode Island

Rhode Island Port Auth. & Econ. Devlpmt. Corp.
1 West Exchange Street
Providence RI 02903
Phone: 401/277-2601   Fax: 401/277-2102

South Carolina

Mr. Craig Lund
National Sales Manager
South Carolina State Ports Authority
P.O. Box 22287

Charleston SC 29413
Phone: 803/723-8651   Fax: 803/577-8710

Utah

Mr. Dan Mabey
Director
Utah Intermountain Port Authority
324 So. State Street Suite 500
Salt Lake City UT 84111
Phone: 801/538-8736

Virginia

Virginia Port Authority
600 World Trade Center
Norfolk VA 23510
Phone: 757/683-8000   Fax: 757/683-8500

Wisconsin

Mr. Alan T. Johnson
Port Director
Port of Green Bay
P.O. Box 23600
Green Bay WI 54305-3600
Phone: 920/448-4290   Fax: 920/448-4487

Mr. Kenneth Szallai
Port Director
Port of Milwaukee
2323 South Lincoln Memorial Drive
Milwaukee WI 53207
Phone: 414/286-3511   Fax: 414/286-8506

Alabama

Alabama World Trade Association
2027 First Avenue North
Birmingham AL 35203
Phone: 205/250-7665   Fax: 205/250-7669

Madison County Commission
International Trade Program
100 Northside Square
Huntsville AL 35801-4820
Phone: 205/532-3505   Fax: 205/532-3704

North Alabama Intl. Trade Association
P.O. Box 2457
Huntsville AL 35804
Phone: 205/536-1854   Fax: 205/539-0945

Center for International Trade and Commerce
250 North Water Street
Station 131
Mobile AL 36602
Phone: 205/441-7012   Fax: 205/438-2711

Arizona

Arizona-Mexico Commission
Suite 180
1700 W. Washington, State Twr. Ofc.
Phoenix AZ 85007
Phone: 602/542-1345   Fax: 602/542-1411

Arkansas

Arkansas International Center
University of Arkansas at Little Rock
2801 South University
Little Rock AR 72204
Phone: 501/569-3282   Fax: 501/569-8347

Mid-South International Trade Association
P.O. Box 888
Little Rock AR 72201
Phone: 501/370-9716   Fax: 501/376-4410

California

Ctr. for Int'l. Trade Development, Chula Vista
Southwestern College CITD
900 Otay Lakes Road, Building 1600
Chula Vista CA 91910
Phone: 619/482-6391   Fax: 619/482-6402

Ctr. for Int'l. Trade Development, Clovis
Fresno City College CITD
390-B West First Avenue
Clovis CA 93611
Phone: 209/323-4689   Fax: 209/323-4811

Ctr. for Int'l. Trade Development, Fountain Valley
Coastline Community College CITD
11460 Warner Avenue
Fountain Valley CA 92708

Phone: 714/241-6258   Fax: 714/241-6207

Ctr. for Int'l. Trade Development, Gilroy
Gavilan College CITD
5055 Santa Teresa Boulevard
Gilroy CA 95020
Phone: 408/847-0373   Fax: 408/847-0393

California Council for International Trade
The Meridian Group
13315 Washington Boulevard, #200
Los Angeles CA 90066
Phone: 310/306-6777   Fax: 310/827-1160

Economic Devlpmt. Corp. of Los Angeles County
515 South Flower Street, 32nd Floor
Los Angeles CA 90071
Phone: 213/622-4300   Fax: 213/622-7100

Export Managers Assoc. of California,
   Los Angeles
110 E. 9th Street, Suite A669
Los Angeles CA 90079
Phone: 213/892-1388   Fax: 213/892-0087

Foreign Trade Assoc. of So. California
900 Wilshire Boulevard, Suite 1434
Los Angeles CA 90017
Phone: 213/627-0634   Fax: 213/627-0398

Japan Business Assoc. of So. California
550 South Hope Street, Suite 176
Los Angeles CA 90071
Phone: 213/485-0160   Fax: 213/626-5526

LA TRADE
350 South Bixel Street
P.O. Box 3696
Los Angeles CA 90051-1696
Phone: 213/580-7569   Fax: 213/580-7511

Ctr. for Int'l. Trade Development, Merced
Merced College CITD
301 West 18th Street, Suite 104
Merced CA 95340
Phone: 209/384-5892   Fax: 209/384-9268

BAYTRADE, Novato
North Bay International Trade Center
330 Ignacio Blvd., Suite 102
Novato CA 94949
Phone: 415/884-4939   Fax: 415/884-4933

BAYTRADE, Oakland
Greater Oakland Intl. Trade Center
530 Water Street, Suite 740
Oakland CA 94607
Phone: 510/251-5900   Fax: 510/251-5902

California-S.E. Asia Business Council
1946 Embarcadero, Suite 200
Oakland CA 94606
Phone: 510/536-1967   Fax: 510/261-9598

Ctr. for Int'l. Trade Development, Oakland
Vista Community College CITD
519 17th Street, Suite 210
Oakland CA 94612
Phone: 510/893-4114   Fax: 510/893-5532

Ctr. for Int'l. Trade Development, Pomona
Citrus College CITD
375 South Main, Suite 101
Pomona CA 91766
Phone: 909/629-2247   Fax: 909/397-5769

Ctr. for Int'l. Trade Development, Riverside
Riverside Community College CITD
3638 University Avenue, Suite 250
Riverside CA 92501
Phone: 909/682-2923   Fax: 909/682-2441

Inland Empire Economic Partnership
Small Business Development Center
2002 Iowa Avenue, Suite 110
Riverside CA 92507
Phone: 909/781-2345   Fax: 909/781-2353

BAYTRADE, Sacramento
World Trade Center Sacramento
917 7th Street
Sacramento CA 95814
Phone: 916/552-6808   Fax: 916/443-2672

Ctr. for Int'l. Trade Development, Sacramento
Sacramento City College CITD
1410 Ethan Way
Sacramento CA 95825
Phone: 916/563-3200   Fax: 916/563-3264

Pan American Pacific Trade Assoc., Sacramento
4280 Armadale Way
Sacramento CA 95823
Phone: 415/788-4764

Asian Business League of San Francisco
233 Samson Street, Suite 515
San Francisco CA 94104
Phone: 415/788-4664   Fax: 415/788-4756

BAYTRADE, San Francisco
Bay Area World Trade Center
725 Front Street, Suite 104 Floor
San Francisco CA 94104
Phone: 415/392-2705   Fax: 415/392-1710

California Council for Int'l. Trade, San Francisco
700 Montgomery Street, Suite 305
San Francisco CA 94111
Phone: 415/788-4127   Fax: 415/788-5356

Custom Brokers & Forwarders Association
   of Northern California
P.O. Box 26269
San Francisco CA 94126
Phone: 510/536-2233   Fax: 510/261-9598

Hong Kong Econ. & Trade Office, San Francisco
222 Kearney Street, Suite 402
San Francisco CA 94108-4510
Phone: 415/397-2215   Fax: 415/421-0646

Intl. Trade Council of San Francisco
465 California Street, 9th Floor
San Francisco CA 94104
Phone: 415/979-8864

Pan American Society of California
c/o: Arbitus National
600 Woodley Street, Suite 350
San Francisco CA 94111
Phone: 415/788-4764   Fax: 415/788-5427

World Affrs. Coun. No. California, San Francisco
312 Sutter Street, Suite 200
San Francisco CA 94108
Phone: 415/982-2541   Fax: 415/982-5028

BAYTRADE, Silicon Valley
Silicon Valley Export Resource Center
101 Park Center Plaza, Suite 1001

San Jose CA 95113
Phone: 408/271-7303   Fax: 408/282-1005

Office of Economic Development, San Jose
City of San Jose
50 W. San Fernando Street, Suite 900
San Jose CA 95113
Phone: 408/277-5880   Fax: 408/277-3615

San Mateo Economic Development
1 Waters Park Drive, Suite 101
San Mateo CA 94403
Phone: 415/345-8300   Fax: 415/345-6896

Contra Costa Council, Northern CA
2694 Bishop Drive, Suite 121
San Ramon CA 94583
Phone: 510/866-6666   Fax: 510/866-8647

BAYTRADE, Santa Cruz
Monterey Bay International Trade Association
725 Front Street, Suite 104
Santa Cruz CA 95060
Phone: 408/469-0148   Fax: 408/469-0917

Ctr. for Int'l. Trade Development, Ventura
Oxnard College CITD
5700 Ralston Street, Suite 310
Ventura CA 93003
Phone: 805/644-9981   Fax: 805/658-2252

Colorado

Metro Denver Network
1445 Market Street
Denver CO 80202
Phone: 303/534-8500   Fax: 303/534-3200

Connecticut

WestConn Intl. Trade Association
2814 Fairfield Avenue, Suite 130
Bridgeport CT 06605
Phone: 203/356-2841

Connecticut Intl. Trade Association
P.O. Box 974
East Gramby CT 06026
Phone: 860/844-8776   Fax: 860/653-2705

Connecticut Foreign Trade Association
P.O. Box 1601
Norwalk CT 06852-1601
Phone: 800/243-4645   Fax: 860/927-4703

District of Columbia

Greater Washington Board of Trade
International Business Council
1129 20th Street, NW, Suite 200
Washington DC 20036
Phone: 202/857-5900   Fax: 202/223-2648

Florida

Greater Miami Chamber of Commerce
Omni International Complex
1601 Biscayne Blvd.
Miami FL 33132-1260
Phone: 305/350-7700   Fax: 305/374-6902

Georgia

Center of Intl. Standards and Quality

Georgia Institute of Technology
143 O'Keefe Building
Atlanta GA 30332
Phone: 404/894-0968   Fax: 404/894-1192

Hawaii

Pacific Basin Development Council
711 Kapiolani Boulevard, Suite 1075
Honolulu HI 96813-5214
Phone: 808/596-7229   Fax: 808/596-7249

Pacific Business Center Program
University of Hawaii at Manoa
2404 Maile Way, A413
Honolulu HI 96822
Phone: 808/956-6286   Fax: 808/956-6278

Small Business Action Center
1130 North Nimitz Highway, Room A-254
Honolulu HI 96817
Phone: 808/586-2545   Fax: 808/586-2544

Illinois

Customs Brkrs. & Foreign Freight Forwarders
    Association of Chicago
9757 West Farragut
P.O. Box 66640
Chicago IL 60018
Phone: 773/992-4100   Fax: 773/992-2323

International Trade Club of Chicago
203 North Wabash Street, Suite 2208
Chicago IL 60601
Phone: 312/368-9197   Fax: 312/368-0673

International Trade Assoc. of Greater Chicago
P.O. Box 454
Elk Grove Village IL 60009-0454
Phone: 847/985-4109   Fax: 847/985-8566

Indiana

Evansville Chambers of Commerce
100 North West 2nd Street, Suite 202
Evansville IN 47708-1242
Phone: 712/425-8147   Fax: 812/421-5883

Forum for Intl. Professional Services
One North Capitol Street, Suite 200
Indianapolis IN 46204-2248
Phone: 317/264-3100   Fax: 317/264-6855

Global Business Information Network
One North Capitol Street, Suite 100
Indianapolis IN 46204
Phone: 812/855-5463

Indiana Manufacturers Association
2400 One American Square
Box 82012
Indianapolis IN 46282
Phone: 317/632-2474   Fax: 317/231-2320

Chamber of Commerce for St. Joseph County
401 E. Colfax Avenue, Suite 310
P.O. Box 1677
South Bend IN 46634-1677
Phone: 219/234-0051   Fax: 219/289-0358

Iowa

International Business Association
314 Main Street

Cedar Falls IA 50613
Phone: 319/277-4700

N.E. Iowa International Trade Council
Cedar Falls Chamber of Commerce
10 Main Street, P. O. Box 367
Cedar Falls IA 50613
Phone: 319/266-3593   Fax: 319/277-4325

International Trade Bureau of Cedar Rapids
Cedar Rapids Area Chamber of Commerce
424 First Avenue, NE, Box 74860
Cedar Rapids IA 52407
Phone: 319/398-5317   Fax: 319/398-5228

International Traders of Iowa
P.O. Box 897
Des Moines IA 50304
Phone: 515/245-5284   Fax: 515/245-5216

Economic Development Council
North Iowa Area Community College
500 College Drive
Mason City IA 50401
Phone: 515/423-1264

Kansas

International Trade Council of Mid-America, Inc.
630 Humboldt
P.O. Box 1588
Manhattan KS 66502
Phone: 785/539-6799   Fax: 785/539-5599

International Trade Institute
Kansas State University
2323 Anderson Avenue, Suite 110
Manhattan KS 66502
Phone: 785/532-6799   Fax: 785/532-5599

The World Trade Council of Wichita, Inc.
The Wichita State University, Clinton Hall
Rm. 205, Campus Box 88, 1845 No. Fairmount
Wichita KS 67208
Phone: 316/978-3176   Fax: 316/978-3770

Kentucky

North Kentucky Intl. Trade Association
P.O. Box 668
Florence KY 41022-0668
Phone: 606/283-1885   Fax: 606/283-8178

Louisville/Jefferson City Office for
    Economic Development
600 West Main Street, Suite 400
Louisville KY 40202-4266
Phone: 502/574-3051   Fax: 502/574-3026

Louisiana

Le Centre International de Lafayette
P.O. Box 4017-C
735 Jefferson Street
Lafayette LA 70501
Phone: 318/291-5474   Fax: 318/291-5480

Jefferson Parish Econ. Devlpmt. Commission
3445 No. Causeway Blvd., Suite 300
Metairie LA 70002
Phone: 504/833-1881

Southern United States Trade Association
World Trade Center, Suite 1540
2 Canal Street
New Orleans LA 70130
Phone: 504/568-5986   Fax: 504/568-6010

Maine

Maine International Trade Center
511 Congress Street
Portland ME 04101-3428
Phone: 207/541-7400   Fax: 207/541-7420

Maryland

Greater Baltimore Committee
Legg Mason Tower
111 South Calvert Street, Suite 1500
Baltimore MD 21202
Phone: 410/727-2820   Fax: 410/539-5705

World Trade Center
6801 Oxen Hill Road
Oxen Hill MD 20745
Phone: 301/839-2477   Fax: 301/839-7868

Baltimore County Dept. of Econ. Devlpmt.
400 Washington Avenue
Courthouse Mezzanine
Towson MD 21204
Phone: 410/887-8000   Fax: 410/887-8017

Massachusetts

Associated Industries of Massachusetts
222 Berkeley Street
Boston MA 02116
Phone: 617/262-1180   Fax: 617/536-6785

Smaller Business Assoc. of New England, Inc.
204 2nd Avenue
Waltham MA 02154
Phone: 617/890-9070   Fax: 617/890-4567

Michigan

City of Detroit
Community and Econ. Devlpmt. Department
150 Michigan Avenue, 9th Floor
Detroit MI 48226
Phone: 313/224-2523   Fax: 313/226-4579

World Trade Club of Detroit
600 West Lafayette
Detroit MI 48226
Phone: 313/596-0340   Fax: 313/964-0168

Minnesota

Red River Trade Corridor
208 Selvig Hall
University of Minnesota
Crookstone MN 56716
Phone: 218/281-8459   Fax: 218/281-8050

Hennepin International Trade Service
012 Government Center
300 South 6th Street
Minneapolis MN 55487
Phone: 612/699-0542   Fax: 612/699-0542

Medical Alley Association
1550 South Utica Avenue, Suite 725
Travelers Express Tower
Minneapolis MN 55416
Phone: 612/542-3077   Fax: 612/542-3088

New Hampshire

Greater Nashua Chamber of Commerce
188 Main Street, Second Floor
Nashua NH 03060
Phone: 603/881-8333   Fax: 603/881-7323

New Mexico

New Mexico Industry Devlpmnt. Corporation
1009 Bradbury, SE
Albuquerque NM 87106
Phone: 505/646-4309

New York

Southern Tier World Commerce Assoc.
Int'l. Bus. Devlpmt. Assistance Project
SUNY-Binghamton, School of Mgmt.
P.O. Box 6000
Binghamton NY 13902-6000
Phone: 607/777-2342   Fax: 907/777-4422

Western New York Trade Council
300 Main Place Tower
Buffalo NY 14202
Phone: 716/852-7160   Fax: 716/852-2761

North Carolina

International Programs Office
North Carolina State University
Box 7112
Raleigh NC 27695-7112
Phone: 919/515-3201   Fax: 919/515-6835

North Dakota

Regional International Trade Roundtable
Tricollege University
209 Engineer Tech. Building, NDSU
Fargo ND 58105
Phone: 701/231-8170   Fax: 701/231-7205

Ohio

International Trade Assistance Center
Akron Regional Development Board
1 Cascade Plaza, 8th Floor
Akron OH 44308-1192
Phone: 800/621-8001   Fax: 330/379-3164

Greater Cincinnati Chamber of Commerce
300 Carew Tower
441 Vine Street
Cincinnati OH 45202
Phone: 513/579-3100   Fax: 513/579-3102

Int'l. Trade Club of North Central Ohio
800 No. Main St.
P.O. Box 1568
Mansfield OH 44901
Phone: 419/524-8388

Toledo Area Intl. Trade Association
Enterprise Suite 200
300 Madison Avenue
Toledo OH 43604-1575
Phone: 419/243-8191   Fax: 419/241-8302

Oklahoma

Oklahoma City Intl. Trade Association
5400 North Grand, Suite 100
Oklahoma City OK 73112
Phone: 405/943-9590   Fax: 405/943-9513

Center for Intl. Trade Development
Oklahoma State University, 204 CITD
Stillwater OK 74078-8084
Phone: 405/744-7693   Fax: 405/744-8973

Tulsa Global Alliance
616 So. Boston Avenue, Suite 401
Tulsa OK 74119
Phone: 918/596-7839   Fax: 918/596-2817

Tulsa World Trade Association
Economic Development
616 South Boston Avenue
Tulsa OK 74119
Phone: 918/560-0234   Fax: 918/585-8386

Oregon

Willamette International Trade Center
1401 Willamette
Eugene OR 97401
Phone: 541/484-1314   Fax: 541/484-4942

Pacific Northwest Intl. Trade Assoc.
One World Trade Center
121 SW Salmon Street, Suite 1100
Portland OR 97204
Phone: 503/221-2991   Fax: 503/464-2299

Pennsylvania

Econ. Devlpmt. Co. of Lancaster County
100 S. Queen Street
P.O. Box 1558
Lancaster PA 17608-1558
Phone: 717/397-4046   Fax: 717/293-3159

Wharton Export Network
Wharton School, University of Pennsylvania
3733 Spruce Street, 433 Vance Hall
Philadelphia PA 19104-6357
Phone: 215/898-4189   Fax: 215/898-1299

World Trade Association of Philadelphia
P.O. Box 58640
Philadelphia PA 19102
Phone: 610/876-3886

Puerto Rico

Puerto Rico Manufacturers Association
P.O. Box 195477
San Juan PR 00919-5477
Phone: 787/759-9445   Fax: 787/756-7670

Puerto Rico Products Association
P.O. Box 363631
San Juan PR 00936-3631
Phone: 787/753-8484   Fax: 787/753-0855

South Carolina

Midlands International Trade Association
P.O. Box 1481
Columbia SC 29202
Phone: 803/926-7926   Fax: 803/926-8412

Tennessee

Memphis World Trade Club
P.O. Box 240021
Memphis TN 38124-0021
Phone: 901/948-4428   Fax: 901/775-9818

World Affairs Council of Memphis
University of Memphis
Dept. of Political Science, 401 Clement Hall
Memphis TN 38152
Phone: 901/678-2395   Fax: 901/678-2983

Middle Tennessee World Trade Council
P.O. Box 198073
Nashville TN 37219
Phone: 615/748-2720   Fax: 615/748-2485

Texas

Greater Asian Chamber of Commerce
International Committee
P.O. Box 1967
Austin TX 78767
Phone: 512/322-5695   Fax: 512/472-6115

Brownsville Economic Development Council
1205 North Expressway
Brownsville TX 78520
Phone: 956/541-1183   Fax: 956/546-3938

Brownsville Navigation District
1000 Faust Road
Brownsville TX 78521
Phone: 210/831-4592   Fax: 210/931-5006

International Trade Resource Center
World Trade Center - Suite 150
2050 Stemmons Frwy., P.O. Box 420829
Dallas TX 75207
Phone: 214/712-1930   Fax: 214/748-5774

Free Trade Alliance San Antonio
100 West Houston, Suite 1411
San Antonio TX 78205
Phone: 210/229-9036   Fax: 210/229-9724

Utah

Commission for Economic Development in Orem
777 So. State Street
Orem UT 84058
Phone: 801/226-1521   Fax: 801/226-2678

Utah Valley Economic Development Association
100 East Center Street, Suite 3200
Provo UT 84606
Phone: 801/370-8100   Fax: 801/370-8105

World Trade Association of Utah
324 So. State Street, Suite 221
Salt Lake City UT 84111
Phone: 801/524-5116   Fax: 801/524-5886

Vermont

Vermont World Trade Office
60 Main Street, Suite 102
Burlington VT 05401
Phone: 802/865-0493   Fax: 802/860-0091

Virginia

Center for Innovative Technology
CIT Building
Suite 600, 2214 Rock Hill Road
Herndon VA 20170
Phone: 703/689-3000   Fax: 703/689-3041

International Trade Assoc. of Northern Virginia
P.O. Box 2982
Reston VA 22090-0982
Phone: 703/860-8795

Washington

Washington Public Ports Association
P.O. Box 1518
Olympia WA 98507-1518
Phone: 360/943-0760   Fax: 360/753-6176

IMPACT (Agricultural Marketing)
Hulbert Hall
Room 123, Washington State University
Pullman WA 99164-6214
Phone: 509/335-6653   Fax: 509/335-3958

Washington Council on Intl. Trade
2615 Fourth Avenue, Suite 350
Seattle WA 98121
Phone: 206/443-3826   Fax: 206/443-3828

Washington State International Trade Fair
999 Third Avenue, Suite 1080
Seattle WA 98104
Phone: 206/682-6900   Fax: 206/682-6190

West Virginia

West Virginia Manufacturers Assoc.
2001 Quarrier Street
Charleston WV 25311
Phone: 304/342-2123   Fax: 304/342-4552

INDEX

A

B

D

E

F

N

O

P

Q

R

U

V

W

Y

Z

ADVERTISERS

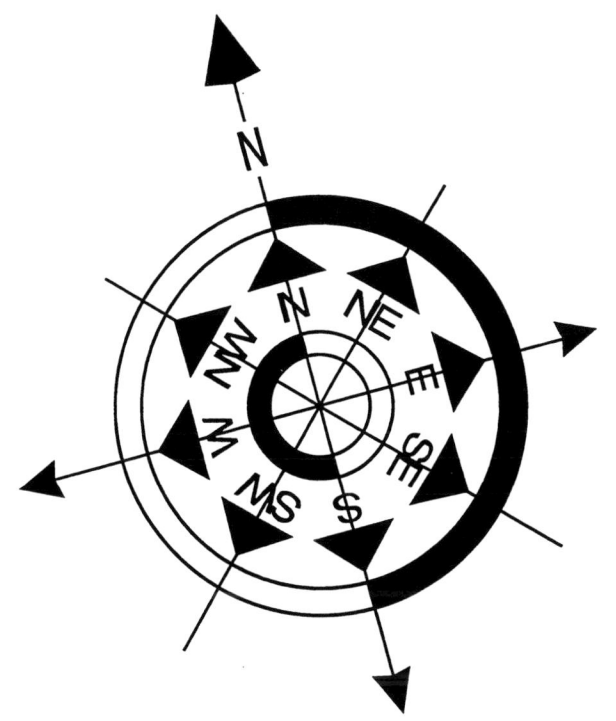

Now Shipping...

Washington State International Trade Directory

➤➤1999 edition

EXPORTERS/IMPORTERS
Alphabetical Listings, Product/SIC Index, Geographic Index

SUPPORT SERVICES
Accounting, Attorneys/Legal Services, Banking, Consultants, Insurance, Trade Organizations, Translators/Cultural Training, Transportation—*Air Cargo, Custom House Brokers & Freight Forwarders, Ports, Shipping, Trucking & Warehousing*

THREE FORMATS
Directory—soft cover
Disk—3.5" floppy in IBM or MAC format; data presented in ASCII text, comma-separated
Mailing Labels—both exporter/importer and support services lists; printed on self-adhesive white labels, zip code order or alphabetical by company name

The Who-What-Where Guide to Washington's International Trade Community since 1982!

SATISFACTION GUARANTEED

ORDER TODAY

☐ **Directory / US$88** shipped

☐ **Disk** (ASCII text, comma-sep.) / **US$165** shipped / Specify: ☐ IBM / ☐ MAC

☐ **Mailing Labels / US$125** shipped / Specify: ☐ Zip order / ☐ Alpha order

Name _____

Title _____ Phone _____

Company _____

Address _____

City _____ State _____ Zip _____

MAIL with Payment: *WSITD*, 6947 Coal Creek Pkwy., #362, Renton, WA, USA 98055-3159
Hirshman Publishing, phone 425-271-6073, fax 425-271-8882

THE CENTRE FOR INTERNATIONAL TRADE

76 Mamaroneck Ave., Suite 6, White Plains, NY 10601 USA
Phone: (914) 946-2734 ☎ Fax: (914) 946-3093 ✉e-mail: gmspub@aol.com
TOLL FREE: 1-800-206-5656
VISIT OUR WEBPAGE: http://www.centretrade.com

EXPORT / IMPORT/ FINANCE/ TRANSPORT LOGISTICS/ PUBLICATIONS/ TRAINING/ MANUALS/ FUNDING/ INVESTMENTS/ SEMINARS/ CONSULTING

📖 **BOOKS, GUIDES AND DIRECTORIES** on International Trade,
Finance and Transportation:
HOW TO EXPORT • EXPORT OPERATIONS & TECHNIQUES
• MANAGING INTERNATIONAL SHIPMENTS
• MAKING CONTACTS TO OPEN DOORS
• GUIDE TO IMPORTING • MARINE INSURANCE
❖ ❖ ❖ ❖ ❖ ❖ ❖ ❖
•MONEY ~ LEARN WHERE IT'S AT! A WORLDWIDE GUIDE
•TRUSTS & ASSET PROTECTION: A DEFINITIVE GUIDE
• PROJECT FUNDING MADE EASY • A TO Z OF FINANCE •
THE FRAUD REPORT•

📑 **MEMBERSHIPS** available to selected firms. Includes substantial benefits.
Request membership details.

📑 **FREE HONORARY MEMBERSHIPS** available to Embassy officials and
ranking government trade officials. Request application forms.

📑 **NEWSLETTERS**
The International Trader-our most popular newsletter covering trade, transportation, finance and much more.
The Vigilance Letter -current information about things we can use in our daily lives and business.
Money Secrets Newsletter-learn about how to handle your money in today's world, covers all aspects of interest.

Become a Certified Member, become informed with our Newsletters, become
educated through our books, become known through our Resources Section,
become an expert with our Network to back you up.

Remember "knowledge itself is power".

Nam et ipsa scientia potestas est.

Also at:
4thFloor, Olympic House, 17/19 Whitworth St. West,
Manchester M1 5WG, U.K.
Phone: (0)161-228-3912 Fax: (0)161-228-7943
Telex: 666682

Octavian House, 40 Victoria Way,
Charlton, London SR7 7QS, U.K.
Phone: (0)181-858-2642 Fax: (0)181-858-1347
Telex: 896102

New business oportunities in Latin America are a lot closer than you think

— at the Institute of the Americas ⊕

When you attend an Institute of the Americas conference in La Jolla, California you'll find out exactly where these new opportunities are — and you'll see just how easy it is to network with US and Latin American government officials and business executives.

Located high above the Pacific Ocean on the campus of the University of California, San Diego, the Institute of the Americas provides a splendid setting to explore the opportunities opened by recent economic and social reforms in Latin America and the region's continually closer relations with the United States and Canada.

Throughout the year, the Institute of the Americas hosts conferences, seminars, as well as small, informal roundtables with government and industry leaders on some of the region's most compelling policy and infrastructure issues. The four major conferences for 1997 include:

▲ **Energy** (June '97). The "La Jolla Conference" as it is now known in the industry — is the largest and most comprehensive high-level energy meeting of its kind in the hemisphere.

▲ **Mining** (Sept. '97). The Institute's mining conference (held this year in Denver) will focus on how to promote the adoption of appropriate policies, technologies, and projects consistent with sustainable development using economic incentives, education, regulation, and enforcement.

▲ **Environment & Water** (Oct. '97). The Latin American Water Infrastructure Conference aims to promote the exchange of ideas and experiences among countries in the hemisphere regarding their initial involvement with regulated private investment in water and wastewater systems.

▲ **Health & Social Security** (Sept. '97). The Institute's healthcare program helps international companies take advantage of the trend toward a greater private role in the provision and financing of health services. The Institute's annual "Salud-Americas" conference, to be held in Orlando, will offer participants detailed information about new projects in the hemisphere as well as provide the latest on hospital management trends, government regulations, expansion financing, and service and equipment sales.

▲ **Telecommunications** (Nov. '97). The Institute's Telecom Americas conference will provide new insights and information to the telecom business sector by comparing and contrasting developments in several Latin American markets. The meeting will also help to build networks and strategic alliances among Latin American investors, equipment and service providers, and their North American counterparts, and will focus specifically on information technologies.

For more information, contact:
The Institute of the Americas
10111 North Torrey Pines Road
La Jolla, California 92037
Tel. 619-453-5560
Fax. 619-453-2165
Internet site: http://ioa.ucsd.edu

An important meeting place where the region's leaders help to define the economic, political, and social agenda for reform throughout the hemisphere.

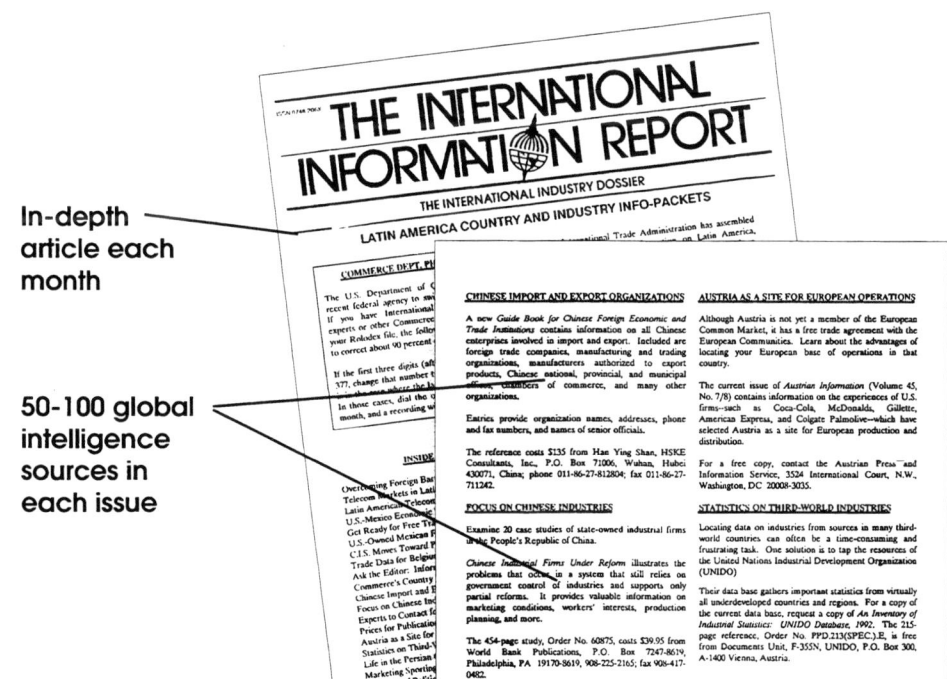